WHITAKER'S CONCISE ALMANACK

2008

A & C BLACK

LONDON

A & C BLACK PUBLISHERS LTD
38 Soho Square, London W1D 3HB

Whitaker's Almanack published annually since 1868
140th edition © 2007 A & C Black Publishers Ltd

STANDARD EDITION
Cloth covers
978–0–7136–8554–1

CONCISE EDITION
Paperback
978–0–7136–8562–6

JACKET PHOTOGRAPHS
1. A helicopter drops water onto forest fires near the ancient city of Olympia in Greece during August 2007. © Louisa Gouliamaki/AFP/Getty Images
2. Residents in Johannesburg, South Africa, some originally from Zimbabwe, demonstrate against Robert Mugabe in March 2007. © Jerome Delay/AP/PA Photos
3. British Formula One driver Lewis Hamilton celebrates victory at the Canadian grand prix in June 2007. © Kerim Okten/epa/Corbis
4. A submerged road sign in Tewkesbury, Gloucestershire, during the July 2007 floods. © Rui Vieira/PA Wire/PA Photos
5. The new British prime minister, Gordon Brown, and his wife Sarah arrive at 10 Downing Street in June 2007. © Andrew Parsons/PA Wire/PA Photos
6. A cigarette stubbed out in an ashtray before the advent of the July 2007 smoking ban. © Matt Morton/PA Wire/PA Photos
7. Revd Ian Paisley and Gerry Adams share a press conference at the Stormont Assembly building in Belfast, in March 2007. © Paul Faith/POOL/PA Wire/PA Photos

Typeset in Great Britain by RefineCatch Ltd, Bungay, Suffolk

Printed and bound in Great Britain by William Clowes Ltd, Beccles, Suffolk

Whitaker's is a Registered trade mark of J. Whitaker and Sons Ltd, Registered Trade Mark Nos. (UK) 1322125/09; 13422126/16 and 1322127/41; (EU) 19960401/09, 16, 41, licensed for use by A & C Black Publishers Ltd.

Whitaker's Almanack was compiled with the assistance of: Christian Research; UK Hydrographic Office; Met Office; Oxford Cartographers; Press Association; WM/Reuters. Crown copyright material is reproduced with the permission of the Controller of Her Majesty's Stationery Office.

The publishers make no representation, express or implied, with regard to the accuracy of the information contained in this book and cannot accept legal responsibility for any errors or omissions that take place. This book is produced using paper that is made from wood grown in managed, sustainable forests. It is natural, renewable and recyclable. The logging and manufacturing processes conform to the environmental regulations of the country of origin.

A CIP catalogue record for this book is available from the British Library.

EDITORIAL STAFF
Editor-in-Chief: Inna Ward
UK Project Editors: Rob Hardy, Ruth Northey
International Project Editor: Mike Jakeman
Editorial Assistant: Clare Slaven

CONTRIBUTORS (where not listed)
Elizabeth Holmes (Education); Gordon Taylor (Astronomy); Hemant Kanitkar (Hindu calendar); John Noi (IT); Karen Harries-Rees (Environment); Clive Longhurst (Insurance); Duncan Murray, Chris Priestley (Legal Notes); Lisa Halborg (Mobile Communications); Jill Papworth (Taxation)

CONTENTS

PREFACE 7

THE YEAR 2008

2008 Calendar 10
2009 Calendar 11
Forthcoming Events 12
Centenaries 14

UNITED KINGDOM

UK in Figures 17
The National Flag 23

ROYAL FAMILY 24
Private Secretaries 26
Finance 29
Military Titles 31
The House of Windsor 34
Descendants of Queen Victoria 35
Kings and Queens 38

PRECEDENCE 43

PEERAGE 45
Hereditary Peers 47
Life Peers 67
Lords Spiritual 76
Courtesy Titles 77
Peers' Surnames 78
Orders of Chivalry 83
Baronetage and Knightage 86
Dames 115
Decorations and Medals 118
Chiefs of Clans in Scotland 121
Privy Council 123

PARLIAMENT 127
Houses of Parliament 128
Political Parties 136
Members of Parliament 139
General Election Results 147
By-elections 183

THE GOVERNMENT AND PUBLIC BODIES 184
Government Departments 186
Executive Agencies 199
Non-ministerial Government Departments 205
Public Bodies Directory 209

REGIONAL GOVERNMENT 238
London 238
Wales 243
Scotland 249
Northern Ireland 260

LOCAL GOVERNMENT 266
Local Government Introduction 266
Political Compositions of Councils 273
England 278

Principal Cities 280
English County Councils 287
District Councils 288
Metropolitan Borough Councils 292
Unitary Councils 293
London 295
The City Guilds 297
London Borough Councils 300
Wales 301
Scotland 304
Northern Ireland 309
Isle of Man 311
Channel Islands 312

EUROPEAN PARLIAMENT 314

LAW AND ORDER 318
Law Courts and Offices 318
Scottish Judicature 326
Northern Ireland Judicature 330
Tribunals 331
Police 337
Prisons 342

DEFENCE 347
Salaries 357
Pensions 359

EDUCATION 360
The Education System 360
Education Directory 379
LEAs 379
Universities 387
Professional Education 397
Independent Schools 405
National Academies 416
Research Councils 418

HEALTH 423
National Health Service 423

SOCIAL WELFARE 430
Social Services 430
National Insurance 432
Pensions 433
War Pensions 435
Tax Credits 437
Benefits 438

UTILITIES AND TRANSPORT 446
Water 446
Energy 449
Transport 454

RELIGION 464
Religion in the UK 464
Churches 471

COMMUNICATIONS 494
Postal Services 494

5

6   Contents

IDD Codes   496
Mobile Communications   498

INFORMATION TECHNOLOGY   501
Glossary   502
Country Web Domain Names   506

THE ENVIRONMENT   508
Conservation and Heritage   512
World Heritage Sites   518
Wildlife and Habitat   519

HERITAGE   523
Historic Buildings and Monuments   523
Museums and Galleries   531
Sights of London   538
Hallmarks   545

BANKING AND FINANCE   548
British Currency   548
Banking and Personal Finance   550
Financial Services Regulation   553
National Savings   555
London Stock Exchange   557
Insurance   558

Economic Statistics   563
Cost of Living and Inflation   568
Taxation   570
Stamp Duty   584

LEGAL NOTES   586
Intellectual Property   610

THE MEDIA   612
Broadcasting   612
  Television   612
  Radio   614
The Press   623
  Newspapers   623
  Periodicals   627

TIME AND SPACE

Astronomy   635
Time Measurement and Calendars   695
Tidal Predictions   711

Index   718
Stop Press   752

PREFACE

Welcome to the 140th edition of *Whitaker's Almanack*. The past year has seen dramatic progress towards peaceful power sharing in Northern Ireland culminating in the reopening of Stormont and the unforgettable image we have chosen for this edition's cover, a photograph that will inspire hope in many nations torn apart by internal conflict.

Britain gained a new prime minister on 27 June. The new cabinet was put to the test almost as soon as it stepped into office, with a terrorist attack, a potentially disastrous foot-and-mouth outbreak and torrential downpours causing widespread flooding across the UK. After such a severe trial, the government's honeymoon period seemed to last and last with both the Tories and the Liberal Democrats lagging in the polls at the time of going to press. Following the reshuffles in all three parties, we have provided an up-to-date account of who is who in the new cabinet and new government departments. However, if the current media speculation about an early autumn election proves to be right, it will be too late to include in this edition.

Outside of the immediate political arena, the closely followed kidnapping of a British journalist (perhaps aided by his place of employment as much as his infallible reportage) ended happily with a smiling Alan Johnston providing a moving account of his imprisonment upon his release. British troops began pulling out of Basra marking the latest phase of Britain's disengagement in the conflict, while the media at large claimed London was experiencing a bigger wave of teenage gun violence than ever before. England, Wales and Northern Ireland followed Scotland by introducing nation-wide public smoking bans and both interest rates and house prices continued to rise, fuelling tabloid speculation of an impending crash. The bubble nearly burst at the end of July when the world stock markets were rocked by severe volatility caused largely by the collapse of the sub-prime debt market in America. Whether it is the lenders or the borrowers behaving irresponsibly, one thing is clear: knowingly or otherwise, we are all part of the world's deeply entwined financial economy, be it through stocks, pensions, employment or home ownership.

As usual, all of the big and the not so big stories of the year are recorded in the *Almanack*. In the main edition, we have added a new section of colour maps showing a few key indicators in various countries of the world and a long overdue list of flags. We have also added a map of the current claims on the Antarctic territory, especially pertinent in view of the recently renewed race for the Arctic. We have expanded our clubs section, which now includes a map of London 'clubland' and, in most cases, a list of notable former members.

In the concise edition, we have added many new sections from the main book, including taxation and legal notes, UK press and broadcasting and an overview of the finance industry. Regional election results for Scotland, Wales and Northern Ireland are listed with details of the previous outcome for each constituency. We have revamped the education section with a new statistical summary, and added diagrams to our environment and architecture articles and countries of the world summaries. As ever, everything has been scrupulously updated using the most authoritative sources available. We are most grateful for the assistance of thousands of organisations and individuals who respond so readily to our requests for information. My personal thanks for their work also go to the Whitaker's team and our contributors, and to everyone involved in ensuring yet another great edition of the *Almanack*.

Inna Ward
Editor-in-Chief
Whitaker's Almanack
38 Soho Square
London
W1D 3HB

THE YEAR 2008

CHRONOLOGICAL CYCLES AND ERAS

Dominical Letter	FE
Epact	22
Golden Number (Lunar Cycle)	XIV
Julian Period	6721
Roman Indiction	1
Solar Cycle	1

	Beginning
Japanese year Heisei 20	1 Jan
Muslim year AH 1429*	10 Jan
Roman year 2761 AUC	14 Jan
Regnal year 57	6 Feb
Chinese year of the Rat	7 Feb
Sikh new year	14 Mar
Indian (Saka) year 1930	21 Mar
Hindu new year (Chaitra)	6 Apr
Jewish year AM 5769*	30 Sep

* Year begins at sunset

RELIGIOUS CALENDARS

CHRISTIAN

Epiphany	6 Jan
Presentation of Christ in the Temple	2 Feb
Ash Wednesday	6 Feb
Maundy Thursday	20 Mar
Good Friday	21 Mar
Easter Day (western churches)	23 Mar
The Annunciation	25 Mar
Easter Day (Eastern Orthodox)	27 Apr
Rogation Sunday	27 Apr
Ascension Day	1 May
Pentecost (Whit Sunday)	11 May
Trinity Sunday	18 May
Corpus Christi	25 May
All Saints' Day	1 Nov
Advent Sunday	30 Nov
Christmas Day	25 Dec

HINDU

Vasant Panchami (Sarasvati Puja)	11 Jan
Makara Sankranti	15 Jan
Mahashivaratri	6 Mar
Holi	21 Mar
Chaitra (Spring new year)	6 Apr
Ramanavami	13 Apr
Raksha Bandhan	16 Aug
Janmashtami	23 Aug
Ganesh Chaturthi	3 Sep
Navaratri festival (Durga Puja)	30 Sep
Dasara	9 Oct
Diwali (New Year festival of lights)	26 Oct

JEWISH

Purim	21 Mar
Pesach (Passover), first day	20 Apr
Shavuoth (Feast of Weeks), first day	9 Jun
Rosh Hashanah (Jewish new year)	30 Sep
Yom Kippur (Day of Atonement)	9 Oct
Succoth (Feast of Tabernacles), first day	14 Oct
Hanukkah, first day	22 Dec

MUSLIM

Muharram (Muslim new year)	10 Jan
Ashura	19 Jan
Ramadan, first day	2 Sep
Eid-ul-Fitr	1 Oct
Hajj	8 Dec
Eid-ul-Adha	11 Dec

SIKH

Birthday of Guru Gobind Singh Ji	5 Jan
Baisakhi Mela (Sikh new year)	14 Mar
Martyrdom of Guru Arjan Dev Ji	16 Jun
Birthday of Guru Nanak Dev Ji	13 Nov
Martyrdom of Guru Tegh Bahadur Ji	24 Nov

CIVIL CALENDAR

Countess of Wessex's birthday	20 Jan
Accession of the Queen	6 Feb
Duke of York's birthday	19 Feb
St David's Day	1 Mar
Earl of Wessex's birthday	10 Mar
Commonwealth Day	10 Mar
St Patrick's Day	17 Mar
Birthday of the Queen	21 Apr
St George's Day	23 Apr
Europe Day	9 May
Coronation Day	2 Jun
Duke of Edinburgh's birthday	10 Jun
The Queen's Official Birthday	14 Jun
Duchess of Cornwall's birthday	17 Jul
Princess Royal's birthday	15 Aug
Lord Mayor's Day	8 Nov
Remembrance Day	9 Nov
Prince of Wales' birthday	14 Nov
Wedding Day of the Queen	20 Nov
St Andrew's Day	30 Nov

LEGAL CALENDAR

LAW TERMS

Hilary Term	11 Jan to 19 Mar
Easter Term	1 Apr to 23 May
Trinity Term	3 Jun to 31 Jul
Michaelmas Term	1 Oct to 20 Dec

QUARTER DAYS
England, Wales and Northern Ireland

Lady – 25 Mar	
Midsummer – 24 Jun	
Michaelmas – 29 Sep	
Christmas – 25 Dec	

TERM DAYS
Scotland

Candlemas – 28 Feb	
Whitsunday – 28 May	
Lammas – 28 Aug	
Martinmas – 28 Nov	

2008

JANUARY

Sunday		6	13	20	27
Monday		7	14	21	28
Tuesday	1	8	15	22	29
Wednesday	2	9	16	23	30
Thursday	3	10	17	24	31
Friday	4	11	18	25	
Saturday	5	12	19	26	

FEBRUARY

Sunday		3	10	17	24
Monday		4	11	18	25
Tuesday		5	12	19	26
Wednesday		6	13	20	27
Thursday		7	14	21	28
Friday	1	8	15	22	29
Saturday	2	9	16	23	

MARCH

Sunday		2	9	16	23	30
Monday		3	10	17	24	31
Tuesday		4	11	18	25	
Wednesday		5	12	19	26	
Thursday		6	13	20	27	
Friday		7	14	21	28	
Saturday	1	8	15	22	29	

APRIL

Sunday		6	13	20	27
Monday		7	14	21	28
Tuesday	1	8	15	22	29
Wednesday	2	9	16	23	30
Thursday	3	10	17	24	
Friday	4	11	18	25	
Saturday	5	12	19	26	

MAY

Sunday		4	11	18	25
Monday		5	12	19	26
Tuesday		6	13	20	27
Wednesday		7	14	21	28
Thursday	1	8	15	22	29
Friday	2	9	16	23	30
Saturday	3	10	17	24	31

JUNE

Sunday	1	8	15	22	29
Monday	2	9	16	23	30
Tuesday	3	10	17	24	
Wednesday	4	11	18	25	
Thursday	5	12	19	26	
Friday	6	13	20	27	
Saturday	7	14	21	28	

JULY

Sunday		6	13	20	27
Monday		7	14	21	28
Tuesday	1	8	15	22	29
Wednesday	2	9	16	23	30
Thursday	3	10	17	24	31
Friday	4	11	18	25	
Saturday	5	12	19	26	

AUGUST

Sunday		3	10	17	24	31
Monday		4	11	18	25	
Tuesday		5	12	19	26	
Wednesday		6	13	20	27	
Thursday		7	14	21	28	
Friday	1	8	15	22	29	
Saturday	2	9	16	23	30	

SEPTEMBER

Sunday		7	14	21	28
Monday	1	8	15	22	29
Tuesday	2	9	16	23	30
Wednesday	3	10	17	24	
Thursday	4	11	18	25	
Friday	5	12	19	26	
Saturday	6	13	20	27	

OCTOBER

Sunday		5	12	19	26
Monday		6	13	20	27
Tuesday		7	14	21	28
Wednesday	1	8	15	22	29
Thursday	2	9	16	23	30
Friday	3	10	17	24	31
Saturday	4	11	18	25	

NOVEMBER

Sunday		2	9	16	23	30
Monday		3	10	17	24	
Tuesday		4	11	18	25	
Wednesday		5	12	19	26	
Thursday		6	13	20	27	
Friday		7	14	21	28	
Saturday	1	8	15	22	29	

DECEMBER

Sunday		7	14	21	28
Monday	1	8	15	22	29
Tuesday	2	9	16	23	30
Wednesday	3	10	17	24	31
Thursday	4	11	18	25	
Friday	5	12	19	26	
Saturday	6	13	20	27	

PUBLIC HOLIDAYS

	England and Wales	Scotland	Northern Ireland
New Year	†1 January	1, †2 January	†1 January
St Patrick's Day	—	—	‡17 March
*Good Friday	21 March	21 March	21 March
Easter Monday	24 March	—	24 March
Early May	†5 May	5 May	†5 May
Spring	26 May	†26 May	26 May
Battle of the Boyne	—	—	‡12 July
Summer	25 August	4 August	25 August
*Christmas	25, 26 December	25, †26 December	25, 26 December

* In England, Wales and Northern Ireland, Christmas Day and Good Friday are common law holidays
† Subject to royal proclamation
‡ Subject to proclamation by the Secretary of State for Northern Ireland
Note: In the Channel Islands, Liberation Day is a bank and public holiday

2009

JANUARY						
Sunday		4	11	18	25	
Monday		5	12	19	26	
Tuesday		6	13	20	27	
Wednesday		7	14	21	28	
Thursday	1	8	15	22	29	
Friday	2	9	16	23	30	
Saturday	3	10	17	24	31	

FEBRUARY					
Sunday	1	8	15	22	
Monday	2	9	16	23	
Tuesday	3	10	17	24	
Wednesday	4	11	18	25	
Thursday	5	12	19	26	
Friday	6	13	20	27	
Saturday	7	14	21	28	

MARCH					
Sunday	1	8	15	22	29
Monday	2	9	16	23	30
Tuesday	3	10	17	24	31
Wednesday	4	11	18	25	
Thursday	5	12	19	26	
Friday	6	13	20	27	
Saturday	7	14	21	28	

APRIL					
Sunday		5	12	19	26
Monday		6	13	20	27
Tuesday		7	14	21	28
Wednesday	1	8	15	22	29
Thursday	2	9	16	23	30
Friday	3	10	17	24	
Saturday	4	11	18	25	

MAY					
Sunday		3	10	17	24	31
Monday		4	11	18	25	
Tuesday		5	12	19	26	
Wednesday		6	13	20	27	
Thursday		7	14	21	28	
Friday	1	8	15	22	29	
Saturday	2	9	16	23	30	

JUNE					
Sunday		7	14	21	28
Monday	1	8	15	22	29
Tuesday	2	9	16	23	30
Wednesday	3	10	17	24	
Thursday	4	11	18	25	
Friday	5	12	19	26	
Saturday	6	13	20	27	

JULY					
Sunday		5	12	19	26
Monday		6	13	20	27
Tuesday		7	14	21	28
Wednesday	1	8	15	22	29
Thursday	2	9	16	23	30
Friday	3	10	17	24	31
Saturday	4	11	18	25	

AUGUST					
Sunday		2	9	16	23	30
Monday		3	10	17	24	31
Tuesday		4	11	18	25	
Wednesday		5	12	19	26	
Thursday		6	13	20	27	
Friday		7	14	21	28	
Saturday	1	8	15	22	29	

SEPTEMBER					
Sunday		6	13	20	27
Monday		7	14	21	28
Tuesday	1	8	15	22	29
Wednesday	2	9	16	23	30
Thursday	3	10	17	24	
Friday	4	11	18	25	
Saturday	5	12	19	26	

OCTOBER					
Sunday		4	11	18	25
Monday		5	12	19	26
Tuesday		6	13	20	27
Wednesday		7	14	21	28
Thursday	1	8	15	22	29
Friday	2	9	16	23	30
Saturday	3	10	17	24	31

NOVEMBER					
Sunday	1	8	15	22	29
Monday	2	9	16	23	30
Tuesday	3	10	17	24	
Wednesday	4	11	18	25	
Thursday	5	12	19	26	
Friday	6	13	20	27	
Saturday	7	14	21	28	

DECEMBER					
Sunday		6	13	20	27
Monday		7	14	21	28
Tuesday	1	8	15	22	29
Wednesday	2	9	16	23	30
Thursday	3	10	17	24	31
Friday	4	11	18	25	
Saturday	5	12	19	26	

PUBLIC HOLIDAYS

	England and Wales	Scotland	Northern Ireland
New Year	†1 January	1, †2 January	†1 January
St Patrick's Day	—	—	‡17 March
*Good Friday	10 April	10 April	10 April
Easter Monday	13 April	—	13 April
Early May	†4 May	4 May	†4 May
Spring	25 May	†25 May	25 May
Battle of the Boyne	—	—	‡13 July
Summer	31 August	3 August	31 August
*Christmas	25, 28 December	25, †28 December	25, 28 December

* In England, Wales and Northern Ireland, Christmas Day and Good Friday are common law holidays

† Subject to royal proclamation

‡ Subject to proclamation by the Secretary of State for Northern Ireland

Note: In the Channel Islands, Liberation Day is a bank and public holiday

FORTHCOMING EVENTS

* Provisional dates
† Venue not confirmed

JANUARY

11–20	London Boat Show, ExCel, Docklands
11–27	London International Mime Festival
13	Russian Winter Festival, Trafalgar Square, London
16–20	London Art Fair, Business Design Centre
23–24	UK Dance Championships, Bournemouth International Centre
31–3 February	London Motorcycle Show, ExCel, Docklands

FEBRUARY

8–17	Leicester Comedy Festival
10	Orange British Academy Film Awards, Royal Opera House, London
23–2 March	Bath Literature Festival
29–1 March	Conservative Party Local Government Conference, Warwickshire
29–2 March	Ceramic Art London, Royal College of Art

MARCH

5–11	BADA Antiques and Fine Art Fair, Duke of York's Square, London
6	World Book Day
6–9	Crufts Dog Show, NEC, Birmingham
7–9	Liberal Democrat Party Spring Conference, Liverpool
7–16	National Science and Engineering Week
8	International Women's Day
14–6 April	Ideal Home Show, Earls Court

APRIL

April–September	Chichester Festival Theatre season
2–6	Oxford Literary Festival
14–16	London Book Fair, Earls Court

MAY

16–18	Battersea Contemporary Art Fair, London
18–31 August	Glyndebourne Festival Opera season
20–24	RHS Chelsea Flower Show, Royal Hospital, London
22–1 June	Hay Festival, Hay-on-Wye, Hereford

JUNE

*9–17 August	Royal Academy of Arts Summer Exhibition, Burlington House, London
14	Trooping the Colour, Horseguards Parade, London
16–29	Aldeburgh Festival of Music and the Arts, Snape, Suffolk
*27–29	Glastonbury Festival of Contemporary Performing Arts, Somerset

JULY

3–6	The Royal Show, Stoneleigh Park, Warwickshire
3–12	York Early Music Festival
3–13	New Designers Exhibition, Business Design Centre, London
4–20	Cheltenham Music Festival
8–13	RHS Hampton Court Palace Flower Show, Surrey
11–27	Buxton Festival, Derbyshire
17–26	The Welsh Proms, St David's Hall, Cardiff
*18–13 September	BBC Promenade Concerts, Royal Albert Hall, London
24–27	RHS Flower Show, Tatton Park, Cheshire
25–27	WOMAD Festival, Charlton Park, Wiltshire
*25–3 August	Edinburgh Jazz and Blues Festival
31–3 August	Cambridge Folk Festival

AUGUST

1–23	Edinburgh Military Tattoo, Edinburgh Castle
2–9	National Eisteddfod of Wales, Cardiff
2–9	Three Choirs Festival, Worcester
*8–31	Edinburgh International Festival
19–21	RHS Wisley Flower Show, RHS Garden, Wisley
*24–25	Notting Hill Carnival, Notting Hill, London
*29–2 November	Blackpool Illuminations, Blackpool Promenade

SEPTEMBER

1	Braemar Royal Highland Gathering, Aberdeenshire
*2	Mercury Music Prize
8	International Literacy Day
8–11	TUC Annual Congress, Brighton Centre, Brighton
12–21	Southampton Boat Show, Mayflower Park

13–18	Liberal Democrat Party Autumn Conference, Bournemouth
27–2 October	Labour Party Conference, Brighton
28–1 October	Conservative Party Conference, Birmingham

OCTOBER

7–4 January	Turner Prize Exhibition, Tate Britain, London
9	National Poetry Day
16–19	Frieze Art Fair, Regent's Park, London
Mid-October	Booker Prize
Mid-October	Classic Motor Show, NEC, Birmingham
Mid-October	London Film Festival

NOVEMBER

2	London to Brighton Veteran Car Run
8	Lord Mayor's Procession and Show, City of London
Mid-November	CBI Annual Conference, Business Design Centre, London
21–30	Huddersfield Contemporary Music Festival

SPORTS EVENTS

JANUARY

| 13–20 | Snooker: Masters, Wembley Arena, London |

FEBRUARY

| 2–15 March | Rugby Union: Six Nations Championship |
| 24 | Football: League Cup Final, Wembley Stadium, London |

MARCH

| 5–26 | Cricket: England Test series vs New Zealand |
| 29 | Rowing: Oxford and Cambridge Boat Race, Putney to Mortlake, London |

APRIL

| 13 | Athletics: London Marathon |
| 19–5 May | Snooker: World Championship, Crucible Theatre, Sheffield |

MAY

1–4	Badminton Horse Trials, Badminton
†4	Football: Welsh FA Cup Final
8–11	Royal Windsor Horse Show, Home Park, Windsor
14	Football: UEFA Cup Final, City of Manchester Stadium
15–9 June	Cricket: England Test series vs New Zealand
17	Football: FA Cup Final, Wembley Stadium, London
*17	Football: Scottish FA Cup Final, Hampden Park, Glasgow

21	Football: UEFA Champions League Final, Luzhniki Stadium, Moscow
*24	Rugby Union: Heineken Cup Final, Millennium Stadium, Cardiff
*24–6 June	Motorcycling: TT Races, Isle of Man

JUNE

7–29	Football: UEFA European Championship, Austria and Switzerland
16–21	British Amateur Golf Championship, Turnberry
23–6 July	Tennis: Wimbledon Championship, All England Lawn Tennis Club, London

JULY

2–6	Rowing: Henley Royal Regatta, Henley-on-Thames
6	Motorsport: British Formula 1 Grand Prix, Silverstone, Northants
10–11 August	Cricket: England Test series vs South Africa
12–26	Shooting: NRA Imperial Meeting, Bisley Camp, Surrey
17–20	Golf: Open Championship, Royal Birkdale
31–3 August	Golf: Women's British Open, Sunningdale

AUGUST

2–19	Sailing: Cowes Week, Isle of Wight
8–24	Olympic Games, Beijing
30	Rugby League: Challenge Cup Final, Wembley Stadium, London

SEPTEMBER

4–7	Burghley Horse Trials, Stamford, Lincolnshire
6–17	Paralympic Games, Beijing
16–21	Golf: Ryder Cup, Valhalla, Kentucky

OCTOBER

| *8–12 | Horse of the Year Show, NEC, Birmingham |
| Mid-October | Rugby League: Super League Final, Old Trafford, Manchester |

HORSE RACING

30 March	Lincoln Handicap, Doncaster
3–5 April	Grand National, Aintree, Liverpool
3 May	Two Thousand Guineas, Newmarket
4 May	One Thousand Guineas, Newmarket
6 June	The Oaks, Epsom Downs
6 June	Coronation Cup, Epsom Downs
7 June	The Derby, Epsom Downs
17–21 June	Royal Ascot
26 July	King George VI and Queen Elizabeth Diamond Stakes, Ascot
10–13 September	St Leger, Doncaster
2–4 October	Cambridgeshire Meeting, Newmarket
17–18 October	Champions Meeting, Newmarket

CENTENARIES

2008

1608
9 Dec — John Milton, poet, born

1708
1 Oct — John Blow, organist and composer, died
15 Nov — William Pitt the Elder, prime minister 1766–8, born

1808
20 Apr — Napoleon III, emperor of France 1852–70, born
29 Dec — Andrew Johnson, president of the USA 1865–9, born

1908
9 Jan — Simone de Beauvoir, French writer and philosopher, born
26 Jan — Stephane Grappelli, French jazz violinist, born
11 Feb — Sir Vivian Fuchs, polar explorer and scientist, born
26 Feb — Frederick 'Tex' Avery, American cartoonist and director, born
5 Mar — Sir Reginald 'Rex' Harrison, actor, born
23 Mar — Joan Crawford, American actor, born
25 Mar — Sir David Lean, film director, born
5 Apr — Bette Davis, American actor, born
5 Apr — Herbert von Karajan, Austrian conductor, born
22 Apr — Sir Henry Campbell-Bannerman, prime minister 1906–8, died
28 Apr — Oskar Schindler, German industrialist who saved Jewish workers from the Holocaust, born
20 May — James Stewart, American actor, born
28 May — Ian Fleming, novelist, born
21 Jun — Nikolay Rimsky-Korsakov, Russian composer, died
24 Jun — Grover Cleveland, president of the USA 1885–9 and 1893–7, died
30 Jun — The Great Siberian Explosion occurred near the Tunguska river, felling an estimated 80 million trees
13 Jul — King Edward VII opened the first Olympic Games held in Britain
22 Jul — Sir William Randal Cremer, MP, pacifist and Nobel Peace Prize winner (1903), died
26 Jul — In the USA, the Federal Bureau of Investigation (FBI) was established
12 Aug — Ford's first Model T car came off the production line
22 Aug — Henri Cartier-Bresson, French photographer, born
27 Aug — Sir Donald Bradman, Australian cricketer, born
27 Aug — Lyndon B. Johnson, president of the USA 1963–9, born
20 Nov — Alistair Cooke, British-born American journalist and broadcaster, born
10 Dec — Olivier Messiaen, French composer, born
25 Dec — Quentin Crisp, author and actor, born

2009

1509
21 Apr — Henry VII, king of England 1485–1509, died
10 Jul — John Calvin, French reformationist, born

1709
18 Sep — Dr Samuel Johnson, lexicographer, critic and poet, born

1809
4 Jan — Louis Braille, French inventor of reading system for the blind, born
19 Jan — Edgar Allen Poe, American author, poet, critic and editor, born
3 Feb — Felix Mendelssohn-Bartholdy, German composer, born
12 Feb — Charles Darwin, naturalist and scientist, born
12 Feb — Abraham Lincoln, president of the USA 1860–5, born
27 Mar — Baron G.-E. Haussmann, French civic planner, financier and architect, born
31 Mar — Nikolai Gogol, Russian writer, born
31 Mar — Edward Fitzgerald, poet and scholar, born
24 May — Dartmoor prison opened to hold prisoners of the Napoleonic Wars
31 May — Franz Joseph Haydn, Austrian composer, died
8 Jun — Thomas Paine, writer, deist and radical, died
6 Aug — Lord Alfred Tennyson, poet, born
29 Dec — William Gladstone, four-time prime minister, born

1909
17 Feb — Geronimo, Apache Indian chief, died
10 Apr — Algernon Swinburne, poet and critic, died
15 May — James Mason, actor, born
18 May — Fred Perry, tennis player, born
26 May — Sir Matt Busby, football player and manager, born
6 Jun — Sir Isaiah Berlin, Latvian-born writer and historian, born
20 Jun — Errol Flynn, Australian actor, born
17 Jul — Sir Hardy Amies, costume designer and the Queen's official dressmaker, born
25 Jul — Louis Bleriot completed the first flight across the English Channel
14 Sep — Sir Peter Scott, conservationist, born
28 Oct — Francis Bacon, Anglo-Irish painter, born
26 Nov — Eugene Ionesco, French-Romanian playwright and dramatist, born
7 Dec — Leo Baekeland was awarded a patent for the first synthetic plastic (Bakelite)
9 Dec — Douglas Fairbanks Jr, American actor, born

THE UNITED KINGDOM

THE UK IN FIGURES

THE NATIONAL FLAG

THE ROYAL FAMILY

PRECEDENCE

THE PEERAGE

THE PRIVY COUNCIL

PARLIAMENT

THE GOVERNMENT

GOVERNMENT DEPARTMENTS AND
PUBLIC OFFICES

REGIONAL GOVERNMENT

LOCAL GOVERNMENT

EUROPEAN PARLIAMENT

LAW COURTS AND OFFICES

TRIBUNALS

POLICE

PRISONS

DEFENCE

EDUCATION

HEALTH

SOCIAL WELFARE

WATER

ENERGY

TRANSPORT

RELIGION

COMMUNICATIONS

INFORMATION TECHNOLOGY

ENVIRONMENT

CONSERVATION AND HERITAGE

FINANCE

LEGAL NOTES

THE MEDIA

THE UK IN FIGURES

The United Kingdom comprises Great Britain (England, Wales and Scotland) and Northern Ireland. The Isle of Man and the Channel Islands are Crown dependencies with their own legislative systems, and not a part of the United Kingdom.

ABBREVIATIONS

AAS	*Annual Abstract of Statistics*
ST	*Social Trends*

All data is for the UK unless otherwise stated.

AREA OF THE UNITED KINGDOM

	sq. km	sq. miles
United Kingdom	242,495	93,627
England	130,279	50,301
Wales	20,733	8,005
Scotland	77,907	30,080
Northern Ireland	13,576	5,242

Source: ONS – *AAS 2006* (Crown copyright)

POPULATION

The first official census of population in England, Wales and Scotland was taken in 1801 and a census has been taken every ten years since, except in 1941 when there was no census because of war. The last official census in the United Kingdom was taken on 29 April 2001 and the next is due in April 2011.

The first official census of population in Ireland was taken in 1841. However, all figures given below refer only to the area which is now Northern Ireland. Figures for Northern Ireland in 1921 and 1931 are estimates based on the censuses taken in 1926 and 1937 respectively.

Estimates of the population of England before 1801, calculated from the number of baptisms, burials and marriages, are:

1570	4,160,221	1670	5,773,646
1600	4,811,718	1700	6,045,008
1630	5,600,517	1750	6,517,035

Further details are available on the Office for National Statistics (ONS) website (W www.statistics.gov.uk)

CENSUS RESULTS *Thousands*

Thousands	United Kingdom Total	*Male*	*Female*	England and Wales Total	*Male*	*Female*	Scotland Total	*Male*	*Female*	Northern Ireland Total	*Male*	*Female*
1801	—	—	—	8,893	4,255	4,638	1,608	739	869	—	—	—
1811	13,368	6,368	7,000	10,165	4,874	5,291	1,806	826	980	—	—	—
1821	15,472	7,498	7,974	12,000	5,850	6,150	2,092	983	1,109	—	—	—
1831	17,835	8,647	9,188	13,897	6,771	7,126	2,364	1,114	1,250	—	—	—
1841	20,183	9,819	10,364	15,914	7,778	8,137	2,620	1,242	1,378	1,649	800	849
1851	22,259	10,855	11,404	17,928	8,781	9,146	2,889	1,376	1,513	1,443	698	745
1861	24,525	11,894	12,631	20,066	9,776	10,290	3,062	1,450	1,612	1,396	668	728
1871	27,431	13,309	14,122	22,712	11,059	11,653	3,360	1,603	1,757	1,359	647	712
1881	31,015	15,060	15,955	25,974	12,640	13,335	3,736	1,799	1,936	1,305	621	684
1891	34,264	16,593	17,671	29,003	14,060	14,942	4,026	1,943	2,083	1,236	590	646
1901	38,237	18,492	19,745	32,528	15,729	16,799	4,472	2,174	2,298	1,237	590	647
1911	42,082	20,357	21,725	36,070	17,446	18,625	4,761	2,309	2,452	1,251	603	648
1921	44,027	21,033	22,994	37,887	18,075	19,811	4,882	2,348	2,535	1,258	610	648
1931	46,038	22,060	23,978	39,952	19,133	20,819	4,843	2,326	2,517	1,243	601	642
1951	50,225	24,118	26,107	43,758	21,016	22,742	5,096	2,434	2,662	1,371	668	703
1961	52,709	25,481	27,228	46,105	22,304	23,801	5,179	2,483	2,697	1,425	694	731
1971	55,515	26,952	28,562	48,750	23,683	25,067	5,229	2,515	2,714	1,536	755	781
1981	55,848	27,104	28,742	49,155	23,873	25,281	5,131	2,466	2,664	1,533*	750	783
1991	56,467	27,344	29,123	49,890	24,182	25,707	4,999	2,392	2,607	1,578	769	809
2001	58,789	28,581	30,208	52,042	25,327	26,715	5,062	2,432	2,630	1,685	821	864

* Figure includes 44,500 non-enumerated persons
Source: ONS – Census Reports (Crown copyright)

RESIDENT POPULATION *Thousands*

	United Kingdom Total	*Male*	*Female*	England and Wales Total	*Male*	*Female*	Scotland Total	*Male*	*Female*	Northern Ireland Total	*Male*	*Female*
2005	60,209	29,479	30,730	53,390	26,179	27,211	5,095	2,456	2,639	1,724	844	880
2006	60,533	29,668	30,864	53,691	26,357	27,334	5,108	2,463	2,646	1,733	848	884
2011	61,892	30,438	31,454	55,005	27,100	27,904	5,120	2,470	2,649	1,767	868	900
2021	64,727	31,943	32,784	57,770	28,572	28,198	5,127	2,471	2,656	1,830	900	930
2026	66,002	32,579	33,423	59,042	29,212	29,831	5,109	2,457	2,652	1,851	911	940

Source: ONS – *AAS 2007* (Crown copyright)

ISLANDS: CENSUS RESULTS

	Isle of Man			Jersey			*Guernsey		
	Total	Male	Female	Total	Male	Female	Total	Male	Female
1901	54,752	25,496	29,256	52,576	23,940	28,636	40,446	19,652	20,794
1911	52,016	23,937	28,079	51,898	24,014	27,884	41,858	20,661	21,197
1921	60,284	27,329	32,955	49,701	22,438	27,263	38,315	18,246	20,069
1931	49,308	22,443	26,865	50,462	23,424	27,038	40,643	19,659	20,984
1951	55,123	25,749	29,464	57,296	27,282	30,014	43,652	21,221	22,431
1961	48,151	22,060	26,091	57,200	27,200	30,000	45,068	21,671	23,397
1971	56,289	26,461	29,828	72,532	35,423	37,109	51,458	24,792	26,666
1981	64,679	30,901	33,778	77,000	37,000	40,000	53,313	25,701	27,612
1991	69,788	33,693	36,095	84,082	40,862	43,220	58,867	28,297	30,570
2001	76,315	37,372	38,943	87,186	42,485	44,701	59,807	29,138	30,669
2006†	80,058	39,523	40,535						

* Population of Guernsey, Herm, Jethou and Lithou
† The Isle of Man conducted a census in 2006
Figures for 1901–71 record all persons present on census night; census figures for 1981–2001 record all persons resident in the islands on census night. The 2001 population census also recorded the population of Alderney as 2,294 and an informal census of Sark gave its population as 591
Source: ONS – Census Reports (Crown copyright)

RESIDENT POPULATION

BY AGE AND SEX

Age Range	Men	Women
		Thousands
Under 1	367	349
1–4	1,389	1,323
5–9	1,823	1,737
10–14	1,962	1,859
15–19	2,038	1,927
20–29	3,847	3,794
30–44	6,645	6,763
45–59	5,746	5,878
60–64	1,519	1,595
65–74	2,389	2,659
75–84	1,403	2,022
85+	352	824

Source: ONS – AAS 2007 (Crown copyright)

BY ETHNIC GROUP

Ethnic group	Thousands
White	
British	48,973
Other	2,570
Mixed	
White and Black Caribbean	211
White and Black African	76
White and Asian	151
Other Mixed	135
Asian	
Indian	1,081
Pakistani	829
Bangladeshi	334
Other Asian	380
Black	
Black Caribbean	583
Black African	653
Black Other	60
Chinese	228
Other	700
ALL*	58,692

* Includes those who did not state their ethnic origin
Source: ONS – AAS 2007 (Crown copyright).

IMMIGRATION

ACCEPTANCES FOR SETTLEMENT IN THE UK

Region*	Number of persons	
	2003	2005
Europe: total†	15,295	20,810
Bulgaria	750	1,225
Russia	2,160	1,795
Serbia and Montenegro	1,165	6,805
Turkey	4,365	5,330
Ukraine	805	1,195
Other former USSR	625	1,015
Americas: total	16,465	13,905
Canada	1,710	1,215
Colombia	1,000	1,555
Jamaica	4,500	2,780
USA	5,620	4,350
Africa: total	44,860	54,080
Angola	620	1,695
Dem. Rep. Congo	1,475	2,960
Ghana	4,015	2,880
Kenya	1,585	2,690
Nigeria	7,570	5,310
Sierra Leone	1,375	3,420
Somalia	6,305	8,255
South Africa	8,805	9,385
Uganda	830	1,065
Zimbabwe	3,675	4,520
Asia: total	54,945	83,740
Indian sub-continent: total	29,490	28,990
Bangladesh	5,590	3,085
India	10,955	16,720
Pakistan	12,945	9,185
Middle East: total	5,020	9,395
Iran	1,585	2,055
Iraq	1,440	4,675
Remainder of Asia: total	20,435	45,355
China	2,540	3,985
Japan	1,850	1,540
Malaysia	1,150	1,945
Philippines	3,810	14,710
Sri Lanka	2,555	5,475
Thailand	2,020	1,945
Oceania: total	7,125	6,335
Australia	4,120	3,740
New Zealand	2,920	2,505

British Overseas Citizens	265	95
Nationality unknown	330	160
ALL NATIONALITIES	139,280	179,120

* Country specified only when the figure for 2003 or 2005 is over 1,000

† Excluding European Economic Area and Swiss nationals

Source: ONS – *AAS 2007* (Crown copyright)

BIRTHS

	Live births	Male	Female	Birth rate*
United Kingdom	723,000	370,000	353,000	12.0
England and Wales	646,000	331,000	315,000	12.1
Scotland	54,000	28,000	26,000	10.7
Northern Ireland	22,000	11,000	11,000	12.9

* Live births per 1,000 population

Source: ONS – *AAS 2007* (Crown copyright)

FERTILITY RATES
Live births per 1,000 women

Age of mother at childbirth	1971	1991	2005
Under 20	50.0	32.9	26.2
20–24	154.4	88.9	70.5
25–29	154.6	119.9	98.3
30–34	79.4	86.5	100.7
35–39	34.3	32.0	50.0
40+	9.2	5.3	10.6
Total fertility rate*	2.41	1.82	1.79
Total births (thousands)	901.6	792.3	722.5

* Number of children that would be born to a woman if current patterns of fertility persisted throughout her child-bearing life. For 1981 onwards, this is based on fertility rates for each single year of age, but for 1971 it is based on the rates for each five-year age group

Source: ONS – *ST 2007* (Crown copyright)

TOP TEN BABY NAMES

	1954		2006	
	Girls	*Boys*	*Girls*	*Boys*
1	Susan	David	Olivia	Jack
2	Linda	John	Grace	Thomas
3	Christine	Stephen	Jessica	Joshua
4	Margaret	Michael	Ruby	Oliver
5	Janet	Peter	Emily	Harry
6	Patricia	Robert	Sophie	James
7	Carol	Paul	Chloe	William
8	Elizabeth	Alan	Lucy	Samuel
9	Mary	Christopher	Lily	Daniel
10	Anne	Richard	Ellie	Charlie

Source: ONS (Crown copyright)

LEGAL ABORTIONS

	2000	2005
England and Wales	175,542	186,416
Scotland	11,997	12,603

Source: ONS – *AAS 2007* (Crown copyright)

DEATHS

Men	*Deaths*	*Death rate* *
United Kingdom	276,803	9.4
England and Wales	243,324	
Scotland	26,522	
Northern Ireland	6,957	

Women	*Deaths*	*Death rate* *
United Kingdom	305,860	10.0
England and Wales	269,368	
Scotland	29,225	
Northern Ireland	7,267	

* Per 1,000 population

Source: ONS – *AAS 2007* (Crown copyright)

INFANT MORTALITY RATE*

United Kingdom	5.1
England and Wales	5.0
Scotland	5.2
Northern Ireland	6.1

* Deaths of infants under one year of age per 1,000 live births

Source: ONS – *AAS 2007* (Crown copyright)

MARRIAGE AND DIVORCE

	Marriages	Divorces
United Kingdom*	283,731	155,052
England and Wales*	244,710	141,750
Scotland	30,881	10,940
Northern Ireland	8,140	2,362

* Provisional data

Source: ONS – *AAS 2007* (Crown copyright)

HOUSEHOLDS

BY TYPE (GREAT BRITAIN)
Percentages

	1971	1991	2006
One Person			
Under state pension age	6	11	14
Over state pension age	12	16	14
One family households			
Couple			
No children	27	28	28
1–2 dependent children	26	20	18
3 or more dependent children	9	5	4
Non-dependent children only	8	8	7
Lone parent			
Dependent children	3	6	7
Non-dependent children only	4	4	3
Two or more unrelated adults	4	3	3
Multi-family households	1	1	1
All households (=100%)	18.6	22.4	24.2
(millions)			

Source: ONS – *ST 2007* (Crown copyright)

BY SIZE (GREAT BRITAIN)
Percentages

	1971	1991	2006
One person	18	27	29
Two people	32	34	36
Three people	19	16	16
Four people	17	16	13
Five people	8	5	4
Six or more people	6	2	2
All households (=100%)	18.6	22.4	24.2
(millions)			
Average household size *(number of people)*	2.9	2.5	2.4

Source: ONS – *ST 2007* (Crown copyright)

DEPENDENT CHILDREN LIVING IN DIFFERENT FAMILY TYPES (GREAT BRITAIN)
Percentages

	1972	1997	2006
Couple families			
1 child	16	17	18
2 children	35	37	36
3 or more children	41	25	22
Lone mother families			
1 child	2	6	7
2 children	2	7	9
3 or more children	2	6	6
Lone father families			
1 child	–	1	1
2 or more children	1	1	1

Source: ONS – ST 2007 (Crown copyright)

ADULTS LIVING WITH THEIR PARENTS (ENGLAND)
Percentages

Age/Gender	1991	2002	2006
Men			
20–24	50	56	58
25–29	19	19	22
30–34	9	8	9
Women			
20–24	32	37	39
25–29	9	10	11
30–34	5	2	3

Source: ONS – ST 2007 (Crown copyright)

MORTGAGES

	1995	2000	2005
Mortgages* (thousands)	10,512	11,173	11,596
Arrears and repossessions* (thousands)			
Loans in arrears at end-period			
By 6–12 months	127	48	35
By 12+ months	85	21	14
Properties repossessed in period	49	23	10
Type of mortgage for house purchase[†] (percentages)			
Standard repayment	33.8	60.1	71.5
Endowment	52.0	17.5	3.8
Other[‡]	14.2	22.5	24.7

* Estimates cover only members of the Council of Mortgage Lenders, which account for 98 per cent of all outstanding mortgages

[†] Includes new mortgages advanced by building societies and other major lenders and includes sitting tenants

[‡] Includes interest only, PEP/ISA and pension

Source: ONS – AAS 2007 (Crown copyright)

TYPE OF ACCOMMODATION (GREAT BRITAIN)
Percentages by tenure 2005

	House or bungalow			Flat or maisonette	
	Detached	Semi-detached	Terraced	Purpose-built	Other
Owner-occupied	30	35	26	7	2
Owned outright	34	35	21	7	2
Owned with mortgage	26	34	30	7	2
Rented from social sector	1	24	30	42	3
Council	1	26	28	42	2
Housing association	1	19	34	41	5
Rented privately	11	19	32	22	16
Furnished	5	14	30	30	20
Unfurnished	14	20	33	18	15
All tenures	22	31	28	16	4

Source: ONS – AAS 2007 (Crown copyright)

HEALTH

All data is for the UK unless otherwise stated.

LIFE EXPECTANCY

	2003	2007 est
Men	76.2	76.2
Women	80.5	81.3

Source: CIA World Factbook

DEATHS BY CAUSE

	England and Wales	Scotland	N. Ireland
Total Deaths	512,692	55,747	14,224
Deaths from natural causes	494,054	53,535	13,463
Certain infectious and parasitic diseases	6,141	719	162
Intestinal infectious diseases	2,221	99	16
Respiratory and other tuberculosis	406	49	4
Meningococcal infection	86	4	1
Viral hepatitis	205	16	2
AIDS (HIV – disease)	230	31	5

Neoplasms	138,454	15,408	3,826
Malignant neoplasms	135,252	15,135	3,735
Malignant neoplasm of oesophagus	6,490	798	162
Malignant neoplasm of stomach	4,927	590	161
Malignant neoplasm of colon	9,076	966	293
Malignant neoplasm of rectum and anus	3,995	367	99
Malignant neoplasm of pancreas	6,509	603	173
Malignant neoplasm of trachea, bronchus and lung	28,792	4,009	824
Malignant neoplasm of skin	1,622	158	43
Malignant neoplasm of breast	11,121	1,151	307
Malignant neoplasm of cervix uteri	911	127	20
Malignant neoplasm of prostate	9,042	765	222
Leukaemia	3,910	351	92
Diseases of the blood and blood-forming organs and certain disorders involving the immune mechanism	1,096	118	36
Endocrine, nutritional and metabolic diseases	7,433	988	302
Diabetes mellitus	5,677	745	224
Mental and behavioural disorders	14,563	2,454	408
Vascular and unspecified dementia	12,995	1,835	316
Alcohol abuse	523	343	86
Drug dependence and non-dependent abuse of drugs	762	217	2
Diseases of the nervous system and sense organs	15,253	1,306	484
Meningitis (excluding meningococcal)	187	18	2
Alzheimer's disease	4,914	415	207
Diseases of the circulatory system	183,997	20,060	5,002
Ischaemic heart diseases	88,271	10,331	2,708
Cerebrovascular diseases	50,772	5,789	1,307
Diseases of the respiratory system	72,517	7,093	1,921
Influenza	44	11	–
Pneumonia	31,443	2,483	895
Bronchitis, emphysema and other chronic obstructive pulmonary diseases	24,230	2,857	596
Asthma	1,186	100	32
Diseases of the digestive system	25,213	3,221	584
Gastric and duodenal ulcer	3,266	230	60
Chronic liver disease	5,873	1,152	150
Diseases of the skin and subcutaneous tissue	1,788	127	20
Diseases of the musculo-skeletal system and connective tissue	4,378	326	95
Rheumatoid arthritis and juvenile arthritis	835	109	28
Osteoporosis	1,416	47	12
Diseases of the genito-urinary system	10,231	1,063	351
Diseases of the kidney and ureter	3,967	617	210
Complications of pregnancy, childbirth and the puerperium	36	4	1
Certain conditions originating in the perinatal period	205*	164	81
Congenital malformations, deformations and chromosomal abnormalities	1,292*	159	82
Congenital malformations of the nervous system	123	15	10
Congenital malformations of the circulatory system	535	58	20
Symptoms, signs and abnormal findings not classified elsewhere	11,457	325	108
Senility without mention of psychosis (old age)	9,785	210	71
Sudden infant death syndrome	164	20	2
Deaths from external causes	16,411	2,212	761
All accidents	11,053	1,284	492
Land transport accidents	2,697	293	175
Accidental falls	3,006	676	99
Accidental poisonings	910	48	40
Suicide and intentional self-harm	3,172	547	186
Homicide and assault	326†	80	32
Event of undetermined intent	1,486	216	27

* Excludes neonatal deaths (those at age under 28 days): for England and Wales neonatal deaths are included in the total number of deaths but excluded from the cause figures
† This will not be a true figure as registration of homicide and assault deaths in England and Wales is often delayed by adjourned inquests

Source: ONS – *AAS 2007* (Crown copyright)

NOTIFICATIONS OF INFECTIOUS DISEASES

	2000	2005
Measles	2,865	2,326
Mumps	3,367	66,541
Rubella	2,064	1,327
Whooping cough	866	679
Scarlet fever	2,544	2,075
Dysentery	1,613	1,346
Food poisoning	98,076	78,959
Typhoid and paratyphoid fevers	205	300
Hepatitis	4,530	5,246
Tuberculosis	7,100	8,017
Malaria	1,166	700

Source: ONS – AAS 2007 (Crown copyright)

IMMUNISATION OF CHILDREN BY THEIR SECOND BIRTHDAY*

Percentage

	1991–2	2004–5
Tetanus	94	94
Diphtheria	94	94
Poliomyelitis	94	94
Whooping cough	88	94
Measles, mumps, rubella (MMR)	90	82

* Excludes Scotland

Source: ONS – ST 2006 (Crown copyright)

ALCOHOL CONSUMPTION* BY AGE (GREAT BRITAIN)

Percentages

	16–24	25–44	45–64	65+	All 16+
Men					
4–8 units	13	17	19	12	16
8+ units	30	25	16	4	19
4+ units	43	42	35	16	35
Women					
3–6 units	14	15	14	3	12
6+ units	22	11	4	1	8
3+ units	36	26	18	4	20

* On at least one day in the previous week. Current Department of Health advice is that consumption of between three and four units a day for men and between two and three units for women should not lead to significant health risks. A unit of alcohol is 8 grams by weight or 10ml by volume of pure alcohol, ie the amount contained in half a pint of ordinary strength beer or lager, a single pub measure of spirits or a small glass of ordinary strength wine.

Source: ONS – ST 2007 (Crown copyright)

DRUG MISUSE BY YOUNG ADULTS* (ENGLAND AND WALES)

Percentages

	Males		Females	
	1996	2004–5	1996	2004–5
Cannabis	30	30	22	18
Ecstasy	9	7	4	3
Cocaine	2	7	–	3
Amphetamines	15	4	9	3
Magic mushrooms or LSD	9	5	2	2
All Class A drugs†	13	11	6	5
Any drug‡	34	33	25	21

* Aged 16–24 years

† Includes heroin, cocaine (powder and crack), ecstasy, magic mushrooms, LSD and unprescribed use of methadone

‡ Includes drugs not listed in the table

Source: ONS – ST 2006 (Crown copyright)

THE NATIONAL FLAG

The national flag of the United Kingdom is the Union Flag, generally known as the Union Jack.

The Union Flag is a combination of the cross of St George, patron saint of England, the cross of St Andrew, patron saint of Scotland and the cross of St Patrick, patron saint of Ireland.

Cross of St George: cross Gules in a field Argent (red cross on a white ground)

Cross of St Andrew: saltire Argent in a field Azure (white diagonal cross on a blue ground)

Cross of St Patrick: saltire Gules in a field Argent (red diagonal cross on a white ground)

The Union Flag was first introduced in 1606 after the union of the kingdoms of England and Scotland under one sovereign. The cross of St Patrick was added in 1801 after the union of Great Britain and Ireland.

See also Flags of the World colour plates.

FLYING THE UNION FLAG

The correct orientation of the Union Flag when flying is with the broader diagonal band of white uppermost in the hoist (ie near the pole) and the narrower diagonal band of white uppermost in the fly (ie furthest from the pole).

It is the practice to fly the Union Flag daily on some customs houses. In all other cases, flags are flown on government buildings by command of the Queen. There is no formal definition of a government building but it is generally accepted to mean a building owned or used by the Crown and predominantly occupied or used by civil servants or the Armed Forces. It is now customary for the Union Flag to be flown at Buckingham Palace, Windsor Castle and Sandringham when the Queen is not in residence. Individuals, local authorities and other organisations may fly the Union Flag whenever they wish, subject to compliance with local planning requirements.

The flying of the Union Flag is decided by the DCMS at the Queen's command.

FLAGS AT HALF-MAST

Flags are flown at half-mast (ie two-thirds up between the top and bottom of the flagstaff) on the following occasions:

- from the announcement of the death up to the funeral of the sovereign, except on Proclamation Day, when flags are hoisted right up from 11am to sunset
- the funerals of members of the royal family*
- the funerals of foreign rulers*
- the funerals of prime ministers and ex-prime ministers of the UK*
- other occasions by special command of the Queen

* Subject to special commands from the Queen in each case

On occasions when days for flying flags coincide with days for flying flags at half-mast, the following rules are observed. Flags are flown at full mast:

- although a member of the royal family, or a near relative of the royal family, may be lying dead, unless special commands are received from the Queen to the contrary
- although it may be the day of the funeral of a foreign ruler

If the body of a very distinguished subject is lying at a government office, the flag may fly at half-mast on that office until the body has left (provided it is a day on which the flag would fly) and then the flag is to be hoisted right up. On all other government buildings the flag will fly as usual.

DAYS FOR FLYING FLAGS

Flags are hoisted from 8am to sunset.

Countess of Wessex's birthday	20 January
Accession of the Queen	6 February
Duke of York's birthday	19 February
St David's Day (in Wales only)*	1 March
Earl of Wessex's birthday	10 March
Commonwealth Day (2008)	10 March
St Patrick's Day (in Northern Ireland only)†	17 March
Birthday of the Queen	21 April
St George's Day (in England only)*	23 April
Europe Day‡	9 May
Coronation Day	2 June
Duke of Edinburgh's birthday	10 June
The Queen's Official Birthday (2008)	14 June
Duchess of Cornwall's birthday	17 July
Princess Royal's birthday	15 August
Remembrance Day (2008)	9 November
Prince of Wales' birthday	14 November
Wedding Day of the Queen	20 November
St Andrew's Day (in Scotland only)*	30 November
Opening of Parliament by the Queen§	
Prorogation of Parliament by the Queen§	

* The appropriate national flag may be flown in addition to the Union Flag, but not in a superior position

† Only the Union Flag should be flown

‡ The Union Flag should fly alongside the European flag. On government buildings that have only one flagpole, the Union Flag should take precedence

§ Flags are flown whether or not the Queen performs the ceremony in person and only in the Greater London area

THE ROYAL STANDARD

The Royal Standard comprises four quarterings – two for England (three lions passant), one for Scotland* (a lion rampant) and one for Ireland (a harp).

The Royal Standard is flown when the Queen is in residence at a royal palace, on transport being used by the Queen for official journeys and from Victoria Tower when the Queen attends parliament. It may also be flown on any building (excluding ecclesiastical buildings) during a visit by the Queen. If the Queen is to be present in a building advice on flag flying can be obtained from the DCMS.

The Royal Standard is never flown at half-mast, even after the death of the Sovereign, as the new monarch immediately succeeds to the throne.

* In Scotland a version with two Scottish quarterings instead of two English quarterings is used

THE ROYAL FAMILY

THE SOVEREIGN

ELIZABETH II, by the Grace of God, of the United Kingdom of Great Britain and Northern Ireland and of her other Realms and Territories Queen, Head of the Commonwealth, Defender of the Faith
Her Majesty Elizabeth Alexandra Mary of Windsor, elder daughter of King George VI and of HM Queen Elizabeth the Queen Mother
Born 21 April 1926, at 17 Bruton Street, London W1
Ascended the throne 6 February 1952
Crowned 2 June 1953, at Westminster Abbey
Married 20 November 1947, in Westminster Abbey, HRH The Prince Philip, Duke of Edinburgh
Official residences: Buckingham Palace, London SW1A 1AA; Windsor Castle, Berks; Palace of Holyroodhouse, Edinburgh
Private residences: Sandringham, Norfolk; Balmoral Castle, Aberdeenshire

HUSBAND OF THE QUEEN

HRH THE PRINCE PHILIP, DUKE OF EDINBURGH, KG, KT, OM, GBE, AC, QSO, PC, Ranger of Windsor Park
Born 10 June 1921, son of Prince and Princess Andrew of Greece and Denmark, naturalised a British subject 1947, created Duke of Edinburgh, Earl of Merioneth and Baron Greenwich 1947

CHILDREN OF THE QUEEN

HRH THE PRINCE OF WALES (Prince Charles Philip Arthur George), KG, KT, GCB, OM and Great Master of the Order of the Bath, AK, QSO, PC, ADC(P)
Born 14 November 1948, created Prince of Wales and Earl of Chester 1958, succeeded as Duke of Cornwall, Duke of Rothesay, Earl of Carrick and Baron Renfrew, Lord of the Isles and Great Steward of Scotland 1952
Married (1) 29 July 1981 Lady Diana Frances Spencer (Diana, Princess of Wales (1961–97), youngest daughter of the 8th Earl Spencer and the Hon. Mrs Shand Kydd), marriage dissolved 1996; (2) 9 April 2005 Mrs Camilla Rosemary Parker Bowles, now HRH The Duchess of Cornwall (*born* 17 July 1947, daughter of Major Bruce Shand and the Hon. Mrs Rosalind Shand)
Residences: Clarence House, London SW1A 1BA; Highgrove, Doughton, Tetbury, Glos GL8 8TN; Birkhall, Ballater, Aberdeenshire
Issue:
1. HRH Prince William of Wales (Prince William Arthur Philip Louis), *born* 21 June 1982
2. HRH Prince Henry of Wales (Prince Henry Charles Albert David), *born* 15 September 1984

HRH THE PRINCESS ROYAL (Princess Anne Elizabeth Alice Louise), KG, KT, GCVO
Born 15 August 1950, declared The Princess Royal 1987
Married (1) 14 November 1973 Captain Mark Anthony Peter Phillips, CVO (*born* 22 September 1948); marriage dissolved 1992; (2) 12 December 1992 Captain Timothy James Hamilton Laurence, MVO, RN (*born* 1 March 1955)
Residence: Gatcombe Park, Minchinhampton, Glos GL6 9AT

Issue:
1. Peter Mark Andrew Phillips, *born* 15 November 1977
2. Zara Anne Elizabeth Phillips, *born* 15 May 1981

HRH THE DUKE OF YORK (Prince Andrew Albert Christian Edward), KG, KCVO, ADC(P)
Born 19 February 1960, created Duke of York, Earl of Inverness and Baron Killyleagh 1986
Married 23 July 1986 Sarah Margaret Ferguson, now Sarah, Duchess of York (*born* 15 October 1959, younger daughter of Major Ronald Ferguson and Mrs Hector Barrantes), marriage dissolved 1996
Residence: Royal Lodge, Windsor Great Park, Berks
Issue:
1. HRH Princess Beatrice of York (Princess Beatrice Elizabeth Mary), *born* 8 August 1988
2. HRH Princess Eugenie of York (Princess Eugenie Victoria Helena), *born* 23 March 1990

HRH THE EARL OF WESSEX (Prince Edward Antony Richard Louis), KG, KCVO
Born 10 March 1964, created Earl of Wessex, Viscount Severn 1999
Married 19 June 1999 Sophie Helen Rhys-Jones, now HRH The Countess of Wessex (*born* 20 January 1965, daughter of Mr and Mrs Christopher Rhys-Jones)
Residence: Bagshot Park, Bagshot, Surrey GU19 5HS
Issue:
1. Lady Louise Windsor (Louise Alice Elizabeth Mary Mountbatten-Windsor), *born* 8 November 2003

NEPHEW AND NIECE OF THE QUEEN

Children of HRH The Princess Margaret, Countess of Snowdon and the Earl of Snowdon (*see* House of Windsor):

DAVID ALBERT CHARLES ARMSTRONG-JONES, VISCOUNT LINLEY, *born* 3 November 1961, *married* 8 October 1993 the Hon. Serena Stanhope, and has issue, Hon. Charles Patrick Inigo Armstrong-Jones, *born* 1 July 1999; Hon. Margarita Elizabeth Alleyne Armstrong-Jones, *born* 14 May 2002

LADY SARAH CHATTO (Sarah Frances Elizabeth), *born* 1 May 1964, *married* 14 July 1994 Daniel Chatto, and has issue, Samuel David Benedict Chatto, *born* 28 July 1996; Arthur Robert Nathaniel Chatto, *born* 5 February 1999

COUSINS OF THE QUEEN

Child of HRH The Duke of Gloucester and HRH Princess Alice, Duchess of Gloucester (*see* House of Windsor):

HRH THE DUKE OF GLOUCESTER (Prince Richard Alexander Walter George), KG, GCVO, Grand Prior of the Order of St John of Jerusalem
Born 26 August 1944
Married 8 July 1972 Birgitte Eva van Deurs, now HRH The Duchess of Gloucester, GCVO (*born* 20 June 1946, daughter of Asger Henriksen and Vivian van Deurs)
Residence: Kensington Palace, London W8 4PU

Issue:
1. Earl of Ulster (Alexander Patrick Gregers Richard), *born* 24 October 1974, *married* 22 June 2002 Dr Claire Booth, and has issue, Lord Culloden (Xan Richard Anders), *born* 12 March 2007
2. Lady Davina Lewis (Davina Elizabeth Alice Benedikte), *born* 19 November 1977, *married* 31 July 2004 Gary Lewis
3. Lady Rose Windsor (Rose Victoria Birgitte Louise), *born* 1 March 1980

Children of HRH The Duke of Kent and Princess Marina, Duchess of Kent (*see* House of Windsor):

HRH THE DUKE OF KENT (Prince Edward George Nicholas Paul Patrick), KG, GCMG, GCVO, ADC(P)
Born 9 October 1935
Married 8 June 1961 Katharine Lucy Mary Worsley, now HRH The Duchess of Kent, GCVO (*born* 22 February 1933, daughter of Sir William Worsley, Bt.)
Residence: Wren House, Palace Green, London W8 4PY
Issue:
1. Earl of St Andrews (George Philip Nicholas), *born* 26 June 1962, *married* 9 January 1988 Sylvana Tomaselli, and has issue, Baron Downpatrick (Edward Edmund Maximilian George), *born* 2 December 1988; Lady Marina-Charlotte Windsor (Marina-Charlotte Alexandra Katharine Helen), *born* 30 September 1992; Lady Amelia Windsor (Amelia Sophia Theodora Mary Margaret), *born* 24 August 1995
2. Lady Helen Taylor (Helen Marina Lucy), *born* 28 April 1964, *married* 18 July 1992 Timothy Taylor, and has issue, Columbus George Donald Taylor, *born* 6 August 1994; Cassius Edward Taylor, *born* 26 December 1996; Eloise Olivia Katharine Taylor, *born* 3 March 2003; Estella Olga Elizabeth Taylor, *born* 21 December 2004
3. Lord Nicholas Windsor (Nicholas Charles Edward Jonathan), *born* 25 July 1970, *married* 4 November 2006 Paola Doimi de Frankopan

HRH PRINCESS ALEXANDRA, THE HON. LADY OGILVY (Princess Alexandra Helen Elizabeth Olga Christabel), KG, GCVO
Born 25 December 1936
Married 24 April 1963 The Rt. Hon. Sir Angus Ogilvy, KCVO (1928–2004), second son of 12th Earl of Airlie
Residence: Thatched House Lodge, Richmond Park, Surrey TW10 5HP
Issue:
1. James Robert Bruce Ogilvy, *born* 29 February 1964, *married* 30 July 1988 Julia Rawlinson, and has issue, Flora Alexandra Ogilvy, *born* 15 December 1994; Alexander Charles Ogilvy, *born* 12 November 1996
2. Marina Victoria Alexandra, Mrs Mowatt, *born* 31 July 1966, *married* 2 February 1990 Paul Mowatt (marriage dissolved 1997), and has issue, Zenouska May Mowatt, *born* 26 May 1990; Christian Alexander Mowatt, *born* 4 June 1993

HRH PRINCE MICHAEL OF KENT (Prince Michael George Charles Franklin), GCVO
Born 4 July 1942

Married 30 June 1978 Baroness Marie-Christine Agnes Hedwig Ida von Reibnitz, now HRH Princess Michael of Kent (*born* 15 January 1945, daughter of Baron Gunther von Reibnitz)
Residence: Kensington Palace, London W8 4PU
Issue:
1. Lord Frederick Windsor (Frederick Michael George David Louis), *born* 6 April 1979
2. Lady Gabriella Windsor (Gabriella Marina Alexandra Ophelia), *born* 23 April 1981

ORDER OF SUCCESSION

1	HRH The Prince of Wales
2	HRH Prince William of Wales
3	HRH Prince Henry of Wales
4	HRH The Duke of York
5	HRH Princess Beatrice of York
6	HRH Princess Eugenie of York
7	HRH The Earl of Wessex
8	Lady Louise Windsor
9	HRH The Princess Royal
10	Peter Phillips
11	Zara Phillips
12	Viscount Linley
13	Hon. Charles Armstrong-Jones
14	Hon. Margarita Armstrong-Jones
15	Lady Sarah Chatto
16	Samuel Chatto
17	Arthur Chatto
18	HRH The Duke of Gloucester
19	Earl of Ulster
20	Lord Culloden
21	Lady Davina Lewis
22	Lady Rose Windsor
23	HRH The Duke of Kent
24	Lady Marina-Charlotte Windsor
25	Lady Amelia Windsor
26	Lady Helen Taylor
27	Columbus Taylor
28	Cassius Taylor
29	Eloise Taylor
30	Estella Taylor
31	Lord Frederick Windsor
32	Lady Gabriella Windsor
33	HRH Princess Alexandra, the Hon. Lady Ogilvy
34	James Ogilvy
35	Alexander Ogilvy
36	Flora Ogilvy
37	Marina Ogilvy, Mrs Mowatt
38	Christian Mowatt
39	Zenouska Mowatt

HRH Prince Michael of Kent, and The Earl of St Andrews both lost the right of succession to the throne through marriage to a Roman Catholic. Lord Nicholas Windsor and Baron Downpatrick renounced their rights to the throne on converting to Roman Catholicism in 2001 and 2003 respectively. Their children remain in succession provided that they are in communion with the Church of England.

PRIVATE SECRETARIES TO THE ROYAL FAMILY

THE QUEEN
Office: Buckingham Palace, London SW1A 1AA
T 020-7930 4832 **W** www.royal.gov.uk
Private Secretary to the Queen, Christopher Geidt, OBE

PRINCE PHILIP, THE DUKE OF EDINBURGH
Office: Buckingham Palace, London SW1A 1AA
T 020-7930 4832
Private Secretary, Brig. Sir Miles Hunt-Davis, KCVO, CBE

THE PRINCE OF WALES AND THE DUCHESS OF
CORNWALL
Office: Clarence House, London SW1A 1BA **T** 020-7930 4832
Principal Private Secretary, Sir Michael Peat, KCVO

PRINCES WILLIAM AND HENRY OF WALES
Office: Clarence House, London SW1A 1BA **T** 020-7930 4832
Private Secretary, James Lowther-Pinkerton, MVO, MBE

THE DUKE OF YORK
Office: Buckingham Palace, London SW1A 1AA
T 020-7930 4832
Private Secretary, Alastair Watson

THE EARL AND COUNTESS OF WESSEX
Office: Bagshot Park, Surrey GU19 5PL **T** 01276-707040
Private Secretary, Brig. J. Smedley

THE PRINCESS ROYAL
Office: Buckingham Palace, London SW1A 1AA
T 020-7930 4832
Private Secretary, Capt. N. P. Wright, LVO, RN

THE DUKE AND DUCHESS OF GLOUCESTER
Office: Kensington Palace, London W8 4PU **T** 020-7368 1000
Private Secretary, Alistair Wood, MBE

THE DUKE OF KENT
Office: St James's Palace, London SW1A 1BQ **T** 020-7930 4872
Private Secretary, N. Adamson, LVO, OBE

THE DUCHESS OF KENT
Office: Wren House, Palace Green, London W8 4PY
T 020-7937 2730
Personal Secretary, Virginia Utley

PRINCE AND PRINCESS MICHAEL OF KENT
Office: Kensington Palace, London W8 4PU **T** 020-7938 3519
W www.princemichael.org.uk
Private Secretary, N. Chance

PRINCESS ALEXANDRA, THE HON. LADY OGILVY
Office: Buckingham Palace, London SW1A 1AA
T 020-7024 4270
Private Secretary, Diane Duke

ROYAL SALUTES

ENGLAND
The basic royal salute is 21 rounds with an extra 20
rounds fired at Hyde Park because it is a royal park. At the
Tower of London 62 rounds are fired on royal
anniversaries (21 plus a further 20 because the Tower is a
royal palace and a further 21 'for the City of London') and
41 on other occasions. Gun salutes occur on the following
royal anniversaries:

- Accession Day
- The Queen's birthday
- Coronation Day
- Duke of Edinburgh's birthday
- The Queen's official birthday
- state opening of parliament

Gun salutes also occur when parliament is prorogued by the
sovereign, on royal births and when a visiting head of state
meets the sovereign in London, Windsor or Edinburgh.
In London, salutes are fired at Hyde Park and the
Tower of London although on some occasions (state
visits, state opening of parliament and the Queen's
birthday parade) Green Park is used instead.

Constable of the Royal Palace and Fortress of London, Gen. Sir
  Roger Wheeler, GCB, CBE
Lieutenant of the Tower of London, Lt.-Gen. Sir Cedric
  Delves, KBE, DSO
Resident Governor and Keeper of the Jewel House, Maj.-Gen.
  Keith Cima, CB
Master Gunner of St James's Park, Gen. Sir Alex Harley,
  KBE, CB
Master Gunner within the Tower, Col. Simon Garrett

SCOTLAND
Royal salutes are authorised at Edinburgh Castle and
Stirling Castle, although in practice Edinburgh Castle is
the only operating saluting station in Scotland. A salute of
21 guns is fired on the following occasions:

- the anniversaries of the birth, accession and coronation
  of the sovereign
- the anniversary of the birth of the Duke of Edinburgh

A salute of 21 guns is fired in Edinburgh on the occasion
of the opening of the general assembly of the Church of
Scotland. A salute of 21 guns may also be fired in
Edinburgh on the arrival of HM The Queen or a member of
the royal family who is a Royal Highness on an official visit.
Other military saluting stations are at Cardiff Castle in
Wales and Hillsborough Castle, County Down in
Northern Ireland.

ROYAL HOUSEHOLD

The PRIVATE SECRETARY is responsible for:

- informing and advising the Queen on constitutional, governmental and political matters in the UK, her other Realms and the wider Commonwealth, including communications with the prime minister and government departments
- organising the Queen's domestic and overseas official programme
- the Queen's speeches, messages, patronage, photographs, portraits and official presents
- communications in connection with the role of the royal family
- dealing with correspondence to the Queen from members of the public
- organising and coordinating royal travel
- coordinating and initiating research to support engagements by members of the royal family

The PRESS SECRETARY is in charge of Buckingham Palace's press office and reports to the private secretary. The press secretary is responsible for:

- developing communications strategies to enhance the public understanding of the role of the monarchy
- briefing the British and international media on the role and duties of the Queen and issues relating to the royal family
- responding to media enquiries
- arranging media facilities in the UK and overseas to support royal functions and engagements
- the management of the royal website

The private secretary is keeper of the Royal Archives and is responsible for the care of the records of the sovereign and the royal household from previous reigns, preserved in the Royal Archives at Windsor. As keeper, it is the private secretary's responsibility to ensure the proper management of the records of the present reign with a view to their transfer to the archives as and when appropriate. The private secretary is an *ex officio* trustee of the Royal Collection Trust.

The KEEPER OF THE PRIVY PURSE AND TREASURER to the Queen is responsible for:

- the Queen's Civil List, which is the money paid from the government's Consolidated Fund to meet official expenditure relating to the Queen's duties as head of state and head of the Commonwealth
- through the director of personnel, the planning and management of personnel policy across the royal household, the administration of all its pension schemes and private estates employees, and the allocation of employee and pensioner housing
- information technology systems
- internal audit services
- health and safety; insurance matters
- the privy purse, which is mainly financed by the net income of the Duchy of Lancaster, and meets both official and private expenditure incurred by the Queen
- liaison with other members of the royal family and their households on financial matters

- the Queen's private estates at Sandringham and Balmoral, the Queen's Racing Establishment and the Royal Studs and liaison with the Ascot Authority
- the Home Park at Windsor and liaison with the Crown Estate Commissioners concerning the Home Park and the Great Park at Windsor
- the Royal Philatelic Collection
- administrative aspects of the Military Knights of Windsor and the Royal Almonry
- administration of the Royal Victorian Order, of which the keeper of the privy purse is secretary, Long and Faithful Service Medals, and the Queen's cups, medals and prizes, and policy on commemorative medals

The keeper of the privy purse is one of three royal trustees (in respect of his responsibilities for the Civil List) and is receiver-general of the Duchy of Lancaster and a member of the Duchy's Council.

The keeper of the privy purse is also responsible for property services at occupied royal palaces in England, comprising Buckingham Palace, St James's Palace, Clarence House, Marlborough House Mews, the residential and office areas of Kensington Palace, Windsor Castle and buildings in the Home and Great Parks of Windsor and Hampton Court Mews and Paddocks. The costs of property services for occupied royal palaces are met from a grant-in-aid from the Department for Culture, Media and Sport.

The DIRECTOR OF PROPERTY SERVICES has day-to-day responsibility for the royal household's property section:

- fire safety issues
- repairs and refurbishment of buildings and new buildings work
- utilities and telecommunications
- putting up stages, tents and other work in connection with ceremonial occasions, garden parties and other official functions

The property section is also responsible, on a sub-contract basis from the DCMS, for the maintenance of Marlborough House (which is occupied by the Commonwealth Secretariat).

The keeper of the privy purse also oversees royal communications and information expenditure, which is met from the property services grant-in-aid, and the financial aspects of royal travel, met from a grant-in-aid provided by the Department for Transport.

The keeper of the privy purse is an *ex officio* trustee of the Historic Royal Palaces Trust and the Royal Collection Trust.

The Queen's Civil List and the grants-in-aid for property services and royal travel are provided by the government in return for the net surplus from the Crown Estate and other hereditary revenues.

The MASTER OF THE HOUSEHOLD is responsible for the staff and domestic arrangements at Buckingham Palace, Windsor Castle, the Palace of Holyroodhouse, Balmoral Castle and Sandringham House when the Queen is in residence. These arrangements include:

- the provision of meals for the Queen and other

members of the royal family, their guests and royal household employees

- service by liveried staff at meals, receptions and other events
- travel arrangements for employees and the movement of baggage between the royal residences
- cleaning and laundry
- furnishings and the internal decorative appearance of occupied royal palaces in collaboration with the director of the Royal Collection
- liaison with the royalty and diplomatic protection department of the Metropolitan Police concerning security procedures at occupied royal palaces
- the Queen's official entertaining, both at home and overseas, and overseeing aspects of the Queen's private entertaining

The COMPTROLLER, LORD CHAMBERLAIN'S OFFICE is responsible for:

- the organisation of all ceremonial engagements, including state visits to the Queen in the UK, royal weddings and funerals, the state opening of parliament, Guards of Honour at Buckingham Palace, investitures, and the Garter and Thistle ceremonies
- garden parties at Buckingham Palace and the Palace of Holyroodhouse (except for catering and tents)
- the Crown Jewels, which are part of the Royal Collection, when they are in use on state occasions
- coordination of the arrangements for the Queen to be represented at funerals and memorial services and at the arrival and departure of visiting heads of state
- advising on matters of precedence, style and titles, dress, flying of flags, gun salutes, mourning and other ceremonial issues
- supervising the applications from tradesmen for Royal Warrants of Appointment
- advising on the commercial use of royal emblems and contemporary royal photographs
- the ecclesiastical household, the medical household, the body guards and certain ceremonial appointments such as Gentlemen Ushers and Pages of Honour
- the lords in waiting, who represent the Queen on various occasions and escort visiting heads of state during incoming state visits
- the Queen's bargemaster and watermen and the Queen's swans

The comptroller is also responsible for the Royal Mews, assisted by the CROWN EQUERRY, who has day-to-day responsibility for:

- the provision of carriage processions for the state opening of parliament, state visits, Trooping of the Colour, Royal Ascot, the Garter Ceremony, the Thistle Service, the presentation of credentials to the Queen by incoming foreign ambassadors and high commissioners, and other state and ceremonial occasions
- the provision of chauffeur-driven cars
- coordinating travel arrangements by road in respect of the Queen's official engagements
- supervision and administration of the Royal Mews at Buckingham Palace, Windsor Castle, Hampton Court and the Palace of Holyroodhouse

The comptroller also has overall responsibility for the MARSHAL OF THE DIPLOMATIC CORPS, who is responsible for the relationship between the royal household and the Diplomatic Heads of Mission in London; and the SECRETARY OF THE CENTRAL CHANCERY OF THE ORDERS OF KNIGHTHOOD, who administers the Orders of Chivalry, makes arrangements for investitures and the distribution of insignia, and ensures the proper public notification of awards through the *London Gazette*.

The DIRECTOR OF THE ROYAL COLLECTION is responsible for:

- the administration and custodial control of the Royal Collection in all royal residences
- the care, display, conservation and restoration of items in the collection
- initiating and assisting research into the collection and publishing catalogues and books on the collection
- making the collection accessible to the public and educating and informing the public about the collection

The Royal Collection, which contains a large number of works of art, is held by the Queen as sovereign in trust for her successors and the nation and is not owned by her as an individual. The administration, conservation and presentation of the Royal Collection are funded by the Royal Collection Trust solely from income from visitors to Windsor Castle, Buckingham Palace and the Palace of Holyroodhouse. The Royal Collection Trust is chaired by the Prince of Wales. The Lord Chamberlain, the private secretary and the keeper of the privy purse are *ex officio* trustees and there are three external trustees appointed by the Queen.

The director of the Royal Collection is also at present the SURVEYOR OF THE QUEEN'S WORKS OF ART and is responsible for pictures and miniatures, the ROYAL LIBRARIAN is responsible for all books, manuscripts, coins and medals, insignia and works of art on paper including the watercolours, prints and drawings in the Print Room at Windsor Castle, and the SURVEYOR OF THE QUEEN'S WORKS OF ART is responsible for furniture, ceramics and the other decorative arts in the collection.

The director of the Royal Collection has overall responsibility for trading activities that fund the Royal Collection Department. These are administered by Royal Collection Enterprises Limited, the trading subsidiary of the Royal Collection Trust. The company, whose chair is the Keeper of the Privy Purse, is responsible for:

- Managing access by the public to Windsor Castle (including Frogmore House), Buckingham Palace (including the Royal Mews and the Queen's Gallery) and the Palace of Holyroodhouse
- Running shops at each location
- Managing the images and intellectual property rights of the Royal Collection

The director of the Royal Collection is also an *ex officio* trustee of the Historic Royal Palaces Trust.

SENIOR MANAGEMENT OF THE ROYAL HOUSEHOLD

Lord Chamberlain, Earl Peel, GCVO, PC
HEADS OF DEPARTMENT
Private Secretary to The Queen, Rt. Hon. Christopher Geidt, OBE
Keeper of the Privy Purse, Sir Alan Reid, KCVO
Master of the Household, Air Vice-Marshal David Walker, OBE, MVO
Comptroller, Lord Chamberlain's Office, Lt.-Col. Andrew Ford
Director of the Royal Collection, Sir Hugh Roberts, KCVO
NON-EXECUTIVE MEMBERS
Private Secretary to the Duke of Edinburgh, Brig. Sir Miles Hunt-Davis, KCVO, CBE

Private Secretary to the Prince of Wales, Sir Michael Peat, KCVO

THE POET LAUREATE

The post of Poet Laureate was officially established when John Dryden was appointed by royal warrant as Poet Laureate and Historiographer Royal in 1668. The post is attached to the royal household and was originally conferred on the holder for life; in 1999 the length of appointment was changed to a ten-year term. It is customary for the Poet Laureate to write verse to mark events of national importance. The postholder currently receives an honorarium of £5,000 a year.
The Poet Laureate, Prof. Andrew Motion, apptd 1999

ROYAL FINANCES

FUNDING

CIVIL LIST

The Civil List dates back to the late 17th century. It was originally used by the sovereign to supplement hereditary revenues for paying the salaries of judges, ambassadors and other government officers as well as the expenses of the royal household. In 1760, on the accession of George III, it was decided that the Civil List would be provided by parliament to cover all relevant expenditure in return for the king surrendering the hereditary revenues of the Crown (principally the net surplus of the Crown Estate). At that time parliament undertook to pay the salaries of judges, ambassadors, etc. In 1831 parliament agreed also to meet the costs of the royal palaces in return for a reduction in the Civil List. Each sovereign has agreed to continue this arrangement. The Civil List now meets the central staff costs and running expenses of the Queen's official household.

Until 1972, the amount of money allocated annually under the Civil List was set for the duration of a reign. The system was then altered to a fixed annual payment for ten years but from 1975 high inflation made an annual review necessary. The system of payments reverted to the practice of a fixed annual payment of £7.9m for a ten year period to 31 December 2000, during this period annual Civil List expenditure reached £6.5m, and a reserve of £35m was established. In order to draw down the reserve, the annual Civil List payment was left at £7.9m for a further ten years to 31 December 2010.

The legislative requirement is for Civil List accounts to be submitted to parliament, in the form of Royal Trustees Reports, at 10-yearly intervals, but from June 2002 accounts have been published annually. The sixth annual accounts for the year ending 31 December 2006 were published in June 2007:

	2005	2006
Civil List payment	£7,900,000	£7,900,000
Draw-down from the Civil List reserve	£3,400,000	£4,100,000
Net Receipts	£11,300,000	£12,000,000
Net Civil List Expenditure	(£11,300,000)	(£12,200,000)

PARLIAMENTARY ANNUITIES

The Civil List Acts provide for other members of the royal family to receive parliamentary annuities from government funds to meet the expenses of carrying out their official duties. Since 1993 the Queen has reimbursed all the annuities except those paid to the late Queen Elizabeth the Queen Mother and the Duke of Edinburgh.

The Prince of Wales does not receive a parliamentary annuity. He derives his income from the revenues of the Duchy of Cornwall and these monies meet the official and private expenses of the Prince of Wales and his family (see Prince of Wales' Funding).

In 2000 the annual amounts payable to members of the royal family, excluding the Earl of Wessex, were reset at their 1990 levels for the next ten years. The Earl of Wessex had his annuity increased by £45,000 to £141,000 on the occasion of his marriage in 1999.

The annual payments remain as follows until December 2010:

The Duke of Edinburgh	£359,000
The Duke of York	£249,000
The Earl of Wessex	£141,000
The Princess Royal	£228,000
The Duke and Duchess of Gloucester	£175,000
The Duke and Duchess of Kent	£236,000
Princess Alexandra	£225,000
Subtotal	£1,613,000
Refunded to the Treasury by the Queen	(£1,254,000)
TOTAL	£359,000

GRANTS-IN-AID

Grants-in-aid are provided to the royal household annually by the Department for Culture, Media and Sport for property services and communications and information, and by the Department for Transport for royal travel. Property services meets the cost of property maintenance, and of utilities, telephones and related services at the occupied royal palaces in England (see Royal Household section for a list of occupied palaces). Communications and Information meets the cost of communication and information services in connection with official royal functions and engagements in England and Scotland. Royal travel meets the cost of official royal travel by air and rail.

GRANTS-IN-AID 2006–7:

	Grant-in-aid voted by parliament	Total net expenditure
Property Services	£15,000,000	£14,500,000
Marlborough House Maintenance	£600,000	£400,000
Communications and Information	£500,000	£500,000
Royal Travel	£6,000,000	£5,600,000

THE PRIVY PURSE AND THE DUCHY OF LANCASTER

The funds received by the privy purse pay for official expenses incurred by the Queen as head of state and for some of the Queen's private expenditure. The revenues of the Duchy of Lancaster are the principal source of income for the privy purse. The revenues of the Duchy were retained by George III in 1760 when the hereditary revenues were surrendered in exchange for the Civil List. The Duchy's affairs are the responsibility of the Duchy Council which reports to the Chancellor of the Duchy of Lancaster, who in turn is accountable directly to the sovereign rather than to parliament. However the chancellor does answer parliamentary questions on matters relating to the Duchy of Lancaster's responsibilities.

THE DUCHY OF LANCASTER, Lancaster Place, London WC2E 7ED E info@duchyoflancaster.co.uk
W www.duchyoflancaster.co.uk
Chancellor of the Duchy of Lancaster, Rt Hon. Hilary Armstrong, MP, *apptd* 2006
Chair of the Council, Lord Shuttleworth
Clerk and Chief Executive, Paul Clarke, FRICS
Receiver-General, Sir Alan Reid, KCVO
Attorney-General, Robert Hildyard, QC

PERSONAL INCOME

The Queen's personal income derives mostly from investments, and is used to meet private expenditure.

EXPENDITURE MET BY GOVERNMENT DEPARTMENTS AND THE CROWN ESTATE 2006–7:

Administration of honours	£500,000
Equerries, orderlies and other personnel	£900,000
Maintenance of Holyroodhouse	£1,300,000
State visits to and by the Queen and liaison with the Diplomatic Corps	£600,000
Ceremonial occasions	£200,000
Maintenance of Home Park, Windsor Castle	£500,000
Other	£100,000
Total	£4,100,000

PRINCE OF WALES' FUNDING

The Duchy Estate was created in 1337 by Edward III for his son and heir Prince Edward (the Black Prince) who became the Duke of Cornwall. The Duchy's primary function is to provide an income from its assets for the Prince of Wales. Under a 1337 charter, confirmed by subsequent legislation, the Prince of Wales is not entitled to the proceeds or profit on the sale of Duchy assets but only to the annual income which is generated from these assets. The Duchy is responsible for the sustainable and commercial management of its properties, investment portfolio and approximately 54,764 hectares of land, based mostly in the southwest of England. The Prince of Wales has chosen to use a proportion of his income to meet the cost of his public and charitable work in addition to providing a private source of income. The Duchy also funds the public, charitable and private activities of the Duchess of Cornwall and princes William and Harry. Proceeds from the Duchy are voluntarily subject to income tax.

THE DUCHY OF CORNWALL, 10 Buckingham Gate, London SW1E 6L
T 0207-834 7346 E London@duchyofcornwall.gov.uk
W www.duchyofcornwall.org
Lord Warden of the Stannaries, Sir Nicholas Bacon, Bt.
Receiver-General, James Leigh-Pemberton
Attorney-General, Jonathan Crow, QC
Secretary and Keeper of the Records, Bertie Ross

TAXATION

The sovereign is not legally liable to pay income tax or capital gains tax. After income tax was reintroduced in 1842, some income tax was paid voluntarily by the sovereign but over a long period these payments were phased out. In 1992 the Queen offered to pay tax on a voluntary basis from 6 April 1993, and the Prince of Wales offered to pay tax on a voluntary basis on his income from the Duchy of Cornwall (he was already taxed in all other respects).

The main provisions for the Queen and the Prince of Wales to pay tax, set out in a Memorandum of Understanding on Royal Taxation presented to parliament on 11 February 1993, are that the Queen will pay income tax and capital gains tax in respect of her private income and assets, and on the proportion of the income and capital gains of the Privy Purse used for private purposes. Inheritance tax will be paid on the Queen's assets, except for those which pass to the next sovereign, whether automatically or by gift or bequest. The Prince of Wales will pay income tax on income from the Duchy of Cornwall used for private purposes.

The Prince of Wales has confirmed that he intends to pay tax on the same basis following his accession to the throne. Other members of the royal family are subject to tax as for any taxpayer.

MILITARY RANKS AND TITLES

THE QUEEN

ROYAL NAVY
Lord High Admiral of the United Kingdom

ARMY
Colonel-in-Chief
The Life Guards; The Blues and Royals (Royal Horse Guards and 1st Dragoons); The Royal Scots Dragoon Guards (Carabiniers and Greys); The Queen's Royal Lancers; Royal Tank Regiment; Corps of Royal Engineers; Grenadier Guards; Coldstream Guards; Scots Guards; Irish Guards; Welsh Guards; The Royal Regiment of Scotland; The Duke of Lancaster's Regiment; The Royal Welsh; Adjutant General's Corps; The Royal Mercian and Lancastrian Yeomanry; The Governor General's Horse Guards (of Canada); The King's Own Calgary Regiment (Royal Canadian Armoured Corps); Canadian Forces Military Engineers Branch; Royal 22e Regiment (of Canada); Governor General's Foot Guards (of Canada); The Canadian Grenadier Guards; Le Régiment de la Chaudière (of Canada); 2nd Battalion Royal New Brunswick Regiment (North Shore); The 48th Highlanders of Canada; The Argyll and Sutherland Highlanders of Canada (Princess Louise's); The Calgary Highlanders; Royal Australian Engineers; Royal Australian Infantry Corps; Royal Australian Army Ordnance Corps; Royal Australian Army Nursing Corps; The Corps of Royal New Zealand Engineers; Royal New Zealand Infantry Regiment; The Malawi Rifles; The Royal Malta Artillery

Affiliated Colonel-in-Chief
The Queen's Gurkha Engineers

Captain-General
Royal Regiment of Artillery; The Honourable Artillery Company; Combined Cadet Force; Royal Regiment of Canadian Artillery; Royal Regiment of Australian Artillery; Royal Regiment of New Zealand Artillery; Royal New Zealand Armoured Corps

Royal Colonel
The Argyll and Sutherland Highlanders, 5th Battalion The Royal Regiment of Scotland

Patron
Royal Army Chaplains' Department

ROYAL AIR FORCE
Air Commodore-in-Chief
Royal Auxiliary Air Force; Royal Air Force Regiment; Air Reserve of Canada; Royal Australian Air Force Reserve; Territorial Air Force (of New Zealand)

Commandant-in-Chief
Royal Air Force College, Cranwell

Royal Honorary Air Commodore
Royal Air Force Marham; 603 (City of Edinburgh) Squadron Royal Auxiliary Air Force

PRINCE PHILIP, DUKE OF EDINBURGH

ROYAL NAVY
Admiral of the Fleet
Admiral of the Fleet, Royal Australian Navy
Admiral of the Fleet, Royal New Zealand Navy
Admiral of the Royal Canadian Sea Cadets

ROYAL MARINES
Captain-General

ARMY
Field Marshal
Field Marshal, Australian Military Forces
Field Marshal, New Zealand Army

Colonel-in-Chief
The Queen's Royal Hussars (Queen's Own and Royal Irish); The Rifles; Corps of Royal Electrical and Mechanical Engineers; Intelligence Corps; Army Cadet Force Association; The Royal Canadian Regiment; The Royal Hamilton Light Infantry (Wentworth Regiment of Canada); The Cameron Highlanders of Ottawa; The Queen's Own Cameron Highlanders of Canada; The Seaforth Highlanders of Canada; The Royal Canadian Army Cadets; The Royal Australian Corps of Electrical and Mechanical Engineers; The Australian Army Cadet Corps

Colonel
Grenadier Guards

Royal Colonel
The Highlanders, 4th Battalion The Royal Regiment of Scotland

Hon. Colonel
City of Edinburgh University Officers' Training Corps; The Trinidad and Tobago Regiment

Member
Honourable Artillery Company

ROYAL AIR FORCE
Marshal of the Royal Air Force
Marshal of the Royal Australian Air Force
Marshal of the Royal New Zealand Air Force

Air Commodore-in-Chief
Air Training Corps; Royal Canadian Air Cadets

Hon. Air Commodore
Royal Air Force Kinloss

THE PRINCE OF WALES

ROYAL NAVY
Admiral
Commodore-in-Chief
Royal Naval Command Plymouth

ARMY
General

Colonel-in-Chief
The Royal Dragoon Guards; The 22nd Cheshire Regiment; The Parachute Regiment; The Royal Gurkha Rifles; Army Air Corps; The Royal Canadian Dragoons; Lord Strathcona's Horse (Royal Canadians); The Royal Regiment of Canada; Royal Winnipeg Rifles; Royal Australian Armoured Corps; The Royal Pacific Islands Regiment; 1st The Queen's Dragoon Guards; The Black Watch (Royal Highland Regiment) of Canada; The Toronto Scottish Regiment (Queen Elizabeth The Queen Mother's Own); The Welsh Guards

Royal Colonel
The Black Watch, 3rd Battalion The Royal Regiment of Scotland; 51st Highland, 7th Battalion The Royal Regiment of Scotland (Territorial Army)

Royal Honorary Colonel
The Queen's Own Yeomanry

ROYAL AIR FORCE
Air Chief Marshal

Hon. Air Commodore
Royal Air Force Valley

Air Commodore-in-Chief
Royal New Zealand Air Force

Colonel-in-Chief
Air Reserve Canada

THE DUCHESS OF CORNWALL

ROYAL NAVY
Commodore-in-Chief
Naval Medical Services

ARMY
Royal Colonel
4th Battalion The Rifles

PRINCE WILLIAM OF WALES

ROYAL NAVY
Commodore-in-Chief
Scotland Command; Submarines Command

ARMY
Second Lieutenant
The Blues and Royals (Royal Horse Guards and 1st Dragoons)

PRINCE HENRY OF WALES

ROYAL NAVY
Commodore-in-Chief
Small Ships and Diving Command

ARMY
Second Lieutenant
The Blues and Royals (Royal Horse Guards and 1st Dragoons)

THE DUKE OF YORK

ROYAL NAVY
Commander
Admiral of the Marine Society and Sea Cadets
Honorary Captain

ARMY
Colonel-in-Chief
The Royal Irish Regiment (27th (Inniskilling), 83rd, 87th and The Ulster Defence Regiment); 9th/12th Royal Lancers (The Prince of Wales's); The Royal Highland Fusiliers, 2nd Battalion The Royal Regiment of Scotland; The Yorkshire Regiment; Small Arms School Corps; The Queen's York Rangers (First Americans); Royal New Zealand Army Logistics Regiment; The Royal Highland Fusiliers of Canada; The Princess Louise Fusiliers (Canada)

ROYAL AIR FORCE
Hon. Air Commodore
Royal Air Force Lossiemouth

THE EARL OF WESSEX

ROYAL NAVY
Commodore-in-Chief
Royal Fleet Auxiliary

Patron
Royal Fleet Auxiliary Association

ARMY
Colonel-in-Chief
Hastings and Prince Edward Regiment; Saskatchewan Dragoons

Royal Hon. Colonel
Royal Wessex Yeomanry

THE COUNTESS OF WESSEX

ARMY
Colonel-in-Chief
Queen Alexandra's Royal Army Nursing Corps; The Lincoln and Welland Regiment

THE PRINCESS ROYAL

ROYAL NAVY
Rear-Admiral (Chief Commandant for Women in the Royal Navy)

ARMY
Colonel-in-Chief
The King's Royal Hussars; Royal Corps of Signals; Royal Logistic Corps; The Royal Army Veterinary Corps; 8th Canadian Hussars (Princess Louise's); Royal Newfoundland Regiment; Canadian Forces Communications and Electronics Branch; The Grey and Simcoe Foresters (Royal Canadian Armoured Corps); The Royal Regina Rifle Regiment; Canadian Forces Medical Branch; Royal Australian Corps of Signals; Royal New Zealand Corps of Signals; Royal New Zealand Nursing Corps

Affiliated Colonel-in-Chief
The Queen's Gurkha Signals; The Queen's Own Gurkha Transport Regiment

Royal Colonel
Royal Scots Borders, 1st Battalion The Royal Regiment of Scotland; 52nd Lowland, 6th Battalion The Royal Regiment of Scotland

Colonel
The Blues and Royals (Royal Horse Guards and 1st Dragoons)

Hon. Colonel
University of London Officers' Training Corps

Commandant-in-Chief
First Aid Nursing Yeomanry (Princess Royal's Volunteer Corps)

ROYAL AIR FORCE
Hon. Air Commodore
Royal Air Force Lyneham; University of London Air Squadron

THE DUKE OF GLOUCESTER

ARMY
Colonel-in-Chief
The Royal Anglian Regiment; Royal Army Medical Corps

Deputy Colonel-in-Chief
The Royal Gloucestershire, Berkshire and Wiltshire Regiment; The Royal Logistic Corps

Hon. Colonel
Royal Monmouthshire Royal Engineers (Militia)

ROYAL AIR FORCE
Hon. Air Marshal

Hon. Air Commodore
Royal Air Force Odiham; No. 501 (County of Gloucester) Squadron Royal Auxiliary Air Force

THE DUCHESS OF GLOUCESTER

ARMY
Colonel-in-Chief
Royal Army Dental Corps; Royal Australian Army Educational Corps; Royal New Zealand Army Educational Corps

Deputy Colonel-in-Chief
Adjutant-General's Corps

Vice-Patron
Adjutant-General's Corps Regimental Association

Patron
Royal Army Educational Corps Association; Army Families Federation

THE DUKE OF KENT

ARMY
Field Marshal

Colonel-in-Chief
The Royal Regiment of Fusiliers; Lorne Scots (Peel, Dufferin and Hamilton Regiment)

Deputy Colonel-in-Chief
The Royal Scots Dragoon Guards (Carabiniers and Greys)

Royal Colonel
1st Battalion The Rifles

Colonel
Scots Guards

ROYAL AIR FORCE
Hon. Air Chief Marshal

Hon. Air Commodore
Royal Air Force Leuchars

THE DUCHESS OF KENT

ARMY
Deputy Colonel-in-Chief
The Royal Dragoon Guards; Adjutant-General's Corps; The Royal Logistic Corps

PRINCE MICHAEL OF KENT

ROYAL NAVY
Honorary Rear Admiral Royal Naval Reserve

ARMY
Major (retd)
The Royal Hussars (Prince of Wales's Own)

Colonel-in-Chief
Essex and Kent Scottish Regiment (Ontario)

ROYAL AIR FORCE
Hon. Air Commodore
RAF Benson

PRINCESS ALEXANDRA, THE HON. LADY OGILVY

ROYAL NAVY
Patron
Queen Alexandra's Royal Naval Nursing Service

ARMY
Colonel-in-Chief
The Queen's Own Rifles of Canada; The Canadian Scottish Regiment (Princess Mary's)

Deputy Colonel-in-Chief
The Queen's Royal Lancers

Royal Colonel
3rd Battalion The Rifles

Honorary Royal Colonel
The Royal Yeomanry

ROYAL AIR FORCE
Patron and Air Chief Commandant
Princess Mary's Royal Air Force Nursing Service

Hon. Air Commodore
Royal Air Force Cottesmore

THE HOUSE OF WINDSOR

King George V assumed by royal proclamation (17 July 1917) for his House and family, as well as for all descendants in the male line of Queen Victoria who are subjects of these realms, the name of Windsor.

KING GEORGE V

(George Frederick Ernest Albert), second son of King Edward VII, *born* 3 June 1865; *married* 6 July 1893 HSH Princess Victoria Mary Augusta Louise Olga Pauline Claudine Agnes of Teck (Queen Mary, *born* 26 May 1867; *died* 24 March 1953); *succeeded* to the throne 6 May 1910; *died* 20 January 1936. *Issue:*

1. HRH PRINCE EDWARD Albert Christian George Andrew Patrick David, *born* 23 June 1894, *succeeded* to the throne as King Edward VIII, 20 January 1936; *abdicated* 11 December 1936; created *Duke of Windsor* 1937; *married* 3 June 1937, Mrs Wallis Simpson (Her Grace The Duchess of Windsor, *born* 19 June 1896; *died* 24 April 1986), *died* 28 May 1972

2. HRH PRINCE ALBERT Frederick Arthur George, *born* 14 December 1895, *created* Duke of York 1920; *married* 26 April 1923, Lady Elizabeth Bowes-Lyon, youngest daughter of the 14th Earl of Strathmore and Kinghorne (HM Queen Elizabeth the Queen Mother, *born* 4 August 1900; *died* 30 March 2002), *succeeded* to the throne as King George VI, 11 December 1936; *died* 6 February 1952. *Issue:*
(1) HRH Princess Elizabeth Alexandra Mary, *succeeded* to the throne as Queen Elizabeth II, 6 February 1952 (*see* Royal Family)
(2) HRH Princess Margaret Rose (later HRH The Princess Margaret, Countess of Snowdon), *born* 21 August 1930; *married* 6 May 1960, Anthony Charles Robert Armstrong-Jones, GCVO, *created* Earl of Snowdon 1961 (marriage dissolved 1978), *died* 9 February 2002, having had issue (*see* Royal Family)

3. HRH PRINCESS (Victoria Alexandra Alice) MARY, *born* 25 April 1897, *created* Princess Royal 1932; *married* 28 February 1922, Viscount Lascelles, later the 6th Earl

of Harewood (1882–1947), *died* 28 March 1965. *Issue:*
(1) George Henry Hubert Lascelles, 7th Earl of Harewood, KBE, *born* 7 February 1923; *married* (1) 1949, Maria (Marion) Stein (marriage dissolved 1967); *issue, (a)* David Henry George, Viscount Lascelles, *born* 1950; *(b)* James Edward, *born* 1953; *(c)* (Robert) Jeremy Hugh, *born* 1955; (2) 1967, Mrs Patricia Tuckwell; *issue, (d)* Mark Hubert, *born* 1964
(2) Gerald David Lascelles (1924–98), *married* (1) 1952, Miss Angela Dowding (marriage dissolved 1978); *issue, (a)* Henry Ulick, *born* 1953; (2) 1978, Mrs Elizabeth Colvin; *issue, (b)* Martin David, *born* 1962

4. HRH PRINCE HENRY William Frederick Albert, *born* 31 March 1900, *created* Duke of Gloucester, Earl of Ulster and Baron Culloden 1928, *married* 6 November 1935, Lady Alice Christabel Montagu-Douglas-Scott, daughter of the 7th Duke of Buccleuch and Queensberry (HRH Princess Alice, Duchess of Gloucester, *born* 25 December 1901; *died* 29 October 2004); *died* 10 June 1974. *Issue:*
(1) HRH Prince William Henry Andrew Frederick, *born* 18 December 1941; *accidentally killed* 28 August 1972
(2) HRH Prince Richard Alexander Walter George (HRH The Duke of Gloucester)

5. HRH PRINCE GEORGE Edward Alexander Edmund, *born* 20 December 1902, *created* Duke of Kent, Earl of St Andrews and Baron Downpatrick 1934, *married* 29 November 1934, HRH Princess Marina of Greece and Denmark (*born* 30 November 1906; *died* 27 August 1968); *killed on active service,* 25 August 1942. *Issue:*
(1) HRH Prince Edward George Nicholas Paul Patrick (HRH The Duke of Kent)
(2) HRH Princess Alexandra Helen Elizabeth Olga Christabel (HRH Princess Alexandra, the Hon. Lady Ogilvy)
(3) HRH Prince Michael George Charles Franklin (HRH Prince Michael of Kent)

6. HRH PRINCE JOHN Charles Francis, *born* 12 July 1905; *died* 18 January 1919

DESCENDANTS OF QUEEN VICTORIA

QUEEN VICTORIA
(Alexandrina Victoria), *born* 24 May 1819; *succeeded* to
the throne 20 June 1837; *married* 10 February 1840
(Francis) Albert Augustus Charles Emmanuel, Duke of
Saxony, Prince of Saxe-Coburg and Gotha (HRH Albert,
Prince Consort, *born* 26 August 1819, *died* 14 December
1861); *died* 22 January 1901. *Issue:*
I. HRH PRINCESS VICTORIA Adelaide Mary
Louisa (Princess Royal) (1840–1901), *m.* 1858,
Friedrich III (1831–88), German Emperor March–
June 1888. *Issue:*
1. HIM Wilhelm II (1859–1941), German
Emperor 1888–1918, *m.* (1) 1881 Princess
Augusta Victoria of Schleswig-Holstein-
Sonderburg-Augustenburg (1858–1921); (2)
1922 Princess Hermine of Reuss (1887–1947).
Issue:
(a) Prince Wilhelm (1882–1951), *Crown Prince*
1888–1918, *m.* 1905 Duchess Cecilie
of Mecklenburg-Schwerin; *issue:* Prince
Wilhelm (1906–40); Prince Louis Ferdinand
(1907–94), *m.* 1938 Grand Duchess Kira;
Prince Hubertus (1909–50); Prince
Friedrich Georg (1911–66); Princess
Alexandrine Irene (1915–80); Princess
Cecilie (1917–75)
(b) Prince Eitel-Friedrich (1883–1942), *m.*
1906 Duchess Sophie of Oldenburg
(marriage dissolved 1926)
(c) Prince Adalbert (1884–1948), *m.* 1914
Princess Adelheid of Saxe-Meiningen; *issue:*
Princess Victoria Marina (1917–81); Prince
Wilhelm Victor (1919–89)
(d) Prince August Wilhelm (1887–1949), *m.*
1908 Princess Alexandra of Schleswig-
Holstein-Sonderburg-Glücksburg (marriage
dissolved 1920); *issue:* Prince Alexander
(1912–85)
(e) Prince Oskar (1888–1958), *m.* 1914
Countess von Ruppin; *issue:* Prince Oskar
(1915–39); Prince Burchard (1917–88);
Princess Herzeleide (1918–89); Prince
Wilhelm-Karl (1922–2007)
(f) Prince Joachim (1890–1920), *m.* 1916
Princess Marie of Anhalt; *issue:* Prince (Karl)
Franz Joseph (1916–75), and has issue
(g) Princess Viktoria Luise (1892–1980), *m.*
1913 Ernst, Duke of Brunswick 1913–18
(1887–1953); *issue:* Prince Ernst (1914–87);
Prince Georg (1915–2006), *m.* 1946
Princess Sophie of Greece and has issue (two
sons, one daughter); Princess Frederika
(1917–81), *m.* 1938 Paul I, King of the
Hellenes; Prince Christian (1919–81);
Prince Welf Heinrich (1923–97)
2. Princess Charlotte (1860–1919), *m.* 1878
Bernhard, Duke of Saxe-Meiningen 1914
(1851–1928). *Issue:* Princess Feodora (1879–
1945), *m.* 1898 Prince Heinrich XXX of Reuss
3. Prince Heinrich (1862–1929), *m.* 1888 Princess
Irene of Hesse. *Issue:*
(a) Prince Waldemar (1889–1945), *m.* Princess
Calixta Agnes of Lippe
(b) Prince Sigismund (1896–1978), *m.* 1919

Princess Charlotte of Saxe-Altenburg; *issue:*
Princess Barbara (1920–94); Prince Alfred
(b. 1924)
(c) Prince Heinrich (1900–4)
4. Prince Sigismund (1864–6)
5. Princess Victoria (1866–1929), *m.* (1) 1890,
Prince Adolf of Schaumburg-Lippe (1859–
1916); (2) 1927, Alexander Zubkov (1900–36)
6. Prince Waldemar (1868–79)
7. Princess Sophie (1870–1932), *m.* 1889
Constantine I (1868–1923), King of the
Hellenes 1913–17, 1920–3. *Issue:*
(a) George II (1890–1947), King of the
Hellenes 1923–47, 1935–47, *m.* 1921
Princess Elisabeth of Roumania (marriage
dissolved 1935)
(b) Alexander I (1893–1920), King of the
Hellenes 1917–20, *m.* 1919 Aspasia Manos;
issue: Princess Alexandra (1921–93), *m.*
1944 King Petar II of Yugoslavia
(c) Princess Helena (1896–1982), *m.* 1921
King Carol of Roumania (marriage
dissolved 1928) (*see* IV.2.(a))
(d) Paul I (1901–64), King of the Hellenes
1947–64, *m.* 1938 Princess Frederika of
Brunswick; *issue:* King Constantine II (b.
1940), *m.* 1964 Princess Anne-Marie of
Denmark, and has issue (three sons, two
daughters); Princess Sophie (b. 1938), *m.*
1962 Juan Carlos I of Spain; Princess Irene
(b. 1942)
(e) Princess Irene (1904–74), *m.* 1939 4th
Duke of Aosta; *issue:* Prince Amedeo, 5th
Duke of Aosta (b. 1943)
(f) Princess Katherine (Lady Katherine
Brandram) (b. 1913), *m.* 1947 Major R. C.
A. Brandram, MC, TD; *issue:* R. Paul G. A.
Brandram (b. 1948)
8. Princess Margarethe (1872–1954), *m.* 1893
Prince Friedrich Karl of Hesse (1868–1940).
Issue:
(a) Prince Friedrich Wilhelm (1893–1916)
(b) Prince Maximilian (1894–1914)
(c) Prince Philipp (1896–1980), *m.* 1925
Princess Mafalda of Italy; *issue:* Prince
Moritz (b. 1926); Prince Heinrich (1927–
99); Prince Otto (1937–98); Princess
Elisabeth (b. 1940)
(d) Prince Wolfgang (1896–1989), *m.* (1) 1924
Princess Marie Alexandra of Baden; (2)
1948 Ottilie Möller
(e) Prince Richard (1901–69)
(f) Prince Christoph (1901–43), *m.* 1930
Princess Sophie of Greece (*see* III.1.(a)) and
has issue (two sons, three daughters)
II. HRH PRINCE ALBERT EDWARD (HM KING
EDWARD VII) (1841–1910), *m.* 1863 HRH
Princess Alexandra of Denmark (1844–1925),
succeeded to the throne 22 January 1901, d. 6 May
1910. *Issue:*
1. Albert Victor, Duke of Clarence and Avondale
(1864–92)
2. George (HM KING GEORGE V) (1865–1936)
(*see* House of Windsor)

3. Louise (1867–1931) Princess Royal 1905–31, *m.* 1889 1st Duke of Fife (1849–1912). *Issue:*
   (a) Princess Alexandra, Duchess of Fife (1891–1959), *m.* 1913 Prince Arthur of Connaught
   (b) Princess Maud (1893–1945), *m.* 1923 11th Earl of Southesk (1893–1992); *issue:* Duke of Fife (*b.* 1929)
4. Victoria (1868–1935)
5. Maud (1869–1938), *m.* 1896 Prince Carl of Denmark (1872–1957), later King Haakon VII of Norway 1905–57. *Issue:*
   (a) Olav V (1903–91), King of Norway 1957–91, *m.* 1929 Princess Märtha of Sweden (1901–54); *issue:* Princess Ragnhild (*b.* 1930); Princess Astrid (*b.* 1932); Harald V, King of Norway (*b.* 1937)
6. Alexander (6–7 April 1871)

III. HRH PRINCESS ALICE Maud Mary (1843–78), *m.* 1862 Prince Ludwig (1837–92), Grand Duke of Hesse 1877–92. *Issue:*
1. Victoria (1863–1950), *m.* 1884 *Admiral of the Fleet* Prince Louis of Battenberg (1854–1921), *cr.* 1st Marquess of Milford Haven 1917. *Issue:*
   (a) Alice (1885–1969), *m.* 1903 Prince Andrew of Greece (1882–1944); *issue:* Princess Margarita (1905–81), *m.* 1931 Prince Gottfried of Hohenlohe-Langenburg (*see* IV.4.(a)); Princess Theodora (1906–69), *m.* Prince Berthold of Baden (1906–63) and has issue (two sons, one daughter); Princess Cecilie (1911–37), *m.* George, Grand Duke of Hesse (*see* III.4.(b)); Princess Sophie (1914–2001), *m.* (1) 1930 Prince Christoph of Hesse (*see* I.8.(f)); (2) 1946 Prince Georg of Hanover; Prince Philip, Duke of Edinburgh (*b.* 1921)
   (b) Louise (1889–1965), *m.* 1923 Gustaf VI Adolf (1882–1973), King of Sweden 1950–73 (*see* VII.1.)
   (c) George, 2nd Marquess of Milford Haven (1892–1938), *m.* 1916 Countess Nadejda, daughter of Grand Duke Michael of Russia; *issue:* Lady Tatiana (1917–88); David Michael, 3rd Marquess (1919–70)
   (d) Louis, 1st Earl Mountbatten of Burma (1900–79), *m.* 1922 Edwina Ashley, daughter of Lord Mount Temple; *issue:* Patricia, Countess Mountbatten of Burma (*b.* 1924); Pamela (*b.* 1929)
2. Elizabeth (1864–1918), *m.* 1884 Grand Duke Sergius of Russia (1857–1905)
3. Irene (1866–1953), *m.* 1888 Prince Heinrich of Prussia
4. Ernst Ludwig (1868–1937), Grand Duke of Hesse 1892–1918, *m.* (1) 1894 Princess Victoria Melita of Saxe-Coburg (*see* IV.3) (marriage dissolved 1901); (2) 1905 Princess Eleonore of Solms-Hohensolmslich. *Issue:*
   (a) Princess Elizabeth (1895–1903)
   (b) George, Hereditary Grand Duke of Hesse (1906–37), *m.* Princess Cecilie of Greece (*see* III.1.(a)), and had issue, two sons, accidentally killed with parents, 1937
   (c) Ludwig, Prince of Hesse (1908–68), *m.* 1937 Margaret, daughter of 1st Lord Geddes
5. Frederick William (1870–3)
6. Alix (Tsaritsa of Russia) (1872–1918), *m.* 1894

Nicholas II (1868–1918) Tsar of All the Russias 1894–1917, assassinated 16 July 1918. *Issue:*
(a) Grand Duchess Olga (1895–1918)
(b) Grand Duchess Tatiana (1897–1918)
(c) Grand Duchess Marie (1899–1918)
(d) Grand Duchess Anastasia (1901–18)
(e) Alexis, Tsarevich of Russia (1904–18)
7. Marie (1874–8)

IV. HRH PRINCE ALFRED Ernest Albert, Duke of Edinburgh, *Admiral of the Fleet* (1844–1900), *m.* 1874 Grand Duchess Marie Alexandrovna of Russia (1853–1920); succeeded as Duke of Saxe-Coburg and Gotha 22 August 1893. *Issue:*
1. Alfred, Prince of Saxe-Coburg (1874–99)
2. Marie (1875–1938), *m.* 1893 Ferdinand (1865–1927), King of Roumania 1914–27. *Issue:*
   (a) Carol II (1893–1953), King of Roumania 1930–40, *m.* (1) 1921 Princess Helena of Greece (*see* I.7.(c)) (marriage dissolved 1928), *issue:* Michael (*b.* 1921), King of Roumania 1927–30, 1940–7; (2) 1948 Princess Anne of Bourbon-Parma, and has issue (five daughters)
   (b) Elisabeth (1894–1956), *m.* 1921 George II, King of the Hellenes
   (c) Marie (1900–61), *m.* 1922 Alexander (1888–1934), King of Yugoslavia 1921–34; *issue:* Petar II (1923–70), King of Yugoslavia 1934–45, *m.* 1944 Princess Alexandra of Greece (*see* I.7.(b)) and has issue (Crown Prince Alexander, *b.* 1945); Prince Tomislav (1928–2000), *m.* (1) 1957 Princess Margarita of Baden (daughter of Princess Theodora of Greece and Prince Berthold of Baden (*see* III.1.(a))); (2) 1982 Linda Bonney; and has issue (three sons, one daughter); Prince Andrej (1929–90), *m.* (1) 1956 Princess Christina of Hesse (daughter of Prince Christoph of Hesse and Princess Sophie of Greece (*see* III.1.(a))); (2) 1963 Princess Kira-Melita of Leiningen (*see* IV.3.(a)); and has issue (three sons, two daughters)
   (d) Prince Nicolas (1903–78)
   (e) Princess Ileana (1909–91), *m.* (1) 1931 Archduke Anton of Austria; (2) 1954 Dr Stefan Issarescu; *issue:* Archduke Stefan (1932–98); Archduchess Maria Ileana (1933–59); Archduchess Alexandra (*b.* 1935); Archduke Dominic (*b.* 1937); Archduchess Maria Magdalena (*b.* 1939); Archduchess Elisabeth (*b.* 1942)
   (f) Prince Mircea (1913–16)
3. Victoria Melita (1876–1936), *m.* (1) 1894 Grand Duke Ernst Ludwig of Hesse (*see* III.4) (marriage dissolved 1901); (2) 1905 the Grand Duke Kirill of Russia (1876–1938). *Issue:*
   (a) Marie Kirillovna (1907–51), *m.* 1925 Prince Friedrich Karl of Leiningen; *issue:* Prince Emich (1926–91); Prince Karl (1928–90); Princess Kira-Melita (1930–2005), *m.* Prince Andrej of Yugoslavia (*see* IV.2.(c)); Princess Margarita (1932–96); Princess Mechtilde (*b.* 1936); Prince Friedrich (1938–98)
   (b) Kira Kirillovna (1909–67), *m.* 1938 Prince Louis Ferdinand of Prussia; *issue:* Prince Friedrich Wilhelm (*b.* 1939); Prince Michael

(b. 1940); Princess Marie (b. 1942); Princess Kira (1943–2004); Prince Louis Ferdinand (1944–77); Prince Christian (b. 1946); Princess Xenia (1949–92)

(c) Vladimir Kirillovich (1917–92), m. 1948 Princess Leonida Bagration-Mukhransky; issue: Grand Duchess Maria (b. 1953), and has issue

4. Alexandra (1878–1942), m. 1896 Ernst, Prince of Hohenlohe Langenburg. Issue:

(a) Gottfried (1897–1960), m. 1931 Princess Margarita of Greece (see III.1.(a)); issue: Prince Kraft (1935–2004), Princess Beatrice (1936–97), Prince Georg Andreas (b. 1938), Prince Ruprecht (1944–76); Prince Albrecht (1944–92)

(b) Maria (1899–1967), m. 1916 Prince Friedrich of Schleswig-Holstein-Sonderburg-Glücksburg; issue: Prince Peter (1922–80); Princess Marie (1927–2000)

(c) Princess Alexandra (1901–63)

(d) Princess Irma (1902–86)

5. Princess Beatrice (1884–1966), m. 1909 Alfonso of Orleans, Infante of Spain. Issue:

(a) Prince Alvaro (1910–97), m. 1937 Carla Parodi-Delfino; issue: Doña Gerarda (b. 1939); Don Alonso (1941–75); Doña Beatriz (b. 1943); Don Alvaro (b. 1947)

(b) Prince Alonso (1912–36)

(c) Prince Ataulfo (1913–74)

V. HRH PRINCESS HELENA Augusta Victoria (1846–1923), m. 1866 Prince Christian of Schleswig-Holstein-Sonderburg-Augustenburg (1831–1917). Issue:

1. Prince Christian Victor (1867–1900)

2. Prince Albert (1869–1931), Duke of Schleswig-Holstein 1921–31

3. Princess Helena (1870–1948)

4. Princess Marie Louise (1872–1956), m. 1891 Prince Aribert of Anhalt (marriage dissolved 1900)

5. Prince Harold (12–20 May 1876)

VI. HRH PRINCESS LOUISE Caroline Alberta (1848–1939), m. 1871 Marquess of Lorne, afterwards 9th Duke of Argyll (1845–1914); without issue

VII. HRH PRINCE ARTHUR William Patrick Albert, Duke of Connaught, Field Marshal (1850–1942), m. 1879 Princess Louisa of Prussia (1860–1917). Issue:

1. Margaret (1882–1920), m. 1905 Crown Prince Gustaf Adolf (1882–1973), afterwards King of Sweden 1950–73 (see III.1.(b)). Issue:

(a) Gustaf Adolf, Duke of Västerbotten (1906–47), m. 1932 Princess Sibylla of Saxe-Coburg-Gotha (see VIII.2.(b)); issue: Princess Margaretha (b. 1934); Princess Birgitta (b. 1937); Princess Désirée (b. 1938); Princess Christina (b. 1943); Carl XVI Gustaf, King of Sweden (b. 1946)

(b) Count Sigvard Bernadotte (1907–2002), m. (1) 1934 Erika Patzeck; (2) 1943 Sonja Robbert; (3) 1961 Marianne Lindberg; issue: Count Michael (b. 1944)

(c) Princess Ingrid (Queen Mother of Denmark) (1910–2000), m. 1935 Frederick IX (1899–1972), King of Denmark 1947–72; issue: Margrethe II, Queen of Denmark (b. 1940); Princess Benedikte (b. 1944); Princess Anne-Marfie (b. 1946), m. 1964 Constantine II of Greece

(d) Prince Bertil, Duke of Halland (1912–97), m. 1976 Mrs Lilian Craig

(e) Count Carl Bernadotte (b. 1916), m. (1) 1946 Mrs Kerstin Johnson; (2) 1988 Countess Gunnila Bussler

2. Arthur (1883–1938), m. 1913 HH Duchess of Fife. Issue: Alastair Arthur, 2nd Duke of Connaught (1914–43)

3. (Victoria) Patricia (1886–1974), m. 1919 Adm. Hon. Sir Alexander Ramsay. Issue: Alexander Ramsay of Mar (1919–2000), m. 1956 Hon. Flora Fraser (Lady Saltoun)

VIII. HRH PRINCE LEOPOLD George Duncan Albert, Duke of Albany (1853–84), m. 1882 Princess Helena of Waldeck (1861–1922). Issue:

1. Alice (1883–1981), m. 1904 Prince Alexander of Teck (1874–1957), cr. 1st Earl of Athlone 1917. Issue:

(a) Lady May (1906–94), m. 1931 Sir Henry Abel-Smith, KCMG, KCVO, DSO; issue: Anne (b. 1932); Richard (1933–2004); Elizabeth (b. 1936)

(b) Rupert, Viscount Trematon (1907–28)

(c) Prince Maurice (March–September 1910)

2. Charles Edward (1884–1954), Duke of Albany 1884 until title suspended 1917, Duke of Saxe-Coburg-Gotha 1900–18, m. 1905 Princess Victoria Adelheid of Schleswig-Holstein-Sonderburg-Glücksburg. Issue:

(a) Prince Johann Leopold (1906–72), and has issue

(b) Princess Sibylla (1908–72), m. 1932 Prince Gustaf Adolf of Sweden (see VII.1.(a))

(c) Prince Dietmar Hubertus (1909–43)

(d) Princess Caroline (1912–83), and has issue

(e) Prince Friedrich Josias (1918–98), and has issue

IX. HRH PRINCESS BEATRICE Mary Victoria Feodore (1857–1944), m. 1885 Prince Henry of Battenberg (1858–96). Issue:

1. Alexander, 1st Marquess of Carisbrooke (1886–1960), m. 1917 Lady Irene Denison. Issue:

(a) Lady Iris Mountbatten (1920–82), m.; issue: Robin A. Bryan (b. 1957)

2. Victoria Eugénie (1887–1969), m. 1906 Alfonso XIII (1886–1941) King of Spain 1886–1931. Issue:

(a) Prince Alfonso (1907–38)

(b) Prince Jaime (1908–75), and has issue

(c) Princess Beatriz (1909–2002), and has issue

(d) Princess Maria (1911–96), and has issue

(e) Prince Juan (1913–93), Count of Barcelona; issue: Princess Maria (b. 1936); Juan Carlos I, King of Spain (b. 1938), m. 1962 Princess Sophie of Greece and has issue (one son, two daughters); Princess Margarita (b. 1939)

(f) Prince Gonzalo (1914–34)

3. Major Lord Leopold Mountbatten (1889–1922)

4. Maurice (1891–1914)

KINGS AND QUEENS

ENGLISH KINGS AND QUEENS 927 TO 1603

HOUSES OF CERDIC AND DENMARK
Reign
927–939 ÆTHELSTAN
Son of Edward the Elder, by Ecgwynn, and grandson of Alfred
Acceded to Wessex and Mercia c.924, established direct rule over Northumbria 927, effectively creating the Kingdom of England
Reigned 15 years
939–946 EDMUND I
Born 921, son of Edward the Elder, by Eadgifu
Married (1) Ælfgifu (2) Æthelflæd
Killed aged 25, *reigned* 6 years
946–955 EADRED
Son of Edward the Elder, by Eadgifu
Reigned 9 years
955–959 EADWIG
Born before 943, son of Edmund and Ælfgifu
Married Ælfgifu
Reigned 3 years
959–975 EDGAR I
Born 943, son of Edmund and Ælfgifu
Married (1) Æthelflæd (2) Wulfthryth (3) Ælfthryth
Died aged 32, *reigned* 15 years
975–978 EDWARD I (the Martyr)
Born c.962, son of Edgar and Æthelflæd
Assassinated aged c.16, *reigned* 2 years
978–1016 ÆTHELRED (the Unready)
Born c.968/969, son of Edgar and Ælfthryth
Married (1) Ælfgifu (2) Emma, daughter of Richard I, Count of Normandy
1013–14 dispossessed of kingdom by Swegn Forkbeard (King of Denmark 987–1014)
Died aged c.47, *reigned* 38 years
1016 EDMUND II (Ironside)
Born before 993, son of Æthelred and Ælfgifu
Married Ealdgyth
Died aged over 23, *reigned* 7 months (April–November)
1016–1035 CNUT (Canute)
Born c.995, son of Swegn Forkbeard, King of Denmark, and Gunhild
Married (1) Ælfgifu (2) Emma, widow of Æthelred the Unready
Gained submission of West Saxons 1015, Northumbrians 1016, Mercia 1016, King of all England after Edmund's death, King of Denmark 1019–35, King of Norway 1028–35
Died aged c.40, *reigned* 19 years
1035–1040 HAROLD I (Harefoot)
Born c.1016/17, son of Cnut and Ælfgifu
Married Ælfgifu
1035 recognised as regent for himself and his brother Harthacnut; 1037 recognised as king
Died aged c.23, *reigned* 4 years

1040–1042 HARTHACNUT (Harthacanute)
Born c.1018, son of Cnut and Emma
Titular king of Denmark from 1028
Acknowledged King of England 1035–7 with Harold I as regent; effective king after Harold's death
died aged c.24, *reigned* 2 years
1042–1066 EDWARD II (the Confessor)
Born between 1002 and 1005, son of Æthelred the Unready and Emma
Married Eadgyth, daughter of Godwine, Earl of Wessex
Died aged over 60, *reigned* 23 years
1066 HAROLD II (Godwinesson)
Born c.1020, son of Godwine, Earl of Wessex, and Gytha
Married (1) Eadgyth (2) Ealdgyth
Killed in battle aged c.46, *reigned* 10 months (January–October)

THE HOUSE OF NORMANDY
1066–1087 WILLIAM I (the Conqueror)
Born 1027/8, son of Robert I, Duke of Normandy; obtained the Crown by conquest
Married Matilda, daughter of Baldwin, Count of Flanders
Died aged c.60, *reigned* 20 years
1087–1100 WILLIAM II (Rufus)
Born between 1056 and 1060, third son of William I; succeeded his father in England only
Killed aged c.40, *reigned* 12 years
1100–1135 HENRY I (Beauclerk)
Born 1068, fourth son of William I
Married (1) Edith or Matilda, daughter of Malcolm III of Scotland (2) Adela, daughter of Godfrey, Count of Louvain
Died aged 67, *reigned* 35 years
1135–1154 STEPHEN
Born not later than 1100, third son of Adela, daughter of William I, and Stephen, Count of Blois
Married Matilda, daughter of Eustace, Count of Boulogne
1141 (February–November) held captive by adherents of Matilda, daughter of Henry I, who contested the crown until 1153
Died aged over 53, *reigned* 18 years

THE HOUSE OF ANJOU (PLANTAGENETS)
1154–1189 HENRY II (Curtmantle)
Born 1133, son of Matilda, daughter of Henry I, and Geoffrey, Count of Anjou
Married Eleanor, daughter of William, Duke of Aquitaine, and divorced queen of Louis VII of France
Died aged 56, *reigned* 34 years
1189–1199 RICHARD I (Coeur de Lion)
Born 1157, third son of Henry II
Married Berengaria, daughter of Sancho VI, King of Navarre
Died aged 42, *reigned* 9 years
1199–1216 JOHN (Lackland)
Born 1167, fifth son of Henry II

Married (1) Isabella or Avisa, daughter of
William, Earl of Gloucester (divorced)
(2) Isabella, daughter of Aymer, Count of
Angoulême
Died aged 48, *reigned* 17 years

1216–1272   HENRY III
Born 1207, son of John and Isabella of
Angoulême
Married Eleanor, daughter of Raymond,
Count of Provence
Died aged 65, *reigned* 56 years

1272–1307   EDWARD I (Longshanks)
Born 1239, eldest son of Henry III
Married (1) Eleanor, daughter of Ferdinand
III, King of Castile (2) Margaret, daughter
of Philip III of France
Died aged 68, *reigned* 34 years

1307–1327   EDWARD II
Born 1284, eldest surviving son of Edward I
and Eleanor
Married Isabella, daughter of Philip IV of
France
Deposed January 1327, *killed* September
1327 aged 43, *reigned* 19 years

1327–1377   EDWARD III
Born 1312, eldest son of Edward II
Married Philippa, daughter of William,
Count of Hainault
Died aged 64, *reigned* 50 years

1377–1399   RICHARD II
Born 1367, son of Edward (the Black
Prince), eldest son of Edward III
Married (1) Anne, daughter of Emperor
Charles IV (2) Isabelle, daughter of Charles
VI of France
Deposed September 1399, *killed* February
1400 aged 33, *reigned* 22 years

THE HOUSE OF LANCASTER

1399–1413   HENRY IV
Born 1366, son of John of Gaunt, fourth son
of Edward III, and Blanche, daughter of
Henry, Duke of Lancaster
Married (1) Mary, daughter of Humphrey,
Earl of Hereford (2) Joan, daughter of
Charles, King of Navarre, and widow of
John, Duke of Brittany
Died aged *c.*47, *reigned* 13 years

1413–1422   HENRY V
Born 1387, eldest surviving son of Henry
IV and Mary
Married Catherine, daughter of Charles VI
of France
Died aged 34, *reigned* 9 years

1422–1471   HENRY VI
Born 1421, son of Henry V
Married Margaret, daughter of René, Duke
of Anjou and Count of Provence
Deposed March 1461, *restored* October 1470
Deposed April 1471, *killed* May 1471 aged
49, *reigned* 39 years

THE HOUSE OF YORK

1461–1483   EDWARD IV
Born 1442, eldest son of Richard of York
(grandson of Edmund, fifth son of
Edward III, and son of Anne,
great-granddaughter of Lionel, third son
of Edward III)
Married Elizabeth Woodville, daughter
of Richard, Lord Rivers, and widow of
Sir John Grey

Acceded March 1461, *deposed* October
1470, *restored* April 1471
Died aged 40, *reigned* 21 years

1483   EDWARD V
Born 1470, eldest son of Edward IV
Deposed June 1483, *died* probably July–
September 1483, aged 12, *reigned* 2
months (April–June)

1483–1485   RICHARD III
Born 1452, fourth son of Richard of York
Married Anne Neville, daughter of
Richard, Earl of Warwick, and widow of
Edward, Prince of Wales, son of Henry
VI
Killed in battle aged 32, *reigned* 2 years

THE HOUSE OF TUDOR

1485–1509   HENRY VII
Born 1457, son of Margaret Beaufort
(great-granddaughter of John of Gaunt,
fourth son of Edward III) and Edmund
Tudor, Earl of Richmond
Married Elizabeth, daughter of Edward IV
Died aged 52, *reigned* 23 years

1509–1547   HENRY VIII
Born 1491, second son of Henry VII
Married (1) Catherine, daughter of
Ferdinand II, King of Aragon, and widow of
his elder brother Arthur (divorced) (2) Anne,
daughter of Sir Thomas Boleyn (executed)
(3) Jane, daughter of Sir John Seymour
(died in childbirth) (4) Anne, daughter of
John, Duke of Cleves (divorced)
(5) Catherine Howard, niece of the Duke of
Norfolk (executed) (6) Catherine, daughter
of Sir Thomas Parr and widow of Lord
Latimer
Died aged 55, *reigned* 37 years

1547–1553   EDWARD VI
Born 1537, son of Henry VIII and Jane
Seymour
Died aged 15, *reigned* 6 years

1553   JANE
Born 1537, daughter of Frances (daughter
of Mary Tudor, the younger daughter of
Henry VII) and Henry Grey, Duke of
Suffolk
Married Lord Guildford Dudley, son of the
Duke of Northumberland
Deposed July 1553, *executed* February 1554
aged 16, *reigned* 14 days

1553–1558   MARY I
Born 1516, daughter of Henry VIII and
Catherine of Aragon
Married Philip II of Spain
Died aged 42, *reigned* 5 years

1558–1603   ELIZABETH I
Born 1533, daughter of Henry VIII and
Anne Boleyn
Died aged 69, *reigned* 44 years

BRITISH KINGS AND QUEENS SINCE 1603

THE HOUSE OF STUART
Reign

1603–1625   JAMES I (VI OF SCOTLAND)
Born 1566, son of Mary, Queen of Scots
(granddaughter of Margaret Tudor, elder
daughter of Henry VII), and Henry Stewart,
Lord Darnley

Married Anne, daughter of Frederick II of
Denmark
Died aged 58, *reigned* 22 years

1625–1649   CHARLES I
Born 1600, second son of James I
Married Henrietta Maria, daughter of Henry
IV of France
Executed 1649 aged 48, *reigned* 23 years

INTERREGNUM 1649–60
1649–53   Government by a council of state
1653–8   Oliver Cromwell, Lord Protector
1658–9   Richard Cromwell, Lord Protector

Reign
1660–1685   CHARLES II
Born 1630, eldest son of Charles I
Married Catherine, daughter of John IV of
Portugal
Died aged 54, *reigned* 24 years

1685–1688   JAMES II (VII OF SCOTLAND)
Born 1633, second son of Charles I
Married (1) Lady Anne Hyde, daughter of
Edward, Earl of Clarendon (2) Mary,
daughter of Alphonso, Duke of Modena
Reign ended with flight from kingdom
December 1688
Died 1701 aged 67, *reigned* 3 years

INTERREGNUM
11 December 1688 to 12 February 1689

Reign
1689–1702   WILLIAM III
Born 1650, son of William II, Prince of
Orange, and Mary Stuart, daughter of
Charles I
Married Mary, elder daughter of James II
Died aged 51, *reigned* 13 years

and
1689–1694   MARY II
Born 1662, elder daughter of James II and
Anne
Died aged 32, *reigned* 5 years

1702–1714   ANNE
Born 1665, younger daughter of James II
and Anne
Married Prince George of Denmark, son of
Frederick III of Denmark
Died aged 49, *reigned* 12 years

THE HOUSE OF HANOVER
1714–1727   GEORGE I (Elector of Hanover)
Born 1660, son of Sophia (daughter of
Frederick, Elector Palatine, and Elizabeth
Stuart, daughter of James I) and Ernest
Augustus, Elector of Hanover
Married Sophia Dorothea, daughter of
George William, Duke of Lüneburg-Celle
Died aged 67, *reigned* 12 years

1727–1760   GEORGE II
Born 1683, son of George I
Married Caroline, daughter of John
Frederick, Margrave of
Brandenburg-Anspach
Died aged 76, *reigned* 33 years

1760–1820   GEORGE III
Born 1738, son of Frederick, eldest son of
George II
Married Charlotte, daughter of Charles
Louis, Duke of Mecklenburg-Strelitz
Died aged 81, *reigned* 59 years

REGENCY 1811–20
Prince of Wales regent owing to the insanity of George III

Reign
1820–1830   GEORGE IV
Born 1762, eldest son of George III
Married Caroline, daughter of Charles,
Duke of Brunswick-Wolfenbüttel
Died aged 67, *reigned* 10 years

1830–1837   WILLIAM IV
Born 1765, third son of George III
Married Adelaide, daughter of George,
Duke of Saxe-Meiningen
Died aged 71, *reigned* 7 years

1837–1901   VICTORIA
Born 1819, daughter of Edward, fourth son
of George III
Married Prince Albert of Saxe-Coburg and
Gotha
Died aged 81, *reigned* 63 years

THE HOUSE OF SAXE-COBURG AND GOTHA
1901–1910   EDWARD VII
Born 1841, eldest son of Victoria and Albert
Married Alexandra, daughter of Christian
IX of Denmark
Died aged 68, *reigned* 9 years

THE HOUSE OF WINDSOR
1910–1936   GEORGE V
Born 1865, second son of Edward VII
Married Victoria Mary, daughter of Francis,
Duke of Teck
Died aged 70, *reigned* 25 years

1936   EDWARD VIII
Born 1894, eldest son of George V
Married (1937) Mrs Wallis Simpson
Abdicated 1936, *died* 1972 aged 77, *reigned*
10 months (20 January to 11 December)

1936–1952   GEORGE VI
Born 1895, second son of George V
Married Lady Elizabeth Bowes-Lyon,
daughter of 14th Earl of Strathmore and
Kinghorne
Died aged 56, *reigned* 15 years

1952–   Elizabeth II
Born 1926, elder daughter of George VI
Married Philip, son of Prince Andrew of
Greece

KINGS AND QUEENS OF SCOTS 1016 TO 1603

Reign
1016–1034   MALCOLM II
Born c.954, son of Kenneth II
Acceded to Alba 1005, secured Lothian
c.1016, obtained Strathclyde for his
grandson Duncan c.1016, thus reigning
over an area approximately the same as that
governed by later rulers of Scotland
Died aged c.80, *reigned* 18 years

THE HOUSE OF ATHOL
1034–1040   DUNCAN I
Son of Bethoc, daughter of Malcolm II, and
Crinan, Mormaer of Atholl
Married a cousin of Siward, Earl of
Northumbria
Reigned 5 years

1040–1057   MACBETH
Born c.1005, son of a daughter of
Malcolm II and Finlaec, Mormaer of Moray
Married Gruoch, granddaughter of
Kenneth III
Killed aged c.52, *reigned* 17 years

1057–1058   LULACH
Born c.1032, son of Gillacomgan, Mormaer
of Moray, and Gruoch (and stepson of
Macbeth)
Died aged c.26, *reigned* 7 months (August–
March)

1058–1093   MALCOLM III (Canmore)
Born c.1031, elder son of Duncan I
Married (1) Ingibiorg (2) Margaret (St
Margaret), granddaughter of Edmund II of
England
Killed in battle aged c.62, *reigned* 35 years

1093–1097   DONALD III BÁN
Born c.1033, second son of Duncan I
Deposed May 1094, *restored* November
1094, *deposed* October 1097, *reigned* 3
years

1094   DUNCAN II
Born c.1060, elder son of Malcolm III and
Ingibiorg
Married Octreda of Dunbar
Killed aged c.34, *reigned* 6 months (May–
November)

1097–1107   EDGAR
Born c.1074, second son of Malcolm III and
Margaret
Died aged c.32, *reigned* 9 years

1107–1124   ALEXANDER I (The Fierce)
Born c.1077, fifth son of Malcolm III and
Margaret
Married Sybilla, illegitimate daughter of
Henry I of England
Died aged c.47, *reigned* 17 years

1124–1153   DAVID I (The Saint)
Born c.1085, sixth son of Malcolm III and
Margaret
Married Matilda, daughter of Waltheof, Earl
of Huntingdon
Died aged c.68, *reigned* 29 years

1153–1165   MALCOLM IV (The Maiden)
Born c.1141, son of Henry, Earl of
Huntingdon, second son of David I
Died aged c.24, *reigned* 12 years

1165–1214   WILLIAM I (The Lion)
Born c.1142, brother of Malcolm IV
Married Ermengarde, daughter of Richard,
Viscount of Beaumont
Died aged c.72, *reigned* 49 years

1214–1249   ALEXANDER II
Born 1198, son of William I
Married (1) Joan, daughter of John, King of
England (2) Marie, daughter of Ingelram de
Coucy
Died aged 50, *reigned* 34 years

1249–1286   ALEXANDER III
Born 1241, son of Alexander II and Marie
Married (1) Margaret, daughter of Henry III
of England (2) Yolande, daughter of the
Count of Dreux
Killed accidentally aged 44, *reigned* 36 years

1286–1290   MARGARET (The Maid of Norway)
Born 1283, daughter of Margaret (daughter
of Alexander III) and Eric II of Norway
Died aged 7, *reigned* 4 years

FIRST INTERREGNUM 1290–2
Throne disputed by 13 competitors. Crown awarded to
John Balliol by adjudication of Edward I of England

THE HOUSE OF BALLIOL
Reign
1292–1296   JOHN (Balliol)
Born c.1250, son of Dervorguilla,
great-great-granddaughter of David I, and
John de Balliol
Married Isabella, daughter of John, Earl of
Surrey
Abdicated 1296, *died* 1313 aged c.63,
reigned 3 years

SECOND INTERREGNUM 1296–1306
Edward I of England declared John Balliol to have
forfeited the throne for contumacy in 1296 and took the
government of Scotland into his own hands

THE HOUSE OF BRUCE
Reign
1306–1329   ROBERT I (Bruce)
Born 1274, son of Robert Bruce and
Marjorie, countess of Carrick, and
great-grandson of the second daughter of
David, Earl of Huntingdon, brother of
William I
Married (1) Isabella, daughter of Donald,
Earl of Mar (2) Elizabeth, daughter of
Richard, Earl of Ulster
Died aged 54, *reigned* 23 years

1329–1371   DAVID II
Born 1324, son of Robert I and Elizabeth
Married (1) Joanna, daughter of Edward II
of England (2) Margaret Drummond,
widow of Sir John Logie (divorced)
Died aged 46, *reigned* 41 years
1332 Edward Balliol, son of John Balliol,
crowned King of Scots September, expelled
December
1333–6 Edward Balliol restored as King of
Scots

THE HOUSE OF STEWART
1371–1390   ROBERT II (Stewart)
Born 1316, son of Marjorie (daughter of
Robert I) and Walter, High Steward of
Scotland
Married (1) Elizabeth, daughter of Sir
Robert Mure of Rowallan (2) Euphemia,
daughter of Hugh, Earl of Ross
Died aged 74, *reigned* 19 years

1390–1406   ROBERT III
Born c.1337, son of Robert II and
Elizabeth
Married Annabella, daughter of Sir John
Drummond of Stobhall
Died aged c.69, *reigned* 16 years

1406–1437   JAMES I
Born 1394, son of Robert III
Married Joan Beaufort, daughter of John,
Earl of Somerset
Assassinated aged 42, *reigned* 30 years

1437–1460   JAMES II
Born 1430, son of James I
Married Mary, daughter of Arnold, Duke of
Gueldres
Killed accidentally aged 29, *reigned* 23 years

1460–1488   JAMES III
Born 1452, son of James II

	Married Margaret, daughter of Christian I of Denmark
	Assassinated aged 36, *reigned* 27 years
1488–1513	JAMES IV
	Born 1473, son of James III
	Married Margaret Tudor, daughter of Henry VII of England
	Killed in battle aged 40, *reigned* 25 years
1513–1542	JAMES V
	Born 1512, son of James IV
	Married (1) Madeleine, daughter of Francis I of France (2) Mary of Lorraine, daughter of the Duc de Guise
	Died aged 30, *reigned* 29 years
1542–1567	MARY
	Born 1542, daughter of James V and Mary
	Married (1) the Dauphin, afterwards Francis II of France (2) Henry Stewart, Lord Darnley (3) James Hepburn, Earl of Bothwell
	Abdicated 1567, prisoner in England from 1568, *executed* 1587, *reigned* 24 years
1567–1625	JAMES VI (and I of England)
	Born 1566, son of Mary, Queen of Scots, and Henry, Lord Darnley
	Acceded 1567 to the Scottish throne, *reigned* 58 years
	Succeeded 1603 to the English throne, so joining the English and Scottish crowns in one person. The two kingdoms remained distinct until 1707 when the parliaments of the kingdoms became conjoined

WELSH SOVEREIGNS AND PRINCES

Wales was ruled by sovereign princes from the earliest times until the death of Llewelyn in 1282. The first English Prince of Wales was the son of Edward I, who was born in Caernarvon town on 25 April 1284. According to a discredited legend, he was presented to the Welsh chieftains as their prince, in fulfilment of a promise that they should have a prince who 'could not speak a word of English' and should be native born. This son, who afterwards became Edward II, was created 'Prince of Wales and Earl of Chester' at the Lincoln Parliament on 7 February 1301.

The title Prince of Wales is borne after individual conferment and is not inherited at birth, though some Princes have been declared and styled Prince of Wales but never formally so created (*s.*). The title was conferred on Prince Charles by the Queen on 26 July 1958. He was invested at Caernarvon on 1 July 1969.

INDEPENDENT PRINCES AD 844 TO 1282

844–878	Rhodri the Great
878–916	Anarawd, son of Rhodri
916–950	Hywel Dda, the Good
950–979	Iago ab Idwal (or Ieuaf)
979–985	Hywel ab Ieuaf, the Bad

985–986	Cadwallon, his brother
986–999	Maredudd ab Owain ap Hywel Dda
999–1008	Cynan ap Hywel ab Ieuaf
1018–1023	Llywelyn ap Seisyll
1023–1039	Iago ab Idwal ap Meurig
1039–1063	Gruffydd Llywelyn ap Seisyll
1063–1075	Bleddyn ap Cynfyn
1075–1081	Trahaern ap Caradog
1081–1137	Gruffydd ap Cynan ab Iago
1137–1170	Owain Gwynedd
1170–1194	Dafydd ab Owain Gwynedd
1194–1240	Llywelyn Fawr, the Great
1240–1246	Dafydd ap Llywelyn
1246–1282	Llywelyn ap Gruffydd ap Llywelyn

ENGLISH PRINCES SINCE 1301

1301	Edward (Edward II)
1343	Edward the Black Prince, son of Edward III
1376	Richard (Richard II), son of the Black Prince
1399	Henry of Monmouth (Henry V)
1454	Edward of Westminster, son of Henry VI
1471	Edward of Westminster (Edward V)
1483	Edward, son of Richard III (*d.* 1484)
1489	Arthur Tudor, son of Henry VII
1504	Henry Tudor (Henry VIII)
1610	Henry Stuart, son of James I (*d.* 1612)
1616	Charles Stuart (Charles I)
*c.*1638 (*s.*)	Charles Stuart (Charles II)
1688 (*s.*)	James Francis Edward Stuart (The Old Pretender), son of James II (*d.* 1766)
1714	George Augustus (George II)
1729	Frederick Lewis, son of George II (*d.* 1751)
1751	George William Frederick (George III)
1762	George Augustus Frederick (George IV)
1841	Albert Edward (Edward VII)
1901	George (George V)
1910	Edward (Edward VIII)
1958	Charles, son of Elizabeth II

PRINCESSES ROYAL

The style Princess Royal is conferred at the sovereign's discretion on his or her eldest daughter. It is an honorary title, held for life, and cannot be inherited or passed on. It was first conferred on Princess Mary, daughter of Charles I, in approximately 1642.

*c.*1642	Princess Mary (1631–60), daughter of Charles I
1727	Princess Anne (1709–59), daughter of George II
1766	Princess Charlotte (1766–1828), daughter of George III
1840	Princess Victoria (1840–1901), daughter of Victoria
1905	Princess Louise (1867–1931), daughter of Edward VII
1932	Princess Mary (1897–1965), daughter of George V
1987	Princess Anne (*b.* 1950), daughter of Elizabeth II

PRECEDENCE

ENGLAND AND WALES

The Sovereign
The Prince Philip, Duke of
  Edinburgh
The Prince of Wales
The Sovereign's younger sons
The Sovereign's grandsons
The Sovereign's cousins
Archbishop of Canterbury
Lord High Chancellor
Archbishop of York
The Prime Minister
Lord President of the Council
Speaker of the House of Commons
Lord Privy Seal
Ambassadors and High
  Commissioners
Lord Great Chamberlain
Earl Marshal
Lord Chamberlain of the Household
Lord Steward of the Household
Master of the Horse
Dukes, according to their patent of
  creation:
  1. of England
  2. of Scotland
  3. of Great Britain
  4. of Ireland
  5. those created since the Union
Eldest sons of Dukes of the Blood
  Royal
Marquesses, according to their patent
  of creation:
  1. of England
  2. of Scotland
  3. of Great Britain
  4. of Ireland
  5. those created since the Union
Dukes' eldest sons
Earls, according to their patent of
  creation:
  1. of England
  2. of Scotland
  3. of Great Britain
  4. of Ireland
  5. those created since the Union
Younger sons of Dukes of Blood Royal
Marquesses' eldest sons
Dukes' younger sons
Viscounts, according to their patent
  of creation:
  1. of England

  2. of Scotland
  3. of Great Britain
  4. of Ireland
  5. those created since the Union
Earls' eldest sons
Marquesses' younger sons
Bishop of London
Bishop of Durham
Bishop of Winchester
Other English Diocesan Bishops
  according to seniority of
  consecration
Suffragan Bishops, according to
  seniority of consecration
Secretaries of State, if of the degree
  of a Baron
Barons, according to their patent of
  creation:
  1. of England
  2. of Scotland
  3. of Great Britain
  4. of Ireland
  5. those created since the Union,
  including Life Barons
Treasurer of the Household
Comptroller of the Household
Vice-Chamberlain of the Household
Secretaries of State under the degree
  of Baron
Viscounts' eldest sons
Earls' younger sons
Barons' eldest sons
Knights of the Garter
Privy Counsellors
Chancellor of the Exchequer
Chancellor of the Duchy of Lancaster
Lord Chief Justice of England and
  Wales
Master of the Rolls
President of the Queen's Bench
  Division
President of the Family Division
Chancellor of the High Court
Lords Justices of Appeal, according to
  seniority of appointment
Judges of the High Court, according
  to seniority of appointment
Viscounts' younger sons
Barons' younger sons
Sons of Life Peers and Lords of
  Appeal in Ordinary
Baronets, according to date of patent
Knights of the Thistle

Knights Grand Cross of the Bath
Knights Grand Commanders of the
  Star of India
Knights Grand Cross of St Michael
  and St George
Knights Grand Commanders of the
  Indian Empire
Knights Grand Cross of the Royal
  Victorian Order
Knights Grand Cross of the British
  Empire
Knights Commanders of the Bath
Knights Commanders of the Star of
  India
Knights Commanders of St Michael
  and St George
Knights Commanders of the Indian
  Empire
Knights Commanders of the Royal
  Victorian Order
Knights Commanders of the British
  Empire
Knights Bachelor
Circuit Judges, according to priority
  and order of their respective
  appointments
Companions of the Bath
Companions of the Star of India
Companions of St Michael and St
  George
Companions of the Indian Empire
Commanders of the Royal Victorian
  Order
Commanders of the British Empire
Companions of the Distinguished
  Service Order
Lieutenants of the Royal Victorian
  Order
Officers of the British Empire
Companions of the Imperial Service
  Order
Eldest sons of younger sons of Peers
Baronets' eldest sons
Eldest sons of Knights, in the same
  order as their fathers
Members of the Royal Victorian
  Order
Members of the British Empire
Younger sons of Baronets
Younger sons of Knights, in the same
  order as their fathers
Esquires
Gentlemen

SCOTLAND

The Sovereign
The Prince Philip, Duke of Edinburgh
The Lord High Commissioner to the General Assembly of the Church of Scotland (while that Assembly is sitting)
The Duke of Rothesay (eldest son of the Sovereign)
The Sovereign's younger sons
Grandsons of the Sovereign
The Sovereign's cousins
Lord-Lieutenants
Lord Provosts of cities being *ex-officio* Lord-Lieutenants of those cities during their term of office
Sheriffs Principal, successively, within their own localities and during holding of office
Lord Chancellor of Great Britain
Moderator of the General Assembly of the Church of Scotland
Keeper of the Great Seal of Scotland (The First Minister)
The Presiding Officer
The Secretary of State for Scotland
Hereditary High Constable of Scotland
Hereditary Master of the Household in Scotland

Dukes, in the same order as in England
Eldest sons of Dukes of the Blood Royal
Marquesses, as in England
Eldest sons of Dukes
Earls, as in England
Younger sons of Dukes of Blood Royal
Eldest sons of Marquesses
Dukes' younger sons
Lord Justice General
Lord Clerk Register
Lord Advocate
The Advocate-General
Lord Justice Clerk
Viscounts, as in England
Eldest sons of Earls
Marquesses' younger sons
Lord-Barons, as in England
Eldest sons of Viscounts
Earls' younger sons
Lord-Barons' eldest sons
Knights of the Garter
Knights of the Thistle
Privy Counsellors
Senators of College of Justice (Lords of Session)
Viscounts' younger sons
Lord-Barons' younger sons
Baronets
Knights Grand Cross and Knights

Grand Commanders of Orders, as in England
Knights Commanders of Orders, as in England
Solicitor-General for Scotland
Lord Lyon King of Arms
Sheriffs Principal, when not within own county
Knights Bachelor
Sheriffs
Companions of Orders, as in England
Commanders of the Royal Victorian Order
Commanders of the British Empire
Companions of the Distinguished Service Order
Lieutenants of the Royal Victorian Order
Officers of the British Empire
Companions of the Imperial Service Order
Eldest sons of younger sons of Peers
Eldest sons of Baronets
Eldest sons of Knights, as in England
Members of the Royal Victorian Order
Members of the British Empire
Baronets' younger sons
Knights' younger sons
Esquires
Gentlemen

WOMEN

Women take the same rank as their husbands or as their brothers; but the daughter of a peer marrying a commoner retains her title as Lady or Honourable. Daughters of peers rank next immediately after the wives of their elder brothers, and before their younger brothers' wives. Daughters of peers marrying peers of a lower degree take the same order of precedence as that of their husbands; thus the daughter of a Duke marrying a Baron becomes of the rank of Baroness only, while her sisters married to commoners retain their rank and take precedence over the Baroness. Merely official rank on the husband's part does not give any similar precedence to the wife.

Peeresses in their own right take the same precedence as peers of the same rank, ie from their date of creation.

LOCAL PRECEDENCE

Scotland
The Lord Provosts of the city districts of Aberdeen, Dundee, Edinburgh and Glasgow are Lord-Lieutenants for those districts *ex officio* and take precedence as such.

THE PEERAGE

The rules which govern the creation and succession of peerages are extremely complicated. There are, technically, five separate peerages, the Peerage of England, of Scotland, of Ireland, of Great Britain, and of the United Kingdom. The Peerage of Great Britain dates from 1707 when an Act of Union combined the two kingdoms of England and Scotland and separate peerages were discontinued. The Peerage of the United Kingdom dates from 1801 when Great Britain and Ireland were combined under an Act of Union. Some Scottish peers have received additional peerages of Great Britain or of the United Kingdom since 1707, and some Irish peers additional peerages of the United Kingdom since 1801.

The Peerage of Ireland was not entirely discontinued from 1801 but holders of Irish peerages, whether pre-dating or created subsequent to the Union of 1801, were not entitled to sit in the House of Lords if they had no additional English, Scottish, Great Britain or United Kingdom peerage. However, they are eligible for election to the House of Commons and to vote in parliamentary elections. An Irish peer holding a peerage of a lower grade which enabled him to sit in the House of Lords was introduced there by the title which enabled him to sit, though for all other purposes he was known by his higher title.

In the Peerage of Scotland there is no rank of Baron; the equivalent rank is Lord of Parliament, abbreviated to 'Lord' (the female equivalent is 'Lady').

All peers of England, Scotland, Great Britain or the United Kingdom who are 21 years or over, and of British, Irish or Commonwealth nationality were entitled to sit in the House of Lords until the House of Lords Act 1999, when hereditary peers lost the right to sit. However, section two of the act provided an exception for 90 hereditary peers plus the holders of the office of Earl Marshal and Lord Great Chamberlain to remain as members of the House of Lords for their lifetime or pending further reform. Of the 90 hereditary peers, 75 were elected by the hereditary peers in their political party, or Crossbench grouping, and the remaining 15 by the whole house. Until 7 November 2002 any vacancy arising due to the death of one of the 90 excepted hereditary peers was filled by the runner-up to the original election. From 7 November 2002 any vacancy due to a death has been filled by holding a by-election. By-elections are conducted in accordance with arrangements made by the Clerk of the Parliaments and have to take place within three months of a vacancy occurring. If the vacancy is among the 75, only the excepted hereditary peers in the relevant party or Crossbench grouping are entitled to vote. If the vacancy is among the other 15, the whole house is entitled to vote.

In the list below, peers currently holding one of the 92 hereditary places in the House of Lords are indicated by **.

HEREDITARY WOMEN PEERS
Most hereditary peerages pass on death to the nearest male heir, but there are exceptions, and several are held by women.

A woman peer in her own right retains her title after marriage, and if her husband's rank is the superior she is designated by the two titles jointly, the inferior one second. Her hereditary claim still holds good in spite of any marriage whether higher or lower. No rank held by a woman can confer any title or even precedence upon her husband but the rank of a hereditary woman peer in her own right is inherited by her eldest son (or in some cases daughter).

After the Peerage Act 1963, hereditary women peers in their own right were entitled to sit in the House of Lords, subject to the same qualifications as men, until the House of Lords Act 1999.

LIFE PEERS
Since 1876 non-hereditary or life peerages have been conferred on certain eminent judges to enable the judicial functions of the House of Lords to be carried out. These lords are known as Lords of Appeal in Ordinary or law lords. In 2004 Baroness Hale of Richmond became the first female law lord.

Since 1958 life peerages have been conferred upon distinguished men and women from all walks of life, giving them seats in the House of Lords in the degree of Baron or Baroness. They are addressed in the same way as hereditary lords and barons, and their children have similar courtesy titles.

PEERAGES EXTINCT SINCE THE LAST EDITION

BARONY: Deramore (cr. 1885)
LIFE PEERAGES: Biffen (cr. 1997); Carter (cr. 1987); Cockfield (cr. 1978); Cooke of Thorndon (cr. 1996); Deedes (cr. 1986); Ewing of Kirkford (cr. 1992); Garden (cr. 2004); Forte (cr. 1982); Harris of High Cross (cr. 1979); Hussey of North Bradley (cr. 1996); Jauncey of Tullichettle (cr. 1988); Jeger (cr. 1979); Jellicoe of Southampton (cr. 1999); Kelvedon (cr. 1997); Nolan (cr. 1994); Peyton of Yeovil (cr. 1983); Renton (cr. 1979); Weatherill (cr. 1992)

DISCLAIMER OF PEERAGES
The Peerage Act 1963 enables peers to disclaim their peerages for life. Peers alive in 1963 could disclaim within twelve months after the passing of the act (31 July 1963); a person subsequently succeeding to a peerage may disclaim within 12 months (one month if an MP) after the date of succession, or of reaching 21, if later. The disclaimer is irrevocable but does not affect the descent of the peerage after the disclaimant's death, and children of a disclaimed peer may, if they wish, retain their precedence and any courtesy titles and styles borne as children of a peer. The disclaimer permitted the disclaimant to sit in the House of Commons if elected as an MP. As the House of Lords Act 1999 removed hereditary peers from the House of Lords, they are now entitled to sit in the House of Commons without having to disclaim their titles.

The following peerages are currently disclaimed:

EARLDOM: Selkirk (1994)
VISCOUNTCY: Stansgate (1963)
BARONIES: Merthyr (1977); Reith (1972); Sanderson of Ayot (1971)

PEERS WHO ARE MINORS (ie under 21 years of age)
EARL: Craven (*b.* 1989)
VISCOUNT: Selby (*b.* 1993)

FORMS OF ADDRESS
Forms of address are given under the style for each
individual rank of the peerage. Both formal and social
forms of address are given where usage differs; nowadays,
the social form is generally preferred to the formal, which
increasingly is used only for official documents and on
very formal occasions.

ABBREVIATIONS AND SYMBOLS

S.	Scottish title
I.	Irish title
**	hereditary peer remaining in the House of Lords
°	there is no 'of' in the title
b.	born
s.	succeeded
m.	married
w.	widower or widow
M.	minor
†	heir not ascertained at time of going to press
F_	represents forename
S_	represents surname

ROLL OF THE PEERAGE

Crown Office, House of Lords, London SW1A 0PW
The Roll of the Peerage is kept at the Crown Office and
maintained by the Registrar and Assistant Registrar of the
Roll of the Perrage in accordance with the terms of a 2004
royal warrant. The roll records the names of all living life
peers and hereditary peers who have proved their
succession to the satisfaction of the Lord Chancellor. The
Roll of the Peerage is maintained in addition to the Clerk
of the Parliaments' register of hereditary peers eligible to
stand for election in House of Lords' by-elections.

A person whose name is not entered on the Roll of
Peerage can not be addressed or mentioned by the title of
a peer in any official document.
Registrar, Ian Denyer, MVO
Assistant Registrar, Grant Bavister

HEREDITARY PEERS

as at 31 August 2007

PEERS OF THE BLOOD ROYAL

Style, His Royal Highness the Duke of _/His Royal Highness the Earl of_
Style of address (formal) May it please your Royal Highness; *(informal)* Sir

Created	Title, order of succession, name, etc	Heir
	Dukes	
1947	Edinburgh (1st), HRH the Prince Philip, Duke of Edinburgh	The Prince of Wales *
1337	Cornwall, HRH the Prince of Wales, s. 1952	‡
1398 S.	Rothesay, HRH the Prince of Wales, s. 1952	‡
1986	York (1st), Prince Andrew, HRH the Duke of York	None
1928	Gloucester (2nd), Prince Richard, HRH the Duke of Gloucester, s. 1974	Earl of Ulster
1934	Kent (2nd),Prince Edward, HRH the Duke of Kent, s. 1942	Earl of St Andrews
	Earl	
1999	Wessex (1st), Prince Edward, HRH the Earl of Wessex	None

* In June 1999 Buckingham Palace announced that the current Earl of Wessex will be granted the Dukedom of Edinburgh when the title reverts to the Crown. The title will only revert to the Crown on both the death of the current Duke of Edinburgh and the Prince of Wales' succession as king
‡ The title is held by the sovereign's eldest son from the moment of his birth or the sovereign's accession

DUKES

Coronet, Eight strawberry leaves

Style, His Grace the Duke of _
    Envelope (formal), His Grace the Duke of _; *(social)*, The Duke of _. *Letter (formal)*, My Lord Duke; *(social)*, Dear Duke.
Spoken (formal), Your Grace; *(social)*, Duke
Wife's style, Her Grace the Duchess of _
    Envelope (formal), Her Grace the Duchess of _; *(social)*, The Duchess of _. *Letter (formal)*, Dear Madam; *(social)*, Dear Duchess. *Spoken*, Duchess
Eldest son's style, Takes his father's second title as a courtesy title *(see* Courtesy Titles)
Younger sons' style, 'Lord' before forename (F_) and surname (S_)
    Envelope, Lord F_ S_. *Letter (formal)*, My Lord; *(social)*, Dear Lord F_. *Spoken (formal)*, My Lord; *(social)*, Lord F_
Daughters' style, 'Lady' before forename (F_) and surname (S_)
    Envelope, Lady F_ S_. *Letter (formal)*, Dear Madam; *(social)*, Dear Lady F_. *Spoken*, Lady F_

Created	Title, order of succession, name, etc	Heir
1868 I.	Abercorn (5th), James Hamilton, KG, b. 1934, s. 1979, m., Lord Steward	Marquess of Hamilton, b. 1969
1701 S.	Argyll (13th), Torquhil Ian Campbell, b. 1968, s. 2001	Marquess of Lorne, b. 2004
1703 S.	Atholl (11th), John Murray, b. 1929, s. 1996, m.	Marquis of Tullibardine, b. 1960
1682	Beaufort (11th), David Robert Somerset, b. 1928, s. 1984, m.	Marquess of Worcester, b. 1952
1694	Bedford (15th), Andrew Ian Henry Russell, b. 1962, s. 2003, m.	Lord Robin L. H. R., b. 1963
1663 S.	Buccleuch (9th) and Queensberry (11th) (S. 1684), Walter Francis John Montagu Douglas Scott, KT, VRD, b. 1923, s. 1973, m.	Earl of Dalkeith, KBE b. 1954
1694	Devonshire (12th), Peregrine Andrew Morny Cavendish, b. 1944, s. 2004, m.	Marquess of Hartington, b. 1969
1900	Fife (3rd), James George Alexander Bannerman Carnegie, b. 1929, s. 1959	Earl of Southesk, b. 1961
1675	Grafton (11th), Hugh Denis Charles FitzRoy, KG, b. 1919, s. 1970, m.	Earl of Euston, b. 1947
1643 S.	Hamilton (15th) and Brandon (12th) (1711), Angus Alan Douglas Douglas-Hamilton, b. 1938, s. 1973 Premier Peer of Scotland	Marquis of Douglas and Clydesdale, b. 1978
1766 I.	Leinster (9th), Maurice FitzGerald, b. 1948, s. 2004, m. Premier Duke, Marquess and Earl of Ireland	Lord John F., b. 1952

1719	*Manchester (13th)*, Alexander Charles David Drogo Montagu, *b.* 1962, *s.* 2002, *m.*	Viscount Mandeville, *b.* 1993
1702	*Marlborough (11th)*, John George Vanderbilt Henry Spencer-Churchill, *b.* 1926, *s.* 1972, *m.*	Marquess of Blandford, *b.* 1955
1707 S.	** *Montrose (8th)*, James Graham, *b.* 1935, *s.* 1992, *m.*	Marquis of Graham, *b.* 1973
1483	** *Norfolk (18th)*, Edward Wiliam Fitzalan-Howard, *b.* 1956, *s.* 2002, *m.* Premier Duke and Earl Marshal	Earl of Arundel and Surrey, *b.* 1987
1766	*Northumberland (12th)*, Ralph George Algernon Percy, *b.* 1956, *s.* 1995, *m.*	Earl Percy, *b.* 1984
1675	*Richmond (10th) and Gordon (5th) (1876)*, Charles Henry Gordon Lennox, *b.* 1929, *s.* 1989, *m.*	Earl of March and Kinrara, *b.* 1955
1707 S.	*Roxburghe (10th)*, Guy David Innes-Ker, *b.* 1954, *s.* 1974, *m.* Premier Baronet of Scotland	Marquis of Bowmont and Cessford, *b.* 1981
1703	*Rutland (11th)*, David Charles Robert Manners, *b.* 1959, *s.* 1999, *m.*	Marquess of Granby, *b.* 1999
1684	*St Albans (14th)*, Murray de Vere Beauclerk, *b.* 1939, *s.* 1988, *m.*	Earl of Burford, *b.* 1965
1547	*Somerset (19th)*, John Michael Edward Seymour, *b.* 1952, *s.* 1984, *m.*	Lord Seymour, *b.* 1982
1833	*Sutherland (7th)*, Francis Ronald Egerton, *b.* 1940, *s.* 2000, *m.*	Marquess of Stafford, *b.* 1975
1814	*Wellington (8th)*, Arthur Valerian Wellesley, KG, LVO, OBE, MC, *b.* 1915, *s.* 1972, *m.*	Marquess of Douro, *b.* 1945
1874	*Westminster (6th)*, Gerald Cavendish Grosvenor, KG, OBE, *b.* 1951, *s.* 1979, *m.*	Earl Grosvenor, *b.* 1991

MARQUESSES

Coronet, Four strawberry leaves alternating with four silver balls

Style, The Most Hon. the Marquess (of) _ . In Scotland the spelling 'Marquis' is preferred for pre-Union creations
    Envelope (formal), The Most Hon. the Marquess of _; *(social),* The Most Hon. the Marquess of _. *Letter (formal),* My Lord; *(social),* Dear Lord _. *Spoken (formal),* My Lord; *(social),* Lord _
Wife's style, The Most Hon. the Marchioness (of) _
    Envelope (formal), The Most Hon. the Marchioness of _; *(social),* The Marchioness of _. *Letter (formal),* Madam; *(social),* Dear Lady _. *Spoken,* Lady _
Eldest son's style, Takes his father's second title as a courtesy title (*see* Courtesy Titles)
Younger sons' style, 'Lord' before forename and surname, as for Duke's younger sons
Daughters' style, 'Lady' before forename and surname, as for Duke's daughter

Created	Title, order of succession, name, etc	Heir
1916	*Aberdeen and Temair (7th)*, Alexander George Gordon, *b.* 1955, *s.* 2002, *m.*	Earl of Haddo, *b.* 1983
1876	*Abergavenny (6th) and 10th Earl, Abergavenny, 1784*, Christopher George Charles Nevill, *b.* 1955, *s.* 2000, *m.*	To Earldom only, David M. R. N., *b.* 1941
1821	*Ailesbury (8th)*, Michael Sidney Cedric Brudenell-Bruce, *b.* 1926, *s.* 1974	Earl of Cardigan, *b.* 1952
1831	*Ailsa (8th)*, Archibald Angus Charles Kennedy, *b.* 1956, *s.* 1994	Lord David Kennedy, *b.* 1958
1815	*Anglesey (7th)*, George Charles Henry Victor Paget, *b.* 1922, *s.* 1947, *m.*	Earl of Uxbridge, *b.* 1950
1789	*Bath (7th)*, Alexander George Thynn, *b.* 1932, *s.* 1992, *m.*	Viscount Weymouth, *b.* 1974
1826	*Bristol (8th)*, Frederick William Augustus Hervey, *b.* 1979, *s.* 1999	Timothy H. H., *b.* 1960
1796	*Bute (7th)*, John Colum Crichton-Stuart, *b.* 1958, *s.* 1993, *m.*	Lord Mount Stuart, *b.* 1989
1812	° *Camden (6th)*, David George Edward Henry Pratt, *b.* 1930, *s.* 1983	Earl of Brecknock, *b.* 1965
1815	** *Cholmondeley (7th)*, David George Philip Cholmondeley, KCVO, *b.* 1960, *s.* 1990, *Lord Great Chamberlain*	Charles G. C., *b.* 1959
1816	° *Conyngham (7th)*, Frederick William Henry Francis Conyngham, *b.* 1924, *s.* 1974, *m.*	Earl of Mount Charles, *b.* 1951
1791 I.	*Donegall (8th)*, Arthur Patrick Chichester, *b.* 1952, *s.* 2007, *m.*	Earl of Belfast, *b.* 1990
1789 I.	*Downshire (9th)*, (Arthur Francis) Nicholas Wills Hill, *b.* 1959, *s.* 2003, *m.*	Earl of Hillsborough, *b.* 1996
1801 I.	*Ely (9th)*, Charles John Tottenham, *b.* 1943, *s.* 2006, *m.*	Lord Timothy C. T., *b.* 1948
1801	*Exeter (8th)*, (William) Michael Anthony Cecil, *b.* 1935, *s.* 1988, *m.*	Lord Burghley, *b.* 1970

1800 I.	*Headfort (7th)*, Thomas Michael Ronald Christopher Taylour, *b.* 1959, *s.* 2005, *m.*	Earl of Bective, *b.* 1989
1793	*Hertford (9th)*, Henry Jocelyn Seymour, *b.* 1958, *s.* 1997, *m.*	Earl of Yarmouth, *b.* 1993
1599 S.	*Huntly (13th)*, Granville Charles Gomer Gordon, *b.* 1944, *s.* 1987, *m.* *Premier Marquess of Scotland*	Earl of Aboyne, *b.* 1973
1784	*Lansdowne (9th)*, Charles Maurice Mercer Nairne Petty-Fitzmaurice, LVO *b.* 1941, *s.* 1999, *m.*	Earl of Kerry, *b.* 1970
1902	*Linlithgow (4th)*, Adrian John Charles Hope, *b.* 1946, *s.* 1987, *m.*	Earl of Hopetoun, *b.* 1969
1816 I.	*Londonderry (9th)*, Alexander Charles Robert Vane-Tempest-Stewart, *b.* 1937, *s.* 1955, *m.*	Viscount Castlereagh, *b.* 1972
1701 S.	*Lothian (13th)*, Michael Andrew Foster Jude Kerr (Michael Ancram), PC, *b.* 1945, *s.* 2004, *m.*	Lord Ralph W. F. J. K., *b.* 1957
1917	*Milford Haven (4th)*, George Ivar Louis Mountbatten, *b.* 1961, *s.* 1970, *m.*	Earl of Medina, *b.* 1991
1838	*Normanby (5th)*, Constantine Edmund Walter Phipps, *b.* 1954, *s.* 1994, *m.*	Earl of Mulgrave, *b.* 1994
1812	*Northampton (7th)*, Spencer Douglas David Compton, *b.* 1946, *s.* 1978, *m.*	Earl Compton, *b.* 1973
1682 S.	*Queensberry (12th)*, David Harrington Angus Douglas, *b.* 1929, *s.* 1954	Viscount Drumlanrig, *b.* 1967
1926	*Reading (4th)*, Simon Charles Henry Rufus Isaacs, *b.* 1942, *s.* 1980, *m.*	Viscount Erleigh, *b.* 1986
1789	*Salisbury (7th) and Baron Gascoyne-Cecil (life peerage, 1999)*, Robert Michael James Gascoyne-Cecil, PC, *b.* 1946, *s.* 2003, *m.*	Viscount Cranborne, *b.* 1970
1800 I.	*Sligo (11th)*, Jeremy Ulick Browne, *b.* 1939, *s.* 1991, *m.*	Sebastian U. B., *b.* 1964
1787	° *Townshend (7th)*, George John Patrick Dominic Townshend, *b.* 1916, *s.* 1921, *w.*	Viscount Raynham, *b.* 1945
1694 S.	*Tweeddale (14th)*, Charles David Montagu Hay, *b.* 1947, *s.* 2005	Lord Andrew A. G. H., *b.* 1959
1789 I.	*Waterford (8th)*, John Hubert de la Poer Beresford, *b.* 1933, *s.* 1934, *m.*	Earl of Tyrone, *b.* 1958
1551	*Winchester (18th)*, Nigel George Paulet, *b.* 1941, *s.* 1968, *m.* *Premier Marquess of England*	Earl of Wiltshire, *b.* 1969
1892	*Zetland (4th)*, Lawrence Mark Dundas, *b.* 1937, *s.* 1989, *m.*	Earl of Ronaldshay, *b.* 1965

EARLS

Coronet, Eight silver balls on stalks alternating with eight gold strawberry leaves

Style, The Right Hon. the Earl (of) _
 Envelope (formal), The Right Hon. the Earl (of) _; *(social),* The Earl (of) _. *Letter (formal),* My Lord; *(social),* Dear Lord _. *Spoken (formal),* My Lord; *(social),* Lord _.
Wife's style, The Right Hon. the Countess (of) _
 Envelope (formal), The Right Hon. the Countess (of) _; *(social),* The Countess (of) _. *Letter (formal),* Madam; *(social),* Lady _. *Spoken (formal),* Madam; *(social),* Lady _.
Eldest son's style, Takes his father's second title as a courtesy title (*see* Courtesy Titles)
Younger sons' style, 'The Hon.' before forename and surname, as for Baron's children
Daughters' style, 'Lady' before forename and surname, as for Duke's daughter

Created	Title, order of succession, name, etc	Heir
1639 S.	*Airlie (13th)*, David George Coke Patrick Ogilvy, KT, GCVO, PC, Royal Victorian Chain, *b.* 1926, *s.* 1968, *m.*	Lord Ogilvy, *b.* 1958
1696	*Albemarle (10th)*, Rufus Arnold Alexis Keppel, *b.* 1965, *s.* 1979, *m.*	Viscount Bury, *b.* 2003
1952	° *Alexander of Tunis (2nd)*, Shane William Desmond Alexander, *b.* 1935, *s.* 1969, *m.*	Hon. Brian J. A., *b.* 1939
1662	*Annandale and Hartfell (11th)*, Patrick Andrew Wentworth Hope Johnstone, *b.* 1941, *s.* 1983, *m.* claim established 1985	Lord Johnstone, *b.* 1971
1789 I.	° *Annesley (11th)*, Philip Harrison Annesley, *b.* 1927, *s.* 2001, *m.*	Hon. Michael R. A., *b.* 1933
1785 I.	*Antrim (9th)*, Alexander Randal Mark McDonnell, *b.* 1935, *s.* 1977, *m.*	Viscount Dunluce, *b.* 1967
1762 I.	** *Arran (9th)*, Arthur Desmond Colquhoun Gore, *b.* 1938, *s.* 1983, *m.*	Paul A. G., CMG, CVO, *b.* 1921
1955	° ** *Attlee (3rd)*, John Richard Attlee, *b.* 1956, *s.* 1991, *m.*	None
1714	*Aylesford (11th)*, Charles Ian Finch-Knightley, *b.* 1918, *s.* 1958, *w.*	Lord Guernsey, *b.* 1947

1937	** *Baldwin of Bewdley (4th)*, Edward Alfred Alexander Baldwin, *b.* 1938, *s.* 1976, *w.*	Viscount Corvedale, *b.* 1973
1922	*Balfour (5th)*, Roderick Francis Arthur Balfour, *b.* 1948, *s.* 2003, *m.*	Charles G. Y. B., *b.* 1951
1772	° *Bathurst (8th)*, Henry Allen John Bathurst, *b.* 1927, *s.* 1943, *m.*	Lord Apsley, *b.* 1961
1919	° *Beatty (3rd)*, David Beatty, *b.* 1946, *s.* 1972, *m.*	Viscount Borodale, *b.* 1973
1797 I.	° *Belmore (8th)*, John Armar Lowry-Corry, *b.* 1951, *s.* 1960, *m.*	Viscount Corry, *b.* 1985
1739 I.	*Bessborough (12th)*, Myles Fitzhugh Longfield Ponsonby, *b.* 1941, *s.* 2002, *m.*	Viscount Duncannon, *b.* 1974
1815	*Bradford (7th)*, Richard Thomas Orlando Bridgeman, *b.* 1947, *s.* 1981, *m.*	Viscount Newport, *b.* 1980
1469	*Buchan (17th)*, Malcolm Harry Erskine, *b.* 1930, *s.* 1984, *m.*	Lord Cardross, *b.* 1960
1746	*Buckinghamshire (10th)*, (George) Miles Hobart-Hampden, *b.* 1944, *s.* 1983, *m.*	Sir John Hobart, Bt., *b.* 1945
1800	° *Cadogan (8th)*, Charles Gerald John Cadogan, *b.* 1937, *s.* 1997, *m.*	Viscount Chelsea, *b.* 1966
1878	° *Cairns (6th)*, Simon Dallas Cairns, CVO, CBE, *b.* 1939, *s.* 1989, *m.*	Viscount Garmoyle, *b.* 1965
1455	** *Caithness (20th)*, Malcolm Ian Sinclair, PC, *b.* 1948, *s.* 1965, *w.*	Lord Berriedale, *b.* 1981
1800 I.	*Caledon (7th)*, Nicholas James Alexander, *b.* 1955, *s.* 1980, *m.*	Viscount Alexander, *b.* 1990
1661	*Carlisle (13th)*, George William Beaumont Howard, *b.* 1949, *s.* 1994	Hon. Philip C. W. H., *b.* 1963
1793	*Carnarvon (8th)*, George Reginald Oliver Molyneux Herbert, *b.* 1956, *s.* 2001, *m.*	Lord Porchester, *b.* 1992
1748 I.	*Carrick (10th)*, David James Theobald Somerset Butler, *b.* 1953, *s.* 1992, *m.*	Viscount Ikerrin, *b.* 1975
1800 I.	° *Castle Stewart (8th)*, Arthur Patrick Avondale Stuart, *b.* 1928, *s.* 1961, *w.*	Viscount Stuart, *b.* 1953
1814	°** *Cathcart (7th)*, Charles Alan Andrew Cathcart, *b.* 1952, *s.* 1999, *m.*	Lord Greenock, *b.* 1986
1647 I.	*Cavan*, The 12th Earl died in 1988.	†Roger C. Lambart, *b.* 1944
1827	° *Cawdor (7th)*, Colin Robert Vaughan Campbell, *b.* 1962, *s.* 1993, *m.*	Viscount Emlyn, *b.* 1998
1801	*Chichester (9th)*, John Nicholas Pelham, *b.* 1944, *s.* 1944, *m.*	Richard A. H. P., *b.* 1952
1803 I.	*Clancarty (9th)*, Nicholas Power Richard Le Poer Trench, *b.* 1952, *s.* 1995	None
1776 I.	*Clanwilliam (7th)*, John Herbert Meade, *b.* 1919, *s.* 1989, *w.*	Lord Gillford, *b.* 1960
1776	*Clarendon (7th)*, George Frederick Laurence Hyde Villiers, *b.* 1933, *s.* 1955, *m.*	Lord Hyde, *b.* 1976
1620 I.	*Cork and Orrery (15th)*, John Richard Boyle, *b.* 1945, *s.* 2003, *m.*	Viscount Dungarvan, *b.* 1978
1850	*Cottenham (9th)*, Mark John Henry Pepys, *b.* 1983, *s.* 2000	Hon. Sam R. P., *b.* 1986
1762 I.	** *Courtown (9th)*, James Patrick Montagu Burgoyne Winthrop Stopford, *b.* 1954, *s.* 1975, *m.*	Viscount Stopford, *b.* 1988
1697	*Coventry (13th)*, George William Coventry, *b.* 1939, *s.* 2004, *m.*	David D. S. C., *b.* 1973
1857	° *Cowley (7th)*, Garret Graham Wellesley, *b.* 1934, *s.* 1975, *m.*	Viscount Dangan, *b.* 1965
1892	*Cranbrook (5th)*, Gathorne Gathorne-Hardy, *b.* 1933, *s.* 1978, *m.*	Lord Medway, *b.* 1968
1801 M.	*Craven (9th)*, Benjamin Robert Joseph Craven, *b.* 1989, *s.* 1990	Rupert J. E. C., *b.* 1926
1398 S.	*Crawford (29th) and Balcarres (12th) (S. 1651) and Baron Balniel (life peerage, 1974)*, Robert Alexander Lindsay, KT, GCVO, PC, *b.* 1927, *s.* 1975, *m. Premier Earl on Union Roll*	Lord Balniel, *b.* 1958
1861	*Cromartie (5th)*, John Ruaridh Blunt Grant Mackenzie, *b.* 1948, *s.* 1989, *m.*	Viscount Tarbat, *b.* 1987
1901	*Cromer (4th)*, Evelyn Rowland Esmond Baring, *b.* 1946, *s.* 1991, *m.*	Viscount Errington, *b.* 1994
1633 S.	*Dalhousie (17th)*, James Hubert Ramsay, *b.* 1948, *s.* 1999, *m.*	Lord Ramsay, *b.* 1981
1725 I.	*Darnley (11th)*, Adam Ivo Stuart Bligh, *b.* 1941, *s.* 1980, *m.*	Lord Clifton, *b.* 1968
1711	*Dartmouth (10th)*, William Legge, *b.* 1949, *s.* 1997	Hon. Rupert L., *b.* 1951
1761	° *De La Warr (11th)*, William Herbrand Sackville, *b.* 1948, *s.* 1988, *m.*	Lord Buckhurst, *b.* 1979
1622	*Denbigh (12th) and Desmond (11th) (I. 1622)*, Alexander Stephen Rudolph Feilding, *b.* 1970, *s.* 1995, *m.*	William D. F, *b.* 1939
1485	*Derby (19th)*, Edward Richard William Stanley, *b.* 1962, *s.* 1994, *m.*	Lord Stanley, *b.* 1998
1553	*Devon (18th)*, Hugh Rupert Courtenay, *b.* 1942, *s.* 1998, *m.*	Lord Courtenay, *b.* 1975
1800 I.	*Donoughmore (8th)*, Richard Michael John Hely-Hutchinson, *b.* 1927, *s.* 1981, *w.*	Viscount Suirdale, *b.* 1952
1661 I.	*Drogheda (12th)*, Henry Dermot Ponsonby Moore, *b.* 1937, *s.* 1989, *m.*	Viscount Moore, *b.* 1983
1837	*Ducie (7th)*, David Leslie Moreton, *b.* 1951, *s.* 1991, *m.*	Lord Moreton, *b.* 1981
1860	*Dudley (4th)*, William Humble David Ward, *b.* 1920, *s.* 1969, *m.*	Viscount Ednam, *b.* 1947
1660 S.	** *Dundee (12th)*, Alexander Henry Scrymgeour, *b.* 1949, *s.* 1983, *m.*	Lord Scrymgeour, *b.* 1982
1669 S.	*Dundonald (15th)*, Iain Alexander Douglas Blair Cochrane, *b.* 1961, *s.* 1986, *m.*	Lord Cochrane, *b.* 1991
1686 S.	*Dunmore (12th)*, Malcolm Kenneth Murray, *b.* 1946, *s.* 1995, *m.*	Hon. Geoffrey C. M., *b.*1949
1822 I.	*Dunraven and Mount-Earl (7th)*, Thady Windham Thomas Wyndham-Quin, *b.* 1939, *s.* 1965, *m.*	None

1833	*Durham (7th)*, Edward Richard Lambton, *b.* 1961, *s.* 2006, *m.*	Viscount Lambton, *b.* 1985
1837	*Effingham (7th)*, David Mowbray Algernon Howard, *b.* 1939, *s.* 1996, *m.*	Lord Howard of Effingham, *b.* 1971
1507 S.	*Eglinton (18th) and Winton (9th) (S. 1600)*, Archibald George Montgomerie, *b.* 1939, *s.* 1966, *m.*	Lord Montgomerie, *b.* 1966
1733 I.	*Egmont (12th)*, Thomas Frederick Gerald Perceval, *b.* 1934, *s.* 2001, *m.*	Hon. Donald W. P., *b.* 1954
1821	*Eldon (5th)*, John Joseph Nicholas Scott, *b.* 1937, *s.* 1976, *m.*	Viscount Encombe, *b.* 1962
1633 S.	*Elgin (11th) and Kincardine (15th) (S. 1647)*, Andrew Douglas Alexander Thomas Bruce, KT, *b.* 1924, *s.* 1968, *m.*	Lord Bruce, *b.* 1961
1789 I.	*Enniskillen (7th)*, Andrew John Galbraith Cole, *b.* 1942, *s.* 1989, *m.*	Arthur G. C., *b.* 1920
1789 I.	*Erne (6th)*, Henry George Victor John Crichton, *b.* 1937, *s.* 1940, *m.*	Viscount Crichton, *b.* 1971
1452 S.	** *Erroll (24th)*, Merlin Sereld Victor Gilbert Hay, *b.* 1948, *s.* 1978, *m.* *Hereditary Lord High Constable and Knight Marischal of Scotland*	Lord Hay, *b.* 1984
1661	*Essex (11th)*, Frederick Paul de Vere Capell, *b.* 1944, *s.* 2005	William J. C., *b.* 1952
1711	° ** *Ferrers (13th)*, Robert Washington Shirley, PC, *b.* 1929, *s.* 1954, *m.*	Viscount Tamworth, *b.* 1952
1789	° *Fortescue (8th)*, Charles Hugh Richard Fortescue, *b.* 1951, *s.* 1993, *m.*	John A. F. F., *b.* 1955
1841	*Gainsborough (5th)*, Anthony Gerard Edward Noel, *b.* 1923, *s.* 1927, *m.*	Viscount Campden, *b.* 1950
1623 S.	*Galloway (13th)*, Randolph Keith Reginald Stewart, *b.* 1928, *s.* 1978, *w.*	Andrew C. S., *b.* 1949
1703 S.	** *Glasgow (10th)*, Patrick Robin Archibald Boyle, *b.* 1939, *s.* 1984, *m.*	Viscount of Kelburn, *b.* 1978
1806 I.	*Gosford (7th)*, Charles David Nicholas Alexander John Sparrow Acheson, *b.* 1942, *s.* 1966, *m.*	Hon. Patrick B. V. M. A., *b.* 1915
1945	*Gowrie (2nd)*, Alexander Patrick Greysteil Hore-Ruthven, PC, *b.* 1939, *s.* 1955, *m.*	Viscount Ruthven of Canberra, *b.* 1964
1684 I.	*Granard (10th)*, Peter Arthur Edward Hastings Forbes, *b.* 1957, *s.* 1992, *m.*	Viscount Forbes, *b.* 1981
1833	° *Granville (6th)*, Granville George Fergus Leveson-Gower, *b.* 1959, *s.* 1996, *m.*	Lord Leveson, *b.* 1999
1806	° *Grey (6th)*, Richard Fleming George Charles Grey, *b.* 1939, *s.* 1963, *m.*	Philip K. G., *b.* 1940
1752	*Guilford (10th)*, Piers Edward Brownlow North, *b.* 1971, *s.* 1999, *m.*	Lord North, *b.* 2002
1619	*Haddington (13th)*, John George Baillie-Hamilton, *b.* 1941, *s.* 1986, *m.*	Lord Binning, *b.* 1985
1919	° *Haig (2nd)*, George Alexander Eugene Douglas Haig, OBE, *b.* 1918, *s.* 1928, *m.*	Viscount Dawick, *b.* 1961
1944	*Halifax (3rd)*, Charles Edward Peter Neil Wood, *b.* 1944, *s.* 1980, *m.*	Lord Irwin, *b.* 1977
1898	*Halsbury (4th)*, Adam Edward Giffard, *b.* 1934, *s.* 2000, *m.*	None
1754	*Hardwicke (10th)*, Joseph Philip Sebastian Yorke, *b.* 1971, *s.* 1974	Charles E. Y., *b.* 1951
1812	*Harewood (7th)*, George Henry Hubert Lascelles, KBE, *b.* 1923, *s.* 1947, *m.*	Viscount Lascelles, *b.* 1950
1742	*Harrington (11th)*, William Henry Leicester Stanhope, *b.* 1922, *s.* 1929, *m.*	Viscount Petersham, *b.* 1945
1809	*Harrowby (7th)*, Dudley Danvers Granville Coutts Ryder, TD, *b.* 1922, *s.* 1987, *m.*	Viscount Sandon, *b.* 1951
1605	** *Home (15th)*, David Alexander Cospatrick Douglas-Home, CVO, CBE, *b.* 1943, *s.* 1995, *m.*	Lord Dunglass, *b.* 1987
1821	° ** *Howe (7th)*, Frederick Richard Penn Curzon, *b.* 1951, *s.* 1984, *m.*	Viscount Curzon, *b.* 1994
1529	*Huntingdon (16th)*, William Edward Robin Hood Hastings Bass, LVO, *b.* 1948, *s.* 1990, *m.*	Hon. Simon A. R. H. H. B., *b.* 1950
1885	*Iddesleigh (5th)*, John Stafford Northcote, *b.* 1957, *s.* 2004, *m.*	Viscount St Cyres, *b.* 1985
1756	*Ilchester (10th)*, Robin Maurice Fox-Strangways, *b.* 1942, *s.* 2006, *m.*	Lord Stavordale, *b.* 1972
1929	*Inchcape (4th)*, (Kenneth) Peter (Lyle) Mackay, *b.* 1943, *s.* 1994, *m.*	Viscount Glenapp, *b.* 1979
1919	*Iveagh (4th)*, Arthur Edward Rory Guinness, *b.* 1969, *s.* 1992	Viscount Elveden, *b.* 2003
1925	° *Jellicoe (3rd)*, Patrick John Bernard Jellicoe, *b.* 1950, *s.* 2007	Viscount Brocas, *b.* 1970
1697	*Jersey (10th)*, George Francis William Child Villiers, *b.* 1976, *s.* 1998 *m.*	Hon. Jamie C. V., *b.* 1994
1822 I.	*Kilmorey (6th)*, Sir Richard Francis Needham, PC, *b.* 1942, *s.* 1977, *m.*, (does not use title)	Viscount Newry and Mourne, *b.* 1966
1866	*Kimberley (5th)*, John Armine Wodehouse, *b.* 1951, *s.* 2002, *m.*	Lord Wodehouse, *b.*1978
1768 I.	*Kingston (12th)*, Robert Charles Henry King-Tenison, *b.* 1969, *s.* 2002, *m.*	Viscount Kingsborough, *b.* 2000
1633 S.	*Kinnoull (15th)*, Arthur William George Patrick Hay, *b.* 1935, *s.* 1938, *m.*	Viscount Dupplin, *b.* 1962
1677 S.	*Kintore (14th)*, James William Falconer Keith, *b.* 1976, *s.* 2004	Hon. Alexander D. B. K., *b.* 1946
1914	° *Kitchener of Khartoum (3rd)*, Henry Herbert Kitchener, TD, *b.* 1919, *s.* 1937	None
1624	*Lauderdale (17th)*, Patrick Francis Maitland, *b.* 1911, *s.* 1968, *w.*	Viscount Maitland, *b.* 1937
1837	*Leicester (7th)*, Edward Douglas Coke, *b.* 1936, *s.* 1994, *m.*	Viscount Coke, *b.* 1965

1641 S.	*Leven (14th) and Melville (13th) (S. 1690)*, Alexander Robert Leslie Melville, *b.* 1924, *s.* 1947, *m.*	Lord Balgonie, *b.* 1984
1831	*Lichfield (6th)*, Thomas William Robert Hugh Anson, *b.* 1978, *s.* 2005	George R. A., *b.* 1960
1803 I.	*Limerick (7th)*, Edmund Christopher Pery, *b.* 1963, *s.* 2003, *m.*	Viscount Glentworth, *b.* 1991
1572	*Lincoln (19th)*, Robert Edward Fiennes-Clinton, *b.* 1972, *s.* 2001	Hon. William R. F.-C., *b.* 1980
1633 S.	** *Lindsay (16th)*, James Randolph Lindesay-Bethune, *b.* 1955, *s.* 1989, *m.*	Viscount Garnock, *b.* 1990
1626	*Lindsey (14th) and Abingdon (9th) (1682)*, Richard Henry Rupert Bertie, *b.* 1931, *s.* 1963, *m.*	Lord Norreys, *b.* 1958
1776 I.	*Lisburne (8th)*, John David Malet Vaughan, *b.* 1918, *s.* 1965, *m.*	Viscount Vaughan, *b.* 1945
1822 I.	** *Listowel (6th)*, Francis Michael Hare, *b.* 1964, *s.* 1997, *m.*	Hon. Timothy P. H., *b.* 1966
1905	** *Liverpool (5th)*, Edward Peter Bertram Savile Foljambe, *b.* 1944, *s.* 1969, *m.*	Viscount Hawkesbury, *b.* 1972
1945	° *Lloyd George of Dwyfor (3rd)*, Owen Lloyd George, *b.* 1924, *s.* 1968, *m.*	Viscount Gwynedd, *b.* 1951
1785 I.	*Longford (8th)*, Thomas Frank Dermot Pakenham, *b.* 1933, *s.* 2001, *m.*	Hon. Edward M. P., *b.* 1970
1807	*Lonsdale (8th)*, Hugh Clayton Lowther, *b.* 1949, *s.* 2006, *m.*	Hon. William J. L., *b.* 1957
1633 S.	*Loudoun (14th)*, Michael Edward Abney-Hastings, *b.* 1942, *s.* 2002, *m.*	Lord Mauchline, *b.* 1974
1838	*Lovelace (5th)*, Peter Axel William Locke King, *b.* 1951, *s.* 1964, *m.*	None
1795 I.	*Lucan (7th)*, Richard John Bingham, *b.* 1934, *s.* 1964, *m.* (missing since 8 November 1974)	Lord Bingham, *b.* 1967
1880	*Lytton (5th)*, John Peter Michael Scawen Lytton, *b.* 1950, *s.* 1985, *m.*	Viscount Knebworth, *b.* 1989
1721	*Macclesfield (9th)*, Richard Timothy George Mansfield Parker, *b.* 1943, *s.* 1992, *m.*	Hon. J. David G. P., *b.* 1945
1800	*Malmesbury (7th)*, James Carleton Harris, *b.* 1946, *s.* 2000, *m.*	Viscount FitzHarris, *b.* 1970
1776	*Mansfield and Mansfield (8th) (1792)*, William David Mungo James Murray, *b.* 1930, *s.* 1971, *m.*	Viscount Stormont, *b.* 1956
1565 S.	*Mar (14th) and Kellie (16th) (S. 1616) and Baron Erskine of Alloa Tower (life peerage, 2000)*, James Thorne Erskine, *b.* 1949, *s.* 1994, *m.*	Hon. Alexander D. E., *b.* 1952
1785 I.	*Mayo (11th)*, Charles Diarmuidh John Bourke, *b.* 1953, *s.* 2006, *m.*	Lord Naas, *b.* 1985
1627 I.	*Meath (15th)*, John Anthony Brabazon, *b.* 1941, *s.* 1998, *m.*	Lord Ardee, *b.* 1977
1766 I.	*Mexborough (8th)*, John Christopher George Savile, *b.* 1931, *s.* 1980, *m.*	Viscount Pollington, *b.* 1959
1813	*Minto (7th)*, Gilbert Timothy George Lariston Elliot-Murray-Kynynmound, *b.* 1953, *s.* 2005, *m.*	Viscount Melgund, *b.* 1984
1562 S.	*Moray (20th)*, Douglas John Moray Stuart, *b.* 1928, *s.* 1974, *m.*	Lord Doune, *b.* 1966
1815	*Morley (6th)*, John St Aubyn Parker, KCVO, *b.* 1923, *s.* 1962, *m.*	Viscount Boringdon, *b.* 1956
1458	*Morton (22nd)*, John Charles Sholto Douglas, *b.* 1927, *s.* 1976, *m.*	Lord Aberdour, *b.* 1952
1789	*Mount Edgcumbe (8th)*, Robert Charles Edgcumbe, *b.* 1939, *s.* 1982	Piers V. E., *b.* 1946
1805	° *Nelson (9th)*, Peter John Horatio Nelson, *b.* 1941, *s.* 1981, *m.*	Viscount Merton, *b.* 1971
1660 S.	*Newburgh (12th)*, Don Filippo Giambattista Camillo Francesco Aldo Maria Rospigliosi, *b.* 1942, *s.* 1986, *m.*	Princess Donna Benedetta F. M. R., *b.* 1974
1827 I.	*Norbury (7th)*, Richard James Graham-Toler, *b.* 1967, *s.* 2000	None
1806 I.	*Normanton (6th)*, Shaun James Christian Welbore Ellis Agar, *b.* 1945, *s.* 1967, *m.*	Viscount Somerton, *b.* 1982
1647 S.	** *Northesk (14th)*, David John MacRae Carnegie, *b.* 1954, *s.* 1994, *m.*	Patrick C. C., *b.* 1940
1801	** *Onslow (7th)*, Michael William Coplestone Dillon Onslow, *b.* 1938, *s.* 1971, *m.*	Viscount Cranley, *b.* 1967
1696 S.	*Orkney (9th)*, (Oliver) Peter St John, *b.* 1938, *s.* 1998, *m.*	Viscount Kirkwall, *b.* 1969
1328 I.	*Ormonde and Ossory (I. 1527)*, The 25th/18th Earl (7th Marquess) died in 1988	†Viscount Mountgarret *b.* 1961 (*see* that title)
1925	*Oxford and Asquith (2nd)*, Julian Edward George Asquith, KCMG, *b.* 1916, *s.* 1928, *w.*	Viscount Asquith, OBE, *b.* 1952
1929	° ** *Peel (3rd)*, William James Robert Peel, GCVO, PC, *b.* 1947, *s.* 1969, *m.*	Viscount Clanfield, *b.* 1976
1551	*Pembroke (18th) and Montgomery (15th) (1605)*, William Alexander Sidney Herbert, *b.* 1978, *s.* 2003	Earl of Carnarvon *b.* 1956 (*see* that title)
1605	*Perth (18th)*, John Eric Drummond, *b.* 1935, *s.* 2002, *m.*	Viscount Strathallan, *b.* 1965
1905	*Plymouth (3rd)*, Other Robert Ivor Windsor-Clive, *b.* 1923, *s.* 1943, *m.*	Viscount Windsor, *b.* 1951
1785	*Portarlington (7th)*, George Lionel Yuill Seymour Dawson-Damer, *b.* 1938, *s.* 1959, *m.*	Viscount Carlow, *b.* 1965
1689	*Portland (12th)*, Count Timothy Charles Robert Noel Bentinck, *b.* 1953, *s.* 1997, *m.*	Viscount Woodstock, *b.* 1984
1743	*Portsmouth (10th)*, Quentin Gerard Carew Wallop, *b.* 1954, *s.* 1984, *m.*	Viscount Lymington, *b.* 1981
1804	*Powis (8th)*, John George Herbert, *b.* 1952, *s.* 1993, *m.*	Viscount Clive, *b.* 1979
1765	*Radnor (8th)*, Jacob Pleydell-Bouverie, *b.* 1927, *s.* 1968, *w.*	Viscount Folkestone, *b.* 1955
1831 I.	*Ranfurly (7th)*, Gerald Françoys Needham Knox, *b.* 1929, *s.* 1988, *m.*	Viscount Northland, *b.* 1957
1771 I.	*Roden (10th)*, Robert John Jocelyn, *b.* 1938, *s.* 1993, *m.*	Viscount Jocelyn, *b.* 1989
1801	*Romney (8th)*, Julian Charles Marsham, *b.* 1948, *s.* 2004, *m.*	Viscount Marsham, *b.* 1977

1703 S.   *Rosebery (7th)*, Neil Archibald Primrose, *b.* 1929, *s.* 1974, *m.*   Lord Dalmeny, *b.* 1967
1806 I.   *Rosse (7th)*, William Brendan Parsons, *b.* 1936, *s.* 1979, *m.*   Lord Oxmantown, *b.* 1969.
1801   ** *Rosslyn (7th)*, Peter St Clair-Erskine, *b.* 1958, *s.* 1977, *m.*   Lord Loughborough, *b.* 1986
1457 S.   *Rothes (22nd)*, James Malcolm David Leslie, *b.* 1958, *s.* 2005, *m.*   Alastair P. L., *b.* 1934
1861   ° *Russell (6th)*, Nicholas Lyulph Russell, *b.* 1968, *s.* 2004   Hon. John F. R., *b.* 1971
1915   ° *St Aldwyn (3rd)*, Michael Henry Hicks Beach, *b.* 1950, *s.* 1992, *m.*   Hon. David S. H. B., *b.* 1955
1815   *St Germans (10th)*, Peregrine Nicholas Eliot, *b.* 1941, *s.* 1988   Lord Eliot, *b.* 2004
1660   ** *Sandwich (11th)*, John Edward Hollister Montagu, *b.* 1943, *s.* 1995, *m.*   Viscount Hinchingbrooke, *b.* 1969

1690   *Scarbrough (13th)*, Richard Osbert Lumley, *b.* 1973, *s.* 2004   Hon. Thomas H. L., *b.* 1980
1701 S.   *Seafield (13th)*, Ian Derek Francis Ogilvie-Grant, *b.* 1939, *s.* 1969, *m.*   Viscount Reidhaven, *b.* 1963
1882   ** *Selborne (4th)*, John Roundell Palmer, KBE, *b.* 1940, *s.* 1971, *m.*   Viscount Wolmer, *b.* 1971
1646 S.   *Selkirk*, Disclaimed for life 1994. *(see* Lord Selkirk of Douglas, Life Peers)   Master of Selkirk, *b.* 1978
1672   *Shaftesbury (12th)*, Nicholas Edmund Anthony Ashley-Cooper, *b.* 1979, *s.* 2005   None
1756 I.   *Shannon (9th)*, Richard Bentinck Boyle, *b.* 1924, *s.* 1963   Viscount Boyle, *b.* 1960
1442   ** *Shrewsbury and Waterford (22nd) (I. 1446)*, Charles Henry John Benedict Crofton Chetwynd Chetwynd-Talbot, *b.* 1952, *s.* 1980, *m. Premier Earl of England and Ireland*   Viscount Ingestre, *b.* 1978

1961   *Snowdon (1st) and Baron Armstrong-Jones (life peerage, 1999)*, Antony Charles Robert Armstrong-Jones, GCVO, *b.* 1930, *m.*   Viscount Linley, *b.* 1961
1765   ° *Spencer (9th)*, Charles Edward Maurice Spencer, *b.* 1964, *s.* 1992, *m.*   Viscount Althorp, *b.* 1994
1703 S.   *Stair (14th)*, John David James Dalrymple, *b.* 1961, *s.* 1996, *m.*   Hon. David H. D., *b.* 1963
1984   *Stockton (2nd)*, Alexander Daniel Alan Macmillan, MEP, *b.* 1943, *s.* 1986, *m.*   Viscount Macmillan of Ovenden, *b.* 1974
1821   *Stradbroke (6th)*, Robert Keith Rous, *b.* 1937, *s.* 1983, *m.*   Viscount Dunwich, *b.* 1961
1847   *Strafford (8th)*, Thomas Edmund Byng, *b.* 1936, *s.* 1984, *m.*   Viscount Enfield, *b.* 1964
1606 S.   *Strathmore and Kinghorne (18th) (S. 1677)*, Michael Fergus Bowes Lyon, *b.* 1957, *s.* 1987, *m.*   Lord Glamis, *b.* 1986
1603   *Suffolk (21st) and Berkshire (14th) (1626)*, Michael John James George Robert Howard, *b.* 1935, *s.* 1941, *m.*   Viscount Andover, *b.* 1974
1955   *Swinton (3rd)*, Nicholas John Cunliffe-Lister, *b.* 1939, *s.* 2006, *m.*   Lord Masham *b.* 1970
1714   *Tankerville (10th)*, Peter Grey Bennet, *b.* 1956, *s.* 1980   Revd the Hon. George A. G. B., *b.* 1925
1822   ° *Temple of Stowe (8th)*, (Walter) Grenville Algernon Temple-Gore-Langton, *b.* 1924, *s.* 1988, *m.*   Lord Langton, *b.* 1955
1815   *Verulam (7th)*, John Duncan Grimston, *b.* 1951, *s.* 1973, *m.*   Viscount Grimston, *b.* 1978
1729   ° *Waldegrave (13th)*, James Sherbrooke Waldegrave, *b.* 1940, *s.* 1995, *m.*   Viscount Chewton, *b.* 1986
1759   *Warwick (9th) and Brooke (9th) (1746)*, Guy David Greville, *b.* 1957, *s.* 1996, *m.*   Lord Brooke, *b.* 1982
1633 S.   *Wemyss (12th) and March (8th)*, Francis David Charteris, KT, *b.* 1912, *s.* 1937, *m.*   Lord Neidpath, *b.* 1948
1621 I.   *Westmeath (13th)*, William Anthony Nugent, *b.* 1928, *s.* 1971, *m.*   Hon. Sean C. W. N., *b.* 1965
1624   *Westmorland (16th)*, Anthony David Francis Henry Fane, *b.* 1951, *s.* 1993, *m.*   Hon. Harry St C. F., *b.* 1953
1876   *Wharncliffe (5th)*, Richard Alan Montagu Stuart Wortley, *b.* 1953, *s.* 1987, *m.*   Viscount Carlton, *b.* 1980
1801   *Wilton (8th)*, Francis Egerton Grosvenor, *b.* 1934, *s.* 1999, *m.*   Viscount Grey de Wilton, *b.*1959
1628   *Winchilsea (17th) and Nottingham (12th) (1681)*, Daniel James Hatfield Finch Hatton, *b.* 1967, *s.* 1999, *m.*   Viscount Maidstone, *b.* 1998
1766   ° *Winterton (8th)*, (Donald) David Turnour, *b.* 1943, *s.* 1991, *m.*   Robert C. T., *b.* 1950
1956   *Woolton (3rd)*, Simon Frederick Marquis, *b.* 1958, *s.* 1969, *m.*   None
1837   *Yarborough (8th)*, Charles John Pelham, *b.* 1963, *s.* 1991, *m.*   Lord Worsley, *b.* 1990

COUNTESSES IN THEIR OWN RIGHT

Style, The Right Hon. the Countess (of) _
   Envelope (formal), The Right Hon. the Countess (of) _; *(social),* The Countess (of) _. *Letter (formal),* Madam; *(social),*
   Lady _. *Spoken (formal),* Madam; *(social),* Lady _.
Husband, Untitled
Children's style, As for children of an Earl

Created	Title, order of succession, name, etc	Heir
1643 S.	Dysart (12th in line), Katherine Grant of Rothiemurchus, b. 1918, s. 2003 w.	Lord Huntingtower, b. 1946
c.1115 S.	** Mar (31st in line), Margaret of Mar, b. 1940, s. 1975, m. Premier Earldom of Scotland	Mistress of Mar, b. 1963
1947	° Mountbatten of Burma (2nd in line), Patricia Edwina Victoria Knatchbull, CBE, b. 1924, s. 1979, w.	Lord Romsey, (also Lord Brabourne (8th) see that title)
c.1235 S.	Sutherland (24th in line), Elizabeth Millicent Sutherland, b. 1921, s. 1963, w.	Lord Strathnaver, b. 1947

VISCOUNTS

Coronet, Sixteen silver balls

Style, The Right Hon. the Viscount _
   Envelope (formal), The Right Hon. the Viscount _; *(social),* The Viscount _. *Letter (formal),* My Lord; *(social),* Dear Lord
   _. *Spoken,* Lord _.
Wife's style, The Right Hon. the Viscountess _
   Envelope (formal), The Right Hon. the Viscountess _; *(social),* The Viscountess _. *Letter (formal),* Madam; *(social),* Dear
   Lady _. *Spoken,* Lady _.
Children's style, 'The Hon.' before forename and surname, as for Baron's children
In Scotland, the heir apparent to a Viscount may be styled 'The Master of _ (title of peer)'

Created	Title, order of succession, name, etc	Heir
1945	Addison (4th), William Matthew Wand Addison, b. 1945, s. 1992, m.	Hon. Paul W. A., b. 1973
1946	Alanbrooke (3rd), Alan Victor Harold Brooke, b. 1932, s. 1972	None
1919	** Allenby (3rd), Lt.-Col. Michael Jaffray Hynman Allenby, b. 1931, s. 1984, m.	Hon. Henry J. H. A., b. 1968
1911	Allendale (4th), Wentworth Peter Ismay Beaumont, b. 1948, s. 2002, m.	Hon. Wentworth A. I. B., b. 1979
1642 S.	Arbuthnott (16th), John Campbell Arbuthnott, KT, CBE, DSC, b. 1924, s. 1966, m.	Master of Arbuthnott, b. 1950
1751 I.	Ashbrook (11th), Michael Llowarch Warburton Flower, b. 1935, s. 1995, m.	Hon. Rowland F. W. F., b. 1975
1917	** Astor (4th), William Waldorf Astor, b. 1951, s. 1966, m.	Hon. William W. A., b. 1979
1781 I.	Bangor (8th), William Maxwell David Ward, b. 1948, s. 1993, m.	Hon. E. Nicholas W., b. 1953
1925	Bearsted (5th), Nicholas Alan Samuel, b. 1950, s. 1996, m.	Hon. Harry R. S., b. 1988
1963	Blakenham (2nd), Michael John Hare, b. 1938, s. 1982, m.	Hon. Caspar J. H., b. 1972
1935	** Bledisloe (3rd), Christopher Hiley Ludlow Bathurst, QC, b. 1934, s. 1979	Hon. Rupert E. L. B., b. 1964
1712	Bolingbroke (7th) and St John (8th) (1716), Kenneth Oliver Musgrave St John, b. 1927, s. 1974	Hon. Henry F. St J., b. 1957
1960	Boyd of Merton (2nd), Simon Donald Rupert Neville Lennox-Boyd, b. 1939, s. 1983, m.	Hon. Benjamin A. L.-B., b. 1964
1717 I.	Boyne (11th), Gustavus Michael Stucley Hamilton-Russell, b. 1965, s. 1995, m.	Hon. Gustavus A. E. H.-R., b. 1999
1929	Brentford (4th), Crispin William Joynson-Hicks, b. 1933, s. 1983, m.	Hon. Paul W. J.-H., b. 1971
1929	** Bridgeman (3rd), Robin John Orlando Bridgeman, b. 1930, s. 1982, m.	Hon. Luke R. O. B., b. 1971

Year	Title	Heir
1868	*Bridport (4th) and 7th Duke, Bronte in Sicily, 1799,* Alexander Nelson Hood, *b.* 1948, *s.* 1969, *m.*	Hon. Peregrine A. N. H., *b.* 1974
1952	** *Brookeborough (3rd),* Alan Henry Brooke, *b.* 1952, *s.* 1987, *m.*	Hon. Christopher A. B., *b.* 1954
1933	*Buckmaster (4th),* Adrian Charles Buckmaster, *b.* 1949, *s.* 2007, *m.*	Hon. Andrew N. B., *b.* 1980
1939	*Caldecote (3rd),* Piers James Hampden Inskip, *b.* 1947, *s.* 1999, *m.*	Hon. Thomas J. H. I., *b.* 1985
1941	*Camrose (4th),* Adrian Michael Berry, *b.* 1937, *s.* 2001, *m.*	Hon. Jonathan W. B., *b.* 1970
1954	*Chandos (3rd) and Baron Lyttelton of Aldershot (life peerage, 2000),* Thomas Orlando Lyttelton, *b.* 1953, *s.* 1980, *m.*	Hon. Oliver A. L., *b.* 1986
1665 I.	*Charlemont (15th),* John Dodd Caulfeild, *b.* 1966, *s.* 2001, *m.*	Hon. Shane A. C., *b.* 1996
1921	*Chelmsford (4th)* Frederic Corin Piers Thesiger, *b.* 1962, *s.* 1999, *m.*	Hon. Frederic T. *b.* 2006
1717 I.	*Chetwynd (10th),* Adam Richard John Casson Chetwynd, *b.* 1935, *s.* 1965, *m.*	Hon. Adam D. C., *b.* 1969
1911	*Chilston (4th),* Alastair George Akers-Douglas, *b.* 1946, *s.* 1982, *m.*	Hon. Oliver I. A.-D., *b.* 1973
1902	*Churchill (3rd) and 5th UK Baron Churchill (1815),* Victor George Spencer, *b.* 1934, *s.* 1973	To Barony only, Richard H. R. S., *b.* 1926
1718	*Cobham (12th),* Christopher Charles Lyttelton, *b.* 1947, *s.* 2006, *m.*	Hon. Oliver C. L., *b.* 1976
1902	** *Colville of Culross (4th),* John Mark Alexander Colville, QC, *b.* 1933, *s.* 1945, *m.*	Master of Colville, *b.* 1959
1826	*Combermere (6th),* Thomas Robert Wellington Stapleton-Cotton, *b.* 1969, *s.* 2000	Hon. David P. D. S.-C., *b.* 1932
1917	*Cowdray (4th),* Michael Orlando Weetman Pearson, *b.* 1944, *s.* 1995, *m.*	Hon. Peregrine J. D. P., *b.* 1994
1927	** *Craigavon (3rd),* Janric Fraser Craig, *b.* 1944, *s.* 1974	None
1943	*Daventry (4th),* James Edward FitzRoy Newdegate, *b.* 1960, *s.* 2000, *m.*	Hon. Humphrey J. F. N., *b.* 1995
1937	*Davidson (2nd),* John Andrew Davidson, *b.* 1928, *s.* 1970, *m.*	Hon. Malcolm W. M. D., *b.* 1934
1956	*De L'Isle (2nd),* Philip John Algernon Sidney, MBE, *b.* 1945, *s.* 1991, *m.*	Hon. Philip W. E. S., *b.* 1985
1776 I.	*De Vesci (7th),* Thomas Eustace Vesey, *b.* 1955, *s.* 1983, *m.*	Hon. Oliver I. V., *b.* 1991
1917	*Devonport (3rd),* Terence Kearley, *b.* 1944, *s.* 1973	Chester D. H. K., *b.* 1932
1964	*Dilhorne (2nd),* John Mervyn Manningham-Buller, *b.* 1932, *s.* 1980, *m.*	Hon. James E. M.-B., *b.* 1956
1622 I.	*Dillon (22nd),* Henry Benedict Charles Dillon, *b.* 1973, *s.* 1982	Hon. Richard A. L. D., *b.* 1948
1785 I.	*Doneraile (10th),* Richard Allen St Leger, *b.* 1946, *s.* 1983, *m.*	Hon. Nathaniel W. R. St J. St L., *b.* 1971
1680 I.	*Downe (12th),* Richard Henry Dawnay, *b.* 1967, *s.* 2002	Thomas P. D., *b.* 1978
1959	*Dunrossil (3rd),* Andrew William Reginald Morrison, *b.* 1953, *s.* 2000, *m.*	Hon. Callum A. B. M., *b.* 1994
1964	** *Eccles (2nd),* John Dawson Eccles, CBE, *b.* 1931, *s.* 1999, *m.*	Hon. William D. E., *b.* 1960
1897	*Esher (5th),* Christopher Lionel Baliol Brett, *b.* 1936, *s.* 2004, *m.*	Hon. Matthew C. A. B., *b.* 1963
1816	*Exmouth (10th),* Paul Edward Pellew, *b.* 1940, *s.* 1970, *m.*	Hon. Edward F. P., *b.* 1978
1620 S.	** *Falkland (15th),* Lucius Edward William Plantagenet Cary, *b.* 1935, *s.* 1984, *m. Premier Scottish Viscount on the Roll*	Master of Falkland, *b.* 1963
1720	*Falmouth (9th),* George Hugh Boscawen, *b.* 1919, *s.* 1962, *w.*	Hon. Evelyn A. H. B., *b.* 1955
1720 I.	*Gage (8th),* (Henry) Nicolas Gage, *b.* 1934, *s.* 1993, *m.*	Hon. Henry W. G., *b.* 1975
1727 I.	*Galway (12th),* George Rupert Monckton-Arundell, *b.* 1922, *s.* 1980, *m.*	Hon. J. Philip M., *b.* 1952
1478 I.	*Gormanston (17th),* Jenico Nicholas Dudley Preston, *b.* 1939, *s.* 1940, *m. Premier Viscount of Ireland*	Hon. Jenico F. T. P., *b.* 1974
1816 I.	*Gort (9th),* Foley Robert Standish Prendergast Vereker, *b.* 1951, *s.* 1995, *m.*	Hon. Robert F. P. V., *b.* 1993
1900	** *Goschen (4th),* Giles John Harry Goschen, *b.* 1965, *s.* 1977, *m.*	Hon. Alexander J. E. G., *b.* 2001
1849	*Gough (5th),* Shane Hugh Maryon Gough, *b.* 1941, *s.* 1951	None
1929	*Hailsham (3rd),* Douglas Martin Hogg, PC, QC, MP, *b.* 1945, *s.* 2001, *m.*	Hon. Quintin J. N. M. H., *b.* 1973
1891	*Hambleden (4th),* William Herbert Smith, *b.* 1930, *s.* 1948, *m.*	Hon. William H. B. S., *b.* 1955
1884	*Hampden (6th),* Anthony David Brand, *b.* 1937, *s.* 1975, *m.*	Hon. Francis A. B., *b.* 1970
1936	*Hanworth (3rd),* David Stephen Geoffrey Pollock, *b.* 1946, *s.* 1996, *m.*	Harold W. C. P., *b.* 1988
1791 I.	*Harberton (11th),* Henry Robert Pomeroy, *b.* 1958, *s.* 2004, *m.*	Hon. Patrick C. P., *b.* 1995
1846	*Hardinge (7th),* Andrew Hartland Hardinge, *b.* 1960, *s.* 2004, *m.*	Hon. Thomas H. de M. H., *b.* 1993
1791 I.	*Hawarden (9th),* (Robert) Connan Wyndham Leslie Maude, *b.* 1961, *s.* 1991, *m.*	Hon. Varian J. C. E. M., *b.* 1997
1960	*Head (2nd),* Richard Antony Head, *b.* 1937, *s.* 1983, *m.*	Hon. Henry J. H., *b.* 1980
1550	*Hereford (19th),* Charles Robin De Bohun Devereux, *b.* 1975, *s.* 2004, *Premier Viscount of England*	Hon. Edward M. de B. D., *b.* 1977
1842	*Hill (9th),* Peter David Raymond Charles Clegg-Hill, *b.* 1945, *s.* 2003	*Hon.* Paul A. R. C.-H., *b.* 1979

1796	*Hood (8th)*, Henry Lyttleton Alexander Hood, *b.* 1958, *s.* 1999, *m.*	Hon. Archibald L. S. H., *b.* 1993
1956	*Ingleby (2nd)*, Martin Raymond Peake, *b.* 1926, *s.* 1966, *w.*	None
1945	*Kemsley (3rd)*, Richard Gomer Berry, *b.* 1951, *s.* 1999, *m.*	Hon. Luke G. B., *b.* 1998
1911	*Knollys (3rd)*, David Francis Dudley Knollys, *b.* 1931, *s.* 1966, *m.*	Hon. Patrick N. M. K., *b.* 1962
1895	*Knutsford (6th)*, Michael Holland-Hibbert, *b.* 1926, *s.* 1986, *m.*	Hon. Henry T. H.-H., *b.* 1959
1954	*Leathers (3rd)*, Christopher Graeme Leathers, *b.* 1941, *s.* 1996, *m.*	Hon. James F. L., *b.* 1969
1781 I.	*Lifford (9th)*, (Edward) James Wingfield Hewitt, *b.* 1949, *s.* 1987, *m.*	Hon. James T. W. H., *b.* 1979
1921	*Long (4th)*, Richard Gerard Long, CBE, *b.* 1929, *s.* 1967, *m.*	Hon. James R. L., *b.* 1960
1957	*Mackintosh of Halifax (3rd)*, (John) Clive Mackintosh, *b.* 1958, *s.* 1980, *m.*	Hon. Thomas H. G. M., *b.* 1985
1955	*Malvern (3rd)*, Ashley Kevin Godfrey Huggins, *b.* 1949, *s.* 1978	Hon. M. James H., *b.* 1928
1945	*Marchwood (3rd)*, David George Staveley Penny, *b.* 1936, *s.* 1979, *w.*	Hon. Peter G. W. P., *b.* 1965
1942	*Margesson (2nd)*, Francis Vere Hampden Margesson, *b.* 1922, *s.* 1965, *m.*	Capt. Hon. Richard F. D. M., *b.* 1960
1660 I.	*Massereene (14th) and Ferrard (7th) (I. 1797)*, John David Clotworthy Whyte-Melville Foster Skeffington, *b.* 1940, *s.* 1992, *m.*	Hon. Charles J. C. W.-M. F. S., *b.* 1973
1802	*Melville (9th)*, Robert David Ross Dundas, *b.* 1937, *s.* 1971, *m.*	Hon. Robert H. K. D., *b.* 1984
1916	*Mersey (5th)*, Edward John Hallam Bigham, *b.* 1966, *s.* 2006, *m.*	Hon. David E. H. B., *b.* 1938
1717 I.	*Midleton (12th)*, Alan Henry Brodrick, *b.* 1949, *s.* 1988, *m.*	Hon. Ashley R. B., *b.* 1980
1962	*Mills (3rd)*, Christopher Philip Roger Mills, *b.* 1956, *s.* 1988, *m.*	None
1716 I.	*Molesworth (12th)*, Robert Bysse Kelham Molesworth, *b.* 1959, *s.* 1997	Hon. William J. C. M., *b.* 1960
1801 I.	*Monck (7th)*, Charles Stanley Monck, *b.* 1953, *s.* 1982 (Does not use title)	Hon. George S. M., *b.* 1957
1957	*Monckton of Brenchley (3rd)*, Christopher Walter Monckton, *b.* 1952, *s.* 2006, *m.*	Hon. Timothy D. R. M., *b.* 1955
1946	** *Montgomery of Alamein (2nd)*, David Bernard Montgomery, CBE, *b.* 1928, *s.* 1976, *m.*	Hon. Henry D. M., *b.* 1954
1550 I.	*Mountgarret (18th)*, Piers James Richard Butler, *b.* 1961, *s.* 2004	Hon. Edmund H. R. B., *b.* 1962
1952	*Norwich (2nd)*, John Julius Cooper, CVO, *b.* 1929, *s.* 1954, *m.*	Hon. Jason C. D. B. C., *b.* 1959
1651 S.	*Oxfuird (14th)*, Ian Arthur Alexander Makgill, *b.* 1969, *s.* 2003	Hon. Robert E. G. M., *b.* 1969
1873	*Portman (10th)*, Christopher Edward Berkeley Portman, *b.* 1958, *s.* 1999, *m.*	Hon. Luke O. B. P., *b.* 1984
1743 I.	*Powerscourt (10th)*, Mervyn Niall Wingfield, *b.* 1935, *s.* 1973, *m.*	Hon. Mervyn A. W., *b.* 1963
1900	*Ridley (4th)*, Matthew White Ridley, KG, GCVO, TD, *b.* 1925, *s.* 1964, *w.*	Hon. Matthew W. R., *b.* 1958
1960	*Rochdale (2nd)*, St John Durival Kemp, *b.* 1938, *s.* 1993, *m.*	Hon. Jonathan H. D. K., *b.* 1961
1919	*Rothermere (4th)*, (Harold) Jonathan Esmond Vere Harmsworth, *b.* 1967, *s.* 1998, *m.*	Hon. Vere R. J. H. H., *b.* 1994
1937	*Runciman of Doxford (3rd)*, Walter Garrison Runciman (Garry), CBE, *b.* 1934, *s.* 1989, *m.*	Hon. David W. R., *b.* 1967
1918	*St Davids (3rd)*, Colwyn Jestyn John Philipps, *b.* 1939, *s.* 1991, *m.*	Hon. Rhodri C. P., *b.* 1966
1801	*St Vincent (8th)*, Edward Robert James Jervis, *b.* 1951, *s.* 2006, *m.*	Hon. James R. A. J., *b.* 1982
1937	*Samuel (3rd)*, David Herbert Samuel, OBE, PHD, *b.* 1922, *s.* 1978, *m.*	Hon. Dan J. S., *b.* 1925
1911	*Scarsdale (4th)*, Peter Ghislain Nathaniel Curzon, *b.* 1949, *s.* 2000, *m.*	Hon. David J. N. C., *b.* 1958
1905 M.	*Selby (6th)*, Christopher Rolf Thomas Gully, *b.* 1993, *s.* 2001	Hon. (James) Edward H. G. G., *b.* 1945
1805	*Sidmouth (8th)*, Jeremy Francis Addington, *b.* 1947, *s.* 2005, *m.*	Hon. Steffan A., *b.* 1966
1940	** *Simon (3rd)*, Jan David Simon, *b.* 1940, *s.* 1993, *m.*	None
1960	** *Slim (2nd)*, John Douglas Slim, OBE, *b.* 1927, *s.* 1970, *m.*	Hon. Mark W. R. S., *b.* 1960
1954	*Soulbury (2nd)*, James Herwald Ramsbotham, *b.* 1915, *s.* 1971, *w.*	Hon. Sir Peter E. R., GCMG, GCVO, *b.* 1919
1776 I.	*Southwell (7th)*, Pyers Anthony Joseph Southwell, *b.* 1930, *s.* 1960, *m.*	Hon. Richard A. P. S., *b.* 1956
1942	*Stansgate*, Anthony Neil Wedgwood Benn, *b.* 1925, *s.* 1960, *w.* Disclaimed for life 1963.	Stephen M. W. B., *b.* 1951
1959	*Stuart of Findhorn (3rd)*, James Dominic Stuart, *b.* 1948, *s.* 1999, *m.*	Hon. Andrew M. S., *b.* 1957
1957	** *Tenby (3rd)*, William Lloyd George, *b.* 1927, *s.* 1983, *m.*	Hon. Timothy H. G. L. G., *b.* 1962
1952	*Thurso (3rd)*, John Archibald Sinclair, *b.* 1953, *s.* 1995, *m.*	Hon. James A. R. S., *b.* 1984
1721	*Torrington (11th)*, Timothy Howard St George Byng, *b.* 1943, *s.* 1961, *m.*	Colin H. C.-B., *b.* 1960
1936	** *Trenchard (3rd)*, Hugh Trenchard, *b.* 1951, *s.* 1987, *m.*	Hon. Alexander T. T., *b.* 1978
1921	** *Ullswater (2nd)*, Nicholas James Christopher Lowther, PC, LVO, *b.* 1942, *s.* 1949, *m.*	Hon. Benjamin J. L., *b.* 1975
1622 I.	*Valentia (15th)*, Richard John Dighton Annesley, *b.* 1929, *s.* 1983, *m.*	Hon. Francis W. D. A., *b.* 1959
1952	** *Waverley (3rd)*, John Desmond Forbes Anderson, *b.* 1949, *s.* 1990	Hon. Forbes A. R. A., *b.* 1996

1938	*Weir (3rd)*, William Kenneth James Weir, *b.* 1933, *s.* 1975, *m.*	Hon. James W. H. W., *b.* 1965
1918	*Wimborne (4th)*, Ivor Mervyn Vigors Guest, *b.* 1968, *s.* 1993	Hon. Julien J. G., *b.* 1945
1923	*Younger of Leckie (5th)*, James Edward George Younger, *b.* 1955, *s.* 2003, *m.*	Hon. Alexander W. G. Y., *b.* 1993

BARONS/LORDS

Coronet, Six silver balls

Style, The Right Hon. the Lord _
  Envelope (formal), The Right Hon. Lord _; *(social)*, The Lord _. *Letter (formal)*, My Lord; *(social)*, Dear Lord _. *Spoken*, Lord _.
In the Peerage of Scotland there is no rank of Baron; the equivalent rank is Lord of Parliament and Scottish peers should always be styled 'Lord', never 'Baron'.
Wife's style, The Right Hon. the Lady _
  Envelope (formal), The Right Hon. Lady _; *(social)*, The Lady _. *Letter (formal)*, My Lady; *(social)*, Dear Lady _. *Spoken*, Lady _
Children's style, 'The Hon.' before forename (F_) and surname (S_)
  Envelope, The Hon. F_ S_. *Letter*, Dear Mr/Miss/Mrs S_. *Spoken*, Mr/Miss/Mrs S_
In Scotland, the heir apparent to a Lord may be styled 'The Master of _ (title of peer)'

Created	Title, order of succession, name, etc	Heir
1911	*Aberconway (4th)*, (Henry) Charles McLaren, *b.* 1948, *s.* 2003, *m.*	Hon. Charles S. M., *b.* 1984
1873	*Aberdare (5th)*, Alastair John Lyndhurst Bruce, *b.* 1947, *s.* 2005, *m.*	Hon. Hector M. N. B., *b.* 1974
1835	*Abinger (9th)*, James Harry Scarlett, *b.* 1959, *s.* 2002, *m.*	Hon. Peter R. S., *b.* 1961
1869	*Acton (4th) and Acton of Bridgnorth (life peerage, 2000)*, Richard Gerald Lyon-Dalberg-Acton, *b.* 1941, *s.* 1989, *m.*	Hon. John C. F. H. L.-D.-A., *b.* 1966
1887	** *Addington (6th)*, Dominic Bryce Hubbard, *b.* 1963, *s.* 1982	Hon. Michael W. L. H., *b.* 1965
1896	*Aldenham (6th) and Hunsdon of Hunsdon (4th) (1923)*, Vicary Tyser Gibbs, *b.* 1948, *s.* 1986, *m.*	Hon. Humphrey W. F. G., *b.* 1989
1962	*Aldington (2nd)*, Charles Harold Stuart Low, *b.* 1948, *s.* 2000, *m.*	Hon. Philip T. A. L., *b.* 1990
1945	*Altrincham (3rd)*, Anthony Ulick David Dundas Grigg, *b.* 1934, *s.* 2001, *m.*	Hon. (Edward) Sebastian G., *b.* 1965
1929	*Alvingham (2nd)*, Maj.-Gen. Robert Guy Eardley Yerburgh, CBE, *b.* 1926, *s.* 1955, *m.*	Capt. Hon. Robert R. G. Y., *b.* 1956
1892	*Amherst of Hackney (4th)*, William Hugh Amherst Cecil, *b.* 1940, *s.* 1980, *m.*	Hon. H. William A. C., *b.* 1968
1881	** *Ampthill (4th)*, Geoffrey Denis Erskine Russell, CBE, PC *b.* 1921, *s.* 1973	Hon. David W. E. R., *b.* 1947
1947	*Amwell (3rd)*, Keith Norman Montague, *b.* 1943, *s.* 1990, *m.*	Hon. Ian K. M., *b.* 1973
1863	*Annaly (6th)*, Luke Richard White, *b.* 1954, *s.* 1990, *m.*	Hon. Luke H. W., *b.* 1990
1885	*Ashbourne (4th)*, Edward Barry Greynville Gibson, *b.* 1933, *s.* 1983, *m.*	Hon. Edward C. d'O. G., *b.* 1967
1835	*Ashburton (7th)*, John Francis Harcourt Baring, KG, KCVO, *b.* 1928, *s.* 1991, *m.*	Hon. Mark F. R. B., *b.* 1958
1892	*Ashcombe (4th)*, Henry Edward Cubitt, *b.* 1924, *s.* 1962, *m.*	Mark E. C., *b.* 1964
1911	*Ashton of Hyde (3rd)*, Thomas John Ashton, TD, *b.* 1926, *s.* 1983, *m.*	Hon. Thomas H. A., *b.* 1958
1800 I.	*Ashtown (7th)*, Nigel Clive Crosby Trench, KCMG, *b.* 1916, *s.* 1990, *m.*	Hon. Roderick N. G. T., *b.* 1944
1956	** *Astor of Hever (3rd)*, John Jacob Astor, *b.* 1946, *s.* 1984, *m.*	Hon. Charles G. J. A., *b.* 1990
1789 I.	*Auckland (10th) and Auckland (10th) (1793)*, Robert Ian Burnard Eden, *b.* 1962, *s.* 1997, *m.*	Hon. Ronald J. E., *b.* 1931
1313	*Audley*, Barony in abeyance between three co-heiresses since 1997	
1900	** *Avebury (4th)*, Eric Reginald Lubbock, *b.* 1928, *s.* 1971, *m.*	Hon. Lyulph A. J. L., *b.* 1954
1718 I.	*Aylmer (14th)*, (Anthony) Julian Aylmer, *b.* 1951, *s.* 2006, *m.*	Hon. Michael H. A., *b.* 1991
1929	*Baden-Powell (3rd)*, Robert Crause Baden-Powell, *b.* 1936, *s.* 1962, *m.*	Hon. David M. B.-P., *b.* 1940
1780	*Bagot (10th)*, (Charles Hugh) Shaun Bagot, *b.* 1944, *s.* 2001, *m.*	Richard C. V. B., *b.* 1941
1953	*Baillieu (3rd)*, James William Latham Baillieu, *b.* 1950, *s.* 1973, *m.*	Hon. Robert L. B., *b.* 1979
1607 S.	*Balfour of Burleigh (8th)*, Robert Bruce, *b.* 1927, *s.* 1967, *m.*	Hon. Victoria B., *b.* 1973
1945	*Balfour of Inchrye (2nd)*, Ian Balfour, *b.* 1924, *s.* 1988, *w.*	None
1924	*Banbury of Southam (3rd)*, Charles William Banbury, *b.* 1953, *s.* 1981, *m.*	None
1698	*Barnard (11th)*, Harry John Neville Vane, TD, *b.* 1923, *s.* 1964	Hon. Henry F. C. V., *b.* 1959

1887	*Basing (5th)*, Neil Lutley Sclater-Booth, *b*. 1939, *s*. 1983, *m*.	Hon. Stuart W. S.-B., *b*. 1969
1917	*Beaverbrook (3rd)*, Maxwell William Humphrey Aitken, *b*. 1951, *s*. 1985, *m*.	Hon. Maxwell F. A., *b*. 1977
1647 S.	*Belhaven and Stenton (13th)*, Robert Anthony Carmichael Hamilton, *b*. 1927, *s*. 1961, *m*.	Master of Belhaven, *b*. 1953
1848 I.	*Bellew (7th)*, James Bryan Bellew, *b*. 1920, *s*. 1981, *w*.	Hon. Bryan E. B., *b*. 1943
1856	*Belper (5th)*, Richard Henry Strutt, *b*. 1941, *s*. 1999, *m*.	Hon. Michael H. S., *b*. 1969
1421	*Berkeley (18th) and Gueterbock (life peerage, 2000)*, Anthony Fitzhardinge Gueterbock, OBE, *b*. 1939, *s*. 1992, *m*.	Hon. Thomas F. G., *b*. 1969
1922	*Bethell (4th)*, Nicholas William Bethell, *b*. 1938, *s*. 1967, *m*.	Hon. James N. B., *b*. 1967
1938	*Bicester (3rd)*, Angus Edward Vivian Smith, *b*. 1932, *s*. 1968	Hugh C. V. S., *b*. 1934
1903	*Biddulph (5th)*, (Anthony) Nicholas Colin Maitland Biddulph, *b*. 1959, *s*. 1988, *m*.	Hon. Robert J. M. B., *b*. 1994
1938	*Birdwood (3rd)*, Mark William Ogilvie Birdwood, *b*. 1938, *s*. 1962, *m*.	None
1958	*Birkett (2nd)*, Michael Birkett, *b*. 1929, *s*. 1962, *w*.	Hon. Thomas B., *b*. 1982
1907	*Blyth (4th)*, Anthony Audley Rupert Blyth, *b*. 1931, *s*. 1977, *m*.	Hon. James A. I. B., *b*. 1970
1797	*Bolton (8th)*, Harry Algar Nigel Orde-Powlett, *b*. 1954, *s*. 2001, *m*.	Hon. Thomas O.-P., *b*. 1979
1452 S.	*Borthwick (24th)*, John Hugh Borthwick, *b*. 1940, *s*. 1996, *m*.	Hon. James H. A. B. of Glengelt, *b*. 1940
1922	*Borwick (5th)*, (Geoffrey Robert) James Borwick, *b*. 1955, *s*. 2007, *m*.	Hon. Edwin D. W. B., *b*. 1984
1761	*Boston (11th)*, George William Eustace Boteler Irby, *b*. 1971, *s*. 2007, *m*.	Hon. Thomas W. G. B. I., *b*. 1999
1942	** *Brabazon of Tara (3rd)*, Ivon Anthony Moore-Brabazon, *b*. 1946, *s*. 1974, *m*.	Hon. Benjamin R. M.-B., *b*. 1983
1880	*Brabourne (8th)*, Norton Louis Philip Knatchbull, *b*. 1947, *s*. 2005, *m*. (*also* Lord Romsey heir to Countess Mountbatten of Burma, *see* that title)	Hon. Nicholas L. C. N. K., *b*. 1981
1925	*Bradbury (3rd)*, John Bradbury, *b*. 1940, *s*. 1994, *m*.	Hon. John B., *b*. 1973
1962	*Brain (2nd)*, Christopher Langdon Brain, *b*. 1926, *s*. 1966, *m*.	Hon. Michael C. B., *b*. 1928
1938	*Brassey of Apethorpe (3rd)*, David Henry Brassey, OBE, *b*. 1932, *s*. 1967, *m*.	Hon. Edward B., *b*. 1964
1788	*Braybrooke (10th)*, Robin Henry Charles Neville, *b*. 1932, *s*. 1990, *m*.	George N., *b*. 1943
1957	** *Bridges (2nd)*, Thomas Edward Bridges, GCMG, *b*. 1927, *s*. 1969, *m*.	Hon. Mark T. B., *b*. 1954
1945	*Broadbridge (4th)*, Martin Hugh Broadbridge, *b*. 1929, *s*. 2000, *w*.	Hon. Richard J. M. B., *b*. 1959
1933	*Brocket (3rd)*, Charles Ronald George Nall-Cain, *b*. 1952, *s*. 1967, *w*.	Hon. Alexander C. C. N.-C., *b*. 1984
1860	** *Brougham and Vaux (5th)*, Michael John Brougham, CBE, *b*. 1938, *s*. 1967	Hon. Charles W. B., *b*. 1971
1776	*Brownlow (7th)*, Edward John Peregrine Cust, *b*. 1936, *s*. 1978, *m*.	Hon. Peregrine E. Q. C., *b*. 1974
1942	*Bruntisfield (3rd)*, Michael John Victor Warrender, *b*. 1949, *s*. 2007, *m*.	Hon. John M. P. C. W., *b*. 1996
1950	*Burden (4th)*, Fraser William Elsworth Burden, *b*. 1964, *s*. 2000, *m*.	Hon. Ian S. B., *b*. 1967
1529	*Burgh (8th)*, (Alexander) Gregory Disney Leith, *b*. 1958, *s*. 2001, *m*.	Hon. Alexander J. S. L., *b*. 1986
1903	*Burnham (7th)*, Harry Frederick Alan Lawson, *b*. 1968, *s*. 2005	None
1897	*Burton (3rd)*, Michael Evan Victor Baillie, *b*. 1924, *s*. 1962, *m*.	Hon. Evan M. R. B., *b*. 1949
1643	*Byron (13th)*, Robert James Byron, *b*. 1950, *s*. 1989, *m*.	Hon. Charles R. G. B., *b*. 1990
1937	*Cadman (3rd)*, John Anthony Cadman, *b*. 1938, *s*. 1966, *m*.	Hon. Nicholas A. J. C., *b*. 1977
1945	*Calverley (3rd)*, Charles Rodney Muff, *b*. 1946, *s*. 1971, *m*.	Hon. Jonathan E. M., *b*. 1975
1383	*Camoys (7th)*, (Ralph) Thomas Campion George Sherman Stonor, GCVO, PC, *b*. 1940, *s*. 1976, *m*.	Hon. R. William R. T. S., *b*. 1974
1715 I.	*Carbery (11th)*, Peter Ralfe Harrington Evans-Freke, *b*. 1920, *s*. 1970, *w*.	Hon. Michael P. E.-F., *b*. 1942
1834 I.	*Carew (7th) and Carew (7th) (1838)*, Patrick Thomas Conolly-Carew, *b*. 1938, *s*. 1994, *m*.	Hon. William P. C.-C., *b*. 1973
1916	*Carnock (4th)*, David Henry Arthur Nicolson, *b*. 1920, *s*. 1982	Adam N., *b*. 1957
1796 I.	*Carrington (6th) and Carrington (6th) (1797) and Carington of Upton (life peerage, 1999)*, Peter Alexander Rupert Carington, KG, GCMG, CH, MC, PC, *b*. 1919, *s*. 1938, *m*.	Hon. Rupert F. J. C., *b*. 1948
1812 I.	*Castlemaine (8th)*, Roland Thomas John Handcock, MBE, *b*. 1943, *s*. 1973, *m*.	Hon. Ronan M. E. H., *b*. 1989
1936	*Catto (3rd)*, Innes Gordon Catto, *b*. 1950, *s*. 2001, *m*.	Hon. Alexander G. C., *b*. 1952
1918	*Cawley (4th)*, John Francis Cawley, *b*. 1946, *s*. 2001, *m*.	Hon. William R. H. C., *b*. 1981
1937	*Chatfield (2nd)*, Ernle David Lewis Chatfield, *b*. 1917, *s*. 1967, *m*.	None
1858	*Chesham (6th)*, Nicholas Charles Cavendish, *b*. 1941, *s*. 1989, *m*.	Hon. Charles G. C. C., *b*. 1974
1945	*Chetwode (2nd)*, Philip Chetwode, *b*. 1937, *s*. 1950, *m*.	Hon. Roger C., *b*. 1968
1945	** *Chorley (2nd)*, Roger Richard Edward Chorley, *b*. 1930, *s*. 1978, *m*.	Hon. Nicholas R. D. C., *b*. 1966
1858	*Churston (5th)*, John Francis Yarde-Buller, *b*. 1934, *s*. 1991, *m*.	Hon. Benjamin F. A. Y.-B., *b*. 1974

1946	*Citrine (3rd)*, Ronald Eric Citrine, *b.* 1919, *s.* 1997, *m.* (Does not use title)	None
1800 I.	*Clanmorris (8th)*, Simon John Ward Bingham, *b.* 1937, *s.* 1988, *m.*	Robert D. de B. B., *b.* 1942
1672	*Clifford of Chudleigh (14th)*, Thomas Hugh Clifford, *b.* 1948, *s.* 1988, *m.*	Hon. Alexander T. H. C., *b.* 1985
1299	*Clinton (22nd)*, Gerard Nevile Mark Fane Trefusis, *b.* 1934, *s.* 1965, *m.*	Hon. Charles P. R. F. T., *b.* 1962
1955	*Clitheroe (2nd)*, Ralph John Assheton, *b.* 1929, *s.* 1984, *m.*	Hon. Ralph C. A., *b.* 1962
1919	*Clwyd (4th)*, (John) Murray Roberts, *b.* 1971, *s.* 2006	Hon. Jeremy T. R., *b.* 1973
1948	*Clydesmuir (3rd)*, David Ronald Colville, *b.* 1949, *s.* 1996, *m.*	Hon. Richard C., *b.* 1980
1960	** *Cobbold (2nd)*, David Antony Fromanteel Lytton Cobbold, *b.* 1937, *s.* 1987, *m.*	Hon. Henry F. L. C., *b.* 1962
1919	*Cochrane of Cults (4th)*, (Ralph Henry) Vere Cochrane, *b.* 1926, *s.* 1990, *m.*	Hon. Thomas H. V. C., *b.* 1957
1954	*Coleraine (2nd)*, (James) Martin (Bonar) Law, *b.* 1931, *s.* 1980, *m.*	Hon. James P. B. L., *b.* 1975
1873	*Coleridge (5th)*, William Duke Coleridge, *b.* 1937, *s.* 1984, *m.*	Hon. James D. C., *b.* 1967
1946	*Colgrain (3rd)*, David Colin Campbell, *b.* 1920, *s.* 1973, *m.*	Hon. Alastair C. L. C., *b.* 1951
1917	** *Colwyn (3rd)*, (Ian) Anthony Hamilton-Smith, CBE, *b.* 1942, *s.* 1966, *m.*	Hon. Craig P. H.-S., *b.* 1968
1956	*Colyton (2nd)*, Alisdair John Munro Hopkinson, *b.* 1958, *s.* 1996, *m.*	Hon. James P. M. H., *b.* 1983
1841	*Congleton (8th)*, Christopher Patrick Parnell, *b.* 1930, *s.* 1967, *m.*	Hon. John P. C. P., *b.* 1959
1927	*Cornwallis (3rd)*, Fiennes Neil Wykeham Cornwallis, OBE, *b.* 1921, *s.* 1982, *m.*	Hon. F. W. Jeremy C., *b.* 1946
1874	*Cottesloe (5th)*, John Tapling Fremantle, *b.* 1927, *s.* 1994, *m.*	Hon. Thomas F. H. F., *b.* 1966
1929	*Craigmyle (4th)*, Thomas Columba Shaw, *b.* 1960, *s.* 1998, *m.*	Hon. Alexander F. S., *b.* 1988
1899	*Cranworth (3rd)*, Philip Bertram Gurdon, *b.* 1940, *s.* 1964, *m.*	Hon. Sacha W. R. G., *b.* 1970
1959	** *Crathorne (2nd)*, Charles James Dugdale, *b.* 1939, *s.* 1977, *m.*	Hon. Thomas A. J. D., *b.* 1977
1892	*Crawshaw (5th)*, David Gerald Brooks, *b.* 1934, *s.* 1997, *m.*	Hon. John P. B., *b.* 1938
1940	*Croft (3rd)*, Bernard William Henry Page Croft, *b.* 1949, *s.* 1997, *m.*	None
1797 I.	*Crofton (7th)*, Guy Patrick Gilbert Crofton, *b.* 1951, *s.* 1989, *m.*	Hon. E. Harry P. C., *b.* 1988
1375	*Cromwell (7th)*, Godfrey John Bewicke-Copley, *b.* 1960, *s.* 1982, *m.*	Hon. David G. B.-C., *b.* 1997
1947	*Crook (3rd)*, Robert Douglas Edwin Crook, *b.* 1955, *s.* 2001, *m.*	Hon. Matthew R. C., *b.* 1990
1920	*Cullen of Ashbourne (3rd)*, Edmund Willoughby Marsham Cokayne, *b.* 1916, *s.* 2000, *w.*	(Hon.) John O'B. M. C., *b.*1920
1914	*Cunliffe (3rd)*, Roger Cunliffe, *b.* 1932, *s.* 1963, *m.*	Hon. Henry C., *b.* 1962
1927	*Daresbury (4th)*, Peter Gilbert Greenall, *b.* 1953, *s.* 1996, *m.*	Hon. Thomas E. G., *b.* 1984
1924	*Darling (3rd)*, (Robert) Julian Henry Darling, *b.* 1944, *s.* 2003, *m.*	Hon. Robert J. C. D., *b.* 1972
1946	*Darwen (3rd)*, Roger Michael Davies, *b.* 1938, *s.* 1988, *m.*	Hon. Paul D., *b.* 1962
1932	*Davies (3rd)*, David Davies, *b.* 1940, *s.* 1944, *m.*	Hon. David D. D., *b.* 1975
1812 I.	*Decies (7th)*, Marcus Hugh Tristram de la Poer Beresford, *b.* 1948, *s.* 1992, *m.*	Hon. Robert M. D. de la P. B., *b.* 1988
1299	*de Clifford (27th)*, John Edward Southwell Russell, *b.* 1928, *s.* 1982, *m.*	Hon. William S. R., *b.* 1930
1851	*De Freyne (7th)*, Francis Arthur John French, *b.* 1927, *s.* 1935, *m.*	Hon. Fulke C. A. J. F., *b.* 1957
1821	*Delamere (5th)*, Hugh George Cholmondeley, *b.* 1934, *s.* 1979, *m.*	Hon. Thomas P. G. C., *b.* 1968
1838	** *de Mauley (7th)*, Rupert Charles Ponsonby, *b.* 1957, *s.* 2002, *m.*	Ashley G. P., *b.* 1959
1937	** *Denham (2nd)*, Bertram Stanley Mitford Bowyer, KBE, PC, *b.* 1927, *s.* 1948, *m.*	Hon. Richard G. G. B., *b.* 1959
1834	*Denman (5th)*, Charles Spencer Denman, CBE, MC, TD, *b.* 1916, *s.* 1971, *w.*	Hon. Richard T. S. D., *b.* 1946
1887	*De Ramsey (4th)*, John Ailwyn Fellowes, *b.* 1942, *s.* 1993, *m.*	Hon. Freddie J. F., *b.* 1978
1264	*de Ros (28th)*, Peter Trevor Maxwell, *b.* 1958, *s.* 1983, *m. Premier Baron of England*	Hon. Finbar J. M., *b.* 1988
1881	*Derwent (5th)*, Robin Evelyn Leo Vanden-Bempde-Johnstone, LVO, *b.* 1930, *s.* 1986, *m.*	Hon. Francis P. H. V.-B.-J., *b.* 1965
1831	*de Saumarez (7th)*, Eric Douglas Saumarez, *b.* 1956, *s.* 1991, *m.*	Hon. Victor T. S., *b.* 1956
1910	*de Villiers (4th)*, Alexander Charles de Villiers, *b.* 1940, *s.* 2001, *m.*	None
1930	*Dickinson (2nd)*, Richard Clavering Hyett Dickinson, *b.* 1926, *s.* 1943, *m.*	Hon. Martin H. D., *b.* 1961
1620 I.	*Digby (12th) and Digby (5th) (1765)*, Edward Henry Kenelm Digby, KCVO, *b.* 1924, *s.* 1964, *m.*	Hon. Henry N. K. D., *b.* 1954
1615	*Dormer (17th)*, Geoffrey Henry Dormer, *b.* 1920, *s.* 1995, *m.*	Hon. William R. D., *b.* 1960
1943	*Dowding (3rd)*, Piers Hugh Tremenheere Dowding, *b.* 1948, *s.* 1992	Hon. Mark D. J. D., *b.* 1949
1439	*Dudley (15th)*, Jim Anthony Hill Wallace, *b.* 1930, *s.* 2002, *m.*	Hon. Jeremy W. G. W., *b.* 1964
1800 I.	*Dufferin and Clandeboye (11th)*, John Francis Blackwood, *b.* 1944, *s.* 1991 (claim to the peerage not yet established), *m.*	*Hon.* Francis S. B., *b.* 1979
1929	*Dulverton (3rd)*, (Gilbert) Michael Hamilton Wills, *b.* 1944, *s.* 1992, *m.*	Hon. Robert A. H. W., *b.* 1983
1800 I.	*Dunalley (7th)*, Henry Francis Cornelius Prittie, *b.* 1948, *s.* 1992, *m.*	Hon. Joel H. P., *b.* 1981
1324 I.	*Dunboyne (29th)*, John Fitzwalter Butler, *b.* 1951, *s.* 2004, *m.*	Hon. Richard P. T. B., *b.* 1983
1892	*Dunleath (6th)*, Brian Henry Mulholland, *b.* 1950, *s.* 1997, *m.*	Hon. Andrew H. M., *b.* 1981

1439 I.	*Dunsany (20th)*, Edward John Carlos Plunkett, *b.* 1939, *s.* 1999, *m.*	Hon. Randal P., *b.* 1983
1780	*Dynevor (9th)*, Richard Charles Uryan Rhys, *b.* 1935, *s.* 1962	Hon. Hugo G. U. R., *b.* 1966
1963	*Egremont (2nd) and Leconfield (7th) (1859)*, John Max Henry Scawen Wyndham, *b.* 1948, *s.* 1972, *m.*	Hon. George R. V. W., *b.* 1983
1643	*Elibank (14th)*, Alan D'Ardis Erskine-Murray, *b.* 1923, *s.* 1973, *w.*	Master of Elibank, *b.* 1964
1802	*Ellenborough (8th)*, Richard Edward Cecil Law, *b.* 1926, *s.* 1945, *m.*	Maj. Hon. Rupert E. H. L., *b.* 1955
1509 S.	*Elphinstone (19th) and Elphinstone (5th) (1885)*, Alexander Mountstuart Elphinstone, *b.* 1980, *s.* 1994, *m.*	Hon. Angus J. E., *b.* 1982
1934	** *Elton (2nd)*, Rodney Elton, TD, *b.* 1930, *s.* 1973, *m.*	Hon. Edward P. E., *b.* 1966
1627 S.	*Fairfax of Cameron (14th)*, Nicholas John Albert Fairfax, *b.* 1956, *s.* 1964, *m.*	Hon. Edward N. T. F., *b.* 1984
1961	*Fairhaven (3rd)*, Ailwyn Henry George Broughton, *b.* 1936, *s.* 1973, *m.*	Maj. Hon. James H. A. B., *b.* 1963
1916	*Faringdon (3rd)*, Charles Michael Henderson, *b.* 1937, *s.* 1977, *m.*	Hon. James H. H., *b.* 1961
1756 I.	*Farnham (13th)*, Simon Kenlis Maxwell, *b.* 1933, *s.* 2001, *m.*	Hon. Robin S. M., *b.* 1965
1856 I.	*Fermoy (6th)*, Patrick Maurice Burke Roche, *b.* 1967, *s.* 1984, *m.*	Hon. E. Hugh B. R., *b.* 1972
1826	*Feversham (6th)*, Charles Antony Peter Duncombe, *b.* 1945, *s.* 1963, *m.*	Hon. Jasper O. S. D., *b.* 1968
1798 I.	*ffrench (8th)*, Robuck John Peter Charles Mario ffrench, *b.* 1956, *s.* 1986, *m.*	Hon. John C. M. J. F. ff., *b.* 1928
1909	*Fisher (3rd)*, John Vavasseur Fisher, DSC, *b.* 1921, *s.* 1955, *m.*	Hon. Patrick V. F., *b.* 1953
1295	*Fitzwalter (22nd)*, Julian Brook Plumptre, *b.* 1952, *s.* 2004, *m.*	Hon. Edward B. P., *b.* 1989
1776	*Foley (8th)*, Adrian Gerald Foley, *b.* 1923, *s.* 1927, *m.*	Hon. Thomas H. F., *b.* 1961
1445	*Forbes (22nd)*, Nigel Ivan Forbes, KBE, *b.* 1918, *s.* 1953, *m. Premier Lord of Scotland*	Master of Forbes, *b.* 1946
1821	*Forester (9th)*, Charles Richard George Weld-Forester, *b.* 1975, *s.* 2004,	Wolstan W. W.-F., *b.* 1941
1922	*Forres (4th)*, Alastair Stephen Grant Williamson, *b.* 1946, *s.* 1978, *m.*	Hon. George A. M. W., *b.* 1972
1917	*Forteviot (4th)*, John James Evelyn Dewar, *b.* 1938, *s.* 1993, *w.*	Hon. Alexander J. E. D., *b.* 1971
1951	** *Freyberg (3rd)*, Valerian Bernard Freyberg, *b.* 1970, *s.* 1993	None
1917	*Gainford (3rd)*, Joseph Edward Pease, *b.* 1921, *s.* 1971, *m.*	Hon. George P., *b.* 1926
1818 I.	*Garvagh (5th)*, (Alexander Leopold Ivor) George Canning, *b.* 1920, *s.* 1956, *m.*	Hon. Spencer G. S. de R. C., *b.* 1953
1942	** *Geddes (3rd)*, Euan Michael Ross Geddes, *b.* 1937, *s.* 1975, *m.*	Hon. James G. N. G., *b.* 1969
1876	*Gerard (5th)*, Anthony Robert Hugo Gerard, *b.* 1949, *s.* 1992, *m.*	Hon. Rupert B. C. G., *b.* 1981
1824	*Gifford (6th)*, Anthony Maurice Gifford, *b.* 1940, *s.* 1961, *m.*	Hon. Thomas A. G., *b.* 1967
1917	*Gisborough (3rd)*, Thomas Richard John Long Chaloner, *b.* 1927, *s.* 1951, *m.*	Hon. T. Peregrine L. C., *b.* 1961
1960	*Gladwyn (2nd)*, Miles Alvery Gladwyn Jebb, *b.* 1930, *s.* 1996	None
1899	*Glanusk (5th)*, Christopher Russell Bailey, *b.* 1942, *s.* 1997, *m.*	Hon. Charles H. B., *b.* 1976
1918	** *Glenarthur (4th)*, Simon Mark Arthur, *b.* 1944, *s.* 1976, *m.*	Hon. Edward A. A., *b.* 1973
1911	*Glenconner (3rd)*, Colin Christopher Paget Tennant, *b.* 1926, *s.* 1983, *m.*	Cody C. E. T., *b.* 1994
1964	*Glendevon (2nd)*, Julian John Somerset Hope, *b.* 1950, *s.* 1996	Hon. Jonathan C. H., *b.* 1952
1922	*Glendyne (3rd)*, Robert Nivison, *b.* 1926, *s.* 1967, *m.*	Hon. John N., *b.* 1960
1939	** *Glentoran (3rd)*, (Thomas) Robin (Valerian) Dixon, CBE, *b.* 1935, *s.* 1995, *m.*	Hon. Daniel G. D., *b.* 1959
1909	*Gorell (4th)*, Timothy John Radcliffe Barnes, *b.* 1927, *s.* 1963, *m.*	Hon. Ronald A. H. B., *b.* 1931
1953	** *Grantchester (3rd)*, Christopher John Suenson-Taylor, *b.* 1951, *s.* 1995, *m.*	Hon. Jesse D. S.-T., *b.* 1977
1782	*Grantley (8th)*, Richard William Brinsley Norton, *b.* 1956, *s.* 1995	Hon. Francis J. H. N., *b.* 1960
1794 I.	*Graves (10th)*, Timothy Evelyn Graves, *b.* 1960, *s.* 2002	None
1445 S.	*Gray (23rd)*, Andrew Godfrey Diarmid Stuart Campbell-Gray, *b.* 1964, *s.* 2003, *m.*	Master of Gray, *b.* 1996
1950	*Greenhill (3rd)*, Malcolm Greenhill, *b.* 1924, *s.* 1989	None
1927	** *Greenway (4th)*, Ambrose Charles Drexel Greenway, *b.* 1941, *s.* 1975, *m.*	Hon. Nigel. P. G., *b.* 1944
1902	*Grenfell (3rd) and Grenfell of Kilvey (life peerage, 2000)*, Julian Pascoe Francis St Leger Grenfell, *b.* 1935, *s.* 1976, *m.*	Francis P. J. G., *b.* 1938
1944	*Gretton (4th)*, John Lysander Gretton, *b.* 1975, *s.* 1989	None
1397	*Grey of Codnor (6th)*, Richard Henry Cornwall-Legh, *b.* 1936, *s.* 1996, *m.*	Hon. Richard S. C. C.-L., *b.* 1976
1955	*Gridley (3rd)*, Richard David Arnold Gridley, *b.* 1956, *s.* 1996, *m.*	Peter A. C. G., *b.* 1940
1964	*Grimston of Westbury (3rd)*, Robert John Sylvester Grimston, *b.* 1951, *s.* 2003, *m.*	Hon. Gerald C. W. G., *b.* 1953
1886	*Grimthorpe (5th)*, Edward John Beckett, *b.* 1954, *s.* 2003, *m.*	Hon. Harry M. B., *b.* 1993
1945	*Hacking (3rd)*, Douglas David Hacking, *b.* 1938, *s.* 1971, *m.*	Hon. Douglas F. H., *b.* 1968
1950	*Haden-Guest (5th)*, Christopher Haden-Guest, *b.* 1948, *s.* 1996, *m.*	Hon. Nicholas H.-G., *b.* 1951

1886	*Hamilton of Dalzell (5th)*, Gavin Goulburn Hamilton, *b.* 1968, *s.* 2006, *m.*	Hon. Robert P. H., *b.* 1971
1874	*Hampton (7th)*, John Humphrey Arnott Pakington, *b.* 1964, *s.* 2003, *m.*	None
1939	*Hankey (3rd)*, Donald Robin Alers Hankey, *b.* 1938, *s.* 1996, *m.*	Hon. Alexander M. A. H., *b.* 1947
1958	*Harding of Petherton (2nd)*, John Charles Harding, *b.* 1928, *s.* 1989, *m.*	Hon. William A. J. H., *b.* 1969
1910	*Hardinge of Penshurst (4th)*, Julian Alexander Hardinge, *b.* 1945, *s.* 1997	Hon. Hugh F. H., *b.* 1948
1876	*Harlech (6th)*, Francis David Ormsby-Gore, *b.* 1954, *s.* 1985, *m.*	Hon. Jasset D. C. O.-G., *b.* 1986
1939	*Harmsworth (3rd)*, Thomas Harold Raymond Harmsworth, *b.* 1939, *s.* 1990, *m.*	Hon. Dominic M. E. H., *b.* 1973
1815	*Harris (8th)*, Anthony Harris, *b.* 1942, *s.* 1996, *m.*	Anthony J. T. H., *b.* 1915
1954	*Harvey of Tasburgh (2nd)*, Peter Charles Oliver Harvey, *b.* 1921, *s.* 1968, *w.*	Charles J. G. H., *b.* 1951
1295	*Hastings (23rd)*, Delaval Thomas Harold Astley, *b.* 1960, *s.* 2007, *m.*	Hon. Jacob A. A., *b.* 1991
1835	*Hatherton (8th)*, Edward Charles Littleton, *b.* 1950, *s.* 1985, *m.*	Hon. Thomas E. L., *b.* 1977
1776	*Hawke (11th)*, Edward George Hawke, TD, *b.* 1950, *s.* 1992, *m.*	Hon. William M. T. H., *b.* 1995
1927	*Hayter (4th)*, George William Michael Chubb, *b.* 1943, *s.* 2003, *m.*	Hon. Thomas F. F. C., *b.*1986
1945	*Hazlerigg (3rd)*, Arthur Grey Hazlerigg, *b.* 1951, *s.* 2002, *m.*	Hon. Arthur W. G. H. *b.* 1987
1943	*Hemingford (3rd)*, (Dennis) Nicholas Herbert, *b.* 1934, *s.* 1982, *m.*	Hon. Christopher D. C. H., *b.* 1973
1906	*Hemphill (5th)*, Peter Patrick Fitzroy Martyn Martyn-Hemphill, *b.* 1928, *s.* 1957, *m.*	Hon. Charles A. M. M.-H., *b.* 1954
1799 I.	** *Henley (8th) and Northington (6th) (1885)*, Oliver Michael Robert Eden, *b.* 1953, *s.* 1977, *m.*	Hon. John W. O. E., *b.* 1988
1800 I.	*Henniker (9th) and Hartismere (6th) (1866)*, Mark Ian Philip Chandos Henniker-Major, *b.* 1947, *s.* 2004, *m.*	Hon. Edward G. M. H.-M., *b.* 1985
1461	*Herbert (19th)*, David John Seyfried Herbert, *b.* 1952, *s.* 2002, *m.*	Hon. Oliver R. S. H., *b.* 1976
1886	*Herschell (3rd)*, Rognvald Richard Farrer Herschell, *b.* 1923, *s.* 1929, *m.*	None
1935	*Hesketh (3rd)*, Thomas Alexander Fermor-Hesketh, KBE, PC, *b.* 1950, *s.* 1955, *m.*	Hon. Frederick H. F.-H., *b.* 1988
1828	*Heytesbury (7th)*, James William Holmes à Court, *b.* 1967, *s.* 2004, *m.*	Peter M. H.. H. à. C., *b.* 1968
1886	*Hindlip (6th)*, Charles Henry Allsopp, *b.* 1940, *s.* 1993, *m.*	Hon. Henry W. A., *b.* 1973
1950	*Hives (3rd)*, Matthew Peter Hives, *b.* 1971, *s.* 1997	Hon. Michael B. H., *b.* 1926
1912	*Hollenden (4th)*, Ian Hampden Hope-Morley, *b.* 1946, *s.* 1999, *m.*	Hon. Edward H.-M., *b.* 1981
1897	*Holm Patrick (4th)*, Hans James David Hamilton, *b.* 1955, *s.* 1991, *m.*	Hon. Ion H. J. H., *b.* 1956
1797 I.	*Hotham (8th)*, Henry Durand Hotham, *b.* 1940, *s.* 1967, *m.*	Hon. William B. H., *b.* 1972
1881	*Hothfield (6th)*, Anthony Charles Sackville Tufton, *b.* 1939, *s.* 1991, *m.*	Hon. William S. T., *b.* 1977
1930	*Howard of Penrith (3rd)*, Philip Esme Howard, *b.* 1945, *s.* 1999, *m.*	Hon. Thomas Philip H., *b.* 1974
1960	*Howick of Glendale (2nd)*, Charles Evelyn Baring, *b.* 1937, *s.* 1973, *m.*	Hon. David E. C. B., *b.* 1975
1796 I.	*Huntingfield (7th)*, Joshua Charles Vanneck, *b.* 1954, *s.* 1994, *m.*	Hon. Gerard C. A. V., *b.* 1985
1866	** *Hylton (5th)*, Raymond Hervey Jolliffe, *b.* 1932, *s.* 1967, *m.*	Hon. William H. M. J., *b.* 1967
1933	*Iliffe (3rd)*, Robert Peter Richard Iliffe, *b.* 1944, *s.* 1996, *m.*	Hon. Edward R. I., *b.* 1968
1543 I.	*Inchiquin (18th)*, Conor Myles John O'Brien, *b.* 1943, *s.* 1982, *m.*	Conor J. A. O'B., *b.* 1952
1962	*Inchyra (2nd)*, Robert Charles Reneke Hoyer Millar, *b.* 1935, *s.* 1989, *m.*	Hon. C. James C. H. M., *b.* 1962
1964	** *Inglewood (2nd)*, (William) Richard Fletcher-Vane, *b.* 1951, *s.* 1989, *m.*	Hon. Henry W. F. F.-V., *b.* 1990
1919	*Inverforth (4th)*, Andrew Peter Weir, *b.* 1966, *s.* 1982	Hon. John V. W., *b.* 1935
1941	*Ironside (2nd)*, Edmund Oslac Ironside, *b.* 1924, *s.* 1959, *m.*	Hon. Charles E. G. I., *b.* 1956
1952	*Jeffreys (3rd)*, Christopher Henry Mark Jeffreys, *b.* 1957, *s.* 1986, *m.*	Hon. Arthur M. H. J., *b.* 1989
1906	*Joicey (5th)*, James Michael Joicey, *b.* 1953, *s.* 1993, *m.*	Hon. William J. J., *b.* 1990
1937	*Kenilworth (4th)*, (John) Randle Siddeley, *b.* 1954, *s.* 1981, *m.*	Hon. William R. J. S., *b.* 1992
1935	*Kennet (2nd)*, Wayland Hilton Young, *b.* 1923, *s.* 1960, *m.*	Hon. W. A. Thoby Y., *b.* 1957
1776 I.	*Kensington (8th) and Kensington (5th) (1886)*, Hugh Ivor Edwardes, *b.* 1933, *s.* 1981, *m.*	Hon. W. Owen A. E., *b.* 1964
1951	*Kenswood (2nd)*, John Michael Howard Whitfield, *b.* 1930, *s.* 1963, *m.*	Hon. Michael C. W., *b.* 1955
1788	*Kenyon (6th)*, Lloyd Tyrell-Kenyon, *b.* 1947, *s.* 1993, *m.*	Hon. Lloyd N. T.-K., *b.* 1972
1947	*Kershaw (4th)*, Edward John Kershaw, *b.* 1936, *s.* 1962, *m.*	Hon. John C. E. K., *b.* 1971
1943	*Keyes (3rd)*, Charles William Packe Keyes, *b.* 1951, *s.* 2005, *m.*	Hon. Leopold R. J. K., *b.* 1956
1909	*Kilbracken (4th)*, Christopher John Godley, *b.* 1945, *s.* 2006, *m.*	Hon. James J. G., *b.* 1972
1900	*Killanin (4th)*, (George) Redmond Fitzpatrick Morris, *b.* 1947, *s.* 1999, *m.*	Hon. Luke M. G. M., *b.* 1975
1943	*Killearn (3rd)*, Victor Miles George Aldous Lampson, *b.* 1941, *s.* 1996, *m.*	Hon. Miles H. M. L., *b.* 1977
1789 I.	*Kilmaine (7th)*, John David Henry Browne, *b.* 1948, *s.* 1978, *m.*	Hon. John F. S. B., *b.* 1983

1831	*Kilmarnock (7th)*, Alastair Ivor Gilbert Boyd, *b.* 1927, *s.* 1975, *m.*	Hon. Robin J. B., *b.* 1941
1941	*Kindersley (3rd)*, Robert Hugh Molesworth Kindersley, *b.* 1929, *s.* 1976, *m.*	Hon. Rupert J. M. K., *b.* 1955
1223 I.	*Kingsale (36th)*, Nevinson Mark de Courcy, *b.* 1958, *s.* 2005, *m.*, *Premier Baron of Ireland*	Joseph K. C. de C., *b.* 1955
1902	*Kinross (5th)*, Christopher Patrick Balfour, *b.* 1949, *s.* 1985, *m.*	Hon. Alan I. B., *b.* 1978
1951	*Kirkwood (3rd)*, David Harvie Kirkwood, PHD, *b.* 1931, *s.* 1970, *m.*	Hon. James S. K., *b.* 1937
1800 I.	*Langford (9th)*, Col. Geoffrey Alexander Rowley-Conwy, OBE, *b.* 1912, *s.* 1953, *m.*	Hon. Owain G. R.-C., *b.* 1958
1942	*Latham (2nd)*, Dominic Charles Latham, *b.* 1954, *s.* 1970	Anthony M. L., *b.* 1954
1431	*Latymer (9th)*, Crispin James Alan Nevill Money-Coutts, *b.* 1955, *s.* 2003, *m.*	Hon. Drummond W. T. M.-C., *b.* 1986
1869	*Lawrence (5th)*, David John Downer Lawrence, *b.* 1937, *s.* 1968	None
1947	*Layton (3rd)*, Geoffrey Michael Layton, *b.* 1947, *s.* 1989, *m.*	Hon. David L., *b.* 1914
1839	*Leigh (6th)*, Christopher Dudley Piers Leigh, *b.* 1960, *s.* 2003, *m.*	Hon. Rupert D. L., *b.* 1994
1962	*Leighton of St Mellons (3rd)*, Robert William Henry Leighton Seager, *b.* 1955, *s.* 1998	Hon. Simon J. L. S., *b.* 1957
1797	*Lilford (8th)*, Mark Vernon Powys, *b.* 1975, *s.* 2005	Robert C. L. P., *b.* 1930
1945	*Lindsay of Birker (3rd)*, James Francis Lindsay, *b.* 1945, *s.* 1994, *m.*	Alexander S. L., *b.* 1940
1758 I.	*Lisle (9th)*, (John) Nicholas Geoffrey Lysaght, *b.* 1960, *s.* 2003	Hon. David J. L., *b.* 1963
1850	*Londesborough (9th)*, Richard John Denison, *b.* 1959, *s.* 1968, *m.*	Hon. James F. D., *b.* 1990
1541 I.	*Louth (16th)*, Otway Michael James Oliver Plunkett, *b.* 1929, *s.* 1950, *m.*	Hon. Jonathan O. P., *b.* 1952
1458 S.	*Lovat (16th) and Lovat (5th) (1837)*, Simon Fraser, *b.* 1977, *s.* 1995	Hon. Jack F., *b.* 1984
1946	*Lucas of Chilworth (3rd)*, Simon William Lucas, *b.* 1957, *s.* 2001, *m.*	Hon. John R. M. L., *b.* 1995
1663	** *Lucas (11th) and Dingwall (14th) (S. 1609)*, Ralph Matthew Palmer, *b.* 1951, *s.* 1991	Hon. Lewis E. P., *b.* 1987
1929	** *Luke (3rd)*, Arthur Charles St John Lawson-Johnston, *b.* 1933, *s.* 1996, *m.*	Hon. Ian J. St J. L.-J., *b.* 1963
1914	** *Lyell (3rd)*, Charles Lyell, *b.* 1939, *s.* 1943	None
1859	*Lyveden (7th)*, Jack Leslie Vernon, *b.* 1938, *s.* 1999, *m.*	Hon. Colin R. V., *b.* 1967
1959	*MacAndrew (3rd)*, Christopher Anthony Colin MacAndrew, *b.* 1945, *s.* 1989, *m.*	Hon. Oliver C. J. M., *b.* 1983
1776 I.	*Macdonald (8th)*, Godfrey James Macdonald of Macdonald, *b.* 1947, *s.* 1970, *m.*	Hon. Godfrey E. H. T. M., *b.* 1982
1937	*McGowan (4th)*, Harry John Charles McGowan, *b.* 1971, *s.* 2003, *m.*	Hon. Dominic J. W. McG., *b.* 1951
1922	*Maclay (3rd)*, Joseph Paton Maclay, *b.* 1942, *s.* 1969, *m.*	Hon. Joseph P. M., *b.* 1977
1955	*McNair (3rd)*, Duncan James McNair, *b.* 1947, *s.* 1989, *m.*	Hon. William S. A. M., *b.* 1958
1951	*Macpherson of Drumochter (2nd)*, (James) Gordon Macpherson, *b.* 1924, *s.* 1965, *m.*	Hon. James A. M., *b.* 1979
1937	** *Mancroft (3rd)*, Benjamin Lloyd Stormont Mancroft, *b.* 1957, *s.* 1987, *m.*	Hon. Arthur L. S. M., *b.* 1995
1807	*Manners (5th)*, John Robert Cecil Manners, *b.* 1923, *s.* 1972, *w.*	Hon. John H. R. M., *b.* 1956
1922	*Manton (4th)*, Miles Ronald Marcus Watson, *b.* 1958, *s.* 2003, *m.*	Hon. Thomas N. C. D. W., *b.* 1985
1908	*Marchamley (4th)*, William Francis Whiteley, *b.* 1968, *s.* 1994	None
1964	*Margadale (3rd)*, Alastair John Morrison, *b.* 1958, *s.* 2003, *m.*	Hon. Declan J. M., *b.* 1993
1961	*Marks of Broughton (3rd)*, Simon Richard Marks, *b.* 1950, *s.* 1998, *m.*	Hon. Michael M., *b.* 1989
1964	*Martonmere (2nd)*, John Stephen Robinson, *b.* 1963, *s.* 1989	David A. R., *b.* 1965
1776 I.	*Massy (10th)*, David Hamon Somerset Massy, *b.* 1947, *s.* 1995	Hon. John H. M., *b.* 1950
1935	*May (4th)*, Jasper Bertram St John May, *b.* 1965, *s.* 2006	None
1928	*Melchett (4th)*, Peter Robert Henry Mond, *b.* 1948, *s.* 1973	None
1925	*Merrivale (3rd)*, Jack Henry Edmond Duke, *b.* 1917, *s.* 1951, *w.*	Hon. Derek J. P. D., *b.* 1948
1911	*Merthyr*, Trevor Oswin Lewis, CBE, *b.* 1935, *s.* 1977, *m.* Disclaimed for life 1977	David T. L., *b.* 1977
1919	*Meston (3rd)*, James Meston, *b.* 1950, *s.* 1984, *m.*	Hon. Thomas J. D. M., *b.* 1977
1838	** *Methuen (7th)*, Robert Alexander Holt Methuen, *b.* 1931, *s.* 1994, *m.*	James P. A. M.-C., *b.* 1952
1711	*Middleton (12th)*, (Digby) Michael Godfrey John Willoughby, MC, *b.* 1921, *s.* 1970	Hon. Michael C. J. W., *b.* 1948
1939	*Milford (4th)*, Guy Wogan Philipps, *b.* 1961, *s.* 1999, *m.*	Hon. Archie S. P., *b.* 1997
1933	*Milne (3rd)*, George Alexander Milne, *b.* 1941, *s.* 2005	Hon. Iain C. L. M., *b.* 1949
1951	*Milner of Leeds (3rd)*, Richard James Milner, *b.* 1959, *s.* 2003, *m.*	None
1947	*Milverton (2nd)*, Revd Fraser Arthur Richard Richards, *b.* 1930, *s.* 1978, *m.*	Hon. Michael H. R., *b.* 1936
1873	*Moncreiff (6th)*, Rhoderick Harry Wellwood Moncreiff, *b.* 1954, *s.* 2002, *m.*	Hon. Harry J. W. M., *b.* 1986

1884	*Monk Bretton (3rd)*, John Charles Dodson, *b.* 1924, *s.* 1933, *m.*	Hon. Christopher M. D., *b.* 1958
1885	*Monkswell (5th)*, Gerard Collier, *b.* 1947, *s.* 1984, *m.*	Hon. James A. C., *b.* 1977
1728	** *Monson (11th)*, John Monson, *b.* 1932, *s.* 1958, *m.*	Hon. Nicholas J. M., *b.* 1955
1885	** *Montagu of Beaulieu (3rd)*, Edward John Barrington Douglas-Scott-Montagu, *b.* 1926, *s.* 1929, *m.*	Hon. Ralph D.-S.-M., *b.* 1961
1839	*Monteagle of Brandon (6th)*, Gerald Spring Rice, *b.* 1926, *s.* 1946, *m.*	Hon. Charles J. S. R., *b.* 1953
1943	** *Moran (2nd)*, (Richard) John (McMoran) Wilson, KCMG, *b.* 1924, *s.* 1977, *m.*	Hon. James M. W., *b.* 1952
1918	*Morris (3rd)*, Michael David Morris, *b.* 1937, *s.* 1975, *m.*	Hon. Thomas A. S. M., *b.* 1982
1950	*Morris of Kenwood (3rd)*, Jonathan David Morris, *b.* 1968, *s.* 2004, *m.*	None
1831	*Mostyn (6th)*, Llewellyn Roger Lloyd-Mostyn, *b.* 1948, *s.* 2000, *m.*	Hon. Gregory P. R. L.-M., *b.* 1984
1933	*Mottistone (4th)*, David Peter Seely, CBE, *b.* 1920, *s.* 1966, *m.*	Hon. Peter J. P. S., *b.* 1949
1945	*Mountevans (3rd)*, Edward Patrick Broke Evans, *b.* 1943, *s.* 1974, *m.*	Hon. Jeffrey de C. R. E., *b.* 1948
1283	*Mowbray (27th), Segrave (28th) (1295) and Stourton (24th) (1448)*, Edward William Stephen Stourton, *b.* 1953, *s.* 2006, *m.*	Hon. James C. P. S., *b.* 1991
1932	*Moyne (3rd)*, Jonathan Bryan Guinness, *b.* 1930, *s.* 1992, *m.*	Hon. Jasper J. R. G., *b.* 1954
1929	** *Moynihan (4th)*, Colin Berkeley Moynihan, *b.* 1955, *s.* 1997, *m.*	Hon. Nicholas E. B. M., *b.* 1994
1781 I.	*Muskerry (9th)*, Robert Fitzmaurice Deane, *b.* 1948, *s.* 1988, *m.*	Hon. Jonathan F. D., *b.* 1986
1627 S.	*Napier (14th) and Ettrick (5th) (1872)*, Francis Nigel Napier, KCVO, *b.* 1930, *s.* 1954, *m.*	Master of Napier, *b.* 1962
1868	*Napier of Magdala (6th)*, Robert Alan Napier, *b.* 1940, *s.* 1987, *m.*	Hon. James R. N., *b.* 1966
1940	*Nathan (3rd)*, Rupert Harry Bernard Nathan, *b.* 1957, *s.* 2007, *m.*	None
1960	*Nelson of Stafford (4th)*, Alistair William Henry Nelson, *b.* 1973, *s.* 2006	Hon. James J. N., *b.* 1947
1959	*Netherthorpe (3rd)*, James Frederick Turner, *b.* 1964, *s.* 1982, *m.*	Hon. Andrew J. E. T., *b.* 1993
1946	*Newall (2nd)*, Francis Storer Eaton Newall, *b.* 1930, *s.* 1963, *m.*	Hon. Richard H. E. N., *b.* 1961
1776 I.	*Newborough (8th)*, Robert Vaughan Wynn, *b.* 1949, *s.* 1998, *m.*	Hon. Charles H. R. W., *b.* 1923
1892	*Newton (5th)*, Richard Thomas Legh, *b.* 1950, *s.* 1992, *m.*	Hon. Piers R. L., *b.* 1979
1930	*Noel-Buxton (3rd)*, Martin Connal Noel-Buxton, *b.* 1940, *s.* 1980, *m.*	Hon. Charles C. N.-B., *b.* 1975
1957	*Norrie (2nd)*, (George) Willoughby Moke Norrie, *b.* 1936, *s.* 1977, *m.*	Hon. Mark W. J. N., *b.* 1972
1884	** *Northbourne (5th)*, Christopher George Walter James, *b.* 1926, *s.* 1982, *m.*	Hon. Charles W. H. J., *b.* 1960
1866	** *Northbrook (6th)*, Francis Thomas Baring, *b.* 1954, *s.* 1990, *m.*	To the Baronetcy, Peter B. *b.* 1939
1878	*Norton (8th)*, James Nigel Arden Adderley, *b.* 1947, *s.* 1993, *m.*	Hon. Edward J. A. A., *b.* 1982
1906	*Nunburnholme (6th)*, Stephen Charles Wilson, *b.* 1973, *s.* 2000	Hon. David M. W., *b.* 1954
1950	*Ogmore (3rd)*, Morgan Rees-Williams, *b.* 1937, *s.* 2004, *m.*	Hon. Tudor D. R.-W., *b.* 1991
1870	*O'Hagan (4th)*, Charles Towneley Strachey, *b.* 1945, *s.* 1961	Hon. Richard T. S., *b.* 1950
1868	*O'Neill (4th)*, Raymond Arthur Clanaboy O'Neill, TD, *b.* 1933, *s.* 1944, *m.*	Hon. Shane S. C. O'N., *b.* 1965
1836 I.	*Oranmore and Browne (5th) and Mereworth (3rd) (1926)*, Dominick Geoffrey Thomas Browne, *b.* 1929, *s.* 2002	Hon. Martin M. D. B., *b.* 1931
1933	** *Palmer (4th)*, Adrian Bailie Nottage Palmer, *b.* 1951, *s.* 1990, *m.*	Hon. Hugo B. R. P., *b.* 1980
1914	*Parmoor (4th)*, (Frederick Alfred) Milo Cripps, *b.* 1929, *s.* 1977	Michael L. S. C., *b.* 1942
1937	*Pender (3rd)*, John Willoughby Denison-Pender, *b.* 1933, *s.* 1965, *m.*	Hon. Henry J. R. D.-P., *b.* 1968
1866	*Penrhyn (7th)*, Simon Douglas-Pennant, *b.* 1938, *s.* 2003, *m.*	Hon. Edward S. D.-P., *b.* 1966
1603	*Petre (18th)*, John Patrick Lionel Petre, *b.* 1942, *s.* 1989, *m.*	Hon. Dominic W. P., *b.* 1966
1918	*Phillimore (5th)*, Francis Stephen Phillimore, *b.* 1944, *s.* 1994, *m.*	Hon. Tristan A. S. P., *b.* 1977
1945	*Piercy (3rd)*, James William Piercy, *b.* 1946, *s.* 1981	Hon. Mark E. P. P., *b.* 1953
1827	*Plunket (8th)*, Robin Rathmore Plunket, *b.* 1925, *s.* 1975, *m.*	Hon. Shaun A. F. S. P., *b.* 1931
1831	*Poltimore (7th)*, Mark Coplestone Bampfylde, *b.* 1957, *s.* 1978, *m.*	Hon. Henry A. W. B., *b.* 1985
1690 S.	*Polwarth (11th)*, Andrew Walter Hepburne-Scott, *b.* 1947, *s.* 2005, *m.*	Master of Polwarth, *b.* 1973
1930	*Ponsonby of Shulbrede (4th) and Ponsonby of Roehampton (life peerage, 2000)*, Frederick Matthew Thomas Ponsonby, *b.* 1958, *s.* 1990	None
1958	*Poole (2nd)*, David Charles Poole, *b.* 1945, *s.* 1993, *m.*	Hon. Oliver J. P., *b.* 1972
1852	*Raglan (5th)*, FitzRoy John Somerset, *b.* 1927, *s.* 1964	Hon. Geoffrey S., *b.* 1932
1932	*Rankeillour (5th)*, Michael Richard Hope, *b.* 1940, *s.* 2005, *m.*	James F. H., *b.* 1968
1953	*Rathcavan (3rd)*, Hugh Detmar Torrens O'Neill, *b.* 1939, *s.* 1994, *m.*	Hon. François H. N. O'N., *b.* 1984
1916	*Rathcreedan (3rd)*, Christopher John Norton, *b.* 1949, *s.* 1990, *m.*	Hon. Adam G. N., *b.* 1952
1868 I.	*Rathdonnell (5th)*, Thomas Benjamin McClintock-Bunbury, *b.* 1938, *s.* 1959, *m.*	Hon. William L. M.-B., *b.* 1966
1911	*Ravensdale (3rd)*, Nicholas Mosley, MC, *b.* 1923, *s.* 1966, *m.*	Hon. Shaun N. M., *b.* 1949

1821	*Ravensworth (9th)*, Thomas Arthur Hamish Liddell, *b.* 1954, *s.* 2004, *m.*	Hon. Henry A. T. L., *b.* 1987
1821	*Rayleigh (6th)*, John Gerald Strutt, *b.* 1960, *s.* 1988, *m.*	Hon. John F. S., *b.* 1993
1937	** *Rea (3rd)*, John Nicolas Rea, MD, *b.* 1928, *s.* 1981, *m.*	Hon. Matthew J. R., *b.* 1956
1628 S.	** *Reay (14th)*, Hugh William Mackay, *b.* 1937, *s.* 1963, *m.*	Master of Reay, *b.* 1965
1902	*Redesdale (6th) and Mitford (life peerage 2000)*, Rupert Bertram Mitford, *b.* 1967, *s.* 1991, *m.*	Hon. Bertram D. M., *b.* 2000
1940	*Reith*, Christopher John Reith, *b.* 1928, *s.* 1971, *m.* Disclaimed for life 1972.	Hon. James H. J. R., *b.* 1971
1928	*Remnant (3rd)*, James Wogan Remnant, CVO, *b.* 1930, *s.* 1967, *m.*	Hon. Philip J. R., *b.* 1954
1806 I.	*Rendlesham (9th)*, Charles William Brooke Thellusson, *b.* 1954, *s.* 1999, *m.*	Hon. Peter R. T., *b.* 1920
1933	*Rennell (4th)*, James Roderick David Tremayne Rodd, *b.* 1978, *s.* 2006	None
1964	*Renwick (2nd)*, Harry Andrew Renwick, *b.* 1935, *s.* 1973, *m.*	Hon. Robert J. R., *b.* 1966
1885	*Revelstoke (6th)*, James Cecil Baring, *b.* 1938, *s.* 2003, *m.*	Hon. Alexander R. B., *b.* 1970
1905	*Ritchie of Dundee (5th)*, (Harold) Malcolm Ritchie, *b.* 1919, *s.* 1978, *m.*	Hon. C. Rupert R. R., *b.* 1958
1935	*Riverdale (3rd)*, Anthony Robert Balfour, *b.* 1960, *s.* 1998	Hon. David R. B., *b.* 1938
1961	*Robertson of Oakridge (2nd)*, William Ronald Robertson, *b.* 1930, *s.* 1974, *m.*	Hon. William B. E. R., *b.* 1975
1938	*Roborough (3rd)*, Henry Massey Lopes, *b.* 1940, *s.* 1992, *m.*	Hon. Massey J. H. L., *b.* 1969
1931	*Rochester (2nd)*, Foster Charles Lowry Lamb, *b.* 1916, *s.* 1955, *w.*	Hon. David C. L., *b.* 1944
1934	*Rockley (3rd)*, James Hugh Cecil, *b.* 1934, *s.* 1976, *m.*	Hon. Anthony R. C., *b.* 1961
1782	*Rodney (10th)*, George Brydges Rodney, *b.* 1953, *s.* 1992, *m.*	Hon. John G. B. R., *b.* 1999
1651 S.	*Rollo (14th) and Dunning (5th) (1869)*, David Eric Howard Rollo, *b.* 1943, *s.* 1997, *m.*	Master of Rollo, *b.* 1972
1959	*Rootes (3rd)*, Nicholas Geoffrey Rootes, *b.* 1951, *s.* 1992, *m.*	William B. R., *b.* 1944
1796 I.	*Rossmore (7th) and Rossmore (6th) (1838)*, William Warner Westenra, *b.* 1931, *s.* 1958, *m.*	Hon. Benedict W. W., *b.* 1983
1939	** *Rotherwick (3rd)*, (Herbert) Robin Cayzer, *b.* 1954, *s.* 1996, *m.*	Hon. H. Robin C., *b.* 1989
1885	*Rothschild (4th)*, (Nathaniel Charles) Jacob Rothschild, OM, GBE, *b.* 1936, *s.* 1990, *m.*	Hon. Nathaniel P. V. J. R., *b.* 1971
1911	*Rowallan (4th)*, John Polson Cameron Corbett, *b.* 1947, *s.* 1993	Hon. Jason W. P. C. C., *b.* 1972
1947	*Rugby (3rd)*, Robert Charles Maffey, *b.* 1951, *s.* 1990, *m.*	Hon. Timothy J. H. M., *b.* 1975
1919	*Russell of Liverpool (3rd)*, Simon Gordon Jared Russell, *b.* 1952, *s.* 1981, *m.*	Hon. Edward C. S. R., *b.* 1985
1876	*Sackville (7th)*, Robert Bertrand Sackville-West, *b.* 1958, *s.* 2004, *m.*	Hon. Arthur S-W., *b.* 2000
1964	*St Helens (2nd)*, Richard Francis Hughes-Young, *b.* 1945, *s.* 1980, *m.*	Hon. Henry T. H.-Y., *b.* 1986
1559	** *St John of Bletso (21st)*, Anthony Tudor St John, *b.* 1957, *s.* 1978, *m.*	Hon. Oliver B. St J., *b.* 1995
1887	*St Levan (4th)*, John Francis Arthur St Aubyn, DSC, *b.* 1919, *s.* 1978, *w.*	James P. S. St. A., *b.* 1950
1885	*St Oswald (6th)*, Charles Rowland Andrew Winn, *b.* 1959, *s.* 1999, *m.*	Hon. Rowland C. S. H. W., *b.* 1986
1960	*Sanderson of Ayot*, Alan Lindsay Sanderson, *b.* 1931, *s.* 1971, *m.* Disclaimed for life 1971.	Hon. Michael S., *b.* 1959
1945	*Sandford (2nd)*, Revd John Cyril Edmondson, DSC, *b.* 1920, *s.* 1959, *m.*	Hon. James J. M. E., *b.* 1949
1871	*Sandhurst (6th)*, Guy Rees John Mansfield, *b.* 1949, *s.* 2002, *m.*	Hon. Edward J. M., *b.* 1982
1802	*Sandys (7th)*, Richard Michael Oliver Hill, *b.* 1931, *s.* 1961, *m.*	The Marquess of Downshire
1888	*Savile (3rd)*, George Halifax Lumley-Savile, *b.* 1919, *s.* 1931	John A. T. L-S., *b.* 1947
1447	*Saye and Sele (21st)*, Nathaniel Thomas Allen Fiennes, *b.* 1920, *s.* 1968, *m.*	Hon. Martin G. F., *b.* 1961
1826	*Seaford (6th)*, Colin Humphrey Felton Ellis, *b.* 1946, *s.* 1999, *m.*	Hon. Benjamin F. T. E., *b.* 1976
1932	** *Selsdon (3rd)*, Malcolm McEacharn Mitchell-Thomson, *b.* 1937, *s.* 1963, *m.*	Hon. Callum M. M. M.-T., *b.* 1969
1489 S.	*Sempill (21st)*, James William Stuart Whitemore Sempill, *b.* 1949, *s.* 1995, *m.*	Master of Sempill, *b.* 1979
1916	*Shaughnessy (4th)*, Michael James Shaughnessy, *b.* 1946, *s.* 2003	Charles, G. P. S., *b.* 1955
1946	*Shepherd (3rd)*, Graham George Shepherd, *b.* 1949, *s.* 2001, *m.*	Hon. Patrick M. S., *b.* 19–
1964	*Sherfield (3rd)*, Dwight William Makins, *b.* 1951, *s.* 2006, *m.*	None
1902	*Shuttleworth (5th)*, Charles Geoffrey Nicholas Kay-Shuttleworth, *b.* 1948, *s.* 1975, *m.*	Hon. Thomas E. K.-S., *b.* 1976
1950	*Silkin (3rd)*, Christopher Lewis Silkin, *b.* 1947, *s.* 2001	Rory L. S., *b.* 1954
1963	*Silsoe (3rd)*, Simon Rupert Trustram Eve, *b.* 1966, *s.* 2005	Hon. Peter N. T. E., *b.* 1930
1947	*Simon of Wythenshawe (3rd)*, Matthew Simon, *b.* 1955, *s.* 2002	Martin S., *b.* 1944
1449 S.	*Sinclair (18th)*, Matthew Murray Kennedy St Clair *b.* 1968, *s.* 2004, *m.*	Hugh A. C. St C., *b.* 1957
1957	*Sinclair of Cleeve (3rd)*, John Lawrence Robert Sinclair, *b.* 1953, *s.* 1985	None
1919	*Sinha (6th)*, Arup Kumar Sinha, *b.* 1966, *s.* 1999	Hon. Dilip K. S., *b.* 1967
1828	** *Skelmersdale (7th)*, Roger Bootle-Wilbraham, *b.* 1945, *s.* 1973, *m.*	Hon. Andrew B.-W., *b.* 1977

1916	*Somerleyton (3rd)*, Savile William Francis Crossley, GCVO, *b.* 1928, *s.* 1959, *m.*	Hon. Hugh F. S. C., *b.* 1971
1784	*Somers (9th)*, Philip Sebastian Somers Cocks, *b.* 1948, *s.* 1995	Alan B. C., *b.* 1930
1780	*Southampton (6th)*, Charles James FitzRoy, *b.* 1928, *s.* 1989, *m.*	Hon. Edward C. F., *b.* 1955
1959	*Spens (4th)*, Patrick Nathaniel George Spens, *b.* 1968, *s.* 2001, *m.*	Hon. Peter L. S., *b.* 2000
1640	*Stafford (15th)*, Francis Melfort William Fitzherbert, *b.* 1954, *s.* 1986, *m.*	Hon. Benjamin J. B. F., *b.* 1983
1938	*Stamp (4th)*, Trevor Charles Bosworth Stamp, MD, *b.* 1935, *s.* 1987, *m.*	Hon. Nicholas C. T. S., *b.* 1978
1839	*Stanley of Alderley (8th), Sheffield (8th) (I. 1738) and Eddisbury (7th) (1848)*, Thomas Henry Oliver Stanley, *b.* 1927, *s.* 1971, *m.*	Hon. Richard O. S., *b.* 1956
1318	** *Strabolgi (11th)*, David Montague de Burgh Kenworthy, *b.* 1914, *s.* 1953, *m.*	Andrew D. W. K., *b.* 1967
1954	*Strang (2nd)*, Colin Strang, *b.* 1922, *s.* 1978, *m.*	None
1628	*Strange (17th)*, Adam Humphrey Drummond of Megginch, *b.* 1953, *s.* 2005 *m.*	Hon. John A. H. D. of M. *b.* 1992
1955	*Strathalmond (3rd)*, William Roberton Fraser, *b.* 1947, *s.* 1976, *m.*	Hon. William G. F., *b.* 1976
1936	*Strathcarron (3rd)*, Ian David Patrick Macpherson, *b.* 1949, *s.* 2006, *m.*	Hon. Rory D. A. M., *b.* 1982
1955	** *Strathclyde (2nd)*, Thomas Galloway Dunlop du Roy de Blicquy Galbraith, PC, *b.* 1960, *s.* 1985, *m.*	Hon. Charles W. du R. de B. G., *b.* 1962
1900	*Strathcona and Mount Royal (4th)*, Donald Euan Palmer Howard, *b.* 1923, *s.* 1959, *m.*	Hon. D. Alexander S. H., *b.* 1961
1836	*Stratheden (6th) and Campbell (6th) (1841)*, Donald Campbell, *b.* 1934, *s.* 1987, *m.*	Hon. David A. C., *b.* 1963
1884	*Strathspey (6th)*, James Patrick Trevor Grant of Grant, *b.* 1943, *s.* 1992, *m.*	Hon. Michael P. F. G., *b.* 1953
1838	*Sudeley (7th)*, Merlin Charles Sainthill Hanbury-Tracy, *b.* 1939, *s.* 1941	D. Andrew J. H.-T., *b.* 1928
1786	*Suffield (11th)*, Anthony Philip Harbord-Hamond, MC, *b.* 1922, *s.* 1951, *w.*	Hon. Charles A. A. H.-H., *b.* 1953
1893	*Swansea (5th)*, Richard Anthony Hussey Vivian, *b.* 1957, *s.* 2005, *m.*	Hon. James H. V., *b.* 1999
1907	*Swaythling (5th)*, Charles Edgar Samuel Montagu, *b.* 1954, *s.* 1998, *m.*	Hon. Anthony T. S. M., *b.* 1931
1919	** *Swinfen (3rd)*, Roger Mynors Swinfen Eady, *b.* 1938, *s.* 1977, *m.*	Hon. Charles R. P. S. E., *b.* 1971
1935	*Sysonby (3rd)*, John Frederick Ponsonby, *b.* 1945, *s.* 1956	None
1831 I.	*Talbot of Malahide (10th)*, Reginald John Richard Arundell, *b.* 1931, *s.* 1987, *m.*	Hon. Richard J. T. A., *b.* 1957
1946	*Tedder (3rd)*, Robin John Tedder, *b.* 1955, *s.* 1994, *m.*	Hon. Benjamin J. T., *b.* 1985
1884	*Tennyson (6th)*, David Harold Alexander Tennyson, *b.* 1960, *s.* 2006	Alan J. D. T., *b.* 1965
1918	*Terrington (6th)*, Christopher Richard James Woodhouse, MB, *b.* 1946, *s.* 2001, *m.*	Hon. Jack H. L. W., *b.* 1978
1940	*Teviot (2nd)*, Charles John Kerr, *b.* 1934, *s.* 1968, *m.*	Hon. Charles R. K., *b.* 1971
1616	*Teynham (20th)*, John Christopher Ingham Roper-Curzon, *b.* 1928, *s.* 1972, *m.*	Hon. David J. H. I. R.-C., *b.* 1965
1964	*Thomson of Fleet (3rd)*, David Kenneth Roy Thomson, *b.* 1957, *s.* 2006, *m.*	Hon. Benjamin T., *b.* 2006
1792	*Thurlow (8th)*, Francis Edward Hovell-Thurlow-Cumming-Bruce, KCMG, *b.* 1912, *s.* 1971, *w.*	Hon. Roualeyn R. H.-T.-C.-B., *b.* 1952
1876	*Tollemache (5th)*, Timothy John Edward Tollemache, *b.* 1939, *s.* 1975, *m.*	Hon. Edward J. H. T., *b.* 1976
1564 S.	*Torphichen (15th)*, James Andrew Douglas Sandilands, *b.* 1946, *s.* 1975, *m.*	Robert P. S., *b.* 1950
1947	** *Trefgarne (2nd)*, David Garro Trefgarne, PC, *b.* 1941, *s.* 1960, *m.*	Hon. George G. T., *b.* 1970
1921	*Trevethin (4th) and Oaksey (2nd) (1947)*, John Geoffrey Tristram Lawrence, OBE, *b.* 1929, *s.* 1971, *m.*	Hon. Patrick J. T. L., *b.* 1960
1880	*Trevor (5th)*, Marke Charles Hill-Trevor, *b.* 1970, *s.* 1997, *m.*	Hon. Iain R. H.-T., *b.* 1971
1461 I.	*Trimlestown (21st)*, Raymond Charles Barnewall, *b.* 1930, *s.* 1997	None
1940	*Tryon (3rd)*, Anthony George Merrik Tryon, *b.* 1940, *s.* 1976	Hon. Charles G. B. T., *b.* 1976
1935	*Tweedsmuir (3rd)*, William de l'Aigle Buchan, *b.* 1916, *s.* 1996, *m.*	Hon. John W. H. de l'A. B., *b.* 1950
1523	*Vaux of Harrowden (11th)*, Anthony William Gilbey, *b.* 1940, *s.* 2002, *m.*	Hon. Richard H. G. G., *b.*1965
1800 I.	*Ventry (8th)*, Andrew Wesley Daubeny de Moleyns, *b.* 1943, *s.* 1987, *m.*	Hon. Francis W. D. de M., *b.* 1965
1762	*Vernon (11th)*, Anthony William Vernon-Harcourt, *b.* 1939, *s.* 2000, *m.*	Hon. Simon A. V.-H., *b.* 1969
1922	*Vestey (3rd)*, Samuel George Armstrong Vestey, *b.* 1941, *s.* 1954, *m.*	Hon. William G. V., *b.* 1983
1841	*Vivian (7th)*, Charles Crespigny Hussey Vivian, *b.* 1966, *s.* 2004	Hon. Victor A. R. B. V., *b.* 1940
1934	*Wakehurst (3rd)*, (John) Christopher Loder, *b.* 1925, *s.* 1970, *m.*	Hon. Timothy W. L., *b.* 1958
1723	** *Walpole (10th) and Walpole of Wolterton (8th) (1756)*, Robert Horatio Walpole, *b.* 1938, *s.* 1989, *m.*	Hon. Jonathan R. H. W., *b.* 1967

1780	*Walsingham (9th)*, John de Grey, MC, *b.* 1925, *s.* 1965, *m.*	Hon. Robert de. G., *b.* 1969
1936	*Wardington (3rd)*, William Simon Pease, *b.* 1925, *s.* 2005, *m.*	None
1792 I.	*Waterpark (7th)*, Frederick Caryll Philip Cavendish, *b.* 1926, *s.* 1948, *m.*	Hon. Roderick A. C., *b.* 1959
1942	*Wedgwood (4th)*, Piers Anthony Weymouth Wedgwood, *b.* 1954, *s.* 1970, *m.*	John W., *b.* 1919
1861	*Westbury (6th)*, Richard Nicholas Bethell, MBE, *b.* 1950, *s.* 2001, *m.*	Hon. Alexander B., *b.* 1986
1944	*Westwood (3rd)*, (William) Gavin Westwood, *b.* 1944, *s.* 1991, *m.*	Hon. W. Fergus W., *b.* 1972
1544/5	*Wharton (12th)*, Myles Christopher David Robertson, *b.* 1964, *s.* 2000, *m.*	Hon. Christopher J. R., *b.* 1969
1935	*Wigram (2nd)*, (George) Neville (Clive) Wigram, MC, *b.* 1915, *s.* 1960, *w.*	Maj. Hon. Andrew F. C. W., *b.* 1949
1491	** *Willoughby de Broke (21st)*, Leopold David Verney, *b.* 1938, *s.* 1986, *m.*	Hon. Rupert G. V., *b.* 1966
1946	*Wilson (2nd)*, Patrick Maitland Wilson, *b.* 1915, *s.* 1964, *w.*	None
1937	*Windlesham (3rd) and Hennessy (life peerage, 1999)*, David James George Hennessy, CVO, PC, *b.* 1932, *s.* 1962, *w.*	Hon. James R. H., *b.* 1968
1951	*Wise (2nd)*, John Clayton Wise, *b.* 1923, *s.* 1968, *m.*	Hon. Christopher J. C. W., *b.* 1949
1869	*Wolverton (7th)*, Christopher Richard Glyn, *b.* 1938, *s.* 1988	Hon. Andrew J. G., *b.* 1943
1928	*Wraxall (3rd)*, Eustace Hubert Beilby Gibbs, KCVO, CMG, *b.* 1929, *s.* 2001, *m.*	Hon. Anthony H. G., *b.* 1958
1915	*Wrenbury (3rd)*, Revd John Burton Buckley, *b.* 1927, *s.* 1940, *m.*	Hon. William E. B., *b.* 1966
1838	*Wrottesley (6th)*, Clifton Hugh Lancelot de Verdon Wrottesley, *b.* 1968, *s.* 1977, *m.*	Hon. Stephen J. W., *b.* 1955
1829	*Wynford (9th)*, John Philip Robert Best, *b.* 1950, *s.* 2002, *m.*	Hon. Harry R. F. B., *b.* 1987
1308	*Zouche (18th)*, James Assheton Frankland, *b.* 1943, *s.* 1965, *m.*	Hon. William T. A. F., *b.* 1984

BARONESSES/LADIES IN THEIR OWN RIGHT

Style, The Right Hon. the Lady _ , *or* The Right Hon. the Baroness _ , according to her preference. Either style may be used, except in the case of Scottish titles (indicated by S.), which are not baronies (*see* page 44) and whose holders are always addressed as Lady

Envelope, may be addressed in same way as a Baron's wife or, if she prefers *(formal)*, The Right Hon. the Baroness _; *(social)*, The Baroness _. Otherwise as for a Baron's wife

Husband, Untitled

Children's style, As for children of a Baron

Created	Title, order of succession, name, etc	Heir
1664	*Arlington,* Jennifer Jane Forwood, *b.* 1939, *s.* 1999, *w.* Title called out of abeyance 1999	Hon. Patrick J. D. F., *b.* 1967
1455	*Berners (16th),* Pamela Vivien Kirkham, *b.* 1929, *s.* 1995, *m.*	Hon. Rupert W. T. K., *b.* 1953
1529	*Braye (8th),* Mary Penelope Aubrey-Fletcher, *b.* 1941, *s.* 1985, *m.*	Two co-heiresses
1321	*Dacre (27th),* Rachel Leila Douglas-Home, *b.* 1929, *s.* 1970, *w.*	Hon. James T. A. D.-H., *b.* 1952
1332	** *Darcy de Knayth (18th),* Davina Marcia Ingrams, DBE, *b.* 1938, *s.* 1943, *w.*	Hon. Caspar D. I., *b.* 1962
1490 S.	*Herries of Terregles (14th),* Anne Elizabeth Fitzalan-Howard, *b.* 1938, *s.* 1975, *w.*	Lady Mary Mumford, *b.* 1940
1597	*Howard de Walden (10th),* Mary Hazel Caridwen Czernin, *b.* 1935, *s.* 2004, *m.* Title called out of abeyance 2004	Hon. Peter J. J. C. *b.* 1966
1602 S.	*Kinloss (12th),* Beatrice Mary Grenville Freeman-Grenville, *b.* 1922, *s.* 1944, *w.*	Master of Kinloss, *b.* 1953
1445 S.	** *Saltoun (20th),* Flora Marjory Fraser, *b.* 1930, *s.* 1979, *w.*	Hon. Katharine I. M. I. F., *b.* 1957
1313	*Willoughby de Eresby (27th),* (Nancy) Jane Marie Heathcote-Drummond-Willoughby, *b.* 1934, *s.* 1983	Two co-heiresses

LIFE PEERS

Style, The Right Hon. the Lord _ /The Right Hon. the
Lady _ , *or* The Right Hon. the Baroness _ , according
to her preference
Envelope (formal), The Right Hon. Lord _/Lady_/
Baroness_; *(social),* The Lord _/Lady_/Baroness_
Letter (formal), My Lord/Lady; *(social),* Dear Lord/
Lady _. *Spoken,* Lord/Lady _
Wife's style, The Right Hon. the Lady _
Husband, Untitled
Children's style, 'The Hon.' before forename (F_) and
surname (S_)
Envelope, The Hon. F_ S_. *Letter,* Dear Mr/Miss/Mrs
S_. *Spoken,* Mr/Miss/Mrs S_

NEW LIFE PEERAGES

1 September 2006 to 31 August 2007:
Prof. Paul Anthony Elliott Bew; Dame Jane Susan
Campbell; Jean Coussins; Sir Ara Warkes Darzi, KBE; Dr
Khalid Hameed, CBE; Sir Robin Berry Janvrin, GCB,
KCVO, PC; Prof. Sir John (Richard) Krebs, FRS; Sir George Mark Malloch Brown,
KCMG, PC; Revd Andrew Mawson, OBE; Rt. Hon. Sir
David Edmond Neuberger; Dame (Lilian) Pauline
Neville-Jones, DCMG; Shriti Vadera; Gen. Sir Michael
John Dawson Walker, GCB, CMG, CBE; Syeeda Warsi;
Adm. Sir Alan William John West, GCB, DSC

SYMBOLS
* Hereditary peer who has been granted a life peerage. For
further details, please refer to the Hereditary Peers
section. For example, life peer *Balniel* can be found
under his hereditary title *Earl of Crawford and Balcarres*
‡ Title not confirmed at time of going to press

CREATED UNDER THE APPELLATE JURISDICTION ACT 1876 (AS AMENDED)

BARONS
Created
1980 *Bridge of Harwich,* Nigel Cyprian Bridge, PC,
b. 1917, m.
2004 *Brown of Eaton-under-Heywood,* Simon Denis
Brown, PC, b. 1937, m., Lord of Appeal in
Ordinary
1991 *Browne-Wilkinson,* Nicolas Christopher Henry
Browne-Wilkinson, PC, b. 1930, m.
2004 *Carswell,* Robert Douglas Carswell, PC, b. 1934,
m., Lord of Appeal in Ordinary
1996 *Clyde,* James John Clyde, PC, b. 1932, m.
1986 *Goff of Chieveley,* Robert Lionel Archibald Goff,
PC, b. 1926, m.
1985 *Griffiths,* (William) Hugh Griffiths, MC, PC,
b. 1923, m.
1995 *Hoffmann,* Leonard Hubert Hoffmann, PC,
b. 1934, m. Second Senior Lord of Appeal in
Ordinary
1997 *Hutton,* (James) Brian (Edward) Hutton, PC,
b. 1931, m.

1993 *Lloyd of Berwick,* Anthony John Leslie Lloyd,
PC, b. 1929, m.
2005 *Mance,* Jonathan Hugh Mance, PC, b. 1943, m.,
Lord of Appeal in Ordinary
1998 *Millett,* Peter Julian Millett, PC, b. 1932, m.
1992 *Mustill,* Michael John Mustill, PC, b. 1931, m.
2007 *Neuberger of Abbotsbury,* David Edmond
Neuberger, PC, b. 1948, m., Lord of Appeal in
Ordinary
1994 *Nicholls of Birkenhead,* Donald James Nicholls,
PC, b. 1933, m.
1986 *Oliver of Aylmerton,* Peter Raymond Oliver, PC,
b. 1921, m.
1999 *Phillips of Worth Matravers,* Nicholas Addison
Phillips, b. 1938, m. Lord Chief Justice of
England and Wales
1997 *Saville of Newdigate,* Mark Oliver Saville, PC,
b. 1936, m. Lord of Appeal in Ordinary
2000 *Scott of Foscote,* Richard Rashleigh Folliott Scott,
PC, b. 1934, m. Lord of Appeal in Ordinary
1992 *Slynn of Hadley,* Gordon Slynn, PC, b. 1930, m.
1995 *Steyn,* Johan van Zyl Steyn, PC, b. 1932, m.
1982 *Templeman,* Sydney William Templeman, MBE,
PC, b. 1920, m.
2003 *Walker of Gestingthorpe,* Robert Walker, PC,
b. 1938, m. Lord of Appeal in Ordinary
1992 *Woolf,* Harry Kenneth Woolf, PC, b. 1933, m.

BARONESSES
2004 *Hale of Richmond,* Brenda Marjorie Hale, DBE,
PC, b. 1945, m., Lord of Appeal in Ordinary

CREATED UNDER THE LIFE PEERAGES ACT 1958

BARONS
Created
2000 **Acton of Bridgnorth,* Lord Acton, b. 1941, m.
(see Hereditary Peers)
2001 *Adebowale,* Victor Olufemi Adebowale, CBE,
b. 1962
2005 *Adonis,* Andrew Adonis, b. 1963, m.
1998 *Ahmed,* Nazir Ahmed, b. 1957, m.
1996 *Alderdice,* John Thomas Alderdice, b. 1955, m.
1976 *Allen of Abbeydale,* Philip Allen, GCB,
b. 1912, w.
1998 *Alli,* Waheed Alli, b. 1964
2004 *Alliance,* David Alliance, CBE, b. 1932
1997 *Alton of Liverpool,* David Patrick Paul Alton,
b. 1951, m.
2005 *Anderson of Swansea,* Donald Anderson, PC,
b. 1939, m.
1992 *Archer of Sandwell,* Peter Kingsley Archer, PC,
QC, b. 1926, m.
1992 *Archer of Weston-super-Mare,* Jeffrey Howard
Archer, b. 1940, m.
1988 *Armstrong of Ilminster,* Robert Temple
Armstrong, GCB, CVO, b. 1927, m.
1999 **Armstrong-Jones,* Earl of Snowdon, GCVO,
b. 1930, m. (see Hereditary Peers)
2000 *Ashcroft,* Michael Anthony Ashcroft, KCMG,

2001   *Ashdown of Norton-sub-Hamdon*, Jeremy John Durham (Paddy) Ashdown, GCMG, KBE, PC, *b.* 1941, *m.*

1992   *Ashley of Stoke,* Jack Ashley, CH, PC, *b.* 1922, *w.*

1993   *Attenborough*, Richard Samuel Attenborough, CBE, *b.* 1923, *m.*

1998   *Bach*, William Stephen Goulden Bach, *b.* 1946, *m.*

1997   *Bagri*, Raj Kumar Bagri, CBE, *b.* 1930, *m.*

1997   *Baker of Dorking*, Kenneth Wilfred Baker, CH, PC, *b.* 1934, *m.*

2004   *Ballyedmond*, Dr Edward Haughey, OBE, *b.* 1944, *m.*

1974   *Balniel*, The Earl of Crawford and Balcarres, *b.* 1927, *m. (see* Hereditary Peers)

1992   *Barber of Tewkesbury*, Derek Coates Barber, *b.* 1918, *m.*

1983   *Barnett*, Joel Barnett, PC, *b.* 1923, *m.*

1997   *Bassam of Brighton*, (John) Steven Bassam, *b.* 1953

1967   *Beaumont of Whitley*, Revd Timothy Wentworth Beaumont, *b.* 1928, *m.*

1998   *Bell*, Timothy John Leigh Bell, *b.* 1941, *m.*

2000   *Bernstein of Craigweil*, Alexander Bernstein, *b.* 1936, *m.*

2001   *Best*, Richard Stuart Best, OBE, *b.* 1945, *m.*

2007   *Bew*, Prof. Paul Anthony Elliott Bew, PC, *b.* 1950, *m.*

2001   *Bhatia*, Amirali Alibhai Bhatia, OBE, *b.* 1932, *m.*

2004   *Bhattacharyya*, Prof. (Sushantha) Kumar Bhattacharyya, CBE *b.* 1932, *m.*

2006   *Bilimoria*, Karan Faridoon Bilimoria, CBE, *b.* 1961, *m.*

2005   *Bilston*, Dennis Turner, *b.* 1942, *m.*

1996   *Bingham of Cornhill*, Thomas Henry Bingham, KG, PC, *b.* 1933, *m. Senior Lord of Appeal in Ordinary*

2000   *Birt*, John Francis Hodgess Birt, *b.* 1944, *m.*

2001   *Black of Crossharbour*, Conrad Moffat Black, OC, PC, *b.* 1944, *m.*

1997   *Blackwell*, Norman Roy Blackwell, *b.* 1952, *m.*

1994   *Blaker*, Peter Allan Renshaw Blaker, KCMG, PC, *b.* 1922, *m.*

1978   *Blease*, William John Blease, *b.* 1914, *m.*

1995   *Blyth of Rowington*, James Blyth, *b.* 1940, *m.*

1996   *Borrie*, Gordon Johnson Borrie, QC, *b.* 1931, *m.*

1976   *Boston of Faversham*, Terence George Boston, QC, *b.* 1930, *m.*

1996   *Bowness*, Peter Spencer Bowness, CBE, *b.* 1943, *m.*

2003   *Boyce*, Michael Boyce, GCB, OBE, *b.* 1943

2006   *Boyd of Duncansby*, Colin David Boyd, PC, *b.* 1953, *m.*

2006   *Bradley*, Keith John Charles Bradley, PC, *b.* 1950, *m.*

1999   *Bradshaw*, William Peter Bradshaw, *b.* 1936, *m.*

1998   *Bragg*, Melvyn Bragg, *b.* 1939, *m.*

1987   *Bramall*, Edwin Noel Westby Bramall, KG, GCB, OBE, MC, *b.* 1923, *m.*

2000   *Brennan*, Daniel Joseph Brennan, QC, *b.* 1942, *m.*

1999   *Brett*, William Henry Brett, *b.* 1942, *m.*

1976   *Briggs*, Asa Briggs, FBA, *b.* 1921, *m.*

2000   *Brittan of Spennithorne*, Leon Brittan, PC, QC, *b.* 1939, *m.*

2004   *Broers*, Prof. Alec (Nigel) Broers, *b.* 1938, *m.*

1997   *Brooke of Alverthorpe*, Clive Brooke, *b.* 1942, *m.*

2001   *Brooke of Sutton Mandeville*, Peter Leonard Brooke, CH, PC, *b.* 1934, *m.*

1998   *Brookman*, David Keith Brookman, *b.* 1937, *m.*

1979   *Brooks of Tremorfa*, John Edward Brooks, *b.* 1927, *m.*

2006   *Browne of Belmont*, Wallace Hamilton Browne, *b.* 1947

2001   *Browne of Madingley*, Edmund John Phillip Browne, *b.* 1948

2006   *Bruce-Lockhart*, Alexander John (Sandy) Bruce-Lockhart, OBE, *b.* 1942, *m.*

1997   *Burlison*, Thomas Henry Burlison, *b.* 1936, *m.*

2006   *Burnett*, John Patrick Aubone Burnett, *b.* 1945, *m.*

1998   *Burns*, Terence Burns, GCB, *b.* 1944, *m.*

1998   *Butler of Brockwell*, (Frederick Edward) Robin Butler, KG, GCB, CVO, PC, *b.* 1938, *m.*

1978   *Buxton of Alsa*, Aubrey Leland Oakes Buxton, KCVO, MC, *b.* 1918, *m.*

2004   *Cameron of Dillington*, Ewen (James Hanning) Cameron, *b.* 1949, *m.*

1984   *Cameron of Lochbroom*, Kenneth John Cameron, PC, *b.* 1931, *m.*

1981   *Campbell of Alloway*, Alan Robertson Campbell, QC, *b.* 1917, *m.*

2001   *Campbell-Savours*, Dale Norman Campbell-Savours, *b.* 1943, *m.*

2002   *Carey of Clifton*, Rt. Revd George Leonard Carey, PC, *b.* 1935, *m.*

1999   *Carington of Upton*, Lord Carrington, GCMG, *b.* 1919, *m. (see* Hereditary Peers)

1999   *Carlile of Berriew*, Alexander Charles Carlile, QC, *b.* 1948, *m.*

1975   *Carr of Hadley*, (Leonard) Robert Carr, PC, *b.* 1916, *m.*

2004   *Carter of Coles*, Patrick Robert Carter, *b.* 1946, *m.*

1990   *Cavendish of Furness*, (Richard) Hugh Cavendish, *b.* 1941, *m.*

1996   *Chadlington*, Peter Selwyn Gummer, *b.* 1942, *m.*

1964   *Chalfont*, (Alun) Arthur Gwynne Jones, OBE, MC, PC, *b.* 1919, *m.*

2005   *Chidgey*, David William George Chidgey, *b.* 1942, *m.*

1987   *Chilver*, (Amos) Henry Chilver, FRS, FRENG, *b.* 1926, *m.*

1977   *Chitnis*, Pratap Chidamber Chitnis, *b.* 1936, *m.*

1998   *Christopher*, Anthony Martin Grosvenor Christopher, CBE, *b.* 1925, *m.*

2001   *Clark of Windermere*, David George Clark, PC, PHD, *b.* 1939, *m.*

1998   *Clarke of Hampstead*, Anthony James Clarke, CBE, *b.* 1932, *m.*

1998   *Clement-Jones*, Timothy Francis Clement-Jones, CBE, *b.* 1949, *m.*

1990   *Clinton-Davis*, Stanley Clinton Clinton-Davis, PC, *b.* 1928, *m.*

2000   *Coe*, Sebastian Newbold Coe, KBE, *b.* 1956, *m.*

2001   *Condon*, Paul Leslie Condon, QPM, *m.*

1992   *Cooke of Islandreagh*, Victor Alexander Cooke, OBE, *b.* 1920, *m.*

1997   *Cope of Berkeley*, John Ambrose Cope, PC, *b.* 1937, *m.*

2001   *Corbett of Castle Vale*, Robin Corbett, *b.* 1933, *m.*

2006   *Cotter*, Brian Joseph Michael Cotter, *b.* 1938, *m.*

1991   *Craig of Radley*, David Brownrigg Craig, GCB, OBE, *b.* 1929, *m.*

1987   *Crickhowell*, (Roger) Nicholas Edwards, PC, *b.* 1934, *m.*

2006   *Crisp*, (Edmund) Nigel (Ramsay) Crisp, KCB, b. 1952, *m.*

1978   *Croham*, Douglas Albert Vivian Allen, GCB, b. 1917, *w.*

1995   *Cuckney*, John Graham Cuckney, b. 1925, *m.*

2003   *Cullen of Whitekirk*, William Douglas Cullen, PC, b. 1935, *m.*

2005   *Cunningham of Felling*, John Anderson Cunningham, PC, b. 1939, *m.*

1996   *Currie of Marylebone*, David Anthony Currie, b. 1946, *m.*

1993   *Dahrendorf*, Ralf Dahrendorf, KBE, PHD, DPHIL, FBA, b. 1929, *m.*

2007   *Darzi of Denham*, Ara Warkes Darzi, KBE, b. 1960, *m.*

2006   *Davidson of Glen Clova*, Neil Forbes Davidson, QC, b. 1950, *m.*

1997   *Davies of Coity*, (David) Garfield Davies, CBE, b. 1935, *m.*

1997   *Davies of Oldham*, Bryan Davies, PC, b. 1939, *m.*

1993   *Dean of Harptree*, (Arthur) Paul Dean, PC, b. 1924, *m.*

2006   *Dear*, Geoffrey (James) Dear, QPM, b. 1937, *m.*

1998   *Dearing*, Ronald Ernest Dearing, b. 1930, *m.*

1991   *Desai*, Prof. Meghnad Jagdishchandra Desai, PHD, b. 1940, *m.*

1997   *Dholakia*, Navnit Dholakia, OBE, b. 1937, *m.*

1997   *Dixon*, Donald Dixon, PC, b. 1929, *m.*

1993   *Dixon-Smith*, Robert William Dixon-Smith, b. 1934, *m.*

1985   *Donoughue*, Bernard Donoughue, DPHIL, b. 1934

2004   *Drayson*, Paul Rudd Drayson, b. 1960, *m.*

1994   *Dubs*, Alfred Dubs, b. 1932, *m.*

2004   *Dykes*, Hugh John Maxwell Dykes, b. 1939, *m.*

1995   *Eames*, Robert Henry Alexander Eames, OM, PHD, b. 1937, *m.*

1992   *Eatwell*, John Leonard Eatwell, PHD, b. 1945

1983   *Eden of Winton*, John Benedict Eden, PC, b. 1925, *m.*

1999   *Elder*, Thomas Murray Elder, b. 1950

1992   *Elis-Thomas*, Dafydd Elis Elis-Thomas, PC, b. 1946, *m.*

1985   *Elliott of Morpeth*, Robert William Elliott, b. 1920, *m.*

1981   *Elystan-Morgan*, Dafydd Elystan Elystan-Morgan, b. 1932, *w.*

2000   **Erskine of Alloa Tower*, Earl of Mar and Kellie, b. 1949, *m. (see* Hereditary Peers)

1997   *Evans of Parkside*, John Evans, b. 1930, *m.*

2000   *Evans of Temple Guiting*, Matthew Evans, CBE, b. 1941, *m.*

1998   *Evans of Watford*, David Charles Evans, b. 1942, *m.*

1983   *Ezra*, Derek Ezra, MBE, b. 1919, *m.*

1997   *Falconer of Thoroton*, Charles Leslie Falconer, QC, b. 1951, *m.*

1999   *Faulkner of Worcester*, Richard Oliver Faulkner, b. 1946, *m.*

2001   *Fearn*, Ronald Cyril Fearn, OBE, b. 1931, *m.*

1996   *Feldman*, Basil Feldman, b. 1926, *m.*

1999   *Fellowes*, Robert Fellowes, GCB, GCVO, PC, b. 1941, *m.*

1999   *Filkin*, David Geoffrey Nigel Filkin, CBE, b. 1944

1979   *Flowers*, Brian Hilton Flowers, FRS, b. 1924, *m.*

1999   *Forsyth of Drumlean*, Michael Bruce Forsyth, b. 1954, *m.*

2005   *Foster of Bishop Auckland*, Derek Foster, PC, b. 1937, *m.*

1999   *Foster of Thames Bank*, Norman Robert Foster, OM, b. 1935, *m.*

2005   *Foulkes of Cumnock*, George Foulkes, PC, b. 1942, *m.*

2001   *Fowler*, (Peter) Norman Fowler, PC, b. 1938, *m.*

1989   *Fraser of Carmyllie*, Peter Lovat Fraser, PC, QC, b. 1945, *m.*

1997   *Freeman*, Roger Norman Freeman, PC, b. 1942, *m.*

2000   *Fyfe of Fairfield*, George Lennox Fyfe, b. 1941, *m.*

1997   *Garel-Jones*, (William Armand) Thomas Tristan Garel-Jones, PC, b. 1941, *m.*

1999*   *Gascoyne-Cecil*, The Marquess of Salisbury, PC , b. 1946, *m. (see* Hereditary Peers)

1999   *Gavron*, Robert Gavron, CBE, b. 1930, *m.*

2004   *George*, Edward (Alan John) George, GBE, PC, b. 1938, *m.*

2004   *Giddens*, Prof. Anthony Giddens, b. 1938, *m.*

1997   *Gilbert*, John William Gilbert, PC, PHD, b. 1927, *m.*

1992   *Gilmour of Craigmillar*, Ian Hedworth John Little Gilmour, PC, b. 1926, *w.*

1977   *Glenamara*, Edward Watson Short, CH, PC, b. 1912, *m.*

1999   *Goldsmith*, Peter Henry Goldsmith, QC, b. 1950, *m.*

1997   *Goodhart*, William Howard Goodhart, QC, b. 1933, *m.*

2005   *Goodlad*, Alastair Robertson Goodlad, KCMG, b. 1943, *m.*

1997   *Gordon of Strathblane*, James Stuart Gordon, CBE, b. 1936, *m.*

2004   *Gould of Brookwood*, Philip Gould b. 1950 *m.*

1999   *Grabiner*, Anthony Stephen Grabiner, QC, b. 1945, *m.*

1983   *Graham of Edmonton*, (Thomas) Edward Graham, b. 1925, *m.*

2000   *Greaves*, Anthony Robert Greaves, b. 1942, *m.*

1975   *Gregson*, John Gregson, b. 1924

2000   **Grenfell of Kilvey*, Lord Grenfell, b. 1935, *m.* (*see* Hereditary Peers)

2004   *Griffiths of Burry Port*, Revd Dr Leslie John Griffiths, b. 1942, *m.*

1991   *Griffiths of Fforestfach*, Brian Griffiths, b. 1941, *m.*

2001   *Grocott*, Bruce Joseph Grocott, PC, b. 1940, *m.*

2000   **Gueterbock*, Lord Berkley, OBE, b. 1939, *m. (see* Hereditary Peers)

2000   *Guthrie of Craigiebank*, Charles Ronald Llewelyn Guthrie, GCB, LVO, OBE b. 1938, *m.*

1995   *Habgood*, Rt. Revd John Stapylton Habgood, PC, PHD, b. 1927, *m.*

2007   *Hameed*, Dr Khalid Hameed, b. 1941, *m.*

2005   *Hamilton of Epsom*, Archibald Gavin Hamilton, PC, b. 1941, *m.*

2001   *Hannay of Chiswick*, David Hugh Alexander Hannay, GCMG, CH, b. 1935, *m.*

1998   *Hanningfield*, Paul Edward Winston White, b. 1940

1997   *Hardie*, Andrew Rutherford Hardie, QC, PC, b. 1946, *m.*

2006   *Harries of Pentregarth*, Rt. Revd Richard Douglas Harries, b. 1936, *m.*

1998   *Harris of Haringey*, (Jonathan) Toby Harris, b. 1953, *m.*

1996 *Harris of Peckham,* Philip Charles Harris,
      b. 1942, *m.*
1999 *Harrison,* Lyndon Henry Arthur Harrison,
      b. 1947, *m.*
2004 *Hart of Chilton,* Garry Richard Rushby Hart,
      b. 1940, *m.*
1993 *Haskel,* Simon Haskel, *b.* 1934, *m.*
1998 *Haskins,* Christopher Robin Haskins,
      b. 1937, *m.*
2005 *Hastings of Scarisbrick,* Michael John Hastings,
      CBE, *b.* 1958, *m.*
1997 *Hattersley,* Roy Sidney George Hattersley, PC,
      b. 1932, *m.*
2004 *Haworth,* Alan Robert Haworth, *b.* 1948, *m.*
1992 *Hayhoe,* Bernard John (Barney) Hayhoe, PC,
      b. 1925, *m.*
1992 *Healey,* Denis Winston Healey, CH, MBE, PC,
      b. 1917, *m.*
1999 *Hennessey,* Lord Windlesham, CVO, *b.* 1932, *m.*
      (*see* Hereditary Peers)
2001 *Heseltine,* Michael Ray Dibdin Heseltine, CH,
      PC, *b.* 1933, *m.*
1997 *Higgins,* Terence Langley Higgins, KBE, PC,
      b. 1928, *m.*
2000 *Hodgson of Astley Abbotts,* Robin Granville
      Hodgson, CBE, *b.* 1942, *m.*
1997 *Hogg of Cumbernauld,* Norman Hogg, *b.* 1938, *m.*
1991 *Hollick,* Clive Richard Hollick, *b.* 1945, *m.*
1990 *Holme of Cheltenham,* Richard Gordon Holme,
      CBE, *b.* 1936, *m.*
1979 *Hooson,* (Hugh) Emlyn Hooson, QC, *b.* 1925, *m.*
2005 *Hope of Thornes,* Rt. Revd David Michael Hope,
      KCVO, PC, *b.* 1940
1995 *Hope of Craighead,* (James Arthur) David Hope,
      PC, *b.* 1938, *m. Lord of Appeal in Ordinary*
2004 *Howard of Rising,* Greville Patrick Charles
      Howard, *b.* 1941, *m.*
2005 *Howarth of Newport,* Alan Thomas Howarth,
      CBE, PC, *b.* 1944
1992 *Howe of Aberavon,* (Richard Edward) Geoffrey
      Howe, CH, PC, QC, *b.* 1926, *m.*
1997 *Howell of Guildford,* David Arthur Russell
      Howell, PC, *b.* 1936, *m.*
1978 *Howie of Troon,* William Howie, *b.* 1924, *w.*
1997 *Hoyle,* (Eric) Douglas Harvey Hoyle, *b.* 1930, *w.*
1997 *Hughes of Woodside,* Robert Hughes, *b.* 1932, *m.*
2000 *Hunt of Chesterton,* Julian Charles Roland Hunt,
      CBE, *b.* 1941, *m.*
1997 *Hunt of Kings Heath,* Philip Alexander Hunt,
      OBE, *b.* 1949, *m.*
1980 *Hunt of Tanworth,* John Joseph Benedict Hunt,
      GCB, *b.* 1919, *w.*
1997 *Hunt of Wirral,* David James Fletcher Hunt,
      MBE, PC, *b.* 1942, *m.*
1997 *Hurd of Westwell,* Douglas Richard Hurd, CH,
      CBE, PC, *b.* 1930, *m.*
1978 *Hutchinson of Lullington,* Jeremy Nicolas
      Hutchinson, QC, *b.* 1915, *m.*
1999 *Imbert,* Peter Michael Imbert, QPM, *b.* 1933, *m.*
1997 *Inge,* Peter Anthony Inge, KG, GCB, PC,
      b. 1935, *m.*
1987 *Irvine of Lairg,* Alexander Andrew Mackay
      Irvine, PC, QC, *b.* 1940, *m.*
1997 *Jacobs,* (David) Anthony Jacobs, *b.* 1931, *m.*
2006 *James of Blackheath,* David Noel James, CBE,
      b. 1937, *m.*
1997 *Janner of Braunstone,* Greville Ewan Janner, QC,
      b. 1928, *w.*

2007 ‡*Janvrin,* Robin Berry Janvrin, GCB, KCVO, PC,
      b. 1946, *m.*
2006 *Jay of Ewelme,* Michael (Hastings) Jay, GCMG,
      b. 1946, *m.*
1987 *Jenkin of Roding,* (Charles) Patrick (Fleeming)
      Jenkin, PC, *b.* 1926, *m.*
2000 *Joffe,* Joel Goodman Joffe, CBE, *b.* 1932, *m.*
2001 *Jones,* (Stephen) Barry Jones, *b.* 1937, *m.*
2007 *Jones of Birmingham,* Digby Marritt Jones,
      b. 1955, *m.*
2005, *Jones of Cheltenham,* Nigel David Jones,
      b. 1948, *m.*
1997 *Jopling,* (Thomas) Michael Jopling, PC,
      b. 1930, *m.*
2000 *Jordan,* William Brian Jordan, CBE, *b.* 1936, *m.*
1991 *Judd,* Frank Ashcroft Judd, *b.* 1935, *m.*
2004 *Kalms,* Harold Stanley Kalms, *b.* 1931 *m.*
2004 *Kerr of Kinlochard,* John (Olav) Kerr, GCMG,
      b. 1942, *m.*
2001 *Kilclooney,* John David Taylor, PC (NI),
      b. 1937, *m.*
1996 *Kilpatrick of Kincraig,* Robert Kilpatrick, CBE,
      b. 1926, *m.*
1985 *Kimball,* Marcus Richard Kimball, *b.* 1928, *m.*
2001 *King of Bridgwater,* Thomas Jeremy King, CH,
      PC, *b.* 1933, *m.*
1999 *King of West Bromwich,* Tarsem King, *b.* 1937
1993 *Kingsdown,* Robert (Robin) Leigh-Pemberton,
      KG, PC, *b.* 1927, *m.*
1994 *Kingsland,* Christopher James Prout, TD, PC,
      QC, *b.* 1942
2005 *Kinnock,* Neil Gordon Kinnock, PC,
      b. 1942, *m.*
1999 *Kirkham,* Graham Kirkham, *b.* 1944, *m.*
1975 *Kirkhill,* John Farquharson Smith, *b.* 1930, *m.*
2005 *Kirkwood of Kirkhope,* Archibald Johnstone
      Kirkwood, *b.* 1946, *m.*
2007 *Krebs,* Prof. John (Richard) Krebs, FRS,
      b. 1945, *m.*
1987 *Knights,* Philip Douglas Knights, CBE, QPM,
      b. 1920, *m.*
2004 *Laidlaw,* Irvine Alan Stewart Laidlaw, *b.* 1942, *m.*
1991 *Laing of Dunphail,* Hector Laing, *b.* 1923, *m.*
1999 *Laird,* John Dunn Laird, *b.* 1944, *m.*
1998 *Laming,* (William) Herbert Laming, CBE,
      b. 1936, *m.*
1998 *Lamont of Lerwick,* Norman Stewart Hughson
      Lamont, PC, *b.* 1942, *m.*
1990 *Lane of Horsell,* Peter Stewart Lane, *b.* 1925, *w.*
1997 *Lang of Monkton,* Ian Bruce Lang, PC,
      b. 1940, *m.*
1992 *Lawson of Blaby,* Nigel Lawson, PC, *b.* 1932, *m.*
2000 *Layard,* Peter Richard Grenville Layard,
      b. 1934, *m.*
1999 *Lea of Crondall,* David Edward Lea, OBE,
      b. 1937
2006 *Leach of Fairford,* Charles Guy Rodney Leach,
      b. 1934, *m.*
2006 *Lee of Trafford,* John Robert Louis Lee, *b.* 1942,
      m.
2004 *Leitch,* Alexander Park Leitch, *b.* 1947, *m.*
1993 *Lester of Herne Hill,* Anthony Paul Lester, QC,
      b. 1936, *m.*
1997 *Levene of Portsoken,* Peter Keith Levene, KBE,
      b. 1941, *m.*
1997 *Levy,* Michael Abraham Levy, *b.* 1944, *m.*
1989 *Lewis of Newnham,* Jack Lewis, FRS, *b.* 1928, *m.*
1999 *Lipsey,* David Lawrence Lipsey, *b.* 1948, *m.*

2001   *Livsey of Talgarth*, Richard Arthur Lloyd Livsey,
        CBE, *b.* 1935, *m.*
1997   *Lloyd-Webber*, Andrew Lloyd Webber,
        b. 1948, *m.*
1997   *Lofthouse of Pontefract*, Geoffrey Lofthouse,
        b. 1925, *w.*
2006   *Low of Dalston*, Prof. Colin Mackenzie Low,
        CBE, *b.* 1942, *m.*
2000   *Luce*, Richard Napier Luce, GCVO, PC,
        b. 1936, *m.*
2005   *Lyell of Markyate*, Nicholas Walter Lyell, PC,
        QC, *b.* 1938, *m.*
2000   **Lyttleton of Aldershot*, The Viscount Chandos,
        b. 1953, *m. (see* Hereditary Peers)
1984   *McAlpine of West Green*, (Robert) Alistair
        McAlpine, *b.* 1942, *m.*
1988   *Macaulay of Bragar*, Donald Macaulay, QC,
        b. 1933, *m.*
1975   *McCarthy*, William Edward John McCarthy,
        DPHIL, *b.* 1925, *m.*
1976   *McCluskey*, John Herbert McCluskey,
        b. 1929, *m.*
1989   *McColl of Dulwich*, Ian McColl, CBE, FRCS,
        FRCSE, *b.* 1933, *m.*
1998   *Macdonald of Tradeston*, Angus John
        Macdonald, CBE, *b.* 1940, *m.*
1991   *Macfarlane of Bearsden*, Norman Somerville
        Macfarlane, KT, FRSE, *b.* 1926, *m.*
2001   *MacGregor of Pulham Market*, John Roddick
        Russell MacGregor, CBE, PC, *b.* 1937, *m.*
1982   *McIntosh of Haringey*, Andrew Robert
        McIntosh, *b.* 1933, *w.*
1979   *Mackay of Clashfern*, James Peter Hymers
        Mackay, KT, PC, FRSE, *b.* 1927, *m.*
1995   *Mackay of Drumadoon*, Donald Sage Mackay,
        PC, *b.* 1946, *m.*
2004   *McKenzie of Luton*, William David McKenzie,
        b. 1946, *m.*
1999   *Mackenzie of Culkein*, Hector Uisdean
        MacKenzie, *b.* 1940
1998   *Mackenzie of Framwellgate*, Brian Mackenzie,
        OBE, *b.* 1943, *m.*
1974   *Mackie of Benshie*, George Yull Mackie, CBE,
        DSO, DFC, *b.* 1919, *m.*
1996   *MacLaurin of Knebworth*, Ian Charter
        MacLaurin, *b.* 1937, *m.*
2001   *Maclennon of Rogart*, Robert Adam Ross
        Maclennan, PC, *b.* 1936, *m.*
1995   *McNally*, Tom McNally, PC, *b.* 1943, *m.*
2001   *Maginnis of Drumglass*, Kenneth Wiggins
        Maginnis, *b.* 1938, *m.*
2007   *Malloch-Brown*, George Mark Malloch Brown,
        KCMG, PC, *b.* 1953, *m.*
2006   *Marland*, Jonathan Peter Marland, *b.* 1956, *m.*
1991   *Marlesford*, Mark Shuldham Schreiber,
        b. 1931, *m.*
1981   *Marsh*, Richard William Marsh, PC,
        b. 1928, *m.*
1998   *Marshall of Knightsbridge*, Colin Marsh
        Marshall, *b.* 1933, *m.*
1987   *Mason of Barnsley*, Roy Mason, PC, *b.* 1924, *m.*
2005   *Mawhinney*, Brian Stanley Mawhinney, PC,
        b. 1940, *m.*
2007   *Mawson*, Revd Andrew Mawson, OBE,
        b. 1954, *m.*
2004   *Maxton*, John Alston Maxton, *b.* 1936, *m.*
2001   *May of Oxford*, Robert McCredie May, OM,
        b. 1936, *m.*

1997   *Mayhew of Twysden*, Patrick Barnabas Burke
        Mayhew, QC, PC, *b.* 1929, *m.*
2000   *Mitchell*, Parry Andrew Mitchell, *b.* 1943, *m.*
2000   **Mitford*, Lord Redesdale, *b.* 1967, *m. (see*
        Hereditary Peers)
1997   *Molyneaux of Killead*, James Henry Molyneaux,
        KBE, PC, *b.* 1920
2005   *Moonie*, Dr. Lewis George Moonie, *b.* 1947, *m.*
1992   *Moore of Lower Marsh*, John Edward Michael
        Moore, PC, *b.* 1937, *m.*
1986   *Moore of Wolvercote*, Philip Brian Cecil Moore,
        GCB, GCVO, CMG, PC, *b.* 1921, *m.*
2000   *Morgan*, Kenneth Owen Morgan, *b.* 1934, *m.*
2001   *Morris of Aberavon*, John Morris, KG, QC,
        b. 1931, *m.*
2006   *Morris of Handsworth*, William Manuel Morris,
        b. 1938, *m.*
1997   *Morris of Manchester*, Alfred Morris, PC,
        b. 1928, *m.*
2006   *Morrow*, Maurice George Morrow, *m.*
2001   *Moser*, Claus Adolf Moser, KCB, CBE,
        b. 1922, *m.*
1979   *Murton of Lindisfarne*, (Henry) Oscar Murton,
        OBE, TD, PC, *b.* 1914, *m.*
1997   *Naseby*, Michael Wolfgang Laurence Morris, PC,
        b. 1936, *m.*
1997   *Neill of Bladen*, (Francis) Patrick Neill, QC,
        b. 1926, *m.*
1997   *Newby*, Richard Mark Newby, OBE, *b.* 1953, *m.*
1997   *Newton of Braintree*, Antony Harold Newton,
        OBE, PC, *b.* 1937, *m.*
1994   *Nickson*, David Wigley Nickson, KBE, FRSE,
        b. 1929, *m.*
1975   *Northfield*, (William) Donald Chapman, *b.* 1923
1998   *Norton of Louth*, Philip Norton, *b.* 1951
2000   *Oakeshott of Seagrove Bay*, Matthew Alan
        Oakeshott, *b.* 1947, *m.*
2005   *O'Neill of Clackmannan*, Martin John O'Neill,
        b. 1945, *m.*
2001   *Ouseley*, Herman George Ouseley, *b.* 1945, *m.*
1992   *Owen*, David Anthony Llewellyn Owen, CH,
        PC, *b.* 1938, *m.*
1999   *Oxburgh*, Ernest Ronald Oxburgh, KBE, FRS,
        PHD, *b.* 1934, *m.*
1991   *Palumbo*, Peter Garth Palumbo, *b.* 1935, *m.*
2000   *Parekh*, Bhikhu Chhotalal Parekh, *b.* 1935, *m.*
1992   *Parkinson*, Cecil Edward Parkinson, PC,
        b. 1931, *m.*
1999   *Patel*, Narendra Babubhai Patel, *b.* 1938
2000   *Patel of Blackburn*, Adam Hafejee Patel, *b.* 1940
2006   *Patel of Bradford*, Prof. Kamlesh Kumar Patel,
        OBE, *b.* 1960 *m.*
2005   *Patten of Barnes*, Christopher Francis Patten, CH,
        PC, *b.* 1944, *m.*
1997   *Patten*, John Haggitt Charles Patten, PC,
        b. 1945, *m.*
1996   *Paul*, Swraj Paul, *b.* 1931, *m.*
1990   *Pearson of Rannoch*, Malcolm Everard MacLaren
        Pearson, *b.* 1942, *m.*
2001   *Pendry*, Thomas Pendry, *b.* 1934, *m.*
1987   *Peston*, Maurice Harry Peston, *b.* 1931, *m.*
1998   *Phillips of Sudbury*, Andrew Wyndham Phillips,
        OBE, *b.* 1939, *m.*
1996   *Pilkington of Oxenford*, Revd Canon Peter
        Pilkington, *b.* 1933, *w.*
1992   *Plant of Highfield*, Prof. Raymond Plant, PHD,
        b. 1945, *m.*
1987   *Plumb*, (Charles) Henry Plumb, *b.* 1925, *m.*

1981   *Plummer of St Marylebone,* (Arthur) Desmond (Herne) Plummer, TD, *b.* 1914, *m.*

2000   **Ponsonby of Roehampton,* Lord Ponsonby of Shulbrede, *b.* 1958 (*see* Hereditary Peers)

2000   *Powell of Bayswater,* Charles David Powell, KCMG, *b.* 1941

1987   *Prior,* James Michael Leathes Prior, PC, *b.* 1927, *m.*

1982   *Prys-Davies,* Gwilym Prys Prys-Davies, *b.* 1923, *m.*

1997   *Puttnam,* David Terence Puttnam, CBE, *b.* 1941, *m.*

1987   *Pym,* Francis Leslie Pym, MC, PC, *b.* 1922, *m.*

1982   *Quinton,* Anthony Meredith Quinton, FBA, *b.* 1925, *m.*

1994   *Quirk,* Prof. (Charles) Randolph Quirk, CBE, FBA, *b.* 1920, *m.*

2001   *Radice,* Giles Heneage Radice, PC, *b.* 1936

2005   *Ramsbotham,* Gen. David John Ramsbotham, GCB, CBE, *b.* 1934, *m.*

2004   *Rana,* Dr Diljit Singh Rana, MBE, *b.* 1938, *m.*

1997   *Randall of St Budeaux,* Stuart Jeffrey Randall, *b.* 1938, *m.*

1997   *Razzall,* (Edward) Timothy Razzall, CBE, *b.* 1943, *m.*

1987   *Rees,* Peter Wynford Innes Rees, PC, QC, *b.* 1926, *m.*

2005   *Rees of Ludlow,* Prof. Martin John Rees, OM, *b.* 1942, *m.*

1988   *Rees-Mogg,* William Rees-Mogg, *b.* 1928, *m.*

1991   *Renfrew of Kaimsthorn,* (Andrew) Colin Renfrew, FBA, *b.* 1937, *m.*

1999   *Rennard,* Christopher John Rennard, MBE, *b.* 1960

1997   *Renton of Mount Harry,* (Ronald) Timothy Renton, PC, *b.* 1932, *m.*

1997   *Renwick of Clifton,* Robin William Renwick, KCMG, *b.* 1937, *m.*

1990   *Richard,* Ivor Seward Richard, PC, QC, *b.* 1932, *m.*

1983   *Richardson of Duntisbourne,* Gordon William Humphreys Richardson, KG, MBE, TD, PC, *b.* 1915, *m.*

1992   *Rix,* Brian Norman Roger Rix, CBE, *b.* 1924, *m.*

2004   *Roberts of Llandudno,* Revd John Roger Roberts, *b.* 1935, *m.*

1997   *Roberts of Conwy,* (Ieuan) Wyn (Pritchard) Roberts, PC, *b.* 1930, *m.*

1999   *Robertson of Port Ellen,* George Islay MacNeill Robertson, KT, GCMG, PC, *b.* 1946, *m.*

1992   *Rodger of Earlsferry,* Alan Ferguson Rodger, PC, QC, FBA, *b.* 1944, *Lord of Appeal in Ordinary*

1992   *Rodgers of Quarry Bank,* William Thomas Rodgers, PC, *b.* 1928, *w.*

1999   *Rogan,* Dennis Robert David Rogan, *b.* 1942, *m.*

1996   *Rogers of Riverside,* Richard George Rogers, RA, RIBA, *b.* 1933, *m.*

2001   *Rooker,* Jeffrey William Rooker, PC, *b.* 1941, *m.*

2000   *Roper,* John Francis Hodgess Roper, PC, *b.* 1935, *m.*

2004   *Rosser,* Richard Andrew Rosser, *b.* 1944, *m.*

2006   *Rowe-Beddoe,* David (Sydney) Rowe-Beddoe, *b.* 1937, *m.*

2004   *Rowlands,* Edward Rowlands, CBE, *b.* 1940, *m.*

1997   *Russell-Johnston,* (David) Russell Russell-Johnston, *b.* 1932, *m.*

1997   *Ryder of Wensum,* Richard Andrew Ryder, OBE, PC, *b.* 1949, *m.*

1996   *Saatchi,* Maurice Saatchi, *b.* 1946, *m.*

1989   *Sainsbury of Preston Candover,* John Davan Sainsbury, KG, *b.* 1927, *m.*

1997   *Sainsbury of Turville,* David John Sainsbury, *b.* 1940, *m.*

1987   *St John of Fawsley,* Norman Antony Francis St John-Stevas, PC, *b.* 1929

1997   *Sandberg,* Michael Graham Ruddock Sandberg, CBE, *b.* 1927, *m.*

1985   *Sanderson of Bowden,* Charles Russell Sanderson, *b.* 1933, *m.*

1998   *Sawyer,* Lawrence (Tom) Sawyer, *b.* 1943

1997   *Selkirk of Douglas,* James Alexander Douglas-Hamilton, MSP, PC, QC, *b.* 1942, *m.*

1996   *Sewel,* John Buttifant Sewel, CBE, *b.* 1946

1999   *Sharman,* Colin Morven Sharman, OBE, *b.* 1943, *m.*

1994   *Shaw of Northstead,* Michael Norman Shaw, *b.* 1920, *m.*

2006   *Sheikh,* Mohamed Iltaf Sheikh, *b.* 1941, *m.*

2001   *Sheldon,* Robert Edward Sheldon, PC, *b.* 1923, *m.*

1994   *Sheppard of Didgemere,* Allan John George Sheppard, KCVO, *b.* 1932, *m.*

2000   *Shutt of Greetland,* David Trevor Shutt, OBE, *b.* 1942

1997   *Simon of Highbury,* David Alec Gwyn Simon, CBE, *b.* 1939, *m.*

1997   *Simpson of Dunkeld,* George Simpson, *b.* 1942, *m.*

1991   *Skidelsky,* Robert Jacob Alexander Skidelsky, DPHIL, *b.* 1939, *m.*

1997   *Smith of Clifton,* Trevor Arthur Smith, *b.* 1937, *m.*

2005   *Smith of Finsbury,* Christopher Robert Smith, PC, *b.* 1951

1999   *Smith of Leigh,* Peter Richard Charles Smith, *b.* 1945, *m.*

2004   *Snape,* Peter Charles Snape, *b.* 1942

2005   *Soley,* Clive Stafford Soley, *b.* 1939

1990   *Soulsby of Swaffham Prior,* Ernest Jackson Lawson Soulsby, PHD, *b.* 1926, *m.*

1983   *Stallard,* Albert William Stallard, *b.* 1921, *m.*

1997   *Steel of Aikwood,* David Martin Scott Steel, KT, KBE, PC, *b.* 1938, *m.*

2004   *Steinberg,* Leonard Steinberg, *b.* 1936

1991   *Sterling of Plaistow,* Jeffrey Maurice Sterling, GCVO, CBE, *b.* 1934, *m.*

2005   *Stevens of Kirkwhelpington,* John Arthur Stevens, *b.* 1942, *m.*

1987   *Stevens of Ludgate,* David Robert Stevens, *b.* 1936, *m.*

1999   *Stevenson of Coddenham,* Henry Dennistoun Stevenson, CBE, *b.* 1945, *m.*

1992   *Stewartby,* (Bernard Harold) Ian (Halley) Stewart, RD, PC, FBA, FRSE, *b.* 1935, *m.*

1983   *Stoddart of Swindon,* David Leonard Stoddart, *b.* 1926, *m.*

1969   *Stokes,* Donald Gresham Stokes, TD, FENG, *b.* 1914, *w.*

1997   *Stone of Blackheath,* Andrew Zelig Stone, *b.* 1942, *m.*

2001   *Sutherland of Houndwood,* Stewart Ross Sutherland, KT, *b.* 1941, *m.*

1971   *Tanlaw,* Simon Brooke Mackay, *b.* 1934, *m.*

1996   *Taverne,* Dick Taverne, QC, *b.* 1928, *m.*

1978   *Taylor of Blackburn,* Thomas Taylor, CBE, *b.* 1929, *m.*

2006	*Taylor of Holbeach*, John Derek Taylor, CBE, b. 1943, m.
1996	*Taylor of Warwick*, John David Beckett Taylor, b. 1952, m.
1992	*Tebbit*, Norman Beresford Tebbit, CH, PC, b. 1931, m.
2001	*Temple-Morris*, Peter Temple-Morris, b. 1938, m.
2006	*Teverson*, Robin Teverson, b. 1952, m.
1996	*Thomas of Gresford*, Donald Martin Thomas, OBE, QC, b. 1937, m.
1987	*Thomas of Gwydir*, Peter John Mitchell Thomas, PC, QC, b. 1920, w.
1997	*Thomas of Macclesfield*, Terence James Thomas, CBE, b. 1937, m.
1981	*Thomas of Swynnerton*, Hugh Swynnerton Thomas, b. 1931, m.
1977	*Thomson of Monifieth*, George Morgan Thomson, KT, PC, b. 1921, m.
1990	*Tombs*, Francis Leonard Tombs, FENG, b. 1924, m.
1998	*Tomlinson*, John Edward Tomlinson, b. 1939
1994	*Tope*, Graham Norman Tope, CBE, b. 1943, m.
1981	*Tordoff*, Geoffrey Johnson Tordoff, b. 1928, m.
2004	*Triesman*, David Maxim Triesman, b. 1943
2006	*Trimble*, William David Trimble, PC, b. 1944, m.
2004	*Truscott*, Dr Peter Derek Truscott, b. 1959 m.
1993	*Tugendhat*, Christopher Samuel Tugendhat, b. 1937, m.
2004	*Tunnicliffe*, Denis Tunnicliffe, CBE, b. 1943, m.
2000	*Turnberg*, Leslie Arnold Turnberg, MD, b. 1934, m.
2005	*Turnbull*, Andrew Turnbull, KCB, CVO, b. 1943, m.
2005	*Turner of Ecchinswell*, Jonathan Adair Turner, b. 1955, m.
2005	*Tyler*, Paul Archer Tyler, CBE, b. 1941, m.
2004	*Vallance of Tummel*, Iain (David Thomas) Vallance, b. 1943, m.
1990	*Varley*, Eric Graham Varley, PC, b. 1932, m.
1996	*Vincent of Coleshill*, Richard Frederick Vincent, GBE, KCB, DSO, b. 1931, m.
1985	*Vinson*, Nigel Vinson, LVO, b. 1931, m.
1990	*Waddington*, David Charles Waddington, GCVO, PC, QC, b. 1929, m.
1990	*Wade of Chorlton*, (William) Oulton Wade, b. 1932, m.
1992	*Wakeham*, John Wakeham, PC, b. 1932, m.
1999	*Waldegrave of North Hill*, William Arthur Waldegrave, PC, b. 1946, m.
2007	*Walker of Aldringham*, Michael John Dawson Walker, GCB, CMG, CBE, b. 1944, m.
1992	*Walker of Worcester*, Peter Edward Walker, MBE, PC, b. 1932, m.
1995	*Wallace of Saltaire*, William John Lawrence Wallace, PHD, b. 1941, m.
1989	*Walton of Detchant*, John Nicholas Walton, TD, FRCP, b. 1922, w.
1998	*Warner*, Norman Reginald Warner, PC, b. 1940, m.
1997	*Watson of Invergowrie*, Michael Goodall Watson, b. 1949, m.
1999	*Watson of Richmond*, Alan John Watson, CBE, b. 1941, m.
1977	*Wedderburn of Charlton*, (Kenneth) William Wedderburn, FBA, QC, b. 1927, m.

1976	*Weidenfeld*, (Arthur) George Weidenfeld, b. 1919, m.
2007	*West of Spithead*, Adm. Alan William John West, GCB, DSC, b. 1948, m.
1996	*Whitty*, John Lawrence (Larry) Whitty, b. 1943, m.
1985	*Williams of Elvel*, Charles Cuthbert Powell Williams, CBE, b. 1933, m.
1999	*Williamson of Horton*, David (Francis) Williamson, GCMG, CB, PC, b. 1934, m.
2002	*Wilson of Dinton*, Richard Thomas James Wilson, GCB, b. 1942, m.
1992	*Wilson of Tillyorn*, David Clive Wilson, KT, GCMG, PHD, b. 1935, m.
1995	*Winston*, Robert Maurice Lipson Winston, FRCOG, b. 1940, m.
1985	*Wolfson*, Leonard Gordon Wolfson, b. 1927, m.
1991	*Wolfson of Sunningdale*, David Wolfson, b. 1935, m.
1999	*Woolmer of Leeds*, Kenneth John Woolmer, b. 1940, m.
1994	*Wright of Richmond*, Patrick Richard Henry Wright, GCMG, b. 1931, m.
2004	*Young of Norwood Green*, Anthony (Ian) Young, b. 1942, m.
1984	*Young of Graffham*, David Ivor Young, PC, b. 1932, m.

BARONESSES
Created

2005	*Adams of Craigielea*, Katherine Patricia Irene Adams, b. 1947, w.
1997	*Amos*, Valerie Ann Amos, b. 1954
2000	*Andrews*, Elizabeth Kay Andrews, OBE, b. 1943, m.
1996	*Anelay of St Johns*, Joyce Anne Anelay, DBE, b. 1947, m.
1999	*Ashton of Upholland*, Catherine Margaret Ashton, PC, b. 1956, m.
1999	*Barker*, Elizabeth Jean Barker, b. 1961
2000	*Billingham*, Angela Theodora Billingham, DPHIL, b. 1939, w.
1987	*Blackstone*, Tessa Ann Vosper Blackstone, PHD, b. 1942
1999	*Blood*, May Blood, MBE, b. 1938
2000	*Boothroyd*, Betty Boothroyd, OM, PC, b. 1929
2004	*Bonham-Carter of Yarnbury*, Jane Bonham Carter, b. 1957, w.
2005	*Bottomley of Nettlestone*, Virginia Hilda Brunette Maxwell Bottomley, PC, b. 1948, m.
1998	*Buscombe*, Peta Jane Buscombe, b. 1954, m.
2006	*Butler-Sloss*, (Ann) Elizabeth (Oldfield) Butler-Sloss, GBE, PC b. 1933, m.
1996	*Byford*, Hazel Byford, DBE, b. 1941, m.
2007	*Campbell of Surbiton*, Jane Susan Campbell, DBE, PC, b. 1959, m.
1982	*Carnegy of Lour*, Elizabeth Patricia Carnegy of Lour, b. 1925
1992	*Chalker of Wallasey*, Lynda Chalker, PC, b. 1942, m.
2004	*Chapman*, Nicola Jane Chapman, b. 1961
2005	*Clark of Calton*, Dr Lynda Margaret Clark, QC, b. 1949
2000	*Cohen of Pimlico*, Janet Cohen, b. 1940, m.
2005	*Corston*, Jean Ann Corston, PC, b. 1942, m.
2007	*Coussins*, Jean Coussins, PC, b. 1950
1982	*Cox*, Caroline Anne Cox, b. 1937, m.
1998	*Crawley*, Christine Mary Crawley, b. 1950, m.

1990   *Cumberlege*, Julia Frances Cumberlege, CBE, *b.* 1943, *m.*

1978   *David*, Nora Ratcliff David, *b.* 1913, *w.*

1993   *Dean of Thornton-le-Fylde*, Brenda Dean, PC, *b.* 1943, *m.*

2005   *Deech*, Ruth Lynn Deech, DBE, *b.* 1943, *m.*

1974   *Delacourt-Smith of Alteryn*, Margaret Rosalind Delacourt-Smith, *b.* 1916, *m.*

2004   *D'Souza*, Dr Frances Gertrude Claire D'Souza, CMG, *b.* 1944 *m.*

1990   *Dunn*, Lydia Selina Dunn, DBE, *b.* 1940, *m.*

1990   *Eccles of Moulton*, Diana Catherine Eccles, *b.* 1933, *m.*

1972   *Elles*, Diana Louie Elles, *b.* 1921, *m.*

1997   *Emerton*, Audrey Caroline Emerton, DBE, *b.* 1935

1974   *Falkender*, Marcia Matilda Falkender, CBE, *b.* 1932

2004   *Falkner of Margravine*, Kishwer Falkner, *b.* 1955, *m.*

1994   *Farrington of Ribbleton*, Josephine Farrington, *b.* 1940, *m.*

2001   *Finlay of Llandaff*, Ilora Gillian Finlay, *b.* 1949, *m.*

1990   *Flather*, Shreela Flather, *m.*

1997   *Fookes*, Janet Evelyn Fookes, DBE, *b.* 1936

2006   *Ford*, Margaret Anne Ford, *b.* 1957, *m.*

2005   *Fritchie*, Irene Tordoff Fritchie, DBE, *b.* 1942, *m.*

1999   *Gale*, Anita Gale, *b.* 1940

1981   *Gardner of Parkes*, (Rachel) Trixie (Anne) Gardner, *b.* 1927, *w.*

2000   *Gibson of Market Rasen*, Anne Gibson, OBE, *b.* 1940, *m.*

2001   *Golding*, Llinos Golding, *b.* 1933, *m.*

1998   *Goudie*, Mary Teresa Goudie, *b.* 1946, *m.*

1993   *Gould of Potternewton*, Joyce Brenda Gould, *b.* 1932, *m.*

2001   *Greenfield*, Susan Adele Greenfield, CBE, *b.* 1950, *m.*

2000   *Greengross*, Sally Ralea Greengross, OBE, *b.* 1935, *m.*

1991   *Hamwee*, Sally Rachel Hamwee, *b.* 1947

1999   *Hanham*, Joan Brownlow Hanham, CBE, *b.* 1939, *m.*

1999   *Harris of Richmond*, Angela Felicity Harris, *b.* 1944

1996   *Hayman*, Helene Valerie Hayman, PC, *b.* 1949, *m.*

2004   *Henig*, Ruth Beatrice Henig, CBE, *b.* 1943, *m.*

1991   *Hilton of Eggardon*, Jennifer Hilton, QPM, *b.* 1936

1995   *Hogg*, Sarah Elizabeth Mary Hogg, *b.* 1946, *m.*

1990   *Hollis of Heigham*, Patricia Lesley Hollis, DPHIL, *b.* 1941, *m.*

1985   *Hooper*, Gloria Dorothy Hooper, CMG, *b.* 1939

2001   *Howarth of Breckland*, Valerie Georgina Howarth, OBE, *b.* 1940

2001   *Howe of Idlicote*, Elspeth Rosamond Morton Howe, CBE, *b.* 1932, *m.*

1999   *Howells of St Davids*, Rosalind Patricia-Anne Howells, *b.* 1931, *m.*

1991   *James of Holland Park*, Phyllis Dorothy White (P. D. James), OBE, *b.* 1920, *w.*

1992   *Jay of Paddington*, Margaret Ann Jay, PC, *b.* 1939, *m.*

2006   *Jones of Whitchurch*, Margaret Beryl Jones, *b.* 1955

1997   *Kennedy of the Shaws*, Helena Ann Kennedy, QC, *b.* 1950, *m.*

2006   *Kingsmill*, Denise Patricia Byrne Kingsmill, CBE, *b.* 1947, *m.*

1997   *Knight of Collingtree*, (Joan Christabel) Jill Knight, DBE, *b.* 1927, *w.*

1997   *Linklater of Butterstone*, Veronica Linklater, *b.* 1943, *m.*

1978   *Lockwood*, Betty Lockwood, *b.* 1924, *w.*

1997   *Ludford*, Sarah Ann Ludford, *b.* 1951

2004   *McDonagh*, Margaret Josephine McDonagh

1979   *McFarlane of Llandaff*, Jean Kennedy McFarlane, *b.* 1926

1999   *McIntosh of Hudnall*, Genista Mary McIntosh, *b.* 1946

1997   *Maddock*, Diana Margaret Maddock, *b.* 1945, *m.*

1991   *Mallalieu*, Ann Mallalieu, QC, *b.* 1945, *m.*

1970   *Masham of Ilton*, Susan Lilian Primrose Cunliffe-Lister, *b.* 1935, *w.*

1999   *Massey of Darwen*, Doreen Elizabeth Massey, *b.* 1938, *m.*

2006   *Meacher*, Molly Christine Meacher, *b.* 1940, *m.*

2001   *Michie of Gallanach*, Janet Ray Michie, *b.* 1934, *m.*

1998   *Miller of Chilthorne Domer*, Susan Elizabeth Miller, *b.* 1954

1993   *Miller of Hendon*, Doreen Miller, MBE, *b.* 1933, *m.*

2004   *Morgan of Drefelin*, Delyth Jane Morgan, *b.* 1961, *m.*

2001   *Morgan of Huyton*, Sally Morgan, *b.* 1959, *m.*

2004   *Morris of Bolton*, Patricia Morris, OBE, *b.* 1953

2005   *Morris of Yardley*, Estelle Morris, PC, *b.* 1952

2004   *Murphy*, Elaine Murphy, *b.* 1947, *m.*

2004   *Neuberger*, Rabbi Julia (Babette Sarah) Neuberger, DBE, *b.* 1950, *m.*

2007   ‡*Neville-Jones*, (Lilian) Pauline Neville-Jones, DCMG, *b.* 1939

1997   *Nicholson of Winterbourne*, Emma Harriet Nicholson, MEP, *b.* 1941, *m.*

1982   *Nicol*, Olive Mary Wendy Nicol, *b.* 1923, *m.*

2000   *Noakes*, Shiela Valerie Masters, DBE, *b.* 1949, *m.*

2000   *Northover*, Lindsay Patricia Granshaw, *b.* 1954

1991   *O'Cathain*, Detta O'Cathain, OBE, *b.* 1938, *m.*

1999   *O'Neill of Bengarve*, Onora Sylvia O'Neill, CBE, PHD, *b.* 1941

1989   *Oppenheim-Barnes*, Sally Oppenheim-Barnes, PC, *b.* 1930, *m.*

2006   *Paisley of St George's*, Eileen Emily Paisley, *m.*

1990   *Park of Monmouth*, Daphne Margaret Sybil Désirée Park, CMG, OBE, *b.* 1921

1991   *Perry of Southwark*, Pauline Perry, *b.* 1931, *m.*

1997   *Pitkeathley*, Jill Elizabeth Pitkeathley, OBE, *b.* 1940

1981   *Platt of Writtle*, Beryl Catherine Platt, CBE, FENG, *b.* 1923, *m.*

1999   *Prashar*, Usha Kumari Prashar, CBE, *b.* 1948, *m.*

2004   *Prosser*, Margaret Theresa Prosser, OBE, *b.* 1937

2006   *Quin*, Joyce Gwendoline Quin, PC *b.* 1944

1996   *Ramsay of Cartvale*, Margaret Mildred (Meta) Ramsay, *b.* 1936

1994   *Rawlings*, Patricia Elizabeth Rawlings, *b.* 1939

1997   *Rendell of Babergh*, Ruth Barbara Rendell, CBE, *b.* 1930, *m.*

1998   *Richardson of Calow*, Kathleen Margaret Richardson, OBE, *b.* 1938, *m.*

2004   *Royall of Blaisdon*, Janet Anne Royall, *b.* 1955, *m.*

1997	*Scotland of Asthal,* Patricia Janet Scotland, QC, *b.* 1955, *m.*
2000	*Scott of Needham Market,* Rosalind Carol Scott, *b.* 1957
1991	*Seccombe,* Joan Anna Dalziel Seccombe, DBE, *b.* 1930, *m.*
1998	*Sharp of Guildford,* Margaret Lucy Sharp, *b.* 1938, *m.*
1973	*Sharples,* Pamela Sharples, *b.* 1923, *m.*
2005	*Shephard of Northwold,* Gillian Patricia Shephard, PC, *b.* 1940, *m.*
1995	*Smith of Gilmorehill,* Elizabeth Margaret Smith, *b.* 1940, *w.*
1999	*Stern,* Vivien Helen Stern, CBE, *b.* 1941
1996	*Symons of Vernham Dean,* Elizabeth Conway Symons, *b.* 1951
2005	*Taylor of Bolton,* Winifred Ann Taylor, PC *b.* 1947, *m.*
1992	*Thatcher,* Margaret Hilda Thatcher, KG, OM, PC, FRS, *b.* 1925, *w.*
1994	*Thomas of Walliswood,* Susan Petronella Thomas, OBE, *b.* 1935, *m.*
2006	*Thomas of Winchester,* Celia Marjorie Thomas, MBE, *b.* 1945
1998	*Thornton,* (Dorothea) Glenys Thornton, *b.* 1952, *m.*

2005	*Tonge,* Dr. Jennifer Louise Tonge, *b.* 1941, *m.*
1980	*Trumpington,* Jean Alys Barker, DCVO, PC, *b.* 1922, *w.*
1985	*Turner of Camden,* Muriel Winifred Turner, *b.* 1927, *m.*
1998	*Uddin,* Manzila Pola Uddin, *b.* 1959, *m.*
2007	*Vadera,* Shriti Vadera
2005	*Valentine,* Josephine Clare Valentine
2006	*Verma,* Sandip Verma, *b.* 1959, *m.*
2004	*Wall of New Barnet,* Margaret Mary Wall, *b.* 1941, *m.*
2000	*Walmsley,* Joan Margaret Walmsley, *b.* 1943
1985	*Warnock,* Helen Mary Warnock, DBE, *b.* 1924, *w.*
2007	‡*Warsi,* Syeeda Warsi, *b.* 1971, *m.*
1999	*Warwick of Undercliffe,* Diana Mary Warwick, *b.* 1945, *m.*
1999	*Whitaker,* Janet Alison Whitaker, *b.* 1936
1996	*Wilcox,* Judith Ann Wilcox, *b.* 1940, *w.*
1999	*Wilkins,* Rosalie Catherine Wilkins, *b.* 1946
1993	*Williams of Crosby,* Shirley Vivien Teresa Brittain Williams, PC, *b.* 1930, *w.*
2004	*Young of Hornsey,* Prof. Margaret Omolola Young, OBE, *b.* 1951, *m.*
1997	*Young of Old Scone,* Barbara Scott Young, *b.* 1948

LORDS SPIRITUAL

The Lords Spiritual are the Archbishops of Canterbury and York and 24 diocesan bishops of the Church of England. The Bishops of London, Durham and Winchester always have seats in the House of Lords; the other 21 seats are filled by the remaining diocesan bishops in order of seniority. The Bishop of Sodor and Man and the Bishop of Gibraltar are not eligible to sit in the House of Lords.

ARCHBISHOPS

Style, The Most Revd and Right Hon. the Lord Archbishop of_
Addressed as Archbishop *or* Your Grace

INTRODUCED TO HOUSE OF LORDS

2003　*Canterbury* (104th), Rowan Douglas Williams, PC, DPHIL, *b.* 1950, *m., cons.* 1992, *elected* 2002

2005　*York* (97th), John Mugabi Tucker Sentamu, PC, PHD, *b.* 1949, *m., cons.* 1996, *elected* 2005, *trans.* 2005

BISHOPS

Style, The Right Revd the Lord Bishop of _
Addressed as My Lord
elected date of confirmation as diocesan bishop

INTRODUCED TO HOUSE OF LORDS
(as at 31 August 2007)

1996　*London* (132nd), Richard John Carew Chartres, *b.* 1947, *m., cons.* 1992, *elected* 1995

2003　*Durham* (71st), Nicholas Thomas Wright, DPHIL, *b.* 1948, *m., cons.* 2003, *elected* 2003

1996　*Winchester* (96th), Michael Charles Scott-Joynt, *b.* 1943, *m., cons.* 1987, *elected* 1995

1997　*Southwark* (9th), Thomas Frederick Butler, *b.* 1940, *m., cons.* 1985, *elected* 1991, *trans.* 1998

1997　*Manchester* (11th), Nigel Simeon McCulloch, *b.* 1942, *m., cons.* 1986, *elected* 1992, *trans.* 2002

1998　*Salisbury* (77th), David Staffurth Stancliffe, *b.* 1942, *m., cons.* 1993, *elected* 1993

1999　*Rochester* (106th), Michael James Nazir-Ali, PHD, *b.* 1949, *m., cons.* 1984, *elected* 1994

1999　*Chelmsford* (9th), John Warren Gladwin, *b.* 1942, *m., cons.* 1994, *elected* 1994, *trans.* 2003

1999　*Portsmouth* (8th), Kenneth William Stevenson, *b.* 1949, *m., cons.* 1995, *elected* 1995

1999　*St Albans* (9th), Christopher William Herbert, *b.* 1944, *m., cons.* 1995, *elected* 1995

2001　*Peterborough* (37th), Ian Patrick Martyn Cundy, *b.* 1945, *m., cons.* 1992, *elected* 1996

2001　*Chester* (40th), Peter Robert Forster, PHD, *b.* 1950, *cons.* 1996, *elected* 1996

2002　*Truro* (14th), William Ind, *b.* 1942, *m., cons.* 1987, *elected* 1997

2003　*Newcastle* (11th), (John) Martin Wharton, *b.* 1944, *m., cons.* 1992, *elected* 1997

2003　*Sheffield* (6th), John Nicholls, *b.* 1943, *m., cons.* 1990, *elected* 1997

2003　*Coventry* (8th), Colin James Bennetts, *b.* 1940, *m., cons.* 1994, *elected* 1998

2003　*Liverpool* (7th), James Stuart Jones, *b.* 1948, *m., cons.* 1994, *elected* 1998

2003　*Leicester* (6th), Timothy John Stevens, *b.* 1946, *m., cons.* 1995, *elected* 1999

2004　*Southwell and Nottingham* (10th), George Henry Cassidy, *b.* 1942, *m., cons.* 1999, *elected* 1999

2004　*Norwich* (71st), Graham Richard James, *b.* 1951, *m., cons.* 1993, *elected* 1999

2005　*Exeter* (70th), Michael Lawrence Langrish, *b.* 1946, *m., cons.* 1993, *elected* 2000

2006　*Ripon and Leeds* (12th), John Richard Packer, *b.* 1946, *m., cons.* 1996, *elected* 2000

2007　*Ely* (68th), Dr Anthony John Russell, *b.* 1943, *m., cons.* 1988, *elected* 2000

2007　*Carlisle* (65th), (Geoffrey) Graham Dow, *b.* 1942, *m., cons.* 1985, *elected* 2000

BISHOPS AWAITING SEATS, in order of seniority
(as at 31 August 2007)

Chichester (102nd), John William Hind, *b.* 1945, *m., cons.* 1991, *elected* 2001

Lincoln (71st), Dr John Charles Saxbee, *b.* 1946, *m., cons.* 1994, *elected* 2001

Bath and Wells (77th), Peter Bryan Price, *b.* 1944, *m., cons.* 1997, *elected* 2002

Bradford (9th), David Charles James, *b.* 1945, *m., cons.* 1998, *elected* 2002

Wakefield (12th), Stephen George Platten, *b.* 1947, *m., cons.* 2003, *elected* 2003

Bristol (55th), Michael Arthur Hill, *b.* 1947, *m., cons.* 1998, *elected* 2003

Lichfield (98th), Jonathan Michael Gledhill, *b.* 1949, *m., cons.* 1996, *elected* 2003

Blackburn (8th), Nicholas Stewart Reade, *b.* 1946, *m., cons.* 2004, *elected* 2004

Hereford (104th), Anthony Martin Priddis, *b.* 1948, *m., cons.* 1996, *elected* 2004

Gloucester (40th), Michael Francis Perham, *b.* 1947, *m., cons.* 2004, *elected* 2004

Guildford (9th), Christopher John Hill, *b.* 1945, *m., cons.* 1996, *elected* 2004

Derby (7th), Alastair Llewellyn John Redfern, *b.* 1948, *m., cons.* 1997, *elected* 2005

Birmingham (9th), David Andrew Urquhart, *b.* 1952, *cons.* 2000, *elected* 2006

Oxford (42nd), John Lawrence Pritchard, *b.* 1948, *m., cons.* 2002, *elected* 2007

St Edmundsbury and Ipswich (10th), (William) Nigel Stock, *b.* 1950, *m., cons.* 2000, *elected* 2007

Worcester (113th), John Geoffrey Inge, PHD, *b.* 1955, *m., cons.* 2003, *elected* 2007

COURTESY TITLES AND PEERS' SURNAMES

COURTESY TITLES

The heir apparent to a Duke, Marquess or Earl uses the highest of his father's other titles as a courtesy title. For example, the Marquess of Blandford is heir to the Dukedom of Marlborough, and Viscount Amberley to the Earldom of Russell. Titles of second heirs (when in use) are also given, and the courtesy title of the father of a second heir is indicated by * eg Earl of Mornington, eldest son of *Marquess of Douro.

The holder of a courtesy title is not styled 'the Most Hon.' or 'the Right Hon.', and in correspondence 'the' is omitted before the title. The heir apparent to a Scottish title may use the title 'Master'.

MARQUESSES

*Blandford – Marlborough, D.
Bowmont and Cessford – Roxburghe, D.
Douglas and Clydesdale – Hamilton, D.
*Douro – Wellington, D.
Graham – Montrose, D.
Hamilton – Abercorn, D.
Hartington – Devonshire, D.
Lorne – Argyll, D.
Stafford – Sutherland, D.
Tullibardine – Atholl, D.
*Worcester – Beaufort, D.

EARLS

Aboyne – Huntly, M.
Arundel and Surrey – Norfolk, D.
Bective – Headfort, M.
Belfast – Donegall, M.
Brecknock – Camden, M.
Burford – St Albans, D.
*Cardigan – Ailesbury, M.
Compton – Northampton, M.
*Dalkeith – Buccleuch, D.
*Euston – Grafton, D.
Glamorgan – *Worcester, M.
Grosvenor – Westminster, D.
Haddo – Aberdeen and Temair, M.
Hillsborough – Downshire, M.
Hopetoun – Linlithgow, M.
Kerry – Lansdowne, M.
March and Kinrara – Richmond, D.
Medina – Milford Haven, M.
*Mount Charles – Conyngham, M.
Mornington – *Douro, M.
Mulgrave – Normanby, M.

Percy – Northumberland, D.
Ronaldshay – Zetland, M.
*St Andrews – Kent, D.
*Southesk – Fife, D.
Sunderland – *Blandford, M.
*Tyrone – Waterford, M.
Ulster – Gloucester, D.
*Uxbridge – Anglesey, M.
Wiltshire – Winchester, M.
Yarmouth – Hertford, M.

VISCOUNTS

Alexander – Caledon, E.
Althorp – Spencer, E.
Andover – Suffolk and Berkshire, E.
Asquith – Oxford and Asquith, E.
Boringdon – Morley, E.
Borodale – Beatty, E.
Boyle – Shannon, E.
Brocas – Jellicoe, E.
Bury – Albermarle, E.
Campden – Gainsborough, E.
Carlow – Portarlington, E.
Carlton – Wharncliffe, E.
Castlereagh – Londonderry, M.
Chelsea – Cadogan, E.
Chewton – Waldegrave, E.
Clanfield – Peel, E.
Clive – Powis, E.
Coke – Leicester, E.
Corry – Belmore, E.
Corvedale – Baldwin of Bewdley, E.
Cranborne – Salisbury, M.
Cranley – Onslow, E.
Crichton – Erne, E.
Curzon – Howe, E.
Dangan – Cowley, E.
Dawick – Haig, E.
Drumlanrig – Queensberry, M.

Duncannon – Bessborough, E.
Dungarvan – Cork and Orrery, E.
Dunluce – Antrim, E.
Dunwich – Stradbroke, E.
Dupplin – Kinnoull, E.
Ednam – Dudley, E.
Elveden – Iveagh, E.
Emlyn – Cawdor, E
Encombe – Eldon, E.
Enfield – Strafford, E.
Erleigh – Reading, M.
Errington – Cromer, E.
FitzHarris – Malmesbury, E.
Folkestone – Radnor, E.
Forbes – Granard, E.
Garmoyle – Cairns, E.
Garnock – Lindsay, E.
Glenapp – Inchcape, E.
Glentworth – Limerick, E.
Grey de Wilton – Wilton, E.
Grimstone – Verulam, E.
Gwynedd – Lloyd George of Dwyfor, E.
Hawkesbury – Liverpool, E.
Hinchingbrooke – Sandwich, E.
Ikerrin – Carrick, E.
Ingestre – Shrewsbury, E.
Ipswich – *Euston, E.
Jocelyn – Roden, E.
Kelburn – Glasgow, E.
Kingsborough – Kingston, E.
Kirkwall – Orkney, E.
Knebworth – Lytton, E.
Lambton – Durham, E.
Lascelles – Harewood, E.
Linley – Snowdon, E.
Lymington – Portsmouth, E.
Macmillan of Ovenden – Stockton, E.
Maidstone – Winchilsea, E
Maitland – Lauderdale, E.
Mandeville – Manchester, D.
Marsham – Romney, E.
Melgund – Minto, E.
Merton – Nelson, E.
Moore – Drogheda, E.
Newport – Bradford, E.
Northland – Ranfurly, E
Newry and Mourne – Kilmorey, E.
Petersham – Harrington, E.
Pollington – Mexborough, E

Raynham – Townshend, M.
Reidhaven – Seafield, E.
Ruthven of Canberra – Gowrie, E.
St Cyres – Iddesleigh, E.
Sandon – Harrowby, E.
Savernake – *Cardigan, E.
Slane – *Mount Charles, E.
Somerton – Normanton, E.
Stopford – Courtown, E.
Stormont – Mansfield, E.
Strathallan – Perth, E.
Stuart – Castle Stewart, E.
Suirdale – Donoughmore, E.
Tamworth – Ferrers, E.
Tarbat – Cromartie, E.
Vaughan – Lisburne, E.
Weymouth – Bath, M.
Windsor – Plymouth, E.
Wolmer – Selborne, E.
Woodstock – Portland, E.

BARONS (LORDS)

Aberdour – Morton, E.
Apsley – Bathurst, E.
Ardee – Meath, E.
Balgonie – Leven and Melville, E.
Balniel – Crawford and Balcarres, E.
Berriedale – Caithness, E.
Bingham – Lucan, E.
Binning – Haddington, E.
Brooke – Warwick, E.
Bruce – Elgin, E.
Burghley – Exeter, M.
Cardross – Buchan, E.
Carnegie – *Southesk, E.
Clifton – Darnley, E.
Cochrane – Dundonald, E.
Courtenay – Devon, E.
Dalmeny – Rosebery, E.
Doune – Moray, E.
Downpatrick – *St Andrews, E.
Dunglass – Home, E.
Eliot – St Germans, E.
Eskdail – *Dalkeith, E.
Formartine – *Haddo, E.
Gillford – Clanwilliam, E.
Glamis – Strathmore, E.
Greenock – Cathcart, E.
Guernsey – Aylesford, E.
Hay – Erroll, E.
Howard of Effingham – Effingham, E.
Huntingtower – Dysart, C.
Hyde – Clarendon, E.
Irwin – Halifax, E.

Johnstone – *Annandale and Hartfell, E.*
Langton – *Temple of Stowe, E.*
La Poer – **Tyrone, E.*
Leveson – *Granville, E*
Loughborough – *Rosslyn, E.*
Masham – *Swinton, E.*
Mauchline – *Loudoun, C.*

Medway – *Cranbrook, E.*
Montgomerie – *Eglinton and Winton, E.*
Moreton – *Ducie, E.*
Mount Stuart – *Bute, M*
Naas – *Mayo, E.*
Neidpath – *Wemyss and March, E.*
Norreys – *Lindsey and Abingdon, E.*

North – *Guilford, E.*
Ogilvy – *Airlie, E.*
Oxmantown – *Rosse, E.*
Paget de Beaudesert – **Uxbridge, E.*
Porchester – *Carnarvon, E.*
Ramsay – *Dalhousie, E.*
Romsey – *Mountbatten of Burma, C.*
Scrymgeour – *Dundee, E.*

Seymour – *Somerset, D.*
Stanley – *Derby, E.*
Stavordale – *Ilchester, E.*
Strathnaver – *Sutherland, C.*
Wodehouse – *Kimberley, E.*
Worsley – *Yarborough, E.*

PEERS' SURNAMES

The following symbols indicate the rank of the peer holding each title:

C.   Countess
D.   Duke
E.   Earl
M.   Marquess
V.   Viscount
*   Life Peer

Where no designation is given, the title is that of a hereditary Baron or Baroness.

Abney-Hastings – *Loudoun, C.*
Acheson – *Gosford, E.*
Adams – *A. of Craigielea**
Adderley – *Norton*
Addington – *Sidmouth, V.*
Adebowale – *A. of Thornes**
Agar – *Normanton, E.*
Aitken – *Beaverbrook*
Akers-Douglas – *Chilston, V.*
Alexander – *A. of Tunis, E.*
Alexander – *Caledon, E.*
Allen – *A. of Abbeydale**
Allen – *Croham**
Allsopp – *Hindlip*
Alton – *A. of Liverpool**
Anderson – *A. of Swansea**
Anderson – *Waverley, V.*
Anelay – *A. of St Johns**
Annesley – *Valentia, V.*
Anson – *Lichfield, E.*
Archer – *A. of Sandwell**
Archer – *A. of Weston-super-Mare**
Armstrong – *A. of Ilminster**
Armstrong-Jones – *Snowdon, E.*
Arthur – *Glenarthur*
Arundell – *Talbot of Malahide*
Ashdown – *A. of Norton-sub-Hamdon**
Ashley – *A. of Stoke**
Ashley-Cooper – *Shaftesbury, E.*
Ashton – *A. of Hyde*
Ashton – *A. of Upholland**

Asquith – *Oxford and Asquith, E.*
Assheton – *Clitheroe*
Astley – *Hastings*
Astor – *A. of Hever*
Aubrey-Fletcher – *Braye*
Bailey – *Glanusk*
Baillie – *Burton*
Baillie Hamilton – *Haddington, E.*
Baker – *B. of Dorking**
Baldwin – *B. of Bewdley, E.*
Balfour – *B. of Inchrye*
Balfour – *Kinross*
Balfour – *Riverdale*
Bampfylde – *Poltimore*
Banbury – *B. of Southam*
Barber – *B. of Tewkesbury**
Baring – *Ashburton*
Baring – *Cromer, E.*
Baring – *Howick of Glendale*
Baring – *Northbrook*
Baring – *Revelstoke*
Barker – *Trumpington**
Barnes – *Gorell*
Barnewall – *Trimlestown*
Bassam – *B. of Brighton**
Bathurst – *Bledisloe, V.*
Beauclerk – *St Albans, D.*
Beaumont – *Allendale, V.*
Beaumont – *B. of Whitley**
Beckett – *Grimthorpe*
Benn – *Stansgate, V.*
Bennet – *Tankerville, E.*
Bentinck – *Portland, E.*
Beresford – *Decies*
Beresford – *Waterford, M.*
Bernstein – *B. of Craigweil**
Berry – *Camrose, V.*
Berry – *Kemsley, V.*
Bertie – *Lindsey, E.*
Best – *Wynford*
Bethell – *Westbury*
Bewicke-Copley – *Cromwell*
Bigham – *Mersey, V.*
Bingham – *B. of Cornhill**
Bingham – *Clanmorris*
Bingham – *Lucan, E.*
Black – *B. of Crossharbour**

Bligh – *Darnley, E.*
Blyth – *B. of Rowington**
Bonham Carter – *B.-C. of Yarnbury**
Bootle-Wilbraham – *Skelmersdale*
Boscawen – *Falmouth, V.*
Boston – *B. of Faversham**
Bottomley – *B. of Nettlestone**
Bourke – *Mayo, E.*
Bowes Lyon – *Strathmore, E.*
Bowyer – *Denham*
Boyd – *Kilmarnock*
Boyd – *B. of Duncansby**
Boyle – *Cork and Orrery, E.*
Boyle – *Glasgow, E.*
Boyle – *Shannon, E.*
Brabazon – *Meath, E.*
Brand – *Hampden, V.*
Brassey – *B. of Apethorpe*
Brett – *Esher, V.*
Bridge – *B. of Harwich**
Bridgeman – *Bradford, E.*
Brittan – *B. of Spennithorne**
Brodrick – *Midleton, V.*
Brooke – *Alanbrooke, V.*
Brooke – *B. of Alverthorpe**
Brooke – *Brookeborough, V.*
Brooke – *B. of Sutton Mandeville**
Brooks – *B. of Tremorfa**
Brooks – *Crawshaw*
Brougham – *Brougham and Vaux*
Broughton – *Fairhaven*
Brown – *B. of Eaton-under-Heywood**
Browne – *B. of Belmont**
Browne – *B. of Madingley**
Browne – *Kilmaine*
Browne – *Oranmore and Browne*
Browne – *Sligo, M.*
Bruce – *Aberdare*
Bruce – *Balfour of Burleigh*
Bruce – *Elgin and Kincardine, E.*

Brudenell-Bruce – *Ailesbury, M.*
Buchan – *Tweedsmuir*
Buckley – *Wrenbury*
Butler – *B. of Brockwell**
Butler – *Carrick, E.*
Butler – *Dunboyne*
Butler – *Mountgarret, V.*
Buxton – *B. of Alsa**
Byng – *Strafford, E.*
Byng – *Torrington, V.*
Cambell-Savours – *C.-S. of Allerdale**
Cameron – *C. of Dillington**
Cameron – *C. of Lochbroom**
Campbell – *Argyll, D.*
Campbell – *C. of Alloway**
Campbell – *C. of Surbiton**
Campbell – *Cawdor, E.*
Campbell – *Colgrain*
Campbell – *Stratheden and Campbell*
Campbell-Gray – *Gray*
Canning – *Garvagh*
Capell – *Essex, E.*
Carey – *C. of Clifton**
Carington – *Carrington*
Carlisle – *C. of Berriew**
Carnegie – *Fife, D.*
Carnegie – *Northesk, E.*
Carr – *C. of Hadley**
Carter – *C. of Coles**
Cary – *Falkland, V.*
Caulfeild – *Charlemont, V.*
Cavendish – *C. of Furness**
Cavendish – *Chesham*
Cavendish – *Devonshire, D.*
Cavendish – *Waterpark*
Cayzer – *Rotherwick*
Cecil – *Amherst of Hackney*
Cecil – *Exeter, M.*
Cecil – *Rockley*
Chalker – *C. of Wallasey**
Chaloner – *Gisborough*
Chapman – *C. of Leeds**
Chapman – *Northfield**
Charteris – *Wemyss and March, E.*
Chetwynd-Talbot – *Shrewsbury, E.*
Chichester – *Donegall, M.*

Child Villiers – *Jersey, E.*
Cholmondeley – *Delamere*
Chubb – *Hayter*
Clark – *C. of Calton**
Clarke – *C. of Hampstead**
Clegg-Hill – *Hill, V.*
Clifford – *C. of Chudleigh*
Cochrane – *C. of Cults*
Cochrane – *Dundonald, E.*
Cocks – *Somers*
Cohen – *C. of Pimlico**
Cokayne – *Cullen of Ashbourne*
Coke – *Leicester, E.*
Cole – *Enniskillen, E.*
Collier – *Monkswell*
Colville – *Clydesmuir*
Colville – *C. of Culross, V.*
Compton – *Northampton, M.*
Conolly-Carew – *Carew*
Cooke – *C. of Islandreagh**
Cooper – *Norwich, V*
Cope – *C. of Berkeley**
Corbett – *C. of Castle Vale*.*
Corbett – *Rowallan*
Cornwall-Leigh – *Grey of Condor*
Courtenay – *Devon, E.*
Craig – *C. of Radley**
Craig – *Craigavon, V.*
Crichton – *Erne, E.*
Crichton-Stuart – *Bute, M.*
Cripps – *Parmoor*
Crossley – *Somerleyton*
Cubitt – *Ashcombe*
Cunliffe-Lister – *Masham of Ilton**
Cunliffe-Lister – *Swinton, E.*
Cunningham – *C. of Felling**
Currie – *C. of Marylebone**
Curzon – *Howe, E.*
Curzon – *Scarsdale, V.*
Cust – *Brownlow*
Czernin – *Howard de Walden*
Dalrymple – *Stair, E.*
Darzi – *D. of Denham**
Daubeny de Moleyns – *Ventry*
Davidson – *D. of Glen Clova**
Davies – *D. of Coity**
Davies – *Darwen*
Davies – *D. of Oldham**
Dawnay – *Downe, V.*
Dawson-Damer – *Portarlington, E.*
Dean – *D. of Harptree**
Dean – *D. of Thornton-le-Fylde**
Deane – *Muskerry*
de Courcy – *Kingsale*
de Grey – *Walsingham*

Delacourt-Smith – *Delacourt Smith of Alteryn**
Denison – *Londesborough*
Denison-Pender – *Pender*
Devereux – *Hereford, V.*
Dewar – *Forteviot*
Dixon – *Glentoran*
Dodson – *Monk Bretton*
Douglas – *Morton, E.*
Douglas – *Queensberry, M.*
Douglas-Hamilton – *Hamilton, D.*
Douglas-Hamilton – *Selkirk, E.*
Douglas-Hamilton – *Selkirk of Douglas**
Douglas-Home – *Dacre*
Douglas-Home – *Home, E.*
Douglas-Pennant – *Penrhyn*
Douglas-Scott-Montagu – *Montagu of Beaulieu*
Drummond – *Perth, E.*
Drummond of Megginch – *Strange*
Dugdale – *Crathorne*
Duke – *Merrivale*
Duncombe – *Feversham*
Dundas – *Melville, V.*
Dundas – *Zetland, M.*
Eady – *Swinfen*
Eccles – *E. of Moulton**
Eden – *Auckland*
Eden – *E. of Winton**
Eden – *Henley*
Edgcumbe – *Mount Edgcumbe, E.*
Edmondson – *Sandford*
Edwardes – *Kensington*
Edwards – *Crickhowell**
Egerton – *Sutherland, D.*
Eliot – *St Germans, E.*
Elliott – *E. of Morpeth**
Elliot-Murray-Kynynmound – *Minto, E.*
Ellis – *Seaford*
Erskine – *Buchan, E.*
Erskine – *Mar and Kellie, E.*
Erskine-Murray – *Elibank*
Evans – *E. of Parkside**
Evans – *E. of Temple Guiting**
Evans – *E. of Watford**
Evans – *Mountevans*
Evans-Freke – *Carbery*
Eve – *Silsoe*
Fairfax – *F. of Cameron*
Falconer – *F. of Thoroton**
Falkner – *F. of Margravine**
Fane – *Westmorland, E.*
Farrington – *F. of Ribbleton**
Faulkner – *F. of Worcester**
Fearn – *F. of Southport**
Feilding – *Denbigh, E.*

Felton – *Seaford*
Fellowes – *De Ramsey*
Fermor-Hesketh – *Hesketh*
Fiennes – *Saye and Sele*
Fiennes-Clinton – *Lincoln, E.*
Finch Hatton – *Winchilsea, E.*
Finch-Knightley – *Aylesford, E.*
Finlay – *F. of Llandaff**
Fitzalan-Howard – *Herries of Terregles*
Fitzalan-Howard – *Norfolk, D.*
FitzGerald – *Leinster, D.*
Fitzherbert – *Stafford*
FitzRoy – *Grafton, D.*
FitzRoy – *Southampton*
FitzRoy Newdegate – *Daventry, V.*
Fletcher-Vane – *Inglewood*
Flower – *Ashbrook, V.*
Foljambe – *Liverpool, E.*
Forbes – *Granard, E*
Forsyth – *F. of Drumlean**
Forwood – *Arlington*
Foster – *F. of Thames Bank**
Foulkes – *F. of Cumnock**
Fowler – *F. of Sutton Caulfield**
Fox-Strangways – *Ilchester, E.*
Frankland – *Zouche*
Fraser – *F. of Carmyllie**
Fraser – *F. of Kilmorack**
Fraser – *Lovat*
Fraser – *Saltoun*
Fraser – *Strathalmond*
Freeman-Grenville – *Kinloss*
Fremantle – *Cottesloe*
French – *De Freyne*
Fyfe – *F. of Fairfield**
Galbraith – *Strathclyde*
Gardner – *G. of Parkes**
Gascoyne-Cecil – *M. of Salisbury**
Gathorne-Hardy – *Cranbrook, E.*
Gibbs – *Aldenham*
Gibbs – *Wraxall*
Gibson – *Ashbourne*
Gibson – *G. of Market Rasen**
Giffard – *Halsbury, E.*
Gilbey – *Vaux of Harrowden*
Gilmour – *G. of Craigmillar**
Glyn – *Wolverton*
Godley – *Kilbracken*
Goff – *G. of Chieveley**
Golding – *G. of Newcastle-under-Lyme**
Gordon – *Aberdeen, M.*

Gordon – *G. of Strathblane**
Gordon – *Huntly, M.*
Gordon Lennox – *Richmond, D.*
Gore – *Arran, E.*
Gould – *G. of Brookwood**
Gould – *G. of Potternewton**
Graham – *G. of Edmonton**
Graham – *Montrose, D.*
Graham-Toler – *Norbury, E.*
Granshaw – *Northover**
Grant of Grant – *Strathspey*
Grant of Rothiemurchus – *Dysart, E.*
Granville – *G. of Eye**
Greenall – *Daresbury*
Greville – *Warwick, E.*
Griffiths – *G. of Burry Port**
Griffiths – *G. of Fforestfach**
Grigg – *Altrincham*
Grimston – *G. of Westbury*
Grimston – *Verulam, E.*
Grosvenor – *Westminster, D.*
Grosvenor – *Wilton and Ebury, E*
Guest – *Wimborne, V*
Gueterbock – *Berkeley*
Guinness – *Iveagh, E.*
Guinness – *Moyne*
Gully – *Selby, V.*
Gummer – *Chadlington**
Gurdon – *Cranworth*
Guthrie – *G. of Craigiebank**
Gwynne Jones – *Chalfont**
Hale – *H. of Richmond**
Hamilton – *Abercorn, D.*
Hamilton – *Belhaven and Stenton*
Hamilton – *H. of Dalzell*
Hamilton – *H. of Epsom**
Hamilton – *Holm Patrick*
Hamilton-Russell – *Boyne, V.*
Hamilton-Smith – *Colwyn*
Hanbury-Tracy – *Sudeley*
Handcock – *Castlemaine*
Hannay – *H. of Chiswick**
Harbord-Hamond – *Suffield*
Harding – *H. of Petherton*
Hardinge – *H. of Penshurst*
Hare – *Blakenham, V.*
Hare – *Listowel, E.*
Harmsworth – *Rothermere, V.*
Harries – *H. of Pentregarth**
Harris – *H. of Haringey**
Harris – *H. of Peckham**
Harris – *H. of Richmond**

Harris – *Malmesbury, E.*
Hart – *H. of Chilton*★
Harvey – *H. of Tasburgh*
Hastings – *H. of Scarisbrick*★
Hastings Bass – *Huntingdon, E.*
Haughey – *Ballyedmond*★
Hay – *Erroll, E.*
Hay – *Kinnoull, E.*
Hay – *Tweeddale, M.*
Heathcote-Drummond-Willoughby – *Willoughby de Eresby*
Hely-Hutchinson – *Donoughmore, E.*
Henderson – *Faringdon*
Hennessy – *Windlesham*
Henniker-Major – *Henniker*
Hepburne-Scott – *Polwarth*
Herbert – *Carnarvon, E.*
Herbert – *Hemingford*
Herbert – *Pembroke, E.*
Herbert – *Powis, E.*
Hervey – *Bristol, M.*
Heseltine – *H. of Thenford*★
Hewitt – *Lifford, V.*
Hicks Beach – *St Aldwyn, E.*
Hill – *Downshire, M.*
Hill – *Sandys*
Hill-Trevor – *Trevor*
Hilton – *H. of Eggardon*★
Hobart-Hampden – *Buckinghamshire, E.*
Hodgson – *H. of Astley Abbotts*★
Hogg – *Hailsham, V.*
Hogg – *H. of Cumbernauld*★
Holland-Hibbert – *Knutsford, V.*
Hollis – *H. of Heigham*★
Holme – *H. of Cheltenham*★
Holmes à Court – *Heytesbury*
Hood – *Bridport, V.*
Hope – *Glendevon*
Hope – *H. of Craighead*★
Hope – *H. of Thornes*★
Hope – *Linlithgow, M.*
Hope – *Rankeillour*
Hope Johnstone – *Annandale and Hartfell, E.*
Hope-Morley – *Hollenden*
Hopkinson – *Colyton*
Hore Ruthven – *Gowrie, E.*
Hovell-Thurlow-Cumming-Bruce – *Thurlow*
Howard – *Carlisle, E.*
Howard – *Effingham, E.*
Howard – *H. of Penrith*
Howard – *H. of Rising*★

Howard – *Strathcona*
Howard – *Suffolk and Berkshire, E.*
Howarth – *H. of Breckland*★
Howarth – *H. of Newport*★
Howe – *H. of Aberavon*★
Howe – *H. of Idlicote*★
Howell – *H. of Guildford*★
Howells – *H. of St. Davids*★
Howie – *H. of Troon*★
Hubbard – *Addington*
Huggins – *Malvern, V.*
Hughes – *H. of Woodside*★
Hughes-Young – *St Helens*
Hunt – *H. of Chesterton*★
Hunt – *H. of Kings Heath*★
Hunt – *H. of Tanworth*★
Hunt – *H. of Wirral*★
Hurd – *H. of Westwell*★
Hutchinson – *H. of Lullington*★
Ingrams – *Darcy de Knayth*
Innes-Ker – *Roxburghe, D.*
Inskip – *Caldecote, V.*
Irby – *Boston*
Irvine – *I. of Lairg*★
Isaacs – *Reading, M.*
James – *J. of Blackheath*★
James – *J. of Holland Park*★
James – *Northbourne*
Janner – *J. of Braunstone*★
Jay – *J. of Ewelme*★
Jay – *J. of Paddington*★
Jebb – *Gladwyn*
Jenkin – *J. of Roding*★
Jervis – *St Vincent, V.*
Jocelyn – *Roden, E.*
Jolliffe – *Hylton*
Jones – *J. of Birmingham*★
Jones – *J. of Cheltenham*★
Jones – *J. of Deeside*★
Jones – *J. of Whitchurch*★
Joynson-Hicks – *Brentford, V.*
Kay-Shuttleworth – *Shuttleworth*
Kearley – *Devonport, V.*
Keith – *Kintore, E.*
Kemp – *Rochdale, V.*
Kennedy – *Ailsa, M*
Kennedy – *K. of the Shaws*★
Kenworthy – *Strabolgi*
Keppel – *Albemarle, E.*
Kerr – *K. of Kinlochard*★
Kerr – *Lothian, M.*
Kerr – *Teviot*
Kilpatrick – *K. of Kincraig*★
King – *Lovelace, E.*
King – *K. of West Bromwich*★
King-Tenison – *Kingston, E.*
Kirkham – *Berners*

Kirkwood – *K. of Kirkhope*★
Kitchener – *K. of Khartoum, E.*
Knatchbull – *Brabourne*
Knatchbull – *Mountbatten of Burma, C.*
Knight – *K. of Collingtree*★
Knox – *Ranfurly, E.*
Laing – *L. of Dunphail*★
Lamb – *Rochester*
Lambton – *Durham, E.*
Lamont – *L. of Lerwick*★
Lampson – *Killearn*
Lane – *L. of Horsell*★
Lang – *L. of Monkton*★
Lascelles – *Harewood, E.*
Law – *Coleraine*
Law – *Ellenborough*
Lawrence – *Trevethin and Oaksey*
Lawson – *Burnham*
Lawson – *L. of Blaby*★
Lawson-Johnston – *Luke*
Lea – *L. of Crondall*★
Leach – *L. of Fairford*★
Lee – *L. of Trafford*★
Legge – *Dartmouth, E.*
Legh – *Grey of Codnor*
Legh – *Newton*
Leigh-Pemberton – *Kingsdown*★
Leith – *Burgh*
Lennox-Boyd – *Boyd of Merton, V.*
Le Poer Trench – *Clancarty, E.*
Leslie – *Rothes, E.*
Leslie Melville – *Leven and Melville, E.*
Lester – *L. of Herne Hill*★
Levene – *L. of Portsoken*★
Leveson-Gower – *Granville, E.*
Lewis – *L. of Newnham*★
Lewis – *Merthyr*
Liddell – *Ravensworth*
Lindesay-Bethune – *Lindsay, E.*
Lindsay – *Crawford, E.*
Lindsay – *L. of Birker*
Linklater – *L. of Butterstone*★
Littleton – *Hatherton*
Lloyd – *L. of Berwick*★
Lloyd George – *Lloyd George of Dwyfor, E.*
Lloyd George – *Tenby, V.*
Lloyd-Mostyn – *Mostyn*
Loder – *Wakehurst*
Lofthouse – *L. of Pontefract*★
Lopes – *Roborough*
Lour – *Carnegy of Lour*★
Low – *Aldington*
Low – *L. of Dalston*★
Lowry-Corry – *Belmore, E.*
Lowther – *Lonsdale, E.*

Lowther – *Ullswater, V.*
Lubbock – *Avebury*
Lucas – *L. of Chilworth*
Lumley – *Scarbrough, E.*
Lumley-Savile – *Savile*
Lyell – *L. of Markyate*★
Lyon-Dalberg-Acton – *Acton*
Lysaght – *Lisle*
Lyttelton – *Chandos, V.*
Lyttelton – *Cobham, V.*
Lytton Cobbold – *Cobbold*
McAlpine – *M. of West Green*★
Macaulay – *M. of Bragar*★
McClintock-Bunbury – *Rathdonnell*
McColl – *M. of Dulwich*★
Macdonald – *M. of Tradeston*★
McDonnell – *Antrim, E.*
Macfarlane – *M. of Bearsden*★
McFarlane – *M. of Llandaff*★
MacGregor – *M. of Pulham Market*★
McIntosh – *M. of Haringey*★
McIntosh – *M. of Hudnall*★
McKenzie – *M. of Luton*★
Mackay – *Inchcape, E.*
Mackay – *M. of Clashfern*★
Mackay – *M. of Drumadoon*★
Mackay – *Reay*
Mackay – *Tanlaw*★
MacKenzie – *M. of Culkein*★
MacKenzie – *M. of Framwellgate*★
Mackenzie – *Cromartie, E.*
Mackie – *M. of Benshie*★
Mackintosh – *M. of Halifax, V.*
McLaren – *Aberconway*
MacLaurin – *M. of Knebworth*★
MacLennan – *M. of Rogart*★
Macmillan – *Stockton, E.*
Macpherson – *M. of Drumochter*
Macpherson – *Strathcarron*
Maffey – *Rugby*
Maginnis – *M. of Drumglass*★
Maitland – *Lauderdale, E.*
Makgill – *Oxfuird, V.*
Makins – *Sherfield*
Manners – *Rutland, D.*
Manningham-Buller – *Dilhorne, V.*
Mansfield – *Sandhurst*
Marks – *M. of Broughton*
Marquis – *Woolton, E.*

Marshall – *M. of Knightsbridge**

Marsham – *Romney, E.*

Martyn-Hemphill – *Hemphill*

Mason – *M. of Barnsley**

Massey – *M. of Darwen**

Masters – *Noakes**

Maude – *Hawarden, V.*

Maxwell – *de Ros*

Maxwell – *Farnham*

May – *M. of Oxford**

Mayhew – *M. of Twysden**

Meade – *Clanwilliam, E.*

Mercer Nairne Petty-Fitzmaurice – *Lansdowne, M.*

Millar – *Inchyra*

Miller – *M. of Chiltorne Domer**

Miller – *M. of Hendon**

Milner – *M. of Leeds*

Mitchell-Thomson – *Selsdon*

Mitford – *Redesdale*

Molyneaux – *M. of Killead**

Monckton – *M. of Brenchley, V.*

Monckton-Arundell – *Galway, V.*

Mond – *Melchett*

Money-Coutts – *Latymer*

Montagu – *Manchester, D.*

Montagu – *Sandwich, E.*

Montagu – *Swaythling*

Montagu Douglas Scott – *Buccleuch, D.*

Montagu Stuart Wortley – *Wharncliffe, E.*

Montague – *Amwell*

Montgomerie – *Eglinton, E.*

Montgomery – *M. of Alamein, E.*

Moore – *Drogheda, E.*

Moore – *M. of Lower Marsh**

Moore – *M. of Wolvercote**

Moore-Brabazon – *Brabazon of Tara*

Moreton – *Ducie, E*

Morgan – *M. of Drefelin**

Morgan – *M. of Huyton**

Morris – *Killanin*

Morris – *M. of Aberavon**

Morris – *M. of Bolton**

Morris – *M. of Handsworth**

Morris – *M. of Manchester**

Morris – *M. of Kenwood*

Morris – *M. of Yardley**

Morris – *Naseby**

Morrison – *Dunrossil, V.*

Morrison – *Margadale*

Moser – *M. of Regents Park**

Mosley – *Ravensdale*

Mountbatten – *Milford Haven, M.*

Muff – *Calverley*

Mulholland – *Dunleath*

Murray – *Atholl, D.*

Murray – *Dunmore, E.*

Murray – *Mansfield and Mansfield, E.*

Murton – *M. of Lindisfarne**

Nall-Cain – *Brocket*

Napier – *Napier and Ettrick*

Napier – *N. of Magdala*

Needham – *Kilmorey, E.*

Neill – *N. of Bladen**

Nelson – *N. of Stafford*

Neuberger – *N. of Abbotsbury**

Nevill – *Abergavenny, M.*

Neville – *Braybrooke*

Newton – *N. of Braintree**

Nicholls – *N. of Birkenhead**

Nicolson – *Carnock*

Nicholson – *N. of Winterbourne**

Nivison – *Glendyne*

Noel – *Gainsborough, E.*

North – *Guilford, E.*

Northcote – *Iddesleigh, E.*

Norton – *Grantley*

Norton – *N. of Louth**

Norton – *Rathcreedan*

Nugent – *Westmeath, E.*

Oakeshott – *O. of Seagrove Bay**

O'Brien – *Inchiquin*

Ogilvie-Grant – *Seafield, E.*

Ogilvy – *Airlie, E.*

Oliver – *O. of Aylmerton**

O'Neill – *O'N. of Bengarve**

O'Neill – *O'N. of Clackmannan**

O'Neill – *Rathcavan*

Orde-Powlett – *Bolton*

Ormsby-Gore – *Harlech*

Ouseley – *O. of Peckham Rye**

Paget – *Anglesey, M.*

Paisley – *P. of St George's**

Pakenham – *Longford, E.*

Pakington – *Hampton*

Palmer – *Lucas and Dingwall*

Palmer – *Selborne, E.*

Park – *P. of Monmouth**

Parker – *Macclesfield, E.*

Parker – *Morley, E.*

Parnell – *Congleton*

Parsons – *Rosse, E.*

Patel – *P. of Blackburn**

Patel – *P. of Bradford**

Patten – *P. of Barnes**

Paulet – *Winchester, M.*

Peake – *Ingleby, V.*

Pearson – *Cowdray, V.*

Pearson – *P. of Rannoch**

Pease – *Gainford*

Pease – *Wardington*

Pelham – *Chichester, E.*

Pelham – *Yarborough, E.*

Pellew – *Exmouth, V*

Pendry – *P. of Stalybridge**.*

Penny – *Marchwood, V.*

Pepys – *Cottenham, E.*

Perceval – *Egmont, E.*

Percy – *Northumberland, D.*

Perry – *P. of Southwark**

Pery – *Limerick, E.*

Philipps – *Milford*

Philipps – *St Davids, V.*

Phillips – *P. of Sudbury**

Phillips – *P. of Worth Matravers**

Phipps – *Normanby, M.*

Pilkington – *P. of Oxenford**

Plant – *P. of Highfield**

Platt – *P. of Writtle**

Pleydell-Bouverie – *Radnor, E.*

Plummer – *P. of St Marylebone**

Plumptre – *Fitzwalter*

Plunkett – *Dunsany*

Plunkett – *Louth*

Pollock – *Hanworth, V.*

Pomeroy – *Harberton, V.*

Ponsonby – *Bessborough, E.*

Ponsonby – *de Mauley*

Ponsonby – *P. of Shulbrede*

Ponsonby – *Sysonby*

Powell – *P. of Bayswater**

Powys – *Lilford*

Pratt – *Camden, M.*

Preston – *Gormanston, V.*

Primrose – *Rosebery, E.*

Prittie – *Dunalley*

Prout – *Kingsland**

Ramsay – *Dalhousie, E.*

Ramsay – *R. of Cartvale**

Ramsbotham – *Soulbury, V.*

Randall – *R. of St. Budeaux**

Rees – *R. of Ludlow**

Rees-Williams – *Ogmore*

Rendell – *R. of Babergh**

Renfrew – *R. of Kaimsthorn**

Renton – *R. of Mount Harry**

Renwick – *R. of Clifton**

Rhys – *Dynevor*

Richards – *Milverton*

Richardson – *R. of Calow**

Richardson – *R. of Duntisbourne**

Ritchie – *R. of Dundee*

Roberts – *Clwyd*

Roberts – *R. of Conway**

Roberts – *R. of Llandudno**

Robertson – *R. of Oakridge*

Robertson – *R. of Port Ellen**

Robertson – *Wharton*

Robinson – *Martonmere*

Roche – *Fermoy*

Rodd – *Rennell*

Rodger – *R. of Earlsferry**

Rodgers – *R. of Quarry Bank**

Rogers – *R. of Riverside**

Roper-Curzon – *Teynham*

Rospigliosi – *Newburgh, E.*

Rous – *Stradbroke, E.*

Rowley-Conwy – *Langford*

Royall – *R. of Blaisdon**

Runciman – *R. of Doxford, V.*

Russell – *Ampthill*

Russell – *Bedford, D.*

Russell – *de Clifford*

Russell – *R. of Liverpool*

Ryder – *Harrowby, E.*

Ryder – *R. of Wensum**

Sackville – *De La Warr, E.*

Sackville-West – *Sackville*

Sainsbury – *S. of Preston Candover**

Sainsbury – *S. of Turville**

St Aubyn – *St Levan*

St Clair – *Sinclair*

St Clair-Erskine – *Rosslyn, E.*

St John – *Bolingbroke and St John, V.*

St John – *St John of Blesto*

St John-Stevas – *St John of Fawsley**

St Leger – *Doneraile, V.*

Samuel – *Bearsted, V.*

Sanderson – *S. of Ayot*

Sanderson – *S. of Bowden**

Sandilands – *Torphichen*

Saumarez – *De Saumarez*

Savile – *Mexborough, E.*

Saville – *S. of Newdigate**

Scarlett – *Abinger*

Schreiber – *Marlesford**

Sclater-Booth – *Basing*

Scotland – *S. of Asthal**

Scott – *Eldon, E*

Scott – *S. of Foscotte**

Scott – *S. of Needham Market**.*

Scrymgeour – *Dundee, E.*

Seager – *Leighton of St Mellons*

Seely – *Mottistone*

Seymour – *Hertford, M.*

Seymour – *Somerset, D.*

Sharp – *S. of Guildford**

Shaw – *Craigmyle*
Shaw – *S. of Northstead**
Shephard – *S. of Northwood**
Sheppard – *S. of Didgemere**
Shirley – *Ferrers, E.*
Short – *Glenamara**
Shutt – *S. of Greetland**
Siddeley – *Kenilworth*
Sidney – *De L'Isle, V.*
Simon – *S. of Highbury**
Simon – *S. of Wythenshawe*
Simpson – *S. of Dunkeld**
Sinclair – *Caithness, E.*
Sinclair – *S. of Cleeve*
Sinclair – *Thurso, V.*
Skeffington – *Massereene, V.*
Slynn – *S. of Hadley**
Smith – *Bicester*
Smith – *Hambleden, V.*
Smith – *Kirkhill**
Smith – *S. of Clifton**
Smith – *Smith of Finsbury**
Smith – *S. of Gilmorehill**
Smith – *S. of Leigh**
Somerset – *Beaufort, D.*
Somerset – *Raglan*
Soulsby – *S. of Swaffham Prior**
Spencer – *Churchill, V.*
Spencer-Churchill – *Marlborough, D.*
Spring Rice – *Monteagle of Brandon*
Stanhope – *Harrington, E.*
Stanley – *Derby, E.*
Stanley – *of Alderley and Sheffield*
Stapleton-Cotton – *Combermere, V.*
Steel – *S. of Aikwood**
Sterling – *S. of Plaistow**
Stevens – *S. of Kirkwhelpington**
Stevens – *S. of Ludgate**
Stevenson – *S. of Coddenham**
Stewart – *Galloway, E.*

Stewart – *Stewartby**
Stoddart – *S. of Swindon**
Stone – *S. of Blackheath**
Stonor – *Camoys*
Stopford – *Courtown, E.*
Stourton – *Mowbray*
Strachey – *O'Hagan*
Strutt – *Belper*
Strutt – *Rayleigh*
Stuart – *Castle Stewart, E.*
Stuart – *Moray, E.*
Stuart – *S. of Findhorn, V.*
Suenson-Taylor – *Grantchester*
Sutherland – *S. of Houndwood**
Symons – *S. of Vernham Dean**
Taylor – *Kilclooney**
Taylor – *T. of Blackburn**
Taylor – *T. of Bolton**
Taylor – *T. of Holbeach**
Taylor – *T. of Warwick**
Taylour – *Headfort, M.*
Temple-Gore-Langton – *Temple of Stowe, E*
Temple-Morris – *Temple-Morris of Llandaff**
Tennant – *Glenconner*
Thellusson – *Rendlesham*
Thesiger – *Chelmsford, V.*
Thomas – *T. of Gresford**
Thomas – *T. of Gwydir**
Thomas – *T. of Macclesfield**
Thomas – *T. of Swynnerton**
Thomas – *T. of Walliswood**
Thomas – *T. of Winchester**
Thomson – *T. of Fleet*
Thomson – *T. of Monifieth**
Thynn – *Bath, M.*
Tottenham – *Ely, M.*
Trefusis – *Clinton*
Trench – *Ashtown*
Tufton – *Hothfield*

Turner – *Bilston**
Turner – *Netherthorpe*
Turner – *T. of Camden**
Turner – *T. of Ecchinswell**
Turnour – *Winterton, E.*
Tyrell-Kenyon – *Kenyon*
Vanden-Bempde-Johnstone – *Derwent*
Vane – *Barnard*
Vane-Tempest-Stewart – *Londonderry, M.*
Vanneck – *Huntingfield*
Vaughan – *Lisburne, E.*
Vereker – *Gort, V.*
Verney – *Willoughby de Broke*
Vernon – *Lyveden*
Vesey – *De Vesci, V.*
Villiers – *Clarendon, E.*
Vincent – *V. of Coleshill**
Vivian – *Swansea*
Wade – *W. of Chorlton**
Waldegrave – *W. of North Hill**
Walker – *W. of Aldringham**
Walker – *W. of Gestingthorpe**
Walker – *W. of Worcester**
Wall – *W. of New Barnett**
Wallace – *Dudley*
Wallace – *W. of Saltaire**
Wallace – *W. of Tummel**
Wallop – *Portsmouth, E.*
Walton – *W. of Detchant**
Ward – *Bangor, V.*
Ward – *Dudley, E.*
Warrender – *Bruntisfield*
Warwick – *W. of Undercliffe**
Watson – *W. of Invergowrie**
Watson – *Manton*
Watson – *W. of Richmond**
Webber – *Lloyd-Webber**
Wedderburn – *W. of Charlton**
Weir – *Inverforth*
Weld-Forester – *Forester*

Wellesley – *Cowley, E.*
Wellesley – *Wellington, D.*
West – *W. of Spithead**
Westenra – *Rossmore*
White – *Annaly*
White – *Hanningfield**
Whiteley – *Marchamley*
Whitfield – *Kenswood*
Williams – *W. of Crosby**
Williams – *W. of Elvel**
Williamson – *Forres*
Williamson – *W. of Horton**
Willoughby – *Middleton*
Wills – *Dulverton*
Wilson – *Moran*
Wilson – *Nunburnholme*
Wilson – *W. of Dinton**
Wilson – *W. of Tillyorn**
Windsor – *Gloucester, D.*
Windsor – *Kent, D.*
Windsor-Clive – *Plymouth, E.*
Wingfield – *Powerscourt, V.*
Winn – *St Oswald*
Wodehouse – *Kimberley, E.*
Wolfson – *W. of Sunningdale**
Wood – *Halifax, E.*
Woodhouse – *Terrington*
Woolmer – *W. of Leeds**
Wright – *W. of Richmond**
Wyndham – *Egremont and Leconfield*
Wyndham-Quin – *Dunraven, E.*
Wynn – *Newborough*
Yarde-Buller – *Churston*
Yerburgh – *Alvingham*
Yorke – *Hardwicke, E.*
Young – *Kennet*
Young – *Y. of Graffham**
Young – *Y. of Hornsey**
Young – *Y. of Norwood Green**
Younger – *Y. of Leckie, V.*

ORDERS OF CHIVALRY

THE MOST NOBLE ORDER OF THE GARTER (1348)

KG
Ribbon, Blue
Motto, Honi soit qui mal y pense
(Shame on him who thinks evil of it)

The number of Knights and Lady Companions is limited to 24

SOVEREIGN OF THE ORDER
The Queen

LADIES OF THE ORDER
HRH The Princess Royal, 1994
HRH Princess Alexandra, The Hon. Lady Ogilvy, 2003

ROYAL KNIGHTS
HRH The Prince Philip, Duke of Edinburgh, 1947
HRH The Prince of Wales, 1958
HRH The Duke of Kent, 1985
HRH The Duke of Gloucester, 1997
HRH The Duke of York, 2006
HRH The Earl of Wessex, 2006

EXTRA KNIGHT COMPANIONS AND LADIES
Grand Duke Jean of Luxembourg, 1972
HM The Queen of Denmark, 1979
HM The King of Sweden, 1983
HM The King of Spain, 1988
HM The Queen of the Netherlands, 1989
HIM The Emperor of Japan, 1998
HM The King of Norway, 2001

KNIGHTS AND LADY COMPANIONS
Duke of Grafton, 1976
Lord Richardson of Duntisbourne, 1983
Lord Carrington, 1985
Duke of Wellington, 1990
Lord Bramall, 1990
Viscount Ridley, 1992
Lord Sainsbury of Preston Candover, 1992
Lord Ashburton, 1994
Lord Kingsdown, 1994
Sir Ninian Stephen, 1994
Baroness Thatcher, 1995
Sir Edmund Hillary, 1995
Sir Timothy Colman, 1996
Duke of Abercorn, 1999
Sir William Gladstone, 1999
Lord Inge, 2001
Sir Anthony Acland, 2001

Duke of Westminster, 2003
Lord Butler of Brockwell, 2003
Lord Morris of Aberavon, 2003
Lady Soames, 2005
Lord Bingham of Cornhill, 2005
Sir John Major, 2005

Prelate, Bishop of Winchester
Chancellor, Lord Carrington, KG, GCMG, CH, MC
Register, Dean of Windsor
Garter King of Arms, Peter Gwynn-Jones, CVO
Gentleman Usher of the Black Rod, Lt.-Gen. Sir Michael Willcocks, KCB
Secretary, P. L. Dickinson, LVO

THE MOST ANCIENT AND MOST NOBLE ORDER OF THE THISTLE (REVIVED 1687)

KT
Ribbon, Green
Motto, Nemo me impune lacessit
(No one provokes me with impunity)

The number of Knights and Ladies of the Thistle is limited to 16

SOVEREIGN OF THE ORDER
The Queen

ROYAL LADY OF THE ORDER
HRH The Princess Royal, 2000

ROYAL KNIGHTS
HRH The Prince Philip, Duke of Edinburgh, 1952
HRH The Prince of Wales, Duke of Rothesay, 1977

KNIGHTS AND LADIES
Earl of Wemyss and March, 1966
Duke of Buccleuch and Queensberry, 1978
Earl of Elgin and Kincardine, 1981
Lord Thomson of Monifieth, 1981
Earl of Airlie, 1985
Viscount of Arbuthnott, 1996
Earl of Crawford and Balcarres, 1996
Lady Marion Fraser, 1996
Lord Macfarlane of Bearsden, 1996
Lord Mackay of Clashfern, 1997
Lord Wilson of Tillyorn, 2000
Lord Sutherland of Houndwood, 2002

Sir Eric Anderson, 2002
Lord Steel of Aikwood, 2004
Lord Robertson of Port Ellen, 2004

Chancellor, Duke of Buccleuch and Queensberry, KT, VRD
Dean, Very Revd Gilleasbuig Macmillan, CVO
Secretary and Lord Lyon King of Arms, Robin Blair, LVO, WS
Gentleman Usher of the Green Rod, Rear-Adm. Christopher Layman, CB, DSO, LVO

THE MOST HONOURABLE ORDER OF THE BATH (1725)

GCB *Military* GCB *Civil*

GCB   Knight (or Dame) Grand Cross
KCB   Knight Commander
DCB   Dame Commander
CB   Companion

Ribbon, Crimson
Motto, Tria juncta in uno
(Three joined in one)

Remodelled 1815, and enlarged many times since. The order is divided into civil and military divisions. Women became eligible for the order from 1 January 1971.

THE SOVEREIGN

GREAT MASTER AND FIRST OR PRINCIPAL KNIGHT GRAND CROSS
HRH The Prince of Wales, KG, KT, GCB, OM

Dean of the Order, Dean of Westminster
Bath King of Arms, Gen. Sir Brian Kenny, GCB, CBE
Registrar and Secretary, Rear-Adm. Iain Henderson, CB, CBE
Genealogist, Peter Gwynn-Jones, CVO
Gentleman Usher of the Scarlet Rod, Maj.-Gen. Charles Vyvyan, CB, CBE
Deputy Secretary, Secretary of the Central Chancery of the Orders of Knighthood

Chancery, Central Chancery of the
Orders of Knighthood, St James's
Palace, London SW1A 1BH

THE ORDER OF MERIT (1902)

OM *Military*   OM *Civil*

OM
Ribbon, Blue and crimson

This order is designed as a special distinction for eminent men and women without conferring a knighthood upon them. The order is limited in numbers to 24, with the addition of foreign honorary members.

THE SOVEREIGN

HRH The Prince Philip, Duke of
Edinburgh, 1968
Revd Prof. Owen Chadwick, KBE,
1983
Sir Andrew Huxley, 1983
Dr Frederick Sanger, 1986
Baroness Thatcher, 1990
Dame Joan Sutherland, 1991
Sir Michael Atiyah, 1992
Lucian Freud, 1993
Sir Aaron Klug, 1995
Lord Foster of Thames Bank, 1997
Sir Denis Rooke, 1997
Sir James Black, 2000
Sir Anthony Caro, 2000
Prof. Sir Roger Penrose, 2000
Sir Tom Stoppard, 2000
HRH The Prince of Wales, 2002
Lord May of Oxford, 2002
Lord Rothschild, 2002
Sir David Attenborough, 2005
Baroness Boothroyd, 2005
Sir Michael Howard, 2005
Sir Timothy Berners-Lee, KBE, 2007
Lord Eames, 2007
Lord Rees of Ludlow, 2007

Honorary Member, Nelson Mandela,
1995

Secretary and Registrar, Lord Fellowes,
GCB, GCVO, PC, QSO
Chancery, Central Chancery of the
Orders of Knighthood, St James's
Palace, London SW1A 1BH

THE MOST DISTINGUISHED ORDER OF ST MICHAEL AND ST GEORGE (1818)

GCMG   KCMG

GCMG   Knight (or Dame)
        Grand Cross
KCMG   Knight Commander
DCMG   Dame Commander
CMG   Companion

Ribbon, Saxon blue, with scarlet centre
Motto, Auspicium melioris aevi
(Token of a better age)

THE SOVEREIGN

GRAND MASTER
HRH The Duke of Kent, KG,
GCMG, GCVO, ADC

Prelate, Rt. Revd David Urquhart
Chancellor, Sir Christopher Mallaby,
GCMG, GCVO
Secretary, Permanent Under-Secretary
of State at the Foreign and
Commonwealth Office and Head
of the Diplomatic Service
Registrar, Lord Wilson of Tillyorn,
KT, GCMG
King of Arms, Sir Ewen Fergusson,
GCMG, GCVO
Gentleman Usher of the Blue Rod, Sir
Anthony Figgis, KCVO, CMG
Dean, Dean of St Paul's
Deputy Secretary, Secretary of the
Central Chancery of the Orders of
Knighthood
Chancery, Central Chancery of the
Orders of Knighthood, St James's
Palace, London SW1A 1BH

THE MOST EMINENT ORDER OF THE INDIAN EMPIRE (1878)

GCIE   Knight Grand Commander
KCIE   Knight Commander
CIE   Companion

Ribbon, Imperial purple
Motto, Imperatricis auspiciis *(Under
the auspices of the Empress)*

THE SOVEREIGN

Registrar, Secretary of the Central
Chancery of the Orders of
Knighthood
No conferments have been made
since 1947

HH Maharaja Shriraj Sahib of
Halvad Dhrangadhara, 1947

THE IMPERIAL ORDER OF THE CROWN OF INDIA (1877) FOR LADIES

CI

Badge, the royal cipher of Queen Victoria in jewels within an oval, surmounted by an heraldic crown and attached to a bow of light blue watered ribbon, edged white

The honour does not confer any rank or title upon the recipient

No conferments have been made since 1947

HM The Queen, 1947

THE ROYAL VICTORIAN ORDER (1896)

GCVO   KCVO

GCVO   Knight or Dame Grand
        Cross
KCVO   Knight Commander
DCVO   Dame Commander
CVO   Commander
LVO   Lieutenant
MVO   Member

Ribbon, Blue, with red and white edges
Motto, Victoria

THE SOVEREIGN
GRAND MASTER
HRH The Princess Royal

Chancellor, Lord Chamberlain
Secretary, Keeper of the Privy Purse
Registrar, Secretary of the
Central Chancery of the Orders of
Knighthood
Chaplain, Chaplain of the Queen's
Chapel of the Savoy
Hon. Genealogist, D. H. B. Chesshyre,
CVO

THE MOST EXCELLENT ORDER OF THE BRITISH EMPIRE (1917)

GBE   KBE

The order was divided into military and civil divisions in December 1918

GBE   Knight or Dame Grand Cross
KBE   Knight Commander
DBE   Dame Commander
CBE   Commander
OBE   Officer
MBE   Member

Ribbon, Rose pink edged with pearl grey with vertical pearl stripe in centre (military division); without vertical pearl stripe (civil division)
Motto, For God and the Empire

THE SOVEREIGN

GRAND MASTER
HRH The Prince Philip, Duke of Edinburgh, KG, KT, OM, GBE, PC

Prelate, Bishop of London
King of Arms, Air Chief Marshal Sir Patrick Hine, GCB, GBE
Registrar, Secretary of the Central Chancery of the Orders of Knighthood
Secretary, Secretary of the Cabinet and Head of the Home Civil Service
Dean, Dean of St Paul's
Gentleman Usher of the Purple Rod, Sir Alexander Michael Graham, GBE, DCL
Chancery, Central Chancery of the Orders of Knighthood, St James's Palace, London SW1A 1BH

ORDER OF THE COMPANIONS OF HONOUR (1917)

CH

Ribbon, Carmine, with gold edges
This order consists of one class only and carries with it no title. The number of awards is limited to 65 (excluding honorary members).

Anthony, Rt. Hon. John, 1981
Ashley of Stoke, Lord, 1975
Attenborough, Sir David, 1995
Baker, Dame Janet, 1993
Baker of Dorking, Lord, 1992
Birtwistle, Sir Harrison, 2000
Brenner, Sydney, 1986
Brook, Peter, 1998
Brooke of Sutton Mandeville, Lord, 1992
Carrington, Lord, 1983
Christie, Sir George, 2001
Davis, Sir Colin, 2001
De Chastelain, Gen. John, 1999
Dench, Dame Judi, 2005
Fraser, Rt. Hon. Malcolm, 1977
Freud, Lucian, 1983
Glenamara, Lord, 1976
Hamilton, Richard, 1999
Hannay of Chiswick, Lord, 2003
Hawking, Prof. Stephen, 1989
Healey, Lord, 1979
Heseltine, Lord, 1997
Hobsbawm, Prof. Eric, 1998
Hockney, David, 1997
Hodgkin, Sir Howard, 2002
Howard, Sir Michael, 2002
Howe of Aberavon, Lord, 1996
Hurd of Westwell, Lord, 1995
Jones, James, 1977
King of Bridgewater, Lord, 1992
Lessing, Doris, 1999
Lovelock, Prof. James, 2002
McKenzie, Prof. Dan Peter, 2003
MacKerras, Sir Charles, 2003
Mahon, Sir Denis, 2002
Major, Rt. Hon. Sir John, 1998
Owen, Lord, 1994
Patten, Rt. Hon. Lord, 1997
Pawson, Prof. Anthony James, 2006
Pinter, Harold, 2002
Riley, Bridget, 1998
Sanger, Dr. Frederick, 1981
Scofield, Paul, 2000
Somare, Rt. Hon. Sir Michael, 1978
Talboys, Rt. Hon. Sir Brian, 1981
Tebbit, Lord, 1987
Varah, Revd Dr Chad, 1999

Honorary Members, Lee Kuan Yew, 1970; Prof. Amartya Sen, 2000; Bernard Haitink, 2002
Secretary and Registrar, Secretary of the Central Chancery of the Orders of Knighthood

THE DISTINGUISHED SERVICE ORDER (1886)

DSO

Ribbon, Red, with blue edges

Bestowed in recognition of especial services in action of commissioned officers in the Navy, Army and Royal Air Force and (since 1942) Mercantile Marine. The members are Companions only. A bar may be awarded for any additional act of service.

THE IMPERIAL SERVICE ORDER (1902)

ISO

Ribbon, Crimson, with blue centre

Appointment as companion of this order is open to members of the civil services whose eligibility is determined by the grade they hold. The order consists of the sovereign and companions to a number not exceeding 1,900, of whom 1,300 may belong to the home civil services and 600 to overseas civil services. The then prime minister announced in March 1993 that he would make no further recommendations for appointments to the order.

Secretary, Secretary of the Cabinet and Head of the Home Civil Service
Registrar, Secretary of the Central Chancery of the Orders of Knighthood

THE ROYAL VICTORIAN CHAIN (1902)

It confers no precedence on its holders

HM THE QUEEN

HM The King of Thailand, 1960
HM The King of Denmark, 1974
HM The King of Sweden, 1975
HM The Queen of the Netherlands, 1982
Gen. Antonio Eanes, 1985
HM The King of Spain, 1986
Dr Richard von Weizsäcker, 1992
HM The King of Norway, 1994
Earl of Airlie, 1997
Rt. Revd and Rt. Hon. Lord Carey of Clifton, 2002

BARONETAGE AND KNIGHTAGE

BARONETS

Style, 'Sir' before forename and surname, followed by 'Bt'.
Envelope, Sir F_ S_, Bt. *Letter (formal)*, Dear Sir; *(social)*, Dear Sir F_. *Spoken*, Sir F_
Wife's style, 'Lady' followed by surname
Envelope, Lady S_. *Letter (formal)*, Dear Madam; *(social)*, Dear Lady S_. *Spoken*, Lady S_
Style of Baronetess, 'Dame' before forename and surname, followed by 'Btss.' (*see also* Dames)

There are five different creations of baronetcies: Baronets of England (creations dating from 1611); Baronets of Ireland (creations dating from 1619); Baronets of Scotland or Nova Scotia (creations dating from 1625); Baronets of Great Britain (creations after the Act of Union 1707 which combined the kingdoms of England and Scotland); and Baronets of the United Kingdom (creations after the union of Great Britain and Ireland in 1801).

Badge of Baronets of the United Kingdom   *Badge of Baronets of Nova Scotia*

Badge of Ulster

The patent of creation limits the destination of a baronetcy, usually to male descendants of the first baronet, although special remainders allow the baronetcy to pass, if the male issue of sons fail, to the male issue of daughters of the first baronet. In the case of baronetcies of Scotland or Nova Scotia, a special remainder of 'heirs male and of tailzie' allows the baronetcy to descend to heirs general, including women. There are four existing Scottish baronets with such a remainder.

The Official Roll of the Baronetage is kept at the Crown Office and maintained by the Registrar and Assistant Registrar of the Baronetage. Anyone who considers that he or she is entitled to be entered on the roll may apply through the Crown Office to prove their succession. Every person succeeding to a baronetcy must exhibit proofs of succession to the Lord Chancellor. A person whose name is not entered on the official roll will not be addressed or mentioned by the title of baronet or baronetess in any official document, nor will he or she be accorded precedence as a baronet of baronetess.

BARONETCIES EXTINCT SINCE THE LAST EDITION
Echlin (cr. (I.) 1721); Prince-Smith (cr. 1911); Warren (cr.1784)

OFFICIAL ROLL OF THE BARONETAGE, Crown Office, House of Lords, London SW1A 0PW T 020-7219 2632
Registrar, Ian Denyer, MVO
Assistant Registrar, Grant Bavister

KNIGHTS

Style, 'Sir' before forename and surname, followed by appropriate post-nominal initials if a Knight Grand Cross, Knight Grand Commander or Knight Commander
Envelope, Sir F_ S_. *Letter (formal)*, Dear Sir; *(social)*, Dear Sir F_. *Spoken*, Sir F_
Wife's style, 'Lady' followed by surname
Envelope, Lady S_. *Letter (formal)*, Dear Madam; *(social)*, Dear Lady S_. *Spoken*, Lady S_

The prefix 'Sir' is not used by knights who are clerics of the Church of England, who do not receive the accolade. Their wives are entitled to precedence as the wife of a knight but not to the style of 'Lady'.

ORDERS OF KNIGHTHOOD
Knight Grand Cross, Knight Grand Commander, and Knight Commander are the higher classes of the Orders of Chivalry (*see* Orders of Chivalry). Honorary knighthoods of these orders may be conferred on men who are citizens of countries of which the Queen is not head of state. As a rule, the prefix 'Sir' is not used by honorary knights.

KNIGHTS BACHELOR

The Knights Bachelor do not constitute a royal order, but comprise the surviving representation of the ancient state orders of knighthood. The Register of Knights Bachelor, instituted by James I in the 17th century, lapsed, and in 1908 a voluntary association under the title of the Society of Knights (now the Imperial Society of Knights Bachelor) was formed with the primary objectives of continuing the various registers dating from 1257 and obtaining the uniform registration of every created Knight Bachelor. In 1926 a design for a badge to be worn by Knights Bachelor was approved and adopted; in 1974 a neck badge and miniature were added.

THE IMPERIAL SOCIETY OF KNIGHTS BACHELOR, 1 Throgmorton Avenue, London EC2N 2BY
Knight Principal, Sir Robert Balchin
Prelate, Rt. Revd and Rt. Hon. Bishop of London
Registrar, Sir Paul Judge
Hon. Treasurer, Sir Colin Berry
Clerk to the Council, Richard Jenkins, LVO, TD

LIST OF BARONETS AND KNIGHTS

as at 31 August 2007

†	Not registered on the Official Roll of the Baronetage at the time of going to press
()	The date of creation of the baronetcy is given in parentheses
I	Baronet of Ireland
NS	Baronet of Nova Scotia
S	Baronet of Scotland

A full entry in italic type indicates that the recipient of a knighthood died during the year in which the honour was conferred. The name is included for purposes of record. Peers are not included in this list.

Aaronson, Sir Michael John, Kt., CBE

Abbott, *Adm.* Sir Peter Charles, GBE, KCB

Abdy, Sir Valentine Robert Duff, Bt. (1850)

Acheson, *Prof.* Sir (Ernest) Donald, KBE

Ackers, Sir James George, Kt.

Ackers-Jones, Sir David, KBE, CMG

Ackroyd, Sir Timothy Robert Whyte, Bt. (1956)

Acland, Sir Antony Arthur, KG, GCMG, GCVO

Acland, *Lt.-Col.* Sir (Christopher) Guy (Dyke), Bt. (1890), MVO

Acland, Sir John Dyke, Bt. (1644)

Adam, Sir Christopher Eric Forbes, Bt. (1917)

Adam, Sir Kenneth Hugo, Kt., OBE

Adams, Sir William James, KCMG

Adsetts, Sir William Norman, Kt., OBE

Adye, Sir John Anthony, KCMG

Aga Khan IV, HH Prince Karim, KBE

Agnew, Sir Crispin Hamlyn, Bt. (S. 1629)

Agnew, Sir John Keith, Bt. (1895)

Agnew, Sir Rudolph Ion Joseph, Kt.

Agnew-Somerville, Sir Quentin Charles Somerville, Bt. (1957)

Ah Koy, Sir James Michael, KBE

Aikens, *Hon.* Sir Richard John Pearson, Kt.

†Ainsworth, Sir Anthony Thomas Hugh, Bt. (1916)

Aird, *Capt.* Sir Alastair Sturgis, GCVO

Aird, Sir (George) John, Bt. (1901)

Airy, *Maj.-Gen.* Sir Christopher John, KCVO, CBE

Aitchison, Sir Charles Walter de Lancey, Bt. (1938)

Ajegbo, Sir Keith Onyema, Kt., OBE

Alberti, *Prof.* Sir Kurt George Matthew Mayer, Kt.

Albu, Sir George, Bt. (1912)

Alcock, *Air Chief Marshal* Sir (Robert James) Michael, GCB, KBE

Aldous, *Rt. Hon.* Sir William, Kt.

Alexander, Sir Charles Gundry, Bt. (1945)

Alexander, Sir Douglas, Bt. (1921)

Allen, *Prof.* Sir Geoffrey, Kt., PHD, FRS

Allen, Sir John Derek, Kt., CBE

Allen, Sir Mark John Spurgeon, Kt., CMG

Allen, *Hon.* Sir Peter Austin Philip Jermyn, Kt.

Allen, Sir Thomas Boaz, Kt., CBE

Allen, *Hon.* Sir William Clifford, KCMG

Allen, Sir William Guilford, Kt.

Alleyne, Sir George Allanmoore Ogarren, Kt.

Alleyne, *Revd* John Olpherts Campbell, Bt. (1769)

Allinson, Sir (Walter) Leonard, KCVO, CMG

Alliott, *Hon.* Sir John Downes, Kt.

Allison, *Air Chief Marshal* Sir John Shakespeare, KCB, CBE

Alun-Jones, Sir (John) Derek, Kt.

Ambo, *Rt. Revd* George, KBE

Amet, *Hon.* Sir Arnold Karibone, Kt.

Amory, Sir Ian Heathcoat, Bt. (1874)

Anderson, Sir John Anthony, KBE

Anderson, *Maj.-Gen.* Sir John Evelyn, KBE

Anderson, Sir Leith Reinsford Steven, Kt., CBE

Anderson, *Vice-Adm.* Sir Neil Dudley, KBE, CB

Anderson, *Prof.* Sir Roy Malcolm, Kt.

Anderson, Sir (William) Eric Kinloch, KT.

Anderson, *Prof.* Sir (William) Ferguson, Kt., OBE

Anderton, Sir (Cyril) James, Kt., CBE, QPM

Andrew, Sir Robert John, KCB

Andrews, Sir Derek Henry, KCB, CBE

Andrews, Sir Ian Charles Franklin, Kt., CBE, TD

Angus, Sir Michael Richardson, Kt.

Annesley, Sir Hugh Norman, Kt., QPM

Anson, *Vice-Adm.* Sir Edward Rosebery, KCB

Anson, Sir John, KCB

Anson, *Rear-Adm.* Sir Peter, Bt. CB (1831)

†Anstruther, Sir Sebastian Paten Campbell, Bt. (S. 1694)

†Anstruther, Sir Tobias Alexander Campbell, Bt. (1798)

Anstruther-Gough-Calthorpe, Sir Euan Hamilton, Bt. (1929)

Antrobus, Sir Edward Philip, Bt. (1815)

Appleyard, Sir Leonard Vincent, KCMG

Appleyard, Sir Raymond Kenelm, KBE

Arbib, Sir Martyn, Kt.

Arbuthnot, Sir Keith Robert Charles, Bt. (1823)

Arbuthnot, Sir William Reierson, Bt. (1964)

Arbuthnott, *Prof.* Sir John Peebles, Kt., PHD, FRSE

Archdale, *Capt.* Sir Edward Folmer, Bt. (1928), DSC, RN

Arculus, Sir Ronald, KCMG, KCVO

Arculus, Sir Thomas David Guy, Kt.

Armitage, *Air Chief Marshal* Sir Michael John, KCB, CBE

Armour, *Prof.* Sir James, Kt., CBE

Armstrong, Sir Christopher John Edmund Stuart, Bt. (1841), MBE

Armstrong, Sir Patrick John, Kt., CBE

Armstrong, Sir Richard, Kt., CBE

Armytage, Sir John Martin, Bt. (1738)

Arnold, Sir Thomas Richard, Kt.

Arnott, Sir Alexander John Maxwell, Bt. (1896)

Arrindell, Sir Clement Athelston, GCMG, GCVO, QC

Arthur, Sir Gavyn Farr, Kt.

Arthur, *Lt.-Gen.* Sir (John) Norman Stewart, KCB

Arthur, Sir Michael Anthony, KCMG

Arthur, Sir Stephen John, Bt. (1841)

Asbridge, Sir Jonathan Elliott, Kt.

Ash, *Prof.* Sir Eric Albert, Kt., CBE, FRS, FRENG

Ashburnham, Sir James Fleetwood, Bt. (1661)

Ashley, Sir Bernard Albert, Kt.

Ashmore, *Admiral of the Fleet* Sir Edward Beckwith, GCB, DSC

Aske, Sir Robert John Bingham, Bt. (1922)

Askew, Sir Bryan, Kt.

Asscher, Prof. Sir (Adolf) William, Kt., MD, FRCP

Astill, *Hon.* Sir Michael John, Kt.

Astley-Cooper, Sir Alexander Paston, Bt. (1821)

Aston, Sir Harold George, Kt., CBE

Astwood, *Hon.* Sir James Rufus, KBE

Atcherley, Sir Harold Winter, Kt.

Atiyah, Sir Michael Francis, Kt., OM, PHD, FRS

Atkins, *Rt. Hon.* Sir Robert James, Kt.

Atkinson, *Prof.* Sir Anthony Barnes, Kt.

Atkinson, *Air Marshal* Sir David William, KBE

Atkinson, Sir Frederick John, KCB

Atkinson, Sir John Alexander, KCB, DFC

Atkinson, Sir Robert, Kt., DSC, FRENG

Atopare, Sir Sailas, GCMG

Attenborough, Sir David Frederick, Kt., OM, CH, CVO, CBE, FRS

Aubrey-Fletcher, Sir Henry Egerton, Bt. (1782)

Audland, Sir Christopher John, KCMG

Audley, Sir George Bernard, Kt.

Augier, *Prof.* Sir Fitz-Roy Richard, Kt.

Auld, *Rt. Hon.* Sir Robin Ernest, Kt.

Austin, Sir Anthony Leonard, Bt. (1894)

Austin, *Air Marshal* Sir Roger Mark, KCB, AFC

Austen-Smith, *Air Marshal* Sir Roy David, KBE, CB, CVO, DFC

Avei, Sir Moi, KBE

Axford, Sir William Ian, Kt.

Ayckbourn, Sir Alan, Kt., CBE

Aykroyd, Sir James Alexander Frederic, Bt. (1929)

†Aykroyd, Sir Michael David, Bt. (1920)

Aylmer, Sir Richard John, Bt. (I. 1622)

Aynsley-Green, *Prof.* Sir Albert, Kt.

Bacha, Sir Bhinod, Kt., CMG

Backhouse, Sir Jonathan Roger, Bt. (1901)

Bacon, Sir Nicholas Hickman Ponsonby, Bt. (1611 and 1627), *Premier Baronet of England*

Bacon, Sir Sidney Charles, Kt., CB, FRENG.

Baddeley, Sir John Wolsey Beresford, Bt. (1922)

Baddiley, *Prof.* Sir James, Kt., PHD, FRS, FRSE

Badge, Sir Peter Gilmour Noto, Kt.

Baer, Sir Jack Mervyn Frank, Kt.

Bagge, Sir (John) Jeremy Picton, Bt. (1867)

Bagnall, *Air Chief Marshal* Sir Anthony, GBE, KCB

Bailey, Sir Alan Marshall, KCB

Bailey, Sir Brian Harry, Kt., OBE

Bailey, Sir Derrick Thomas Louis, Bt. (1919), DFC

Bailey, Sir John Bilsland, KCB

Bailey, *Rt. Revd* Jonathan Sansbury, KCVO

Bailey, Sir Richard John, Kt., CBE

Bailey, Sir Stanley Ernest, Kt., CBE, QPM

Bailhache, Sir Philip Martin, Kt.

Baillie, Sir Adrian Louis, Bt. (1823)

Bain, *Prof.* Sir George Sayers, Kt.

Baird, Sir Charles William Stuart, Bt. (1809)

†Baird, Sir James Andrew Gardiner, Bt. (S. 1695)

Baird, *Air Marshal* Sir John Alexander, KBE

Baird, *Vice-Adm.* Sir Thomas Henry Eustace, KCB

Bairsto, *Air Marshal* Sir Peter Edward, KBE, CB

Baker, Sir Bryan William, Kt.

Baker, *Prof.* Sir John Hamilton, Kt., QC

Baker, Sir John William, Kt., CBE

Baker, *Rt. Hon.* Sir (Thomas) Scott (Gillespie), Kt.

Balchin, Sir Robert George Alexander, Kt.

Balderstone, Sir James Schofield, Kt.

Baldwin, *Prof.* Sir Jack Edward, Kt., FRS

Baldwin, Sir Peter Robert, KCB

Ball, *Air Marshal* Sir Alfred Henry Wynne, KCB, DSO, DFC

Ball, Sir Christopher John Elinger, Kt.

Ball, *Prof.* Sir John Macleod, Kt.

Ball, Sir Richard Bentley, Bt. (1911)

Ball, *Prof.* Sir Robert James, Kt., PHD

Ballantyne, *Dr* Sir Frederick Nathaniel, GCMG

Bamford, Sir Anthony Paul, Kt.

Band, *Adm.* Sir Jonathon, KCB

Banham, Sir John Michael Middlecott, Kt.

Bannerman, Sir David Gordon, Bt., OBE (S. 1682)

Bannister, Sir Roger Gilbert, Kt., CBE, DM, FRCP

Barber, Sir Michael Bayldon, Kt.

Barber, Sir (Thomas) David, Bt. (1960)

Barbour, *Very Revd* Robert Alexander Stewart, KCVO, MC

Barclay, Sir Colville Herbert Sanford, Bt. (S. 1668)

Barclay, Sir David Rowat, Kt.

Barclay, Sir Frederick Hugh, Kt.

Barclay, Sir Peter Maurice, Kt., CBE

Barder, Sir Brian Leon, KCMG

Baring, Sir John Francis, Bt. (1911)

Barker, Sir Colin, Kt.

Barker, *Hon.* Sir (Richard) Ian, Kt.

Barker, Sir Christopher Hilaro, Bt. (1803)

Barlow, Sir Frank, Kt., CBE

Barlow, Sir (George) William, Kt., FRENG

Barlow, Sir James Alan, Bt. (1902)

Barlow, Sir John Kemp, Bt. (1907)

Barnard, Sir Joseph Brian, Kt.

Barnes, *The Most Revd.* Brian James, KBE

Barnes, Sir (James) David (Francis), Kt., CBE

Barnes, Sir Kenneth, KCB

Barnewall, Sir Reginald Robert, Bt. (I. 1623)

Baron, Sir Thomas, Kt., CBE

Barraclough, *Air Chief Marshal* Sir John, KCB, CBE, DFC, AFC

Barran, Sir John Napoleon Ruthven, Bt. (1895)

Barratt, Sir Lawrence Arthur, Kt.

Barratt, Sir Richard Stanley, Kt., CBE, QPM

Barrett, Sir Stephen Jeremy, KCMG

†Barrett-Lennard, Sir Richard Fynes, Bt. (1801)

Barrington, Sir Benjamin, Bt. (1831)

Barrington, Sir Nicholas John, KCMG, CVO

Barrington-Ward, *Rt. Revd* Simon, KCMG

Barron, Sir Donald James, Kt.

Barrow, *Capt.* Sir Richard John Uniacke, Bt. (1835)

Barry, Sir (Lawrence) Edward (Anthony Tress), Bt. (1899)

Barter, Sir Peter Leslie Charles, Kt., OBE

†Bartlett, Sir Andrew Alan, Bt. (1913)

Barttelot, *Col.* Sir Brian Walter de Stopham, Bt. (1875), OBE

Bate, Sir David Lindsay, KBE

†Bates, Sir James Geoffrey, Bt. (1880)

Bates, Sir Malcolm Rowland, Kt.

Bates, Sir Richard Dawson Hoult, Bt. (1937)

Bateson, *Prof.* Sir Patrick, Kt.

Batho, Sir Peter Ghislain, Bt. (1928)

Bathurst, *Admiral of the Fleet* Sir (David) Benjamin, GCB

Batten, Sir John Charles, KCVO

Battersby, *Prof.* Sir Alan Rushton, Kt., FRS

Battishill, Sir Anthony Michael William, GCB

Baxendell, Sir Peter Brian, Kt., CBE, FRENG

Bayly, *Prof.* Sir Christopher Alan, Kt.

Bayne, Sir Nicholas Peter, KCMG

Baynes, Sir Christopher Rory, Bt. (1801)

Bazley, Sir Thomas John Sebastian, Bt. (1869)

Beach, *Gen.* Sir (William Gerald) Hugh, GBE, KCB, MC

Beache, *Hon.* Sir Vincent Ian, KCMG

Beale, *Lt.-Gen.* Sir Peter John, KBE, FRCP

Beamish, Sir Adrian John, KCMG

Bean, *Hon.* Sir David Michael, Kt

Beaumont, *Capt.* the Hon. Sir (Edward) Nicholas (Canning), KCVO

Beaumont, Sir George (Howland Francis), Bt. (1661)

Beaumont, Sir Richard Ashton, KCMG, OBE

Beatson, *Hon.* Sir Jack, Kt.

Beavis, *Air Chief Marshal* Sir Michael Gordon, KCB, CBE, AFC

Beck, Sir Edgar Philip, Kt.

Beckett, Sir Richard Gervase, Bt. (1921), QC

Beckett, Sir Terence Norman, KBE, FRENG

Beckwith, Sir John Lionel, Kt., CBE

Bedser, Sir Alec Victor, Kt., CBE

Beecham, Sir Jeremy Hugh, Kt.

Beecham, Sir John Stratford Roland, Bt. (1914)

Beetham, *Marshal of the Royal Air Force* Sir Michael James, GCB, CBE, DFC, AFC

Beevor, Sir Thomas Agnew, Bt. (1784)

Beldam, *Rt. Hon.* Sir (Alexander) Roy (Asplan), Kt.

Belich, Sir James, Kt.

Bell, Sir Brian Ernest, KBE

Bell, Sir David Charles Maurice, Kt.

Bell, Sir John Lowthian, Bt. (1885)

Bell, *Prof.* Sir Peter Robert Frank, Kt.
Bell, *Hon.* Sir Rodger, Kt.
Bell, Sir Stuart, Kt.
Bellamy, *Hon.* Sir Christopher William, Kt.
Bellingham, Sir Anthony Edward Norman, Bt. (1796)
Bender, Sir Brian Geoffrey, KCB
Benn, Sir (James) Jonathan, Bt. (1914)
Bennett, *Air Vice-Marshal* Sir Erik Peter, KBE, CB
Bennett, *Hon.* Sir Hugh Peter Derwyn, Kt.
Bennett, *Gen.* Sir Phillip Harvey, KBE, DSO
Bennett, Sir Richard Rodney, Kt., CBE
Bennett, Sir Ronald Wilfrid Murdoch, Bt. (1929)
Benson, Sir Christopher John, Kt.
Benyon, Sir William Richard, Kt.
Beresford, Sir (Alexander) Paul, Kt.
Beresford-Peirse, Sir Henry Grant de la Poer, Bt. (1814)
Berghuser, *Hon.* Sir Eric, Kt., MBE
Beringer, *Prof.* Sir John Evelyn, Kt., CBE
Berman, Sir Franklin Delow, KCMG
Berners-Lee, Sir Timothy John, KBE, OM, FRS
Bernard, Sir Dallas Edmund, Bt. (1954)
Bernstein, Sir Howard, Kt.
Berney, Sir Julian Reedham Stuart, Bt. (1620)
Berridge, *Prof.* Sir Michael John, Kt., FRS
Berrill, Sir Kenneth Ernest, GBE, KCB
Berriman, Sir David, Kt.
Berry, *Prof.* Sir Colin Leonard, Kt., FRCPATH
Berry, *Prof.* Sir Michael Victor, Kt., FRS
Berthoud, Sir Martin Seymour, KCVO, CMG
Best, Sir Richard Radford, KCVO, CBE
Best-Shaw, Sir John Michael Robert, Bt. (1665)
Bethel, Sir Baltron Benjamin, KCMG
Bett, Sir Michael, Kt., CBE
Bettison, Sir Norman George, Kt., QPM
Bevan, Sir Martyn Evan Evans, Bt. (1958)
Bevan, Sir Nicolas, Kt., CB
Bevan, Sir Timothy Hugh, Kt.
Beverley, *Lt.-Gen.* Sir Henry York La Roche, KCB, OBE, RM
Bibby, Sir Michael James, Bt. (1959)
Bichard, Sir Michael George, KCB
Bickersteth, *Rt. Revd* John Monier, KCVO
Biddulph, Sir Ian D'Olier, Bt. (1664)
Bide, Sir Austin Ernest, Kt.
Bidwell, Sir Hugh Charles Philip, GBE
Biggam, Sir Robin Adair, Kt.
Biggs, Sir Norman Paris, Kt.

Bilas, Sir Angmai Simon, Kt., OBE
Billière, *Gen.* Sir Peter Edgar de la Cour de la, KCB, KBE, DSO, MC
Bindman, Sir Geoffrey Lionel, Kt.
Bingham, *Hon.* Sir Eardley Max, Kt.
Birch, Sir John Allan, KCVO, CMG
Birch, Sir Roger, Kt., CBE, QPM
Bird, Sir Richard Geoffrey Chapman, Bt. (1922)
Birkin, Sir John Christian William, Bt. (1905)
Birkin, Sir (John) Derek, Kt., TD
Birkmyre, Sir James, Bt. (1921)
Birrell, Sir James Drake, Kt.
Birtwistle, Sir Harrison, Kt., CH
Bischoff, Sir Winfried Franz Wilhelm, Kt.
Bishop, Sir Michael David, Kt., CBE
Bisson, *Rt. Hon.* Sir Gordon Ellis, Kt.
Black, Sir James Whyte, Kt., OM, FRCP, FRS
Black, *Adm.* Sir (John) Jeremy, GBE, KCB, DSO
Black, Sir Robert David, Bt. (1922)
Blackburn, *Vice-Adm.* Sir David Anthony James, KCVO, CB, LVO
Blackburne, *Hon.* Sir William Anthony, Kt.
Blackett, Sir Hugh Francis, Bt. (1673)
Blackham, *Vice-Adm.* Sir Jeremy Joe, KCB
Blackman, Sir Frank Milton, KCVO, OBE
Blair, *Lt.-Gen.* Sir Chandos, KCVO, OBE, MC
†Blair, Sir Patrick David Hunter, Bt. (1786)
Blair, Sir Ian Warwick, Kt., QPM
Blake, Sir Alfred Lapthorn, KCVO, MC
Blake, Sir Francis Michael, Bt. (1907)
Blake, Sir Peter Thomas, Kt., CBE
Blake, Sir (Thomas) Richard (Valentine), Bt. (I. 1622)
Blaker, Sir John, Bt. (1919)
Blakiston, Sir Ferguson Arthur James, Bt. (1763)
Blanch, Sir Malcolm, KCVO
Bland, Sir (Francis) Christopher (Buchan), Kt.
Bland, *Lt.-Col.* Sir Simon Claud Michael, KCVO
Blank, Sir Maurice Victor, Kt.
Blatherwick, Sir David Elliott Spiby, KCMG, OBE
Blelloch, Sir John Nial Henderson, KCB
Blennerhassett, Sir (Marmaduke) Adrian Francis William, Bt. (1809)
Blewitt, *Maj.* Sir Shane Gabriel Basil, GCVO
Blofeld, *Hon.* Sir John Christopher Calthorpe, Kt.
Blois, Sir Charles Nicholas Gervase, Bt. (1686)
Blom-Cooper, Sir Louis Jacques, Kt., QC
Blomefield, Sir Thomas Charles Peregrine, Bt. (1807)

Bloomfield, Sir Kenneth Percy, KCB
Blundell, Sir Thomas Leon, Kt., FRS
Blunden, Sir George, Kt.
Blunden, Sir Philip Overington, Bt. (I. 1766)
Blunt, Sir David Richard Reginald Harvey, Bt. (1720)
Blyth, Sir Charles (Chay), Kt., CBE, BEM
Boardman, *Prof.* Sir John, Kt., FSA, FBA
Bodey, *Hon.* Sir David Roderick Lessiter, Kt.
Bodmer, Sir Walter Fred, Kt., PHD, FRS
Body, Sir Richard Bernard Frank Stewart, Kt.
Bogan, Sir Nagora, KBE
Boileau, Sir Guy (Francis), Bt. (1838)
Boles, Sir Jeremy John Fortescue, Bt. (1922)
Boles, Sir John Dennis, Kt., MBE
Bolland, Sir Edwin, KCMG
Bollers, *Hon.* Sir Harold Brodie Smith, Kt.
Bolt, *Air Marshal* Sir Richard Bruce, KBE, CB, DFC, AFC
Bona, Sir Kina, KBE
Bonallack, Sir Michael Francis, Kt., OBE
Bond, Sir John Reginald Hartnell, Kt.
Bond, *Prof.* Sir Michael Richard, Kt., FRCPSYCH, FRCPGLAS, FRCSE
Bone, Sir Roger Bridgland, KCMG
Bonfield, Sir Peter Leahy, Kt., CBE, FRENG
Bonham, *Maj.* Sir Antony Lionel Thomas, Bt. (1852)
Bonington, Sir Christian John Storey, Kt., CBE
Bonsall, Sir Arthur Wilfred, KCMG, CBE
Bonsor, Sir Nicholas Cosmo, Bt. (1925)
Boord, Sir Nicolas John Charles, Bt. (1896)
Boorman, *Lt.-Gen.* Sir Derek, KCB
Booth, Sir Christopher Charles, Kt., MD, FRCP
Booth, Sir Clive, Kt.
Booth, Sir Douglas Allen, Bt. (1916)
Booth, Sir Gordon, KCMG, CVO
Boothby, Sir Brooke Charles, Bt. (1660)
Bore, Sir Albert, Kt.
Boreel, Sir Stephan Gerard, Bt. (1645)
Borthwick, Sir Anthony Thomas, Bt. (1908)
Borysiewicz, *Prof.* Sir Leszek Krzysztof, Kt.
Bossom, *Hon.* Sir Clive, Bt. (1953)
Boswell, *Lt.-Gen.* Sir Alexander Crawford Simpson, KCB, CBE
Bosworth, Sir Neville Bruce Alfred, Kt., CBE
Botham, Sir Ian Terence, Kt., OBE
Bottoms, *Prof.* Sir Anthony Edward, Kt.
Bottomley, Sir James Reginald Alfred, KCMG

Boughey, Sir John George Fletcher, Bt. (1798)

Boulton, Sir Clifford John, GCB

Boulton, Sir William Whytehead, Bt. (1944), CBE, TD

Bourn, Sir John Bryant, KCB

Bouraga, Sir Phillip, KBE

Bourne, Sir Clive John, Kt.

Bowater, Sir Euan David Vansittart, Bt. (1939)

Bowater, Sir (John) Vansittart, Bt. (1914)

Bowden, Sir Andrew, Kt., MBE

Bowden, Sir Nicholas Richard, Bt. (1915)

Bowen, Sir Geoffrey Fraser, Kt.

Bowen, Sir Mark Edward Mortimer, Bt. (1921)

Bowes Lyon, Sir Simon Alexander, KCVO

Bowett, *Prof.* Sir Derek William, Kt., CBE, QC, FBA

†Bowlby, Sir Richard Peregrine Longstaff, Bt. (1923)

Bowman, Sir Edwin Geoffrey, KCB

Bowman, Sir Jeffery Haverstock, Kt.

Bowman-Shaw, Sir (George) Neville, Kt.

Bowness, Sir Alan, Kt., CBE

Bowyer-Smyth, Sir Thomas Weyland, Bt. (1661)

Boyce, Sir Graham Hugh, KCMG

Boyce, Sir Robert Charles Leslie, Bt. (1952)

Boyd, Sir Alexander Walter, Bt. (1916)

Boyd, Sir John Dixon Iklé, KCMG

Boyd, *Prof.* Sir Robert David Hugh, Kt.

Boyd-Carpenter, Sir (Marsom) Henry, KCVO

Boyd-Carpenter, *Lt.-Gen. Hon.* Sir Thomas Patrick John, KBE

Boyle, Sir Stephen Gurney, Bt. (1904)

Boyson, *Rt. Hon.* Sir Rhodes, Kt.

Brabham, Sir John Arthur, Kt., OBE

Bracewell-Smith, Sir Charles, Bt. (1947)

Bradbeer, Sir John Derek Richardson, Kt., OBE, TD

Bradfield, *Dr* Sir John Richard Grenfell, Kt.

Bradford, Sir Edward Alexander Slade, Bt. (1902)

Bradshaw, Sir Kenneth Anthony, KCB

Brady, *Prof.* Sir John Michael, Kt., FRS

Braithwaite, *Rt. Hon.* Sir Nicholas Alexander, Kt., OBE

Braithwaite, Sir Rodric Quentin, GCMG

Bramley, *Prof.* Sir Paul Anthony, Kt.

Branson, Sir Richard Charles Nicholas, Kt.

Bratza, *Hon.* Sir Nicolas Dušan, Kt.

Breckenridge, *Prof.* Sir Alasdair Muir, Kt., CBE

Brennan, *Hon.* Sir (Francis) Gerard, KBE

Brenton, Sir Anthony Russell, KCMG

Brewer, Sir David William, Kt., CMG

Bridges, *Hon.* Sir Phillip Rodney, Kt., CMG

Brierley, Sir Ronald Alfred, Kt.

Briggs, *Hon.* Sir Michael Townley Featherstone, Kt.

Bright, Sir Graham Frank James, Kt.

Bright, Sir Keith, Kt.

Brigstocke, *Adm.* Sir John Richard, KCB

Brinckman, Sir Theodore George Roderick, Bt. (1831)

†Brisco, Sir Campbell Howard, Bt. (1782)

Briscoe, Sir Brian Anthony, Kt.

Briscoe, Sir John Geoffrey James, Bt. (1910)

Brittan, Sir Samuel, Kt.

†Broadbent, Sir Andrew George, Bt. (1893)

Broadbent, Sir Richard John, KCB

Brocklebank, Sir Aubrey Thomas, Bt. (1885)

Brodie, Sir Benjamin David Ross, Bt. (1834)

Brodie-Hall, Sir Laurence Charles, Kt., AO, CMG

Brooke, Sir Rodney George, Kt., CBE

Brooking, Sir Trevor, Kt., CBE

Bromhead, Sir John Desmond Gonville, Bt. (1806)

Bromley, Sir Michael Roger, KBE

Bromley, Sir Rupert Charles, Bt. (1757)

Brook, *Prof.* Sir Richard John, Kt. OBE

†Brooke, Sir Alistair Weston, Bt. (1919)

Brooke, Sir Francis George Windham, Bt. (1903)

Brooke, *Rt. Hon.* Sir Henry, Kt.

Brooke, Sir (Richard) David Christopher, Bt. (1662)

Brooking, Sir Trevor David, Kt., CBE

Brooks, Sir Timothy Gerald Martin, KCVO

Brooksbank, Sir (Edward) Nicholas, Bt. (1919)

Broomfield, Sir Nigel Hugh Robert Allen, KCMG

†Broughton, Sir David Delves, Bt. (1661)

Broun, Sir Wayne Hercules, Bt. (S. 1686)

Brown, Sir (Austen) Patrick, KCB

Brown, *Adm.* Sir Brian Thomas, KCB, CBE

Brown, Sir (Cyril) Maxwell Palmer, KCB, CMG

Brown, Sir David, Kt.

Brown, *Hon.* Sir Douglas Dunlop, Kt.

Brown, Sir George Francis Richmond, Bt. (1863)

Brown, Sir George Noel, Kt.

Brown, Sir Mervyn, KCMG, OBE

Brown, Sir Peter Randolph, Kt.

Brown, *Rt. Hon.* Sir Stephen, GBE

Brown, Sir Stephen David Reid, KCVO

Browne, Sir Nicholas Walker, KBE, CMG

Brownrigg, Sir Nicholas (Gawen), Bt. (1816)

Browse, *Prof.* Sir Norman Leslie, Kt., MD, FRCS

Bruce, Sir (Francis) Michael Ian, Bt. (S. 1628)

Bruce-Clifton, Sir Hervey James Hugh, Bt. (1804)

Bruce-Gardner, Sir Robert Henry, Bt. (1945)

Brunner, Sir John Henry Kilian, Bt. (1895)

Brunton, Sir (Edward Francis) Lauder, Bt. (1908)

Brunton, Sir Gordon Charles, Kt.

Bryan, Sir Arthur, Kt.

Buchan-Hepburn, Sir John Alastair Trant Kidd, Bt. (1815)

Buchanan, Sir Andrew George, Bt. (1878)

Buchanan, *Vice-Adm.* Sir Peter William, KBE

Buchanan, Sir Robert Wilson (Robin), Kt.

Buchanan-Jardine, *Maj.* Sir (Andrew) Rupert (John), Bt. (1885), MC

Buckland, Sir Ross, Kt.

Buckley, Sir Michael Sidney, Kt.

Buckley, *Lt.-Cdr.* Sir (Peter) Richard, KCVO

Buckley, *Hon.* Sir Roger John, Kt.

Buckworth-Herne-Soame, Sir Charles John, Bt. (1697)

Budd, Sir Alan Peter, Kt.

Budd, Sir Colin Richard, KCMG

Bull, Sir George Jeffrey, Kt.

Bull, Sir Simeon George, Bt. (1922)

Bullock, Sir Stephen Michael, Kt.

Bultin, Sir Bato, Kt., MBE

Bunbury, Sir Michael William, Bt. (1681), KCVO

Bunch, Sir Austin Wyeth, Kt., CBE

Bunyard, Sir Robert Sidney, Kt., CBE, QPM

Burbidge, Sir Peter Dudley, Bt. (1916)

Burden, Sir Anthony Thomas, Kt., QPM

Burdett, Sir Savile Aylmer, Bt. (1665)

Burgen, Sir Arnold Stanley Vincent, Kt., FRS

Burgess, *Gen.* Sir Edward Arthur, KCB, OBE

Burgess, Sir (Joseph) Stuart, Kt., CBE, PHD, FRSC

Burgh, Sir John Charles, KCMG, CB

Burke, Sir James Stanley Gilbert, Bt. (I. 1797)

Burke, Sir (Thomas) Kerry, Kt.

Burnell-Nugent, *Vice-Adm.* Sir James Michael, KCB, CBE, ADC

Burnet, Sir James William Alexander (Sir Alastair Burnet), Kt.

Burnett, *Air Chief Marshal* Sir Brian Kenyon, GCB, DFC, AFC

Burnett, Sir Charles David, Bt., (1913)

Burnett, Sir Walter John, Kt.

Burney, Sir Nigel Dennistoun, Bt. (1921)

Burns, Sir (Robert) Andrew, KCMG

Burnton, *Hon.* Sir Stanley Jeffrey, Kt.

Burrell, Sir John Raymond, Bt. (1774)

Burridge, *Air Chief Marshal* Sir Brian Kevin, KCB, CBE, ADC

Burston, Sir Samuel Gerald Wood, Kt., OBE

Burt, Sir Peter Alexander, Kt.

Burton, Sir Carlisle Archibald, Kt., OBE

Burton, Sir George Vernon Kennedy, Kt., CBE

Burton, *Lt.-Gen.* Sir Edmund Fortescue Gerard, KBE

Burton, Sir Graham Stuart, KCMG

Burton, *Hon.* Sir Michael John, Kt.

Burton, Sir Michael St Edmund, KCVO, CMG

Bush, *Adm.* Sir John Fitzroy Duyland, GCB, DSC

Butler, *Rt. Hon.* Sir Adam Courtauld, Kt.

Butler, *Hon.* Sir Arlington Griffith, KCMG

Butler, Sir Michael Dacres, GCMG

Butler, Sir (Reginald) Michael (Thomas), Bt. (1922)

Butler, Sir Percy James, Kt., CBE

Butler, *Hon.* Sir Richard Clive, Kt.

Butler, Sir Richard Pierce, Bt. (1628)

Butter, *Maj.* Sir David Henry, KCVO, MC

Butterfield, *Hon.* Sir Alexander Neil Logie, Kt.

Butterfill, Sir John Valentine, Kt.

Buxton, Sir Jocelyn Charles Roden, Bt. (1840)

Buxton, *Rt. Hon.* Sir Richard Joseph, Kt.

Buzzard, Sir Anthony Farquhar, Bt. (1929)

Byatt, Sir Hugh Campbell, KCVO, CMG

Byatt, Sir Ian Charles Rayner, Kt.

Byford, Sir Lawrence, Kt., CBE, QPM

Byron, *Rt. Hon.* Sir Charles Michael Dennis, Kt.

†Cable-Alexander, Sir Patrick Desmond William, Bt. (1809)

Cadbury, Sir (George) Adrian (Hayhurst), Kt.

Cadbury, Sir (Nicholas) Dominic, Kt.

Cadogan, *Prof.* Sir John Ivan George, Kt., CBE, FRS, FRSE

Cahn, Sir Albert Jonas, Bt. (1934)

Cain, Sir Henry Edney Conrad, Kt.

Caine, Sir Michael (Maurice Micklewhite), Kt., CBE

Caines, Sir John, KCB

Caldwell, Sir Edward George, KCB

Callaghan, Sir William Henry, Kt.

Callan, Sir Ivan Roy, KCVO, CMG

Calman, *Prof.* Sir Kenneth Charles, KCB, MD, FRCP, FRCS, FRSE

Calne, *Prof.* Sir Roy Yorke, Kt., FRS

Calvert-Smith, Sir David, Kt., QC

Cameron, Sir Hugh Roy Graham, Kt., QPM

Campbell, Sir Alan Hugh, GCMG

Campbell, *Prof.* Sir Colin Murray, Kt.

Campbell, Sir Ian Tofts, Kt., CBE, VRD

Campbell, Sir Ilay Mark, Bt. (1808)

Campbell, Sir James Alexander Moffat Bain, Bt. (S. 1668)

Campbell, Sir Lachlan Philip Kemeys, Bt. (1815)

Campbell, Sir Roderick Duncan Hamilton, Bt. (1831)

Campbell, Sir Robin Auchinbreck, Bt. (S. 1628)

Campbell, *Rt. Hon.* Sir Walter Menzies, Kt., CBE, QC

Campbell, *Rt. Hon.* Sir William Anthony, Kt.

Campbell-Orde, Sir John Alexander, Bt. (1790)

†Carden, Sir Christopher Robert, Bt. (1887)

Carden, Sir John Craven, Bt. (I. 1787)

Carew, Sir Rivers Verain, Bt. (1661)

Carey, Sir de Vic Graham, Kt.

Carey, Sir Peter Willoughby, GCB

Carleton-Smith, *Maj.-Gen.* Sir Michael Edward, Kt., CBE

Carlisle, Sir James Beethoven, GCMG

Carlisle, Sir John Michael, Kt.

Carlisle, Sir Kenneth Melville, Kt.

Carnegie, *Lt.-Gen.* Sir Robin Macdonald, KCB, OBE

Carnegie, Sir Roderick Howard, Kt.

Carnwath, *Rt. Hon.* Sir Robert John Anderson, Kt., CVO

Caro, Sir Anthony Alfred, Kt., OM, CBE

Carr, Sir (Albert) Raymond (Maillard), Kt.

Carr, Sir Peter Derek, Kt., CBE

Carr, *Very Revd Dr* Arthur Wesley, KCVO

Carr-Ellison, *Col.* Sir Ralph Harry, KCVO, TD

Carrick, *Hon.* Sir John Leslie, KCMG

Carrick, Sir Roger John, KCMG, LVO

Carruthers, Sir Ian James, Kt., OBE

Carsberg, *Prof.* Sir Bryan Victor, Kt.

Carter, *Prof.* Sir David Craig, Kt., FRCSE, FRCSGLAS, FRCPE

Carter, Sir John Alexander, Kt.

Carter, Sir John Gordon Thomas, Kt.

Carter, Sir Philip David, Kt., CBE

Carter, Sir Richard Henry Alwyn, Kt.

Cartland, Sir George Barrington, Kt., CMG

Cartledge, Sir Bryan George, KCMG

Cary, Sir Roger Hugh, Bt. (1955)

Casey, *Rt. Hon.* Sir Maurice Eugene, Kt.

Cass, Sir Geoffrey Arthur, Kt.

Cassel, Sir Timothy Felix Harold, Bt. (1920)

Cassels, Sir John Seton, Kt., CB

Cassels, *Adm.* Sir Simon Alastair Cassillis, KCB, CBE

Cassidi, *Adm.* Sir (Arthur) Desmond, GCB

Castell, Sir William Martin, Kt.

Castledine, *Prof.* Sir George, Kt.

Catford, Sir (John) Robin, KCVO, CBE

Catherwood, Sir (Henry) Frederick (Ross), Kt.

Catto, *Prof.* Sir Graeme Robertson Dawson, Kt.

Cave, Sir John Charles, Bt. (1896)

Cave-Browne-Cave, Sir Robert, Bt. (1641)

Cayley, Sir Digby William David, Bt. (1661)

Cayzer, Sir James Arthur, Bt. (1904)

Cazalet, *Hon.* Sir Edward Stephen, Kt.

Cazalet, Sir Peter Grenville, Kt.

Cecil, *Rear-Adm.* Sir (Oswald) Nigel Amherst, KBE, CB

Chadwick, *Revd Prof.* Henry, KBE

Chadwick, *Rt. Hon.* Sir John Murray, Kt.

Chadwick, Sir Joshua Kenneth Burton, Bt. (1935)

Chadwick, *Revd Prof.* (William) Owen, OM, KBE, FBA

Chadwyck-Healey, Sir Charles Edward, Bt. (1919)

Chakrabarti, Sir Sumantra, KCB

Chalmers, Sir Iain Geoffrey, Kt.

Chalmers, Sir Neil Robert, Kt.

Chalstrey, Sir (Leonard) John, Kt., MD, FRCS

Chan, *Rt. Hon.* Sir Julius, GCMG, KBE

Chan, Sir Thomas Kok, Kt., OBE

Chance, Sir (George) Jeremy ffolliott, Bt. (1900)

Chandler, Sir Colin Michael, Kt.

Chandler, Sir Geoffrey, Kt., CBE

Chantler, *Prof.* Sir Cyril, Kt., MD, FRCP

Chaplin, Sir Malcolm Hilbery, Kt., CBE

Chapman, Sir David Robert Macgowan, Bt. (1958)

Chapman, Sir George Alan, Kt.

Chapman, Sir Sidney Brookes, Kt., MP

Chapple, *Field Marshal* Sir John Lyon, GCB, CBE

Charles, *Hon.* Sir Arthur William Hessin, Kt.

Charles, Sir George Frederick Lawrence, KCMG, CBE

Charlton, Sir Robert (Bobby), Kt., CBE

Charnley, Sir (William) John, Kt., CB, FRENG

Chataway, *Rt. Hon.* Sir Christopher, Kt.

Chatfield, Sir John Freeman, Kt., CBE

†Chaytor, Sir Bruce Gordon, Bt. (1831)

Checketts, *Sqn. Ldr.* Sir David John, KCVO

Checkland, Sir Michael, Kt.

Cheshire, *Air Chief Marshal* Sir John Anthony, KBE, CB

Chessells, Sir Arthur David (Tim), Kt.

Chesterton, Sir Oliver Sidney, Kt., MC

Chetwood, Sir Clifford Jack, Kt.

†Chetwynd, Sir Robin John Talbot, Bt. (1795)

Cheyne, Sir Patrick John Lister, Bt. (1908)

†Chichester, Sir James Henry Edward, Bt. (1641)

Chichester-Clark, Sir Robin, Kt.

Chilcot, *Rt. Hon.* Sir John Anthony, GCB

Child, Sir (Coles John) Jeremy, Bt. (1919)

Chilton, *Brig.* Sir Frederick Oliver, Kt., CBE, DSO

Chilwell, *Hon.* Sir Muir Fitzherbert, Kt.

Chinn, Sir Trevor Edwin, Kt., CVO

Chipperfield, Sir Geoffrey Howes, KCB

Chisholm, Sir John Alexander Raymond, Kt., FRENG

Chitty, Sir Thomas Willes, Bt. (1924)

Cholmeley, Sir Hugh John Frederick Sebastian, Bt. (1806)

Chow, Sir Chung Kong, Kt.

Chow, Sir Henry Francis, Kt., OBE

Christie, Sir George William Langham, Kt., CH

Christie, Sir William, Kt., MBE

Christopher, Sir Duncan Robin Carmichael, KBE, CMG

Chung, Sir Sze-yuen, GBE, FRENG

Clark, Sir Francis Drake, Bt. (1886)

Clark, Sir John Arnold, Kt.

Clark, Sir Jonathan George, Bt. (1917)

Clark, Sir Robert Anthony, Kt., DSC

Clark, Sir Terence Joseph, KBE, CMG, CVO

Clarke, *Rt. Hon.* Sir Anthony Peter, Kt.

Clarke, Sir Arthur Charles, Kt., CBE

Clarke, Sir (Charles Mansfield) Tobias, Bt. (1831)

Clarke, *Hon.* Sir Christopher Simon Courtenay Stephenson, Kt.

Clarke, Sir Christopher James, Kt., OBE

Clarke, *Hon.* Sir David Clive, Kt.

Clarke, Sir Ellis Emmanuel Innocent, GCMG

Clarke, Sir Jonathan Dennis, Kt.

Clarke, Sir Robert Cyril, Kt.

†Clarke, Sir Rupert Grant Alexander, Bt. (1882)

Clay, Sir Edward, KCMG

Clay, Sir Richard Henry, Bt. (1841)

Clayton, Sir David Robert, Bt. (1732)

Cleaver, Sir Anthony Brian, Kt.

Clementi, Sir David Cecil, Kt.

Cleminson, Sir James Arnold Stacey, KBE, MC

Clerk, Sir Robert Maxwell, Bt. (1679), OBE

Clerke, Sir John Edward Longueville, Bt. (1660)

Clifford, Sir Roger Joseph, Bt. (1887)

Clifford, Sir Timothy Peter Plint, Kt.

Clothier, Sir Cecil Montacute, KCB, QC

Clucas, Sir Kenneth Henry, KCB

Clutterbuck, *Vice-Adm.* Sir David Granville, KBE, CB

Coates, Sir Anthony Robert Milnes, Bt. (1911)

Coates, Sir David Frederick Charlton, Bt. (1921)

Coats, Sir Alastair Francis Stuart, Bt. (1905)

Coats, Sir William David, Kt.

Cochrane, Sir (Henry) Marc (Sursock), Bt. (1903)

Cockburn, Sir John Elliot, Bt. (S. 1671)

Cockburn-Campbell, Sir Alexander Thomas, Bt. (1821)

Cockshaw, Sir Alan, Kt., FRENG

†Codrington, Sir Christopher George Wayne, Bt. (1876)

Codrington, Sir William Alexander, Bt. (1721)

Coghill, Sir Patrick Kendal Farley, Bt. (1778)

Coghlin, *Hon.* Sir Patrick, Kt.

Cohen, Sir Edward, Kt.

Cohen, Sir Ivor Harold, Kt., CBE, TD

Cohen, *Prof.* Sir Philip, Kt., PHD, FRS

Cohen, Sir Ronald, Kt.

Cole, Sir (Robert) William, Kt.

Coleman, Sir Robert John, KCMG

Coleridge, *Hon.* Sir Paul James Duke, Kt.

Coles, Sir (Arthur) John, GCMG

Colfox, Sir (William) John, Bt. (1939)

Collett, Sir Christopher, GBE

Collett, Sir Ian Seymour, Bt. (1934)

Collins, Sir Alan Stanley, KCVO, CMG

Collins, *Hon.* Sir Andrew David, Kt.

Collins, Sir Bryan Thomas Alfred, Kt., OBE, QFSM

Collins, Sir John Alexander, Kt

Collins, Sir Kenneth Darlingston, Kt.

Collins, *Hon.* Sir Lawrence Antony, Kt.

Collyear, Sir John Gowen, Kt.

Colman, *Hon.* Sir Anthony David, Kt.

Colman, Sir Michael Jeremiah, Bt. (1907)

Colman, Sir Timothy, KG

Colquhoun of Luss, Sir Ivar Iain, Bt. (1786)

Colt, Sir Edward William Dutton, Bt. (1694)

Colthurst, Sir Charles St John, Bt. (1744)

Colvin, Sir Howard Montagu, Kt., CVO, CBE, FBA

Compton, *Rt. Hon.* Sir John George Melvin, KCMG

Conant, Sir John Ernest Michael, Bt. (1954)

Connell, *Hon.* Sir Michael Bryan, Kt.

Connery, Sir Sean, Kt.

Connor, Sir William Joseph, Kt.

Conran, Sir Terence Orby, Kt.

Cons, *Hon.* Sir Derek, Kt.

Constantinou, Sir Georkios, Kt., OBE

Conway, *Prof.* Sir Gordon Richard, KCMG, FRS

Cook, Sir Christopher Wymondham Rayner Herbert, Bt. (1886)

Cook, *Prof.* Sir Peter Frederic Chester, Kt.

Cooke, *Col.* Sir David William Perceval, Bt. (1661)

Cooke, Sir Howard Felix Hanlan, GCMG, GCVO

Cooke, *Hon.* Sir Jeremy Lionel, Kt.

Cooke, *Prof.* Sir Ronald Urwick, Kt.

Cooksey, Sir David James Scott, GBE, Kt.

Cooper, *Gen.* Sir George Leslie Conroy, GCB, MC

Cooper, Sir Henry, Kt.

Cooper, Sir Richard Adrian, Bt. (1905)

Cooper, *Maj.-Gen.* Sir Simon Christie, GCVO

Cooper, Sir William Daniel Charles, Bt. (1863)

Coote, Sir Christopher John, Bt. (I. 1621), *Premier Baronet of Ireland*

Copas, *Most Revd* Virgil, KBE

Copisarow, Sir Alcon Charles, Kt.

Corbett, *Maj.-Gen.* Sir Robert John Swan, KCVO, CB

Corby, Sir (Frederick) Brian, Kt.

Cordy-Simpson, *Lt.-Gen.* Sir Roderick Alexander, KBE, CB

Corfield, Sir Kenneth George, Kt., FRENG

Cormack, Sir Patrick Thomas, Kt.

Cornelius-Wheeler, Sir Charles, Kt., CMG

Corness, Sir Colin Ross, Kt.

Cornforth, Sir John Warcup, Kt., CBE, DPHIL, FRS

Corry, Sir James Michael, Bt. (1885)

Cortazzi, Sir (Henry Arthur) Hugh, GCMG

Cory, Sir (Clinton Charles) Donald, Bt. (1919)

Cory-Wright, Sir Richard Michael, Bt. (1903)

Cossons, Sir Neil, Kt., OBE

Cotter, Sir Patrick Laurence Delaval, Bt. (I. 1763)

Cotterell, Sir John Henry Geers, Bt. (1805)

Cotton, *Hon.* Sir Robert Carrington, KCMG

Cotton, Sir William Frederick, Kt., CBE

Cottrell, Sir Alan Howard, Kt., PHD, FRS, FRENG

†Cotts, Sir Richard Crichton Mitchell, Bt. (1921)

Couper, Sir James George, Bt. (1841)

Court, *Hon.* Sir Charles Walter Michael, KCMG, OBE

Courtenay, Sir Thomas Daniel, Kt.

Cousins, *Air Chief Marshal* Sir David, KCB, AFC

Coville, *Air Marshal* Sir Christopher Charles Cotton, KCB

Cowan, *Gen.* Sir Samuel, KCB, CBE

Coward, *Vice-Adm.* Sir John Francis, KCB, DSO

Cowen, *Rt. Hon. Prof.* Sir Zelman, GCMG, GCVO

Cowie, Sir Thomas (Tom), Kt., OBE

Cowper-Coles, Sir Sherard Louis, KCMG, LVO

Cox, Sir Alan George, Kt., CBE
Cox, *Prof.* Sir David Roxbee, Kt.
Cox, Sir Geoffrey Sandford, Kt., CBE
Cox, Sir George Edwin, Kt.
Cradock, *Rt. Hon.* Sir Percy, GCMG
Craft, *Prof.* Sir Alan William, Kt.
Craig, Sir (Albert) James (Macqueen), GCMG
Craig-Cooper, Sir (Frederick Howard) Michael, Kt., CBE, TD
Crane, *Hon.* Sir Peter Francis, Kt.
Crane, *Prof.* Sir Peter Robert, Kt.
Craufurd, Sir Robert James, Bt. (1781)
Craven, Sir John Anthony, Kt.
Craven, Sir Philip Lee, Kt., MBE
Crawford, *Prof.* Sir Frederick William, Kt., FRENG
Crawford, Sir Robert William Kenneth, Kt. CBE
Crawley-Boevey, Sir Thomas Michael Blake, Bt. (1784)
Crew, Sir (Michael) Edward, Kt., QPM
Crewe, *Prof.* Sir Ivor Martin, Kt.
Cresswell, *Hon.* Sir Peter John, Kt.
Crichton-Brown, Sir Robert, KCMG, CBE, TD
Crick, *Prof.* Sir Bernard, Kt.
Crisp, Sir John Charles, Bt. (1913)
Critchett, Sir Charles George Montague, Bt. (1908)
Crockett, Sir Andrew Duncan, Kt.
Croft, Sir Owen Glendower, Bt. (1671)
Croft, Sir Thomas Stephen Hutton, Bt. (1818)
†Crofton, Sir Hugh Denis, Bt. (1801)
Crofton, *Prof.* Sir John Wenman, Kt.
†Crofton, Sir Julian Malby, Bt. (1838)
Crompton, Sir Dan, Kt., CBE, QPM
Crosby, Sir James Robert, Kt.
Crossland, *Prof.* Sir Bernard, Kt., CBE, FRENG
Crossley, Sir Sloan Nicholas, Bt. (1909)
Crowe, Sir Brian Lee, KCMG
Cruickshank, Sir Donald Gordon, Kt.
Cruthers, Sir James Winter, Kt.
Cubbon, Sir Brian Crossland, GCB
Cubitt, Sir Hugh Guy, Kt., CBE
Cullen, Sir (Edward) John, Kt., FRENG
Culme-Seymour, Sir Michael Patrick, Bt. (1809)
Culpin, Sir Robert Paul, Kt.
Cummins, Sir Michael John Austin, Kt.
Cunliffe, *Prof.* Sir Barrington, Kt., CBE
Cunliffe, Sir David Ellis, Bt. (1759)
Cunliffe-Owen, Sir Hugo Dudley, Bt. (1920)
Cunningham, *Lt.-Gen.* Sir Hugh Patrick, KBE
Cunningham, Sir Roger Keith, Kt., CBE
Cunynghame, Sir Andrew David Francis, Bt. (S. 1702)
†Currie, Sir Donald Scott, Bt. (1847)

Curry, Sir Donald Thomas Younger, Kt., CBE
Curtain, Sir Michael, KBE
Curtis, Sir Barry John, Kt.
Curtis, *Hon.* Sir Richard Herbert, Kt.
Curtis, Sir William Peter, Bt. (1802)
Curtiss, *Air Marshal* Sir John Bagot, KCB, KBE
Curwen, Sir Christopher Keith, KCMG
Cuschieri, *Prof.* Sir Alfred, Kt.
Cutler, Sir Charles Benjamin, KBE
Dain, Sir David John Michael, KCVO
Dales, Sir Richard Nigel, KCVO
Dalrymple-Hay, Sir John Hugh, Bt. (1798)
†Dalrymple-White, Sir Jan Hew, Bt. (1926)
Dalton, *Vice-Adm.* Sir Geoffrey Thomas James Oliver, KCB
Dalton, *Prof.* Sir Howard, Kt.
Dalton, Sir Richard John, KCMG
Dalyell, Sir Tam (Thomas), Bt. (NS 1685)
Daniel, Sir John Sagar, Kt., DSC
Dankworth, Sir John, Kt., CBE
Dannatt, *Lt.-Gen.* Sir Francis Richard, KCB, CBE
Darby, Sir Peter Howard, Kt., CBE, QFSM
Darell, Sir Jeffrey Lionel, Bt. (1795), MC
Darling, Sir Clifford, GCVO
Darrington, Sir Michael John, Kt.
Dasgupta, *Prof.* Sir Partha Sarathi, Kt.
†Dashwood, Sir Edward John Francis, Bt. (1707), *Premier Baronet of Great Britain*
Dashwood, Sir Richard James, Bt. (1684)
Daunt, Sir Timothy Lewis Achilles, KCMG
Davenport-Handley, Sir David John, Kt., OBE
David, Sir Jean Marc, Kt., CBE, QC
David, *His Hon.* Sir Robin (Robert) Daniel George, Kt.
Davies, Sir Alan Seymour, Kt.
Davies, Sir (Charles) Noel, Kt.
Davies, *Prof.* Sir David Evan Naughton, Kt., CBE, FRS, FRENG
Davies, *Hon.* Sir (David Herbert) Mervyn, Kt., MC, TD
Davies, Sir David John, Kt.
Davies, Sir Frank John, Kt., CBE
Davies, *Prof.* Sir Graeme John, Kt., FRENG
Davies, Sir John Howard, Kt.
Davies, Sir John Michael, KCB
Davies, *Vice-Adm.* Sir Lancelot Richard Bell, KBE
Davies, Sir Peter Maxwell, Kt., CBE
Davies, Sir Rhys Everson, Kt., QC
Davis, Sir Andrew Frank, Kt., CBE
Davis, Sir Colin Rex, Kt., CH, CBE
Davis, Sir Crispin Henry Lamert, Kt.
Davis, Sir John Gilbert, Bt. (1946)
Davis, *Hon.* Sir Nigel Anthony Lambert, Kt.

Davis, Sir Peter John, Kt.
Davis, *Hon.* Sir Thomas Robert Alexander Harries, KBE
Davis-Goff, Sir Robert (William), Bt. (1905)
Davison, *Rt. Hon.* Sir Ronald Keith, GBE, CMG
†Davson, Sir George Trenchard Simon, Bt. (1927)
Dawanincura, Sir John Norbert, Kt., OBE
Dawbarn, Sir Simon Yelverton, KCVO, CMG
Dawson, *Hon.* Sir Daryl Michael, KBE, CB
Dawson, Sir Hugh Michael Trevor, Bt. (1920)
Dawtry, Sir Alan (Graham), Kt., CBE, TD
Day, Sir Derek Malcolm, KCMG
Day, *Air Chief Marshal* Sir John Romney, KCB, OBE, ADC
Day, Sir (Judson) Graham, Kt.
Day, Sir Michael John, Kt., OBE
Day, Sir Simon James, Kt.
Deane, *Hon.* Sir William Patrick, KBE
Dearlove, Sir Richard Billing, KCMG, OBE
de Bellaigue, Sir Geoffrey, GCVO
†Debenham, Sir Thomas Adam, Bt. (1931)
de Deney, Sir Geoffrey Ivor, KCVO
Deeny, *Hon.* Sir Donnell Justin Patrick, Kt.
de Hoghton, Sir (Richard) Bernard (Cuthbert), Bt. (1611)
De la Bère, Sir Cameron, Bt. (1953)
de la Rue, Sir Andrew George Ilay, Bt. (1898)
De Silva, Sir George Desmond Lorenz, Kt., QC
Dellow, Sir John Albert, Kt., CBE
Delves, *Lt.-Gen.* Sir Cedric Norman George, KBE
Denholm, Sir John Ferguson (Ian), Kt., CBE
Denison-Smith, *Lt.-Gen.* Sir Anthony Arthur, KBE
Denny, Sir Anthony Coningham de Waltham, Bt. (I. 1782)
Denny, Sir Charles Alistair Maurice, Bt. (1913)
Derbyshire, Sir Andrew George, Kt.
Derham, Sir Peter John, Kt.
de Trafford, Sir Dermot Humphrey, Bt. (1841)
Deverell, *Gen.* Sir John Freegard, KCB, OBE
Devesi, Sir Baddeley, GCMG, GCVO
De Ville, Sir Harold Godfrey Oscar, Kt., CBE
Devitt, Sir James Hugh Thomas, Bt. (1916)
de Waal, Sir (Constant Henrik) Henry, KCB, QC
Dewey, Sir Anthony Hugh, Bt. (1917)
De Witt, Sir Ronald Wayne, Kt.
Dhenin, *Air Marshal* Sir Geoffrey Howard, KBE, AFC, GM, MD
Dhrangadhara, HH Maharaja Shriraj Sahib of Halvad, KCIE

Dick-Lauder, Sir Piers Robert, Bt. (S. 1690)

Dickinson, Sir Harold Herbert, Kt.

Dilke, Sir Charles John Wentworth, Bt. (1862)

Dillwyn-Venables-Llewelyn, Sir John Michael, Bt. (1890)

Dixon, Sir Jeremy, Kt.

Dixon, Sir Jonathan Mark, Bt. (1919)

Djanogly, Sir Harry Ari Simon, Kt., CBE

Dobson, *Vice-Adm.* Sir David Stuart, KBE

Dodds, Sir Ralph Jordan, Bt. (1964)

Dollery, Sir Colin Terence, Kt.

Don-Wauchope, Sir Roger (Hamilton), Bt. (S. 1667)

Donald, Sir Alan Ewen, KCMG

Donald, *Air Marshal* Sir John George, KBE

Donaldson, *Prof.* Sir Liam Joseph, Kt.

Donne, *Hon.* Sir Gaven John, KBE

Donne, Sir John Christopher, Kt.

Donnelly, Sir Joseph Brian, KBE, CMG

Dorey, Sir Graham Martyn, Kt.

Dorman, Sir Philip Henry Keppel, Bt. (1923)

Doughty, Sir Graham Martin, Kt.

Doughty, Sir William Roland, Kt.

Douglas, *Hon.* Sir Roger Owen, Kt.

Dover, *Prof.* Sir Kenneth James, Kt., DLITT, FBA, FRSE

Dowell, Sir Anthony James, Kt., CBE

Dowling, Sir Robert, Kt.

Downes, Sir Edward Thomas, Kt., CBE

Downey, Sir Gordon Stanley, KCB

Downs, Sir Diarmuid, Kt., CBE, FRENG

Downward, *Maj.-Gen.* Sir Peter Aldcroft, KCVO, CB, DSO, DFC

Dowson, Sir Philip Manning, Kt., CBE, PRA

Doyle, Sir Reginald Derek Henry, Kt., CBE

D'Oyly, Sir Hadley Gregory Bt. (1663)

Drake, *Hon.* Sir (Frederick) Maurice, Kt., DFC

Drewry, *Lt.-Gen.* Sir Christopher Francis, KCB, CBE

Drinkwater, Sir John Muir, Kt., QC

Driver, Sir Eric William, Kt.

Drury, Sir (Victor William) Michael, Kt., OBE

Dryden, Sir John Stephen Gyles, Bt. (1733 and 1795)

du Cann, *Rt. Hon.* Sir Edward Dillon Lott, KBE

†Duckworth, Sir James Edward Dyce, Bt. (1909)

du Cros, Sir Claude Philip Arthur Mallet, Bt. (1916)

Dudley-Williams, Sir Alastair Edgcumbe James, Bt. (1964)

Duff, *Prof.* Sir Gordon William, Kt.

Duff-Gordon, Sir Andrew Cosmo Lewis, Bt. (1813)

Duffell, *Lt.-Gen.* Sir Peter Royson, KCB, CBE, MC

Duffy, Sir (Albert) (Edward) Patrick, Kt., PHD

Dugdale, Sir William Stratford, Bt. (1936), MC

Duggin, Sir Thomas Joseph, Kt.

Dummett, *Prof.* Sir Michael Anthony Eardley, Kt., FBA

Dunbar, Sir Archibald Ranulph, Bt. (S. 1700)

Dunbar, Sir Robert Drummond Cospatrick, Bt. (S. 1698)

Dunbar, Sir James Michael, Bt. (S. 1694)

Dunbar of Hempriggs, Sir Richard Francis, Bt. (S. 1706)

Dunbar-Nasmith, *Prof.* Sir James Duncan, Kt., CBE

Duncan, Sir James Blair, Kt.

Dunlop, Sir Thomas, Bt. (1916)

Dunn, *Air Marshal* Sir Eric Clive, KBE, CB, BEM

Dunn, *Rt. Hon.* Sir Robin Horace Walford, Kt., MC

Dunne, Sir Thomas Raymond, KCVO

Dunning, Sir Simon William Patrick, Bt. (1930)

Dunnington-Jefferson, Sir Mervyn Stewart, Bt. (1958)

Dunstan, *Lt.-Gen.* Sir Donald Beaumont, KBE, CB

Dunt, *Vice-Adm.* Sir John Hugh, KCB

Duntze, Sir Daniel Evans Bt. (1774)

Dupre, Sir Tumun, Kt., MBE

Dupree, Sir (Thomas William James) David, Bt. (1921)

Durand, Sir Edward Alan Christopher David Percy, Bt. (1892)

Durant, Sir (Robert) Anthony (Bevis), Kt.

Durie, Sir David Robert Campbell, KCMG

Durrant, Sir William Alexander Estridge, Bt. (1784)

Duthie, *Prof.* Sir Herbert Livingston, Kt.

Duthie, Sir Robert Grieve (Robin), Kt., CBE

Dwyer, Sir Joseph Anthony, Kt.

Dyke, Sir David William Hart, Bt. (1677)

Dyson, Sir James, Kt., CBE

Dyson, *Rt. Hon.* Sir John Anthony, Kt.

Eady, *Hon.* Sir David, Kt.

Eardley-Wilmot, Sir Michael John Assheton, Bt. (1821)

Earle, Sir (Hardman) George (Algernon), Bt. (1869)

Easton, Sir Robert William Simpson, Kt., CBE

Eaton, *Adm.* Sir Kenneth John, GBE, KCB

Eberle, *Adm.* Sir James Henry Fuller, GCB

Ebrahim, Sir (Mahomed) Currimbhoy, Bt. (1910)

Eckersley, Sir Donald Payze, Kt., OBE

Eddington, Sir Roderick Ian, Kt.

Edge, *Capt.* Sir (Philip) Malcolm, KCVO

†Edge, Sir William, Bt. (1937)

Edmonstone, Sir Archibald Bruce Charles, Bt. (1774)

Edward, *Rt. Hon.* Sir David Alexander Ogilvy, KCMG

Edwardes, Sir Michael Owen, Kt.

Edwards, Sir Christopher John Churchill, Bt. (1866)

Edwards, Sir Llewellyn Roy, Kt.

Edwards, *Prof.* Sir Samuel Frederick, Kt., FRS

†Edwards-Moss, Sir David John, Bt. (1868)

Egan, Sir John Leopold, Kt.

Ehrman, Sir William Geoffrey, KCMG

Eichelbaum, *Rt. Hon.* Sir Thomas, GBE

Elias, *Hon.* Sir Patrick, Kt.

Eliott of Stobs, Sir Charles Joseph Alexander, Bt. (S. 1666)

Elliot, Sir Gerald Henry, Kt.

Elliott, Sir Clive Christopher Hugh, Bt. (1917)

Elliott, Sir David Murray, KCMG, CB

Elliott, *Prof.* Sir John Huxtable, Kt., FBA

Elliott, Sir Randal Forbes, KBE

Elliott, *Prof.* Sir Roger James, Kt., FRS

Elphinstone, Sir John, Bt. (S. 1701)

Elphinstone, Sir John Howard Main, Bt. (1816)

Elsmore, Sir Lloyd, Kt., OBE

Elton, Sir Arnold, Kt., CBE

Elton, Sir Charles Abraham Grierson, Bt. (1717)

Elton, Sir Leslie, Kt.

Elvidge, Sir John, KCB

Elwes, Sir Jeremy Vernon, Kt., CBE

Elwood, Sir Brian George Conway, Kt., CBE

Elworthy, *Air Cdre. Hon.* Sir Timothy Charles, KCVO, CBE

Empey, Sir Reginald Norman Morgan, Kt., OBE

Enderby, *Prof.* Sir John Edwin, Kt. CBE, FRS

Engle, Sir George Lawrence Jose, KCB, QC

English, Sir Terence Alexander Hawthorne, KBE, FRCS

Epstein, *Prof.* Sir (Michael) Anthony, Kt., CBE, FRS

Errington, *Col.* Sir Geoffrey Frederick, Bt. (1963), OBE

Errington, Sir Lancelot, KCB

Erskine, Sir (Thomas) Peter Neil, Bt. (1821)

Erskine-Hill, Sir Alexander Rodger, Bt. (1945)

Esmonde, Sir Thomas Francis Grattan, Bt. (I. 1629)

Esplen, Sir John Graham, Bt. (1921)

Essenhigh, *Adm.* Sir Nigel Richard, GCB

Etherton, *Hon.* Sir Terence Michael Elkan Barnet, Kt.

Evans, Sir Anthony Adney, Bt. (1920)

Evans, *Rt. Hon.* Sir Anthony Howell Meurig, Kt., RD

Evans, *Prof.* Sir Christopher Thomas, Kt., OBE

Evans, *Air Chief Marshal* Sir David George, GCB, CBE

Evans, *Hon.* Sir David Roderick, Kt.

Evans, Sir Harold Matthew, Kt.

Evans, *Hon.* Sir Haydn Tudor, Kt.

Evans, *Prof.* Sir John Grimley, Kt., FRCP

Evans, Sir John Stanley, Kt., QPM

Evans, *Prof.* Sir Martin John, Kt., FRS

Evans, Sir Richard Harry, Kt., CBE

Evans, Sir Richard Mark, KCMG, KCVO

Evans, Sir Robert, Kt., CBE, FRENG

Evans-Lombe, *Hon.* Sir Edward Christopher, Kt.

†Evans-Tipping, Sir David Gwynne, Bt. (1913)

Eveleigh, *Rt. Hon.* Sir Edward Walter, Kt., ERD

Everard, Sir Robin Charles, Bt. (1911)

Every, Sir Henry John Michael, Bt. (1641)

Ewans, Sir Martin Kenneth, KCMG

†Ewart, Sir William Michael, Bt. (1887)

Ewbank, *Hon.* Sir Anthony Bruce, Kt.

Eyre, Sir Reginald Edwin, Kt.

Eyre, Sir Richard Charles Hastings, Kt., CBE

Faber, Sir Richard Stanley, KCVO, CMG

Fagge, Sir John Christopher Frederick, Bt. (1660)

Fairbairn, Sir (James) Brooke, Bt. (1869)

Fairhall, *Hon.* Sir Allen, KBE

Fairlie-Cuningham, Sir Robert Henry, Bt. (S. 1630)

Fairweather, Sir Patrick Stanislaus, KCMG

Falconer, *Hon.* Sir Douglas William, Kt., MBE

†Falkiner, Sir Benjamin Simon Patrick, Bt. (I. 1778)

Fall, Sir Brian James Proetel, GCVO, KCMG

Falle, Sir Samuel, KCMG, KCVO, DSC

Fang, *Prof.* Sir Harry, Kt., CBE

Fareed, Sir Djamil Sheik, Kt.

Farmer, Sir Thomas, Kt., CBE

Farquhar, Sir Michael Fitzroy Henry, Bt. (1796)

Farquharson, *Rt. Hon.* Sir Donald Henry, Kt.

Farrell, Sir Terence, Kt., CBE

Farrer, Sir (Charles) Matthew, GCVO

Farrington, Sir Henry William, Bt. (1818)

Fat, Sir (Maxime) Edouard (Lim Man) Lim, Kt.

Faulkner, Sir (James) Dennis (Compton), Kt., CBE, VRD

Fay, Sir (Humphrey) Michael Gerard, Kt.

Fayrer, Sir John Lang Macpherson, Bt. (1896)

Feachem, *Prof.* Sir Richard George Andrew, KBE

Fean, Sir Thomas Vincent, KCVO

Feilden, Sir Bernard Melchior, Kt., CBE

Feilden, Sir Henry Wemyss, Bt., (1846)

Fell, Sir David, KCB

Fender, Sir Brian Edward Frederick, Kt., CMG, PHD

Fenn, Sir Nicholas Maxted, GCMG

Fennell, *Hon.* Sir (John) Desmond Augustine, Kt., OBE

Fennessy, Sir Edward, Kt., CBE

Fergus, Sir Howard Archibald, KBE

Ferguson, Sir Alexander Chapman, Kt., CBE

Ferguson-Davie, Sir Michael, Bt. (1847)

Fergusson of Kilkerran, Sir Charles, Bt. (S. 1703)

Fergusson, Sir Ewan Alastair John, GCMG, GCVO

Fermor, Sir Patrick Michael Leigh, Kt., DSO, OBE

Feroze, Sir Rustam Moolan, Kt., FRCS

Fersht, *Prof.* Sir Alan Roy, Kt., FRS

Ferris, *Hon.* Sir Francis Mursell, Kt., TD

ffolkes, Sir Robert Francis Alexander, Bt. (1774), OBE

Field, Sir Malcolm David, Kt.

Field, *Hon.* Sir Richard Alan, Kt.

Fielding, Sir Colin Cunningham, Kt., CB

Fielding, Sir Leslie, KCMG

Fields, Sir Allan Clifford, KCMG

Fieldsend, *Hon.* Sir John Charles Rowell, KBE

Fiennes, Sir Ranulph Twisleton-Wykeham, Bt. (1916), OBE

Figg, Sir Leonard Clifford William, KCMG

Figgis, Sir Anthony St John Howard, KCVO, CMG

Finch, Sir Robert Gerard, Kt.

Finlay, Sir David Ronald James Bell, Bt. (1964)

Finlayson, Sir Garet Orlando, KCMG, OBE

Finney, Sir Thomas, Kt., OBE

Fison, Sir (Richard) Guy, Bt. (1905), DSC

Fitzalan-Howard, *Maj.-Gen.* Lord Michael, GCVO, CB, CBE, MC

†Fitzgerald, *Revd* Daniel Patrick, Bt. (1903)

FitzGerald, Sir Adrian James Andrew, Bt. (1880)

FitzHerbert, Sir Richard Ranulph, Bt. (1784)

Fitzpatrick, *Air Marshal* Sir John Bernard, KBE, CB

Flanagan, Sir Ronald, GBE

Fletcher, Sir James Muir Cameron, Kt.

Floissac, *Hon.* Sir Vincent Frederick, Kt., CMG, OBE

Floud, *Prof.* Sir Roderick Castle, Kt.

Floyd, Sir Giles Henry Charles, Bt. (1816)

Foley, *Lt.-Gen.* Sir John Paul, KCB, OBE, MC

Follett, *Prof.* Sir Brian Keith, Kt., FRS

Foot, Sir Geoffrey James, Kt.

Foots, Sir James William, Kt.

Forbes, *Maj.* Sir Hamish Stewart, Bt. (1823), MBE, MC

Forbes, *Adm.* Sir Ian Andrew, KCB, CBE

Forbes of Craigievar, Sir Andrew Iain Ochoncar, Bt. (S. 1630)

Forbes, *Vice-Adm.* Sir John Morrison, KCB

Forbes, *Hon.* Sir Thayne John, Kt.

Forbes-Leith, Sir George Ian David, Bt. (1923)

Ford, Sir Andrew Russell, Bt. (1929)

Ford, Sir David Robert, KBE, LVO

Ford, *Prof.* Sir Hugh, Kt., FRS, FRENG

Ford, Sir John Archibald, KCMG, MC

Ford, *Gen.* Sir Robert Cyril, GCB, CBE

Foreman, Sir Philip Frank, Kt., CBE, FRENG

Forestier-Walker, Sir Michael Leolin, Bt. (1835)

Forman, Sir John Denis, Kt., OBE

Forrest, *Prof.* Sir (Andrew) Patrick (McEwen), Kt.

Forte, *Hon.* Sir Rocco John Vincent, Kt.

Forwood, Sir Peter Noel, Bt. (1895)

Foster, Sir Andrew William, Kt.

Foster, *Prof.* Sir Christopher David, Kt.

Foster, Sir John Gregory, Bt. (1930)

Foulkes, Sir Arther Alexander, KCMG

Foulkes, Sir Nigel Gordon, Kt.

Fountain, *Hon.* Sir Cyril Stanley Smith, Kt.

Fowden, Sir Leslie, Kt., FRS

Fowke, Sir David Frederick Gustavus, Bt. (1814)

Fowler, Sir (Edward) Michael Coulson, Kt.

Fox, Sir Christopher, Kt., QPM

Fox, Sir Paul Leonard, Kt., CBE

France, Sir Christopher Walter, GCB

Francis, Sir Horace William Alexander, Kt., CBE, FRENG

Frank, Sir Robert Andrew, Bt. (1920)

Franklin, Sir Michael David Milroy, KCB, CMG

Franks, Sir Arthur Temple, KCMG

Fraser, Sir Alasdair MacLeod, Kt.

Fraser, Sir Charles Annand, KCVO

Fraser, *Gen.* Sir David William, GCB, OBE

Fraser, Sir Iain Michael Duncan, Bt. (1943)

Fraser, Sir James Murdo, KBE

Fraser, Sir William Kerr, GCB

Frayling, *Prof.* Sir Christopher John, Kt.

Frederick, Sir Christopher St John, Bt. (1723)

Freedman, *Prof.* Sir Lawrence David, KCMG, CBE

Freeland, Sir John Redvers, KCMG

Freeman, Sir James Robin, Bt. (1945)

Freer, *Air Chief Marshal* Sir Robert William George, GBE, KCB

French, *Air Marshal* Sir Joseph Charles, KCB, CBE

Frere, *Vice-Adm.* Sir Richard Tobias, KCB

Fretwell, Sir (Major) John (Emsley), GCMG

Freud, Sir Clement Raphael, Kt.

Friend *Prof.* Sir Richard Henry, Kt.

Froggatt, Sir Leslie Trevor, Kt.

Froggatt, Sir Peter, Kt.

Frossard, Sir Charles Keith, KBE

Frost, Sir David Paradine, Kt., OBE

Fry, Sir Graham Holbrook, KCMG

Fry, Sir Peter Derek, Kt.

Fry, *Lt.-Gen.* Sir Robert Allan, KCB, CBE

Fulford, *Hon.* Sir Adrian Bruce, Kt.

Fuller, Sir James Henry Fleetwood, Bt. (1910)

Fuller, *Hon.* Sir John Bryan Munro, Kt.

Fulton, *Lt.-Gen.* Sir Robert Henry Gervase, KBE

Furness, Sir Stephen Roberts, Bt. (1913)

Gage, *Rt. Hon.* Sir William Marcus, Kt.

Gains, Sir John Christopher, Kt.

Gainsford, Sir Ian Derek, Kt.

Gaius, *Rt. Revd* Saimon, KBE

Galsworthy, Sir Anthony Charles, KCMG

Galway, Sir James, Kt., OBE

Gamble, Sir David Hugh Norman, Bt. (1897)

Gambon, Sir Michael John, Kt., CBE

Gammell, Sir William Benjamin Bowring, Kt.

Gardiner, Sir John Eliot, Kt., CBE

Gardner, *Prof.* Sir Richard Lavenham, Kt.

Gardner, Sir Roy Alan, Kt.

Garland, *Hon.* Sir Patrick Neville, Kt.

Garland, *Hon.* Sir Ransley Victor, KBE

Garner, Sir Anthony Stuart, Kt.

Garnett, *Adm.* Sir Ian David Graham, KCB

Garnier, *Rear-Adm.* Sir John, KCVO, CBE

Garrard, Sir David Eardley, Kt.

Garrett, Sir Anthony Peter, Kt., CBE

Garrick, Sir Ronald, Kt., CBE, FRENG

Garrioch, Sir (William) Henry, Kt.

Garrod, *Lt.-Gen.* Sir (John) Martin Carruthers, KCB, OBE

Garthwaite, Sir (William) Mark (Charles), Bt. (1919)

Gaskell, Sir Richard Kennedy Harvey, Kt.

Geno, Sir Makena Viora, KBE

Gent, Sir Christopher Charles, Kt.

George, Sir Arthur Thomas, Kt.

George, *Prof.* Sir Charles Frederick, MD, FRCP

George, Sir Richard William, Kt., CVO

Gerken, *Vice-Adm.* Sir Robert William Frank, KCB, CBE

Gershon, Sir Peter Oliver, Kt., CBE

Gethin, Sir Richard Joseph St Lawrence, Bt. (I. 1665)

Ghurburrun, Sir Rabindrah, Kt.

Gibb, Sir Francis Ross (Frank), Kt., CBE, FRENG

Gibbings, Sir Peter Walter, Kt.

Gibbons, Sir (John) David, KBE

Gibbons, Sir William Edward Doran, Bt. (1752)

Gibbs, *Hon.* Sir Richard John Hedley, Kt.

Gibbs, Sir Roger Geoffrey, Kt.

†Gibson, *Revd* Christopher Herbert, Bt. (1931)

Gibson, Sir Ian, Kt., CBE

Gibson, *Rt. Hon.* Sir Peter Leslie, Kt.

Gibson-Craig-Carmichael, Sir David Peter William, Bt. (S. 1702 and 1831)

Giddings, *Air Marshal* Sir (Kenneth Charles) Michael, KCB, OBE, DFC, AFC

Gieve, Sir Edward John Watson, KCB

Giffard, Sir (Charles) Sydney (Rycroft), KCMG

Gilbart-Denham, *Lt.-Col.* Sir Seymour Vivian, KCVO

Gilbert, *Air Chief Marshal* Sir Joseph Alfred, KCB, CBE

Gilbert, Sir Martin John, Kt., CBE

†Gilbey, Sir Walter Gavin, Bt. (1893)

Gill, Sir Anthony Keith, Kt.

Gill, Sir Arthur Benjamin Norman, Kt., CBE

Gillam, Sir Patrick John, Kt.

Gillen, *Hon.* Sir John de Winter, Kt.

Gillett, Sir Robin Danvers Penrose, Bt. (1959), GBE, RD

Gillinson, Sir Clive Daniel, Kt., CBE

†Gilmour, Sir John, Bt. (1897)

Gina, Sir Lloyd Maepeza, KBE

Gingell, *Air Chief Marshal* Sir John, GBE, KCB, KCVO

Giordano, Sir Richard Vincent, KBE

Girolami, Sir Paul, Kt.

Girvan, *Rt. Hon.* Sir (Frederick) Paul, Kt.

Gladstone, Sir (Erskine) William, Bt. (1846), KG

Glenn, Sir (Joseph Robert) Archibald, Kt., OBE

Glidewell, *Rt. Hon.* Sir Iain Derek Laing, Kt.

Glover, Sir Victor Joseph Patrick, Kt.

Glyn, Sir Richard Lindsay, Bt. (1759 and 1800)

Gobbo, Sir James Augustine, Kt., AC

Godber, Sir George Edward, GCB, DM

Goldberg, *Prof.* Sir Abraham, Kt., MD, DSC, FRCP

Goldberg, *Prof.* Sir David Paul Brandes, Kt.

Goldring, *Hon.* Sir John Bernard, Kt.

Gomersall, Sir Stephen John, KCMG

Gonsalves-Sabola, *Hon.* Sir Joaquim Claudino, Kt

†Gooch, Sir Miles Peter, Bt. (1866)

Gooch, Sir Timothy Robert, Bt. (1746), MBE

Goodall, Sir (Arthur) David Saunders, GCMG

Goodall, *Air Marshal* Sir Roderick Harvey, KBE, CB, AFC

Goode, *Prof.* Sir Royston Miles, Kt., CBE, QC

Goodenough, Sir Anthony Michael, KCMG

Goodenough, Sir William McLernon, Bt. (1943)

Goodhart, Sir Philip Carter, Kt.

Goodhart, Sir Robert Anthony Gordon, Bt. (1911)

Goodison, Sir Nicholas Proctor, Kt.

Goodman, Sir Patrick Ledger, Kt., CBE

Goodson, Sir Mark Weston Lassam, Bt. (1922)

Goodwin, Sir Frederick, KBE

Goodwin, Sir Frederick Anderson, Kt.

Goodwin, Sir Matthew Dean, Kt., CBE

Goody, *Prof.* Sir John Rankine, Kt.

†Goold, Sir George William, Bt. (1801)

Gordon, Sir Charles Addison Somerville Snowden, KCB

Gordon, Sir Donald, Kt.

Gordon, Sir Gerald Henry, Kt., CBE, QC

Gordon, Sir Robert James, Bt. (S. 1706)

Gordon-Cumming, Sir Alexander Penrose, Bt. (1804)

†Gore, Sir Nigel Hugh St George, Bt. (I. 1622)

Gore-Booth, Sir Josslyn Henry Robert, Bt. (I. 1760)

Goring, Sir William Burton Nigel, Bt. (1627)

Gorman, Sir John Reginald, Kt., CVO, CBE, MC

Gorst, Sir John Michael, Kt.

Goschen, Sir (Edward) Alexander, Bt. (1916)

Gosling, Sir (Frederick) Donald, KCVO

Goswell, Sir Brian Lawrence, Kt.

Gough, Sir Charles Brandon, Kt.

Goulden, Sir (Peter) John, GCMG

Goulding, Sir Marrack Irvine, KCMG

Goulding, Sir (William) Lingard Walter, Bt. (1904)

Gourlay, *Gen.* Sir (Basil) Ian (Spencer), KCB, OBE, MC, RM

Gourlay, Sir Simon Alexander, Kt.

Govan, Sir Lawrence Herbert, Kt.

Gow, *Gen.* Sir (James) Michael, GCB

Gowans, Sir James Learmonth, Kt., CBE, FRCP, FRS

Gozney, Sir Richard Hugh Turton, KCMG

†Graaff, Sir David de Villiers, Bt. (1911)

Grabham, Sir Anthony Henry, Kt.

Graham, Sir Alexander Michael, GBE

Graham, Sir James Bellingham, Bt. (1662)

Graham, Sir James Fergus Surtees, Bt. (1783)

Graham, Sir James Thompson, Kt., CMG

Graham, Sir John Alexander Noble, Bt. (1906), GCMG

Graham, Sir John Alistair, Kt.

Graham, Sir John Moodie, Bt. (1964)

Graham, Sir Norman William, Kt., CB

Graham, Sir Peter, KCB, QC

Graham, Sir Peter Alfred, Kt., OBE

Graham, Lt.-Gen. Sir Peter Walter, KCB, CBE

†Graham, Sir Ralph Stuart, Bt. (1629)

Graham-Moon, Sir Peter Wilfred Giles, Bt. (1855)

Graham-Smith, Prof. Sir Francis, Kt.

Granger, Prof. Sir Clive William John, Kt.

Grant, Sir Archibald, Bt. (S. 1705)

Grant, Sir Clifford, Kt.

Grant, Sir (John) Anthony, Kt.

Grant, Sir John Douglas Kelso, KCMG

Grant, Sir Patrick Alexander Benedict, Bt. (S. 1688)

Grant, Lt.-Gen. Sir Scott Carnegie, KCB

Grant-Suttie, Sir James Edward, Bt. (S. 1702)

Granville-Chapman, Lt.-Gen. Sir Timothy John, GBE, KCB, ADC

Gratton-Bellew, Sir Henry Charles, Bt. (1838)

Gray, Hon. Sir Charles Anthony St John, Kt.

Gray, Sir Charles Ireland, Kt., CBE

Gray, Prof. Sir Denis John Pereira, Kt., OBE, FRCGP

Gray, Sir John Archibald Browne, Kt., SCD, FRS

Gray, Dr. Sir John Armstrong Muir, Kt., CBE

Gray, Lt.-Gen. Sir Michael Stuart, KCB, OBE

Gray, Sir Robert McDowall (Robin), Kt.

Gray, Sir William Hume, Bt. (1917)

Graydon, Air Chief Marshal Sir Michael James, GCB, CBE

Grayson, Sir Jeremy Brian Vincent Harrington, Bt. (1922)

Green, Sir Allan David, KCB, QC

Green, Sir Andrew Fleming, KCMG

Green, Sir Edward Patrick Lycett, Bt. (1886)

Green, Sir Gregory David, KCMG

Green, Hon. Sir Guy Stephen Montague, KBE

Green, Sir Kenneth, Kt.

Green, Prof. Sir Malcolm, Kt.

Green, Sir Owen Whitley, Kt.

Green, Sir Philip Green, Kt.

Green-Price, Sir Robert John, Bt. (1874)

Greenaway, Sir John Michael Burdick, Bt. (1933)

Greenbury, Sir Richard, Kt.

Greener, Sir Anthony Armitage, Kt.

Greengross, Sir Alan David, Kt.

Greening, Rear-Adm. Sir Paul Woollven, GCVO

Greenstock, Sir Jeremy Quentin, GCMG

Greenwell, Sir Edward Bernard, Bt. (1906)

Gregson, Sir Peter Lewis, GCB

Greig, Sir (Henry Louis) Carron, KCVO, CBE

Grey, Sir Anthony Dysart, Bt. (1814)

Grey-Egerton, Sir (Philip) John (Caledon), Bt. (1617)

Grierson, Sir Michael John Bewes, Bt. (S. 1685)

Grierson, Sir Ronald Hugh, Kt.

Griffin, Maj. Sir (Arthur) John (Stewart), KCVO

Griffiths, Sir Eldon Wylie, Kt.

Grigson, Hon. Sir Geoffrey Douglas, Kt.

Grimshaw, Sir Nicholas Thomas, Kt., CBE

Grimwade, Sir Andrew Sheppard, Kt., CBE

Grindrod, Most Revd John Basil Rowland, KBE

Grinstead, Sir Stanley Gordon, Kt.

Grose, Vice-Adm. Sir Alan, KBE

Gross, Hon. Sir Peter Henry, Kt.

Grossart, Sir Angus McFarlane McLeod, Kt., CBE

Grotrian, Sir Philip Christian Brent, Bt. (1934)

Grove, Sir Charles Gerald, Bt. (1874)

Grove, Sir Edmund Frank, KCVO

Grugeon, Sir John Drury, Kt.

Grundy, Sir Mark, Kt.

Guinness, Sir Howard Christian Sheldon, Kt., VRD

Guinness, Sir John Ralph Sidney, Kt., CB

Guinness, Sir Kenelm Ernest Lee, Bt. (1867)

†Guise, Sir Christopher James, Bt. (1783)

Gull, Sir Rupert William Cameron, Bt. (1872)

Gumbs, Sir Emile Rudolph, Kt.

Gunn, Sir Robert Norman, Kt.

†Gunning, Sir Charles Theodore, Bt. (1778)

Gunston, Sir John Wellesley, Bt. (1938)

Gurdon, Prof. Sir John Bertrand, Kt., DPHIL, FRS

Guthrie, Sir Malcolm Connop, Bt. (1936)

Haddacks, Vice-Adm. Sir Paul Kenneth, KCB

Hadfield, Sir Ronald, Kt., QPM

Hadlee, Sir Richard John, Kt., MBE

Hagart-Alexander, Sir Claud, Bt. (1886)

Hague, Prof. Sir Douglas Chalmers, Kt., CBE

Haines, Prof. Sir Andrew Paul, Kt.

Haji-Ioannou, Sir Stelios, Kt.

Halberg, Sir Murray Gordon, Kt., MBE

Hall, Sir Basil Brodribb, KCB, MC, TD

Hall, Prof. Sir David Michael Baldock, Kt.

Hall, Sir Ernest, Kt., OBE

Hall, Sir Graham Joseph, Kt.

Hall, Sir Iain Robert, Kt.

Hall, Sir (Frederick) John (Frank), Bt. (1923)

Hall, Sir John, Kt.

Hall, Sir John Bernard, Bt. (1919)

Hall, Sir John Douglas Hoste, Bt. (S. 1687)

Hall, Sir Peter Edward, KBE, CMG

Hall, Prof. Sir Peter Geoffrey, Kt., FBA

Hall, Sir Peter Reginald Frederick, Kt., CBE

Halliday, Vice-Adm. Sir Roy William, KBE, DSC

Halpern, Sir Ralph Mark, Kt.

Halsey, Revd John Walter Brooke, Bt. (1920)

Halstead, Sir Ronald, Kt., CBE

Hambling, Sir (Herbert) Hugh, Bt. (1924)

Hamilton, Sir Andrew Caradoc, Bt. (S. 1646)

Hamilton, Sir Edward Sydney, Bt. (1776 and 1819)

Hamilton, Sir James Arnot, KCB, MBE, FRENG

Hamilton-Dalrymple, Maj. Sir Hew Fleetwood, Bt. (S. 1697), GCVO

Hamilton-Spencer-Smith, Sir John, Bt. (1804)

Hammick, Sir Stephen George, Bt. (1834)

Hammond, Sir Anthony Hilgrove, KCB, QC

Hampel, Sir Ronald Claus, Kt.

Hampson, Sir Stuart, Kt.

Hampton, Sir (Leslie) Geoffrey, Kt.

Hampton, Sir Philip Roy, Kt.

Hanbury-Tenison, Sir Richard, KCVO

Hancock, Sir David John Stowell, KCB

Hanham, Sir Michael William, Bt. (1667), DFC

Hankes-Drielsma, Sir Claude Dunbar, KCVO

Hanley, Rt. Hon. Sir Jeremy James, KCMG

Hanmer, Sir John Wyndham Edward, Bt. (1774)

Hannam, Sir John Gordon, Kt.

Hanson, Sir (Charles) Rupert (Patrick), Bt. (1918)

Hanson, Sir John Gilbert, KCMG, CBE

Harcourt-Smith, Air Chief Marshal Sir David, GBE, KCB, DFC

Hardie Boys, Rt. Hon. Sir Michael, GCMG

Harding, Sir George William, KCMG, CVO

Harding, Marshal of the Royal Air Force Sir Peter Robin, GCB

Harding, Sir Roy Pollard, Kt., CBE

Hardy, Sir David William, Kt.

Hardy, Sir James Gilbert, Kt., OBE

Hardy, Sir Richard Charles Chandos, Bt. (1876)
Hare, Sir David, Kt., FRSL
Hare, Sir Nicholas Patrick, Bt. (1818)
Harford, Sir (John) Timothy, Bt. (1934)
Hargroves, *Brig.* Sir Robert Louis, Kt., CBE
Harington, Sir Nicholas John, Bt. (1611)
Harkness, *Very Revd* James, KCVO, CB, OBE
Harland, *Air Marshal* Sir Reginald Edward Wynyard, KBE, CB
Harley, *Gen.* Sir Alexander George Hamilton, KBE, CB
Harman, *Gen.* Sir Jack Wentworth, GCB, OBE, MC
Harman, *Hon.* Sir Jeremiah LeRoy, Kt.
Harman, Sir John Andrew, Kt.
Harmsworth, Sir Hildebrand Harold, Bt. (1922)
Harper, Sir Ewan William, Kt. CBE
Harper, *Prof.* Sir Peter Stanley, Kt., CBE
Harris, *Prof.* Sir Henry, Kt., FRCP, FRCPATH, FRS
Harris, Sir Jack Wolfred Ashford, Bt. (1932)
Harris, *Air Marshal* Sir John Hulme, KCB, CBE
Harris, *Prof.* Sir Martin Best, Kt., CBE
Harris, Sir Thomas George, KBE, CMG
Harrison, *Prof.* Sir Brian Howard, Kt.
Harrison, Sir David, Kt., CBE, FRENG
Harrison, Sir Ernest Thomas, Kt., OBE
Harrison, *Surgeon Vice-Adm.* Sir John Albert Bews, KBE
Harrison, *Hon.* Sir Michael Guy Vicat, Kt.
Harrison, Sir Michael James Harwood, Bt. (1961)
Harrison, Sir (Robert) Colin, Bt. (1922)
Harrison, Sir Terence, Kt., FRENG
Harrop, Sir Peter John, KCB
Hart, *Hon.* Sir Anthony Ronald, Kt.
Hart, Sir David Michael, Kt., OBE
Hart, Sir Graham Allan, KCB
Hartwell, Sir (Francis) Anthony Charles Peter, Bt. (1805)
Harvey, Sir Charles Richard Musgrave, Bt. (1933)
Harvey-Jones, Sir John Henry, Kt., MBE
Harvie, Sir John Smith, Kt., CBE
Harvie-Watt, Sir James, Bt. (1945)
Haselhurst, *Rt. Hon.* Sir Alan Gordon Barraclough, Kt.
Haskard, Sir Cosmo Dugal Patrick Thomas, KCMG, MBE
Haslam, *Rear-Adm.* Sir David William, KBE, CB
Hassett, *Gen.* Sir Francis George, KBE, CB, DSO, LVO
Hastings, Sir Max Macdonald, Kt.

Hatter, Sir Maurice, Kt.
Havelock-Allan, Sir (Anthony) Mark David, Bt. (1858)
Hawkins, Sir Richard Caesar, Bt. (1778)
Hawley, Sir Donald Frederick, KCMG, MBE
†Hawley, Sir Henry Nicholas, Bt. (1795)
Haworth, Sir Philip, Bt. (1911)
Hawthorne, *Prof.* Sir William Rede, Kt., CBE, SCD, FRS, FRENG
Hay, Sir David Osborne, Kt., CBE, DSO
Hay, Sir David Russell, Kt., CBE, FRCP, MD
Hay, Sir Hamish Grenfell, Kt.
Hay, Sir John Erroll Audley, Bt. (S. 1663)
†Hay, Sir Ronald Frederick Hamilton, Bt. (S. 1703)
Hayes, Sir Brian, Kt., CBE, QPM
Hayes, Sir Brian David, GCB
Hayman-Joyce, *Lt.-Gen.* Sir Robert John, KCB, CBE
Hayter, Sir Paul David Grenville, KCB, LVO
Hayward, Sir Anthony William Byrd, Kt.
Hayward, Sir Jack Arnold, Kt., OBE
Haywood, Sir Harold, KCVO, OBE
Head, Sir Richard Douglas Somerville, Bt. (1838)
Heap, Sir Peter William, KCMG
Heap, *Prof.* Sir Robert Brian, Kt., CBE, FRS
Hearne, Sir Graham James, Kt., CBE
Heathcote, *Brig.* Sir Gilbert Simon, Bt. (1733), CBE
†Heathcote, Sir Timothy Gilbert, Bt. (1733)
Heatley, Sir Peter, Kt., CBE
Hedley, *Hon.* Sir Mark, Kt.
Hegarty, Sir John Kevin, Kt.
Heiser, Sir Terence Michael, GCB
Henao, Revd Ravu, Kt., OBE
Henderson, Sir Denys Hartley, Kt.
Henderson, Sir (John) Nicholas, GCMG, KCVO
Henderson, *Hon.* Sir Launcelot Dinadan James, Kt.
Henderson, *Maj.* Sir Richard Yates, KCVO
Hennessy, Sir James Patrick Ivan, KBE, CMG
†Henniker, Sir Adrian Chandos, Bt. (1813)
Henniker-Heaton, Sir Yvo Robert, Bt. (1912)
Henriques, *Hon.* Sir Richard Henry Quixano, Kt.
Henry, *Rt. Hon.* Sir Denis Robert Maurice, Kt.
Henry, *Hon.* Sir Geoffrey Arama, KBE
†Henry, Sir Patrick Denis, Bt. (1923)
Henry, *Hon.* Sir Trevor Ernest, Kt.
Henshaw, Sir David George, Kt.
Hepple, *Prof.* Sir Bob Alexander, Kt.
Herbecq, Sir John Edward, KCB
Herbert, *Adm.* Sir Peter Geoffrey Marshall, KCB, OBE

Hermon, Sir John Charles, Kt., OBE, QPM
Heron, Sir Conrad Frederick, KCB, OBE
Heron, Sir Michael Gilbert, Kt.
Heron-Maxwell, Sir Nigel Mellor, Bt. (S. 1683)
Hervey, Sir Roger Blaise Ramsay, KCVO, CMG
Hervey-Bathurst, Sir Frederick John Charles Gordon, Bt. (1818)
Heseltine, *Rt. Hon.* Sir William Frederick Payne, GCB, GCVO
Hewetson, Sir Christopher Raynor, Kt., TD
Hewett, Sir Richard Mark John, Bt. (1813)
Hewitt, Sir (Cyrus) Lenox (Simson), Kt., OBE
Hewitt, Sir Nicholas Charles Joseph, Bt. (1921)
Heygate, Sir Richard John Gage, Bt. (1831)
Heywood, Sir Peter, Bt. (1838)
Hezlet, *Vice-Adm.* Sir Arthur Richard, KBE, CB, DSO, DSC
Hibbert, Sir Jack, KCB
Hickey, Sir Justin, Kt.
Hickman, Sir (Richard) Glenn, Bt. (1903)
Hicks, Sir Robert, Kt.
Hidden, *Hon.* Sir Anthony Brian, Kt.
Hielscher, Sir Leo Arthur, Kt.
Higgins, *Rt. Hon.* Sir Malachy Joseph, Kt.
Higginson, Sir Gordon Robert, Kt., PHD, FRENG
Higgs, Sir Derek Alan, Kt.
Hill, Sir Arthur Alfred, Kt., CBE
Hill, Sir Brian John, Kt.
Hill, Sir James Frederick, Bt. (1917)
Hill, Sir John Alfred Rowley, Bt. (I 1779)
Hill, Sir John McGregor, Kt., PHD, FRENG
Hill, *Vice-Adm.* Sir Robert Charles Finch, KBE, FRENG
Hill-Norton, *Vice-Adm. Hon.* Sir Nicholas John, KCB
Hill-Wood, Sir Samuel Thomas, Bt. (1921)
Hillary, Sir Edmund, KG, KBE
Hillhouse, Sir (Robert) Russell, KCB
Hills, Sir Graham John, Kt.
Hine, *Air Chief Marshal* Sir Patrick Bardon, GCB, GBE
Hirsch, *Prof.* Sir Peter Bernhard, Kt., PHD., FRS
Hirst, *Rt. Hon.* Sir David Cozens-Hardy, Kt.
Hirst, Sir Michael William, Kt.
Hoare, *Prof.* Sir Charles Anthony Richard, Kt., FRS
Hoare, Sir David John, Bt. (1786)
Hoare, Sir Timothy Edward Charles, Bt. (I. 1784), OBE
Hobart, Sir John Vere, Bt. (1914)
Hobbs, *Maj.-Gen.* Sir Michael Frederick, KCVO, CBE
Hobday, Sir Gordon Ivan, Kt.
Hobhouse, Sir Charles John Spinney, Bt. (1812)

Hobson, Sir Ronald, KCVO

†Hodge, Sir Andrew Rowland, Bt. (1921)

Hodge, *Hon.* Sir Henry Egar Garfield, Kt.

Hodge, Sir James William, KCVO, CMG

Hodgkin, Sir (Gordon) Howard (Eliot), Kt., CH, CBE

Hodgkinson, Sir Michael Stewart, Kt.

Hodgkinson, *Air Chief Marshal* Sir (William) Derek, KCB, CBE, DFC, AFC

Hodgson, Sir Maurice Arthur Eric, Kt., FRENG

Hodson, Sir Michael Robin Adderley, Bt. (I. 1789)

Hogg, Sir Christopher Anthony, Kt.

†Hogg, Sir Piers Michael James, Bt. (1846)

Holcroft, Sir Peter George Culcheth, Bt. (1921)

Holderness, Sir Martin William, Bt. (1920)

Holden, Sir Paul, Bt. (1893)

Holden, Sir John David, Bt. (1919)

Holden-Brown, Sir Derrick, Kt.

Holder, Sir John Henry, Bt. (1898)

Holdgate, Sir Martin Wyatt, Kt., CB, PHD

Holdsworth, Sir (George) Trevor, Kt., CVO

Holland, *Hon.* Sir Alan Douglas, Kt.

Holland, *Hon.* Sir Christopher John, Kt.

Holland, Sir Clifton Vaughan, Kt.

Holland, Sir Geoffrey, KCB

Holland, Sir John Anthony, Kt.

Holland, Sir Philip Welsby, Kt.

Holliday, *Prof.* Sir Frederick George Thomas, Kt., CBE, FRSE

Hollings, *Hon.* Sir (Alfred) Kenneth, Kt., MC

Hollom, Sir Jasper Quintus, KBE

Holloway, *Hon.* Sir Barry Blyth, KBE

Holman, *Hon.* Sir (Edward) James, Kt.

Holmes, *Prof.* Sir Frank Wakefield, Kt.

Holmes, Sir John Eaton, GCVO, KBE, CMG

Holmes-Sellors, Sir Patrick John, KCVO

Holroyd, *Air Marshal* Sir Frank Martyn, KBE, CB

Holroyd, Sir Michael De Courcy Fraser, Kt., CBE

Holt, *Prof.* Sir James Clarke, Kt.

Holt, Sir Michael, Kt., CBE

Home, Sir William Dundas, Bt. (S. 1671)

Honeycombe, *Prof.* Sir Robert William Kerr, Kt., FRS, FRENG

Honywood, Sir Filmer Courtenay William, Bt. (1660)

†Hood, Sir John Joseph Harold, Bt. (1922)

Hookway, Sir Harry Thurston, Kt.

Hooper, *Rt. Hon.* Sir Anthony, Kt.

Hope, Sir Colin Frederick Newton, Kt.

Hope, Sir John Carl Alexander, Bt. (S. 1628)

Hope-Dunbar, Sir David, Bt. (S. 1664)

Hopkin, Sir Royston Oliver, KCMG

Hopkin, Sir (William Aylsham) Bryan, Kt., CBE

Hopkins, Sir Anthony Philip, Kt., CBE

Hopkins, Sir Michael John, Kt., CBE, RA, RIBA

Hopwood, *Prof.* Sir David Alan, Kt., FRS

Hordern, *Rt. Hon.* Sir Peter Maudslay, Kt.

Horlick, *Vice-Adm.* Sir Edwin John, KBE, FRENG

Horlick, Sir James Cunliffe William, Bt. (1914)

Horlock, *Prof.* Sir John Harold, Kt., FRS, FRENG

Horn, *Prof.* Sir Gabriel, Kt., FRS

Horn-Smith, Sir Julian Michael, Kt.

Hornby, Sir Derek Peter, Kt.

Hornby, Sir Simon Michael, Kt.

Horne, Sir Alan Gray Antony, Bt. (1929)

Horne, *Dr* Sir Alistair Allan, Kt. CBE

Horsbrugh-Porter, Sir John Simon, Bt. (1902)

Horsfall, Sir Edward John Wright, Bt. (1909)

†Hort, Sir Andrew Edwin Fenton, Bt. (1767)

Horton, Sir Robert Baynes, Kt.

Hosker, Sir Gerald Albery, KCB, QC

Hoskins, *Prof.* Sir Brian John, Kt. CBE, FRS

Hoskyns, Sir Benedict Leigh, Bt. (1676)

Hoskyns, Sir John Austin Hungerford Leigh, Kt.

Hotung, Sir Joseph Edward, Kt.

Houghton, Sir John Theodore, Kt., CBE, FRS

Houldsworth, Sir Richard Thomas Reginald, Bt. (1887)

Hourston, Sir Gordon Minto, Kt.

House, *Lt.-Gen.* Sir David George, GCB, KCVO, CBE, MC

Houssemayne du Boulay, Sir Roger William, KCVO, CMG

Houstoun-Boswall, Sir (Thomas) Alford, Bt. (1836)

Howard, Sir David Howarth Seymour, Bt. (1955)

Howard, *Prof.* Sir Michael Eliot, Kt., OM, CH, CBE, MC

Howard-Dobson, *Gen.* Sir Patrick John, GCB

Howard-Lawson, Sir John Philip, Bt. (1841)

Howell, Sir Ralph Frederic, Kt.

Howells, Sir Eric Waldo Benjamin, Kt., CBE

Howes, Sir Christopher Kingston, KCVO, CB

Howlett, *Gen.* Sir Geoffrey Hugh Whitby, KBE, MC

Huggins, *Hon.* Sir Alan Armstrong, Kt.

Hugh-Jones, Sir Wynn Normington, Kt., LVO

Hugh-Smith, Sir Andrew Colin, Kt.

Hughes, *Rt. Hon.* Sir Anthony Philip Gilson, Kt.

Hughes, Sir Thomas Collingwood, Bt. (1773)

Hughes, Sir Trevor Poulton, KCB

†Hughes-Morgan, Sir (Ian) Parry David, Bt. (1925)

Hull, *Prof.* Sir David, Kt.

Hulse, Sir Edward Jeremy Westrow, Bt. (1739)

Hum, Sir Christopher Owen, KCMG

Hunt, Sir John Leonard, Kt.

Hunt, *Adm.* Sir Nicholas John Streynsham, GCB, LVO

Hunt, Sir Rex Masterman, Kt., CMG

Hunt, *Dr* Sir Richard Timothy, Kt.

Hunt-Davis, *Brig.* Sir Miles Garth, KCVO, CBE

Hunter, Sir Alistair John, KCMG

Hunter, *Prof.* Sir Laurence Colvin, Kt., CBE, FRSE

Hunter, Sir Thomas Blane, Kt.

Huntington-Whiteley, Sir Hugo Baldwin, Bt. (1918)

Hurn, Sir (Francis) Roger, Kt.

Hurrell, Sir Anthony Gerald, KCVO, CMG

Hurst, Sir Geoffrey Charles, Kt., MBE

Husbands, Sir Clifford Straugh, GCMG

Hutchinson, *Hon.* Sir Ross, Kt., DFC

Hutchison, Sir James Colville, Bt. (1956)

Hutchison, *Rt. Hon.* Sir Michael, Kt.

Hutchison, Sir Robert, Bt. (1939)

Hutt, Sir Dexter Walter, Kt.

Huxley, *Prof.* Sir Andrew Fielding, Kt., OM, FRS

Huxtable, *Gen.* Sir Charles Richard, KCB, CBE

Ibbs, Sir (John) Robin, KBE

Imbert-Terry, Sir Michael Edward Stanley, Bt. (1917)

Imray, Sir Colin Henry, KBE, CMG

Ingham, Sir Bernard, Kt.

Ingilby, Sir Thomas Colvin William, Bt. (1866)

Inglis, Sir Brian Scott, Kt.

Inglis of Glencorse, Sir Roderick John, Bt. (S. 1703)

Ingram, Sir James Herbert Charles, Bt. (1893)

Ingram, Sir John Henderson, Kt., CBE

Inkin, Sir Geoffrey David, Kt., OBE

†Innes, Sir David Charles Kenneth Gordon, Bt. (NS 1686)

Innes of Edingight, Sir Malcolm Rognvald, KCVO

Innes, Sir Peter Alexander Berowald, Bt. (S. 1628)

Irvine, Sir Donald Hamilton, Kt., CBE, MD, FRCGP

Irving, *Prof.* Sir Miles Horsfall, Kt., MD, FRCS, FRCSE

Irwin, *Lt.-Gen.* Sir Alistair Stuart Hastings, KCB, CBE

Irwin, *Hon.* Sir Stephen John, Kt.
Isaacs, Sir Jeremy Israel, Kt.
Isham, Sir Ian Vere Gyles, Bt. (1627)
Ivory, Sir Brian Gammell, Kt., CBE
Jack, *Hon.* Sir Alieu Sulayman, Kt.
Jack, Sir David, Kt., CBE, FRS, FRSE
Jack, Sir David Emmanuel, GCMG, MBE
Jack, *Hon.* Sir Raymond Evan, Kt.
Jackling, Sir Roger Tustin, KCB, CBE
Jackson, Sir Barry Trevor, Kt.
Jackson, Sir Kenneth Joseph, Kt.
Jackson, *Gen.* Sir Michael David, GCB, CBE
Jackson, Sir Michael Roland, Bt. (1902)
Jackson, Sir Nicholas Fane St George, Bt. (1913)
Jackson, Sir Keith Arnold, Bt. (1815)
Jackson, *Hon.* Sir Rupert Matthew, Kt.
Jackson, Sir (William) Roland Cedric, Bt. (1869)
Jacob, *Rt. Hon.* Sir Robert Raphael Hayim (Robin), Kt.
Jacobi, Sir Derek George, Kt., CBE
Jacobi, *Dr* Sir James Edward, Kt., OBE
Jacobs, Sir Cecil Albert, Kt., CBE
Jacobs, *Rt. Hon.* Sir Francis Geoffrey, KCMG, QC
Jacobs, *Hon.* Sir Kenneth Sydney, KBE
Jacomb, Sir Martin Wakefield, Kt.
Jaffray, Sir William Otho, Bt. (1892)
Jagger, Sir Michael Philip, Kt.
James, Sir Cynlais Morgan, KCMG
James, Sir Jeffrey Russell, KBE
James, Sir John Nigel Courtenay, KCVO, CBE
James, Sir Stanislaus Anthony, GCMG, OBE
Jamieson, *Air Marshal* Sir David Ewan, KBE, CB
Jansen, Sir Ross Malcolm, KBE
Jardine of Applegirth, Sir Alexander Maule, Bt. (S. 1672)
Jardine, Sir Andrew Colin Douglas, Bt. (1916)
Jarman, *Prof.* Sir Brian, Kt., OBE
Jarratt, Sir Alexander Anthony, Kt., CB
Jarvis, Sir Gordon Ronald, Kt.
Jawara, *Hon.* Sir Dawda Kairaba, Kt.
Jay, Sir Antony Rupert, Kt., CVO
Jeewoolall, Sir Ramesh, Kt.
Jefferson, Sir George Rowland, Kt., CBE, FRENG
Jeffreys, *Prof.* Sir Alec John, Kt., FRS
Jeffries, *Hon.* Sir John Francis, Kt.
Jehangir, Sir Cowasji, Bt. (1908)
Jejeebhoy, Sir Jamsetjee, Bt. (1857)
Jenkins, Sir Brian Garton, GBE
Jenkins, Sir Elgar Spencer, Kt., OBE
Jenkins, Sir James Christopher, KCB, QC
Jenkins, Sir Michael Nicholas Howard, Kt., OBE
Jenkins, Sir Michael Romilly Heald, KCMG
Jenkins, Sir Simon, Kt.
Jenkinson, Sir John Banks, Bt. (1661)

Jenks, Sir (Richard) Peter, Bt. (1932)
Jenner, *Air Marshal* Sir Timothy Ivo, KCB
Jennings, Sir John Southwood, Kt., CBE, FRSE
Jennings, Sir Peter Neville Wake, Kt., CVO
Jephcott, Sir Neil Welbourn, Bt. (1962)
Jessel, Sir Charles John, Bt. (1883)
Jewkes, Sir Gordon Wesley, KCMG
Job, Sir Peter James Denton, Kt.
John, Sir David Glyndwr, KCMG
John, Sir Elton Hercules (Reginald Kenneth Dwight), Kt., CBE
Johns, *Air Chief Marshal* Sir Richard Edward, GCB, CBE, LVO
Johnson, Sir Colpoys Guy, Bt. (1755)
Johnson, *Gen.* Sir Garry Dene, KCB, OBE, MC
Johnson, Sir John Rodney, KCMG
†Johnson, Sir Patrick Eliot, Bt. (1818)
Johnson, *Hon.* Sir Robert Lionel, Kt.
Johnson, Sir Vassel Godfrey, Kt., CBE
Johnson-Ferguson, Sir Ian Edward, Bt. (1906)
Johnston, *Lt.-Gen.* Sir Maurice Robert, KCB, CVO, OBE
Johnston, Sir Thomas Alexander, Bt. (S. 1626)
Johnstone, Sir Geoffrey Adams Dinwiddie, KCMG
Johnstone, Sir (George) Richard Douglas, Bt. (S. 1700)
Johnstone, Sir (John) Raymond, Kt., CBE
Jolliffe, Sir Anthony Stuart, GBE
Jolly, Sir Arthur Richard, KCMG
Jonas, Sir John Peter Jens, Kt., CBE
Jones, Sir Alan Jeffrey, Kt.
Jones, Sir Harry George, Kt., CBE
Jones, Sir John Francis, Kt.
Jones, Sir Keith Stephen, Kt.
Jones, Sir Lyndon, Kt.
Jones, Sir (Owen) Trevor, Kt.
Jones, Sir Richard Anthony Lloyd, KCB
Jones, Sir Robert Edward, Kt.
Jones, Sir Roger Spencer, Kt., OBE
Jones, Sir Simon Warley Frederick Benton, Bt. (1919)
†Joseph, *Hon.* Sir James Samuel, Bt. (1943)
Jowitt, *Hon.* Sir Edwin Frank, Kt.
Judge, *Rt. Hon.* Sir Igor, Kt.
Judge, Sir Paul Rupert, Kt.
Jugnauth, *Rt. Hon.* Sir Aneerood, KCMG
Jungius, *Vice-Adm.* Sir James George, KBE
Kaberry, *Hon.* Sir Christopher Donald, Bt. (1960)
Kadoorie, *Hon.* Sir Michael David, Kt.
Kakaraya, Sir Pato, KBE
Kan Yuet-Keung, Sir, GBE
Kapi, *Hon.* Sir Mari, Kt., CBE
Kaputin, Sir John Rumet, KBE, CMG
Kaufman, *Rt. Hon.* Sir Gerald Bernard, Kt.

Kausimae, Sir David Nanau, KBE
Kavali, Sir Thomas, Kt., OBE
Kawharu, *Prof.* Sir Ian Hugh, Kt.
Kay, *Prof.* Sir Andrew Watt, Kt.
Kay, *Rt. Hon.* Sir Maurice Ralph, Kt.
Kaye, Sir Paul Henry Gordon, Bt. (1923)
Keane, Sir Richard Michael, Bt. (1801)
Kearney, *Hon.* Sir William John Francis, Kt., CBE
Keeble, Sir (Herbert Ben) Curtis, GCMG
Keegan, Sir John Desmond Patrick, Kt., OBE
Keene, *Rt. Hon.* Sir David Wolfe, Kt.
Keith, *Hon.* Sir Brian Richard, Kt.
Keith, *Prof.* Sir James, KBE
†Kellett, Sir Stanley Charles, Bt. (1801)
Kelly, Sir Christopher William, KCB
Kelly, Sir David Robert Corbett, Kt., CBE
Kelly, *Rt. Hon.* Sir (John William) Basil, Kt.
Kemakeza, Sir Allan, Kt.
Kemball, *Air Marshal* Sir (Richard) John, KCB, CBE
Kemp, Sir (Edward) Peter, KCB
Kemp-Welch, Sir John, Kt.
Kenilorea, *Rt. Hon.* Sir Peter, KBE
Kennaway, Sir John Lawrence, Bt. (1791)
Kennedy, Sir Francis, KCMG, CBE
Kennedy, *Hon.* Sir Ian Alexander, Kt.
Kennedy, *Prof.* Sir Ian McColl, Kt.
Kennedy, Sir Ludovic Henry Coverley, Kt.
†Kennedy, Sir Michael Edward, Bt. (1836)
Kennedy, *Rt. Hon.* Sir Paul Joseph Morrow, Kt.
Kennedy, *Air Chief Marshal* Sir Thomas Lawrie, GCB, AFC
Kennedy-Good, Sir John, KBE
Kenny, Sir Anthony John Patrick, Kt., DPHIL, DLITT, FBA
Kenny, *Gen.* Sir Brian Leslie Graham, GCB, CBE
Kentridge, Sir Sydney Woolf, KCMG, QC
Kenyon, Sir George Henry, Kt.
Keogh, *Prof.* Sir Bruce Edward, KBE
Kermode, Sir (John) Frank, Kt., FBA
Kerr, *Rt. Hon.* Sir Brian Francis, Kt.
Kerr, *Adm.* Sir John Beverley, GCB
Kerry, Sir Michael James, KCB, QC
Kershaw, *Prof.* Sir Ian, Kt.
Kershaw, Sir (John) Anthony, Kt., MC
Kerslake, Sir Robert Walker, Kt.
Keswick, Sir John Chippendale Lindley, Kt.
Kevau, *Prof.* Sir Isi Henao, Kt., CBE
Kikau, *Ratu* Sir Jone Latianara, KBE
Kimber, Sir Charles Dixon, Bt. (1904)
King, *Prof.* Sir David Anthony, Kt., FRS
King, Sir John Christopher, Bt. (1888)

King, *Vice-Adm.* Sir Norman Ross Dutton, KBE

King, *Hon.* Sir Timothy Roger Alan, Kt.

King, Sir Wayne Alexander, Bt. (1815)

Kingman, *Prof.* Sir John Frank Charles, Kt., FRS

Kingsland, Sir Richard, Kt., CBE, DFC

Kingsley, Sir Ben, Kt.

Kinloch, Sir David, Bt. (S. 1686)

Kinloch, Sir David Oliphant, Bt. (1873)

Kipalan, Sir Albert, Kt.

Kirkpatrick, Sir Ivone Elliott, Bt. (S. 1685)

Kirkwood, *Hon.* Sir Andrew Tristram Hammett, Kt.

Kiszely, *Lt.-Gen.* Sir John Panton, KCB, MC

Kitchin, *Hon.* Sir David James Tyson, Kt.

Kitson, *Gen.* Sir Frank Edward, GBE, KCB, MC

Kitson, Sir Timothy Peter Geoffrey, Kt.

Kleinwort, Sir Richard Drake, Bt. (1909)

Klug, Sir Aaron, Kt., OM

Knight, Sir Harold Murray, KBE, DSC

Knight, Sir Kenneth John, Kt., CBE, QFSM

Knight, *Air Chief Marshal* Sir Michael William Patrick, KCB, AFC

Knight, *Prof.* Sir Peter, Kt.

†Knill, Sir Thomas John Pugin Bartholomew, Bt. (1893)

Knowles, Sir Charles Francis, Bt. (1765)

Knowles, Sir Durward Randolph, Kt., OBE

Knowles, Sir Richard Marchant, Kt.

Knox, Sir David Laidlaw, Kt.

Knox, *Hon.* Sir John Leonard, Kt.

Knox-Johnston, Sir William Robert Patrick (Sir Robin), Kt., CBE, RD

Koraea, Sir Thomas, Kt.

Kornberg, *Prof.* Sir Hans Leo, Kt., DSC, SCD, PHD, FRS

Korowi, Sir Wiwa, GCMG

Kroto, *Prof.* Sir Harold Walter, Kt., FRS

Kulukundis, Sir Elias George (Eddie), Kt., OBE

Kurongku, *Most Revd* Peter, KBE

Kwok-Po Li, *Dr* Sir David, Kt., OBE

Lachmann, *Prof.* Sir Peter Julius, Kt.

Lacon, Sir Edmund Vere, Bt. (1818)

Lacy, Sir Patrick Brian Finucane (1921)

Lacy, Sir John Trend, Kt., CBE

Laddie, *Hon.* Sir Hugh Ian Lang, Kt.

Laidlaw, Sir Christopher Charles Fraser, Kt.

Laing, Sir (John) Martin (Kirby), Kt., CBE

Laing, Sir (John) Maurice, Kt.

Laing, Sir (William) Kirby, Kt., FRENG

Laird, Sir Gavin Harry, Kt., CBE

Lake, Sir (Attwell) Graham, Bt. (1711)

Lakin, Sir Michael, Bt. (1909)

Laking, Sir George Robert, KCMG

Lamb, Sir Albert Thomas, KBE, CMG, DFC

Lambert, Sir John Henry, KCVO, CMG

†Lambert, Sir Peter John Biddulph, Bt. (1711)

Lampl, Sir Frank William, Kt.

Lampl, Sir Peter, Kt., OBE

Lamport, Sir Stephen Mark Jeffrey, KCVO

Landale, Sir David William Neil, KCVO

Landau, Sir Dennis Marcus, Kt.

Lander, Sir Stephen James, KCB

Lane, Prof. Sir David Philip, Kt.

Langham, Sir John Stephen, Bt. (1660)

Langlands, Sir Robert Alan, Kt.

Langley, *Hon.* Sir Gordon Julian Hugh, Kt.

Langley, *Maj.-Gen.* Sir Henry Desmond Allen, KCVO, MBE

Langrishe, Sir James Hercules, Bt. (I. 1777)

Langstaff, *Hon.* Sir Brian Frederick James, Kt.

Lankester, Sir Timothy Patrick, KCB

Lapli, Sir John Ini, GCMG

Large, Sir Andrew McLeod Brooks, Kt.

Latasi, *Rt. Hon.* Sir Kamuta, KCMG, OBE

Latham, *Rt. Hon.* Sir David Nicholas Ramsey, Kt.

Latham, Sir Michael Anthony, Kt.

Latham, Sir Richard Thomas Paul, Bt. (1919)

Latimer, Sir (Courtenay) Robert, Kt., CBE

Latimer, Sir Graham Stanley, KBE

Latour-Adrien, *Hon.* Sir Maurice, Kt.

Laughton, Sir Anthony Seymour, Kt.

Laurence, Sir Peter Harold, KCMG, MC

Laurie, Sir Robert Bayley Emilius, Bt. (1834)

Lauterpacht, Sir Elihu, Kt., CBE, QC

Lauti, *Rt. Hon.* Sir Toaripi, GCMG

Lavan, *Hon.* Sir John Martin, Kt.

Lawes, Sir (John) Michael Bennet, Bt. (1882)

Lawler, Sir Peter James, Kt., OBE

Lawrence, Sir Clive Wyndham, Bt. (1906)

Lawrence, Sir Henry Peter, Bt. (1858)

Lawrence, Sir Ivan John, Kt., QC

Lawrence, Sir John Patrick Grosvenor, Kt., CBE

Lawrence, Sir William Fettiplace, Bt. (1867)

Lawrence-Jones, Sir Christopher, Bt. (1831)

Laws, *Rt. Hon.* Sir John Grant McKenzie, Kt.

Lawson, Sir Charles John Patrick, Bt. (1900)

Lawson, *Gen.* Sir Richard George, KCB, DSO, OBE

Lawson-Tancred, Sir Henry, Bt. (1662)

Lawton, *Prof.* Sir John Hartley, Kt., CBE, FRS

Layard, *Adm.* Sir Michael Henry Gordon, KCB, CBE

Lea, *Vice-Adm.* Sir John Stuart Crosbie, KBE

Lea, Sir Thomas William, Bt. (1892)

Leach, *Admiral of the Fleet* Sir Henry Conyers, GCB

Leahy, Sir Daniel Joseph, Kt.

Leahy, Sir John Henry Gladstone, KCMG

Leahy, Sir Terence Patrick, Kt.

Learmont, *Gen.* Sir John Hartley, KCB, CBE

Leaver, Sir Christopher, GBE

Le Bailly, *Vice-Adm.* Sir Louis Edward Stewart Holland, KBE, CB

Le Cheminant, *Air Chief Marshal* Sir Peter de Lacey, GBE, KCB, DFC

Lechmere, Sir Reginald Anthony Hungerford, Bt. (1818)

Ledger, Sir Philip Stevens, Kt., CBE, FRSE

Lee, *Brig.* Sir Leonard Henry, Kt., CBE

Lee, Sir Quo-wei, Kt., CBE

Leeds, Sir Christopher Anthony, Bt. (1812)

Lees, Sir David Bryan, Kt.

Lees, Sir Thomas Edward, Bt. (1897)

Lees, Sir Thomas Harcourt Ivor, Bt. (1804)

Lees, Sir (William) Antony Clare, Bt. (1937)

Leese, Sir Richard Charles, Kt., CBE

le Fleming, Sir David Kelland, Bt. (1705)

Legard, Sir Charles Thomas, Bt. (1660)

Legg, Sir Thomas Stuart, KCB, QC

Leggatt, *Rt. Hon.* Sir Andrew Peter, Kt.

Leggatt, Sir Hugh Frank John, Kt.

Leggett, *Prof.* Sir Anthony James, KBE

Leigh, Sir Geoffrey Norman, Kt.

Leigh, Sir Richard Henry, Bt. (1918)

Leighton, Sir Michael John Bryan, Bt. (1693)

Leitch, Sir George, KCB, OBE

Leith-Buchanan, Sir Gordon Kelly McNicol, Bt. (1775)

Le Marchant, Sir Francis Arthur, Bt. (1841)

Leng, *Gen.* Sir Peter John Hall, KCB, MBE, MC

Lennox-Boyd, The Hon. Sir Mark Alexander, Kt.

Leon, Sir John Ronald, Bt. (1911)

Leonard, *Rt. Revd Monsignor* and *Rt. Hon.* Graham Douglas, KCVO

Lepping, Sir George Geria Dennis, GCMG, MBE

Le Quesne, Sir (John) Godfray, Kt., QC

Lee-Steere, Sir Ernest Henry, KBE

Leslie, Sir Colin Alan Bettridge, Kt.
Leslie, Sir John Norman Ide, Bt. (1876)
Leslie, Sir Peter Evelyn, Kt.
Lester, Sir James Theodore, Kt.
Lethbridge, Sir Thomas Periam Hector Noel, Bt. (1804)
Lever, Sir Jeremy Frederick, KCMG, QC
Lever, Sir Paul, KCMG
Lever, Sir (Tresham) Christopher Arthur Lindsay, Bt. (1911)
Leveson, Rt. Hon. Sir Brian Henry, Kt.
Levey, Sir Michael Vincent, Kt., LVO
Levine, Sir Montague Bernard, Kt.
Levinge, Sir Richard George Robin, Bt. (I. 1704)
Lewinton, Sir Christopher, Kt.
Lewis, Sir David Courtenay Mansel, KCVO
Lewis, Sir John Anthony, Kt., OBE
Lewis, Sir Leigh Warren, KCB
Lewis, Sir Terence Murray, Kt., OBE, GM, QPM
Lewison, Hon. Sir Kim Martin Jordan, Kt.
Ley, Sir Ian Francis, Bt. (1905)
Li, Sir Ka-Shing, KBE
Lickiss, Sir Michael Gillam, Kt.
Liddington, Sir Bruce, Kt.
Liggins, Prof. Sir Graham Collingwood, Kt., CBE, FRS
Lightman, Hon. Sir Gavin Anthony, Kt.
Lighton, Sir Thomas Hamilton, Bt. (I. 1791)
Likierman, Prof. Sir John Andrew, Kt.
Lilleyman, Prof. Sir John Stuart, Kt.
Limon, Sir Donald William, KCB
Linacre, Sir (John) Gordon (Seymour), Kt., CBE, AFC, DFM
Lindop, Sir Norman, Kt.
Lindsay, Sir James Harvey Kincaid Stewart, Kt.
Lindsay, Hon. Sir John Edmund Frederic, Kt.
†Lindsay, Sir James Martin Evelyn, Bt. (1962)
†Lindsay-Hogg, Sir Michael Edward, Bt. (1905)
Lipton, Sir Stuart Anthony, Kt.
Lipworth, Sir (Maurice) Sydney, Kt.
Lister-Kaye, Sir John Phillip Lister, Bt. (1812)
Lithgow, Sir William James, Bt. (1925)
Little, Most Revd Thomas Francis, KBE
Littler, Sir (James) Geoffrey, KCB
Llewellyn, Sir David St Vincent, Bt. (1922)
Llewellyn-Smith, Prof. Sir Christopher Hubert, Kt.
Lloyd, Prof. Sir Geoffrey Ernest Richard, Kt., FBA
Lloyd, Sir Nicholas Markley, Kt.
Lloyd, Rt. Hon. Sir Peter Robert Cable, Kt.
Lloyd, Sir Richard Ernest Butler, Bt. (1960)

Lloyd, Hon. Sir Timothy Andrew Wigram, Kt.
Lloyd-Hughes, Sir Trevor Denby, Kt.
Lloyd Jones, Sir David, Kt.
Lloyd-Jones, Sir (Peter) Hugh (Jefferd), Kt.
Loader, Air Marshal Sir Clive Robert, KCB, OBE
Loane, Most Revd Marcus Lawrence, KBE
Lobo, Sir Rogerio Hyndman, Kt., CBE
†Loder, Sir Edmund Jeune, Bt. (1887)
Logan, Sir David Brian Carleton, KCMG
Logan, Sir Donald Arthur, KCMG
Lokoloko, Sir Tore, GCMG, GCVO, OBE
Longmore, Rt. Hon. Sir Andrew Centlivres, Kt.
Loram, Vice-Adm. Sir David Anning, KCB, CVO
Lord, Sir Michael Nicholson, Kt.
Lorimer, Sir (Thomas) Desmond, Kt.
Los, Hon. Sir Kubulan, Kt., CBE
Loughran, Sir Gerald Finbar, KCB
Louisy, Rt. Hon. Sir Allan Fitzgerald Laurent, KCMG
Lovell, Sir (Alfred Charles) Bernard, Kt., OBE, FRS
Lovelock, Sir Douglas Arthur, KCB
Loveridge, Sir John Warren, Kt.
Lovill, Sir John Roger, Kt., CBE
Lowe, Air Chief Marshal Sir Douglas Charles, GCB, DFC, AFC
Lowe, Sir Frank Budge, Kt.
Lowe, Sir Thomas William Gordon, Bt. (1918)
Lowson, Sir Ian Patrick, Bt. (1951)
Lowther, Col. Sir Charles Douglas, Bt. (1824)
Lowther, Sir John Luke, KCVO, CBE
Loyd, Sir Julian St John, KCVO
Lu, Sir Tseng Chi, Kt.
Lucas, Prof. Sir Colin Renshaw, Kt.
Lucas, Sir Thomas Edward, Bt. (1887)
Lucas-Tooth, Sir (Hugh) John, Bt. (1920)
Luddington, Sir Donald Collin Cumyn, KBE, CMG, CVO
Lumsden, Sir David James, Kt.
Lushington, Sir John Richard Castleman, Bt. (1791)
Lyall Grant, Sir Mark Justin, KCMG
Lygo, Adm. Sir Raymond Derek, KCB
Lyle, Sir Gavin Archibald, Bt. (1929)
Lynch-Blosse, Capt. Sir Richard Hely, Bt. (1622)
Lynch-Robinson, Sir Dominick Christopher, Bt. (1920)
Lyne, Sir Roderic Michael John, KBE, CMG
Lyons, Sir John, Kt.
Lyons, Sir Michael Thomas, Kt.
McAlpine, Sir William Hepburn, Bt. (1918)
Macara, Sir Alexander Wiseman, Kt., FRCP, FRCGP

†Macara, Sir Hugh Kenneth, Bt. (1911)
McCaffrey, Sir Thomas Daniel, Kt.
McCallum, Sir Donald Murdo, Kt., CBE, FRENG
McCamley, Sir Graham Edward, KBE
McCarthy, Sir Callum, Kt.
McCartney, Sir (James) Paul, Kt., MBE
Macartney, Sir John Ralph, Bt. (I. 1799)
McClay, Dr Sir Allen James, Kt., CBE
McClement, Vice-Admiral Sir Timothy Pentreath, KCB, OBE
McClintock, Sir Eric Paul, Kt.
McColl, Sir Colin Hugh Verel, KCMG
McCollum, Rt. Hon. Sir William, Kt.
McCombe, Hon. Sir Richard George Bramwell, Kt.
McConnell, Sir Robert Shean, Bt. (1900)
MacCormac, Sir Richard Cornelius, Kt., CBE
MacCormick, Prof. Sir Donald Neil, Kt., MEP, QC
†McCowan, Sir David William, Bt. (1934)
McCullough, Hon. Sir (Iain) Charles (Robert), Kt.
MacDermott, Rt. Hon. Sir John Clarke, Kt.
Macdonald, Sir Kenneth Carmichael, KCB
Macdonald, Sir Kenneth Donald John, Kt., QC
Mcdonald, Sir Trevor, Kt., OBE
Macdonald of Sleat, Sir Ian Godfrey Bosville, Bt. (S. 1625)
McDowell, Sir Eric Wallace, Kt., CBE
Mace, Lt.-Gen. Sir John Airth, KBE, CB
McEwen, Sir John Roderick Hugh, Bt. (1953)
McFarland, Sir John Talbot, Bt. (1914)
MacFarlane, Prof. Sir Alistair George James, Kt., CBE, FRS
McFarlane, Sir Andrew Ewart, Kt.
Macfarlane, Sir (David) Neil, Kt.
McFarlane, Sir Ian, Kt.
McGrath, Sir Brian Henry, GCVO
Macgregor, Sir Ian Grant, Bt. (1828)
McGregor, Sir James David, Kt., OBE
MacGregor of MacGregor, Sir Malcolm Gregor Charles, Bt. (1795)
McGrigor, Capt. Sir Charles Edward, Bt. (1831)
McIntosh, Sir Neil William David, Kt., CBE
McIntosh, Sir Ronald Robert Duncan, KCB
McIntyre, Sir Donald Conroy, Kt., CBE
McIntyre, Sir Meredith Alister, Kt.
Mackay, Hon. Sir Colin Crichton, Kt.
MacKay, Prof. Sir Donald Iain, Kt.
MacKay, Sir Francis Henry, Kt.
McKay, Sir William Robert, KCB

Mackay-Dick, *Maj.-Gen.* Sir Iain Charles, KCVO, MBE

Mackechnie, Sir Alistair John, Kt.

McKellen, Sir Ian Murray, Kt., CBE

Mackenzie, Sir (James William) Guy, Bt. (1890)

Mackenzie, *Gen.* Sir Jeremy John George, GCB, OBE

†Mackenzie, Sir Peter Douglas, Bt. (S. 1673)

†Mackenzie, Sir Roderick McQuhae, Bt. (S. 1703)

McKenzie, Sir Roy Allan, KBE

Mackerras, Sir (Alan) Charles (MacLaurin), Kt., CH, CBE

Mackeson, Sir Rupert Henry, Bt. (1954)

McKillop, Sir Thomas Fulton Wilson, Kt.

McKinnon, Sir James, Kt.

McKinnon, *Hon.* Sir Stuart Neil, Kt.

Mackintosh, Sir Cameron Anthony, Kt.

Mackworth, Sir Digby (John), Bt. (1776)

McLaren, Sir Robin John Taylor, KCMG

McLaughlin, Sir Richard, Kt.

Maclean of Dunconnell, Sir Charles Edward, Bt. (1957)

Maclean, Sir Donald Og Grant, Kt.

Maclean, Sir Lachlan Hector Charles, Bt. (NS 1631)

Maclean, Sir Murdo, Kt.

McLeod, Sir Charles Henry, Bt. (1925)

MacLeod, Sir (John) Maxwell Norman, Bt. (1924)

Macleod, Sir (Nathaniel William) Hamish, KBE

McLintock, Sir Michael William, Bt. (1934)

Maclure, Sir John Robert Spencer, Bt. (1898)

McMahon, Sir Brian Patrick, Bt. (1817)

McMahon, Sir Christopher William, Kt.

McMaster, Sir Brian John, Kt., CBE

Macmillan, Sir (Alexander McGregor) Graham, Kt.

MacMillan, *Lt.-Gen.* Sir John Richard Alexander, KCB, CBE

McMullin, *Rt. Hon.* Sir Duncan Wallace, Kt.

McMurtry, Sir David, Kt., CBE

†Macnaghten, Sir Malcolm Francis, Bt. (1836)

McNair-Wilson, Sir Patrick Michael Ernest David, Kt.

McNamara, *Air Chief Marshal* Sir Neville Patrick, KBE

Macnaughton, *Prof.* Sir Malcolm Campbell, Kt.

McNee, Sir David Blackstock, Kt., QPM

McNulty, Sir (Robert William) Roy, Kt., CBE

MacPhail, Sir Bruce Dugald, Kt.

Macpherson, Sir Ronald Thomas Steward (Tommy), CBE, MC, TD

Macpherson of Cluny, *Hon.* Sir William Alan, Kt., TD

McQuarrie, Sir Albert, Kt.

MacRae, Sir (Alastair) Christopher (Donald Summerhayes), KCMG

Macready, Sir Nevil John Wilfrid, Bt. (1923)

MacSween, *Prof.* Sir Roderick Norman McIver, Kt.

Mactaggart, Sir John Auld, Bt. (1938)

McWilliam, Sir Michael Douglas, KCMG

McWilliams, Sir Francis, GBE

Madden, Sir David Christopher Andrew, KCMG

†Madden, Sir Charles Jonathan, Bt. (1919)

Maddox, Sir John Royden, Kt.

Madel, Sir (William) David, Kt.

Magee, Sir Ian Bernard Vaughan, Kt., CB

Magnus, Sir Laurence Henry Philip, Bt. (1917)

Mahon, Sir (John) Denis, Kt., CH, CBE

Mahon, Sir William Walter, Bt. (1819)

Maiden, Sir Colin James, Kt., DPHIL

Main, Sir Peter Tester, Kt., ERD

Maingard de la Ville ès Offrans, Sir Louis Pierre René, Kt., CBE

Maini, *Prof.* Sir Ravinder Nath, Kt.

Maino, Sir Charles, KBE

†Maitland, Sir Charles Alexander, Bt. (1818)

Maitland, Sir Donald James Dundas, GCMG, OBE

Major, *Rt. Hon.* Sir John, KG, CH

Malbon, *Vice-Adm.* Sir Fabian Michael, KBE

Malcolm, Sir James William Thomas Alexander, Bt. (S. 1665)

Malet, Sir Harry Douglas St Lo, Bt. (1791)

Mallaby, Sir Christopher Leslie George, GCMG, GCVO

Mallet, Sir William George, GCMG, CBE

Mallick, *Prof.* Sir Netar Prakash, Kt.

Mallinson, Sir William James, Bt. (1935)

Malpas, Sir Robert, Kt., CBE

Mamo, Sir Anthony Joseph, Kt., OBE

Mancham, Sir James Richard Marie, KBE

†Mander, Sir (Charles) Nicholas, Bt. (1911)

Manduell, Sir John, Kt., CBE

Mann, *Hon.* Sir George Anthony, Kt.

Mann, *Rt. Revd* Michael Ashley, KCVO

Mann, Sir Rupert Edward, Bt. (1905)

Manning, Sir David Geoffrey, KCMG, CVO

Mansel, Sir Philip, Bt. (1622)

Mansfield, *Prof.* Sir Peter, Kt.

Mantell, *Rt. Hon.* Sir Charles Barrie Knight, Kt.

Manuella, Sir Tulaga, GCMG, MBE

Manzie, Sir (Andrew) Gordon, KCB

Margetson, Sir John William Denys, KCMG

Margetts, Sir Robert John, Kt., CBE

Mark, Sir Robert, GBE

Markesinis, *Prof.* Sir Basil Spyridonos, Kt. QC

Markham, Sir (Arthur) David, Bt. (1911)

Marling, Sir Charles William Somerset, Bt. (1882)

Marmot, *Prof.* Sir Michael Gideon, Kt.

Marr, Sir Leslie Lynn, Bt. (1919)

Marriner, Sir Neville, Kt., CBE

†Marsden, Sir Simon Neville Llewelyn, Bt. (1924)

Marsh, *Prof.* Sir John Stanley, Kt., CBE

Marshall, Sir Denis Alfred, Kt.

Marshall, *Prof.* Sir (Oshley) Roy, Kt., CBE

Marshall, Sir Peter Harold Reginald, KCMG

Martin, Sir Clive Haydon, Kt., OBE

Martin, Sir George Henry, Kt., CBE

Martin, *Vice-Adm.* Sir John Edward Ludgate, KCB, DSC

Martin, *Prof.* Sir Laurence Woodward, Kt.

Martin, Sir (Robert) Bruce, Kt., QC

Marychurch, Sir Peter Harvey, KCMG

Masefield, Sir Charles Beech Gordon, Kt.

Mason, *Hon.* Sir Anthony Frank, KBE

Mason, Sir (Basil) John, Kt., CB, DSC, FRS

Mason, *Prof.* Sir David Kean, Kt., CBE

Mason, Sir Frederick Cecil, KCVO, CMG

Mason, Sir Gordon Charles, Kt., OBE

Mason, Sir John Charles Moir, KCMG

Mason, Sir John Peter, Kt., CBE

Mason, Sir Peter James, KBE

Mason, *Prof.* Sir Ronald, KCB, FRS

Massie, Sir Herbert William, Kt., CBE

Matane, HE Sir Paulias Nguna, GCMG, OBE

Mathers, Sir Robert William, Kt.

Matheson of Matheson, Sir Fergus John, Bt. (1882)

Mathewson, Sir George Ross, Kt., CBE, PHD, FRSE

Matthews, Sir Terence Hedley, Kt., OBE

Maud, *Hon.* Sir Humphrey John Hamilton, KCMG

Maughan, Sir Deryck, Kt.

Mawer, Sir Philip John Courtney, Kt.

Maxwell, Sir Michael Eustace George, Bt. (S. 1681)

Maxwell-Hyslop, Sir Robert John (Robin), Kt.

Maxwell-Scott, Sir Dominic James, Bt. (1642)

May, *Rt. Hon.* Sir Anthony Tristram Kenneth, Kt.

Mayhew-Sanders, Sir John Reynolds, Kt.

Maynard, *Hon.* Sir Clement Travelyan, Kt.

Meadow, *Prof.* Sir (Samuel) Roy, Kt., FRCP, FRCPE

Medlycott, Sir Mervyn Tregonwell, Bt. (1808)

Meldrum, Sir Graham, Kt., CBE, QFSM

Melhuish, Sir Michael Ramsay, KBE, CMG

Mellon, Sir James, KCMG

Melmoth, Sir Graham John, Kt.

Melville, *Prof.* Sir David, Kt., CBE

Merifield, Sir Anthony James, KCVO, CB

†Meyer, Sir (Anthony) Ashley Frank, Bt. (1910)

Meyer, Sir Christopher John Rome, KCMG

Meyjes, Sir Richard Anthony, Kt.

†Meyrick, Sir Timothy Thomas Charlton, Bt. (1880)

Miakwe, *Hon.* Sir Akepa, KBE

Michael, Sir Duncan, Kt.

Michael, *Dr* Sir Jonathan, Kt.

Michael, Sir Peter Colin, Kt., CBE

Michels, Sir David Michael Charles, Kt.

Middleton, Sir John Maxwell, Kt.

Middleton, Sir Peter Edward, GCB

Miers, Sir (Henry) David Alastair Capel, KBE, CMG

Milbank, Sir Anthony Frederick, Bt. (1882)

Milborne-Swinnerton-Pilkington, Sir Thomas Henry, Bt. (S. 1635)

Milburn, Sir Anthony Rupert, Bt. (1905)

Miles, Sir Peter Tremayne, KCVO

Miles, Sir William Napier Maurice, Bt. (1859)

Millais, Sir Geoffrey Richard Everett, Bt. (1885)

Millard, Sir Guy Elwin, KCMG, CVO

Miller, Sir Albert Joel, KCMG, MVO, MBE, QPM, CPM

Miller, Sir Donald John, Kt., FRSE, FRENG

Miller, *Air Marshal* Sir Graham Anthony, KBE

Miller, Sir Harry Holmes, Bt. (1705)

Miller, Sir Hilary Duppa (Hal), Kt.

Miller, Sir Jonathan Wolfe, Kt., CBE

Miller, Sir Peter North, Kt.

Miller, Sir Robin Robert William, Kt.

Miller, Sir Ronald Andrew Baird, Kt., CBE

Miller of Glenlee, Sir Stephen William Macdonald, Bt. (1788)

Mills, Sir Ian, Kt.

Mills, Sir Keith, Kt.

Mills, Sir Peter Frederick Leighton, Bt. (1921)

Milman, Sir David Patrick, Bt. (1800)

Milne, Sir John Drummond, Kt.

Milne-Watson, Sir Andrew Michael, Bt. (1937)

Milner, Sir Timothy William Lycett, Bt. (1717)

Milton, Sir Simon, Kt.

Milton-Thompson, *Surgeon Vice-Adm.* Sir Godfrey James, KBE

Mirrlees, *Prof.* Sir James Alexander, Kt., FBA

Mitchell, Sir David Bower, Kt.

Mitchell, Sir Derek Jack, KCB, CVO

Mitchell, *Rt. Hon.* Sir James FitzAllen, KCMG

Mitchell, *Very Revd* Patrick Reynolds, KCVO

Mitchell, *Hon.* Sir Stephen George, Kt.

Mitting, *Hon.* Sir John Edward, Kt.

Moate, Sir Roger Denis, Kt.

Moberly, Sir Patrick Hamilton, KCMG

Moffat, Sir Brian Scott, Kt., OBE

Moffat, *Lt.-Gen.* Sir (William) Cameron, KBE

Mogg, Sir John Frederick, KCMG

Moir, Sir Christopher Ernest, Bt. (1916)

†Molesworth-St Aubyn, Sir William, Bt. (1689)

†Molony, Sir Thomas Desmond, Bt. (1925)

Monck, Sir Nicholas Jeremy, KCB

Money-Coutts, Sir David Burdett, KCVO

Montagu, Sir Nicholas Lionel John, KCB

Montagu-Pollock, Sir Giles Hampden, Bt. (1872)

Montague, Sir Adrian Alastair, Kt., CBE

Montague-Browne, Sir Anthony Arthur Duncan, KCMG, CBE, DFC

Montgomery, Sir (Basil Henry) David, Bt. (1801), CVO

Montgomery, Sir (William) Fergus, Kt.

Montgomery-Cuninghame, Sir John Christopher Foggo, Bt. (NS 1672)

Moody-Stuart, Sir Mark, KCMG

Moollan, Sir Abdool Hamid Adam, Kt.

Moollan, *Hon.* Sir Cassam (Ismael), Kt.

†Moon, Sir Roger, Bt. (1887)

Moore, *Most Revd* Desmond Charles, KBE

Moore, Sir Francis Thomas, Kt.

Moore, *Maj.-Gen.* Sir (John) Jeremy, KCB, OBE, MC

Moore, Sir John Michael, KCVO, CB, DSC

Moore, *Vice Adm.* Sir Michael Antony Claës, KBE, LVO

Moore, *Prof.* Sir Norman Winfrid, Bt. (1919)

Moore, Sir Patrick Alfred Caldwell, Kt., CBE

Moore, Sir Patrick William Eisdell, Kt., OBE

Moore, Sir Roger George, KBE

Moore, Sir William Roger Clotworthy, Bt. (1932), TD

Moore-Bick, *Rt. Hon.* Sir Martin James, Kt.

Moores, Sir Peter, Kt., CBE

Morauta, Sir Mekere, Kt.

Mordaunt, Sir Richard Nigel Charles, Bt. (1611)

Moreton, Sir John Oscar, KCMG, KCVO, MC

Morgan, *Vice-Adm.* Sir Charles Christopher, KBE

Morgan, *Hon.* Sir Charles Declan, Kt.

Morgan, Sir Graham, Kt.

Morgan, Sir John Albert Leigh, KCMG

Morgan-Giles, *Rear-Adm.* Sir Morgan Charles, Kt., DSO, OBE, GM

Morison, *Hon.* Sir Thomas Richard Atkin, Kt.

Morland, *Hon.* Sir Michael, Kt.

Morland, Sir Robert Kenelm, Kt.

Morpeth, Sir Douglas Spottiswoode, Kt., TD

†Morris, Sir Allan Lindsay, Bt. (1806)

Morris, *Air Marshal* Sir Arnold Alec, KBE, CB

Morris, Sir Derek James, Kt.

Morris, Sir (James) Richard (Samuel), Kt., CBE

Morris, Sir Keith Elliot Hedley, KBE, CMG

Morris, *Prof.* Sir Peter John, Kt.

Morris, Sir Trefor Alfred, Kt., CBE, QPM

Morris, *Very Revd* William James, KCVO

Morrison, Sir (Alexander) Fraser, Kt., CBE

Morrison, Sir Howard Leslie, OBE

Morrison, Sir Kenneth Duncan, Kt., CBE

Morrison-Bell, Sir William Hollin Dayrell, Bt. (1905)

Morrison-Low, Sir James Richard, Bt. (1908)

Morritt, *Rt. Hon.* Sir (Robert) Andrew, Kt., CVO

Morse, Sir Christopher Jeremy, KCMG

Mortimer, Sir John Clifford, Kt., CBE, QC

Moseley, Sir George Walker, KCB

Moses, *Rt. Hon.* Sir Alan George, Kt.

Moses, *Very Revd Dr* John Henry, KCVO

Moss, Sir David Joseph, KCVO, CMG

Moss, Sir Stephen Alan, Kt.

Moss, Sir Stirling Craufurd, Kt., OBE

Mostyn, Sir William Basil John, Bt. (1670)

Mott, Sir John Harmer, Bt. (1930)

Mottram, Sir Richard Clive, GCB

†Mount, Sir (William Robert) Ferdinand, Bt. (1921)

†Mountain, Sir Edward Brian Stanford, Bt. (1922)

Mountfield, Sir Robin, KCB

Mowbray, Sir John Robert, Bt. (1880)

Moylan, *Hon.* Sir Andrew John Gregory, Kt.

Muir, Sir Laurence Macdonald, Kt.

†Muir, Sir Richard James Kay, Bt. (1892)

Muir-Mackenzie, Sir Alexander Alwyne Henry Charles Brinton, Bt. (1805)
Mulcahy, Sir Geoffrey John, Kt.
Mullens, Lt.-Gen. Sir Anthony Richard Guy, KCB, OBE
Mummery, Rt. Hon. Sir John Frank, Kt.
Munby, Hon. Sir James Lawrence, Kt.
Munn, Sir James, Kt., OBE
Munro, Sir Alan Gordon, KCMG
†Munro, Sir Kenneth Arnold William, Bt. (S. 1634)
Munro, Sir Alasdair Thomas Ian, Bt. (1825)
Muria, Hon. Sir Gilbert John Baptist, Kt.
Murphy, Sir Leslie Frederick, Kt.
Murray, Sir David Edward, Kt.
Murray, Rt. Hon. Sir Donald Bruce, Kt.
Murray, Sir James, KCMG
Murray, Prof. Sir Kenneth, Kt.
Murray, Sir Nigel Andrew Digby, Bt. (S. 1628)
Murray, Sir Patrick Ian Keith, Bt. (S. 1673)
†Murray, Sir Rowland William, Bt. (S. 1630)
Mursell, Sir Peter, Kt., MBE
Musgrave, Sir Christopher John Shane, Bt. (1782)
Musgrave, Sir Christopher Patrick Charles, Bt. (1611)
Musson, Gen. Sir Geoffrey Randolph Dixon, GCB, CBE, DSO
Myers, Sir Philip Alan, Kt., OBE, QPM
Myers, Prof. Sir Rupert Horace, KBE
Mynors, Sir Richard Baskerville, Bt. (1964)
Naipaul, Sir Vidiadhar Surajprasad, Kt.
Nairn, Sir Michael, Bt. (1904)
Nairne, Rt. Hon. Sir Patrick Dalmahoy, GCB, MC
Naish, Sir (Charles) David, Kt.
Nall, Sir Edward William Joseph Bt. (1954)
Namaliu, Rt. Hon. Sir Rabbie Langanai, KCMG
†Napier, Sir Charles Joseph, Bt. (1867)
Napier, Sir John Archibald Lennox, Bt. (S. 1627)
Napier, Sir Oliver John, Kt.
Naylor-Leyland, Sir Philip Vyvyan, Bt. (1895)
Neal, Sir Eric James, Kt., CVO
Neal, Sir Leonard Francis, Kt., CBE
Neale, Sir Gerrard Anthony, Kt.
Neave, Sir Paul Arundell, Bt. (1795)
Neill, Rt. Hon. Sir Brian Thomas, Kt.
Neill, Sir (James) Hugh, KCVO, CBE, TD
†Nelson, Sir Jamie Charles Vernon Hope, Bt. (1912)
Nelson, Hon. Sir Robert Franklyn, Kt.
Neubert, Sir Michael John, Kt.
New, Maj.-Gen. Sir Laurence Anthony Wallis, Kt., CB, CBE

Newall, Sir Paul Henry, Kt., TD
Newby, Prof. Sir Howard Joseph, Kt., CBE
Newington, Sir Michael John, KCMG
Newman, Sir Francis Hugh Cecil, Bt. (1912)
Newman, Sir Geoffrey Robert, Bt. (1836)
Newman, Hon. Sir George Michael, Kt.
Newman, Sir Kenneth Leslie, GBE, QPM
Newman, Vice-Adm. Sir Roy Thomas, KCB
Newsam, Sir Peter Anthony, Kt.
†Newson-Smith, Sir Peter Frank Graham, Bt. (1944)
Newton, Sir (Charles) Wilfred, Kt., CBE
Newton, Sir (Harry) Michael (Rex), Bt. (1900)
Newton, Sir Kenneth Garnar, Bt. (1924), OBE, TD
Ngata, Sir Henare Kohere, KBE
Nice, Sir Geoffrey, Kt., QC
Nichol, Sir Duncan Kirkbride, Kt., CBE
Nicholas, Sir David, Kt., CBE
Nicholas, Sir John William, KCVO, CMG
Nicholls, Sir Nigel Hamilton, KCVO, CBE
Nichols, Sir Richard Everard, Kt.
Nicholson, Sir Bryan Hubert, GBE, Kt.
†Nicholson, Sir Charles Christian, Bt. (1912)
Nicholson, Rt. Hon. Sir Michael, Kt.
Nicholson, Sir Paul Douglas, Kt.
Nicholson, Sir Robin Buchanan, Kt., PHD, FRS, FRENG
Nicoll, Sir William, KCMG
Nightingale, Sir Charles Manners Gamaliel, Bt. (1628)
Nixon, Sir Simon Michael Christopher, Bt. (1906)
Nixon, Sir Edwin Ronald, Kt., CBE
Noble, Sir David Brunel, Bt. (1902)
Noble, Sir Iain Andrew, Bt., OBE (1923)
Nombri, Sir Joseph Karl, Kt., ISO, BEM
Noon, Sir Gulam Kaderbhoy, Kt., MBE
Norman, Sir Arthur Gordon, KBE, DFC
Norman, Sir Mark Annesley, Bt. (1915)
Norman, Sir Robert Henry, Kt., OBE
Norman, Sir Ronald, Kt., OBE
Norman, Sir Torquil Patrick Alexander, Kt., CBE
Normington, Sir David John, KCB
Norrington, Sir Roger Arthur Carver, Kt., CBE
Norriss, Air Marshal Sir Peter Coulson, KBE, CB, AFC
North, Sir Peter Machin, Kt., CBE, QC, DCL, FBA
North, Sir Thomas Lindsay, Kt.
North, Sir (William) Jonathan (Frederick), Bt. (1920)

Norton-Griffiths, Sir John, Bt. (1922)
Nossal, Sir Gustav Joseph Victor, Kt., CBE
Nott, Rt. Hon. Sir John William Frederic, KCB
Nourse, Rt. Hon. Sir Martin Charles, Kt.
Nugent, Sir John Edwin Lavallin, Bt. (I. 1795)
†Nugent, Sir Christopher George Ridley, Bt. (1806)
†Nugent, Sir (Walter) Richard Middleton, Bt. (1831)
Nunn, Sir Trevor Robert, Kt., CBE
Nunneley, Sir Charles Kenneth Roylance, Kt.
Nursaw, Sir James, KCB, QC
Nurse, Sir Paul Maxime, Kt.
†Nuttall, Sir Harry, Bt. (1922)
Nutting, Sir John Grenfell, Bt. (1903), QC
Oakeley, Sir John Digby Atholl, Bt. (1790)
Oakes, Sir Christopher, Bt. (1939)
†Oakshott, Hon. Sir Michael Arthur John, Bt. (1959)
Oates, Sir Thomas, Kt., CMG, OBE
O'Brien, Sir Frederick William Fitzgerald, Kt.
O'Brien, Sir Richard, Kt., DSO, MC
O'Brien, Sir Timothy John, Bt. (1849)
O'Brien, Adm. Sir William Donough, KCB, DSC
O'Connell, Sir Bernard, Kt.
O'Connell, Sir Maurice James Donagh MacCarthy, Bt. (1869)
O'Dea, Sir Patrick Jerad, KCVO
Odell, Sir Stanley John, Kt.
Odgers, Sir Graeme David William, Kt.
O'Donnell, Sir Augustine Thomas, KCB
O'Donnell, Sir Christopher John, Kt.
O'Donoghue, Lt.-Gen. Sir Kevin, KCB, CBE
O'Dowd, Sir David Joseph, Kt., CBE, QPM
Ogden, Dr Sir Peter James, Kt.
Ogden, Sir Robert, Kt., CBE
Ogilvy, Sir Francis Gilbert Arthur, Bt. (S. 1626)
Ogilvy-Wedderburn, Sir Andrew John Alexander, Bt. (1803)
Ognall, Hon. Sir Harry Henry, Kt.
Ohlson, Sir Brian Eric Christopher, Bt. (1920)
Oldham, Dr Sir John, Kt., OBE
Oliver, Sir James Michael Yorrick, Kt.
Oliver, Sir Stephen John Lindsay, Kt., QC
O'Loghlen, Sir Colman Michael, Bt. (1838)
Olver, Sir Stephen John Linley, KBE, CMG
Omand, Sir David Bruce, GCB
O'Nions, Prof. Sir Robert Keith, Kt., FRS, PHD
Ondaatje, Sir Christopher, Kt., CBE
Onslow, Sir John Roger Wilmot, Bt. (1797)

Oppenheimer, Sir Michael Bernard Grenville, Bt. (1921)
Oppenshaw, Sir Charles Peter Lawford, Kt., QC
Orde, Sir Hugh Stephen Roden, Kt., OBE
O'Regan, *Dr* Sir Stephen Gerard (Tipene), Kt.
O'Reilly, Sir Anthony John Francis, Kt.
O'Reilly, *Prof.* Sir John James, Kt.
Orr, Sir David Alexander, Kt., MC
Orr, Sir John, Kt., OBE
Orr-Ewing, Sir (Alistair) Simon, Bt. (1963)
Orr-Ewing, Sir Archibald Donald, Bt. (1886)
Osborn, Sir John Holbrook, Kt.
Osborn, Sir Richard Henry Danvers, Bt. (1662)
Osborne, Sir Peter George, Bt. (I. 1629)
Osmotherly, Sir Edward Benjamin Crofton, Kt., CB
O'Sullevan, Sir Peter John, Kt., CBE
Oswald, *Admiral of the Fleet* Sir (John) Julian Robertson, GCB
Oswald, Sir (William Richard) Michael, KCVO
Otton, Sir Geoffrey John, KCB
Otton, *Rt. Hon.* Sir Philip Howard, Kt.
Oulton, Sir Antony Derek Maxwell, GCB, QC
Ouseley, *Hon.* Sir Brian Walter, Kt.
Outram, Sir Alan James, Bt. (1858)
Owen, Sir Geoffrey, Kt.
Owen, *Hon.* Sir John Arthur Dalziel, Kt.
Owen, *Hon.* Sir Robert Michael, Kt.
Owen-Jones, Sir Lindsay Harwood, KBE
Packer, Sir Richard John, KCB
Page, Sir (Arthur) John, Kt.
Paget, Sir Julian Tolver, Bt. (1871), CVO
Paget, Sir Richard Herbert, Bt. (1886)
Paine, Sir Christopher Hammon, Kt., FRCP, FRCR
Pakenham, *Hon.* Sir Michael Aiden, KBE, CMG
Palin, *Air Chief Marshal* Sir Roger Hewlett, KCB, OBE
Palliser, *Rt. Hon.* Sir (Arthur) Michael, GCMG
Palmer, Sir Albert Rocky, Kt.
Palmer, Sir (Charles) Mark, Bt. (1886)
Palmer, Sir Geoffrey Christopher John, Bt. (1660)
Palmer, *Rt. Hon.* Sir Geoffrey Winston Russell, KCMG
Palmer, Sir John Edward Somerset, Bt. (1791)
Palmer, *Maj.-Gen.* Sir (Joseph) Michael, KCVO
Palmer, Sir Reginald Oswald, GCMG, MBE
Pantlin, Sir Dick Hurst, Kt., CBE
Parbo, Sir Arvi Hillar, Kt.

Park, *Hon.* Sir Andrew Edward Wilson, Kt.
Parker, Sir Alan William, Kt., CBE
Parker, Sir Eric Wilson, Kt.
Parker, *Rt. Hon.* Sir Jonathan Frederic, Kt.
Parker, *Maj.* Sir Michael John, KCVO, CBE
Parker, Sir Richard (William) Hyde, Bt. (1681)
Parker, *Rt. Hon.* Sir Roger Jocelyn, Kt.
Parker, Sir (Thomas) John, Kt.
Parker, Sir William Peter Brian, Bt. (1844)
Parkes, Sir Edward Walter, Kt., FRENG
Parry, Sir Emyr Jones, GCMG
Parry-Evans, *Air Chief Marshal* Sir David, GCB, CBE
Parsons, Sir John Christopher, KCVO
Parsons, Sir (John) Michael, Kt.
Parsons, Sir Richard Edmund (Clement Fownes), KCMG
Partridge, Sir Michael John Anthony, KCB
Pascoe, *Gen.* Sir Robert Alan, KCB, MBE
Pasley, Sir Robert Killigrew Sabine, Bt. (1794)
Paston-Bedingfeld, *Capt.* Sir Edmund George Felix, Bt. (1661)
Paterson, Sir Dennis Craig, Kt.
Patnick, Sir (Cyril) Irvine, Kt., OBE
Patten, *Hon.* Mr Justice, Sir Nicholas John, Kt.
Pattie, *Rt. Hon.* Sir Geoffrey Edwin, Kt.
Pattison, *Prof.* Sir John Ridley, Kt., DM, FRCPATH
Pattullo, Sir (David) Bruce, Kt., CBE
Pauncefort-Duncombe, Sir Philip Digby, Bt. (1859)
Payne, Sir Norman John, Kt., CBE, FRENG
Payne-Gallwey, Sir Philip Frankland, Bt. (1812)
Peach, Sir Leonard Harry, Kt.
Peacock, *Prof.* Sir Alan Turner, Kt., DSC
Pearce, Sir (Daniel Norton) Idris, Kt., CBE, TD
Pearse, Sir Brian Gerald, Kt.
Pearson, Sir Francis Nicholas Fraser, Bt. (1964)
Pearson, *Gen.* Sir Thomas Cecil Hook, KCB, CBE, DSO
Peart, *Prof.* Sir William Stanley, Kt., MD, FRS
Pease, Sir (Alfred) Vincent, Bt. (1882)
Pease, Sir Richard Thorn, Bt. (1920)
Peat, Sir Gerrard Charles, KCVO
Peat, Sir Michael Charles Gerrard, KCVO
Peck, Sir Edward Heywood, GCMG
Peckham, *Prof.* Sir Michael John, Kt.
Pedelty, Sir Mervyn Kay, Kt.
Peek, *Vice-Adm.* Sir Richard Innes, KBE, CB, DSC
Peek, Sir Richard Grenville, Bt. (1874)

Peirse, *Air Vice-Marshal* Sir Richard Charles Fairfax, KCVO, CB
Pelgen, Sir Harry Friedrich, Kt., MBE
Peliza, Sir Robert John, KBE, ED
Pelly, Sir Richard John, Bt. (1840)
Pemberton, Sir Francis Wingate William, Kt., CBE
Pendry, *Prof.* Sir John Brian, Kt., FRS
Penrose, *Prof.* Sir Roger, Kt., OM, FRS
Penry-Davey, *Hon.* Sir David Herbert, Kt.
Pepper, *Dr.* Sir David Edwin, KCMG
Pepper, *Prof.* Sir Michael, Kt.
Perowne, *Vice-Adm.* Sir James Francis, KBE
Perring, Sir John Raymond, Bt. (1963)
Perris, Sir David (Arthur), Kt., MBE
Perry, Sir David Howard, KCB
Perry, Sir (David) Norman, Kt., MBE
Perry, Sir Michael Sydney, GBE
Pervez, Sir Mohammed Anwar, Kt., OBE
Peters, *Prof.* Sir David Keith, Kt., FRCP
Peterson, Sir Christopher Matthew, Kt., CBE, TD
†Petit, Sir Jehangir, Bt. (1890)
Peto, Sir Henry George Morton, Bt. (1855)
Peto, Sir Michael Henry Basil, Bt. (1927)
Peto, *Prof.* Sir Richard, Kt., FRS
Petrie, Sir Peter Charles, Bt. (1918), CMG
Pettigrew, Sir Russell Hilton, Kt.
Pettit, Sir Daniel Eric Arthur, Kt.
Pettitt, Sir Dennis, Kt.
†Philipson-Stow, Sir (Robert) Matthew, Bt. (1907)
Phillips, Sir Fred Albert, Kt., CVO
Phillips, Sir (Gerald) Hayden, GCB
Phillips, Sir John David, Kt., QPM
Phillips, Sir Peter John, Kt., OBE
Phillips, Sir Robin Francis, Bt. (1912)
Phillis, Sir Robert Weston, Kt.
Pickard, Sir (John) Michael, Kt.
Pickthorn, Sir James Francis Mann, Bt. (1959)
Pidgeon, Sir John Allan Stewart, Kt.
†Piers, Sir James Desmond, Bt. (I. 1661)
Piggott-Brown, Sir William Brian, Bt. (1903)
Pigot, Sir George Hugh, Bt. (1764)
Pigott, *Lt.-Gen.* Sir Anthony David, KCB, CBE
Pigott, Sir Berkeley Henry Sebastian, Bt. (1808)
Pike, *Lt.-Gen.* Sir Hew William Royston, KCB, DSO, MBE
Pike, Sir Michael Edmund, KCVO, CMG
Pike, Sir Philip Ernest Housden, Kt., QC
Pilditch, Sir Richard Edward, Bt. (1929)
Pile, Sir Frederick Devereux, Bt. (1900), MC
Pill, *Rt. Hon.* Sir Malcolm Thomas, Kt.

Pilling, Sir Joseph Grant, KCB
Pinsent, Sir Christopher Roy, Bt. (1938)
Pinsent, Sir Matthew Clive, Kt., CBE
Pippard, *Prof.* Sir (Alfred) Brian, Kt., FRS
Pitakaka, Sir Moses Puibangara, GCMG
Pitcher, Sir Desmond Henry, Kt.
Pitchers, *Hon.* Sir Christopher (John), Kt.
Pitchford, *Hon.* Sir Christopher John, Kt.
Pitman, Sir Brian Ivor, Kt.
Pitoi, Sir Sere, Kt., CBE
Pitt, Sir Michael Edward, Kt.
Pitts, Sir Cyril Alfred, Kt.
Plastow, Sir David Arnold Stuart, Kt.
Platt, Sir Harold Grant, Kt.
Platt, Sir Martin Philip, Bt. (1959)
Pledger, *Air Chief Marshal* Sir Malcolm David, KCB, OBE, AFC
Plumbly, Sir Derek John, KCMG
Pogo, *Most Revd.* Ellison Leslie, KBE
Pohai, Sir Timothy, Kt., MBE
Pole, Sir (John) Richard (Walter Reginald) Carew, Bt. (1628)
Pole, Sir Peter Van Notten, Bt. (1791)
Polkinghorne, *Revd Canon* John Charlton, KBE, FRS
Pollard, Sir Charles, Kt.
†Pollen, Sir Richard John Hungerford, Bt. (1795)
Pollock, Sir George Frederick, Bt. (1866)
Ponsonby, Sir Ashley Charles Gibbs, Bt., KCVO, MC (1956)
Poore, Sir Roger Ricardo, Bt. (1795)
Pope, Sir Joseph Albert, Kt., DSC, PHD
Popplewell, *Hon.* Sir Oliver Bury, Kt.
†Porritt, Sir Jonathon Espie, Bt. (1963)
Portal, Sir Jonathan Francis, Bt. (1901)
Porter, *Rt. Hon.* Sir Robert Wilson, Kt., PC (NI)
Posnett, Sir Richard Neil, KBE, CMG
Potter, *Rt. Hon.* Sir Mark Howard, Kt.
Potts, *Hon.* Sir Francis Humphrey, Kt.
Pound, Sir John David, Bt. (1905)
Povey, Sir Keith, Kt., QPM
Powell, Sir Nicholas Folliott Douglas, Bt. (1897)
Power, Sir Alastair John Cecil, Bt. (1924)
Power, *Hon.* Sir Noel Plunkett, Kt.
Prance, *Prof.* Sir Ghillean Tolmie, Kt., FRS
Prendergast, Sir (Walter) Kieran, KCVO, CMG
Prescott, Sir Mark, Bt. (1938)
†Preston, Sir Philip Charles Henry Hulton, Bt. (1815)
Prevost, Sir Christopher Gerald, Bt. (1805)
Price, Sir David Ernest Campbell, Kt.
Price, Sir Francis Caradoc Rose, Bt. (1815)
Price, Sir Frank Leslie, Kt.

Prickett, *Air Chief Marshal* Sir Thomas Other, KCB, DSO, DFC
Prideaux, Sir Humphrey Povah Treverbian, Kt., OBE
Priestly, Sir Julian Gordon, KCMG
†Primrose, Sir John Ure, Bt. (1903)
Pringle, *Air Marshal* Sir Charles Norman Seton, KBE, FRENG
Pringle, *Hon.* Sir John Kenneth, Kt.
Pringle, *Lt.-Gen.* Sir Steuart (Robert), Bt. (S. 1683), KCB
Pritchard, Sir Neil, KCMG
Prichard-Jones, Sir John, Bt. (1910)
Proby, Sir William Henry, Bt. (1952)
Proctor-Beauchamp, Sir Christopher Radstock, Bt. (1745)
Prosser, Sir David John, Kt.
Prosser, Sir Ian Maurice Gray, Kt.
Pryke, Sir Christopher Dudley, Bt. (1926)
Puapua, *Rt. Hon.* Sir Tomasi, GCMG, KBE
Pugh, Sir Idwal Vaughan, KCB
Pumfrey, *Hon.* Sir Nicholas Richard, Kt.
Pumphrey, Sir (John) Laurence, KCMG
Purves, Sir William, Kt., CBE, DSO
Purvis, *Vice-Adm.* Sir Neville, KCB
Quan, Sir Henry (Francis), KBE
Quicke, Sir John Godolphin, Kt., CBE
Quigley, Sir (William) George (Henry), Kt., CB, PHD
Quilter, Sir Anthony Raymond Leopold Cuthbert, Bt. (1897)
Quinlan, Sir Michael Edward, GCB
Quinton, Sir James Grand, Kt.
Radcliffe, Sir Sebastian Everard, Bt. (1813)
Radda, *Prof.* Sir George Karoly, CBE, FRS
Rae, Sir William, Kt., QPM
Raeburn, Sir Michael Edward Norman, Bt. (1923)
Raikes, *Vice-Adm.* Sir Iwan Geoffrey, KCB, CBE, DSC
Raison, *Rt. Hon.* Sir Timothy Hugh Francis, Kt.
Rake, Sir Michael Derek Vaughan, Kt.
Ralli, Sir Godfrey Victor, Bt., TD (1912)
Ramdanee, Sir Mookteswar Baboolall Kailash, Kt.
Ramphal, Sir Shridath Surendranath, GCMG
Ramphul, Sir Baalkhristna, Kt.
Ramphul, Sir Indurduth, Kt.
Ramsay, Sir Alexander William Burnett, Bt. (1806)
Ramsay, Sir Allan John (Hepple), KBE, CMG
Ramsay-Fairfax-Lucy, Sir Edmund John William Hugh, Bt. (1836)
Ramsbotham, *Hon.* Sir Peter Edward, GCMG, GCVO
Ramsden, Sir John Charles Josslyn, Bt. (1689)
Ramsey, *Dr* Sir Frank Cuthbert, KCMG

Ramsey, *Hon.* Sir Vivian Arthur, Kt.
Rankin, Sir Ian Niall, Bt. (1898)
Rasch, Sir Simon Anthony Carne, Bt. (1903)
Rashleigh, Sir Richard Harry, Bt. (1831)
Ratford, Sir David John Edward, KCMG, CVO
Rattee, *Hon.* Sir Donald Keith, Kt.
Rattle, Sir Simon Dennis, Kt., CBE
Rawlins, *Surgeon Vice-Adm.* Sir John Stuart Pepys, KBE
Rawlins, *Prof.* Sir Michael David, Kt., FRCP, FRCPED
Rawlinson, Sir Anthony Henry John, Bt. (1891)
Rea, *Prof.* Sir Desmond, Kt., OBE
Read, *Air Marshal* Sir Charles Frederick, KBE, CB, DFC, AFC
Read, *Prof.* Sir David John, Kt.
Read, Sir John Emms, Kt.
†Reade, Sir Kenneth Ray, Bt. (1661)
Reardon-Smith, Sir (William) Antony (John), Bt. (1920)
Reay, *Lt.-Gen.* Sir (Hubert) Alan John, KBE
Redgrave, *Maj.-Gen.* Sir Roy Michael Frederick, KBE, MC
Redgrave, Sir Steven Geoffrey, Kt., CBE
Redmayne, Sir Nicholas, Bt. (1964)
Redwood, Sir Peter Boverton, Bt. (1911)
Reece, Sir Charles Hugh, Kt.
Reedie, Sir Craig Collins, Kt., CBE
Rees, Sir Richard Ellis Meuric, Kt., CBE
Reeve, Sir Anthony, KCMG, KCVO
Reeves, *Most Revd* Paul Alfred, GCMG, GCVO
Reffell, *Adm.* Sir Derek Roy, KCB
Refshauge, *Maj.-Gen.* Sir William Dudley, Kt., CBE
Reid, Sir Alexander James, Bt. (1897)
Reid, Sir Hugh, Bt. (1922)
Reid, Sir Norman Robert, Kt.
Reid, Sir (Philip) Alan, KCVO
Reid, Sir Robert Paul, Kt.
Reid, Sir William Kennedy, KCB
Reiher, Sir Frederick Bernard Carl, KBE, CMG
Reilly, *Lt.-Gen.* Sir Jeremy Calcott, KCB, DSO
Renals, Sir Stanley, Bt. (1895)
Renouf, Sir Clement William Bailey, Kt.
Renshaw, Sir John David Bine, Bt. (1903)
Renwick, Sir Richard Eustace, Bt. (1921)
Reporter, Sir Shapoor Ardeshirji, KBE
Reynolds, Sir David James, Bt. (1923)
Reynolds, Sir Peter William John, Kt., CBE
Rhodes, Sir John Christopher Douglas, Bt. (1919)
Rice, *Maj.-Gen.* Sir Desmond Hind Garrett, KCVO, CBE
Rice, Sir Timothy Miles Bindon, Kt.
Richard, Sir Cliff, Kt., OBE

Richards, Sir Brian Mansel, Kt., CBE, PHD

Richards, *Hon.* Sir David Anthony Stewart, Kt.

Richards, Sir David Gerald, Kt.

Richards, *Lt.-Gen.* Sir David, Julian, KCB, CBE, DSO

Richards, Sir Francis Neville, KCMG, CVO

Richards, *Rt. Hon.* Sir Stephen Price, Kt.

Richardson, Sir Anthony Lewis, Bt. (1924)

Richardson, *Rt. Hon.* Sir Ivor Lloyd Morgan, Kt.

Richardson, *Lt.-Gen.* Sir Robert Francis, KCB, CVO, CBE

Richardson, Sir Thomas Legh, KCMG

Richardson-Bunbury, Sir (Richard David) Michael, Bt. (I. 1787)

Richmond, *Prof.* Sir Mark Henry, Kt., FRS

Ricketts, Sir (Robert) Tristram, Bt. (1828)

Riddell, Sir John Charles Buchanan, Bt. (S. 1628), CVO

Ridley, Sir Adam (Nicholas), Kt.

Ridley, Sir Michael Kershaw, KCVO

Rifkind, *Rt. Hon.* Sir Malcolm Leslie, KCMG

Rigby, Sir Anthony John, Bt. (1929)

Rigby, Sir Peter, Kt.

Rimer, *Hon.* Sir Colin Percy Farquharson, Kt.

Ripley, Sir William Hugh, Bt. (1880)

Risk, Sir Thomas Neilson, Kt.

Ritako, Sir Thomas Baha, Kt., MBE

Ritblat, Sir John Henry, Kt.

Rivett-Carnac, Sir Miles James, Bt. (1836)

Rix, *Rt. Hon.* Sir Bernard Anthony, Kt.

Rix, Sir John, Kt., MBE, FRENG

Robati, Sir Pupuke, KBE

Robb, Sir John Weddell, Kt.

Roberts, *Hon.* Sir Denys Tudor Emil, KBE

Roberts, Sir Derek Harry, Kt., CBE, FRS, FRENG

Roberts, *Prof.* Sir Edward Adam, KCMG

Roberts, Sir Gilbert Howland Rookehurst, Bt. (1809)

Roberts, Sir Hugh Ashley, KCVO

Roberts, Sir Ivor Anthony, KCMG

Roberts, *Maj.-Gen.* Sir Sebastian John Lechmere, KCVO, OBE

Roberts, Sir Samuel, Bt. (1919)

Roberts, Sir William James Denby, Bt. (1909)

Robertson, Sir Lewis, Kt., CBE, FRSE

Robins, Sir Ralph Harry, Kt., FRENG

Robinson, Sir Albert Edward Phineas, Kt.

†Robinson, Sir Christopher Philipse, Bt. (1854)

Robinson, Sir Gerrard Jude, Kt.

Robinson, Sir Ian, Kt.

Robinson, Sir John James Michael Laud, Bt. (1660)

Robinson, *Dr* Sir Kenneth, Kt.

Robinson, Sir Wilfred Henry Frederick, Bt. (1908)

Robson, Sir John Adam, KCMG

Robson, Sir Stephen Arthur, Kt., CB

Robson, Sir Robert William, Kt., CBE

Roch, *Rt. Hon.* Sir John Ormond, Kt.

Roche, Sir David O'Grady, Bt. (1838)

Roche, Sir Henry John, Kt.

Rodgers, Sir (Andrew) Piers (Wingate Aikin-Sneath), Bt. (1964)

Rodley, *Prof.* Sir Nigel, KBE

Rodrigues, Sir Alberto Maria, Kt., CBE, ED

Rogers, *Air Chief Marshal* Sir John Robson, KCB, CBE

Rooke, Sir Denis Eric, Kt., OM, CBE, FRS, FRENG

Ropner, Sir John Bruce Woollacott, Bt. (1952)

Ropner, Sir Robert Clinton, Bt. (1904)

Rose, Sir Arthur James, Kt., CBE

Rose, *Rt. Hon.* Sir Christopher Dudley Roger, Kt.

Rose, Sir Clive Martin, GCMG

Rose, Sir David Lancaster, Bt. (1874)

Rose, *Gen.* Sir (Hugh) Michael, KCB, CBE, DSO, QGM

Rose, Sir John Edward Victor, Kt.

Rose, Sir Julian Day, Bt. (1872 and 1909)

Rosenthal, Sir Norman Leon, Kt.

Ross, *Maj.* Sir Andrew Charles Paterson, Bt. (1960)

Ross, *Lt.-Gen.* Sir Robert Jeremy, KCB, OBE

Ross, *Lt.-Col.* Sir Walter Hugh Malcolm, GCVO, OBE

Rossi, Sir Hugh Alexis Louis, Kt.

Rothschild, Sir Evelyn Robert Adrian de, Kt.

Rougier, *Hon.* Sir Richard George, Kt.

Rove, *Revd* Ikan, KBE

Rowe, *Rear-Adm.* Sir Patrick Barton, KCVO, CBE

Rowe-Ham, Sir David Kenneth, GBE

Rowland, Sir (John) David, Kt.

Rowlands, Sir David, KCB

Rowley, Sir Charles Robert, Bt. (1836)

Rowling, Sir John Reginald, Kt.

Rowlinson, *Prof.* Sir John Shipley, Kt., FRS

Royce, *Hon.* Sir Roger John, Kt.

Royden, Sir Christopher John, Bt. (1905)

Rudd, Sir (Anthony) Nigel (Russell), Kt.

Rudge, Sir Alan Walter, Kt., CBE, FRS

Rugge-Price, Sir James Keith Peter, Bt. (1804)

Ruggles-Brise, Sir Timothy Edward, Bt. (1935)

Rumbold, Sir Henry John Sebastian, Bt. (1779)

Runchorelal, Sir (Udayan) Chinubhai Madhowlal, Bt. (1913)

Rusby, *Vice-Adm.* Sir Cameron, KCB, LVO

Rushdie, Sir (Ahmed) Salman, Kt.

†Russell, Sir (Arthur) Mervyn, Bt. (1812)

Russell, Sir Charles Dominic, Bt. (1916)

Russell, Sir George, Kt., CBE

Russell, Sir Muir, KCB

Rutter, *Prof.* Sir Michael Llewellyn, Kt., CBE, MD, FRS

Ryan, Sir Derek Gerald, Bt. (1919)

Rycroft, Sir Richard John, Bt. (1784)

Ryder, *Hon.* Sir Ernest Nigel Ryder, Kt., TD

Ryrie, Sir William Sinclair, KCB

Sacks, *Chief Rabbi Dr* Jonathan, Kt.

Sacranie, Sir Iqbal Abdul Karim Mussa, Kt., OBE

Sainsbury, *Rt. Hon.* Sir Timothy Alan Davan, Kt.

St Clair-Ford, Sir James Anson, Bt. (1793)

St George, Sir John Avenel Bligh, Bt. (I. 1766)

St John-Mildmay, Sir Walter John Hugh, Bt. (1772)

Sainty, Sir John Christopher, KCB

Salisbury, Sir Robert William, Kt.

Salt, Sir Patrick MacDonnell, Bt. (1869)

Salt, Sir (Thomas) Michael John, Bt. (1899)

Salusbury-Trelawny, Sir John Barry, Bt. (1628)

Sampson, Sir Colin, Kt., CBE, QPM

Samuel, Sir John Michael Glen, Bt. (1898)

Samuelson, Sir (Bernard) Michael (Francis), Bt. (1884)

Samuelson, Sir Sydney Wylie, Kt., CBE

Sanders, Sir Robert Tait, KBE, CMG

Sanders, Sir Ronald Michael, KCMG

Sanderson, Sir Frank Linton, Bt. (1920)

Sands, Sir Roger Blakemore, KCB

Sarei, Sir Alexis Holyweek, Kt., CBE

Satchwell, Sir Kevin Joseph, Kt.

Saunders, *Hon.* Sir John Henry Boulton, Kt.

Savile, Sir James Wilson Vincent, Kt., OBE

Savory, Sir Michael Berry, Kt.

Sawers, Sir Robert John, KCMG

Saxby, *Prof.* Sir Robin Keith, Kt.

Scarlett, Sir John McLeod, KCMG, OBE

Scheele, Sir Nicholas Vernon, KCMG

Schiemann, *Rt. Hon.* Sir Konrad Hermann Theodor, Kt.

Scholar, Sir Michael Charles, KCB

Scholey, Sir David Gerald, Kt., CBE

Scholey, Sir Robert, Kt., CBE, FRENG

Scholtens, Sir James Henry, KCVO

Schreier, Sir Bernard, Kt.

Schubert, Sir Sydney, Kt.

Scipio, Sir Hudson Rupert, Kt.

Scoon, Sir Paul, GCMG, GCVO, OBE
Scott, Sir Anthony Percy, Bt. (1913)
Scott, Sir David Aubrey, GCMG
Scott, *Prof.* Sir George Peter, Kt.
Scott, Sir James Jervoise, Bt. (1962)
Scott, Sir Kenneth Bertram Adam, KCVO, CMG
Scott, Sir Oliver Christopher Anderson, Bt. (1909)
Scott, *Prof.* Sir Philip John, KBE
Scott, Sir Ridley, Kt.
Scott, Sir Robert David Hillyer, Kt.
Scott, Sir Walter John, Bt. (1907)
Scott-Lee, Sir Paul Joseph, Kt., QPM
Seale, Sir Clarence David, Kt.
Seale, Sir John Henry, Bt. (1838)
Seaman, Sir Keith Douglas, KCVO, OBE
Sebastian, Sir Cuthbert Montraville, GCMG, OBE
†Sebright, Sir Rufus Hugo Giles, Bt. (1626)
Seccombe, Sir (William) Vernon Stephen, Kt.
Seconde, Sir Reginald Louis, KCMG, CVO
Sedley, *Rt. Hon.* Sir Stephen John, Kt.
Seely, Sir Nigel Edward, Bt. (1896)
Seeto, Sir Ling James, Kt., MBE
Seeyave, Sir Rene Sow Choung, Kt., CBE
Seligman, Sir Peter Wendel, Kt., CBE
Semple, Sir John Laughlin, KCB
Sergeant, Sir Patrick, Kt.
Series, Sir (Joseph Michel) Emile, Kt., CBE
Serota, Sir Nicholas Andrew, Kt.
Serpell, Sir David Radford, KCB, CMG, OBE
†Seton, Sir Charles Wallace, Bt. (S. 1683)
Seton, Sir Iain Bruce, Bt. (S. 1663)
Severne, *Air Vice-Marshal* Sir John de Milt, KCVO, OBE, AFC
Shaffer, Sir Peter Levin, Kt., CBE
Shakerley, Sir Geoffrey Adam, Bt. (1838)
Shakespeare, Sir Thomas William, Bt. (1942)
Sharp, Sir Adrian, Bt. (1922)
Sharp, Sir Kenneth Johnston, Kt., TD
Sharp, Sir Leslie, Kt., QPM
Sharp, Sir Sheridan Christopher Robin, Bt. (1920)
Sharples, Sir James, Kt., QPM
Shattock, Sir Gordon, Kt.
Shaw, Sir Brian Piers, Kt.
Shaw, Sir (Charles) Barry, Kt., CB, QC
Shaw, Sir Charles De Vere, Bt. (1821)
Shaw, *Prof.* Sir John Calman, Kt., CBE
Shaw, Sir Neil McGowan, Kt.
Shaw, Sir Roy, Kt.
Shaw, Sir Run Run, Kt., CBE
Shaw-Stewart, Sir Ludovic Houston, Bt. (S. 1667)
Shearing, Sir George Albert, Kt. OBE
Shebbeare, Sir Thomas Andrew, KCVO

Sheehy, Sir Patrick, Kt.
Sheffield, Sir Reginald Adrian Berkeley, Bt. (1755)
Shehadie, Sir Nicholas Michael, Kt., OBE
Sheil, *Rt. Hon.* Sir John, Kt.
Sheinwald, Sir Nigel Elton, KCMG
Shelley, Sir John Richard, Bt. (1611)
Shepherd, Sir Colin Ryley, Kt.
Shepherd, Sir John Alan, KCVO, CMG
Shepperd, Sir Alfred Joseph, Kt.
Sher, Sir Antony, KBE
Sherbourne, Sir Stephen Ashley, Kt., CBE
Sherston-Baker, Sir Robert George Humphrey, Bt. (1796)
Shields, *Prof.* Sir Robert, Kt., MD
Shiffner, Sir Henry David, Bt. (1818)
Silber, *Hon.* Sir Stephen Robert, Kt.
Shinwell, Sir (Maurice) Adrian, Kt.
Shock, Sir Maurice, Kt.
Short, Sir Apenera Pera, KBE
Shortridge, Sir Jon Deacon, KCB
Shuckburgh, Sir Rupert Charles Gerald, Bt. (1660)
Sieff, *Hon.* Sir David, Kt.
Silber, *Rt. Hon.* Sir Stephen Robert, Kt.
Simeon, Sir Richard Edmund Barrington, Bt. (1815)
Simmonds, *Rt. Hon. Dr* Sir Kennedy Alphonse, KCMG
Simmons, *Air Marshal* Sir Michael George, KCB, AFC
Simmons, Sir Stanley Clifford, Kt.
Simms, Sir Neville Ian, Kt., FRENG
Simon, *Hon.* Sir Peregrine Charles Hugh, Kt.
Simonet, Sir Louis Marcel Pierre, Kt., CBE
Simpson, *Dr* Sir Peter Jeffery, Kt.
Sims, Sir Roger Edward, Kt.
Sinclair, Sir Clive Marles, Kt.
Sinclair, Sir Ian McTaggart, KCMG, QC
Sinclair, Sir Patrick Robert Richard, Bt. (S. 1704)
Sinclair, Sir Robert John, Kt.
Sinclair-Lockhart, Sir Simon John Edward Francis, Bt. (S. 1636)
Sinden, Sir Donald Alfred, Kt., CBE
Singer, *Hon.* Sir Jan Peter, Kt.
Singh, Sir Pritpal, Kt.
Singleton, Sir Roger, Kt., CBE
Sione, Sir Tomu Malaefone, GCMG, OBE
Sitwell, Sir (Sacheverell) Reresby, Bt. (1808)
Skeggs, Sir Clifford George, Kt.
Skehel, Sir John James, Kt., FRS
Skingsley, *Air Chief Marshal* Sir Anthony Gerald, GBE, KCB
Skinner, Sir (Thomas) Keith (Hewitt), Bt. (1912)
Skipwith, Sir Patrick Alexander d'Estoteville, Bt. (1622)
Slack, Sir William Willatt, KCVO, FRCS
Slade, Sir Benjamin Julian Alfred, Bt. (1831)

Slade, *Rt. Hon.* Sir Christopher John, Kt.
Slaney, *Prof.* Sir Geoffrey, KBE
Slater, *Adm.* Sir John (Jock) Cunningham Kirkwood, GCB, LVO
Sleight, Sir Richard, Bt. (1920)
Sloan, Sir Andrew Kirkpatrick, Kt., QPM
Sloman, Sir Albert Edward, Kt., CBE
Smart, Sir Jack, Kt., CBE
Smiley, *Lt.-Col.* Sir John Philip, Bt. (1903)
Smith, Sir Alan, Kt., CBE, DFC
Smith, *Hon.* Sir Andrew Charles, Kt.
Smith, Sir Andrew Thomas, Bt. (1897)
†Smith, Sir Robert Christopher Sydney Winwood, Bt. (1809)
Smith, *Prof.* Sir Colin Stansfield, Kt., CBE
Smith, Sir Cyril, Kt., MBE
Smith, *Prof.* Sir David Cecil, Kt., FRS
Smith, Sir David Iser, KCVO
Smith, Sir Dudley (Gordon), Kt.
Smith, *Prof.* Sir Eric Brian, Kt., PHD
Smith, Sir Geoffrey Johnson, Kt.
Smith, Sir John Alfred, Kt., QPM
Smith, Sir Joseph William Grenville, Kt.
Smith, Sir Kevin, Kt., CBE
Smith, Sir Michael John Llewellyn, KCVO, CMG
Smith, Sir (Norman) Brian, Kt., CBE, PHD
Smith, Sir Paul Brierley, Kt., CBE
Smith, *Hon.* Sir Peter (Winston), Kt.
Smith, Sir Robert Courtney, Kt., CBE
Smith, Sir Robert Haldane, Kt
Smith, Sir Robert Hill, Bt. (1945)
Smith, *Gen.* Sir Rupert Anthony, KCB, DSO, OBE, QGM
Smith-Dodsworth, Sir John Christopher, Bt. (1784)
Smith-Gordon, Sir (Lionel) Eldred (Peter), Bt. (1838)
Smith-Marriott, Sir Hugh Cavendish, Bt. (1774)
Smurfit, *Dr.* Sir Michael William Joseph, KBE
Smyth, Sir Timothy John, Bt. (1955)
Sobers, Sir Garfield St Auburn, Kt.
Solomon, Sir Harry, Kt.
Somare, *Rt. Hon.* Sir Michael Thomas, GCMG, CH
Somerville, *Brig.* Sir John Nicholas, Kt., CBE
Sorrell, Sir Martin Stuart, Kt.
Soulsby, Sir Peter Alfred, Kt.
Soutar, *Air Marshal* Sir Charles John Williamson, KBE
Southby, Sir John Richard Bilbe, Bt. (1937)
Southern, *Prof.* Sir Edwin Mellor, Kt.
Southgate, Sir Colin Grieve, Kt.
Southgate, Sir William David, Kt.
Southward, *Dr* Sir Nigel Ralph, KCVO
Souyave, *Hon.* Sir (Louis) Georges, Kt.

Sowrey, *Air Marshal* Sir Frederick Beresford, KCB, CBE, AFC

Sparrow, Sir John, Kt.

Spearman, Sir Alexander Young Richard Mainwaring, Bt. (1840)

Spedding, *Prof.* Sir Colin Raymond William, Kt., CBE

Speed, Sir (Herbert) Keith, Kt., RD

Speelman, Sir Cornelis Jacob, Bt. (1686)

Speight, *Hon.* Sir Graham Davies, Kt.

Spencer, Sir Derek Harold, Kt., QC

Spencer, *Vice-Adm.* Sir Peter, KCB

Spencer-Nairn, Sir Robert Arnold, Bt. (1933)

Spicer, Sir James Wilton, Kt.

Spicer, Sir Nicholas Adrian Albert, Bt. (1906)

Spicer, Sir (William) Michael Hardy, Kt.

Spiers, Sir Donald Maurice, Kt., CB, TD

Spooner, Sir James Douglas, Kt.

Spratt, *Col.* Sir Greville Douglas, GBE, TD

Spring, Sir Dryden Thomas, Kt.

Squire, *Air Chief Marshal* Sir Peter Ted, GCB, DFC, AFC, ADC

Stainton, Sir (John) Ross, Kt., CBE

Staite, Sir Richard John, Kt., OBE

Stamer, Sir (Lovelace) Anthony, Bt. (1809)

Stanhope, *Adm.* Sir Mark, KCB, OBE

Stanier, Sir Beville Douglas, Bt. (1917)

Stanier, *Field Marshal* Sir John Wilfred, GCB, MBE

Stanley, *Rt. Hon.* Sir John Paul, Kt., MP

Staples, Sir Richard Molesworth, Bt. (I. 1628)

Starkey, Sir John Philip, Bt. (1935)

Staughton, *Rt. Hon.* Sir Christopher Stephen Thomas Jonathan Thayer, Kt.

Staveley, Sir John Malfroy, KBE, MC

Stear, *Air Chief Marshal* Sir Michael James Douglas, KCB, CBE

Steel, *Hon.* Sir David William, Kt.

Steer, Sir Alan William, Kt.

Stephen, *Rt. Hon.* Sir Ninian Martin, KG, GCMG, GCVO, KBE

Stephens, Sir (Edwin) Barrie, Kt.

Stephens, Sir William Benjamin Synge, Kt.

Stephenson, Sir Henry Upton, Bt. (1936)

Stern, *Prof.* Sir Nicholas Herbert, Kt.

Sternberg, Sir Sigmund, Kt.

Stevens, Sir Jocelyn Edward Greville, Kt., CVO

Stevens, Sir Laurence Houghton, Kt., CBE

Stevenson, Sir Simpson, Kt.

Stewart, Sir Alan d'Arcy, Bt. (I. 1623)

Stewart, Sir Brian John, Kt., CBE

Stewart, Sir David James Henderson, Bt. (1957)

Stewart, Sir David John Christopher, Bt. (1803)

Stewart, Sir James Douglas, Kt.

Stewart, Sir James Moray, KCB

Stewart, Sir (John) Simon (Watson), Bt. (1920)

Stewart, Sir John Young, Kt., OBE

Stewart, *Lt.-Col.* Sir Robert Christie, KCVO, CBE, TD

Stewart, Sir Robertson Huntly, Kt., CBE

Stewart, Sir Robin Alastair, Bt. (1960)

Stewart, *Prof.* Sir William Duncan Paterson, Kt., FRS, FRSE

Stewart-Clark, Sir John, Bt. (1918)

Stewart-Richardson, Sir Simon Alaisdair, Bt. (S. 1630)

Stewart-Wilson, *Lt.-Col.* Sir Blair Aubyn, KCVO

Stibbon, *Gen.* Sir John James, KCB, OBE

Stirling, Sir Alexander John Dickson, KBE, CMG

Stirling, Sir Angus Duncan Aeneas, Kt.

Stirling-Hamilton, Sir Malcolm William Bruce, Bt. (S. 1673)

Stirling of Fairburn, Sir Roderick William Kenneth, KCVO

Stirling of Garden, *Col.* Sir James, KCVO, CBE, TD

Stirrup, *Air Chief Marshal* Sir Graham Eric (Jock), GCB, AFC, ADC

Stockdale, Sir Thomas Minshull, Bt. (1960)

Stoddart, *Prof.* Sir James Fraser, Kt.

Stoddart, *Wg Cdr.* Sir Kenneth Maxwell, KCVO, AE

Stoker, *Prof.* Sir Michael George Parke, Kt., CBE, FRCP, FRS, FRSE

Stones, Sir William Frederick, Kt., OBE

Stonhouse, *Revd* Michael Philip, Bt. (1628 and 1670)

Stonor, *Air Marshal* Sir Thomas Henry, KCB

Stoppard, Sir Thomas, Kt., OM, CBE

Storey, *Hon.* Sir Richard, Bt., CBE (1960)

Stothard, Sir Peter Michael, Kt.

Stott, Sir Adrian George Ellingham, Bt. (1920)

Stoute, Sir Michael Ronald, Kt.

Stowe, Sir Kenneth Ronald, GCB, CVO

Stracey, Sir John Simon, Bt. (1818)

Strachan, Sir Curtis Victor, Kt., CVO

Strachey, Sir Charles, Bt. (1801)

Straker, Sir Louis Hilton, KCMG

Strang Steel, Sir (Fiennes) Michael, Bt. (1938)

Street, *Hon.* Sir Laurence Whistler, KCMG

Streeton, Sir Terence George, KBE, CMG

Strickland-Constable, Sir Frederic, Bt. (1641)

Stringer, Sir Donald Edgar, Kt., CBE

Stringer, Sir Howard, Kt.

Strong, Sir Roy Colin, Kt., PHD, FSA

Stronge, Sir James Anselan Maxwell, Bt. (1803)

Stuart, Sir James Keith, Kt.

Stuart, Sir Kenneth Lamonte, Kt.

†Stuart, Sir Phillip Luttrell, Bt. (1660)

†Stuart-Forbes, Sir William Daniel, Bt. (S. 1626)

Stuart-Menteth, Sir James Wallace, Bt. (1838)

Stuart-Paul, *Air Marshal* Sir Ronald Ian, KBE

Stuart-Smith, *Rt. Hon.* Sir Murray, Kt.

Stubbs, Sir William Hamilton, Kt., PHD

Stucley, *Lt.* Sir Hugh George Coplestone Bampfylde, Bt. (1859)

Studd, Sir Edward Fairfax, Bt. (1929)

Studholme, Sir Henry William, Bt. (1956)

Sturridge, Sir Nicholas Anthony, KCVO

†Style, Sir William Frederick, Bt. (1627)

Sugar, Sir Alan Michael, Kt.

Sullivan, *Hon.* Sir Jeremy Mirth, Kt.

Sullivan, Sir Richard Arthur, Bt. (1804)

Sulston, Sir John Edward, Kt.

Sumner, *Hon.* Sir Christopher John, Kt.

Sunderland, Sir John Michael, Kt.

Sutherland, Sir John Brewer, Bt. (1921)

Sutherland, Sir William George MacKenzie, Kt.

Sutton, Sir Frederick Walter, Kt., OBE

Sutton, *Air Marshal* Sir John Matthias Dobson, KCB

Sutton, Sir Richard Lexington, Bt. (1772)

Swaffield, Sir James Chesebrough, Kt., CBE, RD

Swaine, Sir John Joseph, Kt., CBE

Swan, Sir Conrad Marshall John Fisher, KCVO, PHD

Swan, Sir John William David, KBE

Swann, Sir Michael Christopher, Bt. (1906), TD

Swartz, *Hon.* Sir Reginald William Colin, KBE, ED

Sweeney, Sir George, Kt.

Sweeting, *Prof.* Sir Martin Nicholas, Kt., OBE, FRS

Sweetnam, Sir (David) Rodney, KCVO, CBE, FRCS

Swinburn, *Lt.-Gen.* Sir Richard Hull, KCB

Swinnerton-Dyer, *Prof.* Sir (Henry) Peter (Francis), Bt. (1678), KBE, FRS

Swinton, *Maj.-Gen.* Sir John, KCVO, OBE

Swire, Sir Adrian Christopher, Kt.

Swire, Sir John Anthony, Kt., CBE

Sykes, Sir David Michael, Bt. (1921)

Sykes, Sir Francis John Badcock, Bt. (1781)

Sykes, Sir Hugh Ridley, Kt.

Sykes, *Prof.* Sir (Malcolm) Keith, Kt.

Sykes, Sir Richard, Kt.

Sykes, Sir Tatton Christopher Mark, Bt. (1783)

Symington, *Prof.* Sir Thomas, Kt., MD, FRSE
Symons, *Vice-Adm.* Sir Patrick Jeremy, KBE
Synge, Sir Robert Carson, Bt. (1801)
Synnott, Sir Hilary Nicholas Hugh, KCMG
Talboys, *Rt. Hon.* Sir Brian Edward, CH, KCB
Tangaroa, *Hon.* Sir Tangaroa, Kt., MBE
Tapps-Gervis-Meyrick, Sir George Christopher Cadafael, Bt. (1791)
Tapsell, Sir Peter Hannay Bailey, Kt., MP
Tate, Sir (Henry) Saxon, Bt. (1898)
Taureka, *Dr* Sir Reubeh, KBE
Tauvasa, Sir Joseph James, KBE
Tavare, Sir John, Kt., CBE
Tavener, *Prof.* Sir John Kenneth, Kt.
Taylor, Sir (Arthur) Godfrey, Kt.
Taylor, Sir Cyril Julian Hebden, GBE
Taylor, Sir Edward Macmillan (Teddy), Kt.
Taylor, *Rt. Revd* John Bernard, KCVO
Taylor, *Dr.* Sir John Michael, Kt., OBE
Taylor, Sir Nicholas Richard Stuart, Bt. (1917)
Taylor, Sir Robert Richard, KCVO, OBE
Taylor, *Prof.* Sir William, Kt., CBE
Taylor, Sir William George, Kt.
Teagle, *Vice-Adm.* Sir Somerford Francis, KBE
Teare, *Hon.* Sir Nigel John Martin, Kt.
Teasdale, *Prof.* Sir Graham Michael, Kt.
Tebbit, Sir Donald Claude, GCMG
Tebbit, Sir Kevin Reginald, KCB, CMG
Telford, Sir Robert, Kt., CBE, FRENG
Telito, *HE Revd* Filoimea, GCMG, MBE
Temple, *Prof.* Sir John Graham, Kt.
Temple, *Maj.* Sir Richard Anthony Purbeck, Bt. (1876), MC
Templeton, Sir John Marks, Kt.
Tennant, Sir Anthony John, Kt.
Tennyson-D'Eyncourt, Sir Mark Gervais, Bt. (1930)
Terry, *Air Marshal* Sir Colin George, KBE, CB
Terry, *Air Chief Marshal* Sir Peter David George, GCB, AFC
Thatcher, Sir Mark, Bt. (1990)
Thomas, Sir David John Godfrey, Bt. (1694)
Thomas, Sir Derek Morison David, KCMG
Thomas, Sir Gilbert Stanley, Kt., OBE
Thomas, Sir Jeremy Cashel, KCMG
Thomas, Sir (John) Alan, Kt.
Thomas, *Prof.* Sir John Meurig, Kt., FRS
Thomas, Sir Keith Vivian, Kt.
Thomas, Sir Philip Lloyd, KCVO, CMG

Thomas, Sir Quentin Jeremy, Kt., CB
Thomas, *Rt. Hon.* Sir Roger John Laugharne, Kt.
Thomas, *Hon.* Sir Swinton Barclay, Kt.
Thomas, Sir William Michael, Bt. (1919)
Thomas, Sir (William) Michael (Marsh), Bt. (1918)
Thompson, Sir Christopher Peile, Bt. (1890)
Thompson, Sir Clive Malcolm, Kt.
Thompson, Sir David Albert, KCMG
Thompson, Sir Gilbert Williamson, Kt., OBE
Thompson, *Prof.* Sir Michael Warwick, Kt., DSC
Thompson, Sir Nicholas Annesley, Bt. (1963)
Thompson, Sir Nigel Cooper, KCMG, CBE
Thompson, Sir Paul Anthony, Bt. (1963)
Thompson, Sir Peter Anthony, Kt.
Thompson, *Dr* Sir Richard Paul Hepworth, KCVO
Thompson, Sir Thomas d'Eyncourt John, Bt. (1806)
Thomson, Sir (Frederick Douglas) David, Bt. (1929)
Thomson, Sir John Adam, GCMG
Thomson, Sir John (Ian) Sutherland, KBE, CMG
Thomson, Sir Mark Wilfrid Home, Bt. (1925)
Thomson, Sir Thomas James, Kt., CBE, FRCP
Thorn, Sir John Samuel, Kt., OBE
Thorne, Sir Neil Gordon, Kt., OBE, TD
Thornton, *Air Marshal* Sir Barry Michael, KCB
Thornton, Sir (George) Malcolm, Kt.
Thornton, Sir Peter Eustace, KCB
Thornton, Sir Richard Eustace, KCVO, OBE
†Thorold, Sir (Anthony) Oliver, Bt. (1642)
Thorpe, *Rt. Hon.* Sir Mathew Alexander, Kt.
Thurecht, Sir Ramon Richard, Kt., OBE
Thwaites, Sir Bryan, Kt., PHD
Tickell, Sir Crispin Charles Cervantes, GCMG, KCVO
Tikaram, Sir Moti, KBE
Tilt, Sir Robin Richard, Kt.
Tiltman, Sir John Hessell, KCVO
Timmins, *Col.* Sir John Bradford, KCVO, OBE, TD
Tims, Sir Michael David, KCVO
Tindle, Sir Ray Stanley, Kt., CBE
Tirvengadum, Sir Harry Krishnan, Kt.
Tjoeng, Sir James Neng, KBE
Tod, *Vice-Adm.* Sir Jonathan James Richard, KCB, CBE
Todd, *Prof.* Sir David, Kt., CBE
Todd, Sir Ian Pelham, KBE, FRCS
Tollemache, Sir Lyonel Humphry John, Bt. (1793)
Tomkins, Sir Edward Emile, GCMG, CVO

Tomkys, Sir (William) Roger, KCMG
Tomlinson, *Prof.* Sir Bernard Evans, Kt., CBE
Tomlinson, Sir John Rowland, Kt., CBE
Tomlinson, Sir Michael John, Kt., CBE
Tomlinson, *Hon.* Sir Stephen Miles, Kt.
Tooke, *Prof.* Sir John Edward, Kt.
Tooley, Sir John, Kt.
ToRobert, Sir Henry Thomas, KBE
Torpy, *Air Marshal* Sir Glenn Lester, KCB, CBE, DSO
Torry, Sir Peter James, GCVO, KCMG
Tory, Sir Geofroy William, KCMG
Touche, Sir Anthony George, Bt. (1920)
Touche, Sir Rodney Gordon, Bt. (1962)
Toulson, *Rt. Hon.* Sir Roger Grenfell, Kt.
Tovadek, Sir Martin, Kt. CMG
Tovey, Sir Brian John Maynard, KCMG
ToVue, Sir Ronald, Kt., OBE
Towneley, Sir Simon Peter Edmund Cosmo William, KCVO
Townsend, Sir Cyril David, Kt.
Traill, Sir Alan Towers, GBE
Trant, *Gen.* Sir Richard Brooking, KCB
Treacher, *Adm.* Sir John Devereux, KCB
Treacy, *Hon.* Sir Colman Maurice, Kt.
Treacy, *Hon.* Sir (James Mary) Seamus, Kt.
Treitel, *Prof.* Sir Guenter Heinz, Kt., FBA, QC
Trescowthick, Sir Donald Henry, KBE
Trevelyan, Sir Geoffrey Washington, Bt. (1662 and 1874)
Trezise, Sir Kenneth Bruce, Kt., OBE
Trippier, Sir David Austin, Kt., RD
Tritton, Sir Anthony John Ernest, Bt. (1905)
Trollope, Sir Anthony Simon, Bt. (1642)
Trotman-Dickenson, Sir Aubrey Fiennes, Kt.
Trotter, Sir Neville Guthrie, Kt.
Trotter, Sir Ronald Ramsay, Kt.
Troubridge, Sir Thomas Richard, Bt. (1799)
Troup, *Vice-Adm.* Sir (John) Anthony (Rose), KCB, DSC
Trousdell, *Lt.-Gen.* Sir Philip Charles Cornwallis, KCB, CB
Truscott, Sir Ralph Eric Nicholson, Bt. (1909)
Tsang, Sir Donald Yam-keun, KBE
Tuamure-Maoate, *Dr* Sir Terepai, KBE
Tuck, Sir Bruce Adolph Reginald, Bt. (1910)
Tucker, *Hon.* Sir Richard Howard, Kt.
Tuckey, *Rt. Hon.* Sir Simon Lane, Kt.
Tugendhat, *Hon.* Sir Michael George, Kt.
Tuita, Sir Mariano Kelesimalefo, KBE

Tuite, Sir Christopher Hugh, Bt. (1622), PHD

Tuivaga, Sir Timoci Uluiburotu, Kt.

Tully, Sir William Mark, KBE

Tupper, Sir Charles Hibbert, Bt. (1888)

Turbott, Sir Ian Graham, Kt., CMG, CVO

Turing, Sir John Dermot, Bt. (S. 1638)

Turner, Sir Colin William Carstairs, Kt., CBE, DFC

Turner, Hon. Sir Michael John, Kt.

Turnquest, Sir Orville Alton, GCMG, QC

Tusa, Sir John, Kt.

Tuti, Revd Dudley, KBE

Tweedie, Prof. Sir David Philip, Kt.

Tyree, Sir (Alfred) William, Kt., OBE

Tyrwhitt, Sir Reginald Thomas Newman, Bt. (1919)

Underhill, Hon. Sir Nicholas Edward, Kt.

Underwood, Prof. Sir James Cressee Elphinstone, Kt.

Unwin, Sir (James) Brian, KCB

Ure, Sir John Burns, KCMG, LVO

Urquhart, Sir Brian Edward, KCMG, MBE

Urwick, Sir Alan Bedford, KCVO, CMG

Usher, Sir Andrew John, Bt. (1899)

Utting, Sir William Benjamin, Kt., CB

Vallat, Sir Francis Aimé, GBE, KCMG, QC

Vallings, Vice-Adm. Sir George Montague Francis, KCB

Vanderfelt, Sir Robin Victor, KBE

Vardy, Sir Peter, Kt.

Varney, Sir David Robert, Kt.

Vasquez, Sir Alfred Joseph, Kt., CBE, QC

Vassar-Smith, Sir John Rathbone, Bt. (1917)

Vavasour, Sir Eric Michael Joseph Marmaduke, Bt. (1828)

Veness, Sir David, Kt., CBE, QPM

Venner, Sir Kenneth Dwight Vincent, KBE

Vereker, Sir John Michael Medlicott, KCB

†Verney, Sir John Sebastian, Bt. (1946)

Verney, Hon. Sir Lawrence John, Kt., TD

†Verney, Sir Edmund Ralph, Bt. (1818)

Vernon, Sir Nigel John Douglas, Bt. (1914)

Vernon, Sir (William) Michael, Kt.

Vestey, Sir Paul Edmund, Bt. (1921)

Vickers, Sir John Stuart, Kt.

Vickers, Lt.-Gen. Sir Richard Maurice Hilton, KCB, CVO, OBE

Viggers, Lt-Gen. Sir Frederick Richard, KCB, CMG, MBE

Vincent, Sir William Percy Maxwell, Bt. (1936)

Vineall, Sir Anthony John Patrick, Kt.

Vines, Sir William Joshua, Kt., CMG

von Schramek, Sir Eric Emil, Kt.

†Vyvyan, Sir Ralph Ferrers Alexander, Bt. (1645)

Wade-Gery, Sir Robert Lucian, KCMG, KCVO

Waena, Sir Nathaniel Rahumaea, GCMG

Waine, Rt. Revd John, KCVO

Waite, Rt. Hon. Sir John Douglas, Kt.

Waka, Sir Lucas Joseph, Kt., OBE

Wake, Sir Hereward, Bt. (1621), MC

Wakefield, Sir (Edward) Humphry (Tyrell), Bt. (1962)

Wakefield, Sir Norman Edward, Kt.

Wakefield, Sir Peter George Arthur, KBE, CMG

Wakeford, Sir Geoffrey Michael Montgomery, Kt., OBE

Wakeley, Sir John Cecil Nicholson, Bt. (1952), FRCS

†Wakeman, Sir Edward Offley Bertram, Bt. (1828)

Wales, Sir Robert Andrew, Kt.

Waley-Cohen, Sir Stephen Harry, Bt. (1961)

Walford, Sir Christopher Rupert, Kt.

Walker, Gen. Sir Antony Kenneth Frederick, KCB

†Walker, Sir Christopher Robert Baldwin, Bt. (1856)

Walker, Sir David Alan, Kt.

Walker, Sir Harold Berners, KCMG

†Walker, Sir Roy Edward, Bt. (1906)

Walker, Sir James Graham, Kt., MBE

Walker, Sir John Ernest, Kt., DPHIL, FRS

Walker, Air Marshal Sir John Robert, KCB, CBE, AFC

Walker, Sir Miles Rawstron, Kt., CBE

Walker, Sir Patrick Jeremy, KCB

Walker, Hon. Sir Paul James, Kt.

Walker, Sir Rodney Myerscough, Kt.

Walker, Hon. Sir Timothy Edward, Kt.

Walker, Sir Victor Stewart Heron, Bt. (1868)

Walker-Okeover, Sir Andrew Peter Monro, Bt. (1886)

Walker-Smith, Sir John Jonah, Bt. (1960)

Wall, Sir John Anthony, Kt., CBE

Wall, Sir (John) Stephen, GCMG, LVO

Wall, Rt. Hon. Sir Nicholas Peter Rathbone, Kt.

Wall, Sir Robert William, Kt., OBE

Wallace, Lt.-Gen. Sir Christopher Brooke Quentin, KBE

Wallace, Prof. David James, Kt., CBE, FRS

Wallace, Sir Ian James, Kt., CBE

Waller, Rt. Hon. Sir (George) Mark, Kt.

Waller, Sir John Michael, Bt. (I. 1780)

Wallis, Sir Peter Gordon, KCVO

Wallis, Sir Timothy William, Kt.

Walmsley, Vice-Adm. Sir Robert, KCB

†Walsham, Sir Timothy John, Bt. (1831)

Walters, Prof. Sir Alan Arthur, Kt.

Walters, Sir Dennis Murray, Kt., MBE

Walters, Sir Frederick Donald, Kt.

Walters, Sir Peter Ingram, Kt.

Walters, Sir Roger Talbot, KBE, FRIBA

Wamiri, Sir Akapite, KBE

Wan, Sir Wamp, Kt., MBE

Wanless, Sir Derek, Kt.

Ward, Rt. Hon. Sir Alan Hylton, Kt.

Ward, Sir Austin, Kt., QC

Ward, Sir John Devereux, Kt., CBE

Ward, Prof. Sir John MacQueen, Kt., CBE

Ward, Sir Joseph James Laffey, Bt. (1911)

Ward, Sir Timothy James, Kt.

Wardale, Sir Geoffrey Charles, KCB

Wardlaw, Sir Henry (John), Bt. (NS. 1631)

Waring, Sir (Alfred) Holburt, Bt. (1935)

Warmington, Sir Rupert Marshall, Bt. (1908)

Warner, Sir (Edward Courtenay) Henry, Bt. (1910)

Warner, Prof. Sir Frederick Edward, Kt., FRS, FRENG

Warner, Sir Gerald Chierici, KCMG

Warren, Sir (Frederick) Miles, KBE

Warren, Sir Kenneth Robin, Kt.

Warren, Sir Nicholas Roger, Kt.

Wass, Sir Douglas William Gretton, GCB

Waterhouse, Hon. Sir Ronald Gough, GBE

Waterlow, Sir Christopher Rupert, Bt. (1873)

Waterlow, Sir (James) Gerard, Bt. (1930)

Waters, Gen. Sir (Charles) John, GCB, CBE

Waters, Sir (Thomas) Neil (Morris), Kt.

Waterworth, Sir Alan William, KCVO

Wates, Sir Christopher Stephen, Kt.

Watkins, Rt. Hon. Sir Tasker, VC, GBE

Watson, Sir Bruce Dunstan, Kt.

Watson, Prof. Sir David John, Kt., PHD

Watson, Sir (James) Andrew, Bt. (1866)

Watson, Vice-Adm. Sir Philip Alexander, KBE, LVO

Watson, Sir Ronald Matthew, Kt., CBE

Watson, Sir Simon Conran Hamilton, Bt. (1895)

Watt, Gen. Sir Charles Redmond, KCVO, CBE

Watt, Surgeon Vice-Adm. Sir James, KBE, FRCS

Watts, Sir Arthur Desmond, KCMG

Watts, Sir John Augustus Fitzroy, KCMG, CBE

Watts, Sir Philip Beverley, KCMG

Weatherall, Prof. Sir David John, Kt., FRS

Weatherall, Vice-Adm. Sir James Lamb, KCVO, KBE

Weatherstone, Sir Dennis, KBE

Weatherup, Hon. Sir Ronald Eccles, Kt.

Webb, *Prof.* Sir Adrian Leonard, Kt.

Webb-Carter, *Gen.* Sir Evelyn John, KCVO, OBE

Webster, *Very Revd* Alan Brunskill, KCVO

Webster, *Vice-Adm.* Sir John Morrison, KCB

Webster, *Hon.* Sir Peter Edlin, Kt.

Wedgwood, Sir (Hugo) Martin, Bt. (1942)

Weekes, Sir Everton DeCourcey, KCMG, OBE

Weinberg, Sir Mark Aubrey, Kt.

Weir, *Hon.* Sir Reginald George, Kt.

Weir, Sir Roderick Bignell, Kt.

Welby, Sir (Richard) Bruno Gregory, Bt. (1801)

Welch, Sir John Reader, Bt. (1957)

Weldon, Sir Anthony William, Bt. (I. 1723)

Weller, Sir Arthur Burton, Kt., CBE

Wellings, Sir Jack Alfred, Kt., CBE

†Wells, Sir Christopher Charles, Bt. (1944)

Wells, Sir John Julius, Kt.

Wells, Sir William Henry Weston, Kt., FRICS

Wesker, Sir Arnold, Kt.

Westbrook, Sir Neil Gowanloch, Kt., CBE

Westmacott, Sir Peter John, KCMG

Weston, Sir Michael Charles Swift, KCMG, CVO

Weston, Sir (Philip) John, KCMG

Whalen, Sir Geoffrey Henry, Kt., CBE

Wheeler, Sir Harry Anthony, Kt., OBE

Wheeler, *Air Chief Marshal* Sir (Henry) Neil (George), GCB, CBE, DSO, DFC, AFC

Wheeler, *Rt. Hon.* Sir John Daniel, Kt.

Wheeler, Sir John Frederick, Bt. (1920)

Wheeler, *Gen.* Sir Roger Neil, GCB, CBE

Wheeler-Booth, Sir Michael Addison John, KCB

Wheler, Sir Edward Woodford, Bt. (1660)

Whishaw, Sir Charles Percival Law, Kt.

Whitaker, Sir John James Ingham (Jack), Bt. (1936)

Whitchurch, Sir Graeme Ian, Kt., OBE

White, *Prof.* Sir Christopher John, Kt., CVO

White, Sir Christopher Robert Meadows, Bt. (1937)

White, Sir David (David Jason), Kt., OBE

White, Sir David Harry, Kt.

White, *Hon.* Sir Frank John, Kt.

White, Sir George Stanley James, Bt. (1904)

White, *Adm.* Sir Hugo Moresby, GCB, CBE

White, *Hon.* Sir John Charles, Kt., MBE

White, Sir John Woolmer, Bt. (1922)

White, Sir Nicholas Peter Archibald, Bt. (1802)

White, *Adm.* Sir Peter, GBE

White, Sir Willard Wentworth, Kt., CBE

Whitehead, Sir John Stainton, GCMG, CVO

†Whitehead, Sir Philip Henry Rathbone, Bt. (1889)

Whiteley, *Gen.* Sir Peter John Frederick, GCB, OBE, RM

Whitfield, Sir William, Kt., CBE

Whitmore, Sir Clive Anthony, GCB, CVO

Whitmore, Sir John Henry Douglas, Bt. (1954)

Whitney, Sir Raymond William, Kt., OBE

Whitson, Sir Keith Roderick, Kt.

Wickerson, Sir John Michael, Kt.

Wicks, Sir Nigel Leonard, GCB, CVO, CBE

†Wigan, Sir Michael Iain, Bt. (1898)

Wiggin, Sir Alfred William (Jerry), Kt., TD

†Wiggin, Sir Charles Rupert John, Bt. (1892)

†Wigram, Sir John Woolmore, Bt. (1805)

Wilbraham, Sir Richard Baker, Bt. (1776)

Wiles, *Prof.* Sir Andrew John, KBE

Wilkes, *Prof.* Sir Maurice Vincent, Kt.

Wilkes, *Gen.* Sir Michael John, KCB, CBE

Wilkie, *Hon.* Sir Alan Fraser, Kt.

Wilkinson, Sir (David) Graham (Brook) Bt. (1941)

Wilkinson, *Prof.* Sir Denys Haigh, Kt., FRS

Willcocks, Sir David Valentine, Kt., CBE, MC

Willcocks, *Lt.-Gen.* Sir Michael Alan, KCB

Williams, Sir Arthur Dennis Pitt, Kt.

Williams, Sir (Arthur) Gareth Ludovic Emrys Rhys, Bt. (1918)

Williams, *Prof.* Sir Bruce Rodda, KBE

Williams, Sir Charles Othniel, Kt.

Williams, Sir Daniel Charles, GCMG, QC

Williams, *Adm.* Sir David, GCB

Williams, *Prof.* Sir David Glyndwr Tudor, Kt.

Williams, Sir David Innes, Kt.

Williams, Sir David Reeve, Kt., CBE

Williams, *Hon.* Sir Denys Ambrose, KCMG

Williams, Sir Donald Mark, Bt. (1866)

Williams, *Prof.* Sir (Edward) Dillwyn, Kt., FRCP

Williams, Sir Francis Owen Garbett, Kt., CBE

Williams, *Hon.* Sir (John) Griffith, Kt.

Williams, Sir (Lawrence) Hugh, Bt. (1798)

Williams, Sir Osmond, Bt. (1909), MC

Williams, Sir Peter Michael, Kt.

Williams, Sir (Robert) Philip Nathaniel, Bt. (1915)

Williams, Sir Robin Philip, Bt. (1953)

Williams, *Prof.* Sir Roger, Kt.

Williams, Sir (William) Maxwell (Harries), Kt.

Williams, *Hon.* Sir Wyn Lewis

Williams-Bulkeley, Sir Richard Thomas, Bt. (1661)

Williams-Wynn, Sir David Watkin, Bt. (1688)

Williamson, Sir George Malcolm, Kt.

Williamson, *Marshal of the Royal Air Force* Sir Keith Alec, GCB, AFC

Williamson, Sir Robert Brian, Kt., CBE

Willink, Sir Charles William, Bt. (1957)

Willis, *Air Chief Marshal* Sir John Frederick, GBE, KCB

Willison, *Lt.-Gen.* Sir David John, KCB, OBE, MC

Wills, Sir David James Vernon, Bt. (1923)

Wills, Sir David Seton, Bt. (1904)

Wilmot, Sir David, Kt., QPM

Wilmot, Sir Henry Robert, Bt. (1759)

Wilsey, *Gen.* Sir John Finlay Willasey, GCB, CBE

Wilshaw, Sir Michael, Kt.

Wilson, *Prof.* Sir Alan Geoffrey, Kt.

Wilson, Sir Anthony, Kt.

Wilson, *Vice-Adm.* Sir Barry Nigel, KCB

Wilson, Sir David, Bt. (1920)

Wilson, Sir David Mackenzie, Kt.

Wilson, Sir James William Douglas, Bt. (1906)

Wilson, *Brig.* Sir Mathew John Anthony, Bt. (1874), OBE, MC

Wilson, *Rt. Hon.* Sir Nicholas Allan Roy, Kt.

Wilson, Sir Robert Peter, KCMG

Wilson, *Air Chief Marshal* Sir (Ronald) Andrew (Fellowes), KCB, AFC

Wilton, Sir (Arthur) John, KCMG, KCVO, MC

Wingate, *Capt.* Sir Miles Buckley, KCVO

Winkley, Sir David Ross, Kt.

Winnington, Sir Anthony Edward, Bt. (1755)

Winship, Sir Peter James Joseph, Kt., CBE

Winter, *Dr* Sir Gregory Winter, Kt., CBE

Winterton, Sir Nicholas Raymond, Kt.

Winton, Sir Nicholas George, Kt., MBE

Wisdom, Sir Norman, Kt., OBE

Wiseman, Sir John William, Bt. (1628)

Wolfendale, *Prof.* Sir Arnold Whittaker, Kt., FRS

Wolseley, Sir Charles Garnet Richard Mark, Bt. (1628)

†Wolseley, Sir James Douglas, Bt. (I. 1745)

†Wombell, Sir George Philip Frederick, Bt. (1778)

Womersley, Sir Peter John Walter, Bt. (1945)
Woo, Sir Leo Joseph, Kt.
Woo, Sir Po-Shing, Kt.
Wood, Sir Alan Marshall Muir, Kt., FRS, FRENG
Wood, Sir Andrew Marley, GCMG
Wood, Sir Anthony John Page, Bt. (1837)
Wood, Sir Ian Clark, Kt., CBE
Wood, *Hon.* Sir John Kember, Kt., MC
Wood, Sir Martin Francis, Kt., OBE
Wood, Sir Michael Charles, KCMG
Wood, *Hon.* Sir Roderic Lionel James, Kt.
Wood, Sir Russell Dillon, KCVO, VRD
Wood, Sir William Alan, KCVO, CB
Woodard, *Rear Adm.* Sir Robert Nathaniel, KCVO
Woodcock, Sir John, Kt., CBE, QPM
Woodhead, *Vice-Adm.* Sir (Anthony) Peter, KCB
Woodhouse, *Rt. Hon.* Sir (Arthur) Owen, KBE, DSC
Woodroffe, *Most Revd* George Cuthbert Manning, KBE
Woods, Sir Robert Kynnersley, Kt., CBE
Woodward, *Hon.* Sir (Albert) Edward, Kt., OBE
Woodward, Sir Clive Ronald, Kt., OBE
Woodward, *Adm.* Sir John Forster, GBE, KCB
Woodward, Sir Thomas Jones (Tom Jones), Kt., OBE
Worsley, *Gen.* Sir Richard Edward, GCB, OBE

Worsley, Sir (William) Marcus (John), Bt. (1838)
Worsthorne, Sir Peregrine Gerard, Kt.
Wratten, *Air Chief Marshal* Sir William John, GBE, CB, AFC
Wraxall, Sir Charles Frederick Lascelles, Bt. (1813)
Wrey, Sir George Richard Bourchier, Bt. (1628)
Wrigglesworth, Sir Ian William, Kt.
Wright, Sir Allan Frederick, KBE
Wright, Sir David John, GCMG, LVO
Wright, *Hon.* Sir (John) Michael, Kt.
Wright, Sir (John) Oliver, GCMG, GCVO, DSC
Wright, *Prof.* Sir Nicholas Alcwyn, Kt.
Wright, Sir Peter Robert, Kt., CBE
Wright, *Air Marshal* Sir Robert Alfred, KBE, AFC
Wright, Sir Stephen John Leadbetter, KCMG
Wrightson, Sir Charles Mark Garmondsway, Bt. (1900)
Wrigley, *Prof.* Sir Edward Anthony (Sir Tony), Kt., PHD, PBA
Wrixon-Becher, Sir John William Michael, Bt. (1831)
Wu, Sir Gordon Ying Sheung, KCMG
Yacoub, *Prof.* Sir Magdi Habib, Kt., FRCS
Yaki, Sir Roy, KBE
Yang, *Hon.* Sir Ti Liang, Kt.
Yapp, Sir Stanley Graham, Kt.
Yardley, Sir David Charles Miller, Kt., LLD
Yarrow, Sir Eric Grant, Bt. (1916), MBE

Yocklunn, Sir John (Soong Chung), KCVO
Yoo Foo, Sir (François) Henri, Kt.
Young, Sir Brian Walter Mark, Kt.
Young, Sir Colville Norbert, GCMG, MBE
Young, Sir Dennis Charles, KCMG
Young, *Rt. Hon.* Sir George Samuel Knatchbull, Bt. (1813)
Young, *Hon.* Sir Harold William, KCMG
Young, Sir Jimmy Leslie Ronald, Kt., CBE
Young, Sir John Kenyon Roe, Bt. (1821)
Young, *Hon.* Sir John McIntosh, KCMG
Young, Sir John Robertson, GCMG
Young, Sir Leslie Clarence, Kt., CBE
Young, Sir Nicholas Charles, Kt.
Young, Sir Richard Dilworth, Kt.
Young, Sir Robin Urquhart, KCB
Young, Sir Roger William, Kt.
Young, Sir Stephen Stewart Templeton, Bt. (1945)
Young, Sir William Neil, Bt. (1769)
Younger, Sir Julian William Richard, Bt. (1911)
Yuwi, Sir Matiabe, KBE
Zeeman, *Prof.* Sir (Erik) Christopher, Kt., FRS
Zissman, Sir Bernard Philip, Kt.
Zochonis, Sir John Basil, Kt.
Zunz, Sir Gerhard Jacob (Jack), Kt., FRENG
Zurenuoc, Sir Zibang, KBE

BARONETESS

Stirling-Maxwell, Dame Ann Maxwell Macdonald, Btss. (NS 1682)

DAMES

DAMES GRAND CROSS AND DAMES COMMANDERS

Style, 'Dame' before forename and surname, followed by appropriate post-nominal initials. Where such an award is made to a lady already in possession of a higher title, the appropriate initials follow her name
Envelope, Dame F_ S_, followed by appropriate post-nominal letters. *Letter (formal),* Dear Madam; *(social),* Dear Dame F_. *Spoken,* Dame F_
Husband, Untitled

Dame Grand Cross and Dame Commander are the higher classes for women of the Order of the Bath, the Order of St Michael and St George, the Royal Victorian Order, and the Order of the British Empire. Dames Grand Cross rank after the wives of Baronets and before the wives of Knights Grand Cross. Dames Commanders rank after the wives of Knights Grand Cross and before the wives of Knights Commanders.

Honorary Dames Commanders may be conferred on women who are citizens of countries of which the Queen is not head of state.

LIST OF DAMES
As at 31 August 2007

Women peers in their own right and life peers are not included in this list. Female members of the royal family are not included in this list; details of the orders they hold can be found within the Royal Family section.

If a dame has a double barrelled or hyphenated surname, she is listed under the first element of the name. *A full entry in italic type* indicates that the recipient of an honour died during the year in which the honour was conferred. The name is included for the purposes of record.

Abaijah, Dame Josephine, DBE
Airlie, The Countess of, DCVO
Albemarle, The Countess of, DBE
Allen, *Prof.* Dame Ingrid Victoria, DBE
Andrews, Dame Julie, DBE
Anglesey, The Marchioness of, DBE
Anson, Lady (Elizabeth Audrey), DBE
Anstee, Dame Margaret Joan, DCMG
Arden, *Rt. Hon.* Dame Mary Howarth (Mrs Mance), DBE
Atkins, Dame Eileen, DBE
Bainbridge, Dame Beryl, DBE
Baker, Dame Janet Abbott (Mrs Shelley), CH, DBE
Barbour, Dame Margaret (Mrs Ash), DBE
Baron, *Hon.* Dame Florence Jacqueline, DBE
Barrow, Dame Jocelyn Anita (Mrs Downer), DBE
Barstow, Dame Josephine Clare (Mrs Anderson), DBE
Bassey, Dame Shirley, DBE
Beaurepaire, Dame Beryl Edith, DBE
Beer, *Prof.* Dame Gillian Patricia Kempster, DBE, FBA
Bergquist, *Prof.* Dame Patricia Rose, DBE
Bevan, Dame Yasmin, DBE
Bewley, Dame Beulah Rosemary, DBE
Bibby, Dame Enid, DBE
Black, *Prof.* Dame Carol Mary, DBE

Black, *Hon.* Dame Jill Margaret, DBE
Blackadder, Dame Elizabeth Violet, DBE
Blaize, Dame Venetia Ursula, DBE
Blaxland, Dame Helen Frances, DBE
Booth, *Hon.* Dame Margaret Myfanwy Wood, DBE
Bowtell, Dame Ann Elizabeth, DCB
Boyd, Dame Vivienne Myra, DBE
Brain, Dame Margaret Anne (Mrs Wheeler), DBE
Brennan, Dame Maureen, DBE
Bridges, Dame Mary Patricia, DBE
Brittan, Dame Diana (Lady Brittan of Spennithorne), DBE
Browne, Lady Moyra Blanche Madeleine, DBE
Buckland, Dame Yvonne Helen Elaine, DBE
Burnell, *Prof.* Dame Susan Jocelyn Bell, DBE
Burslem, Dame Alexandra Vivien, DBE
Byatt, Dame Antonia Susan, DBE, FRSL
Bynoe, Dame Hilda Louisa, DBE
Caldicott, Dame Fiona, DBE, FRCP, FRCPSYCH
Cameron, *Prof.* Dame Averil Millicent, DBE
Campbell-Preston, Dame Frances Olivia, DCVO
Cartwright, Dame Silvia Rose, DBE
Clark, *Prof.* Dame Jill MacLeod, DBE
Clark, *Prof.* Dame (Margaret) June, DBE, PHD
Clayton, Dame Barbara Evelyn (Mrs Klyne), DBE
Collarbone, Dame Patricia, DBE
Contreras, *Prof.* Dame Marcela, DBE
Corsar, *Hon.* Dame Mary Drummond, DBE
Coward, Dame Pamela Sarah, DBE
Cox, *Hon.* Dame Laura Mary, DBE
Davies, Dame Wendy Patricia, DBE
Davis, Dame Karlene Cecile, DBE
Daws, Dame Joyce Margaretta, DBE
Dawson, *Prof.* Dame Sandra Jane Noble, DBE
Dell, Dame Miriam Patricia, DBE
Dench, Dame Judith Olivia (Mrs Williams), CH, DBE
Descartes, Dame Marie Selipha Sesenne, DBE, BEM
Devonshire, The Duchess of, DCVO
Digby, Lady, DBE
Dobbs, *Hon.* Dame Linda Penelope, DBE
Docherty, Dame Jacqueline, DBE
Douglas, Prof. Dame Margaret Mary, DBE
Dowling, *Prof.* Dame Ann Patricia, DBE
Duffield, Dame Vivien Louise, DBE
Dumont, Dame Ivy Leona, DCMG
Dyche, Dame Rachael Mary, DBE
Elcoat, Dame Catherine Elizabeth, DBE
Ellison, Dame Jill, DBE
Else, Dame Jean, DBE
Engel, Dame Pauline Frances (Sister Pauline Engel), DBE
Esteve-Coll, Dame Elizabeth Anne Loosemore, DBE
Evans, Dame Anne Elizabeth Jane, DBE
Evans, Dame Madeline Glynne Dervel, DBE, CMG
Evison, Dame Helen June Patricia, DBE
Fenner, Dame Peggy Edith, DBE
Fielding, Dame Pauline, DBE
Forgan, Dame Elizabeth Anne Lucy, DBE
Fort, Dame Maeve Geraldine, DCMG, DCVO
Fraser, Dame Dorothy Rita, DBE
Friend, Dame Phyllis Muriel, DBE

Fry, Dame Margaret Louise, DBE
Gallagher, Dame Monica Josephine, DBE
Gardiner, Dame Helen Louisa, DBE, MVO
Glen-Haig, Dame Mary Alison, DBE
Glenn, *Prof.* Dame Hazel Gillian, DBE
Glennie, *Dr* Dame Evelyn Elizabeth Ann, DBE
Gloster, *Hon.* Dame Elisabeth (Lady Popplewell), DBE
Glover, Dame Audrey Frances, DBE, CMG
Goodall, *Dr* Dame (Valerie) Jane, DBE
Goodman, Dame Barbara, DBE
Gordon, Dame Minita Elmira, GCMG, GCVO
Gordon, *Hon.* Dame Pamela Felicity, DBE
Gow, Dame Jane Elizabeth (Mrs Whiteley), DBE
Grafton, The Duchess of, GCVO
Grant, Dame Mavis, DBE
Green, Dame Pauline, DBE
Grey, Dame Beryl Elizabeth (Mrs Svenson), DBE
Grey-Thompson, Dame Tanni Carys Davina, DBE
Griffiths, Dame Anne, DCVO
Grimthorpe, The Lady, DCVO
Guilfoyle, Dame Margaret Georgina Constance, DBE
Guthardt, *Revd Dr* Dame Phyllis Myra, DBE
Hallett, *Rt. Hon.* Dame Heather Carol, DBE
Harbison, Dame Joan Irene, DBE
Harper, Dame Elizabeth Margaret Way, DBE
Harris, Lady Pauline, DBE
Hassan, Dame Anna Patricia Lucy, DBE
Hedley-Miller, Dame Mary Elizabeth, DCVO, CB
Henderson, Dame Fiona Douglas, DCVO
Herbison, Dame Jean Marjory, DBE, CMG
Hercus, *Hon.* Dame (Margaret) Ann, DCMG
Higgins, *Prof.* Dame Joan Margaret, DBE
Higgins, *Prof.* Dame Julia Stretton, DBE, FRS
Higgins, *Prof.* Dame Rosalyn, DBE, QC
Hill, *Air Cdre* Dame Felicity Barbara, DBE
Hine, Dame Deirdre Joan, DBE, FRCP
Hodgson, Dame Patricia Anne, DBE
Hogg, *Hon.* Dame Mary Claire (Mrs Koops), DBE
Hollows, Dame Sharon, DBE
Holmes, Dame Kelly, DBE
Hoodless, Dame Elisabeth Anne, DBE
Hufton, *Prof.* Dame Olwen, DBE
Husband, *Prof.* Dame Janet Elizabeth Siarey, DBE
Hussey, Dame Susan Katharine (Lady Hussey of North
   Bradley), DCVO
Hutton, Dame Deirdre Mary, DBE
Imison, Dame Tamsyn, DBE
Isaacs, Dame Albertha Madeline, DBE
James, Dame Naomi Christine (Mrs Haythorne), DBE
Jenkins, Dame (Mary) Jennifer (Lady Jenkins of Hillhead),
   DBE
Johnson, *Prof.* Dame Louise Napier, DBE, FRS
Jonas, Dame Judith Mayhew
Jones, Dame Gwyneth (Mrs Haberfeld-Jones), DBE
Jordan, *Prof.* Dame Carole, DBE
Keegan, Dame Elizabeth Mary, DBE
Keegan, Dame Geraldine Mary Marcella, DBE
Kekedo, Dame Rosalina Violet, DBE
Kelleher, Dame Joan, DBE
Kellett-Bowman, Dame (Mary) Elaine, DBE
Kelly, Dame Barbara Mary, DBE
Kelly, Dame Lorna May Boreland, DBE
Kershaw, Dame Janet Elizabeth Murray (Dame Betty),
   DBE
Kettlewell, *Comdt.* Dame Marion Mildred, DBE
Kidu, Lady, DBE
Kirby, Dame Carolyn Emma, DBE
Kirby, Dame Georgina Kamiria, DBE

Kramer, *Prof.* Dame Leonie Judith, DBE
Laine, Dame Cleo (Clementine) Dinah (Lady Dankworth),
   DBE
Lamb, Dame Dawn Ruth, DBE
Leather, Dame Susan Catherine, DBE
Leslie, Dame Ann Elizabeth Mary, DBE
Lewis, Dame Edna Leofrida (Lady Lewis), DBE
Lott, Dame Felicity Ann Emwhyla (Mrs Woolf), DBE
Louisy, Dame (Calliopa) Pearlette, GCMG
Lynn, Dame Vera (Mrs Lewis), DBE
MacArthur, Dame Ellen Patricia, DBE
Macdonald, Dame Mary Beaton, DBE
McDonald, Dame Mavis, DCB
Mackinnon, Dame (Una) Patricia, DBE
Macmillan of Ovenden, Katharine, Viscountess, DBE
Macur, *Hon.* Dame Julia Wendy, DBE
Mayhew, Dame Judith, DBE
Major, Dame Malvina Lorraine (Mrs Fleming), DBE
Major, Dame Norma Christina Elizabeth, DBE
Manningham-Buller, *Hon.* Dame Elizabeth, DCB
Marsh, Dame Mary Elizabeth, DBE
Mellor, Dame Julie Thérèse Mellor, DBE
Metge, *Dr* Dame (Alice) Joan, DBE
Middleton, Dame Elaine Madoline, DCMG, MBE
Mills, Dame Barbara Jean Lyon, DBE, QC
Mirren, Dame Helen, DBE
Moores, Dame Yvonne, DBE
Morgan, *Dr* Dame Gillian Margaret, DBE
Morrison, *Hon.* Dame Mary Anne, DCVO
Muirhead, Dame Lorna Elizabeth Fox, DBE
Muldoon, Lady Thea Dale, DBE, QSO
Mullally, *Revd* Dame Sarah Elisabeth, DBE
Mumford, Lady Mary Katharine, DCVO
Munro, Dame Alison, DBE
Murdoch, Dame Elisabeth Joy, DBE
Nelson, *Prof.* Dame Janet Laughland, DBE
Neville, Dame Elizabeth, DBE, QPM
Ogilvie, Dame Bridget Margaret, DBE, PHD, DSC
Oliver, Dame Gillian Frances, DBE
Ollerenshaw, Dame Kathleen Mary, DBE, DPHIL
Oxenbury, Dame Shirley Anne, DBE
Park, Dame Merle Florence (Mrs Bloch), DBE
Pauffley, *Hon.* Dame Anna Evelyn Hamilton, DBE
Penhaligon, Dame Annette (Mrs Egerton), DBE
Perkins, Dame Mary Lesley, DBE
Peters, Dame Mary Elizabeth, DBE
Pindling, Lady (Marguerite M.), DCMG
Platt, Dame Denise, DBE
Plowright, Dame Joan Ann, DBE
Polak, *Prof.* Dame Julia Margaret, DBE
Poole, Dame Avril Anne Barker, DBE
Porter, Dame Shirley (Lady Porter), DBE
Powell, Dame Sally Ann Vickers, DBE
Prendergast, Dame Simone Ruth, DBE
Price, Dame Margaret Berenice, DBE
Pugh, *Dr* Dame Gillian Mary, DBE
Purves, Dame Daphne Helen, DBE
Quinn, Dame Sheila Margaret Imelda, DBE
Rafferty, *Hon.* Dame Anne Judith, DBE
Rawson, *Prof.* Dame Jessica Mary, DBE
Rees, *Prof.* Dame Lesley Howard, DBE
Reeves, Dame Helen May, DBE
Richardson, Dame Mary, DBE
Ridsdale, Dame Victoire Evelyn Patricia (Lady Ridsdale),
   DBE
Rigg, Dame Diana, DBE
Rimington, Dame Stella, DCB
Ritterman, Dame Janet, DBE

Roberts, Dame Jane Elisabeth, DBE
Robins, Dame Ruth Laura, DBE
Robottom, Dame Marlene, DBE
Roe, Dame Marion Audrey, DBE
Roe, Dame Raigh Edith, DBE
Ronson, Dame Gail, DBE
Rothwell, *Prof.* Dame Nancy Jane, DBE
Rumbold, *Rt. Hon.* Dame Angela Claire Rosemary, DBE
Runciman of Doxford, The Viscountess, DBE
Salas, Dame Margaret Laurence, DBE
Salmond, *Prof.* Dame Mary Anne, DBE
Sawyer, *Hon.* Dame Joan Augusta, DBE
Scardino, Dame Marjorie, DBE
Scott, Dame Catherine Margaret (Mrs Denton), DBE
Seward, Dame Margaret Helen Elizabeth, DBE
Shedrick, *Dr* Dame Daphne Marjorie, DBE
Shirley, Dame Stephanie, DBE
Shovelton, Dame Helena, DBE
Sibley, Dame Antoinette (Mrs Corbett), DBE
Silver, *Dr* Dame Ruth Muldoon, DBE
Smith, Dame Dela, DBE
Smith, *Rt. Hon.* Dame Janet Hilary (Mrs Mathieson), DBE
Smith, *Hon.* Dame Jennifer Meredith, DBE
Smith, Dame Margaret Natalie (Maggie) (Mrs Cross), DBE
Soames, Lady Mary, KG, DBE
Southgate, *Prof.* Dame Lesley Jill, DBE
Spencer, Dame Rosemary Jane, DCMG
Steel, *Hon.* Dame (Anne) Heather (Mrs Beattie), DBE
Strachan, Dame Valerie Patricia Marie, DCB
Strathern, *Prof.* Dame Anne Marilyn, DBE
Street, Dame Susan Ruth, DCB
Sutherland, Dame Joan (Mrs Bonynge), OM, DBE
Sutherland, Dame Veronica Evelyn, DBE, CMG

Swift, *Hon.* Dame Caroline Jane (Mrs Openshaw), DBE, QC
Symmonds, Dame Olga Patricia, DBE
Taylor, Dame Elizabeth, DBE
Taylor, Dame Meg, DBE
Te Kanawa, Dame Kiri Janette, DBE
Thomas, *Prof.* Dame Jean Olwen, DBE
Thomas, Dame Maureen Elizabeth (Lady Thomas), DBE
Tinson, Dame Sue, DBE
Tizard, Dame Catherine Anne, GCMG, GCVO, DBE
Tokiel, Dame Rosa, DBE
Trotter, Dame Janet Olive, DBE
Turner-Warwick, Dame Margaret Elizabeth Harvey, DBE, FRCP, FRCPED
Uprichard, Dame Mary Elizabeth, DBE
Varley, Dame Joan Fleetwood, DBE
Wagner, Dame Gillian Mary Millicent (Lady Wagner), DBE
Wall, Dame (Alice) Anne, (Mrs Michael Wall), DCVO
Wallis, Dame Sheila Ann, DBE
Warburton, Dame Anne Marion, DCVO, CMG
Waterhouse, Dame Rachel Elizabeth, DBE, PHD
Waterman, *Dr* Dame Fanny, DBE
Webb, *Prof.* Dame Patricia, DBE
Weir, Dame Gillian Constance (Mrs Phelps), DBE
Weller, Dame Rita, DBE
Weston, Dame Margaret Kate, DBE
Westwood, Dame Vivienne Isabel, DBE
Wheldon, Dame Juliet Louise, DCB, QC
Williams, Dame Josephine, DBE
Wilson-Barnett, *Prof.* Dame Jenifer, DBE
Winstone, Dame Dorothy Gertrude, DBE, CMG
Wong Yick-ming, Dame Rosanna, DBE

DECORATIONS AND MEDALS

PRINCIPAL DECORATIONS AND MEDALS
IN ORDER OF WEAR

VICTORIA CROSS (VC), 1856 (*see* below)
GEORGE CROSS (GC), 1940 (*see* below)

BRITISH ORDERS OF KNIGHTHOOD (*see also* Orders of Chivalry)
Order of the Garter
Order of the Thistle
Order of St Patrick
Order of the Bath
Order of Merit
Order of the Star of India
Order of St Michael and George
Order of the Indian Empire
Order of the Crown of India
Royal Victorian Order (Classes I, II and III)
Order of the British Empire (Classes I, II and III)
Order of the Companions of Honour
Distinguished Service Order
Royal Victorian Order (Class IV)
Order of the British Empire (Class IV)
Imperial Service Order
Royal Victorian Order (Class V)
Order of the British Empire (Class V)

BARONET'S BADGE

KNIGHT BACHELOR'S BADGE

INDIAN ORDER OF MERIT (MILITARY)

DECORATIONS
Conspicuous Gallantry Cross (CGC), 1995
Royal Red Cross Class I (RRC), 1883
Distinguished Service Cross (DSC), 1914
Military Cross (MC), December 1914
Distinguished Flying Cross (DFC), 1918
Air Force Cross (AFC), 1918
Royal Red Cross Class II (ARRC)
Order of British India
Kaisar-i-Hind Medal
Order of St John

MEDALS FOR GALLANTRY AND DISTINGUISHED CONDUCT
Union of South Africa Queen's Medal for Bravery, in Gold
Distinguished Conduct Medal (DCM), 1854
Conspicuous Gallantry Medal (CGM), 1874
Conspicuous Gallantry Medal (Flying)
George Medal (GM), 1940
Queen's Police Medal for Gallantry
Queen's Fire Service Medal for Gallantry
Royal West African Frontier Force Distinguished Conduct Medal
King's African Rifles Distinguished Conduct Medal
Indian Distinguished Service Medal
Union of South Africa Queen's Medal for Bravery, in Silver
Distinguished Service Medal (DSM), 1914
Military Medal (MM), 1916

Distinguished Flying Medal (DFM), 1918
Air Force Medal (AFM)
Constabulary Medal (Ireland)
Medal for Saving Life at Sea (Sea Gallantry Medal)
Indian Order of Merit (Civil)
Indian Police Medal for Gallantry
Ceylon Police Medal for Gallantry
Sierra Leone Police Medal for Gallantry
Sierra Leone Fire Brigades Medal for Gallantry
Colonial Police Medal for Gallantry (CPM)
Queen's Gallantry Medal (QGM), 1974
Royal Victorian Medal (RVM), Gold, Silver and Bronze
British Empire Medal (BEM)
Canada Medal
Queen's Police Medal for Distinguished Service (QPM)
Queen's Fire Service Medal for Distinguished Service (QFSM)
Queen's Volunteer Reserves Medal
Queen's Medal for Chiefs

CAMPAIGN MEDALS AND STARS
Including authorised United Nations, European Community/Union and North Atlantic Treaty Organisation medals (in order of date of campaign for which awarded)

POLAR MEDALS (in order of date)

IMPERIAL SERVICE MEDAL

POLICE MEDALS FOR VALUABLE SERVICE
Indian Police Medal for Meritorious Service
Ceylon Police Medal for Merit
Sierra Leone Police Medal for Meritorious Service
Sierra Leone Fire Brigades Medal for Meritorious Service
Colonial Police Medal for Meritorious Service

BADGE OF HONOUR

JUBILEE, CORONATION AND DURBAR MEDALS
Queen Victoria, King Edward VII, King George V, King George VI, Queen Elizabeth II, Visit Commemoration and Long and Faithful Service Medals

EFFICIENCY AND LONG SERVICE DECORATIONS AND MEDALS
Medal for Meritorious Service
Accumulated Campaign Service Medal
Medal for Long Service and Good Conduct (Military)
Naval Long Service and Good Conduct Medal
Medal for Meritorious Service (Royal Navy 1918–28)
Indian Long Service and Good Conduct Medal
Indian Meritorious Service Medal
Royal Marines Meritorious Service Medal (1849–1947)
Royal Air Force Meritorious Service Medal (1918–1928)
Royal Air Force Long Service and Good Conduct Medal
Medal for Long Service and Good Conduct (Ulster Defence Regiment)
Indian Long Service and Good Conduct Medal
Royal West African Frontier Force Long Service and Good Conduct Medal

Royal Sierra Leone Military Forces Long Service and Good
  Conduct Medal
King's African Rifles and Long Service and Good Conduct
  Medal
Indian Meritorious Service Medal
Police Long Service and Good Conduct Medal
Fire Brigade Long Service and Good Conduct Medal
African Police Medal for Meritorious Service
Royal Canadian Mounted Police Long Service Medal
Ceylon Police Long Service Medal
Ceylon Fire Services Long Service Medal
Sierra Leone Police Long Service Medal
Colonial Police Long Service Medal
Sierra Leone Fire Brigades Long Service Medal
Mauritius Police Long Service and Good Conduct Medal
Mauritius Fire Services Long Service and Good Conduct
  Medal
Mauritius Prisons Service Long Service and Good Conduct
  Medal
Colonial Fire Brigades Long Service Medal
Colonial Prison Service Medal
Hong Kong Disciplined Services Medal
Army Emergency Reserve Decoration (ERD)
Volunteer Officers' Decoration (VD)
Volunteer Long Service Medal
Volunteer Officers' Decoration (for India and the Colonies)
Volunteer Long Service Medal (for India and the Colonies)
Colonial Auxiliary Forces Officers' Decoration
Colonial Auxiliary Forces Long Service Medal
Medal for Good Shooting (Naval)
Militia Long Service Medal
Imperial Yeomanry Long Service Medal
Territorial Decoration (TD), 1908
Ceylon Armed Services Long Service Medal
Efficiency Decoration (ED)
Territorial Efficiency Medal
Efficiency Medal
Special Reserve Long Service and Good Conduct Medal
Decoration for Officers of the Royal Navy Reserve (RD),
  1910
Decoration for Officers of the Royal Naval Volunteer Reserve
  (VRD)
Royal Naval Reserve Long Service and Good Conduct Medal
Royal Naval Volunteer Reserve Long Service and Good
  Conduct Medal
Royal Naval Auxiliary Sick Berth Reserve Long Service and
  Good Conduct Medal
Royal Fleet Reserve Long Service and Good Conduct Medal
Royal Naval Wireless Auxiliary Reserve Long Service and
  Good Conduct Medal
Royal Naval Auxiliary Service Medal
Air Efficiency Award (AE), 1942
Volunteer Reserves Service Medal
Ulster Defence Regiment Medal
Northern Ireland Home Service Medal
Queen's Medal (for Champion Shots of the RN and RM)
Queen's Medal (for Champion Shots of the New Zealand
  Naval Forces)
Queen's Medal (for Champion Shots in the Military
  Forces)
Queen's Medal (for Champion Shots of the Air Forces)
Cadet Forces Medal, 1950
Coastguard Auxiliary Service Long Service Medal
Special Constabulary Long Service Medal
Canadian Forces Decoration
Royal Observer Corps Medal
Civil Defence Long Service Medal

Ambulance Service (Emergency Duties) Long Service and
  Good Conduct Medal
Royal Fleet Auxiliary Service Medal Rhodesia Medal
Royal Ulster Constabulary Service Medal
Northern Ireland Prison Service Medal
Union of South Africa Commemoration Medal
Indian Independence Medal
Pakistan Medal
Ceylon Armed Services Inauguration Medal
Ceylon Police Independence Medal (1948)
Sierra Leone Independence Medal
Jamaica Independence Medal
Uganda Independence Medal
Malawi Independence Medal
Fiji Independence Medal
Papua New Guinea Independence Medal
Solomon Islands Independence Medal
Service Medal of the Order of St John
Badge of the Order of the League of Mercy
Voluntary Medical Service Medal (1932)
Women's Royal Voluntary Service Medal
South African Medal for War Services
Colonial Special Constabulary Medal

HONORARY MEMBERSHIP OF COMMONWEALTH
ORDERS

OTHER COMMONWEALTH MEMBERS' ORDERS,
DECORATIONS AND MEDALS

FOREIGN ORDERS

FOREIGN DECORATIONS

FOREIGN MEDALS

THE VICTORIA CROSS (1856)
FOR CONSPICUOUS BRAVERY

VC

Ribbon, Crimson, for all Services (until 1918 it was blue
  for the Royal Navy)

Instituted on 29 January 1856, the Victoria Cross was
awarded retrospectively to 1854, the first being held by
Lt. C. D. Lucas, RN, for bravery in the Baltic Sea on 21
June 1854 (gazetted 24 February 1857). The first 62
crosses were presented by Queen Victoria in Hyde Park,
London, on 26 June 1857.
   The Victoria Cross is worn before all other decorations,
on the left breast, and consists of a cross-pattée of bronze,
3.8cm in diameter, with the royal crown surmounted by a
lion in the centre, and beneath there is the inscription For
Valour. Holders of the VC currently receive a tax-free
annuity of £1,500, irrespective of need or other
conditions. In 1911, the right to receive the cross was
extended to Indian soldiers, and in 1920 to matrons,
sisters and nurses, the staff of the nursing services and
other services pertaining to hospitals and nursing, and to
civilians of either sex regularly or temporarily under the
orders, direction or supervision of the naval, military, or
air forces of the crown.

SURVIVING RECIPIENTS OF THE VICTORIA CROSS
as at 31 August 2007

Beharry, *Pte.* J. G. (Princess of Wales's Royal Regiment)
2005 *Iraq*

Bhan Bhagta Gurung, *Havildar* (2nd Gurkha Rifles)
1945 *World War*

Cruickshank, *Flt. Lt.* J. A. (RAFVR)
1944 *World War*

Fraser, *Lt.-Cdr.* I. E., DSC, RD and bar (RNR)
1945 *World War*

Kenna, *Pte.* E. (Australian Military Forces, 2/4th (NSW))
1945 *World War*

Lachhiman Gurung, *Havildar* (8th Gurkha Rifles)
1945 *World War*

Payne, *WO* K., DSC (USA) (Australian Army Training
Team)
1969 *Vietnam*

Rambahadur Limbu, *Capt.,* MVO (10th Princess Mary's
Gurkha Rifles)
1965 *Sarawak*

Speakman-Pitts, *Sgt.* W. (Black Watch, attached KOSB)
1951 *Korea*

Tulbahadur Pun, *Lt.* (6th Gurkha Rifles)
1944 *World War*

Watkins, *Maj. Rt. Hon.* Sir Tasker, GBE (Welch Regiment)
1944 *World War*

Wilson, *Lt.-Col.* E. C. T. (East Surrey Regiment)
1940 *World War*

AWARDED POSTHUMOUSLY IN 2006–7
Budd, *Cpl.* B. J. (Parachute Regiment), killed in action
2006 *Afghanistan*

THE GEORGE CROSS (1940)
FOR GALLANTRY

GC

Ribbon, Dark blue, threaded through a bar adorned with
laurel leaves

Instituted 24 September 1940 (with amendments,
3 November 1942)

The George Cross is worn before all other decorations
(except the VC) on the left breast (when worn by a woman
it may be worn on the left shoulder from a ribbon of the
same width and colour fashioned into a bow). It consists
of a plain silver cross with four equal limbs, the cross
having in the centre a circular medallion bearing a design

showing St George and the Dragon. The inscription *For
Gallantry* appears round the medallion and in the angle
of each limb of the cross is the royal cypher 'G VI'
forming a circle concentric with the medallion. The
reverse is plain and bears the name of the recipient and
the date of the award. The cross is suspended by a ring
from a bar adorned with laurel leaves on dark blue
ribbon 3.8cm wide.

The cross is intended primarily for civilians; awards to
the fighting services are confined to actions for which
purely military honours are not normally granted. It is
awarded only for acts of the greatest heroism or of the
most conspicuous courage in circumstances of extreme
danger. From 1 April 1965, holders of the cross have
received a tax-free annuity, which is currently £1,500.
The cross has twice been awarded collectively rather than
to an individual: to Malta (1942) and the Royal Ulster
Constabulary (1999).

In October 1971 all surviving holders of the Albert
Medal and the Edward Medal exchanged those
decorations for the George Cross.

SURVIVING RECIPIENTS OF THE GEORGE
CROSS
as at 31 August 2007

If the recipient originally received the Albert Medal (AM)
or the Edward Medal (EM), this is indicated by the initials
in parentheses.

Archer, *Col.* B. S. T., GC, OBE, ERD, 1941
Bamford, J., GC, 1952
Beaton, J., GC, CVO, 1974
Butson, *Lt.-Col.* A. R. C., GC, CD, MD (AM), 1948
Finney, *Trooper* C., GC, 2003
Flintoff, H. H., GC (EM), 1944
Gledhill, A. J., GC, 1967
Gregson, J. S., GC (AM), 1943
Johnson, *WO1 (SSM)* B., GC, 1990
Kinne, D. G., GC, 1954
Lowe, A. R., GC (AM), 1949
Norton, *Capt.* P. A., GC, 2006
Pratt, M. K., GC, 1978
Purves, Mrs M., GC (AM), 1949
Raweng, Awang anak, GC, 1951
Stevens, H. W., GC, 1958
Walker, C., GC, 1972
Walker, C. H., GC (AM), 1942
Walton, E. W. K., GC (AM), DSO, 1948
Wooding, E. A., GC (AM), 1945

AWARDED POSTHUMOUSLY IN 2006–7
Wright, *Cpl.* M. W., GC, 2006

CHIEFS OF CLANS IN SCOTLAND

Only chiefs of whole Names or Clans are included, except certain special instances (marked *) who, though not chiefs of a whole Name, were or are for some reason (eg the Macdonald forfeiture) independent. Under decision (*Campbell-Gray,* 1950) that a bearer of a 'double or triple-barrelled' surname cannot be held chief of a part of such, several others cannot be included in the list at present.

THE ROYAL HOUSE: HM The Queen
AGNEW: Sir Crispin Agnew of Lochnaw, Bt.
ANSTRUTHER: Tobias Anstruther of Anstruther and Balcaskie
ARBUTHNOTT: Viscount of Arbuthnott, KT, CBE, DSC
BANNERMAN: Sir David Bannerman of Elsick, Bt.
BARCLAY: Peter C. Barclay of Towie Barclay and of that Ilk
BORTHWICK: Lord Borthwick
BOYD: Lord Kilmarnock, MBE
BOYLE: Earl of Glasgow
BRODIE: Alexander Brodie of Brodie
BROUN OF COLSTOUN: Sir Wayne Broun of Colstoun, Bt.
BRUCE: Earl of Elgin and Kincardine, KT
BUCHAN: David Buchan of Auchmacoy
BURNETT: J. C. A. Burnett of Leys
CAMERON: Donald Cameron of Lochiel
CAMPBELL: Duke of Argyll
CARMICHAEL: Richard Carmichael of Carmichael
CARNEGIE: Duke of Fife
CATHCART: Earl Cathcart
CHARTERIS: Earl of Wemyss and March, KT
CLAN CHATTAN: K. Mackintosh of Clan Chattan
CHISHOLM: Hamish Chisholm of Chisholm *(The Chisholm)*
COCHRANE: Earl of Dundonald
COLQUHOUN: Sir Ivar Colquhoun of Luss, Bt.
CRANSTOUN: David Cranstoun of that Ilk
CUMMING: Sir Alastair Cumming of Altyre, Bt.
DARROCH: Capt. Duncan Darroch of Gourock
DAVIDSON: Alister Davidson of Davidston
DEWAR: Michael Dewar of that Ilk and Vogrie
DRUMMOND: Earl of Perth
DUNBAR: Sir James Dunbar of Mochrum, Bt.
DUNDAS: David Dundas of Dundas
DURIE: Andrew Durie of Durie, CBE
ELIOTT: Mrs Margaret Eliott of Redheugh
ERSKINE: Earl of Mar and Kellie
FARQUHARSON: Capt. A. Farquharson of Invercauld, MC
FERGUSSON: Sir Charles Fergusson of Kilkerran, Bt.
FORBES: Lord Forbes, KBE
FORSYTH: Alistair Forsyth of that Ilk
FRASER: Lady Saltoun
*FRASER (OF LOVAT): Lord Lovat
GAYRE: R. Gayre of Gayre and Nigg
GORDON: Marquess of Huntly
GRAHAM: Duke of Montrose
GRANT: Lord Strathspey
GRIERSON: Sir Michael Grierson of Lag, Bt.
GUTHRIE: Alexander Guthrie of Guthrie
HAIG: Earl Haig, OBE

HALDANE: Martin Haldane of Gleneagles
HANNAY: David Hannay of Kirkdale and of that Ilk
HAY: Earl of Erroll
HENDERSON: Alistair Henderson of Fordell
HUNTER: Pauline Hunter of Hunterston
IRVINE OF DRUM: David Irvine of Drum
JARDINE: Sir Alexander Jardine of Applegirth, Bt.
JOHNSTONE: Earl of Annandale and Hartfell
KEITH: Earl of Kintore
KENNEDY: Marquess of Ailsa
KERR: Marquess of Lothian, PC
KINCAID: Madam Arabella Kincaid of Kincaid
LAMONT: Revd Peter Lamont of that Ilk
LEASK: Madam Leask of Leask
LENNOX: Edward Lennox of that Ilk
LESLIE: Earl of Rothes
LINDSAY: Earl of Crawford and Balcarres, KT, GCVO, PC
LIVINGSTONE (or MACLEA): Alastair Livingstone of Bachuil
LOCKHART: Angus Lockhart of the Lee
LUMSDEN: Gillem Lumsden of that Ilk and Blanerne
MACALESTER: William St J. McAlester of Loup and Kennox
MACARTHUR; John MacArthur of that Ilk
MCBAIN: J. H. McBain of McBain
MACDONALD: Lord Macdonald *(The Macdonald of Macdonald)*
*MACDONALD OF CLANRANALD: Ranald Macdonald of Clanranald
MACDONALD OF KEPPOCH: Ranald MacDonald of Keppoch
*MACDONALD OF SLEAT (CLAN HUSTEAIN): Sir Ian Macdonald of Sleat, Bt.
*MACDONELL OF GLENGARRY: Ranald MacDonell of Glengarry
MACDOUGALL: Morag MacDougall of MacDougall
MACDOWALL: Fergus Macdowall of Garthland
MACGREGOR: Sir Malcolm MacGregor of MacGregor, Bt.
MACINTYRE: Donald MacIntyre of Glenoe
MACKAY: Lord Reay
MACKENZIE: Earl of Cromartie
MACKINNON: Anne Mackinnon of Mackinnon
MACKINTOSH: John Mackintosh of Mackintosh *(The Mackintosh of Mackintosh)*
MACLACHLAN: Euan MacLachlan of MacLachlan
MACLAREN: Donald MacLaren of MacLaren and Achleskine
MACLEAN: Hon. Sir Lachlan Maclean of Duart, Bt., CVO
MACLENNAN: Ruaraidh MacLennan of MacLennan
MACLEOD: Hugh MacLeod of MacLeod
MACMILLAN: George MacMillan of MacMillan
MACNAB: J. C. Macnab of Macnab *(The Macnab)*
MACNAGHTEN: Sir Patrick Macnaghten of Macnaghten and Dundarave, Bt.
MACNEACAIL: John Macneacail of Macneacail and Scorrybreac

MACNEIL OF BARRA: Ian Macneil of Barra *(The Macneil of Barra)*

MACPHERSON: Hon. Sir William Macpherson of Cluny, TD

MACTHOMAS: Andrew MacThomas of Finegand

MAITLAND: Earl of Lauderdale

MAKGILL: Viscount of Oxfuird

MALCOLM (MACCALLUM): Robin N. L. Malcolm of Poltalloch

MAR: Countess of Mar

MARJORIBANKS: Andrew Marjoribanks of that Ilk

MATHESON: Maj. Sir Fergus Matheson of Matheson, Bt.

MENZIES: David Menzies of Menzies

MOFFAT: Madam Moffat of that Ilk

MONCREIFFE: Hon. Peregrine Moncreiffe of that Ilk

MONTGOMERIE: Earl of Eglinton and Winton

MORRISON: Dr Iain Morrison of Ruchdi

MUNRO: Hector Munro of Foulis

MURRAY: Duke of Atholl

NESBITT (or NISBET): Mark Nesbitt of that Ilk

NICOLSON: Lord Carnock

OGILVY: Earl of Airlie, KT, GCVO, PC

OLIPHANT: Richard Oliphant of that Ilk

RAMSAY: Earl of Dalhousie

RIDDELL: Sir John Riddell of Riddell, Bt., CVO

ROBERTSON: Alexander Robertson of Struan *(Struan-Robertson)*

ROLLO: Lord Rollo

ROSE: Miss Elizabeth Rose of Kilravock

ROSS: David Ross of that Ilk and Balnagowan

RUTHVEN: Earl of Gowrie, PC

SCOTT: Duke of Buccleuch and Queensberry, KT, VRD

SCRYMGEOUR: Earl of Dundee

SEMPILL: Lord Sempill

SHAW: John Shaw of Tordarroch

SINCLAIR: Earl of Caithness

SKENE: Danus Skene of Skene

STIRLING: Fraser Stirling of Cader

STRANGE: Maj. Timothy Strange of Balcaskie

SUTHERLAND: Countess of Sutherland

SWINTON: John Swinton of that Ilk

TROTTER: Alexander Trotter of Mortonhall

URQUHART: Kenneth Urquhart of Urquhart

WALLACE: Ian Wallace of that Ilk

WEDDERBURN: Master of Dundee

WEMYSS: Michael Wemyss of that Ilk

THE PRIVY COUNCIL

The sovereign in council, or Privy Council, was the chief source of executive power until the system of cabinet government developed in the 18th century. Now the Privy Council's main functions are to advise the sovereign and to exercise its own statutory responsibilities independent of the sovereign in council.

Membership of the Privy Council is automatic upon appointment to certain government and judicial positions in the United Kingdom, eg cabinet ministers must be Privy Counsellors and are sworn in on first assuming office. Membership is also accorded by the Queen to eminent people in the UK and independent countries of the Commonwealth of which she is Queen, on the recommendation of the British prime minister. Membership of the council is retained for life, except for very occasional removals.

The administrative functions of the Privy Council are carried out by the Privy Council Office under the direction of the president of the council, who is always a member of the cabinet.

President of the Council, Rt. Hon. Baroness Ashton of Upholland
Clerk of the Council, Judith Simpson

MEMBERS *as at August 2007*

Style The Right (or Rt.) Hon._
Envelope, The Right (or Rt.) Hon. F_ S_. *Letter,* Dear Mr/Miss/Mrs S_.
Spoken, Mr/Miss/Mrs S_
It is incorrect to use the letters PC after the name in conjunction with the prefix The Right Hon., unless the Privy Counsellor is a peer below the rank of Marquess and so is styled The Right Hon. because of his/her rank. In this case only, the post-nominal letters may be used in conjunction with the prefix The Right Hon.

HRH The Duke of Edinburgh, 1951
HRH The Prince of Wales, 1977

Abernethy, *Hon.* Lord (Alastair Cameron), 2005
Ainsworth, Robert, 2005
Airlie, Earl of, 1984
Aldous, Sir William, 1995
Alebua, Ezekiel, 1988
Alexander, Douglas, 2005
Amos, Baroness, 2003
Ampthill, Lord, 1995

Ancram, Michael, 1996
Anderson of Swansea, Lord, 2000
Angiolini, Elish, 2006
Anthony, Douglas, 1971
Arbuthnot, James, 1998
Archer of Sandwell, Lord, 1977
Arden, Dame Mary, 2000
Armstrong, Hilary, 1999
Arthur, *Hon.* Owen, 1995
Ashdown of Norton-sub-Hamdon, Lord, 1989
Ashley of Stoke, Lord, 1979
Ashton of Upholland, Baroness, 2006
Atkins, Sir Robert, 1995
Auld, Sir Robin, 1995
Baker, Sir Thomas, 2002
Baker of Dorking, Lord, 1984
Balls, Ed, 2007
Barnett, Lord, 1975
Barron, Kevin, 2001
Battle, John, 2002
Beckett, Margaret, 1993
Beith, Alan, 1992
Beldam, Sir Roy, 1989
Benn, Anthony, 1964
Benn, Hilary, 2003
Bew, Lord, 2007
Bingham of Cornhill, Lord, 1986
Birch, William, 1992
Bisson, Sir Gordon, 1987
Blackstone, Baroness, 2001
Blair, Anthony, 1994
Blaker, Lord, 1983
Blanchard, Peter, 1998
Blears, Hazel, 2005
Blunkett, David, 1997
Boateng, Paul, 1999
Bolger, James, 1991
Booth, Albert, 1976
Boothroyd, Baroness, 1992
Boscawen, *Hon.* Robert, 1992
Bottomley of Nettlestone, Baroness, 1992
Boyd of Duncansby, Lord, 2000
Boyson, Sir Rhodes, 1987
Bradley, Lord, 2001
Brathwaite, Sir Nicholas, 1991
Bridge of Harwich, Lord, 1975
Brittan of Spennithorne, Lord, 1981
Brooke, Sir Henry, 1996
Brooke of Sutton Mandeville, Lord, 1988
Brown, Gordon, 1996
Brown, Nicholas, 1997
Brown, Sir Stephen, 1983
Brown of Eaton-under-Heywood, Lord, 1992
Browne, Desmond, 2005
Browne-Wilkinson, Lord, 1983
Bruce, Malcolm, 2006
Burnham, Andy, 2007
Butler, Sir Adam, 1984
Butler of Brockwell, Lord, 2004
Butler-Sloss, Baroness, 1988
Buxton, Sir Richard, 1997
Byers, Stephen, 1998
Bryon, Sir Dennis, 2004
Caborn, Richard, 1999

Caithness, Earl of, 1990
Cameron, David, 2005
Cameron of Lochbroom, Lord, 1984
Camoys, Lord, 1997
Campbell, Sir Walter Menzies, 1999
Campbell, Sir William, 1999
Campbell of Surbiton, Baroness, 2007
Canterbury, Archbishop of, 2002
Carey of Clifton, Lord, 1991
Carnwath, Sir Robert, 2002
Carr of Hadley, Lord, 1963
Carrington, Lord, 1959
Carswell, Lord, 1993
Casey, Sir Maurice, 1986
Chadwick, Sir John, 1997
Chalfont, Lord, 1964
Chalker of Wallasey, Baroness, 1987
Chan, Sir Julius, 1981
Chataway, Sir Christopher, 1970
Chilcot, Sir John, 2004
Christie, Perry, 2004
Clark of Windermere, Lord, 1997
Clark, Helen, 1990
Clarke, Sir Anthony, 1998
Clarke, Charles, 2001
Clarke, Kenneth, 1984
Clarke, Thomas, 1997
Clinton-Davis, Lord, 1998
Clwyd, Ann, 2004
Clyde, Lord, 1996
Colman, Fraser, 1986
Compton, Sir John, 1983
Cope of Berkeley, Lord, 1988
Corston, Baroness, 2003
Cosgrove, *Hon.* Lady (Hazel Cosgrove), 2003
Coulsfield, *Hon.* Lord (John Coulsfield), 2000
Coussins, Baroness, 2007
Cowen, Sir Zelman, 1981
Cradock, Sir Percy, 1993
Crawford and Balcarres, Earl of, 1972
Creech, *Hon.* Wyatt, 1999
Crickhowell, Lord, 1979
Cullen of Whitekirk, *Hon.* Lord, 1997
Cunningham of Felling, Lord, 1993
Curry, David, 1996
Darling, Alistair, 1997
Davies, Denzil, 1978
Davies, Ronald, 1997
Davies of Oldham, Lord, 2006
Davis, David, 1997
Davis, Terence, 1999
Davison, Sir Ronald, 1978
de la Bastide, Michael, 2004
Dean of Harptree, Lord, 1991
Dean of Thornton-le-Fylde, Baroness, 1998
Denham, John, 2000
Denham, Lord, 1981
Dixon, Lord, 1996
Dobson, Frank, 1997
Donaldson, Jeffrey, 2007
Dorrell, Stephen, 1994
du Cann, Sir Edward, 1964
Duncan Smith, Iain, 2001

Dunn, Sir Robin, 1980
Dyson, Sir John, 2001
Eassie, *Hon.* Lord (Ronald Mackay), 2006
East, Paul, 1998
Eden of Winton, Lord, 1972
Edward, Sir David, 2005
Eggar, Timothy, 1995
Eichelbaum, Sir Thomas, 1989
Elias, *Hon.* Dame, Sian, 1999
Elis-Thomas, Lord, 2004
Esquivel, Manuel, 1986
Evans, Sir Anthony, 1992
Eveleigh, Sir Edward, 1977
Falconer of Thoroton, Lord, 2003
Farquharson, Sir Donald, 1989
Fellowes, Lord, 1990
Ferrers, Earl, 1982
Field, Frank, 1997
Floissac, Sir Vincent, 1992
Foot, Michael, 1974
Forsyth of Drumlean, Lord, 1995
Foster of Bishop Auckland, Lord, 1993
Foulkes of Cumnock, Lord, 2002
Fowler, Lord, 1979
Fraser, Malcolm, 1976
Fraser of Carmyllie, Lord, 1989
Freeman, John, 1966
Freeman, Lord, 1993
Gage, Sir William, 2004
Garel-Jones, Lord, 1992
Gault, Thomas, 1992
Geidt, Christopher, 2007
George, Bruce, 2000
George, Lord, 1999
Gibson, Sir Peter, 1993
Gilbert, Lord, 1978
Gill, *Hon.* Lord (Brian Gill), 2002
Gilmour of Craigmillar, Lord, 1973
Girvan, Sir (Frederick) Paul, 2007
Glenamara, Lord, 1964
Glidewell, Sir Iain, 1985
Goff of Chieveley, Lord, 1982
Goldsmith, Lord, 2002
Goodlad, Lord, 1992
Gowrie, Earl of, 1984
Graham, Sir Douglas, 1998
Graham of Edmonton, Lord, 1998
Griffiths, Lord, 1980
Grocott, Lord, 2002
Gummer, John, 1985
Habgood, Rt. Revd Lord, 1983
Hague, William, 1995
Hain, Peter, 2001
Hale of Richmond, Baroness, 1999
Hallett, Dame Heather, 2005
Hameed, Lord, 2007
Hamilton, *Hon.* Lord (Arthur Hamilton), 2002
Hamilton of Epsom, Lord, 1991
Hanley, Sir Jeremy, 1994
Hanson, David, 2007
Hardie, Lord, 1997
Hardie Boys, Sir Michael, 1989
Harman, Harriet, 1997
Harrison, Walter, 1977
Haselhurst, Sir Alan, 1999
Hattersley, Lord, 1975
Hayhoe, Lord, 1985
Hayman, Baroness, 2000
Healey, Lord, 1964
Heathcoat-Amory, David, 1996
Henry, Sir Denis, 1993
Henry, John, 1996
Heseltine, Lord, 1979
Heseltine, Sir William, 1986

Hesketh, Lord, 1991
Hewitt, Patricia, 2001
Higgins, Lord, 1979
Higgins, Sir Malachy, 2007
Hill, Keith, 2003
Hirst, Sir David, 1992
Hodge, Margaret, 2003
Hoffmann, Lord, 1992
Hogg, *Hon.* Douglas, 1992
Hollis of Heigham, Baroness, 1999
Holme of Cheltenham, Lord, 2000
Hoon, Geoffrey, 1999
Hooper, Sir Anthony, 2004
Hope of Craighead, Lord, 1989
Hope of Thornes, Lord, 1991
Hordern, Sir Peter, 1993
Howard, Michael, 1990
Howarth, George, 2005
Howarth of Newport, Lord, 2000
Howe of Aberavon, Lord, 1972
Howell of Guildford, Lord, 1979
Hughes, Sir Anthony, 2006
Hughes, Beverley, 2004
Hunt, Jonathan, 1989
Hunt of Wirral, Lord, 1990
Hurd of Westwell, Lord, 1982
Hutchison, Sir Michael, 1995
Hutton, Lord, 1988
Hutton, John, 2001
Inge, Lord, 2004
Ingraham, Hubert, 1993
Ingram, Adam, 1999
Irvine of Lairg, Lord, 1997
Jack, Michael, 1997
Jacob, Sir Robert, 2004
Jacobs, Francis, 2005
Janvrin, Lord, 1998
Jay of Paddington, Baroness, 1998
Jenkin of Roding, Lord, 1973
Johnson, Alan, 2003
Johnson Smith, Sir Geoffrey, 1996
Johnston, *Hon.* Lord (Alan Johnston), 2005
Jones, Lord, 1999
Jopling, Lord, 1979
Jowell, Tessa, 1998
Judge, Sir Igor, 1996
Jugnauth, Sir Anerood, 1987
Kaufman, Sir Gerald, 1978
Kay, Sir Maurice, 2004
Keene, Sir David, 2000
Keith, Sir Kenneth, 1998
Kelly, Sir Basil, 1984
Kelly, Ruth, 2004
Kenilorea, Sir Peter, 1979
Kennedy, Charles, 1999
Kennedy, Jane, 2003
Kennedy, Sir Paul, 1992
Kerr, Sir Brian, 2004
King of Bridgwater, Lord, 1979
Kingarth, *Hon.* Lord (Derek Emslie)
Kingsdown, Lord, 1987
Kingsland, Lord, 1994
Kinnock, Lord, 1983
Kirkwood, *Hon.* Lord (Ian Kirkwood), 2000
Knight, Gregory, 1995
Lamont of Lerwick, Lord, 1986
Lang of Monkton, Lord, 1990
Latasi, Sir Kamuta, 1996
Latham, Sir David, 2000
Lauti, Sir Toaripi, 1979
Lawrence, John, 2005
Laws, Sir John, 1999
Lawson of Blaby, Lord, 1981
Leggatt, Sir Andrew, 1990
Leonard, Rt. Revd Graham, 1981

Letwin, Oliver, 2002
Leveson, Sir Brian, 2006
Liddell, Mrs Helen, 1998
Lilley, Peter, 1990
Lloyd of Berwick, Lord, 1984
Lloyd, Sir Peter, 1994
Lloyd, Sir Timothy, 2005
London, Bishop of, 1995
Longmore, Sir Andrew, 2001
Louisy, Sir Allan, 1981
Luce, Lord, 1986
Lyell of Markyate, Lord, 1990
Mabon, Dickson, 1977
McAvoy, Thomas, 2003
McCartney, Ian, 1999
McCollum, Sir Liam, 1997
McConnell, Jack, 2001
McCowan, Sir Anthony, 1989
MacDermott, Sir John, 1987
Macdonald of Tradeston, Lord, 1999
Macfadyen, *Hon.* Lord (Donald MacFadyen), 2002
McFall, John, 2004
MacGregor of Pulham Market, Lord, 1985
McIntosh of Haringey, Lord, 2002
Mackay, Andrew, 1998
McKay, Ian, 1992
Mackay of Clashfern, Lord, 1979
Mackay of Drumadoon, Lord, 1996
McKinnon, Donald, 1992
Maclean, David, 1995
Maclean, *Hon.* Lord (Ranald MacLean), 2001
McLeish, Henry, 2000
Maclennan of Rogart, Lord, 1997
McLoughlin, Patrick, 2005
McMullin, Sir Duncan, 1980
McNally, Lord, 2005
McNulty, Anthony, 2007
McShane, Denis, 2005
Major, Sir John, 1987
Malloch-Brown, Lord, 2007
Mance, Lord, 1999
Mandelson, Peter, 1998
Mantell, Sir Charles, 1997
Marnoch, *Hon.* Lord (Michael Marnoch), 2001
Marsh, Lord, 1966
Martin, Michael, 2000
Mason of Barnsley, Lord, 1968
Mates, Michael, 2004
Maude, *Hon.* Francis, 1992
Mawhinney, Lord, 1994
May, Sir Anthony, 1998
May, Theresa, 2003
Mayhew of Twysden, Lord, 1986
Meacher, Michael, 1997
Mellor, David, 1990
Michael, Alun, 1998
Milburn, Alan, 1998
Miliband, David, 2005
Miliband, Ed, 2007
Millan, Bruce, 1975
Millett, Lord, 1994
Mitchell, Sir James, 1985
Mitchell, Dr Keith, 2004
Molyneaux of Killead, Lord, 1983
Moore, Michael, 1990
Moore of Lower Marsh, Lord, 1986
Moore of Wolvercote, Lord, 1977
Moore-Bick, Sir Martin, 2005
Morgan, Rhodri, 2000
Morley, Elliot, 2007
Morris, Charles, 1978
Morris of Aberavon, Lord, 1970
Morris of Manchester, Lord, 1979

Morris of Yardley, Baroness, 1999
Morritt, Sir Robert, 1994
Moses, Sir Alan, 2005
Moyle, Roland, 1978
Mummery, Sir John, 1996
Murphy, Paul, 1999
Murray, *Hon.* Lord (Ronald Murray), 1974
Murray, Sir Donald, 1989
Murton of Lindisfarne, Lord, 1976
Musa, Wilbert, 2005
Mustill, Lord, 1985
Nairne, Sir Patrick, 1982
Namaliu, Sir Rabbie, 1989
Naseby, Lord, 1994
Needham, Sir Richard, 1994
Neill, Sir Brian, 1985
Neuberger of Abbotsbury, Lord, 2004
Newton of Braintree, Lord, 1988
Nicholls of Birkenhead, Lord, 1995
Nicholson, Sir Michael, 1995
Nimmo Smith, *Hon.* Lord (William Nimmo Smith), 2005
Nott, Sir John, 1979
Nourse, Sir Martin, 1985
O'Donnell, Turlough, 1979
Oliver of Aylmerton, Lord, 1980
Oppenheim-Barnes, Baroness, 1979
Osborne, *Hon.* Lord (Kenneth Osborne), 2001
Otton, Sir Philip, 1995
Owen, Lord, 1976
Paeniu, Bikenibeu, 1991
Paisley, Dr Ian, 2005
Palliser, Sir Michael, 1983
Palmer, Sir Geoffrey, 1986
Parker, Sir Jonathan, 2000
Parker, Sir Roger, 1983
Parkinson, Lord, 1981
Paton, *Hon.* Lady (Ann Paton), 2007
Patten, Lord, 1990
Patten of Barnes, Lord, 1989
Patterson, Percival, 1993
Pattie, Sir Geoffrey, 1987
Peel, Earl, 2006
Pendry, Lord, 2000
Penrose, *Hon.* Lord (George Penrose), 2000
Peters, Winston, 1998
Philip, *Hon.* Lord (Alexander Philip), 2005
Phillips of Worth Matravers, Lord, 1995
Pill, Sir Malcolm, 1995
Portillo, Michael, 1992
Potter, Sir Mark, 1996
Prescott, John, 1994
Price, George, 1982
Primarolo, Dawn, 2002
Prior, Lord, 1970
Prosser, *Hon.* Lord (William Prosser), 2000
Puapua, Sir Tomasi, 1982
Purnell, James, 2007
Pym, Lord, 1970
Quin, Baroness, 1998

Radice, Lord, 1999
Raison, Sir Timothy, 1982
Ramsden, James, 1963
Raynsford, Nick, 2001
Redwood, John, 1993
Rees, Lord, 1983
Reid, George, 2004
Reid, John, 1998
Renton of Mount Harry, Lord, 1989
Richard, Lord, 1993
Richards, Sir Stephen, 2005
Richardson, Sir Ivor, 1978
Richardson of Duntisbourne, Lord, 1976
Rifkind, Sir Malcolm, 1986
Rix, Sir Bernard, 2000
Roberts of Conwy, Lord, 1991
Robertson of Port Ellen, Lord, 1997
Robinson, Peter, 2007
Roch, Sir John, 1993
Rodger of Earlsferry, Lord, 1992
Rodgers of Quarry Bank, Lord, 1975
Rooker, Lord, 1999
Roper, Lord, 2005
Rose, Sir Christopher, 1992
Ross, *Hon.* Lord (Donald MacArthur), 1985
Rumbold, Dame Angela, 1991
Ryan, Joan, 2007
Ryder of Wensum, Lord, 1990
Sainsbury, Sir Timothy, 1992
St John of Fawsley, Lord, 1979
Salisbury, Marquess of, 1994
Salmond, Alex, 2007
Sandiford, Erskine, 1989
Saville of Newdigate, Lord, 1994
Sawyer, Dame Joan, 2004
Schiemann, Sir Konrad, 1995
Scotland of Asthal, Baroness, 2001
Scott of Foscote, Lord, 1991
Seaga, Edward, 1981
Sedley, Sir Stephen, 1999
Selkirk of Douglas, Lord, 1996
Sheldon, Lord, 1977
Shephard of Northwold, Baroness, 1992
Sheil, Sir John, 2005
Shipley, Jennifer, 1998
Short, Clare, 1997
Simmonds, Kennedy Sir, 1984
Sinclair, Ian, 1977
Slade, Sir Christopher, 1982
Slynn of Hadley, Lord, 1992
Smith, Andrew, 1997
Smith, Dame Janet, 2002
Smith, Jacqueline, 2003
Smith of Finsbury, Lord, 1997
Somare, Sir Michael, 1977
Spellar, John, 2001
Stanley, Sir John, 1984
Staughton, Sir Christopher, 1988
Steel of Aikwood, Lord, 1977
Stephen, Sir Ninian, 1979
Stewartby, Lord, 1989
Steyn, Lord, 1992
Strang, Gavin, 1997
Strathclyde, Lord, 1995

Straw, Jack, 1997
Stuart-Smith, Sir Murray, 1988
Sutherland, *Hon.* Lord (Ranald Sutherland), 2000
Symons of Vernham Dean, Baroness, 2001
Talboys, Sir Brian, 1977
Taylor of Bolton, Baroness, 1997
Tebbit, Lord, 1981
Templeman, Lord, 1978
Thatcher, Baroness, 1970
Thomas, Edmund, 1996
Thomas of Gwydir, Lord, 1964
Thomas, Sir Roger, 2003
Thomas, Sir Swinton, 1994
Thomson of Monifieth, Lord, 1966
Thorpe, Jeremy, 1967
Thorpe, Sir Matthew, 1995
Timms, Stephen, 2006
Tipping, Andrew, 1998
Tizard, Robert, 1986
Touhig, Don, 2006
Toulson, Sir Roger, 2007
Trefgarne, Lord, 1989
Trimble, Lord, 1997
Trumpington, Baroness, 1992
Tuckey, Sir Simon, 1998
Ullswater, Viscount, 1994
Upton, Simon, 1999
Varley, Lord, 1974
Vaz, Keith, 2006
Waddington, Lord, 1987
Waite, Sir John, 1993
Wakeham, Lord, 1983
Waldegrave of North Hill, Lord, 1990
Walker of Gestingthorpe, Lord, 1997
Walker of Worcester, Lord, 1970
Wall, Sir Nicholas, 2004
Wallace, James, 2000
Waller, Sir Mark, 1996
Ward, Sir Alan, 1995
Warner, Lord, 2006
Watkins, Sir Tasker, 1980
Wheatley, *Hon.* Lord (John Wheatley), 2007
Wheeler, Sir John, 1993
Whitty, Lord, 2005
Widdecombe, Ann, 1997
Wigley, Dafydd, 1997
Williams, Alan, 1977
Williams of Crosby, Baroness, 1974
Williamson of Horton, Lord, 2007
Wilson, Brian, 2003
Wilson, Sir Nicholas, 2005
Windlesham, Lord, 1973
Winterton, Rosie, 2006
Winti, Paias, 1987
Withers, Reginald, 1977
Woodhouse, Sir Owen, 1974
Woodward, Shaun, 2007
Woolf, Lord, 1986
York, Archbishop of, 2005
Young, Sir George, 1993
Young of Graffham, Lord, 1984
Zacca, Edward, 1992

PRIVY COUNCIL OF NORTHERN IRELAND

The Privy Council of Northern Ireland had responsibilities in Northern Ireland similar to those of the Privy Council in Great Britain until the Northern Ireland Act 1974.

Membership of the Privy Council of Northern Ireland is retained for life. Since the Northern Ireland Constitution Act 1973 no further appointments have been made. The postnominal initials PC (NI) are used to differentiate its members from those of the Privy Council.

MEMBERS *as at August 2007*

Bailie, Robin, 1971
Bleakley, David, 1971
Craig, William, 1963
Dobson, John, 1969
Kelly, Sir Basil, 1969
Kilclooney, Lord, 1970
Kirk, Herbert, 1962
Long, William, 1966
Porter, Sir Robert, 1969

PARLIAMENT

The United Kingdom constitution is not contained in any single document but has evolved over time, formed partly by statute, partly by common law and partly by convention. A constitutional monarchy, the United Kingdom is governed by ministers of the crown in the name of the sovereign, who is head both of the state and of the government.

The organs of government are the legislature (parliament), the executive and the judiciary. The executive consists of HM government (the cabinet and other ministers), government departments and local authorities (see Local Government, Government Departments and Public Bodies sections). The judiciary (see Law Courts and Offices section) pronounces on the law, both written and unwritten, interprets statutes and is responsible for the enforcement of the law; the judiciary is independent of both the legislature and the executive.

THE MONARCHY

The sovereign personifies the state and is, in law, an integral part of the legislature, head of the executive, head of the judiciary, commander-in-chief of all armed forces of the crown and supreme governor of the Church of England. The seat of the monarchy is in the United Kingdom. In the Channel Islands and the Isle of Man, which are crown dependencies, the sovereign is represented by a lieutenant-governor. In the member states of the Commonwealth of which the sovereign is head of state, her representative is a governor-general; in UK dependencies the sovereign is usually represented by a governor, who is responsible to the British government.

Although in practice the powers of the monarchy are now very limited, and restricted mainly to the advisory and ceremonial, there are important acts of government which require the participation of the sovereign. These include summoning, proroguing and dissolving parliament, giving royal assent to bills passed by parliament, appointing important office-holders, eg government ministers, judges, bishops and governors, conferring peerages, knighthoods and other honours, and granting pardon to a person wrongly convicted of a crime. The sovereign appoints the prime minister; by convention this office is held by the leader of the political party which enjoys, or can secure, a majority of votes in the House of Commons. In international affairs the sovereign as head of state has the power to declare war and make peace, to recognise foreign states and governments, to conclude treaties and to annex or cede territory. However, as the sovereign entrusts executive power to ministers of the crown and acts on the advice of her ministers, which she cannot ignore, royal prerogative powers are in practice exercised by ministers, who are responsible to parliament.

Ministerial responsibility does not diminish the sovereign's importance to the smooth working of government. She holds meetings of the Privy Council (see below), gives audiences to her ministers and other officials at home and overseas, receives accounts of cabinet decisions, reads dispatches and signs state papers; she must be informed and consulted on every aspect of national life; and she must show complete impartiality.

COUNSELLORS OF STATE

In the event of the sovereign's absence abroad, it is necessary to appoint counsellors of state under letters patent to carry out the chief functions of the monarch, including the holding of Privy Councils and giving royal assent to acts passed by parliament. The normal procedure is to appoint as counsellors three or four members of the royal family among those remaining in the UK.

In the event of the sovereign on accession being under the age of 18 years, or at any time unavailable or incapacitated by infirmity of mind or body for the performance of the royal functions, provision is made for a regency.

THE PRIVY COUNCIL

The sovereign in council, or Privy Council, was the chief source of executive power until the system of cabinet government developed. Its main function today is to advise the sovereign on the approval of various statutory functions and acts of the royal prerogative. These powers are exercised through orders in council and royal proclamations, approved by the Queen at meetings of the Privy Council. The council is also able to exercise a number of statutory duties without approval from the sovereign, including powers of supervision over the registering bodies for the medical and allied professions. These duties are exercised through orders in council.

Although appointment as a privy counsellor is for life, only those who are currently government ministers are involved in the day-to-day business of the council. A full council is summoned only on the death of the sovereign or when the sovereign announces his or her intention to marry. (For a full list of privy counsellors, see the Privy Council section.)

There are a number of advisory Privy Council committees whose meetings the sovereign does not attend. Some are prerogative committees, such as those dealing with legislative matters submitted by the legislatures of the Channel Islands and the Isle of Man or with applications for charters of incorporation; and some are provided for by statute, eg those for the universities of Oxford and Cambridge and the Scottish universities.

The Judicial Committee of the Privy Council is the court of final appeal from courts of the UK dependencies, courts of independent Commonwealth countries which have retained the right of appeal and courts of the Channel Islands and the Isle of Man.

It also has certain jurisdiction within the United Kingdom, the most important of which is that it is the court of final appeal for 'devolution issues', ie issues as to the legal competences and functions of the legislative and executive authorities established in Scotland, Wales and Northern Ireland by the devolution legislation of 1998.

The committee is composed of privy counsellors who hold, or have held, high judicial office, although usually only three or five hear each case.

Administrative work is carried out by the Privy Council Office under the direction of the Lord President of the Council, a cabinet minister.

PARLIAMENT

Parliament is the supreme law-making authority and can legislate for the UK as a whole or for any parts of it separately (the Channel Islands and the Isle of Man are crown dependencies and not part of the UK). The main functions of parliament are to pass laws, to provide (by voting taxation) the means of carrying on the work of government and to scrutinise government policy and administration, particularly proposals for expenditure. International treaties and agreements are by custom presented to parliament before ratification.

Parliament emerged during the late 13th and early 14th centuries. The officers of the king's household and the king's judges were the nucleus of early parliaments, joined by such ecclesiastical and lay magnates as the king might summon to form a prototype 'House of Lords', and occasionally by the knights of the shires, burgesses and proctors of the lower clergy. By the end of Edward III's reign a 'House of Commons' was beginning to appear; the first known Speaker was elected in 1377.

Parliamentary procedure is based on custom and precedent, partly formulated in the standing orders of both houses of parliament, and each house has the right to control its own internal proceedings and to commit for contempt. The system of debate in the two houses is similar; when a motion has been moved, the Speaker proposes the question as the subject of a debate. Members speak from wherever they have been sitting. Questions are decided by a vote on a simple majority. Draft legislation is introduced, in either house, as a bill. Bills can be introduced by a government minister or a private member, but in practice the majority of bills which become law are introduced by the government. To become law, a bill must be passed by each house (for parliamentary stages, *see* Parliamentary Information) and then sent to the sovereign for the royal assent, after which it becomes an act of parliament.

Proceedings of both houses are public, except on extremely rare occasions. The minutes (called *Votes and Proceedings in the Commons,* and *Minutes of Proceedings in the Lords*) and the speeches (*The Official Report of Parliamentary Debates,* Hansard) are published daily. Proceedings are also recorded for transmission on radio and television and stored in the Parliamentary Recording Unit before transfer to the National Sound Archive. Television cameras have been allowed into the House of Lords since 1985 and into the House of Commons since 1989; committee meetings may also be televised.

By the Parliament Act of 1911, the maximum duration of a parliament is five years (if not previously dissolved), the term being reckoned from the date given on the writs for the new parliament. The maximum life has been prolonged by legislation in such rare circumstances as the two World Wars (31 January 1911 to 25 November 1918; 26 November 1935 to 15 June 1945). Dissolution and writs for a general election are ordered by the sovereign on the advice of the prime minister. The life of a parliament is divided into sessions, usually of one year in length, beginning and ending most often in October or November.

DEVOLUTION

The Scottish parliament has legislative power over all devolved matters, ie matters not reserved to Westminster or otherwise outside its powers. The National Assembly for Wales has power to make secondary legislation in the areas where executive functions have been transferred to it. The Northern Ireland Assembly has legislative authority in the fields previously administered by the Northern Ireland departments. The assembly was suspended in October 2002 and dissolved in April 2003, before being reinstated on 8 May 2007. For further information, *see* the Regional Government section.

THE HOUSE OF LORDS

London SW1A 0PW
T 020-7219 3000 Information Office 020-7219 3107
E hlinfo@parliament.uk W www.parliament.uk

The House of Lords is the second chamber, or 'Upper House', of the UK's bicameral parliament. Until the beginning of the twentieth century, the House of Lords had considerable power, being able to veto any bill submitted to it by the House of Commons. Today the main functions of the House of Lords are to revise legislation, to act as a check on the government, to provide a forum of independent expertise and to act as a final court of appeal.

The House of Lords has a number of select committees. Some relate to the internal affairs of the house – such as its management and administration – while others carry out important investigative work on matters of public interest. There are four main areas of work – Europe, science, the economy and the constitution. House of Lords investigative committees look at broader issues and do not mirror government departments as the select committees in the House of Commons do.

The House of Lords has judicial powers as the ultimate court of appeal for courts in Great Britain and Northern Ireland, except for criminal cases in Scotland. These powers are exercised by the Lords of Appeal in Ordinary (the law lords) – (*see* Law Courts and Offices section). On 12 June 2003 the government announced reforms affecting the role of the Lord Chancellor as a judge and Speaker of the House of Lords, and establishing a separate supreme court (*see* Government Departments section). The supreme court is expected to be established in late 2009, when the judicial function of the House of Lords will cease. In 2006 the position of Lord Chancellor was significantly altered by the Constitutional Reform Act 2005. The office holder is no longer speaker of the House of Lords nor head of the judiciary in England and Wales, and is instead a cabinet minister (the Secretary of State for Justice). The function of speaker of the House of Lords was devolved to the newly created post of Lord Speaker. The Rt. Hon. Baroness Hayman was elected as the first Lord Speaker by the house on 4 July 2006.

Members of the House of Lords comprise life peers created under the Life Peerages Act 1958, 92 hereditary peers under the House of Lords Act 1999 and Lords of Appeal in Ordinary, ie law lords, under the Appellate Jurisdiction Act 1876. The Archbishops of Canterbury and York, the Bishops of London, Durham and Winchester, and the 21 senior diocesan bishops of the Church of England are also members.

The House of Lords Act provides for 90 elected hereditary peers to remain in the House of Lords until longer-term reform of the House has been carried out; 42 Conservative, 28 crossbench, three Liberal Democrat and two Labour. Elections for each of the party groups and the crossbenches were held in October and November 1999. Fifteen office holders were elected by the whole house. Two hereditary peers, the Earl Marshal and the Lord Great Chamberlain, are also members.

Peers are disqualified from sitting in the house if they are:

- aliens, ie any peer who is not a British citizen, a Commonwealth citizen (under the British Nationality Act 1981) or a citizen of the Republic of Ireland
- under the age of 21
- undischarged bankrupts or, in Scotland, those whose estate is sequestered
- convicted of treason

Bishops retire at the age of 70 and cease to be members of the house at that time.

Members who do not wish to attend sittings of the House of Lords may apply for leave of absence for the duration of a parliament.

Members of the House of Lords are unpaid but are entitled to allowances for attendance at sittings of the house. The daily maxima, between 1 August 2006 and 31 July 2007, were £159.50 for overnight subsistence, £79.50 for day subsistence and incidental travel, and £69.00 for office costs.

COMPOSITION *as at 2 July 2007*

Archbishops and bishops	26
Life peers under the Appellate Jurisdiction Act 1876	26
Life peers under the Life Peerages Act 1958	603
Peers under the House of Lords Act 1999	92
Total	747

STATE OF THE PARTIES *as at 2 July 2007**

Conservative	204
Labour	211
Liberal Democrat	77
Crossbench	205
Archbishops and bishops	26
Other	12
Total	735

* Excluding 12 peers on leave of absence from the house

HOUSE OF LORDS PAY BANDS

Staff are placed in the following pay bands according to their level of responsibility and taking account of other factors such as experience and marketability.

Judicial group 4	£165,900
Senior band 3	£97,852–£139,974
Senior band 2	£79,433–£129,729
Senior band 1A	£66,771–£108,806
Senior band 1	£57,561–£96,477
Band A1	£53,221–£70,019
Band A2	£44,253–£57,931

OFFICERS AND OFFICIALS

The house is presided over by the Lord Speaker, whose powers differ from those of the Speaker of the House of Commons. The Lord Speaker has no power to maintain order because the House of Lords is self-regulating.

A panel of deputy speakers is appointed by Royal Commission. The first deputy speaker is the chair of committees, appointed at the beginning of each session,

who is a salaried officer of the house. He or she takes the chair when the whole house is in committee and in some select committees. He or she is assisted by a panel of deputy chairs, headed by the salaried principal deputy chair of committees, who is also chair of the European Communities Committee of the house.

The Clerk of the Parliaments is the accounting officer and the chief permanent official responsible for the administration of the house. The Gentleman Usher of the Black Rod is responsible for security and other services and also has royal duties as secretary to the Lord Great Chamberlain.

Lord Speaker (£104,386), Rt. Hon. Baroness Hayman

Chair of Committees (£81,504), Lord Brabazon of Tara

Principal Deputy Chair of Committees (£76,250), Lord Grenfell

Clerk of the Parliaments (Judicial Group 4), Sir Paul Hayter, KCB, LVO

Clerk Assistant (Senior Band 3), M. G. Pownall

Reading Clerk and Clerk of the Overseas Office (Senior Band 2), D. R. Beamish, LLM

Clerk of the Committees (Senior Band 2), Dr R. H. Walters, DPHIL

Finance Director (Senior Band 1A), E. C. Ollard

Head of Human Resources (Senior Band 1A), Dr F. P. Tudor

Clerk of the Judicial Office and Registrar of Lords Interests (Senior Band 1A), B. P. Keith

Director of Information Services and Librarian (Senior Band 2), Dr E. Hallam Smith

Clerk of Public and Private Bill Office and Examiner of Petitions for Private Bills in the House of Lords (Senior Band 1A), T. V. Mohan

Editor of the Official Report (Senior Band 1), A. S. Nicholls

Clerk of the Records (Senior Band 1), S. K. Ellison

Deputy Finance Director and Head of Finance (Senior Band 1), A. D. Underwood

Director of Public Information (Band A1), Miss M. L. Morgan

Counsel to the Chairman of Committees (Senior Band 2), A. Roberts

Second Counsel to the Chairman of Committees (Senior Band 2), Dr C. S. Kerse, CB, PHD

Legal Adviser to the Human Rights Committee (Senior Band 2), M. Hunt

Change Manager (Senior Band 1), Mrs M. E. Ollard

Clerk of the Journals (Senior Band 1), A. Makower

Clerk of the European Union Committee (Senior Band 1A), S. P. Burton

Clerk of Pre-Legislative Scrutiny (Senior Band 1), Mrs K. S. Lawrence

Gentleman Usher of the Black Rod and Serjeant-at-Arms (Senior Band 2), Lt.-Gen. Sir Michael Willcocks, KCB

Yeoman Usher of the Black Rod and Deputy Serjeant-at-Arms (Band A2), Brig. H. D. C. Duncan, MBE

LORD GREAT CHAMBERLAIN'S OFFICE

Lord Great Chamberlain, Marquess of Cholmondeley

Secretary to the Lord Great Chamberlain, Lt.-Gen. Sir Michael Willcocks, KCB

SELECT COMMITTEES

The main House of Lords select committees, *as at June 2007*, are as follows:

European Union – Chair, Lord Grenfell; *Clerk*, S. Burton

European Union – Sub-committees:

    A (Economic and Financial Affairs and International Trade) – Chair, Baroness Cohen of Pimlico; *Clerk*, Simon Blackburn

B *(Internal Market) – Chair,* Lord Freeman; *Clerk,* Judith Brooke

C *(Foreign Affairs, Defence and Development Policy) – Chair,* Lord Roper; *Clerk,* Kathryn Colvin

D *(Agriculture and the Environment) – Chair,* Lord Sewel; *Clerk,* Robert Preston

E *(Law and Institutions) – Chair,* Lord Brown of Eaton-under-Heywood; *Clerk,* Susanna Street

F *(Home Affairs) – Chair,* Lord Wright of Richmond; *Clerk,* Michael Collon

G *(Social and Consumer Affairs) – Chair,* Baroness Thomas of Walliswood; *Clerk,* Barry Werner

Constitution Committee – Chair, Lord Holme of Cheltenham; *Clerk,* Tom Wilson

Delegated Powers and Regulatory Reform – Chair, Lord Goodhart; *Clerk,* A. Mackersie

Economic Affairs – Chair, Lord Wakeham; *Clerk,* Robert Graham-Harrison

Science and Technology – Chair, Lord Broers; *Clerk,* Dr Christopher Johnson

    I *– Chair,* Baroness Finlay of Llandaff; *Clerk,* Sarah Jones

    II *– Chair,* Lord Broers; *Clerk,* Dr Christopher Johnson

Human Rights Joint Committee – Chair, Andrew Dismore, MP; *Lords Clerk,* Bill Sinton

Merits of Statutory Instruments Committee – Chair, Lord Filkin; *Clerk,* A. Mackersie

THE HOUSE OF COMMONS

London SW1A 0AA
T 020-7219 3000
Information Office 020-7219 4272
Forthcoming business 020-7219 5532
E hcinfo@parliament.uk W www.parliament.uk

The members of the House of Commons are elected by universal adult suffrage. For electoral purposes, the United Kingdom is divided into constituencies, each of which returns one member to the House of Commons, the member being the candidate who obtains the largest number of votes cast in the constituency. To ensure equitable representation, the four Boundary Commissions keep constituency boundaries under review and recommend any redistribution of seats which may seem necessary because of population movements, etc. The number of seats was raised to 640 in 1945, reduced to 625 in 1948, and subsequently rose to 630 in 1955, 635 in 1970, 650 in 1983, 651 in 1992 and 659 in 1997, before falling to 646 in 2005. Of the present 646 seats, there are 529 for England, 40 for Wales, 59 for Scotland and 18 for Northern Ireland.

ELECTIONS

Elections are by secret ballot, each elector casting one vote; voting is not compulsory. For entitlement to vote in parliamentary elections, *see* Legal Notes section. When a seat becomes vacant between general elections, a by-election is held.

British subjects and citizens of the Irish Republic can stand for election as MPs provided they are 21 or over and not subject to disqualification. Those disqualified from sitting in the house include:
– undischarged bankrupts
– people sentenced to more than one year's imprisonment
– members of the House of Lords (but hereditary peers not sitting in the Lords are eligible)

– holders of certain offices listed in the House of Commons Disqualification Act 1975, eg members of the judiciary, civil service, regular armed forces, police forces, some local government officers and some members of public corporations and government commissions

A candidate does not require any party backing but his or her nomination for election must be supported by the signatures of ten people registered in the constituency. A candidate must also deposit £500 with the returning officer, which is forfeit if the candidate does not receive more than 5 per cent of the votes cast. All election expenses at a general election, except the candidate's personal expenses, are subject to a statutory limit of £7,150, plus five pence for each elector in a borough constituency or seven pence for each elector in a county constituency.

See pages 139–146 for an alphabetical list of MPs, results of the last general election in 2005 and results of by-elections since the general election.

STATE OF THE PARTIES *as at 1 August 2007**

Labour, 352
Conservative, 196
Liberal Democrats, 63
Democratic Unionist Party, 9
Scottish National Party, 6
Sinn Fein (have not taken their seats), 5
Plaid Cymru, 3
Social Democratic Labour Party, 3
Independent, 2
Independent Labour, 1
Respect, 1
Ulster Unionist, 1
The Speaker and three Deputy Speakers, 4
Total, 646

* Working majority of 67; 352 Labour MPs less 285 of all other parties (excluding the speaker, deputy speakers and Sinn Fein)

BUSINESS

The week's business of the house is outlined each Thursday by the leader of the house, after consultation between the chief government whip and the chief opposition whip. A quarter to a third of the time will be taken up by the government's legislative programme and the rest by other business. As a rule, bills likely to raise political controversy are introduced in the Commons before going on to the Lords, and the Commons claims exclusive control in respect of national taxation and expenditure. Bills such as the finance bill, which imposes taxation, and the consolidated fund bills, which authorise expenditure, must begin in the Commons. A bill of which the financial provisions are subsidiary may begin in the Lords; and the Commons may waive its rights in regard to Lords' amendments affecting finance.

The Commons has a public register of MPs' financial and certain other interests; this is published annually as a House of Commons paper. Members must also disclose any relevant financial interest or benefit in a matter before the house when taking part in a debate, in certain other proceedings of the house, or in consultations with other MPs, with ministers or with civil servants.

MEMBERS' PAY AND ALLOWANCES

Since 1911 members of the House of Commons have received salary payments; facilities for free travel were introduced in 1924. Salary rates since 1911 are as follows:

1911	£400	1987 Jan	£18,500
1931	360	1988 Jan	22,548
1934	380	1989 Jan	24,107
1935	400	1990 Jan	26,701
1937	600	1991 Jan	28,970
1946	1,000	1992 Jan	30,854
1954	1,250	1994 Jan	31,687
1957	1,750	1995 Jan	33,189
1964	3,250	1996 Jan	34,085
1972 Jan	4,500	1996 Jul	43,000
1975 Jun	5,750	1997 Apr	43,860
1976 Jun	6,062	1998 Apr	45,066
1977 Jul	6,270	1999 Apr	47,008
1978 Jun	6,897	2000 Apr	48,371
1979 Jun	9,450	2001 Apr	49,822
1980 Jun	11,750	2002 Apr	55,118
1981 Jun	13,950	2003 Apr	56,358
1982 Jun	14,510	2004 Apr	57,485
1983 Jun	15,308	2005 Apr	59,095
1984 Jan	16,106	2006 Apr	59,686
1985 Jan	16,904	2007 Apr	60,675

Pay Band 1	£56,100–£92,000
Pay Band 1A	£65,280–£104,000
Pay Band 2	£81,600–£123,000
Pay Band 3	£99,960–£137,763

In 1969 MPs were granted an annual allowance for secretarial and research expenses, revised in July 2001. Members receive an incidental expenses provision (£21,339), a staffing allowance (up to £90,505) and a communications allowance (£10,000).

Since 1972 MPs have been able to claim reimbursement for the additional cost of staying overnight away from their main residence while on parliamentary business; this is known as the additional costs allowance and from April 2007 is £23,083 per year.

Members of staff who are paid out of the allowances can benefit from a sum not exceeding 10 per cent of their gross salary which is paid into the Portcullis Pension Plan. This sum comes from a central budget.

MEMBERS' PENSIONS

Pension arrangements for MPs were first introduced in 1964. Under the Parliamentary Contributory Pension Fund (PCPF), MPs receive a pension on retirement based upon their salary in their final year, and upon their number of years' service as an MP. Members may pay a contribution rate of 10 per cent or 6 per cent and build up a pension of 2.5 per cent or 2 per cent of salary for each year of service. Pensions are normally payable at age 65; upon retirement at 65, the pension payable is subject to a maximum of 66.6 per cent inclusive of pensions from employment or self-employment prior to becoming an MP. There are provisions in place for: early retirement for those MPs who cease to serve between the ages of 50 and 65; MPs of any age who retire due to ill health; and pensions for widows/widowers of MPs. All pensions are index-linked. There is an Exchequer contribution to ensure that shortfalls are made up; currently 8.7 per cent of an MP's salary for 15 years from 2006/7.

The House of Commons Members' Fund provides for annual or lump sum grants to ex-MPs, their widows or widowers, and children of those who either ceased to serve as an MP prior to the PCPF being established or who are experiencing hardship. Members contribute £24 a year and the Exchequer £215,000 a year to the fund.

HOUSE OF COMMONS PAY BANDS

Staff are placed in the following Senior Civil Service pay bands. These pay bands apply to the most senior staff in departments and agencies.

OFFICERS AND OFFICIALS

The House of Commons is presided over by the Speaker, who has considerable powers to maintain order. A deputy speaker, called the chairman of ways and means, and two deputy chairs may preside over sittings of the House of Commons; they are elected by the house, and, like the Speaker, neither speak nor vote other than in their official capacity.

The staff of the house are employed by a commission chaired by the Speaker. The heads of the six House of Commons departments are permanent officers of the house, not MPs. The Clerk of the House is the principal adviser to the Speaker on the privileges and procedures of the house, the conduct of the business of the house, and committees. The Serjeant-at-Arms is responsible for security, ceremonial, and for accommodation in the Commons part of the Palace of Westminster.

Speaker (£137,579), Rt. Hon. Michael J. Martin, MP (Glasgow Springburn)
Chairman of Ways and Means (£100,567), Sir Alan Haselhurst, MP (Saffron Walden)
First Deputy Chairman of Ways and Means (£95,736), Sylvia Heal, MP (Halesowen and Rowley Regis)
Second Deputy Chairman of Ways and Means (£95,736), Sir Michael Lord, MP (Suffolk Central and Ipswich North)

OFFICES OF THE SPEAKER AND CHAIRMAN OF WAYS AND MEANS
Speaker's Secretary (£65,280–£104,000), A. Sinclair
Chaplain to the Speaker, Revd Canon R. Wright
Secretary to the Chairman of Ways and Means (£40,723–£55,539), J. Whatley

DEPARTMENT OF THE CLERK OF THE HOUSE
Clerk of the House of Commons (£165,900), Dr M. R. Jack
Clerk Assistant (£99,960–£137,763), D. G. Millar
Clerk of Committees (£99,960–£137,763), Ms H. E. Irwin
Clerk of Legislation (£99,960–£137,763), R. J. Rogers
Principal Clerks (£81,600–£123,000)
    Table Office, D. L. Natzler
    Journals, Ms J. Sharpe
    Principal Clerk and Deputy Head of Committee Office, R. W. G. Wilson
Principal Clerks (£65,280–£104,000)
    Overseas Office, L. C. Laurence Smyth
    Bills, D. W. N. Doig
    Clerk of Domestic Committees / Secretary to the Commission, A. R. Kennon
    Select Committees, P. A. Evans; D. J. Gerhild
    Delegated Legislation, S. J. Patrick
Deputy Principal Clerks (£56,100–£92,000), J. S. Benger, DPHIL; Mrs S. A. R. Davies; A. H. Doherty; Mrs E. J. Flood; K. C. Fox; Miss L. M. Gardner; M. D. Hamlyn; D. F. Harrison; T. W. P. Healey; Ms P. A. Helme; M. Hennessy; B. M. Hutton; Dr R. G. James; C. G. Lee; D. R. Lloyd; S. Mark; Mrs J. N. St J. Mulley; Mrs C. Oxborough; R. I. S. Phillips; S. J. Priestly; F. J. Reid; D. W. Rhys; Ms E. C. Samson; A. Sandall; C. A. Shaw; C. D. Stanton; N. P. Walker; Dr C. R. M. Ward; H. A. Yardley
Senior Clerks (£40,723–£55,539), M. P. Atkins; T. Byrne;

M. Clark; G. K. Clarke; Ms E. Commander; Ms O. Davidson; J. H. Davies; Dr R. Davies; M. Egan; Ms K. Emms; M. Etherton; G. F. J. Farrar; Miss T. S. Garratty; J. Gearson; T. Goldsmith; D. H. Griffiths; Ms S. Griffiths; P. Harborne; M. Hedges; M. Hillyard; Miss S. F. Ioannou; Ms S. Jones; Ms C. A. Littleboy; Ms J. E. McCullogh; G. McKee; Miss F. McLean; Sir Edward Osmotherly; Ms A. Toft; Ms E. Webbon; Ms N. Welfoot; J. D. Whatley; N. P. Wright

Examiners of Petitions for Private Bills, D. W. N. Doig; T. Mohan

Registrar of Members' Interests (£56,100–£92,000), Ms A. Barry

Taxing Officer, D. W. N. Doig

VOTE OFFICE
Deliverer of the Vote (£56,100–£92,000), J. F. Collins
Deputy Deliverers of the Vote (£40,723–£55,539), O. B. T. Sweeney *(Parliamentary)*; R. Brook *(Development)*; Ms J. Pitt *(Production)*; A. Powell *(Systems)*

LEGAL SERVICES OFFICE
Speaker's Counsel and Head of Legal Services Office (£81,600–£123,000), J. E. G. Vaux
Counsel for European Legislation (£65,280–£104,000), M. Carpenter
Counsel for Legislation, (£65,280–£104,000), Peter Davis
Deputy Counsel (£56,100–£92,000), A. Akbar; P. Brooksbank; Ms V. Rose
Assistant Counsel (£40,723–£55,539), Ms H. Emes

DEPARTMENT OF THE SERJEANT-AT-ARMS
Serjeant-at-Arms (£81,600–£123,000), vacant
Deputy Serjeant-at-Arms (£65,280–£104,000), R. M. Morton
Assistant Serjeants-at-Arms, (£40,723–£67,340), Ms R. Beech; Mrs J. Pay; J. M. Robertson

DEPARTMENT OF THE LIBRARY
Librarian (£81,600–£123,000), J. Pullinger
Directors (£56,100–£92,000), R. Clements *(Research Services)*; Ms B. McInnes *(Departmental Services)*; S. Wise *(Service Delivery and Development)*; E. Wood *(Information Services)*
Heads of Sections (£40,723–£67,340), C. Barclay; R. Cracknell; T. Edmonds; O. Gay; Mrs C. Gillie; V. Miller; B. Morgan; Dr C. Pond; Ms P. J. Strickland; A Walker *(acting)*
Senior Library Clerks (£40,723–£55,539), G. Allen; J. Anseau; E. Ares; E. Beale; G. Berman; P. Bolton; P. Bowers; Ms B. Brevitt; A. Brown; L. Butcher; Ms D. Clark; G. Danby; C. Fairbairn; M. Gheera; V. Gialias; Ms D. Gore; V. Griffin; Ms H. Holden; A. Horne; J. Hough; S. Hubble; R. Kelly; S. Kennedy; V. Keter; Dr J. Lunn; L. Maer; S. McGinness; K. Parry; M. Peck; E. Potton; Ms J. Roll; A. Seely; C. Taylor; Ms A. Thorp; D. Thurley; P. Ward; D. Webb; C. Weeds; Ms I. White; M. Whittaker; Ms F. Whittle; Ms W. Wilson; R. Winstone; R. Young; T. Youngs

DEPARTMENT OF FINANCE AND ADMINISTRATION
Director of Finance and Administration (£81,600–£123,000), A. J. Walker
Deputy Director of Finance and Administration (£56,100–£92,000), Ms E. Honer
Director of Operations (£65,280–£104,000), T. M. Bird
Director of Human Resource Management (£56,100–£92,000), Mrs H. Bryson

Director of Finance Policy (£56,100–£92,000), C. Ridley
Director of Internal Review Services (£56,100–£92,000), R. Russell

DEPARTMENT OF THE OFFICIAL REPORT
Editor (£65,280–£104,000), Miss L. Sutherland
Deputy Editors (£56,100–£92,000), Ms C. Fogarty; V. A. Widgery

REFRESHMENT DEPARTMENT
Director of Catering Services (£65,280–£104,000), Mrs S. Harrison
Business Development Manager (£49,392–£67,340), Mrs J. Rissen
Catering Operations Manager (Outbuildings) (£40,723–£55,539), Ms D. Herd
Food and Beverage Operations Manager, Palace of Westminster (£40,723–£55,539), R. Gibbs
Executive Chef (£40,723–£55,539), M. Hill
Retail Manager (£40,723–£55,539), Mrs M. DeSouza
Human Resources and Development Manager (£40,723–£55,539), J. van den Broek

PARLIAMENTARY INFORMATION AND COMMUNICATION TECHNOLOGY (ICT)
Director of Parliamentary ICT (£65,280–£104,000), Ms J. Miller
Director of Business Information Systems Directorate (£56,100–£92,000), I. Montgomery *(acting)*
Director of Operations (£56,100–£92,000), M. Taylor
Director of Resources (£56,100–£92,000), R. Ware
Director of Programmes and Project Development (£56,100–£92,000), Ms N. Woods *(acting)*

NATIONAL AUDIT OFFICE
157–197 Buckingham Palace Road, London SW1W 9SP
T 020-7798 7000 **F** 020-7798 7070
E enquiries@nao.gsi.gov.uk **W** www.nao.org.uk

The National Audit Office came into existence under the National Audit Act 1983 to replace and continue the work of the former Exchequer and Audit Department. The act reinforced the office's total financial and operational independence from the government and brought its head, the Comptroller and Auditor-General, into a closer relationship with parliament as an officer of the House of Commons.

The National Audit Office provides independent information, advice and assurance to parliament and the public about all aspects of the financial operations of government departments and many other bodies receiving public funds. It does this by examining and certifying the accounts of these organisations. It also regularly publishes reports to parliament on the results of its value for money investigations of the economy, namely the efficiency and effectiveness with which public resources have been used. The National Audit Office is also the auditor by agreement of the accounts of certain international and other organisations. In addition, the office authorises the issue of public funds to government departments.

Comptroller and Auditor-General, Sir John Bourn, KCB
Private Secretary, Dean Parker
Deputy Comptroller and Auditor-General, Tim Burr
Assistant Auditors-General, Gabrielle Cohen; Wendy Kenway-Smith; Caroline Mawhood; Jim Rickleton; Anna Simons; Martin Sinclair; Michael Whitehouse

SELECT COMMITTEES
The more significant committees, as at June 2007, are:

DEPARTMENTAL COMMITTEES
Communities and Local Government – *Chair*, Dr Phyllis Starkey, MP; *Clerk*, Jessica Mulley
*Constitutional Affairs** – *Chair*, Rt. Hon. Alan Beith, MP; *Clerk*, Roger Phillips
Culture, Media and Sport – *Chair*, John Whittingdale, MP; *Clerk*, Kenneth Fox
Defence – *Chair*, Rt. Hon. James Arbuthnot, MP; *Clerk*, Philippa Helme
*Education and Skills** – *Chair*, Barry Sheerman, MP; *Clerk*, David Lloyd
Environment, Food and Rural Affairs – *Chair*, Rt. Hon. Michael Jack, MP; *Clerk*, Chris Stanton
Foreign Affairs – *Chair*, Mike Gapes, MP; *Clerk*, Steve Priestley
Health – *Chair*, Rt. Hon. Kevin Barron, MP; *Clerk*, Dr David Harrison
Home Affairs – *Chair*, Rt. Hon. John Denham, MP; *Clerk*, Dr Robin James
International Development – *Chair*, Malcolm Bruce, MP; *Clerk*, Carol Oxborough
Northern Ireland Affairs – *Chair*, Sir Patrick Cormack, MP; *Clerk*, James Rhys
Scottish Affairs – *Chair*, Mohammad Sarwar, MP; *Clerk*, Mike Clark
Standards and Privileges – *Chair*, Rt. Hon. Sir George Young, Bt., MP; *Clerk*, Dr Christopher Ward
*Trade and Industry** – *Chair*, Peter Luff, MP; *Clerk*, Elizabeth Flood
Transport – *Chair*, Gwyneth Dunwoody, MP; *Clerks*, Tom Healey; Annette Toft
Treasury – *Chair*, Rt. Hon. John McFall, MP; *Clerk*, Colin Lee
Welsh Affairs – *Chair*, Dr Hywel Francis, MP; *Clerk*, Nick Wright
Work and Pensions – *Chair*, Terry Rooney, MP; *Clerk*, Sarah Davies
* From the beginning of the parliamentary session on 6 November 2007, these committees were due to be disbanded with four new committees being formed in their place (Business, Enterprise and Regulatory Reform; Children, Schools and Families; Innovation, Universities and Skills; and Justice)

NON-DEPARTMENTAL COMMITTEES
Environmental Audit – *Chair*, Tim Yeo, MP; *Clerk*, Mike Hennessy
European Scrutiny – *Chair*, Michael Connarty, MP; *Clerk*, Alistair Doherty
Finance and Services – *Chair*, Sir Stuart Bell, MP; *Clerk*, Andrew Kennon
Human Rights (Joint Committee) – *Chair*, Andrew Dismore, MP; *Clerks*, Dr Mark Egan; Bill Sinton
Intelligence and Security (Cabinet Office) – *Chair*, Rt. Hon. Paul Murphy, MP; *Clerk*, Emma-Louise Avery
Modernisation of the House of Commons – *Chair*, Rt. Hon. Jack Straw, MP; *Clerk*, Helen Irwin
Procedure – *Chair*, Rt. Hon. Greg Knight, MP; *Clerk*, Mark Hutton
Public Accounts – *Chair*, Edward Leigh, MP; *Clerk*, Mark Etherton
Public Administration – *Chair*, Dr Tony Wright, MP; *Clerk*, Eve Samson
Regulatory Reform – *Chair*, Andrew Miller, MP; *Clerk*, Mick Hillyard
*Science and Technology** – *Chair*, Phil Willis, MP; *Clerk*, Dr Lynn Gardner
Statutory Instruments (Joint Committee) – *Chair*, Rt. Hon. David Maclean, MP; *Clerk*, Mick Hillyard

DOMESTIC COMMITTEE
Administration – *Chair*, Frank Doran, MP; *Clerk*, Steven Mark

PARLIAMENTARY INFORMATION

The following is a short glossary of aspects of the work of parliament. Unless otherwise stated, references are to House of Commons procedures.

BILL – Proposed legislation is termed a bill. The stages of a public bill (for private bills, *see* below) in the House of Commons are as follows:

First Reading: This stage merely constitutes an order to have the bill printed.

Second Reading: The debate on the principles of the bill.

Committee Stage: The detailed examination of a bill, clause by clause. In most cases this takes place in a public bill committee, or the whole house may act as a committee. Public bill committees may take evidence before embarking on detailed scrutiny of the bill. Very rarely, a bill may be examined by a select committee.

Report Stage: Detailed review of a bill as amended in committee, on the floor of the house.

Third Reading: Final debate on a bill. Public bills go through the same stages in the House of Lords, but with important differences: the committee stage is taken in committee of the whole house or in a grand committee, in which any peer may participate. There are no time limits, and no selection of amendments can be made at third reading.

A bill may start in either house, and has to pass through both houses to become law. Both houses have to agree the final text of a bill, so that amendments made by the second house are then considered in the originating house, and if not agreed, sent back or themselves amended, until agreement is reached.

CHILTERN HUNDREDS – A nominal office of profit under the crown, the acceptance of which requires an MP to vacate his/her seat. The Manor of Northstead is similar. These are the only means by which an MP may resign.

CONSOLIDATED FUND BILL – A bill to authorise issue of money to maintain government services. The bill is dealt with without debate.

EARLY DAY MOTION – A motion put on the notice paper by an MP without, in general, the real prospect of its being debated. Such motions are expressions of back-bench opinion.

FATHER OF THE HOUSE – The MP whose continuous service in the House of Commons is the longest. The present Father of the House is the Rt. Hon. Alan Williams, MP.

HOURS OF MEETING – The House of Commons normally meets on Mondays and Tuesdays at 2.30pm, Wednesdays at 11.30am, Thursdays at 10.30am and some Fridays at 9.30am. (*See also* Westminster Hall Sittings, below.) The House of Lords normally meets at 2.30pm Mondays and Tuesdays, 3pm on Wednesdays and at 11am on Thursdays. The House of Lords often sits on Fridays at 11am.

LEADER OF THE OPPOSITION – In 1937 the office of leader of the opposition was recognised and a salary was assigned to the post. Since April 2007 this has been £131,172 (including a parliamentary salary of £60,675).

The present leader of the opposition is the Rt. Hon. David Cameron, MP.

THE LORD CHANCELLOR – The office of Lord High Chancellor of Great Britain was significantly altered by the Constitutional Reform Act 2005. Previously, the Lord Chancellor was (*ex officio*) the Speaker of the House of Lords, and took part in debates and voted in divisions in the House of Lords. The Department for Constitutional Affairs was created in 2003, which became the Ministry of Justice in 2007, incorporating most of the responsibilities of the Lord Chancellor's department. The role of Speaker has been transferred to the newly created post of Lord Speaker. The Constitutional Reform Act 2005 also brought to an end the Lord Chancellor's role as head of the judiciary. A new Judicial Appointments Commission was created in April 2006, and a new supreme court (separate from the House of Lords) is being established (scheduled to open in 2009).

THE LORD SPEAKER – The first Lord Speaker of the House of Lords, the Rt. Hon. Baroness Hayman, took up office on 4 July 2006. Unlike in the case of the Lord Chancellor, the Lord Speaker is independent of the government and elected by members of the House of Lords rather than appointed by the prime minister. Although the Lord Speaker's primary role is to preside over proceedings in the House of Lords, she does not have the same powers as the speaker of the House of Commons. For example, the Lord Speaker is not responsible for maintaining order during debates, as this is the responsibility of the house as a whole. The Lord Speaker sits in the Lords on one of the woolsacks, which are couches covered in red cloth and stuffed with wool.

THE LORD GREAT CHAMBERLAIN – The Lord Great Chamberlain is a Great Officer of State, the office being hereditary since the grant of Henry I to the family of De Vere, Earls of Oxford. It is now a joint hereditary office rotating on the death of the sovereign between the Cholmondeley, Carington and Ancaster families.

The Lord Great Chamberlain, currently the Marquess of Cholmondeley, is responsible for the royal apartments in the Palace of Westminster, the Royal Gallery, the administration of the Chapel of St Mary Undercroft and, in conjunction with the Lord Speaker and the Speaker of the House of Commons, Westminster Hall. The Lord Great Chamberlain has the right to perform specific services at a coronation, he carries out ceremonial duties in the Palace of Westminster when the sovereign visits the palace and has particular responsibility for the internal administrative arrangements within the House of Lords for state openings of parliament.

NORTHERN IRELAND GRAND COMMITTEE – The Northern Ireland Grand Committee consists of all MPs representing constituencies in Northern Ireland, together with not more than 25 other MPs nominated by the committee of selection. The business of the committee includes questions, short debates, ministerial statements, bills, legislative proposals and other matters relating exclusively to Northern Ireland, and delegated legislation.

The Northern Ireland Affairs Committee is one of the departmental select committees, empowered to examine the expenditure, administration and policy of the Northern Ireland Office and the administration and expenditure of the Crown Solicitor's Office.

OPPOSITION DAY – A day on which the topic for debate is chosen by the opposition. There are 20 such days in a normal session. On 17 days, subjects are chosen by the leader of the opposition; on the remaining three days by the leader of the next largest opposition party.

PARLIAMENT ACTS 1911 AND 1949 – Under these acts, bills may become law without the consent of the Lords, though the House of Lords has the power to delay a public bill for a parliamentary session.

PRIME MINISTER'S QUESTIONS – The prime minister answers questions from 12.00 to 12.30pm on Wednesdays.

PRIVATE BILL – A bill promoted by a body or an individual to give powers additional to, or in conflict with, the general law, and to which a special procedure applies to enable people affected to object.

PRIVATE MEMBER'S BILL – A public bill promoted by an MP or peer who is not a member of the government.

PRIVATE NOTICE QUESTION – A question adjudged of urgent importance on submission to the Speaker (in the Lords, the Lord Speaker), answered at the end of oral questions.

PRIVILEGE – The House of Commons has rights and immunities to protect it from obstruction in carrying out its duties. These are known as parliamentary privilege and enable Members of Parliament to debate freely. The most important privilege is that of freedom of speech. MPs cannot be prosecuted for sedition or sued for libel or slander over anything said during proceedings in the house. This enables them to raise in the house questions affecting the public good which might be difficult to raise outside owing to the possibility of being sued. The House of Lords has similar privileges.

QUESTION TIME – Oral questions are answered by ministers in the Commons from 2.30 to 3.30pm on Mondays and Tuesdays, 11.30am to 12.30pm on Wednesdays, and 10.30 to 11.30am on Thursdays. Questions are also taken at the start of the Lords sittings, with a daily limit of four oral questions.

ROYAL ASSENT – The royal assent is signified by letters patent to such bills and measures as have passed both Houses of Parliament (or bills which have been passed under the Parliament Acts 1911 and 1949). The sovereign has not given royal assent in person since 1854. On occasion, for instance in the prorogation of parliament, royal assent may be pronounced to the two houses by Lords Commissioners. More usually royal assent is notified to each house sitting separately in accordance with the Royal Assent Act 1967. The old French formulae for royal assent are then endorsed on the acts by the Clerk of the Parliaments.

The power to withhold assent resides with the sovereign but has not been exercised in the UK since 1707.

SELECT COMMITTEES – Consisting usually of 10 to 15 members of all parties, select committees are a means used by both houses in order to investigate certain matters.

Most select committees in the House of Commons are tied to departments: each committee investigates subjects within a government department's remit. There are other select committees dealing with matters such as public accounts (ie the spending by the government of money voted by parliament) and European legislation, and also committees advising on procedures and domestic administration of the house. Major select committees usually take evidence in public; their evidence and reports are published on the parliament website and in hard copy by TSO (The Stationery Office). House of Commons select committees are reconstituted after a general election.

In the House of Lords, select committees do not mirror

government departments but cover broader issues. There is a select committee on the European Union (EU), which has seven sub-committees dealing with specific areas of EU policy, a select committee on science and technology, which appoints sub-committees to deal with specific subjects, a select committee on economic affairs and also one on the constitution. There is also a select committee on delegated powers and regulatory reform and one on the merits of statutory instruments. In addition, *ad hoc* select committees have been set up from time to time to investigate specific subjects. There are also joint committees of the two houses, eg the committees on statutory instruments and on human rights.

THE SPEAKER – The Speaker of the House of Commons is the spokesperson and chair of the Chamber. He or she is elected by the house at the beginning of each parliament or when the previous Speaker retires or dies. The Speaker neither speaks in debates nor votes in divisions except when the voting is equal.

VACANT SEATS – When a vacancy occurs in the House of Commons during a session of parliament, the writ for the by-election is moved by a whip of the party to which the member whose seat has been vacated belonged. If the house is in recess, the Speaker can issue a warrant for a writ, should two members certify to him that a seat is vacant.

WELSH AFFAIRS COMMITTEE — The Welsh Affairs Committee is one of the Commons departmental select committees, empowered to examine matters within the responsibility of the Secretary of State for Wales (including relations with the National Assembly for Wales).

WESTMINSTER HALL SITTINGS – Following a report by the Modernisation of the House of Commons Select Committee, the Commons decided in May 1999 to set up a second debating forum. It is known as 'Westminster Hall' and sittings are in the Grand Committee Room on Tuesdays from 9.30am to 2pm, Wednesdays from 9.30 to 11.30am and from 2.30 to 5pm, and Thursdays from 2.30 to 5.30pm. Sittings will be open to the public at the times indicated.

WHIPS – In order to secure the attendance of members of a particular party in parliament, particularly on the occasion of an important vote, whips (originally known as 'whippers-in') are appointed. The written appeal or circular letter issued by them is also known as a 'whip', its urgency being denoted by the number of times it is underlined. Failure to respond to a three-line whip is tantamount in the Commons to secession (at any rate temporarily) from the party. Whips are provided with office accommodation in both houses, and government and some opposition whips receive salaries from public funds.

HOUSE OF COMMONS INFORMATION OFFICE
Norman Shaw Building (North), London SW1A 2TT
T 020-7219 4272 E hcinfo@parliament.uk
W www.parliament.uk

PARLIAMENTARY ARCHIVES
Houses of Parliament, London SW1A 0PW
T 020-7219 3074 F 020-7219 2570
E archives@parliament.uk W www.parliament.uk/archives

Since 1497, the records of parliament have been kept within the Palace of Westminster. They are in the custody of the Clerk of the Parliaments. In 1946 the House of Lords Record Office, which became the Parliamentary Archives in 2006, was established to supervise their preservation and their availability to the public. Some three million documents are preserved, including acts of parliament from 1497, journals of the House of Lords from 1510, minutes and committee proceedings from 1610, and papers laid before parliament from 1531. Amongst the records are the Petition of Right, the death warrant of Charles I, the Declaration of Breda, and the Bill of Rights. Records are available through a public search room.
Clerk of the Records, S. K. Ellison

GOVERNMENT OFFICE

The government is the body of ministers responsible for the administration of national affairs, determining policy and introducing into parliament any legislation necessary to give effect to government policy. The majority of ministers are members of the House of Commons but members of the House of Lords, or of neither house, may also hold ministerial responsibility. The Lord Chancellor is always a member of the House of Lords. The prime minister is, by current convention, always a member of the House of Commons.

THE PRIME MINISTER
The office of prime minister, which had been in existence for nearly 200 years, was officially recognised in 1905 and its holder was granted a place in the table of precedence. The prime minister, by tradition also First Lord of the Treasury and Minister for the Civil Service, is appointed by the sovereign and is usually the leader of the party which enjoys, or can secure, a majority in the House of Commons. Other ministers are appointed by the sovereign on the recommendation of the prime minister, who also allocates functions amongst ministers and has the power to obtain their resignation or dismissal individually.

The prime minister informs the sovereign of state on political matters, advises on the dissolution of parliament, and makes recommendations for important crown appointments, ie the award of honours, etc.

As the chair of cabinet meetings and leader of a political party, the prime minister is responsible for translating party policy into government activity. As leader of the government, the prime minister is responsible to parliament and to the electorate for the policies and their implementation.

The prime minister also represents the nation in international affairs, eg summit conferences.

THE CABINET
The cabinet developed during the 18th century as an inner committee of the Privy Council, which was the chief source of executive power until that time. The cabinet is composed of about 20 ministers chosen by the prime minister, usually the heads of government departments (generally known as secretaries of state unless they have a special title, eg Chancellor of the Exchequer), the leaders of the two houses of parliament, and the holders of various traditional offices.

The cabinet's functions are the final determination of policy, control of government and coordination of government departments. The exercise of its functions is dependent upon enjoying majority support in the House of Commons. Cabinet meetings are held in private, taking place once or twice a week during parliamentary sittings and less often during a recess. Proceedings are confidential, the members being bound by their oath as privy counsellors not to disclose information about the proceedings.

The convention of collective responsibility means that the cabinet acts unanimously even when cabinet ministers do not all agree on a subject. The policies of departmental ministers must be consistent with the policies of the government as a whole, and once the government's policy has been decided, each minister is expected to support it or resign.

The convention of ministerial responsibility holds a minister, as the political head of his or her department, accountable to parliament for the department's work. Departmental ministers usually decide all matters within their responsibility, although on matters of political importance they normally consult their colleagues collectively. A decision by a departmental minister is binding on the government as a whole.

POLITICAL PARTIES

Before the reign of William and Mary the principal officers of state were chosen by and were responsible to the sovereign alone, and not to parliament or the nation at large. Such officers acted sometimes in concert with one another but more often independently, and the fall of one did not, of necessity, involve that of others, although all were liable to be dismissed at any moment.

In 1693 the Earl of Sunderland recommended to William III the advisability of selecting a ministry from the political party which enjoyed a majority in the House of Commons, and the first united ministry was drawn in 1696 from the Whigs, to which party the king owed his throne. This group became known as the 'Junto' and was regarded with suspicion as a novelty in the political life of the nation, being a small section meeting in secret apart from the main body of ministers. It may be regarded as the forerunner of the cabinet and in the course of time it led to the establishment of the principle of joint responsibility of ministers, so that internal disagreement caused a change of personnel or resignation of the whole body of ministers.

The accession of George I, who was unfamiliar with the English language, led to a disinclination on the part of the sovereign to preside at meetings of his ministers and caused the emergence of a prime minister, a position first acquired by Robert Walpole in 1721 and retained by him without interruption for 20 years and 326 days.

DEVELOPMENT OF PARTIES

In 1828 the Whigs became known as Liberals, a name originally given by opponents to imply laxity of principles, but gradually accepted by the party to indicate its claim to be pioneers and champions of political reform and progressive legislation. In 1861 a Liberal Registration Association was founded and Liberal Associations became widespread. In 1877 a National Liberal Federation was formed, with its headquarters in London. The Liberal Party was in power for long periods during the second half of the 19th century and for several years during the first quarter of the 20th century, but after a split in the party in 1931, the numbers elected remained small. In 1988, a majority of the Liberals agreed on a merger with the Social Democratic Party under the title Social and Liberal Democrats; since 1989 they have been known as the Liberal Democrats. A minority continue separately as the Liberal Party.

Soon after the change from Whig to Liberal, the Tory Party became known as Conservative, a name believed to have been invented by John Wilson Croker in 1830 and to have been generally adopted around the time of the passing of the Reform Act of 1832 – to indicate that the preservation of national institutions was the leading principle of the party. After the Home Rule crisis of 1886 the dissentient Liberals entered into a compact with the Conservatives, under which the latter undertook not to contest their seats, but a separate Liberal Unionist organisation was maintained until 1912, when it was united with the Conservatives.

Labour candidates for parliament made their first appearance at the general election of 1892, when there were 27 standing as Labour or Liberal-Labour. In 1900 the Labour Representation Committee (LRC) was set up in order to establish a distinct Labour group in parliament, with its own whips, its own policy, and a readiness to cooperate with any party which might be engaged in promoting legislation in the direct interests of labour. In 1906 the LRC became known as the Labour Party.

The Council for Social Democracy was announced by four former Labour cabinet ministers in January 1981 and in March 1981 the Social Democratic Party (SDP) was launched. Later that year the SDP and the Liberal Party formed an electoral alliance. In 1988 a majority of the SDP agreed on a merger with the Liberal Party but a minority continued as a separate party under the SDP title. In 1990 it was decided to wind up the party organisation and its three sitting MPs were known as independent social democrats. None were returned at the 1992 general election.

Plaid Cymru was founded in 1926 to provide an independent political voice for Wales and to campaign for self-government in Wales.

The Scottish National Party was founded in 1934 to campaign for independence for Scotland.

The Social Democratic and Labour Party was founded in 1970, emerging from the civil rights movement of the 1960s, with the aim of promoting reform, reconciliation and partnership across the sectarian divide in Northern Ireland, and of opposing violence from any quarter.

The Democratic Unionist Party was founded in 1971 to resist moves by the Ulster Unionist Party which were considered a threat to the Union. Its aim is to maintain Northern Ireland as an integral part of the UK.

The Ulster Unionist Council first met formally in 1905. Its objectives are to maintain Northern Ireland as an integral part of the UK and to promote the aims of the Ulster Unionist Party.

Sinn Fein first emerged in the 1900s as a federation of nationalist clubs. It is a left-wing republican and labour party that seeks to end British governance in Ireland and achieve a 32-county republic.

GOVERNMENT AND OPPOSITION

The government of the day is formed by the party which wins the largest number of seats in the House of Commons at a general election, or which has the support of a majority of members in the House of Commons. By tradition, the leader of the majority party is asked by the sovereign to form a government, while the largest minority party becomes the official opposition with its own leader and a shadow cabinet. Leaders of the government and opposition sit on the front benches of the Commons with their supporters (the back-benchers) sitting behind them.

FINANCIAL SUPPORT

Financial support for opposition parties in the House of Commons was introduced in 1975 and is commonly known as Short Money, after Edward Short, the leader of the house at that time, who introduced the scheme. Short Money allocation for 2007–8 is:

Conservative	£3,816,074
Liberal Democrats	£1,626,225
Plaid Cymru	£63,378
SNP	£135,103
SDLP	£56,817
Democratic Unionists	£152,448

A specific allocation for the leader of the opposition's office was introduced in April 1999 and has been set at £622,223 for the years 2007–8.

Financial support for opposition parties in the House of Lords was introduced in 1996 and is commonly known as Cranborne Money.

The parties included here are those with MPs sitting in the House of Commons in the present parliament.

CONSERVATIVE PARTY

Conservative Campaign Headquarters, 30 Millbank, London SW1P 4DP
T 020-7222 9000 F 020-7222 1135
E ccoffice@conservatives.com
W www.conservatives.com

SHADOW CABINET *as at July 2007*

Leader of the Opposition, Rt. Hon. David Cameron, MP
Senior Member and Secretary of State for Foreign Affairs, Rt. Hon. William Hague, MP
Chancellor of the Exchequer and General Election Campaign Coordinator, George Osborne, MP
Secretary of State for Home Affairs, Rt. Hon. David Davis, MP
Party Chair, Caroline Spelman, MP
Chair of Policy Review and of Conservative Research Department, Rt. Hon. Oliver Letwin, MP
Minister for the Cabinet Office, Chancellor of the Duchy of Lancaster, Rt. Hon. Francis Maude, MP
Secretary of State for Business, Enterprise and Regulatory Reform, Alan Duncan, MP
Secretary of State for Children, School and Families, Michael Gove, MP
Secretary of State for Communities and Local Government, Eric Pickles, MP
Minister for Community Cohesion, Sayeeda Warsi, MP
Secretary of State for Culture, Media and Sport, Jeremy Hunt, MP
Secretary of State for Defence, Dr Liam Fox, MP
Secretary of State for Environment, Food and Rural Affairs, Peter Ainsworth, MP
Secretary of State for Health, Andrew Lansley, CBE, MP
Secretary of State for Innovation, Universities and Skills, David Willetts, MP
Secretary of State for International Development, Andrew Mitchell, MP
Secretary of State for Justice, Nick Herbert, MP
Leader in the House of Commons, Rt. Hon. Theresa May, MP
Leader in the House of Lords, Rt. Hon. Lord Strathclyde
Secretary of State for Northern Ireland, Owen Paterson, MP
Secretary of State for Scotland, David Mundell, MP
Minister for Security and National Security Adviser to the

Leader of the Opposition, Dame Pauline Neville-Jones, DCMG
Secretary of State for Transport, Theresa Villiers, MP
Chief Secretary to the Treasury, Philip Hammond, MP
Secretary of State for Wales, Cheryl Gillan, MP
Secretary of State for Work and Pensions, Chris Grayling, MP

CONSERVATIVE WHIPS

House of Lords, Baroness Anelay of St Johns, DBE
House of Commons, Rt. Hon. Patrick McLoughlin, MP

LABOUR PARTY

Eldon House, Regent Centre, Newcastle upon Tyne NE3 3PW
T 0870-590 0200 W www.labour.org.uk
Parliamentary Party Leader, Rt. Hon. Gordon Brown, MP
Deputy Party Leader, Leader in the Commons and Party Chair, Rt. Hon. Harriet Harman, QC, MP
Leader in the Lords, Rt. Hon. Baroness Ashton of Upholland
General Secretary, Peter Watt
General Secretary, Scottish Labour Party, Lesley Quinn

LIBERAL DEMOCRATS

4 Cowley Street, London SW1P 3NB
T 020-7222 7999 F 020-7799 2170
E info@libdems.org.uk W www.libdems.org.uk
President and Leader in the Commons, Simon Hughes, MP
Hon. Treasurer, Lord Razzall
Chief Executive, Lord Rennard
Parliamentary Party Leader, Rt. Hon. Sir Menzies Campbell, QC, MP
Leader in the Lords, Rt. Hon. Lord McNally

LIBERAL DEMOCRAT SPOKESMEN *as at July 2007*

Deputy Leader and Shadow Chancellor of the Exchequer, Dr Vincent Cable, MP
Attorney-General, Lord Thomas of Gresford
Business, Enterprise and Regulatory Reform, Lembit Opik, MP
Cabinet Office, Norman Baker, MP
Children, Schools and Families, David Laws, MP
Communities and Local Government, Andrew Stunell, MP
Culture, Media and Sport, Don Foster, MP
Defence, Nick Harvey, MP
Environment, Food and Rural Affairs, Chris Huhne, MP
Foreign and Commonwealth Affairs, Michael Moore, MP
Health, Norman Lamb, MP
Home Affairs, Nick Clegg, MP
Housing, Paul Holmes, MP
Innovation, Universities and Skills, Sarah Teather, MP
International Development, Lynne Featherstone, MP
Justice, David Heath, MP
Scotland and Northern Ireland, Alistair Carmichael, MP
Solicitor-General, David Howarth, MP
Transport, Susan Kramer, MP
Treasury, Julia Goldsworthy, MP
Wales, Roger Williams, MP
Work and Pensions, Danny Alexander, MP
Chair of the Manifesto Group, Prof. Steve Webb, MP
Chair of the Parliamentary Party, Paul Holmes, MP
Chief of Staff and Chair of Campaigns and Communications, Ed Davey, MP
Parliamentary Private Secretary to the Leader, Tim Farron, MP

LIBERAL DEMOCRAT WHIPS
House of Lords, Lord Shutt of Greetland
House of Commons, Paul Burstow, MP

NORTHERN IRELAND DEMOCRATIC UNIONIST PARTY

91 Dundela Avenue, Belfast BT4 3BU
T 028-9065 4479 F 028-9065 4480
E info@dup.org.uk W www.dup2win.com
Parliamentary Party Leader, Dr Ian Paisley, MP, MLA
Deputy Leader, Peter Robinson, MP, MLA
Chair, Lord Morrow, MLA
Hon. Treasurer, Gregory Campbell, MP, MLA
Party Secretary, Nigel Dodds, MP, MLA

PLAID CYMRU – THE PARTY OF WALES

Ty Gwynfor, 18 Park Grove, Cardiff CF10 3BN
T 029-2064 6000
E post@plaidcymru.org W www.plaidcymru.org
Party Leader, Ieuan Wyn Jones, AM
Party President, Dafydd Iwan
Party Vice-President, Jill Evans, MEP
Parliamentary Group Leader, Elfyn Llwyd
Chief Executive, Dafydd Trystan

RESPECT – THE UNITY COALITION

9 Club Row, London E1 6JX
T 0870-850 1978
E office@respectcoalition.org W www.respectcoalition.org
Chair, Linda Smith
Vice-Chair, Salma Yaqoob
National Secretary, John Rees
Treasurer, Elaine Graham-Leigh

SCOTTISH NATIONAL PARTY

107 McDonald Road, Edinburgh EH7 4NW
T 0131-525 8900 F 0131-525 8901
E snp.hq@snp.org W www.snp.org
Westminster Parliamentary Party Leader, Alex Salmond, MP
Westminster Parliamentary Party Chief Whip, Pete Wishart, MP
Scottish Parliamentary Party Leader, Alex Salmond, MSP
Scottish Parliamentary Party Chief Whip, Bruce Crawford, MSP
National Treasurer, Colin Beattie
National Secretary, Dr Duncan Ross
Chief Executive, Peter Murrell

SINN FEIN

53 Falls Road, Belfast BT12 4PD
T 028-9022 3000 F 028-9022 3001
E sfadmin@eircom.net W www.sinnfein.ie
Party President, Gerry Adams, MP, MLA
Vice-President, Pat Doherty, MP, MLA

Chair, Mary Lou McDonald, MEP
Chief Negotiator, Martin McGuinness, MP, MLA
General Secretary, Rita O'Hare

SOCIAL DEMOCRATIC AND LABOUR PARTY

121 Ormeau Road, Belfast BT7 1SH
T 028-9024 7700 F 028-9023 6699
E sdlp@indigo.ie W www.sdlp.ie
Parliamentary Party Leader, Mark Durkan, MP, MLA
Deputy Leader, Dr Alasdair McDonnell, MP, MLA
Chief Whip, John Dallat
Chair, Sean Farren, MLA
Treasurer, Peter McEvoy
General Secretary, Gerry Cosgrove

ULSTER UNIONIST PARTY

429 Holywood Road, Belfast BT4 2LN
T 028-9076 5500 F 028-9076 9419
E uup@uup.org W www.uup.org
Party Leader, Sir Reg Empey, OBE, MLA
Chief Whip, David McNarry, MLA

ULSTER UNIONIST COUNCIL
President, John White, OBE
Leader, Sir Reg Empey, OBE, MLA
Chair of the Executive Committee, David Campbell, CBE
Hon. Treasurer, Lord Maginnis of Drumglass
Vice-Chair, Tom Fleming
Party Officers, Johnny Andrews; Joan Carson; Cllr. Mark Cosgrove; Kenny Donaldson; Richard Holmes; Terry Wright
Officers from Elected Representatives, David McNarry, MLA; Jim Nicholson, MEP; Cllr. Trevor Wilson

The following parties have sitting MEPs, *see* European Parliament section.

GREEN PARTY

1A Waterlow Road, London N19 5NJ
T 020-7272 4474 F 020-7272 6653
E office@greenparty.org.uk W www.greenparty.org.uk
Chair, Richard Mallender
Principal Speakers, Siân Berry; Dr Derek Wall
Registered Treasurer, Khalid Hussenbux

UK INDEPENDENCE PARTY

Lexdrum House, Unit 1, King Charles Industrial Estate, Bovey Tracey, Devon TQ12 6UT
T 01626-831290 F 01626-831348
E mail@ukip.org W www.ukip.org
Party Leader, Nigel Farage, MEP
Chair, Dr John Whittaker, MEP
Party Secretary, Michael Zuckerman

MEMBERS OF PARLIAMENT as at 1 September 2007

* New MP
† Previously MP in another seat
‡ Previously MP for another party

Abbott, Diane (*b.* 1953) *Lab., Hackney North & Stoke Newington,* Maj. 7,427

Adams, Gerry (*b.* 1948) *SF, Belfast West,* Maj. 19,315

***Afriyie**, Adam (*b.* 1965) *C., Windsor,* Maj. 10,292

Ainger, Nick (*b.* 1949) *Lab., Carmarthen West & Pembrokeshire South,* Maj. 1,910

Ainsworth, Peter (*b.* 1956) *C., Surrey East,* Maj. 15,921

Ainsworth, Rt. Hon. Robert (*b.* 1952) *Lab., Coventry North East,* Maj. 14,222

***Alexander**, Danny (*b.* 1972) *LD, Inverness, Nairn, Badenoch & Strathspey,* Maj. 4,148

Alexander, Rt. Hon. Douglas (*b.* 1967) *Lab., Paisley & Renfrewshire South,* Maj. 13,232

Allen, Graham (*b.* 1953) *Lab., Nottingham North,* Maj. 12,171

Amess, David (*b.* 1952) *C., Southend West,* Maj. 8,959

Ancram, Rt. Hon. Michael (*b.* 1945) *C., Devizes,* Maj. 13,194

***Anderson**, David (*b.* 1953) *Lab., Blaydon,* Maj. 5,335

Anderson, Janet (*b.* 1949) *Lab., Rossendale & Darwen,* Maj. 3,676

Arbuthnot, Rt. Hon. James (*b.* 1952) *C., Hampshire North East,* Maj. 12,549

Armstrong, Rt. Hon. Hilary (*b.* 1945) *Lab., Durham North West,* Maj. 13,443

Atkins, Charlotte (*b.* 1950) *Lab., Staffordshire Moorlands,* Maj. 2,438

Atkinson, Peter (*b.* 1943) *C., Hexham,* Maj. 5,020

***Austin**, Ian (*b.* 1965) *Lab., Dudley North,* Maj. 5,432

Austin, John (*b.* 1944) *Lab., Erith & Thamesmead,* Maj. 11,500

Bacon, Richard (*b.* 1962) *C., Norfolk South,* Maj. 8,782

Bailey, Adrian (*b.* 1945) *Lab. (Co-op), West Bromwich West,* Maj. 10,894

Baird, Vera (*b.* 1950) *Lab., Redcar,* Maj. 12,116

Baker, Norman (*b.* 1957) *LD, Lewes,* Maj. 8,474

Baldry, Tony (*b.* 1950) *C., Banbury,* Maj. 10,797

***Balls**, Ed (*b.* 1967) *Lab. (Co-op), Normanton,* Maj. 10,002

***Banks**, Gordon (*b.* 1955) *Lab., Ochil & Perthshire South,* Maj. 688

Barker, Gregory (*b.* 1966) *C., Bexhill & Battle,* Maj. 13,449

***Barlow**, Celia (*b.* 1955) *Lab., Hove,* Maj. 420

Baron, John (*b.* 1959) *C., Billericay,* Maj. 11,206

Barrett, John (*b.* 1954) *LD, Edinburgh West,* Maj. 13,600

Barron, Rt. Hon. Kevin (*b.* 1946) *Lab., Rother Valley,* Maj. 14,224

Battle, Rt. Hon. John (*b.* 1951) *Lab., Leeds West,* Maj. 12,810

Bayley, Hugh (*b.* 1952) *Lab., York, City of,* Maj. 10,472

Beckett, Rt. Hon. Margaret (*b.* 1943) *Lab., Derby South,* Maj. 5,657

Begg, Anne (*b.* 1955) *Lab., Aberdeen South,* Maj. 1,348

Beith, Rt. Hon. Alan (*b.* 1943) *LD, Berwick-upon-Tweed,* Maj. 8,632

Bell, Sir Stuart (*b.* 1938) *Lab., Middlesbrough,* Maj. 12,567

Bellingham, Henry (*b.* 1955) *C., Norfolk North West,* Maj. 9,180

Benn, Rt. Hon. Hilary (*b.* 1953) *Lab., Leeds Central,* Maj. 11,866

Benton, Joe (*b.* 1933) *Lab., Bootle,* Maj. 16,357

***Benyon**, Richard (*b.* 1960) *C., Newbury,* Maj. 3,460

Bercow, John (*b.* 1963) *C., Buckingham,* Maj. 18,129

Beresford, Sir Paul (*b.* 1946) *C., Mole Valley,* Maj. 11,997

Berry, Dr Roger (*b.* 1948) *Lab., Kingswood,* Maj. 7,873

Betts, Clive (*b.* 1950) *Lab., Sheffield Attercliffe,* Maj. 15,967

***Binley**, Brian (*b.* 1942) *C., Northampton South,* Maj. 4,419

Blackman, Liz (*b.* 1949) *Lab., Erewash,* Maj. 7,084

***Blackman-Woods**, Dr Roberta (*b.* 1957) *Lab., Durham, City of,* Maj. 3,274

Blears, Rt. Hon. Hazel (*b.* 1956) *Lab., Salford,* Maj. 7,945

Blizzard, Bob (*b.* 1950) *Lab., Waveney,* Maj. 5,915

Blunkett, Rt. Hon. David (*b.* 1947) *Lab., Sheffield Brightside,* Maj. 13,644

Blunt, Crispin (*b.* 1960) *C., Reigate,* Maj. 10,988

***Bone**, Peter (*b.* 1952) *C., Wellingborough,* Maj. 687

Borrow, David (*b.* 1952) *Lab., Ribble South,* Maj. 2,184

Boswell, Tim (*b.* 1942) *C., Daventry,* Maj. 14,686

Bottomley, Peter (*b.* 1944) *C., Worthing West,* Maj. 9,379

Bradshaw, Ben (*b.* 1960) *Lab., Exeter,* Maj. 7,665

Brady, Graham (*b.* 1967) *C., Altrincham & Sale West,* Maj. 7,159

Brake, Tom (*b.* 1962) *LD, Carshalton & Wallington,* Maj. 1,068

Brazier, Julian (*b.* 1953) *C., Canterbury,* Maj. 7,471

Breed, Colin (*b.* 1947) *LD, Cornwall South East,* Maj. 6,507

Brennan, Kevin (*b.* 1959) *Lab., Cardiff West,* Maj. 8,167

***Brokenshire**, James (*b.* 1968) *C., Hornchurch,* Maj. 480

Brooke, Annette (*b.* 1947) *LD, Dorset Mid & Poole North,* Maj. 5,482

Brown, Rt. Hon. Gordon (*b.* 1951) *Lab., Kirkcaldy & Cowdenbeath,* Maj. 18,216

***Brown**, Lyn (*b.* 1960) *Lab., West Ham,* Maj. 9,801

Brown, Rt. Hon. Nick (*b.* 1950) *Lab., Newcastle upon Tyne East & Wallsend,* Maj. 7,565

Brown, Russell (*b.* 1951) *Lab., Dumfries & Galloway,* Maj. 2,922

Browne, Rt. Hon. Desmond (*b.* 1952) *Lab., Kilmarnock & Loudoun,* Maj. 8,703

***Browne**, Jeremy (*b.* 1970) *LD, Taunton,* Maj. 573

Browning, Angela (*b.* 1946) *C., Tiverton & Honiton,* Maj. 11,051

Bruce, Malcolm (*b.* 1944) *LD, Gordon,* Maj. 11,026

Bryant, Chris (*b.* 1962) *Lab., Rhondda,* Maj. 16,242

Buck, Karen (*b.* 1958) *Lab., Regent's Park & Kensington North,* Maj. 6,131

Burden, Richard (*b.* 1954) *Lab., Birmingham Northfield,* Maj. 6,454

Burgon, Colin (*b.* 1948) *Lab., Elmet,* Maj. 4,528

Burnham, Andy (*b.* 1970) *Lab., Leigh,* Maj. 17,272

Burns, Simon (*b.* 1952) *C., Chelmsford West,* Maj. 9,620

***Burrowes**, David (*b.* 1969) *C., Enfield Southgate,* Maj. 1,747

Burstow, Paul (*b.* 1962) *LD, Sutton & Cheam,* Maj. 2,846

Burt, Alistair (*b.* 1955) *C., Bedfordshire North East,* Maj. 12,251

***Burt**, Lorely (*b.* 1957) *LD, Solihull,* Maj. 279

***Butler**, Dawn (*b.* 1969) *Lab., Brent South,* Maj. 11,326

Butterfill, Sir John (*b.* 1941) *C., Bournemouth West,* Maj. 4,031

Byers, Rt. Hon. Stephen (*b.* 1953) *Lab., Tyneside North,* Maj. 15,037

Byrne, Liam (*b.* 1970) *Lab., Birmingham Hodge Hill,* Maj. 5,449

Cable, Dr Vincent (*b.* 1943) *LD, Twickenham,* Maj. 9,965

Caborn, Rt. Hon. Richard (*b.* 1943) *Lab., Sheffield Central,* Maj. 7,055

Cairns, David (*b.* 1966) *Lab., Inverclyde,* Maj. 11,259

Cameron, Rt. Hon. David (*b.* 1966) *C., Witney,* Maj. 14,156

Campbell, Alan (*b.* 1957) *Lab., Tynemouth,* Maj. 4,143

Campbell, Gregory (*b.* 1953) *DUP, Londonderry East,* Maj. 7,727

Campbell, Rt. Hon. Sir Menzies (*b.* 1941) *LD, Fife North East,* Maj. 12,571

Campbell, Ronnie (*b.* 1943) *Lab., Blyth Valley,* Maj. 8,527

Carmichael, Alistair (*b.* 1965) *LD, Orkney & Shetland,* Maj. 6,627

*****Carswell**, Douglas (*b.* 1971) *C., Harwich,* Maj. 920

Cash, Bill (*b.* 1940) *C., Stone,* Maj. 9,089

Caton, Martin (*b.* 1951) *Lab., Gower,* Maj. 6,703

Cawsey, Ian (*b.* 1960) *Lab., Brigg & Goole,* Maj. 2,894

Challen, Colin (*b.* 1953) *Lab., Morley & Rothwell,* Maj. 12,343

Chapman, Ben (*b.* 1940) *Lab., Wirral South,* Maj. 3,724

Chaytor, David (*b.* 1949) *Lab., Bury North,* Maj. 2,926

Chope, Christopher (*b.* 1947) *C., Christchurch,* Maj. 15,559

Clapham, Michael (*b.* 1943) *Lab., Barnsley West & Penistone,* Maj. 11,314

Clappison, James (*b.* 1956) *C., Hertsmere,* Maj. 11,093

*****Clark**, Greg (*b.* 1967) *C., Tunbridge Wells,* Maj. 9,988

*****Clark**, Katy (*b.* 1967) *Lab., Ayrshire North & Arran,* Maj. 11,296

Clark, Paul (*b.* 1957) *Lab., Gillingham,* Maj. 254

Clarke, Rt. Hon. Charles (*b.* 1950) *Lab., Norwich South,* Maj. 3,653

Clarke, Rt. Hon. Kenneth (*b.* 1940) *C., Rushcliffe,* Maj. 12,974

Clarke, Rt. Hon. Thomas (*b.* 1941) *Lab., Coatbridge, Chryston & Bellshill,* Maj. 19,519

*****Clegg**, Nick (*b.* 1967) *LD, Sheffield Hallam,* Maj. 8,682

Clelland, David (*b.* 1943) *Lab., Tyne Bridge,* Maj. 10,400

Clifton-Brown, Geoffrey (*b.* 1953) *C., Cotswold,* Maj. 9,688

Clwyd, Rt. Hon. Ann (*b.* 1937) *Lab., Cynon Valley,* Maj. 13,259

Coaker, Vernon (*b.* 1953) *Lab., Gedling,* Maj. 3,811

Coffey, Ann (*b.* 1946) *Lab., Stockport,* Maj. 9,163

Cohen, Harry (*b.* 1949) *Lab., Leyton & Wanstead,* Maj. 6,857

Connarty, Michael (*b.* 1947) *Lab., Linlithgow & Falkirk East,* Maj. 11,202

Conway, Derek (*b.* 1953) *C., Old Bexley & Sidcup,* Maj. 9,920

Cook, Frank (*b.* 1935) *Lab., Stockton North,* Maj. 12,437

*****Cooper**, Rosie (*b.* 1950) *Lab., Lancashire West,* Maj. 6,084

Cooper, Yvette (*b.* 1969) *Lab., Pontefract & Castleford,* Maj. 15,246

Corbyn, Jeremy (*b.* 1949) *Lab., Islington North,* Maj. 6,716

Cormack, Sir Patrick (*b.* 1939) *C., Staffordshire South,* Maj. 8,847

Cousins, Jim (*b.* 1944) *Lab., Newcastle upon Tyne Central,* Maj. 3,982

*****Cox**, Geoffrey (*b.* 1960) *C., Devon West & Torridge,* Maj. 3,236

*****Crabb**, Stephen (*b.* 1973) *C., Preseli Pembrokeshire,* Maj. 607

Crausby, David (*b.* 1946) *Lab., Bolton North East,* Maj. 4,103

*****Creagh**, Mary (*b.* 1967) *Lab., Wakefield,* Maj. 5,154

Cruddas, Jonathan (*b.* 1965) *Lab., Dagenham,* Maj. 7,605

Cryer, Ann (*b.* 1939) *Lab., Keighley,* Maj. 4,852

Cummings, John (*b.* 1943) *Lab., Easington,* Maj. 18,636

Cunningham, Jim (*b.* 1941) *Lab., Coventry South,* Maj. 6,255

Cunningham, Tony (*b.* 1952) *Lab., Workington,* Maj. 6,895

Curry, Rt. Hon. David (*b.* 1944) *C., Skipton & Ripon,* Maj. 11,620

Curtis-Thomas, Claire (*b.* 1958) *Lab., Crosby,* Maj. 5,840

Darling, Rt. Hon. Alistair (*b.* 1953) *Lab., Edinburgh South West,* Maj. 7,242

Davey, Edward (*b.* 1965) *LD, Kingston & Surbiton,* Maj. 8,966

David, Wayne (*b.* 1957) *Lab., Caerphilly,* Maj. 15,359

Davidson, Ian (*b.* 1950) *Lab. (Co-op), Glasgow South West,* Maj. 13,896

*****Davies**, Dai (*b.* 1959) *Ind., Blaenau Gwent,* Maj. 2,484

*****Davies**, David (*b.* 1970) *C., Monmouth,* Maj. 4,527

*****Davies**, Philip (*b.* 1972) *C., Shipley,* Maj. 422

‡**Davies**, Quentin (*b.* 1944) *Lab., Grantham & Stamford,* Maj. 7,445

Davis, Rt. Hon. David (*b.* 1948) *C., Haltemprice & Howden,* Maj. 5,116

Dean, Janet (*b.* 1949) *Lab., Burton,* Maj. 1,421

Denham, Rt. Hon. John (*b.* 1953) *Lab., Southampton Itchen,* Maj. 9,302

*****Devine**, Jim (*b.* 1953) *Lab., Livingston,* Maj. 2,680

Dhanda, Parmjit (*b.* 1971) *Lab., Gloucester,* Maj. 4,271

Dismore, Andrew (*b.* 1954) *Lab., Hendon,* Maj. 2,699

Djanogly, Jonathan (*b.* 1965) *C., Huntingdon,* Maj. 12,847

Dobbin, Jim (*b.* 1941) *Lab. (Co-op), Heywood & Middleton,* Maj. 11,083

Dobson, Rt. Hon. Frank (*b.* 1940) *Lab., Holborn & St Pancras,* Maj. 4,787

Dodds, Nigel (*b.* 1958) *DUP, Belfast North,* Maj. 5,188

Doherty, Pat (*b.* 1945) *SF, Tyrone West,* Maj. 5,005

‡**Donaldson**, Jeffrey (*b.* 1962) *DUP, Lagan Valley,* Maj. 14,117

Donohoe, Brian (*b.* 1948) *Lab., Ayrshire Central,* Maj. 10,423

Doran, Frank (*b.* 1949) *Lab., Aberdeen North,* Maj. 6,795

Dorrell, Rt. Hon. Stephen (*b.* 1952) *C., Charnwood,* Maj. 8,809

*****Dorries**, Nadine (*b.* 1958) *C., Bedfordshire Mid,* Maj. 11,355

Dowd, Jim (*b.* 1951) *Lab., Lewisham West,* Maj. 9,932

Drew, David (*b.* 1952) *Lab. (Co-op), Stroud,* Maj. 350

*****Duddridge**, James (*b.* 1971) *C., Rochford & Southend East,* Maj. 5,494

Duncan Smith, Rt. Hon. Iain (*b.* 1954) *C., Chingford & Woodford Green,* Maj. 10,641

Duncan, Alan (*b.* 1957) *C., Rutland & Melton,* Maj. 12,930

*****Dunne**, Philip (*b.* 1958) *C., Ludlow,* Maj. 2,027

Dunwoody, Gwyneth (*b.* 1930) *Lab., Crewe & Nantwich,* Maj. 7,078

*****Durkan**, Mark (*b.* 1960) *SDLP, Foyle,* Maj. 5,957

Eagle, Angela (*b.* 1961) *Lab., Wallasey,* Maj. 9,109

Eagle, Maria (*b.* 1961) *Lab., Liverpool Garston,* Maj. 7,193

Efford, Clive (b. 1958) Lab., Eltham, Maj. 3,276

Ellman, Louise (b. 1945) Lab. (Co-op), Liverpool Riverside, Maj. 10,214

*****Ellwood**, Tobias (b. 1966) C., Bournemouth East, Maj. 5,244

*****Engel**, Natascha (b. 1967) Lab., Derbyshire North East, Maj. 10,065

Ennis, Jeff (b. 1952) Lab., Barnsley East & Mexborough, Maj. 14,125

Etherington, Bill (b. 1941) Lab., Sunderland North, Maj. 9,995

Evans, Nigel (b. 1957) C., Ribble Valley, Maj. 14,171

†**Evennett**, David (b. 1949) C., Bexleyheath & Crayford, Maj. 4,551

Fabricant, Michael (b. 1950) C., Lichfield, Maj. 7,080

Fallon, Michael (b. 1952) C., Sevenoaks, Maj. 12,970

Farrelly, Paul (b. 1962) Lab., Newcastle-under-Lyme, Maj. 8,108

*****Farron**, Tim (b. 1970) LD, Westmorland & Lonsdale, Maj. 267

*****Featherstone**, Lynne (b. 1951) LD, Hornsey & Wood Green, Maj. 2,395

Field, Rt. Hon. Frank (b. 1942) Lab., Birkenhead, Maj. 12,934

Field, Mark (b. 1934) C., Cities of London & Westminster, Maj. 8,095

Fisher, Mark (b. 1944) Lab., Stoke-on-Trent Central, Maj. 9,774

Fitzpatrick, Jim (b. 1952) Lab., Poplar & Canning Town, Maj. 7,129

*****Flello**, Robert (b. 1966) Lab., Stoke-on-Trent South, Maj. 8,681

Flint, Caroline (b. 1961) Lab., Don Valley, Maj. 8,598

Flynn, Paul (b. 1935) Lab., Newport West, Maj. 5,458

Follett, Barbara (b. 1942) Lab., Stevenage, Maj. 3,139

Foster, Don (b. 1947) LD, Bath, Maj. 4,638

Foster, Michael (b. 1946) Lab., Hastings & Rye, Maj. 2,026

Foster, Michael (b. 1963) Lab., Worcester, Maj. 3,144

Fox, Dr Liam (b. 1961) C., Woodspring, Maj. 6,016

Francis, Dr Hywel (b. 1946) Lab., Aberavon, Maj. 13,937

Francois, Mark (b. 1965) C., Rayleigh, Maj. 14,726

†**Fraser**, Christopher (b. 1962) C., Norfolk South West, Maj. 10,086

Gale, Roger (b. 1943) C., Thanet North, Maj. 7,634

†‡**Galloway**, George (b. 1954) Respect, Bethnal Green & Bow, Maj. 823

Gapes, Mike (b. 1952) Lab. (Co-op), Ilford South, Maj. 9,228

Gardiner, Barry (b. 1957) Lab., Brent North, Maj. 5,641

Garnier, Edward (b. 1952) C., Harborough, Maj. 3,892

*****Gauke**, David (b. 1971) C., Hertfordshire South West, Maj. 8,473

George, Andrew (b. 1958) LD, St Ives, Maj. 11,609

George, Rt. Hon. Bruce (b. 1942) Lab., Walsall South, Maj. 7,946

Gerrard, Neil (b. 1942) Lab., Walthamstow, Maj. 7,993

Gibb, Nick (b. 1960) C., Bognor Regis & Littlehampton, Maj. 7,822

Gibson, Dr Ian (b. 1938) Lab., Norwich North, Maj. 5,459

Gidley, Sandra (b. 1957) LD, Romsey, Maj. 125

Gildernew, Michelle (b. 1970) SF, Fermanagh & South Tyrone, Maj. 4,582

Gillan, Cheryl (b. 1952) C., Chesham & Amersham, Maj. 13,798

Gilroy, Linda (b. 1949) Lab. (Co-op), Plymouth Sutton, Maj. 4,109

Godsiff, Roger (b. 1946) Lab., Birmingham Sparkbrook & Small Heath, Maj. 3,289

Goggins, Paul (b. 1953) Lab., Wythenshawe & Sale East, Maj. 10,827

*****Goldsworthy**, Julia (b. 1978) LD, Falmouth & Camborne, Maj. 1,886

*****Goodman**, Helen (b. 1958) Lab., Bishop Auckland, Maj. 10,047

Goodman, Paul (b. 1960) C., Wycombe, Maj. 7,051

*****Goodwill**, Robert (b. 1956) C., Scarborough & Whitby, Maj. 1,245

*****Gove**, Michael (b. 1967) C., Surrey Heath, Maj. 10,845

Gray, James (b. 1954) C., Wiltshire North, Maj. 5,303

Grayling, Chris (b. 1962) C., Epsom & Ewell, Maj. 16,447

Green, Damian (b. 1956) C., Ashford, Maj. 13,298

*****Greening**, Justine (b. 1969) C., Putney, Maj. 1,766

Greenway, John (b. 1946) C., Ryedale, Maj. 10,469

Grieve, Dominic (b. 1956) C., Beaconsfield, Maj. 15,253

*****Griffith**, Nia (b. 1956) Lab., Llanelli, Maj. 7,234

Griffiths, Nigel (b. 1955) Lab., Edinburgh South, Maj. 405

Grogan, John (b. 1961) Lab., Selby, Maj. 467

Gummer, Rt. Hon. John (b. 1939) C., Suffolk Coastal, Maj. 9,685

*****Gwynne**, Andrew (b. 1974) Lab., Denton & Reddish, Maj. 13,498

Hague, Rt. Hon. William (b. 1961) C., Richmond (Yorks), Maj. 17,807

Hain, Rt. Hon. Peter (b. 1950) Lab., Neath, Maj. 12,710

Hall, Mike (b. 1952) Lab., Weaver Vale, Maj. 6,855

Hall, Patrick (b. 1951) Lab., Bedford, Maj. 3,383

Hamilton, David (b. 1950) Lab., Midlothian, Maj. 7,265

Hamilton, Fabian (b. 1955) Lab., Leeds North East, Maj. 5,262

Hammond, Philip (b. 1955) C., Runnymede & Weybridge, Maj. 12,349

*****Hammond**, Stephen (b. 1962) C., Wimbledon, Maj. 2,301

Hancock, Mike (b. 1946) LD, Portsmouth South, Maj. 3,362

*****Hands**, Greg (b. 1965) C., Hammersmith & Fulham, Maj. 5,029

Hanson, David (b. 1957) Lab., Delyn, Maj. 6,644

Harman, Rt. Hon. Harriet (b. 1950) Lab., Camberwell & Peckham, Maj. 13,483

*****Harper**, Mark (b. 1970) C., Forest of Dean, Maj. 2,049

Harris, Dr Evan (b. 1965) LD, Oxford West & Abingdon, Maj. 7,683

Harris, Tom (b. 1964) Lab., Glasgow South, Maj. 10,832

Harvey, Nick (b. 1961) LD, Devon North, Maj. 4,972

Haselhurst, Rt. Hon. Sir Alan (b. 1937) C., Saffron Walden, Maj. 13,008

Havard, Dai (b. 1949) Lab., Merthyr Tydfil & Rhymney, Maj. 13,934

Hayes, John (b. 1958) C., South Holland & The Deepings, Maj. 15,780

Heal, Sylvia (b. 1942) Lab., Halesowen & Rowley Regis, Maj. 4,337

Heald, Oliver (b. 1954) C., Hertfordshire North East, Maj. 9,138

Healey, John (b. 1960) Lab., Wentworth, Maj. 15,056

Heath, David (b. 1954) LD, Somerton & Frome, Maj. 812

Heathcoat-Amory, Rt. Hon. David (b. 1949) C., Wells, Maj. 3,040

*****Hemming**, John (b. 1960) LD, Birmingham Yardley, Maj. 2,672

Henderson, Doug (b. 1949) Lab., Newcastle upon Tyne North, Maj. 7,023

Hendrick, Mark (b. 1958) Lab. (Co-op), Preston, Maj. 9,407

Hendry, Charles (b. 1959) C., Wealden, Maj. 15,921

Hepburn, Stephen (b. 1959) Lab., Jarrow, Maj. 13,904

Heppell, John (b. 1948) Lab., Nottingham East, Maj. 6,939

*Herbert, Nick (b. 1963) C., Arundel & South Downs, Maj. 11,309

Hermon, Lady Sylvia (b. 1956) UUP, Down North, Maj. 4,944

Hesford, Stephen (b. 1957) Lab., Wirral West, Maj. 1,097

Hewitt, Rt. Hon. Patricia (b. 1948) Lab., Leicester West, Maj. 9,070

Heyes, David (b. 1946) Lab., Ashton-under-Lyne, Maj. 13,952

Hill, Rt. Hon. Keith (b. 1943) Lab., Streatham, Maj. 7,466

*Hillier, Meg (b. 1969) Lab. (Co-op), Hackney South & Shoreditch, Maj. 10,204

Hoban, Mark (b. 1964) C., Fareham, Maj. 11,702

Hodge, Rt. Hon. Margaret (b. 1944) Lab., Barking, Maj. 8,883

*Hodgson, Sharon (b. 1966) Lab., Gateshead East & Washington West, Maj. 13,407

Hoey, Kate (b. 1946) Lab., Vauxhall, Maj. 9,977

Hogg, Rt. Hon. Douglas (b. 1945) C., Sleaford & North Hykeham, Maj. 12,705

*Hollobone, Philip (b. 1964) C., Kettering, Maj. 3,301

*Holloway, Adam (b. 1965) C., Gravesham, Maj. 654

Holmes, Paul (b. 1957) LD, Chesterfield, Maj. 3,045

Hood, Jimmy (b. 1948) Lab., Lanark & Hamilton East, Maj. 11,947

Hoon, Rt. Hon. Geoff (b. 1953) Lab., Ashfield, Maj. 10,213

Hope, Phil (b. 1955) Lab. (Co-op), Corby, Maj. 1,517

Hopkins, Kelvin (b. 1941) Lab., Luton North, Maj. 6,487

Horam, John (b. 1939) C., Orpington, Maj. 4,947

*Horwood, Martin (b. 1962) LD, Cheltenham, Maj. 2,303

*Hosie, Stewart (b. 1963) SNP, Dundee East, Maj. 383

Howard, Rt. Hon. Michael (b. 1941) C., Folkestone & Hythe, Maj. 11,680

*Howarth, David (b. 1958) LD, Cambridge, Maj. 4,339

Howarth, Rt. Hon. George (b. 1949) Lab., Knowsley North & Sefton East, Maj. 16,269

Howarth, Gerald (b. 1947) C., Aldershot, Maj. 5,334

Howells, Dr Kim (b. 1946) Lab., Pontypridd, Maj. 13,191

Hoyle, Lindsay (b. 1957) Lab., Chorley, Maj. 7,625

Hughes, Rt. Hon. Beverley (b. 1950) Lab., Stretford & Urmston, Maj. 7,851

Hughes, Simon (b. 1951) LD, Southwark North & Bermondsey, Maj. 5,406

*Huhne, Chris (b. 1954) LD, Eastleigh, Maj. 568

Humble, Joan (b. 1951) Lab., Blackpool North & Fleetwood, Maj. 5,062

*Hunt, Jeremy (b. 1966) C., Surrey South West, Maj. 5,711

*Hunter, Mark (b. 1957) LD, Cheadle, Maj. 3,657

*Hurd, Nick (b. 1962) C., Ruislip-Northwood, Maj. 8,910

Hutton, Rt. Hon. John (b. 1955) Lab., Barrow & Furness, Maj. 6,037

Iddon, Dr Brian (b. 1940) Lab., Bolton South East, Maj. 11,638

Illsley, Eric (b. 1955) Lab., Barnsley Central, Maj. 12,732

Ingram, Rt. Hon. Adam (b. 1947) Lab., East Kilbride, Strathaven & Lesmahagow, Maj. 14,723

Irranca-Davies, Huw (b. 1963) Lab., Ogmore, Maj. 13,703

Jack, Rt. Hon. Michael (b. 1946) C., Fylde, Maj. 12,459

Jackson, Glenda (b. 1936) Lab., Hampstead & Highgate, Maj. 3,729

*Jackson, Stewart (b. 1965) C., Peterborough, Maj. 2,740

*James, Sian (b. 1959) Lab., Swansea East, Maj. 11,249

Jenkin, Bernard (b. 1959) C., Essex North, Maj. 10,903

Jenkins, Brian (b. 1942) Lab., Tamworth, Maj. 2,569

Johnson, Boris (b. 1964) C., Henley, Maj. 12,793

Johnson, Rt. Hon. Alan (b. 1950) Lab., Hull West & Hessle, Maj. 9,450

*Johnson, Diana (b. 1966) Lab., Hull North, Maj. 7,351

*Jones, David (b. 1952) C., Clwyd West, Maj. 133

Jones, Helen (b. 1954) Lab., Warrington North, Maj. 12,204

Jones, Kevan (b. 1964) Lab., Durham North, Maj. 16,781

Jones, Dr Lynne (b. 1951) Lab., Birmingham Selly Oak, Maj. 8,851

Jones, Martyn (b. 1947) Lab., Clwyd South, Maj. 6,348

Jowell, Rt. Hon. Tessa (b. 1947) Lab., Dulwich & West Norwood, Maj. 8,807

Joyce, Eric (b. 1960) Lab., Falkirk, Maj. 13,475

Kaufman, Rt. Hon. Sir Gerald (b. 1930) Lab., Manchester Gorton, Maj. 5,808

*Kawczynski, Daniel (b. 1972) C., Shrewsbury & Atcham, Maj. 1,808

Keeble, Sally (b. 1951) Lab., Northampton North, Maj. 3,960

*Keeley, Barbara (b. 1952) Lab., Worsley, Maj. 9,368

Keen, Alan (b. 1937) Lab. (Co-op), Feltham & Heston, Maj. 6,820

Keen, Ann (b. 1948) Lab., Brentford & Isleworth, Maj. 4,411

Keetch, Paul (b. 1961) LD, Hereford, Maj. 962

Kelly, Rt. Hon. Ruth (b. 1968) Lab., Bolton West, Maj. 2,064

Kemp, Fraser (b. 1958) Lab., Houghton & Washington East, Maj. 16,065

Kennedy, Rt. Hon. Charles (b. 1959) LD, Ross, Skye & Lochaber, Maj. 14,249

Kennedy, Rt. Hon. Jane (b. 1958) Lab., Liverpool Wavertree, Maj. 5,173

Key, Robert (b. 1945) C., Salisbury, Maj. 11,142

*Khan, Sadiq (b. 1970) Lab., Tooting, Maj. 5,381

Kidney, David (b. 1955) Lab., Stafford, Maj. 2,121

Kilfoyle, Peter (b. 1946) Lab., Liverpool Walton, Maj. 15,957

Kirkbride, Julie (b. 1960) C., Bromsgrove, Maj. 10,080

Knight, Rt. Hon. Greg (b. 1949) C., Yorkshire East, Maj. 6,283

Knight, Jim (b. 1965) Lab., Dorset South, Maj. 1,812

*Kramer, Susan (b. 1950) LD, Richmond Park, Maj. 3,731

Kumar, Dr Ashok (b. 1956) Lab., Middlesbrough South & Cleveland East, Maj. 8,000

Ladyman, Dr Stephen (b. 1952) Lab., Thanet South, Maj. 664

Laing, Eleanor (b. 1958) C., Epping Forest, Maj. 14,358

Lait, Jacqui (b. 1947) C., Beckenham, Maj. 8,401

Lamb, Norman (b. 1957) LD, Norfolk North, Maj. 10,606

Lammy, David (b. 1972) Lab., Tottenham, Maj. 13,034

*Lancaster, Mark (b. 1970) C., Milton Keynes North East, Maj. 1,665

Lansley, Andrew (b. 1956) C., Cambridgeshire South, Maj. 8,001

Laws, David (b. 1965) LD, Yeovil, Maj. 8,562

Laxton, Bob (b. 1944) Lab., Derby North, Maj. 3,757

Lazarowicz, Mark (b. 1953) Lab. (Co-op), Edinburgh North & Leith, Maj. 2,153

*Leech, John (b. 1971) LD, Manchester Withington, Maj. 667

Leigh, Edward (b. 1950) C., Gainsborough, Maj. 8,003

Lepper, David (b. 1945) Lab. (Co-op), Brighton Pavilion, Maj. 5,030

Letwin, Rt. Hon. Oliver (b. 1956) C., Dorset West, Maj. 2,461

Levitt, Tom (b. 1954) Lab., High Peak, Maj. 735

Lewis, Ivan (b. 1967) Lab., Bury South, Maj. 8,912

Lewis, Dr Julian (b. 1951) C., New Forest East, Maj. 6,551

Liddell-Grainger, Ian (b. 1959) C., Bridgwater, Maj. 8,469

Lidington, David (b. 1956) C., Aylesbury, Maj. 11,065

Lilley, Rt. Hon. Peter (b. 1943) C., Hitchin & Harpenden, Maj. 11,393

Linton, Martin (b. 1944) Lab., Battersea, Maj. 163

Lloyd, Tony (b. 1950) Lab., Manchester Central, Maj. 9,776

Llwyd, Elfyn (b. 1951) PC, Meirionnydd Nant Conwy, Maj. 6,614

Lord, Sir Michael (b. 1938) C., Suffolk Central & Ipswich North, Maj. 7,856

Loughton, Tim (b. 1962) C., Worthing East & Shoreham, Maj. 8,183

Love, Andy (b. 1949) Lab. (Co-op), Edmonton, Maj. 8,075

Lucas, Ian (b. 1960) Lab., Wrexham, Maj. 6,819

Luff, Peter (b. 1955) C., Worcestershire Mid, Maj. 13,327

McAvoy, Rt. Hon. Thomas (b. 1943) Lab. (Co-op), Rutherglen & Hamilton West, Maj. 16,112

McCabe, Stephen (b. 1955) Lab., Birmingham Hall Green, Maj. 5,714

McCafferty, Christine (b. 1945) Lab., Calder Valley, Maj. 1,367

*McCarthy, Kerry (b. 1965) Lab., Bristol East, Maj. 8,621

*McCarthy-Fry, Sarah (b. 1955) Lab. (Co-op), Portsmouth North, Maj. 1,139

McCartney, Rt. Hon. Ian (b. 1951) Lab., Makerfield, Maj. 18,149

†McCrea, Dr William (b. 1948) DUP, Antrim South, Maj. 3,448

McDonagh, Siobhain (b. 1960) Lab., Mitcham & Morden, Maj. 12,560

*McDonnell, Dr Alasdair (b. 1949) SDLP, Belfast South, Maj. 1,235

McDonnell, John (b. 1951) Lab., Hayes & Harlington, Maj. 10,847

MacDougall, John (b. 1947) Lab., Glenrothes, Maj. 10,664

*McFadden, Pat (b. 1965) Lab., Wolverhampton South East, Maj. 10,495

McFall, Rt. Hon. John (b. 1944) Lab. (Co-op), Dunbartonshire West, Maj. 12,553

*McGovern, James (b. 1956) Lab., Dundee West, Maj. 5,379

McGrady, Edward (b. 1935) SDLP, Down South, Maj. 9,140

McGuinness, Martin (b. 1950) SF, Ulster Mid, Maj. 10,976

McGuire, Anne (b. 1949) Lab., Stirling, Maj. 4,767

McIntosh, Anne (b. 1954) C., Vale of York, Maj. 13,712

McIsaac, Shona (b. 1960) Lab., Cleethorpes, Maj. 2,642

Mackay, Rt. Hon. Andrew (b. 1949) C., Bracknell, Maj. 12,036

McKechin, Ann (b. 1961) Lab., Glasgow North, Maj. 3,338

McKenna, Rosemary (b. 1941) Lab., Cumbernauld, Kilsyth & Kirkintilloch East, Maj. 11,562

Mackinlay, Andrew (b. 1949) Lab., Thurrock, Maj. 6,375

Maclean, Rt. Hon. David (b. 1953) C., Penrith & The Border, Maj. 11,904

McLoughlin, Rt. Hon. Patrick (b. 1957) C., Derbyshire West, Maj. 10,753

*MacNeil, Angus (b. 1970) SNP, Na h-Eileanan an Iar, Maj. 1,441

McNulty, Tony (b. 1958) Lab., Harrow East, Maj. 4,730

MacShane, Rt. Hon. Denis (b. 1948) Lab., Rotherham, Maj. 10,681

Mactaggart, Fiona (b. 1953) Lab., Slough, Maj. 7,851

Mahmood, Khalid (b. 1961) Lab., Birmingham Perry Barr, Maj. 7,948

*Main, Anne (b. 1957) C., St Albans, Maj. 1,361

*Malik, Shahid (b. 1967) Lab., Dewsbury, Maj. 4,615

Malins, Humfrey (b. 1945) C., Woking, Maj. 6,612

Mallaber, Judith (b. 1951) Lab., Amber Valley, Maj. 5,275

Mann, John (b. 1960) Lab., Bassetlaw, Maj. 10,837

Maples, John (b. 1943) C., Stratford-upon-Avon, Maj. 12,184

Marris, Rob (b. 1955) Lab., Wolverhampton South West, Maj. 2,879

Marsden, Gordon (b. 1953) Lab., Blackpool South, Maj. 7,922

Marshall, David (b. 1941) Lab., Glasgow East, Maj. 13,507

Marshall-Andrews, Bob (b. 1944) Lab., Medway, Maj. 213

Martin, Rt. Hon. Michael (b. 1945) The Speaker, Glasgow North East, Maj. 10,134

Martlew, Eric (b. 1949) Lab., Carlisle, Maj. 5,695

Mates, Rt. Hon. Michael (b. 1934) C., Hampshire East, Maj. 5,509

Maude, Rt. Hon. Francis (b. 1953) C., Horsham, Maj. 12,627

May, Rt. Hon. Theresa (b. 1956) C., Maidenhead, Maj. 6,231

Meacher, Rt. Hon. Michael (b. 1939) Lab., Oldham West & Royton, Maj. 10,454

Meale, Alan (b. 1949) Lab., Mansfield, Maj. 11,365

Mercer, Patrick (b. 1956) C., Newark, Maj. 6,464

Merron, Gillian (b. 1959) Lab., Lincoln, Maj. 4,614

Michael, Rt. Hon. Alun (b. 1943) Lab. (Co-op), Cardiff South & Penarth, Maj. 9,237

Milburn, Rt. Hon. Alan (b. 1958) Lab., Darlington, Maj. 10,404

Miliband, Rt. Hon. David (b. 1966) Lab., South Shields, Maj. 12,312

*Miliband, Edward (b. 1969) Lab., Doncaster North, Maj. 12,656

Miller, Andrew (b. 1949) Lab., Ellesmere Port & Neston, Maj. 6,486

*Miller, Maria (b. 1964) C., Basingstoke, Maj. 4,680

*Milton, Anne (b. 1955) C., Guildford, Maj. 347

Mitchell, Andrew (b. 1956) C., Sutton Coldfield, Maj. 12,283

Mitchell, Austin (b. 1934) Lab., Great Grimsby, Maj. 7,654

Moffat, Anne (b. 1958) Lab., East Lothian, Maj. 7,620

Moffatt, Laura (b. 1954) Lab., Crawley, Maj. 37

Mole, Chris (b. 1958) Lab., Ipswich, Maj. 5,332

*Moon, Madeleine (b. 1950) Lab., Bridgend, Maj. 6,523

Moore, Michael (b. 1965) LD, Berwickshire, Roxburgh & Selkirk, Maj. 5,901

Moran, Margaret (b. 1955) Lab., Luton South, Maj. 5,650

*Morden, Jessica (b. 1968) Lab., Newport East, Maj. 6,838

Morgan, Julie (b. 1944) Lab., Cardiff North, Maj. 1,146

Morley, Elliot (b. 1952) Lab., Scunthorpe, Maj. 8,963

Moss, Malcolm (b. 1943) C., Cambridgeshire North East, Maj. 8,901

Mountford, Kali (b. 1954) Lab., Colne Valley, Maj. 1,501

Mudie, George (b. 1945) Lab., Leeds East, Maj. 11,578

*Mulholland, Greg (b. 1970) LD, Leeds North West, Maj. 1,877

Mullin, Chris (b. 1947) Lab., Sunderland South, Maj. 11,059

*Mundell, David (b. 1962) C., Dumfriesshire, Clydesdale & Tweeddale, Maj. 1,738

Munn, Meg (b. 1959) Lab. (Co-op), Sheffield Heeley, Maj. 11,370

*Murphy, Conor (b. 1963) SF, Newry & Armagh, Maj. 8,195

Murphy, Denis (b. 1948) Lab., Wansbeck, Maj. 10,581

Murphy, Jim (b. 1967) Lab., Renfrewshire East, Maj. 6,657

Murphy, Rt. Hon. Paul (b. 1948) Lab., Torfaen, Maj. 14,791

Murrison, Dr Andrew (b. 1961) C., Westbury, Maj. 5,349

Naysmith, Dr Doug (b. 1941) Lab. (Co-op), Bristol North West, Maj. 8,962

*Neill, Bob (b. 1952) C., Bromley & Chislehurst, Maj. 633

*Newmark, Brooks (b. 1958) C., Braintree, Maj. 3,893

Norris, Dan (b. 1960) Lab., Wansdyke, Maj. 1,839

Oaten, Mark (b. 1964) LD, Winchester, Maj. 7,476

O'Brien, Mike (b. 1954) Lab., Warwickshire North, Maj. 7,553

O'Brien, Stephen (b. 1957) C., Eddisbury, Maj. 6,195

O'Hara, Eddie (b. 1937) Lab., Knowsley South, Maj. 17,688

Olner, Bill (b. 1942) Lab., Nuneaton, Maj. 2,280

Opik, Lembit (b. 1965) LD, Montgomeryshire, Maj. 7,173

Osborne, George (b. 1971) C., Tatton, Maj. 11,731

Osborne, Sandra (b. 1956) Lab., Ayr, Carrick & Cumnock, Maj. 9,997

Ottaway, Richard (b. 1945) C., Croydon South, Maj. 13,528

Owen, Albert (b. 1960) Lab., Ynys Mon, Maj. 1,242

Paice, James (b. 1949) C., Cambridgeshire South East, Maj. 8,624

Paisley, Revd Rt. Hon. Ian (b. 1926) DUP, Antrim North, Maj. 17,965

Palmer, Dr Nick (b. 1950) Lab., Broxtowe, Maj. 2,296

Paterson, Owen (b. 1956) C., Shropshire North, Maj. 11,020

Pearson, Ian (b. 1959) Lab., Dudley South, Maj. 4,244

*Pelling, Andrew (b. 1959) C., Croydon Central, Maj. 75

*Penning, Michael (b. 1957) C., Hemel Hempstead, Maj. 499

*Penrose, John (b. 1964) C., Weston-Super-Mare, Maj. 2,079

Pickles, Eric (b. 1952) C., Brentwood & Ongar, Maj. 11,612

Plaskitt, James (b. 1954) Lab., Warwick & Leamington, Maj. 266

Pope, Greg (b. 1960) Lab., Hyndburn, Maj. 5,587

Pound, Stephen (b. 1948) Lab., Ealing North, Maj. 7,059

Prentice, Bridget (b. 1952) Lab., Lewisham East, Maj. 6,751

Prentice, Gordon (b. 1951) Lab., Pendle, Maj. 2,180

Prescott, Rt. Hon. John (b. 1938) Lab., Hull East, Maj. 11,747

Price, Adam (b. 1968) PC, Carmarthen East & Dinefwr, Maj. 6,718

Primarolo, Rt. Hon. Dawn (b. 1954) Lab., Bristol South, Maj. 11,142

Prisk, Mark (b. 1962) C., Hertford & Stortford, Maj. 13,097

*Pritchard, Mark (b. 1966) C., The Wrekin, Maj. 942

Prosser, Gwyn (b. 1943) Lab., Dover, Maj. 4,941

Pugh, Dr John (b. 1948) LD, Southport, Maj. 3,838

Purchase, Ken (b. 1939) Lab. (Co-op), Wolverhampton North East, Maj. 8,156

Purnell, James (b. 1970) Lab., Stalybridge & Hyde, Maj. 8,348

Rammell, Bill (b. 1959) Lab., Harlow, Maj. 97

Randall, John (b. 1955) C., Uxbridge, Maj. 6,171

Raynsford, Rt. Hon. Nick (b. 1945) Lab., Greenwich & Woolwich, Maj. 10,146

Redwood, Rt. Hon. John (b. 1951) C., Wokingham, Maj. 7,240

Reed, Andy (b. 1964) Lab. (Co-op), Loughborough, Maj. 1,996

*Reed, Jamie (b. 1973) Lab., Copeland, Maj. 6,320

Reid, Alan (b. 1954) LD, Argyll & Bute, Maj. 5,636

Reid, Rt. Hon. Dr John (b. 1947) Lab., Airdrie & Shotts, Maj. 14,084

*Rennie, Willie (b. 1967) LD, Dunfermline & Fife West, Maj. 1,800

†Rifkind, Rt. Hon. Sir Malcolm (b. 1946) C., Kensington & Chelsea, Maj. 12,418

*Riordan, Linda (b. 1953) Lab. (Co-op), Halifax, Maj. 3,417

Robathan, Andrew (b. 1951) C., Blaby, Maj. 7,873

Robertson, Angus (b. 1969) SNP, Moray, Maj. 5,676

Robertson, Hugh (b. 1962) C., Faversham & Kent Mid, Maj. 8,720

Robertson, John (b. 1952) Lab., Glasgow North West, Maj. 10,093

Robertson, Laurence (b. 1958) C., Tewkesbury, Maj. 9,892

Robinson, Geoffrey (b. 1938) Lab., Coventry North West, Maj. 9,315

Robinson, Iris (b. 1949) DUP, Strangford, Maj. 13,049

Robinson, Peter (b. 1948) DUP, Belfast East, Maj. 5,877

*Rogerson, Dan (b. 1975) LD, Cornwall North, Maj. 3,076

Rooney, Terry (b. 1950) Lab., Bradford North, Maj. 3,511

Rosindell, Andrew (b. 1966) C., Romford, Maj. 11,589

*Rowen, Paul (b. 1955) LD, Rochdale, Maj. 442

Roy, Frank (b. 1958) Lab., Motherwell & Wishaw, Maj. 15,222

Ruane, Christopher (b. 1958) Lab., Vale of Clwyd, Maj. 4,669

Ruddock, Joan (b. 1943) Lab., Lewisham Deptford, Maj. 11,811

Ruffley, David (b. 1962) C., Bury St Edmunds, Maj. 9,930

Russell, Bob (b. 1946) LD, Colchester, Maj. 6,277

Russell, Christine (b. 1945) Lab., Chester, City of, Maj. 915

Ryan, Joan (b. 1955) Lab., Enfield North, Maj. 1,920

Salmond, Alex (b. 1954) SNP, Banff & Buchan, Maj. 11,837

Salter, Martin (b. 1954) Lab., Reading West, Maj. 4,682

Sanders, Adrian (b. 1959) LD, Torbay, Maj. 2,029

Sarwar, Mohammad (b. 1952) Lab., Glasgow Central, Maj. 8,531

*Scott, Lee (b. 1956) C., Ilford North, Maj. 1,653

*Seabeck, Alison (b. 1954) Lab., Plymouth Devonport, Maj. 8,103

Selous, Andrew (b. 1962) C., Bedfordshire South West, Maj. 8,277

*Shapps, Grant (b. 1968) C., Welwyn Hatfield, Maj. 5,946

Sharma, Virendra (b. 1947) Lab., Ealing Southall, Maj. 5,070

Shaw, Jonathan (b. 1966) Lab., Chatham & Aylesford, Maj. 2,332

Sheerman, Barry (b. 1940) Lab. (Co-op), Huddersfield, Maj. 8,351

Shepherd, Richard (b. 1942) C., Aldridge-Brownhills, Maj. 5,507

Sheridan, James (b. 1952) Lab., Paisley & Renfrewshire North, Maj. 11,001

‡Short, Rt. Hon. Clare (b. 1946) Ind., Birmingham Ladywood, Maj. 6,801

Simmonds, Mark (b. 1964) C., Boston & Skegness, Maj. 5,907

Simon, Sion (b. 1969) Lab., Birmingham Erdington, Maj. 9,575

Simpson, Alan (b. 1948) Lab., Nottingham South, Maj. 7,486

*Simpson, David (b. 1959) DUP, Upper Bann, Maj. 5,298

Simpson, Keith (b. 1949) C., Norfolk Mid, Maj. 7,560

Singh, Marsha (b. 1954) Lab., Bradford West, Maj. 3,026

Skinner, Dennis (b. 1932) Lab., Bolsover, Maj. 18,437

*Slaughter, Andrew (b. 1960) Lab., Ealing, Acton & Shepherd's Bush, Maj. 5,520

Smith, Rt. Hon. Andrew (b. 1951) Lab., Oxford East, Maj. 963

*Smith, Angela C. (b. 1961) Lab., Sheffield Hillsborough, Maj. 11,243

Smith, Angela E. (b. 1959) Lab. (Co-op), Basildon, Maj. 3,142

Smith, Geraldine (b. 1961) Lab., Morecambe & Lunesdale, Maj. 4,768

Smith, Rt. Hon. Jacqui (b. 1962) Lab., Redditch, Maj. 2,716

Smith, John (b. 1951) Lab., Vale of Glamorgan, Maj. 1,808

Smith, Sir Robert (b. 1958) LD, Aberdeenshire West & Kincardine, Maj. 7,471

*Snelgrove, Anne (b. 1957) Lab., Swindon South , Maj. 1,353

Soames, Hon. Nicholas (b. 1948) C., Sussex Mid, Maj. 5,890

*Soulsby, Sir Peter (b. 1948) Lab., Leicester South, Maj. 3,717

Southworth, Helen (b. 1956) Lab., Warrington South, Maj. 3,515

Spellar, Rt. Hon. John (b. 1947) Lab., Warley, Maj. 10,147

Spelman, Caroline (b. 1958) C., Meriden, Maj. 7,009

Spicer, Sir Michael (b. 1943) C., Worcestershire West, Maj. 2,475

Spink, Dr Robert (b. 1948) C., Castle Point, Maj. 8,201

Spring, Richard (b. 1946) C., Suffolk West, Maj. 8,909

Stanley, Rt. Hon. Sir John (b. 1942) C., Tonbridge & Malling, Maj. 13,352

Starkey, Dr Phyllis (b. 1947) Lab., Milton Keynes South West, Maj. 4,010

Steen, Anthony (b. 1939) C., Totnes, Maj. 1,947

Stewart, Ian (b. 1950) Lab., Eccles, Maj. 12,886

Stoate, Dr Howard (b. 1954) Lab., Dartford, Maj. 706

Strang, Rt. Hon. Gavin (b. 1943) Lab., Edinburgh East, Maj. 6,202

Straw, Rt. Hon. Jack (b. 1946) Lab., Blackburn, Maj. 8,009

Streeter, Gary (b. 1955) C., Devon South West, Maj. 10,141

Stringer, Graham (b. 1950) Lab., Manchester Blackley, Maj. 12,027

Stuart, Gisela (b. 1955) Lab., Birmingham Edgbaston, Maj. 2,349

*Stuart, Graham (b. 1962) C., Beverley & Holderness, Maj. 2,580

Stunell, Andrew (b. 1942) LD, Hazel Grove, Maj. 7,748

Sutcliffe, Gerry (b. 1953) Lab., Bradford South, Maj. 9,167

Swayne, Desmond (b. 1956) C., New Forest West, Maj. 17,285

*Swinson, Jo (b. 1980) LD, Dunbartonshire East, Maj. 4,061

Swire, Hugo (b. 1959) C., Devon East, Maj. 7,936

Syms, Robert (b. 1956) C., Poole, Maj. 5,988

Tami, Mark (b. 1963) Lab., Alyn & Deeside, Maj. 8,378

Tapsell, Sir Peter (b. 1930) C., Louth & Horncastle, Maj. 9,896

Taylor, Dari (b. 1944) Lab., Stockton South, Maj. 6,139

Taylor, David (b. 1946) Lab. (Co-op), Leicestershire North West, Maj. 4,477

Taylor, Ian (b. 1945) C., Esher & Walton, Maj. 7,727

Taylor, Matthew (b. 1963) LD, Truro & St Austell, Maj. 7,403

Taylor, Dr Richard (b. 1935) KHHC, Wyre Forest, Maj. 5,250

Teather, Sarah (b. 1974) LD, Brent East, Maj. 2,712

Thomas, Gareth (b. 1967) Lab. (Co-op), Harrow West, Maj. 2,028

*Thornberry, Emily (b. 1960) Lab., Islington South & Finsbury, Maj. 484

Thurso, John (b. 1953) LD, Caithness, Sutherland & Easter Ross, Maj. 8,168

Timms, Stephen (b. 1955) Lab., East Ham, Maj. 13,155

Tipping, Paddy (b. 1949) Lab., Sherwood, Maj. 6,652

Todd, Mark (b. 1954) Lab., Derbyshire South, Maj. 4,495

Touhig, Don (b. 1947) Lab. (Co-op), Islwyn, Maj. 15,740

Tredinnick, David (b. 1950) C., Bosworth, Maj. 5,319

Trickett, Jon (b. 1950) Lab., Hemsworth, Maj. 13,481

Truswell, Paul (b. 1955) Lab., Pudsey, Maj. 5,870

Turner, Andrew (b. 1953) C., Isle of Wight, Maj. 12,978

Turner, Dr Desmond (b. 1939) Lab., Brighton Kemptown, Maj. 2,737

Turner, Neil (b. 1945) Lab., Wigan, Maj. 11,767

Twigg, Derek (b. 1959) Lab., Halton, Maj. 14,606

Tyrie, Andrew (b. 1957) C., Chichester, Maj. 10,860

*Ussher, Kitty (b. 1971) Lab., Burnley, Maj. 5,778

*Vaizey, Ed (b. 1969) C., Wantage, Maj. 8,017

*Vara, Shailesh (b. 1960) C., Cambridgeshire North West, Maj. 9,833

Vaz, Keith (b. 1956) Lab., Leicester East, Maj. 15,876

Viggers, Peter (b. 1938) C., Gosport, Maj. 5,730

*Villiers, Theresa (b. 1968) C., Chipping Barnet, Maj. 5,960

Vis, Dr Rudi (b. 1941) Lab., Finchley & Golders Green, Maj. 741

*Walker, Charles (b. 1967) C., Broxbourne, Maj. 11,509

*Wallace, Ben (b. 1970) C., Lancaster & Wyre, Maj. 4,171

Walley, Joan (b. 1949) Lab., Stoke-on-Trent North, Maj. 10,036

Walter, Robert (b. 1948) C., Dorset North, Maj. 2,244

*Waltho, Lynda (b. 1960) Lab., Stourbridge, Maj. 407

Ward, Claire (b. 1972) Lab., Watford, Maj. 1,148

Wareing, Robert (b. 1930) Lab., Liverpool West Derby, Maj. 15,225

Waterson, Nigel (b. 1950) C., Eastbourne, Maj. 1,124

Watkinson, Angela (b. 1941) C., Upminster, Maj. 6,042

Watson, Tom (b. 1967) Lab., West Bromwich East, Maj. 11,652

Watts, Dave (b. 1951) Lab., St Helens North, Maj. 13,962

Webb, Prof. Steve (b. 1965) LD, Northavon, Maj. 11,033

Weir, Michael (b. 1957) SNP, Angus, Maj. 1,601

Whitehead, Dr Alan (b. 1950) Lab., Southampton Test, Maj. 7,018

Whittingdale, John (*b.* 1959) *C., Maldon & Chelmsford East,* Maj. 12,573

Wicks, Malcolm (*b.* 1947) *Lab., Croydon North,* Maj. 13,888

Widdecombe, Rt. Hon. Ann (*b.* 1947) *C., Maidstone & The Weald,* Maj. 14,856

Wiggin, Bill (*b.* 1966) *C., Leominster,* Maj. 13,187

Willetts, David (*b.* 1956) *C., Havant,* Maj. 6,508

Williams, Rt. Hon. Alan (*b.* 1930) *Lab., Swansea West,* Maj. 4,269

Williams, Betty (*b.* 1944) *Lab., Conwy,* Maj. 3,081

Williams, Hywel (*b.* 1953) *PC, Caernarfon,* Maj. 5,209

*Williams, Mark (*b.* 1966) *LD, Ceredigion,* Maj. 219

Williams, Roger (*b.* 1948) *LD, Brecon & Radnorshire,* Maj. 3,905

*Williams, Stephen (*b.* 1966) *LD, Bristol West,* Maj. 5,128

Willis, Phil (*b.* 1941) *LD, Harrogate & Knaresborough,* Maj. 10,429

*Willott, Jenny (*b.* 1974) *LD, Cardiff Central,* Maj. 5,593

Wills, Michael (*b.* 1952) *Lab., Swindon North,* Maj. 2,571

Wilshire, David (*b.* 1943) *C., Spelthorne,* Maj. 9,936

*Wilson, Phil (*b.* 1959) *Lab., Sedgefield,* Maj. 6,956

*Wilson, Rob (*b.* 1965) *C., Reading East,* Maj. 475

*Wilson, Sammy (*b.* 1953) *DUP, Antrim East,* Maj. 7,304

Winnick, David (*b.* 1933) *Lab., Walsall North,* Maj. 6,640

Winterton, Lady Ann (*b.* 1941) *C., Congleton,* Maj. 8,246

Winterton, Sir Nicholas (*b.* 1938) *C., Macclesfield,* Maj. 9,401

Winterton, Rosie (*b.* 1958) *Lab., Doncaster Central,* Maj. 9,802

Wishart, Peter (*b.* 1962) *SNP, Perth & Perthshire North,* Maj. 1,521

Wood, Mike (*b.* 1946) *Lab., Batley & Spen,* Maj. 5,788

Woodward, Shaun (*b.* 1958) *Lab., St Helens South,* Maj. 9,309

Woolas, Phil (*b.* 1959) *Lab., Oldham East & Saddleworth,* Maj. 3,590

Wright, Anthony (*b.* 1954) *Lab., Great Yarmouth,* Maj. 3,055

Wright, David (*b.* 1967) *Lab., Telford,* Maj. 5,406

Wright, Iain (*b.* 1972) *Lab., Hartlepool,* Maj. 7,478

*Wright, Jeremy (*b.* 1972) *C., Rugby & Kenilworth,* Maj. 1,556

Wright, Dr Tony (*b.* 1948) *Lab., Cannock Chase,* Maj. 9,227

Wyatt, Derek (*b.* 1949) *Lab., Sittingbourne & Sheppey,* Maj. 79

Yeo, Tim (*b.* 1945) *C., Suffolk South,* Maj. 6,606

Young, Rt. Hon. Sir George (*b.* 1941) *C., Hampshire North West,* Maj. 13,264

Younger-Ross, Richard (*b.* 1953) *LD, Teignbridge,* Maj. 6,215

GENERAL ELECTION RESULTS

The results of voting in each parliamentary division at the general election of 5 May 2005 are given below.

SCOTTISH BOUNDARY CHANGES

The number of Scottish constituencies was reduced from 72 to 59 for the 2005 general election, bringing the average electorate of each constituency in line with that of England.

For the majority of constituencies where a boundary change has taken place, it is not appropriate to make a straight comparison between the results of 2001 and 2005. The seat of Dundee East, for example, comprises 80 per cent of the old Dundee East constituency and 30 per cent of the old Angus constituency; it cannot therefore be described as a simple gain for the Scottish National Party from Labour. The term 'notional' used here refers to a theoretical set of results, published by Professors Rallings and Thrasher of Plymouth University, that estimates the way each new constituency might have voted in the 2001 general election.

KEY

* New MP
† Previously MP in another seat
‡ Previously MP for another party
§ Notional result; *see* explanation of Scottish boundary changes
E. Electorate   T. Turnout

Abbreviations of parties standing in the General Election in 2005:

AFC	Alliance for Change
Alliance	Alliance
AP	Alternative Party
Baths	Save the Bristol North Baths Party
Bean	New Millennium Bean
BMG	Blair Must Go Party
BNP	British National Party
BPP	British Public Party
Bridges	Build Duddon and Morecambe Bridges
Burnley	Burnley First Independent
C.	Conservative
CAP	Community Action Party
CG	Community Group
CL	Communist League
Clause 28	Clause 28 Children's Protection Christian Democrats
Comm.	Communist Party
Comm. Brit.	Communist Party of Britain
Community	Community
CP	Civilisation Party
CPA	Christian Peoples Alliance
Croydon	Croydon Pensions Alliance
Currency	Virtue Currency Cognitive Appraisal Party
DDTP	Death, Dungeons & Taxes Party
Dem. Lab.	Democratic Labour Party
Dem. Soc. All.	Democratic Socialist Alliance – People Before Profit
DUP	Democratic Unionist Party
EDP	English Democratic Party
EPP	English Parliamentary Party
Elvis	Church of the Militant Elvis Party
Eng. Dem.	English Democrats Party
Eng. Ind.	English Independence Party
FF	familiesfirst.uk.net
Fit	Fit Party For Integrity And Trust
Forum	Open-Forum
FP	Freedom Party
Free Scot.	Free Scotland Party
FWP	Forward Wales Party
GBB	Get Britain Back Party
Good	Common Good

Green	Green
Green Soc.	Alliance for Green Socialism
Honesty	Demanding Honesty in Politics and Whitehall
Ind. Green	Independent Green Voice
Ind.	Independent
Ind. Pr. Lab.	Independent Progressive Labour
IP	Imperial Party
Iraq	Iraq War, Not in My Name
IWCA	Independent Working Class Association
IZB	Islam Zinda Baad Platform
JP	Justice Party
KHHC	Kidderminster Hospital and Health Concern
Lab.	Labour
Lab. (Co-op)	Labour (Cooperative)
LCA	Legalise Cannabis Alliance
LD	Liberal Democrat
Lib.	Liberal
Local	Local Community Party
Loony	Monster Raving Loony Party
Masts	Removal of Tetra Masts in Cornwall
MC	The Millenium Council
Meb. Ker.	Mebyon Kernow
MNP	Motorcycle News Party
NACVP	Newcastle Academy with Christian Values Party
NEP	New England Party
NF	National Front
Northern	Northern Progress for You
OCV	Operation Christian Vote
OFD	Organisation of Free Democrats
Online	Seeks a Worldwide Online Participatory Directory
Paisley	Pride in Paisley Party
PC	Plaid Cymru
PDP	Progressive Democratic Party
PHF	People of Horsham First
Power	Max Power Party
PPN-V	Peace Party, Non-Violence, Justice, Environment
PPS	Pensioners Party Scotland
Progress	Peace and Progress Party
Protest	Protest Vote Party
PRTYP	Personality and Rational Thinking? Yes! Party
Publican	Publican Party – Free to Smoke (Pubs)

RA	Residents Association
R & R Loony	Rock & Roll Loony Party
Respect	Respect – the Unity Coalition
RP	The Resolutionist Party
St Albans	St Albans Party
Scot. Green	Scottish Green Party
Scot. Ind.	Scottish Independence Party
Scot. Senior	Scottish Senior Citizens Party
Scot. U.	Scottish Unionist
SDLP	Social Democratic and Labour Party
Senior	Senior Citizens Party
SF	Sinn Fein
Silent	Silent Majority Party
SNH	Safeguard the National Health Service
SNP	Scottish National Party
Soc. All.	Socialist Alliance
Soc. Alt.	Socialist Alternative Party
Socialist	Socialist
Soc. Lab.	Socialist Labour Party
Soc. Unity	Socialist Unity Network
SOS	SOS! Voters Against Overdevelopment of Northampton
Speaker	The Speaker
SSCUP	Scottish Senior Citizens Unity Party
SSP	Scottish Socialist Party
Tele.	telepathicpartnership.com
TEPK	Tigers Eye the Party for Kids
Third	Third Way
TP	Their Party
UKC	UK Community Issues Party
UKIP	UK Independence Party
UK Path	UK Pathfinders
UKPP	UK Pensioners Party
UUP	Ulster Unionist Party
Veritas	Veritas
Vote Dream	Vote for Yourself Rainbow Dream Ticket
Wessex Reg.	Wessex Regionalist
Work	The People's Choice Making Politicians Work
WP	Workers' Party
WRP	Workers' Revolutionary Party
XPP	Xtraordinary People Party
YPB	Your Party (Banbury)

PARLIAMENTARY CONSTITUENCIES AS AT MAY 2005 GENERAL ELECTION

ENGLAND

ALDERSHOT
E. 78,553 T. 48,141 (61.28%) C. hold
Gerald Howarth, C.   20,572
Adrian Collett, LD   15,238
Howard Linsley, Lab.   9,895
Derek Rumsey, UKIP   1,182
Gary Cowd, Eng. Dem.   701
Howling Lord Hope, Loony   553
C. maj. 5,334 (11.08%)
1.74% swing C. to LD
(2001: C. maj. 6,564 (14.49%))

ALDRIDGE-BROWNHILLS
E. 61,761 T. 39,556 (64.05%) C. hold
Richard Shepherd, C.   18,744
Jon Phillips, Lab.   13,237
Roy Sheward, LD   4,862
William Vaughan, BNP   1,620
Graham Eardley, UKIP   1,093
C. maj. 5,507 (13.92%)
1.98% swing Lab. to C.
(2001: C. maj. 3,768 (9.97%))

ALTRINCHAM & SALE WEST
E. 67,247 T. 44,310 (65.89%) C. hold
Graham Brady, C.   20,569
John Stockton, Lab.   13,410
Ian Chappell, LD   9,595
Gary Peart, UKIP   736
C. maj. 7,159 (16.16%)
4.70% swing Lab. to C.
(2001: C. maj. 2,941 (6.75%))

AMBER VALLEY
E. 75,376 T. 47,391 (62.87%) Lab. hold
Judy Mallaber, Lab.   21,593
Gillian Shaw, C.   16,318
Kate Smith, LD   6,225
Paul Snell, BNP   1,243
Alexander Stevenson, Veritas   1,224
Hugh Price, UKIP   788
Lab. maj. 5,275 (11.13%)
2.55% swing Lab. to C.
(2001: Lab. maj. 7,227 (16.24%))

ARUNDEL & SOUTH DOWNS
E. 72,535 T. 49,690 (68.50%) C. hold
*Nick Herbert, C.   24,752
Derek Deedman, LD   13,443
Sharon Whitlam, Lab.   8,482
Andrew Moffat, UKIP   2,700
Mark Stack, Protest   313
C. maj. 11,309 (22.76%)
3.55% swing C. to LD
(2001: C. maj. 13,704 (29.86%))

ASHFIELD
E. 73,403 T. 42,051 (57.29%) Lab. hold
Rt. Hon. Geoff Hoon, Lab.   20,433
Giles Inglis-Jones, C.   10,220
Wendy Johnson, LD   5,829
Roy Adkins, Ind.   2,292
Kathryn Allsop, Ind.   1,900
Sarah Hemstock, Veritas   1,108
Eddie Grenfell, Ind.   269
Lab. maj. 10,213 (24.29%)
4.72% swing Lab. to C.
(2001: Lab. maj. 13,268 (33.72%))

ASHFORD
E. 79,493 T. 51,685 (65.02%) C. hold
Damian Green, C.   26,651
Valerie Whitaker, Lab.   13,353
Chris Took, LD   8,308
Richard Boden, Green   1,753
Bernard Stroud, UKIP   1,620
C. maj. 13,298 (25.73%)
5.19% swing Lab. to C.
(2001: C. maj. 7,359 (15.35%))

ASHTON UNDER LYNE
E. 72,000 T. 36,967 (51.34%) Lab. hold
David Heyes, Lab.   21,211
Graeme Brown, C.   7,259
Les Jones, LD   5,108
Anthony Jones, BNP   2,051
Dr John Whittaker, UKIP   768
Jack Crossfield, Local   570
Lab. maj. 13,952 (37.74%)
2.82% swing Lab. to C.
(2001: Lab. maj. 15,518 (43.39%))

AYLESBURY
E. 82,428 T. 51,458 (62.43%) C. hold
David Lidington, C.   25,252
Peter Jones, Lab.   14,187
Mohammed Khaliel, Lab.   9,540
Christopher Adams, UKIP   2,479
C. maj. 11,065 (21.50%)
0.56% swing LD to C.
(2001: C. maj. 10,009 (20.39%))

BANBURY
E. 87,168 T. 56,209 (64.48%) C. hold
Tony Baldry, C.   26,382
Les Sibley, Lab.   15,585
Zoe Patrick, LD   10,076
Alyson Duckmanton, Green   1,590
Dianna Heimann, UKIP   1,241
James Starkey, NF   918
Christopher Rowe, YPB   417
C. maj. 10,797 (19.21%)
4.54% swing Lab. to C.
(2001: C. maj. 5,219 (10.13%))

BARKING
E. 57,658 T. 28,906 (50.13%) Lab. hold
Rt. Hon. Margaret Hodge, Lab.   13,826
Keith Prince, C.   4,943
Richard Barnbrook, BNP   4,916
Toby Wickenden, LD   3,211
Terry Jones, UKIP   803
Laurie Cleeland, Green   618
Demetrious Panton, Ind.   530
Michael Saxby, WRP   59
Lab. maj. 8,883 (30.73%)
3.61% swing Lab. to C.
(2001: Lab. maj. 9,534 (37.94%))

BARNSLEY CENTRAL
E. 60,592 T. 28,615 (47.23%) Lab. hold
Eric Illsley, Lab.   17,478
Miles Crompton, LD   4,746
Peter Morel, C.   3,813
Geoff Broadley, BNP   1,403
Donald Wood, Ind.   1,175
Lab. maj. 12,732 (44.49%)
5.22% swing Lab. to LD
(2001: Lab. maj. 15,130 (54.93%))

BARNSLEY EAST & MEXBOROUGH
E. 66,941 T. 33,026 (49.34%) Lab. hold
Jeff Ennis, Lab.   20,779
Sharron Brook, LD   6,654
Carolyn Abbott, C.   4,853
Terence Robinson, Soc. Lab.   740
Lab. maj. 14,125 (42.77%)
4.44% swing Lab. to LD
(2001: Lab. maj. 16,789 (51.64%))

BARNSLEY WEST & PENISTONE
E. 66,985 T. 36,852 (55.02%) Lab. hold
Michael Clapham, Lab.   20,372
Clive Watkinson, C.   9,058
Alison Brelsford, LD   7,422
Lab. maj. 11,314 (30.70%)
2.52% swing Lab. to C.
(2001: Lab. maj. 12,352 (35.74%))

BARROW & FURNESS
E. 61,883 T. 36,493 (58.97%) Lab. hold
Rt. Hon. John Hutton, Lab.   17,360
Bill Dorman, C.   11,323
Barry Rabone, LD   6,130
Alan Beach, UKIP   758
Timothy Bell, Bridges   409
Brian Greaves, Veritas   306
Helene Young, Ind.   207
Lab. maj. 6,037 (16.54%)
4.40% swing Lab. to C.
(2001: Lab. maj. 9,889 (25.34%))

BASILDON
E. 73,912 T. 43,141 (58.37%)
                          Lab. (Co-op) hold
Angela Smith, Lab. (Co-op)   18,720
Aaron Powell, C.   15,578
Martin Thompson, LD   4,473
Emma Colgate, BNP   2,055
Alix Blythe, UKIP   1,143
Vikki Copping, Green   662
Kim Gandy, Eng. Dem.   510
Lab. (Co-op) maj. 3,142 (7.28%)
5.82% swing Lab. (Co-op) to C.
(2001: Lab. (Co-op) maj. 7,738
(18.93%))

BASINGSTOKE
E. 76,404 T. 48,123 (62.98%) C. gain
*Maria Miller, C.   19,955
Paul Harvey, Lab.   15,275
Jen Smith, LD   9,952
Peter Effer, UKIP   1,044
Darren Shirley, Green   928
Roger Robertson, BNP   821
Roger Macnair, MC   148
C. maj. 4,680 (9.73%)
3.95% swing Lab. to C.
(C. gain because previous MP defected to
DUP in 2004)
(2001: C. maj. 880 (1.83%))

BASSETLAW
E. 69,389 T. 40,342 (58.14%) Lab. hold
John Mann, Lab.   22,847
Jonathan Sheppard, C.   12,010
David Dobbie, LD   5,485
Lab. maj. 10,837 (26.86%)
0.90% swing C. to Lab.
(2001: Lab. maj. 9,748 (25.06%))

BATH
E. 66,824 T. 45,836 (68.59%) LD hold
Don Foster, LD   20,101
Sian Dawson, C.   15,463
Harriet Ajderian, Lab.   6,773
Eric Lucas, Green   2,494
Richard Crowder, UKIP   770
Patrick Cobbe, Ind.   177
Graham Walker, Ind.   58
LD maj. 4,638 (10.12%)
5.63% swing LD to C.
(2001: LD maj. 9,894 (21.37%))

BATLEY & SPEN
E. 62,948 T. 39,208 (62.29%) Lab. hold
Mike Wood, Lab.   17,974
Robert Light, C.   12,186
Neil Bentley, LD   5,731
Colin Auty, BNP   2,668
Clive Lord, Green   649
Lab. maj. 5,788 (14.76%)
0.81% swing C. to Lab.
(2001: Lab. maj. 5,064 (13.14%))

BATTERSEA
E. 69,548 T. 41,049 (59.02%) Lab. hold
Martin Linton, Lab.   16,569
Dominic Schofield, C.   16,406
Norsheen Bhatti, LD   6,006
Hugo Charlton, Green   1,735
Terence Jones, UKIP   333
Lab. maj. 163 (0.40%)
6.67% swing Lab. to C.
(2001: Lab. maj. 5,053 (13.73%))

BEACONSFIELD
E. 68,083 T. 43,523 (63.93%) C. hold
Dominic Grieve, C.   24,126
Peter Chapman, LD   8,873
Alex Sobel, Lab.   8,422
John Fagan, UKIP   2,102
C. maj. 15,253 (35.05%)
1.96% swing LD to C.
(2001: C. maj. 13,065 (31.07%))

BECKENHAM
E. 74,738 T. 48,964 (65.51%) C. hold
Jacqui Lait, C.   22,183
Liam Curran, Lab.   13,782
Jef Foulger, LD   10,862
James Cartwright, UKIP   1,301
Roderick Reed, Ind.   836
C. maj. 8,401 (17.16%)
3.14% swing Lab. to C.
(2001: C. maj. 4,959 (10.88%))

BEDFORD
E. 70,629 T. 42,072 (59.57%) Lab. hold
Patrick Hall, Lab.   17,557
Richard Fuller, C.   14,174
Michael Headley, LD   9,063
Peter Conquest, UKIP   995
John McCready, Ind.   283
Lab. maj. 3,383 (8.04%)
3.57% swing Lab. to C.
(2001: Lab. maj. 6,157 (15.17%))

BEDFORDSHIRE MID
E. 73,768 T. 50,420 (68.35%) C. hold
*Nadine Dorries, C.   23,345
Mark Chapman, LD   11,990
Martin Lindsay, Lab.   11,351
Richard Joselyn, UKIP   1,372
Ben Foley, Green   1,292
Howard Martin, Veritas   769
Saqhib Ali, Ind.   301
C. maj. 11,355 (22.52%)
2.55% swing C. to LD
(2001: C. maj. 8,066 (17.29%))

BEDFORDSHIRE NORTH EAST
E. 72,757 T. 49,505 (68.04%) C. hold
Alistair Burt, C.   24,725
Keith White, Lab.   12,474
Stephen Rutherford, LD   10,320
James May, UKIP   1,986
C. maj. 12,251 (24.75%)
2.9% swing Lab. to C.
(2001: C. maj. 8,577 (18.96%))

BEDFORDSHIRE SOUTH WEST
E. 74,096 T. 45,814 (61.83%) C. hold
Andrew Selous, C.   22,114
Joyce Still, Lab.   13,837
Andy Strange, LD   7,723
Tom Wise, UKIP   1,923
Kenson Gurney, Forum   217
C. maj. 8,277 (18.07%)
8.15% swing Lab. to C.
(2001: C. maj. 776 (1.77%))

BERWICK-UPON-TWEED
E. 56,944 T. 36,090 (63.38%) LD hold
Rt. Hon. Alan Beith, LD   19,052
Mike Elliott, C.   10,420
Glen Reynolds, Lab.   6,618
LD maj. 8,632 (23.92%)
0.31% swing C. to LD
(2001: LD maj. 8,458 (23.30%))

BETHNAL GREEN & BOW
E. 85,950 T. 44,007 (51.20%)
                         Respect gain
†‡George Galloway, Respect   15,801
Oona King, Lab.   14,978
Shahagir Bakth Faruk, C.   6,244
Syed Nurul Islam Dulu, LD   4,928
John Foster, Green   1,950
Ejiro Etefia, AFC   68
Celia Pugh, CL   38
Respect maj. 823 (1.87%)
26.20% swing Lab. to Respect
(2001: Lab. maj. 10,057 (26.14%))

BEVERLEY & HOLDERNESS
E. 77,460 T. 50,202 (64.81%) C. hold
*Graham Stuart, C.   20,434
George McManus, Lab.   17,854
Brian Willie, LD   9,578
Oliver Marriott, UKIP   2,336
C. maj. 2,580 (5.14%)
1.73% swing Lab. to C.
(2001: C. maj. 781 (1.68%))

BEXHILL & BATTLE
E. 69,676 T. 46,834 (67.22%) C. hold
Greg Barker, C.   24,629
Mary Varrall, LD   11,180
Michael Jones, Lab.   8,457
Anthony Smith, UKIP   2,568
C. maj. 13,449 (28.72%)
2.63% swing LD to C.
(2001: C. maj. 10,503 (23.45%))

BEXLEYHEATH & CRAYFORD
E. 65,025 T. 42,580 (65.48%) C. gain
†David Evennett, C.   19,722
Nigel Beard, Lab.   15,171
David Raval, LD   5,144
John Dunford, UKIP   1,302
Jay Lee, BNP   1,241
C. maj. 4,551 (10.69%)
7.17% swing Lab. to C.
(2001: Lab. maj. 1,472 (3.65%))

BILLERICAY
E. 79,537 T. 48,858 (61.43%) C. hold
John Baron, C.   25,487
Anneliese Dodds, Lab.   14,281
Mike Hibbs, LD   6,471
Bryn Robinson, BNP   1,435
Seantino Callaghan, UKIP   1,184
C. maj. 11,206 (22.94%)
5.97% swing Lab. to C.
(2001: C. maj. 5,013 (10.99%))

BIRKENHEAD
E. 57,097 T. 27,786 (48.66%) Lab. hold
Rt. Hon. Frank Field, Lab.   18,059
Stuart Kelly, LD   5,125
Howard Morton, C.   4,602
Lab. maj. 12,934 (46.55%)
5.54% swing Lab. to LD
(2001: Lab. maj. 15,591 (53.82%))

BIRMINGHAM EDGBASTON
E. 64,893 T. 37,631 (57.99%) Lab. hold
Gisela Stuart, Lab.   16,465
Deirdre Alden, C.   14,116
Mike Dixon, LD   5,185
Peter Beck, Green   1,116
Stephen White, UKIP   749
Lab. maj. 2,349 (6.24%)
3.10% swing Lab. to C.
(2001: Lab. maj. 4,698 (12.45%))

BIRMINGHAM ERDINGTON
E. 64,951 T. 31,746 (48.88%) Lab. hold
Sion Simon, Lab.   16,810
Victoria Elvidge, C.   7,235
Jerry Evans, LD   5,027
Sharon Ebanks, BNP   1,512
Rannal Hepburn, UKIP   746
Terry Williams, NF   416
Lab. maj. 9,575 (30.16%)
1.20% swing Lab. to C.
(2001: Lab. maj. 9,962 (32.55%))

BIRMINGHAM HALL GREEN
E. 57,222 T. 34,536 (60.35%) Lab. hold
Stephen McCabe, Lab.   16,304
Eddie Hughes, C.   10,590
Roger Harmer, LD   6,682
David Melhuish, UKIP   960
Lab. maj. 5,714 (16.55%)
1.77% swing Lab. to C.
(2001: Lab. maj. 6,648 (20.09%))

BIRMINGHAM HODGE HILL
E. 53,903 T. 28,417 (52.72%) Lab. hold
Liam Byrne, Lab.   13,822
Nicola Davies, LD   8,373
Deborah Thomas, C.   3,768
Denis Adams, BNP   1,445
Adrian Duffen, UKIP   680
Azmat Begg, Progress   329
Lab. maj. 5,449 (19.18%)
18.29% swing Lab. to LD
(2004 July by-election: Lab. maj. 460
(2.25%))
(2001: Lab. maj. 11,618 (43.90%))

BIRMINGHAM LADYWOOD
E. 70,977 T. 33,246 (46.84%) Lab. hold
Rt. Hon. Clare Short, Lab. 17,262
Ayoub Khan, LD 10,461
Philippa Stroud, C. 3,515
Lynette Nazemi-Afshar, UKIP 2,008
Lab. maj. 6,801 (20.46%)
20.11% swing Lab. to LD
(2001: Lab. maj. 18,143 (57.61%))

BIRMINGHAM NORTHFIELD
E. 54,868 T. 31,056 (56.60%) Lab. hold
Richard Burden, Lab. 15,419
Vicky Ford, C. 8,965
Trevor Sword, LD 4,171
Mark Cattell, BNP 1,278
Gillian Chant, UKIP 641
Richard Rodgers, Good 428
Louise Houldey, Soc. Alt. 120
Francis Sweeney, WRP 34
Lab. maj. 6,454 (20.78%)
2.81% swing Lab. to C.
(2001: Lab. maj. 7,798 (26.40%))

BIRMINGHAM PERRY BARR
E. 70,126 T. 38,911 (55.49%) Lab. hold
Khalid Mahmood, Lab. 18,269
Jon Hunt, LD 10,321
Naweed Khan, C. 6,513
Dr Mohammad Naseem, Respect 2,173
Rajinder Clair, Soc. Lab. 890
Bimla Balu, UKIP 745
Lab. maj. 7,948 (20.43%)
1.61% swing Lab. to LD
(2001: Lab. maj. 8,753 (23.39%))

BIRMINGHAM SELLY OAK
E. 70,162 T. 41,740 (59.49%) Lab. hold
Dr Lynne Jones, Lab. 19,226
Joe Tildesley, C. 10,375
Richard Brighton, LD 9,591
Barney Smith, Green 1,581
Ronan Burnett, UKIP 967
Lab. maj. 8,851 (21.21%)
2.29% swing Lab. to C.
(2001: Lab. maj. 10,339 (25.78%))

BIRMINGHAM SPARKBROOK & SMALL HEATH
E. 73,721 T. 38,192 (51.81%) Lab. hold
Roger Godsiff, Lab. 13,787
Salma Yaqoob, Respect 10,498
Talib Hussain, LD 7,727
Sameer Mirza, C. 3,480
Jennifer Brookes, UKIP 1,342
Ian Jamieson, Green 855
Abdul Chaudhary, Ind. 503
Lab. maj. 3,289 (8.61%)
24.4% swing Lab. to Respect
(2001: Lab. maj. 16,246 (44.33%))

BIRMINGHAM YARDLEY
E. 50,975 T. 29,431 (57.74%) LD gain
*John Hemming, LD 13,648
Jayne Innes, Lab. 10,976
Paul Uppal, C. 2,970
Robert Purcell, BNP 1,523
Mohammed Yaqub, UKIP 314
LD maj. 2,672 (9.08%)
8.83% swing Lab. to LD
(2001: Lab. maj. 2,578 (8.59%))

BISHOP AUCKLAND
E. 67,534 T. 38,128 (56.46%) Lab. hold
*Helen Goodman, Lab. 19,065
Chris Foote-Wood, LD 9,018
Richard Bell, C. 8,736
Margaret Hopson, UKIP 1,309
Lab. maj. 10,047 (26.35%)
8.36% swing Lab. to LD
(2001: Lab. maj. 13,926 (36.12%))

BLABY
E. 75,444 T. 49,388 (65.46%) C. hold
Andrew Robathan, C. 22,487
David Morgan, Lab. 14,614
Jeff Stephenson, LD 9,382
Michael Robinson, BNP 1,704
Delroy Young, UKIP 1,201
C. maj. 7,873 (15.94%)
1.45% swing Lab. to C.
(2001: C. maj. 6,209 (13.03%))

BLACKBURN
E. 73,494 T. 41,805 (56.88%) Lab. hold
Rt. Hon. Jack Straw, Lab. 17,562
Imtiaz Ameen, C. 9,553
Tony Melia, LD 8,608
Nicholas Holt, BNP 2,263
Craig Murray, Ind. 2,082
Dorothy Baxter, UKIP 954
Graham Carter, Green 783
Lab. maj. 8,009 (19.16%)
1.90% swing Lab. to C.
(2001: Lab. maj. 9,249 (22.85%))

BLACKPOOL NORTH & FLEETWOOD
E. 74,975 T. 43,290 (57.74%) Lab. hold
Joan Humble, Lab. 20,620
Gavin Williamson, C. 15,558
Steven Bate, LD 5,533
Roy Hopwood, UKIP 1,579
Lab. maj. 5,062 (11.69%)
0.87% swing Lab. to C.
(2001: Lab. maj. 5,721 (13.44%))

BLACKPOOL SOUTH
E. 73,529 T. 38,342 (52.15%) Lab. hold
Gordon Marsden, Lab. 19,375
Michael Winstanley, C. 11,453
Doreen Holt, LD 5,552
Roy Goodwin, BNP 1,113
John Porter, UKIP 849
Lab. maj. 7,922 (20.66%)
0.32% swing Lab. to C.
(2001: Lab. maj. 8,262 (21.30%))

BLAYDON
E. 62,413 T. 39,053 (62.57%) Lab. hold
*David Anderson, Lab. 20,120
Peter Maughan, LD 14,785
Dorothy Luckhurst, C. 3,129
Norman Endacott, UKIP 1,019
Lab. maj. 5,335 (13.66%)
3.70% swing Lab. to LD
(2001: Lab. maj. 7,809 (21.06%))

BLYTH VALLEY
E. 63,640 T. 35,773 (56.21%) Lab. hold
Ronnie Campbell, Lab. 19,659
Jeffrey Reid, LD 11,132
Michael Windridge, C. 4,982
Lab. maj. 8,527 (23.84%)
5.72% swing Lab. to LD
(2001: Lab. maj. 12,188 (35.28%))

BOGNOR REGIS & LITTLEHAMPTON
E. 65,591 T. 40,747 (62.12%) C. hold
Nick Gibb, C. 18,183
George O'Neill, Lab. 10,361
Simon McDougall, LD 8,927
Adrian Lithgow, UKIP 3,276
C. maj. 7,822 (19.20%)
2.36% swing Lab. to C.
(2001: C. maj. 5,643 (14.48%))

BOLSOVER
E. 67,568 T. 38,699 (57.27%) Lab. hold
Dennis Skinner, Lab. 25,217
Denise Hawksworth, LD 6,780
Hasan Imam, C. 6,702
Lab. maj. 18,437 (47.64%)
4.53% swing Lab. to LD
(2001: Lab. maj. 18,777 (49.06%))

BOLTON NORTH EAST
E. 67,394 T. 36,911 (54.77%) Lab. hold
David Crausby, Lab. 16,874
Paul Brierley, C. 12,771
Adam Killeya, LD 6,044
Kevin Epsom, UKIP 640
Alan Ainscow, Veritas 375
Lynne Lowe, Soc. Lab. 207
Lab. maj. 4,103 (11.12%)
5.25% swing Lab. to C.
(2001: Lab. maj. 8,422 (21.62%))

BOLTON SOUTH EAST
E. 63,697 T. 31,850 (50.00%) Lab. hold
Dr Brian Iddon, Lab. 18,129
Deborah Dunleavy, C. 6,491
Frank Harasiwka, LD 6,047
Florence Bates, UKIP 840
David Jones, Veritas 343
Lab. maj. 11,638 (36.54%)
0.57% swing Lab. to C.
(2001: Lab. maj. 12,871 (37.69%))

BOLTON WEST
E. 63,836 T. 40,543 (63.51%) Lab. hold
Rt. Hon. Ruth Kelly, Lab. 17,239
Philip Allott, C. 15,175
Tim Perkins, LD 7,241
Marjorie Ford, UKIP 524
Michael Ford, Veritas 290
Kate Griggs, XPP 74
Lab. maj. 2,064 (5.09%)
4.15% swing Lab. to C.
(2001: Lab. maj. 5,518 (13.39%))

BOOTLE
E. 53,700 T. 25,622 (47.71%) Lab. hold
Joe Benton, Lab. 19,345
Chris Newby, LD 2,988
Wafik Moustafa, C. 1,580
Paul Nuttall, UKIP 1,054
Peter Glover, Soc. Alt. 655
Lab. maj. 16,357 (63.84%)
2.59% swing Lab. to LD
(2001: Lab. maj. 19,043 (69.01%))

BOSTON & SKEGNESS
E. 71,212 T. 41,869 (58.79%) C. hold
Mark Simmonds, C. 19,329
Paul Kenny, Lab. 13,422
Dr Richard Horsnell, UKIP 4,024
Alan Riley, LD 3,649
Wendy Russell, BNP 1,025
Marcus Petz, Green 420
C. maj. 5,907 (14.11%)
6.42% swing Lab. to C.
(2001: C. maj. 515 (1.28%))

BOSWORTH
E. 71,596 T. 47,499 (66.34%) C. hold
David Tredinnick, C.   20,212
Rupert Herd, Lab.   14,893
James Moore, LD   10,528
Denis Walker, UKIP   1,866
C. maj. 5,319 (11.20%)
3.07% swing Lab. to C.
(2001: C. maj. 2,280 (5.05%))

BOURNEMOUTH EAST
E. 63,426 T. 37,599 (59.28%) C. hold
*Tobias Ellwood, C.   16,925
Andrew Garratt, LD   11,681
David Stokes, Lab.   7,191
Thomas Collier, UKIP   1,802
C. maj. 5,244 (13.95%)
2.18% swing LD to C.
(2001: C. maj. 3,434 (9.59%))

BOURNEMOUTH WEST
E. 63,658 T. 33,924 (53.29%) C. hold
Sir John Butterfill, C.   14,057
Richard Renaut, LD   10,026
Dafydd Williams, Lab.   7,824
Michael Maclaire-Hillier, UKIP   2,017
C. maj. 4,031 (11.88%)
2.90% swing C. to LD
(2001: C. maj. 4,718 (14.02%))

BRACKNELL
E. 80,657 T. 51,141 (63.41%) C. hold
Rt. Hon. Andrew Mackay, C.   25,412
Janet Keene, Lab.   13,376
Lee Glendon, LD   10,128
Vincent Pearson, UKIP   1,818
Dominica Roberts, Ind.   407
C. maj. 12,036 (23.53%)
4.95% swing Lab. to C.
(2001: C. maj. 6,713 (13.64%))

BRADFORD NORTH
E. 64,515 T. 34,397 (53.32%) Lab. hold
Terry Rooney, Lab.   14,622
David Ward, LD   11,111
Teck Khong, C.   5,569
Lynda Cromie, BNP   2,061
Steve Schofield, Green   560
Umit Yildiz, Respect   474
Lab. maj. 3,511 (10.21%)
9.88% swing Lab. to LD
(2001: Lab. maj. 8,969 (25.61%))

BRADFORD SOUTH
E. 67,576 T. 36,605 (54.17%) Lab. hold
Gerry Sutcliffe, Lab.   17,954
Geraldine Carter, C.   8,787
Mike Doyle, LD   5,334
Dr James Lewthwaite, BNP   2,862
Derek Curtis, Green   695
Jason Smith, UKIP   552
Therese Muchewicz, Veritas   421
Lab. maj. 9,167 (25.04%)
1.23% swing Lab. to C.
(2001: Lab. maj. 9,662 (27.50%))

BRADFORD WEST
E. 67,356 T. 36,369 (54.00%) Lab. hold
Marsha Singh, Lab.   14,570
Haroon Rashid, C.   11,544
Mukhtar Ali, LD   6,620
Paul Cromie, BNP   2,525
Parvez Darr, Green   1,110
Lab. maj. 3,026 (8.32%)
1.27% swing Lab. to C.
(2001: Lab. maj. 4,165 (10.85%))

BRAINTREE
E. 80,458 T. 53,055 (65.94%) C. gain
*Brooks Newmark, C.   23,597
Alan Hurst, Lab.   19,704
Peter Turner, LD   7,037
James Abbott, Green   1,308
Roger Lord, UKIP   1,181
Buster Michael Nolan, Ind.   228
C. maj. 3,893 (7.34%)
4.02% swing Lab. to C.
(2001: Lab. maj. 358 (0.71%))

BRENT EAST
E. 56,227 T. 31,068 (55.25%) LD hold
Sarah Teather, LD   14,764
Yasmin Qureshi, Lab.   12,052
Kwasi Kwarteng, C.   3,193
Shahrar Ali, Green   905
Michelle Weininger, Ind.   115
Rainbow George Weiss, Vote Dream   39
LD maj. 2,712 (8.73%)
30.68% swing Lab. to LD
(2003 Sept. by-election: LD maj. 1,118
(5.36%))
(2001: Lab. maj. 13,047 (45.00%))

BRENT NORTH
E. 60,148 T. 35,682 (59.32%) Lab. hold
Barry Gardiner, Lab.   17,420
Bob Blackman, C.   11,779
Havard Hughes, LD   5,672
Babar Ahmad, Progress   685
Rainbow George Weiss, Vote Dream   126
Lab. maj. 5,641 (15.81%)
7.13% swing Lab. to C.
(2001: Lab. maj. 10,205 (30.07%))

BRENT SOUTH
E. 56,508 T. 29,764 (52.67%) Lab. hold
*Dawn Butler, Lab.   17,501
James Allie, LD   6,175
Rishi Saha, C.   4,485
Rowan Langley, Green   957
Shaun Wallace, Ind.   297
Rocky Fernandez, Ind.   288
Rainbow George Weiss, Vote Dream   61
Lab. maj. 11,326 (38.05%)
12.20% swing Lab. to LD
(2001: Lab. maj. 17,380 (60.69%))

BRENTFORD & ISLEWORTH
E. 84,366 T. 46,017 (54.54%) Lab. hold
Ann Keen, Lab.   18,329
Alexander Northcote, C.   13,918
Andrew Dakers, LD   10,477
John Hunt, Green   1,652
Phillip Andrews, Community   1,118
Michael Stoneman, NF   523
Lab. maj. 4,411 (9.59%)
6.80% swing Lab. to C.
(2001: Lab. maj. 10,318 (23.18%))

BRENTWOOD & ONGAR
E. 64,496 T. 44,145 (68.45%) C. hold
Eric Pickles, C.   23,609
Gavin Stollar, LD   11,997
John Adams, Lab.   6,579
Stuart Gulleford, UKIP   1,805
Anthony Appleton, Ind.   155
C. maj. 11,612 (26.30%)
1.91% swing LD to C.
(2001: C. maj. 2,821 (6.48%))

BRIDGWATER
E. 75,790 T. 48,109 (63.48%) C. hold
Ian Liddell-Grainger, C.   21,240
Matthew Burchell, Lab.   12,771
James Main, LD   10,940
Ray Weinstein, UKIP   1,767
Charlie Graham, Green   1,391
C. maj. 8,469 (17.60%)
1.96% swing Lab. to C.
(2001: C. maj. 4,987 (10.42%))

BRIGG & GOOLE
E. 67,364 T. 42,578 (63.21%) Lab. hold
Ian Cawsey, Lab.   19,257
Matthew Bean, C.   16,363
Gary Johnson, LD   5,690
Stephen Martin, UKIP   1,268
Lab. maj. 2,894 (6.80%)
1.43% swing Lab. to C.
(2001: Lab. maj. 3,961 (9.65%))

BRIGHTON KEMPTOWN
E. 65,985 T. 39,719 (60.19%) Lab. hold
Dr Desmond Turner, Lab.   15,858
Judith Symes, C.   13,121
Marina Pepper, LD   6,560
Simon Williams, Green   2,800
Dr James Chamberlain-Webber,
  UKIP   758
Caroline O'Reilly, PPN-V   172
John McLeod, Soc. Lab.   163
Elaine Cook, Ind.   127
Phil Clarke, Soc. Alt.   113
Gene Dobbs, Ind.   47
Lab. maj. 2,737 (6.89%)
2.83% swing Lab. to C.
(2001: Lab. maj. 4,922 (12.56%))

BRIGHTON PAVILION
E. 68,087 T. 43,578 (64.00%)
                          Lab. (Co-op) hold
David Lepper, Lab. (Co-op)   15,427
Mike Weatherley, C.   10,397
Keith Taylor, Green   9,571
Hazel Thorpe, LD   7,171
Kimberley Crisp-Comotto, UKIP   508
Tony Greenstein, Green Soc.   188
Ian Fyvie, Soc. Lab.   152
Christopher Rooke, Ind.   122
Keith Jago, Ind.   42
Lab. (Co-op) maj. 5,030 (11.55%)
6.06% swing Lab. (Co-op) to C.
(2001: Lab. (Co-op) maj. 9,643
(23.68%))

BRISTOL EAST
E. 68,096 T. 41,720 (61.27%) Lab. hold
*Kerry McCarthy, Lab.   19,152
Philip James, LD   10,531
Julia Manning, C.   8,787
Arjuna Krishna-Das, Green   1,586
Jean Smith, UKIP   1,132
Paulette North, Respect   532
Lab. maj. 8,621 (20.66%)
8.59% swing Lab. to LD
(2001: Lab. maj. 13,392 (33.20%))

BRISTOL NORTH WEST
E. 77,703 T. 47,492 (61.12%)
Lab. (Co-op) hold
Dr Doug Naysmith, Lab. (Co-op) 22,192
Alastair Watson, C.   13,230
Bob Hoyle, LD   9,545
Christopher Lees, UKIP   1,132
Michael Blundell, EDP   828
Graeme Jones, Soc. Alt.   565
Lab. (Co-op) maj. 8,962 (18.87%)
2.28% swing Lab. (Co-op) to C.
(2001: Lab. (Co-op) maj. 11,087
(23.74%))

BRISTOL SOUTH
E. 70,835 T. 42,328 (59.76%) Lab. hold
Rt. Hon. Dawn Primarolo, Lab.   20,778
Kay Barnard, LD   9,636
Graham Hill, C.   8,466
Charlie Bolton, Green   2,127
Mark Dent, UKIP   1,321
Lab. maj. 11,142 (26.32%)
7.86% swing Lab. to LD
(2001: Lab. maj. 14,181 (34.61%))

BRISTOL WEST
E. 81,382 T. 57,396 (70.53%) LD gain
*Stephen Williams, LD   21,987
Valerie Davey, Lab.   16,859
David Martin, C.   15,429
Justin Quinnell, Green   2,163
Simon Muir, UKIP   439
Bernard Kennedy, Soc. Lab.   329
Doug Reid, Baths   190
LD maj. 5,128 (8.93%)
8.44% swing Lab. to LD
(2001: Lab. maj. 4,426 (7.95%))

BROMLEY & CHISLEHURST
E. 71,173 T. 46,137 (64.82%) C. hold
Rt. Hon. Eric Forth, C.   23,583
Rachel Reeves, Lab.   10,241
Peter Brooks, LD   9,368
David Hooper, UKIP   1,475
Ann Garrett, Green   1,470
C. maj. 13,342 (28.92%)
4.01% swing Lab. to C.
(2001: C. maj. 9,037 (20.90%))

BROMSGROVE
E. 70,762 T. 47,810 (67.56%) C. hold
Julie Kirkbride, C.   24,387
David Jones, Lab.   14,307
Sue Haswell, LD   7,197
Paul Buckingham, UKIP   1,919
C. maj. 10,080 (21.08%)
1.63% swing Lab. to C.
(2001: C. maj. 8,138 (17.81%))

BROXBOURNE
E. 68,106 T. 40,628 (59.65%) C. hold
*Charles Walker, C.   21,878
Jamie Bolden, Lab.   10,369
Andrew Porrer, LD   4,973
Dr Andrew Emerson, BNP   1,929
Martin Harvey, UKIP   1,479
C. maj. 11,509 (28.33%)
2.28% swing Lab. to C.
(2001: C. maj. 8,993 (23.76%))

BROXTOWE
E. 71,121 T. 48,806 (68.62%) Lab. hold
Dr Nick Palmer, Lab.   20,457
Bob Seely, C.   18,161
David Watts, LD   7,837
Paul Anderson, Green   896
Patricia Wolfe, UKIP   695
Damian Hockney, Veritas   590
Mark Gregory, Ind.   170
Lab. maj. 2,296 (4.70%)
3.64% swing Lab. to C.
(2001: Lab. maj. 5,873 (11.98%))

BUCKINGHAM
E. 70,265 T. 48,307 (68.75%) C. hold
John Bercow, C.   27,748
David Greene, Lab.   9,619
Luke Croydon, LD   9,508
David Williams, UKIP   1,432
C. maj. 18,129 (37.53%)
4.05% swing Lab. to C.
(2001: C. maj. 13,325 (29.43%))

BURNLEY
E. 65,869 T. 38,983 (59.18%) Lab. hold
*Kitty Ussher, Lab.   14,999
Gordon Birtwistle, LD   9,221
Harry Brooks, Burnley   5,786
Yousuf Miah, C.   4,206
Len Starr, BNP   4,003
Dr Jeff Slater, Ind.   392
Robert McDowell, UKIP   376
Lab. maj. 5,778 (14.82%)
9.15% swing Lab. to LD
(2001: Lab. maj. 10,498 (28.46%))

BURTON
E. 78,556 T. 47,882 (60.95%) Lab. hold
Janet Dean, Lab.   19,701
Adrian Pepper, C.   18,280
Sandra Johnson, LD   6,236
Julie Russell, BNP   1,840
Philip Lancaster, UKIP   913
Brian Buxton, Veritas   912
Lab. maj. 1,421 (2.97%)
3.73% swing Lab. to C.
(2001: Lab. maj. 4,849 (10.44%))

BURY NORTH
E. 72,268 T. 44,439 (61.49%) Lab. hold
David Chaytor, Lab.   19,130
David Nuttall, C.   16,204
Wilf Davison, LD   6,514
Stewart Clough, BNP   1,790
Philip Silver, UKIP   476
Ryan O'Neill, Soc. Lab.   172
Ian Upton, Veritas   153
Lab. maj. 2,926 (6.58%)
4.00% swing Lab. to C.
(2001: Lab. maj. 6,532 (14.58%))

BURY SOUTH
E. 66,898 T. 39,154 (58.53%) Lab. hold
Ivan Lewis, Lab.   19,741
Alex Williams, C.   10,829
Victor D'Albert, LD   6,968
Jim Greenhalgh, UKIP   1,059
Yvonne Hossack, Ind.   557
Lab. maj. 8,912 (22.76%)
4.77% swing Lab. to C.
(2001: Lab. maj. 12,772 (32.30%))

BURY ST EDMUNDS
E. 79,658 T. 52,619 (66.06%) C. hold
David Ruffley, C.   24,332
David Monaghan, Lab.   14,402
David Chappell, LD   10,423
Dr John Howlett, UKIP   1,859
Graham Manning, Green   1,603
C. maj. 9,930 (18.87%)
6.95% swing Lab. to C.
(2001: C. maj. 2,503 (4.98%))

CALDER VALLEY
E. 71,325 T. 47,770 (66.98%) Lab. hold
Christine McCafferty, Lab.   18,426
Liz Truss, C.   17,059
Liz Ingleton, LD   9,027
John Gregory, BNP   1,887
Paul Palmer, Green   1,371
Lab. maj. 1,367 (2.86%)
1.83% swing Lab. to C.
(2001: Lab. maj. 3,094 (6.52%))

CAMBERWELL & PECKHAM
E. 55,739 T. 28,991 (52.01%) Lab. hold
Rt. Hon. Harriet Harman, Lab.   18,933
Richard Porter, LD   5,450
Jessica Lee, C.   2,841
Paul Ingram, Green   1,172
Derek Penhallow, UKIP   350
Margaret Sharkey, Soc. Lab.   132
Sanjay Kulkarni, WRP   113
Lab. maj. 13,483 (46.51%)
4.88% swing Lab. to LD
(2001: Lab. maj. 14,123 (56.26%))

CAMBRIDGE
E. 70,154 T. 43,569 (62.10%) LD gain
*David Howarth, LD   19,152
Anne Campbell, Lab.   14,813
Ian Lyon, C.   7,193
Martin Lucas-Smith, Green   1,245
Helene Davies, UKIP   569
Tom Woodcock, Respect   477
Suzon Forscey-Moore, Ind.   60
Graham Wilkinson, Ind.   60
LD maj. 4,339 (9.96%)
14.99% swing Lab. to LD
(2001: Lab. maj. 8,579 (20.03%))

CAMBRIDGESHIRE NORTH EAST
E. 85,079 T. 50,877 (59.80%) C. hold
Malcolm Moss, C.   24,181
Ffinlo Costain, Lab.   15,280
Alan Dean, LD   8,693
Leonard Baynes, UKIP   2,723
C. maj. 8,901 (17.50%)
2.12% swing Lab. to C.
(2001: C. maj. 6,373 (13.26%))

CAMBRIDGESHIRE NORTH WEST
E. 79,694 T. 49,092 (61.60%) C. hold
*Shailesh Vara, C.   22,504
Ayfer Orhan, Lab.   12,671
John Souter, LD   11,232
Robert Brown, UKIP   2,685
C. maj. 9,833 (20.03%)
0.80% swing Lab. to C.
(2001: C. maj. 8,101 (18.43%))

CAMBRIDGESHIRE SOUTH
E. 77,022 T. 52,648 (68.35%) C. hold
Andrew Lansley, C.   23,676
Andrew Dickson, LD   15,675
Sandra Wilson, Lab.   10,189
Robin Page, UKIP   1,556
Simon Saggers, Green   1,552
C. maj. 8,001 (15.20%)
1.09% swing C. to LD
(2001: C. maj. 8,403 (17.38%))

CAMBRIDGESHIRE SOUTH EAST
E. 85,901 T. 56,060 (65.26%) C. hold
James Paice, C.   26,374
Jonathan Chatfield, LD   17,750
Fiona Ross, Lab.   11,936
C. maj. 8,624 (15.38%)
0.97% swing C. to LD
(2001: C. maj. 8,990 (17.33%))

CANNOCK CHASE
E. 75,194 T. 43,155 (57.39%) Lab. hold
Dr Tony Wright, Lab.   22,139
Ian Collard, C.   12,912
Jenny Pinkett, LD   5,934
Roy Jenkins, UKIP   2,170
Lab. maj. 9,227 (21.38%)
2.34% swing Lab. to C.
(2001: Lab. maj. 10,704 (26.07%))

CANTERBURY
E. 72,046 T. 47,587 (66.05%) C. hold
Julian Brazier, C.   21,113
Alex Hilton, Lab.   13,642
Jenny Barnard-Langston, LD   10,059
Geoff Meaden, Green   1,521
John Moore, UKIP   926
Rocky van de Benderskum, LCA   326
C. maj. 7,471 (15.70%)
5.56% swing Lab. to C.
(2001: C. maj. 2,069 (4.58%))

CARLISLE
E. 59,508 T. 35,394 (59.48%) Lab. hold
Eric Martlew, Lab.   17,019
Mike Mitchelson, C.   11,324
Steven Tweedie, LD   5,916
Steven Cochrane, UKIP   792
Lezley Gibson, LCA   343
Lab. maj. 5,695 (16.09%)
0.12% swing Lab. to C.
(2001: Lab. maj. 5,702 (16.33%))

CARSHALTON & WALLINGTON
E. 67,844 T. 43,061 (63.47%) LD hold
Tom Brake, LD   17,357
Ken Andrew, C.   16,289
Andrew Theobald, Lab.   7,396
Francis Day, UKIP   1,111
Bob Steel, Green   908
LD maj. 1,068 (2.48%)
4.36% swing LD to C.
(2001: LD maj. 4,547 (11.20%))

CASTLE POINT
E. 69,480 T. 45,802 (65.92%) C. hold
Dr Robert Spink, C.   22,118
Luke Akehurst, Lab.   13,917
James Sandbach, LD   4,719
Neil Hamper, UKIP   3,431
Irene Willis, Green   1,617
C. maj. 8,201 (17.91%)
7.71% swing Lab. to C.
(2001: C. maj. 985 (2.48%))

CHARNWOOD
E. 76,274 T. 50,616 (66.36%) C. hold
Rt. Hon. Stephen Dorrell, C.   23,571
Richard Robinson, Lab.   14,762
Sue King, LD   9,057
Andrew Holders, BNP   1,737
Jamie Bye, UKIP   1,489
C. maj. 8,809 (17.40%)
0.68% swing Lab. to C.
(2001: C. maj. 7,739 (16.03%))

CHATHAM & AYLESFORD
E. 70,515 T. 42,080 (59.68%) Lab. hold
Jonathan Shaw, Lab.   18,387
Anne Jobson, C.   16,055
Debra Enever, LD   5,744
Jeffrey King, UKIP   1,226
Michael Russell, Eng. Dem.   668
Lab. maj. 2,332 (5.54%)
2.69% swing Lab. to C.
(2001: Lab. maj. 4,340 (10.92%))

CHEADLE
E. 68,123 T. 47,437 (69.63%) LD hold
Patsy Calton, LD   23,189
Stephen Day, C.   19,169
Martin Miller, Lab.   4,169
Vincent Cavanagh, UKIP   489
Richard Chadfield, BNP   421
LD maj. 4,020 (8.47%)
4.20% swing C. to LD
(2001: LD maj. 33 (0.08%))

CHELMSFORD WEST
E. 82,489 T. 51,052 (61.89%) C. hold
Simon Burns, C.   22,946
Stephen Robinson, LD   13,326
Russell Kennedy, Lab.   13,236
Kenneth Wedon, UKIP   1,544
C. maj. 9,620 (18.84%)
0.18% swing C. to LD
(2001: C. maj. 6,261 (13.01%))

CHELTENHAM
E. 71,541 T. 43,621 (60.97%) LD hold
*Martin Horwood, LD   18,122
Dr Vanessa Gearson, C.   15,819
Christopher Evans, Lab.   4,988
Dr Robert Hodges, Ind.   2,651
Keith Bessant, Green   908
Niall Warry, UKIP   608
Dancing Ken Hanks, Loony   525
LD maj. 2,303 (5.28%)
3.64% swing LD to C.
(2001: LD maj. 5,255 (12.56%))

CHESHAM & AMERSHAM
E. 69,217 T. 47,097 (68.04%) C. hold
Cheryl Gillan, C.   25,619
John Ford, LD   11,821
Rupa Huq, Lab.   6,610
Nick Wilkins, Green   1,656
David Samuel-Camps, UKIP   1,391
C. maj. 13,798 (29.30%)
1.53% swing LD to C.
(2001: C. maj. 11,882 (26.24%))

CHESTER, CITY OF
E. 69,785 T. 44,903 (64.34%) Lab. hold
Christine Russell, Lab.   17,458
Paul Offer, C.   16,543
Mia Jones, LD   9,818
Allan Weddell, UKIP   776
Ed Abrams, Eng. Dem.   308
Lab. maj. 915 (2.04%)
6.66% swing Lab. to C.
(2001: Lab. maj. 6,894 (15.36%))

CHESTERFIELD
E. 74,007 T. 44,121 (59.62%) LD hold
Paul Holmes, LD   20,875
Simon Rich, Lab.   17,830
Mark Kreling, C.   3,605
Christopher Brady, UKIP   997
Ian Jerram, Eng. Dem.   814
LD maj. 3,045 (6.90%)
0.54% swing Lab. to LD
(2001: LD maj. 2,586 (5.82%))

CHICHESTER
E. 78,645 T. 52,401 (66.63%) C. hold
Andrew Tyrie, C.   25,302
Alan Hilliar, LD   14,442
Jonathan Austin, Lab.   9,632
Douglas Denny, UKIP   3,025
C. maj. 10,860 (20.72%)
1.09% swing C. to LD
(2001: C. maj. 11,355 (22.93%))

CHINGFORD & WOODFORD GREEN
E. 61,386 T. 38,648 (62.96%) C. hold
Rt. Hon. Iain Duncan Smith, C.   20,555
Simon Wright, Lab.   9,914
John Beanse, LD   6,832
Michael McGough, UKIP   1,078
Barry White, Ind.   269
C. maj. 10,641 (27.53%)
6.35% swing Lab. to C.
(2001: C. maj. 5,487 (14.84%))

CHIPPING BARNET
E. 66,143 T. 42,381 (64.07%) C. hold
*Theresa Villiers, C.   19,744
Pauline Coakley-Webb, Lab.   13,784
Sean Hooker, LD   6,671
Audrey Poppy, Green   1,199
Victor Kaye, UKIP   924
Rainbow George Weiss, Vote Dream   59
C. maj. 5,960 (14.06%)
3.85% swing Lab. to C.
(2001: C. maj. 2,701 (6.36%))

CHORLEY
E. 78,838 T. 49,569 (62.87%) Lab. hold
Lindsay Hoyle, Lab.   25,131
Simon Mallett, C.   17,506
Alexander Wilson-Fletcher, LD   6,932
Lab. maj. 7,625 (15.38%)
1.11% swing Lab. to C.
(2001: Lab. maj. 8,444 (17.61%))

CHRISTCHURCH
E. 74,109 T. 51,565 (69.58%) C. hold
Christopher Chope, C.   28,208
Leslie Coman, LD   12,649
Jim King, Lab.   8,051
David Hughes, UKIP   2,657
C. maj. 15,559 (30.17%)
1.42% swing LD to C.
(2001: C. maj. 13,544 (27.32%))

CITIES OF LONDON &
WESTMINSTER
E. 72,577 T. 36,487 (50.27%)   C. hold
Mark Field, C.   17,260
Hywel Lloyd, Lab.   9,165
Marie-Louise Rossi, LD   7,306
Tristan Smith, Green   1,544
Colin Merton, UKIP   399
Brian Haw, Ind.   298
Jill McLachlan, CPA   246
David Harris, Veritas   218
Cass Jean-Claude Cass-Horne, Ind.   51
C. maj. 8,095 (22.19%)
4.47% swing Lab. to C.
(2001: C. maj. 4,499 (13.24%))

CLEETHORPES
E. 70,746 T. 43,589 (61.61%) Lab. hold
Shona McIsaac, Lab.   18,889
Martin Vickers, C.   16,247
Geoff Lowis, LD   6,437
Bill Hardie, UKIP   2,016
Lab. maj. 2,642 (6.06%)
3.59% swing Lab. to C.
(2001: Lab. maj. 5,620 (13.25%))

COLCHESTER
E. 79,010 T. 44,899 (56.83%) LD hold
Bob Russell, LD   21,145
Kevin Bentley, C.   14,868
Laura Bruni, Lab.   8,886
LD maj. 6,277 (13.98%)
0.64% swing C. to LD
(2001: LD maj. 5,553 (12.70%))

COLNE VALLEY
E. 74,121 T. 48,920 (66.00%) Lab. hold
Kali Mountford, Lab.   17,536
Maggie Throup, C.   16,035
Elisabeth Wilson, LD   11,822
Barry Fowler, BNP   1,430
Lesley Hedges, Green   1,295
Helen Martinek, Veritas   543
Ian Mumford, Loony   259
Lab. maj. 1,501 (3.07%)
3.40% swing Lab. to C.
(2001: Lab. maj. 4,639 (9.87%))

CONGLETON
E. 72,770 T. 46,682 (64.15%) C. hold
Lady Ann Winterton, C.   21,189
Nicholas Milton, Lab.   12,943
Eleanor Key, LD   12,550
C. maj. 8,246 (17.66%)
0.92% swing Lab. to C.
(2001: C. maj. 7,134 (15.82%))

COPELAND
E. 54,206 T. 33,757 (62.28%) Lab. hold
*Jamie Reed, Lab.   17,033
Chris Whiteside, C.   10,713
Frank Hollowell, LD   3,880
Edward Caley-Knowles, UKIP   735
Brian Earley, Ind.   734
Alan Mossop, Eng. Dem.   662
Lab. maj. 6,320 (18.72%)
2.22% swing C. to Lab.
(2001: Lab. maj. 4,964 (14.28%))

CORBY
E. 73,000 T. 48,527 (66.48%)
                        Lab. (Co-op) hold
Phil Hope, Lab. (Co-op)   20,913
Andrew Griffith, C.   19,396
David Radcliffe, LD   6,184
Ian Gillman, UKIP   1,278
Steve Carey, Soc. Lab.   499
John Morris, Ind.   257
Lab. (Co-op) maj. 1,517 (3.13%)
4.47% swing Lab. (Co-op) to C.
(2001: Lab. (Co-op) maj. 5,700
(12.07%))

CORNWALL NORTH
E. 86,841 T. 55,982 (64.46%) LD hold
*Dan Rogerson, LD   23,842
Mark Formosa, C.   20,766
David Acton, Lab.   6,636
David Campbell-Bannerman,
    UKIP   3,063
Dick Cole, Meb. Ker.   1,351
Alan Eastwood, Veritas   324
LD maj. 3,076 (5.49%)
6.36% swing LD to C.
(2001: LD maj. 9,832 (18.21%))

CORNWALL SOUTH EAST
E. 80,704 T. 53,455 (66.24%) LD hold
Colin Breed, LD   24,986
Ashley Gray, C.   18,479
Colin Binley, Lab.   6,069
David Lucas, UKIP   2,693
Graham Sandercock, Meb. Ker.   769
Anne Assheton-Salton, Veritas   459
LD maj. 6,507 (12.17%)
0.89% swing C. to LD
(2001: LD maj. 5,375 (10.39%))

COTSWOLD
E. 71,039 T. 47,351 (66.65%)   C. hold
Geoffrey Clifton-Brown, C.   23,326
Philip Beckerlegge, LD   13,638
Mark Dempsey, Lab.   8,457
Richard Buckley, UKIP   1,538
James Derieg, Ind.   392
C. maj. 9,688 (20.46%)
2.80% swing C. to LD
(2001: C. maj. 11,983 (26.06%))

COVENTRY NORTH EAST
E. 70,225 T. 37,195 (52.97%) Lab. hold
Rt. Hon. Robert Ainsworth, Lab. 21,178
Jaswant Singh Birdi, C.   6,956
Russell Field, LD   6,123
Dave Nellist, Soc. Alt.   1,874
Paul Sootheran, UKIP   1,064
Lab. maj. 14,222 (38.24%)
2.02% swing Lab. to C.
(2001: Lab. maj. 15,751 (42.27%))

COVENTRY NORTH WEST
E. 73,180 T. 43,438 (59.36%) Lab. hold
Geoffrey Robinson, Lab.   20,942
Brian Connell, C.   11,627
Iona Anderson, LD   7,932
David Clarke, BNP   1,556
Sandra List, UKIP   766
Nicola Downes, Soc. Alt.   615
Lab. maj. 9,315 (21.44%)
2.06% swing Lab. to C.
(2001: Lab. maj. 10,874 (25.56%))

COVENTRY SOUTH
E. 68,884 T. 40,685 (59.06%) Lab. hold
Jim Cunningham, Lab.   18,649
Heather Wheeler, C.   12,394
Vincent McKee, LD   7,228
Rob Windsor, Soc. Alt.   1,097
William Brown, UKIP   829
Irene Rogers, Ind.   344
James Rooney, FF   144
Lab. maj. 6,255 (15.37%)
2.64% swing Lab. to C.
(2001: Lab. maj. 8,279 (20.65%))

CRAWLEY
E. 71,911 T. 41,973 (58.37%) Lab. hold
Laura Moffatt, Lab.   16,411
Henry Smith, C.   16,374
Rupert Sheard, LD   6,503
Richard Trower, BNP   1,277
Ronald Walters, UKIP   935
Robin Burnham, Dem. Soc. All.   263
Arshad Khan, JP   210
Lab. maj. 37 (0.09%)
8.52% swing Lab. to C.
(2001: Lab. maj. 6,770 (17.13%))

CREWE & NANTWICH
E. 72,472 T. 43,485 (60.00%) Lab. hold
Gwyneth Dunwoody, Lab.   21,240
Eveleigh Moore-Dutton, C.   14,162
Paul Roberts, LD   8,083
Lab. maj. 7,078 (16.28%)
3.78% swing Lab. to C.
(2001: Lab. maj. 9,906 (23.84%))

CROSBY
E. 54,255 T. 36,194 (66.71%) Lab. hold
Claire Curtis-Thomas, Lab.   17,463
Debi Jones, C.   11,623
Jim Murray, LD   6,298
Dr John Whittaker, UKIP   454
Geoffrey Bottoms, Comm. Brit.   199
David Braid, Clause 28   157
Lab. maj. 5,840 (16.14%)
3.26% swing Lab. to C.
(2001: Lab. maj. 8,353 (22.66%))

CROYDON CENTRAL
E. 80,825 T. 48,957 (60.57%) C. gain
*Andrew Pelling, C.   19,974
Geraint Davies, Lab.   19,899
Jeremy Hargreaves, LD   6,384
Ian Edwards, UKIP   1,066
Bernice Golberg, Green   1,036
Marianne Bowness, Veritas   304
John Cartwright, Loony   193
Janet Stears, Work   101
C. maj. 75 (0.15%)
4.42% swing Lab. to C.
(2001: Lab. maj. 3,984 (8.69%))

CROYDON NORTH
E. 83,796 T. 43,847 (52.33%) Lab. hold
Malcolm Wicks, Lab.   23,555
Tariq Ahmad, C.   9,667
Adrian Gee-Turner, LD   7,560
Shasha Khan, Green   1,248
Henry Pearce, UKIP   770
Peter Gibson, Croydon   394
Winston McKenzie, Veritas   324
Farhan Rasheed, Ind.   197
Michelle Chambers, Work   132
Lab. maj. 13,888 (31.67%)
4.29% swing Lab. to C.
(2001: Lab. maj. 16,858 (40.25%))

CROYDON SOUTH
E. 76,872 T. 48,897 (63.61%) C. hold
Richard Ottaway, C.   25,320
Paul Smith, Lab.   11,792
Sandra Lawman, LD   10,049
James Feisenberger, UKIP   1,054
Graham Dare, Veritas   497
Mark Samuel, Work   185
C. maj. 13,528 (27.67%)
4.18% swing Lab. to C.
(2001: C. maj. 8,697 (19.30%))

DAGENHAM
E. 60,141 T. 30,841 (51.28%) Lab. hold
Jonathan Cruddas, Lab.   15,446
Michael White, C.   7,841
James Kempton, LD   3,106
Lawrence Rustem, BNP   2,870
Gerard Batten, UKIP   1,578
Lab. maj. 7,605 (24.66%)
3.43% swing Lab. to C.
(2001: Lab. maj. 8,693 (31.52%))

DARLINGTON
E. 65,281 T. 39,388 (60.34%) Lab. hold
Rt. Hon. Alan Milburn, Lab.   20,643
Anthony Frieze, C.   10,239
Robert Adamson, LD   7,269
John Hoodless, UKIP   730
Dai Davies, Veritas   507
Lab. maj. 10,404 (26.41%)
0.19% swing C. to Lab.
(2001: Lab. maj. 9,529 (23.38%))

DARTFORD
E. 74,028 T. 46,779 (63.19%) Lab. hold
Dr Howard Stoate, Lab.   19,909
Gareth Johnson, C.   19,203
Peter Bucklitsch, LD   5,036
Mark Croucher, UKIP   1,407
Michael Tibby, NEP   1,224
Lab. maj. 706 (1.51%)
2.94% swing Lab. to C.
(2001: Lab. maj. 3,306 (7.39%))

DAVENTRY
E. 88,758 T. 60,439 (68.09%) C. hold
Tim Boswell, C.   31,206
Andrew Hammond, Lab.   16,520
Hannah Saul, LD   9,964
Barry Mahoney, UKIP   1,927
Barrie Wilkins, Veritas   822
C. maj. 14,686 (24.30%)
3.64% swing Lab. to C.
(2001: C. maj. 9,649 (17.02%))

DENTON & REDDISH
E. 68,267 T. 35,442 (51.92%) Lab. hold
*Andrew Gwynne, Lab.   20,340
Alex Story, C.   6,842
Allison Seabourne, LD   5,814
John Edgar, BNP   1,326
Gerald Price, UKIP   1,120
Lab. maj. 13,498 (38.08%)
3.77% swing Lab. to C.
(2001: Lab. maj. 15,330 (45.63%))

DERBY NORTH
E. 68,173 T. 43,818 (64.27%) Lab. hold
Bob Laxton, Lab.   19,272
Richard Aitken-Davies, C.   15,515
Jeremy Beckett, LD   7,209
Martin Bardoe, Veritas   958
Michelle Medgyesy, UKIP   864
Lab. maj. 3,757 (8.57%)
3.64% swing Lab. to C.
(2001: Lab. maj. 6,982 (15.85%))

DERBY SOUTH
E. 70,397 T. 43,373 (61.61%) Lab. hold
Rt. Hon. Margaret Beckett, Lab.   19,683
Lucy Care, LD   14,026
David Brackenbury, C.   8,211
David Black, UKIP   845
Frank Leeming, Veritas   608
Lab. maj. 5,657 (13.04%)
12.05% swing Lab. to LD
(2001: Lab. maj. 13,855 (32.16%))

DERBYSHIRE NORTH EAST
E. 70,981 T. 43,434 (61.19%) Lab. hold
*Natascha Engel, Lab.   21,416
Dominic Johnson, C.   11,351
Tom Snowdon, LD   8,812
Kenneth Perkins, UKIP   1,855
Lab. maj. 10,065 (23.17%)
2.96% swing Lab. to C.
(2001: Lab. maj. 12,258 (29.10%))

DERBYSHIRE SOUTH
E. 85,049 T. 55,820 (65.63%) Lab. hold
Mark Todd, Lab.   24,823
Simon Spencer, C.   20,328
Deborah Newton-Cook, LD   7,600
David Joines, BNP   1,797
Edward Spalton, Veritas   1,272
Lab. maj. 4,495 (8.05%)
3.53% swing Lab. to C.
(2001: Lab. maj. 7,851 (15.11%))

DERBYSHIRE WEST
E. 73,865 T. 51,143 (69.24%) C. hold
Patrick McLoughlin, C.   24,378
David Menon, Lab.   13,625
Ray Dring, LD   11,408
Michael Cruddas, UKIP   1,322
Nick Delves, Loony   405
Martin Kyslun, Ind.   5
C. maj. 10,753 (21.03%)
3.23% swing Lab. to C.
(2001: C. maj. 7,370 (14.57%))

DEVIZES
E. 86,168 T. 56,146 (65.16%) C. hold
Rt. Hon. Michael Ancram, C.   27,253
Fiona Hornby, LD   14,059
Sharon Charity, Lab.   12,519
Alan Wood, UKIP   2,315
C. maj. 13,194 (23.50%)
0.84% swing C. to LD
(2001: C. maj. 11,896 (22.34%))

DEVON EAST
E. 71,000 T. 49,247 (69.36%) C. hold
Hugo Swire, C.   23,075
Tim Dumper, LD   15,139
James Court, Lab.   7,598
Colin McNamee, UKIP   3,035
Christopher Way, Ind.   400
C. maj. 7,936 (16.11%)
0.51% swing C. to LD
(2001: C. maj. 8,195 (17.13%))

DEVON NORTH
E. 76,203 T. 51,930 (68.15%) LD hold
Nick Harvey, LD   23,840
Orlando Fraser, C.   18,868
Mark Cann, Lab.   4,656
John Browne, UKIP   2,740
Richard Knight, Green   1,826
LD maj. 4,972 (9.57%)
1.76% swing C. to LD
(2001: LD maj. 2,984 (6.06%))

DEVON SOUTH WEST
E. 71,307 T. 48,885 (68.56%) C. hold
Gary Streeter, C.   21,906
Judy Evans, LD   11,765
Christopher Mavin, Lab.   11,545
Hugh Williams, UKIP   3,669
C. maj. 10,141 (20.74%)
3.86% swing C. to LD
(2001: C. maj. 7,144 (15.23%))

DEVON WEST & TORRIDGE
E. 83,489 T. 58,584 (70.17%) C. gain
*Geoffrey Cox, C.   25,013
David Walter, LD   21,777
Rebecca Richards, Lab.   6,001
Matthew Jackson, UKIP   3,790
Peter Christie, Green   2,003
C. maj. 3,236 (5.52%)
3.83% swing LD to C.
(2001: LD maj. 1,194 (2.14%))

DEWSBURY
E. 62,243 T. 38,595 (62.01%) Lab. hold
*Shahid Malik, Lab.   15,807
Sayeeda Warsi, C.   11,192
Kingsley Hill, LD   5,624
David Exley, BNP   5,066
Brenda Smithson, Green   593
Alan Girvan, Ind.   313
Lab. maj. 4,615 (11.96%)
4.18% swing Lab. to C.
(2001: Lab. maj. 7,449 (20.32%))

DON VALLEY
E. 66,993 T. 36,864 (55.03%) Lab. hold
Caroline Flint, Lab.   19,418
Adam Duguid, C.   10,820
Stewart Arnold, LD   6,626
Lab. maj. 8,598 (23.32%)
1.33% swing Lab. to C.
(2001: Lab. maj. 9,520 (25.99%))

DONCASTER CENTRAL
E. 65,731 T. 34,351 (52.26%) Lab. hold
Rosie Winterton, Lab.   17,617
Patrick Wilson, LD   7,815
Stefan Kerner, C.   6,489
John Wilkinson, BNP   1,239
Alan Simmons, UKIP   1,191
Lab. maj. 9,802 (28.53%)
8.80% swing Lab. to LD
(2001: Lab. maj. 11,999 (35.39%))

DONCASTER NORTH
E. 61,741 T. 31,578 (51.15%) Lab. hold
*Ed Miliband, Lab.   17,531
Martin Drake, C.   4,875
Doug Pickett, LD   3,800
Martin Williams, CG   2,365
Lee Hagan, BNP   1,506
Robert Nixon, UKIP   940
Michael Cassidy, Eng. Dem.   561
Lab. maj. 12,656 (40.08%)
4.17% swing Lab. to C.
(2001: Lab. maj. 15,187 (48.42%))

DORSET MID & POOLE NORTH
E. 65,924 T. 45,159 (68.50%) LD hold
Annette Brooke, LD   22,000
Simon Hayes, C.   16,518
Philip Murray, Lab.   5,221
Avril King, UKIP   1,420
LD maj. 5,482 (12.14%)
5.63% swing C. to LD
(2001: LD maj. 384 (0.88%))

DORSET NORTH
E. 74,286　T. 52,815 (71.10%)　C. hold
Robert Walter, C.　23,714
Emily Gasson, LD　21,470
John Yarwood, Lab.　4,596
Richard Frampton Hobbs, UKIP　1,918
Ralph Arliss, Green　1,117
C. maj. 2,244 (4.25%)
1.85% swing C. to LD
(2001: C. maj. 3,797 (7.94%))

DORSET SOUTH
E. 70,668　T. 48,584 (68.75%)　Lab. hold
Jim Knight, Lab.　20,231
Ed Matts, C.　18,419
Graham Oakes, LD　7,647
Hugh Chalker, UKIP　1,571
Vic Hamilton, LCA　282
Bernard Parkes, Respect　219
Andrew Kirkwood, PRTYP　107
Colin Bex, Wessex Reg.　83
David Marchesi, Soc. Lab.　25
Lab. maj. 1,812 (3.73%)
1.70% swing C. to Lab.
(2001: Lab. maj. 153 (0.34%))

DORSET WEST
E. 69,764　T. 53,225 (76.29%)　C. hold
Rt. Hon. Oliver Letwin, C.　24,763
Justine McGuinness, LD　22,302
Dave Roberts, Lab.　4,124
Linda Guest, UKIP　1,084
Susan Greene, Green　952
C. maj. 2,461 (4.62%)
0.89% swing LD to C.
(2001: C. maj. 1,414 (2.85%))

DOVER
E. 70,884　T. 47,884 (67.55%)　Lab. hold
Gwyn Prosser, Lab.　21,680
Paul Watkins, C.　16,739
Antony Hook, LD　7,607
Mike Wiltshire, UKIP　1,252
Vic Matcham, Ind.　606
Lab. maj. 4,941 (10.32%)
0.62% swing Lab. to C.
(2001: Lab. maj. 5,199 (11.56%))

DUDLEY NORTH
E. 68,766　T. 41,408 (60.22%)　Lab. hold
*Ian Austin, Lab.　18,306
Ian Hillas, C.　12,874
Gerry Lewis, LD　4,257
Simon Darby, BNP　4,022
Malcolm Davis, UKIP　1,949
Lab. maj. 5,432 (13.12%)
2.26% swing Lab. to C.
(2001: Lab. maj. 6,800 (17.63%))

DUDLEY SOUTH
E. 65,228　T. 39,276 (60.21%)　Lab. hold
Ian Pearson, Lab.　17,800
Marco Longhi, C.　13,556
Jonathan Bramall, LD　4,808
John Salvage, BNP　1,841
Andrew Benion, UKIP　1,271
Lab. maj. 4,244 (10.81%)
3.98% swing Lab. to C.
(2001: Lab. maj. 6,817 (18.76%))

DULWICH & WEST NORWOOD
E. 72,232　T. 41,989 (58.13%)　Lab. hold
Rt. Hon. Tessa Jowell, Lab.　19,059
Jonathan Mitchell, LD　10,252
Kim Humphreys, C.　9,200
Jenny Jones, Green　2,741
Ralph Atkinson, UKIP　290
David Heather, Veritas　241
Amanda Rose, Soc. Lab.　149
Judy Weleminsky, Fit　57
Lab. maj. 8,807 (20.97%)
9.37% swing Lab. to LD
(2001: Lab. maj. 12,310 (32.19%))

DURHAM NORTH
E. 67,506　T. 37,341 (55.32%)　Lab. hold
Kevan Jones, Lab.　23,932
Philip Latham, LD　7,151
Mark Watson, C.　6,258
Lab. maj. 16,781 (44.94%)
4.12% swing Lab. to LD
(2001: Lab. maj. 18,683 (48.44%))

DURHAM NORTH WEST
E. 68,130　T. 39,509 (57.99%)　Lab. hold
Rt. Hon. Hilary Armstrong, Lab.　21,312
Alan Ord, LD　7,869
Jamie Devlin, C.　6,463
Watts Stelling, Ind.　3,865
Lab. maj. 13,443 (34.03%)
6.80% swing Lab. to LD
(2001: Lab. maj. 16,333 (41.64%))

DURHAM, CITY OF
E. 71,441　T. 44,364 (62.10%)　Lab. hold
*Dr Roberta Blackman-Woods, Lab.　20,928
Carol Woods, LD　17,654
Ben Rogers, C.　4,179
Anthony Martin, Veritas　1,603
Lab. maj. 3,274 (7.38%)
12.51% swing Lab. to LD
(2001: Lab. maj. 13,441 (32.40%))

EALING ACTON & SHEPHERD'S BUSH
E. 70,454　T. 39,623 (56.24%)　Lab. hold
*Andrew Slaughter, Lab.　16,579
Jonathan Gough, C.　11,059
Gary Malcolm, LD　9,986
Geoff Burgess, Green　1,999
Lab. maj. 5,520 (13.93%)
7.54% swing Lab. to C.
(2001: Lab. maj. 10,789 (29.00%))

EALING NORTH
E. 78,298　T. 46,507 (59.40%)　Lab. hold
Stephen Pound, Lab.　20,956
Roger Curtis, C.　13,897
Francesco Fruzza, LD　9,148
Alan Outten, Green　1,319
Robin Lambert, UKIP　692
David Malindine, Veritas　495
Lab. maj. 7,059 (15.18%)
5.58% swing Lab. to C.
(2001: Lab. maj. 11,837 (26.33%))

EALING SOUTHALL
E. 83,738　T. 47,045 (56.18%)　Lab. hold
Piara Khabra, Lab.　22,937
Nigel Bakhai, LD　11,497
Mark Nicholson, C.　10,147
Sarah Edwards, Green　2,175
Malkiat Bilku, WRP　289
Lab. maj. 11,440 (24.32%)
6.59% swing Lab. to LD
(2001: Lab. maj. 13,683 (29.22%))

EASINGTON
E. 61,084　T. 31,855 (52.15%)　Lab. hold
John Cummings, Lab.　22,733
Christopher Ord, LD　4,097
Lucille Nicholson, C.　3,400
Ian McDonald, BNP　1,042
Dave Robinson, Soc. Lab.　583
Lab. maj. 18,636 (58.50%)
4.00% swing Lab. to LD
(2001: Lab. maj. 21,949 (66.49%))

EAST HAM
E. 78,104　T. 39,569 (50.66%)　Lab. hold
Stephen Timms, Lab.　21,326
Abdul Khaliq Mian, Respect　8,171
Sarah Macken, C.　5,196
Ann Haigh, LD　4,296
David Bamber, CPA　580
Lab. maj. 13,155 (33.25%)
19.95% swing Lab. to Respect
(2001: Lab. maj. 21,032 (56.42%))

EASTBOURNE
E. 74,628　T. 48,392 (64.84%)　C. hold
Nigel Waterson, C.　21,033
Stephen Lloyd, LD　19,909
Andrew Jones, Lab.　5,268
Andrew Meggs, UKIP　1,233
Clive Gross, Green　949
C. maj. 1,124 (2.32%)
1.24% swing C. to LD
(2001: C. maj. 2,154 (4.81%))

EASTLEIGH
E. 76,844　T. 49,771 (64.77%)　LD hold
*Christopher Huhne, LD　19,216
Conor Burns, C.　18,648
Chris Watt, Lab.　10,238
Christopher Murphy, UKIP　1,669
LD maj. 568 (1.14%)
2.64% swing LD to C.
(2001: LD maj. 3,058 (6.43%))

ECCLES
E. 69,006　T. 34,632 (50.19%)　Lab. hold
Ian Stewart, Lab.　19,702
Thelma Matuk, C.　6,816
Jane Brophy, LD　6,429
Peter Reeve, UKIP　1,685
Lab. maj. 12,886 (37.21%)
3.29% swing Lab. to C.
(2001: Lab. maj. 14,528 (43.78%))

EDDISBURY
E. 72,249　T. 45,674 (63.22%)　C. hold
Stephen O'Brien, C.　21,181
Mark Green, Lab.　14,986
Joanne Crotty, LD　8,182
Steve Roxborough, UKIP　1,325
C. maj. 6,195 (13.56%)
1.64% swing Lab. to C.
(2001: C. maj. 4,568 (10.29%))

EDMONTON
E. 58,764　T. 34,703 (59.05%)　Lab. (Co-op) hold
Andy Love, Lab. (Co-op)　18,456
Lionel Zetter, C.　10,381
Dr Iarla Kilbane-Dawe, LD　4,162
Nina Armstrong, Green　889
Gwyneth Rolph, UKIP　815
Lab. (Co-op) maj. 8,075 (23.27%)
2.42% swing Lab. (Co-op) to C.
(2001: Lab. (Co-op) maj. 9,772 (28.10%))

ELLESMERE PORT & NESTON
E. 68,249 T. 42,069 (61.64%) Lab. hold
Andrew Miller, Lab.   20,371
Myles Hogg, C.   13,885
Steve Cooke, LD   6,607
Henry Crocker, UKIP   1,206
Lab. maj. 6,486 (15.42%)
5.37% swing Lab. to C.
(2001: Lab. maj. 10,861 (26.15%))

ELMET
E. 68,514 T. 47,146 (68.81%) Lab. hold
Colin Burgon, Lab.   22,260
Andrew Millard, C.   17,732
Madeleine Kirk, LD   5,923
Tracy Andrews, BNP   1,231
Lab. maj. 4,528 (9.60%)
0.26% swing C. to Lab.
(2001: Lab. maj. 4,171 (9.08%))

ELTHAM
E. 57,236 T. 35,305 (61.68%) Lab. hold
Clive Efford, Lab.   15,381
Spencer Drury, C.   12,105
Ian Gerrard, LD   5,669
Jeremy Elms, UKIP   1,024
Barry Roberts, BNP   979
Andrew Graham, Ind.   147
Lab. maj. 3,276 (9.28%)
5.71% swing Lab. to C.
(2001: Lab. maj. 6,996 (20.70%))

ENFIELD NORTH
E. 66,460 T. 40,749 (61.31%) Lab. hold
Joan Ryan, Lab.   18,055
Nick de Bois, C.   16,135
Simon Radford, LD   4,642
Terence Farr, BNP   1,004
Gary Robbens, UKIP   750
Patrick Burns, Ind.   163
Lab. maj. 1,920 (4.71%)
0.63% swing Lab. to C.
(2001: Lab. maj. 2,291 (6.01%))

ENFIELD SOUTHGATE
E. 63,613 T. 42,210 (66.35%) C. gain
*David Burrowes, C.   18,830
Stephen Twigg, Lab.   17,083
Ziz Kakoulakis, LD   4,724
Trevor Doughty, Green   1,083
Brian Hall, UKIP   490
C. maj. 1,747 (4.14%)
8.69% swing Lab. to C.
(2001: Lab. maj. 5,546 (13.23%))

EPPING FOREST
E. 72,776 T. 44,860 (61.64%) C. hold
Eleanor Laing, C.   23,783
Bambos Charalambous, Lab.   9,425
Michael Heavens, LD   8,279
Julian Leppert, BNP   1,728
Andrew Smith, UKIP   1,014
Robin Tilbrook, Eng. Dem.   631
C. maj. 14,358 (32.01%)
6.07% swing Lab. to C.
(2001: C. maj. 8,426 (19.87%))

EPSOM & EWELL
E. 75,515 T. 49,879 (66.05%) C. hold
Chris Grayling, C.   27,146
Jonathan Lees, LD   10,699
Charles Mansell, Lab.   10,265
Peter Kefford, UKIP   1,769
C. maj. 16,447 (32.97%)
3.50% swing LD to C.
(2001: C. maj. 10,080 (21.61%))

EREWASH
E. 78,376 T. 50,553 (64.50%) Lab. hold
Liz Blackman, Lab.   22,472
David Simmonds, C.   15,388
Martin Garnett, LD   7,073
Robert Kilroy-Silk, Veritas   2,957
Sadie Graham, BNP   1,319
Geoffrey Kingscott, UKIP   941
R. U. Seerius, Loony   287
David Bishop, Elvis   116
Lab. maj. 7,084 (14.01%)
0.13% swing Lab. to C.
(2001: Lab. maj. 6,932 (14.26%))

ERITH & THAMESMEAD
E. 72,058 T. 37,651 (52.25%) Lab. hold
John Austin, Lab.   20,483
Chris Bromby, C.   8,983
Steven Toole, LD   5,088
Brian Ravenscroft, BNP   1,620
Barrie Thomas, UKIP   1,477
Lab. maj. 11,500 (30.54%)
1.47% swing Lab. to C.
(2001: Lab. maj. 11,167 (33.48%))

ESHER & WALTON
E. 76,926 T. 47,878 (62.24%) C. hold
Ian Taylor, C.   21,882
Mark Marsh, LD   14,155
Richard Taylor, Lab.   9,309
Bernard Collignon, UKIP   1,582
Chinners Chinnery, Loony   608
Richard Cutler, Soc. Lab.   342
C. maj. 7,727 (16.14%)
5.17% swing C. to LD
(2001: C. maj. 11,538 (25.34%))

ESSEX NORTH
E. 73,037 T. 47,959 (65.66%) C. hold
Bernard Jenkin, C.   22,811
Elizabeth Hughes, Lab.   11,908
James Raven, LD   9,831
Christopher Fox, Green   1,718
George Curtis, UKIP   1,691
C. maj. 10,903 (22.73%)
3.37% swing Lab. to C.
(2001: C. maj. 7,186 (15.99%))

EXETER
E. 84,964 T. 55,068 (64.81%) Lab. hold
Ben Bradshaw, Lab.   22,619
Peter Cox, C.   14,954
Jon Underwood, LD   11,340
Margaret Danks, Lib.   2,214
Tim Brenan, Green   1,896
Mark Fitzgeorge-Parker, UKIP   1,854
John Stuart, Ind.   191
Lab. maj. 7,665 (13.92%)
4.21% swing Lab. to C.
(2001: Lab. maj. 11,759 (22.35%))

FALMOUTH & CAMBORNE
E. 71,509 T. 48,015 (67.15%) LD gain
*Julia Goldsworthy, LD   16,747
Candy Atherton, Lab.   14,861
Ashley Crossley, C.   12,644
Michael Mahon, UKIP   1,820
David Mudd, Ind.   961
Paul Holmes, Lib.   423
Hilda Wasley, Meb. Ker.   370
Peter Gifford, Veritas   128
Richard Smith, Masts   61
LD maj. 1,886 (3.93%)
9.52% swing Lab. to LD
(2001: Lab. maj. 4,527 (9.67%))

FAREHAM
E. 72,599 T. 48,576 (66.91%) C. hold
Mark Hoban, C.   24,151
James Carr, Lab.   12,449
Richard De Ste-Croix, LD   10,551
Peter Mason-Apps, UKIP   1,425
C. maj. 11,702 (24.09%)
4.33% swing Lab. to C.
(2001: C. maj. 7,009 (15.42%))

FAVERSHAM & KENT MID
E. 66,411 T. 43,626 (65.69%) C. hold
Hugh Robertson, C.   21,690
Andrew Bradstock, Lab.   12,970
David Naghi, LD   7,204
Robert Thompson, UKIP   1,152
Norman Davidson, Loony   610
C. maj. 8,720 (19.99%)
4.90% swing Lab. to C.
(2001: C. maj. 4,183 (10.19%))

FELTHAM & HESTON
E. 75,391 T. 37,282 (49.45%)
                        Lab. (Co-op) hold
Alan Keen, Lab. (Co-op)   17,741
Mark Bowen, C.   10,921
Satnam Kaur Khalsa, LD   6,177
Graham Kemp, NF   975
Elizabeth Anstis, Green   815
Leon Mullett, UKIP   612
Warwick Prachar, Ind.   41
Lab. (Co-op) maj. 6,820 (18.29%)
8.35% swing Lab. (Co-op) to C.
(2001: Lab. (Co-op) maj. 12,657
(34.99%))

FINCHLEY & GOLDERS GREEN
E. 69,808 T. 43,214 (61.90%) Lab. hold
Dr Rudi Vis, Lab.   17,487
Andrew Mennear, C.   16,746
Sue Garden, LD   7,282
Noel Lynch, Green   1,136
Jeremy Jacobs, UKIP   453
Rainbow George Weiss, Vote Dream 110
Lab. maj. 741 (1.71%)
3.40% swing Lab. to C.
(2001: Lab. maj. 3,716 (8.51%))

FOLKESTONE & HYTHE
E. 70,914 T. 48,503 (68.40%) C. hold
Rt. Hon. Michael Howard, C.   26,161
Peter Carroll, LD   14,481
Maureen Tomison, Lab.   6,053
Dr Hazel Dawe, Green   688
Petrina Holdsworth, UKIP   619
Lord Toby Jug, Loony   175
Rodney Hylton-Potts, GBB   153
Grahame Leon-Smith, Senior   151
Sylvia Dunn, Progress   22
C. maj. 11,680 (24.08%)
5.60% swing LD to C.
(2001: C. maj. 5,907 (12.88%))

FOREST OF DEAN
E. 67,225 T. 47,640 (70.87%) C. gain
*Mark Harper, C.   19,474
Isabel Owen, Lab.   17,425
Christopher Coleman, LD   8,185
Patricia Hill, UKIP   1,140
Stephen Tweedie, Green   991
Anthony Reeve, Ind.   300
Gerald Morgan, EPP   125
C. maj. 2,049 (4.30%)
4.45% swing Lab. to C.
(2001: Lab. maj. 2,049 (4.59%))

FYLDE
E. 75,703   T. 45,510 (60.12%)   C. hold
Rt. Hon. Michael Jack, C.   24,287
William Parbury, Lab.   11,828
Bill Winlow, LD   7,748
Tim Akeroyd, Lib.   1,647
C. maj. 12,459 (27.38%)
2.95% swing Lab. to C.
(2001: C. maj. 9,610 (21.48%))

GAINSBOROUGH
E. 70,733   T. 45,681 (64.58%)   C. hold
Edward Leigh, C.   20,040
Adrian Heath, LD   12,037
John Knight, Lab.   11,744
Steven Pearson, UKIP   1,860
C. maj. 8,003 (17.52%)
1.02% swing C. to LD
(2001: C. maj. 8,071 (19.07%))

GATESHEAD EAST & WASHINGTON
WEST
E. 61,421   T. 34,668 (56.44%)   Lab. hold
*Sharon Hodgson, Lab.   20,997
Frank Hindle, LD   7,590
Lee Martin, C.   4,812
Jim Batty, UKIP   1,269
Lab. maj. 13,407 (38.67%)
7.29% swing Lab. to LD
(2001: Lab. maj. 17,904 (53.26%))

GEDLING
E. 68,917   T. 44,069 (63.95%)   Lab. hold
Vernon Coaker, Lab.   20,329
Anna Soubry, C.   16,518
Raymond Poynter, LD   6,070
Alan Margerison, UKIP   741
Deborah Johnson, Veritas   411
Lab. maj. 3,811 (8.65%)
2.06% swing Lab. to C.
(2001: Lab. maj. 5,598 (12.78%))

GILLINGHAM
E. 72,223   T. 45,167 (62.54%)   Lab. hold
Paul Clark, Lab.   18,621
Tim Butcher, C.   18,367
Andrew Stamp, LD   6,734
Craig MacKinlay, UKIP   1,191
Gordon Bryan, Ind.   254
Lab. maj. 254 (0.56%)
2.41% swing Lab. to C.
(2001: Lab. maj. 2,272 (5.38%))

GLOUCESTER
E. 82,500   T. 51,803 (62.79%)   Lab. hold
Parmjit Dhanda, Lab.   23,138
Paul James, C.   18,867
Jeremy Hilton, LD   7,825
Gary Phipps, UKIP   1,116
Bryan Meloy, Green   857
Lab. maj. 4,271 (8.24%)
0.10% swing C. to Lab.
(2001: Lab. maj. 3,880 (8.05%))

GOSPORT
E. 71,119   T. 43,034 (60.51%)   C. hold
Peter Viggers, C.   19,268
Richard Williams, Lab.   13,538
Roger Roberts, LD   7,145
John Bowles, UKIP   1,825
Andrea Smith, Green   1,258
C. maj. 5,730 (13.32%)
3.36% swing Lab. to C.
(2001: C. maj. 2,621 (6.59%))

GRANTHAM & STAMFORD
E. 74,074   T. 47,147 (63.65%)   C. hold
Quentin Davies, C.   22,109
Ian Selby, Lab.   14,664
Patrick O'Connor, LD   7,838
Stuart Rising, UKIP   1,498
Benedict Brown, Eng. Dem.   774
John Andrews, OFD   264
C. maj. 7,445 (15.79%)
3.02% swing Lab. to C.
(2001: C. maj. 4,518 (9.76%))

GRAVESHAM
E. 68,705   T. 45,179 (65.76%)   C. gain
*Adam Holloway, C.   19,739
Chris Pond, Lab.   19,085
Bruce Parmenter, LD   4,851
Geoff Coates, UKIP   850
Christopher Nickerson, Eng. Ind.   654
C. maj. 654 (1.45%)
6.29% swing Lab. to C.
(2001: Lab. maj. 4,862 (11.14%))

GREAT GRIMSBY
E. 63,711   T. 32,964 (51.74%)   Lab. hold
Austin Mitchell, Lab.   15,512
Giles Taylor, C.   7,858
Andrew de Freitas, LD   6,356
Stephen Fyfe, BNP   1,338
Martin Grant, UKIP   1,239
David Brooks, Green   661
Lab. maj. 7,654 (23.22%)
5.78% swing Lab. to C.
(2001: Lab. maj. 11,484 (34.78%))

GREAT YARMOUTH
E. 68,887   T. 41,378 (60.07%)   Lab. hold
Anthony Wright, Lab.   18,850
Mark Fox, C.   15,795
Stephen Newton, LD   4,585
Bertie Poole, UKIP   1,759
Michael Skipper, LCA   389
Lab. maj. 3,055 (7.38%)
1.96% swing Lab. to C.
(2001: Lab. maj. 4,564 (11.31%))

GREENWICH & WOOLWICH
E. 64,033   T. 35,615 (55.62%)   Lab. hold
Rt. Hon. Nick Raynsford, Lab.   17,527
Christopher Le Breton, LD   7,381
Alistair Craig, C.   7,142
David Sharman, Green   1,579
Garry Bushell, Eng. Dem.   1,216
Stanley Gain, UKIP   709
Puvarani Nagalingam, Ind.   61
Lab. maj. 10,146 (28.49%)
8.21% swing Lab. to LD
(2001: Lab. maj. 13,433 (41.29%))

GUILDFORD
E. 75,566   T. 51,631 (68.33%)   C. gain
*Anne Milton, C.   22,595
Sue Doughty, LD   22,248
Karen Landles, Lab.   5,054
John Pletts, Green   811
Martin Haslam, UKIP   645
John Morris, PPN-V   166
Victoria Lavin, Ind.   112
C. maj. 347 (0.67%)
0.90% swing LD to C.
(2001: LD maj. 538 (1.12%))

HACKNEY NORTH & STOKE
NEWINGTON
E. 59,260   T. 29,380 (49.58%)   Lab. hold
Diane Abbott, Lab.   14,268
James Blanchard, LD   6,841
Ertan Hurer, C.   4,218
Mischa Borris, Green   2,907
David Vail, Ind.   602
Nusrat Sen, Soc. Lab.   296
Nigel Barrow, Loony   248
Lab. maj. 7,427 (25.28%)
10.84% swing Lab. to LD
(2001: Lab. maj. 13,651 (46.09%))

HACKNEY SOUTH & SHOREDITCH
E. 64,818 T. 32,237 (49.73%)
                        Lab. (Co-op) hold
*Meg Hillier, Lab. (Co-op)   17,048
Gavin Baylis, LD   6,844
John Moss, C.   4,524
Ipemndoh dan Iyan, Green   1,779
Dean Ryan, Respect   1,437
Benjamin Rae, Lib.   313
Monty Goldman, Comm.   200
Jonty Leff, WRP   92
Lab. (Co-op) maj. 10,204 (31.65%)
8.97% swing Lab. (Co-op) to LD
(2001: Lab. (Co-op) maj. 15,049
(49.59%))

HALESOWEN & ROWLEY REGIS
E. 65,748 T. 41,327 (62.86%) Lab. hold
Sylvia Heal, Lab.   19,243
Les Jones, C.   14,906
Martin Turner, LD   5,204
Nikki Sinclaire, UKIP   1,974
Lab. maj. 4,337 (10.49%)
4.12% swing Lab. to C.
(2001: Lab. maj. 7,359 (18.74%))

HALIFAX
E. 64,861 T. 39,659 (61.14%)
                        Lab. (Co-op) hold
*Linda Riordan, Lab. (Co-op)   16,579
Kris Hopkins, C.   13,162
Michael Taylor, LD   7,100
Geoff Wallace, BNP   2,627
Thomas Holmes, NF   191
Lab. (Co-op) maj. 3,417 (8.62%)
3.28% swing Lab. (Co-op) to C.
(2001: Lab. (Co-op) maj. 6,129
(15.17%))

HALTEMPRICE & HOWDEN
E. 68,471   T. 48,029 (70.15%)   C. hold
Rt. Hon. David Davis, C.   22,792
Jon Neal, LD   17,676
Edward Hart, Lab.   6,104
Jonathan Mainprize, BNP   798
Philip Lane, UKIP   659
C. maj. 5,116 (10.65%)
3.16% swing LD to C.
(2001: C. maj. 1,903 (4.33%))

HALTON
E. 64,379   T. 34,183 (53.10%)   Lab. hold
Derek Twigg, Lab.   21,460
Colin Bloom, C.   6,854
Roger Barlow, LD   5,869
Lab. maj. 14,606 (42.73%)
3.92% swing Lab. to C.
(2001: Lab. maj. 17,428 (50.56%))

HAMMERSMITH & FULHAM
E. 79,082 T. 49,327 (62.37%) C. gain
*Greg Hands, C.   22,407
Melanie Smallman, Lab.   17,378
Alan Bullion, LD   7,116
Fiona Harrold, Green   1,933
Giles Fisher, UKIP   493
C. maj. 5,029 (10.20%)
7.35% swing Lab. to C.
(2001: Lab. maj. 2,015 (4.51%))

HAMPSHIRE EAST
E. 79,801 T. 53,139 (66.59%) C. hold
Rt. Hon. Michael Mates, C.   24,273
Ruth Bright, LD   18,764
Marjory Broughton, Lab.   8,519
David Samuel, UKIP   1,583
C. maj. 5,509 (10.37%)
3.66% swing C. to LD
(2001: C. maj. 8,890 (17.68%))

HAMPSHIRE NORTH EAST
E. 72,939 T. 47,287 (64.83%) C. hold
Rt. Hon. James Arbuthnot, C.   25,407
Adam Carew, LD   12,858
Kevin McGrath, Lab.   7,630
Paul Birch, UKIP   1,392
C. maj. 12,549 (26.54%)
1.81% swing C. to LD
(2001: C. maj. 13,257 (30.17%))

HAMPSHIRE NORTH WEST
E. 79,763 T. 51,265 (64.27%) C. hold
Rt. Hon. Sir George Young, C.   26,005
Martin Tod, LD   12,741
Michael Mumford, Lab.   10,594
Peter Sumner, UKIP   1,925
C. maj. 13,264 (25.87%)
1.50% swing C. to LD
(2001: C. maj. 12,009 (24.69%))

HAMPSTEAD & HIGHGATE
E. 68,737 T. 38,173 (55.53%) Lab. hold
Glenda Jackson, Lab.   14,615
Piers Wauchope, C.   10,886
Ed Fordham, LD   10,293
Sian Berry, Green   2,013
Magnus Nielsen, UKIP   275
Rainbow George Weiss, Vote Dream   91
Lab. maj. 3,729 (9.77%)
6.24% swing Lab. to C.
(2001: Lab. maj. 7,876 (22.24%))

HARBOROUGH
E. 74,583 T. 47,922 (64.25%) C. hold
Edward Garnier, C.   20,536
Jill Hope, LD   16,644
Peter Evans, Lab.   9,222
Marietta King, UKIP   1,520
C. maj. 3,892 (8.12%)
1.60% swing C. to LD
(2001: C. maj. 5,252 (11.31%))

HARLOW
E. 63,500 T. 39,733 (62.57%) Lab. hold
Bill Rammell, Lab.   16,453
Robert Halfon, C.   16,356
Lorna Spenceley, LD   5,002
John Felgate, UKIP   981
Anthony Bennett, Veritas   941
Lab. maj. 97 (0.24%)
6.39% swing Lab. to C.
(2001: Lab. maj. 5,228 (13.03%))

HARROGATE & KNARESBOROUGH
E. 65,622 T. 42,858 (65.31%) LD hold
Phil Willis, LD   24,113
Maggie Punyer, C.   13,684
Lorraine Ferris, Lab.   3,627
Chris Royston, UKIP   845
Colin Banner, BNP   466
John Allman, AFC   123
LD maj. 10,429 (24.33%)
1.68% swing C. to LD
(2001: LD maj. 8,845 (20.97%))

HARROW EAST
E. 84,033 T. 50,823 (60.48%) Lab. hold
Tony McNulty, Lab.   23,445
David Ashton, C.   18,715
Pash Nandhra, LD   7,747
Paul Cronin, UKIP   916
Lab. maj. 4,730 (9.31%)
6.92% swing Lab. to C.
(2001: Lab. maj. 11,124 (23.14%))

HARROW WEST
E. 74,228 T. 47,759 (64.34%)
                          Lab. (Co-op) hold
Gareth Thomas, Lab. (Co-op)   20,298
Mike Freer, C.   18,270
Christopher Noyce, LD   8,188
Janice Cronin, UKIP   576
Berjis Daver, Ind.   427
Lab. (Co-op) maj. 2,028 (4.25%)
4.48% swing Lab. (Co-op) to C.
(2001: Lab. (Co-op) maj. 6,156
(13.20%))

HARTLEPOOL
E. 68,776 T. 35,436 (51.52%) Lab. hold
Iain Wright, Lab.   18,251
Jody Dunn, LD   10,773
Amanda Vigar, C.   4,058
George Springer, UKIP   1,256
Frank Harrison, Soc. Lab.   373
Iris Ryder, Green   288
John Hobbs, Ind.   275
Sausage Supremo Headbanger,
   Loony   162
Lab. maj. 7,478 (21.10%)
11.51% swing Lab. to LD
(2004 Sept. by-election: Lab. maj. 2,033
(6.48%))
(2001: Lab. maj. 14,571 (38.29%))

HARWICH
E. 80,474 T. 50,408 (62.64%) C. gain
*Douglas Carswell, C.   21,235
Ivan Henderson, Lab.   20,315
Keith Tully, LD   5,913
Jeffrey Titford, UKIP   2,314
John Tipple, Respect   477
Christopher Humphrey, Ind.   154
C. maj. 920 (1.83%)
3.61% swing Lab. to C.
(2001: Lab. maj. 2,596 (5.40%))

HASTINGS & RYE
E. 72,765 T. 43,004 (59.10%) Lab. hold
Michael Foster, Lab.   18,107
Mark Coote, C.   16,081
Richard Stevens, LD   6,479
Terry Grant, UKIP   1,098
Sally Phillips, Green   1,032
John Ord-Clarke, Loony   207
Lab. maj. 2,026 (4.71%)
2.87% swing Lab. to C.
(2001: Lab. maj. 4,308 (10.45%))

HAVANT
E. 68,545 T. 41,351 (60.33%) C. hold
David Willetts, C.   18,370
Sarah Bogle, Lab.   11,862
Alex Bentley, LD   8,358
Timothy Dawes, Green   1,006
Steve Harris, UKIP   998
Ian Johnson, BNP   562
Russell Thomas, Veritas   195
C. maj. 6,508 (15.74%)
2.67% swing Lab. to C.
(2001: C. maj. 4,207 (10.40%))

HAYES & HARLINGTON
E. 57,493 T. 32,389 (56.34%) Lab. hold
John McDonnell, Lab.   19,009
Richard Worrall, C.   8,162
Jon Ball, LD   3,174
Tony Hazel, BNP   830
Martin Haley, UKIP   552
Brian Outten, Green   442
Paul Goddard, Ind.   220
Lab. maj. 10,847 (33.49%)
4.03% swing Lab. to C.
(2001: Lab. maj. 13,466 (41.56%))

HAZEL GROVE
E. 64,376 T. 39,117 (60.76%) LD hold
Andrew Stunell, LD   19,355
Alan White, C.   11,607
Andrew Graystone, Lab.   6,834
Keith Ryan, UKIP   1,321
LD maj. 7,748 (19.81%)
1.06% swing LD to C.
(2001: LD maj. 8,435 (21.92%))

HEMEL HEMPSTEAD
E. 73,095 T. 47,108 (64.45%) C. gain
*Michael Penning, C.   19,000
Tony McWalter, Lab. (Co-op)   18,501
Dr Richard Grayson, LD   8,089
Barry Newton, UKIP   1,518
C. maj. 499 (1.06%)
4.61% swing Lab. (Co-op) to C.
(2001: Lab. (Co-op) maj. 3,742 (8.16%))

HEMSWORTH
E. 67,339 T. 36,792 (54.64%) Lab. hold
Jon Trickett, Lab.   21,630
Jonathan Mortimer, C.   8,149
David Hall-Matthews, LD   5,766
John Burdon, Veritas   1,247
Lab. maj. 13,481 (36.64%)
3.87% swing Lab. to C.
(2001: Lab. maj. 15,636 (44.39%))

HENDON
E. 71,764 T. 41,839 (58.30%) Lab. hold
Andrew Dismore, Lab.   18,596
Dr Richard Evans, C.   15,897
Nahid Boethe, LD   5,831
David Williams, Green   754
Melvyn Smallman, UKIP   637
Rainbow George Weiss, Vote Dream   68
Michael Stewart, PDP   56
Lab. maj. 2,699 (6.45%)
5.85% swing Lab. to C.
(2001: Lab. maj. 7,417 (18.16%))

HENLEY
E. 68,538   T. 46,537 (67.90%)   C. hold
Boris Johnson, C.   24,894
David Turner, LD   12,101
Kaleem Saeed, Lab.   6,862
Mark Stevenson, Green   1,518
Delphine Gray-Fisk, UKIP   1,162
C. maj. 12,793 (27.49%)
4.22% swing LD to C.
(2001: C. maj. 8,458 (19.05%))

HEREFORD
E. 71,813   T. 46,894 (65.30%)   LD hold
Paul Keetch, LD   20,285
Virginia Taylor, C.   19,323
Tom Calver, Lab.   4,800
Brian Lunt, Green   1,052
Christopher Kingsley, UKIP   1,030
Peter Morton, Ind.   404
LD maj. 962 (2.05%)
0.06% swing LD to C.
(2001: LD maj. 968 (2.17%))

HERTFORD & STORTFORD
E. 73,394   T. 49,692 (67.71%)   C. hold
Mark Prisk, C.   25,074
Richard Henry, Lab.   11,977
James Lucas, LD   9,129
Peter Hart, Green   1,914
David Sodey, UKIP   1,026
Debbie Le May, Veritas   572
C. maj. 13,097 (26.36%)
7.24% swing Lab. to C.
(2001: C. maj. 5,603 (11.88%))

HERTFORDSHIRE NORTH EAST
E. 72,190   T. 47,374 (65.62%)   C. hold
Oliver Heald, C.   22,402
Andrew Harrop, Lab.   13,264
Iain Coleman, LD   10,147
David Hitchman, UKIP   1,561
C. maj. 9,138 (19.29%)
5.79% swing Lab. to C.
(2001: C. maj. 3,444 (7.71%))

HERTFORDSHIRE SOUTH WEST
E. 73,170   T. 50,088 (68.45%)   C. hold
*David Gauke, C.   23,494
Ed Featherstone, LD   15,021
Kerron Cross, Lab.   10,466
Colin Rodden, UKIP   1,107
C. maj. 8,473 (16.92%)
0.54% swing C. to LD
(2001: C. maj. 8,181 (17.31%))

HERTSMERE
E. 67,572   T. 42,572 (63.00%)   C. hold
James Clappison, C.   22,665
Kelly Tebb, Lab.   11,572
Jonathan Davies, LD   7,817
James Dry, Soc. Lab.   518
C. maj. 11,093 (26.06%)
7.12% swing Lab. to C.
(2001: C. maj. 4,902 (11.81%))

HEXHAM
E. 60,374   T. 41,513 (68.76%)   C. hold
Peter Atkinson, C.   17,605
Kevin Graham, Lab.   12,585
Andrew Duffield, LD   10,673
Ian Riddell, Eng. Dem.   521
Thomas Davison, IP   129
C. maj. 5,020 (12.09%)
3.06% swing Lab. to C.
(2001: C. maj. 2,529 (5.96%))

HEYWOOD & MIDDLETON
E. 71,510   T. 39,053 (54.61%)
                        Lab. (Co-op) hold
Jim Dobbin, Lab. (Co-op)   19,438
Stephen Pathmarajah, C.   8,355
Crea Lavin, LD   7,261
Gary Aronsson, BNP   1,855
Phil Burke, Lib.   1,377
Dr John Whittaker, UKIP   767
Lab. (Co-op) maj. 11,083 (28.38%)
0.86% swing Lab. (Co-op) to C.
(2001: Lab. (Co-op) maj. 11,670
(30.09%))

HIGH PEAK
E. 75,275   T. 49,989 (66.41%)   Lab. hold
Tom Levitt, Lab.   19,809
Andrew Bingham, C.   19,074
Marc Godwin, LD   10,000
Michael Schwartz, UKIP   1,106
Lab. maj. 735 (1.47%)
3.93% swing Lab. to C.
(2001: Lab. maj. 4,489 (9.33%))

HITCHIN & HARPENDEN
E. 67,207   T. 47,387 (70.51%)   C. hold
Rt. Hon. Peter Lilley, C.   23,627
Hannah Hedges, LD   12,234
Paul Orrett, Lab.   10,499
John Saunders, UKIP   828
Peter Rigby, Ind.   199
C. maj. 11,393 (24.04%)
2.66% swing C. to LD
(2001: C. maj. 6,663 (14.83%))

HOLBORN & ST PANCRAS
E. 68,237   T. 34,359 (50.35%)   Lab. hold
Rt. Hon. Frank Dobson, Lab.   14,857
Jill Fraser, LD   10,070
Margot James, C.   6,482
Adrian Oliver, Green   2,798
Rainbow George Weiss, Vote Dream   152
Lab. maj. 4,787 (13.93%)
10.98% swing Lab. to LD
(2001: Lab. maj. 11,175 (35.90%))

HORNCHURCH
E. 59,773   T. 38,169 (63.86%)   C. gain
*James Brokenshire, C.   16,355
John Cryer, Lab.   15,875
Nat Green, LD   2,894
Ian Moore, BNP   1,313
Lawrence Webb, UKIP   1,033
Malvin Brown, RA   395
Graham Williamson, Third   304
C. maj. 480 (1.26%)
2.71% swing Lab. to C.
(2001: Lab. maj. 1,482 (4.17%))

HORNSEY & WOOD GREEN
E. 76,621   T. 47,330 (61.77%)   LD gain
*Lynne Featherstone, LD   20,512
Barbara Roche, Lab.   18,117
Peter Forrest, C.   6,014
Jayne Forbes, Green   2,377
Roy Freshwater, UKIP   310
LD maj. 2,395 (5.06%)
14.57% swing Lab. to LD
(2001: Lab. maj. 10,614 (24.09%))

HORSHAM
E. 80,974   T. 54,495 (67.30%)   C. hold
Rt. Hon. Francis Maude, C.   27,240
Rosie Sharpley, LD   14,613
Rehman Chishti, Lab.   9,320
Hugo Miller, UKIP   2,552
Jim Duggan, Ind.   416
Martin Jeremiah, PHF   354
C. maj. 12,627 (23.17%)
1.87% swing C. to LD
(2001: C. maj. 13,666 (26.92%))

HOUGHTON & WASHINGTON EAST
E. 67,089   T. 34,694 (51.71%)   Lab. hold
Fraser Kemp, Lab.   22,310
Mark Greenfield, LD   6,245
Anthony Devenish, C.   4,772
John Richardson, BNP   1,367
Lab. maj. 16,065 (46.30%)
7.20% swing Lab. to LD
(2001: Lab. maj. 19,818 (58.91%))

HOVE
E. 69,939   T. 44,796 (64.05%)   Lab. hold
*Celia Barlow, Lab.   16,786
Nicholas Boles, C.   16,366
Paul Elgood, LD   8,002
Anthea Ballam, Green   2,575
Stuart Bower, UKIP   575
Paddy O'Keeffe, Respect   268
Bob Dobbs, Ind.   95
Richard Franklin, Silent   78
Brian Ralfe, Ind.   51
Lab. maj. 420 (0.94%)
3.31% swing Lab. to C.
(2001: Lab. maj. 3,171 (7.55%))

HUDDERSFIELD
E. 61,723   T. 34,940 (56.61%)
                        Lab. (Co-op) hold
Barry Sheerman, Lab. (Co-op)   16,341
Emma Bone, LD   7,990
David Meacock, C.   7,597
Julie Stewart-Turner, Green   1,651
Karl Hanson, BNP   1,036
Theresa Quarmby, Ind.   325
Lab. (Co-op) maj. 8,351 (23.90%)
7.18% swing Lab. (Co-op) to LD
(2001: Lab. (Co-op) maj. 10,046
(28.39%))

HULL EAST
E. 65,407   T. 31,022 (47.43%)   Lab. hold
Rt. Hon. John Prescott, Lab.   17,609
Andy Sloan, LD   5,862
Katy Lindsay, C.   4,038
Alan Siddle, BNP   1,022
Janet Toker, Lib.   1,018
Graham Morris, Veritas   750
Ronald Noon, Ind.   334
Linda Muir, Soc. Lab.   207
Carl Wagner, LCA   182
Lab. maj. 11,747 (37.87%)
5.88% swing Lab. to LD
(2001: Lab. maj. 15,325 (49.64%))

HULL NORTH
E. 62,590 T. 29,584 (47.27%) Lab. hold
*Diana Johnson, Lab.   15,364
Denis Healy, LD   8,013
Lydia Rivlin, C.   3,822
Martin Deane, Green   858
Brian Wainwright, BNP   766
Tineke Robinson, Veritas   389
Christopher Veasey, Northern   193
Carl Wagner, LCA   179
Lab. maj. 7,351 (24.85%)
6.30% swing Lab. to LD
(2001: Lab. maj. 10,721 (37.44%))

HULL WEST & HESSLE
E. 61,494 T. 27,818 (45.24%) Lab. hold
Rt. Hon. Alan Johnson, Lab.   15,305
David Nolan, LD   5,855
Karen Woods, C.   5,769
Stephen Wallis, Veritas   889
Lab. maj. 9,450 (33.97%)
4.66% swing Lab. to LD
(2001: Lab. maj. 10,951 (37.87%))

HUNTINGDON
E. 83,843 T. 52,418 (62.52%) C. hold
Jonathan Djanogly, C.   26,646
Julian Huppert, LD   13,799
Stephen Sartain, Lab.   9,821
Derek Norman, UKIP   2,152
C. maj. 12,847 (24.51%)
0.78% swing C. to LD
(2001: C. maj. 12,792 (26.06%))

HYNDBURN
E. 67,086 T. 39,449 (58.80%) Lab. hold
Greg Pope, Lab.   18,136
James Mawdsley, C.   12,549
Bill Greene, LD   5,577
Christian Jackson, BNP   2,444
Dr John Whittaker, UKIP   743
Lab. maj. 5,587 (14.16%)
3.66% swing Lab. to C.
(2001: Lab. maj. 8,219 (21.49%))

ILFORD NORTH
E. 70,718 T. 43,000 (60.80%) C. gain
*Lee Scott, C.   18,781
Linda Perham, Lab.   17,128
Mark Gayler, LD   5,896
Andrew Cross, UKIP   902
Martin Levin, Ind.   293
C. maj. 1,653 (3.84%)
4.55% swing Lab. to C.
(2001: Lab. maj. 2,115 (5.26%))

ILFORD SOUTH
E. 79,639 T. 42,693 (53.61%)
                       Lab. (Co-op) hold
Mike Gapes, Lab. (Co-op)   20,856
Stephen Metcalfe, C.   11,628
Matthew Lake, LD   8,761
Kashif Rana, BPP   763
Colin Taylor, UKIP   685
Lab. (Co-op) maj. 9,228 (21.61%)
6.14% swing Lab. (Co-op) to C.
(2001: Lab. (Co-op) maj. 13,997
(33.90%))

IPSWICH
E. 68,825 T. 41,878 (60.85%) Lab. hold
Chris Mole, Lab.   18,336
Paul West, C.   13,004
Richard Atkins, LD   8,464
Alison West, UKIP   1,134
Jervis Kay, Eng. Dem.   641
Sally Wainman, Ind.   299
Lab. maj. 5,332 (12.73%)
4.03% swing Lab. to C.
(2001 Nov. by-election: Lab. maj. 4,087
(14.91%))
(2001: Lab. maj. 8,081 (20.79%))

ISLE OF WIGHT
E. 109,046 T. 66,843 (61.30%) C. hold
Andrew Turner, C.   32,717
Anthony Rowlands, LD   19,739
Mark Chiverton, Lab.   11,484
Michael Tarrant, UKIP   2,352
Edward Corby, Ind.   551
C. maj. 12,978 (19.42%)
7.48% swing LD to C.
(2001: C. maj. 2,826 (4.45%))

ISLINGTON NORTH
E. 58,427 T. 31,494 (53.90%) Lab. hold
Jeremy Corbyn, Lab.   16,118
Laura Willoughby, LD   9,402
Nicola Talbot, C.   3,740
Jon Nott, Green   2,234
Lab. maj. 6,716 (21.32%)
10.78% swing Lab. to LD
(2001: Lab. maj. 12,958 (42.88%))

ISLINGTON SOUTH & FINSBURY
E. 57,748 T. 30,961 (53.61%) Lab. hold
*Emily Thornberry, Lab.   12,345
Bridget Fox, LD   11,861
Melanie McLean, C.   4,594
James Humphries, Green   1,471
Patricia Theophanides, UKIP   470
Andy the Hat Gardner, Loony   189
Chris Gidden, Ind.   31
Lab. maj. 484 (1.56%)
12.12% swing Lab. to LD
(2001: Lab. maj. 7,280 (25.81%))

JARROW
E. 61,814 T. 33,978 (54.97%) Lab. hold
Stephen Hepburn, Lab.   20,554
Bill Schardt, LD   6,650
Linkson Jack, C.   4,807
Alan Badger, UKIP   1,567
Roger Nettleship, SNH   400
Lab. maj. 13,904 (40.92%)
5.06% swing Lab. to LD
(2001: Lab. maj. 17,595 (51.03%))

KEIGHLEY
E. 68,229 T. 46,312 (67.88%) Lab. hold
Ann Cryer, Lab.   20,720
Karl Poulsen, C.   15,868
Nader Fekri, LD   5,484
Nick Griffin, BNP   4,240
Lab. maj. 4,852 (10.48%)
0.62% swing C. to Lab.
(2001: Lab. maj. 4,005 (9.24%))

KENSINGTON & CHELSEA
E. 62,662 T. 31,336 (50.01%) C. hold
†Rt. Hon. Sir Malcolm Rifkind, C.
                                        18,144
Jennifer Kingsley, LD   5,726
Catherine Atkinson, Lab.   5,521
Julia Stephenson, Green   1,342
Mildred Eilorat, UKIP   395
Alfred Bovill, Ind.   107
Eddie Adams, Green Soc.   101
C. maj. 12,418 (39.63%)
0.46% swing LD to C.
(2001: C. maj. 8,771 (31.28%))

KETTERING
E. 81,887 T. 55,646 (67.95%) C. gain
*Philip Hollobone, C.   25,401
Phil Sawford, Lab.   22,100
Roger Aron, LD   6,882
Rosemarie Clark, UKIP   1,263
C. maj. 3,301 (5.93%)
3.58% swing Lab. to C.
(2001: Lab. maj. 665 (1.24%))

KINGSTON & SURBITON
E. 72,671 T. 49,750 (68.46%) LD hold
Edward Davey, LD   25,397
Kevin Davis, C.   16,431
Nick Parrott, Lab.   6,553
Barry Thornton, UKIP   657
John Hayball, Soc. Lab.   366
David Henson, Veritas   200
Rainbow George Weiss, Vote Dream 146
LD maj. 8,966 (18.02%)
6.95% swing LD to C.
(2001: LD maj. 15,676 (31.93%))

KINGSWOOD
E. 84,400 T. 56,311 (66.72%) Lab. hold
Dr Roger Berry, Lab.   26,491
Owen Inskip, C.   18,618
Geoff Brewer, LD   9,089
John Knight, UKIP   1,444
David Burnside, Ind.   669
Lab. maj. 7,873 (13.98%)
6.26% swing Lab. to C.
(2001: Lab. maj. 13,962 (26.51%))

KNOWSLEY NORTH & SEFTON EAST
E. 70,403 T. 37,053 (52.63%) Lab. hold
George Howarth, Lab.   23,461
Flo Clucas, LD   7,192
Naman Purewal, C.   5,064
Michael McDermott, BNP   872
Stephen Whatham, Soc. Lab.   464
Lab. maj. 16,269 (43.91%)
4.52% swing Lab. to LD
(2001: Lab. maj. 18,927 (50.45%))

KNOWSLEY SOUTH
E. 70,726 T. 36,444 (51.53%) Lab. hold
Eddie O'Hara, Lab.   24,820
David Smithson, LD   7,132
Andrea Leadsom, C.   4,492
Lab. maj. 17,688 (48.53%)
4.86% swing Lab. to LD
(2001: Lab. maj. 21,316 (58.26%))

LANCASHIRE WEST
E. 74,777 T. 43,155 (57.71%) Lab. hold
*Rosie Cooper, Lab.   20,746
Alf Doran, C.   14,662
Richard Kemp, LD   6,059
Alan Freeman, UKIP   871
Stephen Garrett, Eng. Dem.   525
David Braid, Clause 28   292
Lab. maj. 6,084 (14.10%)
4.17% swing Lab. to C.
(2001: Lab. maj. 9,643 (22.44%))

LANCASTER & WYRE
E. 80,739   T. 52,061 (64.48%) C. gain
*Ben Wallace, C.   22,266
Anne Sacks, Lab.   18,095
Stuart Langhorn, LD   8,453
Jon Barry, Green   2,278
John Mander, UKIP   969
C. maj. 4,171 (8.01%)
4.47% swing Lab. to C.
(2001: Lab. maj. 481 (0.92%))

LEEDS CENTRAL
E. 62,939 T. 29,186 (46.37%) Lab. hold
Rt. Hon. Hilary Benn, Lab.   17,526
Ruth Coleman, LD   5,660
Brian Cattell, C.   3,865
Mark Collett, BNP   1,201
Peter Sewards, UKIP   494
Mick Dear, Ind.   189
Oluwole Taiwo, Ind.   126
Julian Fitzgerald, AFC   125
Lab. maj. 11,866 (40.66%)
6.53% swing Lab. to LD
(2001: Lab. maj. 14,381 (52.67%))

LEEDS EAST
E. 54,691 T. 30,077 (54.99%) Lab. hold
George Mudie, Lab.   17,799
Andrew Tear, LD   6,221
Dominic Ponniah, C.   5,557
Peter Socrates, Ind.   500
Lab. maj. 11,578 (38.49%)
5.48% swing Lab. to LD
(2001: Lab. maj. 12,643 (43.51%))

LEEDS NORTH EAST
E. 63,304 T. 41,467 (65.50%) Lab. hold
Fabian Hamilton, Lab.   18,632
Matthew Lobley, C.   13,370
Jonathan Brown, LD   8,427
Celia Foote, Green Soc.   1,038
Lab. maj. 5,262 (12.69%)
2.57% swing Lab. to C.
(2001: Lab. maj. 7,089 (17.82%))

LEEDS NORTH WEST
E. 71,644   T. 44,711 (62.41%) LD gain
*Greg Mulholland, LD   16,612
Judith Blake, Lab.   14,735
George Lee, C.   11,510
Martin Hemingway, Green   1,128
Adrian Knowles, Eng. Dem.   545
Jeannie Sutton, Green Soc.   181
LD maj. 1,877 (4.20%)
9.59% swing Lab. to LD
(2001: Lab. maj. 5,236 (12.33%))

LEEDS WEST
E. 62,882 T. 33,718 (53.62%) Lab. hold
Rt. Hon. John Battle, Lab.   18,704
Darren Finlay, LD   5,894
Tim Metcalfe, C.   4,807
David Blackburn, Green   2,519
Julie Day, BNP   1,166
David Sewards, UKIP   628
Lab. maj. 12,810 (37.99%)
6.85% swing Lab. to LD
(2001: Lab. maj. 14,935 (46.54%))

LEICESTER EAST
E. 66,383 T. 41,306 (62.22%) Lab. hold
Keith Vaz, Lab.   24,015
Suella Fernandes, C.   8,139
Susan Cooper, LD   7,052
Colin Brown, Veritas   1,666
Valerie Smalley, Soc. Lab.   434
Lab. maj. 15,876 (38.44%)
2.69% swing C. to Lab.
(2001: Lab. maj. 13,442 (33.06%))

LEICESTER SOUTH
E. 72,310 T. 42,411 (58.65%) Lab. gain
*Sir Peter Soulsby, Lab.   16,688
Parmjit Singh Gill, LD   12,971
Martin McElwee, C.   7,549
Yvonne Ridley, Respect   2,720
Matthew Follett, Green   1,379
Ken Roseblade, Veritas   573
Dave Roberts, Soc. Lab.   315
Paul Lord, Ind.   216
Lab. maj. 3,717 (8.76%)
14.26% swing Lab. to LD
(2004 July by-election: LD maj.1,654
(5.62%))
(2001: Lab. maj. 13,243 (31.43%))

LEICESTER WEST
E. 62,389 T. 33,224 (53.25%) Lab. hold
Rt. Hon. Patricia Hewitt, Lab.   17,184
Sarah Richardson, C.   8,114
Zuffar Haq, LD   5,803
Geoff Forse, Green   1,571
Steve Score, Soc. Alt.   552
Lab. maj. 9,070 (27.30%)
0.86% swing Lab. to C.
(2001: Lab. maj. 9,639 (29.02%))

LEICESTERSHIRE NORTH WEST
E. 70,519 T. 47,140 (66.85%)
                         Lab. (Co-op) hold
David Taylor, Lab. (Co-op)   21,449
Nicola Le Page, C.   16,972
Rod Keyes, LD   5,682
John Blunt, UKIP   1,563
Clive Potter, BNP   1,474
Lab. (Co-op) maj. 4,477 (9.50%)
4.31% swing Lab. (Co-op) to C.
(2001: Lab. (Co-op) maj. 8,157
(18.12%))

LEIGH
E. 72,473 T. 36,488 (50.35%) Lab. hold
Andy Burnham, Lab.   23,097
Laurance Wedderburn, C.   5,825
Dave Crowther, LD   4,962
Ian Franzen, CAP   2,189
Thomas Hampson, LCA   415
Lab. maj. 17,272 (47.34%)
0.49% swing C. to Lab.
(2001: Lab. maj. 16,362 (46.35%))

LEOMINSTER
E. 70,587   T. 48,793 (69.12%) C. hold
Bill Wiggin, C.   25,407
Caroline Williams, LD   12,220
Paul Bell, Lab.   7,424
Felicity Norman, Green   2,191
Peter Venables, UKIP   1,551
C. maj. 13,187 (27.03%)
2.42% swing LD to C.
(2001: C. maj. 10,367 (22.19%))

LEWES
E. 67,073   T. 46,552 (69.40%) LD hold
Norman Baker, LD   24,376
Rory Love, C.   15,902
Richard Black, Lab.   4,169
Susan Murray, Green   1,071
John Petley, UKIP   1,034
LD maj. 8,474 (18.20%)
1.58% swing LD to C.
(2001: LD maj. 9,710 (21.37%))

LEWISHAM DEPTFORD
E. 59,018 T. 30,393 (51.50%) Lab. hold
Joan Ruddock, Lab.   16,902
Columba Blango, LD   5,091
James Cartlidge, C.   3,773
Darren Johnson, Green   3,367
Ian Page, Soc. Alt.   742
Dr David Holland, UKIP   518
Lab. maj. 11,811 (38.86%)
7.21% swing Lab. to LD
(2001: Lab. maj. 15,293 (52.54%))

LEWISHAM EAST
E. 59,135 T. 31,127 (52.64%) Lab. hold
Bridget Prentice, Lab.   14,263
James Cleverly, C.   7,512
Richard Thomas, LD   6,787
Anna Baker, Green   1,243
Arnold Tarling, UKIP   697
Bernard Franklin, NF   625
Lab. maj. 6,751 (21.69%)
4.12% swing Lab. to C.
(2001: Lab. maj. 8,959 (29.82%))

LEWISHAM WEST
E. 58,349 T. 31,923 (54.71%) Lab. hold
Jim Dowd, Lab.   16,611
Alex Feakes, LD   6,679
Evett McAnuff, C.   6,396
Nick Long, Green   1,464
Jens Winton, UKIP   773
Lab. maj. 9,932 (31.11%)
8.25% swing Lab. to LD
(2001: Lab. maj. 11,920 (38.68%))

LEYTON & WANSTEAD
E. 60,444 T. 33,272 (55.05%) Lab. hold
Harry Cohen, Lab.   15,234
Meher Khan, LD   8,377
Julien Foster, C.   7,393
Ashley Gunstock, Green   1,522
Nick Jones, UKIP   591
Marc Robertson, Ind.   155
Lab. maj. 6,857 (20.61%)
10.71% swing Lab. to LD
(2001: Lab. maj. 12,904 (38.27%))

LICHFIELD
E. 65,565   T. 43,744 (66.72%) C. hold
Michael Fabricant, C.   21,274
Nigel Gardner, Lab.   14,194
Ian Jackson, LD   6,804
Malcolm McKenzie, UKIP   1,472
C. maj. 7,080 (16.19%)
2.78% swing Lab. to C.
(2001: C. maj. 4,426 (10.62%))

LINCOLN
E. 65,203 T. 36,857 (56.53%) Lab. hold
Gillian Merron, Lab.   16,724
Karl McCartney, C.   12,110
Lisa Gabriel, LD   6,715
Nicholas Smith, UKIP   1,308
Lab. maj. 4,614 (12.52%)
5.08% swing Lab. to C.
(2001: Lab. maj. 8,420 (22.68%))

LIVERPOOL GARSTON
E. 63,669 T. 34,974 (54.93%) Lab. hold
Maria Eagle, Lab.   18,900
Paula Keaveney, LD   11,707
Amber Rudd, C.   3,424
Kevin Kearney, UKIP   780
David Oatley, WRP   163
Lab. maj. 7,193 (20.57%)
8.85% swing Lab. to C.
(2001: Lab. maj. 12,494 (38.27%))

LIVERPOOL RIVERSIDE
E. 75,171 T. 31,191 (41.49%)
                          Lab. (Co-op) hold
Louise Ellman, Lab. (Co-op)   17,951
Richard Marbrow, LD   7,737
Gabrielle Howatson, C.   2,843
Peter Cranie, Green   1,707
Beth Marshall, Soc. Lab.   498
Ann Irving, UKIP   455
Lab. (Co-op) maj. 10,214 (32.75%)
10.98% swing Lab. (Co-op) to LD
(2001: Lab. (Co-op) maj. 13,950
(54.70%))

LIVERPOOL WALTON
E. 62,044 T. 27,930 (45.02%) Lab. hold
Peter Kilfoyle, Lab.   20,322
Kiron Reid, LD   4,365
Sharon Buckle, C.   1,655
Joseph Moran, UKIP   1,108
Daniel Wood, Lib.   480
Lab. maj. 15,957 (57.13%)
3.05% swing Lab. to LD
(2001: Lab. maj. 17,996 (63.24%))

LIVERPOOL WAVERTREE
E. 69,189 T. 35,171 (50.83%) Lab. hold
Rt. Hon. Jane Kennedy, Lab.   18,441
Colin Eldridge, LD   13,268
Jason Steen, C.   2,331
Mark Bill, UKIP   660
Gary Theys, Soc. Lab.   244
Paul Filby, Dem. Soc. All.   227
Lab. maj. 5,173 (14.71%)
11.81% swing Lab. to LD
(2001: Lab. maj. 12,319 (38.33%))

LIVERPOOL WEST DERBY
E. 64,591 T. 30,464 (47.16%) Lab. hold
Robert Wareing, Lab.   19,140
Patrick Maloney, LD   3,915
Steve Radford, Lib.   3,606
Peter Garrett, C.   2,567
Kai Andersen, Soc. Lab.   698
Peter Baden, UKIP   538
Lab. maj. 15,225 (49.98%)
2.66% swing Lab. to LD
(2001: Lab. maj. 15,853 (51.29%))

LOUGHBOROUGH
E. 72,351 T. 46,140 (63.77%)
                          Lab. (Co-op) hold
Andy Reed, Lab. (Co-op)   19,098
Nicky Morgan, C.   17,102
Graeme Smith, LD   8,258
Bernard Sherratt, UKIP   1,094
John McVay, Veritas   588
Lab. (Co-op) maj. 1,996 (4.33%)
5.04% swing Lab. (Co-op) to C.
(2001: Lab. (Co-op) maj. 6,378
(14.41%))

LOUTH & HORNCASTLE
E. 75,313 T. 46,683 (61.99%) C. hold
Sir Peter Tapsell, C.   21,744
Frank Hodgkiss, Lab.   11,848
Fiona Martin, LD   9,480
Christopher Pain, UKIP   3,611
C. maj. 9,896 (21.20%)
2.10% swing Lab. to C.
(2001: C. maj. 7,554 (16.99%))

LUDLOW
E. 64,572 T. 46,540 (72.07%) C. gain
*Philip Dunne, C.   20,979
Matthew Green, LD   18,952
Nigel Knowles, Lab.   4,974
Jim Gaffney, Green   852
Michael Zuckerman, UKIP   783
C. maj. 2,027 (4.36%)
4.07% swing LD to C.
(2001: LD maj. 1,630 (3.78%))

LUTON NORTH
E. 68,175 T. 39,122 (57.38%) Lab. hold
Kelvin Hopkins, Lab.   19,062
Hannah Hall, C.   12,575
Linda Jack, LD   6,081
Colin Brown, UKIP   1,255
Kayson Gurney, Forum   149
Lab. maj. 6,487 (16.58%)
4.46% swing Lab. to C.
(2001: Lab. maj. 9,977 (25.50%))

LUTON SOUTH
E. 71,949 T. 38,918 (54.09%) Lab. hold
Margaret Moran, Lab.   16,610
Richard Stay, C.   10,960
Qurban Hussain, LD   8,778
Charles Lawman, UKIP   957
Marc Scheimann, Green   790
Mohammed Ilyas, Respect   725
Arthur Lynn, WRP   98
Lab. maj. 5,650 (14.52%)
5.62% swing Lab. to C.
(2001: Lab. maj. 10,133 (25.75%))

MACCLESFIELD
E. 72,267 T. 45,621 (63.13%) C. hold
Sir Nicholas Winterton, C.   22,628
Stephen Carter, Lab.   13,227
Catherine O'Brien, LD   8,918
John Scott, Veritas   848
C. maj. 9,401 (20.61%)
2.41% swing Lab. to C.
(2001: C. maj. 7,200 (15.79%))

MAIDENHEAD
E. 63,978 T. 45,850 (71.67%) C. hold
Rt. Hon. Theresa May, C.   23,312
Kathryn Newbound, LD   17,081
Janet Pritchard, Lab.   4,144
Tim Rait, BNP   704
Douglas Lewis, UKIP   609
C. maj. 6,231 (13.59%)
3.00% swing LD to C.
(2001: C. maj. 3,284 (7.58%))

MAIDSTONE & THE WEALD
E. 74,054 T. 48,755 (65.84%) C. hold
Rt. Hon. Ann Widdecombe, C.   25,670
Beth Breeze, Lab.   10,814
Mark Corney, LD   10,808
Anthony Robertson, UKIP   1,463
C. maj. 14,856 (30.47%)
3.92% swing Lab. to C.
(2001: C. maj. 10,318 (22.64%))

MAKERFIELD
E. 69,039 T. 35,580 (51.54%) Lab. hold
Rt. Hon. Ian McCartney, Lab.   22,494
Kulveer Ranger, C.   4,345
Trevor Beswick, LD   3,789
Peter Franzen, CAP   2,769
Dennis Shambley, BNP   1,221
Gregory Atherton, UKIP   962
Lab. maj. 18,149 (51.01%)
0.04% swing C. to Lab.
(2001: Lab. maj. 17,750 (50.92%))

MALDON & CHELMSFORD EAST
E. 69,502 T. 46,091 (66.32%) C. hold
John Whittingdale, C.   23,732
Sue Tibballs, Lab.   11,159
Matthew Lambert, LD   9,270
Jesse Pryke, UKIP   1,930
C. maj. 12,573 (27.28%)
4.05% swing Lab. to C.
(2001: C. maj. 8,462 (19.19%))

MANCHESTER BLACKLEY
E. 60,229 T. 27,591 (45.81%) Lab. hold
Graham Stringer, Lab.   17,187
Iain Donaldson, LD   5,160
Amar Ahmed, C.   3,690
Roger Bullock, UKIP   1,554
Lab. maj. 12,027 (43.59%)
6.99% swing Lab. to LD
(2001: Lab. maj. 14,464 (54.53%))

MANCHESTER CENTRAL
E. 69,656 T. 29,264 (42.01%) Lab. hold
Tony Lloyd, Lab.   16,993
Marc Ramsbottom, LD   7,217
Tom Jackson, C.   2,504
Steven Durrant, Green   1,292
Richard Kemp, NF   421
Damien O'Connor, Ind. Pr. Lab.   382
Dr John Whittaker, UKIP   272
Ronald Sinclair, Soc. Lab.   183
Lab. maj. 9,776 (33.41%)
9.80% swing Lab. to LD
(2001: Lab. maj. 13,742 (53.00%))

MANCHESTER GORTON
E. 64,696 T. 29,123 (45.02%) Lab. hold
Rt. Hon. Sir Gerald Kaufman, Lab.
　　　　　　　　　　　　　　　　15,480
Qassim Afzal, LD　　　　　　　9,672
Amanda Byrne, C.　　　　　　　2,848
Gregory Beaman, UKIP　　　　　783
Dan Waller, WRP　　　　　　　　181
Matthew Kay, RP　　　　　　　　159
Lab. maj. 5,808 (19.94%)
10.79% swing Lab. to LD
(2001: Lab. maj. 11,304 (41.51%))

MANCHESTER WITHINGTON
E. 67,781 T. 37,458 (55.26%) LD gain
*John Leech, LD　　　　　　　15,872
Rt. Hon. Keith Bradley, Lab.　15,205
Karen Bradley, C.　　　　　　　3,919
Brian Candeland, Green　　　　1,595
Dr Robert Gutfreund-Walmsley,
　UKIP　　　　　　　　　　　　424
Ivan Benett, Ind.　　　　　　　243
Yasmin Zalzala, Ind.　　　　　　153
Richard Reed, TP　　　　　　　　47
LD maj. 667 (1.78%)
17.33% swing Lab. to LD
(2001: Lab. maj. 11,524 (32.88%))

MANSFIELD
E. 69,131 T. 38,276 (55.37%) Lab. hold
Alan Meale, Lab.　　　　　　　18,400
Anne Wright, C.　　　　　　　　7,035
Stewart Rickersey, Ind.　　　　6,491
Roger Shelley, LD　　　　　　　5,316
Michael Harvey, Veritas　　　　1,034
Lab. maj. 11,365 (29.69%)
0.13% swing Lab. to C.
(2001: Lab. maj. 11,038 (29.95%))

MEDWAY
E. 67,251 T. 41,093 (61.10%) Lab. hold
Bob Marshall-Andrews, Lab.　17,333
Mark Reckless, C.　　　　　　17,120
Geoffrey Juby, LD　　　　　　5,152
Robert Oakley, UKIP　　　　　1,488
Lab. maj. 213 (0.52%)
4.64% swing Lab. to C.
(2001: Lab. maj. 3,780 (9.79%))

MERIDEN
E. 77,342 T. 46,503 (60.13%) C. hold
Caroline Spelman, C.　　　　22,416
Jim Brown, Lab.　　　　　　15,407
William Laitinen, LD　　　　7,113
Denis Brookes, UKIP　　　　1,567
C. maj. 7,009 (15.07%)
3.29% swing Lab. to C.
(2001: C. maj. 3,784 (8.49%))

MIDDLESBROUGH
E. 65,924 T. 32,140 (48.75%) Lab. hold
Sir Stuart Bell, Lab.　　　　18,562
Joe Michna, LD　　　　　　5,995
Caroline Flynn-Macleod, C.　5,263
Ron Armes, BNP　　　　　　819
Michael Landers, UKIP　　　768
Jackie Elder, Ind.　　　　　503
Derrick Arnott, Ind.　　　　230
Lab. maj. 12,567 (39.10%)
9.03% swing Lab. to LD
(2001: Lab. maj. 16,330 (48.43%))

MIDDLESBROUGH SOUTH &
CLEVELAND EAST
E. 71,883 T. 43,696 (60.79%) Lab. hold
Dr Ashok Kumar, Lab.　　　21,945
Mark Brooks, C.　　　　　　13,945
Carl Minns, LD　　　　　　6,049
Geoffrey Groves, BNP　　　1,099
Charlotte Bull, UKIP　　　　658
Lab. maj. 8,000 (18.31%)
1.47% swing Lab. to C.
(2001: Lab. maj. 9,351 (21.26%))

MILTON KEYNES NORTH EAST
E. 78,758 T. 50,104 (63.62%) C. gain
*Mark Lancaster, C.　　　　19,674
Brian White, Lab.　　　　　18,009
Jane Carr, LD　　　　　　　9,789
Michael Phillips, UKIP　　　1,400
Peter Richardson, Green　　1,090
Anant Vyas, Ind.　　　　　　142
C. maj. 1,665 (3.32%)
3.60% swing Lab. to C.
(2001: Lab. maj. 1,829 (3.88%))

MILTON KEYNES SOUTH WEST
E. 82,228 T. 48,709 (59.24%) Lab. hold
Dr Phyllis Starkey, Lab.　　20,862
Iain Stewart, C.　　　　　　16,852
Neil Stuart, LD　　　　　　7,909
George Harlock, UKIP　　　1,750
Alan Francis, Green　　　　1,336
Lab. maj. 4,010 (8.23%)
3.57% swing Lab. to C.
(2001: Lab. maj. 6,978 (15.38%))

MITCHAM & MORDEN
E. 65,172 T. 39,868 (61.17%) Lab. hold
Siobhain McDonagh, Lab.　22,489
Andrew Shellhorn, C.　　　9,929
Jo Christie-Smith, LD　　　5,583
Tom Walsh, Green　　　　　1,395
Adrian Roberts, Veritas　　286
Rathy Alagaratnam, Ind.　　186
Lab. maj. 12,560 (31.50%)
2.40% swing Lab. to C.
(2001: Lab. maj. 13,785 (36.31%))

MOLE VALLEY
E. 68,181 T. 49,415 (72.48%) C. hold
Sir Paul Beresford, C.　　　27,060
Nasser Butt, LD　　　　　　15,063
Farmida Bi, Lab.　　　　　　5,310
David Payne, UKIP　　　　　1,475
Roger Meekins, Veritas　　　507
C. maj. 11,997 (24.28%)
1.35% swing LD to C.
(2001: C. maj. 10,153 (21.57%))

MORECAMBE & LUNESDALE
E. 67,775 T. 41,635 (61.43%) Lab. hold
Geraldine Smith, Lab.　　　20,331
James Airey, C.　　　　　　15,563
Alex Stone, LD　　　　　　5,741
Lab. maj. 4,768 (11.45%)
0.39% swing Lab. to C.
(2001: Lab. maj. 5,092 (12.22%))

MORLEY & ROTHWELL
E. 72,248 T. 42,495 (58.82%) Lab. hold
Colin Challen, Lab.　　　　20,570
Nick Vineall, C.　　　　　　8,227
Stewart Golton, LD　　　　6,819
Robert Finnigan, Ind.　　　4,608
Chris Beverley, BNP　　　　2,271
Lab. maj. 12,343 (29.05%)
1.20% swing Lab. to C.
(2001: Lab. maj. 12,090 (31.45%))

NEW FOREST EAST
E. 68,633 T. 45,235 (65.91%) C. hold
Dr Julian Lewis, C.　　　　21,975
Brian Dash, LD　　　　　　15,424
Stephen Roberts, Lab.　　　5,492
Katy Davies, UKIP　　　　　2,344
C. maj. 6,551 (14.48%)
2.70% swing LD to C.
(2001: C. maj. 3,829 (9.08%))

NEW FOREST WEST
E. 69,232 T. 46,067 (66.54%) C. hold
Desmond Swayne, C.　　　26,004
Murari Kaushik, LD　　　　8,719
Janice Hurne, Lab.　　　　7,590
Brian Lawrence, UKIP　　　1,917
Janet Richards, Green　　　1,837
C. maj. 17,285 (37.52%)
3.80% swing LD to C.
(2001: C. maj. 13,191 (29.92%))

NEWARK
E. 72,249 T. 45,696 (63.25%) C. hold
Patrick Mercer, C.　　　　21,946
Jason Reece, Lab.　　　　　15,482
Stuart Thompstone, LD　　7,276
Charlotte Creasy, UKIP　　992
C. maj. 6,464 (14.15%)
2.56% swing Lab. to C.
(2001: C. maj. 4,073 (9.02%))

NEWBURY
E. 75,903 T. 54,673 (72.03%) C. gain
*Richard Benyon, C.　　　26,771
David Rendel, LD　　　　　23,311
Oscar Van Nooijen, Lab.　3,239
David McMahon, UKIP　　857
Nicholas Cornish, Ind.　　409
Barrie Singleton, Ind.　　　86
C. maj. 3,460 (6.33%)
5.54% swing LD to C.
(2001: LD maj. 2,415 (4.75%))

NEWCASTLE-UNDER-LYME
E. 68,414 T. 39,788 (58.16%) Lab. hold
Paul Farrelly, Lab.　　　　18,053
Jeremy Lefroy, C.　　　　　9,945
Trevor Johnson, LD　　　　7,528
David Nixon, UKIP　　　　1,436
John Dawson, BNP　　　　1,390
Prof. Andrew Dobson, Green　918
Marian Harvey-Lover, Veritas　518
Lab. maj. 8,108 (20.38%)
2.72% swing Lab. to C.
(2001: Lab. maj. 9,986 (25.82%))

NEWCASTLE UPON TYNE CENTRAL
E. 62,734 T. 35,920 (57.26%) Lab. hold
Jim Cousins, Lab.　　　　　16,211
Greg Stone, LD　　　　　　12,229
Wendy Morton, C.　　　　5,749
Joe Hulm, Green　　　　　1,254
Clive Harding, NACVP　　477
Lab. maj. 3,982 (11.09%)
11.10% swing Lab. to LD
(2001: Lab. maj. 11,605 (33.28%))

NEWCASTLE UPON TYNE EAST &
WALLSEND
E. 56,900 T. 31,678 (55.67%) Lab. hold
Rt. Hon. Nick Brown, Lab.　17,462
David Ord, LD　　　　　　9,897
Norma Dias, C.　　　　　　3,532
William Hopwood, Soc. Alt.　582
Martin Levy, Comm. Brit.　205
Lab. maj. 7,565 (23.88%)
9.81% swing Lab. to LD
(2001: Lab. maj. 14,223 (43.50%))

NEWCASTLE UPON TYNE NORTH
E. 64,599 T. 38,444 (59.51%) Lab. hold
Doug Henderson, Lab. 19,224
Ron Beadle, LD 12,201
Neil Hudson, C. 6,022
Roland Wood, NF 997
Lab. maj. 7,023 (18.27%)
11.22% swing Lab. to LD
(2001: Lab. maj. 14,450 (39.73%))

NORFOLK MID
E. 81,738 T. 54,734 (66.96%) C. hold
Keith Simpson, C. 23,564
Daniel Zeichner, Lab. 16,004
Vivienne Clifford-Jackson, LD 12,988
Simon Fletcher, UKIP 2,178
C. maj. 7,560 (13.81%)
2.57% swing Lab. to C.
(2001: C. maj. 4,562 (8.68%))

NORFOLK NORTH
E. 80,784 T. 58,965 (72.99%) LD hold
Norman Lamb, LD 31,515
Iain Dale, C. 20,909
Philip Harris, Lab. 5,447
Stuart Agnew, UKIP 978
Justin Appleyard, Ind. 116
LD maj. 10,606 (17.99%)
8.56% swing C. to LD
(2001: LD maj. 483 (0.86%))

NORFOLK NORTH WEST
E. 82,171 T. 50,649 (61.64%) C. hold
Henry Bellingham, C. 25,471
Damien Welfare, Lab. 16,291
Simon Higginson, LD 7,026
Michael Stone, UKIP 1,861
C. maj. 9,180 (18.12%)
5.66% swing Lab. to C.
(2001: C. maj. 3,485 (6.81%))

NORFOLK SOUTH
E. 85,896 T. 58,974 (68.66%) C. hold
Richard Bacon, C. 26,399
Dr Ian Mack, LD 17,617
John Morgan, Lab. 13,262
Philip Tye, UKIP 1,696
C. maj. 8,782 (14.89%)
1.28% swing LD to C.
(2001: C. maj. 6,893 (12.32%))

NORFOLK SOUTH WEST
E. 88,260 T. 55,127 (62.46%) C. hold
†Christopher Fraser, C. 25,881
Charmaine Morgan, Lab. 15,795
April Pond, LD 10,207
Delia Hall, UKIP 2,738
Kim Hayes, Ind. 506
C. maj. 10,086 (18.30%)
0.30% swing Lab. to C.
(2001: C. maj. 9,366 (17.69%))

NORMANTON
E. 65,129 T. 37,424 (57.46%)
Lab. (Co-op) hold
*Ed Balls, Lab. (Co-op) 19,161
Andrew Percy, C. 9,159
Simone Butterworth, LD 6,357
John Aveyard, BNP 1,967
Mark Harrop, Ind. 780
Lab. (Co-op) maj. 10,002 (26.73%)
1.18% swing Lab. (Co-op) to C.
(2001: Lab. (Co-op) maj. 9,937 (29.09%))

NORTHAMPTON NORTH
E. 73,926 T. 42,048 (56.88%) Lab. hold
Sally Keeble, Lab. 16,905
Damian Collins, C. 12,945
Andrew Simpson, LD 10,317
John Howsam, UKIP 1,050
Paul Withrington, SOS 495
Andrew Otchie, CPA 336
Lab. maj. 3,960 (9.42%)
4.80% swing Lab. to C.
(2001: Lab. maj. 7,893 (19.02%))

NORTHAMPTON SOUTH
E. 89,722 T. 54,481 (60.72%) C. gain
*Brian Binley, C. 23,818
Tony Clarke, Lab. 19,399
Kevin Barron, LD 8,327
Derek Clark, UKIP 1,032
Anthony Green, Veritas 508
John Harrisson, SOS 437
John Percival, Loony 354
Fitzy Fitzpatrick, Ind. 346
Tim Webb, CPA 260
C. maj. 4,419 (8.11%)
4.92% swing Lab. to C.
(2001: Lab. maj. 885 (1.73%))

NORTHAVON
E. 81,800 T. 59,056 (72.20%) LD hold
Prof. Steve Webb, LD 30,872
Chris Butt, C. 19,839
Patricia Gardener, Lab. 6,277
Adrian Blake, UKIP 1,032
Alan Pinder, Green 922
Thomas Beacham, Ind. 114
LD maj. 11,033 (18.68%)
0.48% swing C. to LD
(2001: LD maj. 9,877 (17.71%))

NORWICH NORTH
E. 76,992 T. 47,033 (61.09%) Lab. hold
Dr Ian Gibson, Lab. 21,097
James Tumbridge, C. 15,638
Robin Whitmore, LD 7,616
Adrian Holmes, Green 1,252
John Youles, UKIP 1,122
Bill Holden, Ind. 308
Lab. maj. 5,459 (11.61%)
0.62% swing Lab. to C.
(2001: Lab. maj. 5,863 (12.85%))

NORWICH SOUTH
E. 70,409 T. 42,190 (59.92%) Lab. hold
Rt. Hon. Charles Clarke, Lab. 15,904
Andrew Aalders-Dunthorne, LD 12,251
Antony Little, C. 9,567
Adrian Ramsay, Green 3,101
Vandra Ahlstrom, UKIP 597
Christine Constable, Eng. Dem. 466
Don Barnard, LCA 219
Roger Blackwell, WRP 85
Lab. maj. 3,653 (8.66%)
7.09% swing Lab. to LD
(2001: Lab. maj. 8,816 (20.70%))

NOTTINGHAM EAST
E. 60,634 T. 30,091 (49.63%) Lab. hold
John Heppell, Lab. 13,787
Issan Ghazni, LD 6,848
Jim Thornton, C. 6,826
Ashley Baxter, Green 1,517
Anthony Ellwood, UKIP 740
Pete Ratcliff, Soc. Unity 373
Lab. maj. 6,939 (23.06%)
11.44% swing Lab. to LD
(2001: Lab. maj. 10,320 (34.71%))

NOTTINGHAM NORTH
E. 61,894 T. 30,383 (49.09%) Lab. hold
Graham Allen, Lab. 17,842
Priti Patel, C. 5,671
Tim Ball, LD 5,190
Irena Marriott, UKIP 1,680
Lab. maj. 12,171 (40.06%)
0.34% swing Lab. to C.
(2001: Lab. maj. 12,240 (40.74%))

NOTTINGHAM SOUTH
E. 68,921 T. 34,840 (50.55%) Lab. hold
Alan Simpson, Lab. 16,506
Sudesh Mattu, C. 9,020
Tony Sutton, LD 7,961
Ken Browne, UKIP 1,353
Lab. maj. 7,486 (21.49%)
2.90% swing Lab. to C.
(2001: Lab. maj. 9,989 (27.29%))

NUNEATON
E. 73,440 T. 45,280 (61.66%) Lab. hold
Bill Olner, Lab. 19,945
Mark Pawsey, C. 17,665
Ali Asghar, LD 5,884
Keith Tyson, UKIP 1,786
Lab. maj. 2,280 (5.04%)
6.18% swing Lab. to C.
(2001: Lab. maj. 7,535 (17.40%))

OLD BEXLEY & SIDCUP
E. 68,227 T. 44,572 (65.33%) C. hold
Derek Conway, C. 22,191
Gavin Moore, Lab. 12,271
Nickolas O'Hare, LD 6,564
Michael Barnbrook, UKIP 2,015
Claire Sayers, BNP 1,227
Gregory Peters, Ind. 304
C. maj. 9,920 (22.26%)
7.16% swing Lab. to C.
(2001: C. maj. 3,345 (7.94%))

OLDHAM EAST & SADDLEWORTH
E. 75,680 T. 43,367 (57.30%) Lab. hold
Phil Woolas, Lab. 17,968
Tony Dawson, LD 14,378
Keith Chapman, C. 7,901
Michael Treacy, BNP 2,109
Valerie Nield, UKIP 873
Philip O'Grady, Ind. 138
Lab. maj. 3,590 (8.28%)
1.14% swing LD to Lab.
(2001: Lab. maj. 2,726 (6.00%))

OLDHAM WEST & ROYTON
E. 70,496 T. 37,562 (53.28%) Lab. hold
Rt. Hon. Michael Meacher, Lab. 18,452
Sean Moore, C. 7,998
Stuart Bodsworth, LD 7,519
Anita Corbett, BNP 2,606
David Short, UKIP 987
Lab. maj. 10,454 (27.83%)
2.81% swing Lab. to C.
(2001: Lab. maj. 13,365 (33.44%))

ORPINGTON
E. 78,276 T. 54,734 (69.92%) C. hold
John Horam, C. 26,718
Chris Maines, LD 21,771
Emily Bird, Lab. 4,914
Mick Greenhough, UKIP 1,331
C. maj. 4,947 (9.04%)
4.25% swing LD to C.
(2001: C. maj. 269 (0.53%))

OXFORD EAST
E. 72,234 T. 41,790 (57.85%) Lab. hold
Rt. Hon. Andrew Smith, Lab.   15,405
Steve Goddard, LD   14,442
Virginia Morris, C.   6,992
Jacob Sanders, Green   1,813
Honest Blair, Ind.   1,485
Maurice Leen, IWCA   892
Peter Gardner, UKIP   715
Pat Mylvaganam, Ind.   46
Lab. maj. 963 (2.30%)
11.83% swing Lab. to LD
(2001: Lab. maj. 10,344 (25.96%))

OXFORD WEST & ABINGDON
E. 80,195 T. 52,600 (65.59%) LD hold
Dr Evan Harris, LD   24,336
Amanda McLean, C.   16,653
Antonia Bance, Lab.   8,725
Tom Lines, Green   2,091
Marcus Watney, UKIP   795
LD maj. 7,683 (14.61%)
1.60% swing LD to C.
(2001: LD maj. 9,185 (17.81%))

PENDLE
E. 64,917 T. 41,132 (63.36%) Lab. hold
Gordon Prentice, Lab.   15,250
Jane Ellison, C.   13,070
Shazad Anwar, LD   9,528
Thomas Boocock, BNP   2,547
Graham Cannon, UKIP   737
Lab. maj. 2,180 (5.30%)
2.73% swing Lab. to C.
(2001: Lab. maj. 4,275 (10.76%))

PENRITH & THE BORDER
E. 70,922 T. 46,882 (66.10%) C. hold
Rt. Hon. David Maclean, C.   24,046
Geyve Walker, LD   12,142
Michael Boaden, Lab.   8,958
William Robinson, UKIP   1,187
Mark Gibson, LCA   549
C. maj. 11,904 (25.39%)
3.89% swing C. to LD
(2001: C. maj. 14,677 (33.17%))

PETERBOROUGH
E. 67,499 T. 41,204 (61.04%) C. gain
*Stewart Jackson, C.   17,364
Rt. Hon. Helen Clark, Lab.   14,624
Nick Sandford, LD   6,876
Mary Herdman, UKIP   1,242
Terry Blackham, NF   931
Marc Potter, MNP   167
C. maj. 2,740 (6.65%)
6.91% swing Lab. to C.
(2001: Lab. maj. 2,854 (7.17%))

PLYMOUTH DEVONPORT
E. 72,848 T. 42,013 (57.67%) Lab. hold
*Alison Seabeck, Lab.   18,612
Richard Cuming, C.   10,509
Judith Jolly, LD   8,000
Bill Wakeham, UKIP   3,324
Keith Greene, Ind.   747
Robert Hawkins, Soc. Lab.   445
Tony Staunton, Respect   376
Lab. maj. 8,103 (19.29%)
5.98% swing Lab. to C.
(2001: Lab. maj. 13,033 (31.24%))

PLYMOUTH SUTTON
E. 67,202 T. 38,192 (56.83%)
                       Lab. (Co-op) hold
Linda Gilroy, Lab. (Co-op)   15,497
Oliver Colvile, C.   11,388
Karen Gillard, LD   8,685
Robert Cumming, UKIP   2,392
Rob Hawkins, Soc. Lab.   230
Lab. (Co-op) maj. 4,109 (10.76%)
4.24% swing Lab. (Co-op) to C.
(2001: Lab. (Co-op) maj. 7,517
(19.24%))

PONTEFRACT & CASTLEFORD
E. 61,871 T. 32,947 (53.25%) Lab. hold
Yvette Cooper, Lab.   20,973
Simon Jones, C.   5,727
Wesley Paxton, LD   3,942
Suzy Cass, BNP   1,835
Bob Hague, Green Soc.   470
Lab. maj. 15,246 (46.27%)
2.95% swing Lab. to C.
(2001: Lab. maj. 16,378 (52.17%))

POOLE
E. 64,178 T. 40,513 (63.13%) C. hold
Robert Syms, C.   17,571
Mike Plummer, LD   11,583
Darren Brown, Lab.   9,376
John Barnes, UKIP   1,436
Peter Pirnie, BNP   547
C. maj. 5,988 (14.78%)
2.42% swing C. to LD
(2001: C. maj. 7,166 (18.27%))

POPLAR & CANNING TOWN
E. 81,544 T. 39,010 (47.84%) Lab. hold
Jim Fitzpatrick, Lab.   15,628
Tim Archer, C.   8,499
Oliur Rahman, Respect   6,573
Janet Ludlow, LD   5,420
Terry McGrenera, Green   955
Aminul Hoque, Ind.   815
Tony Smith, Veritas   650
Simeon Ademolake, CPA   470
Lab. maj. 7,129 (18.27%)
11.55% swing Lab. to C.
(2001: Lab. maj. 14,104 (41.35%))

PORTSMOUTH NORTH
E. 62,884 T. 37,717 (59.98%)
                       Lab. (Co-op) hold
*Sarah McCarthy-Fry,
   Lab. (Co-op)   15,412
Penny Mordaunt, C.   14,273
Gary Lawson, LD   6,684
Mike Smith, UKIP   1,348
Lab. (Co-op) maj. 1,139 (3.02%)
5.45% swing Lab. (Co-op) to C.
(2001: Lab. (Co-op) maj. 5,134
(13.93%))

PORTSMOUTH SOUTH
E. 70,969 T. 40,374 (56.89%) LD hold
Mike Hancock, LD   17,047
Caroline Dinenage, C.   13,685
Mark Button, Lab.   8,714
Dennis Pierson, UKIP   928
LD maj. 3,362 (8.33%)
3.60% swing LD to C.
(2001: LD maj. 6,094 (15.54%))

PRESTON
E. 63,351 T. 34,081 (53.80%)
                       Lab. (Co-op) hold
Mark Hendrick, Lab. (Co-op)   17,210
Fiona Bryce, C.   7,803
William Parkinson, LD   5,701
Michael Lavalette, Respect   2,318
Ellen Boardman, UKIP   1,049
Lab. (Co-op) maj. 9,407 (27.60%)
3.22% swing Lab. (Co-op) to C.
(2001: Lab. (Co-op) maj. 12,268
(34.04%))

PUDSEY
E. 70,411 T. 46,444 (65.96%) Lab. hold
Paul Truswell, Lab.   21,261
Pamela Singleton, C.   15,391
James Keeley, LD   8,551
David Daniel, UKIP   1,241
Lab. maj. 5,870 (12.64%)
0.09% swing C. to Lab.
(2001: Lab. maj. 5,626 (12.45%))

PUTNEY
E. 61,498 T. 36,574 (59.47%) C. gain
*Justine Greening, C.   15,497
Tony Colman, Lab.   13,731
Jeremy Ambache, LD   5,965
Keith Magnum, Green   993
Anthony Gahan, UKIP   388
C. maj. 1,766 (4.83%)
6.46% swing Lab. to C.
(2001: Lab. maj. 2,771 (8.09%))

RAYLEIGH
E. 71,996 T. 46,193 (64.16%) C. hold
Mark Francois, C.   25,609
Julian Ware-Lane, Lab.   10,883
Sid Cumberland, LD   7,406
Janet Davies, UKIP   2,295
C. maj. 14,726 (31.88%)
6.25% swing Lab. to C.
(2001: C. maj. 8,290 (19.38%))

READING EAST
E. 72,806 T. 43,912 (60.31%) C. gain
*Rob Wilson, C.   15,557
Tony Page, Lab.   15,082
Prof. John Howson, LD   10,619
Rob White, Green   1,548
David Lamb, UKIP   849
Jan Lloyd, Ind.   135
Rex Hora, Ind.   122
C. maj. 475 (1.08%)
6.95% swing Lab. to C.
(2001: Lab. maj. 5,588 (12.81%))

READING WEST
E. 69,011 T. 42,103 (61.01%) Lab. hold
Martin Salter, Lab.   18,940
Ewan Cameron, C.   14,258
Denise Gaines, LD   6,663
Peter Williams, UKIP   1,180
Adrian Windisch, Green   921
Dave Boyle, Veritas   141
Lab. maj. 4,682 (11.12%)
4.98% swing Lab. to C.
(2001: Lab. maj. 8,849 (21.08%))

REDCAR
E. 66,947 T. 38,861 (58.05%) Lab. hold
Vera Baird, Lab.   19,968
Ian Swales, LD   7,852
Jonathan Lehrle, C.   6,954
Christopher McGlade, Ind.   2,379
Andrew Harris, BNP   985
Edward Walker, UKIP   564
John Taylor, Soc. Lab.   159
Lab. maj. 12,116 (31.18%)
8.25% swing Lab. to LD
(2001: Lab. maj. 13,443 (35.19%))

REDDITCH
E. 64,121 T. 40,291 (62.84%) Lab. hold
Rt. Hon. Jacqui Smith, Lab.   18,012
Karen Lumley, C.   15,296
Nigel Hicks, LD   5,602
John Ison, UKIP   1,381
Lab. maj. 2,716 (6.74%)
0.02% swing C. to Lab.
(2001: Lab. maj. 2,484 (6.71%))

REGENT'S PARK & KENSINGTON
NORTH
E. 78,975 T. 40,680 (51.51%) Lab. hold
Karen Buck, Lab.   18,196
Jeremy Bradshaw, C.   12,065
Rabi Martins, LD   7,569
Dr Paul Miller, Green   1,985
Pamela Perrin, UKIP   456
Rezouk Boufas, CP   227
Abby Dharamsey, Ind.   182
Lab. maj. 6,131 (15.07%)
6.32% swing Lab. to C.
(2001: Lab. maj. 10,266 (27.71%))

REIGATE
E. 65,719 T. 42,605 (64.83%) C. hold
Crispin Blunt, C.   20,884
Jane Kulka, LD   9,896
Sam Townend, Lab.   8,896
Jeremy Wraith, UKIP   1,921
Harold Green, EDP   600
Michael Selby, Ind.   408
C. maj. 10,988 (25.79%)
0.46% swing C. to LD
(2001: C. maj. 8,025 (20.33%))

RIBBLE SOUTH
E. 75,357 T. 47,511 (63.05%) Lab. hold
David Borrow, Lab.   20,428
Lorraine Fullbrook, C.   18,244
Mark Alcock, LD   7,634
Kenneth Jones, UKIP   1,205
Lab. maj. 2,184 (4.60%)
1.82% swing Lab. to C.
(2001: Lab. maj. 3,792 (8.22%))

RIBBLE VALLEY
E. 75,692 T. 49,766 (65.75%) C. hold
Nigel Evans, C.   25,834
Julie Young, LD   11,663
Jack Davenport, Lab.   10,924
Kevin Henry, UKIP   1,345
C. maj. 14,171 (28.48%)
2.81% swing LD to C.
(2001: C. maj. 11,238 (22.85%))

RICHMOND (YORKS)
E. 69,521 T. 45,200 (65.02%) C. hold
Rt. Hon. William Hague, C.   26,722
Neil Foster, Lab.   8,915
Jacquie Bell, LD   7,982
Leslie Rowe, Green   1,581
C. maj. 17,807 (39.40%)
1.17% swing Lab. to C.
(2001: C. maj. 16,319 (37.06%))

RICHMOND PARK
E. 70,555 T. 51,374 (72.81%) LD hold
*Susan Kramer, LD   24,011
Marco Forgione, C.   20,280
James Butler, Lab.   4,768
James Page, Green   1,379
Peter Dul, UKIP   458
Peter Flower, CPA   288
Margaret Harrison, Ind.   83
Rainbow George Weiss, Vote Dream   63
Richard Meacock, Ind.   44
LD maj. 3,731 (7.26%)
1.42% swing LD to C.
(2001: LD maj. 4,964 (10.10%))

ROCHDALE
E. 69,894 T. 40,836 (58.43%) LD gain
*Paul Rowen, LD   16,787
Lorna Fitzsimons, Lab.   16,345
Khalid Hussain, C.   4,270
Derek Adams, BNP   1,773
Dr John Whittaker, UKIP   499
Samir Chatterjee, Green   448
Mohammed Salim, IZB   361
Carl Faulkner, Veritas   353
LD maj. 442 (1.08%)
7.72% swing Lab. to LD
(2001: Lab. maj. 5,655 (14.35%))

ROCHFORD & SOUTHEND EAST
E. 71,186 T. 39,462 (55.44%) C. hold
*James Duddridge, C.   17,874
Fred Grindrod, Lab.   12,380
Graham Longley, LD   5,967
John Croft, UKIP   1,913
Andrew Vaughan, Green   1,328
C. maj. 5,494 (13.92%)
2.43% swing C. to Lab.
(2001: C. maj. 7,034 (18.78%))

ROMFORD
E. 58,571 T. 36,482 (62.29%) C. hold
Andrew Rosindell, C.   21,560
Margaret Mullane, Lab.   9,971
Geoffrey Seeff, LD   3,066
John McCaffrey, BNP   1,088
Terry Murray, UKIP   797
C. maj. 11,589 (31.77%)
7.51% swing Lab. to C.
(2001: C. maj. 5,977 (16.74%))

ROMSEY
E. 72,177 T. 50,311 (69.71%) LD hold
Sandra Gidley, LD   22,465
Caroline Nokes, C.   22,340
Matthew Stevens, Lab.   4,430
Michael Wigley, UKIP   1,076
LD maj. 125 (0.25%)
2.32% swing LD to C.
(2001: LD maj. 2,370 (4.89%))

ROSSENDALE & DARWEN
E. 72,207 T. 44,437 (61.54%) Lab. hold
Janet Anderson, Lab.   19,073
Nigel Adams, C.   15,397
Mike Carr, LD   6,670
Anthony Wentworth, BNP   1,736
Graeme McIver, Green   821
David Duthie, UKIP   740
Lab. maj. 3,676 (8.27%)
1.85% swing Lab. to C.
(2001: Lab. maj. 5,223 (12.63%))

ROTHER VALLEY
E. 67,973 T. 39,495 (58.10%) Lab. hold
Rt. Hon. Kevin Barron, Lab.   21,871
Colin Phillips, C.   7,647
Phillip Bristow, LD   6,272
Nicholas Cass, BNP   2,020
Gordon Brown, UKIP   1,685
Lab. maj. 14,224 (36.01%)
2.21% swing Lab. to C.
(2001: Lab. maj. 14,882 (40.44%))

ROTHERHAM
E. 54,410 T. 29,978 (55.10%) Lab. hold
Rt. Hon. Denis MacShane, Lab.   15,840
Timothy Gordon, LD   5,159
Lee Rotherham, C.   4,966
Marlene Guest, BNP   1,986
David Cutts, UKIP   1,122
Richard Penycate, Green   905
Lab. maj. 10,681 (35.63%)
8.83% swing Lab. to C.
(2001: Lab. maj. 13,077 (44.55%))

RUGBY & KENILWORTH
E. 83,303 T. 56,949 (68.36%) C. gain
*Jeremy Wright, C.   23,447
Andy King, Lab.   21,891
Richard Allanach, LD   10,143
John Thurley, UKIP   911
Brian Hadland, Ind.   299
Lillian Pallikaropoulos, Ind.   258
C. maj. 1,556 (2.73%)
4.04% swing Lab. to C.
(2001: Lab. maj. 2,877 (5.35%))

RUISLIP-NORTHWOOD
E. 60,774 T. 39,670 (65.27%) C. hold
*Nick Hurd, C.   18,939
Mike Cox, LD   10,029
Ashley Riley, Lab.   8,323
Graham Lee, Green   892
Ian Edward, NF   841
Roland Courtenay, UKIP   646
C. maj. 8,910 (22.46%)
3.49% swing C. to LD
(2001: C. maj. 7,537 (20.29%))

RUNNYMEDE & WEYBRIDGE
E. 74,172 T. 43,524 (58.68%) C. hold
Philip Hammond, C.   22,366
Paul Greenwood, Lab.   10,017
Henry Bolton, LD   7,771
Anthony Micklethwait, UKIP   1,719
Charles Gilman, Green   1,180
Mad Crab Collett, Loony   358
Katrina Osman, UKC   113
C. maj. 12,349 (28.37%)
4.33% swing Lab. to C.
(2001: C. maj. 8,360 (19.70%))

RUSHCLIFFE
E. 79,913 T. 56,311 (70.47%) C. hold
Rt. Hon. Kenneth Clarke, C.   27,899
Edward Gamble, Lab.   14,925
Karrar Khan, LD   9,813
Simon Anthony, Green   1,692
Matthew Faithfull, UKIP   1,358
Daniel Moss, Veritas   624
C. maj. 12,974 (23.04%)
4.76% swing Lab. to C.
(2001: C. maj. 7,357 (13.51%))

RUTLAND & MELTON
E. 75,823 T. 49,284 (65.00%) C. hold
Alan Duncan, C.	25,237
Linda Arnold, Lab.	12,307
Grahame Hudson, LD	9,153
Peter Baker, UKIP	1,554
Duncan Shelley, Veritas	696
Helen Pender, Ind.	337

C. maj. 12,930 (26.24%)
3.97% swing Lab. to C.
(2001: C. maj. 8,612 (18.30%))

RYEDALE
E. 67,770 T. 44,120 (65.10%) C. hold
John Greenway, C.	21,251
Gordon Beever, LD	10,782
Paul Blanchard, Lab.	9,148
Stephen Feaster, UKIP	1,522
John Clarke, Lib.	1,417

C. maj. 10,469 (23.73%)
6.31% swing LD to C.
(2001: C. maj. 4,875 (11.11%))

SAFFRON WALDEN
E. 77,600 T. 53,020 (68.32%) C. hold
Rt. Hon. Sir Alan Haselhurst, C.	27,263
Elfreda Tealby-Watson, LD	14,255
Swatantra Nandanwar, Lab.	8,755
Raymond Tyler, UKIP	1,412
Raymond Brown, Eng. Dem.	860
Trevor Hackett, Veritas	475

C. maj. 13,008 (24.53%)
0.27% swing LD to C.
(2001: C. maj. 12,004 (23.99%))

ST ALBANS
E. 64,595 T. 45,462 (70.38%) C. gain
*Anne Main, C.	16,953
Kerry Pollard, Lab.	15,592
Michael Green, LD	11,561
Richard Evans, UKIP	707
Janet Girsman, St Albans	430
Mark Reynolds, Ind.	219

C. maj. 1,361 (2.99%)
6.60% swing Lab. to C.
(2001: Lab. maj. 4,466 (10.21%))

ST HELENS NORTH
E. 69,834 T. 39,271 (56.23%) Lab. hold
Dave Watts, Lab.	22,329
John Beirne, LD	8,367
Paul Oakley, C.	7,410
Sylvia Hall, UKIP	1,165

Lab. maj. 13,962 (35.55%)
3.99% swing Lab. to LD
(2001: Lab. maj. 15,901 (42.29%))

ST HELENS SOUTH
E. 65,441 T. 35,473 (54.21%) Lab. hold
Shaun Woodward, Lab.	19,345
Brian Spencer, LD	10,036
Una Riley, C.	4,602
Malcolm Nightingale, UKIP	847
Michael Perry, Soc. Lab.	643

Lab. maj. 9,309 (26.24%)
0.17% swing Lab. to LD
(2001: Lab. maj. 8,985 (26.58%))

ST IVES
E. 74,716 T. 50,417 (67.48%) LD hold
Andrew George, LD	25,577
Christian Mitchell, C.	13,968
Michael Dooley, Lab.	6,583
Michael Faulkner, UKIP	2,551
Katrina Slack, Green	1,738

LD maj. 11,609 (23.03%)
1.31% swing C. to LD
(2001: LD maj. 10,053 (20.41%))

SALFORD
E. 53,294 T. 22,600 (42.41%) Lab. hold
Rt. Hon. Hazel Blears, Lab.	13,007
Norman Owen, LD	5,062
Laetitia Cash, C.	3,440
Lisa Duffy, UKIP	1,091

Lab. maj. 7,945 (35.15%)
6.88% swing Lab. to LD
(2001: Lab. maj. 11,012 (48.91%))

SALISBURY
E. 80,385 T. 54,322 (67.58%) C. hold
Robert Key, C.	25,961
Richard Denton-White, LD	14,819
Clare Moody, Lab.	9,457
Frances Howard, UKIP	2,290
Hamish Soutar, Green	1,555
John Holme, Ind.	240

C. maj. 11,142 (20.51%)
1.98% swing LD to C.
(2001: C. maj. 8,703 (16.54%))

SCARBOROUGH & WHITBY
E. 73,806 T. 46,912 (63.56%) C. gain
*Robert Goodwill, C.	19,248
Lawrence Quinn, Lab.	18,003
Tania Exley-Moore, LD	7,495
Jonathan Dixon, Green	1,214
Paul Abbott, UKIP	952

C. maj. 1,245 (2.65%)
5.10% swing Lab. to C.
(2001: Lab. maj. 3,585 (7.54%))

SCUNTHORPE
E. 62,669 T. 32,664 (52.12%) Lab. hold
Elliot Morley, Lab.	17,355
Julian Sturdy, C.	8,392
Neil Poole, LD	5,556
David Baxendale, UKIP	1,361

Lab. maj. 8,963 (27.44%)
1.70% swing Lab. to C.
(2001: Lab. maj. 10,372 (30.85%))

SEDGEFIELD
E. 66,666 T. 41,483 (62.23%) Lab. hold
Rt. Hon. Tony Blair, Lab.	24,429
Grp Capt Al Lockwood, C.	5,972
Robert Browne, LD	4,935
Reg Keys, Ind.	4,252
William Brown, UKIP	646
Mark Farrell, NF	253
Fiona Luckhurst-Matthews, Veritas	218
Berony Abraham, Ind.	209
Boney Maroney, Loony	157
Jonathan Cockburn, BMG	103
Terry Pattinson, Senior	97
Cherri Gilham, UKPP	82
Helen John, Ind.	68
John Barker, Ind.	45
Julian Brennan, Ind.	17

Lab. maj. 18,457 (44.49%)
0.25% swing C. to Lab.
(2001: Lab. maj. 17,713 (44.00%))

SELBY
E. 78,111 T. 52,549 (67.27%) Lab. hold
John Grogan, Lab.	22,623
Mark Menzies, C.	22,156
Ian Cuthbertson, LD	7,770

Lab. maj. 467 (0.89%)
1.68% swing Lab. to C.
(2001: Lab. maj. 2,138 (4.25%))

SEVENOAKS
E. 65,109 T. 43,298 (66.50%) C. hold
Michael Fallon, C.	22,437
Ben Abbotts, LD	9,467
Tim Stanley, Lab.	9,101
Robert Dobson, UKIP	1,309
John Marshall, Eng. Dem.	751
Mark Ellis, UK Path	233

C. maj. 12,970 (29.96%)
1.09% swing LD to C.
(2001: C. maj. 10,154 (23.83%))

SHEFFIELD ATTERCLIFFE
E. 67,815 T. 37,019 (54.59%) Lab. hold
Clive Betts, Lab.	22,250
Kevin Moore, LD	6,283
Tracy Critchlow, C.	5,329
Jonathan Arnott, UKIP	1,680
Beverley Jones, BNP	1,477

Lab. maj. 15,967 (43.13%)
5.22% swing Lab. to LD
(2001: Lab. maj. 18,844 (52.60%))

SHEFFIELD BRIGHTSIDE
E. 51,379 T. 24,629 (47.94%) Lab. hold
Rt. Hon. David Blunkett, Lab.	16,876
Jonathan Harston, LD	3,232
Tim Clark, C.	2,205
Christopher Hartigan, BNP	1,537
Judith Clarke, UKIP	779

Lab. maj. 13,644 (55.40%)
6.37% swing Lab. to LD
(2001: Lab. maj. 17,049 (66.72%))

SHEFFIELD CENTRAL
E. 59,862 T. 29,985 (50.09%) Lab. hold
Rt. Hon. Richard Caborn, Lab.	14,950
Ali Qadar, LD	7,895
Samantha George, C.	3,094
Bernard Little, Green	1,808
Maxine Bowler, Respect	1,284
Mark Payne, BNP	539
Charlotte Arnott, UKIP	415

Lab. maj. 7,055 (23.53%)
9.09% swing Lab. to LD
(2001: Lab. maj. 12,544 (41.72%))

SHEFFIELD HALLAM
E. 59,606 T. 40,427 (67.82%) LD hold
*Nick Clegg, LD	20,710
Spencer Pitfield, C.	12,028
Mahroof Hussain, Lab.	5,110
Rob Cole, Green	1,331
Sid Cordle, CPA	441
Nigel James, UKIP	438
Ian Senior, BNP	369

LD maj. 8,682 (21.48%)
1.48% swing LD to C.
(2001: LD maj. 9,347 (24.44%))

SHEFFIELD HEELEY
E. 59,748 T. 34,093 (57.06%)
Lab. (Co-op) hold
Meg Munn, Lab. (Co-op)	18,405
Colin Ross, LD	7,035
Aster Crawshaw, C.	4,987
John Beatson, BNP	1,314
Rob Unwin, Green	1,312
Mark Suter, UKIP	775
Mark Dunnell, Soc. Alt.	265

Lab. (Co-op) maj. 11,370 (33.35%)
0.47% swing Lab. (Co-op) to LD
(2001: Lab. (Co-op) maj. 11,704
(34.28%))

SHEFFIELD HILLSBOROUGH
E. 75,706 T. 45,884 (60.61%) Lab. hold
*Angela Smith, Lab.   23,477
John Commons, LD   12,234
Jackie Doyle-Price, C.   6,890
David Wright, BNP   2,010
Maurice Patterson, UKIP   1,273
Lab. maj. 11,243 (24.50%)
4.87% swing Lab. to LD
(2001: Lab. maj. 14,569 (34.25%))

SHERWOOD
E. 75,913 T. 47,117 (62.07%) Lab. hold
Paddy Tipping, Lab.   22,824
Bruce Laughton, C.   16,172
Peter Harris, LD   6,384
Moritz Dawkins, UKIP   1,737
Lab. maj. 6,652 (14.12%)
3.15% swing Lab. to C.
(2001: Lab. maj. 9,373 (20.42%))

SHIPLEY
E. 69,575 T. 47,666 (68.51%) C. gain
*Philip Davies, C.   18,608
Christopher Leslie, Lab.   18,186
John Briggs, LD   7,018
Tom Linden, BNP   2,000
Quentin Deakin, Green   1,665
David Crabtree, Iraq   189
C. maj. 422 (0.89%)
1.99% swing Lab. to C.
(2001: Lab. maj. 1,428 (3.10%))

SHREWSBURY & ATCHAM
E. 73,193 T. 50,296 (68.72%) C. gain
*Daniel Kawczynski, C.   18,960
Michael Ion, Lab.   17,152
Richard Burt, LD   11,487
Peter Lewis, UKIP   1,349
Emma Bullard, Green   1,138
James Gollins, Ind.   126
Nigel Harris, Online   84
C. maj. 1,808 (3.59%)
5.38% swing Lab. to C.
(2001: Lab. maj. 3,579 (7.17%))

SHROPSHIRE NORTH
E. 73,477 T. 46,510 (63.30%) C. hold
Owen Paterson, C.   23,061
Sandra Samuels, Lab.   12,041
Steven Bourne, LD   9,175
Ian Smith, UKIP   2,233
C. maj. 11,020 (23.69%)
5.14% swing Lab. to C.
(2001: C. maj. 6,241 (13.42%))

SITTINGBOURNE & SHEPPEY
E. 62,950 T. 40,803 (64.82%) Lab. hold
Derek Wyatt, Lab.   17,051
Gordon Henderson, C.   16,972
Jane Nelson, LD   5,183
Stephen Dean, UKIP   926
Mad MikeYoung, R & R Loony   479
David Cassidy, Veritas   192
Lab. maj. 79 (0.19%)
4.54% swing Lab. to C.
(2001: Lab. maj. 3,509 (9.27%))

SKIPTON & RIPON
E. 76,485 T. 50,521 (66.05%) C. hold
Rt. Hon. David Curry, C.   25,100
Paul English, LD   13,480
Paul Baptie, Lab.   9,393
Ian Bannister, UKIP   2,274
Robert Leakey, Currency   274
C. maj. 11,620 (23.00%)
1.66% swing C. to LD
(2001: C. maj. 12,930 (26.32%))

SLEAFORD & NORTH HYKEHAM
E. 79,612 T. 53,397 (67.07%) C. hold
Rt. Hon. Douglas Hogg, C.   26,855
Katrina Bull, Lab.   14,150
David Harding-Price, LD   9,710
Guy Croft, UKIP   2,682
C. maj. 12,705 (23.79%)
3.05% swing Lab. to C.
(2001: C. maj. 8,622 (17.70%))

SLOUGH
E. 71,595 T. 37,095 (51.81%) Lab. hold
Fiona Mactaggart, Lab.   17,517
Sheila Gunn, C.   9,666
Thomas McCann, LD   5,739
Ajaz Khan, Respect   1,632
Geoff Howard, UKIP   1,415
David Wood, Green   759
Paul Janik, Ind.   367
Lab. maj. 7,851 (21.16%)
5.45% swing Lab. to C.
(2001: Lab. maj. 12,508 (32.07%))

SOLIHULL
E. 77,910 T. 52,313 (67.15%) LD gain
*Lorely Burt, LD   20,896
John Taylor, C.   20,617
Rory Vaughan, Lab.   8,058
Diane Carr, BNP   1,752
Andrew Moore, UKIP   990
LD maj. 279 (0.53%)
10.01% swing C. to LD
(2001: C. maj. 9,407 (19.49%))

SOMERTON & FROME
E. 77,806 T. 54,102 (69.53%) LD hold
David Heath, LD   23,759
Clive Allen, C.   22,947
Joseph Pestell, Lab.   5,865
William Lukins, UKIP   1,047
Carleton Beaman, Veritas   484
LD maj. 812 (1.50%)
0.12% swing C. to LD
(2001: LD maj. 668 (1.27%))

SOUTH HOLLAND & THE DEEPINGS
E. 77,453 T. 48,249 (62.29%) C. hold
John Hayes, C.   27,544
Linda Woodings, Lab.   11,764
Steve Jarvis, LD   6,244
Jamie Corney, UKIP   1,950
Paul Poll, Ind.   747
C. maj. 15,780 (32.71%)
4.34% swing Lab. to C.
(2001: C. maj. 11,099 (24.02%))

SOUTH SHIELDS
E. 59,403 T. 30,206 (50.85%) Lab. hold
Rt. Hon. David Miliband, Lab.   18,269
Stephen Psallidas, LD   5,957
Richard Lewis, C.   5,207
Nader Afshari-Naderi, Ind.   773
Lab. maj. 12,312 (40.76%)
2.78% swing Lab. to LD
(2001: Lab. maj. 14,090 (46.28%))

SOUTHAMPTON ITCHEN
E. 78,818 T. 43,225 (54.84%) Lab. hold
Rt. Hon. John Denham, Lab.   20,871
Flick Drummond, C.   11,569
David Goodall, LD   9,162
Kim Rose, UKIP   1,623
Lab. maj. 9,302 (21.52%)
2.80% swing Lab. to C.
(2001: Lab. maj. 11,223 (27.13%))

SOUTHAMPTON TEST
E. 72,833 T. 41,783 (57.37%) Lab. hold
Dr Alan Whitehead, Lab.   17,845
Stephen MacLoughlin, C.   10,827
Steve Sollitt, LD   10,368
John Spottiswoode, Green   1,482
Peter Day, UKIP   1,261
Lab. maj. 7,018 (16.80%)
5.08% swing Lab. to C.
(2001: Lab. maj. 11,207 (26.96%))

SOUTHEND WEST
E. 64,915 T. 39,830 (61.36%) C. hold
David Amess, C.   18,408
Peter Wexham, LD   9,449
Jan Etienne, Lab.   9,072
Carole Sampson, UKIP   1,349
Dr Marimuthu Velmurugan, Ind.   745
Jeremy Moss, Eng. Dem.   701
Dan Anslow, Power   106
C. maj. 8,959 (22.49%)
0.55% swing LD to C.
(2001: C. maj. 7,941 (21.25%))

SOUTHPORT
E. 67,977 T. 41,201 (60.61%) LD hold
Dr John Pugh, LD   19,093
Mark Bigley, C.   15,255
Paul Brant, Lab.   5,277
Terry Durrance, UKIP   749
Bill Givens, YPB   589
Harry Forster, Veritas   238
LD maj. 3,838 (9.32%)
1.00% swing C. to LD
(2001: LD maj. 3,007 (7.31%))

SOUTHWARK NORTH & BERMONDSEY
E. 77,084 T. 37,959 (49.24%) LD hold
Simon Hughes, LD   17,874
Kirsty McNeill, Lab.   12,468
David Branch, C.   4,752
Storm Poorun, Green   1,137
Linda Robson, UKIP   791
Paul Winnett, NF   704
Simi Lawanson, CPA   233
LD maj. 5,406 (14.24%)
5.94% swing LD to Lab.
(2001: LD maj. 9,632 (26.13%))

SPELTHORNE
E. 69,650 T. 42,829 (61.49%) C. hold
David Wilshire, C.   21,620
Keith Dibble, Lab.   11,684
Simon James, LD   7,318
Christopher Browne, UKIP   1,968
Caroline Schwark, UKC   239
C. maj. 9,936 (23.20%)
7.70% swing Lab. to C.
(2001: C. maj. 3,262 (7.80%))

STAFFORD
E. 70,359 T. 45,554 (64.75%) Lab. hold
David Kidney, Lab.   19,889
David Chambers, C.   17,768
Barry Stamp, LD   6,390
Frederick Goode, UKIP   1,507
Lab. maj. 2,121 (4.66%)
3.34% swing Lab. to C.
(2001: Lab. maj. 5,032 (11.34%))

STAFFORDSHIRE MOORLANDS
E. 69,136 T. 44,253 (64.01%) Lab. hold
Charlotte Atkins, Lab.	18,126
Marcus Hayes, C.	15,688
John Fisher, LD	6,927
Steve Povey, UKIP	3,512
Lab. maj. 2,438 (5.51%)
4.09% swing Lab. to C.
(2001: Lab. maj. 5,838 (13.69%))

STAFFORDSHIRE SOUTH
Deferred until 23 June 2005 due to the
death of the Liberal Democrat candidate
during the general election campaign (*see*
by-elections)

STALYBRIDGE & HYDE
E. 66,013 T. 35,314 (53.50%) Lab. hold
James Purnell, Lab.	17,535
Lisa Boardman, C.	9,187
Viv Bingham, LD	5,532
Nigel Byrne, BNP	1,399
Mike Smee, Green	1,088
Dr John Whittaker, UKIP	573
Lab. maj. 8,348 (23.64%)
2.00% swing Lab. to C.
(2001: Lab. maj. 8,859 (27.64%))

STEVENAGE
E. 66,889 T. 41,934 (62.69%) Lab. hold
Barbara Follett, Lab.	18,003
George Freeman, C.	14,864
Julia Davies, LD	7,610
Victoria Peebles, UKIP	1,305
Antal Losonczi, Ind.	152
Lab. maj. 3,139 (7.49%)
6.35% swing Lab. to C.
(2001: Lab. maj. 8,566 (20.18%))

STOCKPORT
E. 65,593 T. 35,771 (54.53%) Lab. hold
Ann Coffey, Lab.	18,069
Elizabeth Berridge, C.	8,906
Lyn-Su Floodgate, LD	7,832
Richard Simpson, UKIP	964
Lab. maj. 9,163 (25.62%)
3.54% swing Lab. to C.
(2001: Lab. maj. 11,569 (32.70%))

STOCKTON NORTH
E. 63,271 T. 36,428 (57.57%) Lab. hold
Frank Cook, Lab.	20,012
Harriett Baldwin, C.	7,575
Neil Hughes, LD	6,869
Kevin Hughes, BNP	986
Gordon Parkin, UKIP	986
Lab. maj. 12,437 (34.14%)
3.60% swing Lab. to C.
(2001: Lab. maj. 14,647 (41.34%))

STOCKTON SOUTH
E. 71,286 T. 44,923 (63.02%) Lab. hold
Dari Taylor, Lab.	21,480
James Gaddas, C.	15,341
Mike Barker, LD	7,171
Sandra Allison, UKIP	931
Lab. maj. 6,139 (13.67%)
3.44% swing Lab. to C.
(2001: Lab. maj. 9,086 (20.55%))

STOKE-ON-TRENT CENTRAL
E. 57,643 T. 27,907 (48.41%) Lab. hold
Mark Fisher, Lab.	14,760
John Redfern, LD	4,986
Esther Baroudy, C.	4,823
Michael Coleman, BNP	2,178
Joseph Bonfiglio, UKIP	914
Jim Cessford, Soc. Alt.	246
Lab. maj. 9,774 (35.02%)
5.50% swing Lab. to LD
(2001: Lab. maj. 11,845 (41.86%))

STOKE-ON-TRENT NORTH
E. 58,422 T. 30,760 (52.65%) Lab. hold
Joan Walley, Lab.	16,191
Benjamin Browning, C.	6,155
Henry Jebb, LD	4,561
Spencer Cartlidge, BNP	2,132
Eileen Braithwaite, UKIP	696
Ian Taylor, Veritas	689
Harry Chesters, Ind.	336
Lab. maj. 10,036 (32.63%)
3.25% swing Lab. to C.
(2001: Lab. maj. 11,784 (39.13%))

STOKE-ON-TRENT SOUTH
E. 70,612 T. 37,820 (53.56%) Lab. hold
*Robert Flello, Lab.	17,727
Mark Deaville, C.	9,046
Andrew Martin, LD	5,894
Mark Leat, BNP	3,305
Neville Benson, UKIP	1,043
Grant Allen, Veritas	805
Lab. maj. 8,681 (22.95%)
3.08% swing Lab. to C.
(2001: Lab. maj. 10,489 (29.11%))

STONE
E. 70,359 T. 47,036 (66.85%) C. hold
Bill Cash, C.	22,733
Mark Davis, Lab.	13,644
Peter Stevens, LD	9,111
Michael Nattrass, UKIP	1,548
C. maj. 9,089 (19.32%)
3.05% swing Lab. to C.
(2001: C. maj. 6,036 (13.22%))

STOURBRIDGE
E. 64,479 T. 41,708 (64.68%) Lab. hold
*Lynda Waltho, Lab.	17,089
Diana Coad, C.	16,682
Chris Bramall, LD	6,850
Daniel Pui Chai Mau, UKIP	1,087
Lab. maj. 407 (0.98%)
4.29% swing Lab. to C.
(2001: Lab. maj. 3,812 (9.55%))

STRATFORD-UPON-AVON
E. 84,591 T. 58,240 (68.85%) C. hold
John Maples, C.	28,652
Dr Susan Juned, LD	16,468
Rachel Blackmore, Lab. (Co-op)	10,145
Harry Cottam, UKIP	1,621
Mick Davies, Green	1,354
C. maj. 12,184 (20.92%)
0.29% swing C. to LD
(2001: C. maj. 11,802 (21.49%))

STREATHAM
E. 79,193 T. 40,615 (51.29%) Lab. hold
Rt. Hon. Keith Hill, Lab.	18,950
Darren Sanders, LD	11,484
James Sproule, C.	7,238
Shane Collins, Green	2,245
Trevor Gittings, UKIP	396
William Colvill, WRP	127
Philippa Stone, Ind.	100
Robert West, Ind.	40
Sarah Acheng, Ind.	35
Lab. maj. 7,466 (18.38%)
10.09% swing Lab. to LD
(2001: Lab. maj. 14,270 (38.57%))

STRETFORD & URMSTON
E. 61,979 T. 38,101 (61.47%) Lab. hold
Rt. Hon. Beverley Hughes, Lab.	19,417
Damian Hinds, C.	11,566
Faraz Bhatti, LD	5,323
Mark Krantz, Respect	950
Michael McManus, UKIP	845
Lab. maj. 7,851 (20.61%)
6.71% swing Lab. to C.
(2001: Lab. maj. 13,239 (33.97%))

STROUD
E. 79,748 T. 56,875 (71.32%)
Lab. (Co-op) hold
David Drew, Lab. (Co-op)	22,527
Neil Carmichael, C.	22,177
Peter Hirst, LD	8,026
Martin Whiteside, Green	3,056
Edward Noble, UKIP	1,089
Lab. (Co-op) maj. 350 (0.62%)
4.26% swing Lab. (Co-op) to C.
(2001: Lab. (Co-op) maj. 5,039 (9.13%))

SUFFOLK CENTRAL & IPSWICH NORTH
E. 76,271 T. 50,866 (66.69%) C. hold
Sir Michael Lord, C.	22,333
Neil MacDonald, Lab.	14,477
Andrew Houseley, LD	10,709
John West, UKIP	1,754
Martin Wolfe, Green	1,593
C. maj. 7,856 (15.44%)
4.04% swing Lab. to C.
(2001: C. maj. 3,469 (7.36%))

SUFFOLK COASTAL
E. 77,423 T. 52,557 (67.88%) C. hold
Rt. Hon. John Gummer, C.	23,415
David Rowe, Lab.	13,730
David Young, LD	11,637
Richard Curtis, UKIP	2,020
Paul Whitlow, Green	1,755
C. maj. 9,685 (18.43%)
4.92% swing Lab. to C.
(2001: C. maj. 4,326 (8.58%))

SUFFOLK SOUTH
E. 70,237 T. 48,707 (69.35%) C. hold
Tim Yeo, C.	20,471
Kathy Pollard, LD	13,865
Kevin Craig, Lab.	11,917
James Carver, UKIP	2,454
C. maj. 6,606 (13.56%)
1.45% swing C. to LD
(2001: C. maj. 5,081 (11.22%))

SUFFOLK WEST
E. 72,856 T. 44,205 (60.67%) C. hold
Richard Spring, C.   21,682
Michael Jefferys, Lab.   12,773
Adrian Graves, LD   7,573
Ian Smith, UKIP   2,177
C. maj. 8,909 (20.15%)
5.02% swing Lab. to C.
(2001: C. maj. 4,295 (10.12%))

SUNDERLAND NORTH
E. 58,146 T. 28,913 (49.72%) Lab. hold
Bill Etherington, Lab.   15,719
Stephen Daughton, C.   5,724
James Hollern, LD   4,277
Neil Herron, Ind.   2,057
Debra Hiles, BNP   1,136
Lab. maj. 9,995 (34.57%)
5.11% swing Lab. to C.
(2001: Lab. maj. 13,354 (44.78%))

SUNDERLAND SOUTH
E. 62,256 T. 30,712 (49.33%) Lab. hold
Chris Mullin, Lab.   17,982
Robert Oliver, C.   6,923
Gareth Kane, LD   4,492
David Guynan, BNP   1,166
Rosalyn Warner, Loony   149
Lab. maj. 11,059 (36.01%)
3.91% swing Lab. to C.
(2001: Lab. maj. 13,667 (43.82%))

SURREY EAST
E. 73,948 T. 49,253 (66.60%) C. hold
Peter Ainsworth, C.   27,659
Jeremy Pursehouse, LD   11,738
James Bridge, Lab.   7,288
Tony Stone, UKIP   2,158
Winston Matthews, LCA   410
C. maj. 15,921 (32.32%)
2.13% swing LD to C.
(2001: C. maj. 13,203 (28.06%))

SURREY HEATH
E. 76,090 T. 47,858 (62.90%) C. hold
*Michael Gove, C.   24,642
Rosalyn Harper, LD   13,797
Chris Lowe, Lab.   7,989
Steve Smith, UKIP   1,430
C. maj. 10,845 (22.66%)
0.66% swing C. to LD
(2001: C. maj. 10,819 (23.99%))

SURREY SOUTH WEST
E. 72,977 T. 52,409 (71.82%) C. hold
*Jeremy Hunt, C.   26,420
Simon Cordon, LD   20,709
Thomas Sleigh, Lab.   4,150
Timothy Clark, UKIP   958
Glenn Platt, Veritas   172
C. maj. 5,711 (10.90%)
4.58% swing LD to C.
(2001: C. maj. 861 (1.74%))

SUSSEX MID
E. 72,114 T. 49,494 (68.63%) C. hold
Hon. Nicholas Soames, C.   23,765
Serena Tierney, LD   17,875
Robert Fromant, Lab.   6,280
Harold Piggott, UKIP   1,574
C. maj. 5,890 (11.90%)
1.58% swing C. to LD
(2001: C. maj. 6,898 (15.05%))

SUTTON & CHEAM
E. 63,319 T. 41,932 (66.22%) LD hold
Paul Burstow, LD   19,768
Richard Willis, C.   16,922
Anand Shukla, Lab.   4,954
Rainbow George Weiss, Vote Dream 288
LD maj. 2,846 (6.79%)
2.02% swing LD to C.
(2001: LD maj. 4,304 (10.84%))

SUTTON COLDFIELD
E. 72,995 T. 46,318 (63.45%) C. hold
Andrew Mitchell, C.   24,308
Robert Pocock, Lab.   12,025
Craig Drury, LD   7,710
Stephen Shorrock, UKIP   2,275
C. maj. 12,283 (26.52%)
1.63% swing Lab. to C.
(2001: C. maj. 10,104 (23.25%))

SWINDON NORTH
E. 73,636 T. 44,885 (60.96%) Lab. hold
Michael Wills, Lab.   19,612
Justin Tomlinson, C.   17,041
Mike Evemy, LD   6,831
Robert Tingey, UKIP   998
Andy Newman, Soc. Unity   208
Ernest Reynolds, Ind.   195
Lab. maj. 2,571 (5.73%)
6.71% swing Lab. to C.
(2001: Lab. maj. 8,105 (19.15%))

SWINDON SOUTH
E. 72,267 T. 43,472 (60.15%) Lab. hold
*Anne Snelgrove, Lab.   17,534
Robert Buckland, C.   16,181
Sue Stebbing, LD   7,322
Bill Hughes, Green   1,234
Stephen Halden, UKIP   955
Alan Hayward, Ind.   193
John Williams, Ind.   53
Lab. maj. 1,353 (3.11%)
6.90% swing Lab. to C.
(2001: Lab. maj. 7,341 (16.92%))

TAMWORTH
E. 71,675 T. 43,740 (61.03%) Lab. hold
Brian Jenkins, Lab.   18,801
Christopher Pincher, C.   16,232
Phillip Bennion, LD   6,175
Patrick Eston, Veritas   1,320
Tom Simpson, UKIP   1,212
Lab. maj. 2,569 (5.87%)
2.78% swing Lab. to C.
(2001: Lab. maj. 4,598 (11.42%))

TATTON
E. 64,140 T. 41,414 (64.57%) C. hold
George Osborne, C.   21,447
Justin Madders, Lab.   9,716
Ainsley Arnold, LD   9,016
Diane Bowler, UKIP   996
Michael Gibson, Ind.   239
C. maj. 11,731 (28.33%)
3.73% swing Lab. to C.
(2001: C. maj. 8,611 (20.86%))

TAUNTON
E. 85,466 T. 59,528 (69.65%) LD gain
*Jeremy Browne, LD   25,764
Adrian Flook, C.   25,191
Andrew Govier, Lab.   7,132
Helen Miles, UKIP   1,441
LD maj. 573 (0.96%)
0.69% swing C. to LD
(2001: C. maj. 235 (0.43%))

TEIGNBRIDGE
E. 88,674 T. 60,898 (68.68%) LD hold
Richard Younger-Ross, LD   27,808
Stanley Johnson, C.   21,593
Chris Sherwood, Lab.   6,931
Trevor Colman, UKIP   3,881
Reginald Wills, Lib.   685
LD maj. 6,215 (10.21%)
2.56% swing C. to LD
(2001: LD maj. 3,011 (5.08%))

TELFORD
E. 59,277 T. 34,206 (57.71%) Lab. hold
David Wright, Lab.   16,506
Stella Kyriazis, C.   11,100
Ian Jenkins, LD   4,941
Tom McCartney, UKIP   1,659
Lab. maj. 5,406 (15.80%)
5.67% swing Lab. to C.
(2001: Lab. maj. 8,383 (27.15%))

TEWKESBURY
E. 72,145 T. 45,453 (63.00%) C. hold
Laurence Robertson, C.   22,339
Alistair Cameron, LD   12,447
Charles Mannan, Lab.   9,179
Robert Rendell, Green   1,488
C. maj. 9,892 (21.76%)
0.96% swing LD to C.
(2001: C. maj. 8,663 (19.17%))

THANET NORTH
E. 72,734 T. 43,732 (60.13%) C. hold
Roger Gale, C.   21,699
Iris Johnston, Lab.   14,065
Mark Barnard, LD   6,279
Timothy Stocks, UKIP   1,689
C. maj. 7,634 (17.46%)
0.79% swing Lab. to C.
(2001: C. maj. 6,650 (15.88%))

THANET SOUTH
E. 63,436 T. 41,242 (65.01%) Lab. hold
Dr Stephen Ladyman, Lab.   16,660
Mark MacGregor, C.   15,996
Guy Voizey, LD   5,431
Nigel Farage, UKIP   2,079
Howard Green, Green   888
Maude Kinsella, Ind.   188
Lab. maj. 664 (1.61%)
1.47% swing Lab. to C.
(2001: Lab. maj. 1,792 (4.54%))

THURROCK
E. 79,545 T. 43,692 (54.93%) Lab. hold
Andrew Mackinlay, Lab.   20,636
Garry Hague, C.   14,261
Earnshaw Palmer, LD   4,770
Nick Geri, BNP   2,526
Carol Jackson, UKIP   1,499
Lab. maj. 6,375 (14.59%)
6.08% swing Lab. to C.
(2001: Lab. maj. 9,997 (26.76%))

TIVERTON & HONITON
E. 83,375 T. 58,168 (69.77%) C. hold
Angela Browning, C.   27,838
David Nation, LD   16,787
Fiona Bentley, Lab.   7,944
Robert Edwards, UKIP   2,499
Roy Collins, Lib.   1,701
Colin Matthews, Green   1,399
C. maj. 11,051 (19.00%)
3.87% swing LD to C.
(2001: C. maj. 6,284 (11.26%))

TONBRIDGE & MALLING
E. 68,444 T. 46,063 (67.30%) C. hold
Rt. Hon. Sir John Stanley, C.   24,357
Victoria Hayman, Lab.   11,005
John Barstow, LD   8,980
David Waller, UKIP   1,721
C. maj. 13,352 (28.99%)
4.77% swing Lab. to C.
(2001: C. maj. 8,250 (19.44%))

TOOTING
E. 70,504 T. 41,568 (58.96%) Lab. hold
*Sadiq Khan, Lab.   17,914
James Bethell, C.   12,533
Stephanie Dearden, LD   8,110
Siobhan Vitelli, Green   1,695
Ali Zaidi, Respect   700
Strachan McDonald, UKIP   424
Ian Perkin, Ind.   192
Lab. maj. 5,381 (12.95%)
7.36% swing Lab. to C.
(2001: Lab. maj. 10,400 (27.67%))

TORBAY
E. 76,474 T. 47,303 (61.86%) LD hold
Adrian Sanders, LD   19,317
Marcus Wood, C.   17,288
David Pedrick-Friend, Lab.   6,972
Graham Booth, UKIP   3,726
LD maj. 2,029 (4.29%)
4.91% swing LD to C.
(2001: LD maj. 6,708 (14.10%))

TOTNES
E. 74,744 T. 50,575 (67.66%) C. hold
Anthony Steen, C.   21,112
Michael Treleaven, LD   19,165
Valerie Burns, Lab.   6,185
Roger Knapman, UKIP   3,914
Michael Thompson, Ind.   199
C. maj. 1,947 (3.85%)
1.73% swing C. to LD
(2001: C. maj. 3,597 (7.30%))

TOTTENHAM
E. 66,231 T. 31,664 (47.81%) Lab. hold
David Lammy, Lab.   18,343
Wayne Hoban, LD   5,309
William MacDougall, C.   4,278
Janet Alder, Respect   2,014
Pete McAskie, Green   1,457
Jaamit Durrani, Soc. Lab.   263
Lab. maj. 13,034 (41.16%)
8.39% swing Lab. to LD
(2001: Lab. maj. 16,916 (53.53%))

TRURO & ST AUSTELL
E. 80,256 T. 51,564 (64.25%) LD hold
Matthew Taylor, LD   24,089
Dr Fiona Kemp, C.   16,686
Dr Charlotte Mackenzie, Lab.   6,991
David Noakes, UKIP   2,736
Conan Jenkin, Meb. Ker.   1,062
LD maj. 7,403 (14.36%)
0.84% swing LD to C.
(2001: LD maj. 8,065 (16.04%))

TUNBRIDGE WELLS
E. 64,630 T. 42,482 (65.73%) C. hold
*Greg Clark, C.   21,083
Laura Murphy, LD   11,095
Jacqui Jedrzejewski, Lab.   8,736
Victor Webb, UKIP   1,568
C. maj. 9,988 (23.51%)
0.35% swing C. to LD
(2001: C. maj. 9,730 (24.20%))

TWICKENHAM
E. 72,015 T. 51,687 (71.77%) LD hold
Dr Vincent Cable, LD   26,696
Paul Maynard, C.   16,731
Brian Whitington, Lab.   5,868
Henry Gower, Green   1,445
Douglas Orchard, UKIP   766
Brian Gilbert, Ind.   117
Rainbow George Weiss, Vote Dream   64
LD maj. 9,965 (19.28%)
1.98% swing C. to LD
(2001: LD maj. 7,655 (15.33%))

TYNE BRIDGE
E. 53,565 T. 26,383 (49.25%) Lab. hold
David Clelland, Lab.   16,151
Chris Boyle, LD   5,751
Tom Fairhead, C.   2,962
Kevin Scott, BNP   1,072
Jill Russell, Respect   447
Lab. maj. 10,400 (39.42%)
9.35% swing Lab. to LD
(2001: Lab. maj. 14,889 (57.19%))

TYNEMOUTH
E. 64,023 T. 42,859 (66.94%) Lab. hold
Alan Campbell, Lab.   20,143
Michael McIntyre, C.   16,000
Colin Finlay, LD   6,716
Lab. maj. 4,143 (9.67%)
5.05% swing Lab. to C.
(2001: Lab. maj. 8,678 (19.77%))

TYNESIDE NORTH
E. 64,634 T. 36,939 (57.15%) Lab. hold
Rt. Hon. Stephen Byers, Lab.   22,882
Duncan McLellan, C.   7,845
Gillian Ferguson, LD   6,212
Lab. maj. 15,037 (40.71%)
7.09% swing Lab. to C.
(2001: Lab. maj. 20,668 (55.01%))

UPMINSTER
E. 55,075 T. 34,676 (62.96%) C. hold
Angela Watkinson, C.   16,820
Keith Darvill, Lab.   10,778
Peter Truesdale, LD   3,128
Ronald Ower, RA   1,455
Chris Roberts, BNP   1,173
Alan Hindle, UKIP   701
Melanie Collins, Green   543
David Durant, Third   78
C. maj. 6,042 (17.42%)
6.88% swing C. to LD
(2001: C. maj. 1,241 (3.67%))

UXBRIDGE
E. 57,878 T. 34,378 (59.40%) C. hold
John Randall, C.   16,840
Rod Marshall, Lab.   10,669
Dr Tariq Mahmood, LD   4,544
Cliff Le May, BNP   763
Stephen Young, Green   725
Robert Kerby, UKIP   553
Peter Shaw, NF   284
C. maj. 6,171 (17.95%)
5.84% swing Lab. to C.
(2001: C. maj. 2,098 (6.28%))

VALE OF YORK
E. 76,000 T. 50,378 (66.29%) C. hold
Anne McIntosh, C.   26,025
David Scott, Lab.   12,313
Jeremy Wilcock, LD   12,040
C. maj. 13,712 (27.22%)
0.70% swing Lab. to C.
(2001: C. maj. 12,517 (25.81%))

VAUXHALL
E. 79,637 T. 37,353 (46.90%) Lab. hold
Kate Hoey, Lab.   19,744
Charles Anglin, LD   9,767
Edward Heckels, C.   5,405
Tim Summers, Green   1,705
Robert McWhirter, UKIP   271
Daniel Lambert, Socialist   240
Janus Polenceus, Eng. Dem.   221
Lab. maj. 9,977 (26.71%)
6.14% swing Lab. to LD
(2001: Lab. maj. 13,018 (38.99%))

WAKEFIELD
E. 73,118 T. 43,381 (59.33%) Lab. hold
*Mary Creagh, Lab.   18,802
Alec Shelbrooke, C.   13,648
David Ridgway, LD   7,063
Grant Rowe, BNP   1,328
Derek Hardcastle, Green   1,297
John Upex, UKIP   467
Paul McEnhill, Eng. Dem.   356
Mick Griffiths, Soc. Alt.   319
Linda Sheridan, Soc. Lab.   101
Lab. maj. 5,154 (11.88%)
3.70% swing Lab. to C.
(2001: Lab. maj. 7,954 (19.28%))

WALLASEY
E. 63,764 T. 36,671 (57.51%) Lab. hold
Angela Eagle, Lab.   20,085
Leah Fraser, C.   10,976
Joanna Pemberton, LD   4,770
Philip Griffiths, UKIP   840
Lab. maj. 9,109 (24.84%)
4.02% swing Lab. to C.
(2001: Lab. maj. 12,276 (32.87%))

WALSALL NORTH
E. 63,268 T. 33,428 (52.84%) Lab. hold
David Winnick, Lab.   15,990
Ian Lucas, C.   9,350
Douglas Taylor, LD   4,144
William Locke, BNP   1,992
Anthony Lenton, UKIP   1,182
Peter Smith, Dem. Lab.   770
Lab. maj. 6,640 (19.86%)
4.60% swing Lab. to C.
(2001: Lab. maj. 9,391 (29.06%))

WALSALL SOUTH
E. 60,370 T. 35,315 (58.50%) Lab. hold
Rt. Hon. Bruce George, Lab.   17,633
Kabir Sabar, C.   9,687
Mohamed Hanif Asmal, LD   3,240
Derek Bennett, UKIP   1,833
Kevin Smith, BNP   1,776
Nadia Fazal, Respect   1,146
Lab. maj. 7,946 (22.50%)
2.98% swing Lab. to C.
(2001: Lab. maj. 9,931 (28.46%))

WALTHAMSTOW
E. 63,079 T. 34,444 (54.60%) Lab. hold
Neil Gerrard, Lab.   17,323
Farid Ahmed, LD   9,330
Jane Wright, C.   6,254
Robert Brook, UKIP   810
Nancy Taaffe, Soc. Alt.   727
Lab. maj. 7,993 (23.21%)
12.18% swing Lab. to LD
(2001: Lab. maj. 15,181 (44.09%))

WANSBECK
E. 63,096 T. 36,809 (58.34%) Lab. hold
Denis Murphy, Lab.   20,315
Simon Reed, LD   9,734
Ginny Scrope, C.   5,515
Dr Nic Best, Green   1,245
Lab. maj. 10,581 (28.75%)
3.13% swing Lab. to LD
(2001: Lab. maj. 13,101 (35.01%))

WANSDYKE
E. 70,359 T. 50,933 (72.39%) Lab. hold
Dan Norris, Lab.   20,686
Chris Watt, C.   18,847
Gail Coleshill, LD   10,050
Peter Sandell, UKIP   1,129
Geoffrey Parkes, Ind.   221
Lab. maj. 1,839 (3.61%)
3.86% swing Lab. to C.
(2001: Lab. maj. 5,113 (10.42%))

WANTAGE
E. 76,156 T. 51,931 (68.19%) C. hold
*Ed Vaizey, C.   22,354
Andrew Crawford, LD   14,337
Mark McDonald, Lab.   12,464
Adam Twine, Green   1,332
Nikolai Tolstoy-Miloslavsky, UKIP 798
Gerald Lambourne, Eng. Dem.   646
C. maj. 8,017 (15.44%)
1.92% swing LD to C.
(2001: C. maj. 5,600 (11.40%))

WARLEY
E. 56,171 T. 32,087 (57.12%) Lab. hold
Rt. Hon. John Spellar, Lab.   17,462
Karen Bissell, C.   7,315
Tony Ferguson, LD   4,277
Simon Smith, BNP   1,761
Malcolm Connigale, Soc. Lab.   637
David Matthews, UKIP   635
Lab. maj. 10,147 (31.62%)
3.05% swing Lab. to C.
(2001: Lab. maj. 11,850 (37.72%))

WARRINGTON NORTH
E. 73,352 T. 40,418 (55.10%) Lab. hold
Helen Jones, Lab.   21,632
Andrew Ferryman, C.   9,428
Peter Walker, LD   7,699
John Kirkham, UKIP   1,086
Mike Hughes, CAP   573
Lab. maj. 12,204 (30.19%)
4.38% swing Lab. to C.
(2001: Lab. maj. 15,156 (38.95%))

WARRINGTON SOUTH
E. 75,724 T. 46,797 (61.80%) Lab. hold
Helen Southworth, Lab.   18,972
Fiona Bruce, C.   15,457
Ian Marks, LD   11,111
Gerald Kelley, UKIP   804
Paul Kennedy, Ind.   453
Lab. maj. 3,515 (7.51%)
4.37% swing Lab. to C.
(2001: Lab. maj. 7,387 (16.24%))

WARWICK & LEAMINGTON
E. 81,205 T. 54,784 (67.46%) Lab. hold
James Plaskitt, Lab.   22,238
Chris White, C.   21,972
Linda Forbes, LD   8,119
Ian Davison, Green   1,534
Greville Warwick, UKIP   921
Lab. maj. 266 (0.49%)
5.32% swing Lab. to C.
(2001: Lab. maj. 5,953 (11.12%))

WARWICKSHIRE NORTH
E. 75,435 T. 46,939 (62.22%) Lab. hold
Mike O'Brien, Lab.   22,561
Ian Gibb, C.   15,008
Jerry Roodhouse, LD   6,212
Michaela Mackenzie, BNP   1,910
Iain Campbell, UKIP   1,248
Lab. maj. 7,553 (16.09%)
2.81% swing Lab. to C.
(2001: Lab. maj. 9,639 (21.71%))

WATFORD
E. 76,280 T. 49,394 (64.75%) Lab. hold
Claire Ward, Lab.   16,575
Sal Brinton, LD   15,427
Ali Miraj, C.   14,634
Steve Rackett, Green   1,466
Kenneth Wight, UKIP   1,292
Lab. maj. 1,148 (2.32%)
12.75% swing Lab. to LD
(2001: Lab. maj. 5,555 (11.98%))

WAVENEY
E. 77,138 T. 49,653 (64.37%) Lab. hold
Bob Blizzard, Lab.   22,505
Peter Aldous, C.   16,590
Nick Bromley, LD   7,497
Brian Aylett, UKIP   1,861
Graham Elliott, Green   1,200
Lab. maj. 5,915 (11.91%)
3.11% swing Lab. to C.
(2001: Lab. maj. 8,553 (18.13%))

WEALDEN
E. 82,261 T. 55,653 (67.65%) C. hold
Charles Hendry, C.   28,975
Christopher Wigley, LD   13,054
Dudley Rose, Lab.   9,360
Julian Salmon, Green   2,150
Keith Riddle, UKIP   2,114
C. maj. 15,921 (28.61%)
1.25% swing LD to C.
(2001: C. maj. 13,772 (26.11%))

WEAVER VALE
E. 69,072 T. 39,420 (57.07%) Lab. hold
Mike Hall, Lab.   18,759
Jonathan Mackie, C.   11,904
Nigel Griffiths, LD   7,723
Brenda Swinscoe, UKIP   1,034
Lab. maj. 6,855 (17.39%)
3.58% swing Lab. to C.
(2001: Lab. maj. 9,637 (24.54%))

WELLINGBOROUGH
E. 79,679 T. 53,005 (66.52%) C. gain
*Peter Bone, C.   22,674
Paul Stinchcombe, Lab.   21,987
Richard Church, LD   6,147
James Wrench, UKIP   1,214
Nicholas Alex, Veritas   749
Andy Dickson, Soc. Lab.   234
C. maj. 687 (1.30%)
2.96% swing Lab. to C.
(2001: Lab. maj. 2,355 (4.62%))

WELLS
E. 77,842 T. 52,965 (68.04%) C. hold
Rt. Hon. David
  Heathcoat-Amory, C.   23,071
Tessa Munt, LD   20,031
Dan Whittle, Lab.   8,288
Steven Reed, UKIP   1,575
C. maj. 3,040 (5.74%)
0.15% swing LD to C.
(2001: C. maj. 2,796 (5.45%))

WELWYN HATFIELD
E. 65,617 T. 44,716 (68.15%) C. gain
*Grant Shapps, C.   22,172
Melanie Johnson, Lab.   16,226
Sara Bedford, LD   6,318
C. maj. 5,946 (13.30%)
8.05% swing Lab. to C.
(2001: Lab. maj. 1,196 (2.79%))

WENTWORTH
E. 63,561 T. 35,596 (56.00%) Lab. hold
John Healey, Lab.   21,225
Mark Hughes, C.   6,169
Keith Orrell, LD   4,800
Jonathan Pygott, BNP   1,798
John Wilkinson, UKIP   1,604
Lab. maj. 15,056 (42.30%)
3.20% swing Lab. to C.
(2001: Lab. maj. 16,449 (48.70%))

WEST BROMWICH EAST
E. 60,565 T. 35,512 (58.63%) Lab. hold
Tom Watson, Lab.   19,741
Rosemary Bromwich, C.   8,089
Ian Garrett, LD   4,386
Carl Butler, BNP   2,329
Steven Grey, UKIP   607
Judith Sambrook, Soc. Lab.   200
Margaret Macklin, Ind.   160
Lab. maj. 11,652 (32.81%)
1.46% swing C. to Lab.
(2001: Lab. maj. 9,763 (29.89%))

WEST BROMWICH WEST
E. 66,752 T. 34,917 (52.31%)
                              Lab. (Co-op) hold
Adrian Bailey, Lab. (Co-op)   18,951
Mimi Harker, C.   8,057
Martyn Smith, LD   3,583
James Lloyd, BNP   3,456
Kevin Walker, UKIP   870
Lab. (Co-op) maj. 10,894 (31.20%)
2.23% swing Lab. (Co-op) to C.
(2001: Lab. (Co-op) maj. 11,355
(35.66%))

WEST HAM
E. 62,184 T. 30,966 (49.80%) Lab. hold
*Lyn Brown, Lab.   15,840
Lindsey German, Respect   6,039
Chris Whitbread, C.   3,618
Alexandra Sugden, LD   3,364
Jane Lithgow, Green   894
Stephen Hammond, CPA   437
Henry Mayhew, UKIP   409
Generoso Alcantara, Veritas   365
Lab. maj. 9,801 (31.65%)
19.12% swing Lab. to Respect
(2001: Lab. maj. 15,645 (53.45%))

WESTBURY
E. 83,039 T. 55,604 (66.96%) C. hold
Dr Andrew Murrison, C.   24,749
Duncan Hames, LD   19,400
Phil Gibby, Lab.   9,640
Lincoln Williams, UKIP   1,815
C. maj. 5,349 (9.62%)
0.42% swing C. to LD
(2001: C. maj. 5,294 (10.46%))

WESTMORLAND & LONSDALE
E. 69,363 T. 49,636 (71.56%) LD gain
*Tim Farron, LD 22,569
Tim Collins, C. 22,302
John Reardon, Lab. 3,796
Robert Gibson, UKIP 660
Anthony Kemp, Ind. 309
LD maj. 267 (0.54%)
3.55% swing C. to LD
(2001: C. maj. 3,147 (6.57%))

WESTON-SUPER-MARE
E. 74,900 T. 49,095 (65.55%) C. gain
*John Penrose, C. 19,804
Brian Cotter, LD 17,725
Damien Egan, Lab. 9,169
Paul Spencer, UKIP 1,207
Clive Courtney, BNP 778
William Human, Ind. 225
Paul Hemingway-Arnold, Honesty 187
C. maj. 2,079 (4.23%)
2.48% swing LD to C.
(2001: LD maj. 338 (0.72%))

WIGAN
E. 64,267 T. 34,278 (53.34%) Lab. hold
Neil Turner, Lab. 18,901
John Coombes, C. 7,134
Denise Capstick, LD 6,051
Dr John Whittaker, UKIP 1,166
Kevin Williams, CAP 1,026
Lab. maj. 11,767 (34.33%)
3.29% swing Lab. to C.
(2001: Lab. maj. 13,743 (40.91%))

WILTSHIRE NORTH
E. 80,896 T. 56,061 (69.30%) C. hold
James Gray, C. 26,282
Paul Fox, LD 20,979
David Nash, Lab. 6,794
Neil Dowdney, UKIP 1,428
Philip Allnatt, Ind. 578
C. maj. 5,303 (9.46%)
1.07% swing LD to C.
(2001: C. maj. 3,878 (7.32%))

WIMBLEDON
E. 63,714 T. 43,404 (68.12%) C. gain
*Stephen Hammond, C. 17,886
Roger Casale, Lab. 15,585
Stephen Gee, LD 7,868
Giles Barrow, Green 1,374
Andrew Mills, UKIP 408
Christopher Coverdale, Ind. 211
Alastair Wilson, TEPK 50
Rainbow George Weiss, Vote Dream 22
C. maj. 2,301 (5.30%)
7.20% swing Lab. to C.
(2001: Lab. maj. 3,744 (9.11%))

WINCHESTER
E. 85,810 T. 61,658 (71.85%) LD hold
Mark Oaten, LD 31,225
George Hollingbery, C. 23,749
Patrick Davies, Lab. 4,782
Dr David Abbott, UKIP 1,321
Arthur Uther Pendragon, Ind. 581
LD maj. 7,476 (12.12%)
2.08% swing LD to C.
(2001: LD maj. 9,634 (16.29%))

WINDSOR
E. 68,290 T. 43,693 (63.98%) C. hold
*Adam Afriyie, C. 21,646
Antony Wood, LD 11,354
Mark Muller, Lab. 8,339
David Black, UKIP 1,098
Derek Wall, Green 1,074
Peter Hooper, Ind. 182
C. maj. 10,292 (23.56%)
1.22% swing LD to C.
(2001: C. maj. 8,889 (21.11%))

WIRRAL SOUTH
E. 58,834 T. 39,704 (67.48%) Lab. hold
Ben Chapman, Lab. 16,892
Carl Cross, C. 13,168
Simon Holbrook, LD 8,568
David Scott, UKIP 616
Laurence Jones, Ind. 460
Lab. maj. 3,724 (9.38%)
1.65% swing Lab. to C.
(2001: Lab. maj. 5,049 (12.68%))

WIRRAL WEST
E. 61,050 T. 41,233 (67.54%) Lab. hold
Stephen Hesford, Lab. 17,543
Esther McVey, C. 16,446
Jeff Clarke, LD 6,652
John Moore, UKIP 429
Roger Taylor, AP 163
Lab. maj. 1,097 (2.66%)
3.65% swing Lab. to C.
(2001: Lab. maj. 4,035 (9.97%))

WITNEY
E. 78,053 T. 53,869 (69.02%) C. hold
David Cameron, C. 26,571
Liz Leffman, LD 12,415
Tony Gray, Lab. 11,845
Richard Dossett-Davies, Green 1,682
Paul Wesson, UKIP 1,356
C. maj. 14,156 (26.28%)
0.79% swing LD to C.
(2001: C. maj. 7,973 (16.20%))

WOKING
E. 72,676 T. 46,045 (63.36%) C. hold
Humfrey Malins, C. 21,838
Anne Lee, LD 15,226
Ellie Blagbrough, Lab. 7,507
Matthew Davies, UKIP 1,324
Michael Osman, UKC 150
C. maj. 6,612 (14.36%)
0.70% swing C. to LD
(2001: C. maj. 6,759 (15.75%))

WOKINGHAM
E. 68,614 T. 46,072 (67.15%) C. hold
Rt. Hon. John Redwood, C. 22,174
Prue Bray, LD 14,934
David Black, Lab. 6,991
Frank Carstairs, UKIP 994
Top Cat Owen, Loony 569
Richard Colborne, BNP 376
Michael Hall, Tele. 34
C. maj. 7,240 (15.71%)
1.02% swing LD to C.
(2001: C. maj. 5,994 (13.67%))

WOLVERHAMPTON NORTH EAST
E. 60,595 T. 32,956 (54.39%)
Lab. (Co-op) hold
Ken Purchase, Lab. (Co-op) 17,948
Alexandra Robson, C. 9,792
David Jack, LD 3,845
Lydia Simpson, UKIP 1,371
Lab. (Co-op) maj. 8,156 (24.75%)
3.45% swing Lab. (Co-op) to C.
(2001: Lab. (Co-op) maj. 9,965
(31.64%))

WOLVERHAMPTON SOUTH EAST
E. 54,047 T. 28,251 (52.27%) Lab. hold
*Pat McFadden, Lab. 16,790
James Fairbairn, C. 6,295
David Murray, LD 3,682
Kevin Simmons, UKIP 1,484
Lab. maj. 10,495 (37.15%)
4.26% swing Lab. to C.
(2001: Lab. (Co-op) maj. 12,464
(45.66%))

WOLVERHAMPTON SOUTH WEST
E. 67,096 T. 41,679 (62.12%) Lab. hold
Rob Marris, Lab. 18,489
Sandy Verma, C. 15,610
Colin Ross, LD 5,568
Douglas Hope, UKIP 1,029
Edward Mullins, BNP 983
Lab. maj. 2,879 (6.91%)
0.81% swing Lab. to C.
(2001: Lab. maj. 3,487 (8.53%))

WOODSPRING
E. 71,662 T. 51,618 (72.03%) C. hold
Dr Liam Fox, C. 21,587
Mike Bell, LD 15,571
Chanel Stevens, Lab. 11,249
Rebecca Lewis, Green 1,309
Anthony Butcher, UKIP 1,269
Michael Howson, BNP 633
C. maj. 6,016 (11.65%)
3.90% swing C. to LD
(2001: C. maj. 8,798 (18.04%))

WORCESTER
E. 72,384 T. 46,388 (64.09%) Lab. hold
Michael Foster, Lab. 19,421
Margaret Harper, C. 16,277
Mary Dhonau, LD 7,557
Richard Chamings, UKIP 1,113
Martin Roberts, BNP 980
Chris Lennard, Green 921
Prudence Dowson, Ind. 119
Lab. maj. 3,144 (6.78%)
3.13% swing Lab. to C.
(2001: Lab. maj. 5,766 (13.04%))

WORCESTERSHIRE MID
E. 71,546 T. 48,127 (67.27%) C. hold
Peter Luff, C. 24,783
Matt Gregson, Lab. 11,456
Margaret Rowley, LD 9,796
Tony Eaves, UKIP 2,092
C. maj. 13,327 (27.69%)
2.01% swing Lab. to C.
(2001: C. maj. 10,627 (23.67%))

WORCESTERSHIRE WEST
E. 66,999 T. 47,077 (70.27%)   C. hold
Sir Michael Spicer, C.   20,959
Tom Wells, LD   18,484
Qamar Bhatti, Lab.   4,945
Caroline Bovey, UKIP   1,590
Malcolm Victory, Green   1,099
C. maj. 2,475 (5.26%)
3.37% swing C. to LD
(2001: C. maj. 5,374 (11.99%))

WORKINGTON
E. 61,441 T. 39,737 (64.68%)   Lab. hold
Tony Cunningham, Lab.   19,554
Judith Pattinson, C.   12,659
Kate Clarkson, LD   5,815
Mark Richardson, UKIP   1,328
John Peacock, LCA   381
Lab. maj. 6,895 (17.35%)
4.30% swing Lab. to C.
(2001: Lab. maj. 10,850 (25.94%))

WORSLEY
E. 69,534 T. 36,946 (53.13%)   Lab. hold
*Barbara Keeley, Lab.   18,859
Graham Evans, C.   9,491
Richard Clayton, LD   6,902
Bernard Gill, UKIP   1,694
Lab. maj. 9,368 (25.36%)
3.99% swing Lab. to C.
(2001: Lab. maj. 11,787 (33.33%))

WORTHING EAST & SHOREHAM
E. 72,302 T. 44,543 (61.61%)   C. hold
Tim Loughton, C.   19,548
Daniel Yates, Lab.   11,365
James Doyle, LD   10,844
Richard Jelf, UKIP   2,109
Chris Baldwin, LCA   677
C. maj. 8,183 (18.37%)
2.06% swing Lab. to C.
(2001: C. maj. 6,139 (14.25%))

WORTHING WEST
E. 71,780 T. 44,941 (62.61%)   C. hold
Peter Bottomley, C.   21,383
Claire Potter, LD   12,004
Antony Bignell, Lab.   8,630
Timothy Cross, UKIP   2,374
Chris Baldwin, LCA   550
C. maj. 9,379 (20.87%)
0.02% swing C. to LD
(2001: C. maj. 9,037 (20.91%))

WREKIN, THE
E. 67,291 T. 45,054 (66.95%)   C. gain
*Mark Pritchard, C.   18,899
Peter Bradley, Lab.   17,957
Bill Tomlinson, LD   6,608
Bruce Lawson, UKIP   1,590
C. maj. 942 (2.09%)
5.37% swing Lab. to C.
(2001: Lab. maj. 3,587 (8.65%))

WYCOMBE
E. 71,464 T. 44,427 (62.17%)   C. hold
Paul Goodman, C.   20,331
Julia Wassell, Lab.   13,280
James Oates, LD   8,780
Robert Davis, UKIP   1,735
David Fitton, Ind.   301
C. maj. 7,051 (15.87%)
4.41% swing Lab. to C.
(2001: C. maj. 3,168 (7.04%))

WYRE FOREST
E. 73,192 T. 46,987 (64.20%)
                                        KHHC hold
Dr Richard Taylor, KHHC   18,739
Mark Garnier, C.   13,489
Marc Bayliss, Lab.   10,716
Fran Oborski, LD   2,666
Rustie Lee, UKIP   1,074
Bert Priest, Loony   303
KHHC maj. 5,250 (11.17%)
13.92% swing KHHC to C.
(2001: KHHC maj. 17,630 (35.93%))

WYTHENSHAWE & SALE EAST
E. 71,766 T. 36,184 (50.42%)   Lab. hold
Paul Goggins, Lab.   18,878
Jane Meehan, C.   8,051
Alison Firth, LD   7,766
William Ford, UKIP   1,120
Lynn Worthington, Soc. Alt.   369
Lab. maj. 10,827 (29.92%)
3.02% swing Lab. to C.
(2001: Lab. maj. 12,608 (35.97%))

YEOVIL
E. 77,668 T. 49,913 (64.26%)   LD hold
David Laws, LD   25,658
Ian Jenkins, C.   17,096
Colin Rolfe, Lab.   5,256
Graham Livings, UKIP   1,903
LD maj. 8,562 (17.15%)
4.50% swing C. to LD
(2001: LD maj. 3,928 (8.16%))

YORK, CITY OF
E. 75,555 T. 46,597 (61.67%)   Lab. hold
Hugh Bayley, Lab.   21,836
Clive Booth, C.   11,364
Andrew Waller, LD   10,166
Andy D'Agorne, Green   2,113
Richard Jackson, UKIP   832
Ken Curran, Ind.   121
Damien Fleck, DDTP   93
Andrew Hinkles, Ind.   72
Lab. maj. 10,472 (22.47%)
3.12% swing Lab. to C.
(2001: Lab. maj. 13,779 (28.72%))

YORKSHIRE EAST
E. 76,648 T. 46,925 (61.22%)   C. hold
Rt. Hon. Greg Knight, C.   21,215
Emma Hoddinott, Lab.   14,932
Jim Wastling, LD   9,075
Christopher Tresidder, UKIP   1,703
C. maj. 6,283 (13.39%)
1.29% swing C. to LD
(2001: C. maj. 4,682 (10.81%))

WALES

ABERAVON
E. 51,080 T. 30,104 (58.94%)   Lab. hold
Dr Hywel Francis, Lab.   18,077
Claire Waller, LD   4,140
Philip Evans, PC   3,545
Annunziata Rees-Mogg, C.   3,064
Walter Wright, Veritas   768
Miranda La Vey, Green   510
Lab. maj. 13,937 (46.30%)
3.57% swing Lab. to LD
(2001: Lab. maj. 16,108 (53.36%))

ALYN & DEESIDE
E. 58,939 T. 35,496 (60.22%)   Lab. hold
Mark Tami, Lab.   17,331
Lynne Hale, C.   8,953
Paul Brighton, LD   6,174
Richard Coombs, PC   1,320
William Crawford, UKIP   918
Klaus Armstrong-Braun, FWP   378
Judith Kilshaw, Ind.   215
Glyn Davies, Comm Brit   207
Lab. maj. 8,378 (23.60%)
1.22% swing Lab. to C.
(2001: Lab. maj. 9,222 (26.04%))

BLAENAU GWENT
E. 53,301 T. 35,251 (66.14%)   Ind. gain
*Peter Law, Ind.   20,505
Maggie Jones, Lab.   11,384
Brian Thomas, LD   1,511
John Price, PC   843
Dr Phillip Lee, C.   816
Peter Osborne, UKIP   192
Ind. maj. 9,121 (25.87%)
43.38% swing Lab. to Ind.
(2001: Lab. maj. 19,313 (60.88%))

BRECON & RADNORSHIRE
E. 55,171 T. 38,341 (69.49%)   LD hold
Roger Williams, LD   17,182
Andrew Davies, C.   13,277
Leighton Veale, Lab.   5,755
Mabon ap Gwynfor, PC   1,404
Elizabeth Phillips, UKIP   723
LD maj. 3,905 (10.18%)
4.09% swing C. to LD
(2001: LD maj. 751 (2.00%))

BRIDGEND
E. 63,936 T. 37,859 (59.21%)   Lab. hold
*Madeleine Moon, Lab.   16,410
Helen Baker, C.   9,887
Paul Warren, LD   7,949
Gareth Clubb, PC   2,527
Jonathan Spink, Green   595
Kunnathur Rajan, UKIP   491
Lab. maj. 6,523 (17.23%)
4.96% swing Lab. to C.
(2001: Lab. maj. 10,045 (27.15%))

CAERNARFON
E. 46,393 T. 27,999 (60.35%)   PC hold
Hywel Williams, PC   12,747
Martin Eaglestone, Lab.   7,538
Melfyn ab Owain, LD   3,508
Guy Opperman, C.   3,483
Elwyn Williams, UKIP   723
PC maj. 5,209 (18.60%)
3.26% swing Lab. to PC
(2001: PC maj. 3,511 (12.08%))

CAERPHILLY
E. 66,939 T. 39,229 (58.60%) Lab. hold
Wayne David, Lab.   22,190
Lindsay Whittle, PC   6,831
Stephen Watson, C.   5,711
Ashgar Ali, LD   3,861
Graeme Beard, FWP   636
Lab. maj. 15,359 (39.15%)
1.00% swing PC to Lab.
(2001: Lab. maj. 14,425 (37.15%))

CARDIFF CENTRAL
E. 61,001 T. 36,132 (59.23%) LD gain
*Jenny Willott, LD   17,991
Jon Owen Jones, Lab. (Co-op)   12,398
Gotz Mohindra, C.   3,339
Richard Grigg, PC   1,271
Raja Gul Raiz, Respect   386
Frank Hughes, UKIP   383
Anne Savoury, Ind.   168
Captain Beany, Bean   159
Catherine Taylor-Dawson, Vote
  Dream   37
LD maj. 5,593 (15.48%)
8.69% swing Lab. (Co-op) to LD
(2001: Lab. (Co-op) maj. 659 (1.89%))

CARDIFF NORTH
E. 64,341 T. 45,360 (70.50%) Lab. hold
Julie Morgan, Lab.   17,707
Jonathan Morgan, C.   16,561
John Dixon, LD   8,483
John Rowlands, PC   1,936
Don Hulston, UKIP   534
Alison Hobbs, FWP   138
Catherine Taylor-Dawson, Vote Dream 1
Lab. maj. 1,146 (2.53%)
5.87% swing Lab. to C.
(2001: Lab. maj. 6,165 (14.26%))

CARDIFF SOUTH & PENARTH
E. 65,710 T. 36,912 (56.17%)
                              Lab. (Co-op) hold
Rt. Hon. Alun Michael,
  Lab. (Co-op)   17,447
Victoria Green, C.   8,210
Gavin Cox, LD   7,529
Jason Toby, PC   2,023
John Matthews, Green   729
Jennifer Tuttle, UKIP   522
Dave Bartlett, Soc. Alt.   269
Andrew Taylor, Ind.   104
Catherine Taylor-Dawson, Vote
  Dream   79
Lab. (Co-op) maj. 9,237 (25.02%)
4.67% swing Lab. (Co-op) to C.
(2001: Lab. (Co-op) maj. 12,287
(34.37%))

CARDIFF WEST
E. 59,847 T. 34,561 (57.75%) Lab. hold
Kevin Brennan, Lab.   15,729
Simon Baker, C.   7,562
Alison Goldsworthy, LD   6,060
Neil McEvoy, PC   4,316
Joe Callan, UKIP   727
Catherine Taylor-Dawson, Vote
  Dream   167
Lab. maj. 8,167 (23.63%)
4.79% swing Lab. to C.
(2001: Lab. maj. 11,321 (33.22%))

CARMARTHEN EAST & DINEFWR
E. 53,484 T. 38,291 (71.59%) PC hold
Adam Price, PC   17,561
Ross Hendry, Lab.   10,843
Suzy Davies, C.   5,235
Juliana Hughes, LD   3,719
Mike Squires, UKIP   661
Sid Whitworth, LCA   272
PC maj. 6,718 (17.54%)
5.37% swing Lab. to PC
(2001: PC maj. 2,590 (6.81%))

CARMARTHEN WEST &
PEMBROKESHIRE SOUTH
E. 56,245 T. 37,863 (67.32%) Lab. hold
Nick Ainger, Lab.   13,953
David Morris, C.   12,043
John Dixon, PC   5,582
John Allen, LD   5,399
Josie MacDonald, UKIP   545
Alex Daszak, LCA   237
Nick Turner, Ind.   104
Lab. maj. 1,910 (5.04%)
3.62% swing Lab. to C.
(2001: Lab. maj. 4,538 (12.29%))

CEREDIGION
E. 53,493 T. 35,947 (67.20%) LD gain
*Mark Williams, LD   13,130
Simon Thomas, PC   12,911
John Harrison, C.   4,455
Alun Davies, Lab.   4,337
Dave Bradney, Green   846
Iain Sheldon, Veritas   268
LD maj. 219 (0.61%)
6.00% swing PC to LD
(2001: PC maj. 3,944 (11.40%))

CLWYD SOUTH
E. 52,353 T. 32,931 (62.90%) Lab. hold
Martyn Jones, Lab.   14,808
Tom Biggins, C.   8,460
Deric Burnham, LD   5,105
Mark Strong, PC   3,111
Alwyn Humphreys, FWP   803
Nick Powell, UKIP   644
Lab. maj. 6,348 (19.28%)
3.64% swing Lab. to C.
(2001: Lab. maj. 8,898 (26.56%))

CLWYD WEST
E. 55,642   T. 35,614 (64.01%)   C. gain
*David Jones, C.   12,909
Gareth Thomas, Lab.   12,776
Frank Taylor, LD   4,723
Eilian Williams, PC   3,874
Warwick Nicholson, UKIP   512
Jimmy James, Ind.   507
Patrick Keenan, Soc. Lab.   313
C. maj. 133 (0.37%)
1.80% swing Lab. to C.
(2001: Lab. maj. 1,115 (3.22%))

CONWY
E. 53,987 T. 33,657 (62.34%) Lab. hold
Betty Williams, Lab.   12,479
Guto Bebb, C.   9,398
Gareth Roberts, LD   6,723
Paul Rowlinson, PC   3,730
Jim Killock, Green   512
David Lloyd Jones, Soc. Lab.   324
Kenneth Khambatta, UKIP   298
Tim Evans, LCA   193
Lab. maj. 3,081 (9.15%)
4.47% swing Lab. to C.
(2001: Lab. maj. 6,219 (18.10%))

CYNON VALLEY
E. 45,369 T. 26,647 (58.73%) Lab. hold
Rt. Hon. Ann Clwyd, Lab.   17,074
Geraint Benney, PC   3,815
Margaret Phelps, LD   2,991
Antonia Dunn, C.   2,062
Susan Davies, UKIP   705
Lab. maj. 13,259 (49.76%)
0.77% swing PC to Lab.
(2001: Lab. maj. 12,998 (48.22%))

DELYN
E. 52,766 T. 34,004 (64.44%) Lab. hold
David Hanson, Lab.   15,540
John Bell, C.   8,896
Tudor Jones, LD   6,089
Phil Thomas, PC   2,524
May Crawford, UKIP   533
Nigel Williams, Ind.   422
Lab. maj. 6,644 (19.54%)
2.65% swing Lab. to C.
(2001: Lab. maj. 8,605 (24.84%))

GOWER
E. 60,925 T. 39,542 (64.90%) Lab. hold
Martin Caton, Lab.   16,786
Mike Murray, C.   10,083
Nick Tregoning, LD   7,291
Sian Caiach, PC   3,089
Richard Lewis, UKIP   1,264
Rhodri Griffiths, Green   1,029
Lab. maj. 6,703 (16.95%)
1.42% swing Lab. to C.
(2001: Lab. maj. 7,395 (19.80%))

ISLWYN
E. 50,595 T. 30,865 (61.00%)
                              Lab. (Co-op) hold
Don Touhig, Lab. (Co-op)   19,687
Jim Criddle, PC   3,947
Lee Dillon, LD   3,873
Phillip Howells, C.   3,358
Lab. (Co-op) maj. 15,740 (51.00%)
0.67% swing PC to Lab. (Co-op)
(2001: Lab. (Co-op) maj. 15,309
(48.31%))

LLANELLI
E. 55,678 T. 35,344 (63.48%) Lab. hold
*Nia Griffith, Lab.   16,592
Neil Baker, PC   9,358
Adrian Phillips, C.   4,844
Ken Rees, LD   4,550
Lab. maj. 7,234 (20.47%)
1.39% swing PC to Lab.
(2001: Lab. maj. 6,403 (17.69%))

MEIRIONNYDD NANT CONWY
E. 33,443 T. 20,640 (61.72%) PC hold
Elfyn Llwyd, PC   10,597
Rhodri Jones, Lab.   3,983
Dan Munford, C.   3,402
Adrian Fawcett, LD   2,192
Francis Wykes, UKIP   466
PC maj. 6,614 (32.04%)
2.53% swing Lab. to PC
(2001: PC maj. 5,684 (26.98%))

MERTHYR TYDFIL & RHYMNEY
E. 54,579 T. 29,976 (54.92%) Lab. hold
Dai Havard, Lab. 18,129
Ceirion Rees, LD 4,195
Noel Turner, PC 2,972
Roger Berry, C. 2,680
Neil Greer, FWP 1,030
Gwyn Parry, UKIP 699
Ina Marsden, Soc. Lab. 271
Lab. maj. 13,934 (46.48%)
3.88% swing Lab. to LD
(2001: Lab. maj. 14,923 (47.10%))

MONMOUTH
E. 63,093 T. 45,653 (72.36%) C. gain
*David Davies, C. 21,396
Huw Edwards, Lab. 16,869
Phil Hobson, LD 5,852
Jonathan Clark, PC 993
John Bufton, UKIP 543
C. maj. 4,527 (9.92%)
5.39% swing Lab. to C.
(2001: Lab. maj. 384 (0.86%))

MONTGOMERYSHIRE
E. 46,766 T. 30,097 (64.36%) LD hold
Lembit Opik, LD 15,419
Simon Baynes, C. 8,246
David Tinline, Lab. 3,454
Ellen ap Gwynn, PC 2,078
Clive Easton, UKIP 900
LD maj. 7,173 (23.83%)
1.16% swing C. to LD
(2001: LD maj. 6,234 (21.51%))

NEATH
E. 57,607 T. 35,817 (62.17%) Lab. hold
Rt. Hon. Peter Hain, Lab. 18,835
Geraint Owen, PC 6,125
Sheila Waye, LD 5,112
Harri Lloyd Davies, C. 4,136
Susan Jay, Green 658
Gerry Brienza, Ind. 360
Pat Tabram, LCA 334
Heather Falconer, Respect 257
Lab. maj. 12,710 (35.49%)
3.41% swing Lab. to PC
(2001: Lab. maj. 14,816 (42.31%))

NEWPORT EAST
E. 54,956 T. 31,825 (57.91%) Lab. hold
*Jessica Morden, Lab. 14,389
Ed Townsend, LD 7,551
Matthew Collings, C. 7,459
Mohammad Asghar, PC 1,221
Roger Thomas, UKIP 945
Liz Screen, Soc. Lab. 260
Lab. maj. 6,838 (21.49%)
9.60% swing Lab. to LD
(2001: Lab. maj. 9,874 (31.56%))

NEWPORT WEST
E. 60,287 T. 35,732 (59.27%) Lab. hold
Paul Flynn, Lab. 16,021
Dr William Morgan, C. 10,563
Nigel Flanagan, LD 6,398
Tony Salkeld, PC 1,278
Hugh Moelwyn Hughes, UKIP 848
Peter Varley, Green 540
Saeid Arjomand, Ind. 84
Lab. maj. 5,458 (15.27%)
5.63% swing Lab. to C.
(2001: Lab. maj. 9,304 (26.54%))

OGMORE
E. 52,349 T. 30,278 (57.84%) Lab. hold
Huw Irranca-Davies, Lab. 18,295
Jackie Radford, LD 4,592
Dr Norma Lloyd-Nesling, C. 4,243
John Williams, PC 3,148
Lab. maj. 13,703 (45.26%)
2.01% swing Lab. to LD
(2002 Feb. by-election: Lab maj. 5,721
(31.13%))
(2001: Lab. maj. 14,574 (48.02%))

PONTYPRIDD
E. 65,074 T. 39,634 (60.91%) Lab. hold
Dr Kim Howells, Lab. 20,919
Mike Powell, LD 7,728
Quentin Gwynne Edwards, C. 5,321
Julie Richards, PC 4,420
David Bevan, UKIP 1,013
Robert Griffiths, Comm. 233
Lab. maj. 13,191 (33.28%)
7.91% swing Lab. to LD
(2001: Lab. maj. 17,684 (46.16%))

PRESELI PEMBROKESHIRE
E. 55,502 T. 38,587 (69.52%) C. gain
*Stephen Crabb, C. 14,106
Sue Hayman, Lab. 13,499
Dewi Smith, LD 4,963
Matt Mathias, PC 4,752
James Carver, UKIP 498
Molly Scott-Cato, Green 494
Trish Bowen, Soc. Lab. 275
C. maj. 607 (1.57%)
4.79% swing Lab. to C.
(2001: Lab. maj. 2,946 (8.01%))

RHONDDA
E. 51,041 T. 31,148 (61.03%) Lab. hold
Chris Bryant, Lab. 21,198
Layton Percy Jones, PC 4,956
Karen Roberts, LD 3,264
Paul Stuart-Smith, C. 1,730
Lab. maj. 16,242 (52.14%)
2.48% swing PC to Lab.
(2001: Lab. maj. 16,047 (47.19%))

SWANSEA EAST
E. 58,813 T. 30,834 (52.43%) Lab. hold
*Sian James, Lab. 17,457
Robert Speht, LD 6,208
Ellenor Bland, C. 3,103
Carolyn Shan Couch, PC 2,129
Kevin Holloway, BNP 770
Timothy Jenkins, UKIP 674
Tony Young, Green 493
Lab. maj. 11,249 (36.48%)
9.27% swing Lab. to LD
(2001: Lab. maj. 16,148 (53.70%))

SWANSEA WEST
E. 57,946 T. 33,086 (57.10%) Lab. hold
Rt. Hon. Alan Williams, Lab. 13,833
Rene Kinzett, LD 9,564
Mohammed Abdel-Haq, C. 5,285
Harri Roberts, PC 2,150
Martyn Shrewsbury, Green 738
Martyn Ford, UKIP 609
Yvonne Holley, Veritas 401
Robert Williams, Soc. Alt. 288
Steve Pank, LCA 218
Lab. maj. 4,269 (12.90%)
9.64% swing Lab. to LD
(2001: Lab. maj. 9,550 (29.75%))

TORFAEN
E. 60,669 T. 35,979 (59.30%) Lab. hold
Rt. Hon. Paul Murphy, Lab. 20,472
Nick Ramsay, C. 5,681
Veronica Watkins, LD 5,678
Aneurin Preece, PC 2,242
David Rowlands, UKIP 1,145
Richard Turner-Thomas, Ind. 761
Lab. maj. 14,791 (41.11%)
2.54% swing Lab. to C.
(2001: Lab. maj. 16,280 (46.19%))

VALE OF CLWYD
E. 51,982 T. 32,313 (62.16%) Lab. hold
Christopher Ruane, Lab. 14,875
Felicity Elphick, C. 10,206
Elizabeth Jewkes, LD 3,820
Mark Jones, PC 2,309
Mark Young, Ind. 442
Edna Khambatta, UKIP 375
Jeff Ditchfield, LCA 286
Lab. maj. 4,669 (14.45%)
1.68% swing Lab. to C.
(2001: Lab. maj. 5,761 (17.81%))

VALE OF GLAMORGAN
E. 68,657 T. 47,324 (68.93%) Lab. hold
John Smith, Lab. 19,481
Alun Cairns, C. 17,673
Mark Hooper, LD 6,140
Barry Shaw, PC 2,423
Richard Suchorzewski, UKIP 840
Karl-James Langford, Lib. 605
Paul Mules, Soc. Lab. 162
Lab. maj. 1,808 (3.82%)
3.29% swing Lab. to C.
(2001: Lab. maj. 4,700 (10.40%))

WREXHAM
E. 48,016 T. 30,385 (63.28%) Lab. hold
Ian Lucas, Lab. 13,993
Tom Rippeth, LD 7,174
Dr Therese Coffey, C. 6,079
Sion Owen, PC 1,744
John Walker, BNP 919
Janet Williams, FWP 476
Lab. maj. 6,819 (22.44%)
6.72% swing Lab. to LD
(2001: Lab. maj. 9,188 (30.58%))

YNYS MON
E. 52,512 T. 35,462 (67.53%) Lab. hold
Albert Owen, Lab. 12,278
Eurig Wyn, PC 11,036
Peter Rogers, Ind. 5,216
James Roach, C. 3,915
Sarah Green, LD 2,418
Elaine Gill, UKIP 367
Tim Evans, LCA 232
Lab. maj. 1,242 (3.50%)
0.58% swing PC to Lab.
(2001: Lab. maj. 800 (2.35%))

SCOTLAND

ABERDEEN NORTH
E. 65,714 T. 36,634 (55.75%) Lab. win
Frank Doran, Lab.   15,557
Steve Delaney, LD   8,762
Kevin Stewart, SNP   8,168
David Anderson, C.   3,456
John Connon, SSP   691
Lab. maj. 6,795 (18.55%)
§ 9.25% swing Lab. to LD
(§ 2001 Lab. maj. 9,294 (23.66%))

ABERDEEN SOUTH
E. 67,012 T. 41,621 (62.11%) Lab. win
Anne Begg, Lab.   15,272
Vicki Harris, LD   13,924
Stewart Whyte, C.   7,134
Maureen Watt, SNP   4,120
Rhonda Reekie, Scot. Green   768
Donald Munro, SSP   403
Lab. maj. 1,348 (3.24%)
§ 3.13% swing Lab. to LD
(§ 2001 Lab. maj. 3,931 (9.49%))

ABERDEENSHIRE WEST & KINCARDINE
E. 65,548 T. 41,648 (63.54%) LD win
Sir Robert Smith, LD   19,285
Alex Johnstone, C.   11,814
James Barrowman, Lab.   5,470
Caroline Little, SNP   4,700
Lorna Grant, SSP   379
LD maj. 7,471 (17.94%)
§ 2.25% swing C. to LD
(§ 2001 LD maj. 5,146 (13.44%))

AIRDRIE & SHOTTS
E. 61,955 T. 33,158 (53.52%) Lab. win
Rt. Hon. Dr John Reid, Lab.   19,568
Malcolm Balfour, SNP   5,484
Helen Watt, LD   3,792
Stuart Cottis, C.   3,271
Fraser Coats, SSP   706
Joseph Rowan, Scot. Ind.   337
Lab. maj. 14,084 (42.48%)
§ 1.51% swing SNP to Lab.
(§ 2001 Lab. maj. 13,545 (39.46%))

ANGUS
E. 63,093 T. 38,186 (60.52%) SNP win
Mike Weir, SNP   12,840
Sandy Bushby, C.   11,280
Douglas Bradley, Lab.   6,850
Scott Rennie, LD   6,660
Alan Manley, SSP   556
SNP maj. 1,601 (4.20%)
§ 1.34% swing C. to SNP
(§ 2001 SNP maj. 532 (1.52%))

ARGYLL & BUTE
E. 67,325 T. 43,229 (64.21%) LD win
Alan Reid, LD   15,786
James McGrigor, C.   10,150
Carolyn Manson, Lab.   9,696
Isobel Strong, SNP   6,716
Deirdre Henderson, SSP   881
LD maj. 5,636 (13.04%)
§ 1.94% swing C. to LD
(§ 2001 LD maj. 3,832 (9.16%))

AYR, CARRICK & CUMNOCK
E. 73,448 T. 45,048 (61.33%) Lab. win
Sandra Osborne, Lab.   20,433
Mark Jones, C.   10,436
Colin Waugh, LD   6,341
Charles Brodie, SNP   5,932
Donald Sharp, SSCUP   592
Murray Steele, SSP   554
James McDaid, Soc. Lab.   395
Bryan McCormack, UKIP   365
Lab. maj. 9,997 (22.19%)
§ 2.18% swing Lab. to C.
(§ 2001 Lab. maj. 12,387 (26.56%))

AYRSHIRE CENTRAL
E. 68,643 T. 42,871 (62.46%) Lab. win
Brian Donohoe, Lab.   19,905
Garry Clark, C.   9,482
Iain Kennedy, LD   6,881
Jahangir Hanif, SNP   4,969
Denise Morton, SSP   820
Robert Cochrane, Soc. Lab.   468
Jim Groves, UKIP   346
Lab. maj. 10,423 (24.31%)
§ 0.68% swing C. to Lab.
(§ 2001 Lab. maj. 9,772 (22.96%))

AYRSHIRE NORTH & ARRAN
E. 72,986 T. 44,205 (60.57%) Lab. win
*Katy Clark, Lab.   19,417
Stewart Connell, C.   8,121
Tony Gurney, SNP   7,938
George White, LD   7,264
Colin Turbett, SSP   780
John Pursley, UKIP   382
Louise McDaid, Soc. Lab.   303
Lab. maj. 11,296 (25.55%)
§ 2.68% swing Lab. to C.
(§ 2001 Lab. maj. 12,140 (27.33%))

BANFF & BUCHAN
E. 65,570 T. 37,216 (56.76%) SNP win
Alex Salmond, SNP   19,044
Sandy Wallace, C.   7,207
Eleanor Anderson, LD   4,952
Rami Okasha, Lab.   4,476
Victor Ross, OCV   683
Kathleen Kemp, UKIP   442
Steve Will, SSP   412
SNP maj. 11,837 (31.81%)
§ 2.22% swing C. to SNP
(§ 2001 SNP maj. 9,744 (27.37%))

BERWICKSHIRE, ROXBURGH & SELKIRK
E. 71,702 T. 45,388 (63.30%) LD win
Michael Moore, LD   18,993
John Lamont, C.   13,092
Sam Held, Lab.   7,206
Aileen Orr, SNP   3,885
John Hein, Lib.   916
Graeme McIver, SSP   695
Peter Neilson, UKIP   601
LD maj. 5,901 (13.00%)
§ 5.90% swing LD to C.
(§ 2001 LD maj. 10,770 (24.80%))

CAITHNESS, SUTHERLAND & EASTER ROSS
E. 46,837 T. 27,663 (59.06%) LD win
John Thurso, LD   13,957
Alan Jamieson, Lab.   5,789
Karen Shirron, SNP   3,686
Angus Ross, C.   2,835
Gordon Campbell, Ind.   848
Luke Ivory, SSP   548
LD maj. 8,168 (29.53%)
§ 7.60% swing Lab. to LD
(§ 2001 LD maj. 4,078 (14.33%))

COATBRIDGE, CHRYSTON & BELLSHILL
E. 67,385 T. 38,344 (56.90%) Lab. win
Rt. Hon. Thomas Clarke, Lab.   24,725
Duncan Ross, SNP   5,206
Rodney Ackland, LD   4,605
Lindsay Paterson, C.   2,775
Joan Kinloch, SSP   1,033
Lab. maj. 19,519 (50.90%)
§ 1.82% swing Lab. to SNP
(§ 2001 Lab. maj. 22,092 (54.55%))

CUMBERNAULD, KILSYTH & KIRKINTILLOCH EAST
E. 64,748 T. 39,088 (60.37%) Lab. win
Rosemary McKenna, Lab.   20,251
James Hepburn, SNP   8,689
Hugh O'Donnell, LD   5,817
James Boswell, C.   2,718
Willie O'Neill, SSP   1,141
Patrick Elliott, OCV   472
Lab. maj. 11,562 (29.58%)
§ 1.11% swing Lab. to SNP
(§ 2001 Lab. maj. 12,667 (31.79%))

DUMFRIES & GALLOWAY
E. 74,273 T. 50,891 (68.52%) Lab. win
Russell Brown, Lab.   20,924
Peter Duncan, C.   18,002
Douglas Henderson, SNP   6,182
Keith Legg, LD   4,259
John Schofield, Scot. Green   745
John Dennis, SSP   497
Mark Smith, OCV   282
Lab. maj. 2,922 (5.74%)
§ 2.73% swing C. to Lab.
(§ 2001 Lab. maj. 141 (0.28%))

DUMFRIESSHIRE, CLYDESDALE & TWEEDDALE
E. 66,045 T. 44,616 (67.55%) C. win
*David Mundell, C.   16,141
Sean Marshall, Lab.   14,403
Patsy Kenton, LD   9,046
Andrew Wood, SNP   4,075
Sarah MacTavish, SSP   521
Tony Lee, UKIP   430
C. maj. 1,738 (3.90%)
§ 7.98% swing Lab. to C.
(§ 2001 Lab. maj. 5,254 (12.06%))

DUNBARTONSHIRE EAST
E. 64,763 T. 46,724 (72.15%) LD win
*Jo Swinson, LD   19,533
John Lyons, Lab.   15,472
David Jack, C.   7,708
Chris Sagan, SNP   2,716
Stuart Callison, Scot. Green   876
Pamela Page, SSP   419
LD maj. 4,061 (8.69%)
§ 7.49% swing Lab. to LD
(§ 2001 Lab. maj. 2,601 (6.29%))

DUNBARTONSHIRE WEST
E. 67,805 T. 41,589 (61.34%)
Lab. (Co-op) win
Rt. Hon. John McFall,
Lab. (Co-op) 21,600
Tom Chalmers, SNP 9,047
Niall Walker, LD 5,999
Campbell Murdoch, C. 2,679
Les Robertson, SSP 1,708
Bryan Maher, UKIP 354
Marlon Dawson, OCV 202
Lab. (Co-op) maj. 12,553 (30.18%)
§ 4.65% swing Lab. (Co-op) to SNP
(§ 2001 Lab. (Co-op) maj. 18,169
(39.49%))

DUNDEE EAST
E. 63,335 T. 39,540 (62.43%) SNP win
*Stewart Hosie, SNP 14,708
Iain Luke, Lab. 14,325
Christopher Bustin, C. 5,061
Clive Sneddon, LD 4,498
Harvey Duke, SSP 537
Donald Low, UKIP 292
David Allison, Ind. 119
SNP maj. 383 (0.97%)
§ 1.13% swing Lab. to SNP
(§ 2001 Lab. maj. 496 (1.29%))

DUNDEE WEST
E. 65,857 T. 36,936 (56.09%) Lab. win
*James McGovern, Lab. 16,468
Joe Fitzpatrick, SNP 11,089
Nykoma Garry, LD 5,323
Christopher McKinlay, C. 3,062
Jim McFarlane, SSP 994
Lab. maj. 5,379 (14.56%)
§ 3.99% swing Lab. to SNP
(§ 2001 Lab. maj. 8,410 (22.54%))

DUNFERMLINE & FIFE WEST
E. 70,775 T. 42,394 (59.90%) Lab. win
Rachel Squire, Lab. 20,111
David Herbert, LD 8,549
Douglas Chapman, SNP 8,026
Roger Smillie, C. 4,376
Susan Archibald, SSP 689
Ian Borland, UKIP 643
Lab. maj. 11,562 (27.27%)
§ 6.47% swing Lab. to LD
(§ 2001 Lab. maj. 14,845 (36.64%))

EAST KILBRIDE, STRATHAVEN &
LESMAHAGOW
E. 75,132 T. 47,733 (63.53%) Lab. win
Rt. Hon. Adam Ingram, Lab. 23,264
Douglas Edwards, SNP 8,541
John Oswald, LD 7,904
Tony Lewis, C. 4,776
Kirsten Robb, Scot. Green 1,575
Rose Gentle, Ind. 1,513
John Houston, Ind. 160
Lab. maj. 14,723 (30.84%)
§ 0.78% swing SNP to Lab.
(§ 2001 Lab. maj. 13,999 (29.29%))

EAST LOTHIAN
E. 70,989 T. 45,776 (64.48%) Lab. win
Anne Picking, Lab. 18,983
Chris Butler, LD 11,363
William Stevenson, C. 7,315
Paul McLennan, SNP 5,995
Michael Collie, Scot. Green 1,132
Gary Galbraith, SSP 504
Eric Robb, UKIP 306
William Thompson, OCV 178
Lab. maj. 7,620 (16.65%)
§ 7.54% swing Lab. to LD
(§ 2001 Lab. maj. 14,011 (31.73%))

EDINBURGH EAST
E. 64,826 T. 39,709 (61.25%) Lab. win
Rt. Hon. Gavin Strang, Lab. 15,899
Gordon Mackenzie, LD 9,697
Stefan Tymkewycz, SNP 6,760
Mev Brown, C. 4,093
Cara Gillespie, Scot. Green 2,266
Catriona Grant, SSP 868
Brett Harris, DDTP 89
Peter Clifford, Ind. 37
Lab. maj. 6,202 (15.62%)
§ 8.47% swing Lab. to LD
(§ 2001 Lab. maj. 12,808 (32.56%))

EDINBURGH NORTH & LEITH
E. 68,038 T. 42,640 (62.67%)
Lab. (Co-op) win
Mark Lazarowicz, Lab. (Co-op) 14,597
Mike Crockart, LD 12,444
Iain Whyte, C. 7,969
Davie Hutchison, SNP 4,344
Mark Sydenham, Scot. Green 2,482
Bill Scott, SSP 804
Lab. (Co-op) maj. 2,153 (5.05%)
§ 8.26% swing Lab. (Co-op) to LD
(§ 2001 Lab. (Co-op) maj. 8,688
(21.56%))

EDINBURGH SOUTH
E. 60,993 T. 42,698 (70.00%) Lab. win
Nigel Griffiths, Lab. 14,188
Marilyne MacLaren, LD 13,783
Gavin Brown, C. 10,291
Graham Sutherland, SNP 2,635
Dr Steve Burgess, Scot. Green 1,387
Morag Robertson, SSP 414
Lab. maj. 405 (0.95%)
§ 6.50% swing Lab. to LD
(§ 2001 Lab. maj. 5,785 (13.95%))

EDINBURGH SOUTH WEST
E. 67,135 T. 43,926 (65.43%) Lab. win
Rt. Hon. Alistair Darling, Lab. 17,476
Gordon Buchan, C. 10,234
Simon Clark, LD 9,252
Nick Elliott-Cannon, SNP 4,654
John Blair-Fish, Scot. Green 1,520
Pat Smith, SSP 585
William Boys, UKIP 205
Lab. maj. 7,242 (16.49%)
§ 0.71% swing Lab. to C.
(§ 2001 Lab. maj. 7,951 (17.91%))

EDINBURGH WEST
E. 65,741 T. 45,265 (68.85%) LD win
John Barrett, LD 22,417
David Brogan, C. 8,817
Navraj Singh Ghaleigh, Lab. 8,433
Sheena Cleland, SNP 4,124
Ailsa Spindler, Scot. Green 964
Gary Clark, SSP 510
LD maj. 13,600 (30.05%)
§ 6.71% swing C. to LD
(§ 2001 LD maj. 5,320 (11.86%))

FALKIRK
E. 76,784 T. 45,750 (59.58%) Lab. win
Eric Joyce, Lab. 23,264
Laura Love, SNP 9,789
Callum Chomczuk, LD 7,321
David Potts, C. 4,538
Danny Quinlan, SSP 838
Lab. maj. 13,475 (29.45%)
§ 0.36% swing Lab. to SNP
(§ 2001 Lab. maj. 13,555 (30.17%))

FIFE NORTH EAST
E. 62,057 T. 38,556 (62.13%) LD win
Rt. Hon. Sir Menzies Campbell,
LD 20,088
Mike Scott-Hayward, C. 7,517
Anthony King, Lab. 4,920
Rod Campbell, SNP 4,011
Jim Park, Scot. Green 1,071
Dr Duncan Pickard, UKIP 533
Jack Ferguson, SSP 416
LD maj. 12,571 (32.60%)
§ 3.20% swing C. to LD
(§ 2001 LD maj. 9,686 (26.20%))

GLASGOW CENTRAL
E. 64,053 T. 28,037 (43.77%) Lab. win
Mohammad Sarwar, Lab. 13,518
Isabel Nelson, LD 4,987
Bill Kidd, SNP 4,148
Richard Sullivan, C. 1,757
Gordon Masterton, Scot. Green 1,372
Marie Gordon, SSP 1,110
Walter Hamilton, BNP 671
Ian Johnson, Soc. Lab. 255
Thomas Greig, OCV 139
Elinor McKenzie, Comm. Brit. 80
Lab. maj. 8,531 (30.43%)
§ 7.36% swing Lab. to LD
(§ 2001 Lab. maj. 9,382 (33.82%))

GLASGOW EAST
E. 64,130 T. 30,939 (48.24%) Lab. win
David Marshall, Lab. 18,775
Lachlan McNeill, SNP 5,268
David Jackson, LD 3,665
Carl Thomson, C. 2,135
George Savage, SSP 1,096
Lab. maj. 13,507 (43.66%)
§ 1.48% swing Lab. to SNP
(§ 2001 Lab. maj. 15,238 (46.62%))

GLASGOW NORTH
E. 55,419 T. 27,921 (50.38%) Lab. win
Ann McKechin, Lab. 11,001
Amy Rodger, LD 7,663
Kenneth McLean, SNP 3,614
Brian Pope, C. 2,441
Martin Bartos, Scot. Green 2,135
Nick Tarlton, SSP 1,067
Lab. maj. 3,338 (11.96%)
§ 8.70% swing Lab. to LD
(§ 2001 Lab. maj. 8,023 (29.36%))

GLASGOW NORTH EAST
E. 62,042 T. 28,418 (45.80%)
Speaker win
Rt. Hon. Michael Martin, Speaker 15,153
John McLaughlin, SNP 5,019
Doris Kelly, Soc. Lab. 4,036
Graham Campbell, SSP 1,402
Daniel Houston, Scot. U. 1,266
Scott McLean, BNP 920
Joe Chambers, Ind. 622
Speaker maj. 10,134 (35.66%)
§ 6.62% swing Speaker to SNP
(§ 2001 Speaker maj. 15,203 (48.90%))

GLASGOW NORTH WEST
E. 61,880 T. 34,061 (55.04%) Lab. win
John Robertson, Lab.   16,748
Paul Graham, LD   6,655
Graeme Hendry, SNP   4,676
Murray Roxburgh, C.   3,262
Martha Wardrop, Scot. Green   1,333
Anthea Irwin, SSP   1,108
Colin Muir, Soc. Lab.   279
Lab. maj. 10,093 (29.63%)
§ 6.80% swing Lab. to LD
(§ 2001 Lab. maj. 13,231 (38.83%))

GLASGOW SOUTH
E. 68,837 T. 38,431 (55.83%) Lab. win
Tom Harris, Lab.   18,153
Arthur Sanderson, LD   7,321
Finlay MacLean, SNP   4,860
Dr Janette McAlpine, C.   4,836
Kay Allan, Scot. Green   1,692
Ronnie Stevenson, SSP   1,303
Dorothy Entwistle, Soc. Lab.   266
Lab. maj. 10,832 (28.19%)
§ 4.93% swing Lab. to LD
(§ 2001 Lab. maj. 13,042 (33.15%))

GLASGOW SOUTH WEST
E. 62,005 T. 30,977 (49.96%)
                        Lab. (Co-op) win
Ian Davidson, Lab. (Co-op)   18,653
James Dornan, SNP   4,757
Katy Gordon, LD   3,593
Scott Brady, C.   1,786
Keith Baldassara, SSP   1,666
Alistair McConnachie, Ind. Green   379
Violet Shaw, Soc. Lab.   143
Lab. (Co-op) maj. 13,896 (44.86%)
§ 0.22% swing SNP to Lab. (Co-op)
(§ 2001 Lab. (Co-op) maj. 14,687
(44.42%))

GLENROTHES
E. 66,563 T. 37,366 (56.14%) Lab. win
John MacDougall, Lab.   19,395
John Beare, SNP   8,731
Elizabeth Riches, LD   4,728
Belinda Don, C.   2,651
George Rodger, PPS   716
Morag Balfour, SSP   705
Paul Smith, UKIP   440
Lab. maj. 10,664 (28.54%)
§ 2.71% swing Lab. to SNP
(§ 2001 Lab. maj. 12,988 (33.95%))

GORDON
E. 71,925 T. 44,438 (61.78%) LD win
Malcolm Bruce, LD   20,008
Iain Brotchie, Lab.   8,982
Philip Atkinson, C.   7,842
Joanna Strathdee, SNP   7,098
Tommy Paterson, SSP   508
LD maj. 11,026 (24.81%)
§ 3.73% swing Lab. to LD
(§ 2001 LD maj. 6,845 (17.36%))

INVERCLYDE
E. 59,291 T. 36,098 (60.88%) Lab. win
David Cairns, Lab.   18,318
Stuart McMillan, SNP   7,059
Douglas Herbison, LD   6,123
Gordon Fraser, C.   3,692
David Landels, SSP   906
Lab. maj. 11,259 (31.19%)
§ 2.51% swing Lab. to SNP
(§ 2001 Lab. maj. 11,314 (29.06%))

**INVERNESS, NAIRN, BADENOCH &
STRATHSPEY**
E. 69,636 T. 44,255 (63.55%) LD win
*Danny Alexander, LD   17,830
David Stewart, Lab.   13,682
David Thompson, SNP   5,992
Robert Rowantree, C.   4,579
Donnie MacLeod, Scot. Green   1,065
Donald Lawson, Publican   678
George MacDonald, SSP   429
LD maj. 4,148 (9.37%)
§ 6.01% swing Lab. to LD
(§ 2001 Lab. maj. 1,134 (2.65%))

KILMARNOCK & LOUDOUN
E. 72,851 T. 44,383 (60.92%) Lab. win
Rt. Hon. Desmond Browne, Lab. 20,976
Daniel Coffey, SNP   12,273
Gary Smith, C.   5,026
Kevin Lang, LD   4,945
Hugh Kerr, SSP   833
Ronnie Robertson, UKIP   330
Lab. maj. 8,703 (19.61%)
§ 5.45% swing Lab. to SNP
(§ 2001 Lab. maj. 13,621 (30.51%))

KIRKCALDY & COWDENBEATH
E. 71,606 T. 41,796 (58.37%) Lab. win
Rt. Hon. Gordon Brown, Lab.   24,278
Alan Bath, SNP   6,062
Alex Cole-Hamilton, LD   5,450
Stuart Randall, C.   4,308
Steve West, SSP   666
Peter Adams, UKIP   516
James Parker, Scot. Senior   425
Elizabeth Kwantes, Ind.   47
Pat Sargent, Ind.   44
Lab. maj. 18,216 (43.58%)
§ 1.84% swing SNP to Lab.
(§ 2001 Lab. maj. 16,238 (39.91%))

LANARK & HAMILTON EAST
E. 73,736 T. 43,589 (59.11%) Lab. win
Jimmy Hood, Lab.   20,072
Fraser Grieve, LD   8,125
John Wilson, SNP   7,746
Robert Pettigrew, C.   5,576
Dennis Reilly, SSP   802
Donald Mackay, UKIP   437
Duncan McFarlane, Ind.   416
Robin Mawhinney, OCV   415
Lab. maj. 11,947 (27.41%)
§ 5.89% swing Lab. to LD
(§ 2001 Lab. maj. 12,861 (28.59%))

LINLITHGOW & FALKIRK EAST
E. 76,739 T. 46,389 (60.45%) Lab. win
Michael Connarty, Lab.   22,121
Gordon Guthrie, SNP   10,919
Stephen Glenn, LD   7,100
Michael Veitch, C.   5,486
Ally Hendry, SSP   763
Lab. maj. 11,202 (24.15%)
§ 1.16% swing Lab. to SNP
(§ 2001 Lab. maj. 11,796 (26.46%))

LIVINGSTON
E. 76,353 T. 44,337 (58.07%) Lab. win
Rt. Hon. Robin Cook, Lab.   22,657
Angela Constance, SNP   9,560
Charles Dundas, LD   6,832
Alison Ross, C.   4,499
Steven Nimmo, SSP   789
Lab. maj. 13,097 (29.54%)
§ 1.17% swing Lab. to SNP
(§ 2001 Lab. maj. 13,638 (31.88%))

MIDLOTHIAN
E. 60,644 T. 37,704 (62.17%) Lab. win
David Hamilton, Lab.   17,153
Fred Mackintosh, LD   9,888
Colin Beattie, SNP   6,400
Iain McGill, C.   3,537
Norman Gilfillan, SSP   726
Lab. maj. 7,265 (19.27%)
§ 6.98% swing Lab. to LD
(§ 2001 Lab. maj. 12,017 (31.29%))

MORAY
E. 66,463 T. 38,793 (58.37%) SNP win
Angus Robertson, SNP   14,196
Jamie Halcro-Johnston, C.   8,520
Kevin Hutchens, Lab.   7,919
Linda Gorn, LD   7,460
Norma Anderson, SSP   698
SNP maj. 5,676 (14.63%)
§ 4.07% swing C. to SNP
(§ 2001 SNP maj. 1,852 (5.06%))

MOTHERWELL & WISHAW
E. 66,987 T. 37,109 (55.40%) Lab. win
Frank Roy, Lab.   21,327
Ian MacQuarrie, SNP   6,105
Conor Snowden, LD   4,464
Peter Finnie, C.   3,440
Gregor MacEwan, SSP   1,019
Dallas Carter, Free Scot.   384
Coral Thompson, OCV   370
Lab. maj. 15,222 (41.02%)
§ 2.35% swing SNP to Lab.
(§ 2001 Lab. maj. 13,778 (36.33%))

NA H-EILEANAN AN IAR
E. 21,576 T. 13,836 (64.13%) SNP gain
*Angus MacNeil, SNP   6,213
Calum MacDonald, Lab.   4,772
Dr Jean Davis, LD   1,096
James Hargreaves, OCV   1,048
Andy Maciver, C.   610
Joanne Telfer, SSP   97
SNP maj. 1,441 (10.41%)
9.29% swing Lab. to SNP
(2001: Lab. maj. 1,074 (8.16%))

OCHIL & PERTHSHIRE SOUTH
E. 70,731 T. 46,697 (66.02%) Lab. win
*Gordon Banks, Lab.   14,645
Annabelle Ewing, SNP   13,957
Elizabeth Smith, C.   10,021
Catherine Whittingham, LD   6,218
George Baxter, Scot. Green   978
Iain Campbell, SSP   420
David Bushby, UKIP   275
Maitland Kelly, Free Scot.   183
Lab. maj. 688 (1.47%)
§ 0.18% swing Lab. to SNP
(§ 2001 Lab. maj. 821 (1.83%))

ORKNEY & SHETLAND
E. 33,048 T. 17,742 (53.69%) LD hold
Alistair Carmichael, LD   9,138
Richard Meade, Lab.   2,511
Frank Nairn, C.   2,357
John Mowat, SNP   1,833
John Aberdein, SSP   992
Scott Dyble, UKIP   424
Paul Cruickshank, LCA   311
Brian Nugent, Free Scot.   176
LD maj. 6,627 (37.35%)
8.29% swing Lab. to LD
(2001: LD maj. 3,475 (20.77%))

PAISLEY & RENFREWSHIRE NORTH
E. 63,076 T. 40,885 (64.82%) Lab. win
James Sheridan, Lab.   18,697
Bill Wilson, SNP   7,696
Lewis Hutton, LD   7,464
Philip Lardner, C.   5,566
Angela McGregor, SSP   646
Katharine McGavigan, Soc. Lab.   444
John Pearson, UKIP   372
Lab. maj. 11,001 (26.91%)
§ 1.34% swing Lab. to SNP
(§ 2001 Lab. maj. 12,417 (29.58%))

PAISLEY & RENFREWSHIRE SOUTH
E. 60,181 T. 37,860 (62.91%) Lab. win
Douglas Alexander, Lab.   19,904
Eileen McCartin, LD   6,672
Andrew Doig, SNP   6,653
Thomas Begg, C.   3,188
Iain Hogg, SSP   789
Gordon Matthew, Paisley   381
Robert Rodgers, Ind.   166
Howard Broadbent, Soc. Lab.   107
Lab. maj. 13,232 (34.95%)
§ 6.24% swing Lab. to LD
(§ 2001 Lab. maj. 13,968 (36.10%))

PERTH & PERTHSHIRE NORTH
E. 70,895 T. 45,930 (64.79%) SNP win
Peter Wishart, SNP   15,469
Douglas Taylor, C.   13,948
Doug Maughan, Lab.   8,601
Gordon Campbell, LD   7,403
Philip Stott, SSP   509
SNP maj. 1,521 (3.31%)
§ 3.85% swing SNP to C.
(§ 2001 SNP maj. 5,020 (11.01%))

RENFREWSHIRE EAST
E. 65,714 T. 47,405 (72.14%) Lab. hold
Jim Murphy, Lab.   20,815
Richard Cook, C.   14,158
Dr Gordon Macdonald, LD   8,659
Osama Bhutta, SNP   3,245
Ian Henderson, SSP   528
Lab. maj. 6,657 (14.04%)
2.43% swing Lab. to C.
(2001: Lab. maj. 9,141 (18.90%))

ROSS, SKYE & LOCHABER
E. 50,507 T. 32,538 (64.42%) LD win
Rt. Hon. Charles Kennedy, LD   19,100
Christine Conniff, Lab.   4,851
John Hodgson, C.   3,275
Mhairi Will, SNP   3,119
David Jardine, Scot. Green   1,097
Phillip Anderson, UKIP   500
Anne Macleod, SSP   412
Morris Grant, Ind.   184
LD maj. 14,249 (43.79%)
§ 11.27% swing Lab. to LD
(§ 2001 LD maj. 6,567 (21.26%))

RUTHERGLEN & HAMILTON WEST
E. 73,998 T. 43,261 (58.46%)
                            Lab. (Co-op) win
Rt. Hon. Thomas McAvoy,
Lab. (Co-op)   24,054
Ian Robertson, LD   7,942
Margaret Park, SNP   6,023
Peter Crerar, C.   3,621
Bill Bonnar, SSP   1,164
Janice Murdoch, UKIP   457
Lab. (Co-op) maj. 16,112 (37.24%)
§ 5.37% swing Lab. (Co-op) to LD
(§ 2001 Lab. (Co-op) maj. 18,504
(44.42%))

STIRLING
E. 64,554 T. 43,691 (67.68%) Lab. win
Anne McGuire, Lab.   15,729
Stephen Kerr, C.   10,962
Kelvin Holdsworth, LD   9,052
Frances McGlinchey, SNP   5,503
Duncan Illingworth, Scot. Green   1,302
Rowland Sheret, SSP   458
James McDonald, Ind.   261
Michael Willis, OCV   215
Matthew Desmond, UKIP   209
Lab. maj. 4,767 (10.91%)
§ 4.18% swing Lab. to C.
(§ 2001 Lab. maj. 8,303 (19.28%))

NORTHERN IRELAND

ANTRIM EAST
E. 58,335 T. 31,767 (54.46%)
                                    DUP gain
*Sammy Wilson, DUP   15,766
Roy Beggs, UUP   8,462
Sean Neeson, Alliance   4,869
Danny O'Connor, SDLP   1,695
James McKeown, SF   828
David Kerr, Vote Dream   147
DUP maj. 7,304 (22.99%)
11.67% swing UUP to DUP
(2001: UUP maj. 128 (0.36%))

ANTRIM NORTH
E. 74,450 T. 45,926 (61.69%)
                                    DUP hold
Revd Ian Paisley, DUP   25,156
Philip McGuigan, SF   7,191
Rodney McCune, UUP   6,637
Sean Farren, SDLP   5,585
Jayne Dunlop, Alliance   1,357
DUP maj. 17,965 (39.12%)
0.47% swing DUP to SF
(2001: DUP maj. 14,224 (28.90%))

ANTRIM SOUTH
E. 66,931 T. 37,957 (56.71%)
                                    DUP gain
†Revd William McCrea, DUP   14,507
David Burnside, UUP   11,059
Noreen McClelland, SDLP   4,706
Henry Cushinan, SF   4,407
David Ford, Alliance   3,278
DUP maj. 3,448 (9.08%)
5.69% swing UUP to DUP
(2001: UUP maj. 1,011 (2.29%))

BELFAST EAST
E. 53,176 T. 30,831 (57.98%)
                                    DUP hold
Peter Robinson, DUP   15,152
Sir Reg Empey, UUP   9,275
Naomi Long, Alliance   3,746
Deborah Devenny, SF   1,029
Mary Muldoon, SDLP   844
Alan Greer, C.   434
Joe Bell, WP   179
Lynda Gilby, Vote Dream   172
DUP maj. 5,877 (19.06%)
0.13% swing DUP to UUP
(2001: DUP maj. 7,117 (19.32%))

BELFAST NORTH
E. 52,853 T. 30,540 (57.78%)
                                    DUP hold
Nigel Dodds, DUP   13,935
Gerry Kelly, SF   8,747
Alban Maginness, SDLP   4,950
Fred Cobain, UUP   2,154
Marjorie Hawkins, Alliance   438
Marcella Delaney, WP   165
Lynda Gilby, Vote Dream   151
DUP maj. 5,188 (16.99%)
0.69% swing SF to DUP
(2001: DUP maj. 6,387 (15.60%))

BELFAST SOUTH
E. 52,668 T. 32,028 (60.81%)
                                    SDLP gain
*Dr Alasdair McDonnell, SDLP   10,339
James Spratt, DUP   9,104
Michael McGimpsey, UUP   7,263
Alex Maskey, SF   2,882
Geraldine Rice, Alliance   2,012
Lynda Gilby, Vote Dream   235
Paddy Lynn, WP   193
SDLP maj. 1,235 (3.86%)
11.91% swing UUP to SDLP
(2001: UUP maj. 5,399 (14.23%))

BELFAST WEST
E. 53,831 T. 34,545 (64.17%) SF hold
Gerry Adams, SF   24,348
Alex Attwood, SDLP   5,033
Diane Dodds, DUP   3,652
Chris McGimpsey, UUP   779
John Lowry, WP   432
Lynda Gilby, Vote Dream   154
Liam Kennedy, Ind.   147
SF maj. 19,315 (55.91%)
4.36% swing SDLP to SF
(2001: SF maj. 19,342 (47.20%))

DOWN NORTH
E. 59,748 T. 32,290 (54.04%)

	UUP hold
Lady Sylvia Hermon, UUP	16,268
Peter Weir, DUP	11,324
David Alderdice, Alliance	2,451
Liam Logan, SDLP	1,009
Julian Robertson, C.	822
Christopher Carter, Ind.	211
Janet McCrory, SF	205

UUP maj. 4,944 (15.31%)
20.35% swing UUP to DUP
(2001: UUP maj. 7,324 (19.69%))

DOWN SOUTH
E. 73,668 T. 48,177 (65.40%)

	SDLP hold
Edward McGrady, SDLP	21,557
Caitriona Ruane, SF	12,417
Jim Wells, DUP	8,815
Dermot Nesbitt, UUP	4,775
Julian Crozier, Alliance	613

SDLP maj. 9,140 (18.97%)
3.82% swing SDLP to SF
(2001: SDLP maj. 13,858 (26.61%))

FERMANAGH & SOUTH TYRONE
E. 67,174 T. 48,793 (72.64%) SF hold

Michelle Gildernew, SF	18,638
Arlene Foster, DUP	14,056
Tom Elliott, UUP	8,869
Tommy Gallagher, SDLP	7,230

SF maj. 4,582 (9.39%)
12.35% swing SF to DUP
(2001: SF maj. 53 (0.10%))

FOYLE
E. 69,207 T. 45,609 (65.90%)

	SDLP hold
*Mark Durkan, SDLP	21,119
Mitchel McLaughlin, SF	15,162
William Hay, DUP	6,557
Eammon McCann, Soc EA	1,649
Earl Storey, UUP	1,091
Ben Reel, Vote Dream	31

SDLP maj. 5,957 (13.06%)
5.28% swing SDLP to SF
(2001: SDLP maj. 11,550 (23.63%))

LAGAN VALLEY
E. 70,742 T. 42,572 (60.18%)

	DUP gain
‡Jeffrey Donaldson, DUP	23,289
Basil McCrea, UUP	9,172
Seamus Close, Alliance	4,316
Paul Butler, SF	3,197
Patricia Lewsley, SDLP	2,598

DUP maj. 14,117 (33.16%)
38.13% swing UUP to DUP
(2001: UUP maj. 18,342 (39.93%))

LONDONDERRY EAST
E. 58,861 T. 35,504 (60.32%)

	DUP hold
Gregory Campbell, DUP	15,225
David McClarty, UUP	7,498
John Dallat, SDLP	6,077
Billy Leonard, SF	5,709
Yvonne Boyle, Alliance	924
Malcolm Samuel, Ind.	71

DUP maj. 7,727 (21.76%)
8.50% swing UUP to DUP
(2001: DUP maj. 1,901 (4.77%))

NEWRY & ARMAGH
E. 72,448 T. 50,696 (69.98%) SF gain

*Conor Murphy, SF	20,965
Dominic Bradley, SDLP	12,770
Paul Berry, DUP	9,311
Danny Kennedy, UUP	7,025
Gerry Markey, Ind.	625

SF maj. 8,195 (16.16%)
11.30% swing SDLP to SF
(2001: SDLP maj. 3,575 (6.43%))

STRANGFORD
E. 69,040 T. 37,032 (53.64%)

	DUP hold
Iris Robinson, DUP	20,921
Gareth McGimpsey, UUP	7,872
Kieran McCarthy, Alliance	3,332
Joe Boyle, SDLP	2,496
Terry Dick, C.	1,462
Dermot Kennedy, SF	949

DUP maj. 13,049 (35.24%)
16.34% swing UUP to DUP
(2001: DUP maj. 1,110 (2.57%))

TYRONE WEST
E. 60,286 T. 43,487 (72.13%) SF hold

Pat Doherty, SF	16,910
Dr Kieran Deeny, Ind.	11,905
Thomas Buchanan, DUP	7,742
Eugene McMenamin, SDLP	3,949
Derek Hussey, UUP	2,981

SF maj. 5,005 (11.51%)
14.65% swing SF to Ind.
(2001: SF maj. 5,040 (10.39%))

ULSTER MID
E. 62,666 T. 45,426 (72.49%) SF hold

Martin McGuinness, SF	21,641
Ian McCrea, DUP	10,665
Patsy McGlone, SDLP	7,922
Billy Armstrong, UUP	4,853
Francis Donnelly, WP	345

SF maj. 10,976 (24.16%)
2.12% swing DUP to SF
(2001: SF maj. 9,953 (19.93%))

UPPER BANN
E. 72,402 T. 44,422 (61.35%)

	DUP gain
*David Simpson, DUP	16,679
John O'Dowd, SF	11,381
Dolores Kelly, SDLP	9,305
Alan Castle, Alliance	5,747
Tom French, WP	955
	355

DUP maj. 5,298 (11.93%)
7.98% swing UUP to DUP
(2001: UUP maj. 2,058 (4.03%))

BY-ELECTIONS 2005–7

Abbreviations of parties standing in the 2005–7 by-elections (see also General Election Results):

Money	Money Reform Party
SCP	Scottish Christian Party (formerly Operation Christian Vote)
SPGB	Socialist Party of Great Britain
Tolls	Abolish Forth Bridge Tolls Party

BLAENAU GWENT
E. 52,508 T. 27,165 (51.73%) Ind hold

*Dai Davis, Ind.	12,543
Owen Smith, Lab.	10,059
Steffan Lewis, PC	1,755
Amy Kitcher, LD	1,477
Margrit Williams, C.	1,013
Alan Hope, Loony	318

Ind maj. 2,484 (9.14%)
8.37% swing Ind. to Lab.
(2005: Ind. maj. 9,121 (25.81%))

BROMLEY & CHISLEHURST
E. 71,818 T. 29,052 (40.45%) C. hold

*Bob Neill, C.	11,621
Ben Abbotts, LD	10,988
Nigel Farage, UKIP	2,347
Rachel Reeves, Lab	1,925
Anne Garrett, Green	811
Paul Winnett, NF	476
John Hemming-Clarke, Ind.	442
Stevens Uncles, Eng. Dem.	212
John Cartwright, Loony	132
Nick Hadziannis, Ind.	65
Anne Belsey, Money	33

C. maj. 633 (2.18%)
14.32% swing C. to LD
(2005: C. maj. 13,342 (28.92%))

CHEADLE
E. 68,051 T. 37,567 (55.20%) LD hold

*Mark Hunter, LD	19,593
Stephen Day, C.	15,936
Martin Miller, Lab.	1,739
Leslie Leggett, Veritas	218
John Allman, AFC	81

LD maj. 3,657 (9.73%)
0.63% swing C. to LD
(2005: LD maj. 4,020 (8.47%))

DUNFERMLINE & FIFE WEST
E. 71,017 T. 34,578 (48.69%) LD gain

*Willie Rennie, LD	12,391
Catherine Stihler, Lab.	10,591
Douglas Chapman, SNP	7,261
Carrie Ruxton, C.	2,702
John McAllion, SSP	537
James Hargreaves, SCP	411
Thomas Minogue, Tolls	374
Ian Borland, UKIP	208
Dick Rodgers, Good	103

LD maj. 1,800 (5.21%)
16.24% swing Lab. to LD
(2005: Lab maj. 11,562 (27.27%))

EALING SOUTHALL
E. 85,423 T. 36,618 (42.87%) Lab. hold

*Virendra Sharma, Lab.	15,188
Nigel Bakhai, LD	10,118
Tony Lit, C.	8,230
Sarah Edwards, Green	1,135
Salvinder Dhillon, Respect	588
Dr Kunnathur Rajan, UKIP	285
Yaqub Masih, Christian Party	280
Jasdev Rai, Ind.	275
John Cartwright, Loony	188
Sati Chaggar, Eng. Dem.	152
Gulbash Singh, Ind.	92
Kuldeep Grewal, Ind.	87

Lab. maj. 5,070 (13.85%)
5.24% swing Lab. to LD
(2005: Lab. maj. 11,440 (24.32%))

LIVINGSTON
E. 76,376 T. 29,477 (38.59%) Lab. hold

*Jim Devine, Lab.	12,319
Angela Constance, SNP	9,639
Charles Dundas, LD	4,362
Gordon Lindhurst, C.	1,993
David Robertson, Green	529
Steven Nimmo, SSP	407
Peter Adams, UKIP	108
Melville Brown, Ind.	55
John Allman, AFC	33
Brian Gardner, SPGB	32

Lab. maj. 2,680 (9.09%)
10.22% swing Lab. to SNP
(2005: Lab. maj. 13,097 (29.54%))

SEDGEFIELD
E. 67,339 T. 27,980 (41.55%) Lab. hold

*Phil Wilson, Lab.	12,528
Greg Stone, LD	5,572
Graham Robb, C.	4,082
Andrew Spence, BNP	2,494
Paul Gittins, Ind.	1,885
Toby Horton, UKIP	536
Chris Haine, Green	348
Stephen Gash, Eng. Dem.	177
Tim Grainger, Christian Party	177
Alan Hope, Loony	147
Norman Scarth, Anti-Crime Party	34

Lab. maj. 6,956 (24.86%)
11.06% swing Lab. to LD
(2005: Lab. maj. 18,457 (44.49%))

STAFFORDSHIRE SOUTH
(23 June 2005; not strictly a by-election, the Staffordshire South poll was deferred until this date as a result of the death of the Liberal Democrat candidate during the general election campaign)
E. 68,763 T. 25,635 (37.28%) C. hold

Sir Patrick Cormack, C.	13,343
Paul Kalinauckas, Lab.	4,496
Jo Crotty, LD	3,540
Malcolm Hurst, UKIP	2,675
Garry Bushell, Eng. Dem.	643
Kate Spohrer, Green	437
Adrian Davies, FP	434
The Rev David Braid, Clause 28	67

C. maj. 8,847 (34.51%)
9.10% swing Lab. to C.
(2001: C. maj. 6,881 (16.31%))

THE GOVERNMENT

as at 1 September 2007

THE CABINET

Prime Minister, First Lord of the Treasury and Minister for the Civil Service
Rt. Hon. Gordon Brown, MP (since June 2007)
Chancellor of the Exchequer
Rt. Hon. Alistair Darling, MP (since June 2007)
Chancellor of the Duchy of Lancaster and Minister for the Cabinet Office
Rt. Hon. Ed Miliband, MP (since June 2007)
Chief Secretary to the Treasury
Rt. Hon. Andy Burnham, MP (since June 2007)
Leader of the House of Commons and Lord Privy Seal, Deputy Leader and Chair of Labour Party, and Minister for Women
Rt. Hon. Harriet Harman, QC, MP (since June 2007)
Leader of the House of Lords and Lord President of the Council
Rt. Hon. Baroness Ashton of Upholland (since June 2007)
Parliamentary Secretary to the Treasury and Chief Whip
Rt. Hon. Geoff Hoon, MP (since June 2007)
Secretary of State for Business, Enterprise and Regulatory Reform
Rt. Hon. John Hutton, MP (since June 2007)
Secretary of State for Children, Schools and Families
Rt. Hon. Ed Balls, MP (since June 2007)
Secretary of State for Communities and Local Government
Rt. Hon. Hazel Blears, MP (since June 2007)
Secretary of State for Culture, Media and Sport
Rt. Hon. James Purnell, MP (since June 2007)
Secretary of State for Defence (since May 2006) and Secretary of State for Scotland (since June 2007)
Rt. Hon. Des Browne, MP
Secretary of State for Environment, Food and Rural Affairs
Rt. Hon. Hilary Benn, MP (since June 2007)
Secretary of State for Foreign and Commonwealth Affairs
Rt. Hon. David Miliband, MP (since June 2007)
Secretary of State for Health
Rt. Hon. Alan Johnson, MP (since June 2007)
Secretary of State for the Home Department
Rt. Hon. Jacqui Smith, MP (since June 2007)
Secretary of State for Innovation, Universities and Skills
Rt. Hon. John Denham, MP (since June 2007)
Secretary of State for International Development
Rt. Hon. Douglas Alexander, MP (since June 2007)
Secretary of State for Justice and Lord Chancellor
Rt. Hon. Jack Straw, MP (since June 2007)
Secretary of State for Northern Ireland
Rt. Hon. Shaun Woodward, MP (since June 2007)
Secretary of State for Transport
Rt. Hon. Ruth Kelly, MP (since June 2007)
Secretary of State for Work and Pensions (since June 2007) and Secretary of State for Wales (since October 2002)
Rt. Hon. Peter Hain, MP

The Attorney-General (Rt. Hon. Baroness Scotland of Asthal, QC), the Minister of State for the Olympics and London (Rt. Hon. Tessa Jowell, MP), the Minister of State for Housing (Yvette Cooper, MP), the Minister of State for Africa, Asia and the UN (Lord Malloch Brown, KCMG), the Minister for the North-West (Rt. Hon Beverley Hughes, MP), the Parliamentary Private Secretaries to the Prime Minister (Ian Austin, MP; Angela E. Smith, MP) and the Chief Whip in the House of Lords and Captain of the Gentlemen-at-Arms (Rt. Hon. Lord Grocott) attend cabinet meetings although they are not members of the cabinet.

LAW OFFICERS

Attorney-General
Rt. Hon. Baroness Scotland, QC (since June 2007)
Solicitor-General
Vera Baird, QC, MP (since June 2007)
Advocate-General for Scotland
Lord Davidson of Glen Clova, QC (since May 2006)

MINISTERS OF STATE

Business, Enterprise and Regulatory Reform
Lord Drayson*
Sir Digby Jones†
Pat McFadden, MP
Rt. Hon. Stephen Timms, MP
Malcolm Wicks, MP
Cabinet Office
Rt. Hon. Ed Miliband, MP *(Chancellor of the Duchy of Lancaster)*
Rt. Hon. Tessa Jowell, MP
Children, Schools and Families
Rt. Hon. Beverley Hughes, MP
Jim Knight, MP
Communities and Local Government
Yvette Cooper, MP
John Healey, MP
Culture, Media and Sport
Rt. Hon. Margaret Hodge, MBE, MP
Defence
Rt. Hon. Bob Ainsworth, MP
Environment, Food and Rural Affairs
Rt. Hon. Lord Rooker
Phil Woolas, MP
Foreign and Commonwealth Office
Dr Kim Howells, MP
Lord Malloch Brown, KCMG
Rt. Hon. Jim Murphy, MP
Health
Ben Bradshaw, MP
Rt. Hon. Dawn Primarolo, MP
Home Office
Liam Byrne, MP
Tony McNulty, MP
Innovation, Universities and Skills
Ian Pearson, MP
Bill Rammell, MP
Justice
Rt. Hon. David Hanson, MP
Michael Wills, MP

Northern Ireland Office
Paul Goggins, MP
Scotland Office
David Cairns, MP
Transport
Rt. Hon. Rosie Winterton, MP
Work and Pensions
Mike O'Brien, MP
Caroline Flint, MP

* Also works in the Ministry of Defence
† Also works in the Foreign and Commonwealth Office

UNDER-SECRETARIES OF STATE

Business, Enterprise and Regulatory Reform
Gareth Thomas, MP*
Children, Schools and Families
Lord Adonis
Kevin Brennan, MP
Communities and Local Government
Parmjit Dhanda, MP
Iain Wright, MP
Culture, Media and Sport
Gerry Sutcliffe, MP
Defence
Derek Twigg, MP
Environment, Food and Rural Affairs
Joan Ruddock, MP
Jonathan Shaw, MP
Foreign and Commonwealth Office
Meg Munn, MP
Health
Prof. Sir Ara Darzi
Ann Keen, MP
Ivan Lewis, MP
Home Office
Vernon Coaker, MP
Meg Hillier, MP
Adm. Sir Alan West
Innovation, Universities and Skills
David Lammy, MP
Lord Triesman
International Development
Shahid Malik, MP
Baroness Vadera
Justice
Maria Eagle, MP
Lord Hunt of King's Heath, OBE
Transport
Jim Fitzpatrick, MP
Tom Harris, MP
Wales Office
Huw Irranca-Davies, MP
Work and Pensions
Barbara Follett, MP
Anne McGuire, MP
Lord McKenzie of Luton
James Plaskitt, MP

* Also in the Department for International Development

OTHER MINISTERS

Parliamentary Private Secretary to the Prime Minister
Ian Austin, MP
Cabinet Office
Rt. Hon. Tessa Jowell, MP *(Paymaster-General)*
Phil Hope, MP *(Parliamentary Secretary)*
Gillian Merron, MP *(Parliamentary Secretary)*
Leader of the Commons
Harriet Harman, QC, MP *(Lord Privy Seal, Labour Party Chair and Minister for Women)*
Helen Goodman, MP *(Parliamentary Secretary)*
Treasury
Rt. Hon. Jane Kennedy, MP *(Financial Secretary)*
Kitty Ussher, MP *(Economic Secretary)*
Angela Eagle, MP *(Exchequer Secretary)*

GOVERNMENT WHIPS

HOUSE OF LORDS
Captain of the Honourable Corps of the Gentlemen-at-Arms (Chief Whip)
Rt. Hon. Lord Grocott
Captain of the Queen's Bodyguard of the Yeomen of the Guard (Deputy Chief Whip)
Rt. Hon. Lord Davies of Oldham
Lords-in-Waiting
Lord Bassam of Brighton
Lord Evans of Temple Guiting, CBE
Lord Truscott
Baronesses-in-Waiting
Baroness Crawley
Baroness Farrington of Ribbleton
Baroness Morgan of Drefelin
Baroness Royall of Blaisdon

HOUSE OF COMMONS
Parliamentary Secretary to the Treasury (Chief Whip)
Rt. Hon. Geoff Hoon, MP
Treasurer of HM Household (Deputy Chief Whip)
Rt. Hon. Nicholas Brown, MP
Comptroller of HM Household
Rt. Hon. Thomas McAvoy, MP
Vice-Chamberlain of HM Household
Liz Blackman, MP
Lords Commissioners of HM Treasury
Alan Campbell, MP; Stephen McCabe, MP; Frank Roy, MP; Claire Ward, MP; Dave Watts, MP
Assistant Whips
Bob Blizzard, MP; Tony Cunningham, MP; Wayne David, MP; Michael Foster, MP; Diana R. Johnson, MP; Sadiq Khan, MP; Siobhain McDonagh, MP; Alison Seabeck, MP; Mark Tami, MP

GOVERNMENT DEPARTMENTS

THE CIVIL SERVICE

Under the Next Steps programme, launched in 1988, many semi-autonomous executive agencies were established to carry out much of the work of the civil service. Executive agencies operate within a framework set by the responsible minister which specifies policies, objectives and available resources. All executive agencies are set annual performance targets by their minister. Each agency has a chief executive, who is responsible for the day-to-day operations of the agency and who is accountable to the minister for the use of resources and for meeting the agency's targets. The minister accounts to parliament for the work of the agency. Nearly 75 per cent of civil servants now work in executive agencies. In June 2006 there were about 524,000 permanent civil servants, down from about 537,000 in June 2005.

The Senior Civil Service was created in 1996 and on 1 April 2007 comprised about 4,000 staff from permanent secretary to the former grade 5 level, including all agency chief executives. All government departments and executive agencies are now responsible for their own pay and grading systems for civil servants outside the Senior Civil Service.

SALARIES 2006–7

MINISTERIAL SALARIES *from 1 April 2007*
Ministers who are members of the House of Commons receive a parliamentary salary (£60,675) in addition to their ministerial salary.

Prime minister	£128,174
Cabinet minister (Commons)	£76,704
Cabinet minister (Lords)	£104,386
Minister of state (Commons)	£39,893
Minister of state (Lords)	£81,504
Parliamentary under-secretary (Commons)	£30,280
Parliamentary under-secretary (Lords)	£70,986

SPECIAL ADVISERS' SALARIES *from 1 April 2007*
Special advisers to government ministers are paid out of public funds; their salaries are negotiated individually, but are usually in the range of £38,862 to £102,918.

CIVIL SERVICE SALARIES *from 1 April 2007*

Senior Civil Servants	
Permanent secretary	£139,740–£273,250
Band 3	£99,960–£205,000
Band 2	£81,580–£160,000
Band 1A	£65,280–£127,000
Band 1	£56,100–£116,000

Staff are placed in pay bands according to their level of responsibility and taking account of other factors such as experience and marketability. Movement within and between bands is based on performance. Following the delegation of responsibility for pay and grading to government departments and agencies from 1 April 1996, it is no longer possible to show service-wide pay rates for staff outside the Senior Civil Service.

GOVERNMENT DEPARTMENTS

CABINET OFFICE

70 Whitehall, London SW1A 2AS
Switchboard 020-7276 3000 T 020-7276 1234
W www.cabinet-office.gov.uk

The Cabinet Office, alongside the Treasury, sits at the centre of the government. It has three core functions: to support the prime minister in defining and delivering the government's objectives; to support the cabinet in ensuring the coherence, quality and delivery of policy and operations across departments; and strengthening the Civil Service's capabilities in terms of organisation, leadership and skills. The department is headed by the Chancellor of the Duchy of Lancaster.

Prime Minister and Minister for the Civil Service, Rt. Hon. Gordon Brown, MP
Principal Private Secretary to the Prime Minister, Tom Scholar
Chancellor of the Duchy of Lancaster and Minister for the Cabinet Office, Rt. Hon. Ed Miliband, MP
Parliamentary Private Secretary, Jeffrey Ennis, MP
Principal Private Secretary, Lee O'Rourke
Private Secretary, Louise Coward
Parliamentary Secretary, Phil Hope, MP
Assistant Private Secretaries, Gemma Lobb; Kate Wilson
Parliamentary Secretary, Gillian Merron, MP
Private Secretary, Sarah Goulbourne
Secretary of the Cabinet and Head of the Home Civil Service, Sir Gus O'Donnell, KCB
Principal Private Secretary, Ciaran Martin
Private Secretary, Paul Rennie
Assistant Private Secretary, Jackie Fraser *(Diary)*
Permanent Secretary, Sir Richard Mottram, GCB *(Intelligence, Security and Resilience)*
Principal Private Secretary, Dominic Fagan
Private Secretary, Stephen Knight
Minister for the Olympics and London, Rt. Hon. Tessa Jowell, MP
Private Secretary, Alec Taylor
Parliamentary Private Secretary, John Mann, MP

The TRANSFORMATIONAL GOVERNMENT TEAM comprises Transformational Government, Cabinet Office Management, Business Support Group and Change Team. It was established to provide overall technology leadership in three key areas of government: the transformation of public services for the benefit of citizens, businesses, taxpayers and front-line staff; the efficiency of the corporate services and infrastructure of government organisations; and the steps necessary to achieve the effective delivery of technology for government.

TRANSFORMATIONAL GOVERNMENT

1 Horse Guards Road, London SW1A 2HQ
T 020-7276 3248
HM Government Chief Information Officer, John Suffolk

CABINET OFFICE MANAGEMENT

Admiralty Arch, The Mall, London SW1A 2WH
T 020-7276 3090

Director-General, Transformational Government and Cabinet Office Management, Alexis Cleveland

BUSINESS SUPPORT GROUP
Kirkland House, 22–26 Whitehall, London SW1A 2WH
T 020-7276 0530
Director-General, Strategic Finance and Operations, Roger Marsh

CHANGE TEAM
Kirkland House, 22–26 Whitehall, London SW1A 2WH
T 020-7276 2160
Director, Sarah Cox

The CIVIL SERVICE CAPABILITY GROUP comprises Cabinet Office Human Resources, the Leadership and Development Strategy Directorate and Capability Review. The group is responsible for recruiting and developing staff and raising the capability of HR management throughout the civil service.
Director-General, Leadership, People and Change, Gill Rider

CABINET OFFICE HUMAN RESOURCES
Admiralty Arch South, The Mall, London SW1A 2WH
T 020-7276 6200
Director, Helen Dudley

LEADERSHIP AND DEVELOPMENT STRATEGY DIRECTORATE
Admiralty Arch, The Mall, London SW1A 2WH
T 020-7276 2006
Director, Anne-Marie Lawlor

CAPABILITY REVIEW
1 Horse Guards Road, London SW1A 2HQ
T 020-7270 5884
Director, Peter Thomas

The DOMESTIC POLICY GROUP comprises the Ceremonial Secretariat, the Economic and Domestic Affairs Secretariat, the Office of the Third Sector, the Social Exclusion Task Force and the Strategy Unit.

CEREMONIAL SECRETARIAT
35 Great Smith Street, London SW1P 3BQ
T 020-7276 2777
Ceremonial Officer, Denis Brennan

ECONOMIC AND DOMESTIC AFFAIRS SECRETARIAT
Cabinet Office, 70 Whitehall, London SW1A 2WH
T 020-7276 0055
Director, Paul Britton, CB

OFFICE OF THE THIRD SECTOR
35 Great Smith Street, London SW1P 3BQ
T 020-7276 6400
Director-General, Campbell Robb

SOCIAL EXCLUSION TASK FORCE
Admiralty Arch, The Mall, London SW1A 2WH
T 020-7276 2323
Director, Naomi Eisenstadt

STRATEGY UNIT
Admiralty Arch, The Mall, London SW1A 2WH
T 020-7276 1881 W www.strategy.gov.uk
Director, Stephen Aldridge

EUROPEAN SECRETARIAT
70 Whitehall, London SW1A 2WH
T 020-7276 1234
Prime Minister's Adviser on International Economic Affairs and Europe, Jon Cunliffe

The COMMUNICATION AND INFORMATION GROUP comprises Cabinet Office Communication, Government Communication and the Histories, Openness and Records Unit.

CABINET OFFICE COMMUNICATIONS
22 Whitehall, London SW1A 2WH
T 020-7276 0432/0400
Director, vacant

GOVERNMENT COMMUNICATION
26 Whitehall, London SW1A 2WH
T 020-7276 2712 W www.comms.gov.uk
Permanent Secretary, Howell James, CBE
Director, John Worne

HISTORIES OPENNESS AND RECORDS UNIT
Admiralty Arch, The Mall, London SW1A 2WH
T 020-7276 6326
Departmental Records Officer and Adviser, Tessa Stirling

The INTELLIGENCE, SECURITY AND RESILIENCE GROUP comprises the Civil Contingencies Secretariat, the Emergency Planning College and the Intelligence and Security Secretariat (including the Central Sponsor for Information Assurance).

CIVIL CONTINGENCIES SECRETARIAT
10 Great George Street, London SW1P 3AE
T 020-7276 5117
Director, Bruce Mann

EMERGENCY PLANNING COLLEGE
The Hawkhills, Easingwold, York YO61 3EG
T 01347-822877 W www.epcollege.gov.uk
Chief Executive, Michael Charlton-Weedy

INTELLIGENCE AND SECURITY SECRETARIAT
70 Whitehall, London SW1A 2WH
T 020-7276 0333
Director, Chris Wright

CENTRAL SPONSOR FOR INFORMATION ASSURANCE
2nd Floor, Cabinet Office, 26 Whitehall, London SW1A 2WH
T 020-7276 3108
W www.cabinetoffice.gov.uk/csia
Director, Roger Styles

DEFENCE AND OVERSEAS SECRETARIAT
70 Whitehall, London SW1A 2WH
T 020-7276 1234
Prime Minister's Foreign Policy Adviser and Head of Secretariat, Sir Nigel Sheinwald, KCMG

PRIME MINISTER'S OFFICE
10 Downing Street, London SW1A 2AA
T 020-7270 3000 F 020-7925 0918
W www.number-10.gov.uk
Prime Minister, Rt. Hon Gordon Brown, MP
Parliamentary Private Secretaries, Ian Austin, MP; Angela E. Smith, MP
Chief of Staff and Principal Private Secretary, Tom Scholar

Prime Minister's Spokesman and Director of Communications, Michael Ellam
Deputy Chief of Staff, Gavin Kelly
Directors, Sue Nye *(Government Relations)*; Spencer Livermore *(Political Strategy)*
Heads of Units, Jeremy Heywood *(Domestic Policy and Strategy)*; Simon McDonald *(Foreign and Defence Policy)*; Jon Cunliffe *(International Economic Affairs, Europe and G8 Sherpa)*; Dan Corry *(Policy)*
Special Advisers, Dan Corry; Gavin Kelly; Spencer Livermore; Damian McBride; Sue Nye

CROSS GOVERNMENT UNITS in the Cabinet Office comprises the Committee on Standards in Public Life *(see* Public Bodies section), Independent Offices and the Office of the Parliamentary Counsel.

INDEPENDENT OFFICES

OFFICE OF THE COMMISSIONER FOR PUBLIC APPOINTMENTS (OCPA)
3rd Floor, 35 Great Smith Street, London SW1P 3BQ
T 020-7276 2625 F 020-7276 2633
E ocpa@gtnet.gov.uk W www.ocpa.gov.uk

The Commissioner for Public Appointments is responsible for monitoring, regulating and reporting on ministerial appointments to public bodies. The commissioner can investigate complaints about the way in which appointments were made or applicants treated.
Commissioner for Public Appointments, Janet Gaymer, CBE
Secretary to the Commissioner and Head of the Independent Offices, Jim Barron, CBE

OFFICE OF THE CIVIL SERVICE COMMISSIONERS (OCSC)
35 Great Smith Street, London SW1P 3BQ
T 020-7276 2617 W www.civilservicecommissioners.gov.uk

The Civil Service Commissioners are the custodians of the principle of selection on merit by fair and open competition; they publish a recruitment code and audit departments' and agencies' performance against it. When the most senior posts are opened to people from outside the service, the commissioners normally chair the recruitment process.
First Commissioner, Janet Paraskeva
Commissioners (part-time), Sir Michael Aaronson, CBE; Mark Addison; James Boyle; Dame A. Burslem, DBE; Janet Gaymer, CBE; Ms M. J. Jacobi; Bernard Knight; J. MacAuslan; A. MacDonald, CB; Ms E. McMeikan; Anthea Millett, CBE; Ms S. Pantelides; Ranjit Sondhi; C. Stephens; Libby Watkins
Secretary to the Commissioners and Head of the Independent Offices, Jim Barron, CBE

OFFICE OF THE PARLIAMENTARY COUNSEL
35 Whitehall, London SW1A 2AY
T 020-7210 2588 W www.parliamentary-counsel.gov.uk
First Parliamentary Counsel, Stephen Laws, CB
Chief Executive, John Gilhooly, CB

INTELLIGENCE AND SECURITY COMMITTEE SECRETARIAT
70 Whitehall, London SW1A 2AS
T 020-7276 1215 W www.cabinetoffice.gov.uk/intelligence
Head of Management Unit, Emma-Louise Avery

INTERNAL AUDIT SERVICE
9th Floor, Ashdown House, 123 Victoria Street, London SW1E 6DE
T 020-7944 6882
Head, Steve Simmonds

ATTORNEY-GENERAL'S OFFICE
Attorney-General's Office, 20 Victoria Street, London SW1H 0NF
T 020-7271 2492 F 020-7271 2434
Attorney-General's Chambers, Royal Courts of Justice, Belfast BT1 3JY
T 028-9054 6082 F 028-9054 6049
E correspondenceunit@attorneygeneral.gsi.gov.uk
W www.attorneygeneral.gov.uk
The law officers of the crown for England and Wales are the Attorney-General and the Solicitor-General. The Attorney-General, assisted by the Solicitor-General, is the chief legal adviser to the government and is also ultimately responsible for all crown litigation. He has overall responsibility for the work of the Law Officers' Departments (the Treasury Solicitor's Department, the Crown Prosecution Service, the Serious Fraud Office, the Revenue and Customs Prosecution Office, the Army Prosecuting Authority, HM Crown Prosecution Service Inspectorate and the Attorney-General's Office). He has a specific statutory duty to superintend the discharge of their duties by the Director of Public Prosecutions (who heads the Crown Prosecution Service) and the Director of the Serious Fraud Office. The Director of Public Prosecutions for Northern Ireland and the Crown Solicitor for Northern Ireland are also responsible to the Attorney-General for the performance of their functions. The Attorney-General has specific responsibilities for the enforcement of the criminal law and also performs certain public interest functions, eg protecting charities and appealing unduly lenient sentences. He also deals with questions of law arising in bills and with issues of legal policy.
Attorney-General, Rt. Hon. Lord Goldsmith, QC
Private Secretary, W. Hart
Solicitor-General, Hon. Mike O'Brien, QC, MP
Legal Secretary, J. Jones
Deputy Legal Secretary, H. Heycock

DEPARTMENT FOR BUSINESS, ENTERPRISE AND REGULATORY REFORM
1 Victoria Street, London SW1H 0ET
T 020-7215 5000 F 020-7215 0105
W www.berr.gov.uk
The Department for Business, Enterprise and Regulatory Reform (BERR) was established in June 2007 after the Department of Trade and Industry was disbanded. BERR promotes best practice in design and manufacture, and investment opportunities, and champions different industries' legitimate interests through policy and regulation. The department aims to create the conditions required for business success through competitive and flexible markets that provide value for businesses, consumers and employers. It is responsible for regulatory reform and works across government and the UK's regions to raise levels of UK productivity, and has joint responsibility – with the Department for International Development and the Foreign and Commonwealth Office respectively – for trade policy, and trade promotion and inward investment. BERR also works closely with the

newly established Department for Innovation, Universities and Skills.

Secretary of State for Business, Enterprise and Regulatory Reform, Rt. Hon. John Hutton, MP
Principal Private Secretary, Dr Philippa Lloyd
Senior Private Secretary, Catherine Capon
Private Secretaries, Emily Bourne; Dr Matthew Clarke
Parliamentary Private Secretary, Eric Joyce, MP
Special Advisers, John Williams; John Woodcock
Minister of State, Rt. Hon. Stephen Timms, MP *(Competitiveness)*
Private Secretary, vacant
Parliamentary Private Secretary, Stephen Pound, MP
Minister of State, Malcolm Wicks, MP *(Energy)*
Private Secretary, David Curran
Parliamentary Private Secretary, Dr Nick Palmer, MP
Minister of State, Lord Jones of Birmingham *(Trade and Investment)*
Private Secretary, vacant
Parliamentary Private Secretary, Andy Slaughter, MP
Minister of State, Pat McFadden, MP *(Employment Relation and Postal Affairs)*
Private Secretary, Dominic Scullard
Parliamentary Private Secretary, Jim McGovern, MP
Minister of State, Lord Drayson *(Business and Regulatory Reform; also a minister with MoD)*
Private Secretary, vacant
Parliamentary Private Secretary, Russell Brown, MP
Parliamentary Under-Secretary of State, Gareth Thomas, MP *(Trade and Consumer Affairs; also a minister with DfID)*
Private Secretary, vacant
Permanent Secretary, Sir Brian Bender, KCB
Private Secretary, John Sartin
Head of Parliamentary Unit, Ian Webster

MANAGEMENT BOARD
Chair, Sir Brian Bender
Members, Hilary Douglas *(Chief Operating Officer)*; Vicky Pryce *(Economics, Director-General; Chief Economic Adviser)*; Willy Rickett *(Energy Group, Director-General)*; Mark Gibson *(Enterprise and Business Group, Director-General)*; John Alty *(Fair Markets Group, Director-General)*; Mark Clarke *(Finance and Strategy, Director-General)*; Anthony Inglese *(Legal Services, Director-General; Solicitor and Deputy Chair)*; Sir Keith O'Nions *(Science and Innovation, Director-General)*; Andrew Cahn *(UK Trade and Industry, Chief Executive)*
Independent Members, Arnoud De Meyer; Roger Urwin; Fields Wicker-Miurin; Dr Brian Woods-Scawen

BETTER REGULATION EXECUTIVE
22 Whitehall, London SW1A 2WH
T 020-7276 2828 W www.betterregulation.gov.uk

The Better Regulation Executive works across government to minimise bureaucracy by reducing and removing unnecessary regulation from the public, private and voluntary sectors.
Chair, William Sargent
Chief Executive, Jitinder Kohli

SHAREHOLDER EXECUTIVE
1 Victoria Street, London SW1H 0ET
T 020-7215 6830 F 020-7215 5494
W www.shareholderexecutive.gov.uk

The Shareholder Executive was established in September 2003 to improve the government's performance as a shareholder in government-owned businesses and to provide a source of corporate finance expertise within government; currently the executive's remit covers 27 businesses.
Chair, Philip Remnant
Chief Executive (acting), Stephen Lovegrove

DEPARTMENT FOR CHILDREN, SCHOOLS AND FAMILIES
Sanctuary Buildings, Great Smith Street, London SW1P 3BT
Caxton House, Tothill Street, London SW1H 9NA
Castle View House, East Lane, Runcorn WA7 2GJ
Mowden Hall, Staindrop Road, Darlington DL3 9BG
Moorfoot, Sheffield S1 4PQ
T 0870-001 2345 Public Enquiries 0870-000 2288
F 01928-794248
E info@dcsf.gsi.gov.uk W www.dcsf.gov.uk

The Department for Children, Schools and Families (DCSF) was established in June 2007 in place of the Department for Education and Skills (DfES), in order to achieve better integrated children's services and improved educational standards; higher education and lifelong learning directorates moved to the new Department for Innovation, Universities and Skills.

The DCSF is responsible for everything affecting children and young people under the age of 19, including schools and relevant services. The department's objectives are to raise standards in order to increase the number of children reaching expected standards; help children out of poverty; and re-engage disaffected young people. It also aims to respond to factors affecting children and families, such as demographic and socio-economic change, developing technology and increasing global competition.

Secretary of State for Children, Schools and Families, Rt. Hon. Ed Balls, MP
Principal Private Secretary, Mela Watts
Private Secretary, Hannah Sheehan
Special Advisers, Francine Bates; Alex Belardinelli
Parliamentary Private Secretary, Paul Clark, MP
Minister of State, Jim Knight, MP *(Schools and Learners)*
Private Secretary, Charles Deighton-Fox
Parliamentary Private Secretary, Madeline Moon, MP
Minister of State, Rt. Hon. Beverley Hughes, MP *(Children, Young People and Families)*
Private Secretary, Jo Hawley
Parliamentary Private Secretary, Christine Russell, MP
Parliamentary Under-Secretary of State, Lord Adonis *(Schools and Learners)*
Private Secretary, Dunstan Hadley
Parliamentary Under-Secretary of State, Kevin Brennan, MP *(Children, Young People and Families)*
Private Secretary, Nicola Sams
Parliamentary Clerk, Mike Watts
Spokesperson in the House of Lords, Lord Adonis
Permanent Secretary, David Bell
Private Secretary, Lucy Andrew

BOARD MEMBERS
Chair, David Bell
Directors-General, Tom Jeffrey *(Children and Families)*; Jon Thompson *(Corporate Services)*; Ralph Tabberer *(Schools)*; Lesley Longstone *(Young People)*
Director of Communications, Caroline Wright
Non-Executive Members, Philip Augar; Katherine Kerswell

CORPORATE SERVICES DIRECTORATE
Chief Information Officer, Tim Wright

INTERNAL AUDIT
Head of Internal Audit, Suzanne Orr

LEGAL ADVISER'S OFFICE
Legal Adviser, David Noble

DEPARTMENT FOR COMMUNITIES AND LOCAL GOVERNMENT

Eland House, London SW1E 5DU
T 020-7944 4400 F 020-7944 9645
W www.communities.gov.uk

The Department for Communities and Local Government (DCLG) was formed in May 2006 with a remit to promote community cohesion and equality, as well as responsibility for housing, urban regeneration and planning. It unites the communities and civil renewal functions previously undertaken by the Home Office, with responsibility for regeneration, neighbourhood renewal and local government (previously held by the Office of the Deputy Prime Minister, which was abolished following a cabinet reshuffle in May 2006).

The DCLG also brings together responsibility for equality policy, including policy on race, faith, gender and sexual orientation (functions that were previously split between several government departments). The department will also sponsor the Commission for Equality and Human Rights.

Secretary of State for the Department for Communities and Local Government, Minister for Women, Rt. Hon. Hazel Blears, MP
Private Secretary, Daniel Thornton
Parliamentary Private Secretary, Robert Flello, MP
Minister of State, Rt. Hon. John Healey, MP *(Local Government)*
Private Secretary, Mark Doran
Parliamentary Private Secretary, Chris Mole, MP
Minister of State, Yvette Cooper, MP *(Housing)*
Private Secretary, Mark Livesey
Parliamentary Private Secretary, Angela C. Smith, MP
Parliamentary Under-Secretary of State, Parmjit Dhanda, MP
Private Secretary, Ian Hardy
Parliamentary Under-Secretary of State, Baroness Andrews, OBE
Private Secretary, Alistair MacDonald
Parliamentary Under-Secretary of State, Iain Wright, MP
Private Secretary, Stella Michael
Permanent Secretary, Peter Housden
Private Secretary, Tanya Ferguson
Chief Scientist, Prof. Michael Kelly

DEPARTMENT FOR COMMUNITIES AND LOCAL GOVERNMENT BOARD
Chair, Peter Housden *(Permanent Secretary)*
Members, Susan Scholefield *(Director-General, Equalities)*; Joe Montgomery *(Director-General, Places and Communities)*; Richard McCarthy *(Director-General, Programmes, Policy and Innovation)*

SENIOR STAFF
Directors-General, Susan Scholefield *(Equalities)*; Hunada Nouss *(Finance and Corporate Service Delivery)*; Chris Wormald *(Governance and Communications)*; Joe Montgomery *(Places and Communities)*; Richard McCarthy *(Programmes, Policy and Innovation)*; Alun Evans *(Transformation)*
Directors, Michael Kell *(Analytical Services)*; John Shield *(Communications)*; Peter Betts *(Fire and Resilience)*;

Colin Byrne *(Home Information Packs)*; Terrie Alafat *(Housing Strategy and Support)*; Clive Norris *(Human Resources)*; Roy Marshall *(Knowledge, IT and Working Environment)*; Sandra Unerman *(Legal)*; David Rossington *(Local Democracy)*; Ros Dunn *(Local Development and Renewal)*; Lindsay Bell *(Local Government Finance)*; Andrew Campbell *(Local Strategic Partnerships and Performance)*; Andrew Wells *(New Homes and Sustainable Development)*; Neil McDonald *(Planning Policy)*; Mark Carroll *(Race, Faith and Cohesion)*; Teresa Vokes *(Regional and Cross Government Delivery)*; Mark Kleinman *(Regional, Urban and Economic Policy)*
Chief Executive of Thames Gateway and Olympics, Judith Armitt

DEPARTMENT FOR CULTURE, MEDIA AND SPORT

2–4 Cockspur Street, London SW1Y 5DH
T 020-7211 6200 F 020-7211 6032
E enquiries@culture.gov.uk W www.culture.gov.uk

The Department for Culture, Media and Sport (DCMS) was established in July 1997 and aims to improve the quality of life for all those in the UK through cultural and sporting activities while championing the tourism, creative and leisure industries. It is responsible for government policy relating to the arts, sport, the National Lottery, tourism, libraries, museums and galleries, broadcasting, creative industries – including film and the music industry – press freedom and regulation, licensing, gambling and the historic environment.

The department is also responsible for 63 public bodies that help deliver the department's strategic aims and objectives, the 2012 Olympic Games and Paralympic Games, the listing of historic buildings and scheduling of ancient monuments, the export licensing of cultural goods, and the management of the Government Art Collection and the Royal Parks (its sole executive agency). In May 2005 the DCMS assumed responsibility for fashion design, advertising and the arts market from the then Department for Trade and Industry – now the Department for Business, Enterprise and Regulatory Reform – which it also works jointly with on design issues (including sponsorship of the Design Council) and on relations with the computer games and publishing industries.

Secretary of State for Culture, Media and Sport, Rt. Hon. James Purnell, MP
Principal Private Secretary, Rita Patel
Special Advisers, vacant
Parliamentary Private Secretary, Gordon Banks, MP
Minister of State, Rt. Hon. Margaret Hodge, MBE, MP *(Culture, Creative Industries and Tourism)*
Private Secretary, James Bird
Parliamentary Private Secretary, Derek Wyatt, MP
Parliamentary Under-Secretary of State, Gerry Sutcliffe, MP *(Sport)*
Private Secretary, vacant
Permanent Secretary, Jonathan Stephens
Private Secretary, Sarah Taylor

MANAGEMENT BOARD
Chair, Jonathan Stephens
Directors-General, Andrew Ramsay, CB *(Culture, Creativity and Economy)*; Jeremy Beeton *(Government Olympic Executive)*
Chief Operating Officer, Nicholas Holgate
Directors, Anita Charlesworth *(Active Generation)*; Jon Zeff

(Broadcasting); Paddy Feeny *(Communications)*; Alan Davey *(Culture)*; David Goldstone *(Finance)*; Brian Leonard *(Industry)*; Patrick Kilgarriff *(Legal)*; Andrew Lean *(Olympics)*; Nicky Roche *(Olympics)*; David Roe *(Strategy)*
Non-Executive Directors, Clive Elphick; Parminder Vir
Royal Parks Chief Executive, Mark Camley

MINISTRY OF DEFENCE
see Defence section

DEPARTMENT FOR ENVIRONMENT, FOOD AND RURAL AFFAIRS
Nobel House, 17 Smith Square, London SW1P 3JR
T 020-7238 3000 **F** 020-7238 6591
Helpline 0845-933 5577
E helpline@defra.gsi.gov.uk **W** www.defra.gov.uk
The Department for Environment, Food and Rural Affairs (DEFRA) is responsible for government policy on the environment, rural matters, farming and food production; its central aim is sustainable development. In association with the agriculture departments of the Scottish Executive, the National Assembly for Wales and the Northern Ireland Office, and with the Intervention Board, the department is responsible for negotiations in the EU on the common agricultural and fisheries policies, and for single European market questions relating to its responsibilities. Its remit includes international agricultural and food trade policy.

The department's five strategic priorities, published in *DEFRA's Five-Year Strategy: Delivering the Essentials of Life*, are climate change and energy; sustainable consumption and production; the protection of natural resources and the countryside; sustainable rural communities; and sustainable farming and food, including animal health and welfare. DEFRA is also the lead government department for emergencies in animal and plant diseases, flooding, food and water supply, dealing with the consequences of a chemical, biological, radiological or nuclear incident, and certain other threats to the environment.

Secretary of State for Environment, Food and Rural Affairs, Rt. Hon. Hilary Benn, MP
Principal Private Secretary, Rory O'Donnell
Private Secretaries, Beth Crook; Rebecca Evernden; Sharee Samuel
Parliamentary Private Secretary, Dr Ashok Kumar, MP
Minister of State, Phil Woolas, MP *(Environment)*
Senior Private Secretary, Neil Hornby
Private Secretary, Kathryn Wood
Parliamentary Private Secretary, Nia Griffith, MP
Minister of State, Rt. Hon. Lord Rooker *(Sustainable Food and Farming, and Animal Health)*
Senior Private Secretary, Rhian Mewis
Private Secretaries, Amelia Munn; Vincent Venturotti
Parliamentary Under-Secretary of State, Joan Ruddock, MP *(Climate Change, Biodiversity and Waste)*
Senior Private Secretary, Naomi Matthiessen
Private Secretaries, Liz Kitchen; David Miller
Parliamentary Under-Secretary of State, Jonathan Shaw, MP *(Marine, Landscape and Rural Affairs)*
Senior Private Secretary, Deborah Wells
Private Secretaries, Anna Sanders; Joe Speck
Permanent Secretary, Helen Ghosh
Private Secretary, Jenny McClelland

MANAGEMENT BOARD
Chair, Helen Ghosh *(Permanent Secretary)*

Directors-General, Prof. Howard Dalton *(Chief Scientific Adviser)*; Mike Anderson *(Climate Change)*; Ian Grattidge *(Finance)*; Andy Lebrecht *(Food and Farming)*; Debby Reynolds *(Food and Farming, and Chief Veterinary Officer)*; Gill Aitken *(Legal Services, and Solicitor)*; Peter Unwin *(Natural Environment Group)*; Liz Sands *(Renew Programme)*; Andrew Burchell *(Service Transformation)*; Bill Stow *(Strategy and Evidence)*
Non-Executive Members, Bill Griffiths; Janet Grossman

FOREIGN AND COMMONWEALTH OFFICE
King Charles Street, London SW1A 2AH
T 020-7008 1500 **W** www.fco.gov.uk
The Foreign and Commonwealth Office (FCO) provides, through its staff in the UK and through its diplomatic missions abroad, the means of communication between the British government and other governments – and international governmental organisations – on all matters falling within the field of international relations.

It is responsible for alerting the British government to the implications of developments overseas; promoting British interests overseas; protecting British citizens abroad; explaining British policies to, and cultivating relationships with, governments overseas; the discharge of British responsibilities to the overseas territories; entry clearance UK visas (with the Home Office); and promoting British business overseas (jointly with the Department for Business, Enterprise and Regulatory Reform through UK Trade and Investment).

Secretary of State for Foreign and Commonwealth Affairs, Rt. Hon. David Miliband, MP
Principal Private Secretary, Matthew Gould
Special Advisers, Ravi Gurumurthy; Madlin Sadler; Sarah Schaefer
Parliamentary Private Secretary, Dan Norris, MP
Minister of State, Jim Murphy, MP *(Europe)*
Private Secretary, Nicholas Catsaras
Parliamentary Private Secretary, Neil Turner, MP
Minister of State, Dr Kim Howells, MP *(Middle East)*
Private Secretary, Scott Furssedonn
Parliamentary Private Secretary, John Robertson, MP
Minister of State, Lord Jones of Birmingham *(Trade and Investment)*
Minister of State, Lord Malloch-Brown, KCMG *(Africa, Asia and the UN)*
Private Secretary, Craig Fulton
Parliamentary Private Secretary, Andy Slaughter, MP
Parliamentary Under-Secretary of State, Meg Munn, MP
Private Secretary, Darren James
Permanent Under-Secretary of State and Head of HM Diplomatic Service, Sir Peter Ricketts, CMG
Private Secretary, Jill Parkinson
Group Chief Executive, UK Trade and Investment, Andrew Cahn
Directors-General, Dickie Stagg, CMG *(Change and Delivery)*; David Richmond, CMG *(Defence / Intelligence)*; Nicola Brewer, CMG *(EU Policy)*; Martin Donnelly, CMG *(Europe and Globalisation)*; Keith Luck *(Finance)*; Mark Lyall Grant *(Political)*; Daniel Bethlehem *(Legal Adviser)*
Non-Executive Board Members, Alistair Johnson; Alison Platt

SENIOR PERSONNEL
Directors, Andrew Lloyd *(Africa)*; Chris Wood *(Americas)*; John Dennis *(Asia)*; Sebastian Wood *(Asia Pacific)*;

Lucian Hudson *(Communications, and Press Secretary)*;
Rob Macaire *(Consular Services)*; Mariot Leslie *(Defence
and Strategic Threats)*; Geoff Gillham *(Estates)*; Anthony
Smith *(European Political Affairs)*; Shan Morgan
(European Union); Ric Todd *(Finance)*; Scott Wightman
(Global and Economic Issues); Darren Warren *(Human
Resources)*; Tony Mather *(Information and Technology)*;
Stephen Pattison *(International Security)*; Simon
McDonald *(Iraq)*; Peter Gooderham *(Middle East and
North Africa)*; Judith Gregor *(Migration)*; Sarah Gillot
(Protocol); Simon Smith *(Russia, South Caucasus and
Central Asia)*; Andrew Noble *(Security)*; Adam
Thomson *(South Asia and Afghanistan)*; Anne Pringle,
CMG *(Strategy and Information)*; Mark Sedwell *(UK
Visas)*
Chief Executive, FCO Services, Chris Moxey
Legal Adviser, Sir Michael Wood, KCMG

UK SPECIAL REPRESENTATIVES
Afghanistan, Tom Phillips, CMG
Climate Change, John Ashton
South Caucasus, Sir Brian Fall, KCMG
Sudan, Rod Pullen

UK VISAS (JOINT FCO/HOME OFFICE DIRECTORATE)
Directors-General, Dickie Stagg, CMG *(Corporate Affairs)*;
Lin Homer *(Immigration and Nationality Directorate)*
Director, UK Visas, Mark Sedwill
Head of Directorate, Mandie Campbell

DEPARTMENT OF HEALTH
Richmond House, 79 Whitehall, London SW1A 2NS
T 020-7210 3000
W www.dh.gov.uk
The Department of Health is responsible for the provision
of the National Health Service (NHS) in England and for
social care. The department's aims are to support, protect,
promote and improve the nation's health; to secure the
provision of comprehensive, high-quality care for all
those who need it, regardless of their ability to pay, where
they live or their age; and to provide responsive social care
and child protection for those who lack the support they
need.
The Department of Health is responsible for setting
health and social care policy in England. The department's
work sets standards and drives modernisation across all
areas of the NHS, social care and public health.
Secretary of State for Health, Rt. Hon. Alan Johnson,
MP
Principal Private Secretary, Clara Swinson
Parliamentary Private Secretary, Laura Moffat, MP
Minister of State, Ben Bradshaw, MP *(Health Services)*
Private Secretary, Kirsten Hubble
Parliamentary Private Secretary, Rosie Cooper, MP
Minister of State, Rt. Hon. Dawn Primarolo, MP *(Public
Health)*
Private Secretary, Sarah Hall
Parliamentary Private Secretary, Helen Jones, MP
Parliamentary Under-Secretary of State, Prof. Lord Darzi,
KBE
Private Secretary, Julia Scott
Parliamentary Under-Secretary of State, Ivan Lewis, MP
(Care Services)
Private Secretary, Edward Scully
Parliamentary Under-Secretary of State, Ann Keen, MP
(Health)

Private Secretary, Thomas Strickland
Parliamentary Clerk, Tim Elms

DEPARTMENTAL BOARD MEMBERS
Chief Executive of the NHS, David Nicholson, CBE
Permanent Secretary of State, Hugh Taylor, CB
Chief Medical Officer, Prof. Sir Liam Donaldson, KB
Directors-General, Chan Wheeler *(Commercial)*; Mark
Britnell *(Commissioning and System Management)*; Sian
Jarvis *(Communications)*; Alan Doran *(Departmental
Management)*; Richard Douglas *(Finance and
Investment)*; Richard Granger *(IT)*; David Flory *(NHS
Finance, Performance and Operations)*; Una O'Brien
(Policy and Strategy, acting); David Behan *(Social Care,
Local Government and Care Partnerships)*; Prof.
Christine Beasley, CBE *(Chief Nursing Officer, and
Director-General of User Experience and Involvement,
and Professional Leadership)*; Clare Chapman
(Workforce)
Non-Executive Directors, Julie Baddeley; Derek Myers;
Mike Wheeler

NON-BOARD DIRECTORS
Deputy Chief Medical Officer, Dr Fiona Adshead
Director for Equality and Human Rights, Surinder Sharma
National Director for Social Care, Kathryn Hudson

NATIONAL CLINICAL DIRECTORS
Cancer, Prof. Mike Richards
Children, Dr Sheila Shribman
Diabetes, Dr Sue Roberts
Emergency Access, Prof. Sir George Alberti
Heart Disease and Stroke, Dr Roger Boyle
Kidney Services, Donal J. O'Donoghue
Learning Disabilities, Nicola Smith
Mental Health, Prof. Louis Appleby
Older People's Services, Ian Philp
Pandemic Influenza Preparedness, Prof. Lindsey Davies
Patients and the Public, Harry Cayton
Primary Care, David Colin-Thome
Valuing People, Rob Greig
Widening Participation in Learning, Prof. Bob Fryer, CBE

SOLICITOR'S OFFICE, DEPARTMENT FOR WORK AND
PENSIONS
Solicitor, Richard Heaton
Director of Legal Services, John Catlin; Greer Kerrigan, CB

SPECIAL HEALTH AUTHORITIES

HEALTH PROTECTION AGENCY
W www.hpa.org.uk
MENTAL HEALTH ACT COMMISSION
W www.mhac.org.uk
NATIONAL BLOOD SERVICE
W www.blood.co.uk
NATIONAL CLINICAL ASSESSMENT SERVICE
W www.ncas.nhs.uk
NATIONAL INSTITUTE FOR CLINICAL
EXCELLENCE
W www.nice.org.uk
NATIONAL TREATMENT AGENCY FOR
SUBSTANCE MISUSE
W www.nta.nhs.uk
NATIONAL PATIENT SAFETY AGENCY
W www.npsa.nhs.uk

NHS APPOINTMENTS COMMISSION
W www.appointments.org.uk
NHS BUSINESS SERVICES AUTHORITY
W www.nhsbsa.nhs.uk
NHS LITIGATION AUTHORITY
W www.nhsla.com
UK TRANSPLANT
W www.uktransplant.org.uk

HOME OFFICE
2 Marsham Street, London SW1P 4DF
T 020-7035 4848 F 020-7035 4745
E public.enquiries@homeoffice.gsi.gov.uk
W www.homeoffice.gov.uk
The Home Office deals with those internal affairs in England and Wales which have not been assigned to other government departments. The Secretary of State for the Home Department is the link between the Queen and the public, and exercises certain powers on her behalf, including that of the royal pardon.

The Home Office aims to build a safe, just and tolerant society and to maintain and enhance public security and protection; to support and mobilise communities so that they are able to shape policy and improvement for their locality, overcome nuisance and anti-social behaviour, maintain and enhance social cohesion and enjoy their homes and public spaces peacefully; to deliver departmental policies and responsibilities fairly, effectively and efficiently; and to make the best use of resources. These objectives reflect the priorities of the government and the home secretary in areas of crime, citizenship and communities, namely to reduce crime and the fear of crime through visible, responsive and accountable policing; to reduce organised and international crime; to combat terrorism and other threats to national security; to ensure the effective delivery of justice; to reduce re-offending and protect the public; to reduce the availability and abuse of dangerous drugs; to regulate entry to, and settlement in, the UK in the interests of sustainable growth and social inclusion; and to support strong, active communities in which people of all races and backgrounds are valued and participate on equal terms.

The Home Office delivers these aims through the immigration services, its agencies and non-departmental public bodies, and by working with partners in private, public and voluntary sectors, individuals and communities. The home secretary is also the link between the UK government and the governments of the Channel Islands and the Isle of Man.

Secretary of State for the Home Department, Rt. Hon. Jacqui Smith, MP
Principal Private Secretary, Richard Westlake
Private Secretaries, Chris Felton; Mark Williams; Paul Wylie
Special Adviser, Susan Jackson
Minister of State, Tony McNulty, MP *(Security, Counter-Terrorism, Crime and Policing)*
Private Secretary, Neil Roberts
Minister of State, Liam Byrne, MP *(Borders and Immigration)*
Private Secretary, Thomas Grieg
Parliamentary Under-Secretary of State, Lord West of Spithead *(Security and Counter-Terrorism)*
Private Secretary, Caroline Smith
Parliamentary Under-Secretary of State, Vernon Coaker, MP *(Crime Reduction)*

Private Secretary, Suzanne Jacob
Parliamentary Under-Secretary of State, Meg Hiller, MP *(Identity)*
Private Secretary, Jacob Hawkins
Permanent Secretary of State, Sir David Normington, KCB
Private Secretary, Isobel Arthur
Parliamentary Clerk, Phil Rawlinson

HOME OFFICE BOARD MEMBERS
Permanent Secretary of State, Sir David Normington, KCB *(Chair)*
Chief Executive of Border and Immigration Agency, Lin Homer
Chief Executive of Office for Criminal Justice Reform, Ursula Brennan
Director-General of Crime, Policing and Counter-Terrorism, Moira Wallace
Director-General of Financial and Commercial, Helen Kilpatrick
Director-General of Performance and Reform, Peter Makeham
Group Director of Human Resources, Kevin White
Non-Executive Members, Derrick Anderson; Patrick Carter

COMMUNICATION DIRECTORATE
Director, Julia Simpson
Head of News (Press Office), Michael Winders

SHARED SERVICES DIRECTORATE
Director, David Myers

STRATEGY AND REFORM DIRECTORATE
Director, Peter Makeham

CRIME REDUCTION AND COMMUNITY SAFETY GROUP
Director-General, Moira Wallace
Directors, Vanessa Nicholls *(Crime Drug Strategy)*; Paul Evans *(Police and Crime Standards)*; Vic Hogg *(Policing Policy and Operations)*; Stephen Kershaw *(Police Reform and Resources)*; Alastair Bridges *(Strategic Support)*

OFFICE FOR SECURITY AND COUNTER-TERRORISM
Director-General, Charles Farr
Directors, William Nye; Jaee Samant; Stephen Smith

OFFICE FOR CRIMINAL JUSTICE REFORM
Chief Executive, Ursula Brennan
Directors, Stephen Jenner *(Criminal Justice IT, acting)*; Catherine Lee *(Delivery and Communications, acting)*; David Wood *(Policy and Process)*; Jonathan Sedgwick *(Strategy and Planning)*

Note: The OCJR is a cross-departmental organisation, also reporting to the Ministry of Justice and the Office of the Attorney-General

HUMAN RESOURCES DIRECTORATE
Director, Kevin White
Directors, Dusty Amroliwala *(Services)*; Mandie Campbell *(Leadership and Learning)*

BORDER AND IMMIGRATION AGENCY
Chief Executive, Lin Homer
Deputy Chief Executive, Ken Sutton
Strategic Directors, Matthew Coats *(Asylum)*; Brodie Clark *(Borders)*; Jonathan Lindley *(Enforcement)*; Joe Dugdale *(HR and Organisational Development)*; Paula Higson

(Managed Migration); Justin Holiday *(Resource Management)*

LEGAL ADVISERS' BRANCH
Senior Legal Adviser, David Seymour
Deputy Legal Advisers, Steven Bramley; Iain Macleod

PERFORMANCE AND FINANCE DIRECTORATE
Director, Peter Kane

INTERNATIONAL DIRECTORATE
Director, Peter Storr

COMMERCIAL DIRECTORATE
Director, John Collington

SCIENCE AND RESEARCH GROUP
Director and Chief Scientific Adviser, Prof. Paul Wiles

DEPARTMENT FOR INNOVATION, UNIVERSITIES AND SKILLS

1 Victoria Street, London SW1H 0ET
T 020-7215 5555 W www.dfid.gov.uk
The Department for Innovation, Universities and Skills (DIUS) was established in June 2007, and brings together functions from the former Department for Trade and Industry – including responsibilities for science and innovation – with functions from the former Department for Education and Skills (further and higher education and skills). The DIUS works particularly closely with the Department for Business, Enterprise and Regulatory Reform and with the Department for Children, Schools and Families.

The DIUS aims to sustain and develop a world-class research base; maximise the exploitation of said base to support innovation across all sectors of the economy; increase and widen participation in higher education; raise participation and attainment by young people and adults in post-16 education and learning; reduce the skills gap amongst adults, particularly in terms of numeracy and literacy; and increase the supply of people in the fields of science, technology, engineering and mathematics.
Secretary of State for Innovation, Universities and Skills, Rt. Hon. John Denham, MP
Principal Private Secretary, Claire Burton
Private Secretary, Kate McAleenan
Parliamentary Private Secretary, Lyn Brown, MP
Minister of State, Ian Pearson, MP *(Science and Innovation)*
Private Secretary, Georgiana Glaysher
Parliamentary Private Secretary, Celia Barlow, MP
Minister of State, Bill Rammell, MP *(Lifelong Learning, Further and Higher Education)*
Private Secretary, Lisa Glover
Parliamentary Private Secretary, David Anderson, MP
Parliamentary Under-Secretary of State, David Lammy, MP *(Skills)*
Private Secretary, Luke Owen
Parliamentary Under-Secretary of State, Lord Triesman *(Intellectual Property and Quality)*
Private Secretary, Francesca Orpen

MANAGEMENT BOARD
Permanent Secretary, Ian Watmore *(Chair)*
Government Chief Scientific Adviser and Head of Government Office for Science, Prof. Sir David King
Directors-General, Simon Morys *(Business Operations)*; Nick Edmonds *(Finance and Performance)*; Stephen Marston *(Further Education and Skills)*; Ruth Thompson

(Higher Education); Shirley Pointer *(Human Resources)*; Sir Keith O'Nions *(Science and Innovation)*; Zina Etheridge *(Strategy and Communications)*

SENIOR STAFF
Directors, David Williams *(British National Space Centre)*; Susan Pember *(Further Education and Skills Performance Group)*; Jeremy Clayton *(Government Office for Science)*; Martin Williams *(Higher Education Strategy)*; John Landeryou *(Improvement Group)*; Win Harris *(Joint International Unit)*; Jeff Llewellyn *(National Weights and Measures Laboratory)*; John Neilson *(Research Base)*; Stephen Hillier *(Skills Group)*; Michael Hipkins *(Student Finance Strategy)*; David Evans *(Technology and Innovation)*; Ian Fletcher *(UK Intellectual Property Office)*

DEPARTMENT FOR INTERNATIONAL DEVELOPMENT

1 Palace Street, London SW1 5HE
T 020-7023 0000 F 020-7023 0016
Abercrombie House, Eaglesham Road, East Kilbride, Glasgow G75 8EA T 01355-844000 F 01355-844099
Public Enquiries 0845-300 4100
E enquiry@dfid.gov.uk W www.dfid.gov.uk
The Department for International Development (DFID) is responsible for promoting sustainable development and reducing poverty. The central focus of the government's policy, based on the 1997, 2000 and 2006 white papers on international development, is a commitment to the internationally agreed Millennium Development Goals, to be achieved by 2015. These seek to eradicate extreme poverty and hunger; achieve universal primary education; promote gender equality and empower women; reduce child mortality; improve maternal health; combat HIV/AIDS, malaria and other diseases; ensure environmental sustainability; and encourage a global partnership for development.

DFID's assistance is concentrated in the poorest countries of sub-Saharan Africa and Asia, but also contributes to poverty reduction and sustainable development in middle-income countries, including those in Latin America and Eastern Europe. The department works in partnership with governments committed to the Millennium Development Goals, and with the private sector and the research community. It also works with multilateral institutions, including the World Bank, United Nations agencies and the European Commission. The department has headquarters in London and East Kilbride, offices in many developing countries, and staff based in British embassies and high commissions around the world.
Secretary of State for International Development, Rt. Hon. Douglas Alexander, MP
Principal Private Secretary, Howard Taylor
Private Secretary, Helen Winterton
Special Advisers, Paul Sinclair; Anthony Vigor
Parliamentary Private Secretary, Kerry McCarthy, MP
Parliamentary Clerk, Richard Haviland
Parliamentary Under-Secretary of State, Gareth R. Thomas, MP *(also a minister with BERR)*
Private Secretary, Eleanor Briers
Parliamentary Under-Secretary of State, Shahid Malik, MP
Private Secretary, Charlotte Pierre
Parliamentary Under-Secretary of State, Baroness Vadera
Private Secretary, Hugh Walker
House of Lords Spokesperson, Baroness Amos
Liaison Peer, Baroness Whitaker

Whips, Bob Blizzard, MP *(Commons)*; Baroness Royall *(Lords)*
Permanent Secretary, Suma Chakrabarti

MANAGEMENT BOARD
Directors-General, Sue Owen *(Corporate Performance and Knowledge Sharing)*; Mark Lowcock *(Policy and International)*; Minouche Shafik *(Regional Programmes)*
Non-Executive Directors, Helen Ghosh; Bill Griffiths

DIVISIONS
Directors, Paul Mylrea *(Communications)*; Dave Fish *(East and Central Africa)*; Sue Wardell *(Europe, Middle East, Americas, Central and East Asia Division)*; Sam Sharpe *(Finance and Corporate Performance)*; Owen Barder *(Global Development Effectiveness)*; Liz Davies *(Human Resources)*; Marcus Manuel *(Pan-Africa Strategy and Programmes)*; Andrew Steer *(Policy and Research)*; Jim Drummond *(South Asia)*; Martin Dinham *(UN, Conflict and Humanitarian)*; Beverley Warmington *(West and Southern Africa)*

CDC GROUP
6 Duke Street, London SW1Y 6BN
T 020-7484 7700 W www.cdcgroup.com

Founded in 1948, CDC is a government-owned fund of funds that provides capital to invest through third-party fund managers in private equity funds focused on emerging economies; it covers countries in Africa, Asia and Latin America. CDC is a public limited company with the Department for International Development as its 100 per cent shareholder.
Chair, Sir Malcolm Williamson
Chief Executive, Richard Laing

MINISTRY OF JUSTICE
Selbourne House, 54 Victoria Street, London SW1E 6QW
T 020-7210 8500 E general.enquiries@justice.gsi.gov.uk
W www.justice.gov.uk
The Ministry of Justice (MoJ) was established in May 2007 and the responsibilities of the Department for Constitutional Affairs (DCA) were transferred to it. The MoJ's priorities are to protect the public; reduce reoffending; promote and provide access to justice; engender confidence in the justice system; uphold people's human rights, alongside their information and democratic rights; and to safeguard and modernise the constitution.
The MoJ incorporates the National Offender Management Service, which includes HM Prison Service and the National Probation Service, and the Office for Criminal Justice Reform (a cross-departmental organisation also reporting to the Home Office and the Office of the Attorney-General). In April 2006 the largest central government tribunals were incorporated into the MoJ (then, the DCA) as the Tribunals Service (*see* Tribunals section). The remit of the Lord Chancellor was also altered: he continues to be the government minister responsible to parliament for the judiciary and the courts system, but is no longer the head of the judiciary. The Lord Chief Justice has taken on the role of head of the judiciary and now performs many of the judicial functions formerly undertaken by the Lord Chancellor.
The MoJ established an independent Judicial Appointments Commission and related bodies, and retains its association with several associated departments, non-departmental public bodies and executive agencies, including the Northern Ireland Court Service, Her

Majesty's Land Registry, the National Archives, the Legal Service Commission, and the Public Guardianship Office. The administrative functions of the Scotland Office and the Wales Office transferred to the MoJ in June 2003. Responsibilities for the maintenance of the relationship between Westminster and the devolved administrations in Edinburgh and Cardiff remain with the Secretary of State for Scotland and the Secretary of State for Wales respectively.
Secretary of State for Justice and Lord Chancellor, Rt. Hon. Jack Straw, MP
Principal Private Secretary, Antonia Romeo
Special Advisers, Mark Davies; Declan McHugh
Parliamentary Private Secretary, Mark Hendrick, MP
Minister of State, Rt. Hon. David Hanson, MP
Private Secretary, Philip Lawley
Parliamentary Private Secretary, Lynda Waltho, MP
Minister of State, Michael Wills, MP
Private Secretary, Martyn Taylor
Parliamentary Private Secretary, Gordon Marsden, MP
Parliamentary Under-Secretary of State, Lord Hunt of Kings Heath, OBE
Private Secretary, Alexandra Knapton
Parliamentary Under-Secretary of State, Bridget Prentice, MP
Private Secretary, Adam Rothapel
Parliamentary Under-Secretary of State, Maria Eagle, MP
Private Secretary, Dileeni Daniel-Selvaratnam
Permanent Secretary, Alex Allan
Private Secretary, Jennifer Hepker
Parliamentary Clerk, Ann Nixon

MINISTRY OF JUSTICE BOARD
Chair, Rt. Hon. Jack Straw, MP *(Lord Chancellor and Secretary of State for Justice)*
Members, MoJ Ministers of State; MoJ Parliamentary Under-Secretaries of State; Peter Brook *(Director-General, Financial and Commercial, acting)*; Sir Ron de Witt *(Chief Executive, HM Courts Service)*; Phil Wheatley *(Director-General, HM Prison Service for England and Wales)*; John Lyon, CB *(Director-General, Legal and Judicial)*; Carolyn Regan *(Chief Executive, Legal Services Commission)*; Helen Edwards *(Chief Executive, National Offender Management Service)*; Ursula Brennan *(Chief Executive, Office for Criminal Justice Reform)*; Alex Allan *(Permanent Secretary)*; Rod Clark *(Director-General, Strategy)*
Non-Executive Directors, Sir Peter Bonfield; Prof. George M. Selim

DEPARTMENTAL MANAGEMENT BOARD
Chair, Alex Allan *(Permanent Secretary)*
Members, Yvonne Gallagher *(Chief Information Officer)*; Peter Brook *(Director-General, Financial and Commercial, acting)*; Sir Ron de Witt *(Chief Executive, HM Courts Service)*; Phil Wheatley *(Director-General, HM Prison Service for England and Wales)*; Beverley Shears *(Human Resources, Director)*; John Lyon, CB *(Director-General, Legal and Judicial)*; Carolyn Regan *(Chief Executive, Legal Services Commission)*; Helen Edwards *(Chief Executive, National Offender Management Service)*; Ursula Brennan *(Chief Executive, Office for Criminal Justice Reform)*; Rod Clark *(Director-General, Strategy)*; Peter Handcock, CBE *(Chief Executive, The Tribunals Service)*

LORD CHANCELLOR'S DEPARTMENT
See Ministry of Justice

NORTHERN IRELAND OFFICE

11 Millbank, London SW1P 4PN
T 020-7210 3000
Castle Buildings, Stormont, Belfast BT4 3SG
T 028-9052 0700 E mail@nio.gov.uk
W www.nio.gov.uk

The Northern Ireland Office was established in 1972, when the Northern Ireland (Temporary Provisions) Act transferred the legislative and executive powers of the Northern Ireland parliament and government to the UK parliament and a secretary of state.

The Northern Ireland Office is responsible primarily for security issues, law and order and prisons, and for matters relating to the political and constitutional future of the province. It also deals with international issues as they affect Northern Ireland.

Under the terms of the 1998 Good Friday Agreement, power was devolved to the Northern Ireland Assembly in 1999. The assembly took on responsibility for the relevant areas of work previously undertaken by the departments of the Northern Ireland Office, covering agriculture and rural development, the environment, regional development, social development, education, higher education, training and employment, enterprise, trade and investment, culture, arts and leisure, health, social services, public safety and finance and personnel. In October 2002 the Northern Ireland Assembly was suspended and Northern Ireland returned to direct rule, but despite repeated setbacks, devolution was restored on 8 May 2007. For further details, *see* Regional Government section.

Secretary of State for Northern Ireland, Rt. Hon. Shaun Woodward, MP
Parliamentary Private Secretary, Rob Marris, MP
Minister of State, Paul Goggins, MP
Parliamentary Private Secretary, vacant
Permanent Secretary, Jonathan Phillips
Head of the Northern Ireland Civil Service, Nigel Hamilton

NORTHERN IRELAND INFORMATION SERVICE
Castle Buildings, Stormont Estate, Belfast BT4 3SG
T 028-9052 0700

OFFICE OF THE ADVOCATE-GENERAL FOR SCOTLAND

Dover House, Whitehall, London SW1A 2AU
T 020-7270 6720 F 020-7270 6813
1 Melville Crescent, Edinburgh EH3 7HW
T 0131-244 9033 F 0131-244 9034
E ps/advocategeneral@scotland.gsi.gov.uk
W www.oag.gov.uk

The Advocate-General for Scotland is one of the three law officers of the crown, alongside the Attorney-General and the Solicitor-General for England and Wales. He is the legal adviser to the UK government on Scottish law and is supported by staff in the Office of the Advocate-General for Scotland.

The post was created as a consequence of the constitutional changes set out in the Scotland Act 1998, which created a devolved Scottish parliament. The Lord Advocate and the Solicitor-General for Scotland were then transferred to the Scottish Executive and the Advocate-General took over their previous role as legal adviser to the government on Scottish law. *See also* Regional Government section and Ministry of Justice.

Advocate-General for Scotland, Lord Davidson of Glen Clova, QC
Private Secretary, Chris Fawcett

OFFICE OF THE LEADER OF THE HOUSE OF COMMONS

26 Whitehall, London SW1A 2WH
T 020-7276 1005 F 020-7276 1006
E leader@commonsleader.x.gsi.gov.uk
W www.commonsleader.gov.uk

The Office of the Leader of the House of Commons is responsible for the arrangement of government business in the House of Commons and for planning and supervising the government's legislative programme. The Leader of the House of Commons upholds the rights and privileges of the house and acts as a spokesperson for the government as a whole.

The leader reports regularly to the cabinet on parliamentary business and the legislative programme. In her capacity as leader of the house, she is a member of the Public Accounts Commission and of the House of Commons Commission. She also chairs the cabinet committee on the legislative programme. As Lord Privy Seal, she is chair of the board of trustees of the Chevening Estate.

The Deputy Leader of the House of Commons supports the leader in handling the government's business in the house. She is responsible for monitoring MPs' and peers' correspondence and is a member of several committees, including the Ministerial Committee on the Law Commission.

Leader of the House of Commons and Lord Privy Seal, Rt. Hon. Harriet Harman, QC, MP
Principal Private Secretary, Stephen Hillcoat
Private Secretary, Mike Winter
Deputy Leader of the House of Commons, Helen Goodman, MP
Private Secretary, Frances Slee

PRIVY COUNCIL OFFICE

2 Carlton Gardens, London SW1Y 5AA
T 020-7210 1033 F 020-7210 1071
W www.privy-council.gov.uk

The office is responsible for the arrangements leading to the making of all royal proclamations and orders in council; for certain formalities connected with ministerial changes; for considering applications for the granting (or amendment) of royal charters; for the scrutiny and approval of by-laws and statutes of chartered bodies; and for the appointment of high sheriffs and many crown and Privy Council appointments to governing bodies.

The Lord President of the Council presides at meetings of the Privy Council, is a member of the cabinet and Leader of the House of Lords. She has no departmental portfolio but is a member of several cabinet committees, and supports the Lord Chancellor in his responsibility for the House of Lords reform. She is the Lords' spokesperson on equality and human rights issues, and is responsible to the prime minister for the organisation of government business in the house as well as repeating in the House of Lords statements made by the prime minister in the House of Commons. She also gives guidance to the house on matters of order and procedure.

Lord President of the Council (and Leader of the House of Lords), Baroness Ashton of Upholland, PC
Principal Private Secretary, Tanya Ferguson
Clerk of the Council, Judith Simpson
Head of Secretariat, Ceri King
Senior Clerks, Christopher Berry; Meriel McCullagh
Registrar of the Judicial Committee, Mary MacDonald

SCOTLAND OFFICE

Dover House, Whitehall, London SW1A 2AU
T 020-7270 6754 F 020-7270 6812
1 Melville Crescent, Edinburgh EH3 7HW
T 0131-244 9010 F 0131-244 9028
E scottish.secretary@scotland.gsi.gov.uk
W www.scotlandoffice.gov.uk

The Scotland Office is the department of the Secretary of State for Scotland which represents Scottish interests within the UK government in matters reserved to the UK parliament. The Secretary of State for Scotland also exercises certain specific functions in relation to devolution, including those provided for in the Scotland Act 1998; maintains the stability of the devolution settlement for Scotland; and pays grants to the Scottish Consolidated Fund and manages other financial transactions.

Reserved matters include the constitution, foreign affairs, defence, international development, the civil service, financial and economic matters, national security, immigration and nationality, misuse of drugs, trade and industry, various aspects of energy regulation (eg coal, electricity, oil, gas and nuclear energy), various aspects of transport, social security, employment, abortion, genetics, surrogacy, medicines, broadcasting and equal opportunities. Devolved matters include health and social work, education and training, local government and housing, justice and police, agriculture, forestry, fisheries, the environment, tourism, sports, heritage, economic development and internal transport. *See also* Regional Government section and Ministry of Justice.

Secretary of State for Scotland, Rt. Hon. Des Browne, MP
Private Secretary, Amy Bishop
Parliamentary Private Secretary, Russell Brown, MP
Minister of State, David Cairns, MP
Private Secretary, Amy Bishop
Parliamentary Private Secretary, Mike Lazarowicz, MP
Spokesperson in the House of Lords, Lord Evans of Temple Guiting, CBE

DEPARTMENT FOR TRANSPORT

Great Minster House, 76 Marsham Street, London SW1P 4DR
T 020-7944 8300 W www.dft.gov.uk

The Department for Transport (DfT) was established in May 2002 following the de-merger of the Department of Transport, Local Government and the Regions. The department's role is to oversee the delivery of a reliable, safe and secure transport system and to determine overall transport strategy; its main responsibilities are aviation, freight, health and safety, integrated and local transport, London Underground, maritime, mobility and inclusion, railways, roads and road safety, shipping and vehicles.

The DfT's work is focused around the following tasks: improving the current operation and capacity of transport networks and services, and providing better information for travellers; shaping the future pattern of demand for transport, including through land-use planning and appropriate pricing; tackling the environmental impact of transport through pricing, regulation, technology, consumer information and promoting efficient use of resources; planning and managing long-term investment programmes; regulating and licensing certain transport services and operators; and managing information and delivering services to support wider government objectives.

Secretary of State for Transport, Rt. Hon Ruth Kelly, MP
Principal Private Secretary, Lara Sherwin
Minister of State, Rt. Hon. Rosie Winterton, MP

Private Secretary, Peter Lee
Parliamentary Under-Secretary of State, Tom Harris, MP
Private Secretary, Roy Cahill
Parliamentary Under-Secretary of State, Jim Fitzpatrick, MP
Private Secretary, Eamonn Beirne
Permanent Secretary, Robert Devereux
Private Secretary, Suzanne Roddie

MANAGEMENT BOARD
Chair, Robert Devereux
Members, Ann Hemingway *(Non-Executive)*; Barbara Moorhouse; Archie Robertson; Deborah Williams *(Non-Executive)*

SENIOR STAFF
Directors-General, Bronwyn Hill *(City and Regional Networks Group)*; Barbara Moorhouse *(Corporate Resources)*; Simon Webb *(International Networks and Environment)*; Mike Mitchell *(Rail and National Networks)*; Stephen Hickey *(Safety, Service Delivery and Logistics)*
Director, Legal Services, Christopher Muttukumaru
Chief Scientific Adviser, Brian Collins

HM TREASURY

1 Horse Guards Road, London SW1A 2HQ
T 020-7270 4558 F 020-7270 4861
E public.enquiries@hm-treasury.gov.uk
W www.hm-treasury.gov.uk

HM Treasury is the country's economics and finance ministry, and is responsible for formulating and implementing the government's financial and economic policy. It aims to raise the rate of sustainable growth, boost prosperity, and provide the conditions necessary for universal economic and employment opportunities. The Office of the Lord High Treasurer has been continuously in commission for over 200 years. The Lord High Commissioners of HM Treasury are the First Lord of the Treasury (who is also the prime minister), the Chancellor of the Exchequer and five junior lords. This board of commissioners is assisted at present by the chief secretary, the parliamentary secretary (who is also the government chief whip in the House of Commons), the financial secretary, the economic secretary and the exchequer secretary. The prime minister as first lord is not primarily concerned with the day-to-day aspects of Treasury business; neither are the parliamentary secretary and the junior lords as government whips. Treasury business is managed by the Chancellor of the Exchequer and the other Treasury ministers, assisted by the permanent secretary.

The chief secretary is responsible for public expenditure, including spending reviews and strategic planning; in-year control; public sector pay and pensions; efficiency in public services; capital investment; and public service delivery and performance. He also has responsibility for the Treasury's interest in devolution, assists the Chancellor of the Exchequer where necessary on international and European issues, and oversees the integration of the tax and benefit system.

The financial secretary is the departmental minister for HM Revenue and Customs and the Valuation Office Agency and has strategic oversight of the UK tax system as a whole. She is the lead minister on European and international tax issues, and her responsibilities include the Finance Bill, the voluntary sector and charities, childcare issues and tax credits.

The exchequer secretary is a title only used

occasionally, normally when the post of paymaster-general is allocated to a minister outside of the Treasury (as it is at present; Rt. Hon. Tessa Jowell, MP was appointed paymaster-general as Olympic minister within the Cabinet Office in June 2007). Her responsibilities include enterprise and productivity; competition and better regulation; science, innovation and skills policy; regional economic policy and environmental issues.

The economic secretary's responsibilities include financial services policy, including tax issues; personal savings policy; foreign exchange reserves and debt management policy; stamp duty land tax and real estate investment trusts; and EMU preparations.

Prime Minister and First Lord of the Treasury, Rt. Hon. Gordon Brown, MP
Chancellor of the Exchequer, Rt. Hon. Alistair Darling, MP
Principal Private Secretary, James Bowler
Private Secretaries, Jonathan Black; Lewis Neal
Parliamentary Private Secretary, Ann Coffey, MP
Special Advisers, Emily Thomas; Sam White
Chief Secretary to the Treasury, Rt. Hon. Andy Burnham, MP
Private Secretary, Matthew Style
Parliamentary Private Secretary, Mary Creagh, MP
Financial Secretary to the Treasury, Rt. Hon. Jane Kennedy, MP
Private Secretary, Cerys Morgan
Parliamentary Private Secretary, David Wright, MP
Exchequer Secretary to the Treasury, Angela Eagle, MP
Private Secretary, Su Viner
Economic Secretary to the Treasury, Kitty Ussher, MP
Private Secretary, Hermione Gough
Permanent Secretary to the Treasury, Nick Macpherson
Private Secretary, Dan Mobley
Parliamentary Secretary to the Treasury and Government Chief Whip, Rt. Hon. Geoff Hoon, MP
Parliamentary Private Secretary, Sarah McCarthy-Fry, MP
Economic Adviser, Andrew Maugham
Lords Commissioners of HM Treasury (Whips), Alan Campbell, MP; Stephen McCabe, MP; Frank Roy, MP; Clarie Ward, MP; Dave Watts, MP
Assistant Whips, Bob Blizzard, MP; Tony Cunningham, MP; Wayne David, MP; Michael Foster, MP; Diana R. Johnson, MP; Sadiq Khan, MP; Siobhain McDonagh, MP; Alison Seabeck, MP; Mark Tami, MP; Tom Watson, MP

TREASURY BOARD
Permanent Secretary, Nick Macpherson *(Chair)*
Managing Directors, Mark Neale *(Budget, Tax and Revenue)*; Mary Keegan *(Government Financial Management)*; Stephen Pickford *(International and Finance)*; Dave Ramsden *(Macroeconomic and Fiscal Policy)*; John Kingman *(Public Services and Growth)*
Chief Executive of Office of Government Commerce, Nigel Smith
Directors, Louise Tulett *(Group Finance, Procurement and Operations)*; Sam Beckett *(Policy and Planning)*
Non-Executive Directors, Sir Peter Gershon; Stella Manzie; William Sargent; Sir David Varney

OTHER BODIES

OFFICE OF GOVERNMENT COMMERCE (OGC)
1 Horse Guards Road, London SW1A 2HQ
T 0845-000 4999 E servicedesk@ogc.gsi.gov.uk
W www.ogc.gov.uk

The Office of Government Commerce was set up in April 2000. It is responsible for increasing the government's value for money by improving standards and capability in procurement, for example by commodities buying, delivering major capital projects, and maximising the effective use of 60 per cent of government spending and a £30bn property estate.
Chief Executive, Nigel Smith

WALES OFFICE
Gwydyr House, Whitehall, London SW1A 2ER
T 020-7270 0534
E walesoffice@walesoffice.gsi.gov.uk
W www.walesoffice.gov.uk

The Wales Office was established in 1999 when most of the powers of the Welsh Office were handed over to the National Assembly for Wales. It is the department of the Secretary of State for Wales, who is the key government figure liaising with the devolved government in Wales and who represents Welsh interests in the cabinet and parliament. The secretary of state has the right to attend and speak at sessions of the National Assembly (and must consult the assembly on the government's legislative programme). *See also* Regional Government section and Ministry of Justice.
Secretary of State for Wales, Rt. Hon. Peter Hain, MP
Principal Private Secretary, Glynne Jones
Parliamentary Under-Secretary, Huw Irranca-Davies, MP
Director of Office, Alan Cogbill

DEPARTMENT FOR WORK AND PENSIONS
Caxton House, Tothill Street, London SW1H 9NA
T 020-7962 8000 E enquiries@dwp.gsi.gov.uk
W www.dwp.gov.uk

The Department for Work and Pensions was formed in June 2001 from parts of the former Department of Social Security, the Department for Education and Employment and the Employment Service. The department helps unemployed people of working age into work, helps employers to fill their vacancies and provides financial support to people unable to help themselves, through back-to-work programmes. The department also administers the child support system, social security benefits and the social fund. In addition, the department has reciprocal social security arrangements with other countries.

In April 2002 the Benefits Agency and the Employment Service were replaced by the Jobcentre Plus network (responsible for helping to find jobs and paying benefits to people of working age), and the Pension Service which administers the Benefits Agency's pension-related services.
Secretary of State for Work and Pensions, Rt. Hon. Peter Hain, MP
Principal Private Secretary, John Oliver
Private Secretaries, Helen Bache; Tom Fox; Zoe Rigden; Antonia Williams
Special Advisers, Matthew Burchell; Claire McCarthy
Parliamentary Private Secretary, Natascha Engel, MP
Minister of State, Caroline Flint, MP *(Employment and Welfare Reform)*
Private Secretary, Laura Timms
Parliamentary Private Secretary, vacant
Assistant Private Secretaries, Jessica Hodgson; Linda Reynolds
Minister of State, Mike O'Brien, MP *(Pensions Reform)*
Private Secretary, Jean-Paul Marks

Parliamentary Private Secretary, Jim Cunningham, MP
Assistant Private Secretaries, Michael Cordy; Helen
Hutchings
Parliamentary Under-Secretary of State (Commons), James
Plaskitt, MP
Private Secretary, Robin Gordon-Farleigh
Assistant Private Secretaries, Anahita Easton; Christopher
Raitt
Parliamentary Under-Secretary of State (Lords), Lord
McKenzie of Luton
Private Secretary, Sarah Kelly
Assistant Private Secretaries, Janet Smith; Maxine
Thompson
Parliamentary Under-Secretary of State (Commons), Anne
McGuire, MP *(Disabled People)*
Private Secretary, Lisa Pinnell
Assistant Private Secretaries, Kevin Green; Paul Warren
Parliamentary Under-Secretary of State, Barbara Follett, MP
(Equality)
Permanent Secretary, Leigh Lewis
Private Secretaries, Phil Hall; Judith Tunstall; Lucy Wyatt

PENSIONS CLIENT DIRECTORATE
Director-General, Phil Wynn Owen
Directors, Caroline Rookes *(Private Pensions, Planning for
Retirement and Older People)*; Alan Woods *(State Pensions
and Pensions Reform)*; Robert Laslett *(Strategic Analysis
and Stewardship, Chief Economist)*

GROUP FINANCE DIRECTORATE
Director-General, John Codling
Deputy Director-General, Howard Orme
Directors, David Smith *(Commercial)*; Jeremy Moore
(Planning and Performance Management); Richard Paul
(Risk Assurance)

PROGRAMME AND SYSTEM DELIVERY
Director-General, Chief Information Officer, Joe Harley
Chief Operating Officer, Dean James

HUMAN RESOURCES GROUP
Director-General (acting), Jane Saint
Directors, Debbie Haigh *(Diversity and Equality)*; Alison
Stanley *(HR Policy)*; Jerry Arnott *(Organisational
Capability)*

HEALTH, WORK AND WELLBEING DIRECTORATE
Director, Chief Medical Adviser, Chief Scientist, Dr Bill
Gunnyeon
Deputy Director, Principal Scientific Adviser, Dr Peter
Wright
Principal Occupational Physician, Dr Nerys Williams
Chief Psychologist, David Carew

LAW, GOVERNANCE AND SPECIAL POLICY GROUP
Director-General, Richard Heaton
Directors, Ronald Powell *(Commercial and Employment)*;
Frances Logan *(Legal Services)*; Mark Gidden
(Litigation); Amanda de Blaquiere *(Prosecutions)*; Greer
Kerrigan, CB *(Social Security)*

COMMUNICATIONS NETWORK
Director, Sue Garrard

WORK, WELFARE AND EQUALITY GROUP
Director-General, Adam Sharples

Directors, Shirley Trundle *(Benefit Strategy)*; Hilary
Reynolds *(Child Maintenance Redesign)*; Alan Cave
(Delivery); Bruce Calderwood *(Disability and Carers)*;
Ian Scott *(Finance)*; Dr Bill Gunnyeon *(Health, Work
and Wellbeing)*; Win Harris *(Joint International Unit)*;
Cay Stratton *(National Employment Panel)*; Jonathan
Portes *(Poverty and Analysis)*; Sharon White *(Welfare to
Work)*

EXECUTIVE AGENCIES

Executive agencies are well-defined business units that
carry out services with a clear focus on delivering specific
outputs within a framework of accountability to ministers.
They can be set up or disbanded without legislation, and
they are organisationally independent from the
department they are answerable to. In the following list
the agencies are shown in the accounts of their sponsor
departments. Legally they act on behalf of the relevant
secretary of state. Their chief executives also perform the
role of accounting officers, which means they are
responsible for the money spent by their organisations.
Staff employed by agencies are civil servants.

CABINET OFFICE

COI (CENTRAL OFFICE OF INFORMATION)
Hercules Road, London SE1 7DU
T 020-7928 2345 F 020-7928 5037
W www.coi.gov.uk
The COI is the principal agency within government for
the provision and procurement of marketing and
communications services. Administrative responsibility for
the COI rests with the minister for the Cabinet Office.
Chief Executive, A. Bishop
Deputy Chief Executive, P. Buchanan

MANAGEMENT BOARD
Members, G. Beasant; Ms A. Butler; R. Haslam; I.
Hamilton; G. Hooper; Ms E. Lochhead; A. Wade; Mrs
S. Whetton

ATTORNEY-GENERAL'S OFFICE

TREASURY SOLICITOR'S DEPARTMENT
1 Kemble Street, London WC2B 4TS
T 020-7210 3000 F 020-7210 3004
E thetreasurysolicitor@tsol.gsi.gov.uk
W www.tsol.gov.uk
The Treasury Solicitor's Department, which became an
executive agency in 1996, provides legal services for
many government departments and is answerable to the
Attorney-General. Those departments without their own
lawyers are provided with legal advice, and both they and
other departments are provided with litigation services.
The Treasury Solicitor is also the Queen's Proctor, and is
responsible for collecting ownerless goods *(bona vacantia)*
on behalf of the crown.
*HM Procurator-General and Treasury Solicitor, Permanent
Secretary,* Paul Jenkins

BONA VACANTIA DIVISION
Head of Division, Valerie Cain

CABINET OFFICE AND CENTRAL ADVISORY DIVISION
Head of Division, Peter Fish

DEPARTMENT OF CULTURE, MEDIA AND SPORT
DIVISION
Legal Adviser, Patrick Kilgarriff

DEPARTMENT FOR CHILDREN, SCHOOLS AND
FAMILIES DIVISION
Legal Adviser, David Noble

DIRECTORATE OF CORPORATE STRATEGY
Director, Julie Anderson

EUROPEAN DIVISION
Head of Division, Frances Nash

HM TREASURY ADVISORY DIVISION
Legal Adviser, Stephen Parker

LITIGATION GROUP
Head of Division, David Pearson

DEPARTMENT FOR BUSINESS, ENTERPRISE AND REGULATORY REFORM

COMPANIES HOUSE
Crown Way, Cardiff CF14 3UZ
T 0870-333 3636 F 029-2038 0517
E enquiries@companieshouse.gov.uk
W www.companieshouse.gov.uk
Companies House incorporates companies, registers company documents and provides company information.
Registrar of Companies for England and Wales, Gareth Jones
Registrar of Companies for Scotland, Dorothy Blair

THE INSOLVENCY SERVICE
21 Bloomsbury Street, London WC1B 3QW
Insolvency Enquiry Line 0845-602 9848
Redundancy Enquiry Line 0845-145 0004
W www.insolvency.gov.uk
The role of the service includes administration and investigation of the affairs of bankrupts, partners and companies in compulsory liquidation; dealing with the disqualification of directors in all corporate failures; authorising and regulating the insolvency profession; providing banking and investment services for bankruptcy and liquidation estate funds; assessing and paying statutory entitlement to redundancy payments when an employer cannot, or will not, pay its employees; and advising ministers on insolvency, redundancy and related issues.
Inspector-General and Chief Executive, Stephen Speed
Deputy Inspectors-General, L. T. Cramp; G. Horne
Inspector of Companies, Robert Burns

DEPARTMENT FOR COMMUNITIES AND LOCAL GOVERNMENT

FIRE SERVICE COLLEGE
Moreton-in-Marsh, Gloucestershire GL56 0RH
T 01608-650831 F 01608-651788
W www.fireservicecollege.ac.uk
The Fire Service College provides unique facilities for both practical and theoretical fire fighting, fire safety and accident and emergency training, including urban search and rescue and community safety.
Chief Executive, Gill Newton

ORDNANCE SURVEY
Romsey Road, Southampton SO16 4GU
T 0845-605 0505 F 023-8079 2615
E customerservices@ordnancesurvey.co.uk
W www.ordnancesurvey.co.uk
Ordnance Survey is the national mapping agency for Great Britain. It is a government department and executive agency operating as a trading fund since 1999.
Director-General and Chief Executive, Vanessa Lawrence

PLANNING INSPECTORATE
Temple Quay House, 2 The Square, Temple Quay, Bristol BS1 6PN
T 0117-372 6372 E enquiries@planning-inspectorate.gsi.gov.uk
Crown Buildings, Cathays Park, Cardiff CF10 3NQ
T 029-2082 3866 E wales@planning-inspectorate.gsi.gov.uk
W www.planning-inspectorate.gov.uk
The main work of the inspectorate consists of the processing of planning and enforcement appeals, and holding inquiries into local development plans and frameworks. It also deals with appeals against the decisions of local authorities on planning applications; appeals against local authority enforcement notices; listed building consent appeals; advertisement appeals; rights of way cases; and cases arising from the Environmental Protection and Water acts, the Transport and Works Act 1992 and other highways legislation.
Chief Executive, Katrine Sporle

THE QUEEN ELIZABETH II CONFERENCE CENTRE
Broad Sanctuary, London SW1P 3EE
T 020-7222 5000 F 020-7798 4200
E info@qeiicc.co.uk W www.qeiicc.co.uk
The centre provides secure conference facilities for national and international government and private sector use.
Chief Executive, Ernest Vincent

DEPARTMENT FOR CULTURE, MEDIA AND SPORT

THE ROYAL PARKS
The Old Police House, Hyde Park, London W2 2UH
T 020-7298 2000 F 020-7298 2005
E hq@royalparks.gsi.gov.uk W www.royalparks.org.uk
Royal Parks is responsible for maintaining and developing over 2,000 hectares (5,000 acres) of urban parkland contained within the eight royal parks in London: Bushy Park (with the Longford River); Green Park; Greenwich Park; Hyde Park; Kensington Gardens; Regent's Park (with Primrose Hill); Richmond Park and St James's Park.
Chief Executive, Mark Camley

DEPARTMENT FOR ENVIRONMENT, FOOD AND RURAL AFFAIRS

ANIMAL HEALTH
Corporate Centre, Block C, Government Buildings, Whittington Road, Worcester WR5 2LQ
T 01905-767111 F 01905-768854
E corporate-office@animalhealth.gsi.gov.uk
W www.svs.gov.uk
Animal Health, formerly the State Veterinary Service, is the government's delivery agent for animal health and welfare in England, Scotland and Wales. It is responsible for the prevention, detection and management of diseases in animals; protecting the welfare of farmed animals; the

eradication of endemic disease; import and export certification; animal by-product regulation; preparedness for managing exotic animal diseases; and licensing the trade in endangered species for conservation purposes.
Chief Executive, Glenys Stacey

CENTRAL SCIENCE LABORATORY (CSL)

Sand Hutton, York YO41 1LZ
T 01904-462000 F 01904-462111
E science@csl.gov.uk W www.csl.gov.uk
The Central Science Laboratory specialises in the sciences underpinning sustainable land use, environmental protection and food safety. It provides a wide range of analytical, diagnostic and consultancy services to organisations in both the public and private sectors, designed to support the international land-based and food industries.
Chief Executive, Prof. Michael Roberts

CENTRE FOR ENVIRONMENT, FISHERIES AND AQUACULTURE SCIENCE (CEFAS)

Pakefield Road, Lowestoft, Suffolk NR33 0HT
T 01502-562244 F 01502-513865
W www.cefas.co.uk
Established in April 1997, the agency provides research and consultancy services in fisheries science and management, aquaculture, fish health and hygiene, environmental impact assessment, and environmental quality assessment.
Chief Executive, Richard Judge

GOVERNMENT DECONTAMINATION SERVICE

MoD Stafford, Beaconside, Stafford ST18 0AQ
T 0845-850 1323 F 01785-216363
E gds@gds.gsi.gov.uk W www.gds.gov.uk
The Government Decontamination Service boosts the UK's capacity to resist and recover from deliberate and accidental releases of chemical, biological, radiological and nuclear materials, and from major accidental releases of hazardous materials.
Chief Executive, Robert Bettley-Smith, FRICS

MARINE AND FISHERIES AGENCY

3–8 Whitehall Place, London SW1A 2HH
T 020-7270 8328 F 020-7270 8345
E info@mfa.gsi.gov.uk W www.mfa.gov.uk
The Marine and Fisheries Agency was established in October 2005 to coordinate for the first time the service delivery, inspection and enforcement of activities provided by the government to the fishing industry and other marine stakeholders in England and Wales.
Chief Executive, Nigel Gooding

PESTICIDES SAFETY DIRECTORATE

Mallard House, Kings Pool, 3 Peasholme Green, York YO1 7PX
T 01904-455775 F 01904-455733
E information@psd.defra.gsi.gov.uk W www.pesticides.gov.uk
The Pesticides Safety Directorate aims to ensure the safe use of pesticides and detergents for the public and the environment; to harmonise pesticide regulation within the European Community; and to reduce negative impacts of pesticides on the environment.
Chief Executive, Dr H. K. Wilson

RURAL PAYMENTS AGENCY

Kings House, 33 Kings Road, Reading RG1 3BU
T 0845-603 7777 F 0118-959 7736
E enquiries@rpa.gsi.gov.uk W www.rpa.gov.uk
The RPA was established in 2001. It is the single paying agency responsible for Common Agricultural Policy (CAP) schemes in England and for certain schemes throughout the UK; it intends to deliver over £2bn of payments to farmers and traders per year.
Chief Executive, Tony Cooper
Chief Operating Officer, Hugh Taylor

VETERINARY LABORATORIES AGENCY

Woodham Lane, New Haw, Addlestone, Surrey KT15 3NB
T 01932-341111 F 01932-347046
E enquiries@vla.defra.gov.uk W www.vla.gov.uk
The Veterinary Laboratories Agency is a regional network of 16 veterinary laboratories and two surveillance centres, which provides all sectors of the animal health industry with animal disease surveillance, diagnostic services and veterinary scientific research.
Chief Executive, Prof. S. Edwards

VETERINARY MEDICINES DIRECTORATE

Woodham Lane, New Haw, Addlestone, Surrey KT15 3LS
T 01932-336911 F 01932-336618
W www.vmd.gov.uk
The Veterinary Medicines Directorate is responsible for all aspects of the authorisation and control of veterinary medicines, including post-authorisation surveillance of residues in animals and animal products, and also for the provision of policy advice to ministers.
Chief Executive, Steve Dean

FOREIGN AND COMMONWEALTH OFFICE

FCO SERVICES

Hanslope Park, Milton Keynes MK19 7BH
T 01908-515789 E fco.serv@fco.gov.uk
W www.fcoservices.gov.uk
FCO Services was established in April 2006. It delivers a combination of secure business-to-business services to the FCO in the UK and at its missions overseas, other UK government departments and public bodies, friendly foreign governments and private sector organisations.
The Corps of Queen's Messengers, couriers of confidential and important documents, was transferred to FCO Services in 2006.
Chief Executive, Chris Moxey
Superintendent of the Corps of Queen's Messengers, Sqn. Ldr. J. S. Frizzell
Queen's Messengers, S. J. Addy; P. Allen; R. Allen; Maj. A. N. D. Bols; Maj. S. Cambridge; Maj. P. C. H. Dening-Smitherman; J. A. Hatfield; Sqn. Ldr. P. J. Hearn; Sqn. Ldr. A. Hill; W. Lisle; Maj. K. J. Rowbottom; Maj. J. H. Steele; R. T. Wilson

WILTON PARK CONFERENCE CENTRE

Wiston House, Steyning, W. Sussex BN44 3DZ
T 01903-815020 F 01903-816373
E admin@wiltonpark.org.uk W www.wiltonpark.org.uk
Wilton Park organises international affairs conferences and is hired out to government departments and commercial users.
Chief Executive, Donald Lamont

DEPARTMENT OF HEALTH

MEDICINES AND HEALTHCARE PRODUCTS REGULATORY AGENCY (MHRA)

Market Towers, 1 Nine Elms Lane, London SW8 5NQ
T 020-7084 2000 F 020-7084 2353
E info@mhra.gsi.gov.uk W www.mhra.gov.uk

The MHRA is responsible for protecting and promoting public and patient safety by ensuring that medicines, healthcare products and medical equipment meet appropriate standards of safety, quality, performance and effectiveness, and are used safely.

Chair, Prof. Sir Alasdair Breckenridge, CBE
Chief Executive, Prof. Kent Woods

NHS PURCHASING AND SUPPLY AGENCY

Premier House, 60 Caversham Road, Reading RG1 7EB
T 0118-980 8600 F 0118-980 8650
E pasa@pasa.nhs.uk W www.pasa.nhs.uk
The agency was established in April 2000 and is responsible for ensuring that the NHS makes the most effective use of its resources by getting the best value for money possible when purchasing goods and services. It works with around 400 NHS trusts and health authorities, and manages in the region of 3,000 national purchasing contracts.
Chief Operating Officer, John Cooper

HOME OFFICE

CRIMINAL RECORDS BUREAU

PO Box 110, Liverpool L69 3EF
T 0870-909 0811 W www.crb.gov.uk
The Criminal Records Bureau was launched in March 2002 and provides access to criminal record information to enable organisations in the public, private and voluntary sectors to make safer recruitment decisions by identifying candidates who may be unsuitable for certain work – especially that which involves children or vulnerable adults.
Chief Executive, Vincent Gaskell

FORENSIC SCIENCE SERVICE (FSS)

see Police Service section

HM PRISON SERVICE

see Prison Service section

IDENTITY AND PASSPORT SERVICE

Globe House, 89 Ecclestone Square, London SW1V 1PN
T Advice Line 0870-521 0410
E info@passport.gov.uk W www.passport.gov.uk
The Identity and Passport Service was established on in April 2006 and incorporates the UK Passport Service. Its role is to provide passport services and, in the future (as part of the National Identity Scheme), identity cards for British and foreign nationals resident in the UK.
Chief Executive, James Hall

DEPARTMENT FOR INNOVATION, UNIVERSITIES AND SKILLS

NATIONAL WEIGHTS AND MEASURES LABORATORY

Stanton Avenue, Teddington, Middx TW11 0JZ
T 020-8943 7272 F 020-8943 7270
E info@nwml.gov.uk W www.nwml.gov.uk
The laboratory is responsible for ensuring all trade measurements are accurate, legal and fair to both buyer and seller. It provides the following services: type approval; mass, length and volume calibration; ISO 9001 certification; metrology training; and consultancy. It is also responsible for the implementation of European directives on measuring instruments.
Chief Executive, Dr Jeff Llewellyn

UK INTELLECTUAL PROPERTY OFFICE

Concept House, Cardiff Road, Newport NP10 8QQ
T 0845-950 0505 F 01633-814444
E enquiries@ipo.gov.uk W www.ipo.gov.uk
The UK Intellectual Property Office, formerly known as the Patent Office, was established in 1990 and became a trading fund in 1991. The office is responsible for intellectual property (IP) policy and operation in the UK, and aims to educate business, researchers and the public about the IP system; facilitate the appropriate protection and use of rights; design and provide commercial services to assist business use of the IP system; and create a domestic and international legal and political framework, which balances the interests of rights holders with the need for open competition and free markets.
Comptroller-General and Chief Executive, Ian Fletcher

MINISTRY OF JUSTICE

HER MAJESTY'S COURTS SERVICE

see Law Courts and Offices section

LAND REGISTRY

Lincoln's Inn Fields, London WC2A 3PH
T 020-7917 8888 F 020-7955 0110
E propertyinformationteam@landregistry.gsi.gov.uk
W www.landregistry.gov.uk
The registration of title to land was first introduced in England and Wales by the Land Registry Act 1862. Land Registry keeps and maintains the Land Register for England and Wales, and is an executive agency and trading fund responsible to the Secretary of State for Justice. The Land Register has been open to public inspection since 1990.
Chief Land Registrar and Chief Executive, Peter Collis, CB
Deputy Chief Executive and Business Development Director,
 Ted Beardsall, CBE

NATIONAL ARCHIVES

Kew, Richmond, Surrey TW9 4DU
T 020-8876 3444 F 020-8878 8905
E enquiries@nationalarchives.gov.uk
W www.nationalarchives.gov.uk
The National Archives, a government department and an executive agency reporting to the Secretary of State for Justice, was formed in April 2003 by bringing together the Public Record Office (founded in 1838) and the Historical Manuscripts Commission (founded in 1869).

The National Archives leads on record management policy with government, and provides access to government records at its sites in Kew and Islington and through digital resources available online. The National Archives also oversees information and archive management across the UK, setting standards and providing advice and support to raise the standards of information management. OPSI – with its copyright, legislation and official publishing roles – operates from within the National Archives.

The organisation administers the UK's public records system under the Public Records Acts of 1958 and 1967. The records it holds span 1,000 years – from the Domesday Book to the latest government papers to be released – and fill more than 160km (100 miles) of shelving.
Chief Executive, Ms N. Ceeney
Directors, Dr D. Thomas *(Collections and Technology)*;
 Ms E. Stoddart *(Finance and Corporate Services)*;
 M. Lamb *(Human Resources and Organisational*

Development); Ms C. Tullo *(Public Sector Information)*; J. Strachan *(Public Services and Marketing)*

OFFICE OF PUBLIC SECTOR INFORMATION
St Clements House, 2–16 Colegate, Norwich NR3 1BQ
T 01603-723011 W www.opsi.gov.uk
The Office of Public Sector Information (OPSI) operates from within the National Archives as of October 2006, after previously being attached to the Cabinet Office. It is responsible for policy in relation to access and re-use of UK public sector information. The legal and statutory responsibilities of Her Majesty's Stationery Office (HMSO), in relation to statutory publishing and the management of crown copyright, operate from within the OPSI's wider remit.
Director/Controller, Carol Tullo

OFFICE OF THE PUBLIC GUARDIAN
Archway Tower, 2 Junction Road, London N19 5SZ
T 0845-330 2900 F 020-7664 7705
E customerservices@publicguardian.gsi.gov.uk
W www.publicguardian.gov.uk
The Office of the Public Guardian was established on 1 October 2007, in place of the Public Guardianship Office. It is responsible for providing services that support the financial, property, health and welfare matters of people lacking in the mental capacity to make decisions in a particular area. Capacity is assessed in accordance with the requirements set out in the Mental Capacity Act 2005.
Chief Executive and Public Guardian Designate, Richard Brook

TRIBUNALS SERVICE
see Tribunals section

NORTHERN IRELAND OFFICE

COMPENSATION AGENCY
Royston House, 34 Upper Queen Street, Belfast BT1 6FD
T 028-9024 9944 E comp-agency@nics.gov.uk
W www.compensationni.gov.uk
The Compensation Agency supports the victims of violent crime by providing compensation to those who sustain loss as a result of actions taken under emergency provisions legislation.
Chief Executive, Gareth Johnston

FORENSIC SCIENCE NORTHERN IRELAND
151 Belfast Road, Carrickfergus, Co. Antrim BT38 8PL
T 028-9036 1888 F 028-9036 1900
E forensic.science@fsni.gov.uk W www.fsni.gov.uk
Forensic Science Northern Ireland aims to enhance the delivery of justice by providing scientific support and advice for the police and the legal profession, and training and analytical support for pathologists.
Chief Executive, Stanley Brown

NORTHERN IRELAND PRISON SERVICE
see Prison Service section

YOUTH JUSTICE AGENCY
Corporate Headquarters, 41–43 Waring Street, Belfast BT1 2DY
T 028-9031 6400 F 028-9031 6402/3
E info@yjani.gov.uk W www.youthjusticeagencyni.gov.uk
The Youth Justice Agency aims to prevent children committing criminal offences through provision of community-based services, youth conferencing services, attendance centres and secure custody.
Chief Executive, Bill Lockhart, OBE

DEPARTMENT FOR TRANSPORT

DRIVER AND VEHICLE LICENSING AGENCY (DVLA)
Longview Road, Swansea SA6 7JL
T 01792-782341 W www.dvla.gov.uk
The agency was established as an executive agency in 1990 and became a trading fund in 2004. It is responsible for registering and licensing drivers and vehicles, and the collection and enforcement of vehicle excise duty (some £4.9bn annually). The DVLA also maintains records of all those who are entitled to drive various types of vehicle (currently 39 million people), all vehicles entitled to travel on public roads (currently 32 million), and drivers' endorsements, disqualifications and medical conditions.
Chief Executive, Clive Bennett

DRIVING STANDARDS AGENCY
Stanley House, 56 Talbot Street, Nottingham NG1 5GU
T 0115-901 2500 F 0115-901 2510
E customer.services@dsa.gsi.gov.uk
W www.dsa.gov.uk
The agency is responsible for carrying out theory and practical driving tests for car drivers, motorcyclists, bus and lorry drivers, and for maintaining the registers of approved driving instructors and large goods vehicle instructors. It also supervises Compulsory Basic Training (CBT) for learner motorcyclists. There are two area offices, which manage over 400 practical driving test centres across Britain.
Chief Executive, Rosemary Thew

GOVERNMENT CAR AND DESPATCH AGENCY
46 Ponton Road, London SW8 5AX
T 020-7217 3839 F 020-7217 3859
W www.gcda.gov.uk
The agency provides secure transport and mail distribution to government and the public sector.
Chief Executive, Roy Burke

HIGHWAYS AGENCY
123 Buckingham Palace Road, London SW1W 9HA
T 0845-955 6575 Information Line 0845-750 4030
E ha_info@highways.gsi.gov.uk W www.highways.gov.uk
The agency is responsible for delivering the Department for Transport's road programme and for maintaining the 7,754km (4,818 miles) of strategic road network in England (made up of motorways and trunk roads and valued at over £65bn).
Chief Executive, Archie Robertson

MARITIME AND COASTGUARD AGENCY
Spring Place, 105 Commercial Road, Southampton SO15 1EG
T 023-8032 9100 F 023-8032 9374
W www.mcga.gov.uk
The agency's aims are to prevent loss of life, continuously improve maritime safety and protect the marine environment.
Chief Executive, Peter Cardy
Chief Coastguard, Peter Dymond

VEHICLE CERTIFICATION AGENCY
1 Eastgate Office Centre, Eastgate Road, Bristol BS5 6XX
T 0117-952 4235 F 0117-952 4104
E enquiries@vca.gov.uk W www.vca.gov.uk

The agency is the UK authority responsible for ensuring that vehicles and vehicle parts have been designed and constructed to meet internationally agreed standards of safety and environmental protection.
Chief Executive, P. Markwick

VEHICLE AND OPERATOR SERVICES AGENCY

Berkeley House, Croydon Street, Bristol BS5 0DA
T 0117-954 3200 F 0117-954 3212
Enquiry Line 0870-606 0440
E enquiries@vosa.gov.uk W www.vosa.gov.uk
The Vehicle and Operator Services Agency was formed in April 2003 from the merger of the Vehicle Inspectorate and the Traffic Area Network. The agency works with the independent traffic commissioners to improve road safety and the environment; safeguard fair competition by promoting and enforcing compliance with commercial operator licensing requirements; process applications for licences to operate lorries and buses; register bus services; operate and administer testing schemes for all vehicles, including the supervision of the MOT testing scheme; enforce the law on vehicles to ensure that they comply with legal standards and regulations; enforce drivers' hours and licensing requirements; provide training and advice for commercial operators; and investigate vehicle accidents, defects and recalls.
Chief Executive, Stephen J. Tetlow, MBE

HM TREASURY

NATIONAL SAVINGS AND INVESTMENTS

375 Kensington High Street, London W14 8SD
T 020-7348 9200 F 020-7048 9698
E customerenquiries@nsandi.com
W www.nsandi.com
National Savings and Investments came into being in 1861 when the Palmerston government set up the Post Office Savings Bank, a savings scheme which aimed to encourage ordinary wage earners 'to provide for themselves against adversity and ill health'. National Savings and Investments was established as a government department in 1969. It became an executive agency of the Treasury in 1996 and is responsible for the design, marketing and administration of savings and investment products for personal savers and investors. It has approximately 26 million customers with over £70bn invested. *See also* Finance section.
Chief Executive, Jane Platt

OFFICE FOR NATIONAL STATISTICS

1 Drummond Gate, London SW1V 2QQ
T 0845-601 3034 E info@statistics.gov.uk
W www.statistics.gov.uk
ONS was created in 1996 by the merger of the Central Statistical Office and the Office of Population Censuses and Surveys. It is both a government department and an executive agency of the Treasury and is responsible for preparing, interpreting and publishing key statistics on the government, economy and society of the UK. Its key responsibilities include the provision of population estimates and projections and statistics on health and other demographic matters in England and Wales; the production of the UK National Accounts and other key economic indicators; the organisation of population censuses in England and Wales and surveys of government departments and public bodies.
Following a consultation period that ended in June 2006, plans are underway to establish ONS as a non-ministerial

department fully independent of government, with a governing board that will report directly to parliament.
The General Register Office is part of the ONS and is responsible for ensuring the registration of all births, marriages and deaths in England and Wales, and for maintaining a central archive dating back to 1837.
National Statistician, Director of ONS, Registrar-General for England and Wales, Karen Dunnell

OGC BUYING SOLUTIONS

5th Floor, Royal Liver Building, Pier Head, Liverpool L3 1PE
T 0845-410 2222 F 0151-227 3315
W www.ogcbuyingsolutions.gov.uk
The agency provides a professional procurement service to government departments and other public bodies. From April 2000 it became part of the Office of Government Commerce in the Treasury.
Chief Executive, Alison Littley

ROYAL MINT

Llantrisant, Pontyclun CF72 8YT
T 01443-222111 F 01443-623148
E information.office@royalmint.gov.uk
W www.royalmint.gov.uk
The Royal Mint has operated as a trading fund since 1975, and was established as an executive agency in 1990.
The prime responsibility of the Royal Mint is the provision of United Kingdom coinage, but it actively competes in world markets for a share of the available circulating coin business and about half of the coins and blanks it produces annually are exported. It also manufactures special proof and uncirculated quality coins in gold, silver and other metals; military and civil decorations and medals; commemorative and prize medals; and royal and official seals. In 1999 the Royal Mint was given greater commercial freedom to expand its business into new areas and develop partnerships with the private sector.
Master of the Mint, Chancellor of the Exchequer *(ex officio)*
Chief Executive, D. Barrass

UK DEBT MANAGEMENT OFFICE

Eastcheap Court, 11 Philpot Lane, London EC3M 8UD
T 0845-357 6500 F 0845-357 6509
W www.dmo.gov.uk
The UK Debt Management Office (DMO) was launched as an executive agency of HM Treasury in April 1998. The Chancellor of the Exchequer determines the policy and financial framework within which the DMO operates, but delegates operational decisions on debt and cash management and the day-to-day running of the office to the chief executive. The DMO's remit is to carry out the government's debt management policy of minimising financing costs over the long term, and to minimise the cost of offsetting the government's net cash flows over time, while operating at a level of risk approved by ministers in both cases.
Chief Executive, Robert Stheeman

DEPARTMENT FOR WORK AND PENSIONS

CHILD SUPPORT AGENCY (CSA)

PO Box 55, Brierly Hill, West Midlands DY5 1YL
T 0845-713 3133 F 0845-713 8924
W www.csa.gov.uk

The CSA was set up in April 1993. It is responsible for the administration of the Child Support Act and for the assessment, collection and enforcement of maintenance payments. Government plans to establish a new organisation, the Child Maintenance and Enforcement Commission, were outlined in the Child Maintenance White Paper; the commission was due to be in place, with statutory authority, by the end of 2009.

Chief Executive, Stephen Geraghty

DISABILITY AND CARERS SERVICE

Block 1, Room 112, Government Buildings, Norcross Lane, Blackpool, Lancs FY5 3TA T 0800-882 200
E dbu-customer-service@dwp.gsi.gov.uk
W www.dwp.gov.uk/dcs

The Disability and Carers Service (DCS) aims to enable the independence of disabled people and carers through the financial support available from the disability living allowance, attendance allowance and carer's allowance. The DCS also delivers payments to those who have become disabled as a result of vaccine damage. Currently the service provides in excess of £13bn per year to over 4 million disabled people and carers.

Chief Executive, Terry Moran
Chief Operating Officer, Vivien Hopkins

JOBCENTRE PLUS

First Floor, Steel City House, West Street, Sheffield S1 2GQ
T 0845-606 0234 E contact-us@jobcentreplus.gsi.gov.uk
W www.jobcentreplus.gov.uk

Jobcentre Plus was formed in April 2002 following the merger of the Employment Service and some parts of the Benefits Agency. The agency administers claims for, and payment of, social security benefits to help people gain employment or improve their prospects for work, as well as helping employers to fill their vacancies.

Chief Executive, Lesley Strathie

THE PENSION SERVICE

Room 204, Richmond House, 79 Whitehall, London SW1A 2NS
T 0207-271 2601 Public Enquiries 0845-606 0265
W www.thepensionservice.gov.uk

The Pension Service was launched in April 2002 as an organisation dedicated to understanding the wishes and needs of today's and future pensioners, and to providing state financial support for pensioners.

Chief Executive, Alexis Cleveland

THE RENT SERVICE

5 Welbeck Street, London W1G 9YQ
T 020-7023 6000 F 020-7023 6222
E customer.services@therentservice.gov.uk
W www.therentservice.gov.uk

The Rent Service provides a rental valuation service to local authorities in England, supplying them with a range of valuations to assist them in settling claims for housing benefit. It also provides fair rent determinations for landlords and tenants under the provisions laid down in the Rent Act 1977.

Chief Executive, Patrick Boyle

NON-MINISTERIAL GOVERNMENT DEPARTMENTS

ASSETS RECOVERY AGENCY

PO Box 39992, London EC4M 7XQ
T 020-7029 5700 E enquiries@ara.gsi.gov.uk
W www.assetsrecovery.gov.uk

The Assets Recovery Agency became operational in February 2003. It reports to the home secretary and was established to disrupt organised criminal enterprises through the recovery of criminal assets. It also works to promote the use of financial investigation as an integral part of criminal investigations.

Subject to the passing of the necessary legislation, a proposed merger of the Assets Recovery Agency and the Serious Organised Crime Agency will take place in April 2008.

Director (acting), Alan McQuillan

CHARITY COMMISSION

PO Box 1227, Liverpool L69 3UG
T 0845-300 0218 E enquiries@charitycommission.gsi.gov.uk
W www.charitycommission.gov.uk

The Charity Commission for England and Wales is the government department whose aim is to give the public confidence in the integrity of charities. It also carries out the functions of the registration, monitoring and support of charities and the investigation of alleged wrongdoing. The commission maintains a computerised register of some 187,000 charities. It is accountable to the courts and, for its efficiency, to the home secretary. There are five commissioners appointed by the Home Office for a fixed term and the commission has offices in London, Liverpool, Taunton and Newport.

Chair, Dame Suzi Leather
Chief Executive, Andrew Hind

CROWN ESTATE

16 New Burlington Place, London W1S 2HX
T 020-7851 5000 F 020-7851 5128
W www.thecrownestate.co.uk

The Crown Estate is valued at more than £5bn, and includes substantial blocks of urban property, primarily in London, almost 108,000 hectares (266,800 acres) of rural land, almost half of the foreshore, and the sea bed out to the twelve nautical mile territorial limit throughout the UK. The Crown Estate is part of the hereditary possessions of the sovereign 'in right of the crown', managed under the provisions of the Crown Estate Act 1961. The Crown Estate has a duty to maintain and enhance the capital value of estate and the income obtained from it. Under the terms of the act, the Crown Estate pays its revenue surplus to the Treasury every year.

Chair, Ian Grant, CBE
Chief Executive, Roger Bright
Board Members, Chris Bartram, FRICS; Sir Donald Curry, KB, CBE; Hugh Duberly, CBE; Jenefer Greenwood, FRICS; Martin Moore; Dinah Nichols, CB
Directors, John Lelliot *(Finance and Information Services);* Giles Clarke *(Investment and Asset Management);* Rob Hastings *(Marine Estate);* Chris Bourchier *(Rural Estate)*

CROWN PROSECUTION SERVICE

50 Ludgate Hill, London EC4M 7EX
T 020-7796 8000 F 020-7796 8680
E enquiries@cps.gsi.gov.uk W www.cps.gov.uk

The Crown Prosecution Service (CPS) is the independent body responsible for prosecuting people in England and Wales. The CPS was established as a result of the Prosecution of Offences Act 1985. It works closely with the police to advise on lines of inquiry and to decide on

appropriate charges and other disposals in all but minor cases. *See also* Law Courts and Offices section.
Director of Public Prosecutions, Sir Ken Macdonald, QC
Chief Executive, Peter Lewis

EXPORT CREDITS GUARANTEE DEPARTMENT (ECGD)

PO Box 2200, 2 Exchange Tower, Harbour Exchange Square, London E14 9GS
T 020-7512 7000 F 020-7512 7649
E help@ecgd.gsi.gov.uk W www.ecgd.gov.uk

ECGD is the UK's official export credit agency and was established in 1919. A separate government department reporting to the Secretary of State for Business, Enterprise and Regulatory Reform, it has more than 80 years' experience of working closely with exporters, project sponsors, banks and buyers to help UK exporters of capital equipment and project-related goods and services. ECGD does this by providing help in arranging finance packages for buyers of UK goods by guaranteeing bank loans; insurance against non-payment to UK exporters; and overseas investment insurance – a facility that gives UK investors up to 15 years' insurance against political risks such as war, expropriation and restrictions on remittances.
Chief Executive and Accounting Officer, P. Crawford
Non-Executive Chair, G. Pimlott
Group Directors, S. R. Dodgson *(Business Group)*; David Havelock *(Credit Risk Group)*; Nigel Addison-Smith *(Finance)*; D. N. Ridley *(General Counsel)*; S. Johnson *(Human Resources)*
Non-Executive Directors, D. Godfrey; D. Harrison; P. Haslehurst; K. Letsinger; G. Pimlott

FOOD STANDARDS AGENCY

Aviation House, 125 Kingsway, London WC2B 6NH
T 020-7276 8000 F 020-7276 8004
E helpline@foodstandards.gsi.gov.uk
W www.food.gov.uk

The FSA was established in April 2000 to protect public health from risks arising in connection with the consumption of food, and otherwise to protect the interests of consumers in relation to food. The agency has the general function of developing policy in these areas and provides information and advice to the government, other public bodies and consumers. It also sets standards for and monitors food law enforcement by local authorities. The agency is a UK-wide non-ministerial government body, led by a board which has been appointed to act in the public interest. It has executive offices in Scotland, Wales and Northern Ireland. It is advised by advisory committees on food safety matters of special interest to each of these areas.
Chair, Dame Deirdre Hutton, CBE
Deputy Chair, Dr Ian Reynolds
Chief Executive, John Harwood

FOOD STANDARDS AGENCY NORTHERN IRELAND, 10C Clarendon Road, Belfast BT1 3BG T 028-9041 7700 E infosani@foodstandards.gsi.gov.uk
FOOD STANDARDS AGENCY SCOTLAND, St Magnus House, 6th Floor, 25 Guild Street, Aberdeen AB11 6NJ T 01224-285100 E scotland@foodstandards.gsi.gov.uk
FOOD STANDARDS AGENCY WALES, 11th Floor, Southgate House, Wood Street, Cardiff CF10 1EW T 029-2067 8999 E wales@foodstandards.gsi.gov.uk

MEAT HYGIENE SERVICE

Kings Pool, Peasholme Green, York YO1 7PR
T 01904-455501 F 01904-455502
E mhs.enquiries@mhs.gov.uk
The Meat Hygiene Service was launched in April 1995 as an agency of the former Ministry of Agriculture, Fisheries and Food, and became an executive agency of the Food Standards Agency in April 2000. It protects public health and animal welfare at slaughter through veterinary supervision and meat inspection in approved fresh meat establishments in Great Britain.
Chief Executive, Steve McGrath

FORESTRY COMMISSION

Silvan House, 231 Corstorphine Road, Edinburgh EH12 7AT
T 0131-334 0303 F 0131-334 3047
E enquiries@forestry.gsi.gov.uk W www.forestry.gov.uk

The Forestry Commission is the government department responsible for forestry policy in Great Britain. It reports directly to forestry ministers (ie the Secretary of State for Environment, Food and Rural Affairs, the Scottish ministers and the National Assembly for Wales), to whom it is responsible for advice on forestry policy and for the implementation of that policy.
The commission's principal objectives are to protect Britain's forests and woodlands; expand Britain's forest area; enhance the economic value of forest resources; conserve and improve the biodiversity, landscape and cultural heritage of forests and woodlands; develop opportunities for woodland recreation; and increase public understanding of, and community participation in, forestry.
Chair (part-time), Rt. Hon. Lord Clark of Windermere
Director-General and Deputy Chair, T. Rollinson

FORESTRY COMMISSION ENGLAND, Great Eastern House, Tenison Road, Cambridge CB1 2DU T 01223-314546
FORESTRY COMMISSION SCOTLAND, Silvan House, 231 Corstorphine Road, Edinburgh EH12 7AT T 0131-334 0303
FORESTRY COMMISSION WALES, Victoria Terrace, Aberystwyth, Ceredigion SY23 2DQ T 0845-604 0845
NORTHERN RESEARCH STATION, Roslin, Midlothian EH25 9SY T 0131-445 2176

FOREST ENTERPRISE
Forest Enterprise England, 340 Bristol Business Park, Coldharbour Lane, Bristol BS16 1EJ
T 0117-906 6000 F 0117-931 2859
Forest Enterprise Scotland, 1 Highlander Way, Inverness Business and Retail Park, Inverness IV2 6GB
T 01463-232811 F 01463-243846

Forest Enterprise was established as an executive agency of the Forestry Commission in 1996 to manage the UK's forest estate; it ceased to exist as a single executive agency in March 2003, when three new agencies were created – one each for England, Wales and Scotland. Forest Enterprise Wales has since been wound up, with its responsibilities reabsorbed by the Forestry Commission.
The agencies in England and Scotland take their direction from their respective country governments but their basic remit is to provide environmental, social and economic benefits from the forests they manage.
Chief Executives, Simon Hodgson *(England)*; Dr Hugh Insley *(Scotland)*

FOREST RESEARCH

Alice Holt Lodge, Farnham, Surrey GU10 4LH
T 01420-22255 F 01420-23653
W www.forestresearch.gov.uk

Forest Research is also an executive agency of the Forestry Commissions. Its objectives are to inform and support forestry's contribution to the development and delivery of the policies of the government and devolved administrations; to provide research, development and monitoring services relevant to UK forestry interests; and to transfer knowledge actively and appropriately.
Chief Executive, Prof. Jim Lynch
Research Director, Dr Peter Freer-Smith

HM REVENUE AND CUSTOMS

Board of HM Revenue and Customs, 100 Parliament Street, London SW1A 2BQ
W www.hmrc.gov.uk

HMRC was formed following the integration of the Inland Revenue and HM Customs and Excise, which was made formal by parliament in April 2005. It administers, and advises the Chancellor of the Exchequer on, any matters connected with the following areas: income, corporation, capital gains, inheritance, insurance premium, stamp, land and petroleum revenue taxes; environmental taxes (climate change and aggregates levy, landfill tax); value added tax (VAT); customs duties and frontier protection; excise duties; National Insurance; tax credits, child benefit and the Child Trust Fund; enforcement of the minimum wage; and recovery of student loan repayments.
Chair, Paul Gray, CB
Directors, Stuart Cruickshank; Mike Eland; Mike Hanson, MBE; Dave Hartnett, CB; Steve Heminsley; David Hogg; Chris Hopson; Bernadette Kenny; Steve Lamey

VALUATION OFFICE AGENCY

New Court, 48 Carey Street, London WC2A 2JE
T 020-7506 1700 F 020-7506 1998
E customerservices@voa.gsi.gov.uk W www.voa.gov.uk

Established in 1991, the Valuation Office is an executive agency of HM Revenue and Customs. It is responsible for compiling and maintaining the business rating and council tax valuation lists for England and Wales; valuing property throughout Great Britain for the purposes of taxes administered by the Inland Revenue; providing statutory and non-statutory property valuation services in England, Wales and Scotland; and giving policy advice to ministers on property valuation matters.
Chief Executive, Andrew Hudson

NATIONAL SCHOOL OF GOVERNMENT

Sunningdale Park, Larch Avenue, Ascot, Berks SL5 0QE
T 01344-634000 F 01344-634233
E customer.services@nationalschool.gsi.gov.uk
W www.nationalschool.gov.uk

The National School of Government became a separate non-ministerial department on 1 January 2007. It works both nationally and internationally to help government departments and public sector organisations build capacity in good governance and offer more effective, better value services.
Chair, Sir Brian Bender
Principal and Chief Executive, David Spencer

OFFICE OF FAIR TRADING (OFT)

Fleetbank House, 2–6 Salisbury Square, London EC4Y 8JX
T 020-7211 8000
E enquiries@oft.gsi.gov.uk W www.oft.gov.uk

The OFT is a non-ministerial government department established by statute in 1973, and it is the UK's consumer and competition authority. It encourages businesses to comply with competition and consumer law and to improve their trading practices through self-regulation. It acts decisively to stop hardcore or flagrant offenders, studies markets and recommends action where required, and empowers consumers with the knowledge and skills to make informed choices.
Chair, Philip Collins
Chief Executive Officer, John Fingleton

OFFICE OF GAS AND ELECTRICITY MARKETS (OFGEM)

9 Millbank, London SW1P 3GE
T 020-7901 7295 F 020-7901 7196
E consumeraffairs@ofgem.gov.uk W www.ofgem.gov.uk

OFGEM is the regulator for Britain's gas and electricity industries. Its role is to protect and advance the interests of consumers by promoting competition where possible, and through regulation only where necessary. OFGEM operates under the direction and governance of the Gas and Electricity Markets Authority, which makes all major decisions and sets policy priorities for OFGEM. OFGEM's powers are provided for under the Gas Act 1986 and the Electricity Act 1989, as amended by the Utilities Act 2000. It also has enforcement powers under the Competition Act 1998.
Chair, Sir John Mogg
Chief Executive, Alistair Buchanan

OFFICE OF RAIL REGULATION

1 Kemble Street, London WC2B 4AN
T 020-7282 2000 F 020-7282 2045
E rail.library@orr.gsi.gov.uk W www.rail-reg.gov.uk

The Office of the Rail Regulator was set up under the Railways Act 1993. It became the ORR in July 2004, under the provisions of the Railways and Transport Safety Act 2003. On 1 April 2006, in addition to its role as economic regulator, the ORR became the health and safety regulator for the rail industry. This transfer of responsibility from the Health and Safety Executive was given effect under the Railways Act 2005. The board and chair are appointed by the Secretary of State for Transport. The ORR's key roles are to ensure that Network Rail, the owner and operator of the national railway infrastructure (the track and signalling), manages the network efficiently and in a way that meets the needs of its users; to encourage continuous improvement in health and safety performance while securing compliance with relevant health and safety law, including taking enforcement action as necessary; and to develop policy and enhance relevant railway health and safety legislation. It is also responsible for licensing operators of railway assets, setting the terms for access by operators to the network and other railway facilities, and enforcing competition law in the rail sector.
Chair, Chris Bolt
Chief Executive, Bill Emery

OFFICE FOR STANDARDS IN EDUCATION, CHILDREN'S SERVICES AND SKILLS (OFSTED)

Royal Exchange Buildings, St Ann's Square, Manchester M2 7LA
T 0845-404040 W www.ofsted.gov.uk

OFSTED was established under the Education (Schools Act) 1992 and was relaunched on 1 April 2007 with a wider remit, bringing together four formerly separate inspectorates. It inspects and regulates care for children and young people, and inspects education and training for learners of all ages. *See also* The Education System.
HM Chief Inspector, Christine Gilbert, CBE
Chair, Zenna Atkins

POSTAL SERVICES COMMISSION (POSTCOMM)

Hercules House, 6 Hercules Road, London SE1 7DB
T 020-7593 2100 W www.psc.gov.uk

Postcomm is an independent regulator set up by the Postal Services Act 2000 to secure the universal postal service, improve postal services by introducing competition to the UK postal market, and ensure that postal operators, including Royal Mail, meet the needs of their customers throughout the UK. Postcomm also monitors – and reports to the Department for Business, Enterprise and Regulatory Reform on – the network of post offices in the UK.
Chair, Nigel Stapleton
Chief Executive, Sarah Chambers

REVENUE AND CUSTOMS PROSECUTIONS OFFICE (RCPO)

New Kings Beam House, 22 Upper Ground, London SE1 9BT
E enquiries@rcpo.gsi.gov.uk W www.rcpo.gov.uk

The RCPO prosecutes major drug trafficking and tax fraud cases in the UK, currently at a rate of around 2,500 each year. Prior to the establishment of the RCPO in April 2005, criminal prosecutions were handled separately by Customs and Excise and Inland Revenue Lawyers. The RCPO's director is appointed by the attorney-general.
Director, David Green, QC

SECURITY AND INTELLIGENCE SERVICES

GOVERNMENT COMMUNICATIONS HEADQUARTERS (GCHQ)

Hubble Road, Cheltenham GL51 0EX
T 01242-221491 F 01242-574349
E pressoffice@gchq.gsi.gov.uk W www.gchq.gov.uk

GCHQ produces signals intelligence in support of national security and the UK's economic wellbeing, and in the prevention or detection of serious crime. Additionally, GCHQ Communications-Electronics Security Group (CESG) is the national authority for information assurance, and provides advice and assistance to government departments, the armed forces and other national infrastructure bodies on the security of their communications and information systems. GCHQ was placed on a statutory footing by the Intelligence Services Act 1994 and is headed by a director who is directly accountable to the foreign secretary.
Director, Sir David Pepper

SECRET INTELLIGENCE SERVICE (MI6)

PO Box 1300, London SE1 1BD
W www.mi6.gov.uk

The Secret Intelligence Service produces secret intelligence in support of the government's security, defence, foreign and economic policies. It was placed on a statutory footing by the Intelligence Services Act 1994 and is headed by a chief, known as 'C', who is directly accountable to the foreign secretary.
Chief, Sir J. M. Scarlett, KCMG, OBE

SECURITY SERVICE (MI5)

PO Box 3255, London SW1P 1AE
T 020-7930 9000
W www.mi5.gov.uk

The Security Service is responsible for security intelligence work against covertly organised threats to the UK. These include terrorism, espionage and the proliferation of weapons of mass destruction. The Security Service also provides security advice to a wide range of organisations to help reduce vulnerability to threats from individuals, groups or countries hostile to UK interests. The home secretary has parliamentary accountability for the Security Service.
Director-General, Jonathan Evans

SERIOUS FRAUD OFFICE

Elm House, 10–16 Elm Street, London WC1X 0BJ
T 020-7239 7272 F 020-7837 1689
E public.enquiries@sfo.gsi.gov.uk
W www.sfo.gov.uk

The Serious Fraud Office is an independent government department that investigates and prosecutes serious or complex fraud. It is part of the UK Criminal Justice System. The office is headed by a director who is appointed by and accountable to the Attorney-General, and has jurisdiction over England, Wales and Northern Ireland but not Scotland, the Isle of Man or the Channel Islands.
Director, Robert Wardle

UK TRADE AND INVESTMENT

Kingsgate House, 66–74 Victoria Street, London SW1E 6SW
T 020-7215 8000 W www.uktradeinvest.gov.uk

UK Trade and Investment is a government organisation that aims to enhance the competitiveness of companies in the UK through overseas trade and investments, and to attract high-quality foreign direct investment.
Chief Executive, Andrew Cahn

WATER SERVICES REGULATION AUTHORITY (OFWAT)

Centre City Tower, 7 Hill Street, Birmingham B5 4UA
T 0121-625 1300 F 0121-625 1400
E enquiries@ofwat.gsi.gov.uk W www.ofwat.gov.uk

OFWAT succeeded the director-general of Water Services on 1 April 2006. It is the independent economic regulator of the water and sewerage companies in England and Wales. OFWAT's main duties are to ensure that the companies can finance and carry out the functions specified in the Water Industry Act 1991 and to protect the interests of water customers, by promoting effective competition wherever appropriate.
Chair, Philip Fletcher
Chief Executive, Regina Finn

PUBLIC BODIES

The following section is a listing of public bodies, ombudsman services and selected other civil service organisations.

Whereas executive agencies are either part of a government department or are one in their own right (see Government Departments section), public bodies carry out their functions to a greater or lesser extent at arm's length from central government. Ministers are ultimately responsible to parliament for the activities of the public bodies sponsored by their department and in almost all cases (except where there is separate statutory provision) ministers make the appointments to their boards. Departments are responsible for funding and ensuring good governance of their public bodies.

The term 'public body' is a general one which includes public corporations, such as the BBC; NHS bodies; and non-departmental public bodies (NDPBs). There were 883 public bodies sponsored by UK government departments as at 31 March 2006. This figure is made up of 21 public corporations, the Bank of England, two public broadcasting authorities, 23 NHS bodies and 836 NDPBs. The NDPB group is made up of 199 executive NDPBs, 448 advisory NDPBs, 40 tribunal NDPBs (counted on the basis of tribunal systems rather than individual boards; see Tribunals section) and 149 independent monitoring boards. The following is not a complete listing of these organisations.

ADJUDICATOR'S OFFICE
6th Floor, Haymarket House, 28 Haymarket, London SW1Y 4SP
T 020-7930 2292 F 020-7930 2298
E adjudicators@gtnet.gov.uk W www.adjudicatorsoffice.gov.uk

The Adjudicator's Office opened in 1993 and investigates complaints about the way HM Revenue and Customs, the Valuation Office Agency, the Public Guardianship Office and the Insolvency Service have handled a person's affairs.
The Adjudicator, Dame Barbara Mills, DBE, QC

ADVISORY, CONCILIATION AND ARBITRATION SERVICE (ACAS)
Brandon House, 180 Borough High Street, London SE1 1LW
T 020-7210 3613 Helpline 0845-747 4747 F 020-7210 3708
W www.acas.org.uk

ACAS was set up under the Employment Protection Act 1975 (the provisions now being found in the Trade Union and Labour Relations (Consolidation) Act 1992).

ACAS is funded by the Department for Business, Enterprise and Regulatory Reform and overall guidance is provided by a council consisting of a full-time chair and part-time members from businesses, trade unions and independent sectors. The chair and members are appointed by the Secretary of State for Business, Enterprise and Regulatory Reform. ACAS aims to promote the improvement of industrial relations in general, to provide facilities for conciliation, mediation and arbitration as means of avoiding and resolving industrial disputes, and to provide advisory and information services on industrial relations matters to employers, employees and their representatives.

ACAS has 13 regional offices in Birmingham, Bury St Edmunds, Bristol, Cardiff, Fleet, Glasgow, Leeds, Liverpool, London, Manchester, Newcastle upon Tyne, Nottingham and Paddock Wood.
Chair, Rita Donaghy, CBE
Chief Executive, John Taylor

ADVISORY COUNCIL ON NATIONAL RECORDS AND ARCHIVES
Secretariat : The National Archives, Kew, Surrey TW9 4DU
T 020-8392 5381 F 020-8392 9198
W www.nationalarchives.gov.uk/advisorycouncil

Following the bringing together of the Public Record Office and the Historical Manuscripts Commission to form the National Archives, the advisory council advises on all matters relating to the preservation, use of, and access to historical manuscripts, records and archives of all kinds. The Advisory Council on National Records and Archives encompasses the statutory Advisory Council on Public Records, and advises on public records issues as before.
Chair, Rt. Hon. Sir Anthony Clarke (Master of the Rolls)

ANCIENT MONUMENTS BOARD FOR WALES (CADW)
Plas Carew, Unit 5–7 Cefn Coed, Parc Nantgarw,
Cardiff CF15 7QQ
T 01443-336000 F 01443-336001
E cadw@wales.gsi.gov.uk W www.cadw.wales.gov.uk

The Ancient Monuments Advisory Board for Wales advises the Welsh Assembly Government on its statutory functions in respect of ancient monuments.
Chair, Richard Brewer
Members, Prof. Miranda Aldhouse-Green, FSA; Dr Nancy Edwards; Prof. Ralph Griffiths, DLITT; John Hilling; Christopher Musson, MBE, FSA; Dr Emma Plunkett Dillon; Dr Anthony Ward; Prof. Alasdair Whittle, FBA, DPHIL

ARCHITECTURE AND DESIGN SCOTLAND (A+DS)
Bakehouse Close, 146 Canongate, Edinburgh EH8 8DD
T 0131-556 6699 F 0131-556 6633
E info@ads.org.uk W www.ads.org.uk

Architecture and Design Scotland (A+DS) was established in 2005 by the Scottish Executive as the national champion for good architecture, design and planning in the built environment; it works with a wide range of organisations at national, regional and local levels. A+DS also assumed the independent design review and advisory role of the Royal Fine Art Commission for Scotland.
Chair, Raymond Young
Chief Executive, Sebastian Tombs

ARMED FORCES' PAY REVIEW BODY
6th Floor, Kingsgate House, 66–74 Victoria Street,
London SW1E 6SW
T 020-7215 8534 W www.ome.uk.com

The Armed Forces' Pay Review Body was appointed in 1971. It advises the prime minister and the Secretary of State for Defence on the pay and allowances of members of naval, military and air forces of the crown.

Chair, Prof. David Greenaway

Members, Robert Burgin; Alison Gallico; Dr Peter Knight; Prof. Derek Leslie; Keith McNeish; Neil Sherlock; Air Vice-Marshall (retd) Ian Stewart, CB; Dr Anne Wright; Lord Young of Norwood Green

ARTS COUNCIL ENGLAND

14 Great Peter Street, London SW1P 3NQ
T 0845-300 6200 F 020-7973 6590
E enquiries@artscouncil.org.uk
W www.artscouncil.org.uk

Arts Council England is the national development agency for the arts in England, distributing public money from government and the National Lottery. Between 2006 and 2008 Arts Council England plans to invest £1.1bn of public funds in the arts in England. Arts Council grants are for individuals, arts organisations, national touring and other people who use the arts in their work.

In 2002, the Arts Council of England and nine regional arts boards joined together to form a single development organisation for the arts. The governing council's members and chair are appointed by the Secretary of State for Culture, Media and Sport usually for a term of four years, and meet approximately five times a year.

Chair, Prof. Sir Christopher Frayling

Members, Diran Adebayo; Janet Barnes; Tom Bloxham, MBE; Kentake Chinyelu-Hope; Lady Hollick; Keith Khan; Prof. Alan Livingston; Sir Brian McMaster, CBE; Francois Matarasso; Elsie Owusu, OBE; Alice Rawsthorn; Dr Tom Shakespeare; Prof. Stuart Timperley; Dorothy Wilson

Chief Executive, Peter Hewitt

ARTS COUNCIL OF NORTHERN IRELAND

77 Malone Road, Belfast BT9 6AQ
T 028-9038 5200 F 028-9066 1715
E info@artscouncil-ni.org W www.artscouncil-ni.org

The Arts Council of Northern Ireland is the prime distributor of government funds in support of the arts in Northern Ireland. It is funded by the Department of Culture, Arts and Leisure and from National Lottery funds. In January 2007, the council launched a five-year plan which aims to increase arts funding from £6 to £10 per capita (an increase of approximately £20m for the period up to 2012).

Chair, Rosemary Kelly

Members, Eithne Benson; Kate Bond; Martin Bradley *(Vice-Chair);* Lucy Finnegan; Raymond Fullerton; Anthony Kennedy; Tim Kerr; Jill McEneaney; Bill Montgomery; Sharon O'Connor; Gearoid O'Heara; Peter Spratt

Chief Executive, Roisin McDonough

ARTS COUNCIL OF WALES

9 Museum Place, Cardiff CF10 3NX
T 029-2037 6500 F 029-2022 1447
E feedback@artswales.org.uk
W www.artswales.org.uk

The Arts Council of Wales was established in 1994 by royal charter and is the development body for the arts in Wales. It funds arts organisations with funding from the National Assembly for Wales and is the distributor of National Lottery funds to the arts in Wales. The grant for 2006–7 was £26.6m from the National Assembly and £11.3m from the National Lottery.

Chair, Prof. Dai Smith

Members, Simon Dancey; Maggie Hampton; John Metcalf; Robin Morrison; Christopher O'Neil; Dr Ian J. Rees; Clive Sefia; Ruth Till; David Vokes; Debbie Wilcox; Rhiannon Wyn Hughes

Chief Executive, Peter Tyndall

AUDIT COMMISSION

1st Floor, Millbank Tower, London SW1P 4HQ
T 020-7828 1212 F 020-7976 6187
E enquiries@audit-commission.gov.uk
W www.audit-commission.gov.uk

The Audit Commission was set up in 1983 and is an independent body responsible for ensuring that public money is spent economically, efficiently and effectively, to achieve high-quality local services for the public. Its remit covers around 11,000 bodies in England, which between them spend more than £180bn of public money each year. Its work covers local government, health, criminal justice organisations and public services.

The commission has a chair, a deputy chair and a board of up to 20 commissioners who are appointed by the Department of Communities and Local Government following consultation with key stakeholders.

Chair, Michael Higgins

Members, S. Bundred *(ex officio);* Jim Coulter; Dr Jennifer Dixon; Sheila Drew Smith; Cllr Stephen Houghton; Cllr Peter Jones; Sir Thomas Legg; David Moss; Brian Pomeroy, CBE; Prof. Peter Smith; Cllr Chris White

Chief Executive, Steve Bundred

BANK OF ENGLAND

Threadneedle Street, London EC2R 8AH
T 020-7601 4444 F 020-7601 4771
E enquiries@bankofengland.co.uk
W www.bankofengland.co.uk

The Bank of England was incorporated in 1694 under royal charter. It is the banker of the government and it manages the issue of banknotes. Since 1997 it has been operationally independent and its Monetary Policy Committee has had responsibility for setting short-term interest rates to meet the government's inflation target. As the central reserve bank of the country, the Bank of England keeps the accounts of British banks, who maintain with it a proportion of their cash resources, and of most overseas central banks. The bank's core purposes are monetary stability and financial stability. Its responsibility for banking supervision was transferred to the Financial Services Authority in 1998.

Governor, M. A. King

Deputy Governors, Sir John Gieve, CB; Ms R. Lomax

Non-Executive Directors, B. Barber; Ms A. C. Fawcett, CBE; Mrs M. Francis, LVO; Sir Graham Hall; Hon. Peter Jay; Prof. Sir John Likierman; C. McCarthy; P. Myners; Sir Thomas Parker; Dr D. Potter, CBE; Ms H. Rabbats, CBE; David Rhind; A. Sarin; James Strachan; G. Wilkinson; Bob Wigley

Monetary Policy Committee, The Governor; the Deputy Governors; Mrs K. Barker; C. Bean; Prof. Tim Besley; D. Blanchflower; Dr Andrew Sentance; P. Tucker

Advisers to the Governor, M. Blejer; Juliet Wheldon
Chief Cashier and Executive Director, Banking Services, A. Bailey
The Auditor, S. Brown

BIG LOTTERY FUND

1 Plough Place, London EC4A 1DE
T 020-7211 1800 F 020-7211 1750
Advice Line 0845-410 2030
E general.enquiries@biglotteryfund.org.uk
W www.biglotteryfund.org.uk

The Big Lottery Fund was launched in 2004, merging the New Opportunities Fund and the Community Fund. The fund receives 50 per cent of the proceeds raised for good causes through the sale of lottery tickets, which is currently between £600m and £700m per year (this level of funding is guaranteed until the current Camelot licence expires in 2009). The money is distributed to charitable, benevolent and philanthropic organisations in the voluntary and community sectors, as well as health, education and environmental projects. The Big Lottery Fund also assumed the Millennium Commission's role of supporting large-scale regenerative projects.

Chair, Prof. Sir Clive Booth
Vice-Chair, Anna Southall
Regional Chairs, Sanjay Dighe *(England)*; Breidge Gadd, CBE *(Northern Ireland)*; Alison Magee *(Scotland)*; Huw Vaughan *(Wales)*
General Members, Judith Donovan, CBE; Roland Doven, MBE; John Gartside, OBE; Esther O'Callaghan; Albert Tucker; Diana Whitworth
Chief Executive, Stephen Dunmore
Directors, Walter Rader *(Northern Ireland)*; Dharmendra Kanani *(Scotland)*; Ceri Doyle *(Wales)*

BOUNDARY COMMISSIONS

The commissions, established in 1944, are constituted under the Parliamentary Constituencies Act 1986 (as amended). The Speaker of the House of Commons is *ex officio* chair of all four commissions in the UK. Each of the four commissions is required by law to keep the parliamentary constituencies in their part of the UK under review. The latest Boundary Commission report for England was laid before parliament in February 2007, and the proposals outlined will take effect at the next general election. The latest report from Northern Ireland was published in May 2006, from Wales in January 2005 and the most recent Scottish report was completed in December 2004.

ENGLAND

1 Drummond Gate, London SW1V 2QQ
T 020-7533 5177 F 020-7533 5176
E bcomm.england@ons.gov.uk W www.statistics.gov.uk/pbc/
Deputy Chair, Hon. Mr Justice Sullivan

WALES

1st Floor, Caradog House, 1–6 St Andrews Place, Cardiff CF10 3BE
T 029-2039 5031 F 029-2039 5250
E bcomm.wales@wales.gsi.gov.uk
W www.bcomm-wales.gov.uk
Deputy Chair, Hon. Justice Lloyd Jones

SCOTLAND

3 Drumsheugh Gardens, Edinburgh EH3 7QJ
T 0131-538 7200 F 0131-538 7240

E secretariat@bcomm-scotland.gov.uk
W www.bcomm-scotland.gov.uk
Deputy Chair, Hon. Lord McEwan

NORTHERN IRELAND

Forestview, Purdy's Lane, Newtownbreda, Belfast BT8 7AR
T 028-9069 4800 F 028-9069 4801
E bcni@belfast.org.uk W www.boundarycommission.org.uk
Deputy Chair, Hon. Mr Justice Coghlin

BRITISH BROADCASTING CORPORATION (BBC)

Television Centre, Wood Lane, London W12 7RJ
T 020-8743 8000 BBC Information Line 0870-010 0222
W www.bbc.co.uk

The BBC was incorporated under royal charter in 1926 as successor to the British Broadcasting Company Ltd. The BBC's current charter, which came into force on 1 January 2007 and extends to 31 December 2016, recognises the BBC's editorial independence and sets out its public purposes. The BBC Trust was formed under the new charter and replaces the Board of Governors; it sets the strategic direction of the BBC and has a duty to represent the interests of licence fee payers. The chair, vice-chair and other trustees are appointed by the Queen-in-Council. The BBC is financed by revenue from receiving licences for the home services and by grant-in-aid from parliament for the World Service (radio). *See also* Broadcasting section.

BBC TRUST MEMBERS

Chair, Sir Michael Lyons
Vice-Chair, Chitra Bharucha
National Trustees, Alison Hastings *(England)*; Rotha Johnston *(N. Ireland)*; Janet Lewis-Jones *(Wales)*; Jeremy Peat *(Scotland)*
Trustees, Diane Coyle; Dermot Gleeson; Patricia Hodgson; David Liddiment; Mehmuda Mian Pritchard; Richard Tait

EXECUTIVE BOARD

Director-General and Chair, Mark Thompson
Deputy Director-General, Mark Byford
Directors, Jenny Abramsky *(Audio and Music)*; Jana Bennett *(Vision)*; Tim Davie *(Marketing, Communications and Audiences)*; Ashley Highfield *(Future Media and Technology)*; Stephen Kelly *(People)*; Zarin Patel *(Group Finance)*
Chief Executive, BBC Worldwide, John Smith
Chief Operating Officer, Caroline Thomas
Senior Independent Director, Marcus Agius
Non-Executive Directors, Dr Mike Lynch, OBE; David Robbie; Dr Samir Shah, OBE; Robert Webb, QC

STATION CONTROLLERS

BBC1, Peter Fincham
BBC2, Roly Keating
BBC3, Danny Cohen
BBC4, Janice Hadlow
BBC News 24, Kevin Bakhurst
BBC Parliament, Peter Knowles
BBC Northern Ireland, Peter Johnston
BBC Scotland, Ken MacQuarrie
BBC Wales, Menna Richards
Radio 1, Andy Parfitt
Radio 2, Lesley Douglas
Radio 3, Roger Wright

Radio 4, Mark Damazer
Radio 5 Live, Bob Shennan

BRITISH COUNCIL

Bridgewater House, 58 Whitworth Street, Manchester M1 6BB
T 0161-957 7755 F 0161-957 7762
E general.enquiries@britishcouncil.org
W www.britishcouncil.org

The British Council was established in 1934, incorporated by royal charter in 1940 and granted a supplemental charter in 1993. It is an independent, non-political organisation which promotes Britain abroad and is the UK's international organisation for educational and cultural relations. The British Council is represented in 216 towns and cities in 109 countries. Turnover in 2005–6, including Foreign and Commonwealth Office grants and contracted money, was £512m.
Chair, Lord Kinnock, PC
Chief Executive, Martin Davidson, CMG

BRITISH FILM INSTITUTE (BFI)

21 Stephen Street, London W1T 1LN
T 020-7255 1444 F 020-7436 0165
W www.bfi.org.uk

The BFI, established in 1933, offers opportunities for people throughout the UK to experience, learn and discover more about the world of film and moving image culture. It incorporates the BFI National Archive, the BFI National Library, a range of video and DVD releases, publications and educational materials (including the monthly *Sight and Sound* magazine), BFI Southbank, BFI Distribution, the annual BFI London Film Festival as well as the BFI London Lesbian and Gay Film Festival, and the BFI IMAX cinema, and provides advice and support for regional cinemas and film festivals across the UK.
Chair, Anthony Minghella, CBE
Director, Amanda Nevill

BRITISH LIBRARY

96 Euston Road, London NW1 2DB
T 020-7412 7332 F 020-7412 7340
E visitor-services@bl.uk W www.bl.uk

The British Library was established in 1973. It is the UK's national library and occupies a key position in the library and information network. It aims to serve scholarship, research, industry, commerce and all other major users of information. Its services are based on a collection of 150 million separate items, including books, journals, manuscripts, maps, stamps, music, patents, newspapers and sound recordings in all written and spoken languages. The library is now based at three sites: London (St Pancras and Colindale) and Boston Spa, W. Yorks. The library's sponsoring department is the Department for Culture, Media and Sport.

Access to the reading rooms at St Pancras is limited to holders of a British Library reader's pass; information about eligibility is available from the reader admissions office. The exhibition galleries and public areas are open to all, free of charge.

BRITISH LIBRARY BOARD
Chair, Sir Colin Lucas
Chief Executive and Deputy Chair, Mrs L. Brindley
Members, Ms D. Airey; H. Boyd-Carpenter, KCVO; R. S. Broadhurst, CBE; Prof. R. Burgess; Sir K. Calman; Ms

S. Forbes, CBE; Prof. W. Hall, CBE; Ms E. Mackay, CB; Prof. K. McLuskie; S. Olswang; Dr G. W. Roberts; M. Semple, OBE

SCHOLARSHIP AND COLLECTIONS
Americas Collections, T 020-7412 7743
Asia, Pacific and Africa Collections, T 020-7412 7873
British and Irish Collections, T 020-7412 7538
British Library Newspapers, Colindale Avenue, London NW9 5HE T 020-7412 7353
British Library Sound Archive, T 020-7412 7676
Early Printed Collections, T 020-7412 7676
Map Library, T 020-7412 7702
Music Library, T 020-7412 7772
Philatelic Collections, T 020-7412 7635
Reader Information, T 020-7412 7676
West European Collections, T 020-7412 7572

OPERATIONS AND SERVICES
Permission Clearance, T 020-7412 7755
Research Services, T 020-7412 7797

SCIENCE, TECHNOLOGY AND INNOVATION
Business, T 020-7412 7454
National Preservation Office, T 020-7412 7612
Patents, T 020-7412 7919
Science and Technology, T 020-7412 7494/7288
Social Science, Law and Official Publications, T 020-7412 7536

BRITISH LIBRARY, BOSTON SPA
Boston Spa, Wetherby, W. Yorks LS23 7BQ
T 01937-546000

BRITISH MUSEUM

Great Russell Street, London WC1B 3DG
T 020-7323 8000 F 020-7323 8616
E information@thebritishmuseum.ac.uk
W www.thebritishmuseum.ac.uk

The British Museum houses the national collection of antiquities, ethnography, coins and paper money, medals, prints and drawings. The British Museum may be said to date from 1753, when parliament approved the holding of a public lottery to raise funds for the purchase of the collections of Sir Hans Sloane and the Harleian manuscripts, and for their proper housing and maintenance. The building (Montagu House) was opened in 1759. The existing buildings were erected between 1823 and the present day, and the original collection has increased to its current dimensions by gifts and purchases. Total government grant-in-aid for 2006–7 was in the region of £40m.

BOARD OF TRUSTEES
Appointed by the Sovereign, HRH The Duke of Gloucester, KG, GCVO
Appointed by the Prime Minister, Chief Emeka Anyaoku; Lord Broers; Sir Ronald Cohen; Prof. Sir Barry Cunliffe, CBE; Francis Finlay; Niall FitzGerald, KBE *(Chair);* Val Gooding, OBE; Bonnie Greer; Baroness Kennedy; Richard Lambert; David Lindsell; Dr David Norgrove; Eric Salama; Vikram Seth, CBE
Appointed by the Trustees of the British Museum, Stephen Green; Lord Powell of Bayswater, KCMG; Sir John Tusa
Appointed by the Royal Society, Dr Olga Kennard; Ms Edmee P. Leventis

Appointed by the Royal Academy, Antony Gormley, OBE
Appointed by the British Academy, Sir Keith Thomas, FBA

OFFICERS
Director, Neil MacGregor
Deputy Director, Andrew Burnett
Director of Communications, Joanna Mackle
Director of Marketing and Public Affairs, Gillian Marsh
Director of Operations, Chris Rofe
Heads of Departments, Simon Neale *(Capital Projects);* Joanna Mackle *(Communications);* Xerxes Mazda *(Education);* Stephen Gill *(Facilities);* Zoe Hancock *(Finance, acting);* Carolyn Young *(Membership Development)*

KEEPERS
Keeper of Ancient Near East Antiquities, Dr John Curtis
Keeper of Coins and Medals, Joe Cribb
Keeper of Department of Asia, Jan Stuart
Keeper of Ancient Egypt and Sudan, Vivian Davies
Keeper of Africa, Oceania and the Americas, Jonathan King
Keeper of Greek and Roman Antiquities, Dr Dyfri Williams
Keeper of Prehistory and Europe, Jonathan Williams
Keeper of Prints and Drawings, Antony Griffiths
Conservation, Documentation and Science, David Saunders

BRITISH PHARMACOPOEIA COMMISSION
Market Towers, 1 Nine Elms Lane, London SW8 5NQ
T 020-7084 2561 E bpcom@mhra.gsi.gov.uk
W www.pharmacopoeia.org.uk

The British Pharmacopoeia Commission sets standards for medicinal products used in human and veterinary medicines and is responsible for publication of the *British Pharmacopoeia* (a publicly available statement of the standard that a product must meet throughout its shelf-life), the *British Pharmacopoeia (Veterinary)* and the *British Approved Names*. It has 17 members, including two lay members, who are appointed by the NHS Appointments Commission (the body responsible for appointments to all of the Medicines Act advisory bodies).
Chair, Prof. A. D. Woolfson
Vice-Chair, V'lain Fenton-May
Secretary and Scientific Director, Dr M. G. Lee

BRITISH WATERWAYS
Willow Grange, Church Road, Watford WD17 4QA
T 01923-201120 F 01923-201400
E enquiries.hq@britishwaterways.co.uk
W www.britishwaterways.co.uk

British Waterways conserves and manages the network of over 3,540km (2,200 miles) of canals and rivers in England, Scotland and Wales. Its sponsoring departments are the Department for Environment, Food and Rural Affairs in England and Wales, and the Enterprise, Transport and Lifelong Learning Department in Scotland.
   Its responsibilities include maintaining the waterways and structures on and around them; looking after wildlife and the waterway environment; and ensuring that canals and rivers are safe and enjoyable places to visit.
Chair, Tony Hales
Vice-Chair, Dr Campbell Christie, CBE
Chief Executive, Robin Evans, FRICS

CENTRAL ARBITRATION COMMITTEE (CAC)
PO Box 51547, London SE1 1ZG
T 020-7904 2300 F 020-7904 2301
E enquiries@cac.gov.uk W www.cac.gov.uk

The CAC is a permanent independent body with statutory powers whose main function is to adjudicate on applications relating to the statutory recognition and de-recognition of trade unions for collective bargaining purposes, where such recognition or de-recognition cannot be agreed voluntarily. In addition, the CAC has a statutory role in determining disputes between trade unions and employers over the disclosure of information for collective bargaining purposes, and in resolving applications and complaints under the information and consultation regulations, and performs a similar role in relation to the legislation on the European Works Council, European companies and the European cooperative societies. The CAC also provides voluntary arbitration in industrial disputes.
   The committee consists of a chair and 11 deputy chairs, 29 members experienced as representatives of employers and 26 members experienced as representatives of workers. All members of the committee are appointed by the Secretary of State for Business, Enterprise and Regulatory Reform after consulting ACAS.
Chair, Sir Michael Burton
Chief Executive, Graeme Charles

CERTIFICATION OFFICE FOR TRADE UNIONS AND EMPLOYERS' ASSOCIATIONS
Brandon House, 180 Borough High Street, London SE1 1LW
T 020-7210 3734 F 020-7210 3612
E info@certoffice.org W www.certoffice.org

The Certification Office is an independent statutory authority. The certification officer is appointed by the Secretary of State for Business, Enterprise and Regulatory Reform and is responsible for receiving and scrutinising annual returns from trade unions and employers' associations; for determining complaints concerning trade union elections, certain ballots and certain breaches of trade union rules; for ensuring observance of statutory requirements governing mergers between trade unions and employers' associations; for overseeing the political funds and finances of trade unions and employers' associations; and for certifying the independence of trade unions.
Certification Officer, David Cockburn

SCOTLAND
69A George Street, Edinburgh EH2 2JG
T 0131-220 7660
Certification Officer for Scotland, Christine Stuart

CHURCH COMMISSIONERS
Church House, Great Smith Street, London SW1P 3AZ
T 020-7898 1000 F 020-7898 1131
E commissioners.enquiry@c-of-e.org
W www.cofe.anglican.org/about/churchcommissioners

The Church Commissioners were established in 1948 by the amalgamation of Queen Anne's Bounty (established 1704) and the Ecclesiastical Commissioners (established 1836). They are responsible for the management of some of the Church of England's assets, the income from which is predominantly used to help pay for the stipend and pension of the clergy. The commissioners own over 48,500ha (120,000 acres) of agricultural land, a residential estate in central London, and commercial property across Great Britain. They also carry out administrative duties in connection with pastoral reorganisation and redundant churches.

The commissioners are: the Archbishops of Canterbury and of York; four bishops, three clergy and four lay persons elected by the respective houses of the General Synod; two deans elected by all the deans; three persons nominated by the Queen; three persons nominated by the Archbishops of Canterbury and York; three persons nominated by the archbishops after consultation with others including the Lord Mayors of London and York and the vice-chancellors of the universities of Oxford and Cambridge; the First Lord of the Treasury; the Lord President of the Council; the home secretary; the Lord Chancellor; the Secretary of State for Culture, Media and Sport; and the Speaker of the House of Commons.

CHURCH ESTATES COMMISSIONERS
First, A. Whittam Smith
Second, Sir Stuart Bell, MP
Third, T. E. H. Walker

OFFICERS
Secretary, A. C. Brown

ASSISTANT SECRETARIES
Chief Surveyor, P. Clark
Chief Investments Manager, M. Chaloner
Pastoral and Redundant Churches, P. Lewis
Official Solicitor, S. Jones

CIVIL AVIATION AUTHORITY (CAA)
CAA House, 45–59 Kingsway, London WC2B 6TE
T 020-7379 7311 E infoservices@caa.co.uk
W www.caa.co.uk

The CAA is the UK's specialist aviation regulator. Its responsibilities include ensuring that the aviation industry meets the highest technical and operational safety standards; preventing holidaymakers from being stranded abroad or losing money because of tour operator insolvency; planning and regulating all UK airspace; regulating airports, air traffic services and airlines; and providing advice on aviation policy from an economic standpoint. The government provides no direct funding; the CAA must meet its costs entirely from charges on those whom it regulates.
Chair, Sir Roy McNulty, CBE

THE COAL AUTHORITY
200 Lichfield Lane, Mansfield, Notts NG18 4RG
T 01623-637000 F 01623-622072
E thecoalauthority@coal.gov.uk W www.coal.gov.uk

The Coal Authority was established under the Coal Industry Act 1994 to manage certain functions previously undertaken by British Coal, including ownership of unworked coal. It is responsible for licensing coal mining operations and for providing information on coal reserves and past and future coal mining. It settles subsidence damage claims which are not the reponsibility of licensed coal mining operators. It deals with the management and disposal of property, and with surface hazards such as abandoned coal mine shafts.

Chair, Dr Helen Mounsey
Chief Executive, Philip Lawrence

COLLEGE OF ARMS (HERALDS' COLLEGE)
Queen Victoria Street, London EC4V 4BT
T 020-7248 2762 F 020-7248 6448
E enquiries@college-of-arms.gov.uk
W www.college-of-arms.gov.uk

The Sovereign's Officers of Arms (Kings, Heralds and Pursuivants of Arms) were first incorporated by Richard III in 1484. The powers vested by the crown in the Earl Marshal (the Duke of Norfolk) with regard to state ceremonial are largely exercised through the college. The college is also the official repository of the arms and pedigrees of English, Welsh, Northern Irish and Commonwealth (except Canadian) families and their descendants, and its records include official copies of the records of the Ulster King of Arms, the originals of which remain in Dublin. The 13 officers of the college specialise in genealogical and heraldic work for their respective clients.

Arms have long been, and still are, granted by letters patent from the Kings of Arms. A right to arms can only be established by the registration in the official records of the College of Arms of a pedigree showing direct male line descent from an ancestor already appearing therein as being entitled to arms, or by making application through the College of Arms for a grant of arms. Grants are made to corporations as well as to individuals.
Earl Marshal, Duke of Norfolk

KINGS OF ARMS
Garter, P. L. Gwynn-Jones, CVO, FSA
Clarenceux, D. H. B. Chesshyre, CVO, FSA
Norroy and Ulster, T. Woodcock, LVO, FSA

HERALDS
Richmond (and Earl Marshal's Secretary), P. L. Dickinson, LVO
York, H. E. Paston-Bedingfeld
Chester, T. H. S. Duke
Lancaster, R. J. B. Noel
Windsor (and Registrar), W. G. Hunt, TD
Somerset, D. V. White

PURSUIVANTS
Rouge Dragon, C. E. A. Cheesman
Bluemantle, M. P. D. O'Donoghue

COMMISSION FOR ARCHITECTURE AND THE BUILT ENVIRONMENT (CABE)
1 Kemble Street, London WC2B 4AN
T 020-7070 6700 F 020-7070 6777
E enquiries@cabe.org.uk W www.cabe.org.uk

CABE was established in 1999 and is responsible for promoting the importance of high-quality architecture and urban design, and for encouraging the understanding of architecture through educational and regional initiatives. The commission offers free advice to local authorities, public sector clients and others embarking on building projects of any size or purpose. CABE has a board of 16 commissioners, appointed by the Secretary of State for Culture, Media and Sport for a maximum of two four-year terms.
Chair, John Sorrell
Chief Executive, Richard Simmons

COMMISSION FOR INTEGRATED TRANSPORT (CFIT)

1/F16, Ashdown House, 123 Victoria Street, London SW1E 6DE
T 020-7944 8131 F 020-7944 8643
E cfit@dft.gsi.gov.uk W www.cfit.gov.uk

The CfIT was established in June 1999. Its role is to provide independent expert advice to the government in order to achieve a transport system that supports sustainable development. The CfIT also encourages best practice amongst local authorities and delivery agencies, and assesses both the impact of new technology on future policy options and transport policy initiatives from outside the UK. Members of the commission are appointed by the transport secretary.
Chair, Peter Hendy
Vice-Chair, David Leeder

COMMISSION FOR EQUALITY AND HUMAN RIGHTS (CEHR)

Kingsgate House, 66–74 Victoria Street, London SW1E 6SW
T 020-7215 8415 F 020-7215 8225
W www.cehr.org.uk

The CEHR is a statutory body, established under the Equality Act 2006 and launched in October 2007. It inherited the responsibilities of the Commission for Racial Equality, the Disability Rights Commission and the Equal Opportunities Commission. The CEHR's purpose is to reduce inequality, eliminate discrimination, strengthen relations between people, and promote and protect human rights. It enforces equality legislation on age, disability and health, gender, race, religion and belief, sexual orientation or transgender status, and encourages compliance with the Human Rights Act 1998 throughout England, Wales and Scotland.

The Secretary of State for Communities and Local Government appoints the chair and commissioners of the board, which has a maximum of 15 members including a commissioner each for Wales and Scotland, and one who is or has been a disabled person.
Chair, Trevor Phillips
Deputy Chair, Baroness Prosser, OBE
Commissioners, Morag Alexander; Kay Allen; Dame Jane Campbell, DBE; Kay Carberry; Jeannie Drake, CBE; Baroness Greengross, OBE; Prof. Kay Hampton; Francesca Klug; Sir Bert Massie, CBE; Ziauddin Sardar; Ben Summerskill; Dr Neil Wooding
Chief Executive, Dr Nicola Brewer

COMMISSION FOR RURAL COMMUNITIES

John Dower House, Crescent Place, Cheltenham GL50 3RA
T 01242-521381 E info@ruralcommunities.gov.uk
W www.ruralcommunities.gov.uk

The Commission for Rural Communities was established in October 2006; it was formerly an operating division of the now-defunct Countryside Agency. It is a statutory body under the Natural Environment and Rural Communities Act 2006 and it aims to provide well-informed, independent advice to government and to ensure that policies reflect the needs of people living and working in rural England, with a particular focus on tackling disadvantage. Its three key roles are to be a rural advocate, an expert adviser and an independent watchdog. The commission is funded by an annual grant from the Department for Environment, Food and Rural Affairs and board members are appointed by the secretary of state.
Chair and Rural Advocate, Dr Stuart Burgess
Members, Prof. Sheena Asthana; Richard Burge; Dr Jim Cox, OBE; Elinor Goodman; Alison McLean; Howard Petch, CBE; Prof. Mark Shucksmith; John Varley; Prof. Michael Winter, OBE
Chief Executive, Graham Garbutt

COMMITTEE ON STANDARDS IN PUBLIC LIFE

35 Great Smith Street, London SW1P 3BQ
T 020-7276 2595 F 020-7276 2585
E standards@evidence.x.gsi.gov.uk
W www.public-standards.gov.uk

The Committee on Standards in Public Life was set up in October 1994. It is a standing body whose chair and members are appointed by the prime minister; three members are nominated by the leaders of the three main political parties. The committee's remit is to examine concerns about standards of conduct of all holders of public office, including arrangements relating to financial and commercial activities, and to make recommendations as to any changes in present arrangements which might be required to ensure the highest standards of propriety in public life. It is also charged with reviewing issues in relation to the funding of political parties. The committee does not investigate individual allegations of misconduct.
Chair (acting), Rita Donaghy, CBE
Members, Lloyd Clark, QPM; Prof. Hazel Genn, CBE; Dame Patricia Hodgson, DBE; Baroness Maddock; Rt. Hon. Baroness Shephard of Northwold; Dr Elizabeth Vallance; Dr Brian Woods-Scawen

COMMONWEALTH WAR GRAVES COMMISSION

2 Marlow Road, Maidenhead, Berks SL6 7DX
T 01628-634221 F 01628-771208
E casualty.enq@cwgc.org W www.cwgc.org

The Commonwealth War Graves Commission (formerly Imperial War Graves Commission) was founded by royal charter in 1917. It is responsible for the commemoration of around 1.7 million members of the forces of the Commonwealth who lost their lives in the two world wars. More than one million graves are maintained in 23,274 burial grounds throughout the world. Over three-quarters of a million men and women who have no known grave or who were cremated are commemorated by name on memorials built by the commission.

The funds of the commission are derived from the six participating governments, ie the UK, Canada, Australia, New Zealand, South Africa and India.
President, HRH The Duke of Kent, KG, GCMG, GCVO, ADC
Chair, Secretary of State for Defence (UK)
Vice-Chair, Air Chief Marshal Sir Peter Squire, GCB, DFC, AFC, DSC
Members, High Commissioners in London for Australia, Canada, South Africa, New Zealand and India; Adm. Sir Ian Garnett, KCB; Lt.-Gen. Sir Alistair Irwin, KCB, CBE; Ian Henderson, CBE, FRICS; Sara Jones, CBE; Alan Meale, MP; Hon. Nicholas Soames, MP; Prof. Huw Strachan, FRSE; Sir Rob Young, GCMG

Director-General and Secretary to the Commission, R. E.
Kellaway, CBE
Deputy Director-General, T. V. Reeves
Legal Adviser and Solicitor, G. C. Reddie

COMPETITION COMMISSION

Victoria House, Southampton Row, London WC1B 4AD
T 020-7271 0100
E info@cc.gsi.gov.uk W www.competition-commission.org.uk

The commission was established in 1948 as the
Monopolies and Restrictive Practices Commission (later
the Monopolies and Mergers Commission); it became the
Competition Commission in April 1999 under the
Competition Act 1998. The commission conducts in-
depth inquiries into mergers, markets, and the regulation
of major industries. Every inquiry the commission
undertakes is in response to a reference made to it by
another authority, usually the Office of Fair Trading. The
commission has no power to conduct inquiries on its own
initiative. The Enterprise Act 2002 introduced a new
regime for the assessment of mergers and markets in the
UK – in most related investigations the commission is
responsible for making decisions on the competition
questions and for making and implementing decisions on
appropriate remedies.

The commission has a full-time chair and three deputy
chairs. There are usually around 50 part-time commission
members, who usually carry out investigations in groups
of four or five after appointment by the chair. All are
appointed by the Secretary of State for Business,
Enterprise and Regulatory Reform for eight-year terms.
Chair, Peter Freeman
Deputy Chairs, Christopher Clarke; Dr Peter Davis; Diana
Guy
Members, Jayne Almond; Prof. John Baillie; Christopher
Bright; Laura Carstensen; Dr John Collings; Dr Diane
Coyle; Prof. John Cubbin; Roger Davis; Carolan
Dobson; Barbara Donoghue; Laurence Elks; Richard
Farrant; Christopher Goodall; Prof. Alan Gregory,
FCMA; Ivar Grey; Prof. Alan Hamlin; Prof. Jonathan
Haskel; Peter Hazell; Jill Hill; Richard Holroyd;
Alexander Johnston; Ian Jones; Peter Jones; Prof. Bruce
Lyons; Dame Barbara Mills, DBE, QC; Prof. Peter
Moizer, FCA; Jeremy Peat; Prof. Mahendra Raj;
Christopher Smallwood; John Smith; Anthony Stern;
Peter Stoddart, FCA; Prof. Sudi Sudarsanam; Richard
Taylor; Robert Turgoose; Prof. Catherine Waddams;
Steven Walzer; Prof. Michael Waterson; Jonathan
Whiticar; Prof. Stephen Wilks, FCA; Fiona Woolf, CBE
Non-Executive Directors, Tony Foster; Dame Patricia
Hodgson, DBE
Chief Executive and Secretary, Martin Stanley

COMPETITION SERVICE

Victoria House, Bloomsbury Place, London WC1A 2EB
T 020-7979 7979 F 020-7979 7978
E info@catribunal.org.uk W www.catribunal.org.uk

The Enterprise Act 2002 created the Competition Service,
a non-departmental public body whose purpose is to fund
and provide support services to the Competition Appeal
Tribunal. Support services include everything necessary to
facilitate the carrying out by the Competition Appeal
Tribunal of its statutory functions such as administration,
accommodation and office equipment.
Director, Operations, Jeremy Straker

CONSUMER COUNCIL FOR WATER (CCW)

Victoria Square House, Victoria Square, Birmingham B2 4AJ
T 0121-345 1000 F 0121-345 1001
E enquiries@ccwater.org.uk W www.ccwater.org.uk

The CCW was established in 2005 under the Water Act
2003 to represent customers' interests in respect of price,
service and value for money from their water and
sewerage services, and to investigate complaints from
customers about their water company. There are nine
regional committees in England and one in Wales.
Chair, Dame Yve Buckland, DBE

CORPORATION OF TRINITY HOUSE

Trinity House, Tower Hill, London EC3N 4DH
T 020-7481 6900 F 020-7480 7662
E enquiries@thls.org W www.trinityhouse.co.uk

The Corporation of Trinity House is the general
lighthouse authority for England, Wales and the
Channel Islands, and was granted its first charter by
Henry VIII in 1514. Its remit is to assist the safe passage
of a variety of vessels through some of the busiest sea-
lanes in the world; it does this by deploying and
maintaining approximately 600 aids to navigation,
ranging from lighthouses to a satellite navigation service.
The corporation also has certain statutory jurisdiction
over aids to navigation maintained by local harbour
authorities and is responsible for marking or dispersing
wrecks dangerous to navigation, except those occurring
within port limits or wrecks of HM ships.

The statutory duties of Trinity House are funded by the
General Lighthouse Fund, which is provided from light
duties levied on ships calling at ports of the UK and the
Republic of Ireland. The corporation is a deep-sea
pilotage authority, authorised by the Secretary of State for
Transport to license deep-sea pilots. In addition Trinity
House is a charitable organisation that maintains a
number of retirement homes for mariners and their
dependants, funds a four-year training scheme for those
seeking a career in the merchant navy, and also dispenses
grants to a wide range of maritime charities. The charity
work is wholly funded by its own activities.

The corporation is controlled by a board of Elder
Brethren; a separate board controls the Lighthouse
Service. The Elder Brethren also act as nautical assessors
in marine cases in the Admiralty Division of the High
Court.

ELDER BRETHREN
Master, HRH The Prince Philip, Duke of Edinburgh, KG,
KT, PC
Deputy Master, Rear-Adm. Jeremy de Halpert, CB
Wardens, Cdre. Peter Melson, CBE, RN *(Rental)*; Douglas
Potter *(Nether)*
Elder Brethren, HRH The Prince of Wales, KG, KT, GCB;
HRH The Duke of York, KG, KCVO, ADC; HRH The
Princess Royal, KG, KT, GCVO; Adm. Lord Boyce,
GCB, OBE; Lord Browne of Madingley; Capt. John
Burton-Hall, RD; Rt. Hon. Lord Carrington, KG,
GCMG, CH; Capt. David Cloke; Rt. Hon. Lord
Cuckney of Millbank; Capt. Sir Malcolm Edge, KCVO;
Capt. Ian Gibb; Cdr. Sir Robin Gillett, Bt., GBE, RD;
Capt. Duncan Glass; Lord Greenway; Hon. Christopher
Lyttelton; Rt. Hon. Lord Mackay of Clashfern, KT;
Capt. Peter Mason, CBE; Capt. David Orr; Capt. Nigel
Pryke, MCIT, FNI; Capt. Derek Richards, RD, RNR;

Cdr. Miles Rivett-Carnac, RN; Rt. Hon. Lord Robertson of Port Ellen, KT, GCMG; Rear-Adm. Sir Patrick Rowe, KCVO, CBE; Cdre. Jim Scorer; Sir Brian Shaw; Simon Sherard; Adm. Sir Jock Slater, GCB, LVO; Capt. David Smith, OBE, RN; Capt. David Squire, CBE, RFA; Cdre. Rt. Hon. Lord Sterling of Plaistow, CBE, GCVO, RNR; Capt. Colin Stewart, LVO; Sir Adrian Swire, AE; Capt. Sir Miles Wingate, KCVO; Capt. Thomas Woodfield, OBE

OFFICERS
Secretary, Peter Galloway
Director of Finance, Jerry Wedge
Director of Operations and Asset Management, Cdre. Jim Scorer
Director of Navigation, Capt. Duncan Glass

COUNCIL ON TRIBUNALS

81 Chancery Lane, London WC2A 1BQ
T 020-7855 5200 F 020-7855 5201
E enquiries@cot.gsi.gov.uk
W www.council-on-tribunals.gov.uk

The Council on Tribunals is a permanent standing advisory body that operates under the Tribunals and Inquiries Act 1992. It consists of 17 members appointed by the Secretary of State for Justice and the Scottish ministers; one member is appointed to represent the interests of people in Wales. The Scottish Committee of the Council generally considers Scottish tribunals and matters relating only to Scotland. The Parliamentary Commissioner for Administration is an *ex officio* member of the council and the Scottish Committee.

The council advises on, and keeps under review, the constitution and working of the tribunals listed in the Tribunals and Inquiries Act 1992, and considers and reports on administrative procedures relating to statutory inquiries. Some 80 tribunals are currently under the council's supervision. It is consulted by and advises government departments on a wide range of subjects relating to adjudicative procedures.
Chair, Rt. Hon. Lord Newton of Braintree, OBE
Members, The Parliamentary Commissioner *(ex officio)*, Ann Abraham; Carolyn Berkeley; Prof. Alice Brown *(ex officio)*; Elizabeth Cameron; Sue Davis; Judith Edwards; Susan Howdle; Penny Letts; Prof. Alistair MacLeary; Stephen Mannion, QPM; Bernard Quoroll; Prof. Genevra Richardson, CBE; Dr Jonathan Spencer, CB; Dr Adrian Stokes, OBE; Pat Thomas, CBE; Heather Wilcox

SCOTTISH COMMITTEE OF THE COUNCIL ON TRIBUNALS
George House, 126 George Street, Edinburgh EH2 4HH
T 0131-271 4300 F 0131-271 4309
E sccot@gtnet.gov.uk
Chair, Prof. A. MacLeary
Members, The Parliamentary Commissioner for Administration *(ex officio)*; The Scottish Public Services Ombudsman *(ex officio)*; Elizabeth C. Cameron; Douglas Graham; Stephen Mannion; Lyndy Roberts; Audrey Watson; Mary Wood

COUNTRYSIDE COUNCIL FOR WALES/CYNGOR CEFN GWLAD CYMRU

Maes-y-Ffynnon, Penrhosgarnedd, Bangor, Gwynedd LL57 2DW
T 0845-130 6229 F 01248-355782
E enquiries@ccw.gov.uk W www.ccw.gov.uk

The Countryside Council for Wales is the government's statutory adviser on sustaining natural beauty, wildlife and the opportunity for outdoor enjoyment in Wales and its inshore waters. It is funded by the National Assembly for Wales and accountable to the First Secretary, who appoints its members.
Chair, John Lloyd Jones, OBE
Chief Executive, Roger Thomas
Directors, Dr David Parker *(Science)*; Dr John Taylor *(Policy)*

COVENT GARDEN MARKET AUTHORITY

Covent House, New Covent Garden Market, London SW8 5NX
T 020-7720 2211 F 020-7622 5307
E info@cgma.gov.uk W www.cgma.gov.uk

The Covent Garden Market Authority is constituted under the Covent Garden Market Acts 1961 to 1977, the board being appointed by the Department of Environment, Food and Rural Affairs. The authority owns and operates the 22 hectare (56 acre) New Covent Garden Markets (fruit, vegetables, flowers), which have been trading at the site since 1974.
Chair (part-time), Rt. Hon. Baroness Dean of Thornton-le-Fylde
Chief Executive, Jan Lloyd

CRIMINAL CASES REVIEW COMMISSION

Alpha Tower, Suffolk Street, Queensway, Birmingham B1 1TT
T 0121-633 1800 F 0121-633 1823/1804
E info@ccrc.x.gsi.gov.uk W www.ccrc.gov.uk

The Criminal Cases Review Commission is an independent body set up under the Criminal Appeal Act 1995. It is a non-departmental public body reporting to parliament via the Lord Chancellor and Secretary of State for Justice. It is responsible for investigating possible miscarriages of justice in England, Wales and Northern Ireland, and deciding whether or not to refer cases back to an appeal court. Membership of the commission is by royal appointment; the senior executive staff are appointed by the commission.
Chair, Prof. Graham Zellick
Members, M. Allen; Ms P. Barrett; M. Emerton; J. England; Ms J. Goulding; D. Jessel; A. MacGregor, QC; I. Nicholl; E. Smith; J. Weeden
Principal Director, C. Albert

CRIMINAL INJURIES COMPENSATION AUTHORITY (CICA)

Tay House, 300 Bath Street, Glasgow G2 4LN
T 0141-331 2726 Freephone 0800-358 3601
F 0141-331 2287
E enquiries@cica.gsi.gov.uk W www.cica.gov.uk

All applications for compensation for personal injury arising from crimes of violence in England, Scotland and Wales are dealt with at the above location (separate arrangements apply in Northern Ireland). Applications received up to 31 March 1996 are assessed on the basis of common law damages under the 1990 compensation

scheme. Applications received on or after 1 April 1996 are assessed under a tariff-based scheme, made under the Criminal Injuries Compensation Act 1995, by the CICA. There is a separate avenue of appeal to the Criminal Injuries Compensation Appeals Panel (CICAP – *see* Tribunals section).
Chief Executive, Joanne Drean

CROFTERS COMMISSION

Castle Wynd, Inverness IV2 3EQ
T 01463-663450 F 01463-711820
E info@crofterscommission.org.uk
W www.crofterscommission.org.uk

The Crofters Commission, established in 1955 under the Crofters (Scotland) Act, is a government-funded organisation tasked with overseeing crofting legislation and developing crofting. It works with communities to regulate crofting and assist local development initiatives. It also advises Scottish ministers on crofting matters. The commission administers the Crofting Counties Agricultural Grants Scheme, the Highlands and Islands Croft Entrant Scheme, the Crofters' Cattle Improvement Scheme and the Crofting Community Development Scheme. It also provides a free enquiry service.
Chair, Drew Ratter
Chief Executive, Nick Reiter

DEER COMMISSION FOR SCOTLAND

Great Glen House, Leachkin Road, Inverness IV3 8NW
T 01463-725000 F 01463-725048
E enquiries@deercom.com W www.dcs.gov.uk

The Deer Commission for Scotland has the general functions of furthering the conservation and control of deer in Scotland. It has the statutory duty, with powers, to prevent damage to agriculture, forestry and the habitat by deer. It is funded by the Scottish Executive.
Chair (part-time), Prof. J. Milne, MBE
Director, N. Halfhide

DESIGN COUNCIL

34 Bow Street, London WC2E 7DL
T 020-7420 5200 F 020-7420 5300
E info@designcouncil.org.uk W www.design-council.org.uk

The Design Council is a campaigning organisation which works with partners in business, education and government to promote the effective use of good design; its aim is to make businesses more competitive and public services more effective. It is a registered charity with a royal charter and is funded jointly by grant-in-aid from the Department for Business, Enterprise and Regulatory Reform and the Department for Culture, Media and Sport; the secretaries of state of these two departments appoint the chair and members of the council.
Chair, Sir George Cox
Chief Executive, David Kester

ENGLISH HERITAGE (HISTORIC BUILDINGS AND MONUMENTS COMMISSION FOR ENGLAND)

1 Waterhouse Square, 138–142 Holborn, London EC1N 2ST
T 020-7973 3000 F 020-7973 3001
W www.english-heritage.org.uk

English Heritage was established under the National Heritage Act 1983. On 1 April 1999 it merged with the Royal Commission on the Historical Monuments of England to become the new lead body for England's historic environment. It is sponsored by the Department for Culture, Media and Sport and its duties are to carry out and sponsor archaeological, architectural and scientific surveys and research designed to increase the understanding of England's past and its changing condition; to identify buildings, monuments and landscapes for protection whilst also offering expert advice, skills and grants to conserve these sites; to encourage town planners to make imaginative re-use of historic buildings to aid regeneration of the centres of cities, towns and villages; to manage and curate selected sites; and to curate and make publicly accessible the National Monuments Record, whose records of over one million historic sites and buildings, and extensive collections of photographs, maps, drawings and reports constitute the central database and archive of England's historic environment.
Chair, Sir Neil Cossons, OBE, FSA, FMA
Commissioners, Maria Adebowale; Joyce Bridges, CBE; Bill Bryson; Michael Cairns; Prof. David Cannadine, DPHIL, LITT D, FBA; Manish Chande; Barry Cunliffe, CBE; Gilly Drummond; Marquess of Douro, OBE; Jane Grenville, FSA; Michael Jolly, CBE; Jane Kennedy; Earl of Leicester, CBE; Les Sparks, OBE, FRSA; Elizabeth Williamson, FSA
Chief Executive, Dr Simon Thurley

CUSTOMER SERVICES DEPARTMENT, PO Box 569, Swindon SN2 2YP T 0870-333 1181
    E customers@english-heritage.org.uk
NATIONAL MONUMENTS RECORD CENTRE, Kemble Drive, Swindon SN2 2GZ T 01793-414600
    F 01793-414606

ENVIRONMENT AGENCY

Rio House, Waterside Drive, Aztec West, Almondsbury, Bristol BS32 4UD
T 0870-850 6506 F 01709-312820
E enquiries@environment-agency.gov.uk
W www.environment-agency.gov.uk

The Environment Agency was established in 1996 under the Environment Act 1995 and is a non-departmental public body sponsored by the Department for Environment, Food and Rural Affairs and the National Assembly for Wales – around 60 per cent of the agency's funding is from the government, with the rest raised from various charging schemes. The agency is responsible for pollution prevention and control in England and Wales, helping businesses use resources more effectively, and for the management and use of water resources, including flood defences, fisheries and navigation. It has head offices in London and Bristol, and eight regional offices.

THE BOARD
Chair, Sir John Harman
Members, James Braithwaite, CBE; Peter Bye; Ted Cantle, CBE; John Edmonds; Prof. Ruth Hall; Richard Percy; Dr Lyndon Stanton; Cllr Kay Twitchen, OBE; Dr Malcolm Smith; Lady Warner, OBE; Prof. Lynda Warren; Lord Whitty
Chief Executive, Barbara Young

EQUALITY COMMISSION FOR NORTHERN IRELAND

Equality House, 7–9 Shaftesbury Square, Belfast BT2 7DP
T 028-9050 0600 F 028-9024 8687
E information@equalityni.org W www.equalityni.org

The Equality Commission was set up in 1999 under the Northern Ireland Act 1998 and is responsible for promoting equality, keeping the relevant legislation under review, eliminating discrimination on the grounds of race, disability, sexual orientation, gender, religion and political opinion and for overseeing the statutory duty on public authorities to promote equality of opportunity.

Chief Commissioner, Bob Collins
Deputy Chief Commissioner, Anne O'Reilly
Chief Executive, Evelyn Collins

FOREIGN COMPENSATION COMMISSION (FCC)

Old Admiralty Building, London SW1A 2PA
T 020-7008 1321 F 020-7008 0160
W www.fcc.gov.uk

The FCC was set up by the Foreign Compensation Act 1950 primarily to distribute, under orders in council, funds received from other governments in accordance with agreements to pay compensation for expropriated British property and other losses sustained by British nationals. The FCC carries out both judicial and administrative functions, including the adjudication of claims by applicants and the investment and management of compensation funds. There are no active compensation programmes at present.

Chair, Dr John Barker

GAMBLING COMMISSION

Victoria Square House, Victoria Square, Birmingham B2 4BP
T 0121-230 6666 F 0121-233 6720
E info@gamblingcommission.gov.uk
W www.gamblingcommission.gov.uk

The Gambling Commission was established under the Gambling Act 2005, and took over the role previously occupied by the Gaming Board for Great Britain in regulating and licensing all commercial gambling – apart from spread betting and the National Lottery – ie casinos, bingo, remote gambling, gaming machines and lotteries. It also advises local and central government on related issues, and is responsible for the protection of children and the vulnerable. The commission is sponsored by the Department for Culture, Media and Sport, with its work funded mainly by licence fees paid by the gambling industry.

Chair, Peter Dean, CBE
Chief Executive, Jenny Williams

GOVERNMENT OFFICES FOR THE REGIONS

The nine Government Offices for the Regions (GOs) are the primary means by which a wide range of government policies are delivered in the English regions. The Government Offices bring together the activities and interests of eleven 'sponsor' government departments: the Department for Business, Enterprise and Regulatory Reform; the Cabinet Office; the Department for Children, Schools and Families; the Department for Communities and Local Government; the Department for Culture, Media and Sport; the Department for Environment, Food and Rural Affairs; the Department of Health; the Home Office; the Ministry of Justice; the Department for Transport; and the Department for Work and Pensions.

GOs contribute to the delivery of over 40 public service agreements (PSAs) on behalf of their sponsor departments. These PSAs cover a diverse range of tasks including regenerating communities, fighting crime, tackling housing needs, improving public health, raising standards in education and skills, tackling countryside issues, and reducing unemployment. GOs also manage European funds.

GOs directly manage the spending programmes of the government departments listed above. They oversee budgets and contracts delegated to regional organisations, as well as carrying out regulatory functions and sponsoring Regional Development Agencies. As part of central government, their role also includes providing a regional perspective to inform the development and evaluation of policy.

The Government Office Network comprises the nine regional Government Offices, and the Regional Coordination Unit.

REGIONAL COORDINATION UNIT

2nd Floor, Riverwalk House, 157–161 Millbank, London SW1P 4RR
T 020–7217 3111 F 020–7217 3590
E rcuenquiries@rcu.gsi.gov.uk W www.gos.gov.uk
Director-General, Joe Montgomery

EAST MIDLANDS

The Belgrave Centre, Stanley Place, Talbot Street, Nottingham NG1 5GG
T 0115–971 9971 F 0115–971 2404
E enquiries@goem.gsi.gov.uk
W www.goem.gov.uk
Regional Director, Jane Todd

EAST OF ENGLAND

Eastbrook, Shaftesbury Road, Cambridge CB2 2DF
T 01223–372500 F 01223–372501
W www.go-east.gov.uk
Regional Director, Brian Hackland

LONDON

Riverwalk House, 157–161 Millbank, London SW1P 4RR
T 020–7217 3151 F 020–7217 3450
W www.gol.gov.uk
Regional Director, Liz Meek

NORTH EAST

Citygate, Gallowgate, Newcastle upon Tyne NE1 4WH
T 0191–201 3300 F 0191–202 3998
W www.go-ne.gov.uk
Regional Director, Jonathan Blackie

NORTH WEST

City Tower, Piccadilly Plaza, Manchester M1 4BE
T 0161–952 4000 F 0161–952 4099
W www.go-nw.gov.uk
Regional Director, Keith Barnes

SOUTH EAST

Bridge House, 1 Walnut Tree Close, Guildford GU1 4GA
T 01483–882255 F 01483–882259
W www.go-se.gov.uk
Regional Director, Rolande Anderson

SOUTH WEST

2 Rivergate, Temple Quay, Bristol BS1 6ED
T 0117–900 1700 F 0117–900 1900
W www.gosw.gov.uk
Regional Director (acting), Richard Sheard

WEST MIDLANDS

5 St Phillips Place, Colmore Row, Birmingham B3 2PW
T 0121–352 5050 F 0121–352 1010
W www.go-wm.gov.uk
Regional Director, Trudi Elliot

YORKSHIRE AND THE HUMBER

8 City Walk, Leeds LS11 9AT
T 0113–341 3000 W www.goyh.gov.uk
Regional Director, Felicity Everiss

HEALTH PROTECTION AGENCY (HPA)

7th Floor, Holborn Gate, 330 High Holborn, London WC1V 7PP
T 020-7759 2700 F 020-7759 2733
E webteam@hpa.org.uk W www.hpa.org.uk

The HPA was set up in 2003 and is responsible for providing an integrated approach to protecting public health through the provision of support and advice to the NHS, local authorities, emergency services, other NDPBs, the Department of Health and the devolved administrations.

The HPA works at local, regional, national and international levels to reduce the impact of infectious diseases and reduce exposure to chemicals, radiation and poisons, as well as ensuring a rapid response when hazards occur. The HPA provides services in Northern Ireland and works closely with the devolved administrations, so that there is a coordinated response to incidents, trends and outbreaks on a national level. Research and development projects conducted by HPA scientists are primarily concerned with new methods of treating illness and assessing exposure to chemicals or radiation, ie developing new vaccines and biomarkers of chemical exposure.

Chair, Sir William Stewart
Board Members, Dr Parvaiz Ali; Dr Barbara Bannister, FRCP; Michael Beaumont, CBE, FCA; James T. Brown; Ian Cranston, FCA; Dr Paul Darragh, TD; Prof. Charles Easmon, CBE; Prof. William Gelletly; Prof. Rod Griffiths, CBE; Prof. Andrew Hall; Prof. David Latchman, FRSA; Dr Vanessa Mayatt; Prof. Karl Nicholson; John Wyn Owen, CB; Prof. Sandy Primrose; Dr Geoffrey Schild, CBE; Prof. Richard Wise
Chief Executive, Prof. Pat Troop

HEALTH AND SAFETY COMMISSION

Rose Court, 2 Southwark Bridge, London SE1 9HS
T 0845-345 0055 E hse.infoline@natbrit.com
W www.hse.gov.uk

The Health and Safety Commission was created under the Health and Safety at Work etc Act 1974, and is responsible for health and safety regulation in Great Britain. The Health and Safety Executive and local government are the enforcing authorities who work in support of the commission. Its aim is to ensure risks in the workplace are properly controlled and generally to promote the protection of people at work and the public from hazards arising from industrial and commercial activity, including major industrial accidents and the transportation of hazardous materials.

Its members are appointed by the Secretary of State for Work and Pensions following consultation with representative groups (employers, employees, local authorities and others).

Chair, Sir Bill Callaghan
Members, S. Blair; D. Carrigan; R. Dahlberg; Ms J. Donovan; S. Khan; J. Longworth; H. Robertson; Ms E. Snape; J. Spanswick

HEALTH AND SAFETY EXECUTIVE

Rose Court, 2 Southwark Bridge, London SE1 9HS
T 0845-345 0055 F 0845-408 9566
E hse.infoline@natbrit.com W www.hse.gov.uk

The Health and Safety Executive is the Health and Safety Commission's major instrument. Through its inspectorates it enforces health and safety law in the majority of industrial premises. The executive advises the commission in its major task of laying down safety standards through regulations and practical guidance for many industrial processes. The executive is also the licensing authority for nuclear installations, the reporting officer on the severity of nuclear incidents in Britain, and it is responsible for the Channel Tunnel Safety Authority.

Chief Executive, Geoffrey Podger
Deputy Chief Executive, Operations, Justin McCracken
Deputy Chief Executive, Policy, Jonathan Rees
Director and HM Chief Inspector of the Nuclear Installations Inspectorate, Dr Mike Weightman
Chief Scientist and Director of Corporate Science and Analytical Service Directorate, Dr Patrick McDonald

HIGHLANDS AND ISLANDS ENTERPRISE (HIE)

Cowan House, Inverness Retail and Business Park, Inverness IV2 7GF
T 01463-234171 F 01463-244469
E hie.general@hient.co.uk W www.hie.co.uk

HIE was set up under the Enterprise and New Towns (Scotland) Act 1991. Its role is to design, direct and deliver enterprise development, training and environmental and social projects and services. HIE is made up of a strategic core body and nine local enterprise companies (LECs), to which many of its individual functions are delegated.

Chair, W. Roe
Chief Executive, I. J. R. S. Cumming

HISTORIC ENVIRONMENT ADVISORY COUNCIL FOR SCOTLAND

Longmore House, Salisbury Place, Edinburgh EH9 1SH
T 0131-668 8810 F 0131-668 8987
E heacs@scotland.gsi.gov.uk W www.heacs.org.uk

The Historic Environment Advisory Council for Scotland, established in 2003, is the advisory body set up to provide Scottish ministers with advice on issues affecting the historic environment and how the functions of the Scottish ministers may be exercised effectively for the benefit of said historic environment. In this context the historic environment means any or all structures and places in Scotland of historical, archaeological or architectural interest or importance.

Chair, Elizabeth Burns, CMG, OBE

HISTORIC ROYAL PALACES
Apartment 39A, Hampton Court Palace, Surrey KT8 9AU
T 0870-751 5172 F 020-8781 9754
E operators@hrp.org.uk W www.hrp.org.uk

Historic Royal Palaces was established in 1998 as a royal charter body with charitable status and is contracted by the Secretary of State for Culture, Media and Sport to manage the palaces on her behalf. The palaces – the Tower of London, Hampton Court Palace, the Banqueting House, Kensington Palace and Kew Palace – are owned by the Queen on behalf of the nation.

The organisation is governed by a board comprising a chair and ten non-executive trustees. The chief executive is accountable to the board of trustees and ultimately to parliament. Historic Royal Palaces receives no funding from the government or the crown.

TRUSTEES
Chair, Charles Mackay
Appointed by the Queen, Sir Trevor McDonald, OBE; Sir Alan Reid, KCVO; Sir Hugh Roberts, KCVO, FSA
Appointed by the Secretary of State, Dawn Austwick, OBE; Dr Bridget Cherry, OBE, FSA; Sue Farr; John Hamer; Malcolm Reading
Ex officio, Gen. Sir Roger Wheeler, GCB, CBE *(Constable of the Tower of London)*

OFFICERS
Chief Executive, Michael Day
Resident Governor, HM Tower of London, Maj.-Gen. Keith Cima

HOME-GROWN CEREALS AUTHORITY
Caledonia House, 223 Pentonville Road, London N1 9HY
T 020-7520 3926 F 020-7520 3954
E communications@hgca.com W www.hgca.com

Set up under the Cereals Marketing Act 1965, the Home-Grown Cereals Authority (HGCA) board consists of: seven members representing UK cereal growers; seven representing dealers in, or processors of, grain; and two independent members. HGCA's functions are to improve the production and marketing of UK-grown cereals and oilseeds through a research and development programme, to provide a market information service and to promote UK cereals in export markets.
Chair, J. Page
Chief Executive, J. Cowens

HORSERACE TOTALISATOR BOARD
Douglas House, Chapel Lane, Wigan WN3 4HS
T 01942-617500 F 01942-617701
W www.totesport.com

The Horserace Totalisator Board (the Tote) was established by the Betting, Gaming and Lotteries Act 1963. Its function is to operate totalisators on approved racecourses in Great Britain, and it also provides on and off-course cash and credit offices. Under the Horserace Totalisator and Betting Levy Board Act 1972, it is further empowered to offer bets at starting price (or other bets at fixed odds) on any sporting event, and under the Horserace Totalisator Board Act 1997 to take bets on any event, except the National Lottery. The chair and members of the board are appointed by the Secretary of State for Culture, Media and Sport.

The government announced in March 2001 that the Tote would eventually be sold to a racing trust. The necessary legislation was passed in 2004 and the privatisation of the Tote is expected to be completed during the 2007 financial year.
Chair, P. I. Jones
Chief Executive, T. Beaumont

HOUSING CORPORATION
Maple House, 149 Tottenham Court Road, London W1T 7BN
T 0845-230 7000 F 0113-233 7101
E enquiries@housingcorp.gsx.gov.uk
W www.housingcorp.gov.uk

Established by parliament in 1964, the Housing Corporation funds new affordable housing and is the statutory regulator for housing associations. Under the Housing Act 1996, the corporation's regulatory role was widened to embrace new types of landlords, in particular local housing companies. The corporation is funded by the Department for Communities and Local Government; the £3.9bn programme of investment for 2006–8 is set to create 84,000 new affordable homes.
Chair, Peter Dixon
Chief Executive, Jon Rouse

HUMAN FERTILISATION AND EMBRYOLOGY AUTHORITY (HFEA)
21 Bloomsbury Street, London WC1B 3HF
T 020-7291 8200 F 020-7291 8201
E admin@hfea.gov.uk W www.hfea.gov.uk

The HFEA was established in 1991 under the Human Fertilisation and Embryology Act 1990. It is the UK's independent regulator tasked with overseeing safe and appropriate practice in fertility treatment and embryo research, including licensing and monitoring centres carrying out IVF, donor insemination and human embryo research. HFEA also provides a range of detailed information for patients, professionals and government, and maintains a formal register of information about donors, fertility treatments and children born as a result of those treatments.
Chair, Shirley Harrison
Chief Executive, Angela McNab

HUMAN GENETICS COMMISSION
Area 605, Wellington House, 133–155 Waterloo Road, London SE1 8UG
T 020-7972 4351 F 020-7972 4300
E hgc@dh.gsi.gov.uk W www.hgc.gov.uk

The Human Genetics Commission was established in 1999, subsuming three previous advisory committees. Its remit is to give ministers strategic advice on how developments in human genetics will impact on people and healthcare, focusing in particular on the social and ethical implications.
Chair, Baroness H. Kennedy of the Shaws, QC
Vice Chair, Sir John Sulston
Members, Prof. Emerita Brenda Almond; Prof. Stephen Bain; Dr Celia Brazell; Prof. Angus Clarke; Prof. Sarah Cunningham-Burley; Dr Paul Darragh; Dr Paul Debenham; Dr Frances Flinter; Ros Gardner; Prof. John Harris; Michael Harrison; Shirley Harrison; Prof. Christopher Higgins; Alastair Kent; Dr Rosemary Leonard; Alice Maynard; Lola Oni; Dr Christine Patch; Peter Sayers; Dr Rosalind Skinner; Dr Anita Thomas

HUMAN TISSUE AUTHORITY (HTA)
Ground Floor, Finlaison House, 15–17 Furnival Street,
London EC4A 1AB
T 020-7211 3400 F 020-7211 3430
E enquiries@hta.gov.uk W www.hta.gov.uk

The HTA was established on 1 April 2005 under the Human Tissue Act 2004, and is sponsored and part-funded by the Department of Health. Its role is to inform the public and Secretary of State for Health about issues within its remit, which include the import, export, storage and use of human bodies and tissue for scheduled purposes, and disposal of human tissue following its use in medical treatment or for scheduled purposes. The HTA is the competent authority under the EU Tissues and Cells Directive for regulating human tissue banking for transplant services.

The HTA also supersedes and extends the role that was previously performed by the now-defunct Unrelated Live Transplant Regulatory Authority (ULTRA) in setting out the circumstances in which live 'transplantable material' (from both related and unrelated donors) will be allowed.

Chair, Shirley Harrison
Chief Executive, Adrian McNeil

IMPERIAL WAR MUSEUM
Lambeth Road, London SE1 6HZ
T 020-7416 5320 F 020-7416 5374
E mail@iwm.org.uk W www.iwm.org.uk

The museum, founded in 1917, illustrates and records all aspects of the two world wars and other military operations involving Britain and the Commonwealth since 1914. It was opened in its present home, formerly Bethlem Royal Hospital, in 1936. The museum is a multi-branch organisation that also includes the Churchill Museum and Cabinet War Rooms in Whitehall; HMS *Belfast* in the Pool of London; Imperial War Museum Duxford in Cambridgeshire; and Imperial War Museum North in Trafford, Manchester.

The total grant-in-aid (including grants for special projects) for 2007–8 is £22.18m.

OFFICERS
Chair of Trustees, Air Chief Marshal Sir Peter Squire, GCB, DFC, AFC
Director-General, Sir Robert Crawford, CBE
Directors, Richard Ashton *(Imperial War Museum Duxford)*; Jon Card *(Secretary, Finance)*; Jim Forrester *(Imperial War Museum North)*; Angela Godwin *(Public Services)*; Brad King *(HMS Belfast)*; Phil Reed *(Churchill Museum and Cabinet War Rooms)*; Alan Stoneman *(Corporate Services)*; Mark Whitmore *(Collections)*

INDEPENDENT HOUSING OMBUDSMAN
81 Aldwych, London WC2B 4HN
T 020-7421 3800 F 020-7831 1942
E info@housing-ombudsman.org.uk
W www.housing-ombudsman.org.uk

The Housing Ombudsman Service, established in 1997, deals with complaints from residents concerning shortcomings in the way homes are managed by landlords and housing agents. The ombudsman has a statutory jurisdiction over all registered social landlords in England.

Private and other landlords can join the service on a voluntary basis.

Ombudsman, Dr Mike Biles
Deputy Ombudsman, Rafael Runco

INDEPENDENT POLICE COMPLAINTS COMMISSION (IPCC)
90 High Holborn, London WC1V 6BH
T 0845-300 2002 F 020-7404 0430
E enquiries@ipcc.gsi.gov.uk W www.ipcc.gov.uk

The IPCC succeeded the Police Complaints Authority in 2004. It was established under the Police Reform Act 2002. The IPCC has teams of investigators headed by directors in each of its regions to assist with the supervision and management of some police investigations. They also carry out independent investigations into serious incidents or allegations of misconduct by persons serving with the police. From April 2006 the IPCC took on responsibility for investigating complaints of serious incidents, including death or injury, made against staff of HM Revenue and Customs and the Serious Organised Crime Agency. The 17 commissioners of the IPCC must not previously have worked for the police.

Chair, N. Hardwick
Deputy Chair, J. Wadham
Commissioners, I. Bynoe; J. Crawley; T. Davies; M. Franklin; G. Garland; Ms D. Glass; L. Jackson; N. Long; L. Lustgarten; Ms N. Malik; Ms R. Marsh; D. Petch; Ms M. Mian Pritchard; Ms A. Somal; Ms N. Williams
Chief Executive, Jane Furniss

INDEPENDENT REVIEW SERVICE FOR THE SOCIAL FUND
4th Floor, Centre City Podium, 5 Hill Street, Birmingham B5 4UB
T 0800-096 1926 F 0121-606 2172
E sfc@irs-review.org.uk W www.irs-review.org.uk

The Social Fund Commissioner is appointed by the Secretary of State for Work and Pensions. The commissioner appoints Social Fund Inspectors, who provide an independent review for customers dissatisfied with decisions made in Jobcentre Plus offices throughout England, Scotland and Wales regarding the grants and loans available from the Discretionary Social Fund.

Social Fund Commissioner, Sir Richard Tilt

INDUSTRIAL INJURIES ADVISORY COUNCIL
6th Floor, The Adelphi, 1–11 John Adam Street,
London WC2N 6HT
T 020-7962 8066 F 020-7712 2255
E iiac@dwp.gsi.gov.uk W www.iiac.org.uk

The Industrial Injuries Advisory Council was established under the Social Security Administration Act 1992, with statutory provisions governing its work set out in section 171 of the act. The council consists of 16 members appointed by the Secretary of State for Work and Pensions, and has three roles: to advise on the prescription of diseases; to advise on matters referred to the council by the secretary of state or proposals concerning the Industrial Injuries Disablement Benefit Scheme; and to advise on any other matter relating to industrial injuries benefit or its administration.

Chair, Prof. A. J. Newman Taylor, CB, FRCP

INFORMATION COMMISSIONER'S OFFICE

Wycliffe House, Water Lane, Wilmslow, Cheshire SK9 5AF
T 0845-630 6060 F 01625-524510
E mail@ico.gsi.gov.uk W www.ico.gov.uk

The Information Commissioner's Office is sponsored by the Ministry of Justice and oversees and enforces the Freedom of Information Act 2000 and the Data Protection Act 1998, with the objective of promoting public access to official information and protecting personal information.

The Data Protection Act 1998 sets out rules for the processing of personal information and applies to records held on computers and some paper files. It works in two ways: it dictates that those who record and use personal information (data controllers) must be open about how the information is used and must follow the eight principles of 'good information handling', and it gives individuals certain rights to access their personal information.

The Freedom of Information Act 2000 is designed to help end the culture of unnecessary secrecy and open up the inner workings of the public sector to citizens and businesses. Under the Freedom of Information Act, public authorities must produce a publication scheme that sets out what information the public authority is obliged to publish by law.

The Information Commissioner reports annually to parliament on the performance of his functions under the acts and has obligations to assess breaches of the acts.
Information Commissioner, Richard Thomas

INVESTIGATORY POWERS TRIBUNAL

PO Box 33220, London SW1H 9ZQ
T 020-7035 3711 W www.ipt-uk.com

The Investigatory Powers Tribunal replaced the Interception of Communications Tribunal, the Intelligence Services Tribunal, the Security Services Tribunal and the complaints function of the commissioner appointed under the Police Act 1997.

The Regulation of Investigatory Powers Act 2000 (RIPA) provides for a tribunal made up of senior members of the legal profession, independent of the government and appointed by the Queen, to consider all complaints against the intelligence services and those against public authorities in respect of powers covered by RIPA; and to consider proceedings brought under section 7 of the Human Rights Act 1998 against the intelligence services and law enforcement agencies in respect of these powers.
President, Rt. Hon. Lord Justice John Mummery
Vice-President, Mr Justice Michael Burton
Members, W. Carmichael; Sir Richard Gaskell; Sheriff Principal J. McInnes, QC; P. Scott, QC; R. Seabrook, QC

JOINT NATURE CONSERVATION COMMITTEE

Monkstone House, City Road, Peterborough PE1 1JY
T 01733-562626 F 01733-555948
E comment@jncc.gov.uk W www.jncc.gov.uk

The committee was established under the Environmental Protection Act 1990 and was reconstituted by the Natural Environment and Rural Communities Act 2006. It advises the government and others on UK and international nature conservation issues and disseminates knowledge on these subjects. It establishes common standards for the monitoring of nature conservation and research, and provides guidance to Natural England, Scottish Natural Heritage, the Council for Nature Conservation and the Countryside, and the Countryside Council for Wales.
Chair, Adrian Darby, OBE
Deputy Chair, Prof. David Ingram, OBE

LAW COMMISSION

Conquest House, 37–38 John Street, London WC1N 2BQ
T 020-7453 1220 F 020-7453 1297
E chief.executive@lawcommission.gsi.gov.uk
W www.lawcom.gov.uk

The Law Commission was set up under the Law Commissions Act 1965, to make proposals to the government for the examination of the law in England and Wales and for its revision where it is unsuited for modern requirements, obscure, or otherwise unsatisfactory. It recommends to the Lord Chancellor programmes for the examination of different branches of the law and suggests whether the examination should be carried out by the commission itself or by some other body. The commission is also responsible for the preparation of Consolidation and Statute Law (Repeals) Bills.
Chair, Hon. Mr Justice Etherton
Commissioners, S. Bridge; David Hertzell; Dr Jeremy Horder; Kenneth Parker, QC; Prof. M. Partington, CBE
Chief Executive, S. Humphreys

LEARNING AND SKILLS COUNCIL (LSC)

Cheylesmore House, Quinton Road, Coventry CV1 2WT
T 0870-900 6800 F 02476-823675
E info@lsc.gov.uk W www.lsc.gov.uk

The LSC was established in 2001 to replace the Further Education Funding and the Training and Enterprise Councils. It is a non-departmental public body responsible for the planning and funding of post-16 education and training outside of universities. Its remit is to ensure that high-quality post-16 provision is available to meet the needs of employers, individuals and communities. The LSC operates through a national office based in Coventry and also through local departments, which work to promote the equality of opportunity in the workplace; its budget for 2006–7 was £10.4bn.
Chair, Chris Banks, CBE
Chief Executive, Mark Haysom

LEGAL SERVICES COMMISSION

85 Gray's Inn Road, London WC1X 8TX
T 020-7759 0000
W www.legalservices.gov.uk

The Legal Services Commission was created under the Access to Justice Act 1999 and replaced the Legal Aid Board in April 2000. It is a non-departmental public body which is sponsored by the Ministry of Justice.

The commission is responsible for two schemes. The Community Legal Service funds the delivery of civil legal and advice services, identifies priorities and unmet needs, and develops suppliers and services to meet those needs. The Criminal Defence Service provides free legal advice and representation for people involved in criminal investigations or proceedings.

The commission produces free information leaflets which are available from solicitors' and advisory offices, and from the commission's website.

Chief Executive, Carolyn Regan
Chair, Sir Michael Bichard

MENTAL HEALTH ACT COMMISSION (MHAC)

Maid Marian House, 56 Hounds Gate, Nottingham NG1 6BG
T 0115-943 7100 F 0115-943 7101
E chiefexec@mhac.org.uk W www.mhac.org.uk

The MHAC was established in 1983. Its functions are to keep under review the operation of the Mental Health Act 1983; to visit and meet patients detained under the act; to investigate complaints falling within the commission's remit; to operate the 'consent to treatment' safeguards in the Mental Health Act; to publish a biennial report on its activities; to monitor the implementation of the code of practice; and to advise ministers.

The MHAC is comprised of approximately 100 part-time commission members, who are appointed by the Secretary of State for Health.

Chair, Prof. Lord Patel of Bradford
Vice-Chair, Deborah Jenkins, MBE
Chief Executive, Chris Heginbotham

MUSEUM OF LONDON

150 London Wall, London EC2Y 5HN
T 0870-444 3852 F 0870-444 3853
E info@museumoflondon.org.uk
W www.museumoflondon.org.uk

The Museum of London illustrates the history of London from prehistoric times to the present day. It opened in 1976 and is based on the amalgamation of the former Guildhall Museum and London Museum. The museum is controlled by a board of governors, appointed (nine each) by the government and the Corporation of London. The museum is currently funded by grants from the Department for Culture, Media and Sport and the Corporation of London. The total grant-in-aid for 2007–8 is £13.6m.

Chair of Board of Governors, Michael Cassidy, CBE
Director, Prof. Jack Lohman

MUSEUMS, LIBRARIES AND ARCHIVES COUNCIL (MLA)

Victoria House, Southampton Row, London WC1B 4EA
T 020-7273 1444 F 020-7273 1404
E info@mla.gov.uk W www.mla.gov.uk

The MLA was launched in April 2000 and is the lead strategic agency for museums, libraries and archives. It works with nine regional agencies and is a non-departmental public body sponsored by the Department for Culture, Media and Sport. The MLA replaced the Museums and Galleries Commission (MGC) and the Library and Information Commission (LIC).

Chair, Mark Wood
Chief Executive, Chris Batt, OBE
Board Members, Geoffrey Bond; Sarah Carthew; Roy Clare; Alex Cunningham; Nick Dodd; Yinnon Ezra; Helen Forde; John Hicks; Sir Geoffrey Holland; Glen Lawes; Prof. Sara Selwood; John Tarrant; Michael Walsh; Robert Wand

NATIONAL ARMY MUSEUM

Royal Hospital Road, London SW3 4HT
T 020-7730 0717
E info@national-army-museum.ac.uk
W www.national-army-museum.ac.uk

The National Army Museum was established by royal charter in 1960, and covers the history of five centuries of the British Army. It chronicles the campaigns and battles fought over this time as well as the social history and development of the Army, and its impact on Britain and the world. The museum houses a wide array of artefacts, paintings, photographs, uniforms and equipment.

Chair, General Sir Jack Deverell, KCB, OBE
Director, Dr Alan J. Guy

NATIONAL CONSUMER COUNCIL (NCC)

20 Grosvenor Gardens, London SW1W 0DH
T 020-7730 3469 F 020-7730 0191
E info@ncc.org.uk W www.ncc.org.uk

The NCC was set up by the government in 1975 to give an independent voice to consumers in the UK. Its role is to advocate the consumer interest to decision-makers in national and local government, industry and regulatory bodies, business and the professions. It does this through a combination of research and campaigning. The NCC is a non-profit-making company limited by guarantee and is largely funded by grant-in-aid from the Department for Business, Enterprise and Regulatory Reform, and the secretary of state appoints the chair and board members. The council is not a consumer advice or complaints body.

Chair, Lord Whitty
Chief Executive, Ed Mayo

NATIONAL ENDOWMENT FOR SCIENCE, TECHNOLOGY AND THE ARTS (NESTA)

1 Plough Place, London EC4A 1DE
T 020-7438 2500 F 020-7438 2501
E nesta@nesta.org.uk W www.nesta.org.uk

NESTA was established under the National Lottery Act 1998 with a £200m endowment from the proceeds of the National Lottery. Its endowment is presently over £250m, making it the largest single source of early-stage business funding in the UK. NESTA's aim is to improve the UK's capacity for innovation by investing in ventures that stimulate entrepreneurship and by instigating programmes of business mentoring and support.

Chair, Chris Powell
Chief Executive, Jonathan Kestenbaum

NATIONAL GALLERIES OF SCOTLAND

The Dean Gallery, 73 Belford Road, Edinburgh EH4 3DS
T 0131-624 6200 F 0131-623 7133
E enquiries@nationalgalleries.org W www.nationalgalleries.org

The National Galleries of Scotland comprise the National Gallery of Scotland, the Scottish National Portrait Gallery, the Scottish National Gallery of Modern Art, the Dean Gallery and the Royal Scottish Academy Building. There are also outstations at Paxton House, Berwickshire, and Duff House, Banffshire. Total government grant-in-aid for 2006–7 was £12.43m.

NATIONAL GALLERY

Trafalgar Square, London WC2N 5DN
T 020-7747 2885 F 020-7747 2423
W www.nationalgallery.org.uk

The National Gallery, which houses a permanent
collection of western European painting from the 13th to
the 20th century, was founded in 1824, following a
parliamentary grant of £60,000 for the purchase and
exhibition of the Angerstein collection of pictures. The
present site was first occupied in 1838; an extension to
the north of the building with a public entrance in Orange
Street was opened in 1975; the Sainsbury wing was
opened in 1991; and the Getty Entrance opened off
Trafalgar Square at the east end of the main building in
2004. Total government grant-in-aid for 2007–8 is
£25.57m.

NATIONAL HERITAGE MEMORIAL FUND

7 Holbein Place, London SW1W 8NR
T 020-7591 6042 E enquire@hlf.org.uk
W www.nhmf.org.uk

The National Heritage Memorial Fund was set up under
the National Heritage Act 1980 in memory of people
who have given their lives for the United Kingdom. The
fund is one of 'last resort', focusing on saving heritage
which is under threat – whether from sale overseas, the
break-up of collections or, in the case of land, from
unsympathetic development. The fund is administered by
a chair and 14 trustees who are appointed by the prime
minister.
   The National Lottery etc Act 1993 designated the fund
as distributor of the heritage share of proceeds from the
National Lottery. As a result, the fund now operates a
National Heritage Memorial Fund and a Heritage Lottery
Fund. The National Heritage Memorial Fund receives an
annual grant from the Department for Culture, Media and
Sport.

NATIONAL LIBRARY OF SCOTLAND

George IV Bridge, Edinburgh EH1 1EW
T 0131-623 3700 F 0131-623 3701
E enquiries@nls.uk W www.nls.uk

The library, which was founded as the Advocates' Library
in 1682, became the National Library of Scotland (NLS)
in 1925. It is funded by the Scottish Executive. It contains
about 13 million books and pamphlets, two million maps,
20,000 current periodicals, 350 newspaper titles and
120,000 manuscripts, including the recently acquired
John Murray Archive. It has an unrivalled Scottish
collection as well as online catalogues and digital
resources which can be accessed through the NLS
website.
   Material can be consulted in the reading rooms, which
are open to anyone with a valid reader's ticket.

NATIONAL LIBRARY OF WALES/LLYFRGELL GENEDLAETHOL CYMRU

Aberystwyth SY23 3BU
T 01970-632800 F 01970-615709
E holi@llgc.org.uk W www.llgc.org.uk

The National Library of Wales was founded by royal
charter in 1907, and is funded by the National Assembly
for Wales. It contains about four million printed books,
40,000 manuscripts, four million deeds and documents,
numerous maps, prints and drawings, and a sound and
moving image collection. It specialises in manuscripts and
books relating to Wales and the Celtic peoples. It is the
repository for pre-1858 Welsh probate records, manorial
records and tithe documents, and certain legal records.
Admission is by reader's ticket to the reading rooms but
entry to the exhibition programme is free.

NATIONAL LOTTERY COMMISSION

101 Wigmore Street, London W1U 1QU
T 0845-712 5596 F 020-7016 3401
W www.natlotcomm.gov.uk

The National Lottery Commission replaced the Office of
the National Lottery (OFLOT) in 1999 under the
National Lottery Act 1998. The commission is
responsible for the granting, varying and enforcing of
licences to run the National Lottery. It also runs the
competition to award the next licence. Its duties are to
ensure that the National Lottery is run with all due
propriety, that the interests of players are protected, and,
subject to these two objectives, that returns to the

good causes are maximised. The commission does not have a role in the distribution of funds to good causes, this is undertaken by 14 distributors, visit www.lotteryfunding.org.uk for further information. Gaming and lotteries in the UK are officially regulated and may only be run by licensed operators or in licensed premises.

The Department of Culture, Media and Sport (DCMS) is responsible for gaming and lottery policy and laws. Empowered by the National Lottery Act 1993 (as amended), the DCMS directs the National Lottery Commission, who in turn regulates Camelot, the lottery operator. Camelot, a private company wholly owned by five shareholders, was granted a second seven-year licence to run the Lottery, which began on 27 January 2002 and ends on 31 January 2009.

Chair, Anne Wright, CBE
Chief Executive, Mark Harris

NATIONAL MARITIME MUSEUM

Park Row, Greenwich, London SE10 9NF
T 020-8858 4422 F 020-8312 6632
W www.nmm.ac.uk

Established in 1934, the National Maritime Museum provides information on the maritime history of Great Britain and is the largest institution of its kind in the world, with over two million items in its collections related to seafaring, navigation and astronomy. The museum is in three groups of buildings in Greenwich Park: the main building, the Queen's House (built by Inigo Jones, 1616–35) and the Royal Observatory (including Christopher Wren's Flamsteed House). In 1999 a £20m Heritage Lottery-supported project opened 16 new galleries in a glazed courtyard in the museum's west wing.

Director, Kevin Fewster
Chair, Lord Sterling of Plaistow, GCVO, CBE

NATIONAL MUSEUMS AND GALLERIES NORTHERN IRELAND

Botanic Gardens, Belfast BT9 5AB
T 028-9038 3000 F 028-9038 3006
W www.magni.org.uk

The organisation of National Museums and Galleries of Northern Ireland was established under the Museums and Galleries (Northern Ireland) Order in 1998 and includes the Ulster Museum with Armagh Museum, the Ulster Folk and Transport Museum, the Ulster American Folk Park and W5 at Odyssey (a wholly owned subsidiary).

Legislation requires National Museums and Galleries of Northern Ireland's board of trustees to care for, preserve and add to the collections; ensure that the collections are exhibited to the public; ensure that the significance of the collections is interpreted; and promote the awareness, appreciation and understanding of the public in relation to art, history and science.

Chair, Margaret Elliott, CBE
Vice-Chair, Sir Kenneth Bloomfield
Trustees, Linda Beers; Lt.-Col. Reginald Harvey Bickers; Patricia Flanagan; Dan Harvey; Dame Geraldine Keegan; Prof. Eithne McLaughlin; William Montgomery; Sean Neeson, MLA; Wendy Osborne; Thomas Shaw; Dr Alastair Walker
Chief Executive, Tim Cooke

NATIONAL MUSEUM WALES – AMGUEDDFA CYMRU

Cathays Park, Cardiff CF10 3NP
T 029-2039 7951 F 029-2057 3321
E post@museumwales.ac.uk W www.museumwales.ac.uk

National Museum Wales – Amgueddfa Cymru aims to provide a complete illustration of the geology, mineralogy, zoology, botany, ethnography, archaeology, art, history and special industries of Wales. It is comprised of the National Museum Cardiff; St Fagans National History Museum; Big Pit – National Coal Museum, Blaenafon; the National Roman Legion Museum, Caerleon; the National Slate Museum, Llanberis; the National Wool Museum, Dre-fach Felindre; and the National Waterfront Museum, Swansea. Total funding from the Welsh Assembly government for 2006–7 was £22.45m.

President, Paul E. Loveluck, CBE
Vice-President, Dr Susan J. Davies
Director-General, Michael Houlihan
Trustees, D. Bowen Lewis; Elisabeth Elias; Dr Iolo ap Gwynn; Prof. Colin L. Jones, OBE; Prof. J. W. Last, CBE; Peter W. Morgan; J. E. Peirson Jones; M. C. T. Prichard, CBE; Gareth Williams; H. R. C. Williams; Dr Brian Willott, CB; Rhiannon Wyn Hughes, MBE; J. Wynford Evans, CBE

NATIONAL MUSEUMS LIVERPOOL

127 Dale Street, Liverpool L2 2JH
T 0151-207 0001 F 0151-478 4790
W www.liverpoolmuseums.org.uk

The board of trustees of the National Museums Liverpool (formerly National Museums and Galleries on Merseyside) is responsible for the World Museum Liverpool, the Merseyside Maritime Museum (incorporating HM Customs and Excise National Museum), the Museum of Liverpool, the Lady Lever Art Gallery, the Walker Art Gallery, Sudley House, the National Conservation Centre and the International Slavery Museum. Total government grant-in-aid for 2005–6 was £17.6m.

Chair of the Board of Trustees, Loyd Grossman, OBE
Director, Dr David Fleming
Keeper of Art Galleries, R. King
Keeper, World Museum Liverpool, J. Millard
Keeper, Merseyside Maritime Museum, T. Tibbles
Keeper, Museum of Liverpool, J. Dugdale
Head of Collections Management, National Conservation Centre, Sally Ann Yates
Head of International Slavery Museum, Dr Richard Benjamin

NATIONAL MUSEUMS OF SCOTLAND

Chambers Street, Edinburgh EH1 1JF
T 0131-247 4422 E info@nms.ac.uk W www.nms.ac.uk

National Museums Scotland provides advice and expertise to the museums community across Scotland, and comprise the National Museum of Scotland, the National War Museum, the National Museum of Rural Life, the National Museum of Flight, the National Museum of Costume and the National Museums Collection Centre. Total grant-in-aid funding from the Scottish Executive for 2007–8 is £20.3m.

Trustees are appointed by the Minister for Tourism, Culture and Sport for a term of four years, and may serve a second term.

Chair, Sir Angus Grossart, CBE, LLD, DLITT

Trustees, James Fiddes, OBE, FRICS; Lesley Hart, MBE; Michael Kirwan, FCA; Prof. Michael Lynch, FRSE, FSA (SCOT); Neena Mahal; Sir Neil McIntosh, CBE; Prof. Malcolm McLeod, CBE, FRSE; Dr Stuart Munro, OBE; Ian Ritchie, CBE, FRENG, FRSE; Sir John Ward, CBE, FRSE, FRSA; Iain Watt
Director, Dr Gordon Rintoul

NATIONAL PORTRAIT GALLERY

St Martin's Place, London WC2H 0HE
T 020-7306 0055 F 020-7306 0056
W www.npg.org.uk

The National Portrait Gallery was formed after a grant was made in 1856 to form a gallery of the portraits of the most eminent persons in British history. The present building was opened in 1896 and the Ondaatje Wing (including a new Balcony Gallery, Tudor Gallery, IT Gallery, lecture theatre and roof-top restaurant) opened in May 2000. There are three regional partnerships displaying portraits at Montacute House, Beningbrough Hall and Bodelwyddan Castle. Total government grant-in-aid for 2007–8 is £7.03m.

BOARD OF TRUSTEES

Chair, Prof. David Cannadine, FBA, FRSL
Trustees, Rt. Hon. Baroness Amos; Zeinab Badawi; Nicholas Blake, QC; Prof. R. Boucher, CBE, FRENG; Marchioness of Douro; Amelia Fawcett, CBE; Flora Fraser; Sir Nicholas Grimshaw, CBE, PRA; Prof. Ludmilla Jordanova; David Mach, RA; Sir Christopher Ondaatje, CBE, OC; David Ross; Prof. Sara Selwood; Alexandra Shulman, OBE; Sir John Weston, KCMG
Director, Sandy Nairne

NATURAL ENGLAND

1 East Parade, Sheffield S1 2ET
T 0845-600 3078
E enquiries@naturalengland.org.uk
W www.naturalengland.org.uk

Natural England was established on 1 October 2006 after the Natural Environment and Rural Communities Act received royal assent in March 2006. The organisation encompasses three previous bodies: English Nature, the environmental land management elements of the Rural Development Service and the Countryside Agency's landscape, access and recreation division. It is responsible for enhancing biodiversity, landscapes and wildlife in rural, urban, coastal and marine areas; promoting access, recreation and public wellbeing; designating sites of special scientific interest, national parks and areas of outstanding natural beauty; managing national nature reserves; enforcing associated regulations; and contributing to the way natural resources are managed.
Chief Executive, Dr Helen Phillips

NATURAL HISTORY MUSEUM

Cromwell Road, London SW7 5BD
T 020-7942 5000 W www.nhm.ac.uk

The Natural History Museum originates from the natural history departments of the British Museum, which grew extensively during the 19th century; in 1860 the natural history collection was moved from Bloomsbury to a new location. Part of the site of the 1862 International Exhibition in South Kensington was acquired for the new

museum, and the museum opened to the public in 1881. In 1963 the Natural History Museum became completely independent with its own board of trustees. The Natural History Museum at Tring, bequeathed by the second Lord Rothschild, has formed part of the museum since 1938. The Geological Museum merged with the Natural History Museum in 1985. Total government grant-in-aid for 2006–7 was £42.8m.

Chair, Oliver Stacken
Trustees, Sir William Castell; Prof. Dianne Edwards, CBE, FRS; Prof. M. Hassell, CBE, FRS; Prof. C. Leaver, CBE, FRS; Prof. Georgina Mace, OBE; Dame Judith Mayhew, DBE; Prof. J. McGlade; Lord Palumbo; Prof. Linda Partridge, FRS, FRSE; Sir Richard Sykes, FRS

SENIOR STAFF
Director, Dr Michael Dixon
Director of Estates and Services, David Sanders
Director of Finance, N. Greenwood
Director of Human Resources, P. Brereton
Director, Natural History Museum at Tring, Mrs T. Wild
Director of Public Engagement Group, Sharon Ament
Director of Science, R. Lane
Head of Audit and Review, D. Thorpe
Head of Library and Information Services, G. Higley
Keeper of Botany, Dr J. Vogel
Keeper of Entomology, Dr M. Scoble
Keeper of Mineralogy, Prof. A. Fleet
Keeper of Palaeontology, Dr N. MacLeod
Keeper of Zoology, Prof. P. Rainbow
Museum Manager, I. Jenkinson

NORTHERN IRELAND HUMAN RIGHTS COMMISSION

Temple Court, 39 North Street, Belfast BT1 1NA
T 028-9024 3987 Textphone 028-9024 9066
F 028-9024 7844
E information@nihrc.org W www.nihrc.org

The Northern Ireland Human Rights Commission was set up in March 1999. Its main functions are to keep under review the law and practice relating to human rights in Northern Ireland, to advise the government and to promote an awareness of human rights in Northern Ireland. It can also take cases to court. The members of the commission are appointed by the Secretary of State for Northern Ireland.
Chief Commissioner, Prof. Monica McWilliams
Commissioners, Jonathan Bell; Thomas Duncan; Lady Christine Eames; Prof. Colin Harvey; Alan Henry; Ann Hope; Kevin McLaughlin; Eamonn O'Neill; Geraldine Rice

NORTHERN LIGHTHOUSE BOARD

84 George Street, Edinburgh EH2 3DA
T 0131-473 3100 F 0131-220 2093
E enquiries@nlb.org.uk W www.nlb.org.uk

The Northern Lighthouse Board is the general lighthouse authority for Scotland and the Isle of Man and owes its origin to an act of parliament passed in 1786. At present there are 19 commissioners who operate under the Merchant Shipping Act 1995.

The commissioners control 212 lighthouses, many lighted and unlighted buoys, a DGPS (differential global positioning system) station and a LORAN (long-range navigation) system (class C) on a trial basis. *See also* Transport section.

Chair, Capt. George Sutherland
Commissioners, Lord Advocate; Solicitor-General for Scotland; Lord Provosts of Edinburgh, Glasgow and Aberdeen; Convener of Highland Council; Convener of Argyll and Bute Council; Sheriffs-Principal of North Strathclyde, Tayside, Central and Fife, Grampian, Highlands and Islands, South Strathclyde, Dumfries and Galloway, Lothians and Borders and Glasgow and Strathkelvin; Peter MacKay, CB; Dr Andrew Cubie, CBE, FRSE; Capt. Kenneth MacLeod; Robert Quayle; Alistair Whyte
Chief Executive, Roger Lockwood, CB

OFFICE OF COMMUNICATIONS (OFCOM)

Riverside House, 2A Southwark Bridge Road,
London SE1 9HA
T 020-7981 3000 F 020-7981 3033
E contact@ofcom.org.uk W www.ofcom.org.uk

OFCOM was established in 2003 under the Office of Communications Act 2002 as the independent regulator and competition authority for the UK communications industries with responsibility for television, radio, telecommunications and wireless communications services. It merged the functions of five regulatory bodies: the Independent Television Commission (ITC), the Broadcasting Standards Commission (BSC), the Office of Telecommunications (OFTEL), the Radio Authority (RAu) and the Radiocommunications Agency (RA).
Chief Executive, Ed Richards
Chair, David Currie
Deputy Chair, Philip Graf, CBE
Board Members, Millie Banerjee; Ian Hargreaves; Stephanie Liston; Sara Nathan; Philip Rutnam

OFFICE OF THE LEGAL SERVICES OMBUDSMAN

3rd Floor, Sunlight House, Quay Street, Manchester M3 3JZ
T 0161-839 7262; 0845-601 0794 F 0161-832 5446
E lso@olso.gsi.gov.uk W www.olso.org

The Legal Services Ombudsman oversees the handling of complaints against solicitors, barristers, licensed conveyancers, legal executives and patent agents by their professional bodies. A complainant must first complain to the relevant professional body before raising the matter with the ombudsman, who will then investigate the way the complaint was dealt with. The ombudsman is independent of the legal profession and her services are free of charge, although she is unable to give legal advice.
Legal Services Ombudsman, Zahida Manzoor, CBE
Operations Director, Gavin Brown

OFFICE OF MANPOWER ECONOMICS (OME)

6th Floor, Kingsgate House, 66–74 Victoria Street,
London SW1E 6SW
T 020-7215 8252 F 020-7215 4445
W www.ome.uk.com

OME was set up in 1971. It is an independent non-statutory organisation which is responsible for servicing independent review bodies which advise on the pay of various public service groups, the Police Negotiating Board and the Police Advisory Board for England and Wales. The OME is also responsible for servicing *ad hoc* bodies of inquiry and for undertaking research into pay and associated matters as requested by the government.
OME Director, Ian Jones
Director, Health Secretariats, Research and Analysis Group and OME Deputy Director, David Miner
Director, Armed Forces' and Prison Service Secretariats, Christine Haworth
Director, Senior Salaries Secretariat, Keith Masson
Director, School Teachers', Police Negotiating Board and Police Advisory Board for England and Wales Secretariats, David Wilson

OFFICE OF THE PENSIONS OMBUDSMAN

6th Floor, 11 Belgrave Road, London SW1V 1RB
T 020-7834 9144 F 020-7821 0065
E enquiries@pensions-ombudsman.org.uk
W www.pensions-ombudsman.org.uk

The Pensions Ombudsman is appointed by the Secretary of State for Work and Pensions, under the Pension Schemes Act 1993 as amended by the Pensions Act 1995. He independently investigates and decides complaints and disputes concerning pension schemes. The Pension Ombudsman's decision is final and binding to all parties concerned in the complaint or dispute, and it can be legally enforced.
Pensions Ombudsman, David Laverick

OFFICE OF THE SCOTTISH LEGAL SERVICES OMBUDSMAN

17 Waterloo Place, Edinburgh EH1 3DL
T 0131-556 9123 F 0131-556 9292
E ombudsman@slso.org.uk W www.slso.org.uk

The ombudsman investigates complaints about the way in which Scottish professional bodies have handled a complaint against a practitioner.
The ombudsman also examines complaints about the unwillingness of a professional body to investigate a complaint against a practitioner.
Scottish Legal Services Ombudsman, Jane Irvine

PARADES COMMISSION

Windsor House, 9–15 Bedford Street, Belfast BT2 7EL
T 028-9089 5900 F 028-9032 2988
E info@paradescommission.com
W www.paradescommission.org

The Parades Commission was set up under the Public Processions (Northern Ireland) Act 1998. Its function is to encourage and facilitate local accommodation on contentious parades; where this is not possible, the commission is empowered to make legal determinations about such parades, which may include imposing conditions on aspects of the notified parade (such as restrictions on routes/areas and exclusion of certain groups with a record of bad behaviour).
The chair and members are appointed by the Secretary of State for Northern Ireland; the membership must, as far as is practicable, be representative of the community in Northern Ireland.
Chair, Roger Poole
Vice-Chair, Vilma Patterson, MBE
Members, Kelly Andrews; David Burrows; Dr Joe Hendron; Anne Monaghan; Alison Scott-McKinley

PARLIAMENTARY AND HEALTH SERVICE OMBUDSMAN

Millbank Tower, Millbank, London SW1P 4QP
T 0845-015 4033 F 020-7217 4000
E phso.enquiries@ombudsman.org.uk
W www.ombudsman.org.uk

The Parliamentary Ombudsman is independent of government and is an officer of parliament. She is responsible for investigating complaints referred to her by MPs from members of the public who claim to have sustained injustice in consequence of maladministration by or on behalf of government departments and certain non-departmental public bodies. In 1999 an additional 158 public bodies were brought within the jurisdiction of the Parliamentary Ombudsman. Certain types of action by government departments or bodies are excluded from investigation. The Parliamentary Ombudsman is also responsible for investigating complaints, referred by MPs, alleging that access to official information has been wrongly refused under the Code of Practice on Access to Government Information 1994.

The Health Service Ombudsman for England is responsible for investigating complaints against National Health Service authorities and trusts that are not dealt with by those authorities to the satisfaction of the complainant. Complaints can be referred directly by the member of the public who claims to have sustained injustice or hardship in consequence of the failure in a service provided by a relevant body. The ombudsman's jurisdiction now covers complaints about family doctors, dentists, pharmacists and opticians, and complaints about actions resulting from clinical judgement.

The Health Service Ombudsman is also responsible for investigating complaints that information has been wrongly refused under the Code of Practice on Openness in the National Health Service 1995. The parliamentary and the health offices are presently held by the same person.

Parliamentary Ombudsman and Health Service Ombudsman, Ms A. Abraham

Deputy Parliamentary Commissioner, Ms T. Longdon

PAROLE BOARD FOR ENGLAND AND WALES

Grenadier House, 99–105 Horseferry Road, London SW1P 2DD
T 0870-420 3505 F 020-7217 0118
E info@paroleboard.gov.uk W www.paroleboard.gov.uk

The Parole Board was established under the Criminal Justice Act 1967 and became an independent executive non-departmental public body under the Criminal Justice and Public Order Act 1994. It is the body that protects the public by making risk assessments about prisoners to decide who may safely be released into the community and who must remain in, or be returned to, custody. Board decisions are taken at two main types of three-member panels: 'paper panels' for the vast majority of cases, or oral hearings for finely balanced decisions concerning prisoners serving life or on extended sentences.

Chair, Prof. Sir Duncan Nichol, CBE

Chief Executive, Christine Glenn

PAROLE BOARD FOR SCOTLAND

Saughton House, Broomhouse Drive, Edinburgh EH11 3XD
T 0131-244 8373 F 0131-244 6974
W www.scottishparoleboard.gov.uk

The board directs and advises the Scottish ministers on the release of prisoners on licence, and related matters.

Chair, Prof. Sandy Cameron

Vice-Chair, Sheriff Rita Rae, QC

PENSION PROTECTION FUND (PPF)

Knollys House, 17 Addiscombe Road, Croydon CR0 6SR
T 0845-600 2541 F 020-8633 4903
E information@ppf.gsi.gov.uk
W www.pensionprotectionfund.org.uk

The PPF became operational in 2005. It was established to pay compensation to members of eligible defined-benefit pension schemes where a qualifying insolvency event in relation to the employer occurs, or where there is a lack of sufficient assets in the pension scheme. The PPF is also responsible for the Fraud Compensation Fund (which provides compensation to occupational pension schemes that suffer a loss that can be attributed to dishonesty). The chair and board of the PPF are appointed by, and accountable to, the Secretary of State for Work and Pensions, and are responsible for paying compensation, calculating annual levies (which help fund the PPF), and setting and overseeing investment strategy.

Chair, Lawrence Churchill

Chief Executive, Partha Dasgupta

THE PENSIONS REGULATOR

Napier House, Trafalgar Place, Brighton BN1 4DW
T 0870-606 3636 F 0870-241 1144
E customersupport@thepensionsregulator.gov.uk
W www.thepensionsregulator.gov.uk

The Pensions Regulator was established in 2005 as the regulator of work-based pensions in the UK, replacing the Occupational Pensions Regulatory Authority (OPRA). It aims to protect the benefits of occupational and personal pension scheme members, while reducing the risk of situations leading to claims on the Pension Protection Fund. The regulator is able to collect detailed scheme information, issue improvement notices and third-party notices, disqualify trustees deemed unfit to carry out their duties, issue a contribution notice or financial support direction, and freeze a scheme at risk while it investigates.

Chair, David Norgrove

Chief Executive, Tony Hobman

POLICE ADVISORY BOARD FOR ENGLAND AND WALES

6th Floor, Kingsgate House, 66–74 Victoria Street,
London SW1E 6SW
T 020-7215 8101 F 020-7215 4445
W www.ome.uk.com

The Police Advisory Board for England and Wales was established in 1965 and provides advice to the home secretary on general questions affecting the police in England and Wales. It also considers draft regulations which the secretary of state proposes to make with respect to matters other than hours of duty, leave, pay and allowances or the issue, use and return of police clothing, personal equipment and other effects.

Independent Chair, John Randall

Independent Deputy Chair, Prof. Gillian Morris

POLICE NEGOTIATING BOARD (PNB)

6h Floor, Kingsgate House, 66–74 Victoria Street,
London SW1E 6SW
T 020-7215 8101 F 020-7215 4445
W www.ome.uk.com

The PNB was established in 1980 to negotiate pay, allowances, hours of duty, leave and pensions of United Kingdom police officers and to make recommendations on these matters to the Secretary of State for Home Affairs, Northern Ireland secretary, and Scottish ministers.
Independent Chair, John Randall
Independent Deputy Chair, Prof. Gillian Morris

POLICE OMBUDSMAN FOR NORTHERN IRELAND

New Cathedral Buildings, St Anne's Square, Belfast BT1 1PG
T 028-9082 8600 F 028-9082 8659
E info@policeombudsman.org W www.policeombudsman.org

Founded in November 2000 under the Police (Northern Ireland) Act 1998, the function of the Office of the Police Ombudsman for Northern Ireland is to investigate complaints against the police in an impartial, efficient, effective and (as far as is possible) transparent way, to win the confidence of the public and the police. It must report on trends in complaints and react to incidents involving the police, where it is in the public interest, even if no individual complaint has been made.
Police Ombudsman, N. O'Loan

PRISONS AND PROBATION OMBUDSMAN FOR ENGLAND AND WALES

Ashley House, 2 Monck Street, London SW1P 2BQ
T 020-7035 2876 F 020-7035 2860
E mail@ppo.gsi.gov.uk W www.ppo.gov.uk

The ombudsman provides a free and independent complaints investigation service for prisoners, those held in immigration detention and those under probation supervision who have been unable to resolve their grievances with the Prison, Immigration and Probation Services. He also conducts independent investigations into the deaths of prisoners, residents of probation hostels and people detained by the immigration authorities.
Ombudsman, Stephen Shaw, CBE

PRISON SERVICE PAY REVIEW BODY (PSPRB)

6th Floor, Kingsgate House, 66–74 Victoria Street,
London SW1E 6SW
T 020-7215 8503 F 020-7215 4445
W www.ome.uk.com

The PSPRB was set up in 2001. It makes independent recommendations on the pay of prison governors, operational managers, prison officers and related grades for the Prison Service in England and Wales and for the Northern Ireland Prison Service.
Chair, Jerry Cope
Members, Beryl Brewer; Dr Henrietta Campbell; Richard Childs, QPM; Ray Coughlin; Bronwen Curtis; John Davies; Joseph Magee; Sarah Murray; Dr Peter Riach; Ann Robinson; Peter Tett

REGIONAL DEVELOPMENT AGENCIES (RDAS)

Broadway House, Tothill Street, London SW1H 9NQ
T 020-7222 8180 F 020-7222 8182
E natsec@rda-secretariat.com
W www.englandsrdas.com

RDAs were established to help the English regions improve their relative economic performance and reduce social and economic disparities within and between regions. Their five statutory objectives are to further economic development and regeneration; to promote business efficiency and competitiveness; to promote employment; to enhance the development and application of skills relevant to employment; and to contribute to sustainable development. There are nine RDAs in England, and they are financed through a single fund provided by contributing government departments (BERR, DCSF, DIUS, DEFRA and DCMS). In 2005–6 the RDA's budget was £2.2bn.

RDA REGIONS
NORTH WEST – PO Box 37, Renaissance House, Centre Park, Warrington WA1 1XB T 01925-400100
Chair, Bryan Gray, MBE
YORKSHIRE – Victoria House, 2 Victoria Place, Leeds LS11 5AE T 0113-394 9600 *Chair,* Terry Hodgkinson
NORTH EAST – Stella House, Goldcrest Way, Newburn Riverside, Newcastle upon Tyne NE15 8NY T 0191-229 6200
Chair, Margaret Fay
WEST MIDLANDS – 3 Priestley Wharf, Holt Street, Aston Science Park, Birmingham B7 4BN T 0121-380 3500
Chair, Nick Paul
EAST MIDLANDS – Apex Court, City Link, Nottingham NG2 4LA T 0115-988 8300 *Chair,* Dr Bryan Jackson
EAST OF ENGLAND – The Business Centre, Station Road, Histon, Cambridge CB4 9LQ T 01223-713900
Chair, Richard Ellis
SOUTH WEST – Sterling House, Dix's Field, Exeter EX1 1QA T 01392-214747 *Chair,* Juliet Williams
LONDON – Palestra, 197 Blackfriars Road, London SE1 8AA T 020-7593 8700 *Chair,* Mary Reilly
SOUTH EAST – Cross Lanes, Guildford GU1 1YA T 01483-484200 *Chair,* Jim Braithwaite

REGISTRAR OF PUBLIC LENDING RIGHT

Richard House, Sorbonne Close, Stockton on Tees TS17 6DA
T 01642-604699 F 01642-615641
E authorservices@plr.uk.com W www.plr.uk.com

Under the Public Lending Right system, in operation since 1983, payment is made from public funds to authors whose books are lent out from public libraries. Payment is made once a year and the amount each author receives is proportionate to the number of times (established from a sample) that each registered book has been lent out during the previous year. The registrar of PLR, who is appointed by the Secretary of State for Culture, Media and Sport, compiles the register of authors and books. Authors resident in all EU countries are eligible to apply. (The term 'author' covers writers, illustrators, translators, and some editors/compilers.)

A payment of 5.98 pence was made in 2006–7 for each estimated loan of a registered book, up to a top limit of £6,600 for the books of any one registered author; the money for loans above this level is used to augment the remaining PLR paymensts. In 2007 the sum of £6.81m was paid out to 23,869 registered authors and assignees as the annual payment of PLR.

Registrar, Dr J. G. Parker

Chair of Advisory Committee, S. Brett

REVIEW BODY FOR NURSING AND OTHER HEALTH PROFESSIONS

6th Floor, Kingsgate House, 66–74 Victoria Street, London SW1E 6SW

T 020-7215 4453 F 020-7215 4445

W www.ome.uk.com

The Review Body for Nurses and Allied Health Professions was set up in 1983, and following the Agenda for Change in 2004 the body changed its name to recognise its broader staff remit. It advises the prime minister and the Secretary of State for Health, and ministers of the Scottish Executive and Welsh Assembly on the remuneration of nursing staff and other health professions employed in the National Health Service, which is currently around 700,000 people.

Chair, Prof. Gillian Morris

Members, Philip Ashmore; Lucinda Bolton; Prof. Richard Disney; Wilma MacPherson, CBE; Prof. Alan Manning; Ian McKay; Sharon Whitlam

REVIEW BODY ON DOCTORS' AND DENTISTS' REMUNERATION

6th Floor, Kingsgate House, 66–74 Victoria Street, London SW1E 6SW

T 020-7215 8407 F 020-7215 4445

W www.ome.uk.com

The Review Body on Doctors' and Dentists' Remuneration was set up in 1971. It advises the prime minister and the Secretaries of State for Health, Scotland and Wales on the remuneration of doctors and dentists taking any part in the National Health Service.

Chair, Ronald Amy, OBE

Members, Prof. John Beath; Dr Margaret Collingwood, TD; Hugh Donaldson; Katrina Easterling; David Grafton

ROYAL AIR FORCE MUSEUM

Grahame Park Way, London NW9 5LL

T 020-8205 2266 F 020-8200 1751

E london@rafmuseum.org W www.rafmuseum.org

The museum has two sites, one at the former airfield at Hendon and the second at Cosford, in the West Midlands, both of which illustrate the development of aviation from before the Wright brothers to the present-day RAF with over 100 aircraft, as well as artefacts, aviation memorabilia, fine art and photographs. Total government grant-in-aid for 2005–6, provided by the Ministry of Defence, was £7.03m.

Director-General, Dr M. A. Fopp

ROYAL BOTANIC GARDEN EDINBURGH (RBGE)

20A Inverleith Row, Edinburgh EH3 5LR

T 0131-552 7171 F 0131-248 2901

E info@rbge.org.uk W www.rbge.org.uk

The RBGE originated as the Physic Garden, established in 1670 beside the Palace of Holyroodhouse. The garden moved to its present 28-hectare site at Inverleith, Edinburgh, in 1821. There are also three regional gardens: Benmore Botanic Garden, near Dunoon, Argyll; Logan Botanic Garden, near Stranraer, Wigtownshire; and Dawyck Botanic Garden, near Stobo, Peeblesshire. Since 1986 RBGE has been administered by a board of trustees established under the National Heritage (Scotland) Act 1985. It receives an annual grant from the Environment and Rural Affairs Department of the Scottish Executive.

The RBGE is an international centre for scientific research on plant diversity and for horticulture education and conservation. It has an extensive library, a herbarium with over two million preserved plant specimens, and over 16,500 species in the living collections.

Chair of the Board of Trustees, Dr Paul Nicholson

Regius Keeper, Prof. Stephen Blackmore, FRSE

ROYAL BOTANIC GARDENS (RBG) KEW

Richmond, Surrey TW9 3AB

T 020-8332 5000 F 020-8332 5197

Wakehurst Place, Ardingly, W. Sussex RH17 6TN

T 01444-89000 F 01444-894069

E info@kew.org W www.kew.org

The Royal Botanic Gardens (RBG) Kew were originally laid out as a private garden for Kew House for George III's mother, Princess Augusta, in 1759. The gardens were much enlarged in the 19th century, notably by the inclusion of the grounds of the former Richmond Lodge. In 1965 the garden at Wakehurst Place was acquired; it is owned by the National Trust and managed by RBG Kew. Under the National Heritage Act 1983 a board of trustees was set up to administer the gardens, which in 1984 became an independent body supported by grant-in-aid from the Department of Environment, Food and Rural Affairs.

The functions of RBG Kew are to carry out research into plant sciences, to disseminate knowledge about plants and to provide the public with the opportunity to gain knowledge and enjoyment from the gardens' collections. There are extensive national reference collections of living and preserved plants and a comprehensive library and archive. The main emphasis is on plant conservation and biodiversity; Wakehurst Place houses the Millennium Seed Bank, which is the largest *ex situ* conservation project ever conceived – its aim is to acquire seed from ten per cent of Earth's wild plant species by 2010.

BOARD OF TRUSTEES

Chair, Lord Selborne

Members, Marcus Agius; Tanya Burman; Andrew Cahn; Richard Deverell; Prof. Jonathan Drori, CBE; Prof. Charles Godfray; Dr Sandy Harrison; Richard Lapthorne, CBE; David Norman; Marion Regan; Prof. Sir William Stewart; Sir Richard Sykes

Director, Prof. Stephen Hopper

ROYAL COMMISSION ON ENVIRONMENTAL POLLUTION

3rd Floor, 5–8 The Sanctuary, Westminster, London SW1P 3JS

T 020-7799 8970 F 020-7799 8971

E enquiries@rcep.org.uk W www.rcep.org.uk

The commission was set up in 1970 to advise on national and international matters concerning the pollution of the environment. The commission's advice is mainly in the form of reports which are the outcome of studies, the most recent of which relates to the urban environment.

Members are appointed by the Queen on the advice of the prime minister.

Chair, Prof. Sir John Lawton, CBE, FRS

Members, Prof. Nicholas Cumpsty, FRENG; Prof. Michael H. Depledge; Dr Paul Ekins; Dr I. Graham-Bryce, CBE, FRSE; Prof. Stephen Holgate, FRCP; Prof. J. Jowell, QC; Prof. Peter Liss; Prof. Susan Owens, OBE; Prof. Judith Petts; Prof. S. Rayner; John Speirs, CBE, LVO; Prof. Janet Sprent, OBE, FRSE; Prof. Lynda Warren

ROYAL COMMISSION ON THE ANCIENT AND HISTORICAL MONUMENTS OF SCOTLAND

John Sinclair House, 16 Bernard Terrace, Edinburgh EH8 9NX

T 0131-662 1456 F 0131-662 1477

E info@rcahms.gov.uk W www.rcahms.gov.uk

The Royal Commission was established by a royal warrant in 1908, which was revised in 1992, and is appointed to provide for the survey and recording of ancient and historical monuments connected with the culture, civilisation and conditions of life of the people in Scotland from the earliest times. It is funded by the Scottish Executive. The commission compiles, maintains and makes available the National Monuments Record of Scotland as the national record of the archaeological and historical environment.

Chair, Prof. John Hume, OBE, FSA (SCOT)

Commissioners, Kate Byrne; Mark Hopton, FSA (SCOT); Prof. John Hunter, FSA, FSA (SCOT); Prof. Angus Macdonald, FSA (SCOT); Dr Margaret Mackay, FSA (SCOT); Gordon Masterton; Prof. Christopher Morris, FSA, FRSE, FSA (SCOT); Dr Jane Murray, FSA (SCOT); Dr Stana Nenadic, FSA (SCOT)

Chief Executive, Diana Murray, FSA, FSA (SCOT)

ROYAL COMMISSION ON THE ANCIENT AND HISTORICAL MONUMENTS OF WALES

Crown Building, Plas Crug, Aberystwyth SY23 1NJ

T 01970-621200 F 01970-627701

E nmr.wales@rcahmw.gov.uk W www.rcahmw.gov.uk

The Royal Commission was established in 1908 and is currently empowered by a royal warrant of 2001 to survey, record, publish and maintain a database of ancient and historical and maritime sites and structures, and landscapes, in Wales. The commission is funded by the National Assembly for Wales and is also responsible for the National Monuments Record of Wales, which is open daily for public reference and has a public enquiry service. The commission is responsible for supplying archaeological information to Ordnance Survey, for the coordination of archaeological aerial photography in Wales, and for sponsorship of the regional Sites and Monuments Records.

Chair, Prof. Ralph A. Griffiths, DLITT, FRHISTS

Vice-Chair, Dr Llinos Smith, FRHISTS

Commissioners, Prof. Anthony D. Carr, FSA, FRHISTS; David W. Crossley, FSA; Mrs A. Eastham; Neil Harries; John W. Lloyd, CB; Jonathan Matthews Hudson; John Newman, FSA; Henry Owen-John; Prof. Patrick Sims-Williams, FBA

ROYAL MAIL GROUP

148 Old Street, London EC1V 9HQ

T 020-7250 2888

W www.royalmailgroup.com

Crown services for the carriage of government dispatches were set up in about 1516. The conveyance of public correspondence began in 1635 and the mail service was made a parliamentary responsibility with the setting up of a Post Office in 1657. Telegraphs came under Post Office control in 1870 and the Post Office Telephone Service began in 1880. The National Girobank service of the Post Office began in 1968. The Post Office ceased to be a government department in 1969 when responsibility for the running of the postal, telecommunications, giro and remittance services was transferred to a public authority of the same name.

The British Telecommunications Act 1981 separated the functions of the Post Office, making it solely responsible for postal services and Girobank. Girobank was privatised in 1990. The Postal Services Act 2000 turned the Post Office into a wholly owned public limited company establishing a regulatory regime under the Postal Service Commission. The Post Office Group changed its name to Consignia plc in March 2001 when its new corporate structure took effect; in November 2001 the name was changed to Royal Mail Group plc. As of 1 January 2006 the UK postal service market was fully liberalised, and any licensed operator is now able to deliver mail to businesses and residential customers.

The chair, chief executive and members of the board are appointed by the Secretary of State for Business, Enterprise and Regulatory Reform but responsibility for the running of Royal Mail Group as a whole rests with the board in its corporate capacity.

BOARD

Chair, Allan Leighton

Chief Executive (Royal Mail Group), Adam Crozier

Managing Director, Alan Cook, CBE *(Post Office Ltd)*

Members, David Burden *(Group Technology Director);* Ian Duncan *(Group Finance Director);* Tony McCarthy *(Group Director, People and Organisational Development)*

Non-Executive Directors, David Fish; Richard Handover; Sir Mike Hodgkinson; John Neill, CBE; Baroness Prosser, OBE; Helen Weir

ROYAL NAVAL MUSEUM

HM Naval Base (PP66), Portsmouth PO1 3NH

T 023-9272 7562 F 023-9272 7575

W www.royalnavalmuseum.org

The Royal Naval Museum is a non-departmental public body sponsored by the Ministry of Defence, and is a registered charity governed by a board of trustees. Lord Nelson's flagship, HMS *Victory,* is in dry dock and is part of the museum. The museum aims to provide an effective and accessible repository for the heritage of the Navy, and to raise public awareness, and encourage scholarship and research into, the history and achievements of the Royal Navy.

Chair, Adm. Sir Peter Abbott, GBE, KCB

SCHOOL TEACHERS' REVIEW BODY (STRB)

6th Floor, Kingsgate House, 66–74 Victoria Street, London SW1E 6SW

T 020-7215 8297 F 020-7215 4445

W www.ome.uk.com

The STRB was set up under the School Teachers' Pay and Conditions Act 1991. It is required to examine and report on such matters relating to the statutory conditions of employment of school teachers in England and Wales as may be referred to it by the education secretary.

Chair, Bill Cockburn, CBE, TD

Members, Jennifer Board; Monojit Chatterji; Mark Goodridge; Dewi Jones; Elizabeth Kidd; Esmond Lindop; Bruce Warman; Anne Watts

SCIENCE MUSEUM

Exhibition Road, London SW7 2DD

T 0870-870 4868 E sciencemuseum@nmsi.ac.uk

W www.sciencemuseum.org.uk

The Science Museum, part of the National Museum of Science and Industry (NMSI), houses the national collections of science, technology, industry and medicine. The museum began as the science collection of the South Kensington Museum and first opened in 1857. In 1883 it acquired the collections of the Patent Museum and in 1909 the science collections were transferred to the new Science Museum, leaving the art collections with the Victoria and Albert Museum. The Wellcome Wing was opened in July 2000.

Some of the museum's larger objects, ranging across aircraft, agricultural machinery, computing, mechanical engineering, and road and rail transport collections, are at Science Museum Swindon, Wilts. The NMSI also incorporates the National Railway Museum, York, the National Museum of Photography, Film and Television, Bradford, and Locomotion: the National Railway Museum at Shildon.

Total government grant-in-aid for 2007–8 is £38.61m.

Chair, Rt. Hon. Lord Waldegrave of North Hill

Trustees, Lady Chisholm; Prof. Sir Ron U. Cooke, DSC; Prof. Dame Ann Dowling, CBE, FRENG; Lord Faulkner of Worcester; Dr Douglas Gurr; Richard Haythornthwaite; Lord Rees of Ludlow, FRS; Prof. Sir Howard Newby, KB, CBE; Prof. Simon J. Schaffer; Dr Maggie Semple, OBE; Dr Tony Sewell; Martin G. Smith; Prof. Roderick A. Smith, FRENG; Prof. Kathy Sykes; Sir William Wells; Michael G. Wilson

Director of NMSI, Martin Earwicker

Director of Science Museum, Prof. Chris Rapley, CBE

Director of National Media Museum, Colin Philpott

Director of National Railway Museum, Andrew Scott

SCOTTISH ARTS COUNCIL

12 Manor Place, Edinburgh EH3 7DD

T 0131-226 6051 F 0131-225 9833

E help.desk@scottisharts.org.uk W www.scottisharts.org.uk

The Scottish Arts Council is the main arts development agency in Scotland. It is a non-departmental public body, accountable to the Scottish Executive. The Scottish Arts Council invests funds from the Scottish Executive and National Lottery and works with partners to support and develop artistic excellence and creativity throughout Scotland.

Chair, Richard Holloway

Members, Dinah Caine; Donald Emslie; Steven Grimmond; Charles Lovatt; Ray Macfarlane *(Vice-Chair)*; Barbara McKissack; Jim McSharry; John Mulgrew; Rab Noakes; Ian Smith; Ben Twist

Chief Executive (acting), Jim Tough

SCOTTISH CRIMINAL CASES REVIEW COMMISSION

5th Floor, Portland House, 17 Renfield Street, Glasgow G2 5AH

T 0141-270 7030 F 0141-270 7040/23

E info@sccrc.org.uk W www.sccrc.org.uk

The commission is a non-departmental public body, funded by the Scottish Executive Justice Department, and established in April 1999. It assumed the role previously performed by the Secretary of State for Scotland to consider alleged miscarriages of justice in Scotland and refer cases meeting the relevant criteria to the High Court for determination. Members are appointed by the Queen on the recommendation of the First Minister; senior executive staff are appointed by the commission.

Chair, Very Revd Graham Forbes, CBE

Members, David Belfall; Graham Bell, QC; Prof. Brian Caddy; Stewart Campbell; Sir Gerald Gordon, CBE, QC; Robert Gordon, QC; James Mackay, QPM; Gerard McClay

Chief Executive, Gerard Sinclair

SCOTTISH ENTERPRISE

5 Atlantic Quay, 150 Broomielaw, Glasgow G2 8LU

T 0141-248 2700 Helpline 0845-607 8787 F 0141-221 3217

E network.helpline@scotent.co.uk

W www.scottish-enterprise.com

Scottish Enterprise was established in 1991 and its purpose is to create jobs and prosperity for the people of Scotland. It is funded by the Scottish Executive and is responsible to the Scottish ministers. Working in partnership with the private and public sectors, Scottish Enterprise aims to further the development of Scotland's economy, to enhance the skills of the Scottish workforce and to promote Scotland's international competitiveness. Scottish Enterprise is concerned with attracting firms to Scotland and, through Scottish Trade International, it helps Scottish companies to compete in world export markets. Scottish Enterprise has a network of 12 local enterprise companies that deliver economic development services at local level.

Chair, Sir John Ward, CBE

Chief Executive, Jack Perry

SCOTTISH ENVIRONMENT PROTECTION AGENCY (SEPA)

Erskine Court, Castle Business Park, Stirling FK9 4TR

T 01786-457700 Hotline 0800-807060

F 01786-446885 E info@sepa.org.uk

W www.sepa.org.uk

SEPA was established in 1996 and is the public body responsible for environmental protection in Scotland. It regulates potential pollution to land, air and water; the storage, transport and disposal of controlled waste; and the safekeeping and disposal of radioactive materials. It does this within a complex legislative framework of acts of parliament, EC directives and regulations, granting licences to operations of industrial processes and waste disposal. SEPA also operates Floodline, 0845-988 1188, a public service providing information on the possible risk of flooding 24 hours a day, 365 days a year.

Chair, Sir Ken Collins

Chief Executive, Campbell Gemmell

Directors, Colin Bayes *(Environmental Regulation and Improvement)*; Calum MacDonald *(Environmental and Organisational Development)*; Chris Spray *(Environmental Science)*

SCOTTISH LAW COMMISSION

140 Causewayside, Edinburgh EH9 1PR
T 0131-668 2131 F 0131-662 4900
E info@scotlawcom.gov.uk W www.scotlawcom.gov.uk

The Scottish Law Commission, established in 1965, keeps the law in Scotland under review and makes proposals for its development and reform. It is responsible to the Scottish ministers through the Scottish Executive Justice Department.

Chair (part-time), Hon. Lord Drummond Young
Chief Executive, C. M. A. Lugton
Commissioners, Prof. G. L. Gretton; Prof. G. Maher, QC; Prof. J. M. Thomson; C. J. Tyre, QC

SCOTTISH LEGAL AID BOARD

44 Drumsheugh Gardens, Edinburgh EH3 7SW
T 0131-226 7061 Helpline 0845-122 8686
F 0131-220 4878
E general@slab.org.uk W www.slab.org.uk

The Scottish Legal Aid Board was set up under the Legal Aid (Scotland) Act 1986 to manage legal aid in Scotland. It reports to the Scottish Executive. Board members are appointed by Scottish ministers.

Chair, Iain A. Robertson, CBE
Members, Graham Bell, QC; Les Campbell; William Gallagher; Joseph Hughes; Denise Loney; Paul McBride, QC; Susan McPhee; Ellen Morton; David Nicol; Elaine Rosie; Prof. Mahendra Raj; Sheriff Kenneth Ross; Graham Watson
Chief Executive, Lindsay Montgomery

SCOTTISH NATURAL HERITAGE (SNH)

Great Glen House, Leachkin Road, Inverness IV3 8NW
T 01463-725000 F 01463-725067
E enquiries@snh.gov.uk W www.snh.org.uk

SNH was established in 1992 under the Natural Heritage (Scotland) Act 1991. It provides advice on nature conservation to all those whose activities affect wildlife, landforms and features of geological interest in Scotland, and seeks to develop and improve facilities for the enjoyment and understanding of the Scottish countryside. It is funded by the Scottish Executive.

Chair, Andrew Thin
Chief Executive, I. Jardine
Chief Scientific Adviser, C. Galbraith
Directors of Operations, A. Bachell *(East)*; J. Watson *(North)*; J. Thomson *(West)*
Director of Corporate Services, J. Moore

SCOTTISH PRISONS COMPLAINTS COMMISSION

Government Buildings, Broomhouse Drive, Edinburgh EH11 3XD
T 0131-244 8423 F 0131-244 8430
E spcc@scotland.gsi.gov.uk W www.scotland.gov.uk/spcc

The commission was established in 1994. It is an independent body to which prisoners in Scottish prisons can make applications in relation to any matter where they have failed to obtain satisfaction from the Scottish Prison Service's internal grievance procedures. Clinical judgements made by medical officers, matters which are the subject of legal proceedings and matters relating to sentence, conviction and parole decision-making are excluded from the commission's jurisdiction. The

commissioner is appointed by the Scottish ministers.
Commissioner, Vaughan Barrett

SCOTTISH PUBLIC SERVICES OMBUDSMAN

Freepost EH641, Edinburgh EH3 0BR
T 0800-377 7330 F 0800-377 7331
E ask@spso.org.uk W www.spso.org.uk

The Scottish Public Services Ombudsman was established in 2002. The ombudsman investigates complaints about Scottish Executive departments and agencies, councils, housing associations, the National Health Service (NHS) and other public bodies. The public bodies which the Scottish Public Services Ombudsman may consider investigating are contained in a list outlined in the Scottish Public Services Ombudsman Act 2002. The ombudsman's remit was extended in 2005 to cover Scotland's further education colleges and higher education institutions. Complaints considered by the ombudsman can range from complaints about poor service, failure to provide a service, administrative failure and complaints about the NHS including hospital staff, GPs, dentists and other health professionals.
Scottish Public Services Ombudsman, Prof. Alice Brown

SCOTTISH RECORDS ADVISORY COUNCIL

HM General Register House, Edinburgh EH1 3YY
T 0131-535 1403 F 0131-535 1430
W www.scottishrecordsadvisorycouncil.info

The council was established under the Public Records (Scotland) Act 1937. Its members are appointed by the First Minister and it may submit proposals or make representations to the First Minister, the Lord Justice General or the Lord President of the Court of Session on questions relating to the public records of Scotland.
Chair, Prof. H. MacQueen

SEAFISH INDUSTRY AUTHORITY

18 Logie Mill, Logie Green Road, Edinburgh EH7 4HS
T 0131-558 3331 F 0131-558 1442
E seafish@seafish.co.uk W www.seafish.org

Established under the Fisheries Act 1981, the authority works with all sectors of the UK seafood industry to satisfy consumers, raise standards, improve efficiency and secure a sustainable and profitable future. It is sponsored by the four UK fisheries departments, which appoint the board, and is funded by a levy on seafood.
Chair, Andrew Dewar-Durie
Chief Executive, John Rutherford

SENIOR SALARIES REVIEW BODY

6th Floor, Kingsgate House, 66–74 Victoria Street, London SW1E 6SW
T 020-7215 8276 F 020-7215 4445
W www.ome.uk.com

The Senior Salaries Review Body (formerly the Top Salaries Review Body) was set up in 1971 to advise the prime minister on the remuneration of the judiciary, senior civil servants and senior officers of the armed forces. In 1993 its remit was extended to cover the pay, pensions and allowances of MPs, ministers and others whose pay is determined by the Ministerial and Other Salaries Act 1975, and also the allowances of peers. If asked, it advises on the pay of officers and members of the devolved parliament and assemblies.

Chair, John Baker, CBE

Members, Mark Baker, CBE; Mary Galbraith; Prof. David Greenaway; Michael Langley; Jim McKenna; Mei Sim Lai, OBE; Sir Peter North, CBE, QC; Richard Pearson; Paul Williams

SERIOUS ORGANISED CRIME AGENCY (SOCA)

PO Box 8000, London SE11 5EN
T 020–7238 8000 W www.soca.gov.uk

SOCA was established in April 2006. It took over the functions of the National Criminal Intelligence Service and the National Crime Squad, as well as the role of HM Revenue and Customs in investigating drug trafficking and related criminal finance, and some of the functions of the UK Immigration Service in dealing with organised immigration crime. Its remit is to prevent and detect serious organised crime and to gather, store, analyse and disseminate information on crime. SOCA is also tasked with providing support to law enforcement partners.

The Secretary of State for Home Affairs appoints the chair and director-general, may set SOCA strategies and judges the success of its efforts. Grant-in-aid is provided by the Home Office and for 2006–7 was set provisionally at £416m in resource funding and £41m in capital provision.

Chair, Sir Stephen Lander

Director-General, Bill Hughes

Directors, David Bolt *(Intelligence)*; Malcolm Cornberg *(Corporate Services)*; Paul Evans *(Intervention)*; Trevor Pearce *(Enforcement)*

Non-Executive Directors, Stephen Barrett; Elizabeth France; Ken Jarrold; Janet Paraskeva; Gen. Sir Roger Wheeler

STATISTICS COMMISSION

Artillery House, 11–19 Artillery Row, London SW1P 1RT
T 020-7273 8008 F 020-7273 8019
E statscom@statscom.org.uk W www.statscom.org.uk

The Statistics Commission was set up in 2000 to advise on the quality, quality assurance and priority-setting for official statistics, and on the procedures designed to deliver statistical integrity, to help ensure official statistics are trustworthy and responsive to public needs. It is independent of both ministers and the producers of National Statistics. It operates in a transparent way with the minutes of its meetings, correspondence and evidence it receives, and advice it gives, all normally publicly available for scrutiny.

Chair, Prof. D. Rhind, CBE, FRS, FBA

Vice-Chair, Sir Derek Wanless

Members, Ian Beesley; Miss C. Bowe; H. J. Dixon; Dr Isabelle Low; Mrs J. Trewsdale; M. Weale

STUDENT LOANS COMPANY LTD

100 Bothwell Street, Glasgow G2 7JD
T 0141-306 2000 F 0141-306 2005
W www.slc.co.uk

The Student Loans Company Ltd is wholly owned by the government. It administers the Student Loan Scheme (established in 1990) and the Income Contingent Loans Scheme (established in 1998), and provides loans to eligible students in higher education in the United Kingdom. In the region of £2.95bn of loans were distributed during 2006–7. As at 31 March 2007 there were 2.5 million borrowers, and a total of £18.13bn of outstanding loans to be repaid.

Chair, Keith Bedell-Pearce

Chief Executive, Ralph Seymour-Jackson

TATE BRITAIN

Millbank, London SW1P 4RG
T 020-7887 8888
E visiting.britain@tate.org.uk W www.tate.org.uk

Tate Britain displays the national collection of British art from 1500 to the present day – with special attention and dedicated space given to Blake, Turner and Constable. The gallery opened in 1897, the cost of building (£80,000) being defrayed by Sir Henry Tate, who also contributed the nucleus of the present collection. The Turner wing was opened in 1910, and further galleries and a new sculpture hall followed in 1937. In 1979 a further extension was built, and the Clore Gallery was opened in 1987. The Centenary Development was opened in 2001.

There are four Tate galleries: Tate Britain and Tate Modern in London, Tate Liverpool and Tate St Ives; the entire Tate collection is available to view online.

BOARD OF TRUSTEES

Chair, Paul Myners, CBE

Trustees, Helen Alexander; Victoria Barnsley; Melanie Clore; Sir Howard Davies; Jeremy Deller; Anish Kapoor; Patricia Lankester; Prof. Jennifer Latto; Fiona Rae; Jon Snow; John Studzinski

OFFICERS

Director, Sir Nicholas Serota

Director, Tate Britain, Dr Stephen Deuchar

Director, Tate Liverpool, Dr Christoph Grunenberg

Director, Tate Modern, Vicente Todoli

Director, Tate St Ives, Susan Daniel-McElroy

TATE MODERN

Bankside, London SE1 9TG
T 020-7887 8888 E visiting.modern@tate.org.uk
W www.tate.org.uk

Opened in May 2000, Tate Modern displays the Tate collection of international modern art dating from 1900 to the present day. It includes works by Dalí, Picasso, Matisse and Warhol as well as many contemporary works. It is housed in the former Bankside Power Station in London, which was redesigned by the Swiss architects Herzog and de Meuron.

Director, Vicente Todoli

TOURISM BODIES

Visit Britain, Visit Scotland, the Wales Tourist Board and the Northern Ireland Tourist Board are responsible for developing and marketing the tourist industry in their respective countries.

VISIT BRITAIN

Thames Tower, Blacks Road, London W6 9EL T 020-8846 9000
F 020-8563-0302 W www.visitbritain.com

Chair, Christopher Rodrigues, CBE

Chief Executive, Tom Wright

VISIT SCOTLAND
94 Ocean Drive, Leith, Edinburgh EH6 6JH T 0131-472 2222
E generalenquiries@visitscotland.com
W www.visitscotland.com
Chair, Peter Lederer, CBE
Chief Executive, Philip Riddle

WALES TOURIST BOARD
Brunel House, 2 Fitzalan Road, Cardiff CF24 0UY
T 0870-830 0306 F 0870-121 1259
E info@visitwales.co.uk W www.visitwales.com
Directors, Gareth Hall; Jonathan Jones

NORTHERN IRELAND TOURIST BOARD
59 North Street, Belfast BT1 1NB T 028-9023 1221
F 028-9024 0960 E info@nitb.com
W www.discovernorthernireland.com
Chair, Tom McGrath, OBE
Chief Executive, Alan Clarke

TRAINING AND DEVELOPMENT AGENCY (TDA)
151 Buckingham Palace Road, London SW1W 9SZ
T 020-7023 8001 W www.tda.gov.uk

The TDA was launched in September 2005 and took on the role, and expanded the remit of, the Teacher Training Agency. The TDA aims to attract able and committed people to teaching, concentrating specifically on subjects where teachers are in short supply; provide schools and their staff with good information on training and development opportunities; and ensure that new teachers enter schools with appropriate skills and knowledge, through working closely with providers of initial teacher training.
Chief Executive, Graham Holley

TRANSPORT FOR LONDON (TFL)
Windsor House, 42–50 Victoria Street, London SW1H 0TL
T 020-7222 5600
E enquire@tfl.gov.uk W www.tfl.gov.uk

TfL was formed in July 2000 as a functional body of the Greater London Authority and is responsible for the capital's transport system. Its role is to implement the Mayor of London's transport strategy and manage the transport services across London for which the mayor has responsibility.

As a result, TfL is responsible for London's buses, the Underground, the Docklands Light Railway (DLR) and the management of Croydon Tramlink and London River Services. It also runs Victoria Coach Station and London's Transport Museum, manages the Congestion Charging scheme and regulates the city's taxis and private hire trade.
Chair, Ken Livingstone
Vice-Chair, Dave Wetzel
Commissioner, Peter Hendy

UK ATOMIC ENERGY AUTHORITY (UKAEA)
Harwell Science and Innovation Campus, Oxon OX11 0RA
T 01235-820220 F 01235-436899
W www.ukaea.org.uk

The UKAEA was established by the Atomic Energy Authority Act 1954 and took over responsibility for the research and development of the civil nuclear power programme. The UKAEA is now responsible for the safe management and decommissioning of its radioactive plants and for leading the development of the Harwell Science and Innovation Campus. The UKAEA also undertakes the UK's contribution to the international fusion programme.
Chair, Hon. Barbara Thomas Judge
Chief Executive, Norman Harrison

UK FILM COUNCIL
10 Little Portland Street, London W1W 7JG
T 020-7861 7861 F 020-7861 7862
E info@ukfilmcouncil.org.uk W www.ukfilmcouncil.org.uk

The council was created in April 2000 by the Department for Culture, Media and Sport. The council's board is comprised of 15 directors and has been established as a private company limited by guarantee, with an intention to move it to a statutory basis at a later stage. It invests grant-in-aid and National Lottery funds in film development and production, training, international development and export promotion, distribution and exhibition, and education.

UK Film Council International (formerly the British Film Commission) is part of the same organisation, and was originally established in 1991. Its remit is to attract inward investment by promoting the UK as an international production centre to the film and television industries and encouraging the use of British locations, services, facilities and personnel.
Chair, Stewart Till, CBE
Chief Executive, John Woodward
British Film Commissioner, Colin Brown

UNITED KINGDOM SPORTS COUNCIL (UK SPORT)
40 Bernard Street, London WC1N 1ST
T 020-7211 5100 F 020-7211 5246
E info@uksport.gov.uk W www.uksport.gov.uk

UK Sport was established by royal charter in 1996 and is accountable to parliament through the Department for Culture, Media and Sport. Its role is to lead the UK to sporting excellence by supporting winning athletes, world-class events, world-class standards and ethically fair and drug-free sport. UK Sport is responsible for managing and distributing public investment (£60m annually) and is a statutory distributor of funds raised by the National Lottery.
Chair, Sue Campbell, CBE
Chief Executive, John Steele

VICTORIA AND ALBERT MUSEUM
Cromwell Road, London SW7 2RL
T 020-7942 2000 W www.vam.ac.uk

The Victoria and Albert Museum (V&A) is the national museum of fine and applied art and design. It descends directly from the Museum of Manufactures, which opened in Marlborough House in 1852 after the Great Exhibition of 1851. The museum was moved in 1857 to become part of the South Kensington Museum. It was renamed the Victoria and Albert Museum in 1899. It also houses the National Art Library and Print Room.

The museum administers the V&A Museum of Childhood at Bethnal Green, which was opened in 1872; the building is the most important surviving example of the type of glass and iron construction used by Paxton for the Great Exhibition. Total government grant-in-aid for 2007–8 is £41.7m.

BOARD OF TRUSTEES

Chair, Paula Ridley, OBE
Members, E. Davies, OBE; T. Dixon, OBE; Mrs J. Gordon Clark; Prof. Sir Christopher Frayling, PHD; Ms B. Jackson, MBE; Prof. Lisa Jardine, CBE; R. Mather; P. Rogers, CBE; P. Ruddock; Rt. Hon. Sir Timothy Sainsbury; Dame Marjorie Scardino, DBE; S. Shah, OBE

OFFICERS

Managing Director of V&A Enterprises Ltd, Ms. J. Prosser
Director of the V&A, M. Jones
Deputy Director, I. Blatchford
Directors, Ms B. McKillop *(Collections; Keeper of the Asian Department)*; N. Umney *(Collections Services)*; Ms J. Lawson *(Development)*; A. Ganguli *(Finance)*; A. Hill *(Human Resources)*; D. Anderson, OBE *(Learning and Interpretation)*; Ms M. Gemmill *(Projects and Design)*; P. Catlow *(Property Services)*; D. Whitmore *(Public Affairs)*; Ms S. Ridley *(Security and Visitor Services)*; G. Marsh *(Theatre Collections)*; Ms D. Lees *(V&A Museum of Childhood)*
Keepers of Departments, C. Wilk *(Furniture, Fashion and Textiles)*; Dr P. E. D. Williamson *(Sculpture, Metalwork, Ceramics and Glass)*; J. Bryant *(Word and Image)*

WALLACE COLLECTION

Hertford House, Manchester Square, London W1U 3BN
T 020-7563 9500 F 020-7224 2155
E enquiries@wallacecollection.org
W www.wallacecollection.org

The Wallace Collection was bequeathed to the nation by the widow of Sir Richard Wallace, in 1897, and Hertford House was subsequently acquired by the government. The collection contains works by Titian and Rembrandt, and includes porcelain, furniture and an array of arms and armour. Total government grant-in-aid for 2006–7 was £3.53m.

Director, Rosalind Savill

WOMEN'S NATIONAL COMMISSION

1/F6 Ashdown House, 123 Victoria Street, London SW1E 5DE
T 020-7944 0585 F 020-7944 0583
E wnc@communities.gsi.gov.uk W www.thewnc.org.uk

The Women's National Commission was established in 1969 as an independent advisory committee to the government. It is an umbrella organisation representing women and women's organisations in the UK. Its remit is to ensure that the informed opinions of women are given their due weight in the deliberations of the government and in public debate on matters of public interest, including those of special interest to women. The commission is an advisory NDPB based within the Department for Communities and Local Government alongside the Women and Equality Unit.

Chair (acting), Baroness Gould of Potternewton
Director (acting), Susan Green

REGIONAL GOVERNMENT

LONDON

GREATER LONDON AUTHORITY (GLA)
City Hall, The Queen's Walk, London SE1 2AA
T 020-7983 4000 E mayor@london.gov.uk
W www.london.gov.uk

On 7 May 1998 London voted in favour of the formation of the Greater London Authority (GLA). The first elections to the GLA took place on 4 May 2000 and the new authority took over its responsibilities on 3 July 2000. In July 2002 the GLA moved to one of London's most spectacular buildings, newly built on a brownfield site on the south bank of the Thames, adjacent to Tower Bridge. The second election to the GLA took place on 10 June 2004.

The structure and objectives of the GLA stem from its eight main areas of responsibility. These are transport, planning, economic development and regeneration, the environment, police, fire and emergency planning, culture and health. The bodies that coordinate these functions and report to the GLA are Transport for London (TfL), the London Development Agency (LDA), the Metropolitan Police Authority (MPA), and the London Fire and Emergency Planning Authority (LFEPA). The GLA also absorbed a number of other London bodies, such as the London Planning Advisory Committee, the London Ecology Unit and the London Research Centre.

The GLA consists of a directly elected mayor, the Mayor of London, and a separately elected assembly, the London Assembly. The mayor has the key role of decision making, with the assembly performing the tasks of regulating and scrutinising these decisions. In addition, the GLA has around 600 permanent staff to support the activities of the mayor and the assembly, which are overseen by a head of paid service. The mayor may appoint two political advisers, though does not necessarily exercise this power, but he may not appoint the chief executive, the monitoring officer or the chief finance officer. These must be appointed by the assembly.

Every aspect of the assembly and its activities must be open to public scrutiny and therefore accountable. The assembly holds the mayor to account through scrutiny of his strategies, decisions and actions. This is carried out by direct questioning at assembly meetings and by conducting detailed investigations in committee.

People's Question Time gives Londoners the chance to question the mayor and the London Assembly about plans, priorities and policies for London. It is held twice a year in different areas of London.

The role of the mayor can be broken down into a number of key areas: to represent and promote London at home and abroad and speak up for Londoners; to devise strategies and plans to tackle London-wide issues, such as transport, economic development and regeneration, air quality, environment, noise, waste, bio-diversity, planning and culture; and to set budgets for TFL, the LDA, the MPA and the LFEPA. The mayor is chair of TFL and has the power to appoint the members of their board and those of the LDA; he also makes appointments to the police and fire authorities. With London's successful bid to host the 2012 Olympic and Paralympic Games, the mayor is the signatory to the contract with the International Olympic Committee undertaking that the games will be delivered.

The role of the assembly can be broken down into a number of key areas:
• to check on and balance the mayor
• to scrutinise the mayor
• to have the power to amend the mayor's budget by a majority of two-thirds
• to investigate issues of London-wide significance and make proposals to the mayor
• to provide the deputy mayor and the members serving on the police, fire and emergency planning authorities with advice

Mayor, Ken Livingstone
Deputy Mayor, Nicky Gavron
Chair of the London Assembly, Sally Hamwee
Deputy Chair of the Assembly, Brian Coleman

ELECTIONS AND THE VOTING SYSTEMS
The assembly is elected every four years at the same time as the mayor, and consists of 25 members. There is one member from each of the 14 GLA constituencies topped up with 11 London members who are representatives of political parties or individuals standing as independent candidates. The next election will be on 1 May 2008.

The GLA constituencies are Barnet and Camden; Bexley and Bromley; Brent and Harrow; City and East, covering Barking and Dagenham, the City of London, Newham and Tower Hamlets; Croydon and Sutton; Ealing and Hillingdon; Enfield and Haringey; Greenwich and Lewisham; Havering and Redbridge; North East, covering Hackney, Islington and Waltham Forest; Lambeth and Southwark; West Central, covering Hammersmith and Fulham, Kensington and Chelsea and Westminster; South West, covering Hounslow, Kingston upon Thames and Richmond upon Thames; Merton and Wandsworth.

Two distinct voting systems are used to appoint the existing mayor and the assembly. The mayor is elected using the supplementary vote system (SVS). With SVS, electors have two votes: one to give a first choice for mayor and one to give a second choice. Electors cannot vote twice for the same candidate. If one candidate gets more than half of all the first-choice votes, he or she becomes mayor. If no candidate gets more than half of the first-choice votes, the two candidates with the most first-choice votes remain in the election and all the other candidates drop out. The second-choice votes on the ballot papers of the candidates who drop out are then counted. Where these second-choice votes are for the two remaining candidates they are added to the first-choice votes these candidates already have. The candidate with the most first- and second-choice votes combined becomes the Mayor of London.

The assembly is appointed using the additional member system (AMS). Under AMS, electors have two votes. The first vote is for a constituency candidate. The second vote is for a party list or individual candidate contesting the London-wide assembly seats. The 14 constituency members are elected under the first-past-the-post system, the same system used in general and local elections. Electors vote for one candidate and the candidate with the most votes wins. The additional (London) members are drawn from party lists or are independent candidates who stand as London members.

The Greater London Returning Officer (GLRO) is the independent official responsible for running the election in London. The GLRO has overall responsibility for running a free, fair and efficient election. He is supported in this by returning officers in each of the 14 London constituencies.

GLRO, Anthony Mayer

TRANSPORT FOR LONDON (TfL)

TfL is the integrated body responsible for London's transport system. Its role is to implement the mayor's transport strategy for London and manage transport services across the capital for which the mayor has responsibility. TfL is directed by a management board whose members are chosen for their understanding of transport matters and are appointed by the mayor, who chairs the board. TfL's role is:

- to manage the London Underground, buses, Croydon Tramlink and the Docklands Light Railway (DLR)
- to manage a 580km (360 miles) network of main roads and all of London's 4,600 traffic lights
- to regulate taxis and minicabs
- to run the London River Services, Victoria Coach Station and London's Transport Museum
- to help to coordinate the Dial-a-Ride and Taxicard schemes for door-to-door services for transport users with mobility problems

The London Borough Councils maintain the role of highway and traffic authorities for 95 per cent of London's roads. A £5 congestion charge for motorists driving into central London between the hours of 7am and 6.30pm, Monday to Friday (excluding public holidays) was introduced on 17 February 2003, and was subsequently raised to £8 on 4 July 2005. On 19 February 2007, the charge zone roughly doubled in size after a westward expansion, and the time zone changed to finish earlier at 6pm.

From 11 November 2007, responsibility for running the Silverlink overland train service was due to be transferred to TfL.

Transport Commissioner for London, Peter Hendy

LONDON DEVELOPMENT AGENCY (LDA)

The LDA promotes economic development and regeneration. It is one of the nine regional development agencies set up around the country to perform this task. It is run by a board of 14 members appointed by the mayor. The key aspects of the LDA's role are:

- to promote business efficiency, investment and competitiveness
- to promote employment
- to enhance the skills of local people
- to create sustainable development

The London boroughs retain powers to promote economic development in their local areas.

Chair, Mary Reilly

THE ENVIRONMENT

The mayor is required to formulate strategies to tackle London's environmental issues including the quality of water, air and land; the use of energy and London's contribution to climate change targets; groundwater levels and traffic emissions; and municipal waste management.

METROPOLITAN POLICE AUTHORITY (MPA)

This body, which oversees the policing of London, consists of 23 members; 12 from the assembly, including the deputy mayor, four magistrates and seven independents. One of the independents is appointed directly by the home secretary. The role of the MPA is:

- to maintain an efficient and effective police force
- to publish an annual policing plan
- to set police targets and monitor performance
- to be part of the appointment, discipline and removal of senior officers
- to be responsible for the performance budget
- to oversee formal inquiries and the implementation of their recommendations

The boundaries of the metropolitan police districts have been changed to be consistent with the 32 London boroughs. Areas beyond the GLA remit have been incorporated into the Surrey, Hertfordshire and Essex police areas. The City of London has its own police force.

Chair, Len Duvall

LONDON FIRE AND EMERGENCY PLANNING AUTHORITY (LFEPA)

In July 2000 the London Fire and Civil Defence Authority became the London Fire and Emergency Planning Authority. It consists of 17 members, 9 drawn from the assembly and 8 from the London boroughs. The role of the LFEPA is:

- to set the strategy for the provision of fire services
- to ensure that the fire brigade can meet all the normal requirements efficiently
- to ensure that effective arrangements are made for the fire brigade to receive emergency calls and deal with them promptly
- to ensure that information useful to the development of the fire brigades is gathered
- to assist the boroughs with their emergency planning training and exercises

Chair, Valerie Shawcross

SALARIES *as at June 2007*	
Mayor	£137,579
Deputy Mayor	£90,954
Chair of the Assembly	£60,675
Assembly Member	£50,582

LONDON ASSEMBLY COMMITTEES

Chair, Audit Panel, Peter Hulme Cross

Chair, Budget Committee, Andrew Pelling

Chair, Business Management and Appointments Committee, Elections Review Committee, Brian Coleman

Chair, Economic Development, Culture, Sport and Tourism Committee, Dee Doocey

Chair, Environment Committee, Darren Johnson

Chair, Health and Public Services Committee, Joanne McCartney

Chair, Planning and Spatial Development Committee, Tony Arbour

Chair, Standards Committee, Prof. Malcolm Grant

Chair, Transport Committee, Roger Evans

GLA ORGANISATIONAL STRUCTURE

MAYOR'S OFFICE
Public Affairs (International and European Relations, London Stakeholders, Government and Parliamentary Liaison, Public Consultation, Public Affairs Publications)
Best Value Partnership (Borough Liaison)
Economic and Business Policy (Private Sector, Strategic Evaluation Unit)
Equalities and Policing
Environment
Tourism and Creative Industries
London House (Brussels)
Administration Manager

SECRETARIAT
Assembly Support
Scrutiny and Investigations
Committee Services
Assembly's Media Relations

CHIEF EXECUTIVE'S OFFICE
Governance
Marketing
Mayor's Media Relations

POLICY AND PARTNERSHIPS
Spatial Development Strategy
Planning Decisions
Architecture and Urbanism Unit
Environment
Culture
Policy Support (Health, Housing and Homelessness, Social Inclusion, Sustainable Development)
Business Support

CORPORATE SERVICES
GLA Economics
Information and Communication Technology
Legal
HR and Administration (Facilities Management and Internal Communications)
Research Library
Data Management
Public Liaison
Business Support

FINANCE AND PERFORMANCE
Core Performance and Project Management
Strategic Performance
Core Finance
Strategic Finance

LONDON ASSEMBLY MEMBERS
as at 1 July 2007
Arbour, Anthony, *C., South West,* Maj. 4,067
Arnold, Jennette Sarah Alfreda, *Lab., North East,* Maj. 13,338
Barnes, Richard Michael, *C., Ealing and Hillingdon,* Maj. 11,016
Biggs, John Robert, *Lab., City and East,* Maj. 14,336
Blackman, Robert, *C., Brent and Harrow,* Maj. 4,686
Bray, Angela Lavinia, *C., West Central,* Maj. 29,944
Coleman, Brian, *C., Barnet and Camden,* Maj. 11,519
Doocey, Dee, *LD, London List*
Duvall, Leonard Lloyd, *Lab., Greenwich and Lewisham,* Maj. 14,083

Evans, Jeremy Roger, *C., Havering and Redbridge,* Maj. 16,706
Gavron, Felicia Nicolette, *Lab., London List*
Hamwee, Sally Rachel, *LD, London List*
Hockney, Nicholas Damian, *One London, London List*
Howlett, Elizabeth, *C., Merton and Wandsworth,* Maj. 16,878
Hulme-Cross, Peter Kenneth, *One London, London List*
Johnson, Darren, *Green, London List*
Jones, Jenny, *Green, London List*
McCartney, Joanne, *Lab., Enfield and Haringey,* Maj. 1,574
Neill, Robert James Macgillivray, *C., Bexley and Bromley,* Maj. 34,254
Pelling, Andrew John, *C., Croydon and Sutton,* Maj. 23,694
*Pope, Geoff, *LD, London List*
Qureshi, Murad, *Lab., London List*
Shawcross, Valerie, *Lab., Lambeth and Southwark,* Maj. 5,475
Tope, Graham Norman, *LD, London List*
Tuffrey, Michael William, *LD, London List*

* Lynne Featherstone stepped down after her election to parliament and was replaced by Geoff Pope on 6 June 2005

STATE OF THE PARTIES *as at 1 July 2007*

Party	Seats	Gain/Loss
Conservative (C.)	9	0
Labour (Lab.)	7	-2
Liberal Democrats (LD)	5	+1
Green	2	-1
One London	2	+2

MAYORAL ELECTION RESULTS
10 June 2004
E. 5,197,647 T. 1,920,533 (36.95%)
Change in turnout from 2000: +2.52%
Good votes 1st choice 1,863,671 (97.04%); 2nd choice 1,591,443 (82.86%)
Rejected votes 1st choice 56,862 (2.96%); 2nd choice 329,090 (17.14%)

First	Party	Votes	%
Ken Livingstone	Lab.	685,541	35.70
Steven Norris	C.	542,423	28.24
Simon Hughes	LD	284,645	14.82
Frank Maloney	UKIP	115,665	6.02
Lindsey German	Respect	61,731	3.21
Julian Leppert	BNP	58,405	3.04
Darren Johnson	Green	57,331	2.99
Ram Gidoomal	CPA	41,696	2.17
Lorna Reid	Ind. Working Class	9,542	0.50
Tammy Nagalingam	Ind.	6,692	0.35

Second	Party	Votes	%
Simon Hughes	LD	465,704	24.25
Ken Livingstone	Lab.	250,517	13.04
Steven Norris	C.	222,559	11.59
Darren Johnson	Green	208,686	10.87
Frank Maloney	UKIP	193,157	10.06
Julian Leppert	BNP	70,736	3.68
Lindsey German	Respect	63,294	3.30
Ram Gidoomal	CPA	56,721	2.95
Lorna Reid	Ind. Working Class	39,678	2.07
Tammy Nagalingam	Ind.	20,391	1.06

LONDON ASSEMBLY ELECTION RESULTS
as at June 2004

E. Electorate T. Turnout
See General Election Results for a list of party abbreviations

CONSTITUENCIES

BARNET AND CAMDEN
E. 371,186 T. 38.41%

Brian Coleman, C.	47,640
Lucy Anderson, Lab.	36,121
Jonathan Simpson, LD	23,603
Miranda Dunn, Green	11,921
Magnus Nielsen, UKIP	8,685
Elisabeth Wheatley, Respect	5,150
Humberto Heliotrope, CPA	1,914

C. majority 11,519

BEXLEY AND BROMLEY
E. 397,075 T. 41.48%

Robert Neill, C.	64,246
Duncan Borrowman, LD	29,992
Heather Bennett, UKIP	26,703
Charles Mansell, Lab.	24,848
Ann Garrett, Green	8,069
Miranda Suit, CPA	3,397
Alun Morinan, Respect	1,673

C. majority 34,254

BRENT AND HARROW
E. 332,723 T. 38.03%

Robert Blackman, C.	39,900
Toby Harris, Lab.	35,214
Havard Hughes, LD	20,782
Daniel Moss, UKIP	7,199
Mohammad Ali, Green	6,975
Albert Harriott, Respect	4,586
Gladstone Macaulay, CPA	2,734

C. majority 4,686

CITY AND EAST
E. 437,298 T. 33.43%

John Biggs, Lab.	38,085
Shafi Choudhury, C.	23,749
Oliur Rahman, Respect	19,675
Guy Burton, LD	18,255
Christopher Pratt, UKIP	17,997
Terry McGrenera, Green	8,687
Christopher Gill, CPA	4,461

Lab. majority 14,336

CROYDON AND SUTTON
E. 376,175 T. 37.82%

Andrew Pelling, C.	52,330
Steven Gauge, LD	28,636
Sean Fitzsimons, Lab.	25,861
James Feisenberger, UKIP	15,203
Shasha Khan, Green	6,175
David Campanale, CPA	4,234
Waqas Hussain, Respect	3,108

C. majority 23,694

EALING AND HILLINGDON
E. 397,564 T. 37.28%

Richard Barnes, C.	45,230
Gurcharan Singh, Lab.	34,214
Michael Cox, LD	23,440
David Malindine, UKIP	14,698
Sarah Edwards, Green	9,395
Dalawar Chaudhry, Ind.	5,285
Salvinder Dhillon, Respect	4,229
Genevieve Hibbs, CPA	3,024

C. majority 11,016

ENFIELD AND HARINGEY
E. 343,617 T. 36.14%

Joanne McCartney, Lab.	33,955
Peter Forrest, C.	32,381
Wayne Hoban, LD	19,720
Brian Hall, UKIP	10,652
Jayne Forbes, Green	10,310
Sait Akgul, Respect	6,855
Peter Wolstenholme, CPA	2,365

Lab. majority 1,574

GREENWICH AND LEWISHAM
E. 329,450 T. 35.10%

Leonard Duvall, Lab.	36,251
Gareth Bacon, C.	22,168
Alexander Feakes, LD	19,183
Timothy Reynolds, UKIP	13,454
Susan Luxton, Green	11,271
Stephen Hammond, CPA	3,619
Ian Page, Respect/Soc. Alt.	2,825

Lab. majority 14,083

HAVERING AND REDBRIDGE
E. 350,652 T. 38.96%

Jeremy Evans, C.	44,723
Keith Darvill, Lab.	28,017
Lawrence Webb, UKIP	18,297
Matthew Lake, LD	13,646
Malvin Brown, Residents Assn. of London	6,925
Ashley Gunstock, Green	6,009
Abdurahman Jafar, Respect	5,185
Juliet Hawkins, CPA	2,917
David Stephens, Third Way	2,031
Peter Thorogood, Ind.	1,597

C. majority 16,706

LAMBETH AND SOUTHWARK
E. 373,293 T. 33.38%

Valerie Shawcross, Lab.	36,280
Caroline Pidgeon, LD	30,805
Bernard Gentry, C.	17,379
Shane Collins, Green	11,900
Frank Maloney, UKIP	8,776
Janet Noble, Respect	4,930
Simisola Lawanson, CPA	3,655
Navindh Baburam, Ind.	608

Lab. majority 5,475

MERTON AND WANDSWORTH
E. 340,792 T. 38.55%

Elizabeth Howlett, C.	48,295
Kathryn Smith, Lab.	31,417
Andrew Martin, LD	17,864
Roy Vickery, Green	10,163
Adrian Roberts, UKIP	8,327
Ruairidh Maclean, Respect	4,291
Ellen Greco, CPA	2,782
Rathy Alagaratnam, Ind.	1,240

C. majority 16,878

NORTH EAST
E. 410,719 T. 33.93%

Jennette Arnold, Lab.	37,380
Terry Stacy, LD	24,042
Andrew Boff, C.	23,264
Jon Nott, Green	16,739
Robert Selby, UKIP	11,459
Dean Ryan, Respect	11,184
Andrew Otchie, CPA	3,219
James Beavis, Comm.	1,378

Lab. majority 13,338

SOUTH WEST
E. 384,450 T. 40.31%

Tony Arbour, C.	48,858
Dee Doocey, LD	44,791
Seema Malhotra, Lab.	25,225
Alan Hindle, UKIP	12,477
Judy Maciejowska, Green	9,866
Omar Waraich, Respect	3,785
Peter Flower, CPA	3,008

C. majority 4,067

WEST CENTRAL
E. 352,653 T. 35.28%

Angela Bray, C.	51,884
Ansuya Sodha, Lab.	21,940
Francesco Fruzza, LD	17,478
Julia Stephenson, Green	10,762
Damian Hockney, UKIP	7,219
Kevin Cobham, Respect	4,825
Jillian McLachlan, CPA	1,993

C. majority 29,944

TOP-UP MEMBERS

LABOUR
Felicia Nicolette Gavron
Murad Qureshi

LIBERAL DEMOCRAT
Dee Doocey
Lynne Featherstone*
Sally Hamwee
Graham Tope
Michael Tuffey

ONE LONDON GROUP†
Damian Hockney
Peter Hulme-Cross

GREEN PARTY
Darren Johnson
Jenny Jones

* Lynne Featherstone stepped down after her election to parliament and was replaced by Geoff Pope on 6 June 2005
† On 1 September 2005, Damian Hockney and Peter Hulme-Cross formed the One London Group; both members were originally elected to the assembly as UK Independence Party (UKIP) representatives

WALES

NATIONAL ASSEMBLY FOR WALES

Cardiff Bay, Cardiff CF99 1NA
T 0845-010 5500 E webmaster@assemblywales.org
W www.assemblywales.org

In July 1997 the government announced plans to establish a National Assembly for Wales. In a referendum in September 1997 about 50 per cent of the electorate voted, of whom 50.3 per cent voted in favour of the assembly. Elections are held every four years and the first elections took place on 6 May 1999, the second on 1 May 2003 and the third on 3 May 2007.

Until 2007 the National Assembly for Wales had responsibility in Wales for ministerial functions relating to health and personal social services; education; the Welsh language, arts and culture; local government; housing; water and sewerage; environmental protection; sport; agriculture and fisheries; forestry; land use, including town and country planning and conservation; roads; tourism; and European Union matters.

The Government of Wales Act 2006 introduced a radical change to the functions and status of the National Assembly for Wales. With effect from 25 May 2007 the act formally separated the National Assembly for Wales (the legislature – made up of 60 elected assembly members) and the Welsh Assembly Government (the executive – comprising the first minister, Welsh ministers, deputy Welsh ministers and the counsel general). It also made changes to the electoral process: candidates are no longer permitted to stand for both a constituency and on a regional list. The act enabled the National Assembly for Wales to formulate its own legislation (assembly measures) on devolved matters such as health, education, social services and local government; the assembly is given legislative competence (the legal authority to pass measures) on a case-by-case basis by the UK parliament.

The role of the National Assembly for Wales is to scrutinise and monitor the Welsh Assembly Government. It meets in the Senedd debating chamber. The 60 assembly members examine and approve assembly measures and approve certain items of subordinate legislation; approve budgets for the Welsh Assembly Government's programmes; hold Welsh ministers to account; and analyse and debate their decisions and policies.

Presiding Officer, Lord Dafydd Elis-Thomas, AM

SALARIES *as at 1 April 2007*

First Minister*	£76,996
Minister/Presiding Officer*	£39,939
Deputy Presiding Officer*	£25,121
Assembly Members (AM)†	£46,496

* Also receives the assembly member salary
† Reduced by two-thirds if the member is already an MP or an MEP

WELSH ASSEMBLY GOVERNMENT

Cathays Park, Cardiff CF10 3NQ
T 0845-010 3300 W http://new.wales.gov.uk

The Welsh Assembly Government is comprised of the first minister, the Welsh ministers, the counsel general – a newly created position, the counsel general is the chief legal adviser – and the deputy Welsh ministers. The 60 assembly members delegate their executive powers, including the implementation of policies and legislation,

to the first minister – who is elected by the whole assembly and is therefore usually the leader of the largest political party. In turn, the first minister delegates responsibility for delivering the executive functions to Welsh ministers, who together form the cabinet.

The Welsh Assembly Government has responsibility over the following devolved areas: agriculture, fisheries, forestry and rural development; ancient monuments and historic buildings; culture; economic development; education and training; environment; fire and rescue services; food; health and health services; highways and transport; housing; local government; public administration; social welfare; sport and recreation; tourism; town and county planning; water and flood defence; and the Welsh language.

First Minister for Wales, Rt. Hon. Rhodri Morgan, AM
Minister for Budget and Business Management, Jane Hutt, AM
Minister for the Economy and Transport, Dr Brian Gibbons, AM
Minister for Education, Culture and the Welsh Language, Carwyn Jones, AM
Minister for Health and Social Services, Edwina Hart, MBE, AM
Minister for Social Justice and Public Service Delivery, Andrew Davies, AM
Minister for Sustainability and Rural Development, Jane Davidson, AM
Chief Whip and Deputy Business Minister, Carl Sargeant, AM
Deputy Minister for the Economy and Transport, Huw Lewis, AM
Deputy Minister for Education, Culture and Welsh Language, John Griffiths, AM
Deputy Minister for Health and Social Services, Gwenda Thomas, AM
Deputy Minister for Social Justice and Public Service Delivery, Leighton Andrews, AM
Counsel General, Carwyn Jones, AM
Clerk to the Assembly and Chief Executive of Assembly Commission, Claire Clancy

MANAGEMENT BOARD

Permanent Secretary, Sir Jon Shortridge
Senior Director, Derek Jones
Director, Business Development, June Milligan
Director, Corporate Information and Services, Dr Michael Harrington
Director, Economy and Transport, Gareth Hall
Director, Education, Culture and the Welsh Language, Steven Marshall
Director, Finance, Christine Daws
Director, Health and Social Services, Ann Lloyd
Director, Human Resources, Bernard Galton
Director, Legal Services, Jeff Godfrey
Director, Public Health and Health Professions, and Chief Medical Officer, Dr Tony Jewell
Director, Public Services and Performance, Richard Davies
Director, Social Justice and Local Government, Dr Emyr Roberts
Director, Strategic Policy, Legislation and Communications, Hugh Rawlings
Director, Sustainability and Rural Development, Huw Brodie
Non-Executive Directors, Kathryn Bishop; Adrian Webb

DEPARTMENTS

Economy and Transport
Education, Culture and Welsh Language

Health and Social Services
Public Services and Performance
Social Justice and Local Government
Strategic Policy, Legislation and Communications
Sustainability and Rural Development

EXECUTIVE AGENCIES
Planning Inspectorate
Welsh European Funding Office

COMMITTEES
Audit
Business
Communities and Culture
Enterprise and Learning
Equality of Opportunity
European and External Affairs
Finance
Health, Wellbeing and Local Government
Petitions
Standards of Conduct
Subordinate Legislation
Sustainability

PUBLIC SERVICES OMBUDSMAN FOR WALES
1 Ffordd yr Hen Gae, Pencoed CF35 5LJ
T 01656-641150 F 01656-641199
E ask@ombudsman-wales.org.uk
W www.ombudsman-wales.org.uk
Ombudsman, Adam Peat

MEMBERS OF THE NATIONAL ASSEMBLY FOR WALES
as at 4 May 2007

Andrews, Leighton, *Lab., Rhondda,* Maj. 6,215
Ashgar, Mohammad, *PC, South Wales East region*
Barrett, Lorraine Jayne, *Lab., Cardiff South and Penarth,* Maj. 2,754
Bates, Michael, *LD, Montgomeryshire,* Maj. 1,979
Black, Peter, *LD, South Wales West region*
Bourne, Prof. Nicholas, *C., Mid and West Wales region*
Burnham, Eleanor, *LD, North Wales region*
Burns, Angela, *C., Carmarthen West and South Pembrokeshire,* Maj. 98
Butler, Rosemary Janet Mair, *Lab., Newport West,* Maj. 1,401
Cairns, Alun, *C., South Wales West region*
Chapman, Christine, *Lab., Cynon Valley,* Maj. 5,623
Cuthbert, Jeffrey, *Lab., Caerphilly,* Maj. 2,287
Davidson, Jane Elizabeth, *Lab., Pontypridd,* Maj. 3,347
Davies, Alun, *Lab., Mid and West Wales region*
Davies, Andrew David, *Lab., Swansea West,* Maj. 1,511
Davies, Andrew Robert, *C., South Wales Central region*
Davies, Jocelyn, *PC, South Wales East region*
Davies, Paul, *C., Preseli Pembrokeshire,* Maj. 3,205
Elis-Thomas, Lord Dafydd, *PC, Dwyfor Meirionnydd,* Maj. 8,868
Evans, Nerys, *PC, Mid and West Wales region*
Franks, Christopher, *PC, South Wales Central region*
German, Michael, *LD, South Wales East region*
Gibbons, Brian, *Lab., Aberavon,* Maj. 6,571
Graham, William, *C., South Wales East region*
Gregory, Janice, *Lab., Ogmore,* Maj. 7,900
Griffiths, Albert John, *Lab., Newport East,* Maj. 875
Griffiths, Lesley, *Lab., Wrexham,* Maj. 1,250
Hart, Edwina, *Lab., Gower,* Maj. 1,192
Hutt, Jane, *Lab., Vale of Glamorgan,* Maj. 83
Isherwood, Mark, *C., North Wales region*
James, Irene, *Lab., Islwyn,* Maj. 2,218

Jenkins, Bethan, *PC, South Wales West region*
Jones, Alun, *PC, Arfon,* Maj. 5,018
Jones, Carwyn Howell, *Lab., Bridgend,* Maj. 2,556
Jones, Elin, *PC, Ceredigion,* Maj. 3,955
Jones, Gareth, *PC, Aberconwy,* Maj. 1,693
Jones, Helen Mary, *PC, Llanelli,* Maj. 3,884
Jones, Margaret Ann (Ann), *Lab., Vale of Clwyd,* Maj. 92
Law, Trish, *Ind., Blaenau Gwent,* Maj. 5,357
Lewis, Huw, *Lab., Merthyr Tydfil and Rhymney,* Maj. 4,581
Lloyd, Dr David, *PC, South Wales West region*
Lloyd, Val, *Lab., Swansea East,* Maj. 4,961
Melding, David, *C., South Wales Central region*
Mewies, Sandra Elaine, *Lab., Delyn,* Maj. 511
Millar, Darren, *C., Clwyd West,* Maj. 1,596
Morgan, Hywel Rhodri, *Lab., Cardiff West,* Maj. 3,698
Morgan, Jonathan, *C., Cardiff North,* Maj. 4,844
Neagle, Lynne, *Lab., Torfaen,* Maj. 5,396
Ramsay, Nicholas, *C., Monmouth,* Maj. 8,469
Randerson, Jennifer Elizabeth, *LD, Cardiff Central,* Maj. 6,565
Ryder, Janet, *PC, North Wales region*
Sargeant, Carl, *Lab., Alyn and Deeside,* Maj. 3,362
Sinclair, Karen, *Lab., Clwyd South,* Maj. 1,119
Thomas, Gwenda, *Lab., Neath,* Maj. 1,944
Thomas, Rhodri, *PC, Carmarthen East and Dinefwr,* Maj. 8,469
Watson, Joyce, *Lab., Mid and West Wales region*
Williams, Brynle, *C., North Wales region*
Williams, Kirsty, *LD, Brecon and Radnorshire,* Maj. 5,354
Wood, Leanne, *PC, South Wales Central region*
Wyn Jones, Ieuan, *PC, Ynys Mon,* Maj. 4,392

STATE OF THE PARTIES *as at 4 May 2007*

	Constituency AMs	Regional AMs	AM total
Labour (Lab.)	23*	2	25*
Plaid Cymru (PC)	6*	8	14*
Conservative (C.)	5	7	12
Liberal Democrats (LD)	3	3	6
Others	1	0	1
The Presiding Officer	1	0	1
The Deputy Presiding Officer	1	0	1
Total	40	20	60

* Excludes the presiding officer (PC) and deputy presiding officer (Lab.), who have no party allegiance while in post

NATIONAL ASSEMBLY ELECTION RESULTS
As at May 2007
E. Electorate T. Turnout
See General Election Results for a list of party abbreviations

CONSTITUENCIES

ABERAVON (S. WALES WEST)
E. 51,536 T. 20,528 (39.83%)
Brian Gibbons, Lab.   10,129
Linet Purcell, PC   3,558
Andrew Tutton, Neath Port Talbot Ratepayers
  Association   2,561
Daisy Meyland-Smith, C.   1,990
Claire Waller, LD   1,450
Captain Beany, Bean   840
Lab. majority 6,571 (32.01%)
4.82% swing Lab. to PC

ALYN AND DEESIDE (WALES N.)
E. 59,355 T. 21,095 (35.54%)
Carl Sargeant, Lab.   8,196
Will Gallagher, C.   4,834
Dennis Hutchinson, Ind.   3,241
Paul Brighton, LD   2,091
Dafydd Passe, PC   1,398
William Crawford, UKIP   1,335
Lab. majority 3,362 (15.94%)
3.66% swing Lab. to C.

BLAENAU GWENT (S. WALES EAST)
E. 52,816 T. 23,518 (44.53%)
Trish Law, Ind.   12,722
Keren Bender, Lab.   7,365
Gareth Lewis, LD   1,351
Natasha Asghar, PC   1,129
Bob Hayward, C.   951
Ind. majority 5,357 (22.78%)
46.5% swing Lab. to Ind.

BRECON AND RADNORSHIRE (WALES MID AND W.)
E. 55,428 T. 28,748 (51.87%)
Kirsty Williams, LD   15,006
Suzy Davies, C.   9,652
Neil Stone, Lab.   2,514
Arwel Lloyd, PC   1,576
LD majority 5,354 (18.62%)
0.58% swing LD to C.

BRIDGEND (S. WALES WEST)
E. 59,550 T. 24,552 (41.23%)
Carwyn Jones, Lab.   9,889
Emma Greenow, C.   7,333
Paul Warren, LD   3,730
Nicholas Thomas, PC   3,600
Lab. majority 2,556 (10.41%)
0.71% swing Lab. to C.

CAERNARFON (WALES N.)
E. 39,891 T. 19,573 (49.07%)
Alun Ffred Jones, PC   10,260
Martin Eaglestone, Lab.   5,242
Gerry Frobisher, C.   1,858
Mel ab Owain, LD   1,424
Elwyn Williams, UKIP   789
PC majority 5,018 (25.64%)
3.43% swing Lab. to PC

CAERPHILLY (S. WALES EAST)
E. 62,046 T. 26,922 (43.39%)
Jeff Cuthbert, Lab.   8,937
Lindsay Whittle, PC   7,000
Ron Davies, Ind.   6,071
Richard Foley, C.   3,227
Huw Price, LD   1,687
Lab. majority 1,937 (7.19%)
5.07% swing Lab. to PC

CARDIFF CENTRAL (S. WALES CENTRAL)
E. 62,202 T. 22,397 (36.01%)
Jenny Randerson, LD   11,462
Sue Lent, Lab.   4,897
Andrew Murphy, C.   3,137
Thomas Whitfield, PC   1,855
Frank Hughes, UKIP   1,046
LD majority 6,565 (29.31%)
2.71% swing LD to Lab.

CARDIFF NORTH (S. WALES CENTRAL)
E. 65,687 T. 33,702 (51.31%)
Jonathan Morgan, C.   15,253
Sophie Howe, Lab.   10,409
Ed Bridges, LD   4,287
Wyn Jones, PC   2,491
Dai Llewellyn, UKIP   1,262
C. majority 4,844 (14.37%)
8.16% swing Lab. to C.

CARDIFF SOUTH AND PENARTH (S. WALES CENTRAL)
E. 71,312 T. 26,728 (37.48%)
Lorraine Barrett, Lab.   10,106
Karen Robson, C.   7,352
Dominic Hannigan, LD   5,445
Jason Toby, PC   3,825
Lab. majority 2,754 (10.30%)
4.22% swing Lab. to C.

CARDIFF WEST (S. WALES CENTRAL)
E. 64,588 T. 26,889 (41.63%)
Rhodri Morgan, Lab.   10,390
Craig Williams, C.   6,692
Neil McEvoy, PC   5,719
Alison Goldsworthy, LD   4,088
Lab. majority 3,698 (13.75%)
8.77% swing Lab. to C.

CARMARTHEN EAST AND DINEFWR (WALES MID AND W.)
E. 52,528 T. 29,269 (55.72%)
Rhodri Glyn Thomas, PC   15,655
Kevin Madge, Lab.   7,186
Henrietta Hensher, C.   4,676
Ian Walton, LD   1,752
PC majority 8,469 (28.94%)
5.85% swing Lab. to PC

CARMARTHEN WEST AND SOUTH PEMBROKESHIRE (WALES MID AND W.)
E. 57,477 T. 28,568 (49.70%)
Angela Burns, C.   8,590
Christine Gwyther, Lab.   8,492
John Dixon, PC   8,340
John Gossage, LD   1,806
Malcolm Calver, Ind.   1,340
C. majority 98 (0.34%)
7.45% swing Lab. to C.

CEREDIGION (WALES MID AND W.)
E. 54,071 T. 30,108 (55.68%)
Elin Jones, PC   14,818
John Davies, LD   10,863
Trefor Jones, C.   2,369
Linda Grace, Lab.   1,530
Emyr Morgan, Ind.   528
PC majority 3,955 (13.14%)
2.20% swing PC to LD

CLWYD SOUTH (WALES N.)
E. 51,865 T. 19,498 (37.59%)
Karen Sinclair, Lab.   6,838
John Bell, C.   5,719
Nia Davies, PC   3,894
Frank Biggs, LD   1,838
David Rowlands, UKIP   1,209
Lab. majority 1,119 (5.74%)
6.04% swing Lab. to C.

CLWYD WEST (WALES N.)
E. 57,312 T. 26,205 (45.72%)

Darren Millar, C.	8,905
Alun Pugh, Lab.	7,309
Philip Edwards, PC	7,162
Simon Croft, LD	1,705
Warwick Nicholson, UKIP	1,124

C. majority 1,596 (6.09%)
4.13% swing Lab. to C.

CONWY (WALES N.)
E. 44,143 T. 20,699 (46.89%)

Gareth Jones, PC	7,983
Dylan Jones-Evans, C.	6,290
Denise Idris Jones, Lab.	4,508
Euron Hughes, LD	1,918

PC majority 1,693 (8.18%)
2.86% swing C. to PC

CYNON VALLEY (S. WALES CENTRAL)
E. 50,846 T. 19,517 (38.38%)

Christine Chapman, Lab.	11,058
Liz Walters, PC	5,435
Neill John, C.	2,024
Margaret Phelps, LD	1,000

Lab. majority 5,623 (28.81%)
7.16% swing Lab. to PC

DELYN (WALES N.)
E. 52,733 T. 21,668 (41.09%)

Sandy Mewies, Lab.	7,506
Antoinette Sandbach, C.	6,996
Meg Ellis, PC	3,179
Ian Matthews, LD	2,669
Derek Bigg, UKIP	1,318

Lab. majority 510 (2.35%)
3.63% swing Lab. to C.

GOWER (S. WALES WEST)
E. 61,520 T. 27,545 (44.77%)

Edwina Hart, Lab.	9,406
Byron Davis, C.	8,214
Darren Price, PC	5,106
Nick Tregoning, LD	2,924
Alex Lewis, UKIP	1,895

Lab. majority 1,192 (4.33%)
9.84% swing Lab. to C.

ISLWYN (S. WALES EAST)
E. 54,795 T. 23,564 (43.00%)

Irene James, Lab.	8,883
Kevin Etheridge, Ind.	6,665
Allan Pritchard, PC	5,084
Paul Williams, C.	1,797
Mark Maguire, LD	1,135

Lab. majority 2,218 (9.41%)
23.3% swing Lab. to Ind.

LLANELLI (WALES MID AND W.)
E. 56,154 T. 27,602 (49.15%)

Helen Mary Jones, PC	13,839
Catherine Thomas, Lab.	9,955
Andrew Morgan, C.	2,757
Jeremy Townsend, LD	1,051

PC majority 3,884 (14.07%)
7.08% swing Lab. to PC

MEIRIONNYDD NANT CONWY (WALES MID AND W.)
E. 46,718 T. 22,122 (47.35%)

Dafydd Elis-Thomas, PC	13,201
Mike Wood, C.	4,333
David Phillips, Lab.	2,749
Steve Churchman, LD	1,839

PC majority 8,868 (40.09%)
1.57% swing PC to C.

MERTHYR TYDFIL AND RHYMNEY (S. WALES EAST)
E. 54,025 T. 21,028 (38.92%)

Huw Lewis, Lab.	7,776
Amy Kitcher, LD	3,195
Clive Tovey, Ind.	2,622
Glyndwr Jones, PC	2,519
Jeff Edwards, Ind.	1,950
Giles Howard, C.	1,151
Jock Greer, Ind.	844
Vivienne Hadley, Ind.	809
Richard Williams, Ind.	162

Lab. majority 4,581 (21.79%)
15.77% swing Lab. to LD

MONMOUTH (S. WALES EAST)
E. 63,000 T. 29,565 (46.93%)

Nick Ramsay, C.	15,389
Richard Clark, Lab.	6,920
Jacqui Sullivan, LD	4,359
Jonathan Clark, PC	2,093
Ed Abrams, Eng. Dem.	804

C. majority 8,469 (28.65%)
0.99% swing C. to Lab.

MONTGOMERYSHIRE (WALES MID AND W.)
E. 48,377 T. 22,300 (46.10%)

Mick Bates, LD	8,704
Don Munford, C.	6,725
David Thomas, PC	3,076
Charles Lawson, UKIP	2,251
Rachel Maycock, Lab.	1,544

LD majority 1,979 (8.87%)
1.18% swing LD to C.

NEATH (S. WALES WEST)
E. 57,952 T. 25,200 (43.48%)

Gwenda Thomas, Lab.	10,934
Alun Llewelyn, PC	8,990
Andrew Sivertsen, C.	2,956
Sheila Waye, LD	2,320

Lab. majority 1,944 (7.71%)
7.29% swing Lab. to PC

NEWPORT EAST (S. WALES EAST)
E. 53,060 T. 19,906 (37.52%)

John Griffiths, Lab.	6,395
Ed Townsend, LD	5,520
Peter Fox, C.	4,512
Trefor Puw, PC	1,696
James Harris, Ind.	1,354
Mike Blundell, Eng. Dem.	429

Lab. majority 875 (4.40%)
12.00% swing Lab. to LD

NEWPORT WEST (S. WALES EAST)
E. 58,981 T. 23,659 (40.11%)
Rosemary Butler, Lab.	9,582
Matthew Evans, C.	8,181
Nigel Flanagan, LD	2,813
Brian Hancock, PC	2,449
Andrew Constantine, Eng. Dem.	634

Lab. majority 1,401 (5.92%)
5.79% swing Lab. to C.

OGMORE (S. WALES WEST)
E. 56,973 T. 22,766 (39.96%)
Janice Gregory, Lab.	11,761
Sian Caiach, PC	3,861
Norma Lloyd-Nesling, C.	2,663
Steve Smith, Ind.	2,337
Martin Plant, LD	2,144

Lab. majority 7,900 (34.70%)
2.65% swing Lab. to PC

PONTYPRIDD (S. WALES CENTRAL)
E. 57,512 T. 23,501 (40.86%)
Jane Davidson, Lab.	9,836
Michael Powell, LD	6,449
Richard Grigg, PC	4,181
Janice Charles, C.	3,035

Lab. majority 3,387 (14.41%)
11.08% swing Lab. to LD

PRESELI PEMBROKESHIRE (WALES MID AND W.)
E. 56,435 T. 28,720 (50.89%)
Paul Davies, C.	11,086
Tamsin Dunwoody, Lab.	7,881
John Osmond, PC	7,101
Hywel Davies, LD	2,652

C. majority 3,205 (11.16%)
8.52% swing Lab. to C.

RHONDDA (S. WALES CENTRAL)
E. 52,478 T. 22,107 (42.13%)
Leighton Andrews, Lab.	12,875
Jill Evans, PC	6,660
Karen Roberts, LD	1,441
Howard Parsons, C.	1,131

Lab. majority 6,215 (28.11%)
3.23% swing Lab. to PC

SWANSEA EAST (S. WALES WEST)
E. 59,186 T. 20,717 (35.00%)
Val Lloyd, Lab.	8,590
Helen Clarke, LD	3,629
Danny Bowles, PC	3,218
Bob Dowdle, C.	2,025
David Robinson, Ind.	1,618
Ray Welsby, Ind.	1,177
Gary Evans, Ind.	460

Lab. majority 4,961 (23.95%)
0.49% swing LD to Lab.

SWANSEA WEST (S. WALES WEST)
E. 61,469 T. 22,879 (37.22%)
Andrew Davies, Lab.	7,393
Peter May, LD	5,882
Harri Davies, C.	4,379
Ian Titherington, PC	3,583
Richard Lewis, UKIP	1,642

Lab. majority 1,511 (6.60%)
5.75% swing Lab. to LD

TORFAEN (S. WALES EAST)
E. 62,592 T. 23,215 (37.09%)
Lynne Neagle, Lab.	9,921
Graham Smith, C.	4,525
Ian Williams, Ind.	3,348
Rhys ab Elis, PC	2,762
Patrick Legge, LD	2,659

Lab. majority 5,396 (23.24%)
6.18% swing Lab. to C.

VALE OF CLWYD (WALES N.)
E. 55,234 T. 22,275 (40.33%)
Ann Jones, Lab.	8,104
Matt Wright, C.	8,012
Mark Jones, PC	3,884
Mark Young, LD	2,275

Lab. majority 92 (0.41%)
7.40% swing Lab. to C.

VALE OF GLAMORGAN (S. WALES CENTRAL)
E. 68,856 T. 33,686 (48.92%)
Jane Hutt, Lab.	11,515
Gordon Kemp, C.	11,432
Barry Shaw, PC	4,671
Mark Hooper, LD	3,758
Kevin Mahoney, UKIP	2,310

Lab. majority 83 (0.25%)
4.02% swing Lab. to C.

WREXHAM (WALES N.)
E. 50,759 T. 19,567 (38.55%)
Lesley Griffiths, Lab.	5,633
John Marek, Ind.	4,383
Felicity Elphick, C.	3,372
Bruce Roberts, LD	3,268
Sion Aled Owen, PC	1,878
Peter Lewis, UKIP	1,033

Lab. majority 1,250 (6.39%)
6.0% swing Ind. to Lab.

YNYS MON (WALES N.)
E. 51,814 T. 26,820 (51.76%)
Ieuan Wyn Jones, PC	10,653
Peter Rogers, Ind.	6,261
Jonathan Austin, Lab.	4,681
James Roach, C.	3,480
Mandi Abrahams, LD	912
Francis Wykes, UKIP	833

PC majority 4,392 (16.38%)
10.5% swing PC to Ind.

REGIONS

MID AND WEST WALES
E. 427,188 T. 216,957 (50.79%)
PC	67,258 (31.00%)
C.	49,606 (22.86%)
Lab.	39,979 (18.43%)
LD	28,790 (13.27%)
Green	8,768 (4.04%)
UKIP	8,191 (3.78%)
BNP	6,389 (2.94%)
Soc. Lab.	2,196 (1.01%)
Ind.	1,598 (0.74%)
Welsh Christian Party	1,493 (0.69%)
Ind. Evans	1,108 (0.51%)
Comm. Brit.	666 (0.31%)
Veritas	502 (0.23%)
CPA	413 (0.19%)

PC majority 17,652 (8.14%)
1.16% swing PC to C. (2003 PC majority 5,423)

ADDITIONAL MEMBERS
Nick Bourne, *C.*
Alun Davies, *Lab.*
Joyce Watson, *Lab.*
Nerys Evans, *PC*

NORTH WALES
E. 463,106 T. 196,442 (42.42%)

Lab.	51,831 (26.38%)
PC	50,558 (25.74%)
C.	50,266 (25.59%)
LD	15,275 (7.78%)
BNP	9,986 (5.08%)
UKIP	8,015 (4.08%)
Green	5,660 (2.88%)
Soc. Lab.	2,209 (1.12%)
Welsh Christian Party	1,300 (0.66%)
Comm. Brit.	700 (0.36%)
CPA	642 (0.33%)

Lab. majority 1,273 (0.65%)
4.72% swing Lab. to PC (2003 Lab. majority 13,610)

ADDITIONAL MEMBERS
Brynle Williams, *C.*
Mark Isherwood, *C.*
Eleanor Burnham, *LD*
Janet Ryder, *PC*

SOUTH WALES CENTRAL
E. 493,481 T. 208,294 (42.21%)

Lab.	70,799 (33.99%)
C.	45,147 (21.67%)
PC	32,207 (15.46%)
LD	29,262 (14.05%)
BNP	7,889 (3.79%)
Green	7,831 (3.76%)
UKIP	7,645 (3.67%)
Welsh Christian Party	1,987 (0.95%)
Soc. Lab.	1,744 (0.84%)
Respect	1,079 (0.52%)
Soc. Alt.	838 (0.40%)
Comm. Brit.	817 (0.39%)
CPA	757 (0.36%)
Socialist Equality Party	292 (0.14%)

Lab. majority 25,652 (12.32%)
5.16% swing Lab. to C. (2003 Lab. majority 40,965)

ADDITIONAL MEMBERS
David Melding, *C.*
Andrew Davies, *C.*
Leanne Wood, *PC*
Chris Franks, *PC*

SOUTH WALES EAST
E. 461,315 T. 190,064 (41.20%)

Lab.	67,998 (35.78%)
C.	37,935 (19.96%)
PC	25,915 (13.63%)
LD	20,947 (11.02%)
BNP	8,940 (4.70%)
UKIP	8,725 (4.59%)
Green	5,414 (2.85%)
Ind.	4,876 (2.57%)
Soc. Lab.	3,693 (1.94%)
Welsh Christian Party	2,498 (1.31%)
Eng. Dem.	1,655 (0.87%)
Comm. Brit.	979 (0.52%)
CPA	489 (0.26%)

Lab. majority 30,063 (15.82%)
4.55% swing Lab. to C. (2003 Lab. majority 42,291)

ADDITIONAL MEMBERS
William Graham, *C.*
Michael German, *LD*
Jocelyn Davies, *PC*
Mohammed Asghar, *PC*

SOUTH WALES WEST
E. 408,186 T. 163,127 (39.96%)

Lab.	58,347 (35.77%)
PC	28,819 (17.67%)
C.	26,199 (16.06%)
LD	20,226 (12.40%)
BNP	8,993 (5.51%)
Green	6,130 (3.76%)
UKIP	5,914 (3.63%)
Soc. Lab.	2,367 (1.45%)
Welsh Christian Party	1,685 (1.03%)
Ind. James	1,186 (0.73%)
Soc. Alt.	1,027 (0.63%)
Respect	713 (0.44%)
Ind.	582 (0.36%)
Comm. Brit.	546 (0.33%)
CPA	393 (0.24%)

Lab. majority 29,528 (18.10%)
2.87% swing Lab. to PC (2003 Lab. majority 33,267)

ADDITIONAL MEMBERS
Alun Cairns, *C.*
Peter Black, *LD*
Bethan Jenkins, *PC*
Dai Lloyd, *PC*

SCOTLAND

SCOTTISH PARLIAMENT

Edinburgh EH99 1SP
T 0131-348 5000/0845-278 1999 Textphone 0845-270 0152
F 0131-348 5601
E sp.info@scottish.parliament.uk
W www.scottish.parliament.uk

In July 1997 the government announced plans to establish a Scottish parliament. In a referendum on 11 September 1997 about 60 per cent of the electorate voted. Of those who voted, 74.3 per cent voted in favour of the parliament and 63.5 per cent in favour of it having tax-raising powers. Elections are held every four years. The first elections were held on 6 May 1999, when about 59 per cent of the electorate voted. The first meeting was held on 12 May 1999 and the Scottish parliament was officially opened on 1 July 1999 at the Assembly Hall, Edinburgh. A new building to house parliament was opened, in the presence of the Queen, at Holyrood on 9 October 2004. On 3 May 2007 the third elections to the Scottish parliament took place.

The Scottish parliament has 129 members (including the presiding officer), comprising 73 constituency members and 56 additional regional members, mainly from party lists. It can introduce primary legislation and has the power to raise or lower the basic rate of income tax by up to three pence in the pound.

The areas for which the Scottish parliament is responsible include: education, health, law, environment, economic development, local government, housing, police, fire services, planning, financial assistance to industry, tourism, some transport, heritage and the arts, agriculture, forestry and food standards.

SALARIES *as at 1 April 2007*

First Minister*	£76,907
Ministers*	£39,897
Lord Advocate*	£52,123
Solicitor-General for Scotland*	£37,690
Junior Ministers*	£24,989
MSPs†	£53,091
Presiding Officer*	£39,897
Deputy Presiding Officer*	£24,989

* In addition to the MSP salary
† Reduced by two-thirds if the member is already an MP or an MEP

SCOTTISH EXECUTIVE

St Andrew's House, Regent Road, Edinburgh EH1 3DG
T 0845-774 1741 Enquiry Line 0131-556 8400
E ceu@scotland.gov.uk W www.scotland.gov.uk

The Scottish Executive is the devolved government for Scotland. It is responsible for most of the issues of day-to-day concern to the people of Scotland, including health, education, justice, rural affairs and transport, and manages an annual budget of around £30bn.

The executive was established in 1999, following the first elections to the Scottish parliament, and the current administration was formed after elections in May 2007.

The executive is led by a first minister who is nominated by the parliament and in turn appoints the other Scottish ministers.

Scottish Executive civil servants are accountable to Scottish ministers, who are themselves accountable to the Scottish parliament.

CABINET

First Minister, Rt. Hon. Alex Salmond, MSP
Minister for EU, International and Culture, Linda Fabiani, MSP
Minister for Parliamentary Business, Bruce Crawford, MSP
Deputy First Minister and Cabinet Secretary for Health and Wellbeing, Nicola Sturgeon, MSP
Minister for Communities and Sport, Stewart Maxwell, MSP
Minister for Public Health, Shona Robison, MSP
Cabinet Secretary for Education and Lifelong Learning, Fiona Hyslop, MSP
Minister for Children and Early Years, Adam Ingram, MSP
Minister for Schools and Skills, Maureen Watt, MSP
Cabinet Secretary for Finance and Sustainable Growth, John Swinney, MSP
Minister for Enterprise, Energy and Tourism, Jim Mather, MSP
Minister for Transport, Infrastructure and Climate Change, Stewart Stevenson, MSP
Cabinet Secretary for Justice, Kenny MacAskill, MSP
Minister for Community Safety, Fergus Ewing, MSP
Cabinet Secretary for Rural Affairs and the Environment, Richard Lochhead, MSP
Minister for Environment, Michael Russel, MSP

LAW OFFICERS
Lord Advocate, Elish Angiolini, QC
Solicitor-General for Scotland, John Beckett, QC

STRATEGIC BOARD
Permanent Secretary, Sir John Elvidge, KCB
Director-General, Economy, and Chief Economic Adviser, Dr Andrew Goudie
Director-General, Education, Philip Rycroft
Director-General, Environment, Richard Wakeford
Director-General, Health, and Chief Executive of NHS Scotland, Dr Kevin Woods
Director-General, Justice and Communities, Robert Gordon, CB
Non-Executive Directors, Prof. William Bound; David Fisher; Shonaig Macpherson

CHANGE AND CORPORATE SERVICES
Saughton House, Broomhouse Drive, Edinburgh EH11 3XD
T 0845-774 1741
Director of Change and Corporate Services, Paul Pagliari

ECONOMY DEPARTMENT
Victoria Quay, Edinburgh EH6 6QQ
T 0845-774 1741
Directorates: Europe; External Affairs and Culture; Finance; Inquiry Reporters; Planning; Public Service Reform; Scottish Development International; Transport
Director-General and Chief Economic Adviser, Dr Andrew Goudie

EXECUTIVE AGENCIES
General Register Office of Scotland
Historic Scotland
National Archives for Scotland
Registers of Scotland
Scottish Building Standards Agency
Scottish Public Pensions Agency
Scottish Water
Transport Scotland
Water Industry Commission

EDUCATION DEPARTMENT
Pentland House, 47 Robb's Loan, Edinburgh EH14 1TY
T 0845-774 1741 F 01397-795001
Directorates: Analytical Services; Chief Scientific Adviser;
    Children; Enterprise and Industrial Affairs and
    Tourism; Lifelong Learning; School; Young People and
    Social Care
Director-General, Philip Ryecroft

EXECUTIVE AGENCIES
HM Inspectorate of Education
Social Work Inspection Agency
Student Awards Agency for Scotland

ENVIRONMENT DEPARTMENT
Pentland House, 47 Robb's Loan, Edinburgh EH14 1TY
T 0845-774 1741
Directorates: Environment; Marine; Operations; Rural;
    Science and Analysis
Director-General, Richard Wakeford

EXECUTIVE AGENCIES
Animal Health Agency
Cairngorms National Park Authority
Crofters Commission
Deer Commission Scotland
Fisheries Research Service
Forest Enterprise
Forestry Commission Scotland
Loch Lomond and Trossach National Park Authority
Royal Botanic Gardens
Scottish Agricultural Science Agency
Scottish Agricultural Wages Board
Scottish Environmental Protection Agency
Scottish Fisheries Protection Service

HEALTH DEPARTMENT
St Andrew's House, Regent Road, Edinburgh EH1 3DG
T 0131-244 2440
Directorates: Chief Medical Officer; Chief Nursing
    Officer; Delivery; eHealth; Finance; Health
    Improvement; Primary and Community Care; Service
    Policy and Planning; Workforce
Director-General and Chief Executive of NHS Scotland, Dr
    Kevin Woods

EXECUTIVE AGENCIES
Mental Health Tribunal (Scotland)
Scottish Commission for the Regulation of Care

JUSTICE AND COMMUNITIES DEPARTMENT
St Andrew's House, Regent Road, Edinburgh EH1 3DG
T 0131-244 2040 F 0131-244 2121
Directorates: Courts; Civil and International Justice;
    Constitutional and Legal Services; Criminal Justice;
    Housing and Regeneration; Office of the First Scottish
    Parliamentary Counsel; Police and Community Safety;
    Solicitor
Director-General, Robert Gordon, CB

EXECUTIVE AGENCIES
Accountant in Bankruptcy
Communities Scotland
HM Inspector Constabulary
HMC Inspector Fire Rescue Service
HMC Inspector Prisons
Office of Scottish Charities Regulator
Scottish Courts Service
Scottish Prison Service

CROWN OFFICE AND PROCURATOR FISCAL
SERVICE
29 Chambers Street, Edinburgh EH1 1LD
T 0131-226 4962
Chief Executive and Crown Agent, Norman McFadyen

OFFICE OF THE PERMANENT SECRETARY
St Andrew's House, Regent Road, Edinburgh EH1 3DG
T 0131-244 4028 F 0131-244 2756
Permanent Secretary, Sir John Elvidge, KCB

AUDIT SCOTLAND
110 George Street, Edinburgh EH2 4LH
T 0845-146 1010 F 0845-146 1009
W www.audit-scotland.gov.uk
Auditor-General, Robert W. Black
Accounts Commission Chair, Alastair MacNish

COURT OF THE LORD LYON
HM New Register House, Edinburgh EH1 3YT
T 0131-556 7255 F 0131-557 2148
W www.lyon-court.com
Lord Lyon King of Arms, Robin O. Blair, LVO, WS

MEMBERS OF THE SCOTTISH PARLIAMENT
as at 3 May 2007
Adam, Brian, *SNP, Aberdeen North,* Maj. 3,749
Ahmad, Bashir, *SNP, Glasgow region*
Aitken, Bill, *C., Glasgow region*
Alexander, Wendy, *Lab., Paisley North,* Maj. 5,113
Allan, Alasdair, *SNP, Western Isles,* Maj. 987
Baillie, Jackie, *Lab., Dumbarton,* Maj. 1,611
Baker, Claire, *Lab., Mid Scotland and Fife region*
Baker, Richard, *Lab., North East Scotland region*
Boyack, Sarah, *Lab., Edinburgh Central,* Maj. 1,193
Brankin, Rhona, *Lab., Midlothian,* Maj. 1,702
Brocklebank, Ted, *C., Mid Scotland and Fife region*
Brown, Gavin, *C., Lothians region*
Brown, Keith, *SNP, Ochil,* Maj. 490
Brown, Robert E., *LD, Glasgow region*
Brownlee, Derek, *C., South of Scotland region*
Butler, Bill, *Lab., Glasgow Anniesland,* Maj. 4,306
Campbell, Aileen, *SNP, South of Scotland region*
Carlaw, Jackson, *C., West of Scotland region*
Chisholm, Malcolm, *Lab., Edinburgh North and Leith,*
    Maj. 2,444
Coffey, Willie, *SNP, Kilmarnock and Loudon,* Maj. 1,342
Constance, Angela, *SNP, Livingston,* Maj. 870
Craigie, Cathie, *Lab., Cumbernauld and Kilsyth,* Maj.
    2,079
Crawford, Bruce, *SNP, Stirling,* Maj. 620
Cunningham, Roseanna, *SNP, Perth,* Maj. 2,495
Curran, Margaret, *Lab., Glasgow Baillieston,* Maj. 3,934
Don, Nigel, *SNP, North East Scotland region*
Doris, Bob, *SNP, Glasgow region*
Eadie, Helen, *Lab., Dunfermline East,* Maj. 3,993
Ewing, Fergus, *SNP, Inverness East, Nairn and Lochaber,*
    Maj. 5,471
Fabiani, Linda, *SNP, Central Scotland region*
Ferguson, Patricia, *Lab., Glasgow Maryhill,* Maj. 2,310
Fergusson, Alex, *C., Galloway and Upper Nithsdale,* Maj.
    3,333
Finnie, Ross, *LD, West of Scotland region*
Fitzpatrick, Joe, *SNP, Dundee West,* Maj. 1,946
Foulkes, George, *Lab., Lothians region*
Fraser, Murdo, *C., Mid Scotland and Fife region*
Gibson, Kenneth, *SNP, Cunninghame North,* Maj. 48

Gibson, Rob, *SNP, Highlands and Islands region*
Gillon, Karen, *Lab., Clydesdale,* Maj. 2,893
Glen, Marlyn, *Lab., North East Scotland region*
Godman, Trish, *Lab., Renfrewshire West,* Maj. 2,178
Goldie, Annabel, *C., West of Scotland region*
Gordon, Charlie, *Lab., Glasgow Cathcart,* Maj. 2,189
Grahame, Christine, *SNP, South of Scotland region*
Grant, Rhoda, *Lab., Highlands and Islands region*
Gray, Ian, *Lab., East Lothian,* Maj. 2,448
Harper, Robin, *Scot. Green, Lothians region*
Harvie, Christopher, *SNP, Mid Scotland and Fife region*
Harvie, Patrick, *Scot. Green, Glasgow region*
Henry, Hugh, *Lab., Paisley South,* Maj. 4,230
Hepburn, Jamie, *SNP, Central Scotland region*
Hume, Jim, *LD, South of Scotland region*
Hyslop, Fiona, *SNP, Lothians region*
Ingram, Adam, *SNP, South of Scotland region*
Jamieson, Cathy, *Lab., Carrick, Cumnock and Doon Valley,* Maj. 3,986
Johnstone, Alex, *C., North East Scotland region*
Kelly, James, *Lab., Glasgow Rutherglen,* Maj. 4,378
Kerr, Andy, *Lab., East Kilbride,* Maj. 1,972
Kidd, Bill, *SNP, Glasgow region*
Lamont, Johann, *Lab., Glasgow Pollok,* Maj. 4,393
Lamont, John, *C., Roxburgh and Berwickshire,* Maj. 1,985
Livingstone, Marilyn, *Lab., Kirkcaldy,* Maj. 2,622
Lochhead, Richard, *SNP, Moray,* Maj. 7,924
MacAskill, Kenny, *SNP, Edinburgh East and Musselburgh,* Maj. 1,382
Macdonald, Lewis, *Lab., Aberdeen Central,* Maj. 382
MacDonald, Margo, *Ind., Lothians region*
Macintosh, Kenneth, *Lab., Eastwood,* Maj. 891
McArthur, Liam, *LD, Orkney,* Maj. 2,476
McAveety, Frank, *Lab., Glasgow Shettleston,* Maj. 2,881
McCabe, Tom, *Lab., Hamilton South,* Maj. 3,652
McConnell, Jack, *Lab., Motherwell and Wishaw,* Maj. 5,938
McGrigor, Jamie, *C., Highlands and Islands region*
McInnes, Alison, *LD, North East Scotland region*
McKee, Ian, *SNP, Lothians region*
McKelvie, Christina, *SNP, Central Scotland region*
McLetchie, David, *C., Edinburgh Pentlands,* Maj. 4,525
McMahon, Michael, *Lab., Hamilton North and Bellshill,* Maj. 4,865
McMillan, Stuart, *SNP, West of Scotland region*
McNeil, Duncan, *Lab., Greenock and Inverclyde,* Maj. 3,024
McNeill, Pauline, *Lab., Glasgow Kelvin,* Maj. 1,207
McNulty, Des, *Lab., Clydebank and Milngavie,* Maj. 3,179
Martin, Paul, *Lab., Glasgow Springburn,* Maj. 5,095
Marwick, Tricia, *SNP, Central Fife,* Maj. 1,166
Mather, Jim, *SNP, Argyll and Bute,* Maj. 815
Matheson, Michael, *SNP, Falkirk West,* Maj. 776
Maxwell, Stewart, *SNP, West of Scotland region*
Milne, Nanette, *C., North East Scotland region*
Mitchell, Margaret, *C., Central Scotland region*
Morgan, Alasdair, *SNP, South of Scotland region*
Mulligan, Mary, *Lab., Linlithgow,* Maj. 1,160
Munro, John F., *LD, Ross, Skye and Inverness West,* Maj. 3,486
Murray, Dr Elaine, *Lab., Dumfries,* Maj. 2,839
Neil, Alex, *SNP, Central Scotland region*
O'Donnell, Hugh, *LD, Central Scotland region*
Oldfather, Irene, *Lab., Cunninghame South,* Maj. 2,168
Park, John, *Lab., Mid Scotland and Fife region*

Paterson, Gil, *SNP, West of Scotland region*
Peacock, Peter, *Lab., Highlands and Islands region*
Peattie, Cathy, *Lab., Falkirk East,* Maj. 1,872
Pringle, Mike, *LD, Edinburgh South,* Maj. 1,929
Purvis, Jeremy, *LD, Tweeddale, Ettrick and Lauderdale,* Maj. 598
Robison, Shona, *SNP, Dundee East,* Maj. 4,524
Rumbles, Mike, *LD, Aberdeenshire West and Kincardine,* Maj. 5,170
Russell, Michael, *SNP, South of Scotland region*
Salmond, Alex, *SNP, Gordon,* Maj. 2062
Scanlon, Mary, *C., Highlands and Islands region*
Scott, John, *C., Ayr,* Maj. 3,906
Scott, Tavish, *LD, Shetland,* Maj. 4,909
Simpson, Richard, *Lab., Mid Scotland and Fife region*
Smith, Elaine, *Lab., Coatbridge and Chryston,* Maj. 4,510
Smith, Elizabeth, *C., Mid Scotland and Fife region*
Smith, Iain, *LD, Fife North East,* Maj. 5,016
Smith, Margaret, *LD, Edinburgh West,* Maj. 5,886
Stephen, Nicol, *LD, Aberdeen South,* Maj. 2,732
Stevenson, Stewart, *SNP, Banff and Buchan,* Maj. 10,530
Stewart, David, *Lab., Highlands and Islands region*
Stone, Jamie, *LD, Caithness, Sutherland and Easter Ross,* Maj. 2,323
Sturgeon, Nicola, *SNP, Glasgow Govan,* Maj. 744
Swinney, John, *SNP, North Tayside,* Maj. 7,584
Thompson, Dave, *SNP, Highlands and Islands region*
Tolson, Jim, *LD, Dunfermline West,* Maj. 476
Tymkewycz, Stefan, *SNP, Lothians region*
Watt, Maureen, *SNP, North East Scotland region*
Welsh, Andrew, *SNP, Angus,* Maj. 8,243
White, Sandra, *SNP, Glasgow region*
Whitefield, Karen, *Lab., Airdrie and Shotts,* Maj. 1,446
Whitton, David, *Lab., Strathkelvin and Bearsden,* Maj. 3,388
Wilson, Bill, *SNP, West of Scotland region*
Wilson, John, *SNP, Central Scotland region*

STATE OF THE PARTIES *as at 3 May 2007*

	Constituency MSPs	Regional MSPs	Total
Scottish Labour Party (Lab.)	37	9	46
Scottish National Party (SNP)	21	26	47
Scottish Conservative and Unionist Party (C.)	3	13	16
Scottish Liberal Democrats (LD)	11	5	16
Scottish Green Party (Scot. Green)	0	2	2
Independent (Ind.)*	9	1	1
Presiding Officer†	1	0	1
Total	73	56	129

* Independent MSP is Margo MacDonald
† The presiding officer was elected as a constituency member for the Conservatives but has no party allegiance while in post

The Presiding Officer, Alex Fergusson, MSP
Deputy Presiding Officers, Trish Godman, MSP *(Lab.);* Alasdair Morgan, MSP *(SNP)*

SCOTTISH PARLIAMENT CONSTITUENCIES
as at May 2007
E. Electorate T. Turnout
See General Election Results for a list of party abbreviations

ABERDEEN CENTRAL
(Scotland North East Region)
E. 46,588 T. 21,120 (45.33%)
Lewis Macdonald, Lab.	7,232
Karen Shirron, SNP	6,850
John Stewart, LD	4,693
Andrew Jones, C.	2,345

Lab. majority 382 (1.81%)
2.06% swing Lab. to SNP

ABERDEEN NORTH
(Scotland North East Region)
E. 51,507 T. 24,891 (48.33%)
Brian Adam, SNP	11,406
Elaine Thomson, Lab.	7,657
Steve Delaney, LD	3,836
Carol Garvie, C.	1,992

SNP majority 3,749 (15.06%)
6.62% swing Lab. to SNP

ABERDEEN SOUTH
(Scotland North East Region)
E. 56,700 T. 29,885 (52.71%)
Nicol Stephen, LD	10,843
Maureen Watt, SNP	8,111
Rami Okasha, Lab.	5,499
David Davidson, C.	5,432

LD majority 2,732 (9.14%)
11.21% swing LD to SNP

ABERDEENSHIRE WEST AND KINCARDINE
(Scotland North East Region)
E. 65,233 T. 34,823 (53.38%)
Mike Rumbles, LD	14,314
Dennis Robertson, SNP	9,144
Stewart Whyte, C.	8,604
James Noble, Lab.	2,761

LD majority 5,170 (14.85%)
8.48% swing LD to SNP

AIRDRIE AND SHOTTS
(Scotland Central Region)
E. 57,660 T. 27,160 (47.10%)
Karen Whitefield, Lab.	11,907
Sophia Coyle, SNP	10,461
Iain McGill, C.	2,370
Robert Gorrie, LD	1,452
Mev Brown, Scottish Voice	970

Lab. majority 1,446 (5.32%)
15.23% swing Lab. to SNP

ANGUS
(Scotland North East Region)
E. 61,362 T. 31,960 (52.08%)
Andrew Welsh, SNP	15,686
Alex Johnstone, C.	7,443
Doug Bradley, Lab.	5,032
Scott Rennie, LD	3,799

SNP majority 8,243 (25.79%)
1.67% swing C. to SNP

ARGYLL AND BUTE
(Highlands and Islands Region)
E. 48,846 T. 28,792 (58.94%)
Jim Mather, SNP	9,944
George Lyon, LD	9,129
Jamie McGrigor, C.	5,571
Mary Galbraith, Lab.	4,148

SNP majority 815 (2.83%)
9.17% swing LD to SNP

AYR
(Scotland South Region)
E. 55,034 T. 31,025 (56.37%)
John Scott, C.	12,619
John Duncan, Lab.	8,713
Iain White, SNP	7,952
Stuart Ritchie, LD	1,741

C. majority 3,906 (12.59%)
3.30% swing Lab. to C.

BANFF AND BUCHAN
(Scotland North East Region)
E. 56,324 T. 27,285 (48.44%)
Stewart Stevenson, SNP	16,031
Geordie Burnett-Stuart, C.	5,501
Kay Barnett, Lab.	3,136
Alison McInnes, LD	2,617

SNP majority 10,530 (38.59%)
3.30% swing C. to SNP

CAITHNESS, SUTHERLAND AND EASTER ROSS
(Highlands and Islands Region)
E. 41,789 T. 22,334 (53.44%)
Jamie Stone, LD	8,981
Rob Gibson, SNP	6,658
John McKendrick, Lab.	3,152
Donald MacDonald, C.	2,586
Gordon Campbell, Ind.	957

LD majority 2,323 (10.40%)
4.38% swing LD to SNP

CARRICK, CUMNOCK AND DOON VALLEY
(Scotland South Region)
E. 65,166 T. 33,785 (51.84%)
Cathy Jamieson, Lab.	14,350
Adam Ingram, SNP	10,364
Tony Lewis, C.	6,729
Paul McGreal, LD	1,409
Hugh Hill, Ind.	809
Ray Barry, Equal Parenting Alliance	124

Lab. majority 3,986 (11.80%)
9.61% swing Lab. to SNP

CLYDEBANK AND MILNGAVIE
(Scotland West Region)
E. 48,700 T. 26,765 (54.96%)
Des McNulty, Lab.	11,617
Gil Paterson, SNP	8,438
Murray Roxburgh, C.	3,544
Ashay Ghai, LD	3,166

Lab. majority 3,179 (11.88%)
2.61% swing Lab. to SNP

CLYDESDALE
(Scotland South Region)
E. 66,011 T. 33,332 (50.49%)
Karen Gillon, Lab.	13,835
Aileen Campbell, SNP	10,942
Colin McGavigan, C.	5,604
Fraser Grieve, LD	2,951

Lab. majority 2,893 (8.68%)
5.94% swing Lab. to SNP

COATBRIDGE AND CHRYSTON
(Scotland Central Region)
E. 54,423 T. 25,725 (47.27%)
Elaine Smith, Lab.	11,860
Frances McGlinchey, SNP	7,350
Ross Thomson, C.	2,305
Julie McAnulty, Ind.	1,843
Doreen Nisbet, LD	1,519
Gaille McCann, Scottish Voice	848

Lab. majority 4,510 (17.53%)
9.19% swing Lab. to SNP

CUMBERNAULD AND KILSYTH
(Scotland Central Region)
E. 49,197 T. 26,382 (53.63%)
Cathie Craigie, Lab.	12,672
Jamie Hepburn, SNP	10,593
Hugh O'Donnell, LD	1,670
Anne Harding, C.	1,447

Lab. majority 2,079 (7.88%)
2.87% swing SNP to Lab.

CUNNINGHAME NORTH
(Scotland West Region)
E. 55,925 T. 30,241 (54.07%)
Kenneth Gibson, SNP	9,295
Allan Wilson, Lab.	9,247
Philip Lardner, C.	5,466
Campbell Martin, Ind.	4,423
Lewis Hutton, LD	1,810

SNP majority 48 (0.16%)
5.99% swing Lab. to SNP

CUNNINGHAME SOUTH
(Scotland South Region)
E. 49,969 T. 23,422 (46.87%)
Irene Oldfather, Lab.	10,270
Duncan Ross, SNP	8,102
Pat McPhee, C.	3,073
Iain Dale, LD	1,977

Lab. majority 2,168 (9.26%)
8.71% swing Lab. to SNP

DUMBARTON
(Scotland West Region)
E. 54,023 T. 30,054 (55.63%)
Jackie Baillie, Lab.	11,635
Graeme McCormick, SNP	10,024
Brian Pope, C.	4,701
Alex Mackie, LD	3,385
John Black, Scottish Jacobite Party	309

Lab. majority 1,611 (5.36%)
8.79% swing Lab. to SNP

DUMFRIES
(Scotland South Region)
E. 53,518 T. 33,419 (62.44%)
Elaine Murray, Lab.	13,707
Murray Tosh, C.	10,868
Michael Russell, SNP	6,306
Lynne Hume, LD	2,538

Lab. majority 2,839 (8.50%)
2.54% swing C. to Lab.

DUNDEE EAST
(Scotland North East Region)
E. 53,804 T. 26,869 (49.94%)
Shona Robison, SNP	13,314
Iain Luke, Lab.	8,790
Chris Bustin, C.	2,976
Clive Sneddon, LD	1,789

SNP majority 4,524 (16.84%)
8.25% swing Lab. to SNP

DUNDEE WEST
(Scotland North East Region)
E. 49,711 T. 24,268 (48.82%)
Joe Fitzpatrick, SNP	10,955
Jill Shimi, Lab.	9,009
Michael Charlton, LD	2,517
Belinda Don, C.	1,787

SNP majority 1,946 (8.02%)
6.14% swing Lab. to SNP

DUNFERMLINE EAST
(Scotland Mid and Fife Region)
E. 51,115 T. 24,568 (48.06%)
Helen Eadie, Lab.	10,995
Ewan Dow, SNP	7,002
Graeme Brown, C.	3,718
Karen Utting, LD	2,853

Lab. majority 3,993 (16.25%)
7.62% swing Lab. to SNP

DUNFERMLINE WEST
(Scotland Mid and Fife Region)
E. 56,953 T. 29,525 (51.84%)
Jim Tolson, LD	9,952
Scott Barrie, Lab.	9,476
Len Woods, SNP	7,296
Peter Lyburn, C.	2,363
Susan Archibald, Scottish Voice	438

LD majority 476 (1.61%)
10.77% swing Lab. to LD

EAST KILBRIDE
(Scotland Central Region)
E. 66,935 T. 35,902 (53.64%)
Andy Kerr, Lab.	15,334
Linda Fabiani, SNP	13,362
Graham Simpson, C.	4,114
David Clark, LD	3,092

Lab. majority 1,972 (5.49%)
5.00% swing Lab. to SNP

EAST LOTHIAN
(Scotland South Region)
E. 61,378 T. 34,471 (56.16%)
Iain Gray, Lab.	12,219
Andrew Sharp, SNP	9,771
Judy Hayman, LD	6,249
Bill Stevenson, C.	6,232

Lab. majority 2,448 (7.10%)
10.08% swing Lab. to SNP

EASTWOOD
(Scotland West Region)
E. 67,347 T. 42,187 (62.64%)
Ken Macintosh, Lab.	15,099
Jackson Carlaw, C.	14,186
Stewart Maxwell, SNP	7,972
Gordon MacDonald, LD	3,603
Frank McGhee, Ind.	1,327

Lab. majority 913 (2.16%)
3.68% swing Lab. to C.

EDINBURGH CENTRAL
(Lothians Region)
E. 55,953 T. 29,396 (52.54%)
Sarah Boyack, Lab.	9,155
Siobhan Mathers, LD	7,962
Shirley-Anne Somerville, SNP	7,496
Fiona Houston, C.	4,783

Lab. majority 1,193 (4.06%)
2.73% swing Lab. to LD

EDINBURGH EAST AND MUSSELBURGH
(Lothians Region)
E. 56,578 T. 29,967 (52.97%)
Kenny MacAskill, SNP	11,209
Norman Murray, Lab.	9,827
Gillian Cole-Hamilton, LD	5,473
Christine Wright, C.	3,458

SNP majority 1,382 (4.61%)
12.91% swing Lab. to SNP

EDINBURGH NORTH AND LEITH
(Lothians Region)
E. 60,340 T. 31,685 (52.51%)
Malcolm Chisholm, Lab.	11,020
Mike Crockart, LD	8,576
Davie Hutchison, SNP	8,044
Iain Whyte, C.	4,045

Lab. majority 2,444 (7.71%)
6.92% swing Lab. to LD

EDINBURGH PENTLANDS
(Lothians Region)
E. 57,891 T. 34,377 (59.38%)
David McLetchie, C.	12,927
Sheila Gilmore, Lab.	8,402
Ian McKee, SNP	8,234
Simon Clark, LD	4,814

C. majority 4,525 (13.16%)
3.42% swing Lab. to C.

EDINBURGH SOUTH
(Lothians Region)
E. 57,621 T. 32,573 (56.53%)
Mike Pringle, LD	11,398
Donald Anderson, Lab.	9,469
Robert Holland, SNP	6,117
Gavin Brown, C.	5,589

LD majority 1,929 (5.92%)
2.71% swing Lab. to LD

EDINBURGH WEST
(Lothians Region)
E. 59,814 T. 34,752 (58.10%)
Margaret Smith, LD	13,677
Sheena Cleland, SNP	7,791
Gordon Lindhurst, C.	7,361
Richard Meade, Lab.	5,343
John Wilson, Ind.	580

LD majority 5,886 (16.94%)
7.00% swing LD to SNP

FALKIRK EAST
(Scotland Central Region)
E. 57,663 T. 30,333 (52.60%)
Cathy Peattie, Lab.	13,184
Annabelle Ewing, SNP	11,312
Scott Campbell, C.	3,701
Natalie Maver, LD	2,136

Lab. majority 1,872 (6.17%)
9.00% swing Lab. to SNP

FALKIRK WEST
(Scotland Central Region)
E. 56,254 T. 28,785 (51.17%)
Michael Matheson, SNP	12,068
Dennis Goldie, Lab.	11,292
Stephen O'Rourke, C.	2,887
Callum Chomczuk, LD	2,538

SNP majority 776 (2.70%)
1.13% swing Lab. to SNP

FIFE CENTRAL
(Scotland Mid and Fife Region)
E. 58,215 T. 26,965 (46.32%)
Tricia Marwick, SNP	11,920
Christine May, Lab.	10,754
Elizabeth Riches, LD	2,288
Maurice Golden, C.	2,003

SNP majority 1,166 (4.32%)
7.56% swing Lab. to SNP

FIFE NORTH EAST
(Scotland Mid and Fife Region)
E. 61,078 T. 31,552 (51.66%)
Iain Smith, LD	13,307
Ted Brocklebank, C.	8,291
Roderick Campbell, SNP	6,735
Kenny Young, Lab.	2,557
Tony Campbell, Ind.	662

LD majority 5,016 (15.90%)
0.68% swing LD to C.

GALLOWAY AND UPPER NITHSDALE
(Scotland South Region)
E. 52,583 T. 30,318 (57.66%)

Alex Fergusson, C.	13,387
Alasdair Morgan, SNP	10,054
Stephen Hodgson, Lab.	4,935
Alastair Cooper, LD	1,631
Sandy Richardson, Ind.	311

C. majority 3,333 (10.99%)
5.33% swing SNP to C.

GLASGOW ANNIESLAND
(Glasgow Region)
E. 48,344 T. 22,139 (45.79%)

Bill Butler, Lab.	10,483
Bill Kidd, SNP	6,177
Bill Aitken, C.	3,154
Danica Gilland, LD	2,325

Lab. majority 4,306 (19.45%)
4.38% swing Lab. to SNP

GLASGOW BAILLIESTON
(Glasgow Region)
E. 44,367 T. 17,272 (38.93%)

Margaret Curran, Lab.	9,141
Lachie McNeill, SNP	5,207
Richard Sullivan, C.	1,276
David Jackson, LD	1,060
George Hargreaves, Scottish Christian Party	588

Lab. majority 3,934 (22.78%)
5.52% swing Lab. to SNP

GLASGOW CATHCART
(Glasgow Region)
E. 47,822 T. 21,657 (45.29%)

Charlie Gordon, Lab.	8,476
James Dornan, SNP	6,287
David Smith, Ind.	2,911
Davena Rankin, C.	2,324
Shabnum Mustapha, LD	1,659

Lab. majority 2,189 (10.11%)
6.40% swing Lab. to SNP

GLASGOW GOVAN
(Glasgow Region)
E. 47,405 T. 21,521 (45.40%)

Nicola Sturgeon, SNP	9,010
Gordon Jackson, Lab.	8,266
Chris Young, LD	1,891
Martyn McIntyre, C.	1,680
Asif Nasir, Ind.	423
Elinor McKenzie, Comm. Brit.	251

SNP majority 744 (3.46%)
4.65% swing Lab. to SNP

GLASGOW KELVIN
(Glasgow Region)
E. 55,096 T. 23,500 (42.65%)

Pauline McNeill, Lab.	7,875
Sandra White, SNP	6,668
Martin Bartos, Green	2,971
Katy Gordon, LD	2,843
Brian Cooklin, C.	1,943
Niall Walker, Ind.	744
Isobel Macleod, Scottish Christian Party	456

Lab. majority 1,207 (5.14%)
4.88% swing Lab. to SNP

GLASGOW MARYHILL
(Glasgow Region)
E. 46,060 T. 16,564 (35.96%)

Patricia Ferguson, Lab.	7,955
Bob Doris, SNP	5,645
Kenn Elder, LD	1,936
Heather MacLeod, C.	1,028

Lab. majority 2,310 (13.95%)
7.74% swing Lab. to SNP

GLASGOW POLLOK
(Glasgow Region)
E. 47,189 T. 19,416 (41.15%)

Johann Lamont, Lab.	10,456
Chris Stephens, SNP	6,063
Gerald Michaluk, C.	1,460
Christine Gilmore, LD	1,437

Lab. majority 4,393 (22.63%)
0.85% swing Lab. to SNP

GLASGOW RUTHERGLEN
(Glasgow Region)
E. 50,005 T. 24,252 (48.50%)

James Kelly, Lab.	10,237
Margaret Park, SNP	5,857
Robert Brown, LD	5,516
Christina Harcus, C.	2,094
Tom Greig, Scottish Christian Party	548

Lab. majority 4,380 (18.06%)
6.43% swing Lab. to SNP

GLASGOW SHETTLESTON
(Glasgow Region)
E. 44,278 T. 14,801 (33.43%)

Frank McAveety, Lab.	7,574
John McLaughlin, SNP	4,693
Ross Renton, LD	1,182
William MacNair, C.	946
Bob Graham, Scottish Christian Party	406

Lab. majority 2,881 (19.46%)
9.45% swing Lab. to SNP

GLASGOW SPRINGBURN
(Glasgow Region)
E. 47,021 T. 17,612 (37.46%)

Paul Martin, Lab.	10,024
Anne McLaughlin, SNP	4,929
Katy McCloskey, LD	1,108
Gordon Wilson, C.	1,067
David Johnston, Scottish Christian Party	484

Lab. majority 5,095 (28.93%)
7.09% swing Lab. to SNP

GORDON
(Scotland North East Region)
E. 65,431 T. 35,363 (54.05%)

Alex Salmond, SNP	14,650
Nora Radcliffe, LD	12,588
Nanette Milne, C.	5,348
Neil Cardwell, Lab.	2,276
Donald Marr, Ind.	199
Dave Mathers, Ind.	185
Bob Ingram, Scottish Enterprise Party	117

SNP majority 2,062 (5.83%)
10.66% swing LD to SNP

GREENOCK AND INVERCLYDE
(Scotland West Region)
E. 44,646 T. 23,105 (51.75%)
Duncan McNeil, Lab.	10,035
Stuart McMillan, SNP	7,011
Ross Finnie, LD	3,893
Charles Ferguson, C.	2,166

Lab. majority 3,024 (13.09%)
6.37% swing Lab. to SNP

HAMILTON NORTH AND BELLSHILL
(Scotland Central Region)
E. 53,854 T. 25,366 (47.10%)
Michael McMahon, Lab.	12,334
Alex Neil, SNP	7,469
James Callander, C.	2,835
Douglas Herbison, LD	1,726
Joe Gorman, Scottish Voice	571
Gordon Weir, Ind.	431

Lab. majority 4,865 (19.18%)
6.75% swing Lab. to SNP

HAMILTON SOUTH
(Scotland Central Region)
E. 48,838 T. 23,211 (47.53%)
Tom McCabe, Lab.	10,280
Christina McKelvie, SNP	6,628
Margaret Mitchell, C.	2,929
Michael McGlynn, Ind.	1,764
John Oswald, LD	1,610

Lab. majority 3,652 (15.73%)
3.89% swing Lab. to SNP

INVERNESS EAST, NAIRN AND LOCHABER
(Highlands and Islands Region)
E. 71,609 T. 39,609 (55.31%)
Fergus Ewing, SNP	16,443
Craig Harrow, LD	10,972
Linda Stewart, Lab.	7,559
Jamie Halcro-Johnston, C.	4,635

SNP majority 5,471 (13.81%)
0.48% swing SNP to LD

KILMARNOCK AND LOUDOUN
(Scotland Central Region)
E. 60,753 T. 33,435 (55.03%)
Willie Coffey, SNP	14,297
Margaret Jamieson, Lab.	12,955
Janette McAlpine, C.	4,127
Ron Aitken, LD	2,056

SNP majority 1,342 (4.01%)
3.93% swing Lab. to SNP

KIRKCALDY
(Scotland Mid and Fife Region)
E. 50,761 T. 24,195 (47.66%)
Marilyn Livingstone, Lab.	10,627
Chris Harvie, SNP	8,005
Alice Soper, LD	3,361
David Potts, C.	2,202

Lab. majority 2,622 (10.84%)
5.58% swing Lab. to SNP

LINLITHGOW
(Lothians Region)
E. 56,175 T. 29,637 (52.76%)
Mary Mulligan, Lab.	12,715
Fiona Hyslop, SNP	11,565
Donald Cameron, C.	3,125
Martin Oliver, LD	2,232

Lab. majority 1,150 (3.88%)
1.62% swing Lab. to SNP

LIVINGSTON
(Lothians Region)
E. 66,348 T. 33,224 (50.08%)
Angela Constance, SNP	13,159
Bristow Muldoon, Lab.	12,289
Ernie Walker, Action to Save St John's Hospital	2,814
David Brown, C.	2,804
Evan Bell, LD	2,158

SNP majority 870 (2.62%)
7.31% swing Lab. to SNP

MIDLOTHIAN
(Lothians Region)
E. 48,395 T. 25,111 (51.89%)
Rhona Brankin, Lab.	10,671
Colin Beattie, SNP	8,969
Ross Laird, LD	2,704
P.J. Lewis, C.	2,269
George McCleery, Had Enough Party	498

Lab. majority 1,702 (6.78%)
8.37% swing Lab. to SNP

MORAY
(Highlands and Islands Region)
E. 60,959 T. 30,274 (49.66%)
Richard Lochhead, SNP	15,045
Mary Scanlon, C.	7,121
Lee Butcher, Lab.	4,580
Dominique Rommel, LD	3,528

SNP majority 7,924 (26.17%)
3.24% swing C. to SNP

MOTHERWELL AND WISHAW
(Scotland Central Region)
E. 53,875 T. 26,150 (48.54%)
Jack McConnell, Lab.	12,574
Marion Fellows, SNP	6,636
Diane Huddleston, C.	1,990
John Swinburne, SSCUP	1,702
Stuart Douglas, LD	1,570
Tom Selfridge, Scottish Christian Party	1,491
Richard Leat, Anti-Trident Party	187

Lab. majority 5,938 (22.71%)
6.88% swing Lab. to SNP

OCHIL
(Scotland Mid and Fife Region)
E. 58,104 T. 31,553 (54.30%)
Keith Brown, SNP	12,147
Brian Fearon, Lab.	11,657
George Murray, C.	4,284
Lorraine Caddell, LD	3,465

SNP majority 490 (1.55%)
0.29% swing Lab. to SNP

ORKNEY
(Highlands and Islands Region)
E. 16,195 T. 8,653 (53.43%)
Liam McArthur, LD	4,113
John Mowat, SNP	1,637
Helen Gardiner, C.	1,632
Iain MacDonald, Lab.	1,134
Barrie Johnson, Ind.	137

LD majority 2,476 (28.61%)
1.95% swing LD to SNP

PAISLEY NORTH
(Scotland West Region)
E. 44,081 T. 23,206 (52.64%)
Wendy Alexander, Lab.	12,111
Andy Doig, SNP	6,998
Malcolm MacAskill, C.	1,721
Angela McGarrigle, LD	1,570
Iain Hogg, SSP	525
John Plott, Ind.	281

Lab. majority 5,113 (22.03%)
1.31% swing SNP to Lab.

PAISLEY SOUTH
(Scotland West Region)
E. 49,175 T. 25,527 (51.91%)
Hugh Henry, Lab.	12,123
Fiona McLeod, SNP	7,893
Eileen McCartin, LD	3,434
Tom Begg, C.	2,077

Lab. majority 4,230 (16.57%)
3.38% swing SNP to Lab.

PERTH
(Scotland and Mid Fife Region)
E. 62,220 T. 34,862 (56.03%)
Roseanna Cunningham, SNP	13,751
Liz Smith, C.	11,256
Peter Barrett, LD	4,767
Doug Maughan, Lab.	4,513
Jim Fairlie, Free Scot.	575

SNP majority 2,495 (7.16%)
2.43% swing C. to SNP

RENFREWSHIRE WEST
(Scotland West Region)
E. 50,787 T. 29,129 (57.36%)
Trish Godman, Lab.	10,467
Annabel Goldie, C.	8,289
Bill Wilson, SNP	8,167
Simon Hutton, LD	2,206

Lab. majority 2,178 (7.48%)
1.22% swing Lab. to C.

ROSS, SKYE AND INVERNESS WEST
(Highlands and Islands Region)
E. 59,237 T. 31,719 (53.55%)
John Farquhar Munro, LD	13,501
Dave Thompson, SNP	10,015
Maureen Macmillan, Lab.	4,789
John Hodgson, C.	3,122
Iain Brodie, Scottish Enterprise Party	292

LD majority 3,486 (10.99%)
6.32% swing LD to SNP

ROXBURGH AND BERWICKSHIRE
(Scotland South Region)
E. 47,862 T. 25,680 (53.65%)
John Lamont, C.	10,556
Euan Robson, LD	8,571
Aileen Orr, SNP	4,127
Mary Lockhart, Lab.	2,108
Jesse Rae, No Description	318

C. majority 1,985 (7.73%)
9.40% swing LD to C.

SHETLAND
(Highlands and Islands Region)
E. 17,108 T. 9,795 (57.25%)
Tavish Scott, LD	6,531
Val Simpson, SNP	1,622
Mark Jones, C.	972
Scott Burnett, Lab.	670

LD majority 4,909 (50.12%)
11.99% swing SNP to LD

STIRLING
(Scotland and Mid Fife Region)
E. 52,864 T. 32,625 (61.71%)
Bruce Crawford, SNP	10,447
Sylvia Jackson, Lab.	9,827
Bob Dalrymple, C.	8,081
Alex Cole-Hamilton, LD	3,693
Liz Law, Peace Party	577

SNP majority 620 (1.90%)
9.41% swing Lab. to SNP

STRATHKELVIN AND BEARSDEN
(Scotland West Region)
E. 60,389 T. 36,595 (60.60%)
David Whitton, Lab.	11,396
Robin Easton, SNP	8,008
Jean Turner, Ind.	6,742
Stephanie Fraser, C.	5,178
Cathy McInnes, LD	4,658
Bob Handyside, Scottish Christian Party	613

Lab. majority 3,388 (9.26%)
3.91% swing Lab. to SNP

TAYSIDE NORTH
(Scotland Mid and Fife Region)
E. 62,133 T. 35,396 (56.97%)
John Swinney, SNP	18,281
Murdo Fraser, C.	10,697
Michael Marna, Lab.	3,243
James Taylor, LD	3,175

SNP majority 7,584 (21.43%)
3.96% swing C. to SNP

TWEEDDALE, ETTRICK AND LAUDERDALE
(Scotland South Region)
E. 53,588 T. 30,327 (56.59%)
Jeremy Purvis, LD	10,656
Christine Grahame, SNP	10,058
Derek Brownlee, C.	5,594
Catherine Maxwell-Stuart, Lab.	4,019

LD majority 598 (1.97%)
0.02% swing LD to SNP

WESTERN ISLES
(Highlands and Islands Region)
E. 22,051 T. 13,625 (61.79%)

Alasdair Allan, SNP	6,354
Alasdair Morrison, Lab.	5,667
Ruaraidh Ferguson, LD	852
Dave Petrie, C.	752

SNP majority 687 (5.04%)
5.43% swing Lab. to SNP

REGIONS

GLASGOW
E. 477,587 T. 206,618 (43.26%)

Lab.	78,838 (38.16%)
SNP	55,832 (27.02%)
LD	14,767 (7.15%)
C.	13,781 (6.67%)
Green	10,759 (5.21%)
Solidarity	8,525 (4.13%)
BNP	3,865 (1.87%)
SSCUP	3,703 (1.79%)
Scottish Christian Party	2,991 (1.45%)
Soc. Lab.	2,680 (1.30%)
CPA	2,626 (1.27%)
SSP	2,579 (1.25%)
Scottish Unionist Party	1,612 (0.78%)
Publican Party Smoking-Room in Pubs	952 (0.46%)
Ind. Shoaib	582 (0.28%)
Ind. Green	496 (0.24%)
UKIP	405 (0.20%)
Scottish Voice	389 (0.19%)
Ind. Nasir	317 (0.15%)
Scotland Against Crooked Lawyers	293 (0.14%)
Ind.	286 (0.14%)
Comm. Brit.	260 (0.13%)
Nine Per Cent Growth Party	80 (0.04%)

Lab. majority 23,006 (11.13%)
4.75% swing Lab. to SNP (2003 Lab. majority 42,146)

ADDITIONAL MEMBERS
Bill Aitken, C.
Robert Brown, *LD*
Bashir Ahmad, *SNP*
Sandra White, *SNP*
Bob Doris, *SNP*
Bill Kidd, *SNP*
Patrick Harvie, *Green*

HIGHLANDS AND ISLANDS
E. 337,794 T. 185,773 (55.00%)

SNP	63,979 (34.44%)
LD	37,001 (19.92%)
Lab.	32,952 (17.74%)
C.	23,334 (12.56%)
Green	8,602 (4.63%)
Scottish Christian Party	6,332 (3.41%)
SSCUP	3,841 (2.07%)
BNP	2,152 (1.16%)
Solidarity	1,833 (0.99%)
UKIP	1,287 (0.69%)
Soc. Lab.	1,027 (0.55%)
SSP	973 (0.52%)
Publican Party Smoking-Room in Pubs	914 (0.49%)
CPA	885 (0.48%)
Scottish Voice	450 (0.24%)
Scottish Enterprise Party	211 (0.11%)

SNP majority 26,978 (14.52%)
4.94% swing LD to SNP (2003 SNP majority 1,892)

ADDITIONAL MEMBERS
Mary Scanlon, *C.*
Jamie McGrigor, *C.*
Peter Peacock, *Lab.*
Rhoda Grant, *Lab.*
David Stewart, *Lab.*
Rob Gibson, *SNP*
Dave Thompson, *SNP*

LOTHIANS
E. 519,115 T. 287,039 (55.29%)

SNP	76,019 (26.48%)
Lab.	75,495 (26.30%)
C.	37,548 (13.08%)
LD	36,571 (12.74%)
Green	20,147 (7.02%)
Ind.	19,256 (6.71%)
SSCUP	4,176 (1.45%)
Solidarity	2,998 (1.04%)
BNP	2,637 (0.92%)
Soc. Lab.	2,190 (0.76%)
Scottish Christian Party	2,002 (0.70%)
SSP	1,994 (0.69%)
Publican Party Smoking-Room in Pubs	1,230 (0.43%)
Witchery Tour Party	867 (0.30%)
CPA	848 (0.30%)
UKIP	834 (0.29%)
Had Enough Party	670 (0.23%)
Scottish Voice	661 (0.23%)
Scotland Against Crooked Lawyers	322 (0.11%)
Ind. Scott	189 (0.07%)
Scottish Enterprise Party	183 (0.06%)
Ind. Wilson	129 (0.04%)
Ind. Thorp	73 (0.03%)

SNP majority 524 (0.18%)
4.22% swing Lab. to SNP (2003 Lab. majority 21,960)

ADDITIONAL MEMBERS
Gavin Brown, *C.*
George Foulkes, *Lab.*
Fiona Hyslop, *SNP*
Ian McKee, *SNP*
Stefan Tymkewycz, *SNP*
Robin Harper, *Green*
Margo MacDonald, *Ind.*

SCOTLAND CENTRAL
E. 559,452 T. 284,512 (50.86%)

Lab.	112,596 (39.58%)
SNP	89,210 (31.36%)
C.	24,253 (8.52%)
LD	14,648 (5.15%)
Green	7,204 (2.53%)
SSCUP	7,060 (2.48%)
Scottish Christian Party	5,575 (1.96%)
Solidarity	5,012 (1.76%)
CPA	4,617 (1.62%)
BNP	4,125 (1.45%)
Soc. Lab.	2,303 (0.81%)
SSP	2,188 (0.77%)
Scottish Voice	1,955 (0.69%)
Scottish Unionist Party	1,544 (0.54%)
Publican Party Smoking-Room in Pubs	1,500 (0.53%)
UKIP	722 (0.25%)

Lab. majority 23,386 (8.22%)
4.83% swing Lab. to SNP (2003 Lab. majority 47,044)

ADDITIONAL MEMBERS
Margaret Mitchell, *C.*
Hugh O'Donnell, *LD*
Alex Neil, *SNP*
Linda Fabiani, *SNP*
Jamie Hepburn, *SNP*
Christina McKelvie, *SNP*
John Wilson, *SNP*

SCOTLAND MID AND FIFE
E. 513,443 T. 273,083 (53.19%)
SNP	90,090	(32.99%)
Lab.	71,922	(26.34%)
C.	44,341	(16.24%)
LD	36,195	(13.25%)
Green	10,318	(3.78%)
SSCUP	5,523	(2.02%)
BNP	2,620	(0.96%)
Solidarity	2,468	(0.90%)
Scottish Christian Party	1,698	(0.62%)
UKIP	1,587	(0.58%)
Soc. Lab.	1,523	(0.56%)
Publican Party Smoking-Room in Pubs	1,309	(0.48%)
SSP	1,116	(0.41%)
Scottish Voice	919	(0.34%)
CPA	790	(0.29%)
Free Scotland Party	664	(0.24%)

SNP majority 18,168 (6.65%)
4.45% swing Lab. to SNP (2003 Lab. majority 5,608)

ADDITIONAL MEMBERS
Murdo Fraser, *C.*
Liz Smith, *C.*
Ted Brocklebank, *C.*
John Park, *Lab.*
Claire Baker, *Lab.*
Richard Simpson, *Lab.*
Chris Harvie, *SNP*

SCOTLAND NORTH EAST
E. 506,660 T. 256,282 (50.58%)
SNP	105,265	(41.07%)
Lab.	52,125	(20.34%)
LD	40,934	(15.97%)
C.	37,666	(14.70%)
Green	8,148	(3.18%)
BNP	2,764	(1.08%)
Solidarity	2,004	(0.78%)
Scottish Christian Party	1,895	(0.74%)
CPA	1,173	(0.46%)
SSP	1,051	(0.41%)
UKIP	1,045	(0.41%)
SSCUP	930	(0.36%)
Scottish Voice	569	(0.22%)
Soc. Lab.	491	(0.19%)
Scottish Enterprise Party	222	(0.09%)

SNP majority 53,140 (20.73%)
6.82% swing Lab. to SNP (2003 SNP majority 17,274)

ADDITIONAL MEMBERS
Alex Johnstone, *C.*
Nanette Milne, *C.*
Richard Baker, *Lab.*
Marlyn Glen, *Lab.*
Alison McInnes, *LD*
Maureen Watt, *SNP*
Nigel Don, *SNP*

SCOTLAND SOUTH
E. 514,105 T. 276,910 (53.86%)
Lab.	79,762	(28.80%)
SNP	77,053	(27.83%)
C.	62,475	(22.56%)
LD	28,040	(10.13%)
Green	9,254	(3.34%)
SSCUP	5,335	(1.93%)
Solidarity	3,433	(1.24%)
BNP	3,212	(1.16%)
Scottish Christian Party	2,353	(0.85%)
Soc. Lab.	1,633	(0.59%)
UKIP	1,429	(0.52%)
SSP	1,114	(0.40%)
CPA	839	(0.30%)
Scottish Voice	490	(0.18%)
Ind.	488	(0.18%)

Lab. majority 2,709 (0.98%)
5.32% swing Lab. to SNP (2003 Lab. majority 15,128)

ADDITIONAL MEMBERS
Derek Brownlee, *C.*
Jim Hume, *LD*
Christine Grahame, *SNP*
Michael Russell, *SNP*
Adam Ingram, *SNP*
Alasdair Morgan, *SNP*
Aileen Campbell, *SNP*

SCOTLAND WEST
E. 475,073 T. 268,179 (56.45%)
Lab.	91,725	(34.20%)
SNP	75,953	(28.32%)
C.	40,637	(15.15%)
LD	22,515	(8.40%)
Green	8,152	(3.04%)
SSCUP	5,231	(1.95%)
Solidarity	4,774	(1.78%)
Scottish Christian Party	3,729	(1.39%)
BNP	3,241	(1.21%)
CPA	3,027	(1.13%)
Save Our NHS Group	2,682	(1.00%)
SSP	1,716	(0.64%)
Soc. Lab.	1,557	(0.58%)
Scottish Unionist Party	1,245	(0.46%)
UKIP	888	(0.33%)
Scottish Voice	522	(0.19%)
Scottish Jacobite Party	446	(0.17%)
Socialist Equality Party	139	(0.05%)

Lab. majority 15,772 (5.88%)
2.70% swing Lab. to SNP (2003 Lab. majority 12,351)

ADDITIONAL MEMBERS
Annabel Goldie, *C.*
Jackson Carlaw, *C.*
Ross Finnie, *LD*
Stewart Maxwell, *SNP*
Gil Paterson, *SNP*
Bill Wilson, *SNP*
Stuart McMillan, *SNP*

NORTHERN IRELAND

NORTHERN IRELAND ASSEMBLY

Parliament Buildings, Stormont, Belfast BT4 3XX
T 028-9052 1333 F 028-9052 1961
W www.niassembly.gov.uk

The Northern Ireland Assembly was established as a result of the Belfast Agreement (also known as the Good Friday Agreement) in April 1998. The agreement was endorsed through a referendum held in May 1998 and subsequently given legal force through the Northern Ireland Act 1998.

The Northern Ireland Assembly has full legislative and executive authority for all matters that are the responsibility of the government's Northern Ireland departments – known as transferred matters. Excepted and reserved matters are defined in schedules 2 and 3 of the Northern Ireland Act 1998 and remain the responsibility of UK parliament.

The first assembly election occurred on 25 June 1998 and the 108 members elected met for the first time on 1 July 1998. The 108 members are elected by the single transferable vote system from 18 constituencies – six per constituency. The first minister and deputy first minister head the executive committee of ministers and, acting jointly, determine the total number of ministers in the executive. First and deputy first ministers are elected by members through a formula of parallel consent that requires a majority of designated unionists, a majority of designated nationalists and a majority of the whole assembly. The parties elected to the assembly select ministerial portfolios in proportion to party strengths using the d'Hondt nominating procedure.

On 29 November 1999 the assembly appointed ten ministers as well as the chairs and deputy chairs for the ten statutory departmental committees. Devolution of powers to the Northern Ireland Assembly occurred on 2 December 1999, following several delays concerned with Sinn Fein's inclusion in the executive while Irish Republican Army (IRA) weapons were yet to be decommissioned.

Since the devolution of powers, the assembly has been suspended by the Secretary of State for Northern Ireland on four occasions. The first was between 11 February and 30 May 2000, with two 24-hour suspensions on 10 August and 22 September 2001– all owing to a lack of progress in decommissioning. The final suspension took place on 14 October 2002 after unionists walked out of the executive following a police raid on Sinn Fein's office investigating alleged intelligence gathering.

The assembly was formally dissolved in April 2003 in anticipation of an election, which eventually took place on 26 November 2003. The results of the election changed the balance of power between the political parties, with an increase in the number of seats held by the Democratic Unionist Party (DUP) and Sinn Fein (SF), so that they became the largest parties. The assembly was restored to a state of suspension following the November election while political parties engaged in a review of the Belfast Agreement aimed at fully restoring the devolved institutions.

In July 2005 the leadership of the IRA formally ordered an end to its armed campaign; it authorised a representative to engage with the Independent International Commission on Decommissioning in order to verifiably put the arms beyond use. On 26 September 2005 General John de Chastelain, the chair of the commission, along with two independent church witnesses confirmed that the IRA's entire arsenal of weapons had been decommissioned.

Following the passing of the Northern Ireland Act 2006 the secretary of state created a non-legislative fixed-term assembly, whose membership consisted of the 108 members elected in the 2003 election. It first met on 15 May 2006 with the remit of making preparations for the restoration of devolved government; its discussions informed the next round of talks called by the British and Irish governments held at St Andrews. The St Andrews agreement of 13 October 2006 led to the establishment of the transitional assembly.

The Northern Ireland (St Andrews Agreement) Act 2006 set out a timetable to restore devolution, and also set the date for the third election to the assembly as 7 March 2007. The DUP and SF again had the largest number of Members of the Legislative Assembly (MLAs) elected, and although the initial restoration deadline of 26 March was missed, the leaders of the DUP and SF (Revd Dr Ian Paisley, MP, MLA and Gerry Adams, MLA, respectively) took part in a historic meeting and made a joint commitment to establish an executive committee in the assembly to which devolved powers were restored on 8 May 2007.

SALARIES *as at May 2007*
Assembly Member   £31,817

NORTHERN IRELAND EXECUTIVE

Stormont Castle, Stormont, Belfast BT4 3TT
T 028-9052 0700 F 028-9052 8195
W www.northernireland.gov.uk

The executive committee includes five DUP ministers, four SF ministers, two Ulster Unionist members, one Social Democratic and Labour Party minister alongside the first minister, Ian Paisley MP, MLA, of the DUP, and the deputy first minister, Martin McGuinness, MLA, of SF.

EXECUTIVE COMMITTEE
First Minister, Rt. Hon. Revd Ian Paisley, MP, MLA
Deputy First Minister, Martin McGuinness, MP, MLA
Junior Ministers, Gerry Kelly, MLA; Ian Paisley Jr, MLA
Minister for Agriculture and Rural Development, Michelle Gildernew, MP, MLA
Minister for Culture, Arts and Leisure, Edwin Poots, MLA
Minister for Education, Caitriona Ruane, MLA
Minister for Employment and Learning, Sir Reg Empey, MLA
Minister for Enterprise, Trade and Investment, Nigel Dodds, OBE, MP, MLA
Minister for Environment, Arlene Foster, MLA
Minister for Finance and Personnel, Rt. Hon. Peter Robinson, MP, MLA
Minister for Health, Social Services and Public Safety, Michael McGimpsey, MLA
Minister for Regional Development, Conor Murphy, MP, MLA
Minister for Social Development, Margaret Ritchie, MLA

OFFICE OF THE FIRST MINISTER AND DEPUTY FIRST MINISTER
Stormont Castle, Stormont, Belfast BT4 3TT
T 028-9052 8400 W www.ofmdfmni.gov.uk

DEPARTMENT OF AGRICULTURE AND RURAL DEVELOPMENT
Dundonald House, Upper Newtownards Road, Belfast BT4 3SB
T 028-9052 0100 W www.dardni.gov.uk

EXECUTIVE AGENCIES
Forest Service
Rivers Agency

DEPARTMENT OF CULTURE, ARTS AND LEISURE
Interpoint, 20–24 York Street, Belfast BT15 1AQ
T 028-9025 8825 W www.dcalni.gov.uk

EXECUTIVE AGENCIES
Ordnance Survey of Northern Ireland
Public Record Office of Northern Ireland

DEPARTMENT OF EDUCATION
Rathgael House, Balloo Road, Bangor, Co. Down BT19 7PR
T 028-9127 9279 W www.deni.gov.uk

DEPARTMENT FOR EMPLOYMENT AND LEARNING
Adelaide House, 39–49 Adelaide Street, Belfast BT2 8FD
T 028-9025 7777 W www.delni.gov.uk

DEPARTMENT OF ENTERPRISE, TRADE AND INVESTMENT
Netherleigh, Massey Avenue, Belfast BT4 2JP
T 028-9052 9900 F 028-9052 9550
W www.detini.gov.uk

EXECUTIVE AGENCY
Health and Safety Executive

DEPARTMENT OF THE ENVIRONMENT
Clarence Court, 10–18 Adelaide Street, Belfast BT2 8GB
T 028-9054 0540 W www.doeni.gov.uk

EXECUTIVE AGENCIES
Driver and Vehicle Agency (Northern Ireland)
Environment and Heritage Service
Planning Service

DEPARTMENT OF FINANCE AND PERSONNEL
Rathgael House, Balloo Road, Bangor BT19 7PR
T 028-9185 8111 W www.dfpni.gov.uk

EXECUTIVE AGENCIES
Land Registers of Northern Ireland
Northern Ireland Statistics and Research Agency*
Land and Property Services
* Incorporates the General Register Office (Northern Ireland)

DEPARTMENT OF HEALTH, SOCIAL SERVICES AND PUBLIC SAFETY
Castle Buildings, Stormont, Belfast BT4 3SJ T 028-9052 0500
W www.dhsspsni.gov.uk

EXECUTIVE AGENCY
Northern Ireland Health and Social Services Agency

DEPARTMENT FOR REGIONAL DEVELOPMENT
Clarence Court, 10–18 Adelaide Street, Belfast BT2 8GB
T 028-9054 0540 W www.drdni.gov.uk

EXECUTIVE AGENCY
Roads Agency

DEPARTMENT FOR SOCIAL DEVELOPMENT
Lighthouse Building, 1 Cromac Place, Gasworks Business Park,
Ormeau Road, Belfast BT7 2JB T 028-9082 9028
W www.dsdni.gov.uk

NORTHERN IRELAND AUDIT OFFICE
106 University Street, Belfast BT7 1EU
T 028-9025 1000 F 028-9025 1106

E info@niauditoffice.gov.uk W www.niauditoffice.gov.uk
Comptroller and Auditor-General for Northern Ireland, J. M. Dowdall, CB

NORTHERN IRELAND AUTHORITY FOR ENERGY REGULATION
Queens House, 10–14 Queen Street, Belfast BT1 6ER
T 028-9031 1575 F 028-9031 1740
E ofreg@nics.gov.uk W http://ofreg.nics.gov.uk
Chair, Prof. Peter Matthews

NORTHERN IRELAND ASSEMBLY MEMBERS
as at 8 May 2007
Adams, Gerry, *SF, West Belfast*
Anderson, Martina, *SF, Foyle*
Armstrong, Billy, *UUP, Mid Ulster*
Attwood, Alex, *SDLP, West Belfast*
Beggs, Roy, *UUP, East Antrim*
Boylan, Cathal, *SF, Newry and Armagh*
Bradley, Dominic, *SDLP, Newry and Armagh*
Bradley, Mary, *SDLP, Foyle*
Bradley, P. J., *SDLP, South Down*
Brady, Mickey, *SF, Newry and Armagh*
Bresland, Allan, *DUP, West Tyrone*
Brolly, Francie, *SF, East Londonderry*
Browne of Belmont, Lord, *DUP, East Belfast*
Buchanan, Thomas, *DUP, West Tyrone*
Burns, Thomas, *SDLP, South Antrim*
Burnside, David, *UUP, South Antrim*
Butler, Paul, *SF, Lagan Valley*
Campbell, Gregory, *DUP, East Londonderry*
Clarke, Trevor, *DUP, South Antrim*
Clarke, Willie, *SF, South Down*
Cobain, Fred, *UUP, North Belfast*
Coulter, Revd Dr Robert, *UUP, North Antrim*
Craig, Jonathan, *DUP, Lagan Valley*
Cree, Leslie, *UUP, North Down*
Dallat, John, *SDLP, East Londonderry*
Deeny, Dr Kieran, *Ind., West Tyrone*
Dodds, Nigel, *DUP, North Belfast*
Doherty, Pat, *SF, West Tyrone*
Donaldson, Jeffrey, *DUP, Lagan Valley*
Durkan, Mark, *SDLP, Foyle*
Easton, Alex, *DUP, North Down*
Elliot, Tom, *UUP, Fermanagh and South Tyrone*
Empey, Sir Reg, *UUP, East Belfast*
Farry, Stephen, *All., North Down*
Ford, David, *All., South Antrim*
Foster, Arlene, *DUP, Fermanagh and South Tyrone*
Gallagher, Tommy, *SDLP, Fermanagh and South Tyrone*
Gardiner, Samuel, *UUP, Upper Bann*
Gildernew, Michelle, *SF, Fermanagh and South Tyrone*
Hamilton, Simon, *DUP, Strangford*
Hanna, Carmel, *SDLP, South Belfast*
Hay, William, *DUP, Foyle*
Hilditch, David, *DUP, East Antrim*
Irwin, William, *DUP, Newry and Armagh*
Kelly, Dolores, *SDLP, Upper Bann*
Kelly, Gerry, *SF, North Belfast*
Kennedy, Danny, *UUP, Newry and Armagh*
Lo, Anna, *All., South Belfast*
Long, Naomi, *All., East Belfast*
Lunn, Trevor, *All., Lagan Valley*
Maginness, Alban, *SDLP, North Belfast*
Maskey, Alex, *SF, South Belfast*
Maskey, Paul, *SF, West Belfast*
McCallister, John, *UUP, South Down*
McCann, Fra, *SF, West Belfast*

McCann, Jennifer, *SF, West Belfast*
McCarthy, Kieran, *All., Strangford*
McCartney, Raymond, *SF, Foyle*
McCausland, Nelson, *DUP, North Belfast*
McClarty, David, *UUP, East Londonderry*
McCrea, Basil, *UUP, Lagan Valley*
McCrea, Ian, *DUP, Mid Ulster*
McCrea, Dr William, *DUP, South Antrim*
McDonnell, Dr Alasdair, *SDLP, South Belfast*
McElduff, Barry, *SF, West Tyrone*
McFarland, Alan, *UUP, North Down*
McGill, Claire, *SF, West Tyrone*
McGimpsey, Michael, *UUP, South Belfast*
McGlone, Patsy, *SDLP, Mid Ulster*
McGuinness, Martin, *SF, Mid Ulster*
McHugh, Gerry, *SF, Fermanagh and South Tyrone*
McIlveen, Michelle, *DUP, Strangford*
McKay, Daithí, *SF, North Antrim*
McLaughlin, Mitchel, *SF, South Antrim*
McNarry, David, *UUP, Strangford*
McQuillan, Adrian, *DUP, East Londonderry*
Molloy, Francie, *SF, Mid Ulster*
Morrow, Lord, *DUP, Fermanagh and South Tyrone*
Moutray, Stephen, *DUP, Upper Bann*
Murphy, Conor, *SF, Newry and Armagh*
Neeson, Sean, *All., East Antrim*
Newton, Robin, *DUP, East Belfast*
Ní Chuilín, Carál, *SF, North Belfast*
O'Dowd, John, *SF, Upper Bann*
O'Loan, Declan, *SDLP, North Antrim*
O'Neill, Michelle, *SF, Mid Ulster*
Paisley, Revd Dr Ian, PC, *DUP, North Antrim*
Paisley, Ian Jr, *DUP, North Antrim*
Poots, Edwin, *DUP, Lagan Valley*
Purvis, Dawn, *PUP, East Belfast*
Ramsey, Pat, *SDLP, Foyle*
Ramsey, Sue, *SF, West Belfast*
Ritchie, Margaret, *SDLP, South Down*
Robinson, George, *DUP, East Londonderry*
Robinson, Iris, *DUP, Strangford*
Robinson, Ken, *UUP, East Antrim*
Robinson, Peter, *DUP, East Belfast*
*Ross, Alastair, *DUP, East Antrim*
Ruane, Caitriona, *SF, South Down*
Savage, George, *UUP, Upper Bann*
Shannon, Jim, *DUP, Strangford*
Simpson, David, *DUP, Upper Bann*
Spratt, Jimmy, *DUP, South Belfast*
Storey, Mervyn, *DUP, North Antrim*
Weir, Peter, *DUP, North Down*
Wells, Jim, *DUP, South Down*
Wilson, Brian, *Green, North Down*
Wilson, Sammy, *DUP, East Antrim*

* George Dawson died on 7 May 2007 and was replaced by Alastair Ross, whose appointment was notified by the Chief Electoral Officer with effect from 14 May 2007

POLITICAL COMPOSITION

Democratic Unionist Party (DUP)	36
Sinn Fein (SF)	28
Ulster Unionist Party (UUP)	18
Social Democratic and Labour Party (SDLP)	16
Alliance Party (Alliance)	7
Independent (Ind.)	1
Progressive Unionist Party (PUP)	1
Green Party	1

NORTHERN IRELAND ASSEMBLY ELECTION RESULTS
as at March 2007

E. Electorate T. Turnout
First = first-preference votes
Final = final total for that candidate, after all necessary transfers of lower-preference votes
See General Election Results for a list of party abbreviations

ANTRIM EAST
E. 56,666 T. 30,293

(53.46%)	First	Final	Elected (Round)
Sammy Wilson, DUP	6,755	6,755	First (1)
George Dawson, DUP	4,167	4,777	Second (2)
Sean Neeson, Alliance	3,114	5,191	Fourth (10)
Roy Beggs, UUP	3,076	5,115	Fifth (12)
David Hilditch, DUP	2,732	4,587	Third (3)
Ken Robinson, UUP	1,881	4,195	Sixth (13)
Danny O'Connor, SDLP *(Eliminated last)*	1,769	3,298	
Stewart Dickson, Alliance	1,624		
Mark Dunn, UUP	1,617		
Oliver McMullan, SF	1,168		
Tom Robinson, UK Unionist Party	731		
Mark Bailey, Green	612		
John Anderson, Ind.	398		
Tim Lewis, C.	395		

ANTRIM NORTH
E. 72,814 T. 44,655

(61.33%)	First	Final	Elected (Round)
Revd Ian Paisley, DUP	7,716	7,716	First (1)
Daithi McKay, SF	7,065	7,065	Second (1)
Ian Paisley Jr, DUP	6,106	7,264	Third (2)
Mervyn Storey, DUP	5,171	6,924	Fifth (8)
Revd Robert Coulter, UUP	5,047	6,579	Fourth (7)
Declan O'Loan, SDLP	3,281	6,498	Sixth (10)
Deirdre Nelson, DUP *(Eliminated last)*	2,740	4,092	
Orla Black, SDLP	2,129		
Lyle Cubitt, UK Unionist Party	1,848		
Robert Swann, UUP	1,281		
Jayne Dunlop, Alliance	1,254		
Paul McGlinchey, Ind.	383		
James Gregg, Ind.	310		

ANTRIM SOUTH
E. 65,654 T. 38,481

(58.61%)	First	Final	Elected (Round)
Mitchel McLaughlin, SF	6,313	6,313	First (1)
Revd William McCrea, DUP	6,023	6,023	Second (1)
David Ford, Alliance	5,007	5,495	Third (5)
David Burnside, UUP	4,507	6,926	Fourth (7)
Trevor Clarke, DUP	4,302	5,544	Fifth (8)
Mel Lucas, DUP *(Eliminated last)*	2,840	4,429	
Thomas Burns, SDLP	2,721	5,396	Sixth (8)
Danny Kinahan, UUP	2,391		
Noreen McClelland, SDLP	1,526		
Stephen Nicholl, UUP	927		

Robert McCartney, UK
Unionist Party 893
Pete Whitcroft, Green ... 507
Stephen O'Brien, C. 129
Marcella Delaney, WP 89

BELFAST EAST
E. 49,757 T. 29,873

	First	Final	Elected (Round)
(60.04%)			
Peter Robinson, DUP	5,635	5,635	First (1)
Naomi Long, Alliance	5,585	5,585	Second (1)
Sir Reg Empey, UUP	4,139	4,620	Third (3)
Lord Wallace Browne, DUP	3,185	3,734	Fifth (10)
Dawn Purvis, Progressive Unionist Party	3,045	4,208	Fourth (10)
Robin Newton, DUP	2,335	3,517	Sixth (10)
Michael Copeland, UUP (Eliminated last)	1,557	2,999	
Niall O'Donnghaile, SF	1,055		
Jim Rodgers, UUP	820		
Mary Muldoon, SDLP	816		
Steve Agnew, Green	653		
Glyn Chambers, C.	427		
Thomas Black, Socialist Party	225		
Joe Bell, WP	107		
Rainbow George, Make Politicians History	47		

BELFAST NORTH
E. 49,372 T. 30,067

	First	Final	Elected (Round)
(60.90%)			
Nigel Dodds, DUP	6,973	6,973	First (1)
Gerry Kelly, SF	5,414	5,414	Second (1)
Caral Ni Chuilin, SF	3,680	4,587	Third (3)
Fred Cobain, UUP	2,498	3,967	Fifth (10)
Nelson McCausland, DUP	2,462	3,818	Sixth (10)
Alban Maginness, SDLP	2,212	4,830	Fourth (9)
Pat Convery, SDLP	1,868		
William Humphrey, DUP (Eliminated last)	1,673	3,327	
Raymond McCord, Ind.	1,320		
Peter Emerson, Green	590		
Tommy McCullough, Alliance	486		
Robert McCartney, UK Unionist Party	360		
John Lavery, WP	139		
Rainbow George, Make Politicians History	40		

BELFAST SOUTH
E. 48,923 T. 30,533

	First	Final	Elected (Round)
(62.41%)			
Jimmy Spratt, DUP	4,762	4,762	First (1)
Dr Alasdair McDonnell, SDLP	4,379	4,379	Second (1)
Alex Maskey, SF	3,996	4,167	Sixth (10)
Anna Lo, Alliance	3,829	4,415	Third (8)
Carmel Hanna, SDLP	3,748	4,262	Fifth (10)
Michael McGimpsey, UUP	2,647	4,927	Fourth (10)
Christopher Stalford, DUP (Eliminated last)	2,035	3,275	

Dr Esmond Birnie, UUP 1,804
Bob Stoker, UUP 1,122
Brenda Cooke, Green 737
Andrew Park, Progressive Unionist Party .. 410
David Hoey, UK Unionist Party ... 298
Jim Barbour, Socialist Party ... 248
Paddy Lynn, WP 123
Roger Lomas, C. 108
Rainbow George, Make Politicians History .. 66
Charles Smyth, Pro-Capitalism .. 22
Geoffrey Wilson, Ind. 10

BELFAST WEST
E. 50,792 T. 34,238

	First	Final	Elected (Round)
(67.41%)			
Gerry Adams, SF	6,029	6,029	First (1)
Sue Ramsey, SF	4,715	5,267	Second (2)
Paul Maskey, SF	4,368	5,075	Third (6)
Jennifer McCann, SF	4,265	4,849	Fourth (6)
Fra McCann, SF	4,254	4,647	Sixth (6)
Diane Dodds, DUP (Eliminated last)	3,661	4,166	
Alex Attwood, SDLP	3,036	4,779	Fifth (6)
Margaret Walsh, SDLP	1,074		
Sean Mitchell, People Before Profit	774		
Louis West, UUP	558		
John Lowry, WP	434		
Geraldine Taylor, Republican Sinn Fein	427		
Dan McGuinness, Alliance	127		
Rainbow George, Make Politicians History	68		

DOWN NORTH
E. 57,525 T. 30,930

	First	Final	Elected (Round)
(53.77%)			
Alex Easton, DUP	4,946	4,946	First (1)
Peter Weir, DUP	3,376	4,380	Fifth (10)
Stephen Farry, Alliance	3,131	4,466	Second (8)
Leslie Cree, UUP	2,937	4,687	Third (10)
Brian Wilson, Green	2,839	4,572	Fourth (10)
Alan McFarland, UUP	2,245	3,986	Sixth (10)
Alan Graham, DUP (Eliminated last)	2,147	3,255	
Marion Smith, UUP	2,098		
Robert McCartney, UK Unionist Party	1,806		
Brian Rowan, Ind.	1,194		
Alan Chambers, Ind.	1,129		
Liam Logan, SDLP	1,115		
James Leslie, C.	864		
Deaglan Page, SF	390		
Elaine Martin, Progressive Unionist Party	367		
Chris Carter, Ind.	123		

DOWN SOUTH

E. 71,704 T. 46,623

(65.02%)	First	Final	Elected (Round)
Catriona Ruane, SF	6,334	6,676	First (7)
Margaret Ritchie, SDLP	5,838	6,945	Third (8)
P. J. Bradley, SDLP	5,652	6,650	Fourth (9)
Jim Wells, DUP	5,542	8,463	Fifth (10)
Willie Clarke, SF	5,138	7,382	Second (8)
John McCallister, UUP	4,447	7,721	Sixth (11)
Michael Carr, SDLP (Eliminated last)	2,972	3,883	
Eamonn McConvey, SF	2,662		
William Burns, DUP	2,611		
Ciaran Mussen, Green	1,622		
Henry Reilly, UKIP	1,229		
David Griffin, Alliance	691		
Martin Cunningham, Ind.	434		
Nelson Wharton, UK Unionist Party	424		
Peter Bowles, C.	391		
Malachi Curran, Lab.	123		

FERMANAGH AND SOUTH TYRONE

E. 65,826 T. 46,845

(71.16%)	First	Final	Elected (Round)
Arlene Foster, DUP	7,138	7,138	First (1)
Michelle Gildernew, SF	7,026	7,026	Second (1)
Tom Elliott, UUP	6,603	6,680	Third (2)
Gerry McHugh, SF	5,103	5,777	Sixth (8)
Sean Lynch, SF (Eliminated last)	4,704	5,188	
Lord Morrow, DUP	4,700	7,014	Fifth (8)
Tommy Gallagher, SDLP	4,440	6,640	Fourth (7)
Kenny Donaldson, UUP	2,531		
Vincent Currie, SDLP	2,043		
Gerry McGeough, Ind.	814		
Allan Leonard, Alliance	521		
Michael McManus, Republican Sinn Fein	431		
Robert McCartney, UK Unionist Party	388		

FOYLE

E. 64,889 T. 41,455

(63.89%)	First	Final	Elected (Round)
William Hay, DUP	6,960	6,960	First (1)
Mark Durkan, SDLP	6,401	6,401	Second (1)
Martina Anderson, SF	5,414	5,972	Third (6)
Raymond McCartney, SF	4,321	7,275	Fourth (8)
Pat Ramsey, SDLP	3,242	5,396	Fifth (10)
Lynn Fleming, SF	2,914		
Mary Bradley, SDLP	2,891	4,419	Sixth (10)
Helen Quigley, SDLP (Eliminated last)	2,648		
Eamonn McCann, Socialist Environmental Alliance	2,045		
Peggy O'Hara, Ind.	1,789		
Peter Munce, UUP	1,755		
Adele Corry, Green	359		
Yvonne Boyle, Alliance	224		
Willie Frazer, Ind.	73		

LAGAN VALLEY

E. 70,101 T. 42,058

(60.00%)	First	Final	Elected (Round)
Jeffrey Donaldson, DUP	9,793	9,793	First (1)
Paul Butler, SF	5,098	6,387	Second (6)
Basil McCrea, UUP	4,031	6,712	Third (7)
Trevor Lunn, Alliance	3,765	6,264	Fourth (7)
Jonathan Craig, DUP	3,471	6,147	Fifth (8)
Edwin Poots, DUP	3,457	5,386	Sixth (9)
Paul Givan, DUP (Eliminated last)	3,377	4,728	
Marietta Farrell, SDLP	2,839		
Billy Bell, UUP	2,599		
Ronnie Crawford, UUP	1,147		
Michael Rogan, Green	922		
Robert McCartney, UK Unionist Party	853		
Neil Johnston, C.	387		
John Magee, WP	83		

LONDONDERRY EAST

E. 56,104 T. 34,180

(60.92%)	First	Final	Elected (Round)
Gregory Campbell, DUP	6,845	6,845	First (1)
Francie Brolly, SF	4,476	5,003	Third (7)
George Robinson, DUP	3,991	4,869	Second (5)
David McClarty, UUP	2,875	4,409	Fifth (9)
Adrian McQuillan, DUP	2,650	4,074	Sixth (9)
John Dallat, SDLP	2,638	6,380	Fourth (8)
Billy Leonard, SF	2,321		
Norman Hillis, UUP (Eliminated last)	2,054	3,195	
Orla Beattie, SDLP	1,797		
Barney Fitzpatrick, Alliance	1,401		
Edwin Stevenson, UUP	1,338		
Leslie Cubitt, UK Unionist Party	549		
Phillippe Moison, Green	521		
Michael McGonigle, Republican Sinn Fein	393		
Victor Christie, Ind.	73		

NEWRY AND ARMAGH

E. 70,823 T. 50,165

(70.83%)	First	Final	Elected (Round)
Conor Murphy, SF	7,437	7,437	First (1)
Cathal Boylan, SF	7,105	7,105	Second (1)
Danny Kennedy, UUP	6,517	7,653	Fifth (5)
William Irwin, DUP	6,418	8,008	Fourth (5)
Mickey Brady, SF	6,337	7,514	Third (4)
Dominic Bradley, SDLP	5,318	6,311	Sixth (7)
Sharon Haughey, SDLP (Eliminated last)	4,500	5,368	
Paul Berry, Ind.	2,317		
Davy Hyland, Ind.	2,188		
Willie Frazer, Ind.	605		
Arthur Morgan, Green	599		
Maire Hendron, Alliance	278		

STRANGFORD

E. 66,648 T. 36,340

(54.53%)	First	Final	Elected (Round)
Iris Robinson, DUP	5,917	5,917	First (1)
Jim Shannon, DUP	4,788	5,178	Second (6)
Kieran McCarthy, Alliance	4,085	5,207	Third (9)

	First	Final	Round
Simon Hamilton, DUP	3,889	4,998	Fifth (13)
David McNarry, UUP	3,709	6,036	Fourth (10)
Michelle McIlveen, DUP	3,468	4,579	Sixth (13)
Joe Boyle, SDLP *(Eliminated last)*	3,068	4,548	
Angus Carson, UUP	2,128		
Dermot Kennedy, SF	1,089		
George Ennis, UK Unionist Party	872		
Stephanie Sim, Green	868		
Michael Henderson, UUP	675		
David Gregg, Ind.	650		
Bob Little, C.	508		
Cedric Wilson, Ind.	305		

TYRONE WEST

E. 58,367 T. 41,839 (71.68%)

	First	Final	*Elected (Round)*
Barry McElduff, SF	6,971	6,971	First (1)
Pat Doherty, SF	6,709	6,709	Second (1)
Clare McGill, SF	4,757	6,217	Third (3)
Tom Buchanan, DUP	4,625	6,208	Fourth (6)
Allan Bresland, DUP	4,244	5,543	Sixth (7)
Dr Kieran Deeny, Ind.	3,776	5,616	Fifth (7)
Derek Hussey, UUP	3,686		
Josephine Deehan, SDLP *(Eliminated last)*	2,689	5,186	
Eugene McMenamin, SDLP	2,272		
Seamus Shiels, SDLP	1,057		
Joe O'Neill, Republican Sinn Fein	448		
Robert McCartney, UK Unionist Party	220		

ULSTER MID

E. 61,223 T. 44,728 (73.06%)

	First	Final	*Elected (Round)*
Martin McGuinness, SF	8,065	8,065	First (1)
Ian McCrea, DUP	7,608	7,608	Second (1)
Francie Molloy, SF	6,597	6,597	Third (1)
Michelle O'Neill, SF	6,432	6,432	Fourth (1)
Patsy McGlone, SDLP	4,976	6,430	Fifth (5)
Billy Armstrong, UUP	4,781	6,355	Sixth (7)
Kate Lagan, SDLP *(Eliminated last)*	2,759	3,531	
Walter Millar, UK Unionist Party	1,210		
Ann Forde, DUP	1,021		
Brendan McLaughlin, Republican Sinn Fein	437		
Margaret Marshall, Alliance	221		
Harry Hutchinson, Ind.	170		

UPPER BANN

E. 70,716 T. 43,235 (61.14%)

	First	Final	*Elected (Round)*
John O'Dowd, SF	7,733	7,733	First (1)
David Simpson, DUP	6,828	6,828	Second (1)
Samuel Gardiner, UUP	5,135	7,265	Fourth (9)
Dolores Kelly, SDLP	4,689	6,191	Third (8)
Stephen Moutray, DUP	3,663	7,550	Fifth (11)
Dessie Ward, SF *(Eliminated last)*	3,118	4,732	
Junior McCrum, DUP	2,975		
George Savage, UUP	2,167	5,998	Sixth (12)
Arnold Hatch, UUP	1,815		
David Calvert, No Description	1,332		
Helen Corry, Green	1,156		
Sheila McQuaid, Alliance	798		
Pat McAleenan, SDLP	761		
Barry Toman, Republican Sinn Fein	386		
David Fry, C.	248		
Suzanne Peeples, Ind.	78		

LOCAL GOVERNMENT

Major changes in local government were introduced in England and Wales in 1974 and in Scotland in 1975 by the Local Government Act 1972 and the Local Government (Scotland) Act 1973. Further significant alterations were made in England by the Local Government Acts of 1985, 1992 and 2000.

The structure in England was based on two tiers of local authorities (county councils and district councils) in the non-metropolitan areas; and a single tier of metropolitan councils in the six metropolitan areas of England and London borough councils in London.

Following reviews of the structure of local government in England by the Local Government Commission, 46 unitary (all-purpose) authorities were created between April 1995 and April 1998 to cover certain areas in the non-metropolitan counties. The remaining county areas continue to have two tiers of local authorities. The county and district councils in the Isle of Wight were replaced by a single unitary authority on 1 April 1995; the former counties of Avon, Cleveland, Humberside and Berkshire were replaced by unitary authorities; and Hereford and Worcester was replaced by a new county council for Worcestershire (with district councils) and a unitary authority for Herefordshire.

The Local Government (Wales) Act 1994 and the Local Government etc (Scotland) Act 1994 abolished the two-tier structure in Wales and Scotland with effect from 1 April 1996, replacing it with a single tier of unitary authorities.

ELECTIONS

Local elections are normally held on the first Thursday in May. Generally, all British subjects, citizens of the Republic of Ireland, Commonwealth and other European Union citizens who are 18 years or over and resident on the qualifying date in the area for which the election is being held, are entitled to vote at local government elections. A register of electors is prepared and published annually by local electoral registration officers.

A returning officer has the overall responsibility for an election. Voting takes place at polling stations, arranged by the local authority and under the supervision of a presiding officer specially appointed for the purpose. Candidates, who are subject to various statutory qualifications and disqualifications designed to ensure that they are suitable to hold office, must be nominated by electors for the electoral area concerned.

In England, the Boundary Committee for England is responsible for carrying out periodic reviews of electoral arrangements and making recommendations to the Electoral Commission.

In Wales and Scotland these matters are the responsibility of the Local Government Boundary Commission for Wales and the Boundary Commission for Scotland respectively. The Local Government Act 2000 provided for the secretary of state to change the frequency and phasing of elections.

THE BOUNDARY COMMITTEE FOR ENGLAND,
Trevelyan House, Great Peter Street, London SW1P 2HW
T 020-7271 0500 W www.boundarycommittee.org.uk

LOCAL GOVERNMENT BOUNDARY COMMISSION
FOR WALES, Caradog House, 1–6 St Andrew's Place,
Cardiff CF10 3BE T 029-2039 5031
W www.lgbc-wales.gov.uk
THE BOUNDARY COMMISSION FOR SCOTLAND,
3 Drumsheugh Gardens, Edinburgh EH3 7QJ
T 0131-538 7200 W www.bcomm-scotland.gov.uk

INTERNAL ORGANISATION

The council as a whole is the final decision-making body within any authority. Councils are free to a great extent to make their own internal organisational arrangements. The Local Government Act, given royal assent on 28 July 2000, allows councils to adopt one of three broad categories of a new constitution which include a separate executive.

These three categories are:
- A directly elected mayor with a cabinet selected by that mayor
- A cabinet, either elected by the council or appointed by its leader
- A directly elected mayor and council manager

Normally, questions of policy are settled by the full council, while the administration of the various services is the responsibility of committees of councillors. Day-to-day decisions are delegated to the council's officers, who act within the policies laid down by the councillors.

FINANCE

Local government in England, Wales and Scotland is financed from four sources: the council tax, non-domestic rates, government grants and income from fees and charges for services.

COUNCIL TAX

Under the Local Government Finance Act 1992, from 1 April 1993 the council tax replaced the community charge (which had been introduced in April 1989 in Scotland and April 1990 in England and Wales in place of domestic rates).

The council tax is a local tax levied by each local council. Liability for the council tax bill usually falls on the owner-occupier or tenant of a dwelling which is their sole or main residence. Council tax bills may be reduced because of the personal circumstances of people resident in a property, and there are discounts in the case of dwellings occupied by fewer than two adults.

In England, each county council, each district council and each police authority sets its own council tax rate. The district councils collect the combined council tax, and the county councils and police authorities claim their share from the district councils' collection funds. In Wales, each unitary authority and each police authority sets its own council tax rate. The unitary authorities collect the combined council tax and the police authorities claim their share from the funds. In Scotland, each local authority sets its own rate of council tax.

The tax relates to the value of the dwelling. In England and Scotland each dwelling is placed in one of eight valuation bands, ranging from A to H, based on the property's estimated market value as at 1 April 1991. In Wales there are nine bands, ranging from A to I, based on the estimated market value of property as at 1 April 2003.

The valuation bands and ranges of values in England, Wales and Scotland are:

England

A	Up to £40,000	E	£88,001–£120,000
B	£40,001–£52,000	F	£120,001–£160,000
C	£52,001–£68,000	G	£160,001–£320,000
D	£68,001–£88,000	H	Over £320,001

Wales

A	Up to £44,000	F	£223,001–£324,000
B	£44,001–£65,000	G	£223,001–£324,000
C	£65,001–£91,000	H	£324,001–£424,000
D	£91,001–£123,000	I	Over £424,001
E	£123,001–£162,000		

Scotland

A	Up to £27,000	E	£58,001–£80,000
B	£27,001–£35,000	F	£80,001–£106,000
C	£35,001–£45,000	G	£106,001–£212,000
D	£45,001–£58,000	H	Over £212,001

The council tax within a local area varies between the different bands according to proportions laid down by law. The charge attributable to each band as a proportion of the Band D charge set by the council is approximately:

A	67%	F	144%
B	78%	G	167%
C	89%	H	200%
D	100%	I	233%*
E	122%		

* Wales only

The average Band D council tax bill for each authority area is given in the tables on the following pages. There may be variations from the given figure within each district council area because of different parish or community precepts being levied.

NON-DOMESTIC RATES
Non-domestic (business) rates are collected by billing authorities; these are the district councils in those areas of England with two tiers of local government and unitary authorities in other parts of England, in Wales and in Scotland. In respect of England and Wales, the Local Government Finance Act 1988 provides for liability for rates to be assessed on the basis of a poundage (multiplier) tax on the rateable value of property (hereditaments). Separate multipliers are set by the Department for Communities and Local Government in England, the Welsh Assembly Government and the Scottish Executive. Rates are collected by the billing authority for the area where a property is located. Rate income collected by billing authorities is paid into a national non-domestic rating (NNDR) pool and redistributed to individual authorities on the basis of the adult population figure as prescribed by the Department for Communities and Local Government, the Welsh Assembly Government or the Scottish Executive. The rates pools are maintained separately in England, Wales and Scotland. Actual payment of rates in certain cases is subject to transitional arrangements, to phase in the larger increases and

reductions in rates resulting from the effects of the latest revaluation.

Rateable values for the 2005 rating lists came into effect on 1 April 2005. They are derived from the rental value of property as at 1 April 2003 and determined on certain statutory assumptions by the Valuation Office Agency in England and Wales, and by local area assessors in Scotland. New property which is added to the list, and significant changes to existing property, necessitate amendments to the rateable value on the same basis. Rating lists (valuation rolls in Scotland) remain in force until the next general revaluation. Such revaluations take place every five years, the next being in 2010.

Certain types of property are exempt from rates, eg agricultural land and buildings, certain businesses and places of public religious worship. Charities and other non-profit-making organisations may receive full or partial relief. The owner or leaseholder of an empty property is liable to pay rates but at a reduced level, except for some types of premises, such as factories, which are entirely exempt.

GOVERNMENT GRANTS
In addition to specific grants in support of revenue expenditure on particular services, central government pays a revenue support grant to local authorities. This grant is paid to each local authority so that if each authority spends at the level of its standard spending assessment, all authorities in the same class can set broadly the same council tax.

COMPLAINTS

ENGLAND
In England the Local Government Ombudsmen investigate complaints of injustice arising from maladministration by local authorities and certain other bodies. The Local Government Ombudsman will not usually consider a complaint unless the local authority concerned has had an opportunity to investigate and reply to a complainant. Details about how to make a complaint are given in *Complaint about the Council?* and *How to complain to the Local Government Ombudsman* from the Commission for Local Administration in England (W www.lgo.org.uk).

The Local Government Act 2000 established a Standards Board and an independent tribunal known as the Adjudication Panel for England. The Standards Board's main task is to ensure that standards of ethical conduct are maintained and to investigate any allegations that councillors have breached the council's Code of Conduct. At the end of the investigation, the case may be referred to either the relevant local authority's standards committee or the Adjudication Panel, which has a number of sanctions at its disposal, up to and including the disqualification of a member from holding office for five years. Unlike the ombudsmen, the Standards Board does not deal with issues of corporate maladministration nor seek to secure financial recompense for complainants.
Local Government Ombudsmen, Tony Redmond, Anne Seex, Jerry White

COMMISSION FOR LOCAL ADMINISTRATION IN ENGLAND, 10th Floor, Millbank Tower, Millbank, London SW1P 4QP T 020-7217 4620
THE STANDARDS BOARD FOR ENGLAND, 4th Floor, Griffin House, 40 Lever Street, Manchester M1 1BB T 0161-817 5300
W www.standardsboard.gov.uk

THE ADJUDICATION PANEL FOR ENGLAND,
23 Victoria Avenue, Harrogate, North Yorkshire HG1 5RD
T 01423-538783 W www.adjudicationpanel.co.uk

WALES

The office of Public Services Ombudsman for Wales came into force on 1 April 2006 incorporating the functions of the Local Government Ombudsman for Wales.
Public Service Ombudsman for Wales, Adam Peat
PUBLIC SERVICES OMBUDSMAN FOR WALES,
1 Ffordd yr Hen Gae, Pencoed CF35 5LJ T 01656-641150
W www.ombudsman-wales.org.uk

SCOTLAND

The Scottish Public Services Ombudsman is responsible for complaints regarding the maladaministration of local government in Scotland.
Scottish Public Services Ombudsman, Prof. Alice Brown
SCOTTISH PUBLIC SERVICES OMBUDSMAN,
Freepost EH641, Edinburgh EH3 0BR T 0800-377 7330
W www.spso.org.uk

NORTHERN IRELAND

The Northern Ireland Commissioner for Complaints fulfils a similar function in Northern Ireland, investigating complaints about local authorities and certain public bodies. Complaints are made to the relevant local authority in the first instance but may also be made directly to the Commissioner.
Northern Ireland Commissioner for Complaints, Tom Frawley
NORTHERN IRELAND COMMISSIONER FOR COMPLAINTS, Freepost BEL 1478, Belfast BT1 6LR
T 0800-343424 W www.ni-ombudsman.org.uk

THE QUEEN'S REPRESENTATIVES

The lord-lieutenant of a county is the permanent local representative of the Crown in that county. The appointment of lord-lieutenants is now regulated by the Lieutenancies Act 1997. They are appointed by the sovereign on the recommendation of the prime minister. The retirement age is 75. The office of lord-lieutenant dates from 1551, and its holder was originally responsible for maintaining order and for local defence in the county. The duties of the post include attending on royalty during official visits to the county, performing certain duties in connection with armed forces of the Crown (and in particular the reserve forces), and making presentations of honours and awards on behalf of the Crown. In England, Wales and Northern Ireland, the lord-lieutenant usually also holds the office of *Custos Rotulorum*. As such, he or she acts as head of the county's commission of the peace (which recommends the appointment of magistrates).

The office of sheriff (from the Old English shire-reeve) of a county was created in the tenth century. The sheriff was the special nominee of the sovereign, and the office reached the peak of its influence under the Norman kings. The Provisions of Oxford (1258) laid down a yearly tenure of office. Since the mid-16th century the office has been purely civil, with military duties taken over by the lord-lieutenant of the county. The sheriff (commonly known as 'high sheriff') attends on royalty during official visits to the county, acts as the returning officer during parliamentary elections in county constituencies, attends the opening ceremony when a high court judge goes on circuit, executes high court writs, and appoints under-sheriffs to act as deputies. The appointments and duties of the sheriffs in England and Wales are laid down by the Sheriffs Act 1887.

The serving high sheriff submits a list of names of possible future sheriffs to a tribunal which chooses three names to put to the sovereign. The tribunal nominates the high sheriff annually on 12 November and the sovereign picks the name of the sheriff to succeed in the following year. The term of office runs from 25 March to the following 24 March (the civil and legal year before 1752). No person may be chosen twice in three years if there is any other suitable person in the county.

CIVIC DIGNITIES

District councils in England may petition for a royal charter granting borough or 'city' status to the district. Local councils in Wales may petition for a royal charter granting county borough or 'city' status to the council.

In England and Wales the chairman of a borough or county borough council may be called a mayor, and the chairman of a city council may be called a lord mayor if lord mayoralty has been conferred on that city. Parish councils in England and community councils in Wales may call themselves 'town councils', in which case their chairman is the town mayor.

In Scotland the chairman of a local council may be known as a convenor; a provost is the mayoral equivalent. The chairmen of the councils for the cities of Aberdeen, Dundee, Edinburgh and Glasgow are lord provosts.

ENGLAND

There are currently 34 counties; all are divided into districts. In addition, there are 46 unitary authorities plus the Isles of Scilly and 238 district councils. The populations of most of the unitary authorities are in the range of 100,000 to 300,000. The district councils have populations broadly in the range of 60,000 to 100,000; some, however, have larger populations, because of the need to avoid dividing large towns, and some in mainly rural areas have smaller populations.

The main conurbations outside Greater London – Tyne and Wear, West Midlands, Merseyside, Greater Manchester, West Yorkshire and South Yorkshire – are divided into 36 metropolitan boroughs, most of which have a population of over 200,000.

There are also about 10,000 parishes, in 219 of the district councils and 18 of the metropolitan boroughs.

ELECTIONS

For districts, counties and for about 8,000 parishes, there are elected councils, consisting of directly elected councillors. The councillors elect annually one of their number as chair.

Generally, councillors serve four years and there are no elections of district and parish councillors in county election years. In metropolitan boroughs, one-third of the councillors for each ward are elected each year except in the year when county elections take place elsewhere. District councils can choose whether to have elections by thirds or whole council elections. In the former case, one-third of the council (or as near as possible) is elected in each year of metropolitan borough elections. If whole council elections are chosen, these are held in the year midway between county elections.

FUNCTIONS

In non-metropolitan areas, functions are divided between the districts and counties (those requiring the larger area or population are generally the responsibility of the county). The metropolitan councils, with the larger population in their areas, already had wider functions than non-metropolitan councils, and following the abolition of the metropolitan county councils were also given most of their functions. A few functions continue to be exercised over the larger area by joint bodies, made up of councillors from each district.

The allocation of functions is as follows:

County councils: education; strategic planning; traffic, transport and highways; fire service; consumer protection; refuse disposal; smallholdings; social services; libraries

District councils: local planning; housing; highways (maintenance of certain urban roads and off-street car parks); building regulations; environmental health; refuse collection; cemeteries and crematoria

Unitary and metropolitan councils: their functions are all those listed above, except that the fire service is exercised by a joint body

Concurrently by county and district councils: recreation (parks, playing fields, swimming pools); museums; encouragement of the arts, tourism and industry

The Police and Magistrates Court Act 1994 set up police authorities in England and Wales separate from the local authorities.

PARISH COUNCILS

Parishes with 200 or more electors must generally have parish councils, which means that over three-quarters of the parishes have councils. A parish council comprises at least five members, the number being fixed by the district council. Elections are held every four years, at the time of the election of the district councillor for the ward including the parish. All parishes have parish meetings comprising the electors of the parish. Where there is no council, the meeting must be held at least twice a year.

Parish council functions include: allotments; encouragement of arts and crafts; community halls; recreational facilities (eg open spaces, swimming pools); cemeteries and crematoria; and many minor functions. They must also be given an opportunity to comment on planning applications. They may, like county and district councils, spend limited sums for the general benefit of the parish. They levy a precept on the district councils for their funds. Parish precepts for 2007–8 totalled £299m, an increase of 6.7 per cent on 2006–7.

REGIONAL ASSEMBLIES

Voluntary regional chambers were established in each of the eight english regions outside London under the Regional Development Agencies Act 1998. The chambers operate within the same boundaries as the Government Offices in the Regions and the Regional Development Agencies.

The Regional Assemblies (Preparations) Act received royal assent on 8 May 2003, giving the chambers responsibility to act as regional planning bodies and to receive direct funding from central government for fulfilling this role. Regional assemblies are mainly funded by central government although some assemblies also receive money from other sources such as local authority subscriptions.

The profile and number of assembly members varies from region to region but under guidance issued by the secretary of state, generally comprises 70 per cent elected local authority councillors and 30 per cent drawn from other sectors, including education, business, arts and culture, faith groups, community, voluntary and environmental organisations.

ROLE OF THE CHAMBERS

All assemblies perform four core functions: acting as regional planning bodies and housing boards, advising the government and European institutions on matters of regional strategic and policy development and scrutinising the work of the Regional Development Agencies. They may also engage in other work according to regional circumstances and priorities. Principal areas of policy development include regional planning and transport, the environment, sustainable development, rural issues and equalities.

EAST MIDLANDS REGIONAL ASSEMBLY, First Floor Suite, Council Offices, Nottingham Road, Melton Mowbray, Leicestershire LE13 0UL T 01664-502555 W www.emra.gov.uk

EAST OF ENGLAND REGIONAL ASSEMBLY, Flempton House, Flempton, Bury St Edmunds, Suffolk IP28 6EG T 01284-728151 W www.eera.gov.uk

NORTH EAST ASSEMBLY, The Axis Building, Kingsway North, Team Valley, Gateshead NE11 0NQ T 0845-673 3343 W www.northeastassembly.gov.uk

NORTH WEST REGIONAL ASSEMBLY, Wigan Investment Centre, Waterside Drive, Wigan WN3 5BA T 01942-737916 W www.nwra.gov.uk

SOUTH EAST ENGLAND REGIONAL ASSEMBLY, Berkeley House, Cross Lanes, Guildford, Surrey GU1 1UN T 01483-555200 W www.southeast-ra.gov.uk

SOUTH WEST REGIONAL ASSEMBLY, Dennett House, 11 Middle Street, Taunton, Somerset TA1 1SH T 01823-270101 W www.southwest-ra.gov.uk

WEST MIDLANDS REGIONAL ASSEMBLY, Regional Partnership Centre, Albert House, Quay Place, 92–93 Edward Street, Birmingham B1 2RA T 0121-245 0200 W www.wmra.gov.uk

YORKSHIRE AND HUMBER ASSEMBLY, 18 King Street, Wakefield, West Yorkshire WF1 2SQ T 01924-331555 W www.yhassembly.gov.uk

The English Regions Network is the umbrella organisation for England's eight regional assemblies (c/o West Midlands Regional Assembly)

FINANCE

Budgeted revenue expenditure in 2007–8 is £97.3bn; 24 per cent of this is to be raised through council tax (£23.6bn), 26 per cent from formula grant (comprises revenue support grant £3.1bn, redistributed business rates £18.5bn and £4.0bn police grant) and 44 per cent from specific grants (estimated at £43bn).

In England, the average council tax per dwelling for 2007–8 is £1,101, up from £1,056 in 2006–7, an increase of 4.3 per cent. The average council tax for 2007–8 is £1,148 in shire areas, £1,167 in London and £919 in metropolitan areas. In England, the average council tax bill for a Band D dwelling (occupied by two adults, including parish precepts) for 2007–8 is £1,321, an average increase of 4.2 per cent from 2006–7. The average Band D council tax is £1,348 in shire areas, £1,284 in metropolitan areas and £1,258 in London. Since 2006–7 the London figure includes a levy to fund the 2012 Olympic Games which equates to a £20 a year increase on Band D council tax.

The provisional amount estimated to be raised from national non-domestic rates from central and local lists is £18.5bn. The non-domestic rating multiplier for England for 2007–8 is 44.4p (44.1p for small businesses). The City of London is able to set a different multiplier from the rest of England; for 2007–8 this is 44.8p (44.5p for small businesses).

Under the Local Government and Housing Act 1989, local authorities have four main ways of paying for capital expenditure: borrowing and other forms of extended credit; capital grants from central government towards some types of capital expenditure; 'usable' capital receipts from the sale of land, houses and other assets; and revenue.

The amount of capital expenditure which a local authority can finance by borrowing (or other forms of credit) is effectively limited by the credit approvals issued to it by central government. Most credit approvals can be used for any kind of local authority capital expenditure; these are known as basic credit approvals. Others (supplementary credit approvals) can be used only for the kind of expenditure specified in the approval, and so are often given to fund particular projects or services.

Local authorities can use all capital receipts from the sale of property or assets for capital spending, except in the case of sales of council houses. Generally, the 'usable' part of a local authority's capital receipts consists of 25 per cent of receipts from the sale of council houses and 50 per cent of other housing assets such as shops or vacant land. The balance has to be set aside as provision for repaying debt and meeting other credit liabilities.

EXPENDITURE

Local authority budgeted net expenditure for 2007–8 is:

Service	£ million
Education	39,620
Highways and transport	5,600
Social services	18,469
Housing (excluding HRA)	2,452
Cultural, environment and planning	9,902
Police	11,609
Fire and rescue	2,227
Courts	62
Central services	3,350
Other	248
Mandatory rent allowances	8,365
Mandatory rent rebates	626
Rent rebates granted to HRA tenants	3,803
Net current expenditure	106,333
Capital financing	3,352
Capital expenditure charged to revenue account	1,245
Council tax benefit	3,338
Discretionary non-domestic rate relief	25
Bad debt provision	29
Flood defence payments to Environment Agency	26
Pensions interest cost and expected return on pensions assets	3,531
Less interest receipts	(1,123)
Less specific grants outside AEF	(19,444)
Gross revenue expenditure	97,312
Less specific grants inside AEF	(43,035)
Net revenue expenditure	54,277
Less appropriations from pensions reserves	(3,990)
Less appropriations from other revenue reserves	(890)
Less adjustments	(0)
BUDGET REQUIREMENT	49,398

HRA = Housing Revenue Account
AEF = aggregate external finance

LONDON

The Greater London Council was abolished in 1986 and London was divided into 32 borough councils, which have a status similar to the metropolitan borough councils in the rest of England, and the Corporation of the City of London.

In March 1998 the government announced proposals for a Greater London Authority (GLA) covering the area of the 32 London boroughs and the City of London, which would comprise a directly elected mayor and a 25-member assembly. A referendum was held in London on 7 May 1998; the turnout was approximately 34 per cent and 72 per cent of electors voted in favour of the GLA. The independent candidate for London mayor, Ken Livingstone, was elected on 4 May 2000 and the Authority assumed its responsibilities on 3 July 2000. He was re-elected on 10 June 2004 as a Labour candidate. The next mayoral election is due on 1 May 2008.

The GLA is responsible for transport, economic development, strategic planning, culture, health, the environment, the police and fire and emergency planning. The separately elected assembly scrutinises the mayor's activities and approves plans and budgets. There are 14 constituency assembly members, each representing a separate area of London (each constituency is made up of two or three complete London boroughs). Eleven additional members, making up the total assembly complement of 25 members, are elected on a London-wide basis, either as independents or from party political lists on the basis of proportional representation.

LONDON BOROUGH COUNCILS

The London boroughs have whole council elections every four years, in the year immediately following the county council election year. The most recent elections took place on 4 May 2006.

The borough councils have responsibility for the following functions: building regulations; cemeteries and crematoria; consumer protection; education; youth employment; environmental health; electoral registration; food; drugs; housing; leisure services; libraries; local planning; local roads; museums; parking; recreation (parks, playing fields, swimming pools); refuse collection and street cleansing; social services; town planning; and traffic management.

CORPORATION OF LONDON

The Corporation of London is the local authority for the City of London. Its legal definition is the 'Mayor and Commonalty and Citizens of the City of London'. It is governed by the court of common council, which consists of the lord mayor, 25 other aldermen, and about 100 common councilmen. The lord mayor and two sheriffs are nominated annually by the City guilds (the livery companies) and elected by the court of aldermen. Aldermen and councilmen are elected from the 25 wards into which the City is divided; councilmen must stand for re-election annually. The council is a legislative assembly, and there are no political parties.

The corporation has the same functions as the London borough councils. In addition, it runs the City of London Police; is the health authority for the Port of London; has health control of animal imports throughout Greater London, including at Heathrow airport; owns and manages public open spaces throughout Greater London; runs the central criminal court; and runs Billingsgate, Smithfield and Spitalfields markets.

THE CITY GUILDS (LIVERY COMPANIES)

The livery companies of the City of London grew out of early medieval religious fraternities and began to emerge as trade and craft guilds, retaining their religious aspect, in the 12th century. From the early 14th century, only members of the trade and craft guilds could call themselves citizens of the City of London. The guilds began to be called livery companies, because of the distinctive livery worn by the most prosperous guild members on ceremonial occasions, in the late 15th century.

By the early 19th century the power of the companies within their trades had begun to wane, but those wearing the livery of a company continued to play an important role in the government of the City of London. Liverymen still have the right to nominate the lord mayor and sheriffs, and most members of the court of common council are liverymen.

WALES

The Local Government (Wales) Act 1994 abolished the two-tier structure of eight county and 37 district councils which had existed since 1974, and replaced it, from 1 April 1996, with 22 unitary authorities. The new authorities were elected in May 1995. Each unitary authority inherited all the functions of the previous county and district councils, except fire services (which are provided by three combined fire authorities, composed of representatives of the unitary authorities) and national parks (which are the responsibility of three independent National Park Authorities).

COMMUNITY COUNCILS

In Wales community councils are the equivalent of parishes in England. Unlike England, where many areas are not in any parish, communities have been established for the whole of Wales, approximately 865 communities in all. Community meetings may be convened as and when desired.

Community or town councils exist in 736 of the communities and further councils may be established at the request of a community meeting. Community councils have broadly the same range of powers as English parish councils. Community councillors are elected for a term of four years.

FINANCE

Total budgeted revenue expenditure for 2007–8 is £6.7bn, an increase of 5.5 per cent on 2006–7. Total budget requirement, which excludes expenditure financed by specific and special government grants and any use of reserves, is £5.2bn. This comprises revenue support grant of £3bn, support from the national non-domestic rate pool of £791m, police grant of £225m and £1.1bn to be raised through council tax. The non-domestic rating multiplier for Wales for 2007–8 is 44.8p. The average band D council tax levied in Wales for 2007–8 is £1,005, comprising unitary authorities £829, police authorities £153 and community councils £23.

EXPENDITURE

Local authority budgeted net revenue expenditure for 2007–8 is:

Service	£ million
Education	2,312.7
Social services	1,307.8

	£ million
Council fund housing, including housing benefit	730.7
Local environmental services	358.9
Roads and transport	300.3
Libraries, culture, heritage, sport and recreation	263.0
Planning, economic and community development	111.2
Council tax collection	30.0
Debt financing costs: counties	312.9
Central administrative and other revenue expenditure	239.1
Police	616.4
Fire	137.2
National parks	17.1
Gross revenue expenditure	6,737.3
Less specific and special government grants	(1,489.4)
Net revenue expenditure	5,247.9
Less appropriations from reserves	(42.1)
BUDGET REQUIREMENT	5,205.8

SCOTLAND

The Local Government etc (Scotland) Act 1994 abolished the two-tier structure of nine regional and 53 district councils which had existed since 1975 and replaced it, from 1 April 1996, with 29 unitary authorities on the mainland; the three islands councils remained. The new authorities were elected in April 1995.

In July 1999 the Scottish parliament assumed responsibility for legislation on local government. The government had established a commission on local government and the Scottish parliament (the McIntosh Commission) to make recommendations on the relationship between local authorities and the Scottish parliament and on increasing local authorities' accountability.

The local government in Scotland bill was introduced to the Scottish parliament in May 2002. The bill focused on three integrated core elements:

- A power for local authorities to promote and improve the well-being of their area and/or persons in it
- Statutory underpinning for community planning through the introduction of a duty on local authorities and key partners, including police, health boards and enterprise agencies
- A duty to secure best value

ELECTIONS

The unitary authorities consist of directly elected councillors. The Scottish Local Government (Elections) Act 2002 moved elections from a three-year to a four-year cycle; the last elections took place in May 2007.

FUNCTIONS

The functions of the councils and islands councils are: education; social work; strategic planning; the provision of infrastructure such as roads; consumer protection; flood prevention; coast protection; valuation and rating; the police and fire services; civil defence; electoral registration; public transport; registration of births, deaths and marriages; housing; leisure and recreation; development and building control; environmental health; licensing; allotments; public conveniences; and the administration of district courts.

COMMUNITY COUNCILS

Scottish community councils differ from those in England and Wales. Their purpose as defined in statute is to ascertain and express the views of the communities they represent, and to take in the interests of their communities such action as appears to be expedient or practicable. Around 1,200 community councils have been established under schemes drawn up by local authorities in Scotland.

FINANCE

Budgeted aggregate external finance for 2007–8 is £8.7bn, comprising £6bn revenue support grant, non-domestic rate income of £1.9bn and specific grants of £861m. The non-domestic rate multiplier or poundage for 2007–8 is 44.1p. All non-domestic properties in with a rateable value of £11,500 or less are eligible for a discount of between 5 and 50 per cent in the rate poundage. The average band D council tax for 2007–8 is £1,149.

EXPENDITURE

The 2007–8 net expenditure budget estimates for local authorities in Scotland were:

Service	£ million
Education	4,372.5
Cultural and related services	576.2
Social work services	2,275.6
Police	1,099.2
Roads and transport	473.8
Environmental services	511.8
Fire	291.3
Planning and development services	183.1
Other	1,248.7
TOTAL	11,032.2

NORTHERN IRELAND

For the purpose of local government Northern Ireland has a system of 26 single-tier district councils.

ELECTIONS

Council members are elected for periods of four years at a time on the principle of proportional representation.

FUNCTIONS

The district councils have three main roles. These are:

Executive: responsibility for a wide range of local services including building regulations; community services; consumer protection; cultural facilities; environmental health; miscellaneous licensing and registration provisions, including dog control; litter prevention; recreational and social facilities; refuse collection and disposal; street cleaning; and tourist development

Representative: nominating representatives to sit as members of the various statutory bodies responsible for the administration of regional services such as drainage, education, fire, health and personal social services, housing, and libraries

Consultative: acting as the medium through which the views of local people are expressed on the operation in their area of other regional services – notably conservation (including water supply and sewerage services), planning and roads – provided by those departments of central government which have an obligation, statutory or otherwise, to consult the district councils about proposals affecting their areas

FINANCE

Local government in Northern Ireland is funded by a system of rates. The ratepayer receives a combined tax bill consisting of the regional rate and the district rate, which is set by each district council. The regional and district rates are both collected by the Land and Property Services Agency (formerly the Rate Collection Agency). The product of the district rates is paid over to each council whilst the product of the regional rate supports expenditure by the departments of the executive and assembly.

Since April 2007 domestic rates bills have been based on the capital value of a property, rather than the rental value. The capital value is defined as the price the property might reasonably be expected to realise had it been sold on the open market on 1 January 2005. Non-domestic rates bills are based on 2001 rental values.

Rate bills are calculated by multiplying the property's net annual rental value (NAV) (in the case of non-domestic property), or capital value (in the case of domestic property), by the regional and district rate poundages respectively.

For 2007–8 the overall average domestic poundage is 0.6285p (direct comparisons can not be made between 2007–8 and 2006–7 poundages due to the change from rental to capital values). For 2007–8 the overall average non-domestic rate poundage is 49.37p compared to 47.71p in 2006–7.

POLITICAL COMPOSITION OF LOCAL COUNCILS

as at May 2007

Abbreviations

All.	Alliance
BNP	British National Party
C.	Conservative
DUP	Democratic Unionist Party
Green	Green
Ind.	Independent
Ind. Un.	Independent Unionist
Lab.	Labour
LD	Liberal Democrat
Lib.	Liberal
O.	Other
PC	Plaid Cymru
R	Residents Associations/Ratepayers
SD	Social Democrat
SDLP	Social Democratic and Labour Party
SF	Sinn Fein
SNP	Scottish National Party
Soc.	Socialist
UUP	Ulster Unionist Party
v.	Vacant

Total number of seats is given in parentheses after council name.

ENGLAND

COUNTY COUNCILS

Bedfordshire (52)	C. 35; LD 9; Lab. 7; Ind. 1
Buckinghamshire (57)	C. 44; LD 11; Lab. 2
Cambridgeshire (69)	C. 43; LD 22; Lab. 4
Cheshire (51)	C. 26; Lab. 16; LD 8; Ind. 1
Cornwall (82)	LD 48; Ind. 19; C. 9; Lab. 5; Lib. 1
Cumbria (84)	Lab. 39; C. 32; LD 11; Ind. 2
Derbyshire (64)	Lab. 38; C. 15; LD 10; Ind. 1
Devon (62)	LD 33; C. 23; Lab. 4; Ind. 2
Dorset (45)	C. 24; LD 16; Lab. 4; Ind. 1
Durham (63)	Lab. 53; LD 5; Ind. 3; C. 2
East Sussex (49)	C. 29; LD 13; Lab. 5; Ind. 1; O. 1
Essex (75)	C. 50; Lab. 13; LD 8; Green 2; Ind. 2
Gloucestershire (63)	C. 34; LD 13; Lab. 12; Ind. 3; O. 1
Hampshire (78)	C. 46; LD 28; Lab. 4
Hertfordshire (77)	C. 46; Lab. 16; LD 14; Green 1
Kent (84)	C. 57; Lab. 21; LD 5; v. 1
Lancashire (84)	Lab. 43; C. 31; LD 6; Ind. 2; Green 1; O. 1
Leicestershire (55)	C. 31; Lab. 13; LD 11
Lincolnshire (77)	C. 45; Lab. 20; LD 8; Ind. 3; v. 1
Norfolk (84)	C. 47; Lab. 22; LD 13; Green 2
North Yorkshire (72)	C. 42; LD 19; Lab. 8; Ind. 3
Northamptonshire (73)	C. 45; Lab. 19; LD 8; v. 1
Northumberland (67)	Lab. 35; C. 17; LD 14; Ind. 1
Nottinghamshire (67)	Lab. 36; C. 26; LD 5
Oxfordshire (74)	C. 44; LD 16; Lab. 8; Green 5; Ind. 1
Shropshire (48)	C. 25; LD 12; Lab. 9; Ind. 2
Somerset (58)	LD 30; C. 24; Lab. 4
Staffordshire (62)	Lab. 32; C. 26; LD 2; Ind. 1; v. 1
Suffolk (75)	C. 45; Lab. 21; LD 7; Ind. 1; v. 1
Surrey (80)	C. 58; LD 12; R 8; Lab. 2
Warwickshire (62)	C. 28; Lab. 23; LD 10; Ind. 1
West Sussex (70)	C. 46; LD 16; Lab. 7; v. 1
Wiltshire (49)	C. 29, LD 16; Lab. 3; Ind. 1
Worcestershire (57)	C. 29; Lab. 17; LD 8; Lib. 2; Ind. 1

DISTRICT COUNCILS

Adur (29)	C. 26; Ind. 2; LD 1
Allerdale (56)	O. 33; Lab. 21; Ind. 2
Alnwick (30)	LD 11; C. 9; Ind. 6; Lab. 2; O. 2
Amber Valley (45)	C. 28; Lab. 17
Arun (56)	C. 42; LD 9; Lab. 3; Ind. 2
Ashfield (33)	LD 10; Ind. 9; Lab. 9; C. 3; O. 2
Ashford (43)	C. 28; LD 8; O. 3; Ind. 2; Lab. 2
Aylesbury Vale (59)	C. 37; LD 21; Ind. 1
Babergh (43)	C. 19; LD 16; Ind. 7; O. 1
Barrow-in-Furness (38)	C. 19; Lab. 16; Ind. 2; O. 1
Basildon (42)	C. 28; Lab. 11; LD 3
Basingstoke and Deane (60)	C. 31; LD 15; Lab. 11; Ind. 3
Bassetlaw (48)	C. 28; Lab. 16; Ind. 4
Bedford (54)	C. 19; LD 16; Lab. 12; Ind. 4; O. 3
Berwick-upon-Tweed (29)	LD 13; C. 10; Ind. 6
Blaby (39)	C. 27; LD 7; Lab. 4; Ind. 1
Blyth Valley (50)	Lab. 30; LD 13; Ind. 5; C. 2
Bolsover (37)	Lab. 27; Ind. 7; R 2; O. 1
Boston (32)	O. 25; C. 5; Ind. 2
Braintree (60)	C. 42; Lab. 9; R 5; Green 2; Ind. 1; LD 1
Breckland (54)	C. 48; Ind. 3; Lab. 3
Brentwood (37)	C. 28; LD 6; Lab. 3
Bridgnorth (34)	Ind. 23; C. 6; O. 4; Lab. 1
Broadland (47)	C. 35; LD 9; Ind. 3
Bromsgrove (39)	C. 26; Lab. 6; Ind. 4; R 2; LD 1
Broxbourne (38)	C. 36; Lab. 2
Broxtowe (44)	C. 16; LD 15; Lab. 10; Ind. 2; BNP 1
Burnley (45)	LD 18; Lab. 17; C. 6; BNP 4
Cambridge (42)	LD 28; Lab. 13; Ind. 1
Cannock Chase (41)	Lab. 16; LD 14; C. 10; v. 1
Canterbury (50)	C. 29; LD 19; Lab. 2
Caradon (42)	LD 23; C. 9; Ind. 9; O. 1
Carlisle (52)	Lab. 25; C. 19; LD 7; Ind. 1
Carrick (47)	C. 19; LD 18; Ind. 8; Lab. 1; O. 1
Castle Morpeth (33)	C. 12; LD 12; Lab. 6; Ind. 2; Green 1
Castle Point (41)	C. 26; Ind. 15
Charnwood (52)	C. 32; Lab. 13; LD 5; BNP 1; Ind. 1
Chelmsford (57)	C. 33; LD 24
Cheltenham (40)	C. 17; LD 17; O. 5; Lab. 1
Cherwell (50)	C. 42; Lab. 4; LD 4
Chester (60)	C. 33; Lab. 13; LD 13; Ind. 1
Chester-le-Street (34)	Lab. 26; Ind. 5; C. 2; LD 1
Chesterfield (48)	LD 35; Lab. 12; Ind. 1
Chichester (48)	C. 34; LD 11; Ind. 3
Chiltern (40)	C. 30; LD 9; Ind. 1
Chorley (47)	C. 25; Lab. 15; Ind. 4; LD 3
Christchurch (24)	C. 17; LD 4; Ind. 3
Colchester (60)	C. 30; LD 21; Lab. 6; Ind. 3
Congleton (48)	C. 26; LD 14; O. 6; Ind. 2

Copeland (51) — Lab. 31; C. 19; Ind. 1
Corby (29) — Lab. 16; C. 8; LD 5
Cotswolds (44) — C. 38; LD 4; Ind. 2
Craven (30) — C. 13; Ind. 10; LD 6; v. 1
Crawley (37) — C. 22; Lab. 12; LD 3
Crewe and Nantwich (56) — C. 28; Lab. 17; LD 6; O. 3; Ind. 2
Dacorum (51) — C. 44; LD 5; Lab. 2
Dartford (44) — C. 26; Lab. 12; R 6
Daventry (38) — C. 35; LD 2; Lab. 1
Derbyshire Dales (39) — C. 26; LD 8; Lab. 4; Ind. 1
Derwentside (55) — Lab. 29; Ind. 24; LD 2
Dover (45) — C. 28; Lab. 14; LD 2; v. 1
Durham (50) — LD 30; Lab. 17; Ind. 3
Easington (51) — Lab. 47; Ind. 2; LD 2
East Cambridgeshire (39) — C. 24; LD 13; Ind. 2
East Devon (59) — C. 43; LD 10; Ind. 6
East Dorset (36) — C. 25; LD 11
East Hampshire (44) — C. 30; LD 14
East Hertfordshire (50) — C. 42; LD 4; Ind. 2; O. 2
East Lindsey (60) — C. 28; Ind. 19; Lab. 8; LD 3; O. 2
East Northamptonshire (40) — C. 38; Ind. 1; v. 1
East Staffordshire (39) — C. 25; Lab. 12; LD 2
Eastbourne (27) — LD 20; C. 7
Eastleigh (44) — LD 37; C. 5; Lab. 2
Eden (38) — Ind. 18; C. 14; LD 5; O. 1
Ellesmere Port and Neston (43) — Lab. 24; C. 17; LD 2
Elmbridge (60) — C. 28; R 23; LD 8; O. 1
Epping Forest (58) — C. 32; LD 11; BNP 6; R 5; Ind. 2; Lab. 1; O. 1
Epsom and Ewell (38) — R 25; LD 11; C. 2
Erewash (51) — C. 30; Lab. 18; LD 2; Ind. 1
Exeter (40) — Lab. 14; LD 12; C. 10; Lib. 4
Fareham (31) — C. 22; LD 9
Fenland (40) — C. 39; Ind. 1
Forest Heath (27) — C. 22; LD 2; O. 2; Ind. 1
Forest of Dean (48) — C. 30; Ind. 8; Lab. 8; LD 2
Fylde (51) — C. 29; Ind. 14; R 4; LD 2; O. 2
Gedling (50) — C. 28; Lab. 9; LD 9; Ind. 4
Gloucester (36) — C. 15; LD 12; Lab. 9
Gosport (34) — C. 17; LD 9; Lab. 7; Ind. 1
Gravesham (44) — C. 26; Lab. 16; v. 2
Great Yarmouth (39) — C. 22; Lab. 17
Guildford (48) — C. 26; LD 22
Hambleton (44) — C. 39; Ind. 3; LD 2
Harborough (37) — C. 26; LD 11
Harlow (33) — C. 12; Lab. 12; LD 8; Ind. 1
Harrogate (54) — C. 25; LD 23; Ind. 6
Hart (35) — C. 15; LD 12; O. 6; Ind. 2
Hastings (32) — C. 15; Lab 12; LD 5
Havant (38) — C. 31; Lab 4; LD 3
Hertsmere (39) — C. 28; LD 7; Lab. 4
High Peak (43) — C. 24; Lab. 9; LD 6; Ind. 4
Hinckley and Bosworth (34) — LD 19; C. 13; Lab. 2
Horsham (44) — C. 31; LD 11; Ind. 2
Huntingdonshire (52) — C. 39; LD 11; Ind. 2
Hyndburn (35) — C. 18; Lab. 15; Ind. 2
Ipswich (48) — C. 20; Lab. 18; LD 9; v. 1
Kennet (43) — C. 34; Ind. 5; O. 3; LD 1
Kerrier (44) — Ind. 21; LD 11; C. 5; O. 4; Lab. 2; Lib. 1
Kettering (36) — C. 28; Lab. 6; Ind. 2
King's Lynn and West Norfolk (62) — C. 52; Lab. 4; LD 4; Ind. 2

Lancaster (60) — O. 16; Lab. 14; C. 12; Green 12; LD 5; Ind. 1
Lewes (41) — LD 23; C. 17; Ind. 1
Lichfield (56) — C. 44; Lab. 7; LD 4; Ind. 1
Lincoln City (33) — C. 17; Lab. 15; LD 1
Macclesfield (60) — C. 38; LD 12; Lab. 6; Ind. 2; R 2
Maidstone (55) — C. 26; LD 21; Ind. 4; Lab. 4
Maldon (31) — C. 25; Ind. 4; v. 2
Malvern Hills (38) — C. 29; LD 5; Ind. 3; Green 1
Mansfield (46) — O. 28; Lab. 12; LD 4; C. 1; Ind. 1
Melton (28) — C. 20; Ind. 5; Lab. 3
Mendip (47) — C. 24; LD 23
Mid Bedfordshire (53) — C. 38; LD 11; Ind. 4
Mid Devon (42) — C. 17; Ind. 14; LD 10; v. 1
Mid Suffolk (40) — C. 25; LD 10; Green 2; O. 2; Ind. 1
Mid Sussex (54) — C. 30; LD 23; Lab. 1
Mole Valley (41) — C. 22; LD 16; Ind. 3
New Forest (60) — C. 45; LD 14; Ind. 1
Newark and Sherwood (46) — C. 26; Ind. 10; Lab. 6; LD 4
Newcastle-under-Lyme (60) — C. 20; Lab. 20; LD 18; O. 2
North Cornwall (36) — Ind. 15; LD 14; C. 6; O. 1
North Devon (43) — C. 22; LD 17; Ind. 4
North Dorset (33) — C. 17; LD 13; Lab. 3
North East Derbyshire (53) — Lab. 29; C. 10; Ind. 7; LD 7
North Hertfordshire (49) — C. 30; LD 9; O. 8; Lab. 2
North Kesteven (43) — C. 25; Ind. 14; LD 4
North Norfolk (48) — LD 29; C. 17; Ind. 2
North Shropshire (40) — C. 26; Ind. 12; Lab. 2
North Warwickshire (35) — C. 21; Lab. 14
North West Leicestershire (38) — C. 27; Lab. 5; LD 3; BNP 2; Ind. 1
North Wiltshire (54) — C. 39; LD 14; Lab. 1
Northampton (47) — LD 26; C. 15; Lab. 5; Ind. 1
Norwich (39) — Lab. 15; LD 11; Green 10; C. 3
Nuneaton and Bedworth (34) — Lab. 18; C. 14; LD 1; v. 1
Oadby and Wigston (26) — LD 21; C. 5
Oswestry (29) — C. 17; O. 6; LD 4; Ind. 2
Oxford (48) — Lab. 18; LD 16; Green 8; O. 4; C. 2
Pendle (49) — LD 27; C. 14; Lab. 6; BNP 1; v. 1
Penwith (35) — C. 17; LD 12; Ind. 6
Preston (57) — Lab. 24; C. 20; LD 10; O. 2; Ind. 1
Purbeck (24) — C. 13; LD 9; Ind. 2
Redditch (29) — Lab. 14; C. 11; LD 3; BNP 1
Reigate and Banstead (51) — C. 41; R 6; LD 2; Ind. 1; Lab. 1
Restormel (45) — LD 20; Ind. 13; C. 10; O. 2
Ribble Valley (40) — C. 29; LD 10; Ind. 1
Richmondshire (34) — C. 17; O. 11; LD 6
Rochford (39) — C. 31; LD 5; Ind. 1; R 1; v. 1
Rossendale (36) — C. 22; Lab. 12; Ind. 1; LD 1
Rother (38) — C. 28; LD 8; Ind. 2
Rugby (48) — C. 27; Lab. 11; LD 10
Runnymede (42) — C. 36; R 6
Rushcliffe (50) — C. 34; LD 11; Green 2; Lab. 2; Ind. 1
Rushmoor (42) — C. 28; LD 8; Lab. 5; Ind. 1
Ryedale (30) — C. 14; LD 8; Ind. 5; Lib. 1; R 1; v. 1

St Albans (58) — LD 29; C. 19; Lab. 8; Ind. 2
St Edmundsbury (45) — C. 36; Lab. 3; LD 3; Ind. 2; O. 1
Salisbury (55) — C. 22; LD 19; Lab. 10; Ind. 4
Scarborough (50) — C. 23; Ind. 15; LD 6; Lab. 4; Green 2
Sedgefield (50) — Lab. 28; Ind. 14; LD 6; C. 1; O. 1
Sedgemoor (50) — C. 35; Lab. 11; LD 4
Selby (41) — C. 29; Lab. 9; Ind. 3
Sevenoaks (54) — C. 41; LD 7; Lab. 5; Ind. 1
Shepway (46) — C. 34; LD 10; O. 2
Shrewsbury and Atcham (40) — C. 22; Lab. 10; LD 5; Ind. 3
South Bedfordshire (50) — C. 34; LD 12; Lab. 4
South Bucks (40) — C. 36; Ind. 2; LD 2
South Cambridgeshire (57) — C. 31; LD 16; Ind. 8; O. 2
South Derbyshire (36) — C. 21; Lab. 14; Ind. 1
South Hams (40) — C. 28; LD 9; Ind. 3
South Holland (37) — C. 26; Ind. 11
South Kesteven (58) — C. 35; Ind. 15; LD 6; Lab. 2
South Lakeland (52) — LD 34; C. 15; Lab. 2; Ind. 1
South Norfolk (46) — C. 39; LD 7
South Northamptonshire (42) — C. 35; Ind. 7
South Oxfordshire (48) — C. 38; LD 6; Ind. 2; Lab. 1; R 1
South Ribble (55) — C. 44; Lab. 8; O. 2; LD 1
South Shropshire (34) — C. 18; LD 11; Ind. 3; O. 2
South Somerset (60) — LD 38; C. 17; Ind. 5
South Staffordshire (49) — C. 42; Ind. 3; Lab. 1; LD 1; v. 2
Spelthorne (39) — C. 31; LD 8
Stafford (59) — C. 40; Lab. 13; O. 6
Staffordshire Moorlands (56) — C. 28; Ind. 11; LD 6; Lab. 5; R 3; O. 2; BNP 1
Stevenage (39) — Lab. 32; LD 4; C. 3
Stratford-on-Avon (53) — C. 37; LD 14; Ind. 2
Stroud (51) — C. 31; Lab. 9; Green 5; LD 4; Ind. 1; O. 1
Suffolk Coastal (55) — C. 45; LD 9; Lab. 1
Surrey Heath (40) — C. 30; LD 7; Lab. 2; Ind. 1
Swale (47) — C. 26; Lab. 10; LD 6; Ind. 5
Tamworth (30) — C. 24; Lab. 5; Ind. 1
Tandridge (42) — C. 30; LD 10; Lab. 2; Ind. 1
Taunton Deane (56) — LD 26; C. 25; Ind. 4; Lab. 1
Teesdale (32) — Ind. 16; Lab. 6; O. 6; C. 4
Teignbridge (46) — LD 21; C. 19; Ind. 6
Tendring (60) — C. 28; O. 15; Lab. 6; LD 6; Ind. 5
Test Valley (48) — C. 33; LD 15
Tewkesbury (38) — C. 19; LD 17; Ind. 2
Thanet (56) — C. 33; Lab. 19; Ind. 3; O. 1
Three Rivers (48) — LD 30; C. 11; Lab. 7
Tonbridge and Malling (53) — C. 46; LD 7
Torridge (36) — C. 13; Ind. 12; LD 8; O. 3
Tunbridge Wells (48) — C. 41; LD 7
Tynedale (52) — C. 30; LD 9; Lab. 8; Ind. 5
Uttlesford (44) — C. 26; LD 15; Ind. 3
Vale of White Horse (51) — LD 34; C. 17
Vale Royal (57) — C. 29; Lab. 17; LD 11
Wansbeck (45) — Lab. 26; C. 16; O. 3
Warwick (46) — C. 24; Lab. 9; LD 9; Ind. 4
Watford (37) — LD 29; C. 3; Green 3; Ind. 1; Lab. 1
Waveney (48) — C. 30; Lab. 12; LD 3; Ind. 2; Green 1

Waverley (57) — C. 51; Ind. 3; LD 3
Wealden (55) — C. 34; LD 12; O. 6; Green 2; Ind. 1
Wear Valley (40) — Lab. 18; LD 16; Ind. 6
Wellingborough (36) — C. 30; O. 6
Welwyn and Hatfield (48) — C. 35; Lab. 10; LD 3
West Devon (31) — C. 14; Ind. 10; LD 7
West Dorset (48) — C. 26; LD 16; Ind. 6
West Lancashire (54) — C. 33; Lab. 21
West Lindsey (37) — LD 20; C. 16; Ind. 1
West Oxfordshire (49) — C. 36; LD 8; Ind. 4; Lab. 1
West Somerset (31) — Ind. 16; C. 13; Lab. 1; LD 1
West Wiltshire (44) — C. 26; LD 14; Ind. 2; O. 2
Weymouth and Portland (36) — C. 14; LD 11; Lab. 6; Ind. 5
Winchester (57) — C. 29; LD 23; Ind. 4; Lab. 1
Woking (36) — C. 19; LD 17
Worcester (35) — C. 18; Lab. 12; LD 3; Ind. 1; O. 1
Worthing (37) — C. 24; LD 12; Ind. 1
Wychavon (45) — C. 35; LD 10
Wycombe (60) — C. 49; Lab. 5; LD 4; Ind. 2
Wyre (55) — C. 45; Lab. 9; LD 1
Wyre Forest (42) — C. 18; O. 10; Lib. 7; Lab. 3; Ind. 2; LD 2

LONDON BOROUGH COUNCILS

Barking and Dagenham (51) — Lab. 38; BNP 12; C. 1
Barnet (63) — C. 37; Lab. 20; LD 6
Bexley (63) — C. 54; Lab. 9
Brent (63) — LD 27; Lab. 21; C. 15
Bromley (60) — C. 49; LD 7; Lab. 4
Camden (54) — LD 21; Lab. 17; C. 14; Green 2
Croydon (70) — C. 43; Lab. 27
Ealing (69) — C. 37; Lab. 29; LD 3
Enfield (63) — C. 34; Lab. 27; O. 2
Greenwich (51) — Lab. 36; C. 13; LD 2
Hackney (58) — Lab. 45; C. 9; LD 3; Green 1
Hammersmith and Fulham (46) — C. 33; LD 13
Haringey (57) — Lab. 30; LD 27
Harrow (63) — C. 37; Lab. 24; LD 2
Havering (54) — C. 34; R 16; Lab. 2; BNP 1; O. 1
Hillingdon (65) — C. 45; Lab. 18; LD 2
Hounslow (60) — Lab. 24; C. 23; O. 6; LD 4; Ind. 3
Islington (48) — LD 24; Lab. 23; Green 1
Kensington and Chelsea (54) — C. 45; Lab. 9
Kingston upon Thames (48) — LD 25; C. 21; Lab. 1; Ind. 1
Lambeth (63) — Lab. 39; LD 17; C. 6; Green 1
Lewisham (55) — Lab. 27; LD 16; Green 6; C. 3; Soc. 2; Ind. 1
Merton (60) — C. 30; Lab. 27; R 3
Newham (60) — Lab. 54; O. 6
Redbridge (63) — C. 34; Lab. 18; LD 10; BNP 1
Richmond upon Thames (54) — LD 36; C. 18
Southwark (63) — Lab. 29; LD 27; C. 6; Green 1
Sutton (54) — LD 32; C. 22
Tower Hamlets (51) — Lab. 27; O. 11; C. 7; LD 6
Waltham Forest (60) — Lab. 26; LD 19; C. 15
Wandsworth (60) — C. 51; Lab. 9
Westminster (60) — C. 48; Lab. 12

METROPOLITAN BOROUGHS

Barnsley (63)	Lab. 33; Ind. 21; C. 5; LD 2; O. 2
Birmingham (120)	C. 44; Lab. 41; LD 32; O. 2; Ind. 1
Bolton (60)	Lab. 26; C. 22; LD 12
Bradford (90)	Lab. 39; C. 32; LD 14; Green 3; BNP 2
Bury (51)	C. 23; Lab. 20; LD 8
Calderdale (51)	C. 18; LD 16; Lab. 11; Ind. 4; BNP 1; O. 1
Coventry (54)	C. 28; Lab. 23; Soc. 2; LD 1
Doncaster (63)	Lab. 29; LD 12; Ind. 10; C. 9; O. 3
Dudley (72)	C. 39; Lab. 28; LD 5
Gateshead (66)	Lab. 41; LD 23; Lib. 1; v. 1
Kirklees (69)	Lab. 22; C. 20; LD 18; Green 4; BNP 3; Ind. 2
Knowsley (63)	Lab. 50; LD 13
Leeds (99)	Lab. 43; LD 24; C. 22; O. 5; Green 3; BNP 1; Ind. 1
Liverpool (90)	LD 51; Lab 34; Lib. 3; Green 1; Ind. 1
Manchester (96)	Lab. 61; LD 34; Green 1
Newcastle-upon-Tyne (78)	LD 45; Lab. 31; v. 2
North Tyneside (60)	C. 28; Lab. 23; LD 9
Oldham (60)	Lab. 30; LD 26; C. 3; Ind. 1
Rochdale (60)	LD 32; Lab. 20; C. 8
Rotherham (63)	Lab. 53; C. 7; Ind. 2; v. 1
St Helens (48)	Lab. 21; LD 21; C. 6
Salford (60)	Lab. 42; C. 10; LD 8
Sandwell (72)	Lab. 51; C. 10; LD 6; BNP 4; v. 1
Sefton (66)	LD 26; Lab. 22; C. 18
Sheffield (84)	Lab. 41; LD 39; Green 2; C. 1; Ind. 1
Solihull (51)	C. 24; LD 18; Lab. 7; BNP 1; Ind. 1
South Tyneside (54)	Lab. 35; O. 7; Ind. 6; C. 3; LD 3
Stockport (63)	LD 36; Lab. 15; C. 9; R 3
Sunderland (75)	Lab. 54; C. 16; Ind. 4; LD 1
Tameside (57)	Lab. 45; C. 8; Ind. 3; LD 1
Trafford (63)	C. 39; Lab. 20; LD 4
Wakefield (63)	Lab. 40; C. 16; Ind. 4; LD 3
Walsall (60)	C. 33; Lab. 18; LD 6; Ind. 2; O. 1
Wigan (75)	Lab. 46; C. 10; O. 10; Ind. 5; LD 3; v. 1
Wirral (66)	Lab. 25; C. 21; LD 19; O. 1
Wolverhampton (60)	Lab. 36; C. 19; LD 3; Ind. 1; O. 1

UNITARY COUNCILS

Bath and North East Somerset (65)	LD 29; C. 26; Lab. 6; Ind. 4
Blackburn with Darwen (64)	Lab. 31; C. 17; LD 13; O. 3
Blackpool (42)	C. 26; Lab. 13; LD 3
Bournemouth (54)	C. 41; LD 7; Lab. 3; Ind. 3
Bracknell Forest (42)	C. 39; Lab. 3
Brighton and Hove (54)	C. 26; Lab. 13; Green 12; LD 2; Ind. 1
Bristol (70)	LD 31; Lab. 25; C. 13; Green 1
Darlington (53)	Lab. 29; C. 18; LD 5; Ind. 1
Derby (51)	Lab. 24; LD 13; C. 12; Ind. 2
East Riding of Yorkshire (67)	C. 47; LD 12; Ind. 4; Lab. 3; SD 1
Halton (56)	Lab. 33; LD 15; C. 8
Hartlepool (47)	Lab. 24; O. 12; LD 7; C. 4
Herefordshire (58)	C. 31; Ind. 14; LD 10; Lab. 2; O. 1

Isles of Scilly (21)*	O. 21
Isle of Wight (48)	C. 35; Ind. 4; LD. 4; O. 3; Lab 2
Kingston-upon-Hull (59)	LD 30; Lab. 20; O. 6; C. 2; Ind. 1
Leicester (54)	Lab. 38; C. 8; LD 6; Green 2
Luton (48)	Lab. 26; LD 17; C. 5
Medway (55)	C. 33; Lab. 13; LD 8; Ind. 1
Middlesbrough (48)	Lab. 26; Ind. 10; C. 6; LD 5; O. 1
Milton Keynes (51)	LD 22; C. 15; Lab. 13; O. 1
North East Lincolnshire (42)	LD 19; C. 15; Lab. 6; Ind. 2
North Lincolnshire (43)	Lab. 22; C. 18; Ind. 2; LD 1
North Somerset (61)	C. 46; Ind. 7; LD 5; Lab. 3
Nottingham (55)	Lab. 42; C. 7; LD 6
Peterborough (57)	C. 40; Ind. 6; O. 5; LD 4; Lab. 2
Plymouth (57)	C. 31; Lab. 26
Poole (42)	C. 25; LD 17
Portsmouth (42)	LD 19; C. 17; Lab. 5; Ind. 1
Reading (46)	Lab. 25; C. 14; LD 7
Redcar and Cleveland (59)	Lab. 28; LD 13; C. 11; Ind. 7
Rutland (26)	C. 19; Ind. 5; LD 2
Slough (41)	Lab. 19; C. 7; LD 4; Ind. 3; Lib. 3; R 3; O. 2
South Gloucestershire (70)	C. 34; LD 27; Lab. 9
Southampton (48)	C. 18; Lab. 18; LD 12
Southend-on-Sea (51)	C. 30; LD 10; Lab. 7; Ind. 4
Stockton-on-Tees (56)	Lab. 22; C. 13; Ind. 13; LD 8
Stoke-on-Trent (60)	Lab. 24; O. 13; Ind. 12; BNP 6; LD 5
Swindon (59)	C. 43; Lab. 12; LD 3; Ind. 1
Telford and Wrekin (54)	C. 25; Lab. 19; Ind. 4; LD 3; O. 3
Thurrock (49)	C. 24; Lab. 22; Ind. 2; O. 1
Torbay (36)	C. 24; LD 9; Ind. 3
Warrington (57)	LD 27; Lab. 24; C. 5; Ind. 1
West Berkshire (52)	C. 36; LD 16
Windsor and Maidenhead (57)	C. 36; LD 16; Ind. 5
Wokingham (54)	C. 43; LD 11
York (47)	LD 19; Lab. 18; C. 8; Green 2

* Thirteen councillors are elected by the residents of the isle of St Mary's and two councillors each are elected by the residents of the four other islands (Bryher, St Martins, St Agnes and Tresco)

WALES

Blaenau Gwent (42)	Lab. 29; Ind. 11; LD 1; v. 1
Bridgend (54)	Lab. 22; LD 13; C. 8; O. 6; Ind. 4; PC 1
Caerphilly (73)	Lab. 41; PC 26; Ind. 6
Cardiff (75)	LD 32; Lab. 27; C. 10; PC 4; Ind. 2
Carmarthenshire (74)	Ind. 31; Lab. 25; PC 16; O. 2
Ceredigion (42)	Ind. 16; PC 16; LD 9; Lab. 1
Conwy (59)	Ind. 17; C. 15; Lab. 11; PC 11; LD 4; v. 1
Denbighshire (47)	Ind. 18; C. 9; Lab. 7; PC 7; O. 6
Flintshire (70)	Lab. 36; Ind. 18; LD 10; C. 4; O. 1; PC 1
Gwynedd (75)	PC 44; Ind. 14; Lab. 9; LD 6; O. 2
Merthyr Tydfil (33)	Lab. 16; O. 9; Ind. 8
Monmouthshire (43)	C. 24; Lab. 9; Ind. 3; LD 3; O. 2; PC 2

Neath Port Talbot (64)   Lab. 36; PC 10; R 9; Ind. 4; SD 3; LD 2

Newport (50)   Lab. 31; C. 11; LD 6; Ind. 1; PC 1

Pembrokeshire (60)   Ind. 39; Lab. 11; PC 5; LD 4; O. 1

Powys (73)   Ind. 53; LD 15; Lab. 4; v. 1

Rhondda Cynon Taff (75)   Lab. 57; PC 13; Ind. 2; O. 2; LD 1

Swansea (72)   Lab. 31; O. 31; C. 4; PC 4; Ind. 1; v. 1

Torfaen (44)   Lab. 34; Ind. 7; LD 2; C. 1

Vale of Glamorgan (47)   C. 20; Lab. 16; PC 8; Ind. 3

Wrexham (52)   Lab. 19; LD 15; O. 9; Ind. 5; C. 4

Ynys Mon (Isle of Anglesey) (40)   Ind. 28; PC 6; C. 2; O. 2; Lab. 1; LD 1

SCOTLAND

Aberdeen (43)   LD 15; SNP 12; Lab. 10; C. 5; Ind. 1

Aberdeenshire (68)   LD 24; SNP 22; C. 14; Ind. 8

Angus (29)   SNP 13; Ind. 6; C. 5; LD 3; Lab. 2

Argyll and Bute (36)   Ind. 16; SNP 10; LD 7; C. 3

Clackmannanshire (18)   Lab. 8; SNP 7; C. 1; Ind. 1; LD 1

Dumfries and Galloway (47)   C. 18; Lab. 14; SNP 10; LD 3; Ind. 2

Dundee (29)   SNP 13; Lab. 10; C. 3; LD 2; Ind. 1

East Ayrshire (32)   Lab. 14; SNP 14; C. 3; Ind. 1

East Dunbartonshire (24)   SNP 8; Lab. 6; C. 5; LD 3; Ind. 2

East Lothian (23)   Lab. 7; SNP 7; LD 6; C. 2; Ind. 1

East Renfrewshire (20)   C. 7; Lab. 7; SNP 3; Ind. 2; LD 1

Edinburgh (58)   LD 17; Lab. 15; SNP 12; C. 11; Green 3

Eilean Siar (Western Isles) (31)   Ind. 25; SNP 4; Lab. 2

Falkirk (32)   Lab. 14; SNP 13; Ind. 3; C. 2

Fife (78)   Lab. 24; SNP 23; LD 21; C. 5; Ind. 3; O. 2

Glasgow (79)   Lab. 45; SNP 22; LD 5; Green 5; C. 1; O. 1

Highland (80)   Ind. 34; LD 22; SNP 17; Lab. 7

Inverclyde (20)   Lab. 9; SNP 5; LD 4; C. 1; Ind. 1

Midlothian (18)   Lab. 9; SNP 6; LD 3

Moray (26)   Ind. 12; SNP 9; C. 3; Lab. 2

North Ayrshire (30)   Lab. 12; SNP 8; Ind. 5; C. 3; LD 2

North Lanarkshire (70)   Lab. 40; SNP 23; Ind. 5; C. 1; O. 1

Orkney Islands (21)   Ind. 21

Perth and Kinross (41)   SNP 18; C. 12; LD 8; Lab. 3

Renfrewshire (40)   Lab. 17; SNP 17; LD 4; C. 2

Scottish Borders (34)   C. 11; LD 10; SNP 6; Ind. 5; O. 2

Shetland Islands (22)   O. 12; Ind. 10

South Ayrshire (30)   C. 12; Lab. 9; SNP 8; Ind. 1

South Lanarkshire (67)   Lab. 30; SNP 24; C. 8; Ind. 3; LD 2

Stirling (22)   Lab. 8; SNP 7; C. 4; LD 3

West Dunbartonshire (22)   Lab. 10; SNP 9; Ind. 2; Soc. 1

West Lothian (32)   Lab. 14; SNP 13; O. 3; C. 1; Ind. 1

NORTHERN IRELAND

Antrim (19)   DUP 6; UUP 5; SF 3; All. 2; SDLP 2; Ind. 1

Ards (23)   DUP 11; UUP 6; All. 3; Ind. 1; O. 1; SDLP 1

Armagh City (22)   SDLP 6; DUP 5; SF 5; UUP 5; Ind. Un. 1

Ballymena (24)   DUP 9; O. 6; UUP 4; Ind. 2; SDLP 2; SF 1

Ballymoney (16)   DUP 7; SF 3; Ind. Un. 2; SDLP 2; UUP 2

Banbridge (17)   DUP 6; UUP 5; SDLP 3; All. 1; Ind. Un. 1; SF 1

Belfast (51)   DUP 14; SF 14; SDLP 8; UUP 8; All. 4; O. 2; Ind. 1

Carrickfergus (17)   DUP 8; UUP 4; All. 3; Ind. 1; O. 1

Castlereagh (24)   DUP 13; All. 4; UUP 4; SDLP 3

Coleraine (22)   DUP 8; UUP 8; SDLP 3; All. 1; Ind. Un. 1; SF 1

Cookstown (16)   SDLP 5; SF 5; DUP 3; UUP 3

Craigavon (26)   DUP 8; SF 6; UUP 6; Ind. 3; SDLP 3

Derry City (30)   SDLP 14; SF 10; DUP 5; UUP 1

Down (23)   SDLP 10; SF 5; DUP 3; UUP 3; C. 1; Green 1

Dungannon and South Tyrone (22)   SF 9; DUP 5; SDLP 4; UUP 4

Fermanagh (23)   SF 9; SDLP 5; UUP 5; DUP 4

Larne (15)   DUP 4; UUP 4; Ind. 3; All. 2; SDLP 2

Limavady (15)   SF 6; SDLP 3; DUP 2; O. 2; UUP 2

Lisburn (30)   DUP 12; UUP 7; SF 4; All. 3; SDLP 3; Ind. Un. 1

Magherafelt (16)   SF 6; DUP 4; O. 2; SDLP 2; UUP 2

Moyle (15)   SF 4; DUP 3; Ind. Un. 3; SDLP 3; UUP 2

Newry and Mourne (30)   SF 12; SDLP 9; DUP 2; Ind. 2; UUP 2; Green 1; Ind. Un. 1; O. 1

Newtownabbey (25)   DUP 12; UUP 6; Ind. Un. 3; All. 2; SDLP 1; SF 1

North Down (25)   DUP 8; UUP 8; All. 6; Ind. 2; Green 1

Omagh (21)   SF 10; DUP 3; SDLP 3; UUP 3; Ind. Un. 2

Strabane (16)   SF 8; DUP 3; SDLP 2; UUP 2; Ind. Un. 1

ENGLAND

The Kingdom of England lies between 55° 46' and 49° 57' 30" N. latitude (from a few miles north of the mouth of the Tweed to the Lizard), and between 1° 46' E. and 5° 43' W. longitude (from Lowestoft to Land's End). England is bounded on the north by the Cheviot Hills; on the south by the English Channel; on the east by the Straits of Dover (Pas de Calais) and the North Sea; and on the west by the Atlantic Ocean, Wales and the Irish Sea. It has a total area of 130,432 sq. km (50,360 sq. miles): land 130,279 sq. km (50,301 sq. miles); inland water 153 sq. km (59 sq. miles).

POPULATION

The population at the 2001 census was 49,138,831. The average density of the population in 2001 was 377 persons per sq. km (976 per sq. mile).

FLAG

The flag of England is the cross of St George, a red cross on a white field (cross gules in a field argent). The cross of St George, the patron saint of England, has been used since the 13th century.

RELIEF

There is a marked division between the upland and lowland areas of England. In the extreme north the Cheviot Hills (highest point, the Cheviot, 815m/2,674ft) form a natural boundary with Scotland. Running south from the Cheviots, though divided from them by the Tyne Gap, is the Pennine range (highest point, Cross Fell, 893m/2,930ft), the main orological feature of the country. The Pennines culminate in the Peak District of Derbyshire (Kinder Scout, 636m/2,088ft). West of the Pennines are the Cumbrian mountains, which include Scafell Pike (978m/3,210ft), the highest peak in England, and to the east are the Yorkshire Moors, their highest point being Urra Moor (454m/1,490ft).

In the west, the foothills of the Welsh mountains extend into the bordering English counties of Shropshire (the Wrekin, 407m/1,334ft; Long Mynd, 516m/1,694ft) and Hereford and Worcester (the Malvern Hills – Worcestershire Beacon, 425m/1,394ft). Extensive areas of highland and moorland are also to be found in the south-western peninsula formed by Somerset, Devon and Cornwall, principally Exmoor (Dunkery Beacon, 519m/1,704ft), Dartmoor (High Willhays, 621m/2,038ft) and Bodmin Moor (Brown Willy, 420m/1,377ft). Ranges of low, undulating hills run across the south of the country, including the Cotswolds in the Midlands and south-west, the Chilterns to the north of London, and the North (Kent) and South (Sussex) Downs of the south-east coastal areas.

The lowlands of England lie in the Vale of York, East Anglia and the area around the Wash. The lowest-lying are the Cambridgeshire Fens in the valleys of the Great Ouse and the River Nene, which are below sea-level in places. Since the 17th century extensive drainage has brought much of the Fens under cultivation. The North Sea coast between the Thames and the Humber, low-lying and formed of sand and shingle for the most part, is subject to erosion and defences against further incursion have been built along many stretches.

HYDROGRAPHY

The Severn is the longest river in Great Britain, rising in the north-eastern slopes of Plynlimon (Wales) and entering England in Shropshire, with a total length of 354km (220 miles) from its source to its outflow into the Bristol Channel, where it receives the Bristol Avon on the east and the Wye on the west; its other tributaries are the Vyrnwy, Tern, Stour, Teme and Upper (or Warwickshire) Avon. The Severn is tidal below Gloucester, and a high bore or tidal wave sometimes reverses the flow as high as Tewkesbury (21.75km/13.5 miles above Gloucester). The scenery of the greater part of the river is very picturesque, and the Severn is a noted salmon river, with some of its tributaries being famous for trout. Navigation is assisted by the Gloucester and Berkeley Ship Canal (26km/16.25 miles), which admits vessels of 350 tons to Gloucester. The Severn Tunnel was begun in 1873 and completed in 1886 at a cost of £2m and after many difficulties caused by flooding. It is 7km (4 miles 628 yards) in length (of which 3.67km/2.25 miles are under the river). The Severn road bridge between Haysgate, Gwent, and Almondsbury, Glos, with a centre span of 988m (3,240ft), was opened in 1966.

The longest river wholly in England is the Thames, with a total length of 346km (215 miles) from its source in the Cotswold hills to the Nore, and is navigable by ocean-going ships to London Bridge. The Thames is tidal to Teddington (111km/69 miles from its mouth) and forms county boundaries almost throughout its course; on its banks are situated London, Windsor Castle, Eton College and Oxford University. Of the remaining English rivers, those flowing into the North Sea are the Tyne, Wear, Tees, Ouse and Trent from the Pennine Range, the Great Ouse (257km/160 miles), which rises in Northamptonshire, and the Orwell and Stour from the hills of East Anglia. Flowing into the English Channel are the Sussex Ouse from the Weald, the Itchen from the Hampshire Hills, and the Axe, Teign, Dart, Tamar and Exe from the Devonian hills. Flowing into the Irish Sea are the Mersey, Ribble and Eden from the western slopes of the Pennines and the Derwent from the Cumbrian mountains.

The English Lakes, notable for their picturesque scenery and poetic associations, lie in Cumbria's Lake District; the largest are Windermere (14.7 sq. km/5.7 sq. miles), Ullswater (8.8 sq. km/3.4 sq. miles) and Derwent Water (5.3 sq. km/2.0 sq. miles).

ISLANDS

The Isle of Wight is separated from Hampshire by the Solent. The capital, Newport, stands at the head of the estuary of the Medina, and Cowes (at the mouth) is the chief port. Other centres are Ryde, Sandown, Shanklin, Ventnor, Freshwater, Yarmouth, Totland Bay, Seaview and Bembridge.

Lundy (the name means Puffin Island), 18km (11 miles) north-west of Hartland Point, Devon, is around 5km (3 miles) long and almost 1km (half a mile) wide on average, with a total area of around 452 hectares (1,116 acres), and a population of around 18. It became the property of the National Trust in 1969 and is now principally a bird sanctuary.

The Isles of Scilly comprise around 140 islands and

skerries (total area, 10 sq. km/6 sq. miles) situated 45 km (28 miles) south-west of Land's End in Cornwall. Only five are inhabited: St Mary's, St Agnes, Bryher, Tresco and St Martin's. The population at the 2001 census was 2,153. The entire group has been designated an Area of Outstanding Natural Beauty because of its unique flora and fauna. Tourism and the winter/spring flower trade for the home market form the basis of the economy of the islands. The island group is a recognised rural development area.

EARLY HISTORY

Archaeological evidence suggests that England has been inhabited since at least the Palaeolithic period, though the extent of the various Palaeolithic cultures was dependent upon the degree of glaciation. The succeeding Neolithic and Bronze Age cultures have left abundant remains throughout the country; the best-known of these are the henges and stone circles of Stonehenge (ten miles north of Salisbury, Wilts) and Avebury (Wilts), both of which are believed to have been of religious significance. In the latter part of the Bronze Age the Goidels, a people of the Celtic race, invaded the country and brought with them Celtic civilisation and dialects; as a result place names in England bear witness to the spread of the invasion across the whole kingdom.

THE ROMAN CONQUEST
The Roman conquest of Gaul (57–50 BC) brought Britain into close contact with Roman civilisation, but although Julius Caesar raided the south of Britain in 55 and 54 BC, conquest was not undertaken until nearly 100 years later. In AD 43 the Emperor Claudius dispatched Aulus Plautius, with a well-equipped force of 40,000, and himself followed with reinforcements in the same year. Success was delayed by the resistance of Caratacus (Caractacus), the British leader from AD 48–51, who was finally captured and sent to Rome, and by a great revolt in AD 61 led by Boudicca (Boadicea), Queen of the Iceni, but the south of Britain was secured by AD 70, and Wales and the area north to the Tyne by about AD 80.

In AD 122, the Emperor Hadrian visited Britain and built a continuous rampart, since known as Hadrian's Wall, from Wallsend to Bowness (Tyne to Solway). The work was entrusted by the Emperor Hadrian to Aulus Platorius Nepos, legate of Britain from AD 122 to 126, and it was intended to form the northern frontier of the Roman Empire.

The Romans administered Britain as a province under a governor, with a well-defined system of local government, each Roman municipality ruling itself and its surrounding territory, while London was the centre of the road system and the seat of the financial officials of the Province of Britain. Colchester, Lincoln, York, Gloucester and St Albans stand on the sites of five Roman municipalities, and Wroxeter, Caerleon, Chester, Lincoln and York were at various times the sites of legionary fortresses. Well-preserved Roman towns have been uncovered at or near Silchester *(Calleva Atrebatum)*, ten miles south of Reading, Wroxeter *(Viroconium Cornoviorum)*, near Shrewsbury, and St Albans *(Verulamium)* in Hertfordshire.

Four main groups of roads radiated from London, and a fifth (the Fosse) ran obliquely from Lincoln through Leicester, Cirencester and Bath to Exeter. Of the four groups radiating from London, one ran south-east to Canterbury and the coast of Kent, a second to Silchester and thence to parts of western Britain and south Wales, a third (later known as Watling Street) ran through St Albans to Chester, with various branches, and the fourth reached Colchester, Lincoln, York and the eastern counties.

In the fourth century Britain was subjected to raids along the east coast by Saxon pirates, which led to the establishment of a system of coastal defences from the Wash to Southampton Water, with forts at Brancaster, Burgh Castle (Yarmouth), Walton (Felixstowe), Bradwell, Reculver, Richborough, Dover, Lympne, Pevensey and Porchester (Portsmouth). The Irish (Scoti) and Picts in the north were also becoming more aggressive and from around AD 350 incursions became more frequent and more formidable. As the Roman Empire came increasingly under attack towards the end of the fourth century, many troops were removed from Britain for service in other parts of the empire. The island was eventually cut off from Rome by the Teutonic conquest of Gaul, and with the withdrawal of the last Roman garrison early in the fifth century, the Romano-British were left to themselves.

SAXON SETTLEMENT
According to legend, the British King Vortigern called in the Saxons to defend his lands against the Picts. The Saxon chieftains Hengist and Horsa landed at Ebbsfleet, Kent, and established themselves in the Isle of Thanet, but the events during the one-and-a-half centuries between the final break with Rome and the re-establishment of Christianity are unclear. However, it would appear that over the course of this period the raids turned into large-scale settlement by invaders traditionally known as Angles (England north of the Wash and East Anglia), Saxons (Essex and southern England) and Jutes (Kent and the Weald), which pushed the Romano-British into the mountainous areas of the north and west. Celtic culture outside Wales and Cornwall survives only in topographical names. Various kingdoms established at this time attempted to claim overlordship of the whole country, hegemony finally being achieved by Wessex (with the capital at Winchester) in the ninth century. This century also saw the beginning of raids by the Vikings (Danes), which were resisted by Alfred the Great (871–899), who fixed a limit on the advance of Danish settlement by the Treaty of Wedmore (878), giving him the area north and east of Watling Street on the condition that they adopt Christianity.

In the tenth century the kings of Wessex recovered the whole of England from the Danes, but subsequent rulers were unable to resist a second wave of invaders. England paid tribute *(Danegeld)* for many years, and was invaded in 1013 by the Danes and ruled by Danish kings (including Cnut) from 1016 until 1042, when Edward the Confessor was recalled from exile in Normandy. On Edward's death in 1066 Harold Godwinson (brother-in-law of Edward and son of Earl Godwin of Wessex) was chosen to be King of England. After defeating (at Stamford Bridge, Yorkshire, 25 September) an invading army under Harald Hadraada, King of Norway (aided by the outlawed Earl Tostig of Northumbria, Harold's brother), Harold was himself defeated at the Battle of Hastings on 14 October 1066, and the Norman conquest secured the throne of England for Duke William of Normandy, a cousin of Edward the Confessor.

CHRISTIANITY
Christianity reached the Roman province of Britain from Gaul in the third century (or possibly earlier). Alban, traditionally Britain's first martyr, was put to death as a

Christian during the persecution of Diocletian (22 June 303) at his native town *Verulamium*, and the Bishops of *Londinium*, *Eboracum* (York), and *Lindum* (Lincoln) attended the Council of Arles in 314. However, the Anglo-Saxon invasions submerged the Christian religion in England until the sixth century: conversion was undertaken in the north from 563 by Celtic missionaries from Ireland led by St Columba, and in the south by a mission sent from Rome in 597 which was led by St Augustine, who became the first archbishop of Canterbury. England appears to have been converted again by the end of the seventh century and followed, after the Council of Whitby in 663, the practices of the Roman Church, which brought the kingdom into the mainstream of European thought and culture.

PRINCIPAL CITIES

There are 50 cities in England and space constraints prevent us from including profiles of them all. Below is a selection of England's principal cities with the date on which city status was conferred in parenthesis. Other cities are: Chichester (pre-1900), Derby (1977), Ely (pre-1900), Exeter (pre-1900), Gloucester (pre-1900), Hereford (pre-1900), Lancaster (1937), Lichfield (pre-1900), London (pre-1900), Peterborough (pre-1900), Plymouth (1928), Portsmouth (1926), Preston (2002), Ripon (pre-1900), Salford (1926), Sunderland (1992), Truro (pre-1900), Wakefield (pre-1900), Wells (pre-1900), Westminster (pre-1900), Wolverhampton (2000) and Worcester (pre-1900).

Certain cities have also been granted a lord mayoralty – this grant confers no additional powers or functions and is purely honorific. Cities with lord mayors are: Birmingham, Bradford, Bristol, Canterbury, Chester, Coventry, Exeter, Kingston-upon-Hull, Leeds, Leicester, Liverpool, London, Manchester, Newcastle-upon-Tyne, Norwich, Nottingham, Oxford, Plymouth, Portsmouth, Sheffield, Stoke-on-Trent, Westminster and York.

BATH (PRE-1900)

Bath stands on the River Avon between the Cotswold Hills to the north and the Mendips to the south. In the early 18th century, Bath became England's premier spa town where the rich and celebrated members of fashionable society gathered to 'take the waters' and enjoy the town's theatres and concert rooms. During this period the architect John Wood laid the foundations for a new Georgian city to be built using the honey-coloured stone for which Bath is famous today.

Contemporary Bath is a thriving tourist destination and remains a leading cultural, religious and historical centre with many art galleries and historic sites including the Pump Room (1790); the Royal Crescent (1767); the Circus (1754); the 18th-century Assembly Rooms (housing the Museum of Costume); Pulteney Bridge (1771); the Guildhall and the Abbey, now over 500 years old, which is built on the site of a Saxon monastery. In 2006 the Bath Thermae Spa was completed and the hot springs re-opened to the public for the first time since 1978; combining five historic spa buildings with contemporary architecture, it is the only spa in the UK to utilise naturally occurring thermal waters.

BIRMINGHAM (PRE-1900)

Birmingham is Britain's second largest city, with a population of nearly one million. The generally accepted derivation of 'Birmingham' is the *ham* (dwelling-place) of

the *ing* (family) of *Beorma*, presumed to have been Saxon. During the Industrial Revolution the town grew into a major manufacturing centre and in 1889 was granted city status.

Recent developments include Millennium Point, which houses Thinktank, the Birmingham science museum, and Brindleyplace, a development of shops, offices and leisure facilities on a former industrial site clustered around canals. In 2003 the Bullring shopping centre was officially opened as part of the city's urban regeneration programme.

The principal buildings are the Town Hall (1834–50), the Council House (1879), Victoria Law Courts (1891), the University of Birmingham (1906–9), the 13th-century Church of St Martin-in-the-Bull-Ring (rebuilt 1873), the cathedral (formerly St Philip's Church) (1711), the Roman Catholic cathedral of St Chad (1839–41), the Assay Office (1773), the Rotunda (1964) and the National Exhibition Centre (1976). There is also the Birmingham Museum and Art Gallery which was founded in 1885 and is home to a collection of Pre-Raphaelite paintings.

BRADFORD (PRE-1900)

During the Industrial Revolution of the 18th and 19th centuries Bradford expanded rapidly, largely as a result of the thriving wool industry.

Bradford city centre has a host of buildings with historical and cultural interest, including City Hall, with its 19th-century Lord Mayor's rooms and Victorian law court; Bradford Cathedral; the Priestley, a theatre and arts centre originally established as the Bradford Civic Playhouse by J. B. Priestley and friends; the Colour Museum; the National Museum of Photography, Film and Television which houses five floors of interactive displays and three cinemas; Piece Hall Yard which incorporates the Bradford Club, a Victorian Gothic style building dating from 1837, and the Peace Museum.

BRIGHTON AND HOVE (2000)

Brighton and Hove is situated on the south coast of England, around 96 km (60 miles) south of London. Originally a fishing village called Brighthelmstone, it was transformed into a fashionable seaside resort in the 18th century when Dr Richard Russell popularised the benefits of his 'sea-water cure'; as one of the closest beaches to London, Brighton began to attract wealthy visitors. One of these was the Prince Regent (the future King George IV), who first visited in 1783 and became so fond of the city that in 1807 he bought the former farmhouse he had been renting, and gradually turned it into Brighton's most recognisable building, the Royal Pavilion. The Pavilion is renowned for its Indo-Saracenic exterior, featuring minarets and an enormous central dome designed by John Nash, combined with the lavish chinoiserie of Frederick Crace's and Robert Jones' interiors.

Brighton and Hove's Regency heritage can also be seen in the numerous elegant squares and crescents designed by Amon Wilds and Augustin Busby that dominate the seafront.

Brighton and Hove is once again a fashionable resort, known for its cafe culture, lively nightlife and thriving gay scene.

BRISTOL (PRE-1900)

Bristol was a royal borough before the Norman conquest. The earliest form of the name is *Bricgstow*.

The principal buildings include the 12th-century

Cathedral with Norman chapter house and gateway; the 14th-century Church of St Mary Redcliffe; Wesley's Chapel, Broadmead; the Merchant Venturers' Almshouses; the Council House (1956); the Guildhall; the Exchange (erected from the designs of John Wood in 1743); Cabot Tower; the University and Clifton College. The Roman Catholic cathedral at Clifton was opened in 1973.

The Clifton Suspension Bridge, with a span of 214m (702ft) over the Avon, was projected by Isambard Kingdom Brunel in 1836 but was not completed until 1864. Brunel's SS *Great Britain,* the first ocean-going propeller-driven ship, now forms a museum at the Western Dockyard, from where she was originally launched in 1843. The docks themselves have been extensively restored and redeveloped; the 19th-century two-storey former tea warehouse is now the Arnolfini centre for contemporary arts, and an 18th-century sail loft houses the Architecture Centre. Behind the baroque-domed facade of the former 'E' Shed are shops, cafes, restaurants and the Watershed Media Centre, and on Princes Wharf disused transit sheds house the Industrial Museum.

CAMBRIDGE (1951)

Cambridge, a settlement far older than its ancient university, lies on the River Cam (or Granta). The city is a county town and regional headquarters. Its industries include technology research and development, and biotechnology. Among its open spaces are Jesus Green, Sheep's Green, Coe Fen, Parker's Piece, Christ's Pieces, the University Botanic Garden, and the 'Backs' – lawns and gardens through which the Cam winds behind the principal line of college buildings. Historical sites east of the Cam include King's Parade, Great St Mary's Church, Gibbs' Senate House and King's College Chapel.

University and college buildings provide the outstanding features of Cambridge's architecture but several churches (especially St Benet's, the oldest building in the city, and Holy Sepulchre or the Round Church) are also notable. The Guildhall (1937) stands on a site, of which at least part has held municipal buildings since 1224.

CANTERBURY (PRE-1900)

Canterbury, seat of the Archbishop of Canterbury, the primate of the Church of England, dates back to prehistoric times. It was the Roman *Durovernum Cantiacorum* and the Saxon *Cant-wara-byrig* (stronghold of the men of Kent). It was here in 597 that St Augustine began the conversion of the English to Christianity, when Ethelbert, King of Kent, was baptised.

Of the Benedictine St Augustine's Abbey, burial place of the Jutish Kings of Kent, only ruins remain. St Martin's Church, on the eastern outskirts of the city, is stated by Bede to have been the place of worship of Queen Bertha, the Christian wife of King Ethelbert, before the advent of St Augustine.

In 1170 the rivalry of Church and State culminated in the murder in Canterbury Cathedral, by Henry II's knights, of Archbishop Thomas Becket. His shrine became a great centre of pilgrimage, as described in Chaucer's *Canterbury Tales.* After the Reformation pilgrimages ceased, but the prosperity of the city was strengthened by an influx of Huguenot refugees, who introduced weaving. The poet and playwright Christopher Marlowe was born and raised in Canterbury, and there are also literary associations with Defoe, Dickens, Joseph Conrad and Somerset Maugham.

The cathedral, its architecture ranging from the 11th to the 15th centuries, is famous worldwide. Visitors are attracted particularly to the Martyrdom, the Black Prince's Tomb, the Warriors' Chapel and the many examples of medieval stained glass.

The medieval city walls are built on Roman foundations and the 14th-century West Gate is one of the finest buildings of its kind in the country.

The 1,000-seat Marlowe Theatre is a centre for the Canterbury Arts Festival each autumn.

CARLISLE (PRE-1900)

Carlisle is situated at the confluence of the River Eden and River Caldew, 497km (309 miles) north-west of London and around 16km (10 miles) from the Scottish border. It was granted a charter in 1158.

The city stands at the western end of Hadrian's Wall and dates from the original Roman settlement of *Luguvalium.* Granted to Scotland in the tenth century, Carlisle is not included in the Domesday Book. William Rufus reclaimed the area in 1092 and the castle and city walls were built to guard Carlisle and the western border; the citadel is a Tudor addition to protect the south of the city. Border disputes were common until the problem of the Debateable Lands was settled in 1552. During the Civil War the city remained Royalist; in 1745 Carlisle was besieged for the last time by the Young Pretender (Bonnie Prince Charlie).

The cathedral, originally a 12th-century Augustinian priory, was enlarged in the 13th and 14th centuries after the diocese was created in 1133. To the south is a restored tithe barn and nearby the 18th-century church of St Cuthbert, the third to stand on a site dating from the seventh century.

Carlisle is the major shopping, commercial and agricultural centre for the area, and industries include the manufacture of metal goods, biscuits and textiles. However, the largest employer is the services sector, most notably in central and local government, retailing and transport. The city occupies an important position at the centre of a network of major roads, as a stage on the main west coast rail services, and with its own airport at Crosby-on-Eden.

CHESTER (PRE-1900)

Chester is situated on the River Dee. Its recorded history dates from the first century when the Romans founded the fortress of *Deva.* The city's name is derived from the Latin *castra* (a camp or encampment). During the Middle Ages, Chester was the principal port of north-west England but declined with the silting of the Dee estuary and competition from Liverpool. The city was also an important military centre, notably during Edward I's Welsh campaigns and the Elizabethan Irish campaigns. During the Civil War, Chester supported the King and was besieged from 1643 to 1646. Chester's first charter was granted c.1175 and the city was incorporated in 1506. The office of sheriff is the earliest created in the country (1120s), and in 1992 the mayor was granted the title of Lord Mayor, who also enjoys the title 'Admiral of the Dee'.

The city's architectural features include the city walls (an almost complete two-mile circuit), the unique 13th-century Rows (covered galleries above the street-level shops), the Victorian Gothic Town Hall (1869), the castle (rebuilt 1788 and 1822) and numerous half-timbered buildings. The cathedral was a Benedictine abbey until the Dissolution of the Monasteries. Remaining monastic buildings include the chapter house, refectory and cloisters and there is a modern free-standing bell tower. The Norman church of St John the Baptist was a cathedral church in the early Middle Ages.

COVENTRY (PRE-1900)
Coventry is an important industrial centre, producing vehicles, machine tools, agricultural machinery, man-made fibres, aerospace components and telecommunications equipment. New investment has come from financial services, power transmission, professional services, leisure and education.

The city owes its beginning to Leofric, Earl of Mercia, and his wife Godiva who, in 1043, founded a Benedictine monastery. The guildhall of St Mary and three of the city's churches date from the 14th and 15th centuries, and 16th-century almshouses can still be seen. Coventry's first cathedral was destroyed during the Reformation, its second in the 1940 blitz (the walls and spire remain) and the new cathedral designed by Sir Basil Spence, consecrated in 1962, now draws numerous visitors.

Coventry is the home of the University of Warwick, Coventry University, the Westwood Business Park, the Museum of British Road Transport and the Skydome Arena.

DURHAM (PRE-1900)
The city of Durham is a major tourist attraction and its prominent Norman cathedral and castle are set high on a wooded peninsula overlooking the River Wear. The cathedral was founded as a shrine for the body of St Cuthbert in 995. The present building dates from 1093 and among its many treasures is the tomb of the Venerable Bede (673–735). Durham's prince bishops had unique powers up to 1836, being lay rulers as well as religious leaders. As a palatinate, Durham could have its own army, nobility, coinage and courts. The castle was the main seat of the prince bishops for nearly 800 years; it is now used as a college by the University of Durham. The university, founded in the early 19th century on the initiative of Bishop William Van Mildert, is England's third oldest.

Among other buildings of interest is the Guildhall in the Market Place which dates from the 14th century. Work has been carried out to conserve this area as part of the city's contribution to the Council of Europe's Urban Renaissance Campaign. Annual events include Durham's regatta in June (claimed to be the oldest rowing event in Britain) and the annual Gala (formerly Durham Miners' Gala) in July.

The economy has undergone a significant change with the replacement of mining as the dominant industry by 'white collar' employment. Although still a predominantly rural area, the industrial and commercial sectors are growing and a wide range of manufacturing and service industries are based on industrial estates in and around the city. A research and development centre, linked to the university, also plays an important role in the local economy.

KINGSTON-UPON-HULL (PRE-1900)
Hull (officially Kingston-upon-Hull, so named by Edward I) lies at the junction of the River Hull with the Humber, 35km (22 miles) from the North Sea. It is one of the major seaports of the United Kingdom. The port provides a wide range of cargo services, including ro-ro and container traffic, and handles an estimated million passengers annually on daily sailings to Rotterdam and Zeebrugge. There is a variety of manufacturing and service industries. City status was accorded in 1897 and the office of mayor raised to the dignity of Lord Mayor in 1914.

The city, restored after heavy air raid damage during the Second World War, has good educational facilities with both the University of Hull and the University of Lincoln being within its boundaries. Hull is home to the world's only submarium, The Deep, a £45.5m project which opened in 2002, and the Kingston Communications Stadium, with a seating capacity for 25,000, which was also completed in 2002.

Tourism is a growing industry; the old town area has been renovated and includes museums, a marina and a shopping complex. Just west of the city is the Humber Bridge, the fourth-largest suspension bridge in the world.

LEEDS (PRE-1900)
Leeds, situated in the lower Aire Valley, is a junction for road, rail, canal and air services and an important commercial centre. It was first incorporated by Charles I in 1626. The earliest forms of the name are *Loidis* or *Ledes*, the origins of which are obscure.

The principal buildings are the Civic Hall (1933), the Town Hall (1858), the Municipal Buildings and Art Gallery (1884) with the Henry Moore Gallery (1982), the Corn Exchange (1863) and the University. The parish church (St Peter's) was rebuilt in 1841; the 17th-century St John's Church has a fine interior with a famous English Renaissance screen; the last remaining 18th-century church in the city is Holy Trinity in Boar Lane (1727). Kirkstall Abbey (about three miles from the centre of the city), founded by Henry de Lacy in 1152, is one of the most complete examples of a Cistercian house now remaining. Temple Newsam, birthplace of Lord Darnley and largely rebuilt by Sir Arthur Ingram c.1620, was acquired by the council in 1922. Adel Church, about five miles from the centre of the city, is a fine Norman structure. The Royal Armouries Museum forms part of a group of museums, including the Tower of London, which house the national collection of antique arms and armour.

LEICESTER (1919)
Leicester is situated in central England. The city was an important Roman settlement and also one of the five Danish boroughs of Danelaw. In 1485 Richard III was buried in Leicester following his death at the nearby Battle of Bosworth. In 1589 Queen Elizabeth I granted a charter to the city and the ancient title was confirmed by letters patent in 1919.

The textile industry, responsible for Leicester's early expansion, has declined in recent years, although the city still maintains a strong manufacturing base. Cotton mills and factories are now undergoing extensive regeneration and are being converted into offices, apartments, bars and restaurants. The principal buildings include the two universities (the University of Leicester and De Montfort University), as well as the Town Hall, the 13th-century Guildhall, De Montfort Hall, Leicester Cathedral, the Jewry Wall (the UK's highest standing Roman wall), St Nicholas Church and St Mary de Castro church. The motte and Great Hall of Leicester can be seen from the castle gardens, situated next to the River Soar.

Leicester is now one of the UK's most ethnically diverse cities – home to the only Jain temple in the western world and hosting the country's second-largest Caribbean carnival.

LINCOLN (PRE-1900)

Situated 64km (40 miles) inland on the River Witham, Lincoln derives its name from a contraction of *Lindum Colonia*, the settlement founded in AD 48 by the Romans to command the crossing of Ermine Street and Fosse Way. Sections of the third-century Roman city wall can be seen, including an extant gateway (Newport Arch), and excavations have discovered traces of a sewerage system unique in Britain. The Romans also drained the surrounding fenland and created a canal system, laying the foundations of Lincoln's agricultural prosperity and also the city's importance in the medieval wool trade as a port and staple town.

As one of the five boroughs of Danelaw, Lincoln was an important trading centre in the ninth and tenth centuries and prosperity from the wool trade lasted until the 14th century. This wealth enabled local merchants to build parish churches, of which three survive, and there are also remains of a 12th-century Jewish community (Jew's House and Court, Aaron's House). However, the removal of the staple to Boston in 1369 heralded a decline, from which the city only recovered fully in the 19th century, when improved fen drainage made Lincoln agriculturally important. Improved canal and rail links led to industrial development, mainly in the manufacture of machinery, components and engineering products.

The castle was built shortly after the Norman Conquest and is unusual in having two mounds; on one motte stands a keep (Lucy's Tower) added in the 12th century. It currently houses one of the four surviving copies of the Magna Carta. The cathedral was begun c.1073 when the first Norman bishop moved the see of Lindsey to Lincoln, but was mostly destroyed by fire and earthquake in the 12th century. Rebuilding was begun by St Hugh and completed over a century later. Other notable architectural features are the 12th-century High Bridge, the oldest in Britain still to carry buildings, and the Guildhall, situated above the 15th–16th-century Stonebow gateway.

LIVERPOOL (PRE-1900)

Liverpool, on the north bank of the River Mersey, 5km (3 miles) from the Irish Sea, is the United Kingdom's foremost port for Atlantic trade. Tunnels link Liverpool with Birkenhead and Wallasey.

There are 2,100 acres of dockland on both sides of the river and the Gladstone and Royal Seaforth Docks can accommodate tanker-sized vessels. Liverpool Free Port was opened in 1984.

Liverpool was created a free borough in 1207 and a city in 1880. From the early 18th century it expanded rapidly with the growth of industrialisation and Atlantic trade. Surviving buildings from this period include the Bluecoat Chambers (1717, formerly the Bluecoat School), the Town Hall (1754, rebuilt to the original design 1795), and buildings in Rodney Street, Canning Street and the suburbs. Notable from the 19th and 20th centuries are the Anglican cathedral, built from the designs of Sir Giles Gilbert Scott (the foundation stone was laid in 1904, but the building was only completed in 1980); the Catholic Metropolitan Cathedral (designed by Sir Frederick Gibberd, consecrated 1967) and St George's Hall (1842), regarded as one of the finest modern examples of classical architecture. The refurbished Albert Dock (designed by Jesse Hartley) contains the Merseyside Maritime Museum and Tate Gallery, Liverpool.

In 1852 an act was passed establishing a public library, museum and art gallery; as a result Liverpool had one of the first public libraries in the country. The Brown, Picton and Hornby libraries form one of the country's major collections. The Victoria Building of Liverpool University; the Royal Liver, Cunard and Mersey Docks & Harbour Company buildings at the Pier Head; the Municipal Buildings and the Philharmonic Hall are other examples of the city's fine architecture.

Six areas of Liverpool's maritime mercantile city were designated as UNESCO World Heritage Sites in 2004, and Liverpool has been elected as European Capital of Culture for 2008.

MANCHESTER (PRE-1900)

Manchester (the *Mamucium* of the Romans, who occupied it in AD 79) is a commercial and industrial centre engaged in the engineering, chemical, clothing, food processing and textile industries and in education. Banking, insurance and a growing leisure industry are among the prime commercial activities. The city is connected with the sea by the Manchester Ship Canal, opened in 1894, 57km (35.5 miles) long, and accommodating ships up to 15,000 tons.

The principal buildings are the Town Hall, erected in 1877 from the designs of Alfred Waterhouse, with a large extension of 1938; the Royal Exchange (1869, enlarged 1921); the Central Library (1934); Heaton Hall, the 17th-century Chetham Library; the Rylands Library (1900), which includes the Althorp collection; the university precinct; the 15th-century cathedral (formerly the parish church); the Manchester Central conference and exhibition centre and the Bridgewater Hall (1996) concert venue. Manchester is the home of the Hallé Orchestra, the Royal Northern College of Music, the Royal Exchange Theatre and numerous public art galleries.

To accommodate the Commonwealth Games held in the city in 2002, new sports facilities were built including a stadium, swimming pool complex and the National Cycling Centre.

The town received its first charter of incorporation in 1838 and was created a city in 1853.

NEWCASTLE UPON TYNE (PRE-1900)

Newcastle upon Tyne, on the north bank of the River Tyne, is 13km (8 miles) from the North Sea. A cathedral and university city, it is the administrative, commercial and cultural centre for north-east England and the principal port. It is an important manufacturing centre with a wide variety of industries.

The principal buildings include the Castle Keep (12th century), Black Gate (13th century), Blackfriars (13th century), West Walls (13th century), St Nicholas's Cathedral (15th century, fine lantern tower), St Andrew's Church (12th–14th century), St John's (14th–15th century), All Saints (1786 by Stephenson), St Mary's Roman Catholic Cathedral (1844), Trinity House (17th century), Sandhill (16th-century houses), Guildhall (Georgian), Grey Street (1834–9), Central Station (1846–50), Laing Art Gallery (1904), University of Newcastle Physics Building (1962) and Medical Building (1985), Civic Centre (1963), Central Library (1969) and Eldon Square shopping development (1976). Open spaces include the Town Moor (927 acres) and Jesmond Dene. Ten bridges span the Tyne at Newcastle, including the tilting Millennium Bridge (2001), which links the city with Gateshead to the south.

The city's name is derived from the 'new castle' (1080) erected as a defence against the Scots. In 1400 it was made a county, and in 1882 a city.

NORWICH (PRE-1900)

Norwich grew from an early Anglo-Saxon settlement near the confluence of the rivers Yare and Wensum, and now serves as provincial capital for the predominantly agricultural region of East Anglia. The name is thought to relate to the most northerly of a group of Anglo-Saxon villages or *wics*. The city's first known charter was granted in 1158 by Henry II.

Norwich serves its surrounding area as a market town and commercial centre, with banking and insurance prominent among the city's businesses. From the 14th century until the Industrial Revolution, Norwich was the regional centre of the woollen industry, but now the biggest single industry is financial services and principal trades are engineering, printing, shoemaking, the production of chemicals and clothing, food processing and technology. Norwich is accessible to seagoing vessels by means of the River Yare, entered at Great Yarmouth, 32km (20 miles) to the east.

Among many historic buildings are the cathedral (completed in the 12th century and surmounted by a 15th-century spire 96m (315ft) in height); the keep of the Norman castle (now a museum and art gallery); the 15th-century flint-walled Guildhall; some thirty medieval parish churches; St Andrew's and Blackfriars' Halls; the Tudor houses preserved in Elm Hill and the Georgian Assembly House. The University of East Anglia is on the city's western boundary.

NOTTINGHAM (PRE-1900)

Nottingham stands on the River Trent. *Snotingaham* or *Notingeham,* literally the homestead of the people of Snot, is the Anglo-Saxon name for the Celtic settlement of *Tigguocobauc,* or the house of caves. In 878, Nottingham became one of the five boroughs of Danelaw. William the Conqueror ordered the construction of Nottingham Castle, while the town itself developed rapidly under Norman rule. Its laws and rights were later formally recognised by Henry II's charter in 1155. The castle became a favoured residence of King John. In 1642 King Charles I raised his personal standard at Nottingham Castle at the start of the Civil War.

Nottingham is home to Notts County FC (the world's oldest football league side), Nottingham Forest FC, Nottingham Racecourse, Trent Bridge cricket ground and the National Watersports Centre. The principal industries include textiles, pharmaceuticals, food manufacturing, engineering and telecommunications. There are two universities within the city boundaries.

Architecturally, Nottingham has a wealth of notable buildings, particularly those designed in the Victorian era by T. C. Hine and Watson Fothergill. The city council owns the castle, of Norman origin but restored in 1878, Wollaton Hall (1580–8), Newstead Abbey (home of Lord Byron), the Guildhall (1888) and Council House (1929). St Mary's, St Peter's and St Nicholas' churches are of interest, as is the Roman Catholic cathedral (Pugin, 1842–4). Nottingham was granted city status in 1897.

OXFORD (PRE-1900)

Oxford is a university city, an important industrial centre and a market town. Industry played a minor part in Oxford until the motor industry was established in 1912.

Oxford is known for its architecture, its oldest specimens being the reputedly Saxon tower of St Michael's Church, the remains of the Norman castle and city walls, and the Norman church at Iffley. It also has many Gothic buildings, such as the Divinity Schools, the Old Library at Merton College, William of Wykeham's New College, Magdalen and Christ Church colleges and many other college buildings. Later centuries are represented by the Laudian quadrangle at St John's College, the Renaissance Sheldonian Theatre by Wren, Trinity College Chapel, All Saints Church, Hawksmoor's mock-Gothic at All Souls College, and the 18th-century Queen's College. In addition to individual buildings, High Street and Radcliffe Square both form interesting architectural compositions. Most of the colleges have gardens, those of Magdalen, New College, St John's and Worcester being the largest.

ST ALBANS (PRE-1900)

The origins of St Albans, situated on the River Ver, stem from the Roman town of *Verulamium.* Named after the first Christian martyr in Britain, who was executed there, St Albans has developed around the Norman abbey and cathedral church (consecrated 1115), built partly of materials from the old Roman city. The museums house Iron Age and Roman artefacts and the Roman theatre, unique in Britain, has a stage as opposed to an amphitheatre. Archaeological excavations in the city centre have revealed evidence of pre-Roman, Saxon and medieval occupation.

The town's significance grew to the extent that it was a signatory and venue for the drafting of the Magna Carta. It was also the scene of riots during the Peasants' Revolt, the French King John was imprisoned there after the Battle of Poitiers, and heavy fighting took place there during the Wars of the Roses.

Previously controlled by the Abbot, the town achieved a charter in 1553 and city status in 1877. The street market, first established in 1553, is still an important feature of the city, as are many hotels and inns, surviving from the days when St Albans was an important coach stop. Tourist attractions include historic churches and houses and a 15th-century clock tower.

The city is now home to a wide range of businesses, with special emphasis on information and legal services. In addition, it is home to the Royal National Rose Society and Rothamsted Park, the agricultural research centre.

SALISBURY (PRE-1900)

The history of Salisbury centres around the cathedral and cathedral close. The city evolved from an Iron Age camp a mile to the north of its current position which was strengthened by the Romans and called *Serviodunum.* The Normans built a castle and cathedral on the site and renamed it Sarum. In 1220 Bishop Richard Poore and the architect Elias de Derham decided to build a new Gothic style cathedral. The cathedral was completed 38 years later and a community known as New Sarum, now called Salisbury, grew around it. Originally the cathedral had a squat tower; the 404ft spire that makes the cathedral the tallest medieval structure in the world was added c.1315. A walled close with houses for the clergy was built around the cathedral; the Medieval Hall still stands today, alongside buildings dating from the 13th to the 20th century, some designed by Sir Christopher Wren.

A prosperous wool and cloth trade allowed Salisbury to flourish until the 17th century. When the wool trade declined new crafts were established including cutlery, leather and basket work, saddlery, lacemaking, joinery and malting. By 1750 it had become an important road junction and coaching centre and in the Victorian era the railways enabled a new age of expansion and prosperity. Today Salisbury is a thriving tourist centre.

SHEFFIELD (PRE-1900)

Sheffield is situated at the junction of the Sheaf, Porter, Rivelin and Loxley valleys with the River Don and was created a city in 1893. Though its cutlery, silverware and plate have long been famous, Sheffield has other and now more important industries: special and alloy steels, engineering, tool-making, medical equipment and media-related industries (in its new cultural industries quarter). Sheffield has two universities and is an important research centre.

The parish church of St Peter and St Paul, founded in the 12th century, became the cathedral church of the Diocese of Sheffield in 1914. The Roman Catholic Cathedral Church of St Marie (founded 1847) was created a cathedral for the new diocese of Hallam in 1980. Parts of the present building date from c.1435. The principal buildings are the Town Hall (1897), the Cutlers' Hall (1832), City Hall (1932), Graves Art Gallery (1934), Mappin Art Gallery, the Crucible Theatre and the restored Lyceum theatre, which dates from 1897 and was reopened in 1990. Three major sports venues were opened between 1990 and 1991: Sheffield Arena, Don Valley Stadium and Pond's Forge. The Millennium Galleries opened in 2001.

SOUTHAMPTON (1964)

Southampton is a major seaport on the south coast of England, situated between the mouths of the Test and Itchen rivers. Southampton's natural deep-water harbour has made the area an important settlement since the Romans built the first port (known as *Clausentum*) in the first century, and Southampton's port has witnessed several important departures, including those of King Henry V in 1415 for the Battle of Agincourt, RMS *Titanic* in 1912, and the *Mayflower* in 1620.

The city's strategic importance, not only as a seaport but also as a centre for aircraft production, meant that it was heavily bombed during the Second World War; however, many historically significant structures remain, including the Wool House, dating from 1417 and now used as the Maritime Museum; parts of the Norman city walls which are among the most complete in the UK; the Bargate, which was originally the main gateway into the city; God's House Tower, now the Museum of Archaeology; St Michael's, the city's oldest church; and the Tudor Merchants Hall.

Home to the National Oceanography Centre, the International Boat Show and some of the country's principal watersports venues, Southampton's coastal setting and maritime history remain its main focus, but it also features extensive parks and a thriving entertainment scene.

STOKE-ON-TRENT (1925)

Stoke-on-Trent, standing on the River Trent and familiarly known as 'the potteries', is the main centre of employment for the population of north Staffordshire. The city is the largest clayware producer in the world (china, earthenware, sanitary goods, refractories, bricks and tiles) and also has a wide range of other manufacturing industries, including steel, chemicals, engineering and tyres. Extensive reconstruction has been carried out in recent years.

The city was formed by the federation of the separate municipal authorities of Tunstall, Burslem, Hanley, Stoke, Fenton, and Longton in 1910 and received its city status in 1925.

WINCHESTER (PRE-1900)

Winchester, the ancient capital of England, is situated on the River Itchen. The city is rich in architecture of all types, especially notable is the cathedral. Built in 1079–93 the cathedral exhibits examples of Norman, early English and Perpendicular styles and is the burial place of author Jane Austen. Winchester College, founded in 1382, is one of the country's most famous public schools, and the original building (1393) remains largely unaltered. St Cross Hospital, another great medieval foundation, lies one mile south of the city. The almshouses were founded in 1136 by Bishop Henry de Blois, and Cardinal Henry Beaufort added a new almshouse of 'Noble Poverty' in 1446. The chapel and dwellings are of great architectural interest, and visitors may still receive the 'Wayfarer's Dole' of bread and ale.

Excavations have done much to clarify the origins and development of Winchester. Part of the forum and several of the streets from the Roman town have been discovered. Excavations in the Cathedral Close have uncovered the entire site of the Anglo-Saxon cathedral (known as the Old Minster) and parts of the New Minster which was built by Alfred's son, Edward the Elder, and is the burial place of the Alfredian dynasty. The original burial place of St Swithun, before his remains were translated to a site in the present cathedral, was also uncovered.

Excavations in other parts of the city have thrown much light on Norman Winchester, notably on the site of the Royal Castle (adjacent to which the new Law Courts have been built) and in the grounds of Wolvesey Castle, where the great house built by Bishops Giffard and Henry de Blois in the 12th century has been uncovered. The Great Hall, built by Henry III between 1222 and 1236, survives and houses the Arthurian Round Table.

YORK (PRE-1900)

The city of York is an archiepiscopal seat. Its recorded history dates from AD 71, when the Roman Ninth Legion established a base under Petilius Cerealis that would later become the fortress of *Eburacum*, or *Eboracum*. In Anglo-Saxon times the city was the royal and ecclesiastical centre of Northumbria, and after capture by a Viking army in AD 866 it became the capital of the Viking kingdom of Jorvik. By the 14th century the city had become a great mercantile centre, mainly because of its control of the wool trade, and was used as the chief base against the Scots. Under the Tudors its fortunes declined, although Henry VIII made it the headquarters of the Council of the North. Excavations on many sites, including Coppergate, have greatly expanded knowledge of Roman, Viking and medieval urban life.

With its development as a railway centre in the 19th century the commercial life of York expanded, and today the city is home to the award-winning National Railway Museum. The principal industries are the manufacture of chocolate, scientific instruments and sugar.

The city is rich in examples of architecture of all periods. The earliest church was built in AD 627 and, from the 12th to 15th centuries, the present Minster was built in a succession of styles. Other examples within the city are the medieval city walls and gateways, churches and guildhalls. Domestic architecture includes the Georgian mansions of The Mount, Micklegate and Bootham.

LORD-LIEUTENANTS AND HIGH SHERIFFS

Area	Lord-Lieutenant	High Sheriff (2007–8)
Bedfordshire	S. Whitbread	Dr Vaughan Southgate
Berkshire	P. Wroughton	Harry Henderson
Bristol	Mary Prior, MBE	William Durie
Buckinghamshire	Sir Henry Aubrey-Fletcher	Amanda Nicholson
Cambridgeshire	Hugh Duberly, CBE	Col. Peter Horrell, TD
Cheshire	W. Bromley-Davenport	Nicholas Bromley-Davenport
Cornwall	Lady Mary Holborow	Hon. Evelyn Boscawen
Cumbria	J. Cropper	Claire Hensman
Derbyshire	J. Bather	Roger Wardle
Devon	E. Dancer, CBE	Anthony Mildmay-White
Dorset	Valerie Pitt-Rivers	Adrian Scott
Durham	Sir Paul Nicholson	Ian Dewhirst
East Riding of Yorkshire	Hon. Susan Cunliffe-Lister	Nicholas Hildyard
East Sussex	Mrs P. Stewart-Roberts, OBE	Caroline Mayhew
Essex	Lord Petre	Lady Kemp-Welch
Gloucestershire	Henry Elwes	Jonathan Carr
Greater London	Lord Imbert, QPM	Jan Pethick
Greater Manchester	Warren Smith	Michael Oglesby
Hampshire	Mrs M. Fagan	Sarah Thorne
Herefordshire	Sir Thomas Dunne, KCVO	John Yorke
Hertfordshire	Countess of Verulam	Howard Guard
Isle of Wight	Maj.-Gen. Martin White, CB, CBE	Lt.-Col. David Langford
Kent	Allan Willett, CMG	Nigel Wheeler
Lancashire	Lord Shuttleworth	Ruth Winterbottom
Leicestershire	Lady Gretton	Barry Jackson
Lincolnshire	Mrs B. Cracroft-Eley	Patricia Ware
Merseyside	Dame Lorna Fox Muirhead, DBE	Prof. Philip Love, CBE
Norfolk	Richard Jewson	Earl of Romney
North Yorkshire	Lord Crathorne	Philip Ingham
Northamptonshire	Lady Juliet Townsend	Lady Harper
Northumberland	Sir John Riddell, CVO	Sir Hugh Blackett, Bt.
Nottinghamshire	Sir Andrew Buchanan, Bt.	Cdr. Peter Moore, RD
Oxfordshire	H. Brunner	Thomas Loyd
Rutland	Dr Laurence Howard, OBE	Barbara Gilman
Shropshire	A. Heber-Percy	Meriel Afia, LVO
Somerset	Lady Gass	David Medlock
South Yorkshire	David Moody	Col. Jonathan Hunt, OBE, TD
Staffordshire	J. Hawley, TD	Graham Stow, CBE
Suffolk	Lord Tollemache	Air Marshal Sir Richard Kemball, KCB, CBE
Surrey	Mrs S. Goad	Nicholas Sealy
Tyne and Wear	N. Sherlock, OBE	Hon. Nigel Westwood
Warwickshire	M. Dunne	Andrew Arkwright
West Midlands	Paul Sabapathy, CBE	Robert Tomlinson
West Sussex	H. Wyatt	Colin Field
West Yorkshire	Dr Ingrid Roscoe	Rhona Hartley, MBE
Wiltshire	John Bush, OBE	Hon. Peter Pleydell-Bouverie
Worcestershire	M. Brinton	John Yorke

COUNTY COUNCILS

Council & Administrative Headquarters	Telephone	Population*	Council Tax†	Chief Executive
Bedfordshire, Bedford	01234-363222	397,700	£1,082	Andrea Hill
Buckinghamshire, Aylesbury	01296-395000	481,500	£975	Chris Williams
Cambridgeshire, Cambridge	01223-717111	588,900	£932	Mike Parsons (acting)
Cheshire, Chester	0845-113 3311	679,900	£1,002	Jeremy Taylor
Cornwall, Truro	01872-322000	519,400	£970	Sheila Healy
Cumbria, Carlisle	01228-606060	498,900	£1,070	Peter Stybelski
Derbyshire, Matlock	01629-580000	747,500	£996	Nick Hodgson
Devon, Exeter	01392-382000	731,000	£1,024	Phil Norrey
Dorset, Dorchester	01305-251000	401,100	£1,049	David Jenkins
Durham, Durham	0191-383 3000	499,800	£995	Mark Lloyd
East Sussex, Lewes	01273-481000	497,900	£1,048	Cheryl Miller, CBE
Essex, Chelmsford	01245-492211	1,340,000	£1,004	Joanna Killian
Gloucestershire, Gloucester	01452-425000	575,200	£988	Peter Bungard
Hampshire, Winchester	01962-841841	1,259,500	£956	Peter Robertson
Hertfordshire, Hertford	01992-555555	1,048,200	£1,034	Caroline Tapster
Kent, Maidstone	01622-671411	1,369,900	£964	Peter Gilroy
Lancashire, Preston	0545-053 0000	1,156,100	£1,046	Chris Trinick
Leicestershire, Leicester	0116-232 3232	627,800	£970	John Sinnott
Lincolnshire, Lincoln	01522-552222	678,700	£987	Tony McArdle
Norfolk, Norwich	0844-800 8020	824,200	£1,052	David White
North Yorkshire, Northallerton	01609-780780	582,000	£944	John Marsden
Northamptonshire, Northampton	01604-236236	651,800	£918	Rory Borealis (acting)
Northumberland, Morpeth	01670-533000	311,300	£1,111	Mark Henderson
Nottinghamshire, Nottingham	0115-982 3823	762,700	£1,125	Roger Latham
Oxfordshire, Oxford	01865-792422	626,900	£1,049	Joanna Simons
Shropshire, Shrewsbury	0845-678 9000	289,000	£976	Carolyn Downs
Somerset, Taunton	0845-345 9166	515,600	£963	Alan Jones
Staffordshire, Stafford	01785-223121	816,700	£948	Nigel Pursey
Suffolk, Ipswich	0845-606 6067	692,100	£1,035	Mike More
Surrey, Kingston upon Thames	020-8541 8800	1,075,500	£1,010	Richard Shaw
Warwickshire, Warwick	01926-410410	533,900	£1,045	Jim Graham
West Sussex, Chichester	01243-777100	764,400	£1,051	Mark Hammond
Wiltshire, Trowbridge	01225-713000	446,600	£974	Dr Keith Robinson
Worcestershire, Worcester	01905-763763	555,800	£944	Rob Sykes

* Source: The Office of National Statistics – Mid-2005 Population Estimates (Crown copyright)
† Average 2007–8 Band D council tax in the county area exclusive of precepts for fire and police authorities. County councils claim their share of the combined council tax from the collection funds of the district authorities into whose area they fall. Average Band D council tax bills for the billing authority are given on the following pages

DISTRICT COUNCILS

District Council	Telephone	Population*	Council Tax†	Chief Executive
Adur	01273-263000	59,100	£1,432	Ian Lowrie
Allerdale	01900-326333	96,300	£1,401	Gillian Bishop
Alnwick	01665-510505	32,200	£1,369	William Batey
Amber Valley	01773-570222	118,600	£1,370	Peter Carney
Arun	01903-737500	144,500	£1,373	Ian Sumnall
Ashfield	01623-450000	114,000	£1,489	Alan Mellor
Ashford	01233-637311	110,000	£1,285	David Hill
Aylesbury Vale	01296-585858	168,100	£1,346	Andrew Grant
Babergh	01473-822801	85,100	£1,354	Patricia Rockall
Barrow-in-Furness	01229-894900	70,100	£1,435	Tom Campbell
Basildon	01268-533333	167,000	£1,417	Bala Mahendran
Basingstoke and Deane	01256-844844	156,900	£1,247	Gordon Holdcroft
Bassetlaw	01909-533533	110,700	£1,490	David Hunter
Bedford	01234-267422	153,000	£1,443	Shaun Field
Berwick-upon-Tweed	01289-330044	26,200	£1,370	Jane Pannell
Blaby	0116-275 0555	91,400	£1,340	Sandra Whiles
Blyth Valley	01670-542000	81,600	£1,337	Geoff Paul
Bolsover	01246-240000	73,200	£1,431	Wes Lumley
Boston	01205-314200	58,000	£1,293	Michael Gallagher
Braintree	01376-552525	137,800	£1,358	Allan Reid
Breckland	01362-695333	127,100	£1,327	Trevor Holden
Brentwood	01277-312500	70,900	£1,345	Bob McLintock
Bridgnorth	01746-713100	52,200	£1,375	John Harmeston
Broadland	01603-431133	121,100	£1,372	Colin Bland
Bromsgrove	01527-873232	91,500	£1,355	Kevin Dicks
Broxbourne	01992-785555	86,400	£1,269	Mike Walker
Broxtowe	0115-917 7777	109,100	£1,491	Ruth Hyde
Burnley	01282-425011	87,700	£1,463	Steve Rumbelow
CAMBRIDGE CITY	01223-457000	124,000	£1,283	Rob Hammond
Cannock Chase	01543-462621	93,200	£1,362	Stephen Brown
CANTERBURY CITY	01227-862000	143,700	£1,317	Colin Carmichael
Caradon	01579-341000	82,100	£1,315	Byron Davies
CARLISLE CITY	01228-817000	105,200	£1,430	Maggie Mooney
Carrick	01872-224400	90,600	£1,314	John Winskill
Castle Morpeth	01670-535000	49,900	£1,406	Ken Dunbar
Castle Point	01268-882200	87,000	£1,393	David Marchant
Charnwood	01509-263151	160,100	£1,313	Brian Hayes
Chelmsford	01245-606606	161,100	£1,352	Steve Packham
Cheltenham	01242-262626	111,700	£1,342	Andrew North
Cherwell	01295-252535	134,200	£1,379	Clive Baynes (acting)
CHESTER CITY	01244-324324	118,600	£1,361	Paul Durham
Chesterfield	01246-345345	100,000	£1,333	David Shaw
Chester-le-Street	0191-387 1919	53,200	£1,399	Roy Templeman
Chichester	01243-785166	109,300	£1,332	John Marsland
Chiltern	01494-729000	89,800	£1,359	Alan Goodrum
Chorley	01257-515151	103,700	£1,417	Donna Hall
Christchurch	01202-495000	45,100	£1,416	Michael Turvey
Colchester	01206-282222	163,400	£1,355	Adrian Pritchard
Congleton	01270-763231	91,800	£1,371	Glyn Chambers
Copeland	0845-054 8600	71,500	£1,419	Liam Murphy
Corby	01536-464000	53,500	£1,250	Chris Mallender
Cotswold	01285-623000	83,100	£1,345	Bob Austin
Craven	01756-700600	54,400	£1,368	Gill Dixon
Crawley	01293-438000	98,500	£1,352	Michael Coughlin
Crewe and Nantwich	01270-537777	113,600	£1,331	Paul Ancell
Dacorum	01442-228000	138,500	£1,325	Daniel Zammit
Dartford	01322-343434	87,400	£1,313	Graham Harris

* Source: ONS – Mid-2005 Population Estimates (Crown copyright)
† Average Band D council tax bill for 2007–8

District Council	Telephone	Population*	Council Tax†	Chief Executive
Daventry	01327-871100	75,900	£1,259	Ian Vincent
Derbyshire Dales	01629-761100	69,800	£1,403	David Wheatcroft
Derwentside	01207-218000	86,300	£1,462	Mike Clark
Dover	01304-821199	106,100	£1,326	Nadeem Aziz
DURHAM CITY	0191-386 6111	92,200	£1,409	Brian Spears
Easington	0191-527 0501	93,300	£1,539	Janet Johnson
East Cambridgeshire	01353-665555	78,500	£1,300	John Hill
East Devon	01395-516551	129,800	£1,357	Mark Williams
East Dorset	01202-886201	85,200	£1,459	Alan Breakwell
East Hampshire	01730-266551	111,300	£1,314	Will Godfrey
East Hertfordshire	01279-655261	131,800	£1,365	Anne Freimanis
East Lindsey	01507-601111	137,400	£1,245	Nigel Howells
East Northamptonshire	01832-742000	81,500	£1,253	David Oliver
East Staffordshire	01283-508000	106,900	£1,367	Simon Baker (acting)
Eastbourne	01323-410000	92,900	£1,448	Martin Ray
Eastleigh	023-8068 8000	116,600	£1,311	Bernie Topham
Eden	01768-817817	52,800	£1,413	Kevin Douglas
Ellesmere Port and Neston	0151-356 6789	80,600	£1,353	Stephen Ewbank
Elmbridge	01372-474474	130,300	£1,372	Rob Moran (acting)
Epping Forest	01992-564000	122,000	£1,372	Peter Hayward
Epsom and Ewell	01372-732000	68,500	£1,327	David Smith
Erewash	0115-907 2244	109,800	£1,359	Jeremy Jaroszek
EXETER CITY	01392-277888	117,600	£1,329	Philip Bostock
Fareham	01329-236100	108,500	£1,270	Alan Davies
Fenland	01354-654321	87,200	£1,370	Tim Pilsbury
Forest Heath	01638-719000	63,100	£1,359	David Burnip
Forest of Dean	01594-810000	80,900	£1,360	Tim Perrin
Fylde	01253-658658	76,400	£1,395	Phillip Woodward
Gedling	0115-901 3901	111,200	£1,470	Peter Murdock
GLOUCESTER CITY	01452-522232	111,300	£1,335	Julian Wain
Gosport	023-9258 4242	77,300	£1,328	Ian Lycett
Gravesham	01474-337000	95,200	£1,300	Jim Wintour
Great Yarmouth	01493-856100	92,500	£1,359	Richard Packham
Guildford	01483-505050	132,200	£1,336	David Hill
Hambleton	0845-121 1555	85,000	£1,291	Peter Simpson
Harborough	01858-828282	80,400	£1,342	Sue Smith
Harlow	01279-446611	77,700	£1,416	Malcolm Morley
Harrogate	01423-500600	155,300	£1,396	Michael Walsh
Hart	01252-622122	87,800	£1,325	Geoff Bonner
Hastings	0845-274 1066	84,600	£1,460	Roy Mawford
Havant	023-9247 4174	115,300	£1,314	Gwen Andrews
Hertsmere	020-8207 2277	93,900	£1,333	Eden Lee
High Peak	0845-129 7777	91,100	£1,377	Peter Sloman
Hinckley and Bosworth	01455-238141	102,800	£1,295	Steve Atkinson
Horsham	01403-215100	125,800	£1,337	Tom Crowley
Huntingdonshire	01480-388388	162,000	£1,306	David Monks
Hyndburn	01254-388111	81,600	£1,439	David Welsby
Ipswich	01473-432000	118,200	£1,462	James Hehir
Kennet	01380-724911	77,400	£1,345	Mark Boden
Kerrier	01209-614000	96,200	£1,316	Barry Manning
Kettering	01536-410333	86,000	£1,269	David Cook
King's Lynn and West Norfolk	01553-616200	140,400	£1,358	Ray Harding
LANCASTER CITY	01524-582000	138,000	£1,406	Mark Cullinan
Lewes	01273-471600	93,400	£1,479	John Crawford
Lichfield	01543-308000	95,500	£1,331	Nina Dawes
LINCOLN CITY	01522-881188	87,000	£1,331	Andrew Taylor
Macclesfield	01625-500500	150,500	£1,345	Vivienne Horton
Maidstone	01622-602000	143,400	£1,363	David Petford
Maldon	01621-854477	60,700	£1,375	Steve Watson
Malvern Hills	01684-862151	75,100	£1,337	Chris Bocock
Mansfield	01623-463463	99,000	£1,497	Ruth Marlow
Melton	01664-502502	48,300	£1,338	Lynn Aisbett
Mendip	01749-343399	107,300	£1,357	David Thomson
Mid Bedfordshire	08452-304040	129,400	£1,456	Jaki Salisbury
Mid Devon	01884-255255	73,000	£1,413	David Ablett (acting)
Mid Suffolk	01449-720711	89,900	£1,355	Andrew Good
Mid Sussex	01444-458166	129,000	£1,357	John Jory

District Council	Telephone	Population*	Council Tax†	Chief Executive
Mole Valley	01306-885001	81,100	£1,325	Darren Mepham
New Forest	023-8028 5000	171,700	£1,338	David Yates
Newark and Sherwood	01636-650000	110,800	£1,540	Andrew Muter
Newcastle-under-Lyme	01782-717717	123,400	£1,340	Mark Barrow
North Cornwall	01208-893333	84,100	£1,322	Mark Hall
North Devon	01271-327711	90,200	£1,405	John Sunderland
North Dorset	01258-454111	65,400	£1,411	Elizabeth Goodall
North East Derbyshire	01246-231111	97,300	£1,426	Mrs Lee Adams
North Hertfordshire	01462-474000	120,700	£1,361	John Campbell
North Kesteven	01529-414155	101,700	£1,297	Ian Fytche
North Norfolk	01263-513811	100,200	£1,371	Philip Burton
North Shropshire	01939-232771	59,100	£1,406	Nicola Yates
North Warwickshire	01827-715341	62,300	£1,420	Jeremy Hutchinson
North West Leicestershire	01530-454545	88,800	£1,364	Christine Fisher
North Wiltshire	01249-706111	129,400	£1,381	Delwyn Burbidge
Northampton	01604-837837	195,000	£1,289	John Edwards *(acting)*
NORWICH CITY	01603-212212	127,600	£1,422	Laura McGillivray
Nuneaton and Bedworth	02476-376376	120,700	£1,383	Christine Kerr
Oadby and Wigston	0116-288 8961	56,000	£1,345	Wendy Back
Oswestry	01691-671111	39,200	£1,440	Paul Shevlin
OXFORD CITY	01865-249811	149,800	£1,429	Peter Sloman
Pendle	01282-661661	89,300	£1,466	Stephen Barnes
Penwith	01736-362341	64,000	£1,263	Jim McKenna
PRESTON CITY	01772-906900	131,300	£1,463	Jim Carr
Purbeck	01929-556561	45,100	£1,443	Steve Mackenzie
Redditch	01527-64252	79,600	£1,354	Christopher Smith
Reigate and Banstead	01737-276000	127,200	£1,366	Nigel Clifford
Restormel	01726-223300	100,300	£1,276	Gareth Pinwell
Ribble Valley	01200-425111	56,900	£1,373	David Morris
Richmondshire	01748-829100	50,700	£1,383	Jack Neal
Rochford	01702-546366	79,500	£1,389	Paul Warren
Rossendale	01706-217777	66,000	£1,471	Carolyn Wilkins
Rother	01424-787878	86,000	£1,431	Derek Stevens
Rugby	01788-533533	91,600	£1,369	Simon Warren
Runnymede	01932-838383	79,600	£1,302	Tim Williams
Rushcliffe	0115-981 9911	107,800	£1,488	Allen Graham
Rushmoor	01252-398398	89,200	£1,307	Andrew Lloyd
Ryedale	01653-600666	52,000	£1,379	Janet Waggott
ST ALBANS CITY	01727-866100	133,500	£1,361	Daniel Goodwin
St Edmundsbury	01284-763233	101,500	£1,370	Deborah Cadman
SALISBURY CITY	01722-336272	115,800	£1,323	David Crook *(acting)*
Scarborough	01723-232323	107,000	£1,391	Jim Dillon
Sedgefield	01388-816166	87,800	£1,566	Brian Allen
Sedgemoor	0845-408 2540	109,900	£1,322	Mr Kerry Rickards
Selby	01757-705101	77,600	£1,370	Martin Connor
Sevenoaks	01732-227000	111,100	£1,363	Robin Hales
Shepway	01303-853000	99,500	£1,396	Alistair Stewart
Shrewsbury and Atcham	01743-281000	96,300	£1,366	Robin Hooper
South Bedfordshire	01582-472222	115,300	£1,527	Jon Ruddick
South Bucks	01895-837200	63,500	£1,341	Chris Furness
South Cambridgeshire	08450-450500	137,200	£1,293	Greg Harlock
South Derbyshire	01283-221000	87,700	£1,353	Frank McArdle
South Hams	01803-861234	82,800	£1,379	Ruth Bagley
South Holland	01775-761161	81,200	£1,288	Terry Huggins
South Kesteven	01476-406080	128,500	£1,265	Duncan Kerr
South Lakeland	01539-733333	102,900	£1,421	Peter Ridgway
South Norfolk	01508-533633	115,300	£1,393	Geoff Rivers
South Northamptonshire	0845-230 0226	86,000	£1,287	Jean Morgan
South Oxfordshire	01491-823000	128,200	£1,364	David Buckle
South Ribble	01772-421491	105,800	£1,426	Jean Hunter
South Shropshire	01584-813000	42,300	£1,443	Graham Biggs
South Somerset	01935-462462	156,100	£1,361	Philip Dolan
South Staffordshire	01902-696000	105,300	£1,301	Rolf Levesley
Spelthorne	01784-451499	88,500	£1,335	Roberto Tambini
Stafford	01785-619000	123,600	£1,320	David Rawlings
Staffordshire Moorlands	01538-483483	94,600	£1,340	Simon Baker
Stevenage	01438-242242	79,000	£1,339	Peter Ollis

District Council	Telephone	Population*	Council Tax†	Chief Executive
Stratford-on-Avon	01789-267575	119,000	£1,355	Paul Lankester
Stroud	01453-766321	110,000	£1,388	David Hagg
Suffolk Coastal	01394-383789	119,600	£1,342	Stephen Baker
Surrey Heath	01276-707100	81,500	£1,362	Barry Catchpole
Swale	01795-424341	126,800	£1,303	Mark Bilsborough
Tamworth	01827-709709	74,200	£1,301	David Weatherley
Tandridge	01883-722000	79,400	£1,366	Stephen Weigel
Taunton Deane	01823-356356	106,800	£1,312	Penny James
Teesdale	01833-690000	24,900	£1,433	Neil Stokell
Teignbridge	01626-361101	124,500	£1,383	Nicola Bulbeck
Tendring	01255-686868	141,800	£1,344	John Hawkins
Test Valley	01264-368000	112,300	£1,270	Roger Tetstall
Tewkesbury	01684-295010	78,400	£1,288	Bob Austin
Thanet	01843-577000	128,100	£1,348	Richard Samuel
Three Rivers	01923-776611	84,600	£1,353	Steven Halls
Tonbridge and Malling	01732-844522	112,400	£1,332	David Hughes
Torridge	01237-428700	62,500	£1,385	John van de Laarschot
Tunbridge Wells	01892-526121	106,200	£1,306	Sheila Wheeler
Tynedale	01434-652121	59,800	£1,381	Richard Robson
Uttlesford	01799-510400	71,100	£1,363	Alasdair Bovaird
Vale of White Horse	01235-520202	117,000	£1,336	Terry Stock
Vale Royal	01606-862862	124,600	£1,357	Anne Bingham-Holmes
Wansbeck	01670-532200	61,700	£1,356	Bob Stephenson
Warwick	01926-450000	140,300	£1,342	Chris Elliott
Watford	01923-226400	79,300	£1,409	Alastair Robertson
Waveney	01502-562111	114,700	£1,317	Glen Garrod
Waverley	01483-523333	116,800	£1,365	Mary Orton
Wealden	01892-653311	141,000	£1,470	Charles Lant
Wear Valley	01388-765555	62,100	£1,423	Michael Lainge
Wellingborough	01933-229777	73,900	£1,227	Lyn Martin-Bennison
Welwyn & Hatfield	01707-357000	100,500	£1,383	Michel Saminaden
West Devon	01822-813600	50,600	£1,434	David Incoll
West Dorset	01305-251010	95,800	£1,432	David Clarke
West Lancashire	01695-577177	109,500	£1,416	William Taylor
West Lindsey	01427-676676	84,900	£1,329	Duncan Sharkey
West Oxfordshire	01993-861000	97,700	£1,309	David Neudegg
West Somerset	01643-703704	35,500	£1,334	Tim Howes
West Wiltshire	01225-776655	124,100	£1,369	Andrew Pate
Weymouth and Portland	01305-838000	64,600	£1,501	Tom Grainger
WINCHESTER CITY	01962-840222	112,500	£1,308	Simon Eden
Woking	01483-755855	90,500	£1,372	Ray Morgan
WORCESTER CITY	01905-723471	94,300	£1,314	David Wareing
Worthing	01903-239999	98,100	£1,367	Ian Lowrie
Wychavon	01386-565000	116,900	£1,305	Jack Hegarty
Wycombe	01494-461000	160,200	£1,320	Ms K. Satterford
Wyre	01253-891000	109,900	£1,397	Jim Corry
Wyre Forest	01562-732928	98,500	£1,361	Walter Delin

Councils in CAPITAL LETTERS have city status

METROPOLITAN BOROUGH COUNCILS

Metropolitan Borough Councils	Telephone	Population*	Council Tax†	Chief Executive
Barnsley	01226-770770	222,100	£1,278	Philip Coppard
BIRMINGHAM CITY	0121-303 9944	1,001,200	£1,189	Stephen Hughes
Bolton	01204-333333	265,400	£1,321	Bernard Knight
BRADFORD CITY	01274-432001	485,000	£1,206	Tony Reeves
Bury	0161-253 5000	183,500	£1,289	Mark Sanders
Calderdale	01422-357257	195,300	£1,360	Paul Sheehan
COVENTRY CITY	024-7683 3333	304,200	£1,349	Stella Manzie
Doncaster	01302-734444	289,600	£1,179	Paul Hart *(acting)*
Dudley	01384-812345	305,600	£1,145	Andrew Sparke
Gateshead	0191-433 3000	191,500	£1,468	Roger Kelly
Kirklees	01484-221000	394,600	£1,290	Rob Vincent
Knowsley	0151-489 6000	149,400	£1,297	Sheena Ramsey
LEEDS CITY	0113-234 8080	723,100	£1,188	Paul Rogerson
LIVERPOOL CITY	0151-233 3000	447,500	£1,379	Colin Hilton
MANCHESTER CITY	0161-234 5000	441,200	£1,235	Sir Howard Bernstein
NEWCASTLE UPON TYNE CITY	0191-232 8520	276,400	£1,396	Ian Stratford
North Tyneside	0191-200 6565	192,300	£1,367	Andrew Kerr
Oldham	0161-911 3000	219,200	£1,481	Andrew Kilburn
Rochdale	01706-647474	206,400	£1,317	Roger Ellis
Rotherham	01709-382121	253,200	£1,320	Mike Cuff
St Helens	01744-456000	176,300	£1,279	Carole Hudson
SALFORD CITY	0161-794 4711	216,400	£1,414	Barbara Spicer
Sandwell	0121-569 2200	286,300	£1,248	Allison Fraser
Sefton	0151-922 4040	280,900	£1,351	Graham Haywood
SHEFFIELD CITY	0114-272 6444	520,700	£1,386	Sir Robert Kerslake
Solihull	0121-704 6000	200,900	£1,200	Katherine Kerswell
South Tyneside	0191-427 1717	151,300	£1,331	Irene Lucas
Stockport	0161-480 4949	281,600	£1,376	John Schultz
SUNDERLAND CITY	0191-553 1000	283,700	£1,247	Jed Fitzgerald
Tameside	0161-342 8355	214,100	£1,251	Janet Callender
Trafford	0161-912 1212	213,200	£1,152	David McNulty
WAKEFIELD CITY	01924-306090	320,600	£1,172	John Foster
Walsall	01922-650000	253,500	£1,383	Dave Martin *(acting)*
Wigan	01942-244991	306,700	£1,277	Joyce Redfern
Wirral	0151-638 7070	313,100	£1,330	Stephen Maddox
WOLVERHAMPTON CITY	01902-556556	239,600	£1,348	Richard Carr

* Source: ONS – *Mid-2005 Population Estimates* (Crown copyright)
† Average Band D council tax bill for 2007–8
Councils in CAPITAL LETTERS have city status

UNITARY COUNCILS

Unitary Councils	Telephone	Population*	Council Tax†	Chief Executive
Bath and North East Somerset	01225-477000	173,700	£1,318	John Everitt
Blackburn with Darwen	01254-585585	140,200	£1,381	Graham Burgess
Blackpool	01253-477477	142,900	£1,359	Steve Weaver
Bournemouth	01202-451451	163,600	£1,330	Pam Donnellan
Bracknell Forest	01344-424642	111,200	£1,210	Timothy Wheadon
BRIGHTON AND HOVE CITY	01273-290000	255,000	£1,342	Alan McCarthy
BRISTOL CITY	0117-922 2000	398,300	£1,424	Nick Gurney
Darlington	01325-380651	99,200	£1,278	Ada Burns
DERBY CITY	01332-293111	233,700	£1,217	Ray Cowlishaw
East Riding of Yorkshire	01482-887700	327,400	£1,356	Nigel Pearson
Halton	0151-424 2061	118,800	£1,221	Tony McDermot
Hartlepool	01429-266522	90,000	£1,497	Paul Walker
Herefordshire	01432-260000	178,800	£1,336	Neil Pringle
Isle of Wight	01983-821000	140,000	£1,319	Joe Duckworth
Isles of Scilly‡	01720-422537	2,100	£1,028	Philip Hygate
KINGSTON UPON HULL CITY	01482-609100	249,100	£1,244	Mr Kim Ryley
LEICESTER CITY	0116-254 9922	288,000	£1,248	Rodney Green
Luton	01582-546000	184,900	£1,234	Kevin Crompton
Medway	01634-306000	251,100	£1,178	Neil Davies
Middlesbrough	01642-245432	137,600	£1,337	Jan Richmond
Milton Keynes	01908-691691	218,500	£1,261	John Best
North East Lincolnshire	01472-313131	157,500	£1,407	George Krawiec
North Lincolnshire	01724-296296	157,100	£1,400	Simon Driver
North Somerset	01934-888888	195,100	£1,319	Graham Turner
NOTTINGHAM CITY	0115-915 5555	278,700	£1,418	Michael Frater
PETERBOROUGH CITY	01733-563141	159,700	£1,235	Gillian Beasley
PLYMOUTH CITY	01752-668000	246,100	£1,295	Barry Keel
Poole	01202-633633	137,100	£1,279	John McBride
PORTSMOUTH CITY	023-9282 2251	189,600	£1,226	David Williams
Reading	0118-939 0900	145,100	£1,379	Trish Haines
Redcar and Cleveland	0845-612 6126	138,600	£1,383	Colin Moore
Rutland	01572-722577	37,300	£1,534	Helen Briggs
Slough	01753-475111	117,500	£1,219	Ruth Bagley
South Gloucestershire	01454-868686	248,100	£1,371	Amanda Deeks
SOUTHAMPTON CITY	023-8022 3855	222,000	£1,316	Brad Roynon
Southend-on-Sea	01702-215000	159,300	£1,174	Robert Tinlin
Stockton-on-Tees	01642-393939	186,700	£1,321	George Garlick
STOKE-ON-TRENT CITY	01782-234567	238,300	£1,262	Steve Robinson
Swindon	01793-463000	184,000	£1,271	Gavin Jones
Telford and Wrekin	01952-202100	161,600	£1,296	Steve Wellings
Thurrock	01375-652652	146,600	£1,188	Angie Ridgwell
Torbay	01803-201201	132,800	£1,332	Colin Gamble
Warrington	01925-444400	194,700	£1,217	Diana Terris
West Berkshire	01635-42400	146,300	£1,362	Nick Carter
Windsor and Maidenhead	01628-683800	138,500	£1,215	David Lunn, OBE
Wokingham	0118-974 6000	153,600	£1,308	Doug Patterson
YORK CITY	01904-613161	186,800	£1,232	David Atkinson

* Source: ONS – Mid-2005 Population Estimates (Crown copyright)
† Average Band D council tax bill for 2007–8
‡ Under the Isles of Scilly Clause the council has additional functions to other unitary authorities and certain other functions are performed by Cornwall County Council for the benefit of the Isles of Scilly
Councils in CAPITAL LETTERS have city status

MAP OF COUNCILS IN ENGLAND

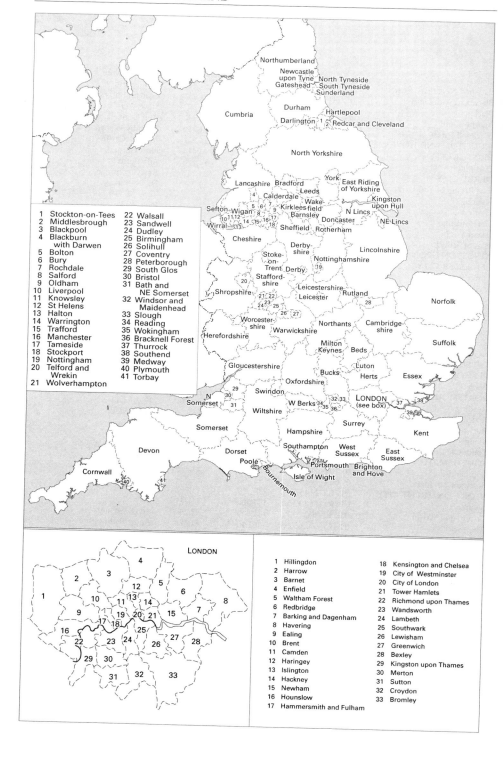

1	Stockton-on-Tees	22	Walsall
2	Middlesbrough	23	Sandwell
3	Blackpool	24	Dudley
4	Blackburn	25	Birmingham
	with Darwen	26	Solihull
5	Bolton	27	Coventry
6	Bury	28	Peterborough
7	Rochdale	29	South Glos
8	Salford	30	Bristol
9	Oldham	31	Bath and
10	Liverpool		NE Somerset
11	Knowsley	32	Windsor and
12	St Helens		Maidenhead
13	Halton	33	Slough
14	Warrington	34	Reading
15	Trafford	35	Wokingham
16	Manchester	36	Bracknell Forest
17	Tameside	37	Thurrock
18	Stockport	38	Southend
19	Nottingham	39	Medway
20	Telford and	40	Plymouth
	Wrekin	41	Torbay
21	Wolverhampton		

LONDON

1	Hillingdon	18	Kensington and Chelsea
2	Harrow	19	City of Westminster
3	Barnet	20	City of London
4	Enfield	21	Tower Hamlets
5	Waltham Forest	22	Richmond upon Thames
6	Redbridge	23	Wandsworth
7	Barking and Dagenham	24	Lambeth
8	Havering	25	Southwark
9	Ealing	26	Lewisham
10	Brent	27	Greenwich
11	Camden	28	Bexley
12	Haringey	29	Kingston upon Thames
13	Islington	30	Merton
14	Hackney	31	Sutton
15	Newham	32	Croydon
16	Hounslow	33	Bromley
17	Hammersmith and Fulham		

LONDON

THE CITY OF LONDON CORPORATION

The City of London is the historic centre at the heart of London known as 'the square mile' around which the vast metropolis has grown over the centuries. The City's residential population is roughly 9,000 and in addition, over 320,000 people work in the City. The civic government is carried on by the City of London Corporation through the court of Common Council.

The City is an international financial and business centre, generating about £30bn a year for the British economy. It includes the head offices of the principal banks, insurance companies and mercantile houses, in addition to buildings ranging from the historic Roman Wall and the 15th-century Guildhall, to the massive splendour of St Paul's Cathedral and the architectural beauty of Wren's spires.

The City of London was described by Tacitus in AD 62 as 'a busy emporium for trade and traders'. Under the Romans it became an important administration centre and hub of the road system. Little is known of London in Saxon times, when it formed part of the kingdom of the East Saxons. In 886 Alfred recovered London from the Danes and reconstituted it a burgh under his son-in-law. In 1066 the citizens submitted to William the Conqueror who in 1067 granted them a charter, which is still preserved, establishing them in the rights and privileges they had hitherto enjoyed.

THE MAYORALTY

The mayoralty was probably established about 1189, the first mayor being Henry Fitz Ailwyn who filled the office for 23 years and was succeeded by Fitz Alan (1212–14). A new charter was granted by King John in 1215, directing the mayor to be chosen annually, which has been done ever since, though in early times the same individual often held the office more than once. A familiar instance is that of 'Whittington, thrice Lord Mayor of London' (in reality four times, 1397, 1398, 1406, 1419); and many modern cases have occurred. The earliest instance of the phrase 'lord mayor' in English is in 1414. It was used more generally in the latter part of the 15th century and became invariable from 1535 onwards. At Michaelmas the liverymen in Common Hall choose two aldermen who have served the office of sheriff for presentation to the Court of Aldermen, and one is chosen to be lord mayor for the following mayoral year.

LORD MAYOR'S DAY

The lord mayor of London was previously elected on the feast of St Simon and St Jude (28 October), and from the time of Edward I, at least, was presented to the King or to the Barons of the Exchequer on the following day, unless that day was a Sunday. The day of election was altered to 16 October in 1346, and after some further changes was fixed for Michaelmas Day in 1546, but the ceremonies of admittance and swearing-in of the lord mayor continued to take place on 28 and 29 October respectively until 1751. In 1752, at the reform of the calendar, the lord mayor was continued in office until 8 November, the 'new style' equivalent of 28 October. The lord mayor is now presented to the lord chief justice at the royal courts of justice on the second Saturday in November to make the final declaration of office, having been sworn in at Guildhall on the preceding day. The procession to the royal courts of justice is popularly known as the Lord Mayor's Show.

REPRESENTATIVES

Aldermen are mentioned in the 11th century and their office is of Saxon origin. They were elected annually between 1377 and 1394, when an act of parliament of Richard II directed them to be chosen for life.

The Common Council was, at an early date, substituted for a popular assembly called the *Folkmote*. At first only two representatives were sent from each ward, but now each of the City's 25 wards is represented by an alderman and at least two Common Councilmen (the number depending on the size of the ward).

OFFICERS

Sheriffs were Saxon officers; their predecessors were the *wic-reeves* and *portreeves* of London and Middlesex. At first they were officers of the Crown, and were named by the Barons of the Exchequer; but Henry I (in 1132) gave the citizens permission to choose their own Sheriffs, and the annual election of Sheriffs became fully operative under King John's charter of 1199. The citizens lost this privilege, as far as the election of the Sheriff of Middlesex was concerned, by the Local Government Act 1888; but the liverymen continue to choose two Sheriffs of the City of London, who are appointed on Midsummer Day and take office at Michaelmas.

The office of Chamberlain is an ancient one, the first contemporary record of which is 1237. The town clerk (or Common Clerk) is first mentioned in 1274.

ACTIVITIES

The work of the City of London Corporation is assigned to a number of committees which present reports to the Court of Common Council. These committees are: Barbican Centre; Barbican Residential; Board of Governors of the City of London Freeman's School, the City of London School, the City of London School for Girls, the Guildhall School of Music and Drama and the Museum of London; City Bridge Trust; City Lands and Bridge House Estates; Community and Children's Services; Court of Alderman; Court of Common Council; Education; Epping Forest and Commons; Establishment; Finance; Freedom Applications; Gresham (city side); Guildhall Improvement; Guildhall Yard East Building; Hampstead Heath Consultative; Hampstead Heath Management; Joint Working Party of the Three Schools; Keats House Management; Libraries, Archives and Guildhall Art Gallery; Licensing; Livery; London Drug Policy Forum; Managers of West Ham Park; Markets; Open Spaces; Planning and Transportation; Police; Policy and Resources; Port Health and Environmental Services; Queen's Park and Highgate Wood Management and Standards Committees.

The City's estate, in the possession of which the City of London Corporation differs from other municipalities, is managed by the City Lands and Bridge House Estates Committee, the chairmanship of which carries with it the title of Chief Commoner.

The Honourable the Irish Society, which manages the City Corporation's estates in Ulster, consists of a governor and five other aldermen, the recorder, and 19 Common Councilmen, of whom one is elected deputy governor.

THE LORD MAYOR 2007–8
The Rt. Hon. the Lord Mayor, David Lewis*
Private Secretary, Kay Brock
* Provisional at time of going to press

THE SHERIFFS 2007–8
Michael Bear (Portsoken); Ian Luder (Castle Baynard)

OFFICERS, ETC
Town Clerk, Chris Duffield
Chamberlain, Chris Bilsland
Chief Commoner (2007), Pauline Halliday
Clerk, The Honourable the Irish Society, C. Fisher

THE ALDERMEN
with office held and date of appointment to that office

Name and Ward	CC	Ald.	Shff	Lord Mayor
Sir Richard Nichols, Candlewick	1983	1984	1994	1997
Lord Levene of Portsoken, KBE, *Aldgate*	1983	1984	1995	1998
Sir David Howard, Bt., Cornhill	1972	1986	1997	2000
Sir Michael Oliver, Bishopsgate	1980	1987	1997	2001
Sir Gavyn Arthur, Cripplegate	1988	1991	1998	2002
Sir Robert Finch, *Coleman Street*	–	1992	1999	2003
Sir Michael Savory, *Bread Street*	1980	1996	2001	2004
Sir David Brewer, *Bassishaw*	1992	1996	2002	2005
John Stuttard, *Lime Street*	–	2001	2005	2006

All the above have passed the Civic Chair

Nicholas Anstee, *Aldersgate*	1987	1996	2003
John Hughesdon, *Billingsgate*	1991	1997	2004
David Lewis, *Broad Street*	–	2001	2007
Dr Andrew Parmley, *Vintry*	1992	2001	
Simon Walsh, *Farringdon Wt.*	1989	2000	
Robert Hall, *Farringdon Wn.*	1995	2002	
Alison Gowman, *Dowgate*	1991	2002	
Richard Walduck, OBE, Tower	–	2003	
Gordon Haines, *Queenhithe*	–	2004	
Colin Hart, *Cheap*	–	2004	
Roger Gifford, *Cordwainer*	–	2004	
David Mauleverer, *Walbrook*	–	2005	2001
Ian Luder, *Castle Baynard*	1998	2005	
Michael Bear, *Portsoken*	2003	2005	
David Wootton, *Langbourn*	2002	2005	
Alan Yarrow, *Bridge*	–	2007	

THE COMMON COUNCIL
Deputy: each Common Councilman so described serves as deputy to the alderman of her/his ward.

Abrahams, G. C. (2000) — *Farringdon Wt.*
Absalom, J. D. (1994) — *Farringdon Wt.*
Altman, L. P., CBE (1996) — *Cripplegate Wn.*
Ayers, K. E. (1996) — *Bassishaw*
Bain-Stewart, A. (2005) — *Farringdon Wn.*
Barker, *Deputy* J. A., OBE (1981) — *Cripplegate*
Bennett, J. A. (2005) — *Broad Street*
Bird, J. L., OBE (1977) — *Tower*
Boleat, M. J. (2002) — *Cordwainer*
Bradshaw, D. J. (1991) — *Cripplegate Wn.*
Brewster, J. W., OBE (1994) — *Bassishaw*
Burleigh, I. B. (2005) — *Portsoken*
Campbell-Taylor, Revd W. G. (2005) — *Portsoken*
Carrington, M. L. (2004) — *Lime Street*
Cassidy, *Deputy* M. J., CBE (1989) — *Coleman Street*
Catt, R. M. (2004) — *Castle Baynard*
Cenci Di Bello, Mrs P. J. (2004) — *Farringdon Wn.*
Chadwick, R. A. H. (1994) — *Tower*
Challis, N. K. (2005) — *Castle Baynard*
Chapman, N. K. (2006) — *Langbourn*
Cohen, Mrs C. M., OBE (1986) — *Lime Street*
Cotgrove, D. (1991) — *Lime Street*
Currie, *Deputy* Miss S. E. M. (1985) — *Cripplegate Wt.*
Day, M. J. (2005) — *Bishopsgate*
Dove, W. H., MBE (1993) — *Bishopsgate*
Duckworth, S. (2000) — *Bishopsgate*
Dudley, Revd Dr M. R. (2002) — *Aldersgate*
Duffield, R. W. (2004) — *Farringdon Wn.*
Eskenzi, *Deputy* A. N., CBE (1970) — *Farringdon Wn.*
Eve, *Deputy* R. A. (1980) — *Cheap*
Everett, K. M. (1984) — *Candlewick*
Farr, M. C. (1998) — *Walbrook*
Farrow, *Deputy* M. W. W. (1996) — *Farringdon Wt.*
FitzGerald, *Deputy* R. C. A. (1981) — *Bread Street*
Fraser, S. J. (1993) — *Coleman Street*
Fraser, *Deputy* W. B., OBE (1981) — *Vintry*
Galloway, *Deputy* A. D., OBE (1981) — *Broad Street*
Gillon, G. M. F. (1995) — *Cordwainer*
Ginsburg, *Deputy* S. (1990) — *Bishopsgate*
Graves, A. C. (1985) — *Bishopsgate*
Haines, Revd S. D. (2005) — *Cornhill*
Halliday, *Deputy* Mrs P. A. (1992) — *Walbrook*
Hardwick, Dr P. B. (1987) — *Aldgate*
Harris, B. N. (2004) — *Bridge*
Henderson-Begg, M. (1977) — *Coleman Street*
Hilliard, N. R. M. (2005) — *Farringdon Wt.*
Hoffman, T. D. D. (2002) — *Vintry*
Holland, *Deputy* J., CBE (1972) — *Aldgate*
Hudson, M. (2007) — *Castle Baynard*
Hughes-Penney, R. C. (2004) — *Farringdon Wn.*
Hunt, W. G. (2004) — *Castle Baynard*
Jackson, L. St J. T. (1978) — *Bread Street*
Jones, H. L. M. (2004) — *Portsoken*
Kellett, Mrs M. W. F. (1986) — *Tower*
Kemp, D. L. (1984) — *Coleman Street*
King, *Deputy* A. J. N. (1999) — *Queenhithe*
Knowles, *Deputy* S. K. (1984) — *Candlewick*
Lawrence, *Deputy* G. A. (2002) — *Farringdon Wt.*
Leck, P. (1998) — *Aldersgate*
Lee, *Deputy* Revd Dr B. J. (2001) — *Portsoken*
Lord, C. E. (2001) — *Coleman Street*
Luder, I. D. (1998) — *Castle Baynard*
McGuinness, *Deputy* C. S. (1997) — *Castle Baynard*
Malins, J. H., QC (1981) — *Farringdon Wt.*
Martinelli, *Deputy* P. J. (1994) — *Bassishaw*
Mayhew, J. P. (1996) — *Aldersgate*
Mead, Mrs W. (1997) — *Farringdon Wt.*
Mobsby, *Deputy* D. J. L. (1985) — *Billingsgate*

Mooney, B. D. F. (1998)   *Queenhithe*
Moss, A. D. (1989)   *Tower*
Moys, Mrs S. D. (2001)   *Aldgate*
Nash, *Deputy* Mrs J. C., OBE (1983)   *Aldersgate*
Newman, Mrs P. B., CBE (1989)   *Aldersgate*
Nove, P. R., CBE (2004)   *Castle Baynard*
Owen, *Deputy* Mrs J., MBE (1975)   *Langbourn*
Owen-Ward, J. R. (1983)   *Bridge*
Page, M. (2002)   *Farringdon Wn.*
Pembroke, *Deputy* Mrs A. M. F. (1978)   *Cheap*
Pollard, J. H. G. (2002)   *Dowgate*
Price, E. E. (1996)   *Farringdon Wt.*
Pulman, *Deputy* G. A. G. (1983)   *Tower*
Punter, C. (1993)   *Cripplegate Wn.*
Quilter, S. D. (1998)   *Cripplegate Wt.*
Regan, R. D. (1998)   *Farringdon Wn.*
Robinson, Mrs D. C. (1989)   *Bishopsgate*
Roney, *Deputy* E. P. T., CBE (1974)   *Bishopsgate*
Scott, J. G. S. (1999)   *Broad Street*
Shalit, *Deputy* D. M. (1972)   *Farringdon Wn.*
Sherlock, *Deputy* M. R. C. (1992)   *Dowgate*
Simons, J. L. (2004)   *Castle Baynard*
Snyder, *Deputy* M. J. (1986)   *Cordwainer*
Spanner, J. H. (2001)   *Farringdon Wt.*
Starling, Mrs A. J. (2006)   *Cripplegate Wt.*
Stevenson, F. P. (1994)   *Cripplegate Wn.*
Thompson, D. J. (2004)   *Aldgate*
Tomlinson, J. (2004)   *Cripplegate Wt.*
Twogood, M. (2004)   *Farringdon Wt.*
Wang, *Deputy* Mrs C. A. M. (2004)   *Cornhill*
Welbank, J. M. (2005)   *Billingsgate*
Willoughby, *Deputy* P. J. (1985)   *Bishopsgate*

THE CITY GUILDS (LIVERY COMPANIES)

The constitution of the livery companies has been unchanged for centuries. There are three ranks of membership: freemen, liverymen and assistants. A person can become a freeman by patrimony (through a parent having been a freeman); by servitude (through having served an apprenticeship to a freeman); or by redemption (by purchase).

Election to the livery is the prerogative of the company, who can elect any of its freemen as liverymen. Assistants are usually elected from the livery and form a Court of Assistants which is the governing body of the company. The master (in some companies called the prime warden) is elected annually from the assistants.

The register for 2007–8 lists 24,344 liverymen of the guilds entitled to vote at elections at Common Hall.

The order of precedence, omitting extinct companies, is given in parentheses after the name of each company in the list below. In certain companies the election of Master or Prime Warden for the year does not take place until the autumn. In such cases the master or prime warden for 2006–7, rather than 2007–8, is given.

THE TWELVE GREAT COMPANIES
In order of civic precedence

MERCERS *(1)*. *Hall*, Mercers' Hall, Ironmonger Lane, London EC2V 8HE *Livery*, 244. *Clerk*, Charles Parker *Master*, Frederick Hohler

GROCERS *(2)*. *Hall*, Grocers' Hall, Princes Street, London EC2R 8AD *Livery*, 349. *Clerk*, Brig. Robert Pridham, OBE *Master*, J. Scott

DRAPERS *(3)*. *Hall*, Drapers' Hall, Throgmorton Avenue, London EC2N 2DQ *Livery*, 293. *Clerk*, Rear-Adm. Alastair Ross, CB, CBE *Master*, Stephen Foakes, TD

FISHMONGERS *(4)*. *Hall*, Fishmongers' Hall, London Bridge, London EC4R 9EL *Livery*, 342. *Clerk*, Keith Waters *Prime Warden*, Sir Matthew Farrer, GCVO

GOLDSMITHS *(5)*. *Hall*, Goldsmiths' Hall, Foster Lane, London EC2V 6BN *Livery*, 260. *Clerk*, R. Melly *Prime Warden*, Prof. R. Himsworth, FRCP

SKINNERS *(6/7)*. *Hall*, Skinners' Hall, 8 Dowgate Hill, London EC4R 2SP *Livery*, 400. *Clerk*, Maj.-Gen. Brian Plummer, CBE *Master*, Patrick Tudor Crosthwaite

MERCHANT TAYLORS *(6/7)*. *Hall*, Merchant Taylors' Hall, 30 Threadneedle Street, London EC2R 8JB *Livery*, 285. *Clerk*, Rear-Adm. Nick Harris, CB, MBE *Master*, H. Stubbs

HABERDASHERS *(8)*. *Hall*, 18 West Smithfield, London EC1A 9HQ *Livery*, 285. *Clerk*, Rear-Adm. Richard Phillips, CB *Master*, M. Jeans (from November 2007, subject to election), MBE

SALTERS *(9)*. *Hall*, Salters' Hall, 4 Fore Street, London EC2Y 5DE *Livery*, 159. *Clerk*, Capt. D. Morris, RN *Master*, D. Blackwell

IRONMONGERS *(10)*. *Hall*, Ironmongers' Hall, 1 Shaftesbury Place, London EC2Y 8AA *Livery*, 133. *Clerk*, Col. Hamon Massey *Master*, Jonathan Hudson

VINTNERS *(11)*. *Hall*, Vintners' Hall, Upper Thames Street, London EC4V 3BG *Livery*, 312. *Clerk*, Brig. Michael Smythe, OBE *Master*, A. Edwards

CLOTHWORKERS *(12)*. *Hall*, Clothworkers' Hall, Dunster Court, Mincing Lane, London EC3R 7AH *Livery*, 228. *Clerk*, Andrew Blessley *Master*, Christopher Jonas

OTHER CITY GUILDS
In alphabetical order

ACTUARIES *(91)*. 3rd Floor Cheapside House, 138 Cheapside, London EC2V 6BW *Livery*, 221. *Clerk*, David Johnson *Master*, Chris Ide

AIR PILOTS AND AIR NAVIGATORS *(81)*. *Hall*, Cobham House, 9 Warwick Court, Gray's Inn, London WC1R 5DJ *Livery*, 600. *Clerk*, Paul Tacon *Grand Master*, HRH The Duke of York, KG, KCVO, ADC(P) *Master*, Gp Capt. R. Gault

APOTHECARIES *(58)*. *Hall*, Apothecaries' Hall, 14 Black Friars Lane, London EC4V 6EJ *Livery*, 1,274. *Clerk*, A. Wallington-Smith *Master*, Ami Paris, FRCS

ARBITRATORS *(93)*. 13 Hall Gardens, Colney Heath, St Albans, Herts AL4 0QF *Livery*, 175. *Clerk*, Gaye Duffy *Master*, Michael Stevens

ARMOURERS AND BRASIERS *(22)*. *Hall*, Armourers' Hall, 81 Coleman Street, London EC2R 5BJ *Livery*, 122. *Clerk*, Cdre Christopher Waite *Master*, Prof. William Bonfield, CBE, FRS, FRENG

BAKERS *(19)*. *Hall*, Bakers' Hall, Harp Lane, London EC3R 6DP *Livery*, 300. *Clerk*, John Tompkins *Master*, J. Renshaw (from 26 November subject to election)

BARBERS *(17)*. *Hall*, Barber-Surgeons' Hall, Monkwell Square, Wood Street, London EC2Y 5BL *Livery*, 210. *Clerk*, Col. Peter Durrant, MBE *Master*, Prof. John Christopher Buckland-Wright, DSC

BASKETMAKERS *(52)*. 29 Ingram House, Park Road, Hampton Wick, Surrey KT1 4BA *Livery*, 300. *Clerk*, Roger de Pilkyngton *Prime Warden*, Richard Walduck, OBE

BLACKSMITHS *(40)*. 48 Upwood Road, London SE12 8AN *Livery*, 235. *Clerk*, Christopher Jeal *Prime Warden*, John McCuin

BOWYERS *(38)*. 5 Archer House, Vicarage Crescent, London SW11 3LF *Livery*, 97. *Clerk*, Richard Wilkinson *Master*, Richard Model

BREWERS *(14)*. *Hall*, Brewers' Hall, Aldermanbury Square, London EC2V 7HR *Livery*, 180. *Clerk*, Brig. D. Ross, CBE *Master*, M. Thomas

BRODERERS *(48)*. Ember House, 35–37 Creek Road, East Molesey, Surrey KT8 9BE *Livery*, 154. *Clerk*, Peter Crouch *Master*, Brig. D. Chaundler, OBE

BUILDERS MERCHANTS *(88)*. 4 College Hill, London EC4R 2RB *Livery*, 202. *Clerk*, T. Statham *Master*, John O'Carroll-Bailey

BUTCHERS *(24)*. *Hall*, Butchers' Hall, 87 Bartholomew Close, London EC1A 7EB *Livery*, 635. *Clerk*, Cdre Anthony Morrow, CVO *Master*, John Tuckwell

CARMEN *(77)*. 5 Kings House, 1 Queen Street Place, London EC4R 1QS *Livery*, 500. *Clerk*, Walter Gill *Master*, Montague Meyer

CARPENTERS *(26)*. *Hall*, Carpenters' Hall, 1 Throgmorton Avenue, London EC2N 2JJ *Livery*, 184. *Clerk*, Brig. T. Gregson *Master*, Michael Mathews

CHARTERED ACCOUNTANTS *(86)*. The Rustlings, Valley Close, Studham, Dunstable LU6 2QN *Livery*, 340. *Clerk*, Clifford Bygrave *Master*, H. P. Gold

CHARTERED ARCHITECTS *(98)*. 82A Muswell Hill Road, London N10 3JR *Livery*, 142. *Clerk*, David Cole-Adams *Master*, Jonathan Ball, MBE

CHARTERED SECRETARIES AND ADMINISTRATORS *(87)*. 3rd Floor, Saddlers' House, 40 Gutter Lane, London EC2V 6BR *Livery*, 261. *Clerk*, Col. Michael Dudding, OBE, TD *Master*, Adèle Thorpe

CHARTERED SURVEYORS *(85)*. 75 Meadway Drive, Horsell, Woking, Surrey GU21 4TF *Livery*, 345. *Clerk*, Amanda Jackson *Master*, David Larkin

CLOCKMAKERS *(61)*. Salters' Hall, 4 Fore Street, London EC2Y 5DE *Livery*, 270. *Clerk*, Joseph Buxton *Master*, David Poole

COACHMAKERS AND COACH-HARNESS MAKERS *(72)*. Elm Tree Cottage, Bottom House Farm Lane, Chalfont St Giles, Buckinghamshire HP8 4EE *Livery*, 400. *Clerk*, Gp Capt. Gerry Bunn, CBE *Master*, Andrew Love

CONSTRUCTORS *(99)*. Forge Farmhouse, Glassenbury, Cranbrook, Kent TN17 2QE *Livery*, 135. *Clerk*, Tim Nicholson *Master*, Martin Wade, FRICS

COOKS *(35)*. Coombe Ridge, Thursley Road, Churt, Farnham, Surrey GU10 2LQ *Livery*, 76. *Clerk*, Michael Thatcher, LLB *Master* (subject to election), Alan Granger Fairbrass

COOPERS *(36)*. *Hall*, Coopers' Hall, 13 Devonshire Square, London EC2M 4TH *Livery*, 260. *Clerk*, Lt.-Col. Adrian Carroll *Master*, Richard Sibley

CORDWAINERS *(27)*. Clothworkers' Hall, Dunster Court, Mincing Lane, London EC3R 7AH *Livery*, 168. *Clerk*, John Miller *Master*, James Calder

CURRIERS *(29)*. Hedgerley, 10 The Leaze, Ashton Keynes, Wiltshire SN6 6PE *Livery*, 93. *Clerk*, Gp Capt. David Moss *Master*, His Hon. Judge Lawson, QC

CUTLERS *(18)*. *Hall*, Cutlers' Hall, Warwick Lane, London EC4M 7BR *Livery*, 100. *Clerk*, J. Allen *Master*, R. Randolph

DISTILLERS *(69)*. 71 Lincoln's Inn Fields, London WC2A 3JF *Livery*, 260. *Clerk*, C. Hughes *Master*, Derek Plant

DYERS *(13)*. *Hall*, Dyers' Hall, 10 Dowgate Hill, London EC4R 2ST *Livery*, 129. *Clerk*, J. Vaizey *Prime Warden*, J. Chambers

ENGINEERS *(94)*. Wax Chandlers' Hall, 6 Gresham Street, London EC2V 7AD *Livery*, 300. *Clerk*, Air Vice-Marshal Graham Skinner, CBE *Master*, Rear-Adm. David Bawtree, CB

ENVIRONMENTAL CLEANERS *(97)*. 6 Grange Meadows, Elmswell, Bury St Edmunds, Suffolk IP30 9GE *Livery*, 268. *Clerk*, Michael Bizley *Master*, Michael Bayless

FAN MAKERS *(76)*. Skinners' Hall, 8 Dowgate Hill, London

EC4R 2SP *Livery*, 202. *Clerk*, Keith Patterson *Master*, His Hon. Judge Connor

FARMERS *(80)*. *Hall*, The Farmers' and Fletchers' Hall, 3 Cloth Street, London EC1A 7LD *Livery*, 300. *Clerk*, Col. David King, OBE *Master*, T. Copas

FARRIERS *(55)*. 19 Queen Street, Chipperfield, Kings Langley, Herts WD4 9BT *Livery*, 321. *Clerk*, Charlotte Clifford *Master*, Col. Richard Kinsella-Bevan

FELTMAKERS *(63)*. Post Cottage, Greywell, Hook, Hampshire RG29 1DA *Livery*, 171. *Clerk*, Maj. J. Coombs *Master*, Derek Bonham

FIREFIGHTERS *(103)*. The Insurance Hall, 20 Aldermanbury, London EC2V 7HY *Livery*, 76. *Clerk*, Martin Bonham *Master*, Vivian Jones

FLETCHERS *(39)*. *Hall*, The Farmers' and Fletchers' Hall, 3 Cloth Street, London EC1A 7LD *Livery*, 143. *Clerk*, Capt. Michael Johnson, RN *Master*, Peter Scott

FOUNDERS *(33)*. *Hall*, Founders' Hall, 1 Cloth Fair, London EC1A 7JQ *Livery*, 155. *Clerk*, A. Gillett *Master*, J. Kelly, RD

FRAMEWORK KNITTERS *(64)*. 86 Park Drive, Upminster, Essex RM14 3AS *Livery*, 215. *Clerk*, Alan Clark *Master*, Hugh Stevenson

FRUITERERS *(45)*. Chapelstones, 84 High Street, Codford St Mary, Warminster BA12 0ND *Livery*, 283. *Clerk*, Lt.-Col. L. French *Master*, I. Robins

FUELLERS *(95)*. 26 Merrick Square, London SE1 4JB *Livery*, 125. *Clerk*, Sir Anthony Reardon Smith, Bt. *Master*, David Bell

FURNITURE MAKERS *(83)*. *Hall*, Furniture Makers' Hall, 12 Austin Friars, London EC2N 2HE *Livery*, 295. *Clerk*, Mrs J. Wright *Master*, George Mitchell

GARDENERS *(66)*. 25 Luke Street, London EC2A 4AR *Livery*, 285. *Clerk*, Trevor Hines *Master*, Alderman Sir Gavyn Arthur

GIRDLERS *(23)*. *Hall*, Girdlers' Hall, Basinghall Avenue, London EC2V 5DD *Livery*, 80. *Clerk*, Brig. I. Rees *Master*, R. Roberts

GLASS SELLERS *(71)*. 57 Witley Court, Coram Street, London WC1N 1HD *Livery*, 230. *Clerk*, Col. Audrey Smith *Master*, Sir Anthony Hammond, KCB, QC

GLAZIERS AND PAINTERS OF GLASS *(53)*. *Hall*, Glaziers' Hall, 9 Montague Close, London SE1 9DD *Livery*, 240. *Clerk*, Alex Galloway, CVO *Master*, David Ball, FRENG

GLOVERS *(62)*. Oscar Court, 17A Tite Street, London SW3 4JR *Livery*, 250. *Clerk*, Carole Blackshaw *Master*, John Brown, CBE

GOLD AND SILVER WYRE DRAWERS *(74)*. Middleton House, Winterslow, Salisbury, Wiltshire SP5 1QR *Livery*, 305. *Clerk*, Cdr. R. House, RN *Master*, J. Simmons

GUNMAKERS *(73)*. The Proof House, 48–50 Commercial Road, London E1 1LP *Livery*, 310. *Clerk*, Col. W. Chesshyre *Master*, S. Urry

HACKNEY CARRIAGE DRIVERS *(104)*. 25 The Grove, Parkfield, Latimer, Buckinghamshire HP5 1UE *Livery*, 98. *Clerk*, Mary Whitworth *Master*, Alan Parker

HORNERS *(54)*. c/o Clergy House, Hide Place, London SW1P 4NJ *Livery*, 224. *Clerk*, Raymond Layard *Master*, David Oxley

INFORMATION TECHNOLOGISTS *(100)*. *Hall*, Information Technologists' Hall, 39A Bartholomew Close, London EC1A 7JN *Livery*, 287. *Clerk*, Michael Grant *Master*, David Morriss

INNHOLDERS *(32)*. *Hall*, Innholders' Hall, 30 College Street, London EC4R 2RH *Livery*, 154. *Clerk*, Dougal Bulger *Master*, Cdr. Hugh Evans

INSURERS *(92)*. The Hall, 20 Aldermanbury, London

EC2V 7HY *Livery*, 380. *Clerk*, L. Walters *Master*, Graham Doswell

INTERNATIONAL BANKERS *(106)*. 12 Austin Friars, London EC2N 2HE *Livery*, 109. *Clerk*, Wg Cdr Tim Woods, BEM *Master*, Angus MacLennan

JOINERS AND CEILERS *(41)*. 75 Meadway Drive, Horsell, Woking, Surrey GU21 4TF *Livery*, 128. *Clerk*, Amanda Jackson *Master*, David Latham

LAUNDERERS *(89)*. *Hall*, Launderers' Hall, 9 Montague Close, London Bridge, London SE1 9DD *Livery*, 240. *Clerk*, Mrs J. Polek *Master*, Selwin Burchhardt

LEATHERSELLERS *(15)*. *Hall*, Leathersellers' Hall, 15 St Helen's Place, London EC3A 6DQ *Livery*, 150. *Clerk*, Jonathan Cooke *Master*, Anthony Collinson

LIGHTMONGERS *(96)*. Crown Wharf, 11A Coldharbour, Blackwall Reach, London E14 9NS *Livery*, 194. *Clerk*, Derek Wheatley *Master*, Martin Tratte

LORINERS *(57)*. Hampton House, High Street, East Grinstead, West Sussex RH19 3AW *Livery*, 344. *Clerk*, Peter Lusty *Master*, Dr Nigel Berman

MAKERS OF PLAYING CARDS *(75)*. 2 Cannon Way, West Molesey, Surrey KT8 2NB *Livery*, 146. *Clerk*, Paul Bowen *Master*, Adrian Maurice

MANAGEMENT CONSULTANTS *(105)*. Copperfield, The Ridgeway, Cranleigh GU6 7HR *Livery*, 170. *Clerk*, Lt.-Col. Dennis Hall *Master*, H. Morris

MARKETORS *(90)*. 13 Hall Gardens, Colney Heath, St Albans, Herts AL4 0QF *Livery*, 298. *Clerk*, Mrs G. Duffy *Master*, Keith Arundale

MASONS *(30)*. 22 Cannon Hill, Southgate, London N14 6LG *Livery*, 132. *Clerk*, P. Clark *Master*, G. Everett

MASTER MARINERS *(78)*. *Hall*, HQS Wellington, Temple Stairs, Victoria Embankment, London WC2R 2PN *Livery*, 197. *Clerk*, Cdr. Rod Craig, RN *Master*, Capt. E. Scott

MUSICIANS *(50)*. 6th Floor, 2 London Wall Building, London EC2M 5PP *Livery*, 381. *Clerk*, Mrs M. Alford *Master*, Leslie East

NEEDLEMAKERS *(65)*. PO Box 3682, Windsor, Berkshire SL4 3WR *Livery*, 200. *Clerk*, Philip Grant *Master*, Dr Simon Fradd

PAINTER-STAINERS *(28)*. *Hall*, Painters' Hall, 9 Little Trinity Lane, London EC4V 2AD *Livery*, 320. *Clerk*, Chris Twyman *Master*, P. Gandy

PATTENMAKERS *(70)*. 3 The High Street, Sutton Valence, Kent ME17 3AG *Livery*, 200. *Clerk*, Col. R. W. Murfin, TD *Master*, Prof. B. A. K. Rider

PAVIORS *(56)*. 3 Ridgemount Gardens, Enfield, Middx EN2 8QL *Livery*, 269. *Clerk*, John White *Master*, Oliver Whitehead

PEWTERERS *(16)*. *Hall*, Pewterers' Hall, Oat Lane, London EC2V 7DE *Livery*, 80. *Clerk*, Capt. Paddy Watson, RN *Master*, Peter Errington Gibbs

PLAISTERERS *(46)*. *Hall*, Plaisterers' Hall, 1 London Wall, London EC2Y 5JU *Livery*, 210. *Clerk*, Hilary Machtus *Master*, Nicholas Carr

PLUMBERS *(31)*. Wax Chandlers' Hall, 6 Gresham Street, London EC2V 7AD *Livery*, 340. *Clerk*, Lt.-Col. Anthony Paterson-Fox *Master*, D. W. Alexander

POULTERS *(34)*. The Old Butchers, Station Road, Groombridge, Kent TN3 9QX *Livery*, 204. *Clerk*, Gwen Butcher *Master*, John Nokes

SADDLERS *(25)*. *Hall*, Saddlers' Hall, 40 Gutter Lane, London EC2V 6BR *Livery*, 75. *Clerk*, Col. N. Lithgow, CBE *Master*, I. Pulley

SCIENTIFIC INSTRUMENT MAKERS *(84)*. 9 Montague Close, London SE1 9DD *Livery*, 230. *Clerk*, Neville Watson *Master*, D. Smith

SCRIVENERS *(44)*. HQS Wellington, Temple Stairs, Victoria

Embankment, London WC2R 2PN *Livery*, 200. *Clerk*, P. Elliott *Master*, Syliva Tutt

SHIPWRIGHTS *(59)*. Ironmongers Hall, Barbican, London EC2Y 8AA *Livery*, 463. *Clerk*, Rear-Adm. Derek Anthony, MBE *Permanent Master*, HRH the Duke of Edinburgh, KG, KT, OM *Prime Warden*, A. Marsh

SOLICITORS *(79)*. 4 College Hill, London EC4R 2RB *Livery*, 350. *Clerk*, Neil Cameron *Master*, William Knight

SPECTACLE MAKERS *(60)*. Apothecaries' Hall, Black Friars Lane, London EC4V 6EL *Livery*, 380. *Clerk*, Lt.-Col. John Salmon, OBE *Master*, Rubin Weathersbee

STATIONERS AND NEWSPAPER MAKERS *(47)*. *Hall*, Stationers' Hall, Ave Maria Lane, London EC4M 7DD *Livery*, 441. *Clerk*, Brig. D. Sharp, AFC *Master*, J. Waterlow

TALLOW CHANDLERS *(21)*. *Hall*, Tallow Chandlers' Hall, 4 Dowgate Hill, London EC4R 2SH *Livery*, 175. *Clerk*, Brig. R. Wilde, CBE *Master*, Philip Edwards

TAX ADVISERS *(107)*. 191 West End Road, Ruislip, Middlesex HA4 6LD *Freemen*, 121. *Clerk*, Paul Herbage *Master*, W. Norris

TIN PLATE WORKERS (ALIAS WIRE WORKERS) *(67)*. Highbanks, Ferry Road, Surlingham, Norwich, Norfolk NR14 7AR *Livery*, 210. *Clerk*, Michael Henderson-Begg *Master*, D. Saunders, RD

TOBACCO PIPE MAKERS AND TOBACCO BLENDERS *(82)*. Green Meadow Island, Steep, Hampshire GU32 1AE *Livery*, 150. *Clerk*, Barbara Hines *Master*, George Lankester

TURNERS *(51)*. 182 Temple Chambers, Temple Avenue, London EC4Y 0HP *Livery*, 175. *Clerk*, Edward Windsor Clive *Master*, G. Kieffer

TYLERS AND BRICKLAYERS *(37)*. 30 Shelley Avenue, Tiptree CO5 0SF *Livery*, 151. *Clerk*, Barry Blumson *Master*, Dr George Bird

UPHOLDERS *(49)*. Hall in the Wood, 46 Quail Gardens, Selsdon Vale, Croydon CR2 8TF *Livery*, 213. *Clerk*, Jean Cody *Master*, Peter Lawton

WATER CONSERVATORS *(102)*. The Lark, 2 Bell Lane, Worlington, Bury St Edmunds, Suffolk IP28 8SE *Livery*, 210. *Clerk*, Ralph Riley *Master*, Colin Drummond

WAX CHANDLERS *(20)*. *Hall*, Wax Chandlers' Hall, 6 Gresham Street, London EC2V 7AD *Livery*, 130. *Clerk*, Richard Percival *Master*, T. Willcox

WEAVERS *(42)*. Saddlers' House, Gutter Lane, London EC2V 6BR *Livery*, 125. *Clerk*, John Snowdon *Upper Bailiff*, Julian Birchall

WHEELWRIGHTS *(68)*. 7 Glengall Road, Bexleyheath, Kent DA7 4AL *Livery*, 218. *Clerk*, Brian François *Master*, K. Davidson

WOOLMEN *(43)*. The Old Post Office, 56 Lower Way, Great Brickhill, Bucks MK17 9AG *Livery*, 141. *Clerk*, Gillian Wilson *Master*, Gavin Hamilton-Deeley

WORLD TRADERS *(101)*. 36 Ladbroke Grove, London W11 2PA *Livery*, 208. *Clerk*, Nigel Pullman *Master*, Robert Alston, CMG

SECURITY PROFESSIONALS *(No Livery)*. 1 Wallis Mews, Guildford Road, Leatherhead, Surrey KT22 9DQ *Freemen*, 282. *Clerk*, John Maddock *Master*, Peter French

PARISH CLERKS *(No Livery*)*. Acreholt, 33 Medstead Road, Beech, Alton, Hampshire GU34 4AD *Members*, 95. *Clerk*, Lt.-Col. Brian Coombes *Master*, R.F. S. Townend

WATERMEN AND LIGHTERMEN *(No Livery*)*. *Hall*, Watermen's Hall, 16 St Mary-at-Hill, London EC3R 8EF *Craft Owning Freemen*, 340. *Clerk*, Colin Middlemiss *Master*, K. Dwan

* Parish Clerks and Watermen and Lightermen have requested to remain with no livery

LONDON BOROUGH COUNCILS

Council	Telephone	Population*	Council Tax†	Chief Executive
Barking and Dagenham	020-8592 4500	164,500	£1,278	Robert Whiteman
Barnet	020-8359 2000	329,700	£1,350	Leo Boland
Bexley	020-8303 7777	220,300	£1,362	Nick Johnson
Brent	020-8937 1234	270,100	£1,299	Gareth Daniel
Bromley	020-8464 3333	301,900	£1,218	Doug Patterson
Camden	020-7278 4444	226,100	£1,301	Moira Gibb, CBE
CITY OF LONDON CORPORATION	020-7606 3030	9,200	£900	Chris Duffield
Croydon	020-8686 4433	342,700	£1,358	Jon Rouse
Ealing	020-8825 5000	301,800	£1,344	Darra Singh
Enfield	020-8379 1000	280,500	£1,337	Rob Leak
Greenwich	020-8854 8888	228,100	£1,266	Mary Ney
Hackney	020-8356 5000	207,700	£1,302	Tim Shields (acting)
Hammersmith and Fulham	020-8748 3020	179,900	£1,193	Geoff Alltimes
Haringey	020-8489 0000	224,500	£1,432	Ita O'Donovan
Harrow	020-8863 5611	214,000	£1,423	Michael Lockwood
Havering	01708-434343	226,200	£1,433	Cheryl Coppell
Hillingdon	01895-250111	252,400	£1,384	Hugh Dunnachie (acting)
Hounslow	020-8583 2000	212,500	£1,395	Mark Gilks
Islington	020-7527 2000	182,600	£1,219	Helen Bailey
Kensington and Chelsea	020-7937 5464	196,200	£1,043	Derek Myers
Kingston upon Thames	020-8547 5757	153,000	£1,523	Bruce McDonald
Lambeth	020-7926 1000	269,100	£1,187	Derrick Anderson
Lewisham	020-8314 6000	247,500	£1,296	Barry Quirk, CBE
Merton	020-8543 2222	194,700	£1,358	Ged Curran
Newham	020-8430 2000	246,200	£1,220	Chris Wood (acting)
Redbridge	020-8554 5000	251,500	£1,331	Roger Hampson
Richmond upon Thames	020-8891 1411	186,300	£1,491	Gillian Norton
Southwark	020-7525 5000	257,700	£1,181	Annie Shepperd
Sutton	020-8770 5000	177,700	£1,376	Paul Martin
Tower Hamlets	020-7364 5000	213,200	£1,140	Martin Smith
Waltham Forest	020-8496 3000	224,100	£1,407	Roger Taylor (acting)
Wandsworth	020-8871 6000	281,400	£681	Gerald Jones
WESTMINSTER	020-7641 6000	244,400	£682	Peter Rogers

* Source: ONS – Mid-2005 Population Estimates (Crown copyright)
† Average Band D council tax bill for 2007–8
Councils in CAPITAL LETTERS have city status

WALES

Cymru

The Principality of Wales (Cymru) occupies the extreme west of the central southern portion of the island of Great Britain, with a total area of 20,778 sq. km (8,022 sq. miles): land 20,733 sq. km (8,005 sq. miles); inland water 45 sq. km (17 sq. miles). It is bordered in the north by the Irish Sea, in the south by the Bristol Channel, in the east by the English counties of Cheshire, Shropshire, Herefordshire and Gloucestershire, and in the west by St George's Channel.

Across the Menai Straits is Ynys Mon (Isle of Anglesey) (715 sq. km/276 sq. miles), communication with which is facilitated by the Menai Suspension Bridge (305m/1,000ft long) built by Telford in 1826, and by the tubular railway bridge (335m/1,100ft long) built by Stephenson in 1850. Holyhead harbour, on Holy Isle (north-west of Anglesey), provides ferry services to Dublin (113km/70 miles).

POPULATION

The population at the 2001 census was 2,903,085 (men 1,403,782; women 1,499,303). The average density of population in 2001 was 140 persons per sq. km (362 per sq. mile).

RELIEF

Wales is a country of extensive tracts of high plateau and shorter stretches of mountain ranges deeply dissected by river valleys. Lower-lying ground is largely confined to the coastal belt and the lower parts of the valleys. The highest mountains are those of Snowdonia in the north west (Snowdon, 1,085m/3,559ft), Berwyn (Aran Fawddwy, 906m/2,971ft), Cader Idris (Pen y Gadair, 892m/2,928ft), Dyfed (Plynlimon, 752m/2,467ft), and the Black Mountains, Brecon Beacons and Black Forest ranges in the south-east (Pen y Fan, 886m/2,906ft; Waun Fâch, 811m/2,660ft; Carmarthen Van, 802m/2,630ft).

HYDROGRAPHY

The principal river in Wales is the Severn, which flows from the slopes of Plynlimon to the English border. The Wye (209km/130 miles) also rises in the slopes of Plynlimon. The Usk (90km/56 miles) flows into the Bristol Channel through Gwent. The Dee (113km/70 miles) rises in Bala Lake and flows through the Vale of Llangollen, where an aqueduct (built by Telford in 1805) carries the Pontcysyllte branch of the Shropshire Union Canal across the valley. The estuary of the Dee is the navigable portion, it is 23km (14 miles) in length and about 8km (5 miles) in breadth. The Towy (109km/68 miles), Teifi (80km/50 miles), Taff (64km/40 miles), Dovey (48km/30 miles), Taf (40km/25 miles) and Conway (39km/24 miles) are wholly Welsh rivers.

The largest natural lake is Bala (Llyn Tegid) in Gwynedd, nearly 7km (4 miles) long and 1.6km (1 mile) wide. Lake Vyrnwy is an artificial reservoir, about the size of Bala, it forms the water supply of Liverpool; Birmingham's water is supplied from reservoirs in the Elan and Claerwen valleys.

WELSH LANGUAGE

According to the 2001 census results, the percentage of people aged three years and over who are able to speak Welsh is:

Blaenau Gwent	9.1	Neath Port Talbot	17.8
Bridgend	10.6	Newport	9.6
Caerphilly	10.9	Pembrokeshire	21.5
Cardiff	10.9	Powys	20.8
Carmarthenshire	50.1	Rhondda Cynon Taf	12.3
Ceredigion	51.8	Swansea	13.2
Conwy	29.2	Torfaen	10.7
Denbighshire	26.1	Vale of Glamorgan	11.1
Flintshire	14.1	Wrexham	14.4
Gwynedd	68.7	Ynys Mon (Isle of	59.8
Merthyr Tydfil	10.0	Anglesey)	
Monmouthshire	9.0	*Total in Wales*	20.5

FLAG

The flag of Wales, the Red Dragon (Y Ddraig Goch), is a red dragon on a field divided white over green (per fess argent and vert a dragon passant gules). The flag was augmented in 1953 by a royal badge on a shield encircled with a riband bearing the words *Ddraig Goch Ddyry Cychwyn* and imperially crowned, but this augmented flag is rarely used.

EARLY HISTORY

The earliest inhabitants of whom there is any record appear to have been subdued or exterminated by the Goidels (a people of Celtic race) in the Bronze Age. A further invasion of Celtic Brythons and Belgae followed in the ensuing Iron Age. The Roman conquest of southern Britain and Wales was for some time successfully opposed by Caratacus (Caractacus or Caradog), chieftain of the Catuvellauni and son of Cunobelinus (Cymbeline). South-east Wales was subjugated and the legionary fortress at Caerleon-on-Usk established by around AD 75–7; the conquest of Wales was completed by Agricola around AD 78. Communications were opened up by the construction of military roads from Chester to Caerleon-on-Usk and Caerwent, and from Chester to Conwy (and thence to Carmarthen and Neath). Christianity was introduced in the fourth century, during the Roman occupation.

ANGLO-SAXON ATTACKS

The Anglo-Saxon invaders of southern Britain drove the Celts into the mountain stronghold of Wales, and into Strathclyde (Cumberland and south-west Scotland) and Cornwall, giving them the name of *Waelisc* (Welsh), meaning 'foreign'. The West Saxons' victory of Deorham (AD 577) isolated Wales from Cornwall and the battle of Chester (AD 613) cut off communication with Strathclyde and northern Britain. In the eighth century the boundaries of the Welsh were further restricted by the annexations of Offa, King of Mercia, and counter-attacks were largely prevented by the construction of an artificial boundary from the Dee to the Wye (Offa's Dyke).

In the ninth century Rhodri Mawr (844–878) united

the country and successfully resisted further incursions of the Saxons by land and raids of Norse and Danish pirates by sea, but at his death his three provinces of Gwynedd (north), Powys (central) and Deheubarth (south) were divided among his three sons, Anarawd, Mervyn and Cadell. Cadell's son Hywel Dda ruled a large part of Wales and codified its laws but the provinces were not united again until the rule of Llewelyn ap Seisyllt (husband of the heiress of Gwynedd) from 1018 to 1023.

THE NORMAN CONQUEST

After the Norman conquest of England, William I created palatine counties along the Welsh frontier, and the Norman barons began to make encroachments into Welsh territory. The Welsh princes recovered many of their losses during the civil wars of Stephen's reign (1135–54), and in the early 13th century Owen Gruffydd, prince of Gwynedd, was the dominant figure in Wales. Under Llywelyn ap Iorwerth (1194–1240) the Welsh united in powerful resistance to English incursions and Llywelyn's privileges and de facto independence were recognised in the Magna Carta. His grandson, Llywelyn ap Gruffydd, was the last native prince; he was killed in 1282 during hostilities between the Welsh and English, allowing Edward I of England to establish his authority over the country. On 7 February 1301, Edward of Caernarvon, son of Edward I, was created Prince of Wales, a title subsequently borne by the eldest son of the sovereign.

Strong Welsh national feeling continued, expressed in the early 15th century in the rising led by Owain Glyndwr, but the situation was altered by the accession to the English throne in 1485 of Henry VII of the Welsh House of Tudor. Wales was politically annexed by England under the Act of Union of 1535, which extended English laws to the principality and gave it parliamentary representation for the first time.

EISTEDDFOD

The Welsh are a distinct nation, with a language and literature of their own; the national bardic festival (Eisteddfod), instituted by Prince Rhys ap Griffith in 1176, is still held annually. These Eisteddfodau (sessions) form part of the Gorsedd (assembly) and are believed to date from the time of Prydian, a ruling prince in an age many centuries before the Christian era.

PRINCIPAL CITIES

There are five cities in Wales (with date city status conferred): Bangor (pre-1900), Cardiff (1905), St David's (1994), Newport (2002) and Swansea (1969).

Cardiff and Swansea have also been granted Lord Mayoralities.

CARDIFF

Cardiff, at the mouth of the rivers Taff, Rhymney and Ely, is the capital city of Wales and at the 2001 census had a population of 305,353. The city has changed dramatically in recent years following the regeneration of Cardiff Bay and construction of a barrage, which has created a permanent freshwater lake and waterfront for the city. As the capital city, Cardiff is home to the National Assembly for Wales and is a major administrative, retail, business and cultural centre.

The city is home to many fine buildings including the City Hall, Cardiff Castle, Llandaff Cathedral, the National Museum of Wales, university buildings, law courts and the Temple of Peace and Health. The Millennium Stadium opened in 1999 and has hosted FA Cup finals and other high-profile English football matches since 2001.

SWANSEA

Swansea (Abertawe) is a seaport with a population of 223,293 at the 2001 census. The Gower peninsula was brought within the city boundary under local government reform in 1974.

The principal buildings are the Norman Castle (rebuilt c.1330), the Royal Institution of South Wales, founded in 1835 (including library), the University of Wales Swansea at Singleton and the Guildhall, containing Frank Brangwyn's British Empire panels. The Dylan Thomas Centre, formerly the old Guildhall, was restored in 1995. More recent buildings include the County Hall, the Maritime Quarter Marina, the Wales National Pool and the National Waterfront Museum.

Swansea was chartered by the Earl of Warwick (1158–84), and further charters were granted by King John, Henry III, Edward II, Edward III and James II, Oliver Cromwell and the Marcher Lord William de Breos. It was formally invested with city status in 1969 by HRH The Prince of Wales.

LORD-LIEUTENANTS AND HIGH SHERIFFS

Area	Lord-Lieutenant	High Sheriff (2007–8)
Clwyd	T. Jones, CBE	Jonathan Major
Dyfed	Hon. Robin Lewis, OBE	Col. David Davies, TD
Gwent	S. Boyle	Lt.-Col. Michael Harry
Gwynedd	Gruffydd Daniel	Dr Dewi Roberts
Mid Glamorgan	Kate Thomas	Charles Knight
Powys	Hon. Mrs E. Legge-Bourke, LVO	John Turner
S. Glamorgan	Capt. N. Lloyd-Edwards	Paul Williams, OBE
W. Glamorgan	R. Hastie, CBE	Martin Trainer

LOCAL COUNCILS

Council	Administrative Headquarters	Telephone	Population*	Council Tax†	Chief Executive
Blaenau Gwent	Ebbw Vale	01495-350555	68,400	£1,215	Robin Morrison
Bridgend	Bridgend	01656-643643	130,800	£1,085	Dr Jo Farrar
Caerphilly	Hengoed	01443-815588	170,200	£993	Stewart Rosser
CARDIFF CITY	Cardiff	029-2087 2000	319,700	£949	Byron Davies
Carmarthenshire	Carmarthen	01267-234567	178,100	£1,033	Mark James
Ceredigion	Aberaeron	01545-570881	78,300	£969	Bronwen Morgan
Conwy	Conwy	01492-574000	111,500	£915	Derek Barker
Denbighshire	Ruthin	01824-706000	96,000	£1,123	Ian Miller
Flintshire	Mold	01352-752121	150,200	£1,006	Colin Everett
Gwynedd	Caernarfon	01286-672255	118,000	£1,060	Harry Thomas
Merthyr Tydfil	Merthyr Tydfil	01685-725000	54,900	£1,169	Alistair Neill
Monmouthshire	Cwmbran	01633-644644	87,700	£1,041	Colin Berg
Neath Port Talbot	Port Talbot	01639-763333	135,600	£1,204	Ken Sawyers
NEWPORT CITY	Newport	01633-656656	139,600	£854	Chris Freegard
Pembrokeshire	Haverfordwest	01437-764551	117,500	£796	Bryn Parry-Jones
Powys	Llandrindod Wells	01597-826000	131,500	£985	Mark Kerr
Rhondda Cynon Taff	Tonypandy	01443-424000	231,600	£1,103	Keith Griffiths
SWANSEA CITY	Swansea	01792-636000	226,400	£990	Paul Smith
Torfaen	Pontypool	01495-762200	90,300	£1,030	Alison Ward
Vale of Glamorgan	Barry	01446-700111	122,900	£959	John Maitland-Evans
Wrexham	Wrexham	01978-292000	130,500	£1,002	Isobel Garner
Ynys Mon (Isle of Anglesey)	Ynys Mon	01248-750057	68,900	£959	Derrick Jones

* *Source:* ONS – *Mid-2005 Population Estimates* (Crown copyright)
† Average Band D council tax bill 2007–8
Councils in CAPITAL LETTERS have city status

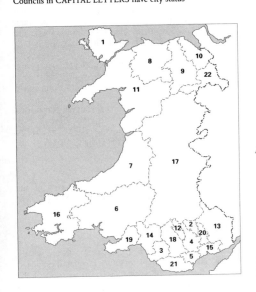

Key	Council	Key	Council
1	Anglesey (Ynys Mon)	12	Merthyr Tydfil
2	Blaenau Gwent	13	Monmouthshire
3	Bridgend	14	Neath Port Talbot
4	Caerphilly	15	Newport
5	Cardiff	16	Pembrokeshire
6	Carmarthenshire	17	Powys
7	Ceredigion	18	Rhondda, Cynon, Taff
8	Conwy	19	Swansea
9	Denbighshire	20	Torfaen
10	Flintshire	21	Vale of Glamorgan
11	Gwynedd	22	Wrexham

SCOTLAND

The Kingdom of Scotland occupies the northern portion of the main island of Great Britain and includes the Inner and Outer Hebrides, Orkney, Shetland and many other islands. It lies between 60° 51′ 30″ and 54° 38′ N. latitude and between 1° 45′ 32″ and 6° 14′ W. longitude, with England to the south, the Atlantic Ocean on the north and west, and the North Sea on the east.

The greatest length of the mainland (Cape Wrath to the Mull of Galloway) is 441km (274 miles), and the greatest breadth (Buchan Ness to Applecross) is 248km (154 miles). The customary measurement of the island of Great Britain is from the site of John o' Groats house, near Duncansby Head, Caithness, to Land's End, Cornwall, a total distance of 970km (603 miles) in a straight line and approximately 1,448km (900 miles) by road.

The total area of Scotland is 78,807 sq. km (30,427 sq. miles): land 77,907 sq. km (30,080 sq. miles), inland water 900 sq. km (347 sq. miles).

POPULATION
The population at the 2001 census was 5,062,011 (men 2,432,494; women 2,629,517). The average density of the population in 2001 was 64 persons per sq. km (166 per sq. mile).

RELIEF
There are three natural orographic divisions of Scotland. The southern uplands have their highest points in Merrick (843m/2,766ft), Rhinns of Kells (814m/2,669ft) and Cairnsmuir of Carsphairn (797m/2,614ft), in the west; and the Tweedsmuir Hills in the east (Broad Law 840m/2,756ft; Dollar Law 817m/2,682ft; Hartfell 808m/2,651ft).

The central lowlands, formed by the valleys of the Clyde, Forth and Tay, divide the southern uplands from the northern Highlands, which extend almost from the extreme north of the mainland to the central lowlands, and are divided into a northern and a southern system by the Great Glen.

The Grampian Mountains, which entirely cover the southern Highland area, include in the west Ben Nevis (1,343m/4,406ft), the highest point in the British Isles, and in the east the Cairngorm Mountains (Ben Macdui 1,309m/4,296ft; Braeriach 1,295m/4,248ft; Cairn Gorm 1,245m/4,084ft). The north-western Highland area contains the mountains of Wester and Easter Ross (Carn Eige 1,183m/3,880ft; Sgurr na Lapaich 1,151m/3,775ft).

Created, like the central lowlands, by a major geological fault, the Great Glen (97km/60 miles long) runs between Inverness and Fort William, and contains Loch Ness, Loch Oich and Loch Lochy. These are linked to each other and to the north-east and south-west coasts of Scotland by the Caledonian Canal, providing a navigable passage between the Moray Firth and the Inner Hebrides.

HYDROGRAPHY
The western coast is fragmented by peninsulas and islands, and indented by fjords (sea-lochs), the longest of which is Loch Fyne (68km/42 miles long) in Argyll. Although the east coast tends to be less fractured and

lower, there are several great drowned inlets (firths), eg Firth of Forth, Firth of Tay and Moray Firth, as well as the Firth of Clyde in the west.

The lochs are the principal hydrographic feature. The largest in Scotland and in Britain is Loch Lomond (70 sq. km/27 sq. miles), in the Grampian valleys and the longest and deepest is Loch Ness (39km/24 miles long and 244m/800ft deep), in the Great Glen.

The longest river is the Tay (188km/117 miles), noted for its salmon. It flows into the North Sea, with Dundee on the estuary, which is spanned by the Tay Bridge (3,136m/10,289ft) opened in 1887 and the Tay Road Bridge (2,245m/7,365ft) opened in 1966. Other noted salmon rivers are the Dee (145km/90 miles) which flows into the North Sea at Aberdeen, and the Spey (177km/110 miles), the swiftest flowing river in the British Isles, which flows into Moray Firth. The Tweed, which gave its name to the woollen cloth produced along its banks, marks in the lower stretches of its 154km (96 mile) course the border between Scotland and England.

The most important river commercially is the Clyde (171km/106 miles), formed by the junction of the Daer and Portrail water, which flows through the city of Glasgow to the Firth of Clyde. During its course it passes over the picturesque Falls of Clyde, Bonnington Linn (9m/30ft), Corra Linn (26m/84ft), Dundaff Linn (3m/10ft) and Stonebyres Linn (24m/80ft), above and below Lanark. The Forth (106km/66 miles), upon which stands Edinburgh, the capital, is spanned by the Forth Railway Bridge (1890), which is 1,625m (5,330ft) long, and the Forth Road Bridge (1964), which has a total length of 1,876m (6,156ft) (over water) and a single span of 914m (3,000ft).

The highest waterfall in Scotland, and the British Isles, is Eas a'Chal Aluinn with a total height of 201m (658ft), which falls from Glas Bheinn in Sutherland. The Falls of Glomach, on a head-stream of the Elchaig in Wester Ross, have a drop of 113m (370ft).

GAELIC LANGUAGE
According to the 2001 census, 1.2 per cent of the population of Scotland, mainly in Eilean Siar (Western Isles), were able to speak the Scottish form of Gaelic.

LOWLAND SCOTTISH LANGUAGE
Several regional lowland Scottish dialects, known variously as Scots, Scotch, Lallans or Doric, are widely spoken. The General Register Office (Scotland) estimated in 1996 that 1.5 million people, or 30 per cent of the population, are Scots speakers. A question on Scots was not included in the 2001 census.

FLAG
The flag of Scotland is known as the Saltire. It is a white diagonal cross on a blue field (saltire argent in a field azure) and represents St Andrew, the patron saint of Scotland.

THE SCOTTISH ISLANDS

ORKNEY

The Orkney Islands (total area 972 sq. km/376 sq. miles) lie about ten km (six miles) north of the mainland, separated from it by the Pentland Firth. Of the 90 islands and islets (holms and skerries) in the group, about one-third are inhabited.

The total population at the 2001 census was 19,245; the 2001 populations of the islands shown here include those of smaller islands forming part of the same council district.

Mainland, 15,339	Rousay, 267
Burray, 357	Sanday, 478
Eday, 121	Shapinsay, 300
Flotta, 81	South Ronaldsay, 854
Hoy, 392	Stronsay, 358
North Ronaldsay, 70	Westray, 563
Papa Westray, 65	

The islands are rich in prehistoric and Scandinavian remains, the most notable being the Stone Age village of Skara Brae, the burial chamber of Maes Howe, the many brochs (towers) and the 12th-century St Magnus Cathedral. Scapa Flow, between the Mainland and Hoy, was the war station of the British Grand Fleet from 1914 to 1919 and the scene of the scuttling of the surrendered German High Seas Fleet (21 June 1919).

Most of the islands are low-lying and fertile, and farming (principally beef cattle) is the main industry. Flotta, to the south of Scapa Flow, is the site of the oil terminal for the Piper, Claymore and Tartan fields in the North Sea.

The capital is Kirkwall (population 6,206) situated on Mainland.

SHETLAND

The Shetland Islands have a total area of 1,427 sq. km (551 sq. miles) and a population at the 2001 census of 21,988. They lie about 80km (50 miles) north of the Orkneys, with Fair Isle about half way between the two groups. Out Stack, off Muckle Flugga, 1.6km (one mile) north of Unst, is the most northerly part of the British Isles (60° 51′ 30″ N. lat.).

There are over 100 islands, of which 16 are inhabited. Populations at the 2001 census were:

Mainland, 17,575	Muckle Roe, 104
Bressay, 384	Trondra, 133
East Burra, 66	Unst, 720
Fair Isle, 69	West Burra, 784
Fetlar, 86	Whalsay, 1,034
Housay, 76	Yell, 957

Shetland's many archaeological sites include Jarlshof, Mousa and Clickhimin, and its long connection with Scandinavia has resulted in a strong Norse influence on its placenames and dialect.

Industries include fishing, knitwear and farming. In addition to the fishing fleet there are fish processing factories, and the traditional handknitting of Fair Isle and Unst is now supplemented with machine-knitted garments. Farming is mainly crofting, with sheep being raised on the moorland and hills of the islands. Latterly the islands have become a centre of the North Sea oil industry, with pipelines from the Brent and Ninian fields running to the terminal at Sullom Voe, the largest of its kind in Europe.

The capital is Lerwick (population 6,830) situated on Mainland. Lerwick is the main centre for supply services for offshore oil exploration and development.

THE HEBRIDES

Until the late 13th century the Hebrides included other Scottish islands in the Firth of Clyde, the peninsula of Kintyre (Argyll), the Isle of Man, and the (Irish) Isle of Rathlin. The origin of the name is probably the Greek *Eboudai*, latinised as *Hebudes* by Pliny, and corrupted to its present form. The Norwegian name *Sudreyjar* (Southern Islands) was latinised as *Sodorenses*, a name that survives in the Anglican bishopric of Sodor and Man.

There are over 500 islands and islets, of which about 100 are inhabited, though mountainous terrain and extensive peat bogs mean that only a fraction of the total area is under cultivation. Stone, Bronze and Iron Age settlement has left many remains, including those at Callanish on Lewis, and Norse colonisation influenced language, customs and placenames. Occupations include farming (mostly crofting and stock-raising), fishing and the manufacture of tweeds and other woollens. Tourism is also an important part of the economy.

The Inner Hebrides lie off the west coast of Scotland and are relatively close to the mainland. The largest and best-known is Skye (area 1,665 sq. km/643 sq. miles; pop. 9,251; chief town, Portree), which contains the Cuillin Hills (Sgurr Alasdair 993m/3,257ft); Bla Bheinn (928m/3,046ft); the Storr (719m/2,358ft) and the Red Hills (Beinn na Caillich 732m/2,403ft). Other islands in the Highland council area include Raasay (pop. 194), Rum, Eigg (pop. 131) and Muck.

Further south the Inner Hebridean islands include Arran (pop. 5,058) containing Goat Fell (874m/2,868ft); Coll and Tiree (pop. 934); Colonsay and Oronsay (pop. 113); Easdale (pop. 58); Gigha (pop. 110); Islay (area 608 sq. km/235 sq. miles; pop. 3,457); Jura (area 414 sq. km/160 sq. miles; pop. 188) with a range of hills culminating in the Paps of Jura (Beinn-an-Oir, 785m/2,576ft, and Beinn Chaolais, 755m/2,477ft); Lismore (pop. 146); Luing (pop. 220); and Mull (area 950 sq. km/367 sq. miles; pop. 2,696; chief town Tobermory) containing Ben More (967m/3,171ft).

The Outer Hebrides, separated from the mainland by the Minch, now form the Eilean Siar (Western Isles) council area (area 2,897 sq. km/1,119 sq. miles; pop. 26,502). The main islands are Lewis with Harris (area 1,994 sq. km/770 sq. miles, pop. 19,918), whose chief town, Stornoway, is the administrative headquarters; North Uist (pop. 1,320); South Uist (pop. 1,818); Benbecula (pop. 1,249) and Barra (pop. 1,078). Other inhabited islands include Bernera (233), Berneray (136), Eriskay (133), Grimsay (201), Scalpay (322) and Vatersay (94).

EARLY HISTORY

There is evidence of human settlement in Scotland dating from the third millennium BC, the earliest settlers being Middle Stone Age hunters and fishermen. Early in the second millennium BC, New Stone Age farmers began to cultivate crops and rear livestock; their settlements were on the west coast and in the north, and included Skara Brae and Maeshowe (Orkney). Settlement by the early Bronze Age 'Beaker Folk', so-called from the shape of their drinking vessels, in eastern Scotland dates from about 1800 BC. Further settlement is believed to have occurred from 700 BC onwards, as tribes were displaced from further south by new incursions from the Continent and the Roman invasions from AD 43.

Julius Agricola, the Roman governor of Britain AD 77–84, extended the Roman conquests in Britain by advancing into Caledonia, culminating with a victory at Mons Graupius, probably in AD 84; he was recalled to Rome shortly afterwards and his forward policy was not pursued. Hadrian's Wall, mostly completed by AD 30, marked the northern frontier of the Roman empire except for the period between about AD 144 and 190 when the frontier moved north to the Forth-Clyde isthmus and a turf wall, the Antonine Wall, was manned.

After the Roman withdrawal from Britain, there were centuries of warfare between the Picts, Scots, Britons, Angles and Vikings. The Picts, believed to be a non-Indo-European race, occupied the area north of the Forth. The Scots, a Gaelic-speaking people of northern Ireland, colonised the area of Argyll and Bute (the kingdom of Dalriada) in the fifth century AD and then expanded eastwards and northwards. The Britons, speaking a Brythonic Celtic language, colonised Scotland from the south from the first century BC; they lost control of south-eastern Scotland (incorporated into the kingdom of Northumbria) to the Angles in the early seventh century but retained Strathclyde (south-western Scotland and Cumbria). Viking raids from the late eighth century were followed by Norse settlement in the western and northern isles, Argyll, Caithness and Sutherland from the mid-ninth century onwards.

UNIFICATION

The union of the areas which now comprise Scotland began in AD 843 when Kenneth mac Alpin, king of the Scots from c.834, also became king of the Picts, joining the two lands to form the kingdom of Alba (comprising Scotland north of a line between the Forth and Clyde rivers). Lothian, the eastern part of the area between the Forth and the Tweed, seems to have been leased to Kenneth II of Alba (reigned 971–995) by Edgar of England c.973, and Scottish possession was confirmed by Malcolm II's victory over a Northumbrian army at Carham c.1016. At about this time Malcolm II (reigned 1005–34) placed his grandson Duncan on the throne of the British kingdom of Strathclyde, bringing under Scots rule virtually all of what is now Scotland.

The Norse possessions were incorporated into the kingdom of Scotland from the 12th century onwards. An uprising in the mid-12th century drove the Norse from most of mainland Argyll. The Hebrides were ceded to Scotland by the treaty of Perth in 1266 after a Norwegian expedition in 1263 failed to maintain Norse authority over the islands. Orkney and Shetland fell to Scotland in 1468–9 as a pledge for the unpaid dowry of Margaret of Denmark, wife of James III, although Danish claims of suzerainty were relinquished only with the marriage of Anne of Denmark to James VI in 1590.

From the 11th century, there were frequent wars between Scotland and England over territory and the extent of England's political influence. The failure of the Scottish royal line with the death of Margaret of Norway in 1290 led to disputes over the throne which were resolved by the adjudication of Edward I of England. He awarded the throne to John Balliol in 1292 but Balliol's refusal to be a puppet king led to war. Balliol surrendered to Edward I in 1296 and Edward attempted to rule Scotland himself. Resistance to Scotland's loss of

independence was led by William Wallace, who defeated the English at Stirling Bridge (1297), and Robert Bruce, crowned in 1306, who held most of Scotland by 1311 and routed Edward II's army at Bannockburn (1314). England recognised the independence of Scotland in the treaty of Northampton in 1328. Subsequent clashes include the disastrous battle of Flodden (1513) in which James IV and many of his nobles fell.

THE UNION

In 1603 James VI of Scotland succeeded Elizabeth I on the throne of England (his mother, Mary Queen of Scots, was the great-granddaughter of Henry VII); his successors reigning as sovereigns of Great Britain. Political union of the two countries did not occur until 1707.

THE JACOBITE REVOLTS

After the abdication (by flight) in 1688 of James VII and II, the crown devolved upon William III (grandson of Charles I) and Mary II (elder daughter of James VII and II). In 1689 Graham of Claverhouse roused the Highlands on behalf of James VII and II, but died after a military success at Killiecrankie.

After the death of Anne (younger daughter of James VII and II), the throne devolved upon George I (great-grandson of James VI and I). In 1715, armed risings on behalf of James Stuart (the Old Pretender, son of James VII and II) led to the indecisive battle of Sheriffmuir, and the Jacobite movement died down until 1745, when Charles Stuart (the Young Pretender) defeated the Royalist troops at Prestonpans and advanced to Derby (1746). From Derby, the adherents of 'James VIII and III' (the title claimed for his father by Charles Stuart) fell back on the defensive and were finally crushed at Culloden (16 April 1746) by an army led by by the Duke of Cumberland, son of George II.

PRINCIPAL CITIES

ABERDEEN

Aberdeen, 209km (130 miles) north-east of Edinburgh, received its charter as a Royal Burgh in 1124. Scotland's third largest city, Aberdeen lies between two rivers, the Dee and the Don, facing the North Sea; the city has a strong maritime history and is today a major centre for offshore oil exploration and production. It is also an ancient university town and distinguished research centre. Other industries include engineering, food processing, textiles, paper manufacturing and chemicals.

Places of interest include King's College, St Machar's Cathedral, Brig o' Balgownie, Duthie Park and Winter Gardens, Hazlehead Park, the Kirk of St Nicholas, Mercat Cross, Marischal College and Marischal Museum, Provost Skene's House, Art Gallery, Gordon Highlanders Museum, Satrosphere Hands-On Discovery Centre, and Aberdeen Maritime Museum.

DUNDEE

The Royal Burgh of Dundee is situated on the north bank of the Tay estuary. The city's port and dock installations are important to the offshore oil industry and the airport also provides servicing facilities. Principal industries include textiles, biotechnology and digital media, lasers, printing, tyre manufacture, food processing, engineering and tourism.

The unique City Churches – three churches under one roof, together with the 15th-century St Mary's Tower – are the most prominent architectural feature. Dundee is home to two historic ships: the Dundee-built RRS *Discovery* which took Capt. Scott to the Antarctic lies alongside Discovery Quay, and the frigate *Unicorn*, the only British-built wooden warship still afloat, is moored in Victoria Dock. Places of interest include Mills Public Observatory, the Tay road and rail bridges, Dundee Contemporary Arts Centre, McManus Galleries, Claypotts Castle, Broughty Castle, Verdant Works (Textile Heritage Centre) and the Sensation Science Centre.

EDINBURGH

Edinburgh is the capital city and seat of government in Scotland. The city is built on a group of hills and contains in Princes Street one of the most beautiful thoroughfares in the world. Edinburgh has many strong literary associations and was named UNESCO city of literature in 2005.

The principal buildings are the castle, which houses the Stone of Scone and also includes St Margaret's Chapel, the oldest building in Edinburgh, and near it, the Scottish National War Memorial; the Palace of Holyroodhouse; Parliament House, the present seat of the judicature; three universities (Edinburgh, Heriot-Watt, Napier); St Giles' Cathedral; St Mary's (Scottish Episcopal) Cathedral (Sir George Gilbert Scott); the General Register House (Robert Adam); the National and Signet libraries; the National Gallery of Scotland; the Royal Scottish Academy; the Scottish National Portrait Gallery and the Edinburgh International Conference Centre.

GLASGOW

Glasgow, a Royal Burgh, is Scotland's largest city and its principal commercial and industrial centre. The city occupies the north and south banks of the Clyde, formerly one of the chief commercial estuaries in the world. The main industries include engineering, electronics, finance, chemicals and printing. The city is also a key tourist and conference destination.

The chief buildings are the 13th-century Gothic cathedral, the university (Sir George Gilbert Scott), the City Chambers, the Royal Concert Hall, St Mungo Museum of Religious Life and Art, Pollok House, the School of Art (Charles Rennie Mackintosh), Kelvingrove Art Galleries, the Gallery of Modern Art, the Burrell Collection museum and the Mitchell Library. The city is home to the Scottish National Orchestra, Scottish Opera, Scottish Ballet and BBC Scotland and Scottish Television.

INVERNESS

Inverness was granted city status in 2000. The city's name is derived from the Gaelic for 'the mouth of the Ness', referring to the river on which it lies. Inverness is recorded as being at the junction of the old trade routes since AD 565. Today the city is the main administrative centre for the north of Scotland and is the capital of the Highlands. Tourism is one of the city's main industries.

Among the city's most notable buildings is Abertarff House, built in 1593 and the oldest secular building remaining in Inverness. Balnain House, built as a town house in 1726, is a fine example of early Georgian architecture. Once a hospital for Hanoverian soldiers after the battle of Culloden and as billets for the Royal Engineers when completing the first Ordnance Survey, today Balnain House is the National Trust for Scotland's regional HQ. The Old High Church, on St Michael's Mount, is the original parish church of Inverness and is built on the site of the earliest Christian church in the city. Parts of the church date back to the 14th century.

Stirling was granted city status in 2002. Aberdeen, Dundee, Edinburgh and Glasgow have also been granted Lord Mayoralty/Lord Provostship.

LORD-LIEUTENANTS

Title	Name	Title	Name
Aberdeen City*	Lord Provost Peter Stephen	Lanarkshire	G. Cox, MBE
Aberdeenshire	A. Farquharson, OBE	Midlothian	Patrick Prenter, CBE
Angus	Mrs G. Osborne	Moray	Grenville Shaw Johnston, OBE, TD
Argyll and Bute	K. Mackinnon		
Ayrshire and Arran	John Duncan, QPM	Nairn	Ewen Brodie of Lethan
Banffshire	Clare Russell	Orkney	Dr Anthony Trickett, MBE
Berwickshire	Maj. A. Trotter	Perth and Kinross	Brig. Melville Jameson, CBE
Caithness	Miss M. Dunnett	Renfrewshire	Guy Clark
Clackmannan	Mrs S. Cruickshank	Ross and Cromarty	Janet Bowen
Dumfries	Jean Tulloch	Roxburgh, Ettrick and	Hon. Capt. Gerald Maitland-
Dunbartonshire	Col. Donald Ross, OBE	Lauderdale	Carew
Dundee City*	Lord Provost John Letford	Shetland	J. Scott
East Lothian	W. Garth Morrison, CBE	Stirling and Falkirk	Mrs M. McLachlan
Edinburgh City*	Rt. Hon. Lord Provost George Grubb	Sutherland	Dr Monica Maitland Main
		The Stewartry of	Lt.-Col. Sir Malcolm Walter
Eilean Siar (Western Isles)	A. Matheson, OBE	Kirkcudbright	Hugh Ross, GCVO, OBE
Fife	Mrs C. Dean	Tweeddale	Capt. D. Younger
Glasgow City*	Rt. Hon. Lord Provost Robert Winter	West Lothian	Mrs I. Brydie, MBE
		Wigtown	Marion Brewis
Inverness	Donald Angus Cameron of Lochiel		
Kincardineshire	Carol Kinghorn		

* The Lord Provosts of the four cities of Aberdeen, Dundee, Edinburgh and Glasgow are Lord-Lieutenants *ex officio* for those districts

LOCAL COUNCILS

Council	Administrative Headquarters	Telephone	Population*	Council Tax†	Chief Executive
ABERDEEN	Aberdeen	01224-522000	202,400	£1,230	Douglas Paterson
Aberdeenshire	Aberdeen	01467-620981	235,400	£1,141	Alan Campbell
Angus	Forfar	01307-461460	109,200	£1,072	David Sawers
Argyll and Bute	Lochgilphead	01546-602127	90,900	£1,178	James McLellan
Clackmannanshire	Alloa	01259-452000	48,600	£1,148	Dave Jones
Dumfries and Galloway	Dumfries	01387-260000	148,300	£1,049	Philip Jones
DUNDEE	Dundee	01382-434000	142,200	£1,211	Alex Stephen
East Ayrshire	Kilmarnock	01563-576000	119,400	£1,189	Fiona Lees
East Dunbartonshire	Kirkintilloch	0141-578 8000	106,000	£1,142	Sue Bruce
East Lothian	Haddington	01620-827827	91,800	£1,118	Alex McCrorie
East Renfrewshire	Giffnock	0141-577 3000	89,600	£1,126	David Dippie
EDINBURGH	Edinburgh	0131-200 2000	457,800	£1,169	Tom Aitchison
Eilean Siar (Western Isles)	Stornoway	01851-703773	26,400	£1,024	Malcolm Burr
Falkirk	Falkirk	01324-506070	149,200	£1,070	Mary Pitcaithly
Fife	Glenrothes	01592-414141	356,700	£1,118	Ronnie Hinds
GLASGOW	Glasgow	0141-287 2000	578,800	£1,213	George Black
Highland	Inverness	01463-702000	213,600	£1,163	Arthur McCourt
Inverclyde	Greenock	01475-717171	82,100	£1,198	John Mundell
Midlothian	Dalkeith	0131-270 7500	79,200	£1,210	Trevor Muir
Moray	Elgin	01343-543451	88,100	£1,135	Alastair Keddie
North Ayrshire	Irvine	0845-324100	135,800	£1,152	Ian Snodgrass
North Lanarkshire	Motherwell	01698-302222	323,400	£1,098	Gavin Whitefield
Orkney	Kirkwall	01856-873535	19,600	£1,037	Alistair Buchan
Perth and Kinross	Perth	01738-475000	138,400	£1,158	Bernadette Malone
Renfrewshire	Paisley	0141-842 5000	170,000	£1,165	David Martin
Scottish Borders	Melrose	01835-824000	109,700	£1,084	David Hume
Shetland	Lerwick	01595-693535	22,000	£1,053	Morgan Goodlad
South Ayrshire	Ayr	01292-612000	111,800	£1,154	Tom Cairns
South Lanarkshire	Hamilton	01698-454444	306,300	£1,101	Archie Streng
STIRLING	Stirling	0845-277 7000	86,900	£1,223	Keith Yates
West Dunbartonshire	Dumbarton	01389-737000	91,400	£1,163	David McMillian
West Lothian	Livingston	01506-777000	163,800	£1,128	Alex Linkston

* *Source:* ONS – *Mid-2005 Population Estimates* (Crown copyright)
† Average Band D council tax bill 2007–8
Councils in CAPITAL LETTERS have city status

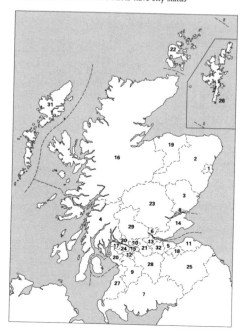

Key	Council		Key	Council
1	Aberdeen City		18	Midlothian
2	Aberdeenshire		19	Moray
3	Angus		20	North Ayrshire
4	Argyll and Bute		21	North Lanarkshire
5	City of Edinburgh		22	Orkney
6	Clackmannanshire		23	Perth and Kinross
7	Dumfries and Galloway		24	Renfrewshire
8	Dundee City		25	Scottish Borders
9	East Ayrshire		26	Shetland
10	East Dunbartonshire		27	South Ayrshire
11	East Lothian		28	South Lanarkshire
12	East Renfrewshire		29	Stirling
13	Falkirk		30	West Dunbartonshire
14	Fife		31	Western Isles (Eilean Siar)
15	Glasgow City		32	West Lothian
16	Highland			
17	Inverclyde			

NORTHERN IRELAND

Northern Ireland has a total area of 14,149 sq. km (5,463 sq. miles): land, 13,576 sq. km (5,242 sq. miles); inland water, 573 sq. km (221 sq. miles).

The population of Northern Ireland at the 2001 census was 1,685,267 (men 821,449; women 863,818). The average density of population in 2001 was 119 persons per sq. km (308 per sq. mile).

In 2001 the number of persons in the various religious denominations (expressed as percentages of the total population) were: Catholic, 40.26; Presbyterian, 20.69; Church of Ireland, 15.30; Methodist Church in Ireland, 3.51; other Christian (including Christian related) 6.07; other religions and philosophies, 0.3; no religion or religion not stated, 13.88.

FLAG

The official national flag of Northern Ireland is now the Union Flag. The flag formerly in use (a white, six-pointed star in the centre of a red cross on a white field, enclosing a red hand and surmounted by a crown) has not been used since the imposition of direct rule.

PRINCIPAL CITIES

BELFAST

Belfast, the administrative centre of Northern Ireland, is situated at the mouth of the River Lagan at its entrance to Belfast Lough. The city grew to be a great industrial centre, owing to its easy access by sea to Scottish coal and iron.

The principal buildings are of a relatively young age and include the parliament buildings at Stormont, the City Hall, Waterfront Hall, the Law Courts, the Public Library and the Museum and Art Gallery.

Belfast received its first charter of incorporation in 1613 and was created a city in 1888; the title of lord mayor was conferred in 1892.

LONDONDERRY

Londonderry (originally Derry) is situated on the River Foyle, and has important associations with the City of London. The Irish Society was created by the City of London in 1610, and under its royal charter of 1613 it fortified the city and was for a long time closely associated with its administration. Because of this connection the city was incorporated in 1613 under the new name of Londonderry.

The city is famous for the great siege of 1688–9, when for 105 days the town held out against the forces of James II. The city walls are still intact and form a circuit of 1.6 km (one mile) around the old city.

Interesting buildings are the Protestant cathedral of St Columb's (1633) and the Guildhall, reconstructed in 1912 and containing a number of beautiful stained glass windows, many of which were presented by the livery companies of London.

Three other places in Northern Ireland have been granted city status: Armagh (1994), Lisburn (2002) and Newry (2002).

CONSTITUTIONAL DEVELOPMENTS

Northern Ireland is subject to the same fundamental constitutional provisions which apply to the rest of the United Kingdom. It had its own parliament and government from 1921 to 1972, but after increasing civil unrest the Northern Ireland (Temporary Provisions) Act 1972 transferred the legislative and executive powers of the Northern Ireland parliament and government to the UK parliament and a secretary of state. The Northern Ireland Constitution Act 1973 provided for devolution in Northern Ireland through an assembly and executive, but a power-sharing executive formed by the Northern Ireland political parties in January 1974 collapsed in May 1974. Following the collapse of the power-sharing executive Northern Ireland returned to direct rule governance under the provisions of the Northern Ireland Act 1974, placing the Northern Ireland department under the direction and control of the Northern Ireland secretary.

In December 1993 the British and Irish governments published the Joint Declaration complementing their political talks, and making clear that any settlement would need to be founded on principles of democracy and consent. The declaration also stated that all democratically mandated parties could be involved in political talks as long as they permanently renounced paramilitary violence.

On 12 January 1998 the British and Irish governments issued a joint document, *Propositions on Heads of Agreement,* proposing the establishment of various new cross-border bodies; further proposals were presented on 27 January. A draft peace settlement was issued by the talks' chairman, US Senator George Mitchell, on 6 April 1998 but was rejected by the Unionists the following day. On 10 April agreement was reached between the British and Irish governments and the eight Northern Ireland political parties still involved in the talks (the Good Friday Agreement). The agreement provided for an elected Northern Ireland Assembly, a North/South Ministerial Council, and a British-Irish Council comprising representatives of the British, Irish, Channel Islands and Isle of Man governments and members of the new assemblies for Scotland, Wales and Northern Ireland. Further points included the abandonment of the Republic of Ireland's constitutional claim to Northern Ireland; the decommissioning of weapons; the release of paramilitary prisoners and changes in policing.

Referendums on the agreement were held in Northern Ireland and the Republic of Ireland on 22 May 1998. In Northern Ireland the turnout was 81 per cent, of which 71.12 per cent voted in favour of the agreement. In the Republic of Ireland, the turnout was about 55 per cent, of which 94.4 per cent voted in favour of both the agreement and the necessary constitutional change. In the UK, the Northern Ireland Act 1998, enshrining the provisions of the agreement, received royal assent in November 1998.

On 28 April 2003 the secretary of state again assumed responsibility for the direction of the Northern Ireland departments on the dissolution of the Northern Ireland Assembly, following its initial suspension from midnight on 14 October 2002. In 2006, following the passing of the Northern Ireland Act, the secretary of state created a non-legislative fixed-term assembly which would cease to operate either when the political parties agreed to restore devolution, or on 24 November 2006 (whichever occurred first). In October 2006 a timetable to restore devolution was drawn up (St Andrews Agreement) and a transitional Northern Ireland Assembly was formed on 24 November. The transitional assembly was dissolved in January 2007 in preparation for elections to be held on 7 March; following the elections a power-sharing executive was formed and the new 108-member Northern Ireland Assembly became operational on 8 May 2007.

See also Regional Government and Events of the Year.

FINANCE

Northern Ireland's expenditure is funded through the Northern Ireland Consolidated Fund (NICF). Up until devolution on 2 December 1999, the NICF was largely financed by Northern Ireland's attributed share of UK taxation and supplemented by a grant-in-aid. From devolution, these separate elements have been subsumed into a single block grant. The Northern Ireland Departmental Expenditure Limit for 2007–8 was set at £8,612m.

LORD-LIEUTENANTS AND HIGH SHERIFFS

County	Lord-Lieutenant	High Sheriff (2007)
Antrim	The Lord O'Neill, TD	Dr Joseph Wilson
Armagh	The Earl of Caledon	Dr Colin Mathews
Belfast City	Lady Carswell, OBE	Thomas Kirkpatrick
Down	William Hall	John Fisher
Fermanagh	The Earl of Erne	Rosemary Forde
Londonderry	Denis Desmond, CBE	Sharyn Griffith
Londonderry City	Dr Donal Keegan, OBE	Richard Sterling, OBE
Tyrone	The Duke of Abercorn	John Little

LOCAL COUNCILS

Council	Telephone	Population*	Chief Executive
Antrim, Co. Down	028-9446 3113	50,500	David McCammick
Ards, Co. Down	028-9182 4000	75,300	Ashley Boreland
ARMAGH CITY, Co. Armagh	028-3752 9600	55,800	John Briggs *(acting)*
Ballymena, Co. Antrim	028-2566 0300	60,700	*vacant*
Ballymoney, Co. Antrim	028-2766 0200	28,700	John Dempsey
Banbridge, Co. Down	028-4066 0600	44,800	Liam Hannaway
BELFAST CITY, Co. Antrim and Co. Down	028-9032 0202	268,000	Peter McNaney
Carrickfergus, Co. Antrim	028-9335 8000	39,200	Alan Cardwell
Castlereagh, Co. Down	028-9046 4500	65,700	Adrian Donaldson
Coleraine, Co. Londonderry	028-7034 7034	56,600	Davy Wreath *(acting)*
Cookstown, Co. Tyrone	028-8676 2205	34,100	Michael McGuckin
Craigavon, Co. Armagh	028-3831 2400	84,700	Francis Rock
DERRY CITY, Co. Londonderry	028-7136 5151	107,300	Anthony McGurk
Down, Co. Down	028-4461 0800	67,400	John McGrillen
Dungannon and South Tyrone, Co. Tyrone	028-8772 0300	50,700	Alan Burke *(acting)*
Fermanagh, Co. Fermanagh	028-6632 5050	59,700	Rodney Connor
Larne, Co. Antrim	028-2827 2313	31,100	Geraldine McGahey
Limavady, Co. Londonderry	028-7772 2226	34,100	Liam Flanigan
LISBURN CITY, Co. Antrim	028-9250 9250	111,500	Norman Davidson
Magherafelt, Co. Londonderry	028-7939 7979	41,800	John McLaughlin
Moyle, Co. Antrim	028-2076 2225	16,500	Richard Lewis
NEWRY and Mourne, Co. Down and Co. Armagh	028-3031 3031	91,600	Thomas McCall
Newtownabbey, Co. Antrim	028-9034 0000	80,800	Norman Dunn
North Down, Co. Down	028-9127 0371	78,300	Trevor Polley
Omagh, Co. Tyrone	028 8224 5321	50,700	Daniel McSorley
Strabane, Co. Tyrone	028-7138 2204	38,700	Philip Faithfull

* *Source:* ONS – *Mid-2005 Population Estimates* (Crown copyright)
Councils in CAPITAL LETTERS have city status

THE ISLE OF MAN

Ellan Vannin

The Isle of Man is an island situated in the Irish Sea, at latitude 54° 3'–54° 25' N. and longitude 4° 18'–4° 47' W., nearly equidistant from England, Scotland and Ireland. Although the early inhabitants were of Celtic origin, the Isle of Man was part of the Norwegian Kingdom of the Hebrides until 1266, when this was ceded to Scotland. Subsequently granted to the Stanleys (Earls of Derby) in the 15th century and later to the Dukes of Atholl, it was brought under the administration of the crown in 1765. The island forms the bishopric of Sodor and Man.

The total land area is 572 sq. km (221 sq. miles). The 2006 census showed a resident population of 80,058 (men, 39,523; women, 40,535). The main language in use is English. There are no remaining native speakers of Manx Gaelic but around 1,550 people are able to speak the language.

CAPITAL – ΨDouglas; population, 26,218 (2006). ΨCastletown (3,109) is the ancient capital; the other towns are ΨPeel (4,280) and ΨRamsey (7,309)

FLAG – A red flag charged with three conjoined armoured legs in white and gold

NATIONAL DAY – 5 July (Tynwald Day)

GOVERNMENT

The Isle of Man is a self-governing crown dependency, with its own parliamentary, legal and administrative system. The British government is responsible for international relations and defence. Under the UK Act of Accession, Protocol 3, the island's relationship with the European Union is limited to trade alone and does not extend to financial aid. The Lieutenant-Governor is the Queen's personal representative on the island.

The legislature, Tynwald, is the oldest parliament in the world in continuous existence. It has two branches: the Legislative Council and the House of Keys. The council consists of the President of Tynwald, the Bishop of Sodor and Man, the Attorney-General (who does not have a vote) and eight members elected by the House of Keys. The House of Keys has 24 members, elected by universal adult suffrage. The branches sit separately to consider legislation and sit together, as Tynwald Court, for most other parliamentary purposes.

The presiding officer of Tynwald Court is the President of Tynwald, elected by the members, who also presides over sittings of the Legislative Council. The presiding officer of the House of Keys is the Speaker, who is elected by members of the house.

The principal members of the Manx government are the chief minister and nine departmental ministers, who comprise the Council of Ministers.

Lieutenant-Governor, HE Vice-Adm. Sir Paul Kenneth Haddacks, KCB
ADC to the Lieutenant-Governor, C. J. Tummon

President of Tynwald, Hon. Noel Cringle
Speaker, House of Keys, Hon. Steve Rodan, SHK
The First Deemster and Clerk of the Rolls, John Michael Kerruish
Clerk of Tynwald, Secretary to the House of Keys and Counsel to the Speaker, Malachy Cornwell-Kelly
Clerk of the Legislative Council and Deputy Clerk of Tynwald, Mrs M. Cullen
Attorney-General, W. J. H. Corlett, QC
Chief Minister, Hon. Tony Brown, MHK
Chief Secretary, Mrs M. Williams

ECONOMY

Most of the income generated in the island is earned in the services sector with financial and professional services accounting for just over half of the national income. Tourism and manufacturing are also major generators of income whilst the island's other traditional industries of agriculture and fishing now play a smaller role in the economy. Under the terms of Protocol 3, the island has tariff-free access to EU markets for its goods.

In May 2007 the island's unemployment rate was 1.4 per cent and inflation (RPI) was 4.2 per cent.

FINANCE

The budget for 2007–8 provides for net revenue expenditure of £538.2m. The principal sources of government revenue are taxes on income and expenditure. Income tax is payable at a rate of 10 per cent on the first £10,500 of taxable income for single resident individuals and 18 per cent on the balance, after personal allowances of £8,850. These bands are doubled for married couples. The rate of income tax for trading companies is zero per cent except for income from banking and land and property, which is taxed at 10 per cent. By agreement with the British government, the island keeps most of its rates of indirect taxation (VAT and duties) the same as those in the UK. However, VAT on tourist accommodation, property, repairs and renovations is charged at 5 per cent. A reciprocal agreement on national insurance benefits and pensions exists between the governments of the Isle of Man and the UK. Taxes are also charged on property (rates), but these are comparatively low.

The major government expenditure items are health, social security, social services and education, which account for 59 per cent of the government budget. The island makes an annual contribution to the UK for defence and other external services.

The island has a special relationship with the European Union and neither contributes money to nor receives funds from the EU budget.

Ψ = sea port

THE CHANNEL ISLANDS

The Channel Islands, situated off the north-west coast of France (at a distance of 16km (10 miles) at their closest point), are the only portions of the Dukedom of Normandy still belonging to the crown, to which they have been attached since the Norman Conquest of 1066. They were the only British territory to come under German occupation during the Second World War, following invasion on 30 June and 1 July 1940. The islands were relieved by British forces on 9 May 1945, and 9 May (Liberation Day) is now observed as a bank and public holiday.

The islands consist of Jersey (11,630ha/28,717 acres), Guernsey (6,340ha/15,654 acres), and the dependencies of Guernsey: Alderney (795ha/1,962 acres), Brecqhou (30ha/74 acres), Great Sark (419ha/1,035 acres), Little Sark (97ha/239 acres), Herm (130ha/320 acres), Jethou (18ha/44 acres) and Lihou (15ha/38 acres) – a total of 19,474ha/48,083 acres, or 194 sq. km/75 sq. miles. The 2001 census showed the population of Jersey as 87,186; Guernsey, 59,807 and Alderney, 2,294. Sark did not complete the same census but a recent informal census gave its population figure as 591. The official languages are English and French. In country districts of Jersey and Guernsey and throughout Sark a Norman-French *patois* is also in use, though to a lesser extent.

GOVERNMENT
The islands are crown dependencies with their own legislative assemblies (the States in Jersey, Guernsey and Alderney and the Chief Pleas in Sark), systems of local administration and law, and their own courts. Acts passed by the States require the sanction of the Queen-in-council. The British government is responsible for defence and international relations. The Channel Islands have trading rights only (not including financial aid) within the European Union.

In both Jersey and Guernsey bailiwicks the Lieutenant-Governor and Commander-in-Chief, who is appointed by the crown, is the personal representative of the Queen and the channel of communication between the crown (via the Privy Council) and the island's government.

In 2001 a ministerial system of government was introduced in Jersey to replace the previous committee system. The executive consists of a chief minister and nine ministers who form the Council of Ministers. Ministers are assisted by up to 13 assistant ministers. Members of the States who are not in the executive are able to sit on a number of scrutiny panels and the Public Accounts Committee to examine the policy of the executive and hold ministers to account. On 1 May 2004 Guernsey also introduced a ministerial governance system – a Policy Council comprising a chief minister and ten departmental ministers. There are also five specialist committees, each led by a chairman, responsible for public sector pay negotiations, parliamentary procedural matters and for scrutinising policy, finance and legislation. Justice is administered by the royal courts of Jersey and Guernsey, each consisting of the bailiff and 12 elected jurats. The bailiffs of Jersey and Guernsey, appointed by the crown, are presidents of the states and of the royal courts of their respective islands.

Each bailiwick constitutes a deanery under the jurisdiction of the Bishop of Winchester.

ECONOMY
A mild climate and good soil have led to the development of intensive systems of agriculture and horticulture, which form a significant part of the economy. Equally important are earnings from tourism and banking and finance: the low rates of income and corporation tax and the absence of death duties and VAT make the islands an important offshore financial centre.

Principal exports are agricultural produce and flowers; imports are chiefly machinery, manufactured goods, food, fuel and chemicals. Trade with the UK is regarded as internal.

British currency is legal tender in the Channel Islands but each bailiwick issues its own coins and notes (*see* Currency section). They also issue their own postage stamps; UK stamps are not valid.

JERSEY

Lieutenant-Governor and Commander-in-Chief of Jersey, HE
    Lt.-Gen. Andrew Peter Ridgway, CB, CBE, *apptd* 2006
Secretary and ADC, Lt.-Col. A. J. C. Woodrow, OBE, MC
Bailiff of Jersey, Sir Philip Bailhache, Kt.
Deputy Bailiff, M. C. St J. Birt
Attorney-General, W. J. Bailhache, QC
Receiver-General, P. Lewin
Solicitor-General, Miss S. C. Nicolle, QC
Greffier of the States, M. N. de la Haye
States Treasurer, Mr I. Black

FINANCE

	2005	2006
Revenue income	£699,100,000	£732,557,000
Revenue expenditure	£652,479,000	£670,749,000
Capital expenditure	£56,686,000	£58,090,000

CHIEF TOWN – Ψ St Helier, on the south coast
FLAG – A white field charged with a red saltire cross, and the arms of Jersey in the upper centre

GUERNSEY AND DEPENDENCIES

Lieutenant-Governor and Commander-in-Chief of the
    Bailiwick of Guernsey and its Dependencies, HE Vice-
    Adm. Sir Fabian Malbon, KBE, *apptd* 2005
Secretary and ADC, Col. R Graham, MBE
Bailiff of Guernsey, Geoffrey Rowland
Deputy Bailiff, Richard Collas
HM Procureur and Receiver-General, John van Leuven, QC
HM Comptroller, Howard Roberts, QC
Chief Minister, Deputy Mike Torode
Chief Executive, Mike Brown

FINANCE

	2005	2006
Revenue	£310,481,250	£325,098,105
Expenditure	£291,604,688	£294,612,476

CHIEF TOWNS – ΨSt Peter Port, on the east coast of Guernsey; St Anne on Alderney

FLAG – White, bearing a red cross of St George, with a gold cross of Normandy overall in the centre

ALDERNEY

President of the States, Sir Norman Browse, OBE

Chief Executive, David Jeremiah, OBE, QC

Greffier, Sarah Kelly

SARK*

Seigneur of Sark, John Beaumont, OBE

Seneschal, Lt.-Col. R Guille, MBE

Greffier, Trevor Hamon

OTHER DEPENDENCIES

Herm and Lihou are owned by the States of Guernsey; Herm is leased. Jethou is leased by the Crown to the States of Guernsey and is sub-let by the States. Brecqhou is within the legislative and judicial territory of Sark.

* On 4 October 2006 the islanders of Sark voted in favour of establishing a 28-member elected assembly from December 2008; *see also* UK Events of the Year

Ψ = sea port

EUROPEAN PARLIAMENT

European parliament elections take place at five-yearly intervals; the first direct elections to the parliament were held in 1979. In mainland Britain, members of the European parliament (MEPs) were elected in all constituencies on a first-past-the-post basis until 1999 when a regional system of proportional representation was introduced; in Northern Ireland three MEPs have been elected by the single transferable vote system of proportional representation since 1979. From 1979 to 1994 the number of seats held by the UK in the European parliament was 81, which increased to 87 in the 1994 election and decreased to 78 (England 64, Wales 4, Scotland 7, Northern Ireland 3) following EU enlargement in 2004.

At the 2004 European parliament elections all UK MEPs were elected under a 'closed-list' regional system of proportional representation, with England being divided into nine regions and Scotland, Wales and Northern Ireland each constituting a region. Since June 2004 residents of Gibraltar vote in the South West region. Parties submitted a list of candidates for each region in their own order of preference. Voters voted for a party or an independent candidate, and the first seat in each region was allocated to the party or candidate with the highest number of votes. The rest of the seats in each region were then allocated broadly in proportion to each party's share of the vote. Each region returned the following number of members: East Midlands, 6; Eastern, 7; London, 9; North East, 3; North West, 9; South East, 10; South West, 7; West Midlands, 7; Yorkshire and the Humber, 6; Wales, 4; Northern Ireland, 3; Scotland, 7.

If a vacancy occurs due to the resignation or death of an MEP, it is filled by the next available person on that party's list. If an independent MEP resigns or dies, a by-election is held. Where an MEP leaves the party on whose list he/she was elected, there is no requirement to resign and he/she can remain in office until the next election.

British subjects and nationals of member states of the European Union are eligible for election to the European parliament provided they are 21 or over and not subject to disqualification. Since 1994, eligible citizens have had the right to vote in elections to the European parliament in the UK as long as they are entered on the electoral register.

MEPs currently receive a salary from the parliaments or governments of their respective member states, set at the level of the national parliamentary salary and subject to national taxation. British MEPs receive a salary of £60,277.

From 2009 a new MEP statute will take effect introducing the same salary for all MEPs at a rate of 38.5 per cent of the basic salary of a European court of justice judge.

The next elections to the European parliament will take place in June 2009. For further information visit the European parliament's website (W www.europarl.org.uk).

UK MEMBERS *as at June 2007*

* Denotes membership of the last European parliament
† Replacements since the last election
‡ Previously a member of UKIP
** Previously a member of DUP

****Allister**, James (b. 1953), *NI, Northern Ireland*
Ashworth, Richard (b. 1947), *C., South East*
***Atkins**, Rt. Hon. Sir Robert (b. 1946), *C., North West*
***Attwooll**, Elspeth M. A. (b. 1943), *LD, Scotland*
Batten, Gerard (b. 1972), *UKIP, London*
***Beazley**, Christopher J. P. (b. 1952), *C., Eastern*
Bloom, Godfrey (b. 1949), *UKIP, Yorkshire and the Humber*
***Booth**, Graham (b. 1940), *UKIP, South West*
***Bowis**, John C., OBE (b. 1945), *C., London*
†**Bowles**, Sharon M. (b. 1953), *LD, South East*
***Bradbourn**, Philip, OBE (b. 1951), *C., West Midlands*
***Bushill-Matthews**, Philip (b. 1943), *C., West Midlands*
***Callanan**, Martin (b. 1961), *C., North East*
***Cashman**, Michael (b. 1950), *Lab., West Midlands*
***Chichester**, Giles B. (b. 1946), *C., South West*
Clark, Derek (b. 1933), *UKIP, East Midlands*
***Corbett**, Richard (b. 1955), *Lab., Yorkshire and the Humber*
***Davies**, Christopher G. (b. 1954), *LD, North West*
de Brún, Bairbre (b. 1954), *SF, Northern Ireland*
***Deva**, Niranjan J. A. (Nirj), FRSA (b. 1948), *C., South East*
***Dover**, Densmore (b. 1938), *C., North West*
***Duff**, Andrew N. (b. 1950), *LD, Eastern*
***Elles**, James E. M. (b. 1949), *C., South East*
***Evans**, Jillian R. (b. 1959), *PC, Wales*
***Evans**, Jonathan P., FRSA (b. 1950), *C., Wales*
***Evans**, Robert J. E. (b. 1956), *Lab., London*
***Farage**, Nigel P. (b. 1964), *UKIP, South East*
***Ford**, Glyn J. (b. 1950), *Lab., South West*
***Gill**, Neena (b. 1956), *Lab., West Midlands*
Hall, Fiona (b. 1955), *LD, North East*
***Hannan**, Daniel J. (b. 1971), *C., South East*
***Harbour**, Malcolm (b. 1947), *C., West Midlands*
***Heaton-Harris**, Christopher (b. 1967), *C., East Midlands*
***Helmer**, Roger (b. 1944), *C., East Midlands*
***Honeyball**, Mary (b. 1952), *Lab., London*
***Howitt**, Richard (b. 1961), *Lab., Eastern*
***Hudghton**, Ian (b. 1951), *SNP, Scotland*
***Hughes**, Stephen (b. 1952), *Lab., North East*
***Jackson**, Caroline F., DPHIL (b. 1946), *C., South West*
†**Kamall**, Syed S. (b. 1967), *C., London*
Karim, Sajjad (b. 1970), *LD, North West*
‡**Kilroy-Silk**, Robert (b. 1942), *NI, East Midlands*
***Kinnock**, Glenys (b. 1944), *Lab., Wales*
***Kirkhope**, Timothy J. R. (b. 1945), *C., Yorkshire and the Humber*
Knapman, Roger (b. 1944), *UKIP, South West*
***Lambert**, Jean D. (b. 1950), *Green, London*
***Lucas**, Dr Caroline (b. 1960), *Green, South East*
***Ludford**, Baroness (b. 1951), *LD, London*
***Lynne**, Elizabeth (b. 1948), *LD, West Midlands*
***McAvan**, Linda (b. 1962), *Lab., Yorkshire and the Humber*

*McCarthy, Arlene (b. 1960), *Lab., North West*
*McMillan-Scott, Edward H. C. (b. 1949), *C., Yorkshire and the Humber*
*Martin, David W. (b. 1954), *Lab., Scotland*
*Moraes, Claude (b. 1965), *Lab., London*
*Morgan, Eluned (b. 1967), *Lab., Wales*
‡Mote, Ashley (b. 1936), *NI, South East*
Nattrass, Mike (b. 1945), *UKIP, West Midlands*
*Newton Dunn, William F. (Bill) (b. 1941), *LD, East Midlands*
*Nicholson, James (b. 1945), *UUP, Northern Ireland*
*Nicholson of Winterbourne, Baroness (b. 1941), *LD, South East*
*Parish, Neil (b. 1956), *C., South West*
*Purvis, John R., CBE (b. 1938), *C., Scotland*
†Simpson, Brian (b. 1953), *Lab., North West*

*Skinner, Peter W. (b. 1959), *Lab., South East*
Smith, Alyn (b. 1973), *SNP, Scotland*
*Stevenson, Struan (b. 1948), *C., Scotland*
*Stihler, Catherine D. (b. 1973), *Lab., Scotland*
*Sturdy, Robert W. (b. 1944), *C., Eastern*
*Sumberg, David (b. 1941), *C., North West*
*Tannock, Dr Charles (b. 1957), *C., London*
*Titford, Jeffrey (b. 1933), *UKIP, Eastern*
*Titley, Gary (b. 1950), *Lab., North West,*
*Van Orden, Geoffrey (b. 1945), *C., Eastern*
*Wallis, Diana (b. 1954), *LD, Yorkshire and the Humber*
*Watson, Graham R. (b. 1956), *LD, South West*
Whittaker, John (b. 1945), *UKIP, North West*
†Willmott, Glenis (b. 1951), *Lab., East Midlands*
Wise, Tom (b. 1948), *UKIP, Eastern*

UK REGIONS *as at 10 June 2004 election*

Abbreviations

AGS	Alliance for Green Socialism
Common	The Common Good
ED	English Democrats
EFP	English Freedom Party
FW	Forward Wales
NI	Non-attached Members
OCV	Operation Christian Vote
Peace	Peace Party
PPBG	People's Party for Better Government
Respect	Respect – Unity Coalition
SEA	Socialist Environmental Alliance
Senior	Senior Citizens
Soc. All.	Socialist Alliance
SSP	Scottish Socialist Party
SWW	Scottish Wind Watch

For other abbreviations, *see* UK General Election Results
For detailed information on which areas of the country are covered by a particular region, please contact the Home Office.

EASTERN
(Bedfordshire, Cambridgeshire, Essex, Hertfordshire, Luton, Norfolk, Peterborough, Southend-on-Sea, Suffolk, Thurrock)

E. 4,137,210	T. 36.73%
C.	465,526 (30.8%)
UKIP	296,160 (19.6%)
Lab.	244,929 (16.2%)
LD	211,378 (14.0%)
Ind.	93,028 (6.2%)
Green	84,068 (5.6%)
BNP	65,557 (4.3%)
ED	26,807 (1.8%)
Respect	13,904 (0.9%)
Ind.	5,137 (0.3%)
ProLife	3,730 (0.3%)
C. majority	169,366
(June 1999, C. maj. 174,959)	

MEMBERS ELECTED
*G. van Orden, *C.*

*J. Titford, *UKIP*
*R. Howitt, *Lab.*
*R. Sturdy, *C.*
A. Duff, *LD*
*C. Beazley, *C.*
T. Wise, *UKIP*

EAST MIDLANDS
(Derby, Derbyshire, Leicester, Leicestershire, Northamptonshire, Nottingham, Nottinghamshire, Rutland)

E. 3,220,019	T. 43.88%
C.	371,362 (26.4%)
UKIP	366,498 (26.1%)
Lab.	294,918 (21.0%)
LD	181,964 (12.9%)
BNP	91,860 (6.5%)
Green	76,633 (5.5%)
Respect	20,009 (1.4%)
Ind.	2,615 (0.2%)
Ind.	847 (0.1%)
C. majority	4,864
(June 1999, C. maj. 78,906)	

MEMBERS ELECTED
*R. Helmer, *C.*
‡R. Kilroy-Silk, *NI*
*P. Whitehead, *Lab.*
*C. Heaton-Harris, *C.*
D. Clark, *UKIP*
*W. Newton Dunn, *LD*

LONDON

E. 5,054,957	T. 37.65%
C.	504,941 (26.5%)
Lab.	466,584 (24.5%)
LD	288,790 (15.2%)
UKIP	232,633 (12.2%)
Green	158,986 (8.4%)
Respect	91,175 (4.8%)
BNP	76,152 (4.0%)
CPA	45,038 (2.4%)
ED	15,945 (0.8%)
PPBG	5,205 (0.3%)
C. majority	38,357
(June 1999, Lab. maj. 26,477)	

MEMBERS ELECTED
†S. Kamall, *C.*
*C. Moraes, *Lab.*
*Baroness Ludford, *LD*
*J. Bowis, *C.*
*M. Honeyball, *Lab.*
G. Batten, *UKIP*
*C. Tannock, *C.*
*J. Lambert, *Green*
*R. Evans, *Lab.*

NORTH EAST
(Co. Durham, Darlington, Hartlepool, Middlesbrough, Northumberland, Redcar and Cleveland, Stockton-on-Tees, Tyne and Wear)

E. 1,905,132	T. 41.54%
Lab.	266,057 (34.1%)
C.	144,969 (18.6%)
LD	138,791 (17.8%)
UKIP	94,887 (12.2%)
BNP	50,249 (6.4%)
Ind.	39,658 (5.1%)
Green	37,247 (4.8%)
Respect	8,633 (1.1%)
Lab. majority	121,088
(June 1999, Lab. maj. 57,000)	

MEMBERS ELECTED
*S. Hughes, *Lab.*
*M. Callanan, *C.*
Ms F. Hall, *LD*

NORTHERN IRELAND
(Northern Ireland forms a three-member seat with a single transferable vote system)

E. 1,072,669	T. 51.72%
Jim Allister, *NI*	175,761 (31.9%)
Bairbre de Brún, *SF*	144,541 (26.3%)
Jim Nicholson, *UUP*	91,164 (16.6%)
Martin Morgan, *SDLP*	87,559 (15.9%)
John Gilliland, *Ind.*	36,270 (6.6%)

Eamonn McCann, 9,172 (1.6%)
SEA
Lindsay Whitcroft, 4,810 (0.9%)
Green

MEMBERS ELECTED
**J. Allister, *NI*
B. de Brún, *SF*
*J. Nicholson, *UUP*

NORTH WEST
(Blackburn-with-Darwen, Blackpool,
Cheshire, Cumbria, Greater
Manchester, Halton, Lancashire,
Merseyside, Warrington)

E. 5,151,488		T. 41.46%
Lab.	576,388 (27.3%)	
C.	509,446 (24.1%)	
LD	335,063 (15.8%)	
UKIP	257,158 (12.2%)	
BNP	134,959 (6.4%)	
Green	117,393 (5.6%)	
Lib.	96,325 (4.6%)	
ED	34,110 (1.6%)	
Respect	24,636 (1.2%)	
Country	11,283 (0.5%)	
ProLife	10,084 (0.5%)	
Ind.	8,318 (0.4%)	
Lab. majority	66,942	

(June 1999, C. maj. 9,516)

MEMBERS ELECTED
*G. Titley, *Lab.*
*D. Dover, *C.*
*C. Davies, *LD*
*A. McCarthy, *Lab.*
J. Whittaker, *UKIP*
*D. Sumberg, *C.*
*T. Wynn, *Lab.*
*Sir Robert Atkins, *C.*
S. Karim, *LD*

SCOTLAND

E. 3,839,952		T. 30.75%
Lab.	310,865 (26.4%)	
SNP	231,505 (19.7%)	
C.	209,028 (17.8%)	
LD	154,178 (13.1%)	
Green	79,695 (6.8%)	
UKIP	78,828 (6.7%)	
SSP	61,356 (5.2%)	
OCV	21,056 (1.8%)	
BNP	19,427 (1.6%)	
SWW	7,255 (0.6%)	
Ind.	3,624 (0.3%)	
Lab. majority	79,360	

(June 1999, Lab. maj. 14,962)

MEMBERS ELECTED
*D. Martin, *Lab.*
*I. Hudghton, *SNP*
*S. Stevenson, *C.*
*C. Stihler, *Lab.*
*E. Attwooll, *LD*
A. Smith, *SNP*
*J. Purvis, *C.*

SOUTH EAST
(Bracknell Forest, Brighton and
Hove, Buckinghamshire, East Sussex,
Hampshire, Isle of Wight, Kent,
Medway, Milton Keynes,
Oxfordshire, Portsmouth, Reading,
Slough, Southampton, Surrey, West
Berkshire, West Sussex, Windsor and
Maidenhead, Wokingham)

E. 6,034,549		T. 36.78%
C.	776,370 (35.2%)	
UKIP	431,111 (19.5%)	
LD	338,342 (15.3%)	
Lab.	301,398 (13.7%)	
Green	173,351 (7.9%)	
BNP	64,877 (2.9%)	
Senior	42,681 (1.9%)	
ED	29,126 (1.3%)	
Respect	13,426 (0.9%)	
Peace	12,572 (0.6%)	
CPA	11,733 (0.5%)	
ProLife	6,579 (0.3%)	
Ind.	5,671 (0.3%)	
C. majority	345,259	

(June 1999, C. maj. 369,785)

MEMBERS ELECTED
*D. Hannan, *C.*
*N. Farage, *UKIP*
*N. Deva, *C.*
†S. Bowles, *LD*
*P. Skinner, *Lab.*
*J. Elles, *C.*
‡A. Mote, *NI*
R. Ashworth, *C.*
*Dr Caroline Lucas, *Green*
*Baroness Nicholson of
Winterbourne, *LD*

SOUTH WEST
(Bath and North East Somerset,
Bournemouth, Bristol, Cornwall,
Devon, Dorset, Gloucestershire,
North Somerset, South
Gloucestershire, Swindon, Torbay,
Wiltshire)

E. 3,845,210		T. 37.80%
C.	457,371 (31.6%)	
UKIP	326,784 (22.5%)	
LD	265,619 (18.3%)	
Lab.	209,908 (14.5%)	
Green	103,821 (7.2%)	
BNP	43,653 (3.0%)	
Country	30,824 (2.1%)	
Respect	10,437 (0.7%)	
C. majority	130,587	

(June 1999, C. maj. 246,283)

MEMBERS ELECTED
*N. Parish, *C.*
G. Booth, *UKIP*
*G. Watson, *LD*
*Dr Caroline Jackson, *C.*
*G. Ford, *Lab.*
R. Knapman, *UKIP*
*G. Chichester, *C.*

WALES

E. 2,218,649		T. 41.86%
Lab.	297,810 (32.1%)	
C.	177,771 (19.1%)	
PC	159,888 (17.2%)	
UKIP	96,677 (10.4%)	
LD	96,116 (10.4%)	
Green	32,761 (3.5%)	
BNP	27,135 (2.9%)	
FW	17,280 (1.9%)	
Ch. D	6,821 (0.7%)	
Respect	5,427 (0.6%)	
Lab. majority	120,039	

(June 1999, Lab. maj. 14,455)

MEMBERS ELECTED
*G. Kinnock, *Lab.*
*J. Evans, *C.*
*J. Evans, *PC*
*E. Morgan, *Lab.*

WEST MIDLANDS
(Herefordshire, Shropshire,
Staffordshire, Stoke-on-Trent,
Telford and Wrekin, Warwickshire,
West Midlands Metropolitan area,
Worcestershire)

E. 3,957,848		T. 36.63%
C.	392,937 (27.3%)	
Lab.	336,613 (23.4%)	
UKIP	251,366 (17.5%)	
LD	197,479 (13.7%)	
BNP	107,794 (7.5%)	
Green	73,991 (5.2%)	
Respect	34,704 (2.4%)	
Pensioner	33,501 (2.3%)	
Common	8,650 (0.6%)	
C. majority	56,324	

(June 1999, C. maj. 84,048)

MEMBERS ELECTED
*P. Bushill-Matthews, *C.*
*M. Cashman, *Lab.*
M. Nattrass, *UKIP*
*E. Lynne, *LD*
*P. Bradbourn, *C.*
*N. Gill, *Lab.*
*M. Harbour, *C.*

YORKSHIRE AND THE HUMBER

(East Riding of Yorkshire, Kingston-upon-Hull, North East Lincolnshire, North Lincolnshire, North Yorkshire, South Yorkshire, West Yorkshire, York)

E. 3,719,717	T. 42.93%
Lab.	413,213 (26.3%)
C.	387,369 (24.6%)
LD	244,607 (15.6%)
UKIP	228,666 (14.0%)
BNP	126,538 (8.0%)
Green	90,337 (5.7%)
Respect	29,865 (1.9%)
ED	24,068 (1.5%)
Ind.	14,762 (0.9%)
AGS	13,776 (0.9%)
Lab. majority	25,844

(June 1999, C. maj. 39,629)

MEMBERS ELECTED
*Linda McAvan, Lab.
*T. Kirkhope, C.
*D. Wallis, LD
G. Bloom, UKIP
*R. Corbett, Lab.
*E. McMillan-Scott, C.

LAW COURTS AND OFFICES

HIERARCHY OF ENGLISH COURTS

Court	Courts it binds	Courts it follows
European Court of Justice	The court making the preliminary reference	None
House of Lords	All English courts	None
Court of Appeal	Divisional Courts High Court Crown Court County courts Magistrates' courts	House of Lords
Divisional Courts	High Court Crown Court County courts Magistrates' courts	House of Lords Court of Appeal
High Court	County courts Magistrates' courts	House of Lords Court of Appeal Divisional Courts
Crown Court	None	House of Lords
County courts	None	Court of Appeal
Magistrates' courts	None	Divisional Courts High Court

JUDICATURE OF ENGLAND AND WALES

The legal system in England and Wales is divided into criminal law and civil law. Criminal law is concerned with acts harmful to the community and the rules laid down by the state for the benefit of citizens, whereas civil law governs the relationships and transactions between individuals. Administrative law is a kind of civil law usually concerning the interaction of individuals and the state, and most cases are heard in tribunals specific to the subject (see Tribunals section). Scotland and Northern Ireland possess legal systems that differ from the system in England and Wales in law, judicial procedure and court structure, but retain the distinction between criminal and civil law.

The appellate committee of the House of Lords is the supreme judicial authority. It is the ultimate court of appeal for all courts in Great Britain and Northern Ireland (except criminal courts in Scotland) for all cases except those concerning the interpretation and application of European Community law, including preliminary rulings requested by British courts and tribunals, which are decided by the European court of justice (see European Union section). As a court of appeal the House of Lords consists of 12 Lords of Appeal in Ordinary (law lords); virtually all appeals concern the meaning of the law, rather than the evidence in a particular case.

Under the provisions of the Criminal Appeal Act 1995, a commission was set up to direct and supervise investigations into possible miscarriages of justice and to refer cases to the courts on the grounds of conviction and sentence; these functions were formerly the responsibility of the home secretary.

SUPREME COURT OF JUDICATURE

The supreme court of judicature comprises the high court of justice, the crown court and the court of appeal. The President of the Courts of England and Wales, a new title given to the Lord Chief Justice under the Constitutional Reform Act 2005, is the head of the judiciary.

The high court was created in 1875 and combined many previously separate courts. Sittings are held at the royal courts of justice in London or at about 120 district registries outside the capital. It is the superior civil court and is split into three divisions – the chancery division, the Queen's bench division and the family division – each of which is further divided. The chancery division is headed by the Chancellor of the High Court and is concerned mainly with equity, trusts, tax and bankruptcy, while also including two specialist courts, the patents court and the companies court. The Queen's bench division (QBD) is the largest of the three divisions, and is headed by its own president, who is also Head of Criminal Justice. It deals with common law (ie tort, contract, debt and personal injuries), some tax law, eg VAT tribunal appeals, and encompasses the admiralty court and the commercial court. The QBD also administers the technology and construction court. The family division was created in 1970 and is headed by its own president, who is also Head of Family Justice, and hears cases concerning divorce, access to and custody of children, and other family matters. The divisional court of the high court sits in the family and chancery divisions, and hears appeals from the magistrates' courts and county courts.

The crown court was set up in 1972 and sits at about 90 centres throughout England and Wales. It deals with more serious (indictable) criminal offences, which are triable before a judge and jury, including treason, murder, rape, kidnapping, armed robbery and Official Secrets Act offences. It also handles cases transferred from the magistrates' courts where the magistrate decides his or her own power of sentence is inadequate, or where someone appeals against a magistrate's decision, or in a case that is triable 'either way' where the accused has chosen a jury trial. The crown court centres are divided into three tiers: high court judges, and sometimes circuit judges and recorders (part-time circuit judges), sit in first-tier centres and deal with the most serious (Class 1) criminal offences (eg murder, treason) and with some civil high court cases; the second-tier centres are presided over by high court judges, circuit judges or recorders and deal with Class 2 criminal offences (eg rape, manslaughter); third-tier courts deal with Class 3 criminal offences, with circuit judges or recorders presiding.

The court of appeal hears appeals against both fact and law, and was last restructured in 1966 when it replaced the court of criminal appeal. It is split into the civil division (which hears appeals from the high court, tribunals and in certain cases, the county courts) and the criminal division (which hears appeals from the crown court). Cases are heard by Lord Justices of Appeal if deemed suitable for reconsideration.

The Constitutional Reform Act 2005 instigated several key changes to the judiciary in England and Wales. These include the provision for the establishment of an independent supreme court, scheduled to open in October 2009; the reform of the post of Lord Chancellor, transferring its judicial functions to the President of the Courts of England and Wales; a duty on government ministers to uphold the independence of the judiciary by barring them from trying to influence judicial decisions through any special access to judges; the formation of a fully transparent and independent Judicial Appointments Commission that is responsible for selecting candidates to recommend for judicial appointment to the Secretary of State for Justice; and the creation of the post of Judicial Appointments and Conduct Ombudsman.

CRIMINAL CASES

In criminal matters the decision to prosecute (in the majority of cases) rests with the Crown Prosecution Service (CPS), which is the independent prosecuting body in England and Wales. The CPS is headed by the director of public prosecutions, who works under the superintendence of the Attorney-General. Certain categories of offence continue to require the Attorney-General's consent for prosecution.

Most minor criminal cases (summary offences) are dealt with in magistrates' courts, usually by a bench of three unpaid lay magistrates (justices of the peace) sitting without a jury and assisted on points of law and procedure by a legally trained clerk. There were around 29,828 justices of the peace in April 2007. In busier courts a full-time, salaried and legally qualified 'district judge (magistrates' court)' – formerly known as a stipendiary judge – presides alone. There were 139 district judges (magistrates' courts) as at 1 April 2007. Magistrates' courts oversee the completion of 95 per cent of all criminal cases. Magistrates' courts also house some family proceedings courts (which deal with relationship breakdown and childcare cases) and youth courts. Cases of medium seriousness (known as 'offences triable either way') where the defendant pleads not guilty can be heard in the crown court for a trial by jury, if the defendant so chooses. Preliminary proceedings in a serious case to decide whether there is evidence to justify committal for trial in the crown court are dealt with in the magistrates' courts.

The 91 centres that the crown court sits in are divided into seven regions; a case is presided over by high court judges, circuit judges or recorders. There were 1,201 recorders as at 1 April 2007; they must sit a minimum of 15 days per year and are usually subject to a maximum of 30. A jury is present in all trials that are contested.

Appeals from magistrates' courts against sentence or conviction are made to the crown court, and appeals upon a point of law are made to the high court, which may ultimately be appealed to the House of Lords. Appeals from the crown court, either against sentence or conviction, are made to the court of appeal (criminal division), presided over by the Lord Chief Justice. Again, these appeals may be brought to the House of Lords if a point of law is contested, and if the house considers it is of sufficient importance.

CIVIL CASES

Most minor civil cases – including contract, tort (especially personal injuries), property, divorce and other family matters, bankruptcy etc – are dealt with by the county courts, of which there are 225 (see the Court Service website, www.hmcourts-service.gov.uk, for further details). Cases are heard by circuit judges, recorders or district judges. For cases involving small claims (with certain exceptions, where the amount claimed is £5,000 or less) there are informal and simplified procedures designed to enable parties to present their cases themselves without recourse to lawyers. Where there are financial limits on county court jurisdiction, claims that exceed those limits may be tried in the county courts with the consent of the parties, subject to the court's agreement, or in certain circumstances on transfer from the high court. Outside London, bankruptcy proceedings can be heard in designated county courts. Magistrates' courts also deal with certain classes of civil case and committees of magistrates license public houses, clubs and betting shops. For the implementation of the Children Act 1989, a new structure of hearing centres was set up in 1991 for family proceedings cases, involving magistrates' courts (family proceedings courts), divorce county courts, family hearing centres and care centres.

Appeals in certain family matters heard in the family proceedings courts go to the family division of the high court. Appeals against decisions made in magistrates' courts are heard in the crown court. Appeals from county courts may be heard in the court of appeal (civil division), presided over by the Master of the Rolls, and may go on to the House of Lords.

CORONERS' COURTS

The coroners' courts investigate violent and unnatural deaths or sudden deaths where the cause is unknown. Doctors, the police, various public authorities or members of the public may bring cases before a local coroner (a senior lawyer or doctor), in order to determine whether further criminal investigation is necessary. Where a death is sudden and the cause is unknown, the coroner may order a post-mortem examination to determine the cause of death rather than hold an inquest in court. An inquest must be held however if a person died in a violent or unnatural way, or died in prison or other unusual circumstances. If the coroner suspects murder, manslaughter or infanticide, he or she must summon a jury.

HOUSE OF LORDS
AS FINAL COURT OF APPEAL

Senior Lord of Appeal in Ordinary (£205,700), Rt. Hon. Lord Bingham of Cornhill, KG, *born* 1933, *apptd* 2000

LORDS OF APPEAL IN ORDINARY *as at 1 July 2007* (each £198,700)
Style, The Rt. Hon. Lord/Lady–

Rt. Hon. Lord Hoffmann, *born* 1934, *apptd* 1995
Rt. Hon. Lord Hope of Craighead, *born* 1938, *apptd* 1996
Rt. Hon. Lord Saville of Newdigate, *born* 1936, *apptd* 1997
Rt. Hon. Lord Scott of Foscote, *born* 1934, *apptd* 2000
Rt. Hon. Lord Rodger of Earlsferry, *born* 1944, *apptd* 2001
Rt. Hon. Lord Walker of Gestingthorpe, *born* 1938, *apptd* 2002
Rt. Hon. Lady Hale of Richmond, *born* 1945, *apptd* 2004
Rt. Hon. Lord Carswell, *born* 1934, *apptd* 2004
Rt. Hon. Lord Brown of Eaton-under-Heywood, *born* 1937, *apptd* 2004
Rt. Hon. Lord Mance, *born* 1943, *apptd* 2005
Rt. Hon. Lord Neuberger, *born* 1948, *apptd* 2007

JUDICIAL OFFICE OF THE HOUSE OF LORDS
House of Lords, London SW1A 0PW T 020-7219 3111
Registrar, Clerk of the Parliaments

SENIOR JUDICIARY OF ENGLAND AND WALES

Lord Chief Justice of England and Wales (£230,400), Rt. Hon. Lord Phillips of Worth Matravers, *born* 1938, *apptd* 2005
Master of the Rolls and Head of Civil Justice (£205,700), Rt. Hon. Sir Anthony Clarke, *born* 1943, *apptd* 2005
President of the Queen's Bench Division and Head of Criminal Justice (£198,700), Rt. Hon. Sir Igor Judge, *born* 1941, *apptd* 2005
President of the Family Division and Head of Family Justice (£198,700), Rt. Hon. Sir Mark Potter, *born* 1937, *apptd* 2005
Chancellor of the High Court (£198,700), Rt. Hon. Sir Robert Morritt, CVO, *born* 1938, *apptd* 2000

SUPREME COURT OF JUDICATURE

COURT OF APPEAL
Master of the Rolls (£205,700), Rt. Hon. Sir Anthony Clarke, *born* 1943, *apptd* 2005
Secretary, Ms J. Sears
Clerk, Dawn Rollason

LORD JUSTICES OF APPEAL *as at 1 July 2007* (each £188,900)
Style, The Rt. Hon. Lord/Lady Justice [surname]

Rt. Hon. Sir Robin Auld, *born* 1937, *apptd* 1995
Rt. Hon. Sir Malcolm Pill, *born* 1938, *apptd* 1995
Rt. Hon. Sir Alan Ward, *born* 1938, *apptd* 1995
Rt. Hon. Sir Mathew Thorpe, *born* 1938, *apptd* 1995
Rt. Hon. Sir George Waller, *born* 1940, *apptd* 1996
Rt. Hon. Sir John Mummery, *born* 1938, *apptd* 1996
Rt. Hon. Sir John Chadwick, ED, *born* 1941, *apptd* 1997
Rt. Hon. Sir Richard Buxton, *born* 1938, *apptd* 1997

Rt. Hon. Sir Anthony May, *born* 1940, *apptd* 1997
Rt. Hon. Sir Simon Tuckey, *born* 1941, *apptd* 1998
Rt. Hon. Sir John Laws, *born* 1945, *apptd* 1999
Rt. Hon. Sir Stephen Sedley, *born* 1939, *apptd* 1999
Rt. Hon. Sir David Latham, *born* 1942, *apptd* 2000
Rt. Hon. Sir Bernard Rix, *born* 1944, *apptd* 2000
Rt. Hon. Dame Mary Arden, DBE, *born* 1947, *apptd* 2000
Rt. Hon. Sir David Keene, *born* 1941, *apptd* 2000
Rt. Hon. Sir John Dyson, *born* 1943, *apptd* 2001
Rt. Hon. Sir Andrew Longmore, *born* 1944, *apptd* 2001
Rt. Hon. Sir Robert Carnwath, CVO, *born* 1945, *apptd* 2002
Rt. Hon. Sir Scott Baker, *born* 1937, *apptd* 2002
Rt. Hon. Dame Janet Smith, DBE, *born* 1940, *apptd* 2002
Rt. Hon. Sir Roger Thomas, *born* 1947, *apptd* 2003
Rt. Hon. Sir Robin Jacob, *born* 1941, *apptd* 2003
Rt. Hon. Sir Nicholas Wall, *born* 1945, *apptd* 2004
Rt. Hon. Sir Maurice Kay, *born* 1942, *apptd* 2004
Rt. Hon. Sir Anthony Hooper, *born* 1937, *apptd* 2004
Rt. Hon. Sir William Gage, *born* 1938, *apptd* 2004
Rt. Hon. Sir Timothy Lloyd, *born* 1946, *apptd* 2005
Rt. Hon. Sir Martin Moore-Bick, *born* 1948, *apptd* 2005
Rt. Hon. Sir Nicholas Wilson, *born* 1945, *apptd* 2005
Rt. Hon. Sir Alan Moses, *born* 1945, *apptd* 2005
Rt. Hon. Sir Stephen Richards, *born* 1950, *apptd* 2005
Rt. Hon. Dame Heather Hallett, DBE, *born* 1949, *apptd* 2005
Rt. Hon. Sir Anthony Hughes, *born* 1948, *apptd* 2006
Rt. Hon. Sir Brian Leveson, *born* 1949, *apptd* 2006
Rt. Hon. Sir Lawrence Collins, *born* 1941, *apptd* 2007
Rt. Hon. Sir Roger Toulson, *born* 1946, *apptd* 2007

Ex Officio Judges, Lord Chief Justice of England and Wales; Master of the Rolls; President of the Queen's Bench Division; President of the Family Division; and Chancellor of the High Court

COURT OF APPEAL (CIVIL DIVISION)
Vice-President, Rt. Hon. Sir Mark Waller

COURT OF APPEAL (CRIMINAL DIVISION)
Vice-President, Rt. Hon. Sir David Latham
Judges, Lord Chief Justice of England and Wales; Master of the Rolls; Lord Justices of Appeal; and Judges of the High Court of Justice

COURTS-MARTIAL APPEAL COURT
Judges, Lord Chief Justice of England and Wales; Master of the Rolls; Lord Justices of Appeal; and Judges of the High Court of Justice

HIGH COURT OF JUSTICE

CHANCERY DIVISION
Chancellor of the High Court (£198,700), Rt. Hon. Sir Andrew Morritt, CVO, *born* 1938, *apptd* 2000
Secretary, Ms E. Harbert
Clerk, Sheila Glasgow

JUDGES *as at 1 July 2007* (each £165,900)
Style, The Hon. Mr/Mrs Justice [surname]

Hon. Sir John Lindsay, *born* 1935, *apptd* 1992
Hon. Sir Edward Evans-Lombe, *born* 1937, *apptd* 1993
Hon. Sir William Blackburne, *born* 1944, *apptd* 1993
Hon. Sir Gavin Lightman, *born* 1939, *apptd* 1994
Hon. Sir Colin Rimer, *born* 1944, *apptd* 1994

Hon. Sir Nicholas Pumfrey, *born* 1951, *apptd* 1997
Hon. Sir Nicholas Patten, *born* 1950, *apptd* 2000
Hon. Sir Terrence Etherton, *born* 1951, *apptd* 2001
Hon. Sir Peter Smith, *born* 1952, *apptd* 2002
Hon. Sir Kim Lewison, *born* 1952, *apptd* 2003
Hon. Sir David Richards, *born* 1951, *apptd* 2003
Hon. Sir George Mann, *born* 1951, *apptd* 2004
Hon. Sir Nicholas Warren, *born* 1949, *apptd* 2005
Hon. Sir David Kitchin, *born* 1955, *apptd* 2005
Hon. Sir Michael Briggs, *born* 1954, *apptd* 2006
Hon. Sir Launcelot Henderson, *born* 1951, *apptd* 2006

The Chancery Division also includes three specialist courts: the Companies Court, the Patents Court and the Bankruptcy Court.

QUEEN'S BENCH DIVISION
Lord Chief Justice of England and Wales (£230,400), Rt. Hon. Lord Phillips of Worth Matravers, *born* 1938, *apptd* 2005
Secretary, Michèle Souris
Clerk, Helen Tyler
President (£198,700), Rt. Hon. Sir Igor Judge, *born* 1941, *apptd* 2005
Vice-President (£188,900), Rt. Hon. Sir Anthony May, *born* 1940, *apptd* 2002

JUDGES *as at 1 July 2007* (each £165,900)
Style, The Hon. Mr/Mrs Justice [surname]

Hon. Sir Stuart McKinnon, *born* 1938, *apptd* 1988
Hon. Sir Peter Cresswell, *born* 1944, *apptd* 1991
Hon. Sir Christopher Holland, *born* 1937, *apptd* 1992
Hon. Sir John Forbes, *born* 1938, *apptd* 1993
Hon. Sir Andrew Collins, *born* 1942, *apptd* 1994
Hon. Sir Alexander Butterfield, *born* 1942, *apptd* 1995
Hon. Sir George Newman, *born* 1941, *apptd* 1995
Hon. Sir Gordon Langley, *born* 1943, *apptd* 1995
Hon. Sir Robert Nelson, *born* 1942, *apptd* 1996
Hon. Sir David Eady, *born* 1943, *apptd* 1997
Hon. Sir Jeremy Sullivan, *born* 1945, *apptd* 1997
Hon. Sir David Penry-Davey, *born* 1942, *apptd* 1997
Hon. Sir David Steel, *born* 1943, *apptd* 1998
Hon. Sir Charles Gray, *born* 1942, *apptd* 1998
Hon. Sir Nicolas Bratza, *born* 1945, *apptd* 1998
Hon. Sir Michael Burton, *born* 1946, *apptd* 1998
Hon. Sir Rupert Jackson, *born* 1948, *apptd* 1999
Hon. Sir Patrick Elias, *born* 1947, *apptd* 1999
Hon. Sir Richard Aikens, *born* 1948, *apptd* 1999
Hon. Sir Stephen Silber, *born* 1944, *apptd* 1999
Hon. Sir John Goldring, *born* 1944, *apptd* 1999
Hon. Dame Anne Rafferty, DBE, *born* 1950, *apptd* 2000
Hon. Sir Geoffrey Grigson, *born* 1944, *apptd* 2000
Hon. Sir Richard Gibbs, *born* 1941, *apptd* 2000
Hon. Sir Richard Henriques, *born* 1943, *apptd* 2000
Hon. Sir Stephen Tomlinson, *born* 1952, *apptd* 2000
Hon. Sir Andrew Smith, *born* 1947, *apptd* 2000
Hon. Sir Stanley Burnton, *born* 1942, *apptd* 2000
Hon. Sir Christopher Pitchford, *born* 1947, *apptd* 2000
Hon. Sir Duncan Ouseley, *born* 1950, *apptd* 2000
Hon. Sir Richard McCombe, *born* 1952, *apptd* 2001
Hon. Sir Raymond Jack, *born* 1942, *apptd* 2001
Hon. Sir Robert Owen, *born* 1944, *apptd* 2001
Hon. Sir Colin Mackay, *born* 1943, *apptd* 2001
Hon. Sir John Mitting, *born* 1947, *apptd* 2001
Hon. Sir Roderick Evans, *born* 1946, *apptd* 2001
Hon. Sir Nigel Davis, *born* 1951, *apptd* 2001
Hon. Sir Peter Gross, *born* 1952, *apptd* 2001

Hon. Sir Brian Keith, *born* 1944, *apptd* 2001
Hon. Sir Jeremy Cooke, *born* 1949, *apptd* 2001
Hon. Sir Richard Field, *born* 1947, *apptd* 2002
Hon. Sir Christopher Pitchers, *born* 1942, *apptd* 2002
Hon. Sir Colman Treacy, *born* 1949, *apptd* 2002
Hon. Sir Peregrine Simon, *born* 1950, *apptd* 2002
Hon. Sir Roger Royce, *born* 1944, *apptd* 2002
Hon. Dame Laura Cox, DBE, *born* 1951, *apptd* 2002
Hon. Sir Adrian Fulford, *born* 1953, *apptd* 2002
Hon. Sir Jack Beatson, *born* 1948, *apptd* 2003
Hon. Sir Michael Tugendhat, *born* 1944, *apptd* 2003
Hon. Sir David Clarke, *born* 1942, *apptd* 2003
Hon. Dame Elizabeth Gloster, DBE, *born* 1949, *apptd* 2004
Hon. Sir David Bean, *born* 1954, *apptd* 2004
Hon. Sir Alan Wilkie, *born* 1947, *apptd* 2004
Hon. Dame Linda Dobbs, DBE, *born* 1951, *apptd* 2004
Hon. Sir Henry Hodge, OBE, *born* 1944, *apptd* 2004
Hon. Sir Paul Walker, *born* 1954, *apptd* 2004
Hon. Sir David Calvert-Smith, *born* 1945, *apptd* 2005
Hon. Sir Christopher Clarke, *born* 1947, *apptd* 2005
Hon. Sir Charles Openshaw, *born* 1947, *apptd* 2005
Hon. Dame Caroline Swift, DBE, *born* 1955, *apptd* 2005
Hon. Sir Brian Langstaff, *born* 1948, *apptd* 2005
Hon. Sir David Jones, *born* 1952, *apptd* 2005
Hon. Sir Vivian Ramsey, *born* 1950, *apptd* 2005
Hon. Sir Nicholas Underhill, *born* 1952, *apptd* 2006
Hon. Sir Stephen Irwin, *born* 1953, *apptd* 2006
Hon. Sir Nigel Teare, *born* 1952, *apptd* 2006
Hon. Sir John Griffith Williams, *born* 1944, *apptd* 2007
Hon. Sir Wyn Williams, *born* 1951, *apptd* 2007
Hon. Sir Timothy King, *born* 1946, *apptd* 2007

The Queen's Bench Division also includes three specialist courts – the Commercial Court, the Admiralty Court and the Administration Court – and administers the Technology and Construction Court.

FAMILY DIVISION
President (£198,700), Rt. Hon. Sir Mark Potter, *born* 1937, *apptd* 2005
Secretary, Mrs S. Leung
Clerk, Miss Ayo Onatade

JUDGES *as at 3 July 2006* (each £165,900)
Style, The Hon. Mr/Mrs Justice [surname]

Hon. Sir Jan Singer, *born* 1944, *apptd* 1993
Hon. Sir Andrew Kirkwood, *born* 1944, *apptd* 1993
Hon. Sir Hugh Bennett, *born* 1943, *apptd* 1995
Hon. Sir Edward Holman, *born* 1947, *apptd* 1995
Hon. Dame Mary Hogg, DBE, *born* 1947, *apptd* 1995
Hon. Sir Christopher Sumner, *born* 1939, *apptd* 1996
Hon. Sir Arthur Charles, *born* 1948, *apptd* 1998
Hon. Sir David Bodey, *born* 1947, *apptd* 1999
Hon. Dame Jill Black, DBE, *born* 1954, *apptd* 1999
Hon. Sir James Munby, *born* 1948, *apptd* 2000
Hon. Sir Paul Coleridge, *born* 1949, *apptd* 2000
Hon. Sir Mark Hedley, *born* 1946, *apptd* 2002
Hon. Dame Anna Pauffley, DBE, *born* 1956, *apptd* 2003
Hon. Sir Roderic Wood, *born* 1951, *apptd* 2004
Hon. Dame Florence Baron, DBE, *born* 1952, *apptd* 2004
Hon. Sir Ernest Ryder, *born* 1957, *apptd* 2004
Hon. Sir Andrew McFarlane, *born* 1954, *apptd* 2005
Hon. Dame Julia Macur, DBE, *born* 1957, *apptd* 2005
Hon. Sir Andrew Moylan, *born* 1953, *apptd* 2007

SUPREME COURT DEPARTMENTS AND OFFICES
Royal Courts of Justice, London WC2A 2LL
T 020-7947 6000

DIRECTOR'S OFFICE
T 020-7947 6159
Director, Alastair Clegg
Area Directors, Loraine Ladlow *(Court of Appeal)*; Stephen Fash *(High Court Group)*; Helen Smith *(Probate Service)*
Managers, Keith Richardson *(Finance)*; Amanda Monsarrat *(Regional Change and Performance)*

ADMIRALTY AND COMMERCIAL REGISTRY AND MARSHAL'S OFFICE
T 020-7947 6112
Registrar (£98,900), P. Miller
Admiralty Marshal and Court Manager, K. Houghton

BANKRUPTCY AND COMPANIES COURT
T 020-7947 6441
Chief Registrar (£123,200), S. Baister
Bankruptcy Registrars (£98,900), C. Derrett; G. W. Jaques; W. Nicholls; P. J. S. Rawson; J. A. Simmonds
Court Manager, Pauline O'Brien

CENTRAL OFFICE OF THE SUPREME COURT
Senior Master of the Supreme Court (QBD), and Queen's Remembrancer (£123,200), R. L. Turner
Masters of the Supreme Court (QBD) (£98,900), P. G. A. Eyre; B. J. F. Fontaine; I. H. Foster; H. J. Leslie; P. Miller; G. H. Rose; J. G. G. Ungley; S. Whitaker; B. Yoxall
Court Manager, M. A. Brown

CHANCERY CHAMBERS
T 020-7947 7785
Chief Master of the Supreme Court (£123,200), J. I. Winegarten
Masters of the Supreme Court (£98,900), T. J. Bowles; N. W. Bragge; J. A. Moncaster; N. S. Price; P. R. Teverson
Court Manager, Jane O'Connor

COURT OF APPEAL CIVIL DIVISION
T 020-7947 6533
Registrar (£98,900), David Gladwell
Court Manager, Michael O'Neill

COURT OF APPEAL CRIMINAL DIVISION
T 020-7947 6011
Registrar (£98,900), R. A. Venne
Deputy Registrar, Ms P. Donnelly
Group Manager, Ann Lee

ADMINISTRATIVE OFFICE OF THE SUPREME COURT
T 020-7947 6655
Master of the Crown Office, and Queen's Coroner and Attorney (£98,900), R. A. Venne
Head of Crown Office, Mrs L. G. Knapman
Group Manager, Ann Lee

EXAMINERS OF THE COURT
Empowered to take examination of witnesses in all divisions of the High Court.
Examiners, M. W. M. Chism; A. G. Dyer; A. W. Hughes; Mrs G. M. Keene; R. M. Planterose

SUPREME COURT COSTS OFFICE
T 020-7947 6423
Senior Cost Judge (£123,200), P. T. Hurst

Masters of the Supreme Court (£98,900), C. D. N. Campbell; A. Gordon-Saker; P. Haworth; J. E. O'Hare; P. R. Rogers; J. Simons; C. C. Wright
Court Manager, vacant

COURT OF PROTECTION
11th Floor, Archway Towers, 2 Junction Road, London N19 5SZ
T 0845-330 2900
Senior Judge (£123,200), Denzil Lush

ELECTION PETITIONS OFFICE
Room E19, Royal Courts of Justice, London WC2A 2LL
T 020-7947 7529

The office accepts petitions and deals with all matters relating to the questioning of parliamentary, European parliament and local government elections, and with applications for relief under the 'representation of the people' legislation.
Prescribed Officer (£123,200), R. L. Turner
Chief Clerk, Ms H. L. Newman

OFFICE OF THE LORD CHANCELLOR'S VISITORS
Archway Towers, 11th Floor, 2 Junction Road, London N19 5SZ
T 020-7664 7317

The Mental Capacity Act 2005 came into force on 1 October 2007, and it makes provision for there to be two panels of court of protection visitors (special visitors or general visitors). At the time of going to press, no appointments had been made to either panel.

OFFICIAL RECEIVERS' DEPARTMENT
21 Bloomsbury Street, London WC1B 3QW
T 020-7637 1110
Inspector-General, Des Flynn
Deputies, L. Gramp; G. Horn

OFFICIAL SOLICITOR'S DEPARTMENT
81 Chancery Lane, London WC2A 1DD
T 020-7911 7127
Official Solicitor to the Supreme Court, Alastair Pitblado
Deputy Official Solicitor, May Maughan
Public Trustee, David Thompson

PRINCIPAL REGISTRY (FAMILY DIVISION)
First Avenue House, 42–49 High Holborn, London WC1V 6NP
T 020-7947 6000
Senior District Judge (£123,200), P. Waller
District Judges (£98,900), A. R. S. Bassett-Cross; M. C. Berry; Ms H. Black; Ms S. M. Bowman; Ms H. C. Bradley; G. C. Brasse; Ms P. Cushing; Ms K. E. Green; P. Greene; R. Harper; Ms H. MacGregor; K. Malik; C. Million; Ms D. Redgrave; Ms C. Reid; Ms L. D. Roberts; R. Robinson; Ms S. Walker; K. J. White
Director for the Probate Service, Helen Smith
Family Business Director, John Miller

DISTRICT PROBATE REGISTRARS
Probate Manager of London, Kevin Donnelly
Birmingham District, Pam Walbeoff
Brighton District, Phil Ellwood
Bristol District, Russell Joyce
Ipswich District, Helen Whitby
Leeds District, Angela Parry
Liverpool District, Karen Clark-Rimmer
Manchester District, Paul Burch
Newcastle District, Christine Riley

Oxford District, Roland D'Costa
Wales District, Paul Curran
Winchester District, Alan Butler

JUDGE ADVOCATES

The Judge Advocates are the officers in supreme control of the courts martial in the armed forces; historically, the Judge Advocate of the Fleet for the Royal Navy and the Judge Advocate-General for the Army and Royal Air Force. However, since 2004 the functions of the Judge Advocate of the Fleet have been largely delegated to the Judge Advocate-General; it is planned that the two offices will be amalgamated by the end of 2008, when the Armed Forces Act 2006 is fully in force.

THE JUDGE ADVOCATE OF THE FLEET
c/o Chichester Combined Court, Southgate, Chichester
PO19 1SX T 01243-520741
Judge Advocate of the Fleet, His Hon. Judge Sessions

OFFICE OF THE JUDGE ADVOCATE-GENERAL OF THE FORCES
81 Chancery Lane, London WC2A 1BQ
T 020-7218 8089
Judge Advocate-General (£133,100), His Hon. Judge Blackett
Vice-Judge Advocate-General (£116,700), Michael Hunter
Judge Advocates (£102,900)*, J. F. T. Bayliss; C. R. Burn; J. P. Camp; M. R. Elsom; R. D. Hill; A. J. B. McGrigor; R. C. C. Seymour
Style for Judge Advocates, Judge Advocate [surname]

* Salary includes £2,000 London salary lead and a London allowance of £2,000

HIGH COURT AND CROWN COURT CENTRES

First-tier centres deal with both civil and criminal cases and are served by high court and circuit judges. Second-tier centres deal with criminal cases only and are served by high court and circuit judges. Third-tier centres deal with criminal cases only and are served only by circuit judges.

LONDON REGION
First-tier – None
Second-tier – Central Criminal Court
Third-tier – Blackfriars, Harrow, Inner London Sessions House, Isleworth, Kingston, Snaresbrook, Southwark, Wood Green, Woolwich & Croydon
Regional Director, Kevin Pogson, 2nd Floor, Rose Court, 2 Southwark Bridge, London SE1 9HS T 020-7921 2010
Area Directors (London Crown), Sarah McAdam *(Central and South);* Sandra Aston *(North and West)*
Area Director (London Civil and Family), Linda Lennon

The High Court in Greater London sits at the Royal Courts of Justice.

MIDLAND REGION
First-tier – Birmingham, Lincoln, Nottingham, Stafford, Warwick
Second-tier – Leicester, Northampton, Shrewsbury, Worcester, Wolverhampton
Third-tier – Coventry, Derby, Hereford, Stoke-on-Trent
Regional Director, Alan Eccles, PO Box 11772, 6th Floor, Temple Court, Bull Street, Birmingham B4 6WF
T 0121-250 6162

Area Directors, Kelvin Launchbury *(Birmingham, Coventry, Solihull and Warwickshire);* Peter Hammersley *(Black Country, Staffordshire and West Mercia);* Mark Swales *(Derbyshire and Nottinghamshire);* Richard Redgrave *(Leicestershire, Lincolnshire and Northamptonshire)*

NORTH-EAST REGION
First-tier – Leeds, Newcastle upon Tyne, Sheffield, Teesside
Second-tier – Bradford, York
Third-tier – Doncaster, Durham, Kingston-upon-Hull, Great Grimsby
Regional Director, S. Caven, 18th Floor, West Riding House, Albion Street, Leeds LS1 5AA T 0113-251 1200
Area Directors, Sheila Proudlock *(Cleveland, Durham and Northumbria);* Paul Bradley *(South Yorkshire and Humber);* Dyfed Foulkes *(North and West Yorkshire)*

NORTH-WEST REGION
First-tier – Carlisle, Chester, Liverpool, Manchester (Crown Square), Preston
Third-tier – Barrow-in-Furness, Bolton, Burnley, Knutsford, Lancaster, Manchester (Minshull Street), Warrington
Regional Director, Christine Mayer, 15 Quay Street, Manchester M60 9FD T 0161-833 1005
Area Directors, Shaun McNally *(Cheshire and Merseyside);* Gill Hague *(Cumbria and Lancashire);* Richard Knott *(Greater Manchester)*

SOUTH-EAST REGION
First-tier – Cambridge, Chelmsford, Lewes, Norwich, Oxford
Second-tier – Ipswich, Luton, Maidstone, Reading, St Albans
Third-tier – Aylesbury, Basildon, Canterbury, Chichester, Croydon, Guildford, King's Lynn, Peterborough, Southend
Regional Director, Keith Budgen, 3rd Floor, Rose Court, 2 Southwark Bridge, London SE1 9HS T 020-7921 2061
Area Directors, Mark Littlewood *(Bedfordshire, Essex and Hertfordshire);* Dave Weston *(Kent);* Pauline Cornford *(Norfolk, Suffolk and Cambridgeshire);* Julia Eeles *(Sussex and Surrey);* Jonathan Lane *(Thames Valley)*

SOUTH-WEST REGION
First-tier – Bristol, Exeter, Truro, Winchester
Second-tier – Dorchester & Weymouth, Gloucester, Plymouth
Third-tier – Barnstaple, Bournemouth, Newport (IoW), Portsmouth, Salisbury, Southampton, Swindon, Taunton
Regional Director, Peter Risk, 5th Floor, Greyfriars, Lewins Mead, Bristol BS1 2NR T 0117-910 3600
Area Directors, Rod White *(Avon and Somerset);* David Gentry *(Devon and Cornwall);* Rod Brummitt *(Dorset, Gloucestershire and Wiltshire);* Simon Townley *(Hampshire and Isle of Wight)*

WALES REGION
First-tier – Caernarfon, Cardiff, Mold, Swansea
Second-tier – Carmarthen, Merthyr Tydfil, Newport, Welshpool
Third-tier – Dolgellau, Haverfordwest
Regional Director, N. Chibnall, Churchill House, Churchill Way, Cardiff CF10 2HH T 029-2041 5505
Area Directors, Luigi Strinati *(Mid and West Wales);* Clare Pillman *(North Wales);* Alan Davies *(South-East Wales)*

CIRCUIT JUDGES

Circuit judges are barristers of at least seven years' standing or recorders of at least five years' standing. Circuit judges serve in the county courts and the crown court.

Style, His/Her Hon. Judge [surname]
Senior Presiding Judge, Rt. Hon. Lord Justice Leveson
Senior Circuit Judges, each £133,100
Circuit Judges at the Central Criminal Court, London (Old Bailey Judges), each £133,100
Circuit Judges, each £123,200

LONDON REGION

Presiding Judges, Hon. Mr Justice Bean; Hon. Mr Justice Calvert-Smith; Hon. Mr Justice Cooke; Hon. Mr Justice Gross

MIDLAND REGION

Presiding Judges, Hon. Mr Justice Gibbs; Hon. Mr Justice Treacy

NORTH-EAST REGION

Presiding Judges, Hon. Mr Justice Simon; Hon. Mr Justice Wilkie

NORTH-WEST REGION

Presiding Judges, Hon. Mr Justice David Clarke; Hon. Mr Justice McCombe

SOUTH-EAST REGION

Presiding Judges, Hon. Mr Justice Bean; Hon. Mr Justice Calvert-Smith; Hon. Mr Justice Cooke; Hon. Mr Justice Gross

SOUTH-WEST REGION

Presiding Judges, Hon. Mr Justice Owen; Hon. Mr Justice Royce

WALES REGION

Presiding Judges, Hon. Mr Justice Roderick Evans; Hon. Mr Justice Davis

DISTRICT JUDGES

District judges, formerly known as registrars of the court, are solicitors of at least seven years' standing and serve in county courts.

District Judges (each £98,900)

DISTRICT JUDGES (MAGISTRATES' COURTS)

District judges (magistrates' courts), formerly known as stipendiary magistrates, must be barristers or solicitors of at least seven years' standing (including at least two years' experience as a deputy district judge), and serve in magistrates' courts. All former provincial and metropolitan stipendiary magistrates can serve nationally within any district.

District Judges, each £102,900 (salary includes £4,000 inner London weighting)

CROWN PROSECUTION SERVICE

50 Ludgate Hill, London EC4M 7EX
T 020-7796 8000 E enquiries@cps.gsi.gov.uk
W www.cps.gov.uk

The Crown Prosecution Service (CPS) is responsible for prosecuting cases investigated by the police in England and Wales, with the exception of cases conducted by the Serious Fraud Office and certain minor offences.

The CPS is headed by the director of public prosecutions (DPP), who works under the superintendence of the attorney-general. The service comprises a headquarters and 43 areas (including two head offices in London and York), with each area corresponding to a police area in England and Wales. Each area is headed by a chief crown prosecutor, supported by an area business manager.

Director of Public Prosecutions, Sir Ken Macdonald, QC
Chief Executive, Peter Lewis
Directors, vacant *(Business Development)*; Ms C. Hamon *(Business Information Systems)*; Sue Hemming *(Counter-Terrorism)*; Seamus Taylor *(Equality and Diversity)*; J. Graham *(Finance)*; Ros McCool *(Human Resources)*; Alison Saunders *(Organised Crime)*; P. Geering *(Policy)*; C. Newell *(Principal Legal Adviser)*; Carmen David *(Special Crime)*
Head of Strategic Communications, P. Teare

CPS AREAS ENGLAND

CPS DIRECT, 6th Floor, United House, Piccadilly, York YO1 9PQ T 01904-545594
Chief Crown Prosecutor, Barry Hughes
AVON AND SOMERSET, 2nd Floor, Froomsgate House, Rupert Street, Bristol BS1 2QJ T 0117-930 2800
Chief Crown Prosecutor, David Archer
BEDFORDSHIRE, Sceptre House, 7–9 Castle Street, Luton LU1 3AJ T 01582-816600
Chief Crown Prosecutor, Richard Newcombe
CAMBRIDGESHIRE, Justinian House, Spitfire Close, Ermine Business Park, Huntingdon, Cambs PE29 6XY T 01480-825200
Chief Crown Prosecutor, Richard Crowley
CHESHIRE, 2nd Floor, Windsor House, Pepper Street, Chester CH1 1TD T 01244-408600
Chief Crown Prosecutor, Ian Rushton
CLEVELAND, 5 Linthorpe Road, Middlesbrough, Cleveland TS1 1TX T 01642-204500
Chief Crown Prosecutor, Martin Goldman
CUMBRIA, 1st Floor, Stocklund House, Castle Street, Carlisle CA3 8SY T 01228-882900
Chief Crown Prosecutor, Claire Lindley
DERBYSHIRE, 7th Floor, St Peter's House, Gower Street, Derby DE1 1SB T 01332-614000
Chief Crown Prosecutor, Brian Gunn
DEVON AND CORNWALL, Hawkins House, Pynes Hill, Rydon Lane, Exeter EX2 5SS T 01392-288000
Chief Crown Prosecutor, Roger Coe-Salazar, OBE
DORSET, Ground Floor, Oxford House, Oxford Road, Bournemouth BH8 8HA T 01202-498700
Chief Crown Prosecutor (acting), Kate Brown
DURHAM, Elvet House, Hallgarth Street, Durham DH1 3AT T 0191-383 5800
Chief Crown Prosecutor, Ms Portia Ragnauth
ESSEX, County House, 100 New London Road, Chelmsford CM2 0RG T 01245-455800
Chief Crown Prosecutor, Paula Abrahams
GLOUCESTERSHIRE, 2 Kimbrose Way, Gloucester GL1 2DB T 01452-872400
Chief Crown Prosecutor, Adrian Foster
GREATER MANCHESTER, PO Box 237, 8th Floor, Sunlight House, Quay Street, Manchester M60 3PS T 0161-827 4700
Chief Crown Prosecutor, John Holt
HAMPSHIRE AND ISLE OF WIGHT, 3rd Floor, Black Horse House, 8–10 Leigh Road, Eastleigh, Hants SO50 9FH T 023-8067 3800
Chief Crown Prosecutor, Nick Hawkins

HERTFORDSHIRE, Queen's House, 58 Victoria Street, St Albans, Herts AL1 3HZ T 01727-798700
Chief Crown Prosecutor, Charles Ingham
HUMBERSIDE, Citadel House, 58 High Street, Kingston-upon-Hull HU1 1QD T 01482-621000
Chief Crown Prosecutor, Nigel Cowgill
KENT, Priory Gate, 29 Union Street, Maidstone ME14 1PT
T 01622-356300
Chief Crown Prosecutor, Elizabeth Howe
LANCASHIRE, 2nd Floor Podium, Unicentre, Lord's Walk, Preston PR1 1OH T 01772-208100
Chief Crown Prosecutor, Robert Marshall
LEICESTERSHIRE, Beaumont Leys Police Station, 2 Beaumont Way, Beaumont Leys, Leicester LE4 1OS
T 0116-222 2222
Chief Crown Prosecutor, Janet Meek, OBE
LINCOLNSHIRE, Crosstrend House, 10A Newport, Lincoln LN1 3DF T 01522-585900
Chief Crown Prosecutor, Colin Chapman
LONDON, 7th Floor, CPS HQ, 50 Ludgate Hill, London EC4M 7EX T 020-7796 8000
Chief Crown Prosecutor, Dru Sharpling
MERSEYSIDE, 7th Floor (South), Royal Liver Building, Pier Head, Liverpool L3 1HN T 0151-239 6400
Chief Crown Prosecutor, Paul Whittaker
NORFOLK, Carmelite House, St James Court, Whitefriars, Norwich NR3 1SL T 01603-693000
Chief Crown Prosecutor, Peter Tidey
NORTH YORKSHIRE, Athena House, Kettlestring Lane, Clifton Moor, York YO30 4XF T 01904-731700
Chief Crown Prosecutor, Robert Turnbull
NORTHAMPTONSHIRE, Beaumont House, Cliftonville, Northampton NN1 5BE T 01604-823600
Chief Crown Prosecutor, Grace Ononiwu
NORTHUMBRIA, St Ann's Quay, 122 Quayside, Newcastle upon Tyne NE1 3BD T 0191-260 4200
Chief Crown Prosecutor, Nicola Reasbeck
NOTTINGHAMSHIRE, 2 King Edward Court, King Edward Street, Nottingham NG1 1EL T 0115-852 3300
Chief Crown Prosecutor, Kate Carty
SOUTH YORKSHIRE, Greenfield House, 32 Scotland Street, Sheffield S3 7DQ T 0114-229 8600
Chief Crown Prosecutor, Judith Walker
STAFFORDSHIRE, Building 3, Etruria Valley Office Village, Etruria, Stoke-on-Trent ST1 5RU T 01782-664560
Chief Crown Prosecutor, Harry Ireland
SUFFOLK, 9th Floor, St Vincent's House, 1 Cutler Street, Ipswich IP1 1UL T 01473-282100
Chief Crown Prosecutor, Ken Caley
SURREY, Saxon House, 3 Onslow Street, Guildford, Surrey GU1 4YA T 01483-468200
Chief Crown Prosecutor, Tracey Easton
SUSSEX, City Gates, 185 Dyke Road, Brighton BN3 1TL
T 01273-765600
Chief Crown Prosecutor, Mrs Sarah Jane Gallagher
THAMES VALLEY, Eaton Court, 112 Oxford Road, Reading RG1 7LL T 01189-513265
Chief Crown Prosecutor, Baljit Ubhey
WARWICKSHIRE, Rossmore House, 10 Newbold Terrace, Leamington Spa CV32 4EA T 01926-455000
Chief Crown Prosecutor, Mark Lynn
WEST MERCIA, Artillery House, Heritage Way, Droitwich, Worcester WR9 8YB T 01905-825000
Chief Crown Prosecutor, Chris Enzor
WEST MIDLANDS, Colmore Gate, 2 Colmore Row, Birmingham B3 2QA T 0121-262 1300
Chief Crown Prosecutor, David Blundell

WEST YORKSHIRE, Oxford House, Oxford Row, Leeds LS1 3BE T 0113-290 2700
Chief Crown Prosecutor, Neil Franklin
WILTSHIRE, 2nd Floor, Fox Talbot House, Bellinger Close, Malmesbury Road, Chippenham SN15 1BN
T 01249-766100
Chief Crown Prosecutor, Karen Harrold

CPS AREAS WALES

DYFED POWYS, Heol Penlanffos, Tanerdy, Carmarthen, Dyfed SA31 2EZ T 01267-242100
Chief Crown Prosecutor, Iwan Jenkins
GWENT, 6th Floor, Chartist Tower, Upper Dock Street, Newport, Gwent NP20 1DW T 01633-261100
Chief Crown Prosecutor, Christopher Woolley
NORTH WALES, Bromfield House, Ellice Way, Wrexham LL13 7YW T 01978-346000
Chief Crown Prosecutor, Ed Beltrami
SOUTH WALES, 20th Floor, Capital House, Greyfriars Road, Cardiff CF10 3PL T 029-2080 3900
Chief Crown Prosecutor, Christopher Woolley

HER MAJESTY'S COURTS SERVICE

5th Floor, Clive House, Petty France, London SW1H 9HD
T 0845-456 8770 F 020-7189 2732
E customerservicecshq@hmcourts-service.gsi.gov.uk
W www.hmcourts-service.gov.uk

Her Majesty's Courts Service (HMCS) was launched on 1 April 2005, bringing together the Magistrates' Courts Service and the Court Service into a single organisation, and is responsible for the administration of the court of appeal, the high court, the crown court, the magistrates' courts, the county courts and the Probate Service. HMCS is an executive agency of the Ministry of Justice, and provides information on procedures and processes for the public, hearing lists, and address details for all relevant courts.
Chief Executive, Sir Ron De Witt, KB

JUDICIAL APPOINTMENTS COMMISSION

Steel House, 11 Tothill Street, London SW1H 9LJ
T 020-7210 1453 E enquiries@jac.gsi.gov.uk
W www.judicialappointments.gov.uk

The Judicial Appointments Commission was established as an independent non-departmental public body in April 2006 by the Constitutional Reform Act 2005. Its role is to select judicial office holders independently of government (a responsibility previously held by the Lord Chancellor). It has a statutory duty to encourage diversity in the range of persons available for selection and is sponsored by the Ministry of Justice and accountable to parliament through the Lord Chancellor. It is made up of 15 commissioners, including a chair.
Chair, Baroness Prashar, CBE
Commissioners, Rt. Hon. Lord Justice Auld; Dame Boreland-Kelly, DBE, FRSA; Dame Prof. Hazel Genn, DBE; Hon. Mr Justice Goldring; Rt. Hon. Lady Justice Hallett, DBE; Sir Geoffrey Inkin, OBE; Her Hon. Judge Kirkham; Edward Nally; Sara Nathan; Charles Newman; His Hon. Judge Pearl; Francis Plowden; Harriet Spicer; Jonathan Sumption, OBE, QC
Chief Executive, Clare Pelham

DIRECTORATE OF JUDICIAL OFFICES

The Directorate of Judicial Offices for England and Wales was established in April 2006 following the implementation of the Constitutional Reform Act 2005, and incorporates the Judicial Office, the Judicial Communications Office and the Judicial Studies Board. It provides the Lord Chief Justice and the judiciary with the support they need to fulfil the new responsibilities which transferred to the judiciary in April 2006. Although part of the directorate is based at the royal courts of justice (which is managed by HM Courts Service), the directorate works independently from government departments and agencies.

DIRECTOR'S OFFICE
T 020-7947 7598
Director, Debora Matthews
Secretary, Sarah Welfoot

JUDICIAL OFFICE
T 020-7073 4858
Heads, Jonathan Creer *(Judicial HR Services)*; Amanda Jeffrey *(Planning and Governance)*
Secretary to the Judges' Council, Barbara Flaxman

JUDICIAL COMMUNICATIONS OFFICE
T 020-7073 4852
Heads, Phillip Golding *(Corporate Communications)*; Mike Wicksteed *(Judicial Communications)*
Chief Public Information Officer, Peter Farr

JUDICIAL STUDIES BOARD
Millbank Tower, London SW1P 4QU
T 020-7217 4708 W www.jsboard.co.uk
Executive Directors, Judith Kilick; Maggy Piggot
Heads, Mark Shore *(Corporate Services)*; Helen Baker *(Judicial Training)*; Lynne McGechie *(Magistrates' Training Unit and Senior Adviser)*; Mary Holmes *(Tribunals and Training Unit and Senior Adviser)*

JUDICIAL COMMITTEE OF THE PRIVY COUNCIL

The Judicial Committee of the Privy Council is the final court of appeal for the United Kingdom overseas territories (*see* UK Overseas Territories section), crown dependencies and those independent Commonwealth countries which have retained this avenue of appeal (Antigua and Barbuda, Bahamas, Barbados, Belize, Brunei, Cook Islands and Niue, Dominica, Grenada, Jamaica, Kiribati, Mauritius, St Christopher and Nevis, St Lucia, St Vincent and the Grenadines, Trinidad and Tobago, and Tuvalu) and the sovereign base areas of Akrotiri and Dhekelia in Cyprus. The committee also hears appeals against pastoral schemes under the Pastoral Measure 1983, and deals with appeals from veterinary disciplinary bodies.

Under the devolution legislation enacted in 1998, the Judicial Committee of the Privy Council is the final arbiter in disputes as to the legal competence of matters done or proposed by the devolved legislative and executive authorities in Scotland, Wales and Northern Ireland.

In 2006 the Judicial Committee dealt with a total of 70 appeals and 60 petitions for special leave to appeal.

The members of the Judicial Committee are the Lords of Appeal in Ordinary, and other Privy Counsellors who hold or have held high judicial office in the United Kingdom or in certain designated courts of Commonwealth countries from which appeals are taken to committee.

JUDICIAL COMMITTEE OF THE PRIVY COUNCIL
Downing Street, London SW1A 2AJ T 020-7276 0483/5
Registrar of the Privy Council, Mary Macdonald
Group Manager, Jackie Lindsay

SCOTTISH JUDICATURE

Scotland has a legal system separate from, and differing greatly from, the English legal system in enacted law, judicial procedure and the structure of courts.

In Scotland the system of public prosecution is headed by the Lord Advocate and is independent of the police, who have no say in the decision to prosecute. The Lord Advocate, discharging his functions through the Crown Office in Edinburgh, is responsible for prosecutions in the high court, sheriff courts and district courts. Prosecutions in the high court are prepared by the Crown Office and conducted in court by one of the law officers, by an advocate-depute, or by a solicitor advocate. In the inferior courts the decision to prosecute is made and prosecution is preferred by procurators fiscal, who are lawyers and full-time civil servants subject to the directions of the Crown Office. A permanent legally qualified civil servant, known as the crown agent, is responsible for the running of the Crown Office and the organisation of the Procurator Fiscal Service, of which he or she is the head.

Scotland is divided into six sheriffdoms, each with a full-time sheriff principal. The sheriffdoms are further divided into sheriff court districts, each of which has a legally qualified resident sheriff or sheriffs, who are the judges of the court.

In criminal cases sheriffs principal and sheriffs have the same powers; sitting with a jury of 15 members, they may try more serious cases on indictment, or, sitting alone, may try lesser cases under summary procedure. Minor summary offences are dealt with in district courts which are administered by the district and the islands local government authorities and presided over by lay justices of the peace (of whom some 500 regularly sit in court) and, in Glasgow only, by stipendiary magistrates. Juvenile offenders (children under 16) may be brought before an informal children's hearing comprising three local lay people. The superior criminal court is the high court of justiciary which is both a trial and an appeal court. Cases on indictment are tried by a high court judge, sitting with a jury of 15, in Edinburgh and on circuit in other towns. Appeals from the lower courts against conviction or sentence are also heard by the high court, which sits as an appeal court only in Edinburgh. There is no further appeal to the House of Lords in criminal cases.

In civil cases the jurisdiction of the sheriff court extends to most kinds of action. Appeals against decisions of the sheriff may be made to the sheriff principal and thence to the court of session, or direct to the court of session, which sits only in Edinburgh. The court of session is divided into the inner and the outer house. The outer house is a court of first instance in which cases are heard by judges sitting singly, sometimes with a jury of 12. The inner house, itself subdivided into two divisions of equal status, is mainly an appeal court. Appeals may be made to the inner house from the outer house as well as from the sheriff court. An appeal may be made from the inner house to the House of Lords.

The judges of the court of session are the same as those

of the high court of justiciary, with the Lord President of the court of session also holding the office of Lord Justice General in the high court. Senators of the College of Justice are Lords Commissioners of Justiciary as well as judges of the court of session. On appointment, a senator takes a judicial title, which is retained for life. Although styled The Hon./Rt. Hon. Lord, the senator is not a peer, although some judges are peers in their own right.

The office of coroner does not exist in Scotland. The local procurator fiscal inquires privately into sudden or suspicious deaths and may report findings to the crown agent. In some cases a fatal accident inquiry may be held before the sheriff.

COURT OF SESSION AND HIGH COURT OF JUSTICIARY

The Lord President and Lord Justice General (£205,700), Rt. Hon. Lord Hamilton, *born* 1942, *apptd* 2005
Private Secretary, A. Maxwell

INNER HOUSE
Lords of Session (each £188,900)

FIRST DIVISION
The Lord President
Rt. Hon. Lord Nimmo Smith (William Nimmo Smith), *born* 1942, *apptd* 1996
Rt. Hon. Lord Philip (Alexander Philip), *born* 1942, *apptd* 1996
Rt. Hon. Lord Kingarth (Derek Emslie), *born* 1945, *apptd* 1997

SECOND DIVISION
Lord Justice Clerk (£198,700), Rt. Hon. Lord Gill (Brian Gill), *born* 1942, *apptd* 2001
Rt. Hon. Lord Osborne (Kenneth Osborne), *born* 1937, *apptd* 1990
Rt. Hon. Lord Abernethy (Alistair Cameron), *born* 1938, *apptd* 1992
Rt. Hon. Lord Johnston (Alan Johnston), *born* 1942, *apptd* 1994
Rt. Hon. Lord MacFadyen (Donald MacFadyen), *born* 1945, *apptd* 1995
Rt. Hon. Lord Eassie (Ronald Mackay), *born* 1945, *apptd* 1997
Rt. Hon. Lord Wheatley (John Wheatley), *born* 1941, *apptd* 2000
Rt. Hon. Lady Paton (Ann Paton), *born* 1952, *apptd* 2000

OUTER HOUSE
Lords of Session (each £165,900)
Hon. Lord Reed (Robert Reed), *born* 1956, *apptd* 1998
Hon. Lord Carloway (Colin Sutherland), *born* 1954, *apptd* 2000
Hon. Lord Clarke (Matthew Clarke), *born* 1947, *apptd* 2000
Rt. Hon. Lord Hardie (Andrew Hardie), *born* 1946, *apptd* 2000
Rt. Hon. Lord Mackay of Drumadoon (Donald Mackay), *born* 1946, *apptd* 2000
Hon. Lord McEwan (Robin McEwan), *born* 1943, *apptd* 2000
Hon. Lord Menzies (Duncan Menzies), *born* 1953, *apptd* 2001
Hon. Lord Drummond Young (James Drummond Young), *born* 1950, *apptd* 2001
Hon. Lord Emslie (Nigel Emslie), *born* 1947, *apptd* 2001
Hon. Lady Smith (Anne Smith), *born* 1955, *apptd* 2001

Hon. Lord Brodie (Philip Brodie), *born* 1950, *apptd* 2002
Hon. Lord Bracadale (Alastair Campbell), *born* 1949, *apptd* 2003
Hon. Lady Dorrian (Leeona Dorrian), *born* 1959, *apptd* 2005
Hon. Lord Hodge (Patrick Hodge), *born* 1953, *apptd* 2005
Hon. Lord Macphail (Iain Macphail), *born* 1938, *apptd* 2005
Hon. Lord Glennie (Angus Glennie), *born* 1950, *apptd* 2005
Hon. Lord Kinclaven (Alexander F. Wylie), *born* 1951, *apptd* 2005
Hon. Lady Clark of Calton (Lynda Clark), *born* 1946, *apptd* 2006
Hon. Lord Turnbull (Alan Turnbull), *born* 1958, *apptd* 2006
Hon. Lord Brailsford (Sidney Brailsford), *born* 1954, *apptd* 2006
Hon. Lord Uist (Roderick Macdonald), *born* 1951, *apptd* 2006
Hon. Lord Malcolm (Colin M. Campbell), *born* 1953, *apptd* 2007
Hon. Lord Matthews (Hugh Matthews), *born* 1953, *apptd* 2007

COURT OF SESSION AND HIGH COURT OF JUSTICIARY
Parliament House, Parliament Square, Edinburgh EH1 1HQ
T 0131-225 2595
Principal Clerk of Session and Justiciary, Graham Marwick
Deputy Principal Clerk of Justiciary, F. Shannly
Deputy Principal Clerk of Session and Principal Extractor, R. Cockburn
Depute in Charge of Offices of Court, Y. Anderson
Keeper of the Rolls, A. Moffat
Depute Clerks of Session and Justiciary, J. Atkinson; D. Bruton; A. Corr; D. Cullen; L. Curran; E. Dickson; W. Dunn; P. Fiddes; A. Finlayson; C. Fyffe; A. Hutchinson; T. Kell; A. Lynch; J. Lynn; L. MacLachlan; D. MacLeod; R. MacPherson; L. MacNamara; I. Martin; A. McArdle; N. McGinley; A. McKay; D. Morrison; J. Moyes; R. Newlands; Q. Oliver; R. Phillips; C. Reid; C. Richardson; N. Robertson; C. Scott; B. Sinclair; R. Sinclair; A. Thompson; K. Todd; C. Truby; P. Weir

SCOTTISH EXECUTIVE COURTS DIRECTORATE
Hayweight House, 23 Lauriston Street, Edinburgh EH3 9DQ
T 0131-229 9200

The Scottish Executive Courts Directorate is responsible for the provision of sufficient judges and sheriffs to meet the needs of the business of the supreme and sheriffs court in Scotland. It is also responsible for the efficient administration of a number of specialist courts and tribunals.
Deputy Director, J. L. Anderson

JUDICIAL APPOINTMENTS BOARD FOR SCOTLAND
9–10 St Andrew Square, Edinburgh EH2 2AF
T 0131-718 6045

The board's remit is to provide the first minister with a list of candidates recommended for appointment to the posts of senator of the court of session, sheriff principal, sheriff and part-time sheriff.
Chair, Sir Neil McIntosh, CBE

SCOTTISH COURT SERVICE

Hayweight House, 23 Lauriston Street, Edinburgh EH3 9DQ
T 0131-229 9200 W www.scotcourts.gov.uk

The Scottish Court Service is an executive agency within the Scottish Executive Justice Department. It is responsible to the Scottish ministers for the provision of staff, courthouses and associated services for the supreme and sheriff courts.
Chief Executive, Eleanor Emberson

SHERIFF COURT OF CHANCERY

27 Chambers Street, Edinburgh EH1 1LB
T 0131-225 2525

The court deals with service of heirs and completion of title in relation to heritable property.
Sheriff Principal, Edward F. Bowen, QC

HM COMMISSARY OFFICE

27 Chambers Street, Edinburgh EH1 1LB
T 0131-225 2525

The office is responsible for issuing confirmation, a legal document entitling a person to execute a deceased person's will, and other related matters.
Commissary Clerk, David Fyfe

SCOTTISH LAND COURT

126 George Street, Edinburgh EH2 4HH
T 0131-271 4360

The court deals with disputes relating to agricultural and crofting land in Scotland.
Chair (£133,100), Hon. Lord McGhie (James McGhie), QC
Members, D. J. Houston; A. Macdonald *(part-time)*; J. A. Smith *(part-time)*
Principal Clerk, K. H. R. Graham, WS

SHERIFFDOMS

SALARIES
Sheriff Principal £133,100
Sheriff £123,200

Floating Sheriffs are denoted with an *.

GLASGOW AND STRATHKELVIN

Sheriff Principal, James A. Taylor
Sheriffdom Business Manager, Stephen Bain

SHERIFFS AND SHERIFF CLERK
Glasgow, J. A. Baird; Mrs P. M. M. Bowman; S. Cathcart; D. Convery; A. F. Deutsch; A. C. Henry; *M. Jones, QC; B. Kearney; *Mrs M. H. Liddell; *A. R. Mackenzie; Miss D. M. MacNeill, QC; C. W. McFarlane, QC; I. H. L. Miller; J. K. Mitchell; S. Murphy; A. W. Noble; A. C. Normand; I. A. S. Peebles, QC; J. Platt; Miss R. E. A. Rae, QC; Miss S. A. O. Raeburn, QC; *N. C. Ritchie, QC; *N. A. Ross; Miss L. M. Ruxton; C. A. L. Scott; W. J. Totten; L. Wood
Sheriff Clerk, Stephen Bain

GRAMPIAN, HIGHLAND AND ISLANDS

Sheriff Principal, Sir Stephen S. T. Young, Bt., QC
Sheriffdom Business Manager, David Fraser

SHERIFFS AND SHERIFF CLERKS
Aberdeen and Stonehaven, G. K. Buchanan; Ms A. M. Cowan; D. J. Cusine; *P. P. Davies; C. J. Harris, QC; A. S. Jessop; K. A. McLernan; *K. M. Stewart; J. K. Tierney; *Sheriff Clerks,* Mrs F. Hendry *(Aberdeen)*; Mrs L. McKnight *(Stonehaven)*
Banff, P. P. Davies; *Sheriff Clerk Depute,* Melissa McLean
Dingwall, A. L. MacFadyen; *Sheriff Clerk Depute,* M. McBey
Dornoch, D. O. Sutherland; *Sheriff Clerk Depute,* Ken Kerr
Elgin, I. A. Cameron; *Sheriff Clerk,* Mrs F. MacPherson
Fort William, W. D. Small *(also Oban)*; *Sheriff Clerk Depute,* S. McKenna
Inverness, Portree, Stornoway, Tain and Wick, D. Booker-Milburn; A. Pollock; *Sheriff Clerk,* A. Bayliss *(Inverness)*; *Sheriff Clerks Depute,* Miss M. Campbell *(Lochmaddy and Portree)*; K. Finnie *(Stornoway)*; R. M. Hughes *(Tain)*; Mrs J. McEwan *(Wick)*
Kirkwall and Lerwick, G. Napier; *Sheriff Clerks Depute,* A. Moore *(Kirkwall)*; Christina Bardsley *(Lerwick)*
Peterhead, *M. Garden; *Sheriff Clerk,* R. Cantwell *(Peterhead)*
Lochmaddy, A. L. MacFadyen; *Sheriff Clerk Depute,* Miss M. Campbell

LOTHIAN AND BORDERS

Sheriff Principal, E. F. Bowen, QC
Sheriffdom Business Manager, David Shand

SHERIFFS AND SHERIFF CLERKS
Edinburgh, J. D. Allan; *F. R. Crowe; J. A. Farrell; J. M. S. Horsburgh, QC; Mrs M. L. E. Jarvie, QC; G. W. M. Liddle; A. Lothian; *Mrs K. E. C. Mackie; K. M. MacIver; I. McColl; *D. W. M. McIntyre; N. McPartlin, QC; N. M. P. Morrison, QC; F. Reith, QC; *J. P. Scott; Miss M. M. Stephen; C. N. Stoddart; *Sheriff Clerk,* David Shand
Linlithgow, *M. G. R. Edington; G. R. Fleming; D. A. Kinloch; W. D. Muirhead; *Sheriff Clerk,* D. Fyffe
Haddington, P. Gillam; *Sheriff Clerk,* I. Munro
Jedburgh and Duns, T. A. K. Drummond, QC; *Sheriff Clerk,* J. O'Donnell
Peebles, Rota system is used; *Sheriff Clerk Depute,* H. Johnston
Selkirk, T. A. K. Drummond, QC; *Interim Sheriff Clerk,* M. McCabe

NORTH STRATHCLYDE

Sheriff Principal, B. A. Kerr, QC
Sheriffdom Business Manager (acting), Christine Cockburn

SHERIFFS AND SHERIFF CLERKS
Campbeltown, *Ms R. Anderson *(also Paisley)*; *Sheriff Clerk Depute,* Ms. E. Harvey
Dumbarton, W. Dunlop; S. W. H. Fraser; S. Pender; *Sheriff Clerk,* K. Carter
Dunoon, Ms C. Kelly; *Sheriff Clerk Depute,* Ms K. Wilson
Greenock, J. Herald *(also Rothesay)*; V. J. Canavan; *Mrs R. Swanney; *Sheriff Clerk,* Ms J. G. Blackstock
Kilmarnock, W. S. Ireland; Mrs I. S. McDonald; Ms E. MacFarlane; A. G. Watson; *Sheriff Clerk,* C. Cockburn
Oban, W. D. Small *(also Fort William)*; *Sheriff Clerk Depute,* G. Whitelaw
Paisley, *Ms R. Anderson *(also Campbeltown)*; N. Douglas; G. C. Kavanagh; D. J. Pender; *C. W. Pettigrew; Ms S. M. Sinclair; J. Spy; *Sheriff Clerk,* C. McGrane
Rothesay, J. Herald *(also Greenock)*; *Sheriff Clerk Depute,* Mrs C. K. McCormick

SOUTH STRATHCLYDE, DUMFRIES AND GALLOWAY

Sheriff Principal, B. A. Lockhart
Sheriffdom Business Manager, Sheila Hindes

SHERIFFS AND SHERIFF CLERKS

Airdrie, P. M. Collins *(also Lanark)*; R. H. Dickson; Mrs M. M. Galbraith; J. C. Morris, QC; A. D. Vannet; *Sheriff Clerk*, J. Hamilton
Ayr, *D. A. Brown; J. McGowan; C. B. Miller; J. Montgomery; *Sheriff Clerk*, Mrs O. McShane
Dumfries, K. G. Barr; K. A. Ross; *Sheriff Clerk*, Ms E. Young
Hamilton, D. M. Bicket; J. Miller; F. L. Pieri; Miss J. Powrie; D. Scullion; H. K. Small; Mrs M. Smart; V. J. Smith; J. H. Stewart; S. A. Waldron; T. Welsh, QC; *Sheriff Clerk*, F. Petrie
Lanark, P. M. Collins *(also Airdrie)*; Ms N. C. Stewart; *Sheriff Clerk*, J. Foy
Stranraer and Kirkcudbright, J. R. Smith; *Sheriff Clerks*, D. Hood *(Kirkcudbright)*; B. Lindsay *(Stranraer)*

TAYSIDE, CENTRAL AND FIFE

Sheriff Principal, R. A. Dunlop, QC
Sheriffdom Business Manager, Gillian Prentice

SHERIFFS AND SHERIFF CLERKS

Alloa, D. M. Mackie; *Sheriff Clerk*, L. Reid
Arbroath, C. N. R. Stein; *Sheriff Clerk*, S. Munro
Cupar, G. J. Evans; *Sheriff Clerk*, C. Donald
Dundee, R. A. Davidson; A. J. M. Duff; T. G. Hughes; A. G. McCulloch; E. Munro; *Sheriff Clerk*, R. McMillan
Dunfermline, I. D. Dunbar; J. C. C. McSherry; *Sheriff Clerk*, J. Murphy
Falkirk, C. Caldwell; N. J. Mackinnon; *Sheriff Clerk*, P. McFarlane
Forfar, K. A. Veal; *Sheriff Clerk*, M. Herbertson
Kirkcaldy, *P. Braid; B. G. Donald; W. H. Holligan; *Sheriff Clerk*, S. Walker
Perth, M. J. Fletcher; L. D. R. Foulis; R. A. McCreadie, QC; *Sheriff Clerk*, A. Nicol
Stirling, A. Cubie; A. W. Robertson; *Sheriff Clerk*, M. McLean

STIPENDIARY MAGISTRATES

GLASGOW

R. B. Christie, *apptd* 1985; Mrs J. A. M. MacLean, *apptd* 1990

CROWN OFFICE AND PROCURATOR FISCAL SERVICE

CROWN OFFICE

25 Chambers Street, Edinburgh EH1 1LA
T 0131-226 2626 W www.crownoffice.gov.uk
Crown Agent, Norman McFadyen
Deputy Crown Agent, James Brisbane

PROCURATORS FISCAL

SALARIES
Area Fiscals   £55,000–£160,000
District Procurator Fiscal   £39,270–£59,464

GRAMPIAN AREA

Area Procurator Fiscal, Ms M. McLaughlin *(Aberdeen)*
Procurators Fiscal, Ms C. Frame; A. B. Hutchinson; Ms S. Ralph

HIGHLAND AND ISLANDS AREA

Area Procurator Fiscal, A. Laing *(Inverness)*
Procurators Fiscal, G. Aitken; Ms S. Foard; A. MacDonald; D. S. Teale; S. T. Swan; Ms A. Wyllie

LANARKSHIRE AREA

Area Procurator Fiscal, Ms J. Cameron *(Hamilton)*
Procurators Fiscal, Mrs A. C. Donaldson; S. Houston; D. Spiers

CENTRAL AREA

Area Procurator Fiscal, Mrs G. W. Watt *(Stirling)*
Procurators Fiscal, K. Donnelly; Ms R. McQuaid

DUNDEE AREA

Area Procurator Fiscal, D. Howdle *(Dundee)*
Procurators Fiscal, A. Grant; Dr David Griffiths; Ms E. Miller

FIFE AREA

Area Procurator Fiscal, C. Ritchie *(Kirkcaldy)*
Procurators Fiscal, J. Robertson; E. B. Russell

LOTHIAN AND BORDERS AREA

Area Procurator Fiscal, F. Mulholland *(Edinburgh)*
Procurators Fiscal, A. R. G. Fraser; M. R. MacLeod; Ms L. Thomson

AYRSHIRE AREA

Area Procurator Fiscal, John Dunn *(Kilmarnock)*
Procurators Fiscal, L. Brown; I. L. Murray

ARGYLL AND CLYDE AREA

Area Procurator Fiscal, J. Watt *(Paisley)*
Procurators Fiscal, J. E. Farrell; A. Miller; S. Pattison; M. Ramage; D. Webster

DUMFRIES AND GALLOWAY AREA

Area Procurator Fiscal, T. Dysart *(Dumfries)*
Procurators Fiscal, K. Grieve; J. Service

GLASGOW AREA

Area Procurator Fiscal, Ms C. Dyer *(Glasgow)*
Procurators Fiscal, A. Currie; D. Green; Ms J. Harrower; M. Watson

NORTHERN IRELAND JUDICATURE

In Northern Ireland the legal system and the structure of courts closely resemble those of England and Wales; there are, however, often differences in enacted law.

The supreme court of judicature of Northern Ireland comprises the court of appeal, the high court of justice and the crown court. The practice and procedure of these courts is similar to that in England. The superior civil court is the high court of justice, from which an appeal lies to the Northern Ireland court of appeal; the House of Lords is the final civil appeal court.

The crown court, served by high court and county court judges, deals with criminal trials on indictment. Cases are heard before a judge and, except those involving offences specified under emergency legislation, a jury. Appeals from the crown court against conviction or sentence are heard by the Northern Ireland court of appeal; the House of Lords is the final court of appeal.

The decision to prosecute in cases tried on indictment and in summary cases of a serious nature rests in Northern Ireland with the director of public prosecutions, who is responsible to the attorney-general. Minor summary offences are prosecuted by the police.

Minor criminal offences are dealt with in magistrates' courts by a legally qualified resident magistrate and, where an offender is under the age of 17, by juvenile courts each consisting of a resident magistrate and two lay members specially qualified to deal with juveniles (at least one of whom must be a woman). On 1 July 2006 there were 800 justices of the peace in Northern Ireland. Appeals from magistrates' courts are heard by the county court, or by the court of appeal on a point of law or an issue as to jurisdiction.

Magistrates' courts in Northern Ireland can deal with certain classes of civil case but most minor civil cases are dealt with in county courts. Judgments of all civil courts are enforceable through a centralised procedure administered by the Enforcement of Judgments Office.

SUPREME COURT OF JUDICATURE

The Royal Courts of Justice, Belfast BT1 3JF
T 028-9023 5111
Lord Chief Justice of Northern Ireland (£205,700), Rt. Hon. Sir Brian Kerr, *born* 1948, *apptd* 2004
Principal Secretary, S. T. A. Rogers

LORD JUSTICES OF APPEAL (£188,900)
Style, The Rt. Hon. Lord Justice [surname]
Rt. Hon. Sir Anthony Campbell, *born* 1936, *apptd* 1998
Rt. Hon. Sir Malachy Higgins, *born* 1944, *apptd* 2007
Rt. Hon. Sir Paul Girvan, *born* 1948, *apptd* 2007

PUISNE JUDGES (£165,900)
Style, The Hon. Mr Justice [surname]
Hon. Sir Patrick Coghlin, *born* 1945, *apptd* 1997
Hon. Sir John Gillen, *born* 1947, *apptd* 1998
Hon. Sir Richard McLaughlin, *born* 1947, *apptd* 1999

Hon. Sir Ronald Weatherup, *born* 1947, *apptd* 2001
Hon. Sir Reginald Weir, *born* 1947, *apptd* 2003
Hon. Sir Declan Morgan, *born* 1952, *apptd* 2004
Hon. Sir Donnell Deeny, *born* 1950, *apptd* 2004
Hon. Sir Anthony Hart, *born* 1946, *apptd* 2005
Hon. Sir Seamus Treacy, *born* 1956, *apptd* 2007
Hon. Sir William Benjamin Synge Stephens, *born* 1954, *apptd* 2007

MASTERS OF THE SUPREME COURT (£98,900)
Master, Queen's Bench and Appeals, C. J. McCorry
Master, Office of Care and Protection, H. Wells
Master, Chancery and Probate, R. A. Ellison
Master, Matrimonial, C. W. G. Redpath
Master, Queen's Bench and Matrimonial, E. Bell
Master, Taxing Office, J. Boullie
Master, Bankruptcy, F. Kelly

OFFICIAL SOLICITOR
Official Solicitor to the Supreme Court of Northern Ireland, Miss B. M. Donnelly

COUNTY COURTS

JUDGES (£123,200)
Style, His/Her Hon. Judge [surname]

Judge Babington; Judge Finnegan; Judge Gibson, QC; Her Hon. Judge Kennedy; Judge Lockie; Judge Loughran; Judge Lynch; Judge McFarland; Judge McKay, QC; Judge McReynolds; Judge Markey, QC; Judge Marrinan, QC; Judge Martin *(Chief Social Security and Child Support Commissioner)*; Judge Rodgers; Judge Smyth, QC

RECORDERS
Belfast (£143,748), Judge Burgess
Londonderry (£123,200), Her Hon. Judge Philpott, QC

MAGISTRATES' COURTS

RESIDENT MAGISTRATES (£98,900)
There are 20 resident magistrates in Northern Ireland.

CROWN SOLICITOR'S OFFICE
PO Box 410, Royal Courts of Justice, Belfast BT1 3JY
T 028-9054 2555
Crown Solicitor, J. Conn

DEPARTMENT OF THE DIRECTOR OF PUBLIC PROSECUTIONS
93 Chichester Street, Belfast BT1 3TR
T 028-9054 2444
Director of Public Prosecutions, Sir Alasdair Fraser, CB, QC

NORTHERN IRELAND COURT SERVICE
Windsor House, Bedford Street, Belfast BT2 7LT
T 028-9032 8594 W www.courtsni.gov.uk
Director, D. A. Lavery

TRIBUNALS

THE TRIBUNALS SERVICE

Victory House, 30–34 Kingsway, London WC2B 6EX
T 0845-600 0877 E customer.services@tribunals.gsi.gov.uk
W www.tribunals.gov.uk

The Tribunals Service, launched in April 2006, is an executive agency within the Ministry of Justice that provides common administrative support to 21 central government tribunals (plus the Adjudicator to HM Land Registry and the Gender Recognition Panel, which are not technically tribunals). The service also aims to deliver greater consistency in practice and procedure, to ensure tribunals are manifestly independent from those whose decisions are being reviewed, and to provide increased access to information for the public.

A number of government tribunals are expected to join the Tribunals Service in the future and all new, non-devolved, central government tribunals will be established as part of the service.

Chief Executive, Peter Handcock

AGRICULTURAL LAND TRIBUNALS

c/o DEFRA, Ergon House, Horseferry Road, London SW1P 2AL
T 0845-933 5577 E helpline@defra.gsi.gov.uk
W www.defra.gov.uk

Agricultural Land Tribunals settle disputes and other issues between agricultural landlords and tenants under the Agricultural Holdings Act 1986, and drainage disputes between neighbours under the Land Drainage Act 1991.

There are seven tribunals covering England and one covering Wales. For each tribunal the Lord Chancellor appoints a chair and one or more deputies (barristers or solicitors of at least seven years' standing). The Lord Chancellor also appoints lay members to three statutory panels: the 'landowners' panel, the 'farmers' panel and the 'drainage' panel.

Each tribunal is an independent statutory body with jurisdiction only within its own geographical area. A separate tribunal is constituted for each case, and consists of a chair and two lay members nominated by the chair.

Chairs (England), Shirley Evans; His Hon. Judge Machin; George Newsom; Paul de la Piquerie; His Hon. Judge Taylor; Nigel Thomas; Martin Wood
Chair (Wales), James Buxton

ASYLUM AND IMMIGRATION TRIBUNAL

PO Box 6987, Leicester LE1 6ZX
T 0845-600 0877 E customer.service@tribunals.gsi.gov.uk
W www.ait.gov.uk

The Asylum and Immigration Tribunal (AIT) is part of the Tribunals Service and hears appeals against decisions made by the Home Office; its powers are derived from the Immigration and Asylum Act 1999. This tribunal replaced the two-tiered Immigration Appellate Authority in 2005 by merging the Immigration Adjudicators and the Immigration Appeal Tribunal under Section 26 of the Asylum and Immigration (Treatment of Claimants, etc) Act 2004. Immigration judges are appointed by the Lord Chancellor and hear appeals against decisions to: refuse asylum under the Refugee Convention; refuse entry into

the UK; refuse to issue or extend a visa; deport a person from the UK; or deprive a person of UK citizenship. An appeal against a decision will go before a hearing, where the appellant, his/her representative and a representative from the Home Office will attend before an immigration judge (or panel, sometimes including non-legal members) who will make a determination on whether the appeal should be allowed or dismissed. In certain circumstances, either side may apply for a reconsideration of the determination. Depending on how the appeal was heard (by a single immigration judge or by a panel) will dictate where any applications for reconsideration will be lodged.
President, Hon. Mr Justice Hodge, OBE
Deputy Presidents, Libby Arfon-Jones; Mark Ockelton

CARE STANDARDS TRIBUNAL

18 Pocock Street, London SE1 0BW
T 020-7960 0660 E cst@tribunals.gsi.gov.uk
W www.carestandardstribunal.gov.uk

The tribunal was established under the Protection of Children Act 1999 and considers appeals in relation to decisions made about the inclusion of individuals' names on the list of those considered unsuitable to work with children, restrictions from teaching and employment in schools/further education institutions, and the registration of independent schools. It also deals with general registration decisions made about care homes, children's homes, nurses' agencies, residential family centres and fostering agencies. The tribunal's president appoints the panels for each case and each appeal is heard by a legally qualified chair and two lay members with expertise in the field.
President, His Hon. Judge Pearl

CIVIL AVIATION AUTHORITY

CAA House, 45–59 Kingsway, London WC2B 6TE
T 020-7453 6162 E legal@caa.co.uk
W www.caa.co.uk

The Civil Aviation Authority (CAA) does not have a separate tribunal department as such, however for certain purposes the CAA must conform to tribunal requirements. For example, to deal with appeals against the refusal or revocation of aviation licences and certificates issued by the CAA, and the allocation of routes outside of the EU to airlines.

The chair and four non-executive members who may sit on panels for tribunal purposes are appointed by the Secretary of State for Transport.
Chair, Sir Roy McNulty, CBE

COMMONS COMMISSIONERS

Room 1/14, Temple Quay House, 2 The Square, Temple Quay, Bristol BS1 6EB
T 0117-372 8973 E commons.commissioners@defra.gsi.gov.uk

The Commons Commissioners are responsible for deciding disputes arising under the Commons Registration Act 1965. They also enquire into the ownership of unclaimed common land and village greens. Commissioners must be barristers or solicitors of at least seven years' standing and are appointed by the Lord Chancellor.
Chief Commons Commissioner, Edward Cousins

COMPETITION APPEAL TRIBUNAL

Victoria House, Bloomsbury Place, London WC1A 2EB
T 020-7979 7979 E info@catribunal.org.uk
W www.catribunal.org.uk

The Competition Appeal Tribunal (CAT) is a specialist tribunal established to hear certain cases in the sphere of UK competition and economic regulatory law. It hears appeals against decisions of the Office of Fair Trading (OFT) and their sectoral regulators under the Competition Act 1998, and also decisions against the OFT, Secretary of State for Trade and Industry and Competition Commission under the merger control and market investigation provisions of the Enterprise Act 2002. The CAT also has jurisdiction under the Competition Act 1998 to award damages in respect of infringements of EC or UK competition law and to hear appeals against decisions of OFCOM under the Communications Act 2003.

Cases are heard before a panel consisting of three members: either the president or a member of the panel of chairs and two ordinary members. The members of the panel are judges of the Chancery Division of the high court and other senior lawyers. The ordinary members have expertise in law and/or related fields. The president and chairs are appointed by the Lord Chancellor; the ordinary members are appointed by the secretary of state.
President, vacant

COPYRIGHT TRIBUNAL

Room 2G31, Concept House, Cardiff Road, Newport NP10 9FU
T 01633-811035 E copyright.tribunal@ipo.gov.uk
W www.ipo.gov.uk/copy/tribunal

The Copyright Tribunal resolves disputes over the terms and conditions of licences offered by, or licensing schemes operated by, collective licensing bodies in the copyright and related rights area. Its decisions are appealable to the high court on points of law only.

The chair and two deputy chairs are appointed by the Lord Chancellor. Up to eight ordinary members are appointed by the Secretary of State for Trade and Industry. The tribunal operates on a panel basis and its members have wide expertise in business, public administration, and the professions.
Chair, Judge Fysh, QC

CRIMINAL INJURIES COMPENSATION APPEALS PANEL

11th Floor, Cardinal Tower, Farringdon Road, London EC1M 3HS
T 020-7549 4600 E enquiries-cicap@tribunals.gsi.gov.uk
W www.cicap.gov.uk

The Criminal Injuries Compensation Appeals Panel determines appeals against review decisions made by the Criminal Injuries Compensation Authority on applications for compensation received from victims of crimes of violence. The chair and members of the panel are appointed by the Secretary of State for the Home Department. Each hearing panel consists of two or three members, one of whom will be a qualified lawyer.
Chair, Roger Goodier

EMPLOYMENT APPEAL TRIBUNAL

London Office: Audit House, 58 Victoria Embankment, London EC4Y 0DS T 020-7273 1041
Edinburgh Office: 52 Melville Street, Edinburgh EH3 7HF
T 0131-225 3963 W www.employmentappeals.gov.uk

The Employment Appeal Tribunal hears appeals (on points of law only) arising from any decision of an employment tribunal. Hearings are conducted by a judge, either alone or accompanied by two lay members who have practical experience in employment relations. Administrative support is provided by the Tribunals Service.
President, Hon. Mr Justice Elias
Scottish Chair, Hon. Lady Smith

EMPLOYMENT TRIBUNALS (ENGLAND AND WALES)

Ground Floor, Victory House, 30–34 Kingsway, London WC2B 6EX
T 0845-795 9775 W www.employmenttribunals.gov.uk

Employment Tribunals for England and Wales sit in 12 regions. The tribunals deal with matters of employment law, redundancy, dismissal, contract disputes, sexual, racial and disability discrimination and related areas of dispute which may arise in the workplace. A public register of judgments is held at 100 Southgate Street, Bury St Edmunds, Suffolk IP33 2AQ.

Chairs, who may be full-time or part-time, are legally qualified. They, along with the tribunal members, are appointed by the Ministry of Justice.
President, His Hon. Judge Meeran

EMPLOYMENT TRIBUNALS (SCOTLAND)

Central Office, Eagle Building, 215 Bothwell Street, Glasgow G2 7TS
T 0141-204 0730

Tribunals in Scotland have the same remit as those in England and Wales. Chairs are appointed by the Lord President of the Court of Session and lay members by the Secretary of State for Trade and Industry.
President, C. M. Milne

FAMILY HEALTH SERVICES APPEAL AUTHORITY

30 Victoria Avenue, Harrogate HG1 5PR
T 01423-530280 E mail@fhsaa.nhs.uk W www.fhsaa.org.uk

The Family Health Services Appeal Authority (FHSAA) is completely independent of the Department of Health and considers appeals against the decisions of primary care trusts (PCTs), for example appeals by GPs, dentists, pharmacists and opticians against action taken against them. The president allocates appeals and applications to panels normally consisting of a legal chair, a professional member and a lay member. The FHSAA's president and members are appointed by the Lord Chancellor.
President, Paul Kelly

FINANCIAL SERVICES AND MARKETS TRIBUNAL

15–19 Bedford Avenue, London WC1B 3AS
T 020-7612 9700 E fs&mt@tribunals.gsi.gov.uk
W www.financeandtaxtribunals.gov.uk

The Financial Services and Markets Tribunal hears cases arising from decisions issued by the Financial Services Authority against financial service providers, including banks, clearing houses, stockbrokers and mortgage advisers. The president, a panel of legally qualified chairs and a panel of lay members are all appointed by the Lord Chancellor.
President, Sir Stephen Oliver, QC

GENERAL COMMISSIONERS OF INCOME TAX

Selborne House, 54–60 Victoria Street, London SW1E 6QW
T 020-7210 0670

General commissioners of income tax operate under the Taxes Management Act 1970. They are unpaid judicial officers who sit in some 350 divisions throughout the UK to hear appeals against decisions by HM Revenue and Customs on a variety of taxation matters. The commissioners' jurisdiction was extended in 1999 to hear National Insurance appeals. The Lord Chancellor appoints general commissioners (except in Scotland, where they are appointed by the Scottish Executive). There are approximately 1,700 general commissioners appointed throughout the United Kingdom. In each division, commissioners appoint a clerk, who is normally legally qualified, who makes the administrative arrangements for appeal hearings and advises the commissioners on points of law and procedure. The Ministry of Justice pays the clerks' remuneration.

Appeals from the general commissioners are by way of case stated, on a point of law, to the high court (the court of session in Scotland or the court of appeal in Northern Ireland).

IMMIGRATION SERVICES TRIBUNAL

Procession House, 55 Ludgate Hill, London EC4M 7JW
T 020-7029 9790 E imset@tribunals.gsi.gov.uk
W www.immigrationservicestribunal.gov.uk

The Immigration Services Tribunal is an independent judicial body established in 2000 to provide a forum in which appeals against decisions of the Immigration Services Commissioner and complaints made by the Immigration Services Commissioner can be heard and determined. The cases exclusively concern people providing advice and representation services in connection with immigration matters.

The tribunal forms part of the Ministry of Justice. There is a president, who is the judicial head; other judicial members, who must be legally qualified; lay members, who must have substantial experience in immigration services or in the law and procedure relating to immigration; and a secretary, who is responsible for administration. The tribunal can sit anywhere in the UK.
President, His Hon. Judge Cripps

INDUSTRIAL TRIBUNALS AND THE FAIR EMPLOYMENT TRIBUNAL (NORTHERN IRELAND)

Long Bridge House, 20–24 Waring Street, Belfast BT1 2EB
T 028-9032 7666 E mail@employmenttribunalsni.org
W www.employmenttribunalsni.co.uk

The industrial tribunal system in Northern Ireland was set up in 1965 and has a similar remit to the employment tribunals in the rest of the UK. There is also a Fair Employment Tribunal, which hears and determines individual cases of alleged religious or political discrimination in employment. Employers can appeal to the Fair Employment Tribunal if they consider the directions of the Equality Commission to be unreasonable, inappropriate or unnecessary, and the Equality Commission can make application to the tribunal for the enforcement of undertakings or directions with which an employer has not complied.

The president, vice-president and part-time chairs of the Fair Employment Tribunal are appointed by the Lord Chancellor. The full-time chair and the part-time chairs of the industrial tribunals and the panel members to both the industrial tribunals and the Fair Employment Tribunal are appointed by the Department for Employment and Learning.
President of the Industrial Tribunals and the Fair Employment Tribunal, Eileen McBride

INFORMATION TRIBUNAL

Arnhem House Support Centre, PO Box 6987, Leicester LE1 6ZX
T 0845-6000 877 E informationtribunal@tribunals.gsi.gov.uk
W www.informationtribunal.gov.uk

The Information Tribunal determines appeals against notices issued by the Information Commissioner. The chair and deputy chair are appointed by the Lord Chancellor and must be legally qualified. Lay members are appointed by the Lord Chancellor to represent the interests of data users or data subjects. A tribunal consists of a chair sitting with equal numbers of the lay members. There is a separate panel of the tribunal which hears national security appeals; the president of this panel is Sir Stephen Mitchell.
Chair, John Angel

LANDS TRIBUNAL

Procession House, 55 Ludgate Hill, London EC4M 7JW
T 020-7029 9780 E lands@tribunals.gsi.gov.uk
W www.landstribunal.gov.uk

The Lands Tribunal is an independent judicial body which determines questions relating to the valuation of land, rating appeals from valuation tribunals, appeals from leasehold valuation tribunals, the discharge or modification of restrictive covenants, and compulsory purchase compensation. The tribunal may also arbitrate under references by consent. The president and members are appointed by the Lord Chancellor. Cases are usually heard by a single member but they may sometimes be heard by two or three members.
President, G. R. Bartlett, QC

LANDS TRIBUNAL FOR SCOTLAND

George House, 126 George Street, Edinburgh EH2 4HH
T 0131-271 4350 E mailbox@lands-tribunal-scotland.org.uk
W www.lands-tribunal-scotland.org.uk

The Lands Tribunal for Scotland has much the same remit as the tribunal for England and Wales but also covers questions relating to tenants' rights to buy their homes under the Housing (Scotland) Act 1987. The president is appointed by the Lord President of the Court of Session.
President, Hon. Lord McGhie, QC

MENTAL HEALTH REVIEW TRIBUNALS

Secretariat: 5th Floor, 11 Belgrave Road, London SW1V 1RS
T 020-7592 1007 W www.mhrt.org.uk

The Mental Health Review Tribunals are independent judicial bodies which review the cases of patients compulsorily detained under the provisions of the Mental Health Act 1983. They have the power to discharge the patient, to recommend leave of absence, to delay discharge, transfer to another hospital or that a guardianship order be made, to reclassify both restricted and unrestricted patients, and to recommend consideration of a supervision application. There are three tribunals in England and Wales, each headed by a regional chair who is appointed by the Lord Chancellor on a

part-time basis. Each tribunal is made up of at least three members, and must include a lawyer, who acts as president, a medical member and a lay member.
Liaison Judge, His Hon. Judge Sycamore

NATIONAL HEALTH SERVICE TRIBUNAL (SCOTLAND)
40 Craiglockhart Road North, Edinburgh EH14 1BT
T 0131-443 2575

The Scottish National Health Service Tribunal considers representations that the continued inclusion of a doctor, dentist, optometrist or pharmacist on a health board's list would be prejudicial to the efficiency of the service concerned, by virtue either of fraudulent practices or unsatisfactory personal or professional conduct. The tribunal sits when required and is composed of a chair, one lay member, and one practitioner member drawn from a representative professional panel. The chair is appointed by the Lord President of the Court of Session, and the lay member and the members of the professional panel are appointed by the Scottish ministers.
Chair, J. Michael D. Graham

NATIONAL PARKING ADJUDICATION SERVICE
Barlow House, Minshull Street, Manchester M1 3DZ
T 0161-242 5252 E npas@parking-adjudication.gov.uk
W www.parking-appeals.gov.uk

The National Parking Adjudication Service considers appeals from motorists against penalty charge notices issued by councils in England and Wales under the Road Traffic Act 1991, including appeals against bus lane contraventions. Parking adjudicators are appointed with the express consent of the Lord Chancellor and must be lawyers of five years' standing. Cases are decided by a single adjudicator, either in a postal, telephone or a personal hearing.
Head of Service, Louise Hutchinson

OFFICE OF THE SOCIAL SECURITY AND CHILD SUPPORT COMMISSIONERS
3rd Floor, Procession House, 55 Ludgate Hill, London EC4M 7JW
T 020-7029 9850 E osscsc@tribunals.gsi.gov.uk
George House, 126 George Street, Edinburgh EH2 4HH
T 0131-271 4310 E ossc@ossc-scotland.org.uk
W www.osscsc.gov.uk

Commissioners are the final statutory authority to decide appeals on points of law in social security, tax credit, child support, housing benefit, council tax benefit and compensation recovery cases. They also decide appeals from Pensions Appeal Tribunals relating to war pensions and cases which have been referred to them under the Forfeiture Act 1982. The commissioners' jurisdiction covers England, Wales and Scotland. There are 18 commissioners, all of whom are qualified lawyers.
Chief Commissioner for Great Britain, His Hon. Judge Hickinbottom
Senior Commissioner for Scotland, D. J. May, QC

OFFICE OF THE SOCIAL SECURITY COMMISSIONERS AND CHILD SUPPORT COMMISSIONERS FOR NORTHERN IRELAND
Headline Building, 10–14 Victoria Street, Belfast BT1 3GG
T 028-9033 2344

E socialsecuritycommissioners@courtsni.gov.uk
W www.courtsni.gov.uk

The role of Northern Ireland Social Security Commissioners and Child Support Commissioners is similar to that of the commissioners in Great Britain; they also have jurisdiction to deal with questions arising under the Forfeiture (Northern Ireland) Order 1982. There are two commissioners for Northern Ireland.
Chief Commissioner, His Hon. Judge Martin, QC
Commissioner, Mrs M. F. Brown, LLB

PENSIONS APPEAL TRIBUNAL
Procession House, 55 Ludgate Hill, London EC4M 7JW
T 020-7029 9800 E pensions.appeal@tribunals.gsi.gov.uk
W www.pensionsappealtribunals.gov.uk

The Pensions Appeal Tribunals are independent from the Service Personnel and Veterans Agency and the Ministry of Defence, and deal with appeals concerning the two schemes that provide compensation for injuries sustained in the armed forces. Established in 1919, the war pensions scheme is applicable in respect of injuries that occurred before 5 April 2005. The tribunals adjudicate on entitlement to a war pension, the percentage at which the War Pensions Agency has assessed a disablement and whether an allowance is justified (ie for mobility needs). For injuries after that date, the armed forces compensation scheme applies, and tribunals decide on entitlement to and amount of the award. The tribunal members are appointed by the Secretary of State for Justice.
President, Dr H. M. G. Concannon, LLM

PENSIONS APPEAL TRIBUNALS FOR SCOTLAND
126 George Street, Edinburgh EH2 4HH
T 0131-271 4340 E info@patscotland.org.uk
W www.patscotland.org.uk
President, C. N. McEachran, QC

RESIDENTIAL PROPERTY TRIBUNAL SERVICE
10 Alfred Place, London WC1E 7LR
T 0845-600 3178 E rptscorporateunit@communities.gsi.gov.uk
W www.rpts.gov.uk

The Residential Property Tribunal Service provides members to sit on panels for the Rent Assessment Committees, Residential Property Tribunals and Leasehold Valuation Tribunals, and serves the private-rented and leasehold property market in England by resolving disputes between leaseholders, tenants and landlords. The president and chair are appointed by the Lord Chancellor and other members are appointed by the Department for Communities and Local Government and the Ministry of Justice.
Senior President, Siobhan McGrath

SOCIAL SECURITY AND CHILD SUPPORT APPEALS
4th Floor, 14 Grays Inn Road, Fox Court, London WC1X 8HN
T 020-7712 2640 W www.appeals-service.gov.uk

The Social Security and Child Support Appeals Tribunal arranges and hears appeals on a range of decisions, including those concerned with social security, child support, child tax credit, pensions credit, housing benefit, council tax benefit, vaccine damage, tax credits and compensation recovery.

Judicial authority rests with the president, while administrative responsibility is exercised by the Tribunals Service, which is an executive agency of the Ministry of Justice.
President, vacant

SOLICITORS' DISCIPLINARY TRIBUNAL
3rd Floor, Gate House, 1 Farringdon Street, London EC4M 7NS
T 020-7329 4808 E enquiries@solicitorsdt.com
W www.solicitorstribunal.org.uk

The Solicitors' Disciplinary Tribunal is an independent statutory body whose members are appointed by the Master of the Rolls. The tribunal considers applications made to it alleging either professional misconduct and/or a breach of the statutory rules by which solicitors are bound against an individually named solicitor, former solicitor, registered foreign lawyer, or solicitor's clerk. The tribunal has around 50 members, two thirds are solicitor members and one third are lay members. The president and solicitor members do not receive remuneration and lay members are remunerated by the Ministry of Justice.
President, A. Isaacs

SOLICITORS' DISCIPLINE TRIBUNAL (SCOTTISH)
Unit 3.5, The Granary Business Centre, Coal Road, Cuper, Fife KY15 5YQ
T 01334-659088 W www.ssdt.org.uk

The Scottish Solicitors' Discipline Tribunal is an independent statutory body with a panel of 22 members, 14 of whom are solicitors; members are appointed by the Lord President of the Court of Session. Its principal function is to consider complaints of misconduct against solicitors in Scotland.
Chair, A. Cockburn

SPECIAL COMMISSIONERS
15–19 Bedford Avenue, London WC1B 3AS
T 020-7612 9700 E sc@tribunals.gsi.gov.uk
W www.financeandtaxtribunals.gov.uk

The Special Commissioners are an independent body appointed by the Lord Chancellor to hear complex appeals against decisions of HM Revenue and Customs relating to direct tax matters.
Presiding Special Commissioner, Sir Stephen Oliver, QC

SPECIAL EDUCATIONAL NEEDS AND DISABILITY TRIBUNAL
Central Office, Procession House, 55 Ludgate Hill, London EC4M 7JW T 0870-241 2555
Darlington Office, Ground Floor, Mowden Hall, Staindrop Road DL3 9BG
E sendistqueries@tribunals.gsi.gov.uk W www.sendist.gov.uk

The Special Educational Needs and Disability Tribunal considers parents' appeals against the decisions of local education authorities (LEAs) about children's special educational needs and claims of disability discrimination in schools. Its president, chairs and specialist members are appointed by the Lord Chancellor.
President, Lady Rosemary Hughes

SPECIAL IMMIGRATION APPEALS COMMISSION
15 Breams Buildings, London EC4A 1DZ
T 0845-600 0877 W www.siac.tribunals.gov.uk

The commission was set up under the Special Immigration Appeals Commission Act 1997. Its main function is to consider appeals against orders for deportations in cases which involve, in the main, considerations of national security or the public interest. The commission also hears appeals against decisions to deprive persons of citizenship status. Members are appointed by the Lord Chancellor.
Chair, Hon. Mr Justice Mitting

TRANSPORT TRIBUNAL
Procession House, 55 Ludgate Hill, London EC4M 7JW
T 020-7029 9780 E transport@tribunals.gsi.gov.uk
W www.transporttribunal.gov.uk

The Transport Tribunal has three jurisdictions: it hears appeals against decisions made by Traffic Commissioners at public inquiries, appeals against decisions of the Registrar of the Driving Standards Agency and is able to resolve disputes under the Postal Services Act 2000. The tribunal consists of a legally qualified president, other judicial members, and lay members. The president and legal members are appointed by the Lord Chancellor and the lay members by the transport secretary. Members of the Transport Tribunal also act as the London Service Permit Appeals Panel.
President, H. B. H. Carlisle, QC

VALUATION TRIBUNAL SERVICE
Chief Executive's Office, Block 1, Angel Square, 1 Torrens Street, London EC1V 1NY
T 020-7841 8700 W www.valuation-tribunals.gov.uk

The Valuation Tribunal Service (VTS) was created as a corporate body by the Local Government Finance Act 2003, and is responsible for providing or arranging the services required for the operation of valuation tribunals in England. The VTS board is comprised of a chair and members appointed by the secretary of state. There are 56 tribunals in England that hear appeals concerning council tax and non-domestic rating and land drainage rates. The VTS is funded by the Department for Communities and Local Government. A separate tribunal is constituted for each hearing, and consists of a chair and two or three other members. A clerk, who is a paid employee of the VTS, is present to advise on points of procedure and law. Members are appointed by a representative of the local authorities and the valuation tribunal president, and serve on a voluntary basis.
Chair, VTS Board, Anne Galbraith, OBE

VALUATION TRIBUNAL SERVICE FOR WALES
Governing Council of VTSW, Dinerth Road, Rhos on Sea, Colwyn Bay LL28 4UL
T 01492-546610 E northwales.vt@vto.gsx.gov.uk

The Valuation Tribunal Service for Wales (VTSW) was created under the Valuation Tribunals (Wales) Regulations 2005, and is responsible for providing or arranging the services required for the operation of the four tribunals in Wales. The governing council of the VTSW is comprised of four regional presidents, one of whom is elected director together with one member who is appointed by the National Assembly for Wales. The VTSW hear appeals concerning council tax and non-domestic rating, and land drainage rates in Wales. An individual tribunal, supported

by a clerk, is constituted for each hearing and is normally serviced by three members, one of whom also chairs.
Director, J. H. Owens

VAT AND DUTIES TRIBUNALS

15–19 Bedford Avenue, London WC1B 3AS
T 020-7612 9700 E vatlon@tribunals.gsi.gov.uk
W www.financeandtaxtribunals.gov.uk

VAT and Duties Tribunals are independent and decide disputes between taxpayers and HM Revenue and Customs. In England and Wales, the president and chairs are appointed by the Lord Chancellor and members by the Treasury. Chairs in Scotland are appointed by the Lord President of the Court of Session.
President, Sir Stephen Oliver, QC
Vice-President, England and Wales, J. D. Demack
Vice-President, Scotland, T. G. Coutts, QC

TRIBUNAL CENTRES
EDINBURGH, 126 George Street, Edinburgh EH2 4HH
T 0131-271 4330
LONDON, 15–19 Bedford Avenue, London WC1B 3AS
T 020-7612 9700
MANCHESTER, 9th Floor, Westpoint, 501 Chester Road, Manchester M16 5HU T 0161-868 6600

THE POLICE SERVICE

There are 52 police forces in the United Kingdom: 43 in England and Wales, including the Metropolitan Police and the City of London Police, eight in Scotland and the Police Service of Northern Ireland. Most forces' areas are coterminous with one or more local authority areas. The Isle of Man, States of Jersey and Guernsey have their own forces responsible for policing in their respective islands and bailiwicks. The Serious Organised Crime Agency (SOCA), which became operational in April 2006, is responsible for the investigation of national and international serious organised crime.

Police authorities are independent bodies, responsible for the supervision of local policing. There are 43 police authorities in England and Wales, plus an additional one for British Transport Police. Most police authorities have 17 members, comprising nine local councillors, five independent members and three magistrates. Authorities which are responsible for larger areas may have more members, such as the Metropolitan Police Authority which has 23 members: 12 drawn from the London Assembly, seven independent members and four magistrates. The Corporation of London acts as the police authority for the City of London Police. In Scotland, six of the forces are maintained by joint police boards, made up of local councillors from each council in the force area; the other two constabularies (Dumfries & Galloway and Fife) are directly administered by their respective councils. The Northern Ireland Policing Board is an independent public body consisting of 19 political and independent members.

Police forces in England, Scotland and Wales are financed by central and local government grants and a precept on the council tax. The Police Service of Northern Ireland is wholly funded by central government. The police authorities, subject to the approval of the home secretary (in England and Wales), the Northern Ireland secretary and to regulations, are responsible for appointing the Chief Constable. In England and Wales the latter are responsible for the force's budget, levying the precept on the council tax, publishing annual policing plans and reports, setting local objectives, monitoring performance targets and appointing or dismissing senior officers. In Scotland the police authorities are responsible for setting the force's budget, providing the resources necessary to police the area adequately and appointing officers of the rank of Assistant Chief Constable and above. In Northern Ireland, the Northern Ireland Policing Board exercises similar functions.

The home secretary, the Northern Ireland secretary and the Scottish Executive are responsible for the organisation, administration and operation of the police service. They regulate police ranks, discipline, hours of duty and pay and allowances. All police forces are subject to inspection by HM Inspectors of Constabulary, who report to the home secretary, Scottish Executive or the Northern Ireland secretary.

COMPLAINTS

The Independent Police Complaints Commission (IPCC) has overall responsibility for the system of complaints against the police in England and Wales. Complaints can be made directly to the local police force or to the IPCC which will contact the police force concerned on the complainant's behalf. All complaints are reviewed by the police force. If the complaint is relatively minor, the police force will attempt to resolve it internally and an official investigation may not be required. Serious complaints are reported to the IPCC immediately and are formerly investigated by a senior officer. The Crown Prosecution Service then decides whether or not to bring criminal charges against the officer(s) involved. The IPCC has the power to initiate, carry out and oversee investigations and is also responsible for the way complaints are handled by local police forces. An officer who is dismissed, required to resign or reduced in rank, whether as a result of a complaint or not, may appeal to a police appeals tribunal established by the relevant police authority.

Under the Police, Public Order and Criminal Justice (Scotland) Act 2006, which came into force on 1 April 2007, the Police Complaints Commissioner for Scotland is responsible for providing independent scrutiny of the way Scottish police forces, authorities and policing agencies handle complaints from the public. The commissioner also has the power to direct police forces to re-examine any complaints which are not considered to have been dealt with satisfactorily. If there is a suggestion of criminal activity, the complaint is investigated by a procurator fiscal.

The Police Ombudsman for Northern Ireland provides an independent police complaints system for Northern Ireland, dealing with all stages of the complaints procedure. Complaints which cannot be resolved informally are investigated and the ombudsman recommends a suitable course of action to the Chief Constable of the Police Service of Northern Ireland or the Northern Ireland Policing Board based on the investigation's findings. The ombudsman may recommend that a police officer be prosecuted although the decision to prosecute a police officer rests with the Director of Public Prosecutions.

RATES OF PAY

London weighting of £2,055 per annum (from 1 July 2006) is awarded to all police officers working in London irrespective of their ranks and in addition to the salaries listed below:

BASIC RATES OF PAY *at 1 September 2006*

Chief Constables of Greater Manchester, Strathclyde and West Midlands*	£161,178–£163,908
Chief Constable*	£114,735–£152,982
Deputy Chief Constable*	£98,346–£125,667
Assistant Chief Constable and Commanders*	£81,954–£95,613
Chief Superintendent	£67,200–£71,031
Superintendent Range 2†	£64,434–£68,571

Superintendent	£56,274–£65,565
Chief Inspector‡§	£46,779 (£48,645)–£48,705 (£50,568)
Inspector‡§	£42,264 (£44,118)–£45,843 (£47,709)
Sergeant‡	£32,985–£37,071
Constable‡	£21,009–£32,985

Metropolitan Police

Commissioner	£234,939
Deputy Commissioner	£193,959

City of London Police

Commissioner	£145,344
Assistant Commissioner	£119,883

Police Service of Northern Ireland

Chief Constable	£174,834
Deputy Chief Constable	£142,053

* Chief Officers may receive a bonus of at least five per cent of pensionable pay if their performance is deemed exceptional

† For Superintendents who were not promoted to the rank of Chief Superintendent on its re-introduction on 1 January 2002

‡ Officers who have been on the highest available salary for one year have access to a competence-related threshold payment of £1,095 per annum

§ London salary in parentheses (applicable only to officers in the Metropolitan and City of London police forces)

POLICE SERVICES

FORENSIC SCIENCE SERVICE

Headquarters: Trident Court, 2920 Solihull Parkway, Birmingham Business Park, Birmingham B37 7YN
T 0121-329 5200 W www.forensic.gov.uk

The Forensic Science Service (FSS) is a government-owned company which provides forensic science and technology services for UK police forces and other law enforcement agencies. Services are also available to defence lawyers and commercial companies. The FSS employs more than 2,500 staff and operates from 12 facilities across the UK.
Chief Executive, David Werrett, PHD

NATIONAL EXTREMISM TACTICAL COORDINATION UNIT

PO Box 525, Huntingdon PE29 9AL
T 01480-425091 E mailbox@netcu.pnn.police.uk
W www.netcu.org.uk

The National Extremism Tactical Coordination Unit (NETCU) provides the police service of England and Wales and other law enforcement agencies with tactical advice and guidance on policing domestic extremism and associated criminality. The unit also supports organisations and companies that are the targets of domestic extremism campaigns. NETCU is funded by the Home Office and accountable to the Association of Chief Police Officers' Terrorism and Allied Matters Committee.

NATIONAL POLICING IMPROVEMENT AGENCY

4th Floor, 10 Victoria Street, London SW1H 0NN
T 020-7084 8841 W www.npia.police.uk

The National Policing Improvement Agency (NPIA) was established under the Police and Justice Act 2006 and became operational on 1 April 2007. NPIA has taken on the functions of the Police Information Technology Organisation (PITO) and the Central Police Training and Development Authority (CENTREX), which have been abolished. In addition NPIA has assumed responsibility for some Home Office and Association of Chief Police Officers (ACPO) functions which relate directly to policing.

The NPIA is a police-owned body whose remit is to ensure that agreed programmes of reforms are implemented and good practice is applied throughout the police service. It is also responsible for the procurement and deployment of information and communications technology systems to support and improve policing and is active in helping to recruit and train police personnel. The NPIA is charged with improving policing in England and Wales but it is also connected to policing bodies in Scotland and Northern Ireland and collaborates with them on some initiatives.
Chairman, Peter Holland, CBE
Director of Policing Policy and Practice, Deputy Chief Constable Chris Sims

SERIOUS ORGANISED CRIME AGENCY

PO Box 8000, London SE11 5EN W www.soca.gov.uk

The Serious Organised Crime Agency (SOCA) is an executive non-departmental public body sponsored by, but operationally independent from, the Home Office. The agency was formed in April 2006 from the amalgamation of the National Crime Squad, National Criminal Intelligence Service, the part of HM Revenue and Customs responsible for dealing with drug trafficking and associated criminal finance and the part of the UK Immigration Service responsible for dealing with organised immigration crime.

SOCA broadly aims to apportion around 40 per cent of its operational effort in tackling primarily Class A drugs trafficking, around 25 per cent of its capabilities towards organised immigration crime, 10 per cent on individual and private sector fraud and 15 per cent to deal with other organised crime. SOCA works closely with other law enforcement agencies and organisations and the remaining 10 per cent of its capabilities is specifically set aside for assisting its law enforcement partners in achieving their objectives.
Chair (non-executive), Sir Stephen Lander
Director-General, Bill Hughes

UK POLICE NATIONAL MISSING PERSONS BUREAU

Room 209, New Scotland Yard, 10 Broadway, London SW1H 0BG
T 0207-230 4029 E pnmpb.enquiries@met.pnn.police.uk
W www.missingpersons.police.uk

The Police National Missing Persons Bureau (PNMPB) acts as a central clearing house for all missing persons information. The bureau receives information on missing person cases that are still outstanding after 14 days (or earlier if it is felt that some harm may have befallen them), unidentified persons who are unable or unwilling to identify themselves and unidentified bodies or remains within 48 hours of being found with a view to cross-matching the missing against the found. Information is forwarded to the PNMPB from all forces in the UK and from foreign police forces via Interpol. The bureau also manages the Missing Kids website.
W http://uk.missingkids.com

POLICE FORCES

Strength: size of force as known at February 2007
Source: Police and Constabulary Almanac 2007, R. Hazell
& Co.

ENGLAND

For the City of London Police and the Metropolitan
Police Service see London Forces.
AVON AND SOMERSET CONSTABULARY PO Box
37, Portishead, Bristol BS20 8QJ T 0845-456 7000
Strength, 3,380
Chief Constable, C. Port
BEDFORDSHIRE POLICE Woburn Road, Kempston,
Bedford MK43 9AX T 01234-841212 Strength, 1,250
Chief Constable, Gillian Parker, QPM
CAMBRIDGESHIRE CONSTABULARY
Hinchingbrooke Park, Huntingdon PE29 6NP
T 0845-456 4564 Strength, 1,414
Chief Constable, Julie Spence
CHESHIRE CONSTABULARY Clemonds Hey,
Oakmere Road, Winsford CW7 2UA T 01244-350000
Strength, 2,292
Chief Constable, P. Fahy, QPM
CLEVELAND POLICE PO Box 70, Ladgate Lane,
Middlesbrough TS8 9EH T 01642-326326
Strength, 1,728
Chief Constable, Sean Price, QPM
CUMBRIA CONSTABULARY Carleton Hall, Penrith
CA10 2AU T 0845-330 0247 Strength, 1,275
Chief Constable, Michael Baxter, QPM
DERBYSHIRE CONSTABULARY Butterley Hall,
Ripley DE5 3RS T 0845-123 3333 Strength, 2,081
Chief Constable, D. Coleman, QPM
DEVON AND CORNWALL
CONSTABULARY Middlemoor, Exeter EX2 7HQ
T 08452-777444 Strength, 3,485
Chief Constable, Stephen Otter
DORSET POLICE Winfrith, Dorchester DT2 8DZ
T 01929-462727 W www.dorset.police.uk Strength, 1,502
Chief Constable, M. Baker, QPM
DURHAM CONSTABULARY Aykley Heads, Durham
DH1 5TT T 0845-606 0365 Strength, 1,733
Chief Constable, Thomas Stoddart QPM
ESSEX POLICE PO Box 2, Springfield, Chelmsford
CM2 6DA T 01245-491491 W www.essex.police.uk
Strength, 3,159
Chief Constable, R. Baker
GLOUCESTERSHIRE CONSTABULARY
1 Waterwells, Waterwells Drive, Quedgeley, Gloucester
GL2 2AN T 0845-090 1234 Strength, 1,354
Chief Constable, Timothy Brain, QPM, PHD
GREATER MANCHESTER POLICE PO Box 22
Chester House, Boyer Street, Manchester M16 0RE
T 0161-872 5050 Strength, 7,930
Chief Constable, Michael Todd, QPM
HAMPSHIRE CONSTABULARY West Hill,
Winchester SO22 5DB T 0845-045 4545 Strength, 3,812
Chief Constable, Paul Kernaghan, CBE, QPM
HERTFORDSHIRE CONSTABULARY Stanborough
Road, Welwyn Garden City AL8 6XF T 01707-354000
Strength, 2,167
Chief Constable, Frank Whiteley
HUMBERSIDE POLICE Priory Road Police Station,
Priory Road, Hull HU1 5SF T 0845-606 0222 Strength,
2,245
Chief Constable, Tim Hollis, QPM
KENT POLICE Sutton Road, Maidstone ME15 9BZ

T 01622-690690 W www.kent.police.uk Strength, 3,732
Chief Constable, Michael Fuller, QPM
LANCASHIRE CONSTABULARY PO Box 77, Hutton, Nr.
Preston PR4 5SB T 01772-614444 Strength, 3,616
Acting Chief Constable, Stephen Finnigan, QPM
LEICESTERSHIRE CONSTABULARY St John's,
Enderby, Leicester LE19 2BX T 0116-222 2222
W www.leics.police.uk Strength, 2,183
Chief Constable, Matthew Baggott, QPM
LINCOLNSHIRE POLICE PO Box 999, Lincoln
LN5 7PH T 01522-532222 Strength, 1,236
Chief Constable, Tony Lake, QPM
MERSEYSIDE POLICE PO Box 59, Liverpool L69 1JD
T 0151-709 6010 Strength, 4,500
Chief Constable, B. Hogan-Howe, QPM
NORFOLK CONSTABULARY Falconers Chase,
Wymondham, NR18 0WW T 0845-456 4567
Strength, 1,568
Chief Constable, Ian McPherson
NORTHAMPTONSHIRE POLICE Wootton Hall,
Northampton NN4 0JQ T 01604-700700 Strength, 1,347
Chief Constable, Peter Maddison
NORTHUMBRIA POLICE Ponteland, Newcastle upon
Tyne NE20 0BL T 01661-872555 Strength, 4,031
Chief Constable, M. Craik, QPM
NORTH YORKSHIRE POLICE Newby Wiske Hall,
Northallerton DL7 9HA T 0845-606 0247 Strength, 1,633
Chief Constable, Ms. D. Cannings, QPM
NOTTINGHAMSHIRE POLICE Sherwood Lodge,
Arnold, Nottingham NG5 8PP T 0115-967 0999
Strength, 2,484
Chief Constable, S. Green, QPM
SOUTH YORKSHIRE POLICE Snig Hill, Sheffield
S3 8LY T 0114-220 2020 Strength, 3,278
Chief Constable, M. Hughes, QPM
STAFFORDSHIRE POLICE Cannock Road, Stafford
ST17 0QG T 0845-330 2010 Strength, 2,332
Acting Chief Constable, David Swift, QPM
SUFFOLK CONSTABULARY Martlesham Heath,
Ipswich IP5 3QS T 01473-613500 Strength, 1,337
Chief Constable, Alastair McWhirter, QPM
SURREY POLICE Mount Browne, Sandy Lane,
Guildford GU3 1HG T 0845-125 2222
W www.surrey.police.uk Strength, 1,778
Chief Constable, Robert Quick, QPM
SUSSEX POLICE Police Headquarters, Lewes BN7 2DZ
T 0845-607 0999 Strength, 3,123
Chief Constable, Joe Edwards, QPM
THAMES VALLEY POLICE Oxford Road, Kidlington
OX5 2NZ T 0845-8505 505 Strength, 4,275
Chief Constable, Sara Thornton
WARWICKSHIRE POLICE PO Box 4, Leek Wootton,
Warwick CV35 7QB T 01926-415000 Strength, 1,042
Chief Constable, Keith Bristow
WEST MERCIA CONSTABULARY Hindlip Hall,
Hindlip, Worcester WR3 8SP T 08457-444888
W www.westmercia.police.uk Strength, 2,524
Chief Constable, Paul West, QPM
WEST MIDLANDS POLICE PO Box 52, Lloyd House,
Colmore Circus, Queensway, Birmingham B4 6NQ
T 0845-113 5000 Strength, 8,311
Chief Constable, Paul Scott-Lee, QPM
WEST YORKSHIRE POLICE PO Box 9, Wakefield
WF1 3QP T 01924-375222 Strength, 5,732
Chief Constable, Sir Norman Bettison
WILTSHIRE CONSTABULARY London Road, Devizes
SN10 2DN T 0845-408 7000 Strength, 1,259
Chief Constable, Martin Richards

WALES

DYFED-POWYS POLICE PO Box 99, Llangunnor,
Carmarthen SA31 2PF **T** 0845-330 2000 *Strength*, 1,201
Chief Constable, T. Grange, QPM
GWENT POLICE Croesyceiliog, Cwmbran NP44 2XJ
T 01633-838111 **W** www.gwent.police.uk *Strength*, 1,483
Chief Constable, Michael Tonge
NORTH WALES POLICE Glan-y-Don, Colwyn Bay
LL29 8AW **T** 0845-607 1001 *Strength*, 1,649
Chief Constable, R. Brunstrom
SOUTH WALES POLICE Cowbridge Road, Bridgend
CF31 3SU **T** 01656-655555 *Strength*, 3,401
Chief Constable, Barbara Wilding, CBE, QPM

SCOTLAND

CENTRAL SCOTLAND POLICE Randolphfield, Stirling
FK8 2HD **T** 01786-456000
W www.centralscotland.police.uk *Strength*, 827
Chief Constable, Andrew Cameron, QPM
DUMFRIES AND GALLOWAY CONSTABULARY
Cornwall Mount, Dumfries DG1 1PZ **T** 0845-600 5701
W www.dumfriesandgalloway.police.uk *Strength*, 509
Chief Constable, David Strang, QPM
FIFE CONSTABULARY Detroit Road, Glenrothes
KY6 2RJ **T** 01592-418888 **W** www.fife.police.uk *Strength*,
1,046
Chief Constable, Peter Wilson, QPM
GRAMPIAN POLICE Queen Street, Aberdeen
AB10 1ZA **T** 0845-600 5700 **W** www.grampian.police.uk
Strength, 1,399
Chief Constable, Colin McKerracher, QPM
LOTHIAN AND BORDERS POLICE Fettes Avenue,
Edinburgh EH4 1RB **T** 0131-311 3131 **W** www.lbp.police.uk
Strength, 2,848
Chief Constable, Paddy Tomkins
NORTHERN CONSTABULARY Old Perth Road,
Inverness IV2 3SY **T** 01463-715555 *Strength*, 705
Chief Constable, Ian Latimer
STRATHCLYDE POLICE 173 Pitt Street, Glasgow G2 4JS
T 0141-532 2000 **W** www.strathclyde.police.uk
Strength, 7,945
Chief Constable, Sir William Rae, QPM
TAYSIDE POLICE PO Box 59, West Bell Street, Dundee
DD1 9JU **T** 01382-223200 **W** www.tayside.police.uk
Strength, 1,173
Chief Constable, John Vine, QPM

NORTHERN IRELAND

POLICE SERVICE OF NORTHERN IRELAND
Brooklyn, 65 Knock Road, Belfast BT5 6LE **T** 028-9065 0222
W www.psni.police.uk *Strength*, 8,888
Chief Constable, Sir Hugh Orde, OBE

ISLANDS

GUERNSEY POLICE Hospital Lane, St Peter Port, Guernsey
GY1 2QN **T** 01481-725111 *Strength*, 177
Chief Officer, G. Le Page
ISLE OF MAN CONSTABULARY Glencrutchery Road,
Douglas IM2 4RG **T** 01624-631212 *Strength*, 236
Chief Constable, Mike Culverhouse
STATES OF JERSEY POLICE PO Box 789, St Helier,
Jersey JE4 8ZD **T** 01534-612612 **W** www.police.gov.je
Strength, 245
Chief Officer, Graham Power, QPM

LONDON FORCES

CITY OF LONDON POLICE

37 Wood Street, London EC2P 2NQ **T** 020-7601 2222
W www.cityoflondon.police.uk

Strength (February 2007), 856
Though small, the City of London has one of the most
important financial centres in the world and the force has
particular expertise in areas such as fraud investigation as
well as the areas required of any police force. The force
has a wholly elected police authority, the police
committee of the Corporation of London, which appoints
the commissioner.
Commissioner (acting), Mike Bowron
Assistant Commissioner (acting), Frank Armstrong
Commander (acting), Patrick Rice

METROPOLITAN POLICE SERVICE

New Scotland Yard, 8–10 Broadway, London SW1H 0BG
T 020-7230 1212 **W** www.met.police.uk

Strength (February 2007), 31,141
The Metropolitan Police Service is divided into three
main areas for operational purposes:

TERRITORIAL POLICING
Most of the day-to-day policing of London is carried out
by 33 borough operational command units; 32 command
units operate within the same boundaries as the London
borough councils, plus there is an additional unit which is
responsible for policing Heathrow airport.

SPECIALIST OPERATIONS
Specialist Operations is divided into three sections known
as commands:
- *Protection Command* is responsible for the protection and
  security of high-profile persons, key public figures and
  official delegations in the UK and overseas. These
  include the current and former prime ministers, foreign
  dignitaries visiting the UK under the Vienna
  Convention, members of the British royal family and
  visiting European royal families, ambassadors,
  diplomats, MPs, peers and others
- *Security Command* is responsible for aviation security at
  Heathrow and London City airports, including policing
  the terminal buildings and local areas, maintaining an
  effective response to terrorist activity and working with
  the airports, airlines, government departments and
  agencies to prevent crime and dismantle organised
  criminal networks
- *Counter Terrorism Command* is responsible for the
  prevention and disruption of terrorist activity, domestic
  extremism and related offences both within London and
  nationally, providing a bomb disposal capability within
  London, assisting the security services in fulfilling their
  roles and providing a single point of contact for
  international partners in counter-terrorism matters

SPECIALIST CRIME DIRECTORATE
The Specialist Crime Directorate's main areas of focus are
dismantling organised criminal networks and seizing their
assets; safeguarding children and young people from
physical, sexual and emotional abuse; and the
investigation and prevention of homicide.

Commissioner, Sir Ian Blair, QPM
Deputy Commissioner, Paul Stephenson, QPM

Assistant Commissioners, Tarique Ghaffur, CBE, QPM *(Central Operations)*; Tim Godwin, OBE *(Territorial Policing)*; Andy Hayman, CBE, QPM *(Specialist Operations)*; Stephen House, QPM *(Specialist Crime Directorate)*; John Yates, QPM *(Operational Services)* Directors, Ailsa Beaton *(Information)*; Sharon Burd *(Resources (acting))*; Dick Fedorico *(Public Affairs and Internal Communication)*; Stephen Rimmer *(Strategy, Modernisation and Performance)*; Martin Tiplady *(Human Resources)*

SPECIALIST FORCES

BRITISH TRANSPORT POLICE
25–27 Camden Road, London NW1 9LN **T** 020-7388 7541
W www.btp.police.uk

Strength (February 2007), 2,177
British Transport Police is the national police force for the railways in England, Wales and Scotland, including the London Underground system, Docklands Light Railway, Midland Metro Tram system and Croydon Tramlink. The chief constable reports to the British Transport Police Authority. The members of the authority are appointed by the transport secretary and include representatives from the rail industry as well as independent members. Officers are paid the same as other police forces.
Chief Constable, Ian Johnston, CBE, QPM
Deputy Chief Constable, Andy Trotter, QPM

CIVIL NUCLEAR CONSTABULARY
Building F6, Culham Science Centre, Abingdon,
Oxfordshire OX14 3DB **T** 01235-466606 **W** www.cnc.police.uk

Strength (March 2007), 670
The Civil Nuclear Constabulary (CNC) operates under the strategic direction of the Department of Trade and Industry. The CNC is a specialised armed force whose role is the protection of civil nuclear sites and nuclear materials. The constabulary is responsible for policing UK civil nuclear industry facilities and for escorting nuclear material between establishments within the UK and worldwide.
Chief Constable (acting), James Smith
Deputy Chief Constable, James Coupland

MINISTRY OF DEFENCE POLICE
Ministry of Defence Police and Guarding Agency, Wethersfield,
Braintree, Essex CM7 4AZ **T** 01371-854000

Strength (January 2007), 3,917
Part of the Ministry of Defence Police and Guarding Agency, the Ministry of Defence Police is a statutory civil police force with particular responsibility for the security and policing of the MoD environment. It contributes to the physical protection of property and personnel within its jurisdiction and provides a comprehensive police service to the MoD as a whole.
Chief Constable/Chief Executive, Steve Love
Deputy Chief Constable, David Ray, QPM
Director of Resources and Planning, Daniel Applegate
Assistant Chief Constables: Director of Professional Development, R. Chidley; *Director of Operational Support,* J. Bligh; *Director of Divisional Operations,* G McAuley; *Director of Regional Operations (MoD Guard Service),* A. MacCormick

THE SPECIAL CONSTABULARY
The Special Constabulary is a force of trained volunteers who support and work with their local police force for a minimum of four hours a week. Special Constables are thoroughly grounded in the basic aspects of police work, such as self-defence, powers of arrest, common crimes and preparing evidence for court, before they can begin to carry out any police duties. Once they have completed their training, they have the same powers as a regular officer and wear a similar uniform.
W http://specials.homeoffice.gov.uk

STAFF ASSOCIATIONS

Police officers are not permitted to join a trade union or to take strike action. All ranks have their own staff associations.
ASSOCIATION OF CHIEF POLICE OFFICERS OF ENGLAND, WALES AND NORTHERN IRELAND, 10 Victoria Street, London SW1H 0NN **T** 020-7084 8950
Secretary, T. Flaherty

ENGLAND AND WALES
POLICE FEDERATION OF ENGLAND AND WALES, 15–17 Langley Road, Surbiton, Surrey KT6 6LP
T 020-8335 1000 **W** www.polfed.org
General Secretary, John Francis
POLICE SUPERINTENDENTS' ASSOCIATION OF ENGLAND AND WALES, 67A Reading Road, Pangbourne, Reading RG8 7JD **T** 0118-984 4005
National Secretary, Chief Supt. Philip Aspey

SCOTLAND
ASSOCIATION OF CHIEF POLICE OFFICERS IN SCOTLAND, Police Headquarters, 173 Pitt Street, Glasgow G2 4JS **T** 0141-532 2052
E secretariat@acpos.pnn.police.uk
Hon. Secretary, Sir William Rae, QPM
ASSOCIATION OF SCOTTISH POLICE SUPERINTENDENTS, Secretariat, 173 Pitt Street, Glasgow G2 4JS **T** 0141-221 5796
E secretariat@scottishpolicesupers.org.uk
W www.asps.org.uk
General Secretary, Carol Forfar
SCOTTISH POLICE FEDERATION, 5 Woodside Place, Glasgow G3 7QF **T** 0141-332 5234 **W** www.spf.org.uk
General Secretary and Treasurer, Joe Grant

NORTHERN IRELAND
POLICE FEDERATION FOR NORTHERN IRELAND, 77–79 Garnerville Road, Belfast BT4 2NX **T** 028-9076 4200
E office.pfni@btconnect.com **W** www.policefed-ni.org.uk
Secretary (acting), Larry Williams
SUPERINTENDENTS' ASSOCIATION OF NORTHERN IRELAND, PSNI College, Garnerville Road, Belfast BT4 2NX **T** 028-9092 2201 **E** mail@psani.org
W www.psani.org
Hon. Secretary, Supt. G. Thomson

THE PRISON SERVICE

The prison services in the United Kingdom are the responsibility of the Secretary of State for Justice, the Scottish Executive Justice Department and the Secretary of State for Northern Ireland. The chief directors-general (chief executive in Scotland, director in Northern Ireland), officers of the Prison Service, the Scottish Prison Service and the Northern Ireland Prison Service are responsible for the day-to-day running of the system.

There are 140 prison establishments in England and Wales, 15 in Scotland and three in Northern Ireland. Convicted prisoners are classified according to their assessed security risk and are housed in establishments appropriate to that level of security. There are no open prisons in Northern Ireland. Female prisoners are housed in women's establishments or in separate wings of mixed prisons. Remand prisoners are, where possible, housed separately from convicted prisoners. Offenders under the age of 21 are usually detained in a Young Offender Institution, which may be a separate establishment or part of a prison. Appellant and failed asylum seekers are held in Immigration Removal Centres, or in separate units of other prisons.

Eleven prisons are now run by the private sector, and in England, Wales and Scotland all escort services have been contracted out to private companies. In Scotland, one prison (Kilmarnock) was built and financed by the private sector and is being operated by private contractors.

There are independent prison inspectorates in England, Wales and Scotland which report annually on conditions and the treatment of prisoners. The Chief Inspector of Criminal Justice in Northern Ireland and HM Chief Inspector of Prisons for England and Wales perform an inspectorate role for prisons in Northern Ireland. Every prison establishment also has an independent monitoring board made up of local volunteers.

Any prisoner whose complaint is not satisfied by the internal complaints procedures may complain to the prisons ombudsman for England and Wales, the Scottish Prisons Complaints Commission or the prisoner ombudsman for Northern Ireland.

The 11 private sector prisons in England and Wales are the direct responsibility of the chief executive of the National Offender Management Service (NOMS). The NOMS was created in January 2004, in order to integrate prisons and probation into a system whereby end-to-end management of offenders is provided; this is expected to reduce re-offending and cut the growth rate of the prison population. The chief executive, Helen Edwards, also has responsibility for public prisons, the National Probation Service, the Youth Justice Board and NOMS policy. In May 2007 NOMS was amalgamated into the Ministry of Justice. The prisons and probation inspectors, the prisons ombudsman and the independent monitoring boards report to the home secretary.

PRISON STATISTICS

PRISON POPULATION (UK)
as at April 2007
The projected 'high scenario' prison population for 2013 in England and Wales is 106,550; the 'low scenario' is 90,250.

	Remand	Sentenced	Other
ENGLAND AND WALES			
Male	11,859	62,591	1,441
Female	918	3,403	49
Total	12,777	65,994	1,490
SCOTLAND*			
Male	1,159	5,364	2
Female	83	251	—
Total	1,242	5,614	2
N. IRELAND			
Male	510	920	—
Female	17	27	—
Total	527	947	—
UK TOTAL	14,546	72,555	1,492

* Figures for Scotland are an average for 2005–6
Sources: Home Office – *Research Development Statistics*; Scottish Prison Service – *Annual Report and Accounts 2005–6*; Northern Ireland Prison Service – www.niprisonservice.gov.uk

SENTENCED PRISON POPULATION BY SEX AND OFFENCE (ENGLAND AND WALES)
as at April 2007

	Male	Female
Violence against the person	17,014	684
Sexual offences	7,240	46
Burglary	7,810	206
Robbery	8,297	304
Theft, handling	3,433	441
Fraud and forgery	1,515	242
Drugs offences	9,639	1,038
Motoring offences	1,608	26
Other offences	5,646	383
Offence not recorded	319	25
*Total**	62,521	3,395

* Figures do not include civil (non-criminal) prisoners or fine defaulters
Source: Home Office – *Research Development Statistics*

SENTENCED POPULATION BY LENGTH OF SENTENCE (ENGLAND AND WALES)
as at April 2007

	Adults	Young offenders
Less than 12 months	6,091	2,022
12 months to less than 4 years	18,042	4,775
4 years to less than life	24,077	1,787
Life	8,494	630
*Total**	56,704	9,214

* Figures do not include civil (non-criminal) prisoners or fine defaulters
Source: Home Office – *Research Development Statistics*

AVERAGE DAILY SENTENCED POPULATION BY LENGTH
OF SENTENCE 2005–6 (SCOTLAND)

	Adults	Young offenders
Less than 4 years	2,266	460
4 years or over (including life)	2,723	165
Total	4,989	625

Source: Scottish Prison Service – Annual Report and Accounts 2005–6

SELF-INFLICTED DEATHS IN PRISON APRIL 2006 –
MARCH 2007 (ENGLAND AND WALES)

Men	68
Women	5
Total	73
Rate per 100,000 prisoners in custody	95.5

Source: Home Office – Research Development Statistics

OPERATING COSTS OF PRISON SERVICE IN ENGLAND
AND WALES 2006–7

Staff costs	£1,586,126,000
Other operating costs	£649,184,000
Operating income	(£299,026,000)
Net operating costs for the year	£1,936,284,000
Average cost per prisoner place	£28,734

Source: HM Prison Service – Annual Report and Accounts 2006–7

OPERATING COSTS OF SCOTTISH PRISON SERVICE
2006–7

Total income	(£2,140,000)
Total expenditure	£264,753,000
Staff costs	£131,984,000
Running costs	£90,947,000
Other current expenditure	£41,822,000
Operating cost	£262,613,000
Cost of capital charges	£18,840,000
Interest payable and similar charges	£16,000
Interest receivable	(£8,000)
Net operating cost	£281,461,000

Source: Scottish Prison Service – Annual Report and Accounts 2006–7

OPERATING COSTS OF NORTHERN IRELAND PRISON
SERVICE 2006–7

Staff costs	£89,443,000
Net running costs	£29,319,000
Depreciation	£8,921,000
Finance charges	£6,231,000
Impairment of fixed assets	£1,804,000
Operating expenditure	£135,718,000
Other current expenditure	£930,000
Net operating costs for the year	£136,648,000

Source: Northern Ireland Prison Service – Annual Report and Accounts 2006–7

THE PRISON SERVICES

HM PRISON SERVICE

Cleland House, Page Street, London SW1P 4LN
T 0870-000 1397 E public.enquiries@hmps.gsi.gov.uk
W www.hmprisonservice.gov.uk

SALARIES
from 1 April 2007

Senior Manager A	£60,442–£78,732
Senior Manager B	£55,528–£76,796
Senior Manager C	£53,357–£69,157
Senior Manager D	£44,589–£63,535
Manager E	£29,184–£43,927
Manager F	£26,280–£37,262
Manager G	£23,434–£30,676

THE PRISON SERVICE MANAGEMENT
Director-General (SCS), Phil Wheatley, CB
Deputy Director-General (SCS), Michael Spurr
Director of High Security Prisons (SCS), Steve Wagstaffe
Director of Operational Policy (SCS), Ian Poree
Director of Finance (SCS), Ann Beasley
Director of Personnel (SCS), Robin Wilkinson
Director of Prison Health (SCS), Richard Bradshaw
Board Secretary and Head of Secretariat (SMB), Ken Everett
Legal Adviser, Andrew Dodsworth
Media Relations, Simon Watts
Race Equality Adviser, Beverley Thompson

AREA MANAGERS
Phil Copple (North-East); Ian Lockwood (North-West); Tony Hassall (Yorkshire and Humberside); Bob Perry (East Midlands); Geoff Hughes (Wales); Sue McAllister (West Midlands); Danny McAllister (Eastern); Alan Scott South-West); Nick Pascoe (London); Colin McConnell (South Central); Adrian Smith (Kent and Sussex); Michelle Jaran-Howe (Contracted Prisons)

PRISON ESTABLISHMENTS – ENGLAND AND WALES

POPULATION STATISTICS
as at 15 June 2007

Male prisoners	76,140
Female prisoners	4,398
Number of prisoners held in police cells under Operation Safeguard	413
Total	80,951
Useable operational capacity	81,058
Spaces available under Operation Safeguard*	400
Total	81,458
Number under home detention curfew supervision	2,296

* These vary from night to night and up to a 400 place ceiling

PRISON ESTABLISHMENTS KEY
* Women's establishment or establishment with units for women
† Remand Centre (other establishments may contain units for remand prisoners)
‡ Young Offender Institution or establishment with units for young offenders
§ Immigration Removal Centre or establishment with units for immigration detainees

as at April 2007

ACKLINGTON, nr. Morpeth, Northumberland NE65 9XF *Prisoners,* 849 *Governor,* Mick Lees

ALBANY, 55 Parkhurst Road, Newport, Isle of Wight PO30 5RS *Prisoners,* 525 *Governor,* Mel Jones

†‡ALTCOURSE (private prison), Higher Lane, Fazakerley, Liverpool L9 7LH *Prisoners,* 1,105 *Director,* John McLaughlin

†‡ASHFIELD (private prison), Shortwood Road, Pucklechurch, Bristol BS16 9QJ *Prisoners,* 386 *Director,* Vicky O'Dea

ASHWELL, Oakham, Rutland, Leics LE15 7LF *Prisoners,* 544 *Governor (acting),* Deborah McGivern

*ASKHAM GRANGE, Askham Richard, York YO23 3FT *Prisoners,* 99 *Governor,* Alec McCrystal

‡AYLESBURY, Bierton Road, Aylesbury, Bucks HP20 1EH *Prisoners,* 443 *Governor,* David Kennedy

‡BEDFORD, St Loyes Street, Bedford MK40 1HG *Prisoners,* 478 *Governor,* Paul Kempster

‡BELMARSH, Western Way, Thamesmead, London SE28 0EB *Prisoners,* 919 *Governor,* Claudia Sturt

‡BIRMINGHAM, Winson Green Road, Birmingham B18 4AS *Prisoners,* 1,452 *Governor,* Mike Shann

‡BLAKENHURST, Hewell Lane, Redditch, Worcs B97 6QS *Prisoners,* 1,070 *Governor,* Terry Witton

BLANTYRE HOUSE, Horden, Goudhurst, Kent TN17 2NH *Prisoners,* 120 *Governor,* Dave Atkinson

BLUNDESTON, Lowestoft, Suffolk NR32 5BG *Prisoners,* 464 *Governor,* Paul Cawkwell

†‡BRINSFORD, New Road, Featherstone, Wolverhampton WV10 7PY *Prisoners,* 476 *Governor,* Pete Knapton

‡BRISTOL, 19 Cambridge Road, Horfield, Bristol BS7 8PS *Prisoners,* 607 *Governor,* Suzy Dymond-White

‡BRIXTON, Jebb Avenue, London SW2 5XF *Prisoners,* 806 *Governor,* Paul McDowell

*†‡BROCKHILL, Hewell Lane, Redditch, Worcs B97 6RD *Prisoners,* 169 *Governor,* Alison Gomme

*‡BRONZEFIELD (private prison), Woodthorpe Road, Ashford, Middlesex TW15 3JZ *Prisoners,* 447 *Director,* Janine McDowell

*†‡BUCKLEY HALL, Buckley Hall Road, Rochdale, Lancs OL12 9DP *Prisoners,* 384 *Governor,* Mick Regan

‡BULLINGDON, PO Box 50, Bicester, Oxon OX25 1WD *Prisoners,* 961 *Governor,* Phil Taylor

*‡BULLWOOD HALL, High Road, Hockley, Essex SS5 4TE *Prisoners,* 182 *Governor,* Roger Plant

CAMP HILL, Newport, Isle of Wight PO30 5PB *Prisoners,* 594 *Governor,* Ian Young

CANTERBURY, 46 Longport, Canterbury, Kent CT1 1PJ *Prisoners,* 276 *Governor,* Chris Bartlett

‡CARDIFF, Knox Road, Cardiff CF24 0UG *Prisoners,* 760 *Governor,* Sian West

‡CASTINGTON, Morpeth, Northumberland NE65 9XG *Prisoners,* 385 *Governor,* Bill Shaw

CHANNINGS WOOD, Denbury, Newton Abbott, Devon TQ12 6DW *Prisoners,* 658 *Governor,* Jeannine Hendrick

†‡CHELMSFORD, 200 Springfield Road, Chelmsford, Essex CM2 6LQ *Prisoners,* 723 *Governor,* Nigel Smith

COLDINGLEY, Shaftesbury Road, Bisley, Woking, Surrey GU24 9EX *Prisoners,* 390 *Governor,* John Robinson

*COOKHAM WOOD, Rochester, Kent ME1 3LU *Prisoners,* 186 *Governor,* Ed Tullet

DARTMOOR, Princetown, Yelverton, Devon PL20 6RR *Prisoners,* 629 *Governor,* Serena Watts

‡DEERBOLT, Bowes Road, Barnard Castle, Co. Durham DL12 9BG *Prisoners,* 403 *Governor,* Debra Baldwin

†‡DONCASTER (private prison), off North Bridge Road, Marshgate, Doncaster DN5 8UX *Prisoners,* 1,142 *Director,* Brian Anderson

‡DORCHESTER, North Square, Dorchester, Dorset DT1 1JD *Prisoners,* 245 *Governor,* Tony Corcoran

DOVEGATE (private prison), Uttoxeter, Staffs ST14 8XR *Prisoners,* 833 *Director,* Wyn Jones

DOVER, The Citadel, Western Heights, Dover, Kent CT17 9DR *Prisoners,* 309 *Governor,* Jim Carmichael

*DOWNVIEW, Sutton Lane, Sutton, Surrey SM2 5PD *Prisoners,* 353 *Governor,* Ian Murray

*DRAKE HALL, Eccleshall, Staffs ST21 6LQ *Prisoners,* 246 *Governor,* John Huntington

*‡DURHAM, Old Elvet, Durham DH1 3HU *Prisoners,* 975 *Governor,* Alan Tallentire

*EAST SUTTON PARK, Sutton Valence, Maidstone, Kent ME17 3DF *Prisoners,* 100 *Governor,* Ed Tullett

*†‡EASTWOOD PARK, Falfield, Wotton-under-Edge, Glos GL12 8DB *Prisoners,* 348 *Governor,* Tim Beeston

†EDMUNDS HILL, Stradishall, Newmarket, Suffolk CB8 9YN *Prisoners,* 366 *Governor,* Norma Harrington

†‡ELMLEY, Church Road, Eastchurch, Sheerness, Kent ME12 4DZ *Prisoners,* 986 *Governor,* Helen Rinaldi

ERLESTOKE, Devizes, Wilts SN10 5TU *Prisoners,* 418 *Governor,* Doug Moon

EVERTHORPE, Beck Road, Brough, E. Yorks HU15 1RB *Prisoners,* 678 *Governor,* Gary Monaghan

‡EXETER, 30 New North Road, Exeter, Devon EX4 4EX *Prisoners,* 495 *Governor,* Mark Flinton

FEATHERSTONE, New Road, Featherstone, Wolverhampton WV10 7PU *Prisoners,* 609 *Governor,* Simon Cartwright

†‡FELTHAM, Bedfont Road, Feltham, Middx TW13 4ND *Prisoners,* 629 *Governor,* vacant

FORD, Arundel, W. Sussex BN18 0BX *Prisoners,* 457 *Governor,* Fiona Radford

‡FOREST BANK (private prison), Agecroft Road, Pendlebury, Manchester M27 8FB *Prisoners,* 1,060 *Director,* Ivor Woods

*‡FOSTON HALL, Foston, Derby DE65 5DN *Prisoners,* 241 *Governor,* Paddy Scriven

FRANKLAND, Brasside, Durham DH1 5YD *Prisoners,* 714 *Governor,* Bob Mullen

FULL SUTTON, York YO41 1PS *Prisoners,* 582 *Governor,* Steve Tilley

GARTH, Ulnes Walton Lane, Leyland, Preston PR26 8NE *Prisoners,* 611 *Governor,* Terry Williams

GARTREE, Gallow Field Road, Market Harborough, Leics LE16 7RP *Prisoners,* 575 *Governor,* Julia Morgan

†‡GLEN PARVA, 10 Tigers Road, Wigston, Leicester LE18 4TN *Prisoners,* 810 *Governor,* Alison Perry

‡GLOUCESTER, Barrack Square, Gloucester GL1 2JN *Prisoners,* 306 *Governor,* David Chalmers

GRENDON, Grendon Underwood, Bucks HP18 0TL *Prisoners,* 547 *Governor,* Dr Peter Bennett

‡GUYS MARSH, Shaftesbury, Dorset SP7 0AH *Prisoners,* 562 *Governor,* Barry Greenberry

§HASLAR, 2 Dolphin Way, Gosport, Hampshire PO12 2AW *Prisoners,* 119 *Manager,* Julia Killick

HAVERIGG, Millom, Cumbria LA18 4NA *Prisoners,* 568 *Governor,* Clive Chatterton

HEWELL GRANGE, Redditch, Worcs B97 6QQ *Prisoners,* 181 *Governor,* Alison Gomme

†‡HIGH DOWN, High Down Lane, Sutton, Surrey SM2 5PJ *Prisoners,* 762 *Governor,* Peter Dawson

†‡HIGHPOINT, Stradishall, Newmarket, Suffolk CB8 9YG *Prisoners,* 812 *Governor,* Sue Doolan

†‡HINDLEY, Gibson Street, Bickershaw, Wigan, Lancs WN2 5TH *Prisoners,* 493 *Governor,* Ray Hill

‡HOLLESLEY BAY, Woodbridge, Suffolk IP12 3JW *Prisoners,* 305 *Governor,* Declan Moore

*†‡HOLLOWAY, Parkhurst Road, London N7 0NU *Prisoners,* 441 *Governor,* Sue Saunders

HOLME HOUSE, Holme House Road, Stockton-on-Tees TS18 2QU *Prisoners,* 1,002 *Governor,* Matt Spencer

‡HULL, Hedon Road, Hull HU9 5LS *Prisoners,* 1,055 *Governor,* Paul Foweather

‡HUNTERCOMBE, Nuffield, Henley-on-Thames, Oxon RG9 5SB *Prisoners,* 362 *Governor,* Kevin Leggett

KENNET, Parkbourn, Maghull, Liverpool, Merseyside L31 1HX *Prisoners,* 350 *Governor,* Steve Lawrence

KINGSTON, 122 Milton Road, Portsmouth PO3 6AS *Prisoners,* 198 *Governor,* Ian Telfer

KIRKHAM, Freckleton Road, Kirkham, Preston, Lancs PR4 2RN *Prisoners,* 508 *Governor,* John Hewitson

KIRKLEVINGTON GRANGE, Yarm, Cleveland TS15 9PA *Prisoners,* 222 *Governor,* Alan Richer

LANCASTER, The Castle, Lancaster LA1 1YL *Prisoners,* 237 *Governor,* Peter Francis

†‡LANCASTER FARMS, Far Moor Lane, Stone Row Head, Off Quernmore Road, Lancaster LA1 3QZ *Prisoners,* 512 *Governor,* Paul Holland

LATCHMERE HOUSE, Church Road, Ham Common, Richmond, Surrey TW10 5HH *Prisoners,* 207 *Governor,* Steve Metcalf

LEEDS, 2 Gloucester Terrace, Stanningley Road, Leeds LS12 2TJ *Prisoners,* 1,019 *Governor,* Rob Kellet

LEICESTER, Welford Road, Leicester LE2 7AJ *Prisoners,* 362 *Governor,* Danny Mulligan

‡LEWES, Brighton Road, Lewes, E. Sussex BN7 1EA *Prisoners,* 532 *Governor,* Eoin McLennan-Murray

LEYHILL, Wotton-under-Edge, Glos GL12 8BT *Prisoners,* 432 *Governor,* Mick Bell

‡LINCOLN, Greetwell Road, Lincoln LN2 4BD *Prisoners,* 534 *Governor,* Lynne Saunders

LINDHOLME, Bawtry Road, Hatfield Woodhouse, Doncaster DN7 6EE *Prisoners,* 1,015 *Governor,* Martin Ward

LITTLEHEY, Perry, Huntingdon, Cambs PE28 0SR *Prisoners,* 697 *Governor,* David Taylor

‡LIVERPOOL, 68 Hornby Road, Liverpool L9 3DF *Prisoners,* 1,347 *Governor,* Alan Brown

LONG LARTIN, South Littleton, Evesham, Worcs WR11 8TZ *Prisoners,* 442 *Governor,* Ferdie Parker

*†‡LOW NEWTON, Brasside, Durham DH1 5YA *Prisoners,* 262 *Governor,* Paddy Fox

LOWDHAM GRANGE (private prison), Lowdham, Notts NG14 7DA *Prisoners,* 609 *Director,* Guy Baulf

MAIDSTONE, 36 County Road, Maidstone, Kent ME14 1UZ *Prisoners,* 575 *Governor,* Jane Galbally

MANCHESTER, 1 Southall Street, Manchester M60 9AH *Prisoners,* 1,247 *Governor,* Chris Sheffield

‡MOORLAND CLOSED, Bawtry Road, Hatfield Woodhouse, Doncaster DN7 6BW *Prisoners,* 784 *Governor,* Jacqui Tilley

‡MOORLAND OPEN, Thorne Road, Hatfield, Doncaster DN7 6EL *Prisoners,* 222 *Governor,* Jacqui Tilley

*MORTON HALL, Swinderby, Lincoln LN6 9PT *Prisoners,* 297 *Governor,* Susan Howard

THE MOUNT, Molyneaux Avenue, Bovingdon, Hemel Hempstead, Herts HP3 0NZ *Prisoners,* 719 *Governor,* Damian Evans

*†‡NEW HALL, Dial Wood, Flockton, Wakefield, W. Yorks WF4 4XX *Prisoners,* 371 *Governor,* Sara Snell

NORTH SEA CAMP, Freiston, Boston, Lincs PE22 0QX *Prisoners,* 303 *Governor,* Norman Warwick

‡NORTHALLERTON, East Road, Northallerton, N. Yorks DL6 1NW *Prisoners,* 244 *Governor,* Norman Griffin

†‡NORWICH, Knox Road, Norwich, Norfolk NR1 4LU *Prisoners,* 611 *Governor,* James Shanley

NOTTINGHAM, Perry Road, Sherwood, Nottingham NG5 3AG *Prisoners,* 550 *Governor,* Tom Wheatley

‡ONLEY, Willoughby, Rugby, Warks CV23 8AP *Prisoners,* 619 *Governor,* Robin Eldridge

†‡PARC (private prison), Heol Hopcyn John, Bridgend, S. Wales CF35 6AR *Prisoners,* 1,128 *Director,* Janet Wallsgrove

‡PARKHURST, Newport, Isle of Wight PO30 5NX *Prisoners,* 525 *Governor,* Carole Draper

‡PENTONVILLE, Caledonian Road, London N7 8TT *Prisoners,* 1,155 *Governor,* Nick Leader

*‡PETERBOROUGH (private prison), Saville Road, Westfield, Peterborough PE3 7PD *Prisoners,* 576 *Director,* Mike Conway

‡PORTLAND, Easton, Portland, Dorset DT5 1DL *Prisoners,* 447 *Governor,* Steve Holland

‡PRESCOED, Coed-y-Paen, Pontypool, Monmouthshire NP4 0TB *Prisoners,* 170 *Governor,* David Ward

‡PRESTON, 2 Ribbleton Lane, Preston, Lancs PR1 5AB *Prisoners,* 737 *Governor,* Richard Vince

RANBY, Retford, Notts DN22 8EU *Prisoners,* 1,024 *Governor,* Louise Taylor

†‡READING, Forbury Road, Reading, Berks RG1 3HY *Prisoners,* 262 *Governor,* Pauline Bryant

RISLEY, Warrington Road, Risley, Warrington, Cheshire WA3 6BP *Prisoners,* 1,081 *Governor,* Bob McColm

‡ROCHESTER, 1 Fort Road, Rochester, Kent ME1 3QS *Prisoners,* 388 *Governor (acting),* John Wilson

RYE HILL (private prison), Willoughby, nr. Rugby, Warks CV23 8SZ *Prisoners,* 646 *Director,* Dave McDonnell

*SEND, Ripley Road, Woking, Surrey GU23 7LJ *Prisoners,* 208 *Governor,* Brian Ritchie

SHEPTON MALLET, Cornhill, Shepton Mallet, Somerset BA4 5LU *Prisoners,* 188 *Governor,* Nick Evans

‡SHREWSBURY, The Dana, Shrewsbury, Shropshire SY1 2HR *Prisoners,* 338 *Governor,* Gerry Hendry

SPRING HILL, Grendon Underwood, nr. Aylesbury, Bucks HP18 0TL *Prisoners,* 314 *Governor,* Dr Peter Bennett

STAFFORD, 54 Gaol Road, Stafford ST16 3AW *Prisoners,* 672 *Governor,* Peter Small

STANDFORD HILL, Church Road, Eastchurch, Sheerness, Kent ME12 4AA *Prisoners,* 419 *Governor,* Kieron Taylor

STOCKEN, Stocken Hall Road, Stretton, nr. Oakham, Leics LE15 7RD *Prisoners,* 621 *Governor,* Steve Turner

‡STOKE HEATH, Market Drayton, Shropshire TF9 2JL *Prisoners,* 661 *Governor,* Teresa Clarke

*†‡STYAL, Wilmslow, Cheshire SK9 4HR *Prisoners,* 432 *Governor,* Steve Hall

SUDBURY, Ashbourne, Derbyshire DE6 5HW *Prisoners,* 500 *Governor,* Chris Davidson

SWALESIDE, Brabazon Road, Eastchurch, Isle of Sheppey, Kent ME12 4AX *Prisoners,* 776 *Governor,* Stephen O'Connell

‡SWANSEA, 200 Oystermouth Road, Swansea SA1 3SR *Prisoners,* 419 *Governor,* Andrea Whitfield

‡SWINFEN HALL, Lichfield, Staffs WS14 9QS *Prisoners*, 618 *Governor*, Tom Watson

‡THORN CROSS, Arley Road, Appleton Thorn, Warrington, Cheshire WA4 4RL *Prisoners*, 223 *Governor*, Derek Harrison

USK, 47 Maryport Street, Usk, Monmouthshire NP15 1XP *Prisoners*, 394 *Governor*, David Ward

THE VERNE, Portland, Dorset DT5 1EQ *Prisoners*, 590 *Governor*, Denise Hodder

WAKEFIELD, 5 Love Lane, Wakefield, West Yorks WF2 9AG *Prisoners*, 745 *Governor*, David Thompson

‡WANDSWORTH, PO Box 757, Heathfield Road, London SW18 3HS *Prisoners*, 1,482 *Governor*, Ian Mulholland

‡WARREN HILL, Hollesley, Woodbridge, Suffolk IP12 3JW *Prisoners*, 217 *Governor*, Ken Kan

WAYLAND, Griston, Thetford, Norfolk IP25 6RL *Prisoners*, 697 *Governor*, Michael Wood

WEALSTUN, Wetherby, W. Yorks LS23 7AZ *Prisoners*, 796 *Governor*, Amy Rice

WELLINGBOROUGH, Millers Park, Doddington Road, Wellingborough, Northants NN8 2NH *Prisoners*, 643 *Governor*, Peter Siddons

‡WERRINGTON, Stoke-on-Trent ST9 0DX *Prisoners*, 156 *Governor*, Frank Flynn

‡WETHERBY, York Road, Wetherby, W. Yorks LS22 5ED *Prisoners*, 323 *Governor*, Will Styles

WHATTON, 14 Cromwell Road, Whatton, Nottingham NG13 9FQ *Prisoners*, 755 *Governor*, Peter Wright

WHITEMOOR, Longhill Road, March, Cambs PE15 0PR *Prisoners*, 448 *Governor*, Steve Rodford

WINCHESTER, Romsey Road, Winchester SO22 5DF *Prisoners*, 544 *Governor*, Andy Lattimore

WOLDS (private prison), Everthorpe, Brough, E. Yorks HU15 2JZ *Prisoners*, 373 *Director*, Dave McDonnell

†‡§WOODHILL, Tattenhoe Street, Milton Keynes, Bucks MK4 4DA *Prisoners*, 826 *Governor*, Luke Serjeant

†WORMWOOD SCRUBS, PO Box 757, Du Cane Road, London W12 0AE *Prisoners*, 1,289 *Governor*, Steve Metcalf

WYMOTT, Ulnes Walton Lane, Leyland, Preston PR26 8LW *Prisoners*, 1,064 *Governor*, Jayne Blake

SCOTTISH PRISON SERVICE (SPS)

Calton House, 5 Redheughs Rigg, Edinburgh EH12 9HW
T 0131-244 8747 E gaolinfo@sps.gov.uk
W www.sps.gov.uk

SALARIES 2007–8

Senior managers in the Scottish Prison Service, including governors and deputy governors of prisons, are paid across three pay bands:

Band I	£50,823–£63,317
Band H	£40,341–£52,465
Band G	£31,765–£43,624

SPS BOARD

Chief Executive, Mike Ewart

Directors, Rachel Gwyon *(Corporate Services)*; Willie Pretswell *(Finance and Business Services)*; Dr Andrew Fraser *(Health and Care)*; Barbara Allison *(Human Resources)*; Eric Murch *(Partnerships and Commissioning)*; Mike Duffy *(Prisons)*

Non-Executive Directors, Bill Carr; Eric Jackson; Elinor Smith

PRISON ESTABLISHMENTS

Average prisoner numbers 2005–6

*ABERDEEN, Craiginches, 4 Grampian Place, Aberdeen AB11 8FN *Prisoners*, 225 *Governor*, Mike Inglis

†BARLINNIE, Glasgow G33 2QX *Prisoners*, 1,195 *Governor*, Bill McKinlay

CASTLE HUNTLY, Longforgan, Dundee DD2 5HL *Prisoners* 155 *Governor*, Ian Whitehead

*‡CORNTON VALE, Cornton Road, Stirling FK9 5NU *Prisoners*, 246 *Governor*, Ian Gunn

†DUMFRIES, Terregles Street, Dumfries DG2 9AX *Prisoners*, 182 *Governor*, Nigel Ironside

‡EDINBURGH, 33 Stenhouse Road, Edinburgh EH11 3LN *Prisoners*, 701 *Governor*, Dan Gunn

GLENOCHIL, King O'Muir Road, Tullibody FK10 3AD *Prisoners*, 485 *Governor*, Audrey Park

‡GREENOCK, Gateside, Greenock PA16 9AH *Prisoners*, 323 *Governor*, Tony Simpson

*INVERNESS, Porterfield, Inverness IV2 3HH *Prisoners*, 150 *Governor*, Eric Fairbairn

‡KILMARNOCK (private prison), Bowhouse, Kilmarnock KA1 5AA *Prisoners*, 583 *Director*, Wendy Sinclair

NORANSIDE, Fern By Forfar, Angus DD8 3QY *Prisoners*, 135 *Governor*, Ian Whitehead

PERTH, 3 Edinburgh Road, Perth PH2 8AT *Prisoners*, 655 *Governor*, Kate Donegan

PETERHEAD, Aberdeenshire AB42 2YY *Prisoners*, 298 *Governor*, vacant

‡POLMONT, Falkirk FK2 0AB *Prisoners*, 632 *Governor*, Derek McGill

SHOTTS, Canthill Road, Lanarkshire ML7 4LE *Prisoners*, 515 *Governor*, Rona Sweeney

NORTHERN IRELAND PRISON SERVICE

Dundonald House, Upper Newtownards Road, Belfast BT4 3SU
T 028-9052 2922
E info@niprisonservice.gov.uk
W www.niprisonservice.gov.uk

SALARIES 2006–7

Governor 1	£66,638–£71,823
Governor 2	£60,612–£64,351
Governor 3	£52,448–£55,962
Governor 4	£45,612–£49,401
Governor 5	£40,066–£44,934

SENIOR STAFF

Director, Robin Masefield, CBE

Deputy Directors, Mark McGuckin *(Finance and Personnel)*; Max Murray *(Operations)*; Anne McCleary *(Services)*

Associate Director of Health and Healthcare, Philip McClements

PRISON ESTABLISHMENTS

*‡§HYDEBANK WOOD, Hospital Road, Belfast BT8 8NA *Governor*, Stephen Davis

§MAGHABERRY, Old Road, Ballinderry Upper, Lisburn, Co. Antrim BT28 2NF *Governor*, Alan Longwell

MAGILLIGAN, Point Road, Limavady, Co. Londonderry BT49 0LR *Governor*, Tom Woods

DEFENCE

The armed forces of the United Kingdom comprise the Royal Navy, the Army and the Royal Air Force (RAF). The Queen is Commander-in-Chief of all the armed forces. The Secretary of State for Defence is responsible for the formulation and content of defence policy and for providing the means by which it is conducted. The formal legal basis for the conduct of defence in the UK rests on a range of powers vested by statute and Letters Patent in the Defence Council, chaired by the Secretary of State for Defence. Beneath the ministers lies the top management of the Ministry of Defence (MoD), headed jointly by the Permanent Secretary and the Chief of Defence Staff. The Permanent Secretary is the government's principal civilian adviser on defence and has the primary responsibility for policy, finance, management and administration. He is also personally accountable to parliament for the expenditure of all public money allocated to defence purposes. The Chief of the Defence Staff is the professional head of the armed forces in the UK and the principal military adviser to the secretary of state and the government.

The Defence Management Board (DMB) is the executive board of the Defence Council. Chaired by the Permanent Secretary, it acts as the main executive board of the Ministry of Defence, providing senior level leadership and strategic management of defence.

The Central Staff, headed by the Vice-Chief of the Defence Staff and the Second Permanent Under-Secretary of State, is the policy core of the department. Defence Equipment and Support, headed by the Chief of Defence Material, is responsible for purchasing defence equipment and providing logistical support to the armed forces.

A permanent Joint Headquarters for the conduct of joint operations was set up at Northwood in 1996. The Joint Headquarters connects the policy and strategic functions of the MoD head office with the conduct of operations and is intended to strengthen the policy/executive division.

The UK pursues its defence and security policies through its membership of NATO (to which most of its armed forces are committed), the European Union, the Organisation for Security and Cooperation in Europe and the UN (*see* International Organisations section).

STRENGTH OF THE ARMED FORCES

	Royal Navy	Army	RAF	All Services
1975 strength	76,200	167,100	95,000	338,300
1990 strength	63,210	152,810	89,680	305,700
2001 strength	42,420	109,530	53,700	205,650
2002 strength	41,630	110,050	53,000	204,680
2003 strength	41,550	112,130	53,240	206,920
2004 strength	40,880	112,750	53,390	207,020
2005 strength	39,940	109,290	51,870	201,100
2006 strength	39,390	107,730	48,730	195,850
2007 strength	38,860*	106,200	45,360*	190,420*

* provisional figures
Source: MoD Defence Analytical Services Agency *National Statistics* (Crown copyright)

SERVICE PERSONNEL BY RANK AND GENDER

	Officers		Other ranks	
	Males	*Females*	*Males*	*Females*
All services	28,410*	3,720*	144,330*	13,960*
Royal Navy	6,900*	680*	28,310*	2,970*
Army	13,040	1,640	84,940	6,590
RAF	8,480*	1,410*	31,080*	4,400*

* provisional figures
Source: MoD Defence Analytical Services Agency *National Statistics* (Crown copyright)

UK regular forces include trained and untrained personnel and nursing services, but exclude Gurkhas, full-time reserve service personnel, the home service battalions of the Royal Irish Regiment, mobilised reservists and naval activated reservists. As at 1 June 2007 these groups number:

All Gurkhas	3,710
Full-time reserve service	1,570*
Royal Irish Regiment (Home Service)	1,230
Mobilised reservists	
Army	1,140
RAF	230*
Naval activated reservists	150*

* provisional figures
Source: MoD Defence Analytical Services Agency *National Statistics* (Crown copyright)

CIVILIAN PERSONNEL

1993 level	159,600
2000 level	121,300
2001 level	118,200
2002 level	110,100
2003 level	107,600
2004 level	108,990
2005 level	107,680
2006 level	102,970
2007 level	95,790

Source: MoD Defence Analytical Services Agency *National Statistics* (Crown copyright)

UK REGULAR FORCES: DEATHS

In 2005 there were a total of 158 deaths among the UK regular armed forces, of which 27 were serving in the Royal Navy and Royal Marines, 91 in the Army and 40 in the RAF. Accidents accounted for 79 deaths (50 per cent) and the largest single cause of death was road traffic accidents, which accounted for 52 deaths (33 per cent) in 2005. Eighteen regular service personnel were killed in action and three died of wounds while in Iraq; accounting for 13 per cent of the total deaths.

NUMBER OF DEATHS AND MORTALITY RATES

	1997	2000	2004	2005	2006
Total number	164	147	169	158	190
Royal Navy	39	25	37	27	33
Army	92	88	95	91	109
RAF	33	34	37	40	48
Mortality rates per thousand					
Tri-service rate	0.81	0.71	0.81	0.78	0.96
Navy	0.87	0.63	0.92	0.69	0.84
Army*	0.93	0.78	0.78	0.81	0.93
RAF	0.47	0.61	0.63	0.71	0.83

* includes personnel deaths in the Brigade of Gurkhas
Source: MoD Defence Analytical Services Agency *National Statistics* (Crown copyright)

NUCLEAR FORCES

The Vanguard Class SSBN (ship submersible ballistic nuclear) provides the UK's strategic nuclear deterrent. Each Vanguard Class submarine is capable of carrying 16 Trident D5 missiles equipped with nuclear warheads.

There is a ballistic missile early warning system station at RAF Fylingdales in North Yorkshire.

ARMS CONTROL

The 1990 Conventional Armed Forces in Europe (CFE) treaty, which commits all NATO and former Warsaw Pact members to limiting their holdings of five major classes of conventional weapons, has been adapted to reflect the changed geo-strategic environment and negotiations continue for its implementation. The Open Skies Treaty, which the UK signed in 1992 and entered into force in 2002, allows for the overflight of States Parties by other States Parties using unarmed observation aircraft.

In 1968 the UK signed and ratified the Nuclear Non-Proliferation Treaty, which came into force in 1970 and was indefinitely and unconditionally extended in 1995. In 1996 the UK signed the Comprehensive Nuclear Test Ban Treaty and ratified it in 1998. The UK is a party to the 1972 Biological and Toxin Weapons Convention, which provides for a worldwide ban on biological weapons, and the 1993 Chemical Weapons Convention, which came into force in 1997 and provides for a verifiable worldwide ban on chemical weapons.

DEFENCE BUDGET DEPARTMENTAL EXPENDITURE
LIMITS (DEL) *(£ billion)*

	Resource budget	Capital budget	Total DEL
2005–6 (outturn)	33.4	6.4	39.8
2006–7 (estimate)	33.7	7.1	40.8
2007–8 (projection)	32.8	7.6	40.4

Source: HM Treasury – *Budget 2007* (Crown copyright)

MINISTRY OF DEFENCE

Main Building, Whitehall, London SW1A 2HB
T 020-7218 9000 W www.mod.uk

Secretary of State for Defence, Rt. Hon. Des Browne, MP
  Private Secretary, Ian Forber
  Special Advisers, Matthew Cavangh; Alena McDonald
  Parliamentary Private Secretary, Dr Roberta Blackman-Woods, MP
Minister of State for the Armed Forces, Rt. Hon. Bob Ainsworth, MP
  Private Secretary, Richard Johnson
  Parliamentary Private Secretary, Adrian Bailey, MP

Minister of State for Defence Equipment and Support, Lord Drayson
  Private Secretary, Conrad Bailey
  Parliamentary Private Secretary, Russell Brown, MP
Under-Secretary of State for Defence and Minister for Veterans, Derek Twigg, MP
  Private Secretary, Jeremy Williams

CHIEFS OF STAFF

Chief of the Defence Staff, Air Chief Marshal Sir Jock Stirrup, GCB, AFC, ADC
Vice Chief of the Defence Staff, Gen. Sir Timothy Granville-Chapman, GBE, KCB, CBE
First Sea Lord and Chief of the Naval Staff, Adm. Sir Jonathon Band, KCB, ADC
Assistant Chief of the Naval Staff, Rear-Adm. Alan Massey, CBE
Chief of the General Staff, Gen. Sir Richard Dannatt, KCB, CBE, MC
Assistant Chief of the General Staff, Maj.-Gen. S. Mayall
Chief of the Air Staff, Air Chief Marshal Sir Glenn Torpy, KCB, CBE, DSO
Assistant Chief of the Air Staff, Air Vice-Marshal T. Anderson, DSO

SENIOR OFFICIALS

Permanent Under-Secretary of State, Bill Jeffrey, CB
Second Permanent Under-Secretary of State, Sir Ian Andrews, CBE, TD
Chief of Defence Material, Gen. Sir Kevin O'Donoghue, KCB, CBE
Chief Scientific Adviser, Prof. Roy Anderson, FRS
Finance Director, Trevor Woolley, CB

THE DEFENCE COUNCIL

The Defence Council is the senior committee of the Ministry of Defence, and was established by royal prerogative under the Letters Patent in April 1964. The Letters Patent confer on the Defence Council the command over all of the armed forces and charge the council with such matters relating to the administration of the armed forces as the Secretary of State for Defence should direct them to execute. It is chaired by the Secretary of State for Defence and consists of the Minister of State for the Armed Forces, the Minister of State for Defence Equipment and Support, the Under-Secretary of State for Defence and the Minister for Veterans, the Chief of Defence Staff, the Permanent Under-Secretary of State, the First Sea Lord and Chief of the Naval Staff, the Chief of the General Staff, the Chief of the Air Staff, the Vice-Chief of Defence Staff, the Second Permanent Under-Secretary of State, the Chief Scientific Adviser and the Finance Director.

CENTRAL STAFF

Vice-Chief of the Defence Staff, Gen. Sir Timothy Granville-Chapman, GBE, KCB, CBE
Second Permanent Under-Secretary of State, Sir Ian Andrews, CBE, TD

PERMANENT JOINT HQ

Chief of Joint Operations, Lt.-Gen. J. Houghton, CBE
Deputy Chief of Joint Operations, Maj.-Gen. J. Dutton, CBE

FLEET COMMAND
Commander-in-Chief Fleet, Adm. Sir James Burnell-Nugent, KCB, CBE
Deputy Commander-in-Chief Fleet, Vice-Adm. Paul Boissier, CB

NAVAL HOME COMMAND
Second Sea Lord and Commander-in-Chief Naval Home Command, Vice-Adm. Adrian Johns, CBE, ADC
Chief of Staff to Second Sea Lord and Commander-in-Chief Naval Home Command, Rear-Adm. Michael Kimmons

LAND COMMAND
Commander-in-Chief Land Command, Gen. Sir Redmond Watt, KCVO, CBE, ADC
Chief of Staff Land Command, Maj.-Gen. J. Shaw, CBE

ADJUTANT-GENERAL'S COMMAND
Adjutant-General, Lt.-Gen. Sir Frederick Viggers, KCB, CMG, MBE
Deputy Adjutant-General and Director-General Service Conditions (Army), Maj.-Gen. M. Mans, CBE

AIR COMMAND
Commander-in-Chief Air Command, Air Chief Marshal Sir Clive Loader, KCB, OBE, DC
Deputy Commander-in-Chief Operations, Air Marshal Iain McNicoll, CB, CBE
Deputy Commander-in-Chief Personnel, Air Marshal Stephen Dalton, CB

DEFENCE EQUIPMENT AND SUPPORT
Chief of Defence Material, Gen. Sir Kevin O'Donoghue, KCB, CBE
Chief Operating Officer, D. Gould
Chief of Corporate Services, T. Flesher
Chief of Material (Fleet), Vice-Adm. Trevor Soar, OBE
Chief of Material (Land), Lt.-Gen. R. Applegate, OBE
Chief of Material (Air), Air Marshal B. Thornton, CB

EXECUTIVE AGENCIES
ARMY BASE REPAIR ORGANISATION (ABRO)
   Portway, Monxton Road, Andover, Hampshire SP11 8HT
   T 01264-383295
BRITISH FORCES POST OFFICE
   Corporate Headquarters, Inglis Barracks, Mill Hill, London
   NW7 1PX T 0845-7769 7978
DEFENCE ANALYTICAL SERVICES AGENCY (DASA)
   Level 32, 1K, Main Building, Whitehall, London SW1A 2HB
   T 020-7218 1474
DEFENCE AVIATION REPAIR AGENCY
   St Athan, Barry, Vale of Glamorgan CF62 4WA
   T 01446-755000
DEFENCE BILLS AGENCY
   Mersey House, Drury Lane, Liverpool L2 7PX
   T 0151-237 6500
DEFENCE COMMUNICATION SERVICES AGENCY
   Building 111, Basil Hill Site, Park Lane, Corsham, Wiltshire
   SN13 9NR T 01225-814750
DEFENCE ESTATES
   St George's House, Kingston Road, Sutton Coldfield, West
   Midlands B75 7RL T 0121-311 2140
DEFENCE MEDICAL EDUCATION AND TRAINING
   AGENCY
   MacKenzie Block, Fort Blockhouse, Gosport, Hampshire
   PO12 2AB T 023-9276 5438
DEFENCE SCIENCE AND TECHNOLOGY LABORATORY
   Porton Down, Salisbury, Wiltshire SP4 0JQ T 01980-613121

DEFENCE STORAGE AND DISTRIBUTION AGENCY
   Ploughley Road, Lower Arncott, Bicester, Oxon OX25 2LD
   T 01869-256804
DEFENCE TRANSPORT AND MOVEMENTS AGENCY
   Building 400, Monxton Road, Andover, Hampshire SP11 8HT
   T 01264-381125
DEFENCE VETTING AGENCY
   Building 107, Imphal Barracks, Fulford Road, York YO10 4AS
   T 01904-662644
DISPOSAL SERVICES AGENCY
   2nd Floor, St George's Court, 2–12 Bloomsbury Way, London
   WC1A 2SH T 020-7305 3156
THE DUKE OF YORK'S ROYAL MILITARY SCHOOL
   Dover, Kent CT15 5EQ T 01304-245024
MET OFFICE
   Fitzroy Road, Exeter EX1 3PB T 0870-900 0100
MINISTRY OF DEFENCE POLICE AND GUARDING
   AGENCY
   Weathersfield, Braintree, Essex CM7 4AZ T 01371-854000
PEOPLE, PAY AND PENSIONS AGENCY
   J Block Foxhill, Combe Down, Bath BA1 5AB
   T 0800-345 7772
SERVICE CHILDREN'S EDUCATION
   HQ SCE, Building 5, Military Complex, Wegberg BFPO 40
   T (+49) (2161) 908 2371
SERVICE PERSONNEL AND VETERANS AGENCY (SPVA)
   Norcross, Blackpool FY5 3WP T 0800-169 2277
UK HYDROGRAPHIC OFFICE
   Admiralty Way, Taunton, Somerset TA1 2DN
   T 01823-337900

ARMED FORCES TRAINING AND RECRUITMENT
In April 2006 the MoD removed agency status from three armed forces training agencies which now function as an integral part of their respective service.

The Naval Training Command provides training at six establishments: Britannia Royal Naval College; Commando Training Centre, RM Lympstone; the Maritime Warfare School (comprising HMS Collingwood; HMS Dryad and HMS Excellent); and HMS Sultan.

The Army Recruiting and Training Division (ARTD) consists of a number of operating groups : Armour Centre; Army Staff Leadership School; Defence College of Electro-Mechanical Engineering; Defence College of Intelligence, Defence College of Logistics; Defence College of Police and Guarding; Defence Medical Education and Training Agency; Initial Training Group; Recruiting Group; Royal Military Academy Sandhurst; Royal School of Artillery; Royal School of Military Engineering; School of Army Aviation and the School of Infantry.

The Royal Air Force No. 22 (Training) Group exists to recruit RAF personnel and provide trained specialist personnel to the armed forces as a whole, such as providing the army air corps with trained helicopter pilots. The group is split into seven areas: RAF College Cranwell and Director of Recruiting; the Directorate of Flying Training (DFT); the Directorate of Joint Technical Training (DJTT); the Air Cadet Organisation; Core Headquarters; the Defence College of Aeronautical Engineering (DCAE) and the Defence College of Communications and Information Systems (DCCIS).

USEFUL WEBSITES
W www.rncom.mod.uk
W www.army.mod.uk
W www.tgda.gov.uk

THE ROYAL NAVY

LORD HIGH ADMIRAL OF THE UNITED KINGDOM
HM The Queen

ADMIRALS OF THE FLEET
HRH The Prince Philip, Duke of Edinburgh, KG, KT, OM, GBE, AC, QSO, PC, *apptd* 1953
Sir Edward Ashmore, GCB, DSC, *apptd* 1977
Sir Henry Leach, GCB, *apptd* 1982
Sir Julian Oswald, GCB, *apptd* 1993
Sir Benjamin Bathurst, GCB, *apptd* 1995

ADMIRALS
(Former Chiefs or Vice Chiefs of Defence Staff and First Sea Lords who remain on the active list)

Slater, Sir Jock, GCB, LVO, *apptd* 1991
Boyce, Lord, GCB, OBE, *apptd* 1995
Abbott, Sir Peter, GBE, KCB, *apptd* 1995
Essenhigh, Sir Nigel, GCB, *apptd* 1998
West of Spithead, Lord, GCB, DSC, *apptd* 2000

ADMIRALS
Band, Sir Jonathon, KCB, ADC *(First Sea Lord and Chief of Naval Staff)*
Stanhope, Sir Mark, KCB, OBE *(Deputy Supreme Allied Commander Transformation)*
Burnell-Nugent, Sir James, KCB, CBE *(Commander-in-Chief Fleet)*
HRH The Prince of Wales, KG, KT, GCB, OM, AK, QSO, PC, ADC

VICE-ADMIRALS
Johns, Adrian, CBE, ADC *(Second Sea Lord and Commander-in-Chief Naval Home Command, Rear-Adm. Fleet Air Arm (Head of Fighting Arm))*
Style, Charles, CBE *(Deputy Chief of Defence Staff (Commitments))*
Dymock, Anthony, CB *(UK Military Representative to NATO and the European Union)*
Boissier, (Robin) Paul, CB *(Deputy Commander-in-Chief Fleet and Chief Naval Warfare Officer)*
Soar, Trevor, OBE *(Chief of Material (Fleet) and Chief of Fleet Support to the Naval Board)*
Laurence, Timothy, CB, MVO *(Chief Executive Defence Estates)*
Wilkinson, Peter *(Deputy Chief of Defence Staff (Personnel))*

REAR-ADMIRALS
HRH The Princess Royal, KG, KT, GCVO *(Chief Commandant for Women in the Royal Navy)*
Ward, Rees, CB *(Director-General Information Systems Services))*
Guild, Nigel, CB *(Director-General Capability (Carrier Strike) and Chief Naval Engineering Officer)*
Spires, Trevor *(Chief Executive Service Personnel and Veterans Agency)*
Wilcocks, Philip, CB, DSC *(Chief of Staff (Capability) to Commander-in-Chief Fleet, Rear-Adm. Surface Ships (Head of Fighting Arm))*
Lambert, Paul *(Capability Manager (Precision Attack), Controller of the Navy)*
Cooke, David, MBE *(Cdr. (Operations) to Commander-in-Chief Fleet, Rear-Adm. Submarines (Head of Fighting Arm))*

Parry, Christopher, CBE *(Director-General Development, Concepts and Doctrine)*
Latham, Neil *(Commandant, College of Management and Technology, Shrivenham)*
Kimmons, Michael *(Chief of Staff (Support and Transformation) to Commander-in-Chief Fleet and Chief Naval Logistics Officer)*
Mathews, Andrew *(Director-General Submarines)*
Ibbotson, Richard, DSC *(Flag Officer Sea Training)*
Massey, Alan, CBE *(Assistant Chief of the Naval Staff)*
Leaman, Richard, OBE *(Deputy Chief of Staff to the Supreme Allied Cdr. Transformation)*
Morisetti, Neil *(Commandant, Joint Services Command and Staff College)*
Rix, Anthony *(Chief of Staff to the Cdr. Allied Naval Forces Southern Europe)*
Zambellas, George, DSC *(Cdr. UK Maritime Forces)*
Cooling, Robert *(Deputy Cdr. Striking Force NATO)*
Hussain, Amjad *(Director-General Weapons)*
Moncrieff, Ian *(National Hydrographer and Deputy Chief Executive UK Hydrographic Office)*
Johnstone-Burt, (Charles) Anthony, OBE (Flag Officer Scotland, Northern England and Northern Ireland and Flag Officer Reserves)
Snow, Christopher *(Senior Naval Member, Royal College of Defence Studies)*
Love, Robert, OBE *(CV(F) Team Leader)*
Montgomery, Charles, CBE *(Naval Secretary and Chief of Staff (Personnel))*
Tibbitt, Ian *(Director-General Safety and Engineering)*
Richards, Alan *(Assistant Chief of Defence Staff (Policy))*

ROYAL MARINES
MAJOR-GENERALS
Dutton, James, CBE *(Deputy Chief of Joint Operations (Operations))*
Rose, John, MBE *(Director-General Intelligence Collection)*
Robison, Garry *(Commandant General Royal Marines and Cdr. UK Amphibious Forces)*
Thomas, Jeremy *(Senior British Military Adviser to US Central Command)*

The Royal Marines were formed in 1664 and are part of the Naval Service. Their primary purpose is to conduct amphibious and land warfare. The principal operational units are

• Three Commando Brigade, an amphibious all-arms brigade trained to operate in arduous environments (a core element of the UK's Joint Rapid Reaction Force). The commando units each have a strength of around 700 and are based in Taunton (40 Commando), Plymouth (42 Commando) and Arbroath (45 Commando)
• Fleet Protection Group, responsible for a wide range of tasks worldwide in support of the Royal Navy. The group is over 500 strong and is based at HM Naval Base Clyde on the west coast of Scotland
• Assault Group, responsible for landing craft training. Based at Poole, Dorset

The Royal Marines also provide detachments for warships and land-based naval parties as required.

ROYAL MARINES RESERVES (RMR)
The Royal Marines Reserve is a commando-trained volunteer force with the principal role, when mobilised, of supporting the Royal Marines. The RMR consists of approximately 600 trained ranks who are distributed between the five RMR centres in the UK. Approximately 10 per cent of the RMR are working with the regular corps on long-term attachments within all of the Royal Marines regular units.

OTHER PARTS OF THE NAVAL SERVICE

FLEET AIR ARM
The Fleet Air Arm (FAA) provides the Royal Navy with a multi-role aviation combat capability able to operate autonomously at short notice worldwide in all environments, over the sea and land. The FAA numbers some 6,200 people, which comprises 11.5 per cent of the total Royal Naval strength. It operates some 200 combat aircraft and more than 50 support/training aircraft.

ROYAL FLEET AUXILIARY SERVICE (RFA)
The Royal Fleet Auxiliary Service is a civilian-manned flotilla of 18 ships. Its primary role is to supply the Royal Navy at sea with fuel, ammunition, food and spares, enabling it to maintain operations away from its home ports. It also provides amphibious support and secure sea transport for Army units and their equipment and aviation support for the Royal Navy.

ROYAL NAVAL RESERVE (RNR)
The Royal Naval Reserve is an integral part of the Naval Service. It comprises up to 3,250 men and women who volunteer to train in their spare time to enable the Royal Navy to meet its operational commitments, at sea and ashore, in crisis or war.

The standard annual training commitment in peacetime is 12 days operational training per annum together with a number of training nights and some weekends. Most new entrants are expected to attend training nights once a week at their nearest RNR unit.

QUEEN ALEXANDRA'S ROYAL NAVAL NURSING SERVICE
The first nursing sisters were appointed to naval hospitals in 1884 and the Queen Alexandra's Royal Naval Nursing Service (QARNNS) gained its current title in 1902. Nursing ratings were introduced in 1960 and men were integrated into the service in 1982; QARNNS recruits qualified nurses as both officers and ratings, and student nurse training can be undertaken in the service.
Patron, HRH Princess Alexandra, the Hon. Lady Ogilvy, KG, GCVO
Director of Naval Nursing Services and Matron-in-Chief, Capt. L. Gibbon, ARRC, QHN, QARNNS

HM FLEET
as at 1 June 2007

Submarines	
Vanguard Class	Vanguard, Vengeance, Victorious, Vigilant
Swiftsure Class	Sceptre, Superb
Trafalgar Class	Talent, Tireless, Torbay, Trafalgar, Trenchant, Triumph, Turbulent
Aircraft Carriers	Ark Royal, Illustrious, Invincible*

Amphibious Assault Ships	Ocean, Albion, Bulwark
Destroyers	
Type 42 Batch 2	Exeter, Liverpool, Nottingham, Southampton
Type 42 Batch 3	Edinburgh, Gloucester, Manchester, York
Frigates	
Type 22	Campbeltown, Chatham, Cornwall, Cumberland
Type 23	Argyll, Iron Duke, Kent, Lancaster, Monmouth, Montrose, Northumberland, Portland, Richmond, St Albans, Somerset, Sutherland, Westminster
Minehunters	
Hunt Class	Atherstone, Brocklesby, Cattistock, Chiddingfold, Hurworth, Ledbury, Middleton, Quorn
Sandown Class	Bangor, Blyth, Grimsby, Pembroke, Penzance, Ramsey, Shoreham, Walney
Patrol Class	
Archer Class P2000 Training Boats	Archer, Biter, Blazer, Charger, Dasher†, Example, Exploit, Explorer, Express, Puncher, Pursuer†, Raider, Ranger, Smiter, Tracker, Trumpeter
Gibraltar Squadron 16m Fast Patrol Class	Sabre, Scimitar
Castle Class Patrol Vessel	Dumbarton Castle‡
River Class Patrol Vessels	Mersey, Severn, Tyne
Survey Vessels	
Antarctic Patrol Ship	Endurance
Ocean Survey Vessels	Scott
Coastal Survey Vessels	Gleaner, Roebuck
Multi-Role Survey Vessels	Echo, Enterprise

* HMS Invincible is currently being held at very low readiness
† HMS Dasher and HMS Pursuer form the Royal Navy Cyprus Squadron
‡ HMS Dumbarton Castle is due to leave service around the end of 2007

ROYAL FLEET AUXILIARY	
Landing Ship Logistic	RFA Sir Bedivere
Landing Ship Dock (Auxiliary)	RFA Cardigan Bay, RFA Mounts Bay, RFA Largs Bay
Wave Class	RFA Wave Knight, RFA Wave Ruler
Rover Class	RFA Black Rover, RFA Gold Rover
Leaf Class	RFA Orangeleaf, RFA Bayleaf, RFA Brambleleaf, RFA Oakleaf
Fort Class	RFA Fort Austin, RFA Fort George, RFA Fort Rosalie, RFA Fort Victoria
Forward Repair Ship	RFA Diligence
Joint Casualty Treatment Ship/Maritime Afloat Training Capability	RFA Angus

THE ARMY

THE QUEEN

FIELD MARSHALS
HRH The Prince Philip, Duke of Edinburgh, KG, KT, OM, GBE, AC, QSO, PC, *apptd* 1953
Lord Bramall, KG, GCB, OBE, MC, *apptd* 1982
Sir John Stanier, GCB, MBE, *apptd* 1985
Lord Vincent of Coleshill, GBE, KCB, DSO, *apptd* 1991
Sir John Chapple, GCB, CBE, *apptd* 1992
HRH The Duke of Kent, KG, GCMG, GCVO, ADC, *apptd* 1993
Lord Inge, KG, GCB *apptd* 1994

FORMER CHIEFS OF STAFF
Gen. Lord Guthrie of Craigiebank, GCB, LVO, OBE, *apptd* 1992
Gen. Sir Roger Wheeler, GCB, CBE, *apptd* 1995
Gen. Sir Michael Walker, GCB, CMG, CBE, *apptd* 1997
Gen. Sir Mike Jackson, GCB, CBE, DSO, *apptd* 2000

GENERALS
Granville-Chapman, Sir Timothy, GBE, KCB, CBE *(Vice-Chief of the Defence Staff)*
Reith, Sir John, KCB, CBE *(held strength pending retirement)*
O'Donoghue, Sir Kevin, KCB, CBE *(Chief of Defence Material)*
Dannatt, Sir Richard, KCB, CBE, MC *(Chief of the General Staff)*
Watt, Sir Redmond, KCVO, CBE, ADC *(Commander-in-Chief Land Command)*
HRH The Prince of Wales, KG, KT, GCB, OM, AK, QSO, PC, ADC
McColl, J., CBE, DSO *(Deputy Supreme Allied Cdr. Europe)*

LIEUTENANT-GENERALS
Kiszely, Sir John, KCB, MC *(Director Defence Academy)*
Richards, Sir David, KCB, CBE, DSO *(Cdr. Allied Rapid Reaction Corps)*
Brims, R., CB, CBE, DSO *(held strength pending retirement)*
Viggers, Sir Frederick, KCB, CMG, MBE *(Adjutant-General)*
Houghton, J., CBE *(Chief of Joint Operations)*
Figgures, A., CBE *(Deputy Chief of the Defence Staff (Equipment Capability))*
Parker, N., CBE *(Cdr. Regional Forces, Land Command)*
Lamb, G., CMG, DSO, OBE *(Cdr. Field Army, Land Command)*
Lillywhite, L., MBE, QHS *(Surgeon General)*
Applegate, R., OBE *(Chief of Material (Land) and Quartermaster General)*
Leakey, A., CMG, CBE *(Director-General European Union Military Staff)*
Baxter, R., CBE *(Deputy Chief of the Defence Staff (Health))*
Rollo, W., CBE *(Deputy Commanding Gen. Multi-National Force, Iraq and Senior British Military Representative, Iraq)*
Pearson, P., CBE *(Deputy Cdr. Allied Joint Force Command, Naples)*
Wall, P., CBE *(Deputy Chief of the Defence Staff (Commitments))*

MAJOR-GENERALS
Gilchrist, P., CB *(Head of British Defence Staff US)*
Howell, D., CB, OBE *(Director Army Legal Services)*
Cottam, N., CB, OBE *(Military Secretary)*
Wood, M., CBE *(Director-General Joint Supply Chain)*
Shirreff, A., CBE *(held strength pending next appointment)*
Roberts, Sir Sebastian, KCVO, OBE *(Senior Army Member, Royal College of Defence Studies)*
Bill, D., CB *(Deputy Cdr. NATO Rapid Deployable Corps, Italy)*
Stewart, A., CB, CBE *(held strength pending retirement)*
Whitley, A., CBE, CMG *(Senior British Loan Service Officer, Oman)*
Brown, C., CBE *(GOC Northern Ireland)*
Graham, A., CBE *(Director-General Army Training and Recruiting)*
Tyler, T. *(Director-General Land Equipment)*
Cooper, J., DSO, MBE *(Director-General Training Support)*
Wilkes, Revd D., OBE, QHC *(Chaplain General)*
Farquhar, A., CBE *(GOC 5th Division)*
Riley, J., DSO *(next appointment not yet announced)*
Wilson, C., CBE *(Capability Manager (Battlespace Manoeuvre) and Master General of the Ordnance)*
Mans, M., CBE *(Deputy Adjutant-General and Director-General Service Conditions (Army))*
White-Spunner, B., CBE *(GOC 3rd (UK) Division)*
Hawley, A., OBE, QHP *(Director-General Army Medical Services)*
Coward, G., OBE *(Cdr. Joint Helicopter Command)*
Steirn, C., CBE *(held strength pending retirement)*
Everson, P., OBE *(GOC 4th Division)*
Newton, P., OBE *(Director-General Engagements Multi-National Force, Iraq)*
Gregory, A. *(HQ Land Command and HQ Adjutant-General Collocation Implementation Team Leader)*
Melvin, R., OBE *(GOC UK Support Command, Germany)*
Mayall, S. *(Assistant Chief of the General Staff)*
Bucknall, J., CBE *(Chief of Staff Allied Rapid Reaction Corps)*
Binns, G., CBE, DSO, MC *(GOC 1st (UK) Armoured Division)*
Von Bertele, M., OBE *(Chief Executive Defence Medical Education and Training Agency)*
Rollo, N., CBE *(GOC Theatre Troops)*
Macklin, A. *(Armoured Fighting Vehicles Group Leader)*
Berragan, G. *(Deputy Commanding Gen. Multi-National Corps, Iraq)*
Shaw, J., CBE *(Chief of Staff Land Command)*
McDowall, D., MBE *(GOC 2nd Division)*
Lalor, S., TD *(Assistant Chief of the Defence Staff (Reserves and Cadets))*
Sykes, R. *(Defence Services Secretary)*
Page, J., OBE *(Cdr. Regional Command (South), Afghanistan)*
Shouesmith, D. *(Assistant Chief of the Defence Staff (Logistic Operations))*
Moore, W., CBE *(Director-General Logistics, Supply and Equipment (Land Command))*
Cubitt, W., CBE *(GOC London District and Maj.-Gen. Commanding The Household Division)*
Rutherford-Jones, D. *(Commandant Royal Military Academy Sandhurst)*
Rutledge, M., OBE *(Kosovo Protection Corps Coordinator)*

CONSTITUTION OF THE ARMY

The army consists of the Regular Army, the Regular Reserve and the Territorial Army (TA). It is commanded by the Chief of the General Staff, who is the professional Head of Service and Chair of the Executive Committee of the Army Board, which provides overall strategic policy and direction to the commands. These are: Land Command, which comprises the Field Army, Regional Forces, the Joint Helicopter Command, the Theatre Troops and Land Support; and the Adjutant General's Command, responsible for army personnel matters and education and training. The army is divided into functional arms and services, sub-divided into regiments and corps (listed below in order of precedence). The army is currently nearing completion of the first phase of a major reform programme known as the Future Army Structure (FAS). The FAS incorporates changes in tactical doctrine, organisational structure, personnel terms and conditions of service and the introduction of new equipment. Under the programme, the infantry has been re-structured into large multi-battalion regiments, which involved amalgamations and changes in title for some regiments. The first phase of FAS is expected to be completed during 2008.

Further information in the public domain on the composition of the Army Board, Headquarters, Arms and Services, including addresses, can be obtained from the Army List, which is published annually by the Stationery Office and held in most public libraries. Members of the public can write for general information to Headquarters Adjutant General Secretariat, Trenchard Lines, Upavon, Wiltshire SN9 6BE. Information on how to make requests for information under the Freedom of Information Act 2000 can be found at www.foi.mod.uk, which includes an electronic request form. All enquiries with regard to records of serving personnel (Regular and Territorial Army) should be directed to The Army Personnel Centre Help Desk, Kentigern House, 65 Brown Street, Glasgow G2 8EX T 0141-224 2023/3303. Enquirers should note that the Army is governed in the release of personal information by various Acts of Parliament.

ORDER OF PRECEDENCE OF CORPS AND REGIMENTS OF THE BRITISH ARMY

ARMS

HOUSEHOLD CAVALRY
The Life Guards
The Blues and Royals (Royal Horse Guards and 1st Dragoons)

ROYAL HORSE ARTILLERY
(when on parade with their guns, the Royal Horse Artillery take precedence over the Household Cavalry)

ROYAL ARMOURED CORPS
1st the Queen's Dragoon Guards
The Royal Scots Dragoon Guards (Carabiniers and Greys)
The Royal Dragoon Guards
The Queen's Royal Hussars (The Queen's Own and Royal Irish)
9th/12th Royal Lancers (Prince of Wales')
The King's Royal Hussars
The Light Dragoons
The Queen's Royal Lancers
Royal Tank Regiment

ROYAL REGIMENT OF ARTILLERY
(with the exception of the Royal Horse Artillery (see above))

CORPS OF ROYAL ENGINEERS

ROYAL CORPS OF SIGNALS

REGIMENTS OF FOOT GUARDS
Grenadier Guards
Coldstream Guards
Scots Guards
Irish Guards
Welsh Guards

REGIMENTS OF INFANTRY
The Royal Regiment of Scotland
The Princess of Wales' Royal Regiment (Queen and Royal Hampshire's)
The Duke of Lancaster's Regiment (King's, Lancashire and Border)
The Royal Regiment of Fusiliers
The Royal Anglian Regiment
The Rifles
The Yorkshire Regiment
The Mercian Regiment
The Royal Welsh
The Royal Irish Regiment
The Parachute Regiment
The Royal Gurkha Rifles

SPECIAL AIR SERVICE

ARMY AIR CORPS

SERVICES

ROYAL ARMY CHAPLAINS' DEPARTMENT

THE ROYAL LOGISTIC CORPS

ROYAL ARMY MEDICAL CORPS

CORPS OF ROYAL ELECTRICAL AND MECHANICAL ENGINEERS

ADJUTANT-GENERAL'S CORPS

ROYAL ARMY VETERINARY CORPS

SMALL ARMS SCHOOL CORPS

ROYAL ARMY DENTAL CORPS

INTELLIGENCE CORPS

ARMY PHYSICAL TRAINING CORPS

QUEEN ALEXANDRA'S ROYAL ARMY NURSING CORPS

CORPS OF ARMY MUSIC

THE ROYAL MONMOUTHSHIRE ROYAL ENGINEERS (MILITIA) (TA)

THE HONOURABLE ARTILLERY COMPANY (TA)

REST OF THE TERRITORIAL ARMY (TA)

ARMY EQUIPMENT

Tanks	386
Challenger 2	386
Reconnaissance vehicles	475
Fuchs	11
Scimitar	327
Sabre	137
Reconnaissance aircraft	3
Armoured Infantry Fighting Vehicle	575
Armoured Personnel Carrier	2,611
Artillery pieces	877
Anti-tank missile	800+
Helicopters	324
Attack	176
Apache	67
Lynx	109
Support	148
Gazelle	133
Scout	15
Unmanned aerial vehicle	8
Surface-to-air missile	339+
Land radar	4+
Miscellaneous boats/craft	4
Amphibious craft	4
Logistics and support vehicles	6

Source: Military Balance 2007

THE TERRITORIAL ARMY (TA)

The Territorial Army is part of the UK's reserve land forces and provides support to the regular army at home and overseas. The TA is divided into three types of unit: national, regional, and sponsored. TA soldiers serving in regional units complete a minimum of 27 days training a year, comprising some evenings, weekends and an annual two-week camp. National units normally specialise in a specific role or trade, such as logistics, IT, communications or medical services. Members of national units have a lower level of training commitment because of the travel involved and complete 19 days training a year, comprising two to three weekends and an annual two-week camp. At the end of 2006 the TA's total strength was 36,260 (the established liability is 42,000).

QUEEN ALEXANDRA'S ROYAL ARMY NURSING CORPS

The Queen Alexandra's Royal Army Nursing Corps (QARANC) was founded in 1902 as Queen Alexandra's Imperial Military Nursing Service and gained its present title in 1949. The QARANC has trained nurses for the register since 1950 and also trains and employs health care assistants to Level 2 NVQ, with the option to train to Level 3. The corps recruits qualified nurses as officers and other ranks and in 1992 male nurses already serving in the army were transferred to the QARANC.

Colonel-in-Chief, HRH The Countess of Wessex
Colonel Commandant, Brig. Jane Arigho, CBE

THE ROYAL AIR FORCE

THE QUEEN

MARSHAL OF THE ROYAL AIR FORCE
HRH The Prince Philip, Duke of Edinburgh, KG, KT, OM, GBE, AC, QSO, PC, *apptd* 1953

FORMER CHIEFS OF THE AIR STAFF

MARSHALS OF THE ROYAL AIR FORCE
Sir Michael Beetham, GCB, CBE, DFC, AFC, *apptd* 1982
Sir Keith Williamson, GCB, AFC, *apptd* 1985
Lord Craig of Radley, GCB, OBE, *apptd* 1988

AIR CHIEF MARSHALS
Sir Michael Graydon, GCB, CBE, *apptd* 1991
Sir Richard Johns, GCB, OBE, LVO *apptd* 1994
Sir Peter Squire, GCB, DFC, AFC *apptd* 1999

AIR RANK LIST

AIR CHIEF MARSHALS
Stirrup, Sir Jock, GCB, AFC, ADC *(Chief of the Defence Staff)*
Torpy, Sir Glenn, KCB, CBE, DSO, ADC *(Chief of the Air Staff)*
HRH The Prince of Wales, KG, KT, GCB, OM, AK, QSO, PC, ADC
Loader, Sir Clive, KCB, OBE, DC *(Commander-in-Chief Air Command)*

AIR MARSHALS
Thornton, Sir Barry, KCB *(Chief of Material (Air) and Air Member for Material)*
Peach, S., CBE *(Chief of Defence Intelligence)*
McNicoll, I., CB, CBE *(Deputy Commander-in-Chief Operations, Air Command)*
Dalton, S., CB *(Deputy Commander-in-Chief Personnel and Air Member for Personnel, Air Command)*
Moran, C., OBE, MVO *(Deputy Cdr. Allied Joint Force Command, Brunssum)*
Walker, D., CBE, AFC *(Deputy Cdr. Allied Air Component Command, Ramstein)*

AIR VICE-MARSHALS
Charles, R., CB *(Director RAF Legal Services)*
Ness, C. *(Director-General Combat (Air))*
Walker, D. A., OBE, MVO *(Master of the Royal Household)*
Cliffe, J., OBE *(Director-General Training and Education, MoD)*
Thornton, E., QHP *(Director-General Healthcare)*
Ruddock, P., CBE *(Director-General Saudi Arabia Armed Forces Project)*
Chisnall, S. *(Senior Directing Staff (Air), Royal College of Defence Studies)*
Leeson, K., CBE *(Assistant Chief of the Defence Staff (Resources and Plans)*
Dougherty, S., QHP *(Chief of Staff (Health) and Director-General RAF Medical Services)*
Ponsonby, J., OBE *(Chief of Staff (Operations) Air Command)*
Dye, P., OBE *(Head of RAF Transformation)*
Nickols, C., CBE *(Assistant Chief of the Defence Staff (Operations), MoD)*

Harper, C., CBE *(Air Officer Commanding No. 1 Group)*
Walton, A., CBE *(Deputy Chief of Joint Operations (Operations Support), Permanent Joint HQ)*
Mills, Revd P., QHC *(Director-General Chaplaincy Services)*
Butler, S. *(Capability Manager (Information Superiority) and Air Member Equipment Capability)*
Lacey, R., CBE *(Cdr. British Forces Cyprus)*
Bryant, S., CBE *(Chief of Staff Personnel and Air Secretary)*
Pulford, A., CBE *(Air Officer Commanding No. 2 Group)*
Allan, R., OBE *(Director-General Information Systems and Services)*
Anderson, T., DSO *(Assistant Chief of the Air Staff)*
Routledge, M. *(Chief of Staff Strategy, Policy and Plans, Air Command)*
Garwood, R., CBE, DFC *(Air Officer Commanding No. 22 Training Group)*
Kurth, N., CBE *(Chief of Staff (Support) Air Command)*
Wiles, M. *(Director-General Joint Supply Chain)*

CONSTITUTION OF THE RAF

The RAF consists of a single command, Air Command, based at RAF High Wycombe. RAF Air Command was formed on 1 April 2007 from the amalgamation of Strike Command and Personnel and Training Command.

Air Command consists of three groups, each organised around specific operational duties, and the Expeditionary Air Wings. No. 1 Group is the coordinating organisation for the tactical fast-jet forces responsible for attack, offensive support and air defence operations. No. 2 Group provides air combat support including air transport and air to air refuelling; intelligence surveillance; targeting and reconnaissance; and force protection. No. 22 (Training) Group recruits personnel and provides trained specialist personnel to the RAF, as well as to the Royal Navy and the Army (*see also* Armed Forces Training and Recruitment).

RAF EQUIPMENT

Aircraft	
BAe 125	5
BAe 146	2
Dominie	9
Firefly	38
Globemaster	4
Harrier	42
Hawk	99
Hercules	44
Islander	2
Jaguar	14
Jetstream	11
King Air (leased)	7
Nimrod	22
Sentinel	1
Sentry	6
Tornado	234
Tristar	8
Tucano	67
Tutor	99
Typhoon	25
VC10	17

Helicopters

Chinook	34
Ecureuil	31
Griffin	14
Merlin	22
Puma	33
Sea King	20

Source: Military Balance 2007

ROYAL AUXILIARY AIR FORCE

The Auxiliary Air Force was formed in 1924 to train an elite corps of civilians to serve their country in flying squadrons in their spare time. In 1947 the force was awarded the prefix 'royal' in recognition of its distinguished war service and the Sovereign's Colour for the Royal Auxiliary Air Force (RAuxAF) was presented in 1989. The RAuxAF continues to recruit civilians who undertake military training in their spare time to support the Royal Air Force in times of emergency or war.

Air Commodore-in-Chief, HM The Queen

Honorary Inspector-General Royal Auxiliary Air Force, Air Vice-Marshal Barry Newton, CB, CVO, OBE

Inspector Royal Auxiliary Air Force, Gp Capt. Gary Bunkell, QVRM, AE, ADC

PRINCESS MARY'S ROYAL AIR FORCE NURSING SERVICE

The Princess Mary's Royal Air Force Nursing Service (PMRAFNS) was formed on 1 June 1918 as the Royal Air Force Nursing Service. In June 1923, His Majesty King George V gave his royal assent for the Royal Air Force Nursing Service to be known as the Princess Mary's Royal Air Force Nursing Service. Men were integrated into the PMRAFNS in 1980 and now serve as officers and other ranks.

Patron and Air Chief Commandant, HRH Princess Alexandra, The Hon. Lady Ogilvy, KG, GCVO

Director of Nursing Services and Matron-in-Chief, Gp Capt. W. B. Williams, RRC, QHN

SERVICE SALARIES

The following rates of pay apply from 1 April 2007.
The pay rates shown are for army personnel. The rates also apply to personnel of equivalent rank and pay band in the other services (*see* below for table of relative ranks).

Rank	Annual salary
SECOND LIEUTENANT	£22,679.76
LIEUTENANT	
On appointment	£27,260.04
After 1 year in rank	£27,980.88
After 2 years in rank	£28,697.76
After 3 years in rank	£29,410.80
After 4 years in rank	£30,131.40
CAPTAIN	
On appointment	£34,934.52
After 1 year in rank	£35,870.28
After 2 years in rank	£36,817.32
After 3 years in rank	£37,768.08
After 4 years in rank	£38,707.56
After 5 years in rank	£39,654.60
After 6 years in rank	£40,594.08
After 7 years in rank	£41,073.24
After 8 years in rank	£41,544.84
MAJOR	
On appointment	£44,004.96
After 1 year in rank	£45,091.56
After 2 years in rank	£46,170.48
After 3 years in rank	£47,264.76
After 4 years in rank	£48,347.76
After 5 years in rank	£49,441.80
After 6 years in rank	£50,528.52
After 7 years in rank	£51,611.28
After 8 years in rank	£52,701.72
LIEUTENANT-COLONEL	
On appointment	£61,760.76
After 1 year in rank	£62,579.52
After 2 years in rank	£63,390.72
After 3 years in rank	£64,202.04
After 4 years in rank	£65,013.12
After 5 years in rank	£65,824.32
After 6 years in rank	£66,635.52
After 7 years in rank	£67,454.28
After 8 years in rank	£68,272.92
COLONEL	
On appointment	£71,521.56
After 1 year in rank	£72,461.04
After 2 years in rank	£73,404.36
After 3 years in rank	£74,343.84
After 4 years in rank	£75,283.32
After 5 years in rank	£76,222.80
After 6 years in rank	£77,162.28
After 7 years in rank	£78,105.48
After 8 years in rank	£79,048.68
BRIGADIER	
On appointment	£85,787.52
After 1 year in rank	£86,700.60
After 2 years in rank	£87,613.68
After 3 years in rank	£88,522.92
After 4 years in rank	£89,443.56

PAY SYSTEM FOR SENIOR MILITARY OFFICERS

Revised pay rates effective from 1 April 2007 for all military officers of 2* rank and above (excluding medical and dental officers).

MAJOR-GENERAL (2*)	Annual salary
Scale 1	£94,749.96
Scale 2	£96,174.96
Scale 3	£98,060.04
Scale 4	£100,310.04
Scale 5	£102,561.00
Scale 6	£104,811.00
Scale 7	£107,060.04
LIEUTENANT-GENERAL (3*)	**Annual salary**
Scale 1	£111,753.96
Scale 2	£118,821.96
Scale 3	£125,889.00
Scale 4	£130,356.96
Scale 5	£134,826.96
Scale 6	£139,295.04
Scale 7	n/a
GENERAL (4*)	**Annual salary**
Scale 1	£151,370.04
Scale 2	£154,386.96
Scale 3	£157,475.04
Scale 4	£160,625.04
Scale 5	£163,836.00
Scale 6	£167,114.04
Scale 7	n/a

Field Marshal – appointments to this rank will not usually be made in peacetime. The salary for holders of the rank is equivalent to the salary of a 5-star General, a salary created only in times of war. In peacetime, the equivalent rank to Field Marshal is the Chief of the Defence Staff. From 1 April 2007, the annual salary range for the Chief of the Defence Staff is: £217,572.00–£230,889.00.

OFFICERS COMMISSIONED FROM THE SENIOR RANKS

Rank	Annual salary
Level 15	£46,695.12
Level 14	£46,389.60
Level 13	£46,068.72
Level 12	£45,446.16
Level 11	£44,827.44
Level 10	£44,201.04
Level 9	£43,578.48
Level 8	£42,956.04
Level 7*	£42,178.80
Level 6	£41,699.52
Level 5	£41,212.80
Level 4†	£40,250.64
Level 3	£39,771.48
Level 2	£39,281.04
Level 1‡	£38,322.72

* Officers commissioned from the ranks with more than 15 years' service enter on level 7
† Officers commissioned from the ranks with between 12 and 15 years' service enter on level 4
‡ Officers commissioned from the ranks with less than 12 years' service enter on level 1

SOLDIERS' SALARIES

Under the Pay 2000 scheme, personnel are paid in either a high or low band in accordance with how their trade has been allocated to those bands at each rank. Pay is based on trade and rank, not on individual appointment, or in response to temporary changes in role.

Rates of pay effective from 1 April 2007 are:

PRIVATE	Lower Band	Higher Band
Level 1	£15,677.04	£15,677.04
Level 2	£16,110.72	£16,899.48
Level 3	£16,544.64	£18,657.72
Level 4	£17,993.52	£20,061.36

LANCE CORPORAL (levels 5–7 also applicable to Privates)

	Lower Band	Higher Band
Level 5	£18,963.24	£22,181.64
Level 6	£19,755.72	£23,260.80
Level 7	£20,600.76	£24,328.44
Level 8	£21,543.96	£25,422.84
Level 9	£22,325.04	£26,664.00

CORPORAL	Lower Band	Higher Band
Level 1	£24,328.44	£25,422.84
Level 2	£25,422.84	£26,664.00
Level 3	£26,664.00	£27,969.48
Level 4	£26,867.76	£28,622.16
Level 5	£27,079.08	£29,312.64
Level 6	£27,294.24	£29,920.20
Level 7	£27,494.16	£30,572.88

SERGEANT	Lower Band	Higher Band
Level 1	£27,652.68	£30,180.48
Level 2	£28,377.00	£30,961.56
Level 3	£29,090.04	£31,746.24
Level 4	£29,384.40	£32,146.32
Level 5	£30,150.36	£32,772.60
Level 6	£31,191.72	£33,398.88
Level 7	£31,429.32	£34,025.16

STAFF SERGEANT	Lower Band	Higher Band
Level 1	£30,610.80	£34,047.84
Level 2	£31,010.52	£34,870.32
Level 3	£32,018.04	£35,704.20
Level 4	£32,768.88	£36,530.52

WARRANT OFFICER II (levels 5–7 also applicable to Staff Sergeants)

	Lower Band	Higher Band
Level 5	£33,213.96	£37,360.68
Level 6	£34,715.76	£38,186.88
Level 7	£35,247.60	£38,737.80
Level 8	£35,704.20	£39,288.60
Level 9	£36,511.68	£39,850.80

WARRANT OFFICER I	Lower Band	Higher Band
Level 1	£35,564.52	£38,771.52
Level 2	£36,255.00	£39,533.88
Level 3	£36,986.88	£40,212.96
Level 4	£37,718.88	£40,952.52
Level 5	£38,454.72	£41,684.52
Level 6	£39,533.88	£42,427.80
Level 7	£40,650.60	£43,076.76

RELATIVE RANK – ARMED FORCES

Royal Navy	Army	Royal Air Force
1 Admiral of the Fleet	1 Field Marshal	1 Marshal of the RAF
2 Admiral (Adm.)	2 General (Gen.)	2 Air Chief Marshal
3 Vice-Admiral (Vice-Adm.)	3 Lieutenant-General (Lt.-Gen.)	3 Air Marshal
4 Rear-Admiral (Rear-Adm.)	4 Major-General (Maj.-Gen.)	4 Air Vice-Marshal
5 Commodore (Cdre)	5 Brigadier (Brig.)	5 Air Commodore (Air Cdre)
6 Captain (Capt.)	6 Colonel (Col.)	6 Group Captain (Gp Capt.)
7 Commander (Cdr)	7 Lieutenant-Colonel (Lt.-Col.)	7 Wing Commander (Wg Cdr)
8 Lieutenant-Commander (Lt.-Cdr)	8 Major (Maj.)	8 Squadron Leader (Sqn Ldr)
9 Lieutenant (Lt.)	9 Captain (Capt.)	9 Flight Lieutenant (Flt Lt)
10 Sub-Lieutenant (Sub-Lt.)	10 Lieutenant (Lt.)	10 Flying Officer (FO)
11 Acting Sub-Lieutenant (Acting Sub-Lt.)	11 Second Lieutenant (2nd Lt.)	11 Pilot Officer (PO)

SERVICE RETIRED PAY
on compulsory retirement

Those who leave the services having served at least five years, but not long enough to qualify for the appropriate immediate pension, now qualify for a preserved pension and terminal grant, both of which are payable at age 60. The tax-free resettlement grants shown below are payable on release to those who qualify for a preserved pension and who have completed nine years' service from age 21 (officers) or 12 years from age 18 (other ranks).

The annual rates for army personnel are given. The rates also apply to personnel of equivalent rank in the other services, including the nursing services.

OFFICERS
Applicable to officers who give full pay service on the active list on or after 31 March 2007. Pensionable earnings for senior officers (*) is defined as the total amount of basic pay received during the year ending on the day prior to retirement, or the amount of basic pay received during any 12-month period within 3 years prior to retirement, whichever is the higher. Figures for senior officers are percentage rates of pensionable earnings on final salary arrangements on or after 31 March 2007.

No. of years reckonable service	Capt. and below	Major	Lt.-Col.	Colonel	Brigadier	Major-General*	Lieutenant-General*	General*
16	£11,569	£13,779	£18,066	£20,920	£24,970	—	—	—
17	£12,103	£14,434	£18,902	£21,888	£25,943	—	—	—
18	£12,636	£15,088	£19,738	£22,856	£26,917	—	—	—
19	£13,169	£15,743	£20,574	£23,823	£27,890	—	—	—
20	£13,702	£16,397	£21,410	£24,791	£28,864	—	—	—
21	£14,236	£17,052	£22,246	£25,759	£29,837	—	—	—
22	£14,769	£17,706	£23,082	£26,726	£30,811	—	—	—
23	£15,302	£18,361	£23,918	£27,694	£31,784	—	—	—
24	£15,835	£19,015	£24,753	£28,662	£32,758	38.5%	—	—
25	£16,369	£19,670	£25,589	£29,629	£33,731	39.7%	—	—
26	£16,902	£20,324	£26,425	£30,597	£34,705	40.8%	—	—
27	£17,435	£20,979	£27,261	£31,565	£35,678	42.0%	42.0%	—
28	£17,968	£21,633	£28,097	£32,532	£36,652	43.1%	43.1%	—
29	£18,502	£22,288	£28,933	£33,500	£37,625	44.3%	44.3%	—
30	£19,035	£22,942	£29,769	£34,468	£38,599	45.4%	45.4%	45.4%
31	£19,568	£23,597	£30,605	£35,436	£39,572	46.6%	46.6%	46.6%
32	£20,102	£24,251	£31,441	£36,403	£40,546	47.7%	47.7%	47.7%
33	£20,635	£24,906	£32,276	£37,371	£41,519	48.9%	48.9%	48.9%
34	£21,168	£25,560	£33,112	£38,339	£42,493	50.0%	50.0%	50.0%

WARRANT OFFICERS, NCOS AND PRIVATES
(Applicable to soldiers who give full pay service on or after 31 March 2007)

No. of years reckonable service	Below Corporal	Corporal	Sergeant	Staff Sergeant	Warrant Officer Level II	Warrant Officer Level I
22	£6,847	£8,833	£9,683	£11,030	£11,776	£12,521
23	£7,086	£9,141	£10,021	£11,415	£12,187	£12,958
24	£7,325	£9,449	£10,359	£11,800	£12,598	£13,395
25	£7,564	£9,757	£10,697	£12,185	£13,009	£13,832
26	£7,803	£10,066	£11,035	£12,570	£13,420	£14,269
27	£8,042	£10,374	£11,373	£12,955	£13,831	£14,706
28	£8,281	£10,682	£11,711	£13,340	£14,242	£15,144
29	£8,520	£10,991	£12,049	£13,725	£14,653	£15,581
30	£8,759	£11,299	£12,387	£14,110	£15,064	£16,018
31	£8,998	£11,607	£12,725	£14,495	£15,475	£16,455
32	£9,237	£11,916	£13,063	£14,880	£15,886	£16,892
33	£9,476	£12,224	£13,401	£15,265	£16,297	£17,329
34	£9,715	£12,532	£13,739	£15,650	£16,708	£17,766
35	£9,954	£12,840	£14,077	£16,035	£17,119	£18,203
36	£10,193	£13,149	£14,415	£16,420	£17,530	£18,640
37	£10,432	£13,457	£14,753	£16,805	£17,941	£19,077

GRANTS AND GRATUITIES
Terminal grants are in each case three times the rate of retired pay or pension. There are special rates of retired pay for certain other ranks not shown above. Lower rates are payable in cases of voluntary retirement.

A gratuity of £3,935 is payable for officers with short service commissions for each year completed. Resettlement grants are £13,531 for officers and £9,249 for other ranks.

THE EDUCATION SYSTEM

Responsibility for education in England lies with the Secretaries of State for Children, Schools and Families (DCSF) and Innovation, Universities and Skills (DIUS); in Wales, with Welsh ministers; in Scotland, with Scottish ministers; and in Northern Ireland with the education minister and the Minister for Employment and Learning.

EXPENDITURE

Most education expenditure is incurred by local authorities, which make their own expenditure decisions according to their local situations and needs. Expenditure for higher and further education in England and Scotland is met by the respective funding agencies; in Wales it is provided directly to post-16 providers; and in Northern Ireland it is met by the Department for Employment and Learning for the Further Education (FE) sector.

The bulk of direct expenditure by the DIUS, the Welsh Assembly Government and the Scottish Executive is directed towards supporting post-16 education. Funding for higher education in universities and colleges is channelled through the Higher Education Funding Councils (HEFCs) and through the Department for Employment and Learning in Northern Ireland. Funding for further education, sixth form provision, work based learning and adult and community education is channelled through the funding councils for that sector, but in Wales is provided directly to post-16 providers through the Welsh Assembly Government's Department for Children, Education, Lifelong Learning and Skills (DCELLS). In addition, the DIUS currently funds student support for students from England and the Welsh Assembly Government is responsible for student support in Wales for students who live in Wales. The DCSF is responsible for the City Technology Colleges, the City College for the Technology of the Arts, and pays grants under the specialist schools programme in England.

LOCAL EDUCATION ADMINISTRATION

In England and Wales the school education service is administered by local authorities, which have day-to-day responsibility for providing state primary and secondary education and special schools for pupils in their areas. They share with the appropriate funding bodies (in Wales with the Assembly Government) the duty to provide adult education to meet local needs.

There are four categories of state-funded mainstream schools: community, foundation, voluntary controlled and voluntary aided. In these schools the role of the governing bodies and ownership of assets varies but they all have a lot in common – they are self-managing and do not charge fees. The majority of pupils go to state schools. Unlike other services, where local authorities are financed largely from the council tax and aggregate external finance from Communities and Local Government in England and the National Assembly for Wales, since 2006–7 funding for schools and other pupil provision in England is provided through the new Dedicated Schools Grant from the DCSF to each local authority. Authority-maintained schools usually manage their own budgets: the local authority allocates funds to the school, largely on the basis of pupil numbers, and the school governing body is responsible for overseeing spending and for most

aspects of staffing, including appointments and dismissals. Local authorities also have intervention powers to add additional governors, take back control of a school's budget or replace the governing body of a school with an interim executive when a school is placed under special measures, is judged to have serious weaknesses or is causing concern and has not complied with a formal warning from the authority. The duty of providing education locally in Scotland rests with the education authorities. They are responsible for the construction of buildings, the employment of teachers and other staff, and the provision of equipment and materials.

Devolved school management is in place for all primary, secondary and special schools. Since August 2007, arrangements for parental involvement in schools have changed, to enable parents to get more involved in their child's education. School Boards were replaced by parent councils. The structure of these councils is decided by parents. Headteachers are involved, and the council can invite members of the school or wider community to attend meetings.

Scotland has primary, secondary and special schools. A select group of secondary schools which have found new ways to inspire pupils to get the most from education are on the Schools of Ambition programme. There are currently 52 schools on the scheme, which allocates them extra funding and support. Scotland has 395 state-funded faith schools: 391 Catholic, one Jewish and three Episcopalian.

Education, with the exception of further and higher education, is administered locally in Northern Ireland by five education and library boards (ELBs), which fund controlled and maintained schools and whose costs are met in full by the Northern Ireland Executive. All grant-aided schools include elected parents and teachers on their boards of governors. All schools and colleges of further education have full responsibility for their own budgets, including staffing costs.

EDUCATION IN FIGURES

EXPENDITURE

UK MANAGED EXPENDITURE ON EDUCATION AND TRAINING *(Percentage of GDP)*

	2004–5 outturn	2005–6 outturn	2006–7 outturn (est)
Education and training	5.4	5.6	5.7
Education	5.3	5.4	5.5

Source: PESA 2007

UK EXPENDITURE ON EDUCATION AND TRAINING *(£m)*

	2005–6 outturn accruals	2006–7 est. outturn accruals
Under-fives	4,299	4,142
Primary schools	18,616	19,426
Secondary schools	21,119	22,136
Post-secondary non-tertiary education	8,033	8,365

Tertiary education	9,069	10,738
Training	2,163	2,408
Other education and training	5,969	6,461
Total	69,268	73,946

Source: PESA 2007

UK MANAGED EXPENDITURE ON EDUCATION AND
TRAINING *(£bn)*

1997–8	46.5	2002–3	58.6
1998–9	47.1	2003–4	63.3
1999–2000	48.6	2004–5	65.8
2000–1	52.2	2005–6	69.3
2001–2	56.9	2006–7	72.2

of which on education (£bn)

1997–8	45.1	2002–3	56.6
1998–9	45.5	2003–4	61.2
1999–2000	47.0	2004–5	63.7
2000–1	50.5	2005–6	67.1
2001–2	55.2	2006–7	69.8

UK EXPENDITURE ON EDUCATION BY THE
GOVERNMENT AND LOCAL AUTHORITIES (2005–6) *(£m)*

Local authorities	
Current	42,292
Capital	3,737
Total	46,029
Central government	
Current	26,326
Capital	3,737
Total	30,039
All public authorities	
Current	68,618
Capital	7,450
TOTAL	76,068

PUPILS AND SCHOOLS

UK PRE-SCHOOL EDUCATION (2006) *(percentage)*

	Public sector	Private and voluntary	Total
UK	64	35	99
England	64	38	102
Wales	83	—	83
Scotland	64	25	89
Northern Ireland	59	13	72

UK SCHOOLS BY CATEGORY (2005–6)

	England	Wales
Maintained nursery schools	455	33
Maintained primary and secondary		
schools	20,871	1,779
Community	13,009	1,500
Voluntary aided	4,302	163
Voluntary controlled	2,667	104
Foundation	893	12
Pupil referral units	449	32
Maintained special schools	1,033	43
Non-maintained special schools	72	—
City Technology Colleges and City		
Colleges for the Technology		
of the Arts	11	—
Academies	27	—
Independent schools	2,261	56
Total	25,179	1,943

Scotland	
Publicly funded schools	2,755
Independent schools	150
Total	2,905

Northern Ireland

Grant-aided mainstream	
Nursery*	99
Primary	879
Secondary	228
grammar	69
other	159
Non-maintained mainstream	18
Special (maintained)	48†
Total	1,272

* Excludes voluntary and private pre-school education centres
† Figure includes three hospital schools

UK PUPILS IN THE MAINTAINED SECTOR (2005–6)

Nursery pupils	150,800
Primary pupils	4,974,900
Secondary pupils	3,987,500
Pupils in special schools	101,300
Pupils in pupil referral units	15,600
Total	9,229,100

SPECIAL NEEDS PUPILS (2005–6)

	Number of pupils	Percentage of all pupils
England	236,700	2.9
Wales	15,800	3.2
Scotland	13,800	1.6
Northern Ireland	12,000	3.5
Total	278,300	2.8

TEACHERS

FULL-TIME QUALIFIED TEACHERS (2005–6 EST)
(THOUSANDS)

	E&W	Scotland	NI	UK
Maintained nursery				
and primary schools	179.0	21.6	7.9	208.5
Maintained secondary				
schools	199.3	23.2	10.0	232.5
Non-maintained				
mainstream schools	53.7	2.5	0.1	56.3
All special schools	17.2	2.1	0.7	19.9
Total	449.1	49.4	18.7	517.2

UK PRIMARY SCHOOL PUPIL–TEACHER RATIOS

	England	Wales	Scotland	NI
2003–4	22.7	20.7	18.2	19.9
2004–5	22.5	20.7	17.6	20.0
2005–6	22.0	19.8	17.1	20.5

* The average size of classes 'as taught' was 25.9 in 2005–6
(Figures refer to 'all classes' rather than 'one-teacher classes'
only).

UK SECONDARY SCHOOLS (2005–6)

	England	Wales	Scotland	NI
No. of pupils	3,306,800	213,000	315,800	151,800
Average class size	21.5	20.6	—	—
Pupil–teacher				
ratio	16.6	16.6	12.3	14.4

POST-16 AND HIGHER EDUCATION

POST-16 STUDENTS IN THE UK (2005–6)

	Full-time	Part-time
UK	1,083,500	3,963,700
England	967,300	3,367,200
Wales	41,400	193,400
Scotland*	47,300	294,400
Northern Ireland	27,500	108,700

* Enrolments, not head count

HIGHER EDUCATION STUDENTS IN THE UK* (2005–6)

	Part-time	Full-time	Total
HE students	–	–	2,336,110
Postgraduate students	311,150	234,220	545,370
Undergraduate students	591,925	1,198,820	1,790,740

*Includes UK, EU and non-EU students

UK HIGHER EDUCATION QUALIFICATIONS AWARDED (2005–6)

	Full-time	Part-time
First degrees	278,385	37,600
Higher degrees	90,895	34,180
Other postgraduate	40,705	32,505
Other graduate	48,565	78,020
Total	458,550	182,300

UK HIGHER EDUCATION INCOME BY SOURCE (2005–6)

	£ thousand	Percentage of total
Funding council grants	7,544,078	38.7
Tuition fees, education grants and contracts	4,640,799	23.8
Research grants and contracts	3,120,606	16.0
Endowment and investment	343,083	1.8
Other	3,854,546	19.7
Total	19,503,112	100

UK HIGHER EDUCATION EXPENDITURE (2005–6)

	£ thousand	Percentage of total
Staff costs	11,188,241	57.9
Other operating expenses	6,908,704	35.8
Depreciation	961,211	5.0
Interest payable	254,012	1.3
Total	17,779,680	100

Statistics are published by each of the home education departments through press notices, bulletins and statistical volumes. These can be found on the following websites:
ENGLAND W www.dcsf.gov.uk
WALES W www.wales.gov.uk
SCOTLAND W www.scotland.gov.uk
NORTHERN IRELAND W www.deni.gov.uk

THE INSPECTORATE

ENGLAND

The Office for Standards in Education, Children's Services and Skills (OFSTED) was created on 1 April 2007. It has responsibility for the regulatory and inspection activities of the former Office for Standards in Education; inspection of adult learning and training formerly undertaken by the Adult Learning Inspectorate; the regulation and inspection of children's social care formerly undertaken by the Commission for Social Care Inspection; and the inspection of the Children and Family Court Advisory and Support Service formerly undertaken by Her Majesty's Inspectorate of Court Administration.

OFSTED is a non-ministerial government department whose executive head is Her Majesty's Chief Inspector of Education, Children's Services and Skills (HMCI). OFSTED is responsible for the registration and inspection of childcare, arrangements for social care and support of children and young people, and the inspection of all maintained and some independent schools. It is also responsible for the inspection of further education, all publicly funded adult education and training and some privately funded training provision, and the inspection of teacher training.

The inspection of the Children and Family Court Advisory and Support Service (CAFCASS) is also undertaken by OFSTED. Joint Area Reviews and Annual Performance Assessments of local children's services provision continue to be led by OFSTED. The post of the Children's Rights Director (CRD) transferred to OFSTED from the Commission for Social Care Inspection on 1 April 2007.

The Education and Inspections Act that established the new OFSTED requires the inspectorate to promote improvement in the public services it inspects and regulates; ensure that these services focus on the interests of children, parents, learners and employers; and ensure that these services are efficient and effective. The act also established a board to provide strategic oversight of OFSTED. The non-executive board has a duty to have regard to the views of service users as well as a statutory purpose to encourage improvement.

WALES

Estyn: Arolygiaeth Ei Mawrhydi dros Addysg a Hyfforddiant yng Nghymru (Her Majesty's Inspectorate for Education and Training in Wales) is responsible for inspecting early years provision in the non-maintained sector, primary schools, secondary schools, special schools (including independent special schools), pupil referral units, independent schools, further education, youth support services, local education authorities, teacher education and training, work-based learning, Careers Wales companies, the education, guidance and training elements of the New Deal and adult community based learning. Its remit from the Welsh Assembly Government also includes providing advice on a wide range of education and training matters.

SCOTLAND

HM Inspectorate of Education (HMIE) is an executive agency of the Scottish Executive. HM Inspectors (HMIs) inspect or review and report on education provision in primary, secondary and special schools, further education institutions (under contract to the Scottish Further Education Funding Council), initial teacher education, community learning and development, care and welfare of pupils, the education functions of local authorities, prison education, children's services and in other contexts as necessary. They work in collaboration with the Care Commission in integrated inspection of pre-school education centres and residential schools. They work with Audit Scotland on the inspection of education authorities and on behalf of the Scottish Further Education Funding Council in the review of Scotland's 43 further education colleges. The HMIs work in teams alongside lay members (who are volunteer members of the public) and associate assessors (who are practising teachers or senior educationalists seconded for the inspection). HMIE is led by the senior chief inspector, supported by six chief inspectors (five of whom head inspectorates) and twelve assistant chief inspectors. The Scottish Higher Education Funding Council has a duty to assess quality in higher education institutions and universities, a responsibility which it sub-contracts to the Quality Assurance Agency for Higher Education (QAA) Scotland office. The Further and Higher Education (Scotland) Act 2005 extends this duty on the council to ensure that provision is made for assessing and enhancing the quality of education provided.

NORTHERN IRELAND

Inspection is carried out in Northern Ireland by the Education and Training Inspectorate, which provides inspection services for the Department of Education Northern Ireland (DENI), the Department for Employment and Learning and the Department of Culture, Arts and Leisure. Schools are currently inspected once every five to seven years. In further education and training, extended inspections are carried out once every eight years and focused inspections at least every four years. In addition, the inspectorate provides evidence-based advice to ministers and departments to assist in the formulation and evaluation of policies in education, training and youth.

SCHOOLS

Full-time education is compulsory in Great Britain for all children between five and 16 years and between four and 16 years in Northern Ireland. About 93 per cent of children in the United Kingdom receive free education from public funds and the rest attend fee-charging schools or are educated at home. Provision is being increased for pre-school children and many pupils remain at school after the minimum leaving age. No fees are charged in any publicly maintained school in England, Wales and Scotland. In Northern Ireland, fees may be charged in voluntary schools and are paid by pupils in preparatory departments of grammar schools, but pupils admitted to the secondary departments of grammar schools, unless they come from outside Northern Ireland, do not pay fees. Students under 19 years of age attending courses at further education colleges are not charged course fees.

ENGLAND AND WALES

There are two main types of school in England and Wales: schools maintained by the state, which charge no fees; and independent schools, which charge fees. Schools maintained by the state, with the exception of the academies and city technology colleges, which exist in England alone, are maintained by local authorities. Schools maintained by the state are classified as community, voluntary or foundation schools. Community schools are owned by local authorities and wholly funded by them (although sixth forms have separate funding arrangements). They are non-denominational and provide primary and secondary education. Schools in the voluntary category provide primary and secondary education and many have a particular religious ethos. Although the school buildings are in many cases provided by the voluntary body (known as the foundation), the authority financially maintains them.

There are two subdivisions in the voluntary category: *voluntary controlled,* and *voluntary aided.* In the case of voluntary controlled schools, the authority bears all the costs. In voluntary aided schools, the governing body is responsible for capital expenditure on the buildings, perimeter walls and fences, playgrounds, furniture fixtures and fittings (including ICT), and the Secretary of State for Children, Schools and Families may pay a capital grant of up to 90 per cent of approved capital expenditure. The local authority is responsible for capital work to playing fields and buildings on those fields related to their use as playing fields, and for all revenue funding. Sixth forms have separate funding arrangements. The arrangements in Wales are similar but the rate of grant support is 85 per cent.

Foundation schools provide primary and secondary education. They can have a religious character, although most do not. They are funded by the local authority, and, via the local authority, by the relevant funding bodies in respect of sixth form provision, although the land and buildings will be owned by a foundation or by the governors. The government's policy is to encourage community and voluntary controlled schools to become self-governing as foundation schools. The government is also encouraging schools to acquire foundations (known as Trusts) as a means of forming permanent relationships with external partners. Foundation schools with foundations are known as Trust schools.

Local authorities are required to provide the schools that they maintain with a delegated budget to cover their running costs, including staffing costs. Authorities can retain funding of various centrally provided services, including transport and some special educational needs. The authority acts as admission authority for most community and some voluntary schools.

Academies (England only) – are all-ability independent state schools with a mission to transform education where the status quo is simply not good enough. They are established and managed by independent sponsors, and funded by the government at a level comparable to other local schools. No fees are paid by parents. There are currently 47 academies open as at April 2007 and a further 37 are scheduled to open by the end of September 2007.

City Technology Colleges (CTCs) and *City Colleges for the Technology of the Arts (CCTAs)* are found in England only, and are state-aided but independent of local authorities. Their aim is to widen the choice of secondary education in disadvantaged urban areas and to teach a broad curriculum with an emphasis on science, technology, business understanding and arts technologies. Capital costs are shared by government and business sponsors, and running costs are covered by a per capita grant from the DCSF in line with an average of the comparable costs in authority-maintained schools in the areas where CTCs are located. CTCs are now being encouraged to convert to academies. To date five have converted and a further seven are considering converting over the next few years.

Education Action Zones (EAZs) were established in England from 1998 to develop local partnerships between schools, parents, the community, businesses and local authorities to find solutions to educational underachievement. They were set up as statutory bodies with a maximum five-year lifespan. After five years EAZs in rural areas changed into *Excellence Clusters* and those in urban areas into *Excellence in Cities (EiC)* action zones.

Education Improvement Partnerships are a way of enabling schools and other education providers to work together to raise standards; extend opportunities; and provide high quality services. They have the potential to become the delivery structure for a child-centred, local community agenda, capable of efficiently and effectively coordinating multi-agency working to ensure the broadest range and richest quality of service provision for every child.

Federations – the term describes groups of two or more governing bodies with a formal agreement for their schools to share governance arrangements and to work together for the benefit of all pupils and their school communities; this could entail sharing the curriculum, teaching resources, staff, ICT facilities, sports facilities or budgets. Federations can involve a mix of primary and secondary schools.

Governing bodies – all publicly maintained schools have a governing body, usually made up of a number of parent and local community representatives, governors appointed by the authority if the school is local authority-maintained, the headteacher (unless he or she chooses otherwise) and serving teachers and other staff. Voluntary schools and some foundation schools (including Trust schools) have foundation governors who are generally appointed to protect the ethos of the school. All schools can also appoint up to two sponsor governors and, since August 2005 in England, maintained secondary schools can appoint up to four sponsor governors. Sponsor governors are persons who give substantial assistance to the school, financially or in kind, or who provide services to the school. Governing bodies are responsible for the overall conduct and policies of schools including their academic aims and objectives.

Independent/State School Partnerships were launched in 1998 to forge links between independent and state schools and enhance the opportunities on offer to pupils. In 2006–7 a £2m government package funded 18 new partnership projects.

The *Leading Edge Partnership Programme* involves secondary schools working together to address some of the most critical learning challenges facing the education system. Partnerships focus on raising the performance of schools which are struggling to improve standards or close the achievement gap by addressing issues of under-performance among groups of pupils from poorer socio-economic backgrounds and from particular ethnic minority groups. There are currently 210 Leading Edge Partnerships already established across nearly 100 local authorities. Participation in the Leading Edge Partnership Programme is open to specialist schools which meet high performance criteria at re-designation.

Specialist Schools Programme – is open to all maintained secondary schools in England, including special schools with secondary aged pupils, that wish to develop a curriculum specialism in one of ten specialist areas: arts, business and enterprise, engineering, humanities, languages, mathematics and computing, music, science, sport, and technology. A new specialism for Special Educational Needs (SEN) for SEN schools was also introduced in 2005. Specialist schools receive additional recurrent funding to support the targets within their plan. This is currently calculated at a rate of £129 per pupil per annum. In addition, they receive a one-off capital grant of £100,000 supplemented by sponsorship, to improve their specialist facilities. Specialist schools are expected to include sponsors, local businesses and/or employers on their governing bodies. In January 2007 there were around 2,700 designated specialist schools, representing over 85 per cent of England's total number of secondary schools. Re-designation to the programme is reviewed at the time the school has an OFSTED section 5 inspection, usually every three years. At this point, schools which

meet certain prescribed criteria are also invited to take on extra roles under the High Performing Specialist School element of the programme. These include the opportunity to take up additional roles to support system-wide reform including taking a second curricular or vocational or SEN/inclusion specialism, raising standards through a focus on underperformance, or a teacher training role. Around 400 have already established their options.

Trust schools are foundation schools supported by a charitable foundation or 'Trust' that shares the school's aspirations for their pupils and can support them in continuing improvement. They are funded on exactly the same basis as other local authority maintained schools. Through the Trust, they employ their own staff, set their own admission arrangements in accordance with the admissions code, and manage their own land and buildings. Trust schools are supported by the Trust through the appointment of governors to the school's governing body. The Trust allows schools to build long-term relationships with partners such as businesses, charities, universities and other schools to help raise standards and widen opportunities for pupils. By May 2007 there were over 200 schools working towards Trust status.

SCOTLAND

Education authority schools (known as publicly-funded schools) are financed by local government, partly through revenue support grants from central government, and partly from local taxation. Devolved management from the local authority to the school is in place for more than 88 per cent of all school-level expenditure. A small number of grant-aided schools, mainly in the special sector, are conducted by boards of managers and receive grants direct from the Scottish Executive Education Department. Independent schools charge fees and receive no direct grant, but are subject to inspection and registration.

NORTHERN IRELAND

Controlled schools are managed by the education and library boards (ELBs) through boards of governors consisting of representatives of transferors (mainly the Protestant churches), parents, teachers and the ELB. Within the controlled sector there is a small number of controlled integrated schools. There are also grant maintained integrated schools which are funded directly by the Department of Education.

Voluntary maintained schools are managed by boards of governors consisting of members nominated by trustees (mainly Roman Catholic) with representatives of teachers, parents and the ELB. Voluntary schools receive grants towards capital costs and running costs in whole or in part. A majority are entitled to capital grants at 100 per cent. Voluntary non-maintained schools are mainly voluntary grammar schools managed by boards of governors consisting of representatives of parents, teachers and, in most cases, the Department of Education and the ELB, as well as those appointed as provided in each school's scheme of management. Integrated schools exist to educate Protestant and Roman Catholic children, as well as those of other faiths and no faith, together. Latest figures show that there are currently 56 integrated schools, comprising 19 integrated second level colleges and 37 integrated primary schools.

There are a number of Irish-language schools and units, and in June 2007 there were 21 freestanding Irish-medium schools (19 of which received recurrent funding from the Department) and 12 Irish-medium units attached to schools in the English language sector. Of the 19 schools, 18 are Irish-medium primary schools. There are also 3 Irish-medium nursery units.

THE STATE SYSTEM

SURE START

Sure Start is a programme in England designed to deliver the best start in life for every child. It increases the availability of childcare; improves health, education and emotional development for young people; and supports parents in their role including increasing their chances to work, train and study. Children's Centres providing integrated services for under-fives are now being rolled out to all communities, with the goal of opening 3,500 across England by 2010. Sure Start's remit is confined to the under-fives, but other Sure Start group programmes are targeted at older children, including as part of the extended schools initiative ensuring that accessible and affordable care is available for all children up to the age of 14, or 16 for children with a special need.

PRE-SCHOOL EDUCATION

Pre-school education is for children from 3 to 5 years of age. It is not compulsory, parents can take as little or as much of their entitlement as they choose, although a free place is available for every 3- and 4-year-old whose parents want one. In England since April 2006 all 3- and 4-year-olds are entitled to 12½ hours per week of free early education over 38 weeks of the year. Children are eligible from 1 January, 1 April or 1 September, following their third birthday. By 2010 the free early education entitlement will increase from 12½ hours per week to 15 hours and parents will be able to use their entitlement for longer periods over a minimum of three days. Free places are funded via local authorities and are delivered by a range of providers in the maintained and non-maintained sectors – nursery schools; nursery classes in primary schools; private schools; private day nurseries; voluntary playgroups; pre-schools and registered childminders (who are part of a network approved to deliver early education). In order to receive funding, providers should be working towards the early learning goals and other features of the Foundation Stage curriculum; they should be inspected on a regular basis by education inspectors appointed by the Office for Standards in Education, Children's Services and Skills (OFSTED) and meet any conditions set by the local authority.

From September 2008 the Foundation Stage curriculum, Birth to Three Matters and relevant elements of the National Daycare Standards will be consolidated into the Early Years Foundation Stage (EYFS). This will be a single quality framework for the development, learning and care of all children in all early years settings. The latest available data (January 2006) shows that around 96 per cent of 3-year-olds and virtually all 4-year-olds in England were receiving at least some free early education. In Wales, a free part-time place in a maintained or funded non-maintained setting is available for each child from the term following their third birthday. In Scotland, councils have a duty to provide pre-school education for all 3- and 4-year-olds whose parents request one. In August 2007, the legal duty for provision increased to 475 hours of free pre-school education per year, although local authorities have the power to provide more if they choose. Most provision is delivered in daily 2.5 hour sessions, but alternative arrangements are possible. In Northern Ireland children who have reached the age of 4 on or before 1 July will commence primary school at the beginning of the September following. In Northern Ireland approximately 30 per cent of pre-school education takes place in voluntary/private sector playgroups funded by the Department of Education.

PRIMARY EDUCATION

Primary education begins at 5 years in Great Britain and 4 years in Northern Ireland. In England, Wales and Northern Ireland the transfer to secondary school is generally made at 11 years.

Primary schools consist mainly of infant schools for children aged 5 to 7, junior schools for those aged 7 to 11, and combined junior and infant schools for both age groups. First schools in some parts of England cater for ages 5 to 10 as the first stage of a three-tier system of first, middle and secondary schools. Unlike England, Scotland has only primary schools.

MIDDLE SCHOOLS

Middle schools take children from first schools, mostly in England, cover varying age ranges between 8 and 14 and usually lead on to comprehensive upper schools.

SECONDARY EDUCATION

Secondary schools are for children aged 11 to 16 and for those who choose to stay on to 18. At 16, many students prefer to move on to tertiary or sixth form colleges or into further education colleges or work-based training. Most secondary schools in England, Wales and Scotland are co-educational. The largest secondary schools have over 1,500 pupils, but only 5.5 per cent of schools in the United Kingdom take over 1,000 pupils.

In England and Wales the main types of maintained secondary schools are: comprehensive schools, whose admission arrangements are without reference to ability or aptitude; deemed middle schools (in England), for children aged between eight and 14 years who then move on to senior comprehensive schools at 12, 13 or 14; and (in England) secondary grammar schools, with selective intake, providing an academic course from 11 to 16–18 years.

In Scotland all pupils in education authority secondary schools attend schools with a comprehensive intake. Most of these schools provide a full range of courses appropriate to all levels of ability from first to sixth year.

In Northern Ireland the process of selection (currently the 11-plus examination) is a key factor of the education system. Children are admitted to either grammar (42 per cent of pupils in 2006) or secondary schools (58 per cent of pupils in 2006) based on the grade they achieve in two tests taken during their seventh year at school when they are 10 or 11 years of age. Following a major review of post-primary education, which included research into the selective education system, extensive consultation and recommendations from the Post-Primary Review Working Group (Costello), Northern Ireland's education system was to embark on a process of major reform. However, following the restoration of the Northern Ireland Assembly a vote by the assembly will be required to end academic selection.

New arrangements for post-primary education, in particular the means by which pupils transfer from primary to post-primary schools, are being introduced. The key aspects of the new arrangements are:
- The last transfer tests will be held in autumn 2008
- Transfer from primary to post-primary will be based on informed parental choice

- A pupil profile will be developed for each child, detailing his or her progress

The new post-primary arrangements will guarantee all pupils access to a much wider range of courses, with a minimum of 24 courses at key stage 4, and 27 at post-16. At least one third of the courses on offer will be general (academic) in nature, and at least one third will be (applied vocational/professional/technical). Legislation has been made to give effect to these changes and to enable schools to enter into collaborative arrangements with other schools, FE colleges or other providers.

SPECIAL EDUCATION

Wherever appropriate, taking parents' wishes into account, children with special educational needs are educated in ordinary schools, which are required to publish their policy for pupils with such needs. Schools and local authorities in England and Wales and education and library boards in Northern Ireland are required to identify and secure provision for children with special educational needs and to involve the parents in decisions.

In Scotland, school placing is a matter of agreement between education authorities and parents. Parents have the right to say which school they want their child to attend, and a right of appeal where their wishes are not being met.

In Northern Ireland grant-aided special schools are funded by local education and library boards (ELBs) and have partially delegated budgets. ELBs can also fund places in a small number of local independent schools, recognised by the Department of Education as providers of special education.

Maintained special schools are run by education authorities which pay all the costs of maintenance, but under the terms of local management, all maintained schools must have a delegated budget including maintained special schools. Non-maintained special schools are run by voluntary bodies; they may receive grants from central government for capital expenditure and for equipment but their current expenditure is met primarily from the fees charged to education authorities for pupils placed in the schools. Some independent schools provide education wholly or mainly for children with special educational needs.

Of all the pupils with statements of special educational needs in 2005–6, 63 per cent were educated in mainstream schools.

ELECTIVE HOME EDUCATION

There is no legal obligation on parents in the UK to educate their children at school provided that the local authority is satisfied that the child is receiving full-time education suited to its age, abilities and aptitudes and any special needs. The education authority need not be informed that a child is being educated at home unless the child is currently attending school. In that case the parents must arrange for the child's name to be removed from the school's register (by writing to the headteacher) before education at home can begin. Failure to do so leaves the parents liable to prosecution for condoning non-attendance. There are no official figures on the numbers of pupils educated outside school.

THE CURRICULUM

ENGLAND

The national curriculum was introduced in England from 1988 for the period of compulsory schooling from 5 to 16. It is mandatory in all maintained schools. Following a review in 1999, a revised curriculum was introduced in schools from September 2000.

The Foundation Stage was introduced in September 2000 for children aged 3–5. It sets out six areas of learning:

- Personal, social and emotional development
- Communication
- Mathematical development
- Knowledge and understanding of the world
- Physical development
- Creative development

The Education Act 2002 extended the national curriculum to include the Foundation Stage. This act also established a single national assessment system for the Foundation Stage called the Foundation Stage Profile.

At key stages 1 and 2, the statutory subjects in the national curriculum are:

Core subjects	Foundation subjects
English	Design and Technology
Mathematics	Information and Communication Technology
Science	History
	Geography
	Art and Design
	Music
	Physical Education

At key stage 3 (11- to 14-year-olds) a modern foreign language and citizenship are introduced. At key stage 4 (14- to 16-year-olds) pupils are required to continue to study the core subjects, plus physical education, information and communication technology and citizenship. Careers and sex education are also statutory subjects for all secondary pupils and work-related learning is statutory for all pupils at key stage 4. In addition, schools must provide access for each key stage 4 pupil to a minimum of one course in the arts (art and design, music, dance, drama and media arts), one course in the humanities (history and geography), at least one modern foreign language and design and technology. Other subjects, such as drama, dance and classical languages, are taught when the resources of individual schools permit. Religious education must be taught across all key stages. Parents have the right to withdraw their children from religious education and sex education classes.

Statutory assessment takes place at the end of the Foundation Stage and national tests and tasks take place in English and mathematics at the end of key stage 1 (seven-year-olds), with the addition of science at the end of key stage 2 (11-year-olds). At key stage 1 the results of tasks and tests are not reported but are used to underpin teachers' overall assessment of pupils. At key stages 2 and 3 separate teacher assessments of pupils' progress are made to set alongside the test results. At key stage 4, the GCSE and vocational equivalents are the main form of assessment.

Each year, the Department for Children, Schools and Families (DCSF) in England publishes four sets of achievement and attainment tables showing performance measures for every school and local authority based on results at key stages 2 and 3, GCSE, A-level and equivalent qualifications.

The Qualifications and Curriculum Authority (QCA) is an independent government agency funded by the DCSF. It is responsible for setting the national curriculum and for ensuring that the curriculum and qualifications available to young people and adults are of high quality, coherent and flexible; its remit ranges from the under-fives to higher level vocational qualifications.

The National Assessment Agency (NAA) was launched in April 2004 by the DfES to develop and deliver high quality national curriculum tests and supervise the delivery and modernisation of GCSE and A-level examinations. The NAA is a subsidiary of the QCA.

WALES

A national curriculum was introduced simultaneously in Wales and, although it is broadly similar to that of England, it has separate and distinctive characteristics which are reflected in the programmes of study where appropriate. Welsh is compulsory for pupils at all key stages, either as a first or as a second language. Between 8 January and 30 March 2007, a series of consultation exercises was undertaken as part of the review of the school curriculum in Wales. Following this consultation, recommendations will be made to the Minister for Education, Lifelong Learning and Skills and it is anticipated that the revised curriculum will be implemented from September 2008.

In July 2003 the minister announced that statutory testing would be removed for pupils in Wales at the end of key stage 2 from 2004–5 and from 2005–6 for key stage 3. Statutory teacher assessment remains and will be strengthened by moderation and accreditation arrangements. It is the only form of statutory assessment from key stages 1–3.

On 1 April 2006, Awdurdod Cymwysterau, Cwricwlwm ac Asesu Cymru (ACCAC – the Qualifications, Curriculum and Assessment Authority for Wales) merged with the Department of Training and Education, ELWa, Dysg and the Welsh Youth Agency to create the Department for Education, Lifelong Learning and Skills.

SCOTLAND

The content and management of the curriculum in Scotland are not prescribed by statute but are the responsibility of education authorities and individual headteachers. Advice and guidance are provided by the Scottish Executive Education Department and Learning and Teaching Scotland, which also has a developmental role. Those bodies have produced guidelines on the structure and balance of the curriculum as well as for each of five broad curriculum areas for the five to 14 age group. There are also guidelines on assessment across the whole curriculum, on reporting to parents, and on the use of national tests for reading, writing and mathematics at six levels. Testing is carried out by the school when the teacher judges that a pupil has completed a level; most pupils are expected to move from one level to the next at roughly 18-month to two-year intervals. Guidance on the curriculum for 14- to 16-year-olds recommends study within each of eight modes: language and communication; mathematical studies; science; technology; social studies; creative activities; physical education; and religious and moral education. There is also a recommended percentage of time to be devoted to each area over the two years. Provision is also made for teaching in Gaelic in many parts of Scotland and the

number of pupils, from nursery to secondary, in Gaelic-medium education is growing. Local authorities must ensure that local education provision meets demand and consider whether they need a Gaelic-medium class, school or unit. For 16- to 18-year-olds, National Qualifications, a unified framework of courses and awards which brings together both academic and vocational courses, was introduced in 1999. The Scottish Qualifications Authority awards the certificates.

NORTHERN IRELAND

The statutory Northern Ireland curriculum is made up of religious education and five broad areas of study at primary level and six at secondary level. Provided the requirements of the statutory curriculum are met, it is for each school to decide what additional subjects should be made available for pupils. Pupils at key stages 1 and 2 study religious education, English, mathematics, science, history and geography (known as the environment and society area of study), art and design, music and PE (the creative and expressive area of study), Irish (in Irish-language schools only) and four educational cross-curricular themes (education for mutual understanding, cultural heritage, health education and information technology). At key stage 3, pupils also study technology and design, plus a foreign language (pupils in Irish-language schools can study a foreign language or continue studying Irish) and two extra cross-curricular themes (economic awareness and careers education). At key stage 4, pupils can drop technology and design, art and design, and music and can choose one subject from history, geography, business studies, home economics, economics, political studies or social and environmental studies.

The government accepted proposals from the Northern Ireland Council for the Curriculum Examinations and Assessment (CCEA) for a revised Northern Ireland curriculum in June 2004. The new curriculum will be phased in over a number of years from September 2007 to allow schools to plan for and implement the changes. A number of elements of the revised curriculum are being piloted in advance of implementation. The revised curriculum will be less prescriptive in terms of content, and more holistic and flexible. There will be greater emphasis on developing skills (such as communication, using mathematics and using ICT, along with thinking skills such as creativity, teamwork and problem-solving) and a new area of Learning for Life and Work at key stages 3 and 4 that will include education for employability, citizenship and personal development. In addition to religious education, the other learning areas (which will replace areas of study) are:

Foundation Stage, Key Stages 1 and 2	Key Stages 3 and 4
The Arts	Learning for Life and Work
Language and Literacy	The Arts
Mathematics and Numeracy	Language and Literacy
Personal Development and Mutual Understanding	Mathematics and numeracy
Physical Education	Modern Languages
The World Around Us	Physical Education
	Science and Technology
	Environment and Society

A new key stage known as the Foundation Stage, which covers years 1 and 2 of primary school, will be introduced. This is to allow a more appropriate learning style for the youngest pupils and to ease the transition from pre-school.

The assessment of pupils is broadly in line with practice in England and Wales and currently takes place at the ages of eight, 11 and 14, ie end of key stage assessment. With the introduction of the revised curriculum, this will be replaced by annual assessment reported to parents in the form of a pupil profile. Teachers will assess pupils in the cross-curricular skills of communication, using mathematics and using ICT. Teachers will also comment on a pupil's progress and areas for future development in the other thinking skills and in the learning areas. Teacher assessment can be suported by objective computer-based diagnostic assessments. The GCSE is used to assess 16-year-olds.

The CCEA is a unique education body in the UK in that it combines the three functions of a curriculum advisory body, an awarding body and a qualifications regulatory body. It monitors and advises the Department of Education and teachers on all matters relating to the curriculum, assessment arrangements and examinations in grant-aided schools. It conducts GCSE, A- and AS-level examinations, pupil assessment at key stages 1, 2 and 3 and administers the transfer procedure tests. It also ensures that qualifications offered by awarding bodies in Northern Ireland are of an appropriate quality and standard.

PUBLIC EXAMINATIONS AND QUALIFICATIONS

ENGLAND, WALES AND NORTHERN IRELAND

In 1988 a single system of examinations, the General Certificate of Secondary Education (GCSE), which is usually taken after five years of secondary education, was introduced. The GCSE is the main method of assessing the performance of pupils on a subject-specific basis. The structure of the examination reflects national curriculum requirements where these apply. GCSE short-course qualifications are available in some subjects. As a rule the syllabus comprises half the content of a full GCSE course. In September 2002 eight GCSEs in vocational subjects were introduced (known as Applied GCSEs) and they are: applied art and design, applied business, engineering, health and social care, applied ICT, leisure and tourism, manufacturing, and applied science.

The GCSE differs from its predecessors in that there are syllabuses based on national criteria covering course objectives, content and assessment methods; differentiated assessment (ie different papers or questions for different ranges of ability) and grade-related criteria (ie grades awarded on absolute rather than relative performance). The GCSE certificates are awarded on an eight-point scale, A* to G. All GCSE syllabuses, assessments and grading procedures are monitored by qualification regulators for England, Wales and Northern Ireland (QCA, DELLS and CCEA) to ensure that they conform to the national criteria. In England in 2005, 56.3 per cent of 15-year-olds (at the beginning of the academic year) gained at least five results at grade C or better at GCSE or General National Vocational Qualification (GNVQ) equivalent (61 per cent in Northern Ireland), while 89.0 per cent achieved five or more at grade G or above. Students are increasingly encouraged to continue their education post-16. For those who do so, in addition to the vocational qualifications outlined below, there are GCE (General Certificate of Education), AS (Advanced Subsidiary) and A (Advanced) Levels and the Advanced Applied A-levels. Since September 2005 Applied A-levels have AS/A2 units, bringing them into line with GCE A-levels. At the same time the formal distinction between GCEs and VCEs was dropped and both vocational and academic qualifications are now known as GCEs. However, a small number of subjects – art and design, business, ICT and science – were available as GCEs and VCEs. In order to distinguish between the different patterns of study and assessment in these qualifications, the term 'applied' was introduced into the current vocational qualification in these subjects: for example, the current VCE in art and design is known as the GCE A-level in applied art and design. A-level courses usually last two years and have traditionally provided the foundation for entry to higher education. AS-level qualifications were introduced in September 2000 and represent the first half of a full A-level and are assessed accordingly. Following extensive consultations in 1996 and 1997 which indicated the need to broaden the post-16 curriculum, new A-level qualifications were introduced in September 2000. The new A-level qualification consists of six units (three AS units and three A2 units). Students who go on to complete the full A-level will be assessed on their attainment in all six units, which may be taken either in stages or at the end of the course. A-levels and AS-levels are marked on a six-point scale from A to E. There is also the opportunity for A-level candidates to take additional papers known as Advanced Extension Awards (which replaced Special papers) and these are designed to challenge the most able A-level students.

VOCATIONAL QUALIFICATIONS

There are two broad categories of vocational qualifications: National Vocational Qualifications (NVQs), which demonstrate competence in a specific occupation (or aspect of an occupation), and vocationally related qualifications, which usually give a broader, more general preparation for an industry or wider occupational area. All vocational qualifications are based upon national occupational standards, which are designed by employers. Vocational qualifications are accredited into the national qualifications framework by the QCA at nine levels:

- Entry level
- Level 1 – Foundation Skills
- Level 2 – Operative/Semiskilled
- Level 3 – Technician/Craft/Skilled/Supervisory
- Level 4 – Technical/Middle Management
- Level 5 – Chartered/Professional/Senior Management
- Level 6 – Knowledge Based Professionals
- Level 7 – High Level Specialist Professional/Senior Professionals
- Level 8 – Leading Experts/Practitioners

General National Vocational Qualifications (GNVQs) are now being replaced by vocational GCSEs (see above). The Advanced Vocational Certificate of Education (VCE), replaced Advanced GNVQs. It is available in different forms: the three-unit Advanced Subsidiary (equivalent to one GCE AS-level), the six-unit Advanced Level (equivalent to one GCE A-level), and the 12-unit Double Award (equivalent to two GCE A-levels).

WELSH BACCALAUREATE

The Welsh Baccalaureate is a new qualification for 16–19 year olds that incorporates current approved qualifications like A-levels, GCSEs and NVQs and adds breadth and balance through a core programme of activities. It is currently being piloted in 31 schools and colleges throughout Wales at both intermediate and advanced level and, subject to ministerial decisions following external evaluation which was reported in the summer of 2006, it was planned to be rolled out nationally from September 2007. In addition, the pilot has now been extended to include the development of a foundation level Welsh Baccalaureate since September 2006. This is being piloted in pre-16 settings along with limited intermediate provision. The Welsh Baccalaureate allows students flexibility of study in the range of traditional qualifications and the opportunity to develop key skills and wider learning experiences.

SCOTLAND

Scotland has its own system of public examinations, and in 1999 a new system of National Qualifications was introduced. Five levels of study are offered: Access, Intermediate 1, Intermediate 2, Higher and Advanced Higher. The new Higher National course and Advanced Higher National course are direct replacements for the old SCE Higher grade and the Certificate of Sixth Year Studies respectively. National Qualifications are included on the Scottish Credit and Qualifications Framework (SCQF) (see below), with Access equating to levels 1 to 3, Intermediate 1 to level 4, Intermediate 2 to level 5, Higher to level 6 and Advanced Higher to level 7.

National courses consist of blocks of study called national units. A unit usually consists of around 40 hours of study and there are three units in a course. Unit awards demonstrate that a learner has achieved competence in a particular area of study. National course awards are graded by external assessment, which consists of an examination, coursework or performance, or a combination of two or more of these. National course awards also require candidates to pass all unit assessments of the course. A typical national course external assessment requires candidates to demonstrate long-term retention of knowledge, high levels of problem solving, integration of knowledge across a whole course and an ability to apply knowledge and skills in novel situations. The range of subjects has been expanded to include vocational qualifications.

A number of schools use the new National Qualifications system for pupils in their fourth year of secondary education, but the majority of this lower age group still take the traditional Standard Grade examinations at the end of a two-year course. Awards at Standard Grade are set at three levels: Credit (leading to awards at grade 1 or 2); General (leading to awards at grade 3 or 4); and Foundation (leading to awards at grade 5 or 6). Grade 7 is awarded to those who, although they have completed the course, have not attained any of these levels. Normally pupils will take examinations covering two pairs of grades, either grades 1–4 or grades 3–6. Most candidates take seven or eight Standard Grade examinations. The three levels of Standard Grade equate to levels 3 to 5 of the SCQF.

INTERNATIONAL BACCALAUREATE

The International Baccalaureate (IB) Organisation is a non-profit foundation that offers three challenging educational programmes – the Primary Years Programme for students aged 3 to 12, the Middle Years Programme for students aged 11 to 16 and the Diploma Programme for students aged 16 to 19. Each programme can be taught in its own right, but, when linked together, they form a continuum of education for students aged 3 to 19. The programmes consist of a curriculum or curriculum

framework and a pedagogy promoting good teaching practice; methods of student assessment appropriate to the age range; professional development and support opportunities for educators; and an ongoing process of school evaluation. The programmes are offered through IB World Schools (of which there are 87 in the UK and over 1,800 worldwide) and are well recognized by governments and universities around the world. More than half of the students currently participating in IB programmes are in state funded schools.

POST-16 EDUCATION

In the UK in 2004–5, 77 per cent of 16-year-olds and 64 per cent of 17-year-olds were in post-compulsory education, either at school or in further education. There were over 5 million further education students in the UK during the academic year 2004–5, of which 79 per cent were part-time. In 2005–6, there were 476 further education colleges in the UK of which 102 were sixth form colleges. In 2004–5, there were 60,000 full-time academic staff in further education institutions.

ENGLAND

The further education (FE) system provides a wide range of education and training opportunities for individuals from age 14 upwards and employers. Learning opportunities are provided at all levels from basic skills to higher education. The central policy aim is to build a further education system that provides the skills the economy needs to sustain quality of life and to contribute to the UK's international standing. The goal is to lead the world in skills development – with virtually all young people staying on in education and training to age 19 and half progressing to higher education; all adults having the support they need to improve their skills throughout life; and all employers seeing skills as key to their success.

In March 2006 a reform strategy *Further Education: Raising Skills, Improving Life Chances* was launched which set out a programme of changes to deliver this aim. Key aspects include:

- a new economic mission for FE
- providers of learning and skills to specialise to supply world class services
- an enhanced role for employers and learners in shaping development
- new entitlements to learning and support for those who most need it – free tuition for first level 3 for 19–25 year olds and learner accounts for adults on level 3 programmes
- a new strategy for raising quality, with intervention to eliminate poor quality provision
- public funding focused on delivery priorities
- less bureaucracy along with more autonomy for effective providers

The English FE system includes independent providers (voluntary and private sector) who offer a range of work-based and personal and community learning. Personal and community development learning takes place in a wide range of settings usually community based and delivered via local authorities. Post-16 education and training (excluding Higher Education) in England is funded through the Learning and Skills Council (LSC).

WORK-BASED LEARNING

Apprenticeships are a way for learners to get practical experience while gaining nationally recognised qualifications. The LSC in England and the Welsh

Assembly Government in Wales contribute towards the cost of the training and assessment. Apprenticeships normally last between one and three years (four in Wales) and there are two levels: apprenticeships and advanced apprenticeships at levels 2 and 3 respectively. Both of these lead to:

- National Vocational Qualifications (NVQs)
- Key Skills qualifications – transferable work-related skills such as IT and communication and problem solving
- Technical certificates – vocationally related qualifications that provide the basic knowledge of the NVQ

There are currently over 250,000 young people aged between 16 to 24 on apprenticeships in England alone, with similar programmes in place in Scotland, Northern Ireland and Wales.

> In May 2004 a new set of apprenticeships was announced, incorporating Young Apprenticeships for 14- to 16-year-olds, which was launched in September 2004 with 1,000 young people. A further 2,000 young people joined the programme from September 2005. The reforms also led to the opening up of adult apprenticeships by scrapping the arbitrary 25-year-old age limit. Following a successful series of trials additional funding has been put in place for around 8,000 adults to take up apprenticeships in 2007–8.

Diplomas are new qualifications which will give young people a real alternative to traditional learning. Combining theoretical and applied learning they provide a package that ensures that young people are both educated and employable. Employers will know that a young person has mastered functional skills in English, Maths and ICT, and can apply these in work situations. Diploma Development Partnerships (DDPs) have been established to explore content development. These DDPs, led by Sector Skills Councils and including employers, higher education, school and college and awarding body representatives, specify the content of the diplomas. Awarding bodies will then develop the qualifications. The diplomas will be available in 14 lines of learning. The content for the first five lines (ICT; health and social care, engineering, creative and media and construction and the built environment) can be accessed via the QCA website. These qualifications will be available for teaching from September 2008. A further five diplomas, in business administration and finance; hair and beauty; hospitality and catering; land-based and environmental; and manufacturing will be available for teaching in 2009. The final four diplomas, in public services; sport and leisure; retail; and travel and tourism will be available in 2010. A new statutory entitlement will be in place for all 14-19 year olds from September 2013.

WALES

In Wales, the aims and makeup of the FE system are very similar to those outlined for England, although, as the education portfolio is devolved to the Welsh Assembly, the policy documents vary. Current thinking is outlined in *The Learning Country: Vision into Action* which was published in October 2006. This document focuses on improving basic skills and aims for 70 per cent of working age adults to be educated to at least level 2, 50 per cent to level 3 and 40 per cent to level 4 and above by 2010.

SCOTLAND

Since Autumn 2005, the Scottish Funding Council has been the statutory body responsible for funding Scotland's 46 further education colleges. The Scottish Qualifications Authority (SQA) is the statutory awarding body for qualifications in the national education and training system. It is both the main awarding body for qualifications for work including Scottish Vocational Qualifications (SVQs) and is also their accrediting body. The SQA is by statute required clearly to separate its awarding and accrediting functions. There are three main qualification 'families' in Scottish further education: National Qualifications; Higher National Qualifications (HNC and HND); and SVQs. In addition to Standard Grade qualifications, National Qualifications are available at five levels. Another feature of the qualifications system is the Scottish Group Award (SGA). SGAs are built up unit by unit and allow opportunity for credit transfer from other qualifications (such as Standard Grade or SVQ), providing a further option, especially for adult learners. SVQs are competence-based qualifications suitable for workplace delivery but they can also be taken in further education colleges and other centres where workplace conditions can be simulated. The Scottish Credit and Qualifications Framework includes qualifications across academic and vocational sectors in a single credit-based framework. It comprises 12 levels, covering all mainstream qualifications from Access level in National Qualifications to postgraduate qualifications, and including SVQs. In the academic year 2004–5 there were 450,435 student enrolments on vocational and non-vocational courses in further education colleges. Of this total, higher education courses accounted for 29 per cent of college activity.

NORTHERN IRELAND

All further education colleges are independent corporate bodies like their counterparts in the rest of the UK. Responsibility for the sector lies with the Department for Employment and Learning (DELNI), which funds the colleges directly. The colleges own their own property, are responsible for their own services and employ their own staff.

The governing bodies of the colleges must include at least 50 per cent membership from those who are engaged or employed in business, industry, or any profession. The composition of governing bodies is being reviewed as part of the planned restructuring of the FE sector from August 2007.

Northern Ireland has 16 institutions of further education. This was reduced to six area-based colleges in August 2007. In 2005–6 there were 33,353 full-time and 133,003 part-time enrolments on vocational further education courses.

STUDENT SUPPORT

Education maintenance allowance (EMA) is an income tested allowance that supports young people in post-16 learning across the UK. EMA consists of a weekly allowance of up to £30, plus periodic bonus payments and is available to learners from low-income households who stay on at school, college, LSC-funded Entry to Employment (E2E) or programme led apprenticeships. EMA is available for up to three years. Also available to students in England aged 16-19 are learner support funds. These funds, which are targeted at those students in greatest need, have four separate strands: transport, childcare (Care2Learn), residential and general funding.

Whilst the funding for both transport and childcare are universal, the discretionary nature of the other funds allows local learning institutions to provide targeted help and support where it is needed. Hardship funds are available to learners in E2E or programme led apprenticeships and replicate the general learner support fund available to learners in further education. For adults (19 and over) in England similar discretionary learner support funds are available for the most disadvantaged students with the greatest need. These provide financial help with the costs of childcare, books, equipment and transport and residential funding. Funds are administered by colleges and other providers. In England, the adult learning grant (ALG) is an income assessed grant of up to £30 per week for adults who are on low incomes. It is paid to learners who are studying full time for their first full level 2 (five GCSEs or equivalent) or level 3 qualification (two A-levels or equivalent). ALG is administered by the LSC and is currently piloted in further education providers across 25 LSC areas. It has been available throughout England since September 2007.

For students over 18 in the UK who choose to fund their course themselves, career development loans are available from three high street banks. Loans of between £300 and £8,000 can be used to pay for the costs of vocational training courses. Interest on the loan is paid by the LSC while the student is completing the course. Eligible Welsh-domiciled students aged 19 years or over on further education courses, whether full-time or part-time (subject to a minimum contact requirement), receive a means-tested non-repayable assembly learning grant. Discretionary financial contingency funds are also available to all students suffering hardship and are administered by the institutions themselves. In addition, individual learning accounts are available in Wales, which provide adults with means-tested support of up to £200 to undertake a wide range of learning. Eligible Scottish-domiciled further education students can apply to their college for discretionary support in the form of bursaries. These can include allowances for maintenance, travel, study, dependants and additional support needs. College students receiving EMAs may also be eligible for the non-maintenance elements. Colleges administer discretionary funds in the form of hardship funds. They also have a childcare fund which is used to pay for registered childcare. Some colleges may offer different methods of childcare support and provision, for example on-site nurseries or childcare vouchers.

Full-time students over 19 years of age, resident in Northern Ireland and on certain vocational courses, may benefit from discretionary non-repayable further education bursaries. The bursaries are administered by the education and library boards. Support includes free tuition to all full-time students up to age 18 and to all full-time students over 18 undertaking a vocational course at level 3 or below. In addition, financial help is provided by colleges through a discretionary support fund for both full-time and part-time students whose access to and participation in further education is inhibited by financial considerations.

TEACHERS

ENGLAND AND WALES

All teachers working in maintained primary, special and secondary schools, non-maintained special schools and pupil referral units are required to register with the General Teaching Council for England (GTCE) in England and the General Teaching Council for Wales (GTCW) in Wales.

New entrants to the teaching profession in state primary and secondary schools are required to be graduates and to have qualified teacher status (QTS). QTS is achieved by successfully completing a course of initial teacher training, traditionally either a Bachelor of Education (BEd) degree, BA with QTS, BSc with QTS or the Postgraduate Certificate of Education (PGCE) at an accredited institution. New entrants are statutorily required to serve a three term (full-time, pro rata part-time) induction period during which they will have a structured programme of support. All initial teacher training has a strong element of practical school-based work, with student teachers spending significant periods of their training in the classroom.

In addition to the traditional routes, in recent years various employment-based routes to QTS have been developed. The Graduate Teacher Programme (GTP) is designed for mature, well-qualified people who can quickly take on teaching responsibilities and who need to earn a living while they train. Trainees are paid a salary and undergo up to a year of school-based training. The Registered Teacher Programme (RTP) is designed for people without a degree or formal teaching qualification but with at least two years of higher education; entrants are paid a salary and complete a degree while undergoing training for up to two years. Employment-based training routes account for about 15 per cent of all teacher training places.

Teachers in further education (FE) are not required to have QTS, though roughly half have a teaching qualification and most have industrial, commercial or professional experience. Since July 2002, all new entrants to FE teaching in Wales are required to have, or to be working towards, a specified FE teaching qualification. A qualification for aspiring headteachers, the National Professional Qualification for Headship (NPQH), has been introduced. The National College for School Leadership administers this qualification and others and acts as a focus for development and support. In Wales, the NPQH and other headship programmes are administered by the Welsh Assembly Government and consideration is being given to establishing a similar scheme in respect of FE principals, in association with powers under the Education Act 2002 allowing the making of regulations requiring FE principals to have a specified qualification.

New financial incentives for trainee teachers were introduced from September 2006. Maths and science postgraduate trainees may be eligible for a £9,000 tax free bursary while they train, and a £5,000 taxable 'golden hello' after successfully completing the induction period. Modern languages, English or drama, design and technology, ICT, music and religious education postgraduate trainees may be eligible for a £9,000 training bursary and a £2,500 'golden hello'. A £6,000 training bursary is available for other postgraduate secondary and primary trainees. In Wales a similar scheme operates, on a pilot basis, for those undertaking the full-time PGCE (FE) or PGCE (PcET) (Post-compulsory Education and Training). Eligible students receive a bursary of £6,000 (£7,000 for mathematics and science courses since September 2005), paid in instalments whilst studying. In England, other training awards may be available through the secondary shortage subject scheme (SSSS). This is an additional, means-tested hardship fund from the Training and Development Agency for Schools. The subjects currently included are: design and technology, geography, information technology, mathematics, modern languages, music, religious education and science.

In Wales, placement grants supported by the Higher Education Funding Council for Wales (HEFCW) provide £1,000 per funded student on undergraduate priority courses – the same subjects that attract the £4,000 training grant – and £600 to students on other undergraduate courses.

The Teacher Training Agency became the Training and Development Agency for Schools (TDA) in September 2005 and in early 2006 it incorporated the work of the National Remodelling Team. In addition to attracting quality people to initial teacher training (ITT), funding universities, colleges and schools to deliver ITT and working to improve the quality of training, the agency's new role is to work with schools to help them develop and train their whole school team. The TDA administers a returners' programme for qualified teachers who wish to refresh their skills before returning to the profession. Participants are entitled to a bursary of up to £150 a week to a total of £1,500 and additional childcare support. The TDA supports the sharing of good practice in teacher training, encourages schools to offer placements for trainee teachers, and funds training and assessment for higher level teaching assistant (HLTA) status.

In Wales funding of ITT is undertaken by the HEFCW. On an integrated England and Wales basis the TDA also acts as a central source of information and advice on entry to teaching.

The General Teaching Council for England (GTCE), an independent professional council, acts as a disciplinary body dealing with cases of misconduct and incompetence in England. The GTCE also hears appeal hearings for registered teachers who have failed their induction year. In addition, it is responsible for promoting the profession and professional standards and for advising the secretary of state. The separate General Teaching Council for Wales (GTCW) fulfils a similar role in Wales and provides advice to the Welsh Assembly Government.

The Specialist Teacher Assistant scheme provides trained support to qualified teachers in the teaching of reading, writing and arithmetic to young pupils.

In January 2003 the DfES, Welsh Assembly Government, employers and teaching unions signed a national agreement, *Raising Standards and Tackling Workload*, setting out a three-year programme of reforms to provide more classroom support for teachers.

SCOTLAND

The General Teaching Council for Scotland (GTCS) advises central government on matters relating to teacher supply and the professional suitability of all teacher training courses. It is also the body responsible for disciplinary procedures in cases of professional misconduct. All teachers in maintained schools must be registered with the GTCS. Only graduates are accepted as entrants to the profession; primary school teachers undertake either a four-year vocational degree course or a one-year postgraduate course, while teachers of academic subjects in secondary schools undertake the latter. There is also a combined degree sometimes known as a concurrent degree.

The Scottish Qualification for Headship has been introduced for aspiring headteachers. Universities with specialist education departments provide both in-service and pre-service training for teachers. The universities are funded by the Scottish Higher Education Funding Council, which also sets intake levels for teacher education courses in line with guidance provided by the Scottish Executive.

NORTHERN IRELAND

All new entrants to teaching in grant-aided schools are graduates and hold an approved teaching qualification. A fully integrated programme of Initial Teacher Education (ITE), induction and early professional development as well as the Professional Qualification for Headship programme, is in place in Northern Ireland. ITE is provided by Queen's University, Belfast, University of Ulster, Stranmillis University College, St Mary's University College and the Open University (NI). The university colleges are concerned with teacher education mainly for the primary school sector and the universities mainly for the post-primary sector. The General Teaching Council for Northern Ireland (GTCNI) advises government on professional issues, maintains a register of professional teachers and acts as a disciplinary body.

SALARIES

Qualified teachers in England and Wales, other than the leadership group (which includes headteachers, deputy headteachers and advanced skills teachers) are paid on a six-point main pay scale. Teachers who demonstrate exceptional ability have the opportunity to be assessed against national standards and moving to the three point upper scale. An 'Excellent Teacher' scheme has been available to schools since September 2006. This allows eligible teachers to access a 'spot' salary. There are teaching and learning responsibility payments for specific posts, special needs work and recruitment and retention factors which may be awarded at the discretion of the relevant body, ie the governing body or the local authority. The advanced skills teacher grade was introduced to enhance prospects in the classroom for the most able teachers. Experienced teachers are assessed against national standards to move onto the upper pay scale, after which they receive performance-related pay increases. There is a statutory superannuation scheme. Teachers working in the London area are paid on separate pay scales. As at September 2007, salary scales for teachers in England and Wales are:

Headteacher	£39,525–£98,022
Advanced skills teacher	£34,938–£53,115
Classroom teacher (upper pay scale)	£31,878–£34,281
Classroom teacher (main pay scale)	£20,133–£29,427
Unqualified teachers	£14,751–£23,331
Inner London	
Headteacher	£46,134–£104,628
Advanced skills teacher	£41,541–£59,724
Classroom teacher (upper pay scale)	£37,809–£41,004
Classroom teacher (main pay scale)	£24,168–£33,936
Unqualified teachers	£18,552–£27,129

Teachers in Scotland are paid on a seven-point scale. The entry point depends on type of qualification and additional allowances are payable under a range of circumstances. As at 1 April 2006, salary scales for teachers in Scotland were:

Headteacher/deputy headteacher	£39,207–£76,527
Principal teacher	£34,566–£44,616
Chartered teacher	£32,688–£38,868
Main grade	£19,878–£31,707

Teachers in Northern Ireland have broadly similar pay and working conditions as teachers in England and Wales, although negotiated through separate local negotiating machinery. There are a few exceptions to this, for example there is no advanced skills teacher grade. As at September 2007, salary scales for teachers in Northern Ireland are:

Principal	£39,525–£98,022
Vice-Principal	From £34,938
Classroom teacher	£20,133–£34,281

HIGHER EDUCATION

The term higher education is used to describe education above A-level, Higher and Advanced Higher Grade and their equivalent, which is provided in universities, colleges of higher education and in some FE colleges.
The main purposes of higher education are:
- to enable people to develop their capabilities and fulfil their potential, both personally and at work
- to advance knowledge and understanding through scholarship and research
- to contribute to an economically successful and culturally diverse nation

Advice to government on matters relating to higher education is provided by the separate Higher Education Funding Councils for England, Wales and Scotland, and by the Northern Ireland Higher Education Council. The former receive a block grant from central government which they allocate to the universities and colleges. In Northern Ireland the grant is allocated directly to institutions by the Department for Employment and Learning.

The Scottish Funding Council (SFC) funds 20 institutions of higher education, including 14 universities. The universities are broadly managed as described above and the remaining colleges are managed by independent governing bodies which include representatives of industrial, commercial, professional and educational interests.

In Northern Ireland higher education is provided in six regional further education colleges, the two universities and the two university colleges. These institutions offer a range of courses, including first and postgraduate degrees, PGCEs, undergraduate diplomas and certificates, foundation degrees, Higher National Diplomas and professional qualifications.

TYPES OF HIGHER EDUCATION INSTITUTION

The Further and Higher Education Act 1992 and parallel legislation in Scotland removed the distinction between higher education provided by the universities and that provided in England, Scotland and Wales by the former polytechnics and colleges of higher education. It allowed all polytechnics, and other higher education institutions which satisfy the necessary criteria, to award their own taught course and research degrees and to adopt the title of university. All the polytechnics have since done so. The change of name does not affect the legal constitution of the institutions. Funding is by the Higher Education Funding Councils for England, Wales and Scotland and directly by the

Department for Employment and Learning in Northern Ireland. There are now 106 universities in the UK, up from the 48 which existed prior to the Further and Higher Education Acts 1992. Of the 106, 88 are in England (including the University of London, which has a federal structure), 13 in Wales, 14 in Scotland (including the Open University) and four (including two university colleges) in Northern Ireland. There are also 46 colleges of higher education in the UK, some of which are multidisciplinary while others specialise, for example, in initial teacher training. Some award their own degrees and qualifications, while others are validated by a university or a national body.

GOVERNANCE OF UNIVERSITIES AND COLLEGES

The pre-1992 universities each have their own system of internal governance but broad similarities exist. They are run by a council which is the executive governing body and is responsible for all the affairs of the university including appointments, promotions and bidding for and allocation of financial resources. At least half the members of the council are drawn from outside the university. Many of the council's functions are carried out through committees. The senate reports to the council and deals primarily with academic issues. It consists of the council and members elected from within the university. The 1992 Act, and the Education Reform Act 1988, set out the system of governance for universities which were formerly polytechnics or other higher education institutions and for the colleges of higher education. Each institution has an instrument and articles of government that are approved by the Privy Council. These post-1992 institutions are run by boards of governors, which are responsible for the mission, finances and all appointments. Much of the board's business is delegated to committees. In particular, there is usually an academic board that deals with all matters relating to teaching and research. Most of the newest universities to be created were originally established by Trust Deed and have become incorporated as companies limited by guarantee. Their memorandum and articles of association incorporate the instrument and articles of government and are subject to Privy Council approval.

OPEN UNIVERSITY AND THE UNIVERSITY FOR INDUSTRY

The non-residential Open University provides a modular programme of courses throughout the UK and most of Europe leading to first and higher degrees, diplomas and certificates. Students are taught through distance learning, using written and audio-visual materials and the internet, supported by tutorials and short residential courses. No qualifications are needed for entry at undergraduate level. In 2005–6 the Open University received £201.1m in public funding and there was a total of 156,000 undergraduate students, 19,000 postgraduate students and a further 32,000 students on programmes at other institutions validated by the university. More than 625,000 degrees, certificates and diplomas have been awarded since the university's first students started to study in 1971. Research across a wide range of disciplines feeds directly into the university's teaching. The university has five Centres of Research Excellence – in citizenship, identities and governance; comparative criminological research; computing; education and educational technology; and earth, planetary, space and astronomical research. In addition, it carries out internationally recognised research in geography, design, art history, music, history, literature, pure mathematics, statistics, materials engineering and biological sciences. The university's new open content initative is making educational resources freely available on the internet, with learning support and collaboration tools to connect students and educators.

- the Open University is the UK's largest university, teaching 33 per cent of all part-time undergraduate students in the UK each year
- thirty-four per cent of new OU undergraduate students in the UK have fewer than two A-levels
- the most popular courses (for 2005–6) were an introduction to the social sciences (7,800 students); an introduction to the humanities (5,200); understanding health and social care (4,900); data, computing and information (4,100); and discovering science (3,900)
- the median age of new undergraduate level students is 32
- in 2005–6, more than 30,000 students received financial help in paying their fees.

The University for Industry (Ufi) Ltd operates Learndirect and UK Online network and is the largest government-backed e-learning organisation in the world. Ufi aims to boost people's employability, by helping them gain skills and qualifications, as well as improve organisations' productivity and competitiveness. Through the national network of over 800 Learndirect centres in England and Wales and 6,000 UK Online centres in England, Ufi provides access and support to a range of services from taster and skills-check activities to e-learning courses which are linked to qualifications. In addition, Learndirect careers advice provides free impartial information and advice to people online and over the telephone on more than 900,000 courses nationally from thousands of providers as well as free careers guidance.

ACADEMIC STAFF

Each university and college appoints its own academic staff. The Universities and Colleges Employers Association (UCEA) is the employers' association for subscribing universities and other higher education institutions in the UK. It provides a framework within which representatives of institutions can discuss salaries, conditions of service, employee relations and all matters connected with the employment of staff and employees. The services of the UCEA include collective bargaining and an annual salary survey. Teaching staff in higher education require no formal teaching qualification. However, the Higher Education Academy leads, supports and informs the professional development and recognition of staff in higher education as well as promoting good practice and providing information, advice and resources. Teacher trainers are required to spend a certain amount of time in schools to ensure that they have sufficient recent practical experience.

In the academic year 2005–6 there were 164,665 academic staff in all higher education institutions in the UK, of which 111,410 were full-time. Of these, 70,665 were male and 40,745 were female.

As a result of the National Framework Agreement, staff working in higher education should be, since August 2006, paid on a single national pay scale, which is used as the basis for locally negotiated pay and grading structures. The framework sought to unify pay arrangements as well as address concerns about equal pay. Since August 2006 the 51-point National Pay Spine has ranged from £11,575 to £49,116 and from February 2008, it will start from £12,461 to £52,628.

COURSES

In the UK all universities and some colleges award their own degrees and other qualifications and may act as awarding and validating bodies for colleges. The power to award degrees is regulated by law and it is an offence to purport to award a UK degree unless authorised to do so. The Quality Assurance Agency for Higher Education advises government on applications for degree-awarding powers.

The Quality Assurance Agency for Higher Education (QAA) was established in 1997 and is an independent public body funded by subscriptions from universities and colleges of higher education, and through contracts with the main higher education funding bodies. Its principal role is to safeguard and help to improve the academic standards and quality of higher education. It does this by working with universities and colleges to define standards for higher education, through a framework known as the academic infrastructure, which includes the qualifications frameworks for the United Kingdom. QAA also carries out reviews of higher education institutions against these standards and publishes their outcomes. It advises governments on applications for the grant of degree awarding powers, university title or designation as a higher education institution. QAA is governed by a board, which has overall responsibility for the conduct and strategic direction of its business. The board has 14 members. Four are appointed by the representative bodies of the heads of higher education institutions; four are appointed by the funding bodies in higher education; and six are independent directors who have wide practical experience of industry, commerce, finance or the practice of a profession, and are appointed by the board as a whole. The chair is appointed by the board from among the independent members.

Facilities exist for full-time and part-time study, day release, sandwich or block release. Credit accumulation and transfer systems allow a student to achieve a final qualification by accumulating credits for courses of study successfully achieved, or even professional experience, over a period of time.

Higher education courses comprise: first degree and postgraduate (including research); Diploma in Higher Education (DipHE); BTEC Higher National Diplomas (HND) and Higher National Certificates (HNC); and preparation for professional examinations.

The DipHE is commonly a two-year diploma usually intended to serve as a stepping stone to a degree course or other further study. The DipHE is awarded by the institution itself if it is accredited or by an accredited institution of its choice if it is not. The HNCs are awarded after two years' part-time study. The HNDs are awarded after two years' full-time, or three years' sandwich-course or part-time study.

The foundation degree, launched in 2001, is a two-year vocational higher education qualification which forms either a self-contained qualification or a basis for further study leading to an honours degree or further professional qualifications.

Undergraduate courses lead to the title of Bachelor, Bachelor of Arts (BA) and Bachelor of Science (BSc) being the most common, except in certain Scottish universities where Master is sometimes used for a first degree in arts subjects. For a higher degree the titles are Master of Arts (MA), Master of Science (MSc) and the research degrees of Master of Philosophy (MPhil) and Doctor of Philosophy (PhD or, at a few universities, DPhil).

Most undergraduate courses at universities and colleges of higher education run for three years, but some take four years or longer. Postgraduate studies vary in length.

Post-experience short courses form a significant part of higher education provision, reflecting the demand for professional and technical training. Most of these courses fund themselves.

ADMISSIONS

The government's target is to increase participation in higher education to 50 per cent of 18- to 30-year-olds by 2010. Institutions suffer financial penalties if the number of students laid down for them by the funding councils is exceeded, but the individual university or college decides which students to accept. The formal entry requirements to most degree courses are two or more A-levels at grade E or above (or equivalent), and to HND courses one A-level (or equivalent). In practice, most offers of places require qualifications in excess of this, higher requirements usually reflecting the popularity of a course or institution. These requirements do not, however, exclude applications from students with a variety of non-GCSE qualifications or unquantified experience and skills.

For admission to a degree, DipHE or HND, potential students apply through UCAS, the organisation responsible for managing applications to higher education courses in the UK. UCAS operates an online application system and provides services to applicants, advisory services, schools, colleges and universities and facilitates and promotes access to higher education. Application services exist across a range of subject areas and for UK universities and colleges. More than 500,000 people wanting to study at a university or college of higher education use the service each year and 100,000 of them use the specialist services: the Graduate Teacher Training Registry (GTTR) and the Conservatoires UK Admissions Service (CUKAS). The Open University conducts its own admissions. Details of initial teacher training courses in Scotland can be obtained from those universities offering such courses, from Universities Scotland, and from the website created by the Scottish Executive to promote teaching: W www.teachinginscotland.com.

For admission as a postgraduate student, universities and colleges normally require a good first degree in a subject related to the proposed course of study or research. Applications can be made to individual institutions, except for teaching and social work. There is also now an alternative to applying to postgraduate courses; UKPASS is an online application service created by UCAS. It was set up in 2007 following demand from the higher education sector to have a centralised admissions service that would not only help institutions to monitor their applicants but would also enable them to get to know more about this particular group, which is the fastest growing sector of the UK higher education marketplace.

FEES AND GRANTS

FEES FOR FULL TIME STUDENTS IN 2007–8
The Higher Education Act 2004 introduced variable tuition fees for full time higher education courses at English and Welsh institutions, and these came into effect for courses starting in September 2006 or later. In Northern Ireland variable tuition fees were introduced under the Higher Education (Northern Ireland) Order 2005. Fees are capped at £3,000 subject only to inflationary increases until 2010. In the academic year 2006–7 the maximum an institution could charge new students was £3,000 a year, and in 2007–8 this rose to £3,070.

However, students who started their course before September 2006 would still be treated under the old student finance regime and make an annual contribution to their tuition fees depending on their own level of income and that of their household. In 2006 this was up to a maximum of £1,200 and in 2007 this could be up to £1,225 (There are a few exceptions to these rules; for example gap year students who started their course in September 2006 instead of September 2005).

From September 2006 no student – no matter when they started – has to pay tuition fees before they start their course or whilst they are studying as student loans for tuition fees are available (*see* below). These cover the full amount of any fees charged.

Welsh Higher Education institutions also charge fees (up to £3,070 in 2007–8). Students who normally live in Wales (and EU students) are entitled to a fee grant up to a maximum of £1,845.

ENGLAND

The following table gives a brief breakdown of what help is available to full time higher education students in England in 2007–8:

Type of support	Old system students*	New system students†
Student loan for tuition fees	Yes	Yes
Student loan for maintenance	Yes	Yes
Extra help for disabled students	Yes	Yes
Extra help for students with dependents	Yes	Yes
Help towards tuition fees	Yes	No
Higher education grant	Yes	No
Maintenance (or special support) grant	No	Yes
Access to learning fund (from institutions)	Yes	Yes

* Old system students are on higher education courses living in England who started (or are treated as starting) their course before September 2006
† New system students are on higher education courses which began in September 2006 or after

A maintenance grant of up to £2,765 to help with living costs is available to new system students only. Any amount due is assessed on income and does not have to be repaid. The full grant is available to students living with a household income lower than £17,910. Partial grants are available for household incomes up to £38,300. For students entitled to benefits, maintenance grants could be replaced by a non-repayable special support grant which will not affect Department for Work and Pensions benefit entitlement.

REPAYMENT OF STUDENT LOANS

Repayment of both student loans for maintenance and student loans for tuition fees does not start until the April after the student has left their course and is earning more than £15,000 a year. Repayments are calculated at 9 per cent of income over the threshold of £15,000, so someone earning £18,000 would pay back around £5.19 a week. If income falls below the threshold, repayments cease until income rises above it again. Those who pay tax through PAYE have repayments deducted from their salaries, whilst the self-employed make repayments through their tax returns.

PART TIME HIGHER EDUCATION STUDENTS

Part-time higher education students on courses in England that are at least 50 per cent of an equivalent full-time course may be entitled to a grant towards their fees, and a grant towards their course costs. This help does not have to be repaid, and entitlement to the fee grant and the course grant depends on the student's income and that of their husband, wife or partner. Students who already have a degree cannot usually apply for this support.

For 2007–8, there are three different rates of fee grant depending on how intensive the course undertaken is:

Course intensity	Maximum fee grant
50–59 per cent of a full time course	£750
60–74 per cent of a full time course	£900
75 per cent or more of a full time course	£1,125

For 2007–8 the maximum course grant is £250 and does not depend on the intensity of the course. Students who receive the part-time grant for fees, but whose tuition fees are more than the amount of support available may be eligible for extra help from their institution. Part-time students with disabilities may be eligible for disabled students allowances.

WALES

Since 2007, students who started in 2006 and 2007 have been charged a deferred flexible fee of up to £3,070. However, students who normally live in Wales and study at a university or college in Wales can apply for a fee grant of up to £1,845 a year which does not have to be repaid. This tuition fee grant is available regardless of family income and is paid directly to the place of study. Since September 2006 eligible full-time undergraduate students who live in Wales have not had to pay fees before starting their course or whilst they are studying. Instead, a student loan for fees can be taken out, which does not have to be repaid until the course is finished and earnings are over £15,000 a year.

Other aspects of Student Finance Wales student support arrangements for 2007 starters include:

• an assembly learning grant worth up to £2,765 for eligible students from low income households
• all eligible students can also apply for a student loan for maintenance of up to £6,320 to help with living costs

Students who normally live in Wales but choose to study elsewhere in the UK will be charged fees according to the fee regime of the country in which they study and that set by the institution. Student Finance Wales will provide a loan to defer this fee but students who live in Wales and are studying elsewhere in the UK will not be entitled to the fee grant.

Fee levels in Wales are the same for students who normally live elsewhere in the UK and began studying in Wales in the academic year 2006–7. However, these students are not eligible to receive Student Finance Wales services. A national bursary scheme is planned for Wales, to commence in the academic year 2007–8. Eligible students will receive a bursary of around £305, which will be additional to other support received and will not be offset by any reductions in other forms of support.

SCOTLAND

The arrangements for Scottish students in Scotland from 2008 are as follows:

Tuition fees – tuition fee contributions have been abolished for all eligible full-time Scottish domiciled and EU students studying in Scotland.

Student Loans – living cost support is mainly provided through a means-tested student loan. An additional loan of £560 is available to young students from low income backgrounds.

Bursaries – the young students' bursary (YSB) is available to young students from low-income backgrounds. It is non-repayable and reduces the level of debt which eligible students accrue during a course of study. In 2007–8 the maximum annual support provided through YSB is £2,510.

SUPPLEMENTARY GRANTS

Depending on eligibility, students in Scotland may also receive: the adult dependants grant; the lone parents grant; childcare fund support; travel costs; the disabled students allowance; the basic allowance; the special equipment allowance; and non-medical personal help.

HARDSHIP FUNDS

Students who are experiencing particular financial difficulty can apply for assistance from their institution's hardship funds.

NORTHERN IRELAND

The arrangements for Northern Ireland are very similar to those for England with these differences:

• the maintenance grant is worth up to £3,265
• the higher education bursary is up to £2,000
• the access to learning fund is known as the support fund in Northern Ireland and is allocated by central government directly to the institution

POSTGRADUATE AWARDS

In general, postgraduate students do not qualify for mandatory support (including student loans and tuition fee assistance). An exception to this is the PGCE.

Awards for postgraduate courses are the responsibility of the Research Councils, depending on the field of study. Research Councils are independent bodies and make their own decisions about expenditure on postgraduate support according to the resources available to them. The fact that a course lies within its remit does not oblige the Research Councils to support every or indeed any student applying for awards.

It is for institutions to decide the level of their fees. The government is raising the levels of award available to postgraduates under the competitive merit-based system provided by the Research Councils: the minimum PhD stipend will be £12,600 in 2007–8.

Targeted support is also available to meet particular needs: postgraduate students can apply through their colleges for discretionary help from the access to learning und. Disabled students allowances are also available to eligible students undertaking postgraduate study.

There is support available to students in Scotland for postgraduate study through the Postgraduate Students' Allowances Scheme (PSAS), which is administered by the Student Awards Agency for Scotland (SAAS). Eligible students can apply for an award consisting of a means tested maintenance grant and payment of tuition fees. Courses supported under PSAS are generally nine-month-long, taught postgraduate diploma courses on largely vocational subjects. Awards from PSAS are discretionary, not mandatory, so there is no guarantee of an award at postgraduate level.

There is support available to students who wish to pursue postgraduate study in Northern Ireland (at either Queen's University of Belfast or University of Ulster). All students should apply to the university for an application form. Students should apply for a place on the course and for an award. As there are always more applicants than awards, not all applicants who secure a place on the courses will be successful in obtaining an award. *See also* Research Councils section

LIFELONG LEARNING

In the UK, the duty of securing adult and continuing education leading to academic or vocational qualifications is statutory. The Learning and Skills Council (LSC) in England, the Welsh Assembly Government and the Scottish Funding Council are responsible for and fund those courses which take place in their sector and lead to academic and vocational qualifications, prepare students to undertake further or higher education courses, or confer basic skills; the Higher Education Funding Councils fund advanced courses of continuing education. Local authorities have the power, although not the duty, to provide those courses which do not fall within the remit of the funding bodies. In Northern Ireland the Department for Employment and Learning is responsible for the funding of the statutory further education sector.

In January 2007 Lord Leitch delivered his interim report into skills. This showed that England lags behind other major economies in terms of skills development. The LSC is working together with the government to raise the nation's skills levels and increase the numbers of adults gaining Level 2 and higher qualifications. The LSC is responsible for funding and planning provision for apprenticeships, adult learning, offender learning and skills, Train to Gain, Basic Skills and leisure learning. It works closely with employers providing vocational education and work based learning. Twelve new national skills academies are to be opened this year in sectors including manufacturing, retail and financial services. Train to Gain provides employers with free and subsidised training for their employees and also provides them with independent advice and guidance via an impartial skills brokerage service. There are currently over 250,000 apprentices working in over 80 subject areas and the LSC has been challenged by government to double this figure to 500,000. In the summer of 2006, the LSC took over responsibility for offender learning across England. The LSC also provides several learner support funds to support those learners who cannot afford to continue in education or training. These include education maintenance allowances (EMA) for young people, the Care2Learn scheme for young parents and adult learning grants.

Of the many voluntary bodies providing adult education, the biggest is the Workers' Educational Association (WEA), which operates throughout England and Scotland to provide over 14,000 courses each year, reaching more than 95,000 adults. The WEA is a charity supported by funding from the LSC in England, and by the Scottish Executive and local authorities in Scotland. Similar but separate organisations operate in Wales and Northern Ireland: Coleg Harlech WEA (covering North Wales), WEA South Wales and WEA Northern Ireland. The National Institute of Adult Continuing Education, has a broad remit to promote lifelong learning opportunities for adults.

NIACE Dysgu Cymru, the Welsh committee, receives financial support from the National Assembly for Wales and support in kind from local authorities, and advises government, voluntary bodies and education providers on adult continuing education and training matters in Wales. In Scotland, policy responsibility for community learning and development lies with Learning Connections and the Directorate General for Education of the Scottish Executive. In Northern Ireland, those functions are undertaken by the Department for Employment and Learning.

CONTACTS

APPRENTICESHIPS T 0800-015 0600
    W www.apprenticeships.co.uk
COUNCIL FOR THE CURRICULUM EXAMINATIONS AND ASSESSMENT (NORTHERN IRELAND) T 028-9026 1200 W www.ccea.org.uk
DEPARTMENT FOR CHILDREN, SCHOOLS AND FAMILIES (ENGLAND) T 0870-000 2288
    W www.dcsf.gov.uk
DEPARTMENT FOR EDUCATION NORTHERN IRELAND T 028-9127 9279 W www.deni.gov.uk
DEPARTMENT FOR EMPLOYMENT AND LEARNING NORTHERN IRELAND T 028 9025 7777
    W www.delni.gov.uk
DEPARTMENT FOR INNOVATION, UNIVERSITIES AND SKILLS (ENGLAND) T 0870-001 0336
    W www.dius.gov.uk
DIPLOMAS T 0870-000 2288 W www.dfes.gov.uk/14-19
EDUCATION DEPARTMENT, SCOTTISH EXECUTIVE T 0845-345 4745
    W www.teachinginscotland.com
EDUCATION OTHERWISE T 0870-730 0074
    W www.education-otherwise.org
EDUCATION AND TRAINING INSPECTORATE (NORTHERN IRELAND) T 028-9127 9726
    W www.etini.gov.uk
EUROPEAN SOCIAL FUND W www.esf.gov.uk
GENERAL TEACHING COUNCIL FOR ENGLAND T 08700-010 308
    W www.gtce.org.uk
GENERAL TEACHING COUNCIL FOR NORTHERN IRELAND T 028-9033 3390 W www.gtcni.org.uk
GENERAL TEACHING COUNCIL FOR SCOTLAND T 0131-314 6000 W www.gtcs.org.uk
GENERAL TEACHING COUNCIL FOR WALES T 029-2055 0350 W www.gtcw.org.uk
HER MAJESTY'S CHIEF INSPECTOR OF EDUCATION AND TRAINING IN WALES T 029-2044 6446 W www.estyn.gov.uk
HER MAJESTY'S INSPECTORATE OF EDUCATION IN SCOTLAND T 01506-600200 W www.hmie.gov.uk
HIGHER EDUCATION ACADEMY T 01904-717500
    W www.heacademy.ac.uk
HIGHER EDUCATION FUNDING COUNCIL FOR ENGLAND T 0117-931 7317 W www.hefce.ac.uk

HIGHER EDUCATION FUNDING COUNCIL FOR WALES T 029-2076 1861 W www.hefcw.ac.uk

HOME EDUCATION ADVISORY SERVICE T 01707-371854 W www.heas.org.uk

INTERNATIONAL BACCALAUREATE ORGANISATION T (+41) (22) 791 7740 W www.ibo.org

LEARNING AND SKILLS COUNCIL (ENGLAND) T 0845-019 4170 W www.lsc.gov.uk

LEARNING AND TEACHING SCOTLAND T 08700-100 297 W www.ltscotland.org.uk

NATIONAL ASSESSMENT AGENCY T 0870-0600 622 W www.naa.org.uk

NATIONAL INSTITUTE OF ADULT CONTINUING EDUCATION T 0116-204 4200 W www.niace.org.uk

OFFICE FOR STANDARDS IN EDUCATION, CHILDREN'S SERVICES AND SKILLS (ENGLAND) T 08456-404045 W www.ofsted.gov.uk

OPEN UNIVERSITY T 0870-333 4340 W www.open.ac.uk

PROFESSIONAL QUALIFICATION FOR HEADSHIP (NORTHERN IRELAND) T 028-9061 8121 W www.rtuni.org/pqhni.cfm

QUALITY ASSURANCE AGENCY T 0141-572 3420 W www.qaa.ac.uk

QUALIFICATIONS AND CURRICULUM AUTHORITY T 020-7509 5556 W www.qca.org.uk

SCOTTISH EXECUTIVE T 08457-741 741 W www.scotland.gov.uk

SCOTTISH FUNDING COUNCIL T 0131-313 6500 W www.sfc.ac.uk

SCOTTISH QUALIFICATION FOR HEADSHIP T 0131-651 6179 W www.sqh.ed.ac.uk

SCOTTISH QUALIFICATIONS AUTHORITY T 0845-279 1000 W www.sqa.org.uk

STUDENT AWARDS AGENCY FOR SCOTLAND T 0845-111 1711 W www.student-support-saas.gov.uk

STUDENT FINANCE DIRECT T 0845-607 7577 W www.studentsupportdirect.co.uk

STUDENT FINANCE WALES T 0845-602 8845 W www.studentfinancewales.co.uk

SURE START T 0870-000 2288 W www.surestart.gov.uk

TRAINING AND DEVELOPMENT AGENCY FOR SCHOOLS T 020-7023 8001 W www.tda.gov.uk

UCAS T 0871-468 0468 W www.ucas.com

UNIVERSITIES AND COLLEGES EMPLOYERS ASSOCIATION T 020-7383 2444 W www.ucea.ac.uk

UNIVERSITY FOR INDUSTRY T 0114-291 5000 W www.ufi.com

WELSH ASSEMBLY T 0845-010 5500 W www.wales.gov.uk

WORKERS' EDUCATION ASSOCIATION T 020-7426 3450 W www.wea.org.uk

LOCAL EDUCATION AUTHORITIES

ENGLAND

COUNTY COUNCILS

BEDFORDSHIRE Children's Services, County Hall, Cauldwell Street, Bedford MK42 9AP **T** 01234-363222
E education@bedscc.gov.uk **W** www.bedfordshire.gov.uk
Director, Malcolm Newsam

BUCKINGHAMSHIRE Children's Services, County Hall, Walton Street, Aylesbury HP20 1UA **T** 01296-395000
E simbriano@buckscc.gov.uk **W** www.buckscc.gov.uk
Director, Sue Imbriano

CAMBRIDGESHIRE **Children and Young People's Services,** ELH 1000, Castle Court, Shire Hall, Cambridge CB3 0AP **T** 01223-717970
E elh.webmaster@cambridgeshire.gov.uk
W www.cambridgeshire.gov.uk
Deputy Chief Executive, Gordon Jeyes

CHESHIRE Children's Services, County Hall, Chester CH1 1SQ **T** 01244-602201 **W** www.cheshire.gov.uk
Director, Joan Feenan

CORNWALL Children, Young People and Families, New County Hall, Treyew Road, Truro TR1 3AY **T** 01872-322003
E childrenservices@cornwall.gov.uk **W** www.cornwall.gov.uk
Director, Dean Ashton

CUMBRIA Children's Services Department, 5 Portland Square, Carlisle CA1 1PU **T** 01228-606877
E education@cumbriacc.gov.uk
W www.cumbria.gov.uk/education
Corporate Director, Moira Swann

DERBYSHIRE Children and Younger Adults Department, County Hall, Matlock DE4 3AG **T** 01629-585814
W www.derbyshire.gov.uk
Strategic Director, Bruce Buckley

DEVON Children and Young People's Services, County Hall, Topsham Road, Exeter EX2 4QG **T** 01392-382000
E edmail@devon.gov.uk **W** www.devon.gov.uk
Director, Anne Whiteley

DORSET Children's Services, County Hall, Dorchester DT1 1XJ **T** 01305-251000 **W** www.dorsetforyou.com
Director, Stephen Prewett

DURHAM Children and Young People's Services, County Hall, Durham DH1 5UL **T** 0191-383 3000
W www.durham.gov.uk
Corporate Director, David Williams

EAST SUSSEX Children's Services, County Hall, St Anne's Crescent, Lewes BN7 1SG **T** 01273-481000
E childrenservices@eastsussex.gov.uk
W www.eastsussex.gov.uk
Director, Matt Dunkley

ESSEX Children and Young People, County Hall, Market Road, Chelmsford CM1 1QH **T** 0845-603 7627
W www.essexcc.gov.uk
Director, Carey Bennet

GLOUCESTERSHIRE Children and Young People's Services, Shire Hall, Westgate Street, Gloucester GL1 2TG
T 01452-425000 **W** www.gloucestershire.gov.uk
Group Director, Jo Davidson

HAMPSHIRE Children's Services, County Office, The Castle, Winchester SO23 8UG **T** 01962-846452
E children.services.enquiries@hants.gov.uk
W www.hants.gov.uk/education
Director, John Coughlan

HERTFORDSHIRE Children, Schools and Families, County Hall, Pegs Lane, Hertford SG13 8DQ **T** 01438-737500
W www.hertsdirect.org
Director, John Harris

KENT Children, Families and Education, Sessions House, County Hall, Maidstone ME14 1XQ **T** 01622-671411
W www.kent.gov.uk
Managing Director, Graham Badman

LANCASHIRE Children's Services, PO Box 61, County Hall, Preston PR1 8RJ **T** 01772-531854 **W** www.lancashire.gov.uk
Executive Director, Pat Jefferson

LEICESTERSHIRE Children and Young People's Service, County Hall, Glenfield, LE3 8RA **T** 0116-265 6631
E childrensservices@leics.gov.uk **W** www.leics.gov.uk
Director, Gareth Williams

LINCOLNSHIRE Children's Services, County Offices, Newland, Lincoln LN1 1YQ **T** 01522-552222
W www.lincolnshire.gov.uk
E customer_services@lincolnshire.gov.uk
Director, Mr P. Duxbury

NORFOLK Children's Services, County Hall, Martineau Lane, Norwich NR1 2DH **T** 0844-800 8001
E information@norfolk.gov.uk **W** www.norfolk.gov.uk
Director, Lisa Christensen

NORTHAMPTONSHIRE Children and Young People's Service, PO Box 93, County Hall, Northampton NN1 1AN
T 01604-237619 **E** citizensfirst@northamptonshire.gov.uk
W www.northamptonshire.gov.uk
Director, Andrew Sortwell

NORTHUMBERLAND Children's Services, County Hall, Morpeth NE61 2EF **T** 01670-533000
E childrensservices@northumberland.gov.uk
W www.northumberland.gov.uk
Executive Director, Trevor Doughty

NORTH YORKSHIRE Children and Young People's Service, County Hall, Northallerton DL7 8AE **T** 01609-780780
E cyp@northyorks.gov.uk **W** www.northyorks.gov.uk
Director, Cynthia Welbourn, FRSA

NOTTINGHAMSHIRE Children and Young People's Services, County Hall, West Bridgford, Nottingham NG2 7QP
T 0115-982 3823 **E** communications.cyp@nottsc.gov.uk
W www.nottinghamshire.gov.uk
Director, Dr Robert Garnett

OXFORDSHIRE Children, Young People and Families, Macclesfield House, New Road, Oxford OX1 1NA
T 01865-815449 **E** learning@oxfordshire.gov.uk
W www.oxfordshire.gov.uk
Director, Janet Tomlinson

SHROPSHIRE Children and Young People, The Shirehall, Abbey Foregate, Shrewsbury SY2 6ND **T** 01743-254307
E children&youngpeople@shropshire-cc.gov.uk
W www.shropshire.gov.uk
Director, Liz Nicholson

SOMERSET Education Service, County Hall, Taunton TA1 4DY **T** 0845-345 9122 **W** www.somerset.gov.uk
Corporate Director, David Taylor

STAFFORDSHIRE Children and Lifelong Learning, Tipping Street, Stafford ST16 2DH **T** 01785-223121
E education@staffordshire.gov.uk
W www.staffordshire.gov.uk
Corporate Director, Peter Traves

SUFFOLK Children and Young People, Endeavour House, Russell Road, Ipswich IP1 2BX **T** 01473-583000 **W** www.suffolk.gov.uk
Director, Rosalind Turner

SURREY Services for Families, County Hall, Penrhyn Road, Kingston upon Thames KT1 2DJ **T** 0845-600 9009 **W** www.surreycc.gov.uk
Strategic Director, Andrew Webster

WARWICKSHIRE Children, Young People and Families, 22 Northgate Street, Warwick CV34 4SP **T** 01926-410410 **E** edcomms@warwickshire.gov.uk **W** www.warwickshire.gov.uk
Strategic Director, Marion Davis

WEST SUSSEX Children and Young People's Services, County Hall, Chichester PO19 1RQ **T** 0845-075 1007 **E** cyps@westsussex.gov.uk **W** www.westsussex.gov.uk
Director, Robert Back

WILTSHIRE Children, Education and Libraries, County Hall, Bythesea Road, Trowbridge BA14 8JB **T** 01225-713000 **E** directorcel@wiltshire.gov.uk **W** www.wiltshire.gov.uk
Director, Carolyn Godfrey

WORCESTERSHIRE Children's Services Directorate, PO Box 73, Worcester WR5 2YA **T** 01905-763763 **W** www.worcestershire.gov.uk
Director, Richard Hubbard

UNITARY AND METROPOLITAN BOROUGH COUNCILS

BARNSLEY Directorate for Children, Young People and Families, Berneslai Close, Barnsley S70 2HS **T** 01226-773500 **E** education@barnsley.gov.uk **W** www.barnsley.gov.uk
Executive Director, E. Sutton

BATH AND NORTH EAST SOMERSET Children's Services, PO Box 25, Riverside, Temple Street, Keynsham BS31 1DN **T** 01225-477000 **E** children's_services@bathnes.gov.uk **W** www.bathnes.gov.uk
Director, Ashley Ayre

BIRMINGHAM Children, Young People and Families, Room 183, Council House Extension, Margaret Street, Birmingham B3 3BU **T** 0121-303 3541 **W** www.bgfl.org
Strategic Director, Tony Howell

BLACKBURN WITH DARWEN Children's Services, Town Hall, Blackburn BB1 7DY **T** 01254-585585 **W** www.blackburn.gov.uk
Director, Peter Morgan

BLACKPOOL Children and Young People's Department, Progress House, Clifton Road, Blackpool FY4 4US **T** 01253-477668 **E** social.services@blackpool.gov.uk **W** www.blackpool.gov.uk
Director, David Lund

BOLTON Children's Services, Paderborn House, Civic Centre, Bolton BL1 1JW **T** 01204-333333 **E** ea.strategy@bolton.gov.uk **W** www.boltonlea.org.uk
Director, Margaret Asquith

BOURNEMOUTH Children's Services, Dorset House, 20–22 Christchurch Road, Bournemouth BH1 3NL **T** 01202-456219 **E** cs@bournemouth.gov.uk **W** www.bournemouth.gov.uk
Corporate Director, J. Portman

BRACKNELL FOREST Education, Children's Services and Libraries, Seymour House, 38 Broadway, Bracknell RG12 1AU **T** 01344-354000 **E** ecsl@bracknell-forest.gov.uk **W** www.bracknell-forest.gov.uk
Director, T. Eccleston

BRADFORD Education Bradford, Future House, Bolling Road, Bradford BD4 7EB **T** 01274-385500 **E** feedback@educationbradford.com **W** www.educationbradford.com
Managing Director, John Gaskin

BRIGHTON AND HOVE Children and Young People's Trust, Kings House, Grand Avenue, Hove BN3 2LS **T** 01273-290000 **E** cis@brighton-hove.gov.uk **W** www.brighton-hove.gov.uk
Director of Children's Services, David Hawker

BRISTOL Children and Young People's Services, The Council House, College Green, Bristol BS99 7EB **T** 0117-903 7900 **W** www.bristol-cyps.org.uk
Director, Heather Tomlinson

BURY Children's Services, Athenaeum House, Market Street, Bury BL9 0BN **T** 0161-253 5652 **E** children.services@bury.gov.uk **W** www.bury.gov.uk
Executive Director, Eleni Ioannides

CALDERDALE Children and Young People's Services, Town Hall, Halifax HX1 1UJ **T** 01422-392500 **E** customer.first@calderdale.gov.uk **W** www.calderdale.gov.uk
Group Director, Carol White

COVENTRY Children, Learning and Young People's Directorate, Civic Centre 1, Earl Street, Coventry CV1 5RS **T** 024-7683 1500 **W** www.coventry.gov.uk
Director, Colin Green

DARLINGTON Children's Services, Town Hall, Darlington DL1 5QT **T** 01325-380651 **E** education.feedback@darlington.gov.uk **W** www.darlington.gov.uk
Director, Murry Rose

DERBY Children and Young People, Middleton House, 27 St Mary's Gate, Derby DE1 3NN **T** 01332-716924 **E** education@derby.gov.uk **W** www.derby.gov.uk
Corporate Director, A. Flack

DONCASTER Children's Services, PO Box 251, Council House, College Road, Doncaster DN1 3AD **T** 01302-737777 **E** general.enquiries@doncaster.gov.uk **W** www.doncaster.gov.uk
Director, Tom Common

DUDLEY Children's Services, Westox House, 1 Trinity Road, Dudley DY1 1JQ **T** 01384-818181 **E** director.children@dudley.gov.uk **W** www.dudley.gov.uk
Director, John Freeman

EAST RIDING OF YORKSHIRE Children, Family and Adult Services, County Hall, Beverley HU17 9BA **T** 01482-392020 **E** june.leech@eastriding.gov.uk **W** www.eastriding.gov.uk
Director, Andrew Williams

GATESHEAD Learning and Children, Civic Centre, Regent Street, Gateshead NE8 1HH **T** 0191-433 3000 **E** enquiries@gateshead.gov.uk **W** www.gateshead.gov.uk
Director, Maggie Atkinson

HALTON Children and Young People, Grosvenor House, Halton Lea, Runcorn WA7 2ED **T** 0151-907 8300 **W** www.halton.gov.uk
Strategic Director, Gerald Meehan

HARTLEPOOL Children's Services, Civic Centre, Victoria Road, Hartlepool TS24 8AY **T** 01429-266522 **E** children@hartlepool.gov.uk **W** www.hartlepool.gov.uk
Director, Adrienne Simcock

HEREFORDSHIRE Children and Young People's Directorate, PO Box 185, Blackfriars Street, Hereford HR4 9ZR **T** 01432-260900 **E** education@herefordshire.gov.uk **W** www.education.herefordshire.gov.uk
Director, S. Menghini

KINGSTON UPON HULL Children and Young People's Services, Essex House, Manor Street, Kingston upon Hull HU1 1YD **T** 01482-613007 **E** childrenandyoungpeople@hullcc.gov.uk **W** www.hullcc.gov.uk
Director, Nigel Richardson

KIRKLEES Children and Young People Service, Oldgate House, 2 Oldgate, Huddersfield HD1 6QW T 01484-225242 E chyps@kirklees.gov.uk W www.kirklees.gov.uk
Director, Alison O'Sullivan

KNOWSLEY Children's Services, Education Offices, Huyton Hey Road, Huyton L36 5YH T 0151-443 3232
W www.knowsley.gov.uk
Executive Director, Damian Allen

LEEDS Education Leeds, 10th Floor East, 110 Merrion Centre, Leeds LS2 8DT T 0113-247 5590
E educ.info@educationleeds.co.uk
W www.educationleeds.co.uk
Chief Executive, Chris Edwards

LEICESTER Children and Young People's Services, Marlborough House, 38 Welford Road, Leicester LE2 7AA
T 0116-252 7807 W www.leicester.gov.uk
Corporate Director, Sheila Lock

LIVERPOOL Education and Lifelong Learning, Municipal Buildings, Dale Street, Liverpool L2 2DH T 0151-233 3000
W www.liverpool.gov.uk
Executive Director, Colin Hilton

LUTON Children and Learning, Unity House, 111 Stuart Street, Luton LU1 5NP T 01582-548005 E feedback@luton.gov.uk
W www.luton.gov.uk
Corporate Director, T. Dessent

MANCHESTER Children's Services, Overseas House, Quay Street, Manchester M3 3BB T 0161-234 5000
E education.enquiries@manchester.gov.uk
W www.manchester.gov.uk/education
Director, Pauline Newman

MEDWAY Children's Services, Civic Centre, Strood, Rochester ME2 4AU T 01634-306000
E childrens.services@medway.gov.uk
W www.medway.gov.uk
Director, Rose Collinson

MIDDLESBROUGH Children, Families and Learning, PO Box 69, Vancouver House, Gurney Street TS1 1EL
T 01642-728301 E jan_douglas@middlesbrough.gov.uk
W www.middlesbrough.gov.uk
Interim Executive Director, Jan Douglas

MILTON KEYNES Learning and Development Directorate, Saxon Court, Avebury Boulevard, Milton Keynes MK9 3HS
T 01908-691691 W www.mkweb.co.uk
Group Director, School Improvement and Planning, David Gamble

NEWCASTLE UPON TYNE Children's Services, Civic Centre, Newcastle upon Tyne NE99 2BN T 0191-232 8520
E education.directorate@newcastle.gov.uk
W www.newcastle.gov.uk
Executive Director, Catherine Fitt

NORTH EAST LINCOLNSHIRE Children's Services, Municipal Offices, Town Hall Square, Grimsby DN31 1HU
T 01472-323021 W www.nelincs.gov.uk
Executive Director, Andrew Samson

NORTH LINCOLNSHIRE Education, Learning and Achievement Service, PO Box 35, Hewson House, Station Road, Brigg DN20 8XJ T 01724-297240
E suzanne.watson@northlincs.gov.uk
W www.northlincs.gov.uk
Head, D. Lea

NORTH SOMERSET Children and Young People's Services, Town Hall, Weston-super-Mare BS23 1UJ T 01934-888888
E colin.diamond@n-somerset.gov.uk
W www.n-somerset.gov.uk
Director, Colin Diamond

NORTH TYNESIDE Education Services, Stephenson House, Stephenson Street, North Shields NE30 1QA
T 0191-200 5006 E gill.alexander@northtyneside.gov.uk
W www.northtyneside.gov.uk
Director, Gill Alexander

NOTTINGHAM Children's Services, Sandfield Centre, Sandfield Road, Nottingham NG7 1HQ T 0115-915 0800
E education@lea.nottinghamcity.gov.uk
W www.nottinghamcity.gov.uk
Director, Edwina Grant

OLDHAM Children, Young People and Families, Civic Centre, West Street, Oldham OL1 1XJ T 0161-770 4260
E general.enquiry@oldham.gov.uk W www.oldham.gov.uk
Executive Director, Ruth M. Baldwin

PETERBOROUGH Children's Services, Bayard Place, Broadway, Peterborough PE1 1FB T 01733-748444
E leonie.owens@peterborough.gov.uk
W www.thelearningcity.co.uk
Director, Mohammed Mehmet

PLYMOUTH Children's Services, Windsor House, Plymouth PL1 2AA T 01752-307400
E childrens.services@plymouth.gov.uk
W www.plymouth.gov.uk
Director, Bronwen Lacey

POOLE Children's Services, Civic Centre, Sandbanks Road, Poole BH15 2RU T 01202-633633
E enquiries@boroughofpoole.com
W www.boroughofpoole.com
Strategic Director, John Nash

PORTSMOUTH Children, Families and Learning, Civic Offices, Guildhall Square, Portsmouth PO1 2AL T 023-9284 1202
W www.portsmouth.gov.uk
Strategic Director, Lynda Fisher

READING Education and Children's Services, Civic Centre, Reading RG1 7WA T 0118-939 0900
W www.reading.gov.uk
Director, Anna Wright

REDCAR AND CLEVELAND Children's Services, Redcar and Cleveland House, Kirkleatham Street, Redcar TS10 1YA
T 01642-441121 E contactus@redcar-cleveland.gov.uk
W www.redcar-cleveland.gov.uk
Director, Jenny Lewis

ROCHDALE Children's Services, Municipal Offices, Smith Street, Rochdale OL16 1YD T 01706-924 7474
E education@rochdale.gov.uk W www.rochdale.gov.uk
Executive Director, Terry Piggott

ROTHERHAM Children and Young People's Services, Norfolk House, Walker Place, Rotherham S65 1AS T 01709-382121
E education@rotherham.gov.uk W www.rotherham.gov.uk
Strategic Director, Sonia Sharp

ROYAL BOROUGH OF WINDSOR AND MAIDENHEAD Education Department, Town Hall, St Ives Road, Maidenhead SL6 1RF T 01628-798888
E jim.gould@rbwm.gov.uk W www.rbwm.gov.uk
Director of Learning and Care, Jim Gould

RUTLAND Children and Young People's Services, Catmose, Oakham LE15 6HP T 01572-722577
E enquiries@rutland.gov.uk W www.rutland.gov.uk
Director, Carol Chambers

SALFORD Children's Services, Minerva House, Pendlebury Road, Swinton M27 4EQ T 0161-778 0123
E sue.atkinson@salford.gov.uk W www.salford.gov.uk
Director, Jill Baker

SANDWELL Education and Children's Services, Shaftesbury House, 402 High Street, West Bromwich B70 9LT
T 0121-569 2200 E education@sandwell.gov.uk
W www.sandwell.gov.uk
Executive Director, Roger Crouch

SEFTON Children's Services, 9th Floor, Merton House, Stanley Road, Bootle L20 3JA T 0845-140 0845

W www.sefton.gov.uk
Director, Bryn Marsh
SHEFFIELD Children and Young People's Service, Town Hall, Pinstone Street, Sheffield S1 2HH T 0114-273 5722
E cypdinformation@sheffield.gov.uk
W www.sheffield.gov.uk
Executive Director, Jonathan Crossley-Holland
SLOUGH Education and Children's Services, Town Hall, Bath Road, Slough SL1 3UQ T 01753-875700
E edhelp@slough.gov.uk W www.slough.gov.uk
Strategic Director, Janet Tomlinson
SOLIHULL Education and Children's Services, PO Box 20, Council House, Homer Road B91 9QU T 0121-704 6000
E childrensservices@solihull.gov.uk W www.solihull.gov.uk
Corporate Director, Mark Rogers
SOUTHAMPTON Children's Services and Learning, Frobisher House, Nelson Gate, Commercial Road, Southampton SO15 1BZ T 023-8083 3466
E education.enquiries@southampton.gov.uk
W www.southampton.gov.uk
Executive Director, Clive Webster
SOUTHEND-ON-SEA Department of Children and Learning, Civic Centre, Victoria Avenue, Southend-on-Sea SS2 6ER
T 01702-215000 W www.southend.gov.uk
Corporate Director, Paul Greenhalgh
SOUTH GLOUCESTERSHIRE Children and Young People, Bowling Hill, Chipping Sodbury BS37 6JX T 01454-868008
E educ_service@southglos.gov.uk W www.southglos.gov.uk
Director, Therese Gillespie
SOUTH TYNESIDE Lifelong Learning and Leisure, Town Hall and Civic Offices, Westoe Road, South Shields NE33 2RL
T 0191-427 1717 W www.southtyneside.info
Executive Director, Kim Bromley-Derry
ST HELENS Children and Young People's Service, Rivington Centre, Rivington Road, St Helens WA10 4ND
T 01744-455328 W www.sthelens.gov.uk
Director, Susan Richardson
STOCKPORT Children and Young People's Directorate, Town Hall, Stockport SK1 3XE T 0161-474 3813
E cypd@stockport.gov.uk W www.stockport.gov.uk
Corporate Director, Andrew Webb
STOCKTON-ON-TEES Children, Education and Social Care, Municipal Buildings, Church Road, Stockton-on-Tees TS18 1LD T 01642-393939 W www.stockton.gov.uk
Director, Ann Baxter
STOKE-ON-TRENT Children and Young People's Services, Civic Centre, Glebe Street, Stoke-on-Trent ST4 1HH
T 01782-234567 E children@stoke.gov.uk
W www.stoke.gov.uk/children
Director, D. Jones
SUNDERLAND Children's Services, Civic Centre, Sunderland SR2 7DN T 0191-520 5555 E enquiries@sunderland.gov.uk
W www.sunderland.gov.uk
Director Dr Helen Paterson
SWINDON Children Services, Sanford House, Sanford Street, Swindon SN1 1QH T 01793-463000
E hpitts@swindon.gov.uk W www.swindon.gov.uk
Group Director, Hilary Pitts
TAMESIDE Education Department, Council Offices, Wellington Road, Ashton under Lyne OL6 6DL T 0161-342 8355 E lifelong.learning@tameside.gov.uk
W www.tameside.gov.uk
Director, Jim Taylor
TELFORD AND WREKIN Children and Young People, Civic Offices, Telford TF3 4WF T 01952-385385
E children&youngpeople@telford.gov.uk
W www.telford.gov.uk
Corporate Director, vacant

THURROCK Children, Education and Families, Civic Offices, New Road, Grays RM17 6SL T 01375-652652
E education@thurrock.gov.uk
W www.thurrock.gov.uk/education
Interim Corporate Director, Julien Kramer
TORBAY Children's Services, Oldway Mansion, Paignton TQ3 2TE T 01803-208227 E csenquiries@torbay.gov.uk
W www.torbay.gov.uk
Strategic Director, Margaret Dennison
TRAFFORD Children and Young People's Service, Sale Waterside, Waterside House, Sale M33 7ZF T 0161-912 2000 E trafford.direct@trafford.gov.uk
W www.trafford.gov.uk
Corporate Director, Chris Pratt
WAKEFIELD Family Services, County Hall, Bond Street, Wakefield WF1 2QL T 01924-306090
W www.wakefield.gov.uk
Corporate Director, Elaine McHale
WALSALL Children's Services, The Civic Centre, Walsall WS1 1TP T 01922-650000 E info@walsall.gov.uk
W www.walsall.gov.uk
Director, David Brown
WARRINGTON Children's Services Directorate, New Town House, Buttermarket Street, Warrington WA1 2NJ
T 01925-444400 E education@warrington.gov.uk
W www.warrington.gov.uk
Strategic Director, Norma Cadwallader
WEST BERKSHIRE Children and Young People, Avonbank House, West Street, Newbury RG14 1BZ T 01635-519027
E mgoldie@westberks.gov.uk W www.westberks.gov.uk
Head of Education Service, Margaret Goldie
WIGAN Children's and Young People's Services, Progress House, Westwood Park Drive, Wigan WN3 4HH
T 01942-486123 E education@wigan.gov.uk
W www.wigan.gov.uk
Director, Ged Rowney
WIRRAL Children and Young People's Department, Hamilton Building, Conway Street, Birkenhead CH41 4FD T 0151-606 2000 E childrens@wirral.gov.uk W www.wirral.gov.uk/ed
Director, Howard Cooper
WOKINGHAM Children's Services, PO Box 156, Shute End, Wokingham RG40 1WN T 0118-974 6134
E childrensservicesreception@wokingham.gov.uk
W www.wokingham.gov.uk
Corporate Head, Wendy Woodcock
WOLVERHAMPTON Children and Young People, Civic Centre, St Peter's Square, Wolverhampton WV1 1RR
T 01902-556556 E educ.mail@wolverhampton.gov.uk
W www.wolverhampton.gov.uk
Director, Roy Lockwood
YORK Learning, Culture and Children's Services, Mill House, North Street, York YO1 6JD T 01904-613161
E education.queries@york.gov.uk W www.york.gov.uk
Director, Pete Dwyer

LONDON
*Inner London borough
BARKING AND DAGENHAM Children's Services, Town Hall, Barking IG11 7LU T 020-8227 3181
E enquiries@lbbd.gov.uk W www.lbbd.gov.uk
Corporate Director, Roger Luxton, OBE
BARNET Barnet Children's Service, Building 4, North London Business Park, Oakleigh Road South, London N11 1NP
T 020-8359 7618 E education.info@barnet.gov.uk
W www.barnet.gov.uk
Director, Gillian Palmer
BEXLEY Children and Young People's Services, Hill View, Hill View Drive, Welling DA16 3RY T 020-8303 7777

E knowledgemanagement@bexley.gov.uk
W www.bexley.gov.uk
Director, Dr Deborah Absalom
BRENT Children and Families Department, Brent House
Annexe, 356–358 High Road, Wembley HA9 6BX
T 020-8937 4715 E childrenandfamilies@brent.gov.uk
W www.brent.gov.uk
Director, Janet Palmer
BROMLEY Children and Young People Services, Civic Centre,
Stockwell Close, Bromley BR1 3UH T 020-8464 3333
W www.bromley.gov.uk
Director, Gillian Pearson
*CAMDEN Education Department, Crowndale Centre, 218
Eversholt Street, London NW1 1BD T 020-7974 1525
W www.camden.gov.uk
Director, Heather Schroeder
*CITY OF LONDON Education Service, Corporation of
London, PO Box 270, Guildhall, London EC2P 2EJ
T 020-7332 1750 E fyi@cityoflondon.gov.uk
Family and Young People's Director, Gillian Humble
CROYDON Education Department, Taberner House, Park
Lane, Croydon CR9 3JS T 020-8726 6400
E contact.thecouncil@croydon.gov.uk
W www.croydon.gov.uk
Director, Peter Wylie
EALING Schools Service, Perceval House, 14–16 Uxbridge
Road, London W5 2HL T 020-8825 5599
E education@ealing.gov.uk W www.ealing.gov.uk
Director, Rachael Black
ENFIELD Education, Children's Services and Leisure, 7th
Floor, Civic Centre, Silver Street, Enfield EN1 3XQ
T 020-8379 1000 W www.enfield.gov.uk
Director, Peter Lewis
*GREENWICH Children's Services, Riverside House, Woolwich
High Street, London SE18 6DF T 020-8854 8888
W www.greenwich.gov.uk
Director, Paul Burnett
*HACKNEY Hackney Technology and Learning Centre,
1 Reading Lane, London E8 1GQ T 020-8820 7000
E info@learningtrust.co.uk W www.learningtrust.co.uk
Chief Executive, Alan Wood
*HAMMERSMITH AND FULHAM Children's Services, Town
Hall, King Street, London W6 9JU T 020-8753 3621
E educationenquiries@lbhf.gov.uk W www.lbhf.gov.uk
Director, Andrew Christie
HARINGEY Children's Service, 48 Station Road, London
N22 7TY T 020-8489 3767
E customer.services@haringey.gov.uk
W www.haringey.gov.uk
Director, Sharon Shoesmith
HARROW Children's Services, PO Box 22, Civic Centre, Station
Road, Harrow HA1 2UW T 020-8863 5611
E info@harrow.gov.uk W www.harrow.gov.uk
Director, Paul Clark
HAVERING Children's Services, Town Hall, Main Road,
Romford RM1 3BB T 01708-434343 E info@havering.gov.uk
W www.havering.gov.uk
Group Director, Andrew Ireland
HILLINGDON Education Department, Civic Centre, High
Street, Uxbridge UB8 1UW T 01895-250529
E cspencer@hillingdon.gov.uk
W www.hillingdon.gov.uk
Corporate Director, Christopher Spencer
HOUNSLOW Children's Services and Lifelong Learning,
Civic Centre, Lampton Road, Hounslow TW3 4DN
T 020-8583 2600 W www.hounslow.gov.uk
Director, Dr Robert Garnett

*ISLINGTON Education Services, Laycock Street, Islington,
London N1 1TH T 020-7527 5800
E admissions.cea@islington.gov.uk W www.islington.gov.uk
Director, Eleanor Schooling
*ROYAL BOROUGH OF KENSINGTON AND CHELSEA
Family and Children's Services, The Town Hall, Hornton
Street, London W8 7NX T 020-7361 3009
E education@rbkc.gov.uk W www.rbkc.gov.uk
Executive Director, Anne Marie Carrie
KINGSTON UPON THAMES Children's Services, Guildhall 2,
Kingston upon Thames KT1 1EU T 020-8546 2121
W www.kingston.gov.uk
Director, P. Leeson
*LAMBETH Children and Young People's Service, International
House, Canterbury Crescent, London SW9 7QE T 020-7926
1000 E infoservice@lambeth.gov.uk
W www.lambeth.gov.uk
Executive Director, Phyllis Dunipace
*LEWISHAM Children and Young People, 3rd Floor, Laurence
House, 1 Catford Road, London SE6 4RU T 020-8314 6000
E frankie.sulke@lewisham.gov.uk W www.lewisham.gov.uk
Executive Director, Frankie Sulke
MERTON Children, Schools and Families, 10th Floor Civic
Centre, London Road, Morden SM4 5DX T 020-8274 4901
E education@merton.gov.uk W www.merton.gov.uk
Director, Dave Hill
NEWHAM Children and Young People's Services, Broadway
House, High Street, Stratford E15 1AJ T 020-8430 2000
W www.newham.gov.uk
Executive Director, Pauline Maddison
REDBRIDGE Children's Services, Lynton House, 255–259
High Road, Ilford IG1 1NN T 020-8478 3020
W www.redbridge.gov.uk
Director, Pat Reynolds
RICHMOND UPON THAMES Education and Leisure
Services, 1st Floor, Regal House, London Road, Twickenham
TW1 3QB T 020-8891 7500 E a.phillips@richmond.gov.uk
W www.richmond.gov.uk
Director, Anji Phillips
*SOUTHWARK Education Department, John Smith House,
144–152 Walworth Road, London SE17 1JL
T 020-7525 5050 E childrens.info@southwark.gov.uk
W www.southwark.gov.uk
Strategic Director, Romi Bowen
SUTTON Learning for Life, The Grove, Carshalton SM5 3AL
T 020-8770 5000 W www.sutton.gov.uk
Strategic Director, Dr I. Birnbaum
*TOWER HAMLETS Children's Services, Mulberry Place,
5 Clove Crescent, London E14 2BG T 020-7364 5006
E childrensservices@towerhamlets.gov.uk
W www.towerhamlets.org.uk
Corporate Director, Kevan Collins
WALTHAM FOREST Children's Services, Silver Birch House,
Uplands Business Park, Blackhorse Lane, London E17 5SD
T 020-8496 3000 W www.walthamforest.gov.uk
E chris.kiernan@walthamforest.gov.uk
Executive Director, Christopher Kiernan
*WANDSWORTH Education Department, Town Hall,
Wandsworth High Street, London SW18 2PU
T 020-8871 8013 E edadmin@wandsworth.gov.uk
W www.wandsworth.gov.uk
Director, Paul Robinson
*CITY OF WESTMINSTER Education Department, City Hall,
13th Floor, 64 Victoria Street, London SW1E 6QP
T 020-7641 6000 W www.westminster.gov.uk
Director of Schools and Learning, Steve Farnsworth

WALES

ANGLESEY County Offices, Llangefni LL77 7TW
T 01248-752900 W www.anglesey.gov.uk
Director, Richard Parry Jones

BLAENAU GWENT Central Depot, Barleyfields, Brynmaur
NP23 4YF T 01495-355294
E education.department@blaenau-gwent.gov.uk
W www.blaenau-gwent.gov.uk
Director, Dr Brett Pugh

BRIDGEND Education Department, Sunnyside, Bridgend
CF31 4AR T 01656-642600 E education@bridgend.gov.uk
W www.bridgend.gov.uk
Executive Director, Hilary Anthony

CAERPHILLY Education Offices, Caerphilly Road, Ystrad
Mynach, Hengoed CF82 7EP T 01443-815588
E info@caerphilly.gov.uk W www.caerphilly.gov.uk
Director, David Hopkins

CARDIFF Schools and Lifelong Learning, County Hall, Atlantic
Wharf, Cardiff CF10 4UW T 029-2087 2000
E cardiff.webmaster@cardiff.gov.uk W www.cardiff.gov.uk
Chief Officer, Chris Jones

CARMARTHENSHIRE Education and Children's Services,
Pibwrlwyd, Carmarthen SA31 2NH T 01267-224532
E lll@carmarthenshire.gov.uk
W www.carmarthenshire.gov.uk
Director, Vernon Morgan

CEREDIGION Education and Community Services, Swyddfa'r
Sir, Glan y Mor, Aberystwyth SY23 2DE T 01970-633600
E education@ceredigion.gov.uk W www.ceredigion.gov.uk
Director, Gareth Jones

CONWY Education Services, Government Buildings, Dinerth
Road, Colwyn Bay LL28 4UL T 01492-575031
E education@conwy.gov.uk W www.conwy.gov.uk
Chief Education Officer, R. Geraint James

DENBIGHSHIRE Lifelong Learning Department, County Hall,
Wynnstay Road, Ruthin LL15 1YN T 01824-706000
E education@denbighshire.gov.uk
W www.denbighshire.gov.uk
Corporate Director, Huw Griffiths

FLINTSHIRE Education and Children's Services, County Hall,
Mold CH7 6ND T 01352-752121 W www.flintshire.gov.uk
Director, Alan Davies

GWYNEDD Schools Services, Council Offices, Caernarfon
LL55 1SH T 01286-672255 E education@gwynedd.gov.uk
W www.gwynedd.gov.uk
Director, Dr Gwynne Jones

MERTHYR TYDFIL Integrated Children's Services, Ty Keir
Hardie, Riverside Court, Avenue De Clichy, Merthyr Tydfil
CF47 8XD T 01685-724600 E officeservices@merthyr.gov.uk
W www.merthyr.gov.uk
Director, C. A. Abbott

MONMOUTHSHIRE Lifelong Learning and Leisure, County
Hall, Cwmbran NP44 2XH T 01633-644644
E andrewkeep@monmouthshire.gov.uk
W www.monmouthshire.gov.uk
Corporate Director, Andrew Keep

NEATH PORT TALBOT Education, Leisure and Lifelong
Learning Directorate, Civic Centre, Port Talbot SA13 1PJ
T 01639-763298 E education@npt.gov.uk
W www.neath-porttalbot.gov.uk
Director, Karl Napieralla

NEWPORT Education Department, Civic Centre, Newport
NP20 4UR T 01633-656656 E education@newport.gov.uk
W www.newport.gov.uk
Chief Education Officer, Dr B. Pugh

PEMBROKESHIRE Education Department, County Hall,
Haverfordwest SA61 1TP T 01437-764551

E enquiries@pembrokeshire.gov.uk
W www.pembrokeshire.gov.uk
Director, Gerson Davies

POWYS Education Department, County Hall, Llandrindod
Wells LD1 5LG T 01597-826422
W www.education.powys.gov.uk
Head of Schools and Inclusion, Douglas Wilson

RHONDDA CYNON TAF Education Department, Ty
Trevithick, Abercynon, Mountain Ash CF45 4UQ
T 01443-744000 W www.rhondda-cynon-taf.gov.uk
Director, Mike Keating

SWANSEA Education Department, County Hall, Oystermouth
Road, Swansea SA1 3SN T 01792-63600
E education.department@swansea.gov.uk
W www.swansea.gov.uk/education
Director, Richard Parry

TORFAEN County Hall, Croesyceiliog, Cwmbran NP44 2WN
T 01495-762200 E your.call@torfaen.gov.uk
W www.torfaen.gov.uk
Chief Education Officer, Catherine Simpson

VALE OF GLAMORGAN Learning and Development, Civic
Offices, Holton Road, Barry CF63 4RU T 01446-700111
W www.valeofglamorgan.gov.uk
Director of Learning and Development, Bryan Jeffreys

WREXHAM Children and Young People Service, Ty Henblas,
Queen's Square, Wrexham LL13 8AZ T 01978-297505
E education@wrexham.gov.uk W www.wrexham.gov.uk
Strategic Director, Terry Garner

SCOTLAND

ABERDEEN Strategic Leadership, Summerhill Centre, Stronsay
Drive, Aberdeen AB15 6JA T 01224-522000
W www.aberdeencity.gov.uk
Director, Abigail Tierney

ABERDEENSHIRE Education and Recreation, Woodhill
House, Westburn Road, Aberdeen AB16 5GB
T 01224-664630 W www.aberdeenshire.gov.uk
Director, Bruce Robertson, OBE

ANGUS Educational Services, County Buildings, Market Street,
Forfar DD8 3WE T 01307-461460
E education@angus.gov.uk W www.angus.gov.uk
Director of Education, Jim Anderson

ARGYLL AND BUTE Community Services, Argyll House,
Alexandra Parade, Dunoon PA23 8AJ T 01369-704000
W www.argyll-bute.gov.uk
Director, Douglas Hendry

CLACKMANNANSHIRE Services to People, Lime Tree House,
Alloa FK10 1EX T 01259-450000
E servicestopeople@clacks.gov.uk
W www.clacksweb.org.uk
Head of Schools, Jim Goodall

DUMFRIES AND GALLOWAY Education and Community
Services, Woodbank, 30 Edinburgh Road, Dumfries
DG1 1NW T 01387-260400 E frasers@dumgal.gov.uk
W www.dumgal.gov.uk
Corporate Director, Fraser Sanderson

DUNDEE Education Department, Tayside House, Crichton
Street, Dundee DD1 3RJ T 01382-434000
E education@dundeecity.gov.uk W www.dundeecity.gov.uk
Director, A. Wilson

EAST AYRSHIRE Education Department, Council
Headquarters, London Road, Kilmarnock KA3 7BU
T 01563-576000 E education@east-ayrshire.gov.uk
W www.east-ayrshire.gov.uk
Executive Director, Graham Short

EAST DUNBARTONSHIRE Community Department, Boclair
House, 100 Milngavie Road, Bearsden, Glasgow G61 2TQ

T 0141-578 8000 E education@eastdunbarton.gov.uk
W www.eastdunbarton.gov.uk
Corporate Director, David Anderson
EAST LOTHIAN Education and Children's Services, John Muir
House, Haddington EH41 3HA T 01620-827631
W www.eastlothian.gov.uk
Director, Alan J. Blackie
EAST RENFREWSHIRE Education Department, Council
Offices, 211 Main Street, Barrhead G78 1SY
T 0141-577 3404 W www.eastrenfrewshire.gov.uk
Director, John Wilson
CITY OF EDINBURGH Children and Families, Waverley
Court, 4 East Market Street, Edinburgh EH8 8BG
T 0131-469 3000 E gillian.tee@edinburgh.gov.uk
W www.edinburgh.gov.uk
Director, Gillian Tee
EILEAN SIAR (WESTERN ISLES) Education Department,
Council Offices, Sandwick Road, Stornoway HS1 2BW
T 01851-709431 E dsmith@cne-siar.gov.uk
W www.cne-siar.gov.uk
Director, Murdo Macleod
FALKIRK Education Services, McLaren House,
Marchmont Avenue, Polmont, Falkirk FK2 0NZ
T 01324-506600 E director.educ@falkirk.gov.uk
W www.falkirk.gov.uk
Director, Julia Swan
FIFE Education Service, Rothesay House, Rothesay Place,
Glenrothes KY7 5PQ T 01592-583372
E education.services@fife.gov.uk W www.fifedirect.co.uk
Executive Director, Kenneth Greer
GLASGOW Education, Training and Young People, Wheatley
House, 25 Cochrane Street, Merchant City, Glasgow G1 1HL
T 0141-287 2000 E education@glasgow.gov.uk
W www.glasgow.gov.uk
Executive Director, Ronnie O'Connor
HIGHLAND Education, Culture and Sport Service, Council
Offices, Glenurquhart Road, Inverness IV3 5NX
T 01463-702074 E ecs@highland.gov.uk
W www.highland.gov.uk
Director, Hugh Fraser
INVERCLYDE Education Services, 105 Dalrymple Street,
Greenock PA15 1HT T 01475-712850
W www.inverclyde.gov.uk
Director, Ian Fraser
MIDLOTHIAN Communications, Midlothian House,
Buccleuch Street, Dalkeith EH22 1DJ T 0131-270 7500
E education.services@midlothian.gov.uk
W www.midlothian.gov.uk
Director, D. MacKay
MORAY Educational Services, Council Offices, High Street,
Elgin IV30 1BX T 01343-563397
E elaine.bain@moray.gov.uk W www.moray.gov.uk
Director, Donald M. Duncan
NORTH AYRSHIRE Educational Services, Cunninghame
House, Friars Croft, Irvine KA12 8EE T 01294-324400
E education@north-ayrshire.gov.uk
W www.north-ayrshire.gov.uk
Corporate Director, John Travers
NORTH LANARKSHIRE Learning and Leisure Services,
Municipal Buildings, Kildonan Street, Coatbridge ML5 3BT
T 01236-812222 E lls.enquiries@northlan.gov.uk
W www.northlan.gov.uk
Executive Director, Christine Pollock
ORKNEY ISLANDS Education and Recreation Services,
Council Offices, School Place, Kirkwall, Orkney KW15 1NY
T 01856-873535 E education@orkney.gov.uk
W www.orkney.gov.uk
Director, Leslie Manson

PERTH AND KINROSS Education and Children's Services,
Pullar House, 35 Kinnoull Street, Perth PH1 5GD
T 01738-476200 E ecsgeneralenquiries@pkc.gov.uk
W www.pkc.gov.uk
Executive Director (interim), David Montgomery
RENFREWSHIRE South Building, Council Headquarters,
Cotton Street, Paisley PA1 1LE T 0141-842 5663
E schools.els@renfrewshire.gov.uk
W www.renfrewshire.gov.uk
Director, John Rooney
SCOTTISH BORDERS Education and Lifelong
Learning, Council Headquarters, Newtown St Boswells,
Melrose TD6 0SA T 01835-824000
E ellinfo@scotborders.gov.uk
W www.scotborders.gov.uk
Director, Glenn Rodger
SHETLAND ISLANDS Education Service, Hayfield
House, Hayfield Lane, Lerwick ZE1 0QD
T 01595-744000
E education.and.social.service@shetland.gov.uk
W www.shetland.gov.uk
Head of Education Service, Helen Budge
SOUTH AYRSHIRE Education, Culture and Lifelong
Learning, County Buildings, Wellington Square, Ayr
KA7 1DR T 01292-612285
E cst@south-ayrshire.gov.uk
W www.south-ayrshire.gov.uk
Director, Mike McCabe
SOUTH LANARKSHIRE Education Resources, Council
Offices, Almada Street, Hamilton ML3 0AE T 01698-454444
E education@southlanarkshire.gov.uk
W www.southlanarkshire.gov.uk
Executive Director, Larry Forde
STIRLING Children's Services, Viewforth, Stirling FK8 2ET
T 01786-442666 E camerond@stirling.gov.uk
W www.stirling.gov.uk
Director, David Cameron
WEST DUNBARTONSHIRE Education and Cultural Services,
Council Offices, Garshake Road, Dumbarton G82 3PU
T 01389-737309
E education.centralregistry@west-dunbarton.gov.uk
Director, Liz McGinlay
WEST LOTHIAN Education and Cultural Services, West
Lothian House, Almondvale Boulevard, Livingston
EH54 6QG T 01506-776000
E education@westlothian.gov.uk
Director, Gordon Ford

NORTHERN IRELAND

BELFAST Education and Library Board, 40 Academy Street,
Belfast BT1 2NQ T 028-9056 4000 E info@belb.co.uk
W www.belb.org.uk
Chief Executive, David Cargo
NORTH EAST North Eastern Education and Library Board,
Library HQ, 25–31 Demesne Avenue, Ballymena BT43 7BG
T 028-2566 4119 W www.neelb.org.uk
Chief Executive, G. Topping
SOUTH Southern Education and Library Board, 3 Charlemont
Place, The Mall, Armagh BT61 9AX T 028-3751 2200
E selb.hq@selb.org W www.selb.org
Chief Executive, Helen McClenaghan
SOUTH EAST South Eastern Education and Library Board,
Headquarters Offices, Grahamsbridge Road, Dundonald,
Belfast BT16 2HS T 028-9056 6200 E info@seelb.org.uk
W www.seelb.org.uk
Chief Executive, I. Knox

WEST Western Education and Library Board, 1 Hospital Road, Omagh BT79 0AW **T** 028-8241 1411 **E** info@welbni.org **W** www.welbni.org
Chief Executive, B. Mulholland

ISLANDS

GUERNSEY Education Department, PO Box 32, The Grange, St Peter Port, Guernsey GY1 3AU **T** 01481-710821 **E** enquiries@education.gov.gg **W** www.education.gg
Director, D. T. Neale

ISLE OF MAN Department of Education, St. George's Court, Upper Church Street, Douglas, Isle of Man IM1 2SG **T** 01624-685808 **E** admin@doe.gov.im **W** www.gov.im
Director, John Cain

ISLE OF WIGHT County Hall, High Street, Newport PO30 1UD **T** 01983-821000 **W** www.iwight.com
Director of Children's Services, Steve Beynon

ISLES OF SCILLY Education Department, Town Hall, Hugh Town, St Mary's TR21 0LW **T** 01720-422537 **E** enquiries@scilly.gov.uk **W** www.scilly.gov.uk
Chief Executive, Philip Hygate

JERSEY Education, Sport and Culture, PO Box 142, Jersey JE4 8QJ **T** 01534-445504 **E** esc@gov.je **W** www.gov.je
Director, T. W. McKeon

UNIVERSITIES

The following is a list of universities, which are those institutions that have been granted degree awarding powers by either a royal charter or an act of parliament and have been granted permission to use the word 'university' (or 'university college') by the Privy Council. There are other recognised bodies in the UK with degree awarding powers, as well as institutions offering courses leading to a degree from a recognised body. Further information is available at W www.dfes.gov.uk.

Where available, student numbers represent the number of full-time undergraduates for the academic year 2006–7, with the exception of the Open University, where all students study part time.

Fees listed are per annum for students beginning full-time undergraduate courses in the academic year 2007–8 (variations apply on certain courses). Whether the fees apply varies depending on where the student is from. English and Northern Irish students pay top-up fees wherever they study in the UK; Welsh students pay top-up fees in England, Scotland and Northern Ireland, but are entitled to a partial tuition fee grant if they remain in Wales or attend a course that is not available at any Welsh university; Scottish students only pay top-up fees in England, Wales and Northern Ireland. EU students pay fees as if they came from the country they are studying in (ie the lowest amount) and international students pay their university's international fees, which are typically much higher than top-up fees.

UNIVERSITY OF ABERDEEN (1495)
King's College, Aberdeen AB24 3FX T 01224-272000
W www.abdn.ac.uk
Students: 8,716 *Fees:* £1,735
Chancellor, Lord Wilson of Tillyorn, KT, GCMG, FRSE
Principal and Vice-Chancellor, Prof. C. Duncan Rice, FRSE
Academic Registrar, Dr Gillian Macintosh

UNIVERSITY OF ABERTAY DUNDEE (1994)
Bell Street, Dundee DD1 1HG T 01382-308000
W www.abertay.ac.uk
Students: 3,165 *Fees:* £1,735
Chancellor, The Rt. Hon. the Earl of Airlie, KT, GCVO
Vice-Chancellor, Prof. Bernard King, CBE
Academic Registrar, Dr Colin Fraser

ANGLIA RUSKIN UNIVERSITY (1992)
Rivermead Campus, Bishop Hall Lane, Chelmsford, Essex CM1 1SQ T 01245-493131 W www.anglia.ac.uk
Students: 9,100 *Fees:* £3,070
Chancellor, Lord Ashcroft, KCMG
Vice-Chancellor, Prof. Michael Thorne, FRSA
The Secretary and Clerk, Stephen Bennett

UNIVERSITY OF THE ARTS LONDON (Formerly The London Institute (1986), University of the Arts London was formed in 2004)
65 Davies Street, London W1K 5DA T 020-7514 6000
W www.arts.ac.uk
Students: 18,797 *Fees:* £3,070
Chancellor, Lord Stevenson of Coddenham, CBE
Rector, Sir Michael Bichard, KCB
University Secretary, Martin Prince

COLLEGES
CAMBERWELL COLLEGE OF ARTS (1898)
Peckham Road, London SE5 8UF T 020-7514 6302
W www.camberwell.arts.ac.uk
Head of College, Chris Wainwright

CENTRAL SAINT MARTINS COLLEGE OF ART & DESIGN (1854)
Southampton Row, London WC1B 4AP T 020-7514 7022
W www.csm.arts.ac.uk
Head of College, Jane Rapley, OBE

CHELSEA COLLEGE OF ART & DESIGN (1895)
Millbank, London SW1P 4RJ T 020-7514 7751
W www.chelsea.arts.ac.uk
Head of College, Chris Wainwright

LONDON COLLEGE OF COMMUNICATION (1894)
Elephant & Castle, London SE1 6SB T 020-7514 6500
W www.lcc.arts.ac.uk
Head of College, Dr William Bridge

LONDON COLLEGE OF FASHION (1963)
20 John Princes Street, London W1G 0BJ T 020-7514 7500
W www.fashion.arts.ac.uk
Head of College, Dr Frances Corner

WIMBLEDON COLLEGE OF ART (1930)
Merton Hall Road, London SW19 3QA T 020-7514 9641
W www.wimbledon.arts.ac.uk
Head of College, Chris Wainwright

ASTON UNIVERSITY (1966)
Aston Triangle, Birmingham B4 7ET T 0121-204 3000
W www.aston.ac.uk
Students: 7,087 *Fees:* £3,070
Chancellor, Prof. Michael Bett, CBE
Vice-Chancellor, Prof. Julia King, CBE, FRENG, FRSA
Registrar, David Packham, FRSA

UNIVERSITY OF BATH (1966)
Bath BA2 7AY T 01225-388388 W www.bath.ac.uk
Students: 8,621 *Fees:* £3,070
Chancellor, Lord Tugendhat
Vice-Chancellor, Prof. Glynis Breakwell, PHD, FRSA
University Secretary, Mark Humphriss

BATH SPA UNIVERSITY (2005)
Newton Park, Newton St Loe, Bath BA2 9BN T 01225-875875
W www.bathspa.ac.uk
Students: 5,500 *Fees:* £3,070
Vice-Chancellor, Prof. Frank Morgan
Academic Registrar, Christopher Ellicott

UNIVERSITY OF BEDFORDSHIRE (1993)
Park Square, Luton LU1 3JU T 01582-734111
W www.beds.ac.uk
Students: 8,298 *Fees:* £3,000
Chancellor, Sir Robin Biggam
Vice-Chancellor, Prof. Les Ebdon
Registrar, Dr Jim Franklin

UNIVERSITY OF BIRMINGHAM (1900)
Edgbaston, Birmingham B15 2TT **T** 0121-414 3344
W www.bham.ac.uk
Students: 16,639 *Fees:* £3,070
Chancellor, Sir Dominic Cadbury
Vice-Chancellor, Prof. M. Sterling
Registrar and Secretary, Mrs G. Ball

UNIVERSITY OF BOLTON (2005)
Deane Road, Bolton BL3 5AB **T** 01204-903903
W www.bolton.ac.uk
Students: 2,760 *Fees:* £3,070
Vice-Chancellor, Dr George Holmes

BOURNEMOUTH UNIVERSITY (1992)
Fern Barrow, Poole, Dorset BH12 5BB **T** 01202-524111
W www.bournemouth.ac.uk
Students: 10,106 *Fees:* £3,070
Chancellor, Lady Digby, DBE, DL
Vice-Chancellor, Prof. Paul Curran
Registrar, Noel Richardson

UNIVERSITY OF BRADFORD (1966)
Richmond Building, Richmond Road, Bradford, W. Yorks
BD7 1DP **T** 01274-232323 **W** www.brad.ac.uk
Students: 7,502 *Fees:* £3,070
Chancellor, Imran Khan
Vice-Chancellor, Prof. Mark Cleary
University Secretary, Mary Rose Millin

UNIVERSITY OF BRIGHTON (1992)
Mithras House, Lewes Road, Brighton BN2 4AT
T 01273-600900 **W** www.bton.ac.uk
Students: 12,649 *Fees:* £3,070
Chancellor, Sir John Mogg
Vice-Chancellor, Prof. Julian Crampton
Registrar and Secretary, Christine Moon

UNIVERSITY OF BRISTOL (1909)
Senate House, Tyndall Avenue, Bristol BS8 1TH **T** 0117-928
9000 **W** www.bristol.ac.uk
Students: 12,000 *Fees:* £3,070
Chancellor, Baroness Hale of Richmond, DBE, PC
Vice Chancellor, Prof. Eric Thomas
Registrar, Derek Pretty

BRUNEL UNIVERSITY (1966)
Uxbridge, Middx UB8 3PH **T** 01895-274000
W www.brunel.ac.uk
Students: 11,000 *Fees:* £3,000
Chancellor, The Rt. Hon. Lord Wakeham
Vice-Chancellor and Principal, Prof. C. Jenks
Secretary and Registrar, J. Weale

UNIVERSITY OF BUCKINGHAM (1983)
Buckingham MK18 1EG **T** 01280-814080
W www.buckingham.ac.uk
Students: 600 *Fees:* £7,500
Chancellor, Sir Martin Jacomb
Vice-Chancellor, Terence Kealey, DPHIL
Registrar, Prof. Len Evans

UNIVERSITY OF CAMBRIDGE (1209)
The Old Schools, Trinity Lane, Cambridge CB2 1TN
T 01223-337733 **W** www.cam.ac.uk
Students: 11,825 *Fees:* £3,000
Chancellor, HRH The Prince Philip, Duke of Edinburgh,
   KG, KT, OM, GBE, PC, FRS

Vice-Chancellor, Prof. Alison Richard (Newnham)
High Steward, Dame Bridget Ogilvie, DBE, FRS (Girton)
Deputy High Steward, Lord Richardson of Duntisbourne,
   KG, MBE, TD, PC (Gonville and Caius)
Commissary, Lord Mackay of Clashfern, KT, PC, FRSE
   (Trinity)
Pro-Vice-Chancellors, Prof. A. D. Cliff (Christ's); Prof. I.
   M. Leslie (Christ's); Prof. M. C. McKendrick (Girton);
   Prof. A. C. Minson (Wolfson); Dr K. B. Pretty
   (Homerton)
Proctors, Revd R. Greeves (Clare), Dr P. Sarris (Trinity)
Orator, A. J. Bowen (Jesus)
Registrary, Dr J. W. Nichols (Emmanuel)
Librarian, P. K. Fox (Selwyn)
Director of the Fitzwilliam Museum, D. D. Robinson
   (Magdalene)
Academic Secretary, G. P. Allen (Wolfson)
Director of Finance, A. M. Reid (Wolfson)

COLLEGES AND HALLS *with dates of foundation*
CHRIST'S (1505)
   Master, Prof. Frank Kelly, FRS
CHURCHILL (1960)
   Master, Prof. Sir David Wallace, CBE, FRS
CLARE (1326)
   Master, Prof. A. J. Badger
CLARE HALL (1966)
   President, Prof. E. K. H. Salje, FRS
CORPUS CHRISTI (1352)
   Master, Prof. Sir Alan Wilson
DARWIN (1964)
   Master, Prof. W. A. Brown, CBE
DOWNING (1800)
   Master, Prof. B. J. Everitt, FRS
EMMANUEL (1584)
   Master, Lord Wilson of Dinton, GCB
FITZWILLIAM (1966)
   Master, Prof. R. D. Lethbridge
GIRTON (1869)
   Mistress, Prof. Dame Marilyn Strathern, DBE, FBA
GONVILLE AND CAIUS (1348)
   Master, Sir Christopher Hum, KCMG
HOMERTON (1824)
   Principal, Dr K. B. Pretty
HUGHES HALL (1985)
   President, Mrs S. Squire
JESUS (1496)
   Master, Prof. R. Mair, FRS, FRENG
KING'S (1441)
   Provost, Prof. T. R. Harrison
LUCY CAVENDISH (1965)
   President, Dame Veronica Sutherland, DBE, CMG
MAGDALENE (1542)
   Master, D. D. Robinson
NEW HALL (1954)
   President, Mrs A. M. Lonsdale, CBE
NEWNHAM (1871)
   Principal, Dame Patricia Hodgson, DBE
PEMBROKE (1347)
   Master, Sir Richard Dearlove, KCMG, OBE
PETERHOUSE (1284)
   Master, Lord Wilson of Tillyorn, KT, GCMG, FRSE
QUEENS' (1448)
   President, Prof. Lord Eatwell
ROBINSON (1977)
   Warden, A. D. Yates
ST CATHARINE'S (1473)
   Master, Prof. Dame Jean Thomas, DBE, FRS

ST EDMUND'S (1896)
  Master, Prof. J. P. Luzio
ST JOHN'S (1511)
  Master, Prof. C. Dobson, FRS
SELWYN (1882)
  Master, Prof. R. J. Bowring
SIDNEY SUSSEX (1596)
  Master, Prof. Dame Sandra Dawson, DBE
TRINITY (1546)
  Master, Prof. Lord Rees of Ludlow, PRS
TRINITY HALL (1350)
  Master, Prof. M. J. Daunton, FBA
WOLFSON (1965)
  President, G. Johnson

CANTERBURY CHRIST CHURCH UNIVERSITY
(2005)
North Holmes Road, Canterbury CT1 1QU T 01227-767700
W www.canterbury.ac.uk
Students: 5,421 *Fees:* £3,070
Chancellor, Most Revd Rowan Williams, PC, DPHIL
Vice-Chancellor and Principal, Prof. Michael Wright
Academic Registrar, Kevin Tomlinson

CARDIFF UNIVERSITY (1883)
Cardiff CF10 3XQ T 029-2087 4000 W www.cardiff.ac.uk
Students: 22,000 *Fees:* £3,000
President, Lord Kinnock, PC
Vice-Chancellor, Dr David Grant, CBE, FRENG
Director of Registry, Prof. Tony Cryer

UNIVERSITY OF CENTRAL LANCASHIRE (1992)
Preston PR1 2HE T 01772-201201 W www.uclan.ac.uk
Students: 18,648 *Fees:* £3,070
Chancellor, Sir Richard Evans, CBE
Vice-Chancellor, Dr Malcolm McVicar
Director of Student Affairs, Ian McMillan

UNIVERSITY OF CHESTER (2005)
Parkgate Road, Chester CH1 4BJ T 01244-511000
W www.chester.ac.uk
Students: 5,768 *Fees:* £3,070
Chancellor, His Grace, The Duke of Westminster
Vice-Chancellor and Principal, Prof. Tim Wheeler, DL
University Secretary/Bursar, David Stevens

UNIVERSITY OF CHICHESTER (2005)
Bishop Otter Campus, College Lane, Chichester PO19 6PE
T 01243-816000 W www.chi.ac.uk
Students: 4,243 *Fees:* £3,100
Vice-Chancellor, Dr Robin Baker

CITY UNIVERSITY (1966)
Northampton Square, London EC1V 0HB T 020-7040 5060
W www.city.ac.uk
Students: 8,550 *Fees:* £3,070
Pro-Chancellor, John Stuttard, BT., DSC
Vice-Chancellor, Prof. Malcolm Gillies
Registrar, Eamon Martin

COVENTRY UNIVERSITY (1992)
Priory Street, Coventry CV1 5FB T 024-7688 7688
W www.coventry.ac.uk
Students: 10,910 *Fees:* £3,070
Chancellor, Sir John Egan
Vice-Chancellor, Prof. Madeleine Atkins, CBE
Academic Registrar and Secretary, Kate Quantrell

DE MONTFORT UNIVERSITY (1992)
The Gateway, Leicester LE1 9BH T 08459-454647
W www.dmu.ac.uk
Students: 14,024 *Fees:* £3,070
Chancellor, Lord Alli
Vice-Chancellor, Prof. Philip Tasker
Registrar, Eugene Critchlow

UNIVERSITY OF DERBY (1992)
Kedleston Road, Derby DE22 1GB T 01332-590500
W www.derby.ac.uk
Students: 9,000 *Fees:* £3,070
Chancellor, Prof. Leslie Wagner, CBE
Vice-Chancellor, Prof. John Coyne
Deputy Vice-Chancellor, Jennifer Fry

UNIVERSITY OF DUNDEE (1967)
Nethergate, Dundee DD1 4HN T 01382-384000
W www.dundee.ac.uk
Students: 9,500 *Fees:* £1,735
Chancellor, Lord Patel, FRSE
Vice-Chancellor, Sir Alan Langlands, FRSE

DURHAM UNIVERSITY (1832)
The University Office, Durham DH1 3HP T 0191-334 2000
W www.dur.ac.uk
Students: 15,057 *Fees:* £3,070
Chancellor, Bill Bryson
Vice-Chancellor and Warden, Prof. C. F. Higgins, FRSE,
  FRSA, FMEDSCI
Registrar and Secretary, L. Sanders

COLLEGES
COLLINGWOOD
  Principal, Prof. J. Taylor until January 2008,
  Prof. E. Corrigan, FRS, thereafter
GEORGE STEPHENSON
  Principal, Prof. A. C. Darnell
GREY
  Master, Prof. J. M. Chamberlain, DPHIL
HATFIELD
  Master, Prof. T. P. Burt, DSC
JOHN SNOW
  Principal, Prof. H. M. Evans
JOSEPHINE BUTLER
  Principal, A. Simpson
ST AIDAN'S
  Principal, Prof. J. S. Ashworth
ST CHAD'S
  Principal, Revd J. P. M. Cassidy, PHD
ST CUTHBERT'S SOCIETY
  Principal, Prof. R. D. Boyne
ST HILD AND ST BEDE
  Principal, J. A. Pearson
ST JOHN'S
  Principal, Revd D. Wilkinson, PHD
ST MARY'S
  Principal (acting), Dr Gillian Boughton
TREVELYAN
  Principal, N. Martin
UNIVERSITY
  Master, Prof. M. E. Tucker
USHAW
  Rector, Revd T. Drainey
USTINOV
  Principal, Penelope B. Wilson, DPHIL
VAN MILDERT
  Master, Prof. P. O'Meara, DPHIL

UNIVERSITY OF EAST ANGLIA (1963)
Norwich NR4 7TJ T 01603-456161 W www.uea.ac.uk
Students: 8,524 Fees: £3,070
Chancellor, Sir Brandon Gough
Vice-Chancellor, Dr Bill Macmillan
Academic Registrar, Brian Summers

UNIVERSITY OF EAST LONDON (1898)
University Way, London E16 2RD T 020-8223 3000
W www.uel.ac.uk
Students: 10,000 Fees: £3,000
Chancellor, Lord Rix, CBE
Vice-Chancellor, Prof. Martin Everett
Registrar and Secretary, Alan Ingle

EDGE HILL UNIVERSITY (2006)
St Helens Road, Ormskirk, Lancs L39 4QP T 01695-575171
W www.edgehill.ac.uk
Students: 12,229 Fees: £3,070
Vice-Chancellor, John Cater
University Secretary, Lesley Munro

UNIVERSITY OF EDINBURGH (1583)
Old College, South Bridge, Edinburgh EH8 9YL T 0131-650
1000 W www.ed.ac.uk
Students: 18,378 Fees: £1,735
Chancellor, HRH The Prince Philip, Duke of Edinburgh,
  KG, KT, OM
Principal and Vice-Chancellor, Prof. Timothy O'Shea,
  FRSE

UNIVERSITY OF ESSEX (1965)
Wivenhoe Park, Colchester CO4 3SQ T 01206-873333
W www.essex.ac.uk
Students: 6,000 Fees: £3,070
Chancellor, Lord Phillips of Sudbury, OBE
Vice-Chancellor, Prof. Colin Riordan
Academic Registrar, Dr Tony Rich

UNIVERSITY OF EXETER (1955)
The Queen's Drive, Exeter EX4 4QJ T 01392-661000
W www.exeter.ac.uk
Students: 9,123 Fees: £3,070
Chancellor, Floella Benjamin, OBE
Vice Chancellor, Prof. Steve Smith
Registrar and Secretary, David Allen

UNIVERSITY OF GLAMORGAN (1992)
Pontypridd CF37 1DL T 0800-716925 W www.glam.ac.uk
Students: 9,833 Fees: £3,070
Chancellor, Lord Morris of Aberavon, KG, PC, QC
Vice-Chancellor, Prof. David Halton
Academic Registrar, John O'Shea

UNIVERSITY OF GLASGOW (1451)
Gilbert Scott Building, University Avenue, Glasgow G12 8QQ
T 0141-330 2000 W www.gla.ac.uk
Students: 14,980 Fees: £1,735–£2,760
Chancellor, Prof. Sir Kenneth Calman, KCB, MD, FRCS
Vice-Chancellor, Sir Muir Russell, KCB, FRSE
Secretary of Court, David Newall

GLASGOW CALEDONIAN UNIVERSITY (1993)
City Campus, 70 Cowcaddens Road, Glasgow G4 0BA
T 0141-331 3000 W www.caledonian.ac.uk
Students: 10,072 Fees: £1,735

Vice-Chancellor and Principal, Prof. Pamela Gillies, FRSA,
  FFPH
Registrar, Alison Rooney

UNIVERSITY OF GLOUCESTERSHIRE (2001)
The Park, Cheltenham GL50 2RH T 08707-210210
W www.glos.ac.uk
Students: 5,375 Fees: £3,070
Chancellor, Lord Carey of Clifton, PC
Vice-Chancellor, Prof. Patricia Broadfoot, CBE
Academic Registrar, Paul Van Rossum

UNIVERSITY OF GREENWICH (1992)
Old Royal Naval College, Park Row, Greenwich, London
SE10 9LS T 020-8331 8000 W www.gre.ac.uk
Students: 12,255 Fees: £2,560
Chancellor, Lord Holme of Cheltenham, CBE, PC
Vice-Chancellor, Baroness Blackstone, PHD
Secretary and Registrar, Linda Cording

HERIOT-WATT UNIVERSITY (1966)
Edinburgh EH14 4AS T 0131-449 5111 W www.hw.ac.uk
Students: 5,298 Fees: £1,700
Chancellor, Susan Greenfield, BT., CBE, FRCP
Principal and Vice-Chancellor, Prof. Anton Muscatelli
Secretary, Peter Wilson

UNIVERSITY OF HERTFORDSHIRE (1992)
College Lane, Hatfield, Herts AL10 9AB T 01707-284000
W www.herts.ac.uk
Students: 18,188 Fees: £3,075
Chancellor, The Marquess of Salisbury, PC
Vice-Chancellor, Prof. Tim Wilson
Registrar and Secretary, Philip Waters

UNIVERSITY OF HUDDERSFIELD (1992)
Queensgate, Huddersfield HD1 3DH T 01484-422288
W www.hud.ac.uk
Students: 6,495 Fees: £3,070
Chancellor, Patrick Stewart, OBE
Vice-Chancellor, Prof. Bob Cryan
Academic Registrar, Kathy Sherlock

UNIVERSITY OF HULL (1927)
Cottingham Road, Hull HU6 7RX T 01482-346311
W www.hull.ac.uk
Students: 10,568 Fees: £3,070
Chancellor, Baroness Bottomley of Nettlestone, PC, LLD
Vice-Chancellor, Prof. David J. Drewry, FRSA
Quality Director, Registrar and Secretary, Frances Owen

IMPERIAL COLLEGE LONDON (1907)
South Kensington, London SW7 2AZ T 020-7589 5111
W www.imperial.ac.uk
Students: 8,050 Fees: £3,070
Rector, Sir Richard Sykes
Deputy Rector, Prof. Sir Leszek Borysiewicz
Academic Registrar, Vernon McClure

KEELE UNIVERSITY (1962)
Keele, Staffs ST5 5BG T 01782-621111 W www.keele.ac.uk
Students: 4,800 Fees: £3,000
Chancellor, Prof. Sir David Weatherall, FRS
Vice-Chancellor, Prof. Janet Finch, CBE
Registrar and Secretary, Mr S. J. Morris

UNIVERSITY OF KENT (1965)
Canterbury, Kent CT2 7NZ T 01227-764000
W www.kent.ac.uk
Students: 11,122 *Fees:* £3,070
Chancellor, Prof. Sir Robert Worcester, KBE
Vice-Chancellor, Prof. Julia Goodfellow, CBE
Secretary of the Council, Karen Griffin

KINGSTON UNIVERSITY (1992)
River House, 53–57 High Street, Kingston upon Thames, Surrey
KT1 1LQ T 020-8547 2000 W www.kingston.ac.uk
Students: 21,059 *Fees:* £3,000
Chancellor, Sir Peter Hall
Vice-Chancellor, Prof. Peter Scott
Academic Registrar, Alison Stokes

UNIVERSITY OF LANCASTER (1964)
Bailrigg, Lancaster LA1 4YW T 01524-65201
W www.lancs.ac.uk
Students: 8,323 *Fees:* £3,070
Chancellor, Sir Christian Bonington, CBE
Vice-Chancellor, Prof. Paul Wellings
University Secretary, Fiona Aiken

UNIVERSITY OF LEEDS (1904)
Leeds LS2 9JT T 0113-243 1751 W www.leeds.ac.uk
Students: 22,391 *Fees:* £3,070
Chancellor, Lord Bragg
Vice-Chancellor, Prof. Michael Arthur
Secretary, Roger Gair

LEEDS METROPOLITAN UNIVERSITY (1992)
Civic Quarter, Leeds LS1 3HE T 0113-283 2600
W www.leedsmet.ac.uk
Students: 14,202 *Fees:* £2,000
Chancellor, Brendan Foster, MBE
Vice-Chancellor, Prof. Simon Lee
Registrar and Secretary, Stephen Denton

UNIVERSITY OF LEICESTER (1957)
University Road, Leicester LE1 7RH T 0116-252 2522
W www.le.ac.uk
Students: 7,426 *Fees:* £3,070
Chancellor, Sir Peter Williams, CBE, FRS, FRENG
Vice-Chancellor, Prof. Robert Burgess
Registrar and Secretary, Dave Hall

UNIVERSITY OF LINCOLN (1992)
Brayford Pool, Lincoln LN6 7TS T 01522-882000
W www.lincoln.ac.uk
Students: 8,236 *Fees:* £3,000
Chancellor, Dame Elizabeth Esteve-Coll
Vice-Chancellor, Prof. David Chiddick
Registrar, Edmund Fitzpatrick

UNIVERSITY OF LIVERPOOL (1903)
Liverpool, Merseyside L69 72X T 0151-794 2000
W www.liv.ac.uk
Students: 13,880 *Fees:* £3,000
Chancellor, Lord Owen, CH, PC, FRCP
Vice-Chancellor, Prof. James Drummond Bone, FRSA
Chief Operating Officer, Ron Calvert

LIVERPOOL HOPE UNIVERSITY (2005)
Hope Park, Liverpool L16 9JD T 0151-291 3000
W www.hope.ac.uk
Students: 6,000 *Fees:* £3,000

Chancellor, Baroness Cox
Vice-Chancellor, Prof. Gerald Pillay, FRSA
University Secretary, Graham Donelan

LIVERPOOL JOHN MOORES UNIVERSITY (1992)
Egerton Court, 2 Rodney Street, Liverpool L3 5UX T 0151-231
2121 W www.ljmu.ac.uk
Students: 14,433 *Fees:* £3,070
Chancellor, vacant
Vice-Chancellor, Prof. Michael Brown
Secretary, Alison Wild

UNIVERSITY OF LONDON (1836)
Senate House, Malet Street, London WC1E 7HU T 020-7862
8000 W www.london.ac.uk
Students: 56,040 *Fees:* variable; contact individual colleges
for details
Chancellor, HRH the Princess Royal, KG, GCVO, FRS
Vice-Chancellor, Prof. Sir Graeme Davies, FRENG, FRSE
Chair of the Council, Lord Sutherland of Houndwood, KT,
FBA
Director of Administration, Catherine Swarbrick

COLLEGES
BIRKBECK COLLEGE
Malet Street, London WC1E 7HX
Master, Prof. D. Latchman

CENTRAL SCHOOL OF SPEECH AND DRAMA
Embassy Theatre, Eton Avenue, London NW3 3HY
Principal, Prof. Gavin Henderson, CBE

COURTAULD INSTITUTE OF ART
North Block, Somerset House, Strand, London WC2R 0RN
Director, Dr Deborah Swallow

GOLDSMITHS COLLEGE
Lewisham Way, New Cross, London SE14 6NW
Warden, Prof. Geoffrey Crossick

HEYTHROP COLLEGE
Kensington Square, London W8 5HQ
Principal, Revd Dr J. McDade, SJ, BD

INSTITUTE OF CANCER RESEARCH
Royal Cancer Hospital, Chester Beatty Laboratories, 237 Fulham
Road, London SW3 6JB
Chief Executive, Prof. P. Rigby

INSTITUTE OF EDUCATION
20 Bedford Way, London WC1H 0AL
Director, Prof. G. Whitty

KING'S COLLEGE LONDON
(includes Guy's, King's and St Thomas's Schools of Medicine,
Dentistry and Biomedical Sciences) Strand, London WC2R 2LS
Principal, Prof. R. Trainor

LONDON BUSINESS SCHOOL
Sussex Place, Regent's Park, London NW1 4SU
Dean, Robin Buchanan

LONDON SCHOOL OF ECONOMICS AND
POLITICAL SCIENCE
Houghton Street, London WC2A 2AE
Director, Sir Howard Davies

LONDON SCHOOL OF HYGIENE AND TROPICAL
MEDICINE
Keppel Street, London WC1E 7HT
Dean, Prof. Sir Andrew Haines

QUEEN MARY
(incorporating St Bartholomew's and the Royal London School
of Medicine and Dentistry) Mile End Road, London E1 4NS
Principal, Prof. A. Smith, FRS

ROYAL ACADEMY OF MUSIC
Marylebone Road, London NW1 5HT
Principal, Prof. Curtis Price, KBE

ROYAL HOLLOWAY
Egham Hill, Egham, Surrey TW20 0EX
Principal, Prof. S. Hill, MPHIL

ROYAL VETERINARY COLLEGE
Royal College Street, London NW1 0TU
Principal and Dean, Prof. Q. McKellar

ST GEORGE'S
Cranmer Terrace, London SW17 0RE
Acting Principal, Prof. Sean Hilton, FRCGP

SCHOOL OF ORIENTAL AND AFRICAN STUDIES
Thornhaugh Street, Russell Square, London WC1H 1AX
Director, Prof. Paul Webley

SCHOOL OF PHARMACY
29–39 Brunswick Square, London WC1N 1AX
Dean, Prof. Anthony Smith

UNIVERSITY COLLEGE LONDON
(including UCL Medical School) Gower Street, London
WC1E 6BT
Provost and President, Prof. Malcolm Grant, CBE

INSTITUTES
UNIVERSITY OF LONDON INSTITUTE IN PARIS
9–11 rue de Constantine, 75340 Paris, Cedex 07
Director, Dr David Shepheard

UNIVERSITY MARINE BIOLOGICAL STATION
Millport, Isle of Cumbrae KA28 0EG
Acting Director, Prof. P. G. Moore

SCHOOL OF ADVANCED STUDY
Senate House, Malet Street, London WC1E 7HU
Dean, vacant

INSTITUTE OF ADVANCED LEGAL STUDIES
Charles Clore House, 17 Russell Square, London WC1B 5DR
Director, Prof. Avrom Sherr

INSTITUTE OF CLASSICAL STUDIES
Senate House, Malet Street, London WC1E 7HU
Director, Prof. M. Edwards

INSTITUTE OF COMMONWEALTH STUDIES
28 Russell Square, London WC1B 5DS
Director, Prof. R. Crook

INSTITUTE OF ENGLISH STUDIES
Senate House, Malet Street, London WC1E 7HU
Director, Prof. W. Gould

INSTITUTE OF GERMANIC AND ROMANCE
STUDIES
Senate House, Malet Street, London WC1E 7HU
Director, Prof. Naomi Segal

INSTITUTE OF HISTORICAL RESEARCH
Senate House, Malet Street, London WC1E 7HU
Director, Prof. David Bates

INSTITUTE OF MUSICAL RESEARCH
Senate House, Malet Street, London WC1E 7HU
Director, Prof. Katharine Ellis

INSTITUTE OF PHILOSOPHY
Senate House, Malet Street, London WC1E 7HU
Director, Prof. Tim Crane

INSTITUTE FOR THE STUDY OF THE AMERICAS
31 Tavistock Square, London WC1H 9HA
Director, Prof. J. Dunkerley

WARBURG INSTITUTE
Woburn Square, London WC1H 0AB
Director, Prof. C. Hope

DISTANCE LEARNING
EXTERNAL PROGRAMME
Senate House, Malet Street, London WC1E 7HU
Director, J. M. McConnell
Dean, Prof. J. Kydd

LONDON METROPOLITAN UNIVERSITY (2002)
31 Jewry Street, London EC3N 2EY **T** 020-7423 0000
W www.londonmet.ac.uk
Students: 21,000 *Fees:* £3,000
Vice-Chancellor and Chief Executive, Brian Roper
Academic Registrar, Dr Ray Smith

LONDON SOUTH BANK UNIVERSITY (1992)
103 Borough Road, London SE1 0AA **T** 020-7815 7815
W www.lsbu.ac.uk
Students: 9,000 *Fees:* £3,000
Chancellor, Jane Newell, OBE
Vice-Chancellor, Prof. Deian Hopkin, FRSA

LOUGHBOROUGH UNIVERSITY (1966)
Ashby Road, Loughborough, Leics LE11 3TU **T** 01509-263171
W www.lboro.ac.uk
Students: 10,505 *Fees:* £3,070
Chancellor, Sir John Jennings, CBE, FRSE
Vice-Chancellor, Prof. Shirley Pearce, CBE
Academic Registrar, John Town

UNIVERSITY OF MANCHESTER (2004)
Oxford Road, Manchester M13 9PL **T** 0161-306 6000
W www.manchester.ac.uk
Students: 26,440 *Fees:* £3,000
Co-Chancellors, Anna Ford and Sir Terry Leahy
President and Vice-Chancellor, Prof. Alan Gilbert
Registrar and Secretary, Albert McMenemy

MANCHESTER METROPOLITAN UNIVERSITY
(1992)
All Saints, Manchester M15 6BH **T** 0161-247 2000
W www.mmu.ac.uk
Students: 24,127 *Fees:* £3,070
Chancellor, Dame Janet Smith, DBE, PC
Vice-Chancellor, Prof. John Brooks, DSC, FINSTP
Registrar, Gwyn Arnold

MIDDLESEX UNIVERSITY (1992)
North London Business Park, Oakleigh Road South, London
N11 1QS **T** 020-8411 5555 **W** www.mdx.ac.uk
Students: 14,230 *Fees:* £3,070
Chancellor, Lord Sheppard of Didgemere, KT, KCVO
Vice-Chancellor, Prof. Michael Driscoll
Registrar, Colin Davis

NAPIER UNIVERSITY (1992)
Craighouse Road, Edinburgh EH10 5LG **T** 0845-260 6040
W www.napier.ac.uk
Students: 11,690 *Fees:* £1,735
Principal and Vice-Chancellor, Prof. Joan Stringer, CBE
Registrar and Secretary, Dr Gerry Webber

UNIVERSITY OF NEWCASTLE UPON TYNE (1963)
6 Kensington Terrace, Newcastle upon Tyne NE1 7RU
T 0191-222 6000 **W** www.ncl.ac.uk
Students: 14,058 *Fees:* £3,070
Chancellor, Rt. Hon. Lord Patten of Barnes, CH
Vice-Chancellor, Prof. Chris Brink, FRS, DPHIL, PHD
Registrar, Dr John Hogan

UNIVERSITY OF NORTHAMPTON (2005)
Park Campus, Boughton Green Road, Northampton NN2 7AL
T 01604-735500 **W** www.northampton.ac.uk
Students: 6,761 *Fees:* £3,070
Vice-Chancellor, Ann Tate
Registrar, Jane Bunce

NORTHUMBRIA UNIVERSITY AT NEWCASTLE
(1992)
Ellison Building, Ellison Place, Newcastle upon Tyne NE1 8ST
T 0191-232 6002 **W** www.northumbria.ac.uk
Students: 19,507 *Fees:* £3,070
Chancellor, Lord Stevens of Kirkwhelpington, QPM,
FRSA
Vice-Chancellor, Prof. Kel Fidler, FRENG
Registrar, Paul Kelly

UNIVERSITY OF NOTTINGHAM (1948)
King's Meadow Campus, Lenton Lane, Nottingham NG7 2NR
T 0115-951 5151 **W** www.nottingham.ac.uk
Students: 20,282 *Fees:* £3,070
Chancellor, Prof. Yang Fujia, LITTD
Vice Chancellor, Prof. Sir Colin Campbell
Registrar, Dr Paul Greatrix

NOTTINGHAM TRENT UNIVERSITY (1992)
Burton Street, Nottingham NG1 4BU **T** 0115-941 8418
W www.ntu.ac.uk
Students: 18,459 *Fees:* £3,070
Senior Pro-Vice-Chancellor, Peter Jones
Vice-Chancellor, Prof. Neil Gorman

OPEN UNIVERSITY (1969)
Walton Hall, Milton Keynes MK7 6AA **T** 01908-274066
W www.open.ac.uk
Students: 150,000 (all part-time) *Fees:* £3,500–£4,000
Chancellor, Lord Puttnam of Queensgate
Vice-Chancellor, Prof. Brenda Gourley
University Secretary, Fraser Woodburn

UNIVERSITY OF OXFORD (c.12th century)
University Offices, Wellington Square, Oxford OX1 2JD
T 01865-270000 **W** www.ox.ac.uk
Students: 11,185 *Fees:* £3,070

Chancellor, Lord Patten of Barnes, CH, PC (Balliol, St
Antony's)
High Steward, Lord Bingham of Cornhill, PC (Balliol,
Nuffield)
Vice-Chancellor, Dr John Hood (All Souls, Templeton,
Worcester)
Pro-Vice-Chancellors, Dame Fiona Caldicott (Somerville);
Dr J. S. Dellandrea (Magdalen); Prof. E. A. Fallaize (St
John's); Prof. E. G. McKendrick (Lady Margaret Hall);
Prof. A. P. Monaco (Merton)
Registrar, Dr J. K. Maxton (University)
Secretary of the Faculties and Academic Registrar, M. D.
Sibly (St Anne's)
Proctors, Dr J. Forder (Balliol); Prof. M. J. Banks
(Wolfson)
Assessor, Dr P. Coones (Hertford)
Public Orator, R. H. A. Jenkyns
*Director of University Library Services and Bodley's
Librarian,* Dr S. E. Thomas (Balliol)
Director of the Ashmolean Museum, Dr C. Brown
(Worcester)
Keeper of Archives, S. Bailey
Director of Estates, Ms J. Wood
Director of Finance, G. F. B. Kerr

COLLEGES AND HALLS *with dates of foundation*
ALL SOULS (1438)
  Warden, Prof. J. Davis, FBA
BALLIOL (1263)
  Master, A. Graham
BLACKFRIARS (1221)
  Regent, Revd Richard Finn
BRASENOSE (1509)
  Principal, Prof. R. Cashmore, FRS
CAMPION HALL (1896)
  Master, Revd Dr P. l'Estrange
CHRIST CHURCH (1546)
  Dean, Very Revd C. A. Lewis
CORPUS CHRISTI (1517)
  President, Timothy Lankester, KCB
EXETER (1314)
  Rector, Ms Frances Cairncross, CBE
GREEN (1979)
  Warden, Dr Colin Bundy
GREYFRIARS (1910)
  Warden, Dr Nicholas Richardson
HARRIS MANCHESTER (1786)
  Principal, Revd R. Waller
HERTFORD (1974)
  Principal, Dr John Landers
JESUS (1571)
  Principal, Lord Krebs, FRS
KEBLE (1868)
  Warden, Prof. A. Cameron, CBE, FBA
KELLOGG (1990)
  President, Dr G. P. Thomas
LADY MARGARET HALL (1878)
  Principal, Dr Frances Lannon
LINACRE (1962)
  Principal, Prof. P. A. Slack, FBA
LINCOLN (1427)
  Rector, Prof. P. Langford
MAGDALEN (1458)
  President, Prof. David Clary, FRS
MANSFIELD (1886)
  Principal, Dr D. Walford, FRCP
MERTON (1264)
  Warden, Prof. Dame J. Rawson, CBE, FBA

NEW COLLEGE (1379)
Warden, Prof. A. J. Ryan, FBA
NUFFIELD (1958)
Warden, Prof. Stephen Nickell, FBA
ORIEL (1326)
Provost, Sir Derek Morris
PEMBROKE (1624)
Master, Giles Henderson, CBE
QUEEN'S (1340)
Provost, Sir Alan Budd
REGENT'S PARK (1820)
Principal, Revd Dr P. S. Fiddes
ST ANNE'S (1952)
Principal, Tim Gardam
ST ANTONY'S (1953)
Warden, Prof. Margaret MacMillan
ST BENET'S HALL (1897)
Master, Father Leo Chamberlain
ST CATHERINE'S (1963)
Master, Prof. Roger Ainsworth
ST CROSS (1965)
Master, Prof. Andrew Goudie
ST EDMUND HALL (c.1278)
Principal, Prof. D. M. P. Mingos, FRS
ST HILDA'S (1893)
Principal, Sheila Forbes, CBE
ST HUGH'S (1886)
Principal, A. Dilnot, CBE
ST JOHN'S (1555)
President, Sir Michael Scholar, KCB
ST PETER'S (1929)
Master, Prof. Bernard Silverman, FRS
ST STEPHEN'S HOUSE (1876)
Principal, Revd Dr Robin Ward
SOMERVILLE (1879)
Principal, Dame Fiona Caldicott, DBE, FRCP, FRCPSYCH
TEMPLETON (1965)
Dean, Prof. Michael Earl
TRINITY (1554)
President, Sir Ivor Roberts, KCMG
UNIVERSITY (1249)
Master, Lord Butler of Brockwell, GCB, CVO
WADHAM (1610)
Warden, Sir Neil Chalmers, CBE
WOLFSON (1966)
President (acting), Prof. John Stallworthy, FBA, FRSL
WORCESTER (1714)
Provost, R. G. Smethurst
WYCLIFFE HALL (1877)
Principal, Revd Dr Richard Turnbull

OXFORD BROOKES UNIVERSITY (1992)
Gipsy Lane, Oxford OX3 0BP T 01865-741111
W www.brookes.ac.uk
Students: 13,670 *Fees:* £3,070
Chancellor, Jon Snow
Vice-Chancellor, Prof. Graham Upton
Academic Registrar, Stephen Marshall

UNIVERSITY OF PAISLEY (1992)
Paisley PA1 2BE T 0141-848 3000 W www.paisley.ac.uk
Students: 5,873 *Fees:* £1,700
Chancellor, Sir Robert Smith, FSA
Principal and Vice-Chancellor, Prof. Seamus McDaid
Secretary, David Rigg
Academic Registrar, Donna McMillan

UNIVERSITY OF PLYMOUTH (1992)
Drake Circus, Plymouth PL4 8AA T 01752-600600
W www.plymouth.ac.uk
Students: 24,250 *Fees:* £3,070
Vice-Chancellor (acting), Prof. Steve Newstead
Academic Registrar and Secretary, Jane Hopkinson

UNIVERSITY OF PORTSMOUTH (1992)
University House, Winston Churchill Avenue, Portsmouth
PO1 2UP T 023-9284 8484 W www.port.ac.uk
Students: 15,287 *Fees:* £3,000
Chancellor, Lord Palumbo
Vice-Chancellor, Prof. John Craven
Academic Registrar, Andy Rees

QUEEN'S UNIVERSITY BELFAST (1908)
University Road, Belfast BT7 1NN T 028-9024 5133
W www.qub.ac.uk
Students: 15,200 *Fees:* £3,070
Chancellor, Senator George Mitchell
Vice-Chancellor, Prof. Peter Gregson, FRENG
Registrar, James O'Kane

UNIVERSITY OF READING (1926)
Whiteknights, PO Box 217, Reading RG6 6AH T 0118-987 5123
W www.reading.ac.uk
Students: 8,840 *Fees:* £3,070
Chancellor, Rt. Hon. Lord Carrington of Upton, KG, GCMG, CH
Vice-Chancellor, Prof. Gordon Marshall, CBE, FBA
Director of Student Services, W. D. Watts

ROBERT GORDON UNIVERSITY (1992)
Schoolhill, Aberdeen AB10 1FR T 01224-262000
W www.rgu.ac.uk
Students: 6,850 *Fees:* £1,735
Chancellor, Sir Ian Wood, CBE
Vice-Chancellor, Prof. R. Michael Pittilo
Academic Registrar, Hilary Douglas

ROEHAMPTON UNIVERSITY (2004)
Erasmus House, Roehampton Lane, London SW15 5PU
T 020-8392 3000 W www.roehampton.ac.uk
Students: 6,351 *Fees:* £3,070
Chancellor, John Simpson, CBE
Vice-Chancellor, Prof. Paul O'Prey
Academic Secretary, Andrew Skinner

ROYAL COLLEGE OF ART (1967)
Kensington Gore, London SW7 2EU T 020-7590 4444
W www.rca.ac.uk
Students: 850 (postgraduate only) *Fees:* £4,250
Provost, Sir Terence Conran
Rector and Vice-Provost, Prof. Sir Christopher Frayling, PHD
Registrar, Alan Selby

ROYAL COLLEGE OF MUSIC (1882)
Prince Consort Road, London SW7 2BS T 020-7589 3643
W www.rcm.ac.uk
Students: 350 *Fees:* £3,000
President, HRH Prince of Wales, KG, KT, GCB
Vice-Chancellor, Dr Colin Lawson, DMUS, FRCM
Registrar and Secretary, Kevin Porter

UNIVERSITY OF ST ANDREWS (1413)
College Gate, St Andrews, Fife KY16 9AJ T 01334-476161
W www.st-andrews.ac.uk

Students: 5,746 *Fees:* £1,735
Chancellor, Rt. Hon. Sir Menzies Campbell, CBE, QC, MP
Principal and Vice-Chancellor, Dr Brian Lang
Secretary and Registrar, Mark Butler

UNIVERSITY OF SALFORD (1967)
Salford, Greater Manchester M5 4WT T 0161-295 5000
W www.salford.ac.uk
Students: 12,753 *Fees:* £3,070
Chancellor, Prof. Sir Martin Harris
Vice-Chancellor, Prof. Michael Harloe
Registrar, Dr Adrian Graves

UNIVERSITY OF SHEFFIELD (1905)
Western Bank, Sheffield S10 2TN T 0114-222 2000
W www.shef.ac.uk
Students: 16,877 *Fees:* £3,070
Chancellor, Sir Peter Middleton, GCB
Vice-Chancellor, Prof. R. F. Boucher, CBE, FRENG
Registrar and Secretary, Dr D. E. Fletcher

SHEFFIELD HALLAM UNIVERSITY (1992)
City Campus, Howard Street, Sheffield S1 1WB T 0114-225 5555 W www.shu.ac.uk
Students: 17,500 *Fees:* £3,070
Chancellor, Prof. Lord Winston, FRCOG, FRCP
Vice-Chancellor, Prof. Philip Jones, LLB, LLM
Secretary and Registrar, Liz Winders

UNIVERSITY OF SOUTHAMPTON (1952)
Building 37, Highfield, Southampton SO17 1BJ T 023-8059 5000 W www.soton.ac.uk
Students: 13,850 *Fees:* £3,070
Chancellor, Sir John Parker
Vice-Chancellor, Prof. William A. Wakeham
Registrar and Chief Operating Officer, Simon Higman

SOUTHAMPTON SOLENT UNIVERSITY (2005)
East Park Terrace, Southampton SO14 0YN T 023-8031 9000
W www.solent.ac.uk
Students: 8,900 *Fees:* £3,070
Chancellor, Sir Alan West, GCB, DSC
Vice-Chancellor, Prof. Van Gore

STAFFORDSHIRE UNIVERSITY (1992)
Federation House, Stoke-on-Trent, Staffs ST4 2DE
T 01782-294000 W www.staffs.ac.uk
Students: 8,895 *Fees:* £3,000
Chancellor, Lord Morris of Handsworth
Vice-Chancellor, Prof. Christine E. King, CBE
University Secretary, Ken Sproston

UNIVERSITY OF STIRLING (1967)
Stirling FK9 4LA T 01786-473171 W www.stir.ac.uk
Students: 6,050 *Fees:* £1,735
Chancellor, Dame Diana Rigg, CBE
Vice-Chancellor, Prof. Christine Hallett, FRSE
Registrar, Joanna Morrow

UNIVERSITY OF STRATHCLYDE (1964)
16 Richmond Street, Glasgow G1 1XQ T 0141-552 4400
W www.strath.ac.uk
Students: 11,400 *Fees:* £1,700
Chancellor, Rt. Hon. Lord Hope of Craighead, FRSE
Vice-Chancellor and Principal, Prof. Andrew Hamnett, DPHIL, FRSC, FRSE
Secretary, Dr Peter West, OBE

UNIVERSITY OF SUNDERLAND (1992)
Edinburgh Building, Chester Road, Sunderland SR1 3SD
T 0191-515 2000 W www.sunderland.ac.uk
Students: 8,500 *Fees:* £3,070
Chancellor, vacant
Vice-Chancellor, Prof. Peter Fidler
Academic Registrar, Beatrice Ollerenshaw

UNIVERSITY OF SURREY (1966)
Guildford, Surrey GU2 7XH T 01483-300800
W www.surrey.ac.uk
Students: 7,000 *Fees:* £3,070
Chancellor, HRH the Duke of Kent, KG, KT, OM
Vice-Chancellor, Prof. Christopher Snowden, FRS, FRENG
Registrar, P. Henry, TD

UNIVERSITY OF SUSSEX (1961)
Sussex House, Falmer, Brighton BN1 9RH T 01273-606755
W www.sussex.ac.uk
Students: 7,427 *Fees:* £3,070
Chancellor, Lord Attenborough, CBE
Vice-Chancellor, Prof. Alasdair Smith
Academic Registrar, Dr Philip Harvey

UNIVERSITY OF TEESSIDE (1992)
Middlesbrough, Tees Valley TS1 3BA T 01642-218121
W www.tees.ac.uk
Students: 8,308 *Fees:* £3,070
Chancellor, Lord Sawyer
Vice-Chancellor, Prof. Graham Henderson
Registrar, Morgan McClintock

THAMES VALLEY UNIVERSITY (1992)
St Mary's Road, Ealing, London W5 5RF T 020-8579 5000
W www.tvu.ac.uk
Students: 6,115 *Fees:* £2,770
Chancellor, Lord Bilimoria, CBE
Vice-Chancellor, Prof. Geoff Crispin
Registrar, Chris Broomfield

UCE BIRMINGHAM (1992) Perry Barr, Birmingham
B42 2SU T 0121-331 5595 W www.uce.ac.uk
Students: 19,628 *Fees:* £3,000
Chancellor, Lord Mayor of Birmingham, Councillor Mike Sharpe
Vice-Chancellor, Prof. David H. Tidmarsh, FIMECHE, FCMI
Registrar, Maxine Penlington

UNIVERSITY OF ULSTER (1984)
Cromore Road, Coleraine, Co. Londonderry BT52 1SA
T 0870-040 0700 W www.ulster.ac.uk
Students: 17,100 *Fees:* £3,070
Chancellor, Sir Richard Nichols
Vice-Chancellor, Prof. Richard Barnett
Director of Corporate and Governance, Irene Aston

UNIVERSITY OF WALES (1893)
King Edward VII Avenue, Cathays Park, Cardiff CF10 3NS
T 029-2038 2656 W www.wales.ac.uk
Students: variable; contact individual institutions for details *Fees:* variable; contact individual institutions for details
Chancellor, HRH The Prince of Wales, KG, KT, GCB
Senior Vice-Chancellor, Prof. A. J. Chapman, FRSA
Secretary-General, Dr L. E. Williams

MEMBER INSTITUTIONS
UNIVERSITY OF WALES, ABERYSTWYTH
Old College, King Street, Aberystwyth SY23 2AX
T 01970-623111
Vice-Chancellor, Prof. N. G. Lloyd

UNIVERSITY OF WALES, BANGOR
Gwynedd LL57 2DG T 01248-351151
Vice-Chancellor, Prof. R. M. Jones

UNIVERSITY OF WALES, LAMPETER
Lampeter SA48 7ED T 01570-422351
Vice-Chancellor, Prof. R. A. Pearce

UNIVERSITY OF WALES, NEWPORT
Caerleon Campus, PO Box 179, Newport NP6 1YG
T 01633-430088
Vice-Chancellor, Dr P. Noyes

UNIVERSITY OF WALES, SWANSEA
Singleton Park SA2 8PP T 01792-205678
Vice-Chancellor, Prof. R. B. Davies

UNIVERSITY OF WALES INSTITUTE, CARDIFF
Llandaff Centre, Western Avenue, Cardiff CF5 2SG
T 029-2041 6070
Vice-Chancellor, Prof. A. J. Chapman

NORTH EAST WALES INSTITUTE OF HIGHER
  EDUCATION
Plas Coch, Mold Road, Wrexham LL11 2AW T 01978-290666
Principal, Prof. M. Scott

SWANSEA INSTITUTE OF HIGHER EDUCATION
Mount Pleasant, Swansea SA1 6ED T 01792-481000
Principal, Prof. D. Warner

TRINITY COLLEGE, CARMARTHEN
Carmarthen SA31 3EP T 01267-676767
Principal, Dr M. Hughes

UNIVERSITY OF WARWICK (1965)
Coventry CV4 7AL T 024-7652 3523 W www.warwick.ac.uk
Students: 11,315 *Fees:* £3,070
Chancellor, Sir Nicholas Scheele
Vice-Chancellor, Prof. Nigel Thrift
Registrar, Jon Baldwin

UNIVERSITY OF WESTMINSTER (1992)
309 Regent Street, London W1B 2UW T 020-7911 5000
W www.wmin.ac.uk
Students: 10,839 *Fees:* £3,070
Chancellor, Lord Paul
Vice-Chancellor, Dr Geoffrey Copland
Academic Registrar, Evelyne Rugg

UNIVERSITY OF THE WEST OF ENGLAND (1992)
Frenchay Campus, Coldharbour Lane, Bristol BS16 1QY
T 0117-965 6261 W www.uwe.ac.uk
Students: 16,891 *Fees:* £3,070
Chancellor, Rt. Hon. Dame Elizabeth Butler-Sloss, CBE
Vice-Chancellor, Sir Howard Newby, KB, CBE
Registrar, Tessa Harrison

UNIVERSITY OF WINCHESTER (2005)
West Hill, Winchester SO22 4NR T 01962-841515
W www.winchester.ac.uk
Students: 3,300 *Fees:* £3,070
Chancellor, Mary Fagan
Vice-Chancellor, Prof. Joy Carter
Registrar, Lyn Black

UNIVERSITY OF WOLVERHAMPTON (1992)
Wulfruna Street, Wolverhampton WV1 1SB T 01902-321000
W www.wlv.ac.uk
Students: 12,534 *Fees:* £3,070
Chancellor, Lord Paul
Vice-Chancellor, Prof. Caroline Gipps
Registrar, Paul Travill

UNIVERSITY OF WORCESTER (2005)
Henwick Grove, Worcester WR2 6AJ T 01905-855000
W www.worcester.ac.uk
Students: 8,000 *Fees:* £3,070
Vice-Chancellor and Chief Executive, Prof. David Green
Registrar and Secretary, John Ryan

UNIVERSITY OF YORK (1963)
Heslington, York YO10 5DD T 01904-430000
W www.york.ac.uk
Students: 7,923 *Fees:* £3,070
Chancellor, Greg Dyke
Vice-Chancellor, Prof. Brian Cantor, FRENG, FIM, FRMS
Registrar, Sally Neocosmos

PROFESSIONAL EDUCATION

The organisations selected below provide specialist training, conduct examinations or are responsible for maintaining a register of those with professional qualifications in their sector, thereby controlling entry into a profession.

EU RECOGNITION
It is possible for those with professional qualifications obtained in the UK to have these recognised in other European countries. Further information can be obtained online (W www.dfes.gov.uk/europeopen) or from:
DEPARTMENT FOR CHILDREN, SCHOOLS AND FAMILIES Sanctuary Buildings, Great Smith Street, London SW1P 3BT T 0870-000 2288 E info@dfes.gsi.gov.uk

ACCOUNTANCY
The vast majority of chartered accountancy trainees are graduates, and entry to the profession is open to graduates of all disciplines. The undergraduate degree is followed by a three-year training contract with an approved employer culminating in professional exams provided by the Institute of Chartered Accountants in England and Wales (ICAEW), the Institute of Chartered Accountants of Scotland (ICAS) or the Institute of Chartered Accountants in Ireland (ICAI). Success in the examination and membership of one of the institutes allows the use of the designation 'chartered accountant' and the letters ACA or CA.

The training route for chartered certified accountants is similar to that of chartered accountants and is taken by students in a range of business sectors and countries. The Association of Chartered Certified Accountants (ACCA) qualification involves up to 14 examinations and a minimum of three years of relevant supervised experience. Chartered certified accountants can use the designatory letters ACCA.

Chartered management accountants focus on accounting for businesses, and most do not work in accountancy practices but in industry, commerce, not-for-profit and public sector organisations. Graduates who have not studied a business or accounting undergraduate degree must gain the Chartered Institute of Management Accountants (CIMA) Certificate in Business Accounting (formerly known as the foundation level) before studying for the CIMA Professional Qualification. The qualification requires three years of practical experience combined with nine examinations and a pass in the Institute's Test of Professional Competence in Management Accounting (TOPCIMA).

Chartered public finance accountants usually work for public bodies, but they can also work in the private sector. To gain chartered public finance accountant status (CPFA), trainees must complete the three parts of the Chartered Institute of Public Finance and Accountancy (CIPFA) Professional Accountancy Qualification (PAQ), which takes approximately three years. The first stage is the certificate level, which leads to affiliate membership of CIPFA, the second is the diploma level which leads to associate membership, and finally completion of the Final Test of Professional Competence leads to full membership of CIPFA.

ASSOCIATION OF CHARTERED CERTIFIED ACCOUNTANTS (ACCA) 29 Lincoln's Inn Fields, London WC2A 3EE T 020-7059 5000 E info@accaglobal.com W www.accaglobal.com *Chief Executive*, Allen Blewitt
CHARTERED INSTITUTE OF MANAGEMENT ACCOUNTANTS (CIMA) 26 Chapter Street, London SW1P 4NP T 020-7663 5441 W www.cimaglobal.com *Chief Executive*, Charles Tilley
CHARTERED INSTITUTE OF PUBLIC FINANCE AND ACCOUNTANCY (CIPFA) 3 Robert Street, London WC2N 6RL T 030-7543 5600 E corporate@cipfa.org W www.cipfa.org.uk *Chief Executive*, Steve Freer
INSTITUTE OF CHARTERED ACCOUNTANTS IN ENGLAND AND WALES (ICAEW) Chartered Accountants' Hall, PO Box 433, London EC2P 2BJ T 020-7920 8100 W www.icaew.com *Chief Executive*, Michael Izza
INSTITUTE OF CHARTERED ACCOUNTANTS IN IRELAND (ICAI) The Linenhall, 32–38 Linenhall Street, Belfast BT2 8BG T 028-9032 1600 E ca@icai.ie W www.icai.ie *Chief Executive*, Pat Costello
INSTITUTE OF CHARTERED ACCOUNTANTS OF SCOTLAND (ICAS) CA House, 21 Haymarket Yards, Edinburgh EH12 5BH T 0131-347 0100 E enquiries@icas.org.uk W www.icas.org.uk *Chief Executive*, Anton Colella

ACTUARIAL SCIENCE
The UK actuarial profession is controlled by the Institute of Actuaries in London and the Faculty of Actuaries in Edinburgh (operating together as 'the actuarial profession'). The faculty and institute together issue technical guidance, develop actuarial techniques and set examinations, professional codes and disciplinary standards, and they develop actuarial techniques and guidance. UK qualified actuaries may be fellows of either organisation. On average, it takes five years to qualify as an actuary; examinations are held twice a year, and applicants to the profession must also have completed three years of actuarial work experience before gaining fellowship.

In March 2005, HM Treasury asked the Financial Reporting Council (FRC) to oversee the actuarial profession. The FRC established a new body, the Board for Actuarial Standards, to set and maintain actuarial standards independently of the profession while the Professional Oversight Board of the FRC oversees the actuarial profession and is responsible for accountancy, audit and corporate reporting and governance.
FACULTY OF ACTUARIES Maclaurin House, 18 Dublin Street, Edinburgh EH1 3PP T 0131-240 1300 E faculty@actuaries.org.uk W www.actuaries.org.uk *Secretary*, Richard Maconachie
FINANCIAL REPORTING COUNCIL (FRC) 5th Floor, Aldwych House, 71–91 Aldwych, London WC2B 4HN T 020-7492 2300 W www.frc.org.uk *Chief Executive*, Paul Boyle

INSTITUTE OF ACTUARIES Staple Inn Hall, High
Holborn, London WC1V 7QJ T 020-7632 2100
E institute@actuaries.org.uk W www.actuaries.org.uk
Chief Executive, Caroline Instance

ARCHITECTURE

It takes a minimum of seven years to become an architect,
involving three stages: a three-year first degree, a two-year
second degree or diploma and two years of professional
experience followed by the successful completion of a
professional practice examination. Architectural
qualifications are validated by the Royal Institute of
British Architects (RIBA).

The Architects Registration Board (ARB) is the
independent regulator for the profession. It was set up by
an act of parliament in 1997 and is responsible for
maintaining the register of UK architects, prescribing
qualifications that lead to registration as an architect, the
conduct and competence of architects, and ensuring only
those who are registered with ARB use the title of
'architect'. It is only following registration with ARB that
an architect can apply for chartered membership of RIBA.
RIBA received its royal charter in 1837 and recognises
courses at 40 schools of architecture in the UK for
exemption from their own examinations as well as courses
at 57 overseas schools.

The Chartered Institute of Architectural Technologists
is the qualifying body for chartered architectural
technologists (MCIAT) and architectural technicians
(TCIAT).

ARCHITECTS REGISTRATION BOARD (ARB) 8
Weymouth Street, London W1W 5BU T 020-7580 5861
E info@arb.org.uk W www.arb.org.uk
Registrar and Chief Executive, Alison Carr
CHARTERED INSTITUTE OF ARCHITECTURAL
TECHNOLOGISTS 397 City Road, London EC1V 1NH
T 020-7278 2206 E info@ciat.org.uk W www.ciat.org.uk
Chief Executive, Francesca Berriman
ROYAL INSTITUTE OF BRITISH ARCHITECTS
(RIBA) 66 Portland Place, London W1B 1AD
T 020-7580 5533 E info@inst.riba.org W www.riba.org
Chief Executive, Richard Hastilow, CBE

ENGINEERING

The Engineering Council UK (ECUK) sets standards of
professional competence and ethics for engineers,
technologists and technicians, and regulates the
profession through the 35 institutions (Licensed
Members) listed below who are licensed to put suitably
qualified members on the ECUK's Register of Engineers.
All candidates for registration as Chartered Engineer,
Incorporated Engineer or Engineering Technician must
satisfy the competence standards set by ECUK and be
members of the appropriate institution. Applicants must
show that they have a satisfactory educational base, have
undergone approved professional development, and, at
interview, must demonstrate their professional
competence against specific criteria.

ENGINEERING COUNCIL 10 Maltravers Street, London
WC2R 3ER T 020-3206 0500 E info@engc.org.uk
W www.engc.org.uk
Chief Executive Officer, Andrew Ramsay

LICENSED MEMBERS
BRITISH COMPUTER SOCIETY
W www.bcs.org.uk
BRITISH INSTITUTE OF NON-DESTRUCTIVE TESTING
W www.bindt.org

CHARTERED INSTITUTION OF BUILDING SERVICES
ENGINEERS W www.cibse.org
CHARTERED INSTITUTION OF WATER AND
ENVIRONMENTAL MANAGEMENT W www.ciwem.org.uk
ENERGY INSTITUTE
W www.energyinst.org.uk
INSTITUTE OF ACOUSTICS
W www.ioa.org.uk
INSTITUTE OF CAST METALS ENGINEERS
W www.icme.org.uk
INSTITUTE OF HEALTHCARE ENGINEERING AND
ESTATE MANAGEMENT W www.iheem.org.uk
INSTITUTE OF HIGHWAY INCORPORATED ENGINEERS
W www.ihie.org.uk
INSTITUTE OF MARINE ENGINEERING, SCIENCE AND
TECHNOLOGY W www.imarest.org
INSTITUTE OF MATERIALS, MINERALS AND MINING
W www.iom3.org
INSTITUTE OF MEASUREMENT AND CONTROL
W www.instmc.org.uk
INSTITUTE OF THE MOTOR INDUSTRY
W www.motor.org.uk
INSTITUTE OF PHYSICS
W www.iop.org
INSTITUTE OF PHYSICS AND ENGINEERING IN
MEDICINE W www.ipem.org.uk
INSTITUTE OF PLUMBING AND HEATING
ENGINEERING W www.iphe.org.uk
INSTITUTION OF AGRICULTURAL ENGINEERS
W www.iagre.org
INSTITUTION OF CHEMICAL ENGINEERS
W www.icheme.org
INSTITUTION OF CIVIL ENGINEERS
W www.ice.org.uk
INSTITUTION OF ENGINEERING DESIGNERS
W www.ied.org.uk
INSTITUTION OF ENGINEERING AND TECHNOLOGY
W www.theiet.org
INSTITUTION OF FIRE ENGINEERS
W www.ife.org.uk
INSTITUTION OF GAS ENGINEERS AND MANAGERS
W www.igem.org.uk
INSTITUTION OF HIGHWAYS AND TRANSPORTATION
W www.iht.org
INSTITUTION OF LIGHTING ENGINEERS
W www.ile.org.uk
INSTITUTION OF MECHANICAL ENGINEERS
W www.imeche.org.uk
INSTITUTION OF NUCLEAR ENGINEERS
W www.inuce.org.uk
INSTITUTION OF RAILWAY SIGNAL ENGINEERS
W www.irse.org
INSTITUTION OF STRUCTURAL ENGINEERS
W www.istructe.org.uk
INSTITUTION OF WATER OFFICERS
W www.iwo.org.uk
ROYAL AERONAUTICAL SOCIETY
W www.raes.org.uk
ROYAL INSTITUTION OF NAVAL ARCHITECTS
W www.rina.org.uk
SOCIETY OF ENVIRONMENTAL ENGINEERS
W www.environmental.org.uk
SOCIETY OF OPERATIONS ENGINEERS
W www.soe.org.uk
WELDING INSTITUTE
W www.twi.co.uk

HEALTHCARE

CHIROPRACTIC
The General Chiropractic Council (GCC) is the statutory regulatory body for chiropractors and its role and remit is defined in the Chiropractors Act 1994. The GCC sets the criteria for the recognition of chiropractic degrees and for standards of proficiency and conduct. Details of the institutions offering degree programmes are available on the GCC website (*see* below). It is illegal for anyone in the UK to use the title 'chiropractor' unless registered with the GCC.

The British Chiropractic Association, McTimoney Chiropractic Association, Scottish Chiropractic Association and the United Chiropractic Association are representative bodies for the profession and are sources of further information about chiropractic.

BRITISH CHIROPRACTIC ASSOCIATION 59 Castle Street, Reading RG1 7SN T 0118-950 5950
E enquiries@chiropractic-uk.co.uk
Executive Director, Sue Wakefield
GENERAL CHIROPRACTIC COUNCIL 44 Wicklow Street, London WC1X 9HL T 020-7713 5155
E enquiries@gcc-uk.org W www.gcc-uk.org
Chief Executive, Margaret Coats
MCTIMONEY CHIROPRACTIC ASSOCIATION Crowmarsh Gifford, Wallingford OX10 8DJ
T 01491-829211 E admin@mctimoney-chiropractic.org
W www.mctimoney-chiropractic.org
Chair, Christina Cunliffe
SCOTTISH CHIROPRACTIC ASSOCIATION Laigh Hatton Farm, Old Greenock Road, Bishopton, Renfrewshire PA7 5BP T 01505-863151 E admin@sca-chiropractic.org
W www.sca-chiropractic.org
Chief Executive, Morag Cairns
UNITED CHIROPRACTIC ASSOCIATION 17 Fore Street, Ivybridge PL21 9AB T 01752-896223
E admin@united-chiropractic.org
W www.united-chiropractic.org
Secretary, Melissa Sandford

DENTISTRY
The General Dental Council (GDC) is the organisation that regulates dental professionals in the United Kingdom. All dentists, dental hygienists, dental therapists, clinical dental technicians and orthodontic therapists must be registered with the GDC to work in the UK, whether they work in the NHS, in private practice or any other form of practice. From July 2008 by law all dental nurses and technicians will need to be registered with the GDC.

There are various different routes to qualify for registration, including holding a degree or licentiate in dental surgery from a UK university or Royal Surgical College; completing the GDC's qualifying examination; or holding a relevant European Economic Area or overseas diploma. The GDC works to set standards of dental practice, behaviour and education, and helps to protect patients by hearing complaints and taking action against professionals where necessary.

The British Dental Association is a membership organisation that provides dentists with professional and educational services. It has over 18,000 qualified members and over 3,500 student members.

BRITISH DENTAL ASSOCIATION 64 Wimpole Street, London W1G 8YS T 020-7935 0875 E enquiries@bda.org
W www.bda.org
Chief Executive, Peter Ward
GENERAL DENTAL COUNCIL 37 Wimpole Street, London W1G 8DQ T 020-7887 3800
E information@gdc-uk.org W www.gdc-uk.org
Chief Executive, Duncan Rudkin

MEDICINE
The General Medical Council (GMC) sets the standard for basic medical education; this covers undergraduate study (usually five years) and the first year of training after graduation. Subsequent training is regulated by the Postgraduate Medical Education and Training Board (PMETB). The first two years of training after graduation are collectively called the 'foundation programme'.

All doctors must be registered with the GMC, which is responsible for protecting the public. It does this by setting standards for professional practice, overseeing medical education, keeping a register of qualified doctors and taking action where a doctor's fitness to practise is in doubt. Doctors are eligible for full registration upon successful completion of the first year of training after graduation.

Following the foundation programme, many doctors then undertake specialist training (provided by the colleges and faculties listed below) to become either a consultant or a GP. Once specialist training has been completed, doctors are awarded the Certificate of Completion of Training (CCT) and are eligible to be placed on either the GMC's specialist register or its GP register. The responsibility for awarding CCTs lies with the PMETB.

GENERAL MEDICAL COUNCIL (GMC) 350 Euston Road, London NW1 3JN T 0845-357 3456
E gmc@gmc-uk.org W www.gmc-uk.org
Chief Executive, Finlay Scott
POSTGRADUATE MEDICAL EDUCATION AND TRAINING BOARD (PMETB) Hercules House, Hercules Road, London SE1 7DU T 020-7160 6100
E info@pmetb.org.uk W www.pmetb.org.uk
Chief Executive, Paul Streets
SOCIETY OF APOTHECARIES OF LONDON Black Friars Lane, London EC4V 6EJ T 020-7236 1189
E clerk@apothecaries.org W www.apothecaries.org
Clerk, A. M. Wallington-Smith

SPECIALIST TRAINING COLLEGES AND FACULTIES
COLLEGE OF EMERGENCY MEDICINE
W www.emergencymed.org.uk
FACULTY OF PHARMACEUTICAL MEDICINE
W www.fpm.org.uk
FACULTY OF PUBLIC HEALTH
W www.fphm.org.uk
ROYAL COLLEGE OF ANAESTHETISTS
W www.rcoa.ac.uk
ROYAL COLLEGE OF GENERAL PRACTITIONERS
W www.rcgp.org.uk
ROYAL COLLEGE OF OBSTETRICIANS AND GYNAECOLOGISTS W www.rcog.org.uk
ROYAL COLLEGE OF OPHTHALMOLOGISTS
W www.rcophth.ac.uk
ROYAL COLLEGE OF PAEDIATRICS AND CHILD HEALTH
W www.rcpch.ac.uk
ROYAL COLLEGE OF PATHOLOGISTS W www.rcpath.org
ROYAL COLLEGE OF PHYSICIANS W www.rcplondon.ac.uk
ROYAL COLLEGE OF PHYSICIANS AND SURGEONS OF GLASGOW W www.rcpsg.ac.uk
ROYAL COLLEGE OF PHYSICIANS OF EDINBURGH
W www.rcpe.ac.uk

ROYAL COLLEGE OF PSYCHIATRISTS
W www.rcpsych.ac.uk
ROYAL COLLEGE OF RADIOLOGISTS
W www.rcr.ac.uk
ROYAL COLLEGE OF SURGEONS OF EDINBURGH
W www.rcsed.ac.uk
ROYAL COLLEGE OF SURGEONS OF ENGLAND
W www.rcseng.ac.uk

MEDICINE, SUPPLEMENTARY PROFESSIONS
The standard of professional education for arts therapists, biomedical scientists, chiropodists and podiatrists, clinical scientists, dietitians, occupational therapists, operating department practitioners, orthoptists, paramedics, physiotherapists, prosthetists and orthotists, radiographers, and speech and language therapists is regulated by the Health Professions Council (HPC), who only register those practitioners who meet certain standards of training, performance and conduct. Other than biomedical science and clinical science, all the professions listed below are described by the NHS as 'allied health professions'. The HPC currently registers over 170,000 professionals.
HEALTH PROFESSIONS COUNCIL Park House, 184 Kennington Park Road, London SE11 4BU T 020-7582 0866 E info@hpc-uk.org W www.hpc-uk.org
Chief Executive and Registrar, Marc Seale

ART, DRAMA AND MUSIC THERAPIES
An art, drama or music therapist encourages people to express their feelings and emotions through art, such as painting and drawing, drama or music. A postgraduate qualification in the relevant therapy is required. Details of accredited training programmes in the UK can be obtained from the following organisations:
ASSOCIATION OF PROFESSIONAL MUSIC THERAPISTS 61 Church Hill Road, East Barnet, Herts EN4 8SY T 020-8440 4153 E apmtoffice@aol.com W www.apmt.org
Administrator, Louise Karena
BRITISH ASSOCIATION OF ART THERAPISTS 24–27 White Lion Street, London N1 9PD T 020-7686 4216 E info@baat.org W www.baat.org
Chief Executive, Val Huet
BRITISH ASSOCIATION OF DRAMA THERAPISTS Waverley, Battledown Approach, Cheltenham, Gloucestershire GL52 6RE T 01242-235515 E enquiries@badth.org.uk W www.badth.org.uk
Chair, Madeleine Andersen-Warren

BIOMEDICAL SCIENCES
Biomedical scientists analyse specimens from patients in order to assist doctors in their diagnoses. Qualifications from higher education establishments and training in medical laboratories are required for membership of the Institute of Biomedical Science, which sets the professional standards of competence for biomedical scientists.
INSTITUTE OF BIOMEDICAL SCIENCE 12 Coldbath Square, London EC1R 5HL T 020-7713 0214 E mail@ibms.org W www.ibms.org
Chief Executive, Alan Potter

CHIROPODY AND PODIATRY
Chiropodists and podiatrists assess, diagnose and treat problems of the lower leg and foot. The Society of Chiropodists and Podiatrists is the professional body and trade union for the profession. Qualifications granted and degrees recognised by the society are approved by the Health Professions Council (HPC). HPC registration is required in order to use the titles chiropodist and podiatrist.
SOCIETY OF CHIROPODISTS AND PODIATRISTS 1 Fellmonger's Path, Tower Bridge Road, London SE1 3LY T 0845-450 3720 E enq@scpod.org W www.feetforlife.org
Chief Executive, Joanna Brown

CLINICAL SCIENCE
Clinical scientists conduct tests in laboratories in order to diagnose and manage disease. The Association of Clinical Scientists is responsible for setting the criteria for competence of applicants to the HPC's register and to present a Certificate of Attainment to candidates following a successful assessment. This certificate will allow direct registration with the HPC.
ASSOCIATION OF CLINICAL SCIENTISTS c/o Association for Clinical Biochemistry, 130–132 Tooley Street, London SE1 2TU T 020-7940 8960 E info@assclinsci.org W www.assclinsci.org
Chair, Derek Pearson

DIETETICS
Dietitians advise patients on how to improve their health and counter specific health problems by eating a healthy diet. The British Dietetic Association, established in 1936, is the professional association for dietitians. Full membership is open to UK registered dietitians, who must also be registered with the Health Professions Council.
BRITISH DIETETIC ASSOCIATION 5th Floor, Charles House, 148–149 Great Charles Street Queensway, Birmingham B3 3HT T 0121-200 8080 E info@bda.uk.com W www.bda.uk.com
Chief Executive, Andy Burman

OCCUPATIONAL THERAPY
Occupational therapists work with people who have physical, mental and/or social problems, either from birth or as a result of accident, illness or ageing, and aim to make them as independent as possible. The professional qualification and eligibility for registration may be obtained upon successful completion of a validated course in any of the educational institutions approved by the College of Occupational Therapists, which is the professional body for occupational therapy in the UK. The courses are normally degree-level courses based in higher education institutions.
COLLEGE OF OCCUPATIONAL THERAPISTS 106–114 Borough High Street, London SE1 1LB T 020-7357 6480 W www.cot.org.uk
Chief Executive, Julia Scott

ORTHOPTICS
Orthoptists undertake the diagnosis and treatment of all types of squint and other anomalies of binocular vision, working in close collaboration with ophthalmologists. The professional body is the British and Irish Orthoptic Society and training is at degree level.
BRITISH AND IRISH ORTHOPTIC SOCIETY Tavistock House North, Tavistock Square, London WC1H 9HX T 020-7387 7992 W www.orthoptics.org.uk
Chair, Rosemary Auld

PARAMEDICAL SERVICES

Paramedics deal with accidents and emergencies, assessing patients and carrying out any specialist treatment and care needed in the first instance. The body that represents ambulance professionals is the British Paramedic Association.

BRITISH PARAMEDIC ASSOCIATION 28 Wilfred Street, Derby DE23 8GF T 01332-746356
E exec.bpa@britishparamedic.org
W www.britishparamedic.org
Chief Executive, Roland Furber

Physiotherapists are concerned with movement and function and deal with problems arising from injury, illness and ageing. Full-time three- or four-year degree courses are available at over 30 higher education institutions in the UK. Information about courses leading to state registration is available from the Chartered Society of Physiotherapy.

CHARTERED SOCIETY OF PHYSIOTHERAPY
14 Bedford Row, London WC1R 4ED T 020-7306 6666
W www.csp.org.uk
Chief Executive, Phil Gray

PROSTHETICS AND ORTHOTICS

Prosthetists provide artificial limbs, while orthotists provide devices to support or control a part of the body. It is necessary to obtain an honours degree to become a prosthetist or orthotist. Training is centred at the universities of Salford and Strathclyde.

BRITISH ASSOCIATION OF PROSTHETISTS AND ORTHOTISTS Sir James Clark Building, Abbey Mill Business Centre, Paisley PA1 1TJ T 0141-561 7217
E admin@bapo.com W www.bapo.org
Chair, Sophie Hill

RADIOGRAPHY

In order to practise both diagnostic and therapeutic radiography in the UK, it is necessary to have successfully completed a course of education and training recognised by the Privy Council. Such courses are offered by universities throughout the UK and lead to the award of a degree in radiography. Further information is available from the Society and College of Radiographers.

SOCIETY AND COLLEGE OF RADIOGRAPHERS
207 Providence Square, Mill Street, London SE1 2EW
T 020-7740 7200 E info@sor.org W www.sor.org
Chief Executive, Richard Evans

SPEECH AND LANGUAGE THERAPY

Speech and language therapists (SLTs) work with people with speech, voice and swallowing problems. The Royal College of Speech and Language Therapists is the professional body for speech and language therapists and support workers. Alongside the Health Professions Council, it accredits education and training courses leading to qualification.

ROYAL COLLEGE OF SPEECH AND LANGUAGE THERAPISTS 2 White Hart Yard, London SE1 1NX
T 020-7378 1200 E info@rcslt.org W www.rcslt.org
Chief Executive, Kamini Gadhok

NURSING

In order to practice in the UK all nurses and midwives must be registered with the Nursing and Midwifery Council (NMC). Courses leading to registration are at a minimum of diploma in higher education, although some are offered at degree level and all are a minimum of three years if undertaken full-time. The NMC approves programmes run jointly by higher education institutions with their healthcare service partners who offer clinical placements. The nursing part of the register has four fields of practice: adult, children's, learning disability and mental health nursing. During the first year of a nursing course, the common foundation programme, students have experience of the first four fields of practice. In addition those studying to become adult nurses have experience of nursing in relation to medicine, surgery, maternity care and nursing in the home. The NMC also sets standards for programmes leading to registration as a midwife and a range of post–registration courses including specialist practice programmes, nurse prescribing and those for teachers of nursing and midwifery. The NMC has a part of the register for specialist community public health nurses and approves programmes for health visitors, occupational health nurses and school nurses.

The Royal College of Nursing is the largest professional union representing nurses, and provides higher education through its institute.

NURSING AND MIDWIFERY COUNCIL 23 Portland Place, London W18 1PZ T 020-7637 7181
E communications@nmc-uk.org W www.nmc-uk.org
Chief Executive and Registrar, Sarah Thewlis
ROYAL COLLEGE OF NURSING 20 Cavendish Square, London W1G 0RN T 020-740 3333 W www.rcn.org.uk
General Secretary, Dr Peter Carter

OPTOMETRY AND DISPENSING OPTICS

There are various routes to qualification as a dispensing optician. Qualification takes three years in total, and can be completed by combining a distance learning course or day release while working as a trainee under the supervision of a qualified and registered optician. Alternatively, students can do a two-year full-time course followed by one year of supervised practice with a qualified and registered optician. Training must be done at a training establishment approved by the regulatory body – the General Optical Council (GOC). There are six training establishments which are approved by the GOC: the Association of British Dispensing Opticians (ABDO), Anglia Ruskin University, Bradford College, the City and Islington College, City University and Glasgow Caledonian University. All routes are concluded by ABDO examinations, successful completion of which leads to registration with the GOC, which is compulsory for all practising dispensing opticians. After qualifying as a dispensing optician and completing training to fit contact lenses, students have the option to take a career progression course at the University of Bradford that allows them to graduate with a degree in optometry in one calendar year.

Optometrists must obtain an undergraduate optometry degree from one of the eight institutions approved by the GOC (Anglia Ruskin University, Aston University, the University of Bradford, Cardiff University, City University, Glasgow Caledonian University, the University of Manchester and the University of Ulster). Following graduation, trainees must complete a year of supervised salaried training with a registered optometrist during which they must successfully complete the assessments within the scheme for registration set by the College of Optometrists. As with dispensing opticians, optometrists must then register with the GOC in order to practise.

ASSOCIATION OF BRITISH DISPENSING OPTICIANS 199 Gloucester Terrace W2 6LD
T 020-7298 5100 E general@abdo.org.uk
W www.abdo.org.uk
General Secretary, Sir Anthony Garrett, CBE

COLLEGE OF OPTOMETRISTS 42 Craven Street,
London WC2N 5NG T 020-7839 6000
E optometry@college-optometrists.org
W www.college-optometrists.org
Chief Executive, Bryony Pawinska
GENERAL OPTICAL COUNCIL (GOC) 1 Harley Street,
London W1G 8DJ T 020-7580 3898 E goc@optical.org
W www.optical.org
Chief Executive and Registrar, Peter Coe

OSTEOPATHY
Osteopathy is a statutorily self-regulated healthcare
profession. The General Osteopathic Council (GOsC)
maintains a register of those entitled to practise
osteopathy in the UK. It is a criminal offence for anyone
to describe themselves as an osteopath unless they are
registered with the GOsC.
To gain entry to the register, applicants must hold a
recognised qualification from an osteopathic education
institute accredited by the GOsC; this involves a four to
five year honours degree programme combined with
clinical training.
GENERAL OSTEOPATHIC COUNCIL Osteopathy
House, 176 Tower Bridge Road, London SE1 3LU
T 020-7357 6655 E info@osteopathy.org.uk
W www.osteopathy.org.uk
Chief Executive and Registrar, Madeleine Craggs

PHARMACY
The Royal Pharmaceutical Society of Great Britain
(RPSGB) is the regulatory and professional body for
pharmacists in all aspects of practice. It has a statutory
duty to maintain the registers of pharmacists and
pharmacy premises. The Pharmaceutical Society of
Northern Ireland performs the same role in Northern
Ireland. In order to register, students must complete a
four-year degree in pharmacy that is accredited by either
the RPSGB or the Pharmaceutical Society of Northern
Ireland followed by one year of pre-registration training
at an approved pharmacy, and must then pass an entrance
examination.
PHARMACEUTICAL SOCIETY OF NORTHERN
IRELAND 73 University Street, Belfast BT7 1HL
T 02890-326927 E mail@psni.org.uk W www.psni.org.uk
Director, Raymond Blaney
ROYAL PHARMACEUTICAL SOCIETY OF GREAT
BRITAIN (RPSGB) 1 Lambeth High Street, London
SE1 7JN T 020-7735 9141 E enquiries@rpsgb.org
W www.rpsgb.org
Secretary and Registrar, Jeremy Holmes

LAW

There are two types of practising lawyers: barristers and
solicitors. Solicitors tend to work as a group in firms, and
can be approached directly by individuals. They advise on
a variety of legal issues and must decide the most
appropriate course of action, if any. Barristers, on the
other hand, are usually self-employed. If a solicitor
believes that a barrister is required, he or she will instruct
one on behalf of the client; the client will not have contact
with the barrister without the solicitor being present.
When specialist expertise is needed, barristers give
opinions on complex matters of law, and when clients
require representation in the higher courts (crown courts,
high courts, the court of appeal and the House of Lords),
barristers provide a specialist advocacy service. However,
solicitors – who represent their clients in the lower courts
such as tribunals, magistrates' courts and county courts –

can also apply for advocacy rights in the higher courts
instead of briefing a barrister.

THE BAR
The governing body of the Bar of England and Wales is
the General Council of the Bar, also known as the Bar
Council. Since January 2006, the regulatory functions of
the Bar Council (including regulating the education and
training requirements for those wishing to enter the
profession) have been undertaken by the Bar Standards
Board.
In the first (or 'academic') stage of training, aspiring
barristers must obtain a law degree of a good standard (at
least second class). Alternatively, a non-law degree (at least
second class) followed by a one-year full-time or two-year
part-time Common Professional Examination (CPE) or an
approved Postgraduate Diploma in Law (PgDL).
The second (vocational) stage is the completion of the
Bar Vocational Course (BVC), which is available at eight
validated institutions in the UK and must be applied for
around one year in advance (W www.bvconline.co.uk). All
barristers must join one of the four Inns of Court prior to
commencing the BVC.
Students are 'called to the Bar' by their Inn after
completion of the vocational stage, but cannot practise as
a barrister until completion of the third stage, which is
called 'pupillage'. Call to the Bar does not entitle a person
to practise as a barrister – successful completion of
pupillage is now a pre-requisite. Pupillage lasts for two
six-month periods: the 'non-practising six' and the
'practising six'. The former consists of shadowing an
experienced barrister, while the latter involves appearing
in court as a barrister.
Admission to the Bar of Northern Ireland is controlled
by the Honorable Society of the Inn of Court of Northern
Ireland; admission as an Advocate to the Scottish Bar is
through the Faculty of Advocates.
BAR STANDARDS BOARD The Bar Council, 289–293
High Holborn, London WC1V 7HZ T 020-7611 1444
W www.barstandardsboard.org.uk
Director of Regulation, Mark Stobbs
FACULTY OF ADVOCATES Parliament House, Edinburgh
EH1 1RF T 0131-226 5071 W www.advocates.org.uk
Chief Executive Officer, Tony Parker
GENERAL COUNCIL OF THE BAR 289–293 High
Holborn, London WC1V 7HZ T 020-7242 0082
E chiefexec@barcouncil.org.uk W www.barcouncil.org.uk
Chief Executive, David Hobart
GENERAL COUNCIL OF THE BAR OF NORTHERN
IRELAND The Bar Library, 91 Chichester Street,
Belfast BT1 3JQ T 028-9056 2349
E chief.executive@barcouncil-ni.org.uk
W www.barlibrary.com
Chief Executive, Brendan Garland
HONOURABLE SOCIETY OF THE INN OF COURT
OF NORTHERN IRELAND The Under-Treasurer's
Office, Room 1–3, Royal Courts of Justice, Belfast BT1 3JF
T 028-9072 4699
Under-Treasurer, J. W. Wilson QC

THE INNS OF COURT
HONOURABLE SOCIETY OF GRAY'S INN 8 South
Square, London WC1R 5ET T 020-7458 7800
W www.graysinn.org.uk
Under-Treasurer, Maj.-Gen. David Jenkins, CB, CBE
HONOURABLE SOCIETY OF LINCOLN'S INN
Treasury Office, Lincoln's Inn, London WC2A 3TL
T 020-7405 1393 E mail@lincolnsinn.org.uk

W www.lincolnsinn.org.uk
Under-Treasurer, Col. D. Hills, MBE
HONOURABLE SOCIETY OF THE INNER TEMPLE
Inner Temple, London EC4Y 7HL T 020-7797 8250
E enquiries@innertemple.org.uk
W www.innertemple.org.uk
Sub-Treasurer, Patrick Maddams
HONOURABLE SOCIETY OF THE MIDDLE TEMPLE
Middle Temple Lane, London EC4Y 9AT T 020-7427 4800
E studentenquiries@middletemple.org.uk
W www.middletemple.org.uk
Under-Treasurer, Air Cdre Peter Hilling

SOLICITORS

Graduates from any discipline can train to be a solicitor; however, if the undergraduate degree is not in law, a one-year conversion course (either the Common Professional Examination (CPE) or the Graduate Diploma in Law (GDL)) must be completed. The next stage, and the beginning of the vocational phase, is the Legal Practice Course (LPC), which takes one year and is obligatory for both law and non-law graduates. The LPC provides professional instruction for prospective solicitors and can be completed on a full-time or part-time basis. Trainee solicitors then enter the final stage, which is a paid period of supervised work that lasts two years for full-time contracts. The employer that provides the training contract must be authorised by the Solicitors Regulation Authority (SRA) (the regulatory body of the Law Society of England and Wales), the Law Society of Scotland, or the Law Society of Northern Ireland. The SRA also monitors the training contract to ensure that it provides the trainee with the necessary expertise to qualify as a solicitor.

THE LAW SOCIETY OF ENGLAND AND WALES The Law Society's Hall, 113 Chancery Lane, London WC2A 1PL
T 020-7242 1222 E enquiries@lawsociety.org.uk
W www.lawsociety.org.uk
Chief Executive, Des Hudson
LAW SOCIETY OF NORTHERN IRELAND 40 Linenhall Street, Belfast BT2 8BA T 028-9023 1614
E info@lawsoc-ni.org W www.lawsoc-ni.org
Chief Executive and Secretary, John Bailie
LAW SOCIETY OF SCOTLAND 26 Drumsheugh Gardens, Edinburgh EH3 7YR T 0131-226 7411
E lawscot@lawscot.org.uk W www.lawscot.org.uk
Chief Executive, Douglas Mill
SOLICITORS REGULATION AUTHORITY Ipsley Court, Berrington Close, Redditch, Worcs B98 0TD
T 0870-606 2555 E info.services@sra.org.uk
W www.sra.org.uk
Chair, Peter Williamson

SURVEYING

The Royal Institution of Chartered Surveyors (RICS) is the professional body that represents and regulates property professionals including land surveyors, valuers, auctioneers, quantity surveyors and project managers. Entry to the institution, following completion of a RICS-accredited degree, is through completion of the Assessment of Professional Competence (APC), which involves a period of practical training concluded by a final assessment of competence. Entry as a technical surveyor requires completion of the Assessment of Technical Competence (ATC), which mirrors the format of the APC. The different levels of RICS membership are MRICS (member) or FRICS (fellow) for chartered surveyors, and TechRICS for technical surveyors.

Relevant courses can also be accredited by the Chartered Institute of Building (CIOB), which represents managers working in a range of construction disciplines; CIOB offers four levels of membership to those who satisfy its requirements: FCIOB (fellow), MCIOB (member), ICIOB (incorporated) and ACIOB (associate).
CHARTERED INSTITUTE OF BUILDING Englemere, King's Ride, Ascot SL5 7TB T 01344-630700
E reception@ciob.org.uk W www.ciob.org.uk
Chief Executive, Chris Blythe
ROYAL INSTITUTION OF CHARTERED SURVEYORS (RICS) 12 Great George Street, Parliament Square, London SW1P 3AD T 0870-333 1600
E contactrics@rics.org W www.rics.org
Chief Executive, J. H. Armstrong

TEACHING
(*See also* Education section)
The General Teaching Councils for England, Northern Ireland, Scotland and Wales maintain registers of qualified teachers in their respective countries, and registration is a legal requirement in order to teach in local authority schools.

Further information on how to become a teacher in England and Wales is available on the Training and Development Agency for Schools website (*see* below). Personal advice is available from the Teaching Information Line (T 0845-600 0991; T 0845-600 0992 for Welsh speakers). Details on courses in Scotland can be obtained from universities and the Graduate Teacher Training Registry. Details of the courses in Northern Ireland can be obtained from individual universities and the Department of Education for Northern Ireland.

The College of Teachers, under the terms of its royal charter, provides professional qualifications in the field of Teaching English to Speakers of Other Languages (TESOL) for teachers based in the UK and overseas.
COLLEGE OF TEACHERS Institute of Education, 20 Bedford Way, London WC1H 0AL T 020-7911 5536
E enquiries@cot.ac.uk W www.cot.ac.uk
President, Prof. Geoff Whitty, FRSA
DEPARTMENT OF EDUCATION NORTHERN IRELAND Rathgael House, Balloo Road, Bangor BT19 7PR
T 028-9127 9279 E mail@deni.gov.uk W www.deni.gov.uk
Permanent Secretary, Will Haire
GENERAL TEACHING COUNCIL FOR ENGLAND Whittington House, 19–30 Alfred Place, London WC1E 7EA
T 0870-001 0308 E info@gtce.org.uk W www.gtce.org.uk
Chief Executive, Keith Bartley
GENERAL TEACHING COUNCIL FOR NORTHERN IRELAND 4th Floor, Albany House, 73–75 Great Victoria Street, Belfast BT2 7AF T 028-9033 3390
E info@gtcni.org.uk W www.gtcni.org.uk
Registrar, Eddie McArdle
GENERAL TEACHING COUNCIL FOR SCOTLAND Clerwood House, 96 Clermiston Road, Edinburgh EH12 6UT
T 0131-314 6000 E gtcs@gtcs.org.uk W www.gtcs.org.uk
Chief Executive, Matthew MacIver
GENERAL TEACHING COUNCIL FOR WALES 4th Floor, Southgate House, Wood Street, Cardiff CF10 1EW
T 029-2055 0350 E information@gtcw.org.uk
W www.gtcw.org.uk
Chief Executive, Gary Brace
GRADUATE TEACHER TRAINING REGISTRY Rosehill, New Barn Lane, Cheltenham GL52 3LZ
T 0871-468 0469 E enquiries@gttr.ac.uk W www.gttr.ac.uk
Chief Executive, Anthony McClaran

TRAINING AND DEVELOPMENT AGENCY FOR
SCHOOLS 151 Buckingham Palace Road, London
SW1W 9SZ T 020-7023 8001 W www.tda.gov.uk
Chief Executive, Graham Holley

VETERINARY MEDICINE

The regulatory body for veterinary surgeons in the UK is
the Royal College of Veterinary Surgeons (RCVS), which
keeps the register of those entitled to practise veterinary
medicine as well as the list of qualified veterinary nurses.
Holders of recognised degrees from any of the six UK
university veterinary schools or from certain EU or
overseas universities are entitled to be registered, and
holders of certain other degrees may take a statutory
membership examination. The UK's veterinary schools
are located at the University of Bristol, the University
of Cambridge, the University of Edinburgh, the
University of Glasgow, the University of Liverpool and
the Royal Veterinary College in London; all veterinary
degrees last for five years except that offered at
Cambridge, which lasts for six. A seventh school at the
University of Nottingham has not received RCVS
accreditation because no student has yet completed the
degree course.

The British Veterinary Association is the professional
body representing veterinary surgeons. The British
Veterinary Nursing Association is the professional body
representing veterinary nurses.

BRITISH VETERINARY ASSOCIATION 7 Mansfield
Street, London W1G 9NQ T 020-7636 6541
E bvahq@bva.co.uk W www.bva.co.uk
Company Secretary, Henrietta Alderman

BRITISH VETERINARY NURSING ASSOCIATION 82
Greenway Business Centre, Harlow Business Park, Harlow
CM19 5QE T 01279-408644 E bvna@bvna.co.uk
W www.bvna.org.uk

ROYAL COLLEGE OF VETERINARY SURGEONS
Belgravia House, 62–64 Horseferry Road, London SW1P 2AF
T 020-7222 2001 E admin@rcvs.org.uk W www.rcvs.org.uk
Registrar, Jane Hern

INDEPENDENT SCHOOLS

Independent schools (non-maintained mainstream schools) charge fees and are owned and managed under special trusts, with profits being used for the benefit of the schools concerned. In 2005–6 there were 2,493 non-maintained mainstream schools (of which 27 were academies) in the United Kingdom, educating over 650,000 pupils, or approximately 7 per cent of the total school-age population. The number of pupils at non-maintained mainstream schools in 2005–6 was:

UK	658,500
England	618,300
Wales	9,600
Scotland	29,700
Northern Ireland	800

The Independent Schools Council (ISC), formed in 1974, acts on behalf of the seven independent schools' associations which constitute it. These associations are: Headmasters' and Headmistresses' Conference, the Girls' Schools Association, the Independent Schools Association, the Society of Headmasters and Headmistresses of Independent Schools, the Incorporated Association of Preparatory Schools, the Association of Governing Bodies of Independent Schools and the Independent Schools Bursars Association. There were 510,000 pupils being educated in 1,275 Independent Schools Council (ISC) accredited schools in 2007. Most of the schools outside ISC membership are likely to be privately owned. The ISC has overall responsibility for the Independent Schools Inspectorate (ISI), which works under a framework agreed with the DfES and OFSTED. A school must pass an ISI accreditation inspection to qualify for membership of an association within ISC. Schools are evaluated on their educational standards (including attainment, learning and behaviour), quality of teaching, assessment and recording, curriculum, staffing, premises and resources, links with parents and the community, pupils' personal development and pastoral care, management, efficiency, aims and ethos. ISC schools are subject to inspection every six years.

In 2006 at GCSE 57.2 per cent of all exams taken by independent school candidates achieve either an A* or A grade (compared to the national average of 19.1 per cent), and at A-level 74.3 per cent of entries were awarded an A or B grade (national average, 48.1 per cent). In 2007 over 125,000 pupils at ISC schools received help with their fees in the form of bursaries and scholarships from the schools. These cost the schools over £300m.

INDEPENDENT SCHOOLS COUNCIL
St Vincent House, 30 Orange Street, London WC2H 7HH
T 020-7766 7070 W www.isc.co.uk

The fees shown below represent the upper limits payable during 2007–8 (fees noted with an * are for 2006–7) for UK pupils who do not qualify for any reduction; please note that scholarships and bursaries are available at many of the listed establishments.

The list was compiled with the assistance of Judy Mott, editor of *Independent Schools Yearbook 2007–8*, published by A&C Black. Further details are available online (W www.isyb.co.uk).

		Termly fees		
School	Web Address	Day	Board	Head
ENGLAND				
Abbey Gate College, Cheshire	www.abbeygatecollege.co.uk	£2,915	–	Mrs L. M. Horner
The Abbey School, Berks	www.theabbey.co.uk	£3,420	–	Mrs B. Stanley
Abbots Bromley School for Girls, Staffs	www.abbotsbromley.staffs.sch.uk	£3,985	£6,670	Mrs P. J. Woodhouse
Abbot's Hill School, Herts	www.abbotshill.herts.sch.uk	£4,145	–	Mrs K. Lewis
Abbotsholme School, Derbyshire	www.abbotsholme.com	£5,200	£7,700	S. Fairclough
Abingdon School, Oxon	www.abingdon.org.uk	£3,980	£7,590	M. Turner
Ackworth School, W. Yorks	www.ackworthschool.com	£3,422	£5,582	P. J. Simpson
Aldenham School, Herts	www.aldenham.com	£5,319	£7,731	J. C. Fowler
Alderley Edge School for Girls, Cheshire	www.aesg.info	£2,627	–	Mrs K. Mills
Alleyn's School, London SE2	www.alleyns.org.uk	£4,095	–	C. Diggory
Amberfield School, Suffolk	www.amberfield.suffolk.sch.uk	£2,905	–	Mrs H. Kay
Ampleforth College, N. Yorks	www.ampleforthcollege.york.sch.uk	£4,682	£8,090	Revd C. G. Everitt
Ardingly College, W. Sussex	www.ardingly.com	£5,900	£7,800	P. Green
Arnold School, Lancs	www.arnoldschool.com	£2,645	–	B. M. Hughes
Ashford School, Kent	www.ashfordschool.co.uk	£4,084	£7,577	M. Buchanan
Ashville College, N. Yorks	www.ashville.co.uk	£3,280	£6,435	A. A. P. Fleck
Austin Friars St Monica's School, Cumbria	www.austinfriars.cumbria.sch.uk	£3,240	–	C. J. Lumb
Bablake School, W. Midlands	www.bablake.com	£2,660	–	J. W. Watson
Badminton School, Bristol	www.badminton.bristol.sch.uk	£4,580	£8,130	Mrs J. A. Scarrow
Bancroft's School, Essex	www.bancrofts.essex.sch.uk	£3,665	–	P. R. Scott
Barnard Castle School, Durham	www.barnardcastleschool.org.uk	£3,220	£5,542	D. H. Ewart
Batley Grammar School, W. Yorks	www.batleygrammar.co.uk	£2,622	–	B. Battye
Battle Abbey School, E. Sussex	www.battleabbeyschool.com	£3,995	£6,585	R. C. Clark

Bearwood College, Berks	www.bearwoodcollege.co.uk	£4,695	£7,905	S. G. G. Aiano
Bedales School, Hants	www.bedales.org.uk	£6,675	£8,547	K. J. Budge
Bedford High School, Beds	www.bedfordhigh.co.uk	£3,386	£6,288	Mrs J. A. Eldridge
Bedford Modern School, Beds	www.bedmod.co.uk	£3,166	–	S. Smith
Bedford School, Beds	www.bedfordschool.org.uk	£4,595	£7,225	I. P. Evans
Bedstone College, Shropshire	www.bedstone.org	£3,390*	£6,200*	M. S. Symonds
Beechwood Sacred Heart, Kent	www.beechwood.org.uk	£4,150	£6,960	N. Beesley
Benenden School, Kent	www.benenden.kent.sch.uk	–	£8,225*	Mrs C. M. Oulton
Berkhamsted Collegiate School, Herts	www.berkhamstedcollegiateschool.org.uk	£4,690	£7,409	Dr P. Chadwick
Bethany School, Kent	www.bethanyschool.org.uk	£4,382	£6,817	N. D. B. Dorey
Birkdale School, S. Yorks	www.birkdaleschool.org.uk	£3,112	–	R. J. Court
Birkenhead High School, Merseyside	www.gdst.net/birkenheadhigh	£2,798	–	Mrs C. H. Evans
Birkenhead School, Merseyside	www.birkenheadschool.co.uk	£2,797	–	D. J. Clark
Bishop's Stortford College, Herts	www.bishops-stortford-college.herts.sch.uk	£4,347	£6,045	J. G. Trotman
Blackheath High School, London SE3	www.blackheathhighschool.gdst.net	£3,490	–	Mrs E. A. Laws
Bloxham School, Oxon	www.bloxhamschool.com	£6,213	£8,040	M. E. Allbrook
Blundell's School, Devon	www.blundells.org	£4,920	£7,625	I. R. Davenport
Bolton School Boys' Division, Lancs	www.boltonschool.org/seniorboys	£2,797	–	M. E. W. Brooker
Bolton School Girls' Division, Lancs	www.boltonschool.org/seniorgirls	£2,797	–	Mrs G. Richards
Bootham School, N. Yorks	www.bootham.york.sch.uk	£4,285	£6,880	J. F. J. Taylor
Box Hill School, Surrey	www.boxhillschool.org.uk	£4,200	£6,940	M. Eagers
Bradfield College, Berks	www.bradfieldcollege.org.uk	£6,500	£8,125	P. J. M. Roberts
Bradford Girls' Grammar School, W. Yorks	www.bggs.com	£3,297	–	Mrs L. J. Warrington
Bradford Grammar School, W. Yorks	www.bradfordgrammar.com	£3,050	–	S. R. Davidson
Brentwood School, Essex	www.brentwoodschool.co.uk	£4,048	£7,142	D. I. Davies
Brighton and Hove High School, E. Sussex	www.gdst.net/bhhs	£2,798	–	Mrs A. Greatorex
Brighton College, E. Sussex	www.brightoncollege.net	£5,178	£8,026	R. J. Cairns
Brigidine School Windsor, Berks	www.brigidine.org.uk	£3,955	–	Mrs J. Dunn
Bristol Cathedral School, Bristol	www.bristolcathedral.bristol.sch.uk	£3,080	–	A. H. Monro
Bristol Grammar School, Bristol	www.bristolgrammarschool.co.uk	£3,099	–	Dr D. J. Mascord
Bromley High School, Kent	www.bromleyhigh.gdst.net	£3,490	–	Mrs L. Duggleby
Bromsgrove School, Worcs	www.bromsgrove-school.co.uk	£3,760	£7,200	C. J. Edwards
Bruton School for Girls, Somerset	www.brutonschool.co.uk	£3,658	£6,141	J. Burrough
Bryanston School, Dorset	www.bryanston.co.uk	–	£8,495	Ms S. J. Thomas
Burgess Hill School for Girls, W. Sussex	www.burgesshill-school.com	£3,800	£6,595	Mrs A. Aughwane
Bury Grammar School Boys, Lancs	www.bgsboys.co.uk	£2,442	–	Revd S. C. Harvey
Bury Grammar School Girls, Lancs	www.bgsg.bury.sch.uk	£2,442	–	Mrs R. Georghiou
Canford School, Dorset	www.canford.com	£6,306	£8,190	J. D. Lever
Casterton School, Lancs	www.castertonschool.co.uk	£3,977	£6,646	P. McLaughlin
Caterham School, Surrey	www.caterhamschool.co.uk	£4,093	£7,636	J. P. Thomas
Central Newcastle High School, Tyne and Wear	www.newcastlehigh.gdst.net	£2,798	–	Mrs H. J. French
Channing School, London N6	www.channing.co.uk	£3,910	–	Mrs B. Elliott
Charterhouse, Surrey	www.charterhouse.org.uk	£7,192	£8,700	Revd J. S. Witheridge
Cheadle Hulme School, Cheshire	www.cheadlehulmeschool.co.uk	£2,759	–	P. V. Dixon
Cheltenham College, Glos	www.cheltcoll.gloucs.sch.uk/cc	£6,455	£8,615	J. S. Richardson
The Cheltenham Ladies' College, Glos	www.cheltladiescollege.org	£5,490	£8,176	Mrs V. Tuck
Chetham's School of Music, Manchester	www.chethams.com	sliding scale		Mrs C. Hickman
Chetwynde School, Cumbria	www.chetwynde.co.uk	£2,215	–	Mrs I. Nixon
Chigwell School, Essex	www.chigwell-school.org	£4,156	£6,316	M. E. Punt
Christ's Hospital, W. Sussex	www.christs-hospital.org.uk	–	£6,392	J. Franklin
Churcher's College, Hants	www.churcherscollege.com	£3,270	–	S. H. L. Williams
City of London Freemen's School, Surrey	www.clfs.surrey.sch.uk	£4,290	£6,822	P. MacDonald

School	Website			Head
City of London School, London EC4	www.clsb.org.uk	£4,008	–	D. R. Levin
City of London School for Girls, London EC2	www.clsg.org.uk	£3,855	–	Miss D. Vernon
Claremont Fan Court School, Surrey	www.claremont-school.co.uk	£3,852	–	Mrs P. B. Farrar
Clayesmore School, Dorset	www.clayesmore.com	£5,788	£7,910	M. G. Cooke
Clifton College, Bristol	www.cliftoncollegeuk.com	£5,415	£8,025	M. J. Moore
Clifton High School, Bristol	www.cliftonhigh.bristol.sch.uk	£2,935	£4,955	Mrs C. Culligan
Cobham Hall, Kent	www.cobhamhall.com	£5,500	£7,950	Mrs H. Davy
Cokethorpe School, Oxon	www.cokethorpe.org.uk	£4,295	–	D. J. Ettinger
Colfe's School, London SE12	www.colfes.com	£3,561*	–	R. F. Russell
Colston's Girls' School, Bristol	www.colstonsgirls.bristol.sch.uk	£2,536*	–	Mrs L. Jones
Colston's School, Bristol	www.colstons.bristol.sch.uk	£2,895	£6,200	P. T. Fraser
Combe Bank School, Kent	www.combebank.kent.sch.uk	£4,075*	–	Mrs R. Martin
Concord College, Shropshire	www.concordcollegeuk.com	£3,323	£6,993	N. G. Hawkins
Cranford House School, Oxon	www.cranfordhouse.oxon.sch.uk	£3,695	–	Mrs C. Hamilton
Cranleigh School, Surrey	www.cranleigh.org	£6,790	£8,330	G. Waller
Croham Hurst School, Surrey	www.crohamhurst.com	£3,475	–	Mrs E. J. Abbotts
Croydon High School, Surrey	www.gdst.net/croydonhigh	£3,490	–	Mrs Z. M. Braganza
Culford School, Suffolk	www.culford.co.uk	£4,610	£7,240	J. F. Johnson-Munday
Dame Alice Harpur School, Beds	www.dahs.co.uk	£3,170	–	Mrs J. Berry
Dame Allan's Boys' School, Tyne and Wear	www.dameallans.co.uk	£2,735	–	Dr J. R. Hind
Dame Allan's Girls' School, Tyne and Wear	www.dameallans.co.uk	£2,735	–	Dr J. R. Hind
Dauntsey's School, Wilts	www.dauntseys.wilts.sch.uk	£4,465	£7,535	S. Roberts
Dean Close School, Glos	www.deanclose.co.uk	£5,870	£8,315	Revd T. M. Hastie-Smith
Denstone College, Staffs	www.denstonecollege.org	£3,290	£5,729	D. M. Derbyshire
Derby High School, Derbyshire	www.derbyhigh.derby.sch.uk	£2,760	–	C. T. Callaghan
Dodderhill School, Worcs	www.dodderhill.co.uk	£2,790	–	Mrs J. M. Mumby
Dover College, Kent	www.dovercollege.org.uk	£3,590	£7,190	S. Jones
Downe House, Berks	www.downehouse.net	£6,267	£8,656	Mrs E. McKendrick
Downside School, Somerset	www.downside.co.uk	£3,630*	£6,954*	Dom Leo Maidlow Davis
Duke of York's Royal Military School, Kent	www.doyrms.mod.uk	–	£2,275	C. H. Johnson
Dulwich College, London SE21	www.dulwich.org.uk	£4,193	£8,443	G. G. Able
Dunottar School, Surrey	www.dunottar.surrey.sch.uk	£3,525	–	Mrs J. Hellier
Durham High School for Girls, Durham	www.dhsfg.org.uk	£2,840	–	Mrs A. J. Templeman
Durham School, Durham	www.durhamschool.co.uk	£4,413	£6,663	N. G. Kern
Eastbourne College, E. Sussex	www.eastbourne-college.co.uk	£4,770*	£7,205*	S. P. Davies
Edgbaston High School, W. Midlands	www.edgbastonhigh.bham.sch.uk	£2,715	–	Dr Ruth A. Weeks
Ellesmere College, Shropshire	www.ellesmere.com	£4,254*	£6,666*	B. J. Wignall
Eltham College, London SE9	www.eltham-college.org.uk	£3,696	–	P. J. Henderson
Emanuel School, London SW11	www.emanuel.org.uk	£4,165	–	M. D. Hanley-Browne
Epsom College, Surrey	www.epsomcollege.org.uk	£5,828	£8,456	S. R. Borthwick
Eton College, Berks	www.etoncollege.com	–	£8,830	A. R. M. Little
Ewell Castle School, Surrey	www.ewellcastle.co.uk	£3,340	–	A. J. Tibble
Exeter School, Devon	www.exeterschool.org.uk	£2,960	–	R. Griffin
Farlington School, W. Sussex	www.farlingtonschool.net	£3,735*	£5,940*	Mrs J. Goyer
Farnborough Hill, Hants	www.farnborough-hill.org.uk	£3,130	–	Mrs S. Buckle
Farringtons School, Kent	www.farringtons.org.uk	£3,390	£6,230	Mrs C. James
Felsted School, Essex	www.felsted.org	£5,596	£7,477	S. C. Roberts
Forest School, London E17	www.forest.org.uk	£3,938	–	A. G. Boggis
Framlingham College, Suffolk	www.framlingham.suffolk.sch.uk	£4,433	£6,897	Mrs G. M. Randall
Francis Holland School, London NW1	www.francisholland.org	£4,065	–	Mrs V. M. Durham
Francis Holland School, London SW1	www.fhs-sw1.org.uk	£3,950*	–	Miss S. J. Pattenden
Frensham Heights, Surrey	www.frensham-heights.org.uk	£4,670	£7,065	A. Fisher

School	Website	Fee 1	Fee 2	Head
Friends' School, Essex	www.friends.org.uk	£4,060	£6,325	G. Wigley
Fulneck School, W. Yorks	www.fulneckschool.co.uk	£3,025	£5,540	T. Kernohan
Gateways School, W. Yorks	www.gatewayschool.co.uk	£2,958	–	Mrs D. Davidson
Giggleswick School, N. Yorks	www.giggleswick.org.uk	£5,272	£7,775	G. P. Boult
The Godolphin and Latymer School, London W6	www.godolphinandlatymer.com	£4,197	–	Miss M. Rudland
The Godolphin School, Wilts	www.godolphin.org	£4,793	£7,097	Miss M. J. Horsburgh
The Grange School, Cheshire	www.grange.org.uk	£2,515	–	C. P. Jeffery
Greenacre School for Girls, Surrey	www.greenacre.surrey.sch.uk	£3,600	–	Mrs P. M. Wood
Grenville College, Devon	www.grenvillecollege.co.uk	£3,250	£6,495	A. Waters
Gresham's School, Norfolk	www.greshams.com	£5,830	£7,595	A. R. Clark
Guildford High School, Surrey	www.guildfordhigh.surrey.sch.uk	£3,705	–	Mrs F. J. Boulton
The Haberdashers' Aske's Boys' School, Herts	www.habsboys.org.uk	£4,025	–	P. B. Hamilton
The Haberdashers' Aske's School for Girls, Herts	www.habsgirls.org.uk	£3,344	–	Mrs E. Radice
Haileybury, Herts	www.haileybury.com	£6,040	£8,040	S. A. Westley
Halliford School, Middx	www.hallifordschool.co.uk	£3,200	–	P. V. Cottam
Hampshire Collegiate School, Hants	www.hampshirecs.org.uk	£3,794	£6,278	D. F. Chapman
Hampton School, Middx	www.hamptonschool.org.uk	£4,040	–	B. R. Martin
Harrogate Ladies' College, N. Yorks	www.hlc.org.uk	£3,910	£6,690	G. F. Hazell
Harrow School, Middx	www.harrowschool.org.uk	–	£8,815	B. J. Lenon
Headington School, Oxon	www.headington.org	£3,750	£7,200	Mrs A. Coutts
Heathfield St Mary's, Berks	www.heathfieldstmarys.net	–	£7,630	Mrs F. King
Heathfield School, Middx	www.heathfield.gdst.net	£3,490	–	Miss C. M. Juett
Hereford Cathedral School, Herefordshire	www.hcsch.org	£3,153	–	P. A. Smith
Hethersett Old Hall School, Norfolk	www.hohs.co.uk	£3,300	£6,195	Mrs J. M. Mark
Highclare School, W. Midlands	www.highclareschool.co.uk	£2,890	–	Mrs M. Viles
Highgate School, London N6	www.highgateschool.org.uk	£4,545	–	A. S. Pettitt
Hipperholme Grammar School, W. Yorks	www.hipperholmegrammar.org.uk	£2,665	–	Dr J. Scarth
Hollygirt School, Notts	www.hollygirt.co.uk	£2,600	–	Mrs P. S. Hutley
Holy Trinity School, Worcs	www.holytrinity.co.uk	£2,795	–	Mrs Y. Wilkinson
Hull Collegiate School, E. Yorks	www.hullcollegiateschool.co.uk	£2,616*	–	R. Haworth
Hurstpierpoint College, W. Sussex	www.hppc.co.uk	£5,495	£7,395	T. J. Manly
Hymers College, E. Yorks	www.hymerscollege.co.uk	£2,469	–	D. C. Elstone
Immanuel College, Herts	www.immanuelcollege.co.uk	£3,832	–	P. Skelker
Ipswich High School, Suffolk	www.ipswichhigh.gdst.net	£2,798	–	Ms E. Purves
Ipswich School, Suffolk	www.ipswich.suffolk.sch.uk	£3,295	£5,752	I. G. Galbraith
James Allen's Girls' School, London SE22	www.jags.org.uk	£3,900	–	Mrs M. Gibbs
The John Lyon School, Middx	www.johnlyon.org	£3,975	–	K. J. Riley
Kelly College, Devon	www.kellycollege.com	£4,250	£7,450	M. S. Steed
Kent College, Kent	www.kentcollege.com	£4,400	£7,570	D. J. Lamper
Kent College Pembury, Kent	www.kent-college.co.uk	£4,630	£7,465	Mrs A. Upton
Kimbolton School, Cambs	www.kimbolton.cambs.sch.uk	£3,610	£5,980	J. Belbin
King Edward VI High School for Girls, W. Midlands	www.kehs.org.uk	£2,810	–	Miss S. H. Evans
King Edward VI School, Hants	www.kes.hants.sch.uk	£3,315	–	A. J. Thould
King Edward VII and Queen Mary School, Lancs	www.keqms.co.uk	£2,492	–	R. J. Karling
King Edward's School, Somerset	www.kesbath.com	£3,119*	–	C. Rowe
King Edward's School, Surrey	www.kesw.surrey.sch.uk	£5,100	£7,100	P. Kerr Fulton-Peebles
King Edward's School, W. Midlands	www.kes.bham.sch.uk	£2,850	–	J. A. Claughton
King Henry VIII School, W. Midlands	www.khviii.com	£2,660	–	G. Fisher
King William's College, Isle of Man	www.kwc.sch.im	£5,289	£7,703	P. D. John
Kingham Hill School, Oxon	www.kingham-hill.oxon.sch.uk	£4,820	£7,110	M. J. Morris

School	Website	Fee 1	Fee 2	Head
King's College School, London SW19	www.kcs.org.uk	£4,775	–	A. C. V. Evans
King's College, Somerset	www.kings-taunton.co.uk	£5,070	£7,490	R. R. Biggs
King's High School, Warks	www.kingshighwarwick.co.uk	£2,900	–	Mrs E. Surber
The King's School, Cambs	www.kingsschoolely.co.uk	£4,955	£7,170	Mrs S. E. Freestone
The King's School, Canterbury, Kent	www.kings-school.co.uk	£6,510	£8,770	N. Clements
The King's School, Chester, Cheshire	www.kingschester.co.uk	£2,975	–	C. D. Ramsey
The King's School, Gloucester	www.thekingsschool.co.uk	£4,322*	–	A. K. Macnaughton
The King's School, Macclesfield, Cheshire	www.kingsmac.co.uk	£2,665	–	S. Coyne
King's School, Rochester, Kent	www.kings-school-rochester.co.uk	£4,920	£8,270	Dr I. R. Walker
King's School, Somerset	www.kingsbruton.com	£5,470	£7,535	N. M. Lashbrook
The King's School, Tyne and Wear	www.kings-tynemouth.org.uk	£2,810	–	P. J. S. Cantwell
The King's School, Worcs	www.ksw.org.uk	£3,261	–	T. H. Keyes
The Kingsley School, Warks	www.thekingsleyschool.com	£3,010	–	Mrs C. A. Mannion Watson
Kingston Grammar School, Surrey	www.kingston-grammar.surrey.sch.uk	£4,078	–	C. D. Baxter
Kingswood School, Somerset	www.kingswood.bath.sch.uk	£3,263	£7,276	G. M. Best
Kirkham Grammar School, Lancs	www.kirkhamgrammar.co.uk	£2,568	£4,783	D. R. Walker
The Lady Eleanor Holles School, Middx	www.lehs.org.uk	£3,900	–	Mrs G. Low
Lancing College, W. Sussex	www.lancingcollege.co.uk	£5,695	£8,200	J. W. J. Gillespie
Langley School, Norfolk	www.langleyschool.co.uk	£3,060	£6,225	D. K. Findlay
La Sagesse School, Tyne and Wear	www.lasagesse.org.uk	£2,985	–	Miss L. Clark
Latymer Upper School, London W6	www.latymer-upper.org	£4,280	–	P. J. Winter
Lavant House, W. Sussex	www.lavanthouse.org.uk	£3,750	£5,930	Mrs M. Scott
Leeds Girls' High School, W. Yorks	www.lghs.org	£2,875*	–	Ms S. Fishburn
The Grammar School at Leeds, W. Yorks	www.gsal.org.uk	£3,075	–	M. Bailey
Leicester Grammar School, Leics	www.leicestergrammar.org.uk	£2,900	–	C. P. M. King
Leicester High School for Girls, Leics	www.leicesterhigh.co.uk	£2,800	–	Mrs J. Burns
Leighton Park School, Berks	www.leightonpark.com	£5,045	£7,700	J. H. Dunston
Leweston School, Dorset	www.leweston.co.uk	£4,565	£6,590	A. J. F. Aylward
The Leys School, Cambs	www.theleys.net	£4,935	£7,634	M. Slater
The Licensed Victuallers' School, Berks	www.lvs.ascot.sch.uk	£3,930	£6,905	G. Best
Lincoln Minster School, Lincs	www.lincolnminsterschool.co.uk	£3,000*	£5,677*	C. Rickart
Liverpool College, Merseyside	www.liverpoolcollege.org.uk	£2,760	–	S. Buglass
Lodge School, Surrey	www.lodgeschool.co.uk	£3,500	–	Miss P. A. Maynard
Longridge Towers School, Northumberland	www.lts.org.uk	£2,995	£6,280	A. E. Clemit
Lord Wandsworth College, Hants	www.lordwandsworth.org	£5,325	£7,505	I. G. Power
Loughborough Grammar School, Leics	www.loughgs.leics.sch.uk	£3,006	£5,338	P. B. Fisher
Loughborough High School, Leics	www.loughhs.leics.sch.uk	£2,787	–	Miss B. A. O'Connor
Luckley-Oakfield School, Berks	www.luckley.wokingham.sch.uk	£3,869	£6,624	Miss V. A. Davis
Magdalen College School, Oxon	www.mcsoxford.org	£3,728	–	A. D. Halls
Malvern College, Worcs	www.malcol.org	£5,591	£8,731	Dr S. J. Welch
Malvern St James, Worcs	www.malvernstjames.co.uk	£3,995*	£7,750*	Mrs R. Hayes
The Manchester Grammar School, Manchester	www.mgs.org	£2,784	–	C. Ray
Manchester High School for Girls, Manchester	www.manchesterhigh.co.uk	£2,720	–	Mrs C. Lee-Jones
Manor House School, Surrey	www.manorhouse.surrey.sch.uk	£3,795	–	Mrs A. Morris
The Marist Senior School, Berks	www.themaristschools.com	£3,095	–	K. McCloskey
Marlborough College, Wilts	www.marlboroughcollege.org	£6,550	£8,730	N. A. Sampson

School	Website	Fee 1	Fee 2	Head
Marymount International School, Surrey	www.marymountlondon.com	£5,350	£8,983	Sr Kathleen Fagan
The Maynard School, Devon	www.maynard.co.uk	£3,010	–	Dr D. West
Merchant Taylors' Boys' School, Merseyside	www.merchanttaylors.com	£2,586	–	D. H. I. Cook
Merchant Taylors' Girls' School, Merseyside	www.mtgs.co.uk	£2,586	–	Mrs L. A. Robinson
Merchant Taylors' School, Middx	www.mtsn.org.uk	£4,470	–	S. N. Wright
Mill Hill School, London NW7	www.millhill.org.uk	£4,849	£7,661	Dr D. Luckett
Millfield, Somerset	www.millfieldschool.com	£5,710	£8,365	P. M. Johnson
Milton Abbey School, Dorset	www.miltonabbey.co.uk	£6,370	£8,490	W. J. Hughes-D'Aeth
Moira House Girls School, E. Sussex	www.moirahouse.co.uk	£4,200	£7,240	Mrs L. Watson
Monkton Senior, Somerset	www.monktoncombeschool.com	£5,261	£7,789	R. P. Backhouse
More House School, London SW1	www.morehouse.org.uk	£3,995	–	R. Carlysle
Moreton Hall, Shropshire	www.moretonhall.org	£6,400	£7,950	J. Forster
The Mount School, London NW7	www.mountschool.com	£3,175	–	Mrs J. K. Jackson
The Mount School, N. Yorks	www.mountschoolyork.co.uk	£4,195	£6,515	Mrs D. J. Gant
Mount St Mary's College, Derbyshire	www.msmcollege.com	£3,135	£5,820	L. E. McKell
New Hall School, Essex	www.newhallschool.co.uk	£4,520	£6,790	Mrs K. Jeffrey
Newcastle-under-Lyme School, Staffs	www.nuls.org.uk	£2,616	–	N. Rugg
The Newcastle upon Tyne Church High School, Tyne and Wear	www.churchhigh.com	£2,885	–	Mrs L. G. Smith
North Cestrian Grammar School, Cheshire	www.ncgs.co.uk	£2,370	–	D. G. Vanstone
North London Collegiate School, Middx	www.nlcs.org.uk	£3,715	–	Mrs B. McCabe
Northampton High School, Northants	www.northamptonhigh.co.uk	£2,990	–	Mrs S. A. Dixon
Northamptonshire Grammar School, Northants	www.ngs-school.com	£3,372	–	N. R. Toone
Northwood College, Middx	www.northwoodcollege.co.uk	£3,610	–	Mrs R. Mercer
Norwich High School, Norfolk	www.gdst.net/norwich	£2,798	–	Mrs V. C. Bidwell
Norwich School, Norfolk	www.norwich-school.org.uk	£3,284	–	J. B. Hawkins
Notre Dame Senior School, Surrey	www.notredame.co.uk	£3,500	–	Mrs B. Williams
Notting Hill and Ealing High School, London W13	www.nhehs.gdst.net	£3,490	–	Mrs S. M. Whitfield
Nottingham High School, Notts	www.nottinghamhigh.co.uk	£3,171	–	K. D. Fear
Nottingham High School for Girls, Notts	www.gdst.net/nottinghamgirlshigh	£2,798	–	Mrs S. Gorham
Oakham School, Rutland	www.oakham.rutland.sch.uk	£4,760	£7,950	Dr J. A. F. Spence
Ockbrook School, Derbyshire	www.ockbrook.derby.sch.uk	£2,780	£5,145	Mrs A. M. Steele
The Old Palace School of John Whitgift, Surrey	www.oldpalace.croydon.sch.uk	£3,190	–	Ms J. Harris
Oldham Hulme Grammar Schools, Lancs	www.hulme-grammar.oldham.sch.uk	£2,475	–	Dr P. G. Neeson
The Oratory School, Berks	www.oratory.co.uk	£5,705	£7,900	C. I. Dytor
Oswestry School, Shropshire	www.oswestryschool.org.uk	£3,775	£6,425	P. D. Stockdale
Oundle School, Northants	www.oundleschool.org.uk	£5,200	£7,980	C. M. P. Bush
Our Lady of Sion School, W. Sussex	www.sionschool.org.uk	£2,935	–	M. Scullion
Our Lady's Convent Senior School, Oxon	www.olcss.org.uk	£3,003	–	Mrs L. Renwick
Oxford High School, Oxon	www.gdst.net/oxfordhigh	£2,798	–	Miss O. F. S. Lusk
Palmers Green High School, London N21	www.pghs.co.uk	£3,265	–	Mrs C. Edmundson
Pangbourne College, Berks	www.pangbournecollege.com	£5,457	£7,780	T. J. C. Garnier
The Perse School, Cambs	www.perse.co.uk	£3,908	–	N. P. V. Richardson
The Perse School for Girls, Cambs	www.perse.cambs.sch.uk	£3,915	–	Miss P. M. Kelleher
Peterborough High School, Cambs	www.peterboroughhigh.co.uk	£3,323	£6,120	A. Meadows
Pipers Corner School, Bucks	www.piperscorner.co.uk	£3,765	£6,225	Mrs H. J. Ness-Gifford

School	Website			Head
Plymouth College, Devon	www.plymouthcollege.com	£3,482	£6,613	Dr S. J. Wormleighton
Pocklington School, E. Yorks	www.pocklingtonschool.com	£3,365	£6,025	N. Clements
Polam Hall School, Durham	www.polamhall.com	£3,290	£6,440	Miss M. Green
The Portsmouth Grammar School, Hants	www.pgs.org.uk	£3,392	–	T. R. Hands
Portsmouth High School, Hants	www.gdst.net/portsmouthhigh	£2,798	–	Mrs J. Clough
The Princess Helena College, Herts	www.phc.herts.sch.uk	£4,845	£6,995	Mrs A-M. Hodgkiss
Princethorpe College, Warks	www.wcisf.co.uk	£2,685	–	J. M. Shinkwin
Prior Park College, Somerset	www.priorparkschools.co.uk	£3,942	£7,108	R. G. G. Mercer
Prior's Field, Surrey	www.priorsfieldschool.com	£4,160	£6,735	Mrs J. A. Roseblade
The Purcell School, Herts	www.purcell-school.org	£7,128*	£9,116*	P. Crook
Putney High School, London SW15	www.gdst.net/putneyhigh	£3,490	–	Dr D. V. Lodge
Queen Anne's School, Berks	www.qas.org.uk	£5,425	£8,005	Mrs J. Harrington
Queen Elizabeth's Grammar School, Lancs	www.qegs.blackburn.sch.uk	£2,816	–	S. A. Corns
Queen Elizabeth Grammar School, W. Yorks	www.wgsf.org.uk	£2,895	–	M. R. Gibbons
Queen Elizabeth's Hospital, Bristol	www.qehbristol.co.uk	£3,035	–	S. W. Holliday
Queen Margaret's School, N. Yorks	www.queenmargaretsschool.co.uk	£4,432	£6,995	G. A. H. Chapman
Queen Mary's School, N. Yorks	www.queenmarys.org	£4,185	£5,450	R. A. McKenzie Johnston
Queen's College, London W1	www.qcl.org.uk	£4,200	–	Miss M. M. Connell
Queen's College, Somerset	www.queenscollege.org.uk	£4,225	£6,494	C. J. Alcock
Queen's Gate School, London SW7	www.queensgate.org	£4,100	–	Mrs R. M. Kamaryc
The Queen's School, Cheshire	www.queens.cheshire.sch.uk	£2,965	–	Mrs C. M. Buckley
Queenswood, Herts	www.queenswood.org	£6,245	£8,090	Mrs P. C. Edgar
Radley College, Oxon	www.radley.org.uk	–	£8,330	A. W. McPhail
Ratcliffe College, Leics	www.ratcliffecollege.com	£3,968	£5,975	P. Farrar
The Read School, N. Yorks	www.readschool.co.uk	£2,543	£5,504	R. A. Hadfield
Reading Blue Coat School, Berks	www.blue-coat.reading.sch.uk	£3,640	–	S. J. W. McArthur
The Red Maids' School, Bristol	www.redmaids.bristol.sch.uk	£2,840	–	Mrs I. Tobias
Redland High School for Girls, Bristol	www.redland.bristol.sch.uk	£2,880	–	Mrs C. P. Bateson
Reed's School, Surrey	www.reeds.surrey.sch.uk	£5,555	£7,350	D. W. Jarrett
Reigate Grammar School, Surrey	www.reigategrammar.org	£4,024	–	D. S. Thomas
Rendcomb College, Glos	www.rendcombcollege.co.uk	£5,235	£7,020	G. Holden
Repton School, Derbyshire	www.repton.org.uk	£5,875	£7,920	R. A. Holroyd
Rishworth School, W. Yorks	www.rishworth-school.co.uk	£3,070	£5,865	R. A. Baker
Roedean School, E. Sussex	www.roedean.co.uk	£5,000	£8,650	Mrs C. Shaw
Rossall School, Lancs	www.rossallschool.org.uk	£3,315	£8,315	T. J. Wilbur
The Royal Grammar School, Surrey	www.rgs-guildford.co.uk	£3,752	–	J. M. Cox
Royal Grammar School, Tyne and Wear	www.rgs.newcastle.sch.uk	£2,610*	–	J. F. X. Miller
RGS Worcester and The Alice Ottley School, Worcs	www.rgsao.org.uk	£2,898	–	A. R. Rattue
The Royal High School, Bath, Somerset	www.gdst.net/royalhighbath	£2,798	£5,486	J. Graham-Brown
The Royal Hospital School, Suffolk	www.royalhospitalschool.org	£3,308	£6,214	H. W. Blackett
The Royal Masonic School for Girls, Herts	www.royalmasonic.herts.sch.uk	£4,040	£6,450	Mrs D. Rose
Royal Russell School, Surrey	www.royalrussell.co.uk	£3,985	£7,880	J. R. Jennings
The Royal School, Surrey	www.royal-school.org	£4,250	£2,624	Mrs L. Taylor-Gooby
Royal School Hampstead, London NW3	www.royalschoolhampstead.net	£2,965	£5,890	Mrs J. Ebner-Landy
The Royal Wolverhampton School, W. Midlands	www.theroyalschool.co.uk	£3,550	£7,420	T. L. Waters
Rugby School, Warks	www.rugbyschool.net	£5,250	£8,305	P. S. J. Derham

School	Website	Fee 1	Fee 2	Head
Ryde School with Upper Chine, Isle of Wight	www.rydeschool.org.uk	£2,865	£5,855	Dr N. J. England
Rye St Antony School, Oxon	www.ryestantony.co.uk	£3,400	£5,700	Miss A. M. Jones
St Albans High School, Herts	www.sahs.org.uk	£3,445	–	Ms Jacqualyn Pain
St Albans School, Herts	www.st-albans.herts.sch.uk	£3,942	–	A. R. Grant
St Andrew's School, Beds	www.standrewsschoolbedford.com	£3,020	–	Mrs J. E. Marsland
St Bede's College, Manchester	www.stbedescollege.co.uk	£2,532	–	J. Byrne
St Bede's School, E. Sussex	www.stbedesschool.org	£4,555	£7,410	S. Cole
St Bees School, Cumbria	www.st-bees-school.org	£4,425	£7,383	P. J. Capes
St Benedict's School, London W5	www.stbenedictsealing.org.uk	£3,670	–	C. J. Cleugh
St Catherine's School, Middx	www.stcatherineschool.co.uk	£3,190	–	Sr Paula Thomas
St Catherine's School, Surrey	www.stcatherines.info	£3,920	£6,450	Mrs A. M. Phillips
St Christopher School, Herts	www.stchris.co.uk	£4,275	£7,500	R. Palmer
St Columba's College, Herts	www.stcolumbascollege.net	£3,180	–	J. Stuart
St David's School, Middx	www.stdavidsschool.com	£3,703	£6,858	Mrs T. Smith
St Dominic's Priory School, Staffs	www.st-dominics.co.uk	£2,586	–	A. Egan
St Dominic's School, Staffs	www.stdominicsschool.co.uk	£2,990*	–	Mrs S. White
St Dunstan's College, London SE6	www.stdunstans.org.uk	£3,854	–	Mrs J. D. Davies
St Edmund's College, Herts	www.stedmundscollege.org	£4,280	£6,940	C. P. Long
St Edmund's School, Kent	www.stedmunds.org.uk	£4,908	£7,601	J. M. Gladwin
St Edward's, Oxford, Oxon	www.stedwards.oxon.sch.uk	£6,795	£8,495	A. F. Trotman
St Edward's School, Glos	www.stedwards.co.uk	£3,598	–	A. J. Nash
Saint Felix School, Suffolk	www.stfelix.co.uk	£3,950	£6,550	D. A. T. Ward
St Francis' College, Herts	www.st-francis.herts.sch.uk	£3,195*	£6,285*	Miss M. Hegarty
St Gabriel's School, Berks	www.st-gabriels.w-berks.sch.uk	£3,620	–	A. Jones
St George's College, Surrey	www.st-georges-college.co.uk	£4,255	–	J. A. Peake
St George's School, Berks	www.stgeorges-ascot.org.uk	£5,170	£7,950	Mrs C. L. Jordan
St George's School, W. Midlands	www.sgse.co.uk	£2,675*	–	Miss H. Phillips
The School of St Helen and St Katharine, Oxon	www.shsk.org.uk	£3,203	–	Mrs C. L. Hall
St Helen's School for Girls, Middx	www.sthelensnorthwood.co.uk	£3,795	£7,038	Mrs M. Morris
St James Independent School for Senior Girls, London W14	www.stjamesschools.co.uk	£3,460	–	Mrs L. Hyde
St John's College, Hants	www.stjohnscollege.co.uk	£2,625	£5,750	N. W. Thorne
St John's School, Surrey	www.stjohnsleatherhead.co.uk	£5,515	£7,580	N. J. R. Haddock
St Joseph's College, Suffolk	www.stjos.co.uk	£3,350	£5,500	Mrs S. Grant
St Joseph's Convent School, Berks	www.st-josephs.reading.sch.uk	£3,300	–	Mrs M. Sheridan
St Lawrence College, Kent	www.slcuk.com	£4,300	£7,342	Revd M. Aitken
St Leonards-Mayfield School, E. Sussex	www.stlm.e-sussex.sch.uk	£4,710	£7,090	Mrs J. Dalton
St Margaret's School, Devon	www.stmargarets-school.co.uk	£2,860	–	Miss R. Edbrooke
St Margaret's School, Herts	www.stmargaretsbushey.org.uk	£3,885	£6,995	Mrs L. Crighton
Saint Martin's, W. Midlands	www.saintmartins-school.com	£2,935	–	Mrs J. Carwithen
St Mary's College, Merseyside	www.stmaryscrosby.co.uk	£2,392*	–	Mrs J. M. Marsh
St Mary's Hall, E. Sussex	www.stmaryshall.co.uk	£3,965	£6,546	Mrs S. M. Meek
St Mary's School, Berks	www.st-marys-ascot.co.uk	£5,925	£8,325	Mrs M. Breen
St Mary's School, Bucks	www.stmarysschool.co.uk	£3,610	–	Mrs F. A. Balcombe
St Mary's School, Cambs	www.stmaryscambridge.co.uk	£3,690	£7,400	Miss C. F. Avery
St Mary's School, Dorset	www.st-marys-shaftesbury.co.uk	£4,750	£6,980	R. James
St Mary's School, Essex	www.stmarysschool.org.uk	£2,705	–	Mrs H. Vipond
St Mary's School, Wilts	www.stmaryscalne.org	£5,850	£8,350	Mrs H. Wright
St Mary's School, Worcs	www.stmarys.org.uk	£2,885	–	Mrs S. K. Cookson
St Nicholas' School, Hants	www.st-nicholas.hants.sch.uk	£3,166	–	Mrs A. V. Whatmough
St Paul's Girls' School, London W6	www.spgs.org	£4,541	–	Ms C. M. Farr
St Paul's School, London SW13	www.stpaulsschool.org.uk	£5,123	£7,624	G. M. Stephen
St Peter's School, N. Yorks	www.st-peters.york.sch.uk	£3,998	£6,760	R. I. Smyth
St Swithun's School, Hants	www.stswithuns.com	£4,425	£7,290	Dr H. L. Harvey
St Teresa's School, Surrey	www.stteresasschool.com	£4,100	£6,970	Mrs L. Falconer
Scarborough College, N. Yorks	www.scarboroughcollege.co.uk	£3,300	£5,633	T. L. Kirkup
Seaford College, W. Sussex	www.seaford.org	£4,650	£7,100	T. J. Mullins
Sedbergh School, Cumbria	www.sedberghschool.org	£5,640	£7,555	C. H. Hirst
Sevenoaks School, Kent	www.sevenoaksschool.org	£5,047	£8,093	Mrs C. L. Ricks
Shebbear College, Devon	www.shebbearcollege.co.uk	£3,025	£5,650	R. S. Barnes
Sheffield High School, S. Yorks	www.sheffieldhighschool.org.uk	£2,798	–	Mrs V. A. Dunsford

School	Website	Fee 1	Fee 2	Head
Sherborne School, Dorset	www.sherborne.org	£6,735	£8,415	S. F. Eliot
Sherborne School for Girls, Dorset	www.sherborne.com	£6,200	£8,500	Mrs J. Dwyer
Shiplake College, Oxon	www.shiplake.org.uk	£4,901	£7,266	A. G. S. Davies
Shrewsbury High School, Shropshire	www.gdst.net/shrewsburyhigh	£2,798	–	Mrs M. Cass
Shrewsbury School, Shropshire	www.shrewsbury.org.uk	£5,800	£8,370	J. W. R. Goulding
Sibford School, Oxon	www.sibford.oxon.sch.uk	£3,195*	£6,208*	M. Goodwin
Sidcot School, Somerset	www.sidcot.org.uk	£3,660	£6,150	J. Walmsley
Silcoates School, W. Yorks	www.silcoates.com	£3,448	–	A. P. Spillane
Sir William Perkins's School, Surrey	www.swps.org.uk	£3,454	–	Mrs S. D. Cooke
Solihull School, W. Midlands	www.solsch.org.uk	£2,943	–	P. J. Griffiths
South Hampstead High School, London NW3	www.gdst.net/shhs	£3,490	–	Mrs J. E. Stephen
Stafford Grammar School, Staffs	www.stafford-grammar.co.uk	£2,676	–	M. R. Darley
Stamford High School, Lincs	www.ses.lincs.sch.uk	£3,380	£6,328	Dr P. R. Mason
Stamford School, Lincs	www.ses.lincs.sch.uk	£3,380	£6,328	Dr P. R. Mason
Stanbridge Earls School, Hants	www.stanbridgeearls.co.uk	£5,600	£7,534	G. P. Link
Stockport Grammar School, Cheshire	www.stockportgrammar.co.uk	£2,571	–	A. H. Chicken
Stonar School, Wilts	www.stonarschool.com	£3,600	£6,350	Mrs S. Shayler
Stonyhurst College, Lancs	www.stonyhurst.ac.uk	£4,553	£7,754	A. R. Johnson
Stover School, Devon	www.stover.co.uk	£2,995	£6,195	Mrs S. Bradley
Stowe School, Bucks	www.stowe.co.uk	£6,305	£8,525	A. K. Wallersteiner
Streatham and Clapham High School, London SW16	www.gdst.net/streathamhigh	£3,490		Mrs S. Mitchell
Sunderland High School, Tyne and Wear	www.sunderlandhigh.co.uk	£2,306*	–	Dr A. Slater
Surbiton High School, Surrey	www.surbitonhigh.com	£3,619	–	Dr J. Longhurst
Sutton High School, Surrey	www.gdst.net/suttonhigh	£3,490	–	S. J. Callaghan
Sutton Valence School, Kent	www.svs.org.uk	£5,010	£7,920	J. S. Davies
Sydenham High School, London SE26	www.gdst.net/sydenhamhigh	£3,490	–	Mrs K. E. Pullen
Talbot Heath, Dorset	www.talbotheath.org.uk	£3,122	£5,199	Mrs C. Dipple
Taunton School, Somerset	www.tauntonschool.co.uk	£4,290*	£6,720*	Dr J. H. Newton
Teesside High School, Cleveland	www.teessidehigh.co.uk	£2,975	–	T. A. Packer
Tettenhall College, W. Midlands	www.tettenhallcollege.co.uk	£3,367*	£5,908*	P. C. Bodkin
Thetford Grammar School, Norfolk	www.thetgram.norfolk.sch.uk	£2,993	–	G. J. Price
Thornton College, Bucks	www.thorntoncollege.com	£2,885*	£4,775*	Miss A. T. Williams
Thorpe House School, Norfolk	www.thorpehouseschool.com	£2,240*	–	A. Todd
Tonbridge School, Kent	www.tonbridge-school.co.uk	£6,575	£8,942	T. H. P. Haynes
Tormead School, Surrey	www.tormeadschool.org.uk	£3,535	–	Mrs S. E. Marks
Trent College, Notts	www.trentcollege.net	£3,999	£4,994	Mrs G. Dixon
Trinity School, Surrey	www.trinity-school.org	£3,622	–	M. J. Bishop
Truro High School for Girls, Cornwall	www.trurohigh.co.uk	£3,065	£5,780	M. A. McDowell
Truro School, Cornwall	www.truroschool.com	£3,200	£6,150	P. K. Smith
Tudor Hall, Oxon	www.tudorhallschool.com	£4,741	£7,354	Miss W. Griffiths
University College School, London NW3	www.ucs.org.uk	£4,620	–	K. J. Durham
Uppingham School, Rutland	www.uppingham.co.uk	£5,810	£8,300	R. Harman
Wakefield Girls' High School, W. Yorks	www.wgsf.org.uk	£2,895	–	Mrs P. A. Langham
Walthamstow Hall, Kent	www.walthamstow-hall.co.uk	£4,280	–	Mrs J. Milner
Warminster School, Wilts	www.warminsterschool.org.uk	£3,730	£6,480	M. J. Priestley
Warwick School, Warks	www.warwickschool.org	£3,106	£6,627	E. B. Halse
Wellingborough School, Northants	www.wellingboroughschool.org	£3,500	–	G. R. Bowe
Wellington College, Berks	www.wellingtoncollege.org.uk	£6,405	£8,540	A. F. Seldon
Wellington School, Somerset	www.wellington-school.org.uk	£3,160	£5,618	M. S. Reader
Wells Cathedral School, Somerset	www.wells-cathedral-school.com	£4,249	£7,102	Mrs E. C. Cairncross
Wentworth College, Dorset	www.wentworthcollege.com	£3,475	£5,725	Miss S. Coe
West Buckland School, Devon	www.westbuckland.devon.sch.uk	£3,390	£5,780	J. F. Vick
Westfield School, Tyne and Wear	www.westfield.newcastle.sch.uk	£2,880	–	Mrs M. Farndale

School	Website			Head
Westholme School, Lancs	www.westholmeschool.com	£2,388	–	Mrs L. Croston
Westminster School, London SW1	www.westminster.org.uk	£5,992	£8,652	M. S. Spurr
Westonbirt, Glos	www.westonbirt.gloucs.sch.uk	£5,460	£7,867	Mrs M. Henderson
Whitgift School, Surrey	www.whitgift.co.uk	£3,940*	–	C. A. Barnett
Wimbledon High School, London SW19	www.gdst.net/wimbledon	£3,490	–	Mrs P. H. Wilkes
Winchester College, Hants	www.winchestercollege.co.uk	£8,385	£8,827	R. D. Townsend
Windermere St Anne's School, Cumbria	www.wsaschool.com	£3,860	£6,970	A. Graham
Wisbech Grammar School, Cambs	www.wgs.cambs.sch.uk	£3,050	–	R. S. Repper
Wispers School for Girls, Surrey	www.wispers.org.uk	£4,405	£6,988	L. H. Beltran
Withington Girls' School, Manchester	www.withington.manchester.sch.uk	£2,680	–	Mrs J. D. Pickering
Woldingham School, Surrey	www.woldinghamschool.co.uk	£4,730	£7,915	Mrs J. Triffitt
Wolverhampton Grammar School, W. Midlands	www.wgs.org.uk	£3,231	–	B. St J. Trafford
Woodbridge School, Suffolk	www.woodbridge.suffolk.sch.uk	£3,828	£6,728	S. H. Cole
Woodhouse Grove School, W. Yorks	www.woodhousegrove.co.uk	£3,110	£5,900	D. C. Humphreys
Worksop College, Notts	www.worksopcollege.notts.sch.uk	£4,640	£6,845	R. A. Collard
Worth School, W. Sussex	www.worthschool.co.uk	£5,707	£7,704	G. G. Carminati
Wrekin College, Shropshire	www.wrekincollege.com	£4,410	£7,282	S. G. Drew
Wychwood School, Oxon	www.wychwood-school.org.uk	£3,325	£5,395	Mrs S. Wingfield Digby
Wycliffe College, Glos	www.wycliffe.co.uk	£4,960	£7,405	Mrs M. E. Burnet Ward
Wycombe Abbey School, Bucks	www.wycombeabbey.com	£6,450	£8,600	Mrs P. E. Davies
Wykeham House School, Hants	www.wykehamhouse.hants.sch.uk	£2,810	–	Mrs L. R. Clarke
Yarm School, Cleveland	www.yarmschool.org	£3,019	–	D. M. Dunn
The Yehudi Menuhin School, Surrey	www.yehudimenuhinschool.co.uk	sliding scale		N. Chisholm

WALES

School	Website			Head
Christ College, Brecon	www.christcollegebrecon.com	£4,155	£6,425	Mrs E. Taylor
Haberdashers' Monmouth School for Girls, Monmouth	www.habs-monmouth.org	£3,303*	£5,893*	Dr B. Despontin
Howell's School, Denbigh	www.howells.org	£3,500	£5,650	Miss R. Hodgson
Howell's School Llandaff, Cardiff	www.gdst.net/howells-llandaff	£2,816	–	Mrs S. Davis
Llandovery College, Llandovery	www.llandoverycollege.com	£4,077	£6,027	P. A. Hogan
Monmouth School, Monmouth	www.habs-monmouth.org	£3,559	£5,991	S. G. Connors
Rougemont School, Newport	www.rougemontschool.co.uk	£2,896	–	Dr J. Tribbick
Ruthin School, Ruthin	www.ruthinschool.co.uk	£3,520	£5,795	J. S. Rowlands
Rydal Penrhos School, Colwyn Bay	www.rydal-penrhos.com	£4,140	£7,100	M. S. James
St David's College, Llandudno	www.stdavidscollege.co.uk	£3,748*	£5,766*	C. Condrup

NORTHERN IRELAND

School	Website			Head
Bangor Grammar School, Bangor	www.bangorgrammarschool.org.uk	–	–	S. D. Connolly
Belfast Royal Academy, Belfast	www.belfastroyalacademy.com	£40	–	W. S. F. Young
Campbell College, Belfast	www.campbellcollege.co.uk	£633	£3,099	J. A. Piggot
Coleraine Academical Institution, Coleraine	www.coleraineai.com	£120	–	Dr D. R. J. Carruthers
Foyle and Londonderry College, Londonderry	www.foylenet.org/foyleandlondonderry	£40	–	W. J. Magill
Methodist College, Belfast	www.methody.org	£40*	£2,433*	J. S. W. Naismith
Portora Royal School, Enniskillen	www.portoraroyal.co.uk	£14	–	J. N. Morton
The Royal Belfast Academical Institution, Belfast	www.rbai.org.uk	£245	–	Miss J. Williamson
The Royal School Dungannon, Dungannon	www.royaldungannon.com	£45	£1,917	P. D. Hewitt

SCOTLAND

School	Website			Head
Dollar Academy, Dollar	www.dollaracademy.org.uk	£2,862	£6,531	J. S. Robertson
The High School of Dundee, Dundee	www.highschoolofdundee.co.uk	£2,904	–	A. M. Duncan
The Edinburgh Academy, Edinburgh	www.edinburghacademy.org.uk	£2,580	£5,790	J. V. Light
Fettes College, Edinburgh	www.fettes.com	£5,632	£7,833	M. C. B. Spens

George Heriot's School, Edinburgh	www.george-heriots.com	£2,774	–	A. G. Hector
George Watson's College, Edinburgh	www.gwc.org.uk	£2,827	–	G. Edwards
The Glasgow Academy, Glasgow	www.theglasgowacademy.org.uk	£2,825	–	P. J. Brodie
Glenalmond College, Perth	www.glenalmondcollege.co.uk	£5,380	£7,885	G. C. Woods
The High School of Glasgow, Glasgow	www.glasgowhigh.com	£2,829	–	C. D. R. Mair
Hutchesons' Grammar School, Glasgow	www.hutchesons.org	£2,748	–	Dr K. M. Greig
Kelvinside Academy, Glasgow	www.kelvinsideacademy.org.uk	£2,965	–	J. L. Broadfoot
Kilgraston, Bridge of Earn	www.kilgraston.com	£4,100	£6,995	M. Farmer
Lomond School, Helensburgh	www.lomond-school.org	£2,590*	£5,540*	A. D. Macdonald
Loretto School, Edinburgh	www.loretto.com	£5,310	£7,825	M. B. Mavor
The Mary Erskine School, Edinburgh	www.esms.edin.sch.uk	£2,728	£5,443	J. N. D. Gray
Merchiston Castle School, Edinburgh	www.merchiston.co.uk	£5,465	£7,615	A. R. Hunter
Morrison's Academy, Crieff	www.morrisonsacademy.org	£2,851	–	G. S. H. Pengelley
Robert Gordon's College, Aberdeen	www.rgc.aberdeen.sch.uk	£2,830	–	H. Ouston
St Aloysius' College, Glasgow	www.staloysius.org	£2,518	–	J. Stoer
St Columba's School, Kilmacolm	www.st-columbas.org	£2,823	–	D. G. Girdwood
St George's School for Girls, Edinburgh	www.st-georges.edin.sch.uk	£3,210	£6,360	Dr J. McClure
St Margaret's School for Girls, Aberdeen	www.st-margaret.aberdeen.sch.uk	£2,860	–	Mrs A. Everest
St Margaret's School, Edinburgh	www.st-margarets.edin.sch.uk	£3,008	£6,512	Mrs E. M. Davis
Stewart's Melville College, Edinburgh	www.esms.edin.sch.uk	£2,728	£5,443	J. N. D. Gray
Strathallan School, Perth	www.strathallan.co.uk	£5,112	£7,535	B. K. Thompson

CHANNEL ISLANDS

Elizabeth College, Guernsey	www.elizcoll.org	£2,178	–	N. D. Argent
The Ladies' College, Guernsey	www.ladiescollege.sch.gg	£1,700	–	Miss M. E. Macdonald
Victoria College, Jersey	www.vcj.sch.je	£1,260	–	R. G. Cook

NATIONAL ACADEMIES OF SCHOLARSHIP

The national academies are self-governing bodies whose members are elected as a result of achievement and distinction in the academy's field. Within their discipline, the academies provide advice, support education and exceptional scholars, stimulate debate, promote UK research worldwide and collaborate with international counterparts.

In addition to income from donations, membership contributions, trading and investments, the English academies receive grant-in-aid funding from the science budget, administered by the Department for Innovation, Universities and Skills*; the allocations for the year 2007–8 are as follows:

	£ thousand
Royal Society	41,072
British Academy	21,385
Royal Academy of Engineering	9,752

* The Academy of Medical Sciences receives grant-in-aid funding from the Department of Health. It was allocated £1.75m spread over five years from 2004.

ACADEMY OF MEDICAL SCIENCES (1998)
10 Carlton House Terrace, London SW1Y 5AH
T 020-7969 5288
W www.acmedsci.ac.uk

The Academy of Medical Sciences was established in 1998 to promote advances in medical science and to ensure these are converted as quickly as possible into healthcare benefits for society.

The academy campaigns for the development, protection and promotion of careers for academics in the biomedical sciences and encourages good practice in training and development.

The academy is independent and self-governing and receives funding from a variety of sources including the fellowship, charitable donations, government and industry.

Fellows are elected from a broad range of medical sciences: biomedical, clinical and population based. The academy includes in its remit vetinary medicine, dentistry, nursing, medical law, economics, sociology and ethics. Elections are from nominations put forward by existing fellows.

At June 2007 there were 881 fellows and 23 honorary fellows.

President, Prof. John Bell, PMedSci
Vice-Presidents, Sir John Skehel, FRS, FMedSci; Sir Michael Rutter, CBE, FRS, FMedSci
Treasurer, Prof. Ian Lauder, FMedSci
Registrar, Prof. Patrick Maxwell, FMedSci
Executive Director, Mary Manning

BRITISH ACADEMY (1902)
10 Carlton House Terrace, London SW1Y 5AH
T 020-7969 5200
W www.britac.ac.uk

The British Academy is an independent, self-governing learned society for the promotion of the humanities and social sciences. It supports advanced academic research and is a channel for the government's support of research in those disciplines.

The fellows are scholars who have attained distinction in one of the branches of study that the academy exists to promote. Candidates must be nominated by existing fellows. There are 770 ordinary fellows, 15 honorary fellows and 306 corresponding fellows overseas.

President, Baroness O'Neill, FBA
Chief Executive, Dr R. Jackson
Treasurer, Prof. R. J. P. Kain, FBA
Foreign Secretary, Prof. D. I. D. Gallie, FBA
Publications Secretary, Dr D. J. McKitterick, FBA

ROYAL ACADEMY OF ENGINEERING (197⬤
29 Great Peter Street, London SW1P 3LW
T 020-7227 0500
W www.raeng.org.uk

The Royal Academy of Engineering was established as the Fellowship of Engineering in 1976. It was granted a royal charter in 1983 and its present title in 1992. It is an independent, self-governing body whose object is the pursuit, encouragement and maintenance of excellence in the whole field of engineering, in order to promote the advancement of science, art and practice of engineering for the benefit of the public.

Election to the fellowship is by invitation only, from nominations supported by the body of fellows. At June 2007 there were 1,339 fellows. The Duke of Edinburgh is the senior fellow and the Duke of Kent is a royal fellow.

President, Lord Browne of Madingley, FRENG
Senior Vice-President, Prof. W. Hall, CBE, FRENG
Vice-Presidents, Prof. W. R. Eatock Taylor, FRENG; Dr S. E. Ion, OBE, FRENG; P. Saraga, OBE, FRENG; Dr R. S. Steedman, FRENG; Prof. R. A. Williams, FRENG
Hon. Treasurer, F. C. Price, FRENG
Hon. Secretaries, P. Saraga, OBE, FRENG (International Activities); Dr D. Grant, CBE, FRENG (Education and Training)
Chief Executive, P. D. Greenish, CBE

ROYAL SOCIETY (1660)
6–9 Carlton House Terrace, London SW1Y 5AG
T 020-7451 2500
W www.royalsoc.ac.uk

The Royal Society is an independent academy promoting the natural and applied sciences. Founded in 1660, the society has three roles, as the UK academy of science, as a learned society and as a funding agency. It is an independent, self-governing body under a royal charter, promoting and advancing all fields of physical and biological sciences, of mathematics and engineering, medical and agricultural sciences and their application.

Fellows are elected for their contributions to science, both in fundamental research resulting in greater understanding, and also in leading and directing scientific and technological progress in industry and research establishments. A maximum of 44 new fellows, who must be citizens or residents of the British Commonwealth countries or Ireland, may be elected annually.

Up to eight foreign members, who are selected from those not eligible to become fellows because of citizenship or residency, are elected annually for their contributions to science.

One honorary fellow may be elected each year from those not eligible for election as fellows or foreign members. There are approximately 1,400 fellows and foreign members covering all scientific disciplines.

President, Prof. Lord Rees of Ludlow, PRS
Treasurer, Prof. Sir D. Wallace, CBE, FRS, FRENG
Biological Secretary, Prof. D. Read, FRS
Physical Secretary, Prof. M. Taylor, FRS
Foreign Secretary, Prof. L. Casselton, FRS
Executive Secretary, S. Cox, CVO

ROYAL SOCIETY OF EDINBURGH (1783)

22–26 George Street, Edinburgh EH2 2PQ
T 0131-240 5000
W www.royalsoced.org.uk

The Royal Society of Edinburgh (RSE) is an educational charity and Scotland's National Academy of Science and Letters. An independent body with charitable status, its multidisciplinary membership of around 1,400 fellows represents a knowledge resource for the people of Scotland. Granted its royal charter in 1783 for the 'advancement of learning and useful knowledge', the society organises conferences, debates and lectures; conducts independent inquiries; facilitates international collaboration and showcases the country's research and development capabilities; provides educational activities for primary and secondary school students and awards prizes and medals. The society also awards over £1.7m annually to Scotland's top researchers and entrepreneurs working in Scotland.

At May 2007 there were 1,462 fellows.

President, Sir Michael Atiyah, OM, PPRS, FRSE
Vice-Presidents, Prof. Janet McDonald, FRSE; Prof. John Mavor, FRSE; Lord Patel, FRSE
Treasurer, Edward Cunningham, CBE, FRSE
General Secretary (acting), Prof. Andrew Miller, CBE, FRSE

PRIVATELY FUNDED ARTS ACADEMIES

The Royal Academy and the Royal Scottish Academy support the visual arts community in the UK, hold educational events and promote interest in the arts. They are entirely privately funded through contributions by 'friends' (regular donors who receive benefits such as free entry, previews and magazines), bequests, corporate donations and exhibitions.

ROYAL ACADEMY OF ARTS (1768)

Burlington House, Piccadilly, London W1J 0BD
T 020-7300 8000
W www.royalacademy.org.uk

The Royal Academy of Arts is an independent, self-governing society devoted to the encouragement and promotion of the fine arts.

Membership of the academy is limited to 80 academicians, all being painters, engravers, sculptors or architects. Candidates are nominated and elected by the existing academicians. There is also a limited class of honorary academicians, of whom as of October 2007 there were 20.

President, Sir Nicholas Grimshaw, PRA
Treasurer, Prof. Paul Huxley, RA
Keeper, Prof. Maurice Cockrill, RA
Secretary and Chief Executive, Charles Saumarez Smith

ROYAL SCOTTISH ACADEMY (1838)

The Mound, Edinburgh EH2 2EL
T 0131-225 6671
W www.royalscottishacademy.org

Founded in 1826 and granted a Royal Charter in 1838, The Royal Scottish Academy is an independent institution led by prominent Scottish artists and architects. It promotes and supports the visual arts through an ongoing exhibitions programme, related educational events and through a series of awards, bursaries and scholarships for artists at all stages of their careers.

Members are elected from the disciplines of art and architecture and elections are from nominations put forward by the existing membership. At mid-2007 there were 20 honorary members and 91 members.

President, I. McKenzie Smith, OBE, PRSA
Secretary, W. Scott, RSA
Treasurer, I. Metzstein, OBE, RSA
Administrative Secretary, B. Laidlaw, ACIS

RESEARCH COUNCILS

The government funds basic and applied civil science research, mostly through seven research councils, which are established under royal charter and supported by the Department for Innovation, Universities and Skills (DIUS). The councils support research and training in universities and other higher education establishments. The science budget, administered by the DIUS, contributes around 30 per cent of public sector investment in research, with funding from other government departments (including higher education funding) and regional development making up the remaining investment. The councils also receive income for research commissioned by government departments and the private sector, in addition to income from charitable sources. The annual science budget has risen from £2.73bn in 2004–5 to almost £3.45bn in 2007–8.

The government science budget for 2007–8 includes the following allocations:

	£ thousand
Arts and Humanities Research Council	97,092
Biotechnology and Biological Sciences Research Council	381,829
Economic and Social Research Council	150,336
Engineering and Physical Sciences Research Council	721,172
Medical Research Council	546,514
Natural Environment Research Council	367,248
Science and Technology Facilities Council	530,000
Higher Education Innovation Fund	85,000
Science Research Investment Fund	300,000

Source: DTI (DIUS) – Science Budget Allocations 2004–5 to 2007–8

ALCOHOL EDUCATION AND RESEARCH COUNCIL

Room 178, Queen Anne Business Centre, 28 Broadway, London SW1H 9JX T 020-7340 9502 F 020-7340 9505
W www.aerc.org.uk

The AERC was established by act of parliament in 1982 to administer the Alcohol Education and Research Fund. The government fund is used in UK education and research projects to develop new ways to help those with drinking problems. The AERC aims to increase awareness of alcohol issues, to reduce alcohol-related harm and to encourage best practice.
Chair, Dr Noel Olsen
Director, Prof. Ray Hodgson

ARTS AND HUMANITIES RESEARCH COUNCIL

Whitefriars, Lewins Mead, Bristol BS1 2AE
T 0117-987 6500 W www.ahrc.ac.uk

Launched in April 2005 as the successor organisation to the Arts and Humanities Research Board, the AHRC funds postgraduate training and research in the arts and humanities, encompassing disciplines such as English literature, history, modern languages, archaeology, music and drama.

With a budget of around £90m, the AHRC provides support for research and postgraduate study within the UK's higher education institutions. In any one year, the AHRC makes approximately 700 research awards and around 1,500 postgraduate awards. Awards are made after a rigorous peer review process, to ensure the quality of applications.
Chair, Prof. Sir Brian Follett
Chief Executive, Prof. Philip Esler

BIOTECHNOLOGY AND BIOLOGICAL SCIENCES RESEARCH COUNCIL

Polaris House, North Star Avenue, Swindon SN2 1UH
T 01793-413200

Established by royal charter in 1994, the BBSRC funds basic and strategic biological research in order to advance UK expertise on the understanding and exploitation of biological systems. It funds research into how all living organisms function and behave. To deliver its mission, the BBRC supports research and training in universities and research centres throughout the UK, including the institutes listed below.
Chair, Dr P. Ringose
Chief Executive, Steve Visscher (acting)

INSTITUTES
BABRAHAM INSTITUTE, Babraham Hall, Babraham, Cambridge CB2 4AT T 01223-496000
Director, Prof. Michael Wakelam
INSTITUTE FOR ANIMAL HEALTH, Compton Laboratory, Compton, Newbury, Berks RG20 7NN
T 01635-578411
Director, Prof. M. Shirley
NEUROPATHOGENESIS UNIT, Ogston Building, West Mains Road, Edinburgh EH9 3JF T 0131-667 5204
IAH PIRBRIGHT LABORATORY, Ash Road, Pirbright, Woking, Surrey GU24 0NF T 01483-232441
Head, Dr David Mackay
ROTHAMSTED RESEARCH, Rothamsted, Harpenden, Herts AL5 2JQ T 01582-763133
Director, Prof. I. R. Crute
ROTHAMSTED RESEARCH, BROOM'S BARN RESEARCH STATION, Higham, Bury St. Edmunds, Suffolk IP28 6NP T 01284-812200
Director, Bill Clark
INSTITUTE OF FOOD RESEARCH, Norwich Research Park, Colney Lane, Norwich NR4 7UA T 01603-255000
Director, Prof. D. White
INSTITUTE OF GRASSLAND AND ENVIRONMENTAL RESEARCH (IGER), Aberystwyth Research Centre, Plas Gogerddan, Aberystwyth SY23 3EB
T 01970-823000
Director (interim), Prof. Mervyn Humphrys
IGER NORTH WYKE RESEARCH STATION, Okehampton, Devon EX20 2SB T 01837-883500
Head, vacant
JOHN INNES CENTRE, Norwich Research Park, Colney, Norwich NR4 7UH T 01603-450000
Director, Prof. C. Lamb

ROSLIN INSTITUTE, Roslin, Midlothian EH25 9PS
T 0131-527 4200
Director, Dr Harry Griffin

ECONOMIC AND SOCIAL RESEARCH COUNCIL
Polaris House, North Star Avenue, Swindon SN2 1UJ
T 01793-413000
E comms@esrc.ac.uk W www.esrcsocietytoday.ac.uk

The purpose of the ESRC is to promote and support research and postgraduate training in the social sciences. It also provides advice, disseminates knowledge and promotes public understanding in these areas.
Chair, Lord A. Turner
Chief Executive, I. Diamond

RESEARCH CENTRES
CENTRE FOR MARKET AND PUBLIC
    ORGANISATION, University of Bristol, Bristol BS8 1TN
    T 0117-928 8436
    Director, Prof. S. Burgess
CENTRE ON MIGRATION, POLICY AND SOCIETY,
    University of Oxford, Oxford OX2 6QS T 01865-274711
    Director, Prof. S. Vertovec
CENTRE FOR MICROECONOMIC ANALYSIS OF
    PUBLIC POLICY, Institute for Fiscal Studies, 7 Ridgmount
    Street, London WC1E 7AE T 020-7291 4800
    Director, Prof. R. Blundell
CENTRE FOR ORGANISATION AND INNOVATION,
    University of Sheffield, Sheffield S10 2TN T 0114-222 3254
    Directors, Prof. C. Clegg; Prof. T. Wall; Prof. S.
    Wood
CENTRE FOR RESEARCH ON INNOVATION AND
    COMPETITION, University of Manchester M13 9QH
    T 0161-275 7374
    Director, Prof. J. Howells
CENTRE FOR RESEARCH ON SOCIO-CULTURAL
    CHANGE, University of Manchester, Manchester M13 9PL
    T 0161-275 8985
    Directors, Prof. M. Savage; Prof. K. Williams
CENTRE ON SKILLS, KNOWLEDGE AND
    ORGANISATIONAL PERFORMANCE, University of
    Oxford, Oxford OX1 3UQ T 01865-276434
    Director, K. Mayhew
CENTRE FOR SOCIAL AND ECONOMIC
    RESEARCH ON THE GLOBAL ENVIRONMENT,
    University of East Anglia, Norwich NR4 7TJ T 01603-592551
    Director, Prof. K. Turner
CENTRE FOR SOCIAL AND ECONOMIC
    RESEARCH ON INNOVATION IN GENOMICS,
    University of Edinburgh, Edinburgh EH1 1LZ
    T 0131-650 9174
    Director, Prof. J. Tait
CENTRE FOR THE STUDY OF GLOBALISATION
    AND REGIONALISATION, University of Warwick,
    Coventry CV4 7AL T 024-7652 4633
    Directors, Prof. R. Higgott; Prof. J. Scholte
COMPLEX PRODUCT SYSTEMS INNOVATION
    CENTRE, University of Sussex, Brighton BN1 9RH
    T 01273-642188
    Directors, Prof. M. Hobday; Prof. H. Rush
ESRC CENTRE FOR GENOMICS IN SOCIETY,
    University of Exeter, Exeter, Devon EX4 4RJ T 01392-262049
    Director, J. Dupré
RESEARCH CENTRE ON MICRO-SOCIAL CHANGE,
    University of Essex, Colchester, Essex CO4 3SQ
    T 01206-872957
    Director, Prof. S. Pudney

TYNDALL CENTRE FOR CLIMATE CHANGE
    RESEARCH, University of East Anglia, Norwich NR4 7TJ
    T 01603-593162
    Directors, Prof. M. Hulme; Prof. J. Schellnhuber

RESOURCE CENTRES
CENTRE FOR LONGITUDINAL STUDIES, Institute of
    Education, London WC1H 0AL T 020-7612 6901
    Director, Prof. H. Joshi
NATIONAL CENTRE FOR RESEARCH METHODS,
    University of Southampton, Southampton SO17 1BJ
    T 023-8059 4539
    Director, Prof. C. Skinner
UK LONGITUDINAL STUDIES CENTRE, University of
    Essex, Colchester CO4 3SQ T 01206-873066
    Director, Prof. N. Buck

ENGINEERING AND PHYSICAL SCIENCES RESEARCH COUNCIL
Polaris House, North Star Avenue, Swindon SN2 1ET
T 01793-444000, Helpline: 01793-444100 W www.epsrc.ac.uk

The EPSRC is the UK government's main funding agency for research and training in engineering and the physical sciences in universities and other organisations throughout the UK. It also provides advice, disseminates knowledge and promotes public understanding in these areas.
Chair, John Armitt, CBE, FRENG
Interim Chief Executive, Prof. Randal Richards

HEALTH PROTECTION AGENCY
7th Floor, Holborn Gate, 330 High Holborn, London WC1V 7PP
T 020-7759 2700 F 020-7759 2733 W www.hpa.org.uk

The Health Protection Agency is a Special Health Authority, established in 2003 (merged with the National Radiological Protection Board in 2005), it gives advice to the public, health authorities and the government. It works to reduce the impact of infectious diseases and exposure to chemicals, poisons and radiation at local, national and regional levels and in emergency situations. The agency researches new ways to combat illness and to assess exposure to chemicals and radiation to determine whether treatment is needed.
Chairman, Sir William Stewart
Chief Executive, Prof. Pat Troop

RESEARCH CENTRES
CENTRE FOR INFECTIONS, 61 Colindale Avenue,
    London NW9 5EQ T 020-8200 4400
    Director, Prof. Peter Borriello
CENTRE FOR EMERGENCY PREPAREDNESS AND
    RESPONSE Porton Down, Salisbury SP4 0JG
    T 01980-612100
    Director, Dr Stephen Chatfield
CENTRE FOR RADIATION, CHEMICAL AND
    ENVIRONMENTAL HAZARDS, Chilton, Didcot
    OX11 0RQ T 01235-831600
    Director, Dr Roger Cox

MEDICAL RESEARCH COUNCIL
20 Park Crescent, London W1B 1AL T 020-7636 5422
W www.mrc.ac.uk

The purpose of the MRC is to promote medical and related biological research. The council employs its own research staff and funds research by other institutions and individuals, complementing the research resources of the universities and hospitals.

Chair, Sir John Chisholm
Chief Executive, Prof. Colin Blakemore
Chair, Neurosciences and Mental Health Board, Prof. C. Kennard
Chair, Molecular and Cellular Medicine Board, Prof. P. Luzio
Chair, Infections and Immunity Board, Prof. D. Smith
Chair, Health Services and Public Health Research Board, Dr D. Armstrong
Chair, Physiological and Clinical Sciences Board, Prof. S. Holgate

MRC RESEARCH CENTRES

MRC/Asthma UK Centre in Allergic Mechanisms of Asthma T 020-7188 1943
Anatomical Neuropharmacology Unit
   W mrcanu.pharm.ox.ac.uk
Biostatistics Unit
   W www.mrc-bsu.cam.ac.uk
Cambridge Behavioural and Clinical Neuroscience Institute
   W www.psychol.cam.ac.uk/bcni
Cancer Cell Unit W www.hutchison-mrc.cam.ac.uk
Cell Biology Unit
   W www.ucl.ac.uk/lmcb
Centre for Developmental Neurobiology at King's College London W www.kcl.ac.uk/depsta/biomedical/mrc
Clinical Sciences Centre
   W www.csc.mrc.ac.uk
MRC/Cancer Research UK/BHF Clinical Trial Service Unit & Epidemiological Studies Unit
   W www.ctsu.ox.ac.uk
Clinical Trials Unit
   W www.ctu.mrc.ac.uk
Cognition and Brain Sciences Unit
   W www.mrc-cbu.cam.ac.uk
Centre for Developmental and Biomedical Genetics
   W cdbg.shef.ac.uk
Dunn Human Nutrition Unit
   W www.mrc-dunn.cam.ac.uk
Epidemiology Resource Centre
   W www.mrc.soton.ac.uk
Epidemiology Unit W www.mrc-epid.cam.ac.uk
Functional Genetics Unit
   W www.mrcfgu.ox.ac.uk
Laboratories, the Gambia
   W www.mrc.gm
MRC/University of Sussex Centre in Genome Damage and Stability W www.sussex.ac.uk/gdsc
Health Services Research Collaboration
   W www.hsrc.ac.uk
Human Genetics Unit
   W www.hgu.mrc.ac.uk
Human Immunology Unit T 01865-222336
Collaborative Centre for Human Nutrition Research
   W www.mrc-hnr.cam.ac.uk
Human Reproductive Sciences Unit
   W www.hrsu.mrc.ac.uk
MRC/University of Birmingham Centre for Immune Regulation W www.bham.ac.uk/mrcbcir
Immunochemistry Unit
   W www2.bioch.ox.ac.uk/immunoch
MRC/University of Edinburgh Centre for Inflammation Research W www.cir.med.ed.ac.uk

Institute of Hearing Research
   W www.ihr.mrc.ac.uk
Mammalian Genetics Unit
   W www.mgu.har.mrc.ac.uk
MRC/UCL Centre for Medical Molecular Virology
   T 020-7504 9343
Laboratory of Molecular Biology
   W www2.mrc-lmb.cam.ac.uk
Molecular Haemotology Unit
   W www.imm.ox.ac.uk/groups/mrc_molhaem
National Institute for Medical Research
   W www.nimr.mrc.ac.uk
Centre for Neurodegenerative Research
   W cnr.iop.kcl.ac.uk
Centre for Nutritional Epidemiology in Cancer Prevention and Survival W www.srl.cam.ac.uk
Centre for Protein Engineering
   W www.mrc-cpe.cam.ac.uk
Prion Unit
   W www.prion.ucl.ac.uk
Protein Phosphorylation Unit
   W www.dundee.ac.uk/lifesciences/mrcppu
Radiation and Genome Damage Stability Unit
   W www.ragsu.har.mrc.ac.uk
Social and Public Health Sciences Unit
   W www.msoc-mrc.gla.ac.uk
Social, Genetic and Developmental Psychiatry Research Centre T 020-7848 0871
Centre for Stem Cell Biology and Medicine
   W www.stemcells.cam.ac.uk
Centre for Stem Cell Research
   W www.iscr.ed.ac.uk
MRC/University of Bristol Centre for Synaptic Plasticity
   W www.bris.ac.uk/depts/synaptic
Toxicology Unit
   W www.le.ac.uk/mrctox
Uganda Research Unit on AIDS
   T (+256) (41) 320272
Virology Unit
   W www.mrcvu.gla.ac.uk

MILK DEVELOPMENT COUNCIL

Stroud Road, Cirencester GL7 6JN T 01285-646500
F 01285-646501 W www.mdc.org.uk

The MDC was founded in 1994 and is funded by the government as an independent public body. It aims to help dairy farmers throughout Britain increase their profits, by offering advice on production efficiency and expertise and opportunities that can increase the demand or value of milk, or stop its value declining. It aims to create better supply chain relationships to ensure that farmers profit as well as retailers.
Chair, Brian Peacock
Chief Executive, Kevin Bellamy

NATIONAL PHYSICAL LABORATORY

Hampton Road, Teddington, Middlesex TW11 0LW T 020-8977 3222 F 020-8943 6458 W www.npl.co.uk

The NPL is the UK's national standards laboratory and has been operating since 1900. It is an independent laboratory for research, development and knowledge transfer in measurement and materials science. The NPL develops the national measurement standards for physical quantities
Managing Director, Steve McQuillan

NATURAL ENVIRONMENT RESEARCH COUNCIL

Polaris House, North Star Avenue, Swindon SN2 1EU
T 01793-411500 W www.nerc.ac.uk

The NERC funds and carries out impartial scientific research in the sciences relating to natural environment. Its work covers the full range of atmospheric, earth, biological, terrestrial and aquatic sciences, from the depths of the oceans to the upper atmosphere. Its mission is to gather and apply knowledge, create understanding and predict the behaviour of the natural environment and its resources.
Chair, Rob Margetts, CBE, FRENG
Chief Executive, Prof. Alan Thorpe

RESEARCH CENTRES
BRITISH ANTARCTIC SURVEY, High Cross, Madingley Road, Cambridge CB3 OET T 01223-221400
Director, Prof. Chris Rapley, CBE
BRITISH GEOLOGICAL SURVEY, Kingsley Dunham Centre, Keyworth, Nottingham NG12 5GG
T 0115-936 3100
Executive Director, Dr John Ludden
CENTRE FOR ECOLOGY AND HYDROLOGY, Polaris House, North Star Avenue, Swindon SN2 1EU
T 01793-442516
Director, Prof. Patricia Nuttall, OBE
PROUDMAN OCEANOGRAPHIC LABORATORY, Joseph Proudman Building, 6 Brownlow Street, Liverpool L3 5DA T 0151-795 4800
Director, Prof. Andrew Willmott

COLLABORATIVE CENTRES
CENTRE FOR OBSERVATION OF AIR-SEA INTERACTIONS AND FLUXES, Plymouth Marine Laboratory, Prospect Place, Plymouth PL1 3DH
T 01752-633429
Director, Prof. Jim Aiken
CENTRE FOR OBSERVATION AND MODELLING OF EARTHQUAKES AND TECTONICS, Department of Earth Sciences, University of Oxford, Parks Road, Oxford OX1 3PR T 01865-272030
Director, Prof. Barry Parsons
CENTRE FOR POLAR OBSERVATION AND MODELLING, Department of Space and Climate Physics, Pearson Building, University College London, Gower Street, London WC1E 6BT T 020-7679 3031
Director, Prof. Duncan Wingham
CENTRE FOR POPULATION BIOLOGY, Imperial College London, Silwood Park Campus, Ascot SL5 7PY
T 020-7594 2475
Director, Prof. Georgina Mace, FRS
CLIMATE AND LAND SURFACE SYSTEMS INTERACTION CENTRE, School of Engineering, Computer Science and Mathematics, Harrison building, North Park Road, University of Exeter EX4 4QF
T 01792-295144
Director, Prof. Peter Cox
DATA ASSIMILATION RESEARCH CENTRE, Department of Meteorology, University of Reading, PO Box 243, Earley Gate, Reading RG6 6BB T 0118-378 6728
Director, Prof. Alan O'Neill
ENVIRONMENTAL SYSTEMS SCIENCE CENTRE, University of Reading, PO Box 238, Harry Pitt Building, 3 Earley Gate, Reading RG6 6AL T 0118-378 8741
Director, Prof. Robert Gurney, OBE

NATIONAL INSTITUTE FOR ENVIRONMENTAL E-SCIENCE, Department of Earth Sciences, University of Cambridge, Downing Street, Cambridge CB2 3EQ
T 01223-764917
Director, Dr Martin Dove
NATIONAL OCEANOGRAPHY CENTRE, SOUTHAMPTON, University of Southampton, Waterfront Campus, European Way, Southampton SO14 3ZH T 023-8059 6666
Director, Prof. Ed Hill
NATIONAL CENTRES FOR ATMOSPHERIC SCIENCE, School of Earth and Environment, University of Leeds LS2 9JT T 0113-343 5158
Director, Prof. Stephen Mobbs
NCAS GLOBAL COMPOSITION AND CLIMATE RESEARCH, Department of Chemistry, University of Cambridge, Lensfield Road, Cambridge CB2 1EW
T 01223-336473
Director, Prof. John Pyle, FRS
NCAS BRITISH ATMOSPHERIC DATA CENTRE, Rutherford Appleton Laboratory, Chilton, Didcot OX11 0QX
T 01235-446432
Director, Dr Bryan Lawrence
NCAS-CLIMATE, Department of Meteorology, University of Reading, PO Box 243, Earley Gate, Reading RG6 6BB
T 0118-378 8424
Director, Prof. Julia Slingo
NCAS DISTRIBUTED INSTITUTE FOR ATMOSPHERIC COMPOSITION, School of Chemistry, University of Leeds, Leeds LS2 9JT
T 0113-343 6450
Director, Prof. Mike Pilling
NCAS FACILITY FOR AIRBORNE ATMOSPHERIC MEASUREMENTS, Building 125, Cranfield University, Cranfield, Bedford MK43 0AL T 01234-754411
Head of Facility, Steve Ball
NCAS UNIVERSITIES FACILITY FOR ATMOSPHERIC MEASUREMENTS, School of Earth and Environment, University of Leeds, Leeds LS2 9JT
T 0113-343 6408
Director, Dr Alan Blyth
NCAS UNIVERSITIES WEATHER RESEARCH NETWORK, Department of Meteorology, University of Reading, PO Box 243, Earley Gate, Reading, RG6 6BB
T 0118-378 8957
Director, Prof. P. Mason
NERC CENTRE FOR TERRESTRIAL CARBON DYNAMICS, University of Sheffield, Hicks Building, Hounsfield Road, Sheffield S3 7RH T 0114-222 3803
Director, Prof. Shaun Quegan
PLYMOUTH MARINE LABORATORY, Prospect Place, Plymouth PL1 3DH T 01752-633100
Director, Prof. Nicholas Owens
SCOTTISH ASSOCIATION FOR MARINE SCIENCE, Dunstaffnage Marine Laboratory, Oban PA37 1QA
T 01631-559000
Director, Prof. Graham Shimmield
SEA MAMMAL RESEARCH UNIT, Gatty Marine Laboratory, University of St Andrews, St Andrews KY16 8LB
T 01334-462630
Director, Prof. Ian Boyd
TYNDALL CENTRE FOR CLIMATE CHANGE RESEARCH, School of Environmental Sciences, University of East Anglia, Norwich, Norfolk NR4 7TJ T 01603-593900
Executive Director, Prof. Mike Hulme

SCIENCE AND TECHNOLOGY FACILITIES COUNCIL

Polaris House, North Star Avenue, Swindon SN2 1SZ
T 01793-442000 F 01793-442002 W www.scitech.ac.uk

Formed by royal charter on 1 April 2007, through the merger of the Council for the Central Laboratory of the Research Councils and the Particle Physics and Astronomy Research Council, the STFC is a non-departmental public body reporting to the Department for Innovation, Universities and Skills.

The STFC invests in large national and international research facilities, whilst delivering science, technology and expertise for the UK. The council is involved in research projects including the Diamond Light Source Synchrotron and the Large Hadron Collider, and develops new areas of science and technology. The EPSRC has transferred its responsibility for nuclear physics to the STFC.

Chair, Peter Warry

Chief Executive, Prof. Keith Mason

CHILBOLTON OBSERVATORY, Stockbridge, Hampshire SO20 6BJ T 01264-860391

DARESBURY LABORATORY, Daresbury Science and Innovation Campus, Daresbury WA4 4AD T 01925-603000

RUTHERFORD APPLETON LABORATORY, Harwell Science and Innovation Campus, Didcot OX11 0QX T 01235-445000

UK ASTRONOMY TECHNOLOGY CENTRE, Royal Observatory, Edinburgh, Blackford Hill, Edinburgh EH9 3HJ T 0131-668 8100

RESEARCH AND TECHNOLOGY ORGANISATIONS

Over 30 industrial and technological research bodies are members of the Association of Independent Research and Technology Organisations Limited (AIRTO). Members' activities span a wide range of disciplines from life sciences to engineering. Their work includes basic research, development and design of innovative products or processes, instrumentation testing and certification, and technology and management consultancy. AIRTO publishes a directory to help clients identify the organisations that might be able to assist them. For a full list of members, see AIRTO's website.

AIRTO LTD, c/o CCFRA, Station Road, Chipping Campden, Glos GL55 6LD T 01386-842247 E airto@campden.co.uk W www.airto.co.uk
President, Prof. R. Brook

HEALTH

NATIONAL HEALTH SERVICE

The National Health Service (NHS) came into being on 5 July 1948 under the National Health Service Act 1946, covering England and Wales and, under separate legislation, Scotland and Northern Ireland. The NHS is now administered by the Secretary of State for Health (in England), the Welsh Assembly Government, the Scottish Executive and the Secretary of State for Northern Ireland.

The function of the NHS is to provide a comprehensive health service designed to secure improvement in the physical and mental health of the people and to prevent, diagnose and treat illness. It was founded on the principle that treatment should be provided according to clinical need rather than ability to pay, and should be free at the point of delivery.

Hospital, mental, dental, nursing, ophthalmic and ambulance services and facilities for the care of expectant and nursing mothers and young children are provided by the NHS to meet all reasonable requirements. Rehabilitation services such as occupational therapy, physiotherapy, speech therapy and surgical and medical appliances are supplied where appropriate. Specialists and consultants who work in NHS hospitals can also engage in private practice, including the treatment of their private patients in NHS hospitals.

STRUCTURE

The structure of the NHS remained relatively stable for the first 30 years of its existence. In 1974, a three-tier management structure comprising regional health authorities, area health authorities and district management teams was introduced in England, and the NHS became responsible for community health services. In 1979 area health authorities were abolished and district management teams were replaced by district health authorities.

The National Health Service and Community Care Act 1990 provided for more streamlined regional health authorities and district health authorities, and for the establishment of family health services authorities (FHSA) and NHS trusts. The concept of the 'internal market' was introduced into health care, whereby care was provided through NHS contracts where health authorities or boards and GP fundholders (the purchasers) were responsible for buying health care from hospitals, non-fundholding GPs, community services and ambulance services (the providers). The Act also paved the way for the community care reforms, which were introduced in April 1993, and changed the way care is administered for older people, the mentally ill, the physically disabled and people with learning disabilities.

ENGLAND

Regional health authorities in England were abolished in April 1996 and replaced by eight regional offices which, together with the headquarters in Leeds, formed the NHS executive (which has since been merged with the Department of Health). In April 2002, as an interim arrangement, the eight regional offices were replaced by

four directorates of health and social care (DHSC). In April 2003, the DHSCs were abolished.

HEALTH AUTHORITIES

In April 1996 the district health authorities and family health service authorities were merged to form 100 unified health authorities (HAs) in England. In April 2002, 28 new health authorities were formed from the existing HAs. In October 2002, as part of the new arrangements set out in the NHS Reform and Health Care Professions Act 2002, these new health authorities were renamed strategic health authorities. The whole of England is now split into 10 strategic health authorities (SHAs) each of which is divided into various types of trusts that take responsibilty for running different NHS services locally. The different types of trusts comprise acute trusts (also known as NHS or foundation trusts), ambulance trusts, care trusts, mental health trusts and primary care trusts. SHAs are charged with improving and monitoring the performance of the trusts in their area.

PRIMARY CARE TRUSTS

The first 17 primary care trusts (PCTs) became operational in England on 1 April 2000. There are currently 152 PCTs in England. PCTs were created to give primary care professionals greater control over how resources are best used to benefit patients. PCTs are free-standing statutory bodies responsible for securing the provision of services and integrating health and social care locally. PCTs receive most of their funding directly from the Department of Health and can use this to purchase hospital and other services from NHS trusts and other healthcare providers. They are also responsible for making payments to independent primary care contractors such as GPs and dentists.

Each PCT is overseen by a board, typically comprising a chair; at least five non-executive directors who are appointed by the Appointments Commission; at least five executive members, including the chief executive, finance director and director of public health; and at least two members of the PCT's professional executive committee (PEC), which is made up of health professionals. Clinical expertise is provided by the PEC with representation from local GPs, nurses, other health professionals and social services. The board concentrates on the overall strategies for the trust and ensures the trust meets its statutory, financial and legal obligations.

ACUTE TRUSTS AND FOUNDATION TRUSTS

Hospitals are managed by acute trusts (also known as NHS trusts) that are responsible for the quality of hospital health care and for spending funds efficiently.

First introduced in April 2004, there are now 73 foundation trusts in England. NHS foundation trusts are NHS hospitals, but have their own accountability and governance systems, which function outside of the Department of Health's framework, giving them greater freedom to run their own affairs. NHS foundation trusts treat patients according to NHS principles and standards and are inspected by the Healthcare Commission. The government's aim is that by 2008, all NHS trusts will have reached a standard which will enable them to apply for NHS foundation trust status.

STRATEGIC HEALTH AUTHORITIES

EAST OF ENGLAND, Victoria House, Capital Park, Fulbourn, Cambridge CB21 5XB **T** 01223-597500 **W** www.eoe.nhs.uk

EAST MIDLANDS, Octavia House, Bostocks Lane, Sandiacre, Nottingham NG10 5QG **T** 0115-968 4444 **W** www.eastmidlands.nhs.uk

LONDON, Southside, 105 Victoria Street, London SW1E 6QT **T** 020-7932 3700 **W** www.london.nhs.uk

NORTH EAST, Riverside House, Goldcrest Way, Newcastle upon Tyne NE15 8NY **T** 0191-210 6400 **W** www.northeast.nhs.uk

NORTH WEST, 7th Floor Gateway House, Piccadilly South, Manchester M60 7LP **T** 0161-236 9456 **W** www.northwest.nhs.uk

SOUTH CENTRAL, 1st Floor Rivergate House, Newbury Business Park, London Road, Newbury, Berks RG14 2PZ **T** 01635-275500 **W** www.southcentral.nhs.uk

SOUTH EAST, York House, 18–20 Masetts Road, Horley, Surrey RH6 7DE, **T** 01293-778899 **W** www.southeastcoast.nhs.uk

SOUTH WEST, Wellsprings Road, Taunton, Somerset TA2 7PQ **T** 01823-333491 **W** www.southwest.nhs.uk

WEST MIDLANDS, St Chad's Court, 213 Hagley Road, Edgbaston, Birmingham B16 9RG **T** 0845-155 1022 **W** www.westmidlands.nhs.uk

YORKSHIRE AND THE HUMBER, Blenheim House, West One, Duncombe Street, Leeds LS1 4PL **T** 0113-295 2000 **W** www.yorkshireandhumber.nhs.uk

Contact details for PCTs and other NHS trusts in England can be found on the NHS Choices website (**W** www.nhs.uk).

WALES
LOCAL HEALTH BOARDS AND COMMUNITY HEALTH COUNCILS

In Wales there were five HAs which replaced the former 17 HAs and FHSAs in April 1996. The HAs set up 22 local health groups (LHGs), coterminous with local authority areas (*see* Local Government section), which began work in April 1999. Originally they advised HAs, but in March 2003 the five HAs were abolished and the LHGs, were renamed local health boards (LHB) and took up a role similar to PCTs, assuming responsibility for commissioning services and devising strategies for improving health. They also integrate the delivery of primary and community care. Each local health board has a governing body made up of local doctors, a nurse, other health professionals, members of the local authority and voluntary organisations and others to represent the interests of patients. There is also a small executive team to take action on decisions and provide services for the public. There are also 19 community health councils (CHCs).

SPECIALISED SERVICES AND PUBLIC HEALTH

Although LHBs plan and fund most hospital and family health services there are a few specialised services which are overseen at national level. These services are the responsibility of the Health Commission Wales (specialised services), which was setup in April 2003. The National Public Health Service for Wales also gives advice and guidance to LHBs on a range of issues such as communicable disease protection and control as well as childhood immunisation.

NHS TRUSTS AND HOSPITALS

There are 14 NHS trusts in Wales, including one all-Wales ambulance trust. Between them, the trusts are responsible for managing 119 hospitals.

REGIONAL OFFICES

There are three regional offices of the Welsh Assembly Government for mid and west Wales, north Wales and south east Wales. The regional offices support coordination at local level between LHBs, local authorities and NHS trusts. They have a specific role in ensuring that Welsh Assembly Government initiatives are carried out.

Contact details for the LHBs, community health councils, NHS trusts and all other NHS national and local services in Wales are available in the *NHS Wales Directory* on the NHS Wales website (**W** www.wales.nhs.uk).

SCOTLAND

In Scotland, the Scottish Executive Health Department leads the central management of the NHS, heading a Management Executive, which oversees the work of 14 area health boards responsible for all health services in their area. On 31 March 2006 Argyll and Clyde health board was dissolved and the administrative boundaries for the Greater Glasgow and Highland health boards were changed to allow them to take responsibility for managing the delivery of health services in relevant parts of the Argyll and Clyde area. Greater Glasgow health board took responsibility for healthcare services in Inverclyde, Renfrewshire, West Dunbartonshire and East Renfrewshire and was re-named the Greater Glasgow and Clyde health board. Highland health board took responsibility for healthcare services in Argyll and Bute.

HEALTH BOARDS

AYRSHIRE AND ARRAN, 3 Lister Street, Crosshouse Hospital, Kilmarnock KA2 0BE **T** 01563-577037 **W** www.nhsayrshireandarran.com

BORDERS, Newstead, Melrose TD6 9BD **T** 01896-828282 **W** www.nhsborders.org.uk

DUMFRIES AND GALLOWAY, Mid North, Crichton Hall, Dumfries DG1 4TG **T** 01387-246246 **W** www.nhsdg.scot.nhs.uk

FIFE, Hayfield House, Hayfield Road, Kirkcaldy, Fife KY2 5AH **T** 01592-643355 **W** www.nhsfife.scot.nhs.uk

FORTH VALLEY, Carseview House, Castle Business Park, Stirling FK9 4SW **T** 01786-463031 **W** www.nhsforthvalley.com

GRAMPIAN, Summerfield House, 2 Eday Road, Aberdeen AB15 6RE **T** 0845-456 6000 **W** www.nhsgrampian.org

GREATER GLASGOW AND CLYDE, Dalian House, 350 St Vincent Street, Glasgow G3 8YZ **T** 0141-201 4444 **W** www.nhsggc.org.uk

HIGHLAND, Assynt House, Beechwood Park, Inverness IV2 3HG **T** 01463-717123 **W** www.nhshighland.scot.nhs.uk

LANARKSHIRE, 14 Beckford Street, Hamilton, Lanarkshire ML3 0TA **T** 01698-281313 **W** www.nhslanarkshire.org.uk

LOTHIAN, Deaconess House, 148 Pleasance, Edinburgh EH8 9RS **T** 0131-536 9000 **W** www.nhslothian.scot.nhs.uk

ORKNEY, Garden House, New Scapa Road, Kirkwall, Orkney KW15 1BQ **T** 01856-888000 **W** www.ohb.scot.nhs.uk

SHETLAND, Brevik House, South Road, Lerwick ZE1 0TG **T** 01595-743060 **W** www.shb.scot.nhs.uk

TAYSIDE, Kings Cross, Clepington Road, Dundee DD3 8EA **T** 01382-818479 **W** www.nhstayside.scot.nhs.uk

WESTERN ISLES, 37 South Beach Street, Stornoway, Isle of Lewis HS1 2BB **T** 01851-702997 **W** www.wihb.scot.nhs.uk

NORTHERN IRELAND

In Northern Ireland there are four health and social services boards responsible for commissioning services to meet the needs of their respective populations. They are also responsible for assessing the needs of that population, establishing objectives and developing policies and priorities to meet these objectives.

EASTERN, Champion House, 12–22 Linenhall Street, Belfast BT2 8BS T 028-9032 1313 W www.ehssb.n-i.nhs.uk

NORTHERN, County Hall, 182 Galgorm Road, Ballymena BT42 1QB T 028-2531 1000 W www.nhssb.n-i.nhs.uk

SOUTHERN, Tower Hill, Armagh BT61 9DR T 028-3741 0041 W www.shssb.org

WESTERN, 15 Gransha Park, Clooney Road, Londonderry BT47 6FN T 028-7186 0086 W www.whssb.n-i.nhs.uk

THE NHS PLAN

In July 2000 the government launched the NHS Plan, a ten-year strategy to modernise the health service. In June 2004 it also launched the NHS Improvement Plan, which set out the next stage of NHS reform, moving the focus from access to services towards the broader issues of public health and chronic disease management. The core aims are to sustain increased levels of investment in the NHS and to continue to focus on the improvements outlined in the NHS Plan, while delivering greater levels of choice and information to patients. In July 2004, the Department of Health published *National Standards, Local Action: Health and Social Care Standards and Planning Framework 2005/6–2007/8*, which cut the number of national targets that NHS providers must comply with from 62 to 20. These national targets, which cover areas such as waiting times for accident and emergency treatment, have become national core standards which all providers of care must maintain from April 2005. Alongside this, NHS providers have been given power to set more locally relevant targets.

FINANCE

The NHS is still funded mainly through general taxation, although in recent years more reliance has been placed on the NHS element of national insurance contributions, patient charges and other sources of income.

In the April 2002 budget, the chancellor announced a five-year spending plan for the NHS. Over the years 2003–4 to 2007–8, these plans mean that expenditure on the NHS in the UK will increase on average by 7.2 per cent a year over and above inflation, 7.4 per cent a year for England. The spending plans are set out in the table below:

	UK £ million	% real terms increase*	England £ million	% real terms increase*
2003–4	74,800	7.0	61,300	7.1
2004–5	82,200	7.1	67,400	7.2
2005–6	90,500	7.4	74,400	7.6
2006–7	99,400	7.2	81,800	7.3
2007–8	109,400	7.4	90,200	7.5

* Calculated using GDP deflator at 27 June 2003
Source: Department of Health

PRIVATE FINANCE INITIATIVE

The Private Finance Initiative (PFI) was launched in 1992, and involves the private sector in designing, building, financing and operating new hospitals and primary care premises, which are then leased to the NHS. The NHS Plan committed the NHS to entering into a new public private partnership, Partnerships for Health, a joint venture between the Department of Health and Partnerships UK plc established in September 2001. Its role is to support the development of NHS Local Improvement Finance Trusts (LIFT) by implementing a standard approach to procurement as well as providing some equity. LIFTs are set up as limited companies with the local NHS, Partnerships for Health and the private sector as shareholders. LIFT schemes build and refurbish primary care premises, which the schemes own and then rent to GPs on a lease basis (as well as other parties such as chemists, opticians, dentists etc).

As at April 2007, there were 49 approved LIFT projects in England; of these, 42 had reached financial close. Forty of these schemes now have buildings open to patients. The total capital cost of all schemes at April 2007 was £1045.35m.

EMPLOYEES AND SALARIES

NHS HEALTH SERVICE STAFF (GREAT BRITAIN)
Full-time equivalent

All hospital and community medical staff	93,532
All hospital and community dental staff	3,680
Nursing and midwifery staff	492,391
General medical practitioners	42,531
General dental practitioners	24,123
Ophthalmic medical practitioners	498
Ophthalmic opticians	9,599

Source: ONS – *Annual Abstract of Statistics 2007* (Crown copyright)

SALARIES

General practitioners (GPs), dentists, optometrists and pharmacists are self-employed, and are employed by the NHS under contract. On 20 June 2003 GPs accepted a new practice-based contract which rewards practices for delivering quality and a wider range of services. Dentists receive payment for items of treatment for individual adult patients and, in addition, a continuing care payment for those registered with them. Optometrists receive approved fees for each sight test they carry out. Pharmacists receive professional fees from the NHS and are refunded the cost of prescriptions supplied. Doctors in training receive additional supplements reflecting the intensity and out-of-hours elements of their duties.

SALARIES FOR HOSPITAL MEDICAL AND DENTAL STAFF* *as at 1 April 2007*

Consultant (2003 contract)	£71,822–£96,831
Consultant (pre-2003 contract)	£59,512–£77,300
Senior Registrar	£33,825–£44,581
Specialist Registrar	£29,364–£44,581
Registrar	£29,364–£35,619
Senior House Officer	£26,270–£36,837
House Officer	£21,052–£23,762

* These figures do not include merit awards, discretionary points or banding supplements

NURSES

From 1 December 2004 a new pay system *Agenda for Change* was introduced throughout the UK for all NHS staff with the exception of medical and dental staff, doctors in public health medicine and the community health service. Nurses' salaries are incorporated in the *Agenda for Change* nine pay band structure, which provides additional payments for flexible working such as providing out-of-hours services, working weekends and nights and being 'on-call'. All employers were expected to have moved their staff to the new pay structure by the end of 2006 and all pay and terms and conditions were backdated to 1 October 2004. Under the nine pay band system the minimum starting salary for a registered nurse is £19,166 per annum.

HEALTH SERVICES

PRIMARY CARE

Primary care comprises the services provided by general practitioners, community health centres, pharmacies, dental surgeries and opticians. Primary nursing care includes the work carried out by practice nurses, community nurses, community midwives and health visitors.

PRIMARY MEDICAL SERVICES

In England, primary medical services are the responsibility of primary care trusts (PCT) who contract with healthcare providers – GPs, dentists, pharmacists etc – to provide the service to the NHS. There are four different contracts available to PCTs: the General Medical Services (GMS) contract, which provides flexibility for GPs; the Personal Medical Services (PMS) contract, which is largely locally determined; the Primary Care Trust Medical Services contract (PCTMS), under which PCTs are able to provide services themselves by directly employing staff and the Alternative Provider Medical Services (APMS) contract, which is particularly useful in areas of under-provision as it allows for substantial restructuring of services.

In Wales, responsibility for primary medical services rests with local health boards (LHB), in Scotland with the 14 health boards and in Northern Ireland with the four health and social services boards.

Any vocationally trained doctor may provide general or personal medical services. GPs may also have private fee-paying patients, but not if that patient is already an NHS patient on that doctor's patient list.

A person who is ordinarily resident in the UK is eligible to register with a GP (or PMS provider) for free primary care treatment. Should a patient have difficulty in registering with a doctor, he or she should contact the local PCT for help. When a person is away from home he/she can still access primary care treatment from a GP if they ask to be treated as a temporary resident. In an emergency any doctor in the service will give treatment and advice.

GPs are responsible for the care of their patients 24 hours a day, seven days a week, but can fulfil the terms of their contract by delegating or transferring responsibility for out-of-hours (OOH) care to an accredited provider. Under the GMS contract, practices can opt out of responsibility for patient care during the OOH period. When they do so it becomes the responsibility of the PCT, who can either provide the OOH cover themselves or commission the service from an OOH provider.

Increasingly, some secondary care services, such as minor operations and consultations, can be provided in a primary care setting. The number of such practitioners is growing and the GMS contract provides a platform for further expansion.

In addition a total of 72 NHS walk-in centres are currently operational across the country, with a further 16 centres under development. Usually open seven days a week, from early in the morning until late in the evening, they are nurse-led and provide treatment for minor ailments and injuries, health information and self-help advice.

HEALTH COSTS

Some people are exempt from, or entitled to help with, health costs such as prescription charges, ophthalmic and dental costs, and in some cases help towards travel costs to and from hospital.

The following list is intended as a general guide to those who may be entitled to help, or who are exempt from some of the charges relating to the above:

- children under 16 and young people in full time education who are under 19
- people aged 60 or over
- pregnant women and women who have had a baby in the last 12 months
- people, or their partners, who are in receipt of income support and/or income-based jobseeker's allowance
- people in receipt of the pension credit guarantee credit
- people with a specified medical condition or disability who have a valid exemption certificate
- diagnosed glaucoma patients, people who have been advised by an ophthalmologist that they are at risk of glaucoma and people aged 40 or over who have an immediate family member who is a diagnosed glaucoma patient
- diagnosed diabetic patients
- NHS in-patients
- NHS out-patients for all prescribed contraceptives, medication given at a hospital, NHS walk-in centre, personally administered by a GP or supplied at a hospital or primary care trust clinic for the treatment of a sexually transmissable infection
- patients of the Community Dental Service or an out-patient of the NHS Hospital Dental Service
- people registered blind or partially sighted
- people who need complex lenses
- war pensioners whose treatment/prescription is for their accepted disablement and who have a valid exemption certificate
- people who are entitled to, or named on, a valid NHS tax credit exemption or HC2 certificate

People in other circumstances may also be eligible for help; Booklet HC11 outlines further details and is available from main post offices, local social security offices or online (W www.direct.gov.uk).

WALES

On 1 April 2007 all prescription charges (including those for medical supports and appliances and wigs) for people living in Wales were abolished. The above guide still applies for NHS dental and optical charges although all people aged under 25 living in Wales are also entitled to free dental examinations.

PHARMACEUTICAL SERVICES

Patients may obtain medicines and appliances under the NHS from any pharmacy whose owner has entered into arrangements with the PCT to provide this service. There are also some suppliers who only provide special appliances. In rural areas, where access to a pharmacy may be difficult, patients may be able to obtain medicines, etc, from a dispensing doctor.

In England, a charge of £6.85 is payable for each item

supplied (except for contraceptives for which there is no charge), unless the patient is exempt and the declaration on the back of the prescription form is completed. Prepayment certificates (£26.85* valid for three months, £98.70 valid for a year) may be purchased by those patients not entitled to exemption who require frequent prescriptions. Prescription charges in Scotland and Northern Ireland are currently the same. In Wales NHS prescription charges were abolished on 1 April 2007.

* In Scotland there is only a four month prepayment certificate available at £35.85

DENTAL SERVICES

Dentists, like doctors, may take part in the NHS and also have private patients. Dentists are responsible to the local health provider in whose areas they provide services. Patients may go to any dentist who is taking part in the NHS and is willing to accept them. On 1 April 2006 the charging system for NHS dentistry in England and Wales was changed. There is now a three-tier payment system based on the individual course of treatment required.

COURSE OF TREATMENT COSTS 2007–8

Examination, diagnosis, preventive care* (eg x-rays, scale and polish)	£15.90/£12.00
Examination, diagnosis, preventive care and basic additional treatment (eg fillings, root canal treatment and extractions)	£43.60/£39.00
Examination, diagnosis, preventive care and all other treatment (eg more complex procedures such as crowns, dentures or bridges)	£194.00/£177.00

* Urgent and out-of-hours treatment will also be charged at this payment tier

The cost of individual treatment plan should be known prior to treatment and some dental practices may require payment in advance. There is no charge for writing a prescription or removing stitches and only one charge is payable for each course of treatment even if more than one visit to the dentist is required. If additional treatment is required within two months of visiting the dentist and this is covered by the course of treatment most recently paid for (eg payment was made for the second tier of treatment but an additional filling is required) then this will be provided free of charge.

SCOTLAND

In Scotland, NHS dental patients pay 80 per cent of the total cost of the treatment up to a maximum of £384 during 2007–8. Basic and extensive examinations are free.

GENERAL OPHTHALMIC SERVICES

General ophthalmic services are administered by local health providers. Testing of sight may be carried out by any ophthalmic medical practitioner or ophthalmic optician (optometrist). The optician must give the prescription to the patient, who can take this to any supplier of glasses to have them dispensed. Only registered opticians can supply glasses to children and to people registered as blind or partially sighted.

As at 1 July 2007 the NHS sight test cost was £18.85 in England and Wales. Free eyesight tests and help towards the cost are available to people in certain

circumstances. Help is also available for the purchase of glasses or contact lenses (see Health Costs section or booklet HC11). In Scotland eye examinations, which include a sight test, are free to all. Help is also available for the purchase of glasses or contact lenses to those entitled to help with health costs in the same way it is available to those in England and Wales.

CHILD HEALTH SERVICES

Pre-school services at GP surgeries or child health clinics provide regular monitoring of children's physical, mental and emotional health and development and advise parents on their children's health and welfare.

NHS DIRECT AND NHS 24

NHS Direct is a 24-hour nurse-led advice telephone service for England and Wales. It provides medical advice as well as directing people to the appropriate part of the NHS for treatment if necessary (T 0845-4647).

NHS 24 provides an equivalent service for Scotland (T 0845-424 2424).

SECONDARY CARE AND OTHER SERVICES

HOSPITALS

NHS hospitals provide acute and specialist care services, treating conditions which normally cannot be dealt with by primary care specialists, and provide for medical emergencies.

NUMBER OF BEDS 2005

In-patients	Average daily	
	available beds	occupation of beds
England	176,000	149,000
Wales	14,000	11,000
Scotland	28,100	22,500
Northern Ireland	8,238	6,887

PATIENT ACTIVITY 2005

Out-patient attendances	New patients	Total
England*	13,370,000	44,768,000
Wales	776,000	2,882,000
Scotland	2,720,000	5,990,000
Northern Ireland	1,043,000	2,221,000

* 2004 figures

Source: ONS – *Annual Abstract of Statistics 2007* (Crown copyright)

HOSPITAL CHARGES

Acute or foundation trusts can provide hospital accommodation in single rooms or small wards, if not required for patients who need privacy for medical reasons. The patient is still an NHS patient, but there may be a charge for these additional facilities. Acute or foundation trusts can charge for certain patient services that are considered to be additional treatments over and above the normal hospital service provision. There is no blanket policy to cover this and each case is considered in the light of the patient's clinical need. However, if an item or service is considered to be an integral part of a patient's treatment by their clinician, then a charge should not be made.

In some NHS hospitals, accommodation and services are available for the treatment of private patients where it does not interfere with care for NHS patients. Income generated by treating private patients is then put back into local NHS services. Private patients undertake to pay the full costs of medical treatment, accommodation, medication and other related services. Charges for private patients are set locally.

WAITING LISTS

England

Under the charter *Your Guide to the NHS*, patients were guaranteed admission within 18 months of being placed on a waiting list. In July 2004 a new target, of an 18 week maximum wait from start time (ie seeing a GP) to treatment, was set to be achieved by 2008. Known as the referral to treatment (RTT) pathway, monthly data is published on the NHS 18-weeks website (W www.18weeks.nhs.uk). In May 2007 the number of patients who completed their RTT pathway totalled 277,540; of which 53 per cent were seen within 18 weeks.

Wales

In Wales the number of patients waiting for in-patient or day case treatment totalled 61,267 on 30 June 2007, a decrease from 67,163 in June 2006; of these, 8,085 had been waiting between 22 and 36 weeks, 15,091 between 13 and 22 weeks and 38,090 under 13 weeks. The number of patients waiting for a first out-patient appointment totalled 171,097 in June 2007, compared with 200,550 in June 2006; of these, 65 had been waiting over 36 weeks, 16,426 had been waiting between 22 and 36 weeks, 36,278 between 13 and 22 weeks and 118,328 under 13 weeks.

Scotland

In 2005 the Scottish Executive Health Department published *Delivering for Health* in which is pledged that by the end of 2007 no patient will wait more than 18 weeks from GP or dentist referral to their first out-patient appointment or between a decision being made to undertake treatment and the start of that treatment. At the end of March 2007 84 per cent of patients had been seen within 18 weeks from point of referral, compared with 78.5 per cent of patients in March 2006, and no patients had been waiting more than 18 weeks for in-patient or day-case treatment at the end of March 2007, compared with 6,117 patients at the end of March 2006.

Northern Ireland

Overall the total number of patients waiting to be admitted to hospitals in Northern Ireland at the end of March 2007 was 37,978, compared with 41,448 in March 2006. The number of patients waiting six months and over for an initial out-patient appointment at the end of March 2007 was 32, a reduction of almost 100 per cent from March 2006, when the figure stood at 73,915. Following the achievement of the waiting time targets for 2006–7 the health minister set new targets to ensure that by March 2008 no patient will wait more than 13 weeks for a first out-patient appointment and no more than 21 weeks for in-patient or day-case treatment.

AMBULANCE SERVICE

The NHS provides emergency ambulance services free of charge via the 999 emergency telephone service. Air ambulances, provided through local charities and partially funded by the NHS, are used throughout the UK. They assist with cases where access may be difficult or heavy traffic could hinder road progress. Non-emergency ambulance services are provided free of charge to patients who are deemed to require them on medical grounds.

In 2006–7 in England approximately 6.3 million emergency calls were made to the ambulance service, an increase of 6.3 per cent on the previous year. There were about 3.6 million emergency patient journeys. Since 1 April 2001 all services have had a system of call prioritisation. The prioritisation procedures require all emergency calls to be classified as either immediately life threatening (category A) or other emergency (category B). Services are expected to reach 75 per cent of Category A (life threatening) calls within eight minutes and 95 per cent of category B calls within 19 minutes (since April 2006 there has been no difference in response time for urban or rural areas). In 2006–7, 74.6 per cent of life threatening calls resulted in emergency response arriving at the scene of the incident within eight minutes. For category B calls, 90.5 per cent of incidents were responded to within 19 minutes.

BLOOD SERVICES

There are four national bodies which coordinate the blood donor programme in the UK. Donors give blood at local centres on a voluntary basis.

NATIONAL BLOOD SERVICE, Oak House, Reeds Crescent, Watford, Herts WD24 4QN T 0845-771 1711
W www.blood.co.uk

WELSH BLOOD SERVICE, Ely Valley Road, Talbot Green, Pontyclun CF72 9WB T 01443-622000
W www.welsh-blood.org.uk

SCOTTISH NATIONAL BLOOD TRANSFUSION SERVICE, 21 Ellen's Glen Road, Edinburgh EH17 7QT T 0845-909 0999
W www.scotblood.co.uk

NORTHERN IRELAND BLOOD TRANSFUSION SERVICE, Belfast City Hospital Complex, Lisburn Road, Belfast BT9 7TS
T 028-9032 1414 W www.nibts.org

HOSPICES

Hospice or palliative care may be available for patients with life-threatening illnesses. It may be provided at the patient's home or in a voluntary or NHS hospice or in hospital, and is intended to ensure the best possible quality of life for the patient during their illness, and to provide help and support to both the patient and the patient's family. The National Council for Palliative Care coordinates NHS and voluntary services in England, Wales and Northern Ireland; the Scottish Partnership for Palliative Care performs the same function in Scotland.

NATIONAL COUNCIL FOR PALLIATIVE CARE, The Fitzpatrick Building, 188–194 York Way, London N7 9AS
T 020-7697 1520 W www.ncpc.org.uk

SCOTTISH PARTNERSHIP FOR PALLIATIVE CARE, 1A Cambridge Street, Edinburgh EH1 2DY
T 0131-229 0538 W www.palliativecarescotland.org.uk

NHS CHARTERS

The original Patient's Charter was published in 1991 and came into force in 1992; an expanded version was published in 1995. The charter set out the rights of patients in relation to the standards of service they should expect to receive at all times and standards of service that the NHS aimed to provide.

The Patient's Charter was replaced nationally in 2001 with *Your Guide to the NHS*, which provided information on how to get treatment and gave specific details on minimum standards for patients, targets for the NHS and improvements in the NHS Plan. It also detailed what patients had a right to expect from the NHS and what is expected from patients.

Information for patients about all aspects of the NHS has now been reorganised and is available on the NHS Choices website (W www.nhs.uk).

COMPLAINTS

Firstly, an attempt must be made to resolve the complaint at a local level directly with the healthcare provider concerned. Patient advice and liaison services (PALS) have been established for every NHS and primary care trust in England. PALS are not part of the complaints procedure itself, but can give advice on local complaints procedure, or resolve concerns informally. Secondly, if the case is not resolved locally, an independent review can be requested by the Healthcare Commission in England or by the relevant health and social services board in Northern Ireland. As a final resort, complainants may approach the Health Service Ombudsman in England, the Scottish Public Services Ombudsman, Public Services Ombudsman for Wales or the Commissioner for Complaints in Northern Ireland.

RECIPROCAL ARRANGEMENTS

UK residents are entitled to medical treatment that becomes necessary, at a reduced cost or free of charge, when temporarily visiting a European Union country, Iceland, Liechtenstein, Norway or Switzerland. Only treatment provided under the country's state scheme is covered. A European Health Insurance Card (EHIC) should be obtained before travelling either from the post office, by telephone (T 0845-606 2030) or online (W www.ehic.org.uk).

The UK also has bilateral agreements with several other countries, including Australia and New Zealand, for the free provision of urgent medical treatment.

European Economic Area nationals visiting the UK and visitors from other countries with which the UK has bilateral health care agreements, are entitled to receive emergency health care on the NHS on the same terms as it is available to UK residents.

SOCIAL WELFARE

SOCIAL SERVICES

The Secretary of State for Health (in England), the National Assembly of Wales, the Scottish Executive and the Secretary of State for Northern Ireland are responsible, under the Local Authority Social Services Act 1970, for the provision of social services for older people, disabled people, families and children, and those with mental disorders. Personal social services are administered by local authorities according to policies, with standards set by central and devolved government. Each authority has a director and a committee responsible for the social services functions placed upon them. Local authorities provide, enable and commission care after assessing the needs of their population. The private and voluntary sectors also play an important role in the delivery of social services, and an estimated six million people in the UK provide substantial regular care for a member of their family.

Under the Health and Social Care (Community Health and Standards) Act 2003 the Commission for Social Care Inspection (CSCI) was established in April 2004. The CSCI was established as a single, regulatory authority, to ensure that local authority, private and voluntary care services throughout England are run in accordance with the national minimum standards and regulations that have been set by the government through a system of inspections and self-assessment. In April 2007 the Office for Standards in Education, Children's Services and Skills (OFSTED) was made responsible for inspecting and regulating all care services for children and young people in England; the CSCI is now only responsible for all adult social care services. Both OFSTED and the CSCI collate information on local care services and make this information available to the public.

The Care and Social Services Inspectorate Wales (CSSIW), an operationally independent part of the Welsh Assembly Government, is reponsible for the regulation and inspection of all social care services in Wales and the Scottish Commission for the Regulation of Care (the Care Commission), established in April 2002 under the Regulation of Care (Scotland) Act 2001, is the independent care services regulator for Scotland. The Department of Health, Social Services and Public Safety is responsible for social care services in Northern Ireland.

COMMISSION FOR SOCIAL CARE INSPECTION (CSCI), 33 Greycoat Street, London SW1P 2QF T 020-7979 2000 E enquiries@csci.gsi.gov.uk W www.csci.org.uk

OFFICE FOR STANDARDS IN EDUCATION, CHILDREN'S SERVICES AND SKILLS (OFSTED), Royal Exchange Buildings, St Ann's Square, Manchester M2 7LA T 0845-640 4040 E enquiries@ofsted.gov.uk W www.ofsted.gov.uk

CARE AND SOCIAL SERVICES INSPECTORATE WALES (CSSIW), Cathays Park, Cardiff CF10 3NQ T 01443-848450 E cssiw@wales.gsi.gov.uk W www.cssiw.org.uk

SCOTTISH COMMISSION FOR THE REGULATION OF CARE, Compass House, 11 Riverside Drive, Dundee DD1 4NY T 01382-207100 W www.carecommission.com

DEPARTMENT OF HEALTH, SOCIAL SERVICES AND PUBLIC SAFETY, Castle Buildings, Stormont, Belfast BT4 3SJ T 028-9052 0500 W www.dhsspsni.gov.uk

STAFF

Total social service staff England and Wales	216,500
Home help service	38,200
Field social workers	40,800
Day care establishments staff	30,600
Residential care staff	52,200

Source: ONS – Annual Abstract of Statistics 2007 (Crown copyright)

OLDER PEOPLE

Services for older people are designed to enable them to remain living in their own homes for as long as possible. Local authority services include advice, domestic help, meals in the home, alterations to the home to aid mobility, emergency alarm systems, day and/or night attendants, laundry services and the provision of day centres and recreational facilities. Charges may be made for these services. Respite care may also be provided in order to allow carers temporary relief from their responsibilities.

Local authorities and the private sector also provide 'sheltered housing' for older people, sometimes with resident wardens.

If an older person is admitted to a residential home, charges are made according to a means test; if the person cannot afford to pay, the costs are met by the local authority.

In March 2001 a National Service Framework for Older People was published. The framework set national standards and service models of care across health and social services for older people whether they live at home, in residential care or are being cared for in hospital.

DISABLED PEOPLE

Services for disabled people are designed to enable them to remain living in their own homes wherever possible. Local authority services include advice, adaptations to the home, meals in the home, help with personal care, occupational therapy, educational facilities and recreational facilities. Respite care may also be provided in order to allow carers temporary relief from their responsibilities.

Special housing may be available for disabled people who can live independently, and residential accommodation for those who cannot.

FAMILIES AND CHILDREN

Local authorities are required to provide services aimed at safeguarding the welfare of children in need and, wherever possible, allowing them to be brought up by their families. Services include advice, counselling, help in the home and the provision of family centres. Many authorities also provide short-term refuge accommodation for women and children.

DAY CARE

In allocating day care places to children, local authorities give priority to children with special needs, whether in terms of their health, learning abilities or social needs. Since September 2001 OFSTED has been responsible for the regulation and registration of all early years childcare and education provision in England (previously the responsibility of the local authorities). All day care and childminding services which care for children under eight years of age for more than two hours a day must register with OFSTED and are inspected at least every two years. As at 30 June 2007 there were 1,551,200 registered childcare places and 104,616 registered childcare providers in England.

CHILD PROTECTION

Children considered to be at risk of physical injury, neglect or sexual abuse are placed on the local authority's child protection register. Local authority social services staff, schools, health visitors and other agencies work together to prevent and detect cases of abuse. In England as at 31 March 2006 there were 26,400 children on child protection registers. Of the children registered during 2005–6, 13,700 were at risk of neglect, 5,100 of physical abuse, 2,600 of sexual abuse and 6,700 of emotional abuse. At 31 March 2006 there were 2,163 children on child protection registers in Wales, 2,288 in Scotland and 1,639 in Northern Ireland.

LOCAL AUTHORITY CARE

Local authorities are required to provide accommodation for children who have no parents or guardians or whose parents or guardians are unable or unwilling to care for them. A family proceedings court may also issue a care order where a child is being neglected or abused, or is not attending school; the court must be satisfied that this would positively contribute to the well-being of the child.

The welfare of children in local authority care must be properly safeguarded. Children may be placed with foster families, who receive payments to cover the expenses of caring for the child or children, or in residential care.

Children's homes may be run by the local authority or by the private or voluntary sectors; all homes are subject to inspection procedures. In England as at 31 March 2006, 60,300 children were in the care of local authorities, of these, 42,000 were in foster placements. In Wales 4,529 children were being looked after by local authorities on 31 March 2006, 12,966 in Scotland and 2,436 children in Northern Ireland.

ADOPTION

Local authorities are required to provide an adoption service, either directly or via approved voluntary societies. In the UK, in 2005, 6,161 children (under 18 years of age) were entered onto the Adopted Children Register: 5,582 in England and Wales, 439 in Scotland and 140 in Northern Ireland.

PEOPLE WITH LEARNING DISABILITIES

Services for people with learning disabilities are designed to enable them to remain living in the community wherever possible. Local authority services include short-term care, support in the home, the provision of day care centres, and help with other activities outside the home. Residential care is provided for the severely or profoundly disabled.

MENTALLY ILL PEOPLE

Under the care programme approach, mentally ill people should be assessed by specialist services, receive a care plan and a key worker should be appointed for each patient. Regular reviews of the person's progress should be conducted. Local authorities provide help and advice to mentally ill people and their families, and places in day centres and social centres. Social workers can apply for a mentally disturbed person to be compulsorily detained in hospital. Where appropriate, mentally ill people are provided with accommodation in special hospitals, local authority accommodation, or at homes run by private or voluntary organisations. Patients who have been discharged from hospitals may be placed on a supervision register. *Mental Health National Service Framework* was published in September 1999 setting national standards on how to prevent and treat mental illness.

NATIONAL INSURANCE

The National Insurance (NI) scheme operates under the Social Security Contributions and Benefits Act 1992 and the Social Security Administration Act 1992, and orders and regulations made thereunder. The scheme is financed by contributions payable by earners, employers and others (*see* below). Money collected under the scheme is used to finance the National Insurance Fund (from which contributory benefits are paid) and to contribute to the cost of the National Health Service.

NATIONAL INSURANCE FUND

Estimated receipts, payments and statement of balances of the National Insurance Fund for 2007–8:

Receipts	£ million
Net national insurance contributions	71,747
Compensation from the Consolidated Fund for statutory sick, maternity, paternity and adoption pay recoveries	1,397
Income from investments	1,799
State scheme premiums	118
Other receipts	69
TOTAL RECEIPTS	75,130

Payments	£ million
Benefits	
At present rates	63,574
Increase due to proposed rate changes	2,170
Personal and stakeholder pensions contracted-out rebates	2,156
Age-related rebates for contracted-out money purchase schemes	205
Administration costs	1,470
Redundancy fund payments	251
Transfer to Northern Ireland	452
Other payments	33
TOTAL PAYMENTS	70,313

Balances	£ million
Opening balance	38,475
Excess of receipts over payments	4,817
BALANCE AT END OF YEAR	43,292

CONTRIBUTIONS

There are six classes of National Insurance contributions (NICs):

Class 1	paid by employees and their employers
Class 1A	paid by employers who provide employees with certain benefits in kind for private use, such as company cars
Class 1B	paid by employers who enter into a pay as you earn (PAYE) settlement agreement with HM Revenue and Customs
Class 2	paid by self-employed people
Class 3	voluntary contributions paid to protect entitlement to the state pension for those who do not pay enough NI contributions in another class
Class 4	paid by the self-employed on their taxable profits over a set limit. These are normally paid by self-employed people in addition to class 2 contributions. Class 4 contributions do not count towards benefits.

The lower and upper earnings limits and the percentage rates referred to below apply from April 2007 to April 2008.

CLASS 1

Class 1 contributions are paid where a person:
- is an employed earner (employee), office holder (eg company director) or employed under a contract of service in Great Britain or Northern Ireland
- is 16 or over and under state pension age
- earns at or above the earnings threshold of £100.00 per week (including overtime pay, bonus, commission, etc, without deduction of superannuation contributions)

Class 1 contributions are made up of primary and secondary contributions. Primary contributions are those paid by the employee and these are deducted from earnings by the employer. Since 6 April 2001 the employee's and employer's earnings thresholds have been the same and are referred to as the earnings threshold. Primary contributions are not paid on earnings below the earnings threshold of £100.00 per week. However, between the lower earnings limit of £87.00 per week and the earnings threshold of £100.00 per week, NI contributions are treated as having been paid to protect the benefit entitlement position of lower earners. Contributions are payable at the rate of 11 per cent on earnings between the earnings threshold and the upper earnings limit of £670.00 per week (9.4 per cent for contracted-out employment). Above the upper earnings limit 1 per cent is payable.

Some married women or widows pay a reduced rate of 4.85 per cent on earnings between the earnings threshold and upper earnings limits and 1 per cent above this. It is no longer possible to elect to pay the reduced rate but those who had reduced liability before 12 May 1977 may retain it for as long as certain conditions are met. *See* leaflet *Married Women Paying Reduced Rate National Insurance Contributions (NICs).*

Secondary contributions are paid by employers of employed earners at the rate of 12.8 per cent on all earnings above the earnings threshold of £97.00 per week. There is no upper earnings limit for employers' contributions. Employers operating contracted-out salary related schemes pay reduced contributions of 9.3 per cent; those with contracted-out money-purchase schemes pay 11.8 per cent. The contracted-out rate applies only to that portion of earnings between the earnings threshold and the upper earnings limits. Employers' contributions below and above those respective limits are assessed at the appropriate not contracted-out rate.

CLASS 2

Class 2 contributions are paid where a person is self-employed and is 16 or over and under state pension age. Contributions are paid at a flat rate of £2.20 per week regardless of the amount earned. However, those with earnings of less than £4,635 a year can apply for small earnings exception, eg exemption from liability to pay class 2 contributions. Those granted exemption from class 2 contributions may pay class 2 or class 3 contributions voluntarily. Self-employed earners (whether or not they pay class 2 contributions) may also be liable to pay class 4 contributions based on profits. There are special rules for those who are concurrently employed and self-employed.

Married women and widows can no longer choose not to pay class 2 contributions but those who elected not to pay class 2 contributions before 12 May 1977 may retain the right for as long as certain conditions are met.

Class 2 contributions are collected by the national insurance contributions department of HM Revenue and Customs (HMRC), by direct debit or quarterly bills. *See* leaflet CA04.

CLASS 3

Class 3 contributions are voluntary flat-rate contributions of £7.80 per week payable by persons over the age of 16 who would otherwise be unable to qualify for retirement pension and certain other benefits because they have an insufficient record of class 1 or class 2 contributions. This may include those who are not working, those not liable for class 1 or class 2 contributions or those excepted from class 2 contributions. Married women and widows who on or before 11 May 1977 elected not to pay class 1 (full rate) or class 2 contributions cannot pay class 3 contributions while they retain this right. Class 3 contributions are collected by HMRC by quarterly bills or direct debit. *See* leaflet CA04.

CLASS 4

Self-employed people whose profits and gains are over £5,225 a year pay class 4 contributions in addition to class 2 contributions. This applies to self-employed earners over 16 and under the state pension age. Class 4 contributions are calculated at 8 per cent of annual profits or gains between £5,225 and £34,840 and 1 per cent above. Class 4 contributions are assessed and collected by HMRC. It is possible, in some circumstances, to apply for exceptions from liability to pay class 4 contributions or to have the amount of contribution reduced.

PENSIONS

Many people will qualify for a state pension; however, there are further pension choices available, such as personal and stakeholder pensions. There are also other non-pension savings and investment options. The following section provides background information on existing pension schemes.

STATE PENSION SCHEME

The state pension scheme consists of:
• basic state pension
• additional state pension

People may be able to get both or either when they reach state pension age and meet the qualifying conditions.

The state pension does not have to be claimed at state pension age, people can delay claiming it to earn extra weekly state pension or a lump sum payment.

Basic State Pension

The amount of basic state pension paid is dependent on the number of 'qualifying years' a person has established during their working life. In 2007–8, the full basic state pension is £87.30 a week and the minimum basic state pension is £21.83 a week (*see also* Benefits, State Pension: Categories A and B).

Qualifying Years

A 'qualifying year' is a tax year in which a person has enough earnings on which they have paid, are treated as having paid, or have been credited with national insurance (NI) contributions (*see* National Insurance Credits section). By state pension age, a person needs to have one qualifying year from NI contributions paid or from NI contributions treated as being paid to be eligible for any basic state pension. The number of qualifying years can be reduced if a person qualifies for home responsibilities protection (*see* below).

National Insurance Credits

Those in receipt of carer's allowance, working tax credit (with a disability element), jobseeker's allowance, incapacity benefit, statutory sick pay or statutory maternity pay may have class 1 NI contributions credited to them. Persons undertaking certain training courses or jury service or who have been wrongly imprisoned for a conviction which is quashed on appeal may also get class 1 NI credits for each week they receive benefit or fulfil certain conditions. Class 1 credits are also available to men for the tax years in which they reach age 60 up to age 64, if they are not liable to pay contributions. Class 1 NI credits count toward all future contributory benefits. A class 3 NI credit for basic state pension and bereavement benefit purposes is awarded, where required, for each week the working tax credit (without a disability element) has been received. Class 3 credits are also awarded automatically to young people aged 16 to 18 if they have not paid enough contributions to gain a qualifying year. However, a state pension will not be paid based on a record of NI credits alone.

Working Life

Working life is counted from the start of the tax year in which a person reaches 16 to the end of the tax year before the one in which they reach state pension age: for men this is normally 49 years and for women this varies between 44 and 49 years depending on their birth date (*see* State Pension Age). To get the full rate (100 per cent) basic state pension a person must normally have qualifying years for about 90 per cent of their working life. To get the minimum basic state pension (25 per cent) a person will normally need ten or eleven qualifying years.

State Pension Age

State pension age is:
• 65 for men
• 60 for women born on or before 5 April 1950
• 65 for women born on or after 6 April 1955

Women born between 6 April 1950 and 5 April 1955 will have a state pension age between 60 and 65 depending on their date of birth. Further information can be obtained from the online state pension calculator (W www.thepensionservice.gov.uk/resourcecentre/statepensioncalc.asp).

Using the NI Contribution Record of Another Person to Claim a State Pension

Married women who are not entitled to a state pension on their own NI contributions may get a basic state pension calculated using their husband's NI contribution record. A basic state pension may be paid of up to 60 per cent of the husband's entitlement (up to £52.30 a week in 2007–8). From 6 April 2010, married men and civil partners will be able to claim a basic state pension based on their wife or civil partner's NI contributions if better than one based on their own record and if their wife or civil partner was born after 6 April 1950. A state pension is also payable to widows, widowers, surviving civil partners, and people who are divorced or whose civil partnership has been dissolved, based on their late or ex-spouse's/civil partner's NI contributions.

Non-contributory State Pensions

A non-contributory state pension may be payable to those aged 80 or over who live in England, Scotland or Wales, and have done so for a total of ten years or more for any continuous period in the 20 years after their 60th birthday, if they are not entitled to another category of state pension, or are entitled to one below the rate of £52.30 a week in 2007–8 (see also Benefits, State Pension: Category D).

Graduated Retirement Benefit

Graduated Retirement Benefit (GRB) is based on the amount of graduated NI contributions paid into the GRB scheme between April 1961 and April 1975.

Home Responsibilities Protection

It is possible for people who have a low income or are unable to work because they care for children or a sick or disabled person at home to reduce the number of qualifying years required. This is called home responsibilities protection (HRP) and can be given for any tax year since April 1978; the number of years for which HRP is given is deducted from the number of qualifying years needed. HRP may, in some cases, also qualify the recipient for additional state pension. Since April 2003, HRP has also been available to approved foster carers.

Additional State Pension

The amount of additional state pension paid depends on the amount of earnings a person has, or is treated as having, between the lower and upper earnings limits for each complete tax year between 6 April 1978 (when the scheme started) and the tax year before they reach state pension age. The right to additional state pension does not depend on the person's right to basic state pension.

From 1978 to 2002, additional state pension was called the State Earnings-Related Pension Scheme (SERPS). SERPS covered all earnings by employees from 6 April 1978 to 5 April 1997 on which standard rate class 1 NI contributions had been paid, and earnings between 6 April 1997 and 5 April 2002 if the standard rate class 1 NI contributions had been contracted-in.

In 2002, SERPS was reformed through the state second pension, by improving the pension available to low and moderate earners and extending access to certain carers and people with long-term illness or disability. If earnings on which class 1 NI contributions have been paid or can be treated as paid are above the annual NI lower earnings limit (£4,524 for 2007–8) but below the statutory low earnings threshold (£13,000 for 2007–8), the state second pension regards this as earnings of £13,000 and it is treated as equivalent. Certain carers and people with long-term illness and disability will be considered as having earned at the low earnings threshold for each complete tax year since 2002–3 even if they do not work at all, or earn less than the annual NI lower earnings limit.

The amount of additional state pension paid also depends on when a person reaches state pension age; changes phased in from 6 April 1999 mean that pensions are calculated differently from that date.

Inheritance

Men or women widowed before 6 October 2002 can inherit all of their late spouse's SERPS pension. From 6 October 2002, the maximum percentage of SERPS pension that a person can inherit from a late spouse or civil partner depends on their late spouse or civil partner's date of birth:

Maximum SERPS entitlement	d.o.b (men)	d.o.b (women)
100%	5/10/37 or earlier	5/10/42 or earlier
90%	6/10/37 to 5/10/39	6/10/42 to 5/10/44
80%	6/10/39 to 5/10/41	6/10/44 to 5/10/46
70%	6/10/41 to 5/10/43	6/10/46 to 5/10/48
60%	6/10/43 to 5/10/45	6/10/48 to 5/7/50
50%	6/10/45 or later	6/7/50 or later

The maximum state second pension a person can inherit from a late spouse or civil partner is 50 per cent.

Pension Forecasts

The Pension Service provides a state pension forecasting service by phone (T 0845-300 0168) or online (W www.thepensionservice.gov.uk).

PRIVATE PENSION SCHEMES

Contracted-Out Appropriate Personal Pension Schemes

Since July 1988 an employee has been able to start a personal pension which, if it meets certain conditions, can be used in place of the additional state pension. These pensions are known as appropriate personal pensions (APPs). The part of an APP derived from the protected rights (rights comprising mainly the NI contribution rebate and its investment return) is intended to provide benefits broadly equivalent to those given up in the additional state pension. At retirement, a contracted-out deduction will be made from additional state pension built up from 6 April 1987 to 5 April 1997. The reduction may be more or less than that part of the pension derived from the protected rights. From 6 April 1997 to 5 April 2002, members of an APP scheme will not have built up any entitlement to additional state pension during the period of their membership. From 6 April 2002, employees contracted-out into a personal pension and earning between the lower earnings limit and the low earnings threshold (£4,524 and £13,000 in 2007–8) will be entitled to a reduced amount of additional state pension.

Contracted-Out Salary-Related (COSR) Scheme

- these schemes (also known as contracted-out defined benefit (DB) schemes) provide a pension related to earnings and the length of pensionable service
- any notional additional state pension built up from 6 April 1978 to 5 April 1997 will be reduced by the amount of guaranteed minimum pension (GMP) built up during that period (the contracted-out deduction)
- from 6 April 1997 these schemes no longer provide a GMP. Instead, as a condition of contracting out they have to satisfy a reference scheme test to ensure that the benefits provided are at least as good as a prescribed standard
- when someone contracts out of the additional state pension through a COSR scheme, both the scheme member and the employer, pay a reduced rate of NI contributions (known as the contracted-out rebate) to compensate for the additional state pension given up

Contracted-Out Money Purchase (COMP) Scheme

- these schemes (also known as contracted-out defined contribution (DC) schemes) provide a pension based on the value of the fund at retirement, ie the money paid in, along with the investment return

- the part of the COMP fund derived from protected rights (rights made up mainly from the contracted-out rebate and its investment return) is intended to provide benefits broadly equivalent to those given up in the additional state pension
- a contracted-out deduction, which may be more or less than that part of the pension derived from the protected rights, will be made from any notional additional pension built up from 6 April 1988 to 5 April 1997
- as with a COSR scheme, when someone contracts out of the additional state pension through a COMP scheme, both the scheme member and the employer pay a reduced rate of NI contributions (the contracted-out rebate) to compensate for the state pension given up. In addition, at the end of each tax year, HM Revenue and Customs pays an additional age-related rebate direct to the scheme for investment on behalf of the employee

Contracted-Out Mixed Benefit (COMB) Scheme

A mixed benefit scheme is a single scheme with both a salary related section and a money purchase section. Scheme rules set out which section individual employees may join and the circumstances (if any), in which members may move between sections. Each section must satisfy the respective contracting-out conditions for COSR and COMP schemes.

For more information on contracted-out pension schemes see the Department for Work and Pensions' leaflet PM7 Contracting out of State Second Pension – Your Guide.

STAKEHOLDER PENSION SCHEMES

Introduced in 2001, stakeholder pensions are available to everyone but are principally for moderate earners who do not have access to a good value company pension scheme. Stakeholder pensions must meet a number of minimum standards to make sure they are flexible, portable and annual management charges are capped. The minimum contribution is £20 per month.

As with personal pensions it is possible to invest up to £3,600 (including tax relief) into stakeholder pensions each year without evidence of earnings. Contributions can be made on someone else's behalf, for example, a non-working partner. If it meets certain conditions, it can be used to contract out of the additional state pension (formerly SERPS). When someone contracts out of the state scheme with either an APP or a stakeholder pension, both the employee and their employers pay NI contributions at the full not contracted-out rate. At the end of the tax year to which those NI contributions relate, HM Revenue and Customs pays an age-related rebate (which increases with age) and tax relief on the employee's share of the rebate directly into the scheme for investment on behalf of the employee.

COMPLAINTS

The Pensions Advisory Service gives free help and advice to people who have problems with occupational or personal pensions. There are two bodies for pension complaints. The Financial Ombudsman Service deals with complaints which predominantly concern the sale and/or marketing of occupational, stakeholder and personal pensions. The Pensions Ombudsman deals with complaints which predominantly concern the management (after sale or marketing) of occupational, stakeholder and personal pensions. The Pensions Regulator is the UK regulator for work-based pension schemes; it concentrates its resources on schemes where there is the greatest risk to the security of members' benefits, promotes good administration practice for all work-based schemes and works with trustees, employers and professional advisers to put things right when necessary.

WAR PENSIONS AND THE ARMED FORCES COMPENSATION SCHEME

The Service Personnel and Veterans Agency (SPVA), formerly the Veterans Agency, is an executive agency of the Ministry of Defence. SPVA was formed on 1 April 2007 from the former Armed Services Personnel Administration Agency and the Veterans Agency to provide services to both serving personnel and veterans. SPVA is responsible for the administration of the war pensions scheme and the armed forces compensation scheme (AFCS) to members of the armed forces in respect of disablement or death due to service. There is also a scheme for civilians and civil defence workers in respect of the Second World War, and other schemes for groups such as merchant seamen and Polish armed forces who served under British command during the Second World War. The agency is also responsible for the administration of the armed forces pension scheme, which provides occupational pensions for ex-service personnel (see Defence).

THE WAR PENSIONS SCHEME

War disablement pension is awarded for the disabling effects of any injury, wound or disease which was the result of, or was aggravated by, conditions of service in the armed forces prior to 6 April 2005. Claims are only considered once the person has left the armed forces. The amount of pension paid depends on the severity of disablement, which is assessed by comparing the health of the claimant with that of a healthy person of the same age and sex. The person's earning capacity or occupation are not taken into account in this assessment. A pension is awarded if the person has a disablement of 20 per cent or more and a lump sum is usually payable to those with a disablement of less than 20 per cent. No award is made for noise-induced sensorineural hearing loss where the assessment of disablement is less than 20 per cent.

A pension is payable to war widows, widowers and surviving civil partners where the spouse's or civil partner's death was due to, or hastened by, service in the armed forces, prior to 6 April 2005, or where the spouse or civil partner was in receipt of a war disablement pension constant attendance allowance (or would have been if not in hospital) at the time of death. A pension is also payable to widows, widowers or surviving civil partners if the spouse or civil partner was receiving the war disablement pension at the 80 per cent rate or higher in conjunction with unemployability supplement at the time of death. War widows, widowers and surviving civil partners receive a standard rank-related rate, but a lower weekly rate is payable to war widows, widowers and surviving civil partners of personnel below the rank of Major who are under the age of 40, without children and capable of maintaining themselves. This is increased to the standard rate at age 40. Allowances are paid for children (in addition to child benefit) and adult dependants. An age allowance is automatically given when the widow, widower or surviving civil partner reaches 65 and increased at ages 70 and 80.

All war pensions and pensions for war widows,

widowers and surviving civil partners are tax-free and pensioners living overseas receive the same amount as those resident in the UK.

SUPPLEMENTARY ALLOWANCES

A number of supplementary allowances may be awarded to a war pensioner which are intended to meet various needs which may result from disablement or death and take account of its particular effect on the pensioner, pensioner's spouse or civil partner. The principal supplementary allowances are unemployability supplement, allowance for lowered standard of occupation and constant attendance allowance. Others include exceptionally severe disablement allowance, severe disablement occupational allowance, treatment allowance, mobility supplement, comforts allowance, clothing allowance, age allowance and widow/widower/surviving civil partner's age allowance. Rent and children's allowances are also available on pensions for war widows, widowers and surviving civil partners.

ARMED FORCES COMPENSATION SCHEME

The armed forces compensation scheme (AFCS) became effective on 6 April 2005 and covers all regular (including Gurkhas) and reserve personnel whose injury, ill health or death is caused by service on or after 6 April 2005. Ex-members of the armed forces who served prior to this date or who are in receipt of any pension under the war pensions scheme will continue to receive their pension and any associated benefits in the normal way. The new scheme affects only those who served after 6 April 2005.

The AFCS provides compensation where service in the armed forces is the only or main cause of injury, illness or death. Compensation can also be paid in certain exceptional circumstances to off-duty personnel, for example, to victims of a terrorist attack targeted due to their position in the armed forces. Under the terms of the scheme a lump sum is payable to service or ex-service personnel based on a 15-level tariff, graduated according to the seriousness of the condition. A guaranteed income payment (GIP), payable for life, is received by those who could be expected to experience a serious loss of earning capability. A GIP will also be paid to surviving partners (including spouses, civil and unmarried partners). GIP is calculated by multiplying the pensionable pay of the service person by a factor which depends on the age of the person's last birthday. The younger the person, the higher the factor, because there are more years to normal retirement age.

DEPARTMENT FOR WORK AND PENSIONS BENEFITS

Most benefits are paid in addition to those in receipt of payments under the AFCS and the war pensions scheme, but may be affected by any supplementary allowances in payment. Any state pension for which a war widow, widower or surviving civil partner qualifies for on their own NI contribution record can be paid in addition to monies received under the war pensions scheme.

CLAIMS AND QUESTIONS

Further information on the war pensions scheme, the armed forces compensation scheme and the nearest War Pensioners' Welfare Office can be obtained from the Service Personnel and Veterans Agency by telephone (T 0800-169 2277, if calling from the UK or, if living overseas, T (+44) (125) 386-6043).

SERVICE PERSONNEL AND VETERANS AGENCY, Norcross, Blackpool FY5 3WP E veterans.help@spva.gsi.gov.uk W www.veterans-uk.info

TAX CREDITS

Tax credits are administered by HM Revenue and Customs and are awarded for up to 12 months, although they can be adjusted during the year to reflect changes in income or circumstances.

WORKING TAX CREDIT

Working tax credit is made up of a basic payment with additional payments for couples, lone parents, people working over 30 hours a week, disabled workers and people aged 50 or over returning to work after a period of benefits. The tax credit is paid with wages to people who are employed and directly to the self-employed. It is available to:

- people with dependent children and/or a disability, working at least 16 hours a week
- people aged 25 or over and working at least 30 hours a week

The aim of the tax credit system is to provide a guaranteed minimum income from full-time work for those aged 25 or over, of £212 a week for couples, and £180 a week for single people. This is increased for those with a disability or for those with children. The system makes assumptions based on the national minimum wage and the number of hours worked per week. An annual income of £8,479 represents the 2007–8 income of an adult working 30 hours a week at the national minimum wage: six months at the 2006-7 rate of £5.35 per hour and six months at the rate of £5.52 per hour (national minimum wage from October 2007).

WORKING TAX CREDIT 2007–8

Annual Income/Status	Tax credit per annum
£5,000*	
Single	–
Couple	–
Single adult with a disability	£4,040
£8,479†	
Single	£1,230
Couple	£2,930
Single adult with a disability	£3,540
£10,000	
Single	£665
Couple	£2,370
Single adult with a disability	£2,980
£15,000	
Single	–
Couple	£520
Single adult with a disability	£1,130

* Those with incomes of £5,000 a year are assumed to work part-time (working between 16 and 30 hours a week).

† Income of £8,479 represents the income of an adult working 30 hours per week at the national minimum wage rate (*see* above for explanation). In families with an income of £8,479 a year or more, at least one adult is assumed to be working 30 or more hours a week.

CHILDCARE

In families with children where a lone parent or both partners in a couple work for at least 16 hours a week, or where one partner works and the other is disabled, the family is entitled to the childcare element of working tax credit. This payment can contribute up to 70 per cent of childcare costs up to a maximum of £175 a week for one child and up to £300 a week for two or more children. Families can only claim if they use an approved or registered childcare provider.

CHILD TAX CREDIT

Child tax credit combines all income-related support for children and is paid direct to the main carer. The credit is made up of a main 'family' payment with additional payments for each extra child in the household, for children with a disability and an extra payment for children who are severely disabled. Child tax credit is available to households where:

- there is at least one dependant under 16-years-old
- there is at least one dependant under 19-years-old and in full-time non-advanced education or registered with the Careers or Connexions Service (does not include Scotland or Northern Ireland)

CHILD TAX CREDIT AND WORKING TAX CREDIT 2007–8 (£ PER YEAR)

	One Child		Two Children	
Annual Income	No Childcare	Maximum Childcare	No Childcare	Maximum Childcare
0	2,390	2,390	4,240	4,240
5,000*	5,825	13,145	7,675	20,220
8,479*	5,325	12,645	7,175	19,720
10,000†	4,760	12,080	6,610	19,160
15,000	2,910	10,230	4,760	17,310
20,000	1,060	8,380	2,910	15,460
25,000	545	6,530	1,060	13,610
30,000	545	4,680	545	11,760
35,000	545	2,830	545	9,910
40,000	545	980	545	8,060
45,000	545	545	545	6,210
50,000	545	545	545	4,360
60,000	–	–	–	660
65,000	–	–	–	230
70,000	–	–	–	–

* At income levels of £5,000 and £8,479 awards are shown for lone parents. At an income level of £5,000 the award is shown for a lone parent working part-time (between 16 and 30 hours a week). At an income level of £8,479 the award is shown for a lone parent working 30 hours a week.

† At an income level of £10,000 awards are shown for two parents working part-time (between 16 and 30 hours per week)

BENEFITS

The following is intended as a general guide to the benefits system. Conditions of entitlement and benefit rates change annually and all prospective claimants should check exact entitlements and rates of benefit directly with their local Jobcentre Plus office, pension centre or online (W www.direct.gov.uk). Leaflets relating to the various benefits and contribution conditions for different benefits are available from local Jobcentre Plus offices; leaflet BRA5DWP *Social Security Benefit Rates* is a general guide to benefit rates and contributions.

CONTRIBUTORY BENEFITS

Entitlement to contributory benefits depends on national insurance contribution conditions being satisfied either by the claimant or by someone on the claimant's behalf (depending on the kind of benefit). The class or classes of national insurance contribution relevant to each benefit are:

Jobseeker's allowance (contribution-based)	Class 1
Incapacity benefit	Class 1 or 2
Widow's benefit and bereavement benefit	Class 1, 2 or 3
State pensions, categories A and B	Class 1, 2 or 3

The system of contribution conditions relates to yearly levels of earnings on which national insurance (NI) contributions have been paid.

JOBSEEKER'S ALLOWANCE

Jobseeker's allowance (JSA) replaced unemployment benefit and income support for unemployed people under state pension age from 7 October 1996. There are two routes of entitlement. Contribution-based JSA is paid at a personal rate (ie additional benefit for dependants is not paid) to those who have made sufficient NI contributions in two particular tax years. Savings and partner's earnings are not taken into account and payment can be made for up to six months. Rates of JSA correspond to income support rates.

Claims are made through Jobcentre Plus. A person wishing to claim JSA must generally be unemployed or working on average less than 16 hours a week, capable of work and available for any work which he or she can reasonably be expected to do, usually for at least 40 hours per week. The claimant must agree and sign a 'jobseeker's agreement', which will set out his or her plans to find work, and must actively seek work. If the claimant refuses work or training the benefit may be sanctioned for between one and 26 weeks.

A person will be sanctioned from JSA for up to 26 weeks if he or she has left a job voluntarily without just cause or through misconduct. In these circumstances, it may be possible to receive hardship payments, particularly where the claimant or the claimant's family is vulnerable, eg if sick or pregnant, or with children or caring responsibilities. *See* leaflet JSAL5 *(JSA – Helping You Back to Work)*.

INCAPACITY BENEFIT

Incapacity benefit is available to those who are incapable of work but cannot get statutory sick pay from their employer. It is not payable to those over state pension age. However, people who are already in receipt of short-term incapacity benefit when they reach state pension age may continue to receive this benefit for up to 52 weeks. Apart from those who qualify under the special provisions for people incapacitated in youth, entitlement is based on a person's NI contribution record. In order to qualify for incapacity benefit, two contribution conditions, based on the last three tax years before the year in which benefit is claimed, must be satisfied. The amount of incapacity benefit payable may be reduced where a claimant receives more than a specified amount of occupational or personal pension. People who became incapable of work before the age of 20 (or 25 for those who were in education or training before the age of 20) may receive incapacity benefit without meeting the NI contribution conditions. There are three rates of incapacity benefit:
• short-term lower rate for the first 28 weeks of sickness
• short-term higher rate from weeks 29 to 52
• long-term rate from week 53 onwards
The terminally ill and those entitled to the highest rate care component of disability living allowance are paid the long-term rate after 28 weeks. Incapacity benefit is taxable after 28 weeks.

Two rates of age addition are paid, with long-term benefit based on the claimant's age when incapacity started. The higher rate is payable where incapacity for work commenced before the age of 35, and the lower rate where incapacity commenced before the age of 45.

Increases are made for claimants over the age of 60 and for adult dependants. Dependent children are provided for through the child tax credit system.

There are two medical tests of incapacity: the 'own occupation' test and the 'personal capability' assessment. Those who worked before becoming incapable of working will be assessed, for the first 28 weeks of incapacity, on their ability to do their own job. After 28 weeks (or from the start of incapacity for those who were not working) claimants are assessed on their ability to carry out a range of work-related activities. *See* leaflets IB1 and IB214. New incapacity benefit claimants will be invited back for work-focused interviews at intervals of not longer than three years. The interviews do not include medical tests, but if the claimant is due for a medical test around the same time, their local office will aim to schedule both together. People who are severely disabled and those who are terminally ill will not be asked to attend these interviews.

BEREAVEMENT BENEFITS

Bereavement benefits replaced widow's benefit on 9 April 2001. Those claiming widow's benefit before this date will continue to receive them under the old scheme for as long as they qualify. The new system provides bereavement benefits for widows, widowers and, from 5 December 2005, surviving civil partners (providing that their deceased spouse or civil partner paid NI contributions). The new system offers benefits in three forms:
• *Bereavement payment* – may be received by a man or woman who is under the state pension age at the time of their spouse or civil partner's death, or whose husband, wife or civil partner was not entitled to a category A retirement pension when he or she died. It is a single tax-free lump sum of £2,000 payable immediately on widowhood or loss of a civil partner
• *Widowed parent's allowance* – a taxable benefit payable to the surviving partner if he or she is entitled or treated as entitled to child benefit, or to a widow if she is expecting her husband's baby at the time of his death
• *Bereavement allowance* – a taxable weekly benefit paid for 52 weeks after the spouse or civil partner's death. If aged over 55 and under state pension age the full

allowance is payable, if aged between 45 and 54 a percentage of the full rate is paid. A widow, widower or surviving civil partner may receive this allowance if his or her widowed parent's allowance ends before 52 weeks.

It is not possible to receive widowed parent's allowance and bereavement allowance at the same time. Bereavement benefits and widow's benefit, in any form, cease upon remarriage or a new civil partnership or are suspended during a period of cohabitation as partners without being legally married or in a civil partnership. *See* leaflets GL14 and D49 (D49S for deaths that occur in Scotland).

STATE PENSION: CATEGORIES A AND B

Category A pension is payable for life to men and women who reach state pension age, who satisfy the contributions conditions and who claim for it. Category B pension is payable for life to married women, widows, widowers and surviving civil partners and is based on their wife, husband or civil partner's contributions. It is payable to a married woman only when both the wife and husband have claimed their state pension and they have both reached state pension age. From April 2010 a married man and civil partner will be able to qualify for a category B pension from their wife's or civil partner's contributions providing the wife or civil partner were born on or after 6 April 1950. Category B pension is also payable on widowhood or death of a civil partner after state pension age. Category B pension is payable to widows regardless of the age of their husband when he died, although at present, it is only paid to widowers and civil partners if their wife or civil partner had reached state pension age when they died. Widowers or surviving civil partners who reach state pension age on or after 6 April 2010 will be able to get a category B pension on the same terms as widows. There are special rules for those whose spouse or civil partner dies before reaching state pension age.

Where a person is entitled to both a category A and category B pension then they can be combined to give a composite pension, but this cannot be more than the full rate pension. Where a person is entitled to more than one category A or category B pension then only one can be paid. In such cases the person can choose which to get; if no choice is made, the most favourable one is paid.

A person may defer claiming their pension beyond state pension age. In doing so they may earn increments which will increase the weekly amount paid by one per cent per five weeks of deferral (equivalent to 10.4 per cent/year) when they claim their state pension. If a person delays claiming for at least 12 months they are given the option of a one-off taxable lump sum, instead of a pension increase, based on the weekly pension deferred, plus interest. If a married man defers his category A pension, his wife cannot claim a category B pension on his contributions but she may earn increments on her state pension during this time. A woman can defer her category B pension, and earn increments, even if her husband is claiming his category A pension.

The basic state pension is £87.30 per week plus any additional (earnings-related) state pension the person may be entitled to. An increase of £52.30 is paid for an adult dependant, providing the dependant's earnings do not exceed the rate of Jobseeker's Allowance for a single person (*see* below) and the couple are living together. If the couple are not living together an increase is payable if the dependant's earnings are not above £52.30. Before

April 2003 it was also possible to get an increase of category A and B pensions for a child or children, since this date provision for children has been made through child tax credits. An age addition of 25p per week is payable with a state pension if a pensioner is aged 80 or over.

The category B pension provides up to £52.30 a week for a married woman and up to £87.30 a week for a widow, widower or surviving civil partner.

Since 1989 pensioners have been allowed to have unlimited earnings without affecting their state pension.

GRADUATED RETIREMENT BENEFIT

Graduated NI contributions were first payable from April 1961 and were calculated as a percentage of earnings between certain bands. The graduated retirement benefit scheme existed until April 1975, however, it is still paid in addition to any state pension, to those who made the relevant contributions. A person will receive graduated retirement benefit based on their own contributions, even if not entitled to a basic state pension. Widows, widowers and surviving civil partners may inherit half of their deceased spouse's or civil partner's entitlement, but none that the deceased spouse or civil partner may have been eligible for from a former spouse or civil partner.

Graduated retirement benefit is calculated using a weekly rate for each 'unit' of graduated contributions paid by the employee (half a unit or more counts as a whole unit); the rate varies from person to person. A unit of graduated retirement benefit can be calculated by adding together all graduated contributions and dividing by 7.5 (men) or 9 (women). If a person defers making a claim beyond state pension age, they may earn an increase or a one-off lump sum payment in respect of their deferred graduated retirement benefit; calculated in the same way as for the category A or B state pension.

WEEKLY RATES OF CONTRIBUTORY BENEFITS
from April 2007

Jobseeker's allowance (JSA) (contribution-based)

Person under 18	£35.65
Person aged 18–24	£46.85
Person aged 25 to state pension age*	£59.15

* Since October 2003 people aged between 60 and state pension age can choose to claim pension credits instead of JSA.

Short-term incapacity benefit

Person under state pension age	
Lower rate	£61.35
Higher rate	£72.55
Increase for adult dependant	£37.90
Person over state pension age	
Lower rate	£78.05
Higher rate	£81.35
Increase for adult dependant	£46.80

Long-term incapacity benefit

Person under state pension age	£81.35
Increase for adult dependant	£48.65
Age addition – lower rate	£8.55
Age addition – higher rate	£17.10

Widow's benefits

Widowed mother's allowance	£87.30
Widow's pension, full entitlement	
(aged 55 or over at time of spouse's death)	£87.30

Amount of widow's pension by age of widow at spouse's death (for deaths occurring before 11 April 1988 refer to the age-points in brackets):

aged 54 (49)	£81.19
aged 53 (48)	£75.08
aged 52 (47)	£68.97
aged 51 (46)	£62.86
aged 50 (45)	£56.75
aged 49 (44)	£50.63
aged 48 (43)	£44.52
aged 47 (42)	£38.41
aged 46 (41)	£32.30
aged 45 (40)	£26.19

Bereavement benefit

Bereavement payment (lump sum)	£2,000
Widowed parent's allowance	£87.30
Bereavement allowance, full entitlement (aged 55 and over at time of spouse's or civil partner's death)	£87.30

Amount of bereavement allowance by age of widow/widower or surviving civil partner at spouse's or civil partner's death:

aged 54	£81.19
aged 53	£75.08
aged 52	£68.97
aged 51	£62.86
aged 50	£56.75
aged 49	£50.63
aged 48	£44.52
aged 47	£38.41
aged 46	£32.30
aged 45	£26.19

State Pension: Categories A and B

Category A or B pension for a single person	£87.30
Category B pension (married women)	£52.30
Increase for adult dependant	£52.30
Age addition at age 80	£0.25

NON-CONTRIBUTORY BENEFITS

These benefits are paid from general taxation and are not dependent on NI contributions.

JOBSEEKER'S ALLOWANCE (INCOME-BASED)

Those who do not qualify for contribution-based jobseeker's allowance (JSA(c)), those who have exhausted their entitlement to contribution-based JSA or those for whom contribution-based JSA provides insufficient income may qualify for income-based JSA. The amount paid depends on age, whether they are single or a couple, number of dependants and amount of income and savings. Income-based JSA is comprised of three parts:

- a personal allowance for the jobseeker and his/her partner*
- premiums for people with special needs
- amounts for housing costs

* Since April 2003, child dependants have been provided for through the child tax credit system, although an increase in JSA for dependent children is still available for existing claimants.

The rules of entitlement are the same as for contribution-based JSA.

If one person in a couple was born after 28 October 1957 and neither person in the couple has responsibility for a child or children, then the couple will have to make a joint claim for JSA if they wish to receive income-based JSA.

MATERNITY ALLOWANCE

Maternity allowance (MA) is a benefit available for pregnant women who are self-employed or otherwise do not qualify for statutory maternity pay (SMP) from their employers. In order to qualify for payment, a woman must have been employed and/or self-employed for at least 26 weeks in the 66 week period up to and including the week before the baby is due (test period). She must also have average weekly earning of at least £30 (maternity allowance threshold) over any 13 weeks of the woman's choice within the test period. Women who are self-employed are deemed to have enough earnings (£125.28 a week) to result in the standard rate of MA being payable. Self-employed women holding a small earnings exception certificate are treated as having earnings equal to the maternity allowance threshold. A woman can choose to start receiving MA from the 11th week before the week in which the baby is due up to the day following the day of birth. The exact date MA starts will depend on when the woman stops work to have her baby or if the baby is born before she stops work. However, where the woman is absent from work wholly or partly due to pregnancy on or after the Sunday of the 4th week before the baby is due to be born, MA will start the day following the first day of absence from work. MA is paid for a maximum of 39 weeks regardless of when the baby is actually born.

For more information *see* leaflet NI17A *A Guide to Maternity Benefits* available on the Department for Work and Pensions website (W www.dwp.gov.uk/advisers/ni17a/).

CHILD BENEFIT

Child benefit is payable for virtually all children aged under 16, for those aged 16 to 18 in full-time education or in a programme of approved training, for those aged 16 or 17 who have registered with Connexions or the Careers Service (or the equivalent in Northern Ireland) and those aged 19 who are in full-time education or approved training which started before their 19th birthday.

GUARDIAN'S ALLOWANCE

Guardian's allowance is payable to a person who is bringing up a child or young person because the child's parents have died, or in some circumstances, where only one parent has died. To receive the allowance the person must be in receipt of child benefit for the child or young person, although they do not have to be the child's legal guardian.

CARER'S ALLOWANCE

Carer's allowance (CA) is a benefit payable to people who spend at least 35 hours per week caring for a severely disabled person. To qualify for CA a person must be caring for someone in receipt of one of the following benefits:

- the middle or highest rate of disability living allowance care component
- either rate of attendance allowance
- constant attendance allowance, paid at not less than the normal maximum rate or basic (full-day) rate, under the industrial injuries or war pension schemes

See leaflet CAA5DCS.

SEVERE DISABLEMENT ALLOWANCE

Since April 2001 severe disablement allowance (SDA) has not been available to new claimants. Those claiming SDA before that date will continue to receive it for as long as they qualify.

ATTENDANCE ALLOWANCE

This may be payable to disabled people who claim after the age of 65 and who need a lot of care or supervision because of physical or mental disability, and who have needed help for a period of at least six months. Attendance allowance has two rates: the lower rate is for day or night care, and the higher rate is for day and night care. People not expected to live for more than six months because of a progressive disease can receive the highest rate of attendance allowance straight away. *See* leaflet *Attendance Allowance.*

DISABILITY LIVING ALLOWANCE

This may be payable to disabled people who claim before the age of 65 who have personal care and/or mobility needs because of an illness or disability for a period of at least three months and are likely to have those needs for a further six months or more. The allowance has two components: the care component, which has three rates, and the mobility component, which has two rates. The rates depend on the care and mobility needs of the claimant. People not expected to live for more than six months because of a progressive disease will automatically receive the highest rate of the care component. *See* leaflets *Disability Living Allowance* and *Disability Living Allowance for Children.*

STATE PENSION: CATEGORY D

Category D pension is provided for people aged 80 and over if they are not entitled to another category of pension or are entitled to a state pension that is less than the category D rate. The person must also normally live in Great Britain and have done so for a continuous period of ten years within any 20-year period since their 60th birthday.

WEEKLY RATES OF NON-CONTRIBUTORY BENEFITS
from April 2007

Jobseeker's allowance (income-based)

Person under 18	£35.65
Person aged 18–24	£46.85
Person aged 25 to state pension age	£59.15
Couple with one or both under 18*	£35.65–£59.15
Couple aged 18 to state pension age	£92.80
Lone parents*	£35.65–£59.15
Dependent children (from birth to the day before 20th birthday)	£47.45
Family premium	£16.43

* depending on circumstances

Maternity allowance

Standard rate	£112.75 or 90 per cent of the women's average weekly earnings if less than £112.75
Increase for adult dependant	£37.90

Child benefit

Eldest/only child	£18.10
Each subsequent child	£12.10

Guardian's allowance

Each child	£12.95

Carer's allowance

	£48.65
Increase for dependent adult	£29.05

Severe disablement allowance

Basic rate	£49.15
Age related addition*:	
Under 40	£17.10
40–49	£11.00
50–59	£5.50

* The age addition applies to the age when incapacity began

Attendance allowance

Higher rate	£64.50
Lower rate	£43.15

Disability living allowance

Care component	
Higher rate	£64.50
Middle rate	£43.15
Lowest rate	£17.10
Mobility component	
Higher rate	£45.00
Lower rate	£17.10

State pension: category D

Single person	£52.30
Age addition to State Pension at age 80	£0.25

INCOME SUPPORT

Income support is a benefit for those aged 16 and over whose income is below a certain level. It can be paid to people who are not expected to sign on as unemployed (income support for unemployed people was replaced by jobseeker's allowance in October 1996) and who are:

- incapable of work due to sickness or disability
- bringing up children alone
- looking after a person who has a disability
- registered blind

Pension credit replaced income support for people aged 60 or over on 6 October 2003. Some people who are not in the above categories may also be able to claim income support.

Income support is also payable to people who work fewer than 16 hours a week on average (or 24 hours for a partner). Some people can claim income support if they work longer hours.

Income support is not payable if the claimant, or claimant and partner, have capital or savings in excess of £16,000. For capital and savings in excess of £6,000, a deduction of £1 a week is made for every £250 or part of £250 held. Different limits apply to people permanently in residential care and nursing homes: the upper limit is £16,000 and deductions apply for capital in excess of £10,000.

Sums payable depend on fixed allowances laid down by law for people in different circumstances. If both partners are eligible for income support, either may claim it for the couple. People receiving income support may be able to receive housing benefit, help with mortgage or home loan interest and help with healthcare. They may also be eligible for help with exceptional expenses from the Social Fund. Special rates may apply to some people living in residential care or nursing homes. Leaflet IS20 (only available online) gives a detailed explanation of income support.

In October 1998 the government's voluntary *New Deal for Lone Parents* programme became available throughout the UK. All lone parents receiving income support are assigned a personal adviser at a Jobcentre who will provide guidance and support with a view to enabling the claimant to find work.

INCOME SUPPORT PREMIUMS

Income support premiums are additional weekly payments for those with special needs. People qualifying for more than one premium will normally only receive the highest single premium for which they qualify. However, family premium, disabled child premium, severe disability premium and carer premium are payable in addition to other premiums.

People with children may qualify for:
- the family premium if they have at least one child (a higher rate is paid to lone parents whose claim was made prior to 6 April 1998)
- the disabled child premium if they have a child who receives disability living allowance or is registered blind

Carers may qualify for:
- the carer premium if they or their partner are in receipt of carer's allowance

Long-term sick or disabled people may qualify for:
- the disability premium if they or their partner are receiving certain benefits because they are disabled or cannot work; are registered blind; or if the claimant has been incapable of work or receiving statutory sick pay for at least 364 days (196 days if the person is terminally ill), including periods of incapacity separated by eight weeks or less
- the severe disability premium if the person lives alone and receives attendance allowance or the middle or higher rate of disability living allowance care component and no one receives carer's allowance for caring for that person. This premium is also available to couples where both partners meet the above conditions

WEEKLY RATES OF INCOME SUPPORT
From April 2007
Single person

under 18	£35.65
under 18 (higher)	£46.85
aged 18–24	£46.85
aged 25 and over	£59.15
aged under 18 and a single parent (lower)	£35.65
aged under 18 and a single parent (higher)	£46.85
aged 18 and over and a single parent	£59.15

Couples

Both under 18	£35.65
Both under 18, one disabled	£46.85
Both under 18 with responsibility for a child	£70.70
One under 18, one aged 18–24	£46.85
One under 18, one aged 25+	£59.15
Both aged 18+	£92.80
For each child in a family from birth to day before 19th birthday	£47.45

Dependent children

From birth to September following 16th birthday	£47.75
From September following 16th birthday to day before 20th birthday	£47.75

Premiums

Family premium	£16.43
Family (lone parent) premium	£16.43
Disabled child premium	£46.69
Carer premium	£27.15
Disability premium	
Single person	£25.25
Couples	£17.75
Enhanced disability premium	
Single person	£12.30
Couples	£17.75
Enhanced disabled child premium	£18.76
Severe disability premium	
Lower rate (single person and some couples)	£48.45
Higher rate (couples)	£96.90

PENSION CREDIT

Pension credit was introduced on 6 October 2003 and replaced income support for those aged 60 and over. There are two elements to pension credit:

THE GUARANTEE CREDIT

The guarantee credit provides a guaranteed minimum income, with additional elements for people who have:
- eligible housing costs
- severe disabilities
- caring responsibilities

Income from state pension, private pensions, earnings and certain benefits are taken into account when calculating the guarantee credit. For savings and capital in excess of £6,000 a deduction of £1 per week is made for every £500 or part of £500 held.

People receiving the guarantee credit element of pension credit will be able to receive housing benefit, council tax benefit and help with healthcare costs.

THE SAVINGS CREDIT

Single people aged 65 or over (and couples where one member is 65 or over) may be entitled to a savings credit which will reward pensioners who have modest income and savings. The savings credit is calculated by taking into account any qualifying income above the savings credit threshold. For 2007–8 the threshold is £87.30 for single people and £139.60 for couples. The savings credit gives pensioners a cash addition calculated at 60p for every pound of qualifying income they have between the savings credit threshold and the guarantee credit. After this, the maximum reward will be reduced by 40p for every pound of income above the guarantee level. The maximum savings credit is £19.05 per week (£25.26 a week for couples).

Income that qualifies towards the savings credit includes state pensions, earnings, second pensions and capital above £6,000.

Some people will be entitled to the guarantee credit, some to the savings credit and some to both.

Where only the savings credit is in payment, people need to claim standard housing benefit or council tax benefit. Although local authorities take any savings credit into account in the housing benefit or council tax benefit assessment, for people aged 65 and over housing benefit or council tax benefit is enhanced to ensure that gains in pension credit are not depleted.

WEEKLY RATES OF PENSION CREDIT
from April 2007
Standard minimum guarantee

Single	£119.05
Couple	£181.70

Additional amount for

Severe disability	£48.45
Carers	£27.15

HOUSING BENEFIT

Housing benefit is designed to help people with rent (including rent for accommodation in guesthouses, lodgings or hostels). It does not cover mortgage payments. The amount of benefit paid depends on:

- the income of the claimant, and partner if there is one, including earned income, unearned income (any other income including some other benefits) and savings
- number of dependants
- certain extra needs of the claimant, partner or any dependants
- number and gross income of people sharing the home who are not dependent on the claimant
- how much rent is paid

Housing benefit is not payable if the claimant, or claimant and partner, have savings in excess of £16,000. The amount of benefit is affected if savings held exceed £6,000 (£10,000 for pensioners and people living in care homes). Housing benefit is not paid for meals, fuel or certain service charges that may be included in the rent. Deductions are also made for most non-dependants who live in the same accommodation as the claimant (and their partner).

The maximum amount of benefit (which is not necessarily the same as the amount of rent paid) may be paid where the claimant is in receipt of income support, income-based jobseeker's allowance, the guarantee element of pension credit or where the claimant's income is less than the amount allowed for their needs. Any income over that allowed for their needs will mean that their benefit is reduced. *See* leaflets HBA5DWP and RR2 (only available online).

COUNCIL TAX BENEFIT

Nearly all the rules which apply to housing benefit apply to council tax benefit, which helps people on low incomes to pay council tax bills. The amount payable depends on how much council tax is paid and who lives with the claimant. The benefit may be available to those receiving income support, income-based jobseeker's allowance, the guarantee element of pension credit or to those whose income is less than that allowed for their needs. Any income over that allowed for their needs will mean that their council tax benefit is reduced. Deductions are made for non-dependants.

The maximum amount that is payable for those living in properties in council tax bands A to E is 100 per cent of the claimant's council tax liability. This also applies to those living in properties in bands F to H who were in receipt of the benefit at 31 March 1998 if they have remained in the same property.

If a person shares a home with one or more adults (not their partner) who are on a low income, it may be possible to claim a second adult rebate. Those who are entitled to both council tax benefit and second adult rebate will be awarded whichever is the greater. Second adult rebate may be claimed by those not in receipt of or eligible for council tax benefit.

THE SOCIAL FUND

REGULATED PAYMENTS
Sure Start Maternity Grant
The Sure Start maternity grant (SSMG) is a one-off payment of £500 to help people on low incomes pay for essential items for new babies that are expected, born, adopted, the subject of a parental order (following a surrogate birth) or, in certain circumstances, the subject of a residency order. SSMG can be claimed any time from the 29th week of pregnancy up to three months after the birth, adoption or date of parental or residency order. Those eligible are people in receipt of income support, income-based jobseeker's allowance, pension credit, child tax credit at a rate higher than the family element or working tax credit where a disability or severe disability element is in payment.

Funeral Payments
Payable to help cover the necessary cost of burial or cremation, plus certain other funeral expenses incurred up to £700. Those eligible are people receiving income support, income-based jobseeker's allowance, pension credit, child tax credit at a higher rate than the family element, working tax credit where a disability or severe disability element is in payment, council tax benefit or housing benefit who have good reason for taking responsibility for the funeral expenses. These payments are recoverable from any estate of the deceased.

Cold Weather Payments
A payment of £8.50 when the average temperature is recorded at or forecast to be 0°C or below over seven consecutive days in the qualifying person's area. Payments are made to people on pension credit, income support and those on income-based jobseeker's allowance who have a child who is disabled or under the age of five, or whose benefit includes a pensioner or disability premium. Payments are made automatically and do not have to be repaid.

Winter Fuel Payments
An annual payment of at least £200 per household paid to most people aged 60 or over. Where the household includes someone aged 80 or over, the amount is £300. The majority of eligible people are paid automatically before Christmas, although a few need to claim. Payments do not have to be repaid.

DISCRETIONARY PAYMENTS
Community Care Grants
These are intended to help people on income support, income-based jobseeker's allowance, in receipt of pension credit, or receiving payments on account of such benefits (or those likely to receive these benefits on leaving residential or institutional accommodation) to live as independently as possible in the community; ease exceptional pressures on families; care for a prisoner or young offender released on temporary licence; help people set up home as part of a resettlement programme and/or assist with certain travelling expenses. They do not have to be repaid.

Budgeting Loans
These are interest-free loans to people who have been receiving income support, income-based jobseeker's allowance, pension credit or payments on account of such

benefits for at least 26 weeks, for intermittent expenses that may be difficult to budget for.

Crisis Loans
These are interest-free loans to anyone, whether receiving benefits or not, who is without resources in an emergency or due to a disaster, where there is no other means of preventing serious damage or serious risk to their, or their family members' health or safety.

SAVINGS
Savings over £500 (£1,000 for people aged 60 or over) are taken into account for community care grants and savings of £1,000 (£2,000 for people aged 60 or over) are taken into account for budgeting loans. All savings are taken into account for crisis loans. Savings are not taken into account for Sure Start maternity grant, funeral payments, cold weather or winter fuel payments.

INDUSTRIAL INJURIES AND DISABLEMENT BENEFITS
The Industrial Injuries Scheme, administered under the Social Security Contributions and Benefits Act 1992, provides a range of benefits designed to compensate for disablement resulting from an industrial accident (ie an accident arising out of and in the course of an earner's employment) or from a prescribed disease due to the nature of a person's employment. Those who are self-employed are not covered by this scheme.

INDUSTRIAL INJURIES DISABLEMENT BENEFIT
A person must be at least 14 per cent disabled (except for certain respiratory diseases) in order to qualify for this benefit. The amount paid depends on the degree of disablement:
- those assessed as 14–19 per cent disabled are paid at the 20 per cent rate
- those with disablement of over 20 per cent will have the percentage rounded up or down to the nearest 10 per cent, eg a disablement of 44 per cent will be paid at the 40 per cent rate while a disablement of 45 per cent will be paid at the 50 per cent rate

Except for certain respiratory diseases for which industrial injuries disablement benefit is paid immediately, most benefit is payable 15 weeks (90 days) after the date of the accident or onset of the disease (subject to backdating limits) and may be payable for a limited period or for life. The benefit is payable whether the person works or not and those who are incapable of work are entitled to draw statutory sick pay or incapacity benefit in addition to industrial injuries disablement benefit. It may also be possible to claim the following allowances:
- reduced earnings allowance for those who are unable to return to their regular work or work of the same standard and who had their accident (or whose disease started) before 1 October 1990. At state pension age this is converted to retirement allowance
- constant attendance allowance for those with a disablement of 100 per cent who need constant care. There are four rates of allowance depending on how much care the person needs
- exceptionally severe disablement allowance for those who are entitled to constant care attendance allowance at one of the higher rates and who need constant care permanently

See leaflets IIDBAA5JP, IIDBASA5JP and IIDBDA5JP.

OTHER BENEFITS
People who are disabled because of an accident or disease that was the result of work that they did before 5 July 1948 are not entitled to industrial injuries disablement benefit. They may, however, be entitled to payment under the Workmen's Compensation Scheme or the Pneumoconiosis, Byssinosis and Miscellaneous Diseases Benefit Scheme. *See* leaflet GL23. People who suffer from certain industrial diseases caused by dust, or their dependants, can make a claim for an additional payment under the Pneumoconiosis etc (Workers' Compensation) Act 1979 if they are unable to get damages from the employer who caused or contributed to the disease.

WEEKLY RATES OF BENEFIT *FROM APRIL 2007*
Disablement benefit/pension[*]
Degree of disablement:

100 per cent	£137.70
90	£118.53
80	£105.36
70	£92.19
60	£79.02
50	£65.85
40	£52.68
30	£39.51
20	£26.34
Unemployability supplement	£81.35
Addition for adult dependant (subject to earnings rule)	£48.65
Reduced earnings allowance (maximum)	£52.68
Retirement allowance (maximum)	£13.17
Constant attendance allowance (normal maximum rate)	£52.70
Exceptionally severe disablement allowance	£52.70

[*] There is a weekly benefit for those under 18 with no dependants which is set at a lower rate

CLAIMS AND QUESTIONS
Entitlement to benefit and regulated Social Fund payments is determined by a decision maker on behalf of the Secretary of State for the Department for Work and Pensions. A claimant who is dissatisfied with that decision can ask for an explanation. He or she can dispute the decision by applying to have it revised or, in particular circumstances, superseded. The claimant can go to the Appeals Service where the case will be heard by an independent tribunal. There is a further right of appeal to a social security commissioner against the tribunal's decision but this is on a point of law only and leave to appeal must first be obtained.

Decisions on claims and applications for housing benefit and council tax benefit are made by local authorities. The explanation, dispute and appeals process is the same as for other benefits. *See* leaflets GL24DWP and NI260DMA.

All decisions on applications to the discretionary Social Fund are made by Jobcentre Plus Social Fund decision makers. Applicants can ask for a review of the decision within 28 days of the date on the decision letter. The Social Fund review officer will review the case and there is a further right of review by an independent Social Fund inspector.

EMPLOYER PAYMENTS

STATUTORY MATERNITY PAY

Employers pay statutory maternity pay (SMP) to pregnant women who have been employed by them full or part-time continuously for at least 26 weeks into the 15th week before the week the baby is due, and whose earnings on average at least equal the lower earnings limit applied to NI contributions (£87 per week from April 2007). All women who meet these conditions receive payment of 90 per cent of their average earnings for the first six weeks; the remaining weeks are paid at £112.75 or 90 per cent of the woman's average weekly earnings if this is less than £112.75. SMP can be paid, at the earliest, 11 weeks before the week in which the baby is due, up to the day following the birth. Women can decide when they wish their maternity leave to start and can work until the baby is born. However, where the woman is absent from work wholly or partly due to pregnancy on or after the Sunday of the 4th week before the baby is due to be born, SMP will start the day following the first day of absence from work. SMP is paid for a maximum of 39 weeks regardless of when the baby is actually born.

Employers are reimbursed for 92 per cent of the SMP they pay. Small employers with annual gross NI payments of £45,000 or less recover 100 per cent of the SMP paid plus 4.5 per cent in compensation for the secondary NI contributions paid on SMP.

For more information *see* leaflet NI7A *A Guide to Maternity Benefits* available on the Department for Work and Pensions website (W www.dwp.gov.uk/advisers/ni17a/).

STATUTORY PATERNITY PAY

Employers pay statutory paternity pay (SPP) to employees who are taking leave when a child is born or placed for adoption. To qualify the employee must:

- have responsibility for the child's upbringing
- be the biological father of the child (or the child's adopter), or the spouse/civil partner/partner of the mother or adopter
- be taking time off work to care for the child and/or support the mother or adopter
- have been employed by the same employer for at least 26 weeks ending with the 15th week before the baby is due (or the week in which the adopter is notified of having been matched with a child)
- continue working for the employer up to the child's birth (or placement for adoption)
- have earnings on average at least equal to the lower earnings limit applied to NI contributions (£87 per week from April 2007)

Employees who meet these conditions receive payment of £112.75 or 90 per cent of the employee's average weekly earnings if this is less than £112.75. The employee can choose to be paid for one or two consecutive weeks. The earliest the SPP period can begin is the date of the child's birth or placement for adoption. The SPP period must be completed within eight weeks of that date. SPP is not payable for any week in which the employee works. Employers are reimbursed in the same way as for statutory maternity pay. *See* Department for Business, Enterprise and Regulatory Reform leaflet *Working fathers: rights to leave and pay available* online (W www.berr.gov.uk).

STATUTORY ADOPTION PAY

Employers pay statutory adoption pay (SAP) to employees taking adoption leave from their employers. To qualify for SAP the employee must:

- be newly matched with a child by an adoption agency
- have been employed by the same employer for at least 26 weeks ending the week in which they have been notified of being matched with a child
- have earnings at least equal to the lower earnings limit applied to NI contributions (£87 per week from April 2007)

Employees who meet these conditions receive payment of £112.75 or 90 per cent of their average weekly earnings if this is less than £112.75 for up to 39 weeks. The SAP period can start from the date of the child's placement. SAP is not payable for any week in which the employee works. Where a couple adopt a child, only one of them may receive SAP, the other may be able to receive statutory paternity pay (SPP) if they meet the eligibility criteria. Employers are reimbursed in the same way as for statutory maternity pay. *See* Department for Business, Enterprise and Regulatory Reform leaflet *Adoptive parents: rights to leave and pay available* online (W www.berr.gov.uk).

STATUTORY SICK PAY

Employers pay statutory sick pay (SSP) for up to a maximum of 28 weeks to any employee incapable of work for four or more consecutive days, who has average earnings, in a specified period, at or above the point at which earnings become relevant for NI purposes (£87 from April 2007). SSP is paid at £72.55 per week and is subject to PAYE and NI contributions. Employees who cannot obtain SSP may be able to claim incapacity benefit. Employers may be able to recover some SSP costs. *See* HM Revenue and Customs Leaflets CA86 *Employees Guide to Statutory Sick Pay,* available online (W www.hmrc.gov.uk).

THE WATER INDUSTRY

Water services in England and Wales are provided by private companies. In Scotland there is a single authority, Scottish Water, that is answerable to the Scottish Executive, and in Northern Ireland all services are provided by the Water Service, which remains in the public sector as an executive agency within Northern Ireland's Department for Regional Development. In the UK the water industry provides services to over 20 million properties and has an annual turnover of £7bn. It also manages assets that include over 2,500 water and 9,000 sewerage treatment plants, 1,000 reservoirs and over 700,000km of water mains and sewers.

ENGLAND AND WALES

The water industry supplies around 18,000 million litres of water every day. In 2002 water companies in England and Wales carried out around 2.9 million tests on drinking water samples, of which 99.87 per cent met all British and European standards. In England and Wales the Secretary of State for Environment, Food and Rural Affairs and the National Assembly for Wales have overall responsibility for water policy and oversee environmental standards for the water industry.

Water UK is the industry association that represents all UK water and wastewater service suppliers at national and European level and is funded directly by its members who are the service suppliers for England, Scotland, Wales and Northern Ireland; every member has a seat on the Water UK Council.

WATER UK, 1 Queen Anne's Gate, London SW1H 9BT
T 020-7344 1844 W www.water.org.uk
Chief Executive, Pamela Taylor

WATER SERVICE COMPANIES
(members of Water UK)
ANGLIAN WATER SERVICES LTD, Customer Services, PO Box 770, Lincoln LN5 7WX T 08457-145145
W www.anglianwater.co.uk
BOURNEMOUTH & WEST HAMPSHIRE WATER PLC, George Jessel House, Francis Avenue, Bournemouth, Dorset BH11 8NX T 01202-590059
W www.bwhwater.co.uk
BRISTOL WATER PLC, PO Box 218, Bridgwater Road, Bristol BS99 7AU T 0117-966 5881
W www.bristolwater.co.uk
CAMBRIDGE WATER PLC, 90 Fulbourn Road, Cambridge CB1 9JN T 01223-706050 W www.cambridge-water.co.uk
CHOLDERTON & DISTRICT WATER COMPANY, Estate Office, Cholderton, Salisbury, Wiltshire SP4 0DR T 01980-629203
DEE VALLEY WATER PLC, Packsaddle, Wrexham Road, Rhostyllen, Wrexham LL14 4EH T 01978-846946
W www.deevalleygroup.com
DWR CYMRU CYFYNGEDIG (WELSH WATER), Pentwyn Road, Nelson, Treharris, Mid Glamorgan CF46 6LY T 0800-052 0145 W www.dwrcymru.co.uk
ESSEX & SUFFOLK WATER PLC (subsidiary of

Northumbrian Water Ltd), Hall Street, Chelmsford, Essex CM2 0HH T 0845-782 0999 W www.eswater.co.uk
FOLKESTONE & DOVER WATER SERVICES LTD, Cherry Garden Lane, Folkestone, Kent CT19 4QB T 0845-888 5888 W www.fdws.co.uk
MID KENT WATER PLC, Snodland, Kent ME6 5AH T 0845-850 6060 W www.midkentwater.co.uk
NORTHUMBRIAN WATER LTD, Abbey Road, Pity Me, Durham DH1 5FJ T 0845 717 1100 W www.nwl.co.uk
PORTSMOUTH WATER PLC, PO Box 8, West Street, Havant, Hampshire PO9 1LG T 023-9249 9888
W www.portsmouthwater.co.uk
SEVERN TRENT PLC, 2297 Coventry Road, Birmingham B26 3PU T 0121-722 4000 W www.severntrent.com
SOUTH EAST WATER PLC, 3 Church Road, Haywards Heath, West Sussex RH16 3NY T 0845-301 0845
W www.southeastwater.co.uk
SOUTH STAFFORDSHIRE WATER PLC, PO Box 63, Walsall WS2 7PJ T 0845-607 0456
W www.south-staffs-water.co.uk
SOUTH WEST WATER LTD, Peninsula House, Rydon Lane, Exeter EX2 7HS T 0800-169 1144
W www.swwater.co.uk
SOUTHERN WATER, Southern House, Yeoman Road, Worthing, W. Sussex BN13 3NX T 0845-278 0845
W www.southernwater.co.uk
SUTTON AND EAST SURREY WATER PLC, London Road, Redhill, Surrey RH1 1LJ T 01737-772000
W www.waterplc.com
TENDRING HUNDRED WATER SERVICES LTD, Mill Hill, Manningtree, Essex CO11 2AZ T 01206-399200
W www.thws.co.uk
THAMES WATER UTILITIES LTD, PO Box 436, Swindon SN38 ITU T 0845-920 0888 W www.thameswater.com
THREE VALLEYS WATER PLC, PO Box 48, Bishops Rise, Hatfield, Hertfordshire AL10 9HL T 01707-268111
W www.3valleys.co.uk
UNITED UTILITIES WATER PLC, Haweswater House, Lingley Mere Business Park, Lingley Green Avenue, Great Sankey, Warrington, WA5 3LP T 0845-7462222
W www.unitedutilities.com
WESSEX WATER SERVICES LTD, Claverton Down Road, Bath BA2 7WW T 01225-526000 W wessexwater.co.uk
YORKSHIRE WATER SERVICES LTD, PO Box 52, Bradford BD3 7YD T 0845-124 2424
W www.yorkshirewater.com

ISLAND WATER AUTHORITIES
(not members of Water UK)
COUNCIL OF THE ISLES OF SCILLY, Town Hall, St Mary's, Isles of Scilly TR21 0LW T 01720-422537
ISLE OF MAN WATER AUTHORITY, Tromode Road, Douglas, Isle of Man IM2 5PA T 01624-695949
W www.gov.im/water
JERSEY WATER, PO Box 69, Mulcaster House, Westmount Road, St. Helier, Jersey JE4 9PN T 01534-707301
W www.jerseywater.je
STATES OF GUERNSEY WATER BOARD, PO Box 30, South Esplanade, St Peter Port, Guernsey GY1 3AS T 01481-724552 W www.gov.gg

WATER SUPPLY AND CONSUMPTION 2005–6

	Supply		Consumption			
	Supply from Treatment Works (megalitres/day)	Total Leakage (megalitres/day)	Household (litres/head/day) Unmetered	Metered	Non-household (litres/property/day) Unmetered	Metered
WATER AND SEWERAGE COMPANIES						
Anglian	1,164	214	160	128	229	2,889
Dwr Cymru	866	224	154	129	426	2,247
Northumbrian	722	157	148	143	786	3,432
Severn Trent	1,946	542	137	118	535	2,239
South West	450	84	165	139	1,003	1,602
Southern	582	93	157	139	705	2,524
Thames	2,801	862	167	154	807	3,297
United Utilities	1,940	477	144	132	739	2,692
Wessex	371	73	157	136	3,251	2,232
Yorkshire	1,295	297	148	134	127	2,757
Total	12,135	3,024	—	—	—	—
Average	—	—	154	135	861	2,591
WATER ONLY COMPANIES						
Total	3,221	553	—	—	—	—
Average	—	—	162	141	747	2,558

Source: OFWAT

REGULATORY BODIES

The Water Services Regulation Authority (OFWAT) was set up under the Water Act 1989 and is the independent economic regulator of the water and sewerage companies in England and Wales. Overall responsibility for water policy and overseeing environmental standards for the water industry lies with DEFRA and the Welsh Assembly. OFWAT's main duties are to ensure that the companies can finance and carry out their statutory functions and to protect the interests of water customers. OFWAT is a non-ministerial government department headed by a board following a change in legislation set out in the Water Act 2003.

Under the Competition Act 1998, from 1 March 2000 the Competition Appeal Tribunal has heard appeals against the regulator's decisions regarding anti-competitive agreements and abuse of a dominant position in the marketplace. The Water Act 2003 placed a new duty on OFWAT to have regard to sustainable development.

The Environment Agency was set up by the Environment Act 1995 as a non-departmental public body and is sponsored largely by DEFRA and the Welsh Assembly. The Environment Agency has statutory duties and powers in relation to water resources, pollution control, flood defence, fisheries, recreation, conservation and navigation in England and Wales. They are also responsible for issuing permits, licences, consents and registrations such as industrial licences to extract water and fishing licences.

The Drinking Water Inspectorate (DWI) is the drinking water quality regulator for England and Wales, responsible for assessing the quality of the drinking water supplied by the water companies and investigating any incidents affecting drinking water quality, initiating prosecution where necessary. The DWI also provides scientific advice on drinking water policy issues to DEFRA and the Welsh Assembly.

OFWAT, Centre City Tower, 7 Hill Street, Birmingham B5 4UA
T 0121-625 1300 E enquiries@ofwat.gsi.gov.uk
W www.ofwat.gov.uk
Chairman, Philip Fletcher

METHODS OF CHARGING

In England and Wales, most domestic customers still pay for domestic water supply and sewerage services through charges based on the rateable value of their property. Overall, companies expect about 33 per cent of household customers in England and Wales to have metered supplies in 2007–8. Industrial and most commercial customers are charged according to consumption.

Under the Water Industry Act 1999, water companies can continue basing their charges on the old rateable value of property. Domestic customers can continue paying on an unmeasured basis unless they choose to pay according to consumption. After having a meter installed (which is free of charge), a customer can revert to unmeasured charging within 12 months. Domestic, school and hospital customers cannot be disconnected for non-payment.

Price limits for the period 2005–10 were set by OFWAT in December 2004.

AVERAGE HOUSEHOLD WATER BILLS (2007–8)

	Unmetered (£)	Metered (£)
Water	157	134
Sewerage	167	151
Combined	325	285

SCOTLAND

Overall responsibility for national water policy in Scotland rests with the Scottish ministers. Until the Local Government (Scotland) Act 1994, water supply and sewerage services were local authority responsibilities. The Central Scotland Water Development Board had the function of developing new sources of water supply for the purpose of providing water in bulk to water authorities whose limits of supply were within the board's area. Under the act, three new public water authorities, covering the north, east and west of Scotland respectively, took over the provision of water and sewerage services from April 1996. The Central Scotland Water Development Board was then abolished. The act also established the Scottish Water and Sewerage Customers Council representing consumer interests. It monitored the performance of the authorities; approved charges schemes; investigated complaints; and advised the secretary of state. The Water Industry Act 1999, whose Scottish provisions were accepted by the Scottish Executive, abolished the Scottish Water and Sewerage Customers Council and replaced it in November 1999 with a Water Industry Commissioner.

The Water Industry (Scotland) Act 2002 resulted from the Scottish Executive's proposal that a single authority was better placed than three separate authorities to harmonise changes across the Scottish water industry. In 2002 the three existing water authorities (East of Scotland Water, North of Scotland Water and West of Scotland Water) merged to form Scottish Water. Scottish Water is a public sector company, structured and managed like a private company, but remains answerable to the Scottish Parliament. Scottish Water is regulated by the Water Industry Commissioner for Scotland, the Scottish Environment Protection Agency (SEPA), and the Drinking Water Quality Regulator for Scotland. The Water Industry Commissioner is responsible for regulating all aspects of economic and customer service performance, including water and sewerage charges. SEPA is responsible for environmental issues, including controlling pollution and promoting the cleanliness of Scotland's rivers, lochs and coastal waters.

METHODS OF CHARGING
Scottish Water sets charges for domestic and non-domestic water and sewerage provision through charges schemes which are regulated by the Water Industries Commissioner for Scotland. In February 2004 the harmonisation of all household charges across the country was completed following the merger of the separate authorities under Scottish Water.

SCOTTISH WATER, PO Box 8855, Edinburgh EH10 6YQ
   T 0845-601 8855 W www.scottishwater.co.uk
SCOTTISH ENVIRONMENT PROTECTION
   AGENCY, Erskine Court, Castle Business Park, Stirling
   FK9 4TR T 01786-457700 W www.sepa.org.uk
WATER INDUSTRY COMMISSIONER FOR
   SCOTLAND, Ochil House, Springkerse Business Park,
   Stirling FK7 7XE T 01786-430200
   W www.watercommissioner.co.uk

NORTHERN IRELAND

In Northern Ireland ministerial responsibility for water services lies with the minister of the Department for Regional Development. The Water Service, which is an executive agency of the Department for Regional Development, is responsible for policy and coordination with regard to supply, distribution and cleanliness of water, and the provision and maintenance of sewerage services.

The Water Service comprises four divisions: Eastern, Northern, Western and Southern. The main divisional offices are based in Belfast, Ballymena, Londonderry and Craigavon.

METHODS OF CHARGING
The Water Service is currently funded from public funds and direct charges. The department's policy is to meter all properties that are not exclusively domestic. They are, however, granted an allowance of 200 cubic metres per annum to reflect domestic usage, known as the domestic usage allowance. Customers are charged only for water used in excess of this allowance together with a standing charge, which is intended to cover the costs of meter provision, maintenance, reading and billing. This allowance is not granted if rates are not paid on the property. Traders operating from de-rated, rate exempt or rate rebated premises are required to pay for the treatment and disposal of trade effluent which they discharge into the public sewer.

Water and sewerage services in Northern Ireland became self-financed in 2006. Under new legislation domestic customers are charged directly for water and sewerage services, currently a proportion of the rates paid on domestic properties. Following a public consultation document *The Reform of the Water and Sewerage Services In Northern Ireland* the initial conclusion from the Department for Regional Development was that the new domestic charge would include a fixed element and a variable element, the latter determined by property value or consumption.

NORTHERN IRELAND WATER SERVICE, PO Box 126,
   Belfast BT1 9DJ T 08457-440088 W www.waterni.gov.uk

ENERGY

The main primary sources of energy in Britain are oil, natural gas, coal, nuclear power and water power. The main secondary sources (ie sources derived from the primary sources) are electricity, coke and smokeless fuels and petroleum products. The Department for the Environment, Food and Rural Affairs (DEFRA) is responsible for promoting energy efficiency.

INDIGENOUS PRODUCTION OF PRIMARY FUELS
Million tonnes of oil equivalent

	2006
Coal	11.4
Primary oils	84.0
Natural gas	80.0
Primary electricity	17.7
Renewable and waste	3.6
Total	196.7

Source: Department for Business, Enterprise and Regulatory Reform

INLAND ENERGY CONSUMPTION BY PRIMARY FUEL
Million tonnes of oil equivalent, seasonally adjusted

	2006
Coal	43.4
Petroleum	77.1
Natural gas	89.2
Nuclear electricity	17.0
Hydro electricity	0.8
Net Imports	0.6
Renewables and waste	4.1
Total	232.1

Source: Department for Business, Enterprise and Regulatory Reform

TRADE IN FUELS AND RELATED MATERIALS (2006)

	Quantity million tonnes of oil equivalent	Value £m
Imports		
Coal and other solid fuel	34.6	2,203
Crude petroleum	60.8	14,580
Petroleum products	35.3	10,019
Natural gas	21.0	2,512
Electricity	0.8	445
Total	152.5	29,759
Exports		
Coal and other solid fuel	0.4	49
Crude petroleum	51.8	12,849
Petroleum products	37.3	9,571
Natural gas	10.4	1,315
Electricity	0.2	92
Total	100.1	23,876

Source: HM Customs & Excise

OIL

Until the 1960s Britain imported almost all its oil supplies. In 1969 oil was discovered in the Arbroath field of the UK Continental Shelf (UKCS). The first oilfield to be brought into production was the Argyll field in 1975, and since the mid-1970s Britain has been a major producer of crude oil.

Licences for exploration and production are granted to companies by the Department for Business, Enterprise and Regulatory Reform; the leading British oil companies are BP and Shell. At the end of 2004, 565 seaward production licences and 101 onshore petroleum exploration and development licences had been awarded, and there were a total of 264 offshore oil and gas fields in production. In 2003 there were 9 oil refineries and three smaller refining units processing crude and process oils. Oil remaining in the UKCS is estimated at 1,267 million tonnes. Royalties are payable on fields approved before April 1982 and petroleum revenue tax is levied on fields approved between 1975 and March 1993.

DRILLING ACTIVITY (2006)
by number of wells started

	Offshore	Onshore
Exploration	29	8
Appraisal	40	7
Development	211	12

Source: Department for Business, Enterprise and Regulatory Reform

INDIGENOUS PRODUCTION AND REFINERY RECEIPTS
Thousand tonnes

	2005	2006
Indigenous production	84,721	76,579
Crude oil	77,179	69,666
NGLs*	7,543	6,913
Refinery receipts	80,221	75,844

* Natural Gas Liquids: condensates and petroleum gases derived at onshore treatment plants
Source: Department for Business, Enterprise and Regulatory Reform

DELIVERIES OF PETROLEUM PRODUCTS FOR INLAND CONSUMPTION BY ENERGY USE
Thousand tonnes

	2005	2006
Industry	6,424	6,553
Transport	52,908	53,457
Domestic	2,782	2,926
Other	1,603	1,399
Total	63,717	64,335

Source: Department for Business, Enterprise and Regulatory Reform

COAL

Coal has been mined in Britain for centuries and the availability of coal was crucial to the industrial revolution of the 18th and 19th centuries. Mines were in private ownership until 1947 when they were nationalised and came under the management of the National Coal Board, later the British Coal Corporation. The corporation held a monopoly on coal production until 1994 when the industry was restructured. Under the Coal Industry Act 1994, the Coal Authority was established to take over ownership of coal reserves and to issue licences to private mining companies. The Coal Authority was also given the responsibility of dealing with the physical legacy of mining, eg subsidence damage claims, and is responsible for holding and making available all existing records.

UK mines were sold as five separate businesses in 1994 and coal production is now undertaken entirely in the private sector. Coal output was around 50 million tonnes a year in 1994. Since then coal output has declined and today there are 7 major deep mines, 11 smaller mines and 30 opencast sites. In 2003 the government launched Coal Investment Aid with a budget of up to £60m to be allocated to coal producers for projects that maintain access to coal reserves.

The main consumer of coal in the UK is the electricity supply industry. Coal still supplies a third of the UK's electricity needs but as indigenous production has declined, imports have risen to make up the shortfall. An energy white paper, published in 2003, had four policy goals, one of which was to cut carbon dioxide emissions by 60 per cent by 2050. This recognised that for a low-carbon economy the development of cleaner coal technologies is required. In November 2005 the government announced an energy policy review and published a report in July 2006. This was the foundation for a further energy white paper published on 23 May 2007 which set out the government's international and domestic energy strategy to meet the long-term challenges posed by climate change to ensure secure, clean and affordable energy. Coal continues to play an important role in the future generating mix, but there is a need to tackle carbon emissions through the introduction of abatement technologies and, in the long term, the introduction of carbon capture and storage.

INLAND COAL USE
Thousand tonnes

	2005	2006
Fuel producers		
Electricity generators	52,084	57,323
Heat generation	450	450
Coke manufacture	5,564	5,929
Blast furnaces	1,039	1,121
Other conversion industries†	266	276
Final consumption		
Industry	1,791	1,714
Domestic	614	547
Public administration	22	9
Commerce	6	6
Agriculture	9	5

† Mainly recycled products
Source: Department for Business, Enterprise and Regulatory Reform

COAL PRODUCTION AND FOREIGN TRADE
Thousand tonnes

	2005	2006
Deep-mined	9,563	9,444
Opencast	10,445	8,635
Imports	43,968	50,456
Exports	536	−443
Total supply	61,802*	67,267*
TOTAL	61,853	67,387

* Includes an estimate for slurry and stock change
Source: Department for Business, Enterprise and Regulatory Reform

GAS

From the late 18th century gas in Britain was produced from coal. In the 1960s town gas began to be produced from oil-based feedstocks using imported oil. In 1965 gas was discovered in the North Sea in the West Sole field, which became the first gasfield in production in 1967, and from the late 1960s natural gas began to replace town gas. Britain is the world's sixth largest producer of gas and in 1998 only 1.5 per cent of gas available for consumption in the UK was imported. From October 1998 Britain was connected to the continental European gas system via a pipeline from Bacton, Norfolk to Zeebrugge, Belgium. Gas is transported through 275,000km of mains pipeline including 6,400km of high-pressure gas pipelines owned and operated in the UK by National Grid Gas plc.

The gas industry in Britain was nationalised in 1949 and operated as the Gas Council. The Gas Council was replaced by the British Gas Corporation in 1972 and the industry became more centralised. The British Gas Corporation was privatised in 1986 as British Gas plc. In 1993 the Monopolies and Mergers Commission found that British Gas' integrated business in Great Britain as a gas trader and the owner of the gas transportation system could operate against the public interest. In February 1997, British Gas demerged its trading arm to become two separate companies, BG plc and Centrica plc. BG Group, as the company is now known, is an international natural gas company whose principal business is finding and developing gas reserves and building gas markets. Its core operations are located in the UK, South America, Egypt, Trinidad and Tobago, Kazakhstan and India. Centrica runs the trading and services operations under the British Gas brand name in Great Britain. In October 2000 BG demerged its pipeline business, Transco, which became part of Lattice Group, finally merging with the National Grid Group in 2002 to become National Grid Transco plc.

In July 2005 National Grid Transco plc changed its name to National Grid plc and Transco plc became National Grid Gas plc. In the same year National Grid Gas also completed the sale of four of its eight gas distribution networks. The distribution networks transport gas at lower pressures, which eventually supply the consumers such as domestic customers. The Scotland and south-east of England networks were sold to Scotia Gas Networks. The Wales and south-west network was sold to Wales &

West Utilities and the network in the north-east to Northern Gas Networks. This was the biggest change in the corporate structure of gas infrastructure since privatisation in 1986.

Competition was gradually introduced into the industrial gas market from 1986. Supply of gas to the domestic market was opened to companies other than British Gas, starting in April 1996 with a pilot project in the West Country and Wales, with the rest of the UK following soon after. Since competition was introduced in domestic retail of gas, around half of Britain's 20 million gas customers have changed their supplier.

BG GROUP PLC, Thames Valley Park, Reading RG6 1PT
T 0118-935 3222 W www.bg-group.com
Chairman, Sir Robert Wilson
Chief Executive, Frank Chapman

CENTRICA PLC, Millstream, Maidenhead Road, Windsor, Berkshire SL4 5GD T 01753-494000 W www.centrica.co.uk
Chairman, Roger Carr
Chief Executive, Sam Laidlaw

NATIONAL GRID TRANSCO PLC, 1–3 Strand, London WC2N 5EH T 020-7004 3000 W www.ngtgroup.com
Chairman, Sir John Parker
Deputy Group Chief Executive, Steve Holliday

UK NATURAL GAS PRODUCTION
GWh

	2004	2005
Power stations	341,111	333,834
Petroleum refineries	1,797	1,987
Nuclear fuel production	201	202
Production and distribution of other energy	721	715
Total final producers	343,830	336,738

Source: Annual Abstract of Statistics 2007 (Crown copyright)

UK GAS CONSUMPTION BY INDUSTRY
GWh

	2004	2005
Iron and steel industry	9,715	8,410
Other industries	143,959	140,271
Domestic	396,411	381,879
Public administration	50,934	49,385
Agriculture	2,355	2,201
Miscellaneous	68,797	64,788
Total final users	672,171	646,990

Source: Annual Abstract of Statistics 2007 (Crown copyright)

ELECTRICITY

The first power station in Britain generating electricity for public supply began operating in 1882. In the 1930s a national transmission grid was developed and it was reconstructed and extended in the 1950s and 1960s. Power stations were operated by the Central Electricity Generating Board.

Under the Electricity Act 1989, 12 regional electricity companies, responsible for the distribution of electricity from the national grid to consumers, were formed from the former area electricity boards in England and Wales. Four companies were formed from the Central Electricity

Generating Board: three generating companies (National Power plc, Nuclear Electric plc and Powergen plc) and the National Grid Company plc, which owned and operated the transmission system in England and Wales. National Power and Powergen were floated on the stock market in 1991.

National Power was demerged in October 2000 to form two separate companies: International Power plc and Innogy plc, which manages the bulk of National Power's UK assets. Nuclear Electric was split into two parts in 1996: British Energy (*see* Nuclear Energy) and Magnox Electric, which owns the magnox nuclear reactors, remained in the public sector. Magnox was integrated into British Nuclear Fuels (BNFL) in 1998.

The National Grid Company was floated on the stock market in 1995 and formed a new holding company, National Grid Group. National Grid Group completed a merger with Lattice in 2002 to form National Grid Transco, a public limited company. National Grid Transco has since undergone a series of name changes (*see* Gas).

Following privatisation, generators and suppliers in England and Wales traded via the Electricity Pool. A competitive wholesale trading market known as NETA (New Electricity Trading Arrangements) replaced the Electicity Pool in March 2001, which was extended to include Scotland via the British Electricity Transmissions and Trading Arrangements (BETTA) in 2005. As part of BETTA, National Grid became the system operator for all transmission. The introduction of competition into the domestic electricity market was completed in May 1999. With the gas market also open, most suppliers now offer their customers both gas and electricity. Since competition was introduced, around half of Britain's 26 million electricity customers have switched their supplier.

In Scotland, three new companies were formed under the Electricity Act 1989: Scottish Power plc and Scottish Hydro-Electric plc, which were responsible for generation, transmission, distribution and supply; and Scottish Nuclear Ltd. Scottish Power and Scottish Hydro-Electric were floated on the stock market in 1991. Scottish Hydro-Electric merged with Southern Electric in 1998 to become Scottish and Southern Energy plc. Scottish Nuclear was incorporated into British Energy in 1996. BETTA opened the Scottish market to the same competition that had applied in England and Wales.

In Northern Ireland, Northern Ireland Electricity plc was set up in 1993 under a 1991 Order in Council. In 1993 it was floated on the stock market and in 1998 it became part of the Viridian Group and is responsible for distribution and supply.

On 30 September 2003 the Electricity Association, the industry's main trade association, was replaced with three separate trade bodies:

ASSOCIATION OF ELECTRICITY PRODUCERS, 1st Floor, 17 Waterloo Place, London SW1Y 4AR
T 020-7930 9390 W www.aepuk.com
ENERGY NETWORKS ASSOCIATION, 18 Stanhope Place, London W2 2HH T 020-7706 5100
W www.energynetworks.org
ENERGY RETAIL ASSOCIATION, 4th Floor, 17 Waterloo Place, London SW1Y 4AR T 020-7930 9175
W www.energy-retail.org.uk

ELECTRICITY GENERATION, SUPPLY AND
CONSUMPTION
GWh

	2004	2005
Electricity generated		
Conventional thermal and other*	130,882	136,348
Combined cycle gas turbine		
stations	139,405	136,084
Nuclear stations	79,999	81,618
Hydroelectric stations		
Natural flow	4,000	3,993
Pumped storage	2,649	2,930
Renewables other than hydro	1,471	1,406
Major power producers: total	358,406	362,379
Other generators	36,900	38,145
Electricity used on works: total	17,081	17,832
Electricity supplied (gross)		
Conventional thermal and other*	124,052	129,156
Combined cycle gas turbine		
stations	137,170	133,713
Nuclear stations	73,682	75,172
Hydroelectric stations		
Natural flow	3,993	3,987
Pumped storage	2,559	2,776
Renewables other than hydro	1,367	1,309
Major power producers: total	342,824	346,113
Other generators total	35,401	36,579
Electricity used in pumping	3,497	3,707
Electricity consumed		
Fuel industries	8,491	9,162
Final users total	339,641	345,926
Industrial sector	116,531	119,515
Domestic sector	115,526	116,811
Other sectors	107,584	109,600
Total	348,134	355,088

* Includes electricity supplied by gas turbines, oil engines and
plants producing electricity from renewable resources other
than hydro
Source: *Annual Abstract of Statistics 2007* (Crown copyright)

GAS AND ELECTRICITY SUPPLIERS

With the gas and electricity markets open, most suppliers
offer their customers both services. The majority of
gas/electricity companies have become part of larger
multi-utility companies, often operating internationally.
The following list comprises a selection of suppliers
offering gas and electricity. Organisations in italics are
subsidiaries of the companies listed in capital letters
directly above.

ENGLAND, SCOTLAND AND WALES
CE ELECTRIC UK, W www.ce-electricuk.com
   Northern Electric Distribution Ltd, Manor House, Station
   Road, New Penshaw, Houghton-le-Spring DH4 7LA
   T 0800-668877
   Yorkshire Electricity Distribution, 161 Gelderd Road, Leeds
   LS1 1QZ T 0800-375675
CENTRICA PLC, Millstream, Maidenhead Road, Windsor,
   Berkshire SL4 5GD T 01753-494000 W www.centrica.com
   British Gas/Scottish Gas, T 0845-955 5200
   W www.house.co.uk
EDF ENERGY, 40 Grosvenor Place, Victoria, London
   SW1X 7EN T 020-7242 9050 W www.edfenergy.com
E.ON, Westwood Way, Westwood Business Park, Coventry,
   CV4 8LG T 024-7642 4000 W www.eon-uk.com

Powergen, PO Box 7750, Nottingham NG1 6WR
   T 0800-052 0346
NPOWER, PO Box 93, Peterlee SR8 2XX T 08457-7145 146
   W www.npower.com
SCOTTISH AND SOUTHERN ENERGY PLC,
   Inveralmond House, 200 Dunkeld Road, Perth PH1 3AQ
   T 01738 456000 W www.scottish-southern.co.uk
   Scottish Hydro Electric, PO Box 7506, Perth PH1 3QR
   T 0845-300 2141 W www.hydro.co.uk
   Southern Electric, PO Box 7506, Perth PH1 3QR
   T 0845-744 4555 W www.southern-electric.co.uk
   SWALEC, PO Box 7506, Perth PH1 3QR T 0800-052 5252
   W www.swalec.co.uk
SCOTTISHPOWER, Cathcart House, Cathcart Business
   Park, Spean Street, Glasgow G44 4BE T 0845-273 4444
   W www.scottishpower.co.uk

NORTHERN IRELAND
VIRIDIAN GROUP PLC, 120 Malone Road, Belfast
   BT9 5HT T 028-9066 8416 W www.viridiangroup.co.uk
   Energia, Energia House, 62 Newforge Lane, Belfast BT9 5NF
   T 028-9068 5900 W www.viridianenergia.co.uk
   Northern Ireland Electricity, 120 Malone Road, Belfast
   BT9 5HT T 028-9066 1100 W www.nie.co.uk

REGULATION OF THE GAS AND ELECTRICITY INDUSTRIES

The Office of the Gas and Electricity Markets (OFGEM)
regulates the gas and electricity industries in Great
Britain. It was formed in 1999 by the merger of the Office
of Gas Supply and the Office of Electricity Regulation.
OFGEM's overriding aim is to protect and promote the
interests of all gas and electricity customers by promoting
competition and regulating monopolies. It is governed by
an authority and its powers are provided for under the
Gas Act 1986, the Electricity Act 1989 and the Utilities
Act 2000.

THE OFFICE OF THE GAS AND ELECTRICTY
   MARKETS (OFGEM), 9 Millbank, London SW1 3GE
   T 020-7901 7000 W www.ofgem.gov.uk

NUCLEAR POWER

Nuclear reactors began to supply electricity to the
national grid in 1956; in 2006 nuclear power generated
26 per cent of the UK electricity at six magnox reactors,
seven advanced gas-cooled reactors (AGR) and one
pressurised water reactor (PWR), Sizewell 'B' in Suffolk.
In 1989 nuclear stations were withdrawn from
privatisation. In 1996 Nuclear Electric Ltd and Scottish
Nuclear Ltd became operating subsidiaries of British
Energy and the magnox stations were transferred to
Nuclear Electric which became Magnox Electric, later part
of British Nuclear Fuels Ltd. British Energy manages
eight nuclear power stations (seven AGRs and one PWR)
and generates around one-fifth of the UK's electricity.
In April 2005 the responsibility for the
decommissioning of civil nuclear reactors and other
nuclear facilities used in research and development was
handed from the UK Atomic Energy Authority (UKAEA)
to a new body, the Nuclear Decommissioning Authority
(NDA). The NDA is a non-departmental public body,
funded mainly by the Department for Business, Enterprise
and Regulatory Reform. UK Nirex, which was set up by
the nuclear generating companies with the agreement of
the government, is responsible for the disposal of

intermediate and some low-level nuclear waste. The UKAEA now operates on a private contractor basis and is currently decommissioning the nuclear power stations at Dounreay, Harwell, Windscale, Withrin and the JET facilities at Culham.

SAFETY AND REGULATION

The Nuclear Safety Directorate of the Health and Safety Executive is the nuclear industry's regulator. Operations at all UK nuclear power stations are governed by a site licence which is issued under the Nuclear Installations Act. The Nuclear Installations Inspectorate (NII) monitors compliance with each licence through an NII inspector that is assigned to each station and has the jurisdiction to close down a reactor if the terms of the licence are breached. The Department for Business, Enterprise and Regulatory Reform is responsible for security at all the UK's nuclear power stations which are policed by the Civil Nuclear Constabulary, a specialised armed force created in April 2005.

THE NUCLEAR DILEMMA

In February 2007 the high court ruled that the consultation conducted during the government's 2006 review on nuclear energy, which advocated the building of new power plants to provide up to 40 per cent of the country's energy, was 'misleading' and 'seriously flawed'. This ruling has brought energy back into public consideration. Both the former prime minister Tony Blair and the former trade and industry secretary, Alistair Darling, have endorsed nuclear power as the best immediate option.

There are a number of factors which have affected the government's backing of nuclear power: domestic gas supplies are running low, oil and gas prices are rising, carbon emissions must be cut to comply with EU legislation and a number of coal-fired power stations that fail to meet clean air requirements are due to be closed. The government has long foreseen an energy gap in the country's future generating capacity due to the decommissioning of current nuclear stations and the necessity of cutting back on fossil fuels.

- Nuclear power provides over 16 per cent of the world's electricity, almost 24 per cent of electricity in OECD countries, and 34 per cent in the EU.
- All but one of the UK nuclear power stations are set to close by 2023. They produce 20 per cent of the UK electricity.

Nuclear power has a number of advantages: reactors emit virtually no carbon dioxide, uranium prices have remained steady for decades and supply does not depend on agreements with unstable foreign regimes. The advantages of low emissions are countered by the high costs of construction. There are difficulties in disposing of nuclear waste; currently the only method is to store it securely until it has slowly decayed to safe levels. Countries that have sought to develop nuclear weapons in the last 50 years – including North Korea and Iran – have done so through manipulating their nuclear power programmes to create an undeniable and difficult link between nuclear energy and warfare. Finally, public distrust persists with the images of disasters such as Chernobyl difficult to forget, despite the advances in safety technology.

RENEWABLE SOURCES

Renewable sources of energy principally include biofuels, hydro, wind and solar. Renewable sources produced over 4.4 million tonnes of oil equivalent for primary energy usage in 2006; of this, about 3.9 million tonnes was used to generate electricity and 0.5 million tonnes to generate heat. In 2006, the UK generated 4.5 per cent of its total energy production from renewable sources.

The government's principal mechanism for developing renewable energy sources are Non-Fossil Fuel Obligation Renewables Orders. Under the terms of the orders, regional electricity companies are required to buy specified amounts of electricity from specified non-fossil fuel sources. The Renewables Obligation (RO) aims to increase the contribution of electricity from renewables in the UK, so that 10 per cent of licensed UK electricity sales should be from renewable sources eligible for the RO by 2010, and 15 per cent should be eligible by 2015.

A renewables obligation has been in place in England and Wales since April 2002 to give incentives to generators to supply progressively higher levels of renewable energy over time. These measures included exempting renewable energy sources from the climate change levy, capital grants, enhanced research funding and regional planning to meet renewables targets. These developments prompted the British government to approve an EU-wide agreement in March 2007 to generate 20 per cent of energy production from renewable sources by 2020. Former prime minister Tony Blair described the deal as 'groundbreaking, bold and ambitious'. A document produced by the Department for Business, Enterprise and Regulatory Reform in the summer of 2007 cast doubt on the government's ability to achieve its ambitions, suggesting that the UK is capable only of generating 9 per cent by the end of the target period.

RENEWABLE ENERGY SOURCES (2006)

	Percentage
Biofuels and wastes	82.0
Landfill gas	33.1
Sewage gas	4.5
Wood combustion	6.4
Waste combustion	11.6
Other biofuels	7.7
Hydro	9.0
Large-scale	8.0
Small-scale	1.0
Wind and wave	8.2
Geothermal and active solar heating	0.7
Total	100

Source: Department for Business, Enterprise and Regulatory Reform

TRANSPORT

CIVIL AVIATION

Since the privatisation of British Airways in 1987, UK airlines have been operated entirely by the private sector. In 2006, total capacity of British airlines amounted to 50 billion tonne km, of which 39 billion tonne km was on scheduled services. British airlines carried 127 million passengers, 98 million on scheduled services and 30 million on charter flights. Overall, passenger traffic grew by 3 per cent. Traffic at the five main London airports grew by 2 per cent over 2006 and regional airlines saw a growth of 4 per cent, largely due to the expansion of 'no-frills' airlines. Leading British airlines include BMI, British Airways, EasyJet, First Choice Airways, Monarch, My Travel Airways, Thomas Cook Airlines, Thomsonfly and Virgin Atlantic. Irish airline Ryanair also operates frequent flights from Britain.

There are around 140 licensed civil aerodromes in Britain, with Heathrow and Gatwick handling the highest volume of passengers. BAA plc owns and operates the seven major airports: Heathrow, Gatwick, Stansted, Southampton, Glasgow, Edinburgh and Aberdeen, which between them handle about 63 per cent of air passengers and a high percentage of air cargo traffic in Britain. Other airports are controlled by local authorities or private companies.

The Civil Aviation Authority (CAA), an independent statutory body, is responsible for the regulation of UK airlines. This includes economic and airspace regulation, air safety, consumer protection and environmental research and consultancy. All commercial airline companies must be granted an air operator's certificate, which is issued by the CAA to operators meeting the required safety standards. The CAA issues airport safety licences, which must be obtained by any airport used for public transport and training flights. All British-registered aircraft must be granted an airworthiness certificate, and the CAA issues professional licences to pilots, flight crew, ground engineers and air traffic controllers. The CAA also manages the Air Travel Organiser's Licence (ATOL), the UK's principal travel protection scheme. The CAA's costs are met entirely from charges on those whom it regulates; there is no direct government funding of the CAA's work.

The Transport Act, passed by parliament on 29 November 2000, separated the CAA from its subsidiary, National Air Traffic Services (NATS), which provides air traffic control services to aircraft flying in UK airspace and over the eastern part of the North Atlantic. In March 2001 the Airline Group, a consortium of seven UK airlines (British Airways, BMI, Virgin Atlantic, Britannia, Monarch, EasyJet and Airtours), was selected by the government as its strategic partner for NATS. Financial restructuring of NATS was completed in March 2003 with additional equity investment of £65m each from BAA and the government. The new structure enabled NATS to begin a ten-year £1bn investment programme, to increase its flight handling capability to three million flights per annum by 2010. NATS is a public private partnership between the Airline Group, which holds 42 per cent of the shares; NATS staff, who hold 5 per cent; BAA, which holds 4 per cent, and the government, which

holds 49 per cent and a golden share. In 2006 NATS handled a total of 2,386,105 flights, an increase of 3.5 per cent on 2005.

AIR PASSENGERS 2006

ALL UK AIRPORTS: TOTAL	235,139,346
Aberdeen (BAA)	3,162,624
Barra (HIAL)†	9,808
Belfast City	2,105,597
Belfast International	5,015,264
Benbecula (HIAL)†	33,433
Biggin Hill	220
Birmingham	9,056,004
Blackpool	552,641
Bournemouth	960,773
Bristol	5,710,222
Cambridge	1,391
Campbeltown (HIAL)†	8,928
Cardiff	1,993,097
City of Derry (Eglinton)	341,719
Coventry	609,859
Doncaster Sheffield	899,307
Dundee	51,496
Durham Tees Valley	900,107
Edinburgh (BAA)	8,606,651
Exeter	970,614
Gatwick (BAA)	34,080,345
Glasgow (BAA)	8,820,462
Gloucestershire	166
Hawarden*	–
Heathrow (BAA)	67,339,227
Humberside	515,889
Inverness (HIAL)†	670,894
Islay (HIAL)†	26,218
Isle of Man	782,734
Isles of Scilly (St Mary's)	128,093
Isles of Scilly (Tresco)	41,906
Kent International	9,845
Kirkwall (HIAL)†	116,837
Lands End (St Just)	23,380
Leeds Bradford	2,787,217
Lerwick (Tingwall)	4,438
Liverpool	4,962,460
London City	2,358,159
Luton	9,414,829
Lydd	2,754
Manchester	22,123,762
Newcastle	5,407,362
Newquay	343,143
Norwich	745,192
Nottingham East Midlands International	4,720,819
Penzance Heliport	93,958
Plymouth	76,568
Prestwick	2,394,928
Scatsta	255,147
Shoreham	4,508
Southampton (BAA)	1,912,702
Southend	30,222
Stansted (BAA)	23,680,352
Stornoway (HIAL)†	120,288

Sumburgh (HIAL)†	128,233
Tiree (HIAL)†	7,016
Wick (HIAL)†	19,538
CHANNEL ISLANDS AIRPORTS: TOTAL	2,420,723
Alderney	76,806
Guernsey	864,764
Jersey	1,479,153

* Figure not supplied by airport
† Highlands and Islands Airports Ltd (HIAL)
Source: Civil Aviation Authority

CAA, CAA House, 45–59 Kingsway, London WC2B 6TE
   T 020-7379 7311 W www.caa.co.uk
BAA, Belgrave House, London SW1W 9TQ T 020-7834 9449
   W www.baa.com

Gatwick Airport	T 0870-000 2468
Heathrow Airport	T 0870-000 0123
Southampton Airport	T 0870-040 0009
Stansted Airport	T 0870-000 0303
Aberdeen Airport	T 0870-040 0006
Edinburgh Airport	T 0870-040 0007
Glasgow Airport	T 0870-040 0008

BMI, Donington Hall, Castle Donington, Derby DE74 2SB
   T 01332-854000 W www.flybmi.com
BRITISH AIRWAYS, Waterside, PO Box 365,
   Harmondsworth UB7 0GB T 0870-850 9850
   W www.britishairways.com
EASYJET, Hangar 89, London Luton Airport LU2 9PF
   T 0871-244 2366 W www.easyjet.com
FIRST CHOICE AIRWAYS, Diamond House, Peel Cross
   Road, Salford, Manchester M5 4DT T 0871-664 0144
   W www.firstchoice.co.uk
MONARCH, Prospect House, Prospect Way, London Luton
   Airport LU2 9NU T 0870-040 5040
   W www.flymonarch.com
MY TRAVEL AIRWAYS, Holiday House, Sandbrook Park,
   Sandbrook Way, Rochdale OL11 1SA T 0161-498 4498
   W www.mytravel.com
THOMAS COOK AIRLINES, Thomas Cook Business Park,
   Coningsby Road, Peterborough PE3 8SB T 0870-243 0416
   W www.thomascookairlines.com
THOMSONFLY, Wigmore House, Wigmore Lane, Luton
   LU2 9TN T 0870-1900 737 W www.thomsonfly.com
VIRGIN ATLANTIC, The Office, Crawley, Sussex RH10 9NU
   T 01293-562345 W www.virgin-atlantic.com

RAILWAYS

The railway network in Britain was developed by private companies in the 19th century. In 1948 the main railway companies were nationalised and were run by a public authority, the British Transport Commission. The commission was replaced by the British Railways Board in 1963, operating as British Rail. On 1 April 1994, responsibility for managing the track and railway infrastructure passed to a newly formed company, Railtrack plc. In October 2001 Railtrack was put into administration under the Railways Act 1993 and Ernst and Young was appointed as administrator. In October 2002 Railtrack was taken out of administration and replaced by the not-for-profit company Network Rail. The British Railways Board continued as operator of all train services until 1996–7, when they were sold or franchised to the private sector.

The Strategic Rail Authority (SRA) was created to provide strategic leadership to the rail industry and formally came into being on 1 February 2001 following the passing of the Transport Act 2000. In January 2002 it published its first strategic plan, setting out the strategic priorities for Britain's railways over the next ten years. In addition to its coordinating role, the SRA was responsible for allocating government funding to the railways and awarding and monitoring the franchises for operating rail services.

On 15 July 2004 the transport secretary announced a new structure for the rail industry in the white paper *The Future of Rail*. These proposals were implemented under the Railways Act 2005, which abolished the Strategic Rail Authority, passing most of its functions to the Department for Transport; established the Rail Passengers Council (RPC) as a single national body, dissolving the regional committees; and gave devolved governments in Scotland and Wales more say in decisions at a local level. In addition, responsibility for railway safety regulation was transferred to the Office of Rail Regulation from the Health and Safety Executive.

OFFICE OF RAIL REGULATION
The Office of Rail Regulation (ORR) was established on 5 July 2004 by the Railways and Transport Safety Act 2003, replacing the Office of the Rail Regulator. As the railway industry's economic and safety regulator, the ORR's principal function is to regulate Network Rail's stewardship of the national network. The ORR also licenses operators of railway assets, approves agreements for access by operators to track, stations and light maintenance depots, and enforces domestic competition law. The ORR is led by a board appointed by the Secretary of State for Transport, under the chairmanship of Chris Bolt. Mr Bolt also fulfils the role of International Rail Regulator (IRR), a statutory office separate from the ORR, which licenses both the operation of certain international rail services in the European Economic Area and access to railway infrastructure in Great Britain for the purpose of operating international services.

SERVICES
For privatisation, under the Railways Act 1993, domestic passenger services were divided into 25 train operating units, which were franchised to private sector operators via a competitive tendering process. The train operators formed the Association of Train Operating Companies (ATOC) to act as the official voice of the passenger rail industry and provide its members with a range of services enabling them to comply with conditions imposed on them through their franchise agreements and operating licences.

As at June 2007 there were 24 passenger train operating companies (TOCs): Arriva Trains Wales; c2c; Central Trains; Chiltern Railways; Eurostar; First Capital Connect; First Great Western; First ScotRail; Gatwick Express; GNER; Heathrow Connect; Heathrow Express; Hull Trains; Island Line (Isle of Wight); Merseyrail; Midland Mainline; Northern Rail; One; Silverlink; South West Trains; Southeastern; Southern; TransPennine Express and Virgin Trains.

Network Rail publishes a national timetable which contains details of rail services operated over the UK network and sea ferry services which provide connections with Ireland, the Isle of Man, the Isle of Wight, the Channel Islands and some European destinations.

The national rail enquiries service offers information about train times and fares for any part of the country,

Transport for London (TfL) provides London-specific travel information for all modes of travel and Eurostar provides information for international channel tunnel rail services:

NATIONAL RAIL ENQUIRIES
T 08457-484950
W www.nationalrail.co.uk
TRANSPORT FOR LONDON
T 020-7222 1234
W www.tfl.gov.uk
EUROSTAR
T 08705-186 186
W www.eurostar.com

PASSENGER FOCUS AND LONDON TRAVELWATCH

Passenger Focus is the operating name of the Rail Passengers' Council, a single national consumer body for rail, which is funded by the Department for Transport but whose independence is guaranteed by an act of parliament. Rail Users' Consultative Committees were set up under the Railways Act 1993 to protect the interests of users of the services and facilities provided on Britain's rail network. The Transport Act 2000 changed their name to Rail Passenger Committees (RPCs) and brought the committees under the overall sponsorship of the Strategic Rail Authority. There were eight RPCs nationwide, one for each of the six English regions and one each for Scotland and Wales. Under the Railways Act 2005, the eight regional committees were disbanded in June 2005 and their functions and duties transferred to the Rail Passengers' Council , the Strategic Rail Authority was abolished and sponsorship for the Rail Passengers' Council transferred to the Department for Transport.

Established in July 2000, London TravelWatch is the operating name of the official watchdog organisation representing the interests of transport users in and around the capital. Officially known as the London Transport Users' Committee, it is sponsored and funded by the London Assembly and is independent of the transport operators. London TravelWatch represents users of buses, the Underground, river and rail services in and around London, including Eurostar and Heathrow Express, Croydon Tramlink and the Docklands Light Railway. The interests of pedestrians, cyclists and motorists are also represented, as are those of taxi users.

FREIGHT

Rail freight services are provided by a small number of companies. On privatisation, British Rail's bulk freight operations were sold to English, Welsh and Scottish Railways (EWS). The other major companies in the rail freight sector are Freightliner Ltd (formerly the British Rail container business), Direct Rail Service (DRS) and GB Railfreight. In 2005 22.1 billion tonne kilometres of freight was moved by rail.

NETWORK RAIL

Network Rail is responsible for the tracks, bridges, tunnels, level crossings, viaducts and 17 main stations that form Britain's rail network. In addition to providing the timetables for the passenger and freight operators, Network Rail is also responsible for all the signalling and electrical control equipment needed to operate the rail network and for monitoring and reporting performance across the industry.

Network Rail is a private company run as a commercial business; it is directly accountable to its members and regulated by the ORR. The members have similar rights to those of shareholders in a public company except they do not receive dividends or share capital and thereby have no financial or economic interest in Network Rail. All of Network Rail's profits are reinvested into maintaining and upgrading the rail infrastructure.

ASSOCIATION OF TRAIN OPERATING
COMPANIES, 3rd Floor, 40 Bernard Street, London
WC1N 1BY T 020-7841 8000 W www.atoc.org
LONDON TRAVELWATCH, 6 Middle Street, London
EC1A 7JA T 020-7505 9000
W www.londontravelwatch.org.uk
NETWORK RAIL, 40 Melton Street, London NW1 2EE
T 020-7557 8000 W www.networkrail.co.uk
OFFICE OF RAIL REGULATION, 1 Kemble Street,
London WC2B 4AN T 020-7282 2000
W www.rail-reg.gov.uk
Chair / International Rail Regulator, Chris Bolt
PASSENGER FOCUS, Freepost WA1521, Warrington
WA4 6GP T 0845-3022 022
W www.railpassengers.org.uk

RAIL SAFETY

On 1 April 2006 responsibility for health and safety policy and enforcement on the railways transferred from the Health and Safety Executive to the Office of Rail Regulation.

In 2006 a total of 20 passengers, railway staff and other members of the public were fatally injured in rail incidents, compared with 33 in 2005. There were no passenger fatalities resulting from train incidents in 2006.

ACCIDENTS ON RAILWAYS

	2005	2006
Total train incidents	1,057	1,061
Total train incident fatalities	7	0
Passengers	0	0
Railway employees	1	0
Others	6	0
Total train incident injuries	51	43
Passengers	22	20
Railway staff	20	19
Others	9	4

TRESPASSERS, SUICIDES AND ATTEMPTED SUICIDES
2006*

Total fatalities	321
Total injuries	140

*Includes all incidents on rail (network rail, London Underground and other rail systems, such as trams). Fatality data is subject to change pending the outcome of Coroners' inquests
Source: Office of Rail Regulation – *Railway Safety Statistical Report 2006*

OTHER RAIL SYSTEMS

Responsibility for the London Underground passed from the government to the Mayor and Transport for London on 15 July 2003, with a public-private partnership (PPP) already in place. Plans for a public-private partnership for London Underground were pushed through by the government in February 2002 despite opposition from the Mayor of London and a range of transport organisations. Under the PPP, long-term contracts with private companies were estimated to enable around £16bn to be invested in renewing and upgrading the Underground's infrastructure over 15 years. Responsibility for stations, trains, operations, signalling and safety remains in the public sector. In 2005–6 there were 970 million passenger journeys on the London Underground, a decrease of 0.6 per cent on the previous year.

Britain has nine other light rail, tram or underground systems: Blackpool Tramway, Croydon Tramlink, Docklands Light Railway (DLR), Glasgow Subway, Manchester Metrolink, Midland Metro, Nottingham Express Transit (NET), Sheffield Supertram and Tyne and Wear Metro.

Light rail and metro systems in Great Britain contributed to the growth in public transport, with 175 million passenger journeys in 2005–6, an increase of 1.7 per cent on the previous year. In England there were 162 million passenger journeys in 2005–6, compared with 124 million in 2000–1. The government's ten-year Transport Plan target is to double light rail use in England (measured by number of passenger journeys) by 2010 compared to 2000 levels.

THE CHANNEL TUNNEL

The earliest recorded scheme for a submarine transport connection between Britain and France was in 1802. Tunnelling began simultaneously on both sides of the Channel three times: in 1881, in the early 1970s, and on 1 December 1987, when construction workers bored the first of the three tunnels which form the Channel Tunnel. Engineers 'holed through' the first tunnel (the service tunnel) on 1 December 1990 and tunnelling was completed in June 1991. The tunnel was officially inaugurated by the Queen and President Mitterrand of France on 6 May 1994.

The submarine link comprises two rail tunnels, each carrying trains in one direction, which measure 7.6m (24.93ft) in diameter. Between them lies a smaller service tunnel, measuring 4.8m (15.75ft) in diameter. The service tunnel is linked to the rail tunnels by 130 cross-passages for maintenance and safety purposes. The tunnels are 50km (31 miles) long, 38km (24 miles) of which is under the seabed at an average depth of 40m (132ft). The rail terminals are situated at Folkestone and Calais, and the tunnels go underground at Shakespeare Cliff, Dover, and Sangatte, west of Calais.

Eurostar is the high-speed passenger train service connecting London with Paris in 2 hours 15 minutes and Brussels in 1 hours 51 minutes, via the Channel Tunnel (from 14 November 2007). Some trains stop en route at Ashford (Kent) and Calais, Disneyland Paris and Lille in France.

RAIL LINKS

The route for the British Channel Tunnel Rail Link will run from Folkestone to a new terminal at St Pancras station, London, with new intermediate stations at Ebbsfleet, Kent, and Stratford, east London. International services presently running into a terminal at Waterloo station, London, will discontinue.

Construction of the rail link is being financed by the private sector with a substantial government contribution. A private sector consortium, London and Continental Railways Ltd (LCR), is responsible for the design, construction and ownership of the rail link, and comprises Union Railways and the UK operator of Eurostar. Construction was expected to be completed in 2003, but on 28 January 1998 LCR informed the government that it was unable to fulfil its obligations. On 3 June 1998 the government announced a new funding agreement with LCR. The rail link will be constructed in two phases: phase one, from the Channel Tunnel to Fawkham Junction, North Kent, began in October 1998 and opened to fare-paying passengers on 28 September 2003; phase two, from Southfleet Junction to St Pancras, was due to be completed in November 2007. Infrastructure developments in France have been completed and high-speed trains run from Calais to Paris and from Lille to the south of France.

ROADS

HIGHWAY AUTHORITIES

The powers and responsibilities of highway authorities in England and Wales are set out in the Highways Act 1980; for Scotland there is separate legislation.

Responsibility for trunk road motorways and other trunk roads in Great Britain rests in England with the Secretary of State for Transport, in Scotland with the Scottish Executive, and in Wales with the Welsh Assembly. The costs of construction, improvement and maintenance are paid for by central government in England and by the Welsh Assembly Government in Wales. The highway authority for non-trunk roads in England, Wales and Scotland is, in general, the local authority in whose area the roads lie. With the establishment of the Greater London Authority in July 2000, Transport for London became the highway authority for roads in London.

In Northern Ireland the Department of Regional Development is the statutory road authority responsible for public roads and their maintenance and construction; the Roads Service executive agency carries out these functions on behalf of the department.

FINANCE

In England all aspects of trunk road and motorway funding are provided directly by the government to the Highways Agency, which operates, maintains and improves a network of motorways and trunk roads over 7,200km (4,500 miles) long, on behalf of the secretary of state. Since 2001 the length of the network that the Highways Agency is responsible for has been decreasing due to a policy of de-trunking, which transfers responsibility for non-core roads to local authorities. For the financial year 2007–8 the Highways Agency's total planned expenditure is £6,470m: £839m for maintenance, £789m for major improvements, £197m revenue support for major private investment, £312m for existing network improvements and technology and the remainder for other programmes and administration costs.

Government support for local authority capital expenditure on roads and other transport infrastructure is provided through grant and credit approvals as part of the Local Transport Plan (LTP). Local authorities bid for resources on the basis of a five-year programme built around delivering integrated transport strategies. As well as covering the structural maintenance of local roads and the construction of major new road schemes, LTP funding also includes smaller-scale safety and traffic management measures with associated improvements for public transport, cyclists and pedestrians.

For the financial year 2007–8, planned expenditure in the form of LTP funding for local authorities is £1.7bn. £683m for road maintenance, £571m for small-scale integrated transport measures and £481m for new and existing major projects.

Total expenditure by the Welsh Assembly Government on trunk roads, motorways, rail, bus and other transport services (including grants to local authorities) in 2006–7 was £537m. Planned expenditure for 2007–8 is £542m.

Until 1999 the Scottish Office received a block vote from parliament and the Secretary of State for Scotland determined how much was spent on roads. Since 1 July 1999 all decisions on transport expenditure have been devolved to the Scottish Executive. Total expenditure on motorways and trunk roads in Scotland during 2006–7 was £907.2m, including depreciation and cost of capital charge. Planned expenditure for 2007–8 is £895m.

In Northern Ireland total expenditure by the Roads Service on all roads in 2006–7 was £121.1m, with £118.8m spent on trunk roads and motorways. Planned expenditure for 2007–8 is £101.8m, with £85.5m allocated for trunk roads and motorways.

The Transport Act 2000 gave English and Welsh local authorities (outside London) powers to introduce road-user charging or workplace parking levy schemes. The act requires that the net revenue raised is used to improve local transport services and facilities for at least ten years. The aim is to reduce congestion and encourage greater use of alternative modes of transport. Schemes developed by local authorities require government approval. The government's 2000 Ten Year Plan for Transport assumes that eight large road user charging schemes and 12 large workplace parking levy schemes will be developed by 2010. The UK's first toll road, the M6 Toll, opened in December 2003 and runs for 43.5km (27 miles) around Birmingham from junction 3a to junction 11a on the M6.

Charging schemes in London are allowed under the 1999 Greater London Authority Act. The Central London Congestion Charge Scheme began on 17 February 2003 (*see also* Regional Government).

TARGETED PROGRAMME OF IMPROVEMENTS

The Targeted Programme of Improvements constitutes the Highway Agency's investment programme in the trunk road and motorway networks. The programme comprises 80 major road schemes, each costing more than £5m, funded either conventionally or by public-private partnerships.

ROAD LENGTHS 2005
Kilometres

	England	Wales	Scotland	Great Britain
Motorways	2,992	141	386	3,519
Dual carriageway	6,569	553	783	7,905
Single carriageway	25,646	3,619	9,487	38,752
B roads	19,863	2,981	7,345	30,189
C roads	64,294	9,841	10,324	84,459
Unclassified roads	178,548	16,098	28,538	223,184
TOTAL	297,912	33,233	56,864	388,008

Source: Department for Transport

ROAD USE

ROAD TRAFFIC BY TYPE OF VEHICLE (GREAT BRITAIN) 2005
Million vehicle kilometres

All motor vehicles	499,400
Cars and taxis	397,200
Motorcycles	5,400
Buses and coaches	5,200
Light vans	62,600
Other goods vehicles	29,000
Pedal cycles	4,400

Source: Department for Transport

FREIGHT TRANSPORT BY ROAD (GREAT BRITAIN) 2005

GOODS MOVED
By mode of working (billion tonne kilometres)

All modes	153
Own account	43
Public haulage	110

By gross weight of vehicle (billion tonne kilometres)

All vehicles	153
3.5–25 tonnes	17
Over 25 tonnes	136

GOODS LIFTED
By mode of working (million tonnes)

All modes	1,746
Own account	667
Public haulage	1,079

By gross weight of vehicle (million tonnes)

All vehicles	1,746
3.5–25 tonnes	257
Over 25 tonnes	1,489

Source: Department for Transport

BUSES

Nearly all bus and coach services in Great Britain are provided by private sector companies. The Transport Act 2000 outlines a ten-year transport plan intended to promote bus use, through agreements between local authorities and bus operators, and to improve the standard and efficiency of services. The ten-year plan sets targets for bus patronage and reliability of services. There are a number of ways in which the government supports bus services:

- Bus Service Operators Grant (BSOG) is paid directly to bus operators and reimburses the major part of the excise duty paid on the fuel used in operating locally registered bus services
- Rural Bus Subsidy Grant (RBSG) is paid to local authorities with rural areas to fund socially necessary bus services that are not provided commercially
- Payments to local authorities to fund existing Rural and Urban Bus Challenge (RUBC) schemes aimed at providing innovative and flexible transport solutions, such as taxi bus services, in public transport deprived rural and urban areas.

In 2007–8 planned expenditure by central government on BSOG is £405m and £67m on RBSG and RUBC schemes.

Since April 2006 it has been a statutory minimum requirement for all local authorities to provide free local bus travel between 9.30am and 11pm, and all day at weekends and bank holidays, to people aged 60 and over and disabled people who qualify under the categories listed in the Transport Act 2000. Local authorities recompense operators for the reduced fare revenue.

In London, Transport for London (TfL) has overall responsibility for setting routes, service standards and fares for the bus network. Almost all routes are competitively tendered to commercial operators.

In Northern Ireland, passenger transport services are provided by Ulsterbus and Metro (formerly Citybus), two wholly owned subsidiaries of the Northern Ireland Transport Holding Company. Along with Northern Ireland Railways, Ulsterbus and Metro operate under the brand name of Translink and are publicly owned. Ulsterbus is responsible for virtually all bus services in Northern Ireland except Belfast city services, which are operated by Metro.

BUS PASSENGER JOURNEYS 2005–6 (GREAT BRITAIN)
No. of journeys (millions)

England	4,125
London	1,810
Wales	117
Scotland	477
TOTAL	4,719
Source: Department for Transport	

TAXIS AND PRIVATE HIRE VEHICLES

A taxi is a public transport vehicle with fewer than nine passenger seats, which is licensed to 'ply for hire'. This distinguishes taxis from private hire vehicles which must be booked in advance through an operator. In London, taxis and private hire vehicles are licensed by the Public Carriage Office (PCO), part of TfL. Outside of London, local authorities are responsible for the licensing of taxis and private hire vehicles operational in their respective administrative areas. At the end of March 2005 there were 63,957 taxis and 79,305 licensed private hire vehicles in England, of these, 20,750 taxis and 40,000 private hire vehicles were licensed by the PCO in London.

ROAD SAFETY

In March 2000, the government published a new road safety strategy, *Tomorrow's Roads – Safer for Everyone*, which set new casualty reduction targets for 2010. The new targets include a 40 per cent reduction in the overall number of people killed or seriously injured in road accidents, a 50 per cent reduction in the number of children killed or seriously injured and a 10 per cent reduction in the slight casualty rate (per 100 million vehicle kilometres), all compared with the average for 1994–8.

There were 258,404 reported casualties on roads in Great Britain in 2006, 5 per cent less than in 2005. Child casualties fell by 9 per cent with 169 child fatalities, an increase of 20 per cent compared to 2005 figures. Car user casualties decreased by 4 per cent on the 2005 level to 171,000 and fatalities decreased by 4 per cent to 1,612 from 1,675. Pedestrian casualties were 30,982 in 2006, 7 per cent less than 2005, although pedestrian deaths were 1 per cent higher compared to 2005 at 675. Compared to 2005, pedal cyclist casualties fell by 2 per cent to 16,196 and the number of pedal cyclists killed on British roads decreased by 1 per cent from 148 to 146.

ROAD ACCIDENT CASUALTIES 2006

	Fatal	Serious	Slight	All Severities
Average for 1994–8	3,578	44,078	272,272	319,928
England	2,695	24,856	201,026	228,577
Wales	163	1,210	11,319	12,692
Scotland	314	2,607	14,214	17,135
Great Britain	3,172	28,673	226,559	258,404

	Killed	Injured
1965	7,952	389,985
1970	7,499	355,869
1975	6,366	318,584
1980	6,010	323,000
1985	5,165	312,359
1990	5,217	335,924
1995	3,621	306,885
2000	3,409	316,872
2005	3,201	267,816
2006	3,172	255,232
Source: Department for Transport		

DRIVING LICENCES

It is necessary to hold a valid full licence in order to drive unaccompanied on public roads in the UK. Learner drivers must obtain a provisional driving licence before starting to learn to drive and must then pass theory and practical tests to obtain a full driving licence.

There are separate tests for driving motorcycles, cars, passenger-carrying vehicles (PCVs) and large goods vehicles (LGVs). Drivers must hold full car entitlement before they can apply for PCV or LGV entitlements.

The Driver and Vehicle Licensing Agency (DVLA) ceased the issue of paper licences in March 2000, however, those currently in circulation will remain valid until they expire or the details on them change. The photocard driving licence was introduced to comply with the second EC directive on driving licences. This requires a photograph of the driver to be included on all UK licences issued from July 2001.

To apply for a first photocard driving licence, individuals are required to complete the form *Application for a Driving Licence* (D1).

The minimum age for driving motor cars, light goods vehicles up to 3.5 tonnes and motorcycles is 17 (moped, 16). Since June 1997, drivers who collect six or more penalty points within two years of qualifying lose their licence and are required to take another test. All forms and leaflets including *What You Need to Know About Driving Licences* (D100), are available from post offices, DVLA local offices and online (W www.dvla.gov.uk or W www.direct.gov.uk).

The DVLA is responsible for issuing driving licences, registering and licensing vehicles, and collecting excise duty in Great Britain. Driver and Vehicle Licensing Northern Ireland (DVLNI), part of the Driver and Vehicle Agency (DVA), has similar responsibilities in Northern Ireland.

DRIVING LICENCE FEES*
valid from February 2007 to March 2008

Provisional licence	
Car, motorcycle or moped	£45.00
Bus or lorry	Free
After disqualification until passing re-test	Free
Changing a provisional licence to a full licence	Free
Renewal	
At age 70 and over	Free
For medical reasons	Free
Bus or lorry licence	Free
After disqualification	£60.00
After disqualification for some drink driving offences†	£85.00
After revocation	£45.00
Replacing a lost or stolen licence	£22.00
Adding an entitlement to a full licence	Free
Removing expired endorsements	
from a photocard licence	£22.00
from a paper licence (while exchanging it for a photocard licence)	£10.00
Exchanging	
a paper licence for a photocard licence	£10.00
a photocard for a photocard licence	£22.00
a full GB licence for a full Northern Ireland licence	Free
a full GB licence for a full EC/EEA or other foreign licence (including Channel Islands and Isle of Man)	Free
a full EC/EEA or other foreign licence (including Channel Islands and Isle of Man) for a full GB licence	£45.00

Change of name or address (existing licence   Free
    must be surrendered)

* If the application involves two separate fees only the higher
  fee is payable
† For an alcohol-related offence where the DVLA needed to
  arrange medical enquiries

DRIVING TESTS

The Driving Standards Agency (DSA) is responsible for
carrying out driving tests and approving driving
instructors in Great Britain. Driver and Vehicle Testing,
part of the Driver and Vehicle Agency, is responsible for
testing drivers and vehicles in Northern Ireland.

DRIVING TESTS TAKEN AND PASSED
April 2006–March 2007

Type of Test	Number Taken	Percentage Passed
Practical Test		
Car	1,789,882	43
Motorcycle	77,007	65
Large goods vehicle	78,140	46
Passenger-carrying vehicle	9,922	46
Theory Test		
Car	1,306,335	68
Motorcycle	71,831	84
Large goods vehicle	41,725	75
Passenger-carrying vehicle	8,919	70

Source: DSA

The theory and practical driving tests can be booked
with a postal application, online (W www.dsa.gov.uk or
W www.direct.gov.uk) or by phone (T 0870-010 1372).

DRIVING TEST FEES (Weekday rate/evening* and weekend
rate)
from September 2007

Theory tests	
Car and motorcycle	£28.50
Lorry and bus	£32.00
Practical tests:	
Car	£48.50/£58.00
Tractors and other specialist vehicles	£48.50/£58.00
Motorcycle	£60.00/£70.00
Lorry and bus	£89.00/£107.00
Car and trailer	£89.00/£107.00
Extended tests for disqualified drivers:	
Car	£97.00/£116.00
Motorcycle	£120.00/£140.00

* after 4.30pm

VEHICLE LICENCES

Registration and first licensing of vehicles is through local
offices of the DVLA in Swansea. Local facilities for
relicensing are available at any post office which deals
with vehicle licensing. Applicants will need to take their
vehicle registration document (V5C) or, if this is not
available, the applicant must complete form V62. Postal
applications can be made to the post offices shown in the
V100 booklet, which also provides guidance on
registering and licensing vehicles. All forms and booklets
are available at post offices, DVLA local offices and online
(W www.dvla.gov.uk or W www.direct.gov.uk)

MOTOR VEHICLES LICENSED 2006 (GREAT BRITAIN)

	Thousands
All cars	27,830
Taxis (black cabs only)	43
Motorcycles, mopeds and scooters	1,224
Buses and coaches	181
Light goods vehicles	3,053
Heavy goods vehicles	419
Other vehicles	619
TOTAL	33,369

Source: Department for Transport

VEHICLE EXCISE DUTY

Details of the present duties chargeable on motor vehicles
are available at DVLA local offices, post offices and online
(W www.dvla.gov.uk or W www.direct.gov.uk). The Vehicle
Excise and Registration Act 1994 provides *inter alia* that
any vehicle kept on a public road but not used on roads is
chargeable to excise duty as if it were in use. All non-
commercial vehicles constructed before 1 January 1973
are exempt from vehicle excise duty. Any vehicle licensed
on or after 31 January 1998, not in use and not kept on
public roads must be registered as SORN (Statutory Off
Road Notification) to be exempted from vehicle excise
duty. From 1 January 2004 the registered keeper of a
vehicle remains responsible for taxing a vehicle or making
a SORN declaration until that liability is formally
transferred to a new keeper.

	12 months rate £	6 months rate £
Private/light goods vehicles registered before 1 March 2001 (not over 3,500kg)		
Under 1,549cc	115.00	63.25
Over 1,549cc	180.00	99.00
Motorcycles (with or without sidecar)		
Not over 150cc	15.00	–
151–400cc	32.00	–
401–600cc	47.00	–
600cc+	64.00	35.20
Tricycles		
Not over 150cc	15.00	–
All others	64.00	35.20
Light goods vehicles (not over 3,500kg) registered on or after 1 March 2001	175.00	96.25
Euro 4 light goods vehicles registered between 1 March 2003 and 31 December 2006	115.00	63.25
Buses *		
Seating 10–17 persons	165.00 (165.00)	90.75 (90.75)
Seating 18–36 persons	220.00 (165.00)	121.00 (90.75)
Seating 37–61 persons	330.00 (165.00)	181.50 (90.75)
Seating 61+ persons	500.00 (165.00)	275.00 (90.75)

* Figures in parentheses refer to reduced pollution vehicles.
  Seating capacity includes driver

RATES OF EXCISE DUTY *from March 2007*

Band	CO_2 Emissions (g/km)	Diesel Car 12 months	6 months	Petrol Car 12 months	6 months	Alternative Fuel Car 12 months	6 months
Private vehicles registered on or after 1 March 2001							
A	Up to 100	£0.00	–	£0.00	–	£0.00	–
B	101–120	£35.00	–	£35.00	–	£15.00	–
C	121–150	£115.00	£63.25	£115.00	£63.25	£95.00	£52.25
D	151–165	£140.00	£77.00	£140.00	£77.00	£120.00	£66.00
E	166–185	£165.00	£90.75	£165.00	£90.75	£145.00	£79.75
F	186–225	£205.00	£112.75	£205.00	£112.75	£190.00	£104.50
Private vehicles registered on or after 23 March 2006							
G	225+	£300.00	£165.00	£300.00	£165.00	£285.00	£156.75

MOT TESTING

Cars, motorcycles, motor caravans, light goods and dual-purpose vehicles more than three years old must be covered by a current MOT test certificate. However, some vehicles (ie minibuses, ambulances and taxis) may require a certificate at one year old. All certificates must be renewed annually. The MOT testing scheme is administered by the Vehicle and Operator Services Agency (VOSA) on behalf of the Secretary of State for Transport.

A fee is payable to MOT testing stations, which must be authorised to carry out tests. The maximum fees, which are prescribed by regulations as at 7 November 2006, are:

For cars and public service vehicles (up to eight seats), motor caravans, dual purpose, ambulances and taxis	£50.35	
For motorcycles	£27.15	
For motorcycles with sidecar	£34.65	
For three-wheeled vehicles	£34.65	
Private passenger vehicles and ambulances with:		
9–12 passenger seats	£52.60	£58.75†
13–16 passenger seats	£54.65	£74.10†
16+ passenger seats	£73.95	£114.45†
Goods vehicles (3,000–3,500kg)	£53.80	

† Including seatbelt installation check

SHIPPING AND PORTS

Sea trade has always played a central role in Britain's economy. By the 17th century Britain had built up a substantial merchant fleet and by the early 20th century it dominated the world shipping industry. Until the late 1990s the size and tonnage of the UK-registered trading fleet had been steadily declining. In December 1998 the government published *British Shipping: Charting a New Course*, which outlined strategies to promote the long-term interests of British shipping. By the end of 2006 the number of ships in the UK fleet had increased by 66 per cent whilst tonnage had more than tripled. The UK-flagged merchant fleet now constitutes 1.3 per cent of the world fleet in terms of vessels and 1.7 per cent in terms of tonnage.

Freight is carried by liner and bulk services, almost all scheduled liner services being containerised. About 95 per cent by weight of Britain's overseas trade is carried by sea; this amounts to 75 per cent of its total value. Passengers and vehicles are carried by roll-on, roll-off ferries, hovercraft, hydrofoils and high-speed catamarans.

There were about 45 million ferry passengers in 2006, of whom 23 million travelled internationally.

Lloyd's of London provides the most comprehensive shipping intelligence service in the world. *Lloyd's Shipping Index,* published daily, lists some 25,000 ocean-going vessels and gives the latest known report of each.

PORTS

There are more than 650 ports in Great Britain for which statutory harbour powers have been granted. Of these about 120 are commercially significant ports. In 2006* the largest ports in terms of freight tonnage were Grimsby and Immingham (64.0 million tonnes), Tees and Hartlepool (53.3 million tonnes), London (51.9 million tonnes), Southampton (40.5 million tonnes), Milford Haven (34.3 million tonnes), Liverpool (33.6 million tonnes), Forth (31.1 million tonnes), Felixstowe (24.4 million tonnes), Dover (23.8 million tonnes) and Sullom Voe (19.4 million tonnes). Belfast is the principal freight port in Northern Ireland.

Broadly speaking, ports are owned and operated by private companies, local authorities or trusts. The largest operator is Associated British Ports which owns 21 ports. Provisional port traffic results show that 580 million tonnes were handled by UK ports in 2006, an decrease of 1.0 per cent on the previous year's figure of 585 million tonnes.

* Provisional data

MARINE SAFETY

The Maritime and Coastguard Agency is an executive agency of the Department for Transport. Working closely with the shipping industry and the public its aims are to:
• reduce accidents and accident related deaths within UK search and rescue waters and coastline
• reduce accidents and accident related deaths from UK registered merchant ships and fishing vessels
• reduce the number of incidents of pollution from shipping activities in the UK pollution control zone

HM Coastguard maintains a 24-hour search and rescue response and coordination capability for the whole of the UK coast and the internationally agreed search and rescue region. HM Coastguard is responsible for mobilising and organising resources in response to people in distress at sea, or at risk of injury or death on the UK's cliffs or shoreline. There are around 500 coastguards and a further 3,000 voluntary auxiliary coastguards that form over 400 local coastguard rescue teams. In 2006 HM Coastguard rescued 4,809 people whose life was at risk and gave assistance to a further 23,113 people whose life was not at risk. Of the total number of 371 deaths recorded by the coastguard, 124 resulted from maritime accidents.

Locations hazardous to shipping in coastal waters are marked by lighthouses and other lights and buoys. The lighthouse authorities are the Corporation of Trinity House (for England, Wales and the Channel Islands), the Northern Lighthouse Board (for Scotland and the Isle of Man), and the Commissioners of Irish Lights (for Northern Ireland and the Republic of Ireland). Trinity House maintains 72 lighthouses, 10 light vessels/floats, 412 buoys, 19 beacons, 48 radar beacons and seven DGPS (Differential Global Positioning System) stations*. The Northern Lighthouse Board maintains 215 lighthouses, 157 buoys, 40 beacons, 26 radar beacons, four DGPS stations and one LORAN (long-range navigation) station; and Irish Lights looks after 80 lighthouses, 149 buoys, 47 beacons, 22 radar beacons, three DGPS stations, two LANBYs (large automatic navigational buoys) and one light float.

Harbour authorities are responsible for pilotage within their harbour areas; and the Ports Act 1991 provides for the transfer of lights and buoys to harbour authorities where these are used for mainly local navigation.

* DGPS is a satellite-based navigation system

UK-OWNED TRADING VESSELS
100 gross tons and over, as at end 2005

Type of vessel	No.	Gross tonnage
Liquid	169	4,147,000
Dry bulk	60	2,753,000
Specialised carrier	19	263,000
Container	75	3,297
Ro-Ro	137	1,413
Other general cargo	179	920,000
Passenger	49	926,000
All trading vessels	688	13,719
of which registered in the UK	382	5,739

Source: Department for Transport

UK SEA PASSENGER MOVEMENTS 2006
Type of journey	*No. of passenger movements**
International†	23,465,000
Domestic	3,476,000

* Passengers are included at both departure and arrival if their journeys begin and end at a UK seaport
† Routes to Belgium, Denmark, Faroe Islands, Finland, France, Germany, Ireland, the Netherlands, Norway, Spain and Sweden
Source: Department for Transport

MARINECALL WEATHER FORECAST SERVICE

Marinecall offers a wide range of inshore, offshore and European forecasts from the Met Office which include gale and strong wind warnings, the general situation, wind speed and direction, probability and strength of gusts, developing weather conditions, visibility and sea state. Information is provided by various means including telephone, fax, SMS etc. Marinecall 10-day forecasts contain a 48-hour inshore/offshore sea area summary, followed by a 1–5 day forecast for the local sea area, 6–10 day national forecast and an outlook for the month ahead. In addition fax forecasts provide a synoptic chart. Other services such as area specific, current weather reports and 6-hour forecasts are also available.

MARINECALL 10-DAY FORECAST

	By Phone 09068-500+	By Fax 09065-300+
INSHORE AREA		
Cape Wrath – Rattray Head	451	251
Rattray Head – Berwick	452	252
Berwick – Whitby	453	253
Whitby – Gibraltar Point	454	254
Gibraltar Point – North Foreland	455	255
North Foreland – Selsey Bill	456	256
Selsey Bill – Lyme Regis	457	257
Lyme Regis – Hartland Point	458	258
Hartland Point – St David's Head	459	259
St David's Head – Great Ormes Head	460	260
Great Ormes Head – Mull of Galloway	461	261
Mull of Galloway – Mull of Kintyre	462	262
Mull of Kintyre – Ardnamurchan	463	263
Ardnamurchan – Cape Wrath	464	264
Lough Foyle – Carlingford Lough	465	265
Channel Islands	432	–
OFFSHORE AREA		
English Channel	992	270
Southern North Sea	991	271
Irish Sea	954	273
Biscay	953	274
North-west Scotland	955	275
Northern North Sea	985	276

Marinecall by UK landline is charged at 60p per minute and Marinecall by fax at £1.50 per minute. Calls from mobiles may be subject to network operator surcharges.

UK SHIPPING FORECAST AREAS

Weather bulletins for shipping are broadcast daily on BBC Radio 4 at the following times: 0048 and 0520, 1201 and 1754 on long wave at 1515m (198kHz). The bulletins consist of a gale warning summary, general synopsis, sea-area forecasts and coastal station reports. In addition, gale warnings are broadcast at the first available programme break after receipt. If this does not coincide with a news bulletin, the warning is repeated after the next news bulletin. Shipping forecasts and gale warnings are also available online (W www.bbc.co.uk/weather/coast/shipping).

RELIGION IN THE UK

The 2001 census included a voluntary question on religion for the first time (although the question had been included in previous censuses in Northern Ireland); 92 per cent of people chose to answer the question. In the UK, 71.6 per cent of people in Britain identified themselves as Christian (42.1 million people). After Christianity, the next most prevalent faith was Islam with 2.7 per cent describing their religion as Muslim (1.6 million people). The next largest religious groups were Hindus (559,000), followed by Sikhs (336,000), Jews (267,000), Buddhists (152,000) and people from other religions (179,000). Together, these groups accounted for less than 3 per cent of the total UK population. People in Northern Ireland were most likely to say that they identified with a religion (86 per cent) compared with 77 per cent in England and Wales and 67 per cent in Scotland. The English counties with the highest proportion of Christians are Durham, Merseyside and Cumbria, each with 82 per cent or more; in Wales it is Ynys Mon (Isle of Anglesey) (79 per cent). London has the highest proportion of Muslims (8.5 per cent), Hindus (4.1 per cent), Jews (2.1 per cent), Buddhists (0.8 per cent) and people of other religions (0.5 per cent). Around 16 per cent of the UK population stated that they had no religion. The districts with the highest proportions of people with no religion were Norwich, Brighton and Hove and Cambridge, all with over 25 per cent. This category included those who identified themselves as agnostics, atheists, heathens and Jedi Knights.

CENSUS 2001 RESULTS – RELIGIONS IN THE UK

	thousand	per cent
Christian	42,079	71.6
Buddhist	152	0.3
Hindu	559	1.0
Jewish	267	0.5
Muslim	1,591	2.7
Sikh	336	0.6
Other religion	179	0.3
All religions	45,163	76.8
No religion	9,104	15.5
Not stated	4,289	7.3
All no religion / not stated	13,626	23.2
TOTAL	58,789	100

Source: Census 2001

ADHERENTS TO RELIGIONS IN THE UK
(million people)

	1975	1985	1995	2000
Christian (Trinitarian)	40.2	39.1	38.1	37.5
Non-Trinitarian	0.7	1.0	1.3	1.3
Hindu	0.3	0.4	0.4	0.5
Jew	0.4	0.3	0.3	0.3
Muslim	0.4	0.9	1.2	1.4
Sikh	0.2	0.3	0.6	0.6
Other	0.1	0.3	0.3	0.4
Total	42.3	42.3	42.2	42.0

Source: Christian Research – UK Christian Handbook
Religious Trends 3

INTER-CHURCH AND INTER-FAITH COOPERATION

The main umbrella body for the Christian churches in the UK is Churches Together in Britain and Ireland. There are also ecumenical bodies in each of the constituent countries of the UK: Churches Together in England, Action of Churches Together in Scotland, CYTUN (Churches Together in Wales), and the Irish Council of Churches. The Free Churches Group (formerly the Free Churches Council), which is closely associated with Churches Together in England, represents most of the free churches in England and Wales, and the Evangelical Alliance represents evangelical Christians.

The Inter Faith Network for the United Kingdom promotes cooperation between faiths, and the Council of Christians and Jews works to improve relations between the two religions. Churches Together in Britain and Ireland also has a commission on inter faith relations.

ACTION OF CHURCHES TOGETHER IN
  SCOTLAND, 7 Forrester Lodge, Inglewood, Alloa
  FK10 2HU T 01259-216980
  E ecumenical@acts-scotland.org W www.acts-scotland.org
  General Secretary, Brother Stephen Smyth
CHURCHES TOGETHER IN BRITAIN AND
  IRELAND, Bastille Court, 2 Paris Garden, London SE1 8ND
  T 020-7654 7254 E info@ctbi.org.uk W www.ctbi.org.uk
  General Secretary, Revd Bob Fyffe
CHURCHES TOGETHER IN ENGLAND, 27 Tavistock
  Square, London WC1H 9HH T 020-7529 8131
  E office@cte.org.uk W www.churches-together.org.uk
  General Secretary, Revd Bill Snelson
COUNCIL OF CHRISTIANS AND JEWS, 1st Floor,
  Camelford House, 87–89 Albert Embankment, London
  SE1 7TP T 020-7820 0090 E cjrelations@ccj.org.uk
  W www.ccj.org.uk
  Chief Executive, David Gifford
CYTUN (CHURCHES TOGETHER IN WALES), 58
  Richmond Road, Cardiff CF24 3UR T 029-2046 4204
  E post@cytun.org.uk W www.cytun.org.uk
  Chief Executive, Revd Aled Edwards
EVANGELICAL ALLIANCE, 186 Kennington Park Road,
  London SE11 4BT T 020-7207 2100 E info@eauk.org
  W www.eauk.org
  General Director, Revd Joel Edwards
FREE CHURCHES GROUP, 27 Tavistock Square, London
  WC1H 9HH T 020-7529 8131 E freechurch@cte.org.uk
  Executive Secretary, Revd Mark Fisher
INTER-FAITH NETWORK FOR THE UNITED
  KINGDOM, 8A Lower Grosvenor Place, London
  SW1W 0EN T 020-7931 7766 E ifnet@interfaith.org.uk
  W www.interfaith.org.uk
  Director, Dr Harriet Crabtree
IRISH COUNCIL OF CHURCHES, Inter-Church Centre,
  48 Elmwood Avenue, Belfast BT9 6AZ T 028-9066 3145
  E irish.churches@btconnect.com W www.irishchurches.org
  General Secretary, Michael Earle

CHRISTIANITY

Christianity is a monotheistic faith based on the person and teachings of Jesus Christ, and all Christian denominations claim his authority. Central to its teaching is the concept of God and his son Jesus Christ, who was crucified and resurrected in order to enable mankind to attain salvation.

The Jewish scriptures predicted the coming of a *Messiah*, an 'anointed one', who would bring salvation. To Christians, Jesus of Nazareth, a Jewish rabbi (teacher) who was born in Palestine, was the promised Messiah. Jesus' birth, teachings, crucifixion and subsequent resurrection are recorded in the *Gospels*, which, together with other scriptures that summarise Christian belief, form the *New Testament*. This, together with the Hebrew scriptures – entitled the *Old Testament* by Christians – makes up the Bible, the sacred texts of Christianity.

BELIEFS

Christians believe that sin distanced mankind from God, and that Jesus was the son of God, sent to redeem mankind from sin by his death. In addition, many believe that Jesus will return again at some future date, triumph over evil and establish a kingdom on earth, thus inaugurating a new age. The Gospel assures Christians that those who believe in Jesus and obey his teachings will be forgiven their sins and will be resurrected from the dead.

PRACTICES

Christian practices vary widely between different Christian churches, but prayer, charity and giving (for the maintenance of the church buildings, for the work of the church, and to the poor and needy) are common to all. In addition, certain days of observance, ie the *Sabbath, Easter* and *Christmas,* are celebrated by most Christians. The Orthodox, Roman Catholic and Anglican churches celebrate many more days of observance, based on saints and significant events in the life of Jesus. The belief in sacraments, physical signs believed to have been ordained by Jesus Christ to symbolise and convey spiritual gifts, varies greatly between Christian denominations; *baptism* and the *Eucharist* are practised by most Christians. Baptism, symbolising repentance and faith in Jesus, is an act marking entry into the Christian community; the Eucharist, the ritual re-enactment of the Last Supper, Jesus' final meal with his disciples, is also practised by most denominations. Other sacraments, such as anointing the sick; the laying on of hands to symbolise the passing on of the office of priesthood or to heal the sick and speaking in tongues, where it is believed that the person is possessed by the Holy Spirit, are less common. In denominations where infant baptism is practised, confirmation (where the person repeats the commitments made for him or her at infancy) is common. Matrimony and the ordination of priests are also widely believed to be sacraments. Many Protestants regard only baptism and the Eucharist to be sacraments; the Quakers and the Salvation Army reject the use of sacraments.

Most Christians believe that God actively guides the church.

THE EARLY CHURCH

The Apostles were Jesus' first converts and are recognised by Christians as the founders of the Christian community. The new faith spread rapidly throughout the eastern provinces of the Roman Empire. Early Christianity was subjected to great persecution until AD 313, when Emperor Constantine's Edict of Toleration confirmed its right to exist and it was established as the religion of the Roman Empire in AD 381.

The Christian faith was slowly formulated in the first millennium of the Christian era. Between AD 325 and 787 there were seven Oecumenical Councils at which bishops from the entire Christian world assembled to resolve various doctrinal disputes. The estrangement between East and West began after Constantine moved the centre of the Roman Empire from Rome to Constantinople, and it grew after the division of the Roman Empire into eastern and western halves. Linguistic and cultural differences between Greek East and Latin West served to encourage separate ecclesiastical developments which became pronounced in the tenth and early 11th centuries.

Administration of the church was divided between five ancient patriarchates: Rome and all the West, Constantinople (the imperial city – the 'New Rome'), Jerusalem and all of Palestine, Antioch and all the East and Alexandria and all of Africa. Of these, only Rome was in the Latin West and after the schism in 1054, Rome developed a structure of authority centralised on the Papacy, while the Orthodox East maintained the style of localised administration.

Papal authority over the doctrine and jurisdiction of the church in Western Europe was unrivalled after the split with the Eastern Orthodox Church until the Protestant Reformation in the 16th century.

CHRISTIANITY IN BRITAIN

An English church already existed when Pope Gregory sent Augustine to evangelise the English in AD 596. Conflicts between Church and State during the Middle Ages culminated in the Act of Supremacy in 1534, which repudiated papal supremacy and declared King Henry VIII to be the supreme head of the church in England. Since 1559 the English monarch has been termed the Supreme Governor of the Church of England.

In 1560 the jurisdiction of the Roman Catholic Church in Scotland was abolished and the first assembly of the Church of Scotland ratified the Confession of Faith, drawn up by a committee led by John Knox. In 1592 parliament passed an act guaranteeing the liberties of the church and its Presbyterian government. King James VI (James I of England) and later Stuart monarchs attempted to reintroduce episcopacy, but a Presbyterian church was finally restored in 1690 and secured by the Act of Settlement (1690) and the Act of Union (1707).

PORVOO DECLARATION

The Porvoo Declaration was drawn up by representatives of the British and Irish Anglican churches and the Nordic and Baltic Lutheran churches and was approved by the General Synod of the Church of England in July 1995. Churches that approve the declaration regard baptised members of each other's churches as members of their own, and allow free interchange of episcopally ordained ministers within the rules of each church.

NON-CHRISTIAN RELIGIONS AND BELIEFS

BAHA'I FAITH

Mirza Husayn-'Ali, known as *Baha'u'llah* (Glory of God) was born in Iran in 1817 and became a follower of the *Bab,* a religious reformer and prophet who was imprisoned for his beliefs and executed on the grounds of heresy in 1850. Baha'u'llah was himself imprisoned in 1852, and in 1853 he had a vision that he was the 'promised one' foretold by the Bab. He was exiled after his release from prison and eventually arrived in Acre, now in Israel, where he continued to compose the Baha'i sacred scriptures. He died in 1892 and was succeeded by his son, Abdu'l-Baha, as spiritual leader, under whose guidance the faith spread to Europe and North America. He was followed by Shoghi Effendi, his grandson, who translated many of Baha'u'llah's works into English. Upon his death in 1957, a democratic system of leadership was brought into operation.

The Baha'i faith espouses the unity and relativity of religious truth and teaches that there is only one God, whose will has been revealed to mankind by a series of messengers, such as Zoroaster, Abraham, Moses, Buddha, Krishna, Christ, Muhammad, the Bab and Baha'u'llah, who were seen as the founders of separate religions, but whose common purpose was to bring God's message to mankind. It teaches that all races and both sexes are equal and deserving of equal opportunities and treatment, that education is a fundamental right and encourages a fair distribution of wealth. In addition, the faith exhorts mankind to establish a world federal system to promote peace and tolerance.

A feast is held every 19 days, which consists of prayer and readings of Baha'i scriptures, consultation on community business, and social activities. Music, food and beverages usually accompany the proceedings. There is no clergy; each local community elects a local assembly, which coordinates community activities, enrols new members, counsels and assists members in need, and conducts Baha'i marriages and funerals. A national assembly is elected annually by locally elected delegates, and every five years the national spiritual assemblies meet together to elect the Universal House of Justice, the supreme international governing body of the Baha'i Faith. Worldwide there are over 13,000 local spiritual assemblies; there are around five million members residing in about 235 countries, of which 179 have national organisations.

THE BAHA'I OFFICE OF PUBLIC INFORMATION,
27 Rutland Gate, London SW7 1PD T 020-7584 2566
E nsa@bahai.org.uk W www.bahai.org.uk
Secretary of the National Spiritual Assembly, Dr Kishan Manocha
Secretary for External Affairs, Robert Weinberg

BUDDHISM

Buddhism originated in what is now the Bihar area of northern India in the teachings of Siddhartha Gautama, who became the *Buddha* (Enlightened One). The Buddhist era is dated from his passing away 45 years after his enlightenment; the year 2008 is 2551 by the Buddhist reckoning.

Fundamental to Buddhism is the concept of rebirth, whereby each life carries with it the consequences of the conduct of earlier lives (known as the law of *karma*) and this cycle of death and rebirth is broken only when the state of *nirvana* has been reached. Buddhism steers a middle path between belief in personal continuity and the belief that death results in total extinction.

While doctrine does not have a pivotal position in Buddhism, a statement of four 'Noble Truths' is common to all its schools and varieties. These are: suffering is inescapable in even the most fortunate of existences; craving is the root cause of suffering; abandonment of the selfish mindset is the way to end suffering; and bodily and mental discipline, accompanied by the cultivation of wisdom and compassion, provides the spiritual path ('Noble Eightfold Path') to accomplish this. Buddhists deny the idea of a creator and prefer to emphasise the practical aspects of moral and spiritual development.

The schools of Buddhism can be broadly divided into three: *Theravada,* the generally monastic-led tradition practised in Sri Lanka and south-east Asia; *Mahayana,* the philosophical and popular traditions of the Far East; *Esoteric,* the Tantric-derived traditions found in Tibet and Mongolia and, to a lesser extent, China and Japan. The extensive Theravada scriptures are contained in the *Pali Canon,* which dates in its written form from the first century BC. Mahayana and Esoteric schools have Sanskrit-derived translations of these plus many more additional scriptures as well as exegetical material.

In the East the new and full moons and the lunar quarter days were (and to a certain extent, still are) significant in determining the religious calendar. Most private homes contain a shrine where offerings, worship and other spiritual practices (such as meditation, chanting or mantra recitation) take place on a daily basis. Buddhist festivals vary according to local traditions within the different schools and there is very little uniformity – even in commemorating the birth, enlightenment and death of the Buddha.

There is no governing authority for Buddhism in the UK. Communities representing all schools of Buddhism operate independently. The Buddhist Society was established in 1924; it runs courses, lectures and meditation groups, and publishes books about Buddhism. The Network of Buddhist Organisations was founded in 1993 to promote fellowship and dialogue between Buddhist organisations and to facilitate cooperation in matters of common interest.

There are estimated to be at least 300 million Buddhists worldwide. Of the 152,000 Buddhists in the UK (according to the 2001 census), 60,000 are white British (the majority are converts), 36,000 Chinese, 15,000 Asian and 36,000 'other ethnic'.

THE BUDDHIST SOCIETY, 58 Eccleston Square, London SW1V 1PH T 020-7834 5858 E info@thebuddhistsociety.org
W www.thebuddhistsociety.org

FRIENDS OF THE WESTERN BUDDHIST ORDER,
The London Buddhist Centre, 51 Roman Road, London E2 0HU T 0845-458 4716 E info@lbc.org.uk
W www.lbc.org.uk

THE NETWORK OF BUDDHIST ORGANISATIONS,
6 Tyne Road, Bishopston, Bristol BS7 8EE T 0845-345 8978
E secretary@nbo.org.uk W www.nbo.org.uk

TIBET HOUSE TRUST, Tibet House, 1 Culworth Street, London NW8 7AF T 020-7722 5378
E secretary@tibet-house-trust.co.uk
W www.tibet-house-trust.co.uk

SOKA GAKKAI UK, Taplow Court Grand Cultural Centre, Taplow, Maidenhead, Berkshire SL6 0ER
T 01628-773163
W www.sgi-uk.org

HINDUISM

Hinduism has no historical founder but had become highly developed in India by c.2500 BC. Its adherents originally called themselves Aryans; Muslim invaders first called the Aryans 'Hindus' (derived from 'Sindhu', the name of the river Indus) in the eighth century.

Most Hindus hold that *satya* (truthfulness), honesty, sincerity and devotion to God are essential for good living. They believe in one supreme spirit *(Brahman)*, and in the transmigration of *atman* (the soul). Most Hindus accept the doctrine of *karma* (consequences of actions), the concept of *samsara* (successive lives) and the possibility of all atmans achieving *moksha* (liberation from samsara) through *jnana* (knowledge), *yoga* (meditation), *karma* (work or action) and *bhakti* (devotion).

Most Hindus offer worship to *murtis* (images of deities) representing different incarnations or aspects of Brahman, and follow their *dharma* (religious and social duty) according to the traditions of their *varna* (social class), *ashrama* (stage in life), *jaiti* (caste) and *kula* (family).

Hinduism's sacred texts are divided into *shruti* ('that which is heard'), including the *Vedas*, and *smriti* ('that which is remembered'), including the *Ramayana*, the *Mahabharata*, the *Puranas* (ancient myths), and the sacred law books. Most Hindus recognise the authority of the *Vedas*, the oldest holy books, and accept the philosophical teachings of the *Upanishads*, the *Vedanta Sutras* and the *Bhagavad-Gita*.

Hindus believe Brahman to be omniscient, omnipotent, limitless and all-pervading. Brahman is usually worshipped in its deity form. Brahma, Vishnu and Shiva are the most important deities or aspects of Brahman worshipped by Hindus; their respective consorts are Saraswati, Lakshmi and Durga or Parvati, also known as Shakti. There are believed to have been ten *avatars* (incarnations) of Vishnu, of whom the most important are Rama and Krishna. Other popular gods are Ganesha, Hanuman and Subrahmanyam. All Hindu gods are seen as aspects of the supreme spirit (Brahman), not as competing deities.

Orthodox Hindus revere all gods and goddesses equally, but there are many denominations, including the Hare-Krishna movement (ISKCon), the Arya Samaj and the Swaminarayan Hindu mission, in which worship is concentrated on one deity. The *guru* (spiritual teacher) is seen as the source of spiritual guidance.

Hinduism does not have a centrally trained and ordained priesthood. The pronouncements of the *shankaracharyas* (heads of monasteries) of Shringeri, Puri, Dwarka and Badrinath are heeded by the orthodox but may be ignored by the various sects.

The commonest form of worship is *puja*, in which water, flowers, food, fruit, incense and light are offered to the deity. Puja may be done either in a home shrine or a *mandir* (temple). Many British Hindus celebrate *samskars* (purification rites), for example to name a baby, the sacred thread (an initiation ceremony), marriage and cremation.

The largest communities of Hindus in Britain are in Leicester, London, Birmingham and Bradford, and developed as a result of immigration from India, eastern Africa and Sri Lanka.

There are an estimated 800 million Hindus worldwide; there are around 559,000 adherents, according to the 2001 UK census, and over 140 temples in the UK.

ARYA SAMAJ LONDON, 69A Argyle Road, London
W13 0LY T 020-8991 1732
E aryasamajlondon@yahoo.co.uk
General Secretary, Amrit Lal Bhardwaj

BHARATIYA VIDYA BHAVAN, Institute of Indian Art and Culture, 4A Castletown Road, London W14 9HE
T 020-7381 3086 E info@bhavan.net W www.bhavan.net
Executive Director, Dr M. N. Nandakumara
INTERNATIONAL SOCIETY FOR KRISHNA CONSCIOUSNESS (ISKCON), Bhaktivedanta Manor, Dharam Marg, Hilfield Lane, Aldenham, Watford, Herts WD25 8EZ T 01923-857244
E bhaktivedanta.manor@pamho.net
W www.krishnatemple.com
Temple President, Gauri das
NATIONAL COUNCIL OF HINDU TEMPLES (UK), Shree Sanatan Mandir, 84 Weymoth Street, Leicester LE4 6FQ T 0116-266 1402 E info@nchtuk.org
W www.nchtuk.org
General Secretary, Sanjay Jagatia
SWAMINARAYAN HINDU MISSION (SHRI SWAMINARAYAN MANDIR), 105–119 Brentfield Road, London NW10 8LD T 020-8965 2651
E info@mandir.org W www.mandir.org

HUMANISM

Humanism traces its roots back to ancient times, with Indian, Chinese, Greek and Roman philosophers expressing Humanist ideas some 2,500 years ago. Confucius, the Chinese philosopher who lived c.500 BC, believed that religious observances should be replaced with moral values as the basis of social and political order and that 'the true way' is based on reason and humanity. He also stressed the importance of benevolence and respect for others, and believed that the individual situation should be considered rather than the global application of traditional rules.

Humanists believe that there is no God or other supernatural being, that humans have only one life (Humanists do not believe in an after-life or reincarnation) and that humans can live ethical and fulfilling lives without religious beliefs through a moral code derived from a shared history, personal experience and thought. There are no sacred Humanist texts. Particular emphasis is placed on science as the only reliable source of knowledge of the universe. Many Humanists recognise a need for ceremonies to mark important occasions in life and the British Humanist Association has a network of officiants and celebrants who are trained and accredited to conduct baby namings, weddings and funerals. The British Humanist Association's campaigns for a secular society (a society based on freedom of religious or non-religious belief with no privileges for any particular set of beliefs) are based on equality and human rights, and the association also campaigns for inclusive schools that meet the needs of all parents and pupils, regardless of their religious or non-religious beliefs.

BRITISH HUMANIST ASSOCIATION, 1 Gower Street, London WC1E 6HD T 020-7079 3580 F 020-7079 3588
E info@humanism.org.uk W www.humanism.org.uk
Chief Executive, Hanne Stinson

ISLAM

Islam (which means 'peace arising from submission to the will of Allah' in Arabic) is a monotheistic religion which was taught in Arabia by the Prophet Muhammad, who was born in Mecca (Al-Makkah) in 570 AD. Islam spread to Egypt, north Africa, Spain and the borders of China in the century following the Prophet's death, and is now the predominant religion in Indonesia, the near and Middle East, northern and parts of western Africa, Pakistan, Bangladesh, Malaysia and some of the former Soviet republics. There are also large Muslim communities in other countries.

For Muslims (adherents of Islam), there is one God *(Allah)*, who holds absolute power. Muslims believe that Allah's commands were revealed to mankind through the prophets, who include Abraham, Moses and Jesus, but that Allah's message was gradually corrupted until revealed finally and in perfect form to Muhammad through the angel *Jibril* (Gabriel) over a period of 23 years. This last, incorruptible message is said to have been recorded in the *Qur'an* (Koran), which contains 114 divisions called *surahs*, each made up of *ayahs* of various lengths, and is held to be the essence of all previous scriptures. The *Ahadith* are the records of the Prophet Muhammad's deeds and sayings (the *Sunnah*) as practised and recounted by his immediate followers. A culture and a system of law and theology gradually developed to form a distinctive Islamic civilisation. Islam makes no distinction between sacred and worldly affairs and provides rules for every aspect of human life. The *Shariah* is the sacred law of Islam based primarily upon prescriptions derived from the *Qur'an* and the *Sunnah* of the Prophet.

The 'five pillars of Islam' are *shahadah* (a declaration of faith in the oneness and supremacy of Allah and the messengership of Muhammad); *salat* (formal prayer, to be performed five times a day facing the *Ka'bah* (the most sacred shrine in the holy city of Mecca)); *zakat* (welfare due, paid annually on all savings at the rate of 2.5 per cent); *sawm* (fasting during the month of Ramadan from dawn until sunset); and *hajj* (pilgrimage to Mecca made once in a lifetime if the believer is financially and physically able). Some Muslims would add *jihad* as the sixth pillar (striving for the cause of good and resistance to evil).

Two main groups developed among Muslims. *Sunni* Muslims accept the legitimacy of Muhammad's first four *caliphs* (successors as head of the Muslim community) and of the authority of the Muslim community as a whole. About 90 per cent of Muslims are Sunni Muslims.

Shi'ites recognise only Muhammad's son-in-law Ali as his rightful successor and the *Imams* (descendants of Ali, not to be confused with *imams,* who are prayer leaders or religious teachers) as the principal legitimate religious authority. The largest group within Shi'ism is *Twelver Shi'ism*, which has been the official school of law and theology in Iran since the 16th century; other subsects include the *Ismailis*, the *Druze* and the *Alawis,* the latter two differing considerably from the main body of Muslims. The *Ibadis* of Oman are neither Sunni nor Shia, deriving from the strictly observant *Khariji* (Seceeders). There is no organised priesthood, but learned men such as imams, *ulama,* and *ayatollahs* are accorded great respect. The *Sufis* are the mystics of Islam. Mosques are centres for worship and teaching and also for social and welfare activities.

Islam was first recorded in western Europe in the eighth century AD when 800 years of Muslim rule began in Spain. Later, Islam spread to eastern Europe. More recently, Muslims came to Europe from Africa, the Middle East and Asia in the late 19th century. Both the Sunni and Shi'a traditions are represented in Britain, but the majority of Muslims in Britain adhere to Sunni Islam. Efforts to establish a representative national body for Muslims in Britain resulted in the founding, in 1997, of the Muslim Council of Britain. In addition, there are many other Muslim organisations in the UK. There are around 1,200 million Muslims worldwide, with nearly two million adherents and about 1,632 mosques in the UK.

IMAMS AND MOSQUES COUNCIL, 20–22 Creffield Road, London W5 3RP **T** 020-8992 6636
E msraza@muslimcollege.ac.uk
Executive Secretary, Moulana M. S. Raza
ISLAMIC CULTURAL CENTRE – THE LONDON CENTRAL MOSQUE, 146 Park Road, London NW8 7RG
T 020-7724 3363 **E** info@iccuk.org **W** www.iccuk.org
Director, Dr Ahmad Al-Dubayan
MUSLIM COUNCIL OF BRITAIN, PO Box 57330, London E1 2WJ **T** 0845-262 6786 **E** admin@mcb.org.uk
W www.mcb.org.uk
Secretary-General, Dr Muhammad Abdul Bari
MUSLIM WORLD LEAGUE LONDON, 46 Goodge Street, London W1T 4LU **T** 020-7636 7568
Director, Abdul Aziz al-Harbi
UNION OF MUSLIM ORGANISATIONS OF THE UK AND EIRE, 109 Campden Hill Road, London W8 7TL
T 020-7221 6608
Secretary-General, Dr Syed A. Pasha

JAINISM

Jainism traces its history to Vardhamana Jnatriputra, known as *Tirthankara Mahavira* (The Great Hero) whose traditional dates were 599–527 BC. He was the last of a series of 24 *Jinas* (those who overcome all passions and desires) or *Tirthankaras* (those who show a way across the ocean of life) stretching back to remote antiquity. Born to a noble family in north-eastern India, he renounced the world for the life of a wandering ascetic and after 12 years of austerity and meditation he attained enlightenment. He then preached his message until, at the age of 72, he passed away and reached *moksha,* total liberation from the cycle of death and rebirth.

Jains declare that the Hindu rituals of transferring merit are not acceptable as each living being is responsible for its own actions. They recognise some of the minor deities of the Hindu pantheon, but the supreme objects of worship are the Tirthankaras. The pious Jain does not ask favours from the Tirthankaras, but seeks to emulate their example in his or her own life.

Jains believe that the universe is eternal and self-subsisting, that there is no omnipotent creator God ruling it and the destiny of the individual is in his or her own hands. *Karma,* the fruit of past actions, is believed to determine the place of every living being and rebirth may be in the heavens, on earth as a human, an animal or other lower being, or in the hells. The ultimate goal of existence for Jains is *moksha* or *nirvana,* a state of perfect knowledge and tranquility for each individual soul, which can be achieved only by gaining enlightenment.

The Jainist path to liberation is defined by the Three Jewels, *samyak darshana* (right perception), *samyak jnana* (right knowledge) and *samyak charitra* (right conduct). Of the five fundamental precepts of the Jains, *Ahimsa* (non-injury to any form of being, in any mode) is the first and foremost, and was popularised by Gandhi as *Ahimsa paramo dharma.*

There are around 25,000 Jains in Britain, sizeable communities in North America and east Africa and smaller groups in many other countries.

INSTITUTE OF JAINOLOGY, Unit 18, Silicon Business Centre, 28 Wadsworth Road, Perivale, Greenford, Middx UB6 7JZ **T** 020-8997 2300 **E** enquiries@jainology.org
W www.jainology.org
Secretary, Harshad Sanghrajka

JUDAISM

Judaism is the oldest monotheistic faith. The primary text of Judaism is the Hebrew bible or *Tanakh*, which records how the descendants of Abraham were led by Moses out of their slavery in Egypt to Mount Sinai where God's law *(Torah)* was revealed to them as the chosen people. The *Talmud*, which consists of commentaries on the *Mishnah* (the first text of rabbinical Judaism), is also held to be authoritative, and may be divided into two main categories: the *halakah* (dealing with legal and ritual matters) and the *aggadah* (dealing with theological and ethical matters not directly concerned with the regulation of conduct). The *midrash* comprises rabbinic writings containing biblical interpretations in the spirit of the aggadah. The halakah has become a source of division: orthodox Jews regard Jewish law as derived from God and therefore unalterable; progressive Jews seek to interpret it in the light of contemporary considerations; and conservative Jews aim to maintain most of the traditional rituals but to allow changes in accordance with tradition. Reconstructionist Judaism, a 20th-century movement, regards Judaism as a culture rather than a theological system and accepts all forms of Jewish practice.

The family is the basic unit of Jewish ritual, with the synagogue playing an important role as the centre for public worship and religious study. A synagogue is led by a group of laymen who are elected to office. The Rabbi is primarily a teacher and spiritual guide. The Sabbath is the central religious observance. Most British Jews are descendants of either the *Ashkenazim* of central and eastern Europe or the *Sephardim* of Spain, Portugal and the Middle East.

The Chief Rabbi of the United Hebrew Congregations of the Commonwealth is appointed by a Chief Rabbinate Conference, and is the rabbinical authority of the mainstream Orthodox sector of the Ashkenazi Jewish community, the largest body of which is the United Synagogue. His formal ecclesiastical authority is not recognised by the Reform Synagogues of Great Britain (the largest progressive group), the Union of Liberal and Progressive Synagogues, the Sephardi community or the Assembly of Masorti Synagogues. He is, however, generally recognised both outside the Jewish community and within it as the public religious representative of the totality of British Jewry. The Chief Rabbi is President of the London *Beth Din* (Court of Judgement), a rabbinic court. The *Dayanim* (Assessors) adjudicate in disputes or on matters of Jewish law and tradition; they also oversee dietary law administration, marriage, divorce and issues of personal status.

The Board of Deputies of British Jews, established in 1760, is the representative body of British Jewry. The basis of representation is through the election of deputies by synagogues and communal organisations. It protects and promotes the interests of British Jewry, acts as the central voice of the community and seeks to counter anti-Jewish discrimination and anti-Semitic activities.

There are over 12.5 million Jews worldwide; in Great Britain and Ireland there are an estimated 285,000 adherents and about 365 synagogues. Of these, 191 congregations and about 175 rabbis and ministers are under the jurisdiction of the Chief Rabbi; 99 orthodox congregations have a more independent status; and 79 congregations are outside the jurisdiction of the Chief Rabbi.

OFFICE OF THE CHIEF RABBI, Adler House, 735 High Road, London N12 0US T 020-8343 6301 F 020-8343 6310 E info@chiefrabbi.org W www.chiefrabbi.org
Chief Rabbi, Sir Jonathan Sacks
BETH DIN (COURT OF THE CHIEF RABBI), 735 High Road, London N12 0US T 020-8343 6270
E info@bethdin.org.uk W www.theus.org.uk
Registrar, David Frei
Dayanim, Rabbi Chanoch Ehrentreu *(Consultant Dayan)*; Menachem Gelley *(Senior Dayan)*; Ivan Binstock; Yonason Abraham; Shmuel Simons
ASSEMBLY OF MASORTI SYNAGOGUES, Alexander House, 3 Shakespeare Road, London N3 1XE
T 020-8349 6650 E enquiries@masorti.org.uk
W www.masorti.org.uk
Executive Director, Michael Gluckman
BOARD OF DEPUTIES OF BRITISH JEWS, 6 Bloomsbury Square, London WC1A 2LP T 020-7543 5400 F 020-7543 0010 E info@bod.org.uk W www.bod.org.uk
President, Henry Grunwald, QC
FEDERATION OF SYNAGOGUES, 65 Watford Way, London NW4 3AQ T 020-8202 2263
E info@federationofsynagogues.com
W www.federationofsynagogues.com
President, Alan Finlay
LIBERAL JUDAISM, The Montagu Centre, 21 Maple Street, London W1T 4BE T 020-7580 1663
E montagu@liberaljudaism.org W www.liberaljudaism.org
Chief Executive, Rabbi Danny Rich
THE MOVEMENT FOR REFORM JUDAISM, The Sternberg Centre for Judaism, 80 East End Road, London N3 2SY T 020-8349 5640 E admin@reformjudaism.org.uk
W www.reformjudaism.org.uk
Head of Movement, Rabbi Tony Bayfield
SPANISH AND PORTUGUESE JEWS' CONGREGATION, 2 Ashworth Road, London W9 1JY
T 020-7289 2573 E howardmiller@spsyn.org.uk
W www.sandp.org
Chief Executive, Howard Miller
UNION OF ORTHODOX HEBREW CONGREGATIONS, 140 Stamford Hill, London N16 6QT
T 020-8802 6226 F 020-8809 6590
Principal Rabbinical Authority, Rabbi Ephraim Padwa
UNITED SYNAGOGUE HEAD OFFICE, Adler House, 735 High Road, London N12 0US T 020-8343 8989
F 020-8343 6262 E info@unitedsynagogue.org.uk
W www.theus.org.uk
Chief Executive, Rabbi Saul Zneimer

PAGANISM

Paganism draws on the ideas of the Celtic people of pre-Roman Europe and is closely linked to Druidism. The first historical record of Druidry comes from classical Greek and Roman writers of the third century BC, who noted the existence of Druids among a people called the Keltoi who inhabited central and southern Europe. The word druid may derive from the Indo-European 'dreo-vid', meaning 'one who knows the truth'. In practice it was probably understood to mean something like 'wise-one' or 'philosopher-priest'.

Paganism is a pantheistic nature-worshipping religion which incorporates beliefs and ritual practices from ancient times. Pagans place much emphasis on the natural world and the ongoing cycle of life and death is central to their beliefs. Most Pagans believe that they are part of nature and not separate from, or superior to it, and seek to live in a way that minimises harm to the natural environment (the word Pagan derives from the Latin

Paganus, meaning 'rural'). Paganism strongly emphasises the equality of the sexes, with women playing a prominent role in the modern Pagan movement and goddess worship featuring in most ceremonies. Paganism cannot be defined by any principal beliefs because it is shaped by each individual's experiences.

The Pagan Federation was founded in 1971 to provide information on Paganism, campaigns on issues which affect Paganism and provides support to members of the Pagan community. Within the UK the Pagan Federation is divided into 13 districts each with a district manager, regional and local coordinators. Local meetings are called 'moots' and take place in private homes, pubs or coffee bars. The Pagan Federation publishes a quarterly journal, *Pagan Dawn,* formerly *The Wiccan* (founded in 1968). The federation also publishes other material, arranges members-only and public events and maintains personal contact by letter with individual members and the wider Pagan community. An annual conference is held at the end of each November and there are regional gatherings throughout the year.

THE PAGAN FEDERATION, BM Box 7097, London WC1N 3XX T 0798-603 4378 E secretary@paganfed.org
W www.paganfed.org
President, Lindsey Heffern

SIKHISM

The Sikh religion dates from the birth of Guru Nanak in the Punjab in 1469. 'Guru' means teacher but in Sikh tradition has come to represent the divine presence of God giving inner spiritual guidance. Nanak's role as the human vessel of the divine guru was passed on to nine successors, the last of whom (Guru Gobind Singh) died in 1708. The immortal guru is now held to reside in the sacred scripture, *Guru Granth Sahib,* and so to be present in all Sikh gatherings.

Guru Nanak taught that there is one God and that different religions are like different roads leading to the same destination. He condemned religious conflict, ritualism and caste prejudices. The fifth Guru, Guru Arjan Dev, largely compiled the Sikh Holy scripture, a collection of hymns *(gurbani)* known as the *Adi Granth.* It includes the writings of the first five gurus and the ninth guru, and selected writings of Hindu and Muslim saints whose views are in accord with the gurus' teachings. Guru Arjan Dev also built the Golden Temple at Amritsar, the centre of Sikhism. The tenth guru, Guru Gobind Singh, passed on the guruship to the sacred scripture, Guru Granth Sahib and founded the *Khalsa,* an order intended to fight against tyranny and injustice. Male initiates to the order added 'Singh' to their given names and women added 'Kaur'. Guru Gobind Singh also made the wearing of five symbols obligatory: *kaccha* (a special undergarment), *kara* (a steel bangle), *kirpan* (a small sword), *kesh* (long unshorn hair, and consequently the wearing of a turban) and *kangha* (a comb). These practices are still compulsory for those Sikhs who are initiated into the Khalsa (the *Amritdharis*). Those who do not seek initiation are known as *Sehajdharis.*

There are no professional priests in Sikhism; anyone with a reasonable proficiency in the Punjabi language can conduct a service. Worship can be offered individually or communally, and in a private house or a *gurdwara*

(temple). Sikhs are forbidden to eat meat prepared by ritual slaughter; they are also asked to abstain from smoking, alcohol and other intoxicants. Such abstention is compulsory for the Amritdharis.

There are about 20 million Sikhs worldwide and, according to the 2001 census, there are 336,000 adherents in the UK. Every gurdwara manages its own affairs; there is no central body in the UK. The Sikh Missionary Society provides an information service.

SIKH MISSIONARY SOCIETY UK, 10 Featherstone Road, Southall, Middx UB2 5AA T 020-8574 1902
E info@sikhmissionarysociety.org
W www.sikhmissionarysociety.org
Hon. General Secretary, Surinder Singh Purewal

ZOROASTRIANISM

Zoroastrians are followers of the Iranian prophet Spitaman Zarathushtra (or Zoroaster in its hellenised form) who lived *c.*1200 BC. Zoroastrians were persecuted in Iran following the Arab invasion of Persia in the seventh century AD and a group (who are known as Parsis) migrated to India in the eighth century AD to avoid harassment and persecution. Zarathushtra's words are recorded in five poems called the *Gathas,* which, together with other scriptures, forms the *Avesta.*

Zoroastrianism teaches that there is one God, *Ahura Mazda* (the Wise Lord), and that all creation stems ultimately from God; the Gathas teach that human beings have free will, are responsible for their own actions and can choose between good and evil. It is believed that choosing *Asha* (truth or righteousness), with the aid of *Vohu Manah* (good mind), leads to happiness for the individual and society, whereas choosing evil leads to unhappiness and conflict. The *Gathas* also encourage hard work, good deeds and charitable acts. Zoroastrians believe that after death the immortal soul is judged by God, and is then sent to paradise or hell, where it will stay until the end of time to be resurrected for the final judgement.

In Zoroastrian places of worship, an urn containing fire is the central feature; the fire symbolises purity, light and truth and is a visible symbol of the *Fravashi* or *Farohar,* the presence of Ahura Mazda in every human being. Zoroastrians respect nature and much importance is attached to cultivating land and protecting air, earth and water.

The Zoroastrian Trust Funds of Europe is the main body for Zorastrians in the UK. Founded in 1861 as the Relgious Funds of the Zorastrians of Europe, it disseminates information on the Zoroastrian faith, provides a place of worship and maintains separate burial grounds for Zoroastrians. It also holds religious and social functions and provides assistance to Zoroastrians as considered necessary, including the provision of loans and grants to students of Zoroastrianism.

There are approximately 140,000 Zoroastrians worldwide, of which around 7,000 reside in Britain, mainly in London and the South East.

ZOROASTRIAN TRUST FUNDS OF EUROPE, Zoroastrian Centre, 440 Alexandra Avenue, Harrow, Middx HA2 9TL T 020-8866 0765 E secretary@ztfe.com
W www.ztfe.com
President, Paurushasp B. Jila

CHURCHES

There are two established (ie state) churches in the United Kingdom: the Church of England and the Church of Scotland. There are no established churches in Wales or Northern Ireland, though the Church in Wales, the Scottish Episcopal Church and the Church of Ireland are members of the Anglican Communion.

CHURCH OF ENGLAND

The Church of England is the established (ie national) church in England and is organised locally into dioceses and parishes. It traces its life back to the first coming of Christianity to England. Its position is defined by the ancient creeds of the church and by the 39 Articles of Religion (1571), the Book of Common Prayer (1662) and the Ordinal. The Church of England is thus both catholic and reformed. It is the mother church of the Anglican Communion.

THE ANGLICAN COMMUNION
The Anglican Communion consists of 38 independent provincial or national Christian churches throughout the world, many of which are in Commonwealth countries and originate from missionary activity by the Church of England. Every ten years all the bishops in the Communion meet at the Lambeth Conference, convened by the Archbishop of Canterbury. The conference has no policy-making authority but is an important forum for discussing and forming consensus around issues of common concern. The Anglican Consultative Council was formed following a resolution of the 1968 Lambeth Conference which discerned the need for more frequent and representative contact than was possible through a once-a-decade conference of bishops. The council came into being in 1969 and meets every two to three years to liaise between the member churches and provinces of the Anglican Communion.

There are about 70 million Anglicans organised into 500 dioceses and 64,000 individual congregations worldwide.

STRUCTURE
The Church of England is divided into the two provinces of Canterbury and York, each under an archbishop. The two provinces are subdivided into 44 dioceses.

Legislative provision for the Church of England is made by the General Synod, established in 1970. It also discusses and expresses opinion on any other matter of religious or public interest. The General Synod has 467 members in total, divided between three houses: the House of Bishops, the House of Clergy and the House of Laity. It is presided over jointly by the Archbishops of Canterbury and York and normally meets twice a year. The synod has the power, delegated by parliament, to frame statute law (known as a 'measure') on any matter concerning the Church of England. A measure must be laid before both houses of parliament, who may accept or reject it but cannot amend it. Once accepted the measure is submitted for royal assent and then has the full force of law. In addition to the General Synod, there are synods at diocesan level.

The Archbishops' Council was established in January 1999. Its creation was the result of changes to the Church of England's national structure proposed in 1995 and subsequently approved by the synod and parliament. The council's purpose, set out in the National Institutions Measure 1998, is 'to coordinate, promote and further the work and mission of the Church of England'. It reports to the General Synod. The Archbishops' Council comprises the Archbishops of Canterbury and York, *ex officio,* the prolocutors elected by the convocations of Canterbury and York, the chair and vice-chair of the House of Laity, elected by that house, two bishops, two clergy and two lay persons elected by their respective houses of General Synod, and up to six persons appointed jointly by the two archbishops with the approval of the General Synod.

There are also a number of national boards, councils and other bodies working on matters such as social responsibility, mission, Christian unity and education which report to the General Synod through the Archbishops' Council.

GENERAL SYNOD OF THE CHURCH OF ENGLAND, Church House, Great Smith Street, London SW1P 3NZ
T 020-7898 1000
Joint Presidents, Archbishops of Canterbury and York
HOUSE OF BISHOPS: *Chair,* Archbishop of Canterbury; *Vice-Chair,* Archbishop of York
HOUSE OF CLERGY: *Chairs (alternating),* Ven. Norman Russell; Canon Glyn Webster
HOUSE OF LAITY: *Chair,* Dr Christina Baxter; *Vice-Chair,* Dr Philip Giddings
ARCHBISHOPS' COUNCIL, Church House, Great Smith Street, London SW1P 3NZ T 020-7898 1000
Joint Presidents, Archbishops of Canterbury and York; *Secretary-General,* William Fittall

THE ORDINATION OF WOMEN
The canon making it possible for women to be ordained to the priesthood was promulgated in the General Synod in February 1994 and the first 32 women priests were ordained on 12 March 1994.

MEMBERSHIP
In 2005, 140,700 people were baptised, the Church of England had an electoral roll membership of 1.3 million, and each week about 1.2 million people attended services. As at December 2006 there were over 16,000 churches and places of worship. At December 2006 there were 354 dignitaries (including bishops, archdeacons and cathedral clergy); 7,890 full-time parochial stipendiary clergy; 337 full-time non parochial stipendiary clergy; 1,230 chaplains etc; 410 lay workers and Church Army evangelists; 8,010 licensed readers and 2,210 readers with permission to officiate and active emeriti; and approximately 4,446 active retired ordained clergy.

	Full-time Diocesan Clergy 2006		Electoral Roll Membership 2005
	Male	Female	
Bath and Wells	175	42	39,000
Birmingham	141	33	18,900
Blackburn	196	21	35,800
Bradford	87	15	12,200
Bristol	113	22	17,000
Canterbury	131	19	22,300
Carlisle	115	24	22,000
Chelmsford	333	68	50,100
Chester	207	40	48,700
Chichester	295	18	55,700
Coventry	109	21	16,900
Derby	134	26	20,100
Durham	157	38	24,900
Ely	109	31	19,500
Europe	80	5	10,400
Exeter	198	28	32,200
Gloucester	111	29	24,100
Guildford	138	29	30,800
Hereford	76	26	18,600
Leicester	109	34	17,700
Lichfield	252	52	47,800
Lincoln	153	39	28,600
Liverpool	168	46	29,800
London	447	69	69,400
Manchester	218	49	35,800
Newcastle	114	28	16,900
Norwich	152	33	23,400
Oxford	298	88	57,400
Peterborough	124	30	18,800
Portsmouth	99	16	18,300
Ripon and Leeds	99	31	18,200
Rochester	186	34	31,700
St Albans	202	64	41,800
St Edmundsbury and Ipswich	115	24	24,700
Salisbury	175	39	45,100
Sheffield	133	35	20,000
Sodor and Man	17	2	2,700
Southwark	275	68	47,300
Southwell and Nottingham	115	36	19,200
Truro	92	18	17,000
Wakefield	120	34	21,700
Winchester	200	22	39,800
Worcester	116	29	20,400
York	197	45	35,900
Total	7,081	1,500	1,268,600

STIPENDS 2007–8*

Archbishop of Canterbury	£66,750
Archbishop of York	£57,210
Bishop of London	£52,440
Other diocesan bishops	£36,230
Suffragan bishops	£29,560
Assistant bishops (full-time)	£28,610
Deans	£30,200
Archdeacons (recommended)	£28,610
Residentiary canons	£22,880†
Incumbents and clergy of similar status	£20,980†

* Rates are for those appointed on or after 1 April 2004, transitional arrangements are in place for those appointed prior to this date.

† National Stipend Benchmark (adjusted regionally to reflect variations in the cost of living)

CANTERBURY

104TH ARCHBISHOP AND PRIMATE OF ALL ENGLAND

Most Revd and Rt. Hon. Rowan Williams, *cons.* 1992, *apptd* 2002; Lambeth Palace, London SE1 7JU

Signs Rowan Cantuar:

BISHOPS SUFFRAGAN

Dover, Rt. Revd Stephen Venner, *cons.* 1994, *apptd* 1999; Upway, St Martin's Hill, Canterbury, Kent CT1 1PR

Maidstone, Rt. Revd Graham Cray, *cons.* 2001, *apptd* 2001; Bishop's House, Pett Lane, Charing, Ashford, Kent TN27 0DL

Ebbsfleet, Rt. Revd Andrew Burnham, *cons.* 2000, *apptd* 2000 (provincial episcopal visitor); Bishop's House, Dry Sandford, Abingdon, Oxon OX13 6JP

Richborough, Rt. Revd Keith Newton, *cons.* 2002, *apptd* 2002 (provincial episcopal visitor); 6 Mellis Gardens, Woodford Green, Essex IG8 0BH

DEAN

Very Revd Robert Willis, *apptd* 2001

Organist, D. Flood, FRCO, *apptd* 1988

ARCHDEACONS

Canterbury, Ven. Sheila Watson, *apptd* 2007

Maidstone, Ven. Philip Down, *apptd* 2002

Vicar-General of Province and Diocese, Chancellor Sheila Cameron, QC

Commissary-General, His Hon. Richard Walker

Joint Registrars of the Province, Canon John Rees; Stephen Slack

Diocesan Registrar and Legal Adviser, Richard Sturt

Diocesan Secretary, Julian Hills, Diocesan House, Lady Wootton's Green, Canterbury CT1 1NQ T 01227-459401

YORK

97TH ARCHBISHOP AND PRIMATE OF ENGLAND

Most Revd and Rt. Hon. Dr John Sentamu, *cons.* 1996, *trans.* 2005; Bishopthorpe, York YO23 2GE

Signs Sentamu Ebor:

BISHOPS SUFFRAGAN

Beverley, Rt. Revd Martyn Jarrett (provincial episcopal visitor), *cons.* 1994, *apptd* 2000; 3 North Lane, Roundhay, Leeds LS8 2QJ

Hull, Rt. Revd Richard Frith, *cons.* 1998, *apptd* 1998; Hullen House, Woodfield Lane, Hessle, Hull HU13 0ES

Selby, Rt. Revd Martin Wallace, *cons.* 2003, *apptd* 2003; Bishop's House, Barton le Street, Malton, York YO17 6PL

Whitby, Rt. Revd Robert Ladds, *cons.* 1999, *apptd* 1999; 60 West Green, Stokesley, Middlesbrough TS9 5BD

DEAN

Very Revd Keith Jones, *apptd* 2004

Master of the Music, Philip Moore, FRCO, *apptd* 1983

ARCHDEACONS

Cleveland, Ven. Paul Ferguson, *apptd* 2001

East Riding, Ven. David Butterfield, *apptd* 2006

York, Ven. Richard Seed, *apptd* 1999

Chancellor of the Diocese, Revd Peter Collier, QC, *apptd* 2006

Registrar and Legal Secretary, Lionel Lennox

Diocesan Secretary, Peter Warry, Diocesan House, Aviator Court, Clifton Moor, York YO30 4WJ T 01904-699500

LONDON *(Canterbury)*

132ND BISHOP
Rt. Revd and Rt. Hon Richard Chartres, *cons.* 1992, *apptd* 1995; The Old Deanery, Dean's Court, London EC4V 5AA
Signs Richard Londin:

AREA BISHOPS
Edmonton, Rt. Revd Peter Wheatley, *cons.* 1999, *apptd* 1999; 27 Thurlow Road, London NW3 5PP
Kensington, Rt. Revd Michael Colclough, *cons.* 1996, *apptd* 1996; Dial House, Riverside, Twickenham, Middx TW1 3DT
Stepney, Rt. Revd Canon Stephen Oliver, *cons.* 2003, *apptd* 2003; 63 Coborn Road, London E3 2DB
Willesden, Rt. Revd Peter Broadbent, *cons.* 2001, *apptd* 2001; 173 Willesden Lane, London NW6 7YN

BISHOP SUFFRAGAN
Fulham, Rt. Revd John Broadhurst, *cons.* 1996, *apptd* 1996; 26 Canonbury Park South, London N1 2FN

DEAN OF ST PAUL'S
Rt. Revd Graeme Knowles, *apptd* 2007

Organist, Malcolm Archer, *apptd* 2004

ARCHDEACONS
Charing Cross, Ven. Dr William Jacob, *apptd* 1996
Hackney, Ven. Lyle Dennen, *apptd* 1999
Hampstead, Ven. Michael Lawson, *apptd* 1999
London, Ven. Peter Delaney, *apptd* 1999
Middlesex, Ven. Stephen Welch, *apptd* 2006
Northolt, Ven. Rachel Treweek, *apptd* 2006

Chancellor, Nigel Seed, QC, *apptd* 2002
Registrar and Legal Secretary, Paul Morris
Diocesan Secretary, Keith Robinson, London Diocesan House, 36 Causton Street, London SW1P 4AU T 020-7932 1226

DURHAM *(York)*

71ST BISHOP
Rt. Revd Dr N. Thomas Wright, *cons.* 2003, *apptd* 2003; Auckland Castle, Bishop Auckland DL14 7NR
Signs Thomas Dunelm:

BISHOP SUFFRAGAN
Jarrow, Rt. Revd Mark Bryant, *cons.* 2007, *apptd* 2007; Bishop's House, Ivy Lane, Low Fell, Gateshead NE9 6QD

DEAN
Very Revd Michael Sadgrove, *apptd* 2003

Organist, James Lancelot, FRCO, *apptd* 1985

ARCHDEACONS
Auckland, Ven. Nicholas Barker, *apptd* 2007
Durham, Ven. Ian Jagger, *apptd* 2006
Sunderland, Ven. Stuart Bain, *apptd* 2002

Chancellor, The Worshipful Revd Dr Rupert Bursell, QC, *apptd* 1989
Registrar and Legal Secretary, Hilary Monckton-Milnes
Diocesan Secretary, Ian Boothroyd, Diocesan Office, Auckland Castle, Bishop Auckland, Co. Durham DL14 7QJ T 01388-604515

WINCHESTER *(Canterbury)*

96TH BISHOP
Rt. Revd Michael C. Scott-Joynt, *cons.*1987, *trans.* 1995; Wolvesey, Winchester SO23 9ND
Signs Michael Winton:

BISHOPS SUFFRAGAN
Basingstoke, Rt. Revd Trevor Willmott, *cons.* 2002, *apptd* 2002; Bishopswood End, Kingswood Rise, Four Marks, Alton, Hants GU34 5BD
Southampton, Rt. Revd Paul Butler, *cons.* 2004, *apptd* 2004; Ham House, The Crescent, Romsey SO51 7NG

DEAN
Very Revd James Atwell, *apptd* 2005
Dean of Jersey (A Peculiar), Very Revd Robert Key, *apptd* 2005
Dean of Guernsey (A Peculiar), Very Revd Paul Mellor, *apptd* 2003
Director of Music, Andrew Lumsden, *apptd* 2002

ARCHDEACONS
Bournemouth, Ven. Adrian Harbidge, *apptd* 1998
Winchester, vacant

Chancellor, Christopher Clark, *apptd* 1993
Registrar and Legal Secretary, Peter White
Diocesan Secretary, Andrew Howard, Church House, 9 The Close, Winchester, Hants SO23 9LS T 01962-624742

BATH AND WELLS *(Canterbury)*

78TH BISHOP
Rt. Revd Peter Price, *cons.* 1997, *apptd* 2002; The Palace, Wells BA5 2PD
Signs Peter Bath & Wells

BISHOP SUFFRAGAN
Taunton, Rt. Revd Peter Maurice, *cons.* 2006, *apptd* 2006; The Palace, Wells BA5 2PD

DEAN
Very Revd John Clarke, *apptd* 2004

Organist, Matthew Owens, *apptd* 2005

ARCHDEACONS
Bath, Ven. Andrew Piggott, *apptd* 2005
Taunton, Ven. John Reed, *apptd* 1999
Wells, Ven. Nicola Sullivan, *apptd* 2006

Chancellor, Timothy Briden, *apptd* 1993
Registrar and Legal Secretary, Tim Berry
Diocesan Secretary, Nicholas Denison, The Old Deanery, Wells, Somerset BA5 2UG T 01749-670777

BIRMINGHAM *(Canterbury)*

8TH BISHOP
Rt. Revd David Urquhart, *cons.* 2000, *apptd* 2006; Bishop's Croft, Old Church Road, Harborne, Birmingham B17 0BG
Signs David Birmingham

BISHOP SUFFRAGAN
Aston, vacant

DEAN
Very Revd Bob Wilkes, *apptd* 2006

Organist, Marcus Huxley, FRCO, *apptd* 1986

ARCHDEACONS
Aston, Ven. Dr Brian Russell, *apptd* 2005
Birmingham, Ven. Hayward Osborne, *apptd* 2001
Chancellor, Martin Cardinal, *apptd* 2005
Registrar and Legal Secretary, Hugh Carslake
Diocesan Secretary, Jim Drennan, 175 Harborne Park Road,
   Harborne, Birmingham B17 0BH T 0121-426 0400

BLACKBURN *(York)*
8TH BISHOP
Rt. Revd Nicholas Reade, *apptd* 2003, *cons.* March 2004;
   Bishop's House, Ribchester Road, Blackburn BB1 9EF
   Signs Nicholas Blackburn

BISHOPS SUFFRAGAN
Burnley, Rt. Revd John Goddard, *cons.* 2000, *apptd* 2000;
   Dean House, 449 Padiham Road, Burnley BB12 6TE
Lancaster, Rt. Revd Geoffrey Pearson, *cons.* 2006, *apptd*
   2006; The Vicarage, Whinney Brow Lane, Shireshead,
   Forton, Preston PR3 0AE

DEAN
Very Revd Christopher Armstrong, *apptd* 2001

Organist, Richard Tanner, *apptd* 1998

ARCHDEACONS
Blackburn, Ven. John Hawley, *apptd* 2002
Lancaster, Ven. Peter Ballard, *apptd* 2006

Chancellor, John Bullimore, *apptd* 1990
Registrar and Legal Secretary, Thomas Hoyle
Diocesan Secretary, Graeme Pollard, Diocesan Office,
   Cathedral Close, Blackburn BB1 5AA T 01254-54421

BRADFORD *(York)*
9TH BISHOP
Rt. Revd David James, *apptd* 2002; Bishopscroft, Ashwell
   Road, Heaton, Bradford BD9 4AU
   Signs David Bradford

DEAN
Very Revd Dr David Ison, *apptd* 2005

Organist, Andrew Teague, FRCO, *apptd* 2003

ARCHDEACONS
Bradford, Ven. David Lee, *apptd* 2004
Craven, Ven. Paul Slater, *apptd* 2005

Chancellor, John de G. Walford, *apptd* 1999
Registrar and Legal Secretary, Peter Foskett
Diocesan Secretary, Malcolm Halliday, Kadugli House,
   Elmsley Street, Steeton, Keighley BD20 6SE T 01535-650555

BRISTOL *(Canterbury)*
55TH BISHOP
Rt. Revd Michael Hill, *cons.* 1998, *apptd* 2003; Wethered
   House, 11 The Avenue, Clifton, Bristol BS8 3HG
   Signs Michael Bristol

BISHOP SUFFRAGAN
Swindon, Rt. Revd Dr Lee Rayfield, *cons.* 2005, *apptd*
   2005; Mark House, Field Rise, Swindon, Wiltshire,
   SN1 4HP

DEAN
Very Revd Robert W. Grimley, *apptd* 1997

Organist and Director of Music, Mark Lee, *apptd* 1998

ARCHDEACONS
Bristol, Ven. Tim McClure, *apptd* 1999
Malmesbury, Ven. Alan Hawker, *apptd* 1998

Chancellor, Dr James Behrens, *apptd* 2005
Registrar and Legal Secretary, Tim Berry
Diocesan Secretary, Lesley Farrall, Diocesan Church House,
   23 Great George Street, Bristol BS1 5QZ T 0117-906 0100

CARLISLE *(York)*
66TH BISHOP
Rt. Revd Graham Dow, *cons.* 1985, *apptd* 2000; Rose
   Castle, Dalston, Carlisle CA5 7BZ
   Signs Graham Carlisle:

BISHOP SUFFRAGAN
Penrith, Rt. Revd James Newcome, *cons.* 2002, *apptd*
   2002; Holm Croft, Castle Road, Kendal, Cumbria LA9 7AU

DEAN
Very Revd Mark Boyling, *apptd* 2004

Organist, Jeremy Suter, FRCO, *apptd* 1991

ARCHDEACONS
Carlisle, Ven. David Thomson, *apptd* 2002
West Cumberland, Ven. Colin Hill, *apptd* 2004
Westmorland and Furness, Ven. George Howe, *apptd* 2000

Chancellor, Geoffrey Tattersall, QC, *apptd* 2003
Registrar and Legal Secretary, Jane Lowdon
Diocesan Secretary, Derek Hurton, Church House, West
   Walls, Carlisle CA3 8UE T 01228-522573

CHELMSFORD *(Canterbury)*
9TH BISHOP
Rt. Revd John Warren Gladwin, *cons.* 1994, *apptd* 2003,
   trans. 2004; Bishopscourt, Margaretting, Ingatestone
   CM4 0HD
   Signs John Chelmsford

BISHOPS SUFFRAGAN
Barking, Rt. Revd David Hawkins, *apptd* 2003; Barking
   Lodge, Verulam Avenue, London E17 8ES
Bradwell, Rt. Revd Laurence Green, *cons.* 1993, *apptd*
   1993; Bishop's House, Orsett Road, Horndon-on-the-Hill,
   Stanford-le-Hope, Essex SS17 8NS
Colchester, Rt. Revd Christopher Morgan, *cons.* 2001,
   apptd 2001; 1 Fitzwalter Road, Colchester, Essex CO3 3SS

DEAN
Very Revd Peter S. M. Judd, *apptd* 1997

Master of Music, Peter Nardone, *apptd* 2000

ARCHDEACONS
Colchester, Ven. Annette Cooper, *apptd* 2004
Harlow, Ven. Peter Taylor, *apptd* 1996
Southend, Ven. David Lowman, *apptd* 2001
West Ham, Ven. Elwin Cockett, *apptd* 2007

Chancellor, George Pulman, QC, *apptd* 2001
Registrar and Legal Secretary, Brian Hood
Chief Executive, Steven Webb, 53 New Street, Chelmsford,
   Essex CM1 1AT T 01245-294400

CHESTER *(York)*
40TH BISHOP
Rt. Revd Peter R. Forster, PHD, *cons.* 1996, *apptd* 1996;
   Bishop's House, Chester CH1 2JD
   Signs Peter Cestr:

BISHOPS SUFFRAGAN
Birkenhead, Rt. Revd Keith Sinclair, *cons.* 2007, *apptd*
2007; Bishop's Lodge, 67 Bidston Road, Prenton CH43 6TR
Stockport, vacant

DEAN
Very Revd Dr Gordon McPhate, *apptd* 2002

Organist and Director of Music, David Poulter, FRCO,
apptd 1997

ARCHDEACONS
Chester, Ven. Donald Allister, *apptd* 2002
Macclesfield, Ven. Richard Gillings, *apptd* 1994

Chancellor, His Hon. Judge Turner, QC, *apptd* 1998
Registrar and Legal Secretary, Alan McAllester
Diocesan Secretary, Dr John Mason, Church House, Lower
Lane, Aldford, Chester CH3 6HP T 01244-620444

CHICHESTER *(Canterbury)*
102ND BISHOP
Rt. Revd John Hind, *cons.* 1991, *apptd* 2001; The Palace,
Chichester PO19 1PY
Signs John Cicestr:

BISHOPS SUFFRAGAN
Horsham, Rt. Revd Lindsay G. Urwin, *cons.* 1993, *apptd*
1993; Bishop's House, 21 Guildford Road, Horsham,
W. Sussex RH12 1LU
Lewes, Rt. Revd Wallace P. Benn, *cons.* 1997, *apptd* 1997;
Bishop's Lodge, 16A Prideaux Road, Eastbourne, E. Sussex
BN21 2NB

DEAN
Very Revd Nicholas Frayling, *apptd* 2002

Organist, Alan Thurlow, FRCO, *apptd* 1980

ARCHDEACONS
Chichester, Ven. Douglas McKittrick, *apptd* 2002
Horsham, Ven. Roger Combes, *apptd* 2003
Lewes and Hastings, Ven. Philip Jones, *apptd* 2005

Chancellor, Mark Hill
Registrar and Legal Secretary, John Stapleton
Diocesan Secretary, Jonathan Prichard, Diocesan Church
House, 211 New Church Road, Hove, E. Sussex BN3 4ED
T 01273-421021

COVENTRY *(Canterbury)*
8TH BISHOP
Rt. Revd Colin J. Bennetts, *cons.* 1994, *apptd* 1997; The
Bishop's House, 23 Davenport Road, Coventry CV5 6PW
Signs Colin Coventry

BISHOP SUFFRAGAN
Warwick, Rt. Revd John Stroyan, *cons.* 2005, *apptd* 2005;
Warwick House, 139 Kenilworth Road, Coventry CV4 7AP

DEAN
Very Revd John Irvine, *apptd* 2001

Director of Music, Mr Kerry Beaumont, *apptd* 2006

ARCHDEACONS
Coventry, Ven. Mark Bryant, *apptd* 2001
Warwick, Ven. Michael Paget-Wilkes, *apptd* 1990

Chancellor, Sir William Gage, *apptd* 1980
Registrar and Legal Secretary, David Dumbleton
Diocesan Secretary, Simon Lloyd, Cathedral & Diocesan
Offices, 1 Hilltop, Coventry CV1 5AB T 024-7652 1200

DERBY *(Canterbury)*
7TH BISHOP
Rt. Revd Alastair Redfern, *cons.*1997, *apptd* 2005;
Bishop's House, 6 King Street, Duffield, Belper, Derbyshire
DE56 4EU
Signs Alastair Derby

BISHOP SUFFRAGAN
Repton, Rt. Revd Humphrey Southern, *cons.* 2007, *apptd*
2007; Repton House, Lea, Matlock, Derbyshire DE4 5JP

DEAN
Very Revd Martin Kitchen, PHD, *apptd* 2005

Organist, Peter Gould, *apptd* 1982

ARCHDEACONS
Chesterfield, Ven. David Garnett, *apptd* 1996
Derby, Ven. Christopher Cunliffe, *apptd* 2006

Chancellor, His Hon. Judge John Bullimore, *apptd* 1981
Registrar and Legal Secretary, Mrs Nadine Waldron
Diocesan Secretary, Bob Carey, Derby Church House, Full
Street, Derby DE1 3DR T 01332-388650

ELY *(Canterbury)*
68TH BISHOP
Rt. Revd Dr Anthony Russell, *cons.* 1988, *apptd* 2000;
The Bishop's House, Ely, Cambs CB7 4DW
Signs Anthony Ely

BISHOP SUFFRAGAN
Huntingdon, vacant

DEAN
Very Revd Dr Michael Chandler, *apptd* 2003

Director of Music, Paul Trepte, FRCO, *apptd* 1991

ARCHDEACONS
Cambridge, Ven. John Beer, *apptd* 2004
Huntingdon and Wisbech, Ven. Hugh McCurdy, *apptd*
2005

Chancellor, The Hon. Mr Justice Gage, QC
Registrar, Peter Beesley
Diocesan Secretary, Dr Matthew Lavis, Bishop Woodford
House, Barton Road, Ely, Cambs CB7 4DX T 01353-652701

EXETER *(Canterbury)*
70TH BISHOP
Rt. Revd Michael Langrish, *cons.* 1993, *apptd* 2000; The
Palace, Exeter EX1 1HY
Signs Michael Exon:

BISHOPS SUFFRAGAN
Crediton, Rt. Revd Robert Evens, *cons.* 2004, *apptd* 2004;
32 The Avenue, Tiverton EX16 4HW
Plymouth, Rt. Revd John Ford, *cons.* 2006, *apptd* 2005;
31 Riverside Walk, Tamerton Foliot, Plymouth PL5 4AQ

DEAN
Very Revd Cyril Meyrick, *apptd* 2005

Director of Music, Andrew Millington, *apptd* 1999

ARCHDEACONS
Barnstaple, Ven. David Gunn-Johnson, *apptd* 2003
Exeter, Ven. Penny Driver, *apptd* 2006
Plymouth, Ven. Tony Wilds, *apptd* 2001
Totnes, Ven. John Rawlings, *apptd* 2006

Chancellor, Hon. Sir Andrew McFarlane

Registrar and Legal Secretary, C. Butcher
Diocesan Secretary, Mark Beedell, The Old Deanery,
The Cloisters, Exeter EX1 1HS **T** 01392-272686

GIBRALTAR IN EUROPE *(Canterbury)*
BISHOP
Rt. Revd Dr Geoffrey Rowell, *cons.* 1994, *apptd* 2001;
Bishop's Lodge, Church Road, Worth, Crawley, West Sussex
RH10 7RT

BISHOP SUFFRAGAN
In Europe, Rt. Revd David Hamid, *cons.* 2002, *apptd*
2002; 14 Tufton Street, London SW1P 3QZ
Dean, Cathedral Church of the Holy Trinity, Gibraltar, Very
Revd Alan Woods
Chancellor, Pro-Cathedral of St Paul, Valletta, Malta,
Canon Thomas Mendel
Chancellor, Pro-Cathedral of the Holy Trinity, Brussels,
Belgium, Canon Dr Robert Innes

ARCHDEACONS
Eastern, Ven. Patrick Curran
North-West Europe, Ven. Dirk Van Leeuwen
France, Ven. Kenneth Letts
Gibraltar, Very Revd Alan Woods
Italy, Ven. Arthur Siddall
Scandinavia and Germany, Ven. Mark Oakley
Switzerland, Ven. Arthur Siddall

Chancellor, Mark Hill
Registrar and Legal Secretary, John Underwood
Diocesan Secretary, Adrian Mumford, 14 Tufton Street,
London SW1P 3QZ **T** 020-7898 1155

GLOUCESTER *(Canterbury)*
40TH BISHOP
Rt. Revd Michael Perham, *cons.* 2004, *apptd* 2004;
Bishopscourt, Pitt Street, Gloucester GL1 2BQ
Signs Michael Gloucestr

BISHOP SUFFRAGAN
Tewkesbury, Rt. Revd John S. Went, *cons.* 1995, *apptd*
1995; Bishop's House, Staverton, Cheltenham GL51 0TW

DEAN
Very Revd Nicholas Bury, *apptd* 1997

Director of Music, Adrian Partington, *apptd* 2007

ARCHDEACONS
Cheltenham, Ven. Hedley Ringrose, *apptd* 1998
Gloucester, Ven. Geoffrey Sidaway, *apptd* 2000

Chancellor and Vicar-General, June Rodgers, *apptd* 1990
Registrar and Legal Secretary, Chris Peak
Diocesan Secretary, Dr Kevin Brown, Church House, College
Green, Gloucester GL1 2LY **T** 01452-410022

GUILDFORD *(Canterbury)*
9TH BISHOP
Rt. Revd Christopher Hill, *cons.* 1996, *apptd* 2004;
Willow Grange, Woking Road, Guildford GU4 7QS
Signs Christopher Guildford

BISHOP SUFFRAGAN
Dorking, Rt. Revd Ian Brackley, *cons.* 1996, *apptd* 1995;
Dayspring, 13 Pilgrims Way, Guildford GU4 8AD

DEAN
Very Revd Victor Stock, *apptd* 2002

Organist, Stephen Farr, FRCO, *apptd* 1999

ARCHDEACONS
Dorking, Ven. Julian Henderson, *apptd* 2005
Surrey, Ven. Stuart Beake, *apptd* 2005

Chancellor, Andrew Jordan
Registrar and Legal Secretary, Peter Beesley
Diocesan Secretary, Stephen Marriott, Diocesan House,
Quarry Street, Guildford GU1 3AG **T** 01483-571826

HEREFORD *(Canterbury)*
104TH BISHOP
Rt. Revd Anthony Priddis, *cons.* 1996, *apptd* 2004; The
Bishop's House, Hereford HR4 9BN
Signs Anthony Hereford

BISHOP SUFFRAGAN
Ludlow, Rt. Revd Michael Wrenford Hooper, *cons.* 2002,
apptd 2002; Bishop's House, Corvedale Road, Craven
Arms, Shropshire SY7 9BT

DEAN
Very Revd Michael Tavinor, *apptd* 2002

Organist, Geraint Bowen, FRCO, *apptd* 2001

ARCHDEACONS
Hereford, Ven. Malcom Colmer, *apptd* 2005
Ludlow, Rt. Revd Michael Hooper, *apptd* 2002

Chancellor, Roger Kaye
Registrar and Legal Secretary, Tom Jordan; Peter Beesley
Diocesan Secretary, John Clark, The Palace, Hereford HR4 9BL
T 01432-373300

LEICESTER *(Canterbury)*
6TH BISHOP
Rt. Revd Timothy J. Stevens, *cons.* 1995, *apptd* 1999;
Bishop's Lodge, 10 Springfield Road, Leicester LE2 3BD
Signs Timothy Leicester

DEAN
Very Revd Vivienne F. Faull, *apptd* 2000

Master of Music, Jonathan Gregory, *apptd* 1994

ARCHDEACONS
Leicester, Ven. Richard Atkinson, *apptd* 2002
Loughborough, Ven. Paul Hackwood, *apptd* 2005

Chancellor, Dr James Behrens
Registrar and Legal Secretary, Trevor Kirkman
Diocesan Secretary, Jane Easton, Church House, 3–5 St
Martin's East, Leicester LE1 5FX **T** 0116-248 7400

LICHFIELD *(Canterbury)*
98TH BISHOP
Rt. Revd Jonathan Gledhill *cons.* 1996, *apptd* 2003;
Bishop's House, The Close, Lichfield WS13 7LG
Signs Jonathan Lichfield

BISHOPS SUFFRAGAN
Shrewsbury, Rt. Revd Dr Alan Smith, *cons.* 2001, *apptd*
2002; 68 London Road, Shrewsbury SY2 6PG
Stafford, Rt. Revd A. Gordon Mursell, *cons.* 2005, *apptd*
2005; Ash Garth, 6 Broughton Crescent, Barlaston, Stoke
on Trent, ST12 9DD

Wolverhampton, Rt. Revd Clive Gregory, *cons.* 2007, *apptd* 2007

DEAN
Very Revd Adrian Dorber, *apptd* 2005

Organist, Philip Scriven, *apptd* 2002

ARCHDEACONS
Lichfield, Ven. Christopher Liley, *apptd* 2001
Salop, Ven. John Hall, *apptd* 1998
Stoke-on-Trent, Ven. Godfrey Owen Stone, *apptd* 2002
Walsall, Revd Robert Jackson, *apptd* 2004

Chancellor, His Hon. Judge Marten Coates
Joint Registrars and Legal Secretaries, J. P. Thorneycroft;
    N. Blackie
Diocesan Secretary, D. R. Taylor, St Mary's House, The Close,
    Lichfield, Staffs WS13 7LD T 01543-306030

LINCOLN *(Canterbury)*
71ST BISHOP
Rt. Revd Dr John Saxbee, *cons.* 1994, *apptd* 2002;
    Bishop's House, Eastgate, Lincoln LN2 1QQ
    Signs John Lincoln

BISHOPS SUFFRAGAN
Grantham, Rt. Revd Dr Timothy Ellis, *cons.* 2006, *apptd*
    2006; Saxonwell Vicarage, Church Street, Long
    Bennington, Newark NG23 5ES
Grimsby, Rt. Revd David D. J. Rossdale, *cons.* 2000, *apptd*
    2000; Bishop's House, Church Lane, Irby-upon-Humber,
    Grimsby DN37 7JR

DEAN
Very Revd Philip Buckler, *apptd* 2007

Director of Music, A. Prentice, *apptd* 2003

ARCHDEACONS
Lincoln, Ven. Arthur Hawes, *apptd* 1995
Lindsey and Stow, Ven. Jane Sinclair, *apptd* 2007

Chancellor, Mark Bishop, QC, *apptd* 2007
Registrar and Legal Secretary, Derek Wellman
Diocesan Secretary, Max Manin, The Old Palace, Lincoln
    LN2 1PU T 01522-504050

LIVERPOOL *(York)*
7TH BISHOP
Rt. Revd James Jones, *cons.* 1994, *apptd* 1998; Bishop's
    Lodge, Woolton Park, Liverpool L25 6DT *Signs* James
    Liverpool

BISHOP SUFFRAGAN
Warrington, Rt. Revd David Jennings, *cons.* 2000, *apptd*
    2000; 34 Central Avenue, Eccleston Park, Prescot,
    Merseyside L34 2QP

DEAN
Revd Justin Welby, *apptd* 2007

Organist, Prof. Ian Tracey, *apptd* 1980

ARCHDEACONS
Liverpool, Ven. Richard Panter, *apptd* 2002
Warrington, Ven. Peter Bradley, *apptd* 2001

Chancellor, Hon. Sir Mark Hedley
Registrar and Legal Secretary, Roger Arden
Diocesan Secretary, Mike Eastwood, Church House,
    1 Hanover Street, Liverpool L1 3DW T 0151-709 9722

MANCHESTER *(York)*
11TH BISHOP
Rt. Revd Nigel McCulloch, *cons.* 1986, *apptd* 2002, *trans.*
    2002; Bishopscourt, Bury New Road, Manchester M7 4LE
    Signs Nigel Manchester

BISHOPS SUFFRAGAN
Bolton, Rt. Revd David Gillett, *cons.* 1999, *apptd* 1999;
    4 Bishop's Lodge, Bolton Road, Hawkshaw, Bury BL8 4JN
Hulme, Rt. Revd Stephen Lowe, *cons.* 1999, *apptd*
    1999; 14 Moorgate Avenue, Withington, Manchester
    M20 1HE
Middleton, Rt. Revd Michael Lewis, *cons.* 1999,
    apptd 1999; The Hollies, Manchester Road, Rochdale
    OL11 3QY

DEAN
Revd Rogers Govender, *apptd* 2006

Organist, Christopher Stokes, *apptd* 1992

ARCHDEACONS
Bolton, Ven. John Applegate, *apptd* 2002
Manchester, Ven. Andrew Ballard, *apptd* 2005
Rochdale, Ven. Mark Davies, *apptd* 2005

Chancellor, G. Tattersall
Registrar and Legal Secretary, Michael Darlington
Diocesan Secretary, Nigel Spraggins, Diocesan Church House,
    90 Deansgate, Manchester M3 2GH T 0161-828 1400

NEWCASTLE *(York)*
11TH BISHOP
Rt. Revd J. Martin Wharton, *cons.* 1992, *apptd* 1997;
    Bishop's House, 29 Moor Road South, Gosforth, Newcastle
    upon Tyne NE3 1PA
    Signs Martin Newcastle

ASSISTANT BISHOP
Rt. Revd Paul Richardson, *cons.* 1987, *apptd* 1999

DEAN
Very Revd Christopher C. Dalliston, *apptd* 2003

Director of Music, Scott Farrell, *apptd* 2002

ARCHDEACONS
Lindisfarne, Ven. Robert Langley, *apptd* 2001
Northumberland, Ven. Geoffrey Miller, *apptd* 2004

Chancellor, Prof. David McClean, *apptd* 1998
Registrar and Legal Secretary, Jane Lowdon
Diocesan Secretary, Philip Davies, Church House, St John's
    Terrace, North Shields NE29 6HS T 0191-270 4100

NORWICH *(Canterbury)*
71ST BISHOP
Rt. Revd Graham R. James, *cons.* 1993, *apptd* 2000;
    Bishop's House, Norwich NR3 1SB *Signs* Graham Norvic:

BISHOPS SUFFRAGAN
Lynn, Rt. Revd James Langstaff, *cons.* 2004, *apptd* 2004;
    The Old Vicarage, Castle Acre, King's Lynn PE32 2AA
Thetford, Rt. Revd David J. Atkinson, *cons.* 2001, *apptd*
    2001; The Red House, 53 Norwich Road, Stoke Holy Cross,
    Norwich NR14 8AB

DEAN
Very Revd Graham Smith, *apptd* 2004

Organist, David Dunnett, *apptd* 1996

ARCHDEACONS

Lynn, Ven. Martin Gray, *apptd* 1999
Norfolk, Ven. David Hayden, *apptd* 2002
Norwich, Ven. Clifford Offer, *apptd* 1994

Chancellor, His Hon. Judge Paul Downes, *apptd* 2007
Registrar and Legal Secretary, Ian Mayers
Diocesan Secretary, Revd Canon Richard Bowett, Diocesan House, 109 Dereham Road, Easton, Norwich, Norfolk NR9 5ES **T** 01603-880853

OXFORD *(Canterbury)*
42ND BISHOP
Rt. Revd John Pritchard *cons.* 2002, *apptd* 2007; Diocesan Church House, North Hinksey Lane, Oxford OX2 0NB
Signs John Oxon:

AREA BISHOPS
Buckingham, Rt. Revd Dr Alan Wilson *cons.* 2003, *apptd* 2003; Sheridan, Grimms Hill, Great Missenden, Bucks HP16 9BD
Dorchester, Rt. Revd Colin Fletcher, *cons.* 2000, *apptd* 2000; Arran House, Sandy Lane, Yarnton, Oxon OX5 1PB
Reading, Rt. Revd Stephen Cottrell, *cons.* 2004, *apptd* 2004; Bishop's House, Tidmarsh Lane, Tidmarsh, Reading RG8 8HA

DEAN OF CHRIST CHURCH
Very Revd Dr Christopher Lewis, *apptd* 2003

Organist, Dr Stephen Darlington, FRCO, *apptd* 1985

ARCHDEACONS
Berkshire, Ven. Norman Russell, *apptd* 1998
Buckingham, vacant
Oxford, Ven. Julian Hubbard, *apptd* 2005

Chancellor, Revd Dr Rupert Bursell, *apptd* 2001
Registrars and Legal Secretaries, Dr F. E. Robson and Revd. Canon John Rees
Diocesan Secretary, Rosemary Pearce, Diocesan Church House, North Hinksey, Oxford OX2 0NB **T** 01865-208202

PETERBOROUGH *(Canterbury)*
37TH BISHOP
Rt. Revd Ian P. M. Cundy, *cons.* 1992, *apptd* 1996;
Bishop's Lodging, The Palace, Peterborough PE1 1YA
Signs Ian Petriburg:

BISHOP SUFFRAGAN
Brixworth, Rt. Revd Frank White, *cons.* 2002, *apptd* 2002; 4 The Avenue, Dallington, Northampton NN1 4RZ

DEAN
Very Revd Charles Taylor, *apptd* 2007

Organist, Andrew Reid, *apptd* 2004

ARCHDEACONS
Northampton, Ven. Christine Allsopp, *apptd* 2005
Oakham, Ven. David Painter, *apptd* 2000

Chancellor, David Pittaway, QC, *apptd* 2005
Registrar and Legal Secretary, Revd Canon Raymond Hemingray
Diocesan Secretary, Canon Richard Pestell, Diocesan Office, The Palace, Peterborough PE1 1YB **T** 01733-887000

PORTSMOUTH *(Canterbury)*
8TH BISHOP
Rt. Revd Dr Kenneth Stevenson, *cons.* 1995, *apptd* 1995;
Bishopsgrove, 26 Osborn Road, Fareham, Hants PO16 7DQ
Signs Kenneth Portsmouth

DEAN
Very Revd David Brindley, *apptd* 2002

Organist, David Price, *apptd* 1996

ARCHDEACONS
Isle of Wight, Ven. Caroline Baston, *apptd* 2006
Portsdown, Ven. Trevor Reader, *apptd* 2006
The Meon, Ven. Peter Hancock, *apptd* 1999

Chancellor, C. Clark, QC
Registrar and Legal Secretary, Hilary Tyler
Diocesan Secretary, Wendy Kennedy, Diocesan Offices, 1st Floor, Peninsular House, Wharf Road, Portsmouth PO2 8HB **T** 023-9289 9664

RIPON AND LEEDS *(York)*
12TH BISHOP
Rt. Revd John Packer, *cons.* 1996, *apptd* 2000; Bishop Mount, Ripon HG4 5DP
Signs John Ripon and Leeds

BISHOP SUFFRAGAN
Knaresborough, Rt. Revd James Bell, *cons.* 2004, *apptd* 2004; Thistledown, Main Street, Exelby, Bedale DL8 2HD

DEAN
Revd Keith Jukes, *apptd* 2007

Director of Music, Andrew Bryden, *apptd* 2003

ARCHDEACONS
Leeds, Ven. Peter Burrows, *apptd* 2005
Richmond, Ven. Janet Henderson, *apptd* 2007

Chancellor, His Hon. Judge Grenfell, *apptd* 1992
Registrars and Legal Secretaries, Christopher Tunnard; Nichola Harding
Diocesan Secretary, Philip Arundel, Diocesan Office, St Mary's Street, Leeds LS9 7DP **T** 0113-200 0540

ROCHESTER *(Canterbury)*
106TH BISHOP
Rt. Revd Dr Michael Nazir-Ali, *cons.* 1984, *apptd* 1994;
Bishopscourt, Rochester ME1 1TS
Signs Michael Roffen:

BISHOP SUFFRAGAN
Tonbridge, Rt. Revd Dr Brian C. Castle, *cons.* 2002, *apptd* 2002; Bishop's Lodge, 48 St Botolph's Road, Sevenoaks TN13 3AG

DEAN
Very Revd Adrian Newman, *apptd* 2004

Director of Music, Roger Sayer, FRCO, *apptd* 1995

ARCHDEACONS
Bromley, Ven. Paul Wright, *apptd* 2003
Rochester, Ven. Peter Lock, *apptd* 2000
Tonbridge, Ven. Clive Mansell, *apptd* 2002

Chancellor, John Gallagher, *apptd* 2006
Registrar and Legal Secretary, Owen Carew-Jones
Diocesan Secretary, Canon Louise Gilbert, St Nicholas Church, Boley Hill, Rochester ME1 1SL **T** 01634-560000

ST ALBANS *(Canterbury)*
9TH BISHOP
Rt. Revd Christopher W. Herbert, *cons.* 1995, *apptd* 1995; Abbey Gate House, St Albans AL3 4HD
Signs Christopher St Albans

BISHOPS SUFFRAGAN
Bedford, Rt. Revd Richard N. Inwood, *cons.* 2003, *apptd* 2003; Bishop's Lodge, Bedford Road, Cardington, Bedford MK44 3SS
Hertford, Rt. Revd Christopher R. J. Foster, *cons.* 2001, *apptd* 2001; Hertford House, Abbey Mill Lane, St Albans AL3 4HE

DEAN
Very Revd Dr Jeffrey John, *apptd* 2004

Organist, Andrew Lucas, *apptd* 1998

ARCHDEACONS
Bedford, Ven. Paul Hughes, *apptd* 2004
Hertford, Ven. Trevor Jones, *apptd* 1997
St Albans, Ven. Helen Cunliffe, *apptd* 2003

Chancellor, Roger Kaye, *apptd* 2002
Registrar and Legal Secretary, David Cheetham
Diocesan Secretary, Susan Pope, Holywell Lodge, 41 Holywell Hill, St Albans AL1 1HE **T** 01727-854532

ST EDMUNDSBURY AND IPSWICH *(Canterbury)*
10TH BISHOP
Rt. Revd Nigel Stock, *cons.* 2000, *apptd* 2007; Bishop's House, 4 Park Road, Ipswich IP1 3ST
Signs Nigel St Edmundsbury and Ipswich

BISHOP SUFFRAGAN
Dunwich, Rt. Revd Clive Young, *cons.* 1999, *apptd* 1999; 28 Westerfield Road, Ipswich IP4 2UJ

DEAN
Very Revd Neil Collings, *apptd* 2006

Organist, James Thomas, *apptd* 1997

ARCHDEACONS
Ipswich, vacant
Sudbury, Ven. David Brierley, *apptd* 2006
Suffolk, Ven. Geoffrey Arrand, *apptd* 1994

Chancellor, The Hon. Mr Justice Blofeld, *apptd* 1974
Registrar and Legal Secretary, James Hall
Diocesan Secretary, Nicholas Edgell, Diocesan Office, St Nicholas Centre, 4 Cutler Street, Ipswich IP1 1UQ **T** 01473-298500

SALISBURY *(Canterbury)*
77TH BISHOP
Rt. Revd Dr David S. Stancliffe, *cons.* 1993, *apptd* 1993; South Canonry, The Close, Salisbury SP1 2ER
Signs David Sarum

BISHOPS SUFFRAGAN
Ramsbury, Rt. Revd Stephen Conway, *cons.* 2006, *apptd* 2006; Southbroom House, London Road, Devizes, Wiltshire SN10 1LT
Sherborne, Rt. Revd Timothy M. Thornton, *cons.* 2001, *apptd* 2001; Sherborne Office, Little Bailie, Dullar Lane, Sturminster Marshall, Wimborne, Dorset BH21 4AD

DEAN
Very Revd June Osborne, *apptd* 2004

Organist, David Halls, *apptd* 2005

ARCHDEACONS
Dorset, Ven. Alistair Magowan, *apptd* 2000
Sherborne, Ven. Paul Taylor, *apptd* 2004
Wilts, Ven. John Wraw, *apptd* 2004
Sarum, Ven. Alan Jeans, *apptd* 2003

Chancellor, His Hon. Judge Samuel Wiggs, *apptd* 1997
Registrar and Legal Secretary, Andrew Johnson
Diocesan Secretary, Lucinda Herklots, Church House, Crane Street, Salisbury SP1 2QB **T** 01722-411922

SHEFFIELD *(York)*
6TH BISHOP
Rt. Revd John (Jack) Nicholls, *cons.* 1990, *apptd* 1997; Bishopscroft, Snaithing Lane, Sheffield S10 3LG
Signs Jack Sheffield

BISHOP SUFFRAGAN
Doncaster, Rt. Revd Cyril Guy Ashton, *cons.* 2000, *apptd* 2000; Bishop's House, 3 Farrington Court, Wickersley, Rotherham S66 1JQ

DEAN
Very Revd Peter Bradley, *apptd* 2003

Master of Music, Neil Taylor, *apptd* 1997

ARCHDEACONS
Doncaster, Ven. Robert Fitzharris, *apptd* 2001
Sheffield and Rotherham, Ven. Richard Blackburn, *apptd* 1999

Chancellor, Prof. David McClean, *apptd* 1992
Registrar and Legal Secretary, Miranda Myers
Diocesan Secretary, Malcolm Fair, Diocesan Church House, 95–99 Effingham Street, Rotherham S65 1BL **T** 01709-309100

SODOR AND MAN *(York)*
81st BISHOP
vacant

ARCHDEACON OF MAN
Ven. Brian Smith, *apptd* 2005

Vicar-General and Chancellor, Clare Faulds
Registrar and Legal Secretary, Jonathan Kewley
Diocesan Secretary, Barbara Brereton, Silverdene, Station Road, Ballasalla, Isle of Man IM9 2DQ **T** 01624-827644

SOUTHWARK *(Canterbury)*
9TH BISHOP
Rt. Revd Dr Tom F. Butler, *cons.* 1985, *apptd* 1998; Bishop's House, 38 Tooting Bec Gardens, London SW16 1QZ
Signs Thomas Southwark

AREA BISHOPS
Croydon, Rt. Revd Nicholas Baines, *cons.* 2003, *apptd* 2003; St Matthew's House, 100 George Street, Croydon, Surrey CR0 1PE
Kingston upon Thames, Rt. Revd Richard Cheetham, *cons.* 2002, *apptd* 2002; Kingston Episcopal Area Office, St Cecilia's, Sutherland Grove, London SW18 5JR
Woolwich, Rt. Revd Christopher Chessun, *cons.* 2005, *apptd* 2005; Diocesan Office (*see* below)

DEAN
Very Revd Colin B. Slee, OBE, *apptd* 1994

Organist, Peter Wright, FRCO, *apptd* 1989

ARCHDEACONS
Croydon, Ven. Tony Davies, *apptd* 1994
Lambeth, Ven. Christopher Skilton, *apptd* 2003
Lewisham, Ven. Christine Hardman, *apptd* 2001
Reigate, Ven. Daniel Kajumba, *apptd* 2001
Southwark, Revd Dr Michael Ipgrave, *apptd* 2004
Wandsworth, Ven. Stephen Roberts, *apptd* 2005

Chancellor, Charles George, QC
Registrar and Legal Secretary, Paul Morris
Diocesan Secretary, Simon Parton, Trinity House, 4 Chapel Court, Borough High Street, London SE1 1HW T 020-7939 9400

SOUTHWELL AND NOTTINGHAM *(York)*
10TH BISHOP
Rt. Revd George H. Cassidy, *cons.* 1999, *apptd* 1999; Bishop's Manor, Southwell NG25 0JR
Signs George Southwell

BISHOP SUFFRAGAN
Sherwood, Rt. Revd Anthony Porter, *cons.* 2006, *apptd* 2006; Dunham House, 8 Westgate, Southwell NG25 0JL

DEAN
Very Revd John Guille, *apptd* 2007

Organist, Paul Hale, *apptd* 1989

ARCHDEACONS
Newark, Ven. Nigel Peyton, *apptd* 1999
Nottingham, Ven. Peter Hill, *apptd* 2007

Chancellor, Linda Box, *apptd* 2005
Registrar and Legal Secretary, Christopher Hodson
Diocesan Secretary, Dunham House, Westgate, Southwell, Notts NG25 0JL T 01636-817204

TRURO *(Canterbury)*
14TH BISHOP
Rt. Revd William Ind, *cons.* 1987, *apptd* 1997; Lis Escop, Truro TR3 6QQ
Signs William Truro

BISHOP SUFFRAGAN
St Germans, Rt. Revd Royden Screech, *cons.* 2000, *apptd* 2000; Royden Screech, 32 Falmouth Road, Truro, Cornwall TR1 2HX

DEAN
Very Revd Dr Christopher Hardwick, *apptd* 2005

Organist, Robert Sharpe, *apptd* 2002

ARCHDEACONS
Cornwall, Ven. Roger Bush, *apptd* 2006
Bodmin, Ven. Clive Cohen, *apptd* 2000

Chancellor, Timothy Briden, *apptd* 1998
Registrar and Legal Secretary, Martin Follett
Diocesan Secretary, Sheri Sturgess, Diocesan House, Kenwyn, Truro TR1 1JQ T 01872-274351

WAKEFIELD *(York)*
12TH BISHOP
Rt. Revd Stephen Platten, *cons.* 2003, *apptd* 2003; Bishop's Lodge, Woodthorpe Lane, Wakefield WF2 6JL
Signs Stephen Wakefield

BISHOP SUFFRAGAN
Pontefract, Rt. Revd Anthony William Robinson, *cons.* 2003, *apptd* 2002; Pontefract House, 181A Manygates Lane, Wakefield WF2 7DR

DEAN
vacant

Organist, Jonathan Bielby, FRCO, *apptd* 1972

ARCHDEACONS
Halifax, Ven. Robert Freeman, *apptd* 2003
Pontefract, Ven. Jonathan Greener, *apptd* 2003

Chancellor, Paul Downes, *apptd* 2006
Registrar and Legal Secretaries, Julian Gill; Julia Wilding
Diocesan Secretary, Ashley Ellis, Church House, 1 South Parade, Wakefield WF1 1LP T 01924-371802

WORCESTER *(Canterbury)*
113TH BISHOP
Rt. Revd Dr John Inge, *cons.* 2003, *apptd* 2007; The Bishop's House, Hartlebury Castle, Kidderminster DY11 7XX
Signs John Wigorn

SUFFRAGAN BISHOP
Dudley, Rt. Revd Dr David S. Walker, *cons.* 2000, *apptd* 2000; The Bishop's House, Bishop's Walk, Cradley Heath B64 7JF

DEAN
Revd Peter Atkinson, *apptd* 2006

Organist, Adrian Lucas, *apptd* 1996

ARCHDEACONS
Dudley, Ven. Fred Trethewey, *apptd* 2001
Worcester, Ven. Dr Joy Tetley, *apptd* 1999

Chancellor, Charles Mynors, *apptd* 1999
Registrar and Legal Secretary, Michael Huskinson
Diocesan Secretary, Robert Higham, The Old Palace, Deansway, Worcester WR1 2JE T 01905-20537

ROYAL PECULIARS *(Canterbury)*
WESTMINSTER
The Collegiate Church of St Peter
Dean, Canon John Hall
Sub Dean and Archdeacon, Canon Robert Wright, *apptd* 2005
Chapter Clerk and Receiver-General, Maj.-Gen. David Burden, CB, CBE, Chapter Office, 20 Dean's Yard, London SW1P 3PA
Organist, James O'Donnell, *apptd* 1999
Registrar, Stuart Holmes, MVO
Legal Secretary, Christopher Vyse, *apptd* 2000

WINDSOR
The Queen's Free Chapel of St George within Her Castle of Windsor
Dean, Rt. Revd David Conner, *apptd* 1998
Chapter Clerk, Charlotte Manley, LVO, OBE, *apptd* 2003; Chapter Office, The Cloisters, Windsor Castle, Windsor, Berks SL4 1NJ
Director of Music, Timothy Byram-Wigfield, *apptd* 2004

OTHER ANGLICAN CHURCHES

THE CHURCH IN WALES

The Anglican Church was the established church in Wales from the 16th century until 1920, when the estrangement of the majority of Welsh people from Anglicanism resulted in disestablishment. Since then the Church in Wales has been an autonomous province consisting of six sees. The bishops are elected by an electoral college comprising elected lay and clerical members, who also elect one of the diocesan bishops as Archbishop of Wales.

The legislative body of the Church in Wales is the Governing Body, which has 207 members divided between the three orders of bishops, clergy and laity. Its president is the Archbishop of Wales and it meets twice annually. Its decisions are binding upon all members of the church. The church's property and finances are the responsibility of the Representative Body. There are about 68,700 members of the Church in Wales, with 584 stipendiary clergy and 977 parishes.

THE GOVERNING BODY OF THE CHURCH IN
  WALES, 39 Cathedral Road, Cardiff CF11 9XF
  T 029-2034 8200 *Lay Secretary*, John Shirley
12th ARCHBISHOP OF WALES, Most Revd Dr Barry
  Morgan (Bishop of Llandaff), *elected* 2003 *Signs* Barry
  Cambrensis

BISHOPS
Bangor (80th), Rt. Revd Anthony Crockett, *b.* 1945, *cons.*
  2004, *elected* 2004; Ty'r Esgob, Bangor, Gwynedd
  LL57 2SS *Signs* Anthony Bangor. *Stipendiary clergy*, 51
Llandaff (102nd), Most Revd Dr Barry Morgan (*also*
  Archbishop of Wales), *b.* 1947, *cons.* 1993, *trans.* 1999;
  Llys Esgob, The Cathedral Green, Llandaff, Cardiff CF5 2YE
  Signs Barry Cambrensis. *Stipendiary clergy*, 143
Monmouth (9th), Rt. Revd Dominic Walker, *b.* 1948, *cons.*
  1997, *elected* 2003; Bishopstow, Stow Hill, Newport
  NP20 4EA *Signs* Dominic Monmouth. *Stipendiary
  clergy*, 90
St Asaph (74th), Rt. Revd John Davies, *b.* 1943, *cons.*
  1999, *elected* 1999; Esgobty, Upper Denbigh Road, St
  Asaph, Denbighshire LL17 0TW *Signs* John St Asaph.
  Stipendiary clergy, 102
St David's (127th), Rt. Revd Carl Cooper, *b.* 1960, *cons.*
  2002, *elected* 2002; Llys Esgob, Abergwili, Carmarthen
  SA31 2JG *Signs* Carl St Davids. *Stipendiary clergy*, 126
Swansea and Brecon (8th), Rt. Revd Anthony Pierce,
  b. 1941, *cons.* 1999, *elected* 1999; Ely Tower, Brecon,
  Powys LD3 9DE *Signs* Anthony Swansea & Brecon.
  Stipendiary clergy, 76

The stipend for a diocesan bishop of the Church in Wales is £35,073 a year for 2007–8.

SCOTTISH EPISCOPAL CHURCH

The Scottish Episcopal Church was founded after the Act of Settlement (1690) established the presbyterian nature of the Church of Scotland. The Scottish Episcopal Church is a member of the worldwide Anglican Communion. The governing authority is the General Synod, an elected body of approximately 140 members which meets once a year. The bishop who convenes and presides at meetings of the General Synod is called the 'primus' and is elected by his fellow bishops.

There are 42,290 members of the Scottish Episcopal Church, of whom 28,589 are communicants. There are seven bishops, approximately 482 serving clergy, and 313 churches and places of worship.

THE GENERAL SYNOD OF THE SCOTTISH
  EPISCOPAL CHURCH, 21 Grosvenor Crescent,
  Edinburgh EH12 5EE T 0131-225 6357
  W www.scotland-anglican.org
  Secretary-General, J. F. Stuart
PRIMUS OF THE SCOTTISH EPISCOPAL CHURCH,
  Most Revd Dr Idris Jones (Bishop of Glasgow and
  Galloway), *elected* 2006

BISHOPS
Aberdeen and Orkney, Very Revd Bob Gillies, *b.* 1951, *cons.*
  2007, *elected* 2007. *Clergy*, 54
Argyll and the Isles, Rt. Revd Martin Shaw, *b.* 1944, *cons.*
  2004, *elected* 2004. *Clergy* 22
Brechin, Rt. Revd John Mantle, *b.* 1946, *cons.* 2005,
  elected 2005. *Clergy*, 35
Edinburgh, Rt. Revd Brian Smith, *b.* 1943, *cons.* 1993,
  elected 2001. *Clergy*, 162
Glasgow and Galloway, Most Revd Idris Jones, *b.* 1943,
  cons. 1998, *elected* 1998. *Clergy*, 99
Moray, Ross and Caithness, Rt. Revd John Crook, *b.* 1940,
  cons. 1999, *elected* 1999. *Clergy*, 31
St Andrews, Dunkeld and Dunblane, Rt. Revd Mark
  Strange, *b.* 1961, *cons.* 2007, *elected* 2007. *Clergy*, 86

The minimum stipend of a diocesan bishop of the Scottish Episcopal Church for 2007 is £31,470 (ie 1.5 times the standard clergy stipend of £20,980).

CHURCH OF IRELAND

The Anglican Church was the established church in Ireland from the 16th century but never secured the allegiance of the majority and was disestablished in 1871. The Church of Ireland is divided into the provinces of Armagh and Dublin, each under an archbishop. The provinces are subdivided into 12 dioceses.

The legislative body is the General Synod, which has 660 members in total, divided between the House of Bishops and the House of Representatives. The Archbishop of Armagh is elected by the House of Bishops; other episcopal elections are made by an electoral college.

There are about 400,000 members of the Church of Ireland, with two archbishops, ten bishops, about 600 clergy and about 1,100 churches and places of worship.
CENTRAL OFFICE, Church of Ireland House, Church
  Avenue, Rathmines, Dublin 6 T (+353) (1) 497 8422
  *Chief Officer and Secretary of the Representative Church
  Body*, D. C. Reardon

PROVINCE OF ARMAGH
ARCHBISHOP OF ARMAGH, PRIMATE OF ALL
  IRELAND AND METROPOLITAN, Most Revd Alan
  Harper, OBE, *b.* 1944, *cons.* 2002, *trans.* 2007.
  Clergy, 55

BISHOPS
Clogher, Rt. Revd Michael Jackson, PHD, DPHIL,
  b. 1956, *cons.* 2002, *apptd* 2002. *Clergy*, 32
Connor, Rt. Revd Alan Abernethy, *b.* 1957, *cons.* 2007,
  apptd 2007. *Clergy*, 106
Derry and Raphoe, Rt. Revd Kenneth Good, *b.* 1952, *cons.*
  2002, *apptd* 2002. *Clergy*, 51
Down and Dromore, Rt. Revd Harold Miller, *b.* 1950, *cons.*
  1997, *apptd* 1997. *Clergy*, 116

Kilmore, Elphin and Ardagh, Rt. Revd Kenneth Clarke, *b.* 1949, *cons.* 2001, *apptd* 2001. *Clergy,* 21
Tuam, Killala and Achonry, Rt. Revd Richard Henderson, DPHIL, *b.* 1957, *cons.* 1998, *apptd* 1998. *Clergy,* 13

PROVINCE OF DUBLIN
ARCHBISHOP OF DUBLIN, BISHOP OF GLENDALOUGH, PRIMATE OF IRELAND AND METROPOLITAN, Most Revd John R. W. Neill, *b.* 1945, *apptd* 2002. *Clergy,* 86

BISHOPS
Cashel and Ossory, Rt. Revd Michael Burrows, *b.* 1961, *cons.* 2006, *apptd* 2006. *Clergy,* 42
Cork, Cloyne and Ross, Rt. Revd W. Paul Colton, *b.* 1960, *cons.* 1999, *apptd* 1999. *Clergy,* 30
Limerick and Killaloe, Rt. Revd Michael Mayes, *b.* 1941, *cons.* 1993, *trans.* 2000. *Clergy,* 19
Meath and Kildare, Most Revd Richard Clarke, PHD, *b.* 1949, *cons.* 1996, *apptd* 1996. *Clergy,* 26

OVERSEAS

PRIMATES
PRIMATE AND PRESIDING BISHOP OF AOTEAROA, NEW ZEALAND AND POLYNESIA, Most Revd William Brown Turei
PRIMATE OF AUSTRALIA, Most Revd Phillip Aspinall
PRIMATE OF BRAZIL, Most Revd Maurício Araújo de Andrade
ARCHBISHOP OF THE PROVINCE OF BURUNDI, Most Revd Bernard Ntahoturi
ARCHBISHOP AND PRIMATE OF CANADA, Most Revd Andrew Sandford Hutchison
ARCHBISHOP OF THE PROVINCE OF CENTRAL AFRICA, Most Revd Bernard Amos Malango
PRIMATE OF THE CENTRAL REGION OF AMERICA, Most Revd Martin de Jesus Barahona
ARCHBISHOP OF THE PROVINCE OF CONGO, Most Revd Dr Dirokpa Balufuga Fidèle
PRIMATE OF THE PROVINCE OF HONG KONG SHENG KUNG HUI, Most Revd Paul Kwong
ARCHBISHOP OF THE PROVINCE OF THE INDIAN OCEAN, Most Revd Gerald James Ernest
PRIMATE OF JAPAN (NIPPON SEI KO KAI), Most Revd Nathaniel Makoto Uematsu
PRESIDENT-BISHOP OF JERUSALEM AND THE MIDDLE EAST, Most Revd Dr Mouneer Hanna Anis
ARCHBISHOP OF THE PROVINCE OF KENYA, Most Revd Benjamin M. P. Nzimbi
ARCHBISHOP OF THE PROVINCE OF KOREA, Most Revd Francis Kyung Jo Park
ARCHBISHOP OF THE PROVINCE OF MELANESIA, Most Revd Sir Ellison Leslie Pogo, KBE
ARCHBISHOP OF MEXICO, Most Revd Carlos Touche-Porter
ARCHBISHOP OF THE PROVINCE OF MYANMAR, Most Revd Samuel San Si Htay
ARCHBISHOP OF THE PROVINCE OF NIGERIA, Most Revd Peter Akinola
ARCHBISHOP OF PAPUA NEW GUINEA, Most Revd James Ayong
PRIME BISHOP OF THE PHILIPPINES, Most Revd Ignacio Capuyan Soliba
ARCHBISHOP OF THE PROVINCE OF RWANDA, Most Revd Emmanuel Musaba Kolini
PRIMATE OF THE PROVINCE OF SOUTH EAST ASIA, Most Revd Dr John Chew

METROPOLITAN OF THE PROVINCE OF SOUTHERN AFRICA, Most Revd Njongonkulu W. H. Ndungane
PRESIDING BISHOP OF THE SOUTHERN CONE OF AMERICA, Most Revd Gregory James Venables
ARCHBISHOP OF THE PROVINCE OF THE SUDAN, Most Revd Joseph Biringi Hassan Marona
ARCHBISHOP OF THE PROVINCE OF TANZANIA, Most Revd Donald Leo Mtetemela
ARCHBISHOP OF THE PROVINCE OF UGANDA, Most Revd Henry Luke Orombi
PRESIDING BISHOP AND PRIMATE OF THE USA, Most Revd Katharine Jefferts Schori
ARCHBISHOP OF THE PROVINCE OF WEST AFRICA, Most Revd Justice Ofei Akrofi
ARCHBISHOP OF THE PROVINCE OF THE WEST INDIES, Most Revd Drexel Wellington Gomez

OTHER CHURCHES AND EXTRA-PROVINCIAL DIOCESES
ANGLICAN CHURCH OF BERMUDA, *extra-provincial to Canterbury*
Bishop, Rt. Revd Ewen Ratteray
CHURCH OF CEYLON, *extra-provincial to Canterbury*
Bishop of Colombo, Rt. Revd Duleep de Chickera
Bishop of Kurunagala, Rt. Revd Kumara Illangasinghe
EPISCOPAL CHURCH OF CUBA, Rt. Revd Miguel Tamayo *(interim)*
FALKLAND ISLANDS, *extra-provincial to Canterbury*
Episcopal Commissary, Rt. Revd Stephen Venner (Bishop of Dover)
LUSITANIAN CHURCH *(Portuguese Episcopal Church), extra-provincial to Canterbury*
Bishop, Rt. Revd Fernando Soares
REFORMED EPISCOPAL CHURCH OF SPAIN, *extra-provincial to Canterbury*
Bishop, Rt. Revd Carlos López-Lozano

MODERATION OF CHURCHES IN FULL COMMUNION WITH THE ANGLICAN COMMUNION
CHURCH OF BANGLADESH, Rt. Revd Michael Baroi
CHURCH OF NORTH INDIA, Most Revd Joel Vidyasagar Mal
CHURCH OF SOUTH INDIA, Most Revd Badda Peter Sugandhar
CHURCH OF PAKISTAN, Rt. Revd Dr Alexander John Malik

CHURCH OF SCOTLAND

The Church of Scotland is the established (ie national) church of Scotland. The church is reformed in doctrine, and presbyterian in constitution, ie based on a hierarchy of councils of ministers and elders and, since 1990, of members of a diaconate. At local level the Kirk Session consists of the parish minister and ruling elders. At district level the presbyteries, of which there are 44 in Britain, consist of all the ministers in the district, one ruling elder from each congregation, and those members of the diaconate who qualify for membership. The General Assembly is the supreme authority, and is presided over by a Moderator chosen annually by the Assembly. The sovereign, if not present in person, is represented by a Lord High Commissioner who is appointed each year by the crown.

The Church of Scotland has about 504,363 members, 1,004 ministers and 1,191 churches. There are about 21 ministers and other personnel working overseas.

Lord High Commissioner (2007–8), HRH The Duke of York, KG, KCVO

Moderator of the General Assembly (2007–8), Rt. Revd Sheilagh Kesting

Principal Clerk, Very Revd Dr F. Macdonald

Depute Clerk, Revd. Dr M. MacLean

Procurator, L. Dunlop

Law Agent and Solicitor of the Church, Mrs J. Wilson

Parliamentary Agent, I. McCulloch *(London)*

General Treasurer, I. Grimmond

Secretary, Church and Society Council, Revd Dr David Sinclair

CHURCH OFFICE, 121 George Street, Edinburgh EH2 4YN
T 0131-225 5722

PRESBYTERIES AND CLERKS

Edinburgh, Revd W. Graham

West Lothian, Revd D. Shaw

Lothian, J. McCulloch

Melrose and Peebles, Jack Stewart

Duns, Peter Johnson

Jedburgh, Revd W. Frank Campbell

Annandale and Eskdale, Revd C. Haston

Dumfries and Kirkcudbright, Revd G. Savage

Wigtown and Stranraer, Revd D. Dutton

Ayr, Revd J. Crichton

Irvine and Kilmarnock, Revd C. Brockie

Ardrossan, Revd J. Mackay

Lanark, Revd J. Cutler

Greenock and Paisley, Revd A. Ward

Glasgow, Revd D. Lunan

Hamilton, Revd S. Paterson

Dumbarton, Revd C. Caskie

Argyll, I. Maclagan

Falkirk, Revd I. Black

Stirling, Revd M. MacCormick

Dunfermline, Revd E. Kenny

Kirkcaldy, Rosemary Frew

St Andrews, Dr R. Mackie

Dunkeld and Meigle, Revd J. Russell

Perth, Revd D. Main

Dundee, Revd J. Wilson

Angus, Revd M. Bicket

Aberdeen, Revd I. MacLean

Kincardine and Deeside, Revd J. Holt

Gordon, Revd Euan Glen

Buchan, George Berstan

Moray, Revd Hugh Smith

Abernethy, Revd J. MacEwan

Inverness, Revd A. Younger

Lochaber, Revd D. Anderson

Ross, Revd T. McWilliam

Sutherland, Revd J. Goskirk

Caithness, J. Houston

Lochcarron-Skye, Revd A. MacArthur

Uist, Revd M. Smith

Lewis, Revd T. Sinclair

Orkney, Revd T. Hunt

Shetland, Revd C. Greig

England, Revd Scott Brown

Europe, Revd J. Cowie

The stipends for ministers in the Church of Scotland in 2007 range from £21,466–£28,500, depending on length of service. In addition, congregations can make extra payments.

ROMAN CATHOLIC CHURCH

The Roman Catholic Church is one worldwide Christian church acknowledging as its head the Bishop of Rome, known as the Pope (Father). He leads a communion of followers of Christ, who believe they continue his presence in the world as servants of faith, hope and love to all society. The Pope is held to be the successor of St Peter and thus invested with the power which was entrusted to St Peter by Jesus Christ. A direct line of succession is therefore claimed from the earliest Christian communities. With the fall of the Roman Empire the Pope also became an important political leader. His territory is now limited to the 0.44 sq. km. (0.17 sq. miles) of the Vatican City State, created to provide some independence to the Pope from Italy and other nations.

The Pope exercises spiritual authority over the church with the advice and assistance of the Sacred College of Cardinals, the supreme council of the church. He is also advised by bishops in communion with him, by a group of officers which form the Roman Curia and by his ambassadors, called Apostolic Nuncios, who liaise with the Bishops' Conference in each country.

Those members of the College of Cardinals who are under the age of 80 elect a successor of the Pope following his death. The assembly of the cardinals called to the Vatican for the election of a new Pope is known as the conclave. In complete seclusion the cardinals vote by a secret ballot; a two-thirds majority is necessary before the vote can be accepted as final. When a cardinal receives the necessary number of votes, the Dean of the Sacred College formally asks him if he will accept election and the name by which he wishes to be known. On his acceptance of the office of Supreme Pontiff, the conclave is dissolved and the first Cardinal Deacon announces the election to the assembled crowd in St Peter's Square.

The number of cardinals was fixed at 70 by Pope Sixtus V in 1586 but has been steadily increased since the pontificate of John XXIII and at the end of March 2005 stood at 183, plus one cardinal 'in pectore' (their name kept secret by the Pope for fear of persecution). At the end of March 2005, 117 of the 183 cardinals were cardinal electors, who took part in the election of Pope Benedict XVI, following the death of Pope John Paul II in April 2005.

The Pope has full legislative, judicial and administrative power over the whole church. He is aided in his administration by the curia, which is made up of a number of departments. The Secretariat of State is the central office for carrying out the Pope's instructions and is presided over by the Cardinal Secretary of State. It maintains relations with the departments of the curia, with the episcopate, with the representatives of the Holy See in various countries, governments and private persons. The congregations and pontifical councils are the Pope's ministries and include departments such as the Congregation for the Doctrine of Faith, whose field of competence concerns faith and morals; the Congregation for the Clergy and the Congregation for the Evangelisation of Peoples, the Pontifical Council for the Family and the Pontifical Council for the Promotion of Christian Unity.

The Vatican State does not have diplomatic representatives. The Holy See, composed of the Pope and those who help him in his mission for the church, is recognised by the Conventions of Vienna as an international moral body. The representatives of the Holy See are known as Apostolic Nuncios. Where representation is only to the local churches and not to the government of a country, the papal representative is known as an apostolic delegate. The Roman Catholic Church has an estimated 840 million adherents under the care of some 2,500 diocesan bishops worldwide.

SOVEREIGN PONTIFF
His Holiness Pope Benedict XVI (Joseph Ratzinger), *born* Bavaria, Germany, 16 April 1927; *ordained priest* 1951; *appointed Archbishop* (of Munich), March 1977; *created Cardinal* June 1977; *assumed pontificate* 19 April 2005

SECRETARIAT OF STATE
Secretary of State, HE Cardinal Tarcisio Bertone
First Section (General Affairs), Most Revd Leonardo Sandri (Titular Archbishop of Cittanova)
Second Section (Relations with Other States), Most Revd Dominique Mamberti (Titular Archbishop of Sagona)

BISHOPS' CONFERENCE
The Catholic Church in England and Wales consists of a total of 22 dioceses. The Bishops' Conference, which coordinates the church, includes the diocesan bishops, the Apostolic Exarch of the Ukrainians, the Bishop of the Forces and the auxiliary bishops. The conference is headed by the president (HE Cardinal Cormac Murphy-O'Connor, Archbishop of Westminster) and vice-president (The Most Revd Patrick Kelly, Archbishop of Liverpool). There are six departments, each with an episcopal chair: the Department for Christian Life and Worship (the Bishop of Leeds), the Department for Dialogue and Unity (the Archbishop of Southwark), the Department for Catholic Education and Formation (the Archbishop of Birmingham), the Department for Christian Responsibility and Citizenship (the Archbishop of Cardiff), the Department for International Affairs (the Bishop of Portsmouth) and the Department for Evangelisation and Catechesis (the Bishop of Nottingham).

The Bishops' Conference Standing Committee is made up of two directly elected bishops in addition to the Metropolitan Archbishops and chairs from each of the above departments. The committee has general responsibility for continuity of policy between the plenary sessions of the conference, preparing the conference agenda and implementing its decisions.

The administration of the Bishops' Conference is funded by a levy on each diocese, according to income. A general secretariat in London coordinates and supervises the Bishops' Conference administration activities. There are also other agencies and consultative bodies affiliated to the conference.

The Bishops' Conference of Scotland is the permanently constituted assembly of the bishops of Scotland. The conference is headed by the president (HE Cardinal Keith Patrick O'Brien, Archbishop of St. Andrews and Edinburgh). The conference establishes various agencies which have an advisory function in relation to the conference. The more important of these agencies are called commissions and each one has a bishop president who, with the other members of the commissions, are appointed by the conference.

The Irish Episcopal Conference has as its president Archbishop Brady of Armagh. Its membership comprises all the archbishops and bishops of Ireland and it appoints various commissions to assist it in its work. There are three types of commissions: (a) those made up of lay and clerical members chosen for their skills and experience,

and staffed by full-time expert secretariats; (b) commissions whose members are selected from existing institutions and whose services are supplied on a part-time basis; and (c) commissions of bishops only.

The Catholic Church in the UK has an estimated 5,631,449 members, 6,583 priests and 4,475 churches.
Bishops' Conferences secretariats:
ENGLAND AND WALES, 39 Eccleston Square, London SW1V 1BX T 020-7630 8220 F 020-7901 4821
E secretariat@cbcew.org.uk W www.catholicchurch.org.uk
General Secretary, Mgr Andrew Summersgill
SCOTLAND, 64 Aitken Street, Airdrie, Lanarkshire ML6 6LT
T 01236-764061 E gensec@bpsconfscot.com
General Secretary, Revd Paul Conroy
IRELAND, Columba Centre, Maynooth, County Kildare
T (+353) (1) 505 3000 W www.catholiccommunications.ie
Secretary, Most Revd William Lee (Bishop of Waterford and Lismore)
Executive Secretary, Revd Aidan O'Boyle

GREAT BRITAIN
APOSTOLIC NUNCIO TO GREAT BRITAIN
Most Revd Faustino Sainz Muñoz, 54 Parkside, London SW19 5NE T 020-8944 7189

ENGLAND AND WALES
THE MOST REVD ARCHBISHOPS
Westminster, HE Cardinal Cormac Murphy-O'Connor, *cons.* 1977, *apptd* 2000 *Auxiliaries,* George Stack, *cons.* 2001; Bernard Longley *cons.* 2003; Alan Hopes *cons.* 2003; John Arnold *cons.* 2006. *Clergy,* 690.
Archbishop's Residence, Archbishop's House, Ambrosden Avenue, London SW1P 1QJ T 020-7798 9033
Birmingham, Vincent Nichols, *cons.* 1992, *apptd* 2000 *Auxiliaries,* Philip Pargeter, *cons.* 1990; David McGough, *cons.* 2005; William Kenney, *cons.* 1987. *Clergy,* 443. *Archbishop's Residence,* Archbishop's House, 8 Shadwell Street, Birmingham B4 6EY
T 0121-236 9090
Cardiff, Peter Smith, *cons.* 1995, *apptd* 2001. *Clergy,* 96. *Archbishop's Residence,* Archbishop's House, 43 Cathedral Road, Cardiff CF11 9HD T 029-2022 0411
Liverpool, Patrick Kelly, *cons.* 1984, *apptd* 1996 *Auxiliary,* Thomas Williams, *cons.* 2003. *Clergy,* 474. *Diocesan Curia,* Archdiocese of Liverpool, Centre for Evangelisation, Croxteth Drive, Sefton Park, Liverpool L17 1AA T 0151-522 1000
Southwark, Kevin McDonald, *cons.* 2001, *apptd* 2003 *Auxiliaries,* John Hine, *cons.* 2001; Patrick Lynch, *cons.* 2006; Paul Hendricks, *cons.* 2006. *Clergy,* 518. *Diocesan Curia,* Archbishop's House, 150 St George's Road, London SE1 6HX T 020-7928 5592

THE RT. REVD BISHOPS
Arundel and Brighton, Kieran Conry, *cons.* 2001, *apptd* 2001. *Clergy,* 105. *Diocesan Curia,* Bishop's House, The Upper Drive, Hove, E. Sussex BN3 6NE T 01273-506387
Brentwood, Thomas McMahon, *cons.* 1980, *apptd* 1980. *Clergy,* 121. *Bishop's Office,* Cathedral House, Ingrave Road, Brentwood, Essex CM15 8AT T 01277-232266
Clifton, Declan Lang, *cons.* 2001, *apptd* 2001. *Clergy,* 251. *Bishop's House,* St Ambrose, North Road, Leigh Woods, Bristol BS8 3PW T 0117-973 3072
East Anglia, Michael Evans, *cons* 2003, *apptd* 2003. *Clergy,* 129. *Diocesan Curia,* The White House, 21 Upgate, Poringland, Norwich NR14 7SH T 01508-492202
Hallam, John Rawsthorne, *cons.* 1981, *apptd* 1997. *Clergy,* 75. *Bishop's House,* 75 Norfolk Road, Sheffield S2 2SZ T 0114-278 7988

Hexham and Newcastle, Kevin Dunn, *cons.* 2004, *apptd* 2004. *Clergy,* 211. *Diocesan Curia,* Bishop's House, East Denton Hall, 800 West Road, Newcastle upon Tyne NE5 2BJ T 0191-228 0003

Lancaster, Patrick O'Donoghue, *cons.* 1993, *apptd* 2001. *Clergy,* 248. *Bishop's Residence,* Bishop's Apartment, Cathedral House, Balmoral Road, Lancaster LA1 3BT T 01524-596050

Leeds, Arthur Roche, *cons.* 2001, *apptd* 2004. *Clergy,* 226. *Diocesan Curia,* Hinsley Hall, 62 Headingley Lane, Leeds LS6 2BX T 0113-261 8022

Menevia (Wales), Mark Jabalé, *cons.* 2001, *apptd* 2001. *Clergy,* 60. *Diocesan Curia,* 27 Convent Street, Swansea SA1 2BX T 01792-644017

Middlesbrough, vacant. *Clergy,* 113. *Diocesan Curia,* 50A The Avenue, Linthorpe, Middlesbrough TS5 6QT T 01642-850505

Northampton, Peter Doyle, *Clergy,* 163. *Diocesan Curia,* Bishop's House, Marriott Street, Northampton NN2 6AW T 01604-715635

Nottingham, Malcolm McMahon, *cons.* 2000, *apptd* 2000. *Clergy,* 162. *Bishop's House,* 27 Cavendish Road East, The Park, Nottingham NG7 1BB T 0115-947 4786

Plymouth, Christopher Budd, *cons.* 1986, *apptd* 1985. *Clergy,* 132. *Bishop's Residence,* Bishop's House, 31 Wyndham Street West, Plymouth PL1 5RZ T 01752-224414

Portsmouth, Crispian Hollis, *cons.* 1987, *apptd* 1989. *Clergy,* 282. *Bishop's Residence,* Bishop's House, Edinburgh Road, Portsmouth, Hants PO1 3HG T 023-9282 0894

Salford, Terence Brain, *cons.* 1991, *apptd* 1997. *Clergy,* 387. *Diocesan Curia,* 5 Gerald Road, Pendleton, Salford M6 6DL T 0161-736 1421

Shrewsbury, Brian Noble, *cons.* 1995, *apptd* 1995. *Clergy* 203. *Diocesan Curia,* 2 Park Road South, Prenton, Wirral CH43 4UX T 0151-652 9855

Wrexham (Wales), Edwin Regan, *cons.*1994, *apptd* 1994. *Clergy,* 45. *Diocesan Curia,* Bishop's House, Sontley Road, Wrexham LL13 7EW T 01978-262726

SCOTLAND
THE MOST REVD ARCHBISHOPS
St Andrews and Edinburgh, HE Cardinal Keith Patrick O'Brien, *cons.* 1985, *apptd* 1985, *elevated* 2003. *Clergy,* 150. *Diocesan Office,* 100 Strathearn Road, Edinburgh EH9 1BB T 0131-623 8900

Glasgow, Mario Joseph Conti, *cons.* 1977, *apptd* 2002. *Clergy,* 233. *Diocesan Curia,* 196 Clyde Street, Glasgow G1 4JY T 0141-226 5898

THE RT. REVD BISHOPS
Aberdeen, Peter Moran, *cons.* 2003, *apptd* 2003. *Clergy,* 43. *Diocesan Curia,* Bishop's House, 3 Queen's Cross, Aberdeen AB15 4XU T 01224-319154

Argyll and the Isles, Ian Murray, *cons.* 1999, *apptd* 1999. *Clergy,* 32. *Bishop's House,* Esplanade, Oban, Argyll PA34 5AB T 01631-571395

Dunkeld, Vincent Logan, *cons.* 1981. *Clergy,* 42. *Diocesan Curia,* 24–28 Lawside Road, Dundee DD3 6XY T 01382-225453

Galloway, John Cunningham, *cons.* 2004, *apptd* 2004. *Clergy* 56. *Diocesan Curia,* Candida Casa, 8 Corsehill Road, Ayr KA7 2ST T 01292-266750

Motherwell, Joseph Devine, *cons.* 1977, *apptd* 1983. *Clergy,* 123. *Diocesan Curia,* Coursington Road, Motherwell ML1 1PP T 01698-269114

Paisley, Philip Tartaglia, *cons.* 2005, *apptd* 2005. *Clergy,* 85. *Diocesan Curia,* Diocesan Centre, Cathedral Precincts, Incle Street, Paisley PA1 1HR T 0141-847 6130

BISHOPRIC OF THE FORCES
Rt. Revd Thomas Matthew Burns, *cons.* 2002, *apptd* 2002. *Administration,* Bishopric of the Forces, Middle Hill, Aldershot, Hants GU11 1PP T 01252-349004

IRELAND
There is one hierarchy for the whole of Ireland. Several of the dioceses have territory partly in the Republic of Ireland and partly in Northern Ireland.

APOSTOLIC NUNCIO TO IRELAND
HE Most Revd Dr Giuseppe Lazzarotto (Titular Archbishop of Numana), 183 Navan Road, Dublin 7 T (+353) (1) 838 0577 F (+353) (1) 838 0276

THE MOST REVD ARCHBISHOPS
Armagh, Seán Brady (*also* Primate of all Ireland), *cons.* 1995, *apptd* 1996. *Archbishop Emeritus,* HE Cardinal Cahal Daly *cons.* 1967, *elevated* 1991. *Auxiliary Bishop,* Most Revd Gerard Clifford, *cons.* 1991. *Clergy,* 165. *Bishop's Residence,* Ara Coeli, Armagh BT61 7QY T 028-3752 2045

Cashel and Emly, Dermot Clifford, *cons.* 1986, *apptd* 1988. *Clergy,* 103. *Archbishop's Residence,* Archbishop's House, Thurles, Co. Tipperary T (+353) (504) 21512

Dublin, Diarmuid Martin, *cons.* 1999, *apptd* Coadjutor Archbishop 2003, *succeeded as Archbishop* 2004. *Emeritus Archbishop,* HE Cardinal Desmond Connell, *cons.* 1988, *elevated* 2001. *Auxiliaries,* Eamonn Walsh, *cons.* 1990; Fiachra O'Ceallaigh, *cons* 1994; Raymond Field, *cons.* 1997. *Clergy,* 994. *Communications Office,* Archbishop's House, Drumcondra, Dublin 9 T (+353) (1) 836 0723

Tuam, Michael Neary, *cons.* 1992, *apptd* 1995. *Clergy,* 141. *Archbishop's Residence,* Archbishop's House, Tuam, Co. Galway T (+353) (93) 24166

THE RT. REVD BISHOPS
Achonry, Thomas Flynn, *cons.* 1977, *apptd* 1976. *Clergy,* 53. *Diocesan Office,* The Presbytery, Ballaghaderreen, Co. Roscommon T (+353) (94) 986 0011

Ardagh and Clonmacnois, Colm O'Reilly, *cons.* 1983, *apptd* 1983. *Clergy,* 65. *Diocesan Office,* Ballinalee Road, Longford, Co. Longford T (+353) (43) 46432

Clogher, Joseph Duffy, *cons.* 1979, *apptd* 1979. *Clergy,* 74. *Bishop's Residence,* Bishop's House, Monaghan T (+353) (47) 81019

Clonfert, John Kirby, *cons.* 1988 *apptd* 1988. *Clergy,* 46. *Bishop's Residence,* St Brendan's, Coorheen, Loughrea, Co. Galway T (+353) (91) 841560

Cloyne, John Magee, *cons.* 1987, *apptd* 1987. *Clergy,* 145. *Diocesan Centre,* Cobh, Co. Cork T (+353) (21) 481 1430

Cork and Ross, John Buckley, *cons.* 1984, *apptd* 1998. *Clergy,* 136. *Diocesan Office,* Cork and Ross Offices, Redemption Road, Cork T (+353) (21) 430 1717

Derry, Seamus Hegarty, *cons.* 1982, *apptd* 1994. *Auxiliary,* Francis Lagan, *cons.* 1988. *Clergy,* 138. *Bishop's Residence,* PO Box 227, Bishop's House, St Eugene's Cathedral, Derry BT48 9YG T 028-7126 2894

Down and Connor, Patrick Walsh, *cons.* 1983, *apptd* 1991. *Auxiliaries,* Anthony Farquhar, *cons.* 1983; Donal McKeown, *cons.* 2001. *Clergy,* 240. *Bishop's Residence,* Lisbreen, 73 Somerton Road, Belfast, Co. Antrim BT15 4DE T 028-9077 6185

Dromore, John McAreavey, *cons.* 1999, *apptd* 1999. *Clergy,* 43. *Bishop's Residence,* Bishop's House, 44 Armagh Road, Newry, Co. Down BT35 6PN T 028-3026 2444

Elphin, Christopher Jones, *cons.* 1994, *apptd* 1994. *Clergy,* 70. *Bishop's Residence*, St Mary's, Sligo T (+353) (71) 916 2670

Ferns, Denis Brennan, *cons.* 2006, *apptd* 2006. *Clergy,* 130. *Bishop's Residence*, Bishop's House, Summerhill, Wexford T (+353) (53) 912 2177

Galway, Kilmacduagh and Kilfenora, Martin Drennan, *cons.* 1997, *apptd* 2005. *Clergy,* 81. *Bishop's Residence*, Mount Saint Mary's, Taylor's Hill, Galway T (+353) (91) 563566

Kerry, William Murphy, *cons.* 1995, *apptd* 1995. *Clergy,* 126. *Bishop's Residence*, Bishop's House, Killarney, Co. Kerry T (+353) (64) 31168

Kildare and Leighlin, James Moriarty, *cons.* 1991, *apptd* 2002. *Clergy,* 110. *Bishop's Residence*, Bishop's House, Dublin Road, Carlow T (+353) (59) 917 6725

Killala, John Fleming, *cons.* 2002, *apptd* 2002. *Clergy,* 54. *Bishop's Residence*, Bishop's House, Ballina, Co. Mayo T (+353) (96) 21518

Killaloe, William Walsh, *cons.* 1994 *apptd* 1994. *Clergy,* 149. *Bishop's Residence*, Westbourne, Ennis, Co. Clare T (+353) (65) 682 8638

Kilmore, Leo O'Reilly, *cons.* 1997, *apptd* 1998. *Clergy,* 98. *Bishop's Residence*, Bishop's House, Cullies, Co. Cavan T (+353) (49) 433 1496

Limerick, Donal Murray, *cons.* 1982, *apptd* 1996. *Clergy,* 110. *Diocesan Office*, Social Service Centre, Henry Street, Limerick T (+353) (61) 315856

Meath, Michael Smith, *cons.* 1984, *apptd* 1990. *Clergy,* 141. *Bishop's Residence*, Bishop's House, Dublin Road, Mullingar, Co. Westmeath T (+353) (44) 934 8841

Ossory, Laurence Forristal, *cons.* 1980, *apptd* 1981. *Clergy,* 91. *Bishop's Residence*, Sion House, Kilkenny T (+353) (56) 62448

Raphoe, Philip Boyce, *cons.* 1995, *apptd* 1995. *Clergy,* 82. *Bishop's Residence*, Ard Adhamhnáin, Letterkenny, Co. Donegal T (+353) (74) 912 1208

Waterford and Lismore, William Lee, *cons.* 1993, *apptd* 1993. *Clergy,* 114. *Bishop's Residence*, John's Hill, Waterford T (+353) (51) 874463

OTHER CHURCHES IN THE UK

AFRICAN AND AFRO-CARIBBEAN CHURCHES

There are more than 160 Christian churches or groups of African or Afro-Caribbean origin in the UK. These include the Apostolic Faith Church, the Cherubim and Seraphim Church, the New Testament Church Assembly, the New Testament Church of God, the Wesleyan Holiness Church and the Aladura Churches. The Afro-West Indian United Council of Churches and the Council of African and Afro-Caribbean Churches UK (which was initiated as the Council of African and Allied Churches in 1979) are the media through which the member churches can work jointly to provide services they cannot easily provide individually.

There are about 70,000 adherents of African and Afro-Caribbean churches in the UK, and over 1,000 congregations. The Council of African and Afro-Caribbean Churches UK has about 17,000 members, 250 ministers and 125 congregations.

There are also numerous African and Caribbean Pentecostal churches and ministries which are members of the African Caribbean Evangelical Alliance.

COUNCIL OF AFRICAN AND AFRO-CARIBBEAN CHURCHES UK, 31 Norton House, Sidney Road, London SW9 0UJ T 020-7274 5589 E olu_abiola@lineone.net *Chair*, HG Most Revd Father Olu A. Abiola, OBE

ASSOCIATED PRESBYTERIAN CHURCHES OF SCOTLAND

The Associated Presbyterian Churches came into being in 1989 as a result of a division within the Free Presbyterian Church of Scotland. Following two controversial disciplinary cases, the culmination of deepening differences within the church, a presbytery was formed calling itself the Associated Presbyterian Churches (APC). The Associated Presbyterian Churches has about 900 members, 9 ministers and 16 churches.

ASSOCIATED PRESBYTERIAN CHURCHES OF SCOTLAND, APC Manse, Polvinster Road, Oban PA34 5TN T 01631-567076 E archibald.mcphail@ntlworld.com W www.apchurches.org *Clerk of Presbytery*, Revd A. N. McPhail

BAPTIST CHURCH

Baptists trace their origins to John Smyth, who in 1609 in Amsterdam reinstituted the baptism of conscious believers as the basis of the fellowship of a gathered church. Members of Smyth's church established the first Baptist church in England in 1612. They came to be known as 'General' Baptists and their theology was Arminian, whereas a later group of Calvinists who adopted the baptism of believers came to be known as 'Particular' Baptists. The two sections of the Baptists were united into one body, the Baptist Union of Great Britain and Ireland, in 1891. In 1988 the title was changed to the Baptist Union of Great Britain.

Baptists emphasise the complete autonomy of the local church, although individual churches are linked in various kinds of associations. There are international bodies (such as the Baptist World Alliance) and national bodies, but some Baptist churches belong to neither. However, in Great Britain the majority of churches and associations belong to the Baptist Union of Great Britain. There are also Baptist Unions in Wales, Scotland and Ireland which are much smaller than the Baptist Union of Great Britain, and there is some overlap of membership.

There are currently some 150,000 members and 2,150 churches associated with the Baptist Union of Great Britain. The Baptist Union of Great Britain is one of the founder members of the European Baptist Federation (1948) and the Baptist World Alliance (1905) which represents nearly 150,000 churches and over 40 million members worldwide.

In the Baptist Union of Scotland there are 13,625 members, 140 pastors and 173 churches.

In the Baptist Union of Wales (Undeb Bedyddwyr Cymru) there are about 15,500 members, 100 pastors and 450 churches, including those in England.

BAPTIST UNION OF GREAT BRITAIN, Baptist House, PO Box 44, 129 Broadway, Didcot, Oxon OX11 8RT T 01235-517700 E mail@baptist.org.uk W www.baptist.org.uk *General Secretary*, Revd Jonathan Edwards

BAPTIST UNION OF SCOTLAND, 14 Aytoun Road, Glasgow G41 5RT T 0141-423 6169 F 0141-424 1422 E director@scottishbaptist.org.uk *General Director*, Revd William Slack

BAPTIST UNION OF WALES, 94 Mansel Street, Swansea SA1 5TZ T 01792-655468 *President of the English Assembly (2007–8)*, Revd Richard Harrison

President of the Welsh Assembly (2007–8), Revd Alwyn Daniels
General Secretary of the Baptist Union of Wales, Revd Peter Thomas

CONGREGATIONAL FEDERATION

The Congregational Federation was founded by members of Congregational churches in England and Wales who did not join the United Reformed Church in 1972. There are also churches in Scotland and France affiliated to the federation. The federation exists to encourage congregations of believers to worship in free assembly, but it has no authority over them and emphasises their right to independence and self-governance.

The federation has 9,286 members, 80 accredited ministers and 293 churches in England, Wales and Scotland.

CONGREGATIONAL FEDERATION, 8 Castle Gate, Nottingham NG1 7AS T 0115-911 1460
E admin@congregational.org.uk
W www.congregational.org.uk
President of the Federation (2007–8), Revd Dr Alan Argent
General Secretary, Revd M. Heaney

FELLOWSHIP OF INDEPENDENT EVANGELICAL CHURCHES

The Fellowship of Independent Evangelical Churches was founded by Revd E. J. Poole-Connor (1872–1962) in 1922. In 1923 the fellowship published its first register of non-denominational pastors, evangelists and congregations who had accepted the doctrinal basis for the fellowship.

Members of the fellowship have two primary convictions, firstly to defend the evangelical faith, and secondly that evangelicism is the bond that unites the fellowship, rather than forms of worship or church government.

The Fellowship of Independent Evangelical Churches exists to promote the welfare of non-denominational bible churches and to give expression to the fundamental doctrines of evangelical Christianity. It supports individual churches by gathering and disseminating information and resources, advising churches on current theological, moral, social and practical issues and seeking to uphold the quality and integrity of church leaders through the Pastors' Association.

More than 480 churches are linked through the fellowship, which has 11 regions covering the whole of the UK. There are more than 330 pastors and approximately 35,000 people worship in fellowship churches every Sunday.

FELLOWSHIP OF INDEPENDENT EVANGELICAL CHURCHES, 39 The Point, Market Harborough, Leics LE16 7QU T 01858-434540 E admin@fiec.org.uk
W www.fiec.org.uk
President, Revd Rupert Bentley-Taylor
General Secretary, Richard Underwood

FREE CHURCH OF ENGLAND

The Free Church of England, otherwise called the Reformed Episcopal Church, is an independent church, constituted according to the historic faith, tradition and practice of the Church of England. Its roots lie in the 18th century, but most of its growth took place from the 1840s onwards, as clergy and congregations joined it from the established church in protest against the Oxford Movement. The historic episcopate was conferred on the

English church in 1876 through bishops of the Reformed Episcopal Church (which had broken away from the Protestant Episcopal Church in the USA in 1873). A branch of the Reformed Episcopal Church was founded in the UK and this merged with the Free Church of England in 1927 to create the present church.

Worship is according to the *Book of Common Prayer* and some modern liturgy is permissible. Only men are ordained to the orders of deacon, presbyter and bishop.

The Free Church of England has 25 congregations, now mainly confined to England. It also has a few members in New Zealand and one congregation in St Petersburg, Russia.

THE FREE CHURCH OF ENGLAND, 329 Wolverhampton Road West, Willenhall WV13 2RL
T 01902-607335 W www.fcofe.org.uk
General Secretary, Rt. Revd Paul Hunt

FREE CHURCH OF SCOTLAND

The Free Church of Scotland was formed in 1843 when over 400 ministers withdrew from the Church of Scotland as a result of interference in the internal affairs of the church by the civil authorities. In 1900, all but 26 ministers joined with others to form the United Free Church (most of which rejoined the Church of Scotland in 1929). In 1904 the remaining 26 ministers were recognised by the House of Lords as continuing the Free Church of Scotland.

The church maintains strict adherence to the Westminster Confession of Faith (1648) and accepts the Bible as the sole rule of faith and conduct. Its general assembly meets annually. It also has links with reformed churches overseas. The Free Church of Scotland has about 12,000 members, 90 ministers and 100 congregations.

FREE CHURCH OF SCOTLAND, 15 North Bank Street, The Mound, Edinburgh EH1 2LS T 0131-226 5286
E offices@freechurchofscotland.org.uk
Chief Administrative Officer, R. M. Morrison

FREE PRESBYTERIAN CHURCH OF SCOTLAND

The Free Presbyterian Church of Scotland was formed in 1893 by two ministers of the Free Church of Scotland who refused to accept a Declaratory Act passed by the Free Church General Assembly in 1892. The Free Presbyterian Church of Scotland is Calvinistic in doctrine and emphasises observance of the Sabbath. It adheres strictly to the Westminster Confession of Faith of 1648.

The church has about 3,000 members in Scotland and about 4,000 in overseas congregations. It has 20 ministers and 50 churches in the UK.

FREE PRESBYTERIAN CHURCH OF SCOTLAND, Free Presbyterian Manse, Laide, Ross-shire IV22 2NB
T 0141-332 9283
Moderator, Revd D. A. Ross
Clerk of the Synod, Revd John MacLeod

HOLY APOSTOLIC CATHOLIC ASSYRIAN CHURCH OF THE EAST

The Holy Apostolic Catholic Assyrian Church of the East traces its beginnings to the middle of the first century. It spread from Upper Mesopotamia throughout the territories of the Persian Empire. The Assyrian Church of the East became theologically separated from the rest of the Christian community following the Council of Ephesus in 431. The church is headed by the Catholicos Patriarch and is episcopal in government. The liturgical language is Syriac (Aramaic). The Assyrian Church of the

East and the Roman Catholic Church agreed a common Christological declaration in 1994 and a process of dialogue between the Assyrian Church of the East and the Chaldean Catholic Church, which is in communion with Rome but shares the Syriac liturgy, was instituted in 1996.

The church has about 400,000 members in the Middle East, India, Europe, North America and Australasia.

The church in Great Britain forms part of the diocese of Europe under Mar Odisho Oraham.

HOLY APOSTOLIC CATHOLIC ASSYRIAN CHURCH OF THE EAST, 66 Montague Road, London W7 3PQ T 020-8579 7259
Representative in Great Britain, Very Revd Younan Y. Younan

INDEPENDENT METHODIST CHURCHES

The Independent Methodist Churches were formed in 1805 and remained independent when the Methodist Church in Great Britain was formed in 1932. They are mainly concentrated in the industrial areas of the north of England.

The churches are Methodist in doctrine but their organisation is congregational. All the churches are members of the Independent Methodist Connexion of Churches. The controlling body of the Connexion is the Annual Meeting, to which churches send delegates. The Connexional President is elected annually. Between annual meetings the affairs of the Connexion are handled by departmental committees. Ministers are appointed by the churches and trained through the Connexion. The ministry is open to both men and women and is unpaid.

There are 2,000 members, 90 ministers and 86 churches in Great Britain.

INDEPENDENT METHODIST RESOURCE CENTRE, Fleet Street, Pemberton, Wigan, WN5 0DS T 01942-223526
E resourcecentre@imcgb.org.uk
General Secretary, W. C. Gabb

LUTHERAN CHURCH

Lutheranism is based on the teachings of Martin Luther, the German leader of the Protestant Reformation. The authority of the scriptures is held to be supreme over church tradition. The teachings of Lutheranism are explained in detail in 16th-century confessional writings, particularly the Augsburg Confession. Lutheranism is one of the largest Protestant denominations and it is particularly strong in northern Europe and the USA. Some Lutheran churches are episcopal, while others have a synodal form of organisation; unity is based on doctrine rather than structure. Most Lutheran churches are members of the Lutheran World Federation, based in Geneva.

Lutheran services in Great Britain are held in 18 languages to serve members of different nationalities. Services usually follow ancient liturgies. English-language congregations are members either of the Lutheran Church in Great Britain or of the Evangelical Lutheran Church of England. The Lutheran Church in Great Britain and other Lutheran churches in Britain are members of the Lutheran Council of Great Britain, which represents them and coordinates their common work.

There are over 70 million Lutherans worldwide; in Great Britain there are about 100,000 members, 50 clergy and 100 congregations.

THE LUTHERAN COUNCIL OF GREAT BRITAIN, 30 Thanet Street, London WC1H 9QH T 020-7554 2900
F 020-7383 3081 E enquiries@lutheran.org.uk
W www.lutheran.org.uk
General Secretary, Revd Thomas Bruch

METHODIST CHURCH

The Methodist movement started in England in 1729 when the Revd John Wesley, an Anglican priest, and his brother Charles met with others in Oxford and resolved to conduct their lives and study by 'rule and method'. In 1739 the Wesleys began evangelistic preaching and the first Methodist chapel was founded in Bristol in the same year. In 1744 the first annual conference was held, at which the Articles of Religion were drawn up. Doctrinal emphases included repentance, faith, the assurance of salvation, social concern and the priesthood of all believers. After John Wesley's death in 1791 the Methodists withdrew from the established church to form the Methodist Church. Methodists gradually drifted into many groups, but in 1932 the Wesleyan Methodist Church, the United Methodist Church and the Primitive Methodist Church united to form the Methodist Church of Great Britain.

The governing body of the Methodist Church is the conference. The conference is held in June each year and consists of three parts: the diaconal, ministerial and representative sessions. In addition, there are 32 district synods whose purpose is to decide policy for the district and be the link between the conference and the circuits. The circuit is the basic structure of the Methodist Church and is usually formed from the local churches in a defined area; a number of circuits make up each district. There are over 60 million Methodists worldwide; in Great Britain in 2007 there were 272,500 members, 3,603 ministers and 239 deacons.

THE METHODIST CHURCH OF GREAT BRITAIN, Methodist Church House, 25 Marylebone Road, London NW1 5JR T 020-7486 5502
E generalsecretary@methodistchurch.org.uk
W www.methodist.org.uk
President of the Conference (2007–8), Revd Dr Martyn Atkins
Vice-President of the Conference (2007–8), Ruby Beech
Secretary of the Conference, Revd David Deeks

IRELAND

The Methodist Church in Ireland is autonomous but has close links with British Methodism. It has a community roll of 54,079, 15,600 members, 230 ministers, 218 lay preachers and 220 churches.

METHODIST CHURCH IN IRELAND, 1 Fountainville Avenue, Belfast BT9 6AN T 028-9032 4554
E secretary@irishmethodist.org W www.irishmethodist.org
President (2007–8), Revd Roy Cooper
Secretary, Revd Donald Ker

ORTHODOX CHURCHES

EASTERN ORTHODOX CHURCH

The Eastern (or Byzantine) Orthodox Church is a communion of self-governing Christian churches that recognises the honorary primacy of the Oecumenical Patriarch of Constantinople.

The position of Orthodox Christians is that the faith was fully defined during the period of the Oecumenical Councils. In doctrine it is strongly trinitarian, and stresses the mystery and importance of the sacraments. It is episcopal in government. The structure of the Orthodox Christian year differs from that of western churches.

Orthodox Christians throughout the world are estimated to number about 300 million; there are an estimated 271,158 in the UK.

GREEK ORTHODOX CHURCH (PATRIARCHATE OF ANTIOCH)

There are sixteen parishes in the UK. The Diocese of Western and Central Europe is led by HE Metropolitan Gabriel.

DIOCESE OF WESTERN AND CENTRAL EUROPE,
22 Avenue Kleber, 75116 Paris T (+33) (145) 01 8356
Bishop, HE Metropolitan Gabriel
PATRIARCHATE OF ANTIOCH IN THE UK, St
George's Cathedral, 1A Redhill Street, London NW1 4BG
T 020-7383 0403 E info@antiochgreekorth.co.uk
W www.antiochgreekorth.co.uk
Priest, Fr. Samir Gholam

GREEK ORTHODOX CHURCH (PATRIARCHATE OF CONSTANTINOPLE)

The presence of Greek Orthodox Christians in Britain dates back at least to 1677 when Archbishop Joseph Geogirenes of Samos fled from Turkish persecution and came to London. The present Greek cathedral in Moscow Road, Bayswater, was opened for public worship in 1879 and the Diocese of Thyateira and Great Britain was established in 1922. There are now 120 parishes and other communities (including monasteries) in the UK, served by five bishops, 105 clergy, nine cathedrals and about 93 churches.

THE PATRIARCHATE OF CONSTANTINOPLE IN GREAT BRITAIN, Thyateira House, 5 Craven Hill, London W2 3EN
T 020-7723 4787 F 020-7224 9301 E mail@thyateira.org.uk
W www.thyateira.org.uk
Archbishop, Gregorios of Thyateira and Great Britain

RUSSIAN ORTHODOX CHURCH

The records of Russian Orthodox Church activities in Britain date from the visit to England of Tsar Peter I in the early 18th century. Clergy were sent from Russia to serve the chapel established to minister to the staff of the Imperial Russian Embassy in London.

In 2007, after an 80-year division, the Russian Orthodox Church Outside Russia agreed to become an autonomous part of the Russian Orthodox Church, Patriarchate of Moscow. The reunification agreement was signed by Patriarch Alexy II, Patriarch of the Russian Orthodox Church and Metropolitan Lavy, leader of the Russian Orthodox Church Outside Russia on 17 May at a ceremony at Christ the Saviour Cathedral in Moscow.

The diocese of Sourozh is the diocese of the Russian Orthodox Church in Great Britain and Ireland and is currently led by Archbishop Innokenty of Korsun. The local administration of the diocese is the responsibility of Bishop Elisey of Bogorodsk and 19 diocesan clergy.

DIOCESE OF SOUROZH, Diocesan Office, Cathedral of the Dormition and All Saints, 67 Ennismore Gardens, London SW7 1NH T 020-7584 0096 W www.sourozh.org
Bishop of Bogorodsk, Rt. Revd Elisey

SERBIAN ORTHODOX CHURCH (PATRIARCHATE OF SERBIA)

There are around 40,000 members in the UK served by 11 clergy. The Patriarchate of Serbia is represented by Bishop Dositej of Great Britain and Scandinavia.

SERBIAN ORTHODOX CHURCH IN GREAT BRITAIN, Saint Sava, 89 Lancaster Road, London W11 1QQ T 020-7727 8367 E crkva@spclondon.org
W www.spclondon.org
Representative, Very Revd Milun Kostic

OTHER NATIONALITIES

The Patriarchates of Romania and Bulgaria have memberships of around 3,000 and 86 respectively, while the Ukrainian Autocephalous Patriarchate has around 1,000 members. The Belarusian (membership estimated at 2,300) and Latvian (membership of around 110) Orthodox churches are part of the Patriarchate of Constantinople.

ORIENTAL ORTHODOX CHURCHES

The term 'Oriental Orthodox Churches' is now generally used to describe a group of six ancient eastern churches which reject the Christological definition of the Council of Chalcedon (AD 451) and use Christological terms in different ways from the Eastern Orthodox Church. There are estimated to be around 50 million members worldwide of the Oriental Orthodox Churches and about 22,020 in the UK.

ARMENIAN ORTHODOX CHURCH (PATRIARCHATE OF ETCHMIADZIN)

The Armenian Orthodox Church is led by HH Karekin II, Catholicos of All Armenians. Bishop Nathan Hovhannisian is the Primate of the Armenian Church of Great Britain and President of the Armenian Community and Church Council.

ARMENIAN CHURCH OF GREAT BRITAIN, The Armenian Vicarage, Iverna Gardens, London W8 6TP
T 020-7937 0152 E arajnortaran@aol.com
W www.accc.org.uk
Primate, Bishop Nathan Hovhannisian

COPTIC ORTHODOX CHURCH

The Coptic Orthodox Church is led by HH Pope Shenouda III and is represented in Great Britain by Bishop Angaelos at the Coptic Orthodox Cathedral of St George at the Coptic Orthodox Church Centre. The Coptic Orthodox Church is the largest Oriental Orthodox community in Great Britain.

COPTIC ORTHODOX CHURCH CENTRE, Shephalbury Manor, Broadhall Way, Stevenage, Herts SG2 8RH T 01438-745232 E info@copticcentre.com
W www.copticcentre.com
Bishop, Bishop Angaelos

BRITISH ORTHODOX CHURCH

The British Orthodox Church is canonically part of the Coptic Orthodox Patriarchate of Alexandria. As it ministers to British people all its services are in English.

THE BRITISH ORTHODOX CHURCH, 10 Heathwood Gardens, Charlton, London SE7 8EP T 020-8854 3090
E boc@nildram.co.uk W www.britishorthodox.org
Metropolitan, Abba Seraphim

INDIAN ORTHODOX CHURCH

The Indian Orthodox Church, also known as the Malankara Orthodox Church, is part of the Diocese of Europe, UK and Canada under Metropolitan Thomas Mar Makarios. The church in Great Britain can be contacted via Fr. Abraham Thomas.

INDIAN ORTHODOX CHURCH, St Gregorios Indian Orthodox Church, Cranfield Road, Brockley, London SE4 1UF T 020-8691 9456 E vicar@indian-orthodox.co.uk
W www.indian-orthodox.co.uk
Vicar, Fr. Abraham Thomas

SYRIAN ORTHODOX CHURCH

The Patriarchate Vicariate of the Syrian Orthodox Church

in the United Kingdom is represented by HE Archbishop Athanasius Toma Dawod.

SYRIAN ORTHODOX CHURCH IN THE UK, 5 Canning Road, Croydon CR0 6QA **T** 020-8654 7531 **E** info-uk@syrianorthodoxchurch.net **W** www.syrianorthodoxchurch.net *Archbishop,* HE Athanasius Toma Dawod

PENTECOSTAL CHURCHES

Pentecostalism is inspired by the descent of the Holy Spirit upon the apostles at Pentecost. The movement began in Los Angeles, USA, in 1906 and is characterised by baptism with the Holy Spirit, divine healing, speaking in tongues (glossolalia), and a literal interpretation of the scriptures.

The Pentecostal movement in Britain dates from 1907. Initially, groups of Pentecostalists were led by laymen and did not organise formally. However, in 1915 the Elim Foursquare Gospel Alliance (more usually called the Elim Pentecostal Church) was founded in Ireland by George Jeffreys and currently has about 550 churches, 68,500 adherents and 650 accredited ministers. In 1924 about 70 independent assemblies formed a fellowship, the Assemblies of God in Great Britain and Ireland, which now incorporates around 600 churches and is known as the Assemblies of God.

The Apostolic Church grew out of the 1904–5 revivals in South Wales and was established in 1916. The Apostolic Church of Great Britain and Northern Ireland has around 116 churches, 5,500 adherents and 76 ministers. The New Testament Church of God was established in England in 1953 and has about 120 congregations, around 40,000 followers and more than 300 ministers across England and Wales. In recent years many aspects of Pentecostalism have been adopted by the growing charismatic movement within the Roman Catholic, Protestant and Eastern Orthodox churches. There are about 105 million Pentecostalists worldwide, with about 280,260 adherents in Great Britain and Ireland.

THE APOSTOLIC CHURCH OF GREAT BRITAIN AND NORTHERN IRELAND, International Administration Offices, PO Box 389, Swansea SA7 9LA **T** 01792-790300 **E** admin@apostolic-church.org *National Leader,* Warren Jones

THE ASSEMBLIES OF GOD INCORPORATED, PO Box 7634, Nottingham NG11 6ZY **T** 0115-921 7272 **E** info@aog.org.uk **W** www.aog.org.uk *General Superintendent,* Paul C. Weaver

THE ELIM PENTECOSTAL CHURCH, PO Box 38, Cheltenham, Glos GL50 3HN **T** 01242-519904 **E** info@elimhq.net **W** www.elim.org.uk *General Superintendent,* Revd John Glass

THE NEW TESTAMENT CHURCH OF GOD, Main House, Overstone Park, Overstone, Northampton NN6 0AD **T** 01604-643311 **E** bigmove@ntcg.org.uk **W** www.ntcg.org.uk *Administrative Bishop,* Bishop Eric Arthur Brown

PLYMOUTH BRETHREN

The Brethren was founded in Dublin in 1827–8. It rejected denominationalism and clericalism and based itself on the structures and practices of the early church. Many groups sprang up and that at Plymouth became the best known, which resulted in the designation by others as Plymouth Brethren.

Early worship had a prescribed form but quickly assumed an unstructured, non-liturgical format. There were services devoted to worship, usually involving the breaking of bread, and separate preaching meetings. There is no salaried ministry.

A theological dispute led in 1848 to schism between the Open Brethren and the Closed or Exclusive Brethren, each branch later suffering further divisions.

Open Brethren churches are completely independent, but freely cooperate with each other. Open Brethren churches are run by appointed elders. Exclusive Brethren churches believe in a universal fellowship between congregations. They do not have elders, but appoint respected members of their congregation to perform certain administrative functions.

The Brethren are established throughout the UK, Ireland, Europe, India, Africa and Australasia. They do not maintain lists of their members. There are a few publishing houses which publish Brethren related literature. Chapter Two is the main supplier of such literature in the UK and also has a Brethren history archive which is available for use by appointment.

CHAPTER TWO, Conduit Mews, London SE18 7AP **T** 020-8316 5389 **E** chapter2uk@aol.com **W** www.chaptertwobooks.org.uk

PRESBYTERIAN CHURCH IN IRELAND

The Presbyterian Church in Ireland is reformed in doctrine and presbyterian in constitution. Presbyterianism was established in Ireland as a result of the Ulster plantation in the early 17th century when English and Scottish Protestants settled in the north of Ireland.

There are 21 presbyteries under the chief court known as the general assembly. The general assembly meets annually and is presided over by a moderator who is elected for one year. The ongoing work of the church is undertaken by 15 boards under which there are specialist committees.

There are around 300,000 Presbyterians in Ireland and Northern Ireland, forming over 560 congregations.

THE PRESBYTERIAN CHURCH IN IRELAND, Church House, Belfast BT1 6DW **T** 028-9032 2284 **E** info@presbyterianireland.org **W** www.presbyterianireland.org *Moderator (2007–8),* Rt. Revd Dr John Finlay *Clerk of Assembly and General Secretary,* Revd Dr Donald Watts

PRESBYTERIAN CHURCH OF WALES

The Presbyterian Church of Wales or Calvinistic Methodist Church of Wales is Calvinistic in doctrine and presbyterian in constitution. It was formed in 1811 when Welsh Calvinists severed the relationship with the established church by ordaining their own ministers. It secured its own confession of faith in 1823 and a Constitutional Deed in 1826, and since 1864 the General Assembly has met annually, presided over by a moderator elected for a year. The doctrine and constitutional structure of the Presbyterian Church of Wales was confirmed by act of parliament in 1931–2.

The Church has around 33,363 members, 89 ministers and 745 churches.

THE PRESBYTERIAN CHURCH OF WALES, Tabernacle Chapel, 81 Merthyr Road, Whitchurch, Cardiff CF14 1DD **T** 029-2062 7465 **E** swyddfa.office@ebcpcw.org.uk **W** www.ebcpcw.org.uk *Moderator (2007–8),* Revd John Owen *General Secretary,* Revd Ifan Roberts

RELIGIOUS SOCIETY OF FRIENDS (QUAKERS)

Quakerism is a religious denomination which was founded in the 17th century by George Fox and others in an attempt to revive what they saw as the original 'primitive Christianity'. The movement, at first called Friends of the Truth, started in the Midlands, Yorkshire and north-west England, but there are now Quakers all over Britain and in 36 countries around the world. The colony of Pennsylvania, founded by William Penn, was originally Quaker.

Emphasis is placed on the experience of God in daily life rather than on sacraments or religious occasions. There is no church calendar. Worship is largely silent and there are no appointed ministers; the responsibility for conducting a meeting is shared equally among those present. Religious tolerance and social reform have always been important to Quakers, together with a commitment to peace and non-violence in resolving disputes.

There are more than 27,000 'friends' or Quakers in Great Britain. There are about 500 places where Quaker meetings are held, many of them Quaker owned Friends Meeting Houses. The Britain Yearly Meeting is the name given to the central organisation of Quakers in Britain.

THE RELIGIOUS SOCIETY OF FRIENDS (QUAKERS) IN BRITAIN, Friends House, 173–177 Euston Road, London NW1 2BJ T 020-7663 1000
E enquiries@quaker.org.uk W www.quaker.org.uk
Recording Clerk, Elsa Dicks

SALVATION ARMY

The Salvation Army is an international Christian organisation working in 111 countries worldwide. As a church and registered charity, the Salvation Army is funded through donations from its members, the general public and, where appropriate, government grants.

The Salvation Army was founded by a Methodist minister, William Booth, in the East End of London in 1865, and now has 755 local church centres, 50 residential centres for the homeless, 18 elderly care centres and six substance misuse centres. It also runs a clothing recycling programme, charity shops, a prison visiting service and a family tracing service. In 1878 it adopted a quasi-military command structure intended to inspire and regulate its endeavours and to reflect its view that the church was engaged in spiritual warfare. Salvationists emphasise evangelism and the provision of social welfare.

UK TERRITORIAL HEADQUARTERS, 101 Newington Causeway, London SE1 6BN T 0845-634 0101
E press.office@salvationarmy.org.uk
W www.salvationarmy.org.uk
International Leader, Gen. Shaw Clifton
UK Territorial Commander, Commissioner John Matear

SEVENTH-DAY ADVENTIST CHURCH

The Seventh-day Adventist Church was founded in 1863 in the USA and the first church in the UK was established in 1886. It is a worldwide Christian church with 14.75 million members worshipping in 121,564 congregations in 202 countries. Slightly more than 70 per cent of all Seventh-day Adventists live in Africa, the Caribbean and Central and South America. In the UK there are 27,079 members worshipping in 279 churches and companies.

The beliefs and practices of the church are rooted in the Bible and are summarised under 28 core beliefs. The mission of the church is to proclaim to all people the everlasting gospel of the three angels' messages of Revelation 14:6–12, leading them to accept Jesus as their personal saviour and to prepare for his imminent return.

The world church is divided administratively into 13 divisions, each made up of 'unions' of churches. The British Isles headquarters is known as the British Union Conference of Seventh-day Adventists.

BRITISH UNION CONFERENCE OF SEVENTH-DAY ADVENTISTS, Stanborough Park, Watford WD25 9JZ
T 01923-672251 W www.adventist.org.uk
President, Don McFarlane

THE (SWEDENBORGIAN) NEW CHURCH

The New Church is based on the teachings of the 18th century Swedish scientist and theologian Emanuel Swedenborg (1688–1772), who believed that Jesus Christ appeared to him and instructed him to reveal the spiritual meaning of the Bible. He claimed to have visions of the spiritual world, including heaven and hell, and conversations with angels and spirits. He published several theological works, including descriptions of the spiritual world and a Bible commentary.

The second coming of Jesus Christ is believed to have already taken place and is still taking place, being not an actual physical reappearance of Christ, but rather his return in spirit. It is also believed that concurrent with our life on earth is life in a parallel spiritual world, of which we are usually unconscious until death. There are around 30,000 Swedenborgians worldwide, with 850 members, 24 Churches and 10 ministers in the UK.

THE GENERAL CONFERENCE OF THE NEW CHURCH, Swedenborg House, 20 Bloomsbury Way, London WC1A 2TH T 020-7229 9340
E enquiries@generalconference.org.uk
W www.thenewchurch.org.uk
Chief Executive, Michael Hindley

UNDEB YR ANNIBYNWYR CYMRAEG

Undeb Yr Annibynwyr Cymraeg, the Union of Welsh Independents, was formed in 1872 and is a voluntary association of Welsh Congregational churches and personal members. It is mainly Welsh-speaking. Congregationalism in Wales dates back to 1639 when the first Welsh Congregational church was opened in Gwent. Member churches are traditionally Calvinistic in doctrine, although a wide range of interpretations are permitted, and congregationalist in organisation. Each church has complete independence in the government and administration of its affairs.

The Union has 28,892 members, 98 ministers and 449 member churches.

UNDEB YR ANNIBYNWYR CYMRAEG, 5 Axis Court, Riverside Business Park, Swansea Vale, Swansea SA7 0AJ
T 01792-795888 E undeb@annibynwyr.org
W www.annibynwyr.org
President of the Union (2007–8), Revd Dewi Myrddin Hughes
General Secretary, Revd Dr Geraint Tudur

UNITED REFORMED CHURCH

The United Reformed Church (URC) was first formed by the union of most of the Congregational churches in England and Wales with the Presbyterian Church of England in 1972. Congregationalism dates from the mid-16th century. It is Calvinistic in doctrine, and its followers form independent self-governing congregations bound under God by covenant, a principle laid down in the writings of Robert Browne (1550–1633). From the late 16th century the movement was driven underground by persecution, but the cause was defended at the Westminster Assembly in 1643 and the Savoy Declaration of 1658 laid down its principles. Congregational churches formed county associations for mutual support and in 1832 these associations merged to form the Congregational Union of England and Wales.

Presbyterianism in England also dates from the mid 16th century, and was Calvinistic and evangelical in its doctrine. It was governed by a hierarchy of courts.

In the 1960s there was close cooperation locally and nationally between congregational and presbyterian churches. This led to union negotiations and a Scheme of Union, supported by act of parliament in 1972. In 1981 a further unification took place, with the Reformed Association of Churches of Christ becoming part of the URC. In 2000 a third union took place, with the Congregational Union of Scotland. In its basis the United Reformed Church reflects local church initiative and responsibility with a conciliar pattern of oversight. The general assembly is the central body, and is made up of equal numbers of ministers and lay members.

The United Reformed Church is divided into 81 district councils which form 13 Synods, each with a Synod Moderator. There are around 1,800 congregations which serve around 150,000 adults and 100,000 children and young people. There are around 1,000 serving ministers.

The General Assembly is the central body, and comprises around 700 representatives, mainly appointed by the district councils, of which half are lay persons and half are ministers. Each year the General Assembly elects a Moderator, either lay or ordained, who then becomes the national representative of the URC.

UNITED REFORMED CHURCH, 86 Tavistock Place, London WC1H 9RT T 020-7916 2020 E urc@urc.org.uk W www.urc.org.uk
Moderator of the General Assembly (2007–8), Revd Stephen Orchard
General Secretary, Revd Dr David Cornick

WESLEYAN REFORM UNION

The Wesleyan Reform Union was founded by Methodists who left or were expelled from Wesleyan Methodism in 1849 following a period of internal conflict. Its doctrine is conservative evangelical and its organisation is congregational, each church having complete independence in the government and administration of its affairs. The union has 1,843 members, 15 ministers, 115 lay preachers and 108 churches.

THE WESLEYAN REFORM UNION, Wesleyan Reform Church House, 123 Queen Street, Sheffield S1 2DU
T 0114-272 1938 E admin@thewru.co.uk
W www.thewru.com
President (2007–8), Revd David Mills
General Secretary, Revd Colin Braithwaite

NON-TRINITARIAN CHURCHES

CHRISTADELPHIAN

Christadelphians believe that the Bible is the word of God and that it reveals both God's dealings with mankind in the past and his plans for the future. These plans centre on the work of Jesus Christ, who it is believed will return to Earth to establish God's kingdom. Christadelphians have existed since the 1850s, beginning in the USA through the work of an Englishman, Dr John Thomas.

THE CHRISTADELPHIAN MAGAZINE AND PUBLISHING ASSOCIATION, 404 Shaftmoor Lane, Birmingham B28 8SZ T 0121-777 6324 F 0121-778 5024
E enquiries@thechristadelphian.com
W www.thechristadelphian.com

CHURCH OF CHRIST, SCIENTIST

The Church of Christ, Scientist was founded by Mary Baker Eddy in the USA in 1879 to 'reinstate primitive Christianity and its lost element of healing'. Christian Science teaches the need for spiritual regeneration and salvation from sin, but is best known for its reliance on prayer alone in the healing of sickness. Adherents believe that such healing is a law, or divine science, and is in direct line with that practised by Jesus Christ (revered, not as God, but as the son of God) and by the early Christian church.

The denomination consists of The First Church of Christ, Scientist, in Boston, Massachusetts, USA (the 'mother church') and its branch churches in almost 80 countries worldwide. The Bible and Mary Baker Eddy's book, *Science and Health with Key to the Scriptures,* are used for daily spiritual guidance and healing by all members and are read at services; there are no clergy. Those engaged in full-time healing are called practitioners, of whom there are 1,500 worldwide. The church also publishes *The Christian Science Monitor.*

No membership figures are available, since Mary Baker Eddy felt that numbers are no measure of spiritual vitality and ruled that such statistics should not be published. There are almost 2,000 branch churches worldwide, including over 100 in the UK.

CHRISTIAN SCIENCE COMMITTEE ON PUBLICATION, Claridge House, 29 Barnes High Street, London SW13 9LW T 020-8282 1645 E londoncs@csps.com
W www.christianscience.com
District Manager for the UK and the Republic of Ireland, Tony Lobl

CHURCH OF JESUS CHRIST OF LATTER-DAY SAINTS

The Church of Jesus Christ of Latter-Day Saints (often referred to as 'Mormons') was founded in New York State, USA, in 1830, and came to Britain in 1837. The oldest continuous congregation of the church is in Preston, Lancashire.

Mormons are Christians who claim to belong to the 'restored church' of Jesus Christ. They believe that true Christianity died when the last original apostle died, but that it was given back to the world by God and Christ through Joseph Smith, the church's founder and first president. They accept and use the Bible as scripture, but believe in continuing revelation from God and use additional scriptures, including *The Book of Mormon: Another Testament of Jesus Christ.* The importance of the family is central to the church's beliefs and practices. Church members set aside Monday evenings as family home evenings when Christian family values are taught. Polygamy was formally discontinued in 1890.

The church has no paid ministry: local congregations are headed by a leader chosen from amongst their number. The world governing body, based in Utah, USA, is led by a president, believed to be the chosen prophet, and his two counsellors. There are more than 12.5 million members worldwide, with over 190,000 adherents and 411 congregations in the UK.

CHURCH OF JESUS CHRIST OF LATTER-DAY
   SAINTS, British Headquarters, 751 Warwick Road, Solihull,
   W. Midlands B91 3DQ T 0121-712 1200 W www.lds.org.uk

JEHOVAH'S WITNESSES

The movement now known as Jehovah's Witnesses grew from a Bible study group formed by Charles Taze Russell in 1872 in Pennsylvania, USA. In 1896 it adopted the name of the Watch Tower Bible and Tract Society, and in 1931 its members became known as Jehovah's Witnesses.

Jehovah's (God's) Witnesses believe in the Bible as the word of God, and consider it to be inspired and historically accurate. They take the scriptures literally, except where there are obvious indications that they are figurative or symbolic, and reject the doctrine of the Trinity. Witnesses also believe that the earth will remain for ever and that all those approved of by Jehovah will have eternal life on a cleansed and beautified earth; only 144,000 will go to heaven to rule with Christ. They believe that the second coming of Christ began in 1914 and his thousand-year reign on earth is imminent, and that armageddon (a final battle in which evil will be defeated) will precede Christ's rule of peace. They refuse to take part in military service and do not accept blood transfusions.

The nine-member world governing body is based in New York, USA. There is no paid ministry, but each congregation has elders assigned to look after various duties and every Witness is assigned homes to visit in their congregation. There are over 6.7 million Jehovah's Witnesses worldwide, with 130,000 Witnesses in the UK organised into more than 1,500 congregations.

BRITISH ISLES HEADQUARTERS, Watch Tower House,
   The Ridgeway, London NW7 1RN T 020-8906 2211
   E opi@wtbts.org.uk W www.watchtower.org

UNITARIAN AND FREE CHRISTIAN CHURCHES

Unitarianism has its historical roots in the Judaeo-Christian tradition but rejects the deity of Christ and the doctrine of the Trinity. It allows the individual to embrace insights from all the world's faiths and philosophies, as there is no fixed creed. It is accepted that beliefs may evolve in the light of personal experience.

Unitarian communities first became established in Poland and Transylvania in the 16th century. The first avowedly Unitarian place of worship in the British Isles opened in London in 1774. The General Assembly of Unitarian and Free Christian Churches came into existence in 1928 as the result of the amalgamation of two earlier organisations.

There are about 4,400 Unitarians in Great Britain and Ireland and about 72 Unitarian ministers. Nearly 200 self-governing congregations and fellowship groups, including a small number overseas, are members of the General Assembly.

GENERAL ASSEMBLY OF UNITARIAN AND FREE
   CHRISTIAN CHURCHES, Essex Hall, 1–6 Essex Street,
   London WC2R 3HY T 020-7240 2384
   E ga@unitarian.org.uk W www.unitarian.org.uk
   President 2007–8, Revd Celia Midgley

COMMUNICATIONS

POSTAL SERVICES

The Royal Mail Group plc operates Parcelforce Worldwide, Post Office and Royal Mail, which handles around 84 million items of mail each day. The Postal Services Commission (Postcomm), an independent regulator accountable to parliament, oversees postal operations in the UK. It is responsible for the smooth introduction of competition into postal services, and the market was opened to full competition in January 2006. All postal operators, including Royal Mail, are licensed by Postcomm; the licence requires the operators to ensure that the mail they handle is always secure and to maintain certain standards. Postwatch is the consumer organisation responsible for postal services and takes up complaints on behalf of consumers against any licensed provider of postal services.

POSTCOMM, Hercules House, 6 Hercules Road, London SE1 7DB T 020-7593 2100 W www.psc.gov.uk

POSTWATCH, Freepost, Postwatch T 08456-013265 W www.postwatch.co.uk

PRICING IN PROPORTION

In August 2006 Royal Mail introduced a new pricing system, whereby the pricing of mail depends upon its size as well as its weight. The system is designed to rebalance postage prices to reflect the fact that larger, bulkier items cost more to handle than smaller, lighter ones. There are three basic categories of correspondence:

LETTER
Length up to 240mm, *width* up to 165mm, *thickness* up to 5mm, *weight* up to 100g, eg most cards, postcards and bills

LARGE LETTER
Length up to 353mm, *width* up to 250mm, *thickness* up to 25mm, *weight* up to 750g, eg most A4 documents, CDs and magazines

PACKET
Length over 353mm, *width* over 250mm, *thickness* over 25mm, *weight* over 750g, eg VHS cassettes, books, prints and posters in cylindrical packaging

INLAND POSTAL SERVICES

Below are details of a number of popular postal services along with prices correct as at August 2007.

INLAND POST RATES

Format	Maximum weight	First class	Second class†
Letter*	100g	£0.34	£0.24
Large letter	100g	£0.48	£0.40
	250g	£0.70	£0.60
	500g	£0.98	£0.83
	750g	£1.42	£1.20
Packet	100g	£1.09	£0.92
	250g	£1.38	£1.20
	500g	£1.84	£1.52
	750g	£2.38	£1.92
	1,000g‡	£2.92	£2.30

* Includes postcards
† First class post is normally delivered on the following working day and second class within three working days
‡ Packets weighing over 1kg cost £4.25 plus £0.75 for every additional 250g or part thereof and can only be sent by first class post

UK PARCEL RATES

Maximum weight	Standard tariff*
1kg	£3.85
1.5kg	£4.95
2kg	£5.68
4kg	£8.24
6kg	£9.35
8kg	£10.67
10kg	£11.45
20kg	£13.33

* Standard parcels are normally delivered within three to five working days

OVERSEAS POSTAL SERVICES

Royal Mail divides the world into three zones: **Europe** (Albania, Andorra, Armenia, Austria, Azerbaijan, Azores, Balearic Islands, Belarus, Belgium, Bosnia and Hercegovina, Bulgaria, Canary Islands, Corsica, Croatia, Cyprus, Czech Republic, Denmark, Estonia, Faroe Islands, Finland, France, Georgia, Germany, Gibraltar, Greece, Greenland, Hungary, Iceland, Ireland, Italy, Kazakhstan, Kyrgyzstan, Latvia, Liechtenstein, Lithuania, Luxembourg, Macedonia, Madeira, Malta, Moldova, Monaco, Montenegro, the Netherlands, Norway, Poland, Portugal, Romania, Russian Federation, San Marino, Serbia, Slovakia, Slovenia, Spain, Spitzbergen, Sweden, Switzerland, Tajikistan, Turkey, Turkmenistan, Ukraine, Uzbekistan, Vatican City State); **World Zone 1** (All countries that are not listed under Europe or World Zone 2); **World Zone 2** (American Samoa, Australia, China, East Timor, Fiji, French Polynesia, French Southern and Antarctic Territories*, Guam, Japan, Kiribati, Democratic People's Republic of Korea, Republic of Korea, Marshall Islands, Micronesia, Mongolia, Nauru, New Caledonia, New Zealand and Territories, Norfolk Island, Northern Mariana Islands, Palau, Papua New Guinea, Philippines, Pitcairn Island, Solomon Islands, Taiwan, Tonga, Tuvalu, Vanuatu, Wake Island, Wallis and Futuna Island, Western Samoa).

* There are no Airmail services to the French Southern and Antarctic Territories

OVERSEAS SURFACE MAIL RATES (WORLD ZONES 1 & 2*)

Letters

Maximum weight		Maximum weight	
20g†	£0.46	150g	£1.55
60g	£0.78	200g	£1.99
100g	£1.10	250g	£2.43

300g	£2.86	1,000g	£8.88
350g	£3.29	1,250g	£11.03
400g	£3.72	1,500g	£13.18
450g	£4.15	1,750g	£15.33
500g	£4.58	2,000g	£17.48
750g	£6.73		

* Letters and postcards to Europe are sent by Airmail
† Includes postcards

Small packets and printed papers

Maximum weight		*Maximum weight*	
100g	£0.77	450g	£2.60
150g	£1.04	500g	£2.86
200g	£1.30	750g	£4.16
250g	£1.56	1,000g	£5.46
300g	£1.82	1,500g	£8.06
350g	£2.08	2,000g*	£10.66
400g	£2.34		

* Maximum weight. For printed papers only: add £0.26 for each additional 50g up to maximum weight of 5kg

AIRMAIL LETTERS

Europe

Maximum weight		*Maximum weight*	
20g*	£0.48	300g	£3.34
40g	£0.69	320g	£3.52
60g	£0.90	340g	£3.70
80g	£1.10	360g	£3.88
100g	£1.31	380g	£4.06
120g	£1.52	400g	£4.24
140g	£1.73	420g	£4.42
160g	£1.94	440g	£4.60
180g	£2.15	460g	£4.78
200g	£2.35	480g	£4.96
220g	£2.54	500g	£5.14
240g	£2.74	1,000g	£9.64
260g	£2.94	2,000g	£18.64
280g	£3.13		

* Includes postcards

World Zones 1 and 2

Maximum weight	*World zone 1*	*World zone 2*
Postcards	£0.54	£0.54
20g	£0.78	£0.78
40g	£1.17	£1.24
60g	£1.58	£1.74
80g	£2.00	£2.24
100g	£2.42	£2.74
500g	£10.14	£11.91
1,000g	£19.39	£22.91
2,000g	£37.89	£44.91

Note that there are different rates for small packets and printed matter. *See* W www.royalmail.com for further details.

SPECIAL DELIVERY SERVICES

SPECIAL DELIVERY NEXT DAY
A guaranteed next working day delivery service by 1pm to 99 per cent of the UK for first class letters and packets (maximum item weight is 10kg). Prices start at £4.30. There is also a service which guarantees delivery by 9am (maximum item weight is 2kg). Prices start at £9.35.

INTERNATIONAL SIGNED FOR AND AIRSURE
Express airmail services (maximum weight 2kg) that include £34 compensation in case of loss or damage. The fee for International Signed For is £3.50 plus airmail postage. The fee for Airsure is £4.20 plus airmail postage.

RECORDED SIGNED FOR
Provides a record of posting and delivery of letters and ensures a signature on delivery. This service is recommended for items of little or no monetary value. All packets must be handed to the post office and a receipt issued as proof of posting. *Charge:* 70p plus the standard first or second class postage.

OTHER SERVICES

BUSINESS SERVICES
A range of postal services are available to businesses including business collection, freepost, business reply services, business packaging for special deliveries and international bulk mailing options.

COMPENSATION
Compensation for loss or damage to an item sent varies according to the service used to send the item.

PASSPORT APPLICATIONS
Around 2,000 post offices process passport applications. To find out your nearest office, and for further information, see W www.postoffice.co.uk.

TRACK AND TRACE
This online service, accessible from www.royalmail.com and www.postoffice.co.uk, enables customers to track the progress of items sent using the special delivery services listed above.

REDIRECTION
A printed form obtainable from the Post Office or from www.royalmail.com must be signed by the person to whom the letters are to be addressed. A fee is payable for each different surname on the application form. *Charges:* one month, £7.10 (abroad via airmail, £14.30); three months, £15.55 (£31.10); six months, £23.95 (£47.90); 12 months, £35.95 (£71.90).

KEEPSAFE
Mail is held for up to two months while the addressee is away and is delivered when the addressee returns. Prices start at £5.70. Perishable items are returned to the sender. Recorded items are held for a week before being returned to the sender, and Special Delivery items for three weeks beyond the keepsafe expiry date.

POST OFFICE BOX
A PO Box provides a short and memorable alternative address. Mail is held at a local delivery office until the addressee is ready to collect it. A PO Box costs £46.95 for six months or £57.85 for a year.

CONTACTS
Royal Mail general enquiries: T 08457-740740
W www.royalmail.com
Royal Mail business enquiries: T 08457-950950
Postcode enquiry line: T 0906-302 1222 / 08457-111222
Parcelforce Worldwide: T 08708-501150
W www.parcelforce.com
Post Office enquiries: T 08457-223344
W www.postoffice.co.uk

INTERNATIONAL DIRECT DIALLING

International dialling (IDD) codes are composed of four elements which are dialled in sequence:

(i)   the international code
(ii)   the country code
(iii)   the area code
(iv)   the telephone number

Calls to Midway Island, Tristan da Cunha and Wake Island must be made by calling the international operator on 155.

* Varies depending on area and/or carrier

	IDD from UK	IDD to UK
Afghanistan	00 93	00 44
Albania	00 355	00 44
Algeria	00 213	00 44
American Samoa	00 1 684	011 44
Andorra	00 376	00 44
Angola	00 244	00 44
Anguilla	00 1 264	011 44
Antigua and Barbuda	00 1 268	011 44
Argentina	00 54	00 44
Armenia	00 374	00 44
Aruba	00 297	00 44
Ascension Island	00 247	00 44
Australia	00 61	00 11 44
Austria	00 43	00 44
Azerbaijan	00 994	810 44
Azores	00 351	00 44
Bahamas	00 1 242	011 44
Bahrain	00 973	00 44
Balearic Islands	00 34	00 44
Bangladesh	00 880	00 44
Barbados	00 1 246	011 44
Belarus	00 375	810 44
Belgium	00 32	00 44
Belize	00 501	00 44
Benin	00 229	00 44
Bermuda	00 1 441	011 44
Bhutan	00 975	00 44
Bolivia	00 591	0010 44*
		0011 44*
		0012 44*
		0013 44*
Bosnia and Hercegovina	00 387	00 44
Botswana	00 267	00 44
Brazil	00 55	0014 44*
		0015 44*
		0021 44*
		0023 44*
		0031 44*
British Virgin Islands	00 1 284	011 44
Brunei	00 673	00 44
Bulgaria	00 359	00 44
Burkina Faso	00 226	00 44
Burundi	00 257	00 44
Cambodia	00 855	001 44
Cameroon	00 237	00 44
Canada	00 1	011 44
Canary Islands	00 34	00 44
Cape Verde	00 238	0 44
Cayman Islands	00 1 345	011 44
Central African Republic	00 236	19 44
Chad	00 235	15 44
Chile	00 56	00 44
China	00 86	00 44
Colombia	00 57	009 44
The Comoros	00 269	00 44
Congo, Dem. Rep. of	00 243	00 44
Congo, Rep. of	00 242	00 44
Cook Islands	00 682	00 44
Costa Rica	00 506	00 44
Côte d'Ivoire	00 225	00 44
Croatia	00 385	00 44
Cuba	00 53	119 44
Cyprus	00 357	00 44
Czech Rep.	00 420	00 44
Denmark	00 45	00 44
Djibouti	00 253	00 44
Dominica	00 1 767	011 44
Dominican Rep.	00 1 809	011 44
	00 1 829	
East Timor	00 670	00 44
Ecuador	00 593	00 44
Egypt	00 20	00 44
El Salvador	00 503	00 44
Equatorial Guinea	00 240	00 44
Eritrea	00 291	00 44
Estonia	00 372	00 44
Ethiopia	00 251	00 44
Falkland Islands	00 500	00 44
Faeroe Islands	00 298	00 44
Fiji	00 679	00 44
Finland	00 358	00 44*
France	00 33	00 44
French Guiana	00 594	00 44
French Polynesia	00 689	00 44
Gabon	00 241	00 44
The Gambia	00 220	00 44
Georgia	00 995	810 44
Germany	00 49	00 44
Ghana	00 233	00 44
Gibraltar	00 350	00 44
Greece	00 30	00 44
Greenland	00 299	00 44
Grenada	00 1 473	011 44
Guadeloupe	00 590	00 44
Guam	00 1 671	011 44
Guatemala	00 502	00 44
Guinea	00 224	00 44
Guinea-Bissau	00 245	00 44
Guyana	00 592	001 44
Haiti	00 509	00 44
Honduras	00 504	00 44
Hong Kong	00 852	001 44
Hungary	00 36	00 44
Iceland	00 354	00 44
India	00 91	00 44
Indonesia	00 62	001 44*
		007 44*
Iran	00 98	00 44
Iraq	00 964	00 44
Ireland	00 353	00 44
Israel	00 972	00 44*
Italy	00 39	00 44
Jamaica	00 1 876	011 44
Japan	00 81	001 010 44*
		0033 010 44*
		0041 010 44*
		0061 010 44*
		010 44*

Jordan	00 962	00 44*		Puerto Rico	00 1 787	011 44
Kazakhstan	00 7	810 44			00 1 939	
Kenya	00 254	000 44		Qatar	00 974	00 44
Kiribati	00 686	00 44		Réunion	00 262	00 44
Korea, Dem. People's				Romania	00 40	00 44
Rep. of	00 850	00 44		Russian Federation	00 7	810 44
Korea, Republic of	00 82	001 44*		Rwanda	00 250	00 44
		002 44*		St Christopher and		
Kuwait	00 965	00 44		Nevis	00 1 869	011 44
Kyrgyzstan	00 996	00 44		St Helena	00 290	00 44
Laos	00 856	00 44		St Lucia	00 1 758	011 44
Latvia	00 371	00 44		St Pierre and		
Lebanon	00 961	00 44		Miquelon	00 508	00 44
Lesotho	00 266	00 44		St Vincent and the		
Liberia	00 231	00 44		Grenadines	00 1 784	011 44
Libya	00 218	00 44		Samoa	00 685	0 44
Liechtenstein	00 423	00 44		San Marino	00 378	00 44
Lithuania	00 370	00 44		Sao Tome and		
Luxembourg	00 352	00 44		Principe	00 239	00 44
Macao	00 853	00 44		Saudi Arabia	00 966	00 44
Macedonia	00 389	00 44		Senegal	00 221	00 44
Madagascar	00 261	00 44		Serbia	00 381	00 44
Madeira	00 351	00 44		Seychelles	00 248	00 44
Malawi	00 265	00 44		Sierra Leone	00 232	00 44
Malaysia	00 60	00 44		Singapore	00 65	001 44
Maldives	00 960	00 44		Slovakia	00 421	00 44
Mali	00 223	00 44		Slovenia	00 386	00 44
Malta	00 356	00 44		Solomon Islands	00 677	00 44
Marshall Islands	00 692	011 44		Somalia	00 252	00 44
Martinique	00 596	00 44		South Africa	00 27	00 44
Mauritania	00 222	00 44		Spain	00 34	00 44
Mauritius	00 230	00 44		Sri Lanka	00 94	00 44
Mayotte	00 269	10 44		Sudan	00 249	00 44
Mexico	00 52	98 44		Suriname	00 597	00 44
Micronesia, Federated				Swaziland	00 268	00 44
States of	00 691	011 44		Sweden	00 46	00 44
Moldova	00 373	00 44		Switzerland	00 41	00 44
Monaco	00 377	00 44		Syria	00 963	00 44
Mongolia	00 976	001 44		Taiwan	00 886	002 44
Montenegro	00 382	00 44		Tajikistan	00 992	810 44
Montserrat	00 1 664	011 44		Tanzania	00 255	000 44
Morocco	00 212	00 44		Thailand	00 66	001 44
Mozambique	00 258	00 44		Tibet	00 86	00 44
Myanmar	00 95	00 44		Togo	00 228	00 44
Namibia	00 264	00 44		Tokelau	00 690	00 44
Nauru	00 674	00 44		Tonga	00 676	00 44
Nepal	00 977	00 44		Trinidad and Tobago	00 1 868	011 44
The Netherlands	00 31	00 44		Tunisia	00 216	00 44
Netherlands Antilles	00 599	00 44		Turkey	00 90	00 44
New Caledonia	00 687	00 44		Turkmenistan	00 993	810 44
New Zealand	00 64	00 44		Turks and Caicos		
Nicaragua	00 505	00 44		Islands	00 1 649	011 44
Niger	00 227	00 44		Tuvalu	00 688	00 44
Nigeria	00 234	009 44		Uganda	00 256	000 44
Niue	00 683	00 44		Ukraine	00 380	810 44
Norfolk Island	00 672	00 44		United Arab Emirates	00 971	00 44
Northern Mariana				United States of		
Islands	00 1 670	011 44		America	00 1	011 44
Norway	00 47	00 44		Uruguay	00 598	00 44
Oman	00 968	00 44		Uzbekistan	00 998	810 44
Pakistan	00 92	00 44		Vanuatu	00 678	00 44
Palau	00 680	011 44		Vatican City State	00 39	00 44
Panama	00 507	00 44		Venezuela	00 58	00 44
Papua New Guinea	00 675	05 44		Vietnam	00 84	00 44
Paraguay	00 595	002 44		Virgin Islands	00 1 340	011 44
Peru	00 51	00 44		Yemen	00 967	00 44
The Philippines	00 63	00 44		Zambia	00 260	00 44
Poland	00 48	00 44		Zimbabwe	00 263	00 44
Portugal	00 351	00 44				

MOBILE COMMUNICATIONS

In *The Telecommunications Market 2006* report, UK regulator OFCOM revealed that year-on-year growth in mobile revenues continued during 2005, with income from users totalling £13.1bn and representing 34 per cent of all retail telecoms revenue. Moreover, for the first time, revenue from mobile calls surpassed that from fixed lines. This is largely due to a rise in the number of mobile subscriptions in the UK, which, at its current level of 66.2 million, exceeds the size of the UK population. This is due to a number of people having more than one mobile subscription, either for a second mobile phone or a substitute wireless device such as a Blackberry.

UK MOBILE SUBSCRIBER STATISTICS (MILLIONS)

Date	1999	2001	2003	2004	2005	2006
Subscriber base	13.0	40.1	46.9	50.2	61.2	65.7

Source: OFCOM Telecommunications Reviews 2005 and 2006

INDUSTRY STRUCTURE

With various technologies converging, the structure of the mobile communications industry is becoming increasingly complex. This has resulted in new services being delivered to consumers over multiple platforms, thereby blurring the industry structure somewhat. In spite of this, two main types of players can be identified in the mobile sector, namely network operators, such as Vodafone and Orange, who own the infrastructure, set tariffs and bill customers; and service providers, who lease network capacity from the operators, with Mobile Virtual Network Operators (MVNOs), such as Virgin Mobile, being the most common service provider in the UK. OFCOM is responsible for setting the controls in this market and for ensuring that industry players do not behave in an anti-competitive manner. Unlike in other European countries, where the regulator forced operators to sell capacity, UK operators originally opened their networks voluntarily, with no regulatory intervention required.

NETWORK OPERATORS
There were five licensed network operators in the UK at the end of 2006:

Operator	Owned by	Subscriber numbers (millions)
Hutchison 3G	Hutchison Whampoa Ltd	3.8
O2	Telefónica O2 Europe	19.0*
Orange	France Telecom SA	15.3
T-Mobile	100Deutsche Telekom AG	16.8
Vodafone	Vodafone Group Plc	14.7

Source: Ofcom operators
* O2 subscriber figures include Tesco Mobile subscribers

ALTERNATIVE SERVICE PROVIDERS
Service providers were introduced into the UK market as a means of stimulating competition, with Singlepoint (acquired by Vodafone in 2003) being an early example.

These players buy wholesale airtime from network operators and sell it on to users at a discount. They do not own any infrastructure or SIM cards. Service providers still exist in the UK market, though the business model has changed somewhat, with MVNOs now representing the most significant service provider model in the UK. As with their predecessors, they also resell wholesale minutes purchased from network operators, but are distinct insofar as they may – under the conditions of their agreement with the operator – set prices, manage accounts, own the customer database, perform customer service activities and manage distribution, marketing and branding. Moreover, MVNOs typically own, issue and activate SIM cards.

The world's first MVNO was Virgin Mobile, which launched in 1999. By the end of 2005 it had an estimated active subscriber base of four million. MVNOs have also been launched by existing telecoms companies such as BT, and by companies in non-related sectors such as supermarkets. There are now an estimated 230 MVNOs worldwide.

MVNO (launched)	Network operator	Active subscribers (est)	Further information
Virgin (1999)	T-Mobile	4,000,000	Virgin Mobile merged with NTL Telewest in July 2006
Tesco (2003)	O2	1,000,000	Joint venture with O2
BT Mobile (2003)	Vodafone	250,000	Deal for a five-year period
Sainsbury's (2004)	O2	30,000	Controlled by Carphone Warehouse
Easy (2005)	T-Mobile	23,000	Joint venture with TDC

Source: OFCOM, Interim Review of the Telecommunications Market 2006

TYPES OF MOBILE SUBSCRIPTIONS

There are two basic types of mobile subscriptions: contracts and pre-paid, also known as pay-as-you-go or PAYG. A contract, generally paid on a monthly basis and fixed to a minimum contract term, requires the user to pay a fixed subscription fee each month entitling him or her to a certain number of services. More recently, there has been a trend towards 18-month contracts by operators through the offer of reduced line rental or complimentary services for the contract duration. Such moves are designed to reduce customer switching between operators, thereby reducing the cost of new customer acquisition. Operators have also introduced more generous service bundles to those customers signing up directly, in an effort to reduce payments to third-party retailers.

By contrast, pre-paid subscribers have access to the same services but pay in advance and simply top up their account when credit is running low. New payment channels, such as bank ATMs, have emerged for PAYG customers to encourage additional spending. The introduction of pre-paid services has allowed the industry to target new areas of the market that would otherwise be ineligible for a contract, either for age or credit rating reasons. PAYG contracts have moved towards more comprehensive packages of multimedia services such as downloadable games, access to news and information updates, and typically offer a certain amount of complimentary airtime.

There has been little change over the past years in terms of the proportion of contract to PAYG customers in the UK; OFCOM's 2006 *Telecommunications Review* reports that at the end of 2005 there were 22.2 million total active contract subscribers and 43.2 million pre-pay customers.

NETWORK TECHNOLOGY

Network technology has improved dramatically since the launch in 1985 of the first-generation 900 MHz analogue GSM service (known as TACS), which offered little or no data capability. In 1992 Vodafone launched a new digital GSM network, usually referred to as 2G or second generation. This technology used digital encoding and allowed voice and low-speed data communications. 2G technology was later extended to 2.5G, allowing additional features such as an enhanced data transfer rate.

More recently, the development of 3G technology has provided increased data transmission speeds, supporting multimedia applications such as video-conferencing and internet access. Since 3G uses an entirely new network, operators are required to hold a licence to offer it. The UK was the third European country to license 3G operators, after Finland and Spain, with five licences being granted to Hutchinson 3G, O2, Orange, T-Mobile and Vodafone. Under the terms of the licence, operators are required to offer a service with coverage for at least 80 per cent of the population by the end of 2007.

MOBILE SERVICES

The upgrade from analogue to 2G brought clearer voice quality, while later moves to 2.5G and 3G opened the door for new data services. In a mature market mobile revenues are expected to come from enhanced mobile services, so pressure is on operators to provide innovative solutions and to encourage upgrades to new handsets with added functionality. This section outlines the array of mobile services available to today's consumer and gives examples by operator, where appropriate.

Aside from voice services, which represent 80 per cent of all mobile retail revenues, SMS, or more colloquially, text messaging, is the secondary source of mobile retail revenue, accounting for 16 per cent of mobile retail revenues, according to OFCOM's *Telecommunications Review 2006*. The number of SMS messages has been increasing dramatically year-on-year, with 3.5 billion text messages sent in 2005.

The technological move to 2G and 2.5G enabled mobile phones to access the internet, thereby allowing for emails and photos to be sent, and for downloading ringtones and games. Such services are referred to as multimedia messaging (MMS). The use of MMS remains relatively low compared to SMS, despite the increasing number of camera phones in circulation.

3G technology provides higher quality audio and video content, so that consumers can access information, entertainment and communication on the move, eg live mobile internet, music downloads and TV streaming. The

table below shows the monthly consumption of services by UK mobile subscribers and highlights the continuing dominance of SMS.

UK CONSUMPTION OF MOBILE CONTENT AND APPLICATIONS (AS AT DECEMBER 2006)

Activity	Subscribers (per cent)
Sent text message	86.3
Used photo messaging	30.3
Browsed news and information	14.5
Used email	11.1
Downloaded mobile game	4.9
Purchased ringtone	4.8
Used instant messenger	4.2
Purchased wallpaper or screensaver	2.1

Source: M:Metrics Inc Benchmark Survey, Dec. 2006

Technological developments have merged the previously distinct areas of television, internet and telephony. During the second half of 2005, operators introduced live streaming television over 3G networks, with deals struck between broadcasters (including BSkyB, Granada and Disney) and mobile operators. In May 2005 Orange was the first operator in the UK to launch a mobile television service, through which subscribers could access a variety of entertainment channels, including ITV and Cartoon Network. Rival operators have since introduced similar services. The pricing structure of mobile TV varies by operator, but subscribers typically pay to view a bundle of programmes.

The convergence of technologies has also encouraged online businesses to offer services to mobile customers. Examples of recent deals include Vodafone's agreement with the social networking site MySpace.com, to distribute software that allows consumers to update their MySpace page from their mobile. Similarly, 3 launched a music download service and SeeMeTV, enabling users to upload videos shot on their phones. 3G handsets also allow users to search the internet, although this process is still slow compared to equivalent searches on personal computers. Advertisers, too, have begun to explore the possibilities of improved mobile technology. Where phone advertising used to be limited to the sending of text messages, in the last year Orange announced a full-scale mobile advertising trial across its Orange World portal, with advertising banners appearing on Orange World web pages as users browsed the internet via their phone. Likewise, Yahoo! announced a deal to create mobile advertising for Vodafone. Meanwhile, Unilever, Coca-Cola and Land Rover were among the brands to launch the first ad-supported mobile content trial across multiple network operators.

REGULATION

Competition in the UK telecommunications market is regulated by OFCOM, a statutory corporation established by Act of Parliament and independent of government. OFCOM replaced the former communications and broadcasting regulators, OFTEL and the Radio-communications Agency. The Communications Act of 2003 governs regulation of the telecoms market and OFCOM's responsibilities cover television, radio, telecoms and wireless communications services. The regulator's principal duty under the Communications Act is to further the interests of (i) citizens in relation to communications matters and (ii) consumers in relevant markets, where appropriate by promoting competition.

Competition in the communications market is also regulated by the Office of Fair Trading (OFT), the main UK regulator. The OFT and OFCOM consult one another, however OFCOM takes the lead in competition investigations in the UK market. The Competition Appeals Tribunal (CAT) hears appeals against OFCOM's decisions, while price-related appeals are referred to the Competition Commission.

HEALTH

The possible health implications of mobile phone use have received a great deal of media coverage. The widespread use of mobile phones is still relatively recent and technologies are continuing to develop at a pace that is outstripping analyses of any potential impact on health. A report produced by the National Radiological Protection Board (NRPB) in 2004 identified a possible danger concerning mobiles with a high specific energy absorption rate (SAR) – a measure of the energy absorbed by the user's head while he or she is using the phone. Different phones have different SAR values, but the SAR also depends on the proximity of a user to a mobile phone mast and the length of time the handset is in use. Presently, the long-term effects are unknown. The NRPB's report concluded that while 'there is as yet no hard evidence of adverse health effects on the general public', the discussion about SAR and mobile phone safety is ongoing.

SAFETY WHILE DRIVING

Numerous studies have shown that motorists risk a higher chance of collision and losing control of their vehicle if talking on a mobile phone while driving, even when using a hands-free kit. In 2003, a new regulation came into force making it an offence to use a hand-held phone, or similar hand-held device, when driving a motor vehicle on the road. The term hand-held refers to a mobile telephone or similar device held at some point during the course of making or receiving a call or performing any other interactive function. The penalty was a £30 fixed fine or up to £1,000 on conviction in court (£2,500 for drivers of goods vehicles, buses or coaches). Tougher penalties were introduced to clamp down on this offence in 2007; the maximum penalty is now a £60 fine and offenders risk three points being added to their licence.

CONTACTS

COMPETITION APPEAL TRIBUNAL (CAT)
Victoria House, Bloomsbury Place, London WC1A 2EB
T 020-7979 7979 W www.catribunal.org.uk

DEPARTMENT FOR BUSINESS, ENTERPRISE AND
REGULATORY REFORM
1 Victoria Street, London SW1V 0ET
T 020-7215 5000 W www.berr.gov.uk

OFCOM
Riverside House, 2A Southwark Bridge Road, London SE1 9HA
T 020-7981 3000 W www.ofcom.org.uk

OFFICE OF FAIR TRADING (OFT)
Fleetbank House, 2-6 Salisbury Square, London EC4Y 8JX
T 020-7211 8000 W www.oft.gov.uk

INFORMATION TECHNOLOGY

POPULAR WEBSITES OF 2007

DAILYMOTION.COM: A video-sharing website that allows users to share personal videos, privately or publicly, with a video-blogging component

DEL.ICIO.US: A social bookmarking website allowing users to store bookmarks online, allowing them access to the same bookmarks from any computer and the ability to add them from anywhere

DIGG.COM: A user-driven social content website where 100 per cent of the news stories are submitted by their community of users. Popular submissions are promoted to the front page through a system of votes – 'diggs'

FACEBOOK.COM: A social networking website that connects people with friends, allowing them to upload photos, and share links and videos

FLICKR.COM: An online photo-management and sharing website which allows users to make their personal photos available through the web, RSS feeds, email and blogs

LAST.FM: A social music website that through a user's music collection creates personal recommendations, music lists, and allows connection with other users who share similar music tastes

LIVEJOURNAL.COM: An online blogging community where people from around the world share stories, discuss topics and keep in touch with friends

MYSPACE.COM: A social networking website that allows users to create private communities and blogs where photos, music and video can be shared with friends

SENDSPACE.COM: A file-sharing website used to send large files too big for email attachments to friends, family and businesses

WIKIPEDIA.ORG: A multilingual, web-based, free content encyclopaedia project written collaboratively by volunteers from all around the world. Articles can be edited by anyone with access to the internet

YOUTUBE.COM: A video-sharing website used to watch and share videos worldwide. YouTube allows people to upload and share videos through websites, mobile devices, blogs and email

A SHORT HISTORY OF THE INTERNET

Prior to the advent of the internet, computers tended to be connected together by hardware and protocols that were specific to each particular connection. Typically, links were point-to-point (physically established between the two computers). In 1969 ARPANET was formed by the US department of defence to establish a way for the computer capability of the military to be dispersed so that no single centre was critical to the operation of the network as a whole. This was achieved by interconnecting computers both directly and by way of other intermediary computers; thus if one computer was destroyed, other pathways of communication could be established. These interconnections, when drawn, appeared as a net or web. ARPANET was extended to non-military users such as universities early in the 1970s, with initial international links appearing in 1972.

The introduction of domain names (eg www.whitakersalmanack.com) in 1984 offered an easier means of using the web. Prior to domain names, IP addresses (eg 192.168.1.100) were used for accessing destination computers. However, before 1989 the internet was still primarily limited to government agencies, the military, academic and research organisations and some big businesses.

In 1989, what most people perceive as 'the internet' was born. It was effectively invented at CERN (the European Particle Physics Laboratory) by Tim Berners-Lee as a way for scientists to share information by placing it in a prescribed format on a server. Initially text only, development of computer capability allowed the inclusion of images.

The internet is effectively a very large network of computers, connected through various telecommunications links. Millions of routers (see Glossary) around the world link together massive networks of computers to form a backbone to the internet. Most home and business users will connect up to an ISP (internet service provider) via a telephone or a digital line. ISPs have their own routers, which all the lines connect to. The internet 'traffic' is then routed to another (often larger) telecommunications company, which is also connected by fibre-optic lines to other such companies across the globe. Websites are stored on servers that are designed for hosting, running a special program that 'serves' up the content.

As use of technology has increased, the downloading of music, pictures and video from the internet has become faster and more practical. Analogue media, such as music stored on a tape, or a painting, loses quality in reproduction. Digital media on the other hand can be copied flawlessly between computers, as it is the simple process of replicating a string of zeros and ones.

The Data Protection Act 1984 (revised 1998) was introduced to ensure the correct and proper handling of personal and sensitive data held on computer databases. During the 1980s computer hacking was still not illegal, but the number of serious computer attacks was rapidly increasing. Failed attempts to prosecute these hackers brought about the Computer Misuse Act, passed in 1990 to protect computer systems from unauthorised access. Copyright law has also been amended to encompass the concept of 'digital property' and include criminal sanctions for breaching the copyright of protected music, video, books, software and website material.

INTERNET TRENDS

While the internet has always been used as a key method of dispersing information, increased internet speeds and accessibility of cheaper broadband have prompted the advent of Web 2.0, a second generation of web-based services enabling more people to reach higher quality content online. Music, high-resolution images and video files can be downloaded in seconds, compared to hours when accessed via telephone modems.

This new era has led to a wave of new photo-sharing websites such as Flickr.com and YouTube.com that allow users to upload photographs and share multimedia files online, and also of file-sharing services such as Sendpsace.com and Bittorrent.com. Websites that promote social networking and user-generated content are also on the rise. Myspace.com and Facebook.com have created international communities of millions of people where users interact and converse via photo and music sharing, blogs and even popularity contests.

The number of web office applications has grown with the merging of traditional desktop applications and web-based technology. Often utilising AJAX, many web-based applications such as Google's Docs and Spreadsheets, Zoho, and Thinkfree, offer free alternatives to Microsoft's Office.

RSS feeds are expected to continue to play an important role in the growth of the internet, and directly related to Web 2.0 is the increase in the use of mobile web. Cheaper internet access plans, mobile banking, mobile-linked user-generated content and even the appearance of the iPhone, Apple's much-touted webphone, are helping make mobile phones a popular browsing device.

INTERNET STATISTICS

- Between 2002 and 2006 the proportion of adults in Great Britain who had used the internet in the last three months increased by almost one-quarter, from 48 per cent to 60 per cent.
- 59 per cent of internet users over the age of 16 went online every day or almost every day in 2006, while 4 per cent went online less than once a month.
- Internet use declines with age. In 2006, 84 per cent of people aged 16 to 24 had used the internet within the last three months, compared with 52 per cent of people aged 55 to 64 and 15 per cent of those aged 65 and over.
- For users aged 16 and over the most common location to access the internet was at home. In 2006, 85 per cent of internet users aged 16 and over who had accessed the internet in the last three months had done so at home.
- For those who did not have household access to the internet, the most common places to go online were at work (46 per cent) and at another person's home (also 46 per cent).
- Information research and using email were the two most common online activities of internet users in 2006.
- Two in five adults said they had purchased items online for private or personal reasons. The most common items bought online were travel and holidays (51 per cent), followed by films, videos and DVDs (42 per cent). 18 per cent of internet users had sold goods or services online in 2006, more than double that in 2004.
- The majority (70 per cent) of those who had shopped online had not encountered any problems doing so. For those who had, the most common problem was that delivery took longer than expected.

Source: National Statistics Omnibus Survey

TOP 10 BROADBAND SUBSCRIBERS BY COUNTRY

Country	2005	2006
1. USA	46,110,191	57,330,216
2. China	37,504,000	51,899,000
3. Japan	22,647,830	26,095,919
4. Germany	10,706,648	14,660,084
5. South Korea	12,199,666	14,042,698
6. France	9,958,086	13,983,900
7. UK	9,828,900	13,116,600
8. Italy	6,977,404	8,826,803
9. Canada	6,854,994	7,876,487
10. Spain	4,852,388	6,726,756

Source: www.dslforum.org

GLOSSARY OF INTERNET TERMS

The following is a selected list of modern computing terms. It is by no means exhaustive but is intended to cover those that the average computer user might encounter.

3G: Third Generation wireless – a term commonly used to describe high-bandwidth (2 Mbps) wireless technologies for mobile phones. 3G is still in its infancy, but when fully deployed 3G technology will offer high speed and capacity transmission of sound, vision and data to and from wireless devices and networks. *See also* Mobile Communications section.

ADSL: Asymmetric Digital Subscriber Line – high-speed internet connection, four or more times faster than a modem, but using the same standard cables as a regular telephone. Faster at downloading than uploading.

AJAX: Asynchronous JavaScript and XML – a way of including content in a web page in which JavaScript code in the web page fetches some data from a server and displays it without re-fetching the entire surrounding page at the same time (hence 'asynchronous'). The intention is to make web pages feel more responsive by exchanging small amounts of data with the server behind the scenes, so that an entire web page does not have to be reloaded each time the user makes a change, thereby increasing its interactivity, speed and usability.

APACHE: The most common web server (or HTTP server) software on the internet. Apache is an open-source application originally created from a series of changes ('patches') made to a web server written at the National Centre for Supercomputing Applications in the USA. It is designed as a set of modules, enabling administrators to choose which features they wish to use to meet specific needs, including handling protocols other than the web-standard HTTP.

ASCII: American Standard Code for Information Interchange – a widely used character-encoding system, expressing letters, numbers and other symbols as binary numbers. It employs a string of eight binary digits or bits to represent 128 characters, enough for all the letters of the Roman alphabet and various permutations of every number between zero and nine.

BANDWIDTH: Determines how much data can be sent through a connection. Usually measured in bits-per-second (bps). A full page of English text is about 16,000 bits. A fast modem can move about 57,000bps. Full-motion, full-screen video would require roughly 10,000,000bps, depending on compression.

BLOG: A blog (short for web log) is an online personal journal that is frequently updated and intended to be read by the public. Blogs generally represent the personality of the author and may include philosophy, commentary on the internet and other social issues and links to favourite websites. Blogs are kept by 'bloggers' and are commonly available as RSS feeds.

BLUETOOTH: Standard for short-range (10m) wireless connectivity between devices such as laptops, cell phones and printers to interact without cables. Bluetooth can presently operate at speeds of up to 2Mbps.

BROADBAND: Generic term to describe high-speed internet-using technologies such as ISDN, ADSL etc as opposed to narrowband connections via modem.

BROWSER: Typically referring to a 'web browser' program that allows a computer user to view web page content on their computer, eg Microsoft Explorer, Netscape Navigator, AOL or Safari.

COOKIE: A piece of information sent by a web server to a web browser which is then saved and sent back to the server whenever the browser makes requests from the server. Cookies contain information such as login, registration or online 'shopping cart' data, user preferences, etc and are usually set to expire after a predetermined length of time.

CSS: Cascading Style Sheet – a standard for specifying the appearance of text and other elements. CSS was developed for use with HTML in web pages, but can be used in other contexts. CSS provides a single 'library' of styles that are used over and over throughout a large number of related documents. A CSS file might specify for example that all numbered lists are to appear in italics.

DIGERATI: The elite of the computer industry and online communities. Famous computer scientists, magazine writers and well-known bloggers are included among the digerati.

DNS: Domain Name Server – a server that translates domain names into the IP addresses used by programs to directly access computers on the internet. Each server has an IP address and a name. DNS is analogous to the telephone directory enquiry service, providing a means of looking up and locating a computer connected to the internet.

DOMAIN: A set of words, numbers and letters separated by dots used to identify an internet server or group of servers, eg www.whitakersalmanack.co.uk, where 'www' denotes a web (http) server, 'whitakersalmanack' denotes the organisation name, 'co' denotes that the organisation is a company and 'uk' indicates United Kingdom. (For a complete list of country suffixes see Internet Domain Names section.)

EMAIL: Electronic mail – an email message is a document that is addressed to one or more persons from an individual address. Usually containing a message, it can also include other documents. It has superseded the telex, telegram, postcard and letter for rapidly exchanging information. The advent of the internet has seen an explosion in the use of email in modern life. Without encryption or digital signature, an email is not secure.

EXTRANET: An extranet is a secure and private subset of the internet, protected by security protocols and typically used for exchanging information and services within a specific group.

FILE SERVER: A computer on a network that stores computer files which users can access from other computers on the network. Popular modern systems include Microsoft Windows, UNIX, Novell NetWare, and MacOS Server.

FIREWALL: Computer or device to protect a network from security risks posed by the internet. Just as a firewall protects parts of a building from a fire raging on the other side, a network firewall stops risks posed by the internet from egressing into a private network.

FLAME: Flaming (or trolling) has come to refer to any kind of derogatory comment, no matter how witless or crude, which takes place in an online discussion. A situation where an online discussion degenerates into a series of personal attacks against the debaters, rather than a discussion of their positions, is known as a 'flame war'.

FTP: File Transfer Protocol – an internet protocol whereby an FTP client program can exchange files with a remote server.

GBPS: Gigabits per second – denoting 1,000 million bits transmitted per second.

GPRS: General Packet Radio Services – a service for continuous wireless communication over the internet from mobile phones and computers. Presently available in data rates of between 56 and 114Kbps, GPRS tends to be charged by volume of information transferred rather than by time, which allows a more economic continuous connection compared with direct dial over a modem.

GZIP: Compression – a common mechanism on UNIX and Linux operating systems to compress information in order to save resources.

HIT: In reference to the internet, a 'hit' means a single request from a web browser for a single item from a web server; thus in order for a web browser to display a page that contains three graphics, four 'hits' would occur at the server: one for the HTML page, and one for each of the three graphics. The number of hits on a website is not synonymous with the number of distinct visitors.

HTML: HyperText Mark-up Language – a small programming language used to denote or mark-up how an internet page should be presented to a user from an HTTP server via a web browser. HTML is an evolving standard that has grown greatly from its first version to accommodate new types of web content and features provided by the different web browsers (eg Netscape and Internet Explorer).

HTTP: HyperText Transfer Protocol – an internet protocol whereby a web server sends web pages, images and files to a web browser.

IMAP: Internet Mail Access Protocol – allows a user to review, manipulate and store email on a central server from one or more workstations without necessitating message removal from the server.

INTRANET: Subset of the internet, using internet protocols over a local area network, common today for publishing information and services within an organisation.

IRC: Internet Relay Chat – a protocol that allows users to 'chat' online using their keyboards. Under IRC a user can log into various chat rooms under their own name or an alias and have a text 'conversation' in real time.

JAVA: a high-level, object-orientated computer language developed by Sun Microsystems, especially designed for use via the web.

KBPS: Kilobits per second – measure of transmission speed, denoting 1,000 bits transmitted per second.

LINUX: A UNIX-like operating system first developed as a free or low-cost system for personal computers. See also Operating Systems in main article.

MASHUP: A web page or site made by automatically combining content from other sources, usually by using material available via RSS feeds.

MBPS: Megabits per second – denoting 1 million bits transmitted per second.

META TAG: A specific kind of HTML tag that contains information not normally displayed to the user. Meta tags contain information about the page itself, hence the name (meta means 'about this subject'). Meta tags are typically used to include information for search engines to help them better categorise a page and can be viewed in the source code.

MODEM: Modulator-Demodulator – a device that modulates digital signals from a computer into analogue signals for transmission over a standard telephone line, and demodulates an incoming analogue signal and converts it to a digital signal for the computer.

MP3: A popular format for compressing audio information for transmission over the internet for later playback on personal computers, music players and other devices.

MPEG: Motion Picture Encoding Group – popular format standard for compressing video and audio information for transmission over the internet for later playback on personal computers and on hand-held devices.

MS-DOS: Microsoft Corporation's Disk Operating System – an early OS commercially developed, but not invented, by Microsoft for use on early Intel-based personal computers. *See also* Operating System.

NETIQUETTE: Conventions of politeness on electronic forums such as internet message boards.

NETIZEN: A person actively involved in online communications. The term implies civic responsibility and participation in improving and developing the internet, while encouraging free speech and open access.

OPEN CONTENT: Copyrighted information that is made available by the owner to the general public under licence terms that allow reuse of the material, often with the requirement that the reuser grant the public the same rights to the modified version. Information that is in the 'public domain' might also be considered a form of open content.

OPEN-SOURCE: A computer program that has its source-code (the instructions that make up a program) freely available for viewing and modification is said to be open-source.

OPERATING SYSTEM (OS): Computer software developed to provide computer programs with standard facilities to interact with users and with computer hardware (via drivers). *See also* MS-DOS, UNIX, MacOS.

PDF: Portable Document Format – a file format designed to enable printing and viewing of documents with all their formatting (typefaces, images, layout, etc.) appearing the same regardless of what operating system is used. The PDF format is based on the widely used Postscript document-description language. Both PDF and Postscript were developed by the Adobe Corporation.

PODCASTING: A form of audio broadcasting using the internet, podcasting takes its name from a combination of 'iPod' and broadcasting, though it does not require the use of an iPod. Podcasting involves making one or more audio files available as 'enclosures' in an RSS feed. A podcaster creates a list of music and/or other sound files and makes that list available in the RSS 2.0 format. The list can then be obtained using various podcast 'retriever' software which makes the audio files available to digital audio devices (including, but not limited to, iPods) where users may then listen to them at their convenience.

POP3: Post Office Protocol 3 – an internet protocol whereby a workstation can collect email from a personal mailbox on an email server and move it to a user's own machine.

RAM: Random Access Memory – the main memory that is used by a computer to store temporary data (while accessing or altering individual storage locations) that is lost when the computer is turned off.

ROUTER: Where multiple networks are joined together, a router acts like a fast sorting office, examining the destination address of each information packet and passing or routing it to the appropriate network. Routers can select the most efficient route for packets.

RSS: Rich Site Summary or RDF Site Summary or Real Simple Syndication – a commonly used protocol for syndication and sharing of content, originally developed to facilitate the syndication of news articles, now widely used to share the contents of blogs. Mashups are often made using RSS feeds.

SERVER: A node on a network that provides service to the terminals on the network. These computers have higher hardware specifications, ie more resources and greater speed, in order to handle large amounts of data.

SOCIAL BOOKMARKING: Web-based service to share internet bookmarks.

SPAM: A term used for unsolicited, generally junk, email. To spam someone is to send them (multiple) junk emails. Junk email is becoming a major issue with some estimates suggesting that spam is becoming more prevalent than legitimate email. Most spam contains offers of pornography, get-rich schemes, prescription drugs, low-cost finance or discount goods or services. Many legislatures around the globe are taking steps to ban or regulate spam.

TAG: As a noun, a tag is a basic element of the languages used to create web pages (HTML) and similar languages such as XML.

TCP/IP: Transmission Control Protocol/Internet Protocol – the lifeblood of the internet, TCP/IP defines how information and requests generated by all other protocols are transmitted over the internet. Information on the internet is chopped up into small chunks or packets which are addressed with a destination and origination address. It sometimes happens that a packet gets lost and TCP/IP dictates how such a loss is handled.

UNIX: *See* Operating Systems in main article. Modern versions include Linux, MacOS X, Solaris, FreeBSD.

USB: Universal Serial Bus – standard for connecting serial devices such as scanners, digital cameras, keyboards, modems and printers to computers. With USB, speeds of 10Mbps and higher are possible.

URL: Uniform Resource Locator – address of an internet file accessible on the internet, eg
http://www.whitakersalmanack.com

USER-GENERATED CONTENT (UGC): Refers to various media content produced or primarily influenced by end-users, as opposed to traditional media producers such as licensed broadcasters and production companies. These forms of media include digital video, blogging, podcasting, mobile phone photography and wikis.

VIRUS: A computer program or script written for the express purpose of replicating itself onto as many machines as possible (much like its biological namesake), often with negative side effects to the host computer and computer network. Such effects vary from harmless screen messages to corruption of document integrity, network overload or the compromising of data security or privacy. Historically transmitted slowly by floppy disk and over networks within offices, the prevalence of email means viruses can spread globally within minutes.

VOIP: Voice Over IP – various technologies used to make telephone calls over IP networks, especially the internet. Just as modems allow computers to connect to the internet over regular telephone lines, VOIP technology allows humans to talk over internet connections. Costs for VOIP calls can be much lower than for traditional telephone calls. Because the IP networks are packet-switched, this allows for vastly different ways of handling connections and more efficient use of network resources.

VPN: Virtual Private Network – usually refers to a network parts of which are connected using the public internet, but the data sent across the internet is encrypted, so the entire network is 'virtually' private.

WAP: Wireless Application Protocol – a set of standards to define how portable devices connected via radio waves (such as mobile phones) can access internet services.

WEBDAV: Web-based Distributed Authoring and Versioning – a set of extensions to the HTTP protocol that allows multiple users not only to read but also to add, delete and change documents residing on a web server.

WEB 2.0: Generally refers to a second generation of services available on the web that lets people collaborate and share information online. In contrast to the first generation, Web 2.0 gives users an experience closer to desktop applications than traditional static web pages. The term was popularised as the name for a series of web development conferences that started in October 2004. Web 2.0 applications often use a combination of techniques including AJAX and web syndication. They also allow for mass publishing (web-based social software).

WI-FI: Industry brand name for the increasingly popular high frequency wireless local area Ethernet networking technology. Wi-Fi is also a popular term for a form of wireless data communication.

WIKI: Software that allows users to freely create and edit web pages' content using any web browser. Theoretically this encourages democratic use of the internet and promotes content composition by non-technical users.

WLAN: Wireless Local Area Network – a network where information is transferred by radio frequency rather than wires between computers and base stations. As radio waves can pass through objects such as walls, it is becoming increasingly important for WLANs to be secured by encryption against unauthorised access.

XHTML: eXtensible HyperText Mark-up Language – essentially HTML expressed as valid XML. XHTML is intended to be used for the same purpose as HTML (creating web pages) but is much more strictly defined, which makes it easier to create software that can read, edit and check it for errors. XHTML is expected to eventually replace HTML.

XML: eXtensible Mark-up Language – similar to HTML but more powerful, XML allows information to be encoded or tagged in a manner that is both human and computer readable. The advent of XML has greatly

simplified the exchange of information between many formerly incompatible systems.

DEVELOPMENT OF COMPUTERS

The abacus was the first true calculating machine and was probably invented in China around 500 BC. The invention of the first mechanical calculating machine in 1623 is credited to Wilhelm Schickard, a friend of the astronomer Johannes Kepler. Unfortunately there are no surviving examples of this machine, so the machine built by French scientist and philosopher Blaise Pascal between 1642 and 1645 tends to be credited as the first true mechanical calculator. This was a device that used cogs and wheels to perform addition and subtraction over eight columns of digits. In 1673 Gottfried Leibniz invented an improved calculator that could be used to multiply, divide and find square roots.

The next significant step towards the modern computer occurred in 1804 when Joseph-Marie Jacquard invented an automated loom. Patterns in cloth woven on the loom were dictated by a series of punchcards. This was the first time that data had been stored on cards and then processed in a machine.

The closest ancestors of the modern computer are the Difference Engine and the Analytical Engine devised by mathematician Charles Babbage 30 years after the Jacquard Loom. The Difference Engine, a clockwork-like mechanism, designed to compute mathematical tables, was abandoned by Babbage in the 1840s due to limitations of the technology of the period and a lack of funds. Unlike the Difference Engine, the Analytical Engine was designed as a general-purpose tool capable of storing information. Babbage's work relied heavily on mechanics and physical machinery and it was not until the 20th-century invention of the electrical vacuum tube, and then the transistor, that computers became a feasible means of solving problems.

FIRST GENERATION

War has played a significant role in the development of the computer. In 1943, during the Second World War, British and American scientists started work on electro-mechanical computers. Colossus, a British effort, was specifically developed to crack German coding ciphers, whilst the US machine, Harvard Mark I, was developed as a more general-purpose electro-mechanical programmable computer (partly intended for atom bomb research). Regarded as early 'first generation' computers, these machines primarily comprised wired circuits and vacuum tubes. Punched cards and paper tape were largely employed as the input, output and main storage systems. In 1946 ENIAC (Electronic Numerical Integrator and Computer) was completed at the University of Pennsylvania, USA. Capable of carrying out 100,000 calculations a second, it was remarkable for its day despite weighing 30 tons.

SECOND GENERATION

Similar to light bulbs, vacuum tubes (more commonly known as 'valves') were prone to failure, requiring tedious checks to resolve problems (ENIAC alone contained 18,000 vacuum valves). In 1947 the transistor was invented, initially to replace vacuum tubes used in amplifiers. Performing the same role as a vacuum tube but less prone to failure, smaller and more efficient, the transistor allowed smaller 'second generation' computers to be developed throughout the 1950s and early 1960s.

THIRD GENERATION

In 1958 Jack St Claire Kilby, of Texas Instruments, invented the first integrated circuit (or 'microchip'). Six months later Robert Noyce of Fairchild Semiconductors independently produced a similar integrated circuit. A microchip is comprised of a large number of transistors and other components fabricated from a wafer ('chip') of silicon, interconnected by a surface film of conductive material rather than by wires. By reducing distance between components, savings are made in both size and electricity. In 1963 the first 'third generation' computers based on microchip technology appeared.

FOURTH GENERATION

In 1971 Intel produced the first 'microprocessor', heralding a 'fourth generation' of computers. The Intel 4004 (capable of 60,000 instructions per second) grouped much of the processing functions onto a single microchip. Around the same time, Intel invented the RAM (random access memory) chip, which grouped significant amounts of memory onto a single chip. Supercomputers and mainframes, utilising scores of microprocessors, had terrific power, capable of 150 million instructions per second. Developments such as multi-layer circuits, and the use of copper instead of gold in microchips, yielded improvements in size and performance through miniaturisation. The size of the transistor was scaled down from thumb size to far smaller than the thickness of a human hair, allowing for greater density and thus exponentially increasing the total power of the computer.

NEXT GENERATION

Most modern computers are still regarded as 'fourth generation' as they use essentially the same technology, albeit highly miniaturised. Gordon Moore, co-founder of Intel, observed in 1965 that the number of transistors per square inch had doubled every 12 months since the inception of the integrated circuit. The widely recognised current definition of the so-called 'Moore's Law' is that the number of transistors on a microprocessor doubles every 18 months and is likely to do so for the next few decades. Moore underestimated the improvement in microprocessing power that has occurred since then – microprocessing 'clock' speeds are now measured in mega- and even gigahertz.

Processor	Clock speed	Year of launch
Intel 80286	8MHz	1982
Intel 80386	16MHz	1985
Intel 80486	25Mhz	1989
Intel Pentium	60MHz	1993
Intel Pentium II	350MHz	1997
Intel Pentium 4	1,500MHz	2000

There are many technological paradigms currently in research that could shape the next generation of computers. The future of computer technology could for example be dependent on the physics of light. Already used extensively in the computer industry for high-speed communications, light offers future possibilities for both calculation and storage. Another strong candidate is the use of quantum computing, where data is not held in bits (zeros and ones) but 'qubits' that, when combined, can hold a greater magnitude of information. Next generation computers may also utilise technology such as neural interfaces, joining the human central nervous system to a computer input and output system. Nanotechnology, a new manufacturing technology that works on a molecular level, is fast becoming a major subject of research. Continuing miniaturisation in computer architecture has a great deal of scope to advance many areas of science, such as medicine, robotics and materials. Theorised applications in medicine include the ability to produce cell-like structures that combat certain diseases or even destroy cancerous cells. Nanorobotics also presents the ability to construct devices that can regenerate when damaged, particularly useful in space exploration. With the current high investment in research, nanotechnology seems likely to become one of the next technological revolutions.

INTERNET DOMAIN NAMES

Internet top-level domains names are two-letter codes that appear at the end of a website address to identify its origin. Websites that use a country code top-level domain must be registered with the individual country or dependent territory. The list below is of active domain names for countries only.*

ad	Andorra	bg	Bulgaria	cl	Chile
ae	United Arab Emirates	bh	Bahrain	cm	Cameroon
af	Afghanistan	bi	Burundi	cn	China
aq	The Antarctic	bj	Benin	co	Colombia
ag	Antigua and Barbuda	bn	Brunei	cr	Costa Rica
al	Albania	bo	Bolivia	cs	Serbia; Montenegro
am	Armenia	br	Brazil	cu	Cuba
ao	Angola	bt	Bhutan	cv	Cape Verde
ar	Argentina	bw	Botswana	cy	Cyprus
at	Austria	by	Belarus	cz	Czech Republic
au	Australia	bz	Belize	de	Germany
az	Azerbaijan	ca	Canada	dj	Djibouti
ba	Bosnia and Hercegovina	cd	Congo, Dem. Republic of	dk	Denmark
bb	Barbados	cf	Central African Republic	dm	Dominica
bd	Bangladesh	cg	Congo, Republic of	do	Dominican Republic
be	Belgium	ch	Switzerland	dz	Algeria
bf	Burkina Faso	ci	Côte d'Ivoire	ec	Ecuador

* North Korea has no internet country code top-level domain, but .kp is reserved for the country

ee	Estonia	li	Liechtenstein	sa	Saudi Arabia
eg	Egypt	lk	Sri Lanka	sb	Solomon Islands
er	Eritrea	lr	Liberia	sc	Seychelles
es	Spain	ls	Lesotho	sd	Sudan
et	Ethiopia	lt	Lithuania	se	Sweden
eu	European Union	lu	Luxembourg	sg	Singapore
fi	Finland	lv	Latvia	si	Slovenia
fj	Fiji	ly	Libya	sk	Slovakia
fm	Micronesia, Federated States of	ma	Morocco	sl	Sierra Leone
fr	France	mc	Monaco	sn	Senegal
ga	Gabon	md	Moldova	so	Somalia
gd	Grenada	mg	Madagascar	sr	Suriname
ge	Georgia	mh	Marshall Islands	st	São Tomé and Príncipe
gh	Ghana	mk	Macedonia	sv	El Salvador
gm	The Gambia	ml	Mali	sy	Syria
gn	Guinea	mm	Myanmar	sz	Swaziland
gq	Equatorial Guinea	mn	Mongolia	td	Chad
gr	Greece	mr	Mauritania	tg	Togo
gt	Guatemala	mt	Malta	th	Thailand
gw	Guinea-Bissau	mu	Mauritius	tj	Tajikistan
gy	Guyana	mv	Maldives	tl	East Timor
hn	Honduras	mw	Malawi	tm	Turkmenistan
hr	Croatia	mx	Mexico	tn	Tunisia
ht	Haiti	my	Malaysia	to	Tonga
hu	Hungary	mz	Mozambique	tp	East Timor
id	Indonesia	na	Namibia	tr	Turkey
ie	Ireland	ne	Niger	tt	Trinidad and Tobago
il	Israel	ng	Nigeria	tv	Tuvalu
in	India	ni	Nicaragua	tw	Taiwan
iq	Iraq	nl	The Netherlands	tz	Tanzania
ir	Iran	no	Norway	ua	Ukraine
is	Iceland	np	Nepal	ug	Uganda
it	Italy	nz	New Zealand	uk	United Kingdom
jm	Jamaica	om	Oman	us	United States of America
jo	Jordan	pa	Panama	uy	Uruguay
jp	Japan	pe	Peru	uz	Uzbekistan
ke	Kenya	pg	Papua New Guinea	va	Vatican City State (Holy See)
kg	Kyrgyzstan	ph	The Philippines	vc	St Vincent and the Grenadines
kh	Cambodia	pk	Pakistan	ve	Venezuela
ki	Kiribati	pl	Poland	vn	Vietnam
km	The Comoros	pt	Portugal	vu	Vanuatu
kn	St Christopher and Nevis	pw	Palau	ws	Samoa
kr	Korea, Republic of	py	Paraguay	ye	Yemen
kw	Kuwait	qa	Qatar	yu	Montenegro; Serbia†
kz	Kazakhstan	ro	Romania	za	South Africa
la	Laos	ru	Russian Federation	zm	Zambia
lb	Lebanon	rw	Rwanda	zw	Zimbabwe

† Montenegro and Serbia have been assigned new codes, me and rs. They are not yet active as of April 2007

THE ENVIRONMENT

The 11 warmest years on record have all occurred in the last 12 years. The second half of the 20th century was the warmest period in the northern hemisphere for 1,300 years and Europe has warmed by about 1°C over the past 100 years according to the United Nations latest climate change report. The report also concludes that the frequency of extreme weather events has increased and regional climate patterns are changing. Heat waves and changes in storm tracks and precipitation can now be traced back to climate change caused by human activity. The European Environment Agency (EEA) has described climate change as Europe's most pressing challenge. Other areas of concern include biodiversity, marine ecosystems and land and water resources air pollution.

This year marks 35 years of environmental legislation. There is strong evidence that past regulation has worked. Water and air have been cleaned up, ozone-depleting substances have been phased out, and waste recycling has risen.

GLOBAL PRODUCTION OF CFCs: 1986–2004

Thousand (ODP) tonnes

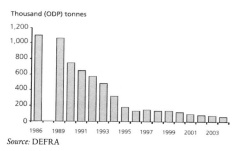

Source: DEFRA

However, these successes have been overshadowed by changes in personal consumption patterns. Europeans are living longer and more live alone, putting greater demands on living space. They travel further and more frequently and are consuming the planet's natural resources at twice the average global rate. Transport is the fastest growing contributor to greenhouse gas emissions and will continue to be for the foreseeable future. It is currently responsible for 21 per cent of total greenhouse gas emissions. Between 1990 and 2003, passenger transport volumes in Europe grew by 20 per cent and emissions from aviation increased by 86 per cent between 1990 and 2004.

With this in mind, attention is turning to individuals and to what they can do to reduce their carbon footprint. This is a measure of the amount of carbon dioxide emitted through the burning of fossil fuels as part of a person's daily life or, in the case of an organisation, as part of its everyday operations. The UK's carbon footprint is currently 648 million tonnes of CO_2 per year, according to the Carbon Trust. This means the average Briton's annual carbon footprint is 10.92 tonnes. By contrast, the average American generates 20 tonnes of carbon dioxide each year. Initiatives aimed at individuals are being launched, such as the UK's *We're in this together* campaign which aims to provide people with practical solutions to reduce their household emissions by a target of one tonne each over the next three years.

SELECTED UK TARGETS

AIR QUALITY AND ATMOSPHERE
• Reduce carbon dioxide emissions to 26–32 per cent below 1990 levels by 2020, and by 60 per cent by 2050
• Reduce emissions of volatile organic compounds by 40 per cent below 1990 levels by 2010
• UK to reduce greenhouse gas emission by 12.5 per cent below 1990 levels by 2008–12

FRESH WATER AND SEA
• All inland and coastal water to reach good status (ecological, chemical and quantitative) by 2015

WASTE
• Recycle or compost 40 per cent of household waste by 2010, 45 per cent by 2015 and 50 per cent by 2020.
• Reduce residual household waste by 29 per cent by 2010, 35 per cent by 2015 and 45 per cent by 2020 from 2000 levels
• Reduce commercial and industrial waste landfilled by 20 per cent by 2010, based on 2004 levels

ENERGY
• Provide 10 per cent of UK electricity from renewable sources by 2010 and 20 per cent by 2020
• Scotland to generate 18 per cent of electricity by 2010 from renewable sources, rising to 40 per cent by 2020
• 10 per cent use of bio-fuels by 2020

EUROPEAN UNION MEASURES

The EU is developing an interlinked set of policies – the sixth environment action programme, the Cardiff Process and the EU sustainable development strategy – that form the framework for more detailed strategies. The European Commission (EC) is also diversifying the methods it uses, in particular to include market-based instruments such as environmental taxes and voluntary measures. These are increasingly being used across Europe. At EU level, several are in use, such as the emissions trading scheme for greenhouse gas emissions.

The environment action programme began in the 1970s. The sixth of these, *Environment 2010: our future, our choice,* was adopted in 2001 and represents the cornerstone of EU policy. It focuses on four topics: climate change, nature and biodiversity, environment and health, and natural resources and waste.

EU environmental legislation is based on the principle that the polluter pays. The environmental liability directive, adopted in 2004, will be used to hold polluters financially liable for damage they cause. The EU is also attempting to look beyond current legislation. The prospective environmental analysis of land use development in Europe (PRELUDE) project looks at what Europe's society and environment might be like 30 years from now with the aim of illustrating key trends to support strategic decision making.

SUSTAINABLE DEVELOPMENT

The environmental agenda has become part of a wider move to address sustainability that incorporates social, environmental and economic development. During the world summit on sustainable development, held in Johannesburg in 2002, governments agreed on a series of commitments in five priority areas: water and sanitation, energy, health, agriculture and biodiversity. Targets and timetables approved included halving the number of people who lack access to clean water or proper sanitation by 2015, and reducing the rate of biodiversity loss by 2010. Following the summit, the UN commission on sustainable development agreed its programme for the next 15 years. In addition, 2005–15 has been named as 'water for life' decade.

The EU's latest sustainable development strategy, launched in 2005, focuses on climate change and clean energy; public health threats; social exclusion, demography and migration; management of natural resources; sustainable transport and global poverty and development. There are multiple links between these challenges; for example between the use of renewable energy and climate change or climate change and poverty.

In 2005, the UK government published *Securing the future*, its revised sustainable development strategy, alongside *Framework for sustainable development across the UK, our future – different paths*, shared between the government, the devolved administrations and the Northern Ireland office. The key aspects of the UK strategy include: a task force on sustainable public procurement that published a national action plan – *Procuring our future*, a scheme to enable government departments to offset the carbon impacts of their air travel; and *Together we can,* which enables groups to help influence authorities' sustainability strategies and development plans at a local level.

The Scottish Executive's vision, priorities and indicators for sustainable development are set out in *Choosing our future*, published in 2005. In October 2006, a new set of indicators was published to reflect the key outcomes in the strategy, including new measures on carbon emissions. The indicators are also more closely aligned to the joint UK framework for sustainable development.

The Welsh National Assembly published sustainability schemes in 2000 and 2004. Its programme for putting the new scheme into effect is set out in its *Sustainable development action plan 2004–2007.* Recommendations for a full set of sustainable development indicators were accepted in 2006.

WASTE

Waste policy in the UK follows a number of principles: the waste hierarchy of reduce, reuse, recycle, dispose; the proximity principle of disposing of waste close to its generation; and national self-sufficiency. EU directives play an important role in driving UK policy, particularly regarding commercial and industrial waste. For example, in response to the landfill directive, adopted in July 1999, the government established a landfill allowance trading scheme, under which the amount of biodegradable municipal waste local authorities can dispose of in landfill sites is limited. These landfill allowances are tradable and authorities can buy, sell or save surplus allowances.

The proposed European integrated products policy aims to internalise the environmental costs of products throughout their life cycle using market forces, by focusing on eco-design and incentives to ensure increased demand for greener products. The policy will culminate in 2007 with the identification of a first set of products with the greatest potential for environmental improvement.

The EU is already addressing greater responsibility for end-of-life products. Producer responsibility directives, which had to be enacted in member states by August 2004, include: the directive for packaging waste; the end-of-life vehicle directive; and directives on waste from electrical and electronic equipment (and on the restriction of the use of certain hazardous substances in such equipment). The directive on batteries has also been adopted, requiring all batteries on the EU market to be collected and recycled.

The proportion of household waste recycled (including composting) in the UK has been steadily increasing, from 22.5 per cent in 2004–5 to 26.7 per cent in 2005–6. Scotland recycled 24.4 per cent of municipal waste in 2005–6, up from 17.3 per cent in the previous year. However, the total amount of waste produced per person per year has grown from 450kg in 1995–6 to 517 in 2004–5.

UK HOUSEHOLD WASTE AND RECYCLING

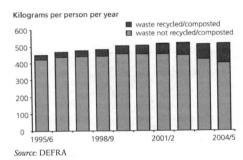

Kilograms per person per year

■ waste recycled/composted
▨ waste not recycled/composted

Source: DEFRA

In May 2007, the UK government published a new waste strategy. Targets for household recycling have been increased significantly and there is a strong emphasis on waste prevention with a new target to help measure waste reduction. Businesses will also have a greater responsibility to minimise and recycle packaging. In addition, the government aims to increase the amount of energy produced from waste schemes. Meanwhile, in March 2006, Northern Ireland launched a new waste management strategy – *Towards resource management* – that outlines plans to modernise waste management policies.

CLIMATE CHANGE AND AIR POLLUTION

The UK's response to climate change has been driven by the UN framework convention on climate change. This is a binding agreement that came into force in March 1994. It aims to reduce the risks of global warming by limiting greenhouse gas emissions.

Progress towards the convention's targets is assessed at regular conferences. In 1997, the Kyoto protocol was adopted. It covers the six main greenhouse gases – carbon dioxide, methane, nitrous oxide, hydrofluorocarbons (HFCs), perfluorocarbons (PFCs) and sulphur hexafluoride. Under the protocol, industrialised countries agreed to legally binding targets for cutting emissions of greenhouse gases by 5.2 per cent below 1990 levels by 2008–12. EU members agreed to an 8 per cent reduction and the UK to 12.5 per cent. The new EU member states have all ratified the protocol and have their own targets of between 6 and 8 per cent. The protocol entered into force in 2005 after it was ratified by Russia; the USA and Australia have stated that they will not ratify the treaty. The EC expects the EU to meet its Kyoto targets, provided all the measures in the pipeline are implemented. The UK is currently on course to meet its Kyoto target. In 2005, emissions of the six greenhouse gases were 15.3 per cent below 1990 levels, and 18.8 per cent below when the effect of the EU emissions trading scheme is taken into account, against the Kyoto target of 12.5 per cent.

In the new member states, emissions have declined substantially. In 2004, emissions were 23 per cent below 1990 levels. This is mainly due to the restructuring or closure of heavily polluting and energy-intensive industries. Greenhouse gas emissions from transport decreased by 5 per cent between 1990 and 1995 but increased after 1995. In 2004, they exceeded 1990 levels by 28 per cent.

EU EMISSIONS OF GREENHOUSE GASES AGAINST KYOTO PROTOCOL TARGET

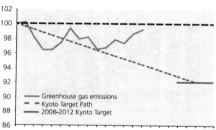

Source: DEFRA

The EC launched a second European climate change programme in 2005 that places a greater emphasis on adaptation to climate change. There are five working groups in this programme: review of the first climate change programme; carbon dioxide capture and geological storage; impacts and adaptation; aviation; and carbon dioxide and cars.

In January, the EC set out proposals and options for keeping climate change to manageable levels in *Limiting global climate change to 2° Celsius: the way ahead for 2020 and beyond*. This is part of a package of measures to establish a new energy policy for Europe. It also contributes to the international discussions on a future global agreement to combat climate change after 2012, when the Kyoto emissions targets expire. An EC impact assessment says investment in a low-carbon economy will require about 0.5 per cent of global GDP over the period 2013–20, compared with the government commissioned Stern Review's estimate that uncontrolled climate change will cost 5–20 per cent of GDP in the longer term.

The EU's national emission ceilings directive sets upper limits for each member state for the total emissions in 2010 of the four pollutants responsible for acidification, eutrophication and ground-level ozone pollution (sulphur dioxide, nitrogen oxides, volatile organic compounds and ammonia), but leaves it largely to the member states to decide which measures to take in order to comply.

In March 2007, the EU heads of state and government agreed a firm target of cutting 20 per cent of the EU's greenhouse gas emissions by 2020, rising to 30 per cent if the USA, Canada and India make similar commitments.

Current measures to tackle climate change in the UK are covered by a programme launched in March 2006. The measures to reduce emissions target every sector of the economy and include: a stricter cap for industry; measures to encourage the uptake of biofuels in petrol; tighter building regulations; measures to improve household energy efficiency; a renewed emphasis on encouraging and enabling the general public, businesses and public authorities to help achieve the government's targets; and increased levels of micro-generation. The programme is expected to reduce the UK's emissions of greenhouse gases to 23–25 per cent below base year levels and reduce the UK's carbon dioxide emissions to 15–18 per cent below 1990 levels by 2010. However, higher than anticipated levels of economic growth and the recent rises in global energy prices, which in turn have altered the relative price of coal and gas, have led to increased emissions and have made the target more challenging. The government recently admitted that the 2010 target is looking increasingly difficult to achieve.

In March, the UK government issued a draft climate change bill. The bill, and the accompanying strategy, set out a framework to move the UK to a low-carbon economy. The bill proposes a legally binding target of a 60 per cent reduction in carbon dioxide emissions below 1990 levels by 2050 with an interim target of a reduction of 26–32 per cent over the period 2008–12. It also proposes five-year carbon budgets. These will require the government to set binding limits on CO_2 emissions during five-year budget periods.

Scotland launched its new climate change programme – *Changing our ways* – in March 2006. It quantifies in carbon terms the contribution Scotland must make towards UK commitments to reduce greenhouse gases. The Scottish share has been calculated at 1.7 million tonnes of carbon savings by 2010. The Scottish Executive will report annually on progress with the climate change programme. The first report was published in March 2007 and showed that in the first year, Scotland had increased investment in renewable technology and met its renewable energy target for 2010 ahead of schedule.

WATER

Water quality targets are set at both EU and UK level for drinking water sources, wastewater discharges, rivers, coastal water and bathing water. The EU's water framework directive, which entered into force in 2000, aims to achieve 'good' water status throughout the EU by 2015. Member states are obliged to monitor and assess groundwater quality on the basis of common criteria and to identify and reverse trends in groundwater pollution. Information on local water quality can be obtained from the water information system for Europe (WISE), a new interactive internet tool, run by the EC.

Under the UK Water Act of 2003, a new water services regulatory authority replaced OFWAT in April 2006, although it carries the same name. The Water Environment and Water Services Bill for Scotland also completed its passage through the Scottish parliament in 2003. It established a source-to-sea planning framework for river basin management.

The EC has adopted a new bathing water directive in February, which sets a tighter bathing water quality standard than the previous directive. Results for 2006 show that only two out of the 413 bathing areas monitored in the UK failed to meet the directive's minimum requirements, while 75 per cent met the tighter standard. These figures show a great improvement since the early 1990s, when less than a third of England's beaches reached the toughest standards. Scotland has a new better bathing waters strategy to raise standards to meet the European directive.

UK COMPLIANCE WITH BATHING WATER STANDARDS

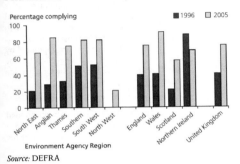

Percentage complying ■ 1996 □ 2005

Environment Agency Region

Source: DEFRA

The Environment Agency sets river quality objectives for each stretch of river. In 2005, 72 per cent of rivers were of good quality, compared with 69 per cent in 2000. Between 1990 and 2005, the biological quality of 31 per cent of rivers improved. Most of this improvement occurred in the first five years and has since levelled off. In some places, such as parts of Wales, biological quality has deteriorated since 1995.

The European urban waste water treatment directive sets minimum standards for sewage treatment before discharge into coastal waters, with the levels of treatment needed depending on the sensitivity of the receiving water.

ENERGY

Energy used in the home is responsible for 25 per cent of the UK's carbon dioxide emissions. In 2003, the UK government published a white paper, *Our energy future – creating a low carbon economy*, setting out a long-term strategy for UK energy policy to 2050, combining environmental, competitiveness, social and security of supply goals. It built on the Performance and Innovation Unit's *Energy review*, published a year earlier. An energy bill was also introduced in 2003.

In 2004 the government launched its *UK international priorities – the energy strategy*, which set out how it plans to meet the international energy challenge over the next five to ten years. The UK has a target to increase the contribution of renewables to 10 per cent of electricity by 2010, with an aspiration to reach 20 per cent by 2020. Renewables capacity is increasing. By the beginning of 2006, the UK installed over 1,300MW of wind capacity.

In July 2006, the UK government published its third annual report on the implementation of the white paper. This detailed the progress made and summarised the way ahead to achieving the four energy policy goals – cutting carbon dioxide emissions, maintaining reliable energy supplies, promoting competitive energy markets, and ensuring homes are affordably heated.

Also in July, the government published its report on the *Energy review – The energy challenge*. Proposals to tackle climate change by reducing carbon dioxide emissions and to deliver secure, clean energy and affordable prices will feed into the energy white paper. The paper was due in 2007, but was delayed by a court ruling, following legal action by Greenpeace, which found that consultation on nuclear power prior to the review being published was inadequate.

A new framework directive for eco-design for energy-using products will set efficiency standards for household items such as boilers, computers and washing machines, as well as commercial equipment and component parts. The EU's renewables directive has been in place since 2001. It aims to increase the EU's share of electricity produced from renewable energy sources to 21 per cent by 2010 (up from 15.2 per cent in 2001). However, current figures show it will fall short, reaching 19 per cent by 2010.

ENVIRONMENT AND HEALTH

Concerns about the impact of pollution on health are covered in the *Environment and health action plan 2004–10*, launched in 2004. The plan proposes an integrated approach involving closer cooperation between the health, environment and research areas.

A new chemicals policy, under which industry will have to provide information on the effects of chemicals on human health and the environment, as well as on safe ways of handling them, has also been set up. It replaces 40 existing pieces of legislation and will be managed by a new European Chemicals Agency, in Helsinki. It will enter into force in 2007.

CONTACTS

DEPARTMENT OF ENVIRONMENT, FOOD AND RURAL AFFAIRS
Eastbury House, 30–34 Albert Embankment, London SE1 7TL
T 08459-335577 W www.defra.gov.uk

DEPARTMENT OF THE ENVIRONMENT, NORTHERN IRELAND
Clarence Court, 10–18 Adelaide Street, Belfast BT2 8GB
T 028-9054 0540 W www.doeni.gov.uk

ENVIRONMENT AGENCY
Rio House, Almondsbury, Bristol BS32 4UD T 08708-506506
W www.environment-agency.gov.uk

EUROPEAN ENVIRONMENT AGENCY
Kongens Nytorv 6, DK-1050 Copenhagen K, Denmark
W www.eea.europa.eu

ROYAL COMMISSION ON ENVIRONMENTAL POLLUTION
Third Floor, The Sanctuary, London SW1P 3JS T 020-7799 8970
W www.rcep.org.uk

SCOTTISH EXECUTIVE, ENVIRONMENT AND RURAL AFFAIRS DEPARTMENT
Pentland House, 47 Robb's Loan, Edinburgh EH14 1TY
T 0131-556 8400 W www.scotland.gov.uk

CONSERVATION AND HERITAGE

NATIONAL PARKS

ENGLAND AND WALES

With the designation of the New Forest as a national park on 1 March 2005, there are now eight national parks in England and three in Wales. In addition, the Norfolk and Suffolk Broads are considered to have equivalent status to a national park. Under the provisions of the National Parks and Access to the Countryside Act 1949, as clarified by the Natural Environment and Rural Communities Act 2006, areas designated as national parks have a statutory requirement to conserve and protect scenic landscapes from inappropriate development and to provide access to the land for public enjoyment.

Natural England (formerly the Countryside Agency) is the statutory body which has the power to designate national parks in England, and the Countryside Council for Wales is responsible for national parks in Wales. Designations in England are confirmed by the Secretary of State for Environment, Food and Rural Affairs and those in Wales by the National Assembly for Wales. The designation of a national park does not affect the ownership of the land or remove the rights of the local community. The majority of the land in the national parks is owned by private landowners (74 per cent) or by bodies such as the National Trust (7 per cent) and the Forestry Commission (7 per cent). The national park authorities own only around 2 per cent of the land.

The Environment Act 1995 replaced the existing national park boards and committees with free-standing national park authorities (NPAs). NPAs are the sole local planning authorities for their areas and as such influence land use and development, and deal with planning applications. Their duties include conserving and enhancing the natural beauty, wildlife and cultural heritage of the parks; promoting opportunities for public understanding and enjoyment; and fostering the economic and social well-being of the communities within national parks. The NPAs publish management plans as statements of their policies and appoint their own officers and staff.

The Broads Authority was established under the Norfolk and Suffolk Broads Act 1998 and meets the requirement for the authority to have a navigation function in addition to a regard for the needs of agriculture, forestry and the economic and social interests of those who live or work in the Broads.

The New Forest NPA was established on 1 April 2005. Following an interim year, in which the authority had a limited range of statutory powers and functions, it became fully operational on 1 April 2006.

MEMBERSHIP

Membership of English NPAs comprises local authority appointees, members directly appointed by the environment secretary of state and members appointed by him after a consultation with local parishes. Under the Natural Environment and Rural Communities Act 2006 every district, county or unitary authority with land in a national park is entitled to appoint at least one member unless it chooses to opt out. The total number of local authority and parish members must exceed the number of national members. Since 1 April 2007 all NPAs have 22 members, except for the Peak District which has 30.

The Broads Authority has 21 members: nine appointed by the constituent local authorities, two appointed by the Navigation Committee and ten appointed by the Secretary of State. The Secretary of State's appointees include at least three which are appointed after consultation with representatives of boating interests and at least two which are appointed after consultation with representatives of landowning and farming interests.

In Wales two-thirds of NPA members are appointed by the constituent local authorities and one-third by the Welsh Assembly Government, advised by the Countryside Council for Wales.

FUNDING

The English NPAs and the Broads Authority are funded by central government. In the financial year 2007–8 a core grant totalling £44.24m was allocated between the authorities.

In Wales, national parks are funded via a grant from the National Assembly. In addition, the three Welsh NPAs can levy a further third of their monies from their constituent local authorities.

All NPAs and the Broads Authority can take advantage of grants from other bodies including lottery and European grants.

The national parks (with date designation confirmed) are:

BRECON BEACONS (1957), Powys (66 per cent)/Carmarthenshire/Rhondda, Cynon and Taff/Merthyr Tydfil/Blaenau Gwent/Monmouthshire, 1,344 sq. km/519 sq. miles – The park is centred on the Beacons, Pen y Fan, Corn Du and Cribyn, but also includes the valley of the Usk, the Black Mountains to the east and the Black Mountain to the west. There are information centres at the national park visitor centre near Libanus, Abergavenny, Llandovery and Craig-y-nos Country Park.
National Park Authority, Plas y Ffynnon, Cambrian Way, Brecon, Powys LD3 7HP T 01874-624437
E enquiries@breconbeacons.org
W www.breconbeacons.org
Chief Executive, Christopher Gledhill

BROADS (1989), Norfolk/Suffolk, 303 sq. km/117 sq. miles – The Broads are located between Norwich and Great Yarmouth on the flood plains of the six rivers flowing through the area to the sea. The area is one of fens, winding waterways, woodland and marsh. The 60 or so broads are man-made, and many are connected to the rivers by dykes, providing over 200km of navigable waterways. There are information centres at Beccles, Hoveton, Potter Heigham, Ranworth, Whitlingham and Toad Hole Cottage at How Hill.
Broads Authority, 18 Colegate, Norwich NR3 1BQ
T 01603-610734 E broads@broads-authority.gov.uk
W www.broads-authority.gov.uk
Chief Executive, Dr John Packman

DARTMOOR (1951), Devon, 954 sq. km/368 sq. miles – The park consists of moorland and rocky granite tors, and is rich in prehistoric remains. There are information centres at Haytor, Newbridge, Princetown (main visitor centre) and Postbridge.

National Park Authority, Parke, Bovey Tracey, Devon TQ13 9JQ T 01626-832093 E hq@dartmoor-npa.gov.uk W www.dartmoor-npa.gov.uk

Chief Executive, Kevin Bishop, PHD

EXMOOR (1954), Somerset (71 per cent)/Devon, 693 sq. km/267 sq. miles – Exmoor is a moorland plateau inhabited by wild Exmoor ponies and red deer. There are many ancient remains and burial mounds. There are national park centres at Dunster, Dulverton and Combe Martin.

National Park Authority, Exmoor House, Dulverton, Somerset TA22 9HL T 01398-323665 E info@exmoor-nationalpark.gov.uk W www.exmoor-nationalpark.gov.uk

Chief Executive/National Park Officer, Dr Nigel Stone

LAKE DISTRICT (1951), Cumbria, 2,292 sq. km/885 sq. miles – The Lake District includes England's highest mountains (Scafell Pike, Helvellyn and Skiddaw) but it is most famous for its glaciated lakes. There are national park information centres at Bowness Bay, Keswick, Glenridding and a visitor centre at Brockhole, Windermere.

National Park Authority, Murley Moss, Oxenholme Road, Kendal, Cumbria LA9 7RL T 01539-724555 E hq@lake-district.gov.uk W www.lake-district.gov.uk

National Park Officer, Richard Leafe

NEW FOREST (2005), Hampshire, 567 sq. km/219 sq. miles – The forest has been protected since 1079 when it was declared a royal hunting forest. The area consists of forest, ancient woodland and heathland. Much of the forest is managed by the Forestry Commission, which provides several campsites. The main villages are Brockenhurst, Burley and Lyndhurst, which has a visitor centre.

National Park Authority, South Efford House, Milford Road, Lymington, Hants SO41 0JD T 01590-646600 E enquiries@newforestnpa.gov.uk W www.newforestnpa.gov.uk

Chief Executive, Lindsay Cornish

NORTH YORK MOORS (1952), North Yorkshire (96 per cent)/Redcar and Cleveland, 1,432 sq. km/554 sq. miles – The park consists of woodland and moorland, and includes the Hambleton Hills and the Cleveland Way. There are information centres at Danby, Sutton Bank and at the Old Coastguard Station in Robin Hood's Bay.

National Park Authority, The Old Vicarage, Bondgate, Helmsley, York YO6 5BP T 01439-770657 E general@northyorkmoors-npa.gov.uk W www.moors.uk.net

Chief Executive/National Park Officer, Andrew Wilson

NORTHUMBERLAND (1956), Northumberland, 1,049 sq. km/405 sq. miles – The park is an area of hill country stretching from Hadrian's Wall to the Scottish border. There are information centres at Ingram, Once Brewed and Rothbury.

National Park Authority, Eastburn, South Park, Hexham, Northumberland NE46 1BS T 01434-605555 E admin@nnpa.org.uk W www.northumberlandnationalpark.org.uk

Chief Executive, Tony Gates

PEAK DISTRICT (1951), Derbyshire (64 per cent)/Staffordshire/South Yorkshire/Cheshire/West Yorkshire/Greater Manchester, 1,438 sq. km/555 sq. miles – The Peak District includes the gritstone moors of the 'Dark Peak' and the limestone dales of the 'White Peak'. There are information centres at Bakewell, Castleton, Edale and Upper Derwent.

National Park Authority, Aldern House, Baslow Road, Bakewell, Derbyshire DE45 1AE T 01629-816200 E customer.service@peakdistrict.gov.uk W www.peakdistrict.gov.uk

Chief Executive, Jim Dixon

PEMBROKESHIRE COAST (1952 and 1995), Pembrokeshire, 620 sq. km/240 sq. miles – The park includes cliffs, moorland and a number of islands, including Skomer. There are information centres at St David's, Newport and Tenby.

National Park Authority, Llanion Park, Pembroke Dock, Pembrokeshire SA72 6DY T 0845-345 7275 E info@pembrokeshirecoast.org.uk W www.pcnpa.org.uk

Chief Executive (National Park Officer), Nic Wheeler

SNOWDONIA/ERYRI (1951), Gwynedd/Conwy, 2,132 sq. km/823 sq. miles – Snowdonia is an area of deep valleys and rugged mountains. There are information centres at Aberdyfi, Beddgelert, Betws y Coed, Blaenau Ffestiniog, Dolgellau and Harlech.

National Park Authority, Penrhyndeudraeth, Gwynedd LL48 6LF T 01766-770274 E parc@eryri-npa.gov.uk W www.eryri-npa.gov.uk

Chief Executive, Aneurin Phillips

YORKSHIRE DALES (1954), North Yorkshire (88 per cent)/Cumbria, 1,762 sq. km/680 sq. miles – The Yorkshire Dales are composed primarily of limestone overlaid in places by millstone grit. The three peaks of Ingleborough, Whernside and Pen-y-Ghent are within the park. There are information centres at Grassington, Hawes, Aysgarth Falls, Malham and Reeth.

National Park Authority, Yoredale, Bainbridge, Leyburn, N. Yorks DL8 3EL T 0870-1666333 E info@yorkshiredales.org.uk W www.yorkshiredales.org.uk

Chief Executive, David Butterworth

In 1999 the Countryside Agency began the process of designating the South Downs (within the Sussex Downs and East Hampshire 'Areas of Outstanding Natural Beauty') as a national park. A designation order for a South Downs national park was submitted by the Countryside Agency to the Secretary of State on 27 January 2003. In February 2006 the designation process was indefinitely postponed following a high court judgement (the 'Meyrick' judgement) regarding part of the 2005 New Forest designation which changed the way in which criteria for national park status had generally been understood. The Department for Environment, Food and Rural Affairs (DEFRA) clarified the national parks legislation through the Natural Environment and Rural Communities Act 2006 and the South Downs designation process was restarted in March 2007.

THE SOUTH DOWNS, West Sussex/Hampshire,1,637 sq. km/632 sq. miles – The South Downs contains a diversity of natural habitats, including flower-studded chalk grassland, ancient woodland, flood meadow, lowland heath and rare chalk heathland.

South Downs Joint Committee, Victorian Barn, Victorian Business Centre, Ford Lane, Ford, Arundel, W. Sussex BN18 0EF T 01243-558700 E comms@southdowns-aonb.gov.uk

South Downs Officer, Martin Beaton

SCOTLAND
On 9 August 2000 the national parks (Scotland) bill received royal assent, giving parliament the ability to

create national parks in Scotland. The first two Scottish national parks, Loch Lomond and the Trossachs and the Cairngorms, became operational in 2002 and 2003 respectively. The Act gives Scottish parks wider powers than in England and Wales, including statutory responsibilities for the economy and rural communities. The board of each Scottish NPA consists of 25 members, of which five are directly elected by a postal ballot of the local electorate. The remaining 20 members, ten of which are nominated by the constituent local authorities, are chosen by the Scottish ministers. In Scotland, the national parks are central government bodies and wholly funded by the Scottish Executive. Funding for 2007–8 totals £11.4m with £6.9m allocated to Loch Lomond and the Trossachs and £4.5m to the Cairngorms.

CAIRNGORMS (2003), Morayshire, 3,800 sq. km/1,466 sq. miles – The Cairngorms national park is the largest in the UK. It displays a vast collection of landforms and includes four of Scotland's highest mountains.
National Park Authority, 14 The Square, Grantown-on-Spey, Morayshire PH26 3HG T 01479-873535
E enquiries@cairngorms.co.uk W www.cairngorms.co.uk
Chief Executive, Jane Hope
LOCH LOMOND AND THE TROSSACHS (2002), Argyll and Bute/Perth and Kinross/Stirling/West Dunbartonshire, 1,865 sq. km/720 sq. miles – The park boundaries encompass lochs, rivers, forests, 20 mountains above 3,000ft including Ben More and a further 20 mountains between 2,500ft and 3,000ft.
National Park Authority, The Old Station, Balloch Road, Balloch G83 8BF T 01389-722600
E info@lochlomond-trossachs.org
W www.lochlomond-trossachs.org
Chief Executive, William Dalrymple

NORTHERN IRELAND
There is a power to designate national parks in Northern Ireland under the Nature Conservation and Amenity Lands Order (Northern Ireland) 1985, but there are currently no national parks in Northern Ireland.

AREAS OF OUTSTANDING NATURAL BEAUTY

ENGLAND AND WALES
Under the National Parks and Access to the Countryside Act 1949, provision was made for the designation of areas of outstanding natural beauty (AONBs). Natural England (formerly the Countryside Agency) is responsible for AONBs in England and the Countryside Council for Wales for the Welsh AONBs. Designations in England are confirmed by the Secretary of State for Environment, Food and Rural Affairs and those in Wales by the National Assembly for Wales. The Countryside and Rights of Way (CROW) Act 2000 placed greater responsibility on local authorities to protect AONBs and made it a statutory duty for relevant authorities to produce a management plan for their AONB area. The CROW Act also provided for the creation of conservation boards for larger and more complex AONBs. The first two conservation boards for the Cotswolds and Chilterns AONBs were established in July 2004 following confirmation by the secretary of state.

The primary objective of the AONB designation is to conserve and enhance the natural beauty of the area. Where an AONB has a conservation board, it has the additional purpose of increasing public understanding and enjoyment of the special qualities of the area, with the first purpose having greater weight, if there should be a conflict of interests between the two. In addition to the above, the board is also required to foster the economic and social well-being of the local communities but without incurring significant expenditure in doing so. Overall responsibility for AONBs lies with the relevant local authorities or conservation board. To coordinate planning and management responsibilities between local authorities in whose area they fall, AONBs are overseen by a joint advisory committee (or similar body) which includes representatives from the local authorities, landowners, farmers, residents and conservation and recreation groups. In addition, an AONB officer is appointed to oversee matters. Core funding for AONBs is provided by central government through Natural England and the Countryside Council for Wales.

The 40 Areas of Outstanding Natural Beauty (with date designation confirmed) are:

ARNSIDE AND SILVERDALE (1972), Cumbria/Lancashire, 75 sq. km/29 sq. miles
BLACKDOWN HILLS (1991), Devon/Somerset, 370 sq. km/143 sq. miles
CANNOCK CHASE (1958), Staffordshire, 68 sq. km/26 sq. miles
CHICHESTER HARBOUR (1964), Hampshire/West Sussex, 74 sq. km/29 sq. miles
CHILTERNS (1965; extended 1990), Bedfordshire/Buckinghamshire/Herefordshire/Oxfordshire, 833 sq. km/322 sq. miles
CLWYDIAN RANGE (1985), Denbighshire/Flintshire, 157 sq. km/61 sq. miles
CORNWALL (1959; Camel Estuary 1983), 958 sq. km/370 sq. miles
COTSWOLDS (1966; extended 1990), Gloucestershire/Oxfordshire/Warwickshire/Wiltshire/Worcestershire, 2,038 sq. km/787 sq. miles
CRANBORNE CHASE AND WEST WILTSHIRE DOWNS (1983), Dorset/Hampshire/Somerset/Wiltshire, 983 sq. km/380 sq. miles
DEDHAM VALE (1970; extended 1978, 1991), Essex/Suffolk, 90 sq. km/35 sq. miles
DORSET (1959), Dorset/Somerset, 1,129 sq. km/436 sq. miles
EAST DEVON (1963), 268 sq. km/103 sq. miles
EAST HAMPSHIRE (1962), 383 sq. km/148 sq. miles
FOREST OF BOWLAND (1964), Lancashire/North Yorkshire, 802 sq. km/310 sq. miles
GOWER (1956), Swansea, 188 sq. km/73 sq. miles
HIGH WEALD (1983), East Sussex/Kent/Surrey/West Sussex, 1,460 sq. km/564 sq. miles
HOWARDIAN HILLS (1987), North Yorkshire, 204 sq. km/79 sq. miles
ISLE OF WIGHT (1963), 189 sq. km/73 sq. miles
ISLES OF SCILLY (1976), 16 sq. km/6 sq. miles
KENT DOWNS (1968), 878 sq. km/339 sq. miles
LINCOLNSHIRE WOLDS (1973), 558 sq. km/215 sq. miles
LLEYN (1957), Gwynedd, 161 sq. km/62 sq. miles
MALVERN HILLS (1959), Gloucestershire/Worcestershire, 150 sq. km/58 sq. miles
MENDIP HILLS (1972; extended 1989), Somerset, 198 sq. km/76 sq. miles
NIDDERDALE (1994), North Yorkshire, 603 sq. km/233 sq. miles

NORFOLK COAST (1968), 451 sq. km/174 sq. miles
NORTH DEVON (1960), 171 sq. km/66 sq. miles
NORTH PENNINES (1988), Cumbria/Durham/North
   Yorkshire/Northumberland, 1,983 sq. km/766 sq.
   miles
NORTH WESSEX DOWNS (1972), Hampshire/
   Oxfordshire/Wiltshire, 1,730 sq. km/668 sq. miles
NORTHUMBERLAND COAST (1958), 135 sq. km/52
   sq. miles
QUANTOCK HILLS (1957), Somerset, 99 sq. km/38 sq.
   miles
SHROPSHIRE HILLS (1959), 804 sq. km/310 sq. miles
SOLWAY COAST (1964), Cumbria, 115 sq. km/44 sq.
   miles
SOUTH DEVON (1960), 337 sq. km/130 sq. miles
SUFFOLK COAST AND HEATHS (1970), 403 sq.
   km/156 sq. miles
SURREY HILLS (1958), 419 sq. km/162 sq. miles
SUSSEX DOWNS (1966), 983 sq. km/379 sq. miles
TAMAR VALLEY (1995), Cornwall/Devon, 195 sq.
   km/75 sq. miles
WYE VALLEY (1971), Gloucestershire/
   Herefordshire/Monmouthshire, 326 sq. km/126 sq.
   miles
YNYS MON (ISLE OF ANGLESEY) (1967), 221 sq.
   km/85 sq. miles

NORTHERN IRELAND
The Department of the Environment for Northern
Ireland, with advice from the Council for Nature
Conservation and the Countryside, designates Areas of
Outstanding Natural Beauty in Northern Ireland. At
present there are nine and these cover a total area of 2,849
sq. km (1,100 sq. miles). Dates given are those of
designation.

ANTRIM COAST AND GLENS (1988), Co. Antrim, 706
   sq. km/272 sq. miles
BINEVENAGH (2006), Co. Londonderry, 166 sq.
   km/64 sq. miles
CAUSEWAY COAST (1989), Co. Antrim, 42 sq. km/16
   sq. miles
LAGAN VALLEY (1965), Co. Down, 21 sq. km/8 sq.
   miles
LECALE COAST (1967), Co. Down, 31 sq. km/12 sq.
   miles
MOURNE (1986), Co. Down, 570 sq. km/220 sq. miles
RING OF GULLION (1991), Co. Armagh, 154 sq.
   km/59 sq. miles
SPERRIN (1968), Co. Tyrone/Co. Londonderry, 1,010
   sq. km/390 sq. miles
STRANGFORD LOUGH (1972), Co. Down, 186 sq.
   km/72 sq. miles

NATIONAL SCENIC AREAS

In Scotland, national scenic areas have a broadly
equivalent status to AONBs. Scottish Natural Heritage
recognises areas of national scenic significance. At the end
of June 2007 there were 40, covering a total area of
1,001,800 hectares (2,475,443 acres).

Development within national scenic areas is dealt with
by local authorities, who are required to consult Scottish
Natural Heritage concerning certain categories of
development. Disagreements between Scottish Natural
Heritage and local authorities are referred to the Scottish
Executive. Land management uses can also be modified in
the interest of scenic conservation.

ASSYNT-COIGACH, Highland, 90,200 ha/222,884
   acres
BEN NEVIS AND GLEN COE, Highland, 101,600
   ha/251,053 acres
CAIRNGORM MOUNTAINS, Highland/
   Aberdeenshire/Moray, 67,200 ha/166,051 acres
CUILLIN HILLS, Highland, 21,900 ha/54,115 acres
DEESIDE AND LOCHNAGAR, Aberdeenshire, 40,000
   ha/98,840 acres
DORNOCH FIRTH, Highland, 7,500 ha/18,532 acres
EAST STEWARTRY COAST, Dumfries and Galloway,
   4,500 ha/11,119 acres
EILDON AND LEADERFOOT, Borders, 3,600
   ha/8,896 acres
FLEET VALLEY, Dumfries and Galloway, 5,300
   ha/13,096 acres
GLEN AFFRIC, Highland, 19,300 ha/47,690 acres
GLEN STRATHFARRAR, Highland, 3,800 ha/9,390
   acres
HOY AND WEST MAINLAND, Orkney Islands, 14,800
   ha/36,571 acres
JURA, Argyll and Bute, 21,800 ha/53,868 acres
KINTAIL, Highland, 15,500 ha/38,300 acres
KNAPDALE, Argyll and Bute, 19,800 ha/48,926 acres
KNOYDART, Highland, 39,500 ha/97,604 acres
KYLE OF TONGUE, Highland, 18,500 ha/45,713 acres
KYLES OF BUTE, Argyll and Bute, 4,400 ha/10,872
   acres
LOCH NA KEAL, Mull, Argyll and Bute, 12,700
   ha/31,382 acres
LOCH LOMOND, Argyll and Bute, 27,400 ha/67,705
   acres
LOCH RANNOCH AND GLEN LYON, Perthshire and
   Kinross, 48,400 ha/119,596 acres
LOCH SHIEL, Highland, 13,400 ha/33,111 acres
LOCH TUMMEL, Perthshire and Kinross, 9,200
   ha/22,733 acres
LYNN OF LORN, Argyll and Bute, 4,800 ha/11,861
   acres
MORAR, MOIDART AND ARDNAMURCHAN,
   Highland, 13,500 ha/33,358 acres
NITH ESTUARY, Dumfries and Galloway, 9,300
   ha/22,980 acres
NORTH ARRAN, North Ayrshire, 23,800 ha/58,810
   acres
NORTH-WEST SUTHERLAND, Highland, 20,500
   ha/50,655 acres
RIVER EARN, Perthshire and Kinross, 3,000 ha/7,413
   acres
RIVER TAY, Perthshire and Kinross, 5,600 ha/13,838
   acres
ST KILDA, Eilean Siar (Western Isles), 900 ha/2,224
   acres
SCARBA, LUNGA AND THE GARVELLACHS, Argyll
   and Bute, 1,900 ha/4,695 acres
SHETLAND, Shetland Isles, 11,600 ha/28,664 acres
SMALL ISLANDS, Highland, 15,500 ha/38,300 acres
SOUTH LEWIS, HARRIS AND NORTH UIST, Eilean
   Siar (Western Isles), 109,600 ha/270,822 acres
SOUTH UIST MACHAIR, Eilean Siar (Western Isles),
   6,100 ha/15,073 acres
THE TROSSACHS, Stirling, 4,600 ha/11,367 acres
TROTTERNISH, Highland, 5,000 ha/12,355 acres
UPPER TWEEDDALE, Borders, 10,500 ha/25,945
   acres
WESTER ROSS, Highland, 145,300 ha/359,036
   acres

THE NATIONAL FOREST

The National Forest is being planted across 517 sq. km (200 sq. miles) of Derbyshire, Leicestershire and Staffordshire. Seven million trees, of mixed species but mainly broadleaved, covering over 5,400 hectares (13,300 acres) have been planted. The aim is to eventually cover about one-third of the designated area.

The project was developed in 1992–5 by the Countryside Commission and is now run by the National Forest Company, which was established in April 1995. The National Forest Company is responsible for the delivery of the government-approved National Forest Strategy and is funded by the DEFRA.

NATIONAL FOREST COMPANY, Enterprise Glade, Bath Lane, Moira, Swadlincote, Derbyshire DE12 6BD
T 01283-551211 E enquiries@nationalforest.org
W www.nationalforest.org
Chief Executive, Sophie Churchill

SITES OF SPECIAL SCIENTIFIC INTEREST

Site of special scientific interest (SSSI) is a legal notification applied to land in England, Scotland or Wales which Natural England (NE) (formerly English Nature), Scottish Natural Heritage (SNH) or the Countryside Council for Wales (CCW) identifies as being of special interest because of its flora, fauna, geological, geomorphological or physiographical features. In some cases, SSSIs are managed as nature reserves.

NE, SNH and CCW must notify the designation of an SSSI to the local planning authority, every owner/occupier of the land, and the environment secretary, the Scottish ministers or the National Assembly for Wales. Forestry and agricultural departments and a number of other interested parties are also formally notified.

Objections to the notification of an SSSI can be made and ultimately considered at a full meeting of the Council of NE or CCW. In Scotland an objection will be dealt with by the main board of SNH or an appropriate subgroup, depending on the nature of the objection. Unresolved objections on scientific grounds from those with a legal interest in the land must be referred to the Advisory Committee on SSSI.

The protection of these sites depends on the cooperation of individual landowners and occupiers. Owner/occupiers must consult NE, SNH or CCW and gain written consent before they can undertake certain listed activities on the site. Funds are available through management agreements and grants to assist owners and occupiers in conserving sites' interests. As a last resort a site can be purchased.

The number and area of SSSIs in Britain as at May 2007 was:

	Number	*Hectares*	*Acres*
England	4,113	1,076,496	2,658,945
Scotland	1,455	1,036,577	2,561,347
Wales	1,016	264,531	653,682

NORTHERN IRELAND
In Northern Ireland 241 Areas of Special Scientific Interest (ASSIs) have been declared by the Department of the Environment for Northern Ireland.

NATIONAL NATURE RESERVES

National nature reserves are defined in the National Parks and Access to the Countryside Act 1949 as modified by the Natural Environment and Rural Communities Act (2006). National nature reserves may be managed solely for the purpose of conservation, or for both the purposes of conservation and recreation, providing this does not compromise the conservation purpose.

Natural England (NE), Scottish Natural Heritage (SNH) or the Countryside Council for Wales (CCW) can declare as a national nature reserve land which is held and managed as a nature reserve under an agreement; land held and managed by NE, SNH or CCW; or land held and managed as a nature reserve by an approved body. NE, SNH or CCW can make by-laws to protect reserves from undesirable activities; these are subject to confirmation by the Secretary of State for Environment, Food and Rural Affairs, the National Assembly for Wales or the Scottish ministers in Scotland.

The number and area of national nature reserves in Britain as at May 2007 was:

	Number	*Hectares*	*Acres*
England	222	93,001	229,805
Scotland	63	111,913	276,533
Wales	68	24,156	59,691

NORTHERN IRELAND
Nature reserves are established and managed by the Department of the Environment for Northern Ireland, with advice from the Council for Nature Conservation and the Countryside. Nature reserves are declared under the Nature Conservation and Amenity Lands (Northern Ireland) order 1985; to date, 47 nature reserves have been declared.

LOCAL NATURE RESERVES

Local nature reserves are defined in the National Parks and Access to the Countryside Act 1949 as land designated for the study and preservation of flora and fauna, or of geological or physiographical features. The Act gives local authorities in England, Scotland and Wales the power to acquire, declare and manage reserves in consultation with Natural England (formerly English Nature), Scottish Natural Heritage and the Countryside Council for Wales. There is similar legislation in Northern Ireland where the consulting organisation is the Environment and Heritage Service.

Any organisation, such as water companies, educational trusts, local amenity groups and charitable nature conservation bodies, such as wildlife trusts, may manage local nature reserves, provided that a local authority has a legal interest in the land. This means that the local authority must either own it, lease it or have a management agreement with the landowner.

The number and area of designated local nature reserves in Britain as at May 2007 was:

	Number	*Hectares*	*Acres*
England	1,366	35,000	86,450
Scotland	48	9,791	24,193
Wales	69	4,999	12,354

FOREST NATURE RESERVES

The Forestry Commission is the government department responsible for forestry policy throughout Great Britain. Forestry is a devolved matter, with the separate Forestry Commissions for England, Scotland and Wales reporting directly to their appropriate minister. The Forestry Commission in each country is led by a director who is also a member of the GB Board of Commissioners. As at March 2006 Forestry Commission managed woodland amounted to 772,000 hectares: 204,000 hectares in England, 108,000 hectares in Wales and 460,000 hectares in Scotland.

NORTHERN IRELAND

There are 34 forest nature reserves in Northern Ireland, covering 1,512 hectares (3,736 acres). They are designated and administered by the Forest Service, an agency of the Department of Agriculture and Rural Development for Northern Ireland. There are also 16 national nature reserves on Forest Service-owned property.

MARINE NATURE RESERVES

The Secretary of State for Environment, Food and Rural Affairs, the National Assembly for Wales and the Scottish Executive have the power to designate marine nature reserves. Natural England, Scottish Natural Heritage and the Countryside Council for Wales select and manage these reserves. Marine nature reserves may be established in Northern Ireland under a 1985 Order.

Marine nature reserves provide protection for marine flora and fauna, and geological and physiographical features on land covered by tidal waters or parts of the sea in or adjacent to the UK. Reserves also provide opportunities for study and research.

The three statutory marine nature reserves are:
LUNDY (1986), Bristol Channel
SKOMER (1990), Dyfed
STRANGFORD LOUGH (1995), Northern Ireland

WORLD HERITAGE SITES

The Convention Concerning the Protection of the World Cultural and Natural Heritage was adopted by the United Nations Educational Scientific and Cultural Organisation (UNESCO) in 1972 and ratified by the UK in 1984. As at 25 October 2006 184 states were party to the convention. The convention provides for the identification, protection and conservation of cultural and natural sites of outstanding universal value.

Cultural sites may be:
• monuments
• groups of buildings
• sites of historic, aesthetic, archaeological, scientific, ethnologic or anthropologic value
• historic areas of towns
• 'cultural landscapes', ie sites whose characteristics are marked by significant interactions between human populations and their natural environment

Natural sites may be:
• those with remarkable physical, biological or geological formations
• those with outstanding universal value from the point of view of science, conservation or natural beauty
• the habitat of threatened species and plants

Governments which are party to the convention nominate sites in their country for inclusion in the World Cultural and Natural Heritage List. Nominations are considered by the World Heritage Committee, an inter-governmental committee composed of 21 representatives of the parties to the convention. The committee is advised by the International Council on Monuments and Sites (ICOMOS), the International Centre for the Study of the Preservation and Restoration of Cultural Property (ICCROM) and the World Conservation Union (IUCN). ICOMOS evaluates and reports on proposed cultural and mixed sites, ICCROM provides expert advice and training on how to conserve the listed sites and IUCN provides technical evaluations of natural sites and reports on the state of conservation of listed sites. The Department for Culture, Media and Sport represents the UK government in matters relating to the convention.

A prerequisite for inclusion in the World Cultural and Natural Heritage List is the existence of an effective legal protection system in the country in which the site is situated (eg listing, conservation areas and planning controls in the UK) and a detailed management plan to ensure the conservation of the site. Inclusion in the list does not confer any greater degree of protection on the site than that offered by the national protection framework.

If a site is considered to be in serious danger of decay or damage, the committee may add it to a complementary list, the World Heritage in Danger List. Sites on this list may benefit from particular attention or emergency measures.

Financial support for the conservation of sites on the World Cultural and Natural Heritage List is provided by the World Heritage Fund. This is administered by the World Heritage Committee, which determines the financial and technical aid to be allocated. The fund's income is derived from compulsory and voluntary contributions from the states party to the convention and from private donations.

DESIGNATED SITES

As at 2 July 2007, following the 31st session of the World Heritage Committee, 851 sites were inscribed on the World Cultural and Natural Heritage List. Of these, 24 are in the United Kingdom and three in British overseas territories; 22 are listed for their cultural significance (†), four for their natural significance (*) and one for both cultural and natural significance. The year in which sites were designated appears in parentheses. In 2005 Hadrian's Wall, a World Heritage Site in its own right since 1987, was joined by the upper German-Raetian Limes to form the first section of a trans-national world heritage site, Frontiers of the Roman Empire.

UNITED KINGDOM

†Bath – the city (1987)
†Blaenarvon industrial landscape, Wales (2000)
†Blenheim Palace and Park, Oxfordshire (1987)
†Canterbury Cathedral, St Augustine's Abbey, St Martin's Church, Kent (1988)
†Castle and town walls of King Edward I, north Wales – Beaumaris, Caernarfon Castle, Conwy Castle, Harlech Castle, Ynys Mon (Isle of Anglesey) (1986)
†Cornwall and west Devon mining landscape (2006)
†Derwent Valley Mills, Derbyshire (2001)
*Dorset and east Devon coast (2001)
†Durham Cathedral and Castle (1986)
†Edinburgh old and new towns (1995)
†Frontiers of the Roman Empire, Hadrian's Wall, northern England (1987, 2005)
*Giant's Causeway and Causeway coast, Co. Antrim (1986)
†Greenwich, London – maritime Greenwich, including the Royal Naval College, Old Royal Observatory, Queen's House, town centre (1997)
†Heart of Neolithic Orkney (1999)
†Ironbridge Gorge, Shropshire – the world's first iron bridge and other early industrial sites (1986)
†Liverpool – six areas of the maritime mercantile city (2004)
†New Lanark, South Lanarkshire, Scotland (2001)
†Royal Botanic Gardens, Kew (2003)
†*St Kilda, Eilean Siar (Western Isles) (1986)
†Saltaire, West Yorkshire (2001)
†Stonehenge, Avebury and related megalithic sites, Wiltshire (1986)
†Studley Royal Park, Fountains Abbey, St Mary's Church, N. Yorkshire (1986)
†Tower of London (1988)
†Westminster Abbey, Palace of Westminster, St Margaret's Church, London (1987)

BRITISH OVERSEAS TERRITORIES

*Henderson Island, Pitcairn Islands, South Pacific Ocean (1988)
*Gough Island and Inaccessible Island (part of Tristan da Cunha), South Atlantic Ocean (1995)
†St George town and related fortifications, Bermuda (2000)

WORLD HERITAGE CENTRE, UNESCO, 7 Place de Fontenoy, 75352 Paris 07 SP, France
W http://whc.unesco.org

CONSERVATION OF WILDLIFE AND HABITATS

The UK is party to a number of international conventions.

RAMSAR CONVENTION

The 1971 Ramsar Convention on Wetlands of International Importance especially as Waterfowl Habitat entered into force in the UK in May 1976. As at July 2007, 155 countries were party to the convention.

The aim of the convention is the conservation and wise use of wetlands and their resources. Governments that are party to the convention must designate wetlands and include wetland conservation considerations in their land-use planning. 1,671 wetland sites, totalling 151 million hectares, have been designated for inclusion in the list of wetlands of international importance. The UK currently has 165 designated sites covering 895,144 hectares. The member countries meet every three years to assess the progress of the convention and the next meeting is scheduled for November 2008.

The UK has set targets under the Ramsar Strategic Plan, 2003–8. Progress towards these is monitored by the UK Ramsar Committee, known as the Joint Working Party. The UK and the Republic of Ireland have established a formal protocol to ensure common monitoring standards for waterbirds in the two countries.

RAMSAR CONVENTION SECRETARIAT, rue Mauverney 28, CH-1196 Gland, Switzerland T (+41) (22) 999 0170 W www.ramsar.org

BIODIVERSITY

The UK ratified the Convention on Biological Diversity in June 1994. As at July 2007 there were 190 parties to the convention.

The objectives are the conservation of biological diversity, the sustainable use of its components and the fair and equitable sharing of the benefits arising out of the use of genetic resources. There are seven thematic work programmes addressing agricultural biodiversity, marine and coastal biodiversity and the biodiversity of inland waters, dry and sub-humid lands, islands, mountains and forests. The Conference of the Parties to the Convention on Biological Diversity adopted a supplementary agreement to the convention known as the Cartagena Protocol on Biosafety on 29 January 2000. The protocol seeks to protect biological diversity from potential risks that may be posed by introducing modified living organisms, resulting from biotechnology, into the environment. As at July 2007, 141 countries were party to the protocol; the UK joined on 17 February 2004.

The UK Biodiversity Action Plan (UKBAP) is the UK government's response to the Convention on Biological Diversity and constitutes a record of UK biological resources and a detailed plan for their protection. UKBAP currently consists of 391 species action plans, 45 habitat action plans and 162 local biodiversity plans. The UK Biodiversity Partnership Standing Committee guides and supports the UK Biodiversity Partnership in implementing UKBAP; it also coordinates between the four UK country groups which form the partnership and are responsible for implementing UKBAP at a national level. In addition, the UK Biodiversity Partnership includes two support groups: the Biodiversity Research

Advisory Group and the Biodiversity Reporting and Information Group.

BIODIVERSITY POLICY UNIT, Zone 1/10B, Temple Quay House, 2 The Square, Temple Quay, Bristol BS1 6EB T 0117-372 6276 W www.ukbap.org.uk

CITES

The 1973 Convention on International Trade in Endangered Species of Wild Fauna and Flora (CITES) is an agreement between governments to ensure that international trade in specimens of wild animals and plants does not threaten their survival. The UK became party to the convention in July 1975 and there are currently 172 member countries. Countries party to the convention ban commercial international trade in an agreed list of endangered species and regulate and monitor trade in other species that might become endangered. The convention accords varying degrees of protection to more than 30,000 species of animals and plants whether they are traded as live specimens or as products derived from them, such as fur coats and dried herbs.

The Conference of the Parties to CITES meets every two to three years to review the convention's implementation. The Wildlife Species Conservation Division at the Department for Environment, Food and Rural Affairs in Bristol (see address above) carries out the government's responsibilities under CITES.

CITES SECRETARIAT, International Environment House, Chemin des Anémones, CH-1219 Châtelaine, Geneva, Switzerland T (+41) (22) 917 8139/8140 E info@cites.org W www.cites.org

BONN CONVENTION

The 1979 Convention on Conservation of Migratory Species of Wild Animals came into force in the UK in October 1979. As at 1 January 2007, 101 countries were party to the convention.

It requires the protection of listed endangered migratory species and encourages international agreements covering these and other threatened species. International agreements can range from legally binding treaties to less formal memorandums of understanding.

Six agreements have been concluded to date under the convention. They aim to conserve seals in the Wadden Sea; bat populations in Europe; small cetaceans of the Baltic and North Seas; African-Eurasian migratory waterbirds; cetaceans of the Mediterranean Sea, Black Sea and contiguous Atlantic area; and albatrosses and petrels. A further ten memorandums of understanding have been agreed for the Siberian crane, slender-billed curlew, marine turtles of the Atlantic coast of Africa, Indian Ocean and South-East Asia, the middle-European population of the great bustard, bukhara deer, aquatic warbler, West African populations of the African elephant, the saiga antelope and cetaceans of the Pacific Islands.

UNEP/CMS SECRETARIAT, United Nations Premises, Hermann-Ehlers-Str. 10, 53113 Bonn, Germany T (+49) (228) 815 2401/2 E secretariat@cms.int W www.cms.int

BERN CONVENTION

The 1979 Bern Convention on the Conservation of European Wildlife and Natural Habitats came into force in the UK in June 1982. Currently there are 45 contracting parties and a number of other states attend meetings as observers.

The aims are to conserve wild flora and fauna and their natural habitats, especially where this requires the cooperation of several countries, and to promote such cooperation. The convention gives particular emphasis to endangered and vulnerable species.

All parties to the convention must promote national conservation policies and take account of the conservation of wild flora and fauna when setting planning and development policies. Reports on contracting parties' conservation policies must be submitted to the standing committee every four years.

SECRETARIAT OF THE BERN CONVENTION
STANDING COMMITTEE, Council of Europe, Avenue de l'Europe, 67075 Strasbourg-Cedex, France
T (+33) (3) 8841 2000 W www.coe.int

EUROPEAN WILDLIFE TRADE REGULATION

The Council (EC) Regulation on the Protection of Species of Wild Fauna and Flora by Regulating Trade Therein came into force in the UK on 1 June 1997. It is intended to standardise wildlife trade regulations across Europe and to improve the application of CITES.

UK LEGISLATION

The Wildlife and Countryside Act 1981 gives legal protection to a wide range of wild animals and plants. Subject to parliamentary approval, the environment secretary may vary the animals and plants given legal protection. The most recent variation of schedules 5 and 8 came into effect in March and April 1998. The fourth quinquennial review of species listed in schedules 5 and 8 is ongoing.

Under section 9 of the act it is an offence to kill, injure, take, possess or sell (whether alive or dead) any wild animal included in schedule 5 of the act and to disturb its place of shelter and protection or to destroy that place. However certain species listed on schedule 5 are protected against some, but not all, of these activities.

Under section 13 of the act it is illegal without a licence to pick, uproot, sell or destroy plants listed in schedule 8. Since January 2001, under the Countryside and Rights of Way Act 2000, persons found guilty of an offence under part 1 of the Wildlife and Countryside Act 1981 face a maximum penalty of up to £5,000 and/or up to six months custodial sentence per specimen.

The act lays down a close season for birds (listed on Schedule 2, part 1) from 1 February to 31 August inclusive, each year. Exceptions to these dates are made for:
Capercaillie and (except Scotland) Woodcock – 1 February to 30 September
Snipe – 1 February to 11 August
Birds listed on schedule 2, part 1 (below high water mark) (see below) – 21 February to 31 August
Birds listed on schedule 2, part 1, which may be killed or taken outside the close season (except on Sundays and on Christmas Day in Scotland, and on Sundays in prescribed areas of England and Wales) are capercaillie, coot, certain wild duck (gadwall, goldeneye, mallard, pintail, pochard, shoveler, teal, tufted duck, wigeon), certain wild geese (Canada, greylag, pink-footed, white-fronted (in England and Wales only)), moorhen, golden plover and woodcock.

Section 16 of the 1981 act allows licences to be issued on either an individual or general basis, to allow the killing, taking and sale of certain birds for specified reasons such as public health and safety. All other wild birds are fully protected by law throughout the year.

ANIMALS PROTECTED BY SCHEDULE 5

Adder *(Vipera berus)**
Allis Shad *(Alosa alosa)**
Atlantic Stream Crayfish *(Austropotomobius pallipes)**
Anemone, Ivell's Sea *(Edwardsia ivelli)*
Anemone, Starlet Sea *(Nematosella vectensis)*
Bat, Horseshoe *(Rhinolophidae, all species)*
Bat, Typical *(Vespertilionidae, all species)*
Beetle *(Hypebaeus flavipes)*
Beetle, Lesser Silver Water *(Hydrochara caraboides)*
Beetle, Mire Pill *(Curimopsis nigrita)**
Beetle, Rainbow Leaf *(Chrysolina cerealis)*
Beetle, Spangled Water *(Graphoderus zonatus)*
Beetle, Stag *(Lucanus cervus)**
Beetle, Violet Click *(Limoniscus violaceus)*
Beetle, Water *(Paracymus aeneus)*
Burbot *(Lota lota)*
Butterfly, Adonis Blue *(Lysandra bellargus)*
Butterfly, Black Hairstreak *(Strymonidia pruni)*
Butterfly, Brown Hairstreak *(Thecla betulae)*
Butterfly, Chalkhill Blue *(Lysandra coridon)*
Butterfly, Chequered Skipper *(Carterocephalus palaemon)*
Butterfly, Duke of Burgundy Fritillary *(Hamearis lucina)*
Butterfly, Glanville Fritillary *(Melitaea cinxia)*
Butterfly, Heath Fritillary *(Mellicta athalia* or *Melitaea athalia)*
Butterfly, High Brown Fritillary *(Argynnis adippe)*
Butterfly, Large Blue *(Maculinea arion)*
Butterfly, Large Copper *(Lycaena dispar)*
Butterfly, Large Heath *(Coenonympha tullia)*
Butterfly, Large Tortoiseshell *(Nymphalis polychloros)*
Butterfly, Lulworth Skipper *(Thymelicus acteon)*
Butterfly, Marsh Fritillary *(Eurodryas aurinia)*
Butterfly, Mountain Ringlet *(Erebia epiphron)*
Butterfly, Northern Brown Argus *(Aricia artaxerxes)*
Butterfly, Pearl-bordered Fritillary *(Boloria euphrosyne)*
Butterfly, Purple Emperor *(Apatura iris)*
Butterfly, Silver Spotted Skipper *(Hesperia comma)*
Butterfly, Silver-studded Blue *(Plebejus argus)*
Butterfly, Small Blue *(Cupido minimus)*
Butterfly, Swallowtail *(Papilio machaon)*
Butterfly, White Letter Hairstreak *(Stymonida w-album)*
Butterfly, Wood White *(Leptidea sinapis)*
Cat, Wild *(Felis silvestris)*
Cicada, New Forest *(Cicadetta montana)*
Cricket, Field *(Gryllus campestris)*
Cricket, Mole *(Gryllotalpa gryllotalpa)*
Damselfly, Southern *(Coenagrion mercuriale)*
Dolphin, all species *(Cetacea)*
Dormouse *(Muscardinus avellanarius)*
Dragonfly, Norfolk Aeshna *(Aeshna isosceles)*
Frog, Common *(Rana temporaria)**
Goby, Couch's *(Gobius couchii)*
Goby, Giant *(Gobius cobitis)*
Grasshopper, Wart-biter *(Decticus verrucivorus)*
Hatchet Shell, Northern *(Thyasira gouldi)*
Hydroid, Marine *(Clavopsella navis)*

Lagoon Snail *(Paludinella littorina)*
Lagoon Snail, De Folin's *(Caecum armoricum)*
Lagoon Worm, Tentacled *(Alkmaria romijni)*
Leech, Medicinal *(Hirudo medicinalis)*
Lizard, Sand *(Lacerta agilis)*
Lizard, Viviparous *(Lacerta vivipara)*
Marten, Pine *(Martes martes)*
Moth, Barberry Carpet *(Pareulype berberata)*
Moth, Black-veined *(Siona lineata* or *Idaea lineata)*
Moth, Essex Emerald *(Thetidia smaragdaria)*
Moth, Fiery Clearwing *(Bembecia chrysidiformis)*
Moth, Fisher's Estuarine *(Gortyna borelii)*
Moth, New Forest Burnet *(Zygaena viciae)*
Moth, Reddish Buff *(Acosmetia caliginosa)*
Moth, Sussex Emerald *(Thalera fimbrialis)*
Mussel, Fan *(Atrina fragilis)*
Mussel, Pearl Freshwater *(Margaritifera margaritifera)*
Newt, Great Crested (or Warty) *(Triturus cristatus)*
Newt, Palmate *(Triturus helveticus)*
Newt, Smooth *(Triturus vulgaris)*
Otter, Common *(Lutra lutra)*
Porpoise, all species *(Phocaena Phocaena)*
Sandworm, Lagoon *(Armandia cirrhosa)*
Sea Fan, Pink *(Eunicella verrucosa)*
Sea Slug, Lagoon *(Tenellia adspersa)*
Sea-mat, Trembling *(Victorella pavida)*
Shad, Twaite *(Alosa fallax)*
Shark, Basking *(Cetorhinus maximus)*
Shrimp, Fairy *(Chirocephalus diaphanus)*
Shrimp, Lagoon Sand *(Gammarus insensibilis)*
Shrimp, Tadpole *(Triops cancriformis)*
Slow-worm *(Anguis fragilis)*
Snail, Glutinous *(Myxas glutinosa)*
Snail, Sandbowl *(Catinella arenaria)*
Snake, Grass *(Natrix natrix* or *Natrix helvetica)*
Snake, Smooth *(Coronella austriaca)*
Spider, Fen Raft *(Dolomedes plantarius)*
Spider, Ladybird *(Eresus niger)*
Squirrel, Red *(Sciurus vulgaris)*
Sturgeon *(Acipenser sturio)*
Toad, Common *(Bufo bufo)*
Toad, Natterjack *(Bufo calamita)*
Turtle, Marine *(Dermochelyidae* and *Cheloniidae,* all species*)*
Vendace *(Coregonus albula)*
Vole, Water *(Arvicola terrestris)*
Walrus *(Odobenus rosmarus)*
Whale, all species *(Cetacea)*
Whitefish *(Coregonus lavaretus)*

* These species are protected against some, but not all, of the activities listed under section 9 of the Wildlife and Countryside Act 1981

PLANTS PROTECTED BY SCHEDULE 8

Adder's Tongue, Least *(Ophioglossum lusitanicum)*
Alison, Small *(Alyssum alyssoides)*
Anomodon, Long-leaved *(Anomodon longifolius)*
Beech-lichen, New Forest *(Enterographa elaborata)*
Blackwort *(Southbya nigrella)*
Bluebell *(Hyacinthoides non-scripta)*
Bolete, Royal *(Boletus regius)*
Broomrape, Bedstraw *(Orobanche caryophyllacea)*
Broomrape, Oxtongue *(Orobanche loricata)*
Broomrape, Thistle *(Orobanche reticulata)*
Cabbage, Lundy *(Rhynchosinapis wrightii)*
Calamint, Wood *(Calamintha sylvatica)*
Caloplaca, Snow *(Caloplaca nivalis)*
Catapyrenium, Tree *(Catapyrenium psoromoides)*

Catchfly, Alpine *(Lychnis alpina)*
Catillaria, Laurer's *(Catellaria laureri)*
Centaury, Slender *(Centaurium tenuiflorum)*
Cinquefoil, Rock *(Potentilla rupestris)*
Cladonia, Convoluted *(Cladonia convoluta)*
Cladonia, Upright Mountain *(Cladonia stricta)*
Clary, Meadow *(Salvia pratensis)*
Club-rush, Triangular *(Scirpus triquetrus)*
Colt's-foot, Purple *(Homogyne alpina)*
Cotoneaster, Wild *(Cotoneaster integerrimus)*
Cottongrass, Slender *(Eriophorum gracile)*
Cow-wheat, Field *(Melampyrum arvense)*
Crocus, Sand *(Romulea columnae)*
Crystalwort, Lizard *(Riccia bifurca)*
Cudweed, Broad-leaved *(Filago pyramidata)*
Cudweed, Jersey *(Gnaphalium luteoalbum)*
Cudweed, Red-tipped *(Filago lutescens)*
Cut-grass *(Leersia oryzoides)*
Diapensia *(Diapensia lapponica)*
Dock, Shore *(Rumex rupestris)*
Earwort, Marsh *(Jamesoniella undulifolia)*
Eryngo, Field *(Eryngium campestre)*
Fern, Dickie's Bladder *(Cystopteris dickieana)*
Fern, Killarney *(Trichomanes speciosum)*
Flapwort, Norfolk *(Leiocolea rutheana)*
Fleabane, Alpine *(Erigeron borealis)*
Fleabane, Small *(Pulicaria vulgaris)*
Fleawort, South Stack*(Tephroseris integrifolia ssp maritima)*
Frostwort, Pointed *(Gymnomitrion apiculatum)*
Fungus, Hedgehog *(Hericium erinaceum)*
Galingale, Brown *(Cyperus fuscus)*
Gentian, Alpine *(Gentiana nivalis)*
Gentian, Dune *(Gentianella uliginosa)*
Gentian, Early *(Gentianella anglica)*
Gentian, Fringed *(Gentianella ciliata)*
Gentian, Spring *(Gentiana verna)*
Germander, Cut-leaved *(Teucrium botrys)*
Germander, Water *(Teucrium scordium)*
Gladiolus, Wild *(Gladiolus illyricus)*
Goblin Lights *(Catolechia wahlenbergii)*
Goosefoot, Stinking *(Chenopodium vulvaria)*
Grass-poly *(Lythrum hyssopifolia)*
Grimmia, Blunt-leaved *(Grimmia unicolor)*
Gyalecta, Elm *(Gyalecta ulmi)*
Hare's-ear, Sickle-leaved *(Bupleurum falcatum)*
Hare's-ear, Small *(Bupleurum baldense)*
Hawk's-beard, Stinking *(Crepis foetida)*
Hawkweed, Northroe *(Hieracium northroense)*
Hawkweed, Shetland *(Hieracium zetlandicum)*
Hawkweed, Weak-leaved *(Hieracium attenuatifolium)*
Heath, Blue *(Phyllodoce caerulea)*
Helleborine, Red *(Cephalanthera rubra)*
Helleborine, Young's *(Epipactis youngiana)*
Horsetail, Branched *(Equisetum ramosissimum)*
Hound's-tongue, Green *(Cynoglossum germanicum)*
Knawel, Perennial *(Scleranthus perennis)*
Knotgrass, Sea *(Polygonum maritimum)*
Lady's-slipper *(Cypripedium calceolus)*
Lecanactis, Churchyard *(Lecanactis hemisphaerica)*
Lecanora, Tarn *(Lecanora archariana)*
Lecidea, Copper *(Lecidea inops)*
Leek, Round-headed *(Allium sphaerocephalon)*
Lettuce, Least *(Lactuca saligna)*
Lichen, Arctic Kidney *(Nephroma arcticum)*
Lichen, Ciliate Strap *(Heterodermia leucomelos)*
Lichen, Coralloid Rosette *(Heterodermia propagulifera)*
Lichen, Ear-lobed Dog *(Peltigera lepidophora)*
Lichen, Forked Hair *(Bryoria furcellata)*

Lichen, Golden Hair *(Teloschistes flavicans)*
Lichen, Orange-fruited Elm *(Caloplaca luteoalba)*
Lichen, River Jelly *(Collema dichotomum)*
Lichen, Scaly Breck *(Squamarina lentigera)*
Lichen, Stary Breck *(Buellia asterella)*
Lily, Snowdon *(Lloydia serotina)*
Liverwort, Lindenberg's Leafy *(Adelanthus lindenbergianus)*
Marsh-mallow, Rough *(Althaea hirsuta)*
Marshwort, Creeping *(Apium repens)*
Milk-parsley, Cambridge *(Selinum carvifolia)*
Moss, Alpine Copper *(Mielichoferia mielichoferi)*
Moss, Baltic Bog *(Sphagnum balticum)*
Moss, Blue Dew *(Saelania glaucescens)*
Moss, Blunt-leaved Bristle *(Orthotrichum obtusifolium)*
Moss, Bright Green Cave *(Cyclodictyon laetevirens)*
Moss, Cordate Beard *(Barbula cordata)*
Moss, Cornish Path *(Ditrichum cornubicum)*
Moss, Derbyshire Feather *(Thamnobryum angustifolium)*
Moss, Dune Thread *(Bryum mamillatum)*
Moss, Flamingo *(Desmatodon cernuus)*
Moss, Glaucous Beard *(Barbula glauca)*
Moss, Green Shield *(Buxbaumia viridis)*
Moss, Hair Silk *(Plagiothecium piliferum)*
Moss, Knothole *(Zygodon forsteri)*
Moss, Large Yellow Feather *(Scorpidium turgescens)*
Moss, Millimetre *(Micromitrium tenerum)*
Moss, Multi-fruited River *(Cryphaea lamyana)*
Moss, Nowell's Limestone *(Zygodon gracilis)*
Moss, Polar Feather *(Hygrohypnum polare)*
Moss, Rigid Apple *(Bartramia stricta)*
Moss, Round-leaved Feather *(Rhyncostegium rotundifolium)*
Moss, Schleicher's Thread *(Bryum schleicheri)*
Moss, Slender Green Feather *(Drepanocladus vernicosus)*
Moss, Triangular Pygmy *(Acaulon triquetrum)*
Moss, Vaucher's Feather *(Hypnum vaucheri)*
Mudwort, Welsh *(Limosella australis)*
Naiad, Holly-leaved *(Najas marina)*
Naiad, Slender *(Najas flexilis)*
Orache, Stalked *(Halimione pedunculata)*
Orchid, Early Spider *(Ophrys sphegodes)*
Orchid, Fen *(Liparis loeselii)*
Orchid, Ghost *(Epipogium aphyllum)*
Orchid, Lapland Marsh *(Dactylorhiza lapponica)*
Orchid, Late Spider *(Ophrys fuciflora)*
Orchid, Lizard *(Himantoglossum hircinum)*
Orchid, Military *(Orchis militaris)*
Orchid, Monkey *(Orchis simia)*
Pannaria, Caledonia *(Panneria ignobilis)*
Parmelia, New Forest *(Parmelia minarum)*
Parmentaria, Oil Stain *(Parmentaria chilensis)*
Pear, Plymouth *(Pyrus cordata)*
Penny-cress, Perfoliate *(Thlaspi perfoliatum)*
Pennyroyal *(Mentha pulegium)*
Pertusaria, Alpine Moss *(Pertusaria bryontha)*

Petalwort *(Petallophyllum ralfsi)*
Physcia, Southern Grey *(Physcia tribacioides)*
Pigmyweed *(Crassula aquatica)*
Pine, Ground *(Ajuga chamaepitys)*
Pink, Cheddar *(Dianthus gratianopolitanus)*
Pink, Childing *(Petroraghia nanteuilii)*
Pink, Deptford (England and Wales only) *(Dianthus armeria)*
Polypore, Oak *(Buglossoporus pulvinus)*
Pseudocyphellaria, Ragged *(Pseudocyphellaria lacerata)*
Psora, Rusty Alpine *(Psora rubiformis)*
Puffball, Sandy Stilt *(Battarraea phalloides)*
Ragwort, Fen *(Senecio paludosus)*
Ramping-fumitory, Martin's *(Fumaria martinii)*
Rampion, Spiked *(Phyteuma spicatum)*
Restharrow, Small *(Ononis reclinata)*
Rock-cress, Alpine *(Arabis alpina)*
Rock-cress, Bristol *(Arabis stricta)*
Rustwort, Western *(Marsupella profunda)*
Sandwort, Norwegian *(Arenaria norvegica)*
Sandwort, Teesdale *(Minuartia stricta)*
Saxifrage, Drooping *(Saxifraga cernua)*
Saxifrage, Yellow Marsh *(Saxifrage hirulus)*
Saxifrage, Tufted *(Saxifraga cespitosa)*
Solenopsora, Serpentine *(Solenopsora liparina)*
Solomon's-seal, Whorled *(Polygonatum verticillatum)*
Sow-thistle, Alpine *(Cicerbita alpina)*
Spearwort, Adder's-tongue *(Ranunculus ophioglossifolius)*
Speedwell, Fingered *(Veronica triphyllos)*
Speedwell, Spiked *(Veronica spicata)*
Spike-rush, Dwarf *(Eleocharis parvula)*
Star-of-Bethlehem, Early *(Gagea bohemica)*
Starfruit *(Damasonium alisma)*
Stonewort, Bearded *(Chara canescens)*
Stonewort, Foxtail *(Lamprothamnium papulosum)*
Strapwort *(Corrigiola litoralis)*
Sulphur-tresses, Alpine *(Alectoria ochroleuca)*
Threadmoss, Long-leaved *(Bryum neodamense)*
Turpswort *(Geocalyx graveolens)*
Violet, Fen *(Viola persicifolia)*
Viper's-grass *(Scorzonera humilis)*
Water-plantain, Floating *(Luronium natans)*
Water-plantain, Ribbon-leaved *(Alisma gramineum)*
Wood-sedge, Starved *(Carex depauperata)*
Woodsia, Alpine *(Woodsia alpina)*
Woodsia, Oblong *(Woodsia ilvenis)*
Wormwood, Field *(Artemisia campestris)*
Woundwort, Downy *(Stachys germanica)*
Woundwort, Limestone *(Stachys alpina)*
Yellow-rattle, Greater *(Rhinanthus serotinus)*

* Protected against some, but not all, of the activities listed under section 13 of the Wildlife and Countryside Act 1981

HISTORIC BUILDINGS AND MONUMENTS

ENGLAND

Under the Planning (Listed Buildings and Conservation Areas) Act 1990, the Secretary of State for Culture, Media and Sport has a statutory duty to compile lists of buildings or groups of buildings in England which are of special architectural or historic interest. Under the Ancient Monuments and Archaeological Areas Act 1979 as amended by the National Heritage Act 1983, the secretary of state is also responsible for compiling a schedule of ancient monuments. Decisions are taken on the advice of English Heritage. On 1 April 2005 responsibility for the administration of the listing system was transferred from the secretary of state to English Heritage. This marked the start of a programme of changes designed to increase the involvement and awareness of the property owner and make the listing process more straightforward and more accountable.

LISTED BUILDINGS

Listed buildings are classified into Grade I, Grade II* and Grade II. There are currently around 372,000 individual listed buildings in England, of which approximately 92 per cent are Grade II listed. Almost all pre-1700 buildings are listed, as are most buildings of 1700 to 1840. English Heritage carries out thematic surveys of particular types of buildings with a view to making recommendations for listing, and members of the public may propose a building for consideration. The main purpose of listing is to ensure that care is taken in deciding the future of a building. No changes which affect the architectural or historic character of a listed building can be made without listed building consent (in addition to planning permission where relevant). Applications for listed building consent are normally dealt with by the local planning authority, although English Heritage is always consulted about proposals affecting Grade I and Grade II* properties. It is a criminal offence to demolish a listed building, or alter it in such a way as to affect its character, without consent.

SCHEDULED MONUMENTS

There are currently around 19,700 scheduled monuments in England. English Heritage is carrying out a Monuments Protection Programme assessing archaeological sites with a view to making recommendations for scheduling, and members of the public may propose a monument for consideration. All monuments proposed for scheduling are considered to be of national importance. Where buildings are both scheduled and listed, ancient monuments legislation takes precedence. The main purpose of scheduling a monument is to preserve it for the future and to protect it from damage, destruction or any unnecessary interference. Once a monument has been scheduled, scheduled monument consent is required before any works can be carried out. The scope of the control is more extensive and more detailed than that applied to listed buildings, but certain minor works, as detailed in the Ancient Monuments (Class Consents) Order 1994, may be carried out without consent. It is a criminal offence to carry out unauthorised work to scheduled monuments.

WALES

Under the Planning (Listed Buildings and Conservation Areas) Act 1990 and the Ancient Monuments and Archaeological Areas Act 1979, the Secretary of State for Wales is responsible for listing buildings and scheduling monuments in Wales on the advice of Cadw (the Welsh Assembly's historic environment division), the Historic Buildings Advisory Council for Wales, the Ancient Monuments Advisory Board for Wales and the Royal Commission on the Ancient and Historical Monuments of Wales (RCAHMW). The criteria for evaluating buildings are similar to those in England and the same listing system is used. There are approximately 29,900 listed buildings and approximately 3,900 scheduled monuments in Wales.

SCOTLAND

Under the Planning (Listed Buildings and Conservation Areas) (Scotland) Act 1997 and the Ancient Monuments and Archaeological Areas Act 1979, Scottish ministers are responsible for listing buildings and scheduling monuments in Scotland on the advice of Historic Scotland, the Historic Environment Advisory Council for Scotland (HEACS) and the Royal Commission on the Ancient and Historical Monuments of Scotland (RCAHMS). The criteria for evaluating buildings are similar to those in England but an A, B, C categorisation is used. There are approximately 46,900 listed buildings and 8,000 scheduled monuments in Scotland.

NORTHERN IRELAND

Under the Planning (Northern Ireland) Order 1991 and the Historic Monuments and Archaeological Objects (Northern Ireland) Order 1995, the Department of the Environment of the Northern Ireland Executive is responsible for listing buildings and scheduling monuments in Northern Ireland on the advice of the Historic Buildings Council for Northern Ireland and the Historic Monuments Council for Northern Ireland. The criteria for evaluating buildings are similar to those in England but an A, B+, B1 and B2 categorisation is used. There are approximately 8,500 listed buildings and 1,733 scheduled monuments in Northern Ireland.

ENGLAND

For more information on any of the English Heritage properties listed below, the official website is www.english-heritage.org.uk

For more information on any of the National Trust properties listed below, the official website is www.nationaltrust.org.uk

(EH) English Heritage property

(NT) National Trust property

A LA RONDE (NT), Exmouth, Devon EX8 5BD
T 01395-265514
Unique 16-sided house completed c.1796

ALNWICK CASTLE, Alnwick, Northumberland NE66 1NQ
T 01665-510777 W www.alnwickcastle.com
Seat of the Dukes of Northumberland since 1309; Italian Renaissance-style interior; gardens with spectacular water features

ALTHORP, Northants NN7 4HQ T 01604-770107
W www.althorp.com
Spencer family seat; Diana, Princess of Wales memorabilia

ANGLESEY ABBEY (NT), Lode, Cambs CB25 9EJ
T 01223-810080
House built c.1600; houses many paintings and a unique clock collection; gardens and Lode Mill

APSLEY HOUSE (EH), London W1J 7NT T 020-7499 5676
Built by Robert Adam 1771–8, home of the Dukes of Wellington since 1817 and known as 'No. 1 London'; collection of fine and decorative arts

ARUNDEL CASTLE, Arundel, W. Sussex BN18 9AB
T 01903-882173 W www.arundelcastle.org
Castle dating from the Norman Conquest; seat of the Dukes of Norfolk

AVEBURY (NT), Wilts SN8 1RF T 01672-539250
Remains of stone circles constructed 4,000 years ago surrounding the later village of Avebury

BANQUETING HOUSE, Whitehall, London SW1A 2ER
T 0870-751 5178 W www.hrp.org.uk
Designed by Inigo Jones; ceiling paintings by Rubens; site of the execution of Charles I

BASILDON PARK (NT), Reading, Berks RG8 9NR
T 0118-984 3040
Palladian house built in 1776–83 by John Carr

BATTLE ABBEY (EH), Battle, E. Sussex TN33 0AD
T 01424-773792
Remains of the abbey founded by William the Conqueror on the site of the Battle of Hastings

BEAULIEU, Brockenhurst, Hants SO42 7ZN T 01590-612345
W www.beaulieu.co.uk
House and gardens; Beaulieu Abbey and exhibition of monastic life; National Motor Museum

BEESTON CASTLE (EH), Cheshire CW6 9TX
T 01829-260464
13th-century inner ward with gatehouse and towers, and remains of outer ward built by Ranulf, sixth Earl of Chester

BELTON HOUSE (NT), Grantham, Lincs NG32 2LS
T 01476-566116
17th-century house; formal gardens in landscaped park

BELVOIR CASTLE, Grantham, Leics NG32 1PD
T 01476-871000 W www.belvoircastle.com
Seat of the Dukes of Rutland; 19th-century Gothic-style castle

BERKELEY CASTLE, Glos GL13 9BQ T 01453-810332
W www.berkeley-castle.com
Completed 1153; site of the murder of Edward II (1327)

BLENHEIM PALACE, Woodstock, Oxon OX20 1PX
T 0870-060 2080 W www.blenheimpalace.com
Seat of the Dukes of Marlborough and Winston Churchill's birthplace; designed by Vanbrugh

BLICKLING HALL (NT), Blickling, Norfolk NR11 6NF
T 01263-738030
Jacobean house with state rooms; temple and 18th-century orangery

BODIAM CASTLE (NT), Bodiam, E. Sussex TN32 5UA
T 01580-830436
Well-preserved medieval moated castle built in 1385

BOLSOVER CASTLE (EH), Bolsover, Derbys S44 6PR
T 01246-822844
17th-century buildings on site of medieval castle

BOSCOBEL HOUSE (EH), Bishops Wood, Shrops
ST19 9AR T 01902-850244
Timber-framed 17th-century hunting lodge; refuge of fugitive Charles II

BOUGHTON HOUSE, Kettering, Northants NN14 1BJ
T 01536-515731 W www.boughtonhouse.org.uk
A 17th-century house with French-style additions; home of the Dukes of Buccleuch and Queensbury

BOWOOD HOUSE, Calne, Wilts SN11 0LZ
T 01249-812102 W www.bowood-house.co.uk
An 18th-century house in Capability Brown park, with lake, temple and arboretum

BROADLANDS, Romsey, Hants SO51 9ZD T 01794-505010
W www.broadlands.net
Palladian mansion in Capability Brown park; Mountbatten exhibition

BRONTË PARSONAGE, Haworth, W. Yorks BD22 8DR
T 01535-642323 W www.bronte.org.uk
Home of the Brontë sisters; museum and memorabilia

BUCKFAST ABBEY, Buckfastleigh, Devon TQ11 0EE
T 01364-645550 W www.buckfast.org.uk
Benedictine monastery on medieval foundations

BUCKINGHAM PALACE, London SW1A 1AA
T 020-7766 7300 W www.royal.gov.uk
Purchased by George III in 1761, and the Sovereign's official London residence since 1837; 18 state rooms, including the Throne Room, and Picture Gallery

BUCKLAND ABBEY (NT), Yelverton, Devon PL20 6EY
T 01822-853607
13th-century Cistercian monastery; home of Sir Francis Drake

BURGHLEY HOUSE, Stamford, Lincs PE9 3JY
T 01780-752451 W www.burghley.co.uk
Late Elizabethan house built by William Cecil, first Lord Burghley

CALKE ABBEY (NT), Ticknall, Derbys DE73 7LE
T 01332-863822
Baroque 18th-century mansion

CARISBROOKE CASTLE (EH), Newport, Isle of Wight
PO30 1XY T 01983-522107
W www.carisbrookecastlemuseum.org.uk
Norman castle; prison of Charles I 1647–8

CARLISLE CASTLE (EH), Carlisle, Cumbria CA3 8UR
T 01228-591922
Medieval castle; prison of Mary Queen of Scots

CARLYLE'S HOUSE (NT), Cheyne Row, London SW3 5HL
T 020-7352 7087
Home of Thomas Carlyle

CASTLE ACRE PRIORY (EH), Swaffham, Norfolk
PE32 2XD T 01760-755394
Remains include 12th-century church and prior's lodgings

CASTLE DROGO (NT), Drewsteignton, Devon EX6 6PB
T 01647-433306
Granite castle designed by Lutyens

CASTLE HOWARD, N. Yorks YO60 7DA T 01653-648444
W www.castlehoward.co.uk
Designed by Vanbrugh 1699–1726; mausoleum
designed by Hawksmoor

CASTLE RISING CASTLE (EH), King's Lynn, Norfolk
PE31 6AH T 01553-631330
12th-century keep in a massive earthwork with
gatehouse and bridge

CHARTWELL (NT), Westerham, Kent TN16 1PS
T 01732-868381
Home of Sir Winston Churchill

CHATSWORTH, Bakewell, Derbys DE45 1PP
T 01246-565300 W www.chatsworth.org
Tudor mansion in magnificent parkland

CHESTERS ROMAN FORT (EH), Chollerford,
Northumberland NE46 3EU T 01434-681379
Roman cavalry fort

CHYSAUSTER ANCIENT VILLAGE (EH), Penzance,
Cornwall TR20 8XA T 07831-757934
Remains of Celtic settlement; eight stone-walled
homesteads

CLIFFORD'S TOWER (EH), York YO1 9SA
T 01904-646940
13th-century tower built on a mound

CLIVEDEN (NT), Taplow, Berks SL6 0JA
T 01628-605069
Former home of the Astors, now a hotel set in garden
and woodland

CORBRIDGE ROMAN SITE (EH), Corbridge,
Northumberland NE45 5NT T 01434-632349
Excavated central area of a Roman town and successive
military bases

CORFE CASTLE (NT), Wareham, Dorset BH20 5EZ
T 01929-481294
Ruined former royal castle dating from the
11th century

CROFT CASTLE (NT), Herefordshire HR6 9PW
T 01568-780246
Pre-Conquest border castle with Georgian-Gothic
interior

DEAL CASTLE (EH), Deal, Kent CT41 7BA
T 01304-372762
Largest of the coastal defence forts built by Henry VIII

DICKENS HOUSE, Doughty Street, London WC1N 2LX
T 020-7405 2127 W www.dickensmuseum.com
House occupied by Dickens 1837–9; manuscripts,
furniture and portraits

DOVE COTTAGE, Grasmere, Cumbria LA22 9SH
T 01539-435544 W www.wordsworth.org.uk
Wordsworth's home 1799–1808; museum

DOVER CASTLE (EH), Dover, Kent CT16 1HU
T 01304-211067
Castle with Roman, Saxon and Norman features;
wartime operations rooms

DR JOHNSON'S HOUSE, Gough Square, London
EC4A 3DE T 020-7353 3745 W www.drjohnsonshouse.org
Home of Samuel Johnson

DUNSTANBURGH CASTLE (EH), Craster, nr Alnwick,
Northumberland NE66 3TT T 01665-576231
14th-century castle on a cliff with a substantial
gatehouse-keep

ELTHAM PALACE (EH), Eltham, London SE9 5QE
T 020-8294 2548
Combines an Art Deco country house and remains of
medieval palace set in moated gardens

FARLEIGH HUNGERFORD CASTLE (EH), Somerset
BA2 7RS T 01225-754026
Late 14th-century castle with two courts; chapel with
tomb of Sir Thomas Hungerford

FARNHAM CASTLE KEEP (EH), Farnham, Surrey
GU9 0JA T 01252-713393
Large 12th-century motte and bailey

FOUNTAINS ABBEY (NT), nr Ripon, N. Yorks HG4 3DY
T 01765-608888 W www.fountainsabbey.org.uk
Deer park; St Mary's Church; ruined
Cistercian monastery; 18th-century landscaped
gardens of Studley Royal estate

FRAMLINGHAM CASTLE (EH), Woodbridge, Suffolk
IP13 9BP T 01728-724189
Castle (c.1200) with high curtain walls enclosing an
almshouse (1639)

FURNESS ABBEY (EH), Barrow-in-Furness, Cumbria
LA13 0PS T 01229-823420
Remains of church and conventual buildings founded
in 1123

GLASTONBURY ABBEY, Glastonbury, Somerset BA6 9EL
T 01458-832267 W www.glastonburyabbey.com
Ruins of a 12th-century abbey rebuilt after fire; site of
an early Christian settlement

GOODRICH CASTLE (EH), Ross-on-Wye, Herefordshire
HR9 6HY T 01600-890538
Remains of 13th- and 14th-century castle with
12th-century keep

GREENWICH, London SE10 9NF T 020-8858 4422
W www.rog.nmm.ac.uk
Former Royal Observatory (founded 1675)
housing the time ball and zero meridian of
longitude; the Queen's House, designed
for Queen Anne, wife of James I, by Inigo
Jones; Painted Hall and Chapel (Royal
Naval College)

GRIMES GRAVES (EH), Brandon, Norfolk IP26 5DE
T 01842-810656
Neolithic flint mines; one shaft can be descended

GUILDHALL, London EC2P 2EJ T 020-7606 3030
W www.cityoflondon.gov.uk
Centre of civic government of the City built c.1441;
facade built 1788–9

HADDON HALL, Bakewell, Derbys DE45 1LA
T 01629-812855 W www.haddonhall.co.uk
Well-preserved 12th-century manor house

HAILES ABBEY (EH), Cheltenham, Glos GL54 5PB
T 01242-602398
Ruins of a 13th-century Cistercian monastery

HAM HOUSE (NT), Richmond-upon-Thames, Surrey
TW10 7RS T 020-8940 1950
Stuart house with lavish interiors and formal
gardens

HAMPTON COURT PALACE, East Molesey,
Surrey KT8 9AU T 0870-751 5175
W www.hrp.org.uk
16th-century palace with additions by Wren;
gardens with maze; Tudor tennis court

HARDWICK HALL (NT), Chesterfield, Derbys S44 5QJ
T 01246-850430
Built 1591–7 for Bess of Hardwick

HARDY'S COTTAGE (NT), Higher Bockhampton, Dorset
DT2 8QJ T 01297-561900
Birthplace and home of Thomas Hardy

HAREWOOD HOUSE, Harewood, W. Yorks LS17 9LG
T 0113-218 1010 W www.harewood.org
18th-century house designed by John Carr and Robert
Adam; park by Capability Brown

HATFIELD HOUSE, Hatfield, Herts AL9 5NQ
T 01707-287010 W www.hatfield-house.co.uk
Jacobean house built by Robert Cecil; surviving wing
of Royal Palace of Hatfield (c.1485)

HELMSLEY CASTLE (EH), Helmsley, N. Yorks YO62 5AB
T 01439-770442
12th-century keep and curtain wall with 16th-century
buildings; spectacular earthwork defences

HEVER CASTLE, nr Edenbridge, Kent TN8 7NG
T 01732-865224 W www.hever-castle.co.uk
13th-century double-moated castle; childhood home
of Anne Boleyn

HOLKER HALL, Cumbria LA11 7PL T 01539-558328
W www.holker-hall.co.uk
Former home of the Dukes of Devonshire; award-
winning gardens

HOLKHAM HALL, Wells-next-the-Sea, Norfolk NR23 1AB
T 01328-710227 W www.holkham.co.uk
Palladian mansion; notable fine art collection

HOUSESTEADS ROMAN FORT (EH), Hexham,
Northumberland NE47 6NN T 01434-344363
Excavated infantry fort on Hadrian's Wall with
extra-mural civilian settlement

HUGHENDEN MANOR (NT), High Wycombe, Bucks
HP14 4LA T 01494-755573
Home of Disraeli; small formal garden

JANE AUSTEN'S HOUSE, Chawton, Hants
GU34 1SD T 01420-83262
W www.jane-austens-house-museum.org.uk
Jane Austen's home from 1809 to 1817

KEDLESTON HALL (NT), Derbys DE22 5JH
T 01332-842191
Classical Palladian mansion built 1759–65; complete
Robert Adam interiors

KELMSCOTT MANOR, nr Lechlade, Glos GL7 3HJ
T 01367-252486 W www.kelmscottmanor.org.uk
Summer home of William Morris, with products of
Morris and Co.

KENILWORTH CASTLE (EH), Kenilworth, Warks CV8 1NE
T 01926-864152
Largest castle ruin in England

KENSINGTON PALACE, Kensington Gardens, London
W8 4PX T 0870-751 5170 W www.hrp.org.uk
Built in 1605 and enlarged by Wren; birthplace of
Queen Victoria; Royal Ceremonial Dress Collection

KENWOOD HOUSE (EH), Hampstead Lane, London
NW3 7JR T 020-8348 1286
Adam villa housing the Iveagh bequest of paintings
and furniture

KEW PALACE, Richmond-upon-Thames, Surrey TW9 3AB
T 0870-751 5179 W www.hrp.org.uk
Includes Queen Charlotte's Cottage, used by King
George III and family as a summerhouse

KINGSTON LACY (NT), Wimborne Minster, Dorset
BH21 4EA T 01202-883402
17th-century house with 19th-century alterations;
important art collection

KNEBWORTH HOUSE, Knebworth, Herts SG3 6PY
T 01438-812661 W www.knebworthhouse.com
Tudor manor house concealed by 19th-century Gothic
decoration; Lutyens gardens

KNOLE (NT), Sevenoaks, Kent TN15 0RP T 01732-462100
House dating from 1456 set in parkland; fine art
collection

LAMBETH PALACE, London SE1 7JU T 020-7898 1200
W www.archbishopofcanterbury.org
Official residence of the Archbishop of Canterbury;
partly dating from the 12th century

LANERCOST PRIORY (EH), Brampton, Cumbria
CA8 2HQ T 01697-73030
The nave of the Augustinian priory church, c.1166, is
still used; remains of other claustral buildings

LANHYDROCK (NT), Bodmin, Cornwall PL30 5AD
T 01208-265950
House dating from the 17th century; 45 rooms,
including kitchen and nursery

LEEDS CASTLE, nr Maidstone, Kent ME17 1PL
T 01622-765400 W www.leeds-castle.com
Castle dating from 9th century, on two islands in lake

LEVENS HALL, Kendal, Cumbria LA8 0PD T 01539-560321
W www.levenshall.co.uk
Elizabethan house with unique topiary garden (1694);
steam engine collection

LINCOLN CASTLE, Lincoln, Lincs LN1 3AA
T 01522-511068 W www.lincolnshire.gov.uk
Built by William the Conqueror in 1068

LINDISFARNE PRIORY (EH), Holy Island,
Northumberland TD15 2RX T 01289-389200
Founded in AD 635; re-established in the 12th century
as a Benedictine priory, now ruined

LITTLE MORETON HALL (NT), Congleton, Cheshire
CW12 4SD T 01260-272018
Timber-framed moated manor house with knot
garden

LONGLEAT HOUSE, Warminster, Wilts BA12 7NW
T 01985-844400 W www.longleat.co.uk
Elizabethan house in Italian Renaissance style; safari
park

LULLINGSTONE ROMAN VILLA (EH), Eynsford, Kent
DA4 0JA T 01322-863467
Large villa occupied for much of the Roman period;
fine mosaics

MANSION HOUSE, London EC4N 8BH
W www.cityoflondon.gov.uk
The official residence of the Lord Mayor of
London

MARBLE HILL HOUSE (EH), Twickenham, Middx
TW1 2NL T 020-8892 5115
English Palladian villa with Georgian paintings and
furniture

MICHELHAM PRIORY, Hailsham, E. Sussex BN27 3QS
T 01323-844224 W www.sussexpast.co.uk
Tudor house built onto an Augustinian priory

MIDDLEHAM CASTLE (EH), Leyburn, N. Yorks DL8 4QR
T 01969-623899
12th-century keep within later fortifications;
childhood home of Richard III

MONTACUTE HOUSE (NT), Montacute, Somerset
TA15 6XP T 01935-823289
Elizabethan house with National Portrait Gallery
collection of portraits from the period

MOUNT GRACE PRIORY (EH), Northallerton, N. Yorks
DL6 3JG T 01609-883494
Carthusian priory with remains of monastic
buildings

NETLEY ABBEY (EH), Hants T 01424-775705
Remains of Cistercian abbey; used as house in Tudor
period

OLD SARUM (EH), Salisbury, Wilts SP1 3SD
T 01722-335398
Earthworks enclosing remains of castle and 11th-
century cathedral

ORFORD CASTLE (EH), Orford, Suffolk IP12 2ND
T 01394-450472
Circular keep of c.1170 and remains of coastal defence
castle built by Henry II

OSBORNE HOUSE (EH), East Cowes, Isle of Wight
PO32 6JY T 01983-200022
Queen Victoria's seaside residence

OSTERLEY PARK (NT), Isleworth, Middx TW7 4RB
T 020-8232 5050 W www.osterleypark.org.uk
Elizabethan mansion set in parkland

PENDENNIS CASTLE (EH), Falmouth, Cornwall TR11 4LP
T 01326-316594
Well-preserved 16th-century coastal defence castle

PENSHURST PLACE, Penshurst, Kent TN11 8DG
T 01892-870307 W www.penshurstplace.com
House with medieval Baron's Hall and 14th-century
gardens

PETWORTH HOUSE (NT), Petworth, W. Sussex GU28 0AE
T 01798-342207
Late 17th-century house set in Capability Brown
landscaped park

PEVENSEY CASTLE (EH), Pevensey, E. Sussex BN24 5LE
T 01323-762604
Walls of a 4th-century Roman fort; remains of an
11th-century castle

PEVERIL CASTLE (EH), Castleton, Derbys S33 8WQ
T 01433-620613
12th-century castle defended on two sides by
precipitous rocks

POLESDEN LACEY (NT), nr Dorking, Surrey RH5 6BD
T 01372-452048
Regency villa remodelled in the Edwardian era; fine
paintings and furnishings

PORTCHESTER CASTLE (EH), Portchester, Hants
PO16 9QW T 02392-378291
Walls of a late Roman fort enclosing a Norman keep
and an Augustinian priory church

POWDERHAM CASTLE, Kenton, Devon EX6 8JQ
T 01626-890243 W www.powderham.co.uk
Medieval castle with 18th- and 19th-century
alterations; historic home of the Earl of
Devon

RABY CASTLE, Staindrop, Co. Durham DL2 3AH
T 01833-660202 W www.rabycastle.com
14th-century castle with walled gardens

RAGLEY HALL, Alcester, Warks B49 5NJ T 01789-762090
W www.ragleyhall.com
17th-century house with gardens, park and lake

RICHBOROUGH ROMAN FORT (EH), Richborough,
Kent CT13 9JW T 01304-612013
Landing-site of the Claudian invasion in AD 43

RICHMOND CASTLE (EH), Richmond, N. Yorks
DL10 4QW T 01748-822493
12th-century keep with 11th-century curtain wall

RIEVAULX ABBEY (EH), nr Helmsley, N. Yorks YO62 5LB
T 01439-798228
Remains of a Cistercian abbey founded c.1132

ROCHESTER CASTLE (EH), Rochester, Kent ME1 1SW
T 01634-402276
11th-century castle partly on the Roman city wall, with
a square keep of c.1130

ROCKINGHAM CASTLE, Market Harborough,
Leics LE16 8TH T 01536-770240
W www.rockinghamcastle.com
Built by William the Conqueror

ROYAL PAVILION, Brighton BN1 1EE T 01273-290900
W www.royalpavilion.org.uk
Palace of George IV, in Chinese style with Indian
exterior and Regency gardens

RUFFORD OLD HALL (NT), nr Ormskirk, Lancs L40 1SG
T 01704-821254
16th-century hall with unique screen

ST AUGUSTINE'S ABBEY (EH), Canterbury, Kent CT1 1TF
T 01227-767345
Remains of Benedictine monastery on site of abbey
founded AD 598

ST MAWES CASTLE (EH), St Mawes, Cornwall TR2 3AA
T 01326-270526
Coastal defence castle built by Henry VIII

ST MICHAEL'S MOUNT (NT), Cornwall TR17 0HS
T 01736-710507
12th-century castle with later additions, off the coast at
Marazion

SANDRINGHAM, Norfolk PE35 6EN T 01553-612908
W www.sandringhamestate.co.uk
The Queen's private residence; a neo-Jacobean house
built in 1870

SCARBOROUGH CASTLE (EH), Scarborough, N. Yorks
YO11 1HY T 01723-372451
Remains of 12th-century keep and curtain walls

SHERBORNE CASTLE, Sherborne, Dorset DT9 3PY
T 01935-813182 W www.sherbornecastle.com
16th-century castle built by Sir Walter Raleigh set in
landscaped gardens

SHUGBOROUGH (NT), Milford, Staffs ST17 0XB
T 01889-881388
House set in 18th-century park with monuments,
temples and pavilions in the Greek Revival style; seat of
the Earls of Lichfield

SKIPTON CASTLE, Skipton, N. Yorks BD23 1AW
T 01756-792442 W www.skiptoncastle.co.uk
D-shaped castle, six round towers and inner courtyard

SMALLHYTHE PLACE (NT), Tenterden, Kent TN30 7NG
T 01580-762334
Half-timbered 16th-century house; home of Ellen
Terry 1899–1928; the Barn Theatre

STANFORD HALL, Lutterworth, Leics LE17 6DH
T 01788-860250 W www.stanfordhall.co.uk
William and Mary house with Stuart portraits;
motorcycle museum

STONEHENGE (EH), nr Amesbury, Wilts SP4 7DE
T 0870-333 1181
Prehistoric monument consisting of concentric
stone circles surrounded by a ditch and bank

STONOR PARK, Henley-on-Thames, Oxon RG9 6HF
T 01491-638587 W www.stonor.com
Medieval house with Georgian facade; centre of
Roman Catholicism after the Reformation

STOURHEAD (NT), Stourton, Wilts BA12 6QD
T 01747-841152
English Palladian mansion with famous gardens

STRATFIELD SAYE HOUSE, Hants RG7 2BZ
T 01256-882882 W www.stratfield-saye.co.uk
House built 1630–40; home of the Dukes of
Wellington since 1817

STRATFORD-UPON-AVON, Warks T 01789-204016
W www.shakespeare.org.uk
Shakespeare's Birthplace Trust with Shakespeare
Centre; Anne Hathaway's Cottage, home of
Shakespeare's wife; Mary Arden's House, home of
Shakespeare's mother; grammar school attended by
Shakespeare; Holy Trinity Church, where Shakespeare
is buried; Royal Shakespeare Theatre (burnt down
1926, rebuilt 1932) and Swan Theatre (opened 1986)

SUDELEY CASTLE, Winchcombe, Glos GL54 5JD
T 01242-602308 W www.sudeleycastle.co.uk
Castle built in 1442; restored in the 19th century

SULGRAVE MANOR, nr Banbury, Oxon OX17 2SD
T 01295-760205 W www.sulgravemanor.org.uk
Home of George Washington's family

SYON HOUSE, Brentford, Middx TW8 8JF T 020-8560 0881
W www.syonpark.co.uk
Built on the site of a former monastery; Adam interior;
Capability Brown park

TILBURY FORT (EH), Tilbury, Essex RM18 7NR
T 01375-858489
17th-century coastal fort

TINTAGEL CASTLE (EH), Tintagel, Cornwall PL34 0HE
T 01840-770328
12th-century cliff-top castle and Dark Age settlement
site; linked with Arthurian legend

TOWER OF LONDON, London EC3N 4AB
T 0870-756 6060 W www.hrp.org.uk
Royal palace and fortress begun by William the
Conqueror in 1078; houses the Crown Jewels

TRERICE (NT), nr Newquay, Cornwall TR8 4PG
T 01637-875404
Elizabethan manor house

TYNEMOUTH PRIORY AND CASTLE (EH), Tyne and
Wear NE30 4BZ T 0191-257 1090
Remains of a Benedictine priory, founded c.1090, on
Saxon monastic site

UPPARK (NT), South Harting, W. Sussex GU31 5QR
T 01730-825415
Late 17th-century house, completely restored after fire;
Fetherstonhaugh art collection

WALMER CASTLE (EH), Walmer, Kent CT14 7LJ
T 01304-364288
One of Henry VIII's coastal defence castles, now the
residence of the Lord Warden of the Cinque Ports

WALTHAM ABBEY (EH), Waltham Abbey, Essex EN9 1DJ
T 01992-702200
Ruined abbey including the nave of the abbey church,
'Harold's Bridge' and late 14th-century gatehouse;
traditionally the burial place of Harold II (1066)

WARKWORTH CASTLE (EH), Warkworth,
Northumberland NE65 0UJ T 01665-711423
15th-century keep amidst earlier ruins, with
14th-century hermitage upstream

WARWICK CASTLE, Warwick, Warks CV34 4QU
T 0870-442 2000 W www.warwick-castle.co.uk
Medieval castle with Madame Tussaud's waxworks, in
Capability Brown park

WHITBY ABBEY (EH), Whitby, N. Yorks YO22 4JT
T 01947-603568
Remains of Norman church on the site of a monastery
founded in AD 657

WILTON HOUSE, nr Salisbury, Wilts SP2 0BJ
T 01722-746714 W www.wiltonhouse.co.uk
17th-century house on the site of a Tudor house and
ninth-century nunnery

WINDSOR CASTLE, Windsor, Berks SL4 1NJ
T 020-7766 7304 W www.royal.gov.uk
Official residence of the Queen; oldest royal residence
still in regular use; largest inhabited castle in the world.
Also St George's Chapel

WOBURN ABBEY, Woburn, Beds MK17 9WA
T 01525-290333 W www.woburnabbey.co.uk
Built on the site of a Cistercian abbey; seat of the Dukes
of Bedford; important art collection; antiques centre

WROXETER ROMAN CITY (EH), nr Shrewsbury,
Shropshire SY5 6PH T 01743-761330
Second-century public baths and part of the forum of
the Roman town of Viroconium

WALES

For more information on any of the Cadw properties
listed below, the official website is www.cadw.wales.gov.uk
For more information on any of the National Trust
properties listed below, the official website is
www.nationaltrust.org.uk
(C) Property of Cadw: Welsh Historic Monuments
(NT) National Trust property

BEAUMARIS CASTLE (C), Anglesey LL58 8AP
T 01248-810361
Concentrically planned castle, still virtually intact

CAERLEON ROMAN BATHS AND AMPHITHEATRE
(C), nr Newport NP18 1AE T 01633-422518
Rare example of a legionary bath-house and late first-
century arena surrounded by bank for spectators

CAERNARFON CASTLE (C), Gwynedd LL55 2AY
T 01286-677617 W www.caernarfon.com
Important castle built between 1283 and 1330,
initially for King Edward I of England

CAERPHILLY CASTLE (C), Caerphilly CF83 1JD
T 029-2088 3143
Concentrically-planned castle (c.1270) notable for its
scale and use of water defences

CARDIFF CASTLE, Cardiff CF10 3RB T 029-2087 8100
W www.cardiffcastle.com
Castle built on the site of a Roman fort; spectacular
towers and rich interior

CASTELL COCH (C), nr Cardiff CF15 7JS T 029-2081 0101
'Fairytale castle' rebuilt 1875–90 on medieval
foundations

CHEPSTOW CASTLE (C), Monmouthshire NP16 5EZ
T 01291-624065
Rectangular keep amid extensive fortifications

CONWY CASTLE (C), Gwynedd LL32 8AY
T 01492-592358
Built by Edward I, 1283–7

CRICCIETH CASTLE (C), Gwynedd LL55 0DP
T 01766-522227
Native Welsh 13th-century castle, altered by Edward I

DENBIGH CASTLE (C), Denbighshire LL16 3NB
T 01745-813385
Remains of the castle (begun 1282), including
triple-towered gatehouse

HARLECH CASTLE (C), Gwynedd LL46 2YH
T 01766-780552
Well-preserved Edwardian castle, constructed
1283–90, on an outcrop above the former shoreline

PEMBROKE CASTLE, Dyfed SA71 4LA T 01646-681510
W www.pembrokecastle.co.uk
Castle founded in 1093; Great Tower built 1200;
birthplace of King Henry VII

PENRHYN CASTLE (NT), Bangor, Gwynedd LL57 4HN
T 01248-353084
Neo-Norman castle built in the 19th-century;
industrial railway museum

PORTMEIRION, Gwynedd LL48 6ET T 01766-770228
W www.portmeirion-village.com
Village in Italianate style

POWIS CASTLE (NT), nr Welshpool, Powys SY21 8RF
T 01938-551929
Medieval castle with interior in variety of styles;
17th-century gardens; Clive of India museum

RAGLAN CASTLE (C), Monmouthshire NP15 2BT
T 01291-690228
Remains of 15th-century castle with moated hexagonal
keep

ST DAVIDS BISHOP'S PALACE (C), Dyfed SA62 6PE
T 01437-720517
   Remains of residence of Bishops of St Davids built
   1328–47
TINTERN ABBEY (C), nr Chepstow, Monmouthshire
NP16 6SE T 01291-689251
   Remains of 13th-century church and conventual
   buildings of a Cistercian monastery
TRETOWER COURT AND CASTLE (C), nr Crickhowell,
Powys NP8 1RF T 01874-730279
   Medieval house with remains of 12th-century castle
   nearby

SCOTLAND

For more information on any of the Historic Scotland
properties listed below, the official website is
www.historic-scotland.gov.uk
   For more information on any of the National Trust for
Scotland properties listed below, the official website is
www.nts.org.uk
(HS) Historic Scotland property
(NTS) National Trust for Scotland property

ABBOTSFORD HOUSE, Melrose, Roxburghshire TD6 9BQ
T 01896-752043 W www.scottsabbotsford.co.uk
   Home of Sir Walter Scott
ANTONINE WALL, between the Clyde and the Forth
   Built around AD 142; consists of ditch, turf rampart,
   road and forts at regular intervals
BALMORAL CASTLE, nr Braemar, Aberdeenshire AB35 5TB
T 01339-742534 W www.balmoralcastle.com
   Baronial-style castle built for Victoria and Albert; the
   Queen's private residence
BLACK HOUSE, ARNOL (HS), Lewis, Western Isles
HS2 9DB T 01851-710395
   Traditional Lewis thatched house
BLAIR CASTLE, Blair Atholl, Perthshire PH18 5TL
T 01796-481207 W www.blair-castle.co.uk
   Mid-18th-century mansion with 13th-century tower;
   seat of the Dukes and Earls of Atholl
BONAWE IRON FURNACE (HS), Taynuilt, Argyll
PA35 1JQ T 01866-822432
   Charcoal-fuelled ironworks founded in 1753
BOWHILL, Selkirkshire TD7 5ET T 01750-22204
   Seat of the Dukes of Buccleuch and Queensberry;
   fine collection of paintings, including portrait
   miniatures
BROUGH OF BIRSAY (HS), Orkney KW17 2NH
T 01856-841815
   Remains of Norse church and village on the tidal island
   of Birsay
CAERLAVEROCK CASTLE (HS), Glencaple, Dumfriesshire
DG1 4RU T 01387-770244
   Triangular 13th-century castle with classical
   Renaissance additions
CAIRNPAPPLE HILL (HS), Torphichen, West Lothian
T 01506-634622
   Neolithic and Bronze Age burial chambers and henge
CALANAIS STANDING STONES (HS), Lewis, Western
Isles HS2 9DY T 01851-621422
   Standing stones in a cross-shaped setting, dating from
   2900–2600 BC
CATERTHUNS (BROWN AND WHITE) (HS), Menmuir,
nr Brechin, Angus T 0131-668 8800
   Two large Iron Age hill forts

CAWDOR CASTLE, Nairn, Moray IV12 5RD
T 01667-404401 W www.cawdorcastle.com
   14th-century keep with 15th- and 17th-century
   additions
CLAVA CAIRNS (HS), nr Inverness, Inverness-shire
T 01667-460232
   Late Neolithic or early Bronze Age cairns
CRATHES CASTLE (NTS), nr Banchory, Aberdeenshire
AB31 5QJ T 01330-844525
   16th-century baronial castle in woodland, fields and
   gardens
CULZEAN CASTLE (NTS), Maybole, Ayrshire KA19 8LE
T 0870-118 1945 W www.culzeanexperience.org
   18th-century Adam castle with oval staircase and
   circular saloon
DRYBURGH ABBEY (HS), nr Melrose, Roxburghshire
TD6 0RQ T 01835-822381
   12th-century abbey containing tomb of Sir Walter Scott
DUNVEGAN CASTLE, Skye IV55 8WF T 01470-521206
W www.dunvegancastle.com
   13th-century castle with later additions; home of the
   chiefs of the Clan MacLeod; trips to seal colony
EDINBURGH CASTLE (HS) EH1 2NG T 0131-225 9846
   Includes the Scottish Crown Jewels, Scottish National
   War Memorial, Scottish United Services Museum and
   historic apartments
EDZELL CASTLE (HS), nr Brechin, Angus DD9 7UE
T 01356-648631
   Medieval tower house; walled garden
EILEAN DONAN CASTLE, Dornie, Ross and Cromarty
IV40 8DX T 01599-555202 W www.eileandonancastle.com
   13th-century castle with Jacobite relics
ELGIN CATHEDRAL (HS), Moray IV30 1EL
T 01343-547171
   13th-century cathedral and chapterhouse
FLOORS CASTLE, Kelso, Roxburghshire TD5 7SF
T 01573-223333 W www.floorscastle.com
   Largest inhabited castle in Scotland; seat of the Dukes
   of Roxburghe; built 1721 by William Adam
FORT GEORGE (HS), Ardersier, Inverness-shire IV2 7TE
T 01667-460232
   18th-century fort
GLAMIS CASTLE, Forfar, Angus DD8 1RJ T 01307-840393
W www.glamis-castle.co.uk
   Seat of the Lyon family (later Earls of Strathmore and
   Kinghorne) since 1372
GLASGOW CATHEDRAL (HS), Lanarkshire G4 0QZ
T 0141-552 6891 W www.glasgowcathedral.org.uk
   Medieval cathedral with elaborately vaulted crypt
GLENELG BROCHS (HS), Shielbridge, Ross and Cromarty
T 01667-460232
   Two broch towers with well-preserved structural
   features
HOPETOUN HOUSE, South Queensferry, W. Lothian
EH30 9SL T 0131-331 2451 W www.hopetounhouse.com
   House designed by Sir William Bruce, enlarged by
   William Adam
HUNTLY CASTLE (HS), Aberdeenshire AB54 4SH
T 01466-793191
   Ruin of a 16th- and 17th-century house
INVERARAY CASTLE, Argyll PA32 8XE T 01499-302203
W www.inveraray-castle.com
   Gothic-style 18th-century castle; seat of the Dukes of
   Argyll
IONA ABBEY (HS), Iona, Inner Hebrides PA76 6SQ
T 01681-700512
   Monastery founded by St Columba in AD 563

JARLSHOF (HS), Sumburgh, Shetland ZE3 9JN
T 01950-460112
Prehistoric and Norse settlement
JEDBURGH ABBEY (HS), Scottish Borders TD8 6JQ
T 01835-863925
Romanesque and early Gothic church founded c.1138
KELSO ABBEY (HS), Kelso, Scottish Borders TD5 7JD
Remains of great abbey church founded 1128
KISIMUL CASTLE (HS), Castlebay, Barra, Western Isles
T 01871-810313
Medieval home of the Clan MacNeil
LINLITHGOW PALACE (HS), Kirkgate, Linlithgow, W.
Lothian EH49 7AL T 01506-842896
Ruin of royal palace in park setting; birthplace of
James V and Mary, Queen of Scots
MAES HOWE (HS), Stenness, Orkney KW16 3HA
T 01856-761606
Neolithic tomb
MEIGLE SCULPTURED STONES (HS), Meigle,
Perthshire PH12 8SB T 01828-640612
Twenty-six Celtic Christian stones
MELROSE ABBEY (HS), Melrose, Roxburghshire TD6 9LG
T 01896-822562
Ruin of Cistercian abbey founded c.1136 by David I
MOUSA BROCH (HS), Mousa, Shetland T 01856-841815
Finest surviving Iron Age broch tower
NEW ABBEY CORN MILL (HS), Dumfriesshire DG2 8BX
T 01387-850260
Working water-powered mill
PALACE OF HOLYROODHOUSE, Edinburgh EH8 8DX
T 0131-556 5100 W www.royal.gov.uk
The Queen's official Scottish residence; main part of
the palace built 1671–9
RING O' BRODGAR (HS), nr Stromness, Orkney
T 01856-841815
Neolithic circle of upright stones with an enclosing
ditch
ROSSLYN CHAPEL, Roslin, Midlothian EH25 9PU
T 0131-440 2159 W www.rosslynchapel.org.uk
Historic church with unique stone carvings
RUTHWELL CROSS (HS), Ruthwell, Dumfriesshire
T 01387-870249
Seventh-century Anglian cross
ST ANDREWS CASTLE AND CATHEDRAL (HS),
Fife KY16 9AR T 01334-477196 (castle);
01334-472563 (cathedral)
Ruins of 13th-century castle and remains of the largest
cathedral in Scotland
SCONE PALACE, Perth, Perthshire PH2 6BD
T 01738-552300 W www.scone-palace.net
House built 1802–13 on the site of a medieval palace
SKARA BRAE (HS), nr Stromness, Orkney KW16 3LR
T 01856-841815
Stone Age village with adjacent 17th-century house
SMAILHOLM TOWER (HS), nr Kelso, Roxburghshire
TD5 7PG T 01573-460365
Well-preserved 15th-century tower-house
STIRLING CASTLE (HS), Stirlingshire FK8 1EJ
T 01786-450000
Great Hall and gatehouse of James IV, palace of James
V, Chapel Royal remodelled by James VI
TANTALLON CASTLE (HS), North Berwick, E. Lothian
EH39 5PN T 01620-892727
Fortification with earthwork defences; and a
14th-century curtain wall with towers

THREAVE CASTLE (HS), Castle Douglas,
Kirkcudbrightshire T 07711-223101
Late 14th-century tower on an island; accessible only
by boat
URQUHART CASTLE (HS), Drumnadrochit, Inverness-shire
IV63 6XJ T 01456-450551
13th-century castle remains on the banks of Loch Ness

NORTHERN IRELAND

For the Northern Ireland Environment and Heritage
Service, the official website is www.ehsni.gov.uk
For more information on any of the National Trust
properties listed below, the official website is
www.nationaltrust.org.uk
(EHS) Property in the care of the Northern Ireland
Environment and Heritage Service
(NT) National Trust property

CARRICKFERGUS CASTLE (EHS), Carrickfergus,
Co. Antrim BT38 7BG T 028-9335 1273
Castle begun in 1180 and garrisoned until 1928
CASTLE COOLE (NT), Enniskillen, Co. Fermanagh
BT74 6JY T 028-6632 2690
18th-century mansion by James Wyatt in parkland
CASTLE WARD (NT), Strangford, Co. Down BT30 7LS
T 028-4488 1204
18th-century house with Classical and Gothic facades
DEVENISH ISLAND (EHS), nr Enniskillen,
Co. Fermanagh T 028-9054 6518
Island monastery founded in the sixth century by St
Molaise
DOWNHILL DEMESNE (NT), Castlerock, Co.
Londonderry BT51 4RP T 028-2073 1582
Ruins of palatial house in landscaped estate including
Mussenden Temple
DUNLUCE CASTLE (EHS), Bushmills, Co. Antrim
BT57 8QG T 028-2073 1938
Ruins of 16th-century stronghold of the MacDonnells
FLORENCE COURT (NT), Enniskillen, Co. Fermanagh
BT92 1DB T 028-6634 8249
Mid-18th-century house with Rococo decoration
GREY ABBEY (EHS), Greyabbey, Co. Down
T 028-9054 6552
Substantial remains of a Cistercian abbey founded in
1193
HILLSBOROUGH FORT (EHS), Hillsborough, Co. Down
BT26 6AG T 028-9054 6552
Square keep built in 1650
MOUNT STEWART (NT), Newtownards, Co. Down
BT22 2AD T 028-4278 8387
18th century house; childhood home of Lord
Castlereagh
NENDRUM MONASTERY (EHS), Mahee Island,
Co. Down T 028-9181 1491
Founded in the fifth century by St Machaoi
TULLY CASTLE (EHS), Co. Fermanagh T 028-9054 6552
Fortified house and bawn built in 1613
WHITE ISLAND (EHS), Co. Fermanagh
Tenth-century monastery; 12th-century church
featuring stone figures dating from the sixth century

MUSEUMS AND GALLERIES

There are approximately 2,500 museums and galleries in the United Kingdom. Around 1,800 are accredited by the Museums, Libraries and Archives Council (MLA), which indicates that they have an appropriate constitution, are soundly financed, have adequate collection management standards and public services, and have access to professional curatorial advice. Applications for accreditation are assessed by either the relevant regional agency in England, Museums Archives and Libraries Wales (CyMAL), the Scottish Museums Council or the Northern Ireland Museums Council.

The following is a selection of museums and art galleries in the United Kingdom. Opening hours and admission charges vary. Further information about museums and galleries in the UK is available from the Museums Association (T 020-7426 6970 W www.museumsassociation.org). W www.24hourmuseum.org.uk is the UK's national virtual museum and includes a database of all the museums and galleries in the UK.

ENGLAND

* Receives government funding directly from the DCMS. These institutions are deemed to have collections of national importance, and the government is able to call upon their staff for expert advice

BARNARD CASTLE, Co. Durham – *The Bowes Museum,* Newgate DL12 8NP T 01833-690606
W www.thebowesmuseum.org.uk
European art from the late medieval period to the 19th century; English period rooms from Elizabeth I to Victoria; local archaeology
BATH – *American Museum,* Claverton Manor BA2 7BD
T 01225-460503 W www.americanmuseum.org
American decorative arts from the 17th to 19th century
Museum of Costume, Bennett Street BA1 2QH
T 01225-477173 W www.museumofcostume.co.uk
Fashion from the 16th century to the present day
Roman Baths Museum, Pump Room, Stall Street BA1 1LZ
T 01225-477785 W www.romanbaths.co.uk
Museum adjoins the remains of a Roman baths and temple complex
Victoria Art Gallery, Bridge Street BA2 4AT T 01225-477233
W www.victoriagal.org.uk
European Old Masters and British art since the 18th century
BEAMISH, Co. Durham – *Beamish, The North of England Open Air Museum,* DH9 0RG T 0191-370 4000
W www.beamish.org.uk
Recreated northern town c.1900, with rebuilt local buildings, colliery village, farm, railway station, tramway, Pockerley Manor and horse-yard (set c.1800)
BEAULIEU, Hants – *National Motor Museum,* SO42 7ZN
T 01590-612345 W www.beaulieu.co.uk
Over 250 vehicles dating from 1895 to the present day
BIRMINGHAM – *Aston Hall,* Trinity Road B6 6JD
T 0121-327 0062 W www.bmag.org.uk/aston_hall
Jacobean House containing paintings, furniture and tapestries from the 17th to 19th century
Barber Institute of Fine Arts, University of Birmingham, Edgbaston B15 2TS T 0121-414 7333
W www.barber.org.uk
Fine arts, including Old Masters

Birmingham Museum and Art Gallery, Chamberlain Square B3 3DH T 0121-303 2834 W www.bmag.org.uk
Includes notable collection of Pre-Raphaelite art
Museum of the Jewellery Quarter, Vyse Street, Hockley B18 6HA T 0121-554 3598 W www.bmag.org.uk
Built around a real jewellery workshop
BOVINGTON, Dorset – *Tank Museum,* BH20 6JG
T 01929-405096 W www.tankmuseum.co.uk
Collection of 300 tanks from the earliest days of tank warfare to the present
BRADFORD – *Cartwright Hall Art Gallery,* Lister Park BD9 4NS T 01274-431212 W www.bradfordmuseums.org
British 19th- and 20th-century fine art
Bradford Industrial Museum and Horses at Work, Moorside Road, Eccleshill BD2 3HP T 01274-435900
W www.bradfordmuseums.org
Engineering, textiles, transport and social history exhibits, including recreated back-to-back cottages, shire horses and horse tram-rides
National Museum of Photography, Film & Television, Princes Way BD1 1NQ T 0870-7010200
W www.nationalmediamuseum.org.uk
Photography, film and television interactive exhibits; features the UK's first IMAX cinema and the only public Cinerama screen in the world
BRIGHTON – *Booth Museum of Natural History,* Dyke Road BN1 5AA T 01273-292777
W www.booth.virtualmuseum.info
Zoology, botany and geology collections; British birds in recreated habitats
Brighton Museum and Art Gallery, Royal Pavilion Gardens BN1 1EE T 01273-290900
W www.brighton.virtualmuseum.info
Includes fine art and design, fashion, non-Western art, Brighton history
BRISTOL – *Arnolfini,* Narrow Quay BS1 4QA
T 0117-917 2300 W www.arnolfini.org.uk
Contemporary visual arts, dance, performance, music, talks and workshops
Blaise Castle House Museum, Henbury BS10 7QS
T 0117-903 9818 W www.bristol-city.gov.uk/museums
Agricultural and social history collections in an 18th-century mansion
Bristol Industrial Museum, Princes Wharf, Wapping Road BS1 4RN T 0117-903 1569
W www.bristol-city.gov.uk/museums
Industrial, maritime and transport collections
City Museum and Art Gallery, Queen's Road BS8 1RL
T 0117-922 3571 W www.bristol-city.gov.uk/museums
Includes fine and decorative art, oriental art, Egyptology and Bristol ceramics and paintings
CAMBRIDGE – *Fitzwilliam Museum,* Trumpington Street CB2 1RB T 01223-332900
W www.fitzmuseum.cam.ac.uk
Antiquities, fine and applied arts, clocks, ceramics, manuscripts, furniture, sculpture, coins and medals
Imperial War Museum Duxford, Duxford CB22 4QR
T 01223-835000 W http://duxford.iwm.org.uk
Displays of military and civil aircraft, tanks, guns and naval exhibits
Sedgwick Museum of Earth Sciences, Downing Street CB2 3EQ
T 01223-333456 W www.sedgwickmuseum.org
Extensive geological collection

University Museum of Archaeology and Anthropology, Downing Street CB2 3DZ T 01223-333516
W http://museum.archanth.cam.ac.uk
Archaeology and anthropology from all parts of the world

University Museum of Zoology, Downing Street CB2 3EJ
T 01223-336600 W www.zoo.cam.ac.uk
Extensive zoological collection

Whipple Museum of the History of Science, Free School Lane CB2 3RH T 01223-330906 W www.hps.cam.ac.uk/whipple
Scientific instruments from the 14th century to the present

CARLISLE — *Tullie House Museum and Art Gallery,* Castle Street CA3 8TP T 01228-534781 W www.tulliehouse.co.uk
Prehistoric archaeology, Hadrian's Wall, Viking and medieval Cumbria, and the social history of Carlisle; British 19th- and 20th-century art; English porcelain

CHATHAM — *Dickens World,* Leviathan Way ME4 4LL
T 0870-241 1415 W www.dickensworld.co.uk
Theme park based on the life, books and era of Charles Dickens

The Historic Dockyard, ME4 4TZ T 01634-823800
W www.chdt.org.uk
Maritime attractions including HMS *Cavalier,* the UK's last Second World War destroyer

Royal Engineers Museum of Military Engineering, Prince Arthur Road, Gillingham ME4 4UG T 01634-822839
W www.remuseum.org.uk
Regimental history, ethnography, decorative art and photography

CHELTENHAM — *Art Gallery and Museum,* Clarence Street GL50 3TJ T 01242-237431 W www.cheltenham.gov.uk
Paintings, arts and crafts

CHESTER — *Grosvenor Museum,* Grosvenor Street CH1 2DD
T 01244-402008 W www.chester.gov.uk
Roman collections, natural history, art, Chester silver, local history and costume

CHICHESTER — *Weald and Downland Open Air Museum,* Singleton PO18 0EU T 01243-811363
W www.wealddown.co.uk
Rebuilt vernacular buildings from south-east England; includes medieval houses, agricultural and rural craft buildings and a working watermill

COLCHESTER — *Colchester Castle Museum,* Castle Park CO1 1TJ T 01206-282939
W www.colchestermuseums.org.uk
Largest Norman keep in Europe standing on foundations of the Roman Temple of Claudius; tours of the Roman vaults, castle walls and chapel

COVENTRY — *Coventry Transport Museum,* Hales Street CV1 1PN T 024-7623 4270 W www.transport-museum.com
Hundreds of motor vehicles and bicycles

Herbert Art Gallery and Museum, Jordan Well CV1 5QP
T 024-7683 2386 W www.theherbert.org
Local history, archaeology and industry; fine and decorative art

DERBY — *Derby Museum and Art Gallery,* The Strand DE1 1BS T 01332-716659 W www.derby.gov.uk
Includes paintings by Joseph Wright of Derby and Derby porcelain

Pickford's House Museum, Friar Gate DE1 1DA
T 01332-255363 W www.derby.gov.uk
Georgian town house by architect Joseph Pickford; reconstructed period rooms and garden

The Silk Mill, Derby's Museum of Industry and History, Full Street DE1 3AF T 01332-255308 W www.derby.gov.uk
Rolls-Royce aero engine collection and railway engineering gallery

DEVIZES — *Wiltshire Heritage Museum,* Long Street SN10 1NS T 01380-727369
W www.wiltshireheritage.org.uk
Natural and local history, art gallery, archaeological finds from Bronze Age, Iron Age, Roman and Saxon sites

DORCHESTER — *Dorset County Museum,* High West Street DT1 1XA T 01305-262735
W www.dorsetcountymuseum.org
Includes a collection of Thomas Hardy's manuscripts, books, notebooks and drawings

DOVER — *Dover Museum,* Market Square CT16 1PB
T 01304-201066 W www.dovermuseum.co.uk
Contains Dover Bronze Age Boat Gallery and archaeological finds from Bronze Age, Roman and Saxon sites

EXETER — *Royal Albert Memorial Museum and Art Gallery,* Queen Street EX4 3RX T 01392-665858
W www.exeter.gov.uk/ramm
Natural history, archaeology, worldwide fine and decorative art including Exeter silver

GATESHEAD — *Baltic Centre for Contemporary Art,* South Shore Road NE8 3BA T 0191-478 1810
W www.balticmill.com
Contemporary art exhibitions and events

Shipley Art Gallery, Prince Consort Road NE8 4JB
T 0191-477 1495 W www.twmuseums.org.uk/shipley
Contemporary crafts

GAYDON, Warks — *Heritage Motor Centre,* Banbury Road CV35 0BJ T 01926-641188
W www.heritage-motor-centre.co.uk
History of British motor industry from 1895 to present; classic vehicles; engineering gallery; Corgi and Lucas collections

GLOUCESTER — *National Waterways Museum,* Gloucester Docks GL1 2EH T 01452-318200 W www.nwm.org.uk
Two-hundred-year history of Britain's canals and inland waterways

GOSPORT, Hants — *Royal Navy Submarine Museum,* Haslar Jetty Road PO12 2AS T 023-9252 9217
W www.rnsubmus.co.uk
Underwater warfare, including the submarine *Alliance;* first Royal Navy submarine

GRASMERE, Cumbria — *Dove Cottage* and the *Wordsworth Museum,* LA22 9SH T 01539-435544
W www.wordsworth.org.uk
William Wordsworth's home and garden

HULL — *Ferens Art Gallery,* Queen Victoria Square HU1 3RA
T 01482-300300 W www.hullcc.gov.uk/museums
European art, especially Dutch 17th-century paintings, British portraits from 17th to 20th century, and marine paintings

Hull Maritime Museum, Queen Victoria Square HU1 3DX
T 01482-300300 W www.hullcc.gov.uk/museums
Whaling, fishing and navigation exhibits

HUNTINGDON — *The Cromwell Museum,* Grammar School Walk PE29 3LF T 01480-375830
W www.cambridgeshire.gov.uk/cromwell
Portraits and memorabilia relating to Oliver Cromwell

IPSWICH — *Christchurch Mansion* and *Wolsey Art Gallery,* Christchurch Park IP4 2BE T 01473-433554
W www.ipswich.gov.uk
Tudor house with paintings by Gainsborough, Constable and other Suffolk artists; furniture and 18th-century ceramics; temporary exhibitions

LEEDS — *Armley Mills, Leeds Industrial Museum,* Canal Road, Armley LS12 2QF T 0113-263 7861
W www.leeds.gov.uk/armleymills
World's largest woollen mill

Leeds City Art Gallery, The Headrow LS1 3AA
T 0113-247 8248 W www.leeds.gov.uk/artgallery
British and European paintings including English
watercolours; modern sculpture; Henry Moore gallery;
print room

Lotherton Hall, Aberford LS25 3EB T 0113-281 3259
W www.leeds.gov.uk/lothertonhall
Costume and oriental collections in furnished
Edwardian house; deer park and bird garden

*Royal Armouries Museum, Armouries Drive LS10 1LT
T 0113-220 1916 W www.royalarmouries.org
National collection of arms and armour from BC to
present; demonstrations of foot combat in museum's
five galleries; falconry and mounted combat in the tiltyard

Temple Newsam, LS15 0AE T 0113-264 5535
W www.leeds.gov.uk/templenewsam
Old Masters and 17th- and 18th-century decorative art
in furnished Jacobean/Tudor house

LEICESTER – Jewry Wall Museum, St Nicholas Circle
LE1 4LB T 0116-225 4971 W www.leicestermuseums.ac.uk
Archaeology; Roman Jewry Wall and baths; mosaics

New Walk Museum and Art Gallery, New Walk LE1 7EA
T 0116-255 4900 W www.leicestermuseums.ac.uk
Natural history and geology; ancient Egypt gallery;
European art and decorative arts

LINCOLN – Museum of Lincolnshire Life, Burton Road
LN1 3LY T 01522-528448 W www.lincolnshire.gov.uk
Social history and agricultural collection

Usher Gallery, Lindum Road LN2 1NN T 01522-527980
W www.lincolnshire.gov.uk
Watches, miniatures, porcelain, silver; collection of
Peter de Wint works; Lincolnshire topography; Royal
Lincs Regiment memorabilia

LIVERPOOL – *Lady Lever Art Gallery, Wirral CH62 5EQ
T 0151-478 4136 W www.liverpoolmuseums.org/ladylever
Paintings, furniture and porcelain

*Merseyside Maritime Museum, Albert Dock L3 4AQ
T 0151-478 4499
W www.liverpoolmuseums.org.uk/maritime
Floating exhibits, working displays and craft
demonstrations; incorporates HM Customs and Excise
National Museum

*Sudley House, Mossley Hill Road L18 8BX T 0151-724 3245
W www.liverpoolmuseums.org/sudley
Late 18th- and 19th-century paintings in former
shipowner's home

*Tate Liverpool, Albert Dock L3 4BB T 0151-702 7400
W www.tate.org.uk/liverpool
Twentieth-century paintings and sculpture

*Walker Art Gallery, William Brown Street L3 8EL
T 0151-478 4199 W www.liverpoolmuseums.org.uk/walker
Paintings from the 14th to 20th century

*World Museum Liverpool, William Brown Street L3 8EN
T 0151-478 4393 W www.liverpoolmuseums.org.uk/wml
Includes Egyptian mummies, weapons and classical
sculpture; planetarium, aquarium, vivarium and natural
history centre

LONDON: GALLERIES – Barbican Art Gallery, Barbican
Centre, Silk Street EC2Y 8DS T 020-7638 4141
W www.barbican.org.uk
Temporary exhibitions

Courtauld Institute of Art Gallery, Somerset House, Strand
WC2R 0RN T 020-7848 2777 W www.courtauld.ac.uk
Impressionist and Post-Impressionist paintings

Dulwich Picture Gallery, Gallery Road, Dulwich Village
SE21 7AD T 020-8693 5254
W www.dulwichpicturegallery.org.uk
England's first public art gallery; built by Sir

John Soane to house 17th- and 18th-century
paintings

Hayward Gallery, Belvedere Road SE1 8XZ T 0870-165 6000
W www.southbankcentre.co.uk
Temporary exhibitions

*National Gallery, Trafalgar Square WC2N 5DN
T 020-7747 2885 W www.nationalgallery.org.uk
Western painting from the 13th to 20th century;
early Renaissance collection in the Sainsbury
Wing

*National Portrait Gallery, St Martin's Place WC2H 0HE
T 020-7306 0055 W www.npg.org.uk
Portraits of eminent people in British history

Percival David Foundation of Chinese Art, Gordon Square
WC1H 0PD T 020-7387 3909 W www.pdfmuseum.org.uk
Chinese ceramics from 10th to 18th century

Photographers' Gallery, Great Newport Street WC2H 7HY
T 020-7831 1772 W www.photonet.org.uk
Temporary exhibitions

The Queen's Gallery, Buckingham Palace SW1A 1AA
T 020-7766 7301 W www.royal.gov.uk
Art from the Royal Collection

Royal Academy of Arts, Burlington House, Piccadilly W1J 0BD
T 020-7300 8000 W www.royalacademy.org.uk
British art since 1750 and temporary exhibitions;
annual Summer Exhibition

Saatchi Gallery, Sloane Square SW3 4RY
T 020-7823 2363 W www.saatchi-gallery.co.uk
Contemporary art including paintings, photographs,
sculpture and installations

Serpentine Gallery, Kensington Gardens W2 3XA
T 020-7402 6075 W www.serpentinegallery.org
Temporary exhibitions of British and international
contemporary art

*Tate Britain, Millbank SW1P 4RG T 020-7887 8888
W www.tate.org.uk/britain
British painting and 20th-century painting and
sculpture

*Tate Modern, Bankside SE1 9TG T 020-7887 8888
W www.tate.org.uk/modern
International modern art from 1900 to the present

*Wallace Collection, Manchester Square W1U 3BN
T 020-7563 9500 W www.wallacecollection.org
Paintings and drawings, French 18th-century furniture,
armour, porcelain, clocks and sculpture

Whitechapel Art Gallery, Whitechapel High Street E1 7QX
T 020-7522 7888 W www.whitechapel.org
Temporary exhibitions of modern art

LONDON: MUSEUMS – Bank of England Museum,
Threadneedle Street EC2R 8AH (entrance on Bartholomew
Lane) T 020-7601 5545
W www.bankofengland.co.uk/museum
History of the Bank of England since 1694

*British Museum, Great Russell Street WC1B 3DG
T 020-7323 8000 W www.thebritishmuseum.ac.uk
Antiquities, coins, medals, prints and drawings

*Cabinet War Rooms, King Charles Street SW1A 2AQ
T 020-7930 6961 W www.cwr.iwm.org.uk
Underground rooms used by Churchill and the
government during the Second World War

Cutty Sark, Greenwich SE10 9HT T 020-8858 3445
W www.cuttysark.org.uk
Damaged by fire in May 2007; temporary exhibition
next to the ship while closed

Design Museum, Shad Thames SE1 2YD T 0870-833 9955
W www.designmuseum.org
The development of design and the mass-production of
consumer objects

Firepower, the Royal Artillery Museum, Royal Arsenal,
Woolwich SE18 6ST **T** 020-8855 7755
W www.firepower.org.uk
The history and development of artillery over the last
700 years including the collections of the Royal
Regiment of Artillery

Geffrye Museum, Kingsland Road E2 8EA **T** 020-7739 9893
W www.geffrye-museum.org.uk
English urban domestic interiors from 1600 to present
day; also paintings, furniture, decorative arts, walled
herb garden and period garden rooms

Gilbert Collection, Strand WC2R 1LA **T** 020-7420 9400
W www.gilbert-collection.org.uk
Collection comprising some 800 works of art
including European silver, gold snuff boxes and Italian
mosaics

*HMS Belfast, Morgan's Lane, Tooley Street SE1 2JH
T 020-7940 6300 **W** http://hmsbelfast.iwm.org.uk
Life on a Second World War cruiser

Horniman Museum, London Road SE23 3PQ **T** 020-8699 1872
W www.horniman.ac.uk
Museum of ethnography, musical instruments and
natural history; aquarium; reference library; sunken,
water and flower gardens

*Imperial War Museum, Lambeth Road SE1 6HZ
T 020-7416 5320 **W** http://london.iwm.org.uk
All aspects of the two world wars and other military
operations involving Britain and the Commonwealth
since 1914

Jewish Museum, Camden Town, Albert Street NW1 7NB
T 020-7284 1997 **W** www.jewishmuseum.org.uk
Jewish life, history and religion

London's Transport Museum, Wellington Street WC2E 7BB
T 020-7379 6344 **W** www.ltmuseum.co.uk
Vehicles, photographs and graphic art relating to the
history of transport in London

MCC Museum, Lord's, St John's Wood NW8 8QN
T 020-7616 8656 **W** www.lords.org
Cricket museum; conducted tours by appointment

*Museum in Docklands, West India Quay, Hertsmere Road
E14 4AL **T** 0870-444 3857
W www.museumindocklands.org.uk
Explores the story of London's river, port and people
over 2,000 years, from Roman times through to the
recent regeneration of London's Docklands

*Museum of Childhood at Bethnal Green (V&A), Cambridge
Heath Road E2 9PA **T** 020-8983 5200
W www.museumofchildhood.org.uk
Toys, games and exhibits relating to the social history
of childhood

Museum of Garden History, Lambeth Palace Road SE1 7LB
T 020-7401 8865 **W** www.museumgardenhistory.org
History and development of gardens and gardening;
recreated 17th-century garden

*Museum of London, London Wall EC2Y 5HN
T 0870-444 3852 **W** www.museumoflondon.org.uk
History of London from prehistoric times to present
day

National Army Museum, Royal Hospital Road SW3 4HT
T 020-7730 0717 **W** www.national-army-museum.ac.uk
Five-hundred-year history of the British soldier;
exhibits include model of the Battle of Waterloo and
recreated First World War trench

*National Maritime Museum, Greenwich SE10 9NF
T 020-8858 4422 **W** www.nmm.ac.uk
Maritime history of Britain; collections include globes,
clocks, telescopes and paintings; comprises the main
building, the Royal Observatory and the Queen's House

*Natural History Museum, Cromwell Road SW7 5BD
T 020-7942 5000 **W** www.nhm.ac.uk
Natural history collections

Petrie Museum of Egyptian Archaeology, University College
London, Malet Place WC1E 6BT **T** 020-7679 2884
W www.petrie.ucl.ac.uk
Egyptian archaeology collection

Royal Air Force Museum, Hendon NW9 5LL **T** 020-8205 2266
W www.rafmuseum.org.uk
Aviation from before the Wright brothers to the
present-day RAF; features more than 70 full-size
aircraft

Royal Mews, Buckingham Palace SW1A 1AA **T** 020-7766 7302
W www.royal.gov.uk
State vehicles, including the Queen's gold state
coach; home to the Queen's horses

*Science Museum, Exhibition Road SW7 2DD
T 0870 870 4868 **W** www.sciencemuseum.org.uk
Science, technology, industry and medicine
collections

Shakespeare's Globe Exhibition, Bankside SE1 9DT
T 020-7902 1400 **W** www.shakespeares-globe.org
Recreation of Elizabethan theatre using
16th-century techniques; includes a tour
of the theatre

*Sir John Soane's Museum, Lincoln's Inn Fields WC2A 3BP
T 020-7405 2107 **W** www.soane.org
Art and antiquities

*Theatre Museum, Russell Street WC2E 7PR **T** 020-7943 4700
W www.theatremuseum.org.uk
History of the performing arts

Tower Bridge Experience, SE1 2UP **T** 020-7403 3761
W www.towerbridge.org.uk
History of the bridge and display of Victorian steam
machinery; panoramic views from walkways

*Victoria and Albert Museum, Cromwell Road SW7 2RL
T 020-7942 2000 **W** www.vam.ac.uk
Includes National Art Library and Print Room; fine and
applied art and design; furniture, glass, textiles and
dress collections

Wimbledon Lawn Tennis Museum, Church Road SW19 5AE
T 020-8946 6131 **W** www.wimbledon.org/museum
Tennis trophies, fashion and memorabilia; view of
Centre Court

MALTON, N. Yorks – *Eden Camp,* YO17 6RT
T 01653 697777 **W** www.edencamp.co.uk
Restored POW camp and Second World War
memorabilia

MANCHESTER – *Gallery of Costume,* Platt Hall, Rusholme
M14 5LL **T** 0161-224 5217 **W** www.manchestergalleries.org
Exhibits from the 16th to the 20th century

*Imperial War Museum North, Trafford Wharf, Trafford Park
M17 1TZ **T** 0161-836 4000 **W** http://north.iwm.org.uk

Manchester Art Gallery, Mosley Street M2 3JL
T 0161-235 8888 **W** www.manchestergalleries.org
Six centuries of European fine and decorative art

Manchester Museum, Oxford Road M13 9PL **T** 0161-275 2634
W www.museum.man.ac.uk
Collections include archaeology, decorative arts,
Egyptology, natural history and zoology

Museum of Science and Industry, Liverpool Road, Castlefield
M3 4FP **T** 0161-832 2244 **W** www.msim.org.uk
On site of world's oldest passenger railway station;
galleries relating to space, energy, power, transport,
aviation, textiles and social history

People's History Museum, The Pump House, Bridge Street
M3 3ER **T** 0161-839 6061 **W** www.phm.org.uk
Political and working life history

Whitworth Art Gallery, Oxford Road M15 6ER
T 0161-275 7450 W www.whitworth.man.ac.uk
Watercolours, drawings, prints, textiles, wallpapers and
20th-century British art
MILTON KEYNES – *Bletchley Park National Codes Centre,*
Bucks MK3 6EB T 01908-640404
W www.bletchleypark.org.uk
Home of British codebreaking during the Second
World War; Enigma machine; computer museum;
wartime toys and memorabilia
MONKWEARMOUTH, Sunderland – *Monkwearmouth
Station Museum,* North Bridge Street SR5 1AP
T 0191-567 7075
W www.twmuseums.org.uk/monkwearmouth
Victorian train station
NEWCASTLE UPON TYNE – *Discovery Museum,*
Blandford Square NE1 4JA T 0191-232 6789
W www.twmuseums.org.uk/discovery
Science and industry, local history, fashion; Tyneside's
maritime history; *Turbinia* (first steam-driven vessel)
gallery
Laing Art Gallery, New Bridge Street NE1 8AG
T 0191-232 7734 W www.twmuseums.org.uk/laing
British and European art, ceramics, glass, silver, textiles
and costume; Art on Tyneside display
NEWMARKET – *National Horseracing Museum,* High Street
CB8 8JL T 01638-667333 W www.nhrm.co.uk
Horseracing simulator, temporary exhibitions and tours
of local trainers' yards and studs
NORTH SHIELDS – *Stephenson Railway Museum,* Middle
Engine Lane NE29 8DX T 0191-200 7146
W www.twmuseums.org.uk/stephenson
Locomotive engines and rolling stock
NOTTINGHAM – *Brewhouse Yard Museum,* Castle
Boulevard NG7 1FB T 0115-915 3600
W www.nottinghamcity.gov.uk
Daily life from the 17th to 20th century
Castle Museum and Art Gallery, Friar Lane NG1 6EL
T 0115-915 3700 W www.nottinghamcity.gov.uk
Paintings, ceramics, silver and glass; history of Nottingham
Industrial Museum, Wollaton NG8 2AE T 0115-915 3900
W www.nottinghamcity.gov.uk
Lacemaking machinery, steam engines and transport
exhibits
Natural History Museum, Wollaton NG8 2AE T 0115-915 3900
W www.nottinghamcity.gov.uk
Local natural history and wildlife dioramas
OXFORD – *Ashmolean Museum,* Beaumont Street OX1 2PH
T 01865-278000 W www.ashmolean.org
European and oriental fine and applied arts,
archaeology, Egyptology and numismatics
Museum of Modern Art, Pembroke Street OX1 1BP
T 01865-722733 W www.modernartoxford.org.uk
Temporary exhibitions
Museum of the History of Science, Broad Street OX1 3AZ
T 01865-277280 W www.mhs.ox.ac.uk
Displays include early scientific instruments, chemical
apparatus, clocks and watches
Oxford University Museum of Natural History, Parks Road
OX1 3PW T 01865-272950 W www.oum.ox.ac.uk
Entomology, geology, mineralogy and zoology
Pitt Rivers Museum, South Parks Road OX1 3PP
T 01865-270927 W www.prm.ox.ac.uk
Ethnographic and archaeological artefacts
PLYMOUTH – *City Museum and Art Gallery,* Drake Circus
PL4 8AJ T 01752-304774 W www.plymouthmuseum.gov.uk
Local and natural history; ceramics; silver; Old Masters;
temporary exhibitions

Plymouth Dome, Hoe Road PL1 2NZ T 01752-603300
W www.plymouthdome.info
Maritime history museum
PORTSMOUTH – *Charles Dickens Birthplace,* Old
Commercial Road PO1 4QL T 023-9282 7261
W www.charlesdickensbirthplace.co.uk
Dickens memorabilia
D-Day Museum, Clarence Esplanade, Southsea PO5 3NT
T 023-9282 7261 W www.ddaymuseum.co.uk
Includes the Overlord embroidery
Portsmouth Historic Dockyard, HM Naval Base PO1 3LJ
T 023-9283 9766 W www.historicdockyard.co.uk
Incorporates the *Royal Naval Museum* (PO1 3NH
T 023-9272 7562 W www.royalnavalmuseum.org),
HMS *Victory* (PO1 3NH T 023-9286 1533
W www.hms-victory.com), HMS *Warrior* (PO1 3QX
T 023-9277 8609 W www.hmswarrior.org),
the *Mary Rose* (PO1 3LX T 023-9281 2931
W www.maryrose.org) and *Action Stations* (PO1 3LJ
T 023-9289 3316 W www.actionstations.org)
History of the Royal Navy and of the dockyard;
warships and technology spanning 500 years
PRESTON – *Harris Museum and Art Gallery,* Market Square
PR1 2PP T 01772-258248 W www.harrismuseum.org.uk
British art since the 18th century; ceramics, glass,
costume and local history; contemporary exhibitions
National Football Museum, Deepdale PR1 6RU
T 01772-908442 W www.nationalfootballmuseum.com
Home to the FIFA museum collection; FA, Football
League and Wembley collections on long-term loan
ST ALBANS – *Verulamium Museum,* St Michael's Street
AL3 4SW T 01727-751810 W www.verulamium.com
Remains of Iron Age settlement and the third-largest
city in Roman Britain; exhibits include Roman wall
plasters, jewellery, mosaics and room reconstructions
ST IVES, Cornwall – **Tate St Ives,* Porthmeor Beach TR26 1TG
T 01736-796226 W www.tate.org.uk/stives
Modern art, much by artists associated with St Ives;
includes the Barbara Hepworth Museum and Sculpture
Garden
SALISBURY – *Salisbury & South Wiltshire Museum,* The
Close SP1 2EN T 01722-332151
W www.salisburymuseum.org.uk
Archaeology collection
SHEFFIELD – *Graves Art Gallery,* Surrey Street S1 1XZ
T 0114-278 2600 W www.sheffieldgalleries.org.uk
20th-century British art, Grice Collection of
Chinese ivories
Millennium Galleries, Arundel Gate S1 2PP T 0114-278 2600
W www.sheffieldgalleries.org.uk
Incorporates four different galleries: the Special
Exhibition Gallery, the Craft and Design Gallery, the
Metalwork Gallery and the Ruskin Gallery, which
houses John Ruskin's collection of paintings, drawings,
books and medieval manuscripts
Weston Park Museum, Western Bank S10 2TP T 0114-278 2600
W www.sheffieldgalleries.org.uk
World history for families
SOUTHAMPTON – *City Art Gallery,* Commercial
Road SO14 7LP T 023-8083 2277
W www.southampton.gov.uk/art
Fine art, especially 20th-century British
Maritime Museum, Town Quay Road SO14 2NY
T 023-8063 5904 W www.southampton.gov.uk
Southampton maritime history
Museum of Archaeology, Winkle Street SO14 2NY
T 023-8063 5904 W www.southampton.gov.uk
Roman, Saxon and medieval archaeology

SOUTH SHIELDS – *Arbeia Roman Fort,* Baring Street NE33 2BB **T** 0191-456 1369 **W** www.twmuseums.org.uk/arbeia Excavated ruins

South Shields Museum and Art Gallery, Ocean Road NE33 2JA **T** 0191-456 8740 **W** www.twmuseums.org.uk/southshields South Tyneside history, including reconstructed street

STOKE-ON-TRENT – *Etruria Industrial Museum,* Lower Bedford Street ST4 7AF **T** 01782-233144 **W** www.stoke.gov.uk/museums Britain's sole surviving steam-powered potter's mill

Gladstone Pottery Museum, Longton ST3 1PQ **T** 01782-237777 **W** www.stoke.gov.uk/museums A working Victorian pottery

Potteries Museum and Art Gallery, Hanley ST1 3DW **T** 01782-232323 **W** www.stoke.gov.uk/museums Pottery, china and porcelain collections and a Mark XVI Spitfire

SUNDERLAND – *Sunderland Museum & Winter Gardens,* Burdon Road SR1 1PP **T** 0191-553 2323 **W** www.twmuseums.org.uk/sunderland Fine and decorative art, local history and gardens

TELFORD – *Ironbridge Gorge Museums,* TF8 7DQ **T** 01952-884391 **W** www.ironbridge.org.uk World's first iron bridge; Blists Hill (late Victorian working town); Museum of Iron; Jackfield Tile Museum; Coalport China Museum; Tar Tunnel; Broseley Pipeworks

WAKEFIELD – *National Coal Mining Museum for England,* Overton WF4 4RH **T** 01924-848806 **W** www.ncm.org.uk Underground tours of one of Britain's oldest working mines

Yorkshire Sculpture Park, West Bretton WF4 4LG **T** 01924-832631 **W** www.ysp.co.uk Open-air sculpture gallery including works by Moore, Hepworth, Frink and others in 121 hectares (300 acres) of parkland

WEYBRIDGE – *Brooklands Museum,* KT13 0QN **T** 01932-857381 **W** www.brooklandsmuseum.com Birthplace of British motorsport; world's first purpose-built motor racing circuit

WILMSLOW – *Quarry Bank Mill,* Styal SK9 4LA **T** 01625-527468 **W** www.quarrybankmill.org.uk Working mill owned by the National Trust illustrating history of cotton industry; costumed guides at restored Apprentice House

WORCESTER – *City Museum and Art Gallery,* Foregate Street WR1 1DT **T** 01905-25371 **W** www.worcestercitymuseums.org.uk Includes a military museum, 19th-century chemist shop and changing art exhibitions

Museum of Worcester Porcelain, Severn Street WR1 2NE **T** 01905-746000 **W** www.worcesterporcelainmuseum.org.uk Worcester porcelain from 1751 to the present day. Also the *Royal Worcester Visitor Centre* (**W** www.royal-worcester.co.uk)

WROUGHTON, nr Swindon, Wilts – *Science Museum,* SN4 9NS **T** 01793-846200 **W** www.sciencemuseum.org.uk/wroughton Aircraft displays and some of the Science Museum's transport and agricultural collection

YEOVIL, Somerset – *Fleet Air Arm Museum,* Royal Naval Air Station, Yeovilton BA22 8HT **T** 01935-840565 **W** www.fleetairarm.com History of naval aviation; historic aircraft, including Concorde 002

YORK – *Beningbrough Hall,* Beningbrough YO30 1DD **T** 01904-472027 **W** www.nationaltrust.org.uk Portraits from the National Portrait Gallery

Jorvik – The Viking City, Coppergate YO1 9WT **T** 01904-543400 **W** www.jorvik-viking-centre.co.uk Reconstruction of Viking York

National Railway Museum, Leeman Road YO26 4XJ **T** 01904-214001 **W** www.nrm.org.uk Includes locomotives, rolling stock and carriages

York Castle Museum, Eye of York YO1 9RY **T** 01904-687687 **W** www.yorkcastlemuseum.org.uk Reconstructed streets; costume and military collections

York Art Gallery, Exhibition Square YO1 7EW **T** 01904-687687 **W** www.yorkartgallery.org.uk European and British painting spanning seven centuries; modern pottery

Yorkshire Museum & Gardens, Museum Gardens YO1 7FR **T** 01904-687687 **W** www.yorkshiremuseum.org.uk Yorkshire life from Roman to medieval times; geology gallery

WALES

* Members of National Museum Wales, a public body that receives its funding through grant-in-aid from the Welsh Assembly

BLAENAFON, Torfaen – *Big Pit National Coal Museum,* NP4 9XP **T** 01495-790311 **W** www.museumwales.ac.uk Colliery with underground tour

BODELWYDDAN, Denbighshire – *Bodelwyddan Castle,* LL18 5YA **T** 01745-584060 **W** www.bodelwyddan-castle.co.uk Portraits from the National Portrait Gallery; furniture from the Victoria and Albert Museum; sculptures from the Royal Academy

CAERLEON – *National Roman Legion Museum,* NP18 1AE **T** 01633-423134 **W** www.museumwales.ac.uk Material from the site of the Roman fortress of Isca and its suburbs

CARDIFF – *National Museum Cardiff,* Cathays Park CF10 3NP **T** 029-2039 7951 **W** www.museumwales.ac.uk Includes natural sciences, archaeology and Impressionist paintings

St Fagans: National History Museum, St Fagans CF5 6XB **T** 029-2057 3500 **W** www.museumwales.ac.uk Open-air museum with re-erected buildings, agricultural equipment and costume

DRE-FACH FELINDRE, nr Llandysul – *National Wool Museum,* SA44 5UP **T** 01559-370929 **W** www.museumwales.ac.uk Exhibitions, a working woollen mill and craft workshops

LLANBERIS, nr Caernarfon – *National Slate Museum,* LL55 4TY **T** 01286-870630 **W** www.museumwales.ac.uk Former slate quarry with original machinery and plant; slate crafts demonstrations

LLANDRINDOD WELLS – *National Cycle Collection,* Automobile Palace, Temple Street LD1 5DL **T** 01597-825531 **W** www.cyclemuseum.org.uk Over 200 bicycles on display, from 1818 to the present day

SWANSEA – *Glynn Vivian Art Gallery,* Alexandra Road SA1 5DZ **T** 01792-516900 **W** www.swansea.gov.uk/glynnvivian Paintings, ceramics, Swansea pottery and porcelain, clocks, glass and Welsh art

National Waterfront Museum, Oystermouth Road SA1 3RD **T** 01792-638950 **W** www.museumwales.ac.uk Wales during the Industrial Revolution

Swansea Museum, Victoria Road SA1 1SN T 01792-653763
W www.swansea.gov.uk
Archaeology, social history, Swansea pottery

SCOTLAND

* Members of National Museums of Scotland or National Galleries of Scotland, which are non-departmental public bodies funded by, and accountable to, the Scottish Executive

ABERDEEN – Aberdeen Art Gallery, Schoolhill AB10 1FQ
T 01224-523700 W www.aagm.co.uk
Art from the 18th to 20th century
Aberdeen Maritime Museum, Shiprow AB11 5BY
T 01224-337700 W www.aagm.co.uk
Maritime history, including shipbuilding and North Sea oil
EDINBURGH – Britannia, Leith EH6 6JJ T 0131-555 5566
W www.royalyachtbritannia.co.uk
Former royal yacht with royal barge and royal family picture gallery
City Art Centre, Market Street EH1 1DE T 0131-529 3993
W www.cac.org.uk
Late 19th- and 20th-century art and temporary exhibitions
*Dean Gallery, Belford Road EH4 3DS T 0131-624 6200
W www.nationalgalleries.org
Dada, Surrealism and sculpture – particularly works by Sir Eduardo Paolozzi
Museum of Childhood, High Street EH1 1TG T 0131-529 4142
W www.cac.org.uk
Toys, games, clothes and exhibits relating to the social history of childhood
Museum of Edinburgh, Canongate EH8 8DD T 0131-529 4143
W www.cac.org.uk
Local history, silver, glass and Scottish pottery
*Museum of Flight, East Fortune Airfield, East Lothian
EH39 5LF T 01620-897240 W www.nms.ac.uk/flight
Display of aircraft
*Museum of Scotland, Chambers Street EH1 1JF
T 0131-247 4422 W www.nms.ac.uk/scotland
Scottish history from prehistoric times to the present
*National Gallery of Scotland, The Mound EH2 2EL
T 0131-624 6200 W www.nationalgalleries.org
Paintings, drawings and prints from the 16th to the 20th century; the national collection of Scottish art
*National War Museum of Scotland, Edinburgh Castle
EH1 2NG T 0131-247 4413 W www.nms.ac.uk/war
History of Scottish military and conflicts
*Royal Museum, Chambers Street EH1 1JF
T 0131-247 4422 W www.nms.ac.uk/royal
Decorative arts; natural history; science and industry; part of the museum will be closed from spring 2008
*Scottish National Gallery of Modern Art, Belford Road
EH4 3DR T 0131-624 6200 W www.nationalgalleries.org
20th-century painting, sculpture and graphic art
*Scottish National Portrait Gallery, Queen Street EH2 1JD
T 0131-624 6200 W www.nationalgalleries.org
Portraits of eminent people in Scottish history; the national collection of photography
The Writers' Museum, Lawnmarket EH1 2PA T 0131-529 4901
W www.cac.org.uk
Robert Louis Stevenson, Walter Scott and Robert Burns exhibits

FORT WILLIAM – West Highland Museum, Cameron
Square PH33 6AJ T 01397-702169
W www.westhighlandmuseum.org.uk
Tartan collections; exhibits relating to 1745 uprising
GLASGOW – Burrell Collection, Pollokshaws Road G43 1AT
T 0141-287 2550 W www.glasgowmuseums.com
Paintings, textiles, furniture, ceramics, stained glass and silver from classical times to the 19th century
Gallery of Modern Art, Royal Exchange Square G1 3AH
T 0141-229 1996 W www.glasgowmuseums.com
Collection of contemporary Scottish and world art
Hunterian Museum & Art Gallery, University of Glasgow
G12 8QQ T 0141-330 4221 W www.hunterian.gla.ac.uk
Rennie Mackintosh and Whistler collections; Old Masters; Scottish paintings; modern paintings; sculpture; prints
Kelvingrove Art Gallery & Museum, Argyle Street G3 8AG
T 0141-287 2699 W www.glasgowmuseums.com
Old Masters; 19th-century French paintings; armour collection
*Museum of Piping, McPhater Street G4 0HW
T 0141-353 0220 W www.thepipingcentre.co.uk
The history and origins of bagpiping
*Museum of Rural Life, East Kilbride G76 9HR
T 0131-247 4377 W www.nms.ac.uk/museumofrurallife
History of rural life and work
Museum of Transport, Bunhouse Road G3 8DP
T 0141-287 2720 W www.glasgowmuseums.com
Includes a reproduction of a 1938 Glasgow street, cars since the 1930s, trams and a Glasgow subway station
People's Palace and Winter Gardens, Glasgow Green G40 1AT
T 0141-271 2962 W www.glasgowmuseums.com
History of Glasgow since 1175; objects from all the main world religions

NORTHERN IRELAND

* Members of National Museums Northern Ireland, a non-departmental public body of the Northern Ireland Office

ARMAGH – *Armagh County Museum, The Mall East
BT61 9BE T 028-3752 3070
W www.armaghcountymuseum.org.uk
Local history; archaeology; crafts
BELFAST – *WhoWhatWhenWhereWhy, Odyssey, Queen's
Quay BT3 9QQ T 028-9046 7700 W www.w5online.co.uk
Interactive science and technology centre
HOLYWOOD, Co. Down – *Ulster Folk and Transport
Museum, Cultra BT18 0EU T 028-9042 8428
W www.uftm.org.uk
Open-air museum with original buildings from Ulster town and rural life c.1900; indoor galleries including Irish rail and road transport and Titanic exhibitions
LONDONDERRY – The Tower Museum, Union Hall Place
BT48 6LU T 028-7137 2411 W www.derrycity.gov.uk/museums
Tells the story of Ireland through the history of Londonderry
OMAGH, Co. Tyrone – *Ulster American Folk Park,
Castletown BT78 5QY T 028-8224 3292
W www.folkpark.com
Open-air museum telling the story of Ulster's emigrants to America; restored or recreated dwellings and workshops; ship and dockside gallery

SIGHTS OF LONDON

For historic buildings, museums and galleries in London, *see* the Historic Buildings and Monuments and Museums and Galleries sections.

BRIDGES

The bridges over the Thames in London, from east to west, are:

Queen Elizabeth II Bridge (2,872m/9423ft), designed by Sir William Halcrow and partners, opened 1991

Tower Bridge (268m/880ft by 18m/60ft), designed by John Wolfe Barry, opened 1894

London Bridge (262m/860ft by 32m/105ft), original 13th-century stone bridge rebuilt by John Rennie and opened 1831, reconstructed in Arizona when current London Bridge opened 1973

Cannon Street Railway Bridge (261m/855ft), designed by Sir John Hawkshaw and John Wolfe Barry, originally named the Alexandra Bridge, opened 1866; renovated 1979–82

Southwark Bridge (244m/800ft by 17m/55ft), designed by John Rennie opened 1819; rebuilt 1912–21 (Mott, Hay and Anderson)

Millennium Bridge (325m/1,066ft by 5m/14 ft), designed by Ove Arup and Partners, opened 2000; reopened after modification 2002

Blackfriars Railway Bridge (284m/933ft), designed by John Wolfe Barry and Henri Marc Brunel, opened 1886

(*London, Chatham and Dover Railway Bridge* (234m/933ft), designed by Joseph Cubitt and opened in 1864, only the columns remain; the rest of the structure was removed in 1985)

Blackfriars Bridge (294m/963ft by 32m/105ft), designed by Robert Mylne, opened 1769; rebuilt 1869 (Joseph Cubitt); widened 1909

Waterloo Bridge (366m/1,200ft by 24m/80ft), designed by John Rennie, opened 1817; rebuilt (Sir Giles Gilbert Scott) 1945

Golden Jubilee Bridges (325m/1,066ft by 4.7m/15ft), designed by WSP Group, opened 2002; commonly known as the Hungerford Footbridges

Hungerford Railway Bridge (366m/1,200ft), designed by Isambard Kingdom Brunel, suspension bridge opened 1845; present railway bridge (Sir John Hawkshaw) opened 1864; widened in 1886

Westminster Bridge (228m/748ft by 26m/85ft), designed by Charles Labelye, opened 1750; rebuilt 1862 by Thomas Page

Lambeth Bridge (237m/776ft by 18m/60ft), designed by Peter W. Barlow, original suspension bridge opened 1862; current structure by George W. Humphreys opened 1932

Vauxhall Bridge (231m/759ft by 24m/80ft), designed by James Walker, opened 1816; redesigned by Sir Alexander Binnie and opened 1906

Grosvenor Railway Bridge (213m/700ft), designed by John Fowler, opened 1860; rebuilt 1965; also known as the Victoria Railway Bridge

Chelsea Bridge (213m/698ft by 25m/83ft), original suspension bridge designed by Thomas Page opened 1858; rebuilt by Rendel, Palmer and Triton in 1937

Albert Bridge (216m/710ft, by 12m/40ft) designed by Rowland M. Ordish, opened 1873; restructured by Sir Joseph Bazalgette in 1884; strengthened 1971–3

Battersea Bridge (204m/670ft by 17m/55ft), designed by Henry Holland, opened 1771; rebuilt by Bazalgette in 1890

Battersea Railway Bridge (204m/670ft), designed by William Baker, opened 1863

Wandsworth Bridge (189m/619ft by 18m/60ft), designed by Julian Tolmé, opened 1873; rebuilt 1940 (Sir T Peirson Frank)

Putney Railway Bridge (229m/750ft), also known as the Fulham Railway Bridge or the Iron Bridge – it has no official name, designed by William Jacomb and opened 1889

Putney Bridge (213m/700ft by 23m/74ft), designed by Sir Jacob Ackworth, original wooden bridge opened in 1729; current granite structure by Bazalgette completed in 1886

Hammersmith Bridge (210m/688ft by 10m/33ft), designed by William Tierney Clarke, the first suspension bridge in London, originally built 1827; rebuilt by Bazalgette in 1887

Barnes Railway Bridge (also footbridge, 110m/360ft), designed by Joseph Locke and opened in 1849; rebuilt 1895 by Head, Wrightson and co.; the original structure stands unused

Chiswick Bridge (137m/450ft by 21m/70ft), designed by Alfred Dryland, opened 1933

Kew Railway Bridge (175m/575ft), designed by W. R. Galbraith, opened 1869

Kew Bridge (110m/360ft by 17m/56ft), designed by Robert Tunstall, original timber bridge built 1759; replaced by a Portland stone structure by James Paine in 1789. Current granite bridge designed by Sir John Wolfe Barry and Cuthbert Brereton and renamed King Edward VII Bridge in 1903, but still known as Kew Bridge

Richmond Lock (91m/300ft by 11m/36ft), designed by FGM Stoney, lock and footbridge opened 1894

Twickenham Bridge (85m/280ft by 21m/70ft), designed by Alfred Dryland, opened 1933

Richmond Railway Bridge (91m/300ft), designed by Joseph Locke, opened 1848; restructured 1906–8

Richmond Bridge (85m/280ft by 9m/36ft), designed by Kenton Couse, built 1777; widened 1939

Teddington Lock (198m/650ft), designed by G. Pooley, two footbridges opened 1889; marks the end of the tidal reach of the Thames

Kingston Railway Bridge, designed by J. E. Errington and W. R. Galbraith, opened 1863

Kingston Bridge (116m/382ft), designed by Edward Lapidge, built 1825–8; widened 1911–14 (Mott and Hay) and 1999–2001

Hampton Court Bridge designed by Samuel Stevens and Benjamin Ludgator, built 1753; replaced by iron bridge 1865; present bridge by W. P. Robinson and Sir Edwin Lutyens opened in 1933

CEMETERIES

In 1832, in response to the overcrowding of burial grounds in London, the government authorised the establishment of seven non-denominational cemeteries hat would encircle the city. These large cemeteries, known as the 'magnificent seven', were seen by many Victorian families as places in which to demonstrate their wealth and stature, and as a result there are some highly ornate graves and tombs.

THE MAGNIFICENT SEVEN

Abney Park, Stamford Hill, N16 (13 hectares/32 acres), established 1840; tomb of General Booth, founder of the Salvation Army, and memorials to many nonconformists and dissenters

Brompton, Old Brompton Road, SW10 (16 hectares/40 acres), established 1840; graves of Sir Henry Cole, Emmeline Pankhurst, John Wisden

Highgate, Swains Lane, N6 (15 hectares/38 acres), established 1839; graves of Douglas Adams, George Eliot, Michael Faraday, Karl Marx, Christina Rossetti and Radclyffe Hall; western side only accessible as part of a guided tour

Kensal Green, Harrow Road, W10 (31.5 hectares/79 acres), established 1832; tombs of William Makepeace Thackeray, Anthony Trollope, Sydney Smith, Wilkie Collins, Tom Hood, George Cruikshank, Leigh Hunt, Isambard Kingdom Brunel and Charles Kemble

Nunhead, Linden Grove, SE15 (21 hectares/52 acres), established 1840; closed in 1969, subsequently restored and opened for burials

Tower Hamlets, Southern Grove, E3 (11 hectares/27 acres), established 1841; bombed heavily during the Second World War and closed to burials in 1966; now a nature reserve

West Norwood Cemetery and Crematorium, Norwood High Street, SE27 (17 hectares/42 acres), established 1837; tombs of Sir Henry Bessemer, Mrs Beeton, Sir Henry Tate and Joseph Whitaker *(Whitaker's Almanack)*

OTHER CEMETERIES

Bunhill Fields, City Road, EC1 (1.6 hectares/4 acres), 17th-century nonconformist burial ground containing the graves of William Blake, John Bunyan and Daniel Defoe

City of London Cemetery and Crematorium, Aldersbrook Road, E12 (81 hectares/200 acres), established 1856

Golders Green Crematorium, Hoop Lane, NW11 (5 hectares/12 acres), established 1902; retains the ashes of Kingsley Amis, Peter Sellers, Marc Bolan, Sigmund Freud, Ivor Novello, Bram Stoker, H. G. Wells, Anna Pavlova and Joe Orton

Hampstead, Fortune Green Road, NW6 (10.5 hectares/26 acres), established 1876; graves of Kate Greenaway, Lord Lister, Marie Lloyd

MARKETS

Billingsgate (fish), a market site for over 1,000 years, with the Lower Thames Street site dating from 1876; moved to the Isle of Dogs (Trafalgar Way, E14) in 1982; owned and run by the Corporation of London.

Borough, Southwark Street, SE1 (vegetables, fruit, flowers, etc), established on present site in 1756; privately owned and run.

Camden Lock, NW1 (second-hand clothing, jewellery, alternative fashion, crafts), established in 1973

Columbia Road, E2 (flowers), dates from 19th century; became dedicated flower market in the 20th century

Covent Garden (vegetables, fruit, flowers, etc), established in 1670 under a charter of Charles II; owned and run by the Covent Garden Market Authority, whose board

is appointed by DEFRA; moved in 1974 to Nine Elms, SW8

Leadenhall, Leadenhall Street, EC3 (meat, poultry, fish, etc), site of market since 14th century; present hall built 1881; owned and run by the Corporation of London

Petticoat Lane, Middlesex Street, E1, a market has existed on the site for over 500 years, now a Sunday morning market selling almost anything

Portobello Road, W11, originally for herbs and horse-trading from 1870; became famous for antiques after the closure of the Caledonian Market in 1948

Smithfield, EC1 (meat, poultry), built 1866–8, refurbished 1993–4; the site of St Bartholomew's Fair from 12th to 19th century; owned and run by the Corporation of London

New Spitalfields, E10 (vegetables, fruit, etc), established 1682, modernised 1928, moved out of the City to Leyton in 1991

Old Spitalfields, E1, continues to trade on the original Spitalfields site on Commercial Street, selling arts, crafts, books, clothes, organic food and antiques on Sundays

MONUMENTS

CENOTAPH, Whitehall, SW1. The Cenotaph (from the Greek meaning 'empty tomb') was built to commemorate 'The Glorious Dead' and is a memorial to all ranks of the sea, land and air forces who gave their lives in the service of the Empire during the First World War. Designed by Sir Edwin Lutyens and constructed in plaster as a temporary memorial in 1919, it was replaced by a permanent structure of Portland stone and unveiled by George V on 11 November 1920, Armistice Day. An additional inscription was made in 1946 to commemorate those who gave their lives in the Second World War.

FOURTH PLINTH, Trafalgar Square, WC2. The fourth plinth (1841) was designed for an equestrian statue that was never built due to lack of funds. From 1999 temporary works have been displayed on the plinth including *Ecce Homo* (Mark Wallinger), *Regardless of History* (Bill Woodrow), *Monument* (Rachel Whiteread), and *Alison Lapper Pregnant* (Marc Quinn). *Hotel for the Birds* by Thomas Schütte was installed in 2007.

LONDON MONUMENT (commonly called the Monument), Monument Street, EC3. Built to designs by Sir Christopher Wren and Robert Hooke between 1671 and 1677, the Monument commemorates the Great Fire of London, which broke out in Pudding Lane on 2 September 1666. The fluted Doric column is 36.6m (120ft) high, the moulded cylinder above the balcony supporting a flaming vase of gilt bronze is an additional 12.8 m (42ft), and the column is based on a square plinth 12.2m (40ft) high (with fine carvings on the west face), making a total height of 61.6m (202ft) – the tallest isolated stone column in the world, with views of London from a gallery at the top (311 steps).

OTHER MONUMENTS (sculptor's name in parentheses):

Albert Memorial (Scott), Kensington Gore

Royal Air Force (Blomfield), Victoria Embankment

Viscount Alanbrooke (Roberts-Jones), Whitehall

Beatty (Wheeler), Trafalgar Square

Belgian Gratitude (setting by Blomfield, statue by Rousseau), Victoria Embankment

Boadicea (or *Boudicca*), *Queen of the Iceni* (Thornycroft), Westminster Bridge

Brunel (Marochetti), Victoria Embankment

Burghers of Calais (Rodin), Victoria Tower Gardens, Westminster

Burns (Steell), Embankment Gardens

Canada Memorial (Granche), Green Park

Carlyle (Boehm), Chelsea Embankment

Cavalry (Jones), Hyde Park

Edith Cavell (Frampton), St Martin's Place

Charles I (Le Sueur), Trafalgar Square

Charles II (Gibbons), Royal Hospital, Chelsea

Churchill (Roberts-Jones), Parliament Square

Cleopatra's Needle (20.9m/68.5ft high, c.1500 BC, erected in 1878; the sphinxes are Victorian), Thames Embankment

Clive (Tweed), King Charles Street

Captain Cook (Brock), The Mall

Oliver Cromwell (Thornycroft), outside Westminster Hall

Cunningham (Belsky), Trafalgar Square

Gen. Charles de Gaulle (Conner), Carlton Gardens

Disraeli, Earl of Beaconsfield (Raggi), Parliament Square

Lord Dowding (Winter), Strand

Duke of Cambridge (Jones), Whitehall

Duke of York (37.8m/124ft column, with statue by Westmacott), Carlton House Terrace

Edward VII (Mackennal), Waterloo Place

Elizabeth I (Kerwin, 1586, oldest outdoor statue in London; from Ludgate), Fleet Street

Eros (Shaftesbury Memorial) (Gilbert), Piccadilly Circus

Marechal/Marshall Foch (Mallisard, copy of one in Cassel, France), Grosvenor Gardens

Charles James Fox (Westmacott), Bloomsbury Square

George III (Cotes Wyatt), Cockspur Street

George IV (Chantrey), Trafalgar Square

George V (Reid Dick and Scott), Old Palace Yard

George VI (Macmillan), Carlton Gardens

Gladstone (Thornycroft), Strand

Guards' (Crimea) (Bell), Waterloo Place

Guards Division (Ledward, figures, Bradshaw, cenotaph), Horse Guards' Parade

Haig (Hardiman), Whitehall

Sir Arthur (Bomber) Harris (Winter), Strand

Gen. Henry Havelock (Behnes), Trafalgar Square

Irving (Brock), north side of National Portrait Gallery

James II (Gibbons), Trafalgar Square

Jellicoe (Macmillan), Trafalgar Square

Samuel Johnson (Fitzgerald), opposite St Clement Danes

Kitchener (Tweed), Horse Guards' Parade

Abraham Lincoln (Saint-Gaudens, copy of one in Chicago), Parliament Square

Milton (Montford), St Giles, Cripplegate

Mountbatten (Belsky), Foreign Office Green

Gen. Charles James Napier (Adams), Trafalgar Square

Nelson (Railton), Trafalgar Square, with Landseer's lions (cast from guns recovered from the wreck of the *Royal George*)

Florence Nightingale (Walker), Waterloo Place

Palmerston (Woolner), Parliament Square

Peel (Noble), Parliament Square

Pitt (Chantrey), Hanover Square

Portal (Nemon), Embankment Gardens

Prince Albert (Bacon), Holborn Circus

Queen Elizabeth Gate (Lund and Wynne), Hyde Park Corner

Raleigh (Macmillan), Greenwich

Richard I (Coeur de Lion) (Marochetti), Old Palace Yard

Roberts (Bates), Horse Guards' Parade

Franklin D. Roosevelt (Reid Dick), Grosvenor Square

Royal Artillery (Jagger and Pearson), Hyde Park Corner

Royal Artillery (South Africa) (Colton), The Mall

Captain Scott (Lady Scott), Waterloo Place

Shackleton (Jagger), Kensington Gore

Shakespeare (Fontana, copy of one by Scheemakers in Westminster Abbey), Leicester Square

Smuts (Epstein), Parliament Square

Sullivan (Goscombe John), Victoria Embankment

Trenchard (Macmillan), Victoria Embankment

Victoria Memorial (Webb and Brock), in front of Buckingham Palace

Raoul Wallenberg (Jackson), Great Cumberland Place

George Washington (Houdon copy), Trafalgar Square

Wellington (Boehm), Hyde Park Corner

Wellington (Chantrey), outside Royal Exchange

John Wesley (Adams Acton), City Road

Westminster School (Crimea) (Scott), Broad Sanctuary

William III (Bacon), St James's Square

Wolseley (Goscombe John), Horse Guards' Parade.

PARKS, GARDENS AND OPEN SPACES

CORPORATION OF LONDON OPEN SPACES

Ashtead Common (200 hectares/500 acres), Surrey

Burnham Beeches and *Fleet Wood* (220 hectares/540 acres), Bucks. Purchased by the Corporation for the benefit of the public in 1880, Fleet Wood (26 hectares/65 acres) being presented in 1921

Coulsdon Common (51 hectares/127 acres), Surrey

Epping Forest (2,428 hectares/6,000 acres), Essex. Purchased by the Corporation and opened to the public in 1882. The present forest is 19.3km (12 miles) long by around 3km (2 miles) wide, approximately one-tenth of its original area

Farthing Downs and New Hill (95 hectares/235 acres), Surrey

Hampstead Heath (319 hectares/791 acres), NW3. Including Golders Hill (15 hectares/36 acres) and Parliament Hill (110 hectares/271 acres)

Highgate Wood (28 hectares/70 acres), N6/N10

Kenley Common (56 hectares/139 acres), Surrey

Queen's Park (12 hectares/30 acres), NW6

Riddlesdown (43 hectares/107 acres), Surrey

Spring Park (21 hectares/51 acres), Kent

West Ham Park (31 hectares/77 acres), E15

West Wickham Common (10 hectares/26 acres), Kent

Woodredon and Warlies Park Estate (299 hectares/740 acres), Waltham Abbey

Also over 150 smaller open spaces within the City of London, including *Finsbury Circus* and *St Dunstan-in-the-East*

OTHER PARKS AND GARDENS

CHELSEA PHYSIC GARDEN, 66 Royal Hospital Road SW3 4HS **T** 020-7352 5646

W www.chelseaphysicgarden.co.uk A garden of general botanical research and education, maintaining a wide range of rare and unusual plants; established in 1673 by the Society of Apothecaries

HAMPTON COURT PARK AND GARDENS (303.5 hectares/750 acres), Surrey KT8 9AU **T** 0870-751 5175 **W** www.hrp.org.uk Also known as Home Park, the park lies beyond the palace's formal gardens. It contains a herd of deer and a 1,000-year-old oak tree from the original park

ROYAL PARKS

W www.royalparks.gov.uk

Bushy Park (445 hectares/1,099 acres), Middx. Adjoins Hampton Court; contains avenue of horse-chestnuts enclosed in a fourfold avenue of limes planted by William III

Green Park (19 hectares/47 acres), W1 Between Piccadilly and St James's Park, with Constitution Hill leading to Hyde Park Corner

Greenwich Park (74 hectares/183 acres), SE10

Hyde Park (142 hectares/350 acres), W1/W2 From Park Lane to Kensington Gardens and incorporating the Serpentine lake, Apsley House, the Achilles Statue, Rotten Row and the Ladies' Mile; fine gateway at Hyde Park Corner. To the north-east is Marble Arch, originally erected by George IV at the entrance to Buckingham Palace and re-erected in the present position in 1851

Kensington Gardens (111 hectares/275 acres), W2/W8 From the western boundary of Hyde Park to Kensington Palace; contains the Albert Memorial, Serpentine Gallery and Peter Pan statue

Kew, Royal Botanic Gardens, Richmond, Surrey TW9 3AB T 020-8332 5655 W www.rbgkew.org.uk Officially inscribed on the UNESCO list of World Heritage Sites

Regent's Park and *Primrose Hill* (197 hectares/487 acres), NW1 From Marylebone Road to Primrose Hill surrounded by the Outer Circle; divided by the Broad Walk leading to the Zoological Gardens

Richmond Park (1,000 hectares/2,500 acres), Surrey

St James's Park (23 hectares/58 acres), SW1 From Whitehall to Buckingham Palace; ornamental lake of 4.9 hectares (12 acres); the Mall leads from Admiralty Arch to Buckingham Palace, Birdcage Walk from Storey's Gate to Buckingham Palace

PLACES OF HISTORICAL AND CULTURAL INTEREST

1 CANADA SQUARE, Canary Wharf, E14 5DY T 020-7418 2000 W www.canarywharf.com Also known as 'Canary Wharf', the steel and glass skyscraper is the tallest structure in London and the tallest habitable building in the UK

30 ST MARY AXE, EC3A 8EP W www.30stmaryaxe.com Completed in 2004 and commonly known as the 'Gherkin', it is the second-tallest building in the City of London

ALEXANDRA PALACE, Alexandra Palace Way, Wood Green, N22 7AY T 020-8365 2121 W www.alexandra palace.com The Victorian palace was severely damaged by fire in 1980 but was restored, and reopened in 1988. Alexandra Palace now provides modern facilities for exhibitions, conferences, banquets and leisure activities. There is an ice rink, a boating lake, the Phoenix Bar and a conservation area

BARBICAN CENTRE, Silk Street, EC2Y 8DS T 020-7638 4141 W www.barbican.org.uk Owned, funded and managed by the Corporation of London, the Barbican Centre opened in 1982 and houses the Barbican Theatre, a studio theatre called The Pit and the Barbican Hall; it is also home to the London Symphony Orchestra. There are three cinemas, six conference rooms, two art galleries, a sculpture court, a lending library, trade and banqueting facilities, a conservatory, shops, restaurants, cafes and bars

CENTRAL CRIMINAL COURT, Old Bailey, EC4M 7EH T 020-7248 3277 W www.cityoflondon.gov.uk The highest criminal court in the UK, the 'Old Bailey' was built in 1907 on the site of the old Newgate Prison. Trials held there have included those of Oscar Wilde, Dr Crippen and the Yorkshire Ripper

CHARTERHOUSE, Charterhouse Square, EC1M 6AN T 020-7253 9503 A Carthusian monastery from 1371 to 1537, purchased in 1611 by Thomas Sutton, who endowed it as a residence for aged men 'of gentle birth' and a school for poor scholars (removed to Godalming in 1872)

DOWNING STREET, SW1 Number 10 Downing Street is the official town residence of the Prime Minister, number 11 of the Chancellor of the Exchequer and number 12 is the office of the Government Whips. The street was named after Sir George Downing, Bt., soldier and diplomat, who was MP for Morpeth from 1660 to 1684

GEORGE INN, Borough High Street, SE1 1NH T 020-7407 2056 W www.nationaltrust.org.uk The last galleried inn in London, built in 1677. Now owned by the National Trust and run as an ordinary public house

GREENWICH, SE10 *Royal Naval College* T 020-8269 4747 W www.greenwichfoundation.org.uk The building was the Greenwich Hospital until 1873. It was built by Charles II, largely from designs by John Webb, and by Queen Mary II and William III, from designs by Wren. It stands on the site of an ancient abbey, a royal house and Greenwich Palace, which was constructed by Henry VII. Henry VIII, Mary I and Elizabeth I were born in the royal palace and Edward VI died there

Greenwich Park (74 hectares/183 acres), T 020-8858 2608, W www.royalparks.gov.uk Enclosed by Humphrey, Duke of Gloucester, and laid out by Charles II from the designs of Le Nôtre. On a hill in Greenwich Park is the *Royal Observatory* (founded 1675). Its buildings are now managed by the *National Maritime Museum,* T 020-8858 4422 W www.nmm.ac.uk and the earliest building is named Flamsteed House, after John Flamsteed (1646–1719), the first Astronomer Royal

The Cutty Sark, T 020-8858 2698, W www.cuttysark.org.uk The last of the famous tea clippers, it was moved into a specially constructed dry dock in 1954 and opened to the public in 1957

HORSE GUARDS, Whitehall, SW1 Archway and offices built about 1753. The changing of the guard takes place daily at 11am (10am on Sundays) and the inspection at 4pm. Only those with the Queen's permission may drive through the gates and archway into *Horse Guards' Parade*, where the colour is 'trooped' on the Queen's official birthday

HOUSES OF PARLIAMENT

House of Commons, Westminster, SW1A 0AA T 020-7219 4272 E hcinfo@parliament.uk W www.parliament.uk

House of Lords, Westminster, SW1A 0PW T 020-7219 3107 E hlinfo@parliament.uk W www.parliament.uk

The royal palace of Westminster, originally built by Edward the Confessor, was the normal meeting place of Parliament from about 1340. St Stephen's Chapel was used from about 1550 for the meetings of the House of Commons, which had previously been held in the Chapter House or Refectory of Westminster Abbey. The House of Lords met in an apartment of the royal palace. The fire of 1834 destroyed much of the palace, and the present Houses of Parliament were erected on the site from the designs of Sir Charles Barry and Augustus Welby Pugin between 1840 and 1867. The chamber of the House of Commons was destroyed by bombing in 1941, and a new chamber designed by Sir Giles Gilbert Scott was used for the first time in 1950. *Westminster Hall and the Crypt Chapel* was the only part of the old palace of Westminster to survive the fire of 1834. It was built by William II from 1097 to 1099 and altered by Richard II between 1394 and 1399. The hammerbeam roof of carved oak dates from 1396–8. The Hall was the scene of the trial of Charles I. *The Victoria Tower* of the House of Lords is 98.5m (323ft) high, and when Parliament is sitting, the Union flag flies by day from its flagstaff. *The Clock Tower* of the House of Commons is 96.3m (316ft) high and contains 'Big Ben', the hour bell said to be named after Sir Benjamin Hall, First Commissioner of Works when the original bell was cast in 1856. This bell, which weighed 16 tons 11 cwt, was found to be cracked in 1857. The present bell (13.5 tons) is a recasting of the original and was first brought into use in 1859. The dials of the clock are 7m (23ft) in diameter, the hands being 2.7m (9ft) and 4.3m (14ft) long (including balance piece). A light is displayed from the Clock Tower at night when parliament is sitting

During session, tours of the Houses of Parliament are only available to UK residents who have made advance arrangements through an MP or peer. Overseas visitors are no longer provided with permits to tour the Houses of Parliament during session, although they can tour during the summer opening and attend debates for both houses in the Strangers' Galleries. During the summer recess tickets for tours of the Houses of Parliament can be booked by telephone (T 0870-906 3773) or bought on site at the ticket office on Abingdon Green opposite Parliament and the Victoria Tower Gardens. The Strangers' Gallery of the House of Commons is open to the public when the house is sitting. To acquire tickets in advance UK residents should write to their local MP and overseas visitors should apply to their embassy or high commission in the UK for a permit. If none of these arrangements have been made, visitors should join the public queue outside St Stephen's Entrance, where there is also a queue for entry to the House of Lords Gallery

INNS OF COURT

The Inns of Court are ancient unincorporated bodies of lawyers which for more than five centuries have had the power to call to the Bar those of their members who have qualified for the rank or degree of Barrister-at-Law. There are four Inns of Court as well as many lesser inns

Lincoln's Inn, Chancery Lane/Lincoln's Inn Fields, WC2A 3TL T 020-7405 1393 W www.lincolnsinn.org.uk
The most ancient of the inns with records dating back to 1422. The hall and library buildings are of 1845, although the library is first mentioned in 1474; the old hall (late 15th century) and the chapel were rebuilt c.1619–23

Inner Temple, King's Bench Walk, EC4Y 7HL T 020-7797 8250 W www.innertemple.org.uk

Middle Temple, Middle Temple Lane, EC4Y 9AT T 020-7427 4800 W www.middletemple.org.uk
Records for the Middle and Inner Temple date back to the beginning of the 16th century. The site was originally occupied by the Order of Knights Templar c.1160–1312. The two inns have separate halls thought to have been formed c.1350. The division between the two societies was formalised in 1732 with Temple Church and the Masters House remaining in common. The Inner Temple Garden is normally open to the public on weekdays between 12.30pm and 3pm

Temple Church, EC4Y 7BB T 020-7353 3470 W www.templechurch.com The nave forms one of five remaining round churches in England

Gray's Inn, South Square, WC1R 5ET T 020-7458 7800 W www.graysinn.org.uk Founded early 14th century. Hall 1556–8 No other 'Inns' are active, but there are remains of *Staple Inn,* a gabled front on Holborn (opposite Gray's Inn Road). *Clement's Inn* (near St Clement Danes Church), *Clifford's Inn,* Fleet Street, and *Thavies Inn,* Holborn Circus, are all rebuilt. *Serjeants' Inn,* Fleet Street, and another (demolished 1910) of the same name in Chancery Lane, were composed of Serjeants-at-Law, the last of whom died in 1922

INSTITUTE OF CONTEMPORARY ARTS, The Mall, SW1Y 5AH T 020-7930 3647 W www.ica.org.uk
Exhibitions of modern art in the fields of film, theatre, new media and the visual arts

LLOYD'S, Lime Street, EC3M 7HA T 020-7327 1000 W www.lloydsoflondon.com International insurance market which evolved during the 17th century from Lloyd's Coffee House. The present building was opened for business in May 1986, and houses the Lutine Bell. Underwriting is on three floors with a total area of 10,591 sq. m (114,000 sq. ft). The Lloyd's building is not open to the general public

LONDON CENTRAL MOSQUE AND THE ISLAMIC CULTURAL CENTRE, Park Road, NW8 7RG T 020-7724 3363 W www.iccuk.org The focus for London's Muslims; established in 1944 but not completed until 1977, the mosque can accommodate about 5,000 worshippers; guided tours are available

LONDON EYE, South Bank, SE1 7PB T 0870-990 0600 W www.londoneye.com Opened in February 2000 as London's millennium landmark, this 450ft observation wheel is the capital's fourth-largest structure. The wheel provides a 30-minute ride offering panoramic views of the capital

LONDON ZOO, Regent's Park, NW1 4RY T 020-7722 3333 W www.londonzoo.org

MADAME TUSSAUD'S AND THE LONDON PLANETARIUM, Marylebone Road, NW1 5LR T 0870-400 3000 W www.madame-tussauds.co.uk
Waxwork exhibition and interactive star show

MARLBOROUGH HOUSE, Pall Mall, SW1Y 5HX T 020-7747 6491 Built by Wren for the first Duke of Marlborough and completed in 1711, the house reverted to the Crown in 1835. In 1863 it became the London house of the Prince of Wales and was the London home of Queen Mary until her death in 1953. In 1959 Marlborough House was given by the Queen as the headquarters for the Commonwealth Secretariat and it was opened as such in 1965. The Queen's Chapel, Marlborough Gate, was begun in 1623 from the designs of Inigo Jones for the Infanta Maria of Spain, and completed for Queen Henrietta Maria. Marlborough House is not open to the public

PORT OF LONDON, Port of London Authority, Bakers' Hall, 7 Harp Lane, EC3R 6LB T 020-7743 7900 W www.portoflondon.co.uk The Port of London covers the tidal section of the River Thames from Teddington to the seaward limit (the outer Tongue buoy and the Sunk light vessel), a distance of 150km. The governing body is the Port of London Authority (PLA). Cargo is handled at privately operated riverside terminals between Fulham and Canvey Island, including the enclosed dock at Tilbury, 40km below London Bridge. Passenger vessels and cruise liners can be handled at moorings at Greenwich, Tower Bridge and Tilbury

ROMAN REMAINS

The city wall of Roman *Londinium* was largely rebuilt during the medieval period but sections may be seen near the White Tower in the Tower of London; at Tower Hill; at Coopers' Row; at All Hallows, London Wall, its vestry being built on the remains of a semi-circular Roman bastion; at St Alphage, London Wall, showing a succession of building repairs from the Roman until the late medieval period; and at St Giles, Cripplegate. Sections of the great forum and basilica, more than 165m^2, have been encountered during excavations in the area of Leadenhall, Gracechurch Street and Lombard Street. Traces of Roman activity along the river include a massive riverside wall built in the late Roman period, and a succession of Roman timber quays along Lower and Upper Thames Street. Finds from these sites can be seen at the Museum of London

Other major buildings are the amphitheatre at Guildhall, remains of bath-buildings in Upper and Lower Thames Street, and the temple of Mithras in Walbrook

ROYAL ALBERT HALL, Kensington Gore, SW7 2AP T 020-7589 8212   W www.royalalberthall.com   The elliptical hall, one of the largest in the world, was completed in 1871; since 1941 it has been the venue each summer for the Promenade Concerts founded in 1895 by Sir Henry Wood. Other events include pop and classical music concerts, dance, opera, sporting events, conferences and banquets

ROYAL COURTS OF JUSTICE, Strand, WC2A 2LL T 020-7947 6000 Victorian Gothic building that is home to the High Court. Visitors are free to watch proceedings

ROYAL HOSPITAL, CHELSEA, Royal Hospital Road, SW3 4SR   T 020-7881 5200   W www.chelsea-pensioners. co.uk Founded by Charles II in 1682, and built by Wren; opened in 1692 for old and disabled soldiers. The extensive grounds include the former Ranelagh Gardens and are the venue for the Chelsea Flower Show each May

ROYAL OPERA HOUSE, Covent Garden, WC2E 9DD T 020-7240 1200 W www.royalopera.org Home of The Royal Ballet (1931) and The Royal Opera (1946). The Royal Opera House is the third theatre to be built on the site, opening 1858; the first was opened in 1732

ST JAMES'S PALACE, Pall Mall, SW1A 1BQ T 020-7930 4832 W www.royal.gov.uk Built by Henry VIII, only the Gatehouse and Presence Chamber remain; later alterations were made by Wren and Kent. Representatives of foreign powers are still accredited 'to the Court of St James's'. *Clarence House* (1825), the official London residence of the Prince of Wales and his sons, stands within the St James's Palace estate

ST PAUL'S CATHEDRAL, St Paul's Churchyard, EC4M 8AD T 020-7236 4128 E chapter@stpaulscathedral.org.uk W www.stpauls.co.uk Built 1675–1710. The cross on the dome is 111m (365ft) above ground level, the inner cupola 66.4 m (218ft) above the floor. 'Great Paul' in the south-west tower weighs nearly 17 tons. The organ by Father Smith (enlarged by Willis and rebuilt by Mander) is in a case carved by Grinling Gibbons, who also carved the choir stalls

SOMERSET HOUSE, Strand, WC2R 1LA T 020 7845 4600 W www.somerset-house.org.uk   The river facade (183m/600ft long) was built in 1776–1801 from the designs of Sir William Chambers; the eastern extension, which houses part of King's College, was built by

Smirke in 1829–35. Somerset House was the property of Lord Protector Somerset, at whose attainder in 1552 the palace passed to the Crown, and it was a royal residence until 1692. Somerset House has recently undergone extensive renovation and is home to the Gilbert Collection, Hermitage Rooms and the Courtauld Institute Gallery. Open-air concerts and ice-skating (Dec–Jan) are held in the courtyard

SOUTH BANK, SE1 Arts complex on the south bank of the River Thames which consists of

The *Royal Festival Hall* T 08703-600400 W www.southbankcentre.co.uk Opened in 1951 for the Festival of Britain, adjacent are the 917-seat *Queen Elizabeth Hall*, the *Purcell Room*, and the *Voice Box.*

The *National Film Theatre*, T 020-7928 3535 W www.bfi.org.uk Opened in 1952 and is administered by the British Film Institute, has three auditoria showing over 2,000 films a year. The London Film Festival is held here every November. There is also an IMAX cinema with 477 seats

The *Royal National Theatre*, T 020-7452 3000 W www.nationaltheatre.org.uk opened in 1976 and stages classical, modern, new and neglected plays in its three auditoria: the Olivier, the Lyttelton and the Cottesloe theatres

SOUTHWARK CATHEDRAL, London Bridge, SE1 9DA T 020-7367 6700 E cathedral@southwark.anglican.org W www.dswark.org Mainly 13th century, but the nave is largely rebuilt. The tomb of John Gower (1330–1408) is between the Bunyan and Chaucer memorial windows in the north aisle; Shakespeare's effigy, backed by a view of Southwark and the Globe Theatre, is in the south aisle; the tomb of Bishop Andrewes (died 1626) is near the screen. The Lady Chapel was the scene of the consistory courts of the reign of Mary (Gardiner and Bonner) and is still used as a consistory court. John Harvard, after whom Harvard University is named, was baptised here in 1607, and the chapel by the north choir aisle is his memorial chapel

THAMES EMBANKMENTS

Sir Joseph Bazalgette (1819–91) constructed the *Victoria Embankment,* on the north side from Westminster to Blackfriarsfor the Metropolitan Board of Works, 1864–70; (the seats, of which the supports of some are a kneeling camel, laden with spicery, and of others a winged sphinx, were presented by the Grocers' Company and by W. H. Smith, MP, in 1874); the *Albert Embankment,* on the south side from Westminster Bridge to Vauxhall, 1866–9, and the Chelsea Embankment, 1871–4. The total cost exceeded £2m. Bazalgette also inaugurated the London main drainage system, 1858–65. A medallion *(Flumini vincula posuit)* has been placed on a pier of the *Victoria Embankment* to commemorate the engineer

THAMES FLOOD BARRIER

Officially opened in May 1984, though first used in February 1983, the barrier consists of ten rising sector gates which span approximately 570 yards from bank to bank of the Thames at Woolwich Reach. When not in use the gates lie horizontally, allowing shipping to navigate the river normally; when the barrier is closed, the gates turn through 90 degrees to stand vertically more than 50 feet above the river bed. The barrier took eight years to complete and can be raised within about 30 minutes

WESTMINSTER ABBEY, Broad Sanctuary, SW1P 3PA T 0207-222 5152 E info@westminster-abbey.org W www.westminster-abbey.org Founded as a Benedictine monastery over 1,000 years ago, the church was rebuilt by Edward the Confessor in 1065 and again by Henry III in the 13th century. The abbey is the resting place for monarchs including Edward I, Henry III, Henry V, Henry VII, Elizabeth I, Mary I and Mary Queen of Scots, and has been the setting of coronations since that of William the Conqueror in 1066. In Poets' Corner there are memorials to many literary figures, and many scientists and musicians are also remembered here. The grave of the Unknown Warrior is to be found in the nave

WESTMINSTER CATHEDRAL, Francis Street, SW1P 1QW T 020-7798 9090   W www.westminstercathedral.org.uk Roman Catholic cathedral built 1895–1903 from the designs of J. F. Bentley. The campanile is 284 feet high

LONDON THEATRES

Adelphi Theatre, Strand, WC2E 7NA T 020-7344 0055 ⊖ Charing Cross
Aldwych Theatre, Aldwych, WC2B 4DF T 020-7379 3367 ⊖ Covent Garden/Holborn
Almeida Theatre, Almeida Street, N1 1TA T 020-7359 4404 ⊖ Angel/Highbury & Islington
Apollo Theatre, Shaftesbury Avenue, W1V 7DH T 020-7494 5700 ⊖ Piccadilly Circus
Apollo Victoria Theatre, Wilton Road, SW1V 1LL T 0207-834 63184 ⊖ Victoria
Barbican Theatre, Barbican Centre, EC2Y 8DS T 020-7638 8891 ⊖ Barbican/Moorgate
Cambridge Theatre, Earlham Street, WC2 9HU T 020-7850 8710 ⊖ Covent Garden/Leicester Square
Chelsea Theatre, World's End Place, SW10 0DR T 020-7352 1967 ⊖ Sloane Square
Comedy Theatre, Panton Street, SW1Y 4DN T 0870-060 6637 ⊖ Leicester Square/Piccadilly Circus
Criterion Theatre, Jermyn Street, SW1Y 4XA T 0870-060 2313 ⊖ Piccadilly Circus
Dominion Theatre, Tottenham Court Road, W1T 7AQ T 020-7636 2295 ⊖ Tottenham Court Road
Donmar Warehouse, Earlham Street, WC2H 9LX T 020-7240 4882 ⊖ Covent Garden
Duchess Theatre, Catherine Street, WC2B 5LA T 020-7494 5075 ⊖ Covent Garden
Duke Of York's Theatre, St Martin's Lane, WC2N 4BG T 0870-060 6623 ⊖ Leicester Square/Piccadilly Circus
Fortune Theatre, Russell Street, WC2B 5HH T 0870-060 6626 ⊖ Covent Garden
Garrick Theatre, Charing Cross Road, WC2H 0HH T 020-7520 5690 ⊖ Charing Cross/Leicester Square
Gielgud Theatre, Shaftesbury Avenue, W1D 6AR T 020-7494 5065 ⊖ Piccadilly Circus
Globe Theatre, New Globe Walk, SE1 9DT T 020-7902 1400 ⊖ Mansion House
Hackney Empire, Mare Street, E8 1EJ T 020-8510 4500 ⊖ Bethnal Green
Her Majesty's Theatre, Haymarket, SW1Y 4QL T 020-7494 5400 ⊖ Piccadilly Circus
Jermyn Street Theatre, Jermyn Street, SW1Y 6ST T 020-7287 2875 ⊖ Piccadilly Circus
London Coliseum, St Martin's Lane, WC2N 4ES T 020-7836 0111 ⊖ Charing Cross
London Palladium, Argyll Street, W1F 7TF T 020-7494 5020 ⊖ Oxford Circus

Lyceum Theatre, Wellington Street, WC2E 7RQ T 0870-243 9000 ⊖ Covent Garden
Lyric Theatre, Shaftesbury Avenue, W1D 7ES T 020-7494 5045 ⊖ Piccadilly Circus
Lyric Theatre Hammersmith, King Street, W6 0QL T 020-8741 2311 ⊖ Hammersmith
National Theatre, South Bank, SE1 9PX T 020-7452 3000 ⊖ Waterloo
New Ambassadors Theatre, West Street, WC2H 9ND T 0870-060 6627 ⊖ Leicester Square
New London Theatre, Drury Lane, WC2B 5PW T 020-7242 9802 ⊖ Holborn
Noël Coward (formerly Albery), St Martin's Lane, WC2N 4BW T 0870-950 0920 ⊖ Leicester Square
Novello Theatre, Aldwych, WC2B 4LD T 020-7759 9640 ⊖ Charing Cross
Old Vic Theatre, The Cut, SE1 8NB T 020-7928 2651 ⊖ Waterloo
Palace Theatre, Shaftesbury Avenue, W1V 8AY T 020-7434 0909 ⊖ Leicester Square/Piccadilly Circus
Phoenix Theatre, Charing Cross Road, WC2H 0JP T 0870-060 6629 ⊖ Tottenham Court Road
Piccadilly Theatre, Denman Street, W1D 7DY T 020-8544 7424 ⊖ Piccadilly Circus
Playhouse Theatre, Northumberland Avenue, WC2N 5DE T 0870-060 6631 ⊖ Embankment
Prince Edward Theatre, Old Compton Street, W1D 4HS T 0870-850 9191 ⊖ Leicester Square
Prince of Wales Theatre, Coventry Street, W1D 6AS T 0870-850 0393 ⊖ Piccadilly Circus
Queen's Theatre, Shaftesbury Avenue, W1D 6BA T 0870-950 0930 ⊖ Piccadilly Circus
Royal Albert Hall, Kensington Gore, SW7 2AP T 020-7589 8212 ⊖ South Kensington
Royal Court Theatre, Sloane Square, SW1W 8AS T 020-7565 5000 ⊖ Sloane Square
Royal Festival Hall, South Bank SE1 8XX T 0871-663 2500 ⊖ Waterloo
Sadler's Wells, Rosebery Avenue, EC1R 4TN T 020-7863 8198 ⊖ Angel
St Martin's Theatre, West Street, WC2H 9NZ T 0870-162 8787 ⊖ Leicester Square
Savoy Theatre, Strand, WC2R 0ET T 0870-164 8787 ⊖ Charing Cross
Shaftesbury Theatre, Shaftesbury Avenue, WC2H 8DP T 020-7379 5399 ⊖ Holborn/Tottenham Court Road
Soho Theatre, Dean Street, W1D 3NE T 020-7287 5060 ⊖ Tottenham Court Road
Southwark Playhouse, Southwark Bridge Road, SE1 0BL T 020-7620 3494 ⊖ Southwark
Theatre Royal Drury Lane, Catherine Street, WC2B 5JF T 020-7494 5000 ⊖ Covent Garden
Theatre Royal Haymarket, Haymarket, SW1Y 4HT T 020-7930 8890 ⊖ Piccadilly Circus
Trafalgar Studios, Whitehall, SW1A 2DY T 020-8544 7424 ⊖ Charing Cross/Embankment
Tricycle Theatre, Kilburn High Road, NW6 7JR T 020-7372 6611 ⊖ Kilburn
Vaudeville Theatre, Strand, WC2R 0NH T 020-7836 3191 ⊖ Charing Cross
Venue Theatre, Leicester Place, WC2H 7BP T 020-7734 6004 ⊖ Leicester Square
Victoria Palace Theatre, Victoria Street, SW1E 5EA T 020-7834 3034 ⊖ Victoria
Wyndham's Theatre, Charing Cross Road, WC2H 0DA T 0870-060 6633 ⊖ Leicester Square
Young Vic, The Cut, SE1 8LZ T 020-7922 2922 ⊖ Waterloo

HALLMARKS

Hallmarks are the symbols stamped on gold, silver or platinum articles to indicate that they have been tested at an official Assay Office and that they conform to one of the legal standards. With certain exceptions, all gold, silver or platinum articles are required by law to be hallmarked before they are offered for sale. The marking of gold and silver articles to identify the maker was instituted in England in 1363 under a statute of Edward III. In 1478 the Assay Office in Goldsmiths' Hall was established and all gold and silversmiths were required to bring their wares to be date-marked by the Hall, hence the term 'hallmarked'.

MODERN HALLMARKS

Since 1 January 1999, UK hallmarks have consisted of three compulsory symbols – the sponsor's mark, the fineness (purity) mark and the assay office mark. Traditional marks such as the year date letter, the Britannia for 958 silver, the lion passant for 925 silver (lion rampant in Scotland) and the orb for 950 platinum may be added voluntarily. The distinction between UK and foreign articles has been removed, and more finenesses are now legal, reflecting the more common finenesses elsewhere in Europe.

SPONSOR'S MARK
Instituted in England in 1363, the sponsor's mark was originally a device such as a bird or fleur-de-lis. Now it consists of the initial letters of the name or names of the manufacturer or firm. Where two or more sponsors have the same initials, there is a variation in the surrounding shield or style of letters.

FINENESS (PURITY) MARK
The fineness (purity) mark indicates that the content of the precious metal in the alloy, from which the article is made, is not less than the legal standard. The legal standard is the minimum content of precious metal by weight in parts per thousand, and the standards are:

Gold	999	
	990	
	916.6	(22 carat)
	750	(18 carat)
	585	(14 carat)
	375	(9 carat)
Silver	999	
	958.4	(Britannia)
	925	(sterling)
	800	
Platinum	999	
	950	
	900	
	850	

ASSAY OFFICE MARK
This mark identifies the particular assay office at which the article was tested and marked. The British assay offices are:

LONDON, Goldsmiths' Hall, Gutter Lane, London EC2V 8AQ
T 020-7606 8971 W www.thegoldsmiths.co.uk

BIRMINGHAM, PO Box 151, Newhall Street, Birmingham B3 1SB T 0121-236 6951 W www.theassayoffice.co.uk

SHEFFIELD, Guardians' Hall, 137 Portobello Street, Sheffield S1 4DS T 0114-275 5111 W www.assayoffice.co.uk

EDINBURGH, Goldsmiths' Hall, 24a Broughton Street, Edinburgh EH1 3RH T 0131-556 1144
W www.assayofficescotland.com

Assay offices formerly existed in other towns, eg Chester, Exeter, Glasgow, Newcastle, Norwich and York, each having its own distinguishing mark.

DATE LETTER

The date letter shows the year in which an article was assayed and hallmarked. Each alphabetical cycle has a distinctive style of lettering or shape of shield. The date letters were different at the various assay offices and the particular office must be established from the assay office mark before reference is made to tables of date letters. Date letter marks became voluntary from 1 January 1999.

The table which follows shows one specimen shield and letter used by the London Assay Office on silver articles for each alphabetical cycle from 1498. The same letters are found on gold articles but the surrounding shield may differ. Until 1 January 1975 two calendar years are given for each specimen date letter as the letter changed annually in May on St Dunstan's Day (the patron saint of silversmiths). Since 1 January 1975, each date letter has indicated a calendar year from January to December and each office has used the same style of date letter and shield for all articles:

LONDON (GOLDSMITHS' HALL) DATE LETTERS FROM 1498

	from	to		from	to
	1498–9	1517–8		1756–7	1775–6
	1518–9	1537–8		1776–7	1795–6
	1538–9	1557–8		1796–7	1815–6
	1558–9	1577–8		1816–7	1835–6
	1578–9	1597–8		1836–7	1855–6
	1598–9	1617–8		1856–7	1875–6
	1618–9	1637–8		1876–7 [A to M square shield, N to Z as shown]	1895–6
	1638–9	1657–8		1896–7	1915–6
	1658–9	1677–8		1916–7	1935–6
	1678–9	1696–7		1936–7	1955–6
	1697	1715–6		1956–7	1974
	1716–7	1735–6		1975	1999
	1736–7	1738–9		2000	
	1739–40	1755–6			

OTHER MARKS

FOREIGN GOODS
Foreign goods imported into the UK are required to be hallmarked before sale, unless they already bear a convention mark (*see* below) or a hallmark struck by an independent assay office in the European Economic Area which is deemed to be equivalent to a UK hallmark.

The following are the assay office marks used for gold until the end of 1998. For silver and platinum the symbols remain the same but the shields differ in shape.

 London   *Sheffield*

 Birmingham   *Edinburgh*

CONVENTION HALLMARKS
Special marks at authorised assay offices of the signatory countries of the International Convention on Hallmarking (Austria, the Czech Republic, Denmark, Finland, Hungary, Ireland, Latvia, Lithuania, the Netherlands, Norway, Poland, Portugal, Sweden, Switzerland, UK and Ukraine) are legally recognised in the United Kingdom as approved hallmarks. These consist of a sponsor's mark, a common control mark, a fineness mark (arabic numerals showing the standard in parts per thousand), and an assay office mark. There is no date letter.

The common control marks are:

GOLD	SILVER	PLATINUM

COMMEMORATIVE MARKS
There are other marks to commemorate special events: the silver jubilee of King George V and Queen Mary in 1935, the coronation of Queen Elizabeth II in 1953, and her silver jubilee in 1977. During 1999 and 2000 there was a voluntary additional Millennium Mark. A mark to commemorate the golden jubilee of Queen Elizabeth II was available during 2002.

BRITISH CURRENCY

The unit of currency is the pound sterling (£) of 100 pence. The decimal system was introduced on 15 February 1971.

COIN

Gold Coins
One hundred pounds £100*
Fifty pounds £50*
Twenty-five pounds £25*
Ten pounds £10*
Five pounds £5
Two pounds £2
Sovereign £1
Half-sovereign 50p

Silver Coins
(Britannia coins)*
Two pounds £2
One pound £1
Fifty pence 50p
Twenty pence 20p

Maundy Money†
Fourpence 4p
Threepence 3p
Twopence 2p
Penny 1p

Bi-colour Coins ‡
Two pounds £2

Nickel-Brass Coins
Two pounds £2 (pre-1997)§
One pound £1

Cupro-Nickel Coins
Crown £5 (since 1990)
Fifty pence 50p
Crown 25p (pre-1990)
Twenty pence 20p
Ten pence 10p
Five pence 5p

Bronze Coins
Two pence 2p
One penny 1p

Copper-plated Steel Coins¶
Two pence 2p
One penny 1p

* Britannia coins: gold bullion coins introduced 1987; silver coins introduced 1997
† Gifts of special money distributed by the sovereign annually on Maundy Thursday to the number of aged poor men and women corresponding to the sovereign's own age
‡ Cupro-nickel centre and nickel-brass outer ring
§ Commemorative coins; not intended for general circulation
¶ Since September 1992, although in 1998 the 2p was struck in both copper-plated steel and bronze

GOLD COIN

Gold ceased to circulate during the First World War. Since then controls on buying, selling and holding gold coin have been imposed at various times but have subsequently been revoked. Under the Exchange Control (Gold Coins Exemption) Order 1979, gold coins may now be imported and exported without restriction, except gold coins which are more than 50 years old and valued at a sum in excess of £8,000; these cannot be exported without specific authorisation from the Department for Business, Enterprise and Regulatory Reform.

Value Added Taxation on the sale of gold coins was revoked in 2000.

SILVER COIN

Prior to 1920 silver coins were struck from sterling silver, an alloy of which 925 parts in 1,000 were silver. In 1920 the proportion of silver was reduced to 500 parts. From 1 January 1947 all 'silver' coins, except Maundy money, have been struck from cupro-nickel, an alloy of 75 parts copper and 25 parts nickel, except for the 20p, composed of 84 parts copper, 16 parts nickel. Maundy coins continue to be struck from sterling silver.

BRONZE COIN

Bronze, introduced in 1860 to replace copper, is an alloy of 97 parts copper, 2.5 parts zinc and 0.5 part tin. Bronze was replaced by copper-plated steel in September 1992 with the exception of 1998 when the 2p was made in both copper-plated steel and bronze.

LEGAL TENDER

Gold (dated 1838 onwards, if not below least current weight)	to any amount
£5 (Crown since 1990)*	to any amount
£2	to any amount
£1	to any amount
50p	up to £10
25p (Crown pre-1990)	up to £10
20p	up to £10
10p	up to £5
5p	up to £5
2p	up to 20p
1p	up to 20p

* Only redeemable at the Post Office

The £1 coin was introduced in 1983 to replace the £1 note. The following coins have ceased to be legal tender:

Farthing	31 December 1960
Halfpenny (½d)	1 July 1969
Half-crown	1 January 1970
Threepence	31 August 1971
Penny (1d)	31 August 1971
Sixpence	30 June 1980
Halfpenny (½p)	31 December 1984
Old 5 pence	31 December 1990
Old 10 pence	30 June 1993
Old 50 pence	28 February 1998

The Channel Islands and the Isle of Man issue their own coinage, which are legal tender only in the island of issue.

	Metal	Standard weight (g)	Standard diameter (mm)
1p	bronze	3.564	20.3
1p	copper-plated steel	3.564	20.3
2p	bronze	7.128	25.9
2p	copper-plated steel	7.128	25.9
5p	cupro-nickel	3.25	18.0
10p	cupro-nickel	6.5	24.5
20p	cupro-nickel	5.0	21.4
25p Crown	cupro-nickel	28.28	38.6
50p	cupro-nickel	8.00	27.3
£1	nickel-brass	9.5	22.5
£2	nickel-brass	15.98	28.4
£2	cupro-nickel, nickel-brass	12.00	28.4
£5 Crown	cupro-nickel	28.28	38.6

The 'remedy' is the amount of variation from standard permitted in weight and fineness of coins when first issued from the Mint.

THE TRIAL OF THE PYX

The Trial of the Pyx is the examination by a jury to ascertain that coins made by the Royal Mint, which have been set aside in the pyx (or box), are of the proper weight, diameter and composition required by law. The trial is held annually, presided over by the Queen's Remembrancer (the Senior Master of the Supreme Court), with a jury of freemen of the Company of Goldsmiths.

BANKNOTES

Bank of England notes are currently issued in denominations of £5, £10, £20 and £50 for the amount of the fiduciary note issue, and are legal tender in England and Wales. No £1 notes have been issued since 1984 and in March 1998 the outstanding notes were written off in accordance with the provision of the Currency Act 1983.

The current E series of notes was introduced from June 1990, replacing the D series (*see* below). A new-style £20 note, the first in series F, was introduced on 13 March 2007. The historical figures portrayed in these series are:

£5	May 2002–date	Elizabeth Fry
£5	June 1990–2003	George Stephenson*
£10	November 2000–date	Charles Darwin*
£10	April 1992–2003	Charles Dickens*
£20	March 2007–date	Adam Smith
£20	June 1999–date	Sir Edward Elgar
£20	June 1991–2001	Michael Faraday*
£50	April 1994–date	Sir John Houblon

* These notes have been withdrawn from circulation: George Stephenson on 21 November 2003; Charles Dickens on 31 July 2003; Michael Faraday on 28 February 2001

NOTE CIRCULATION

Note circulation is highest at the two peak spending periods of the year, around Christmas and during the summer holiday period.

The value of notes in circulation (£million) at the end of February 2005 and 2006 was:

	2006	2007
£5	1,051	1,100
£10	5,591	5,886
£20	22,690	23,740
£50	6,510	6,705
Other notes*	1,071	1,108
TOTAL	36,914	38,449

* Includes higher value notes used internally in the Bank of England, eg as cover for the note issues of banks in Scotland and Northern Ireland in excess of their permitted issue

LEGAL TENDER

Banknotes which are no longer legal tender are payable when presented at the head office of the Bank of England in London.

The white notes for £10, £20, £50, £100, £500 and £1,000, which were issued until April 1943, ceased to be legal tender in May 1945, and the white £5 note in March 1946.

The white £5 note issued between October 1945 and September 1956, the £5 notes issued between 1957 and 1963 (bearing a portrait of Britannia) and the first series to bear a portrait of the queen, issued between 1963 and

1971, ceased to be legal tender in March 1961, June 1967 and September 1973 respectively.

The series of £1 notes issued during the years 1928 to 1960 and the 10 shilling notes issued from 1928 to 1961 (those without the royal portrait) ceased to be legal tender in May and October 1962 respectively. The £1 note first issued in March 1960 (bearing on the back a representation of Britannia) and the £10 note first issued in February 1964 (bearing a lion on the back), both bearing a portrait of the Queen on the front, ceased to be legal tender in June 1979. The £1 note first issued in 1978 ceased to be legal tender on 11 March 1988. The 10 shilling note was replaced by the 50p coin in October 1969, and ceased to be legal tender on 21 November 1970.

The D series of banknotes was introduced from 1970 and ceased to be legal tender from the dates shown below. The predominant identifying feature of each note was the portrayal on the back of a prominent figure from British history:

£1	Feb. 1978–March 1988	Sir Isaac Newton
£5	Nov. 1971–Nov. 1991	Duke of Wellington
£10	Feb. 1975–May 1994	Florence Nightingale
£20	July 1970–March 1993	William Shakespeare
£50	March 1981–Sept. 1996	Sir Christopher Wren

The £1 coin was introduced on 21 April 1983 to replace the £1 note.

OTHER BANKNOTES

SCOTLAND – Banknotes are issued by three Scottish banks. The Royal Bank of Scotland issues notes for £1, £5, £10, £20, £50 and £100. Bank of Scotland and the Clydesdale Bank issue notes for £5, £10, £20, £50 and £100. Scottish notes are not legal tender in the UK but they are an authorised currency.

NORTHERN IRELAND – Banknotes are issued by four banks in Northern Ireland. The Bank of Ireland, the Northern Bank and the Ulster Bank issue notes for £5, £10, £20, £50 and £100. The First Trust Bank issues notes for £10, £20, £50 and £100. Northern Ireland notes are not legal tender in Northern Ireland but they circulate widely and enjoy a status comparable to that of Bank of England notes.

CHANNEL ISLANDS – The States of Guernsey issues its own currency notes and coinage. The notes are for £1, £5, £10, £20 and £50, and the coins are for 1p, 2p, 5p, 10p, 20p, 50p, £1, £2 and £5. The States of Jersey issues its own currency notes and coinage. The notes are for £1, £5, £10, £20 and £50, and the coins are for 1p, 2p, 5p, 10p, 20p, 50p, £1 and £2.

THE ISLE OF MAN – The Isle of Man government issues notes for £1, £5, £10, £20 and £50. Although these notes are only legal tender in the Isle of Man, they are accepted at face value in branches of the clearing banks in the UK. The Isle of Man issues coins for 1p, 2p, 5p, 10p, 20p, 50p, £1, £2 and £5.

Although none of the series of notes specified above is legal tender in the UK, they are generally accepted by banks irrespective of their place of issue. At one time banks made a commission charge for handling Scottish and Irish notes but this was abolished some years ago.

BANKING AND PERSONAL FINANCE

There are two main types of deposit-taking institutions: banks and building societies, although National Savings and Investments also provides savings products. Banks and building societies are supervised by the Financial Services Authority and National Savings and Investments is accountable to the Treasury. As a result of the conversion of several building societies into banks in the 1990s, the size of the banking sector, which was already substantially greater than the non-bank deposit-taking sector, increased further.

The main institutions within the British banking system are the Bank of England (the central bank), retail banks, investment banks and overseas banks. In its role as the central bank, the Bank of England acts as banker to the government and as a note-issuing authority; it also oversees the efficient functioning of payment and settlement systems.

Since May 1997, the Bank of England has had operational responsibility for monetary policy. At monthly meetings of its monetary policy committee the bank sets the interest rate at which it will lend to the money markets.

OFFICIAL INTEREST RATES 2001–7

8 November 2001	4.00%
6 February 2003	3.75%
10 July 2003	3.50%
6 November 2003	3.75%
5 February 2004	4.00%
6 May 2004	4.25%
10 June 2004	4.50%
5 August 2004	4.75%
4 August 2005	4.50%
3 August 2006	4.75%
9 November 2006	5.00%
11 January 2007	5.25%
10 May 2007	5.50%
5 July 2007	5.75%

RETAIL BANKING

Retail banks offer a wide variety of financial services to individuals and companies, including current and deposit accounts, loan and overdraft facilities, automated teller (cash dispenser) machines, cheque guarantee cards, credit and debit cards, investment services, pensions, insurance and mortgages. All banks offer telephone and internet banking facilities in addition to traditional branch services.

The Financial Ombudsman Service provides independent and impartial arbitration in disputes between banks and their customers (*see* Financial Services Regulation).

PAYMENT CLEARINGS

The Association for Payment Clearing Services (APACS) is the UK trade association for payments and for those institutions that deliver payment services to customers. It is also the banking industry's voice on payment issues regarding plastic cards, card fraud, cheques, electronic payments and cash. Membership of APACS is open to any member of a payment scheme which is widely used or significant in the UK. As at April 2007 APACS had 31 members, comprising the major banks, one building society and Royal Mail Group.

There are three separate companies which manage the majority of payment clearings in the UK (and which are contactable through APACS):

- BACS Payment Schemes Ltd manages the schemes under which electronic payments are made, processing direct debits, direct credits and standing orders
- CHAPS Ltd provides electronic same-day clearing for sterling and euro payments
- Cheque and Credit Clearing Company Ltd oversees the clearing of cheques and paper credits in Great Britain

APACS, Mercury House, Triton Court, 14 Finsbury Square, London EC2A 1LQ T 020-7711 6200 W www.apacs.org.uk

MAJOR RETAIL BANKS' FINANCIAL RESULTS 2006

Bank group	Profit before taxation £ million	Profit after taxation £ million	Total assets £ million
Abbey	183	68	191,805
Alliance and Leicester	569	450	68,557
Barclays	7,136	5,195	996,787
HBOS	5,706	3,934	591,029
HSBC	11,993	9,161	947,126
Lloyds TSB	4,248	2,907	343,598
Northern Rock	627	443	101,011
RBS Group	9,186	6,497	871,432

GLOSSARY OF FINANCIAL TERMS

AER (ANNUAL EQUIVALENT RATE) – A notional rate quoted on savings and investment products which demonstrates the return on interest, when compounded and paid annually.

APR (ANNUAL PERCENTAGE RATE) – Calculates the total amount of interest payable over the whole term of a product (such as investment or loan), allowing consumers to compare rival products on a like-for-like basis. Companies offering loans, credit cards, mortgages or overdrafts are required by law to provide the APR rate. Where typical APR is shown, it refers to the company's typical borrower and so is given as a best example; rate and costs may vary depending on individual circumstances.

ANNUITY – A type of insurance policy that provides regular income in exchange for a lump sum. Everyone who has a pension and has built up a lump sum with their provider must buy an annuity by the time they reach 75. The annuity can be bought from a company other than the existing pension provider.

ASU – Accident, sickness and unemployment insurance taken out by a borrower to protect against being unable to work for these reasons. The policy will usually pay a percentage of the normal monthly mortgage repayment if the borrower is unable to work.

ATM (AUTOMATED TELLER MACHINE) – Commonly referred to as cash machines. Users can access their bank accounts using a card for simple transactions such as withdrawing and depositing cash. Some banks and independent ATM deployers charge for transactions.

BANKER'S DRAFT – A cheque drawn on a bank against a cash deposit. Considered to be a secure way of receiving money in instances where a cheque could 'bounce' or where it is not desirable to receive cash.

BASE RATE – The minimum rate at which banks are prepared to lend money. This acts as a benchmark for all other interest rates.

BASIS POINT – Unit of measure (usually one-hundredth of a percentage point) used to express movements in interest rates, foreign rates or bond yields.

BUY-TO-LET – The purchase of a residential property for the sole purpose of letting to a tenant. Not all lenders provide mortgage finance for this purpose. Buy-to-let mortgages typically require at least a 15–25 per cent deposit and the loan agreed is based on a combination of the borrower's income in addition to the rental value of the property. Because of the higher risks involved in letting property, buy-to-let mortgages are more expensive.

CAPITAL GAIN/LOSS – Increase/decrease in the value of a capital asset when it is sold or transferred compared to its initial worth.

CAPPED RATE MORTGAGE – The interest rate applied to a loan is guaranteed not to rise above a certain rate for a set period of time; the rate can therefore fall but will not rise above the capped rate. The level at which the cap is fixed is usually higher than for a fixed rate mortgage for a comparable period of time. The lender normally imposes early redemption penalties within the first few years.

CASH CARD – Issued by banks and building societies for withdrawing cash from ATMs.

CHARGE CARD – Charge cards, eg American Express and Diners Club, can be used in a similar way to credit cards but the debt must be settled in full each month.

CHIP AND PIN CARD – A credit/debit card which incorporates an embedded chip containing unique owner details. When used with a PIN number, such cards offer greater security as they are less prone to fraud. Since 14 February 2006, most card transactions in the UK have required the use of a chip and pin card.

CREDIT CARD – Normally issued with a credit limit, credit cards can be used for purchases until the limit is reached. There is normally an interest-free period on the outstanding balance of up to 56 days. Charges can be avoided if the balance is paid off in full within the interest-free period. Alternatively part of the balance can be paid and in most cases there is a minimum amount set by the issuer (normally a percentage of the outstanding balance) which must be paid on a monthly basis. Some card issuers charge an annual fee and most issuers belong to a least one major credit card network, eg Mastercard or Visa.

CREDIT RATING – Overall credit worthiness of a borrower based on information from a credit reference agency, such as Experian or Equifax, which holds details of credit agreements, payment records, county court judgements etc for all adults in the UK. This information is supplied to lenders who use it in their credit scoring or underwriting systems to calculate the risk of granting a loan to an individual and the probability that it will be repaid. Each lender sets their own criteria for credit worthiness and may accept or reject a credit application based on an individual's credit rating.

CRITICAL ILLNESS COVER – Insurance that covers borrowers against critical illnesses such as stroke, heart attack or cancer and is designed to protect mortgage or other loan payments.

DEBIT CARD – Debit cards were introduced on a large scale in the UK in the mid-1980s, replacing cash and cheques to purchase goods and services. They can be used to withdraw cash from ATMs in the UK and abroad and may also function as a cheque guarantee card. Funds are automatically withdrawn from an individual's bank account after making a purchase and no interest is charged.

DISCOUNTED MORTGAGE – Discounted mortgages guarantee an interest rate set at a margin below the standard variable rate for a period of time. The discounted rate will move up or down with the standard variable rate, but the payment rate will retain the agreed differential below the standard variable rate. The lender normally imposes early redemption penalties within the first few years.

EARLY REDEMPTION PENALTY – see Redemption Penalty

ENDOWMENT MORTGAGE – Only the interest on a property loan is paid back to the lender each month as long as an endowment life insurance policy is taken out for an agreed amount of time, typically 25 years. When the policy matures the lender will take repayment of the money owed on the property loan and any surplus goes to the policyholder. If the endowment policy shows a shortfall on projected returns, the policy holder must make further provision to pay off the mortgage.

EQUITY – When applied to real estate, equity is the difference between the value of a property and the amount outstanding on any loan secured against it. Negative equity occurs when the loan is greater than the market value of the property.

FIXED RATE MORTGAGE – A repayment mortgage

where the interest rate on the loan is fixed for a set amount of time, normally a period of between one and ten years. The interest rate does not vary with changes to the base rate resulting in the monthly mortgage payment remaining the same for the duration of the fixed period. The lender normally imposes early redemption penalties within the first few years.

INTEREST ONLY MORTGAGE – Only interest is paid by the borrower and capital remains constant for the term of the loan. The onus is on the borrower to make provision to repay the capital at the end of the term. This is usually achieved through an investment vehicle such as an endowment policy or pension.

ISA – The individual savings account is a means by which investors can save and invest without paying any tax on the proceeds. Money can be invested across three investment elements: cash, stocks and shares and life insurance products. There are limits on the amount that can be invested during any given tax year.

LOAN TO VALUE – This is the ratio between the size of a mortgage loan sought and the mortgage lender's valuation. On a loan of £55,000, for example, on a property valued at £100,000 the loan to value is 55 per cent. This means that there is sufficient equity in the property for the lender to be reassured that if interest or capital repayments were stopped, it could sell the property and recoup the money owed. Fewer options are available to borrowers requiring high LTV.

MIG (MORTGAGE INDEMNITY GUARANTEE) – An insurance policy designed to protect the lender against loss in the event of the borrower defaulting or ceasing to repay a mortgage. It offers no protection to the borrower. Not all lenders charge MIG premiums.

ONLINE BANKING – Also known as internet or e-banking, where a range of banking transactions from paying bills, transferring funds to arranging overdrafts can be carried out online.

PERSONAL PENSION PLAN (PPP) – Designed for the self-employed or those in non-pensionable employment. Contributions made to a PPP are exempt from tax and the retirement age may be selected at any time from age 50 to 75. Up to 25 per cent of the pension fund may be taken as a tax-free cash sum on retirement.

PHISHING – A fraudulent attempt to obtain bank account details and security codes through an email. The email purports to come from a *bona fide* bank or building society and attempts to steer the recipient, usually under the pretext that the banking institution is updating its security arrangements, to a website which requests personal details.

PIN (PERSONAL IDENTIFICATION NUMBER) – A PIN is issued alongside a cash card to allow the user to access a bank account via an ATM. PINs are also issued with smart, credit and debit cards and, since 14 February 2006, have been requested in the majority of shops and restaurants as a further security measure when making a purchase.

PORTABLE MORTGAGE – A mortgage product that can be transferred to a different property in the event of a house move. Preferable where early redemption penalties are charged.

REDEMPTION PENALTY – A charge levied for paying off a loan, debt balance or mortgage before a date agreed with the lender.

REPAYMENT MORTGAGE – In contrast to the interest only mortgage, the monthly repayment includes an element of the capital sum borrowed in addition to the interest charged.

SELF-CERTIFICATION – Several lenders allow borrowers to self-certify their income. This type of scheme is useful to the self-employed who may not have accounts available or any other person who has difficulty proving their regular income.

SHARE – A share is a divided-up unit of the value of a company. If a company is worth £100 million, and there are 50 million shares in issue, then each share is worth £2 (usually listed as pence). As the overall value of the company fluctuates so does the share price.

SMART CARD – A new generation of cashless payment system. They carry more information than debit cards including mortgage and health details and a fixed number of units of real money. The card is used in conjunction with a PIN and once the money on the card is spent, it must be loaded again by transferring money to it from a bank account via an ATM or telephone.

TELEPHONE BANKING – Banking facilities which can be accessed via the telephone.

UNIT TRUST – A 'pooled' fund of assets, usually shares, owned by a number of individuals. Managed by professional, authorised fund-management groups, unit trusts have traditionally delivered better returns than average cash deposits, but do rise and fall in value as their underlying investment varies in value.

WITH-PROFITS – Usually applies to pensions, endowments, savings schemes or bonds. The intention is to smooth out the rises and falls in the stock market for the benefit of the investor. Actuaries working for the insurance company, or fund managers, hold back some profits in good years in order to make up the difference in years when shares perform badly.

VARIABLE RATE MORTGAGE – Repayment mortgages where the interest rate set by the lender increases or decreases in relation to the base interest rate which can result in fluctuating monthly repayments.

FINANCIAL SERVICES REGULATION

FINANCIAL SERVICES AUTHORITY

The FSA has been the single regulator for financial services in the UK since 1 December 2001, when the Financial Services and Markets Act 2000 (FSMA) came into force. The FSA's aim is to promote efficient, orderly and fair financial markets and help retail consumers to receive a fair deal.

The FSA is required to pursue four statutory objectives:
* maintaining market confidence
* raising public awareness
* protecting consumers
* reducing financial crime

The legislation also requires the FSA to have regard to the following principles while carrying out its general functions:
* using its resources in an economic and efficient way
* the responsibilities of regulated firms' own management
* being proportionate in imposing burdens or restrictions on the industry
* facilitating innovation
* the international character of financial services and the competitive position of the United Kingdom
* not impeding or distorting competition unnecessarily

ORGANISATION AND STRUCTURE
The FSA is a company limited by guarantee and financed by levies on the industry. It receives no funds from the public purse. It is accountable to treasury ministers and, through them, to parliament. The FSA must report annually on the achievement of its statutory objectives to the Treasury, which is required to lay the report before parliament.

The FSA's budgeted costs for 2007–8 are £301.7m.

FSA REGISTER OF AUTHORISED FIRMS AND PERSONS
The FSA maintains a register of all firms that are authorised to carry out regulated activities. The entry for each firm gives its name, address and telephone number; a reference number; its authorisation status (outlining exactly what regulated activities the firm is authorised to carry out), stating which organisation regulates it, and whether it can handle client money. In addition the FSA keeps a list of approved persons in the industry who are authorised to carry out functions regulated by the FSA. Each entry includes a list of controlled functions an individual is authorised to perform and for which firms.

FINANCIAL SERVICES AUTHORITY
25 the North Colonnade, Canary Wharf, London E14 5HS
T 020-7066 1000 **Helpline** 0845-606 1234
W www.fsa.gov.uk
Chair, Sir Callum McCarthy
Chief Executive, vacant

COMPENSATION

FINANCIAL SERVICES COMPENSATION SCHEME
The Financial Services Compensation Scheme (FSCS) is an independent statutory body created under the FSMA.

It provides compensation if a firm authorised by the FSA is unable or likely to be unable to pay claims against it. This is usually when a firm becomes insolvent. The FSCS covers deposits, insurance policies, insurance broking (for business on or after 14 January 2005), investment business and mortgage advice and arranging (for business on or after 31 October 2004). The FSCS is independent of the FSA, with separate staff and premises. However, the FSA appoints the board of the FSCS and sets its guidelines. The FSCS is funded by levies on authorised firms.

FINANCIAL SERVICES COMPENSATION SCHEME
7th Floor, Lloyds Chambers, Portsoken Street, London E1 8BN
T 020-7892 7300 E enquiries@fscs.org.uk
W www.fscs.org.uk
Chair, David Hall
Chief Executive, Loretta Minghella

PENSION PROTECTION FUND
The Pension Protection Fund (PPF) is a statutory fund established under the Pensions Act 2004 that became operational on 6 April 2005. The fund was set-up to pay compensation to members of eligible defined benefit pension schemes, where there is a qualifying insolvency event in relation to the employer and where there are insufficient assets in the pension scheme to cover PPF levels of compensation. Compulsory annual levies are charged on all eligible schemes to help fund the PPF, in addition to investment of PPF assets.

PENSION PROTECTION FUND
Knollys House, 17 Addiscombe Road, Croydon, Surrey
CR0 6SR T 0845-600 2541 E information@ppf.gsi.gov.uk
W www.pensionprotectionfund.org.uk
Chair, Lawrence Churchill
Chief Executive, Partha Dasgupta

DESIGNATED PROFESSIONAL BODIES

Professional firms are exempt from requiring direct regulation by the FSA if they carry out only certain restricted activities that arise out of, or are complementary to, the provision of professional services, such as arranging the sale of shares on the instructions of executors or trustees or providing services to small, private companies. These firms are, however, supervised by designated professional bodies (DPBs). There are a number of safeguards to protect consumers dealing with firms that do not require direct regulation. These arrangements include:
* the FSA's power to ban a specific firm from taking advantage of the exemption and to restrict the regulated activities permitted to the firms
* rules which require professional firms to ensure that their clients are aware that they are not authorised persons
* a requirement for the DPBs to supervise and regulate the firms and inform the FSA on how the professional firms carry on their regulated activities

See Professional Education section for the contact details of the following DPBs:

Institute of Chartered Accountants in England and Wales
Institute of Chartered Accountants in Scotland
Institute of Chartered Accountants in Ireland
Association of Chartered Certified Accountants
Institute of Actuaries
Law Society of England and Wales
Law Society of Northern Ireland
Law Society of Scotland

RECOGNISED INVESTMENT EXCHANGES

The FSA currently supervises six recognised investment exchanges (RIEs); under the FSMA, recognition confers an exemption from the need to be authorised to carry out regulated activities in the UK. The RIEs are organised markets on which member firms can trade investments such as equities and derivatives. As a regulator the FSA must focus on the impact of changes brought about by the continued growth in electronic trading by exchanges and other organisations. Issues such as how these changes affect market quality, reliability and access are important and the FSA works with the exchanges to ensure that new systems meet regulatory requirements. The RIEs are listed with their year of recognition in parentheses:

EUROPEAN DERIVATIVES EXCHANGE (EDX)
LONDON (2003), 10 Paternoster Square, London EC4M 7LS T 020-7797 1000
W www.londonstockexchange.com/edx
(see also London Stock Exchange)

INTERCONTINENTAL EXCHANGE (ICE) FUTURES (2001)*, International House, 1 St Katharine's Way, London E1W 1UY T 020-7265 3648 W www.theice.com

LONDON INTERNATIONAL FINANCIAL FUTURES (LIFFE) ADMINISTRATION AND MANAGEMENT (2001), Cannon Bridge House, 1 Cousin Lane, London EC4R 3XX T 020-7623 0444 W www.liffe.com

LONDON STOCK EXCHANGE (LSE) (2001),
10 Paternoster Square, London EC4M 7LS
T 020-7797 1000 W www.londonstockexchange.com

NEW YORK MERCANTILE EXCHANGE (NYMEX) EUROPE (2005), 131 Finsbury Pavement, London EC2A 1NT T 020-7131 3001 W www.nymex.com

LONDON METAL EXCHANGE
(2001), 56 Leadenhall Street, London EC3A 2BJ
T 020-7264 5555 W www.lme.co.uk

VIRT-X EXCHANGE (2001), 34th Floor, One Canada Square, Canary Wharf, London E14 5AA T 020-7864 4310 W www.virt-x.com
* Formerly the International Petroleum Exchange (IPE)

RECOGNISED CLEARING HOUSES

The FSA is also responsible for recognising and supervising recognised clearing houses (RCHs), which organise the settlement of transactions on recognised investment exchanges. There are two RCHs:

CREST CO LTD (2001), Watling House, 33 Cannon Street, London EC4M 5SB T 020-7849 0000 W www.crestco.co.uk

LONDON CLEARING HOUSE CLEARNET LTD (LCH.CLEARNET) (2001), Aldgate House, 33 Aldgate High Street, London EC3N 1EA T 020-7426 7000 W www.lchclearnet.com

OMBUDSMAN SCHEMES

The Financial Ombudsman Service was set up by the Financial Services and Markets Act 2000 to provide consumers with a free, independent service for resolving disputes with authorised financial firms. The Financial Ombudsman Service can consider complaints about most financial matters including: banking; credit cards and store cards; financial advice; hire purchase and pawnbroking; insurance; loans and credit; mortgages; pensions; savings and investments; stocks, shares, unit trusts and bonds.

Complainants must first complain to the firm involved. They do not have to accept the ombudsman's decision and are free to go to court if they wish, but if a decision is accepted, it is binding for both the complainant and the firm.

The Pensions Ombudsman can investigate and decide complaints and disputes about the way that occupational and personal pension schemes are administered and managed. The Pensions Ombudsman is also the Ombudsman for the board of the Pension Protection Fund (PPF) and as such can deal with disputes regarding decisions made by the board of the actions of PPF staff.

FINANCIAL OMBUDSMAN SERVICE, South Quay Plaza, 183 Marsh Wall, London E14 9SR **Helpline:** 0845-080 1800 T 020-7964 1000
E complaint.info@financial-ombudsman.org.uk
W www.financial-ombudsman.org.uk
Chief Ombudsman, Walter Merricks
Principal Ombudsmen, Tony Boorman; David Thomas

PENSIONS OMBUDSMAN, 11 Belgrave Road, London SW1V 1RB T 020-7834 9144
E www.enquiries@pensions-ombudsman.org.uk
W www.pensions-ombudsman.org.uk
Pensions Ombudsman / Pension Protection Fund Ombudsman, David Laverick

PANEL ON TAKEOVERS AND MERGERS

The Panel on Takeovers and Mergers is an independent body, established in 1968, whose main functions are to issue and administer the City code on takeovers and mergers. Its principal objective is to ensure equality of treatment and opportunity for all shareholders in takeover bids and mergers.

The panel comprises up to 34 members drawn from major financial and business institutions. The chair, deputy chair and up to 20 independent members are nominated by the panel's own nomination committee. The remaining members are nominated by professional bodies representing the banking, insurance, investment, pension and accountancy industries and the CBI.

PANEL ON TAKEOVERS AND MERGERS,
10 Paternoster Square, London EC4M 7DY
T 020-7382 9026 W www.thetakeoverpanel.org.uk
Chair, Peter Scott, QC

NATIONAL SAVINGS AND INVESTMENTS

National Savings and Investments (formerly National Savings) is one of the largest savings organisations in the UK, and is an executive agency of HM Treasury. Savings and investment products are offered to personal savers and investors and the money is used to manage the national debt more effectively. When people invest in National Savings and Investments they are lending money to the government which pays them interest or prizes in return.

TAX-FREE PRODUCTS

NATIONAL SAVINGS AND INVESTMENT CERTIFICATES

INDEX-LINKED SAVING CERTIFICATES
Otherwise known as inflation-beating savings, index-linked saving certificates are fixed rate investments that pay tax-free returns guaranteed to be above inflation. They are available in three- and five-year terms and are sold in issues. The minimum investment for each issue is £100 and the maximum £15,000.

FIXED INTEREST SAVING CERTIFICATES
Fixed interest saving certificates are fixed rate investments that pay tax-free returns. They are available in two- and five-year terms and are sold in issues for which the minimum investment is £100 and the maximum £15,000.

PREMIUM BONDS
Introduced in 1956, premium bonds are an integral part of the government's management of national debt. They enable savers to enter a regular draw for tax-free prizes, while retaining the right to get their money back. A sum equivalent to interest on each bond is put into a prize fund and distributed by monthly prize draws. The prizes are drawn by ERNIE (electronic random number indicator equipment) and are free of all UK income tax and capital gains tax. The top prize is £1m.

Bonds are in units of £1, with a minimum purchase of £100; above this, purchases must be in multiples of £10, up to a maximum holding limit of £30,000 per person. Bonds become eligible for prizes once they have been held for one clear calendar month following the month of purchase. Each £1 unit can win only one prize per draw, but it will be awarded the highest for which it is drawn. Bonds remain eligible for prizes until they are repaid. When a holder dies, bonds remain eligible for prizes up to and including the twelfth monthly draw after the month in which the holder dies.

The scheme offers a facility to reinvest prize wins automatically. Upon completion of an automatic prize reinvestment mandate, holders receive new bonds which are immediately eligible for future prize draws. Bonds can only be held in the name of an individual and not by organisations.

As at March 2007, 149.75 million prizes totalling £9.5bn had been distributed since the first prize draw in 1957.

CHILDREN'S BONUS BONDS
Children's bonus bonds were introduced in 1991. They can be bought for any child under 16 and will go on growing in value until he or she is 21. The bonds are sold in five-year issues at multiples of £25. For each issue the minimum holding is £25 and the maximum holding is £3,000 per child. Bonds for children under 16 must be held by a parent or guardian. All returns are totally exempt from UK income tax and a bonus is payable if the bond is held for the full five years.

OTHER PRODUCTS

GUARANTEED EQUITY BONDS
Guaranteed equity bonds are five-year investments where the returns are linked to the performance of the FTSE-100 index with a guarantee that the original capital invested will be returned even if the FTSE-100 index falls over the five years. They are sold in limited issues with a minimum investment of £1,000 and a maximum of £1m. The returns are subject to income tax on maturity, unless they are held in a self-invested pension plan (SIPP).

SAVINGS AND INVESTMENT ACCOUNTS
The easy access savings account was launched in January 2004 replacing the ordinary account (also known as the Post Office savings account). The easy access savings account offers access to savings via Post Office counters, an ATM card, telephone and online. It can be opened with a minimum balance of £100 and has a maximum limit of £2m (£4m jointly). The interest is paid without deduction of tax at source. Holders of the ordinary account can no longer undertake transactions except for closing the account or transferring the funds to an easy access savings account or the investment account.

The investment account is a passbook account which pays tiered rates of interest and requires one month's notice for withdrawals. Repayments are made without notice or penalty. It can be opened with a minimum balance of £20 and has a maximum limit of £100,000. The interest is paid without deduction of tax at source.

Since April 1999 National Savings and Investments has offered cash mini individual savings accounts (ISAs). A cash mini ISA can be opened online, by post, telephone and in post offices with a minimum investment of £10. A direct ISA was launched in April 2006 which can be opened by telephone and online with a minimum investment of £1,000. Interest for both ISAs is calculated daily and is free of tax.

INCOME BONDS
National Savings and Investments income bonds were introduced in 1982. They are suitable for those who want to receive regular monthly payments of interest while preserving the full cash value of their capital. The bonds are sold in multiples of £500. The minimum holding is £500 and the maximum £1m (sole or joint holding). Interest is calculated on a day-to-day basis and paid monthly. Interest is taxable but is paid without deduction of tax at source. Since August 2005, there is no penalty or notice required for making withdrawals.

PENSIONERS GUARANTEED INCOME BONDS

Pensioners guaranteed income bonds were introduced in January 1994 and are designed for people aged 60 and over who wish to receive regular monthly payments with a rate of interest that is fixed for a period whilst preserving the full cash value of their investment. Five-, two- and one-year terms are available and are sold in issues. The minimum limit for each issue is £500. The maximum holding is £1m (sole or joint holding) with the rate of interest fixed and guaranteed for each bond purchased. Interest is taxable but is paid without deduction of tax at source. The original capital investment is repaid in full at the end of the term.

FIXED RATE SAVINGS BOND

Fixed rate savings bonds are investments that earn fixed rates of interest. Five-, three- and one-year terms are available and are sold in issues. The minimum investment is £500 and the maximum £1m. Interest, from which basic rate tax is deducted at source, can be paid out or reinvested into the bond monthly, annually or at the end of the term. Holders can also choose where the interest is paid. The original capital investment is repaid in full at the end of the term.

CAPITAL BONDS

National Savings and Investments capital bonds were introduced in 1989. Five-year capital bonds are sold in issues. The interest is taxable each year (for those who pay income tax) but is not deducted at source. For each issue, the minimum investment is £100 and the maximum £1m. Capital bonds are repaid in full with all interest gained at the end of five years.

TREASURER'S ACCOUNT

The treasurer's account, introduced in September 1996, offers attractive rates and security to non-profit making organisations such as charities, friendly societies and clubs. The minimum holding is £10,000 and the maximum is £2m.

FURTHER INFORMATION

Further information can be obtained from the Post Office, by telephone (T 0845-964 5000) or online (W www.nsandi.com).

THE LONDON STOCK EXCHANGE

The London Stock Exchange serves the needs of industry and investors by providing facilities for raising capital and a central market place for securities trading. This market place covers government stocks (called gilts), UK and overseas company shares (called equities and fixed interest stocks), and other instruments such as covered warrants and exchange traded funds (ETFs).

PRIMARY MARKETS

The London Stock Exchange enables companies to raise capital for development and growth through the issue of securities. For a company entering the market for the first time there is a choice of exchange markets, depending upon the size, history and requirements of the company. The first is the main market. A company's securities are admitted to the official list by the Financial Services Authority (FSA), which acts as the UK Listing Authority.

The Alternative Investment Market (AIM) was established in June 1995. It enables small, young and growing companies to raise capital, widen their investor base and have their shares traded on a regulated market without the expense of a full London Stock Exchange listing. Many companies use AIM as a stepping-stone to a full listing.

A third market, the Professional Securities Market (PSM), was established in July 2005, to coincide with the introduction of the FSA's new listing rules. PSM provides a solution to issuers who want to list their debt securities or depository receipts in London without having to re-state their financial information to conform with international financial reporting standards.

Once admitted, all companies are obliged to keep their shareholders informed of their progress, making announcements of a price-sensitive nature through a primary information provider approved by the FSA.

At 31 December 2006 there were 3,256 companies listed on the London Stock Exchange: 1,276 were main market UK-listed, with an equity market value of £1,931.9bn; 330 main market internationally listed, with an equity market value of £2,373.7bn; 1,634 listed on AIM, with a market value of £90.7bn; and 16 equity only companies listed on PSM.

UK equity turnover in 2006 was £3,210.5bn with a total number of 89.6 million equity bargains. International equity turnover in 2006 totalled £3,447.7bn with a total number of 21.8 million equity bargains.

'BIG BANG'

During 1986 the London Stock Exchange went through the greatest period of change in its 200-year history. In March 1986 it opened its doors for the first time to overseas and corporate membership, allowing banks, insurance companies and overseas securities houses to become members of the exchange and to buy existing member firms. On 27 October 1986, three major reforms took place and became known as Big Bang:
• the abolition of scales of minimum commissions, allowing clients to negotiate freely with their brokers about the charge for their services
• the abolition of the separation of member firms into

brokers and jobbers: firms are now broker/dealers, able to act as agents on behalf of clients; to act as principals buying and selling shares for their own account; and to become registered market makers, making continuous buying and selling prices in specific securities
• the introduction of the Stock Exchange automated quotations system (SEAQ)

Since the introduction of SEAQ in 1986, dealing in stocks and shares has taken place by telephone in the firms' own dealing rooms, rather than face to face on the floor of the exchange. The Stock Exchange electronic trading service (SETS), launched in 1997, introduced order-driven trading in which deals are executed electronically on an electronic order book. SETS runs alongside SEAQ and allows remote access to the exchange. The new systems also provide increased investor protection. All deals taking place via the exchange systems are recorded on a database which can be used to resolve disputes or to carry out investigations.

Firms trading on the London Stock Exchange buy and sell shares on behalf of the public, as well as institutions such as pension funds or insurance companies. In return for transacting the deal, the broker will charge a commission, which is usually based upon the value of the transaction. The market makers, or wholesalers, in each security do not charge a commission for their services, but will quote the broker two prices, a price at which they will buy and a price at which they will sell. It is the middle of these two prices which is published in lists of share prices in newspapers.

REGULATION

The FSA has overall responsibility for regulating the UK's financial industry under the provisions of the Financial Services and Markets Act 2000. The Act compels business to be conducted through a recognised investment exchange (RIE). The London Stock Exchange is an RIE, regulating three main markets: UK equities, international equities and gilts.

DEVELOPMENTS

On 15 March 2000, the 298 members voted to become shareholders in a demutualised London Stock Exchange, making possible the further commercialisation of the company.

At the end of May 2001 the exchange announced its intention to list on its own main market. The exchange was listed on 20 July 2001 following an annual general meeting the previous day. The full listing is intended to enable the exchange to exploit business opportunities with greater flexibility.

In 2003 the London Stock Exchange created EDX London (European derivatives exchange), a recognised investment exchange for international equity derivatives.

LONDON STOCK EXCHANGE, 10 Paternoster Square, London EC4M 7LS T 020-7797 1000
W www.londonstockexchange.com
Chair, Chris Gibson-Smith
Chief Executive, Clara Furse

INSURANCE

AUTHORISATION AND REGULATION OF INSURANCE COMPANIES

Since 2001, the Financial Services Authority (FSA) has been the authorising, enforcement, supervisory and rule-making body of insurers. Since 2005, this has also included insurance brokers.

The FSA's powers are primarily conferred by the Financial Services and Markets Act 2000, which unified the previous sectoral arrangements and regulators.

AUTHORISATION

The FSA's role is to ensure that firms to which it grants authorisation satisfy the necessary financial criteria, that the senior management of the company are 'fit and proper persons' and that unauthorised firms are not permitted to trade. This part of the FSA's role was previously undertaken by HM Treasury under the Insurance Companies Act 1982, which was repealed when the Financial Services and Markets Act came fully into force. At the end of 2006 there were over 1,000 insurance organisations and friendly societies with authorisation from the FSA to transact one or more classes of insurance business in the UK. However, the single European insurance market, established in 1994, gave insurers authorised in any other European Union country automatic UK authorisation without further formality. This means a potential market of over 5,000 insurance companies.

REGULATION

All life insurers, general insurers, reinsurers, insurance and reinsurance brokers, and composite firms are statutorily regulated. This is achieved through the formulation (after consultation) by the FSA of rules and guidance for regulated organisations. The FSA is also responsible for consumer education and the reduction of financial crime, particularly money laundering.

FINANCIAL SERVICES AUTHORITY, 25 The North Colonnade, London E14 5HS T 020-7066 1000 W www.fsa.gov.uk

COMPLAINTS

Disputes between policyholders and insurers can be referred to the Financial Ombudsman Service (FOS). Policyholders with a complaint against their financial services provider must firstly take the matter to the highest level within the company. Thereafter, if it remains unresolved and it involves an amount below £100,000, they can refer, free of charge, to the Ombudsman Bureau, which examines the facts of a complaint and delivers a decision binding on the insurer (but not the policyholder). Small businesses with a turnover of up to £1m also have access to the scheme. The Financial Ombudsman Service also covers other areas of the financial services industry including banks, building societies and investment firms.

FINANCIAL SERVICES OMBUDSMAN SERVICE, South Quay Plaza, 183 Marsh Wall, London E14 9SR T 020-7964 1000 F 020-7964 1002 W www.financial-ombudsman.org.uk
Chief Ombudsman, Walter Merricks

ASSOCIATION OF BRITISH INSURERS

Over 94 per cent of the domestic business of UK insurance companies is transacted by the 380 members of the Association of British Insurers (ABI). ABI is a trade association which protects and promotes the interests of all its insurance company members. Only insurers authorised in EU countries are eligible for membership. Brokers, intermediaries and claims handlers may not join ABI but may have their own trade associations.

ASSOCIATION OF BRITISH INSURERS (ABI), 51 Gresham Street, London EC2V 7HQ W www.abi.org.uk
Chair, Archie Kane
Director-General, Stephen Haddrill

BALANCE OF PAYMENTS

The financial services industry contributes 8.5 per cent to the UK's gross domestic product (GDP). In 2005 insurance companies generated net exports of £1.6bn, a drop of two-thirds on 2004 caused largely by claims in the aftermath of Hurricane Katrina and a fall in reinsurance business.

TAKEOVERS AND MERGERS

2006 continued to be a very quiet period for takeovers and mergers in the insurance sector. The most significant development was the takeover of GE Insurance by Swiss Reinsurance.

GENERAL INSURANCE

In recent years, measures to combat fraud and guard against climate change have dominated every annual review of general insurance. After the heavy flooding in the UK in 1953, home and property insurers responded to consumer demand by offering flood insurance cover to all areas of the UK. At the time, the comparatively rare instance of flooding meant the average cost of such cover was minimal.

Times and circumstances have since changed and although insurers are still able to offer flood cover, they maintain they can only do so as long as the government is able to continue adequate funding for flood defences. During 2006 and 2007, it became clear that government funding for defences needed a ten per cent increase to prevent breaches by rising sea levels causing substantial damage. Managing risks relating to climate change remains a top priority for general insurers.

Insurance fraud also remains a problem. In 2005, insurers exposed and stopped frauds worth over £400m, an increase of 50 per cent on 2004. To tackle this, after a pilot period of six months, the Insurance Fraud Bureau (W www.insurancefraudbureau.org.uk) was launched in July 2006. This new body was designed to combat insurance fraud in all its forms, whether opportunist – policyholders who exaggerate claims – or organised – premeditated and planned by criminal gangs with proceeds used to fund other crimes. It is not clear how quickly the results of the Bureau's work can be quantified, but some early successes have been recorded.

With average premiums rising for all types of private motorists during the year, the spotlight fell on two types of driver most likely to face higher premiums: newly qualified and older drivers. Pressure groups such as Age Concern and Help the Aged argued that increased premiums may force older drivers to give up driving and rob them of much of their mobility. Insurers countered these concerns by citing statistical data demonstrating that the frequency of accidents increases heavily once a driver passes 70.

An report produced for ABI, published in July 2006, highlighted that younger drivers are ten times more likely to be involved in a serious or fatal accident than a driver aged 40. The report called for measures to reduce road deaths in this age group. These included limiting the times of day when a young driver can be on the road, restricting the number of passengers he or she can carry and creating a 12-month probationary period for newly qualified drivers. Although popular with media and road safety groups, there has been no sign the government is willing to introduce these proposals.

Claims figures were unremarkable with no striking rises of falls. The highest change was a 34.2 per cent increase in the cost of domestic subsidence claims.

LONDON INSURANCE MARKET

The London Insurance Market is a unique wholesale marketplace and a distinct, separate sector of the UK insurance and reinsurance industry. It is the world's leading market for internationally traded insurance and reinsurance, its business comprising mainly overseas non-life large and high-exposure risks. The market is centred on the City of London, which provides the required financial, banking, legal and other support services. Over 50 per cent of London market business is transacted at Lloyd's, 44 per cent through insurance companies and 3 per cent through protection and indemnity clubs. In 2005, the market had a written gross premium income of over £28bn. Around 150 Lloyd's brokers service the market.

The trade association for the international insurers and reinsurers writing primarily non-marine insurance and all classes of reinsurance business in the London market is the International Underwriting Association (IUA).

INTERNATIONAL UNDERWRITING ASSOCIATION, London Underwriting Centre, 3 Mincing Lane, London EC3R 7DD
W www.iua.co.uk

BRITISH INSURANCE COMPANIES

The following insurance company figures refer to members and certain non-members of the ABI.

WORLDWIDE GENERAL BUSINESS UNDERWRITING RESULTS (£m)

| | 2004 | | | 2005 | | |
	UK	Overseas	Total	UK	Overseas	Total
Motor						
Premiums	10,154	3,326	13,480	10,397	3,412	13,809
Profit (loss)	(72)	(48)	(24)	(191)	221	30
Percentage of premiums	0.7	1.4	0.18	1.8	6.5	0.2
Non-motor						
Premiums	19,340	5,343	24,646	20,081	6,055	26,136
Profit (loss)	1,370	(139)	1,079	1,371	607	1,978
Percentage of premiums	7.1	2.6	4.4	6.8	10.0	7.6

CLAIMS STATISTICS (£m)

	2002	2003	2004	2005	2006
Theft	728	630	512	475	517
Fire	1,045	1,067	812	1,128	1,139
Weather	1,258	610	424	735	475
Domestic subsidence	183	390	199	225	302
Business interruption	236	92	108	267	168
Total	3,490	2,738	2,052	2,851	2,601

NET PREMIUM INCOME BY SECTOR 2005 (£m)

	UK	Overseas
Motor	10,397	3,412
Non-motor	20,081	6,055
Marine, aviation and transport	576	223
Reinsurance	910	204
Total general business	31,964	9,894
Ordinary long-term	99,270	24,984
Industrial long-term	303	–
Total long-term business	99,572	24,984

WORLDWIDE GENERAL BUSINESS TRADING RESULTS (£m)

	2004	2005
Net written premiums	40,204	42,103
Underwriting results	1,321	1,831
Investment income	4,133	6,198
Overall trading profit	5,454	8,029
Profit as percentage of premium income	13.6	19.1

LLOYD'S OF LONDON

Lloyd's of London is an international market for almost all types of general insurance. Lloyd's currently has a capacity to accept insurance premiums of around £13.7bn. Much of this business comes from outside Great Britain and makes a valuable contribution to the balance of payments.

A policy is underwritten at Lloyd's by a mixture of private and corporate members, corporate members having been admitted for the first time in 1992. Specialist underwriters accept insurance risks at Lloyd's on behalf of members (referred to as 'Names') grouped in syndicates. There are currently 62 syndicates of varying sizes, each managed by an underwriting agent approved by the Council of Lloyd's.

Individual members are still in the majority at Lloyd's with a total of 1,124 individuals as opposed to 1,017 corporate members. In 2006, the market capacity of the corporate sector was £14,989m (93.1 per cent) while individuals represented £1,111m (6.9 per cent) of capacity.

Lloyd's is incorporated by an act of parliament (Lloyd's Acts 1971 onwards) and is governed by an 18-person council, made up of six working, six external and six nominated members. The structure immediately below this changed when, in 2002, Lloyd's members voted at an extraordinary general meeting to implement a new franchise system for the market with the aim of improving profitability. The first move was the introduction of a new governance structure, replacing the Lloyd's Market Board and the Lloyd's Regulatory Board with a new 11-person Lloyd's Franchise Board. Four main committees report to this new board.

The corporation is a non-profit making body chiefly financed by its members' subscriptions. It provides the premises, administrative staff and services enabling Lloyd's underwriting syndicates to conduct their business. It does not, however, assume corporate liability for the risks accepted by its members. Individual members are responsible to the full extent of their personal means for their underwriting affairs unless they have converted to limited liability companies (known as NameCos).

Lloyd's syndicates have no direct contact with the public. All business is transacted through insurance brokers accredited by the Corporation of Lloyd's. In addition, non-Lloyd's brokers in the UK, when guaranteed by Lloyd's brokers, are able to deal directly with Lloyd's motor syndicates, a facility which has made the Lloyd's market more accessible to the insuring public.

The FSA has ultimate responsibility for the regulation of the Lloyd's market. However, in situations where Lloyd's internal regulatory and compensation arrangements are more far-reaching – as for example with the Lloyd's Central Fund which safeguards claim payments to policyholders – the regulatory role is delegated to the Council of Lloyd's.

Lloyd's also provides the most comprehensive shipping intelligence service in the world. The shipping and other information received from Lloyd's agents, shipowners, news agencies and other sources throughout the world is collated and distributed to the media as well as to the maritime and commercial sectors in general. *Lloyd's List* is London's oldest daily newspaper and contains news of general commercial interest as well as shipping information. It has been independent of Lloyd's since a management buy-out in 1992. *Lloyd's Shipping Index*, also published daily, lists some 25,000 ocean-going vessels in alphabetical order and gives the latest known report of each.

DEVELOPMENTS IN 2006

After the small loss of £103m in 2005, Lloyd's recorded a profit of £3,662m in 2006. This was largely due to the lack of serious losses during the hurricane season. The only reported major event was Hurricane Kyrill with estimates of £1.4–5.4bn. However, the loss to the Lloyd's market is estimated at only £200m.

Claims from damage caused by Hurricane Katrina in 2005 pushed up premium rates in the United States. Elsewhere there was evidence that the market was softening. Gross premiums rose by 9.6 per cent.

Despite the profits recorded in all segmental areas, increased capacity and new syndicates joining the market, some experts believe that increased hurricane activity and the ever-present terrorist threat could ensure that the 2006 result is the exception rather than the rule for the future.

LLOYD'S OF LONDON, One Lime Street, London EC3M 7HA
T 020-7327 1000 W www.lloydsoflondon.co.uk
Chair, Lord Levene of Portsoken
Chief Executive, Richard Ward

LLOYD'S MEMBERSHIP

	2005	2006
Individual	1,497	1,124
Corporate	714	1,017

TOTAL MARKET CAPACITY *(£m)*

	2005	2006
Individual (unlimited liability)	1,445	1,124
Individual (limited liability)	927	927
Corporate	11,328	12,427
Total	13,700	14,788

LLOYD'S SEGMENTAL RESULTS 2006 *(£m)*

	Gross premiums written	Net earned premium	Result
Reinsurance	5,547	4,186	802
Casualty	3,572	2,964	327
Property	3,638	2,730	495
Marine	1,153	921	105
Motor	923	829	30
Energy	1,125	737	9
Aviation	393	278	97
Life	50	40	2
Total from syndicate operations	16,411	12,685	1,867

LIFE AND LONG-TERM INSURANCE AND PENSIONS

Pensions and savings were the dominant issues for life and pensions insurers during 2006. April saw the publication of the final report from the Pensions Commission, a body set up to review pension provision in the UK. Although the report dealt mainly with state provision, there were some important proposals for the private sector. A delivery authority is to be responsible for introducing a new type of pension, which is designed to help those on lower incomes make adequate provision for their retirement.

Among the measures proposed by Lord Turner's reports were mandatory employer contributions and automatic enrolment for every person with no other form of pension provision. This latter proposal was widely welcomed but still faces some barriers as the EU distance marketing directive prohibits use of such measures. The test of success for personal accounts will not be the number of people who enrol into them but the amount of new money they attract, as many fear that investors may simply transfer their existing savings into these new accounts for a better deal.

A number of new regulatory initiatives were announced by the FSA during the year. These were designed to move the regulatory emphasis away from prescriptive rulebooks to a more principles-based approach, a move welcomed by the industry.

In June, the FSA announced a distribution review designed to examine the way the financial services industry markets and sells its products. Issues to be covered include the professionalism and reputation of the industry; access to financial products; the impact of insurers paying commission to sales staff and intermediaries; and the sustainability of the market. The results of the review were expected to be announced in June 2007.

Although the issues of genetic testing and insurance continued to be discussed in the media during 2006, no alteration to the existing moratorium between life insurers and the government's genetic and insurance advisory committee was sought. In February 2006, the ABI wrote to the government confirming that they would not be applying to use predictive genetic test results in underwriting during 2006 or 2007.

The year ended with a warning from life insurers for policyholders who had complaints about mis-sold endowment policies. A survey had revealed that policyholders who used claims management companies to help them with their claims received, on average, £1,400 in compensation after their fees were deducted. Customers who used the process without help received £3,200. The total amount of compensation paid to the 1.8 million customers that were mis-sold endowments had reached £2.7bn by the end of 2006. Overall, the industry had a better year in 2006 with increases recorded in both single premium and regular premium new business.

PAYMENTS TO POLICYHOLDERS *(£m)*

	2004	2005
Payments to UK policyholders	93,653	108,798
Payments to overseas policyholders	13,766	13,447
Total	107,301	122,245

WORLDWIDE LONG-TERM PREMIUM INCOME *(£m)*

	2001	2002	2003	2004	2005
UK Life Insurance					
Regular Premium	12,226	12,015	11,777	10,507	10,544
Single Premium	25,340	23,731	17,010	20,516	25,488
Total	37,566	35,746	28,787	31,023	36,032
Individual Pensions					
Regular Premium	7,821	8,547	8,059	8,973	7,959
Single Premium	17,702	19,443	14,278	12,036	11,642
Total	25,523	27,990	22,337	21,009	19,601
Other Pensions					
Regular Premium	3,563	3,744	4,239	4,183	4,717
Single Premium	24,981	26,682	29,052	25,836	34,822
Total	28,544	30,426	33,291	30,019	39,539
Other (eg Income					
protection, Annuities)	1,806	1,922	5,502	4,994	4,400
TOTAL UK PREMIUM INCOME	93,439	96,084	89,917	87,045	99,572
Overseas Premium Income					
Regular Premium	6,933	7,436	7,958	7,692	8,089
Single Premium	17,069	17,833	14,464	16,075	16,890
Total	24,002	25,269	22,422	23,767	24,979
TOTAL WORLDWIDE					
PREMIUM INCOME	117,441	121,353	112,339	110,812	124,551

PRIVATE MEDICAL INSURANCE

	2002	2003	2004	2005	2006
Number of people covered (thousand)	6,191	6,080	5,820	5,820	5,879
Corporate	4,304	4,207	4,084	4,125	4,188
Personal	1,887	1,873	1,736	1,695	1,691
Gross Earned Premiums (£m)	2,710	2,816	2,855	2,942	3,070
Corporate	1,341	1,394	1,433	1,493	1,561
Personal	1,369	1,422	1,422	1,449	1,509
Gross Claims Incurred (£m)	2,136	2,203	2,188	2,255	2,376

INVESTMENTS OF INSURANCE COMPANIES 2005

Investment of funds	Long-term business (£m)	General business (£m)
Index-linked British government securities	38,687	2,401
Non-index-linked British government securities	120,277	15,310
Other UK public sector debt securities	21,384	507
Overseas government, provincial and municipal securities	38,039	11,986
Debentures, loan shares, preference and guaranteed stocks and shares		
UK	137,666	11,885
Overseas	98,891	14,878
Ordinary stocks and shares UK	293,783	9,258
Overseas	164,578	3,552
Unit trusts		
Equities	107,290	1,759
Fixed interest	27,012	479
Loans secured on property	20,634	3,080
Real property and ground rents	66,564	1,623
Other invested assets	86,610	31,398
Total invested assets	1,221,414	108,116
NET INVESTMENT INCOME	62,744	6,198

NEW BUSINESS

	2002	2003	2004	2005	2006
New regular premiums					
Investment and savings	253	186	109	85	70
Collective investment schemes	417	337	463	535	620
Other stakeholder products	n/a	n/a	n/a	31	22
Individual protection	1,055	1,117	977	1,046	1,033
Group protection	284	273	385	387	314
Individual pension	2,233	1,859	1,864	2,127	3,023
Group pension	804	862	802	766	753
Offshore business	n/a	n/a	n/a	26	22
TOTAL REGULAR	5,047	4,633	4,599	5,004	5,858
New single premiums					
Investments and savings	22,894	16,372	20,150	23,957	30,326
Collective investment schemes	7,314	7,643	8,380	10,866	17,670
Other stakeholder products	n/a	n/a	n/a	164	201
Individual protection	1,001	1,264	1,606	1,698	1,634
Individual pension	11,766	10,551	10,621	12,164	18,757
Pension annuities					
and income drawdown	9,577	9,208	9,022	9,375	12,207
Group pension	7,609	5,760	4,385	6,544	8,428
Offshore business	n/a	n/a	n/a	4,804	7,150
TOTAL SINGLE	60,161	50,800	54,161	69,572	96,374

ECONOMIC STATISTICS

All data is for the UK unless otherwise stated.

ABBREVIATIONS
AAS   *Annual Abstract of Statistics*
ST   *Social Trends*

THE BUDGET (2007)

GOVERNMENT RECEIPTS

	Outturn 2005–6	Estimate 2006–7	£ billion Projection 2007–8
HM Revenue and Customs (HMRC)			
Income tax (gross of tax credits)	135.0	146.9	156.9
Income tax credits	−4.5	−4.7	−4.4
National insurance contributions (NIC)	85.5	88.0	95.1
Value added tax	72.9	77.3	80.0
Corporation tax[1]	42.4	44.9	50.0
Corporation tax credits[2]	−0.5	−0.5	−0.5
Petroleum revenue tax	2.0	2.2	1.6
Fuel duties	23.4	23.6	25.1
Capital gains tax	3.0	3.9	4.6
Inheritance tax	3.3	3.6	4.0
Stamp duties	10.9	13.4	14.3
Tobacco duties	8.0	8.1	8.1
Spirits duties	2.3	2.2	2.3
Wine duties	2.3	2.4	2.5
Beer and cider duties	3.2	3.3	3.4
Betting and gaming duties	1.4	1.4	1.4
Air passenger duty	0.9	1.0	2.1
Insurance premium tax	2.3	2.3	2.4
Landfill tax	0.7	0.8	0.9
Climate change levy	0.7	0.7	0.7
Aggregates levy	0.3	0.3	0.3
Customs duties and levies	2.3	2.3	2.4
TOTAL HMRC	398.0	423.6	453.4
Vehicle excise duties	5.0	5.1	5.6
Business rates	19.9	21.3	22.1
Council tax[3]	21.4	22.4	23.5
Other taxes and royalties[4]	12.7	13.4	14.5
NET TAXES AND NIC[5]	456.8	485.7	519.2
Accruals adjustments on taxes	1.4	3.4	2.4
Less own resources contribution to European Commission (EC) budget	−4.3	−4.7	−4.1
Less private company corporation tax payments	−0.2	−0.2	−0.2
Tax credits adjustment[6]	0.6	0.5	0.6
Interest and dividends	6.7	6.0	7.1
Other receipts[7]	24.7	26.5	28.0
CURRENT RECEIPTS	485.7	517.2	553.0
North Sea revenues[8]	9.7	9.1	8.1

[1] National accounts measure: gross of enhanced and payable tax credits
[2] Includes enhanced company tax credits
[3] Council tax figures are projections based on stylised assumptions and are not government forecasts as increases are determined annually by local authorities
[4] Includes VAT refunds and money paid into the National Lottery Distribution Fund
[5] Includes VAT and 'traditional own resources' contributions to EC budget
[6] Tax credits which are scored as negative tax in the calculation of net taxes and NIC but expenditure in the national accounts
[7] Includes gross operating surplus and rent; net of oil royalties and business rate payments by local authorities
[8] Consists of North Sea corporation tax, petroleum revenue tax and royalties
Source: HM Treasury – *Budget 2007* (Crown copyright)

GOVERNMENT EXPENDITURE

The Economic and Fiscal Strategy Report in June 1998 introduced changes to the public expenditure control regime. Three-year departmental expenditure limits (DELs) now apply to most government departments. Spending which cannot easily be subject to three-year planning is reviewed annually in the budget as annually managed expenditure (AME). Current and capital expenditure are treated separately.

DEPARTMENTAL EXPENDITURE LIMITS (DEL)

RESOURCE AND CAPITAL BUDGETS	Outturn 2005–6	Estimate 2006–7	£ billion Projection 2007–8
Resource Budget			
Education and Skills[1]	25.1	53.6	57.4
Health	76.4	81.1	89.7
of which NHS	74.2	79.2	87.6
Transport	6.1	6.9	6.7
Department for Communities and Local Government	3.5	3.7	4.3
Local Government	46.2	22.5	22.8
Home Office	12.7	13.2	13.5
Department for Constitutional Affairs*	3.6	3.7	4.0
Law Officers' Departments	0.7	0.7	0.7
Defence	33.4	33.7	32.8
Foreign and Commonwealth Office	1.9	2.0	1.9
International Development	4.1	4.3	4.6
Trade and Industry*	5.2	5.8	6.2
Environment, Food and Rural Affairs	2.8	3.3	3.0
Culture, Media and Sport	1.4	1.6	1.6
Work and Pensions	7.8	7.7	7.7
Scotland[2]	20.8	22.3	23.5
Wales[2]	11.0	11.9	12.4
Northern Ireland Executive[2]	6.7	7.2	7.6
Northern Ireland Office	1.2	1.3	1.1

Chancellor's departments	4.9	5.2	5.0
Cabinet Office	2.2	2.4	2.4
Invest to Save Budget	0.0	0.0	0.0
Reserve	0.0	0.0	0.6
Unallocated special reserve[3]	0.0	0.0	0.4
Allowance for shortfall	0.0	−0.7	0.0
TOTAL RESOURCE BUDGET DEL	277.8	293.4	310.0
Capital Budget			
Education and Skills[1]	5.7	5.2	7.0
Health	2.2	3.8	4.3
of which NHS	2.2	3.7	4.2
Transport	5.0	6.5	6.6
Department for Communities and Local Government	5.5	5.4	5.9
Local Government	0.3	0.2	0.1
Home Office	1.0	1.3	1.3
Departments for Constitutional Affairs[1]	0.1	0.2	0.1
Law Officers' Departments	0.0	0.0	0.0
Defence	6.4	7.1	7.6
Foreign and Commonwealth Office	0.1	0.1	0.1
International Development	0.4	0.7	0.6
Trade and Industry[1]	1.2	1.2	1.2
Environment, Food and Rural Affairs	0.8	0.9	0.9
Culture, Media and Sport	0.1	0.2	0.4
Work and Pensions	0.4	0.2	0.1
Scotland[2]	2.4	3.1	3.1
Wales[2]	1.2	1.4	1.6
Northern Ireland Executive[2]	0.8	0.9	1.0
Northern Ireland Office	0.1	0.1	0.1
Chancellor's departments	0.4	0.3	0.3
Cabinet Office	0.3	0.4	0.3
Invest to Save Budget	0.0	0.0	0.0
Reserve	0.0	0.0	1.5
Allowance for shortfall	0.0	−0.4	0.0
TOTAL CAPITAL BUDGET DEL	34.6	38.8	44.3
Less depreciation	(9.5)	(10.5)	(10.6)
TOTAL DEL	302.9	321.7	343.7

[1] Due to changes announced as part of the government reshuffle on 28 June 2007, estimate and projection figures may no longer be accurate for the new departments

[2] For Scotland, Wales and Northern Ireland, the split between current and capital budgets is indicative and reflects the consequentials of the application of the Barnett formula to planned changes in UK departments' spending

[3] This represents provision for the costs of military operations in Iraq and Afghanistan, as well as the UK's other international obligations

Source: HM Treasury – *Budget 2007* (Crown copyright)

ANNUALLY MANAGED EXPENDITURE (AME)			£ billion
	Outturn	Estimate	Projection
	2005–6	2006–7	2007–8
Social security benefits[1]	127.4	132.0	139.2
Tax credits[1]	15.5	16.2	16.5
Net public service pensions[2]	0.2	1.1	1.7
National Lottery	1.8	1.7	1.6
BBC domestic services	3.2	3.3	3.3
Other departmental expenditure	3.3	3.6	3.1
Net expenditure transfers to EU institutions[3]	4.4	4.7	5.0
Locally financed expenditure[4]	25.8	25.9	27.8
Central government gross debt interest	25.8	27.4	29.1
Public corporations' own-financed capital expenditure	5.4	4.3	4.6
AME margin	0.0	0.0	1.0
Accounting adjustments[5]	7.6	10.4	10.0
AME	220.5	230.5	242.9

[1] Includes Income Support and Jobseekers' Allowance child allowances, which are paid as part of the Child Tax Credit
[2] Reported on a national accounts basis
[3] AME spending component only
[4] This expenditure is mainly financed by council tax revenues
[5] Excludes depreciation

Source: HM Treasury – *Budget 2007* (Crown copyright)

PUBLIC SECTOR FINANCES

PUBLIC SECTOR CAPITAL EXPENDITURE			£ billion
	Outturn	Estimate	Projection
	2005–6	2006–7	2007–8
Capital Budget DEL	34.6	38.8	44.3
Locally financed expenditure	1.2	2.0	1.9
National Lottery	1.0	1.0	0.8
Public corporations' own-financed capital expenditure	5.4	4.3	4.6
Other capital spending in AME	0.8	0.3	0.4
AME margin	0.0	0.0	0.1
Accounting adjustments	−3.8	−3.2	−4.2
PUBLIC SECTOR GROSS INVESTMENT[1]	39.2	43.2	48.0
Less depreciation	(16.5)	(17.7)	(18.7)
PUBLIC SECTOR NET INVESTMENT	22.7	25.5	29.4
Proceeds from the sale of fixed assets[2]	6.1	6.2	6.2

[1] This and previous lines are all net of sales of fixed assets
[2] Projections of total receipts from the sale of fixed assets by public sector

Source: HM Treasury – *Budget 2007* (Crown copyright)

SIZE OF THE ECONOMY

GNI	US$2,272.7bn (2005)
GNI, per capita	US$37,740 (2005)
GDP	US$2,198.8bn (2005)
GDP, annual growth	1.8 per cent (2004–5)

Source: The World Bank – *World Development Indicators 2007*

EMPLOYMENT

DISTRIBUTION OF THE WORKFORCE

Claimant count	944,100
Workforce jobs	31,409,000
HM forces	204,000
Self-employment jobs	4,073,000
Employees jobs	27,067,000
Government-supported trainees	66,000

Source: ONS – *AAS 2007* (Crown copyright)

EMPLOYMENT

	Thousands	
Age	*Male*	*Female*
16–17	263	300
18–24	1,867	1,699
25–34	3,408	2,853
35–49	5,819	5,121
50–64(m)/59(f)	3,830	2,616
65+(m)/60+(f)	392	763
All aged 16+	15,578	13,352

m = male, f = female

Source: ONS – *AAS 2007* (Crown copyright)

UNEMPLOYMENT

	Thousands	
Age	*Male*	*Female*
16–17	104	74
18–24	313	207
25–34	182	149
35–49	228	187
50–64(m)/59(f)	137	74
65+(m)/60+(f)	11	16
All aged 16+	975	708

Source: ONS – *AAS 2007* (Crown copyright)

DURATION OF UNEMPLOYMENT

	Thousands
All unemployed	1,683
Duration of unemployment	
Less than 6 months	1,024
6 months–1 year	303
1 year +	356
1 year + as percentage of total	21.2

Source: ONS – *AAS 2007* (Crown copyright)

AVERAGE EARNINGS AND HOURS OF FULL-TIME EMPLOYEES

	All	*Male*	*Female*
Average weekly earnings (£)	537.4	591.6	453.6
Average hours	37.5	40.7	37.6
Average hourly earnings (£)			
Including overtime	13.62	14.54	12.08
Excluding overtime	13.67	14.62	12.11

Source: ONS – *AAS 2007* (Crown copyright)

LABOUR DISPUTES BY DURATION

Under 5 days	102
5–10 days	8
10–20 days	3
20–30 days	–
30–50 days	3
50+ days	–

Source: ONS – *AAS 2007* (Crown copyright)

WORKING DAYS LOST THROUGH LABOUR DISPUTES BY INDUSTRY

Mining, quarrying, electricity, gas and water	6,000
Manufacturing	16,000
Construction	2,000
Transport, storage and communications	33,000
Public administration and defence	23,000
Education	43,000
Health and social work	–
Other community, social and personal services	6,000
All other industries and services	29,000

Source: ONS – *AAS 2007* (Crown copyright)

TRADE UNIONS

Year	*No. of unions*	*Total membership*
1997	252	7,801,000
1998	238	7,851,904
1999	237	7,897,519
2000	226	7,779,393
2001	216	7,750,990
2002	210	7,735,983
2003	206	7,559,062
2004	193	7,473,000

Source: ONS – *AAS 2007* (Crown copyright)

TRADE

TRADE IN GOODS

			£ million
	Exports	*Imports*	*Balance*
1996	167,196	180,918	–13,722
1997	171,923	184,265	–12,342
1998	164,056	185,869	–21,813
1999	166,166	195,217	–29,051
2000	187,936	220,912	–32,976
2001	189,093	230,305	–41,212
2002	186,524	234,229	–47,705
2003	188,320	236,927	–48,607
2004	190,877	251,770	–60,893
2005	211,616	280,399	–68,783
2006	244,542	328,233	–83,691

Source: ONS – *AAS 2007* (Crown copyright)

BALANCE OF PAYMENTS

	£ million
CURRENT ACCOUNT	
Trade in goods and services	
Trade in goods	–83,691
Trade in services	29,605
Total trade in goods and services	–54,086
Income	
Compensation of employees	58
Investment income	22,743
Total income	22,801
Current transfers	
Central government	–9,968
Other sectors	–2,136
Total current transfers	–12,104
TOTAL (CURRENT BALANCE)	–43,389

Source: ONS – *AAS 2007* (Crown copyright)

HOUSEHOLD INCOME AND EXPENDITURE

AVERAGE ANNUAL HOUSEHOLD INCOME

Number of households in the UK	24,431,000
Original income (before state benefits)	£27,569
Gross income (after state benefits)	£31,884
Disposable income	£25,360
Post-tax income	£20,627

Source: ONS – *AAS 2007* (Crown copyright)

AVERAGE WEEKLY HOUSEHOLD INCOME BY SOURCE

		Percentage of total
Wages and salaries	£414.80	67
Self-employment	£50.80	8
Investments	£19.50	3
Annuities and pensions (other than social security benefits)	£45.50	7
Social security benefits	£78.00	13
Other sources	£7.40	1
Total	£616.90	100

Source: ONS – *AAS 2007* (Crown copyright)

PERCEPTION OF ADEQUACY OF INCOME (GREAT BRITAIN)

	Percentages		
	1986	1994	2004
Living comfortably	24	29	40
Coping	50	49	46
Finding it difficult to manage	18	15	11
Finding it very difficult to manage	8	6	3

Source: ONS – *ST 2006* (Crown copyright)

NUMBER OF TAXPAYERS BY ANNUAL INCOME[1]

Number of taxpayers (thousands)

£5,035[2]–£7,499	2,700
£7,500–£9,999	3,370
£10,000–£14,999	5,970
£15,000–£19,999	4,890
£20,000–£29,999	6,440
£30,000–£49,999	4,450
£50,000–£99,999	1,460
£100,000–£199,999	350
£200,000–£499,999	100
£500,000–£999,999	18
£1,000,000+	6
All incomes	29,700

[1] Includes investment income
[2] Basic personal tax-free allowance (*see* Taxation)
Source: ONS – *ST 2007* (Crown copyright)

HOUSEHOLD OWNERSHIP OF SELECTED DURABLE GOODS

		Percentages
	2000–1	2005–6
Car	72	74
One	44	46
Two	22	23
Three+	6	5
Central heating, full or partial	91	94
Washing machine	92	95
Fridge/freezer or deep freezer	94	97
Dishwasher	25	35
Telephone	93	92
Mobile phone	47	79
Home computer	44	65
Video recorder	87	86
Digital television service[1]	40	65
Internet connection	32	55

[1] Includes digital, satelite and cable receivers
Source: ONS – *AAS 2007* (Crown copyright)

HOUSEHOLD EXPENDITURE £ per week

	Couple		Single				
	With children	No children	With children	No children	Retired couple	Retired single	All households
Food and non-alcoholic drink	62.80	46.70	38.60	22.50	46.00	23.70	45.30
Alcohol and tobacco	13.00	13.90	8.70	7.60	9.00	3.90	10.80
Clothing and footwear	33.60	24.50	23.30	11.50	14.00	6.10	22.70
Housing, fuel and power[1]	48.50	46.90	44.70	41.30	31.80	28.80	44.20
Household goods and services	39.00	38.80	25.50	15.00	31.40	14.50	30.00
Health	5.60	7.00	2.10	5.30	5.90	2.80	5.50
Transport	85.60	77.80	30.80	38.70	45.20	12.40	61.70
Communication	15.10	12.70	11.50	8.90	7.00	5.10	11.90
Recreation and culture	79.00	68.10	39.60	34.90	52.90	21.10	57.50
Education	14.30	3.90	6.10	2.40	–	–	6.60
Restaurants and hotels[2]	47.20	45.50	22.80	23.20	24.40	9.50	36.70
Miscellaneous goods and services	50.40	38.70	24.10	18.50	26.90	17.50	34.60
Other expenditure items	120.40	102.80	42.60	58.30	37.70	21.20	75.80
All household expenditure (=100%)	614.20	527.30	320.40	288.20	333.50	166.60	443.40

[1] Excludes mortgage payments, water charges and council tax (domestic rates in Northern Ireland) – these are included in *Other expenditure items*
[2] Includes purchases of alcoholic drink in restaurants and hotels
Source: ONS – *ST 2007* (Crown copyright)

SAVINGS AND WEALTH

	Men by age				Women by age				Percentages All individuals aged 16+
	16–24	25–64	65+	All 16+	16–24	25–64	65+	All 16+	
Current account	81.0	89.9	86.1	88.2	84.1	89.3	80.8	86.9	87.5
ISAs	10.2	26.8	35.1	26.3	13.5	29.0	30.5	27.6	26.9
Basic bank account	2.9	3.8	5.2	3.9	4.2	4.9	6.1	5.1	4.5
TESSA	0.1	4.1	9.2	4.5	–	4.2	7.7	4.5	4.5
Post Office account	2.3	2.5	3.3	2.6	2.8	3.3	4.6	3.5	3.1
Other bank/building society account	23.4	44.9	49.4	43.0	27.2	47.3	48.8	45.4	44.2
Stocks and shares	3.2	18.7	23.0	17.5	2.2	14.7	17.2	13.9	15.6
PEPs	0.3	5.4	10.0	5.6	0.1	4.7	7.0	4.7	5.2
Unit trusts	0.4	3.8	6.5	3.9	0.5	2.9	4.5	3.0	3.4
Endowment policy (not linked)	0.1	3.1	0.3	2.2	–	2.4	0.2	1.7	1.9
Gilts	–	0.3	1.3	0.4	–	0.3	1.4	0.5	0.5
Premium bonds	4.7	16.1	24.4	16.2	4.5	15.6	22.1	15.8	16.0
National Savings bonds	0.8	1.3	6.5	2.2	0.5	1.6	7.5	2.7	2.5
Guaranteed equity bonds	–	0.2	0.6	0.2	–	0.3	0.6	0.3	0.3
Company share scheme	0.6	4.7	0.4	3.4	0.6	2.7	0.1	1.9	2.6
Credit unions	0.3	0.7	0.1	0.5	0.4	0.8	0.1	0.6	0.5
Save as you earn	0.2	0.6	–	0.4	0.2	0.6	0.1	0.4	0.4
Any form of wealth	86.5	94.2	93.7	93.1	90.1	94.6	92.4	93.6	93.4
No form of wealth	13.5	5.9	6.3	6.9	9.9	5.4	7.7	6.4	6.6

Source: ONS – *ST 2007* (Crown copyright)

AVERAGE DWELLING PRICES BY REGION

	2003	2005
UK	£155,485	£183,966
England	£165,834	£193,097
North East	£94,950	£131,814
North West	£108,956	£146,111
Yorkshire and the Humber	£107,325	£143,281
East Midlands	£133,215	£159,249
West Midlands	£132,898	£163,945
East	£181,494	£204,215
London	£236,476	£266,328
South East	£213,115	£233,069
South West	£170,560	£199,230
Wales	£104,140	£145,825
Scotland	£92,006	£124,390
Northern Ireland	£102,348	£129,580

Source: ONS – *ST 2006 and 2007* (Crown copyright)

COST OF LIVING AND INFLATION RATES

The first cost of living index to be calculated took July 1914 as 100 and was based on the pattern of expenditure of working-class families in 1914. The cost of living index was superseded in 1947 by the general index of retail prices (RPI), although the older term is still popularly applied.

The Harmonised Index of Consumer Prices (HICP) was introduced in 1997 to enable comparisons within the European Union using an agreed methodology. In 2003 the National Statistician renamed the HICP as the Consumer Prices Index (CPI) to reflect its role as the main target measure of inflation for macroeconomic purposes. The RPI and indices based on it will continue to be published alongside the CPI. Pensions, benefits and index-linked gilts continue to be calculated with reference to RPI or its derivatives.

CPI AND RPI

The RPI and CPI measure the changes month by month in the average level of prices of goods and services

purchased by households in the UK. The indices are compiled using a selection of around 650 goods and services, and the prices charged for these items are collected at regular intervals at about 150 locations throughout the country. The Office for National Statistics (ONS) reviews the components of the indices once every year to reflect changes in consumer preferences and the establishment of new products. The table below shows changes made by the ONS to the CPI 'shopping basket' in 2007.

CPI excludes a number of items that are included in RPI, mainly related to housing such as council tax and a range of owner-occupier housing costs, such as mortgage payments. The CPI covers all private households, whereas RPI excludes the top 4 per cent by income and pensioner households who derive at least three-quarters of their income from state benefits. The two indices use different methodologies to combine the prices of goods and services, which means that since 1996 the CPI inflation measure is on average less than the RPI inflation measure.

'SHOPPING BASKET' OF GOODS AND SERVICES

Changes to the CPI* 2007 basket of goods and services include:

Goods and Services Group	Removed items	New items
Food and non-alcoholic beverages	vegetable oil; brie; Brussels sprouts; pre-packed fresh vegetables	olive oil; pro-biotic drink; courgettes; broccoli
Clothing and footwear	child's wellington boots; men's leather boots	–
Housing and household services	–	shower head
Furniture and household goods	–	portable or free-standing electric fan
Health	UV protection sunglasses (non-designer frames); designer spectacle frames	–
Transport	–	satellite navigation system
Communication	–	mobile downloads (eg ringtones)
Recreation and culture	portable colour television (CRT); VHS video recorder; portable CD radio cassette; car CD/radio auto-changer; widescreen (CRT) television; blank VHS cassette; pre-recorded video; 35mm compact camera; mail order develop and print photography services; digital television installation fee; decorative outdoor plant pot	flat panel television (14–25″); digital (DAB) radio; pre-recorded DVD (non-film) from chart; recordable DVD (price per DVD from pack of 5–25); digital photography processing (print of up to 50 photographs)
Restaurants and hotels (catering)	–	onboard catering (rail, sea and air); vending machine canned/bottled fizzy drink
Miscellaneous goods and services	gemstone cluster ring	diamond solitaire ring; credit card charges; mortgage fees; toothbrush

* RPI goods and services are grouped together under different classifications

INFLATION RATE

The twelve-monthly percentage change in the 'all items' index of the RPI or CPI is referred to as the rate of inflation. As the most familiar measure of inflation, RPI is often referred to as the 'headline rate of inflation'. CPI is the main measure of inflation for macroeconomic purposes and forms the basis for the government's inflation target, which is currently 2 per cent. The percentage change in prices between any two months/years can be obtained using the following formula:

$$\frac{\text{Later date RPI/CPI} - \text{Earlier date RPI/CPI}}{\text{Earlier date RPI/CPI}} \times 100$$

eg to find the CPI rate of inflation for 2006, using the annual averages for 2005 and 2006:

$$\frac{102.3 - 100.0}{100.0} \times 100 = 2.3$$

From 14 February 2006 the reference year for CPI was re-based to 2005=100 to improve price comparison clarity across the EU. None of the underlying data, from which the re-referenced series was calculated, was revised. Historical rates of change (such as annual inflation figures), calculated from the re-based rounded index levels, were revised due to the effect of rounding. The CPI rate of inflation figure given in the table below may differ by plus or minus 0.1 percentage points from the figure calculated by the above equation. The change of reference period and revision due to rounding does not apply to the RPI which remains unchanged.

The RPI and CPI figures are published by the Office for National Statistics on either the second or third Tuesday of each month in an Indices bulletin and electronically on the National Statistics website (W www.statistics.gov.uk). They are also available as a recorded telephone message (T 020-7533 5866).

PURCHASING POWER OF THE POUND

Changes in the internal purchasing power of the pound may be defined as the 'inverse' of changes in the level of prices: when prices go up, the amount which can be purchased with a given sum of money goes down. To find the purchasing power of the pound in one month or year, given that it was 100p in a previous month or year, the calculation would be:

$$100p \times \frac{\text{Earlier month/year RPI}}{\text{Later month/year RPI}}$$

Thus, if the purchasing power of the pound is taken to be 100p in 1975, the comparable purchasing power in 2000 would be:

$$100p \times \frac{34.2}{170.3} = 20.1p$$

For longer term comparisons, it has been the practice to use an index which has been constructed by linking together the RPI for the period 1962 to date; an index derived from the consumers expenditure deflator for the period from 1938 to 1962; and the pre-war 'cost of living' index for the period 1914 to 1938. This long-term index enables the internal purchasing power of the pound to be calculated for any year from 1914 onwards. It should be noted that these figures can only be approximate.

	Annual average RPI (1987 = 100)	Purchasing power of £ (1998 = 1.00)	Annual average CPI (2005 = 100)*	Rate of inflation (RPI/CPI)
1914	2.8	58.18		
1915	3.5	46.54		
1920	7.0	23.27		
1925	5.0	32.58		
1930	4.5	36.20		
1935	4.0	40.72		
1938	4.4	37.02		
There are no official figures for 1939–45				
1946	7.4	22.01		
1950	9.0	18.10		
1955	11.2	14.54		
1960	12.6	12.93		
1965	14.8	11.00		
1970	18.5	8.80		
1975	34.2	4.76		
1980	66.8	2.44	18.0	
1985	94.6	1.72	6.1	
1990	126.1	1.29	71.5	9.5/7.0
1995	149.1	1.09	86.0	3.5/2.6
1998	162.9	1.0	91.1	3.4/1.6
2000	170.3	0.96	93.1	3.0/0.8
2005	192.0	0.85	100	2.8/2.1
2006	198.1	0.82	102.3	3.2/2.3

* In accordance with an EU Commission regulation all published CPI figures were re-based to 2005 = 100 with effect from 14 February 2006, replacing the 1996 = 100 series

TAXATION

The government raises money to pay for public services such as education, health and the social security system through tax. Each year the Chancellor of the Exchequer's Budget sets out how much it will cost to provide these services and how much tax is therefore needed to pay for them. HM Revenue and Customs (HMRC) is the government department that collects it. There are several different types of tax. The varieties that individuals may have to pay include income tax payable on earnings, pensions, state benefits, savings and investments; capital gains tax (CGT) payable on the disposal of certain assets; inheritance tax (IHT) payable on estates upon death and certain lifetime gifts; stamp duty payable when purchasing property and shares; and value added tax (VAT) payable on goods and services, plus certain other duties such as fuel duty on petrol and excise duty on alcohol and tobacco. Government funds are also raised from companies and small businesses through corporation tax.

HELP AND INFORMATION ON TAXATION

For detailed information on any aspect of taxation individuals may contact their local tax office or enquiry centre. The HMRC website at www.hmrc.gov.uk provides a wide range of information online. All HMRC forms, leaflets and guides are listed on, and can be downloaded from, the website or ordered by telephone. A list of all HMRC telephone helplines can also be found on the website. Those most relevant to topics covered in this section on taxation have been included at pertinent points throughout. Information on taxation is also available in the Money, Tax and Benefits section of the government's public information website www.direct.gov.uk.

INCOME TAX

Income tax is a tax paid on different sorts of income. Not all types of income are taxable, however, and individuals are only taxed on their 'taxable income' above a certain level. Even then, there are other reliefs and allowances that can reduce or, in some cases, cancel out an individual's income tax bill.

An individual's taxable income is assessed each tax year, starting on 6 April one year and ending on 5 April the following year. The following information relates specifically to the year of assessment 2007–8 ending on 5 April 2008 and has only limited application to earlier years. Changes due to come into operation at a later date are briefly mentioned where information is available. Types of income that are taxable include:

- earnings from employment or self-employment
- most pensions income including state, company and personal pensions
- interest on most savings
- income (dividends) from shares and income from unit trusts
- income from property
- income received from a trust
- certain state benefits
- an individual's share of any joint income

There are certain sorts of income on which individuals never pay tax. These are ignored altogether when working out how much income tax an individual may need to pay. Types of income that are not taxable include

- certain state benefits and tax credits such as working tax credit and child tax credit, attendance allowance and disability living allowance, income support and war widow(er)'s pension
- cold weather payments
- income from tax-free National Savings and Investments, such as savings certificates
- interest and terminal bonuses under Save As You Earn schemes
- interest, dividends and other income from various tax-free investments, notably individual savings accounts (ISAs)
- premium bond, national lottery and gambling prizes

PERSONAL ALLOWANCE

Every individual resident in the UK for tax purposes has a personal allowance. This is an amount of taxable income an individual is allowed to earn or receive each year tax-free. This tax year (2007–8) the basic personal allowance or tax-free amount is £5,225. Individuals may be entitled to a higher personal allowance if they are 65 or over. Income tax is only due on an individual's taxable income that is above his or her tax-free allowance. Husbands and wives are taxed separately, with each entitled to his or her personal allowance. Each spouse may obtain other allowances and reliefs where the required conditions are satisfied.

The amount of personal allowance depends on an individual's age on 5 April 2007 and, if he or she is 65 or over, the total income received from all taxable sources. There are three age-related levels of personal allowance – see table below. If an individual turns 65 or 75 during the year to 5 April 2007, he or she is entitled to the allowance for that age group.

If an individual's income is over the income limit, then the age-related allowance reduces by half the amount (£1 for every £2) he or she has over that limit, until the basic rate allowance is reached. For a 66-year-old with an income of £21,300 (£400 over the limit), for example, the age-related allowance would reduce by £200 to £20,700.

Individuals always receive the basic allowance whatever the level of their income. The age-related allowances mean that in 2007–8 no one aged 65 or over need pay tax on income of up to £145 a week. Around half of all pensioners pay no tax on their income according to HMRC. Further information is available in leaflet *IR121: Approaching Retirement – A Guide to Tax and National Insurance Contributions*.

LEVELS OF PERSONAL ALLOWANCE FOR 2007–8

	Personal allowance	Income limit
Basic rate	£5,225	none
Age 65–74	£7,550	£20,900
Age 75 and over	£7,690	£20,900

BLIND PERSON'S ALLOWANCE

If an individual is registered blind or is unable to perform any work for which eyesight is essential, he or she can claim blind person's allowance, an extra amount of tax-free income added to the personal allowance. In 2007–8 the blind person's allowance is £1,730. It is the same for everyone who can claim it, whatever his or her age or level of income. If an individual is married or in a civil partnership and cannot use all of his or her blind person's allowance because of insufficient income, the unused part of the allowance can be passed to the spouse or civil partner.

Other deductible allowances and reliefs that have the effect of reducing an income tax bill are available to tax payers in certain circumstances and will be explained in more detail later in this section.

CALCULATING INCOME TAX DUE

Individuals' liability to pay income tax is determined by establishing their level of taxable income for the year. For married couples and civil partners income must be allocated between the couple by reference to the individual who is beneficially entitled to that income. Where income arises from jointly held assets, it is normally apportioned equally between the partners. If, however, the beneficial interests in jointly held assets are not equal, in most cases couples can make a special declaration to have income apportioned by reference to the actual interests in that income.

To work out an individual's liability for tax, his or her taxable income must be allocated between three different types: earned income (excluding income from savings and dividends); income from savings; and company dividends from shares and other equity-based investments.

After the tax-free allowance plus any deductible allowances and reliefs have been taken into account, the amount of tax an individual pays is calculated using different tax rates and a series of tax bands. The tax band applies to an individual's income after tax allowances and any reliefs have been taken into account. Individuals are not taxed on all of their income.

INCOME TAX RATES (PER CENT) FOR 2007–8

Income tax band	Income tax rate on earned income	Income tax rate on savings	Income tax rate on dividends
Starting rate: £1–2,230	10	10	10
Starting rate: £2,231–34,600	22	20	10
Higher rate: £34,601 and above	40	40	32.5

The first calculation is applied to earned income which includes income from employment or self-employment, most pension income and rental income plus the value of a wide range of employee fringe benefits such as company cars, living accommodation and private medical insurance (for more information on fringe benefits, see later section on payment of income tax). In working out the amount of an individual's net taxable earnings, all expenses incurred 'wholly, exclusively and necessarily' in the performance of his or her work duties, together with the cost of business travel, may be deducted. Fees and subscriptions to certain professional bodies may also be deducted. Redundancy payments and other sums paid on the termination of an employment are assessable to income tax, but the first £30,000 is normally tax-free

provided the payment is not linked with the recipient's retirement or performance.

The first £2,230 of taxable income remaining is taxed at the starting rate of 10 per cent. The next £32,370 is taxed at the basic rate of 22 per cent. Any excess over £34,600 (£2,230 plus £32,370) is taxed at the higher rate of 40 per cent.

Savings and dividend income is added to an individual's other taxable income and taxed last. This means that tax on these sorts of income is based on an individual's highest income tax band.

The chancellor announced in the 2007 Budget that from April 2008 the basic rate of income tax will go down from 22 per cent to 20 per cent and the starting rate band of 10 per cent will be removed as part of the government's ongoing programme of reform to the UK tax and benefit system. This will create a simpler structure of two rates: a 20 pence (in the pound) basic rate and a 40 pence (in the pound) higher rate.

SAVINGS INCOME

The second calculation is applied to any income from savings received by an individual. The appropriate rate at which it must be taxed is determined by adding income from savings to an individual's other taxable income, excluding dividends. It is then taxed as follows:

- savings income that falls within the £2,230 starting rate income tax band is taxed at 10 per cent. In most cases it is likely to fall above this limit unless the individual has little or no other income
- savings income that falls above the £2,230 band but within the £34,600 basic rate band is taxable at 20 per cent
- savings income that falls above the £34,600 band is taxable at 40 per cent
- if it falls on both sides of a tax band, the relevant amounts are taxed at the rates for each tax band

Most savings income, such as interest paid on bank and building society accounts, already has tax at a rate of 20 per cent deducted from it 'at source' – that is, before it is paid out to individuals. This is confirmed by the entry 'net interest' on bank and building society statements.

Basic rate (22 per cent) taxpayers need to take no further action because they owe no extra tax on their savings income even though tax was only deducted at 20 per cent.

Higher rate taxpayers whose income is sufficient to pay 40 per cent tax on their savings income must let their tax office know what savings income they have received so that the extra tax they owe can be collected.

Non-taxpayers – that is, individuals, including most children, whose taxable income is less than their tax allowances – can register to have their savings interest paid 'gross' without any tax being deducted from it at source. To do this, they must complete Form R85, available at all banks and building societies. Parents or guardians need to fill in this form on behalf of those under 16.

Non-taxpayers who have already had tax deducted from their savings interest can claim it back from HMRC by filling in Form R40. Similarly, people whose level of taxable income is low enough for them to pay income tax only at the 10 per cent starting rate can use Form R40 to claim back the difference on savings interest already taxed at 20 per cent. For help or information about registering to get interest paid tax-free or to claim tax back on savings interest, individuals may call a dedicated helpline on 0845-980 0645. Further information is available in the leaflet *IR111: Bank and building society interest – Are you paying tax when you don't need to?*

DIVIDEND INCOME

The third and final income tax calculation is on UK dividends, which means income from shares in UK companies and other share-based investments including unit trusts and open-ended investment companies (OEICs).

Tax on dividends differs from tax on savings income. There are two different rates which depend on whether the individual's overall taxable income (after allowances) falls within or above the basic rate income tax limit, which is £34,600 for the 2007–8 tax year. All dividend income that falls within this limit is taxable at 10 per cent while any that falls above is taxable at 32.5 per cent.

When dividends are paid, a voucher is sent that shows the dividend paid and the amount of associated 'tax credit'. Companies pay dividends out of profits on which they have already paid or are due to pay tax. The tax credit takes account of this and is available to the shareholder to offset against any income tax that may be due on their dividend income. The dividend paid represents 90 per cent of their dividend income. The remaining 10 per cent is made up of the tax credit. In other words the tax credit represents 10 per cent of the dividend income.

Individuals who pay tax at or below the basic rate have no tax to pay on their dividend income because the tax liability is 10 per cent – the same amount as the tax credit. Higher rate taxpayers pay a total of 32.5 per cent tax on dividend income that falls above the £34,600 basic rate income tax limit, but because the first 10 per cent of the tax due on their dividend income is already covered by the tax credit, in practice they owe only 22.5 per cent.

Non-taxpayers cannot claim the 10 per cent tax credit. This is because income tax has not been deducted from the dividends paid to them. The view is that they have simply been given a 10 per cent credit against any income tax due.

If there is significant change to an individual's savings or other income, whatever his or her current tax bracket, it is the individual's responsibility to contact the relevant tax office immediately, even if he or she does not normally complete a tax return. This enables the tax office to work out whether extra or less tax should be paid.

INDIVIDUAL SAVINGS ACCOUNTS (ISAs)

There is a small selection of savings and investment products that are tax-free, meaning that there is no tax to pay on any income they generate in the form of interest or dividends nor on any increase in the value of the capital invested. Their tax-efficient status has been granted by the government in order to give people an incentive to save more. For this reason there are usually limits and restrictions on the amount of money that an individual may invest in such savings and investments. Individual savings accounts (ISAs) are the best known among tax-efficient savings and investments. They were introduced in 1999 to replace other similar schemes called PEPs and TESSAs. Individuals can use an ISA to save cash, or invest in stocks and shares. They may save up to £7,000 each tax year in an ISA and receive all profits free of tax provided that they are UK residents and are over 18 (over 16 for cash ISAs). An ISA must be in an individual's name and cannot be held jointly with another person.

ISAs can include one or more components:
- cash (bank and building society savings accounts, National Savings and Investments)
- stocks and shares (unit trusts, shares, bonds, investment-type life insurance and so on)

There are strict rules regarding the maximum amount allowed for each component and the overall amount individuals can invest in any one tax year.

At present, ISAs come in two types. Maxi ISAs may contain cash and stocks and shares, and all the investments in a maxi ISA must be with the same management company. Mini ISAs can contain either stocks and shares or cash. Each tax year individuals put money into either one maxi ISA or two mini ISAs. They may not have both. They may save up to £7,000 in a maxi ISA invested only in stocks and shares or in a maxi ISA with a maximum of £3,000 in cash and the remainder in stocks and shares. Alternatively, individuals can invest up to £3,000 in one cash mini ISA and up to £4,000 in one stocks and shares mini ISA. They cannot invest in more than one mini cash ISA, or more than one mini stocks and shares ISA in the same tax year.

The government has announced that new rules to simplify ISAs will come into force in April 2008. The reforms will remove the distinction between maxi and mini ISAs and allow transfers from a previous year's cash ISA into a stocks and shares version. Also from April 2008 the annual ISA investment limit will go up to £7,200 with an increase in the cash limit to £3,600.

Further details are available via HMRC's ISA helpline on 0845-604 1701.

DEDUCTIBLE ALLOWANCES AND RELIEFS

Income tax payers may be entitled to certain tax-deductible allowances and reliefs as well as their personal allowances. Examples include the married couple's allowance and maintenance payments relief, both of which are explained below. Unlike the tax-free allowances, these are not amounts of income that an individual can receive tax-free but amounts by which their tax bill can be reduced.

MARRIED COUPLE'S ALLOWANCE

A married couple's allowance (MCA) is available to taxpayers who are married or in a civil partnership only where one or other partner was born before 6 April 1935. Eligible couples can start to claim the MCA from the year of marriage or civil partnership registration.

The MCA is restricted to give relief at a fixed rate of 10 per cent which means that, unlike the personal allowance, it is not income that can be received without paying tax. Instead, it reduces an individual's tax bill by up to a fixed amount calculated as 10 per cent of the amount of the allowance to which they are entitled.

In 2007–8 there are two different levels of MCA:
- £6,285 at 10 per cent – if either partner was born before 6 April 1935 but is aged under 75. This is worth up to £628.50 off their tax bill
- £6,365 at 10 per cent – if either partner is aged 75 or over. This is worth up to £636.50 off their tax bill

The MCA is made up of two parts: a minimum amount (£2,440 in 2007–8); and a second amount dependent on the age bracket of the individual or his or her partner. For a couple where one or other was born before 6 April 1935 but is under 75, this second amount is £3,845. Where one or the other is aged 75 or over, it is £3,925.

For married couples, the minimum amount will always be due whatever the level of the husband's income. The age-related amount can be reduced if the husband's income exceeds certain limits. Whatever the level of the allowance, it is normally reduced in the year of marriage to take account of the months elapsed before the marriage.

The husband will normally receive the allowance but the couple can jointly decide which of them will get the minimum amount of the allowance. Alternatively, they can decide to have the minimum amount of the allowance split equally between them. They must inform their tax office of their decision by completing Form 18 before the start of the new tax year in which they want the decision to become effective. Once this is done, the change will apply until the couple decides to alter it, so there is no need to complete a new form every year. If there is no such decision, the husband will normally get the allowance. The remaining part of the allowance due because of age must go to the husband unless he does not have sufficient income to use it.

If an individual does not have enough income to use all his or her share of the married couple's allowance, the tax office can transfer the unused part of it to his or her spouse or civil partner.

Like the personal allowance, the MCA can be gradually reduced at the rate of £1 of the allowance for every £2 of income above the income limit (£20,900 in 2007–8). The amount of MCA can only be affected by the husband's income, and it only starts to be affected if his personal allowance has already been reduced back to the basic level for people under 65. The wife's income never affects the amount of the MCA. It does not matter whether all or part of the minimum amount of the allowance has been transferred to her. Whatever the level of the husband's income, the MCA can never be reduced below a minimum level. In 2007–8 this minimum amount is £2,440 at 10 per cent.

The same system of allowance allocation applies to civil partners based on the income of the highest earner. *See* leaflets *FS1 (MCA): Married couple's allowance restrictions*; and *REV BN 28: Tax and civil partners.*

MAINTENANCE PAYMENTS RELIEF

An allowance is available to reduce an individual's tax bill for maintenance payments he or she makes to his or her ex spouse or former civil partner in certain circumstances. To be eligible one or other partner must have been born before 6 April 1935; the couple must be legally separated or divorced; the maintenance payments being made must be under a court order; and the payments must be for the maintenance of an ex spouse or former civil partner (provided he or she is not now remarried or in a new civil partnership) or for children who are under 21. This allowance enables individuals to reduce their tax bill by the lower of 10 per cent of £2,350 (maximum £235) or 10 per cent of the amount actually paid in maintenance payments.

To claim maintenance payments relief individuals should contact their tax office and request Form IR41.

CHARITABLE DONATIONS

A number of charitable donations qualify for tax relief. Individuals can increase the value of regular or one-off charitable gifts, however small, by using the Gift Aid scheme that allows charities to reclaim basic rate tax relief on donations they receive. The gift is treated as being paid from net income – that is, after income tax at the basic rate of 22 per cent has been deducted from it. The effect is that, for every £10 a donor gives, the charity actually

receives £12.82 once it reclaims the tax at the basic rate. Higher rate taxpayers also benefit. They can reclaim the 18 per cent difference to give the full 40 per cent relief.

For gifts to qualify for Gift Aid, an individual must pay at least as much income tax as the recipient charities will reclaim on the gifts in the tax year in which they are made. Non-taxpayers should not use Gift Aid. The scheme is only for monetary gifts and there are rules limiting the value of benefits individuals may receive in return for their charitable donations.

For employees or those in receipt of an occupational pension, a tax-efficient way of making regular donations to charities is to make them straight from a salary or pension before income tax is deducted under the Payroll Giving scheme. This effectively increases the value of an individual's contributions, meaning more money for the recipient charity at less cost to the donor. For example, it costs a basic-rate taxpayer only £7.80 in take-home pay to give £10 to charity from their pre-tax pay. Higher rate taxpayers can claim an additional 18 per cent relief, reducing the cost of a £10 donation to £6. Anyone who pays tax through PAYE can give in this way, providing his or her employer or pension provider offers a payroll giving scheme, and there is no limit to the amount individuals can donate.

TAX RELIEF ON PENSION CONTRIBUTIONS

Pensions are long-term investments designed to help ensure that people have enough income in retirement. The government encourages individuals to save towards a pension by offering tax relief on their contributions.

For each pound individuals contribute to their scheme, whether it be an occupational pension or a private or stakeholder plan, the pension provider claims tax back from the government at the basic rate of 22 per cent and reinvests it on behalf of the individual into the scheme. In practice, this means that for every £78 taxpayers pay into their pension, they end up with £100 in their pension fund.

Higher rate taxpayers get 40 per cent tax relief on money they put into a pension, but the way that the money is given back is different. The first 22 per cent is claimed back from HMRC by the pension scheme in the same way as for a lower rate taxpayer. It is then up to individuals to claim back the other 18 per cent from their tax office, either when they fill in their annual tax return or by letter.

The most non-taxpayers can pay into a pension is £2,808 a year; since they receive basic rate 22 per cent tax relief on this sum, the government effectively tops up their contribution to make it £3,600.

Until April 2006 there were various restrictions – based on age and salary – limiting the amounts an individual could save and get tax relief on in personal and company pension schemes. But on 6 April 2006 a new, simplified pensions regime came into effect that included the introduction of just one, more generous annual allowance applied to all types of pension scheme.

In any one tax year, individuals can now get tax relief on pension contributions of 100 per cent of their annual earnings, irrespective of age, up to a maximum 'annual allowance' (£225,000 for 2007–8). Everyone now also has a 'lifetime allowance' (£1.6m for 2007–8) which means taxpayers can save up to this amount in their pension fund and still get tax relief at their highest income tax rate on all their contributions. Individuals may also now pay concurrently into as many different types of pension as they wish and get tax relief on all their contributions, provided they do not exceed the annual allowance.

For information and leaflets on pensions and tax relief, contact the government's Pensions Service on 0845-606 0265 or visit www.thepensionservice.gov.uk.

PAYMENT OF INCOME TAX

Employees have their income tax deducted from their wages throughout the year by their employer who sends it on to HMRC. Those in receipt of a company pension have their due tax deducted in the same way by their pension provider. This system of collecting income tax is known as 'pay as you earn' (PAYE).

BENEFITS IN KIND

The PAYE system is also used to collect tax on certain fringe benefits or 'benefits in kind' that employees or directors receive from their employer but that are not included in their salary cheque or wages. These include company cars, private medical insurance paid for by the employer or cheap or free loans from the employer. Some fringe benefits are tax-free, including employer-paid contributions into an employee's pension fund, cheap or free canteen meals, works buses, in-house sports facilities, relocation expenses up to £8,000, provision of a mobile phone, and workplace nursery places provided for the children of employees and certain other employer-supported childcare up to £50 per week.

For taxable fringe benefits tax is paid on the 'taxable value' of the benefit. The way this is worked out depends on whether or not the benefit is given to a director or 'higher-paid' employee defined as an individual earning £8,500 gross or more per year, including the value of his or her taxable fringe benefits. Company directors normally count as higher-paid, however much they earn.

Employers submit returns for individual employees to the tax office on the Form P11D, with details of any fringe benefits they have been given. Employees should get a copy of this form by 6 July following the end of the tax year and must enter the value of the fringe benefits they have received on their tax return for the relevant year, even if tax has already been paid on them under PAYE. Fringe benefits may be taxed under PAYE by being offset against personal tax allowances in an individual's PAYE code. Otherwise tax will be collected after the end of the tax year by the issue of an assessment on the fringe benefits.

SELF-ASSESSMENT

Individuals who are not on PAYE, notably the self-employed, need to complete a self-assessment tax return each year, in paper form or online at the HMRC website (W www.hmrc.gov.uk), and pay any income tax owed in twice-yearly instalments. Some individuals with more complex tax affairs such as those who earn money from rents or investments above a certain level, even if they are on PAYE, may also need to fill out a self--assessment return. HMRC uses the figures supplied on the tax return to work out the individual's tax bill, or they can choose to work it out themselves. It is called self--assessment because individuals are responsible for making sure the details they provide are correct.

Tax returns are usually sent out in early April, following the end of the tax year to which they apply. They may also go out at other times, for example if an individual wants to claim an allowance or repayment or to register for self-assessment for the first time.

Individuals with simple tax affairs, or with self-employment or rental income of less than £15,000, receive a short four-page return. Those with more complex affairs must fill out a full return that has 10 core pages plus extra pages, depending on the sorts of income received.

Central to the self-assessment system is the requirement for individuals to contact their tax office if they do not receive a self-assessment return but think they should or if their financial circumstances change. Individuals have six months from when the tax year ends to report any new income, for example, and three months to tell HMRC if they become self-employed.

TAX RETURN FILING AND PAYMENT DEADLINES

There are also key deadlines for filing (sending in) completed tax returns and paying the tax due. Failure to do so can incur penalties, interest charges and surcharges. The deadlines are more generous for individuals who do not want to calculate the tax due themselves and file their tax return online.

KEY FILING DATES FOR SELF-ASSESSMENT RETURNS

Date	Why the deadline is important
31 January*	Formal deadline for filing tax return received by the previous 31 October. Late filing incurs an automatic £100 penalty.
30 September†	Paper tax returns for tax year ended the previous 5 April must reach the HMRC by this date if the taxpayer wishes HMRC to: • calculate the tax • notify the taxpayer what to pay by the following 31 January • collect tax through the taxpayer's PAYE tax code (if possible) where the amount owed is less than £2,000.
29 December	Where a taxpayer's agent (eg an accountant) submits his or her tax return via electronic lodgement service (ELS), it must be sent back by this date if the taxpayer wants HMRC to collect tax through his or her tax code (if possible) where the amount owed is less than £2,000.
30 December	Where a taxpayer files the return online, he or she must do so by this date if HMRC is to collect tax through his or her tax code (if possible) where the amount owed is less than £2,000. Otherwise it can be filed up to 31 January.

* It was announced in the 2007 Budget that new filing dates for paper and online self-assessment tax returns will be introduced applying to tax returns that are issued on or after 6 April 2008 and relate to the tax year 2007–8 and subsequent years. For paper returns, the date will be 31 October (for tax year 2007–8 that will be 31 October 2008). For returns filed online, the date will remain at 31 January (for tax year 2007–8 that will be 31 January 2009). For taxpayers filing paper returns who want HMRC to calculate their tax liability for them, the new cut off date will move from 30 September to 31 October to align with the new paper return filing deadline.

† If HMRC receives the paper tax return after 30 September and processes it by 30 December, it will still calculate the tax owed and try to collect it through the taxpayer's tax code but it cannot guarantee to inform the taxpayer what to pay by 31 January. A calculation of tax liability is automatically provided when a return is filed online.

Date	What payments or penalties are due?
31 January	If a tax return was sent by the previous 31 October, this is the deadline for paying the balance of any tax owed – the 'balancing payment'. HMRC will charge daily interest after this date until it receives the payment. It is also the date by which a taxpayer must make any first 'payment on account' for the current tax year. For example on 31 January 2008 a taxpayer will have to pay both the balancing payment for the year 2006–7 and the first payment on account for 2007–8.
28 February	If the balancing payment is not paid by 31 January, there is an automatic 5 per cent surcharge incurred on top of the amount outstanding. This is in addition to any interest payments.
31 July	The deadline for making a second payment on account for tax owing for the preceding tax year. If tax is still owed that was due by the previous 31 January, there is a second automatic 5 per cent surcharge levied on top of the amount owed.

TAX CREDITS

Child tax credit and working tax credit are paid to qualifying individuals. Although the title of both credits incorporates the word 'tax', neither affects the amount of income tax payable or repayable. Both are forms of social security benefits. *See* Social Welfare

CAPITAL GAINS TAX

Capital gains tax (CGT) is a tax on increases in value of capital. When an individual disposes of an asset – that is, something he or she owns such as shares, land or buildings – by selling it or giving it away, CGT may have to be paid on the gain or profit. An individual is potentially chargeable to CGT on gains that accrue from disposals made during a year of tax assessment. The following information relates to the year of assessment 2007–8 ending on 5 April 2008 and has only limited relevance to earlier years.

Liability extends to individuals who are either resident or ordinarily resident in the UK for the tax year, but special rules apply where a person permanently leaves the UK or comes to this country for the purpose of acquiring residence. Non-residents are not usually liable to CGT unless they carry on a business in the UK through a branch or agency. However, individuals who left the UK after 16 March 1998 and who have been resident or ordinarily resident in at least four of the seven years preceding departure may remain liable to CGT unless they reside overseas over a period of five complete tax years. Exceptions to this may apply where there is a disposal of assets acquired in the period of absence. Individuals should consult their tax office for details, which are available in leaflet *IR20: Residents and Non-residents: Liability to Tax in the United Kingdom*.

EXAMPLES OF CAPITAL GAINS CHARGEABLE TO CGT

Typically, individuals have made a gain if they sell an asset for more than they paid for it. It is the gain that is taxed, not the amount the individual receives for the asset. For example, a man buys shares for £1,000 and later sells them for £3,000. He has made a gain of £2,000. If someone gives an asset away, the gain will be based on the difference between what the asset was worth when originally acquired compared with its worth at the time of disposal. The same is true when an asset is sold for less than its full worth in order to give away part of the value. For example, a woman buys a property for £120,000 and three years later, when the property's market value has risen to £180,000, she gives it to her son. The son may pay nothing for the property or pay less than its true worth, eg £100,000. Either way, she has made a gain of £60,000.

If an individual disposes of an asset he or she received as a gift, the gain is worked out according to the market value of the asset when it was received. For example, a man gives his sister a painting worth £8,000. She pays nothing for it. Later she sells the painting for £10,000. For CGT purposes, she is treated as making a gain of £2,000. If an individual inherits an asset, the estate of the person who died does not pay CGT at the time. If the inheritor later disposes of the asset, the gain is worked out by looking at the market value at the time of the death. For example, a woman acquires some shares for £5,000 and leaves them to her niece when she dies. No CGT is payable at the time of death when the shares are worth £8,000. Later the niece sells the shares for £10,000. She has made a gain of £2,000 (£10,000 less £8,000). Individuals may also have to pay CGT if they dispose of part of an asset or exchange one asset for another. Similarly, CGT may be payable if an individual receives a capital sum of money from an asset without disposing of it, for example where he or she receives compensation when an asset is damaged.

Assets that may lead to a CGT charge when they are disposed of include:

- shares in a company
- units in a unit trust
- land and buildings (though not normally an individual's main home – *see* 'disposal of a home' section for details)
- higher value jewellery, paintings, antiques and other personal effects assets used in business such as goodwill

EXEMPT GAINS

Certain kinds of assets do not give rise to a chargeable gain when they are disposed of. Assets exempt from CGT include:

- an individual's private car
- an individual's main home, provided certain conditions are met
- tax-free investments such as assets held in an individual savings account (ISA) or personal equity plan (PEP)
- UK government gilts or 'bonds'
- personal belongings including jewellery, paintings, antiques individually worth £6,000 or less
- cash in sterling or foreign currency held for an individual or his/her family's own personal use
- betting, lottery or pools winnings
- personal injury compensation

DISPOSAL OF A HOME: PRIVATE RESIDENCE RELIEF

Individuals do not have to pay CGT when they sell their main home if all the following conditions are met:

- they bought it and made any expenditure on it, primarily for use as their home rather than with a view to making a profit

- the property was their only home throughout the period they owned it (ignoring the last three years of ownership)
- the property was actually used as their home all the time that they owned it and, throughout the period, it was not used for any purpose other than as a home for the individual, his or her family and no more than one lodger
- the garden and area of grounds sold with the property does not exceed 5,000 sq. m (1.24 acres) including the site of the property

Even if all these conditions are not met, individuals may still be entitled to CGT relief when they sell the home. They may, for example, qualify for relief if they lived away from home temporarily while working abroad. Married couples or couples in a civil partnership may have relief from CGT on only one home. There is a special exception, however, where the spouse or partner each had a qualifying home before marriage or civil partnership and both live together in one of these homes after marriage or civil partnership and sell the other. Provided that it is sold within three years of marriage or the civil partnership, they may not have to pay any CGT (subject to the normal rules for this relief). If they sell it after more than three years it may qualify for partial relief. There are special rules on divorce and separation. Further details are available in HMRC help sheet *IR283: Private Residence Relief.*

Certain other kinds of disposal similarly do not give rise to a chargeable gain. For example, individuals who are married or in a civil partnership and who live together may sell or give assets to their spouse or civil partner without having to pay CGT. Individuals may not, however, give or sell assets cheaply to their children without having to consider CGT. There is no CGT to pay on assets given to a registered charity. See HMRC help sheet *IR178: Giving Shares and Securities to Charity.*

CALCULATING CGT

CGT is worked out for each tax year and is charged on the total of an individual's taxable gains after taking into account certain costs and reliefs that can reduce or defer chargeable gains, allowable losses made on assets to which CGT normally applies and an annual exempt (tax-free) amount that applies to every individual. If the total of an individual's net gains in a tax year is less than the annual exempt amount (AEA), the individual will not have to pay CGT. For the tax year 2007–8 the AEA is £9,200. If an individual's net gains are more than the AEA, they pay CGT on the excess. Should any part of the exemption remain unused, this cannot be carried forward to a future year. A smaller exemption limit applies to most trusts. There are many reliefs available that may eliminate, reduce or defer CGT. Some reliefs are available to many people. For example, taper relief (*see* below) reduces the amount of a gain charged to tax the longer an asset has been held. Other reliefs are available only in special circumstances. Some reliefs are given automatically while others are given only if they are claimed. Some of the costs of buying, selling and improving assets may be deducted from total gains when working out an individual's chargeable gain.

RATES OF TAX

The net gains remaining, if any, calculated after deduction of costs, taking into account all CGT reliefs and subtracting the annual exemption, incur liability to capital gains tax. The rate of CGT individuals pay depends on their overall income. Their total taxable gains are added to their taxable income for the year and treated as the top part of that total. The gains are then charged to CGT at the following rates for the 2007–8 tax year:

- 10 per cent where they fall below the starting rate limit for income tax of £2,230
- 20 per cent where they fall between the starting rate and basic rate limits for income tax (£2,231 to £34,600)
- 40 per cent where they fall above the basic rate limit for income tax (£34,600 and above)

Although income tax rates are used for this purpose liability arises only at the starting rate of 10 per cent, the lower rate of 20 per cent, the higher rate of 40 per cent or a combination of the three rates. Unlike some income tax commitments, there is no liability at the basic rate of 22 per cent. Despite the use of some income tax rates, CGT remains an entirely separate tax. CGT for 2007–8 falls due for payment in full on 31 January 2009. If payment is delayed, interest or surcharges may be imposed. A husband and wife or registered civil partners who live together are separately assessed to CGT. Each partner must independently calculate his or her gains and losses, with each entitled to the benefit of taper relief, if any, and the AEA of £9,200 for 2007–8.

VALUATION OF ASSETS

The disposal proceeds – that is the amount received as consideration for the disposal of an asset – are the sum used to establish the gain or loss once certain allowable costs have been deducted. In most cases this is straightforward because the disposal proceeds are the amount actually received for disposing of the asset. This may include cash payable now or in the future and the value of any asset received in exchange for the asset disposed of. However, in certain circumstances, the disposal proceeds may not accurately reflect the value of the asset and the individual may be treated as disposing of an asset for an amount other than the actual amount (if any) that they received. This applies, in particular, where an asset is transferred as a gift or sold for a price known to be below market value. Disposal proceeds in such transactions are deemed to be equal to the market value of the asset at the time it was disposed of rather than the actual amount (if any) received for it.

Market value represents the price that an asset might reasonably be expected to fetch upon sale in the open market. In the case of unquoted shares or securities, it is to be assumed that the hypothetical purchaser in the open market would have available all the information that a prudent prospective purchaser of shares or securities might reasonably require if that person were proposing to purchase them from a willing vendor by private treaty and at arm's length. The market value of unquoted shares or securities will often be established following negotiations with the HM Revenue and Customs: Shares Valuation. The valuation of land and interests in land in the UK is dealt with by District Valuer Services, part of the Valuation Office Agency. Special rules apply to determine the market value of shares quoted on the London Stock Exchange.

ALLOWABLE COSTS

When working out a chargeable gain, once the actual or notional disposal proceeds have been determined, five kinds of allowable costs may be deducted. There is a general rule that no costs that could be taken into account when working out income or losses for income tax purposes may be deducted. Subject to this, allowable costs are:

- acquisition costs – the actual amount spent on acquiring the asset or, in certain circumstances, the equivalent market value
- incidental costs of acquiring the asset such as fees paid for professional advice, valuation costs, stamp duty and advertising costs to find a seller
- enhancement costs – incurred for the purpose of enhancing the value of the asset (not including normal maintenance and repair costs)
- expenditure on defending or establishing a person's rights over the asset
- incidental costs of disposing of the asset such as fees paid for professional advice, valuation costs, stamp duty and advertising costs to find a buyer

If an individual disposes of part of his or her interest in an asset, or part of a holding of shares of the same class in the same company, or part of a holding of units in the same unit trust, he or she can deduct part of the allowable costs of the asset or holding when working out the chargeable gain. Allowable costs may also be reduced by some reliefs.

INDEXATION ALLOWANCE

For many years an indexation allowance could be inserted when calculating a gain on the disposal of an asset. The allowance was based on percentage increases in the retail prices index between the month of March 1982, or the month in which expenditure was incurred if later, and the month of disposal.

Taper relief has largely replaced the indexation allowance for disposals made after 5 April 1998. However, where an asset was acquired before this date, the indexation allowance will be calculated to the month of April 1998 and frozen. The frozen allowance then enters into the calculation of chargeable gain, if any, when the asset is disposed of at some later date. The adjustment for the indexation allowance must be made before calculating taper relief on the net sum remaining.

TAPER RELIEF

Taper relief, an important and potentially valuable relief from CGT, was introduced with effect from 6 April 1998 to replace the former indexation allowance and to encourage long-term investment. It has been extended substantially since its introduction. The taper relief rules are potentially complex and individuals are advised to seek professional advice if uncertain.

Taper relief is available to individuals, partnerships, estates and trusts but cannot be claimed by companies to whom other tax rules apply. This relief reduces the proportion of a capital gain charged to tax according to the period of ownership since April 1998 and whether the asset disposed of is a business or non-business asset. Business assets, which have a higher rate of relief than non-business assets, are broadly identified as assets used for business purposes and shares in both trading and non-trading companies. The maximum abatement is achieved after a holding period of two years for business assets and ten years for non-business assets. The holding period is normally the number of complete years (not tax years) after 5 April 1998 that the asset is held. For non-business assets acquired before 17 March 1998, however, the period is deemed to be increased by one bonus year. For example, a non-business asset acquired on 16 March 1998 and sold on 6 April 2007 would have a holding period for taper relief of ten years – that is, nine

years' ownership post 5 April 1998 plus the extra bonus year because the asset was held on 17 March 1998. Where an inter-spouse or inter-registered civil partner transfer is involved, the holding period is the combined ownership period of both spouses/partners.

Taper relief reduces the gains on non-business assets by 5 per cent per year, once the asset has been held for three years with a maximum reduction amounting to 40 per cent. Business assets attract a maximum taper relief of 75 per cent of the gain after two years of ownership. The percentages of gains remaining chargeable for disposals taking place on and after 6 April 2007 are shown in the table below .

No. of whole years of ownership	Percentage of gains chargeable	
	Business assets	Non-business assets
	%	%
1	50	100
2	25	100
3	25	95
4	25	90
5	25	85
6	25	80
7	25	75
8	25	70
9	25	65
10 or more	25	60

If an asset has been used partly as a business asset and partly as a non-business asset (ie during different periods of ownership, and/or at the same time) during the 10 years of ownership leading up to disposal, the chargeable gain is calculated and apportioned between business and non-business use of the asset. Business asset taper relief is applied to the business element of the gain, and non-business asset taper relief to the remainder, as if two separate gains had arisen on the disposal of different assets. The two gains are then added together.

If only chargeable gains arise from disposals carried out in 2007–8 the taper relief, if any, must be calculated by reference to each disposal. The aggregate sum of taper relief will then be subtracted from the total chargeable gains to produce the net gains for the year. Where disposals made in 2007–8 give rise to both gains and losses, the losses must be subtracted from the gains and taper relief calculated on the net sum remaining. It is necessary to allocate the losses between the gains where there are two or more disposals producing gains. Losses brought forward from an earlier year must also be subtracted when calculating the net gains qualifying for taper relief. However, the losses brought forward are not to reduce the net gains below the annual exemption limit of £9,200 which applies for 2007–8.

BUSINESS ASSET ROLL-OVER RELIEF

A capital gain on the disposal of certain types of asset used in a person's business may be deferred or 'rolled over' if the proceeds are reinvested in new qualifying trading assets. The gain is deducted from the base cost of the new asset and only becomes chargeable to CGT on the eventual disposal of that replacement asset unless a further roll-over situation then develops. Full relief is available if all the proceeds from the original asset (the old asset) are reinvested in the qualifying replacement asset (the new asset). If only part of the proceeds is reinvested, the difference represents an immediately chargeable gain.

If the amount not reinvested is greater than the gain, no roll-over relief is due.

Relief is only available if the acquisition of the new asset takes place within a period commencing 12 months before, and ending three years after, the disposal of the old asset. However, HMRC may extend this time limit at their discretion where there is a clear intention to acquire a replacement asset. The most common types of business assets that qualify for roll-over relief are land, buildings occupied and used for the purposes of trade, fixed plant and machinery. Roll-over relief is also available for assets used for the commercial letting of furnished holiday accommodation if certain conditions are satisfied. For details, see help sheet *IR290: Business Asset Roll-over Relief*. Roll-over relief is also available where shares in a company are transferred to trustees administering an employees' share incentive plan for the benefit of persons employed by that company. For details, see help sheet *IR287: Employee Share Schemes and Capital Gains Tax*. A similar relief, known as business transfer relief or incorporation relief, is available to defer a gain where business people transfer their business to a company in return for shares.

GIFTS HOLD-OVER RELIEF

The gift of an asset is treated as a disposal made for a consideration equal to market value, with a corresponding acquisition by the transferee at an identical value. In the case of gifts made by individuals and a limited range of trustees to a transferee resident in the UK, a form of hold-over relief may be available. This relief, which must be claimed, in effect enables liability for CGT to be deferred and passed to the person to whom the gift is made. Relief is limited to the transfer of certain assets including the following:

- gifts of assets used for the purposes of a business carried on by the donor or his or her personal company
- gifts of shares in trading companies that are not listed on a stock exchange
- gifts of shares or securities in the donor's personal trading company
- gifts of agricultural land and buildings that would qualify for inheritance tax agricultural property relief
- gifts that are chargeable transfers for inheritance tax purposes
- certain types of gifts that are specifically exempted from inheritance tax

Hold-over relief is automatically due on certain sorts of gifts including gifts to charities and community amateur sports clubs, and gifts of works of art where certain undertakings have been given. There are certain rules to prevent gifts hold-over relief being used for tax-avoidance purposes. For example, restrictions may apply where an individual gifts assets to trustees administering a trust in which the individual retains an interest or where the assets transferred comprise a dwelling-house. Subject to these exceptions, the effect of a valid claim for hold-over relief is similar to that following a claim for roll-over relief on the disposal of business assets. Adjustments may be necessary where some consideration (less than market value) is given for a gift or where a gifted asset has not been used for business purposes throughout the period of ownership. Further information is available in help sheet *IR295: Relief for Gifts and Similar Transactions*.

OTHER CGT RELIEFS

Enterprise investment scheme (EIS) deferral relief allows the deferral of gains on the disposal of an asset when an individual subscribes for shares in an EIS company; see help sheet *IR297: Enterprise Investment Scheme and Capital Gains Tax*. Similarly, venture capital trust (VCT) deferral relief allows the deferral of gains on the disposal of an asset when an individual subscribes for shares in a VCT; see help sheet *IR298: Venture Capital Trusts and Capital Gains Tax*. Halving relief reduces by half certain gains deferred from before April 1988; see help sheet *IR280: Rebasing – Assets Held at 31 March 1982*. For more general guidance on CGT, see HMRC booklet *CGT1: Capital Gains Tax – An Introduction*.

INHERITANCE TAX

Inheritance tax (IHT) is a tax on the value of a person's estate on death and on certain gifts made by an individual during his or her lifetime, usually payable within six months of death. Broadly speaking, a person's estate is everything he or she owned at the time of death including property, possessions, money and investments, less his or her debts. Not everyone pays IHT. It only applies if the taxable value of an estate is above the current inheritance tax threshold. If an estate, including any assets held in trust and gifts made within seven years of death, is less than the threshold, no IHT will be due. See table for the lower threshold limit, known as the nil rate band.

2006–7	£285,000
2007–8	£300,000
2008–9	£312,000
2009–10	£325,000
2010–11	£350,000

IHT used to be something only very wealthy individuals needed to consider. This is no longer the case. A dramatic rise in house prices over recent years coupled with the fact that the IHT threshold has not kept pace with house price inflation means that the estates of an increasing number of taxpayers who would not consider themselves wealthy, are now becoming liable for IHT purely because of the value of their home. However, there are a number of ways that individuals – while still alive – can legally reduce the IHT bill that will apply to their estates on death. Several valuable IHT exemptions are available (explained further below) which allow individuals to pass on assets during their lifetime or in their will without any IHT being due. IHT forms and information leaflets can be downloaded from the HMRC website (W www.hmrc.gov.uk). The main guide is entitled, *HMRC Inheritance Tax: Customer Guide*. Paper versions and further help are available from the probate and IHT helpline on 0845-302 0900.

DOMICILE

Liability to IHT depends on an individual's domicile at the time of any gift or on death. Domicile is a complex legal concept and what follows explains some of the main issues. An individual is domiciled in the country where he or she has a permanent home. Domicile is different from nationality or residence, and an individual can only have one domicile at any given time.

A domicile of origin is normally acquired from the individual's father on birth, though this may not be the country in which he or she is born. For example, a child born in Germany while his or her father is working there, but whose permanent home is in the UK, will have the UK as his or her domicile of origin. Until a person legally changes his or her domicile, it will be the same as that of the person on whom they are legally dependent.

Individuals can legally acquire a new domicile – a domicile of choice – from the age of 16 by leaving the current country of domicile and settling in another country and providing strong evidence of intention to live there permanently or indefinitely. Women who were married before 1974 acquired their husband's domicile and still retain it until they legally acquire a new domicile.

For IHT purposes, there is a concept of deemed domicile. This means that even if a person is not domiciled in the UK under general law, he or she is treated as domiciled in the UK at the time of a transfer (ie at the time of a lifetime gift or on death) if he or she (a) was domiciled in the UK within the three years immediately before the transfer, or (b) was resident in the UK in at least 17 of the 20 income tax years of assessment ending with the year in which a transfer is made. Where a person is domiciled, or treated as domiciled, in the UK at the time of a gift or on death, the location of assets is immaterial and full liability to IHT arises. A non-UK domiciled individual is also liable to IHT but only on chargeable property in the UK. The assets of husband and wife and registered civil partners are not merged for IHT purposes. Each spouse or partner is treated as a separate individual entitled to receive the benefit of his or her exemptions, reliefs and rates of tax.

IHT EXEMPTIONS

There are some important exemptions that allow individuals to legally pass assets on to others, both before and after their death – without being subject to IHT.

Exempt beneficiaries

Assets can be given away to certain people and organisations without any IHT having to be paid. These gifts, which are exempt whether individuals make them during their lifetime or in their will, include gifts to:

- a husband, wife or civil partner, even if the couple is legally separated (but not if they are divorced or the civil partnership has dissolved), as long as both partners have a permanent home in the UK. Note that gifts to an unmarried partner or a partner with whom the donor has not formed a civil partnership are not exempt
- UK charities, including the National Trust
- some national institutions, including national museums and universities
- UK political parties

Annual exemption

The first £3,000 of gifts made each tax year by each individual is exempt from IHT. If this exemption is not used, or not wholly used in any year, the balance may be carried forward to the following year only. A couple, therefore, may give away a total of £6,000 per tax year between them or £12,000 if they haven't used their previous year's annual exemptions.

Wedding gifts / civil partnership ceremony gifts

Some gifts are exempt from IHT because of the type of gift or reason for making it. Wedding or civil partnership ceremony gifts made to either of the couple are exempt from IHT up to certain amounts:

- gifts by a parent, £5,000
- gifts by a grandparent or other relative, £2,500
- gifts by anyone else, £1,000

The gift must be made on or shortly before the date of the wedding or civil partnership ceremony. If it is called off and the gift is still made, this exemption will not apply.

Small gifts

An individual can make small gifts, up to the value of £250, to any number of people in any one tax year without them being liable for IHT. However, a larger sum such as £500 cannot be given and exemption claimed for the first £250. In addition, this exemption cannot be used with any other exemption when giving to the same person. For example, a parent cannot combine a small gifts exemption with a wedding/civil partnership ceremony gift exemption to give a child £5,250 when he or she gets married or forms a civil partnership. Neither may an individual combine a small gifts exemption with the annual exemption to give someone £3,250. Note that it is possible to use the annual exemption with any other exemption, such as the wedding/civil partnership ceremony gift exemption. For example, if a child marries or forms a civil partnership, the parent can give him or her a total IHT-free gift of £8,000 by combining £5,000 under the wedding/civil partnership gift exemption and £3,000 under the annual exemption.

Normal expenditure

Any gifts made out of individuals' after-tax income (not capital) are exempt from IHT if they are part of their normal expenditure and do not result in a fall in their standard of living. These can include regular payments to someone, such as an allowance or gifts for Christmas or a birthday and regular premiums paid on a life insurance policy for someone else.

Maintenance gifts

An individual can make IHT-free maintenance payments to his or her spouse or registered civil partner, ex-spouse or former civil partner, relatives dependent because of old age or infirmity, and children (including adopted children and step-children) who are under 18 or in full-time education.

POTENTIALLY EXEMPT TRANSFERS

If an individual makes a gift to either another individual or certain types of trust and it is not covered by one of the above exemptions, it is known as a potentially exempt transfer (PET). A PET is only free of IHT on two strict conditions: (a) the gift must be made at least seven years before the donor's death. If the donor does not survive seven years after making the gift, it will be liable for IHT and (b) the gift must be made as a true gift with no strings attached (technically known as a gift with reservation of benefit). This means that the donor must give up all rights to the gift and stop benefiting from it in any way.

If a gift is made and the donor does retain some benefit from it then it will still count as part of his or her estate no matter how long he or she lives after making it. For example, a father could make a lifetime gift of his home to his child. HMRC would not accept this as a true gift, however, if the father continued to live in the home (unless he paid his child a full commercial rent to do so) because he would be considered to still have a material interest in the gifted home. Its value, therefore, would still be liable for IHT.

In some circumstances a gift with strings attached might give rise to an income tax charge on the donor based on the value of the benefit he or she retains. In this case the donor can choose whether to pay the income tax or have the gift treated as a gift with reservation.

CHARGEABLE TRANSFERS

Any remaining lifetime gifts that are not (potentially or otherwise) exempt transfers are chargeable transfers or 'chargeable gifts', meaning that they incur liability to IHT. Chargeable transfers comprise mainly gifts to or from companies and gifts to particular types of trust called discretionary trusts. There is an immediate claim for IHT on chargeable gifts, and additional tax may be payable if the donor dies within seven years of making a chargeable gift.

DEATH

Immediately before the time of death an individual is deemed to make a transfer of value. This transfer will comprise the value of assets forming part of the deceased's estate after subtracting most liabilities. Any exempt transfers may be excluded such as transfers for the benefit of a surviving spouse or civil partner, and charities. Death may also trigger three additional liabilities:

- a PET made within the seven years before the death loses its potential status and becomes chargeable to IHT
- the value of gifts made with reservation may incur liability if any benefit was enjoyed within the seven years before the death
- additional tax may become payable for chargeable lifetime transfers made within the seven years before the death

The personal representative (the person nominated to handle the affairs of the deceased person) arranges to value the estate and pay any IHT that is due. One or more personal representatives can be nominated in a person's will, in which case they are known as the executors. If a person dies without leaving a will a court can nominate the personal representative, who is then known as the administrator. Valuing the deceased person's estate is one of the first things his or her personal representative needs to do. The representative will not normally be able to take over management of the estate (called 'applying for probate') until all or some of any IHT that is due has been paid.

VALUATIONS

When valuing a deceased person's estate all assets (property, possessions and money) owned at the time of death and certain assets given away during the seven years before death must be included. The valuation must accurately reflect what those assets would reasonably fetch in the open market at the date of death. The value of all of the assets that the deceased owned should include:

- his or her share of any assets owned jointly with someone else, for example a house owned with a partner
- any assets that are held in a trust, from which the deceased had the right to benefit
- any assets given away, but in which he or she kept an interest (gifts with reservation)
- PETs given away within the last seven years

Most estate assets can be valued quite easily, for example money in bank accounts or stocks and shares. In other instances the help of a professional valuer may be needed. Advice on how to value different assets including joint or trust assets is available at www.hmrc.gov.uk. When valuing an estate, special relief is made available for certain assets. The two main reliefs are business relief and agricultural property relief outlined below. Once all assets have been valued, the next step is to deduct from the total assets everything that the deceased person owed such as unpaid bills, outstanding mortgages and other loans plus their funeral expenses. The value of all of the assets, less the deductible debts, is their estate. IHT is only payable on any value above £300,000 for the tax year 2007–8 at the current rate of 40 per cent.

RELIEF FOR SELECTED ASSETS

Agricultural Property
Relief from IHT is available on the agricultural value of agricultural property that is transferred. Agricultural property generally includes land or pasture used in the growing of crops or intensive rearing of animals for food consumption. It can also include farmhouses and farm cottages. The agricultural property can be owner-occupied or let. Relief is only due if the transferor has owned the property and it has been occupied for agricultural purposes for a minimum period.

The value transferred, either on a lifetime gift or on death, must be determined. This value may then be reduced by a percentage. Under current rates, a 100 per cent deduction will be available if the transferor retained vacant possession or could have obtained that possession within a period of 12 months following the transfer. In other cases, notably including land let to tenants, a lower deduction of 50 per cent is usually available. However, this lower deduction may be increased to 100 per cent if the letting was made after 31 August 1995.

To qualify for the relief, the agricultural property must either have been occupied by the transferor for the purposes of agriculture throughout a two-year period ending on the date of the transfer, or have been owned by the transferor throughout a period of seven years ending on that date and also occupied for agricultural purposes.

Business Relief
Business relief is available on transfers of certain types of business and of business assets if they qualify as relevant business property and the transferor has owned them for a minimum period. The relief can be claimed for transfers made during the person's lifetime and on death and on chargeable occasions arising on relevant business property held in trust. Where the value transferred is attributable to relevant business property, the business relief reduces that value by a percentage. Business relief may be claimed on relevant business property including:

- a business or an interest in a business such as a partnership
- unquoted shares and securities
- shares or securities of a quoted company which themselves or with other listed shares or securities give the transferor control of a company
- any land, buildings, plant or machinery owned by a partner or controlling shareholder and used wholly or mainly in the business of the partnership or company immediately before the transfer; this applies only if the partnership interest or shareholding would itself, if it were transferred, qualify for business relief
- any land, buildings, machinery or plant that were used wholly or mainly for the purpose of a business carried on by the transferor

If an asset qualifies for business relief, the rates (percentage) at which it is currently allowed are as follows:

A business or interest in a business	100
A holding of shares in an unquoted company	100
Control holding of shares in a quoted company	50
(more than 50 of the voting rights)	
Land, buildings or plant and machinery used in a business of which the deceased was a partner at the date of death or used by a company controlled by the deceased	50
Land, buildings, plant and machinery held in a trust where the deceased had the right to benefit from the trust and the asset was used in a business carried on by the deceased	50

It is a general requirement that the property must have been retained for a period of two years before the transfer or death, and restrictions may be necessary if the property has not been used wholly for business purposes. The same property cannot obtain both business property relief and the relief available for agricultural property.

CALCULATION OF TAX PAYABLE

The calculation of IHT payable adopts the use of a cumulative or 'running' total. Looking back seven years from the death the chargeable value of gifts in that period is added to the total value of the estate at death. The gifts will use up all or part of the inheritance tax threshold (the 'nil rate band' above which IHT becomes payable) first.

Lifetime Chargeable Transfers

The value transferred by lifetime chargeable transfers must be added to the seven-year running total to calculate whether any IHT is due. If the nil rate band is exceeded, tax will be imposed on the excess at the rate of 20 per cent. However, if the donor dies within a period of seven years from the date of the chargeable lifetime transfer, additional tax may be due. This is calculated by applying tax at the full rate of 40 per cent in substitution for the rate of 20 per cent previously used. The amount of tax is then reduced to a percentage by applying tapering relief. This percentage is governed by the number of years from the date of the lifetime gift to the date of death, as follows:

PERIOD OF YEARS BEFORE DEATH

Not more than 3	100%
More than 3 but not more than 4	80%
More than 4 but not more than 5	60%
More than 5 but not more than 6	40%
More than 6 but not more than 7	20%

Should this exercise produce liability greater than that previously paid at the 20 per cent rate on the lifetime transfer, additional tax, representing the difference, must be paid. Where the calculation shows an amount falling below tax paid on the lifetime transfer, no additional liability can arise nor will the shortfall become repayable.

Tapering relief is, of course, only available if the calculation discloses a liability to IHT. There is no liability if the lifetime transfer falls within the nil rate band.

Potentially Exempt Transfers

Where a PET loses immunity from liability to IHT because the donor dies within seven years of making the transfer, the value transferred by that transfer enters into the running total. Any liability to IHT will be calculated by applying the full rate of 40 per cent, reduced to the percentage governed by tapering relief if the original transfer occurred more than three years before death. Again, liability to IHT can only arise if the nil rate band is exceeded.

Death

On death, IHT is due on the value of the deceased's estate plus the running total of gifts made in the seven years before death if they come to more than the nil-rate band. IHT is then charged at the full rate of 40 per cent on the amount in excess of the nil rate band.

Settled Property and Trusts

Trusts are special legal arrangements that can be used by individuals to control how their assets are distributed to their beneficiaries and minimise their IHT liability. Complex rules apply to establish IHT liability on settled property which includes property held in trust, and individuals are advised to take expert legal advice when setting up trusts.

RATES OF TAX

In earlier times there were several rates of IHT that progressively increased as the value transferred grew in size. However, since 1988 there have been only three rates:

- a nil rate
- a lifetime rate of 20 per cent
- a full rate of 40 per cent

The nil rate band usually changes on an annual basis, and for events taking place after 5 April 2007 applies to the first £300,000. Any excess over this level is taxable at 20 per cent or 40 per cent as the case may be. The IHT threshold will be increased to £312,000 for 2008–9 and £325,000 for 2009–10.

PAYMENT OF TAX

IHT is normally due six months after the end of the month in which the death occurs or the chargeable transaction takes place. This is referred to as the due date. Tax on some assets such as business property, certain shares and securities and land and buildings (including the deceased person's home) can be deferred and paid in equal instalments over ten years, though interest will be charged in most cases. If IHT is due on lifetime gifts and transfers, the person or transferee who received the gift or assets is normally liable to pay the IHT, though any IHT already paid at the time of a transfer into a trust or company will be taken into account. If tax owed is not paid by the due date, interest is charged on any unpaid IHT, no matter what caused the delay in payment.

CORPORATION TAX

Corporation tax is a tax on a company's profits, including all its income and gains. This tax is payable by UK resident companies and by non-resident companies carrying on a trade in the UK through a permanent establishment. The following comments are confined to companies resident in the UK. The word company is also used to include:

- members' clubs, societies and associations
- trade associations
- housing associations
- groups of individuals carrying on a business but not as a partnership (for example, cooperatives)

A company's taxable income is charged by reference to income or gains arising in its accounting period, which is normally 12 months long. In some circumstances accounting periods can be shorter than 12 months, but never longer. The accounting period is also normally the period for which a company's accounts are drawn up, but the two periods do not have to coincide.

If a company is liable to pay corporation tax on its profits, several things must be done. HMRC must be informed that the company exists and is liable for tax. A self-assessment company tax return plus full accounts and calculation of tax liability must be filed by the statutory filing date, normally 12 months after the end of the accounting period. Companies have to work out their own tax liability and have to pay their tax without prior assessment by HMRC. Records of all company expenditure and income must be kept in order to work out the tax liability correctly. Companies are liable to penalties if they fail to carry out these obligations.

Measures to reform the business tax system were announced in the 2007 Budget with a staged introduction over the next few years. The major elements of the reform package will apply from 2008–9.

Extensive corporation tax information is available on the HMRC website and companies may file their company tax returns online at the HMRC's Corporation Tax Online service at www.hmrc.gov.uk/ctsa/ct-online.htm.

RATE OF TAX

The rate of corporation tax is fixed for a financial year starting on 1 April and ending on the following 31 March. If a company's accounting period does not coincide with the financial year, its profits must be apportioned between the financial years and the tax rates for each financial year applied to those profits. The corporation tax liability is the total tax for both financial years.

The main rate of corporation tax for 2007–8 is 30 per cent, as it has been for the past nine years. It has been announced in advance that the rate will go down to 28 per cent from April 2008 (North Sea oil and gas ring fence activities will retain a main corporation tax rate of 30 per cent).

SMALL COMPANIES' RATE

Where the profits of a company do not exceed stated limits, corporation tax becomes payable at the small companies' rate. It is the amount of profits and not the size of the company that governs the application of the small companies' rate.

For each of the three financial years ending on 31 March 2000, 31 March 2001 and 31 March 2002 the small companies' rate was 20 per cent. It was then reduced to 19 per cent for ensuing years but has been increased once again to 20 per cent from April 2007. It has been announced that there will be a staged increase in the small companies' rate from 20 per cent to 21 per cent from April 2008 and to 22 per cent from April 2009. (North Sea oil and gas ring activities will retain a small companies' rate of 19 per cent).

A company can make profits of up to £300,000 without losing the benefit of the small companies' rate. If, however, its profits exceed £300,000 but fall below £1,500,000, then marginal small companies' rate relief applies. The effect of marginal relief is that the average rate of corporation tax imposed on all profits steadily increases from the lower small companies' rate of 20 per cent to the main rate of 30 per cent, with tax being imposed on profits in the margin at an increased rate. Where a change in the rate of tax is introduced and the accounting period of a company overlaps 31 March, profits must be apportioned to establish the appropriate rate for each part of those profits.

The lower limit of £300,000 and the upper limit of £1,500,000 apply to a period of 12 months and must be proportionately reduced for shorter periods. Some restriction in the small companies' rate and the marginal rate may be necessary if there are two or more associated companies, namely companies under common control. Prior to 1 April 2006 there was a corporation tax starting rate of zero for very small companies where profits for a 12-month period were below £10,000, with marginal relief available where profits were between £10,001 and £50,000. There was also a non-corporate distribution rate (NCDR) set at 19 per cent for the financial year to 31

March 2006. This was a minimum rate of corporation tax that could apply to company profits distributed to persons who were not companies (ie individuals or trustees) if the company's underlying rate of tax on profits was less than the NCDR. From 1 April 2006, both the starting rate and non-corporate distribution rate were replaced with a single banding for small companies.

CORPORATION TAX ON PROFITS

£ per year	2006–7	2007–8
£0–£300,000	19%	20%
£300,001–£1,500,000	Marginal relief	Marginal relief
£1,500,000 or more	30%	30%

CAPITAL ALLOWANCES

Businesses can claim tax allowances, called capital allowances, on certain purchases or investments. This means that a proportion of these costs can be deducted from a business' taxable profits and reduce its tax bill. Capital allowances are currently available on plant and machinery, buildings and research and development. The amount of the allowance depends on what is being claimed for. As part of the staged business tax reform package announced in the 2007 Budget, changes to the capital allowances regime are to be introduced, mainly from April 2008.

Detailed information on capital allowances is available from the Enhanced Capital Allowances website (W www.eca.gov.uk).

PAYMENT OF TAX

Corporation tax liabilities are normally due and payable in a single lump sum not later than nine months and one day after the end of the accounting period. For large companies – those with profits over £1.5m which pay corporation tax at the main rate – there is a requirement to pay corporation tax in four quarterly instalments. Where a company is a member of a group, the profits of the entire group must be merged to establish whether the company is large.

CAPITAL GAINS

Chargeable gains arising to a company are calculated in a manner similar to that used for individuals. However, the withdrawal of the indexation allowance after April 1998 and the introduction of taper relief from the same date have no application to companies. Nor are companies entitled to the CGT annual exemption of £9,200. Companies do not suffer capital gains tax on chargeable gains but incur liability to corporation tax instead. Tax is due on the full chargeable gain of an accounting period after subtracting relief for losses, if any.

GROUPS OF COMPANIES

Each company within a group is separately charged to corporation tax on profits, gains and income. However, where one group member realises a loss for which special rules apply, other than a capital loss, a claim may be made to offset the deficiency against profits of some other member of the same group. The transfer of capital assets from one member of a group to a fellow member will usually incur no liability to tax on chargeable gains.

SPORTS CLUBS

Though corporation tax is payable by unincorporated associations including most clubs, a substantial exemption from liability to corporation tax, introduced in April

2002, is available to qualifying registered community amateur sports clubs (CASCs). Sports clubs that are registered as CASCs are exempt from liability to corporation tax on:

- profits from trading where the turnover of the trade is less than £30,000 in a 12-month period (limit was £15,000 prior to 1 April 2004)
- income from property where gross rental income is less than £20,000 in a 12-month period (limit was £10,000 prior to 1 April 2004)
- bank and building society interest received
- chargeable gains

All of the exemptions depend upon the club having been a registered CASC for the whole of the relevant accounting period and the income or gains being used only for qualifying purposes. If the club has only been a registered CASC for part of an accounting period the exemption amounts of £30,000 (for trading) and £20,000 (for income from property) are reduced proportionately. Only interest and gains received after the club is registered are exempted.

Among other advantages available to registered clubs is that donations may be received under the Gift Aid arrangements. Charities are also generally exempt from corporation tax where they operate through a company structure.

VALUE ADDED TAX

Value added tax (VAT) is a tax on consumer expenditure charged when an individual buys goods and services in the European Union including the UK. It is normally included in the sale price of goods and services and paid at the point of purchase. Each EU country has its own rate of VAT. From a business point of view, VAT is charged on most business transactions involving the supply of goods and services by a registered trader in the UK and Isle of Man. It is also charged on goods, and some services, imported from places outside the EU and on goods and some services coming into the UK from the other EU countries. VAT is administered by HM Revenue and Customs. A wide range of information on VAT, including VAT forms, is available online (W www.hmrc.gov.uk). HMRC notice 700: The VAT Guide is the main guide to VAT rules and procedures. HMRC runs a national advice service enquiry line dealing with VAT queries on 0845-010 9000.

RATES OF TAX

There are three rates of VAT in the UK. The standard rate – currently 17.5 per cent – is payable on most goods and services in the UK. The reduced rate – currently 5 per cent – is payable on certain goods and services including, for example, domestic fuel and power, children's car seats, women's sanitary products, contraceptive products and the installation of energy-saving materials such as wall insulation and solar panels. The 5 per cent rate will also be introduced on 'over the counter' sales of smoking cessation products. It will apply for one year and will take effect alongside the introduction of the ban on smoking in public places in England starting on 1 July 2007. A zero, or nil, rate applies to certain items including, for example, children's clothes, books, newspapers, most food and drink, and drugs and aids for disabled people. There are numerous exceptions to the zero-rated categories however. While most food and drink is zero-rated, items including ice creams, chocolates, sweets, potato crisps and alcoholic drinks are not. Neither are drinks or items sold for consumption in a restaurant or cafe. Takeaway cold items such as sandwiches are zero-rated, while takeaway hot foods like fish and chips are not.

REGISTRATION

All traders, including professional persons and companies, must register for VAT if they are making 'taxable supplies' of a value exceeding stated limits. All goods and services that are VAT-rated are defined as taxable supplies including zero-rated items which must be included when calculating the total value of a trader's taxable supplies – his or her taxable turnover. The limits that govern mandatory registration are amended periodically.

From 1 April 2007, an unregistered trader must register for VAT if:

- at the end of any month the total value of his or her taxable turnover (not just profit) for the past 12 months or less is more than the current VAT threshold of £64,000 – and
- at any time he or she has reasonable grounds to expect that his or her taxable turnover will be more than the current registration threshold of £64,000 in the next thirty days alone

To register for VAT, form VAT 1 must be completed and sent to HMRC within 30 days of any of the above. Traders who do not register at the correct time can be fined. Traders must charge VAT on their taxable supplies from the date they first need to be registered. Traders who only supply zero-rated goods may not have to register for VAT even if their taxable turnover goes above the registration threshold. However, a trader in this position must inform HMRC first and apply to be exempt from registration. A trader whose taxable turnover does not reach the mandatory registration limit may choose to register for VAT voluntarily if what he or she does counts as a business for VAT purposes. This step may be thought advisable to recover input tax (see below) or to compete with other registered traders. Registered traders may submit an application for deregistration if their taxable turnover subsequently falls. An application for deregistration can be made if the taxable turnover for the year beginning on the application date is not expected to exceed £62,000.

INPUT TAX

Registered traders suffer input tax when buying in goods or services for the purposes of their business. It is the VAT that traders pay out to their suppliers on goods and services coming in to their business. Relief can usually be obtained for input tax suffered, either by setting that tax against output tax due or by repayment. Most items of input tax can be relieved in this manner. Where a registered trader makes both exempt supplies and taxable supplies to his customers or clients, there may be some restriction in the amount of input tax that can be recovered.

OUTPUT TAX

When making a taxable supply of goods or services, registered traders must account for output tax, if any, on the value of that supply. Output tax is the term used to describe the VAT on the goods and services that they supply or sell – the VAT on supplies going out of the business and collected from customers on each sale made. Usually the price charged by the registered trader will be increased by adding VAT, but failure to make the required addition will not remove liability to account for output tax. The liability to account for output tax, and also relief for input tax, may be affected where a trader is using a special second-hand goods scheme.

EXEMPT SUPPLIES

VAT is not chargeable on certain goods and services because the law deems them exempt from VAT. These include the provision of burial and cremation facilities, insurance, loans of money, certain types of education and training and some property transactions. The granting of a lease to occupy land or the sale of land will usually comprise an exempt supply, for example, but there are numerous exceptions. Exempt supplies do not enter into the calculation of taxable turnover that governs liability to mandatory registration (*see* above). Such supplies made by a registered trader may, however, limit the amount of input tax that can be relieved. It is for this reason that the exemption may be useful.

COLLECTION OF TAX

Registered traders submit VAT returns for accounting periods usually of three months in duration, but arrangements can be made to submit returns on a monthly basis. Very large traders must account for tax on a monthly basis, but this does not affect the three-monthly return. The return will show both the output tax due for supplies made by the trader in the accounting period and also the input tax for which relief is claimed. If the output tax exceeds input tax the balance must be remitted with the VAT return. Where input tax suffered exceeds the output tax due, the registered trader may claim recovery of the excess from HMRC.

This basis for collecting tax explains the structure of VAT. Where supplies are made between registered traders the supplier will account for an amount of tax that will usually be identical to the tax recovered by the person to whom the supply is made. However, where the supply is made to a person who is not a registered trader there can be no recovery of input tax, and it is on this person that the final burden of VAT eventually falls. Where goods are acquired by a UK trader from a supplier within the EU, the trader must also account for the tax due on acquisition. There are a number of simplified arrangements to make VAT accounting easier for businesses, particularly small businesses:

Cash accounting
Since April 1 2004, if taxable turnover is under £660,000 a year, the trader has been able to arrange to account to HMRC for VAT on the basis of cash received and paid, rather than the invoice date or time of supply. If a trader opts to use this scheme, he or she has been able to do so until the taxable turnover reaches £825,000. From 1 April 2007 the threshold for the cash accounting scheme has more than doubled to £1.35m.

Annual accounting
If taxable turnover is under £1,350,000 a year, the trader may join the annual accounting scheme and send in just one return a year. Traders in the scheme must make nine interim payments of VAT on account throughout the year, with a final balancing payment accompanying submission of the return. The number of interim payments may be reduced if turnover is small. Once a trader has joined the annual accounting scheme, membership may continue until the annual taxable turnover reaches £1,600,000.

Flat rate scheme
Introduced in the 2002 Budget, this scheme allows small businesses with an annual taxable turnover under £150,000 excluding VAT (£187,500 including VAT) to save on administration by paying VAT as a set flat percentage of their annual turnover instead of accounting internally for VAT on each individual 'in and out'. The percentage rate used is governed by the trade sector into which the business falls. The scheme can no longer be used once VAT-inclusive turnover exceeds £225,000.

Retail schemes
There are special schemes that offer retailers an alternative if it is impractical for them to issue invoices for a large number of supplies direct to the public. These schemes include a provision to claim relief from VAT on bad debts where goods or services are supplied to a customer who does not pay for them.

VAT FACT SUMMARY
from 1 April 2007

Standard rate	17.5%
Reduced rate	5%
Registration (last 12 months or next 30 days)	£64,000
Deregistration (next 12 months under)	£62,000
Cash accounting scheme – up to	£660,000
Flat rate scheme – up to	£150,000*
Annual accounting scheme – up to	£1,350,000

* Excluding VAT

STAMP DUTY

For the majority of people, contact with stamp duty arises when they buy a property. Stamp duty is payable by the buyer as a way of raising revenue for the government based on the purchase price of a property, stocks and shares. This section aims to provide a broad overview of stamp duty as it may affect the average person.

STAMP DUTY LAND TAX

Stamp duty land tax was introduced on 1 December 2003 and covers the purchase of houses, flats and other land, buildings and certain leases in the UK.

Before 1 December 2003 property purchasers had to submit documents providing all details of the purchase to the Stamp Office for 'stamping'. The purchaser's solicitor or licensed conveyancer would then send the stamped documentation to the appropriate land registry to register ownership of the property. Under stamp duty land tax, purchasers do not have to send documents for stamping. Instead, a land transaction return form SDLT1, which contains all information regarding the purchase that is relevant to HMRC, is signed by the purchaser. Buyers of property are responsible for completing the land transaction return and payment of stamp duty, though the solicitor or licensed conveyancer acting for them in a land transaction will normally complete the relevant paperwork. Once HMRC has received the completed land transaction return and the payment of any stamp duty due, a certificate will be issued that enables a solicitor or licensed conveyancer to register the property in the new owner's name at the Land Registry.

RATES OF STAMP DUTY LAND TAX

The following table shows the rates of stamp duty that apply on a property purchase price. A change in 2005, welcomed by many first-time buyers, was the doubling of the threshold from £60,000 to £120,000, below which no stamp duty is payable on residential property purchases. The new threshold took effect from 17 March 2005. This was increased again to £125,000 from 23 March 2006:

Purchase price	Rate of tax (% of purchase price)
£125,000 or less*	0%
£125,001 to £250,000	1%
£250,001 to £500,000	3%
£500,001 or more	4%

* For transactions of non-residential land and property, the zero per cent rate applies for purchases of up to £150,000. A 1 per cent rate is payable for transactions of £150,001–£250,000; thereafter, rates are as per residential property transactions. The zero per cent band for residential property transactions in certain designated disadvantaged areas is £150,000. A full list of these areas can be found at www.hmrc.gov.uk

When assessing how much stamp duty is payable, the entire purchase price must be taken into account so the relevant stamp duty rate is paid on the whole sum, not just on the amount over each tax threshold. For example, on a property bought for £250,000, 1 per cent – £2,500 – is payable in stamp duty. On a property bought for £250,001, however, 3 per cent of the whole price – £7,500 – is payable.

RELIEF FOR NEW ZERO CARBON HOMES
A new relief from stamp duty land tax was to be introduced on 1 October 2007 for the vast majority of new 'zero carbon' homes in the UK. The relief will be time limited for five years and will therefore expire on 30 September 2012. Qualifying criteria for the relief will require zero carbon emissions from all energy use in the home over a year. To achieve this, the fabric of the home will be required to reach a very high energy efficiency standard and to be able to provide onsite renewable heat and power. New homes which are liable to stamp duty land tax on the first will be eligible to qualify. The relief will provide complete removal of stamp duty liabilities for all homes up to a purchase price of £500,000. Where the purchase price is in excess of £500,000 then the stamp duty liability will be reduced by £15,000. The balance of the stamp duty will be due in the normal way. Relief will not be available on second and subsequent sales of new zero carbon homes.

FIXTURES AND CHATTELS
As well as buying a property a purchaser may buy items inside the property. Some things inside a property are, in law, part of the land. These are called fixtures. Examples are fitted kitchen units and bathroom suites. Because these fixtures are part of the land, any price paid for them must be taken into account for stamp duty purposes. Other items inside a property are not part of the land. These are called chattels. Examples are free-standing cookers, curtains and fitted carpets. The purchase of chattels is not chargeable to stamp duty. However, where both a property and chattels are purchased, the amount shown on the land transaction return as the purchase price of the property must be a just and reasonable apportionment of the total amount paid. As with other entries on the form, the purchaser is responsible for the accuracy of this information. HMRC pays especial attention to residential property purchases just below stamp duty thresholds to prevent arrangements between buyer and seller to hand over cash so that the purchase price on paper looks lower or to pay unreasonably high amounts to buy chattels.

STAMP DUTY RESERVE TAX
Stamp duty or stamp duty reserve tax (SDRT) is payable at the rate of 0.5 per cent when shares are purchased. Stamp duty is payable when the shares are transferred using a stock transfer form, whereas SDRT is payable on paperless share transactions where the shares are transferred electronically without using a stock transfer form. Most share transactions nowadays are paperless and settled by stockbrokers through CREST (the electronic settlement and registration system). SDRT therefore now accounts for the majority of taxation collected on share transactions effected through the London Stock Exchange.

The flat rate of 0.5 per cent is based on the amount paid for the shares, not what they are worth. If, for example, shares are bought for £1,000, £5 SDRT is payable, whatever the value of the shares themselves. If shares are transferred for free, no SDRT is payable.

A higher rate of 1.5 per cent is payable if shares are transferred into a depositary receipt scheme or a clearance service. These are special arrangements where the shares are held by a third party.

CREST automatically deducts the SDRT and sends it to the HMRC. A stockbroker will settle up with CREST for the cost of the shares and the SDRT and then bill the purchaser for these and the broker's fees. If shares are not purchased through CREST, the stamp duty must be paid by the purchaser to HMRC.

UK stamp duty or SDRT is not payable on the purchase of foreign shares, though there may be foreign taxes to pay. SDRT is already accounted for in the price paid for units in unit trusts or shares in open-ended investment companies.

HELP AND INFORMATION
Further information on stamp duty land tax is available via the stamp taxes helpline on 0845-603 0135 (open 8.30am to 5.00pm Monday to Friday) or the HMRC website at www.hmrc.gov.uk, where a stamp duty calculator for both shares and land and property can be found. For buyers wishing to undertake their own conveyancing, copies of the land transaction return (SDLT1) and guidance notes (SDLT6) can be obtained by calling 0845-302 1472.

LEGAL NOTES

These notes outline certain aspects of the law as they might affect the average person. They are intended only as a broad guideline and are by no means definitive. The law is constantly changing so expert advice should always be taken. In some cases, sources of further information are given in these notes.

It is always advisable to consult a solicitor without delay. Anyone who does not have a solicitor already can contact the following for assistance in finding one: Citizens Advice Bureau (W www.nacab.org.uk), the Community Legal Service (W www.legalservices.gov.uk), the Law Society of England and Wales For assistance in Scotland, contact the Scottish Citizens Advice Bureau (W www.cas.org.uk) or the Law Society of Scotland.

The community legal service fund and legal aid and assistance schemes exist to make the help of a lawyer available to those who would not otherwise be able to afford one. Entitlement depends on an individual's means but a solicitor or Citizens Advice Bureau will be able to advise about entitlement.

LAW SOCIETY OF ENGLAND AND WALES
113 Chancery Lane, London WC2A 1PL **T** 020-7242 1222 **W** www.lawsociety.co.uk

LAW SOCIETY OF SCOTLAND
26 Drumsheugh Gardens, Edinburgh EH3 7YR **T** 0131-1226 7411 **W** www.lawscot.org.uk

ABORTION

Abortion is governed by the Abortion Act 1967. This act is currently under review by the Common Select Committee on science and technology. The provisions below are accurate at the time of writing.

Under the provisions of the Abortion Act 1967, a legally induced abortion must be:
- performed by a registered medical practitioner
- carried out in an NHS hospital or other approved premises
- certified by two registered medical practitioners as justified on one or more of the following grounds:
(a) that the pregnancy has not exceeded its twenty-fourth week and that the continuance of the pregnancy would involve risk, greater than if the pregnancy were terminated, of injury to the physical or mental health of the pregnant woman or any existing children of her family
(b) that the termination is necessary to prevent grave permanent injury to the physical or mental health of the pregnant woman
(c) that the continuance of the pregnancy would involve risk to the life of the pregnant woman, greater than if the pregnancy were terminated
(d) that there is a substantial risk that if the child were born it would suffer from such physical or mental abnormalities as to be seriously handicapped.
In determining whether the continuance of a pregnancy would involve such risk of injury to health as is mentioned in grounds (a) or (b), account may be taken of the pregnant woman's actual or reasonably foreseeable environment.

The requirements relating to the opinion of two registered medical practitioners and to the performance of the abortion at an NHS hospital or other approved place cease to apply in circumstances where a registered medical practitioner is of the opinion, formed in good faith, that a termination is immediately necessary to save the life, or to prevent grave permanent injury to the physical or mental health, of the pregnant woman.

Further information and advice can be obtained from:

FAMILY PLANNING ASSOCIATION (UK)
50 Featherstone Street, London EC1Y 8QU **T** 0845 122 8690 **W** www.fpa.org.uk

FAMILY PLANNING ASSOCIATION (SCOTLAND)
Unit 10, Firhill Business Centre, 76 Firhill Road, Glasgow G20 7BA **T** 0141-576 5088 **W** www.fpa.org.uk

BRITISH PREGNANCY ADVISORY SERVICE (BPAS)
T 08457-304030 **W** www.bpas.org

ADOPTION OF CHILDREN

The Adoption and Children Act 2002 reforms the framework for domestic and intercountry adoption in England and Wales and some parts of it extend to Scotland and Northern Ireland.

WHO MAY APPLY FOR AN ADOPTION ORDER
A couple (whether married or two people living as partners in an enduring family relationship) may apply for an adoption order where both of them are over 21 or where one is only 18 but the natural parent and the other is 21. An adoption order may be made for one applicant where that person is 21 and: a) the court is satisfied that person is the partner of a parent of the person to be adopted; or b) they are not married and are not civil partners; or c) married or in a civil partnership but they are separated from their spouse or civil partner and living apart with the separation likely to be permanent; or d) their spouse/civil partner is either unable to be found, or their spouse/civil partner is incapable by reason of ill-health of making an application. There are certain qualifying conditions an applicant must meet eg residency in the British Isles.

ARRANGING AN ADOPTION
Adoptions may generally only be arranged by an adoption agency or by way of an order from the high court; breach of the restrictions on who may arrange an adoption would constitute a criminal offence. When deciding whether a child should be placed for adoption, the court or adoption agency must consider all the factors set out in the 'welfare checklist'. These factors include amongst other things the child's wishes, needs and any harm which the child has suffered or is likely to suffer, and the interest of the child is paramount. The parents must consent to the adoption, although the need for consent can be dispensed with by the court.

ADOPTION ORDER

Once an adoption has been arranged, a court order is necessary to make it legal; this may be obtained from the high court, county court or magistrates court (including family proceedings court). An adoption order may not be given unless the court is either satisfied that the consent of the child's natural parents (or guardians) has correctly been given or that consent should be dispensed with, eg where the parent or guardian cannot be found or is incapable of giving consent or where the welfare of the child so demands.

An adoption order has the effect of extinguishing the parental responsibility that a person other than the adopters (or adopter) has for the child, although where an order is made on the application of the partner of the parent, that parent keeps parental responsibility. This means that once adopted the child has the same status as a child born to the adoptive parents and will be treated as such for the purposes of intestate succession, National Insurance, child benefit etc. In addition the child may lose rights to the estates of those losing their parental responsibility.

REGISTRATION AND CERTIFICATES

All adoption orders made in England and Wales are required to be registered in the Adopted Children Register which also contains particulars of children adopted under registrable foreign adoptions. The General Register Office keeps this register from which certificates may be obtained in a similar way to birth certificates. The General Register Office also has equivalents in Scotland and Northern Ireland.

TRACING NATURAL PARENTS OR CHILDREN WHO HAVE BEEN ADOPTED

An adult adopted person may apply to the Registrar-General to obtain a certified copy of his/her birth certificate. For those adopted before 12 November 1975 it is obligatory to receive counselling services before this information is given. In any event, adoption agencies and adoption support agencies should provide services to adopted persons to assist them in obtaining information about their adoption and facilitate contact with their relatives. There is an Adoption Contact Register which provides a safe and confidential way for birth parents and other relatives to assure an adopted person that contact would be welcome. The BAAF (*see* below) can provide addresses of organisations which offer advice, information and counselling to adopted people, adoptive parents and people who have had their children adopted. Further information can be obtained from:

BRITISH ASSOCIATION FOR ADOPTION AND
FOSTERING (BAAF)
Saffron House, 6–10 Kirkby Street, London EC1N 8TS
T 020-7421 2600 W www.baaf.org.uk

SCOTLAND

The relevant legislation is the Adoption (Scotland) Act 1978 (as amended by the Children Act 1995 and the Adoption and Children (Scotland) Act 2007) and the provisions are similar to those described above. In Scotland, petitions for adoption are made to the sheriff court or the court of session.

Further information can be obtained from:

BRITISH ASSOCIATION FOR ADOPTION AND
FOSTERING (BAAF)
BAAF Scottish Centre, 40 Shandwick Place, Edinburgh EH2 4RT
T 0131-220 4749

SCOTTISH ADOPTION ADVICE SERVICE
Suite 5/3, Skypark SP5, 45 Finnieston Street, Glasgow G3 8JU
T 0141-248 7530

BIRTHS (REGISTRATION)

It is the duty of the parents of a child born in England or Wales to register the birth within 42 days of the date of birth at the register office in the district in which the baby was born. If it is inconvenient to go to the district where the birth took place, the information for the registration may be given to a registrar in another district. Failure to register the birth within 42 days without reasonable cause may leave the parents liable to a penalty. If a birth has not been registered within 12 months of its occurrence it is possible for the late registration of the birth to be authorised by the Registrar-General, provided certain requirements can be met.

If the parents of the child were married to each other at the time of the birth (or conception), either parent may register the birth. If the parents were not married to each other at the time of the child's birth (or conception), the father's particulars may be entered in the register only where he attends the register office with the mother and they sign the birth register together. Where an unmarried parent is unable to attend the register office either parent may submit to the registrar a statutory declaration acknowledging the father's paternity (this form may be obtained from any registrar in England or Wales); alternatively a parental responsibility agreement or appropriate court order may be produced to the registrar.

If the parents do not register the birth of their child the following people may do so:
- the occupier of the house or hospital where the child was born
- a person who was present at the birth
- a person who is responsible for the child

Upon registration of the birth a short certificate is issued.

BIRTHS ABROAD

There are certain countries where birth registrations may be made for British subjects overseas. The British consul or high commission may register the births and issue certificates which are then sent to the General Register Office. If a birth is registered by the British consul or high commission, the registration would show the person's claim to British citizenship, British dependent territories citizenship or British overseas citizenship.

SCOTLAND

In Scotland the birth of a child must be registered within 21 days at the register office of either the district in which the baby was born or the district in which the mother was resident at the time of the birth.

If the child is born, either in or out of Scotland, on a ship, aircraft or land vehicle that ends its journey at any place in Scotland, the child, in most cases, will be registered as if born in that place.

CERTIFICATES OF BIRTHS, DEATHS OR MARRIAGES

Certificates of births, deaths or marriages that have taken place in England and Wales since 1837 can be obtained from the General Register Office or the Family Records Centre.

Certificates of births, marriages and deaths may be obtained in any of the following ways:
- by a personal visit to the Family Records Centre
- by post, telephone, fax or online (details of which may be obtained by calling T 0845-603 7788 or visiting W www.gro.gov.uk)
- locally from the register office where the event was originally registered

Marriage or death certificates may be obtained from the minister of the church in which the marriage or funeral took place. Any register office can advise about the best way to obtain certificates.

The fees for certificates are:

By personal application:
- full certificate of birth, marriage, death or adoption, £7.00
- short certificate of birth, £7.00
- short certificate of adoption, £5.50

By postal/phone/fax application:
- full certificate of birth, marriage, death or adoption, £11.50
- full certificate of birth, marriage, death or adoption with GRO reference supplied, £8.50
- short certificate of birth, £11.50
- short certificate of adoption, £10.00
- extra copies of the same birth, marriage or death certificate issued at the same time, £7.00

A priority service is also available with certificates despatched on the working day following receipt of your application at an additional cost. Visit W www.gro.gov.uk or call T 0845-603 7788 for further information.

Indexes prepared from the registers are available for searching by the public at the Family Records Centre in London or at a Superintendent Registrar's Office; indexes at the latter relate only to births, deaths and marriages which occurred in that registration district. There is no charge for searching the indexes in the Public Search Room at the Family Records Centre but a general search fee is charged for searches at a Superintendent Registrar's Office. A fee is charged for verifying index references against the records.

The Society of Genealogists has many records of baptisms, marriages and deaths prior to 1837.

SCOTLAND

Certificates of births, deaths or marriages that have taken place in Scotland since 1855 can be obtained from the General Register Office for Scotland or from the appropriate local registrar. The General Register Office for Scotland also keeps the Register of Divorces (including decrees of declaration of nullity of marriage), and holds parish registers dating from before 1855.

Fee for each particular search is:
- personal application: £3.00
- postal, telephone or fax order: £5.00
- internet order: £6.00

Document fee for each extract or abbreviated certificate of birth, death, marriage or adoption:
- personal application: £8.00
- postal, telephone or fax order: £8.00
- internet order: £10.00

A priority service for a response within 24 hours is available for an additional fee of £10.00

General search in the indexes to the statutory registers and parochial registers, per day or part thereof:
- full day (ie 9am to 4.30pm) search, £17.00
- afternoon (ie 1pm to 4.30pm) search, £10.00
- one-week search, £65.00
- four-week search, £220.00
- one-quarter search, £500.00
- one-year search, £1,500.00

Online searching is also available. For more information, visit W www.scotlandspeople.gov.uk Further information can be obtained from:

THE GENERAL REGISTER OFFICE
General Register Office, Trafalgar Road, Southport PR8 2HH
T 0845-603 7788 W www.gro.gov.uk

FAMILY RECORDS CENTRE
1 Myddelton Street, London EC1R 1UW

THE GENERAL REGISTER OFFICE FOR SCOTLAND
New Register House, 3 West Register Street, Edinburgh EH1 3YT
T 0131-334 0380 W www.gro-scotland.gov.uk

THE SOCIETY OF GENEALOGISTS
14 Charterhouse Buildings, Goswell Road, London EC1M 7BA
T 020-7251 8799

BRITISH CITIZENSHIP

Almost everyone who was a citizen of the UK and colonies and had a right of abode in the UK prior to the British Nationality Act 1981 became British citizens when the act came into force. British citizens have the right to live permanently in the UK and are free to leave and re-enter the UK at any time.

A person born on or after 1 January 1983 in the UK (including, for this purpose, the Channel Islands and the Isle of Man) is entitled to British citizenship if he/she falls into one of the following categories:
- he/she has a parent who is a British citizen
- he/she has a parent who is settled in the UK
- he/she is a newborn infant found abandoned in the UK
- his/her parents subsequently settle in the UK or become British citizens and an application is made before he/she is 18
- he/she lives in the UK for the first ten years of his/her life and is not absent for more than 90 days in each of those years
- he/she is adopted in the UK and one of the adopters is a British citizen
- if he/she has always been stateless and lives in the UK for a period of five years before his/her 22nd birthday

A person born outside the UK may acquire British citizenship if he/she falls into one of the following categories:
- he/she has a parent who is a British citizen otherwise than by descent, eg a parent who was born in the UK
- he/she has a parent who is a British citizen serving the crown overseas
- the home secretary consents to his/her registration while he/she is a minor
- he/she is a British dependent territories citizen, a British overseas citizen, a British subject or a British protected person and has been lawfully resident in the UK for five years
- he/she is a British dependent territories citizen who

acquired that citizenship from a connection with Gibraltar

• he/she is adopted or naturalised

Where parents are married, the status of either may confer citizenship on their child. If a child is illegitimate, the status of the mother determines the child's citizenship.

Under the 1981 act, Commonwealth citizens and citizens of the Republic of Ireland were entitled to registration as British citizens before 1 January 1988. In 1985, citizens of the Falkland Islands were granted British citizenship.

Renunciation of British citizenship must be registered with the home secretary and will be revoked if no new citizenship or nationality is acquired within six months. If the renunciation was required in order to retain or acquire another citizenship or nationality, the citizenship may be reacquired once. The secretary of state may deprive a person of a citizenship status if he or she is satisfied that the person has done anything seriously prejudicial to the vital interests of the United Kingdom, or a British overseas territory, unless making the order would have the effect of rendering a person stateless. A person may also be deprived of a citizenship status which results from his registration or naturalisation if the secretary of state is satisfied that the registration or naturalisation was obtained by means of fraud, false representation or concealment of a material fact.

BRITISH DEPENDENT TERRITORIES CITIZENSHIP

Under the 1981 act, this type of citizenship was conferred on citizens of the UK and colonies by birth, naturalisation or registration in British dependent territories. British dependent territories citizens may be entitled to registration as British citizens on completion of five years' legal residence in the UK.

On 1 July 1997 citizens of Hong Kong who did not qualify to register as British citizens under the British Nationality (Hong Kong) Act 1990 lost their British dependent territories citizenship on the handover of sovereignty to China; they may, however, have applied to register as British nationals (overseas).

BRITISH OVERSEAS CITIZENSHIP

Under the 1981 act, as amended by the British Overseas Territories Act 2002, this type of citizenship was conferred on any UK and colonies citizens who did not qualify for British citizenship or citizenship of the British dependent territories. British overseas citizenship may be acquired by the wife, civil partner and minor children of a British overseas citizen in certain circumstances. British overseas citizens may be entitled to registration as British citizens on completion of five years' legal residence in the UK.

RESIDUAL CATEGORIES

British subjects, British protected persons and British nationals (overseas) may be entitled to registration as British citizens on completion of five years' legal residence in the UK.

Citizens of the Republic of Ireland who were also British subjects before 1 January 1949 can retain that status if they fulfil certain conditions.

EUROPEAN UNION CITIZENSHIP

British citizens (including Gibraltarians who are registered as such) are also EU citizens and are entitled to travel freely to other EU countries to work, study, reside and set up a business. EU citizens have the same rights with respect to the United Kingdom.

NATURALISATION

Naturalisation is granted at the discretion of the home secretary. The basic requirements are five years' residence (three years if the applicant is married to, or is the civil partner of a British citizen), good character, adequate knowledge of the English, Welsh or Scottish Gaelic language, passing the UK citizenship test and an intention to reside permanently in the UK.

STATUS OF ALIENS

Aliens may not hold public office or vote in Britain and they may not own a British ship or aircraft. Citizens of the Republic of Ireland are not deemed to be aliens. Certain provisions of the Immigration and Asylum Act 1999 make provision about immigration and asylum and about procedures in connection with marriage by superintendent registrar's certificate.

CONSUMER LAW

SALE OF GOODS

A sale of goods contract is the most common type of contract. It is governed by the Sale of Goods Act 1979 (as amended by the Sale and Supply of Goods Act 1994). The act provides protection for buyers by implying terms into every sale of goods contract. These terms include:

• an implied term that the seller will pass good title to the buyer (unless the seller agrees to transfer only such title as he has)

• where the seller sells goods by reference to a description, an implied term that the goods will match that description and, where the sale is by sample and description, it will not be sufficient that the bulk of the goods corresponds with the sample if the goods do not also correspond with the description

• where goods are sold by a business seller, an implied term that the goods will be of satisfactory quality if they meet the standard that a reasonable person would regard as satisfactory, taking into account any description of the goods, the price, and all other relevant circumstances. The quality of the goods includes their state and condition, relevant aspects being whether they are fit for the purposes for which such goods are commonly supplied, their appearance and finish, freedom from minor defects and their safety and durability. This term will not be implied, however, if a buyer has examined the goods and should have noticed the defect or if the seller specifically drew the buyer's attention to the defect

• where goods are sold by a business seller, an implied term that the goods are reasonably fit for any purpose made known to the seller by the buyer (either expressly or by implication), unless it is shown that the buyer does not rely on the seller's judgement, or it is not reasonable for him/her to do so

• where goods are sold by sample, implied terms that the bulk of the sample will correspond with the sample in quality, and that the goods are free from any defect rendering them unsatisfactory which would have been apparent on a reasonable examination of the sample

Some of the above terms can be excluded from contracts by the seller. The seller's right to do this is, however, restricted by the Unfair Contract Terms Act 1977. The act offers more protection to a buyer who 'deals as a consumer', (that is where the seller is selling in the course of a business, the goods are of a type ordinarily bought for private use and the goods are bought by a buyer who is not a business buyer, though not allowing any liability for breach of the implied terms described above to be excluded). In a sale by auction or competitive tender, a buyer never deals as consumer. Also, a seller can never exclude the implied term as to title mentioned above.

HIRE-PURCHASE AGREEMENTS
Terms similar to those implied in contracts of sales of goods are implied into contracts of hire-purchase, under the Supply of Goods (Implied Terms) Act 1973. The 1977 act limits the exclusion of these implied terms as before.

SUPPLY OF GOODS AND SERVICES
Under the Supply of Goods and Services Act 1982, similar terms are also implied in other types of contract under which ownership of goods passes, eg a contract for 'work and materials' such as supplying new parts while servicing a car, and contracts for the hire of goods (though not hire-purchase agreements). These types of contracts have additional implied terms:
- that the supplier will use reasonable care and skill in carrying out the service
- that the supplier will carry out the service in a reasonable time (unless the time has been agreed)
- that the supplier will make a reasonable charge (unless the charge has already been agreed)

The 1977 act limits the exclusion of these implied terms in a similar manner as before.

UNFAIR TERMS
The Unfair Terms in Consumer Contracts Regulations 1999 apply to contracts between business sellers (or suppliers of goods and services) and consumers. Where the terms have not been individually negotiated, ie where the terms were drafted in advance so that the consumer was unable to influence those terms, there will be an unfair term where a term operates to the detriment of the consumer (ie carries a significant imbalance in the parties' rights and obligations arising under the contract). An unfair term does not bind the consumer but the contract will continue to bind the parties if it is capable of existing without the unfair term. The regulations contain a non-exhaustive list of terms which are regarded as unfair. Whether a term is regarded as fair or not will depend on many factors, including the nature of the goods or services, the surrounding circumstances (such as the bargaining strength of both parties) and the other terms in the contract.

TRADE DESCRIPTIONS
It is a criminal offence under the Trade Descriptions Act 1968 for a business seller to apply a false trade description of goods or to supply or offer to supply any goods to which a false description has been applied. A 'trade description' includes descriptions of quality, size, composition, fitness for purpose, performance, method of manufacture, and place and date of manufacture of the goods.

FAIR TRADING
The Fair Trading Act 1973 is designed to protect the consumer. It provides for the appointment of a Director-General of Fair Trading, one of whose duties is to review commercial activities in the UK relating to the supply of goods and services to consumers. An example of a practice which has been prohibited by a reference made under this act is that of business sellers posing in advertisements as private sellers.

CONSUMER PROTECTION
Under the Consumer Protection Act 1987, producers of goods are liable for any injury or for any damage exceeding £275 caused by a defect in their product (subject to certain defences).

The Consumer Protection (Cancellation of Contracts Concluded Away from Business Premises) Regulations 1987 allow consumers a seven-day period in which to cancel contracts for the supply of goods and services, where the contracts were made during an unsolicited visit by a trader to the consumer's home or workplace. A contract will not be enforceable at all in this situation unless the trader has written to the consumer to notify them of the right to cancel within seven days.

Consumers are also afforded protection under the Consumer Protection (Distance Selling) Regulations 2000 in relation to cancellation periods, for example.

CONSUMER CREDIT
In matters relating to the provision of credit (or the supply of goods on hire or hire-purchase), consumers are also protected by the Consumer Credit Act 1974. Under this act a licence, issued by the Director-General of Fair Trading, is required to conduct a consumer credit or consumer hire business or an ancillary credit business. Any 'fit' person as defined within the act may apply to the Director-General of Fair Trading for a licence, which is normally renewable after five years. A licence is not necessary if only exempt agreements are involved. The provisions of the act only apply to 'regulated' agreements, ie those that are with individuals or partnerships, those that are not exempt (certain local authority and building society loans will be exempt), and those where the total credit does not exceed £25,000. Provisions include:
- the terms of the regulated agreement can be altered by the creditor, provided the agreement gives him/her the right to do so; in such cases the debtor must be given proper notice of this
- in order for a creditor to enforce a regulated agreement, the agreement must comply with certain formalities and must be properly executed. The debtor must also be given specified information by the creditor or his/her broker or agent during the negotiations which take place before the signing of the agreement. The agreement must state certain information such as the amount of credit, the annual interest rate, and the amount and timing of repayments
- if an agreement is signed other than at the creditor's (or credit broker's or negotiator's) place of business and oral representations were made in the debtor's presence during discussions pre-agreement, the debtor has a right to cancel the agreement. Time for cancellation expires five clear days after the debtor receives a second copy of the agreement. The agreement must inform the debtor of his right to cancel and how to cancel
- if the debtor is in arrears (or otherwise in breach of the agreement), the creditor must serve a default notice before taking any action such as repossessing the goods
- if the agreement is a hire-purchase or conditional sale agreement, the creditor cannot repossess the goods without a court order if the debtor has paid one third of the total price of the goods
- in agreements where the debtor is required to make grossly exorbitant payments or where the agreement grossly contravenes the ordinary principles of fair

trading, the debtor may request that the court alter or set aside some of the terms of the agreement. The agreement can also be reopened during enforcement proceedings by the court itself

Where a credit reference agency has been used to check the debtor's financial standing, the creditor must give the agency's name to the debtor, who is entitled to see the agency's file on him. A fee of £1 is payable to the agency.

SCOTLAND

The legislation governing the sale and supply of goods applies to Scotland as follows:

- the Sale of Goods Act 1979 applies with some modifications and it has been amended by the Sale and Supply of Goods Act 1994
- the Supply of Goods (Implied Terms) Act 1973 applies
- the Supply of Goods and Services Act 1982 does not extend to Scotland but some of its provisions were introduced by the Sale and Supply of Goods Act 1994
- only Parts II and III of the Unfair Contract Terms Act 1977 apply
- the Trade Descriptions Act 1968 applies with minor modifications
- the Consumer Credit Act 1974 applies
- the Consumer Protection Act 1987 applies
- the General Product Safety Regulations 2005 apply
- the Unfair Terms in Consumer Contracts Regulations 1999 apply
- the Unfair Terms in Consumer Contracts (Amendment) Regulations 2001 apply
- the Consumer Protection (Distance Selling) Regulations 2000 apply
- the Sale and Supply of Goods to Consumers Regulations 2002 apply

PROCEEDINGS AGAINST THE CROWN

Until 1947, proceedings against the crown were generally possible only by a procedure known as a petition of right, which put the litigant at a considerable disadvantage. The Crown Proceedings Act 1947 placed the crown (not the sovereign in his/her private capacity, but as the embodiment of the state) largely in the same position as a private individual. The act did not however, extinguish or limit the crown's prerogative or statutory powers, and it granted immunity to HM ships and aircraft. It also left certain crown privileges unaffected. The act largely abolished the special procedures which previously applied to civil proceedings by and against the crown. Civil proceedings may be instituted against the appropriate government department or if there is doubt regarding which is the appropriate department, then against the attorney-general.

In Scotland proceedings against the crown founded on breach of contract could be taken before the 1947 act and no special procedures applied. The crown could, however, claim certain special pleas. The 1947 act applies in part to Scotland and brings the practice of the two countries as closely together as the different legal systems permit. As a result of the Scotland Act 1998 actions against government departments should be raised against the Lord Advocate or the advocate-general. Actions should be raised against the Lord Advocate where the department involved administers a devolved matter. Devolved matters include agriculture, education, housing, local government, health and justice. Actions should be raised against the advocate-general where the department is dealing with a reserved matter. Reserved matters include defence, foreign affairs and social security.

DEATHS

WHEN A DEATH OCCURS

If the death (including stillbirth) was expected, the doctor who attended the deceased during their final illness should be contacted. If the death was sudden or unexpected, the family doctor (if known) and police should be contacted. If the cause of death is quite clear the doctor will provide:

- a medical certificate that shows the cause of death
- a formal notice that states that the doctor has signed the medical certificate and that explains how to get the death registered

If the death was known to be caused by a natural illness but the doctor wishes to know more about the cause of death, he/she may ask the relatives for permission to carry out a post–mortem examination.

In England and Wales a coroner is responsible for investigating deaths occurring in the following circumstances:

- where there is no doctor who can issue a medical certificate of cause of death
- when no doctor has treated the deceased during his or her last illness or when the doctor attending the patient did not see him or her within 14 days before death, or after death
- when the death occurred during an operation or before recovery from the effect of an anaesthetic
- when the death was sudden and unexplained or attended by suspicious circumstances
- when the death might be due to an industrial injury or disease, or to accident, violence, neglect or abortion, attended by suspicious circumstances
- the death occurred in prison or in police custody

The doctor will write on the formal notice that the death has been referred to the coroner; if the post-mortem shows that death was due to natural causes, the coroner may issue a notification which gives the cause of death so that the death can be registered. If the cause of death was violent or unnatural, the coroner is obliged to hold an inquest.

In Scotland the office of coroner does not exist. The local procurator fiscal inquires into sudden or suspicious deaths. A fatal accident inquiry will be held before the sheriff where the death has resulted from an accident during the course of the employment of the person who has died, or where the person who has died was in legal custody, or where the Lord Advocate deems it in the public interest that an inquiry be held.

REGISTERING A DEATH

In England and Wales the death must be registered by the registrar of births and deaths for the district in which it occurred; details can be obtained from the doctor or local council, or at a post office or police station. From April 1997, information concerning a death can be given before any registrar of births and deaths in England and Wales. The registrar will pass the relevant details to the registrar for the district where the death occurred, who will then register the death.

In England and Wales the death must normally be registered within five days; in Scotland it must be registered within eight days. If the death has been referred to the coroner/local procurator fiscal it cannot be registered until the registrar has received authority from the coroner/local procurator fiscal to do so. Failure to register a death involves a penalty in England and Wales and may lead to a court decree being granted by a sheriff in Scotland.

If the death occurred at a house or hospital, the death may be registered by:
- any relative of the deceased
- any person present at the death
- the occupier or any inmate of the house or hospital if he/she knew of the occurrence of the death
- any person making the funeral arrangements
- in Scotland, the deceased's executor or legal representative

For deaths that took place elsewhere, the death may be registered by:
- any relative of the deceased
- someone present at the death
- someone who found the body
- a person in charge of the body
- any person making the funeral arrangements

The majority of deaths are registered by a relative of the deceased. The registrar would normally allow one of the other listed persons to register the death only if there were no relatives available.

The person registering the death should take the medical certificate of the cause of death with them; it is also useful, though not essential, to take the deceased's birth and marriage certificates, NHS medical card (if possible), pension documents and life assurance details. The details given to the registrar must be absolutely correct, otherwise it may be difficult to change them later. The person registering the death should check the entry very carefully before it is signed. The registrar will issue a certificate for burial or cremation and a certificate of registration of death; both are free of charge. A death certificate is a certified copy of the entry in the death register; these can be provided on payment of a fee and may be required for the following purposes:
- the will
- bank and building society accounts
- savings bank certificates and premium bonds
- insurance policies
- pension claims
- certificate for applicable Social Security Benefits

If the death occurred abroad or on a foreign ship or aircraft, the death should be registered according to the local regulations of the relevant country and a death certificate should be obtained. The death can also be registered with the British consul in that country and a record will be kept at the General Register Office. This avoids the expense of bringing the body back.

After 12 months (three months in Scotland) of death or the finding of a dead body, no death can be registered without the consent of the registrar-general.

BURIAL AND CREMATION

In most circumstances in England and Wales a certificate for burial or cremation must be obtained from the registrar before the burial or cremation can take place. If the death has been referred to the coroner, an order for burial or a certificate for cremation must be obtained. In Scotland a body may be buried (but not cremated) before the death is registered.

Funeral costs can normally be repaid out of the deceased's estate and will be given priority over any other claims. If the deceased has left a will it may contain directions concerning the funeral; however, these directions need not be followed by the executor.

The deceased's papers should also indicate whether a grave space had already been arranged. This information will be contained in a document known as a 'Deed of Grant'. Most town churchyards and many suburban churchyards are no longer open for burial because they are full. Most cemeteries are non-denominational and may be owned by local authorities or private companies; fees vary.

If the body is to be cremated, an application form, two cremation certificates (for which there is a charge) or a certificate for cremation if the death was referred to the coroner, and a certificate signed by the medical referee must be completed in addition to the certificate for burial or cremation (the form is not required if the coroner has issued a certificate for cremation). All the forms are available from the funeral director or crematorium. Most crematoria are run by local authorities; the fees usually include the medical referee's fee and the use of the chapel. Ashes may be scattered, buried in a churchyard or cemetery, or kept.

The registrar must be notified of the date, place and means of disposal of the body within 96 hours (England and Wales) or three days (Scotland).

If the death occurred abroad or on a foreign ship or aircraft, a local burial or cremation may be arranged. If the body is to be brought back to England or Wales, a death certificate from the relevant country or an authorisation for the removal of the body from the country of death from the coroner or relevant authority will be required. To arrange a funeral in England or Wales, an authenticated translation of a foreign death certificate or a death certificate issued in Scotland or Northern Ireland which must show the cause of death, is needed, together with a certificate of no liability to register from the registrar in England and Wales in whose sub-district it is intended to bury or cremate the body. If it is intended to cremate the body, a cremation order will be required from the Home Office or a certificate for cremation.

Further information can be obtained from:

THE GENERAL REGISTER OFFICE
General Register Office, Trafalgar Road, Southport PR8 2HH
T 0845-603 7788 W www.gro.gov.uk

THE GENERAL REGISTER OFFICE FOR SCOTLAND
New Register House, 3 West Register Street, Edinburgh EH1 3YT
T 0131-314 4452

DIVORCE AND RELATED MATTERS

There are three types of matrimonial suit: annulment of marriage, judicial separation and divorce. To obtain an annulment, judicial separation or divorce in England and Wales (provided a European Union court (except Denmark) has jurisdiction) the one commencing the proceedings (the petitioner) and the one defending the proceedings (the respondent) must be habitually resident in England and Wales; or the petitioner and the respondent must have last been habitually resident in England and Wales and one of them must continue to reside there; or the respondent must be habitually resident in England and Wales; or the petitioner must have been habitually resident in England and Wales throughout the period of at least one year ending with the start of proceedings; or the petitioner must be domiciled in England and Wales and must have been habitually resident in England and Wales throughout the period of at least six months, ending with the start of the proceedings; or both parties must be domiciled in England and Wales. If no European Union court (except Denmark) has jurisdiction, one or both parties must be domiciled in England and Wales. All cases are commenced in a divorce county court or in the Principal Registry in London. If a suit is defended, it may be transferred to the high court.

NULLITY OF MARRIAGE

Various circumstances have the potential to render a marriage void or voidable in nullity proceedings including: if there has been wilful non-consummation of the marriage; one partner has a venereal disease at the time of the marriage and the other did not know about it; the female partner was pregnant at the time of the marriage with another person's child and the male partner did not know of the pregnancy; the parties were within prohibited degrees of consanguinity, affinity or adoption; the parties were not male and female; either of the parties was already married or had entered a civil partnership; either of the parties was under the age of 16; the formalities of the marriage were defective, eg the marriage did not take place in an authorised building and both parties knew of the defect.

SEPARATION

A couple may enter into a private agreement to separate by consent without getting divorced but for the agreement to be valid it must be followed by an immediate separation; a solicitor should be contacted.

Another form of separation is judicial separation. Judicial separation does not dissolve a marriage and it is not necessary to prove that the marriage has irretrievably broken down. Either party can petition for a judicial separation at any time; the grounds listed below as grounds for divorce are also grounds for judicial separation. To petition for judicial separation, the parties do not have to prove that they have been married for 12 months or more.

A financial settlement between spouses in a separation agreement or which accompanies a judicial separation is not binding on the court and will not necessarily be upheld by the court after the commencement of divorce proceedings.

DIVORCE

Neither party can petition for divorce until at least one year after the date of the marriage. The sole ground for divorce is the irretrievable breakdown of the marriage; this must be proved on one or more of the following facts:

- the respondent has committed adultery and the petitioner finds it intolerable to live with him/her; however, the petitioner cannot rely on an act of adultery by the respondent if they have lived together as husband and wife for more than six months after the discovery of the adultery
- the respondent has behaved in such a way that the petitioner cannot reasonably be expected to continue living with him/her
- the respondent has deserted the petitioner for two years immediately before the petition
- the petitioner and the respondent have lived separately for two years immediately before the petition and the respondent consents to the divorce
- the petitioner and the respondent have lived separately for five years immediately before the petition

A total period of less than six months during which the parties have resumed living together is disregarded in determining whether the prescribed period of separation or desertion has been continuous (but may not be included as part of the period of separation).

The Matrimonial Causes Act 1973 requires the solicitor for the petitioner to certify whether the possibility of a reconciliation has been discussed with the petitioner.

THE DECREE NISI

A decree nisi does not dissolve or annul the marriage, but must be obtained before a divorce or annulment can take place.

Where the suit is undefended, the evidence normally takes the form of a sworn written statement made by the petitioner which is considered by a district judge. If the judge is satisfied that the petitioner has proved the contents of the petition, a date will be set for the pronouncement of the decree nisi in open court: neither party need attend.

If the suit is defended, the petition will be heard in open court with parties giving oral evidence.

THE DECREE ABSOLUTE

The decree nisi is capable of being made absolute on the application of the petitioner six weeks after the decree nisi. If the petitioner does not apply, the respondent must wait for a further three months before application may be made. In exceptional circumstances the granting of the decree absolute may be delayed, for example if matters regarding children are not capable of resolution. A decree absolute is unlikely to be applied for until the financial matters have been resolved. The decree absolute dissolves or annuls the marriage. Where the couple have been married in accordance with Jewish or other religious usages, the court may require them to produce a declaration that they have taken such steps as are required to dissolve the marriage in accordance with those usages before the decree absolute is issued.

MAINTENANCE

Either party may be liable to pay maintenance to a spouse or former spouse. If there are any children of the marriage, both parties have a legal responsibility to support them financially if they can afford to do so.

The courts are responsible for assessing maintenance for a spouse or former spouse, taking into account each party's income and essential outgoings and other aspects of the case. The court also deals with any maintenance for a child that has been treated by the spouses as a child of the family, such as a step-child.

The law relating to child support is currently under review. The intention is to replace the Child Support Agency (CSA) with the Child Maintenance and Enforcement Commission (C-MEC). At the time of writing the CSA is still responsible for assessing the maintenance that non-resident parents shall pay for their natural or adopted children (whether or not a marriage has taken place).

The CSA accepts applications only when all the people involved are habitually resident in the UK; the courts will continue to deal with cases where one of the individuals lives abroad. The CSA deals with all new cases unless it is agreed by the spouses that the court may grant an order for child support (but even in agreed jurisdiction cases one parent may give the other 14 months' notice to have the case dealt with by the CSA).

A formula is used to work out how much child maintenance is payable under CSA jurisdiction. The formula requires the non-resident parent to pay 15 per cent net of post-tax, national insurance and pension contributions for one child, 20 per cent for two and 25 per cent for more than two. An earnings cap of £104,000 net a year applies. The parent with care's income is not taken into account. Deductions are applied for staying contact and for further children in the non-resident parent's household. In court jurisdiction cases, the CSA formula is adopted as a guideline only.

Some cases involving unusual circumstances are treated as special cases and the assessment is modified, and in some cases the court retains jurisdiction (for educational costs and high income cases, for example). Where there is financial need (eg because of disability or continual education) maintenance may be ordered by the court for children even beyond the age of 18.

CSA maintenance is reviewed automatically every two years. Either parent can report a change of circumstances and request a review at any time. An independent complaints examiner for the CSA has been appointed.

If the non-resident parent does not pay CSA maintenance, the CSA may make an order for payments to be deducted directly from his/her salary; if all other methods fail, the CSA may take court action to enforce payment.

OTHER FINANCIAL RELIEF

Unlike in some other jurisdictions, there is no algebraic formula for division of assets on divorce. The courts must exercise their powers so as to achieve an outcome which is fair between the parties. In determining what is 'fair' the court must have regard to all the circumstances of the case, first consideration being given to the welfare of any minor child(ren) of the family. Beyond this, the court must have particular regard to a prescribed list of statutory factors, being:

- the income, earning capacity, property and other financial resources which each of the parties to the marriage has or is likely to have in the foreseeable future, including in the case of earning capacity, any increase in that capacity which it would, in the opinion of the court, be reasonable to expect a party to the marriage to take steps to acquire
- the financial needs, obligations and responsibilities which each of the parties to the marriage has or is likely to have in the foreseeable future
- the standard of living enjoyed by the family before the breakdown of the marriage
- the age of each party to the marriage and the duration of the marriage
- any physical or mental disability of either of the parties to the marriage
- the contribution which each of the parties has made or is likely in the foreseeable future to make to the welfare of the family, including any contribution by looking after the home or caring for the family
- the conduct of each of the parties, if that conduct is such that it would, in the opinion of the court, be inequitable to disregard it
- in the case of proceedings for divorce or nullity of marriage, the value to each of the parties to the marriage of any benefit (for example a pension) which by reason of the dissolution of the marriage that party will lose the chance of acquiring.

The court also has a duty to consider making an order which will settle once and for all the parties financial responsibilities towards each other. This is known as a financial 'clean break'. Where a clean break is not possible, the court will combine provision of capital via a lump sum and/or property adjustment order and/or pension sharing/attachment order with an ongoing income order, known as maintenance (alimony).

Maintenance can be for a 'term' (ie for a limited period only) or it can be for the joint lives of the parties. In some cases, the courts use nominal maintenance to leave a party's income claims open. It is possible for either party to apply to court to vary the amount or duration of the maintenance at a future date.

Prior to 2000, in considering the above factors, the courts considered the 'reasonable financial requirements' of the applicant, usually the wife, and treated this as determinative of the extent of the applicant's award. In the landmark case of *White v White* in 2000 the House of Lords re-evaluated the court's approach to dividing assets on divorce. The law lords enunciated three key principles. Firstly, the outcome has to be as fair as possible in all the circumstances with each party being entitled to a fair share of the available property. Secondly, in seeking to achieve a fair outcome there is no space for discriminating between the breadwinner and the homemaker in their respective roles. Thirdly, having considered all the circumstances of the case, and the statutory checklist, the judge should consider his view against the 'yardstick of equality of division'.

More recently, the law lords have offered further guidance as to how to achieve a fair division of assets on divorce in the cases of *Miller* and *McFarlane*. In determining fairness, the court must now consider three strands or principles, being each party's respective needs, the possibility of compensating the financially weaker party for any 'relationship' generated disadvantage, which will be relevant where one party has given up a career, and 'equal sharing' of family assets, which is applicable as much to short marriages as to long marriages, and which will apply unless there is good reason to the contrary.

In assessing whether there is a good reason to depart from the concept of equal sharing, the court will consider the nature of property and whether the property was acquired during the marriage otherwise than by inheritance or gift, known as matrimonial property, such as the matrimonial home, or other property to which the other spouse has not contributed. Whilst the yardstick of equality will apply to matrimonial assets to give full effect to the sharing entitlement, it will apply less readily to non-matrimonial assets, particularly in short marriages. Additionally, conduct and special contributions will be relevant in assessing whether there should be a departure from equality, but only in exceptional cases, where such conduct or contribution is 'gross and obvious'.

COHABITING COUPLES

Rights of unmarried couples are not the same as for married couples. Agreements, whether express or inferred by conduct, often determine interests in money and property. Reliance upon inferences is problematic. By virtue of this, it is important to consider entering into a contract which establishes how money and property should be divided in the event of a relationship breakdown. These contracts are commonly known as 'separation deeds' or 'cohabitation contracts'. The law relating to cohabiting couples is under review. The Law Commission published its recommendations to parliament at the end of July 2007, which were expected to lead to legislative reform.

CIVIL PARTNERSHIP

The Civil Partnership Act 2004 came into force on 5 December 2005; it has UK-wide status. Same-sex couples, by registering as civil partners, are able to gain legal recognition of their relationship and thereby obtain rights and obligations broadly equivalent to those of married couples. These rights and responsibilities include a duty to provide reasonable maintenance for your civil partner and any children of the family, equitable treatment in respect of life assurance and pension benefits, recognition under intestacy rules and domestic violence protection. In addition, inheritance tax is waived as with married couples and there is a right of succession for tenancy. A civil partnership which has irretrievably broken down may be dissolved by the court on the application of either civil partner. The irretrievable breakdown of the partnership must be proved on one of four facts. These facts are the same as those for divorce (see above), save for a civil partner may not seek dissolution of the partnership on the basis of the other's adultery.

DOMESTIC VIOLENCE
If one spouse has been subjected to violence at the hands of the other, it is possible to obtain a court order very quickly to restrain further violence and if necessary to have the other spouse excluded from the home. Such orders may also relate to unmarried couples and to a range of other relationships including parents and children.

SCOTLAND
Although some provisions are similar to those for England and Wales, there is separate legislation for Scotland covering nullity of marriage, judicial separation, divorce and ancillary matters. The principal legislation in relation to family law in Scotland is the Family Law (Scotland) Act 1985. The Family Law (Scotland) Act 2006 came in to force on 4 May 2006, and introduced reforms to various aspects of Scottish family law. The following is confined to major points on which the law in Scotland differs from that of England and Wales.

An action for judicial separation or divorce may be raised in the court of session; it may also be raised in the sheriff court if either party was resident in the sheriffdom for 40 days immediately before the date of the action or for 40 days ending not more than 40 days before the date of the action. The fee for starting a divorce petition in the sheriff court is £81.

The grounds for raising an action of divorce in Scotland have been subject to reform in terms of the 2006 act. The current grounds for divorce are:
- the defender has committed adultery. When adultery is cited as proof that the marriage has broken down irretrievably, it is not necessary in Scotland to prove that it is also intolerable for the pursuer to live with the defender
- the defender's behaviour is such that the pursuer cannot reasonably be expected to cohabit with the defender
- there has been no cohabitation between the parties for one year prior to the raising of the action for divorce, and the defender consents to the granting of decree of divorce
- there has been no cohabitation between the parties for two years prior to the raising of the action for divorce

The previously available ground of desertion has been abolished by the 2006 act.

A simplified procedure for 'do-it-yourself divorce' was introduced in 1983 for certain divorces. If the action is based on one or two years' separation and will not be opposed, and if there are no children under 16 and no

financial claims, and there is no sign that the applicant's spouse is unable to manage his or her affairs through mental illness or handicap, the applicant can write directly to the local sheriff court or to the court of session for the appropriate forms to enable him or her to proceed. The fee is £62, unless the applicant receives income support, family credit or legal advice and assistance, in which case there is no fee.

Where a divorce action has been raised, it may be sisted or put on hold for a variety of reasons. In all actions for divorce an extract decree, which brings the marriage to an end, will be made available 14 days after the divorce has been granted. Unlike in England, there is no decree nisi, only a final decree of divorce. Parties must ensure that all financial issues have been resolved prior to divorce, as it is not possible to seek further financial provision after divorce has been granted.

FINANCIAL PROVISION
In relation to financial provision on divorce, the first, and most important, principle is fair sharing of the matrimonial property. In terms of Scots law matrimonial property is defined as all property acquired by either spouse from the date of marriage up to the date of separation. Property acquired before the marriage is not deemed to be matrimonial unless it was acquired for use by the parties as a family home or as furniture for that home. Property acquired after the date of separation is not matrimonial property. Any property acquired by either of the parties by way of gift or inheritance during the marriage is excluded and does not form part of the matrimonial property.

When considering whether to make an award of financial provision a court shall also take account of any economic advantage derived by either party to the marriage as a result of contributions, financial or otherwise, by the other, and of any economic disadvantage suffered by either party for the benefit of the other party. The court must also ensure that the economic burden of caring for a child under the age of 16 is shared fairly between the parties.

A court can also consider making an order requiring one party to pay the other party a periodical allowance for a certain period of time following divorce. Such an order may be appropriate in cases where there is insufficient capital to effect a fair sharing of the matrimonial property. Orders for periodical allowance are uncommon, as courts will favour a 'clean break' where possible.

CHILDREN
The court has the power to award a residence order in respect of any children of the marriage or to make an order regulating the child's contact with the non-resident parent. The court will only make such orders if it is deemed better for the child to do so than to make no order at all, and the welfare of the children is of paramount importance. The fact that a spouse has caused the breakdown of the marriage does not in itself preclude him/her from being awarded residence.

NULLITY
An action for 'declaration of nullity' can be brought if someone with a legitimate interest is able to show that the marriage is void or voidable. The action can only be brought in the court of session. Although the grounds on which a marriage may be void or voidable are similar to those on which a marriage can be declared invalid in England, there are some differences. Where a spouse is

capable of sexual intercourse but refuses to consummate the marriage, this is not a ground for nullity in Scots law, though it could be a ground for divorce. Where a spouse was suffering from venereal disease at the time of marriage and the other spouse did not know, this is not a ground for nullity in Scots law, neither is the fact that a wife was pregnant by another man at the time of marriage without the knowledge of her husband.

COHABITING COUPLES

The law in Scotland now provides certain financial and property rights for cohabiting couples in terms of the Family Law (Scotland) Act 2006, or 'the 2006 act'. The relevant 2006 act provisions do not place cohabitants in Scotland on an equal footing with married couples or civil partners, but provide some rights for cohabitants in the event that the relationship is terminated by separation or death. The provisions relate to couples who cease to cohabit after 4 May 2006.

The legislation provides for a presumption that any contents of the home shared by the cohabitants are owned in equal shares. A former cohabitee can also seek financial provision on termination of the relationship in the form of a capital payment if they can successfully demonstrate that they have been financially disadvantaged, and that conversely the other cohabitant has been financially advantaged, as a consequence of contributions made (financial or otherwise).

The 2006 act also provides that a cohabitant may make a claim on their partner's estate in the event of that partner's death, providing that there is no will.

Further information can be obtained from:

THE PRINCIPAL REGISTRY
First Avenue House, 42-49 High Holborn, London WC2V 6NP

THE COURT OF SESSION
Parliament House, Parliament Square, Edinburgh EH1 1RQ
T 0131-225 2595

THE CHILD SUPPORT AGENCY
National Enquiry Line 08457-133133 W www.csa.gov.uk

EMPLOYMENT LAW

PAY AND CONDITIONS

The Employment Rights Act 1996 consolidates the statutory provisions relating to employees' rights. Employers must give each employee employed for one month or more a written statement containing the following information:

- names of employer and employee
- date when employment began and the date on which the employee's period of *continuous* employment began (taking into account any employment with a previous employer which counts towards that period)
- remuneration and intervals at which it will be paid
- job title or description of job
- hours and place(s) of work
- holiday entitlement and holiday pay
- provisions concerning incapacity for work due to sickness and injury, including provisions for sick pay
- details of pension scheme(s)
- length of notice period that employer and employee need to give to terminate employment
- if the employment is not intended to be permanent, the period for which it is expected to continue or, if it is for a fixed term, the end date of the contract

- details of any collective agreement which affects the terms of employment
- details of disciplinary and grievance procedures
- if the employee is to work outside the UK for more than one month, the period of such work and the currency in which payment is made
- a note stating whether a contracting out certificate is in force

This must be given to the employee within two months of the start of their employment. The Working Time Regulations 1998, the National Minimum Wage Act 1998, the Employment Rights (Dispute Resolution) Act 1998 and the Employment Relations Act 1999 now supplement the 1996 act. If the employer does not provide the written statement within two months then the employee can complain to an employment tribunal, which can specify the information that the employer should have given. The Employment Act 2002 provides that when, in the context of an employee's successful tribunal claim, the employer is also found to have been in breach of the duty to provide the written statement at the time proceedings were commenced, the tribunal must award the employee two weeks' pay, and may award four weeks' pay, unless it is unjust or inequitable to do so.

FLEXIBLE WORKING

The Employment Act 2002 (and regulations made under it) gives employees who are responsible for the upbringing of a child the right to apply for a flexible working pattern for the purpose of caring for that child. The right was extended to carers of adults in 2006. If an application under the act is rejected, it is open to the employee to complain to an employment tribunal.

SICK PAY

Employees absent from work through illness or injury are entitled to receive Statutory Sick Pay (SSP) from the employer for a maximum period of 28 weeks in any three-year period. Where average earnings (before deductions such as tax and National Insurance) are £87 a week or more, the standard rate of SSP is £72.55 per week.

MATERNITY AND PARENTAL RIGHTS

Under the Employment Relations Act 1999, the Employment Act 2002 and the Maternity and Parental Leave Regulations 1999 (as amended in 2002 and 2006), both men and women are entitled to take leave when they become a parent. Women are protected from discrimination, detriment or dismissal by reason of their pregnancy. Men are protected from suffering a detriment or dismissal for taking paternity or parental leave.

All women are entitled to a maximum period of maternity leave of 52 weeks. This comprises 26 weeks' ordinary maternity leave, followed immediately by 26 weeks' additional maternity leave. A woman who takes ordinary maternity leave normally has the right to return to the job in which she was employed before her absence. If she takes additional maternity leave, she is entitled to return to the same job or, if that is not reasonably practicable, to another job that is suitable and appropriate for her to do.

A woman will qualify for Statutory Maternity Pay (SMP), which is payable for up to 39 weeks, if she has been continuously employed for not less than 26 weeks at the beginning of the 14th week before the expected week of childbirth. The first six weeks of SMP are paid at 90 per cent of the employee's average weekly earnings, and the remaining 33 weeks are paid at the rate of £122.75

per week, or 90 per cent of weekly earnings, whichever is lower.

Employees are entitled to adoption leave and adoption pay subject to fulfillment of criteria similar (but not identical) to those in relation to maternity leave and pay. Where a couple is adopting a child, one may take adoption leave, and the other may take paternity leave.

Certain employees are entitled to paternity leave on the birth or adoption of a child. To be eligible, the employee must be the child's father, or the partner of the mother or adopter, and meet other conditions. One of those conditions is that they must have been continuously employed for not less than 26 weeks at the beginning of the 14th week before the expected week of childbirth (or, in the case of adoptions, 26 weeks ending with the week in which notification of the adoption match is given). The employee may take either one week's leave, or two consecutive weeks' leave. This leave may be taken at any time between the date of the child's birth (or placement of adoption) and 56 days later. During paternity leave, most employees will be entitled to Statutory Paternity Pay, which is paid at the same rate as the second stage rate of SMP (ie £122.75 per week or 90 per cent of weekly earnings, whichever is lower).

Any employee with one year's service who has, or expects to have, responsibility for a child may take parental leave to care for the child. Each parent is entitled to a total of 13 weeks' parental leave for each of their children (or 18 weeks if the child is disabled) but this leave must be taken (at the rate of no more than four weeks per year, and in blocks of whole weeks only) before the child's fifth birthday (or 18th birthday if the child is disabled).

In May 2007 the government issued a consultation paper on certain proposed modifications to statutory paternity leave and pay. The proposed scheme would allow a father to take some of the mother's statutory maternity leave (and pay) where the mother wants to return to work before the end of her ordinary or additional maternity leave entitlement. At the time of writing the consultation is still underway.

SUNDAY TRADING
The Sunday Trading Act 1994 allows shops to open on Sunday for serving retail customers. The Employment Rights Act 1996 gives shop workers and betting workers the right not to be dismissed, selected for redundancy or to suffer any detriment (such as the denial of overtime, promotion or training) if they refuse to work on Sundays. This does not apply to those who, under their contracts, are employed to work on Sundays.

TERMINATION OF EMPLOYMENT
An employee may be dismissed without notice if guilty of gross misconduct but in other cases a period of notice must be given by the employer. The minimum periods of notice specified in the Employment Rights Act 1996 are:
- one week if the employee has been continuously employed for one month or more but for less than two years
- two weeks if the employee has been continuously employed for at least two years
- a week is added for every additional complete year of continuous employment up to 12 years (making the maximum statutory notice period 12 weeks after 12 years' continuous employment)
- longer periods apply if these are specified in the contract of employment

If an employee is dismissed with less notice than he/she is entitled to by statute, or under their contract if longer, he/she will have a wrongful dismissal claim (unless the employer paid the employee in lieu of notice in accordance with a contractual provision entitling it to do so). This claim for wrongful dismissal can be brought by the employee either in the court system or the employment tribunal, but if brought in the tribunal the maximum amount that can be awarded is £25,000. This claim can also be brought by an employee whose fixed-term contract has been terminated prematurely, and without justification, by the employer.

REDUNDANCY
An employee dismissed because of redundancy may be entitled to redundancy pay. This applies if:
- the employee has at least two years' continuous service
- the employee is dismissed by the employer (this can include cases of voluntary redundancy)
- dismissal is due to redundancy. Redundancy can mean closure of the entire business, closure of a particular site of the business, or a reduction in the need for employees to carry out work of a particular kind (eg as a result of over-manning or a reduction in work).

An employee may not be entitled to a redundancy payment if offered a suitable alternative job by the same employer. The amount of statutory redundancy pay depends on the length of service, age, and their earnings, subject to a weekly maximum of (currently) £310. The maximum payment that can be awarded is £9,300. The redundancy payment is guaranteed by the State in cases where the employer becomes insolvent (subject to the conditions above).

UNFAIR DISMISSAL
Complaints of unfair dismissal are dealt with by an employment tribunal. Any employee with one year's continuous service (subject to exceptions, including in relation to whistleblowers – see below) can make a complaint to the tribunal. At the tribunal, it is for the employer to prove that the dismissal was due to one or more of the following six potentially fair reasons:
- the employee's capability or qualifications for the job he/she was employed to do
- the employee's conduct
- redundancy
- retirement
- a legal restriction preventing the continuation of the employee's contract
- some other substantial reason

If the employer succeeds in showing this, the tribunal must then decide whether the employer acted reasonably in dismissing the employee for that reason. If the employee is found to have been unfairly dismissed, the tribunal can order that he/she be reinstated, re-engaged or compensated. Any person believing that they may have been unfairly dismissed should contact their local Citizens Advice Bureau or seek legal advice. A claim must be brought within three months of the date of termination of employment.

The normal maximum compensatory award for unfair dismissal is £60,600 (as at 1 February 2007). Where an employer has failed to follow the statutory dismissal procedures which came into force on 1 October 2004, the tribunal must usually increase the compensatory award by 10 per cent and it may increase by up to 50 per cent.

WHISTLEBLOWING

Under the whistleblowing legislation (Public Interest Disclosure Act 1998, which inserted provisions into the Employment Rights Act 1996) dismissal of an employee is automatically unfair if the reason or principal reason for the dismissal is that the employee has made a protected disclosure. The legislation also makes it unlawful to subject workers (a broad category that includes employees and certain other individuals, such as agency workers) who have made a protected disclosure to any detriment on the ground that they have done so.

For a disclosure to qualify for protection, the claimant must show that he has disclosed information, which in his reasonable belief tends to show one or more of the following six categories of wrongdoing:

- criminal offences
- breach of any legal obligation
- miscarriages of justice
- danger to the health and safety of any individual
- damage to the environment
- the deliberate concealing of information about any of the above

The malpractices can be past, present, prospective or merely alleged.

A qualifying disclosure will only be protected if the manner of the disclosure fulfills certain conditions, including being made in good faith and being made to a defined category of persons, which varies according to the type of disclosure.

Any whistleblower claim in the employment tribunal must normally be brought within three months of the date of dismissal or other act leading to a detriment.

An individual does not need to have been working with the employer for any particular period of time to be able to bring such a claim and compensation is uncapped (and can include an amount for injury to feelings).

DISCRIMINATION

Discrimination in employment on the grounds of sex (including gender reassignment), sexual orientation, race, colour, nationality, ethnic or national origins, religion or belief, married status, age or (subject to wide exceptions) disability is unlawful. Discrimination legislation generally covers direct discrimination, indirect discrimination, harassment and victimisation. Only in limited circumstances can such discrimination be justified (rendering it lawful).

An individual does not need to be employed for any particular period of time to be able to claim discrimination, and discrimination compensation is uncapped (and can include an amount for injury to feelings). These features distinguish the discrimination laws from, for example, the unfair dismissal laws.

The following legislation applies to those employed in Great Britain but not to employees in Northern Ireland or (subject to EC exceptions) to those who work mainly abroad:

- the Equal Pay Act 1970 (as amended) entitles men and women to equality in matters related to their contracts of employment
- the Sex Discrimination Act 1975 (as amended) makes it unlawful to discriminate on grounds of sex or marital/civil partner status. This covers all aspects of employment (including advertising for recruits, terms offered, opportunities for promotion and training, and dismissal procedures) and protects job applicants, employees and other types of worker, as well as ex-workers

- the Race Relations Act 1976 gives individuals the right not to be discriminated against on the grounds of race, colour, nationality, or ethnic or national origins. It applies to all aspects of employment
- the Disability Discrimination Act 1995 makes discrimination against a disabled person in all aspects of employment unlawful. In certain circumstances, the employer may show that the less favourable treatment is justified. The act also imposes a duty on employers to make 'reasonable adjustments' to the arrangements and physical features of the workplace if these place disabled people at a substantial disadvantage compared with those who are not disabled. The definition of a 'disabled person' is wide and now includes people diagnosed with HIV, cancer and multiple sclerosis. Since early 2007 there has been a new positive duty on public bodies to promote equality of opportunity for disabled people
- the Employment Equality (Religion or Belief) Regulations 2003 make discrimination against a person on the grounds of religion or belief, in all aspects of employment, unlawful
- the Employment Equality (Sexual Orientation) Regulations 2003 make discrimination against an individual on the grounds of sexual orientation, in all aspects of employment, unlawful
- The Employment Equality (Age) Regulations 2006 outlaw age discrimination in the workplace. This legislation is having profound implications for employers' policies and practices and has required major changes to selection procedures, recruitment policies, terms and conditions, benefits, dismissals and retirements

The Equal Opportunities Commission, the Commission for Racial Equality and the Disability Rights Commission (which will soon all be merged into the new Commission for Equality and Human Rights) have, as part of their roles, the function of eliminating such discrimination in the workplace, and can provide further information and assistance.

In Northern Ireland similar provisions exist but are contained in separate legislation (although the Disability Discrimination Act does extend to Northern Ireland).

In Northern Ireland there is one combined body working towards equality and eliminating discrimination, the Equality Commission for Northern Ireland.

WORKING TIME

The Working Time Regulations 1998 impose rules that limit working hours and provide for rest breaks and holidays. The regulations apply to workers and so cover not only employees but also other individuals who undertake to perform personally any work or services (eg freelancers). The regulations are complex and subject to various exceptions and qualifications but the basic provisions relating to adult day workers are as follows:

No worker is permitted to work more than an average of 48 hours per week (unless they opt out of this limit), and a worker is entitled to the following breaks:

- 11 consecutive hours' rest in every 24-hour period
- an uninterrupted rest period of at least 24 hours in each 7 day period (in addition to the daily rest period)
- 20 minutes' rest break provided that the working day is longer than 6 hours
- 4 weeks' paid annual leave (this is to increase to 4.8 weeks (24 days full-time) on 1 October 2007 and 5.6 weeks (28 days full-time) on 1 April 2009). 5.6 weeks equates to 4 weeks plus public holidays

There are specific provisions relating to night work and young workers (ie those over school leaving age but under 18).

HUMAN RIGHTS

On 2 October 2000 the Human Rights Act 1998 came into force. This act incorporates the European Convention on Human Rights into the law of the United Kingdom. The main principles of the act are as follows:

- all legislation must be interpreted and given effect by the courts as compatible with the Convention so far as it is possible to do so. Before the second reading of a new bill the minister responsible for the bill must provide a statement regarding the compatibility of the bill with the Human Rights Act
- subordinate legislation (eg statutory instruments) which are incompatible with the Convention can be struck down by the courts
- primary legislation (eg acts of parliament) which is incompatible with the Convention cannot be struck down by a court, but the higher courts can make a declaration of incompatibility which is a signal to parliament to change the law
- all public authorities (including courts and tribunals) must not act in a way which is incompatible with the Convention
- individuals whose Convention rights have been infringed by a public authority may bring proceedings against that authority, but the act is not intended to create new rights as between individuals

The main human rights protected by the Convention are the right to life (article 2); protection from torture and inhuman or degrading treatment (article 3); protection from slavery or forced labour (article 4); the right to liberty and security of the person (article 5); the right to a fair trial (article 6); the right not to be subject to retrospective criminal offences (article 7); the right to respect for private and family life (article 8); freedom of thought, conscience and religion (article 9); freedom of expression (article 10); freedom of peaceful association and assembly (article 11); the right to marry and found a family (article 12); protection from discrimination (article 14); the right to property (article 1 Protocol No.1); the right to free election (article 3 Protocol No.1); and the right to education (article 2 Protocol No.1). Most of the Convention rights are subject to limitations which deem the breach of the right acceptable on the basis it is 'necessary in a democratic society'.

PARENTAL RESPONSIBILITY

The Children Act 1989 gives the mother parental responsibility for the child. There are different rules for unmarried fathers obtaining parental responsibility depending on whether the child was born before or after 1 December 2003. For babies born after 1 December 2003, unmarried fathers can get parental responsibility by: (a) registering the child's birth jointly with the mother at the time of birth or (b) re-registering the birth if you are the natural father or (c) marrying the mother of their child or (d) by obtaining a parental responsibility order from the court or (e) registering with the court for parental responsibility. The Adoption and Children Act 2002 also makes provision for a father who is not married to the child's mother to acquire parental responsibility for the child if he becomes registered as the child's father. The consent of a father without parental responsibility is not required for adoption. However, adoption agencies and local authorities must be careful to establish if possible the identity of the father, as the father then has an opportunity to apply for parental responsibility within the proceedings.

In Scotland, the relevant legislation is the Children (Scotland) Act 1995, which also gives the mother parental responsibility for her child whether or not she is married to the child's father. A father who is married to the mother, either at the time of the child's conception or subsequently, will also have automatic parental rights. Section 23 of the 2006 act provides that an unmarried father will obtain automatic parental responsibilities and rights if he is registered as the father on the child's birth certificate. For unmarried fathers who are not named on the birth certificate, or whose children were born before the 2006 act came into force, it is possible to acquire parental responsibilities and rights by applying to the court or by entering into a parental responsibilities and rights agreement with the mother. The father of any child, regardless of parental rights, has a duty to aliment that child until he/she is 18 (25 if the child is still in full-time education).

LEGITIMATION

Under the Legitimacy Act 1976, an illegitimate person automatically becomes legitimate when his/her parents marry. This applies even where one of the parents was married to a third person at the time of the birth. In such cases it is necessary to re-register the birth of the child. In Scotland, the status of illegitimacy has finally been abolished by section 21 of the 2006 act. The Law Reform Act 1987 reformed the law so as to remove so far as possible the legal disadvantages of illegitimacy.

JURY SERVICE

In England and Wales a person charged with more serious criminal offences and more complex civil cases is entitled to be tried by jury. No such right exists in Scotland, although more serious offences are heard before a jury. In England and Wales there are 12 members of a jury in a criminal case and eight members in a civil case. In Scotland there are 12 members of a jury in a civil case in the court of session (the civil jury being confined to the court of session and a restricted number of actions), and 15 in a criminal trial in the high court of justiciary. Jurors are normally asked to serve for ten working days, although jurors selected for longer cases are expected to sit for the duration of the trial.

Every 'registered' parliamentary or local government elector between the ages of 18 and 70 who has lived in the UK (including, for this purpose, the Channel Islands and the Isle of Man) for any period of at least five years since reaching the age of 13 is qualified to serve on a jury unless he/she is 'mentally disordered' or disqualified.

Those disqualified from jury service include:

- those who have at any time been sentenced by a court in the UK (including, for this purpose, the Channel Islands and the Isle of Man) to a term of imprisonment or youth custody of five years or more
- those who have been imprisoned or detained for public protection
- those who have within the previous ten years served any part of a sentence of imprisonment, youth custody or detention, been detained in a young offenders' institution, received a suspended sentence of

imprisonment or order for detention, or received a community service order
• those who are on bail in criminal proceedings

The court has the discretion to excuse a juror from service, or defer the date of service, if the juror can show there is good reason why he/she should be excused from attending or good reason why his attendance should be deferred. It is an offence to fail to attend when summoned or to make false representations in an attempt to evade service. The defendant can object to any juror if he/she can show cause.

A juror may claim travelling expenses, a subsistence allowance and an allowance for other financial loss (eg loss of earnings or benefits, fees paid to carers or child-minders) up to a stated limit. It is a contempt of court for a juror to disclose what happened in the jury room even after the trial is over. A jury's verdict need not be unanimous. In criminal proceedings the agreement of ten jurors will suffice (when there are at least 11 jurors remaining). In civil proceedings the agreement of seven jurors will suffice. However the court must be satisfied that the jury had reasonable time to consider its verdict based on the nature and complexity of the case. In criminal proceedings this must be no less than two hours.

SCOTLAND

Qualification criteria for jury service in Scotland are similar to those in England and Wales, except that the maximum age for a juror is 65, members of the judiciary are ineligible for ten years after ceasing to hold their post, and others concerned with the administration of justice are only eligible for service five years after ceasing to hold office. Certain persons who have the right to be excused include full-time members of the medical, dental, nursing, veterinary and pharmaceutical professions, full-time members of the armed forces, ministers of religion, persons who have served on a jury within the previous five years, members of the Scottish parliament, members of the Scottish Executive and junior Scottish ministers. Those convicted of a serious crime are automatically disqualified. Those who are incapable by reason of a mental disorder may also be excused. The maximum fine for a person serving on a jury knowing himself/herself to be ineligible is £1,000. The maximum fine for failing to attend without good cause is also £1,000.

Further information can be obtained from:

THE COURT SERVICE
Southside, 105 Victoria Street, London SW1E 6QT
T 020-7210 2266

SCOTTISH COURTS SERVICE
Courts of Session, Parliament House, Parliament Square,
Edinburgh EH1 1RQ T 0131-225 2595

THE CLERK OF JUSTICIARY
High Court of Justiciary, Lawnmarket, Edinburgh EH2 2NS
T 0131-240 6900

LANDLORD AND TENANT

RESIDENTIAL LETTINGS

The provisions outlined here apply only where the tenant lives in a separate dwelling from the landlord and where the dwelling is the tenant's only or main home. It does not apply to licensees such as lodgers, guests or service occupiers.

The 1996 Housing Act radically changed certain aspects of the legislation referred to below; in particular, the grant of assured and assured shorthold tenancies under the Housing Act 1988.

ASSURED SHORTHOLD TENANCIES

If a tenancy was granted on or after 15 January 1989 and before 28 February 1997, the tenant would have an assured tenancy unless the landlord served notice under section 20 in the prescribed form prior to the commencement of the tenancy, stating that the tenancy is to be an assured shorthold tenancy and the tenancy is for a minimum fixed term period of six months (see below). An assured tenancy gives that tenant greater rights of security. The tenant could, for example, stay in possession of the dwelling for as long as the tenant observed the terms of the tenancy. The landlord cannot obtain possession from such a tenant unless the landlord can establish a specific ground for possession (set out in Housing Act 1988) and obtains a court order. The rent payable is that agreed with the landlord at the start of the tenancy. The landlord has the right to increase the rent annually by serving a notice. If that happens the tenant can apply to have the rent fixed by the rent assessment committee of the local authority. The tenant or the landlord may request that the committee sets the rent in line with open market rents for that type of property.

Under the Housing Act 1996, all new lettings entered into on or after 28 February 1997 (for whatever term) will be assured shorthold tenancies unless the landlord serves a notice stating that the tenancy is not to be an assured shorthold tenancy. This means that the landlord is entitled to possession at the end of the tenancy provided he serves a notice under section 21 Housing Act 1988 and commences the proceedings in accordance with the correct procedure. The landlord must obtain a court order, however, to obtain possession if the tenant refuses to vacate at the end of the tenancy. If the tenancy is an assured shorthold tenancy, the court must grant the order. For both assured and assured shorthold tenancies, if the tenant is more than eight weeks in arrears, the landlord can serve notice and, if the tenant is still in arrears at the date of the hearing, the court must make an order for possession.

REGULATED TENANCIES

Before the Housing Act 1988 came into force (15 January 1989) there were regulated tenancies; some are still in existence and are protected by the Rent Act 1977. Under this act it is possible for the landlord or the tenant to apply to the local rent officer to have a 'fair' rent registered. The fair rent is then the maximum rent payable.

SECURE TENANCIES

Secure tenancies are generally given to tenants of local authorities, housing associations (before 15 January 1989) and certain other bodies. This gives the tenant security of tenure unless the terms of the agreement are broken by the tenant and it is reasonable to make an order for possession. Those with secure tenancies may have the right to buy their property. In practice this right is generally only available to council tenants.

AGRICULTURAL PROPERTY

Tenancies in agricultural properties are governed by the Agricultural Holdings Act 1986, the Agricultural Tenancies Act 1995 (both amended by the Regulatory Reform (Agricultural Tenancies) (England and Wales) Order 2006) and the Rent (Agriculture) Act 1976, which give similar protections to those described above, eg security of tenure, right to compensation for disturbance, etc. The Agricultural Holdings (Scotland) Act 1991 along with Agricultural Holdings (Scotland) Act 2003 apply similar provisions to Scotland.

EVICTION

The Protection from Eviction Act 1977 (as amended by the Housing Act 1988) sets out the procedure a landlord must follow in order to obtain possession of property. It is unlawful for a landlord to evict a tenant otherwise than in accordance with the law. For common law tenancies and for Rent Act tenants a Notice to Quit in the prescribed form giving 28 days is required. For secure and assured tenancies a Notice Seeking Possession must be served. It is unlawful for the landlord to evict a person by putting their belongings onto the street, by changing the locks and so on. It is also unlawful for a landlord to harass a tenant in any way in order to persuade him/her to give up the tenancy. The tenant may be able to obtain an injunction to restrain the actions of the landlord and get back into the property and be awarded damages.

LANDLORD RESPONSIBILITIES

Under the Landlord and Tenant Act 1985, where the term of the lease is less than seven years, the landlord is responsible for maintaining the structure and exterior of the property, for sanitation, for heating and hot water, and all installations for the supply of water, gas and electricity.

LEASEHOLDERS

Strictly speaking, leaseholders have bought a long lease rather than a property and in certain limited circumstances the landlord can end the tenancy. Under the Leasehold Reform Act 1967 (as amended by the Housing Acts 1969, 1974 and 1980), leaseholders of houses may have the right to buy the freehold or to take an extended lease for a term of 50 years. This applies to leases where the term of the lease is over 21 years and where the leaseholder has occupied the house as his/her main residence for the last two years, or for a total of two years over the last ten.

The Leasehold Reform, Housing and Urban Development Act came into force in 1993 and allows the leaseholders of flats in certain circumstances to buy the freehold of the building in which they live.

Responsibility for maintenance of the structure, exterior and interior of the building should be set out in the lease. Usually the upkeep of the interior of his/her part of the property is the responsibility of the leaseholder, and responsibility for the structure, exterior and common interior areas is shared between the freeholder and the leaseholder(s).

If leaseholders are in any way dissatisfied with treatment from their landlord or with charges made in respect of lease extensions, they are entitled to have their situation evaluated by the Leasehold Valuation Tribunal.

The Commonhold and Leasehold Reform Act 2002 makes provision for the freehold estate in land to be registered as commonhold land and for the legal interest in the land to be vested in a 'commonhold association' ie a private limited company.

BUSINESS LETTINGS

The Landlord and Tenant acts 1927 and 1954 (as amended) give security of tenure to the tenants of most business premises. The landlord can only evict the tenant on one of the grounds laid down in the 1954 act, and in some cases where the landlord repossesses the property the tenant may be entitled to compensation.

SCOTLAND

In Scotland assured and short assured tenancies exist for lettings after 2 January 1989 and are similar to assured tenancies in England and Wales. The relevant legislation is the Housing (Scotland) Act 1988.

Most tenancies created before 2 January 1989 were regulated tenancies and the Rent (Scotland) Act 1984 still applies where these exist. The act defines, among other things, the circumstances in which a landlord can increase the rent when improvements are made to the property. The provisions of the Rent Act do not apply to tenancies where the landlord is the Crown, a local authority or a housing corporation.

The Housing (Scotland) Acts of 1987 and 2001 relate to local authority responsibilities for housing, the right to buy, and local authority secured tenancies. The provisions are broadly similar to England and Wales.

In Scotland, business premises are not controlled by statute to the same extent as in England and Wales, although the Tenancy of Shops (Scotland) Act 1949 gives some security to tenants of shops. Tenants of shops can apply to the sheriff, within 21 days of being served a notice to quit, for a renewal of tenancy if threatened with eviction. This application may be dismissed on various grounds including where the landlord has offered to sell the property to the tenant at an agreed price or, in the absence of agreement as to price, at a price fixed by a single arbiter appointed by the parties or the sheriff. The act extends to properties where the Crown or government departments are the landlords or the tenants.

Under the Leases Act 1449 the landlord's successors (either purchasers or creditors) are bound by the agreement made with any tenants so long as the following conditions are met:
- the lease, if for more than one year, must be in writing
- there must be a rent
- there must be a term of expiry
- the tenant must have entered into possession
- the subjects of the lease must be land
- the landlord, if owner, must be the proprietor with a recorded title, ie the title deeds are recorded in the Register of Sasines or registered in the Land Register

The Antisocial Behaviour (Scotland) Act 2001 provides that all landlords letting property in Scotland must register with the local authority in which the let property is situated. It is a criminal offence to fail to do this. Exceptions apply to holiday lets, owner-occupied accommodation and agricultural holdings. The act applies to partnerships, trusts and companies as well as to individuals.

LEGAL AID

The Access to Justice Act 1999 has transformed what used to be known as the Legal Aid system. The Legal Aid Board has been replaced by the Legal Services Commission, which is responsible for the development and administration of two legal funding schemes in England and Wales, namely the Criminal Defence Service and the Community Legal Service fund. The Community Legal Service is designed to increase access to legal information and advice by involving a much wider network of funders and providers in giving publicly funded legal services. In Scotland, provision of legal aid is governed by the Legal Aid (Scotland) Act 1986 and administered by the Scottish Legal Aid Board.

LEGAL SERVICES COMMISSION

(85 Gray's Inn Road, London WC1X 8TX T 020-7759 000 W www.legalservices.gov.uk)

CIVIL LEGAL AID

From 1 January 2000, only organisations (such as solicitors or Citizens Advice Bureaux) with a contract with the Legal Services Commission have been able to give initial help in any civil matter. Moreover, from that date decisions about funding were devolved from the Legal Services Commission to contracted organisations in relation to any level of publicly funded service in family and immigration cases. For other types of case, applications for public funding are made through a solicitor (or other contracted legal services providers) in much the same way as the former Legal Aid. On 1 April 2001 the so-called civil contracting scheme was extended to cover all levels of service for all types of cases.

Under the new civil funding scheme there are broadly seven levels of service available:
- legal help
- help at court
- general family help
- legal representation – either investigative help or full representation
- help with mediation
- family mediation
- such other services as authorised by specific orders

ELIGIBILITY

Eligibility for funding from the Community Legal Service depends broadly on five factors:
- the level of service sought (see above)
- whether the applicant qualifies financially
- the merits of the applicant's case
- a costs-benefits analysis (if the costs are likely to outweigh any benefit that might be gained from the proceedings, funding may be refused)
- whether there is any public interest in the case being litigated (ie whether the case has a wider public interest beyond that of the parties involved – for example, a human rights case)

The limits on capital and income above which a person is not entitled to public funding vary with the type of service sought.

CONTRIBUTIONS

Some of those who qualify for Community Legal Service funding will have to contribute towards their legal costs. Contributions must be paid by anyone who has a disposable income or disposable capital exceeding a prescribed amount. The rules relating to applicable contributions are complex and detailed information can be obtained from the Legal Services Commission.

STATUTORY CHARGE

A statutory charge is made if a person keeps or gains money or property in a case for which they have received legal aid. This means that the amount paid by the Community Legal Service fund on their behalf is deducted from the amount that the person receives. This does not apply if the court has ordered that the costs be paid by the other party (unless the amount paid by the other party does not cover all of the costs). In certain circumstances, the Legal Services Commission may waive or postpone payment.

CONTINGENCY OR CONDITIONAL FEES

This system was introduced by the Courts and Legal Services Act 1990. It offers legal representation on a 'no win, no fee' basis. It provides an alternative form of assistance, especially for those cases which are ineligible for funding by the Community Legal Service. The main area for such work is in the field of personal injuries.

Not all solicitors offer such a scheme and different solicitors may well have different terms. The effect of the agreement is that solicitors will not make any charges until the case is concluded successfully. If a case is won then the losing party will usually have to pay towards costs, with the winning party contributing around one third.

SCOTLAND

Civil legal aid is available for cases in the following:
- the sheriff courts
- the court of session
- the House of Lords
- the lands valuation appeal court
- the Scottish land court
- the Lands Tribunal for Scotland
- the Employment Appeal Tribunals
- the Judicial Committee of the Privy Council
- the Proscribed Organisations Appeal Commissioner
- proceedings before the Social Security Commissioners
- proceedings before the Child Support Commissioners

Civil legal aid is not available for defamation actions, small claims or simplified divorce procedures or petitions by a debtor for his own sequestration.

Eligibility for civil legal aid is assessed in a similar way to that in England and Wales, though the financial limits differ in some respects and are as follows:
- a person is eligible and will not have to pay a contribution if his yearly disposable income is £2,995 or less and disposable capital is £6,640 or less
- if disposable income exceeds £9,781, the person is not eligible for legal aid
- if disposable income is between £2,995 and £9,781, contributions are payable
- if disposable capital exceeds £11,070, the person is not eligible for legal aid
- if disposable capital is between £6,640 and £11,070, contributions are payable
- those receiving income support or income-related job seeker's allowance qualify automatically

CRIMINAL LEGAL AID

The Legal Services Commission provides defendants facing criminal charges with free legal representation if they pass a merits test and a means test.

Criminal legal aid covers the cost of preparing a case and legal representation in criminal proceedings. It is also available for appeals against verdicts or sentences in magistrates' courts, the crown court or the court of appeal. It is not available for bringing a private prosecution in a criminal court.

If granted criminal legal aid, either the person may choose their own solicitor or the court will assign one. Contributions to the legal costs may be required if the case proceeds to the crown court. The rules relating to applicable contributions are complex and detailed information can be obtained from the Legal Services Commission.

DUTY SOLICITORS

The Legal Aid Act 1988 also provides free advice and assistance to anyone questioned by the police (whether under arrest or helping the police with their enquiries). No means test or contributions are required for this.

SCOTLAND

Legal advice and assistance operates in a similar way in Scotland. A person is eligible:

- if disposable income does not exceed £215 a week. If disposable income is between £91 and £215 a week, contributions are payable
- if disposable capital does not exceed £1,502 (if the person has dependent relatives, the savings allowance is higher)
- if receiving income support or income-related job seeker's allowance they qualify automatically provided they have no savings over the limit

The procedure for application for criminal legal aid depends on the circumstances of each case. In solemn cases (more serious cases, such as murder) heard before a jury, a person is automatically entitled to criminal legal aid until they are given bail or placed in custody. Thereafter, it is for the court to decide whether to grant legal aid. The court will do this if the person accused cannot meet the expenses of the case without undue hardship on him or his dependants. In less serious cases the procedure depends on whether the person is in custody:

- anyone taken into custody has the right to free legal aid from the duty solicitor up to and including the first court appearance
- if the person is not in custody and wishes to plead guilty, they are not entitled to criminal legal aid but may be entitled to legal advice and assistance, including assistance by way of representation
- if the person is not in custody and wishes to plead not guilty, they can apply for criminal legal aid. This must be done within 14 days of the first court appearance at which they made the plea

The criteria used to assess whether or not criminal legal aid should be granted is similar to the criteria for England and Wales. When meeting with your solicitor, take evidence of your financial position such as details of savings, bank statements, pay slips, pension book or benefits book.

Further information can be obtained from:

THE SCOTTISH LEGAL AID BOARD
44 Drumsheugh Gardens, Edinburgh EH3 7SW
T 0131-226 7061 W www.slab.org.uk

MARRIAGE

Any two persons may marry provided that:

- they are at least 16 years old on the day of the marriage (in England and Wales persons under the age of 18 must generally obtain the consent of their parents; if consent is refused an appeal may be made to the high court, the county court or a court of summary jurisdiction)
- they are not related to one another in a way which would prevent their marrying
- they are unmarried (a person who has already been married must produce documentary evidence that the previous marriage has been ended by death, divorce or annulment)
- they are not of the same sex (though same sex couples can register a civil partnership instead)

- they are capable of understanding the nature of a marriage ceremony and of consenting to marriage

The marriage may be valid in England and Wales and void by the law of the domicile of both or either of the parties. The parties should check the marriage will be recognised as valid in their home country if either is not a British citizen.

DEGREES OF RELATIONSHIP

A marriage between persons within the prohibited degrees of consanguinity, affinity or adoption is void.

A man may not marry his mother, daughter, grandmother, granddaughter, sister, aunt, niece, great-grandmother, adoptive mother, former adoptive mother, adopted daughter or former adopted daughter.

A woman may not marry her father, son, grandfather, grandson, brother, uncle, nephew, great-grandfather, adoptive father, former adoptive father, adopted son or former adopted son. Under the Marriage Act 1983, some exceptions to the law permit a man or a woman to marry certain step-relatives or in-laws.

ENGLAND AND WALES
TYPES OF MARRIAGE CEREMONY

It is possible to marry by either religious or civil ceremony. A religious ceremony can take place at a church or chapel of the Church of England or the Church in Wales, or at any other place of worship which has been formally registered by the Registrar-General.

A civil ceremony can take place at a register office, a registered building or any other premises approved by the local authority.

An application for an approved premises licence must be made by the owners or trustees of the building concerned; it cannot be made by the prospective marriage couple. Approved premises must be regularly open to the public so that the marriage can be witnessed; the venue must be deemed to be a permanent and immovable structure. Open-air ceremonies are prohibited.

Non-Anglican marriages may also be solemnised following the issue of a Registrar-General's licence in unregistered premises where one of the parties is seriously ill, is not expected to recover, and cannot be moved to registered premises. Detained and housebound persons may be married at their place of residence.

MARRIAGE IN THE CHURCH OF ENGLAND OR THE CHURCH IN WALES
Marriage by banns

The marriage must take place in a parish in which one of the parties lives, or in a church in another parish if it is the usual place of worship of either or both of the parties. The banns must be called in the parish in which the marriage is to take place on three Sundays before the day of the ceremony; if either or both of the parties lives in a different parish the banns must also be called there. After three months the banns are no longer valid. The minister will not perform the marriage unless he or she is satisfied that the banns have been properly called.

Marriage by common licence

The vicar who is to conduct the marriage will arrange for a common licence to be issued by the diocesan bishop; this dispenses with the necessity for banns. One of the parties must have lived in the parish for 15 days immediately before the issuing of the licence or must usually worship at the church. Eligibility requirements vary from diocese to diocese, but it is not normally required that the parties should have been baptised. The licence is valid for three months.

Marriage by special licence

A special licence is granted by the Archbishop of Canterbury in special circumstances for the marriage to take place at any place, with or without previous residence in the parish, or at any time. Application must be made to the registrar of the Faculty Office (1 The Sanctuary, London SW1P 3JT T 020-7222 5381).

Marriage by certificate

The marriage can be conducted on the authority of the superintendent registrar's certificate, provided that the vicar's consent is obtained (there is no obligation upon the vicar to accept the certificate). One of the parties must live in the parish or must usually worship at the church.

MARRIAGE BY OTHER RELIGIOUS CEREMONY

One of the parties must normally live in the registration district where the marriage is to take place. In addition to giving notice to the superintendent registrar it may also be necessary to book a registrar to be present at the ceremony.

CIVIL MARRIAGE

A marriage may be solemnised at any register office, registered building or approved premises in England and Wales. The superintendent registrar of the district should be contacted, and, if the marriage is to take place at approved premises, the necessary arrangements at the venue must also be made.

NOTICE OF MARRIAGE

Unless it is to take place by banns or under common or special licence in the Church of England or the Church in Wales, a notice of the marriage must be given in person to the superintendent registrar. Notice of marriage may be given in the following ways:

- by certificate. Both parties must have lived in a registration district in England or Wales for at least seven days immediately before giving notice at the local register office. If they live in different registration districts, notice must be given in both districts. The marriage can take place in any register office or other approved premises in England and Wales no sooner than 16 days after notice has been given, when the superintendent registrar issues a certificate.
- by licence (often known as 'special licence'). One of the parties must have lived in a registration district in England or Wales for at least 15 days before giving notice at the register office; the other party need only be a resident of, or be physically in, England and Wales on the day notice is given. The marriage can take place one clear day (other than a Sunday, Christmas Day or Good Friday) after notice has been given.

A notice of marriage is valid for 12 months, unless it is for the marriage of a detained or housebound person, when it will usually only be accepted within three months of publication. Notice for marriages taking place within the Church of England or Church of Wales should also only be valid within three months of publication. It should be possible to make an advance (provisional) booking 12 months before the ceremony. In this case it is still necessary to give formal notice three months before the marriage. When giving notice of the marriage it is necessary to produce official proof, if relevant, that any

previous marriage has ended in divorce or death by producing a decree absolute or death certificate; it is also necessary to provide proof of age, identity and nationality for each of the parties, for example, with a passport. If either party is under 18 years old, evidence of consent by their parent or guardian is required. There are special procedures for those wishing to get married in the UK that are subject to immigration control; the register office will be able to advise on these.

SOLEMNISATION OF THE MARRIAGE

On the day of the wedding there must be at least two other people present who are prepared to act as witnesses and sign the marriage register. A registrar of marriages must be present at a marriage in a register office or at approved premises, but an authorised person may act in the capacity of registrar in a registered building.

If the marriage takes place at approved premises, the room must be separate from any other activity on the premises at the time of the ceremony, and no food or drink can be sold or consumed in the room during the ceremony or for one hour beforehand.

The marriage must be solemnised between 8am and 6pm, with open doors. At some time during the ceremony the parties must make a declaration that they know of no legal impediment to the marriage and they must also say the contracting words; the declaratory and contracting words may vary according to the form of service. A civil marriage cannot contain any religious aspects, but it may be possible for non-religious music and/or readings to be included. It may also be possible to embellish the marriage vows taken by the couple.

CIVIL FEES

Marriage at a Register Office

By superintendent registrar's certificate, £30 per person for the notice of the marriage (which is not refundable if the marriage does not in fact take place) and £40 for the ceremony at the register office.

Marriage on Approved Premises

By superintendent registrar's certificate, £30 per person for the ceremony at the register office.

An additional fee will also be payable for the superintendent registrar's and registrar's attendance at the marriage. This is set locally by the local authority responsible. A further charge is likely to be made by the owners of the building for the use of the premises. For marriages taking place in a religious building other than the Church of England or Church of Wales, an additional fee of £47 is payable for the registrar's attendance at the marriage unless an 'Authorised Person' appointed by the trustees of the building has agreed to register the marriage. Additional fees may be charged by the trustees of the building for the wedding and by the person who performs the ceremony.

ECCLESIASTICAL FEES

(Church of England and Church in Wales*)

Marriage by banns

For publication of banns, £19
For certificate of banns issued at time of publication, £12.00
For marriage service, £240

Marriage by common licence

Fee for licence, £70

Marriage by special licence

Fee for licence, £140
* These fees are revised from 1 April each calendar year. Some may not apply to the Church in Wales

SCOTLAND
REGULAR MARRIAGES

A regular marriage is one which is celebrated by a minister of religion or authorised registrar or other celebrant. Each of the parties must complete a marriage notice form and return it to the district registrar for the area in which they are to be married, irrespective of where they live, at least 15 days before the ceremony is due to take place. The district registrar must then enter the date of receipt and certain details in a marriage book kept for this purpose, and must also enter the names of the parties and the proposed date of marriage in a list which is displayed in a conspicuous place at the registration office until the date of the marriage has passed. All persons wishing to enter into a regular marriage in Scotland must follow the same preliminary procedure regardless of whether they intend to have a religious or civil ceremony. Before the marriage ceremony takes place any person may submit an objection in writing to the district registrar.

A marriage schedule, which is prepared by the registrar, will be issued to one or both of the parties in person up to seven days before a religious marriage; for a civil marriage the schedule will be available at the ceremony. The schedule must be handed to the celebrant before the ceremony starts; it must be signed immediately after the wedding and the marriage must be registered within three days.

The authority to conduct a religious marriage is deemed to be vested in the authorised celebrant rather than the building in which it takes place; open-air religious ceremonies are therefore permissible in Scotland.

From 10 June 2002 it has been possible, under the Marriage (Scotland) Act 2002, for venues or couples to apply to the local council for a licence to allow a civil ceremony to take place at a venue other than a registration office. To obtain further information, a venue or couple should contact the district registrar in the area they wish to marry. A list of licensed venues is also available on the General Registers of Scotland website (W www.gro-scotland.gov.uk).

MARRIAGE BY COHABITATION WITH HABIT AND REPUTE

Prior to the enactment of the 2006 act, if two people had lived together constantly as husband and wife and were generally held to be such by the neighbourhood and among their friends and relations, a presumption could arise from which marriage could be inferred. Before such a marriage could be registered, however, a decree of declarator of marriage had to be obtained from the court of session. Section 3 of the 2006 act provides that it will no longer be possible for a marriage to be constituted by cohabitation with habit and repute, but it will still be possible for couples whose period of cohabitation began before commencement of the 2006 act to seek a declarator under the old rule of law.

CIVIL FEES

The fee for submitting a notice of marriage to the district registrar is £25. Solemnisation of a civil marriage costs £45, whilst the extract of the entry in the register of marriages attracts a fee of £8.50. The costs of religious marriage ceremonies can vary.

Further information can be obtained from:

THE GENERAL REGISTER OFFICE
Trafalgar Road, Southport PR8 2HH
T 0845-603 7788 W www.gro.gov.uk

THE GENERAL REGISTER OFFICE FOR SCOTLAND
New Register House, 3 West Register Street, Edinburgh EH1 3YT
T 0131-314 4452

TOWN AND COUNTRY PLANNING

The planning system can help to protect the environment and assist individuals in assessing their land rights. There are a number of acts governing the development of land and buildings in England and Wales and advice should always be sought from a Citizens Advice Bureau or local planning authority before undertaking building works on any land or to property. If development takes place which requires planning permission without permission being given, enforcement action may take place and the situation may need to be rectified.

PLANNING PERMISSION

Planning permission is needed if the work involves:
- making a material change in use, such as dividing off part of the house so that it can be used as a separate home or dividing off part of the house for commercial use, eg for a workshop
- going against the terms of the original planning permission, eg there may be a restriction on fences in front gardens on an open-plan estate
- building, engineering for mining, except for the permissions below
- new or wider access to a main road
- additions or extensions to flats or maisonettes

Planning permission is not needed to carry out internal alterations or work which does not affect the external appearance of the building, and are not works for making good damage or works begun after 5 December 1968 for the alteration of a building by providing additional space in it underground.

There are certain types of development for which the Secretary of State for the Environment, Food and Rural Affairs has granted general permissions (permitted development rights). These include:
- house extensions and additions (including conservatories, loft conversions, garages and dormer windows). Up to 10 per cent or up to 50 cubic metres (whichever is the greater) can be added to the original house for terraced houses or houses on land designated as an area of outstanding natural beauty or in a conservation area. Up to 15 per cent or 70 cubic metres (whichever is the greater) to other kinds of houses. The maximum that can be added to any house is 115 cubic metres
- buildings such as garden sheds and greenhouses so long as they are no more than 3 metres high (or 4 metres if the roof is ridged), are no nearer to a highway than the house or 20 metres (whichever is nearer), and at least half the ground around the house remains uncovered by buildings
- adding a porch with a ground area of less than 3 square metres and that is less than 3 metres in height and not within 2 metres of any boundary of the curtilage of the dwelling house with a highway
- putting up fences, walls and gates of under 1 metre in height if next to a road and under 2 metres elsewhere
- laying patios, paths or driveways for domestic use

However, before carrying out any of the above permitted

developments you should contact your local authority to find out whether the general permission has been modified in your area.

OTHER RESTRICTIONS

It may be necessary to obtain other types of permissions before carrying out any development. These permissions are separate from planning permission and apply regardless of whether or not planning permission is needed, eg:

- building regulations will probably apply if a new building is to be erected, if an existing one is to be altered or extended, or if the work involves building over a drain or sewer. The building control department of the local authority will advise on this
- any alterations to a listed building or the grounds of a listed building must be approved by the local authority. Listing will include not only the main building but everything in the curtilage of the building
- local authority approval is necessary if a building (or, in some circumstances, gates, walls, fences or railings) in a conservation area is to be demolished; each local authority keeps a register of all local buildings that are in conservation areas
- many trees are protected by tree preservation orders and must not be pruned or taken down without local authority consent
- bats and many other species are protected, and Natural England, the Countryside Council for Wales or Scottish National Heritage must be notified before any work is carried out that will affect the habitat of protected species, eg timber treatment, renovation or extensions of lofts
- any development in areas designated as a national park, an area of outstanding natural beauty, a national scenic area or in the Norfolk or Suffolk Broads is subject to greater restrictions. The local planning authority will advise or refer enquirers to the relevant authority

The local authority should be contacted if a planning permission is required. There may also be restriction on development contained in the title to the property which should be considered when works are planned.

VOTERS' QUALIFICATIONS

Those entitled to vote at parliamentary, and local government elections are those who are:
- on the electoral roll
- aged 18 years or older
- British citizens, Commonwealth citizens or citizens of the Irish Republic who are resident in the UK
- In Northern Ireland electors must have been resident in Northern Ireland during the whole of the three-month period prior to the relevant date

British citizens resident abroad are entitled to vote for 15 years after leaving Britain, as overseas electors in parliamentary and EU elections in the constituency in which they were last resident. Members of the armed forces, Crown servants and employees of the British Council who are overseas and their spouses are entitled to vote regardless of how long they have been abroad. British citizens who had never been registered as an elector in the UK are not eligible to register as an overseas voter unless they left the UK before they were 18, providing they left the country no more than 15 years ago.

The main categories of people who are not entitled to vote at general elections are:

- sitting peers in the House of Lords
- convicted persons detained in pursuance of their sentences (though remand prisoners, unconvicted prisoners and civil prisoners can vote if on the electoral register)
- those convicted within the previous five years of corrupt or illegal election practices
- EU citizens (who may only vote in EU and local government elections)

Under the Representation of the Peoples Act 2000, several new groups of people are permitted to vote for the first time. These include: people who live on barges; people in mental health hospitals (other than those with criminal convictions) and homeless people who have made a 'declaration of local connection'.

REGISTERING TO VOTE

Voters must be entered on an electoral register. The Electoral Registration Officer (ERO) for each council area is responsible for preparing and publishing the register for his area by 1 December each year. Names may be added to the register to reflect changes in people's circumstances as they occur and each month during December to August, the ERO publishes a list of alterations to the published register.

A registration form is sent to all households in the autumn of each year and the householder is required to provide details of all occupants who are eligible to vote, including ones who will reach their 18th birthday in the year covered by the register. Anyone failing to supply information to the ERO when requested, or supplying false information, may be fined. Application forms and more information are available from the Electoral Commission on W www.electoralcommision.org.uk.

VOTING

Voting is not compulsory in the UK. Those who wish to vote do so in person at the allotted polling station. Postal votes are now available to anyone on request. Those who will be away at the time of the election, those who will not be able to attend in person due to physical incapacity or the nature of their occupation, and those who have changed address during the period for which the register is valid, may apply for a postal vote or nominate a proxy to vote for them. Overseas electors who wish to vote must do so by proxy.

Further information can be obtained from the local authority's ERO in England and Wales or the electoral registration office in Scotland, or the Chief Electoral Officer in Northern Ireland.

WILLS

In a will a person leaves instructions as to the disposal of their property after they die. A will is also used to appoint executors (who will administer the estate), give directions as to the disposal of the body, appoint guardians for children and, for larger estates, can operate to reduce the level of inheritance tax. It is best to have a will drawn up by a solicitor, but if a solicitor is not employed the following points must be taken into account:

- if possible the will must not be prepared on behalf of another person by someone who is to benefit from it or who is a close relative of a major beneficiary
- the language used must be clear and unambiguous and it is better to avoid the use of legal terms where the same thing can be expressed in plain language

- it is better to rewrite the whole document if a mistake is made. If necessary, alterations can be made by striking through the words with a pen, and the signature or initials of the testator and the witnesses must be put in the margin opposite the alteration. No alteration of any kind should be made after the will has been executed
- if the person later wishes to change the will or part of it, it is better to write a new will revoking the old. The use of codicils (documents written as supplements or containing modifications to the will) should be left to a solicitor
- the will should be typed or printed, or if handwritten be legible and preferably in ink. Commercial will forms can be obtained from some stationers

The form of a will varies to suit different cases – a solicitor will be able to advise as to wording, however, 'DIY' will-writing kits can be purchased from good stationery shops and many banks offer a will-writing service.

LAPSED LEGATEES
If a person who has been left property in a will dies before the person who made the will, the gift fails and will pass to the person entitled to everything not otherwise disposed of (the residuary estate).

If the person left the residuary estate dies before the person who made the will, their share will generally pass to the closest relative(s) of the person who made the will (as in intestacy), unless the will names a beneficiary such as a charity who will take as a 'long stop' if this gift is unable to take effect for any reason. It is always better to draw up a new will if a beneficiary predeceases the person who made the will.

EXECUTORS
It is usual to appoint two executors, although one is sufficient. No more than four persons can deal with the estate of the person who has died. The name and address of each executor should be given in full (the addresses are not essential but including them adds clarity to the document). Executors should be 18 years of age or over. An executor may be a beneficiary of the will.

WITNESSES
A person who is a beneficiary of a will, or the spouse of a beneficiary at the time the will is signed, must not act as a witness or else he/she will be unable to take his/her gift. Husband and wife can both act as witnesses provided neither benefits from the will.

It is better that a person does not act as an executor and as a witness, as he/she can take no benefit under a will to which he/she is witness. The identity of the witnesses should be made as explicit as possible.

EXECUTION OF A WILL
The person making the will should sign his/her name at the foot of the document, in the presence of the two witnesses. The witnesses must then sign their names while the person making the will looks on. If this procedure is not adhered to, the will will be considered invalid. There are certain exceptional circumstances where these rules are relaxed, eg where the person may be too ill to sign.

CAPACITY TO MAKE A WILL
Anyone aged 18 or over can make a will. However, if there is any suspicion that the person making the will is not, through reasons of infirmity or age, fully in command of his/her faculties, it is advisable to arrange for a medical practitioner to examine the person making the will at the time it is to be executed (to verify his/her mental capacity and to record that medical opinion in writing), and to ask the examining practitioner to act as a witness. If a person is not mentally able to make a will, the court may do this for him/her by virtue of the Mental Health Act 1983.

REVOCATION
A will may be revoked or cancelled in a number of ways:
- a later will revokes an earlier one if it says so; otherwise the earlier will is by implication revoked by the later one to the extent that it contradicts or repeats the earlier one
- a will is also revoked if the physical document on which it is written is destroyed by the person whose will it is. There must be an intention to revoke the will and it may not be sufficient to obliterate the will with a pen
- a will is revoked when the person marries or forms a civil partnership, unless it is clear from the will that the person intended the will to stand after the marriage or civil partnership
- where a marriage or civil partnership ends in divorce or dissolution or is annulled or declared void, gifts to the spouse or civil partner and the appointment of the spouse or civil partner as executor fail unless the will says that this is not to happen. A former spouse or civil partner is treated as having predeceased the testator. A separation does not change the effect of a married person's will.

PROBATE AND LETTERS OF ADMINISTRATION
Probate is granted to the executors named in a will and once granted, the executors are obliged to carry out the instructions of the will. Letters of administration are granted where no executor is named in a will or is unwilling or able to act or where there is no will or no valid will; this gives a person, often the next of kin, similar powers and duties to those of an executor.

Applications for probate or for letters of administration can be made to the Principal Registry of the Family Division, to a district probate registry or to a probate sub-registry. Applicants will need the following documents: the original will (if any); a certificate of death; oath for executors or administrators; particulars of all property and assets left by the deceased; and a list of debts and funeral expenses. Certain property, up to the value of £5,000, may be disposed of without a grant of probate or letters of administration.

WHERE TO FIND A PROVED WILL
Since 1858 wills which have been proved, that is wills on which probate or letters of administration have been granted, must have been proved at the Principal Registry of the Family Division or at a district probate registry. The Lord Chancellor has power to direct where the original documents are kept but most are filed where they were proved and may be inspected there and a copy obtained. The Principal Registry also holds copies of all wills proved at district probate registries and these may be inspected at First Avenue House, High Holborn. An index of all grants, both of probate and of letters of administration, is compiled by the Principal Registry and may be seen either at the Principal Registry or at a district probate registry.

It is also possible to discover when a grant of probate or letters of administration is issued by requesting a standing search. In response to a request and for a small fee, a district probate registry will supply the names and addresses of executors or administrators and the registry in which the grant was made, of any grant in the estate of a specified person made in the previous 12 months or following six months. This is useful for applicants who may be beneficiaries to a will but who have lost contact with the deceased and for creditors of the deceased.

INTESTACY

Intestacy occurs when someone dies without leaving a will or leaves a will which is invalid or which does not take effect for some reason. Intestacy can be partial, for instance, if there is a will which disposes of some but not all of the testator's property. In such cases the person's estate (property, possessions, other assets following the payment of debts) passes to certain members of the family. The relevant legislation is the Administration of Estates Act 1925, as amended by various legislation including the Intestates Estates Act 1952, the Law Reform (Succession) Act 1995, and the Trusts of Land and Appointment of Trustees Act 1996 and Orders made thereunder. Some of the provisions of this legislation are described below. If a will has been written that disposes of only part of a person's property, these rules apply to the part which is undisposed of.

If the person (intestate) leaves a spouse or a civil partner who survives for 28 days and children (legitimate, illegitimate and adopted children and other descendants), the estate is divided as follows:

- the spouse or civil partner takes the 'personal chattels' (household articles, including cars, but nothing used for business purposes), £125,000 tax-free (with interest payable at six per cent from the time of the death until payment) and a life interest in half of the rest of the estate (which can be capitalised by the spouse or civil partner if he/she wishes)
- the rest of the estate goes to the children*

If the person leaves a spouse or civil partner who survives for 28 days but no children:

- the spouse or civil partner takes the personal chattels, £200,000 tax-free (interest payable as before) and full ownership of half of the rest of the estate
- the other half of the rest of the estate goes to the parents (equally, if both alive) or, if none, to the brothers and sisters of the whole blood*
- if there are no parents or brothers or sisters of the whole blood or their children, the spouse or civil partner takes the whole estate

If there is no surviving spouse or civil partner, the estate is distributed among those who survive the intestate as follows:

- to surviving children*, but if none to
- parents (equally, if both alive), but if none to
- brothers and sisters of the whole blood* (including issue of deceased ones), but if none to
- brothers and sisters of the half blood* (including issue of deceased ones), but if none to
- grandparents (equally, if more than one), but if none to
- aunts and uncles of the whole blood*, but if none to
- aunts and uncles of the half blood*, but if none to
- the crown, Duchy of Lancaster or the Duke of Cornwall (*bona vacantia*)

* To inherit, a member of these groups must survive the intestate and attain the age of 18, or marry under that age. If they die under the age of 18 (unless married under that age), their share goes to others, if any, in the same group. If any member of these groups predeceases the intestate leaving children, their share is divided equally among their children.

In England and Wales the provisions of the Inheritance (Provision for Family and Dependants) Act 1975 may allow other people to claim provision from the deceased's assets. This act also applies to cases where a will has been made and allows a person to apply to the court if they feel that the will or rules of intestacy or both do not make adequate provision for them. The court can order payment from the deceased's assets or the transfer of property from them if the applicant's claim is accepted. The application must be made within six months of the grant of probate or letters of administration and the following people can make an application:

- the spouse or civil partner
- a former spouse or civil partner who has not remarried or formed a subsequent civil partnership
- a child of the deceased
- someone treated as a child of the deceased's family
- someone maintained by the deceased
- someone who has cohabited for two years before the death in the same household as the deceased and as the husband or wife or civil partner of the deceased

SCOTLAND

In Scotland any person over 12 and of sound mind can make a will. The person making the will can only freely dispose of the heritage and what is known as the 'dead's part' of the estate because:

- the spouse or civil partner has the right to inherit one-third of the moveable estate if there are children or other descendants, and one-half of it if there are not
- children are entitled to one-third of the moveable estate if there is a surviving spouse or civil partner, and one-half of it if there is not

The remaining portion is the dead's part, and legacies and bequests are payable from this. Debts are payable out of the whole estate before any division.

From August 1995, wills no longer needed to be 'holographed' and it is now only necessary to have one witness. The person making the will still needs to sign each page. It is better that the will is not witnessed by a beneficiary although the attestation would still be sound and the beneficiary would not have to relinquish the gift.

Subsequent marriage or civil partnership does not revoke a will but the birth of a child who is not provided for may do so. A will may be revoked by a subsequent will, either expressly or by implication, but in so far as the two can be read together both have effect. If a subsequent will is revoked, the earlier will is revived.

Wills may be registered in the sheriff court Books of the Sheriffdom in which the deceased lived or in the Books of Council and Session at the Registers of Scotland.

CONFIRMATION

Confirmation (the Scottish equivalent of probate) is obtained in the sheriff court of the sheriffdom in which the deceased was resident at the time of death. Executives are either 'nominate' (named by the deceased in the will) or 'dative' (appointed by the court in cases where no executor is named in a will or in cases of intestacy). Applicants for confirmation must first provide an inventory of the deceased's estate and a schedule of debts, with an affidavit. In estates under £30,000 gross, confirmation can be obtained under a simplified procedure at reduced fees, with no need for a solicitor. The local sheriff clerk's office can provide assistance.

Further information can be obtained from:

PRINCIPAL REGISTRY (FAMILY DIVISION)
First Avenue House, 42–49 High Holborn, London WC2V 6NP
T 020-7947 6980

REGISTERS OF SCOTLAND
Meadowbank House, 153 London Road, Edinburgh EH8 7AU
T 0131-659 6111

INTESTACY

The rules of distribution are contained in the Succession (Scotland) Act 1964 and are extended to include civil partners by the Civil Partnership Act 2004.

A surviving spouse or civil partner is entitled to 'prior rights'. This means that the spouse or civil partner has the right to inherit:

- the matrimonial or family home up to a value of £300,000, or one matrimonial or family home if there is more than one, or, in certain circumstances, the value of the home
- the furnishings and contents of that home, up to the value of £24,000
- a cash sum of £42,000 if the deceased left children or other descendants, or £75,000 if not

These figures are increased from time to time by regulations.

Once prior rights have been satisfied legal rights are settled. Legal rights are:

Jus relicti(ae) and rights under the section 131 of the Civil Partnership Act 2004 – the right of a surviving spouse or civil partner to one-half of the net moveable estate, after satisfaction of prior rights, if there are no surviving children; if there are surviving children, the spouse or civil partner is entitled to one-third of the net moveable estate

Legitim and rights under the section 131 of the Civil Partnership Act 2004 – the right of surviving children to one-half of the net moveable estate if there is no surviving spouse or civil partner; if there is a surviving spouse or civil partner, the children are entitled to one-third of the net moveable estate after the satisfaction of prior rights

Where there is no surviving spouse, civil partner or children, half of the estate is taken by the parents and half by the brothers and sisters. Failing that, the lines of succession, in general, are:

- to descendants
- if no descendants, then to collaterals (ie brothers and sisters) and parents
- surviving spouse or civil partner
- if no collaterals, parents, spouse or civil partner, then to ascendants collaterals (ie aunts and uncles), and so on in an ascending scale
- if all lines of succession fail, the estate passes to the crown. Relatives of the whole blood are preferred to relatives of the half blood. The right of representation, ie the right of the issue of a person who would have succeeded if he/she had survived the intestate, also applies

INTELLECTUAL PROPERTY

Intellectual property is a broad term covering a number of legal rights provided by the government to help people protect their creative works and encourage further innovation. By using these legal rights people can own the things they create and control the way in which others use their innovations. Intellectual property owners can take legal action to stop others using their intellectual property, they can license their intellectual property to others or they can sell it on. Different types of intellectual property utilise different forms of protection including copyright, designs, patents and trademarks which are all covered below in more detail.

COPYRIGHT

Copyright protects all original literary, dramatic, musical and artistic works (including photographs, maps and plans), published editions of works, computer programs, sound recordings, films (including video and DVD) and broadcasts (including cable, radio, satellite broadcasts, and transmissions on the internet). Under copyright the creators of these works can control the various ways in which their material may be exploited, the rights broadly covering copying, adapting, issuing (including renting and lending) copies to the public, performing in public, and broadcasting the material. The transfer of copyright works to formats accessible to visually impaired persons without infringement of copyright was enacted in 2002.

Copyright protection in the United Kingdom is automatic and there is no official registration system. Steps can be taken by the work's creator to provide evidence that he/she had the work at a particular time (eg by depositing a copy with a bank or solicitor). The main legislation is the Copyright, Designs and Patents Act 1988, which has been amended by other acts and by statutory instrument to take account of EU directives. As a result of an EU directive effective from January 1996, the term of copyright protection for literary, dramatic, musical and artistic works lasts for 70 years after the death of the author. For film copyright lasts for 70 years after the death of the director, authors of the screenplay and dialogue or the composer of any music specially created for the film. Sound recordings are protected for 50 years after their publication, and broadcasts for 50 years from the end of the year in which the first broadcast/transmission was made. Published editions remain under copyright protection for 25 years from the end of the year in which the edition was published.

The main international treaties protecting copyright are the Berne Convention for the Protection of Literary and Artistic Works (administered by the World Intellectual Property Organisation (WIPO)), the Rome Convention for the Protection of Performers, Producers of Phonograms and Broadcasting Organisations (administered jointly by UNESCO and the International Labour Organisation), and the Universal Copyright Convention (developed by UNESCO); the UK is a signatory to these conventions. Copyright material created by UK nationals or residents is protected in each country that is a member of the conventions by the national law of that country. A list of participating countries may be obtained from the UK Intellectual Property Office, previously known as the UK Patent Office.

Two treaties which strengthen and update international standards of protection, particularly in relation to new technologies, were agreed in December 1996: the WIPO copyright treaty, and the WIPO performance and phonograms treaty. In May 2001 the European Union passed a new directive (which in 2003 became law in the UK) aimed at harmonising copyright law throughout the EU to take account of the internet and other technologies. More information can be found online (W www.ipo.gov.uk).

LICENSING

Use of copyright material without seeking permission in each instance may be permitted under 'blanket' licences available from copyright licensing agencies. The International Federation of Reproduction Rights Organisations facilitates agreements between its member licensing agencies and on behalf of its members with organisations such as the WIPO, UNESCO, the European Union and the Council of Europe.

DESIGN PROTECTION

Design protection covers the outward appearance of an article and in the UK takes two forms: registered design and design right, which are not mutually exclusive. Registered design protects the aesthetic appearance of an article, including shape, configuration, pattern or ornament, although artistic works such as sculptures are excluded, being generally protected by copyright. In order to qualify for protection, a design must be new and materially different from earlier UK published designs. The owner of the design must apply to the UK Intellectual Property Office. Initial registration lasts for five years and can be extended in five-year increments to a maximum of 25 years. The current legislation is the Registered Designs Act 1949 which has been amended several times, most recently by the Registered Designs Regulations 2003.

UK applicants wishing to protect their designs in the EU can do so by applying for a Registered Community Design with the Office of Harmonisation in the Internal Market. Outside the EU separate applications must be made in each country in which protection is sought.

Design right is an automatic right which applies to the shape or configuration of articles and does not require registration. Unlike registered design, two-dimensional designs do not qualify for protection but designs of semiconductor chips (topographies) are protected by design right. Designs must be original and non-commonplace. The term of design right is ten years from first marketing of the design and the right is effective only in the UK. The current legislation is Part 3 of the Copyright, Designs and Patents Act 1988, amended on 9 December 2001 to incorporate the European Designs Directive.

PATENTS

A patent is a document issued by the UK Intellectual Property Office relating to an invention and giving the proprietor the right for a limited period to stop others from making, using or selling the invention without the inventor's permission. In return the patentee pays a fee to cover the costs of processing the patent and publicly discloses details of the invention.

To qualify for a patent an invention must be new, must exhibit an inventive step, and must be capable of industrial application. The patent is valid for a maximum of 20 years from the date on which the application was filed, subject to payment of annual fees from the end of the fourth year.

The UK Intellectual Property Office, established in 1852, is responsible for ensuring that all stages of an application comply with the Patents Act 1977, and that the invention meets the criteria for a patent.

The WIPO is responsible for administering many of the international conventions on intellectual property. The Patent Cooperation Treaty allows inventors to file a single application for patent rights in some or all of the contracting states. This application is searched by an International Searching Authority and published by the International Bureau of WIPO. It may also be the subject of an (optional) international preliminary examination. Applicants must then deal directly with the patent offices in the countries where they are seeking patent rights. The European Patent Convention allows inventors to obtain patent rights in all the contracting states by filing a single application with the European Patent Office. More information can be found online (W www.ipo.gov.uk).

RESEARCH DISCLOSURES

Research disclosures are publicly disclosed details of inventions. Once published, an invention is considered no longer novel and becomes prior art. Publishing a disclosure is significantly cheaper than applying for a patent, however unlike a patent, it does not entitle the author to exclusive rights to use or license the invention. Instead, research disclosures are primarily published to ensure the inventor freedom to use the invention. This works because publishing legally prevents other parties from patenting the disclosed innovation and in the UK, patent law dictates that by disclosing, even the inventor relinquishes their right to a patent.

In theory, publishing details of an invention anywhere should be enough to make a research disclosure. However to be effective a research disclosure really needs to be published in a location which patent examiners will include in their prior art searches. To ensure global legal precedent it must be included in a publication with a recognised date stamp and made publicly available across the world.

The *Research Disclosure* journal established in 1960, published by KMP Ltd, is the primary publisher of research disclosures. It is the only disclosure service recognised by the Patent Cooperation Treaty as a mandatory search resource which must be consulted by the international search authorities. More information can be found online (W www.researchdisclosure.com).

TRADE MARKS

Trade marks are a means of identification, whether a word or device or a combination of both, a logo, or the shape of goods or their packaging, which enable traders to make their goods or services readily distinguishable from those supplied by other traders. Registration prevents other traders using the same or similar trade marks for similar products or services for which the mark is registered.

In the UK trade marks are registered at the UK Intellectual Property Office. In order to qualify for registration a mark must be capable of distinguishing its proprietor's goods or services from those of other undertakings; it should be non-deceptive, should not be contrary to law or morality and should not be similar or identical to any earlier marks for the same or similar goods or services. The relevant current legislation is the Trade Marks Act 1994.

It is possible to obtain an international trade mark registration, effective in 80 countries, under the Madrid Agreement or the Madrid Protocol, to which the UK is party. British companies can obtain international trade mark registration through a single application to the WIPO in those countries party to the protocol.

EC trade mark regulation is now in force and is administered by the Office for Harmonisation in the Internal Market (Trade Marks and Designs) in Alicante, Spain. The office registers EC trade marks, which are valid throughout the European Union. The national registration of trade marks in member states continues in parallel with EC trade mark standards.

DOMAIN NAMES

A domain name is a name by which a company or organisation is known on the internet and is a shorthand way of identifying a company's website. A domain name has to be registered separately from a trade mark. Although there are many registrars prepared to register domain names, each country has a central registry to store unique names and addresses used on the internet. A list of accredited registrars can be found online (W www.icann.org).

CONTACTS

THE UK INTELLECTUAL PROPERTY OFFICE, Cardiff Road, Newport NP10 8QQ T 0845-950 0505
   W www.ipo.gov.uk
COPYRIGHT LICENSING AGENCY LTD, 90 Tottenham Court Road, London W1T 0LP T 020-7631 5555
   W www.cla.co.uk
EUROPEAN PATENT OFFICE, Headquarters, Erhardtstrasse 27, D-8000, Munich 2, Germany
   T (+49) 892 3990 W www.epo.org
WORLD INTELLECTUAL PROPERTY ORGANISATION, 34 chemin des Colombettes, CH-1211 Geneva 20, Switzerland T (+41) 22 338 9111
   W www.wipo.int

BROADCASTING

CROSS-MEDIA OWNERSHIP

The Communications Act, which received royal assent on 17 July 2003, overhauled the rules surrounding cross-media ownership. They were simplified and relaxed to encourage dispersion of ownership and new market entry while preventing the most influential media in any community being controlled by too narrow a range of interests. However, transfers and mergers are not solely subject to examination on competition grounds by the competition authorities. The secretary of state has a broad remit to intervene and decide if a transaction is permissible on public interest grounds (relating both to newspapers and cross-media criteria, if broadcasting interests are also involved). The Office of Communications (OFCOM) has an advisory role. Government and parliamentary assurances were given that any intervention into local newspaper transfers would be rare and exceptional.

REGULATION

OFCOM is the regulator for the communication industries in the UK and has responsibility for television, radio, telecommunications and wireless communications services. It replaced the Broadcasting Standards Commission, the Independent Television Commission, the Radio Authority, the Radio Communications Agency and OFTEL. OFCOM is required to report annually to parliament and exists to further the interests of consumers by balancing choice and competition with the duty to foster plurality; protect viewers and listeners and promote cultural diversity in the media; and ensuring full and fair competition between communications providers.

OFFICE OF COMMUNICATIONS (OFCOM)
Riverside House, 2A Southwark Bridge Road, London SE1 9HA
T 020-7981 3000 E enquiries@ofcom.org.uk
W www.ofcom.org.uk
Chief Executive, Stephen Carter

COMPLAINTS

Under the Communications Act 2003 OFCOM's licensees are obliged to adhere to the provisions of its codes (including advertising, programme standards, fairness, privacy and sponsorship). OFCOM also inherited the Broadcasting Standards Commission's Standards Code and is transitionally applying it in respect of BBC/S4C programmes. Complainants should contact the broadcaster in the first instance (details can be found on OFCOM's website), however, if the complainant wishes the complaint to be considered by OFCOM, it will do so. Complaints should be made within a reasonable time as broadcasters are only required to keep recordings for the following periods of time: radio, 42 days; television, 90 days; and cable and satellite, 60 days.

TELEVISION

There are six major television broadcasters operating in the UK. Four of these – the BBC, ITV, Channel 4 and Five – are free-to-air analogue terrestrial networks. BSkyB and Virgin Media Television provide satellite television services.

The BBC is the oldest broadcaster in the world. The corporation began a London-only television service from Alexandra Palace in 1936 and achieved nationwide coverage 15 years later. A second station, BBC Two, was launched in 1964. The BBC's digital services comprise BBC Three, BBC Four, BBC News 24 and BBC Parliament; the children's channels, CBeebies and CBBC; and the interactive channel BBCi. The services are funded by the licence fee. The corporation also has a commercial arm, BBC Worldwide, which was formed in 1994 and exists to maximise the value of the BBC's programme and publishing assets for the benefit of the licence payer. Its businesses include international programming distribution, magazines, other licensed products, live events and media monitoring.

The ITV (Independent Television) network was set up on a regional basis in 1955 to provide competition to the BBC. It comprised a number of independent licensees, the majority of which have now merged to form ITV plc. The network generates funds through broadcasting television advertisements. Its flagship analogue channel was renamed ITV1 in 2001 as part of a rebranding exercise to coincide with the creation of a number of digital-only channels. These now include ITV2, ITV3, ITV4 and CITV. ITV Network Centre is wholly owned by the ITV companies and undertakes commissioning and scheduling of programmes shown across the ITV network and, as with the other terrestrial channels, 25 per cent of programmes must come from independent producers.

Channel Four and S4C were launched in 1982 to provide programmes with a distinctive character that appeal to interests not catered for by ITV. Although state-owned, Channel 4 receives no public funding and is financed by commercial activities, including advertising. S4C has announced that after the digital switchover, it will become a Welsh-only channel. Channel 4 has expanded to create the digital stations E4, More4 and Film4.

Channel 5 (later renamed Five) began broadcasting in 1997. Despite initial problems with coverage, it now reaches about 80 per cent of the population. Digital stations Five US and Five Life were launched in October 2006.

BSkyB was formed after the merger in 1990 of Sky Television and British Sky Broadcasting. The company operates a satellite television service and around 40 television channels, including the Sky Sports and Sky Movies ranges. It is part-owned by Rupert Murdoch's News Corporation. BSkyB's digital package, Sky Digital, was launched in 1998 and offers access to 530 channels. With the 2005 acquisition of Easynet, an internet access provider and network operator, BSkyB now offers voice over IP (VoIP) telephony, video on demand and internet-based TV.

Virgin Media Television was founded in February 2007 as the television production arm of Virgin Media. It was previously known as NTL:Telewest. It owns a number of channels available via satellite, digital and cable platforms, including Bravo, Trouble and Living and runs a single branded channel, Virgin Central.

THE TELEVISION LICENCE

In the United Kingdom and its dependencies, a television licence is required to receive any publicly broadcast television service, regardless of its source, including commercial, satellite and cable programming.

The TV licence is classified as a tax, therefore non-payment is a criminal offence. A fine of up to £1,000 can be imposed on those successfully prosecuted. The Broadcasting Act 1990 made the BBC responsible for licence administration. TV Licensing is the name of the agent contracted to collect the licence fee on behalf of the BBC. Total licence fee income for 2006 was £3,124.8m. In 2007 an annual colour television licence cost £135.50 and a black and white licence £45.50. Concessions are available for the elderly and the disabled. Further details can be found at W www.tvlicensing.co.uk/information

HOW THE LICENCE FEE IS SPENT

	Percentage
Television (terrestrial and digital)	57.3
Local television and radio	16.3
Network radio	10.6
Transmission costs and licence fee collection	10.2
New media	3.4
BBC jam	1.3
Interactive TV	0.7

Source: BBC Online

DIGITAL SWITCHOVER

The digital switchover involves the turning off of the analogue terrestrial transmissions network that has been in place since the 1930s and replacing it with an all-digital terrestrial network. Viewers who receive television through an aerial will need to upgrade their sets with a set-top box (typically costing between £20 and £100) or use integrated digital television (iDTV), cable or satellite digital services. The switchover will take place between 2008 and 2012. The old analogue frequencies are likely to be sold to mobile telephone companies. For more information, *see* W www.digitaluk.co.uk

Region	Expected switchover date
Border	2008–9
West Country, Granada	2009
Wales	2009–10
West, STV North	2010
STV Central	2010–11
Central, Yorkshire, Anglia	2011
Meridian, London, Tyne Tees, Ulster	2012

Source: Digital UK

DIGITAL TELEVISION

Digital broadcasting has dramatically increased the number and reception quality of television channels. Sound and pictures are converted into a digital format and compressed, using as few bits as possible to convey the information on a digital signal. This technique enables several television channels to be carried in the space used by the current analogue signals to carry one channel. Digital signals can be received by standard aerials using

Freeview (*see* below), satellite dishes or cable. The signals are decoded and turned back into sound and pictures by either a set-top box or a decoder built into the television set (iDTV). A basic package of channels is available without charge and services are also offered by cable and satellite companies.

The Broadcasting Act 1996 provided for the licensing of 20 or more digital terrestrial television channels (on six frequency channels or 'multiplexes'). The first digital services went on air in autumn 1998.

In June 2002, following the collapse of ITV Digital, the digital terrestrial television licence was awarded to a consortium made up of the BBC, BSkyB and transmitter company Crown Castle by the Independent Television Commission. Freeview, a new digital network, was launched on 30 October 2002. Freeview offers around 30 digital channels and requires the purchase of a set-top box, but is subsequently free of charge.

By 2006 70 per cent of British homes had access to multi-channel TV. Freeview, cable and satellite channels now account for over a third of all TV viewing. The digital channels combined have a greater share of viewing than any of the five main channels and continue to increase this lead.

The advent of digital television has coincided with the emergence of the internet as a viable alternative means of watching TV. Channel 4's 4oD (4 on Demand) service allows views to revisit and download programmes shown in the previous 28 days and access an archive of older footage using their PC. At the time of writing, the BBC was preparing to launch its iPlayer, which will provide a similar service to 4oD; viewers will be able to download most of the programmes broadcast in the previous week and store each episode for 30 days. Eventually, the iPlayer will be offered through Freeview and satellite. ITV dramas and soaps can also be viewed online through the ITV website and there are plans to extend this service to the sport, entertainment and news sectors.

ESTIMATED AUDIENCE SHARE

	Percentage of all homes		
	2004–5	2005–6	2006–7
BBC One	24.4	22.9	22.7
BBC Two	9.6	9.4	8.6
ITV1	22.3	21.1	19.4
Channel 4	9.8	9.8	9.6
five	6.5	6.3	5.6
BBC Three	0.5	0.6	0.8
BBC Four	0.2	0.2	0.3
BBC News 24	0.4	0.4	0.5
ITV2	1.2	1.5	1.7
ITV3	0.7	0.3	1.1
ITV4*	–	–	0.4
E4	0.6	1.4	1.5
More4†	–	–	0.5
Film4‡	–	–	0.8
Sky One	1.5	1.4	1.3
Sky News	0.4	0.4	0.4
All BBC channels (total)	36.2	34.9	34.3
All Sky channels (total)	6.5	6.3	6.8
Cable, satellite and digital channels (total)	27.3	30.5	34.1

* Commenced broadcasting in November 2005
† Commenced broadcasting in October 2005
‡ Launched on Freeview in July 2006
Source: BBC Annual Report and Accounts/BARB

CONTACTS
THE BRITISH BROADCASTING CORPORATION
BBC TV CENTRE, Wood Lane, London W12 7RJ
T 020-8743 8000 W www.bbc.co.uk
Chair, Sir Michael Lyons

BBC WORLDWIDE LTD, Woodlands, 80 Wood Lane, London
W12 0TT T 020-8433 2000 W www.bbcworldwide.com

INDEPENDENT TELEVISION NETWORK
ITV NETWORK CENTRE/ITV ASSOCIATION, 200 Gray's Inn Road,
London WC1X 8HF T 020-7843 8000 W www.itv.com
Chair, Michael Grade

INDEPENDENT TELEVISION NETWORK REGIONS AND COMPANIES
ANGLIA *(eastern England),* Anglia House, Rose Lane,
Norwich NR1 3JG T 01603-615151
W www.itvregions.com/anglia
BORDER *(Borders and the Isle of Man),* The Television
Centre, Carlisle CA1 3NT T 01228-525101
W www.itvregions.com/border
CENTRAL *(east, west and south Midlands),* Gas Street,
Birmingham B1 2JT T 0870-600 6766
W www.itvregions.com/central
CHANNEL *(Channel Islands),* The Television Centre, St
Helier, Jersey JE1 3ZD T 01534-816816
W www.channelonline.tv
GRANADA *(north-west England),* Quay Street, Manchester
M60 9EA T 0161-832 7211
W www.itvregions.com/granada
LONDON *(London),* London Television Centre, Upper
Ground, London SE1 9LT T 020-7261 8163
W www.itvregions.com/london
MERIDIAN *(south and south-east England),* Solent Business
Park, Whiteley, Hants PO15 7PA T 01489-442000
W www.meridiantv.com
STV *(Scotland),* 200 Renfield Street, Glasgow G2 3PR
T 0141-300 3000 W www.stv.tv
TYNE TEES *(north-east England),* Television House, The
Watermark, Gateshead, Tyne and Wear NE11 9SZ
T 0191-404 8700 W www.itvregions.com/tyne_tees
ULSTER *(Northern Ireland),* Havelock House, Belfast BT7
1EB T 02890-328122 W www.u.tv
WALES The Television Centre, Culverhouse Cross, Cardiff CF5
6XJ T 029-2059 0590 W www.itvregions.com/wales
WEST Television Centre, Bath Road, Bristol BS4 3HG
T 0117-972 2722 W www.itvregions.com/west
WEST COUNTRY *(south-west England),* Langage Science
Park, Western Wood Way, Plymouth PL7 5BQ
T 01752-333333 W www.itvregions.com/westcountry
YORKSHIRE *(Yorkshire),* 96–104 Kirkstall Road, Leeds LS3
1JS T 0113-243 8283 W www.itvregions.com/yorkshire

OTHER TELEVISION COMPANIES
CHANNEL FOUR TELEVISION, 124 Horseferry Road,
London SW1P 2TX T 020-7396 4444
W www.channel4.com
FIVE BROADCASTING LTD, 22 Long Acre, London WC2E
9LY T 0845-705 0505 W www.five.tv
GMTV, The London Television Centre, Upper Ground, London
SE1 9TT T 020-7827 7000 W www.gm.tv
Owned by ITV and Disney, with 75 per cent and 25
per cent respectively, GMTV provides breakfast
television and sells its own advertising.

INDEPENDENT TELEVISION NEWS, 200 Gray's Inn
Road, London WC1X 8XZ T 020-7833 3000
W www.itn.co.uk
TELETEXT LTD, Building 10, Chiswick Park, 566 Chiswick
High Road London W4 5TS T 0870-731 3000
Provides teletext services for the ITV companies and
Channel 4 and offers holiday, car rental and mobile
telecom services.
WELSH FOURTH CHANNEL AUTHORITY, (Sianel
Pedwar Cymru/Channel Four Wales), Parc Ty Glas,
Llanishen, Cardiff CF14 5DU T 029-2074 7444
W www.s4c.co.uk
S4C schedules Welsh language and most Channel 4
programmes.

DIRECT BROADCASTING BY SATELLITE TELEVISION
BRITISH SKY BROADCASTING GROUP, Grant Way,
Isleworth, Middx TW7 5QD T 020-7705 3000
W www.sky.com
Chair, Rupert Murdoch
VIRGIN MEDIA TELEVISION, 160 Great Portland Street,
London W1W 5QA T 020-7299 5000
W www.virginmediatv.co.uk
Chair, Jim Mooney

RADIO

UK domestic radio services are broadcast across three
wavebands: FM, medium wave and long wave (used by
BBC Radio 4). In the UK the FM waveband extends in
frequency from 87.5MHz to 108MHz and the medium
waveband from 531kHz to 1602kHz. A number of radio
stations are now being broadcast in both analogue and
digital as well as a growing number in digital alone. As at
March 2007, the BBC Radio network controlled 56 per
cent of the listening market (*see* BBC Radio section), with
the independent sector (*see* Independent Radio section)
recording 42 per cent.

ESTIMATED AUDIENCE SHARE

| | | | *Percentage* |
| | Apr–Jun | Jan–Mar | Jan–Mar |
	2005	2006	2007
BBC Radio 1	9.2	9.1	10.1
BBC Radio 2	16.0	16.0	15.8
BBC Radio 3	1.1	1.3	1.2
BBC Radio 4	11.2	11.7	12.2
BBC Radio Five Live	4.4	4.6	4.2
Five Live Sports Extra	0.1	0.1	0.1
6 Music	0.1	0.2	0.3
BBC7	0.2	0.3	0.4
Asian Network	0.2	0.2	0.2
1Xtra	0.1	0.2	0.2
BBC Local/Regional	10.9	11.1	10.6
BBC World Service	0.5	0.6	0.7
All BBC	54.0	55.4	56.0
All independent	44.0	42.6	42.1
All national independent	10.2	10.5	10.7
All local independent	33.8	32.2	31.4
Other	2.0	2.0	1.8

Source: RAJAR/Ipsos-MORI

DIGITAL RADIO

DAB (Digital Audio Broadcasting) allows more services to be broadcast to a higher technical quality and provides the data facility for text and pictures. It improves the robustness of high fidelity radio services, especially compared with current FM and AM radio transmissions. It was developed in a collaborative research project under the pan-European Eureka 147 initiative and has been adopted as a world standard by the International Telecommunication Union for new digital radio systems. The frequencies allocated for terrestrial digital radio in the UK are 217.5 to 230MHz. More spectrum (in the 'L-Band' range: 1452–1467.5MHz) was planned for digital radio in the UK in 2007.

It is necessary to possess a digital radio set in order to receive digital broadcasts. Digital radios are available in several different forms: as standalone portable units, hi-fi stacks, car radios and PC cards, and inbuilt within a mobile phone. Newer DAB radios allow the listener to rewind, pause and record broadcasts and can be uploaded to a computer using a USB cable. Some portable sets now combine MP3 playback with DAB. An alternative method is to listen to digital radio through television sets via Freeview, cable or satellite.

LICENSING
The Broadcasting Act 1996 provided for the licensing of digital radio services (on multiplexes, where a number of stations share one frequency to transmit their services). To allocate the multiplexes, OFCOM advertises licences for which interested parties can bid. Once the licence has been awarded, the new owner seeks out services to broadcast on the multiplex. There is one national commercial multiplex owner (Digital One) operating eight digital services. The BBC has a separate national multiplex for its services. There are local multiplexes around the country, each broadcasting an average of seven services, plus the local BBC station. There are also several regional multiplexes covering a wider area and broadcasting up to 11 services each.

INNOVATIONS
As with television, the opportunities offered by digital services and the internet have made important changes to radio. Programmes are now more readily available and more interactive than ever before. Listeners can tune in to any BBC radio station live on the internet or listen again online for seven days after broadcast. Since 2005 increasing numbers of radio stations offer all or part of their programmes as downloadable files to listen to on computers or mobile devices such as MP3 players or phones. These files are known as podcasts.

Podcasting technology allows the listener to automatically receive latest episodes of regularly transmitted programmes as soon as they become available. The user usually needs to subscribe to receive the updates, in the same way as a magazine. While some radio stations and newspapers charge for updates, all of the BBC's podcasts are free.

The relationship between a radio presenter and his or her audience is also undergoing change. Listeners have long been given the opportunity to request songs to be played on air, but the quantity and easy availability of music on the internet has led to the creation of shows dedicated entirely to music sent in by listeners, much of which can be previously unknown to the presenter.

BBC RADIO

BBC Radio broadcasts network services to the UK, Isle of Man and the Channel Islands. There is also a tier of national services in Wales, Scotland and Northern Ireland and 40 local radio stations in England and the Channel Islands. In Wales and Scotland there are also dedicated language services in Welsh and Gaelic respectively. The frequency allocated for digital BBC broadcasts is 225.648MHz.

BBC RADIO Broadcasting House, Portland Place, London W1A 1AA T 020-7580 4468

BBC NETWORK RADIO STATIONS

RADIO 1 (contemporary pop music and entertainment news) – 24 hours a day, *frequencies:* 97–99 FM

RADIO 2 (popular music, entertainment, comedy and the arts) – 24 hours a day, *frequencies:* 88–91 FM

RADIO 3 (classical music, classic drama, documentaries and features) – 24 hours a day, *frequencies:* 90–93 FM

RADIO 4 (news, documentaries, drama, entertainment and cricket on long wave in season) – 5.20am–1am daily, with BBC World Service overnight, *frequencies:* 92–95 FM and 198 LW

RADIO FIVE LIVE (news and sport) – 24 hours a day, *frequencies:* 693/909 MW

FIVE LIVE SPORTS EXTRA (live sport) – schedule varies, digital only

6 MUSIC (contemporary and classic pop and rock music) – 24 hours a day, digital only

BBC7 (comedy, drama and children's) – 24 hours a day, digital only

Asian Network (news, music and sport) – 5am–1am Monday–Friday and Sunday; 5am–2am Saturday, with Radio Five Live overnight

1Xtra (urban music: drum & bass, garage, hip hop, R&B) – 24 hours a day, digital only

BBC NATIONAL RADIO STATIONS

RADIO CYMRU (Welsh-language), *frequencies:* 93.6–96.8 FM and 103.5–105 FM, coverage 97 per cent

RADIO FOYLE, *frequencies:* 792 AM and 93.1 MW

RADIO NAN GAIDHEAL (Gaelic service), *frequencies:* 103.5–105 FM plus 990 MW, coverage 90 per cent

RADIO SCOTLAND, *frequencies:* 810/585 MW and 92.4–94.7 FM, coverage 99 per cent. Local programmes for: Highlands and Islands; North East; Borders; South West; Orkney; and Shetland

RADIO ULSTER, *frequencies:* 1341 MW and 92.4–95.4 FM, coverage 96 per cent. Local programmes on Radio Foyle

RADIO WALES, *frequencies:* 882 MW and 93.9–95.9 FM, coverage 97 per cent

BBC LOCAL RADIO STATIONS

There are 40 local stations serving England and the Channel Islands:

BERKSHIRE, PO Box 1044, Reading RG4 8FH T 08459-001041 *Frequencies:* 94.6/95.4/104.1/104.4 FM and digital

BRISTOL, Whiteladies Road, Bristol BS8 2LR T 0117-974 2211 *Frequencies:* 94.9/95.5 FM and 1548 MW and digital

CAMBRIDGESHIRE, 104 Hills Road, Cambridge CB2 1LD T 01223-259696 *Frequencies:* 95.7/96 FM

CLEVELAND, Broadcasting House, Newport Road, Middlesbrough TS1 5DG T 01642-225211 *Frequency:* 95 FM and digital

CORNWALL, Phoenix Wharf, Truro TR1 1UA T 01872-275421 *Frequencies:* 95.2/96.0/103.9 FM and digital

COVENTRY AND WARWICKSHIRE, Priory Place, Coventry CV1 5SQ T 024-7655 1000 *Frequencies:* 94.8/104/103.7 FM and digital

CUMBRIA, Annetwell Street, Carlisle CA3 8BB T 01228-592444 *Frequencies:* 95.2/95.6/96.1/104.1/104.2 FM, 756/837/1458 MW

DERBY, 56 St Helen's Street, Derby DE1 3HY T 01332-361111 *Frequencies:* 95.3/96.0/104.5 FM, 1116 MW

DEVON, Broadcasting House, Seymour Road, Plymouth PL3 5BD T 01752-260323 *Frequencies:* 94.8/95.7/95.8/96.0/103.4/104.3 FM, 801/855/990/1458 MW and digital

ESSEX, PO Box 765, Chelmsford CM2 9XB T 01245-616000 *Frequencies:* 95.3/103.5 FM, 729/765/1530 MW and digital

GLOUCESTERSHIRE, London Road, Gloucester GL1 1SW T 01452-308585 *Frequencies:* 95.0/95.8/104.7 FM, 1413 MW

GUERNSEY, Broadcasting House, Bulwer Avenue, St Sampson's GY2 4LA T 01481-200600 *Frequencies:* 93.2/99 FM, 1116 AM

HEREFORD AND WORCESTER, Hylton Road, Worcester WR2 5WW T 01905-748485 *Frequencies:* 94.7/104.0/104.6 FM, 738/1584 MW

HUMBERSIDE, Queen's Court, Hull HU1 3RH T 01482-323232 *Frequency:* 95.9 FM, 1485 MW and digital

JERSEY, 18 Parade Road, St Helier JE2 3PL T 01534-837228 *Frequency:* 88.8 FM and digital

KENT, The Great Hall, Mount Pleasant, Tunbridge Wells TN1 1QQ T 01892-670000 *Frequencies:* 96.7/97.6/104.2 FM, 774/1602 MW

LANCASHIRE, 20–26 Darwen Street, Blackburn BB2 2EA T 01254-262411 *Frequencies:* 95.5/103.9/104.5 FM, 855/1557 MW and digital

LEEDS, 2 St Peter's Square, Leeds LS9 8AH T 0113-244 2131 *Frequency:* 92.4 FM, 774 MW and digital

LEICESTER, 9 St Nicholas Place, Leicester LE1 5LB T 0116-251 6688 *Frequency:* 104.9 FM and digital

LINCOLNSHIRE, PO Box 219, Lincoln LN1 3XY T 01522-511411 *Frequencies:* 94.9/104.7 FM, 1368 MW and digital

LONDON, PO Box 949, Marylebone High Street, London W1A 6FL T 020-7224 2424 *Frequency:* 94.9 FM and digital

MANCHESTER, PO Box 951, Oxford Road, Manchester M60 1SD T 0161-200 2020 *Frequencies:* 95.1/104.6 FM and digital

MERSEYSIDE, 55 Paradise Street, Liverpool L1 3BP T 0151-708 5500 *Frequency:* 95.8 FM and digital

NEWCASTLE, Broadcasting Centre, Barrack Road, Newcastle upon Tyne NE99 1RN T 0191-232 4141 *Frequency:* 95.4 and digital

NORFOLK, The Forum, Millennium Plain, Norwich NR2 1BH T 01603-617411 *Frequencies:* 95.1/95.6/104.4 FM and digital

NORTHAMPTON, Broadcasting House, Abington Street, Northampton NN1 2BH T 01604-239100 *Frequencies:* 103.6/104.2 FM

NOTTINGHAM, London Road, Nottingham NG2 4UU T 0115-955 0500 *Frequencies:* 95.5/103.8 FM and digital

OXFORD, 269 Banbury Road, Oxford OX2 7DW T 08459-311 444 *Frequency:* 95.2 FM

SHEFFIELD, 54 Shoreham Street, Sheffield S1 4RS T 0114-273 1177 *Frequencies:* 88.6/94.7/104.1 FM and digital

SHROPSHIRE, 2–4 Boscobel Drive, Harlescott, Shrewsbury SY1 3TT T 01743-237019 *Frequency:* 96 FM and digital

SOLENT, Havelock Road, Southampton SO14 7PW T 0845-313 0961 *Frequencies:* 96.1/103.8 FM

SOMERSET SOUND, Broadcasting House, Park Street, Taunton TA1 4DA T 01823-323956 *Frequency:* 1566 MW

SOUTHERN COUNTIES, Broadcasting Centre, Guildford GU2 7AP T 01483-306306 *Frequencies:* 95–95.3/104–104.8 FM and digital

STOKE, Cheapside, Hanley, Stoke-on-Trent ST1 1JJ T 01782-208080 *Frequencies:* 94.6/104.1 FM, 1503 MW and digital

SUFFOLK, Broadcasting House, St Matthew's Street, Ipswich IP1 3EP T 01473-250000 *Frequencies:* 95.5/95.9/103.9/104.6 FM

SWINDON, Broadcasting House, 56–58 Prospect Place, Swindon SN1 3RW T 01793-513626 *Frequency:* 103.6 FM and digital

THREE COUNTIES, 1 Hastings Street, Luton LU1 5XL T 01582-637400 *Frequencies:* 94.7/95.5/98.0/103.8/104.5 FM, 630/1161 MW

WILTSHIRE, Broadcasting House, 56–58 Prospect Place, Swindon SN1 3RW T 01793-513626 *Frequencies:* 103.5/104.3/104.9 FM and digital

WM (WEST MIDLANDS), The Mailbox, Birmingham B1 1RF T 0121-567 6000 *Frequency:* 95.6 FM and digital

YORK, 20 Bootham Row, York YO30 7BR T 01904-641351 *Frequencies:* 95.5/103.7/104.3 FM

BBC WORLD SERVICE

The BBC World Service broadcasts to an estimated weekly audience of 163 million worldwide, in 33 languages including English, and is now available in 150 capital cities. It no longer broadcasts in Dutch, French for Europe, German, Hebrew, Italian, Japanese or Malay because it was found that most speakers of these languages preferred to listen to the English broadcasts. In 2006 services in ten languages (Bulgarian, Croatian, Czech, Greek, Hungarian, Kazakh, Polish, Slovak, Slovene, and Thai) were terminated to provide funding for a new Arabic television channel, which was to be launched in late 2007. The BBC World Service website offers interactive news services in English, Arabic, Chinese, Hindi, Persian, Portuguese for Brazil, Russian, Spanish and Urdu with audiostreaming available in 33 languages:

Albanian, Arabic, Azeri, Bengali, Burmese, Caribbean-English, Cantonese, French for Africa, Hausa, Hindi, Indonesian, Kinyarwanda/Kirundi, Kyrgyz, Macedonian, Mandarin, Nepali, Pashto, Persian, Portuguese for Brazil, Romanian, Russian, Serbian, Sinhala, Somali, Spanish, Swahili, Tamil, Turkish, Ukrainian, Urdu, Uzbek and Vietnamese.

UK frequencies: 648 MW in southern England and overnight on BBC Radio 4, BBC Radio Ulster, BBC Radio Wales or the Asian Network.

BBC LEARNING ENGLISH teaches English worldwide through radio, television and a wide range of published and online courses.

BBC MONITORING tracks the global media for the latest news reports emerging around the world.

BBC WORLD SERVICE TRUST is a registered charity established in 1999 by BBC World Service. It promotes development through the innovative use of the media in the developing world. The trust presently works in over 30 countries worldwide, tackling health, education and good governance.

BBC WORLD SERVICE Bush House, Strand, London WC2B 4PH T 020-7557 2462

INDEPENDENT RADIO

Until 1973, the BBC had a legal monopoly on radio broadcasting in the UK. During this time, the corporation's only competition came from pirate stations located abroad, such as Radio Luxembourg. Christopher Chataway, Minister for Post and Telecommunications in Edward Heath's government, changed this by creating the first licences for commercial radio stations. The Independent Broadcasting Authority (IBA) awarded the first of these licences to the London Broadcasting Company (LBC) to provide London's news and information service. LBC was followed by Capital Radio, to offer the city's entertainment service, Radio Clyde in Glasgow and BRMB in Birmingham.

The IBA was dissolved when the Broadcasting Act of 1990 de-regulated broadcasting, to be succeeded by the less rigid Radio Authority (RA). The RA began advertising new licences for the development of independent radio in January 1991. It awarded national and local radio, satellite and cable services licences, and long-term restricted service licences for stations serving non-commercial establishments such as hospitals and universities. The first national commercial digital multiplex licence was awarded in October 1998 and a number of local digital multiplex licences followed.

At the end of 2003 the RA was replaced by OFCOM, which now carries out the licensing administration.

The RadioCentre was formed in July 2006 as a result of the merger between the Radio Advertising Bureau (RAB) and the Commercial Radio Companies Association (CRCA), the former non-profit trade body for commercial radio companies in the United Kingdom, to operate essentially as a union for commercial radio stations.

THE RADIOCENTRE, 77 Shaftesbury Avenue, London W1D 5DU T 020-7306 2603 W www.radiocentre.org

Chief Executive, Andrew Harrison

INDEPENDENT NATIONAL RADIO STATIONS

CLASSIC FM, 30 Leicester Square, London WC2H 7LA
T 020-7343 9000 – 24 hours a day, *Frequencies:* 100–102 FM

TALK SPORT, 18 Hatfields, London SE1 8DJ
T 020-7959 7800 – 24 hours a day, *Frequencies:* 1053/1071/1089/1107 AM

VIRGIN 1215, 1 Golden Square, London W1F 9DJ
T 020-7434 1215 – 24 hours a day, *Frequencies:* 1197/1215/1233/1242/1260 AM

INDEPENDENT LOCAL RADIO STATIONS ENGLAND

2BR, Lomeshaye Business Village, Nelson, Lancs BB9 7DR
T 01282-690000 *Frequency:* 99.8 FM

2CR FM, 5–7 Southcote Road, Bournemouth BH1 3LR
T 01202-234900 *Frequency:* 102.3 FM

2-TEN FM, PO Box 2020, Reading, Berks RG31 7FG
T 0118-945 4400 *Frequencies:* 97.0/102.9/103.4 FM

3FM, 45 Victoria Street, Douglas, IOM IM1 3RS
T 01624-616333 *Frequencies:* 104–106 FM

3TR FM, Riverside Studios, Warminster, Wilts BA12 9HQ
T 01985-211111 *Frequency:* 107.5 FM

95.8 CAPITAL RADIO, 30 Leicester Square, London WC2H 7LA T 020-7766 6000 *Frequency:* 95.8 FM

96 TRENT FM, Maid Marian Way, Nottingham NG1 6JR
T 0115-873 1500 *Frequencies:* 96.2/96.5 FM

96.2 THE REVOLUTION, Sarah Moor Studios, Henshaw Street, Oldham OL1 3JF T 0161-621 6500 *Frequency:* 96.2 FM

96.2 TOUCH FM, Watch Close, Spon Street, Coventry CV1 3LN T 024-7652 5656 *Frequency:* 96.2 FM

96.3 RADIO AIRE, 51 Burley Road, Leeds LS3 1LR
T 0113-283 5500 *Frequency:* 96.3 FM

96.4 FM BRMB, Nine Brindleyplace, 4 Oozells Square, Birmingham B1 2DJ T 0121-566 5200 *Frequency:* 96.4 FM

96.4 THE EAGLE, Dolphin House, North Street, Guildford, Surrey GU1 4AA T 01483-300964 *Frequency:* 96.4 FM

96.9 CHILTERN FM, 5 Abbey Court, Fraser Road, Priory Business Park, Bedford MK44 3WH T 01234-235010 *Frequency:* 96.9 FM

96.9 VIKING FM, The Boathouse, Commercial Road, Hull, E. Yorks HU1 2SG T 01482-325141 *Frequency:* 96.9 FM

97 FM PLYMOUTH SOUND, Earl's Acre, Plymouth PL3 4HX T 01752-275600 *Frequencies:* 96.6/97 FM

97.2 STRAY FM, The Hamlet, Hornbeam Park Avenue, Harrogate HG2 8RE T 01423-522972 *Frequency:* 97.2 FM

97.4 ROCK FM, PO Box 974, St. Paul's Square, Preston, Lancs PR1 1YE T 01772-477700 *Frequency:* 97.4 FM

97.6 CHILTERN FM, Chiltern Road, Dunstable LU6 1HQ T 01582-676200 *Frequency:* 97.6 FM

100–102 CENTURY FM, Century House, PO Box 100, Gateshead NE8 2YY T 0191-556 3000 *Frequencies:* 96.2/94.6/100.7/101.8 FM

100.7 HEART FM, 1 The Square, 111 Broad Street, Birmingham B15 1AS T 0121-695 0000 *Frequency:* 100.7 FM

102 TOUCH FM, The Guard House Studios, Banbury Road, Stratford-upon-Avon, Warks CV37 7HX
T 01789-262636 *Frequency:* 102.0 FM

102.2 SMOOTH FM, 26–27 Castlereagh Street, London W1H 5DL T 020-7706 4100 *Frequency:* 102.2 FM

102.4 WISH FM, Orrell Lodge, Orrell Road, Wigan, Lancs WN5 8HJ T 01942-761024 *Frequency:* 102.4 FM

102.7 HEREWARD FM, PO Box 225, Queensgate Centre, Peterborough PE1 1XJ T 01733-460460 *Frequency:* 102.7 FM

102.7 MERCURY FM, 9 The Stanley Centre, Kelvin Way, Crawley, W. Sussex RH10 9SE T 01293-519161 *Frequencies:* 97.5/102.7 FM

103.2 ALPHA FM, Radio House, 11 Woodland Road, Darlington, Co. Durham DL3 7BJ T 01325-255552 *Frequency:* 103.2 FM

103.2 POWER FM, Radio House, Whittle Avenue, Segensworth West, Fareham, Hants PO15 5SH
T 01489-579000 *Frequency:* 103.2 FM

103.4 SUN FM, PO Box 1034, Sunderland, Tyne and Wear SR5 2YL T 0191-548 1034 *Frequency:* 103.4 FM

105.4 CENTURY FM, Laser House, Waterfront Quays, Manchester M50 3XW T 0161-662 4701 *Frequency:* 105.4 FM

107.2 WIN FM, The Brooks, Winchester, Hants SO23 8FT
T 01962-841071 *Frequency:* 107.2 FM

107.2 THE WYRE, Foley House, 123 Stourport Road, Kidderminster DY11 7BW T 01562-641072 *Frequency:* 107.2 FM

107.4 THE QUAY, Flagship Studios, PO Box 1074, Portsmouth PO2 8YG T 023-9236 4141 *Frequency:* 107.4 FM

107.5 SOVEREIGN RADIO, 14 St Mary's Walk, Hailsham, E. Sussex BN27 1AF T 01323-442700 *Frequency:* 107.5 FM

107.6 FM JUICE LIVERPOOL, 27 Fleet Street, Liverpool L1 4AR T 0151-707 3107 *Frequency:* 107.6 FM

107.6 TOUCH BANBURY, Unit 9A, Manor Park, Banbury, Oxfordshire OX16 3TB T 0129-566 1076 *Frequency:* 107.6 FM

107.7 SPLASH FM, The Guildbourne Centre, Worthing, W. Sussex BN11 1LZ T 01903-233005 *Frequency:* 107.7 FM

107.7 THE WOLF, 10th Floor, Mander House, Wolverhampton WV1 3NB T 01902-571070 *Frequency:* 107.7 FM

107.8 ARROW FM, Priory Meadow Centre, Hastings, E. Sussex TN34 1PJ T 01424-461177 *Frequency:* 107.8 FM

107.8 RADIO JACKIE, 110–112 Tolworth Broadway, Surbiton, Surrey KT6 7JD T 020-8288 1300 *Frequency:* 107.8 FM

107.9 DUNE FM, The Power Station, Victoria Way, Southport, Merseyside PR8 1RR T 01704-502500 *Frequency:* 107.9 FM

1548 AM CAPITAL GOLD, 30 Leicester Square, London WC2H 7LA T 020-7054 8000 *Frequency:* 1548 AM

ASIAN SOUND RADIO, Globe House, Southall Street, Manchester M3 1LG T 0161-288 1000 *Frequencies:* 963/1377 AM

ATLANTIC FM, Unit 10, Wheal Kitty Workshops, St Agnes, Cornwall TR5 0RD T 01872-554400 *Frequencies:* 105.1/107.0 FM

BATH FM, Station House, Ashley Avenue, Lower Weston, Bath BA1 3DS T 01225-471571 *Frequency:* 107.9 FM

THE BAY, PO Box 969, St George's Quay, Lancaster LA1 3LD T 01524-848747 *Frequencies:* 96.9/102.3/103.2 FM

THE BEACH, PO Box 103.4, Lowestoft, Suffolk NR32 2TL T 0845-345 1035 *Frequencies:* 97.4/103.4 FM

BEACON FM, 267 Tettenhall Road, Wolverhampton WV6 0DE T 01902-461300 *Frequencies:* 97.2/103.1 FM

THE BEAR 102, The Guard House Studios, Banbury Road, Stratford upon Avon, Warks CV37 7HX T 01789 262636 *Frequency:* 102.0 FM

BRIDGWATER'S 107.4 BCR FM, Royal Clarence House, High Street, Bridgwater, Somerset TA6 3AT T 01278-727701 *Frequency:* 107.4 FM

BRIGHT 106.4, 11A The Market Place Shopping Centre, Burgess Hill, W. Sussex RH15 9NP T 01444-248127 *Frequency:* 106.4 FM

CAPITAL GOLD (1152), Nine Brindleyplace, 4 Oozells Square, Birmingham B1 2DJ T 0121-245 5000 *Frequency:* 1152 AM

CAPITAL GOLD (1242/603), Radio House, John Wilson Business Park, Whitstable, Kent CT5 3QX T 01227-772004 *Frequencies:* 603/1242 AM

CAPITAL GOLD (1323/945), Radio House, PO Box 2000, Brighton BN41 2SS T 01273-430111 *Frequencies:* 945/1323 AM

CAPITAL GOLD 1458 AM, Laser House, Waterfront Quays, Manchester M5 2XW T 0161-662 4700 *Frequency:* 1458 AM

CAPITAL GOLD (1557/1170), Radio House, Whittle Avenue, Segensworth West, Farnham, Hants PO15 5SH T 01489-589911 *Frequencies:* 1170/1557 AM

CFM (CARLISLE AND WEST CUMBRIA), PO Box 964, Carlisle, Cumbria CA1 3NG T 01228-818964 *Frequencies:* 96.4/102.5 FM (Carlisle) (west Cumbria); 102.2/103.4 FM

CHESHIRE'S 106.9 SILK FM, Radio House, Bridge Street, Macclesfield, Cheshire SK11 6DJ T 01625-268000 *Frequency:* 106.9 FM

CHOICE 96.9/107.1 FM, 30 Leicester Square, London WC2H 7LA T 020-7766 6810 *Frequency:* 96.9/107.1 FM

CLASSIC GOLD (666/954), Hawthorn House, Exeter Business Park, Exeter EX1 3QS T 01392-444444 *Frequencies:* 666/954 AM

CLASSIC GOLD (774), Bridge Studios, Eastgate Centre, Gloucester GL1 1SS T 01452-572400 *Frequency:* 774 AM

CLASSIC GOLD (828), 5–7 Southcote Road, Bournemouth, Dorset BH1 3LR T 01202-234900 *Frequency:* 828 AM

CLASSIC GOLD (828/792), Chiltern Road, Dunstable, Beds LU6 1HQ T 01582-676200 *Frequencies:* 792/828 AM

CLASSIC GOLD (936/1161), 1st Floor, Chiseldon House, Stonehill Green, Westlea, Swindon, Wilts SN5 7HB T 01793-663000 *Frequencies:* 936/1161 AM

CLASSIC GOLD (990/1017), 267 Tettenhall Road, Wolverhampton WV6 0DQ T 01902-461200 *Frequencies:* 990/1017 AM

CLASSIC GOLD (1152), Earl's Acre, Plymouth PL3 4HX T 01752-275600 *Frequency:* 1152 AM

CLASSIC GOLD (1260), PO Box 2000, One Passage Street, Bristol BS99 7SN T 0117-984 3200 *Frequency:* 1260 AM

CLASSIC GOLD (1332), PO Box 225, Queensgate Centre, Peterborough, Cambridge PE1 1XJ T 01733-460460 *Frequency:* 1332 AM

CLASSIC GOLD (1359), Hertford Place, Coventry CV1 3TT T 024-7686 8200 *Frequency:* 1359 AM

CLASSIC GOLD (1359/1431), 31 Glebe Road, Chelmsford, Essex CM1 1QG T 01245-524549, *Frequencies:* 1359/1431 AM

CLASSIC GOLD (1431/1485), The Chase, Calcot, Reading, Berks RG3 7RB T 0118-945 4400 *Frequencies:* 1431/1485 AM

CLASSIC GOLD (1521), 9 The Stanley Centre, Kelvin Way, Crawley, W. Sussex RH10 9SE T 01293-519161 *Frequency:* 1521 AM

CLASSIC GOLD (1557), 19–21 St Edmunds Road, Northampton NN1 5DY T 01604-795600 *Frequency:* 1557 AM

CLASSIC GOLD AMBER (NORFOLK), St George's Plain, 47–49 Colegate, Norwich NR3 1DB T 01603-630621 *Frequency:* 1152 AM

CLASSIC GOLD AMBER (SUFFOLK), Alpha Business Park, 6–12 White House Road, Ipswich IP1 5LT T 01473-461000 *Frequency:* 1170/1251 AM

CLASSIC GOLD GEM, 29–31 Castle Gate, Nottingham NG1 7AP T 0115-873 1500 *Frequencies:* 945/999 AM

CLASSIC HITS (954/1530), PO Box 262, Worcester WR6 5ZE T 01905-740600 *Frequencies:* 954/1530 AM

CLUB ASIA, Asia House, 227–247 Gascoigne Road, Barking, Essex IG11 7LN T 020-8594 6662 *Frequencies:* 963/972 AM

COMPASS FM, 26A Wellowgate, Grimsby, Lincs DN32 0RA T 01472-346666 *Frequency:* 96.4 FM

CONNECT FM, Unit 1, Centre 2000, Robinson Close, Telford Way Industrial Estate, Kettering, Northants NN16 8PU T 01536-412413 *Frequencies:* 97.2/107.4 FM

COUNTY SOUND RADIO 1566 AM, Dolphin House, North Street, Guildford, Surrey GU1 4AA T 01483-300964 *Frequency:* 1566 AM

CTR FM, 6–8 Mill Street, Maidstone, Kent ME15 6XH T 01622-662500 *Frequency:* 105.6 FM

DEARNE FM, Unit 7, Network Centre, Zenith Park, Whaley Road, Barnsley S75 1HT T 01226-321733 *Frequencies:* 97.1/102.0 FM

DEE 106.3, 2 Chantry Court, Chester CH1 4QN T 01244-391000 *Frequency:* 106.3 FM

DELTA FM, Tindle House, High Street, Bordon, Hants GU35 0AY T 01420-473473 *Frequencies:* 97.1/101.6/101.8/102.0 FM

DREAM 100 FM, Northgate House, St Peter's Street, Colchester, Essex CO1 1HT T 01206-764466 *Frequency:* 100.2 FM

DREAM 107.7 FM, 12 Bentalls Shopping Centre, Colchester Road, Heybridge, Maldon, Essex CM9 4GD T 01473-836100 *Frequency:* 107.7 FM

EASY RADIO LONDON (1035), Radio House, Merrick Road, Southall, Middlesex UB2 4AU, T 020-8574 6666, *Frequency:* 1035 AM

ENERGY FM, 100 Market Street, Douglas, IOM IM1 2PH T 01624-611936 *Frequencies:* 91.2 FM (Laxey); 93.4 FM (north Isle of Man); 98.4 FM (Ramsey); 98.6 FM

ESSEX FM, Radio House, 31, Glebe House, Chelmsford, Essex CM1 1QG T 01245-524500 *Frequencies:* 96.3/97.5/102.6 FM

FEN RADIO 107.5, Quadrant Studios, Old Christchurch Road, Bournemouth BH1 2AD T 01202-318100 *Frequency:* 107.5 FM

FIRE 107.6 FM, Quadrant Studios, Old Christchurch Road, Bournemouth BH1 2AD T 01202-318100 *Frequency:* 107.6 FM

FOSSEWAY RADIO, Suite 1, 1 Castle Street, Hinckley, Leics LE10 1DA T 01455-614151 *Frequency:* 107.9 FM

FOX FM, Brush House, Pony Road, Oxford OX4 2XR T 01865-871000 *Frequencies:* 97.4/102.6 FM

FRESH RADIO, Firth Mill, Firth Street, Skipton, N. Yorks BD23 2PT T 01756-799991 *Frequencies:* 936/1413/1431 AM

GALAXY BIRMINGHAM, 1 The Square, 111 Broad Street, Birmingham, West Midlands B15 1AS T 0121-695 0000 *Frequency:* 102.2 FM

GALAXY MANCHESTER, 5th Floor, The Triangle, Hanging Ditch, Manchester M4 3TR T 0161-279 0300 *Frequency:* 102.0 FM

GALAXY NORTH EAST, Kingfisher Way, Silverlink Business Park, Wallsend, Tyne and Wear NE28 9NX T 0191-206 8000 *Frequencies:* 105.3/105.6/105.8/106.4 FM

GALAXY YORKSHIRE, Joseph's Well, Hanover Walk, Leeds LS3 1AB T 0113-213 0105 *Frequencies:* 105.1/105.6/105.8 FM

GEMINI FM, Hawthorn House, Exeter Business Park, Exeter EX1 3QS T 01392-444444 *Frequencies:* 96.4/97.0/103.0 FM

GWR FM (Bristol and Bath), PO Box 2000, One Passage Street, Bristol BS99 7SN T 0117-984 3200 *Frequencies:* 96.3/103.0 FM

GWR FM (Swindon and West Wiltshire), Chiseldon House, Stonehill Green, Westlea, Swindon, Wilts SN5 7HB T 01793-842600 *Frequencies:* 96.5/97.2/102.2 FM

HALLAM FM, Radio House, 900 Herries Road, Sheffield S6 1RH T 0114-209 1000 *Frequencies:* 97.4/102.9/103.4 FM

HEART 106, City Link, Nottingham NG2 4NG T 0115-910 6100 *Frequency:* 106 FM

HEART 106.2, The Chrysalis Building, Bramley Road, London W10 6SP T 020-7468 1062 *Frequency:* 106.2 FM

HERTBEAT FM, The Pump House, Knebworth Park, Herts SG3 6HQ T 01438-810900 *Frequencies:* 106.7/106.9 FM

HERTFORDSHIRE'S MERCURY 96.6, St Albans and Watford Broadcasting Company Ltd, 9 Nelson Street, Southend on Sea, Essex SS1 1EH; Unit 5, The Metro Centre, Dwight Road, Watford WD18 9UP T 01923-205470 *Frequency:* 96.9 FM

HIGH PEAK RADIO, The Studios, Smithbrook Close, Chapel-en-le-Frith, High Peak, Derbys SK23 0QD T 01298-813144 *Frequencies:* 103.3/106.4 FM

HOME 107.9, The Old Stable Block, Lockwood Park, Huddersfield HD1 3UR T 01484-321107 *Frequency:* 107.9 FM

HORIZON RADIO, 14 Vincent Avenue, Crowhill, Milton Keynes MK8 0AB, T 01908-269111 *Frequency:* 103.3 FM

IMAGINE FM, Regent House, Heaton Lane, Stockport, Cheshire SK4 1BX T 0161-609 1400 *Frequency:* 104.9 FM

INVICTA FM, Radio House, John Wilson Business Park, Whitstable, Kent CT5 3QX T 01227-772004 *Frequencies:* 95.9/96.1/97.0/102.8/103.1 FM

ISLE OF WIGHT RADIO, Dodnor Park, Newport, IOW PO30 5XE T 01983-822557 *Frequencies:* 102.0/107.0 FM

IVEL FM, The Studios, Middle Street, Yeovil, Somerset BA20 1DJ T 01935-848488 *Frequencies:* 105.6/106.6 FM

KCR FM, The Studios, Cables Retail Park, Prescot, Merseyside LS4 5SW T 0151-290 1501 *Frequency:* 106.7 FM

KERRANG! 105.2 FM, Kerrang House, 20 Lionel Street, Birmingham B3 1AQ T 0845-053 1052 *Frequency:* 105.2 FM

KESTREL FM, 2nd Floor, Paddington House, Festival Place, Basingstoke, Hants RG21 7LJ T 01256-694000 *Frequency:* 107.6 FM

KEY 103, Castle Quay, Castlefield, Manchester M15 4PR T 0161-288 5000 *Frequency:* 103.0 FM

KICK FM, The Studios, 42 Bone Lane, Newbury, Berks RG14 5SD T 01635-841600 *Frequencies:* 105.6/107.4 FM

KISMAT, Radio House, Merrick Road, Southall, Middx UB2 4AU T 020-8843 5330 *Frequency:* 1035 AM

KISS 100 FM, Mappin House, 4 Winsley Street, London W1W 8HF T 020-7975 8100 *Frequency:* 100.0 FM

KISS 101 FM, 26 Baldwin Street, Bristol BS1 1SE T 0117-901 0101 *Frequency:* 97.2/101.0 FM

KISS FM 105–108, Reflection House, The Anderson Centre Olding Road, Bury St Edmunds IP33 3TA T 01284-715300 *Frequency:* 105.6/106.1/106.4/107.7 FM

KL.FM 96.7, 18 Blackfriars Street, King's Lynn, Norfolk PE30 1NN T 01553-772777 *Frequency:* 96.7 FM

KMFM FOR ASHFORD, Express House, 34–36 North Street, Ashford, Kent TN24 8JR T 01233-623232 *Frequency:* 107.7 FM

KMFM FOR CANTERBURY, 9 St George's Place, Canterbury, Kent CT1 1UU T 01227-475950 *Frequency:* 106.0 FM

KMFM FOR MEDWAY, Medway House, Ginsbury Close, Sir Thomas Longley Road, Medway City Estate, Strood, Rochester, Kent ME2 4DU T 01634-711079 *Frequencies:* 100.4/107.9 FM

KMFM FOR SHEPWAY AND WHITE CLIFFS COUNTRY, 93–95 Sandgate Road, Folkstone, Kent CT20 2BQ T 01303-220303 *Frequencies:* 96.4/106.8 FM

KMFM FOR THANET, 183 Northdown Road, Cliftonville, Margate, Kent CT9 2TA T 01843-220222 *Frequency:* 107.2 FM

KMFM FOR WEST KENT, 1 East Street, Tonbridge, Kent TN9 1AR T 01732-369200 *Frequencies:* 96.2/101.6 FM

LAKELAND RADIO, Unit 4, Lakelands Food Park, Plumgarths, Crook Road, Kendal, Cumbria LA8 8QJ T 01539-737390 *Frequencies:* 100.1/100.8 FM

LANTERN FM, Unit 2B, Lauder Lane, Roundswell Business Park, Barnstaple EX31 3TA T 01271-366350 *Frequencies:* 96.2/97.3 FM

LBC 97.3 FM, The Chrysalis Building, 13 Bramley Road, London W10 6SP T 020-7314 7300 *Frequency:* 97.3 FM

LBC NEWS 1152 AM, The Chrysalis Building, 13 Bramley Road, London W10 6SP T 020-7221 2213 *Frequency:* 1152 AM

LEICESTER SOUND, 6 Dominus Way, Meridian Business Park, Leicester LE19 1RP T 0116-256 1300 *Frequency:* 105.4 FM

LINCS FM, Witham Park, Waterside South, Lincoln LN5 7JN T 01522-549900 *Frequencies:* 96.7/102.2/97.6 FM

LITE FM, 2nd Floor, 5 Church Street, Peterborough PE1 1XB T 01733-898106 *Frequency:* 106.8/96.4 FM

LONDON GREEK RADIO, LGR House, 437 High Road, London N12 0AP T 020-8349 6950 *Frequency:* 103.3 FM

LONDON TURKISH RADIO, 185B High Road, Wood Green, London N22 6BA T 020-8881 0606 *Frequency:* 1584 AM

MAGIC 105.4 FM, Mappin House, 4 Winsley Street, London W1 8HF T 020-7182 8000 *Frequency:* 105.4 FM

MAGIC 828, 51 Burley Road, Leeds LS3 1LR T 0113-283 5500 *Frequency:* 828 AM

MAGIC 999, St Paul's Square, Preston, Lancs PR1 1YE T 01772-477700 *Frequency:* 999 AM

MAGIC 1152 (TYNE & WEAR), 50 Degrees North, Pilgrim Street, Newcastle upon Tyne NE1 6BF T 0191-230 6100 *Frequency:* 1152 AM

MAGIC 1161 AM, Commercial Road, Hull, E. Yorks HU1 2SG T 01482-325141 *Frequency:* 1161 AM

MAGIC 1170, Radio House, Yale Crescent, Thornaby, Stockton-on-Tees TS17 6AA T 01642-888222 *Frequency:* 1170 AM

MAGIC 1548 AM, St John's Beacon, 1 Houghton Street, Liverpool L1 1RL T 0151-472 6800 *Frequency:* 1548 AM

MAGIC AM, Radio House, 900 Herries Road, Sheffield S6 1RH T 0114-209 1000 *Frequencies:* 990/1305/1548 AM

MANCHESTER'S MAGIC 1152, Castle Quay, Castlefield, Manchester M1 4AW T 0161-288 5000 *Frequency:* 1152 AM

MANSFIELD 103.2 FM, The Media Suite, Brunts Business Centre, Samuel Brunts Way, Mansfield, Notts NG18 2AH T 01623-646666 *Frequency:* 103.2 FM

MANX RADIO, PO Box 1368, Broadcasting House, Douglas, IOM IM99 1SW T 01624-682600 *Frequencies:* 89.0/97.2/103.7 FM, 1368 AM

MERCIA FM, Hertford Place, Coventry CV1 3TT T 024-7686 8200 *Frequencies:* 97.0/102.9 FM

METRO RADIO, Longrigg, Swalwell, Newcastle upon Tyne NE99 1BB T 0191-420 0971 *Frequencies:* 97.1/102.6/103.0/103.2 FM

MINSTER FM, PO Box 123, Dunnington, York YO1 5ZX T 01904-488888 *Frequencies:* 102.3/104.7 FM

MIX 96, Friars Square Studios, 11 Bourbon Street, Aylesbury, Bucks HP20 2PZ T 01296-399396 *Frequency:* 96.2 FM

MIX 107, 11 Duke Street, High Wycombe, Bucks HP13 6EE T 01494-446611 *Frequencies:* 107.4/107.7 FM

NORTH NORFOLK RADIO, The Studio, Breck Farm, Stody, Norfolk NR24 2ER T 01263-860808 *Frequencies:* 96.2/103.2 FM

NORTHANTS 96, 19–21 St Edmunds Road, Northampton NN1 5DY T 01604-795600 *Frequency:* 96.6 FM

OAK 107, 7 Waldron Court, Prince William Road, Loughborough, Leics LE11 5GD T 01509-211711 *Frequency:* 107.0 FM

OCEAN FM, Radio House, Whittle Avenue, Segensworth West, Fareham, Hants PO15 5SH T 01489-589911 *Frequencies:* 96.7/97.5 FM

ORCHARD FM, Haygrove House, Shoreditch Road, Taunton, Somerset TA3 7BT T 01823-338448 *Frequencies:* 96.5/97.1/102.6 FM

OXFORD'S FM 1079, 270 Woodstock Road, Oxford OX2 7NW T 01865-315980 *Frequency:* 107.9 FM

PALM (105.5), Marble Court, Lymington Road, Torquay TQ1 4AU T 01803-321 055 *Frequency:* 105.5 FM

PEAK 107 FM, Radio House, Foxwood Road, Chesterfield, Derbys S41 9RF T 01246-269107 *Frequencies:* 102.0/107.4 FM

PIRATE FM, Carn Brea Studios, Wilson Way, Redruth, Cornwall TR15 3XX T 01209-314400 *Frequencies:* 102.2/102.8 FM

PREMIER CHRISTIAN RADIO, 22 Chapter Street, London SW1P 4NP T 020-7316 1300 *Frequencies:* 1305/1332/1413 AM

THE PULSE OF WEST YORKSHIRE, Forster Square, Bradford, W. Yorks BD1 5NE T 01274-203040 *Frequencies:* 97.5/102.5 FM

PULSE CLASSIC GOLD, Forster Square, Bradford, W. Yorks BD1 5NE T 01274-203040 *Frequencies:* 1278/1530 AM

Q103 FM, Enterprise House, The Vision Park, Chivers Way, Histon, Cambridge CB4 9WW T 01223-235255 *Frequencies:* 97.4/103.0 FM

QUAY 102.4 FM, Harbour Studios, The Esplanade, Watchet, Somerset TA23 0AJ T 01984-634900 *Frequencies:* 100.8/102.4 FM

RADIO BROADLAND 102.4, St George's Plain, 47–49

Colegate, Norwich NR3 1DB T 01603-630621 *Frequency:* 102.4 FM

RADIO CITY 96.7, St John's Beacon, 1 Houghton Street, Liverpool L1 1RL T 0151-472 6800 *Frequency:* 96.7 FM

RADIO WAVE 96.5 FM, 965 Mowbray Drive, Blackpool, Lancs FY3 7JR T 01253-304965 *Frequency:* 96.5 FM

RADIO XL 1296 AM, KMS House, Bradford Street, Birmingham B12 0JD T 0121-753 5353 *Frequency:* 1296 AM

RAM FM, 35/36 Irongate, Derby DE1 3GA T 01332-324000 *Frequency:* 102.8 FM

READING 107 FM, Radio House, Madejski Stadium, Reading, Berks RG2 0FN T 0118-986 2555 *Frequency:* 107.0 FM

REAL RADIO (YORKSHIRE), 1 Sterling Court, Capitol Park, Leeds WF3 1EL T 0113-238 1114 *Frequencies:* 106.2/107.6/107.7 FM

RIDINGS FM, 2 Thornes Office Park, Monckton Road, Wakefield WF2 7AN T 01924-367177 *Frequency:* 106.8 FM

ROTHER FM, Aspen Court, Bessemer Way, Rotherham S60 1FB T 01709-369993 *Frequency:* 96.1 FM

RUGBY FM, Suites 4–6, Dunsmore Business Centre, Spring Street, Rugby, Warks CV21 3HH T 01788-541100 *Frequency:* 107.1 FM

RUTLAND RADIO, 40 Melton Road, Oakham, Rutland, Leics LE15 6AY T 01572-757868 *Frequencies:* 97.4/107.2 FM

SABRAS RADIO, Radio House, 63 Melton Road, Leicester LE4 6PN T 0116-261 0666 *Frequency:* 1260 AM

THE SAINT, The Friends Provident, St. Mary's Stadium, Britannia Road, Southampton SO14 5FP T 023-8033 0300 *Frequency:* 107.8 FM

THE SEVERN, Abbey Studios, 13–14 Abbey Foregate, Shrewsbury SY2 6AE T 01743-284940 *Frequencies:* 106.5/ 107.1 FM

SEVERN SOUND, Bridge Studios, Eastgate Centre, Gloucester GL1 1SS T 01452-572400 *Frequencies:* 102.4/103.0 FM

SGR COLCHESTER, Abbeygate Two, 9 Whitewell Road, Colchester, Essex CO2 7DE T 01206-575859 *Frequency:* 96.1 FM

SGR-FM, Alpha Business Park, 6–12 White House Road, Ipswich, Suffolk IP1 5LT T 01473-461000 *Frequencies:* 96.4/97.1 FM

SIGNAL 1, Stoke Road, Stoke-on-Trent ST4 2SR T 01782-441300 *Frequencies:* 96.4/96.9/102.6 FM

SIGNAL 2, Stoke Road, Stoke-on-Trent ST4 2SR T 01782-441300 *Frequency:* 1170 AM

SMOOTH 100.4, 8 Exchange Quay, Manchester M5 3EJ T 0845-050 1004 *Frequency:* 100.4 FM

SMOOTH 105.7, 3rd Floor, Crown House, Beaufort Court 123 Hagley Road, Birmingham B16 8LD T 0121-452 1057, *Frequency:* 105.7 FM

SMOOTH 106.6, Saga Radio House, Unit 2, Alder Court, Rennie Hogg Road, Riverside Retail Park, Nottingham NG2 1RX T 0115-986 1066, *Frequencies:* 101.4/106.6 FM

SOUTH HAMS RADIO, Unit 1G, South Hams Business Park, Churchstow, Kingsbridge, Devon TQ7 3QH T 01548-854595 *Frequency:* 100.5/100.8/101.2/101.9 FM

SOUTHERN FM, PO Box 2000, Franklin Road, Brighton BN41 2SS T 01273-430111 *Frequencies:* 96.9/102.0/102.4/103.5 FM

SPECTRUM RADIO, 4 Ingate Place, Battersea, London SW8 3NS T 020-7627 4433 *Frequency:* 558 AM

SPIRE FM, City Hall Studios, Malthouse Lane, Salisbury, Wilts SP2 7QQ T 01722-416644 *Frequency:* 102.0 FM

SPIRIT FM, 9–10 Dukes Court, Bognor Road, Chichester,

W. Sussex PO19 8FX **T** 01243-773600 *Frequencies:*
96.6/102.3/106.6 FM

STAR 106.6, The Observatory, Slough, Berks SL1 1LH
T 01753-551066 *Frequency:* 106.6 FM

STAR RADIO IN BRISTOL, Bristol Evening Post Building,
Temple Way, Bristol BS99 7HD **T** 0117-910 6600 *Frequency:*
107.2 FM

STAR RADIO IN CAMBRIDGE, 20 Mercers Row,
Cambridge CB5 8HY **T** 01223-722300 *Frequencies:*
107.1/107.9 FM

STAR RADIO IN CHELTENHAM, Cheltenham Film
Studios, 1st Floor, West Suite, Arle Court, Cheltenham, Glos
GL51 6PN **T** 01242-699555 *Frequency:* 107.5 FM

STAR RADIO IN SOMERSET, 11 Beaconsfield Road,
Weston-super-Mare BS23 1YE **T** 01934-624455 *Frequency:*
107.7 FM

STAR RADIO IN STROUD, Brunel Mall, London Road,
Stroud GL5 2BP **T** 01453-767369 *Frequencies:*
107.3/107.9 FM

SUNRISE FM, Sunrise House, 30 Chapel Street, Little
Germany, Bradford BD1 5DN **T** 01274-735043 *Frequency:*
103.2 FM

SUNRISE RADIO, Sunrise House, Sunrise Road, Southall,
Middx UB2 4AU **T** 020-8574 6666 *Frequency:* 1458 AM

SUNSHINE 855, Unit 11, Burway Trading Estate, Ludlow,
Shropshire SY8 1EN **T** 01584-873795 *Frequency:*
855 AM

TELFORD FM, c/o The Shropshire Star, Waterloo Road,
Ketley TF1 5HU **T** 01952-280011 *Frequency:* 107.4 FM

TEN 17, Latton Bush Centre, Southern Way, Harlow, Essex
CM18 7BB **T** 01279-431017 *Frequency:* 101.7 FM

TFM, Radio House, Yale Crescent, Thornaby, Stockton-on-Tees
TS17 6AA **T** 01642-888222 *Frequency:* 96.6 FM

TIME 106.6, The Observatory, Slough, Berks SL1 1LH
T 01753-551066 *Frequency:* 106.6 FM

TIME 106.8, 2–6 Basildon Road, Abbey Wood, London
SE2 0EW **T** 020-8311 3112 *Frequency:* 106.8 FM

TIME 107.3, 2–6 Basildon Road, Abbey Wood, London
SE2 0EW **T** 020-8311 3112 *Frequency:* 107.3 FM

TIME 107.5, 7th Floor, Lambourne House, 7 Western Road,
Romford, Essex RM1 3LD **T** 01708-731 643 *Frequency:*
107.5 FM

TOUCH FM, 5/6 Aldergate, Hamworth, Staffordshire B79
7DJ **T** 01827-318000 *Frequencies:* 101.6/ 102.4 FM

TOWER FM, The Mill, Brownlow Way, Bolton BL1 2RA
T 01204-387000 *Frequency:* 107.4 FM

TOWN FM, First Floor, Radio House Prion Court, Great
Blakenham, Ipswich, Suffolk IP6 0LW **T** 0845-3651102
Frequency: 102.0 FM

TRAX FM (BASSETLAW), White Hart Yard, Bridge Street,
Worksop, Notts S80 1HR **T** 01909-500611 *Frequency:*
107.9 FM

TRAX FM (DONCASTER), 5 Sidings Court, White Rose
Way, Doncaster DN4 5NU **T** 01302-341166 *Frequency:*
107.1 FM

VALE FM, Longmead Studios, Shaftesbury, Dorset SP7 8QQ
T 01747-855711 *Frequencies:* 96.6/97.4 FM

VIRGIN RADIO 105.8 FM, 1 Golden Square, London
W1F 9DJ **T** 020-7434 1215 *Frequency:* 105.8 FM

WAVE 105 FM, 5 Manor Court, Barnes Wallis Road,
Segensworth East, Fareham, Hampshire PO15 5TH
T 01489-481050 *Frequencies:* 105.2/105.8 FM

WESSEX FM, Radio House, Trinity Street, Dorchester, Dorset
DT1 1DJ **T** 01305-250333 *Frequencies:* 96.0/97.2 FM

WIRE FM, Warrington Business Park, Long Lane, Warrington
WA2 8TX **T** 01925-445545 *Frequency:* **107.2 FM**

WYVERN FM, 5–6 Barbourne Terrace, Worcester WR1 3JZ
T 01905-545500 *Frequencies:* 96.7/97.6/102.8 FM

XFM MANCHESTER, Laser House, Waterfront Quay,
Salford Quays, Manchester M50 3XW **T** 0161-662 4701
Frequency: 97.7 FM

XFM UK, 30 Leicester Square, London WC2H 7LA
T 020-7054 8000 *Frequency:* 104.9 FM

YORKSHIRE COAST RADIO (BRIDLINGTON), The
Old Harbour Master's Office, Harbour Road, Bridlington,
E. Yorks YO15 2NR **T** 01262-404400 *Frequency:* 102.4 FM

YORKSHIRE COAST RADIO (SCARBOROUGH), Unit
2B, Newchase Business Centre, Hopper Hill Road,
Scarborough, N. Yorks YO11 3YS **T** 01723-581700
Frequencies: 96.2/103.1 FM

WALES

96.4 FM THE WAVE, PO Box 964, Victoria Road, Gowerton,
Swansea SA4 3AB **T** 01792-511964 *Frequency:* 96.4 FM

97.1 RADIO CARMARTHENSHIRE, Unit 14, The Old
School Estate, Station Road, Narberth, Pembrokeshire
SA67 7DU **T** 0845-355 0570 *Frequencies:* 97.1/97.5 FM

97.5 SCARLET FM, Unit 14, The Old School Estate, Station
Road, Narberth, Pembrokeshire SA67 7DU **T** 0845-355 0570
Frequency: 97.5 FM

106.3 BRIDGE FM, PO Box 1063, Bridgend CF35 6WF
T 0845-890 4000 *Frequency:* 106.3 FM

102.5 RADIO PEMBROKESHIRE, Unit 14, The Old
School Estate, Station Road, Narberth, Pembrokeshire
SA67 7DU **T** 01834-869384 *Frequencies:* 102.5/107.5 FM

CAPITAL GOLD (1359/1305), Red Dragon Centre,
Atlantic Wharf, Cardiff CF10 4DJ **T** 029-2066 2066
Frequencies: 1305/1359 AM

CHAMPION FM 103, Llys-Y-Dderwen, Parc Menai, Bangor,
Gwynedd LL55 4BN **T** 01248-673400 *Frequency:* 103.0 FM

CLASSIC GOLD MARCHER (1260), The Studios, Mold
Road Gwersyllt, Wrexham LL11 4AF **T** 01978-752202
Frequency: 1260 AM

COAST 96.3, PO Box 963, Bangor LL57 4ZR **T** 01248-673272
Frequency: 96.3 FM

MFM 103.4, The Studios, Mold Road, Gwersyllt, Wrexham
LL11 4AF **T** 01978-752200 *Frequency:* 103.4 FM

RADIO CEREDIGION, Yr Hen Ysgol Gymraeg,
Aberystwyth, Ceredigion SY23 1LF **T** 01970-627999
Frequencies: 96.6/97.4/103.3/FM

RADIO MALDWYN, The Studios, The Park, Newtown,
Powys SY16 2NZ **T** 01686-623555 *Frequency:* 756 AM

REAL RADIO, Unit 1, Ty-Nant Court, Ty-Nant Road,
Morganstown, Cardiff CF15 8LW **T** 029-2031 5100
Frequencies: 105.2/105.4/105.7/105.9/106/106.2 FM

RED DRAGON FM, Atlantic Wharf, Cardiff CF10 4DJ
T 029-2066 2066 *Frequencies:* 97.4/103.2 FM

SWANSEA SOUND, Victoria Road, Gowerton, Swansea
SA4 3AB **T** 01792-511170 *Frequency:* 1170 AM

VALLEYS RADIO, PO Box 1116, Ebbw Vale, Gwent
NP23 8XW **T** 01495-301116 *Frequencies:* 999/1116 AM

SCOTLAND

ARGYLL FM, 27–29 Longrow, Campbeltown, Argyll
PA28 8ER **T** 01586-551800 *Frequencies:*
106.5/107.1/107.7 FM

CENTRAL 103.1 FM, 201–203 High Street, Falkirk FK1 1DU
T 01324-611164 *Frequency:* 103.1 FM

CLYDE 1, Clydebank Business Park, Clydebank, Glasgow
G81 2RX **T** 0141-565 2200 *Frequencies:* 97/102.5/103.3 FM

CLYDE 2, Clydebank Business Park, Clydebank, Glasgow
G81 2RX **T** 0141-565 2200 *Frequency:* 1152 AM

CUILLIN FM, Stormyhill Road, Portree, Isle of Skye IV51 9DY
T 01478-611234 *Frequency:* 106.2 FM

FORTH ONE, Forth House, Forth Street, Edinburgh EH1 3LE
T 0131-556 9255 *Frequencies:* 97.3/97.6/102.2 FM

FORTH 2, Forth House, Forth Street, Edinburgh EH1 3LE
T 0131-556 9255 *Frequency:* 1548 AM

HEARTLAND FM, Atholl Curling Rink, Lower Oakfield, Pitlochry, Perthshire PH16 5HQ T 01796-474040 *Frequency:* 97.5 FM

ISLES FM, PO Box 333, Stornoway, Isle of Lewis HS1 2PU T 01851-703333 *Frequency:* 103.0 FM

KINGDOM FM, Haig House, Haig Business Park, Balgonie Road, Markinch, Fife KY7 6AQ T 01592-753753 *Frequencies:* 95.2/96.1/96.6/105.4/106.3 FM

LANARKSHIRE'S L107, Media Corp House, 2 Caird Park, Hamilton, Lanarkshire ML3 0EU T 01698-303420 *Frequencies:* 107.5/107.9 FM

LOCHBROOM FM, Radio House, Mill Street, Ullapool, Ross-shire IV26 2UN T 01854-613131 *Frequencies:* 96.8/102.2 FM

MORAY FIRTH RADIO (MFR), Scorguie Place, Inverness IV3 8UJ T 01463-224433 *Frequencies:* 97.4 FM, 1107 AM

NECR, The Shed, School Road, Kintore, Iveruie, Aberdeenshire AB51 0US T 01467-632909 *Frequencies:* 97.1/101.9/102.1/102.6/103.2/106.4 FM

NEVIS RADIO, Ben Nevis Estate, Claggan, Fort William PH33 6PR T 01397-700007 *Frequencies:* 96.6/97.0/102.3/102.4 FM

NORTHSOUND 1, Abbotswell Road, West Tullos, Aberdeen AB12 3AJ T 01224-337000 *Frequencies:* 96.9/97.6/103.0 FM

NORTHSOUND 2, Abbotswell Road, West Tullos, Aberdeen AB12 3AJ T 01224-337000 *Frequency:* 1035 AM

OBAN FM, 132 George Street, Oban, Argyll PA34 5NT T 01631-570057 *Frequency:* 103.3 FM

RADIO BORDERS, Tweeside Park, Galashiels TD1 3TD T 01896-759444 *Frequencies:* 96.8/97.5/103.1/103.4 FM

REAL RADIO (SCOTLAND), Parkway Court, Glasgow Business Park, Glasgow G69 6GA T 0141-781 1011 *Frequencies:* 100.3/101.1 FM

RIVER FM, Stadium House, Alderstone Road, Livingston EH54 7DN T 01506-410411 *Frequency:* 103.4/107.7 FM

RNA FM, Radio North Angus Ltd, Rosemount Road, Arbroath, Angus DD1 2AT T 01241-879660 *Frequencies:* 100.3 /101.1 FM

ROCK RADIO, 65 Sussex Street, Kinning Park, Glasgow, G41 1XD T 0141 429 9430 *Frequency:* 96.3 FM

SIBC, Market Street, Lerwick, Shetland ZE1 0JN T 01595-695299 *Frequencies:* 96.2/102.2 FM

SMOOTH 105.2, City Park Alexandra Parade, Glasgow G31 3AU T 0141-551 1052, *Frequency:* 105.2 FM

SOUTH WEST SOUND FM, Unit 40, The Loreburne Centre, High St, Dumfries DG1 4DA T 01387-250999 *Frequencies:* 96.5/97.0/103.0 FM

TALK 107, 9 South Gyle Crescent, Edinburgh EH12 9EB T 0131-316 3107 *Frequency:* 107.0 FM

TAY AM, 6 North Isla Street, Dundee DD3 7JQ T 01382-200800 *Frequencies:* 1161/1584 AM

TAY FM, 6 North Isla Street, Dundee DD3 7JQ T 01382-200800 *Frequencies:* 96.4/102.8 FM

TWO LOCHS RADIO, Gairloch, Ross-shire IV21 2BQ T 0870-741 4657 *Frequencies:* 106.0/106.6 FM

UCA, University Campus Ayr, Beech Grove, Ayr, S. Ayrshire KA8 0SR T 01292-886385 *Frequency:* 87.7 FM

WAVE 102, 8 South Tay Street, Dundee DD1 1PA T 01382-901000 *Frequency:* 102.0 FM

WAVES RADIO, 7 Blackhouse Circle, Blackhouse Industrial Estate, Peterhead, Aberdeenshire AB42 1BW T 01779-491012 *Frequency:* 101.2 FM

WEST FM, Radio House, 54A Holmston Road, Ayr KA7 3BE T 01292-283662 *Frequency:* 96.7/97.5 FM

WEST SOUND AM, Radio House, 54A Holmston Road, Ayr KA7 3BE T 01292-283662 *Frequency:* 1035 AM

XFM SCOTLAND, Four Winds Pavilion, Pacific Quay, Glasgow G51 1EB T 0141-566 6109 *Frequencies:* 105.7/106.1 FM

YOURRADIO, Pioneer Park Studios, Unit 3, 80 Castlegreen Street, Dumbarton G82 1JB T 01389-734422 *Frequencies:* 103.0 (Dumbarton), 106.9 (Helensburgh) FM

NORTHERN IRELAND

CITY BEAT 96.7 FM, 46 Stranmillis Embankment, Belfast BT9 5FN T 028-9020 5967 *Frequency:* 96.7 FM

COOL FM, PO Box 974, Belfast BT1 1RT T 028-9181 7181 *Frequency:* 97.4 FM

DOWNTOWN RADIO, Newtownards, Co. Down BT23 4ES T 028-9181 5555 *Frequencies:* 96.4 FM (Limavady); 96.6 FM (Enniskillen); 97.1 FM (Larne); 102.3 FM (Ballymena); 102.4 FM (Londonderry)

Q97.2 FM, 24 Cloyfin Road, Coleraine, Co. Londonderry BT52 2NU T 028-7035 9100 *Frequency:* 97.2 FM

Q101.2 WEST FM, 42A Market Street, Omagh, Co. Tyrone BT78 1EH T 028-8224 5777 *Frequency:* 101.2 FM

Q102.9 FM, The Riverview Suite, 87 Rossdowney Road, Waterside, Londonderry BT47 5SU T 028-7134 4449/346666 *Frequency:* 102.9 FM

SEVEN FM, 1 Millenium Park, Woodside Industrial Estate, Woodside Road, Ballymena, Co. Antrim BT42 4QT T 028-2564 8777 *Frequency:* 107.0 FM

SIX FM, 2C Park Avenue, Cookstown, Co. Tyrone BT80 5AH T 028-8675 8696 *Frequencies:* 106.0/107.2 FM

U105, Ulster Television plc, Unit 105, Havelock House Ormeau Road, Belfast BT7 1EB T 028-9032 8122 / 028 9033 3105 *Frequency:* 105.8 FM

CHANNEL ISLANDS

CHANNEL 103 FM, 6 Tunnell Street, St Helier, Jersey JE2 4LU T 01534-888103 *Frequency:* 103.7 FM

ISLAND FM, 12 Westerbrook, St Sampsons, Guernsey GY2 4QQ T 01481-242000 *Frequencies:* 93.7/104.7 FM

THE PRESS

The newspaper and periodical press in the UK is large and diverse, catering for a wide variety of views and interests. There is no state control or censorship of the press; however, it is subject to the laws on publication, and the Press Complaints Commission (PCC) was set up by the industry as a means of self-regulation.

The press is not state-subsidised and receives few tax concessions. The income of most newspapers and periodicals is derived largely from sales and from advertising; the press is the largest advertising medium in Britain.

SELF-REGULATION

The PCC was founded by the newspaper and magazine industry in January 1991 to replace the Press Council (established in 1953). It is a voluntary, non-statutory body set up to operate the press' self-regulation system following the Calcutt report in 1990 on privacy and related matters, when the industry feared that failure to regulate itself might lead to statutory regulation of the press. The performance of the PCC was reviewed after 18 months of operation (the *Calcutt Review of Press Self-Regulation,* presented to parliament in January 1993) to determine whether statutory measures were required. No proposals for replacing the self-regulation system have been made to date. The commission is funded by the industry through the Press Standards Board of Finance.

COMPLAINTS

The PCC's aims are to consider, adjudicate, conciliate, and resolve complaints of unfair treatment by the press; and to ensure that the press maintains the highest professional standards and shows respect for generally recognised freedoms, including freedom of expression, the public's right to know, and the right of the press to operate free from improper pressure. The commission judges newspaper and magazine conduct by a code of practice drafted by editors, agreed by the industry and ratified by the commission.

Six of the commission's members are editors of national, regional and local newspapers and magazines, and ten, including the chair, are drawn from other fields. At the time of writing there was one vacancy for a 'press member' (working as an editor in newspaper or magazine publishing) on the commission. The PCC received 1,647 complaints in the six months to March 2007.

PRESS COMPLAINTS COMMISSION
Halton House, 20–23 Holborn, London EC1N 2JD
T 020-7831 0022 F 020-7831 0025
E complaints@pcc.org.uk
W www.pcc.org.uk
Chair, Sir Christopher Meyer, KCMG

NEWSPAPERS

Newspapers are mostly financially independent of any political party, though most adopt a political stance in their editorial comments, usually reflecting proprietorial influence. Ownership of the national and regional daily newspapers is concentrated in the hands of large corporations whose interests cover publishing and communications. The rules on cross-media ownership, as

amended by the Broadcasting Act 1996, which limited the extent to which newspaper organisations may become involved in broadcasting, have been relaxed by the Communications Act 2003: newspapers with over 20 per cent share of national circulation may own national and/or local radio licences.

There are around 15 daily and 15 Sunday national papers and several hundred local papers that are published daily, weekly or twice-weekly. Scotland, Wales and Northern Ireland all have at least one daily and one Sunday national paper.

Newspapers are usually published in either broadsheet or smaller, tabloid format. The 'quality' daily papers, ie those providing detailed coverage of a wide range of public matters, have traditionally used a broadsheet format, while the tabloid papers typically take a more populist approach and are more illustrated. In 2004 this correlation between format and content was abandoned when three traditionally broadsheet newspapers, *The Times, The Independent* and *The Scotsman,* switched to tabloid-sized editions, while *The Guardian* launched a new 'Berliner' format in September 2005. In October 2005 *The Independent on Sunday* became the first Sunday broadsheet to be published in the tabloid (or 'compact') size, and *The Observer,* like its daily counterpart *The Guardian,* began publishing in the Berliner format in January 2006.

UK CIRCULATION *net average for June 2006/7*

National Daily Newspapers	2006	2007
The Sun	2,949,697	2,852,952
Daily Mail	2,157,567	2,123,008
Daily Mirror	1,499,404	1,433,954
The Daily Telegraph	847,959	841,555
Daily Express	782,749	720,386
Daily Star	667,012	666,343
The Times	612,998	597,899
Daily Record	416,152	389,152
The Guardian	330,496	314,519
The Independent	200,957	188,986
Financial Times	134,337	136,697
The Herald	71,510	69,218
The Scotsman	60,696	56,979

National Sunday Newspapers	2006	2007
News of the World	3,211,961	3,021,301
The Mail on Sunday	2,165,890	2,033,504
Sunday Mirror	1,311,578	1,312,198
The Sunday Times	1,132,118	1,008,168
Sunday Express	759,941	668,997
The People	740,366	669,056
The Sunday Telegraph	611,032	620,255
Sunday Mail	504,028	486,534
Sunday Post	—	411,317
The Observer	414,657	401,959
Daily Star Sunday	319,477	320,383
The Independent on Sunday	176,335	204,138
Sunday Sport	114,526	97,281
Scotland on Sunday	71,736	72,815
Sunday Herald	52,455	53,964

Source: Audit Bureau of Circulations Ltd. For further information see W www.abc.org.uk

NATIONAL DAILY NEWSPAPERS

DAILY EXPRESS
Northern & Shell Building, 10 Lower Thames Street, London
EC3R 6EN **T** 0871-434 1010 **W** www.express.co.uk
Editor, Peter Hill

DAILY MAIL
Northcliffe House, 2 Derry Street, London W8 5TT
T 020-7938 6000 **W** www.dailymail.co.uk
Editor, Paul Dacre

DAILY MIRROR
1 Canada Square, Canary Wharf, London E14 5AP
T 020-7293 3000 **W** www.mirror.co.uk
Editor, Richard Wallace

DAILY RECORD
1 Central Quay, Glasgow G3 8DA **T** 0141-309 3000
W www.dailyrecord.co.uk
Editor, Bruce Waddell

DAILY SPORT
19 Great Ancoats Street, Manchester M60 4BT
T 0161-236 4466 **W** www.dailysport.co.uk
Editor, David Beevers

DAILY STAR
Northern & Shell Building, 10 Lower Thames Street, London
EC3R 6EN **T** 0871-434 1010 **W** www.dailystar.co.uk
Editor, Dawn Neesom

THE DAILY TELEGRAPH
1 Canada Square, Canary Wharf, London E14 5DT
T 020-7931 2000 **W** www.telegraph.co.uk
Editor, John Bryant

FINANCIAL TIMES
1 Southwark Bridge, London SE1 9HL **T** 020-7873 3000
W www.ft.com
Editor, Lionel Barber

THE GUARDIAN
119 Farringdon Road, London EC1R 3ER **T** 020-7278 2332
W www.guardian.co.uk
Editor, Alan Rusbridger

THE HERALD
200 Renfield Street, Glasgow G2 3QB **T** 0141-302 7000
W www.theherald.co.uk
Editor, Charles McGhee

THE INDEPENDENT
Independent House, 191 Marsh Wall, London E14 9RS
T 020-7005 2000 **W** www.independent.co.uk
Editor-in-Chief, Simon Kelner

MORNING STAR
William Rust House, 52 Beachy Road, London E3 2NS
T 020-8510 0815 **W** www.morningstaronline.co.uk
Editor, John Haylett

THE SCOTSMAN
Barclay House, 108 Holyrood Road, Edinburgh EH8 8AS
T 0131-620 8620 **W** www.scotsman.com
Editor, Mike Gilson

THE SUN
1 Virginia Street, London E1 9XP **T** 020-7782 4000
W www.the-sun.co.uk
Editor, Rebekah Wade

THE TIMES
1 Pennington Street, London E98 1TT **T** 020-7782 5000
W www.timesonline.co.uk
Editor, Robert Thomson

WEEKLY NEWSPAPERS

DAILY STAR SUNDAY
Northern & Shell Building, 10 Lower Thames Street,
London EC3R 6EN **T** 0871-434 1010
W www.dailystarsunday.co.uk
Editor, Gareth Morgan

THE INDEPENDENT ON SUNDAY
Independent House, 191 Marsh Wall, London E14 9RS
T 020-7005 2000 **W** www.independent.co.uk
Editor, Tristan Davies

THE MAIL ON SUNDAY
Northcliffe House, 2 Derry Street, London W8 5TS
T 020-7938 6000 **W** www.mailonsunday.co.uk
Editor, Peter Wright

NEWS OF THE WORLD
1 Virginia Street, London E98 1NW **T** 020-7782 4000
W www.newsoftheworld.co.uk
Editor, Colin Myler

THE OBSERVER
3–7 Herbal Hill, London EC1R 5EJ **T** 020-7278 2332
W www.observer.co.uk
Editor, Roger Alton

THE PEOPLE
1 Canada Square, Canary Wharf, London E14 5AP
T 020-7293 3000 **W** www.people.co.uk
Editor, Mark Thomas

SCOTLAND ON SUNDAY
108 Holyrood Road, Edinburgh EH8 8AS **T** 0131-620 8620
W www.scotlandonsunday.co.uk
Editor, Les Snowdon

SUNDAY EXPRESS
Northern & Shell Building, 10 Lower Thames Street, London
EC3R 6EN **T** 0871-434 1010 **W** www.express.co.uk
Editor, Martin Townsend

SUNDAY HERALD
200 Renfield Street, Glasgow G2 3QB **T** 0141-302 7800
W www.sundayherald.com
Editor, Richard Walker

SUNDAY MAIL
1 Central Quay, Glasgow G3 8DA **T** 0141-309 3000
W www.sundaymail.com
Editor, Allan Rennie

SUNDAY MIRROR
1 Canada Square, Canary Wharf, London E14 5AP
T 020-7293 3000 **W** www.sundaymirror.co.uk
Editor, Tina Weaver

THE SUNDAY POST
144 Port Dundas Road, Glasgow G4 0HZ **T** 0141-332 9933
W www.sundaypost.com
Editor, David Pollington

THE SUNDAY TELEGRAPH
111 Buckingham Palace Road, London SW1W 0DT
T 020-7931 2000 **W** www.telegraph.co.uk
Editor, Patience Wheatcroft

THE SUNDAY TIMES
1 Pennington Street, London E98 1ST **T** 020-7782 5000
W www.timesonline.co.uk
Editor, John Witherow

THE SUNDAY TIMES SCOTLAND
124 Portman Street, Kinning Park, Glasgow G41 1EJ
T 0141-420 5100 **W** www.timesonline.co.uk
Editor, Carlos Alba

WALES ON SUNDAY
Thomson House, Havelock Street, Cardiff CF10 1XR
T 029-2058 3583 **W** www.icwales.co.uk
Editor, Tim Gordon

REGIONAL DAILY NEWSPAPERS

EAST ANGLIA
CAMBRIDGE EVENING NEWS
Winship Road, Milton, Cambs CB24 6PP T 01223-434437
W www.cambridge-news.co.uk
Editor, Murray Morse
EAST ANGLIAN DAILY TIMES
30 Lower Brook Street, Ipswich, Suffolk IP4 1AN
T 01473-230023 W www.eadt.co.uk
Editor, Terry Hunt
EASTERN DAILY PRESS
Prospect House, Rouen Road, Norwich NR1 1RE
T 01603-628311 W www.edp24.co.uk
Editor, Peter Franzen, OBE
EVENING STAR
Press House, 30 Lower Brook Street, Ipswich, Suffolk IP4 1AN
T 01473-230023 W www.eveningstar.co.uk
Editor, Jess Gallagher
THE EVENING TELEGRAPH
Telegraph House, 57 Priestgate, Peterborough PE1 1JW
T 01733-555111 W www.peterboroughtoday.co.uk
Editor, Rebecca Stephens
NORWICH EVENING NEWS
Prospect House, Rouen Road, Norwich NR1 1RE
T 01603-628311 W www.eveningnews24.co.uk
Editor (acting), Tim Williams

EAST MIDLANDS
BURTON MAIL
65–68 High Street, Burton on Trent DE14 1LE
T 01283-512345 W www.burtonmail.co.uk
Editor, Paul Hazeldine
EVENING TELEGRAPH
Northcliffe House, Meadow Road, Derby DE1 2DW
T 01332-291111 W www.thisisderbyshire.co.uk
Editor, Steve Hall
LEICESTER MERCURY
St George Street, Leicester LE1 9FQ T 0116-251 2512
W www.thisisleicestershire.co.uk
Editor, Nick Carter
LINCOLNSHIRE ECHO
Brayford Wharf East, Lincoln LN5 7AT T 01522-820000
W www.thisislincolnshire.co.uk
Editor, Jon Grubb
NORTHAMPTON CHRONICLE & ECHO
Upper Mounts, Northampton NN1 3HR T 01604-467000
W www.northamptonchron.co.uk
Editor, Mark Edwards
NOTTINGHAM EVENING POST
Castle Wharf House, Nottingham NG1 7EU
T 0115-948 2000 W www.thisisnottingham.co.uk
Editor, Malcolm Pheby

LONDON
EVENING STANDARD
Northcliffe House, 2 Derry Street, London W8 5EE
T 020-7938 6000 W www.thisislondon.com
Editor, Veronica Wadley
METRO
Northcliffe House, 2 Derry Street, London W8 5TT
T 020-7651 5200 W www.metro.co.uk
Editor, Kenny Campbell

NORTH EAST
EVENING CHRONICLE
Groat Market, Newcastle upon Tyne NE1 1ED
T 0191-232 7500 W www.chroniclelive.co.uk
Editor, Paul Robertson

EVENING GAZETTE
Borough Road, 105–111 Middlesbrough TS1 3AZ
T 01642-245401 W www.gazettelive.co.uk
Editor, Darren Thwaites
HARTLEPOOL MAIL
New Clarence House, Wesley Square, Hartlepool TS24 8BX
T 01429-239333 W www.hartlepoolmail.co.uk
Editor, Joy Yates
THE JOURNAL
Groat Market, Newcastle upon Tyne NE1 1ED
T 0191-232 7500 W www.icnewcastle.co.uk
Editor, Brian Aitken
THE NORTHERN ECHO
Priestgate, Darlington, Co. Durham DL1 1NF
T 01325-381313 W www.thenorthernecho.co.uk
Editor, Peter Barron
THE SHIELDS GAZETTE
Chapter Row, South Shields, Tyne & Wear NE33 1BL
T 0191-455 4661 W www.shieldsgazette.com
Editor, John Szymanski
SUNDERLAND ECHO
Echo House, Pennywell, Sunderland, Tyne & Wear SR4 9ER
T 0191-501 5800 W www.sunderlandecho.com
Editor, Rob Lawson

NORTH WEST
THE BOLTON NEWS
Newspaper House, Churchgate, Bolton, Lancs BL1 1DE
T 01204-522345 W www.theboltonnews.co.uk
Editor-in-Chief, Steve Hughes
THE GAZETTE
Avroe House, Avroe Crescent, Blackpool Business Park,
Squires Gate, Blackpool FY4 2DP T 01253-400888
W www.blackpoolgazette.co.uk
Editor, David Helliwell
LANCASHIRE EVENING POST
Unit 4, Fulwood Business Park, Caxton Road, Fulwood,
Preston, Lancs PR2 9NZ T 01772-254841 W www.lep.co.uk
Editor, Simon Reynolds
LANCASHIRE TELEGRAPH
Newspaper House, High Street, Blackburn, Lancs BB1 1HT
T 01254-678678 W www.thisislancashire.co.uk
Editor, Kevin Young
LIVERPOOL DAILY POST
PO Box 48, Old Hall Street, Liverpool L69 3EB
T 0151-227 2000 W www.liverpooldailypost.co.uk
Editor, Mark Thomas
LIVERPOOL ECHO
PO Box 48, Old Hall Street, Liverpool L69 3EB
T 0151-227 2000 W www.icliverpool.co.uk
Editor, Alastair Machray
MANCHESTER EVENING NEWS
164 Deansgate, Manchester M60 2RD T 0161-832 7200
W www.manchesteronline.co.uk
Editor, Paul Horrocks
NEWS & STAR
Newspaper House, Dalston Road, Carlisle CA2 5UA
T 01228-612600 W www.news-and-star.co.uk
Editor, Neil Hodgkinson
NORTH-WEST EVENING MAIL
Newspaper House, Abbey Road, Barrow-in-Furness, Cumbria
LA14 5QS T 01229-840150 W www.nwemail.co.uk
Editor, Steve Brauner
OLDHAM EVENING CHRONICLE
PO Box 47, Union Street, Oldham, Lancs OL1 1EQ
T 0161-633 2121 W www.oldham-chronicle.co.uk
Editor, Jim Williams

SOUTH

THE ARGUS
Argus House, Crowhurst Road, Hollingbury, Brighton
BN1 8AR **T** 01273-544544 **W** www.theargus.co.uk
Editor, Michael Beard

ECHO
Newspaper House, Chester Hall Lane, Basildon, Essex
SS14 3BL **T** 01268-522792 **W** www.echo-news.co.uk
Editor, Martin McNeill

MEDWAY MESSENGER
Medway House, Ginsbury Close, Sir Thomas Longley Road,
Medway City Estate, Strood, Kent ME2 2DU
T 01634-227800 **W** www.kentonline.co.uk

THE NEWS
The News Centre, Hilsea, Portsmouth PO2 9SX
T 023-9266 4488 **W** www.portsmouth.co.uk
Editor (acting), Mark Acheson

OXFORD MAIL
Newspaper House, Osney Mead, Oxford OX2 0EJ
T 01865-425262 **W** www.oxfordmail.net
Editor, Simon O'Neill

READING EVENING POST
8 Tessa Road, Reading, Berks RG1 8NS **T** 0118-918 3000
W www.getreading.co.uk
Editor, Andy Murrill

SOUTHERN DAILY ECHO
Newspaper House, Test Lane, Redbridge, Southampton
SO16 9JX **T** 023-8042 4777 **W** www.dailyecho.co.uk
Editor, Ian Murray

SWINDON ADVERTISER
100 Victoria Road, Old Town, Swindon SN1 3BE
T 01793-528144 **W** www.swindonadvertiser.co.uk
Editor, Mark Waldron

SOUTH WEST

THE CITIZEN
1 Clarence Parade, Cheltenham GL50 3NY **T** 01242-271900
W www.nng.co.uk
Editor, Ian Mean

DAILY ECHO
Richmond Hill, Bournemouth BH2 6HH **T** 01202-554601
W www.bournemouthecho.co.uk
Editor, Neal Butterworth

DORSET ECHO
Fleet House, Hampshire Road, Weymouth, Dorset DT4 9XD
T 01305-830930 **W** www.dorsetecho.co.uk
Editor, David Murdock

EVENING POST
Temple Way, Bristol BS99 7HD **T** 0117-934 3000
W www.thisisbristol.co.uk
Editor-in-chief, Mike Norton

EXPRESS & ECHO
Heron Road, Sowton, Exeter EX2 7NF **T** 01392-442211
W www.thisisexeter.co.uk
Editor, Marc Astley

GLOUCESTERSHIRE ECHO
1 Clarence Parade, Cheltenham, Glos GL50 3NY
T 01242-271900 **W** www.thisisgloucestershire.co.uk
Editor, Anita Syvret

THE HERALD
17 Brest Road, Derriford Business Park, Plymouth PL6 5AA
T 01752-765500 **W** www.thisisplymouth.co.uk
Editor, Bill Martin

HERALD EXPRESS
Harmsworth House, Barton Hill Road, Torquay, Devon
TQ2 8JN **T** 01803-676000 **W** www.thisissouthdevon.co.uk
Editor, Andy Phelan

WESTERN DAILY PRESS
Temple Way, Bristol BS99 7HD **T** 0117-934 3000
W www.westpress.co.uk
Editor, Andy Wright

WESTERN MORNING NEWS
17 Brest Road, Derriford, Plymouth PL6 5AA
T 01752-765500 **W** www.westernmorningnews.co.uk
Editor, Alan Qualtrough

WEST MIDLANDS

BIRMINGHAM MAIL
PO Box 78, Weaman Street, Birmingham B4 6AY
T 0121-236 3366 **W** www.icbirmingham.co.uk
Editor, Steve Dyson

THE BIRMINGHAM POST
PO Box 78, Weaman Street, Birmingham B4 6AT
T 0121-236 3366 **W** www.icbirmingham.co.uk
Editor, Mark Reeves

COVENTRY EVENING TELEGRAPH
Corporation Street, Coventry CV1 1FP **T** 024-7663 3633
W www.iccoventry.co.uk
Editor, Alan Kirby

EXPRESS & STAR
Queen Street, Wolverhampton WV1 1ES **T** 01902-313131
W www.expressandstar.com
Editor, Adrian Faber

THE SENTINEL
Sentinel House, Etruria, Stoke-on-Trent ST1 5SS
T 01782-602525 **W** www.thisisthesentinel.co.uk
Editor, Michael Sassi

SHROPSHIRE STAR
Ketley, Telford TF1 5HU **T** 01952-242424
W www.shropshirestar.com
Editor, Sarah Jane Smith

WORCESTER NEWS
Berrows House, Hylton Road, Worcester WR2 5JX
T 01905-742244 **W** www.thisisworcester.co.uk
Editor, Stewart Gilbert

YORKSHIRE AND HUMBERSIDE

EVENING COURIER
PO Box 19, King Cross Street, Halifax HX1 2SF
T 01422-260200 **W** www.halifaxcourier.co.uk
Editor, John Furbisher

GRIMSBY TELEGRAPH
80 Cleethorpe Road, Grimsby, North East Lincolnshire
DN31 3EH **T** 01472-360360 **W** www.thisisgrimsby.co.uk
Editor, Michelle Lalor

THE HUDDERSFIELD DAILY EXAMINER
PO Box A26, Queen Street South, Huddersfield HD1 2TD
T 01484-430000 **W** www.examiner.co.uk
Editor, Roy Wright

HULL DAILY MAIL
Blundell's Corner, Beverley Road, Hull HU3 1XS
T 01482-327111 **W** www.thisishullandeastriding.co.uk
Editor, John Meehan

THE PRESS
PO Box 29, 76–86 Walmgate, York YO1 9YN
T 01904-653051 **W** www.yorkpress.co.uk
Editor, Kevin Booth

SCARBOROUGH EVENING NEWS
17–23 Aberdeen Walk, Scarborough, North Yorkshire
YO11 1BB **T** 01723-363636
W www.scarboroughveveningnews.co.uk
Editor, Ed Asquith

THE STAR
York Street, Sheffield S1 1PU **T** 0114-276 7676
W www.thestar.co.uk
Editor, Alan Powell
TELEGRAPH & ARGUS
Hall Ings, Bradford BD1 1JR **T** 01274-729511
W www.thisisbradford.co.uk
Editor, Perry Austin-Clarke
YORKSHIRE EVENING POST
PO Box 168, Wellington Street, Leeds LS1 1RF
T 0113-243 2701 **W** www.ypn.co.uk
Editor, Paul Napier
YORKSHIRE POST
Wellington Street, Leeds LS1 1RF **T** 0113-243 2701
W www.yorkshirepost.co.uk
Editor, Peter Charlton

SCOTLAND
THE COURIER
80 Kingsway East, Dundee DD4 8SL **T** 01382-223131
W www.thecourier.co.uk
Editor, Bill Hutchin
EVENING TELEGRAPH AND POST
80 Kingsway East, Dundee DD4 8SL **T** 01382-223131
W www.eveningtelegraph.co.uk
EVENING EXPRESS
PO Box 43, Lang Stracht, Mastrick, Aberdeen AB15 6DF
T 01224-690222 **W** www.thisisaberdeen.co.uk
Editor, Damian Bates
EVENING NEWS
108 Holyrood Road, Edinburgh EH8 8AS **T** 0131-620 8620
W www.edinburghnews.com
Editor, John McLellan
EVENING TIMES
200 Renfield Street, Glasgow G2 3PR **T** 0141-302 7000
W www.eveningtimes.co.uk
Editor, Donald Martin
THE INVERNESS COURIER
New Century House, Stadium Road, Inverness IV1 1FF
T 01463-732222 **W** www.inverness-courier.co.uk
Editor, Robert Taylor
PAISLEY DAILY EXPRESS
14 New Street, Paisley, Renfrewshire PA1 1YA
T 0141-887 7911 **W** www.icrenfrewshire.co.uk
Editor, Anne Dalrymple
THE PRESS AND JOURNAL
Lang Stracht, Aberdeen AB15 6DF **T** 01224-690222
W www.thisisnorthscotland.co.uk
Editor, Derek Tucker

WALES
EVENING LEADER
Centenary Buildings, King Street, Wrexham, Clwyd LL11 1PN
T 01978-355151 **W** www.eveningleader.co.uk
Editor, Barrie Jones
SOUTH WALES ARGUS
Cardiff Road, Maesglas, Newport, Gwent NP20 3QN
T 01633-777219
Editor, Gerry Keighley
SOUTH WALES ECHO
Thomson House, Havelock Street, Cardiff CF10 1XR
T 029-2058 3622 **W** www.icwales.co.uk
Editor, Richard Williams
SOUTH WALES EVENING POST
PO Box 14, Adelaide Street, Swansea SA1 1QT
T 01792-510000 **W** www.thisissouthwales.co.uk
Editor-in-Chief, Spencer Feeney

WESTERN MAIL
Thomson House, Havelock Street, Cardiff CF10 1XR
T 029-2058 3583 **W** www.icwales.co.uk
Editor, Alan Edmunds

NORTHERN IRELAND
BELFAST TELEGRAPH
124–144 Royal Avenue, Belfast BT1 1EB **T** 028-9026 4000
W www.belfasttelegraph.co.uk
Editor, Martin Lindsay
THE IRISH NEWS
113–117 Donegall Street, Belfast BT1 2GE **T** 028-9032 2226
W www.irishnews.com
Editor, Noel Doran
NEWS LETTER
2 Esky Drive, Portadown, Craigaron, Belfast BT63 5WD
T 028-3839 3939 **W** www.newsletter.co.uk
Editor, Darwin Templeton

CHANNEL ISLANDS
THE GUERNSEY PRESS AND STAR
PO Box 57, Braye Road, Vale, Guernsey GY1 3BW
T 01481-240240 **W** www.guernseypress.com
Editor, Richard Digard
JERSEY EVENING POST
PO Box 582, Five Oaks, St Saviour, Jersey JE4 8XQ
T 01534-611611 **W** www.thisisjersey.com
Editor, Chris Bright

PERIODICALS

ACCOUNTANCY AGE
VNU Business Publications, VNU House, 32–34 Broadwick
Street, London W1A 2HG **T** 020-7316 9236
W www.accountancyage.com
Editor, Gavin Hinks
AEROPLANE MONTHLY
The Blue Fin Building, 110 Southwark Street, London
SE1 0SU **T** 020-7261 5849 **W** www.aeroplanemonthly.com
Editor, Michael Oakey
AMATEUR PHOTOGRAPHER
The Blue Fin Building, 110 Southwark Street, London
SE1 0SU **T** 020-3148 5000
Editor, Damien Demolder
ANGLING TIMES
Bushfield House, Orton Centre, Peterborough PE2 5UW
T 01733-232600 **W** www.anglingtimes.co.uk
Editor, Richard Lee
THE ARCHITECTS' JOURNAL
151 Rosebery Avenue, London EC1R 4GB **T** 020-7505 6700
W www.ajplus.co.uk
Editor, Keiron Long
THE ARCHITECTURAL REVIEW
151 Rosebery Avenue, London EC1R 4GB **T** 020-7505 6725
W www.arplus.com
Editor, Paul Finch
ARCHITECTURE TODAY
161 Rosebery Avenue, London EC1R 4QX **T** 020-7837 0143
W www.architecturetoday.co.uk
Editor, Ian Latham
ARENA
Endeavour House, 189 Shaftesbury Avenue, London
WC2H 8JG **T** 020-7437 9011
Editor, Giles Hattersley
ART MONTHLY
4th Floor, 28 Charing Cross Road, London WC2H 0DB
T 020-7240 0389 **W** www.artmonthly.co.uk
Editor, Patricia Bickers

THE ART NEWSPAPER
70 South Lambeth Road, London SW8 1RL **T** 020-7735 3331
W www.theartnewspaper.com
Editor, Christina Ruiz

ART REVIEW
1 Sekforde Street, 23–24 Smithfield Street, London EC1R 0BE
T 020-7107 2760 **W** www.artreview.com
Editor, Mark Rappolt

ATTITUDE
Northern Shell Tower, City Harbour, London E14 9GL
T 020-7308 5090 **W** www.attitude.co.uk
Editor, Adam Mattera

AUTO EXPRESS
30 Cleveland Street, London W1T 4JD **T** 020-7907 6200
W www.autoexpress.co.uk
Editor, David Johns

THE BANKER
1 Southwark Bridge, London SE1 9HL **T** 020-7775 6359
W www.thebanker.com
Editor-in-Chief, Stephen Timewell

THE BEANO
Albert Square, Dundee DD1 9QJ **T** 01382-223131
Editor, Alan Dogby

BELLA
Academic House, 24–28 Oval Road, London NW1 7DT
T 020-7241 8000
Editor, Jayne Marsden

BEST
33 Broadwick Street, London W1F 0DQ **T** 020-7339 4500
Editor, Michelle Hather

THE BIG ISSUE
1–5 Wandsworth Road, London SW8 2LN **T** 020-7526 3200
W www.bigissue.com
Editor-in-Chief, John Bird

BIKE
Media House, Lynchwood, Peterborough PE2 6EA
T 01733-468000 **W** www.emapbikes.com
Editor, John Westlake

BIRD WATCHING
Bretton Court, Bretton, Peterborough PE3 8DZ
T 01733-264666 **W** www.birdwatchingmagazine.co.uk
Editor, Kevin Wilmott

BIZARRE
30 Cleveland Street, London W1T 4JD **T** 020-7907 6000
W www.bizarremag.com
Editor, Alex Godfrey

BLISS
Panini House, Coach and Horses Passage, The Pantiles,
Tunbridge Wells, Kent TN2 5OT **T** 01892-500106
W www.blissmag.co.uk
Editor, Leslie Sinoway

THE BOOKSELLER
5th Floor, Endeavour House, 189 Shaftesbury Avenue,
London WC2H 8TJ **T** 020-7420 6006
W www.thebookseller.com
Editor-in-Chief, Neill Denny

BRITISH MEDICAL JOURNAL
BMA House, Tavistock Square, London WC1H 9JR
T 020-7387 4499 **W** www.bmj.com
Editor, Dr Fiona Godlee

BROADCAST
33–39 Bowling Green Lane, London EC1R 0DA
T 020-7505 8014 **W** www.broadcastnow.co.uk
Editor, Lisa Campbell

BUILDING
8th Floor, 245 Blackfriars Road, London SE1 9UY
T 020-7560 4000
Editor, Denise Chevin

THE BURLINGTON MAGAZINE
14–16 Duke's Road, London WC1H 9SZ **T** 020-7388 8157
W www.burlington.org.uk
Editor, Richard Shone

THE BUSINESS
22 Old Queen Street, London SW1H 9HP **T** 020-7961 0000
W www.thebusiness.co.uk
Editor, Andrew Neil

CAMPAIGN
174 Hammersmith Road, London W6 7JP **T** 020-8943 5000
W www.brandrepublic.com
Editor, Claire Beale

CAR
3rd Floor, Media House, Lynchwood, Peterborough PE2 6EA
T 01733-468000
Editor, Greg Fountain

CARAVAN MAGAZINE
Leon House, 233 High Street, Croydon CR9 1HZ
T 020-8726 8000 **W** www.caravanmagazine.co.uk
Editor, Victoria Heath

CATERER AND HOTELKEEPER
Quadrant House, The Quadrant, Sutton, Surrey SM2 5AS
T 020-8652 3221
Editor, Mark Lewis

THE CATHOLIC HERALD
Herald House, Lambs Passage, Bunhill Row, London
EC1Y 8TQ **T** 020-7448 3603 **W** www.catholicherald.co.uk
Editor, Luke Coppen

CATHOLIC TIMES
1st Floor, St James's Buildings, Oxford Street, Manchester
M1 6FP **T** 0161-236 8856
Editor, Kevin Flaherty

CHAT
The Blue Fin Building, 110 Southwark Street, London
SE1 0SU **T** 020-3148 5000 **W** www.ipcmedia.com
Editor, Gilly Sinclair

CHURCH TIMES
33 Upper Street, London N1 0PN **T** 020-7359 4570
W www.churchtimes.co.uk
Editor, Paul Handley

CLASSIC CARS
Media House, Lynchwood, Peterborough
PE2 6EA **T** 01733-468219
W www.classiccarsmagazine.co.uk
Editor, Phil Bell

CLASSICAL MUSIC
241 Shaftesbury Avenue, London WC2H 8TF
T 020-7333 1742 **W** www.rhinegold.co.uk
Editor, Keith Clarke

CLASSICS MONTHLY
30 Monmouth Street, Bath BA1 2BW **T** 01225-442244
Editor, Gary Streatham

CLOSER
Endeavour House, 189 Shaftesbury Avenue, London
WC2H 8JG **T** 020-7437 9011 **W** www.closermag.co.uk
Editor, Jane Johnson

COMPANY
National Magazine House, 72 Broadwick Street, London
W1V 2BP **T** 020-7439 5000 **W** www.company.co.uk
Editor, Victoria White

CONDÉ NAST TRAVELLER
Vogue House, Hanover Square, London W1S 1JU
T 020-7499 9080 **W** www.cntraveller.com
Editor, Sarah Miller

COSMOPOLITAN
National Magazine House, 72 Broadwick Street, London
W1F 9EP **T** 020-7439 5000
Editor-in-Chief, Louise Court

COUNTRY HOMES AND INTERIORS
The Blue Fin Building, 110 Southwark Street, London
SE1 0SU T 020-3261 5000
Editor, Rhoda Parry

COUNTRY LIFE
The Blue Fin Building, 110 Southwark Street, London
SE1 0SU T 020-3261 6400 W www.countrylife.co.uk
Editor, Mark Hedges

COUNTRY LIVING
National Magazine House, 72 Broadwick Street, London
W1F 9EP T 020-7439 5000 W www.countryliving.co.uk
Editor, Susy Smith

CYCLING WEEKLY
Leon House, 233 High Street, Croydon CR9 1HZ
T 020-8726 8463 W www.cyclingweekly.co.uk
Editor, Robert Garbutt

DANCING TIMES
45–47 Clerkenwell Green, London EC1R 0EB
T 020-7250 3006 W www.dancing-times.co.uk
Editor, Mary Clarke

THE DANDY
Albert Square, Dundee DD1 9QJ T 01382-223131

DECANTER
The Blue Fin Building, 110 Southwark Street, London
SE1 0SU T 020-3148 5000 W www.decanter.com
Editor (acting), Guy Woodward

EASTERN EYE
Unit 2, 65 Whitechapel Road, London E1 1DU
T 020-7650 2000 W www.easterneyeonline.co.uk
Editor, Hamant Verma

THE ECOLOGIST
Unit 102, Lana House Studios, 116–118 Commercial Street,
London E1 6NF T 020-7422 8100
Editor, Pat Thomas

THE ECONOMIST
25 St James's Street, London SW1A 1HG T 020-7830 7000
W www.economist.com
Editor, John Micklethwait

EDINBURGH REVIEW
22A Buccleugh Place, Edinburgh EH8 9LN T 0131-651 1415
W www.edinburghreview.org.uk
Editor, Brian McCabe

ELLE
64 North Row, London W1K 7LL T 020-7150 7000
W www.elleuk.com
Editor, Lorraine Candy

EMPIRE
Mappin House, 4 Winsley Street, London W1W 8HF
T 020-7182 8781 W www.empireonline.com
Editor, Mark Dinning

THE ENGINEER
St Giles House, 50 Poland Street, London W1F 7AX
T 020-7970 4000 W www.theengineer.com
Editor, Andrew Lee

THE EROTIC REVIEW
1st Floor, 17 Harwood Road, London SW4 4QP
T 020-7736 5800 W www.eroticreviewmagazine.com
Editor, Jamie Maclean

ESQUIRE
National Magazine House, 72 Broadwick Street, London
W1F 9EP T 020-7439 5000 W www.esquire.co.uk
Editor, Jeremy Langmead

ESSENTIALS
The Blue Fin Building, 110 Southwark Street, London
SE1 0SU T 020-3148 7211
Editor, Julie Barton-Breck

EVE
174 Hammersmith Road, London W6 7JP
W www.evemagazine.co.uk

EVENTING
The Blue Fin Building, 110 Southwark Street, London
SE1 0SU T 020-3148 5000
Editor, Julie Harding

FARMERS WEEKLY
Quadrant House, The Quadrant, Sutton, Surrey SM2 5AS
T 020-8652 4911 W www.fwi.co.uk
Editor, Jane King

FHM
Mappin House, 4 Winsley Street, London W1W 8HF
T 020-7182 8028 W www.fhm.com
Editor, Anthony Naguera

THE FIELD
The Blue Fin Building, 110 Southwark Street, London
SE1 0SU T 020-3148 5000 W www.thefield.co.uk
Editor, Jonathan Young

FINANCIAL ADVISER
Tabernacle Court, 16–28 Tabernacle Street, London
EC2A 4DD T 020-7382 8000 W www.ftadviser.com
Editor, Hal Austin

FISHING NEWS
Telephone House, 69–77 Paul Street, London EC2A 4LQ
T 020-7017 4531 W www.fishingnews.co.uk
Editor, Tim Oliver

FLIGHT INTERNATIONAL
Quadrant House, The Quadrant, Sutton, Surrey SM2 5AS
T 020-8652 3842 W www.flightglobal.com
Editor, Kieran Daly

FORTEAN TIMES
Box 2409, London NW5 4NP T 020-7907 6235
W www.forteantimes.com
Editor, David Sutton

FOURFOURTWO
38–42 Hampton Road, Teddington TW11 0JE
T 020-8267 5337 W www.fourfourtwo.co.uk
Editor, Hugh Sleight

THE FRIEND
173 Euston Road, London NW1 2BJ T 020-7663 1010
W www.thefriend.org
Editor, Judy Kirby

GARDEN NEWS
Bretton Court, Bretton Centre, Peterborough PE3 8DZ
T 01733-264666
Editor, Neil Pope

GAY TIMES
Spectrum House, 32–34 Gordon House Road, London
NW5 1LP T 020-7424 7400 W www.gaytimes.co.uk
Editor, Joseph Galliano

GEOGRAPHICAL JOURNAL
Kensington Gore, London SW7 2AR T 020-7591 3026
Editor, Prof. John Briggs

GLAMOUR
Vogue House, Hanover Square, London W1S 1JU
T 020-7499 9080 W www.glamourmagazine.com
Editor, Jo Elvin

GOLF WORLD
Bushfield House, Orton Centre, Peterborough PE2 5UW
T 01733-237111 W www.golfworld-magazine.com
Editor, Paul Hamblin

GOOD HOUSEKEEPING
National Magazine House, 72 Broadwick Street, London
W1F 9EP T 020-7439 5000 W www.natmags.co.uk
Editor-in-Chief, Louise Chunn

GQ
Vogue House, Hanover Square, London W1S 1JU
T 020-7499 9080 W www.gq-magazine.co.uk
Editor, Dylan Jones

GRANTA
2–3 Hanover Yard, Noel Road, London N1 8BE
T 020-7704 9776 W www.granta.com
Editor, Jason Cowley

GRAZIA
Endeavour House, 189 Shaftesbury Avenue, London
WC2H 8JG W www.graziamagazine.co.uk
Editor, Jane Bruton

THE GROCER
Broadfield Park, Crawley, West Sussex RH11 9RT
T 01293-613400 W www.thegrocer.co.uk
Editor, Adam Leyland

GUITARIST
30 Monmouth Street, Bath BA1 2BW T 01225-442244
W www.futurenet.co.uk
Editor, Michael Leonard

HARPER'S BAZAAR
National Magazine House, 72 Broadwick Street, London
W1F 9EP T 020-7439 5000 W www.natmags.co.uk
Editor, Lucy Yeomans

HEALTH AND FITNESS MAGAZINE
2 Balcombe Street, London NW1 6NW T 020-7042 4000
W www.healthandfitnessonline.co.uk
Editor, Mary Comber

HEAT
Endeavour House, 189 Shaftesbury Avenue, London
WC2H 8JG T 020-7859 8657
Editor, Mark Frith

HELLO!
Wellington House, 69–71 Upper Ground, London SE1 9PQ
T 020-7667 8700
Editor, Ronnie Whelan

HOMES AND GARDENS
The Blue Fin Building, 110 Southwark Street, London
SE1 0SU T 020-3148 5000 W www.homesandgardens.com
Editor, Deborah Barker

HORSE AND HOUND
The Blue Fin Building, 110 Southwark Street, London
SE1 0SU T 020-3148 4562 W www.horseandhound.co.uk
Editor, Lucy Higginson

HOUSE AND GARDEN
Vogue House, Hanover Square, London W1S 1JU
T 020-7499 9080
Editor, Susan Crewe

HOUSE BEAUTIFUL
National Magazine House, 72 Broadwick Street, London
W1F 9EP T 020-7439 5000 W www.housebeautiful.co.uk
Editor, Julia Goodwin

HOUSEBUILDER
Byron House, 7–9 St James's Street, London SW1A 1DW
T 020-7960 1630 W www.house-builder.co.uk
Editor, Allison Heller

IDEAL HOME
The Blue Fin Building, 110 Southwark Street, London
SE1 0SU T 020-3148 5000
Editor, Susan Rose

IN STYLE
The Blue Fin Building, 110 Southwark Street, London
SE1 0SU T 020-3148 5000
Editor, Trish Halpin

INSURANCE AGE
Haymarket House, 28–29 Haymarket, London SW1Y 4RX
T 020-7484 9776 W www.insuranceage.com
Editor, Michelle Worvell

JANE'S DEFENCE WEEKLY
Sentinel House, 163 Brighton Road, Coulsdon, Surrey
CR5 2YH T 020-8700 3700 W jdw.janes.com
Editor, Peter Felstead

THE JEWISH QUARTERLY
PO Box 37645, London NW7 1WB T 020-8343 4675
W www.jewishquarterly.org
Editor, Matthew Reisz

KERRANG!
Mappin House, 4 Winsley Street, London W1W 8HF
T 020-7436 1515 W www.kerrang.com
Editor, Paul Brannigan

THE LADY
39–40 Bedford Street, London WC2E 9ER T 020-7379 4717
W www.lady.co.uk
Editor, Arline Usden

LANCET
32 Jamestown Road, London NW1 7BY T 020-7424 4910
W www.thelancet.com
Editor, Dr Richard Horton

LEGAL WEEK
28–29 Haymarket, London SW1Y 4RX T 020-7484 9700
W www.legalweek.com
Editor, John Malpas

LITERARY REVIEW
44 Lexington Street, London W1F 0LW T 020-7437 9392
W www.literaryreview.co
Editor, Nancy Sladek

LOADED
The Blue Fin Building, 110 Southwark Street, London
SE1 0SU T 020-3148 5000 W www.loaded.co.uk
Editor, Martin Daubney

LONDON REVIEW OF BOOKS
28 Little Russell Street, London WC1A 2HN T 020-7209 1101
Editor, Mary-Kay Wilmers

MACUSER
30 Cleveland Street, London W1T 4JD T 020-7907 6000
W www.macuser.co.uk
Editor, Nik Rawlinson

MARIE CLAIRE
7th Floor, The Blue Fin Building, 110 Southwark Street,
London SE1 0LU T 020-3148 7513
Editor, Marie O'Riordan

MARKETING WEEK
50 Poland Street, London W1F 7AX T 020-7970 6328
W www.marketingweek.co.uk
Editor, Stuart Smith

MAXIM
30 Cleveland Street, London W1T 4JD T 020-7907 6410
W www.maxim-magazine.co.uk
Editor, Derek Harbinson

MEDIA WEEK
174 Hammersmith Road, London W6 7JP T 020-8267 8026
Editor, Steve Barrett

MEN'S HEALTH
33 Broadwick Street, London W1F 9EP T 020-7339 4400
W www.menshealth.co.uk
Editor, Morgan Rees

MIXMAG
90–92 Pentonville Road, London N1 9HS T 020-7520 8625
W www.mixmag.net
Editor, Andrew Harrison

MOJO
Mappin House, 4 Winsley Street, London W1W 8HF
T 020-7436 1515 W www.mojo4music.com
Editor, Phil Alexander

MORE
Endeavour House, 189 Shaftesbury Avenue, London
WC2H 8JG T 020-7208 3165 W www.moremagazine.co.uk
Editor, Lisa Smosarski
MOTHER AND BABY
Greater London House, Hampstead Road, London NW1 7EJ
T 020-7347 1869 W www.motherandbabymagazine.com
Editor, Elena Dalrymple
MUSIC WEEK
1st Floor, Ludgate House, 245 Blackfriars Road, London
SE1 9UR T 020-7921 8348
Editor, Martin Talbot
THE NATIONAL TRUST MAGAZINE
Heelis, Kemble Drive, Swindon SN2 2NA T 01793-817400
W www.nationaltrust.org.uk
Editor, Sue Herdman
NATURE
The Macmillan Building, 4 Crinan Street, London N1 9XW
T 020-7833 4000 W www.nature.com/nature
Editor, Philip Campbell
NME
The Blue Fin Building, 110 Southwark Street, London
SE1 0SU T 020-3148 5000
Editor, Conor McNicholas
NEW SCIENTIST
Lacon House, 84 Theobalds Road, London WC1X 8NS
T 020-7611 1200 W www.newscientist.com
Editor, Jeremy Webb
NEW STATESMAN
3rd Floor, 52 Grosvenor Gardens, London SW1W 0AU
T 020-7730 3444 W www.newstatesman.com
Editor, John Kampfner
NEW WOMAN
Endeavour House, 189 Shaftesbury Avenue, London
WC2H 8JG T 020-7437 9011 W www.nwdaily.co.uk
Editor, Lauren Libbert
NURSING TIMES
Greater London House, Hampstead Road, London NW1 7EJ
T 020-7874 0500
Editor, Rachel Downey
OK!
10 Lower Thames Street, London EC3R 6EN
T 0871-434 1010
Editor, Lisa Byrne
THE OLDIE
65 Newman Street, London W1T 3EG T 020-7436 8801
W www.theoldie.co.uk
Editor, Richard Ingrams
OPERA
36 Black Lion Lane, London W6 9BE T 020-8563 8893
W www.opera.co.uk
Editor, John Allison
PC ADVISOR
99 Gray's Inn Road, London WC1X 8TY T 020-7071 3615
W www.pcadvisor.co.uk
Editor, Paul Trotter
PERIOD LIVING
50 Poland Street, London W1F 7AX T 020-7970 4433
Editor, Sarah Whelan
PERSONAL COMPUTER WORLD
32–34 Broadwick Street, London W1A 2HG
T 020-7316 9000 W www.pcw.co.uk
Editor, Kelvyn Taylor
THE PINK PAPER
Spectrum House, 32–34 Gordon House Road, London
NW5 1LP T 020-7424 7400 W www.pinkpaper.com
Editor, Tris Reid-Smith

POETRY REVIEW
22 Betterton Street, London WC2H 9BX T 020-7420 9883
W www.poetrysociety.org.uk
Editor, Fiona Sampson
PR WEEK
174 Hammersmith Road, London W6 7JP T 020-8267 5000
W www.prweek.com
Editor, Daniel Rogers
PRACTICAL FISHKEEPING
Bretton Court, Bretton, Peterborough PE3 8DZ
T 01733-264666 W www.practicalfishkeeping.co.uk
Editor, Karen Youngs
PRACTICAL PHOTOGRAPHY
Bretton Court, Bretton, Peterborough PE3 8DZ
T 01733-264666 W www.practicalphotography.co.uk
Editor, Andrew James
PRIMA
72 Broadwick Street, London W1F 9EP T 020-7439 5000
Editor, Maire Fahey
PRIVATE EYE
6 Carlisle Street, London W1D 3BN T 020-7437 4017
W www.private-eye.co.uk
Editor, Ian Hislop
PROSPECT MAGAZINE
2 Bloomsbury Place, London WC1A 2QA T 020-7255 1281
W www.prospect-magazine.co.uk
Editor, David Goodhart
PUBLISHING NEWS
7 John Street, London WC1N 2ES T 0870-870 2345
W www.publishingnews.co.uk
Editor, Liz Thomson
Q MAGAZINE
Mappin House, 4 Winsley Street, London W1W 8HF
T 020-7182 8000 W www.q4music.com
Editor, Paul Rees
RA MAGAZINE
Royal Academy of Arts, Burlington House, Piccadilly, London
W1J 0BD T 020-7300 5820 W www.ramagazine.org.uk
Editor, Sarah Greenberg
RACING POST
Floor 23, 1 Canada Square, Canary Wharf, London E14 5AP
T 020-7293 3000 W www.racingpost.co.uk
Editor, Chris Smith
RADIO TIMES
80 Wood Lane, London W12 0TT T 020-8433 3400
W www.radiotimes.com
Editor, Gill Hudson
RAILWAY GAZETTE INTERNATIONAL
Quadrant House, The Quadrant, Sutton, Surrey SM2 5AS
T 020-8652 8608 W www.railwaygazette.com
Editor, Chris Jackson
RAILWAY MAGAZINE
The Blue Fin Building, 110 Southwark Street, London
SE1 0SU T 020-3148 5000
Editor, Nick Pigott
READER'S DIGEST
11 Westferry Circus, Canary Wharf, London E14 4HE
T 020-7715 8000 W www.readersdigest.co.uk
Editor-in-Chief, Katherine Walker
RECORD COLLECTOR
Wales Farm Road, London W3 6UG T 0870-732 8080
W www.recordcollectormag.com
Editor-in-Chief, Alan Lewis
RED
64 North Row, London W1K 7LL T 020-7150 7000
W www.redmagazine.co.uk
Editor, Sam Baker

RUNNER'S WORLD
33 Broadwick Street, London W1F 0DG **T** 020-7339 4400
W www.runnersworld.co.uk
Editor, Andy Dixon

SAGA MAGAZINE
The Saga Building, Enbrook Park, Sandgate, Folkestone, Kent
CT20 3SE **T** 01303-771523
Editor, Emma Soames

SCREEN INTERNATIONAL
33–39 Bowling Green Lane, London EC1R 0DA
T 020-7505 8000 **W** www.screendaily.com
Editor, Michael Gubbins

SHE
National Magazine House, 72 Broadwick Street, London
W1F 9EP **T** 020-7439 5000

SIGHT AND SOUND
British Film Institute, 21 Stephen Street, London W1T 1LN
T 020-7255 1444 **W** www.bfi.org.uk/sightandsound
Editor, Nick James

SKI AND BOARD
The White House, 57–63 Church Road, London SW19 5SB
T 0845-458 0780 **W** www.skiclub.co.uk
Editor, Arnie Wilson

THE SPECTATOR
22 Old Queen Street, London SW1H 9HP **T** 020-7961 0200
W www.spectator.co.uk
Editor, Matthew d'Ancona

THE STAGE
Stage House, 47 Bermondsey Street, London SE1 3XT
T 020-7403 1818 **W** www.thestage.co.uk
Editor, Brian Attwood

STAMP MAGAZINE
Leon House, 233 High Street, Croydon CR9 1HZ
T 020-8726 8241
Editor, Guy Thomas

STUFF
Teddington Studios, Broom Road, Teddington, Middlesex
TW11 9BE **T** 020-8267 5036 **W** www.stuffmag.co.uk
Editor, Fraser MacDonald

THE TABLET
1 King Street Cloisters, Clifton Walk, London W6 0QZ
T 020-8748 8484 **W** www.thetablet.co.uk
Editor, Catherine Pepinster

TAKE A BREAK
Academic House, 24–28 Oval Road, London NW1 7DT
T 020-7241 8000 **W** www.bauer.com
Editor, John Dale

TATLER
Vogue House, Hanover Square, London W1S 1JU
T 020-7499 9080 **W** www.tatler.co.uk
Editor, Geordie Greig

THAT'S LIFE!
Academic House, 24–28 Oval Road, London NW1 7DT
T 020-7241 8000
Editor, Jo Checkley

TIME OUT
Universal House, 251 Tottenham Court Road, London
W1T 7AB **T** 020-7813 3000 **W** www.timeout.com
Editor, Gordon Thomson

THE TIMES EDUCATIONAL SUPPLEMENT
Admiral House, 66–68 East Smithfield, London E1W 1BX
T 020-7782 3000 **W** www.tes.co.uk
Editor, Gerard Kelly

THE TIMES LITERARY SUPPLEMENT
Times House, 1 Pennington Street, London E98 1BS
T 020-7782 5000 **W** www.thetls.co.uk
Editor, Peter Stothard

TOTAL FILM
2 Balcombe Street, London NW1 6NW **T** 020-7042 4000
W www.futurenet.com
Editor, Nev Pierce

TRAVELLER
45 Brompton Road, London SW3 1DE **T** 020-7589 0500
W www.traveller.org.uk
Editor, Amy Sohanpaul

TVTIMES MAGAZINE
The Blue Fin Building, 110 Southwark Street, London
SE1 0SU **T** 020-3148 5615 **W** www.tvtimes.co.uk
Editor, Ian Abbott

VANITY FAIR
Vogue House, Hanover Square, London W1S 1JU
T 020-7499 9080 **W** www.vanityfair.co.uk
Editor-in-Chief, Graydon Carter

VIZ
30 Cleveland Street, London W1T 4JD **T** 020-7687 7000
W www.viz.co.uk
Editor, Simon Donald

VOGUE
Vogue House, Hanover Square, London W1S 1JU
T 020-7499 9080 **W** www.vogue.co.uk
Editor, Alexandra Shulman

WALLPAPER
The Blue Fin Building, 110 Southwark Street, London
SE1 0SU **T** 020-3148 5000 **W** www.wallpaper.com
Editor-in-Chief, Tony Chambers

WANDERLUST
PO Box 1832, Windsor SL4 1YT **T** 01753-620426
W www.wanderlust.co.uk
Editor, Dan Linstead

WHAT CAR?
Teddington Studios, Broom Road, Teddington, Middlesex
TW11 9BE **T** 020-8267 5000 **W** www.whatcar.com
Group Editor, Steve Fowler

WOMAN'S OWN
The Blue Fin Building, 110 Southwark Street, London
SE1 0SU **T** 020-3148 5000
Editor, Karen Livermore

THE WORLD OF INTERIORS
Vogue House, Hanover Square, London W1S 1JU
T 020-7499 9080 **W** www.worldofinteriors.co.uk
Editor, Rupert Thomas

WORLD SOCCER
The Blue Fin Building, 110 Southwark Street, London
SE1 0SU **T** 020-3148 5000 **W** www.worldsoccer.com
Editor, Gavin Hamilton

YACHTING MONTHLY
The Blue Fin Building, 110 Southwark Street, London
SE1 0SU **T** 020-3261 6040
Editor, Paul Gelder

ZEST
72 Broadwick Street, London W1F 9EP **T** 020-7439 5000
Editor, Alison Pylkkanen

TIME AND SPACE

ASTRONOMY

TIME MEASUREMENT AND CALENDARS

TIDAL PREDICTIONS

ASTRONOMY

The following pages give astronomical data for each month of the year 2008. There are four pages of data for each month. All data are given for 0h Greenwich Mean Time (GMT), ie at the midnight at the beginning of the day named. This applies also to data for the months when British Summer Time is in operation (for dates, *see* below).

The astronomical data are given in a form suitable for observation with the naked eye or with a small telescope. These data do not attempt to replace the *Astronomical Almanac* for professional astronomers.

A fuller explanation of how to use the astronomical data is given on pages 687–89.

CALENDAR FOR EACH MONTH

The calendar for each month comprises dates of general interest plus the dates of birth or death of well-known people. For key religious, civil and legal dates *see* page 9. For details of flag-flying days *see* page 23. For royal birthdays *see* pages 23 and 24–5. Public holidays are given in italics. *See* also pages 10 and 11.

Fuller explanations of the various calendars can be found under Time Measurement and Calendars.

The zodiacal signs through which the Sun is passing during each month are illustrated. The date of transition from one sign to the next, to the nearest hour, is given under Astronomical Phenomena.

JULIAN DATE

The Julian date on 2008 January 0.0 is 2454465.5. To find the Julian date for any other date in 2008 (at 0h GMT), add the day-of-the-year number on the extreme right of the calendar for each month to the Julian date for January 0.0.

SEASONS

The seasons are defined astronomically as follows:

Spring from the vernal equinox to the summer solstice
Summer from the summer solstice to the autumnal equinox
Autumn from the autumnal equinox to the winter solstice
Winter from the winter solstice to the vernal equinox

The time when seasons start in 2008 (to the nearest hour) are:

Northern Hemisphere

Vernal equinox	March 20d 06h GMT
Summer solstice	June 21d 00h GMT
Autumnal equinox	September 22d 16h GMT
Winter solstice	December 21d 12h GMT

Southern Hemisphere

Autumnal equinox	March 20d 06h GMT
Winter solstice	June 21d 00h GMT
Vernal equinox	September 22d 16h GMT
Summer solstice	December 21d 12h GMT

The longest day of the year, measured from sunrise to sunset, is at the summer solstice. The longest day in the United Kingdom will fall on 20 June in 2008.

The shortest day of the year is at the winter solstice. The shortest day in the United Kingdom will fall on 21 December in 2008.

The equinox is the point at which day and night are of equal length all over the world.

In popular parlance, the seasons in the northern hemisphere comprise the following months:

Spring	March, April, May
Summer	June, July, August
Autumn	September, October, November
Winter	December, January, February

BRITISH SUMMER TIME

British Summer Time is the legal time for general purposes during the period in which it is in operation (*see also* pages 691–2). During this period, clocks are kept one hour ahead of Greenwich Mean Time. The hour of changeover is 01h Greenwich Mean Time. The duration of Summer Time in 2008 is from March 30 01h GMT to October 26 01h GMT.

JANUARY 2008

FIRST MONTH, 31 DAYS. *Janus*, god of the portal, facing two ways, past and future

1	*Tuesday*	The UK joined the EEC with Ireland and Denmark, bringing the number of members to nine 1973	day 1
2	*Wednesday*	Gilbert Murray, British diplomat b. 1866 Henry Booth, English politician d. 1694	2
3	*Thursday*	Clement Attlee, British prime minister b. 1883 Herbert Morrison, British statesman b. 1888	3
4	*Friday*	Burma gained independence from the United Kingdom 1948	4
5	*Saturday*	Konrad Adenauer, German chancellor b. 1876 Juan Carlos, king of Spain b. 1938	5
6	*Sunday*	King Richard II b. 1367 Yahya Ayyash, Palestinian leader d. 1996	6

7	*Monday*	Millard Fillmore, US president b. 1800 Hirohito Michinomiya, emperor of Japan d. 1989	week 1 day 7
8	*Tuesday*	James Craig, prime minister of Northern Ireland b. 1871 François Mitterrand, president of France d. 1996	8
9	*Wednesday*	Richard Nixon, US president b. 1913 Napoleon III, emperor of France d. 1873	9
10	*Thursday*	Harold Macmillan became prime minister of Britain 1957	10
11	*Friday*	John A. Macdonald, prime minister of Canada b. 1815 Zenko Suzuki, prime minister of Japan b. 1911	11
12	*Saturday*	Hermann Goering, German Nazi leader b. 1893 Leopoldo Galtieri, president of Argentina d. 2003	12
13	*Sunday*	Henry II, king of Castile b. 1334 Chiang Ching-kuo, Chinese statesman d. 1988	13

14	*Monday*	Anthony Eden, British prime minister d. 1977 Frederick IX, king of Denmark d. 1972	week 2 day 14
15	*Tuesday*	Gamal Nasser, president of Egypt b. 1918 Martin Luther King Jr, US political activist b. 1929	15
16	*Wednesday*	Johannes Rau, German politician b. 1931 Laurent Kabila, president of the DR Congo d. 2001	16
17	*Thursday*	David Lloyd-George, British prime minister b. 1863 Benjamin Franklin, American statesman b. 1706	17
18	*Friday*	John Tyler, US president d. 1862 Hugh Gaitskell, British politician d. 1963	18
19	*Saturday*	Indira Gandhi became the first female prime minister of India 1966	19
20	*Sunday*	Herbert Bowden, British politician b. 1905 King George V d. 1936	20

21	*Monday*	Louis XVI, king of France d. 1793 Vladimir Lenin, Russian revolutionary d. 1924	week 3 day 21
22	*Tuesday*	Queen Victoria d. 1901 Lyndon B. Johnson, US president d. 1973	22
23	*Wednesday*	Richard Nixon announced a peace deal between the USA and Vietnam after a decade of conflict 1973	23
24	*Thursday*	Winston Churchill, British prime minister d. 1965 Caligula, Roman emperor d. AD 41	24
25	*Friday*	Paul-Henri Spaak, prime minister of Belgium b. 1899 Eduard Shevardnadze, Georgian politician b. 1928	25
26	*Saturday*	The Republic of India was proclaimed with Rajendra Prasad as president 1950	26
27	*Sunday*	Wilhelm II, German emperor b. 1859 Rauf Denktash, Turkish-Cypriot politician b. 1924	27

28	*Monday*	King Henry VII b. 1457 King Henry VIII d. 1547	week 4 day 28
29	*Tuesday*	William McKinley, US president b. 1843 King George III d. 1820	29
30	*Wednesday*	Franklin D. Roosevelt, US president b. 1882 Mahatma Gandhi, Indian leader d. 1948	30
31	*Thursday*	Guy Fawkes was executed for his involvement in the Gunpowder Plot 1606	31

ASTRONOMICAL PHENOMENA

d	h	
3	00	Earth at perihelion (147 million km.)
5	03	Venus in conjunction with Moon. Venus 7°N.
7	10	Jupiter in conjunction with Moon. Jupiter 4°N.
9	16	Mercury in conjunction with Moon. Mercury 0°.3N.
20	00	Mars in conjunction with Moon. Mars 1°S.
20	17	Sun's longitude 300° ≈≈≈
22	05	Mercury at greatest elongation E. 19°
25	04	Saturn in conjunction with Moon. Saturn 3°N.
28	21	Mercury at stationary point
30	23	Mars at stationary point

MINIMA OF ALGOL

d	h	d	h	d	h
1	15.2	13	02.5	24	13.8
4	12.1	15	23.3	27	10.6
7	08.9	18	20.2	30	07.4
10	05.7	21	17.0		

CONSTELLATIONS

The following constellations are near the meridian at

	d	h		d	h
December	1	24	January	16	21
December	16	23	February	1	20
January	1	22	February	15	19

Draco (below the Pole), Ursa Minor (below the Pole), Camelopardus, Perseus, Auriga, Taurus, Orion, Eridanus and Lepus

THE MOON

Phases, Apsides and Node	d	h	m
● New Moon	8	11	37
☽ First Quarter	15	19	46
○ Full Moon	22	13	35
☾ Last Quarter	30	05	03

Apogee (405,298km)	3	08	11
Perigee (366,455km)	19	08	41
Apogee (404,493km)	31	04	27

Mean longitude of ascending node on January 1, 330°

THE SUN

s.d. 16′.3

Day	Right Ascension			Dec. −		Equation of time		Rise 52°		Rise 56°		Transit		Set 52°		Set 56°		Sidereal time			Transit of First Point of Aries		
	h	m	s	°	′	m	s	h	m	h	m	h	m	h	m	h	m	h	m	s	h	m	s
1	18	43	12	23	04	−3	04	8	08	8	31	12	03	15	59	15	35	6	40	08	17	17	02
2	18	47	37	22	59	−3	33	8	08	8	31	12	04	16	00	15	37	6	44	04	17	13	06
3	18	52	02	22	54	−4	01	8	08	8	31	12	04	16	01	15	38	6	48	01	17	09	10
4	18	56	26	22	48	−4	29	8	08	8	30	12	05	16	02	15	39	6	51	57	17	05	14
5	19	00	50	22	42	−4	56	8	07	8	30	12	05	16	03	15	41	6	55	54	17	01	18
6	19	05	14	22	36	−5	23	8	07	8	29	12	06	16	04	15	42	6	59	50	16	57	23
7	19	09	37	22	29	−5	50	8	07	8	29	12	06	16	06	15	44	7	03	47	16	53	27
8	19	14	00	22	21	−6	16	8	06	8	28	12	06	16	07	15	45	7	07	43	16	49	31
9	19	18	22	22	13	−6	42	8	06	8	28	12	07	16	08	15	47	7	11	40	16	45	35
10	19	22	44	22	05	−7	07	8	05	8	27	12	07	16	10	15	48	7	15	37	16	41	39
11	19	27	05	21	56	−7	32	8	05	8	26	12	08	16	11	15	50	7	19	33	16	37	43
12	19	31	25	21	47	−7	56	8	04	8	25	12	08	16	13	15	52	7	23	30	16	33	47
13	19	35	45	21	37	−8	19	8	03	8	24	12	09	16	14	15	53	7	27	26	16	29	51
14	19	40	05	21	27	−8	42	8	03	8	23	12	09	16	16	15	55	7	31	23	16	25	55
15	19	44	23	21	16	−9	04	8	02	8	22	12	09	16	17	15	57	7	35	19	16	21	59
16	19	48	41	21	06	−9	25	8	01	8	21	12	10	16	19	15	59	7	39	16	16	18	03
17	19	52	59	20	54	−9	46	8	00	8	20	12	10	16	20	16	01	7	43	12	16	14	08
18	19	57	15	20	43	−10	06	7	59	8	18	12	10	16	22	16	03	7	47	09	16	10	12
19	20	01	31	20	30	−10	25	7	58	8	17	12	11	16	24	16	05	7	51	06	16	06	16
20	20	05	46	20	18	−10	44	7	57	8	16	12	11	16	25	16	07	7	55	02	16	02	20
21	20	10	01	20	05	−11	02	7	56	8	14	12	11	16	27	16	09	7	58	59	15	58	24
22	20	14	14	19	52	−11	19	7	55	8	13	12	11	16	29	16	11	8	02	55	15	54	28
23	20	18	27	19	38	−11	35	7	53	8	11	12	12	16	30	16	13	8	06	52	15	50	32
24	20	22	39	19	24	−11	51	7	52	8	10	12	12	16	32	16	15	8	10	48	15	46	36
25	20	26	50	19	10	−12	06	7	51	8	08	12	12	16	34	16	17	8	14	45	15	42	40
26	20	31	01	18	55	−12	20	7	50	8	07	12	12	16	36	16	19	8	18	41	15	38	44
27	20	35	11	18	40	−12	33	7	48	8	05	12	13	16	38	16	21	8	22	38	15	34	48
28	20	39	20	18	25	−12	45	7	47	8	03	12	13	16	39	16	23	8	26	35	15	30	53
29	20	43	28	18	09	−12	57	7	45	8	02	12	13	16	41	16	25	8	30	31	15	26	57
30	20	47	35	17	53	−13	08	7	44	8	00	12	13	16	43	16	27	8	34	28	15	23	01
31	20	51	42	17	37	−13	18	7	43	7	58	12	13	16	45	16	29	8	38	24	15	19	05

DURATION OF TWILIGHT (in minutes)

Latitude	52°	56°	52°	56°	52°	56°	52°	56°
	1 January		11 January		21 January		31 January	
Civil	41	47	40	45	38	43	37	41
Nautical	84	96	82	93	80	90	78	87
Astronomical	125	141	123	138	120	134	117	130

THE NIGHT SKY

Mercury is unsuitably placed for observation during the first half of the month but thereafter emerges from the evening twilight to be visible low in the south-western sky at the end of evening civil twilight, until the last couple of days of the month. During this period its magnitude fades from −0.8 to +0.9.

Venus, magnitude −4.0, is a brilliant object in the south-eastern sky before dawn, though the duration of its period of visibility shortens noticeably during the month.

Mars, just past opposition, is a brilliant evening object in the southern sky as soon as it gets dark and still easily visible for several hours after midnight. Mars is in retrograde motion in Taurus until the 30th when it resumes its direct motion. During January its magnitude fades from −1.5 to −0.6. The waxing gibbous Moon passes only 1 degree north of the planet on the night of the 19th–20th.

Jupiter is not visible at first but is gradually emerging from the morning twilight. It may be detected during the last few days of the month, very low above the south-eastern horizon about half an hour before sunrise. Its magnitude is −1.9. Jupiter is in the constellation of Sagittarius. Venus can be used as an aid to finding Jupiter during the last few days of January as it moves eastwards towards Jupiter, being less than 2 degrees from that planet on the 31st.

Saturn, magnitude +0.4, is retrograding in Leo, and by the end of the month is visible from the mid-evening when it rises above the eastern horizon right through until dawn. The Moon, just after Full, passes 3 degrees south of the planet on the morning of the 25th. The rings of Saturn are now closing, and as a result, the planet is not quite as bright as it was in the previous two oppositions. The south pole is presented towards the Earth, but the far side of the rings no longer appears clear of the body of the planet.

THE MOON

Day	R.A. h	R.A. m	Dec. °	Hor. Par. '	Semi-diam. '	Sun's Co-Long. °	PA of Br. Limb °	Ph. %	Age d	Rise 52° h	Rise 52° m	Rise 56° h	Rise 56° m	Transit h	Transit m	Set 52° h	Set 52° m	Set 56° h	Set 56° m
1	12	58	−10.3	54.5	14.9	183	112	44	22.3	1	16	1	26	6	29	11	29	11	17
2	13	42	−15.4	54.2	14.8	195	110	34	23.3	2	28	2	43	7	11	11	42	11	25
3	14	28	−19.8	54.1	14.7	207	106	26	24.3	3	41	4	03	7	55	11	59	11	36
4	15	17	−23.4	54.1	14.7	220	101	18	25.3	4	54	5	22	8	41	12	22	11	53
5	16	08	−26.1	54.3	14.8	232	95	11	26.3	6	05	6	39	9	31	12	54	12	19
6	17	01	−27.6	54.6	14.9	244	87	6	27.3	7	07	7	45	10	23	13	38	13	00
7	17	56	−27.9	54.9	15.0	256	76	2	28.3	7	59	8	35	11	16	14	37	14	01
8	18	51	−26.7	55.4	15.1	268	51	0	29.3	8	37	9	08	12	10	15	48	15	18
9	19	46	−24.2	55.8	15.2	281	286	0	0.5	9	05	9	29	13	01	17	07	16	43
10	20	39	−20.4	56.3	15.3	293	261	2	1.5	9	25	9	43	13	51	18	28	18	11
11	21	30	−15.6	56.8	15.5	305	253	7	2.5	9	41	9	53	14	38	19	49	19	39
12	22	19	−10.0	57.3	15.6	317	248	13	3.5	9	54	10	00	15	24	21	09	21	05
13	23	07	−3.9	57.8	15.7	329	246	21	4.5	10	05	10	06	16	09	22	30	22	32
14	23	55	+2.4	58.2	15.9	341	245	30	5.5	10	17	10	13	16	55	23	53	—	
15	0	44	+8.8	58.7	16.0	354	246	41	6.5	10	30	10	20	17	44	—		0	00
16	1	36	+14.8	59.1	16.1	6	249	52	7.5	10	46	10	30	18	36	1	19	1	33
17	2	31	+20.1	59.4	16.2	18	253	63	8.5	11	08	10	45	19	32	2	48	3	09
18	3	30	+24.3	59.7	16.3	30	259	74	9.5	11	39	11	08	20	33	4	18	4	47
19	4	33	+27.1	59.8	16.3	42	266	84	10.5	12	25	11	49	21	37	5	41	6	18
20	5	38	+28.0	59.8	16.3	54	275	91	11.5	13	31	12	54	22	41	6	50	7	27
21	6	43	+27.0	59.6	16.2	66	284	97	12.5	14	52	14	21	23	42	7	38	8	10
22	7	45	+24.2	59.2	16.1	79	302	100	13.5	16	20	15	57	—		8	11	8	35
23	8	43	+20.0	58.6	16.0	91	88	100	14.5	17	47	17	32	0	38	8	33	8	51
24	9	37	+14.8	57.9	15.8	103	107	97	15.5	19	10	19	01	1	29	8	50	9	01
25	10	27	+9.0	57.2	15.6	115	113	93	16.5	20	29	20	26	2	16	9	02	9	08
26	11	13	+3.0	56.4	15.4	127	115	87	17.5	21	45	21	47	3	00	9	13	9	14
27	11	58	−2.9	55.7	15.2	139	116	79	18.5	22	58	23	06	3	42	9	24	9	20
28	12	42	−8.6	55.1	15.0	151	115	71	19.5	—		—		4	23	9	35	9	25
29	13	27	−13.9	54.6	14.9	164	113	62	20.5	0	11	0	24	5	05	9	47	9	33
30	14	13	−18.5	54.3	14.8	176	110	52	21.5	1	25	1	44	5	48	10	02	9	42
31	15	00	−22.5	54.2	14.8	188	106	43	22.5	2	38	3	04	6	34	10	23	9	56

MERCURY

Day	R.A. h	R.A. m	Dec. °	Diam. "	Phase %	Transit h	Transit m	5° high 52° h	52° m	5° high 56° h	56° m
1	19	20	−24.3	5	97	12	42	15	35	14	55
3	19	35	−23.8	5	96	12	48	15	46	15	08
5	19	49	−23.3	5	94	12	54	15	57	15	22
7	20	02	−22.6	5	93	13	00	16	09	15	36
9	20	16	−21.8	5	90	13	06	16	22	15	51
11	20	29	−21.0	5	88	13	11	16	34	16	06
13	20	42	−20.0	6	84	13	16	16	47	16	20
15	20	55	−19.0	6	80	13	20	16	59	16	34
17	21	06	−17.9	6	75	13	24	17	10	16	48
19	21	17	−16.8	6	68	13	26	17	20	16	59
21	21	26	−15.6	7	61	13	27	17	28	17	09
23	21	33	−14.5	7	53	13	26	17	34	17	17
25	21	39	−13.5	8	43	13	23	17	37	17	21
27	21	42	−12.7	8	34	13	18	17	36	17	21
29	21	43	−12.0	9	24	13	09	17	31	17	16
31	21	40	−11.6	9	15	12	58	17	22	17	07

VENUS

Day	R.A. h	R.A. m	Dec. °	Diam. "	Phase %	Transit h	Transit m	5° high 52° h	52° m	5° high 56° h	56° m
1	15	59	−18.5	15	76	9	20	5	41	6	05
6	16	24	−19.7	14	78	9	25	5	55	6	22
11	16	50	−20.8	14	79	9	31	6	09	6	38
16	17	16	−21.6	13	81	9	37	6	22	6	53
21	17	40	−22.1	13	82	9	44	6	33	7	06
26	18	09	−22.4	13	83	9	51	6	42	7	15
31	18	35	−22.4	13	84	9	58	6	49	7	22

MARS

Day	R.A. h	R.A. m	Dec. °	Diam. "	Phase %	Transit h	Transit m	5° high 52° h	52° m	5° high 56° h	56° m
1	5	59	+26.9	15	100	23	14	7	16	7	39
6	5	52	+27.0	15	99	22	47	6	49	7	12
11	5	45	+27.0	15	98	22	21	6	22	6	46
16	5	40	+26.9	14	98	21	56	5	57	6	21
21	5	36	+26.8	13	97	21	33	5	34	5	57
26	5	34	+26.8	13	96	21	12	5	11	5	34
31	5	34	+26.7	12	95	20	52	4	50	5	13

SUNRISE AND SUNSET

d	London 0° 05' 51° 30'			Bristol 2° 35' 51° 28'			Birmingham 1° 55' 52° 28'			Manchester 2° 15' 53° 28'			Newcastle 1° 37' 54° 59'			Glasgow 4° 14' 55° 52'			Belfast 5° 56' 54° 35'		
	h	m	h	m	h	m	h	m	h	m	h	m	h	m	h	m	h	m	h	m
1	8	06	16	01	8	16	16	12	8	18	16	04	8	25	16	00	8	31	15	48	8	47	15	53	8	46	16	08
2	8	06	16	02	8	16	16	13	8	18	16	05	8	25	16	01	8	31	15	50	8	47	15	54	8	46	16	09
3	8	06	16	04	8	16	16	14	8	18	16	06	8	25	16	02	8	31	15	51	8	47	15	56	8	46	16	10
4	8	06	16	05	8	15	16	15	8	18	16	07	8	24	16	03	8	31	15	52	8	47	15	57	8	45	16	12
5	8	05	16	06	8	15	16	16	8	17	16	08	8	24	16	05	8	30	15	53	8	46	15	58	8	45	16	13
6	8	05	16	07	8	15	16	17	8	17	16	10	8	24	16	06	8	30	15	55	8	46	16	00	8	45	16	14
7	8	05	16	08	8	15	16	19	8	17	16	11	8	23	16	07	8	29	15	56	8	45	16	01	8	44	16	16
8	8	04	16	10	8	14	16	20	8	16	16	12	8	23	16	09	8	29	15	58	8	44	16	03	8	44	16	17
9	8	04	16	11	8	14	16	21	8	16	16	14	8	22	16	10	8	28	15	59	8	44	16	04	8	43	16	19
10	8	03	16	12	8	13	16	23	8	15	16	15	8	22	16	11	8	27	16	01	8	43	16	06	8	42	16	20
11	8	03	16	14	8	13	16	24	8	15	16	17	8	21	16	13	8	26	16	02	8	42	16	08	8	41	16	22
12	8	02	16	15	8	12	16	25	8	14	16	18	8	20	16	15	8	26	16	04	8	41	16	09	8	41	16	23
13	8	01	16	17	8	11	16	27	8	13	16	20	8	19	16	16	8	25	16	06	8	40	16	11	8	40	16	25
14	8	01	16	18	8	10	16	28	8	12	16	21	8	18	16	18	8	24	16	07	8	39	16	13	8	39	16	27
15	8	00	16	20	8	10	16	30	8	11	16	23	8	18	16	19	8	23	16	09	8	38	16	15	8	38	16	28
16	7	59	16	21	8	09	16	31	8	11	16	24	8	17	16	21	8	22	16	11	8	37	16	17	8	37	16	30
17	7	58	16	23	8	08	16	33	8	10	16	26	8	16	16	23	8	21	16	13	8	36	16	18	8	36	16	32
18	7	57	16	24	8	07	16	35	8	09	16	28	8	15	16	24	8	19	16	14	8	35	16	20	8	35	16	34
19	7	56	16	26	8	06	16	36	8	08	16	29	8	13	16	26	8	18	16	16	8	33	16	22	8	34	16	36
20	7	55	16	28	8	05	16	38	8	07	16	31	8	12	16	28	8	17	16	18	8	32	16	24	8	32	16	37
21	7	54	16	29	8	04	16	40	8	05	16	33	8	11	16	30	8	16	16	20	8	31	16	26	8	31	16	39
22	7	53	16	31	8	03	16	41	8	04	16	35	8	10	16	32	8	14	16	22	8	29	16	28	8	30	16	41
23	7	52	16	33	8	02	16	43	8	03	16	36	8	09	16	33	8	13	16	24	8	28	16	30	8	28	16	43
24	7	51	16	35	8	00	16	45	8	02	16	38	8	07	16	35	8	11	16	26	8	26	16	32	8	27	16	45
25	7	49	16	36	7	59	16	46	8	00	16	40	8	06	16	37	8	10	16	28	8	25	16	34	8	25	16	47
26	7	48	16	38	7	58	16	48	7	59	16	42	8	04	16	39	8	08	16	30	8	23	16	36	8	24	16	49
27	7	47	16	40	7	57	16	50	7	58	16	43	8	03	16	41	8	07	16	32	8	21	16	38	8	22	16	51
28	7	45	16	42	7	55	16	52	7	56	16	45	8	02	16	43	8	05	16	34	8	20	16	41	8	21	16	53
29	7	44	16	43	7	54	16	53	7	55	16	47	8	00	16	45	8	04	16	36	8	18	16	43	8	19	16	55
30	7	43	16	45	7	52	16	55	7	53	16	49	7	58	16	47	8	02	16	38	8	16	16	45	8	18	16	57
31	7	41	16	47	7	51	16	57	7	52	16	51	7	57	16	49	8	00	16	40	8	14	16	47	8	16	16	59

JUPITER

Day	R.A.		Dec.		Transit		5° high			
							52°		56°	
	h	m	°	′	h	m	h	m	h	m
1	18	13.1	−23	14	11	32	8	31	9	07
11	18	23.0	−23	11	11	02	8	01	8	37
21	18	32.8	−23	05	10	32	7	30	8	06
31	18	42.2	−22	58	10	03	6	59	7	34

Diameters – equatorial 32″ polar 30″

SATURN

Day	R.A.		Dec.		Transit		5° high			
							52°		56°	
	h	m	°	′	h	m	h	m	h	m
1	10	42.8	+9	58	4	02	21	40	21	35
11	10	41.7	+10	08	3	22	20	59	20	54
21	10	39.9	+10	20	2	40	20	17	20	12
31	10	37.7	+10	36	1	59	19	34	19	28

Diameters – equatorial 19″ polar 17″
Rings – major axis 44″ minor axis 5″

URANUS

Day	R.A.		Dec.		Transit		10° high			
							52°		56°	
	h	m	°	′	h	m	h	m	h	m
1	23	07.3	−6	28	16	25	20	42	20	29
11	23	08.6	−6	20	15	47	20	05	19	52
21	23	10.1	−6	10	15	09	19	28	19	15
31	23	11.8	−5	59	14	31	18	52	18	39

Diameter 4″

NEPTUNE

Day	R.A.		Dec.		Transit		5° high			
							52°		56°	
	h	m	°	′	h	m	h	m	h	m
1	21	31.0	−15	00	14	49	18	10	17	44
11	21	32.3	−14	54	14	10	17	33	17	07
21	21	33.7	−14	48	13	33	16	56	16	30
31	21	35.1	−14	41	12	55	16	19	15	54

Diameter 2″

FEBRUARY 2008

SECOND MONTH, 28 or 29 DAYS. *Februa*, Roman festival of Purification

1	*Friday*	Boris Yeltsin, president of the Russian Federation b. 1931 Shahabuddin Ahmed, president of Bangladesh b. 1930	32
2	*Saturday*	The US supreme court convened for the first time 1790	33
3	*Sunday*	Robert Gascoyne-Cecil, British prime minister b. 1830 Woodrow Wilson, US president d. 1924	34
4	*Monday*	Slavery was banned in the French Republic 1794 week 5 day	35
5	*Tuesday*	Robert Peel, British prime minister b. 1788 Andreas Papandreou, prime minister of Greece b. 1919	36
6	*Wednesday*	Queen Anne b. 1665 Ronald Reagan, US president b. 1911	37
7	*Thursday*	Thomas More, English statesman b. 1478 Daniel Malan, prime minister of South Africa d. 1959	38
8	*Friday*	Yaroslav II, grand prince of Vladimir b. 1191 Mary I, queen of Scotland d. 1587	39
9	*Saturday*	Garrett Fitzgerald, prime minister of Ireland b. 1926 Yuri Andropov, Soviet leader d. 1984	40
10	*Sunday*	Harold Macmillan, British prime minister b. 1894 Maurice Schumann, French statesman d. 1998	41
11	*Monday*	Nelson Mandela was released from prison after 27 years 1990 week 6 day	42
12	*Tuesday*	Francis II, Holy Roman emperor b. 1768 Lady Jane Grey d. 1554	43
13	*Wednesday*	Francis Pym, British politician b. 1922 Catherine Howard, queen consort of Henry VIII d. 1542	44
14	*Thursday*	Rafik Hariri, prime minister of Lebanon d. 2005 Yusuf Salman Yusuf, Iraqi communist leader d. 1949	45
15	*Friday*	H. H. Asquith, British prime minister d. 1928 Henry Hunt, British politician d. 1835	46
16	*Saturday*	Fidel Castro was sworn in as premier of Cuba 1959	47
17	*Sunday*	William III, king of the Netherlands b. 1817 Geronimo, Native American leader d. 1909	48
18	*Monday*	Queen Mary I b. 1516 Kublai Khan, Mongol and Chinese emperor d. 1294 week 7 day	49
19	*Tuesday*	Alvaro Obregon, president of Mexico b. 1880 Deng Xiaoping, Chinese leader d. 1997	50
20	*Wednesday*	Hundreds were killed in election violence in Assam, north-east India 1983	51
21	*Thursday*	Robert Mugabe, president of Zimbabwe b. 1924 Malcolm X, US civil rights campaigner d. 1965	52
22	*Friday*	George Washington, US president b. 1732 Jean-Bédel Bokassa, ruler of the Central African Republic b. 1921	53
23	*Saturday*	Konstantin Päts, president of Estonia b. 1874 William McMahon, prime minister of Australia b. 1908	54
24	*Sunday*	Joe Lieberman, US politician b. 1942 Joseph I, king of Portugal d. 1777	55
25	*Monday*	Néstor Kirchner, president of Argentina b. 1950 William IV, grand duke of Luxembourg week 8 day d. 1912	56
26	*Tuesday*	Ferdinand I, king of Bulgaria b. 1861 Levi Eshkol, prime minister of Israel d. 1969	57
27	*Wednesday*	The German parliamentary building, the Reichstag, was set on fire 1933	58
28	*Thursday*	Robin Cook, British politician b. 1946 Olof Palme, prime minister of Sweden d. 1986	59
29	*Friday*	Morarji Desai, prime minister of India b. 1896 Carlos Romero, president of El Salvador b. 1924	60

ASTRONOMICAL PHENOMENA

d h
1 12 Jupiter in conjunction with Venus. Jupiter 0°.6S.
4 06 Jupiter in conjunction with Moon. Jupiter 4°N.
4 12 Venus in conjunction with Moon. Venus 4°N.
6 18 Mercury in inferior conjunction
7 02 Mercury in conjunction with Moon. Mercury 5°N.
7 04 Annular eclipse of Sun
11 02 Neptune in conjunction
16 08 Mars in conjunction with Moon. Mars 2°S.
19 03 Mercury at stationary point
19 07 Sun's longitude 330° ♓
21 03 Total eclipse of Moon
21 10 Saturn in conjunction with Moon. Saturn 3°N.
24 10 Saturn at opposition
26 18 Venus in conjunction with Mercury. Venus 1°S.

MINIMA OF ALGOL

d	h	d	h	d	h
2	04.3	13	15.6	25	02.8
5	01.1	16	12.4	27	23.7
7	21.9	19	09.2		
10	18.7	22	06.0		

CONSTELLATIONS

The following constellations are near the meridian at

	d	h		d	h
January	1	24	February	15	21
January	16	23	March	1	20
February	1	22	March	16	19

Draco (below the Pole), Camelopardalis, Auriga, Taurus Gemini, Orion, Canis Minor, Monoceros, Lepus, Canis Major and Puppis

THE MOON

Phases, Apsides and Node		d	h	m
●	New Moon	7	03	44
☽	First Quarter	14	03	33
○	Full Moon	21	03	30
☾	Last Quarter	29	02	18
Perigee (370,256km)		14	00	56
Apogee (404,403km)		28	01	25

Mean longitude of ascending node on February 1, 329°

THE SUN

s.d. 16′.2

Day	Right Ascension			Dec. −		Equation of time		Rise 52°		Rise 56°		Transit		Set 52°		Set 56°		Sidereal time			Transit of first point of Aries		
	h	m	s	°	′	m	s	h	m	h	m	h	m	h	m	h	m	h	m	s	h	m	s
1	20	55	48	17	20	−13	27	7	41	7	56	12	14	16	47	16	32	8	42	21	15	15	09
2	20	59	53	17	03	−13	35	7	39	7	54	12	14	16	49	16	34	8	46	17	15	11	13
3	21	03	57	16	46	−13	43	7	38	7	52	12	14	16	50	16	36	8	50	14	15	07	17
4	21	08	00	16	28	−13	50	7	36	7	50	12	14	16	52	16	38	8	54	10	15	03	21
5	21	12	03	16	11	−13	56	7	35	7	48	12	14	16	54	16	40	8	58	07	14	59	25
6	21	16	04	15	52	−14	01	7	33	7	46	12	14	16	56	16	43	9	02	04	14	55	29
7	21	20	05	15	34	−14	05	7	31	7	44	12	14	16	58	16	45	9	06	00	14	51	33
8	21	24	06	15	15	−14	09	7	29	7	42	12	14	17	00	16	47	9	09	57	14	47	37
9	21	28	05	14	56	−14	12	7	28	7	40	12	14	17	02	16	49	9	13	53	14	43	42
10	21	32	03	14	37	−14	14	7	26	7	38	12	14	17	03	16	51	9	17	50	14	39	46
11	21	36	01	14	18	−14	15	7	24	7	36	12	14	17	05	16	54	9	21	46	14	35	50
12	21	39	58	13	58	−14	15	7	22	7	34	12	14	17	07	16	56	9	25	43	14	31	54
13	21	43	54	13	38	−14	15	7	20	7	31	12	14	17	09	16	58	9	29	39	14	27	58
14	21	47	50	13	18	−14	14	7	18	7	29	12	14	17	11	17	00	9	33	36	14	24	02
15	21	51	44	12	58	−14	12	7	16	7	27	12	14	17	13	17	02	9	37	33	14	20	06
16	21	55	38	12	37	−14	09	7	14	7	25	12	14	17	15	17	05	9	41	29	14	16	10
17	21	59	32	12	16	−14	06	7	12	7	22	12	14	17	17	17	07	9	45	26	14	12	14
18	22	03	24	11	56	−14	02	7	10	7	20	12	14	17	18	17	09	9	49	22	14	08	18
19	22	07	16	11	34	−13	57	7	08	7	18	12	14	17	20	17	11	9	53	19	14	04	22
20	22	11	07	11	13	−13	51	7	06	7	15	12	14	17	22	17	13	9	57	15	14	00	27
21	22	14	57	10	52	−13	45	7	04	7	13	12	14	17	24	17	16	10	01	12	13	56	31
22	22	18	47	10	30	−13	38	7	02	7	10	12	14	17	26	17	18	10	05	08	13	52	35
23	22	22	36	10	08	−13	31	7	00	7	08	12	13	17	28	17	20	10	09	05	13	48	39
24	22	26	24	9	46	−13	23	6	58	7	06	12	13	17	29	17	22	10	13	02	13	44	43
25	22	30	12	9	24	−13	14	6	56	7	03	12	13	17	31	17	24	10	16	58	13	40	47
26	22	33	59	9	02	−13	05	6	54	7	01	12	13	17	33	17	26	10	20	55	13	36	51
27	22	37	46	8	39	−12	55	6	52	6	58	12	13	17	35	17	28	10	24	51	13	32	55
28	22	41	32	8	17	−12	45	6	50	6	56	12	13	17	37	17	31	10	28	48	13	28	59
29	22	45	18	7	54	−12	34	6	47	6	53	12	12	17	38	17	33	10	32	44	13	25	03

DURATION OF TWILIGHT (in minutes)

Latitude	52°	56°	52°	56°	52°	56°	52°	56°
	1 February		11 February		21 February		31 February	
Civil	37	41	35	39	34	38	34	37
Nautical	77	86	75	83	74	81	73	80
Astronomical	117	130	114	126	113	124	112	124

THE NIGHT SKY

Mercury passes through inferior conjunction on the 6th and remains too close to the Sun for observation throughout the month.

Venus continues to be visible as a splendid object in the early morning skies, magnitude −3.9, though it will only be seen low above the south-eastern horizon, for a short period of time, just before sunrise.

Mars, its magnitude fading from −0.6 to +0.2 during the month, continues to be visible as an evening object in the south-western quadrant of the sky, in the constellation of Taurus. The waxing gibbous Moon will be seen in the vicinity of the planet on the evenings of the 15th and 16th.

Jupiter, magnitude −1.9, is now emerging from the morning twilight and becoming more easily visible as a brilliant object in the south-eastern sky in the mornings, albeit at a low altitude. Venus passes less than 1 degree north of Jupiter on the 1st.

Saturn reaches opposition on the 24th and thus is visible throughout the hours of darkness. Its magnitude is +0.2.

Zodiacal Light. The evening cone may be observed stretching up from the western horizon, along the ecliptic, after the end of twilight, from the beginning of the month to the 7th and again after the 21st. This faint phenomenon is only visible under good conditions and in the absence of both moonlight and artificial lighting.

THE MOON

Day	R.A. h	m	Dec. °	Hor. par. '	Semi-diam. '	Sun's Co-long. °	PA of Br. Limb °	Ph. %	Age d	Rise 52° h	m	Rise 56° h	m	Transit h	m	Set 52° h	m	Set 56° h	m
1	15	50	−25.5	54.3	14.8	200	101	34	23.5	3	50	4	22	7	23	10	50	10	18
2	16	43	−27.4	54.5	14.8	212	95	25	24.5	4	56	5	33	8	14	11	29	10	52
3	17	37	−28.0	54.9	14.9	224	88	17	25.5	5	52	6	30	9	07	12	23	11	45
4	18	33	−27.3	55.3	15.1	237	81	10	26.5	6	35	7	09	10	00	13	30	12	56
5	19	28	−25.2	55.9	15.2	249	75	5	27.5	7	07	7	34	10	53	14	46	14	20
6	20	22	−21.8	56.5	15.4	261	68	2	28.5	7	30	7	50	11	43	16	08	15	49
7	21	14	−17.2	57.1	15.6	273	43	0	29.5	7	47	8	01	12	32	17	31	17	18
8	22	04	−11.7	57.7	15.7	285	249	1	0.8	8	01	8	10	13	20	18	53	18	47
9	22	54	−5.6	58.2	15.8	298	244	4	1.8	8	13	8	16	14	06	20	16	20	16
10	23	43	+0.9	58.6	16.0	310	243	10	2.8	8	25	8	23	14	53	21	40	21	46
11	0	32	+ 7.4	58.9	16.0	322	244	17	3.8	8	38	8	30	15	41	23	06	23	18
12	1	24	+13.6	59.1	16.1	334	246	26	4.8	8	53	8	39	16	32	—		—	
13	2	18	+19.1	59.2	16.1	346	249	37	5.8	9	12	8	51	17	27	0	34	0	53
14	3	15	+23.5	59.2	16.1	358	255	48	6.8	9	40	9	11	18	25	2	03	2	31
15	4	16	+26.6	59.2	16.1	11	261	60	7.8	10	19	9	44	19	27	3	28	4	03
16	5	20	+28.0	59.1	16.1	23	268	71	8.8	11	16	10	39	20	29	4	40	5	18
17	6	23	+27.5	58.9	16.0	35	276	80	9.8	12	30	11	56	21	30	5	34	6	09
18	7	25	+25.3	58.6	16.0	47	282	89	10.8	13	54	13	28	22	26	6	12	6	39
19	8	23	+21.7	58.2	15.9	59	288	95	11.8	15	21	15	02	23	19	6	37	6	57
20	9	17	+16.9	57.8	15.7	71	292	98	12.8	16	45	16	33	—		6	55	7	09
21	10	08	+11.3	57.2	15.6	83	284	100	13.8	18	05	17	59	0	07	7	09	7	17
22	10	55	+5.4	56.6	15.4	96	120	99	14.8	19	22	19	22	0	52	7	20	7	23
23	11	41	−0.7	56.0	15.3	108	119	96	15.8	20	37	20	42	1	35	7	31	7	29
24	12	26	−6.5	55.5	15.1	120	118	92	16.8	21	51	22	02	2	17	7	42	7	35
25	13	11	−12.0	55.0	15.0	132	117	85	17.8	23	05	23	22	2	59	7	53	7	41
26	13	56	−17.0	54.6	14.9	144	114	78	18.8	—		—		3	42	8	07	7	50
27	14	43	−21.2	54.3	14.8	156	110	69	19.8	0	20	0	42	4	27	8	25	8	02
28	15	33	−24.6	54.2	14.8	168	105	60	20.8	1	33	2	02	5	14	8	50	8	19
29	16	24	−26.9	54.3	14.8	181	99	51	21.8	2	41	3	17	6	04	9	23	8	48

MERCURY

Day	R.A. h	m	Dec. °	Diam. "	Phase %	Transit h	m	5° high 52° h	m	5° high 56° h	m
1	21	38	−11.5	9	12	12	52	17	15	17	01
3	21	31	−11.5	10	6	12	37	16	59	16	45
5	21	23	−11.8	10	2	12	20	16	41	16	26
7	21	14	−12.3	10	1	12	03	16	20	16	05
9	21	04	−12.9	10	2	11	46	7	32	7	48
11	20	56	−13.6	10	6	11	30	7	21	7	37
13	20	49	−14.3	10	11	11	16	7	10	7	28
15	20	44	−14.9	10	16	11	04	7	02	7	21
17	20	41	−15.5	9	22	10	54	6	55	7	15
19	20	40	−16.0	9	28	10	46	6	50	7	10
21	20	42	−16.3	9	33	10	39	6	46	7	07
23	20	45	−16.6	8	38	10	35	6	43	7	04
25	20	49	−16.7	8	43	10	31	6	40	7	02
27	20	55	−16.8	8	47	10	29	6	38	7	00
29	21	01	−16.7	8	51	10	28	6	37	6	58
31	21	09	−16.5	7	55	10	28	6	35	6	56

VENUS

Day	R.A. h	m	Dec. °	Diam. "	Phase %	Transit h	m	5° high 52° h	m	5° high 56° h	m
1	18	41	−22.4	12	85	9	59	6	50	7	23
6	19	07	−22.0	12	86	10	06	6	54	7	26
11	19	34	−21.4	12	87	10	13	6	56	7	26
16	20	00	−20.6	12	88	10	19	6	55	7	24
21	20	26	−19.5	12	89	10	25	6	53	7	19
26	20	51	−18.1	11	90	10	31	6	49	7	12
31	21	16	−16.6	11	91	10	36	6	43	7	04

MARS

Day	R.A. h	m	Dec. °	Diam. "	Phase %	Transit h	m	5° high 52° h	m	5° high 56° h	m
1	5	34	+26.7	12	95	20	48	4	46	5	09
6	5	35	+26.6	11	94	20	29	4	27	4	50
11	5	37	+26.5	11	93	20	12	4	09	4	32
16	5	40	+26.5	10	92	19	56	3	53	4	16
21	5	45	+26.4	10	92	19	41	3	37	4	00
26	5	50	+26.3	9	91	19	27	3	23	3	45
31	5	57	+26.2	9	91	19	14	3	09	3	31

SUNRISE AND SUNSET

d	London 0° 05′	51° 30′	Bristol 2° 35′	51° 28′	Birmingham 1° 55′	52° 28′	Manchester 2° 15′	53° 28′	Newcastle 1° 37′	54° 59′	Glasgow 4° 14′	55° 52′	Belfast 5° 56′	54° 35′
	h m	h m	h m	h m	h m	h m	h m	h m	h m	h m	h m	h m	h m	h m
1	7 40	16 49	7 50	16 59	7 50	16 53	7 55	16 51	7 58	16 42	8 12	16 49	8 14	17 01
2	7 38	16 50	7 48	17 01	7 49	16 55	7 53	16 53	7 57	16 44	8 11	16 51	8 12	17 03
3	7 37	16 52	7 46	17 02	7 47	16 57	7 52	16 54	7 55	16 46	8 09	16 54	8 10	17 05
4	7 35	16 54	7 45	17 04	7 45	16 58	7 50	16 56	7 53	16 49	8 07	16 56	8 09	17 07
5	7 33	16 56	7 43	17 06	7 44	17 00	7 48	16 58	7 51	16 51	8 05	16 58	8 07	17 09
6	7 32	16 58	7 42	17 08	7 42	17 02	7 46	17 00	7 49	16 53	8 03	17 00	8 05	17 11
7	7 30	17 00	7 40	17 10	7 40	17 04	7 45	17 02	7 47	16 55	8 01	17 02	8 03	17 14
8	7 28	17 01	7 38	17 12	7 38	17 06	7 43	17 04	7 45	16 57	7 59	17 04	8 01	17 16
9	7 27	17 03	7 36	17 13	7 37	17 08	7 41	17 06	7 43	16 59	7 56	17 07	7 59	17 18
10	7 25	17 05	7 35	17 15	7 35	17 10	7 39	17 08	7 41	17 01	7 54	17 09	7 57	17 20
11	7 23	17 07	7 33	17 17	7 33	17 12	7 37	17 10	7 39	17 03	7 52	17 11	7 55	17 22
12	7 21	17 09	7 31	17 19	7 31	17 14	7 35	17 12	7 37	17 05	7 50	17 13	7 53	17 24
13	7 19	17 11	7 29	17 21	7 29	17 16	7 33	17 14	7 35	17 08	7 48	17 15	7 51	17 26
14	7 17	17 12	7 27	17 23	7 27	17 17	7 31	17 16	7 33	17 10	7 46	17 18	7 49	17 28
15	7 16	17 14	7 25	17 24	7 25	17 19	7 29	17 18	7 30	17 12	7 43	17 20	7 47	17 30
16	7 14	17 16	7 24	17 26	7 23	17 21	7 27	17 20	7 28	17 14	7 41	17 22	7 44	17 32
17	7 12	17 18	7 22	17 28	7 21	17 23	7 25	17 22	7 26	17 16	7 39	17 24	7 42	17 34
18	7 10	17 20	7 20	17 30	7 19	17 25	7 23	17 24	7 24	17 18	7 36	17 26	7 40	17 36
19	7 08	17 22	7 18	17 32	7 17	17 27	7 21	17 26	7 22	17 20	7 34	17 28	7 38	17 38
20	7 06	17 23	7 16	17 33	7 15	17 29	7 18	17 28	7 19	17 22	7 32	17 31	7 36	17 40
21	7 04	17 25	7 14	17 35	7 13	17 31	7 16	17 30	7 17	17 24	7 29	17 33	7 33	17 42
22	7 02	17 27	7 12	17 37	7 11	17 33	7 14	17 32	7 15	17 26	7 27	17 35	7 31	17 44
23	7 00	17 29	7 10	17 39	7 09	17 34	7 12	17 34	7 12	17 28	7 25	17 37	7 29	17 47
24	6 58	17 31	7 07	17 41	7 07	17 36	7 10	17 36	7 10	17 31	7 22	17 39	7 26	17 49
25	6 55	17 32	7 05	17 42	7 04	17 38	7 07	17 38	7 08	17 33	7 20	17 41	7 24	17 51
26	6 53	17 34	7 03	17 44	7 02	17 40	7 05	17 40	7 05	17 35	7 17	17 44	7 22	17 53
27	6 51	17 36	7 01	17 46	7 00	17 42	7 03	17 42	7 03	17 37	7 15	17 46	7 19	17 55
28	6 49	17 38	6 59	17 48	6 58	17 44	7 01	17 44	7 00	17 39	7 12	17 48	7 17	17 57
29	6 47	17 39	6 57	17 50	6 56	17 46	6 58	17 46	6 58	17 41	7 10	17 50	7 15	17 59

JUPITER

Day	R.A.		Dec.		Transit		5° high			
							52°		56°	
	h	m	°	′	h	m	h	m	h	m
1	18	43.1	−22	57	10	00	6	56	7	31
11	18	52.1	−22	47	9	29	6	24	6	59
21	19	00.6	−22	37	8	58	5	52	6	26
31	19	08.4	−22	26	8	27	5	19	5	52

Diameters – equatorial 33″ polar 31″

SATURN

Day	R.A.		Dec.		Transit		5° high			
							52°		56°	
	h	m	°	′	h	m	h	m	h	m
1	10	37.4	+10	37	1	55	19	29	19	24
11	10	34.7	+10	55	1	13	18	46	18	40
21	10	31.7	+11	14	0	30	18	02	17	56
31	10	28.7	+11	32	23	44	17	18	17	12

Diameters – equatorial 20″ polar 18″
Rings – major axis 45″ minor axis 6″

URANUS

Day	R.A.		Dec.		Transit		10° high			
							52°		56°	
	h	m	°	′	h	m	h	m	h	m
1	23	12.0	−5	58	14	27	18	48	18	35
11	23	13.8	−5	45	13	50	18	12	17	59
21	23	15.9	−5	33	13	13	17	36	17	24
31	23	17.9	−5	19	12	35	17	00	16	48

Diameter 4″

NEPTUNE

Day	R.A.		Dec.		Transit		10° high			
							52°		56°	
	h	m	°	′	h	m	h	m	h	m
1	21	35.3	−14	40	12	51	9	27	9	52
11	21	36.7	−14	33	12	13	8	48	9	13
21	21	38.2	−14	26	11	35	8	09	8	34
31	21	39.7	−14	18	10	57	7	30	7	55

Diameter 2″

✕ MARCH 2008

THIRD MONTH, 31 DAYS. *Mars*, Roman god of battle

1	*Saturday*	The USA tested the most explosive bomb produced to date, at Bikini in the Pacific ocean 1954	61
2	*Sunday*	Mikhail Gorbachev, Soviet leader b. 1931 Horace Walpole, English politician d. 1797	62

3	*Monday*	The German-Russian treaty of Brest-Litovsk was signed 1918	week 9 day 63
4	*Tuesday*	Robert Mugabe became Zimbabwe's first black prime minister 1980	64
5	*Wednesday*	Zhou Enlai, Chinese premier b. 1898 Joseph Stalin, Soviet leader d. 1953	65
6	*Thursday*	Francesco Guicciardini, Italian statesman b. 1483 Philip Yorke, English politician d. 1764	66
7	*Friday*	Ghulam Nabi Azad, Indian politician b. 1949 Aristide Briand, prime minister of France d. 1932	67
8	*Saturday*	Juvénal Habyarimana, president of Rwanda b. 1937 King William III d. 1702	68
9	*Sunday*	Ernest Bevin, British politician b. 1881 Jules Mazarin, Italian-born politician d. 1661	69

10	*Monday*	Alexander III, tsar of Russia b. 1845 Jan Masaryk, Czechoslovak diplomat d. 1948	week 10 day 70
11	*Tuesday*	191 people were killed and over 1,500 injured in three train station explosions in Madrid 2004	71
12	*Wednesday*	John Abbott, prime minister of Canada b. 1821 Zoran Djindjic, prime minister of Serbia d. 2003	72
13	*Thursday*	Charles Grey, British prime minister b. 1764 Alexander II, tsar of Russia d. 1881	73
14	*Friday*	Mustafa Barzani, Kurdish nationalist activist b. 1903 Karl Marx, German revolutionary d. 1883	74
15	*Saturday*	Andrew Jackson, US president b. 1767 Julius Caesar, emperor of Rome d. 44 BC	75
16	*Sunday*	Pat Nixon, US first lady b. 1912 Austen Chamberlain, British politician d. 1937	76

17	*Monday*	Margaret Bondfield, British politician b. 1873 Ramon Magsaysay, president of the Philippines d. 1957	week 11 day 77
18	*Tuesday*	The Tolpuddle Martyrs were sentenced to transportation to Australia 1834	78
19	*Wednesday*	Adolf Eichmann, German Nazi officer b. 1906 Arthur Balfour, British prime minister d. 1930	79
20	*Thursday*	Abdul Hamid I, sultan of the Ottoman empire b. 1725 King Henry IV d. 1413	80
21	*Friday*	Benito Juárez, president of Mexico b. 1806 Guadalupe Victoria, president of Mexico d. 1843	81
22	*Saturday*	Cheddi Jagan, president of Guyana b. 1918 A. K. Gopalan, Indian Communist leader d. 1977	82
23	*Sunday*	Benito Mussolini founded the Fascist movement in Milan, Italy 1919	83

24	*Monday*	Union of English and Scottish crowns after Queen Elizabeth I's death 1603	week 12 day 84
25	*Tuesday*	Joachim Murat, king of Naples b. 1767 Frederick I, king of Sweden d. 1751	85
26	*Wednesday*	Xenophon Zolotas, prime minister of Greece b. 1904 Cecil Rhodes, coloniser of Rhodesia d. 1902	86
27	*Thursday*	James McNeill, Irish politician b. 1869 Michael Joseph Savage, prime minister of New Zealand d. 1940	87
28	*Friday*	Neil Kinnock, British politician b. 1942 Frank Baker, Australian politician d. 1939	88
29	*Saturday*	John Major, British prime minister b. 1943 Barthelemy Boganda, prime minister of the Central African Republic b. 1959	89
30	*Sunday*	Censu Tabone, president of Malta b. 1913 Léon Blum, French statesman d. 1950	90

31	*Monday*	The Greater London Council was abolished 1986	week 13 day 91

ASTRONOMICAL PHENOMENA

d	h	
3	02	Jupiter in conjunction with Moon. Jupiter 4°N.
3	11	Mercury at greatest elongation W. 27°
5	14	Mercury in conjunction with Moon. Mercury 0°.2N.
5	19	Venus in conjunction with Moon. Venus 0°.2S.
8	20	Uranus in conjunction
15	03	Mars in conjunction with Moon. Mars 2°S.
19	14	Saturn in conjunction with Moon. Saturn 2°N.
20	06	Sun's longitude 0° ♈
24	13	Venus in conjunction with Mercury. Venus 1°N.
30	18	Jupiter in conjunction with Moon. Jupiter 3°N.

MINIMA OF ALGOL

d	h	d	h	d	h
1	20.5	13	07.8	24	19.1
4	17.3	16	04.6	27	15.9
7	14.1	19	01.4	30	12.7
10	10.9	21	22.2		

CONSTELLATIONS

The following constellations are near the meridian at

	d	h		d	h
February	1	24	March	16	21
February	15	23	April	1	20
March	1	22	April	15	19

Cepheus (below the Pole), Camelopardalis, Lynx, Gemini, Cancer, Leo, Canis Minor, Hydra, Monoceros, Canis Major and Puppis

THE MOON

Phases, Apsides and Node	d	h	m
● New Moon	7	17	14
☽ First Quarter	14	10	46
○ Full Moon	21	18	40
☾ Last Quarter	29	21	47

Perigee (366,323km)	10	21	31
Apogee (405,058km)	26	20	07

Mean longitude of ascending node on March 1, 327°

THE SUN

s.d. 16'.1

Day	Right Ascension			Dec.		Equation of time		Rise 52°		Rise 56°		Transit		Set 52°		Set 56°		Sidereal time			Transit of first point of Aries		
	h	m	s	°	'	m	s	h	m	h	m	h	m	h	m	h	m	h	m	s	h	m	s
1	22	49	03	−7	31	−12	22	6	45	6	51	12	12	17	40	17	35	10	36	41	13	21	07
2	22	52	48	−7	09	−12	10	6	43	6	48	12	12	17	42	17	37	10	40	37	13	17	12
3	22	56	32	−6	46	−11	58	6	41	6	46	12	12	17	44	17	39	10	44	34	13	13	16
4	23	00	16	−6	23	−11	45	6	39	6	43	12	12	17	46	17	41	10	48	31	13	09	20
5	23	03	59	−5	59	−11	32	6	36	6	41	12	11	17	47	17	43	10	52	27	13	05	24
6	23	07	42	−5	36	−11	18	6	34	6	38	12	11	17	49	17	45	10	56	24	13	01	28
7	23	11	24	−5	13	−11	04	6	32	6	35	12	11	17	51	17	48	11	00	20	12	57	32
8	23	15	06	−4	49	−10	50	6	30	6	33	12	11	17	53	17	50	11	04	17	12	53	36
9	23	18	48	−4	26	−10	35	6	27	6	30	12	10	17	55	17	52	11	08	13	12	49	40
10	23	22	29	−4	02	−10	19	6	25	6	28	12	10	17	56	17	54	11	12	10	12	45	44
11	23	26	10	−3	39	−10	04	6	23	6	25	12	10	17	58	17	56	11	16	06	12	41	48
12	23	29	51	−3	15	−9	48	6	20	6	22	12	10	18	00	17	58	11	20	03	12	37	53
13	23	33	31	−2	52	−9	32	6	18	6	20	12	09	18	02	18	00	11	24	00	12	33	57
14	23	37	12	−2	28	−9	15	6	16	6	17	12	09	18	03	18	02	11	27	56	12	30	01
15	23	40	51	−2	04	−8	59	6	14	6	15	12	09	18	05	18	04	11	31	53	12	26	05
16	23	44	31	−1	41	−8	42	6	11	6	12	12	09	18	07	18	06	11	35	49	12	22	09
17	23	48	10	−1	17	−8	24	6	09	6	09	12	08	18	09	18	08	11	39	46	12	18	13
18	23	51	49	−0	53	−8	07	6	07	6	07	12	08	18	10	18	10	11	43	42	12	14	17
19	23	55	28	−0	29	−7	49	6	04	6	04	12	08	18	12	18	12	11	47	39	12	10	21
20	23	59	07	−0	06	−7	32	6	02	6	01	12	07	18	14	18	14	11	51	35	12	06	25
21	0	02	46	+0	18	−7	14	6	00	5	59	12	07	18	15	18	17	11	55	32	12	02	29
22	0	06	24	+0	42	−6	56	5	57	5	56	12	07	18	17	18	19	11	59	29	11	58	33
23	0	10	03	+1	05	−6	38	5	55	5	54	12	06	18	19	18	21	12	03	25	11	54	38
24	0	13	41	+1	29	−6	20	5	53	5	51	12	06	18	21	18	23	12	07	22	11	50	42
25	0	17	19	+1	53	−6	01	5	50	5	48	12	06	18	22	18	25	12	11	18	11	46	46
26	0	20	58	+2	16	−5	43	5	48	5	46	12	06	18	24	18	27	12	15	15	11	42	50
27	0	24	36	+2	40	−5	25	5	46	5	43	12	05	18	26	18	29	12	19	11	11	38	54
28	0	28	15	+3	03	−5	07	5	43	5	40	12	05	18	28	18	31	12	23	08	11	34	58
29	0	31	53	+3	26	−4	49	5	41	5	38	12	05	18	29	18	33	12	27	04	11	31	02
30	0	35	31	+3	50	−4	30	5	39	5	35	12	04	18	31	18	35	12	31	01	11	27	06
31	0	39	10	+4	13	−4	13	5	37	5	32	12	04	18	33	18	37	12	34	58	11	23	10

DURATION OF TWILIGHT (in minutes)

Latitude	52°	56°	52°	56°	52°	56°	52°	56°
	1 March		11 March		21 March		31 March	
Civil	34	37	34	37	34	37	34	38
Nautical	73	80	73	80	74	81	75	84
Astronomical	112	124	113	125	115	128	120	135

THE NIGHT SKY

Mercury remains too close to the Sun for observation throughout the month.

Venus, magnitude −3.9, continues to be visible as a brilliant object at first, but only visible low in the east-south-eastern sky for a short period before dawn. After the first week of the month the planet will be too close to the Sun for observation.

Mars remains visible in the south-western sky in the evenings, and is still visible well after midnight even by the end of the month. Its magnitude fades during March from +0.2 to +0.8, as it moves steadily eastwards from Taurus into Gemini. During the early hours of the 15th the Moon, at First Quarter, passes 1 degree north of the planet

Jupiter, magnitude −2.0, continues to be visible as a brilliant morning object, low in the south-eastern sky, rising around 1.5 to 2 hours before sunrise. On the morning of the 3rd the thin waning crescent Moon passes south of the planet. On the last two mornings of the month the old waning Moon, just after Last Quarter, will again be seen in the vicinity of Jupiter.

Saturn, magnitude +0.3, is visible above the eastern horizon as soon as darkness falls and remains visible for the greater part of the night. Saturn is in Leo. The rings of Saturn present a beautiful spectacle to the observer armed with a small telescope. The diameter of the minor axis is now only 7 arcseconds, considerably less than the polar diameter of the planet itself. The rings were last at their maximum opening in 2002 and will next appear edge-on in 2009.

Zodiacal Light. The evening cone may be observed stretching up from the western horizon, along the ecliptic, after the end of twilight, from the beginning of the month until the 8th and again after the 22nd. This faint phenomenon is only visible under good conditions and in the absence of both moonlight and artificial lighting.

THE MOON

Day	R.A.		Dec.	Hor. par.	Semi-diam.	Sun's Co-long.	PA of Br. Limb	Ph.	Age	Rise				Transit		Set			
										52°		56°				52°		56°	
	h	m	°	'	'	°	°	%	d	h	m	h	m	h	m	h	m	h	m
1	17	18	−28.0	54.5	14.9	193	93	42	22.8	3	42	4	20	6	56	10	10	9	32
2	18	12	−27.7	55.0	15.0	205	87	32	23.8	4	30	5	06	7	48	11	10	10	35
3	19	07	−26.1	55.5	15.1	217	81	23	24.8	5	06	5	36	8	41	12	23	11	53
4	20	01	−23.2	56.2	15.3	229	76	15	25.8	5	32	5	56	9	32	13	42	13	20
5	20	54	−19.1	57.0	15.5	242	72	9	26.8	5	52	6	09	10	22	15	05	14	49
6	21	45	−13.9	57.7	15.7	254	70	4	27.8	6	07	6	18	11	10	16	28	16	19
7	22	35	−7.9	58.5	15.9	266	74	1	28.8	6	20	6	26	11	58	17	52	17	50
8	23	25	−1.4	59.1	16.1	278	217	0	0.3	6	33	6	32	12	46	19	18	19	21
9	0	16	+5.2	59.5	16.2	290	236	2	1.3	6	45	6	39	13	35	20	45	20	55
10	1	08	+11.7	59.8	16.3	303	241	7	2.3	7	00	6	48	14	26	22	15	22	32
11	2	03	+17.6	59.9	16.3	315	245	14	3.3	7	18	7	00	15	21	23	47	—	
12	3	01	+22.5	59.8	16.3	327	250	23	4.3	7	43	7	17	16	20	—		0	12
13	4	02	+26.0	59.5	16.2	339	257	34	5.3	8	19	7	46	17	21	1	15	1	48
14	5	05	+27.8	59.2	16.1	351	264	45	6.3	9	11	8	33	18	23	2	33	3	10
15	6	09	+27.7	58.8	16.0	4	271	56	7.3	10	19	9	44	19	24	3	32	4	08
16	7	10	+26.0	58.3	15.9	16	278	67	8.3	11	40	11	11	20	21	4	14	4	43
17	8	08	+22.7	57.9	15.8	28	284	77	9.3	13	04	12	43	21	13	4	42	5	04
18	9	03	+18.2	57.4	15.6	40	288	85	10.3	14	27	14	13	22	02	5	01	5	17
19	9	53	+13.0	56.9	15.5	52	290	92	11.3	15	47	15	39	22	47	5	16	5	26
20	10	41	+7.3	56.4	15.4	64	289	97	12.3	17	04	17	01	23	30	5	28	5	33
21	11	26	+1.3	55.9	15.2	77	280	99	13.3	18	19	18	22	—		5	39	5	39
22	12	11	−4.6	55.5	15.1	89	164	100	14.3	19	33	19	41	0	12	5	50	5	45
23	12	55	−10.2	55.0	15.0	101	128	98	15.3	20	47	21	01	0	54	6	01	5	51
24	13	41	−15.3	54.7	14.9	113	121	95	16.3	22	01	22	21	1	36	6	14	5	59
25	14	28	−19.8	54.4	14.8	125	115	90	17.3	23	15	23	42	2	21	6	31	6	09
26	15	17	−23.5	54.2	14.8	137	110	84	18.3	—		—		3	07	6	52	6	25
27	16	08	−26.1	54.1	14.7	149	104	76	19.3	0	26	0	59	3	56	7	22	6	48
28	17	00	−27.6	54.2	14.8	162	98	68	20.3	1	30	2	07	4	47	8	03	7	25
29	17	54	−27.8	54.5	14.9	174	91	59	21.3	2	22	2	59	5	39	8	57	8	20
30	18	48	−26.7	54.9	15.0	186	85	49	22.3	3	03	3	36	6	30	10	03	9	31
31	19	41	−24.3	55.5	15.1	198	80	39	23.3	3	32	3	59	7	21	11	18	10	53

MERCURY

Day	R.A.		Dec.	Diam.	Phase	Transit		5° high			
								52°		56°	
	h	m	°	"	%	h	m	h	m	h	m
1	21	05	−16.6	7	53	10	28	6	36	6	57
3	21	13	−16.4	7	57	10	28	6	35	6	55
5	21	21	−16.1	7	60	10	29	6	33	6	53
7	21	30	−15.7	7	63	10	31	6	32	6	51
9	21	40	−15.2	7	65	10	32	6	30	6	49
11	21	50	−14.6	6	68	10	35	6	28	6	46
13	22	01	−13.9	6	70	10	37	6	27	6	44
15	21	11	−13.1	6	72	10	40	6	25	6	41
17	22	22	−12.3	6	74	10	43	6	22	6	37
19	22	33	−11.3	6	76	10	47	6	20	6	34
21	22	45	−10.3	6	78	10	50	6	18	6	30
23	22	57	− 9.2	6	80	10	54	6	15	6	27
25	23	09	− 8.0	5	82	10	58	6	12	6	23
27	23	21	− 6.8	5	84	11	03	6	10	6	19
29	23	33	− 5.4	5	86	11	07	6	07	6	15
31	23	46	− 4.0	5	88	11	12	6	04	6	11

VENUS

Day	R.A.		Dec.	Diam.	Phase	Transit		5° high			
								52°		56°	
	h	m	°	"	%	h	m	h	m	h	m
1	21	12	−16.9	11	91	10	35	6	44	7	05
6	21	36	−15.2	11	91	10	40	6	38	6	56
11	22	01	−13.3	11	92	10	45	6	30	6	46
16	22	24	−11.2	11	93	10	49	6	22	6	36
21	22	48	−9.0	11	94	10	53	6	13	6	24
26	23	11	−6.7	11	94	10	56	6	04	6	13
31	23	34	−4.4	10	95	10	59	5	54	6	01

MARS

Day	R.A.		Dec.	Diam.	Phase	Transit		5° high			
								52°		56°	
	h	m	°	"	%	h	m	h	m	h	m
1	5	55	+26.3	9	91	19	17	3	11	3	34
6	6	02	+26.2	9	91	19	04	2	58	3,	20
11	6	10	+26.1	8	90	18	52	2	45	3	07
16	6	18	+25.9	8	90	18	41	2	33	2	55
21	6	27	+25.8	8	90	18	30	2	21	2	42
26	6	36	+25.6	7	90	18	19	2	09	2	30
31	6	45	+25.3	7	90	18	09	1	57	2	18

SUNRISE AND SUNSET

	London 0° 05' 51° 30'		Bristol 2° 35' 51° 28'		Birmingham 1° 55' 52° 28'		Manchester 2° 15' 53° 28'		Newcastle 1° 37' 54° 59'		Glasgow 4° 14' 55° 52'		Belfast 5° 56' 54° 35'	
d	h m	h m	h m	h m	h m	h m	h m	h m	h m	h m	h m	h m	h m	h m
1	6 45	17 41	6 55	17 51	6 53	17 47	6 56	17 47	6 56	17 43	7 07	17 52	7 12	18 01
2	6 43	17 43	6 53	17 53	6 51	17 49	6 54	17 49	6 53	17 45	7 05	17 54	7 10	18 03
3	6 41	17 45	6 50	17 55	6 49	17 51	6 51	17 51	6 51	17 47	7 02	17 56	7 08	18 05
4	6 38	17 47	6 48	17 57	6 47	17 53	6 49	17 53	6 48	17 49	7 00	17 58	7 05	18 07
5	6 36	17 48	6 46	17 58	6 44	17 55	6 47	17 55	6 46	17 51	6 57	18 00	7 03	18 09
6	6 34	17 50	6 44	18 00	6 42	17 57	6 44	17 57	6 43	17 53	6 55	18 03	7 00	18 11
7	6 32	17 52	6 42	18 02	6 40	17 58	6 42	17 59	6 41	17 55	6 52	18 05	6 58	18 13
8	6 30	17 53	6 39	18 04	6 38	18 00	6 40	18 01	6 38	17 57	6 50	18 07	6 55	18 15
9	6 27	17 55	6 37	18 05	6 35	18 02	6 37	18 03	6 36	17 59	6 47	18 09	6 53	18 17
10	6 25	17 57	6 35	18 07	6 33	18 04	6 35	18 04	6 33	18 01	6 44	18 11	6 50	18 19
11	6 23	17 59	6 33	18 09	6 31	18 06	6 33	18 06	6 31	18 03	6 42	18 13	6 48	18 20
12	6 21	18 00	6 31	18 10	6 28	18 07	6 30	18 08	6 28	18 05	6 39	18 15	6 45	18 22
13	6 18	18 02	6 28	18 12	6 26	18 09	6 28	18 10	6 26	18 07	6 37	18 17	6 43	18 24
14	6 16	18 04	6 26	18 14	6 24	18 11	6 25	18 12	6 23	18 09	6 34	18 19	6 40	18 26
15	6 14	18 06	6 24	18 16	6 21	18 13	6 23	18 14	6 21	18 11	6 31	18 21	6 38	18 28
16	6 12	18 07	6 21	18 17	6 19	18 14	6 21	18 16	6 18	18 13	6 29	18 23	6 35	18 30
17	6 09	18 09	6 19	18 19	6 17	18 16	6 18	18 17	6 16	18 15	6 26	18 25	6 33	18 32
18	6 07	18 11	6 17	18 21	6 14	18 18	6 16	18 19	6 13	18 17	6 24	18 27	6 30	18 34
19	6 05	18 12	6 15	18 22	6 12	18 20	6 13	18 21	6 11	18 19	6 21	18 29	6 28	18 36
20	6 02	18 14	6 12	18 24	6 10	18 22	6 11	18 23	6 08	18 21	6 18	18 31	6 25	18 38
21	6 00	18 16	6 10	18 26	6 07	18 23	6 08	18 25	6 06	18 23	6 16	18 33	6 23	18 40
22	5 58	18 17	6 08	18 27	6 05	18 25	6 06	18 27	6 03	18 25	6 13	18 35	6 20	18 42
23	5 56	18 19	6 06	18 29	6 03	18 27	6 04	18 29	6 00	18 27	6 11	18 37	6 18	18 44
24	5 53	18 21	6 03	18 31	6 00	18 29	6 01	18 30	5 58	18 29	6 08	18 40	6 15	18 46
25	5 51	18 22	6 01	18 32	5 58	18 30	5 59	18 32	5 55	18 31	6 05	18 42	6 13	18 48
26	5 49	18 24	5 59	18 34	5 56	18 32	5 56	18 34	5 53	18 32	6 03	18 44	6 10	18 49
27	5 46	18 26	5 56	18 36	5 53	18 34	5 54	18 36	5 50	18 34	6 00	18 46	6 08	18 51
28	5 44	18 27	5 54	18 37	5 51	18 36	5 51	18 38	5 48	18 36	5 57	18 48	6 05	18 53
29	5 42	18 29	5 52	18 39	5 48	18 37	5 49	18 39	5 45	18 38	5 55	18 50	6 03	18 55
30	5 40	18 31	5 50	18 41	5 46	18 39	5 47	18 41	5 43	18 40	5 52	18 52	6 00	18 57
31	5 37	18 33	5 47	18 42	5 44	18 41	5 44	18 43	5 40	18 42	5 50	18 54	6 58	18 59

JUPITER

Day	R.A. h m	Dec. ° '	Transit h m	5° high 52° h m	56° h m
1	19 07.7	−22 27	8 30	5 22	5 56
11	19 14.8	−22 16	7 58	4 48	5 21
21	19 21.2	−22 05	7 25	4 14	4 46
31	19 26.6	−21 55	6 51	3 39	4 10

Diameters – equatorial 36" polar 33"

SATURN

Day	R.A. h m	Dec. ° '	Transit h m	5° high 52° h m	56° h m
1	10 29.0	+11 30	23 48	6 18	6 24
11	10 26.1	+11 48	23 06	5 37	5 44
21	10 23.4	+12 03	22 24	4 57	5 03
31	10 21.0	+12 16	21 42	4 16	4 23

Diameters – equatorial 20" polar 18"
Rings – major axis 45" minor axis 7"

URANUS

Day	R.A. h m	Dec. ° '	Transit h m	10° high 52° h m	56° h m
1	23 17.7	−5 21	12 39	8 15	8 27
11	23 19.8	−5 07	12 02	7 36	7 48
21	23 21.9	−4 54	11 25	6 58	7 09
31	23 24.0	−4 41	10 47	6 19	6 31

Diameter 4"

NEPTUNE

Day	R.A. h m	Dec. ° '	Transit h m	10° high 52° h m	56° h m
1	21 39.5	−14 19	11 01	7 34	7 59
11	21 40.9	−14 12	10 23	6 55	7 20
21	21 42.2	−14 06	9 45	6 17	6 41
31	21 43.4	−14 00	9 07	5 38	6 02

Diameter 2"

APRIL 2008

FOURTH MONTH, 30 DAYS. *Aperire*, to open; Earth opens to receive seed.

1	*Tuesday*	Otto von Bismarck, German chancellor b. 1815 George II, king of Greece d. 1947	92
2	*Wednesday*	Jim Allister, Northern Irish politician b. 1953 Georges Pompidou, president of France d. 1974	93
3	*Thursday*	Philip III, king of France b. 1245 Miina Sillanpaa, Finnish politician d. 1952	94
4	*Friday*	Hun Sen, prime minister of Cambodia b. 1951 Zulfikar Ali Bhutto, prime minister of Pakistan d. 1979	95
5	*Saturday*	Georges Danton, French revolutionary d. 1794 Chiang Kai-shek, president of China d. 1975	96
6	*Sunday*	Ian Paisley, Northern Irish politician b. 1926 King Richard I d. 1199	97

7	*Monday*	Gerhard Schroder, German chancellor b. 1944 Alexandre Millerand, president of France d. 1943	week 14 day 98
8	*Tuesday*	Ian Smith, prime minister of Rhodesia b. 1919 Kofi Annan, UN secretary-general b. 1938	99
9	*Wednesday*	Emily Hobhouse, British campaigner b. 1860 Lorenzo de Medici, ruler of Florence d. 1492	100
10	*Thursday*	The Good Friday Agreement was signed at the Northern Ireland peace talks 1998	101
11	*Friday*	George Canning, British prime minister b. 1770 Enver Hoxha, Albanian leader d. 1985	102
12	*Saturday*	James I of England (James VI of Scotland) combined the flags of the two countries 1606	103
13	*Sunday*	Thomas Jefferson, US president b. 1743 Boris Godunov, emperor of Russia d. 1605	104

14	*Monday*	Philip III, king of Spain b. 1578 Ernest Bevin, British politician d. 1951	week 15 day 105
15	*Tuesday*	Il-sung Kim, North Korean leader b. 1912 Pol Pot, prime minister of Cambodia d. 1998	106
16	*Wednesday*	Bonnie Prince Charlie was defeated at the Battle of Culloden 1746	107
17	*Thursday*	Nikita Khrushchev, Soviet leader b. 1894 Sirimavo Bandaranaike, prime minister of Sri Lanka b. 1916	108
18	*Friday*	Adolphe Thiers, president of France b. 1797 Arturo Frondizi, president of Argentina d. 1995	109
19	*Saturday*	Joseph Estrada, president of the Philippines b. 1937 Benjamin Disraeli, British prime minister d. 1881	110
20	*Sunday*	Adolf Hitler, German Nazi leader b. 1889 Pontiac, Native American leader d. 1769	111

21	*Monday*	Queen Elizabeth II b. 1926 François Duvalier, president of Haiti d. 1971	week 16 day 112
22	*Tuesday*	Troops stormed the Japanese embassy in Peru, ending the four-month siege by anti-government rebels 1997	113
23	*Wednesday*	James Buchanan, US president b. 1791 Brian Boru, High King of Ireland d. 1014	114
24	*Thursday*	Stafford Cripps, British politician b. 1889 Oliver Tambo, South African leader d. 1993	115
25	*Friday*	Oliver Cromwell, English political leader b. 1599 King Edward II b. 1284	116
26	*Saturday*	Syrian soldiers withdrew from Lebanon after 29 years 2005	117
27	*Sunday*	Ulysses S. Grant, US president b. 1822 John Trenchard, English politician d. 1695	118

28	*Monday*	Saddam Hussein, president of Iraq b. 1937 Benito Mussolini, prime minister of Italy d. 1945	week 17 day 119
29	*Tuesday*	Jeremy Thorpe, British politician b. 1929 Bernardino Machado, president of Portugal d. 1944	120
30	*Wednesday*	Queen Mary II b. 1662 Renzong, emperor of China d. 1063	121

ASTRONOMICAL PHENOMENA

d h
2 09 Pluto at stationary point
4 22 Venus in conjunction with Moon. Venus 4°S.
5 08 Mercury in conjunction with Moon. Mercury 5°S.
12 06 Mars in conjunction with Moon. Mars 1°S.
15 17 Saturn in conjunction with Moon. Saturn 2°N.
16 07 Mercury in superior conjunction
19 17 Sun's longitude 30° ♉
27 06 Jupiter in conjunction with Moon. Jupiter 3°N.

MINIMA OF ALGOL

d	h	d	h	d	h
2	09.5	13	20.8	25	08.1
5	06.3	16	17.6	28	04.9
8	03.2	19	14.4		
11	00.0	22	11.2		

CONSTELLATIONS

The following constellations are near the meridian at

	d	h		d	h
March	1	24	April	15	21
March	16	23	May	1	20
April	1	22	May	16	19

Cepheus (below the Pole), Cassiopeia (below the Pole), Ursa Major, Leo Minor, Leo, Sextans, Hydra and Crater

THE MOON

Phases, Apsides and Node	d	h	m
● New Moon	6	03	55
☽ First Quarter	12	18	32
○ Full Moon	20	10	25
☾ Last Quarter	28	14	12

Perigee (361,093 km)	7	19	23
Apogee (405,921 km)	23	09	23

Mean longitude of ascending node on April 1, 326°

THE SUN

s.d. 16'.0

Day	Right Ascension			Dec. +		Equation of time		Rise 52°		Rise 56°		Transit		Set 52°		Set 56°		Sidereal time			Transit of First point of Aries		
	h	m	s	°	'	m	s	h	m	h	m	h	m	h	m	h	m	h	m	s	h	m	s
1	0	42	49	4	36	−3	55	5	34	5	30	12	04	18	34	18	39	12	38	54	11	19	14
2	0	46	28	4	59	−3	37	5	32	5	27	12	03	18	36	18	41	12	42	51	11	15	18
3	0	50	06	5	22	−3	19	5	30	5	25	12	03	18	38	18	43	12	46	47	11	11	23
4	0	53	46	5	45	−3	02	5	27	5	22	12	03	18	39	18	45	12	50	44	11	07	27
5	0	57	25	6	08	−2	45	5	25	5	19	12	03	18	41	18	47	12	54	40	11	03	31
6	1	01	04	6	31	−2	27	5	23	5	17	12	02	18	43	18	49	12	58	37	10	59	35
7	1	04	44	6	53	−2	11	5	21	5	14	12	02	18	45	18	51	13	02	33	10	55	39
8	1	08	24	7	16	−1	54	5	18	5	12	12	02	18	46	18	53	13	06	30	10	51	43
9	1	12	04	7	38	−1	38	5	16	5	09	12	01	18	48	18	55	13	10	26	10	47	47
10	1	15	44	8	01	−1	21	5	14	5	06	12	01	18	50	18	57	13	14	23	10	43	51
11	1	19	25	8	23	−1	06	5	12	5	04	12	01	18	51	18	59	13	18	20	10	39	55
12	1	23	06	8	45	−0	50	5	09	5	01	12	01	18	53	19	01	13	22	16	10	35	59
13	1	26	47	9	06	−0	35	5	07	4	59	12	00	18	55	19	03	13	26	13	10	32	03
14	1	30	29	9	28	−0	20	5	05	4	56	12	00	18	57	19	05	13	30	09	10	28	08
15	1	34	11	9	50	−0	05	5	03	4	54	12	00	18	58	19	07	13	34	06	10	24	12
16	1	37	53	10	11	+0	10	5	01	4	51	12	00	19	00	19	10	13	38	02	10	20	16
17	1	41	35	10	32	+0	24	4	58	4	49	11	59	19	02	19	12	13	41	59	10	16	20
18	1	45	18	10	53	+0	37	4	56	4	46	11	59	19	03	19	14	13	45	55	10	12	24
19	1	49	01	11	14	+0	51	4	54	4	44	11	59	19	05	19	16	13	49	52	10	08	28
20	1	52	45	11	34	+1	03	4	52	4	41	11	59	19	07	19	18	13	53	49	10	04	32
21	1	56	29	11	55	+1	16	4	50	4	39	11	59	19	09	19	20	13	57	45	10	00	36
22	2	00	14	12	15	+1	28	4	48	4	36	11	58	19	10	19	22	14	01	42	9	56	40
23	2	03	59	12	35	+1	39	4	46	4	34	11	58	19	12	19	24	14	05	38	9	52	44
24	2	07	44	12	55	+1	50	4	44	4	32	11	58	19	14	19	26	14	09	35	9	48	48
25	2	11	30	13	15	+2	01	4	42	4	29	11	58	19	15	19	28	14	13	31	9	44	53
26	2	15	17	13	34	+2	11	4	40	4	27	11	58	19	17	19	30	14	17	28	9	40	57
27	2	19	04	13	53	+2	21	4	38	4	25	11	58	19	19	19	32	14	21	24	9	37	01
28	2	22	51	14	12	+2	30	4	36	4	22	11	57	19	20	19	34	14	25	21	9	33	05
29	2	26	39	14	31	+2	38	4	34	4	20	11	57	19	22	19	36	14	29	18	9	29	09
30	2	30	28	14	49	+2	46	4	32	4	18	11	57	19	24	19	38	14	33	14	9	25	13

DURATION OF TWILIGHT (in minutes)

Latitude	52°	56°	52°	56°	52°	56°	52°	56°
	1 April		11 April		21 April		31 April	
Civil	34	38	35	39	37	42	39	44
Nautical	76	84	79	89	83	96	89	106
Astronomical	120	136	127	147	137	165	152	204

THE NIGHT SKY

Mercury passes through superior conjunction on the 16th and remains too close to the Sun for observation until the last few days of the month, when it becomes visible low in the west-north-western sky at the end of evening civil twilight. During this short period its magnitude is from −1.2 to −0.9.

Venus is unsuitably placed for observation throughout the month.

Mars continues to be visible in the western sky in the evenings, and even by the end of the month should still be observable for a short while after midnight. Mars remains in the constellation of Gemini, as its magnitude fades during April from +0.8 to +1.2. Towards the end of the month Mars passes 5 degrees south of Pollux. The Moon, approaching First Quarter, is near Mars on the evenings of the 11th and 12th.

Jupiter continues to be visible as a conspicuous morning object and by the end of the month is crossing the meridian around the time of sunrise. Its magnitude is −2.2. The waning gibbous Moon passes 3 degrees south of Jupiter on the morning of the 27th.

Saturn, magnitude +0.5, is still visible as an evening object in the south-western quadrant of the sky until well after midnight. The waxing gibbous Moon passes 3 degrees south of Saturn on the evening of the 15th.

THE MOON

Day	R.A. h	R.A. m	Dec. °	Hor. Par. '	Semi-diam. '	Sun's Co-Long. °	PA of Br. Limb °	Ph. %	Age d	Rise 52° h	Rise 52° m	Rise 56° h	Rise 56° m	Transit h	Transit m	Set 52° h	Set 52° m	Set 56° h	Set 56° m
1	20	33	−20.7	56.3	15.3	210	75	30	24.3	3	54	4	14	8	11	12	38	12	19
2	21	24	−16.0	57.1	15.6	223	71	21	25.3	4	11	4	25	8	59	13	59	13	47
3	22	14	−10.4	58.0	15.8	235	70	13	26.3	4	25	4	33	9	46	15	22	15	17
4	23	04	− 4.2	58.9	16.0	247	70	6	27.3	4	38	4	41	10	34	16	47	16	47
5	23	55	+2.5	59.7	16.3	259	76	2	28.3	4	51	4	48	11	22	18	14	18	21
6	0	47	+9.1	60.3	16.4	272	126	0	29.3	5	05	4	56	12	14	19	45	19	59
7	1	42	+15.4	60.6	16.5	284	228	1	0.8	5	22	5	07	13	09	21	19	21	41
8	2	40	+20.8	60.7	16.5	296	242	5	1.8	5	45	5	22	14	08	22	53	23	22
9	3	43	+24.9	60.5	16.5	308	251	12	2.8	6	17	5	47	15	11	—		—	
10	4	47	+27.3	60.1	16.4	320	259	20	3.8	7	05	6	29	16	15	0	18	0	54
11	5	53	+27.7	59.6	16.2	333	267	31	4.8	8	10	7	33	17	17	1	26	2	02
12	6	56	+26.4	58.9	16.0	345	275	42	5.8	9	28	8	57	18	16	2	13	2	45
13	7	55	+23.4	58.2	15.9	357	281	53	6.8	10	52	10	29	19	10	2	45	3	10
14	8	51	+19.2	57.5	15.7	9	286	63	7.8	12	15	11	59	20	00	3	08	3	25
15	9	41	+14.1	56.9	15.5	21	289	73	8.8	13	35	13	26	20	45	3	24	3	35
16	10	29	+8.6	56.3	15.3	34	291	82	9.8	14	52	14	48	21	28	3	37	3	43
17	11	15	+2.8	55.8	15.2	46	291	89	10.8	16	06	16	07	22	10	3	48	3	49
18	11	59	−3.0	55.3	15.1	58	288	94	11.8	17	19	17	26	22	51	3	58	3	55
19	12	43	−8.7	54.9	15.0	70	280	98	12.8	18	33	18	44	23	33	4	09	4	01
20	13	28	−13.9	54.6	14.9	82	250	100	13.8	19	46	20	04	—		4	22	4	09
21	14	14	−18.5	54.3	14.8	94	147	100	14.8	21	00	21	24	0	17	4	37	4	18
22	15	02	−22.4	54.1	14.7	107	122	98	15.8	22	12	22	43	1	03	4	57	4	32
23	15	53	−25.3	54.0	14.7	119	111	94	16.8	23	18	23	54	1	51	5	24	4	53
24	16	45	−27.1	54.0	14.7	131	103	89	17.8	—		—		2	41	6	01	5	25
25	17	38	−27.7	54.2	14.8	143	96	82	18.8	0	15	0	52	3	32	6	50	6	13
26	18	32	−27.0	54.5	14.8	155	89	74	19.8	0	59	1	33	4	23	7	51	7	17
27	19	25	−25.0	54.9	15.0	168	83	66	20.8	1	32	2	01	5	14	9	02	8	34
28	20	16	−21.8	55.5	15.1	180	77	56	21.8	1	57	2	19	6	02	10	18	9	57
29	21	06	−17.6	56.2	15.3	192	73	46	22.8	2	15	2	31	6	50	11	36	11	22
30	21	55	−12.5	57.0	15.5	204	70	36	23.8	2	30	2	40	7	36	12	56	12	48

MERCURY

Day	R.A. h	R.A. m	Dec. °	Diam. "	Phase %	Transit h	Transit m	5° high 52° h	5° high 52° m	5° high 56° h	5° high 56° m
1	23	52	−3.3	5	89	11	14	6	03	6	09
3	0	05	−1.8	5	91	11	20	6	00	6	04
5	0	18	−0.2	5	93	11	25	5	57	6	00
7	0	32	+1.5	5	95	11	31	5	54	5	56
9	0	46	+3.2	5	96	11	37	5	52	5	52
11	1	00	+4.9	5	98	11	44	5	49	5	48
13	1	15	+6.7	5	99	11	50	5	47	5	44
15	1	30	+8.5	5	100	11	58	5	45	5	41
17	1	45	+10.3	5	100	12	05	18	30	18	36
19	2	01	+12.1	5	99	12	13	18	48	18	55
21	2	17	+13.9	5	98	12	21	19	05	19	14
23	2	33	+15.6	5	95	12	30	19	23	19	33
25	2	49	+17.2	5	91	12	38	19	40	19	52
27	3	05	+18.7	6	87	12	46	19	56	20	10
29	3	21	+20.0	6	81	12	54	20	11	20	26
31	3	36	+21.2	6	75	13	01	20	25	20	41

VENUS

Day	R.A. h	R.A. m	Dec. °	Diam. "	Phase %	Transit h	Transit m	5° high 52° h	5° high 52° m	5° high 56° h	5° high 56° m
1	23	39	−3.9	10	95	11	00	5	52	5	59
6	0	01	−1.5	10	96	11	03	5	43	5	47
11	0	24	+1.0	10	96	11	06	5	33	5	35
16	0	47	+3.4	10	97	11	09	5	23	5	24
21	1	09	+5.8	10	98	11	12	5	14	5	12
26	1	32	+8.2	10	98	11	15	5	05	5	02
31	1	55	+10.5	10	98	11	19	4	57	4	51

MARS

Day	R.A. h	R.A. m	Dec. °	Diam. "	Phase %	Transit h	Transit m	5° high 52° h	5° high 52° m	5° high 56° h	5° high 56° m
1	6	47	+25.3	7	90	18	07	1	55	2	16
6	6	57	+25.0	7	90	17	57	1	43	2	04
11	7	08	+24.7	7	90	17	48	1	32	1	52
16	7	18	+24.3	6	90	17	39	1	20	1	40
21	7	29	+23.9	6	90	17	30	1	08	1	27
26	7	40	+23.4	6	90	17	21	0	56	1	15
31	7	51	+22.9	6	91	17	12	0	44	1	02

SUNRISE AND SUNSET

	London				Bristol				Birmingham				Manchester				Newcastle				Glasgow				Belfast			
	0°05′		51°30′		2°35′		51°28′		1°55′		52°28′		2°15′		53°28′		1°37′		54°59′		4°14′		55°52′		5°56′		54°35′	
d	h	m	h	m	h	m	h	m	h	m	h	m	h	m	h	m	h	m	h	m	h	m	h	m	h	m	h	m
1	5	35	18	34	5	45	18	44	5	41	18	43	5	42	18	45	5	38	18	44	5	47	18	56	5	55	19	01
2	5	33	18	36	5	43	18	46	5	39	18	44	5	39	18	47	5	35	18	46	5	44	18	58	5	53	19	03
3	5	31	18	38	5	41	18	48	5	37	18	46	5	37	18	49	5	32	18	48	5	42	19	00	5	50	19	05
4	5	28	18	39	5	38	18	49	5	34	18	48	5	35	18	50	5	30	18	50	5	39	19	02	5	48	19	07
5	5	26	18	41	5	36	18	51	5	32	18	50	5	32	18	52	5	27	18	52	5	37	19	04	5	45	19	09
6	5	24	18	43	5	34	18	53	5	30	18	51	5	30	18	54	5	25	18	54	5	34	19	06	5	43	19	11
7	5	22	18	44	5	32	18	54	5	28	18	53	5	27	18	56	5	22	18	56	5	31	19	08	5	40	19	12
8	5	19	18	46	5	29	18	56	5	25	18	55	5	25	18	58	5	20	18	58	5	29	19	10	5	38	19	14
9	5	17	18	48	5	27	18	58	5	23	18	56	5	23	19	00	5	17	19	00	5	26	19	12	5	35	19	16
10	5	15	18	49	5	25	18	59	5	21	18	58	5	20	19	01	5	15	19	02	5	24	19	14	5	33	19	18
11	5	13	18	51	5	23	19	01	5	18	19	00	5	18	19	03	5	12	19	04	5	21	19	16	5	30	19	20
12	5	11	18	53	5	21	19	03	5	16	19	02	5	16	19	05	5	10	19	06	5	19	19	18	5	28	19	22
13	5	08	18	54	5	18	19	04	5	14	19	03	5	13	19	07	5	08	19	08	5	16	19	20	5	26	19	24
14	5	06	18	56	5	16	19	06	5	12	19	05	5	11	19	09	5	05	19	09	5	14	19	22	5	23	19	26
15	5	04	18	58	5	14	19	08	5	09	19	07	5	09	19	10	5	03	19	11	5	11	19	24	5	21	19	28
16	5	02	18	59	5	12	19	09	5	07	19	09	5	06	19	12	5	00	19	13	5	09	19	26	5	18	19	30
17	5	00	19	01	5	10	19	11	5	05	19	10	5	04	19	14	4	58	19	15	5	06	19	28	5	16	19	32
18	4	58	19	03	5	08	19	13	5	03	19	12	5	02	19	16	4	55	19	17	5	04	19	30	5	14	19	34
19	4	56	19	04	5	06	19	14	5	01	19	14	5	00	19	18	4	53	19	19	5	01	19	32	5	11	19	35
20	4	53	19	06	5	04	19	16	4	58	19	16	4	57	19	20	4	51	19	21	4	59	19	34	5	09	19	37
21	4	51	19	08	5	01	19	18	4	56	19	17	4	55	19	21	4	48	19	23	4	56	19	36	5	07	19	39
22	4	49	19	09	4	59	19	19	4	54	19	19	4	53	19	23	4	46	19	25	4	54	19	38	5	04	19	41
23	4	47	19	11	4	57	19	21	4	52	19	21	4	51	19	25	4	44	19	27	4	51	19	40	5	02	19	43
24	4	45	19	13	4	55	19	23	4	50	19	23	4	49	19	27	4	41	19	29	4	49	19	42	5	00	19	45
25	4	43	19	14	4	53	19	24	4	48	19	24	4	46	19	29	4	39	19	31	4	47	19	44	4	58	19	47
26	4	41	19	16	4	51	19	26	4	46	19	26	4	44	19	30	4	37	19	33	4	44	19	46	4	55	19	49
27	4	39	19	18	4	49	19	27	4	44	19	28	4	42	19	32	4	35	19	35	4	42	19	48	4	53	19	51
28	4	37	19	19	4	47	19	29	4	42	19	30	4	40	19	34	4	32	19	37	4	40	19	50	4	51	19	53
29	4	35	19	21	4	46	19	31	4	40	19	31	4	38	19	36	4	30	19	39	4	37	19	52	4	49	19	54
30	4	34	19	23	4	44	19	32	4	38	19	33	4	36	19	38	4	28	19	41	4	35	19	54	4	47	19	56

JUPITER

Day	R.A.		Dec.		Transit		5° high			
							52°		56°	
	h	m	°	′	h	m	h	m	h	m
1	19	27.1	−21	54	6	47	3	35	4	07
11	19	31.3	−21	46	6	12	2	59	3	30
21	19	34.4	−21	41	5	36	2	22	2	53
31	19	36.2	−21	38	4	58	1	44	2	15

Diameters – equatorial 39″ polar 37″

SATURN

Day	R.A.		Dec.		Transit		5° high			
							52°		56°	
	h	m	°	′	h	m	h	m	h	m
1	10	20.8	+12	17	21	38	4	12	4	19
11	10	19.1	+12	26	20	57	3	32	3	39
21	10	17.9	+12	32	20	17	2	52	2	59
31	10	17.4	+12	33	19	37	2	12	2	19

Diameters – equatorial 19″ polar 17″
Rings – major axis 43″ minor axis 7″

URANUS

Day	R.A.		Dec.		Transit		10° high			
							52°		56°	
	h	m	°	′	h	m	h	m	h	m
1	23	24.2	−4	40	10	44	6	15	6	27
11	23	26.1	−4	27	10	06	5	37	5	48
21	23	28.0	−4	16	9	29	4	58	5	09
31	23	29.6	−4	06	8	51	4	20	4	30

Diameter 4″

NEPTUNE

Day	R.A.		Dec.		Transit		10° high			
							52°		56°	
	h	m	°	′	h	m	h	m	h	m
1	21	43.5	−14	00	9	03	5	34	5	58
11	21	44.5	−13	55	8	25	4	55	5	19
21	21	45.3	−13	51	7	46	4	16	4	40
31	21	46.0	−13	48	7	08	3	37	4	01

Diameter 2″

MAY 2008

FIFTH MONTH, 31 DAYS. *Maia*, goddess of growth and increase

1	*Thursday*	Albert I of Habsburg, king of Germany d. 1308 Joseph Goebbels, German Nazi officer d. 1945	122
2	*Friday*	Moshoeshoe II, king of Lesotho b. 1938 Shomu, emperor of Japan d. 756	123
3	*Saturday*	Golda Meir, prime minister of Israel b. 1898 Niccolù Machiavelli, Italian statesman b. 1469	124
4	*Sunday*	Margaret Thatcher became UK's first woman prime minister 1979	125

5	*Monday*	Leopold II, Holy Roman Emperor b. 1747 Natalija Obrenovic, queen of Serbia d. 1941	week 18 day 126
6	*Tuesday*	Tony Blair, British prime minister b. 1953 Maximilien Robespierre, French revolutionary b. 1758	127
7	*Wednesday*	Josip Broz Tito, president of Yugoslavia b. 1892 Eva Peron, first lady of Argentina b. 1919	128
8	*Thursday*	Ali Hassan Mwinyi, president of Tanzania b. 1925 Kamehameha I, king of Hawaii d. 1819	129
9	*Friday*	Glenda Jackson, British politician b. 1936 Aldo Moro, prime minister of Italy d. 1978	130
10	*Saturday*	Nelson Mandela became South Africa's first black president 1994	131
11	*Sunday*	Spencer Perceval, British prime minister d. 1812 William Pitt (the elder), British prime minister d. 1778	132

12	*Monday*	Johan Vilhelm Snellman, Finnish statesman b. 1806 Thomas Wentworth, English statesman d. 1641	week 19 day 133
13	*Tuesday*	Asgeir Asgeirsson, president of Iceland b. 1894 Fridtjof Nansen, Norwegian statesman d. 1930	134
14	*Wednesday*	Eight Communist states signed the Warsaw Pact 1955	135
15	*Thursday*	Prince Klemens Metternich, Austrian statesman b. 1773 Charles VIII, king of Sweden d. 1470	136
16	*Friday*	Mao Zedong launched the Cultural Revolution in the People's Republic of China 1966	137
17	*Saturday*	Hazel R. O' Leary, US politician b. 1937 Charles-Maurice de Talleyrand, French politician d. 1838	138
18	*Sunday*	India detonated its first nuclear weapon 1974	139

19	*Monday*	Nancy Astor, British politician b. 1879 Ho Chi-Minh, Vietnamese statesman b. 1890	week 20 day 140
20	*Tuesday*	Faisal I of Iraq b. 1883 Ecgfrith, king of Northumbria d. 685	141
21	*Wednesday*	Mary Robinson, president of Ireland b. 1944 Conrad IV, king of Germany d. 1254	142
22	*Thursday*	Daniel Malan, prime minister of South Africa b. 1874 Giorgio Almirante, Italian politician d. 1988	143
23	*Friday*	The marriage of King Henry VIII to Catherine of Aragon was annulled 1533	144
24	*Saturday*	Jan Smuts, prime minister of South Africa b. 1870 Harold Wilson, British prime minister d. 1995	145
25	*Sunday*	Max Aitken, Canadian-British politician b. 1879 Sunil Dutt, Indian politician d. 2005	146

26	*Monday*	The last public hanging in England took place 1868	week 21 day 147
27	*Tuesday*	Henry Kissinger, US politician b. 1923 Jawaharlal Nehru, prime minister of India d. 1964	148
28	*Wednesday*	William Pitt (the younger), British prime minister b. 1759 King Edward VIII d. 1972	149
29	*Thursday*	King Charles XI b. 1630 Erich Honecker, East German leader d. 1994	150
30	*Friday*	Henry Addington, British prime minister b. 1757 Rama VII, king of Siam d. 1941	151
31	*Saturday*	South Africa left the Commonwealth 1961	152

ASTRONOMICAL PHENOMENA

d	h	
3	03	Saturn at stationary point
4	20	Venus in conjunction with Moon. Venus 6°S.
6	22	Mercury in conjunction with Moon. Mercury 2°S.
9	12	Jupiter at stationary point
10	14	Mars in conjunction with Moon. Mars 0°.2S.
12	22	Saturn in conjunction with Moon. Saturn 3°N.
14	04	Mercury at greatest elongation E. 22°
20	16	Sun's longitude 60° ♊
24	12	Jupiter in conjunction with Moon. Jupiter 2°N.
26	16	Mercury at stationary point
26	16	Neptune at stationary point

MINIMA OF ALGOL

Algol is inconveniently situated for observation during May

CONSTELLATIONS

The following constellations are near the meridian at

	d	h		d	h
April	1	24	May	16	21
April	15	23	June	1	20
May	1	22	June	15	19

Cepheus (below the Pole), Cassiopeia (below the Pole), Ursa Minor, Ursa Major, Canes Venatici, Coma Berenices, Bootes, Leo, Virgo, Crater, Corvus and Hydra

THE MOON

Phases, Apsides and Node		d	h	m
●	New Moon	5	12	18
☽	First Quarter	12	03	47
○	Full Moon	20	02	11
☾	Last Quarter	28	02	57
	Perigee (357,777 km)	6	03	12
	Apogee (406,398 km)	20	14	11

Mean longitude of ascending node on May 1, 324°

THE SUN

s.d. 15′.8

Day	Right Ascension			Dec. +		Equation of time		Rise 52°		Rise 56°		Transit		Set 52°		Set 56°		Sidereal time			Transit of first point of Aries		
	h	m	s	°	′	m	s	h	m	h	m	h	m	h	m	h	m	h	m	s	h	m	s
1	2	34	17	15	08	+2	54	4	30	4	15	11	57	19	25	19	40	14	37	11	9	21	17
2	2	38	07	15	26	+3	01	4	28	4	13	11	57	19	27	19	42	14	41	07	9	17	21
3	2	41	57	15	43	+3	07	4	26	4	11	11	57	19	29	19	44	14	45	04	9	13	25
4	2	45	48	16	01	+3	13	4	24	4	09	11	57	19	30	19	46	14	49	00	9	09	29
5	2	49	39	16	18	+3	18	4	22	4	07	11	57	19	32	19	48	14	52	57	9	05	33
6	2	53	31	16	35	+3	23	4	21	4	04	11	57	19	34	19	50	14	56	53	9	01	38
7	2	57	23	16	52	+3	27	4	19	4	02	11	57	19	35	19	52	15	00	50	8	57	42
8	3	01	17	17	08	+3	30	4	17	4	00	11	56	19	37	19	54	15	04	47	8	53	46
9	3	05	10	17	24	+3	33	4	15	3	58	11	56	19	39	19	56	15	08	43	8	49	50
10	3	09	04	17	40	+3	35	4	14	3	56	11	56	19	40	19	58	15	12	40	8	45	54
11	3	12	59	17	55	+3	37	4	12	3	54	11	56	19	42	20	00	15	16	36	8	41	58
12	3	16	54	18	11	+3	39	4	10	3	52	11	56	19	43	20	02	15	20	33	8	38	02
13	3	20	50	18	26	+3	39	4	09	3	50	11	56	19	45	20	04	15	24	29	8	34	06
14	3	24	46	18	40	+3	39	4	07	3	48	11	56	19	46	20	05	15	28	26	8	30	10
15	3	28	43	18	54	+3	39	4	06	3	47	11	56	19	48	20	07	15	32	22	8	26	14
16	3	32	41	19	08	+3	38	4	04	3	45	11	56	19	50	20	09	15	36	19	8	22	18
17	3	36	39	19	22	+3	37	4	03	3	43	11	56	19	51	20	11	15	40	16	8	18	23
18	3	40	37	19	35	+3	35	4	01	3	41	11	56	19	53	20	13	15	44	12	8	14	27
19	3	44	37	19	48	+3	32	4	00	3	40	11	56	19	54	20	15	15	48	09	8	10	31
20	3	48	36	20	01	+3	29	3	59	3	38	11	57	19	55	20	16	15	52	05	8	06	35
21	3	52	36	20	13	+3	25	3	57	3	36	11	57	19	57	20	18	15	56	02	8	02	39
22	3	56	37	20	25	+3	21	3	56	3	35	11	57	19	58	20	20	15	59	58	7	58	43
23	4	00	38	20	37	+3	16	3	55	3	33	11	57	20	00	20	21	16	03	55	7	54	47
24	4	04	40	20	48	+3	11	3	54	3	32	11	57	20	01	20	23	16	07	51	7	50	51
25	4	08	43	20	59	+3	06	3	52	3	30	11	57	20	02	20	25	16	11	48	7	46	55
26	4	12	45	21	09	+2	59	3	51	3	29	11	57	20	04	20	26	16	15	45	7	42	59
27	4	16	49	21	19	+2	53	3	50	3	28	11	57	20	05	20	28	16	19	41	7	39	03
28	4	20	52	21	29	+2	45	3	49	3	26	11	57	20	06	20	29	16	23	38	7	35	07
29	4	24	57	21	39	+2	38	3	48	3	25	11	57	20	07	20	31	16	27	34	7	31	12
30	4	29	01	21	48	+2	29	3	47	3	24	11	58	20	08	20	32	16	31	31	7	27	16
31	4	33	07	21	56	+2	21	3	47	3	23	11	58	20	10	20	34	16	35	27	7	23	20

DURATION OF TWILIGHT (in minutes)

Latitude	52°	56°	52°	56°	52°	56°	52°	56°
	1 May		11 May		21 May		31 May	
Civil	39	44	41	48	44	53	46	57
Nautical	89	106	97	120	106	141	115	187
Astronomical	152	204	176	TAN	TAN	TAN	TAN	TAN

THE NIGHT SKY

Mercury continues to be visible low above the west-north-western horizon at the end of evening civil twilight, until just after the middle of the month. During this period its magnitude fades from −0.8 to +1.1. This evening apparition is the most suitable one of the year for observers in northern temperate latitudes.

Venus remains too close to the Sun for observation throughout the month.

Mars is still visible as an evening object in the western sky, though no longer visible after midnight, even at the beginning of the month. Its magnitude fades slowly from +1.2 to +1.5 during the month. Early in May, Mars moves from Gemini into Cancer.

Jupiter, magnitude −2.5, continues to be visible as a brilliant morning object low in the south-eastern sky. By the end of the month it is becoming visible low on the horizon by midnight. It reaches its first stationary point on the 9th, and then moves retrograde, in the constellation of Sagittarius. The Galilean satellites are readily observable with a small telescope or even a good pair of binoculars provided that they are held rigidly.

Saturn, magnitude +0.7, is still visible as an evening object in the south-western sky in the evenings, though by the end of the month it will not be visible for long after midnight. Saturn reaches its second stationary point on the 3rd, resuming its direct motion.

THE MOON

Day	R.A. h	R.A. m	Dec. °	Hor. Par. '	Semi-diam. '	Sun's Co-Long. °	PA of Bright Limb °	Ph. %	Age d	Rise 52° h	Rise 52° m	Rise 56° h	Rise 56° m	Transit h	Transit m	Set 52° h	Set 52° m	Set 56° h	Set 56° m
1	22	44	−6.6	58.0	15.8	216	69	26	24.8	2	43	2	48	8	22	14	17	14	15
2	23	33	−0.3	58.9	16.1	229	69	17	25.8	2	55	2	55	9	09	15	41	15	45
3	0	23	+6.3	59.8.	16.3	241	72	9	26.8	3	09	3	03	9	58	17	09	17	19
4	1	17	+12.7	60.6	16.5	253	79	4	27.8	3	24	3	12	10	52	18	42	18	59
5	2	14	+18.6	61.1	16.6	265	104	1	28.8	3	44	3	26	11	49	20	18	20	43
6	3	16	+23.3	61.3	16.7	278	219	1	0.5	4	13	3	46	12	52	21	50	22	23
7	4	22	+26.4	61.2	16.7	290	248	4	1.5	4	54	4	21	13	58	23	09	23	45
8	5	29	+27.6	60.7	16.6	302	261	9	2.5	5	54	5	17	15	04	—	—	—	—
9	6	36	+26.8	60.1	16.4	314	270	17	3.5	7	10	6	38	16	07	0	07	0	40
10	7	38	+24.2	59.3	16.2	326	278	27	4.5	8	36	8	11	17	04	0	45	1	12
11	8	36	+20.2	58.4	15.9	339	284	38	5.5	10	02	9	44	17	56	1	11	1	31
12	9	29	+15,2	57.5	15.7	351	288	48	6.5	11	24	11	13	18	44	1	30	1	43
13	10	18	+9.7	56.7	15.5	3	291	59	7.5	12	42	12	36	19	28	1	44	1	52
14	11	04	+3.9	56.0	15.3	15	292	69	8.5	13	57	13	56	20	10	1	56	1	58
15	11	48	−1.9	55.4	15.1	28	292	78	9.5	15	10	15	15	20	51	2	07	2	05
16	12	32	−7.5	54.9	15.0	40	290	85	10.5	16	22	16	32	21	32	2	18	2	11
17	13	17	−12.7	54.5	14.9	52	286	91	11.5	17	35	17	51	22	15	2	30	2	18
18	14	02	−17.5	54.3	14.8	64	279	96	12.5	18	49	19	10	23	00	2	44	2	27
19	14	50	−21.5	54.1	14.7	76	265	99	13.5	20	01	20	29	23	47	3	02	2	40
20	15	40	−24.6	54.0	14.7	88	205	100	14.5	21	09	21	43	—	—	3	27	2	58
21	16	31	−26.7	54.0	14.7	101	124	99	15.5	22	09	22	45	0	37	4	01	3	26
22	17	24	−27.5	54.0	14.7	113	105	97	16.5	22	57	23	32	1	28	4	46	4	09
23	18	18	−27.1	54.2	14.8	125	94	92	17.5	23	33	—	—	2	19	5	44	5	09
24	19	11	−25.4	54.5	14.9	137	86	87	18.5	—	—	0	03	3	09	6	52	6	22
25	20	02	−22.5	54.9	15.0	149	80	80	19.5	0	00	0	24	3	58	8	05	7	43
26	20	52	−18.6	55.5	15.1	162	75	71	20.5	0	20	0	37	4	45	9	22	9	05
27	21	40	−13.8	56.1	15.3	174	71	62	21.5	0	35	0	47	5	31	10	39	10	28
28	22	28	−8.3	56.9	15.5	186	68	51	22.5	0	48	0	55	6	15	11	57	11	52
29	23	15	−2.3	57.8	15.7	198	67	41	23.5	1	01	1	02	7	00	13	17	13	18
30	0	03	+4.0	58.7	16.0	211	68	30	24.5	1	13	1	10	7	47	14	40	14	47
31	0	54	+10.3	59.6	16.2	223	70	20	25.5	1	27	1	18	8	36	16	08	16	21

MERCURY

Day	R.A. h	R.A. m	Dec. °	Diam. "	Phase %	Transit h	Transit m	5° high 52° h	5° high 52° m	5° high 56° h	5° high 56° m
1	3	36	+21.2	6	75	13	01	20	25	20	41
3	3	51	+22.2	6	69	13	07	20	38	20	55
5	4	04	+23.1	6	63	13	13	20	48	21	07
7	4	17	+23.8	7	57	13	18	20	57	21	16
9	4	29	+24.3	7	51	13	22	21	04	21	23
11	4	40	+24.7	7	45	13	25	21	08	21	29
13	4	50	+24.9	8	40	13	26	21	11	21	32
15	4	59	+25.1	8	35	13	27	21	12	21	32
17	5	06	+25.1	9	30	13	26	21	10	21	31
19	5	12	+24.9	9	25	13	24	21	07	21	27
21	5	17	+24.7	10	21	13	20	21	01	21	21
23	5	21	+24.4	10	17	13	15	20	54	21	13
25	5	22	+24.0	10	14	13	09	20	44	21	03
27	5	23	+23.5	11	10	13	01	20	33	20	52
29	5	22	+23.0	11	7	12	52	20	21	20	38
31	5	20	+22.4	12	5	12	42	20	07	20	23

VENUS

Day	R.A. h	R.A. m	Dec. °	Diam. "	Phase %	Transit h	Transit m	5° high 52° h	5° high 52° m	5° high 56° h	5° high 56° m
1	1	55	+10.5	10	98	11	19	4	57	4	51
6	2	19	+12.7	10	99	11	22	4	49	4	42
11	2	43	+14.7	10	99	11	27	4	42	4	33
16	3	07	+16.6	10	99	11	31	4	36	4	25
21	3	32	+18.4	10	100	11	36	4	32	4	19
26	3	57	+19.9	10	100	11	42	4	28	4	14
31	4	23	+21.2	10	100	11	48	4	26	4	11

MARS

Day	R.A. h	R.A. m	Dec. °	Diam. "	Phase %	Transit h	Transit m	5° high 52° h	5° high 52° m	5° high 56° h	5° high 56° m
1	7	51	+22.9	6	91	17	12	0	44	1	02
6	8	02	+22.3	6	91	17	04	0	32	0	49
11	8	13	+21.7	5	91	16	55	0	20	0	36
16	8	24	+21.0	5	91	16	47	0	07	0	23
21	8	35	+20.3	5	92	16	38	23	52	0	09
26	8	47	+19.5	5	92	16	30	23	39	23	53
31	8	58	+18.7	5	92	16	22	23	26	23	39

SUNRISE AND SUNSET

	London				Bristol				Birmingham				Manchester				Newcastle				Glasgow				Belfast			
	0° 05'		51° 30'		2° 35'		51° 28'		1° 55'		52° 28'		2° 15'		53° 28'		1° 37'		54° 59'		4° 14'		55° 52'		5° 56'		54° 35'	
d	h	m	h	m	h	m	h	m	h	m	h	m	h	m	h	m	h	m	h	m	h	m	h	m	h	m	h	m
1	4	32	19	24	4	42	19	34	4	36	19	35	4	34	19	39	4	26	19	42	4	33	19	56	4	45	19	58
2	4	30	19	26	4	40	19	36	4	34	19	36	4	32	19	41	4	24	19	44	4	31	19	58	4	42	20	00
3	4	28	19	27	4	38	19	37	4	32	19	38	4	30	19	43	4	22	19	46	4	28	20	00	4	40	20	02
4	4	26	19	29	4	36	19	39	4	30	19	40	4	28	19	45	4	19	19	48	4	26	20	02	4	38	20	04
5	4	24	19	31	4	34	19	41	4	28	19	41	4	26	19	47	4	17	19	50	4	24	20	04	4	36	20	06
6	4	23	19	32	4	33	19	42	4	27	19	43	4	24	19	48	4	15	19	52	4	22	20	06	4	34	20	08
7	4	21	19	34	4	31	19	44	4	25	19	45	4	22	19	50	4	13	19	54	4	20	20	08	4	32	20	09
8	4	19	19	35	4	29	19	45	4	23	19	46	4	20	19	52	4	11	19	56	4	18	20	10	4	30	20	11
9	4	18	19	37	4	28	19	47	4	21	19	48	4	18	19	53	4	09	19	58	4	16	20	12	4	28	20	13
10	4	16	19	39	4	26	19	48	4	19	19	50	4	17	19	55	4	08	19	59	4	14	20	14	4	27	20	15
11	4	14	19	40	4	24	19	50	4	18	19	51	4	15	19	57	4	06	20	01	4	12	20	16	4	25	20	17
12	4	13	19	42	4	23	19	52	4	16	19	53	4	13	19	59	4	04	20	03	4	10	20	18	4	23	20	18
13	4	11	19	43	4	21	19	53	4	14	19	55	4	12	20	00	4	02	20	05	4	08	20	20	4	21	20	20
14	4	10	19	45	4	20	19	55	4	13	19	56	4	10	20	02	4	00	20	07	4	06	20	22	4	19	20	22
15	4	08	19	46	4	18	19	56	4	11	19	58	4	08	20	04	3	58	20	08	4	04	20	24	4	18	20	24
16	4	07	19	48	4	17	19	58	4	10	19	59	4	07	20	05	3	57	20	10	4	02	20	25	4	16	20	25
17	4	05	19	49	4	15	19	59	4	08	20	01	4	05	20	07	3	55	20	12	4	01	20	27	4	14	20	27
18	4	04	19	51	4	14	20	01	4	07	20	02	4	04	20	08	3	53	20	14	3	59	20	29	4	13	20	29
19	4	02	19	52	4	13	20	02	4	05	20	04	4	02	20	10	3	52	20	15	3	57	20	31	4	11	20	30
20	4	01	19	53	4	11	20	03	4	04	20	05	4	01	20	12	3	50	20	17	3	56	20	33	4	10	20	32
21	4	00	19	55	4	10	20	05	4	03	20	07	3	59	20	13	3	49	20	19	3	54	20	34	4	08	20	34
22	3	59	19	56	4	09	20	06	4	01	20	08	3	58	20	15	3	47	20	20	3	52	20	36	4	07	20	35
23	3	57	19	58	4	08	20	07	4	00	20	10	3	56	20	16	3	46	20	22	3	51	20	38	4	05	20	37
24	3	56	19	59	4	06	20	09	3	59	20	11	3	55	20	17	3	44	20	23	3	49	20	39	4	04	20	38
25	3	55	20	00	4	05	20	10	3	58	20	12	3	54	20	19	3	43	20	25	3	48	20	41	4	03	20	40
26	3	54	20	01	4	04	20	11	3	57	20	14	3	53	20	20	3	42	20	26	3	47	20	42	4	01	20	41
27	3	53	20	03	4	03	20	13	3	56	20	15	3	52	20	22	3	40	20	28	3	45	20	44	4	00	20	43
28	3	52	20	04	4	02	20	14	3	55	20	16	3	50	20	23	3	39	20	29	3	44	20	45	3	59	20	44
29	3	51	20	05	4	01	20	15	3	54	20	17	3	49	20	24	3	38	20	31	3	43	20	47	3	58	20	46
30	3	50	20	06	4	00	20	16	3	53	20	19	3	48	20	25	3	37	20	32	3	42	20	48	3	57	20	47
31	3	49	20	07	4	00	20	17	3	52	20	20	3	48	20	27	3	36	20	33	3	41	20	50	3	56	20	48

JUPITER

Day	R.A.		Dec.		Transit		5° high		
							52°		56°
	h	m	°	'	h	m	h	m	h	m
1	19	36.2	−21	38	4	58	1	44	2	15
11	19	36.7	−21	38	4	19	1	05	1	36
21	19	35.8	−21	41	3	39	0	25	0	57
31	19	33.7	−21	48	2	58	23	41	0	16

Diameters – equatorial 43″ polar 40″

SATURN

Day	R.A.		Dec.		Transit		5° high		
							52°		56°
	h	m	°	'	h	m	h	m	h	m
1	10	17.4	+12	33	19	37	2	12	2	19
11	10	17.6	+12	31	18	58	1	33	1	40
21	10	18.4	+12	25	18	19	0	54	1	01
31	10	19.9	+12	16	17	42	0	15	0	22

Diameters – equatorial 18″ polar 16″
Rings – major axis 41″ minor axis 7″

URANUS

Day	R.A.		Dec.		Transit		10° high		
							52°		56°
	h	m	°	'	h	m	h	m	h	m
1	23	29.6	−4	06	8	51	4	20	4	30
11	23	31.0	−3	57	8	13	3	41	3	52
21	23	32.2	−3	49	7	35	3	02	3	13
31	23	33.2	−3	44	6	57	2	23	2	34

Diameter 4″

NEPTUNE

Day	R.A.		Dec.		Transit		10° high		
							52°		56°
	h	m	°	'	h	m	h	m	h	m
1	21	40.0	−13	48	7	08	3	37	4	01
11	21	46.4	−13	46	6	29	2	58	3	22
21	21	46.6	−13	45	5	50	2	19	2	42
31	21	46.7	−13	45	5	10	1	39	2	03

Diameter 2″

JUNE 2008

SIXTH MONTH, 30 DAYS. *Junius*, Roman *gens* (family)

1	Sunday	Robert Cecil, English statesman b. 1563 Ion Antonescu, prime minister of Romania d. 1946		153
2	Monday	Constantine II, king of Greece b. 1940 Giuseppe Garibaldi, Italian military campaigner d. 1882	week 22 day 154	
3	Tuesday	King George V b. 1865 Eisaku Sato, prime minister of Japan d. 1975		155
4	Wednesday	C. G. E. Mannerheim, president of Finland b. 1867 Johan Rudolf Thorbecke, Dutch politician d. 1872		156
5	Thursday	Joe Clark, prime minister of Canada b. 1939 Ronald Reagan, US president d. 2004		157
6	Friday	Sukarno, president of Indonesia b. 1901 Camillo Cavour, Italian statesman d. 1861		158
7	Saturday	Queen Elizabeth II's Silver Jubilee procession 1977		159
8	Sunday	Barbara Bush, US first lady b. 1925 Harthacanute, king of Denmark and England d. 1042		160

9	Monday	Peter I, tsar of Russia b. 1672 Jeanne III, queen of Navarre d. 1572	week 23 day 161	
10	Tuesday	Prince Philip, the Duke of Edinburgh b. 1921 Hafez al-Assad, president of Syria d. 2000		162
11	Wednesday	The UN officially declared a famine in Sudan with over a million people facing starvation 1998		163
12	Thursday	George H. W. Bush, US president b. 1924 Masayoshi Ohira, prime minister of Japan d. 1980		164
13	Friday	Ban Ki-moon, UN secretary-general b. 1944 Charles Haughey, prime minister of Ireland d. 2006		165
14	Saturday	Che Guevara, Argentine revolutionary b. 1928 Frederick Stanley, governor-general of Canada d. 1908		166
15	Sunday	King John signed the Magna Carta at Runnymede in Surrey 1215		167

16	Monday	Enoch Powell, British politician b. 1912 Imre Nagy, prime minister of Hungary d. 1958	week 24 day 168	
17	Tuesday	King Edward I b. 1239 Agha Mohammad Khan, shah of Persia d. 1797		169
18	Wednesday	Robert Stewart, British foreign secretary b. 1769 John Aislabie, British politician d. 1742		170
19	Thursday	Douglas Haig, British military commander b. 1861 Vaclav Klaus, Czech president b. 1941		171
20	Friday	John A. Costello, prime minister of Ireland b. 1891 King William IV d. 1837		172
21	Saturday	Prince William of Wales b. 1982 Tage Erlander, prime minister of Sweden d. 1985		173
22	Sunday	Jerry Rawlings, president of Ghana b. 1947 Armand Fallières, president of France d. 1931		174

23	Monday	Gamal Abdel Nasser was elected the first president of the Republic of Egypt 1956	week 25 day 175	
24	Tuesday	Horatio Kitchener, British statesman b. 1850 Marie François Carnot, president of France d. 1894		176
25	Wednesday	Louis Mountbatten, viceroy of India b. 1900 Warren Burger, US chief justice d. 1995		177
26	Thursday	Robert Laird Borden, prime minister of Canada b. 1854 Francisco Pizarro, Spanish conquistador d. 1541		178
27	Friday	Charles Stewart Parnell, Irish politician b. 1846 Georgios Papadopoulos, prime minister of Greece d. 1999		179
28	Saturday	Chris Hani, South African politician b. 1942 Franz Ferdinand, archduke of Austria d. 1914		180
29	Sunday	Pedro Santana Lopes, prime minister of Portugal b. 1956 Ignacy Jan Paderewski, prime minister of Poland d. 1941		181

30	Monday	Hitler ordered the assassination of hundreds of Nazis; now known as the Night of the Long Knives 1934	week 26 day 182	

ASTRONOMICAL PHENOMENA

d h

3 17 Venus in conjunction with Moon. Venus 5°S.
4 04 Mercury in conjunction with Moon. Mercury 6°S
7 15 Mercury in inferior conjunction
7 21 Venus in conjunction with Mercury. Venus 3°N.
8 02 Mars in conjunction with Moon. Mars 1°N.
9 04 Venus in superior conjunction
9 07 Saturn in conjunction with Moon. Saturn 3°N.
19 15 Mercury at stationary point
20 13 Jupiter in conjunction with Moon. Jupiter 2°N.
20 20 Pluto at opposition
21 00 Sun's longitude 90° ♋
27 00 Uranus at stationary point

MINIMA OF ALGOL

Algol is inconveniently situated for observation during June

CONSTELLATIONS

The following constellations are near the meridian at

	d	*h*		*d*	*h*
May	1	24	June	15	21
May	16	23	July	1	20
June	1	22	July	16	19

Cassiopeia (below the Pole), Ursa Minor, Draco, Ursa Major, Canes Venatici, Bootes, Corona, Serpens, Virgo and Libra

THE MOON

Phases, Apsides and Node		*d*	*h*	*m*
●	New Moon	3	19	23
☽	First Quarter	10	15	04
○	Full Moon	18	17	30
☾	Last Quarter	26	12	10
Perigee (357,249km)		3	13	05
Apogee (406,243km)		16	17	20

Mean longitude of ascending node on June 1, 322°

THE SUN

s.d. 15′.8

Day	Right Ascension			Dec. +		Equation of time		Rise 52°		Rise 56°		Transit		Set 52°		Set 56°		Sidereal time			Transit of first point of Aries		
	h	m	s	°	′	m	s	h	m	h	m	h	m	h	m	h	m	h	m	s	h	m	s
1	4	37	12	22	05	+2	12	3	46	3	22	11	58	20	11	20	35	16	39	24	7	19	24
2	4	41	18	22	13	+2	02	3	45	3	21	11	58	20	12	20	36	16	43	21	7	15	28
3	4	45	25	22	20	+1	52	3	44	3	20	11	58	20	13	20	38	16	47	17	7	11	32
4	4	49	31	22	27	+1	42	3	43	3	19	11	58	20	14	20	39	16	51	14	7	07	36
5	4	53	39	22	34	+1	32	3	43	3	18	11	59	20	15	20	40	16	55	10	7	03	40
6	4	57	46	22	40	+1	21	3	42	3	17	11	59	20	16	20	41	16	59	07	6	59	44
7	5	01	54	22	46	+1	10	3	42	3	16	11	59	20	17	20	42	17	03	03	6	55	48
8	5	06	02	22	52	+0	58	3	41	3	16	11	59	20	17	20	43	17	07	00	6	51	52
9	5	10	10	22	57	+0	46	3	41	3	15	11	59	20	18	20	44	17	10	56	6	47	57
10	5	14	18	23	01	+0	35	3	40	3	15	12	00	20	19	20	45	17	14	53	6	44	01
11	5	18	27	23	06	+0	23	3	40	3	14	12	00	20	20	20	46	17	18	50	6	40	05
12	5	22	36	23	10	+0	10	3	40	3	14	12	00	20	20	20	46	17	22	46	6	36	09
13	5	26	45	23	13	−0	02	3	40	3	13	12	00	20	21	20	47	17	26	43	6	32	13
14	5	30	54	23	16	−0	15	3	39	3	13	12	00	20	21	20	48	17	30	39	6	28	17
15	5	35	03	23	19	−0	27	3	39	3	13	12	01	20	22	20	48	17	34	36	6	24	21
16	5	39	13	23	21	−0	40	3	39	3	13	12	01	20	22	20	49	17	38	32	6	20	25
17	5	43	22	23	23	−0	53	3	39	3	13	12	01	20	23	20	49	17	42	29	6	16	29
18	5	47	32	23	25	−1	06	3	39	3	13	12	01	20	23	20	50	17	46	25	6	12	33
19	5	51	41	23	26	−1	19	3	39	3	13	12	01	20	23	20	50	17	50	22	6	08	37
20	5	55	51	23	26	−1	32	3	40	3	13	12	02	20	24	20	50	17	54	19	6	04	42
21	6	00	00	23	26	−1	45	3	40	3	13	12	02	20	24	20	51	17	58	15	6	00	46
22	6	04	10	23	26	−1	58	3	40	3	13	12	02	20	24	20	51	18	02	12	5	56	50
23	6	08	19	23	26	−2	11	3	40	3	14	12	02	20	24	20	51	18	06	08	5	52	54
24	6	12	28	23	25	−2	24	3	41	3	14	12	03	20	24	20	51	18	10	05	5	48	58
25	6	16	38	23	23	−2	36	3	41	3	15	12	03	20	24	20	51	18	14	01	5	45	02
26	6	20	47	23	21	−2	49	3	42	3	15	12	03	20	24	20	50	18	17	58	5	41	06
27	6	24	56	23	19	−3	02	3	42	3	16	12	03	20	24	20	50	18	21	54	5	37	10
28	6	29	05	23	16	−3	14	3	43	3	16	12	03	20	24	20	50	18	25	51	5	33	14
29	6	33	14	23	13	−3	26	3	43	3	17	12	04	20	24	20	50	18	29	48	5	29	18
30	6	37	22	23	10	−3	38	3	44	3	18	12	04	20	23	20	49	18	33	44	5	25	22

DURATION OF TWILIGHT (in minutes)

Latitude	52°	56°	52°	56°	52°	56°	52°	56°
	1 June		11 June		21 June		31 June	
Civil	46	58	48	61	49	63	48	61
Nautical	116	TAN	124	TAN	127	TAN	124	TAN
Astronomical	TAN	TAN	TAN	TAN	TAN	TAN	TAN	TAN

THE NIGHT SKY

Mercury passes through inferior conjunction on the 7th but the long duration of twilight means that it remains unsuitably placed for observation throughout the month.

Venus passes through superior conjunction on the 9th, actually passing behind the disk of the Sun, and thus remaining too close to that body for observation throughout June. It is interesting to note that at this conjunction it is exactly halfway between the only two transits of the planet which occur this century – in 2004 and 2012.

Mars, magnitude +1.6, is no longer a conspicuous object, but continues to be visible in the western sky in the evenings. The planet moves from Cancer back into Leo towards the end of the month. It will be noticed that Mars is moving towards Saturn, being only 5 degrees away from it by the end of June, when it will be seen passing less than 1 degree north of Regulus. By the end of the month Mars will not be visible after about 22h. The 4-day-old crescent Moon will be seen approaching the planet on the evening of the 7th, though closest approach will not occur until after both bodies have set.

Jupiter, magnitude −2.7, continues to be visible as a conspicuous object in the night sky, becoming visible above the south-eastern horizon shortly before midnight at the beginning of the month, and two hours earlier by the end of the month. Jupiter is in the constellation of Sagittarius. The Moon, almost full, will be seen in the vicinity of the planet during the night of the 20th and 21st.

Saturn, magnitude +0.9, continues to be visible low in the western sky in the evenings. Saturn is in the constellation of Leo. The waxing crescent Moon is in the vicinity of the planet on the evenings of the 8th and 9th.

THE MOON

Day	R.A. h	R.A. m	Dec. °	Hor. Par. '	Semi-diam. '	Sun's Co-Long. °	PA of Br. Limb °	Ph. %	Age d	Rise 52° h	Rise 52° m	Rise 56° h	Rise 56° m	Transit h	Transit m	Set 52° h	Set 52° m	Set 56° h	Set 56° m
1	1	49	+16.3	60.4	16.5	235	75	12	26.5	1	44	1	29	9	31	17	40	18	01
2	2	48	+21.4	61.0	16.6	247	83	5	27.5	2	08	1	45	10	30	19	15	19	44
3	3	52	+25.3	61.3	16.7	260	101	1	28.5	2	42	2	12	11	35	20	42	21	17
4	4	59	+27.3	61.3	16.7	272	205	0	0.2	3	33	2	58	12	42	21	51	22	26
5	6	08	+27.2	61.0	16.6	284	258	2	1.2	4	44	4	09	13	49	22	39	23	09
6	7	14	+25.2	60.4	16.5	296	273	7	2.2	6	09	5	41	14	51	23	11	23	34
7	8	15	+21.5	59.6	16.2	308	281	14	3.2	7	39	7	18	15	47	23	33	23	49
8	9	12	+16.7	58.7	16.0	321	287	23	4.2	9	06	8	52	16	38	23	50	23	59
9	10	03	+11.2	57.7	15.7	333	291	33	5.2	10	27	10	20	17	24	—	—	—	—
10	10	51	+5.3	56.8	15.5	345	293	44	6.2	11	45	11	43	18	08	0	03	0	07
11	11	36	−0.6	56.0	15.3	357	293	54	7.2	12	59	13	02	18	49	0	14	0	13
12	12	21	−6.3	55.3	15.1	10	292	64	8.2	14	12	14	21	19	31	0	25	0	20
13	13	05	−11.7	54.8	14.9	22	290	73	9.2	15	25	15	39	20	13	0	37	0	27
14	13	51	−16.5	54.4	14.8	34	287	81	10.2	16	38	16	58	20	58	0	51	0	35
15	14	38	−20.7	54.1	14.8	46	282	88	11.2	17	51	18	17	21	44	1	08	0	46
16	15	27	−24.0	54.0	14.7	58	276	93	12.2	19	00	19	33	22	33	1	30	1	03
17	16	18	−26.3	54.0	14.7	71	266	97	13.2	20	03	20	39	23	23	2	01	1	28
18	17	11	−27.4	54.1	14.7	83	246	99	14.2	20	55	21	31	—	—	2	43	2	06
19	18	05	−27.3	54.2	14.8	95	142	100	15.2	21	34	22	06	0	15	3	37	3	02
20	18	58	−25.8	54.5	14.8	107	96	98	16.2	22	04	22	29	1	06	4	43	4	12
21	19	50	−23.2	54.8	14.9	119	84	95	17.2	22	25	22	45	1	56	5	56	5	31
22	20	40	−19.5	55.2	15.0	132	77	90	18.2	22	42	22	56	2	43	7	11	6	53
23	21	29	−14.9	55.7	15.2	144	72	84	19.2	22	55	23	04	3	29	8	28	8	16
24	22	16	−9.6	56.3	15.3	156	68	75	20.2	23	08	23	11	4	13	9	45	9	38
25	23	02	−3.7	56.9	15.5	168	67	66	21.2	23	19	23	18	4	57	11	02	11	01
26	23	49	+2.4	57.7	15.7	180	66	56	22.2	23	32	23	25	5	41	12	21	12	26
27	0	38	+8.5	58.4	15.9	193	67	45	23.2	23	47	23	35	6	28	13	44	13	55
28	1	29	+14.4	59.2	16.1	205	70	34	24.2	—	—	23	48	7	19	15	12	15	30
29	2	25	+19.7	59.9	16.3	217	74	23	25.2	0	07	—	—	8	14	16	43	17	08
30	3	25	+24.0	60.5	16.5	229	81	14	26.2	0	35	0	08	9	14	18	12	18	45

MERCURY

Day	R.A. h	R.A. m	Dec. °	Diam. "	Phase %	Transit h	Transit m	5° high 52° h	5° high 52° m	5° high 56° h	5° high 56° m
1	5	19	+22.1	12	4	12	37	19	59	20	16
3	5	16	+21.4	12	2	12	25	19	44	20	00
5	5	12	+20.8	12	1	12	13	19	28	19	43
7	5	07	+20.2	12	0	12	01	19	12	19	26
9	5	03	+19.6	12	1	11	49	4	40	4	26
11	4	58	+19.0	12	1	11	37	4	31	4	18
13	4	55	+18.6	12	3	11	25	4	22	4	09
15	4	52	+18.3	12	5	11	15	4	13	4	00
17	4	50	+18.1	11	8	11	05	4	04	3	52
19	4	49	+18.0	11	11	10	56	3	56	3	44
21	4	49	+18.0	10	14	10	49	3	48	3	36
23	4	50	+18.1	10	18	10	43	3	41	3	29
25	4	53	+18.4	9	21	10	38	3	34	3	22
27	4	57	+18.7	9	26	10	35	3	29	3	16
29	5	03	+19.1	9	30	10	32	3	24	3	11
31	5	09	+19.6	8	35	10	31	3	20	3	06

VENUS

Day	R.A. h	R.A. m	Dec. °	Diam. "	Phase %	Transit h	Transit m	5° high 52° h	5° high 52° m	5° high 56° h	5° high 56° m
1	4	28	+21.5	10	100	11	49	19	13	19	29
6	4	54	+22.5	10	100	11	56	19	25	19	43
11	5	21	+23.3	10	100	12	02	19	37	19	55
16	5	47	+23.7	10	100	12	09	19	47	20	05
21	6	14	+23.9	10	100	12	17	19	55	20	14
26	6	41	+23.8	10	100	12	24	20	01	20	20
31	7	08	+23.4	10	99	12	31	20	05	20	23

MARS

Day	R.A. h	R.A. m	Dec. °	Diam. "	Phase %	Transit h	Transit m	5° high 52° h	5° high 52° m	5° high 56° h	5° high 56° m
1	9	00	+18.6	5	92	16	20	23	24	23	36
6	9	12	+17.7	5	93	16	12	23	10	23	22
11	9	23	+16.8	5	93	16	03	22	57	23	07
16	9	34	+15.8	5	93	15	55	22	43	22	53
21	9	46	+14.8	5	94	15	46	22	29	22	38
26	9	57	+13.8	5	94	15	38	22	15	22	23
31	10	08	+12.7	4	94	15	30	22	01	22	08

SUNRISE AND SUNSET

d	London 0°05' 51°30'		Bristol 2°35' 51°28'		Birmingham 1°55' 52°28'		Manchester 2°15' 53°28'		Newcastle 1°37' 54°59'		Glasgow 4°14' 55°52'		Belfast 5°56' 54°35'	
	h m	h m	h m	h m	h m	h m	h m	h m	h m	h m	h m	h m	h m	h m
1	3 49	20 08	3 59	20 18	3 51	20 21	3 47	20 28	3 35	20 35	3 39	20 51	3 55	20 49
2	3 48	20 09	3 58	20 19	3 50	20 22	3 46	20 29	3 34	20 36	3 38	20 52	3 54	20 51
3	3 47	20 11	3 57	20 20	3 49	20 23	3 45	20 30	3 33	20 37	3 38	20 54	3 53	20 52
4	3 46	20 11	3 57	20 21	3 49	20 24	3 44	20 31	3 32	20 38	3 37	20 55	3 52	20 53
5	3 46	20 12	3 56	20 22	3 48	20 25	3 44	20 32	3 31	20 39	3 36	20 56	3 51	20 54
6	3 45	20 13	3 55	20 23	3 47	20 26	3 43	20 33	3 31	20 40	3 35	20 57	3 51	20 55
7	3 45	20 14	3 55	20 24	3 47	20 27	3 42	20 34	3 30	20 41	3 34	20 58	3 50	20 56
8	3 44	20 15	3 55	20 25	3 46	20 28	3 42	20 35	3 29	20 42	3 34	20 59	3 49	20 57
9	3 44	20 16	3 54	20 26	3 46	20 29	3 41	20 36	3 29	20 43	3 33	21 00	3 49	20 58
10	3 44	20 16	3 54	20 26	3 45	20 29	3 41	20 37	3 28	20 44	3 33	21 01	3 48	20 59
11	3 43	20 17	3 53	20 27	3 45	20 30	3 40	20 37	3 28	20 45	3 32	21 02	3 48	20 59
12	3 43	20 18	3 53	20 28	3 45	20 31	3 40	20 38	3 28	20 46	3 32	21 02	3 48	21 00
13	3 43	20 18	3 53	20 28	3 45	20 31	3 40	20 39	3 27	20 46	3 31	21 03	3 47	21 01
14	3 43	20 19	3 53	20 29	3 44	20 32	3 40	20 39	3 27	20 47	3 31	21 04	3 47	21 01
15	3 43	20 19	3 53	20 29	3 44	20 32	3 40	20 40	3 27	20 47	3 31	21 04	3 47	21 02
16	3 42	20 20	3 53	20 30	3 44	20 33	3 39	20 40	3 27	20 48	3 31	21 05	3 47	21 02
17	3 42	20 20	3 53	20 30	3 44	20 33	3 39	20 41	3 27	20 48	3 31	21 05	3 47	21 03
18	3 43	20 21	3 53	20 30	3 44	20 34	3 39	20 41	3 27	20 49	3 31	21 06	3 47	21 03
19	3 43	20 21	3 53	20 31	3 44	20 34	3 40	20 41	3 27	20 49	3 31	21 06	3 47	21 03
20	3 43	20 21	3 53	20 31	3 45	20 34	3 40	20 42	3 27	20 49	3 31	21 06	3 47	21 04
21	3 43	20 21	3 53	20 31	3 45	20 34	3 40	20 42	3 27	20 49	3 31	21 06	3 47	21 04
22	3 43	20 22	3 53	20 31	3 45	20 34	3 40	20 42	3 27	20 50	3 31	21 07	3 47	21 04
23	3 44	20 22	3 54	20 31	3 45	20 35	3 40	20 42	3 28	20 50	3 32	21 07	3 48	21 04
24	3 44	20 22	3 54	20 31	3 46	20 35	3 41	20 42	3 28	20 50	3 32	21 07	3 48	21 04
25	3 44	20 22	3 54	20 31	3 46	20 35	3 41	20 42	3 29	20 50	3 33	21 07	3 49	21 04
26	3 45	20 22	3 55	20 31	3 46	20 34	3 42	20 42	3 29	20 49	3 33	21 06	3 49	21 04
27	3 45	20 22	3 55	20 31	3 47	20 34	3 42	20 42	3 30	20 49	3 34	21 06	3 50	21 04
28	3 46	20 21	3 56	20 31	3 48	20 34	3 43	20 42	3 30	20 49	3 34	21 06	3 50	21 04
29	3 46	20 21	3 57	20 31	3 48	20 34	3 43	20 41	3 31	20 49	3 35	21 06	3 51	21 03
30	3 47	20 21	3 57	20 31	3 49	20 34	3 44	20 41	3 32	20 48	3 36	21 05	3 52	21 03

JUPITER

Day	R.A.		Dec.		Transit		5° high 52°		56°	
	h	m	°	'	h	m	h	m	h	m
1	19	33.4	−21	48	2	53	23	37	0	12
11	19	29.9	−21	57	2	11	22	55	23	27
21	19	25.5	−22	08	1	27	22	13	22	45
31	19	20.4	−22	20	0	43	21	30	22	03

Diameters – equatorial 46" polar 43"

SATURN

Day	R.A.		Dec.		Transit		5° high 52°		56°	
	h	m	°	'	h	m	h	m	h	m
1	10	20.1	+12	14	17	38	0	11	0	18
11	10	22.2	+12	01	17	01	23	29	23	36
21	10	24.9	+11	45	16	24	22	51	22	57
31	10	28.0	+11	26	15	48	22	13	22	19

Diameters – equatorial 17" polar 15"
Rings – major axis 39" minor axis 6"

URANUS

Day	R.A.		Dec.		Transit		10° high 52°		56°	
	h	m	°	'	h	m	h	m	h	m
1	23	33.2	−3	43	6	53	2	19	2	30
11	23	33.9	−3	40	6	14	1	40	1	51
21	23	34.2	−3	38	5	35	1	01	1	11
31	23	34.2	−3	38	4	56	0	22	0	32

Diameter 4"

NEPTUNE

Day	R.A.		Dec.		Transit		10° high 52°		56°	
	h	m	°	'	h	m	h	m	h	m
1	21	46.7	−13	45	5	06	1	35	1	59
11	21	46.4	−13	46	4	27	0	56	1	20
21	21	46.0	−13	48	3	47	0	17	0	40
31	21	45.5	−13	52	3	07	23	33	0	01

Diameter 2"

JULY 2008

SEVENTH MONTH, 31 DAYS. *Julius* Caesar, formerly *Quintilis*, fifth month of Roman pre-Julian calendar

1	Tuesday	Diana Spencer, Princess of Wales b. 1961 Juan Peron, president of Argentina d. 1974	183
2	Wednesday	David Owen, leader of the SDP Party b. 1938 Robert Peel, British prime minister d. 1850	184
3	Thursday	A US warship shot down an Iranian passenger aircraft, mistaking it for a fighter jet 1988	185
4	Friday	Thomas Jefferson, US president d. 1826 John Adams, US president d. 1826	186
5	Saturday	Stamford Raffles, British colonial administrator d. 1826 Hugh Shearer, prime minister of Jamaica d. 2004	187
6	Sunday	Nicholas I, tsar of Russia b. 1796 King Edward VI d. 1553	188

7	Monday	Michael Howard, British politician b. 1941 Talal bin Abdullah, king of Jordan d. 1972　week 27 day	189
8	Tuesday	Micheline Calmy-Rey, Swiss politician b. 1945 Fatima Jinnah, Pakistani politician d. 1967	190
9	Wednesday	Donald Rumsfeld, US secretary of defence b. 1932 Philip V, king of Spain d. 1746	191
10	Thursday	Ahmet Taner Kislali, Turkish politician b. 1939 Hadrian, emperor of Rome d. 138	192
11	Friday	Robert the Bruce, king of Scotland b. 1274 Narai, king of Siam d. 1688	193
12	Saturday	Lionel Jospin, prime minister of France b. 1937 Douglas Hyde, president of Ireland d. 1949	194
13	Sunday	Patrice de MacMahon, president of France b. 1808 Seretse Khama, president of Botswana d. 1980	195

14	Monday	Gerald Ford, US president b. 1913 Paul Kruger, South African revolutionary d. 1904　week 28 day	196
15	Tuesday	Hassanal Bolkiah, sultan of Brunei b. 1946 Hammer DeRoburt, president of Nauru d. 1992	197
16	Wednesday	Trygve Lie, UN secretary-general b. 1896 Nicholas II, tsar of Russia d. 1918	198
17	Thursday	Allied leaders held a conference in Potsdam to decide on the future of Germany 1945	199
18	Friday	The body of the government weapons expert Dr David Kelly was discovered 2003	200
19	Saturday	Francisco Sá Carneiro, prime minister of Portugal b. 1934 Syngman Rhee, president of South Korea d. 1965	201
20	Sunday	Miron Cristea, prime minister of Romania b. 1868 Wilhelm, crown prince of Germany d. 1951	202

21	Monday	Thomas Penham-Holles, British prime minister b. 1693 Albert Lutuli, South African politician d. 1967　week 29 day	203
22	Tuesday	Saddam Hussein's sons, Uday and Qusay Hussein, were killed by US troops in Iraq 2003	204
23	Wednesday	Haile Selassie, emperor of Ethiopia b. 1892 Cordell Hull, US secretary of state d. 1955	205
24	Thursday	Gibraltar was captured from the Spanish by the British 1704	206
25	Friday	Arthur Balfour, British prime minister b. 1848 Engelbert Dollfuss, chancellor of Austria d. 1934	207
26	Saturday	Vladimir Meciar, prime minister of Slovakia b. 1942 Sam Houston, president of the Republic of Texas d. 1863	208
27	Sunday	The Battle of Ushant between British and French fleets took place 1778	209

28	Monday	Jacqueline Onassis, US first lady b. 1929 Thomas Cromwell, English statesman d. 1540　week 30 day	210
29	Tuesday	Henry II, count of Champagne b. 1166 William Wilberforce, British politician d. 1833	211
30	Wednesday	Hongzhi, emperor of China b. 1470 Bao Dai, emperor of Vietnam d. 1997	212
31	Thursday	Maximilian II, Holy Roman Emperor b. 1527 Baudouin I, king of Belgium d. 1993	213

ASTRONOMICAL PHENOMENA

d　h
- 1　14　Mercury in conjunction with Moon. Mercury 8°S.
- 1　18　Mercury at greatest elongation W. 22°
- 3　14　Venus in conjunction with Moon. Venus 2°S.
- 4　08　Earth at aphelion (152 million km.)
- 6　16　Mars in conjunction with Moon. Mars 2°N.
- 6　20　Saturn in conjunction with Moon. Saturn 3°N.
- 9　08　Jupiter at opposition
- 10　18　Saturn in conjunction with Mars. Saturn 0°.6N.
- 17　13　Jupiter in conjunction with Moon. Jupiter 3°N.
- 22　11　Sun's longitude 120° ♌
- 29　20　Mercury in superior conjunction

MINIMA OF ALGOL

d	h	d	h	d	h
3	03.6	14	14.9	26	02.1
6	00.4	17	11.7	28	22.9
8	21.2	20	08.5	31	19.7
11	18.0	23	05.3		

CONSTELLATIONS

The following constellations are near their meridian at

	d	h		d	h
June	1	24	July	16	21
June	15	23	August	1	20
July	1	22	August	16	19

Ursa Minor, Draco, Corona, Hercules, Lyra, Serpens, Ophiuchus, Libra, Scorpius and Sagittarius

THE MOON

Phases, Apsides and Node	d	h	m
● New Moon	3	02	19
☽ First Quarter	10	04	35
○ Full Moon	18	07	59
☾ Last Quarter	25	18	42
Perigee (359,503 km)	1	21	20
Apogee (405,480 km)	14	04	07
Perigee (363,863 km)	29	23	16

Mean longitude of ascending node on July 1, 321°

THE SUN

s.d. 15′.8

Day	Right Ascension			Dec. +		Equation of time		Rise 52°		Rise 56°		Transit		Set 52°		Set 56°		Sidereal time			Transit of first point of Aries		
	h	m	s	°	′	m	s	h	m	h	m	h	m	h	m	h	m	h	m	s	h	m	s
1	6	41	31	23	06	−3	50	3	45	3	19	12	04	20	23	20	49	18	37	41	5	21	26
2	6	45	39	23	02	−4	01	3	45	3	19	12	04	20	23	20	48	18	41	37	5	17	31
3	6	49	47	22	57	−4	13	3	46	3	20	12	04	20	22	20	48	18	45	34	5	13	35
4	6	53	54	22	52	−4	24	3	47	3	21	12	04	20	22	20	47	18	49	30	5	09	39
5	6	58	01	22	46	−4	34	3	48	3	22	12	05	20	21	20	46	18	53	27	5	05	43
6	7	02	08	22	40	−4	45	3	49	3	24	12	05	20	21	20	45	18	57	24	5	01	47
7	7	06	15	22	34	−4	54	3	50	3	25	12	05	20	20	20	45	19	01	20	4	57	51
8	7	10	21	22	27	−5	04	3	51	3	26	12	05	20	19	20	44	19	05	17	4	53	55
9	7	14	26	22	20	−5	13	3	52	3	27	12	05	20	18	20	43	19	09	13	4	49	59
10	7	18	31	22	13	−5	22	3	53	3	28	12	05	20	18	20	42	19	13	10	4	46	03
11	7	22	36	22	05	−5	30	3	54	3	30	12	06	20	17	20	41	19	17	06	4	42	07
12	7	26	40	21	57	−5	38	3	55	3	31	12	06	20	16	20	39	19	21	03	4	38	11
13	7	30	44	21	48	−5	45	3	56	3	32	12	06	20	15	20	38	19	24	59	4	34	16
14	7	34	48	21	39	−5	52	3	57	3	34	12	06	20	14	20	37	19	28	56	4	30	20
15	7	38	50	21	30	−5	58	3	58	3	35	12	06	20	13	20	36	19	32	53	4	26	24
16	7	42	53	21	20	−6	04	4	00	3	37	12	06	20	12	20	34	19	36	49	4	22	28
17	7	46	54	21	10	−6	09	4	01	3	38	12	06	20	11	20	33	19	40	46	4	18	32
18	7	50	56	21	00	−6	13	4	02	3	40	12	06	20	10	20	32	19	44	42	4	14	36
19	7	54	56	20	49	−6	18	4	03	3	42	12	06	20	08	20	30	19	48	39	4	10	40
20	7	58	56	20	38	−6	21	4	05	3	43	12	06	20	07	20	28	19	52	35	4	06	44
21	8	02	56	20	26	−6	24	4	06	3	45	12	06	20	06	20	27	19	56	32	4	02	48
22	8	06	55	20	15	−6	27	4	07	3	46	12	06	20	05	20	25	20	00	28	3	58	52
23	8	10	54	20	02	−6	29	4	09	3	48	12	06	20	03	20	24	20	04	25	3	54	56
24	8	14	51	19	50	−6	30	4	10	3	50	12	07	20	02	20	22	20	08	22	3	51	00
25	8	18	49	19	37	−6	31	4	12	3	52	12	07	20	00	20	20	20	12	18	3	47	05
26	8	22	45	19	24	−6	31	4	13	3	53	12	07	19	59	20	18	20	16	15	3	43	09
27	8	26	42	19	11	−6	30	4	15	3	55	12	07	19	57	20	17	20	20	11	3	39	13
28	8	30	37	18	57	−6	29	4	16	3	57	12	06	19	56	20	15	20	24	08	3	35	17
29	8	34	32	18	43	−6	28	4	18	3	59	12	06	19	54	20	13	20	28	04	3	31	21
30	8	38	27	18	28	−6	26	4	19	4	01	12	06	19	53	20	11	20	32	01	3	27	25
31	8	42	21	18	14	−6	23	4	21	4	03	12	06	19	51	20	09	20	35	57	3	23	29

DURATION OF TWILIGHT (in minutes)

Latitude	52°	56°	52°	56°	52°	56°	52°	56°
	1 July		11 July		21 July		31 July	
Civil	48	61	47	58	44	53	42	49
Nautical	124	TAN	117	TAN	107	146	98	123
Astronomical	TAN	TAN	TAN	TAN	TAN	TAN	182	TAN

THE NIGHT SKY

Mercury passes through superior conjunction on the 29th and remains too close to the Sun for observation throughout the month.

Venus is too close to the Sun for observation during July but will become visible at the beginning of August.

Mars, magnitude +1.7, is now coming to the end of its period of visibility and is only likely to be visible low above the western horizon for the first week or ten days of the month, as the long evening twilight will hinder observation. After this Mars will not be seen again before 2009. On the evening of the 6th the three-day-old crescent Moon can be used to help locate two planets, both of which will be 4 degrees from the Moon's centre. Saturn, the brighter planet, is almost 4 degrees higher than the Moon, and about 1.5 degrees to the right, while Mars is about 2 degrees to the right and below Saturn.

Jupiter, magnitude −2.7, reaches opposition on the 9th and is therefore visible in the southern skies throughout the hours of darkness. As it is in the constellation of Sagittarius it is never at any great altitude. Even from southern England its maximum altitude is only 16 degrees, while from Scotland it is never more than 11 degrees. On the evenings of the 17th and 18th the Full Moon will be in the vicinity of the planet.

Saturn, magnitude +0.9, may still be seen for a short while low in the western sky in the evenings but will soon get lost in the long evening twilight. Mars passes close by around the 6th, see the note for Mars above.

Twilight. Reference to the section above shows that astronomical twilight lasts all night for a period around the summer solstice (ie in June and July), even in southern England. Under these conditions the sky never gets completely dark as the Sun is always less than 18 degrees below the horizon.

THE MOON

Day	R.A. h	R.A. m	Dec. °	Hor. Par. '	Semi-diam. '	Sun's Co-Long. °	PA of Br. Limb °	Ph. %	Age d	Rise 52° h	Rise 52° m	Rise 56° h	Rise 56° m	Transit h	Transit m	Set 52° h	Set 52° m	Set 56° h	Set 56° m
1	4	30	+26.7	60.9	16.6	242	90	7	27.2	1	16	0	43	10	20	19	30	20	06
2	5	38	+27.5	61.0	16.6	254	103	2	28.2	2	17	1	41	11	27	20	28	21	01
3	6	45	+26.3	60.8	16.6	266	162	0	29.2	3	36	3	04	12	31	21	08	21	34
4	7	49	+23.2	60.3	16.4	278	271	1	0.9	5	06	4	42	13	32	21	35	21	53
5	8	49	+18.7	59.6	16.3	291	284	5	1.9	6	37	6	20	14	26	21	53	22	05
6	9	43	+13.2	58.8	16.0	303	290	11	2.9	8	04	7	54	15	16	22	08	22	14
7	10	34	+7.3	57.9	15.8	315	293	19	3.9	9	25	9	21	16	02	22	20	22	22
8	11	21	+1.2	56.9	15.5	327	294	28	4.9	10	43	10	44	16	45	22	32	22	28
9	12	07	−4.7	56.1	15.3	340	294	38	5.9	11	58	12	05	17	28	22	44	22	35
10	12	52	−10.3	55.4	15.1	352	293	48	6.9	13	12	13	24	18	10	22	57	22	43
11	13	38	−15.4	54.8	14.9	4	291	58	7.9	14	26	14	44	18	54	23	12	22	53
12	14	24	−19.8	54.4	14.8	16	287	67	8.9	15	39	16	03	19	40	23	33	23	08
13	15	13	−23.3	54.2	14.8	29	282	76	9.9	16	50	17	21	20	28	—		23	29
14	16	04	−25.9	54.1	14.7	41	277	83	10.9	17	56	18	31	21	18	0	01	—	
15	16	57	−27.3	54.1	14.7	53	270	90	11.9	18	51	19	28	22	10	0	39	0	03
16	17	50	−27.5	54.3	14.8	65	263	95	12.9	19	35	20	08	23	01	1	29	0	53
17	18	44	−26.3	54.5	14.9	77	254	98	13.9	20	07	20	35	23	52	2	32	1	59
18	19	37	−24.0	54.9	15.0	90	229	100	14.9	20	31	20	52	—		3	43	3	17
19	20	28	−20.4	55.3	15.1	102	86	100	15.9	20	49	21	05	0	40	4	59	4	39
20	21	17	−16.0	55.7	15.2	114	73	97	16.9	21	04	21	13	1	27	6	17	6	03
21	22	05	−10.8	56.2	15.3	126	68	93	17.9	21	16	21	21	2	12	7	34	7	26
22	22	51	−5.0	56.7	15.5	138	65	87	18.9	21	28	21	27	2	56	8	51	8	49
23	23	38	+1.1	57.3	15.6	151	64	79	19.9	21	40	21	34	3	40	10	10	10	13
24	0	26	+7.2	57.8	15.8	163	65	69	20.9	21	54	21	43	4	26	11	30	11	39
25	1	16	+13.1	58.4	15.9	175	67	59	21.9	22	11	21	54	5	14	12	55	13	10
26	2	09	+18.5	58.9	16.1	187	70	48	22.9	22	34	22	10	6	06	14	22	14	45
27	3	06	+22.9	59.5	16.2	199	76	36	23.9	23	08	22	37	7	02	15	50	16	20
28	4	08	+26.1	59.9	16.3	212	82	26	24.9	23	59	23	23	8	04	17	11	17	47
29	5	13	+27.5	60.2	16.4	224	90	16	25.9	—		—		9	08	18	16	18	52
30	6	19	+27.1	60.3	16.4	236	98	8	26.9	1	09	0	34	10	13	19	03	19	32
31	7	23	+24.7	60.1	16.4	248	106	3	27.9	2	33	2	05	11	14	19	34	19	56

MERCURY

Day	R.A. h	R.A. m	Dec. °	Diam. "	Phase %	Transit h	Transit m	5° high 52° h	5° high 52° m	5° high 56° h	5° high 56° m
1	5	09	+19.6	8	35	10	31	3	20	3	06
3	5	17	+20.1	8	40	10	32	3	17	3	03
5	5	26	+20.7	7	45	10	33	3	15	3	00
7	5	37	+21.2	7	51	10	36	3	15	2	59
9	5	48	+21.7	7	56	10	40	3	15	2	59
11	6	01	+22.2	6	62	10	45	3	18	3	01
13	6	15	+22.6	6	69	10	52	3	22	3	04
15	6	30	+22.8	6	75	10	59	3	27	3	09
17	6	46	+23.0	6	81	11	07	3	34	3	16
19	7	03	+23.0	6	86	11	17	3	43	3	25
21	7	21	+22.9	5	91	11	26	3	54	3	36
23	7	39	+22.5	5	95	11	37	4	06	3	49
25	7	57	+22.0	5	97	11	47	4	20	4	03
27	8	15	+21.4	5	99	11	57	4	34	4	18
29	8	32	+20.5	5	100	12	07	19	22	19	37
31	8	50	+19.5	5	100	12	16	19	26	19	39

VENUS

Day	R.A. h	R.A. m	Dec. °	Diam. "	Phase %	Transit h	Transit m	5° high 52° h	5° high 52° m	5° high 56° h	5° high 56° m
1	7	08	+23.4	10	99	12	31	20	05	20	23
6	7	34	+22.7	10	99	12	38	20	07	20	24
11	8	01	+21.7	10	99	12	44	20	07	20	23
16	8	26	+20.5	10	98	12	50	20	06	20	20
21	8	52	+19.0	10	98	12	56	20	02	20	15
26	9	17	+17.3	10	97	13	01	19	58	20	09
31	9	41	+15.4	10	97	13	06	19	52	20	01

MARS

Day	R.A. h	R.A. m	Dec. °	Diam. "	Phase %	Transit h	Transit m	5° high 52° h	5° high 52° m	5° high 56° h	5° high 56° m
1	10	08	+12.7	4	94	15	30	22	01	22	08
6	10	20	+11.6	4	94	15	21	21	47	21	53
11	10	31	+10.4	4	95	15	13	21	32	21	37
16	10	42	+9.3	4	95	15	05	21	18	21	22
21	10	54	+8.1	4	95	14	56	21	03	21	06
26	11	05	+6.8	4	96	14	48	20	49	20	51
31	11	16	+5.6	4	96	14	39	20	34	20	35

SUNRISE AND SUNSET

d	London 0°05' 51°30' rise h m	set h m	Bristol 2°35' 51°28' rise h m	set h m	Birmingham 1°55' 52°28' rise h m	set h m	Manchester 2°15' 53°28' rise h m	set h m	Newcastle 1°37' 54°49' rise h m	set h m	Glasgow 4°14' 55°52' rise h m	set h m	Belfast 5°56' 54°35' rise h m	set h m
1	3 48	20 21	3 58	20 30	3 50	20 33	3 45	20 41	3 32	20 48	3 37	21 05	3 52	21 03
2	3 48	20 20	3 59	20 30	3 50	20 33	3 46	20 40	3 33	20 47	3 37	21 04	3 53	21 02
3	3 49	20 20	3 59	20 30	3 51	20 32	3 46	20 40	3 34	20 47	3 38	21 04	3 54	21 02
4	3 50	20 19	4 00	20 29	3 52	20 32	3 47	20 39	3 35	20 46	3 39	21 03	3 55	21 01
5	3 51	20 19	4 01	20 29	3 53	20 31	3 48	20 39	3 36	20 46	3 40	21 02	3 56	21 00
6	3 52	20 18	4 02	20 28	3 54	20 31	3 49	20 38	3 37	20 45	3 41	21 01	3 57	21 00
7	3 53	20 18	4 03	20 27	3 55	20 30	3 50	20 37	3 38	20 44	3 43	21 01	3 58	20 59
8	3 53	20 17	4 04	20 27	3 56	20 29	3 51	20 36	3 39	20 43	3 44	21 00	3 59	20 58
9	3 54	20 16	4 05	20 26	3 57	20 29	3 52	20 36	3 40	20 42	3 45	20 59	4 00	20 57
10	3 56	20 15	4 06	20 25	3 58	20 28	3 53	20 35	3 42	20 41	3 46	20 58	4 01	20 56
11	3 57	20 15	4 07	20 24	3 59	20 27	3 55	20 34	3 43	20 40	3 47	20 57	4 03	20 55
12	3 58	20 14	4 08	20 24	4 00	20 26	3 56	20 33	3 44	20 39	3 49	20 56	4 04	20 54
13	3 59	20 13	4 09	20 23	4 01	20 25	3 57	20 32	3 45	20 38	3 50	20 54	4 05	20 53
14	4 00	20 12	4 10	20 22	4 02	20 24	3 58	20 31	3 47	20 37	3 52	20 53	4 07	20 52
15	4 01	20 11	4 11	20 21	4 04	20 23	4 00	20 30	3 48	20 36	3 53	20 52	4 08	20 51
16	4 02	20 10	4 12	20 20	4 05	20 22	4 01	20 28	3 50	20 35	3 55	20 50	4 09	20 49
17	4 04	20 09	4 14	20 19	4 06	20 21	4 02	20 27	3 51	20 33	3 56	20 49	4 11	20 48
18	4 05	20 08	4 15	20 17	4 07	20 20	4 04	20 26	3 53	20 32	3 58	20 48	4 12	20 47
19	4 06	20 06	4 16	20 16	4 09	20 18	4 05	20 25	3 54	20 30	3 59	20 46	4 14	20 45
20	4 07	20 05	4 18	20 15	4 10	20 17	4 06	20 23	3 56	20 29	4 01	20 45	4 15	20 44
21	4 09	20 04	4 19	20 14	4 11	20 16	4 08	20 22	3 57	20 28	4 03	20 43	4 17	20 43
22	4 10	20 03	4 20	20 13	4 13	20 14	4 09	20 21	3 59	20 26	4 04	20 41	4 18	20 41
23	4 11	20 01	4 22	20 11	4 14	20 13	4 11	20 19	4 00	20 24	4 06	20 40	4 20	20 40
24	4 13	20 00	4 23	20 10	4 16	20 12	4 12	20 18	4 02	20 23	4 08	20 38	4 21	20 38
25	4 14	19 59	4 24	20 08	4 17	20 10	4 14	20 16	4 04	20 21	4 09	20 36	4 23	20 36
26	4 16	19 57	4 26	20 07	4 19	20 09	4 15	20 14	4 05	20 19	4 11	20 35	4 25	20 35
27	4 17	19 56	4 27	20 06	4 20	20 07	4 17	20 13	4 07	20 18	4 13	20 33	4 26	20 33
28	4 19	19 54	4 29	20 04	4 22	20 05	4 19	20 11	4 09	20 16	4 15	20 31	4 28	20 31
29	4 20	19 53	4 30	20 02	4 23	20 04	4 20	20 10	4 11	20 14	4 17	20 29	4 30	20 29
30	4 21	19 51	4 32	20 01	4 25	20 02	4 22	20 08	4 12	20 12	4 18	20 27	4 32	20 28
31	4 23	19 49	4 33	19 59	4 26	20 01	4 23	20 06	4 14	20 10	4 20	20 25	4 33	20 26

JUPITER

Day	R.A. h m	Dec. ° '	Transit h m	5° high 52° h m	5° high 56° h m
1	19 20.4	−22 20	0 43	3 51	3 18
11	19 14.9	−22 31	23 53	3 05	2 31
21	19 09.5	−22 42	23 09	2 18	1 44
31	19 04.5	−22 51	22 24	1 33	0 58

Diameters – equatorial 47″ polar 44″

SATURN

Day	R.A. h m	Dec. ° '	Transit h m	5° high 52° h m	5° high 56° h m
1	10 28.0	+11 26	15 48	22 13	22 19
11	10 31.6	+11 04	15 12	21 36	21 41
21	10 35.5	+10 41	14 37	20 58	21 03
31	10 39.7	+10 15	14 02	20 21	20 26

Diameters – equatorial 16″ polar 15″
Rings – major axis 37″ minor axis 5″

URANUS

Day	R.A. h m	Dec. ° '	Transit h m	10° high 52° h m	10° high 56° h m
1	23 34.2	−3 38	4 56	0 22	0 32
11	23 34.0	−3 40	4 16	23 39	23 49
21	23 33.4	−3 44	3 36	22 59	23 09
31	23 32.7	−3 49	2 56	22 19	22 30

Diameter 4″

NEPTUNE

Day	R.A. h m	Dec. ° '	Transit h m	10° high 52° h m	10° high 56° h m
1	21 45.5	−13 52	3 07	23 33	0 01
11	21 44.7	−13 56	2 27	22 54	23 18
21	21 43.8	−14 00	1 47	22 14	22 38
31	21 42.9	−14 05	1 07	21 34	21 59

Diameter 2″

AUGUST 2008

EIGHTH MONTH, 31 DAYS. *Augustus,* formerly *Sextilis,* sixth month of Roman pre-Julian calendar

1	*Friday*	Kurmanbek Bakiyev, president of Kyrgyzstan b. 1949 Louis VI, king of France d. 1137	214
2	*Saturday*	Philippe II, regent of France b. 1674 Paul von Hindenburg, president of the Weimar Republic d. 1934	215
3	*Sunday*	Stanley Baldwin, British prime minister b. 1867 James II, king of Scotland d. 1460	216

4	*Monday*	Queen Elizabeth, the Queen Mother b. 1900 William Cecil, English politician d. 1598 week 31 day	217
5	*Tuesday*	C. V. Devan Nair, president of Singapore b. 1923 Frederick North, British prime minister d. 1792	218
6	*Wednesday*	The first atomic bomb was dropped at Hiroshima, Japan 1945	219
7	*Thursday*	Idi Amin ordered that all non-citizen Asians leave Uganda within 90 days 1972	220
8	*Friday*	Emiliano Zapata, Mexican revolutionary b. 1879 George Canning, British prime minister d. 1827	221
9	*Saturday*	Joop den Uyl, prime minister of the Netherlands b. 1919 Romano Prodi, prime minister of Italy b. 1939	222
10	*Sunday*	Herbert Hoover, US president b. 1874 Yahya Khan, president of Pakistan d. 1980	223

11	*Monday*	The constitution of the German Weimar Republic was signed into law 1919 week 32 day	224
12	*Tuesday*	Mohammad Hatta, vice-president of Indonesia b. 1902 Robert Stewart, British politician d. 1822	225
13	*Wednesday*	Fidel Castro, president of Cuba b. 1926 Ikeda Hayato, prime minister of Japan d. 1965	226
14	*Thursday*	Francis I, king of the Two Sicilies b. 1777 Jonathan Clarkson Gibbs, US politician d. 1874	227
15	*Friday*	Napoleon Bonaparte, emperor of France b. 1769 Macbeth, king of Scotland d. 1057	228
16	*Saturday*	The Peterloo Massacre at St. Peter's Fields, Manchester 1819	229
17	*Sunday*	Menelik II, emperor of Ethiopia b. 1844 Rudolph Hess, German Nazi officer d. 1987	230

18	*Monday*	John Russell, British prime minister b. 1792 Genghis Khan, Mongol leader d. 1227 week 33 day	231
19	*Tuesday*	Bill Clinton, US president b. 1946 Augustus, emperor of Rome d. AD 14	232
20	*Wednesday*	Raymond Poincaré, president of France b. 1860 Johan de Witt, Dutch politician d. 1672	233
21	*Thursday*	King William IV b. 1765 Sobhuza II, king of Swaziland d. 1982	234
22	*Friday*	Jomo Kenyatta, prime minister of Kenya d. 1978 Michael Collins, Irish revolutionary d. 1922	235
23	*Saturday*	Louis XVI, king of France b. 1754 William Wallace, Scottish resistance leader d. 1305	236
24	*Sunday*	Charles IX ordered the St Bartholomew's Day Massacre of the Huguenots in France 1572	237

25	*Monday*	Sean O' Kelly, president of Ireland b. 1882 Stanley Bruce, prime minister of Australia d. 1967 week 314 day	238
26	*Tuesday*	Prince Albert, consort of Queen Victoria b. 1819 Louis-Philippe, king of France d. 1850	239
27	*Wednesday*	Lord Mountbatten was killed by a bomb detonated on his boat by the IRA 1979	240
28	*Thursday*	Paul Martin, prime minister of Canada b. 1938 Prince William, son of King George V d. 1972	241
29	*Friday*	Andrew Fisher, prime minister of Australia b. 1862 Eamon de Valera, president of Ireland d. 1975	242
30	*Saturday*	Denis Healey, British chancellor of the exchequer b. 1917 Grigory Semyonov, Russian counter-revolutionary d. 1946	243
31	*Sunday*	Wilhelmina, queen of the Netherlands b. 1880 King Henry V d. 1422	244

ASTRONOMICAL PHENOMENA

d	h	
1	10	Total eclipse of Sun
1	16	Mercury in conjunction with Moon. Mercury 1°N.
2	13	Venus in conjunction with Moon. Venus 2°N.
3	11	Saturn in conjunction with Moon. Saturn 3°N.
4	09	Mars in conjunction with Moon. Mars 4°N.
13	15	Jupiter in conjunction with Moon. Jupiter 3°N.
13	17	Saturn in conjunction with Venus. Saturn 0°.2N.
15	08	Neptune at opposition
15	20	Saturn in conjunction with Mercury. Saturn 0°.6N.
16	21	Partial eclipse of Moon
21	16	Venus in conjunction with Mercury. Venus 1°N.
22	18	Sun's longitude 150° ♍
31	02	Saturn in conjunction with Moon. Saturn 4°N.

MINIMA OF ALGOL

d	h	d	h	d	h
3	16.5	15	03.8	26	15.0
6	13.3	18	00.6	29	11.8
9	10.1	20	21.4		
12	07.0	23	18.2		

CONSTELLATIONS

The following constellations are near their meridian at

	d	h		d	h
July	1	24	August	16	21
July	16	23	September	1	20
August	1	22	September	15	19

Draco, Hercules, Lyra, Cygnus, Sagitta, Ophiuchus, Serpens, Aquila and Sagittarius

THE MOON

Phases, Apsides and Node	d	h	m
● New Moon	1	10	13
☽ First Quarter	8	20	20
○ Full Moon	16	21	16
☾ Last Quarter	23	23	49
● New Moon	30	19	58
Apogee (404,594 km)	10	20	15
Perigee (368,664 km)	26	03	51

Mean longitude of ascending node on August 1, 319°

THE SUN

s.d. 15′.8

Day	Right Ascension h	m	s	Dec. + °	′	Equation of time m	s	Rise 52° h	m	Rise 56° h	m	Transit h	m	Set 52° h	m	Set 56° h	m	Sidereal time h	m	s	Transit of first point of Aries h	m	s
1	8	46	14	17	59	−6	20	4	22	4	04	12	06	19	49	20	07	20	39	54	3	19	33
2	8	50	06	17	43	−6	16	4	24	4	06	12	06	19	48	20	05	20	43	51	3	15	37
3	8	53	58	17	28	−6	11	4	25	4	08	12	06	19	46	20	03	20	47	47	3	11	41
4	8	57	50	17	12	−6	06	4	27	4	10	12	06	19	44	20	01	20	51	44	3	07	45
5	9	01	41	16	56	−6	00	4	28	4	12	12	06	19	42	19	59	20	55	40	3	03	50
6	9	05	31	16	39	−5	54	4	30	4	14	12	06	19	41	19	56	20	59	37	2	59	54
7	9	09	20	16	22	−5	47	4	32	4	16	12	06	19	39	19	54	21	03	33	2	55	58
8	9	13	09	16	06	−5	39	4	33	4	18	12	06	19	37	19	52	21	07	30	2	52	02
9	9	16	57	15	48	−5	31	4	35	4	20	12	05	19	35	19	50	21	11	26	2	48	06
10	9	20	45	15	31	−5	22	4	36	4	22	12	05	19	33	19	48	21	15	23	2	44	10
11	9	24	32	15	13	−5	13	4	38	4	24	12	05	19	31	19	45	21	19	20	2	40	14
12	9	28	19	14	55	−5	03	4	40	4	26	12	05	19	29	19	43	21	23	16	2	36	18
13	9	32	05	14	37	−4	52	4	41	4	28	12	05	19	27	19	41	21	27	13	2	32	22
14	9	35	50	14	19	−4	41	4	43	4	29	12	05	19	25	19	38	21	31	09	2	28	26
15	9	39	35	14	00	−4	30	4	44	4	31	12	04	19	23	19	36	21	35	06	2	24	30
16	9	43	20	13	41	−4	17	4	46	4	33	12	04	19	21	19	34	21	39	02	2	20	35
17	9	47	04	13	22	−4	05	4	48	4	35	12	04	19	19	19	31	21	42	59	2	16	39
18	9	50	47	13	03	−3	51	4	49	4	37	12	04	19	17	19	29	21	46	55	2	12	43
19	9	54	30	12	43	−3	38	4	51	4	39	12	04	19	15	19	26	21	50	52	2	08	47
20	9	58	12	12	24	−3	23	4	53	4	41	12	03	19	13	19	24	21	54	49	2	04	51
21	10	01	54	12	04	−3	09	4	54	4	43	12	03	19	11	19	21	21	58	45	2	00	55
22	10	05	35	11	44	−2	54	4	56	4	45	12	03	19	09	19	19	22	02	42	1	56	59
23	10	09	16	11	23	−2	38	4	57	4	47	12	03	19	06	19	17	22	06	38	1	53	03
24	10	12	57	11	03	−2	22	4	59	4	49	12	02	19	04	19	14	22	10	35	1	49	07
25	10	16	37	10	42	−2	06	5	01	4	51	12	02	19	02	19	12	22	14	31	1	45	11
26	10	20	17	10	21	−1	49	5	02	4	53	12	02	19	00	19	09	22	18	28	1	41	15
27	10	23	56	10	00	−1	32	5	04	4	55	12	01	18	58	19	06	22	22	24	1	37	20
28	10	27	36	9	39	−1	15	5	06	4	57	12	01	18	55	19	04	22	26	21	1	33	24
29	10	31	14	9	18	−0	57	5	07	4	59	12	01	18	53	19	01	22	30	18	1	29	28
30	10	34	53	8	57	−0	39	5	09	5	01	12	00	18	51	18	59	22	34	14	1	25	32
31	10	38	31	8	35	−0	20	5	11	5	03	12	00	18	49	18	56	22	38	11	1	21	36

DURATION OF TWILIGHT (in minutes)

Latitude	52°	56°	52°	56°	52°	56°	52°	56°
	1 August		11 August		21 August		31 August	
Civil	41	49	39	45	37	42	35	40
Nautical	97	121	90	107	84	97	79	90
Astronomical	179	TAN	154	210	139	168	128	148

THE NIGHT SKY

Mercury is unsuitably placed for observation throughout the month, though observers with binoculars or small telescopes might like to attempt an observation using Venus as a guide on the evening of the 21st when Mercury is only about 1 degree below Venus.

Venus, magnitude −3.9, becomes visible as an evening object at the beginning of the month, shortly after sunset, very low above the western horizon. Only under exceptionally good conditions, including a sea horizon, is it likely to be visible from as far north as Scotland.

Mars remains unsuitably placed for observation.

Jupiter, magnitude −2.6, continues to be visible as a conspicuous object in the south-western quadrant of the sky in the evenings. The waxing gibbous Moon passes 3 degrees south of the planet on the 13th. By the end of the month it is not visible after 23h from southern England, while the time is an hour earlier for Scotland.

Saturn is unsuitably placed for observation as it approaches conjunction early next month.

Neptune is at opposition on the 15th, in the constellation of Capricornus. It is not visible to the naked-eye since its magnitude is +7.9.

Meteors. The maximum of the famous Perseid meteor shower occurs on the morning of the 12th and will be best seen from the late evening of the 11th onwards, though there will be interference from the waxing gibbous Moon until shortly before midnight (observers should refer to the moonset times on the next page).

THE MOON

Day	R.A. h	m	Dec. °	Hor. Par. ′	Semi-diam. ′	Suns Co-Long. °	PA of Br. Limb °	Ph. %	Age d	Rise 52° h	m	Rise 56° h	m	Transit h	m	Set 52° h	m	Set 56° h	m
1	8	24	+20.7	59.8	16.3	261	117	0	28.9	4	04	3	44	12	12	19	56	20	11
2	9	21	+15.6	59.2	16.1	273	287	0	0.6	5	33	5	20	13	04	20	13	20	22
3	10	13	+9.7	58.5	15.9	285	294	3	1.6	6	59	6	52	13	52	20	26	20	30
4	11	03	+3.6	57.7	15.7	297	296	8	2.6	8	20	8	18	14	37	20	38	20	37
5	11	50	-2.6	56.9	15.5	310	297	15	3.6	9	37	9	42	15	21	20	50	20	43
6	12	36	-8.5	56.1	15.3	322	296	23	4.6	10	53	11	03	16	04	21	03	20	51
7	13	22	-13.8	55.4	15.1	334	294	32	5.6	12	09	12	25	16	49	21	17	21	00
8	14	09	-18.5	54.9	15.0	346	291	42	6.6	13	23	13	45	17	34	21	36	21	13
9	14	58	-22.4	54.5	14.8	359	286	52	7.6	14	36	15	05	18	22	22	01	21	32
10	15	48	-25.3	54.3	14.8	11	281	61	8.6	15	44	16	19	19	11	22	35	22	00
11	16	40	-27.1	54.2	14.8	23	276	70	9.6	16	44	17	21	20	02	23	20	22	43
12	17	34	-27.6	54.3	14.8	35	270	78	10.6	17	32	18	07	20	54	—		23	44
13	18	28	-26.9	54.5	14.9	47	264	86	11.6	18	09	18	39	21	45	0	19	—	
14	19	21	-24.8	54.9	15.0	60	258	92	12.6	18	35	18	59	22	35	1	28	0	58
15	20	13	-21.6	55.4	15.1	72	253	96	13.6	18	55	19	13	23	22	2	43	2	20
16	21	03	-17.4	55.9	15.2	84	251	99	14.6	19	11	19	23	—		4	01	3	45
17	21	51	-12.3	56.4	15.4	96	44	100	15.6	19	24	19	31	0	09	5	19	5	09
18	22	39	-6.6	56.9	15.5	108	60	99	16.6	19	36	19	38	0	54	6	38	6	34
19	23	26	-0.5	57.4	15.7	120	61	95	17.6	19	48	19	45	1	38	7	57	7	58
20	0	14	+5.7	57.9	15.8	133	62	89	18.6	20	02	19	53	2	24	9	18	9	25
21	1	04	+11.8	58.3	15.9	145	64	81	19.6	20	18	20	03	3	11	10	42	10	55
22	1	56	+17.3	58.7	16.0	157	67	72	20.6	20	39	20	17	4	02	12	08	12	29
23	2	52	+22.0	59.0	16.1	169	72	61	21.6	21	09	20	40	4	57	13	36	14	04
24	3	52	+25.4	59.2	16.1	181	78	50	22.6	21	52	21	17	5	56	14	58	15	32
25	4	55	+27.3	59.4	16.2	194	85	39	23.6	22	53	22	17	6	58	16	07	16	44
26	5	59	+27.4	59.5	16.2	206	92	28	24.6	—		23	39	8	01	16	59	17	31
27	7	03	+25.7	59.4	16.2	218	99	18	25.6	0	10	—		9	02	17	35	18	00
28	8	03	+22.3	59.3	16.1	230	104	10	26.6	1	37	1	13	9	59	18	00	18	18
29	9	00	+17.6	58.9	16.1	243	108	4	27.6	3	06	2	49	10	53	18	18	18	30
30	9	53	+12.1	58.5	15.9	255	106	1	28.6	4	32	4	22	11	42	18	32	18	38
31	10	44	+6.0	57.9	15.8	267	334	0	0.2	5	54	5	50	12	28	18	45	18	46

MERCURY

Day	R.A. h	m	Dec. °	Diam. ″	Phase %	Transit h	m	5° high 52° h	m	5° high 56° h	m
1	8	58	+19.0	5	99	12	20	19	27	19	40
3	9	15	+17.8	5	98	12	29	19	28	19	40
5	9	30	+16.6	5	97	12	37	19	29	19	39
7	9	46	+15.3	5	95	12	44	19	29	19	38
9	10	00	+13.9	5	94	12	51	19	28	19	35
11	10	14	+12.5	5	92	12	57	19	26	19	33
13	10	28	+11.0	5	90	13	02	19	24	19	29
15	10	41	+9.6	5	88	13	07	19	21	19	25
17	10	53	+8.1	5	86	13	11	19	18	19	20
19	11	05	+6.6	5	84	13	15	19	14	19	16
21	11	16	+5.2	5	82	13	19	19	10	19	10
23	11	28	+3.7	6	80	13	22	19	06	19	05
25	11	38	+2.3	6	78	13	24	19	01	18	59
27	11	48	+0.8	6	76	13	27	18	56	18	53
29	11	58	-0.5	6	74	13	29	18	51	18	46
31	12	08	-1.9	6	71	13	30	18	45	18	40

VENUS

Day	R.A. h	m	Dec. °	Diam. ″	Phase %	Transit h	m	5° high 52° h	m	5° high 56° h	m
1	9	46	+15.0	10	97	13	06	19	50	19	59
6	10	10	+12.9	10	96	13	10	19	43	19	50
11	10	33	+10.7	10	95	13	14	19	35	19	40
16	10	56	+8.3	10	95	13	17	19	26	19	29
21	11	19	+5.9	11	94	13	20	19	16	19	17
26	11	41	+3.4	11	93	13	23	19	06	19	05
31	12	04	+0.8	11	92	13	26	18	55	18	52

MARS

Day	R.A. h	m	Dec. °	Diam. ″	Phase %	Transit h	m	5° high 52° h	m	5° high 56° h	m
1	11	19	+5.3	4	96	14	38	20	31	20	32
6	11	30	+4.1	4	96	14	30	20	16	20	16
11	11	42	+2.8	4	97	14	21	20	01	20	00
16	11	53	+1.5	4	97	14	13	19	47	19	44
21	12	05	+0.2	4	97	14	05	19	32	19	28
26	12	16	-1.2	4	97	13	57	19	17	19	12
31	12	28	-2.5	4	98	13	49	19	02	18	57

SUNRISE AND SUNSET

d	London 0°05′, 51°30′				Bristol 2°35′, 51°28′				Birmingham 1°55′, 52°28′				Manchester 2°15′, 53°28′				Newcastle 1°37′, 54°59′				Glasgow 4°14′, 55°52′				Belfast 5°56′, 54°35′			
	h	m	h	m	h	m	h	m	h	m	h	m	h	m	h	m	h	m	h	m	h	m	h	m	h	m	h	m
1	4	24	19	48	4	35	19	58	4	28	19	59	4	25	20	04	4	16	20	08	4	22	20	23	4	35	20	24
2	4	26	19	46	4	36	19	56	4	30	19	57	4	27	20	02	4	18	20	07	4	24	20	21	4	37	20	22
3	4	27	19	44	4	38	19	54	4	31	19	55	4	28	20	01	4	19	20	05	4	26	20	19	4	38	20	20
4	4	29	19	43	4	39	19	53	4	33	19	54	4	30	19	59	4	21	20	03	4	28	20	17	4	40	20	18
5	4	31	19	41	4	41	19	51	4	34	19	52	4	32	19	57	4	23	20	01	4	30	20	15	4	42	20	16
6	4	32	19	39	4	42	19	49	4	36	19	50	4	34	19	55	4	25	19	58	4	32	20	13	4	44	20	14
7	4	34	19	37	4	44	19	47	4	38	19	48	4	35	19	53	4	27	19	56	4	33	20	11	4	46	20	12
8	4	35	19	36	4	45	19	45	4	39	19	46	4	37	19	51	4	29	19	54	4	35	20	08	4	47	20	10
9	4	37	19	34	4	47	19	44	4	41	19	44	4	39	19	49	4	30	19	52	4	37	20	06	4	49	20	08
10	4	38	19	32	4	48	19	42	4	43	19	42	4	40	19	47	4	32	19	50	4	39	20	04	4	51	20	06
11	4	40	19	30	4	50	19	40	4	44	19	40	4	42	19	45	4	34	19	48	4	41	20	02	4	53	20	04
12	4	41	19	28	4	52	19	38	4	46	19	38	4	44	19	43	4	36	19	46	4	43	19	59	4	55	20	01
13	4	43	19	26	4	53	19	36	4	47	19	36	4	46	19	41	4	38	19	43	4	45	19	57	4	57	19	59
14	4	45	19	24	4	55	19	34	4	49	19	34	4	47	19	39	4	40	19	41	4	47	19	55	4	58	19	57
15	4	46	19	22	4	56	19	32	4	51	19	32	4	49	19	37	4	42	19	39	4	49	19	52	5	00	19	55
16	4	48	19	20	4	58	19	30	4	52	19	30	4	51	19	34	4	43	19	37	4	51	19	50	5	02	19	53
17	4	49	19	18	5	00	19	28	4	54	19	28	4	53	19	32	4	45	19	34	4	53	19	48	5	04	19	50
18	4	51	19	16	5	01	19	26	4	56	19	26	4	54	19	30	4	47	19	32	4	55	19	45	5	06	19	48
19	4	53	19	14	5	03	19	24	4	57	19	24	4	56	19	28	4	49	19	30	4	57	19	43	5	07	19	46
20	4	54	19	12	5	04	19	22	4	59	19	22	4	58	19	26	4	51	19	27	4	59	19	40	5	09	19	43
21	4	56	19	10	5	06	19	20	5	01	19	20	4	59	19	23	4	53	19	25	5	01	19	38	5	11	19	41
22	4	57	19	08	5	07	19	18	5	02	19	17	5	01	19	21	4	55	19	23	5	03	19	36	5	13	19	39
23	4	59	19	06	5	09	19	16	5	04	19	15	5	03	19	19	4	56	19	20	5	04	19	33	5	15	19	36
24	5	01	19	03	5	11	19	13	5	06	19	13	5	05	19	17	4	58	19	18	5	06	19	31	5	17	19	34
25	5	02	19	01	5	12	19	11	5	07	19	11	5	06	19	14	5	00	19	15	5	08	19	28	5	18	19	32
26	5	04	18	59	5	14	19	09	5	09	19	08	5	08	19	12	5	02	19	13	5	10	19	26	5	20	19	29
27	5	05	18	57	5	15	19	07	5	11	19	06	5	10	19	10	5	04	19	10	5	12	19	23	5	22	19	27
28	5	07	18	55	5	17	19	05	5	12	19	04	5	12	19	07	5	06	19	08	5	14	19	21	5	24	19	24
29	5	09	18	53	5	19	19	03	5	14	19	02	5	13	19	05	5	08	19	06	5	16	19	18	5	26	19	22
30	5	10	18	50	5	20	19	00	5	16	18	59	5	15	19	03	5	10	19	03	5	18	19	15	5	28	19	20
31	5	12	18	48	5	22	18	58	5	17	18	57	5	17	19	00	5	11	19	01	5	20	19	13	5	29	19	17

JUPITER

Day	R.A.		Dec.		Transit		5° high 52°		56°	
	h	m	°	′	h	m	h	m	h	m
1	19	04.0	−22	52	22	20	1	28	0	54
11	18	59.9	−22	59	21	37	0	44	0	09
21	18	56.9	−23	05	20	55	0	01	23	21
31	18	55.1	−23	08	20	14	23	15	22	39

Diameters – equatorial 45″ polar 42″

SATURN

Day	R.A.		Dec.		Transit		5° high 52°		56°	
	h	m	°	′	h	m	h	m	h	m
1	10	40.2	+10	13	13	58	20	17	20	22
11	10	44.6	+9	46	13	23	19	40	19	45
21	10	49.2	+9	18	12	49	19	03	19	07
31	10	53.9	+8	50	12	14	18	26	18	30

Diameters – equatorial 16″ polar 14″
Rings – major axis 36″ minor axis 4″

URANUS

Day	R.A.		Dec.		Transit		10° high 52°		56°	
	h	m	°	′	h	m	h	m	h	m
1	23	32.6	−3	50	2	52	22	15	22	26
11	23	31.5	−3	57	2	12	21	36	21	46
21	23	30.3	−4	05	1	31	20	56	21	07
31	23	28.9	−4	14	0	51	20	16	20	27

Diameter 4″

NEPTUNE

Day	R.A.		Dec.		Transit		10° high 52°		56°	
	h	m	°	′	h	m	h	m	h	m
1	21	42.8	−14	06	1	03	4	31	4	07
11	21	41.7	−14	11	0	22	3	50	3	26
21	21	40.7	−14	17	23	38	3	09	2	44
31	21	39.6	−14	22	22	58	2	28	2	03

Diameter 2″

SEPTEMBER 2008

NINTH MONTH, 30 DAYS. *Septem* (seven), seventh month of Roman pre-Julian calendar

1	*Monday*	Abdur Rahman Biswas, president of Bangladesh b. 1926 Louis XIV, king of France d. 1715	week 35 day 245
2	*Tuesday*	Daniel arap Moi, president of Kenya b. 1924 Dawit II, emperor of Ethiopia d. 1540	246
3	*Wednesday*	Gaston Thorn, president of the EC b. 1928 Edvard Benes, president of Czechoslovakia d. 1948	247
4	*Thursday*	Carlos Romero Barcelo, governor of Puerto Rico b. 1932 Robert Dudley, English statesman d. 1588	248
5	*Friday*	Benita Ferrero-Waldner, Austrian politician b. 1948 Crazy Horse, Native American leader d. 1877	249
6	*Saturday*	11 Israeli hostages, 5 terrorists and a German police officer were killed in the Munich Massacre 1972	250
7	*Sunday*	Queen Elizabeth I b. 1533 Mobutu Sese Seko, president of Zaire d. 1997	251
8	*Monday*	The Former Yugoslav Republic of Macedonia gained independence from Yugoslavia 1991	week 36 day 252
9	*Tuesday*	Susilo Bambang Chinese leader d. 1976	253
10	*Wednesday*	Nicolás Bravo, president of Mexico b. 1786 Taufa'ahau Tupou IV, king of Tonga d. 2006	254
11	*Thursday*	Ferdinand Marcos, president of the Philippines b. 1917 Salvador Allende, president of Chile d. 1973	255
12	*Friday*	H. H. Asquith, British prime minister b. 1852 Steve Biko, South African anti-apartheid activist d. 1977	256
13	*Saturday*	John II Komnenos, Byzantine emperor b. 1087 Charles James Fox, British foreign secretary d. 1806	257
14	*Sunday*	Jacobo Arbenz Guzmán, president of Guatemala b. 1913 Arthur Wellesley, British prime minister d. 1852	258
15	*Monday*	Joseph Lyons, prime minister of Australia b. 1879 Andre Tardieu, prime minister of France d. 1945	week 35 day 259
16	*Tuesday*	Andrew Bonar Law, British prime minister b. 1858 Louis XVIII, king of France d. 1824	260
17	*Wednesday*	Tessa Jowell, British politician b. 1947 Spiro Agnew, US vice-president d. 1996	261
18	*Thursday*	Jorge Sampaio, president of Portugal b. 1939 Dag Hammarskjüld, UN secretary-general d. 1961	262
19	*Friday*	Giuseppe Saragat, president of Italy b. 1898 James Garfield, US president d. 1881	263
20	*Saturday*	Ananda Mahidol, king of Thailand b. 1925 Gareth Williams, British politician d. 2003	264
21	*Sunday*	Girolamo Savonarola, ruler of Florence b. 1452 King Edward II d. 1327	265
22	*Monday*	Anne of Cleves, wife of King Henry VIII b. 1515 Kaarlo Juho Stahlberg, president of Finland d. 1952	week 38 day 266
23	*Tuesday*	Augustus, emperor of Rome b. 63 BC Louis-Joseph Papineau, French-Canadian politician d. 1871	267
24	*Wednesday*	Konstantin Chernenko, Soviet leader b. 1911 Pedro I, emperor of Brazil d. 1834	268
25	*Thursday*	King Harold II defeated Harold Hardrada, king of Norway, at the Battle of Stamford Bridge 1066	269
26	*Friday*	Christian X, king of Denmark b. 1870 James Keir Hardie, British politician d. 1915	270
27	*Saturday*	The Taliban took control of Kabul, Afghanistan, after three days of fighting 1996	271
28	*Sunday*	Augustus Fitzroy, British prime minister b. 1735 Wenceslas I, Duke of Bohemia d. 929	272
29	*Monday*	Robert Clive, British statesman b. 1725 Nguyen Van Thieu, president of South Vietnam d. 2001	week 38 day 273
30	*Tuesday*	Henry Bolingbroke proclaimed himself King Henry IV upon the abdication of Richard II 1399	274

ASTRONOMICAL PHENOMENA

d	h	
1	16	Venus in conjunction with Moon. Venus 5°N.
1	21	Mercury in conjunction with Moon. Mercury 3°N.
2	04	Mars in conjunction with Moon. Mars 5°N.
4	02	Saturn in conjunction
8	04	Jupiter at stationary point
8	18	Mars in conjunction with Mercury. Mars 3°N.
9	03	Pluto at stationary point
9	21	Jupiter in conjunction with Moon. Jupiter 3°N.
11	04	Mercury at greatest elongation E. 27°
12	02	Mars in conjunction with Venus. Mars 0°.3S.
13	02	Uranus at opposition
15	02	Venus in conjunction with Mercury. Venus 4°N.
22	16	Sun's longitude 180° ♎
23	11	Mars in conjunction with Mercury. Mars 4° N.
24	07	Mercury at stationary point
27	16	Saturn in conjunction with Moon. Saturn 4°N.
30	10	Mercury in conjunction with Moon. Mercury 1°N.

MINIMA OF ALGOL

d	h	d	h	d	h
1	08.6	12	19.9	24	07.1
4	05.4	15	16.7	27	03.9
7	02.2	18	13.5	30	00.7
9	23.0	21	10.3		

CONSTELLATIONS

The following constellations are near their meridian at

d	h		d	h
August	1	24	September 15	21
August	16	23	October 1	20
September	1	22	October 16	19

Draco, Cepheus, Lyra, Cygnus, Vulpecula, Sagitta, Delphinus, Equuleus, Aquila, Aquarius and Capricornus

THE MOON

Phases, Apsides and Node		d	h	m
☽	First Quarter	7	14	04
○	Full Moon	15	09	13
☾	Last Quarter	22	05	04
●	New Moon	29	08	12
Apogee (404,254km)		7	14	57
Perigee (368,854km)		20	03	35

Mean longitude of ascending node on September 1, 317°

THE SUN

s.d. 15′.9

Day	Right Ascension			Dec.		Equation of time		Rise 52°		Rise 56°		Transit		Set 52°		Set 56°		Sidereal time			Transit of first point of Aries		
	h	m	s	°	′	m	s	h	m	h	m	h	m	h	m	h	m	h	m	s	h	m	s
1	10	42	08	+8	13	−0	01	5	12	5	05	12	00	18	46	18	54	22	42	07	1	17	40
2	10	45	46	+7	51	+0	18	5	14	5	07	12	00	18	44	18	51	22	46	04	1	13	44
3	10	49	23	+7	29	+0	37	5	15	5	09	11	59	18	42	18	48	22	50	00	1	09	48
4	10	53	00	+7	07	+0	57	5	17	5	11	11	59	18	40	18	46	22	53	57	1	05	52
5	10	56	37	+6	45	+1	17	5	19	5	13	11	59	18	37	18	43	22	57	53	1	01	56
6	11	00	13	+6	23	+1	37	5	20	5	15	11	58	18	35	18	41	23	01	50	0	58	00
7	11	03	49	+6	00	+1	57	5	22	5	16	11	58	18	33	18	38	23	05	47	0	54	05
8	11	07	25	+5	38	+2	18	5	24	5	18	11	58	18	30	18	35	23	09	43	0	50	09
9	11	11	01	+5	15	+2	39	5	25	5	20	11	57	18	28	18	33	23	13	40	0	46	13
10	11	14	36	+4	53	+3	00	5	27	5	22	11	57	18	26	18	30	23	17	36	0	42	17
11	11	18	12	+4	30	+3	21	5	28	5	24	11	56	18	23	18	27	23	21	33	0	38	21
12	11	21	47	+4	07	+3	42	5	30	5	26	11	56	18	21	18	25	23	25	29	0	34	25
13	11	25	23	+3	44	+4	03	5	32	5	28	11	56	18	19	18	22	23	29	26	0	30	29
14	11	28	58	+3	21	+4	25	5	33	5	30	11	55	18	16	18	19	23	33	22	0	26	33
15	11	32	33	+2	58	+4	46	5	35	5	32	11	55	18	14	18	17	23	37	19	0	22	37
16	11	36	08	+2	35	+5	08	5	37	5	34	11	55	18	12	18	14	23	41	16	0	18	41
17	11	39	43	+2	12	+5	29	5	38	5	36	11	54	18	09	18	11	23	45	12	0	14	45
18	11	43	18	+1	49	+5	51	5	40	5	38	11	54	18	07	18	09	23	49	09	0	10	50
19	11	46	53	+1	25	+6	12	5	41	5	40	11	54	18	05	18	06	23	53	05	0	06	54
20	11	50	28	+1	02	+6	34	5	43	5	42	11	53	18	02	18	04	23	57	02	{ 0	02	58
																				23	59	02
21	11	54	03	+0	39	+6	55	5	45	5	44	11	53	18	00	18	01	0	00	58	23	55	06
22	11	57	39	+0	15	+7	16	5	46	5	46	11	53	17	58	17	58	0	04	55	23	51	10
23	12	01	14	−0	08	+7	37	5	48	5	48	11	52	17	55	17	56	0	08	51	23	47	14
24	12	04	50	−0	31	+7	58	5	50	5	50	11	52	17	53	17	53	0	12	48	23	43	18
25	12	08	26	−0	55	+8	19	5	51	5	52	11	52	17	51	17	50	0	16	45	23	39	22
26	12	12	02	−1	18	+8	40	5	53	5	54	11	51	17	48	17	48	0	20	41	23	35	26
27	12	15	38	−1	42	+9	00	5	55	5	56	11	51	17	46	17	45	0	24	38	23	31	31
28	12	19	14	−2	05	+9	20	5	56	5	58	11	51	17	44	17	42	0	28	34	23	27	35
29	12	22	51	−2	28	+9	40	5	58	6	00	11	50	17	41	17	40	0	32	31	23	23	39
30	12	26	28	−2	52	+10	00	6	00	6	02	11	50	17	39	17	37	0	36	27	23	19	43

DURATION OF TWILIGHT (in minutes)

Latitude	52°	56°	52°	56°	52°	56°	52°	56
	1 September		11 September		21 September		31 September	
Civil	35	39	34	38	34	37	34	37
Nautical	79	89	76	85	74	82	73	80
Astronomical	127	147	120	136	116	129	113	125

THE NIGHT SKY

Mercury remains too close to the Sun for observation throughout September even though it is at its greatest eastern elongation on the 11th.

Venus, magnitude −3.9, continues to be visible as a difficult evening object for a very short time after sunset, very low above the western horizon. Although it is farther from the Sun at the end of the month compared with the beginning, its rapid southward motion in declination negates this increase in elongation so that the time available for observation remains almost exactly the same throughout September. It is still unlikely to be glimpsed by observers as far north as Scotland.

Mars continues to be unsuitably placed for observation.

Jupiter continues to be visible as a brilliant object in the south-western sky in the evenings, magnitude −2.4. On the 8th Jupiter reaches its second stationary point and resumes its direct motion, while on the following evening the waxing gibbous Moon passes 3 degrees south of the planet.

Saturn, magnitude +0.9, is still too close to the Sun for observation at first, but gradually becomes visible as a difficult morning object during the last few days of September, low above the eastern horizon before the morning twilight inhibits observation. The thin waning crescent Moon is near the planet on the mornings of the 27th and 28th.

Uranus is at opposition on the 13th, in the constellation of Aquarius. Uranus is barely visible to the naked eye as its magnitude is +5.7, but it is readily located with only small optical aid.

Zodiacal Light. The morning cone may be observed stretching up from the eastern horizon, along the ecliptic, before the beginning of morning twilight, from the beginning of the month until the 13th. This faint phenomenon is only visible under good conditions and in the absence of both moonlight and artificial lighting.

THE MOON

Day	R.A. h m	Dec. °	Hor. Par. '	Semi-diam. '	Sun's Co-Long. °	PA. of Br. Limb °	Ph. %	Age d	Rise 52° h m	Rise 56° h m	Transit h m	Set 52° h m	Set 56° h m
1	11 31	−0.2	57.3	15.6	279	305	2	1.2	7 14	7 15	13 13	18 57	18 53
2	12 18	−6.2	56.6	15.4	292	301	5	2.2	8 31	8 39	13 57	19 09	19 00
3	13 05	−11.9	55.9	15.2	304	298	11	3.2	9 48	10 01	14 41	19 23	19 08
4	13 52	−16.9	55.3	15.1	316	295	18	4.2	11 04	11 23	15 27	19 40	19 20
5	14 41	−21.1	54.8	14.9	328	291	26	5.2	12 18	12 44	16 14	20 02	19 36
6	15 31	−24.4	54.5	14.8	340	286	35	6.2	13 29	14 01	17 03	20 32	20 00
7	16 23	−26.5	54.3	14.8	353	280	45	7.2	14 33	15 09	17 54	21 13	20 37
8	17 16	−27.5	54.3	14.8	5	274	54	8.2	15 26	16 02	18 45	22 06	21 30
9	18 09	−27.2	54.4	14.8	17	268	63	9.2	16 07	16 39	19 36	23 10	22 39
10	19 03	−25.6	54.7	14.9	29	262	72	10.2	16 37	17 03	20 26	–	23 57
11	19 55	−22.8	55.2	15.0	41	257	81	11.2	16 59	17 20	21 14	0 23	–
12	20 45	−19.0	55.8	15.2	54	254	88	12.2	17 17	17 31	22 01	1 40	1 21
13	21 34	−14.1	56.4	15.4	66	252	94	13.2	17 31	17 40	22 47	2 58	2 46
14	22 23	−8.6	57.1	15.6	78	253	98	14.2	17 44	17 47	23 33	4 17	4 11
15	23 11	−2.5	57.7	15.7	90	275	100	15.2	17 56	17 55	–	5 37	5 36
16	23 59	+3.8	58.3	15.9	102	42	99	16.2	18 09	18 02	0 19	6 59	7 04
17	0 50	+10.0	58.8	16.0	115	56	97	17.2	18 25	18 12	1 06	8 24	8 35
18	1 42	+15.9	59.2	16.1	127	62	91	18.2	18 45	18 25	1 57	9 52	10 09
19	2 38	+20.9	59.4	16.2	139	67	84	19.2	19 12	18 45	2 52	11 21	11 46
20	3 38	+24.7	59.4	16.2	151	74	75	20.2	19 51	19 18	3 50	12 46	13 18
21	4 41	+26.9	59.4	16.2	163	81	64	21.2	20 46	20 10	4 52	14 00	14 36
22	5 45	+27.4	59.3	16.2	175	88	53	22.2	21 58	21 25	5 54	14 57	15 30
23	6 48	+26.1	59.1	16.1	188	95	41	23.2	23 21	22 55	6 55	15 36	16 04
24	7 48	+23.2	58.8	16.0	200	101	30	24.2	–	–	7 53	16 04	16 24
25	8 45	+18.9	58.4	15.9	212	106	21	25.5	0 47	0 28	8 46	16 24	16 38
26	9 38	+13.7	58.1	15.8	224	108	12	26.2	2 12	2 00	9 36	16 39	16 47
27	10 28	+8.0	57.6	15.7	236	109	6	27.2	3 34	3 28	10 22	16 52	16 55
28	11 15	+1.9	57.1	15.6	249	104	2	28.2	4 53	4 52	11 07	17 04	17 02
29	12 02	−4.1	56.6	15.4	261	72	0	29.2	6 10	6 15	11 51	17 16	17 09
30	12 49	−9.9	56.0	15.3	273	322	1	0.7	7 27	7 38	12 35	17 30	17 17

MERCURY

Day	R.A. h m	Dec. °	Diam. "	Phase %	Transit h m	5° high 52° h m	5° high 56° h m
1	12 12	−2.5	6	70	13 31	18 42	18 36
3	12 21	−3.8	6	68	13 32	18 37	18 30
5	12 30	−5.1	6	65	13 32	18 30	18 22
7	12 38	−6.2	7	63	13 32	18 24	18 15
9	12 46	−7.4	7	60	13 32	18 18	18 08
11	12 53	−8.4	7	57	13 31	18 11	18 00
13	12 59	−9.4	7	53	13 29	18 04	17 52
15	13 05	−10.2	7	50	13 27	17 57	17 44
17	13 10	−11.0	8	46	13 24	17 50	17 36
19	13 14	−11.6	8	42	13 20	17 42	17 27
21	13 17	−12.1	8	37	13 14	17 34	17 19
23	13 18	−12.3	9	32	13 08	17 26	17 11
25	13 19	−12.4	9	26	13 00	17 18	17 03
27	13 17	−12.2	9	20	12 50	17 10	16 55
29	13 14	−11.8	10	15	12 38	17 01	16 47
31	13 09	−11.1	10	9	12 25	16 53	16 40

VENUS

Day	R.A. h m	Dec. °	Diam. "	Phase %	Transit h m	5° high 52° h m	5° high 56° h m
1	12 08	+0.3	11	92	13 26	18 53	18 50
6	12 30	−2.3	11	91	13 29	18 42	18 37
11	12 53	−4.8	11	90	13 31	18 31	18 23
16	13 15	−7.4	11	89	13 34	18 20	18 10
21	13 38	−9.8	12	88	13 37	18 09	17 57
26	14 01	−12.2	12	87	13 40	17 59	17 43
31	14 24	−14.5	12	86	13 44	17 48	17 30

MARS

Day	R.A. h m	Dec. °	Diam. "	Phase %	Transit h m	5° high 52° h m	5° high 56° h m
1	12 30	−2.7	4	98	13 47	18 59	18 53
6	12 42	−4.1	4	98	13 40	18 44	18 37
11	12 54	−5.4	4	98	13 32	18 30	18 21
16	13 06	−6.7	4	98	13 24	18 15	18 06
21	13 19	−8.0	4	99	13 17	18 00	17 50
26	13 31	−9.3	4	99	13 10	17 46	17 34
31	13 44	−10.5	4	99	13 03	17 31	17 18

SUNRISE AND SUNSET

d	London 0°05' h	m	51°30' h	m	Bristol 2°35' h	m	51°28' h	m	Birmingham 1°55' h	m	52°28' h	m	Manchester 2°15' h	m	53°28' h	m	Newcastle 1°37' h	m	54°59' h	m	Glasgow 4°14' h	m	55°52' h	m	Belfast 5°56' h	m	54°35' h	m
1	5	13	18	46	5	23	18	56	5	19	18	55	5	19	18	58	5	13	18	58	5	22	19	10	5	31	19	15
2	5	15	18	44	5	25	18	54	5	21	18	53	5	20	18	56	5	15	18	56	5	24	19	08	5	33	19	12
3	5	17	18	41	5	27	18	51	5	22	18	50	5	22	18	53	5	17	18	53	5	26	19	05	5	35	19	10
4	5	18	18	39	5	28	18	49	5	24	18	48	5	24	18	51	5	19	18	51	5	28	19	03	5	37	19	07
5	5	20	18	37	5	30	18	47	5	26	18	46	5	26	18	48	5	21	18	48	5	30	19	00	5	39	19	05
6	5	21	18	35	5	31	18	45	5	27	18	43	5	27	18	46	5	23	18	46	5	32	18	57	5	40	19	02
7	5	23	18	32	5	33	18	42	5	29	18	41	5	29	18	44	5	24	18	43	5	34	18	55	5	42	19	00
8	5	24	18	30	5	35	18	40	5	31	18	39	5	31	18	41	5	26	18	40	5	36	18	52	5	44	18	57
9	5	26	18	28	5	36	18	38	5	32	18	36	5	33	18	39	5	28	18	38	5	38	18	49	5	46	18	55
10	5	28	18	26	5	38	18	36	5	34	18	34	5	34	18	36	5	30	18	35	5	39	18	47	5	48	18	52
11	5	29	18	23	5	39	18	33	5	36	18	32	5	36	18	34	5	32	18	33	5	41	18	44	5	50	18	50
12	5	31	18	21	5	41	18	31	5	37	18	29	5	38	18	31	5	34	18	30	5	43	18	42	5	51	18	47
13	5	32	18	19	5	42	18	29	5	39	18	27	5	40	18	29	5	36	18	28	5	45	18	39	5	53	18	45
14	5	34	18	16	5	44	18	26	5	41	18	24	5	41	18	26	5	37	18	25	5	47	18	36	5	55	18	42
15	5	36	18	14	5	46	18	24	5	42	18	22	5	43	18	24	5	39	18	23	5	49	18	34	5	57	18	39
16	5	37	18	12	5	47	18	22	5	44	18	20	5	45	18	22	5	41	18	20	5	51	18	31	5	59	18	37
17	5	39	18	10	5	49	18	19	5	46	18	17	5	46	18	19	5	43	18	17	5	53	18	28	6	01	18	34
18	5	40	18	07	5	50	18	17	5	47	18	15	5	48	18	17	5	45	18	15	5	55	18	26	6	02	18	32
19	5	42	18	05	5	52	18	15	5	49	18	13	5	50	18	14	5	47	18	12	5	57	18	23	6	04	18	29
20	5	44	18	03	5	54	18	13	5	51	18	10	5	52	18	12	5	49	18	10	5	59	18	20	6	06	18	27
21	5	45	18	00	5	55	18	10	5	52	18	08	5	53	18	09	5	51	18	07	6	01	18	18	6	08	18	24
22	5	47	17	58	5	57	18	08	5	54	18	05	5	55	18	07	5	52	18	05	6	03	18	15	6	10	18	22
23	5	48	17	56	5	58	18	06	5	56	18	03	5	57	18	04	5	54	18	02	6	05	18	12	6	12	18	19
24	5	50	17	53	6	00	18	03	5	57	18	01	5	59	18	02	5	56	17	59	6	07	18	10	6	13	18	17
25	5	52	17	51	6	02	18	01	5	59	17	58	6	00	18	00	5	58	17	57	6	09	18	07	6	15	18	14
26	5	53	17	49	6	03	17	59	6	01	17	56	6	02	17	57	6	00	17	54	6	11	18	05	6	17	18	12
27	5	55	17	46	6	05	17	56	6	02	17	54	6	04	17	55	6	02	17	52	6	12	18	02	6	19	18	09
28	5	57	17	44	6	07	17	54	6	04	17	51	6	06	17	52	6	04	17	49	6	14	17	59	6	21	18	07
29	5	58	17	42	6	08	17	52	6	06	17	49	6	08	17	50	6	06	17	47	6	16	17	57	6	23	18	04
30	6	00	17	40	6	10	17	50	6	08	17	47	6	09	17	47	6	07	17	44	6	18	17	54	6	25	18	02

JUPITER

Day	R.A. h	m	Dec. °	'	Transit h	m	5° high 52° h	m	56° h	m
1	18	55.0	−23	08	20	09	23	11	22	35
11	18	54.7	−23	09	19	30	22	31	21	56
21	18	55.7	−23	08	18	52	21	53	21	18
31	18	58.2	−23	06	18	15	21	17	20	42

Diameters – equatorial 42″ polar 39″

SATURN

Day	R.A. h	m	Dec. °	'	Transit h	m	5° high 52° h	m	56° h	m
1	10	54.4	+8	47	12	11	5	59	5	55
11	10	59.1	+8	19	11	36	5	27	5	23
21	11	03.8	+7	51	11	01	4	55	4	51
31	11	08.4	+7	23	10	26	4	22	4	19

Diameters – equatorial 16″ polar 14″
Rings – major axis 36″ minor axis 3″

URANUS

Day	R.A. h	m	Dec. °	'	Transit h	m	10° high 52° h	m	56° h	m
1	23	28.8	−4	15	0	47	5	17	5	06
11	23	27.3	−4	24	0	06	4	35	4	24
21	23	25.8	−4	34	23	21	3	54	3	42
31	23	24.4	−4	43	22	40	3	12	3	01

Diameter 4″

NEPTUNE

Day	R.A. h	m	Dec. °	'	Transit h	m	10° high 52° h	m	56° h	m
1	21	39.5	−14	23	22	54	2	24	1	59
11	21	38.6	−14	28	22	13	1	43	1	18
21	21	37.7	−14	32	21	33	1	02	0	37
31	21	37.0	−14	36	20	53	0	22	23	53

Diameter 2″

OCTOBER 2008

TENTH MONTH, 31 DAYS. *Octo* (eighth), eighth month of Roman pre-Julian calendar

1	*Wednesday*	The People's Republic of China was formally established 1949	275
2	*Thursday*	Charles Albert, king of Sardinia b. 1798 William Cavendish, British prime minister d. 1764	276
3	*Friday*	John Ross, Cherokee chief b. 1790 Gustav Stresemann, chancellor of the Weimar Republic d. 1929	277
4	*Saturday*	Ann Widdecombe, British politician b. 1947 Vladimir Yaroslavich, prince of Novgorod d. 1052	278
5	*Sunday*	Eduardo Duhalde, president of Argentina b. 1941 Henry III, Holy Roman Emperor d. 1056	279

6	*Monday*	Gerry Adams, Irish Republican politician b. 1948 Anwar al-Sadat, president of Egypt d. 1981	week 40 day 280
7	*Tuesday*	Fernando Belaunde Terry, president of Peru b. 1912 Alfred Deakin, prime minister of Australia d. 1919	281
8	*Wednesday*	Betty Boothroyd, British politician b. 1929 Willy Brandt, chancellor of West Germany d. 1992	282
9	*Thursday*	Che Guevara, the Marxist revolutionary, was executed by the Bolivian army 1967	283
10	*Friday*	Radu Vasile, prime minister of Romania b. 1942 Édouard Daladier, prime minister of France d. 1970	284
11	*Saturday*	Arthur Phillip, British colonialist b. 1738 Donald Dewar, first minister of Scotland d. 2000	285
12	*Sunday*	Ramsay Macdonald, British prime minister b. 1866 Anthony Berry, British politician d. 1984	286

13	*Monday*	Margaret Thatcher, British prime minister b. 1925 Le Duc Tho, Vietnamese politician d. 1990	week 41 day 287
14	*Tuesday*	King James II of England and Ireland, and VII of Scotland b. 1633 King Harold II d. 1066	288
15	*Wednesday*	Sali Berisha, president of Albania b. 1944 Pierre Laval, prime minister of France d. 1945	289
16	*Thursday*	David Ben-Gurion, Israeli prime minister b. 1886 Marie Antoinette, queen consort of France d. 1793	290
17	*Friday*	John Wilkes, English politician b. 1725 Philip Sidney, English statesman d. 1586	291
18	*Saturday*	Violeta Chamorro, president of Nicaragua b. 1929 Bess Truman, US first lady d. 1982	292
19	*Sunday*	Myeongseong, empress of Korea b. 1851 King John d. 1216	293

20	*Monday*	Henry Temple, British prime minister b. 1784 Charles VI, Holy Roman Emperor d. 1740	week 42 day 294
21	*Tuesday*	Alphonse de Lamartine, French statesman b. 1790 Horatio Nelson, British naval commander d. 1805	295
22	*Wednesday*	US president John F. Kennedy announced the discovery of Soviet nuclear weapons in Cuba 1962	296
23	*Thursday*	Fatmir Sejdiu, president of Kosovo b. 1951 Edward Smith-Stanley, British prime minister d. 1869	297
24	*Friday*	Domitian, emperor of Rome b. AD 51 Jo Grimond, leader of the Liberal Party d. 1993	298
25	*Saturday*	Michael I, king of Romania b. 1921 King George II d. 1760	299
26	*Sunday*	Thorvald Stauning, prime minister of Denmark b. 1873 Alfred, king of Wessex d. 899	300

27	*Monday*	Theodore Roosevelt, US president b. 1858 Athelstan, king of England d. 939	week 43 day 301
28	*Tuesday*	Mahmoud Ahmadinejad, president of Iran b. 1956 Jahangir, ruler of the Mughal Empire d. 1627	302
29	*Wednesday*	Ellen Johnson-Sirleaf, president of Liberia b. 1938 Walter Raleigh, English courtier d. 1618	303
30	*Thursday*	R. B. Sheridan, Irish politician b. 1751 William Cavendish-Bentinck, British prime minister d. 1809	304
31	*Friday*	Norodom Sihanouk, king of Cambodia b. 1922 Michael Stasinopoulos, president of Greece d. 2002	305

ASTRONOMICAL PHENOMENA

d h
1 00 Mars in conjunction with Moon. Mars 5°N.
1 23 Venus in conjunction with Moon. Venus 5°N.
6 21 Mercury in inferior conjunction
7 08 Jupiter in conjunction with Moon. Jupiter 2°N.
15 20 Mercury at stationary point
22 09 Mercury at greatest elongation W. 18°
23 01 Sun's longitude 210° ♏
25 04 Saturn in conjunction with Moon. Saturn 4°N.
27 12 Mercury in conjunction with Moon. Mercury 7°N.
29 22 Mars in conjunction with Moon. Mars 5°N.

MINIMA OF ALGOL

d	h	d	h	d	h
2	21.5	14	08.8	25	20.0
5	18.3	17	05.6	28	16.8
8	15.2	20	02.4	31	13.7
11	12.0	22	23.2		

CONSTELLATIONS

The following constellations are near their meridian at

	d	h		d	h
September	1	24	October	16	21
September	15	23	November	1	20
October	1	22	November	15	19

Ursa Major (below the Pole), Cepheus, Cassiopeia, Cygnus, Lacerta, Andromeda, Pegasus, Capricornus, Aquarius and Piscis Austrinus

THE MOON

Phases, Apsides and Node	d	h	m
☽ First Quarter	7	09	04
○ Full Moon	14	20	02
☾ Last Quarter	21	11	55
● New Moon	28	23	14

Apogee (404,758 km)	5	10	37
Perigee (363,802 km)	17	06	17

Mean longitude of ascending node on October 1, 316°

THE SUN

s.d. 16'.1

Day	Right Ascension			Dec.		Equation of time		Rise 52°		Rise 56°		Transit		Set 52°		Set 56°		Sidereal time			Transit of first point of Aries		
	h	m	s	°	'	m	s	h	m	h	m	h	m	h	m	h	m	h	m	s	h	m	s
1	12	30	05	3	15	+10	19	6	01	6	04	11	50	17	37	17	34	0	40	24	23	15	47
2	12	33	42	3	38	+10	38	6	03	6	05	11	49	17	34	17	32	0	44	20	23	11	51
3	12	37	20	4	01	+10	57	6	05	6	07	11	49	17	32	17	29	0	48	17	23	07	55
4	12	40	58	4	24	+11	16	6	06	6	09	11	49	17	30	17	27	0	52	13	23	03	59
5	12	44	36	4	48	+11	34	6	08	6	12	11	48	17	28	17	24	0	56	10	23	00	03
6	12	48	15	5	11	+11	52	6	10	6	14	11	48	17	25	17	21	1	00	07	22	56	07
7	12	51	54	5	34	+12	09	6	11	6	16	11	48	17	23	17	19	1	04	03	22	52	11
8	12	55	34	5	57	+12	26	6	13	6	18	11	47	17	21	17	16	1	08	00	22	48	16
9	12	59	14	6	19	+12	43	6	15	6	20	11	47	17	19	17	14	1	11	56	22	44	20
10	13	02	54	6	42	+12	59	6	17	6	22	11	47	17	16	17	11	1	15	53	22	40	24
11	13	06	35	7	05	+13	15	6	18	6	24	11	47	17	14	17	09	1	19	49	22	36	28
12	13	10	16	7	27	+13	30	6	20	6	26	11	46	17	12	17	06	1	23	46	22	32	32
13	13	13	58	7	50	+13	45	6	22	6	28	11	46	17	10	17	04	1	27	42	22	28	36
14	13	17	40	8	12	+13	59	6	23	6	30	11	46	17	07	17	01	1	31	39	22	24	40
15	13	21	23	8	34	+14	13	6	25	6	32	11	46	17	05	16	59	1	35	36	22	20	44
16	13	25	06	8	56	+14	26	6	27	6	34	11	45	17	03	16	56	1	39	32	22	16	48
17	13	28	50	9	18	+14	38	6	29	6	36	11	45	17	01	16	54	1	43	29	22	12	52
18	13	32	35	9	40	+14	50	6	30	6	38	11	45	16	59	16	51	1	47	25	22	08	56
19	13	36	20	10	02	+15	02	6	32	6	40	11	45	16	57	16	49	1	51	22	22	05	01
20	13	40	06	10	24	+15	12	6	34	6	42	11	45	16	55	16	46	1	55	18	22	01	05
21	13	43	53	10	45	+15	22	6	36	6	44	11	45	16	53	16	44	1	59	15	21	57	09
22	13	47	40	11	06	+15	32	6	37	6	46	11	44	16	51	16	41	2	03	11	21	53	13
23	13	51	28	11	27	+15	40	6	39	6	49	11	44	16	48	16	39	2	07	08	21	49	17
24	13	55	16	11	48	+15	48	6	41	6	51	11	44	16	46	16	37	2	11	05	21	45	21
25	13	59	06	12	09	+15	56	6	43	6	53	11	44	16	44	16	34	2	15	01	21	41	25
26	14	02	56	12	30	+16	02	6	45	6	55	11	44	16	42	16	32	2	18	58	21	37	29
27	14	06	46	12	50	+16	08	6	46	6	57	11	44	16	40	16	30	2	22	54	21	33	33
28	14	10	38	13	10	+16	13	6	48	6	59	11	44	16	39	16	28	2	26	51	21	29	37
29	14	14	30	13	30	+16	17	6	50	7	01	11	44	16	37	16	25	2	30	47	21	25	41
30	14	18	23	13	50	+16	20	6	52	7	03	11	44	16	35	16	23	2	34	44	21	21	46
31	14	22	17	14	09	+16	23	6	54	7	05	11	44	16	33	16	21	2	38	40	21	17	50

DURATION OF TWILIGHT (in minutes)

Latitude	52°	56°	52°	56°	52°	56°	52°	56°
	1 October		11 October		21 October		31 October	
Civil	34	37	34	37	34	38	35	39
Nautical	73	80	73	80	74	81	75	83
Astronomical	113	125	112	124	113	124	114	126

THE NIGHT SKY

Mercury passes through inferior conjunction on the 6th and is too close to the Sun for observation until the middle of the month. Thereafter it is visible as a morning object, low in the east-south-eastern sky around the beginning of morning civil twilight. During this time its magnitude brightens from +0.9 to −0.9. On the morning of the 27th the thin waning crescent Moon passes almost 8 degrees south of the planet. This morning apparition is the most suitable one of the year for observers in the British Isles.

Venus, magnitude −4.0, is a brilliant object in the early evenings, though still very low in the south-western sky. For observers in southern England it is visible for about half-an-hour after sunset, by the end of October. It continues to be a very difficult object to observe, even by the end of the month, for observers in Scotland.

Mars remains unsuitably placed for observation.

Jupiter, magnitude −2.2, is still visible in the south-western sky in the early part of the evening. The Moon, at First Quarter, is in the vicinity of the planet on the evenings of the 7th and 8th.

Saturn, magnitude +1.0, is slowly emerging from the morning twilight and becoming visible low above the eastern horizon for a short while, before being lost in the brightening sky before sunrise. On the morning of the 25th the thin waning crescent Moon passes 5 degrees south of the planet. Saturn is still in Leo. Because the rings are slowly closing, before the Earth passes through the ring plane next year, this is the first occasion since 1997 that the planet's magnitude has faded to this level.

THE MOON

Day	R.A.		Dec.	Hor. Par.	Semi- diam.	Sun's Co- Long.	PA of Br. Limb	Ph.	Age	Rise				Transit		Set			
										52°		56°				52°		56°	
	h	m	°	'	'	°	°	%	d	h	m	h	m	h	m	h	m	h	m
1	13	36	−15.1	55.5	15.1	285	305	3	1.7	8	43	9	00	13	20	17	45	17	28
2	14	24	−19.6	55.0	15.0	298	297	7	2.7	9	59	10	22	14	07	18	06	17	42
3	15	14	−23.3	54.6	14.9	310	291	13	3.7	11	12	11	41	14	55	18	33	18	03
4	16	06	−25.8	54.3	14.8	322	285	20	4.7	12	19	12	53	15	45	19	09	18	34
5	16	58	−27.2	54.2	14.8	334	278	28	5.7	13	16	13	52	16	36	19	57	19	21
6	17	52	−27.3	54.2	14.8	346	272	37	6.7	14	02	14	35	17	27	20	56	20	23
7	18	44	−26.1	54.4	14.8	359	266	47	7.7	14	36	15	04	18	17	22	05	21	37
8	19	36	−23.8	54.7	14.9	11	260	56	8.7	15	01	15	24	19	05	23	18	22	57
9	20	27	−20.3	55.3	15.1	23	256	66	9.7	15	20	15	37	19	52	—		—	
10	21	16	−15.9	55.9	15.2	35	253	75	10.7	15	36	15	47	20	38	0	35	0	20
11	22	04	−10.7	56.7	15.4	47	251	83	11.7	15	49	15	55	21	23	1	53	1	43
12	22	51	−4.9	57.5	15.7	59	251	90	12.7	16	02	16	03	22	09	3	12	3	08
13	23	40	+1.3	58.3	15.9	72	254	96	13.7	16	15	16	11	22	56	4	33	4	35
14	0	30	+7.6	59.1	16.1	84	266	99	14.7	16	30	16	20	23	47	5	57	6	05
15	1	23	+13.7	59.7	16.3	96	4	100	15.7	16	48	16	32	—		7	25	7	40
16	2	19	+19.2	60.1	16.4	108	54	98	16.7	17	14	16	50	0	41	8	56	9	18
17	3	19	+23.5	60.3	16.4	120	66	93	17.7	17	49	17	19	1	40	10	26	10	56
18	4	23	+26.3	60.2	16.4	132	76	86	18.7	18	40	18	05	2	43	11	47	12	22
19	5	28	+27.3	60.0	16.3	145	84	77	19.7	19	49	19	15	3	47	12	51	13	25
20	6	33	+26.4	59.6	16.2	157	92	67	20.7	21	10	20	42	4	49	13	37	14	05
21	7	35	+23.8	59.1	16.1	169	99	56	21.7	22	35	22	15	5	49	14	08	14	30
22	8	32	+19.8	58.5	15.9	181	104	45	22.7	—		23	46	6	43	14	30	14	45
23	9	25	+14.8	58.0	15.8	193	108	34	23.7	0	00	—		7	33	14	46	14	56
24	10	15	+9.3	57.4	15.6	205	110	24	24.7	1	21	1	13	8	20	15	00	15	04
25	11	03	+3.4	56.9	15.5	218	110	16	25.7	2	39	2	37	9	04	15	12	15	11
26	11	49	−2.6	56.3	15.4	230	108	9	26.7	3	56	3	59	9	47	15	24	15	19
27	12	35	−8.3	55.9	15.2	242	103	4	27.7	5	11	5	20	10	30	15	37	15	26
28	13	21	−13.6	55.4	15.1	254	89	1	28.7	6	27	6	41	11	15	15	52	15	36
29	14	09	−18.3	55.0	15.0	267	16	0	0.0	7	42	8	02	12	01	16	10	15	49
30	14	58	−22.1	54.6	14.9	279	309	1	1.0	8	56	9	22	12	49	16	35	16	08
31	15	50	−25.0	54.3	14.8	291	294	4	2.0	10	05	10	37	13	38	17	08	16	35

MERCURY

Day	R.A.		Dec.	Diam.	Phase	Transit		5° high			
								52°		56°	
	h	m	°	"	%	h	m	h	m	h	m
1	13	09	−11.1	10	9	12	25	16	53	16	40
3	13	03	−10.0	10	5	12	11	16	45	16	33
5	12	55	−8.7	10	1	11	55	7	15	7	24
7	12	48	−7.3	10	0	11	40	6	52	7	01
9	12	40	−5.8	10	2	11	25	6	29	6	37
11	12	34	−4.4	10	6	11	12	6	08	6	15
13	12	31	−3.3	9	12	11	00	5	51	5	57
15	12	29	−2.5	9	20	10	52	5	38	5	43
17	12	30	−2.0	8	29	10	45	5	29	5	34
19	12	33	−2.0	8	39	10	41	5	25	5	30
21	12	39	−2.3	7	49	10	39	5	24	5	30
23	12	46	−2.8	7	58	10	39	5	27	5	33
25	12	55	−3.6	6	66	10	40	5	32	5	39
27	13	05	−4.6	6	73	10	43	5	40	5	47
29	13	15	−5.7	6	79	10	45	5	49	5	57
31	13	27	−6.9	6	83	10	49	5	59	6	08

VENUS

Day	R.A.		Dec.	Diam.	Phase	Transit		5° high			
								52°		56°	
	h	m	°	"	%	h	m	h	m	h	m
1	14	24	−14.5	12	86	13	44	17	48	17	30
6	14	48	−16.6	12	85	13	48	17	38	17	17
11	15	12	−18.5	13	84	13	53	17	29	17	05
16	15	36	−20.3	13	83	13	58	17	21	16	53
21	16	02	−21.9	13	81	14	03	17	15	16	42
26	16	27	−23.2	13	80	14	09	17	10	16	33
31	16	53	−24.2	14	79	14	15	17	07	16	27

MARS

Day	R.A.		Dec.	Diam.	Phase	Transit		5° high			
								52°		56°	
	h	m	°	"	%	h	m	h	m	h	m
1	13	44	−10.5	4	99	13	03	17	31	17	18
6	13	57	−11.8	4	99	12	56	17	17	17	03
11	14	10	−13.0	4	99	12	49	17	03	16	47
16	14	23	−14.2	4	99	12	43	16	50	16	32
21	14	36	−15.3	4	99	12	36	16	36	16	17
26	14	50	−16.4	4	100	12	30	16	23	16	02
31	15	04	−17.4	4	100	12	25	16	10	15	47

SUNRISE AND SUNSET

d	London 0°05' 51°30'				Bristol 2°35' 51°28'				Birmingham 1°55' 52°28'				Manchester 2°15' 53°28'				Newcastle 1°37' 54°59'				Glasgow 4°14' 55°52'				Belfast 5°56' 54°35'			
	h	m	h	m	h	m	h	m	h	m	h	m	h	m	h	m	h	m	h	m	h	m	h	m	h	m	h	m
1	6	01	17	37	6	11	17	47	6	09	17	44	6	11	17	45	6	09	17	42	6	20	17	51	6	26	17	59
2	6	03	17	35	6	13	17	45	6	11	17	42	6	13	17	43	6	11	17	39	6	22	17	49	6	28	17	56
3	6	05	17	33	6	15	17	43	6	13	17	39	6	15	17	40	6	13	17	36	6	24	17	46	6	30	17	54
4	6	06	17	31	6	16	17	41	6	14	17	37	6	16	17	38	6	15	17	34	6	26	17	44	6	32	17	52
5	6	08	17	28	6	18	17	38	6	16	17	35	6	18	17	35	6	17	17	31	6	28	17	41	6	34	17	49
6	6	10	17	26	6	20	17	36	6	18	17	33	6	20	17	33	6	19	17	29	6	30	17	38	6	36	17	47
7	6	11	17	24	6	21	17	34	6	20	17	30	6	22	17	31	6	21	17	26	6	32	17	36	6	38	17	44
8	6	13	17	22	6	23	17	32	6	21	17	28	6	24	17	28	6	23	17	24	6	34	17	33	6	40	17	42
9	6	15	17	19	6	25	17	29	6	23	17	26	6	26	17	26	6	25	17	21	6	36	17	31	6	42	17	39
10	6	16	17	17	6	26	17	27	6	25	17	23	6	27	17	24	6	27	17	19	6	38	17	28	6	43	17	37
11	6	18	17	15	6	28	17	25	6	27	17	21	6	29	17	21	6	29	17	17	6	40	17	26	6	45	17	34
12	6	20	17	13	6	30	17	23	6	28	17	19	6	31	17	19	6	31	17	14	6	42	17	23	6	47	17	32
13	6	21	17	11	6	31	17	21	6	30	17	17	6	33	17	17	6	33	17	12	6	44	17	21	6	49	17	30
14	6	23	17	09	6	33	17	19	6	32	17	14	6	35	17	14	6	35	17	09	6	46	17	18	6	51	17	27
15	6	25	17	06	6	35	17	16	6	34	17	12	6	36	17	12	6	36	17	07	6	49	17	16	6	53	17	25
16	6	26	17	04	6	36	17	14	6	35	17	10	6	38	17	10	6	38	17	04	6	51	17	13	6	55	17	22
17	6	28	17	02	6	38	17	12	6	37	17	08	6	40	17	07	6	40	17	02	6	53	17	11	6	57	17	20
18	6	30	17	00	6	40	17	10	6	39	17	06	6	42	17	05	6	42	17	00	6	55	17	08	6	59	17	18
19	6	32	16	58	6	42	17	08	6	41	17	04	6	44	17	03	6	44	16	57	6	57	17	06	7	01	17	15
20	6	33	16	56	6	43	17	06	6	42	17	01	6	46	17	01	6	46	16	55	6	59	17	03	7	03	17	13
21	6	35	16	54	6	45	17	04	6	44	16	59	6	48	16	59	6	48	16	53	7	01	17	01	7	05	17	11
22	6	37	16	52	6	47	17	02	6	46	16	57	6	50	16	56	6	50	16	50	7	03	16	59	7	07	17	09
23	6	39	16	50	6	48	17	00	6	48	16	55	6	51	16	54	6	52	16	48	7	05	16	56	7	09	17	06
24	6	40	16	48	6	50	16	58	6	50	16	53	6	53	16	52	6	54	16	46	7	07	16	54	7	11	17	04
25	6	42	16	46	6	52	16	56	6	52	16	51	6	55	16	50	6	56	16	44	7	09	16	52	7	13	17	02
26	6	44	16	44	6	54	16	54	6	53	16	49	6	57	16	48	6	59	16	41	7	11	16	49	7	15	17	00
27	6	46	16	42	6	55	16	52	6	55	16	47	6	59	16	46	7	01	16	39	7	14	16	47	7	17	16	58
28	6	47	16	40	6	57	16	50	6	57	16	45	7	01	16	44	7	03	16	37	7	16	16	45	7	19	16	55
29	6	49	16	38	6	59	16	48	6	59	16	43	7	03	16	42	7	05	16	35	7	18	16	43	7	21	16	53
30	6	51	16	36	7	01	16	46	7	01	16	41	7	05	16	40	7	07	16	33	7	20	16	40	7	23	16	51
31	6	53	16	35	7	03	16	45	7	03	16	39	7	07	16	38	7	09	16	31	7	22	16	38	7	25	16	49

JUPITER

Day	R.A.		Dec.		Transit		5° high 52°		56°	
	h	m	°	'	h	m	h	m	h	m
1	18	58.2	−23	06	18	15	21	17	20	42
11	19	01.9	−23	01	17	39	20	42	20	07
21	19	06.7	−22	54	17	05	20	09	19	34
31	19	12.6	−22	45	16	32	19	37	19	03

Diameters – equatorial 38" polar 35"

SATURN

Day	R.A.		Dec.		Transit		5° high 52°		56°	
	h	m	°	'	h	m	h	m	h	m
1	11	08.4	+7	23	10	26	4	22	4	19
11	11	12.7	+6	57	9	52	3	49	3	47
21	11	16.9	+6	33	9	16	3	16	3	14
31	11	20.6	+6	11	8	41	2	42	2	41

Diameters – equatorial 16" polar 15"
Rings – major axis 37" minor axis 2"

URANUS

Day	R.A.		Dec.		Transit		10° high 52°		56°	
	h	m	°	'	h	m	h	m	h	m
1	23	24.4	−4	43	22	40	3	12	3	01
11	23	23.1	−4	51	22	00	2	31	2	19
21	23	21.9	−4	58	21	19	1	50	1	38
31	23	21.0	−5	04	20	39	1	09	0	57

Diameter 4"

NEPTUNE

Day	R.A.		Dec.		Transit		10° high 52°		56°	
	h	m	°	'	h	m	h	m	h	m
1	21	37.0	−14	36	20	53	0	22	23	53
11	21	36.4	−14	38	20	13	23	38	23	12
21	21	36.0	−14	40	19	34	22	58	22	32
31	21	35.9	−14	41	18	54	22	18	21	53

Diameter 2"

NOVEMBER 2008

ELEVENTH MONTH, 30 DAYS. *Novem* (nine), ninth month of Roman pre-Julian calendar

1	*Saturday*	Rudolf IV, duke of Austria b. 1339 Mamie Eisenhower, US first lady d. 1979	306
2	*Sunday*	Pat Buchanan, US politician b. 1938 Peter III, king of Aragon d. 1285	307

3	*Monday*	Alfredo Stroessner, president of Paraguay b. 1912 Peter II, king of Yugoslavia d. 1970 week 44 day	308
4	*Tuesday*	Thomas Klestil, president of Austria b. 1932 Yitzhak Rabin, prime minister of Israel d. 1995	309
5	*Wednesday*	Saddam Hussein, former president of Iraq, was sentenced to death 2006	310
6	*Thursday*	Ignacy Paderewski, prime minister of Poland b. 1860 Khai Dinh, emperor of Vietnam d. 1925	311
7	*Friday*	Leon Trotsky, Russian revolutionary b. 1879 Jaja Wachuku, Nigerian statesman d. 1996	312
8	*Saturday*	Nguyen Khanh, prime minister of South Vietnam b. 1927 Vyacheslav Molotov, Soviet politician d. 1986	313
9	*Sunday*	King Edward VII b. 1841 Neville Chamberlain, British prime minister d. 1940	314

10	*Monday*	Screaming Lord Sutch, British politician b. 1940 Mustafa Kemal Ataturk, Turkish revolutionary d. 1938 week 45 day	315
11	*Tuesday*	Daniel Ortega, president of Nicaragua b. 1945 Liliuokalani, queen of Hawaii d. 1917	316
12	*Wednesday*	Sun Yat-sen, president of China b. 1866 Dolores Ibarruri, Spanish Communist leader d. 1989	317
13	*Thursday*	King Edward III b. 1312 Malcolm III, king of Scotland d. 1093	318
14	*Friday*	Prince Charles b. 1948 Miguel I, king of Portugal d. 1866	319
15	*Saturday*	Brazil became a republic when the second and last emperor, Pedro II, was deposed in a military coup 1889	320
16	*Sunday*	Oswald Mosley, British politician b. 1896 King Henry III d. 1272	321

17	*Monday*	Bernard Montgomery, British Army commander b. 1887 Lala Lajpat Raj, Indian politician d. 1928 week 46 day	322
18	*Tuesday*	Russia ratified the Kyoto Protocol on climate change 2004	323
19	*Wednesday*	King Charles I b. 1600 Indira Gandhi, prime minister of India b. 1917	324
20	*Thursday*	Wilfrid Laurier, prime minister of Canada b. 1841 Francisco Franco, prime minister of Spain d. 1975	325
21	*Friday*	Richard Durbin, US senator b. 1944 Garret Hobart, US vice-president d. 1899	326
22	*Saturday*	Charles de Gaulle, president of France b. 1890 John F. Kennedy, US president d. 1963	327
23	*Sunday*	Hjalmar Branting, prime minister of Sweden b. 1860 Sean O'Kelly, president of Ireland d. 1966	328

24	*Monday*	Zachary Taylor, US president b. 1784 Georges Clemenceau, prime minister of France d. 1929 week 47 day	329
25	*Tuesday*	Charles Kennedy, British politician b. 1959 Hastings Banda, president of Malawi d. 1997	330
26	*Wednesday*	Go-Daigo, emperor of Japan b. 1288 Isabella, queen regnant of Castile and Leon d. 1504	331
27	*Thursday*	Alexander Dubcek, leader of Czechoslovakia b. 1921 Clovis I, king of the Franks d. 511	332
28	*Friday*	Women were allowed to vote for the first time in a general election in New Zealand 1893	333
29	*Saturday*	William Tubman, president of Liberia b. 1895 Philip IV, king of France d. 1314	334
30	*Sunday*	Winston Churchill, British prime minister b. 1874 King Edmund II d. 1016	335

ASTRONOMICAL PHENOMENA

d	h	
1	08	Venus in conjunction with Moon. Venus 3°N.
2	07	Neptune at stationary point
3	22	Jupiter in conjunction with Moon. Jupiter 2°N.
21	14	Saturn in conjunction with Moon. Saturn 5°N.
21	23	Sun's longitude 240° ♐
25	17	Mercury in superior conjunction
27	16	Uranus at stationary point
27	20	Mercury in conjunction with Moon. Mercury 4°N.
27	22	Mars in conjunction with Moon. Mars 4°N.
29	04	Mars in conjunction with Mercury. Mars 0°.6N.

MINIMA OF ALGOL

d	h	d	h	d	h
3	10.5	14	21.7	26	09.0
6	07.3	17	18.5	29	05.8
9	04.1	20	15.4		
12	00.9	23	12.2		

CONSTELLATIONS

The following constellations are near their meridian at

	d	h		d	h
October	1	24	November	15	21
October	16	23	December	1	20
November	1	22	December	16	19

Ursa Major (below the Pole), Cepheus, Cassiopeia, Andromeda, Pegasus, Pisces, Aquarius and Cetus

THE MOON

Phases, Apsides and Node		d	h	m
☽	First Quarter	6	04	03
○	Full Moon	13	06	17
☾	Last Quarter	19	21	31
●	New Moon	27	16	55

	d	h	m
Apogee (405,753 km)	2	05	03
Perigee (358,961 km)	14	10	07
Apogee (406,494 km)	29	17	08

Mean longitude of ascending node on November 1, 314°

THE SUN

s.d. 16′.2

Day	Right Ascension			Dec.		Equation of time		Rise 52°		Rise 56°		Transit		Set 52°		Set 56°		Sidereal time			Transit of first point of Aries		
	h	m	s	°	′	m	s	h	m	h	m	h	m	h	m	h	m	h	m	s	h	m	s
1	14	26	12	14	29	+16	25	6	55	7	08	11	44	16	31	16	19	2	42	37	21	13	54
2	14	30	07	14	48	+16	26	6	57	7	10	11	44	16	29	16	17	2	46	34	21	09	58
3	14	34	04	15	07	+16	26	6	59	7	12	11	44	16	27	16	14	2	50	30	21	06	02
4	14	38	01	15	25	+16	26	7	01	7	14	11	44	16	26	16	12	2	54	27	21	02	06
5	14	41	59	15	43	+16	25	7	03	7	16	11	44	16	24	16	10	2	58	23	20	58	10
6	14	45	57	16	02	+16	22	7	04	7	18	11	44	16	22	16	08	3	02	20	20	54	14
7	14	49	57	16	19	+16	20	7	06	7	20	11	44	16	21	16	06	3	06	16	20	50	18
8	14	53	57	16	37	+16	16	7	08	7	23	11	44	16	19	16	04	3	10	13	20	46	22
9	14	57	58	16	54	+16	11	7	10	7	25	11	44	16	17	16	02	3	14	09	20	42	26
10	15	02	00	17	11	+16	06	7	12	7	27	11	44	16	16	16	00	3	18	06	20	38	31
11	15	06	03	17	28	+16	00	7	13	7	29	11	44	16	14	15	59	3	22	03	20	34	35
12	15	10	07	17	44	+15	52	7	15	7	31	11	44	16	13	15	57	3	25	59	20	30	39
13	15	14	11	18	00	+15	45	7	17	7	33	11	44	16	11	15	55	3	29	56	20	26	43
14	15	18	16	18	16	+15	36	7	19	7	35	11	44	16	10	15	53	3	33	52	20	22	47
15	15	22	23	18	31	+15	26	7	20	7	37	11	45	16	08	15	52	3	37	49	20	18	51
16	15	26	30	18	46	+15	16	7	22	7	39	11	45	16	07	15	50	3	41	45	20	14	55
17	15	30	38	19	01	+15	04	7	24	7	41	11	45	16	06	15	48	3	45	42	20	10	59
18	15	34	46	19	16	+14	52	7	26	7	43	11	45	16	04	15	47	3	49	38	20	07	03
19	15	38	56	19	30	+14	39	7	27	7	45	11	45	16	03	15	45	3	53	35	20	03	07
20	15	43	06	19	43	+14	25	7	29	7	47	11	46	16	02	15	44	3	57	32	19	59	11
21	15	47	18	19	57	+14	10	7	31	7	49	11	46	16	01	15	42	4	01	28	19	55	15
22	15	51	30	20	10	+13	55	7	32	7	51	11	46	16	00	15	41	4	05	25	19	51	20
23	15	55	43	20	22	+13	39	7	34	7	53	11	47	15	59	15	39	4	09	21	19	47	24
24	15	59	56	20	35	+13	22	7	35	7	55	11	47	15	58	15	38	4	13	18	19	43	28
25	16	04	11	20	47	+13	04	7	37	7	57	11	47	15	57	15	37	4	17	14	19	39	32
26	16	08	26	20	58	+12	45	7	39	7	59	11	47	15	56	15	36	4	21	11	19	35	36
27	16	12	42	21	09	+12	25	7	40	8	00	11	48	15	55	15	35	4	25	07	19	31	40
28	16	16	59	21	20	+12	05	7	42	8	02	11	48	15	54	15	33	4	29	04	19	27	44
29	16	21	16	21	30	+11	44	7	43	8	04	11	48	15	53	15	32	4	33	01	19	23	48
30	16	25	34	21	40	+11	23	7	45	8	06	11	49	15	53	15	32	4	36	57	19	19	52

DURATION OF TWILIGHT (in minutes)

Latitude	52°	56°	52°	56°	52°	56°	52°	56°
	1 November		11 November		21 November		31 November	
Civil	36	40	37	41	38	43	40	45
Nautical	75	84	78	87	80	90	82	93
Astronomical	115	127	117	130	120	134	123	138

THE NIGHT SKY

Mercury is unsuitably placed for observation throughout the month.

Venus continues to be visible as a brilliant object for a short time after sunset, low above the south-western horizon, magnitude −4.1. The thin crescent Moon, only 3 days old, passes 3 degrees south of the planet on the 1st. By the end of the month observers in England will notice that it sets about two hours after sunset. Observers in Scotland should be able to detect the planet for the first time since February.

Mars continues to be unsuitably placed for observation.

Jupiter, magnitude −2.1, is still visible low in the south-western sky in the early evening, though by the end of the month it is lost to view within two hours after sunset. During the evening of the 3rd the waxing crescent Moon passes 3 degrees south of the planet. Venus has been moving rapidly outwards from the Sun and by the end of the month will again be seen about 2 degrees south of Jupiter.

Saturn, magnitude +0.9, is still visible as a morning object in the south-eastern quadrant of the sky. By the end of the month it may be seen rising above the eastern horizon shortly after midnight.

THE MOON

Day	R.A. h	R.A. m	Dec. °	Hor. Par. '	Semi-diam. '	Sun's Co-Long. °	PA. of Br. Limb °	Ph. %	Age d	Rise 52° h	Rise 52° m	Rise 56° h	Rise 56° m	Transit h	Transit m	Set 52° h	Set 52° m	Set 56° h	Set 56° m
1	16	42	−26.7	54.1	14.7	303	284	9	3.0	11	06	11	41	14	29	17	51	17	16
2	17	35	−27.1	54.0	14.7	315	276	15	4.0	11	56	12	30	15	20	18	46	18	12
3	18	28	−26.4	54.1	14.7	328	269	22	5.0	12	34	13	04	16	10	19	51	19	22
4	19	20	−24.4	54.3	14.8	340	263	30	6.0	13	02	13	26	16	58	21	02	20	38
5	20	10	−21.3	54.6	14.9	352	258	39	7.0	13	23	13	42	17	44	22	16	21	58
6	20	58	−17.3	55.1	15.0	4	254	48	8.0	13	40	13	53	18	29	23	31	23	19
7	21	45	−12.5	55.8	15.2	16	251	58	9.0	13	54	14	02	19	13	—		—	
8	22	32	−7.1	56.6	15.4	28	249	68	10.0	14	07	14	10	19	58	0	47	0	41
9	23	19	−1.1	57.6	15.7	41	249	77	11.0	14	19	14	17	20	43	2	05	2	04
10	0	08	+5.0	58.5	15.9	53	250	86	12.0	14	33	14	26	21	32	3	26	3	31
11	0	59	+11.2	59.4	16.2	65	255	93	13.0	14	50	14	37	22	24	4	51	5	02
12	1	54	+16.9	60.2	16.4	77	265	98	14.0	15	12	14	52	23	22	6	21	6	39
13	2	53	+21.8	60.8	16.6	89	307	100	15.0	15	43	15	16	—		7	54	8	20
14	3	57	+25.3	61.1	16.6	101	54	99	16.0	16	28	15	55	0	24	9	22	9	55
15	5	04	+27.0	61.0	16.6	113	76	95	17.0	17	32	16	58	1	30	10	37	11	11
16	6	11	+26.7	60.7	16.5	126	87	89	18.0	18	52	18	22	2	36	11	31	12	02
17	7	16	+24.5	60.2	16.4	138	96	81	19.0	20	20	19	57	3	39	12	08	12	32
18	8	17	+20.7	59.5	16.2	150	102	71	20.0	21	47	21	31	4	37	12	34	12	51
19	9	12	+15.9	58.7	16.0	162	107	60	21.0	23	10	23	01	5	30	12	52	13	03
20	10	04	+10.3	57.9	15.8	174	110	49	22.0	—		—		6	18	13	07	13	13
21	10	52	+4.5	57.1	15.6	186	112	38	23.0	0	30	0	26	7	03	13	19	13	20
22	11	38	−1.4	56.4	15.4	198	112	29	24.0	1	46	1	48	7	46	13	32	13	28
23	12	24	−7.1	55.8	15.2	211	110	20	25.0	3	01	3	08	8	29	13	44	13	35
24	13	10	−12.4	55.3	15.1	223	107	13	26.0	4	15	4	28	9	13	13	58	13	44
25	13	57	−17.2	54.9	15.0	235	102	7	27.0	5	30	5	48	9	58	14	16	13	56
26	14	45	−21.2	54.5	14.9	247	93	3	28.0	6	43	7	08	10	45	14	38	14	13
27	15	36	−24.3	54.3	14.8	259	72	1	29.0	7	54	8	24	11	33	15	08	14	37
28	16	28	−26.3	54.1	14.7	272	333	0	0.3	8	58	9	32	12	24	15	48	15	14
29	17	21	−27.0	54.0	14.7	284	289	2	1.3	9	51	10	26	13	15	16	40	16	05
30	18	14	−26.5	53.9	14.7	296	275	5	2.3	10	33	11	04	14	05	17	42	17	11

MERCURY

Day	R.A. h	R.A. m	Dec. °	Diam. "	Phase %	Transit h	Transit m	5° high 52° h	5° high 52° m	5° high 56° h	5° high 56° m
1	13	32	−7.6	6	85	10	51	6	04	6	14
3	13	44	−8.8	5	89	10	55	6	15	6	27
5	13	56	−10.1	5	91	10	59	6	27	6	40
7	14	08	−11.4	5	94	11	03	6	39	6	53
9	14	20	−12.7	5	95	11	07	6	51	7	06
11	14	33	−13.9	5	97	11	12	7	03	7	20
13	14	45	−15.1	5	98	11	16	7	15	7	34
15	14	58	−16.3	5	98	11	21	7	28	7	48
17	15	11	−17.4	5	99	11	26	7	40	8	03
19	15	23	−18.4	5	99	11	31	7	52	8	17
21	15	36	−19.4	5	100	11	36	8	05	8	31
23	15	49	−20.3	5	100	11	41	8	17	8	45
25	16	02	−21.2	5	100	11	46	8	29	8	59
27	16	15	−22.0	5	100	11	51	8	40	9	13
29	16	28	−22.7	5	100	11	57	8	52	9	27
31	16	42	−23.4	5	100	12	02	15	01	14	24

VENUS

Day	R.A. h	R.A. m	Dec. °	Diam. "	Phase %	Transit h	Transit m	5° high 52° h	5° high 52° m	5° high 56° h	5° high 56° m
1	16	58	−24.4	14	79	14	17	17	06	16	26
6	17	25	−25.1	14	77	14	23	17	07	16	23
11	17	51	−25.5	15	76	14	30	17	10	16	24
16	18	18	−25.6	15	74	14	37	17	16	16	30
21	18	44	−25.3	16	73	14	44	17	25	16	40
26	19	10	−24.8	16	71	14	50	17	37	16	55
31	19	36	−24.0	17	70	14	56	17	51	17	13

MARS

Day	R.A. h	R.A. m	Dec. °	Diam. "	Phase %	Transit h	Transit m	5° high 52° h	5° high 52° m	5° high 56° h	5° high 56° m
1	15	07	−17.6	4	100	12	23	16	07	15	45
6	15	21	−18.6	4	100	12	18	15	55	15	30
11	15	35	−19.5	4	100	12	13	15	43	15	17
16	15	50	−20.4	4	100	12	08	15	32	15	04
21	16	05	−21.1	4	100	12	03	15	21	14	51
26	16	20	−21.8	4	100	11	59	15	11	14	39
31	16	36	−22.4	4	100	11	54	15	02	14	28

SUNRISE AND SUNSET

	London				Bristol				Birmingham				Manchester				Newcastle				Glasgow				Belfast			
	0°05′		51°30′		2°35′		51°28′		1°55′		52°28′		2°15′		53°28′		1°37′		54°59′		4°14′		55°52′		5°56′		54°35′	
d	h	m	h	m	h	m	h	m	h	m	h	m	h	m	h	m	h	m	h	m	h	m	h	m	h	m	h	m
1	6	54	16	33	7	04	16	43	7	04	16	37	7	09	16	36	7	11	16	29	7	24	16	36	7	27	16	47
2	6	56	16	31	7	06	16	41	7	06	16	36	7	11	16	34	7	13	16	26	7	26	16	34	7	29	16	45
3	6	58	16	29	7	08	16	39	7	08	16	34	7	12	16	32	7	15	16	24	7	28	16	32	7	31	16	43
4	7	00	16	27	7	10	16	38	7	10	16	32	7	14	16	30	7	17	16	22	7	30	16	30	7	33	16	41
5	7	01	16	26	7	11	16	36	7	12	16	30	7	16	16	28	7	19	16	20	7	33	16	28	7	35	16	39
6	7	03	16	24	7	13	16	34	7	14	16	28	7	18	16	26	7	21	16	19	7	35	16	26	7	37	16	37
7	7	05	16	22	7	15	16	33	7	15	16	27	7	20	16	25	7	23	16	17	7	37	16	24	7	39	16	35
8	7	07	16	21	7	17	16	31	7	17	16	25	7	22	16	23	7	25	16	15	7	39	16	22	7	41	16	34
9	7	08	16	19	7	18	16	29	7	19	16	23	7	24	16	21	7	27	16	13	7	41	16	20	7	43	16	32
10	7	10	16	18	7	20	16	28	7	21	16	22	7	26	16	19	7	29	16	11	7	43	16	18	7	45	16	30
11	7	12	16	16	7	22	16	26	7	23	16	20	7	28	16	18	7	31	16	09	7	45	16	16	7	47	16	28
12	7	14	16	15	7	24	16	25	7	24	16	19	7	30	16	16	7	33	16	08	7	47	16	14	7	49	16	26
13	7	15	16	13	7	25	16	23	7	26	16	17	7	31	16	15	7	35	16	06	7	49	16	12	7	51	16	25
14	7	17	16	12	7	27	16	22	7	28	16	16	7	33	16	13	7	37	16	04	7	51	16	11	7	53	16	23
15	7	19	16	11	7	29	16	21	7	30	16	14	7	35	16	12	7	39	16	03	7	53	16	09	7	55	16	22
16	7	21	16	09	7	30	16	19	7	32	16	13	7	37	16	10	7	41	16	01	7	56	16	07	7	56	16	20
17	7	22	16	08	7	32	16	18	7	33	16	11	7	39	16	09	7	43	15	59	7	58	16	06	7	58	16	19
18	7	24	16	07	7	34	16	17	7	35	16	10	7	41	16	07	7	45	15	58	8	00	16	04	8	00	16	17
19	7	26	16	05	7	35	16	16	7	37	16	09	7	42	16	06	7	47	15	57	8	02	16	03	8	02	16	16
20	7	27	16	04	7	37	16	14	7	39	16	08	7	44	16	05	7	49	15	55	8	04	16	01	8	04	16	14
21	7	29	16	03	7	39	16	13	7	40	16	06	7	46	16	03	7	51	15	54	8	05	16	00	8	06	16	13
22	7	30	16	02	7	40	16	12	7	42	16	05	7	48	16	02	7	52	15	52	8	07	15	58	8	08	16	12
23	7	32	16	01	7	42	16	11	7	44	16	04	7	49	16	01	7	54	15	51	8	09	15	57	8	10	16	10
24	7	34	16	00	7	44	16	10	7	45	16	03	7	51	16	00	7	56	15	50	8	11	15	56	8	11	16	09
25	7	35	15	59	7	45	16	09	7	47	16	02	7	53	15	59	7	58	15	49	8	13	15	55	8	13	16	08
26	7	37	15	58	7	47	16	08	7	48	16	01	7	54	15	58	8	00	15	48	8	15	15	53	8	15	16	07
27	7	38	15	57	7	48	16	08	7	50	16	00	7	56	15	57	8	01	15	47	8	17	15	52	8	16	16	06
28	7	40	15	57	7	50	16	07	7	52	16	00	7	58	15	56	8	03	15	46	8	18	15	51	8	18	16	05
29	7	41	15	56	7	51	16	06	7	53	15	59	7	59	15	55	8	05	15	45	8	20	15	50	8	20	16	04
30	7	43	15	55	7	53	16	05	7	54	15	58	8	01	15	54	8	06	15	44	8	22	15	49	8	21	16	03

JUPITER

Day	R.A.		Dec.		Transit		5° high			
							52°		56°	
	h	m	°	′	h	m	h	m	h	m
1	19	13.2	−22	44	16	28	19	34	18	59
11	19	20.1	−22	32	15	56	19	03	18	29
21	19	27.8	−22	17	15	24	18	33	18	01
31	19	36.1	−21	59	14	53	18	05	17	33

Diameters – equatorial 35″ polar 33″

SATURN

Day	R.A.		Dec.		Transit		5° high			
							52°		56°	
	h	m	°	′	h	m	h	m	h	m
1	11	21.0	+6	09	8	37	2	39	2	37
11	11	24.4	+5	50	8	01	2	05	2	03
21	11	27.3	+5	34	7	25	1	30	1	28
31	11	29.6	+5	21	6	48	0	54	0	53

Diameters – equatorial 17″ polar 15″
Rings– major axis 39″ minor axis 1″

URANUS

Day	R.A.		Dec.		Transit		10° high			
							52°		56°	
	h	m	°	′	h	m	h	m	h	m
1	23	20.9	−5	04	20	35	1	05	0	53
11	23	20.3	−5	08	19	55	0	24	0	13
21	23	19.9	−5	10	19	15	23	41	23	29
31	23	19.8	−5	10	18	36	23	01	22	49

Diameter 4″

NEPTUNE

Day	R.A.		Dec.		Transit		10° high			
							52°		56°	
	h	m	°	′	h	m	h	m	h	m
1	21	35.9	−14	41	18	50	22	14	21	49
11	21	35.9	−14	41	18	11	21	35	21	10
21	21	36.2	−14	39	17	32	20	56	20	31
31	21	36.8	−14	36	16	53	20	18	19	53

Diameter 2″

DECEMBER 2008

TWELFTH MONTH, 31 DAYS. *Decem* (ten), tenth month of Roman pre-Julian calendar

1	Monday	Sebastian Pinera, Chilean politician b. 1949 King Henry I d. 1135	week 48 day 336
2	Tuesday	Ibrahim Rugova, president of Kosovo b. 1944 Hernan Cortés, Spanish conquistador d. 1547	337
3	Wednesday	Mikhail Gorbachev and George Bush announced the end of the Cold War at the Malta summit 1989	338
4	Thursday	Barbara, queen consort of Spain b. 1711 Robert Jenkinson, British prime minister d. 1828	339
5	Friday	Martin Van Buren, US president b. 1782 Roy Welensky, African politician d. 1991	340
6	Saturday	King Henry VI b. 1421 Joao Goulart, president of Brazil d. 1976	341
7	Sunday	Joseph Cook, prime minister of Australia b. 1860 Felix Houphouet-Boigny, president of Côte d'Ivoire d. 1993	342

8	Monday	Francis I, Holy Roman emperor b. 1708 Sarit Dhanarajata, prime minister of Thailand d. 1963	week 49 day 343
9	Tuesday	Carlo Azeglio Ciampi, president of Italy b. 1920 Edward Hyde, English statesman d. 1674	344
10	Wednesday	James I, king of Scotland b. 1394 Franjo Tudman, president of Croatia d. 1999	345
11	Thursday	Aquilino Pimentel Jr, Philippine politician b. 1933 Llywelyn the Last, prince of Wales d. 1282	346
12	Friday	Kenya became independent from the United Kingdom 1963	347
13	Saturday	B. J. Vorster, prime minister of South Africa b. 1915 Hannes Hafstein, prime minister of Iceland d. 1922	348
14	Sunday	King George VI b. 1895 George Washington, US president d. 1799	349

15	Monday	Nero, emperor of Rome b. AD 37 Sitting Bull, Native American leader d. 1890	week 50 day 350
16	Tuesday	The Boston Tea Party in protest against taxation brought in by the British parliament took place 1773	351
17	Wednesday	Mackenzie King, prime minister of Canada b. 1874 Harold Holt, prime minister of Australia d. 1967	352
18	Thursday	Christina, queen of Sweden b. 1626 Alfonso II, king of Naples d. 1495	353
19	Friday	Margaret Thatcher signed an agreement 1984 to return Hong Kong to China in 1997	354
20	Saturday	Robert Menzies, prime minister of Australia b. 1894 Émile Loubet, president of France d. 1929	355
21	Sunday	Mikheil Saakashvili, president of Georgia b. 1967 Saparmurat Niyazov, president of Turkmenistan d. 2006	356

22	Monday	Frank B. Kellogg, US politician b. 1856 Desmond Hoyte, president of Guyana d. 2002	week 51 day 357
23	Tuesday	Wesley Clark, NATO military officer b. 1944 Hideki Tojo, prime minister of Japan d. 1948	358
24	Wednesday	Hamid Karzai, president of Afghanistan b. 1957 Karl Dünitz, president of Germany d. 1980	359
25	Thursday	Anwar Sadat, president of Egypt b. 1918 Nicolae Ceausescu, president of Romania d. 1989	360
26	Friday	José Ramos Horta, prime minister of East Timor b. 1949 Harry S. Truman, US president d. 1972	361
27	Saturday	Ernesto Zedillo, president of Mexico b. 1951 Hafizullah Amin, president of Afghanistan d. 1979	362
28	Sunday	Milton Obote, president of Uganda b. 1924 Queen Mary II d. 1694	363

29	Monday	William Gladstone, British prime minister b. 1809 Harold Macmillan, British prime minister d. 1986	week 52 day 364
30	Tuesday	Omar Bongo, president of Gabon b. 1935 Saddam Hussein, president of Iraq d. 2006	365
31	Wednesday	Bonnie Prince Charlie, claimant to the English throne b. 1720 Léon Gambetta, French statesman d. 1882	366

ASTRONOMICAL PHENOMENA

d   h
1   09   Jupiter in conjunction with Venus. Jupiter 2°N.
1   15   Jupiter in conjunction with Moon. Jupiter 1°N.
1   16   Venus in conjunction with Moon. Venus 0°.8S.
5   22   Mars in conjunction
18 23   Saturn in conjunction with Moon. Saturn 5°N.
21 12   Sun's longitude 270° ♑
22 09   Pluto in conjunction
26 23   Mars in conjunction with Moon. Mars 3°N.
29 04   Mercury in conjunction with Moon. Mercury 0°.6S.
29 09   Jupiter in conjunction with Moon. Jupiter 0°.6N.
31 12   Jupiter in conjunction with Mercury. Jupiter 1°N.
31 18   Saturn at stationary point
31 19   Venus in conjunction with Moon. Venus 3°S.

MINIMA OF ALGOL

d	h	d	h	d	h
2	02.6	13	13.9	25	01.2
4	23.4	16	10.7	27	22.0
7	20.3	19	07.5	30	18.8
10	17.1	22	04.4		

CONSTELLATIONS

The following constellations are near their meridian at

	d	h		d	h
November	1	24	January	1	20
December	16	21	December	1	22
November	15	23	January	16	19

Ursa Major (below the Pole), Ursa Minor (below the Pole), Cassiopeia, Andromeda, Perseus, Triangulum, Aries, Taurus, Cetus and Eridanus

THE MOON

Phases, Apsides and Node	d	h	m
☽ First Quarter	5	21	26
○ Full Moon	12	16	37
☾ Last Quarter	19	10	29
● New Moon	27	12	22

Perigee (356,564 km)	12	21	45
Apogee (406,596 km)	26	18	03

Mean longitude of ascending node on December 1, 313°

THE SUN

s.d. 16′.3

Day	Right Ascension			Dec.		Equation of time		Rise 52°		Rise 56°		Transit		Set 52°		Set 56°		Sidereal time			Transit of first point of Aries		
	h	m	s	°	′	m	s	h	m	h	m	h	m	h	m	h	m	h	m	s	h	m	s
1	16	29	53	21	49	+11	01	7	46	8	07	11	49	15	52	15	31	4	40	54	19	15	56
2	16	34	12	21	59	+10	38	7	47	8	09	11	50	15	51	15	30	4	44	50	19	12	00
3	16	38	32	22	07	+10	14	7	49	8	11	11	50	15	51	15	29	4	48	47	19	08	05
4	16	42	53	22	15	+9	50	7	50	8	12	11	50	15	50	15	28	4	52	43	19	04	09
5	16	47	14	22	23	+9	26	7	51	8	14	11	51	15	50	15	28	4	56	40	19	00	13
6	16	51	36	22	31	+9	01	7	53	8	15	11	51	15	49	15	27	5	00	37	18	56	17
7	16	55	58	22	37	+8	35	7	54	8	16	11	52	15	49	15	27	5	04	33	18	52	21
8	17	00	21	22	44	+8	09	7	55	8	18	11	52	15	49	15	26	5	08	30	18	48	25
9	17	04	44	22	50	+7	43	7	56	8	19	11	53	15	49	15	26	5	12	26	18	44	29
10	17	09	07	22	55	+7	16	7	57	8	20	11	53	15	48	15	25	5	16	23	18	40	33
11	17	13	31	23	01	+6	48	7	58	8	21	11	53	15	48	15	25	5	20	19	18	36	37
12	17	17	55	23	05	+6	21	7	59	8	23	11	54	15	48	15	25	5	24	16	18	32	41
13	17	22	20	23	09	+5	53	8	00	8	24	11	54	15	48	15	25	5	28	12	18	28	45
14	17	26	45	23	13	+5	24	8	01	8	25	11	55	15	48	15	25	5	32	09	18	24	50
15	17	31	10	23	16	+4	55	8	02	8	26	11	55	15	49	15	25	5	36	06	18	20	54
16	17	35	36	23	19	+4	26	8	03	8	26	11	56	15	49	15	25	5	40	02	18	16	58
17	17	40	01	23	22	+3	57	8	04	8	27	11	56	15	49	15	25	5	43	59	18	13	02
18	17	44	27	23	24	+3	28	8	04	8	28	11	57	15	49	15	26	5	47	55	18	09	06
19	17	48	53	23	25	+2	58	8	05	8	29	11	57	15	50	15	26	5	51	52	18	05	10
20	17	53	20	23	26	+2	29	8	05	8	29	11	58	15	50	15	26	5	55	48	18	01	14
21	17	57	46	23	26	+1	59	8	06	8	30	11	58	15	51	15	27	5	59	45	17	57	18
22	18	02	13	23	26	+1	29	8	06	8	30	11	59	15	51	15	27	6	03	41	17	53	22
23	18	06	39	23	26	+0	59	8	07	8	31	11	59	15	52	15	28	6	07	38	17	49	26
24	18	11	06	23	25	+0	29	8	07	8	31	12	00	15	52	15	29	6	11	35	17	45	30
25	18	15	32	23	24	−0	01	8	08	8	31	12	00	15	53	15	29	6	15	31	17	41	34
26	18	19	58	23	22	−0	31	8	08	8	31	12	01	15	54	15	30	6	19	28	17	37	39
27	18	24	25	23	19	−1	00	8	08	8	32	12	01	15	55	15	31	6	23	24	17	33	43
28	18	28	51	23	16	−1	30	8	08	8	32	12	02	15	55	15	32	6	27	21	17	29	47
29	18	33	17	23	13	−1	59	8	08	8	32	12	02	15	56	15	33	6	31	17	17	25	51
30	18	37	42	23	09	−2	28	8	08	8	32	12	03	15	57	15	34	6	35	14	17	21	55
31	18	42	08	23	05	−2	57	8	08	8	31	12	03	15	58	15	35	6	39	10	17	17	59

DURATION OF TWILIGHT (in minutes)

Latitude	52°	56°	52°	56°	52°	56°	52°	56°
	1 December		11 December		21 December		31 December	
Civil	40	45	41	47	41	47	41	47
Nautical	82	93	84	96	85	97	84	96
Astronomical	123	138	125	141	126	142	125	141

THE NIGHT SKY

Mercury remains too close to the Sun for observation throughout December.

Venus, magnitude −4.2, is a magnificent object in the early evening sky, low above the south-western horizon. Shortly before sunset on the evening of the 1st the waxing crescent Moon will blot out the light of the planet to naked-eye observers, while observers with telescopes will see an actual occultation. By the end of the month Venus is visible for over three hours after sunset.

Mars passes through conjunction on the 5th and therefore remains unsuitably placed for observation.

Jupiter, magnitude −2.0, is still a bright object in the south-western sky in the early evening, though by the end of the month it is lost to view before the end of evening civil twilight. On the 1st the crescent Moon, barely 4 days old, passes 2 degrees south of the planet. A similar situation occurs on the evenings of the 28th and 29th though this will be a much more difficult event to observe in twilight conditions. Jupiter remains in Sagittarius throughout the month, entering Capricornus in the New Year. Venus is now moving away from Jupiter during the month and by the end of the year is about 20 degrees east of Jupiter.

Saturn, continues to be visible as a morning object and by mid-December may be seen above the eastern horizon before midnight.

Meteors. The maximum of the well-known Geminid meteor shower occurs on the 13th, and will be best seen on the evening of that day, though the full Moon will cause serious interference.

THE MOON

Day	R.A.		Dec.	Hor. Par.	Semi-diam.	Sun's Co-Long.	PA. of Br. Limb	Ph.	Age	Rise 52°		Rise 56°		Transit		Set 52°		Set 56°	
	h	m	°	'	'	°	°	%	d	h	m	h	m	h	m	h	m	h	m
1	19	06	−24.8	54.0	14.7	308	267	9	3.3	11	04	11	30	14	54	18	51	18	25
2	19	56	−22.1	54.2	14.8	320	260	16	4.3	11	27	11	47	15	40	20	03	19	44
3	20	44	−18.3	54.6	14.9	333	255	23	5.3	11	45	11	59	16	25	21	16	21	03
4	21	31	−13.8	55.0	15.0	345	251	32	6.3	11	59	12	09	17	08	22	30	22	22
5	22	17	−8.7	55.7	15.2	357	249	41	7.3	12	12	12	17	17	51	23	44	23	42
6	23	02	−3.0	56.4	15.4	9	247	51	8.3	12	24	12	24	18	34	—	—	—	—
7	23	48	+2.9	57.3	15.6	21	247	62	9.3	12	37	12	32	19	19	1	01	1	03
8	0	37	+8.8	58.3	15.9	33	249	72	10.3	12	51	12	41	20	08	2	21	2	29
9	1	29	+14.6	59.2	16.1	45	252	81	11.3	13	10	12	54	21	02	3	46	4	01
10	2	25	+19.8	60.1	16.4	58	258	89	12.3	13	36	13	12	22	01	5	16	5	38
11	3	26	+23.9	60.9	16.6	70	267	96	13.3	14	13	13	43	23	06	6	47	7	16
12	4	32	+26.4	61.4	16.7	82	285	99	14.3	15	08	14	33	—		8	10	8	44
13	5	41	+27.0	61.5	16.8	94	49	100	15.3	16	22	15	50	0	13	9	16	9	49
14	6	49	+25.5	61.3	16.7	106	87	97	16.3	17	51	17	25	1	20	10	02	10	29
15	7	53	+22.2	60.8	16.6	118	99	92	17.3	19	22	19	04	2	23	10	34	10	54
16	8	53	+17.5	60.0	16.4	130	106	85	18.3	20	51	20	39	3	20	10	56	11	09
17	9	47	+11.9	59.1	16.1	143	110	75	19.3	22	14	22	09	4	12	11	12	11	20
18	10	38	+6.0	58.2	15.8	155	113	65	20.3	23	34	23	34	4	59	11	26	11	28
19	11	26	−0.1	57.2	15.6	167	114	55	21.3	—		—		5	44	11	39	11	36
20	12	12	−5.9	56.4	15.4	179	113	44	22.3	0	50	0	56	6	28	11	51	11	44
21	12	58	−11.4	55.7	15.2	191	111	34	23.3	2	05	2	16	7	11	12	05	11	52
22	13	45	−16.3	55.1	15.0	203	108	25	24.3	3	20	3	36	7	56	12	21	12	03
23	14	33	−20.5	54.6	14.9	215	104	18	25.3	4	34	4	56	8	42	12	42	12	18
24	15	23	−23.7	54.3	14.8	228	98	11	26.3	5	45	6	13	9	30	13	09	12	40
25	16	14	−25.9	54.1	14.7	240	91	6	27.3	6	51	7	24	10	20	13	46	13	12
26	17	07	−27.0	54.0	14.7	252	82	2	28.3	7	47	8	22	11	11	14	34	13	59
27	18	00	−26.7	53.9	14.7	264	59	0	29.3	8	32	9	05	12	01	15	33	15	01
28	18	53	−25.3	54.0	14.7	276	290	0	0.5	9	06	9	34	12	50	16	41	16	14
29	19	43	−22.8	54.1	14.8	289	265	2	1.5	9	32	9	54	13	38	17	53	17	32
30	20	32	−19.2	54.4	14.8	301	256	5	2.5	9	51	10	07	14	23	19	06	18	51
31	21	19	−14.8	54.7	14.9	313	251	11	3.5	10	06	10	17	15	06	20	19	20	09

MERCURY

Day	R.A.		Dec.	Diam.	Phase	Transit		5° high 52°		5° high 56°	
	h	m	°	"	%	h	m	h	m	h	m
1	16	42	−23.4	5	100	12	02	15	01	14	24
3	16	55	−23.9	5	99	12	08	15	02	14	22
5	17	09	−24.4	5	99	12	14	15	03	14	22
7	17	23	−24.8	5	99	12	20	15	05	14	22
9	17	36	−25.1	5	98	12	25	15	08	14	24
11	17	50	−25.3	5	97	12	31	15	12	14	27
13	18	04	−25.5	5	96	12	37	15	17	14	31
15	18	18	−25.5	5	95	12	43	15	23	14	37
17	18	32	−25.4	5	94	12	49	15	30	14	45
19	18	45	−25.3	5	93	12	55	15	38	14	54
21	18	59	−25.0	5	91	13	01	15	47	15	04
23	19	13	−24.6	5	89	13	07	15	57	15	16
25	19	26	−24.1	6	86	13	12	16	07	15	28
27	19	39	−23.6	6	83	13	17	16	17	15	40
29	19	51	−22.9	6	79	13	21	16	27	15	53
31	20	03	−22.2	6	74	13	24	16	37	16	05

VENUS

Day	R.A.		Dec.	Diam.	Phase	Transit		5° high 52°		5° high 56°	
	h	m	°	"	%	h	m	h	m	h	m
1	19	36	−24.0	17	70	14	56	17	51	17	13
6	20	01	−23.0	17	68	15	01	18	07	17	32
11	20	26	−21.6	18	66	15	06	18	23	17	52
16	20	49	−20.1	18	64	15	10	18	39	18	12
21	21	12	−18.3	19	62	15	13	18	55	18	32
26	21	34	−16.3	20	60	15	15	19	11	18	51
31	21	56	−14.3	21	58	15	17	19	27	19	09

MARS

Day	R.A.		Dec.	Diam.	Phase	Transit		5° high 52°		5° high 56°	
	h	m	°	"	%	h	m	h	m	h	m
1	16	36	−22.4	4	100	11	54	8	47	9	20
6	16	51	−23.0	4	100	11	50	8	47	9	22
11	17	07	−23.4	4	100	11	46	8	47	9	24
16	17	23	−23.7	4	100	11	43	8	46	9	24
21	17	39	−24.0	4	100	11	39	8	45	9	24
26	17	56	−24.1	4	100	11	36	8	43	9	22
31	18	12	−24.1	4	100	11	33	8	40	9	19

SUNRISE AND SUNSET

	London 0°05'	51°30'	Bristol 2°35'	51°28'	Birmingham 1°55'	52°28'	Manchester 2°15'	53°28'	Newcastle 1°37'	54°59'	Glasgow 4°14'	55°52'	Belfast 5°56'	54°35'
d	h m	h m	h m	h m	h m	h m	h m	h m	h m	h m	h m	h m	h m	h m
1	7 44	15 55	7 54	16 05	7 56	15 57	8 02	15 54	8 08	15 43	8 24	15 48	8 23	16 03
2	7 45	15 54	7 55	16 04	7 57	15 57	8 04	15 53	8 09	15 42	8 25	15 47	8 24	16 02
3	7 47	15 53	7 57	16 04	7 59	15 56	8 05	15 52	8 11	15 42	8 27	15 47	8 26	16 01
4	7 48	15 53	7 58	16 03	8 00	15 56	8 07	15 52	8 12	15 41	8 28	15 46	8 27	16 00
5	7 49	15 53	7 59	16 03	8 01	15 55	8 08	15 51	8 14	15 40	8 30	15 45	8 29	16 00
6	7 51	15 52	8 00	16 02	8 03	15 55	8 09	15 51	8 15	15 40	8 31	15 45	8 30	15 59
7	7 52	15 52	8 02	16 02	8 04	15 54	8 10	15 50	8 17	15 39	8 32	15 44	8 31	15 59
8	7 53	15 52	8 03	16 02	8 05	15 54	8 12	15 50	8 18	15 39	8 34	15 44	8 33	15 59
9	7 54	15 51	8 04	16 02	8 06	15 54	8 13	15 50	8 19	15 39	8 35	15 44	8 34	15 58
10	7 55	15 51	8 05	16 01	8 07	15 54	8 14	15 50	8 20	15 38	8 36	15 43	8 35	15 58
11	7 56	15 51	8 06	16 01	8 08	15 54	8 15	15 50	8 21	15 38	8 38	15 43	8 36	15 58
12	7 57	15 51	8 07	16 01	8 09	15 54	8 16	15 49	8 23	15 38	8 39	15 43	8 37	15 58
13	7 58	15 51	8 08	16 01	8 10	15 54	8 17	15 49	8 24	15 38	8 40	15 43	8 38	15 58
14	7 59	15 51	8 09	16 01	8 11	15 54	8 18	15 49	8 25	15 38	8 41	15 43	8 39	15 58
15	8 00	15 51	8 10	16 02	8 12	15 54	8 19	15 50	8 25	15 38	8 42	15 43	8 40	15 58
16	8 01	15 52	8 10	16 02	8 13	15 54	8 20	15 50	8 26	15 38	8 42	15 43	8 41	15 58
17	8 01	15 52	8 11	16 02	8 14	15 54	8 21	15 50	8 27	15 38	8 43	15 43	8 42	15 58
18	8 02	15 52	8 12	16 02	8 14	15 54	8 21	15 50	8 28	15 39	8 44	15 43	8 43	15 58
19	8 03	15 53	8 12	16 03	8 15	15 55	8 22	15 51	8 28	15 39	8 45	15 44	8 43	15 59
20	8 03	15 53	8 13	16 03	8 16	15 55	8 22	15 51	8 29	15 39	8 45	15 44	8 44	15 59
21	8 04	15 53	8 14	16 04	8 16	15 56	8 23	15 52	8 30	15 40	8 46	15 45	8 44	16 00
22	8 04	15 54	8 14	16 04	8 17	15 56	8 23	15 52	8 30	15 40	8 46	15 45	8 45	16 00
23	8 05	15 55	8 14	16 05	8 17	15 57	8 24	15 53	8 30	15 41	8 47	15 46	8 45	16 01
24	8 05	15 55	8 15	16 05	8 17	15 58	8 24	15 53	8 31	15 42	8 47	15 46	8 46	16 01
25	8 05	15 56	8 15	16 06	8 18	15 58	8 25	15 54	8 31	15 42	8 47	15 47	8 46	16 02
26	8 06	15 57	8 15	16 07	8 18	15 59	8 25	15 55	8 31	15 43	8 48	15 48	8 46	16 03
27	8 06	15 58	8 16	16 08	8 18	16 00	8 25	15 56	8 32	15 44	8 48	15 49	8 46	16 04
28	8 06	15 58	8 16	16 09	8 18	16 01	8 25	15 57	8 32	15 45	8 48	15 50	8 46	16 05
29	8 06	15 59	8 16	16 09	8 18	16 02	8 25	15 57	8 32	15 46	8 48	15 51	8 46	16 06
30	8 06	16 00	8 16	16 10	8 18	16 03	8 25	15 58	8 32	15 47	8 48	15 52	8 46	16 07
31	8 06	16 01	8 16	16 11	8 18	16 04	8 25	16 00	8 31	15 48	8 47	15 53	8 46	16 08

JUPITER

Day	R.A.		Dec.		Transit		5° high 52°		56°	
	h	m	°	'	h	m	h	m	h	m
1	19	36.1	−21	59	14	53	18	05	17	33
11	19	44.9	−21	39	14	23	17	37	17	06
21	19	54.1	−21	15	13	53	17	10	16	40
31	20	03.6	−20	49	13	23	16	44	16	15

Diameters – equatorial 33" polar 31"

SATURN

Day	R.A.		Dec.		Transit		5° high 52°		56°	
	h	m	°	'	h	m	h	m	h	m
1	11	29.6	+5	21	6	48	0	54	0	53
11	11	31.4	+5	13	6	10	0	17	0	16
21	11	32.5	+5	09	5	32	23	35	23	34
31	11	33.0	+5	09	4	53	22	56	22	55

Diameters – equatorial 18" polar 16"
Rings – major axis 41" minor axis 1"

URANUS

Day	R.A.		Dec.		Transit		5° high 52°		56°	
	h	m	°	'	h	m	h	m	h	m
1	23	19.8	−5	10	18	36	23	01	22	49
11	23	20.1	−5	08	17	57	22	22	22	11
21	23	20.6	−5	04	17	18	21	44	21	32
31	23	21.5	−4	58	16	40	21	06	20	55

Diameter 4"

NEPTUNE

Day	R.A.		Dec.		Transit		5° high 52°		56°	
	h	m	°	'	h	m	h	m	h	m
1	21	36.8	−14	36	16	53	20	18	19	53
11	21	37.5	−14	33	16	15	19	40	19	15
21	21	38.4	−14	28	15	36	19	02	18	37
31	21	39.5	−14	23	14	58	18	24	18	00

Diameter 2"

RISING AND SETTING TIMES

TABLE 1. SEMI-DIURNAL ARCS (HOUR ANGLES AT RISING/SETTING)

Dec.	Latitude												Dec.
	0°	10°	20°	30°	40°	45°	50°	52°	54°	56°	58°	60°	
	h m	h m	h m	h m	h m	h m	h m	h m	h m	h m	h m	h m	
0°	6 00	6 00	6 00	6 00	6 00	6 00	6 00	6 00	6 00	6 00	6 00	6 00	0°
1°	6 00	6 01	6 01	6 02	6 03	6 04	6 05	6 05	6 06	6 06	6 06	6 07	1°
2°	6 00	6 01	6 03	6 05	6 07	6 08	6 10	6 10	6 11	6 12	6 13	6 14	2°
3°	6 00	6 02	6 04	6 07	6 10	6 12	6 14	6 15	6 17	6 18	6 19	6 21	3°
4°	6 00	6 03	6 06	6 09	6 13	6 16	6 19	6 21	6 22	6 24	6 26	6 28	4°
5°	6 00	6 04	6 07	6 12	6 17	6 20	6 24	6 26	6 28	6 30	6 32	6 35	5°
6°	6 00	6 04	6 09	6 14	6 20	6 24	6 29	6 31	6 33	6 36	6 39	6 42	6°
7°	6 00	6 05	6 10	6 16	6 24	6 28	6 34	6 36	6 39	6 42	6 45	6 49	7°
8°	6 00	6 06	6 12	6 19	6 27	6 32	6 39	6 41	6 45	6 48	6 52	6 56	8°
9°	6 00	6 06	6 13	6 21	6 31	6 36	6 44	6 47	6 50	6 54	6 59	7 04	9°
10°	6 00	6 07	6 15	6 23	6 34	6 41	6 49	6 52	6 56	7 01	7 06	7 11	10°
11°	6 00	6 08	6 16	6 26	6 38	6 45	6 54	6 58	7 02	7 07	7 12	7 19	11°
12°	6 00	6 09	6 18	6 28	6 41	6 49	6 59	7 03	7 08	7 13	7 20	7 26	12°
13°	6 00	6 09	6 19	6 31	6 45	6 53	7 04	7 09	7 14	7 20	7 27	7 34	13°
14°	6 00	6 10	6 21	6 33	6 48	6 58	7 09	7 14	7 20	7 27	7 34	7 42	14°
15°	6 00	6 11	6 22	6 36	6 52	7 02	7 14	7 20	7 27	7 34	7 42	7 51	15°
16°	6 00	6 12	6 24	6 38	6 56	7 07	7 20	7 26	7 33	7 41	7 49	7 59	16°
17°	6 00	6 12	6 26	6 41	6 59	7 11	7 25	7 32	7 40	7 48	7 57	8 08	17°
18°	6 00	6 13	6 27	6 43	7 03	7 16	7 31	7 38	7 46	7 55	8 05	8 17	18°
19°	6 00	6 14	6 29	6 46	7 07	7 21	7 37	7 45	7 53	8 03	8 14	8 26	19°
20°	6 00	6 15	6 30	6 49	7 11	7 25	7 43	7 51	8 00	8 11	8 22	8 36	20°
21°	6 00	6 16	6 32	6 51	7 15	7 30	7 49	7 58	8 08	8 19	8 32	8 47	21°
22°	6 00	6 16	6 34	6 54	7 19	7 35	7 55	8 05	8 15	8 27	8 41	8 58	22°
23°	6 00	6 17	6 36	6 57	7 23	7 40	8 02	8 12	8 23	8 36	8 51	9 09	23°
24°	6 00	6 18	6 37	7 00	7 28	7 46	8 08	8 19	8 31	8 45	9 02	9 22	24°
25°	6 00	6 19	6 39	7 02	7 32	7 51	8 15	8 27	8 40	8 55	9 13	9 35	25°
26°	6 00	6 20	6 41	7 05	7 37	7 57	8 22	8 35	8 49	9 05	9 25	9 51	26°
27°	6 00	6 21	6 43	7 08	7 41	8 03	8 30	8 43	8 58	9 16	9 39	10 08	27°
28°	6 00	6 22	6 45	7 12	7 46	8 08	8 37	8 52	9 08	9 28	9 53	10 28	28°
29°	6 00	6 22	6 47	7 15	7 51	8 15	8 45	9 01	9 19	9 41	10 10	10 55	29°
30°	6 00	6 23	6 49	7 18	7 56	8 21	8 54	9 11	9 30	9 55	10 30	12 00	30°
35°	6 00	6 28	6 59	7 35	8 24	8 58	9 46	10 15	10 58	12 00	12 00	12 00	35°
40°	6 00	6 34	7 11	7 56	8 59	9 48	12 00	12 00	12 00	12 00	12 00	12 00	40°
45°	6 00	6 41	7 25	8 21	9 48	12 00	12 00	12 00	12 00	12 00	12 00	12 00	45°
50°	6 00	6 49	7 43	8 54	12 00	12 00	12 00	12 00	12 00	12 00	12 00	12 00	50°
55°	6 00	6 58	8 05	9 42	12 00	12 00	12 00	12 00	12 00	12 00	12 00	12 00	55°
60°	6 00	7 11	8 36	12 00	12 00	12 00	12 00	12 00	12 00	12 00	12 00	12 00	60°
65°	6 00	7 29	9 25	12 00	12 00	12 00	12 00	12 00	12 00	12 00	12 00	12 00	65°
70°	6 00	7 56	12 00	12 00	12 00	12 00	12 00	12 00	12 00	12 00	12 00	12 00	70°
75°	6 00	8 45	12 00	12 00	12 00	12 00	12 00	12 00	12 00	12 00	12 00	12 00	75°
80°	6 00	12 00	12 00	12 00	12 00	12 00	12 00	12 00	12 00	12 00	12 00	12 00	80°

Note: If latitude and declination are of the same sign, take out the respondent directly. If they are of opposite signs, subtract the respondent from 12h.

Table 1 gives the complete range of declinations in case any user wishes to calculate semi-diurnal arcs for bodies other than the Sun and Moon.

Example:

Lat.	Dec.	Semi-diurnal arc
+52°	+20°	7h 51m
+52°	−20°	4h 09m

TABLE 2. CORRECTION FOR REFRACTION AND SEMI-DIAMETER

	m	m	m	m	m	m	m	m	m	m	m	m	
0°	3	3	4	4	4	5	5	5	6	6	6	7	0°
10°	3	3	4	4	4	5	5	6	6	6	7	7	10°
20°	4	4	4	4	5	5	6	7	7	8	8	9	20°
25°	4	4	4	4	5	6	7	8	8	9	11	13	25°
30°	4	4	4	5	6	7	8	9	11	14	21	—	30°

SUNRISE AND SUNSET

The local mean time of sunrise or sunset may be found by obtaining the hour angle from Table 1 and applying it to the time of transit. The hour angle is negative for sunrise and positive for sunset. A small correction to the hour angle, which always has the effect of increasing it numerically, is necessary to allow for the Sun's semi-diameter (16′) and for refraction (34′); it is obtained from Table 2. The resulting local mean time may be converted into the standard time of the country by taking the difference between the longitude of the standard meridian of the country and that of the place, adding it to the local mean time if the place is west of the standard meridian, and subtracting it if the place is east.

Example – Required the New Zealand Mean Time (12h fast on GMT) of sunset on May 23 at Auckland, latitude 36° 50′ S. (or minus), longitude 11h 39m E. Taking the declination as +20°.6 (page 653), we find

		h	m
New Zealand Standard Time		+ 12	00
Longitude		− 11	39
Longitudinal Correction		+ 0	21
Tabular entry for Lat. 30° and Dec. 20°, opposite signs		+ 5	11
Proportional part for 6° 50′ of Lat.		−	15
Proportional part for 0°.6 of Dec.		−	2
Correction (Table 2)		+	4
Hour angle		4	58
Sun transits (page 653)		11	57
Longitudinal correction		+	21
New Zealand Mean Time		17	16

MOONRISE AND MOONSET

It is possible to calculate the times of moonrise and moonset using Table 1, though the method is more complicated because the apparent motion of the Moon is much more rapid and also more variable than that of the Sun.

The parallax of the Moon, about 57′, is near to the sum of the semi-diameter and refraction but has the opposite effect on these times. It is thus convenient to neglect all three quantities in the method outlined below.

Notation

ϕ	= latitude of observer
λ	= longitude of observer (measured positively towards the west)
T_{-1}	= time of transit of Moon on previous day
T_0	= time of transit of Moon on day in question
T_1	= time of transit of Moon on following day
δ_0	= approximate declination of Moon
δ_R	= declination of Moon at moonrise
δ_S	= declination of Moon at moonset
h_0	= approximate hour angle of Moon
h_R	= hour angle of Moon at moonrise
h_S	= hour angle of Moon at moonset
t_R	= time of moonrise
t_S	= time of moonset

Method

1. With arguments ϕ, δ_0 enter Table 1 on page 684 to determine h_0 where h_0 is negative for moonrise and positive for moonset.

2. Form approximate times from
$$t_R = T_0 + \lambda + h_0$$
$$t_S = T_0 + \lambda + h_0$$

3. Determine δ_R, δ_S for times t_R, t_S respectively.

4. Re-enter Table 1 on page 684 with
(a) arguments ϕ, δ_R to determine h_R
(b) arguments ϕ, δ_S to determine h_S

5. Form $t_R = T_0 + \lambda + h_R + AX$
$t_S = T_0 + \lambda + h_S + AX$

where $A = (\lambda + h)$

and $X = (T_0 - T_{-1})$ if $(\lambda + h)$ is negative
$X = (T_1 - T_0)$ if $(\lambda + h)$ is positive

AX is the respondent in Table 3.

Example – To find the times of moonrise and moonset at Vancouver ($\phi = +49°$, $\lambda = +8h$ 12m) on 2008 January 3. The starting data (page 638) are

T_{-1} = 7h 11m
T_0 = 7h 55m
T_1 = 8h 41m
δ_0 = −22°

1. h_0 = 4h 09m
2. Approximate values
t_R = 3d 07h 55m + 8h 12m + (−4h 09m)
= 3d 11h 58m
t_S = 3d 07h 55m + 8h 12m + (+4h 09m)
= 3d 20h 16m
3. δ_R = −21°.5
δ_S = −22°.8
4. h_R = − 4h 12m
h_S = +4h 04m
5. t_R = 3d 07h 55m + 8h 12m + (−4h 12m) + 8m
= 3d 12h 03m
t_S = 3d 07h 55m + 8h 12m + (+4h 04m) + 24m
= 3d 20h 35m

To get the LMT of the phenomenon the longitude is subtracted from the GMT thus:

Moonrise = 3d 12h 03m − 8h 12m = 3d 03h 51m
Moonset = 3d 20h 35m − 8h 12m = 3d 12h 23m

TABLE 3. LONGITUDE CORRECTION

X A h	40m m	45m m	50m m	55m m	60m m	65m m	70m m
1	2	2	2	2	3	3	3
2	3	4	4	5	5	5	6
3	5	6	6	7	8	8	9
4	7	8	8	9	10	11	12
5	8	9	10	11	13	14	15
6	10	11	13	14	15	16	18
7	12	13	15	16	18	19	20
8	13	15	17	18	20	22	23
9	15	17	19	21	23	24	26
10	17	19	21	23	25	27	29
11	18	21	23	25	28	30	32
12	20	23	25	28	30	33	35
13	22	24	27	30	33	35	38
14	23	26	29	32	35	38	41
15	25	28	31	34	38	41	44
16	27	30	33	37	40	43	47
17	28	32	35	39	43	46	50
18	30	34	38	41	45	49	53
19	32	36	40	44	48	51	55
20	33	38	42	46	50	54	58
21	35	39	44	48	53	57	61
22	37	41	46	50	55	60	64
23	38	43	48	53	58	62	67
24	40	45	50	55	60	65	70

ECLIPSES 2008

ECLIPSES

During 2008 there will be four eclipses, two of the Sun and two of the Moon. (Penumbral eclipses of the Moon are not mentioned in this section as they are so difficult to observe).

1. An annular eclipse of the Sun on February 7 is visible as a partial eclipse from the western part of the South Pacific Ocean, New Zealand, and eastern Australia. The partial phase begins at 01h 38m and ends at 06h 12m. The path of annularity starts in the South Pacific Ocean and ends in Antarctica. Annularity begins at 03h 20m and ends at 04h 31m. The maximum duration of annularity is 2m 12s.

2. A total eclipse of the Moon on February 21 is visible from central and western Asia, the Indian Ocean, Africa, Europe, the Atlantic Ocean, Iceland, Greenland, the Americas, and the extreme north-east of Asia. The partial phase begins at 01h 43m and ends at 05h 09m. The total phase begins at 03h 00m and ends at 03h 51m.

3. A total eclipse of the Sun on August 1 is visible as a partial eclipse from north-east Canada, northern Europe, and Asia. The partial phase begins at 08h 04m and ends at 12h 38m. The path of totality starts in the northern islands of Canada, and then crosses northern Greenland, Novaya Zemlya and extreme western Mongolia, before ending in China. Totality begins at 09h 21m and ends at 11h 21m. The maximum duration of totality is 2m 27s.

At Greenwich the eclipse begins at 08h 33m and ends at 10h 05m, with a maximum magnitude of 22 per cent, while at Edinburgh the eclipse begins at 08h 24m and ends at 10h 11m, with a maximum magnitude of 35 per cent.

4. A partial eclipse of the Moon on August 16 is visible from Australasia, Asia (except the extreme north-east), the Indian Ocean, Antarctica, Africa, Europe, Iceland, the Atlantic Ocean, the southern tip of Greenland, the north-east of North America, Central America, and South America. The eclipse begins at 19h 35m and ends at 22h 44m. At maximum eclipse 81 per cent of the Moon's surface is obscured.

POSITIONS OF STARS

The positions of heavenly bodies on the celestial sphere are defined by two co-ordinates, right ascension and declination, which are analogous to longitude and latitude on the surface of the Earth. If we imagine the plane of the terrestrial equator extended indefinitely, it will cut the celestial sphere in a great circle known as the celestial equator. Similarly the plane of the Earth's orbit, when extended, cuts in the great circle called the ecliptic. The two intersections of these circles are known as the First Point of Aries and the First Point of Libra. If from any star a perpendicular is drawn to the celestial equator, the length of this perpendicular is the star's declination. The arc, measured eastwards along the equator from the First Point of Aries to the foot of this perpendicular, is the right ascension. An alternative definition of right ascension is that it is the angle at the celestial pole (where the Earth's axis, if prolonged, would meet the sphere) between the great circles to the First Point of Aries and to the star.

The plane of the Earth's equator has a slow movement, so that our reference system for right ascension and declination is not fixed. The consequent alteration in these quantities from year to year is called precession. In right ascension it is an increase of about 3 seconds a year for equatorial stars, and larger or smaller changes in either direction for stars near the poles, depending on the right ascension of the star. In declination it varies between +20″ and −20″ according to the right ascension of the star.

A star or other body crosses the meridian when the sidereal time is equal to its right ascension. The altitude is then a maximum, and may be deduced by remembering that the altitude of the elevated pole is numerically equal to the latitude, while that of the equator at its intersection with the meridian is equal to the co-latitude, or complement of the latitude.

Thus in London (lat. 51° 30′) the meridian altitude of Sirius is found as follows:

	°	′
Altitude of equator	38	30
Declination south	16	43
Difference	21	47

The altitude of Capella (Dec. +46° 00′) at lower transit is:

Altitude of pole	51	30
Polar distance of star	44	00
Difference	7	30

The brightness of a heavenly body is denoted by its magnitude. Omitting the exceptionally bright stars Sirius and Canopus, the twenty brightest stars are of the first magnitude, while the faintest stars visible to the naked eye are of the sixth magnitude. The magnitude scale is a precise one, as a difference of five magnitudes represents a ratio of 100 to 1 in brightness. Typical second magnitude stars are Polaris and the stars in the belt of Orion. The scale is most easily fixed in memory by comparing the stars with Norton's *Star Atlas*. The stars Sirius and Canopus and the planets Venus and Jupiter are so bright that their magnitudes are expressed by negative numbers. A small telescope will show stars down to the ninth or tenth magnitude, while stars fainter than the twentieth magnitude may be photographed by long exposures with the largest telescopes.

MEAN AND SIDEREAL TIME

The length of a sidereal day in mean time is 23h 56m 04s.09. Hence 1h MT = 1h+9^s.86 ST and 1h ST = 1h − 9^s.83 MT.

Acceleration						Retardation					
h	m	s	m	s	s	h	m	s	m	s	s
1	0	10	0	00		1	0	10	0	00	
2	0	20	3	02	0	2	0	20	3	03	0
3	0	30	9	07	1	3	0	29	9	09	1
4	0	39	15	13	2	4	0	39	15	15	2
5	0	49	21	18	3	5	0	49	21	21	3
6	0	59	27	23	4	6	0	59	27	28	4
7	1	09	33	28	5	7	1	09	33	34	5
8	1	19	39	34	6	8	1	19	39	40	6
9	1	29	45	39	7	9	1	28	45	46	7
10	1	39	51	44	8	10	1	38	51	53	8
11	1	48	57	49	9	11	1	48	57	59	9
12	1	58	60	00	10	12	1	58	60	00	10
13	2	08				13	2	08			
14	2	18				14	2	18			
15	2	28				15	2	27			
16	2	38				16	2	37			
17	2	48				17	2	47			
18	2	57				18	2	57			
19	3	07				19	3	07			
20	3	17				20	3	17			
21	3	27				21	3	26			
22	3	37				22	3	36			
23	3	47				23	3	46			
24	3	57				24	3	56			

To convert an interval of mean time to the corresponding interval of sidereal time, enter the acceleration table with the given mean time (taking the hours and the minutes and seconds separately) and add the acceleration obtained to the given mean time. To convert an interval of sidereal time to the corresponding interval of mean time, take out the retardation for the given sidereal time and subtract.

The columns for the minutes and seconds of the argument are in the form known as critical tables. To use these tables, find in the appropriate left-hand column the two entries between which the given number of minutes and seconds lies; the quantity in the right-hand column between these two entries is the required acceleration or retardation. Thus the acceleration for 11m 26s (which lies between the entries 9m 07s and 15m 13s) is 2s. If the given number of minutes and seconds is a tabular entry, the required acceleration or retardation is the entry in the right-hand column above the given tabular entry, eg the retardation for 45m 46s is 7s.

Example – Convert 14h 27m 35s from ST to MT

	h	m	s
Given ST	14	27	35
Retardation for 14h		2	18
Retardation for 27m 35s			5
Corresponding MT	14	25	12

For further explanation, *see* pages 689 and 690.

EXPLANATION OF ASTRONOMICAL DATA

Positions of the heavenly bodies are given only to the degree of accuracy required by amateur astronomers for setting telescopes, or for plotting on celestial globes or star atlases. Where intermediate positions are required, linear interpolation may be employed. Definitions of the terms used cannot be given here. They must be sought in astronomical literature and textbooks.

A special feature has been made of the times when the various heavenly bodies are visible in the British Isles. Since two columns, calculated for latitudes 52° and 56°, are devoted to risings and settings, the range 50° to 58° can be covered by interpolation and extrapolation. The times given in these columns are Greenwich Mean Times for the meridian of Greenwich. An observer west of this meridian must add his/her longitude (in time) and vice versa.

In accordance with the usual convention in astronomy, + and − indicate respectively north and south latitudes or declinations.

All data are, unless otherwise stated, for 0h Greenwich Mean Time (GMT), ie at the midnight at the beginning of the day named. Allowance must be made for British Summer Time during the period that this is in operation.

PAGE ONE OF EACH MONTH

The calendar for each month is explained on page 635.

Under the heading Astronomical Phenomena will be found particulars of the more important conjunctions of the Sun, Moon and planets with each other, and also the dates of other astronomical phenomena of special interest.

Times of Minima of Algol are approximate times of the middle of the period of diminished light.

The Constellations listed each month are those that are near the meridian at the beginning of the month at 22h local mean time. Allowance must be made for British Summer Time if necessary. The fact that any star crosses the meridian 4m earlier each night or 2h earlier each month may be used, in conjunction with the lists given each month, to find what constellations are favourably placed at any moment. The table preceding the list of constellations may be extended indefinitely at the rate just quoted.

The principal phases of the Moon are the GMTs when the difference between the longitude of the Moon and that of the Sun is 0°, 90°, 180° or 270°. The times of perigee and apogee are those when the Moon is nearest to, and farthest from, the Earth, respectively. The nodes or points of intersection of the Moon's orbit and the ecliptic make a complete retrograde circuit of the ecliptic in about 19 years. From a knowledge of the longitude of the ascending node and the inclination, whose value does not vary much from 5°, the path of the Moon among the stars may be plotted on a celestial globe or star atlas.

PAGE TWO OF EACH MONTH

The Sun's semi-diameter, in arc, is given once a month.

The right ascension and declination (Dec.) is that of the true Sun. The right ascension of the mean Sun is obtained by applying the equation of time, with the sign given, to the right ascension of the true Sun, or, more easily, by applying 12h to the Sidereal Time. The direction in which the equation of time has to be applied in different problems is a frequent source of confusion and error. Apparent Solar Time is equal to the Mean Solar Time plus the Equation of Time. For example, at 12h GMT on August 8 the Equation of Time is −5m 35s and thus at 12h Mean Time on that day the Apparent Time is 12h − 5m 35s = 11h 54m 25s.

The Greenwich Sidereal Time at 0h and the Transit of the First Point of Aries (which is really the mean time when the sidereal time is 0h) are used for converting mean time to sidereal time and vice versa.

The GMT of transit of the Sun at Greenwich may also be taken as the local mean time (LMT) of transit in any longitude. It is independent of latitude. The GMT of transit in any longitude is obtained by adding the longitude to the time given if west, and vice versa.

LIGHTING-UP TIME

The legal importance of sunrise and sunset is that the Road Vehicles Lighting Regulations 1989 (SI 1989 No. 1796) as amended make the use of front and rear position lamps on vehicles compulsory during the period between sunset and sunrise. Headlamps on vehicles are required to be used during the hours of darkness on unlit roads, on lit roads with a speed limit exceeding 30mph, or whenever visibility is seriously reduced. The hours of darkness are defined in these regulations as the period between half an hour after sunset and half an hour before sunrise.

In all laws and regulations 'sunset' refers to the local sunset, ie the time at which the Sun sets at the place in question. This common-sense interpretation has been upheld by legal tribunals. Thus the necessity for providing for different latitudes and longitudes, as already described, is evident.

SUNRISE AND SUNSET

The times of sunrise and sunset are those when the Sun's upper limb, as affected by refraction, is on the true horizon of an observer at sea-level. Assuming the mean refraction to be 34′, and the Sun's semi-diameter to be 16′, the time given is that when the true zenith distance of the Sun's centre is 90°+34'+16' or 90° 50', or, in other words, when the depression of the Sun's centre below the true horizon is 50'. The upper limb is then 34' below the true horizon, but is brought there by refraction. An observer on a ship might see the Sun for a minute or so longer, because of the dip of the horizon, while another viewing the sunset over hills or mountains would record an earlier time. Nevertheless, the moment when the true zenith distance of the Sun's centre is 90° 50' is a precise time dependent only on the latitude and longitude of the place, and independent of its altitude above sea-level, the contour of its horizon, the vagaries of refraction or the small seasonal change in the Sun's semi-diameter; this moment is suitable in every way as a definition of sunset (or sunrise) for all statutory purposes.

(For further information, *see* footnote on page 689.)

TWILIGHT

Light reaches us before sunrise and continues to reach us for some time after sunset. The interval between darkness and sunrise or sunset and darkness is called twilight. Astronomically speaking, twilight is considered to begin or end when the Sun's centre is 18° below the horizon, as no light from the Sun can then reach the observer. As thus defined twilight may last several hours; in high latitudes at the summer solstice the depression of 18° is not reached, and twilight lasts from sunset to sunrise.

The need for some sub-division of twilight is met by dividing the gathering darkness into four stages.

(1) *Sunrise or Sunset,* defined as above
(2) *Civil twilight,* which begins or ends when the Sun's centre is 6° below the horizon. This marks the time when operations requiring daylight may commence or must cease. In England it varies from about 30 to 60 minutes after sunset and the same interval before sunrise
(3) *Nautical twilight,* which begins or ends when the Sun's centre is 12° below the horizon. This marks the time when it is, to all intents and purposes, completely dark
(4) *Astronomical twilight,* which begins or ends when the Sun's centre is 18° below the horizon. This marks theoretical perfect darkness. It is of little practical importance, especially if nautical twilight is tabulated

To assist observers the durations of civil, nautical and astronomical twilights are given at intervals of ten days. The beginning of a particular twilight is found by subtracting the duration from the time of sunrise, while the end is found by adding the duration to the time of sunset. Thus the beginning of astronomical twilight in latitude 52°, on the Greenwich meridian, on March 11 is found as 06h 23m − 113m = 04h 30m and similarly the end of civil twilight as 17h 58m +34m = 18h 32m. The letters TAN (twilight all night) are printed when twilight lasts all night.

Under the heading The Night Sky will be found notes describing the position and visibility of the planets and other phenomena.

PAGE THREE OF EACH MONTH

The Moon moves so rapidly among the stars that its position is given only to the degree of accuracy that permits linear interpolation. The right ascension (RA) and declination (Dec.) are geocentric, ie for an imaginary observer at the centre of the Earth. To an observer on the surface of the Earth the position is always different, as the altitude is always less on account of parallax, which may reach 1°.

The lunar terminator is the line separating the bright from the dark part of the Moon's disk. Apart from irregularities of the lunar surface, the terminator is elliptical, because it is a circle seen in projection. It becomes the full circle forming the limb, or edge, of the Moon at New and Full Moon. The selenographic longitude of the terminator is measured from the mean centre of the visible disk, which may differ from the visible centre by as much as 8°, because of libration.

Instead of the longitude of the terminator the Sun's selenographic co-longitude (Sun's co-long.) is tabulated. It is numerically equal to the selenographic longitude of the morning terminator, measured eastwards from the mean centre of the disk. Thus its value is approximately 270° at New Moon, 360° at First Quarter, 90° at Full Moon and 180° at Last Quarter.

The Position Angle (PA) of the Bright Limb is the position angle of the midpoint of the illuminated limb, measured eastwards from the north point on the disk. The Phase column shows the percentage of the area of the Moon's disk illuminated; this is also the illuminated percentage of the diameter at right angles to the line of cusps. The terminator is a semi-ellipse whose major axis is the line of cusps, and whose semi-minor axis is determined by the tabulated percentage; from New Moon to Full Moon the east limb is dark, and vice versa.

The times given as moonrise and moonset are those when the upper limb of the Moon is on the horizon of an observer at sea-level. The Sun's horizontal parallax (Hor. par.) is about 9", and is negligible when considering sunrise and sunset, but that of the Moon averages about 57'. Hence the computed time represents the moment when the true zenith distance of the Moon is 90° 50' (as for the Sun) minus the horizontal parallax. The time required for the Sun or Moon to rise or set is about four minutes (except in high latitudes).

See also page 685 and footnote on page 689.

The GMT of transit of the Moon over the meridian of Greenwich is given; these times are independent of latitude but must be corrected for longitude. For places in the British Isles it suffices to add the longitude if west, and vice versa. For other places a further correction is necessary because of the rapid movement of the Moon relative to the stars. The entire correction is conveniently determined by first finding the west longitude λ of the place. If the place is in west longitude, λ is the ordinary west longitude; if the place is in east longitude λ is the complement to 24h (or 360°) of the longitude and will be greater than 12h (or 180°). The correction then consists of two positive portions, namely λ and the fraction $\lambda/24$ (or $\lambda°/360$) multiplied by the difference between consecutive transits. Thus for Christchurch, New Zealand, the longitude is 11h 31m east, so λ = 12h 29m and the fraction $\lambda/24$ is 0.52. The transit on the local date 5 March 2008 is found as follows:

		d	h	m
GMT of transit at Greenwich	March	5	10	22
λ			12	29
$0.52 \times (10\text{h } 22\text{m} - 9\text{h } 32\text{m})$				25
GMT of transit at Christchurch		5	23	16
Corr. to NZ Standard Time			12	00
Local standard time of transit	March	6	11	16

As is evident, for any given place the quantities λ and the correction to local standard time may be combined permanently, being here 24h 29m.

Positions of Mercury are given for every second day, and those of Venus and Mars for every fifth day; they may be interpolated linearly. The diameter (Diam.) is given in seconds of arc. The phase is the illuminated percentage of the disk. In the case of the inner planets this approaches 100 at superior conjunction and 0 at inferior conjunction. When the phase is less than 50 the planet is crescent-shaped or horned; for greater phases it is gibbous. In the case of the exterior planet Mars, the phase approaches 100 at conjunction and opposition, and is a minimum at the quadratures.

Since the planets cannot be seen when on the horizon, the actual times of rising and setting are not given; instead, the time when the planet has an apparent altitude of 5° has been tabulated. If the time of transit is between 00h and 12h the time refers to an altitude of 5° above the eastern horizon; if between 12h and 24h, to the western horizon. The phenomenon tabulated is the one that occurs between sunset and sunrise. The times given may be interpolated for latitude and corrected for longitude, as in the case of the Sun and Moon.

PAGE FOUR OF EACH MONTH

The GMTs of sunrise and sunset for seven cities, whose adopted positions in longitude (W.) and latitude (N.) are given immediately below the name, may be used not only for these phenomena, but also for lighting-up times (*see* page 687 for a fuller explanation).

The particulars for the four outer planets resemble those for the planets on Page Three of each month, except that, under Uranus and Neptune, times when the planet is 10° high instead of 5° high are given; this is because of the inferior brightness of these planets. The diameters given for the rings of Saturn are those of the major axis (in the plane of the planet's equator) and the minor axis respectively. The former has a small seasonal change due to the slightly varying distance of the Earth from Saturn, but the latter varies from zero when the Earth passes through the ring plane every 15 years to its maximum opening half-way between these periods. The rings were last open at their widest extent (and Saturn at its brightest) in 2002; this will occur again in 2017. The Earth passed through the ring plane in 1995–6 and will do so again in 2009.

TIME

From the earliest ages, the natural division of time into recurring periods of day and night has provided the practical time-scale for the everyday activities of the

SUNRISE, SUNSET, MOONRISE AND MOONSET

The tables have been constructed for the meridian of Greenwich and for latitudes 52° and 56°. They give Greenwich Mean Time (GMT) throughout the year. To obtain the GMT of the phenomenon as seen from any other latitude and longitude in the British Isles, first interpolate or extrapolate for latitude by the usual rules of proportion. To the time thus found, the longitude (expressed in time) is to be added if west (as it usually is in Great Britain) or subtracted if east. If the longitude is expressed in degrees and minutes of arc, it must be converted to time at the rate of 1° = 4m and 15′ = 1m. A method of calculating rise and set time for other places in the world is given on page 685.

The GMT at which the planet transits the Greenwich meridian is also given. The times of transit are to be corrected to local meridians in the usual way, as already described.

human race. Indeed, if any alternative means of time measurement is adopted, it must be capable of adjustment so as to remain in general agreement with the natural time-scale defined by the diurnal rotation of the Earth on its axis. Ideally the rotation should be measured against a fixed frame of reference; in practice it must be measured against the background provided by the celestial bodies. If the Sun is chosen as the reference point, we obtain Apparent Solar Time, which is the time indicated by a sundial. It is not a uniform time but is subject to variations which amount to as much as a quarter of an hour in each direction. Such wide variations cannot be tolerated in a practical time-scale, and this has led to the concept of Mean Solar Time in which all the days are exactly the same length and equal to the average length of the Apparent Solar Day.

The positions of the stars in the sky are specified in relation to a fictitious reference point in the sky known as the First Point of Aries (or the Vernal Equinox). It is therefore convenient to adopt this same reference point when considering the rotation of the Earth against the background of the stars. The time-scale so obtained is known as Apparent Sidereal Time.

GREENWICH MEAN TIME

The daily rotation of the Earth on its axis causes the Sun and the other heavenly bodies to appear to cross the sky from east to west. It is convenient to represent this relative motion as if the Sun really performed a daily circuit around a fixed Earth. Noon in Apparent Solar Time may then be defined as the time at which the Sun transits across the observer's meridian. In Mean Solar Time, noon is similarly defined by the meridian transit of a fictitious Mean Sun moving uniformly in the sky with the same average speed as the true Sun. Mean Solar Time observed on the meridian of the transit circle telescope of the Royal Observatory at Greenwich is called Greenwich Mean Time (GMT). The mean solar day is divided into 24 hours and, for astronomical and other scientific purposes, these are numbered 0 to 23, commencing at midnight. Civil time is usually reckoned in two periods of 12 hours, designated am (*ante meridiem*, ie before noon) and pm (*post meridiem*, ie after noon), although the 24 hour clock is increasingly being used.

UNIVERSAL TIME

Before 1925 January 1, GMT was reckoned in 24 hours commencing at noon; since that date it has been reckoned from midnight. To avoid confusion in the use of the designation GMT before and after 1925, since 1928 astronomers have tended to use the term Universal Time (UT) or Weltzeit (WZ) to denote GMT measured from Greenwich Mean Midnight.

In precision work it is necessary to take account of small variations in Universal Time. These arise from small irregularities in the rotation of the Earth. Observed astronomical time is designated UT0. Observed time corrected for the effects of the motion of the poles (giving rise to a 'wandering' in longitude) is designated UT1. There is also a seasonal fluctuation in the rate of rotation of the Earth arising from meteorological causes, often called the annual fluctuation. UT1 corrected for this effect is designated UT2 and provides a time-scale free from short-period fluctuations. It is still subject to small secular and irregular changes.

APPARENT SOLAR TIME

As mentioned above, the time shown by a sundial is called

Apparent Solar Time. It differs from Mean Solar Time by an amount known as the Equation of Time, which is the total effect of two causes which make the length of the apparent solar day non-uniform. One cause of variation is that the orbit of the Earth is not a circle but an ellipse, having the Sun at one focus. As a consequence, the angular speed of the Earth in its orbit is not constant; it is greatest at the beginning of January when the Earth is nearest the Sun.

The other cause is due to the obliquity of the ecliptic; the plane of the equator (which is at right angles to the axis of rotation of the Earth) does not coincide with the ecliptic (the plane defined by the apparent annual motion of the Sun around the celestial sphere) but is inclined to it at an angle of 23° 26'. As a result, the apparent solar day is shorter than average at the equinoxes and longer at the solstices. From the combined effects of the components due to obliquity and eccentricity, the equation of time reaches its maximum values in February (−14 minutes) and early November (+16 minutes). It has a zero value on four dates during the year, and it is only on these dates (approximately April 15, June 14, September 1 and December 25) that a sundial shows Mean Solar Time.

SIDEREAL TIME

A sidereal day is the duration of a complete rotation of the Earth with reference to the First Point of Aries. The term sidereal (or 'star') time is a little misleading since the time-scale so defined is not exactly the same as that which would be defined by successive transits of a selected star, as there is a small progressive motion between the stars and the First Point of Aries due to the precession of the Earth's axis. This makes the length of the sidereal day shorter than the true period of rotation by 0.008 seconds. Superimposed on this steady precessional motion are small oscillations (nutation), giving rise to fluctuations in apparent sidereal time amounting to as much as 1.2 seconds. It is therefore customary to employ Mean Sidereal Time, from which these fluctuations have been removed. The conversion of GMT to Greenwich sidereal time (GST) may be performed by adding the value of the GST at 0h on the day in question (page two of each month) to the GMT converted to sidereal time using the table on page 686.

Example – To find the GST at August 8d 02h 41m 11s GMT

	h	m	s
GST at 0h	21	07	30
GMT	2	41	11
Acceleration for 2h			20
Acceleration for 41m 11s			7
Sum = GST =	23	49	08

If the observer is not on the Greenwich meridian then his/her longitude, measured positively westwards from Greenwich, must be subtracted from the GST to obtain Local Sidereal Time (LST). Thus, in the above example, an observer 5h east of Greenwich, or 19h west, would find the LST as 4h 47m 05s.

EPHEMERIS TIME

An analysis of observations of the positions of the Sun, Moon and planets taken over an extended period is used in preparing ephemerides. (An ephemeris is a table giving the apparent position of a heavenly body at regular intervals of time, eg one day or ten days, and may be used to compare current observations with tabulated positions.) Discrepancies between the positions of heavenly bodies observed over a 300-year period and their predicted positions arose because the time-scale to which the observations were related was based on the assumption that the rate of rotation of the Earth is uniform. It is now known that this rate of rotation is variable. A revised time-scale, Ephemeris Time (ET), was devised to bring the ephemerides into agreement with the observations.

The second of ET is defined in terms of the annual motion of the Earth in its orbit around the Sun (1/31556925.9747 of the tropical year for 1900 January 0d 12h ET). The precise determination of ET from astronomical observations is a lengthy process as the requisite standard of accuracy can only be achieved by averaging over a number of years.

In 1976 the International Astronomical Union adopted Terrestrial Dynamical Time (TDT), a new dynamical time-scale for general use whose scale unit is the SI second (see Atomic Time, below). TDT was renamed Terrestrial Time (TT) in 1991. ET is now of little more than historical interest.

TERRESTRIAL TIME

The uniform time system used in computing the ephemerides of the solar system is Terrestrial Time (TT), which has replaced ET for this purpose. Except for the most rigorous astronomical calculations, it may be assumed to be the same as ET. During 2008 the estimated difference TT − UT is about 65 seconds.

ATOMIC TIME

The fundamental standards of time and frequency must be defined in terms of a periodic motion adequately uniform, enduring and measurable. Progress has made it possible to use natural standards, such as atomic or molecular oscillations. Continuous oscillations are generated in an electrical circuit, the frequency of which is then compared or brought into coincidence with the frequency characteristic of the absorption or emission by the atoms or molecules when they change between two selected energy levels. Since the 13th General Conference on Weights and Measures in October 1967, the unit of time, the second, has been defined in the International System of units (SI) as 'the duration of 9 192 631 770 periods of the radiation corresponding to the transition between the two hyperfine levels of the ground state of the caesium-133 atom.'

In the UK, the national time scale is maintained by the National Physical Laboratory (NPL), using an ensemble of atomic clocks based on either caesium or hydrogen atoms. In addition the NPL (along with several other national laboratories) has constructed and operates a caesium fountain primary frequency standard, which utilises the cooling of caesium atoms by laser light to determine the duration of the SI second at the highest attainable level of accuracy. Caesium fountain primary standards typically achieve an accuracy of around 1 part in 1,000 000 000 000 000, which is equivalent to one second in 30 million years.

Timekeeping worldwide is based on two closely related atomic time scales that are established through international collaboration. International Atomic Time (TAI) is formed by combining the readings of more than 250 atomic clocks located in about 55 institutes and was set close to the astronomically-based Universal Time (UT) near the beginning of 1958. It was formally recognised in

1971 and since 1988 January 1 has been maintained by the International Bureau of Weights and Measures (BIPM). Civil time in almost all countries is now based on Co-ordinated Universal Time (UTC), which differs from TAI by an integer number of seconds and was designed to make both atomic time and UT available with accuracy appropriate for most users. On 1 January 1972 UTC was set to be exactly 10 seconds behind TAI, and since then the UTC time-scale has been adjusted by the insertion (or, in principle, omission) of leap seconds in order to keep it within ±0.9 s of UT. These leap seconds are introduced, when necessary, at the same instant throughout the world, either at the end of December or at the end of June. The last leap second occurred immediately prior to 0h UTC on 2006 January 1 and was the 23rd leap second. All leap seconds so far have been positive, with 61 seconds in the final minute of the UTC month. The time 23h 59m 60s UTC is followed one second later by 0h 0m 00s of the first day of the following month. Notices concerning the insertion of leap seconds are issued by the International Earth Rotation and Reference Systems Service at the Observatoire de Paris.

The computation of UTC is carried out monthly by the BIPM and takes place in three stages. First, a weighted average known as Echelle Atomique Libre (EAL) is calculated from all of the contributing atomic clocks. In the second stage, TAI is generated by applying small corrections, derived from the results contributed by primary frequency standards, to the scale interval of EAL to maintain its value close to that of the SI second. Finally, UTC is formed from TAI by the addition of an integer number of seconds. The results are published monthly in the BIPM Circular T in the form of offsets at 5-day intervals between UTC and the time scales of contributing organisations.

RADIO TIME-SIGNALS

UTC is made generally available through time-signals and standard frequency broadcasts such as MSF in the UK, CHU in Canada and WWV and WWVH in the USA. These are based on national time-scales that are maintained in close agreement with UTC and provide traceability to the national time-scale and to UTC. The markers of seconds in the UTC scale coincide with those of TAI.

To disseminate the national time-scale in the UK, special signals (call-sign MSF) are broadcast by the National Physical Laboratory. From 2007 April 1 the MSF service, previously broadcast from British Telecom's radio station at Rugby, has been transmitted from Anthorn radio station in Cumbria. The signals are controlled from a caesium beam atomic frequency standard and consist of a precise frequency carrier of 60 kHz which is switched off, after being on for at least half a second, to mark every second. The first second of the minute begins with a period of 500 ms with the carrier switched off, to serve as a minute marker. In the other seconds the carrier is always off for at least one tenth of a second at the start and then it carries an on-off code giving the British clock time and date, together with information identifying the start of the next minute. Changes to and from summer time are made following government announcements. Leap seconds are inserted as announced by the IERS and information provided by them on the difference between UTC and UT is also signalled. Other broadcast signals in the UK include the BBC six pips signal, the BT Timeline ('speaking clock'), the NPL telephone and internet time services for computers, and a coded time-signal on the

BBC 198 kHz transmitters which is used for timing in the electricity supply industry. From 1972 January 1 the six pips on the BBC have consisted of five short pips from second 55 to second 59 (six pips in the case of a leap second) followed by one lengthened pip, the start of which indicates the exact minute. From 1990 February 5 these signals have been controlled by the BBC with seconds markers referenced to the satellite-based US navigation system GPS (Global Positioning System) and time and day referenced to the MSF transmitter. Formerly they were generated by the Royal Greenwich Observatory. The NPL telephone and internet services are directly connected to the national time scale.

Accurate timing may also be obtained from the signals of international navigation systems such as the ground-based LORAN-C, or the satellite-based American GPS or Russian GLONASS systems.

STANDARD TIME

Since 1880 the standard time in Britain has been Greenwich Mean Time (GMT); a statute that year enacted that the word 'time' when used in any legal document relating to Britain meant, unless otherwise specifically stated, the mean time of the Greenwich meridian. Greenwich was adopted as the universal meridian on 13 October 1884. A system of standard time by zones is used worldwide, standard time in each zone differing from that of the Greenwich meridian by an integral number of hours or, exceptionally, half-hours or quarter-hours, either fast or slow. The large territories of the USA and Canada are divided into zones approximately 7.5° on either side of central meridians.

Variations from the standard time of some countries occur during part of the year; they are decided annually and are usually referred to as Summer Time or Daylight Saving Time.

At the 180th meridian the time can be either 12 hours fast on Greenwich Mean Time or 12 hours slow, and a change of date occurs. The internationally recognised date or calendar line is a modification of the 180th meridian, drawn so as to include islands of any one group on the same side of the line, or for political reasons. The line is indicated by joining up the following coordinates:

Lat.	Long.	Lat.	Long.
90° S.	180°	48° N.	180°
51° S.	180°	53° N.	170° E.
45° S.	172.5° W.	65.5° N.	169° W.
15° S.	172.5° W.	68° N.	169° W.
5° S.	180°	90° N.	180°

Changes to the date line would require an international conference.

BRITISH SUMMER TIME

In 1916 an Act ordained that during a defined period of that year the legal time for general purposes in Great Britain should be one hour in advance of Greenwich Mean Time. The Summer Time Acts 1922 and 1925 defined the period during which Summer Time was to be in force, stabilising practice until the Second World War.

During World War 2 (1941–5) and in 1947 Double Summer Time (two hours in advance of Greenwich Mean Time) was used for the period in which ordinary Summer Time would have been in force. During these years clocks were also kept one hour in advance of Greenwich Mean Time in the winter. After the war, ordinary Summer Time was invoked each year from 1948–68.

Between 1968 October 27 and 1971 October 31 clocks were kept one hour ahead of Greenwich Mean Time throughout the year. This was known as British Standard Time.

The most recent legislation is the Summer Time Act 1972, which enacted that 'the period of summer time for the purposes of this Act is the period beginning at two o'clock, Greenwich mean time, in the morning of the day after the third Saturday in March or, if that day is Easter Day, the day after the second Saturday in March, and ending at two o'clock, Greenwich mean time, in the morning of the day after the fourth Saturday in October.'

The duration of Summer Time can be varied by Order in Council and in recent years alterations have been made to synchronise the period of Summer Time in Britain with that used in Europe. The rule for 1981–94 defined the period of Summer Time in the UK as from the last Sunday in March to the day following the fourth Saturday in October and the hour of changeover was altered to 01h Greenwich Mean Time.

There was no rule for the dates of Summer Time between 1995–7. Since 1998 the 9th European Parliament and Council Directive on Summer Time has harmonised the dates on which Summer Time begins and ends across member states as the last Sundays in March and October respectively. Under the directive Summer Time begins and ends at 01hr Greenwich Mean Time in each member state. Amendments to the Summer Time Act to implement the directive came into force in 2002.

The duration of Summer Time in 2008 is:
March 30 01h GMT to October 26 01h GMT

MEAN REFRACTION

Alt. ° ′	Ref. ′	Alt. ° ′	Ref. ′	Alt. ° ′	Ref. ′
1 20		3 12		7 54	
	21		13		6
1 30		3 34		9 27	
	20		12		5
1 41		4 00		11 39	
	19		11		4
1 52		4 30		15 00	
	18		10		3
2 05		5 06		20 42	
	17		9		2
2 19		5 50		32 20	
	16		8		1
2 35		6 44		62 17	
	15		7		0
2 52		7 54		90 00	
	14				
3 12					

The refraction table is in the form of a critical table (*see* page 686).

ASTRONOMICAL CONSTANTS

Solar parallax	8″.794
Astronomical unit	149597870 km
Precession for the year 2008	50″.291
Precession in right ascension	3ˢ.075
Precession in declination	20″.043
Constant of nutation	9″.202
Constant of aberration	20″.496
Mean obliquity of ecliptic (2008)	23° 26′ 18″
Moon's equatorial hor. parallax	57′ 02″.70
Velocity of light in vacuo per second	299792.5 km
Solar motion per second	20.0 km
Equatorial radius of the Earth	6378.140 km
Polar radius of the Earth	6356.755 km
North galactic pole (IAU standard)	
	RA 12h 49m (1950.0). Dec.+27°.4 N.
Solar apex	RA 18h 06m Dec. + 30°

Length of year (in mean solar days)

Tropical	365.24219
Sidereal	365.25636
Anomalistic (perihelion to perihelion)	365.25964
Eclipse	346.62003

Length of month (mean values)	d	h	m	s
New Moon to New	29	12	44	02.9
Sidereal	27	07	43	11.5
Anomalistic (perigee to perigee)	27	13	18	33.2

THE EARTH

The shape of the Earth is that of an oblate spheroid or solid of revolution whose meridian sections are ellipses not differing much from circles, whilst the sections at right angles are circles. The length of the equatorial axis is about 12,756 km, and that of the polar axis is 12,714 km. The mean density of the Earth is 5.5 times that of water, although that of the surface layer is less. The Earth and Moon revolve about their common centre of gravity in a lunar month; this centre in turn revolves round the Sun in a plane known as the ecliptic, that passes through the Sun's centre. The Earth's equator is inclined to this plane at an angle of 23.4°. This tilt is the cause of the seasons. In mid-latitudes, and when the Sun is high above the Equator, not only does the high noon altitude make the days longer, but the Sun's rays fall more directly on the Earth's surface; these effects combine to produce summer. In equatorial regions the noon altitude is large throughout the year, and there is little variation in the length of the day. In higher latitudes the noon altitude is lower, and the days in summer are appreciably longer than those in winter.

The average velocity of the Earth in its orbit is 30 km a second. It makes a complete rotation on its axis in about 23h 56m of mean time, which is the sidereal day. Because of its annual revolution round the Sun, the rotation with respect to the Sun, or the solar day, is more than this by about four minutes (*see* page 689–90). The extremity of the axis of rotation, or the North Pole of the Earth, is not rigidly fixed, but wanders over an area roughly 20 metres in diameter.

ELEMENTS OF THE SOLAR SYSTEM

Orb	Mean distance from Sun (Earth = 1)	km 10⁶	Sidereal period days	Synodic period days	Incl. of orbit to ecliptic ° '	Diameter km	Mass (Earth = 1)	Period of rotation on axis days
Sun	—	—	—	—	—	1,392,530	332,981	25–35*
Mercury	0.39	58	88.0	116	7 00	4,879	0.0553	58.646
Venus	0.72	108	224.7	584	3 24	12,104	0.8150	243.019r
Earth	1.00	150	365.3	—	—	12,756e	1.0000	0.997
Mars	1.52	228	687.0	780	1 51	6,794e	0.1074	1.026
Jupiter	5.20	778	4,332.6	399	1 18	142,984e 133,708p	317.83	0.410e
Saturn	9.55	1429	10,759.2	378	2 29	120,536e 108,728p	95.16	0.426e
Uranus	19.22	2875	30,684.6	370	0 46	51,118e	14.54	0.718r
Neptune	30.11	4504	60,191.2	367	1 46	49,528e	17.15	0.671
Pluto†	39.80	5954	91,708.2	367	17 09	2,302	0.002	6.387

e equatorial, *p* polar, *r* retrograde, * depending on latitude, † reclassified as a dwarf planet since August 2006

THE SATELLITES

Name		Star mag.	Mean distance from primary km	Sidereal period of revolution d
EARTH				
I	Moon	—	384,400	27.322
MARS				
I	Phobos	11	9,378	0.319
II	Deimos	12	23,459	1.262
JUPITER				
XVI	Metis	17	127,960	0.295
XV	Adrastea	19	128,980	0.298
V	Amalthea	14	181,300	0.498
XIV	Thebe	16	221,900	0.675
I	Io	5	421,600	1.769
II	Europa	5	670,900	3.552
III	Ganymede	5	1,070,000	7.155
IV	Callisto	6	1,883,000	16.689
XIII	Leda	20	11,165,000	240.92
VI	Himalia	15	11,460,000	250.57
X	Lysithea	18	11,717,000	259.20
VII	Elara	17	11,741,000	259.64
XII	Ananke	19	21,276,000	629.77r
XI	Carme	18	23,404,000	734.17r
VIII	Pasiphae	17	23,624,000	743.68r
IX	Sinope	18	23,939,000	758.90r
SATURN				
XVIII	Pan	20	133,583	0.575
XV	Atlas	18	137,640	0.602
XVI	Prometheus	16	139,353	0.613
XVII	Pandora	16	141,700	0.629
XI	Epimetheus	15	151,422	0.695
X	Janus	14	151,472	0.695
I	Mimas	13	185,520	0.942
II	Enceladus	12	238,020	1.370
III	Tethys	10	294,660	1.888
XIII	Telesto	19	294,660	1.888
XIV	Calypso	19	294,660	1.888
IV	Dione	10	377,400	2.737
XII	Helene	18	377,400	2.737
V	Rhea	10	527,040	4.518
VI	Titan	8	1,221,850	15.945

Name		Star mag.	Mean distance from primary km	Sidereal period of revolution d
SATURN				
VII	Hyperion	14	1,464,100	21.277
VIII	Iapetus	11	3,560,800	79.330
IX	Phoebe	16	12,944,300	550.48r
URANUS				
VI	Cordelia	24	49,750	0.335
VII	Ophelia	24	53,760	0.376
VIII	Bianca	23	59,170	0.435
IX	Cressida	22	61,780	0.464
X	Desdemona	22	62,660	0.474
XI	Juliet	21	64,360	0.493
XII	Portia	21	66,100	0.513
XIII	Rosalind	22	69,930	0.558
XIV	Belinda	22	75,260	0.624
XV	Puck	20	86,000	0.762
V	Miranda	16	129,900	1.413
I	Ariel	14	190,900	2.520
II	Umbriel	15	266,000	4.144
III	Titania	14	436,300	8.706
IV	Oberon	14	583,600	13.463
XVI	Caliban	22	7,231,000	579.5r
XX	Stephano	24	8,004,000	676.5r
XVII	Sycorax	21	12,179,000	1,283.4r
XVIII	Prospero	23	16,256,000	1,992.8r
XIX	Setebos	23	17,418,000	2,203.3r
NEPTUNE				
III	Naiad	25	48,230	0.294
IV	Thalassa	24	50,070	0.311
V	Despina	23	52,530	0.335
VI	Galatea	22	61,950	0.429
VII	Larissa	22	73,550	0.555
VIII	Proteus	20	117,650	1.122
I	Triton	13	354,760	5.877
II	Nereid	19	5,513,400	360.136
PLUTO				
I	Charon	17	19,600	6.387

Currently the total number of satellites of the outer planets are: Jupiter 62, Saturn 59, Uranus 27, Neptune 13, Pluto 3.

TERRESTRIAL MAGNETISM

The Earth's main magnetic field corresponds approximately to that of a very strong small bar magnet near the centre of the Earth, but with appreciable smooth spatial departures. The origin of the main field is generally ascribed to electric currents associated with fluid motions in the Earth's core. As a result not only does the main field vary in strength and direction from place to place, but also with time. Superimposed on the main field are local and regional anomalies whose magnitudes may in places approach that of the main field; these are due to the influence of mineral deposits in the Earth's crust. A small proportion of the field is of external origin, mostly associated with electric currents in the ionosphere. The configuration of the external field and the ionisation of the atmosphere depend on the incident particle and radiation flux from the Sun. There are, therefore, short-term and non-periodic as well as diurnal, 27-day, seasonal and 11-year periodic changes in the magnetic field, dependent upon the position of the Sun and the degree of solar activity.

A magnetic compass points along the horizontal component of a magnetic line of force. These lines of force converge on the 'magnetic dip-poles', the places where the Earth's magnetic field is vertical. These poles move with time, and their present approximate adopted mean positions are 84.5° N., 126.5° W. and 64.5° S., 137.6° E.

There is also a 'magnetic equator', at all points of which the vertical component of the Earth's magnetic field is zero and a magnetised needle remains horizontal. This line runs between 2° and 12° north of the geographical equator in Asia and Africa, turns sharply south off the west African coast, and crosses South America through Brazil, Bolivia and Peru; it re-crosses the geographical equator in mid-Pacific.

Reference has already been made to secular changes in the Earth's field. The following table indicates the changes in magnetic declination (or variation of the compass). Declination is the angle in the horizontal plane between the direction of true north and that in which a magnetic compass points. Similar, though much smaller, changes have occurred in 'dip' or magnetic inclination. Secular changes differ throughout the world. Although the London observations suggest a cycle with a period of several hundred years, an exact repetition is unlikely.

London			Greenwich			
1580	11°	15′	E.	1900	16°	29′	W.
1622	5°	56′	E.	1925	13°	10′	W.
1665	1°	22′	W.	1950	9°	07′	W.
1730	13°	00′	W.	1975	6°	39′	W.
1773	21°	09′	W.	1998	3°	32′	W.
1850	22°	24′	W.				

In order that up-to-date information on declination may be available, many governments publish magnetic charts on which there are lines (isogonic lines) passing through all places at which specified values of declination will be found at the date of the chart.

In the British Isles, isogonic lines now run approximately north-east to south-west. Though there are considerable local deviations due to geological causes, a rough value of magnetic declination may be obtained by assuming that at 50° N. on the meridian of Greenwich, the value in 2008 is 1° 24′ west and allowing an increase of 12′ for each degree of latitude northwards and one of 27′ for each degree of longitude westwards. For example at 53° N., 5° W., declination will be about 1°24′ + 36′ + 135′, ie 4° 15′ west. The average annual change at the present time is about 10′ decrease.

The number of magnetic observatories is about 180 irregularly distributed over the globe. There are three in Great Britain, run by the British Geological Survey: at Hartland, north Devon; at Eskdalemuir, Dumfries and Galloway; and at Lerwick, Shetland Islands. The following are some recent annual mean values of the magnetic elements for Hartland.

Year	Declination West ° ′	Dip or inclination ° ′	Horizontal intensity nanoTesla (nT)	Vertical intensity nT
1960	9 58.8	66 43.9	18707	43504
1965	9 30.1	66 34.0	18872	43540
1970	9 06.5	66 26.1	19033	43636
1975	8 32.3	66 17.0	19212	43733
1980	7 43.8	66 10.3	19330	43768
1985	6 56.1	66 07.9	19379	43796
1990	6 15.0	66 09.7	19539	43896
1995	5 33.2	66 07.3	19457	43951
2000	4 43.6	66 06.9	19508	44051
2005	3 56.4	66 06.0	19576	44177
2006	3 47.9	66 04.9	19599	44190

As well as navigation at sea, in the air and on land by compass the oil industry depends on the Earth's magnetic field as a directional reference. They use magnetic survey tools when drilling well-bores and require accurate estimates of the local magnetic field, taking into account the crustal and external fields.

MAGNETIC STORMS

Occasionally, sometimes with great suddenness, the Earth's magnetic field is subject for several hours to marked disturbance. During a severe storm in October 2003 the declination at Eskdalemuir changed by over 5° in six minutes. In many instances such disturbances are accompanied by widespread displays of aurorae, marked changes in the incidence of cosmic rays, an increase in the reception of 'noise' from the Sun at radio frequencies, and rapid changes in the ionosphere and induced electric currents within the Earth which adversely affect satellite operations, telecommunications and electric power transmission systems. The disturbances are caused by changes in the stream of ionised particles which emanates from the Sun and through which the Earth is continuously passing. Some of these changes are associated with visible eruptions on the Sun, usually in the region of sun-spots. There is a marked tendency for disturbances to recur after intervals of about 27 days, the apparent period of rotation of the Sun on its axis, which is consistent with the sources being located on particular areas of the Sun.

TIME MEASUREMENT AND CALENDARS

MEASUREMENTS OF TIME

Measurements of time are based on the time taken by the earth to rotate on its axis (day); by the moon to revolve around the earth (month); and by the earth to revolve around the sun (year). From these, which are not commensurable, certain average or mean intervals have been adopted for ordinary use.

THE DAY
The day begins at midnight and is divided into 24 hours of 60 minutes, each of 60 seconds. The hours are counted from midnight up to 12 noon (when the sun crosses the meridian), and these hours are designated am *(ante meridiem)*; and again from noon up to 12 midnight, which hours are designated pm *(post meridiem)*, except when the 24-hour reckoning is employed. The 24-hour reckoning ignores am and pm, numbering the hours 0 to 23 from midnight.

Colloquially the 24 hours are divided into day and night, day being the time while the sun is above the horizon (including the four stages of twilight defined in the Astronomy section). Day is subdivided into morning, the early part of daytime, ending at noon; afternoon, from noon to about 6pm; and evening, which may be said to extend from 6pm until midnight. Night begins at the close of astronomical twilight (*see* the Astronomy section) and extends beyond midnight to sunrise the next day.

The names of the days are derived from Old English translations or adaptations of the Roman titles.

Sunday	Sun	Sol
Monday	Moon	Luna
Tuesday	Tiw/Tyr (god of war)	Mars
Wednesday	Woden/Odin	Mercury
Thursday	Thor	Jupiter
Friday	Frigga/Freyja (goddess of love)	Venus
Saturday	Saeterne	Saturn

THE MONTH
The month in the ordinary calendar is approximately the twelfth part of a year, but the lengths of the different months vary from 28 (or 29) days to 31.

THE YEAR
The equinoctial or tropical year is the time that the earth takes to revolve around the sun from equinox to equinox, ie 365.24219 mean solar days, or 365 days 5 hours 48 minutes and 45 seconds.

The calendar year usually consists of 365 days but a year containing 366 days is called a bissextile (*see* Roman calendar) or leap year, one day being added to the month of February so that a date 'leaps over' a day of the week. In the Roman calendar the day that was repeated was the sixth day before the beginning of March, the equivalent of 24 February.

A year is a leap year if the date of the year is divisible by four without remainder, unless it is the last year of the century. The last year of a century is a leap year only if its number is divisible by 400 without remainder, eg the years 1800 and 1900 had only 365 days but the year 2000 had 366 days.

THE SOLSTICE
A solstice is the point in the tropical year at which the sun attains its greatest distance, north or south, from the Equator. In the northern hemisphere the furthest point north of the Equator marks the summer solstice and the furthest point south – the winter solstice.

The date of the solstice varies according to locality. For example, if the summer solstice falls on 21 June late in the day by Greenwich time, that day will be the longest of the year at Greenwich though it may be by only a second, but it will fall on 22 June, local date, in Japan, and so 22 June will be the longest day there. The date of the solstice is also affected by the length of the tropical year, which is 365 days 6 hours less about 11 minutes 15 seconds. If a solstice happens late on 21 June in one year, it will be nearly 6 hours later in the next (unless the next year is a leap year), ie early on 22 June, and that will be the longest day.

This delay of the solstice does not continue because the extra day in a leap year brings it back a day in the calendar. However, because of the 11 minutes 15 seconds mentioned above, the additional day in a leap year brings the solstice back too far by 45 minutes, and the time of the solstice in the calendar is earlier, in a four-year pattern, as the century progresses. The last year of a century is in most cases not a leap year, and the omission of the extra day puts the date of the solstice later by about 6 hours. Compensation for this is made by the fourth centennial year being a leap year. The solstice has become earlier in date throughout the last century and, because the year 2000 was a leap year, the solstice will get earlier still throughout the 21st century.

The date of the winter solstice, the shortest day of the year, is affected by the same factors as the longest day.

At Greenwich the sun sets at its earliest by the clock about ten days before the shortest day. The daily change in the time of sunset is due in the first place to the sun's movement southwards at this time of the year, which diminishes the interval between the sun's transit and its setting. However, the daily decrease of the Equation of Time causes the time of apparent noon to be continuously later day by day, which to some extent counteracts the first effect. The rates of the change of these two quantities are not equal or uniform; their combination causes the date of earliest sunset to be 12 or 13 December at Greenwich. In more southerly latitudes the effect of the movement of the sun is less, and the change in the time of sunset depends on that of the Equation of Time to a greater degree, and the date of earliest sunset is earlier than it is at Greenwich, eg on the Equator it is about 1 November.

THE EQUINOX
The equinox is the point at which the sun crosses the Equator and day and night are of equal length all over the world. This occurs in March and September.

DOG DAYS
The days about the heliacal rising of the Dog Star, noted from ancient times as the hottest period of the year in the northern hemisphere, are called the Dog Days. Their incidence has been variously calculated as depending on the Greater or Lesser Dog Star (Sirius or Procyon) and their duration has been reckoned as from 30 to 54 days. A generally accepted period is from 3 July to 15 August.

CHRISTIAN CALENDAR

In the Christian chronological system the years are distinguished by cardinal numbers before or after the birth of Christ, the period being denoted by the letters BC (Before Christ) or, more rarely, AC *(Ante Christum),* and AD *(Anno Domini* – In the Year of Our Lord). The correlative dates of the epoch are the fourth year of the 194th Olympiad, the 753rd year from the foundation of Rome, AM 3761 in Jewish chronology, and the 4714th year of the Julian period. The actual date of the birth of Christ is somewhat uncertain.

The system was introduced into Italy in the sixth century. Though first used in France in the seventh century, it was not universally established there until about the eighth century. It has been said that the system was introduced into England by St Augustine (AD 596), but it was probably not generally used until some centuries later. It was ordered to be used by the bishops at the Council of Chelsea (AD 816).

THE JULIAN CALENDAR

In the Julian calendar (adopted by the Roman Empire in 45 BC) all the centennial years were leap years, and for this reason towards the close of the 16th century there was a difference of ten days between the tropical and calendar years; the equinox fell on 11 March of the calendar, whereas at the time of the Council of Nicaea (AD 325), it had fallen on 21 March. In 1582 Pope Gregory ordained that 5 October should be called 15 October and that of the end-century years only the fourth should be a leap year.

THE GREGORIAN CALENDAR

The Gregorian calendar was adopted by Italy, France, Spain and Portugal in 1582, by Prussia, the Roman Catholic German states, Switzerland, Holland and Flanders on 1 January 1583, by Poland in 1586, Hungary in 1587, the Protestant German and Netherland states and Denmark in 1700, and by Great Britain and its Dominions (including the North American colonies) in 1752, by the omission of 11 days (3 September being reckoned as 14 September). Sweden omitted the leap day in 1700 but observed leap days in 1704 and 1708, and reverted to the Julian calendar by having two leap days in 1712; the Gregorian calendar was adopted in 1753 by the omission of 11 days (18 February being reckoned as 1 March). Japan adopted the calendar in 1872, China in 1912, Bulgaria in 1915, Turkey and Soviet Russia in 1918, Yugoslavia and Romania in 1919, and Greece in 1923.

In the same year that the change was made in England from the Julian to the Gregorian calendar, the beginning of the new year was also changed from 25 March to 1 January.

THE ORTHODOX CHURCHES

Some Orthodox churches still use the Julian reckoning but the majority of Greek Orthodox churches and the Romanian Orthodox Church have adopted a modified 'New Calendar', observing the Gregorian calendar for fixed feasts and the Julian for movable feasts.

The Orthodox Church year begins on 1 September. There are four fast periods and, in addition to Pascha (Easter), twelve great feasts, as well as numerous commemorations of the saints of the Old and New Testaments throughout the year.

THE DOMINICAL LETTER

The dominical letter is one of the letters A–G which are used to denote the Sundays in successive years. If the first day of the year is a Sunday the letter is A; if the second, B; the third, C; and so on. A leap year requires two letters, the first for 1 January to 29 February, the second for 1 March to 31 December.

EPIPHANY

The feast of the Epiphany, commemorating the manifestation of Christ, later became associated with the offering of gifts by the Magi. The day was of great importance from the time of the Council of Nicaea (AD 325), as the primate of Alexandria was charged at every Epiphany feast with the announcement in a letter to the churches of the date of the forthcoming Easter. The day was also of importance in Britain as it influenced dates, ecclesiastical and lay, eg Plough Monday, when work was resumed in the fields, fell on the Monday in the first full week after Epiphany.

LENT

The Teutonic word *Lent,* which denotes the fast preceding Easter, originally meant no more than the spring season; but from Anglo-Saxon times, at least, it has been used as the equivalent of the more significant Latin term *Quadragesima,* meaning the 'forty days' or, more literally, the fortieth day. Ash Wednesday is the first day of Lent, which ends at midnight before Easter Day.

PALM SUNDAY

Palm Sunday, the Sunday before Easter and the beginning of Holy Week, commemorates the triumphal entry of Christ into Jerusalem and is celebrated in Britain (when palm is not available) by branches of willow gathered for use in the decoration of churches on that day.

MAUNDY THURSDAY

Maundy Thursday is the day before Good Friday, the name itself being a corruption of *dies mandati* (day of the mandate) when Christ washed the feet of the disciples and gave them the mandate to love one another.

EASTER DAY

Easter Day is the first Sunday after the full moon which happens on, or next after, the 21st day of March; if the full moon happens on a Sunday, Easter Day is the Sunday after.

This definition is contained in an Act of Parliament (24 Geo. II c. 23) and explanation is given in the preamble to the Act that the day of full moon depends on certain tables that have been prepared. These tables are summarised in the early pages of the Book of Common Prayer. The moon referred to is not the real moon of the heavens, but a hypothetical moon on whose 'full' the date of Easter depends, and the lunations of this 'calendar' moon consist of 29 and 30 days alternately, with certain necessary modifications to make the date of its full agree as nearly as possible with that of the real moon, which is known as the Paschal Full Moon.

A FIXED EASTER

In 1928 the House of Commons agreed to a motion for the third reading of a bill proposing that Easter Day shall, in the calendar year next but one after the commencement of the Act and in all subsequent years, be the first Sunday after the second Saturday in April. Easter would thus fall on the second or third Sunday in April, ie between 9 and 15 April (inclusive). A clause in the bill provided that before it shall come into operation, regard shall be had to ny opinion expressed officially by the various Christian churches. Efforts by the World Council of Churches to secure a unanimous choice of date for Easter by its member churches have so far been unsuccessful.

ROGATION DAYS

Rogation Days are the Monday, Tuesday and Wednesday preceding Ascension Day and from the fifth century were observed as public fasts with solemn processions and supplications. The processions were discontinued as religious observances at the Reformation, but survive in the ceremony known as 'beating the parish bounds'. Rogation Sunday is the Sunday before Ascension Day.

EMBER DAYS

The Ember Days at the four seasons are the Wednesday,

Friday and Saturday *(a)* before the third Sunday in Advent, *(b)* before the second Sunday in Lent, and *(c)* before the Sundays nearest to the festivals of St Peter and of St Michael and All Angels.

TRINITY SUNDAY

Trinity Sunday is eight weeks after Easter Day, on the Sunday following Pentecost (Whit Sunday). Subsequent Sundays are reckoned in the Book of Common Prayer calendar of the Church of England as 'after Trinity'.

Thomas Becket (1118–70) was consecrated Archbishop of Canterbury on the Sunday after Whit Sunday and his first act was to ordain that the day of his consecration should be held as a new festival in honour of the Holy Trinity. This observance spread from Canterbury throughout the whole of Christendom.

MOVEABLE FEASTS TO THE YEAR 2035

Year	Ash Wednesday	Easter	Ascension	Pentecost (Whit Sunday)	Advent Sunday
2008	6 February	23 March	1 May	11 May	30 November
2009	25 February	12 April	21 May	31 May	29 November
2010	17 February	4 April	13 May	23 May	28 November
2011	9 March	24 April	2 June	12 June	27 November
2012	22 February	8 April	17 May	27 May	2 December
2013	13 February	31 March	9 May	19 May	1 December
2014	5 March	20 April	29 May	8 June	30 November
2015	18 February	5 April	14 May	24 May	29 November
2016	10 February	27 March	5 May	15 May	27 November
2017	1 March	16 April	25 May	4 June	3 December
2018	14 February	1 April	10 May	20 May	2 December
2019	6 March	21 April	30 May	9 June	1 December
2020	26 February	12 April	21 May	31 May	29 November
2021	17 February	4 April	13 May	23 May	28 November
2022	2 March	17 April	26 May	5 June	27 November
2023	22 February	9 April	18 May	28 May	3 December
2024	14 February	31 March	9 May	19 May	1 December
2025	5 March	20 April	29 May	8 June	30 November
2026	18 February	5 April	14 May	24 May	29 November
2027	10 February	28 March	6 May	16 May	28 November
2028	1 March	16 April	25 May	4 June	3 December
2029	14 February	1 April	10 May	20 May	2 December
2030	6 March	21 April	30 May	9 June	1 December
2031	26 February	13 April	22 May	1 June	30 November
2032	11 February	28 March	6 May	16 May	28 November
2033	2 March	17 April	26 May	5 June	27 November
2034	22 February	9 April	18 May	28 May	3 December
2035	7 February	25 March	3 May	13 May	2 December

NOTES

Ash Wednesday (first day in Lent) can fall at earliest on 4 February and at latest on 10 March

Mothering Sunday (fourth Sunday in Lent) can fall at earliest on 1 March and at latest on 4 April

Easter Day can fall at earliest on 22 March and at latest on 25 April

Ascension Day is forty days after Easter Day and can fall at earliest on 30 April and at latest on 3 June

Pentecost (Whit Sunday) is seven weeks after Easter and can fall at earliest on 10 May and at latest on 13 June

Trinity Sunday is the Sunday after Whit Sunday

Corpus Christi falls on the Thursday after Trinity Sunday

Sundays after Pentecost – there are not less than 18 and not more than 23

Advent Sunday is the Sunday nearest to 30 November

EASTER DAYS AND DOMINICAL LETTERS 1500 TO 2035

Dates up to and including 1752 are according to the Julian calendar. For dominical letters in leap years, *see* note below

			1500–1599	1600–1699	1700–1799	1800–1899	1900–1999	2000–2035
March								
d	22		1573	1668	1761	1818		
e	23		1505/16	1600	1788	1845/56	1913	2008
f	24		1611/95	1706/99	1940			
g	25		1543/54	1627/38/49	1722/33/44	1883/94	1951	2035
A	26		1559/70/81/92	1654/65/76	1749/58/69/80	1815/26/37	1967/78/89	
b	27		1502/13/24/97	1608/87/92	1785/96	1842/53/64	1910/21/32	2005/16
c	28		1529/35/40	1619/24/30	1703/14/25	1869/75/80	1937/48	2027/32
d	29		1551/62	1635/46/57	1719/30/41/52	1807/12/91	1959/64/70	
e	30		1567/78/89	1651/62/73/84	1746/55/66/77	1823/34	1902/75/86/97	
f	31		1510/21/32/83/94	1605/16/78/89	1700/71/82/93	1839/50/61/72	1907/18/29/91	2002/13/24
April								
g	1		1526/37/48	1621/32	1711/16	1804/66/77/88	1923/34/45/56	2018/29
A	2		1553/64	1643/48	1727/38	1809/20/93/99	1961/72	
b	3		1575/80/86	1659/70/81	1743/63/68/74	1825/31/36	1904/83/88/94	
c	4		1507/18/91	1602/13/75/86/97	1708/79/90	1847/58	1915/20/26/99	2010/21
d	5		1523/34/45/56	1607/18/29/40	1702/13/24/95	1801/63/74/85/96	1931/42/53	2015/26
e	6		1539/50/61/72	1634/45/56	1729/35/40/60	1806/17/28/90	1947/58/69/80	
f	7		1504/77/88	1667/72	1751/65/76	1822/33/44	1901/12/85/96	
g	8		1509/15/20/99	1604/10/83/94	1705/87/92/98	1849/55/60	1917/28	2007/12
A	9		1531/42	1615/26/37/99	1710/21/32	1871/82	1939/44/50	2023/34
b	10		1547/58/69	1631/42/53/64	1726/37/48/57	1803/14/87/98	1955/66/77	
c	11		1501/12/63/74/85/96	1658/69/80	1762/73/84	1819/30/41/52	1909/71/82/93	2004
d	12		1506/17/28	1601/12/91/96	1789	1846/57/68	1903/14/25/36/98	2009/20
e	13		1533/44	1623/28	1707/18	1800/73/79/84	1941/52	2031
f	14		1555/60/66	1639/50/61	1723/34/45/54	1805/11/16/95	1963/68/74	
g	15		1571/82/93	1655/66/77/88	1750/59/70/81	1827/38	1900/06/79/90	2001
A	16		1503/14/25/36/87/98	1609/20/82/93	1704/75/86/97	1843/54/65/76	1911/22/33/95	2006/17/28
b	17		1530/41/52	1625/36	1715/20	1808/70/81/92	1927/38/49/60	2022/33
c	18		1557/68	1647/52	1731/42/56	1802/13/24/97	1954/65/76	
d	19		1500/79/84/90	1663/74/85	1747/67/72/78	1829/35/40	1908/81/87/92	
e	20		1511/22/95	1606/17/79/90	1701/12/83/94	1851/62	1919/24/30	2003/14/25
f	21		1527/38/49	1622/33/44	1717/28	1867/78/89	1935/46/57	2019/30
g	22		1565/76	1660	1739/53/64	1810/21/32	1962/73/84	
A	23		1508	1671		1848	1905/16	2000
b	24		1519	1603/14/98	1709/91	1859		2011
c	25		1546	1641	1736	1886	1943	

No dominical letter is placed against the intercalary day 29 February, but since it is still counted as a weekday and given a name, the series of letters moves back one day every leap year after intercalation. Thus, a leap year beginning with the dominical letter C will change to a year with the dominical letter B on 1 March

HINDU CALENDAR

The Hindu calendar is a luni-solar calendar of 12 months, each containing 29 days, 12 hours. Each month is divided into a light fortnight (Shukla or Shuddha) and a dark fortnight (Krishna or Vadya) based on the waxing and waning of the moon. In most parts of India the month starts with the light fortnight, ie the day after the new moon, although in some regions it begins with the dark fortnight, ie the day after the full moon.

The new year according to the civil calendar begins in the month of Chaitra (March/April) and ends in the month of Phalgun (March). The 12 months – Chaitra, Vaishakh, Jyeshtha, Ashadh, Shravan, Bhadrapad, Ashvin, Kartik, Margashirsh, Paush, Magh and Phalgun – have Sanskrit names derived from 12 asterisms (constellations). There are regional variations to the names of the months but the Sanskrit names are understood throughout India.

Every lunar month must have a solar transit and is termed pure *(shuddha)*. The lunar month without a solar transit is impure *(mala)* and called an intercalary month. An intercalary month occurs approximately every 32 lunar months, whenever the difference between the Hindu year of 360 lunar days (354 days 8 hours solar time) and the 365 days 6 hours of the solar year reaches the length of one Hindu lunar month (29 days 12 hours).

The leap month may be added at any point in the Hindu year. The name given to the month varies according to when it occurs but is taken from the month immediately following it. There is no leap month in 2008.

The days of the week are called Raviwar (Sunday), Somawar (Monday), Mangalwar (Tuesday), Budhawar (Wednesday), Guruwar (Thursday), Shukrawar (Friday) and Shaniwar (Saturday). The names are derived from the Sanskrit names of the sun, the moon and five planets, Mars, Mercury, Jupiter, Venus and Saturn.

Most fasts and festivals are based on the lunar calendar but a few are determined by the apparent movement of the sun, eg Sankranti and Pongal (in southern India), which are celebrated on 14/15 January to mark the start of the Sun's apparent journey northwards and a change of season.

Festivals celebrated throughout India are Chaitra (the New Year), Raksha-bandhan (the renewal of the kinship bond between brothers and sisters), Navaratri (a nine-night festival dedicated to the goddess Parvati), Dasara (the victory of Rama over the demon army), Diwali (a festival of lights), Makara Sankranti, Shivaratri (dedicated to Shiva), and Holi (a spring festival). British Hindus commonly celebrate the festival of Diwali as the start of the new year instead of observing it at the beginning of Chaitra.

Regional festivals are Durga-puja (dedicated to the goddess Durga (Parvati)), Sarasvati-puja (dedicated to the goddess Sarasvati), Ganesh Chaturthi (worship of Ganesh on the fourth day (Chaturthi) of the light half of Bhadrapad), Ramanavami (the birth festival of the god Rama) and Janmashtami (the birth festival of the god Krishna).

The main festivals celebrated in Britain are Navaratri, Dasara, Durga-puja, Diwali, Holi, Sarasvati-puja, Ganesh Chaturthi, Raksha-bandhan, Ramanavami and Janmashtami.

For dates of the main festivals in 2008, *see* page 9.

JEWISH CALENDAR

The story of the Flood in the Book of Genesis indicates the use of a calendar of some kind and that the writers recognised 30 days as the length of a lunation. However, after the diaspora, Jewish communities were left in considerable doubt as to the times of fasts and festivals. This led to the formation of the Jewish calendar as used today. It is said that this was done in AD 358 by Rabbi Hillel II, though some assert that it did not happen until much later.

The calendar is luni-solar, and is based on the lengths of the lunation and of the tropical year as found by Hipparchus (c.120 BC), which differ little from those adopted at the present day. The year AM 5768 (2007–2008) is the 11th year of the 304th Metonic (Minor or Lunar) cycle of 19 years and the 28th year of the 206th Solar (or Major) cycle of 28 years since the Era of the Creation. Jews hold that the Creation occurred at the time of the autumnal equinox in the year known in the Christian calendar as 3760 BC (954 of the Julian period). The epoch or starting point of Jewish chronology corresponds to 7 October 3761 BC. At the beginning of each solar cycle, the Tekufah of Nisan (the vernal equinox) returns to the same day and to the same hour.

The hour is divided into 1,080 minims, and the month between one new moon and the next is reckoned as 29 days 12 hours 793 minims. The normal calendar year, called a Regular Common year, consists of 12 months of 30 days and 29 days alternately. Since 12 months such as these comprise only 354 days, in order that each of them shall not diverge greatly from an average place in the solar year, a 13th month is occasionally added after the fifth month of the civil year (which commences on the first day of the month Tishri), or as the penultimate month of the ecclesiastical year (which commences on the first day of the month Nisan). The years when this happens are called Embolismic or leap years.

Of the 19 years that form a Metonic cycle, seven are leap years; they occur at places in the cycle indicated by the numbers 3, 6, 8, 11, 14, 17 and 19, these places being chosen so that the accumulated excesses of the solar years should be as small as possible.

A Jewish year is of one of the following six types:

Minimal Common	353 days
Regular Common	354 days
Full Common	355 days
Minimal Leap	383 days
Regular Leap	384 days
Full Leap	385 days

The Regular year has alternate months of 30 and 29 days. In a Full year, whether common or leap, Marcheshvan, the second month of the civil year, has 30 days instead of 29; in Minimal years Kislev, the third month, has 29 instead of 30. The additional month in leap years is called Adar I and precedes the month called Adar in common years. Adar II is called Adar Sheni in leap years, and the usual Adar festivals are kept in Adar Sheni. Adar I and Adar II always have 30 days, but neither this, nor the other variations mentioned, is allowed to change the number of days in the other months, which still follow the alternation of the normal 12.

These are the main features of the Jewish calendar, which must be considered permanent because as a Jewish law it cannot be altered except by a Great Sanhedrin.

The Jewish day begins between sunset and nightfall. The time used is that of the meridian of Jerusalem, which is 2h 21m in advance of Greenwich Mean Time. Rules for the beginning of sabbaths and festivals were laid down for the latitude of London in the 18th century and hours for nightfall are now fixed annually by the Chief Rabbi.

JEWISH CALENDAR 5768–9
AM 5768 (768) is a Minimal Leap year of 13 months 51 sabbaths and 383 days.

Month (length)	AM 5768	AM 5769
Tishri 1 (30)	13 September 2007	30 September
Marcheshvan 1 (29)	3 October	30 October
Kislev 1 (29/30)	11 November	28 November
Tebet 1 (29)	10 December	28 December
Shebat 1 (30)	8 January 2008	26 January 2009
*Adar 1 (30/29)	7 February	
†Adar II (29)	8 March	
Nisan 1 (30)	6 April	
Iyar 1 (29)	6 May	
Sivan 1 (30)	4 June	
Tammuz 1 (29)	4 July	
Ab 1 (30)	2 August	
Elul 1 (29)	1 September	

* Known as Adar Rishon in leap years
† Known as Adar Sheni in leap years

JEWISH FASTS AND FESTIVALS
For dates of principal festivals in 2008, *see* page 9.

Tishri 1–2	Rosh Hashanah (New Year)
Tishri 3	*Fast of Gedaliah
Tishri 10	Yom Kippur (Day of Atonement)
Tishri 15–21	Succoth (Feast of Tabernacles)
Tishri 21	Hoshana Rabba
Tishri 22	Shemini Atseret (Solemn Assembly)
Tishri 23	Simchat Torah (Rejoicing of the Law)
Kislev 25	Hanukkah (Dedication of the Temple) begins
Tebet 10	Fast of Tebet
†Adar 13	§Fast of Esther
†Adar 14	Purim
†Adar 15	Shushan Purim
Nisan 15–22	Pesach (Passover)
Sivan 6–7	Shavuoth (Feast of Weeks)
Tammuz 17	*Fast of Tammuz
Ab 9	*Fast of Ab

* If these dates fall on the sabbath the fast is kept on the following day
† Adar Sheni in leap years
§ This fast is observed on Adar 11 (or Adar Sheni 11 in leap years) if Adar 13 falls on a sabbath

MUSLIM CALENDAR

The Muslim era is dated from the *Hijrah,* or flight of the Prophet Muhammad from Mecca to Medina, the corresponding date of which in the Julian calendar is 16 July AD 622. The lunar *hijri* calendar is used principally in Iran, Egypt, Malaysia, Pakistan, Mauritania, various Arab states and certain parts of India. Iran uses the solar hijri calendar as well as the lunar hijri calendar. The dating system was adopted about AD 639, commencing with the first day of the month Muharram.

The lunar calendar consists of 12 months containing an alternate sequence of 30 and 29 days, with the intercalation of one day at the end of the 12th month at stated intervals in each cycle of 30 years. The object of the intercalation is to reconcile the date of the first day of the month with the date of the actual new moon.

Some adherents still take the date of the evening of the first physical sighting of the crescent of the new moon as that of the first of the month. If cloud obscures the moon the present month may be extended to 30 days, after which the new month will begin automatically regardless of whether the moon has been seen. (Under religious law a month must have less than 31 days.) This means that the beginning of a new month and the date of religious festivals can vary from the published calendars.

In each cycle of 30 years, 19 years are common and contain 354 days, and 11 years are intercalary (leap years) of 355 days, the latter being called *kabisah.* The mean length of the Hijrah years is 354 days 8 hours 48 minutes and the period of mean lunation is 29 days 12 hours 44 minutes.

To ascertain if a year is common or kabisah, divide it by 30: the quotient gives the number of completed cycles and the remainder shows the place of the year in the current cycle. If the remainder is 2, 5, 7, 10, 13, 16, 18, 21, 24, 26 or 29, the year is kabisah and consists of 355 days.

MUSLIM CALENDAR 1428–9
Hijrah 1428 AH (remainder 18) is a kabisah year. 1429 AH (remainder 19) is a common year. Calendar dates below are estimates based on calculations of moon phases.

Month (length)	1428 AH	1429 AH
Muharram 1 (30)	10 January 2008	29 December
Safar 1 (29)	9 February	28 January 2009
Rabi' I 1 (30)	9 March	
Rabi' II 1 (29)	8 April	
Jumada I 1 (30)	7 May	
Jumada II 1 (29)	6 June	
Rajab 1 (30)	5 July	
Sha'ban 1 (29)	4 August	
Ramadan 1 (30)	2 September	
Shawwal 1 (29)	2 October	
Dhu'l-Qa'da 1 (30)	31 October	
Dhu'l-Hijjah 1 (30/29)	30 November	

MUSLIM FESTIVALS
Ramadan is a month of fasting for all Muslims because it is the month in which the revelation of the *Qur'an* (Koran) began. During Ramadan, Muslims abstain from food, drink and sexual pleasure from dawn until after sunset throughout the month.

The two major festivals are *Eid ul-Fitr* and *Eid ul-Adha.* Eid ul-Fitr marks the end of the Ramadan fast and is celebrated on the day after the sighting of the new moon of the following month. Eid ul-Adha, the festival of sacrifice (also known as the great festival), celebrates the submission of the Prophet Ibrahim (Abraham) to God. Eid ul-Adha falls on the tenth day of Dhu'l-Hijjah, coinciding with the day when those on *hajj* (pilgrimage to Mecca) sacrifice animals.

Other days accorded special recognition are:

Muharram 1	New Year's Day
Muharram 10	Ashura (the day Prophet Noah left the Ark and Prophet Moses was saved from Pharaoh (Sunni), the death of the Prophet's grandson Husain (Shi'ite))
Rabi'u-l-Awwal (Rabi' I) 12	Mawlid ul-Nabi (birthday of the Prophet Muhammad)
Rajab 27	Laylat ul-Isra' wa'l-Mi'raj (The Night of Journey and Ascension)
Ramadan*	Laylat ul-Qadr (Night of Power)
Dhu'l-Hijjah 10	Eid ul-Adha (Festival of Sacrifice)
* Moveable feast	

For dates of the major celebrations in 2008, *see* page 9.

SIKH CALENDAR

The Sikh calendar is a lunar calendar of 365 days divided into 12 months. The length of the months varies between 29 and 32 days.

There are no prescribed feast days and no fasting periods. The main celebrations are Baisakhi Mela (the new year and the anniversary of the founding of the Khalsa), Diwali Mela (festival of light), Hola Mohalla Mela (a spring festival held in the Punjab), and the Gurpurbs (anniversaries associated with the ten Gurus).

For dates of the major celebrations in 2008, *see* page 9.

THAI CALENDAR

Thailand adopted the Suriyakati calendar, a modified version of the Gregorian calendar during the reign of King Rama V in 1888, using 1 April as the first day of the year. In 1940 the date of the new year was changed to 1 January. The years are counted from the beginning of the Buddhist era (BE), which is calculated to have commenced upon the death of the Lord Buddha, taken to have occurred in 543 BC, so AD 2008 is BE 2551. The Chinese system of associating years with one of twelve animals is also in use in Thailand. The Chantarakati lunar calendar is used to determine religious holidays; the new year begins on the first day of the waxing moon in November or, if there is a leap month, in December.

CIVIL AND LEGAL CALENDAR

THE HISTORICAL YEAR
Before 1752, two calendar systems were used in England. The civil or legal year began on 25 March and the historical year on 1 January. Thus the civil or legal date 24 March 1658 was the same day as the historical date 24 March 1659; a date in that portion of the year is written as 24 March 1658/9, the lower figure showing the historical year.

THE NEW YEAR
In England in the seventh century, and as late as the 13th, the year was reckoned from Christmas Day, but in the 12th century the Church in England began the year with the feast of the Annunciation of the Blessed Virgin ('Lady Day') on 25 March, and this practice was adopted generally in the 14th century. The civil or legal year in the

British dominions (exclusive of Scotland) began with Lady Day until 1751. But in and since 1752 the civil year has begun with 1 January. New Year's Day in Scotland was changed from 25 March to 1 January in 1600.

Elsewhere in Europe, 1 January was adopted as the first day of the year by Venice in 1522, German states in 1544, Spain, Portugal and the Roman Catholic Netherlands in 1556, Prussia, Denmark and Sweden in 1559, France in 1564, Lorraine in 1579, the Protestant Netherlands in 1583, Russia in 1725, and Tuscany in 1751.

REGNAL YEARS
Regnal years are the years of a sovereign's reign and each begins on the anniversary of his or her accession, eg regnal year 57 of the present queen begins on 6 February 2008.

The system was used for dating Acts of Parliament until 1962. The Summer Time Act 1925, for example, is quoted as 15 and 16 Geo. V c. 64, because it became law in the parliamentary session which extended over part of both of these regnal years. Acts of a parliamentary session during which a sovereign died were usually given two year numbers, the regnal year of the deceased sovereign and the regnal year of his or her successor, eg those passed in 1952 were dated 16 Geo. VI and 1 Elizabeth II. Since 1962 Acts of Parliament have been dated by the calendar year.

QUARTER AND TERM DAYS
Holy days and saints days were the usual means in early times for setting the dates of future and recurrent appointments. The quarter days in England and Wales are the feast of the Nativity (25 December), the feast of the Annunciation (25 March), the feast of St John the Baptist (24 June) and the feast of St Michael and All Angels (29 September).

The term days in Scotland are Candlemas (the feast of the Purification), Whitsunday, Lammas (Loaf Mass) and Martinmas (St Martin's Day). These fell on 2 February, 15 May, 1 August and 11 November respectively. However, by the Term and Quarter Days (Scotland) Act 1990, the dates of the term days were changed to 28 February (Candlemas), 28 May (Whitsunday), 28 August (Lammas) and 28 November (Martinmas).

RED-LETTER DAYS
Red-letter days were originally the holy days and saints days indicated in early ecclesiastical calendars by letters printed in red ink. The days to be distinguished in this way were approved at the Council of Nicaea in AD 325.

These days still have a legal significance, as judges of the Queen's Bench Division wear scarlet robes on red-letter days falling during the law sittings. The days designated as red-letter days for this purpose are:

Holy and saints days
The Conversion of St Paul, the Purification, Ash Wednesday, the Annunciation, the Ascension, the feasts of St Mark, SS Philip and James, St Matthias, St Barnabas, St John the Baptist, St Peter, St Thomas, St James, St Luke, SS Simon and Jude, All Saints, St Andrew.

Civil calendar (for dates, *see* page 9)
The anniversaries of the Queen's accession, the Queen's birthday and the Queen's coronation, the Queen's official birthday, the birthday of the Duke of Edinburgh, the birthday of the Prince of Wales, St David's Day and Lord Mayor's Day.

PUBLIC HOLIDAYS
Public holidays are divided into two categories, common law and statutory. Common law holidays are holidays 'by habit and custom'; in England, Wales and Northern Ireland these are Good Friday and Christmas Day.

Statutory public holidays, known as bank holidays, were first established by the Bank Holidays Act 1871. They were, literally, days on which the banks (and other public institutions) were closed and financial obligations due on that day were payable the following day. The legislation currently governing public holidays in the UK, which is the Banking and Financial Dealings Act 1971, stipulates the days that are to be public holidays in England, Wales, Scotland and Northern Ireland.

Certain holidays (indicated by * below) are granted annually by royal proclamation, either throughout the UK or in any place in the UK. The public holidays are:

England and Wales
*New Year's Day
Good Friday
Easter Monday
*The first Monday in May
The last Monday in May
The last Monday in August
26 December, if it is not a Sunday
27 December when 25 or 26 December is a Sunday

Scotland
New Year's Day, or if it is a Sunday, 2 January
2 January, or if it is a Sunday, 3 January
Good Friday
The first Monday in May
*The last Monday in May
The first Monday in August
Christmas Day, or if it is a Sunday, 26 December
*Boxing Day – if Christmas Day falls on a Sunday, 26 December is given in lieu and an alternative day is given for Boxing Day

Northern Ireland
*New Year's Day
17 March, or if it is a Sunday, 18 March
Easter Monday
*The first Monday in May
The last Monday in May
*12 July, or if it is a Sunday, 13 July
The last Monday in August
26 December, if it is not a Sunday
27 December if 25 or 26 December is a Sunday
For dates of public holidays in 2008 and 2009, *see* pages 10–11.

CHRONOLOGICAL CYCLES AND ERAS

SOLAR (OR MAJOR) CYCLE
The solar cycle is a period of 28 years in any corresponding year of which the days of the week recur on the same day of the month.

METONIC (LUNAR, OR MINOR) CYCLE
In 432 BC, Meton, an Athenian astronomer, found that 235 lunations are very nearly, though not exactly, equal in duration to 19 solar years and so after 19 years the phases of the Moon recur on the same days of the month (nearly). The dates of full moon in a cycle of 19 years were inscribed in figures of gold on public monuments in

Athens, and the number showing the position of a year in the cycle is called the golden number of that year.

JULIAN PERIOD
The Julian period was proposed by Joseph Scaliger in 1582. The period is 7,980 Julian years, and its first year coincides with the year 4713 BC. The figure of 7980 is the product of the number of years in the solar cycle, the Metonic cycle and the cycle of the Roman indiction (28 × 19 × 15).

ROMAN INDICTION
The Roman indiction is a period of 15 years, instituted for fiscal purposes about AD 300.

EPACT
The epact is the age of the calendar Moon, diminished by one day, on 1 January, in the ecclesiastical lunar calendar.

CHINESE CALENDAR
A lunar calendar was the sole calendar in use in China until 1911, when the government adopted the new (Gregorian) calendar for official and most business activities. The Chinese tend to follow both calendars, the lunar calendar playing an important part in personal life, eg birth celebrations, festivals, marriages; and in rural villages the lunar calendar dictates the cycle of activities, denoting the change of weather and farming activities.

The lunar calendar is used in Hong Kong, Singapore, Malaysia, Tibet and elsewhere in south-east Asia. The calendar has a cycle of 60 years. The new year begins at the first new moon after the sun enters the sign of Aquarius, ie the new year falls between 21 January and 19 February in the Gregorian calendar.

Each year in the Chinese calendar is associated with one of 12 animals: the rat, the ox, the tiger, the rabbit, the dragon, the snake, the horse, the goat or sheep, the monkey, the chicken or rooster, the dog, and the pig.

The date of the Chinese new year and the astrological sign for the years 2008–11 are:

2008	7 February	Rat
2009	26 January	Ox
2010	14 February	Tiger
2011	3 February	Rabbit

COPTIC CALENDAR
In the Coptic calendar, which is used in parts of Egypt and Ethiopia, the year is made up of 12 months of 30 days each, followed, in general, by five complementary days. Every fourth year is an intercalary or leap year and in these years there are six complementary days. The intercalary year of the Coptic calendar immediately precedes the leap year of the Julian calendar. The era is that of Diocletian or the Martyrs, the origin of which is fixed at 29 August AD 284 (Julian date).

INDIAN ERAS
In addition to the Muslim reckoning, other eras are used in India. The Saka era of southern India, dating from 3 March AD 78, was declared the national calendar of the Republic of India with effect from 22 March 1957, to be used concurrently with the Gregorian calendar. As revised, the year of the new Saka era begins at the spring equinox, with five successive months of 31 days and seven of 30 days in ordinary years, and six months of each length in leap years. The year AD 2008 is 1930 of the revised Saka era.

The year AD 2008 corresponds to the following years in other eras:

Year 2065 of the Vikram Samvat era
Year 1415 of the Bengali San era
Year 1184 of the Kollam era
Year 5109 of the Kaliyuga era
Year 2551 of the Buddha Nirvana era

JAPANESE CALENDAR
The Japanese calendar is essentially the same as the Gregorian calendar, the years, months and weeks being of the same length and beginning on the same days as those of the Gregorian calendar. The numeration of the years is different, based on a system of epochs or periods, each of which begins at the accession of an emperor or other important occurrence. The method is not unlike the British system of regnal years, except that each year of a period closes on 31 December. The Japanese chronology begins about AD 650 and the three latest epochs are defined by the reigns of emperors, whose actual names are not necessarily used:

Epoch
Taisho – 1 August 1912 to 25 December 1926
Showa – 26 December 1926 to 7 January 1989
Heisei – 8 January 1989

The year Heisei 20 begins on 1 January 2008.

The months are known as First Month, Second Month, etc, First Month being equivalent to January. The days of the week are Nichiyobi (Sun-day), Getsuyobi (Moon-day), Kayobi (Fire-day), Suiyobi (Water-day), Mokuyobi (Wood-day), Kinyobi (Metal-day) and Doyobi (Earth-day).

THE MASONIC YEAR
Two dates are quoted in warrants, dispensations, etc, issued by the United Grand Lodge of England, those for the current year being expressed as *Anno Domini* 2008 – *Anno Lucis* 6008. This *Anno Lucis* (year of light) is based on the Book of Genesis 1:3, the 4,000-year difference being derived, in modified form, from *Ussher's Notation*, published in 1654, which places the Creation of the World in 4004 BC.

OLYMPIADS
Ancient Greek chronology was reckoned in Olympiads, cycles of four years corresponding with the periodic Olympic Games held on the plain of Olympia, in Elis, once every four years. The intervening years were the first, second, etc, of the Olympiad, which received the name of the victor at the Games. The first recorded Olympiad is that of Choroebus, 776 BC.

ZOROASTRIAN CALENDAR
Zoroastrians, followers of the Iranian prophet Zarathushtra (known to the Greeks as Zoroaster) are mostly to be found in Iran and in India, where they are known as Parsees.

The Zoroastrian era dates from the coronation of the last Zoroastrian Sasanian king in AD 631. The Zoroastrian calendar is divided into 12 months, each comprising 30 days, followed by five holy days of the Gathas at the end of each year to make the year consist of 365 days.

In order to synchronise the calendar with the solar year of 365 days, an extra month was intercalated once every

20 years. However, this intercalation ceased in the 12th century and the new year, which had fallen in the spring, slipped back to August. Because intercalation ceased at different times in Iran and India, there was one month's difference between the calendar followed in Iran (Kadmi calendar) and that followed by the Parsees (Shenshai calendar). In 1906 a group of Zoroastrians decided to bring the calendar back in line with the seasons again and restore the new year to 21 March each year (Fasli calendar).

The Shenshai calendar (new year in August) is mainly used by Parsees. The Fasli calendar (new year, 21 March) is mainly used by Zoroastrians living in Iran, in the Indian subcontinent, or away from Iran.

ROMAN CALENDAR

Roman historians adopted as an epoch the foundation of Rome, which is believed to have happened in the year 753 BC. The ordinal number of the years in Roman reckoning is followed by the letters AUC *(ab urbe condita)*, so that the year 2008 is 2761 AUC (MMDCCLXI). The calendar that we know has developed from one said to have been established by Romulus using a year of 304 days divided into ten months, beginning with March. To this Numa added January and February, making the year consist of 12 months of 30 and 29 days alternately, with

an additional day so that the total was 355. It is also said that Numa ordered an intercalary month of 22 or 23 days in alternate years, making 90 days in eight years, to be inserted after 23 February.

However, there is some doubt as to the origination and the details of the intercalation in the Roman calendar. It is certain that some scheme of this kind was inaugurated and not fully carried out, for in the year 46 BC Julius Caesar found that the calendar had been allowed to fall into some confusion. He sought the help of the Egyptian astronomer Sosigenes, which led to the construction and adoption (45 BC) of the Julian calendar, and, by a slight alteration, to the Gregorian calendar now in use. The year 46 BC was made to consist of 445 days and is called the Year of Confusion.

In the Roman (Julian) calendar the days of the month were counted backwards from three fixed points, or days, and an intervening day was said to be so many days before the next coming point, the first and last being counted. These three points were the Kalends, the Nones, and the Ides. Their positions in the months and the method of counting from them will be seen in the table below. The year containing 366 days was called *bissextilis annus*, as it had a doubled sixth day *(bissextus dies)* before the March Kalends on 24 February – *ante diem sextum Kalendas Martias*, or a.d. VI Kal. Mart.

Present days of the month	March, May, July, October have thirty-one days		January, August, December have thirty-one days		April, June, September, November have thirty days		February has twenty-eight days, and in leap year twenty-nine	
1	Kalendis		Kalendis		Kalendis		Kalendis	
2	VI		IV	ante	IV	ante	IV	ante
3	V	ante	III	Nonas	III	Nonas	III	Nonas
4	IV	Nonas	pridie Nonas		pridie Nonas		pridie Nonas	
5	III		Nonis		Nonis		Nonis	
6	pridie Nonas		VIII		VIII		VIII	
7	Nonis		VII		VII		VII	
8	VIII		VI	ante	VI	ante	VI	ante
9	VII		V	Idus	V	Idus	V	Idus
10	VI	ante	IV		IV		IV	
11	V	Idus	III		III		III	
12	IV		pridie Idus		pridie Idus		pridie Idus	
13	III		Idibus		Idibus		Idibus	
14	pridie Idus		XIX		XVIII		XVI	
15	Idibus		XVIII		XVII		XV	
16	XVII		XVII		XVI		XIV	
17	XVI		XVI		XV		XIII	
18	XV		XV		XIV		XII	
19	XIV		XIV		XIII		XI	
20	XIII		XIII		XII	ante Kalendas	X	ante Kalendas
21	XII		XII	ante Kalendas	XI	(of the month	IX	Martias
22	XI	ante Kalendas	XI	(of the month	X	following)	VIII	
23	X	(of the month	X	following)	IX		VII	
24	IX	following)	IX		VIII		*VI	
25	VIII		VIII		VII		V	
26	VII		VII		VI		IV	
27	VI		VI		V		III	
28	V		V		IV		pridie Kalendas	
29	IV		IV		III		Martias	
30	III		III		pridie Kalendas			
31	pridie Kalendas (Aprilis, Iunias, Sextilis, Novembris)		pridie Kalendas (Februarias, Septembris, Ianuarias)		(Maias, Quinctilis, Octobris, Decembris)		* (repeated in leap year)	

CALENDAR FOR ANY YEAR 1780–2040

To select the correct calendar for any year between 1780 and 2040, consult the index below

*leap year

1780 N*	1813 K	1846 I	1879 G	1912 D*	1945 C	1978 A	2011 M
1781 C	1814 M	1847 K	1880 J*	1913 G	1946 E	1979 C	2012 B*
1782 E	1815 A	1848 N*	1881 M	1914 I	1947 G	1980 F*	2013 E
1783 G	1816 D*	1849 C	1882 A	1915 K	1948 J*	1981 I	2014 G
1784 J*	1817 G	1850 E	1883 C	1916 N*	1949 M	1982 K	2015 I
1785 M	1818 I	1851 G	1884 F*	1917 C	1950 A	1983 M	2016 L*
1786 A	1819 K	1852 J*	1885 I	1918 E	1951 C	1984 B*	2017 A
1787 C	1820 N*	1853 M	1886 K	1919 G	1952 F*	1985 E	2018 C
1788 F*	1821 C	1854 A	1887 M	1920 J*	1953 I	1986 G	2019 E
1789 I	1822 E	1855 C	1888 B*	1921 M	1954 K	1987 I	2020 H*
1790 K	1823 G	1856 F*	1889 E	1922 A	1955 M	1988 L*	2021 K
1791 M	1824 J*	1857 I	1890 G	1923 C	1956 B*	1989 A	2022 M
1792 B*	1825 M	1858 K	1891 I	1924 F*	1957 E	1990 C	2023 A
1793 E	1826 A	1859 M	1892 L*	1925 I	1958 G	1991 E	2024 D*
1794 G	1827 C	1860 B*	1893 A	1926 K	1959 I	1992 H*	2025 G
1795 I	1828 F*	1861 E	1894 C	1927 M	1960 L*	1993 K	2026 I
1796 L*	1829 I	1862 G	1895 E	1928 B*	1961 A	1994 M	2027 K
1797 A	1830 K	1863 I	1896 H*	1929 E	1962 C	1995 A	2028 N*
1798 C	1831 M	1864 L*	1897 K	1930 G	1963 E	1996 D*	2029 C
1799 E	1832 B*	1865 A	1898 M	1931 I	1964 H*	1997 G	2030 E
1800 G	1833 E	1866 C	1899 A	1932 L*	1965 K	1998 I	2031 G
1801 I	1834 G	1867 E	1900 C	1933 A	1966 M	1999 K	2032 J*
1802 K	1835 I	1868 H*	1901 E	1934 C	1967 A	2000 N*	2033 M
1803 M	1836 L*	1869 K	1902 G	1935 E	1968 D*	2001 C	2034 A
1804 B*	1837 A	1870 M	1903 I	1936 H*	1969 G	2002 E	2035 C
1805 E	1838 C	1871 A	1904 L*	1937 K	1970 I	2003 G	2036 F*
1806 G	1839 E	1872 D*	1905 A	1938 M	1971 K	2004 J*	2037 I
1807 I	1840 H*	1873 G	1906 C	1939 A	1972 N*	2005 M	2038 K
1808 L*	1841 K	1874 I	1907 E	1940 D*	1973 C	2006 A	2039 M
1809 A	1842 M	1875 K	1908 H*	1941 G	1974 E	2007 C	2040 B*
1810 C	1843 A	1876 N*	1909 K	1942 I	1975 G	2008 F*	
1811 E	1844 D*	1877 C	1910 M	1943 K	1976 J*	2009 I	
1812 H*	1845 G	1878 E	1911 A	1944 N*	1977 M	2010 K	

A

	January	February	March
Sun.	1 8 15 22 29	5 12 19 26	5 12 19 26
Mon.	2 9 16 23 30	6 13 20 27	6 13 20 27
Tue.	3 10 17 24 31	7 14 21 28	7 14 21 28
Wed.	4 11 18 25	1 8 15 22	1 8 15 22 29
Thur.	5 12 19 26	2 9 16 23	2 9 16 23 30
Fri.	6 13 20 27	3 10 17 24	3 10 17 24 31
Sat.	7 14 21 28	4 11 18 25	4 11 18 25

	April	May	June
Sun.	2 9 16 23 30	7 14 21 28	4 11 18 25
Mon.	3 10 17 24	1 8 15 22 29	5 12 19 26
Tue.	4 11 18 25	2 9 16 23 30	6 13 20 27
Wed.	5 12 19 26	3 10 17 24 31	7 14 21 28
Thur.	6 13 20 27	4 11 18 25	1 8 15 22 29
Fri.	7 14 21 28	5 12 19 26	2 9 16 23 30
Sat.	1 8 15 22 29	6 13 20 27	3 10 17 24

	July	August	September
Sun.	2 9 16 23 30	6 13 20 27	3 10 17 24
Mon.	3 10 17 24 31	7 14 21 28	4 11 18 25
Tue.	4 11 18 25	1 8 15 22 29	5 12 19 26
Wed.	5 12 19 26	2 9 16 23 30	6 13 20 27
Thur.	6 13 20 27	3 10 17 24 31	7 14 21 28
Fri.	7 14 21 28	4 11 18 25	1 8 15 22 29
Sat.	1 8 15 22 29	5 12 19 26	2 9 16 23 30

	October	November	December
Sun.	1 8 15 22 29	5 12 19 26	3 10 17 24 31
Mon.	2 9 16 23 30	6 13 20 27	4 11 18 25
Tue.	3 10 17 24 31	7 14 21 28	5 12 19 26
Wed.	4 11 18 25	1 8 15 22 29	6 13 20 27
Thur.	5 12 19 26	2 9 16 23 30	7 14 21 28
Fri.	6 13 20 27	3 10 17 24	1 8 15 22 29
Sat.	7 14 21 28	4 11 18 25	2 9 16 23 30

EASTER DAYS

March 26	1815, 1826, 1837, 1967, 1978, 1989
April 2	1809, 1893, 1899, 1961
April 9	1871, 1882, 1939, 1950, 2023, 2034
April 16	1786, 1797, 1843, 1854, 1865, 1911
	1922, 1933, 1995, 2006, 2017
April 23	1905

B (LEAP YEAR)

	January	February	March
Sun.	1 8 15 22 29	5 12 19 26	4 11 18 25
Mon.	2 9 16 23 30	6 13 20 27	5 12 19 26
Tue.	3 10 17 24 31	7 14 21 28	6 13 20 27
Wed.	4 11 18 25	1 8 15 22 29	7 14 21 28
Thur.	5 12 19 26	2 9 16 23	1 8 15 22 29
Fri.	6 13 20 27	3 10 17 24	2 9 16 23 30
Sat.	7 14 21 28	4 11 18 25	3 10 17 24 31

	April	May	June
Sun.	1 8 15 22 29	6 13 20 27	3 10 17 24
Mon.	2 9 16 23 30	7 14 21 28	4 11 18 25
Tue.	3 10 17 24	1 8 15 22 29	5 12 19 26
Wed.	4 11 18 25	2 9 16 23 30	6 13 20 27
Thur.	5 12 19 26	3 10 17 24 31	7 14 21 28
Fri.	6 13 20 27	4 11 18 25	1 8 15 22 29
Sat.	7 14 21 28	5 12 19 26	2 9 16 23 30

	July	August	September
Sun.	1 8 15 22 29	5 12 19 26	2 9 16 23 30
Mon.	2 9 16 23 30	6 13 20 27	3 10 17 24
Tue.	3 10 17 24 31	7 14 21 28	4 11 18 25
Wed.	4 11 18 25	1 8 15 22 29	5 12 19 26
Thur.	5 12 19 26	2 9 16 23 30	6 13 20 27
Fri.	6 13 20 27	3 10 17 24 31	7 14 21 28
Sat.	7 14 21 28	4 11 18 25	1 8 15 22 29

	October	November	December
Sun.	7 14 21 28	4 11 18 25	2 9 16 23 30
Mon.	1 8 15 22 29	5 12 19 26	3 10 17 24 31
Tue.	2 9 16 23 30	6 13 20 27	4 11 18 25
Wed.	3 10 17 24 31	7 14 21 28	5 12 19 26
Thur.	4 11 18 25	1 8 15 22 29	6 13 20 27
Fri.	5 12 19 26	2 9 16 23 30	7 14 21 28
Sat.	6 13 20 27	3 10 17 24	1 8 15 22 29

EASTER DAYS

April 1	1804, 1888, 1956, 2040
April 8	1792, 1860, 1928, 2012
April 22	1832, 1984

C

	January	February	March
Sun.	7 14 21 28	4 11 18 25	4 11 18 25
Mon.	1 8 15 22 29	5 12 19 26	5 12 19 26
Tue.	2 9 16 23 30	6 13 20 27	6 13 20 27
Wed.	3 10 17 24 31	7 14 21 28	7 14 21 28
Thur.	4 11 18 25	1 8 15 22	1 8 15 22 29
Fri.	5 12 19 26	2 9 16 23	2 9 16 23 30
Sat.	6 13 20 27	3 10 17 24	3 10 17 24 31

	April	May	June
Sun.	1 8 15 22 29	6 13 20 27	3 10 17 24
Mon.	2 9 16 23 30	7 14 21 28	4 11 18 25
Tue.	3 10 17 24	1 8 15 22 29	5 12 19 26
Wed.	4 11 18 25	2 9 16 23 30	6 13 20 27
Thur.	5 12 19 26	3 10 17 24 31	7 14 21 28
Fri.	6 13 20 27	4 11 18 25	1 8 15 22 29
Sat.	7 14 21 28	5 12 19 26	2 9 16 23 30

	July	August	September
Sun.	1 8 15 22 29	5 12 19 26	2 9 16 23 30
Mon.	2 9 16 23 30	6 13 20 27	3 10 17 24
Tue.	3 10 17 24 31	7 14 21 28	4 11 18 25
Wed.	4 11 18 25	1 8 15 22 29	5 12 19 26
Thur.	5 12 19 26	2 9 16 23 30	6 13 20 27
Fri.	6 13 20 27	3 10 17 24 31	7 14 21 28
Sat.	7 14 21 28	4 11 18 25	1 8 15 22 29

	October	November	December
Sun.	7 14 21 28	4 11 18 25	2 9 16 23 30
Mon.	1 8 15 22 29	5 12 19 26	3 10 17 24 31
Tue.	2 9 16 23 30	6 13 20 27	4 11 18 25
Wed.	3 10 17 24 31	7 14 21 28	5 12 19 26
Thur.	4 11 18 25	1 8 15 22 29	6 13 20 27
Fri.	5 12 19 26	2 9 16 23 30	7 14 21 28
Sat.	6 13 20 27	3 10 17 24	1 8 15 22 29

EASTER DAYS

March 25	1883, 1894, 1951, 2035
April 1	1866, 1877, 1923, 1934, 1945, 2018, 2029
April 8	1787, 1798, 1849, 1855, 1917, 2007
April 15	1781, 1827, 1838, 1900, 1906, 1979, 1990, 2001
April 22	1810, 1821, 1962, 1973

E

	January	February	March
Sun.	6 13 20 27	3 10 17 24	3 10 17 24 31
Mon.	7 14 21 28	4 11 18 25	4 11 18 25
Tue.	1 8 15 22 29	5 12 19 26	5 12 19 26
Wed.	2 9 16 23 30	6 13 20 27	6 13 20 27
Thur.	3 10 17 24 31	7 14 21 28	7 14 21 28
Fri.	4 11 18 25	1 8 15 22	1 8 15 22 29
Sat.	5 12 19 26	2 9 16 23	2 9 16 23 30

	April	May	June
Sun.	7 14 21 28	5 12 19 26	2 9 16 23 30
Mon.	1 8 15 22 29	6 13 20 27	3 10 17 24
Tue.	2 9 16 23 30	7 14 21 28	4 11 18 25
Wed.	3 10 17 24	1 8 15 22 29	5 12 19 26
Thur.	4 11 18 25	2 9 16 23 30	6 13 20 27
Fri.	5 12 19 26	3 10 17 24 31	7 14 21 28
Sat.	6 13 20 27	4 11 18 25	1 8 15 22 29

	July	August	September
Sun.	7 14 21 28	4 11 18 25	1 8 15 22 29
Mon.	1 8 15 22 29	5 12 19 26	2 9 16 23 30
Tue.	2 9 16 23 30	6 13 20 27	3 10 17 24
Wed.	3 10 17 24 31	7 14 21 28	4 11 18 25
Thur.	4 11 18 25	1 8 15 22 29	5 12 19 26
Fri.	5 12 19 26	2 9 16 23 30	6 13 20 27
Sat.	6 13 20 27	3 10 17 24 31	7 14 21 28

	October	November	December
Sun.	6 13 20 27	3 10 17 24	1 8 15 22 29
Mon.	7 14 21 28	4 11 18 25	2 9 16 23 30
Tue.	1 8 15 22 29	5 12 19 26	3 10 17 24 31
Wed.	2 9 16 23 30	6 13 20 27	4 11 18 25
Thur.	3 10 17 24 31	7 14 21 28	5 12 19 26
Fri.	4 11 18 25	1 8 15 22 29	6 13 20 27
Sat.	5 12 19 26	2 9 16 23 30	7 14 21 28

EASTER DAYS

March 24	1799
March 31	1782, 1793, 1839, 1850, 1861, 1907
	1918, 1929, 1991, 2002, 2013
April 7	1822, 1833, 1901, 1985
April 14	1805, 1811, 1895, 1963, 1974
April 21	1867, 1878, 1889, 1935, 1946, 1957, 2019, 2030

D (LEAP YEAR)

	January	February	March
Sun.	7 14 21 28	4 11 18 25	3 10 17 24 31
Mon.	1 8 15 22 29	5 12 19 26	4 11 18 25
Tue.	2 9 16 23 30	6 13 20 27	5 12 19 26
Wed.	3 10 17 24 31	7 14 21 28	6 13 20 27
Thur.	4 11 18 25	1 8 15 22 29	7 14 21 28
Fri.	5 12 19 26	2 9 16 23	1 8 15 22 29
Sat.	6 13 20 27	3 10 17 24	2 9 16 23 30

	April	May	June
Sun.	7 14 21 28	5 12 19 26	2 9 16 23 30
Mon.	1 8 15 22 29	6 13 20 27	3 10 17 24
Tue.	2 9 16 23 30	7 14 21 28	4 11 18 25
Wed.	3 10 17 24	1 8 15 22 29	5 12 19 26
Thur.	4 11 18 25	2 9 16 23 30	6 13 20 27
Fri.	5 12 19 26	3 10 17 24 31	7 14 21 28
Sat.	6 13 20 27	4 11 18 25	1 8 15 22 29

	July	August	September
Sun.	7 14 21 28	4 11 18 25	1 8 15 22 29
Mon.	1 8 15 22 29	5 12 19 26	2 9 16 23 30
Tue.	2 9 16 23 30	6 13 20 27	3 10 17 24
Wed.	3 10 17 24 31	7 14 21 28	4 11 18 25
Thur.	4 11 18 25	1 8 15 22 29	5 12 19 26
Fri.	5 12 19 26	2 9 16 23 30	6 13 20 27
Sat.	6 13 20 27	3 10 17 24 31	7 14 21 28

	October	November	December
Sun.	6 13 20 27	3 10 17 24	1 8 15 22 29
Mon.	7 14 21 28	4 11 18 25	2 9 16 23 30
Tue.	1 8 15 22 29	5 12 19 26	3 10 17 24 31
Wed.	2 9 16 23 30	6 13 20 27	4 11 18 25
Thur.	3 10 17 24 31	7 14 21 28	5 12 19 26
Fri.	4 11 18 25	1 8 15 22 29	6 13 20 27
Sat.	5 12 19 26	2 9 16 23 30	7 14 21 28

EASTER DAYS

March 24	1940
March 31	1872, 2024
April 7	1844, 1912, 1996
April 14	1816, 1968

F (LEAP YEAR)

	January	February	March
Sun.	6 13 20 27	3 10 17 24	2 9 16 23 30
Mon.	7 14 21 28	4 11 18 25	3 10 17 24 31
Tue.	1 8 15 22 29	5 12 19 26	4 11 18 25
Wed.	2 9 16 23 30	6 13 20 27	5 12 19 26
Thur.	3 10 17 24 31	7 14 21 28	6 13 20 27
Fri.	4 11 18 25	1 8 15 22 29	7 14 21 28
Sat.	5 12 19 26	2 9 16 23	1 8 15 22 29

	April	May	June
Sun.	6 13 20 27	4 11 18 25	1 8 15 22 29
Mon.	7 14 21 28	5 12 19 26	2 9 16 23 30
Tue.	1 8 15 22 29	6 13 20 27	3 10 17 24
Wed.	2 9 16 23 30	7 14 21 28	4 11 18 25
Thur.	3 10 17 24	1 8 15 22 29	5 12 19 26
Fri.	4 11 18 25	2 9 16 23 30	6 13 20 27
Sat.	5 12 19 26	3 10 17 24 31	7 14 21 28

	July	August	September
Sun.	6 13 20 27	3 10 17 24 31	7 14 21 28
Mon.	7 14 21 28	4 11 18 25	1 8 15 22 29
Tue.	1 8 15 22 29	5 12 19 26	2 9 16 23 30
Wed.	2 9 16 23 30	6 13 20 27	3 10 17 24
Thur.	3 10 17 24 31	7 14 21 28	4 11 18 25
Fri.	4 11 18 25	1 8 15 22 29	5 12 19 26
Sat.	5 12 19 26	2 9 16 23 30	6 13 20 27

	October	November	December
Sun.	5 12 19 26	2 9 16 23 30	7 14 21 28
Mon.	6 13 20 27	3 10 17 24	1 8 15 22 29
Tue.	7 14 21 28	4 11 18 25	2 9 16 23 30
Wed.	1 8 15 22 29	5 12 19 26	3 10 17 24 31
Thur.	2 9 16 23 30	6 13 20 27	4 11 18 25
Fri.	3 10 17 24 31	7 14 21 28	5 12 19 26
Sat.	4 11 18 25	1 8 15 22 29	6 13 20 27

EASTER DAYS

March 23	1788, 1856, 2008
April 6	1828, 1980
April 13	1884, 1952, 2036
April 20	1924

G

	January	February	March
Sun.	5 12 19 26	2 9 16 23	2 9 16 23 30
Mon.	6 13 20 27	3 10 17 24	3 10 17 24 31
Tue.	7 14 21 28	4 11 18 25	4 11 18 25
Wed.	1 8 15 22 29	5 12 19 26	5 12 19 26
Thur.	2 9 16 23 30	6 13 20 27	6 13 20 27
Fri.	3 10 17 24 31	7 14 21 28	7 14 21 28
Sat.	4 11 18 25	1 8 15 22	1 8 15 22 29

	April	May	June
Sun.	6 13 20 27	4 11 18 25	1 8 15 22 29
Mon.	7 14 21 28	5 12 19 26	2 9 16 23 30
Tue.	1 8 15 22 29	6 13 20 27	3 10 17 24
Wed.	2 9 16 23 30	7 14 21 28	4 11 18 25
Thur.	3 10 17 24	1 8 15 22 29	5 12 19 26
Fri.	4 11 18 25	2 9 16 23 30	6 13 20 27
Sat.	5 12 19 26	3 10 17 24 31	7 14 21 28

	July	August	September
Sun.	6 13 20 27	3 10 17 24 31	7 14 21 28
Mon.	7 14 21 28	4 11 18 25	1 8 15 22 29
Tue.	1 8 15 22 29	5 12 19 26	2 9 16 23 30
Wed.	2 9 16 23 30	6 13 20 27	3 10 17 24
Thur.	3 10 17 24 31	7 14 21 28	4 11 18 25
Fri.	4 11 18 25	1 8 15 22 29	5 12 19 26
Sat.	5 12 19 26	2 9 16 23 30	6 13 20 27

	October	November	December
Sun.	5 12 19 26	2 9 16 23 30	7 14 21 28
Mon.	6 13 20 27	3 10 17 24	1 8 15 22 29
Tue.	7 14 21 28	4 11 18 25	2 9 16 23 30
Wed.	1 8 15 22 29	5 12 19 26	3 10 17 24 31
Thur.	2 9 16 23 30	6 13 20 27	4 11 18 25
Fri.	3 10 17 24 31	7 14 21 28	5 12 19 26
Sat.	4 11 18 25	1 8 15 22 29	6 13 20 27

EASTER DAYS
March 23	1845, 1913
March 30	1823, 1834, 1902, 1975, 1986, 1997
April 6	1806, 1817, 1890, 1947, 1958, 1969
April 13	1800, 1873, 1879, 1941, 2031
April 20	1783, 1794, 1851, 1862, 1919, 1930, 2003, 2014, 2025

I

	January	February	March
Sun.	4 11 18 25	1 8 15 22	1 8 15 22 29
Mon.	5 12 19 26	2 9 16 23	2 9 16 23 30
Tue.	6 13 20 27	3 10 17 24	3 10 17 24 31
Wed.	7 14 21 28	4 11 18 25	4 11 18 25
Thur.	1 8 15 22 29	5 12 19 26	5 12 19 26
Fri.	2 9 16 23 30	6 13 20 27	6 13 20 27
Sat.	3 10 17 24 31	7 14 21 28	7 14 21 28

	April	May	June
Sun.	5 12 19 26	3 10 17 24 31	7 14 21 28
Mon.	6 13 20 27	4 11 18 25	1 8 15 22 29
Tue.	7 14 21 28	5 12 19 26	2 9 16 23 30
Wed.	1 8 15 22 29	6 13 20 27	3 10 17 24
Thur.	2 9 16 23 30	7 14 21 28	4 11 18 25
Fri.	3 10 17 24	1 8 15 22 29	5 12 19 26
Sat.	4 11 18 25	2 9 16 23 30	6 13 20 27

	July	August	September
Sun.	5 12 19 26	2 9 16 23 30	6 13 20 27
Mon.	6 13 20 27	3 10 17 24 31	7 14 21 28
Tue.	7 14 21 28	4 11 18 25	1 8 15 22 29
Wed.	1 8 15 22 29	5 12 19 26	2 9 16 23 30
Thur.	2 9 16 23 30	6 13 20 27	3 10 17 24
Fri.	3 10 17 24 31	7 14 21 28	4 11 18 25
Sat.	4 11 18 25	1 8 15 22 29	5 12 19 26

	October	November	December
Sun.	4 11 18 25	1 8 15 22 29	6 13 20 27
Mon.	5 12 19 26	2 9 16 23 30	7 14 21 28
Tue.	6 13 20 27	3 10 17 24	1 8 15 22 29
Wed.	7 14 21 28	4 11 18 25	2 9 16 23 30
Thur.	1 8 15 22 29	5 12 19 26	3 10 17 24 31
Fri.	2 9 16 23 30	6 13 20 27	4 11 18 25
Sat.	3 10 17 24 31	7 14 21 28	5 12 19 26

EASTER DAYS
March 22	1818
March 29	1807, 1891, 1959, 1970
April 5	1795, 1801, 1863, 1874, 1885, 1931, 1942, 1953, 2015, 2026, 2037
April 12	1789, 1846, 1857, 1903, 1914, 1925, 1998, 2009
April 19	1829, 1835, 1981, 1987

H (LEAP YEAR)

	January	February	March
Sun.	5 12 19 26	2 9 16 23	1 8 15 22 29
Mon.	6 13 20 27	3 10 17 24	2 9 16 23 30
Tue.	7 14 21 28	4 11 18 25	3 10 17 24 31
Wed.	1 8 15 22 29	5 12 19 26	4 11 18 25
Thur.	2 9 16 23 30	6 13 20 27	5 12 19 26
Fri.	3 10 17 24 31	7 14 21 28	6 13 20 27
Sat.	4 11 18 25	1 8 15 22 29	7 14 21 28

	April	May	June
Sun.	5 12 19 26	3 10 17 24 31	7 14 21 28
Mon.	6 13 20 27	4 11 18 25	1 8 15 22 29
Tue.	7 14 21 28	5 12 19 26	2 9 16 23 30
Wed.	1 8 15 22 29	6 13 20 27	3 10 17 24
Thur.	2 9 16 23 30	7 14 21 28	4 11 18 25
Fri.	3 10 17 24	1 8 15 22 29	5 12 19 26
Sat.	4 11 18 25	2 9 16 23 30	6 13 20 27

	July	August	September
Sun.	5 12 19 26	2 9 16 23 30	6 13 20 27
Mon.	6 13 20 27	3 10 17 24 31	7 14 21 28
Tue.	7 14 21 28	4 11 18 25	1 8 15 22 29
Wed.	1 8 15 22 29	5 12 19 26	2 9 16 23 30
Thur.	2 9 16 23 30	6 13 20 27	3 10 17 24
Fri.	3 10 17 24 31	7 14 21 28	4 11 18 25
Sat.	4 11 18 25	1 8 15 22 29	5 12 19 26

	October	November	December
Sun.	4 11 18 25	1 8 15 22 29	6 13 20 27
Mon.	5 12 19 26	2 9 16 23 30	7 14 21 28
Tue.	6 13 20 27	3 10 17 24	1 8 15 22 29
Wed.	7 14 21 28	4 11 18 25	2 9 16 23 30
Thur.	1 8 15 22 29	5 12 19 26	3 10 17 24 31
Fri.	2 9 16 23 30	6 13 20 27	4 11 18 25
Sat.	3 10 17 24 31	7 14 21 28	5 12 19 26

EASTER DAYS
March 29	1812, 1964
April 5	1896
April 12	1868, 1936, 2020
April 19	1840, 1908, 1992

J (LEAP YEAR)

	January	February	March
Sun.	4 11 18 25	1 8 15 22 29	7 14 21 28
Mon.	5 12 19 26	2 9 16 23	1 8 15 22 29
Tue.	6 13 20 27	3 10 17 24	2 9 16 23 30
Wed.	7 14 21 28	4 11 18 25	3 10 17 24 31
Thur.	1 8 15 22 29	5 12 19 26	4 11 18 25
Fri.	2 9 16 23 30	6 13 20 27	5 12 19 26
Sat.	3 10 17 24 31	7 14 21 28	6 13 20 27

	April	May	June
Sun.	4 11 18 25	2 9 16 23 30	6 13 20 27
Mon.	5 12 19 26	3 10 17 24 31	7 14 21 28
Tue.	6 13 20 27	4 11 18 25	1 8 15 22 29
Wed.	7 14 21 28	5 12 19 26	2 9 16 23 30
Thur.	1 8 15 22 29	6 13 20 27	3 10 17 24
Fri.	2 9 16 23 30	7 14 21 28	4 11 18 25
Sat.	3 10 17 24	1 8 15 22 29	5 12 19 26

	July	August	September
Sun.	4 11 18 25	1 8 15 22 29	5 12 19 26
Mon.	5 12 19 26	2 9 16 23 30	6 13 20 27
Tue.	6 13 20 27	3 10 17 24 31	7 14 21 28
Wed.	7 14 21 28	4 11 18 25	1 8 15 22 29
Thur.	1 8 15 22 29	5 12 19 26	2 9 16 23 30
Fri.	2 9 16 23 30	6 13 20 27	3 10 17 24
Sat.	3 10 17 24 31	7 14 21 28	4 11 18 25

	October	November	December
Sun.	3 10 17 24 31	7 14 21 28	5 12 19 26
Mon.	4 11 18 25	1 8 15 22 29	6 13 20 27
Tue.	5 12 19 26	2 9 16 23 30	7 14 21 28
Wed.	6 13 20 27	3 10 17 24	1 8 15 22 29
Thur.	7 14 21 28	4 11 18 25	2 9 16 23 30
Fri.	1 8 15 22 29	5 12 19 26	3 10 17 24 31
Sat.	2 9 16 23 30	6 13 20 27	4 11 18 25

EASTER DAYS
March 28	1880, 1948, 2032
April 4	1920
April 11	1784, 1852, 2004
April 18	1824, 1976

K

	January	February	March
Sun.	3 10 17 24 31	7 14 21 28	7 14 21 28
Mon.	4 11 18 25	1 8 15 22	1 8 15 22 29
Tue.	5 12 19 26	2 9 16 23	2 9 16 23 30
Wed.	6 13 20 27	3 10 17 24	3 10 17 24 31
Thur.	7 14 21 28	4 11 18 25	4 11 18 25
Fri.	1 8 15 22 29	5 12 19 26	5 12 19 26
Sat.	2 9 16 23 30	6 13 20 27	6 13 20 27

	April	May	June
Sun.	4 11 18 25	2 9 16 23 30	6 13 20 27
Mon.	5 12 19 26	3 10 17 24 31	7 14 21 28
Tue.	6 13 20 27	4 11 18 25	1 8 15 22 29
Wed.	7 14 21 28	5 12 19 26	2 9 16 23 30
Thur.	1 8 15 22 29	6 13 20 27	3 10 17 24
Fri.	2 9 16 23 30	7 14 21 28	4 11 18 25
Sat.	3 10 17 24	1 8 15 22 29	5 12 19 26

	July	August	September
Sun.	4 11 18 25	1 8 15 22 29	5 12 19 26
Mon.	5 12 19 26	2 9 16 23 30	6 13 20 27
Tue.	6 13 20 27	3 10 17 24 31	7 14 21 28
Wed.	7 14 21 28	4 11 18 25	1 8 15 22 29
Thur.	1 8 15 22 29	5 12 19 26	2 9 16 23 30
Fri.	2 9 16 23 30	6 13 20 27	3 10 17 24
Sat.	3 10 17 24 31	7 14 21 28	4 11 18 25

	October	November	December
Sun.	3 10 17 24 31	7 14 21 28	5 12 19 26
Mon.	4 11 18 25	1 8 15 22 29	6 13 20 27
Tue.	5 12 19 26	2 9 16 23 30	7 14 21 28
Wed.	6 13 20 27	3 10 17 24	1 8 15 22 29
Thur.	7 14 21 28	4 11 18 25	2 9 16 23 30
Fri.	1 8 15 22 29	5 12 19 26	3 10 17 24 31
Sat.	2 9 16 23 30	6 13 20 27	4 11 18 25

EASTER DAYS
March 28	1869, 1875, 1937, 2027
April 4	1790, 1847, 1858, 1915, 1926, 1999, 2010, 2021
April 11	1819, 1830, 1841, 1909, 1971, 1982, 1993
April 18	1802, 1813, 1897, 1954, 1965
April 25	1886, 1943, 2038

M

	January	February	March
Sun.	2 9 16 23 30	6 13 20 27	6 13 20 27
Mon.	3 10 17 24 31	7 14 21 28	7 14 21 28
Tue.	4 11 18 25	1 8 15 22	1 8 15 22 29
Wed.	5 12 19 26	2 9 16 23	2 9 16 23 30
Thur.	6 13 20 27	3 10 17 24	3 10 17 24 31
Fri.	7 14 21 28	4 11 18 25	4 11 18 25
Sat.	1 8 15 22 29	5 12 19 26	5 12 19 26

	April	May	June
Sun.	3 10 17 24	1 8 15 22 29	5 12 19 26
Mon.	4 11 18 25	2 9 16 23 30	6 13 20 27
Tue.	5 12 19 26	3 10 17 24 31	7 14 21 28
Wed.	6 13 20 27	4 11 18 25	1 8 15 22 29
Thur.	7 14 21 28	5 12 19 26	2 9 16 23 30
Fri.	1 8 15 22 29	6 13 20 27	3 10 17 24
Sat.	2 9 16 23 30	7 14 21 28	4 11 18 25

	July	August	September
Sun.	3 10 17 24 31	7 14 21 28	4 11 18 25
Mon.	4 11 18 25	1 8 15 22 29	5 12 19 26
Tue.	5 12 19 26	2 9 16 23 30	6 13 20 27
Wed.	6 13 20 27	3 10 17 24 31	7 14 21 28
Thur.	7 14 21 28	4 11 18 25	1 8 15 22 29
Fri.	1 8 15 22 29	5 12 19 26	2 9 16 23 30
Sat.	2 9 16 23 30	6 13 20 27	3 10 17 24

	October	November	December
Sun.	2 9 16 23 30	6 13 20 27	4 11 18 25
Mon.	3 10 17 24 31	7 14 21 28	5 12 19 26
Tue.	4 11 18 25	1 8 15 22 29	6 13 20 27
Wed.	5 12 19 26	2 9 16 23 30	7 14 21 28
Thur.	6 13 20 27	3 10 17 24	1 8 15 22 29
Fri.	7 14 21 28	4 11 18 25	2 9 16 23 30
Sat.	1 8 15 22 29	5 12 19 26	3 10 17 24 31

EASTER DAYS
March 27	1785, 1842, 1853, 1910, 1921, 2005
April 3	1825, 1831, 1983, 1994
April 10	1803, 1814, 1887, 1898, 1955, 1966, 1977, 2039
April 17	1870, 1881, 1927, 1938, 1949, 2022, 2033
April 24	1791, 1859, 2011

L (LEAP YEAR)

	January	February	March
Sun.	3 10 17 24 31	7 14 21 28	6 13 20 27
Mon.	4 11 18 25	1 8 15 22 29	7 14 21 28
Tue.	5 12 19 26	2 9 16 23	1 8 15 22 29
Wed.	6 13 20 27	3 10 17 24	2 9 16 23 30
Thur.	7 14 21 28	4 11 18 25	3 10 17 24 31
Fri.	1 8 15 22 29	5 12 19 26	4 11 18 25
Sat.	2 9 16 23 30	6 13 20 27	5 12 19 26

	April	May	June
Sun.	3 10 17 24	1 8 15 22 29	5 12 19 26
Mon.	4 11 18 25	2 9 16 23 30	6 13 20 27
Tue.	5 12 19 26	3 10 17 24 31	7 14 21 28
Wed.	6 13 20 27	4 11 18 25	1 8 15 22 29
Thur.	7 14 21 28	5 12 19 26	2 9 16 23 30
Fri.	1 8 15 22 29	6 13 20 27	3 10 17 24
Sat.	2 9 16 23 30	7 14 21 28	4 11 18 25

	July	August	September
Sun.	3 10 17 24 31	7 14 21 28	4 11 18 25
Mon.	4 11 18 25	1 8 15 22 29	5 12 19 26
Tue.	5 12 19 26	2 9 16 23 30	6 13 20 27
Wed.	6 13 20 27	3 10 17 24 31	7 14 21 28
Thur.	7 14 21 28	4 11 18 25	1 8 15 22 29
Fri.	1 8 15 22 29	5 12 19 26	2 9 16 23 30
Sat.	2 9 16 23 30	6 13 20 27	3 10 17 24

	October	November	December
Sun.	2 9 16 23 30	6 13 20 27	4 11 18 25
Mon.	3 10 17 24 31	7 14 21 28	5 12 19 26
Tue.	4 11 18 25	1 8 15 22 29	6 13 20 27
Wed.	5 12 19 26	2 9 16 23 30	7 14 21 28
Thur.	6 13 20 27	3 10 17 24	1 8 15 22 29
Fri.	7 14 21 28	4 11 18 25	2 9 16 23 30
Sat.	1 8 15 22 29	5 12 19 26	3 10 17 24 31

EASTER DAYS
March 27	1796, 1864, 1932, 2016
April 3	1836, 1904, 1988
April 17	1808, 1892, 1960

N (LEAP YEAR)

	January	February	March
Sun.	2 9 16 23 30	6 13 20 27	5 12 19 26
Mon.	3 10 17 24 31	7 14 21 28	6 13 20 27
Tue.	4 11 18 25	1 8 15 22 29	7 14 21 28
Wed.	5 12 19 26	2 9 16 23	1 8 15 22 29
Thur.	6 13 20 27	3 10 17 24	2 9 16 23 30
Fri.	7 14 21 28	4 11 18 25	3 10 17 24 31
Sat.	1 8 15 22 29	5 12 19 26	4 11 18 25

	April	May	June
Sun.	2 9 16 23 30	7 14 21 28	4 11 18 25
Mon.	3 10 17 24	1 8 15 22 29	5 12 19 26
Tue.	4 11 18 25	2 9 16 23 30	6 13 20 27
Wed.	5 12 19 26	3 10 17 24 31	7 14 21 28
Thur.	6 13 20 27	4 11 18 25	1 8 15 22 29
Fri.	7 14 21 28	5 12 19 26	2 9 16 23 30
Sat.	1 8 15 22 29	6 13 20 27	3 10 17 24

	July	August	September
Sun.	2 9 16 23 30	6 13 20 27	3 10 17 24
Mon.	3 10 17 24 31	7 14 21 28	4 11 18 25
Tue.	4 11 18 25	1 8 15 22 29	5 12 19 26
Wed.	5 12 19 26	2 9 16 23 30	6 13 20 27
Thur.	6 13 20 27	3 10 17 24 31	7 14 21 28
Fri.	7 14 21 28	4 11 18 25	1 8 15 22 29
Sat.	1 8 15 22 29	5 12 19 26	2 9 16 23 30

	October	November	December
Sun.	1 8 15 22 29	5 12 19 26	3 10 17 24 31
Mon.	2 9 16 23 30	6 13 20 27	4 11 18 25
Tue.	3 10 17 24 31	7 14 21 28	5 12 19 26
Wed.	4 11 18 25	1 8 15 22 29	6 13 20 27
Thur.	5 12 19 26	2 9 16 23 30	7 14 21 28
Fri.	6 13 20 27	3 10 17 24	1 8 15 22 29
Sat.	7 14 21 28	4 11 18 25	2 9 16 23 30

EASTER DAYS
March 26	1780
April 2	1820, 1972
April 9	1944
April 16	1876, 2028
April 23	1848, 1916, 2000

GEOLOGICAL TIME

The earth is thought to have come into existence approximately 4,600 million years ago, but for nearly half this time, the Archean era, it was uninhabited. Life is generally believed to have emerged in the succeeding Proterozoic era. The Archean and the Proterozoic eras are often together referred to as the Precambrian.

Although primitive forms of life, eg algae and bacteria, existed during the Proterozoic era, it is not until the strata of Palaeozoic rocks are reached that abundant fossilised remains appear. Since the Precambrian, there have been three great geological eras:

PALAEOZOIC ('ANCIENT LIFE')
*c.*542–*c.*251 million years ago
Cambrian – Mainly sandstones, slate and shales; limestones in Scotland. Shelled fossils and invertebrates, eg trilobites and brachiopods appear, as do the earliest known vertebrates (jawless fish)
Ordovician – Mainly shales and mudstones, eg in north Wales; limestones in Scotland. First fishes
Silurian – Shales, mudstones and some limestones, found mostly in Wales and southern Scotland
Devonian – Old red sandstone, shale, limestone and slate, eg in south Wales and the West Country
Carboniferous – Coal-bearing rocks, millstone grit, limestone and shale. First traces of land-living creatures
Permian – Marls, sandstones and clays. First reptile fossils

There were two great phases of mountain building in the Palaeozoic era: the Caledonian, characterised in Britain by NE–SW lines of hills and valleys; and the later Hercyian, widespread in west Germany and adjacent areas, and in Britain exemplified in E–W lines of hills and valleys.

The end of the Palaeozoic era was marked by the extensive glaciations of the Permian period in the southern continents and the decline of amphibians. It was succeeded by an era of warm conditions.

MESOZOIC ('MIDDLE FORMS OF LIFE')
*c.*251–*c.*65.5 million years ago
Triassic – Mostly sandstone, eg in the West Midlands; primitive mammals appear
Jurassic – Mainly limestones and clays, typically displayed in the Jura mountains, and in England in a NE–SW belt from Lincolnshire and the Wash to the Severn and the Dorset coast
Cretaceous – Mainly chalk, clay and sands, eg in Kent and Sussex

Giant reptiles were dominant during the Mesozoic era, but it was at this time that marsupial mammals first appeared, as well as *Archaeopteryx lithographica,* the earliest known species of bird. Coniferous trees and flowering plants also developed during the era and, with the birds and the mammals, were the main species to survive into the Cenozoic era. The giant reptiles became extinct.

CENOZOIC ('RECENT LIFE')
from *c.*65.5 million years ago
Palaeocene ⎤ The emergence of new forms of life,
Eocene ⎦ including existing species; primates appear
Oligocene – Fossils of a few still existing species
Miocene – Fossil remains show a balance of existing and extinct species
Pliocene – Fossil remains show a majority of still existing species

Pleistocene – The majority of remains are those of still existing species
Holocene – The present, post-glacial period. Existing species only, except for a few exterminated by humans

In the last 25 million years, from the Miocene through the Pliocene periods, the Alpine-Himalayan and the circum-Pacific phases of mountain building reached their climax. During the Pleistocene period ice-sheets repeatedly locked up masses of water as land ice; its weight depressed the land, but the locking-up of the water lowered the sea level by 100–200 metres. The glaciations and interglacials of the Ice Age are difficult to date and classify, but recent scientific opinion considers the Pleistocene period to have begun approximately 1.64 million years ago. The last glacial retreat, merging into the Holocene period, was *c.*10,000 years ago.

HUMAN DEVELOPMENT

Any consideration of the history of humans must start with the fact that all members of the human race belong to one species of animal, ie *Homo sapiens,* the definition of a species being in biological terms that all its members can interbreed. As a species of mammal it is possible to group humans with other similar types, known as the primates. Amongst these are found a sub-group, the apes, which includes, in addition to humans, the chimpanzees, gorillas, orang-utans and gibbons. All lack a tail, have shoulder blades at the back, and a Y-shaped chewing pattern on the surface of their molars, as well as showing the more general primate characteristics of four incisors, a thumb which is able to touch the fingers of the same hand, and finger and toe nails instead of claws. The factors available to scientific study suggest that human beings have chimpanzees and gorillas as their nearest relatives in the animal world. However, there remains the possibility that there once lived creatures, now extinct, which were closer to modern man than the chimpanzees and gorillas, and which shared with modern man the characteristics of having flat faces (ie the absence of a pronounced muzzle), being bipedal, and possessing large brains.

There are two broad groups of extinct apes recognised by specialists. The ramapithecines – the remains of which, mainly jaw fragments, have been found in east Africa, Asia and Turkey – lived about 14 to 8 million years ago, and from the evidence of their teeth it seems they chewed more in the manner of modern humans than the other presently living apes. The second group, the austra-lopithecines, have left more numerous remains amongst which sub-groups may be detected, although the geographic spread is limited to south and east Africa. Living between 5 and 1.5 million years ago, they were closer relatives of modern humans to the extent that they walked upright, did not have an extensive muzzle and had similar types of pre-molars. The first australopithecine remains were recognised at Taung in South Africa in 1924 and named *Australopithecus africanus,* dating between 3.3 and 2.3 million years ago. The most impressive discovery was made at Hadar, Ethiopia, in 1974 when about half a skeleton of *Australopithecus afarensis,* known as 'Lucy', was found. Some 3.2 million years ago, 'Lucy' certainly walked upright.

Also in east Africa, especially at Olduvai Gorge in Tanzania, between *c.*2.5 and 1.8 million years ago, lived a hominid group which not only walked upright, had a flat face, and a large brain case, but also made simple pebble and flake stone tools. On present evidence these habilines seem to have been the first people to make tools, however crude. This facility is related to the larger brain size and human beings are the only animals to make implements to be used in other processes. These early pebble tool users, because of their distinctive characteristics, have been grouped as a separate sub-species, now extinct, of the genus *Homo* and are known as *Homo habilis* or 'handy man'.

The use of fire, again a human characteristic, is associated with another group of extinct hominids whose remains, about a million years old, are found in south and east Africa, China, Indonesia, north Africa and Europe. Mastery of the techniques of making fire probably helped the colonisation of the colder northern areas and in this respect the site of Vertesszollos in Hungary is of particular importance. *Homo ergaster* in Africa and *Homo erectus* in Asia are the names given to this group of fossils and they relate to a number of famous individual discoveries, eg Solo Man, Heidelberg Man, and especially Peking Man who lived at the cave site at Choukoutien which has yielded evidence of fire and burnt bone.

The well-known group Neanderthal Man, or *Homo neanderthalensis*, is an extinct form of man that lived between about 350,000 and 24,000 years ago, thus spanning the last Ice Age. Indeed, its ability to adapt to the cold climate on the edge of the ice-sheets is one of its characteristic features, the remains being found only in Europe, Asia and the Middle East. Complete neanderthal skeletons were found during excavations at Tabun in Israel, together with evidence of tool-making and the use of fire. Distinguished by very large brains, it seems that neanderthal man was the first to develop recognisable social customs, especially deliberate burial rites. Why the neanderthals became extinct is not clear but it may be connected with the climatic changes at the end of the Ice Ages, which would have seriously affected their food supplies; possibly they became too specialised for their own good.

The shin bone of Boxgrove Man found in 1993 – *Homo heidelbergensis* – and the Swanscombe skull are the best known early human fossil remains found in England. Some specialists prefer to group Swanscombe Man (or, more probably, woman) together with the Steinheim skull from Germany, seeing both as a separate sub-species. There is too little evidence as yet on which to form a final judgement.

Modern humans – *Homo sapiens* – had evolved to our present physical condition and had colonised much of the world by about 40,000 years ago. There are many previously distinguished individual specimens, eg Cromagnon Man, which may now be grouped together as *Homo sapiens*. It was modern humans who spread to the American continent by crossing the landbridge between Siberia and Alaska and thence moved south through North America and into South America. Equally it is modern humans who over the last 40,000 years have been responsible for the major developments in technology, art and civilisation generally.

One of the problems for those studying human fossils is the lack in many cases of sufficient quantities of fossil bone for analysis. It is important that theories should be tested against evidence, rather than the evidence being made to fit the theory. The Piltdown hoax of 1912 (and not fully exposed until the 1970s) is a well-known example of 'fossils' being forged to fit what was seen in some quarters as the correct theory of human evolution.

The discovery of the structure of DNA in 1953 has come to have a profound effect upon the study of human evolution. For example, it was claimed in 1987 that a common ancestor of all human beings was a person who lived in Africa some 200,000 years ago, thus encouraging the 'out of Africa' theory of hominid migration from east Africa to the Middle East and then throughout the world. There is no doubt that the studies based on DNA have vast potential to elucidate further the course of human evolution.

CULTURAL DEVELOPMENT

The Eurocentric bias of early archaeologists meant that the search for a starting point for the development and transmission of cultural ideas, especially by migration, trade and warfare, concentrated unduly on Europe and the Near East. The Three Age system, whereby prehistory was divided into a Stone Age, a Bronze Age and an Iron Age, was devised by Christian Thomsen, curator of the National Museum of Denmark in the early 19th century, to facilitate the classification of the museum's collections. The descriptive adjectives referred to the materials from which the implements and weapons were made and came to be regarded as the dominant features of the societies to which they related. The refinement of the Three Age system once dominated archaeological thought and remains a generally accepted concept in the popular mind. However, it is now seen by archaeologists as an inadequate model for human development.

Common sense suggests that there were no complete breaks between one so-called Age and another, any more than contemporaries would have regarded 1485 as a complete break between medieval and modern English history. Nor can the Three Age system be applied universally. In some areas it is necessary to insert a Copper Age, while in Africa south of the Sahara there would seem to be no Bronze Age at all; in Australia, Old Stone Age societies survived, while in South America, New Stone Age communities existed into modern times. The civilisations in other parts of the world clearly invalidate a Eurocentric theory of human development.

The concept of the 'Neolithic revolution', associated with the domestication of plants and animals, was a development of particular importance in the human cultural pattern. It reflected change from the primitive hunter/gatherer economies to a more settled agricultural way of life and therefore, so the argument goes, made possible the development of urban civilisation. However, it can no longer be argued that this 'revolution' took place only in one area from which all development stemmed. Though it appears that the cultivation of wheat and barley was first undertaken, together with the domestication of cattle and goats/sheep, in the Fertile Crescent (the area bounded by the rivers Tigris and Euphrates), there is evidence that rice was first deliberately planted and pigs domesticated in south-east Asia, maize first cultivated in Central America and llamas first domesticated in South America. It has been recognised in recent years that cultural changes can take place independently of each other in different parts of the world at different rates and different times. There is no need for a general diffusionist theory.

Although scholars will continue to study the particular societies which interest them, it may be possible to obtain a reliable chronological framework, in absolute terms of years, against which the cultural development of any particular area may be set. The development and refinement of radio-carbon dating and other scientific methods of producing absolute chronologies is enabling the cross-referencing of societies to be undertaken. As the techniques of dating become more rigorous in application and the number of scientifically obtained dates increases, the attainment of an absolute chronology for prehistoric societies throughout the world comes closer to being achieved.

GEOLOGICAL TIME

Era	Period	Epoch	Dates	Evolutionary stages
Cenozoic	Quaternary	Holocene	9,600 BC –present	Humans
		Pleistocene	1,808,000– 9,600 BC	
	Tertiary	Pliocene	5,332,000– 1,806,000	
		Miocene	23,030,000–5,332,000	
		Oligocene	34–23 Ma*	
		Eocene	–33.9 Ma	
		Palaeocene	–55.8 Ma	
Mesozoic	Cretaceous		145.5–65.5 Ma	
	Jurassic		199.6–145.5 Ma	First birds
	Triassic		251–199.6 Ma	First mammals
Palaeozoic	Permian		299–251 Ma	First reptiles
	Carboniferous		359.2–299 Ma	First amphibians and insects
	Devonian		416–359.2 Ma	
	Silurian		443.7–416 Ma	
	Ordovician		488.3–443.7 Ma	First fishes
	Cambrian		542–488.3 Ma	First invertebrates
Precambrian	Proterozoic		2500–542 M	First primitive life forms, eg algae and bacteria
	Archaean		3800–2500 M	
	Hadean		4500–3800 M	

* Ma = millions of years ago

TIDAL PREDICTIONS

CONSTANTS

The constant tidal difference may be used in conjunction with the time of high water at a standard port shown in the predictions data below to find the time of high water at any of the ports or places listed.

These tidal differences are very approximate and should be used only as a guide to the time of high water at the places below. More precise local data should be obtained for navigational and other nautical purposes.

All data allow high water time to be found in Greenwich Mean Time: this applies to data for the months when British Summer Time is in operation and the hour's time difference should be allowed for. Ports marked * are in a different time zone and the standard time zone difference also needs to be added/subtracted to give local time.

EXAMPLE

Required: time of high water at Stranraer on 2 January 2008. Appropriate time of high water at Greenock

Afternoon tide 2 January	19h 01m
Tidal difference	– 00h 20m
High water at Stranraer	18h 41m

The columns headed 'Springs' and 'Neaps' show the height, in metres, of the tide above datum for mean high water springs and mean high water neaps respectively.

Port		Diff.		Springs	Neaps
		h	min	m	m
Aberdeen	Leith	−1	19	4.4	3.4
*Antwerp	London	+0	50	5.8	4.8
Ardrossan	Greenock	−0	15	3.2	2.6
Ayr	Greenock	−0	25	3.0	2.5
Belfast	London	−2	47	3.5	3.0
Blackpool	Liverpool	−0	10	8.9	7.0
*Boulogne	London	−2	44	8.9	7.2
*Calais	London	−2	04	7.2	5.9
*Cherbourg	London	−6	00	6.4	5.0
Cobh	Liverpool	−5	55	4.2	3.2
Cowes	London	−2	38	4.2	3.5
Dartmouth	London	+4	25	4.9	3.8
*Dieppe	London	−3	03	9.3	7.3
Douglas, IoM	Liverpool	−0	04	6.9	5.4
Dover	London	−2	52	6.7	5.3
Dublin	London	−2	05	4.1	3.4
Dun Loaghaire	London	−2	10	4.1	3.4
*Dunkirk	London	−1	54	6.0	4.9
Fishguard	Liverpool	−4	01	4.8	3.4
Fleetwood	Liverpool	0	00	9.2	7.3
*Flushing	London	−0	15	4.7	3.9
Folkestone	London	−3	04	7.1	5.7
Galway	Liverpool	−6	08	5.1	3.9
Glasgow	Greenock	+0	26	4.7	4.0
Harwich	London	−2	06	4.0	3.4
*Le Havre	London	−3	55	7.9	6.6
Heysham	Liverpool	+0	05	9.4	7.4
Holyhead	Liverpool	−0	50	5.6	4.4
*Hook of Holland	London	−0	01	2.1	1.7

Port		Diff.		Springs	Neaps
		h	min	m	m
Hull (Albert Dock)	London	−7	40	7.5	5.8
Immingham	London	−8	00	7.3	5.8
Larne	London	−2	40	2.8	2.5
Lerwick	Leith	−3	48	2.2	1.6
Londonderry	London	−5	37	2.7	2.1
Lowestoft	London	−4	25	2.4	2.1
Margate	London	−1	53	4.8	3.9
Milford Haven	Liverpool	−5	08	7.0	5.2
Morecambe	Liverpool	+0	07	9.5	7.4
Newhaven	London	−2	46	6.7	5.1
Oban	Greenock	+5	43	4.0	2.9
*Ostend	London	−1	32	5.1	4.2
Plymouth	London	+4	05	5.5	4.4
Portland	London	+5	09	2.1	1.4
Portsmouth	London	−2	38	4.7	3.8
Ramsgate	London	−2	32	5.2	4.1
Richmond Lock	London	+1	00	4.9	3.7
Rosslare Harbour	Liverpool	−5	24	1.9	1.4
Rosyth	Leith	+0	09	5.8	4.7
*Rotterdam	London	+1	45	2.0	1.7
*St Helier	London	+4	48	11.0	8.1
*St Malo	London	+4	27	12.2	9.2
St Peter Port	London	+4	54	9.3	7.0
Scrabster	Leith	−6	06	5.0	4.0
Sheerness	London	−1	19	5.8	4.7
Shoreham	London	−2	44	6.3	4.9
Southampton (1st high water)	London	−2	54	4.5	3.7
Spurn Head	London	−8	25	6.9	5.5
Stornoway	Liverpool	−4	16	4.8	3.7
Stranraer	Greenock	−0	20	3.0	2.4
Stromness	Leith	−5	26	3.6	2.7
Swansea	London	−7	35	9.5	7.2
Tees (River Entrance)	Leith	+1	09	5.5	4.3
Tilbury	London	−0	49	6.4	5.4
Tobermory	Liverpool	−5	11	4.4	3.3
Tyne River (North Shields)	London	−10	30	5.0	3.9
Ullapool	Leith	−7	40	5.2	3.9
Walton-on-the-Naze	London	−2	10	4.2	3.4
Wick	Leith	−3	26	3.5	2.8
*Zeebrugge	London	−0	55	4.8	3.9

PREDICTIONS

The following data are daily predictions of the time and height of high water at London Bridge, Liverpool, Greenock and Leith. The time of the data is Greenwich Mean Time; this applies also to data for the months when British Summer Time is in operation and the hour's time difference should be allowed for. The datum of predictions for each port shows the difference of height, in metres from Ordnance data (Newlyn).

JANUARY 2008   *High Water*   GMT

	LONDON BRIDGE*Datum of Predictions3.20m below				LIVERPOOL (Alfred Dock)*Datum of Predictions4.93m below				GREENOCK*Datum of Predictions1.62m below				LEITH*Datum of Predictions2.90m below			
	hr	m	hr	m	hr	m	hr	m	hr	m	hr	m	hr	m	hr	m
		ht		ht		ht		ht		ht		ht		ht		ht
TU 1	07 12	6.0	19 58	5.9	04 57	7.5	17 20	7.6	06 20	2.9	18 07	3.2	08 43	4.4	21 12	4.5
W 2	08 12	5.7	20 54	5.7	06 00	7.3	18 25	7.4	07 12	2.9	19 01	3.0	09 38	4.3	22 11	4.4
TH 3	09 23	5.6	21 57	5.7	07 09	7.3	19 35	7.4	08 15	2.9	20 06	2.9	10 37	4.3	23 14	4.4
F 4	10 32	5.7	22 58	5.8	08 12	7.6	20 37	7.6	09 23	3.0	21 19	2.9	11 39	4.4	—	—
SA 5	11 32	5.9	23 53	6.0	09 05	7.9	21 29	7.9	10 22	3.1	22 24	3.0	00 16	4.5	12 37	4.6
SU 6	12 24	6.1	—	—	09 50	8.3	22 13	8.2	11 11	3.3	23 15	3.1	01 10	4.7	13 23	4.8
M 7	00 41	6.3	13 11	6.4	10 31	8.6	22 52	8.4	11 52	3.4	23 59	3.1	01 53	4.9	14 03	5.0
TU 8	01 25	6.4	13 53	6.5	11 09	8.8	23 29	8.6	12 28	3.5	—	—	02 32	5.0	14 39	5.1
W 9	02 06	6.5	14 33	6.6	11 46	9.0	—	—	00 40	3.2	13 02	3.6	03 08	5.1	15 14	5.3
TH 10	02 43	6.5	15 12	6.6	00 06	8.7	12 23	9.1	01 20	3.2	13 35	3.6	03 44	5.2	15 48	5.3
F 11	03 19	6.5	15 51	6.7	00 44	8.8	13 01	9.2	01 59	3.2	14 10	3.6	04 20	5.3	16 23	5.4
SA 12	03 55	6.6	16 30	6.7	01 23	8.8	13 41	9.2	02 38	3.3	14 47	3.6	04 58	5.3	17 00	5.4
SU 13	04 31	6.6	17 12	6.7	02 02	8.8	14 22	9.2	03 17	3.3	15 26	3.6	05 38	5.2	17 39	5.3
M 14	05 10	6.7	17 55	6.6	02 44	8.7	15 05	9.0	03 57	3.3	16 08	3.5	06 21	5.1	18 22	5.2
TU 15	05 54	6.6	18 42	6.4	03 29	8.4	15 54	8.8	04 38	3.2	16 53	3.4	07 08	4.9	19 10	5.1
W 16	06 42	6.5	19 34	6.1	04 22	8.1	16 50	8.4	05 22	3.1	17 44	3.3	08 02	4.7	20 09	4.9
TH 17	07 40	6.2	20 36	5.9	05 25	7.8	17 57	8.1	06 11	3.0	18 47	3.1	09 07	4.6	21 24	4.8
F 18	08 52	6.0	21 49	5.7	06 39	7.7	19 12	8.0	07 14	2.9	20 15	3.0	10 19	4.6	22 46	4.8
SA 19	10 13	5.9	23 03	5.8	07 58	7.9	20 32	8.2	08 52	2.9	21 49	3.0	11 30	4.7	—	—
SU 20	11 29	6.1	—	—	09 08	8.4	21 39	8.6	10 14	3.1	23 01	3.1	00 02	4.9	12 36	5.0
M 21	00 09	6.1	12 36	6.4	10 05	8.9	22 35	9.0	11 12	3.3	23 59	3.2	01 08	5.2	13 32	5.2
TU 22	01 07	6.4	13 33	6.7	10 55	9.3	23 24	9.2	12 02	3.5	—	—	02 04	5.4	14 22	5.5
W 23	01 58	6.6	14 25	6.9	11 41	9.6	—	—	00 52	3.3	12 48	3.6	02 52	5.5	15 07	5.6
TH 24	02 45	6.7	15 13	7.0	00 08	9.3	12 24	9.7	01 41	3.3	13 31	3.7	03 36	5.5	15 51	5.7
F 25	03 27	6.8	15 56	7.0	00 50	9.3	13 04	9.6	02 25	3.3	14 11	3.7	04 19	5.5	16 33	5.6
SA 26	04 04	6.8	16 35	6.9	01 28	9.1	13 42	9.4	03 04	3.2	14 49	3.7	05 00	5.3	17 14	5.5
SU 27	04 37	6.7	17 09	6.8	02 04	8.9	14 19	9.1	03 39	3.2	15 26	3.6	05 39	5.1	17 54	5.3
M 28	05 09	6.7	17 42	6.6	02 39	8.6	14 56	8.7	04 12	3.2	16 02	3.5	06 18	4.9	18 35	5.0
TU 29	05 42	6.5	18 15	6.4	03 16	8.2	15 34	8.2	04 46	3.1	16 40	3.4	06 58	4.6	19 19	4.7
W 30	06 20	6.3	18 52	6.1	03 57	7.7	16 18	7.7	05 24	3.0	17 22	3.2	07 43	4.4	20 11	4.4
TH 31	07 06	5.9	19 38	5.8	04 48	7.3	17 15	7.2	06 07	2.9	18 09	2.9	08 36	4.2	21 12	4.2

FEBRUARY 2008   *High Water*   GMT

	LONDON BRIDGE				LIVERPOOL (Alfred Dock)				GREENOCK				LEITH			
F 1	08 04	5.5	20 36	5.5	05 58	7.0	18 31	6.9	07 01	2.8	19 06	2.8	09 36	4.1	22 21	4.1
SA 2	09 23	5.3	21 56	5.5	07 25	7.1	20 01	7.0	08 20	2.7	20 19	2.7	10 44	4.2	23 38	4.2
SU 3	10 55	5.5	23 17	5.7	08 38	7.5	21 08	7.5	09 52	2.9	22 01	2.7	11 59	4.4	—	—
M 4	12 00	5.9	—	—	09 30	8.0	21 56	7.9	10 50	3.1	23 03	2.9	00 46	4.5	13 00	4.6
TU 5	00 17	6.1	12 51	6.3	10 13	8.5	22 37	8.4	11 33	3.3	23 48	3.0	01 35	4.7	13 45	4.9
W 6	01 06	6.4	13 35	6.6	10 52	8.9	23 14	8.7	12 09	3.4	—	—	02 13	5.0	14 22	5.1
TH 7	01 49	6.6	14 17	6.7	11 29	9.2	23 51	9.0	00 28	3.1	12 44	3.4	02 49	5.2	14 56	5.4
F 8	02 29	6.6	14 56	6.8	12 06	9.4	—	—	01 07	3.1	13 17	3.5	03 24	5.4	15 29	5.5
SA 9	03 05	6.7	15 34	6.9	00 27	9.1	12 43	9.6	01 43	3.2	13 53	3.6	03 58	5.5	16 02	5.6
SU 10	03 39	6.8	16 13	6.9	01 04	9.3	13 22	9.7	02 19	3.3	14 31	3.6	04 35	5.5	16 38	5.7
M 11	04 15	6.9	16 51	6.8	01 42	9.2	14 01	9.6	02 55	3.3	15 10	3.6	05 13	5.4	17 17	5.6
TU 12	04 52	6.9	17 31	6.7	02 21	9.1	14 42	9.3	03 32	3.4	15 50	3.6	05 55	5.2	18 00	5.4
W 13	05 33	6.9	18 13	6.5	03 02	8.7	15 28	8.9	04 09	3.3	16 32	3.5	06 39	5.0	18 48	5.2
TH 14	06 18	6.9	19 00	6.1	03 50	8.2	16 22	8.3	04 49	3.2	17 18	3.2	07 30	4.7	19 46	4.8
F 15	07 12	6.2	19 57	5.6	04 53	7.7	17 33	7.7	05 34	3.1	18 15	2.9	08 35	4.5	21 07	4.6
SA 16	08 23	5.7	21 19	5.4	06 15	7.3	19 03	7.4	06 28	2.9	19 56	2.7	09 56	4.4	22 40	4.5
SU 17	10 01	5.6	22 48	5.5	07 51	7.5	20 34	7.8	08 21	2.8	22 00	2.8	11 20	4.5	—	—
M 18	11 26	5.9	23 59	5.9	09 05	8.1	21 38	8.3	10 08	2.9	23 04	3.0	00 05	4.7	12 33	4.8
TU 19	12 31	6.4	—	—	10 00	8.8	22 28	8.9	11 06	3.2	23 56	3.2	01 15	5.0	13 28	5.2
W 20	00 57	6.3	13 26	6.8	10 45	9.3	23 11	9.2	11 52	3.4	—	—	02 00	5.3	14 13	5.4
TH 21	01 46	6.7	14 13	7.0	11 26	9.6	23 50	9.3	00 42	3.2	12 36	3.5	02 41	5.4	14 53	5.6
F 22	02 29	6.8	14 55	7.1	12 04	9.7	—	—	01 24	3.3	13 15	3.6	03 19	5.4	15 31	5.7
SA 23	03 06	6.9	15 33	7.0	00 26	9.3	12 40	9.6	02 01	3.2	13 52	3.6	03 54	5.4	16 08	5.6
SU 24	03 39	6.9	16 04	6.9	00 59	9.2	13 14	9.4	02 33	3.2	14 26	3.6	04 29	5.3	16 44	5.5
M 25	04 08	6.8	16 32	6.8	01 31	9.0	13 46	9.1	03 02	3.2	14 58	3.5	05 03	5.1	17 19	5.3
TU 26	04 37	6.8	17 01	6.7	02 02	8.8	14 18	8.8	03 32	3.2	15 32	3.5	05 38	4.9	17 55	5.0
W 27	05 09	6.7	17 33	6.6	02 35	8.4	14 52	8.3	04 04	3.2	16 07	3.3	06 14	4.7	18 36	4.7
TH 28	05 46	6.4	18 09	6.3	03 10	8.0	15 32	7.7	04 39	3.1	16 46	3.1	06 55	4.5	19 24	4.4
F 29	06 28	6.1	18 53	6.0	03 53	7.4	16 22	7.1	05 18	2.9	17 32	2.8	07 44	4.3	20 23	4.1

MARCH 2008   *High Water*   GMT

Datum of Predictions:
- LONDON BRIDGE: 3.20m below
- LIVERPOOL (Alfred Dock): 4.93m below
- GREENOCK: 1.62m below
- LEITH: 2.90m below

	LONDON BRIDGE hr m	ht m	hr m	ht m	LIVERPOOL hr m	ht m	hr m	ht m	GREENOCK hr m	ht m	hr m	ht m	LEITH hr m	ht m	hr m	ht m
SA 1	07 19	5.6	19 45	5.6	04 54	6.9	17 35	6.6	06 07	2.7	18 28	2.6	08 45	4.1	21 33	4.0
SU 2	08 25	5.3	20 55	5.3	06 30	6.8	19 24	6.7	07 15	2.6	19 38	2.5	09 58	4.0	22 53	4.1
M 3	10 07	5.3	22 38	5.5	08 06	7.1	20 43	7.2	09 14	2.7	21 41	2.6	11 18	4.2	—	—
TU 4	11 32	5.8	23 49	5.9	09 03	7.8	21 32	7.8	10 22	2.9	22 44	2.8	00 14	4.3	12 29	4.5
W 5	12 25	6.3	—	—	09 47	8.4	22 12	8.4	11 05	3.1	23 27	3.0	01 07	4.7	13 17	4.9
TH 6	00 40	6.3	13 11	6.6	10 26	8.9	22 49	8.9	11 41	3.3	—	—	01 46	5.0	13 55	5.2
F 7	01 24	6.6	13 53	6.9	11 03	9.4	23 26	9.2	00 06	3.1	12 17	3.4	02 22	5.3	14 29	5.5
SA 8	02 04	6.7	14 32	7.0	11 41	9.7	—	—	00 43	3.1	12 53	3.4	02 57	5.5	15 02	5.7
SU 9	02 41	6.9	15 11	7.0	00 02	9.5	12 20	9.9	01 19	3.2	13 32	3.5	03 32	5.6	15 38	5.8
M 10	03 17	7.0	15 49	7.0	00 41	9.6	12 59	9.9	01 55	3.3	14 12	3.6	04 09	5.6	16 16	5.8
TU 11	03 55	7.1	16 28	6.9	01 19	9.5	13 40	9.7	02 31	3.4	14 53	3.6	04 48	5.5	16 58	5.7
W 12	04 34	7.1	17 07	6.7	01 58	9.3	14 22	9.3	03 07	3.5	15 33	3.6	05 30	5.3	17 44	5.5
TH 13	05 16	7.0	17 48	6.4	02 40	8.8	15 09	8.7	03 44	3.4	16 16	3.4	06 15	5.0	18 36	5.1
F 14	06 02	6.6	18 33	6.0	03 29	8.2	16 06	8.0	04 24	3.3	17 03	3.1	07 07	4.7	19 39	4.7
SA 15	06 58	6.0	19 29	5.5	04 34	7.6	17 25	7.3	05 09	3.1	18 03	2.8	08 18	4.4	21 06	4.4
SU 16	08 19	5.6	21 06	5.2	06 08	7.2	19 06	7.2	06 04	2.8	20 29	2.6	09 47	4.3	22 39	4.4
M 17	10 01	5.5	22 35	5.5	07 44	7.5	20 27	7.7	08 20	2.7	21 59	2.8	11 12	4.5	—	—
TU 18	11 17	6.0	23 41	6.0	08 52	8.1	21 24	8.3	09 55	2.9	22 54	3.0	00 03	4.7	12 22	4.8
W 19	12 16	6.5	—	—	09 43	8.7	22 10	8.8	10 49	3.2	23 39	3.2	01 03	5.0	13 14	5.1
TH 20	00 36	6.5	13 07	6.9	10 26	9.2	22 49	9.1	11 33	3.4	—	—	01 46	5.2	13 55	5.4
F 21	01 23	6.8	13 51	7.1	11 04	9.4	23 25	9.2	00 19	3.2	12 14	3.4	02 22	5.3	14 32	5.5
SA 22	02 04	6.9	14 30	7.1	11 39	9.4	23 57	9.2	00 57	3.2	12 52	3.5	02 55	5.3	15 07	5.5
SU 23	02 40	6.9	15 04	6.9	12 12	9.3	—	—	01 29	3.2	13 26	3.4	03 27	5.3	15 42	5.5
M 24	03 12	6.8	15 32	6.8	00 28	9.1	12 44	9.2	01 57	3.3	13 57	3.4	03 58	5.2	16 15	5.3
TU 25	03 40	6.8	15 57	6.7	00 58	9.0	13 14	8.9	02 26	3.3	14 29	3.4	04 30	5.1	16 50	5.2
W 26	04 09	6.7	16 26	6.7	01 28	8.8	13 46	8.6	02 56	3.3	15 02	3.3	05 02	5.0	17 26	4.9
TH 27	04 42	6.6	16 58	6.6	02 00	8.5	14 19	8.2	03 27	3.3	15 37	3.2	05 37	4.8	18 06	4.7
F 28	05 18	6.4	17 35	6.4	02 34	8.1	14 58	7.7	04 00	3.2	16 17	3.0	06 16	4.6	18 51	4.4
SA 29	06 00	6.1	18 18	6.1	03 15	7.6	15 46	7.1	04 37	3.0	17 03	2.8	07 02	4.3	19 46	4.2
SU 30	06 49	5.7	19 09	5.7	04 11	7.1	16 53	6.7	05 23	2.8	17 59	2.6	08 01	4.1	20 52	4.0
M 31	07 50	5.4	20 13	5.4	05 33	6.8	18 34	6.6	06 27	2.6	19 07	2.5	09 14	4.0	22 08	4.1

APRIL 2008   *High Water*   GMT

	LONDON BRIDGE hr m	ht m	hr m	ht m	LIVERPOOL hr m	ht m	hr m	ht m	GREENOCK hr m	ht m	hr m	ht m	LEITH hr m	ht m	hr m	ht m
TU 1	09 10	5.3	21 42	5.4	07 16	7.1	20 01	7.1	08 01	2.6	20 53	2.6	10 33	4.2	23 25	4.3
W 2	10 50	5.7	23 07	5.8	08 21	7.7	20 54	7.8	09 36	2.8	22 09	2.8	11 44	4.5	—	—
TH 3	11 50	6.2	—	—	09 09	8.3	21 37	8.4	10 25	3.0	22 53	3.0	00 24	4.7	12 36	4.9
F 4	00 03	6.2	12 38	6.6	09 51	9.0	22 16	9.0	11 04	3.2	23 32	3.1	01 10	5.1	13 18	5.2
SA 5	00 49	6.6	13 22	6.9	10 32	9.4	22 55	9.4	11 44	3.3	—	—	01 49	5.4	13 56	5.5
SU 6	01 31	6.9	14 04	7.1	11 13	9.8	23 35	9.6	00 10	3.2	12 26	3.4	02 26	5.6	14 33	5.8
M 7	02 12	7.0	14 44	7.1	11 55	9.9	—	—	00 49	3.3	13 09	3.5	03 04	5.7	15 14	5.9
TU 8	02 54	7.2	15 25	7.1	00 15	9.7	12 38	9.9	01 28	3.4	13 54	3.6	03 43	5.7	15 57	5.9
W 9	03 36	7.2	16 05	6.9	00 57	9.6	13 22	9.6	02 07	3.5	14 38	3.6	04 25	5.5	16 43	5.7
TH 10	04 20	7.2	16 47	6.7	01 40	9.3	14 09	9.1	02 46	3.5	15 22	3.4	05 09	5.3	17 34	5.4
F 11	05 06	6.9	17 30	6.4	02 26	8.8	15 00	8.6	03 25	3.5	16 08	3.2	05 58	5.0	18 31	5.0
SA 12	05 58	6.5	18 15	5.9	03 20	8.2	16 02	7.8	04 07	3.3	17 02	2.9	06 56	4.7	19 41	4.7
SU 13	07 01	6.0	19 25	5.5	04 30	7.7	17 24	7.3	04 54	3.1	18 22	2.7	08 13	4.5	21 03	4.5
M 14	08 25	5.7	20 57	5.4	05 58	7.4	18 50	7.3	05 57	2.9	20 24	2.6	09 36	4.5	22 26	4.5
TU 15	09 46	5.9	22 11	5.7	07 19	7.7	20 00	7.7	08 03	2.8	21 36	2.8	10 52	4.6	23 41	4.7
W 16	10 52	6.2	23 12	6.2	08 22	8.1	20 56	8.2	09 26	3.0	22 27	3.0	11 57	4.9	—	—
TH 17	11 49	6.7	—	—	09 14	8.6	21 41	8.6	10 20	3.2	23 10	3.1	00 38	4.9	12 49	5.1
F 18	00 05	6.5	12 38	6.9	09 58	8.9	22 20	8.9	11 05	3.3	23 48	3.2	01 21	5.0	13 30	5.2
SA 19	00 52	6.8	13 21	7.0	10 37	9.0	22 55	9.0	11 45	3.3	—	—	01 56	5.1	14 08	5.3
SU 20	01 34	6.9	14 00	6.9	11 12	9.0	23 27	9.0	00 23	3.2	12 22	3.3	02 28	5.3	14 43	5.3
M 21	02 12	6.8	14 33	6.8	11 44	9.0	23 57	9.0	00 54	3.3	12 56	3.3	02 58	5.2	15 17	5.3
TU 22	02 46	6.7	15 00	6.6	12 15	8.8	—	—	01 24	3.3	13 28	3.3	03 29	5.2	15 51	5.2
W 23	03 16	6.6	15 27	6.6	00 28	8.9	12 46	8.7	01 53	3.4	14 00	3.3	04 00	5.1	16 26	5.0
TH 24	03 46	6.5	15 57	6.6	01 00	8.7	13 19	8.4	02 24	3.4	14 35	3.2	04 33	5.0	17 03	4.9
F 25	04 20	6.5	16 31	6.5	01 33	8.5	13 55	8.1	02 56	3.4	15 12	3.1	05 08	4.8	17 43	4.7
SA 26	04 57	6.3	17 08	6.4	02 09	8.2	14 34	7.8	03 29	3.3	15 53	3.0	05 47	4.6	18 27	4.5
SU 27	05 40	6.2	17 51	6.1	02 52	7.8	15 22	7.3	04 05	3.1	16 39	2.8	06 31	4.5	19 17	4.3
M 28	06 29	5.9	18 42	5.8	03 45	7.4	16 23	7.0	04 49	2.9	17 35	2.7	07 25	4.3	20 17	4.2
TU 29	07 26	5.7	19 41	5.6	04 54	7.2	17 41	6.9	05 49	2.7	18 38	2.6	08 31	4.2	21 25	4.3
W 30	08 35	5.6	20 55	5.6	06 14	7.3	19 03	7.2	07 04	2.7	19 53	2.7	09 46	4.3	22 35	4.4

MAY 2008   *High Water*   GMT

	LONDON BRIDGE *Datum of Predictions 3.20m below				LIVERPOOL (Alfred Dock) *Datum of Predictions 4.93m below				GREENOCK *Datum of Predictions 1.62m below				LEITH *Datum of Predictions 2.90m below			
	hr	m	hr	ht m	hr	m	hr	ht m	hr	m	hr	ht m	hr	m	hr	ht m
TH 1	09 56	5.8	22 13	5.9	07 26	7.8	20 05	7.8	08 29	2.8	21 12	2.8	10 53	4.6	23 36	4.7
F 2	11 05	6.2	23 17	6.2	08 23	8.3	20 55	8.4	09 34	3.0	22 08	3.0	11 50	4.9	—	—
SA 3	12 00	6.6	—	—	09 13	8.9	21 41	9.0	10 24	3.2	22 53	3.1	00 28	5.1	12 38	5.2
SU 4	00 10	6.6	12 49	6.9	10 00	9.4	22 25	9.4	11 11	3.3	23 37	3.2	01 13	5.3	13 23	5.5
M 5	01 00	6.9	13 35	7.1	10 46	9.7	23 08	9.6	11 59	3.4	—	—	01 55	5.5	14 08	5.7
TU 6	01 47	7.1	14 20	7.1	11 33	9.8	23 53	9.6	00 20	3.4	12 48	3.5	02 37	5.6	14 54	5.8
W 7	02 34	7.2	15 04	7.0	12 20	9.7	—	—	01 04	3.5	13 38	3.5	03 21	5.6	15 43	5.8
TH 8	03 22	7.2	15 48	6.9	00 39	9.5	13 10	9.4	01 47	3.5	14 27	3.4	04 06	5.5	16 34	5.6
F 9	04 11	7.1	16 33	6.7	01 28	9.3	14 01	9.0	02 29	3.6	15 17	3.3	04 55	5.3	17 28	5.4
SA 10	05 02	6.9	17 20	6.4	02 19	8.9	14 55	8.5	03 12	3.5	16 11	3.1	05 48	5.1	18 28	5.1
SU 11	05 58	6.6	18 14	6.1	03 15	8.4	15 56	8.0	03 57	3.4	17 13	2.9	06 50	4.9	19 35	4.8
M 12	07 01	6.2	19 20	5.8	04 21	8.0	17 05	7.6	04 48	3.2	18 28	2.8	08 02	4.7	20 45	4.6
TU 13	08 11	6.1	20 32	5.8	05 32	7.8	18 17	7.5	05 55	3.0	19 47	2.7	09 13	4.7	21 54	4.5
W 14	09 18	6.1	21 37	6.0	06 41	7.8	19 21	7.6	07 23	2.9	20 52	2.8	10 20	4.7	23 01	4.6
TH 15	10 18	6.3	22 36	6.2	07 44	8.0	20 17	7.9	08 42	3.0	21 46	2.9	11 21	4.8	—	—
F 16	11 13	6.5	23 30	6.5	08 38	8.2	21 05	8.2	09 41	3.1	22 31	3.0	00 00	4.7	12 16	4.9
SA 17	12 03	6.7	—	—	09 25	8.4	21 47	8.5	10 29	3.1	23 11	3.1	00 47	4.8	13 02	5.0
SU 18	00 19	6.6	12 48	6.7	10 07	8.5	22 24	8.6	11 12	3.2	23 48	3.2	01 26	4.9	13 42	5.0
M 19	01 04	6.6	13 28	6.7	10 44	8.6	22 58	8.7	11 50	3.2	—	—	02 00	5.0	14 20	5.0
TU 20	01 46	6.6	14 03	6.6	11 19	8.6	23 31	8.8	00 22	3.3	12 25	3.1	02 32	5.0	14 56	5.0
W 21	02 23	6.5	14 34	6.5	11 51	8.5	—	—	00 55	3.4	12 59	3.1	03 03	5.1	15 31	5.0
TH 22	02 57	6.4	15 04	6.5	00 04	8.7	12 25	8.4	01 27	3.4	13 34	3.1	03 36	5.1	16 07	5.0
F 23	03 30	6.4	15 36	6.5	00 38	8.6	13 00	8.3	01 59	3.4	14 11	3.1	04 10	5.0	16 45	4.9
SA 24	04 05	6.3	16 11	6.4	01 14	8.5	13 38	8.2	02 32	3.4	14 51	3.1	04 47	4.9	17 24	4.8
SU 25	04 43	6.3	16 49	6.4	01 53	8.3	14 18	8.0	03 06	3.3	15 33	3.0	05 25	4.8	18 06	4.7
M 26	05 25	6.3	17 31	6.3	02 36	8.1	15 04	7.7	03 43	3.2	16 19	2.9	06 08	4.7	18 52	4.6
TU 27	06 13	6.2	18 19	6.1	03 25	7.9	15 57	7.5	04 25	3.1	17 10	2.9	06 55	4.6	19 44	4.5
W 28	07 06	6.0	19 14	6.0	04 22	7.8	16 59	7.4	05 17	2.9	18 06	2.8	07 51	4.5	20 44	4.5
TH 29	08 06	6.0	20 18	5.9	05 27	7.8	18 07	7.5	06 22	2.9	19 06	2.8	08 55	4.6	21 49	4.6
F 30	09 15	6.0	21 29	6.0	06 32	8.0	19 14	7.9	07 34	2.9	20 12	2.9	10 03	4.7	22 51	4.8
SA 31	10 24	6.2	22 36	6.3	07 36	8.4	20 14	8.3	08 46	3.0	21 18	3.0	11 05	4.9	23 48	5.0

JUNE 2008   *High Water*   GMT

	LONDON BRIDGE				LIVERPOOL (Alfred Dock)				GREENOCK				LEITH			
SU 1	11 25	6.5	23 37	6.6	08 35	8.8	21 08	8.8	09 48	3.2	22 16	3.1	12 03	5.1	—	—
M 2	12 20	6.7	—	—	09 31	9.1	21 58	9.2	10 44	3.3	23 08	3.2	00 41	5.2	12 57	5.4
TU 3	00 34	6.8	13 11	6.9	10 25	9.4	22 48	9.4	11 38	3.3	23 57	3.4	01 30	5.4	13 50	5.6
W 4	01 28	7.0	14 00	7.0	11 17	9.5	23 37	9.5	12 33	3.4	—	—	02 17	5.5	14 42	5.7
TH 5	02 20	7.2	14 48	6.9	12 09	9.4	—	—	00 45	3.5	13 29	3.3	03 05	5.6	15 34	5.7
F 6	03 12	7.2	15 36	6.9	00 27	9.5	13 01	9.3	01 32	3.6	14 23	3.3	03 54	5.5	16 27	5.6
SA 7	04 04	7.1	16 23	6.7	01 18	9.3	13 52	9.0	02 17	3.6	15 17	3.2	04 45	5.5	17 21	5.4
SU 8	04 56	7.0	17 12	6.6	02 09	9.1	14 43	8.7	03 02	3.6	16 11	3.1	05 39	5.3	18 16	5.2
M 9	05 49	6.8	18 02	6.4	03 01	8.8	15 36	8.3	03 48	3.5	17 06	3.0	06 36	5.1	19 14	4.9
TU 10	06 43	6.6	18 55	6.2	03 56	8.4	16 31	7.9	04 38	3.3	18 01	2.9	07 37	5.0	20 12	4.7
W 11	07 40	6.3	19 54	6.1	04 53	8.1	17 31	7.6	05 32	3.2	18 55	2.8	08 38	4.8	21 11	4.5
TH 12	08 39	6.2	20 54	6.0	05 55	7.8	18 33	7.5	06 33	3.0	19 51	2.8	09 38	4.7	22 10	4.4
F 13	09 36	6.1	21 54	6.0	06 57	7.7	19 32	7.6	07 40	2.9	20 48	2.8	10 38	4.6	23 09	4.5
SA 14	10 32	6.2	22 51	6.1	07 56	7.7	20 27	7.8	08 47	2.9	21 43	2.9	11 36	4.6	—	—
SU 15	11 24	6.3	23 46	6.3	08 50	7.9	21 14	8.1	09 47	2.9	22 32	3.0	00 05	4.6	12 31	4.7
M 16	12 13	6.4	—	—	09 38	8.0	21 57	8.3	10 37	3.0	23 16	3.1	00 53	4.7	13 19	4.8
TU 17	00 36	6.4	12 57	6.5	10 21	8.2	22 35	8.5	11 20	3.0	23 56	3.3	01 34	4.8	14 01	4.8
W 18	01 22	6.4	13 38	6.5	10 59	8.3	23 12	8.6	11 59	3.0	—	—	02 10	4.9	14 39	4.9
TH 19	02 04	6.4	14 14	6.5	11 35	8.3	23 47	8.7	00 32	3.4	12 37	3.0	02 44	5.0	15 15	5.0
F 20	02 42	6.4	14 49	6.4	12 11	8.3	—	—	01 06	3.4	13 14	3.0	03 19	5.1	15 50	5.0
SA 21	03 18	6.4	15 24	6.4	00 23	8.7	12 47	8.4	01 39	3.4	13 53	3.1	03 54	5.1	16 27	5.0
SU 22	03 54	6.4	15 58	6.4	01 01	8.7	13 24	8.3	02 12	3.4	14 33	3.1	04 30	5.1	17 04	5.0
M 23	04 32	6.4	16 35	6.4	01 39	8.6	14 03	8.3	02 47	3.4	15 14	3.1	05 06	5.0	17 44	4.9
TU 24	05 12	6.4	17 14	6.4	02 20	8.6	14 44	8.2	03 24	3.4	15 57	3.1	05 45	5.0	18 26	4.8
W 25	05 55	6.4	17 57	6.4	03 04	8.5	15 30	8.1	04 04	3.3	16 42	3.0	06 28	4.9	19 13	4.7
TH 26	06 43	6.3	18 46	6.3	03 53	8.4	16 22	7.9	04 49	3.2	17 30	3.0	07 15	4.9	20 06	4.7
F 27	07 36	6.1	19 44	6.2	04 49	8.2	17 22	7.8	05 43	3.1	18 22	2.9	08 10	4.8	21 06	4.6
SA 28	08 39	6.0	20 50	6.1	05 51	8.2	18 29	7.8	06 48	3.0	19 20	2.9	09 16	4.8	22 11	4.7
SU 29	09 47	6.0	22 01	6.1	06 57	8.2	19 37	8.1	08 04	3.0	20 31	2.9	10 28	4.8	23 15	4.8
M 30	10 55	6.2	23 11	6.3	08 06	8.4	20 42	8.4	09 20	3.0	21 45	3.0	11 37	5.0	—	—

JULY 2008 *High Water* GMT

	LONDON BRIDGE *Datum of Predictions 3.20m below				LIVERPOOL (Alfred Dock) *Datum of Predictions 4.93m below				GREENOCK *Datum of Predictions 1.62m below				LEITH *Datum of Predictions 2.90m below			
	hr	m	hr	m	hr	m	hr	m	hr	m	hr	m	hr	m	hr	m
TU 1	11 57	6.4	—	—	09 12	8.7	21 42	8.9	10 28	3.1	22 48	3.2	00 16	5.0	12 42	5.2
W 2	00 16	6.6	12 54	6.6	10 13	9.0	22 36	9.2	11 30	3.2	23 43	3.3	01 12	5.2	13 41	5.4
TH 3	01 16	6.8	13 47	6.8	11 08	9.2	23 27	9.5	12 28	3.2	—	—	02 04	5.4	14 35	5.6
F 4	02 12	7.0	14 37	6.9	12 00	9.3	—	—	00 33	3.5	13 25	3.2	02 54	5.6	15 26	5.7
SA 5	03 04	7.1	15 25	6.9	00 16	9.6	12 50	9.3	01 21	3.5	14 19	3.2	03 43	5.6	16 16	5.6
SU 6	03 55	7.2	16 11	6.9	01 05	9.5	13 36	9.2	02 07	3.6	15 09	3.2	04 32	5.6	17 04	5.5
M 7	04 42	7.1	16 54	6.8	01 51	9.4	14 21	8.9	02 50	3.6	15 55	3.1	05 21	5.5	17 53	5.2
TU 8	05 28	6.9	17 35	6.7	02 36	9.1	15 04	8.6	03 33	3.6	16 38	3.1	06 11	5.3	18 41	5.0
W 9	06 12	6.7	18 16	6.6	03 20	8.7	15 47	8.1	04 15	3.5	17 18	3.0	07 01	5.1	19 29	4.7
TH 10	06 56	6.4	19 00	6.3	04 06	8.3	16 34	7.7	04 58	3.3	17 58	2.9	07 54	4.9	20 20	4.5
F 11	07 43	6.1	19 52	6.0	04 56	7.8	17 30	7.4	05 43	3.1	18 42	2.8	08 49	4.6	21 13	4.4
SA 12	08 37	5.9	20 56	5.8	05 57	7.4	18 36	7.2	06 33	2.9	19 34	2.8	09 47	4.4	22 10	4.3
SU 13	09 39	5.7	22 07	5.7	07 07	7.2	19 45	7.4	07 33	2.8	20 41	2.8	10 51	4.3	23 14	4.3
M 14	10 41	5.8	23 14	5.8	08 16	7.3	20 44	7.7	08 48	2.7	21 54	2.9	11 58	4.4	—	—
TU 15	11 39	6.0	—	—	09 14	7.6	21 34	8.1	10 05	2.7	22 51	3.1	00 17	4.5	12 57	4.5
W 16	00 11	6.1	12 31	6.3	10 02	7.9	22 17	8.4	11 01	2.8	23 36	3.2	01 10	4.7	13 43	4.7
TH 17	01 02	6.3	13 17	6.5	10 44	8.1	22 56	8.6	11 45	2.9	—	—	01 52	4.9	14 22	4.9
F 18	01 46	6.5	13 58	6.6	11 21	8.3	23 33	8.8	00 14	3.3	12 23	3.0	02 28	5.0	14 57	5.0
SA 19	02 26	6.6	14 37	6.6	11 57	8.5	—	—	00 48	3.4	13 00	3.0	03 03	5.2	15 32	5.1
SU 20	03 04	6.6	15 12	6.5	00 08	8.9	12 32	8.6	01 20	3.4	13 36	3.0	03 37	5.3	16 06	5.2
M 21	03 40	6.6	15 45	6.5	00 44	9.0	13 07	8.7	01 53	3.5	14 14	3.1	04 10	5.3	16 42	5.2
TU 22	04 16	6.6	16 18	6.6	01 21	9.0	13 43	8.7	02 28	3.5	14 52	3.1	04 45	5.3	17 19	5.2
W 23	04 53	6.6	16 54	6.7	01 59	9.0	14 21	8.7	03 05	3.5	15 31	3.2	05 21	5.3	17 59	5.1
TH 24	05 32	6.6	17 33	6.7	02 39	9.0	15 02	8.5	03 44	3.4	16 11	3.2	06 01	5.2	18 43	5.0
F 25	06 15	6.4	18 18	6.6	03 24	8.8	15 48	8.2	04 25	3.3	16 54	3.1	06 45	5.1	19 31	4.8
SA 26	07 03	6.2	19 10	6.3	04 16	8.4	16 45	7.9	05 11	3.2	17 40	3.0	07 37	4.9	20 28	4.7
SU 27	08 01	5.9	20 14	6.0	05 18	8.1	17 54	7.7	06 09	3.0	18 35	2.9	08 43	4.8	21 38	4.6
M 28	09 12	5.7	21 32	5.9	06 30	7.8	19 13	7.7	07 27	2.8	19 48	2.9	10 05	4.7	22 52	4.7
TU 29	10 31	5.8	22 56	6.0	07 52	7.9	20 31	8.1	09 08	2.8	21 27	2.9	11 26	4.8	—	—
W 30	11 42	6.1	—	—	09 08	8.3	21 35	8.7	10 30	3.0	22 40	3.1	00 02	4.9	12 38	5.1
TH 31	00 09	6.3	12 44	6.4	10 09	8.8	22 29	9.2	11 31	3.1	23 35	3.3	01 04	5.2	13 38	5.4

AUGUST 2008 *High Water* GMT

	LONDON BRIDGE				LIVERPOOL (Alfred Dock)				GREENOCK				LEITH			
	hr	m	hr	m	hr	m	hr	m	hr	m	hr	m	hr	m	hr	m
F 1	01 11	6.7	13 37	6.7	11 01	9.1	23 17	9.5	12 26	3.2	—	—	01 56	5.4	14 28	5.6
SA 2	02 04	7.0	14 25	6.9	11 48	9.3	—	—	00 24	3.5	13 17	3.2	02 43	5.7	15 14	5.7
SU 3	02 53	7.2	15 10	7.0	00 02	9.7	12 32	9.4	01 10	3.6	14 04	3.2	03 27	5.8	15 57	5.6
M 4	03 38	7.2	15 50	7.0	00 45	9.7	13 13	9.3	01 52	3.6	14 46	3.2	04 11	5.8	16 40	5.5
TU 5	04 19	7.2	16 27	7.0	01 25	9.5	13 50	9.0	02 32	3.6	15 23	3.1	04 54	5.7	17 21	5.3
W 6	04 57	7.0	17 00	6.9	02 03	9.2	14 26	8.7	03 09	3.6	15 56	3.1	05 37	5.4	18 02	5.0
TH 7	05 30	6.8	17 33	6.8	02 40	8.8	15 02	8.3	03 45	3.5	16 28	3.1	06 20	5.2	18 44	4.8
F 8	06 02	6.5	18 09	6.5	03 18	8.3	15 40	7.9	04 22	3.4	17 04	3.0	07 06	4.8	19 28	4.5
SA 9	06 38	6.2	18 51	6.1	04 01	7.7	16 27	7.4	05 02	3.1	17 45	2.9	07 57	4.5	20 19	4.3
SU 10	07 21	5.8	19 46	5.7	04 54	7.2	17 31	7.1	05 47	2.9	18 34	2.8	08 57	4.3	21 18	4.2
M 11	08 19	5.5	21 05	5.4	06 10	6.8	19 01	7.0	06 41	2.7	19 38	2.7	10 04	4.1	22 24	4.2
TU 12	09 49	5.4	22 43	5.5	07 45	6.9	20 19	7.4	07 52	2.6	21 18	2.8	11 21	4.2	23 40	4.4
W 13	11 07	5.7	23 48	5.9	08 53	7.3	21 14	7.9	09 45	2.6	22 30	3.0	12 33	4.4	—	—
TH 14	12 06	6.1	—	—	09 43	7.8	21 58	8.4	10 50	2.8	23 15	3.2	00 44	4.6	13 23	4.7
F 15	00 40	6.3	12 55	6.5	10 24	8.2	22 37	8.8	11 32	2.9	23 52	3.3	01 30	4.9	14 01	5.0
SA 16	01 25	6.6	13 38	6.6	11 01	8.5	23 12	9.0	12 08	3.0	—	—	02 07	5.1	14 35	5.2
SU 17	02 05	6.8	14 16	6.7	11 36	8.7	23 46	9.2	00 26	3.4	12 42	3.0	02 41	5.3	15 08	5.3
M 18	02 42	6.8	14 51	6.7	12 09	8.9	—	—	00 58	3.4	13 15	3.1	03 13	5.5	15 41	5.4
TU 19	03 18	6.8	15 24	6.7	00 21	9.3	12 44	9.0	01 32	3.5	13 50	3.2	03 45	5.6	16 16	5.5
W 20	03 53	6.8	15 56	6.8	00 57	9.4	13 19	9.0	02 08	3.5	14 27	3.2	04 19	5.6	16 52	5.4
TH 21	04 28	6.7	16 30	6.9	01 34	9.4	13 55	9.0	02 46	3.6	15 04	3.3	04 56	5.6	17 31	5.3
F 22	05 05	6.7	17 09	6.9	02 14	9.2	14 35	8.8	03 24	3.6	15 42	3.3	05 37	5.5	18 14	5.1
SA 23	05 46	6.5	17 53	6.7	02 58	8.8	15 20	8.4	04 04	3.4	16 23	3.3	06 23	5.2	19 02	4.9
SU 24	06 30	6.1	18 44	6.3	03 50	8.3	16 17	7.8	04 48	3.2	17 08	3.1	07 17	4.9	20 00	4.6
M 25	07 24	5.7	19 48	5.9	04 56	7.7	17 33	7.4	05 42	3.0	18 01	3.0	08 29	4.7	21 17	4.5
TU 26	08 40	5.4	21 17	5.6	06 21	7.4	19 07	7.5	07 05	2.7	19 17	2.8	10 00	4.6	22 41	4.6
W 27	10 17	5.5	22 53	5.8	07 56	7.6	20 30	8.0	09 23	2.7	21 25	2.9	11 27	4.7	23 57	4.9
TH 28	11 32	5.9	—	—	09 07	8.2	21 30	8.7	10 35	3.0	22 34	3.2	12 38	5.1	—	—
F 29	00 04	6.3	12 32	6.4	10 01	8.8	22 18	9.3	11 28	3.1	23 24	3.4	00 56	5.2	13 32	5.4
SA 30	01 02	6.9	13 22	6.8	10 47	9.2	23 02	9.6	12 15	3.2	—	—	01 44	5.5	14 15	5.5
SU 31	01 51	7.2	14 06	7.1	11 29	9.4	23 41	9.8	00 09	3.5	12 58	3.3	02 26	5.7	14 54	5.6

SEPTEMBER 2008   *High Water*   GMT

		LONDON BRIDGE *Datum of Predictions 3.20m below				LIVERPOOL (Alfred Dock) *Datum of Predictions 4.93m below				GREENOCK *Datum of Predictions 1.62m below				LEITH *Datum of Predictions 2.90m below			
		hr	m	hr	m	hr	m	hr	m	hr	m	hr	m	hr	m	hr	m
M	1	02	35 7.3	14	47 7.1	12	07 9.4	—	—	00	51 3.6	13	38 3.2	03	06 5.8	15	32 5.6
TU	2	03	14 7.3	15	23 7.1	00	19 9.7	12	42 9.3	01	30 3.6	14	12 3.6	03	45 5.8	16	10 5.5
W	3	03	49 7.1	15	55 7.0	00	55 9.5	13	15 9.1	02	06 3.6	14	42 3.2	04	24 5.6	16	46 5.3
TH	4	04	19 6.9	16	25 6.9	01	28 9.2	13	47 8.8	02	40 3.6	15	12 3.2	05	03 5.4	17	23 5.1
F	5	04	47 6.8	16	56 6.8	02	01 8.8	14	20 8.5	03	14 3.5	15	44 3.2	05	42 5.1	18	00 4.9
SA	6	05	16 6.6	17	31 6.5	02	36 8.3	14	55 8.0	03	49 3.4	16	19 3.1	06	25 4.8	18	42 4.6
SU	7	05	50 6.3	18	12 6.1	03	15 7.7	15	37 7.5	04	27 3.1	17	00 3.0	07	14 4.5	19	32 4.4
M	8	06	31 6.0	19	01 5.7	04	05 7.1	16	34 7.1	05	11 2.9	17	48 2.8	08	12 4.2	20	32 4.2
TU	9	07	22 5.5	20	06 5.3	05	17 6.6	18	12 6.8	06	07 2.6	18	52 2.7	09	20 4.1	21	42 4.2
W	10	08	36 5.3	22	02 5.2	07	15 6.7	19	49 7.2	07	18 2.5	20	34 2.8	10	37 4.1	22	59 4.3
TH	11	10	32 5.5	23	19 5.7	08	28 7.2	20	46 7.8	09	27 2.6	21	59 3.0	11	58 4.4	—	—
F	12	11	36 5.9	—	—	09	16 7.8	21	30 8.4	10	27 2.8	22	45 3.2	00	09 4.6	12	51 4.7
SA	13	00	11 6.3	12	26 6.4	09	56 8.3	22	08 8.9	11	07 3.0	23	22 3.3	00	58 4.9	13	29 5.1
SU	14	00	56 6.6	13	08 6.6	10	32 8.7	22	43 9.2	11	43 3.1	23	55 3.4	01	36 5.2	14	04 5.3
M	15	01	36 6.8	13	46 6.7	11	06 9.0	23	18 9.5	12	15 3.2	—	—	02	10 5.5	14	38 5.5
TU	16	02	13 6.9	14	21 6.8	11	40 9.2	23	53 9.6	00	30 3.5	12	48 3.2	02	42 5.7	15	11 5.6
W	17	02	50 6.9	14	56 6.9	12	15 9.3	—	—	01	08 3.6	13	24 3.3	03	16 5.8	15	47 5.6
TH	18	03	25 6.9	15	31 7.0	00	31 9.7	12	53 9.3	01	47 3.6	14	01 3.4	03	53 5.8	16	24 5.6
F	19	04	02 6.9	16	10 7.0	01	11 9.6	13	31 9.2	02	27 3.6	14	39 3.5	04	34 5.7	17	05 5.4
SA	20	04	40 6.7	16	51 6.9	01	53 9.2	14	13 8.9	03	08 3.6	15	18 3.5	05	19 5.5	17	49 5.2
SU	21	05	19 6.5	17	37 6.7	02	39 8.7	15	01 8.4	03	49 3.4	15	59 3.4	06	09 5.2	18	40 4.9
M	22	06	03 6.1	18	31 6.2	03	35 8.1	16	01 7.8	04	35 3.2	16	44 3.2	07	09 4.9	19	44 4.6
TU	23	06	57 5.6	19	42 5.7	04	49 7.4	17	26 7.4	05	33 2.9	17	41 3.0	08	29 4.6	21	10 4.5
W	24	08	27 5.3	21	21 5.6	06	26 7.3	19	05 7.6	07	29 2.7	19	13 2.9	10	00 4.6	22	34 4.7
TH	25	10	06 5.5	22	45 6.0	07	53 7.7	20	19 8.2	09	28 2.8	21	16 3.0	11	24 4.8	23	46 5.0
F	26	11	14 6.0	23	49 6.5	08	54 8.3	21	13 8.8	10	26 3.1	22	17 3.3	12	29 5.1	—	—
SA	27	12	09 6.6	—	—	09	43 8.8	21	59 9.3	11	11 3.2	23	04 3.5	00	41 5.3	13	17 5.3
SU	28	00	41 7.0	12	57 6.9	10	25 9.2	22	40 9.6	11	52 3.3	23	47 3.6	01	26 5.6	13	56 5.5
M	29	01	28 7.3	13	40 7.1	11	03 9.3	23	17 9.6	12	30 3.3	—	—	02	05 5.7	14	31 5.5
TU	30	02	09 7.3	14	19 7.1	11	38 9.3	23	51 9.5	00	26 3.6	13	05 3.3	02	43 5.7	15	05 5.5

OCTOBER 2008   *High Water*   GMT

		LONDON BRIDGE				LIVERPOOL (Alfred Dock)				GREENOCK				LEITH			
W	1	02	45 7.1	14	54 7.0	12	10 9.2	—	—	01	03 3.6	13	35 3.3	03	20 5.7	15	39 5.4
TH	2	03	16 7.0	15	25 6.9	00	23 9.3	12	41 9.1	01	38 3.6	14	04 3.4	03	56 5.5	16	13 5.3
F	3	03	42 6.8	15	55 6.8	00	55 9.0	13	12 8.8	02	11 3.5	14	35 3.4	04	34 5.3	16	47 5.1
SA	4	04	09 6.7	16	27 6.7	01	27 8.6	13	44 8.6	02	45 3.5	15	08 3.4	05	12 5.0	17	22 4.9
SU	5	04	39 6.6	17	02 6.4	02	02 8.2	14	20 8.2	03	20 3.3	15	43 3.3	05	53 4.8	18	02 4.7
M	6	05	14 6.4	17	43 6.1	02	41 7.7	15	01 7.7	03	59 3.2	16	22 3.2	06	40 4.5	18	49 4.5
TU	7	05	54 6.1	18	30 5.7	03	29 7.2	15	55 7.2	04	44 2.9	17	09 3.0	07	34 4.3	19	48 4.3
W	8	06	42 5.7	19	29 5.4	04	35 6.7	17	13 6.9	05	40 2.7	18	12 2.8	08	39 4.1	21	00 4.2
TH	9	07	46 5.4	20	48 5.3	06	22 6.6	18	59 7.1	06	50 2.6	19	36 2.8	09	51 4.2	22	14 4.3
F	10	09	26 5.3	22	30 5.6	07	46 7.1	20	04 7.7	08	38 2.7	21	10 3.0	11	04 4.4	23	22 4.6
SA	11	10	51 5.7	23	30 6.1	08	37 7.7	20	50 8.3	09	49 2.9	22	02 3.2	12	04 4.8	—	—
SU	12	11	44 6.2	—	—	09	18 8.3	21	30 8.9	10	33 3.1	22	42 3.3	00	14 5.0	12	49 5.1
M	13	00	17 6.6	12	29 6.6	09	56 8.8	22	09 9.3	11	09 3.2	23	21 3.5	00	57 5.3	13	28 5.4
TU	14	01	00 6.8	13	09 6.8	10	32 9.2	22	47 9.6	11	44 3.3	—	—	01	35 5.6	14	05 5.6
W	15	01	41 7.0	13	49 7.0	11	10 9.5	23	27 9.8	00	01 3.6	12	20 3.4	02	11 5.8	14	41 5.7
TH	16	02	20 7.1	14	29 7.1	11	49 9.6	—	—	00	44 3.6	12	58 3.5	02	50 5.9	15	19 5.7
F	17	02	59 7.0	15	11 7.2	00	08 9.8	12	30 9.5	01	28 3.7	13	38 3.6	03	32 5.9	16	00 5.7
SA	18	03	39 6.9	15	55 7.1	00	53 9.6	13	13 9.3	02	12 3.7	14	19 3.6	04	18 5.8	16	43 5.5
SU	19	04	20 6.8	16	41 7.0	01	39 9.2	13	59 8.9	02	57 3.6	15	00 3.6	05	07 5.6	17	31 5.3
M	20	05	02 6.5	17	32 6.6	02	30 8.6	14	52 8.5	03	43 3.4	15	43 3.5	06	02 5.2	18	26 5.0
TU	21	05	49 6.1	18	32 6.2	03	31 8.0	15	57 8.0	04	35 3.1	16	31 3.3	07	07 4.9	19	37 4.7
W	22	06	50 5.7	19	47 5.8	04	48 7.5	17	20 7.7	05	47 2.9	17	33 3.1	08	27 4.7	21	01 4.7
TH	23	08	23 5.5	21	11 5.9	06	15 7.5	18	43 7.8	07	39 2.8	19	11 3.0	09	48 4.7	22	17 4.8
F	24	09	42 5.8	22	21 6.2	07	29 7.8	19	51 8.2	09	04 2.9	20	47 3.1	11	04 4.8	23	23 5.1
SA	25	10	45 6.2	23	20 6.6	08	27 8.3	20	46 8.7	09	59 3.1	21	48 3.3	12	05 5.0	—	—
SU	26	11	38 6.6	—	—	09	16 8.7	21	33 9.0	10	43 3.3	22	36 3.5	00	17 5.3	12	53 5.2
M	27	00	12 6.9	12	27 6.9	09	58 9.0	22	14 9.2	11	22 3.4	23	19 3.5	01	03 5.4	13	31 5.3
TU	28	00	58 7.1	13	11 7.0	10	35 9.1	22	51 9.2	11	58 3.4	23	59 3.6	01	43 5.5	14	06 5.4
W	29	01	39 7.1	13	51 7.0	11	09 9.2	23	24 9.1	12	31 3.5	—	—	02	21 5.5	14	38 5.4
TH	30	02	15 6.9	14	28 6.8	11	40 9.1	23	56 9.0	00	35 3.5	13	02 3.5	02	57 5.4	15	11 5.3
F	31	02	45 6.7	15	01 6.7	12	11 9.0	—	—	01	10 3.5	13	33 3.6	03	34 5.3	15	43 5.3

NOVEMBER 2008   *High Water*   GMT

	LONDON BRIDGE *Datum of Predictions 3.20m below				LIVERPOOL (Alfred Dock) *Datum of Predictions 4.93m below				GREENOCK *Datum of Predictions 1.62m below				LEITH *Datum of Predictions 2.90m below			
	hr	ht m	hr	ht m	hr	ht m	hr	ht m	hr	ht m	hr	ht m	hr	ht m	hr	ht m
SA 1	03 11	6.6	15 32	6.5	00 27	8.8	12 44	8.9*	01 44	3.5	14 05	3.6	04 10	5.2	16 16	5.2
SU 2	03 38	6.6	16 04	6.5	01 01	8.5	13 18	8.6	02 20	3.4	14 39	3.6	04 48	5.0	16 51	5.0
M 3	04 10	6.6	16 41	6.3	01 37	8.2	13 55	8.3	02 57	3.3	15 14	3.5	05 28	4.8	17 30	4.8
TU 4	04 46	6.4	17 21	6.2	02 17	7.8	14 37	8.0	03 37	3.2	15 52	3.3	06 12	4.6	18 15	4.6
W 5	05 26	6.2	18 07	6.0	03 04	7.4	15 27	7.6	04 22	3.0	16 37	3.1	07 02	4.4	19 08	4.5
TH 6	06 12	5.9	19 01	5.7	04 01	7.1	16 30	7.3	05 15	2.9	17 34	3.0	07 59	4.3	20 12	4.4
F 7	07 09	5.6	20 04	5.6	05 16	6.9	17 46	7.4	06 18	2.8	18 42	2.9	09 04	4.3	21 23	4.5
SA 8	08 20	5.5	21 20	5.7	06 39	7.2	19 00	7.7	07 34	2.8	19 59	3.0	10 10	4.5	22 29	4.6
SU 9	09 44	5.7	22 34	6.0	07 43	7.7	19 58	8.2	08 52	3.0	21 07	3.2	11 11	4.7	23 26	4.9
M 10	10 51	6.1	23 33	6.4	08 33	8.3	20 48	8.8	09 48	3.1	22 00	3.3	12 04	5.0	—	—
TU 11	11 45	6.5	—	—	09 17	8.8	21 34	9.2	10 32	3.3	22 47	3.5	00 15	5.2	12 51	5.3
W 12	00 23	6.8	12 34	6.8	10 00	9.2	22 19	9.6	11 13	3.4	23 35	3.6	01 01	5.5	13 33	5.5
TH 13	01 09	7.0	13 21	7.1	10 43	9.5	23 05	9.7	11 54	3.5	—	—	01 45	5.7	14 14	5.7
F 14	01 54	7.1	14 08	7.2	11 27	9.6	23 52	9.7	00 23	3.6	12 37	3.6	02 30	5.9	14 57	5.7
SA 15	02 38	7.1	14 56	7.2	12 13	9.6	—	—	01 13	3.6	13 21	3.7	03 18	5.9	15 41	5.7
SU 16	03 22	7.0	15 45	7.2	00 41	9.5	13 02	9.5	02 03	3.6	14 04	3.8	04 07	5.8	16 28	5.6
M 17	04 06	6.8	16 35	7.0	01 32	9.2	13 53	9.2	02 53	3.5	14 48	3.7	05 00	5.6	17 19	5.4
TU 18	04 53	6.5	17 30	6.7	02 26	8.7	14 47	8.8	03 45	3.4	15 34	3.7	05 57	5.3	18 17	5.2
W 19	05 44	6.2	18 30	6.4	03 25	8.3	15 48	8.4	04 42	3.2	16 25	3.5	07 01	5.0	19 26	5.0
TH 20	06 46	6.0	19 36	6.2	04 31	7.9	16 56	8.1	05 51	3.0	17 27	3.3	08 10	4.8	20 39	4.9
F 21	07 59	5.9	20 44	6.2	05 43	7.7	18 07	8.0	07 07	2.9	18 42	3.2	09 20	4.7	21 47	4.9
SA 22	09 08	6.0	21 47	6.3	06 51	7.8	19 14	8.1	08 18	3.0	20 01	3.2	10 28	4.7	22 50	5.0
SU 23	10 09	6.2	22 45	6.4	07 52	8.0	20 12	8.3	09 17	3.1	21 08	3.3	11 29	4.8	23 47	5.1
M 24	11 04	6.4	23 37	6.6	08 43	8.3	21 03	8.5	10 06	3.2	22 03	3.3	12 21	4.9	—	—
TU 25	11 55	6.6	—	—	09 28	8.6	21 48	8.7	10 49	3.3	22 50	3.4	00 37	5.1	13 05	5.0
W 26	00 25	6.7	12 43	6.7	10 08	8.8	22 27	8.8	11 28	3.4	23 32	3.4	01 22	5.2	13 42	5.1
TH 27	01 08	6.7	13 26	6.7	10 44	8.9	23 03	8.8	12 04	3.5	—	—	02 03	5.2	14 17	5.2
F 28	01 46	6.6	14 06	6.6	11 18	9.0	23 36	8.7	00 11	3.4	12 38	3.6	02 41	5.2	14 49	5.2
SA 29	02 19	6.5	14 42	6.5	11 51	8.9	—	—	00 48	3.3	13 11	3.6	03 17	5.2	15 21	5.2
SU 30	02 48	6.5	15 16	6.4	00 09	8.6	12 25	8.9	01 24	3.3	13 44	3.7	03 53	5.1	15 55	5.2

DECEMBER 2008   *High Water*   GMT

	LONDON BRIDGE				LIVERPOOL (Alfred Dock)				GREENOCK				LEITH			
M 1	03 18	6.5	15 49	6.4	00 44	8.5	13 01	8.7	02 01	3.3	14 18	3.6	04 29	5.0	16 30	5.1
TU 2	03 50	6.5	16 26	6.4	01 21	8.3	13 39	8.6	02 39	3.3	14 53	3.6	05 07	4.9	17 07	5.0
W 3	04 26	6.4	17 05	6.3	02 00	8.1	14 19	8.4	03 19	3.2	15 30	3.5	05 48	4.8	17 48	4.9
TH 4	05 05	6.3	17 48	6.3	02 43	7.9	15 04	8.1	04 02	3.1	16 11	3.3	06 32	4.7	18 33	4.7
F 5	05 48	6.2	18 36	6.1	03 31	7.6	15 55	7.9	04 49	3.0	16 59	3.2	07 21	4.6	19 24	4.7
SA 6	06 38	6.0	19 30	6.0	04 28	7.4	16 55	7.8	05 41	3.0	17 56	3.1	08 17	4.5	20 24	4.6
SU 7	07 38	5.9	20 32	5.9	05 33	7.4	17 59	7.9	06 39	2.9	19 01	3.1	09 19	4.5	21 31	4.7
M 8	08 48	5.9	21 42	6.0	06 41	7.6	19 04	8.2	07 44	3.0	20 12	3.1	10 22	4.7	22 36	4.8
TU 9	10 01	6.1	22 50	6.2	07 45	8.0	20 06	8.5	08 54	3.1	21 19	3.2	11 21	4.9	23 36	5.0
W 10	11 06	6.4	23 49	6.5	08 41	8.5	21 03	8.9	09 54	3.2	22 20	3.4	12 16	5.1	—	—
TH 11	12 05	6.7	—	—	09 33	9.0	21 58	9.3	10 46	3.4	23 16	3.4	00 33	5.3	13 07	5.4
F 12	00 43	6.8	13 01	7.0	10 24	9.4	22 50	9.5	11 35	3.5	—	—	01 26	5.5	13 54	5.5
SA 13	01 34	6.9	13 54	7.1	11 13	9.6	23 42	9.6	00 10	3.5	12 22	3.6	02 18	5.7	14 41	5.7
SU 14	02 22	7.0	14 46	7.2	12 03	9.7	—	—	01 05	3.5	13 08	3.7	03 09	5.8	15 28	5.7
M 15	03 10	6.9	15 38	7.2	00 33	9.5	12 53	9.7	01 59	3.5	13 55	3.8	04 00	5.8	16 17	5.7
TU 16	03 57	6.8	16 30	7.1	01 24	9.4	13 44	9.6	02 52	3.4	14 41	3.8	04 52	5.7	17 09	5.6
W 17	04 44	6.7	17 21	7.0	02 15	9.1	14 34	9.3	03 43	3.4	15 27	3.8	05 45	5.4	18 03	5.4
TH 18	05 33	6.6	18 14	6.7	03 06	8.7	15 26	8.9	04 35	3.3	16 15	3.7	06 41	5.2	19 02	5.2
F 19	06 23	6.4	19 07	6.5	03 59	8.3	16 20	8.5	05 27	3.1	17 07	3.5	07 39	4.9	20 05	5.0
SA 20	07 19	6.2	20 04	6.3	04 56	7.9	17 19	8.1	06 20	3.0	18 02	3.3	08 40	4.7	21 07	4.9
SU 21	08 21	6.0	21 03	6.1	06 00	7.6	18 24	7.8	07 16	3.0	19 03	3.2	09 40	4.5	22 09	4.8
M 22	09 25	6.0	22 01	6.0	07 06	7.6	19 31	7.8	08 18	2.9	20 11	3.1	10 42	4.5	23 11	4.7
TU 23	10 26	6.0	22 58	6.1	08 07	7.8	20 32	7.9	09 20	3.0	21 22	3.1	11 43	4.6	—	—
W 24	11 24	6.2	23 50	6.2	09 00	8.1	21 24	8.1	10 16	3.2	22 22	3.1	00 11	4.7	12 37	4.7
TH 25	12 17	6.3	—	—	09 46	8.4	22 09	8.3	11 04	3.3	23 13	3.1	01 04	4.8	13 23	4.9
F 26	00 38	6.3	13 06	6.4	10 26	8.7	22 49	8.4	11 45	3.5	23 57	3.2	01 49	4.9	14 01	5.0
SA 27	01 22	6.4	13 49	6.5	11 03	8.8	23 24	8.5	12 22	3.5	—	—	02 28	5.0	14 35	5.1
SU 28	02 00	6.4	14 29	6.5	11 39	8.9	23 58	8.6	00 35	3.2	12 57	3.6	03 04	5.1	15 08	5.2
M 29	02 35	6.4	15 04	6.4	12 13	8.9	—	—	01 12	3.2	13 29	3.6	03 38	5.1	15 41	5.2
TU 30	03 07	6.4	15 38	6.4	00 32	8.6	12 49	8.9	01 48	3.2	14 01	3.6	04 12	5.1	16 14	5.2
W 31	03 39	6.4	16 12	6.5	01 08	8.6	13 25	8.9	02 25	3.2	14 35	3.6	04 47	5.1	16 49	5.2

INDEX

A
2008 calendar 10
2009 calendar 11
Aberavon
  constituencies
    UK Parliament 175
    Welsh Assembly 244
Aberdeen 306
  airport 454, 455
  Bishop (RC) 485
  constituencies
    Scottish Parliament 252
    UK Parliament 178
  education authority 384
  museums and art galleries 537
  unitary authority 277, 308
  universities 387, 394
Aberdeen and Orkney, Bishop 481
Aberdeenshire
  education authority 384
  unitary authority 277, 308
Aberdeenshire West & Kincardine
  constituencies, Scottish
    Parliament 252
  constituency, UK Parliament 178
Abertay Dundee, university 387
Aberystwyth, University of Wales 396
ABI (Association of British Insurers)
  558
abortion
  legal notes 586
abuse of children 431
academic staff 374
  see also teachers
academies (England only) 363
academies of scholarship 416
Academy of Medical Sciences 416
ACAS (Advisory, Conciliation and
  Arbitration Service) 209
ACCAC (Qualifications, Curriculum
  and Assessment Authority for
  Wales) 367
accidents
  on railways 456
  road 459
accountancy, professional education
  397
Achonry, Bishop (RC) 485
Action of Churches Together in
  Scotland 464
actuarial science, professional
  education 397
acute Trusts 423
Additional Adoption Leave 597
Additional Maternity Leave 596
Additional Member System (AMS)
  238
additional State Pension 434
Adjudication Panel 267
Adjudicator's Office 209
Administration Court 321
Admirals of the Fleet 350
Admiralty Court 321
admissions and course information for
  education 375
Adopted Children Register 587
adoption 586
  local authority service 431
Adoption Contact Register 587

adoption orders 586
Adoption Pay 597
A+DS (Architecture and Design
  Scotland) 209
adult and continuing education see
  lifelong learning
Adult Apprenticeships 370
Adult Learning Grants (ALGs) 370
adults living with parents, statistics 20
Adur, district council 273, 288
Advanced Extension Awards 368
Advanced Higher National Course
  369
'advanced skills teacher' grade 372
Advanced Subsidiary (AS) level
  examinations 368
Advanced Vocational Certificates of
  Education (AVCEs) 368
Advent Sunday 697
Advisory, Conciliation and Arbitration
  Service (ACAS) 209
Advisory Council on National Records
  and Archives 209
Advocate-General for Scotland, Office
  of 196
AEP (Association of Electricity
  Producers) 451
AFCS (Armed Forces Compensation
  Scheme) 436
African churches in the UK 486
Afro-Caribbean churches in the UK
  486
Agricultural Land Tribunals 331
agricultural properties
  and inheritance tax 580
  tenancies 600
AHRC (Arts and Humanities Research
  Council) 418
AIM (Alternative Investment Market)
  557
Airdrie & Shotts
  constituencies
    Scottish Parliament 252
    UK Parliament 178
air force see Royal Air Force
airlines 454, 455
airmail letter rates 495
air passenger numbers 454
air pollution 509
  UK targets 508
airports 454
Airsure 495
AIRTO (Association of Independent
  Research and Technology
  Organisations Limited) 422
air transport 454
AIT (Asylum and Immigration
  Tribunal) 331
alcohol consumption, statistics 22
Alcohol Education and Research
  Council 418
aldermen 270, 295
Alderney 313
  airport 455
Aldershot, constituency 148
Aldridge-Brownhills, constituency
  148
A-levels 368
Alexandra, Princess 25

funding 29
  military ranks and titles 33
  Private Secretary 26
Alexandra Palace 541
algol, minima of see months of the year
  eg January, minima of algol
ALGs (Adult Learning Grants) 370
aliens, status of 589
Allerdale, district council 273, 288
Alnwick, district council 273, 288
Alternative Investment Market (AIM)
  557
Altrincham & Sale West, constituency
  148
Alyn & Deeside
  constituencies
    UK Parliament 175
    Welsh Assembly 245
Amber Valley
  constituency 148
  district council 273, 288
ambulance service 428
  see also Central America; North
    America; South America
  see also treaty of Amsterdam
Ancient Monuments Advisory Board
  for Wales see CADW
Andrew, Prince 24
  funding 29
  military ranks and titles 32
  Private Secretary 26
Anglesey
  constituencies
    UK Parliament 177
    Welsh Assembly 247
  education authority 384
  unitary authority 277, 303
Anglia Ruskin University 387
Anglican churches 471
Anglican Communion 471
Anglican Consultative Council 471
Angus
  constituencies
    Scottish Parliament 252
    UK Parliament 178
  education authority 384
  unitary authority 277, 308
Animal Health 200
animals, protected 520
Anjou, House of 38
Anne, Princess 24
  funding 29
  military ranks and titles 32
  Private Secretary 26
annulment of marriage 593
  in Scotland 595, 596
Antrim
  constituencies
    Northern Ireland Assembly
      262
    UK Parliament 181
  district council 277, 310
AONBs (Areas of Outstanding Natural
  Beauty) 514
APACS (Association for Payment
  Clearing Services) 550
Apostolic Nuncios 483
  to Great Britain 484
  to Ireland 485

Apparent Sidereal Time 689
Apparent Solar Time 690
appeal courts *see* Court of Appeal
Apprenticeships 369
Appropriate Personal Pensions (APPs) 434
April 648
  astronomical phenomena 648
  calendar 648
  constellations 648
  duration of twilight 649
  high water 713
  minima of algol 648
  night sky 649
  sunrise and sunset 651
  Moon 648
    position 650
  Sun 649
  Jupiter in 649
  Mars in 649
  Mercury in 649
  Neptune in 651
  Saturn in 649
  Uranus in 651
  Venus in 649
Archbishop of Canterbury 471, 472
Archbishop of Wales 481
Archbishop of York 471, 472
archbishops
  Church of England 472
  Church of Ireland 481, 482
  Lords Spiritual 76
  overseas 482
  Roman Catholic Church
    England and Wales 484
    Ireland 485
Archbishops' Council 471
archdeacons, listing 472
architecture
  professional education 398
  see also listed buildings
Architecture and Design Scotland (A+DS) 209
Architecture and the Built Environment, Commission for (CABE) 214
Ardagh and Clonmacnois, Bishop (RC) 485
Ards, district council 277, 310
area
  of the UK 17
Areas of Outstanding Natural Beauty (AONBs) 514
Areas of Special Scientific Interest (ASSIs) 516
Argyll and Bute
  constituencies
    Scottish Parliament 252
    UK Parliament 178
  education authority 384
  unitary authority 277, 308
Argyll and the Isles
  Bishop (Anglican) 481
  Bishop (RC) 485
Armagh
  Archbishop 481
  Archbishop (RC) 485
  district council 277, 310
armed forces 347
  pay and pensions 357
  relative rank 358
  strength 347

Armed Forces Compensation Scheme (AFCS) 436
Armed Forces' Pay Review Body 209
Armenian Orthodox Church 489
arms control 348
Army 352
  constitution 353
  equipment holdings 354
  ranks 358
  salaries 357
  staff appointments 352
  strength 347
art galleries 531
  England 531
  Northern Ireland 537
  Scotland 537
  Wales 536
  see also names of individual art galleries eg National Gallery
arts academies, privately funded 417
Arts and Humanities Research Council (AHRC) 418
Arts Councils
  England 210
  Northern Ireland 210
  Scotland 233
  Wales 210
Arts London, University of the 387
art therapies, professional education 400
Arun, district council 273, 288
Arundel & South Downs, constituency 148
Arundel and Brighton, Bishop (RC) 484
AS (Advanced Subsidiary) level examinations 368
Ascension Day 697
Ashfield
  constituency 148
  district council 273, 288
Ashford
  constituency 148
  district council 273, 288
Ashton under Lyne, constituency 148
Ash Wednesday 697
Asian Network 615
assay office marks 545
Assembly Learning Grants 370, 371, 376
Assessment Appeal Tribunals 334
assessment in education 366, 368
  see also public examinations and qualifications
Assets Recovery Agency 205
ASSIs (Areas of Special Scientific Interest) 516
Associated Presbyterian Churches of Scotland 486
Association for Payment Clearing Services (APACS) 550
Association of British Insurers (ABI) 558
Association of Electricity Producers (AEP) 451
Association of Independent Research and Technology Organisations Limited (AIRTO) 422
Association of Train Operating Companies (ATOC) 455, 456
assured shorthold tenancies 600
Aston, Bishop Suffragan 473
Aston University 387
astronomical constants 692

astronomical phenomena 687
  see also months of the year eg January, astronomical phenomena
astronomical twilight 688
  see also months of year eg January, twilight
astronomy 635
  explanation of data 687
Asylum and Immigration Tribunal (AIT) 331
Atholl, House of 40
ATOC (Association of Train Operating Companies) 455, 456
Atomic Time 690
Attendance Allowance 441
  weekly rates 441
Attorney-General 188
Attorney-General's Office 188
  executive agencies 199
Audit Commission 210
August 664
  astronomical phenomena 664
  calendar 664
  constellations 664
  duration of twilight 665
  high water 715
  meteors 665
  minima of algol 664
  night sky 665
  sunrise and sunset 667
  Moon 664
    position 666
  Sun 665
  Jupiter in 665
  Mars in 665
  Mercury in 665
  Neptune in 665
  Saturn in 665
  Uranus in 667
  Venus in 665
Autumn 635
AVCEs (Advanced Vocational Certificates of Education) 368
Aylesbury, constituency 148
Aylesbury Vale, district council 273, 288
Ayr, Carrick & Cumnock, UK Parliament constituency 178
Ayr, Scottish Parliament constituency 252
Ayrshire, UK Parliament constituencies 178

B
BAA 454, 455
Babergh, district council 273, 288
BACS Payment Schemes Ltd 550
Baha'i faith 466
balance of payments, UK 565
Balliol, House of 41
Ballymena, district council 277, 310
Ballymoney, district council 277, 310
Banbridge, district council 277, 310
Banbury, constituency 148
Banff & Buchan
  constituencies
    Scottish Parliament 252
    UK Parliament 178
Bangor
  Bishop 481
  University of Wales 396
bank holidays *see* public holidays

banking and personal finance 550
  glossary of financial terms 551
banknotes 549
Bank of England 210, 550
  banknotes 549
Bankruptcy Court 321
banns, marriage by 603
Baptist church 486
the Bar 402
Barbican Centre 541
Barking
  Bishop Suffragan 474
  constituency 148
Barking and Dagenham
  education authority 382
  London borough council 275,
    300
Barnet
  education authority 382
  London borough council 275,
    300
Barnet and Camden, GLA
  constituency 241
Barnsley
  constituencies 148
  education authority 380
  metropolitan borough council
    276, 292
baronesses
  forms of address 66
  hereditary 66
  life 67, 73
baronetage and knightage 86
baronetcies, extinct 86
baronets
  forms of address 86
  listing 87
barons
  courtesy titles 77
  forms of address 57, 66
  hereditary 57
  life 67
Barrow and Furness, constituency 148
Barrow-in-Furness, district council
  273, 288
Basildon
  constituency 148
  district council 273, 288
Basingstoke
  Bishop Suffragan 473
  constituency 148
Basingstoke and Deane, district
  council 273, 288
Bassetlaw
  constituency 148
  district council 273, 288
Bath 280
  constituency 149
  museums and art galleries 531
  universities 387
Bath, Most Honourable Order 83
Bath and North-East Somerset
  education authority 380
  unitary authority 276, 293
Bath and Wells, Bishop 473
Bath Spa University 387
Batley & Spen, constituency 149
Battersea, constituency 149
BBC 211, 612, 614
  estimated audience share 613
BBC 1 612
BBC 1Xtra 615
BBC 2 612
BBC 6 Music 615

BBC 7 615
BBC Asian Network 615
BBC Radio 615
  local stations 615
  national services 615
  network services 615
  estimated audience share 614
BBC Radio 1 615
BBC Radio 2 615
BBC Radio 3 615
BBC Radio 4 615
BBC Radio Five Live 615
BBC Radio Five Live Sports Extra
  615
BBC six pips signal 691
BBC Television 612
BBC World Service 616
BBC Worldwide Ltd 612, 614
BBSRC (Biotechnology and
  Biological Sciences Research
  Council) 418
Beaconsfield, constituency 149
Beckenham, constituency 149
Bedford
  Bishop Suffragan 479
  constituency 149
  district council 273, 288
Bedfordshire
  constituencies 149
  county council 273, 287
  education authority 379
  university 387
Belfast 309
  constituencies
    Northern Ireland Assembly
      263
    UK Parliament 181
  district council 277, 310
  Education and Library Board
    385
  university 394
benefits 438
  claims and questions 444
  contributory see contributory
    benefits
  for industrial injuries and
    disablement 444
  non-contributory see
    non-contributory benefits
benefits in kind 574
Bereavement Allowance 438
  weekly rates 440
bereavement benefits 438
  weekly rates 440
Bereavement Payment 438, 440
Bern Convention (1979) 520
BERR (Department for Business,
  Enterprise and Regulatory Reform)
  188
Berwickshire, Roxburgh & Selkirk,
  UK Parliament constituency 178
Berwick-upon-Tweed
  constituency 149
  district council 273, 288
Bethnal Green & Bow, constituency
  149
Better Regulation Executive (BRE)
  189
Beverley & Holderness, constituency
  149
Beverley, Bishop Suffragan 472
Bexhill & Battle, constituency 149
Bexley
  education authority 382

  London borough council 275,
    300
Bexley and Bromley, GLA
  constituency 241
Bexleyheath & Crayford,
  constituency 149
BFC (British Film Commission) see UK
  Film Council International
BFI (British Film Institute) 212
BG Group 451
Big Bang (London Stock Exchange)
  557
Big Ben 541
Big Lottery Fund 211
Billericay, constituency 149
bills see consolidated fund bills; private
  bills; private member's bills; public
  bills
biodiversity 519
biomedical sciences, professional
  education 400
Biotechnology and Biological
  Sciences Research Council
  (BBSRC) 418
Birkenhead
  Bishop Suffragan 475
  constituency 149
Birmingham 280
  Archbishop (RC) 484
  Bishop 473
  constituencies 149
  education authority 380
  metropolitan borough council
    276, 292
  museums and art galleries 531
  universities 388, 395
birth certificates 588
births
  registration 587
  statistics 19
Bishop Auckland, constituency 150
Bishop of Rome 483
bishops
  Church of England 472
  Church of Ireland 481, 485
  Church in Wales 481
  Lords Spiritual 76
  Roman Catholic Church
    England And Wales 484
    Ireland 485
    Scotland 485
  Scottish Episcopal Church 481
Bishops' Conference of England and
  Wales 484
Bishops' Conference of Scotland
  484
bishops suffragan, listing 472
bissextile year 695
Blaby
  constituency 150
  district council 273, 288
Blackburn
  Bishop 474
  constituency 150
Blackburn with Darwen
  education authority 380
  unitary authority 276, 293
Blackpool
  constituencies 150
  education authority 380
  unitary authority 276, 293
Blaenau Gwent
  constituencies
    UK Parliament 175

by-election (2006) result 183
Welsh Assembly 245
education authority 384
unitary authority 276, 303
Blaydon, constituency 150
blood services 428
Blyth Valley
constituency 150
district council 273, 288
BNFL (British Nuclear Fuels) 451,
452
Bognor Regis & Littlehampton,
constituency 150
Bolsover
constituency 150
district council 273, 288
Bolton
Bishop Suffragan 477
constituencies 150
education authority 380
metropolitan borough council
276, 292
university 388
Bonn Convention (1979) 519
Bootle, constituency 150
borough councils see London borough
councils; metropolitan borough
councils
Boston & Skegness, constituency 150
Boston, district council 273, 288
Bosworth, constituency 151
boundary changes for Scottish
parliamentary constituencies 147
Boundary Commission for Scotland
266
Boundary Commissions 211
Boundary Committee for England
266
Bournemouth
constituencies 151
education authority 380
unitary authority 276, 293
university 388
Bracknell, constituency 151
Bracknell Forest
education authority 380
unitary authority 276, 293
Bradford 280
Bishop 474
constituencies 151
education authority 380
metropolitan borough council
276, 292
museums and art galleries 531
university 388
Bradwell, Bishop Suffragan 474
Braintree
constituency 151
district council 273, 288
BRE (Better Regulation Executive)
189
Brechin, Bishop 481
Breckland, district council 273, 288
Brecon & Radnorshire
constituencies
UK Parliament 175
Welsh Assembly 245
Brecon Beacons National Park 512
Brecqhou 312
Brent
constituencies 151
education authority 383
London borough council 275,
300

Brent and Harrow, GLA constituency
241
Brentford & Isleworth, constituency
151
Brentwood & Ongar, constituency
151
Brentwood
Bishop (RC) 484
district council 273, 288
The Brethren 490
Bridgend
constituencies
UK Parliament 175
Welsh Assembly 245
education authority 384
unitary authority 276, 303
bridges
in London 538
Bridgnorth, district council 273, 288
Bridgwater, constituency 151
Brigg & Goole, constituency 151
Brighton, university 388
Brighton and Hove 280
constituencies 151
education authority 380
unitary authority 276, 293
museums and art galleries 531
Bristol 280
Bishop 474
constituencies 151
education authority 380
museums and art galleries 531
unitary authority 276, 293
universities 388, 396
Britain see UK
British Academy 416
British Broadcasting Corporation see
BBC
British Channel Tunnel Rail Link 457
British citizenship 588
British Council 212
British Dependent Territories
citizenship 589
British Empire, Most Excellent Order
85
British Energy 451, 452
British Film Commission (BFC) see UK
Film Council International
British Film Institute (BFI) 212
British Gas 450, 451
British Library 212
British Museum 212
British Nationals (Overseas) 589
British Nuclear Fuels (BNFL) 451,
452
British Overseas citizenship 589
British Pharmacopoeia Commission
213
British protected persons 589
British Sky Broadcasting (BSkyB)
612, 614
British Summer Time 691
British Transport Police 341
British Waterways 213
Brixworth, Bishop Suffragan 478
broadband subscribers 502
broadcasting 612
complaints 612
see also radio; television
Broadcasting Standards Commission's
Standards Code 612
Broadland, district council 273,
288
The Broads National Park 512

Bromley
education authority 383
London borough council 275,
300
Bromley & Chislehurst
constituency 152
by-election (2006) result 183
Bromsgrove
constituency 152
district council 273, 288
bronze coin 548
Broxbourne
constituency 152
district council 273, 288
Broxtowe
constituency 152
district council 273, 288
Bruce, House of 41
Brunel University 388
BSkyB (British Sky Broadcasting) 612
BTEC qualifications 374
Buckingham
Area Bishop 478
constituency 152
university 388
Buckinghamshire
county council 273, 287
education authority 379
Buddhism 466
adherents in the UK 464
Budgeting Loans 443
budget
year 2007 563
buildings
listed see listed buildings
see also historic buildings and
monuments
building societies 550
burial 592
Burnley
Bishop Suffragan 474
constituency 152
district council 273, 288
Burton, constituency 152
Bury
constituencies 152
education authority 380
metropolitan borough council
276, 292
Bury St Edmunds, constituency 152
Bushy Park 540
business lettings 601
business rates 267, 270
business services for postal needs 495
bus services 458
by-elections, UK Parliament 183
Byzantine Orthodox Church
see Eastern Orthodox Church

C
CAA (Civil Aviation Authority) 214,
331, 454, 455
CABE (Commission for Architecture
and the Built Environment) 214
Cabinet 135
listing 184
Cabinet Office 186
executive agencies 199
cable television 613
CAC (Central Arbitration Committee)
213
CADW (Ancient Monuments Advisory
Board for Wales) 209
list of properties 528

Caernarfon
  constituencies
    UK Parliament 175
    Welsh Assembly 245
Caerphilly
  constituencies
    UK Parliament 176
    Welsh Assembly 245
  education authority 384
  unitary authority 276, 303
Cairngorms National Park 514
Caithness, Sutherland and Easter Ross
  constituencies
    Scottish Parliament 252
    UK Parliament 178
Calderdale
  education authority 380
  metropolitan borough council
    276, 292
Calder Valley, constituency 152
calendars 696, 9
  year 2008 10
  year 2009 11
  for any year 1780 to 2040 704
  civil and legal 700
  Chinese 702
  Christian 696
  Coptic 702
  Gregorian 696
  Hindu 698
  Japanese 702
  Jewish 699
  Julian 696
  Muslim 700
  Roman 703
  Sikh 700
  Thai 700
  Zoroastrian 702
  see also months of the year eg
    January, calendar
calendar year 695
Calvinistic Methodist Church of
  Wales 490
Camberwell & Peckham, constituency
  152
Camberwell College of Arts 387
Cambridge 281
  constituency 152
  district council 273, 288
  museums and art galleries 531
  university 388
Cambridgeshire
  constituencies 152
  county council 273, 287
  education authority 379
Camden
  education authority 383
  London borough council 275,
    300
Camilla, Duchess of Cornwall 24
  military ranks and titles 32
  Private Secretary 26
Canada Square 541
Canary Wharf 541
Cannock Chase
  constituency 153
  district council 273, 288
Canterbury 281
  Archbishop of 472
  constituency 153
  district council 273, 288
Canterbury Christ Church University
  389
capital bonds 556

capital gains tax 575
  and companies 582
  exemptions 575
  liability 575
  rates 576
  relief 577
Caradon, district council 273, 288
carbon footprint 508
Cardiff 302
  Archbishop (RC) 484
  constituencies
    UK Parliament 176
    Welsh Assembly 245
  education authority 384
  museums and art galleries 536
  unitary authority 276, 303
  University of Wales Institute 396
  university 389
Care Programme Approach 431
Carer's Allowance (CA) 441
Care Standards Tribunal 331
Carlisle 281
  Bishop 474
  constituency 153
  district council 273, 288
Carmarthen
  constituencies
    UK Parliament 176
    Welsh Assembly 245
  Trinity College 396
Carmarthenshire
  education authority 384
  unitary authority 276, 303
Carrick, Cumnock & Doon Valley,
  constituencies, Scottish Parliament
  252
Carrick, district council 273, 288
Carrickfergus, district council 277,
  310
cars see motor vehicles
Carshalton & Wallington,
  constituency 153
Cashel and Emly, Archbishop (RC)
  485
Cashel and Ossory, Bishop 482
Castle Morpeth, district council 273,
  288
Castle Point
  constituency 153
  district council 273, 288
Castlereagh, district council 277,
  310
CAT (Competition Appeal Tribunal)
  332
Catholic Church see Roman Catholic
  Church
CATS (credit accumulation and
  transfer systems) 374
CCEA (Northern Ireland Council for
  the Curriculum, Examinations and
  Assessment) 367
CCLRC (Council for the Central
  Laboratory of the Research
  Councils) see STFC
CCTAs (City Colleges for the
  Technology of the Arts) 363
CCW (Consumer Council for Water)
  216
CCW (Countryside Council for
  Wales) 217, 514, 516
CDC Group 195
CEFAS (Centre for Environment,
  Fisheries and Aquaculture Science)
  201

CEHR (Commission for Equality and
  Human Rights) 215
cemeteries in London 538
Cenotaph 539
Cenozoic era 708
census results 17, 18
centenaries
  year 2008 14
  year 2009 14
Central Arbitration Committee (CAC)
  213
central bank see Bank of England
Central Criminal Court (Old Bailey)
  541
Central England in Birmingham,
  university 395
Central Lancashire, university 389
Central London Congestion Charge
  Scheme 458
Central Office of Information 199
Central Saint Martins College of Art &
  Design 387
Central Science Laboratory (CSL)
  201
Central Sponsor for Information
  Assurance (CSIA) 187
Centre for Environment, Fisheries and
  Aquaculture Science (CEFAS) 201
Centrica plc 451
Cerdic and Denmark, Houses of 38
Ceredigion
  constituencies
    UK Parliament 176
    Welsh Assembly 245
  education authority 384
  unitary authority 276, 303
certificate, marriage by 604
certificates of birth, death or marriage
  588
Certification Office for Trade Unions
  and Employers' Associations 213
Chairman of Ways and Means 131
Chamberlains 295, 296
Chancellor of the Exchequer 184
Chancery Division of the High Court
  of Justice 318, 320
Channel 3 see ITV
Channel 4 612, 614
  estimated audience share 613
Channel 5 see Five
Channel Islands 312
  airports 455
  area 312
  currency 548, 549
  see also Guernsey; Jersey
Channel Tunnel 457
  rail links 457
CHAPS Ltd 550
charges, NHS 426
charitable donations, tax relief on 573
Charity Commission 205
Charles, Prince of Wales 24, 42
  funding 30
  military ranks and titles 31
  Private Secretary 26
  taxation 30
Charnwood
  constituency 153
  district council 273, 288
Charterhouse 541
Chatham & Aylesford, constituency
  153
Chatham, museums and art galleries
  532

chattels (stamp duty) 585
Chatto, Lady Sarah 24
Cheadle
    constituency 153
        by-election (2005) result 183
Chelmsford
    Bishop 474
    district council 273, 288
Chelmsford West, constituency 153
Chelsea College of Art & Design 387
Chelsea Physic Garden 540
Cheltenham
    constituency 153
    district council 273, 288
Cheque and Credit Clearing Company
    Ltd 550
Cherwell, district council 273, 288
Chesham & Amersham, constituency
    153
Cheshire
    county council 273, 287
    education authority 379
Chester 281
    Bishop 474
    constituency 153
    district council 273, 288
    university 389
Chesterfield
    constituency 153
    district council 273, 288
Chester-le-Street, district council 273,
    288
Chichester
    Bishop 475
    constituency 153
    district council 273, 288
    university 389
Chief Commoner 296
Chief Constables
    listing 339
    rates of pay 337
Chief of the Defence Staff 347, 348
    salary 357
Chiefs of Clans 121
Child Benefit 440
    weekly rates 441
child care payments 437
child health services, NHS 427
child protection 431
children
    adoption 586
    immunisation of 22
    local authority services 430
    percentage living in different
        family types 20
    registration of births 587
    with special education needs
        (SEN) 366
    tracing adopted 587
    see also infant mortality
children's bonus bonds 555
children's hearings 326
Child Support Agency (CSA) 204,
    593
Child Support Commissioners 334
    for Northern Ireland 334
Child Tax Credit 437
Chiltern, district council 273, 288
Chiltern Hundreds 133
Chinese calendar 702
Chinese new year 702
Chingford & Woodford Green,
    constituency 153
Chipping Barnet, constituency 153

chiropody, professional education
    400
chiropractic, professional education
    399
Chivalry, Orders of 83
Chorley
    constituency 153
    district council 273, 288
Christ, Scientist, Church of 492
Christadelphian 492
Christchurch
    constituency 153
    district council 273, 288
Christian calendar 696
    year 2008 9
Christianity 465
    adherents in UK 464
    early English 279
chronological cycles and eras 701
    year 2008 9
Church Commissioners 213
churches 471
    cooperation between 464
Churches Together in Britain and
    Ireland 464
Churches Together in England 464
Churches Together in Wales
    (CYTUN) 464
Church in Wales 481
    marriage in 603
Church of Christ, Scientist 492
Church of England 471
    dioceses 472
    marriage in 603
    membership 471
    provinces 472
    stipends 472
    structure 471
Church of Ireland 481
Church of Jesus Christ of Latter-Day
    Saints 492
Church of Scotland 482
CICA (Criminal Injuries
    Compensation Authority) 217
CICAP (Criminal Injuries
    Compensation Appeals Panel) 332
circuit judges 318, 319, 324
    banknotes 549
    newspapers 623
CITES (Convention on International
    Trade in Endangered Species of
    Wild Fauna and Flora (1973))
    519
Cities of London & Westminster,
    constituency 154
citizenship of the UK 588
City and East, GLA constituency 241
City Colleges for the Technology of
    the Arts (CCTAs) 363
city guilds 271, 297
City Lands and Bridge House Estates
    Committee 296
City of London 295
    education authority 383
City of London Police 340
    rates of pay 338
City Technology Colleges (CTCs) 363
City University 389
civic dignities, local government 268
civil aviation 454
Civil Aviation Authority (CAA) 214,
    331, 454, 455
civil calendar 700
    year 2008 9

civil cases
    England and Wales 319
    Northern Ireland 330
    Scotland 326
civil fees for marriages
    in Scotland 605
civil legal aid 602
Civil List 29
civil marriage 604
Civil Nuclear Constabulary 341
civil partnership 594
Civil Service 186
Civil Service Capability Group 187
Civil Service Commissioners 188
civil twilight 688
    see also months of year eg January,
        twilight
civil year 700
Clackmannanshire
    education authority 384
    unitary authority 277, 308
Clans, Chiefs of 121
class sizes in schools 361
Cleethorpes, constituency 154
clergy
    Church of England 471
    Church of Ireland 481
    Church of Scotland 482
    Church in Wales 481
    overseas 482
    Roman Catholic Church 484
    Scottish Episcopal Church 481
Clifton, Bishop (RC) 484
climate change 509
clinical science, professional
    education 400
Clogher
    Bishop (Anglican) 481
    Bishop (RC) 485
Clonfert, Bishop (RC) 485
Cloyne, Bishop (RC) 485
Clwyd
    constituencies
        UK Parliament 176
        Welsh Assembly 245
Clydebank & Milngavie,
    constituencies, Scottish Parliament
    252
Clydesdale, constituencies, Scottish
    Parliament 253
coach services 458
coal 450
Coal Authority 214
coastguards 461
Coatbridge & Chryston, Scottish
    Parliament constituency 253
Coatbridge, Chryston & Bellshill, UK
    Parliament constituency 178
cohabitation 594
    marriage by 605
'cohabitation contracts' 594
COI Communications 199
coinage, UK 548
Colchester
    Bishop Suffragan 474
    constituency 154
    district council 273, 288
Cold Weather Payments 443
Coleraine, district council 277, 310
College of Arms 214
colleges of higher education 373
    and adult and continuing
        education 373, 377
    governance 373

Colne Valley, constituency 154
COMB (Contracted-Out Mixed
    Benefit) Schemes 435
commemorative marks 547
Commercial Court 321
commercial radio see independent
    radio
Commercial Radio Companies
    Association (CRCA) 617
Commissary Office, HM 328
Commissioner for Public
    Appointments 188
Commissioners of Irish Lights 462
Commission for Architecture and the
    Built Environment (CABE) 214
Commission for Equality and Human
    Rights (CEHR) 215
Commission for Integrated Transport
    (CfIT) 215
Commission for Racial Equality
    (CRE) see Commission for Equality
    and Human Rights (CEHR)
Commission for Rural Communities
    215, 512, 514
Commission for Social Care
    Inspection (CSCI) 430
Committee on Standards in Public
    Life 215
Common Clerk 295, 296
Common Council 270, 295
    listing of councilmen 296
common law holidays 701
common licence, marriage by 603
Commons see House of Commons
Commons Commissioners 331
Commonwealth War Graves
    Commission 215
Communication, London College of
    387
communications 494
    mobile see mobile communications
Community Care Grants 443
community councils
    Scotland 272
    Wales 271
community healthcare, primary and
    426
Community Legal Service fund 601
community schools 363
Companies Court 321
Companies House 200
Companions of Honour, Order of 85
COMP (Contracted-Out Money
    Purchase) Schemes 434
compensation 553
    postal 495
Compensation Agency, Northern
    Ireland 203
Competition Appeal Tribunal (CAT)
    332
Competition Commission 216
Competition Service 216
complaints see ombudsmen
Comptroller, Lord Chamberlain's
    Office 28
computers
    ancestry and development 505
    capacity units 506
conditional fees 602
confirmation of wills 608
Congleton
    constituency 154
    district council 273, 288
Congregational Federation 487

Connor, Bishop 481
conservation and heritage 512
    see also habitat conservation;
        wildlife conservation
Conservative Party 137
    development 136
    financial support 137
    representation in House of
        Commons 130
    Whips 137
consolidated fund bills 133
constellations 687
    see also months of the year eg
        January, constellations
constituencies
    UK Parliament 130, 148
        boundary changes 147
        England 148
        Northern Ireland 181
        Scotland 178
        Wales 175
    GLA 238, 241
    Northern Ireland Assembly 262
    Scottish Parliament 252
    Welsh Assembly 244
Constitutional Affairs, Department
    for see Ministry of Justice
Constitutional Reform Act 2005 318
constitution of the UK 127
Consumer Council for Water (CCW)
    216
consumer credit 590
consumer law 589
    Scotland 591
Consumer Prices Index (CPI) 568
consumer protection 590
contingency fees 602
Contracted-Out Mixed Benefit
    (COMB) Schemes 435
Contracted-Out Money Purchase
    (COMP) Schemes 434
contracted-out pension schemes 434
Contracted-Out Salary Related
    (COSR) Schemes 434
contract services for mobiles 498
contribution-based Jobseeker's
    Allowance (JSA) 438
contributory benefits 438
    weekly rates 439
convenors 268
convention hallmarks 547
Convention on International Trade in
    Endangered Species of Wild Fauna
    and Flora (CITES) (1973) 519
Conwy
    constituencies
        UK Parliament 176
        Welsh Assembly 246
    education authority 384
    unitary authority 276, 303
Cookstown, district council 277, 310
Coordinated Universal Time (UTC)
    690
Copeland
    constituency 154
    district council 274, 288
Coptic calendar 702
Coptic Orthodox Church 489
copyright 610
Copyright Tribunal 332
Corby
    constituency 154
    district council 274, 288
Cork, Cloyne and Ross, Bishop 482

Cork and Ross, Bishop (RC) 485
Cornwall
    constituencies 154
    county council 273, 287
    education authority 379
    see also Duchy of Cornwall
Cornwall, Duchess of see Camilla,
    Duchess of Cornwall
coroners' courts 319
Corporation of London 270, 295,
    300
Corporation of London open spaces
    540
Corporation of Trinity House 216,
    462
corporation tax 581
    payment 582
    rates 582
Corps of Queen's Messengers 201
Corpus Christi 697
COSR (Contracted-Out Salary
    Related) Schemes 434
cost of living 568
Cotswold
    constituency 154
    district council 274, 288
Council for the Central Laboratory of
    the Research Councils (CCLRC) see
    STFC
Council for the Curriculum,
    Examinations and Assessment 367
Council of Christians and Jews 464
Council on Tribunals 217
council tax 266
    see also individual councils eg
        Westminster, London borough
        council
council tax benefit 443
Counsellors of State 127
countesses in own right 54
    forms of address 54
counties
    England 286
        map 294
    Northern Ireland 310
    Wales 302
Countryside Agency see Natural
    England
Countryside Council for Wales
    (CCW) 217, 514, 516
county councils 266, 287
    functions 269
    map 294
    political composition 273
county courts
    England and Wales 319
    Northern Ireland 330
courtesy titles 77
    forms of address 77
Court of Aldermen 270
Court of Appeal
    England and Wales 319, 320
    House of Lords as final 128, 319,
        320
    Northern Ireland 330
    in Scotland 326
Court of Common Council see
    Common Council
Court of Session 327
courts see Inns of Court; law courts
    and offices
Courts-Martial Appeal Court 320
Covent Garden Market Authority
    217

Coventry 282
  Bishop 475
  constituencies 154
  education authority 380
  metropolitan borough council 276, 292
  university 389
  museums and art galleries 532
CPI (Consumer Prices Index) 568
CPS (Crown Prosecution Service) 205, 319, 324
Craigavon, district council 277, 310
Cranborne Money 137
Craven, district council 274, 288
Crawley
  constituency 154
  district council 274, 288
CRCA (Commercial Radio Companies Association) 617
credit 590
credit accumulation and transfer systems (CATS) 374
Crediton, Bishop Suffragan 475
cremation 592
Crewe and Nantwich
  constituency 154
  district council 274, 288
cricket
  forthcoming events 13
criminal cases
  England and Wales 319
  Northern Ireland 330
  Scotland 326
Criminal Cases Review Commission 217
Criminal Defence Service 601
Criminal Injuries Compensation Appeals Panel (CICAP) 332
Criminal Injuries Compensation Authority (CICA) 217
criminal legal aid 602
Criminal Records Bureau 202
Crisis Loans 444
Crofters Commission 218
Crosby, constituency 154
cross-media ownership 612, 623
Crown, proceedings against 591
Crown Agent 326
Crown Court
  England and Wales 318
    centres 323
  Northern Ireland 330
Crown Estate 205
Crown Office 326, 329
Crown of India (1877) for Ladies, Imperial Order 84
Crown Prosecution Service (CPS) 205, 319, 324
Crown Solicitor's Office, Northern Ireland 330
Croydon
  Area Bishop 479
  constituencies 154
  education authority 383
  London borough council 275, 300
Croydon and Sutton, GLA constituency 241
CSA (Child Support Agency) 204, 593
CSCI (Commission for Social Care Inspection) 430
CSIA (Central Sponsor for Information Assurance) 187

CSL (Central Science Laboratory) 201
CTCs (City Technology Colleges) 363
cultural development of man 709
Culture, Media and Sport, Department for 190
Cumbernauld & Kilsyth, Scottish Parliament constituency 253
Cumbernauld, Kilsyth & Kirkintilloch East, UK Parliament constituency 178
Cumbria
  county council 273, 287
  education authority 379
Cunninghame, Scottish Parliament constituencies 253
currency, UK 548
curriculum 366
cycles and eras, chronological see chronological cycles and eras
Cymru see Wales
Cynon Valley
  constituencies
    UK Parliament 176
    Welsh Assembly 246
CYTUN (Churches Together in Wales) 464

D
DAB (Digital Audio Broadcasting) 615
Dacorum, district council 274, 288
Dagenham, constituency 155
daily newspapers
  national 624
    circulation 623
  regional 625
dames 115
  forms of address 115
Dames Commanders 115
Dames Grand Cross 115
Darlington
  constituency 155
  education authority 380
  unitary authority 276, 293
Dartford
  constituency 155
  district council 274, 288
Dartmoor National Park 512
date letters 546
  London (Goldsmiths' Hall) 546
Daventry
  constituency 155
  district council 274, 289
day care, local authority services 430
Daylight Saving Time 691
days
  definition 695
  for flying flags 23
  Hindu 698
  Jewish 699
  longest and shortest 635
  names of 695
  see also Dog Days; Easter Days; Ember Days; Opposition days; quarter days; red-letter days; Rogation Days; term days
DCA see Ministry of Justice
DCLG see Department for Communities and Local Government
DCS (Disability and Carers Service) 205

DCSF (Department for Children, Schools and Families) 189
DE&S (Defence Equipment and Support) 349
deans, listing 472
death certificates 588
deaths
  and inheritance tax 580
  legal notes 591
  statistics 19
    analysis by cause 20
Debt Management Office, UK 204
December 680
  astrological phenomena 680
  calendar 680
  constellations 680
  duration of twilight 681
  high water 717
  meteors 681
  minima of algol 680
  night sky 681
  sunrise and sunset 683
  Moon 680
    position 682
  Sun 681
  Jupiter in 681
  Mars in 681
  Mercury in 681
  Neptune in 683
  Saturn in 681
  Uranus in 683
  Venus in 681
decorations and medals 118
decree absolute 593
decree nisi 593
'Deed of Grant' 592
Deer Commission for Scotland 218
defence 347
  budget 348
  Ministry of 347, 348
Defence Council 347, 348
Defence Equipment and Support (DE&S) 349
Defence Logistics Organisation (DLO) 347 see Defence Equipment and Support
Defence Management Board (DMB) 347
Defence Procurement Agency (DPA) 347 see Defence Equipment and Support
DEFRA see Department for Environment, Food and Rural Affairs
degree courses 375
Delyn
  constituencies
    UK Parliament 176
    Welsh Assembly 246
Democratic Unionist Party 138
  development 136
  financial support 137
  representation in House of Commons 130
De Montfort University 389
Denbighshire
  education authority 384
  unitary authority 276, 303
Denmark and Cerdic, Houses of 38
dental services, NHS 427
dentists
  professional education 399
  salaries 425

Dentists' and Doctors' Remuneration Review Body 231
Denton & Reddish, constituency 155
Department for Business, Enterprise and Regulatory Reform 188
  executive agencies 200
Department for Children, Schools and Families 189
Department for Communities and Local Government 190
  executive agencies 200
Department for Constitutional Affairs *see* Ministry of Justice
Department for Culture, Media and Sport 190
  executive agency 200
Department for Education, Lifelong Learning and Skills (DELLS) 360, 367
Department for Education and Skills *see* Department for Children, Schools and Families *or* Department for Innovation, Universities and Skills
Department for Environment, Food and Rural Affairs 191, 449
  executive agencies 200
Department for Innovation, Universities and Skills 194
  executive agencies 202
Department for International Development (DFID) 194
Department for Transport 197
  executive agencies 203
Department for Work and Pensions 198
  executive agencies 204
Department of Education Northern Ireland (DENI) 363
Department of Health 192
  executive agencies 201
Department of HM Procurator-General and Treasury Solicitor 199
Department of Trade and Industry *see* Department for Business, Enterprise and Regulatory Reform *or* Department for Innovation, Universities and Skills
Derby
  Bishop 475
  constituencies 155
  education authority 380
  unitary authority 276, 293
  university 389
  museums and art galleries 532
Derbyshire
  constituencies 155
  county council 273, 287
  education authority 379
Derbyshire Dales, district council 274, 289
Derry
  Bishop (RC) 485
  district council 277, 310
Derry and Raphoe, Bishop 481
Derwentside, district council 274, 289
descendants of Queen Victoria 35
Designated Professional Bodies (DPBs) 553
Design Council 218
design protection 610
design right 610
Devizes, constituency 155

devolution 128
Devolved School Management 360
Devon
  constituencies 155
  county council 273, 287
  education authority 379
Dewsbury, constituency 155
DFID (Department for International Development) 194
Diana, Princess of Wales 24
dietetics, professional education 400
Digital Audio Broadcasting (DAB) 615
digital multiplexes 615
digital penetration 613
digital radio 615
digital switchover 613
digital television 613
Digital Terrestrial Television (DTT) licence 613
diocesan clergy *see* clergy
dioceses of the Church of England 472
Diploma Development Partnerships 370
Diploma in Higher Education (DipHE) 374
Directorate of Judicial Offices for England and Wales 326
Director of Public Prosecutions
  England and Wales 319, 324
  Northern Ireland 330
Disability and Carers Service (DCS) 205
Disability Living Allowance 441
  weekly rates 441
Disability Rights Commission (DRC) *see* Commission for Equality and Human Rights (CEHR)
disabled people
  benefits for 444
  local authority services 430
disclaimer of peerages 45
Discretionary Financial Contingency Funds 371
discretionary payments, Social Fund 443
discrimination in employment 598
Distinguished Service Order 85
district councils
  England 266, 268, 288
    functions 269
    political composition 273
  Northern Ireland 272, 310
    political composition 277
district courts 326
district judges 319, 324
district judges (magistrates' courts)
  England and Wales 319, 324
  Scotland 326
DIUS (Department for Innovation, Universities and Skills) 194
dividends 572
divorce 592, 593
  financial relief *see* financial relief in divorces
  Scotland 595
  statistics 19
DLO (Defence Logistics Organisation) 347 *see* Defence Equipment and Support
DMB (Defence Management Board) 347

DMO (Debt Management Office) 204
Doctors' and Dentists' Remuneration Review Body 231
Dog Days 695
'do-it-yourself' divorce 595
domain names *see* web domain names
Domestic Policy Group 187
domestic violence 595
dominical letters 696
  years 1500–2035 698
Doncaster
  Bishop Suffragan 479
  constituencies 155
  education authority 380
  metropolitan borough council 276, 292
Don Valley, constituency 155
Dorchester, Area Bishop 478
Dorking, Bishop Suffragan 476
Dorset
  constituencies 155
  county council 273, 287
  education authority 379
Douglas 311
Dover
  Bishop Suffragan 472
  constituency 156
  district council 274, 289
Down
  constituencies
    Northern Ireland Assembly 263
    UK Parliament 182
  district council 277, 310
Down and Connor, Bishop (RC) 485
Down and Dromore, Bishop 481
Downing Street 541
DPA (Defence Procurement Agency) 347 *see* Defence Equipment and Support
DPBs (Designated Professional Bodies) 553
DPP *see* Director of Public Prosecutions
drama therapies, professional education 400
Drinking Water Inspectorate (DWI) 447
Drinking Water Quality Regulator for Scotland 448
Driver and Vehicle Licensing Agency (DVLA) 203, 459, 460
Driver and Vehicle Testing Agency (Northern Ireland) 459
driving licences 459
Driving Standards Agency 203, 460
driving tests 460
Dromore, Bishop (RC) 485
drug misuse, statistics 22
DTI *see* Department for Business, Enterprise and Regulatory Reform *or* Department for Innovation, Universities and Skills
Dublin
  Archbishop 482
  Archbishop (RC) 485
duchesses *see individual duchesses* eg Kent, Duchess of
Duchy of Cornwall 30
Duchy of Lancaster 30
Dudley
  Bishop Suffragan 480
  constituencies 156

education authority 380
metropolitan borough council
276, 292
dukes 47
forms of address 47
see also individual dukes eg Kent,
Duke of
Dulwich & West Norwood,
constituency 156
Dumbarton, Scottish Parliament
constituency 253
Dumfries, Scottish Parliament
constituency 253
Dumfries and Galloway
education authority 384
UK Parliament constituency
178
unitary authority 277, 308
Dumfriesshire, Clydesdale &
Tweeddale, UK Parliament
constituency 178
Dunbartonshire, UK Parliament
constituencies 178
Dundee 306
constituencies
Scottish Parliament 253
UK Parliament 179
education authority 384
unitary authority 277, 308
universities 387, 389
Dunfermline & Fife West
UK Parliament constituency 179
by-election (2006) result 183
Dunfermline, Scottish Parliament
constituencies 253
Dungannon and South Tyrone, district
council 277, 310
Dunkeld, Bishop (RC) 485
Dunwich, Bishop Suffragan 479
Durham 282
Bishop 473
constituencies 156
county council 273, 287
district council 274, 289
education authority 379
university 389
duty solicitors 603
DVLA (Driver and Vehicle Licensing
Agency) 203, 459, 460
dwelling-houses
average prices 567
and capital gains tax 575
DWI (Drinking Water Inspectorate)
447

E
Ealing
constituencies 156
by-election (2007) result
183
education authority 383
London borough council 275,
300
Ealing and Hillingdon, GLA
constituency 241
earls 49
courtesy titles 77
forms of address 49
early day motions 133
the Earth 692
satellites 693
Easington
constituency 156
district council 274, 289

East Anglia
Bishop (RC) 484
university 390
East Ayrshire
education authority 384
unitary authority 277, 308
Eastbourne
constituency 156
district council 274, 289
East Cambridgeshire, district council
274, 289
East Devon, district council 274, 289
East Dorset, district council 274, 289
East Dunbartonshire
education authority 384
unitary authority 277, 308
Easter Day 696
1500–2035 698
Eastern Orthodox Church 488
East Ham, constituency 156
East Hampshire, district council 274,
289
East Herts, district council 274, 289
East Kilbride, Scottish Parliament
constituency 253
East Kilbride, Strathaven &
Lesmahagow, UK Parliament
constituency 179
Eastleigh
constituency 156
district council 274, 289
East Lindsey, district council 274, 289
East London, university 390
East Lothian
constituencies
Scottish Parliament 254
UK Parliament 179
education authority 385
unitary authority 277, 308
East Midlands European Parliament
Region 315
East Northamptonshire, district
council 274, 289
East Renfrewshire
education authority 385
unitary authority 277, 308
East Riding of Yorkshire
education authority 380
unitary authority 276, 293
East Staffordshire, district council
274, 289
East Sussex
county council 273, 287
education authority 379
Eastwood, Scottish Parliament
constituency 254
easy access savings accounts 555
Ebbsfleet, Bishop Suffragan 472
Eccles, constituency 156
ecclesiastical fees for marriages 604
ECGD (Export Credit Guarantee
Department) 206
eclipses 686
Economic and Social Research
Council (ESRC) 419
economic statistics 563
ECUK (Engineering Council (UK))
398
Eddisbury, constituency 156
Eden, district council 274, 289
Edge Hill University 390
Edinburgh 307
airport 454, 455
Bishop 481

constituencies
Scottish Parliament 254
UK Parliament 179
education authority 385
museums and art galleries 537
unitary authority 277, 308
universities 390, 393
Edinburgh, Duke of *see* Philip, Prince
Edmonton
Area Bishop 473
constituency 156
education 360
the curriculum 366
elective home 366
expenditure 360
fees 363
higher *see* higher education
inspection framework 362
lifelong learning 377
local education administration
360
pre-school 365
primary *see* primary education
post-16 *see* post-16 education
professional 397
responsibility for 360
schools and pupils 363
secondary *see* secondary education
special 366
statistics 360
Education Action Zones (EAZs) 363
Education and Library Boards (ELBs)
360, 364, 385
Education and Training Inspectorate
363
education authorities *see* LEAs
Education Improvement Partnerships
363
Education Maintenance Allowance
(EMA) 370, 371
Edward, Prince 24
funding 29
military ranks and titles
32
Private Secretary 26
EDX London 557
EH *see* English Heritage
Eilean Siar *see* Western Isles
Eisteddfod 302
ELBs (Education and Library Boards)
360, 364, 385
elderly people, local authority
services 430
elections
European Parliament 314
local government 266
England 268
Scotland 271
London Assembly and Mayor of
London 238
UK Parliament 130
see also by-elections; general
election (2005); voting
elective home education 366
electoral register 606
Electoral Registration Officer (ERO)
606
electricity 451
suppliers 452
Elizabeth II 24
funding 29
military ranks and titles 31
Private Secretary 26
taxation 30

Ellesmere Port and Neston
  constituency 157
  district council 274, 289
Elmbridge, district council 274, 289
Elmet, constituency 157
Elphin, Bishop (RC) 486
Eltham, constituency 157
ELWa (National Council for Education
  and Training) 367
Ely, Bishop 475
EMA (Education Maintenance
  Allowance) 370, 371
Ember Days 697
employer payments 445
employment
  discrimination 598
  pay and conditions 596
  termination 597
  UK statistics 565
Employment Appeal Tribunal 332
employment law 596
Employment Tribunals (England and
  Wales) 332
Employment Tribunals (Scotland) 332
ENA (Energy Networks Association)
  451
endowment policies 561
energy 449
  coal 450
  electricity see electricity
  environmental policies 511
  gas see gas
  nuclear power 452
  oil see oil
  renewable sources 453
Energy Networks Association (ENA)
  451
Energy Retail Association 451
Enfield
  constituencies 157
  education authority 383
  London borough council 275,
    300
Enfield and Haringey, GLA
  constituency 241
engineering, professional education
  398
Engineering and Physical Sciences
  Research Council (EPSRC) 419
Engineering Council (UK) (ECUK)
  398
England
  area 17, 278
  Areas of Outstanding Natural
    Beauty (AONBs) 514
  banknotes 549
  constituencies 148
  early history 279
  European Parliament regions 315
  flag 278
  historic buildings and monuments
    524
  hydrography 278
  islands 278
  judicature 318
  Kings and Queens (927 to 1603)
    38
  LEAs (local education authorities)
    379
  local government see local
    government
  museums and art galleries 531
  National Parks 512
  NHS structure 423

police forces 339
population statistics 17, 278
precedence 43
principal cities 280
prison establishments 343
public holidays 10, 11, 701
relief 278
water industry 446
  see also Bank of England; Church
    of England
English Heritage (EH) 218, 523
  list of properties 524
English Nature (EN), see Natural
  England
English Regions Network 269
Enterprise Investment Scheme 578
Entitlement Appeal Tribunals 334
environment 508
  air pollution see air pollution
  climate change 509
  contacts 511
  and health 511
  London issues 239
  sustainable development 509
  UK targets 508
  waste see waste
  water see water, quality targets
Environment, Fisheries and
  Aquaculture Science, Centre for
  201
Environment, Food and Rural Affairs,
  Department for see Department for
  Environment, Food and Rural
  Affairs
Environment Agency 218, 447, 511
epact 702
Ephemeris Time (ET) 690
Epiphany 696
Epping Forest
  constituency 157
  district council 274, 289
Epsom and Ewell
  constituency 157
  district council 274, 289
EPSRC (Engineering and Physical
  Sciences Research Council) 419
Equality Commission for Northern
  Ireland 218
Equal Opportunities Commission see
  Commission for Equality and
  Human Rights (CEHR)
equinoctial year 695
equinox 695
eras see chronological cycles and eras;
  Indian eras
Erewash
  constituency 157
  district council 274, 289
Erith & Thamesmead, constituency
  157
ERO (Electoral Registration Officer)
  606
Eryri/Snowdonia National Park 513
Esher & Walton, constituency 157
ESRC (Economic and Social Research
  Council) 419
Essex
  county council 273, 287
  education authority 379
  university 390
Essex North, constituency 157
ethnic groups in the UK 18
EU
  environmental measures 508

recognition of professional
  qualifications 397
European Derivatives Exchange
  (EDX) 557
European Parliament (EP) 314
  elections 314
  UK members 314
  UK regions 315
European Patent Office 611
European Union see EU
European wildlife trade regulation
  520
Eurostar 457
eviction 601
examinations and qualifications see
  public examinations and
  qualifications
'Excellent Teacher' scheme 372
Exchange markets 557
executive agencies 186
executors of wills 607
exempt supplies 584
Exeter
  Bishop 475
  constituency 157
  district council 274, 289
  university 390
Exmoor National Park 513
expenditure
  government 563
  household 566
  local government 270, 271,
    272
Export Credit Guarantee Department
  (ECGD) 206
exports, UK statistics 565
eyesight tests 427

F
FAA (Fleet Air Arm) 351
Faculty of Actuaries 397
Faculty of Advocates 402
Fair Employment Tribunal (Northern
  Ireland) 333
fair trading 590
  see also Office of Fair Trading
faith see religion
Falkirk
  constituencies
    Scottish Parliament 254
    UK Parliament 179
  education authority 385
  unitary authority 277, 308
Falmouth & Camborne, constituency
  157
families
  local authority services 430
  see also children
Family Division of the High Court of
  Justice 318, 319, 321
Family Health Services Appeal
  Authority (FHSAA) 332
Family Health Services Authorities
  (FHSAs) 423
family proceedings cases 319
Family Records Centre 588
Fareham
  constituency 157
  district council 274, 289
Fashion, London College of 387
Fasli calendar 702
fasts
  Hindu 698
  Jewish 699

Muslim 700
Sikh 700
Father of the House 133
Faversham & Kent Mid, constituency 157
FCC (Foreign Compensation Commission) 219
FCO see Foreign and Commonwealth Office
FCO Services 201
feasts
moveable 697
see also festivals
February 640
astronomical phenomena 640
calendar 640
constellations 640
duration of twilight 641
high water 712
minima of algol 640
night sky 641
sunrise and sunset 643
zodiacal light 641
Moon 640
position 642
Sun 641
Jupiter in 641
Mars in 641
Mercury in 641
Neptune in 643
Saturn in 641
Uranus in 643
Venus in 641
FE Bursaries 371
Federations (schools) 364
Feltham & Heston, constituency 157
Fenland, district council 274, 289
Ferguson, Sarah 24
Fermanagh & South Tyrone
constituencies
Northern Ireland Assembly 264
UK Parliament 182
Fermanagh, district council 277, 310
Ferns, Bishop (RC) 486
festivals
Hindu 698
Jewish 699
Muslim 700
Sikh 700
FHSAA (Family Health Services Appeal Authority) 332
FHSAs (Family Health Services Authorities) 423
Field Marshals 352
salaries 357
Fife
constituencies, Scottish Parliament 254
education authority 385
unitary authority 277, 308
Fife North East, UK Parliament constituency 179
finance
government 563
higher education 362
local government 266
England 269
Northern Ireland 272, 310
Scotland 272
Wales 271
Channel Islands 312
Isle of Man 311
NHS 425

opposition parties 137
personal see banking and personal finance
roads 457
royal family 29
Financial Ombudsman Service 435, 550, 554, 558
financial relief in divorces 594
in Scotland 595
Financial Reporting Council (FRC) 397
Financial Services and Markets Tribunal 332
Financial Services Authority see FSA
Financial Services Compensation Scheme (FSCS) 553
financial services regulation 553
financial terms, glossary 551
Finchley & Golders Green, constituency 157
fineness (purity) marks 545
Fire Service College 200
first class post 494
Five 612, 614
estimated audience share 613
fixed Easter 696
fixed interest saving certificates 555
fixed rate savings bonds 556
fixtures (stamp duty) 585
flags
England 278
Northern Ireland 309
Scotland 304
Wales 301
Guernsey 313
Jersey 312
Isle of Man 311
see also national flag of the UK
Fleet Air Arm (FAA) 351
flexible working 596
Flintshire
education authority 384
unitary authority 276, 303
flying the Union Flag (or Jack) 23
Folkestone & Hythe, constituency 157
Food, Department for Environment, Rural Affairs and see Department for Environment, Food and Rural Affairs
Food Standards Agency (FSA) 206
Foreign and Commonwealth Office 191
executive agencies 201
Foreign Compensation Commission (FCC) 219
foreign goods, hallmarks 547
Forensic Science Northern Ireland 203
Forensic Science Service (FSS) 338
Forest Enterprise 206
Forest Heath, district council 274, 289
Forest Nature Reserves 517
Forest of Dean
constituency 157
district council 274, 289
Forest Research 207
Forestry Commission 206, 517
Forest Service 517
forthcoming events 12
foundation degrees 375
foundation schools 363
foundation trusts 423
Fourth Plinth 539

Foyle
constituencies
Northern Ireland Assembly 264
UK Parliament 182
Free Churches' Council
see Free Churches Group
Free Churches Group 464
Free Church of England 487
Free Church of Scotland 487
Free Presbyterian Church of Scotland 487
Freeview 613
FSA (Financial Services Authority) 550, 553, 557, 558, 560
FSA (Food Standards Agency) 206
FSCS (Financial Services Compensation Scheme) 553
FSS (Forensic Science Service) 338
Fulham, Bishop Suffragan 473
funding councils for education
see Learning and Skills Council (LSC); Training and Development Agency for Schools (TDA)
funding of the royal family 29
Funeral Payments 443
further education see post-16 education
Fylde
constituency 158
district council 274, 289

G
Gaelic languages 304, 311, 367
Gainsborough, constituency 158
Galloway & Upper Nithsdale, Scottish Parliament constituency 255
Galloway, Bishop (RC) 485
Galway and Kilmacduagh, Bishop (RC) 486
Gambling Commission 219
gardens of London 540
Garter, Most Noble Order 83
gas 449, 450
suppliers 452
Gateshead
education authority 380
metropolitan borough council 276, 292
museums and art galleries 532
Gateshead East & Washington West, constituency 158
Gatwick Airport 454, 455
GCC (General Chiropractic Council) 399
GCE A-level examinations see A-levels
GCHQ (Government Communications Headquarters) 208
GCSE 368
GDP of the UK 565
Gedling
constituency 158
district council 274, 289
Genealogists, Society of 588
General Assembly 482
General Assembly of the Church of Scotland 482
General Certificate of Education (GCE) Advanced (A-level) examinations see A-levels
General Certificate of Secondary Education see GCSE

General Chiropractic Council (GCC)
399
General Commissioners of Income
Tax 333
General Council of the Bar 402
General Council of the Bar of
Northern Ireland 402
General Dental Council 399
general election (2005) results 147
general index of retail prices 568
general insurance 558
General Medical Council (GMC) 399
general medical services (GMS) 426
General National Vocational
Qualification (GNVQ) 368
General Ophthalmic Services, NHS
427
General Optical Council (GOC) 402
General Osteopathic Council (GOsC)
402
General Practitioners see GPs
General Register Office 588
General Register Office for Scotland
588
General Synod
Church of England 471
Church of Ireland 481
Scottish Episcopal Church 481
General Teaching Councils (GTCs)
371, 372
Gentleman Usher of the Black Rod,
Department of 129
geological time 708
George Cross 120
George Inn 541
George V 34
Gibraltar in Europe, Bishop 476
Gift Aid scheme 573, 583
gifts
and capital gains tax 578
and inheritance tax 578, 579
Gillingham, constituency 158
GLA 238, 270
constituencies 238, 241
Glamorgan, university 390
Glasgow 307
airport 454, 455
Archbishop (RC) 485
constituencies
Scottish Parliament 255
UK Parliament 179
education authority 385
museums and art galleries 537
Scottish Parliament Region 258
unitary authority 277, 308
universities 390, 395
Glasgow and Galloway, Bishop 481
Glasgow Caledonian University 390
Glenrothes, UK Parliament
constituency 180
Gloucester
Bishop 476
constituency 158
district council 274, 289
Gloucester, Duchess of 24
funding 29
military ranks and titles 33
Private Secretary 26
Gloucester, Duke of 24
funding 29
military ranks and titles 33
Private Secretary 26
Gloucestershire
county council 273, 287

education authority 379
university 390
GMC (General Medical Council) 399
GMS (general medical services) 426
GMT (Greenwich Mean Time) 689,
691
GMTV 614
GNVQ (General National Vocational
Qualification) 368
GOC (General Optical Council) 402
gold coin 548
gold hallmarks 545
Good Friday Agreement 309
goods
sale 589
supply 590
transport
by rail 456
by road 458
by sea 461
Gordon
constituencies
Scottish Parliament 255
UK Parliament 180
GOsC (General Osteopathic Council)
402
Gosport
constituency 158
district council 274, 289
governing bodies of schools 364
Governing Body of the Church in
Wales 481
government 135
current administration 184
departments 186
finance 563
formation 136
organs 127
see also local government; regional
government
Government Car and Despatch
Agency 203
Government Communications
Headquarters (GCHQ) 208
Government Decontamination
Service 201
government grants to local authorities
267
Government Offices for the Regions
219
Government Whips 185
Gower
constituencies
UK Parliament 176
Welsh Assembly 246
GPs 426
salaries 425
Graduated Retirement Benefit (GRB)
434, 439
Graduate Teacher Programme (GTP)
371, 403
Graduate Teacher Training Registry
(GTTR) 375, 403
grant-aided schools 360
Grantham & Stamford, constituency
158
Grantham, Bishop Suffragan 477
grants
for students 375
to local authorities 267
grants-in-aid 29
Gravesham
constituency 158
district council 274, 289

Gray's Inn 402, 542
GRB (Graduated Retirement Benefit)
434, 439
Great Britain see UK
Greater London Authority see GLA
Greater London Returning Officer
(GLRO) 239
Great Grimsby, constituency 158
Great Yarmouth
constituency 158
district council 274, 289
Greek Orthodox Church 489
calendar 696
greenhouse gases, emissions 508
Greenock & Inverclyde, Scottish
Parliament constituency 256
Green Park 541
Green Party 138
Greenwich & Woolwich, constituency
158
Greenwich
education authority 383
London borough council 275,
300
sights 541
university 390
Greenwich and Lewisham, GLA
constituency 241
Greenwich Mean Time (GMT) 689,
691
Greenwich Park 541
Gregorian calendar 696
Grimsby, Bishop Suffragan 477
GTCs (General Teaching Councils)
371, 372
GTP (Graduate Teacher Programme)
371, 403
GTTR (Graduate Teacher Training
Registry) 375, 403
guarantee credit 442
guaranteed equity bonds 555
Guardian's Allowance 440
weekly rates 441
Guernsey 312
airport 455
area 312
currency 549
education authority 386
flag 313
police force 340
population 18, 312
water authority 446
Guildford
Bishop 476
constituency 158
district council 274, 289
Gwynedd
education authority 384
unitary authority 276, 303

H
habitat conservation 519
UK legislation 520
Hackney
constituencies 158
education authority 383
London borough council 275,
300
Halesowen & Rowley Regis,
constituency 158
half-mast, flags at 23
Halifax, constituency 158
Hallam, Bishop (RC) 484
hallmarks 545

Haltemprice & Howden, constituency 158
Halton
 constituency 158
 education authority 380
 unitary authority 276, 293
Hambleton, district council 274, 289
Hamilton, Scottish Parliament constituencies 256
Hammersmith and Fulham
 constituency 159
 education authority 383
 London borough council 275, 300
Hampshire
 constituencies 159
 county council 273, 287
 education authority 379
Hampstead & Highgate, constituency 159
Hampton Court Park and Gardens 541
Hanover, House of 40
Harborough
 constituency 159
 district council 274, 289
harbour authorities 462
Haringey
 education authority 383
 London borough council 275, 300
Harlow
 constituency 159
 district council 274, 289
Harmonised Index of Consumer Prices (HICP) 568
Harrogate & Knaresborough, constituency 159
Harrogate, district council 274, 289
Harrow
 constituencies 159
 education authority 383
 London borough council 275, 300
Harry, Prince see Henry, Prince
Hart, district council 274, 289
Hartlepool
 constituency 159
 education authority 380
 unitary authority 276, 293
Harwich, constituency 159
Hastings & Rye, constituency 159
Hastings, district council 274, 289
Havant
 constituency 159
 district council 274, 289
Havering
 education authority 383
 London borough council 275, 300
Havering and Redbridge, GLA constituency 241
Hayes & Harlington, constituency 159
Hazel Grove, constituency 159
headteachers
 qualifications 371, 372
 salary 372
Health
 Department of see Department of Health
 and the environment 511
 and mobile phone use 500
 statistics 20

Health and Safety Commission 220
Health and Safety Executive 220
Health and Social Services Boards 425, 426
Health Boards 424, 426
healthcare, professional education 399
Health Commission Wales (Specialised Services) 424
health costs 426
Health Professions Council (HPC) 400
Health Protection Agency (HPA) 220
Health Service Ombudsman 229, 429
health services, NHS 426
Heathrow Airport 454, 455
the Hebrides 305
HEFCs (Higher Education Funding Councils) 360, 372, 377
Hemel Hempstead, constituency 159
Hemsworth, constituency 159
Hendon, constituency 159
Henley, constituency 160
Henry, Prince 24
 Military Ranks and Titles 32
 Private Secretary 26
Heralds' College 214
hereditary peers 45, 47
hereditary women peers 45
Hereford
 Bishop 476
 constituency 160
Herefordshire
 education authority 380
 unitary authority 276, 293
Heriot-Watt University 390
Heritage Sites, World see World Heritage Sites
Herm 312
Her Majesty's Courts Service (HMCS) 325
Her Majesty's Inspectorate for Education and Training in Wales 362
Hertford & Stortford, constituency 160
Hertford, Bishop Suffragan 479
Hertfordshire
 constituencies 160
 county council 273, 287
 education authority 379
 university 390
Hertsmere
 constituency 160
 district council 274, 289
Hexham, constituency 160
Hexham and Newcastle, Bishop (RC) 485
Heywood & Middleton, constituency 160
HFEA (Human Fertilisation and Embryology Authority) 221
HGCA (Home-Grown Cereals Authority) 221
HICP (Harmonised Index of Consumer Prices) 568
HIE (Highlands and Islands Enterprise) 220
High Court judges 318, 320
High Court of Justice
 England and Wales 318, 320
 centres 323
 Northern Ireland 330
High Court of Justiciary (Scotland) 326, 327

higher education 373
 admissions 375
 courses 374
 expenditure 360
 fees 375
 finance 362
 student support 375
 types of institution 373
Higher Education Academy 374
Higher Education Funding Councils (HEFCs) 360, 372, 377
higher level teaching assistant (HLTA) status 372
Higher National Certificate (HNC) 370, 374
Higher National Course 369
Higher National Diploma (HND) 370, 374
Higher National Qualifications 370
Highland
 education authority 385
 unitary authority 277, 308
Highlands and Islands Enterprise (HIE) 220
Highlands and Islands Scottish Parliament Region 258
High Peak
 constituency 160
 district council 274, 289
High Sheriffs 268
 England 286
 Northern Ireland 310
 Wales 302
high water, predictions 711
highway authorities 457
Highways Agency 203, 457
Hillingdon
 education authority 383
 London borough council 275, 300
Hinckley and Bosworth, district council 274, 289
Hindu calendar 698
 year 2008 9
Hinduism 467
 adherents in UK 464
hire-purchase agreements 590
historical year 700
historic buildings and monuments 523
 England 524
 Northern Ireland 530
 Scotland 529
 Wales 528
 listing see listed buildings
Historic Buildings and Monuments Commission for England 218
Historic Environment Advisory Council for Scotland 220
Historic Royal Palaces 221
Historic Scotland
 list of properties 529
Hitchin & Harpenden, constituency 160
HLTAs (higher level teaching assistants) 372
HM Coastguard (HMCG) 461
HM Commissary Office 328
HMCS (Her Majesty's Courts Service) 325
HM Fleet 351
HM Inspectorate of Education (HMIE) 362
HM Inspectors (HMIs) 362

HM Prison Service 343
  operating costs 343
  salaries 343
HM Procurator-General and Treasury
  Solicitor, Department of 199
HM Revenue and Customs (HMRC)
  207
HM Treasury 197
  executive agencies 204
HNC (Higher National Certificate)
  370, 374
HND (Higher National Diploma) 370,
  374
Holborn & St Pancras, constituency
  160
hold-over relief on capital gains tax
  578
holidays see public holidays
Holy Apostolic Catholic Assyrian
  Church of the East 487
holy days 701
Holy See 483
home education 366
Home-Grown Cereals Authority
  (HGCA) 221
Home Office 193
  executive agencies 202
Home Responsibilities Protection
  (HRP) 434
homo sapiens, development 708
Honorary Dames Commanders 115
honorary knights 86
The Honourable the Irish Society 296
  Clerk 296
Hornchurch, constituency 160
Hornsey & Wood Green, constituency
  160
Horse Guards 541
Horserace Totalisator Board (the Tote)
  221
horse racing
  forthcoming events 13
Horsham
  Bishop Suffragan 475
  constituency 160
  district council 274, 289
hospices 428
hospitals
  NHS 427
Houghton & Washington East,
  constituency 160
Hounslow
  education authority 383
  London borough council 275,
    300
household
  income and expenditure 566
  ownership of durable goods 566
  statistics 19
  water bills 447
House of Commons 130, 541
  business 130
  elections 130
  Government Whips 185
  hours of meeting 133
  Members see MPs
  officers and officials 131
  party representation 130
  select committees 133, 134
  Speaker 131, 135
House of Commons Members' Fund
  131
House of Lords 128, 541
  composition 128, 129, 45

as final Court of Appeal 128, 319,
    320
  Government Whips 185
  officers 129
  party representation 129
  select committees 128, 129,
    134
  Speaker 129
houses see dwelling-houses
Houses of Parliament
  tours 542
  see also House of Commons; House
    of Lords
Housing Benefit 443
Housing Corporation 221
Hove, constituency 160
HPA (Health Protection Agency) 220
HPC (Health Professions Council)
  400
HRP (Home Responsibilities
  Protection) 434
HTA (Human Tissue Authority) 222
Huddersfield
  constituency 160
  university 390
Hull see Kingston upon Hull
Hulme, Bishop Suffragan 477
human development 708
Human Fertilisation and Embryology
  Authority (HFEA) 221
Human Genetics Commission 221
Humanism 467
human rights 599
Human Tissue Authority (HTA) 222
Huntingdon
  Bishop Suffragan 475
  constituency 161
Huntingdonshire, district council 274,
  289
Hyde Park 541
Hyndburn
  constituency 161
  district council 274, 289

I
ICA (Institute of Contemporary Arts)
  542
IDD (international direct dialling)
  codes 496
Identity and Passport Service 202
Ilford, constituencies 161
illegitimacy 599
Immigration Services Tribunal 333
immigration statistics 18
immunisation
  of children 22
Imperial College London 390
Imperial Service Order 85
Imperial Society of Knights Bachelor
  86
Imperial War Graves Commission see
  Commonwealth War Graves
  Commission
Imperial War Museum 222
imports, UK statistics 565
Incapacity Benefit 438
  weekly rates 439
income, household 566
income-based Jobseeker's Allowance
  (JSA) 440
  weekly rates 441
income bonds 555
income support 441
  weekly rates 442

income support premiums 442
  weekly rates 442
income tax 570
  allowances 570
  relief 572
  self-assessment 574
Independent Housing Ombudsman
  222
Independent Methodist Churches
  488
Independent Police Complaints
  Commission (IPCC) 222, 337
independent radio 617
  estimated audience share 614
  local stations 617
  national stations 617
Independent Review Service for the
  Social Fund 222
independent schools 405
  listing 405
Independent Schools Council (ISC)
  405
Independent Schools Inspectorate
  (ISI) 405
Independent/State School
  Partnerships 364
independent television see ITV
Independent Television News 614
indexation allowance 577
  see also taper relief
index-linked savings certificates 555
Indian Empire, Most Eminent Order
  84
Indian eras 702
Individual Savings Accounts see ISAs
industrial and technological research
  bodies 422
Industrial Injuries Advisory Council
  222
industrial injuries disablement benefit
  444
industrial stoppages 565
industrial tribunals (Northern Ireland)
  333
in Europe, Bishop Suffragan 476
infant mortality 19
infectious diseases, notifications 22
inflation rate 569
Information Commissioner's Office
  223
information technology 501
Information Tribunal 333
inheritance tax 578
  calculation 581
  liability 578
  payment 581
  rates 581
  relief 579
Initial Teacher Education (ITE) 372
initial teacher training (ITT) 372
inland postal services 494
Inner House, Court of Session 327
Inner Temple 403, 542
Inns of Court 402, 542
input tax 583
Insolvency Service 200
Institute of Actuaries 398
Institute of Contemporary Arts (ICA)
  542
insurance 558
insurance companies
  authorisation and regulation 558
  investments 562
  new business 562

takeovers and mergers 558
UK figures 559
integrated schools in Northern
Ireland 364
Integrated Transport, Commission for
(CfIT) 215
intellectual property 610
intellectual property organisations
611
intelligence and security services 208
inter-church cooperation 464
interest rates 550
Inter Faith Network for the United
Kingdom 464
'internal market' in the NHS 423
International Atomic Time (TAI) 690
International Baccalaureate 369
International Development,
Department for 194
international direct dialling (IDD)
codes 496
International Federation of
Reproduction Rights
Organisations 610
International Power plc 451
International Rail Regulator (IRR)
455
International Signed For (airmail
services) 495
International Underwriting
Association (IUA) 559
Internet 501
glossary of terms 502
trends and statistics 501
see also web domain names
intestacy 608, 609
Inverclyde
education authority 385
UK Parliament constituency 180
unitary authority 277, 308
Inverness 307
Inverness, Nairn, Badenoch &
Strathspey, UK Parliament
constituency 180
Inverness East, Nairn & Lochaber,
Scottish Parliament constituency
256
Investigatory Powers Tribunal 223
investment accounts 555
IPCC (Independent Police Complaints
Commission) 222, 337
Ipswich
constituency 161
district council 274, 289
Irish Council of Churches 464
Irish Episcopal Conference 484
Irish-medium schools 364
IRR (International Rail Regulator)
455
ISAs (Individual Savings Accounts)
555
income tax on 572
Islam 467
adherents in UK 464
see also Muslim calendar
Islamic Cultural Centre, London
Central Mosque and 542
islands
England 278
Scotland 305
Isle of Anglesey see Anglesey
Isle of Man see Man, Isle of
Isle of Wight see Wight, Isle of
Isles of Scilly see Scilly, Isles of

Islington
constituencies 161
education authority 383
London borough council 275,
300
Islwyn
constituencies
UK Parliament 176
Welsh Assembly 246
ITE (Initial Teacher Education) 372
ITT (initial teacher training) 372
ITV 612, 614
estimated audience share 613
regions and companies 614
ITV Network Centre/ITV
Association 612, 614
IUA (International Underwriting
Association) 559

J
Jainism 468
January 636
astronomical phenomena 636
calendar 636
constellations 636
duration of twilight 637
high water 712
minima of algol 636
night sky 637
sunrise and sunset 639
Moon 636
position 638
Sun 637
Jupiter in 637
Mars in 637
Mercury in 637
Neptune in 639
Saturn in 637
Uranus in 639
Venus in 637
Japanese calendar 702
Jarrow
Bishop Suffragan 473
constituency 161
Jehovah's Witnesses 493
Jersey 312
airport 455
area 312
currency 549
education authority 386
flag 312
police force 340
population 18, 312
water authority 446
Jesus Christ of Latter-Day Saints,
Church of 492
Jethou 312
Jewish calendar 699
year 2008 9
Jobcentre Plus 205
Jobseeker's Allowance (JSA)
contribution-based 438
weekly rates 439
income-based 440
weekly rates 441
Joint Nature Conservation Committee
223
JSA see Jobseeker's Allowance
Judaism 469
adherents in UK 464
see also Jewish calendar
Judge Advocates 323
judges
circuit 318, 319, 324

district 319, 324
district (magistrates' courts) see
district judges (magistrates'
courts)
High Court 318, 320
judicature
England and Wales 318
Northern Ireland 330
Scotland 326
Judicial Appointments Board for
Scotland 327
Judicial Appointments Commission
325
Judicial Committee of the Privy
Council 326
judicial separation 592, 593
in Scotland 595
Julian calendar 696
see also Roman calendar
Julian date 635
Julian period 702
July 660
astronomical phenomena 660
calendar 660
constellations 660
duration of twilight 661
high water 715
minima of algol 660
night sky 661
sunrise and sunset 663
twilight 661
Moon 660
position 662
Sun 661
Jupiter in 661
Mars in 661
Mercury in 661
Neptune in 663
Saturn in 661
Uranus in 663
Venus in 661
June 656
astronomical phenomena 656
calendar 656
constellations 656
duration of twilight 657
high water 714
minima of algol 656
night sky 657
sunrise and sunset 659
Moon 656
position 658
Sun 657
Jupiter in 657
Mars in 657
Mercury in 657
Neptune in 659
Saturn in 657
Uranus in 659
Venus in 657
Jupiter 693
satellites 693
see also months of the year eg
January, Jupiter in
jury service 599
justices of the peace
England and Wales 319
Northern Ireland 330
Scotland 326
juvenile courts 330

K
Kadmi calendar 702
Keele University 390

Keeper of the Privy Purse 27
Keepsafe 495
Keighley, constituency 161
Kennet, district council 274, 289
Kensington, Area Bishop 473
Kensington and Chelsea
    constituency 161
    education authority 383
    London borough council 275,
        300
Kensington Gardens 541
Kent
    county council 273, 287
    education authority 379
Kent, Duchess of 25
    funding 29
    military ranks and titles 33
    Private Secretary 26
Kent, Duke of 25
    funding 29
    military ranks and titles 33
    Private Secretary 26
Kent, Prince Michael of 25
    military ranks and titles 33
    Private Secretary 26
Kent, Princess Michael of 25
    Private Secretary 26
Kent at Canterbury, University of 391
Kerrier, district council 274, 289
Kerry, Bishop (RC) 486
Kettering
    constituency 161
    district council 274, 289
Kew Royal Botanical Gardens (RBG)
    231, 541
Kildare and Leighlin, Bishop (RC)
    486
Killala, Bishop (RC) 486
Killaloe, Bishop (RC) 486
Kilmarnock & Loudoun
    constituencies
        Scottish Parliament 256
        UK Parliament 180
Kilmore, Bishop (RC) 486
Kilmore, Elphin and Ardagh, Bishop
    482
Kings
    British (since 1603) 39
    of England (927 to 1603) 38
    of Scotland (1016 to 1603) 40
King's Lynn and West Norfolk, district
    council 274, 289
Kingston & Surbiton, constituency
    161
Kingston University 391
Kingston upon Hull 282
    Bishop Suffragan 472
    constituencies 160
    education authority 380
    unitary authority 276, 293
    university 390
    museums and art galleries 532
Kingston upon Thames
    Area Bishop 479
    education authority 383
    London borough council 275,
        300
Kingswood, constituency 161
Kirkcaldy & Cowdenbeath, UK
    Parliament constituency 180
Kirkcaldy, Scottish Parliament
    constituency 256
Kirklees
    education authority 381

metropolitan borough council
    276, 292
Kirkwall 305
Knaresborough, Bishop Suffragan
    478
Knighthood, Orders of 86
knights 86
    forms of address 86
    listing 87
Knights Bachelor 86
Knowsley
    constituencies 161
    education authority 381
    metropolitan borough council
        276, 292

L
Labour Party 137
    development 136
    representation in House of
        Commons 130
ladies in their own right 66
    forms of address 66
Lagan Valley
    constituencies
        Northern Ireland Assembly
            264
        UK Parliament 182
Lake District National Park 513
Lambeth
    education authority 383
    London borough council 275,
        300
Lambeth and Southwark, GLA
    constituency 241
Lambeth Conference 471
Lampeter, University of Wales 396
Lanark & Hamilton East, UK
    Parliament constituency 180
Lancashire
    county council 273, 287
    education authority 379
Lancashire West, constituency 162
Lancaster & Wyre, constituency 162
Lancaster
    Bishop (RC) 485
    Bishop Suffragan 474
    district council 274, 289
    university 391
Lancaster, House of 39
land, UK environmental targets 508
landlords 600
    responsibilities 601
Land Registry 202
Lands Tribunal 333
Lands Tribunal for Scotland 333
languages
    Manx Gaelic 311
    Scottish 304, 367
    Welsh 301, 367
lapsed legatees 607
Larne, district council 277, 310
Laurence, Timothy 24
law
    professional education 402
    see also consumer law; employment
        law
Law Commission 223
law courts and offices 318
    England and Wales 318
    Northern Ireland 330
    Scotland 326
law lords see Lords of Appeal in
    Ordinary

Law Officers 184, 188
Law Officers' Departments 188
Law Society 403
law terms 9
lay magistrates see justices of the peace
LDA (London Development Agency)
    239
Leader of the House of Commons,
    Office of 196
Leader of the Opposition 133
    financial support 137
Leading Edge Partnership
    Programme 364
leap year 695
Learner Support Funds 370
Learning & Teaching Scotland 367
Learning and Skills Council (LSC)
    223, 369, 377
learning disabilities, local authority
    services 431
leaseholders 601
LEAs (local education authorities)
    360, 363, 379
    England 379
    Scotland 384
    Wales 384
    expenditure 360
Leeds 282
    Bishop (RC) 485
    constituencies 162
    education authority 381
    metropolitan borough council
        276, 292
    museums and art galleries 532
    universities 391
Leeds Metropolitan University 391
legal abortion, statistics 19
Legal Aid 601
legal calendar 700
    year 2008 9
legal notes 586
Legal Services Commission 223, 601,
    602
Legal Services Ombudsman 228
Legal Services Ombudsman (Scottish)
    228
legal tender
    banknotes 549
    coins 548
legal year 700
legatees, lapsed 607
legitimation 599
Leicester 282
    Bishop 476
    constituencies 162
    education authority 381
    unitary authority 276, 293
    universities 389, 391
    museums and art galleries 533
Leicestershire
    county council 273, 287
    education authority 379
Leicestershire North West,
    constituency 162
Leigh, constituency 162
length
    of roads 458
Lent 696
Leominster, constituency 162
Lerwick 305
letters of administration 607
lettings
    business 601
    residential 600

Lewes
  Bishop Suffragan 475
  constituency 162
  district council 274, 289
Lewisham
  constituencies 162
  education authority 383
  London borough council 275,
    300
Leyton & Wanstead, constituency 162
LFEPA (London Fire and Emergency
  Planning Authority) 239
LHBs (Local Health Boards) 424, 426
Liberal Democrats 137
  development 136
  financial support 137
  representation in House of
    Commons 130
  spokesmen 137
  Whips 138
Liberal Party 136
licence, marriage by 604
licences
  driving 459
  motor vehicles 460
  television 613
licensing use of copyright material
  610
Lichfield
  Bishop 476
  constituency 162
  district council 274, 289
life expectancy 20
life insurance 560
lifelong learning 377
life peers 45, 67
  forms of address 67
LIFTs (Local Improvement Finance
  Trusts) 425
lighthouse authorities 462
lighting-up time 687
light rail systems 457
Lihou 312
Limavady, district council 277, 310
Limerick, Bishop (RC) 486
Limerick and Killaloe, Bishop 482
Lincoln 283
  Bishop 477
  constituency 163
  district council 274, 289
  university 391
  museums and art galleries 533
Lincolnshire
  county council 273, 287
  education authority 379
Lincoln's Inn 402, 542
Linley, Viscount David Albert Charles
  24
Linlithgow & Falkirk East, UK
  Parliament constituency 180
Linlithgow, Scottish Parliament
  constituency 256
Lisburn, district council 277, 310
listed buildings 523
Liverpool 283
  Archbishop (RC) 484
  Bishop 477
  constituencies 163
  education authority 381
  metropolitan borough council
    276, 292
  museums and art galleries 533
  universities 391
Liverpool Hope University 391

Liverpool John Moores University 391
livery companies 271, 297
Livingston
  constituencies
    Scottish Parliament 256
    UK Parliament 180
    by-election (2005) result 183
Llandaff, Bishop 481
Llanelli
  constituencies
    UK Parliament 176
    Welsh Assembly 246
Lloyd's List 560
Lloyd's of London 461, 542, 560
Lloyd's Shipping Index 560
loans for students 375
local authority care 431
local education authorities *see* LEAs
local government 266
  civic dignities 268
  complaints 267
  Channel Islands 312
  elections 266
  England 268, 278
    changes 266
    political composition of
      councils 273
  finance 266
  internal organisation 266
  Isle of Man 311
  London 270, 295
  Northern Ireland 272, 309, 310
    political composition of
      councils 277
  Queen's representatives 268
  Scotland 271, 304, 308
    changes 266
    political composition of
      councils 277
  Wales 271, 301, 303
    changes 266
    political composition of
      councils 276
Local Government Boundary
  Commission for Wales 266
Local Government Ombudsmen
  England 267
  Wales 268
  Scotland 268
Local Health Boards (LHBs) 424, 426
Local Improvement Finance Trusts
  (LIFTs) 425
Local Nature Reserves 516
local precedence in Scotland 44
Local Transport Plan (LTP) 457
Loch Lomond and the Trossachs
  National Park 514
lochs *see* lakes
London
  airports 454, 455
  art galleries 533
  Bishop 473
  environmental issues 239
  LEAs 382
  local government 270, 295
  museums 533
  regional government 238
  sights 538
  theatres 544
  universities 387, 389, 390, 391,
    394, 395
  see also City of London;
    Corporation of London; Port of
    London

London Assembly 238, 270
  committees 239
  constituencies 241
  members 240
  organisational structure 240
  party representation 240
  role 238
  top-up members 242
  voting system 238
London borough councils 266, 270,
  300
  map 294
  political composition 275
London Central Mosque and the
  Islamic Cultural Centre 542
Londonderry (city) 309
Londonderry East
  constituencies
    Northern Ireland Assembly
      264
    UK Parliament 182
London Development Agency (LDA)
  239
London European Parliament Region
  315
London Eye 542
London Fire and Emergency Planning
  Authority (LFEPA) 239
London (Goldsmiths' Hall) date
  letters 546
London Insurance Market 559
London Metropolitan University
  392
London Monument 539
London Planetarium 542
London South Bank University 392
London Stock Exchange 557
London Transport Users' Committee
  456
London Underground 456
London Zoo 542
longest day 635
long-term incapacity benefit 439
long-term insurance 560
Lord Advocate 326
Lord Chamberlain's Office 28
Lord Chancellor 129, 134, 318
Lord Chancellor's Department *see*
  Ministry of Justice
Lord Chief Justice of England and
  Wales 318
Lord Great Chamberlain 134
Lord High Admiral of the UK 350
Lord High Commissioner 483
Lord Justices of Appeal
  England and Wales 320
  Northern Ireland 330
Lord-Lieutenants 268
  England 286
  Northern Ireland 310
  Scotland 307
  Wales 302
Lord Mayors 268
Lord Mayor's Day 295
Lord Mayors of London 270, 295,
  296
Lord President of the Council 196
Lord Privy Seal *see* Office of the
  Leader of the House of Commons
Lord Provosts 268, 307
lords 57
  courtesy titles 77
  forms of address 57
  see also House of Lords

Lords of Appeal in Ordinary 318, 320, 45
Lords of Session 327
Lord Speaker 134
Lords Spiritual 76
Lothians Scottish Parliament Region 258
Loughborough
    constituency 163
    university 392
Louth & Horncastle, constituency 163
Lowland Scottish language 304
LSC (Learning and Skills Council) 223, 369, 377
LTP (Local Transport Plan) 457
Ludlow
    Bishop Suffragan 476
    constituency 163
lunar cycle 701
Lundy 278
Lutheran Church 488
Luton
    constituencies 163
    education authority 381
    unitary authority 276, 293
    see Bedfordshire, university of
Lynn, Bishop Suffragan 477

M
Macclesfield
    constituency 163
    district council 274, 289
Madame Tussaud's 542
Magherafelt, district council 277, 310
magistrates see justices of the peace; resident magistrates; stipendiary magistrates
magistrates' courts
    England and Wales 319
    Northern Ireland 330
magnetic storms 694
magnetism, terrestrial 694
Maidenhead, constituency 163
Maidstone & The Weald, constituency 163
Maidstone
    Bishop Suffragan 472
    district council 274, 289
mail see postal services
Maintenance Grant 375
maintenance payments 593
    tax relief on 573, 579
major cycle 701
Makerfield, constituency 163
Malankara Orthodox Syrian Church 489
Maldon & Chelmsford East, constituency 163
Maldon, district council 274, 289
Malvern Hills, district council 274, 289
man, development of 708
Man, Isle of 311
    area 311
    currency 548, 549
    education authority 386
    flag 311
    police force 340
    population 18
    water authority 446
Manchester 283
    Bishop 477
    constituencies 163
    education authority 381

metropolitan borough council 276, 292
museums and art galleries 534
universities 392, 395
Manchester Metropolitan University 392
Manpower Economics, Office of (OME) 228
Mansfield
    constituency 164
    district council 274, 289
Manx Gaelic 311
March 644
    astronomical phenomena 644
    calendar 644
    constellations 644
    duration of twilight 645
    high water 713
    minima of algol 644
    night sky 645
    sunrise and sunset 647
    zodiacal light 645
    Moon 644
        position 646
    Sun 645
    Jupiter in 645
    Mars in 645
    Mercury in 645
    Neptune in 647
    Saturn in 645
    Uranus in 647
    Venus in 645
Marine and Fisheries Agency 201
Marinecall 462
Marine Nature Reserves 517
marine safety 461
Maritime and Coastguard Agency (MCA) 203, 461
markets in London 539
Marlborough House 542
marquesses 48
    courtesy titles 77
    forms of address 48
marriage 603
    certificates of 588
    in England and Wales 603
        fees 604
        nullity of 593
    notice of 604
    prohibition 603
    in Scotland 605
        fees 605
        nullity of 595, 596
    solemnisation 604
    statistics 19
Mars 689
    satellites 693
    see also months of the year eg January, Mars in
Marshals of the RAF 355
masonic year 702
Master of the Household's Department 27
Master of the Rolls 319, 320
Maternity Allowance (MA) 440
    weekly rates 441
Maternity Leave 596
maternity pay 596
maternity rights 596
Maundy Money 548
Maundy Thursday 696
May 652
    astronomical phenomena 652
    calendar 652

constellations 652
duration of twilight 653
high water 714
minima of algol 652
night sky 653
sunrise and sunset 655
Moon 652
    position 654
Sun 653
Jupiter in 653
Mars in 653
Mercury in 653
Neptune in 655
Saturn in 653
Uranus in 655
Venus in 653
Mayor of London 238
    election results (2004) 240
    role 238
    salary 239
    voting system 238
mayors 268
MCA (Maritime and Coastguard Agency) 203, 461
MDC (Milk Development Council) 420
mean and sidereal time 686
mean refraction 692
Mean Solar Time 689
measurement of time 695
Meath, Bishop (RC) 486
Meath and Kildare, Bishop 482
Meat Hygiene Service 206
medals, decorations and 118
media 612
Media, Department for Culture, Sport and see Department for Culture, Media and Sport
medical insurance 561
Medical Research Council (MRC) 419
medicine
    professional education 399
    professions supplementary to, professional education 400
Medicines and Healthcare Products Regulatory Agency (MHRA) 201
Medway
    constituency 164
    education authority 381
    unitary authority 276, 293
Meirionnydd Nant Conwy
    constituencies
        UK Parliament 176
        Welsh Assembly 246
Melton, district council 274, 289
Members of Parliament see MPs
Members of the European Parliament see MEPs
Mendip, district council 274, 289
Menevia, Bishop (RC) 485
mental handicaps see learning disabilities
Mental Health Act Commission 224
Mental Health Review Tribunals 333
mentally ill people, local authority services 431
MEPs
    UK 314
Mercury 689
    see also months of the year eg January, Mercury in
Meriden, constituency 164
Merit, Order of 118

Merthyr Tydfil & Rhymney
  constituencies
    UK Parliament 177
    Welsh Assembly 246
Merthyr Tydfil
  education authority 384
  unitary authority 276, 303
Merton
  education authority 383
  London borough council 275,
    300
Merton and Wandsworth, GLA
  constituency 242
Mesozoic era 708
meteors
  in August 665
  in December 681
Methodist Church 488
Methodist Church in Ireland 488
metonic (lunar, or minor) cycle 701
metropolitan borough councils 266,
  269, 292
  functions 269
  map 294
  political composition 276
Metropolitan Police Authority (MPA)
  239
Metropolitan Police Service 340
  rates of pay 338
metro systems 457
MHRA (Medicines and Healthcare
  Products Regulatory Agency) 201
MI5 (Security Service) 208
MI6 (Secret Intelligence Service) 208
Mid and West Wales Welsh Assembly
  Region 247
Mid Bedfordshire, district council
  274, 289
Mid Devon, district council 274, 289
Middlesbrough
  Bishop (RC) 485
  constituencies 164
  education authority 381
  unitary authority 276, 293
middle schools 365
Middlesex University 393
Middle Temple 403, 542
Middleton, Bishop Suffragan 477
Midlothian
  constituencies
    Scottish Parliament 256
    UK Parliament 180
  education authority 385
  unitary authority 277, 308
Mid Suffolk, district council 274, 289
Mid Sussex, district council 274, 289
military officers see officers
military ranks and titles of the royal
  family 31
Milk Development Council (MDC)
  420
Milton Keynes
  constituencies 164
  education authority 381
  unitary authority 276, 293
minima of algol 687
  see also months of the year eg
    January, minima of algol
Ministers of State 184
  salaries 186
Ministry of Defence 347, 348
Ministry of Defence Police 341
Ministry of Justice (MoJ) 195
  executive agencies 202

minor cycle 701
Mitcham & Morden, constituency 164
MLA (Museums, Libraries and
  Archives Council) 224, 531
mobile communications 498
  health implications of mobile
    phone use 500
  industry players 498
  network technology 499
  phone use and driving 500
  regulation 499
  types of service 498, 499
Mobile Virtual Network Operators
  (MVNOs) 498
MOD see Ministry of Defence
Moderator of the General Assembly
  482, 483
MoJ (Ministry of Justice) 195
Mole Valley
  constituency 164
  district council 274, 290
the monarchy 127
  see also royal family
Monmouth
  Bishop 481
  constituencies
    UK Parliament 177
    Welsh Assembly 246
Monmouthshire
  education authority 384
  unitary authority 276, 303
Montgomeryshire
  constituencies
    UK Parliament 177
    Welsh Assembly 246
months
  definition 695
  Hindu 698
  Jewish 699
  Muslim 700
The Monument 539
monuments
  in London 539
  see also historic buildings and
    monuments
Moon 687, 688
  see also months of the year eg
    January, Moon
moonrise 689
  calculation 685
moonset 689
  calculation 685
Moray
  constituencies
    Scottish Parliament 256
    UK Parliament 180
  education authority 385
  unitary authority 277, 308
Moray, Ross and Caithness, Bishop
  481
Morecambe & Lunesdale,
  constituency 164
Morley & Rothwell, constituency 164
Mormons 492
Mothering Sunday 697
Motherwell & Wishaw
  constituencies
    Scottish Parliament 256
    UK Parliament 180
Motherwell, Bishop (RC) 485
motor vehicles
  licences 459
  road use 458
MOT testing 461

moveable feasts to year 2035 697
Moyle, district council 277, 310
MPA (Metropolitan Police Authority)
  239
MPs
  eligibility 130
  listing 139
  pay and allowances 130
  pensions 131
MRC (Medical Research Council) 419
MSPs 250
Museum of London 224
museums 531
  England 531
  Northern Ireland 537
  Scotland 537
  Wales 536
  see also names of individual museums
    eg British Museum
Museums, Libraries and Archives
  Council (MLA) 224
Museums Association 531
music therapies, professional
  education 400
Muslim calendar 700
  year 2008 9
  see also Islam
MVNOs (Mobile Virtual Network
  Operators) 498

N
Na h-Eileanan an Iar, constituency
  180
nanotechnology 506
Napier University 393
national academies of scholarship 416
National Air Traffic Services (NATS)
  454
National Archives 202
National Army Museum 224
National Assembly for Wales see Welsh
  Assembly
National Assessment Agency (NAA)
  367
National Audit Office 132
National Care Standards Commission
  (NCSC) 430
National College for School
  Leadership 371
National Consumer Council (NCC)
  224
National Council for Education and
  Training (ELWa) 367
National Courses 369
National Crime Squad (NCS) see
  Serious Organised Crime Agency
National Criminal Intelligence Service
  (NCIS) see Serious Organised Crime
  Agency
national curriculum 366
  assessment 366
national daily newspapers
  circulation 623
  listing 624
National Endowment for Science,
  Technology and the Arts (NESTA)
  224
National Film Theatre 543
national flag of the UK 23
National Forest 516
National Forest Company 516
National Galleries of Scotland 224
National Gallery 225
National Grid Transco plc 451

National Health Service see NHS
National Heritage Memorial Fund 225
National Institute of Adult Continuing Education (NIACE) 377
National Insurance (NI) 432
National Library of Scotland 225
National Library of Wales 225
National Lottery Commission 225
National Maritime Museum 226
national museums and art galleries 531
    see also names of individual museums and galleries eg British Museum
National Museums and Galleries Northern Ireland 226
National Museums Liverpool 226
National Museums Scotland 226
National Museum Wales – Amgueddfa Cymru 226
National Nature Reserves 516
National Offender Management Service (NOMS) 342
National Park Authorities (NPAs) 512
National Parking Adjudication Service 334
National Parks 512
    funding 512
    membership 512
National Physical Laboratory (NPL) 420
National Policing Improvement Agency (NPIA) 338
National Portrait Gallery 227
National Professional Qualification for Headship (NPQH) 371
National Physical Laboratory (NPL) 690, 691
National Public Health Service 424
National Qualifications 369, 370
National Rail Enquiries 456
National Savings and Investments 204, 550, 555
National Scenic Areas 515
National School of Government 207
National Statistics, Office for 569
national Sunday newspapers, circulation 623
National Trust, list of properties 530
National Trust for Scotland, list of properties 529
National Vocational Qualifications (NVQs) 368
National Weights and Measures Laboratory 202
NATS (National Air Traffic Services) 454
Natural England 227, 512, 514, 516
Natural Environment Research Council (NERC) 421
natural gas see gas
Natural History Museum 227
naturalisation 589
natural parents, tracing 587
nature reserves 516
nautical twilight 688
    see also months of the year eg January, twilight
navy see Merchant Navy training schools; Royal Navy
NCC (National Consumer Council) 224
NCSC (National Care Standards Commission) 430

NDA (Nuclear Decommissioning Authority) 452
Neath
    constituencies
        UK Parliament 177
        Welsh Assembly 246
Neath Port Talbot
    education authority 384
    unitary authority 277, 303
Neptune 689
    satellites 693
    see also months of the year eg January, Neptune in
NERC (Natural Environment Research Council) 421
NESTA (National Endowment for Science, Technology and the Arts) 224
NETA (New Electricity Trading Arrangements) 451
network operators 498
Network Rail 455, 456
    timetabling service 456
Newark, constituency 164
Newark and Sherwood, district council 274, 290
Newbury, constituency 164
Newcastle-under-Lyme
    constituency 164
    district council 274, 290
Newcastle upon Tyne 283
    Bishop 477
    constituencies 164
    education authority 381
    metropolitan borough council 276, 292
    museums and art galleries 535
    universities 393
New Church 491
New Deal for Lone Parents 442
New Forest, constituencies 164
New Forest, district council 274, 290
New Forest National Park 512, 513
Newham
    education authority 383
    London borough council 275, 300
Newport
    constituencies
        UK Parliament 177
        Welsh Assembly 246
    education authority 384
    unitary authority 277, 303
    University of Wales 396
Newry & Armagh
    constituencies
        Northern Ireland Assembly 264
        UK Parliament 182
Newry and Mourne, district council 277, 310
newspapers 623
Newtownabbey, district council 277, 310
New Year 700
Next Steps programme 186
NFFO (Non-Fossil Fuel Obligation Renewables Orders) 453
NHS 423
    complaints procedure 429
    employees and salaries 425
    finance 425
    health services 426

reciprocal arrangements 429
    structure 423
    waiting lists 428
NHS 24 427
NHS Charters 428
NHS Direct 427
NHS Plan 425
NHS Purchasing and Supply Agency 202
NHS Tribunal (Scotland) 334
NHS Trusts 423
    in Wales 424
NHS Walk-in Centres 426
NIACE (National Institute of Adult Continuing Education) 377
NICF (Northern Ireland Consolidated Fund) 310
night, definition 695
night sky see months of the year eg January, night sky
NMC (Nursing and Midwifery Council) 401
NOMS (National Offender Management Service) 342
Non-Christian religions and beliefs 466
non-contributory benefits 440
    weekly rates 441, 442
non-domestic rates 267, 270
Non-Fossil Fuel Obligation (NFFO) Renewables Orders 453
non-hereditary peers see life peers
non-ministerial government departments 205
Non-Trinitarian churches 492
    adherents in UK 464
Norfolk
    constituencies 165
    county council 273, 287
    education authority 379
Normandy, House of 38
Normanton, constituency 165
Northampton
    Bishop (RC) 485
    constituencies 165
    district council 274, 290
    university 393
Northamptonshire
    county council 273, 287
    education authority 379
Northavon, constituency 165
North Ayrshire
    education authority 385
    unitary authority 277, 308
North Cornwall, district council 274, 290
North Devon, district council 274, 290
North Dorset, district council 274, 290
North Down, district council 277, 310
North East, GLA constituency 242
North East Derbyshire, district council 274, 290
North East Education and Library Board 385
North East European Parliament Region 315
North East Lincolnshire
    education authority 381
    unitary authority 276, 293
North East Wales Institute of Higher Education 396

Northern Ireland
  area 17, 309
  Areas of Outstanding Natural
    Beauty (AONBs) 515
  banknotes 549
  constituencies (UK Parliament)
    181
  constitutional developments 309
  Education and Library Boards
    (ELBs) 385
  flag 309
  historic buildings and monuments
    530
  judicature 330
  local government see local
    government
  museums and art galleries 537
  National Parks 514
  NHS structure 425
  passenger transport services 458
  police force see Police Service of
    Northern Ireland
  population statistics 17, 309
  principal cities 309
  prison establishments 346
  public holidays 10, 11, 701
  regional government 260
  water industry 448
Northern Ireland Affairs Committee
  134
Northern Ireland Assembly 128,
  260
  constituencies 262
  departments and executive
    agencies 260
  members 261
  political composition 262
  salaries 260
Northern Ireland Commissioner for
  Complaints 268
Northern Ireland Consolidated Fund
  (NICF) 310
Northern Ireland Council for the
  Curriculum, Examinations and
  Assessment (CCEA) 367
Northern Ireland Court Service 330
Northern Ireland Democratic Unionist
  Party see Democratic Unionist Party
Northern Ireland Electricity plc 451
Northern Ireland Environment and
  Heritage Service, list of properties
  530
Northern Ireland European Parliament
  Region 315
Northern Ireland Executive 260
Northern Ireland Grand Committee
  134
Northern Ireland Human Rights
  Commission 227
Northern Ireland Office 196
  executive agencies 203
Northern Ireland Prison Service 346
  operating costs 343
  salaries 346
Northern Ireland Tourist Board 235
Northern Lighthouse Board 227,
  462
North Hertfordshire, district council
  274, 290
North Kesteven, district council 274,
  290
North Lanarkshire
  education authority 385
  unitary authority 277, 308

North Lincolnshire
  education authority 381
  unitary authority 276, 293
North Norfolk, district council 274,
  290
North Shropshire, district council
  274, 290
North Somerset
  education authority 381
  unitary authority 276, 293
North Tyneside
  education authority 381
  metropolitan borough council
    276, 292
Northumberland
  county council 273, 287
  education authority 379
Northumberland National Park 513
Northumbria University at Newcastle
  393
North Wales Welsh Assembly Region
  248
North Warwickshire, district council
  274, 290
North West European Parliament
  Region 316
North West Leicestershire, district
  council 274, 290
North Wiltshire, district council 274,
  290
North York Moors National Park 513
North Yorkshire
  county council 273, 287
  education authority 379
Norwich 284
  Bishop 477
  constituencies 165
  district council 274, 290
notice of marriage 604
Nottingham 284
  Bishop (RC) 485
  constituencies165
  education authority 381
  museums and art galleries 535
  unitary authority 276, 293
  universities 393
Nottinghamshire
  county council 273
  education authority 379
Nottingham Trent University 393
November 676
  astronomical phenomena 676
  calendar 676
  constellations 676
  duration of twilight 677
  high water 717
  meteors 677
  minima of algol 676
  night sky 677
  sunrise and sunset 679
  Moon 676
    position 678
  Sun 677
  Jupiter in 677
  Mars in 677
  Mercury in 677
  Neptune in 679
  Saturn in 677
  Uranus in 679
  Venus in 677
NPAs (National Park Authorities)
  512
NPIA (National Policing Improvement
  Agency) 338

NPL (National Physical Laboratory)
  420
NPQH (National Professional
  Qualification for Headship)
  371
nuclear forces 348
nuclear power 452
NPL (National Physical Laboratory)
  690, 691
Nuclear Safety Directorate 453
nullity of marriage 593
  in Scotland 595, 596
Nuneaton, constituency 165
Nuneaton and Bedworth, district
  council 274, 290
Nursing and Midwifery Council
  (NMC) 401
Nursing and Other Health Professions
  Review Body 231
nursing staff
  professional education 401
  salaries 425
NVQs (National Vocational
  Qualifications) 368

O
Oadby and Wigston, district council
  274, 290
Occupational Pensions Regulatory
  Authority (OPRA) see Pensions
  Regulator
occupational therapy, professional
  education 400
Ochil & Perthshire South, UK
  Parliament constituency 180
Ochil, Scottish Parliament
  constituency 256
OCPA (Office of the Commissioner
  for Public Appointments) 188
OCSC (Office of the Civil Service
  Commissioners) 188
October 672
  astronomical phenomena 672
  calendar 672
  constellations 672
  duration of twilight 673
  high water 716
  minima of algol 672
  night sky 673
  sunrise and sunset 675
  Moon 672
    position 674
  Sun 673
  Jupiter in 673
  Mars in 673
  Mercury in 673
  Neptune in 675
  Saturn in 673
  Uranus in 675
  Venus in 673
OFCOM (Office of Communications)
  228, 500, 612, 617
Office for National Statistics (ONS)
  204, 569
Office for Standards in Education,
  Children's Services and Skills
  (OFSTED) 208, 362, 430
Office of Communications (OFCOM)
  228, 500, 612, 617
Office of Fair Trading (OFT) 207
Office of Gas and Electricity Markets
  (OFGEM) 207, 452
Office of Government Commerce
  (OGC) 198

Office of Manpower Economics
(OME) 228
Office of Public Sector Information
(OPSI) 203
Office of Rail Regulation (ORR) 207,
455, 456
Office of the Advocate-General for
Scotland 196
Office of the Civil Service
Commissioners (OCSC) 188
Office of the Commissioner for Public
Appointments (OCPA) 188
Office of the Deputy Prime
Minister See Department for Local
Communities and Government
Office of the Leader of the House of
Commons 196
Office of the Legal Services
Ombudsman 228
Office of the Public Guardian 203
Office of the Scottish Legal Services
Ombudsman 228
officers
salaries 357
service retired pay 359
Offices of the Royal Household 27
Official Roll of the Baronetage 86
OFGEM (Office of Gas and Electricity
Markets) 207, 452
Oflot (Office of the National
Lottery) see National Lottery
Commission
OFSTED (Office for Standards in
Education, Children's Services and
Skills) 208, 362, 430
OFT (Office of Fair Trading) 207
OFWAT (Water Services Regulation
Authority) 208, 447
OGC Buying Solutions 204
OGC (Office of Government
Commerce) 198
Ogilvy, the Hon. Lady see Alexandra,
Princess
Ogilvy, the Rt. Hon. Sir Angus 25
Ogmore
constituencies
UK Parliament 177
Welsh Assembly 247
oil 449
'Old Bailey' 541
Old Bexley & Sidcup, constituency
165
older people, local authority services
430
Oldham
constituencies 165
education authority 381
metropolitan borough council
276, 292
Olympiads 702
Omagh, district council 277, 310
Ombudsmen
Financial 435, 550, 554, 558
Health Service 229, 429
Housing 222
Legal Services 228
Scotland 228
Local Government 267
Northern Ireland Police 230, 337
Parliamentary 229
Pensions 228, 435, 554
Prisons and Probation 230
Public Services
Scotland 234

OME (Office of Manpower
Economics) 228
online art museum 531
ONS (Office for National Statistics)
204
OPAS (Pensions Advisory Service)
435
open spaces of London 540
Open University 373, 393
admissions 375
ophthalmic services, NHS 427
Opposition 136
Leader see Leader of the
Opposition
Shadow Cabinet 137
Opposition days 134
opposition parties, financial support
137
OPRA (Occupational Pensions
Regulatory Authority) see Pensions
Regulator
OPSI (Office of Public Sector
Information) 203
optometrists, salaries 425
optometry and dispensing optics,
professional education 401
order of succession 25
Orders of Chivalry 83
Orders of Knighthood 86
Ordinary Adoption Leave 597
Ordinary Maternity Leave 596
ordination of women 471
Ordnance Survey 200
Oriental Orthodox Churches 489
Orkney & Shetland, UK Parliament
constituency 180
Orkney 305
education authority 385
Scottish Parliament constituency
257
unitary authority 277, 308
Orpington, constituency 165
ORR (Office of Rail Regulation) 207,
455, 456
Orthodox churches 488
calendar 696
orthoptics, professional education 400
orthotics, professional education 401
Ossory, Bishop (RC) 486
osteopathy, professional education
402
Oswestry, district council 274, 290
Outer House, Court of Session 327
out-of-hours (OOH) care 426
output tax 583
overseas clergy 482
overseas postal services 494
Oxford 284
Bishop 478
constituencies 166
district council 274, 290
museums and art galleries 535
universities 393
Oxford Brookes University 394
Oxfordshire
county council 273
education authority 379

P
Paganism 469
Paisley & Renfrewshire, UK
Parliament constituencies 181
Paisley
Bishop (RC) 485

Scottish Parliament constituencies
257
university 394
Palaeozoic era 708
palliative care 428
Palm Sunday 696
PALS (Patients Advice and Liaison
Service) 429
Panel on Takeovers and Mergers 554
Parades Commission 228
paramedical services, professional
education 401
Parcelforce Worldwide 494, 495
parcel rates 494
parental leave 596
parental responsibility 599
parental rights 596
parents
adults living with 20
tracing natural 587
parish councils 268, 269
Parker Bowles, Camilla see Camilla,
Duchess of Cornwall
parks of London 540
Parliament 127
glossary of aspects of work 133
see also Houses of Parliament
Parliament Acts 1911 and 1949 134
parliamentary annuities 29
Parliamentary Archives 135
Parliamentary Commissioner for
Administration 229
parliamentary constituencies see
constituencies
Parliamentary Ombudsman 229
parliamentary privilege 134
Parole Board for England and Wales
229
Parole Board for Scotland 229
Particle Physics and Astronomy
Research Council (PPARC) see
STFC
parties, political see political parties
Partnerships for Health 425
Party of Wales see Plaid Cymru
passenger numbers
by air 454
by sea 462
Passport Service 202
Patent Office see UK Intellectual
Property Office
patents 611
Patents Court 321
paternity leave 597
paternity pay 597
Patients Advice and Liaison Service
(PALS) 429
Patient's Charter 428
Patriarchates
of the Eastern Orthodox Church
488
of the Oriental Orthodox
Churches 489
pay as you earn (PAYE) system 574
payment clearings 550
PCC (Press Complaints Commission)
623
PCTs see Primary Care Trusts
Peak District National Park 513
peerage 45
disclaimed 45
extinct since last edition 45
hereditary 45, 47
hereditary women 45

life 45, 67
membership of the House of
Lords 128
minors 46
Peers of the Blood Royal 47
forms of address 47
peers' surnames 78
Pembrokeshire
education authority 384
unitary authority 277, 303
Pembrokeshire Coast National Park
513
Pendle
constituency 166
district council 274, 290
Penrith & The Border, constituency
166
Penrith, Bishop Suffragan 474
Pension Credit 441, 442
pensioners guaranteed income bonds
556
Pension Protection Fund (PPF) 229,
553
pensions 433, 560
armed forces 359
complaints 435
MPs 131
tax relief on contributions 573
see also state pension scheme; war
pensions
Pensions, Department for Work
and see Department for Work and
Pensions
Pensions Advisory Service (OPAS)
435
Pensions Appeal Tribunals 334
Pensions Appeal Tribunals for
Scotland 334
Pension Service 205, 434
Pensions Ombudsman 228, 435,
554
Pensions Regulator 229, 435
Pentecost 697
Sunday after 697
Pentecostal Churches 490
Penwith, district council 274, 290
People's Question Time 238
PEPs (personal equity plans) 572
periodicals 627
personal equity plans (PEPs) 572
personal medical service (PMS) pilots
426
personal pension schemes 434
Personal Social Services 430
staff 430
Perth & Perthshire North, UK
Parliament constituency 181
Perth, Scottish Parliament
constituency 257
Perth and Kinross
education authority 385
unitary authority 277, 308
Pesticides Safety Directorate 201
Peterborough
Bishop 478
constituency 166
education authority 381
unitary authority 276, 293
PFI (Private Finance Initiative) 425
PGCE (Postgraduate Certificate in
Education) 371, 376, 403
pharmaceutical services, NHS 426
pharmacists, salaries 425
pharmacy, professional education 402

Philip, Prince 24
funding 29
military ranks and titles 31
Private Secretary 26
Philips, Mark 24
physiotherapy, professional education
401
Plaid Cymru 138
development 136
financial support 137
representation in House of
Commons 130
planets see individual planets eg
Mercury; transit of
planning, town and country 605
Planning Inspectorate 200
Plantagenets 38
plants, protected 521
PLA (Port of London Authority) 542
platinum hallmarks 545
Pluto 693
satellites 693
Plymouth
Bishop (RC) 485
Bishop Suffragan 475
constituencies 166
education authority 381
unitary authority 276, 293
university 394
museums and art galleries 535
Plymouth Brethren 490
PMRAFNS (Princess Mary's Royal Air
Force Nursing Service) 356
PMS (personal medical service) pilots
426
PNB (Police Negotiating Board) 230
Pneumoconiosis, Byssinosis and
Miscellaneous Diseases Benefit
Scheme 444
PNMPB (Police National Missing
Persons Bureau) 338
podcasting 615
podiatry, professional education 400
Poet Laureate 29
Police Advisory Board for England
and Wales 229
Police Complaints Authority see
Independent Police Complaints
Commission (IPCC)
Police Complaints Commissioner for
Scotland 337
Police National Missing Persons
Bureau (PNMPB) 338
Police Negotiating Board (PNB) 230
Police Ombudsman for Northern
Ireland 230, 337
police service 337
complaints 337
national police services 338
police authorities 337
police forces 339
rates of pay 337
staff associations 341
Police Service of Northern Ireland
340
rates of pay 338, 340
political parties 136
development 136
representation in House of
Commons 130
representation in House of Lords
129
Pontefract & Castleford, constituency
166

Pontefract, Bishop Suffragan 480
Pontypridd
constituencies
UK Parliament 177
Welsh Assembly 247
Poole
constituency 166
education authority 381
unitary authority 276, 293
the Pope (Father) 483
Poplar & Canning Town,
constituency 166
population
UK statistics 17
England 17, 278
Northern Ireland 17, 309
Scotland 17, 304
Wales 17, 301
of prisons 342
Port of London 542
Port of London Authority (PLA) 542
ports 461
Portsmouth
Bishop 478
Bishop (RC) 485
constituencies 166
education authority 381
unitary authority 276, 293
university 394
museums and art galleries 535
Porvoo Declaration 465
post-16 education 369
expenditure 360
financial support 370
postal services 494
Postal Services Commission
(Postcomm) 208, 494
postal votes 606
postcode enquiries 495
Postcomm (Postal Services
Commission) 208
post-experience short courses 375
Postgraduate Certificate in Education
(PGCE) 371, 403
Postgraduate Students' Allowances
Scheme (PSAS) 377
postgraduate studies 375
admissions 375
awards 376
Post Office 495
Post Office (PO) Box 495
Postwatch 494
pound sterling 548
purchasing power 569
Powys
education authority 384
unitary authority 277, 303
PPARC (Particle Physics and
Astronomy Research Council) see
STFC
PPF (Pension Protection Fund) 229,
553
PQH(NI) (Professional Qualification
for Headship in Northern Ireland)
372
precedence 43
premium bonds 555
pre-paid services for mobiles 498
Presbyterian Church in Ireland 490
Presbyterian Church of Wales 490
presbyteries of the Church of
Scotland 483
pre-school education 365
prescription charge system 426

Preseli Pembrokeshire
  constituencies
    UK Parliament 177
    Welsh Assembly 247
President of the Courts of England
    and Wales 318
the press 623
  complaints 623
  newspapers 623
  periodicals 627
  self-regulation 623
Press Complaints Commission (PCC)
    623
Preston
  constituency 166
  district council 274, 290
  museums and art galleries 535
'Pricing in Proportion' 494
primary and community healthcare
    426
Primary Care Trusts 423, 426
primary education 365
  expenditure 360
primary fuels 449
primary medical services 426
primates
  overseas 482
  see also archbishops
Prime Minister 184
  office of 135
  residence 541
  salary 186
Prime Minister's Office 187
Prime Minister's Questions 134
Primus of the Scottish Episcopal
    Church 481
princes see individual princes eg
    Andrew, Prince
princes of Wales 42
  see also Charles, Prince of Wales
princesses see individual princesses eg
    Kent, Princess Michael of
princesses Royal 42
  see also Anne, Princess
Princess Mary's Royal Air Force
    Nursing Service (PMRAFNS) 356
Prisons and Probation Ombudsman
    for England and Wales 230
prison service 342
  complaints 342
  inmate population 342
  inspectorates 342
  operating costs 343
  prison establishments 342, 343
  private sector 342
  self-inflicted deaths 343
Prison Service Pay Review Body
    (PSPRB) 230
private bills 134
Private Finance Initiative (PFI) 425
private medical insurance 561
private member's bills 134
private notice questions 134
private patients in the NHS 427
Private Pension Schemes 434
Private Secretaries to the Royal
    Family 26
Private Secretary's Office 27
privilege of Parliament 134
Privy Council 123, 127
  members 123
    forms of address 123
  see also Judicial Committee of the
    Privy Council

Privy Council Office 196
Privy Council of Northern Ireland
    126
Privy Purse 27, 30
probate 607
proceedings against the Crown 591
Procurator Fiscal Service 326, 327,
    329
professional education 397
  EU recognition 397
Professional Qualification for
    Headship (PQH(NI)) 372
prosthetics, professional education
    401
protection of children 431
provosts 268
proxy, voting by 606
PSAS (Postgraduate Students'
    Allowances Scheme) 377
PSPRB (Prison Service Pay Review
    Body) 230
public bills 134
public bodies 209
public examinations and qualifications
  higher education 362
  secondary education 368
  for teachers 371
  vocational 368, 369
Public Guardianship Office (PGO) see
    Office of the Public Guardian
public holidays 701
  year 2008 10
  year 2009 11
Public Lending Right system 230
Public Prosecutions, Director of see
    Director of Public Prosecutions
    (DPP)
public sector finances 564
Pudsey, constituency 166
Puffin Island 278
pupils 361
  number at independent schools
    405
  with statements of special needs
    366
pupil-teacher ratios 361
Purbeck, district council 274, 290
purchasing power of the pound 569
Putney, constituency 166

Q
QAA (Quality Assurance Agency for
    Higher Education) 362, 374
QARANC (Queen Alexandra's Royal
    Army Nursing Corps) 354
QARNNS (Queen Alexandra's Royal
    Naval Nursing Service) 351
QCA (Qualifications and Curriculum
    Authority) 367, 368
QTS (Qualified Teacher Status) 371
Quakerism 491
qualifications see public examinations
    and qualifications
Qualifications, Curriculum and
    Assessment Authority for Wales
    (ACCAC) 367
Qualifications and Curriculum
    Authority (QCA) 367, 368
Qualified Teacher Status (QTS) 371
Quality Assurance Agency for Higher
    Education (QAA) 362, 374
quarter days 701
  year 2008 9
Queen, the see Elizabeth II

Queen Alexandra's Royal Army
    Nursing Corps (QARANC) 354
Queen Alexandra's Royal Naval
    Nursing Service (QARNNS) 351
Queen Elizabeth II Conference
    Centre 200
Queens
  of England (927–1603) 38
  of Scotland (1016 to 1603) 40
  British (since 1603) 39
Queen's Bench Division of the High
    Court of Justice 318, 321
Queen's Messengers, Corps of 201
Queen's representatives in local
    government 268
Queen's University Belfast 394
question time 134

R
RAB (Radio Advertising Bureau) 617
radio 614
Radio 1 615
Radio 2 615
Radio 3 615
Radio 4 615
Radio Advertising Bureau (RAB) 617
Radio Authority (RA) 617
RadioCentre 617
Radio Five Live 615
Radio Five Live Sports Extra 615
radiography, professional education
    401
radio time-signals 691
RAF (Royal Air Force) 355
  constitution 355
  equipment 355
  ranks 358
  salaries 357
  staff appointments 355
  strength 347
Rail Passengers Council (RPC) 455,
    456
Rail Regulator see ORR
railways 455
  Channel Tunnel link 457
  freight 456
  safety 456
  services 455
Ramadan 700
Ramsar Convention (1971) 519
Ramsbury, Bishop Suffragan 479
ranks of the armed forces 358
Raphoe, Bishop (RC) 486
rates
  non-domestic 267, 270
  Northern Ireland 272
RAUXAF (Royal Auxiliary Air Force)
    356
Rayleigh
  constituency 166
RBGE (Royal Botanic Garden
    Edinburgh) 231
RBG (Royal Botanic Gardens) Kew
    231, 541
RCHs (Recognised Clearing Houses)
    554
RCPO (Revenue and Customs
    Prosecutions Office) 208
RDAs (Regional Development
    Agencies) 230
Reading
  Area Bishop 478
  constituencies 166
  education authority 381

unitary authority 276, 293
university 394
Recognised Clearing Houses (RCHs) 554
Recognised Investment Exchanges (RIEs) 554
Recorded Signed For 495
recorders
England and Wales 318
Northern Ireland 330
Redbridge
education authority 383
London borough council 275, 300
Redcar, constituency 167
Redcar and Cleveland
education authority 381
unitary authority 276, 293
Redditch
constituency 167
district council 274, 290
redirection of post 495
red-letter days 701
redundancy 597
refraction, mean 692
regencies 127
Regent's Park & Kensington North, constituency 167
Regent's Park and Primrose Hill 541
regional assemblies, establishment of 266
Regional Chambers/Assemblies 269
regional daily newspapers 625
Regional Development Agencies (RDAs) 230
regional government 238
London 238
Northern Ireland 260
Scotland 249
Wales 243
regions
European Parliament 315
Scottish Parliament 258
Welsh Assembly 247
Registered Community Design 610
registered design 610
Registered Teacher Programme (RTP) 371
Registrar of Public Lending Right 230
registration
of births 587
of deaths 591
regnal years 701
regular marriages 605
regulated payments, Social Fund 443
regulated tenancies 600
Reigate, constituency 167
Reigate and Banstead, district council 274, 290
religion in the UK 464
religious calendars 9
see also types of religion eg Hindu calendar
Religious Society of Friends 491
renewable energy sources 453
targets for 508
Renfrewshire
education authority 385
unitary authority 277, 308
Renfrewshire East, UK Parliament constituency 181
Renfrewshire West, Scottish Parliament constituency 257

Rent Service 205
Repton, Bishop Suffragan 475
research and technology organisations 422
research councils 418
Research Disclosure Journal 611
Research Disclosures 611
resettlement grants 359
residential lettings 600
Residential Property Tribunal Service 334
resident magistrates 330
resident population statistics 18
Respect – the Unity Coalition 138
representation in House of Commons 130
Restormel, district council 274, 290
retail banking 550
Retail Price Index (RPI) 568
retirement pension see state pension scheme
revenue, government 563
Revenue and Customs 207
Revenue and Customs Prosecutions Office (RCPO) 208
revocation of wills 607
RFA (Royal Fleet Auxiliary Service) 351
Rhondda
constituencies
UK Parliament 177
Welsh Assembly 247
Rhondda Cynon Taff
education authority 384
unitary authority 277, 303
RIBA (Royal Institute of British Architects) 398
Ribble South, constituency 167
Ribble Valley
constituency 167
district council 274, 290
Richborough, Bishop Suffragan 472
Richmond Park 541
constituency 167
Richmondshire, district council 274, 290
Richmond upon Thames
education authority 383
London borough council 275, 300
Richmond (Yorks), constituency 167
RICS (Royal Institution of Chartered Surveyors) 403
RIEs (Recognised Investment Exchanges) 554
Ripon and Leeds, Bishop 478
rising and setting times 684
rivers
in England 278
in Scotland 304
in Wales 301
water quality targets 508
RMR (Royal Marines Reserve) 351
RNR (Royal Naval Reserve) 351
roads 457
finance 457
length 458
safety 459
road use 458
road user charging 458
Robert Gordon University 394
Rochdale
constituency 167
education authority 381

metropolitan borough council 276, 292
Rochester, Bishop 478
Rochford & Southend East, constituency 167
Rochford, district council 274, 290
Roehampton University 394
Rogation Days 697
roll-over relief on capital gains tax 577
Roman calendar 703
see also Julian calendar
Roman Catholic Church 483
England and Wales 484
Ireland 485
Scotland 485
Romanian Orthodox Church calendar 696
Roman indiction 702
Roman remains in London 543
Romford, constituency 167
Romsey, constituency 167
Ross, Skye & Inverness West, Scottish Parliament constituency 257
Ross, Skye & Lochaber, UK Parliament constituency 181
Rossendale & Darwen, constituency 167
Rossendale, district council 274, 290
Rother, district council 274, 290
Rotherham
constituency 167
education authority 381
metropolitan borough council 276, 292
Rother Valley, constituency 167
Roxburgh & Berwickshire, Scottish Parliament constituency 257
Royal Academy of Arts 417
Royal Academy of Engineering 416
Royal Air Force see RAF
Royal Air Force Museum 231
Royal Albert Hall 543
royal archives 27
royal assent 134
Royal Auxiliary Air Force (RAUXAF) 356
Royal Botanic Garden Edinburgh (RBGE) 231
Royal Botanic Gardens (RBG) Kew 231, 541
Royal College of Art 394
Royal College of Music 394
Royal College of Veterinary Surgeons 404
Royal Commission on Environmental Pollution 231
Royal Commission on the Ancient and Historical Monuments of Scotland 232
Royal Commission on the Ancient and Historical Monuments of Wales 232
Royal Courts of Justice 543
royal family 24
finances 29
military ranks and titles 31
Private Secretaries 26
taxation 30
Royal Fleet Auxiliary Service (RFA) 351
Royal Hospital, Chelsea 543
Royal Household, Offices of 27

Royal Institute of British Architects (RIBA) 398
Royal Institution of Chartered Surveyors (RICS) 403
Royal Mail Group 232, 494, 495
Royal Marines 350
Royal Marines Reserves (RMR) 351
Royal Mint 204
Royal National Theatre 543
Royal Naval College 541
Royal Naval Museum 232
Royal Naval Reserve (RNR) 351
Royal Navy 350
  fleet 351
  ranks 358
  salaries 357
  staff appointments 350
  strength 347
Royal Observatory 541
Royal Opera House 543
The Royal Parks 200
royal parks 540
Royal Peculiars 480
Royal Pharmaceutical Society of Great Britain 402
royal salutes 26
Royal Scottish Academy 417
Royal Society 416
Royal Society of Edinburgh (RSE) 417
Royal Standard 23
Royal Victorian Chain 85
Royal Victorian Order 84
RPA (Rural Payments Agency) 201
RPC (Rail Passengers Council) 455, 456
RPI (Retail Price Index) 568
RSE (Royal Society of Edinburgh) 417
RTP (Registered Teacher Programme) 371
Rugby & Kenilworth, constituency 167
Rugby, district council 274, 290
Ruislip-Northwood, constituency 167
Runnymede & Weybridge, constituency 167
Runnymede, district council 274, 290
Rural Affairs, Department for Food, Environment and see Department for Environment, Food and Rural Affairs
Rural Payments Agency (RPA) 201
Rushcliffe
  constituency 167
  district council 274, 290
Rushmoor, district council 274, 290
Russian Orthodox Church 489
Rutherglen & Hamilton West, UK Parliament constituency 181
Rutland & Melton, constituency 168
Rutland
  education authority 381
  unitary authority 276, 293
Ryedale
  constituency 168
  district council 274, 290

S
S4C Wales 614
SAAS (Student Award Agency for Scotland) 377
safety
  marine 461

rail 456
  on roads 459
Saffron Walden, constituency 168
St Albans 284
  Bishop 479
  constituency 168
  district council 275, 290
St Andrews and Edinburgh, Archbishop (RC) 485
St Andrews, Dunkeld and Dunblane, Bishop 481
St Andrews, university 394
St Anne 313
St Asaph, Bishop 481
St David's, Bishop 481
St Edmundsbury and Ipswich, Bishop 479
St Edmundsbury, district council 275, 290
St Germans, Bishop Suffragan 480
St Helens
  constituencies 168
  education authority 382
  metropolitan borough council 276, 292
St Helier 312
St James's Palace 543
St Ives, constituency 168
St James's Park 541
St Mary Axe 541
St Michael and St George, Most Distinguished Order 84
St Paul's Cathedral 543
St Peter Port 313
saints days 701
Saka era 702
sale of goods 589
Salford
  Bishop (RC) 485
  constituency 168
  education authority 381
  metropolitan borough council 276, 292
  university 395
Salisbury 284
  Bishop 479
  constituency 168
  district council 275, 290
Saltire 304
salutes, royal 26
Salvation Army 491
same-sex couples 594
Sandwell
  education authority 381
  metropolitan borough council 276, 292
SAP (Statutory Adoption Pay) 445
Sark 313
satellites 693
Saturn 689
  satellites 693
  see also months of the year eg January, Saturn in
savings
  effect on Social Fund payments 444
  income from 571
savings credit 442
Saxe-Coburg and Gotha, House of 40
Scarborough & Whitby, constituency 168
Scarborough, district council 275, 290
scheduled monuments 523

scholarship, national academies of 416
school boards 360
School-Centred Initial Teacher Training 403
schools 363
  primary 365
  middle 365
  secondary 365
  class sizes 361
  independent see independent schools
  numbers by category 361, 364
  special 366
  grammar 365
School Teachers' Review Body (STRB) 232
science
  government budget (2006–7) 418
Science and Technology Facilities Council (STFC) 422
Science Museum 233
Scilly, Isles of 278
  education authority 386
  water authority 446
  unitary authority 293
Scotland
  area 17, 304
  banknotes 549
  Chiefs of Clans 121
  constituencies (UK Parliament) 178
  early history 305
  flag 304
  historic buildings and monuments 529
  hydrography 304
  islands 305
  judicature 326
  Kings and Queens (1016 to 1603) 40
  languages 304, 367
  LEAs 384
  local government see local government
  museums and art galleries 537
  National Parks 513
  National Scenic Areas 515
  NHS structure 424
  police forces 340
  population statistics 17, 304
  precedence 44
  principal cities 306
  prison establishments 346
  public holidays 10, 11, 701
  regional government 249
  relief 304
  water industry 448
  see also Church of Scotland
Scotland Central Scottish Parliament Region 258
Scotland European Parliament Region 316
Scotland Mid and Fife Scottish Parliament Region 259
Scotland North East Scottish Parliament Region 259
Scotland Office 197
Scotland South Scottish Parliament Region 259
Scotland West Scottish Parliament Region 259
Scottish and Southern Energy plc 451
Scottish Arts Council 233

Scottish Borders
  education authority 385
  unitary authority 277, 308
Scottish Court Service 328
Scottish Credit and Qualifications
  Framework (SCQF) 370
Scottish Criminal Cases Review
  Commission 233
Scottish Enterprise 233
Scottish Environment Protection
  Agency (SEPA) 233, 448
Scottish Episcopal Church 481
Scottish Executive 249
Scottish Executive Courts Directorate
  327
Scottish Funding Council (SFC) 370,
  373
Scottish Group Awards (SGAs) 370
Scottish Land Court 328
Scottish Law Commission 234
Scottish Legal Aid Board 234
Scottish National Party see SNP
Scottish Natural Heritage (SNH) 234,
  516
Scottish Parliament 128, 249
  constituencies 252
  departments and executive
    agencies 249
  members 250
  political composition 251
  regions 258
  salaries 249
Scottish Power plc 451
Scottish Prisons Complaints
  Commission 234
Scottish Prison Service (SPS) 346
  operating costs 343
  salaries 346
Scottish Public Services Ombudsman
  234
Scottish Qualification for Headship
  372
Scottish Qualifications Authority
  (SQA) 367, 370
Scottish Records Advisory Council
  234
Scottish Records Office see National
  Archives of Scotland
Scottish Solicitors' Discipline
  Tribunal 335
Scottish Vocational Qualifications
  (SVQs) 370
Scottish Water 446, 448
SCQF (Scottish Credit and
  Qualifications Framework) 370
Scunthorpe, constituency 168
SDA see Severe Disablement
  Allowance
SDLP (Social Democratic and Labour
  Party) 138
  development 136
  financial support 137
  representation in House of
    Commons 130
SDRT (stamp duty reserve tax) 585
Seafish Industry Authority 234
seas
  UK environmental targets 508
seasons 635
seats in House of Commons
  number 130
  vacancies 135
secondary education 365
  expenditure 360

public examinations and
  qualifications 368
secondary health care services 427
Secondary Shortage Subject Scheme
  (SSSS) 371
second class post 494
Secretaries of State 184
  salaries 186
Secret Intelligence Service (MI6) 208
secure tenancies 600
security and intelligence services 208
Security Service (MI5) 208
Sedgefield
  constituency 168
    by-election (2007) result 183
  district council 275, 290
Sedgemoor, district council 275, 290
Sefton
  education authority 381
  metropolitan borough council
    276, 292
Selby
  Bishop Suffragan 472
  constituency 168
  district council 275, 290
select committees
  House of Commons 133, 134
  House of Lords 128, 129, 134
selective education in Northern
  Ireland 365
self-assessment
  for corporation tax 581
  for income tax 574
Senior Civil Service 186
Senior Judiciary of England and
  Wales 320
senior military officers pay system 357
Senior Salaries Review Body 234
separation 593
'separation deeds' 594
SEPA (Scottish Environment
  Protection Agency) 233, 448
September 668
  astronomical phenomena 668
  calendar 668
  constellations 668
  duration of twilight 669
  high water 716
  minima of algol 668
  night sky 669
  sunrise and sunset 671
  zodiacal light 669
  Moon 668
    position 670
  Sun 669
  Jupiter in 669
  Mars in 669
  Mercury in 669
  Neptune in 671
  Saturn in 669
  Uranus in 669
  Venus in 669
Serbian Orthodox Church 489
Serious Fraud Office 208
Serious Organised Crime Agency
  (SOCA) 338
SERPS (State Earnings-Related
  Pension Scheme) 434
Service Personnel and Veterans
  Agency (SPVA) 435
service providers 498
service retired pay 359
services
  supply of 590

service salaries 357
setting times, rising and 684
Sevenoaks
  constituency 168
  district council 275, 290
Seventh-Day Adventist Church 491
Severe Disablement Allowance (SDA)
  441
  weekly rates 441
Severn river 278
sewage treatment 511
SGAs (Scottish Group Awards) 370
Shadow Cabinet 137
Shareholder Executive 189
SHAs (Strategic Health Authorities)
  423, 424
Sheffield 285
  Bishop 479
  constituencies 168
  education authority 382
  metropolitan borough council
    276, 292
  museums and art galleries 535
  universities 395
Sheffield Hallam University 395
Shenshai calendar 702
Shepway, district council 275, 290
Sherbourne, Bishop Suffragan 479
Sheriff Court of Chancery 328
sheriff courts 326
sheriffdoms (Scottish judicature) 326,
  328
Sheriffs (City of London) 270, 295,
  296
Sheriffs (county) see High Sheriffs
sheriffs (Scottish judicature) 328
Sherwood
  Bishop Suffragan 480
  constituency 169
Shetland 305
  education authority 385
  Scottish Parliament constituency
    257
  unitary authority 277, 308
Shipley, constituency 169
shipping 461
  Lloyd's intelligence service 560
  UK owned vessels 462
shipping forecast areas 463
shires of England 286
  map 294
shortest day 635
Short Money 137
short-term incapacity benefit 439
Shrewsbury & Atcham
  constituency 169
  district council 275, 290
Shrewsbury
  Bishop (RC) 485
  Bishop Suffragan 476
Shropshire
  county council 273
  education authority 379
Shropshire North, constituency 169
sick pay 596
sidereal time 690
  conversion of mean time to 686
sights of London 538
sight tests 427
Sikh calendar 700
  year 2008 9
Sikhism 470
  adherents in UK 464
silver coin 548

silver hallmarks 545
Sinn Fein 138
    representation in House of
        Commons 130
Sites of Special Scientific Interest
    (SSSIs) 516
Sittingbourne & Sheppey,
    constituency 169
six pips signal 691
sixth form colleges see post-16
    education
Skipton & Ripon, constituency 169
Sky, estimated audience share 613
Sleaford & North Hykeham,
    constituency 169
Slough
    constituency 169
    education authority 382
    unitary authority 276, 293
SMP (Statutory Maternity Pay) 445,
    596
SNH (Scottish Natural Heritage) 234,
    516
Snowdonia/Eryri National Park 513
SNP (Scottish National Party) 138
    development 136
    financial support 137
    representation in House of
        Commons 130
SOCA (Serious Organised Crime
    Agency) 338
Social Democratic and Labour
    Party see SDLP
Social Democratic Party (SDP) 136
Social Fund 443
Social Fund Commissioner 222
Social Security and Child Support
    Appeals Tribunal 334
social security benefits see benefits
Social Security Commissioners 334
    for Northern Ireland 334
social welfare 423
Society of Genealogists 588
Society of Knights see Imperial Society
    of Knights Bachelor
Sodor and Man, Bishop 479
solar (or major) cycle 701
solar system 693
    see also individual planets eg Mars
soldiers
    salaries 358
    service retired pay 359
solemnisation of marriages 604
solicitors
    professional education 403
    see also duty solicitors
Solicitors' Disciplinary Tribunal 335
Solihull
    constituency 169
    education authority 382
    metropolitan borough council
        276, 292
solstice 695
Somerset
    county council 273
    education authority 379
Somerset House 543
Somerton & Frome, constituency 169
Sophie, Countess of Wessex
    military ranks and titles 32
    Private Secretary 26
Southampton 285
    airport 454, 455
    Bishop Suffragan 473

constituencies 169
    education authority 382
    museums and art galleries 535
    unitary authority 276, 293
    universities 395
South Ayrshire
    education authority 385
    unitary authority 277, 308
South Bank 543
South Bedfordshire, district council
    275, 290
South Bucks, district council 275, 290
South Cambridgeshire, district
    council 275, 290
South Derbyshire, district council
    275, 290
South Downs, designation as a
    National Park 513
South East Education and Library
    Board 385
South East European Parliament
    Region 316
South Education and Library Board
    385
Southend-on-Sea
    education authority 382
    unitary authority 276, 293
Southend West, constituency 169
South Gloucestershire
    education authority 382
    unitary authority 276
South Hams, district council 275, 290
South Holland & The Deepings,
    constituency 169
South Holland, district council 275,
    290
South Kesteven, district council 275,
    290
South Lakeland, district council 275,
    290
South Lanarkshire
    education authority 385
    unitary authority 277, 308
South Norfolk, district council 275,
    290
South Northamptonshire, district
    council 275, 290
South Oxfordshire, district council
    275, 290
Southport, constituency 169
South Ribble, district council 275,
    290
South Shields
    constituency 169
    museums and art galleries 536
South Shropshire, district council 275,
    290
South Somerset, district council 275,
    290
South Staffordshire, district council
    275, 290
South Tyneside
    education authority 382
    metropolitan borough council
        276, 292
South Wales Central Welsh Assembly
    Region 248
South Wales East Welsh Assembly
    Region 248
South Wales West Welsh Assembly
    Region 248
Southwark
    Archbishop (RC) 484
    Bishop 479

education authority 383
    London borough council 275,
        300
Southwark Cathedral 543
Southwark North & Bermondsey,
    constituency 169
Southwell and Nottingham, Bishop
    480
South West, GLA constituency 242
South West European Parliament
    Region 316
the sovereign 127
    see also Crown; Elizabeth II
Sovereign in Council see Privy Council
Sovereign Pontiff 484
sovereigns and princes of Wales 42
    see also Charles, Prince of Wales
Speakers
    House of Commons 131, 135
    House of Lords 129
special advisers to Government
    Ministers, salaries 186
Special Commissioners 335
special constabulary 341
Special Delivery Next Day 495
special delivery services 495
special education 366
Special Educational Needs and
    Disability Tribunal 335
Special Immigration Appeals
    Commission 335
Specialist Schools Programme 364
Specialist Teacher Assistant (STA)
    scheme 372
special licence, marriage by 604
speech and language therapy,
    professional education 401
Spelthorne
    constituency 169
    district council 275, 290
sponsor's marks 545
Sport, Department for Culture, Media
    and see Department for Culture,
    Media and Sport
sports
    forthcoming events 13
SPP (Statutory Paternity Pay) 445,
    597
Spring 635
SPVA (Service Personnel and Veterans
    Agency) 435
SQA (Scottish Qualifications
    Authority) 367, 370
SRA (Strategic Rail Authority) 455
SSMG (Sure Start Maternity Grant)
    443
SSP (Statutory Sick Pay) 445
SSSIs (Sites of Special Scientific
    Interest) 516
SSSS (Secondary Shortage Subject
    Scheme) 371
staff associations, police service 341
Stafford
    Bishop Suffragan 476
    constituency 169
    district council 275, 290
Staffordshire
    constituencies 170
        by-election (2005) result 183
    county council 273
    education authority 379
    university 395
Staffordshire Moorlands, district
    council 275, 290

stakeholder pension schemes 435
Stalybridge & Hyde, constituency 170
stamp duty 584
stamp duty land tax 584
stamp duty reserve tax (SDRT) 585
Standard Grade examinations 369
Standards Board 267
Standards in Public Life, Committee
    on 215
Standard Time 691
    see also Greenwich Mean Time
        (GMT)
Stansted airport 455
stars, position of 686
State Earnings-Related Pension
    Scheme (SERPS) 434
state pension scheme 433, 439,
    441
    weekly rate 440, 441
State Second Pension 434
state system of education 365
State Veterinary Service (SVS) *see*
    Animal Health
Statistics Commission 235
Statutory Adoption Pay (SAP) 445
Statutory Maternity Pay (SMP) 445,
    596
Statutory Paternity Pay (SPP) 445,
    597
statutory public holidays 701
Statutory Sick Pay (SSP) 445
Stepney, Area Bishop 473
Stevenage
    constituency 170
    district council 275, 290
Stewart, House of 41
STFC (Science and Technology
    Facilities Council) 422
stipendiary magistrates
    Scotland 329
    see also district judges (magistrates'
        courts)
stipends
    Church of England 472
    Church of Scotland 483
    Church in Wales 481
    Scottish Episcopal Church 481
Stirling
    constituencies
        Scottish Parliament 257
        UK Parliament 181
    education authority 385
    unitary authority 277, 308
    university 395
Stock Exchange *see* London Stock
    Exchange
Stockport
    Bishop Suffragan 475
    constituency 170
    education authority 382
    metropolitan borough council
        276, 292
Stockton, constituencies 170
Stockton-on-Tees
    education authority 382
    unitary authority 276, 293
Stoke-on-Trent 285
    constituencies 170
    education authority 382
    unitary authority 276, 293
    museums and art galleries 536
Stone, constituency 170
storms, magnetic 694
Stourbridge, constituency 170

Strabane, district council 277,
    310
Strangford
    constituencies
        Northern Ireland Assembly
            264
        UK Parliament 182
Strategic Health Authorities (SHAs)
    423, 424
Strategic Rail Authority (SRA) 455
Stratford-on-Avon, district council
    275, 291
Stratford-upon-Avon, constituency
    170
Strathclyde, university 395
Strathkelvin & Bearsden, Scottish
    Parliament constituency 257
STRB (School Teachers' Review
    Body) 232
Streatham, constituency 170
Stretford & Urmston, constituency
    170
strikes 565
Stroud
    constituency 170
    district council 275, 291
Stuart, House of 39
Student Award Agency for Scotland
    (SAAS) 377
Student Finance Wales 376
Student Loans Company Ltd 235
students
    higher education
        financial support 360
        number of 362
    post-16 education
        financial support 360,
            370
        number of 369
    succession, order of 25
Suffolk
    constituencies 170
    county council 273
    education authority 380
Suffolk Coastal, district council 275,
    291
suffragan bishops, listing 472
Summer 635
Summer Time 691
Sun 687
    see also months of the year eg
        January, Sun
Sunday national newspapers,
    circulation 623
Sundays after Pentecost 697
Sunday trading 597
Sunderland
    constituencies 171
    education authority 382
    metropolitan borough council
        276, 292
    university 395
sunrise 687, 689
    calculation of 685
    see also months of the year eg
        January, sunrise and sunset
sunset 687, 689
    calculation of 685
    see also months of the year eg
        January, sunrise and sunset
Superintendent Registrar's Offices
    588
Supplementary Vote System (SVS)
    238

Supreme Court of Judicature
    England and Wales 318, 320
    departments and offices 322
    Northern Ireland 330
Sure Start 365
Sure Start Maternity Grant (SSMG)
    443
surface mail rates 494
Suriyakati calendar 700
Surrey
    constituencies 171
    county council 273
    education authority 380
    university 395
Surrey Heath, district council 275,
    291
surveying, professional education 403
Sussex, university 395
Sussex Mid, constituency 171
sustainable development 509
Sutton & Cheam, constituency 171
Sutton
    education authority 383
    London borough council 275,
        300
Sutton Coldfield, constituency 171
SVQs (Scottish Vocational
    Qualifications) 370
Swale, district council 275, 291
Swansea 302
    constituencies
        UK Parliament 177
        Welsh Assembly 247
    education authority 384
    museums and art galleries 536
    unitary authority 277, 303
    University of Wales 396
        Institute of Higher Education 396
Swansea and Brecon, Bishop 481
Swedenborgian New Church 491
Swindon
    Bishop Suffragan 474
    constituencies 171
    education authority 382
    unitary authority 276, 293
Syrian Orthodox Church 489

T
TAI (International Atomic Time) 690
Takeover Panel, *see* Panel on Takeovers
    and Mergers
Tameside
    education authority 382
    metropolitan borough council
        276, 292
Tamworth
    constituency 171
    district council 275, 291
Tandridge, district council 275, 291
taper relief 577
Targeted Programme of Improvements
    (TPI) for roads 458
Tate Britain 235
Tate Modern 235
TA (Territorial Army) 354
Tatton, constituency 171
Taunton
    Bishop Suffragan 473
    constituency 171
Taunton Deane, district council 275,
    291
taxation 570
    capital gains tax *see* capital gains
        tax

corporation tax *see* corporation tax
council tax
see also individual councils eg.
Westminster, London borough
council
income tax *see* income tax
inheritance tax *see* inheritance tax
royal family 30
stamp duty 584
VAT (value added tax) *see* VAT
(value added tax)
Tax Credits 437
effect on income tax 575
tax exempt special savings accounts
(TESSAs) 572
tax-free products, National Savings
and Investments 555
taxis 459
tax return filing 574
Tayside North, Scottish Parliament
constituency 257
TDA (Training and Development
Agency for Schools) 236, 372
teachers 371
numbers 361
pupil-teacher ratios 361
salaries 372
training 371, 403
application for courses 375
financial incentives 371
see also academic staff
Teacher Training Agency (TTA) *see*
Training and Development Agency
for Schools (TDA)
technological research bodies 422
Technology and Construction Court
318, 321
Teesdale, district council 275, 291
Teesside, university 395
Teignbridge
constituency 171
district council 275, 291
Teletext Ltd 614
television 612
licences 613
see also broadcasting (2006–7)
Telford, constituency 171
Telford and Wrekin
education authority 382
unitary authority 276, 293
tenancies 600
Tendring, district council 275, 291
tenure, type of accommodation by 20
term days 701
year 2008 9
termination of employment 597
terrestrial magnetism 694
Terrestrial Time (TT) 690
Territorial Army (TA) 354
TESSAs (tax exempt special savings
accounts) 572
Test Valley, district council 275, 291
Tewkesbury
Bishop Suffragan 476
constituency 171
district council 275, 291
TfL (Transport for London) 236,
239
bus services 458
Thai calendar 700
Thames Embankments 543
Thames Flood Barrier 543
Thames river 278
Thames Valley University 395

Thanet
constituencies 171
district council 275, 291
theatres in London 544
Thetford, Bishop Suffragan 477
Thistle, Most Ancient and Most Noble
Order 118
Three Rivers, district council 275,
291
Thurrock
constituency 171
education authority 382
unitary authority 276, 293
tidal predictions 711
time 689
measurement of 695
see also lighting-up time
time-signals, radio 691
Tiverton & Honiton, constituency
171
TOCs (train operating companies)
455
toll roads 458
Tonbridge & Malling
constituency 172
district council 275, 291
Tonbridge, Bishop Suffragan 478
Tooting, constituency 172
Top Salaries Review Body *see* Senior
Salaries Review Body
Torbay
constituency 172
education authority 382
unitary authority 276, 293
Torfaen
constituencies
UK Parliament 177
Welsh Assembly 247
education authority 384
unitary authority 277, 303
Torridge, district council 275, 291
the Tote (Horserace Totalisator Board)
221
Totnes, constituency 172
Tottenham, constituency 172
tourism bodies 235
Tower Hamlets
education authority 383
London borough council 275,
300
town and country planning 605
Town Clerk 295, 296
town mayors 268
TPI (Targeted Programme of
Improvements) for roads 458
Track and Trace postal service 495
trade, UK statistics 565
Trade and Industry, Department of *see*
Department for Business Enterprise
and Regulatory Reform *or*
Department for Innovation,
Universities and Skills
trade descriptions 590
trade marks 611
number and membership 565
Trafford
education authority 382
metropolitan borough council
276, 292
Training and Development Agency for
Schools (TDA) 236, 372
train operating companies (TOCs)
455
Transco *see* National Grid Transco

Transformational Government Team
186
transport 454
air transport 454
rail *see* railways
roads *see* roads
shipping *see* shipping
Transport, Department for *see*
Department for Transport
Transport for London *see* TfL
Transport Tribunal 335
Treasurer's account 556
Treasurer's Office 27
Treasury *see* HM Treasury
Treasury Solicitor's Department 199
Trial of the Pyx 549
tribunals 331
Tribunals Service 331
Trinity House Lighthouse Service
216, 462
Trinity Sunday 697
tropical year 695
Truro & St Austell, constituency 172
Truro, Bishop 480
Trusts, NHS *see* NHS Trusts
Trust schools 364
TTA (Teacher Training Agency) *see*
Training and Development Agency
for Schools (TDA)
Tuam, Archbishop (RC) 485
Tuam, Killala and Achonry, Bishop
482
Tudor, House of 39
Tunbridge Wells
constituency 172
district council 275, 291
tunnels
see also Channel Tunnel; Thames
tunnels
TV Licensing 613
Tweeddale, Ettrick & Lauderdale,
Scottish Parliament constituency
257
Twickenham, constituency 172
twilight 688
see also months of the year eg
January, twilight
Tyne Bridge, constituency 172
Tynedale, district council 275,
291
Tynemouth, constituency 172
Tyneside North, constituency 172
Tynwald 311
Tynwald Day 311
Tyrone West
constituencies
Northern Ireland Assembly
265
UK Parliament 182

U
UCAS (Universities and Colleges
Admission Service) 375
UCEA (Universities and Colleges
Employers Association) 374
UK
area 17
citizenship 588
constitution 127
currency 548
economic statistics 563
environmental targets 508
European Parliament regions 315
flag 23

Kings and Queens (since 1603) 39
MEPs 314
population 17
religion 464
shipping forecast areas 463
statistics 17
World Heritage Sites 518
see also England; Northern Ireland; Scotland; Wales
UKAEA (UK Atomic Energy Authority) 236
UK Atomic Energy Authority (UKAEA) 236, 452
UK Debt Management Office 204
UK Film Council 236
UK Independence Party 138
UK Intellectual Property Office 202
UK Listing Authority (UKLA) 557
UK Nirex 452
UK Police National Missing Persons Bureau (PNMPB) 338
UK Sports Council 236
UK Trade and Investment 208
Ulster, university 395
Ulster Mid
   constituencies
      Northern Ireland Assembly 265
      UK Parliament 182
Ulster Unionist Council 136, 138
Ulster Unionist Party 136, 138
   representation in House of Commons 130
Undeb Yr Annibynwyr Cymraeg 491
undergraduate courses 375
underground systems 456
Under-Secretaries of State 185
   salaries 186
unemployment statistics 565
unfair dismissal 597
unfair terms 590
Union Flag (or Jack) 23
Union of Welsh Independents 491
Unitarian and Free Christian Churches 493
unitary authorities 266
   England 268, 293
      functions 269
      map 294
      political composition 276
      map 308
      political composition 277
   Wales 271, 303
      map 303
      political composition 276
Unitary Awarding Bodies see UABs
United Kingdom see UK
United Reformed Church 491
Universal Time (UT) 689
universities 373
   governance 373
Universities and Colleges Admission Service (UCAS) 375
Universities and Colleges Employers Association (UCEA) 374
University for Industry (Ufi) Ltd 373
Upminster, constituency 172
Upper Bann
   constituencies
      Northern Ireland Assembly 265
      UK Parliament 182

Uranus 689
   satellites 693
   see also months of the year eg January, Uranus in
UTC (Coordinated Universal Time) 690
Uttlesford, district council 275, 291
Uxbridge, constituency 172

V
Veterans Agency see Service Personnel and Veterans Agency
vacant seats in the House of Commons 135
   see also by-elections
Vale of Clwyd
   constituencies
      UK Parliament 177
      Welsh Assembly 247
Vale of Glamorgan
   constituencies
      UK Parliament 177
      Welsh Assembly 247
   education authority 384
   unitary authority 277, 303
Vale of White Horse, district council 275, 291
Vale of York, constituency 172
Vale Royal, district council 275, 291
Valuation Office Agency 207
Valuation Tribunal Service for Wales (VTSW) 335
Valuation Tribunal Service (VTS) 335
VAT and Duties Tribunals 336
Vatican City State 483
VAT (value added tax) 583
   collection 584
Vauxhall, constituency 172
VCEs (Vocational Certificates of Education) 368
Vehicle and Operator Services Agency (VOSA) 204, 461
Vehicle Certification Agency 203
vehicle excise duty 460
vehicles see motor vehicles
Venus 689
   see also months of the year eg January, Venus in
Veterinary Laboratories Agency 201
veterinary medicine, professional education 404
Veterinary Medicines Directorate 201
Victoria, Queen 35
   descendants 35
Victoria and Albert Museum 236
Victoria Cross 119
Virgin Media Television 612, 614
viscounts 54
   courtesy titles 77
   forms of address 54
Visit Britain 235
Visit Scotland 235
Vocational Certificates of Education (VCEs) 368
vocational qualifications 368
voluntary schools 363
VOSA (Vehicle and Operator Services Agency) 204, 461
voting
   for the London Assembly 238
   for the Mayor of London 238
   qualifications 606
   registration 606
   see also elections

VTS (Valuation Tribunal Service) 335
VTSW (Valuation Tribunal Service for Wales) 335

W
waiting lists, NHS 428
Wakefield
   Bishop 480
   constituency 172
   education authority 382
   metropolitan borough council 276, 292
   museums and art galleries 536
Wales
   Archbishop 481
   area 17, 301
   Areas of Outstanding Natural Beauty (AONBs) 514
   constituencies (UK Parliament) 175
   early history 301
   flag 301
   historic buildings and monuments 528
   hydrography 301
   judicature 318
   language 301, 367
   LEAs 384
   local government see local government
   museums and art galleries 536
   National Parks 512
   NHS structure 424
   police forces 340
   population statistics 17
   precedence 43
   princes of 42
   principal cities 302
   prison establishments 343
   public holidays 10, 11, 701
   regional government 243
   relief 301
   university 395
   water industry 446
   see also Church in Wales
Wales, Prince of
   title 42
   see also Charles, Prince of Wales
Wales, Princess of see Diana, Princess of Wales
Wales European Parliament Region 316
Wales Office 198
Wales Tourist Board 235
Walk-in Centres, NHS 426
Wallace Collection 237
Wallasey, constituency 172
Walsall
   constituencies 172
   education authority 382
   metropolitan borough council 276, 292
Waltham Forest
   education authority 383
   London borough council 275, 300
Walthamstow, constituency 172
Wandsworth
   education authority 383
   London borough council 275, 300
Wansbeck
   constituency 173
   district council 275, 291

Wansdyke, constituency 173
Wantage, constituency 173
war disablement pension 435
Warley, constituency 173
war pensions 435
    claims and questions 436
    effect on benefits 436
    supplementary allowances 436
Warrington
    Bishop Suffragan 477
    constituencies 173
    education authority 382
    unitary authority 276, 293
Warwick & Leamington, constituency
    173
Warwick
    Bishop Suffragan 475
    district council 275, 291
    university 396
Warwickshire
    county council 273
    education authority 380
Warwickshire North, constituency
    173
war widow/widower's pension 435
waste 509
    UK targets 508
water
    quality targets 510
    UK 508
    see also high water
waterfalls
    in Scotland 304
Waterford and Lismore, Bishop (RC)
    486
water industry 446
    England and Wales 446
    Northern Ireland 448
    Scotland 448
Water Industry Commissioner for
    Scotland 448
Water Service 446, 448
Water Services Regulation Authority
    (OFWAT) 208
Water UK 446
Watford
    constituency 173
    district council 275, 291
Waveney
    constituency 173
    district council 275, 291
Waverley, district council 275, 291
Wealden
    constituency 173
    district council 275, 291
Wear Valley, district council 275, 291
Weaver Vale, constituency 173
WEA (Workers' Education
    Association) 377
the Web see Internet
web domain names 611
    of countries 506
weekly newspapers 624
Wellingborough
    constituency 173
    district council 275, 291
Wells, constituency 173
Welsh Affairs Committee 135
Welsh Assembly 128, 243
    committees 244
    constituencies 244
    departments and offices 243
    executive agencies 244
    members 244

political composition 244
    regions 247
    salaries 243
Welsh Assembly Government 243
Welsh Baccalaureate 368
Welsh Fourth Channel Authority see
    S4C Wales
Welsh language 301, 367
Welwyn & Hatfield, district council
    275, 291
Welwyn Hatfield, constituency 173
Wentworth, constituency 173
Wesleyan Reform Union 492
Wessex, Countess of see Sophie,
    Countess of Wessex
Wessex, Earl of see Edward, Prince
West Berkshire
    education authority 382
    unitary authority 276, 293
West Bromwich, constituencies 173
Westbury, constituency 173
West Central, GLA constituency 242
West Devon, district council 275, 291
West Dorset, district council 275, 291
West Dunbartonshire
    education authority 385
    unitary authority 277, 308
West Education and Library Board
    386
Western Isles
    education authority 385
    Scottish Parliament constituency
        258
    unitary authority 277, 308
West Ham, constituency 173
West Lancashire, district council 275,
    291
West Lindsey, district council 275,
    291
West Lothian
    education authority 385
    unitary authority 277, 308
West Midlands European Parliament
    Region 316
Westminster
    Archbishop (RC) 484
    education authority 383
    London borough council 275,
        300
    Royal Peculiar 480
    university 396
Westminster Abbey 543
Westminster Cathedral 544
Westminster Hall Sittings 135
Westmorland & Lonsdale,
    constituency 174
West of England, university 396
Weston-Super-Mare, constituency 174
West Oxfordshire, district council
    275, 291
West Somerset, district council 275,
    291
West Sussex
    county council 273
    education authority 380
West Wiltshire, district council 275,
    291
wetlands, conservation 519
Weymouth and Portland, district
    council 275, 291
Whips 135
    Government 185
    Liberal Democrat 138
    Opposition 137

whistleblowing legislation 598
Whitby, Bishop Suffragan 472
Whit Sunday 697
Widowed Parent's Allowance 438
    weekly rates 440
widow's benefits 439
Wigan
    constituency 174
    education authority 382
    metropolitan borough council
        276, 292
Wight, Isle of 278
    constituency 161
    education authority 386
    unitary authority 276, 293
wildlife conservation 519
    UK legislation 520
Willesden, Area Bishop 473
William, Prince 24
    Military Ranks and Titles 32
    Private Secretary 26
wills 606
    capacity to make 607
    execution 607
    revocation 607
    in Scotland 606
    where to find proved 607
Wilton Park Conference Centre 201
Wiltshire
    county council 273
    education authority 380
Wiltshire North, constituency 174
Wimbledon, constituency 174
Wimbledon College of Art 387
Winchester 285
    Bishop 473
    constituency 174
    district council 275, 291
    university 396
wind farms 453
Windsor
    constituency 174
    Royal Peculiar 480
Windsor, House of 34, 40
Windsor and Maidenhead
    education authority 381
    unitary authority 276, 293
Winter 635
Winter Fuel Payments 443
WIPO (World Intellectual Property
    Organisation) 610, 611
Wirral
    constituencies 174
    education authority 382
    metropolitan borough council
        276, 292
witnesses for wills 607
Witney, constituency 174
Woking
    constituency 174
    district council 275, 291
Wokingham
    constituency 174
    education authority 382
    unitary authority 276, 293
Wolverhampton
    Bishop Suffragan 477
    constituencies 174
    education authority 382
    metropolitan borough council
        276, 292
    university 396
women
    hereditary peers 45